STAGES OF DRAMA

STAGES OF DRAMA
Classical to Contemporary Theater

CARL H. KLAUS
University of Iowa

MIRIAM GILBERT
University of Iowa

BRADFORD S. FIELD, JR.
Wayne State University

Theatrical Illustrations by A. G. Smith
University of Windsor

SCOTT, FORESMAN AND COMPANY
Glenview, Illinois

Dallas, Tex.   Oakland, N.J.   Palo Alto, Cal.
Tucker, Ga.   London, England

Copyright © 1981 Scott, Foresman and Company

Printed in the United States of America

Library of Congress Cataloging in Publication Data:

Main entry under title:

Stages of drama.

Includes index.
1. Drama—Collections.   I. Klaus, Carl H.
II. Gilbert, Miriam.   III.   Field, Bradford S.
PN6112.S687   808.82   80-26187

ISBN 0-673-15686-9

89101112131415–WKK–9594939291908988

PREFACE

"The play's the thing" in *Stages of Drama*. In the spirit of that commitment, we have put together a collection of thirty plays representing major dramatists, forms, and styles of western theater from the classical Greek period to the present. Our choice of plays has been guided by a desire to present only works of dramatic excellence from each period—from *Agamemnon, Oedipus Rex,* and *Lysistrata* to *The Threepenny Opera, Endgame,* and *Equus.*

We also have provided two kinds of introductory essays that we hope will contribute to understanding and enjoying these plays. For each period of drama, we have prepared an introduction to the cultural and theatrical situations that influenced the writing and staging of plays during that time. These essays are illustrated with detailed line drawings of theaters typical of each period, so that every play can be seen in the context of the stage on which it was originally performed. For all of the dramatists, we have prepared introductions that focus on their theatrical careers and their major works. These essays also suggest various approaches to understanding each play, as well as various issues related to its staging.

Above all, plays are meant to be staged and witnessed. Given that truth, we have provided two special kinds of supplementary material that we hope will evoke the excitement and significance of drama on stage. Following each play, we have reproduced photographs from a challenging contemporary production of it. These ninety production shots illustrate important dramatic moments in each play as performed by major actors, actresses, or repertory groups from the United States, Canada, England, and Europe. We also have reprinted provocative reviews of each illustrated production and, in some cases, interviews with its director. From dramatist, to play, to performance, *Stages of Drama* is an invitation to experience the world of theater.

CARL H. KLAUS
MIRIAM GILBERT
BRADFORD S. FIELD, JR.

ACKNOWLEDGMENTS

During ten years of gathering and preparing material for this book, we have received valuable help from many people.

For their expert advice about the table of contents and the introductory essays, we are grateful to Professors Rosemarie Bank (Purdue University), Lester Beaurline (University of Virginia, Charlottesville), Oscar L. Brownstein (Yale University), John M. Clum (Duke University), Charles Brooks Dodson (University of North Carolina, Wilmington), Alan Ehmann (University of Texas, El Paso), Mary Lee Field (Wayne State University), Charles A. Hallett (Fordham University), Barbara Hodgdon (Drake University), David Knauf (University of Massachusetts, Amherst), Harry Mahnken (University of Massachusetts, Amherst), Michael Manheim (University of Toledo), Edythe McGovern (Los Angeles Valley College), Judith Milhous (University of Iowa), Robert Scholes (Brown University), and Sanford Sternlicht (SUNY College at Oswego), as well as to Kate Franks (Iowa City) and Frank Gagnard (*The Times-Picayune*, New Orleans).

For their generous assistance in locating and identifying production photographs, we are grateful to Anne K. Ames (Harvard Theatre Collection), Peter Ansorge (*Plays and Players*, London), William Baker (Yale School of Drama), Jean Beaulieu (Services Culturel Français, Chicago), Robert Brustein (Yale School of Drama), Melissa Cohen (The Guthrie Theater), Joan Crawford (The Royal Shakespeare Company, Stratford-upon-Avon), Connie Dawson (The Prospect Theatre Company, London), Cheryle Elliott (The American Conservatory Theater, San Francisco), Anne Goodrich (Yale School of Drama), Charlotte Solomon Guindon (The Guthrie Theater), Arthur Hartney (Theatre Communications Group, New York), Stella Jackson (The Mermaid Theatre, London), Caroline J. Keely (The National Theatre, London), Alan K. Lathrop (The University of Minnesota Libraries), Martha R. Mahard (Harvard Theatre Collection), Sir Bernard Miles (The Mermaid Theatre, London), Paul B. Myers (Lincoln Center Library and Museum of the Performing Arts), Jeanne Newlin (Harvard Theatre Collection), Sue Rolfe (The Mermaid Theatre, London), Nicholas Rudall (University of Chicago Theatre), Craig Sherfenberg (The Guthrie Theater), Ann Selby (The Stratford Festival, Canada), Dorothy Spellman (American National Theatre Association, New York), Marilyn Sturtridge (Canadian Broadcasting Company, Toronto), Helen Willard (Harvard Theatre Collection), and J. Roland Wilson (The University of Michigan Professional Theater Program).

For their generous help in preparing the manuscript, we are grateful to Dorothy Corder (University of Iowa), Jeff Hopkins (University of Iowa), and Nancy Jones (University of Iowa). And for their expert work in bringing this book into print, we are indebted to all the fine people at John Wiley and Sons, who originally published the book, particularly Elizabeth Doble, Production Supervisor, Malcolm Easterlin, Manager of College Editing, Rafael Hernandez, Assistant Design Director, Geraldine Ivins, Administrative Assistant, Rick

Leyh, College Marketing Manager, Rosemary Wellner, Senior Editor, and above all the two persons who have kept their faith in the project through all the difficulties of bringing it to completion, Thomas O. Gay, Executive Editor, and Clifford Mills, our Sponsoring Editor.

C.H.K.
M.G.
B.S.F.

CONTENTS

RENAISSANCE ENGLISH THEATER 175

NEOCLASSICAL THEATER 381

MODERN THEATER 509

CONTEMPORARY THEATER   781

CLASSICAL GREEK THEATER

During the fifth century B.C., the age of classical Greek drama, the theater in Athens stood empty almost 360 days a year, and yet the theater has probably never commanded quite so much attention as it did in fifth century Athens, the home of classical Greek drama. Drama occupied a unique place in the culture of ancient Athenians, for it was intimately related to one of their most important religious celebrations, and it was vigorously supported by their most powerful political institution. It was, in fact, produced under the auspices of the Athenian government, and during the greater part of the fifth century it was performed only once a year in connection with the *City Dionysia,* the major festival honoring Dionysus, the Greek god of fertility.

Dionysus had for centuries been worshipped in choric rituals known as *dithyrambs,* and these religious ceremonies are thought to be the principal source from which Greek tragedy emerged sometime in the mid-sixth century. It was during this period that Thespis, reputedly the first playwright, added an actor to the dithyrambic chorus, thereby bringing dramatic impersonation into ritual ceremonies that had previously consisted of narrative hymns chanted by a choric leader together with refrains sung and danced by a chorus. The Dionysian heritage of Greek tragedy probably accounts for the special status it achieved at the City Dionysia in 534 B.C., when the Athenian government established a prize, won appropriately by Thespis, for the best tragedy to be presented at the festival. By 486 B.C., when the contest was expanded to include comedy, the City Dionysia had become the most prestigious of the four annual celebrations of Dionysus. Thousands came from everywhere in the Greek world to attend the festival, which was held in late March or early April to insure a fruitful spring. Obviously, theatrical productions constituted a major event in the rhythm of Athenian life, an event uniting the entire community in an expression of its civic pride and sacred convictions.

The magnitude of that event is revealed by the elaborate arrangements connected with the festival productions. The sole responsibility for supervising the contest was entrusted to a state official chosen by lot from the Athenian public. Dramatists who wished to enter the contest were required to submit their plays to him almost a year in advance of the festival, and he chose the three tragic as well as the three comic playwrights who had the honor of competing for each prize. This official also appointed wealthy citizens to serve as producers for each contestant, and these citizens financed the training and costuming of the chorus, the largest and most complex element of Greek theater. The balance of the costs, such as salaries for the actors and prizes for the winners, was paid by the government of Athens. This dramatic festival was the climax of nearly a year of activity on the part of hundreds of Athenian citizens.

The contest was preceded by a splendid public ceremony, featuring a lengthy procession of officials, priests, theatrical sponsors, and citizens who carried ritual offerings that they presented at the altar of Dionysus located in the theater. Once the contest began, it ran for three days, starting early in the morning and continuing throughout the afternoon. Each tragic dramatist needed almost an entire day to produce the three or four plays he was required to submit, and the remainder of each day was taken up by a single comedy each comic dramatist was required to submit. During those three days, the city of Athens became the center of a spectacular drama festival at which a total of twelve to fifteen new plays were produced.

The climax of the contest, when the prizes were awarded, was a moment of extraordinary honor for the winning dramatist and his producer. This honor was so important that the contest was judged by a panel of citizens chosen according to a very elaborate procedure that prevented bribery or any other form of unfair influence on their decision. The honor was so prestigious, in fact, that the government maintained records of all the contests, and many of the producers in turn commissioned monuments to be built as enduring records of their victories. By the middle of the fifth century, prizes had also been established for actors, and the profession of acting came to be so highly regarded that eminent actors were frequently given special public appointments and privileges. Classical Greek drama was neither a commercial enterprise as it is on Broadway, nor a coterie activity as it so often is off Broadway. It was a major public institution commanding the respect and support of the entire city-state.

The prestige of the dramatic contest was matched by the magnitude of the theater where it took place, the Theater of Dionysus, which was a sanctuary restricted to worship and celebration of the god. The design of this theater (see Figures 1 and 2), like the drama performed there, reflected its ritual origin. Its central element was the *orchestra* (literally, the dancing place), a circular area sixty-four feet in diameter where the dithyrambic choruses had performed their hymns to Dionysus and where the altar of Dionysus, the *thymele,* retained its focal location. The *orchestra* was surrounded by the *theatron* (literally, the seeing place), a semicircular sloping hillside that was terraced and equipped with benches capable of seating approximately 15,000 spectators. Facing the *theatron* was the *skene* (literally, the hut), which probably originated as a temporary dressing room for actors and then developed into a scenic structure possibly one-hundred feet long, with three openings on to the *orchestra,* wings projecting toward the *orchestra,* and a slightly raised stage-like platform extending between the wings. Though the theater was frequently remodelled, its basic three-part structure—*theatron, orchestra,* and *skene*—was never altered and, in fact, served as the pattern for others in the ancient Greek world. The classical simplicity of that structure and the magnitude of its parts are unparalleled in the history of the theater.

The 15,000 people who attended the Theater of Dionysus were treated to a unique dramatic spectacle—a spectacle perfectly suited to the size, shape, and ceremonial heritage of that theater. For example, the typical Greek play whether tragedy or comedy contained not only units of dramatic action, known as episodes, but also choral odes following each episode. The performance included not only dialogue and action, but also song and dance that amplified the mood and significance of the action. The chorus typically made its entrance, the *parados,* after a brief expository episode, the *prologos,* and the *parados* must have been a splendid event, for the members of the chorus, using either the stately

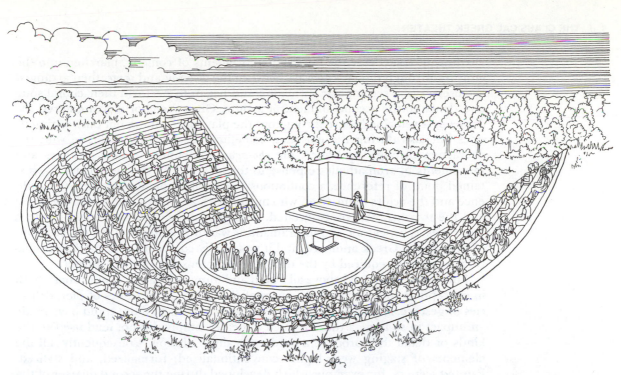

Figure 1. The classical Greek theater.

Figure 2. The classical Greek theater at Epidaurus, in its restored state, during a production of *Agamemnon* by the National Theatre Company of Greece, 1965. (Photograph: D.A. Harissiadis.)

rhythms of tragedy or the burlesque movements of comedy, marched into the *orchestra* through the passageways between the *theatron* and *skene,* then arranged themselves in a rectangular formation and began to perform their choral song and dance to the accompaniment of a flute. Once the chorus had entered the *orchestra,* it remained there throughout the play, performing not only during its odes but also during the episodes, sometimes exchanging dialogue with the characters through its leader, the *choragos,* sometimes making gestures and movements in sympathetic response to the action. The chorus provided a sustained point of reference, a continuous source of mediation between the audience and the actors themselves, who moved back and forth between the *orchestra* and the *skene* as their parts dictated. Although the chorus may strike modern audiences as unrealistic and undramatic, it was in keeping with the expectations of the ancient Greek audience, and it was totally consistent with the ceremonial form of drama required by the design and dimensions of their theater.

This theater required above all a bold and monumental form of drama—both in conception and execution. Nuances of character, complexities of plot, delicacies of gesture, subtleties of inflection—none of these qualities could have made an impact in so large a theater. Such a theater simply did not lend itself to the kinds of detail that produce a modern realistic illusion. Consequently, all the elements of staging were highly conventionalized, formalized, and stylized. Painted scenery, for example, which developed during the second quarter of the fifth century, probably consisted only of a few generalized locales, such as a palace, a temple, a cave, or a forest, represented on the areas between the entrances to the *skene.* Only a few props or machines were available to assist the imagination of the audience, such as a crane by which characters might be suspended as if in flight from the roof of the *skene,* or a tableau wheeled out of the *skene* to suggest offstage action, or a horse-drawn chariot wheeled into the *orchestra* to mark the arrival of a hero, or a torch held up to signify nighttime— props and machines, which, like the painted scenes, were capable of making a clear visual impact.

Actors also required special techniques and equipment. They made large gestures with their arms, for small movements of the hands would have been indetectable by the audience. They also delivered their lines with a clear and strong inflection; no matter how good the acoustics may have been, the actors still had to contend with sounds in the audience, and 15,000 people even when they are trying to be quiet can generate a great deal of noise. Because facial movements would have been invisible to almost everyone in the audience, the actors wore large stylized masks representing basic character types and, as their fortunes and emotions changed, they changed their masks to suit the situation. No doubt their costumes were also designed to accentuate their stature, to make them appear larger than life. In fact, after the fifth century, actors were even equipped with elevated shoes to increase the impression of their height. The chorus also wore masks and probably used lightweight costumes and shoes to facilitate the various dance movements it performed while singing choral odes. Taken as a whole—the choric singing and dancing, the simplified setting, the bold acting—dramatic productions in ancient Greece must have matched the epic dimensions of the theater and of the plays that were written for it by Aeschylus, Sophocles, Euripides, and Aristophanes.

AESCHYLUS

ca. 524—456 B.C.

The tragedies of Aeschylus are the oldest works of Greek drama, and thus of western drama, that have survived. Although they date from the early period of Greek drama, they are by no means primitive either in conception or execution. Aeschylus, in fact, is generally credited with transforming the semidramatic elements he inherited from his predecessors into an authentically dramatic form, and he is, therefore, regarded as having created the structure and style of classical Greek tragedy. He was born near Athens less than ten years after the inauguration of the dramatic contests, which he entered for the first time in 499, but did not win until 484. Subsequently, however, he was so successful and influential a dramatist in Athens that he was honored after his death by an exceptional decree of the state permitting his plays to be revived in the festival contests. He won the contest thirteen times during his life, and after his death he continued to win prizes even though his plays were competing with new works by living dramatists. He reportedly wrote more than ninety plays, and the titles of seventy-nine have been recovered from Athenian records, but only seven of his tragedies have survived.

These seven plays reveal a comprehensive vision of experience, for their action always takes into account not simply the lives of individual men and women but also the destinies of entire families, communities, nations, and sometimes even cosmic forces. In *The Persians* (472), for example, which is the earliest of his extant plays and the only one based completely on historical experience, Aeschylus shows the majestic suffering in defeat of those people who only a few years earlier had invaded Greece and threatened to replace Athenian democracy with Persian tyranny. In *Prometheus Bound* (ca. 460), he dramatizes a cosmic experience, a conflict between the gods, represented by the defiant refusal of Prometheus, though chained to a desolate mountain and threatened with endless torture, to give in to the will of Zeus.

Events and conflicts of a Promethean magnitude could not have been worked out within the limits of a single play. Thus it is not surprising that Aeschylus developed and perfected the trilogy, for its grand scope—three full length plays joined to one another by their treatment of a single subject or theme—was ideally suited to his cosmic view of experience. His only surviving trilogy is *The Oresteia* (458), but it exemplifies the large-scale movements through time and space that are possible within the form. The three plays that make up this trilogy—*Agamemnon, The Libation Bearers,* and *The Eumenides*—dramatize a synoptic history of cultural progress, a history encompassing two generations of a family, during which men and the gods are shown advancing from a barbaric to a civilized form of justice, from the personal vengeance enacted in *Agamemnon* and *The Libation Bearers* to the public trial by jury conducted in *The Eumenides.* Drama so large in scope had not been attempted before Aeschylus, but since his time the trilogy and other multiplay structures have been used by many dramatists, such as Shakespeare in *Henry VI,* Eugene O'Neill in *Mourning Becomes Electra,* which is based on *The Oresteia,* and Ed Bullins in *The Twentieth Century Cycle.*

Aeschylus could never have achieved the dramatic power of his trilogies, or even of the individual plays that constitute them, had he limited himself to the rudimentary theatrical elements he inherited from Thespis: a chorus and a single actor. Given these conditions, tragedy before the time of Aeschylus must have been heavily dominated by the chorus, punctuated occasionally by the single actor impersonating a character and reciting a set speech or exchanging a few lines with the leader of the chorus. But early in his career, as early certainly as *The Persians,* Aeschylus made the revolutionary and dramatically essential innovation of using a second actor. Aeschylus thus made it possible to show characters interacting with one another, as well as with the chorus. He could then dramatize conflict and through conflict show character in action and plot in motion. In his later plays, such as *Agamemnon,* Aeschylus followed the precedent of Sophocles and used three actors.

Once it became possible to represent multiple characters, it was only a matter of time before the actors became as important as the chorus, then more important, then solely important. Aeschylus never went beyond the first stage in this process, for in his plays the chorus continues to have an important dramatic role, not only observing events and meditating on them, but also interacting continuously with the characters, questioning them, prodding them, rebuking them, praising them—taking part in events as they take place. In Aeschylean drama the chorus is not a minor or detachable element. In *Agamemnon,* in fact, the chorus has nearly as many lines as the characters, and without the chorus the play would be only an abbreviated melodrama, consisting of a few sensational incidents from the aftermath of the Trojan War.

Although *Agamemnon* is the first play of a trilogy, it stands alone as a consummately tragic expression of the cultural issues resolved by the remaining two plays. Its plot, as in all the plays of Aeschylus, is remarkably spare and simple, consisting of a few bold events—the return of Agamemnon with Cassandra and the slaying of them by Clytemnestra and Aegisthus. From all the events of the Trojan War, from all the stories about Agamemnon, his ancestors, and his children, Aeschylus chooses to dramatize only the events of a single day. But through the dialogue and lyrical reflections of the chorus, these events are made to symbolize an enduring problem in the life of Agamemnon, his ancestors, his country, and his world—the problem of vengeance, that primitive form of justice, which, rather than ending crime, endlessly renews it. The cyclical nature of revenge is discovered and expressed by the chorus, which repeatedly makes the past vividly present in its recollections—of "hearts howling in boundless bloodlust," of "a war for a runaway wife," of "a virgin's blood upon the altar," of "barbarous building of hates and disloyalties grown on the family." In mingling reflection with memory, the chorus seeks both to justify revenge and to find moral alternatives to it. Through its wavering attitude, its dilemma, its repeated questionings, rememberings, and meditations, the chorus becomes a character in its own right, as dramatically compelling as Agamemnon with all his grandeur and pride, or Clytemnestra with all her bitterness and hate, or Cassandra with all her foresight and all her helplessness.

These characters and the stories about them were, of course, standard items of

Greek legend, readily available to Aeschylus and totally familiar to all the members of his audience. Homer had told about them several hundred years earlier, and his tales had been retold by a long line of Greek poets and storytellers, but those stories took on a strikingly new meaning in the hands of Aeschylus. Just how new (and how different) can be seen by comparing the way that Agamemnon is viewed in Homer's *Odyssey* with the way he is represented in the work of Aeschylus. Whereas Homer had presented Agamemnon as a completely sympathetic character, Aeschylus shows him to be a morally ambiguous character. Their differing conceptions of Agamemnon are, at last, the consequence of their differing ideas of justice. Vengeance, which Homer takes for granted, Aeschylus calls into question.

Because it raises such large questions about the conduct of men, of families, of communities, of nations—and because neither men, nor families, nor communities, nor nations conduct themselves much differently now from the way they have for thousands of years—*Agamemnon* remains a perennially compelling play, a permanently tragic statement about the condition of things. In conjunction with the other two plays that make up *The Oresteia,* it offers actors and directors an extraordinary theatrical challenge, for its grand scope calls for a correspondingly grand form of staging. Grandness, of course, is difficult to achieve within the intimate space of most contemporary theaters, not to mention the naturalistic style of much contemporary acting. But modern productions of *The Oresteia* have sought to meet this challenge either by staging the work in a classical Greek theater (see Figures 2 and 3), or by performing it in costumes, masks, and styles of acting modelled on classical Greek practices (see Figures 4 and 5). Judging from photographs and reviews of these performances, the heroic theater of Aeschylus can be reclaimed, or at least approximated, even in an unheroic age.

AGAMEMNON

BY AESCHYLUS / TRANSLATED BY LOUIS MACNEICE

CHARACTERS*

- WATCHMAN
- CHORUS OF OLD MEN OF THE CITY
- CLYTEMNESTRA
- HERALD
- AGAMEMNON
- CASSANDRA
- AEGISTHUS

SCENE

A space in front of the palace of Agamemnon in Argos. Night. A WATCHMAN *on the roof of the palace.*

WATCHMAN: The gods it is I ask to release me from this watch
A year's length now, spending my nights like a dog,
Watching on my elbow on the roof of the sons of Atreus
So that I have come to know the assembly of the nightly stars

*THE FAMILY TREE

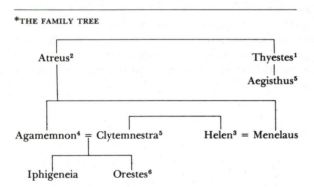

THE CHAIN OF CRIMES

The chain of crimes in this play is as follows (see Family Tree above):

Past
(1) Thyestes seduced Atreus' wife.
(2) Atreus killed Thyestes' young children and gave him them as meat.
(3) Helen forsook her husband and went to Troy with Paris.
(4) Agamemnon, to promote the Trojan War, sacrificed his daughter Iphigeneia.

Present.
(5) Aegisthus and Clytemnestra murder Agamemnon.

Future.
(6) Orestes will kill Aegisthus and his mother Clytemnestra.

Those which bring storm and those which bring summer to men,
The shining Masters riveted in the sky—   10
I know the decline and rising of those stars.
And now I am waiting for the sign of the beacon,
The flame of fire that will carry the report from Troy,
News of her taking. Which task has been assigned me
By a woman of sanguine heart but a man's mind.
Yet when I take my restless rest in the soaking dew,
My night not visited with dreams—   20
For fear stands by me in the place of sleep
That I cannot firmly close my eyes in sleep—
Whenever I think to sing or hum to myself
As an antidote to sleep, then every time I groan
And fall to weeping for the fortunes of this house
Where not as before are things well ordered now.
But now may a good chance fall, escape from pain,
The good news visible in the midnight fire.

(Pause. A light appears, gradually increasing, the light of the beacon.)

Ha! I salute you, torch of the night whose light
Is like the day, an earnest of many dances   30
In the city of Argos, celebration of Peace.
I call to Agamemnon's wife; quickly to rise
Out of her bed and in the house to raise
Clamour of joy in answer to this torch
For the city of Troy is taken—
Such is the evident message of the beckoning flame.
And I myself will dance my solo first
For I shall count my master's fortune mine
Now that this beacon has thrown me a lucky throw.   40
And may it be when he comes, the master of this house,
That I grasp his hand in my hand.
As to the rest, I am silent. A great ox, as they say,
Stands on my tongue. The house itself, if it took voice,

8

Could tell the case most clearly. But I will only speak
To those who know. For the others I remember
50 nothing.

(Enter CHORUS OF OLD MEN. *During the following chorus the day begins to dawn.)*

CHORUS: The tenth year it is since Priam's high
Adversary, Menelaus the king
And Agamemnon, the double-throned and
      sceptred
Yoke of the sons of Atreus
Ruling in fee from God,
From this land gathered an Argive army
On a mission of war a thousand ships,
Their hearts howling in boundless bloodlust
60 In eagles' fashion who in lonely
Grief for nestlings above their homes hang
Turning in cycles
Beating the air with the oars of their wings,
      Now to no purpose
      Their love and task of attention.

But above there is One,
Maybe Pan, maybe Zeus or Apollo,
Who cries the harsh cries of the birds
Guests in his kingdom,
70 Wherefore, though late, in requital
He sends the Avenger.
Thus Zeus our master
Guardian of guest and of host
Sent against Paris the sons of Atreus
For a woman of many men
Many the dog-tired wrestlings
Limbs and knees in the dust pressed—
      For both the Greeks and Trojans
      An overture of breaking spears.

80 Things are where they are, will finish
In the manner fated and neither
Fire beneath nor oil above can soothe
The stubborn anger of the unburnt offering.
As for us, our bodies are bankrupt,
The expedition left us behind
And we wait supporting on sticks
Our strength—the strength of a child;
For the marrow that leaps in a boy's body
Is no better than that of the old
90 For the War God is not in his body;
While the man who is very old
And his leaf withering away
Goes on the three-foot way
No better than a boy, and wanders
A dream in the middle of the day.

But you, daughter of Tyndareus,
Queen Clytemnestra,

What is the news, what is the truth, what have you
      learnt,
On the strength of whose word have you thus   100
Sent orders for sacrifice round?
All the gods, the gods of the town,
Of the worlds of Below and Above,
By the door, in the square,
Have their altars ablaze with your gifts,
From here, from there, all sides, all corners,
Sky-high leap the flame-jets fed
By gentle and undeceiving
Persuasion of sacred unguent,
Oil from the royal stores.   110
Of these things tell
That which you can, that which you may,
Be healer of this our trouble
Which at times torments with evil
Though at times by propitiations
A shining hope repels
The insatiable thought upon grief
Which is eating away our hearts.

Of the omen which powerfully speeded
That voyage of strong men, by God's grace even I   120
Can tell, my age can still
Be galvanized to breathe the strength of song,
To tell how the kings of all the youth of Greece
Two-throned but one in mind
Were launched with pike and punitive hand
Against the Trojan shore by angry birds.
Kings of the birds to our kings came,
One with a white rump, the other black,
Appearing near the palace on the spear-arm side
Where all could see them,   130
Tearing a pregnant hare with the unborn young
Foiled of their courses.
      Cry, cry upon Death; but may the good prevail.

But the diligent prophet of the army seeing the
      sons
Of Atreus twin in temper knew
That the hare-killing birds were the two
Generals, explained it thus—
'In time this expedition sacks the town
Of Troy before whose towers   140
By Fate's force the public
Wealth will be wasted.
Only let not some spite from the gods benight the
      bulky battalions,
The bridle of Troy, nor strike them untimely;
For the goddess feels pity, is angry
With the winged dogs of her father
Who killed the cowering hare with her unborn
      young;
Artemis hates the eagles' feast.'   150
      Cry, cry upon Death; but may the good prevail.

'But though you are so kind, goddess,
To the little cubs of lions
And to all the sucking young of roving beasts
In whom your heart delights,
Fulfil us the signs of these things,
The signs which are good but open to blame,
And I call on Apollo the Healer
That his sister raise not against the Greeks
160 Unremitting gales to baulk their ships,
Hurrying on another kind of sacrifice, with no
      feasting,
Barbarous building of hates and disloyalties
Grown on the family. For anger grimly returns
Cunningly haunting the house, avenging the death
      of a child, never forgetting its due.'
So cried the prophet—evil and good together,
Fate that the birds foretold to the king's house.
In tune with this
170   Cry, cry upon Death; but may the good prevail.

Zeus, whoever He is, if this
Be a name acceptable,
By this name I will call him.
There is no one comparable
When I reckon all of the case
Excepting Zeus, if ever I am to jettison
The barren care which clogs my heart.

Not He who formerly was great
With brawling pride and mad for broils
180 Will even be said to have been.
And He who was next has met
His match and is seen no more,
But Zeus is the name to cry in your triumph-song
And win the prize for wisdom.

Who setting us on the road
Made this a valid law—
   'That men must learn by suffering.'
Drop by drop in sleep upon the heart
Falls the laborious memory of pain,
190 Against one's will comes wisdom;
The grace of the gods is forced on us
   Throned inviolably.

So at that time the elder
Chief of the Greek ships
Would not blame any prophet
Nor face the flail of fortune;
For unable to sail, the people
Of Greece were heavy with famine,
Waiting in Aulis where the tides
200   Flow back, opposite Chalcis.

But the winds that blew from the Strymon,
Bringing delay, hunger, evil harbourage,
Crazing men, rotting ships and cables,
By drawing out the time

Were shredding into nothing the flower of Argos,
When the prophet screamed a new
Cure for that bitter tempest
And heavier still for the chiefs,
Pleading the anger of Artemis so that the sons of
      Atreus   210
Beat the ground with their sceptres and shed tears.

Then the elder king found voice and answered:
'Heavy is my fate, not obeying,
And heavy it is if I kill my child, the delight of my
      house,
And with a virgin's blood upon the altar
Make foul her father's hands.
Either alternative is evil.
How can I betray the fleet
And fail the allied army?   220
It is right they should passionately cry for the winds
      to be lulled
By the blood of a girl. So be it. May it be well.'

But when he had put on the halter of Necessity
Breathing in his heart a veering wind of evil
Unsanctioned, unholy, from that moment forward
He changed his counsel, would stop at nothing.
For the heart of man is hardened by infatuation,
A faulty adviser, the first link of sorrow.
Whatever the cause, he brought himself to slay   230
His daughter, an offering to promote the voyage
To a war for a runaway wife.

Her prayers and her cries of father,
Her life of a maiden,
Counted for nothing with those militarists;
But her father, having duly prayed, told the
      attendants
To lift her, like a goat, above the altar
With her robes falling about her,
To lift her boldly, her spirit fainting,   240
And hold back with a gag upon her lovely mouth
By the dumb force of a bridle
The cry which would curse the house.

Then dropping on the ground her saffron dress,
Glancing at each of her appointed
Sacrificers a shaft of pity,
Plain as in a picture she wished
To speak to them by name, for often
At her father's table where men feasted
She had sung in celebration for her father   250
With a pure voice, affectionately, virginally,
The hymn for happiness at the third libation.

The sequel to this I saw not and tell not
But the crafts of Calchas gained their object.
To learn by suffering is the equation of Justice; the
      Future
Is known when it comes, let it go till then.

To know in advance is sorrow in advance.
The facts will appear with the shining of the dawn.

(*Enter* CLYTEMNESTRA.)

260 But may good, at the least, follow after
As the queen here wishes, who stands
Nearest the throne, the only
Defence of the land of Argos.

LEADER OF THE CHORUS: I have come, Clytemnestra,
reverencing your authority.
For it is right to honour our master's wife
When the man's own throne is empty.
But you, if you have heard good news for certain,
or if
270 You sacrifice on the strength of flattering hopes,
I would gladly hear. Though I cannot cavil at
silence.
CLYTEMNESTRA: Bearing good news, as the proverb
says, may Dawn
Spring from her mother Night.
You will hear something now that was beyond your
hopes.
The men of Argos have taken Priam's city.
LEADER OF THE CHORUS: What! I cannot believe it. It
280 escapes me.
CLYTEMNESTRA: Troy in the hands of the Greeks. Do
I speak plain?
LEADER OF THE CHORUS: Joy creeps over me, calling
out my tears.
CLYTEMNESTRA: Yes. Your eyes proclaim your loyalty.
LEADER OF THE CHORUS: But what are your grounds?
Have you a proof of it?
CLYTEMNESTRA: There is proof indeed—unless God
has cheated us.
290 LEADER OF THE CHORUS: Perhaps you believe the
inveigling shapes of dreams?
CLYTEMNESTRA: I would not be credited with a dozing
brain!
LEADER OF THE CHORUS: Or are you puffed up by
Rumour, the wingless flyer?
CLYTEMNESTRA: You mock my common sense as if I
were a child.
LEADER OF THE CHORUS: But at what time was the city
given to sack?
300 CLYTEMNESTRA: In this very night that gave birth to
this day.
LEADER OF THE CHORUS: What messenger could come
so fast?
CLYTEMNESTRA: Hephaestus, launching a fine flame
from Ida,
Beacon forwarding beacon, despatch-riders of fire,
Ida relayed to Hermes' cliff in Lemnos
And the great glow from the island was taken over
third
310 By the height of Athos that belongs to Zeus,
And towering then to straddle over the sea
The might of the running torch joyfully tossed

The gold gleam forward like another sun,
Herald of light to the heights of Mount Macistus,
And he without delay, nor carelessly by sleep
Encumbered, did not shirk his intermediary role,
His farflung ray reached the Euripus' tides
And told Messapion's watchers, who in turn
Sent on the message further
Setting a stack of dried-up heather on fire. 320
And the strapping flame, not yet enfeebled, leapt
Over the plain of Asopus like a blazing moon
And woke on the crags of Cithaeron
Another relay in the chain of fire.
The light that was sent from far was not declined
By the look-out men, who raised a fiercer yet,
A light which jumped the water of Gorgopis
And to Mount Aegiplanctus duly come
Urged the reveille of the punctual fire.
So then they kindle it squanderingly and launch 330
A beard of flame big enough to pass
The headland that looks down upon the Saronic
gulf,
Blazing and bounding till it reached at length
The Arachnaean steep, our neighbouring heights;
And leaps in the latter end on the roof of the sons
of Atreus
Issue and image of the fire on Ida.
Such was the assignment of my torch-racers,
The task of each fulfilled by his successor, 340
And victor is he who ran both first and last.
Such is the proof I offer you, the sign
My husband sent me out of Troy.
LEADER OF THE CHORUS: To the gods, queen, I shall
give thanks presently.
But I would like to hear this story further,
To wonder at it in detail from your lips.
CLYTEMNESTRA: The Greeks hold Troy upon this
day.
The cries in the town I fancy do not mingle. 350
Pour oil and vinegar into the same jar,
You would say they stand apart unlovingly;
Of those who are captured and those who have
conquered
Distinct are the sounds of their diverse fortunes,
For *these* having flung themselves about the bodies
Of husbands and brothers, or sons upon the bodies
Of aged fathers from a throat no longer
Free, lament the fate of their most loved.
But *those* a night's marauding after battle 360
Sets hungry to what breakfast the town offers
Not billeted duly in any barracks order
But as each man has drawn his lot of luck.
So in the captive homes of Troy already
They take their lodging, free of the frosts
And dews of the open. Like happy men
They will sleep all night without sentry.
But if they respect duly the city's gods,
Those of the captured land and the sanctuaries of
the gods, 370

They need not, having conquered, fear reconquest.
But let no lust fall first upon the troops
To plunder what is not right, subdued by gain,
For they must still, in order to come home safe,
Get round the second lap of the doubled course.
So if they return without offence to the gods
The grievance of the slain may learn at last
A friendly talk—unless some fresh wrong falls.
Such are the thoughts you hear from me, a woman.
380 But may the good prevail for all to see.
We have much good. I only ask to enjoy it.
LEADER OF THE CHORUS: Woman, you speak with
    sense like a prudent man.
I, who have heard your valid proofs, prepare
To give the glory to God.
Fair recompense is brought us for our troubles.

(CLYTEMNESTRA *goes back into the palace.*)

CHORUS: O Zeus our king and Night our friend
    Donor of glories;
    Night who cast on the towers of Troy
390 A close-clinging net so that neither the grown
    Nor any of the children can pass
    The enslaving and huge
    Trap of all-taking destruction.
Great Zeus, guardian and host and guest,
I honour who has done his work and taken
A leisured aim at Paris so that neither
Too short nor yet over the stars
    He might shoot to no purpose.

From Zeus is the blow they can tell of,
400 This at least can be established,
They have fared according to his ruling. For some
Deny that the gods deign to consider those among
    men
Who trample on the grace of inviolate things;
It is the impious man says this,
For Ruin is revealed the child
Of not to be attempted actions
When men are puffed up unduly
And their houses are stuffed with riches.
410 Measure is the best. Let danger be distant,
This should suffice a man
With a proper part of wisdom.
    For a man has no protection
    Against the drunkenness of riches
    Once he has spurned from his sight
    The high altar of Justice.

Sombre Persuasion compels him,
Intolerable child of calculating Doom;
All cure is vain, there is no glozing it over
420 But the mischief shines forth with a deadly light
And like bad coinage
By rubbings and frictions
He stands discoloured and black

Under the test—like a boy
Who chases a winged bird.
He has branded his city for ever.
His prayers are heard by no god.
Who makes such things his practice
The gods destroy him.
    This way came Paris   430
    To the house of the sons of Atreus
    And outraged the table of friendship
    Stealing the wife of his host.

Leaving to her countrymen clanging of
Shields and of spears and
Launching of warships
And bringing instead of a dowry destruction to
    Troy
Lightly she was gone through the gates daring
Things undared. Many the groans   440
Of the palace spokesmen on this theme—
'O the house, the house, and its princes,
O the bed and the imprint of her limbs;
One can see him crouching in silence
Dishonoured and unreviling.'
Through desire for her who is overseas, a ghost
Will seem to rule the household.
    And now her husband hates
    The grace of shapely statues;
    In the emptiness of their eyes   450
    All their appeal is departed.

But appearing in dreams persuasive
Images come bringing a joy that is vain,
Vain for when in fancy he looks to touch her—
Slipping through his hands the vision
Rapidly is gone
Following on wings the walks of sleep.
Such are his griefs in his house on his hearth,
Such as these and worse than these,
But everywhere through the land of Greece which   460
    men have left
Are mourning women with enduring hearts
To be seen in all houses; many
Are the thoughts which stab their hearts;
    For those they sent to war
    They know, but in place of men
    That which comes home to them
    Is merely an urn and ashes.

But the money-changer War, changer of bodies,
Holding his balance in the battle   470
Home from Troy refined by fire
Sends back to friends the dust
That is heavy with tears, stowing
A man's worth of ashes
In an easily handled jar.
And they wail speaking well of the men how that
    one

Was expert in battle, and one fell well in the
 carnage—
480 But for another man's wife.
Muffled and muttered words;
And resentful grief creeps up against the sons
Of Atreus and their cause.
 But others there by the wall
 Entombed in Trojan ground
 Lie, handsome of limb,
 Holding and hidden in enemy soil.

Heavy is the murmur of an angry people
Performing the purpose of a public curse;
490 There is something cowled in the night
That I anxiously wait to hear.
For the gods are not blind to the
Murderers of many and the black
Furies in time
When a man prospers in sin
By erosion of life reduce him to darkness,
Who, once among the lost, can no more
Be helped. Over-great glory
Is a sore burden. The high peak
500 Is blasted by the eys of Zeus.
 I prefer an unenvied fortune,
 Not to be a sacker of cities
 Nor to find myself living at another's
 Ruling, myself a captive.

AN OLD MAN: From the good news' beacon a swift
 Rumour is gone through the town.
 Who knows if it be true
 Or some deceit of the gods?
ANOTHER OLD MAN: Who is so childish or broken in
510 wit
 To kindle his heart at a new-fangled message of
 flame
 And then be downcast
 At a change of report?
ANOTHER OLD MAN: It fits the temper of a woman
 To give her assent to a story before it is proved.
ANOTHER OLD MAN: The over-credulous passion of
 women expands
 In swift conflagration but swiftly declining is gone
520 The news that a woman announced.
LEADER OF THE CHORUS: Soon we shall know about
 the illuminant torches,
 The beacons and the fiery relays,
 Whether they were true or whether like dreams
 That pleasant light came here and hoaxed our wits.
 Look: I see, coming from the beach, a herald
 Shadowed with olive shoots; the dust upon him,
 Mud's thirsty sister and colleague, is my witness
 That he will not give dumb news nor news by
530 lighting
 A flame of fire with the smoke of mountain timber;
 In words he will either corroborate our joy—

But the opposite version I reject with horror.
To the good appeared so far may good be added.
ANOTHER SPEAKER: Whoever makes other prayers for
 this our city,
 May he reap himself the fruits of his wicked heart.

(Enter the HERALD, *who kisses the ground before speaking.)*

HERALD: Earth of my fathers, O the earth of Argos,
 In the light of the tenth year I reach you thus
 After many shattered hopes achieving one,   540
 For never did I dare to think that here in Argive
 land
 I should win a grave in the dearest soil of home;
 But now hail, land, and hail, light of the sun,
 And Zeus high above the country and the Pythian
 king—
 May he no longer shoot his arrows at us
 (Implacable long enough beside Scamander)
 But now be saviour to us and be healer,
 King Apollo. And all the Assembly's gods   550
 I call upon, and him my patron, Hermes,
 The dear herald whom all heralds adore,
 And the Heroes who sped our voyage, again with
 favour
 Take back the army that has escaped the spear.
 O cherished dwelling, palace of royalty,
 O august thrones and gods facing the sun,
 If ever before, now with your bright eyes
 Gladly receive your king after much time,
 Who comes bringing light to you in the night time, 560
 And to all these as well—King Agamemnon.
 Give him a good welcome as he deserves,
 Who with the axe of judgment-awarding God
 Has smashed Troy and levelled the Trojan land;
 The altars are destroyed, the seats of the gods,
 And the seed of all the land is perished from it.
 Having cast this halter round the neck of Troy
 The King, the elder son of Atreus, a blessed man,
 Comes, the most worthy to have honour of all
 Men that are now. Paris nor his guilty city   570
 Can boast that the crime was greater than the
 atonement.
 Convicted in a suit for rape and robbery
 He has lost his stolen goods and with consummate
 ruin
 Mowed down the whole country and his father's
 house.
 The sons of Priam have paid their account with
 interest.
LEADER OF THE CHORUS: Hail and be glad, herald of 580
 the Greek army.
HERALD: Yes. Glad indeed! So glad that at the god's
 demand
 I should no longer hesitate to die.
LEADER OF THE CHORUS: Were you so harrowed by
 desire for home?

HERALD: Yes. The tears come to my eyes for joy.

LEADER OF THE CHORUS: Sweet then is the fever which afflicts you.

590 HERALD: What do you mean? Let me learn your drift.

LEADER OF THE CHORUS: Longing for those whose love came back in echo.

HERALD: Meaning the land was homesick for the army?

LEADER OF THE CHORUS: Yes. I would often groan from a darkened heart.

HERALD: This sullen hatred—how did it fasten on you?

LEADER OF THE CHORUS: I cannot say. Silence is my
600 stock prescription.

HERALD: What? In your masters' absence were there some you feared?

LEADER OF THE CHORUS: Yes. In your phrase, death would now be a gratification.

HERALD: Yes, for success is ours. These things have taken time.

Some of them we could say have fallen well,
While some we blame. Yet who except the gods
Is free from pain the whole duration of life?
610 If I were to tell of our labours, our hard lodging,
The sleeping on crowded decks, the scanty blankets,
Tossing and groaning, rations that never reached us—
And the land too gave matter for more disgust,
For our beds lay under the enemy's walls.
Continuous drizzle from the sky, dews from the marshes,
Rotting our clothes, filling our hair with lice.
620 And if one were to tell of the bird-destroying winter
Intolerable from the snows of Ida
Or of the heat when the sea slackens at noon
Waveless and dozing in a depressed calm—
But why make these complaints? The weariness is over;
Over indeed for some who never again
Need even trouble to rise.
Why make a computation of the lost?
630 Why need the living sorrow for the spites of fortune?
I wish to say a long goodbye to disasters.
For us, the remnant of the troops of Argos,
The advantage remains, the pain can not outweigh it;
So we can make our boast to this sun's light,
Flying on words above the land and sea:
'Having taken Troy the Argive expedition
Has nailed up throughout Greece in every temple
640 These spoils, these ancient trophies.'
Those who hear such things must praise the city
And the generals. And the grace of God be honoured

Which brought these things about. You have the whole story.

LEADER OF THE CHORUS: I confess myself convinced by your report.
Old men are always young enough to learn.

(Enter CLYTEMNESTRA from the palace.)

This news belongs by right first to the house
And Clytemnestra—though I am enriched also. 650

CLYTEMNESTRA: Long before I shouted at joy's command
At the coming of the first night-messenger of fire
Announcing the taking and capsizing of Troy.
And people reproached me saying, 'Do mere beacons
Persuade you to think that Troy is already down?
Indeed a woman's heart is easily exalted.'
Such comments made me seem to be wandering but yet 660
I began my sacrifices and in the women's fashion
Throughout the town they raised triumphant cries
And in the gods' enclosures
Lulling the fragrant, incense-eating flame.
And now what need is there for you to tell me more?
From the King himself I shall learn the whole story.
But how the best to welcome my honoured lord
I shall take pains when he comes back—For what
Is a kinder light for a woman to see than this, 670
To open the gates to her man come back from war
When God has saved him? Tell this to my husband,

To come with all speed, the city's darling;
May he returning find a wife as loyal
As when he left her, watchdog of the house,
Good to *him* but fierce to the ill-intentioned,
And in all other things as ever, having destroyed
No seal or pledge at all in the length of time,
I know no pleasure with another man, no scandal,
More than I know how to dye metal red. 680
Such is my boast, bearing a load of truth,
A boast that need not disgrace a noble wife.

(Exit.)

LEADER OF THE CHORUS: Thus has she spoken; if you take her meaning,
Only a specious tale to shrewd interpreters.
But do you, herald, tell me; I ask after Menelaus
Whether he will, returning safe preserved,
Come back with you, our land's loved master.

HERALD: I am not able to speak the lovely falsehood
To profit you, my friends, for any stretch of time. 690

LEADER OF THE CHORUS: But if only the true tidings could be also good!
It is hard to hide a division of good and true.

HERALD: The prince is vanished out of the Greek fleet,

Himself and ship. I speak no lie.
LEADER OF THE CHORUS: Did he put forth first in the
    sight of all from Troy,
    Or a storm that troubled all sweep him apart?
700 HERALD: You have hit the target like a master archer,
    Told succinctly a long tale of sorrow.
LEADER OF THE CHOURS: Did the rumours current
    among the remaining ships
    Represent him as alive or dead?
HERALD: No one knows so as to tell for sure
    Except the sun who nurses the breeds of earth.
LEADER OF THE CHORUS: Tell me how the storm came
    on the host of ships
    Through the divine anger, and how it ended.
710 HERALD: Day of good news should not be fouled by
    tongue
    That tells ill news. To each god his season.
    When, despair in his face, a messenger brings to a
    town
    The hated news of a fallen army—
    One general wound to the city and many men
    Outcast, outcursed, from many homes
    By the double whip which War is fond of,
    Doom with a bloody spear in either hand,
720   One carrying such a pack of grief could well
    Recite this hymn of the Furies at your asking.
    But when our cause is saved and a messenger of
    good
    Comes to a city glad with festivity,
    How am I to mix good news with bad, recounting
    The storm that meant God's anger on the Greeks?
    For they swore together, those inveterate enemies,
    Fire and sea, and proved their alliance, destroying
    The unhappy troops of Argos.
730   In night arose ill-waved evil,
    Ships on each other the blasts from Thrace
    Crashed colliding, which butting with horns in the
    violence
    Of big wind and rattle of rain were gone
    To nothing, whirled all ways by a wicked shepherd.
    But when there came up the shining light of the
    sun
    We saw the Aegean sea flowering with corpses
    Of Greek men and their ships' wreckage.
740   But for us, our ship was not damaged,
    Whether someone snatched it away or begged it
    off,
    Some god, not a man, handling the tiller;
    And Saving Fortune was willing to sit upon our
    ship
    So that neither at anchor we took the tilt of waves
    Nor ran to splinters on the crag-bound coast.
    But then having thus escaped death on the sea,
    In the white day, not trusting our fortune,
750   We pastured this new trouble upon our thoughts,
    The fleet being battered, the sailors weary,
    And now if any of *them* still draw breath,

They are thinking no doubt of us as being lost
And we are thinking of them as being lost.
May the best happen. As for Menelaus
The first guess and most likely is a disaster.
But still—if any ray of sun detects him
Alive, with living eyes, by the plan of Zeus
Not yet resolved to annul the race completely,
There is some hope then that he will return home. 760
So much you have heard. Know that it is the truth.

(Exit.)

CHORUS: Who was it named her thus
    In all ways appositely
    Unless it was Someone whom we do not see,
    Fore-knowing fate
    And plying an accurate tongue?
    Helen, bride of spears and conflict's
    Focus, who as was befitting
    Proved a hell to ships and men,
    Hell to her country, sailing 770
    Away from delicately-sumptuous curtains,
    Away on the wind of a giant Zephyr,
    And shielded hunters mustered many
    On the vanished track of the oars,
    Oars beached on the leafy
    Banks of a Trojan river
    For the sake of bloody war.

But on Troy was thrust a marring marriage
By the Wrath that working to an end exacts
In time a price from guests 780
Who dishonoured their host
And dishonoured Zeus of the Hearth,
From those noisy celebrants
Of the wedding hymn which fell
To the brothers of Paris
To sing upon that day.
But learning this, unlearning that,
Priam's ancestral city now
Continually mourns, reviling
Paris the fatal bridegroom. 790
The city has had much sorrow,
Much desolation in life,
From the pitiful loss of her people.

So in his house a man might rear
A lion's cub caught from the dam
In need of suckling,
In the prelude of its life
Mild, gentle with children,
For old men a playmate,
Often held in the arms 800
Like a new-born child,
Wheedling the hand,
Fawning at belly's bidding.

But matured by time he showed
The temper of his stock and payed
Thanks for his fostering
With disaster of slaughter of sheep
Making an unbidden banquet
And now the house is a shambles,
810   Irremediable grief to its people,
Calamitous carnage;
For the pet they had fostered was sent
By God as a priest of Ruin.

So I would say there came
To the city of Troy
A notion of windless calm,
Delicate adornment of riches,
Soft shooting of the eyes and flower
Of desire that stings the fancy.
820   But swerving aside she achieved
A bitter end to her marriage,
Ill guest and ill companion,
Hurled upon Priam's sons, convoyed
By Zeus, patron of guest and host,
Dark angel dowered with tears.

Long current among men an old saying
Runs that a man's prosperity
When grown to greatness
Comes to the birth, does not die childless—
830   His good luck breeds for his house
Distress that shall not be appeased.
I only, apart from the others,
Hold that the unrighteous action
Breeds true to its kind,
Leaves its own children behind it.
But the lot of a righteous house
Is a fair offspring always.

Ancient self-glory is accustomed
To bear to light in the evil sort of men
840   A new self-glory and madness,
Which sometime or sometime finds
The appointed hour for its birth,
And born therewith is the Spirit, intractable,
   unholy, irresistible,
The reckless lust that brings black Doom upon the
   house,
A child that is like its parents.

But Honest Dealing is clear
Shining in smoky homes,
850   Honours the god-fearing life.
Mansions gilded by filth of hands she leaves,
Turns her eyes elsewhere, visits the innocent
   house,
Not respecting the power
Of wealth mis-stamped with approval,
But guides all to the goal.

(Enter AGAMEMNON *and* CASSANDRA *on chariots.)*

CHORUS: Come then my King, stormer of Troy,
Offspring of Atreus,
How shall I hail you, how give you honour
Neither overshooting nor falling short   860
   Of the measure of homage?
There are many who honour appearance too much
Passing the bounds that are right.
To condole with the unfortunate man
Each one is ready but the bite of the grief
   Never goes through to the heart.
And they join in rejoicing, affecting to share it,
Forcing their face to a smile.
But he who is shrewd to shepherd his sheep
Will not fail to notice the eyes of a man   870
Which seem to be loyal but lie,
   Fawning with watery friendship.
Even you, in my thought, when you marshalled the
   troops
For Helen's sake, I will not hide it,
Made a harsh and ugly picture,
Holding badly the tiller of reason,
Paying with the death of men
   Ransom for a willing whore.
But now, not unfriendly, not superficially,   880
I offer my service, well-doers' welcome.
In time you will learn by inquiry
Who has done rightly, who transgressed
   In the work of watching the city.
AGAMEMNON: First to Argos and the country's gods
My fitting salutations, who have aided me
To return and in the justice which I exacted
From Priam's city. Hearing the unspoken case
The gods unanimously had cast their vote
Into the bloody urn for the massacre of Troy;   890
But to the opposite urn
Hope came, dangled her hand, but did no more.
Smoke marks even now the city's capture.
Whirlwinds of doom are alive, the dying ashes
Spread on the air the fat savour of wealth.
For these things we must pay some memorable
   return
To Heaven, having exacted enormous vengeance
For wife-rape; for a woman
The Argive monster ground a city to powder,   900
Sprung from a wooden horse, shield-wielding folk,
Launching a leap at the setting of the Pleiads,
Jumping the ramparts, a ravening lion,
Lapped its fill of the kingly blood.
To the gods I have drawn out this overture
But as for your concerns, I bear them in my mind
And say the same, you have me in agreement.
To few of men does it belong by nature
To congratulate their friends unenviously,
For a sullen poison fastens on the heart,   910
Doubling the pain of a man with this disease;

He feels the weight of his own griefs and when
He sees another's prosperity he groans.
I speak with knowledge, being well acquainted
With the mirror of comradeship—ghost of a
   shadow
Were those who seemed to be so loyal to me.
Only Odysseus, who sailed against his will,
Proved, when yoked with me, a ready tracehorse;
920 I speak of him not knowing if he is alive.
But for what concerns the city and the gods
Appointing public debates in full assembly
We shall consult. That which is well already
We shall take steps to ensure it remain well.
But where there is need of medical remedies,
By applying benevolent cautery or surgery
We shall try to deflect the dangers of disease.
But now, entering the halls where stands my
   hearth,
930 First I shall make salutation to the gods
Who sent me a far journey and have brought me
   back.
And may my victory not leave my side.

(Enter CLYTEMNESTRA, *followed by women slaves carrying purple tapestries.*)

CLYTEMNESTRA: Men of the city, you the aged of
      Argos,
   I shall feel no shame to describe to you my love
   Towards my husband. Shyness in all of us
   Wears thin with time. Here are the facts first hand.
   I will tell you of my own unbearable life
940 I led so long as this man was at Troy.
   For first that the woman separate from her man
   Should sit alone at home is extreme cruelty,
   Hearing so many malignant rumours—First
   Comes one, and another comes after, bad news to
      worse,
   Clamour of grief to the house. If Agamemnon
   Had had so many wounds as those reported
   Which poured home through the pipes of hearsay,
      then—
950 Then he would be gashed fuller than a net has
      holes!
   And if only he had died . . . as often as rumour told
      us,
   He would be like the giant in the legend,
   Three-bodied. Dying once for every body,
   He should have by now three blankets of earth
      above him—
   All that above him; I care not how deep the
      mattress under!
960 Such are the malignant rumours thanks to which
   They have often seized me against my will and
      undone
   The loop of a rope from my neck.
   And this is why our son is not standing here,
   The guarantee of your pledges and mine,

As he should be, Orestes. Do not wonder;
He is being brought up by a friendly ally and host,
Strophius the Phocian, who warned me in advance
Of dubious troubles, both your risks at Troy
And the anarchy of shouting mobs that might   970
Overturn policy, for it is born in men
To kick the man who is down.
This is not a disingenuous excuse.
For me the outrushing wells of weeping are dried
   up,
There is no drop left in them.
My eyes are sore from sitting late at nights
Weeping for you and for the baffled beacons,
Never lit up. And, when I slept, in dreams
I have been waked by the thin whizz of a buzzing   980
Gnat, seeing more horrors fasten on you
Than could take place in the mere time of my
   dream.
Having endured all this, now, with unsorrowed
   heart
I would hail this man as the watchdog of the farm,
Forestay that saves the ship, pillar that props
The lofty roof, appearance of an only son
To a father or of land to sailors past their hope,
The loveliest day to see after the storm,   990
Gush of well-water for the thirsty traveller.
Such are the metaphors I think befit him,
But envy be absent. Many misfortunes already
We have endured. But now, dear head, come down
Out of that car, not placing upon the ground
Your foot, O King, the foot that trampled Troy.
Why are you waiting, slaves, to whom the task is
   assigned
To spread the pavement of his path with
   tapestries?   1000
At once, at once let his way be strewn with purple
That Justice lead him toward his unexpected
   home.
The rest a mind, not overcome by sleep
Will arrange rightly, with God's help, as destined.
AGAMEMNON: Daughter of Leda, guardian of my
      house,
   You have spoken in proportion to my absence.
   You have drawn your speech out long. Duly to
      praise me,   1010
   That is a duty to be performed by others.
   And further—do not by women's methods make
      me
   Effeminate nor in barbarian fashion
   Gape ground-grovelling acclamations at me
   Nor strewing my path with cloths make it invidious.
   It is the gods should be honoured in this way.
   But being mortal to tread embroidered beauty
   For me is no way without fear.
   I tell you to honour me as a man, not god.   1020
   Footcloths are very well—Embroidered stuffs
   Are stuff for gossip. And not to think unwisely

Is the greatest gift of God. Call happy only him
Who has ended his life in sweet prosperity.
I have spoken. This thing I could not do with
   confidence.
CLYTEMNESTRA: Tell me now, according to your
   judgment.
1030 AGAMEMNON: I tell you you shall not override my
   judgment.
CLYTEMNESTRA: Supposing you had feared
   something . . .
Could you have vowed to God to do this thing?
AGAMEMNON: Yes. If an expert had prescribed that
   vow.
CLYTEMNESTRA: And how would Priam have acted in
   your place?
AGAMEMNON: He would have trod the cloths, I think,
   for certain.
1040 CLYTEMNESTRA: Then do not flinch before the blame
   of men.
AGAMEMNON: The voice of the multitude is very
   strong.
CLYTEMNESTRA: But the man none envy is not
   enviable.
AGAMEMNON: It is not a woman's part to love
   disputing.
CLYTEMNESTRA: But it is a conqueror's part to yield
   upon occasion.
1050 AGAMEMNON: You think such victory worth fighting
   for?
CLYTEMNESTRA: Give way. Consent to let me have the
   mastery.
AGAMEMNON: Well, if such is your wish, let someone
   quickly loose
My vassal sandals, underlings of my feet,
And stepping on these sea-purples may no god
Shoot me from far with the envy of his eye.
Great shame it is to ruin my house and spoil
1060 The wealth of costly weavings with my feet.
But of this matter enough. This stranger woman
   here
Take in with kindness. The man who is a gentle
   master
God looks on from far off complacently.
For no one of his will bears the slave's yoke.
This woman, of many riches being the chosen
Flower, gift of the soldiers, has come with me.
But since I have been prevailed on by your words
1070 I will go to my palace home, treading on purples.

*(He dismounts from the chariot and begins to walk up the
tapestried path. During the following speech he enters the
palace.)*

CLYTEMNESTRA: There is the sea and who shall drain
   it dry? It breeds
Its wealth in silver of plenty of purple gushing
And ever-renewed, the dyeings of our garments.

The house has its store of these by God's grace,
   King.
This house is ignorant of poverty
And I would have vowed a pavement of many
   garments
Had the palace oracle enjoined that vow   1080
Thereby to contrive a ransom for his life.
For while there is root, foliage comes to the house
Spreading a tent of shade against the Dog Star.
So now that you have reached your hearth and
   home
You prove a miracle—advent of warmth in winter;
And further this—even in the time of heat
When God is fermenting wine from the bitter
   grape,
Even then it is cool in the house if only   1090
Its master walk at home, a grown man, ripe.
O Zeus the Ripener, ripen these my prayers;
Your part it is to make the ripe fruit fall.

(She enters the palace.)

CHORUS: Why, why at the doors
Of my fore-seeing heart
Does this terror keep beating its wings?
And my song play the prophet
Unbidden, unhired—
Which I cannot spit out
Like the enigmas of dreams   1100
Nor plausible confidence
Sit on the throne of my mind?
It is long time since
The cables let down from the stern
Were chafed by the sand when the seafaring army
   started for Troy.

And I learn with my eyes
And witness myself their return;
But the hymn without lyre goes up,
The dirge of the Avenging Fiend,   1110
In the depths of my self-taught heart
Which has lost its dear
Possession of the strength of hope.
But my guts and my heart
Are not idle which seethe with the waves
Of trouble nearing its hour.
But I pray that these thoughts
May fall out not as I think
   And not be fulfilled in the end.

Truly when health grows much   1120
It respects not limit; for disease,
Its neighbour in the next door room,
Presses upon it.
A man's life, crowding sail,
Strikes on the blind reef:
But if caution in advance
Jettison part of the cargo

With the derrick of due proportion,
The whole house does not sink,
1130 Though crammed with a weight of woe
The hull does not go under.
The abundant bounty of God
And his gifts from the year's furrows
Drive the famine back.

But when upon the ground there has fallen once
The black blood of a man's death,
Who shall summon it back by incantations?
Even Asclepius who had the art
To fetch the dead to life, even to him
1140 Zeus put a provident end.
But, if of the heaven-sent fates
One did not check the other,
Cancel the other's advantage,
My heart would outrun my tongue
In pouring out these fears.
But now it mutters in the dark,
Embittered, no way hoping
To unravel a scheme in time
    From a burning mind.

(CLYTEMNESTRA *appears in the door of the palace.*)

1150 CLYTEMNESTRA: Go in too, you; I speak to you,
        Cassandra,
    Since God in his clemency has put you in this house
    To share our holy water, standing with many slaves
    Beside the altar that protects the house,
    Step down from the car there, do not be
        overproud.
    Heracles himself they say was once
    Sold, and endured to eat the bread of slavery.
    But should such a chance inexorably fall,
1160 There is much advantage in masters who have long
        been rich.
    Those who have reaped a crop they never expected
    Are in all things hard on their slaves and overstep
        the line.
    From us you will have the treatment of tradition.
LEADER OF THE CHORUS: You, it is you she has
        addressed, and clearly.
    Caught as you are in these predestined toils
    Obey her if you can. But should you disobey . . .
1170 CLYTEMNESTRA: If she has more than the gibberish of
        the swallow,
    An unintelligible barbaric speech,
    I hope to read her mind, persuade her reason.
LEADER OF THE CHORUS: As things now stand for you,
        she says the best.
    Obey her; leave that car and follow her.
CLYTEMNESTRA: I have no leisure to waste out here,
        outside the door.
    Before the hearth in the middle of my house
1180 The victims stand already, wait the knife.
    You, if you will obey me, waste no time.

But if you cannot understand my language—

(*To* CHORUS LEADER)

You make it plain to her with the brute and
    voiceless hand.
LEADER OF THE CHORUS: The stranger seems to need a
    clear interpreter.
    She bears herself like a wild beast newly captured.
CLYTEMNESTRA: The fact is she is mad, she listens to
    evil thoughts,
    Who has come here leaving a city newly captured 1190
    Without experience how to bear the bridle
    So as not to waste her strength in foam and blood.
    I will not spend more words to be ignored.

(*She re-enters the palace.*)

CHORUS: But I, for I pity her, will not be angry.
    Obey, unhappy woman. Leave this car.
    Yield to your fate. Put on the untried yoke.
CASSANDRA: Apollo! Apollo!
CHORUS: Why do you cry like this upon Apollo?
    He is not the kind of god that calls for dirges.
CASSANDRA: Apollo! Apollo!   1200
CHORUS: Once more her funeral cries invoke the god
    Who has no place at the scene of lamentation.
CASSANDRA: Apollo! Apollo!
    God of the Ways! My destroyer!
    Destroyed again—and this time utterly!
CHORUS: She seems about to predict her own
    misfortunes.
    The gift of the god endures, even in a slave's mind.
CASSANDRA: Apollo! Apollo!
    God of the Ways! My destroyer!   1210
    Where? To what house? Where, where have you
        brought me?
CHORUS: To the house of the sons of Atreus. If you
        do not know it,
    I will tell you so. You will not find it false.
CASSANDRA: No, no, but to a god-hated, but to an
    accomplice
    In much kin-killing, murdering nooses,
    Man-shambles, a floor asperged with blood.
CHORUS: The stranger seems like a hound with a   1220
    keen scent,
    Is picking up a trail that leads to murder.
CASSANDRA: Clues! I have clues! Look! They are
    these.
    These wailing, these children, butchery of
    children;
    Roasted flesh, a father sitting to dinner.
CHORUS: Of your prophetic fame we have heard
    before
    But in this matter prophets are not required.   1230
CASSANDRA: What is she doing? What is she
    planning?
    What is this new great sorrow?
    Great crime . . . within here . . . planning

Unendurable to his folk, impossible
Ever to be cured. For help
  Stands far distant.
CHORUS: This reference I cannot catch. But the children
1240 I recognized; that refrain is hackneyed.
CASSANDRA: Damned, damned, bringing this work to completion—
  Your husband who shared your bed
  To bathe him, to cleanse him, and then—
  How shall I tell of the end?
  Soon, very soon, it will fall.
    The end comes hand over hand
    Grasping in greed.
CHORUS: Not yet do I understand. After her former
1250 riddles
  Now I am baffled by these dim pronouncements.
CASSANDRA: Ah God, the vision! God, God, the vision!
  A net, is it? Net of Hell!
  But herself is the net; shared bed; shares murder.
  O let the pack ever-hungering after the family
  Howl for the unholy ritual, howl for the victim.
CHORUS: What black Spirit is this you call upon the house—
1260 To raise aloft her cries? Your speech does not lighten me.
  Into my heart runs back the blood
  Yellow as when for men by the spear fallen
  The blood ebbs out with the rays of the setting life
    And death strides quickly.
CASSANDRA: Quick! Be on your guard! The bull—
  Keep him clear of the cow.
  Caught with a trick, the black horn's point,
  She strikes. He falls; lies in the water.
1270 Murder; a trick in a bath. I tell what I see.
CHORUS: I would not claim to be expert in oracles
  But these, as I deduce, portend disaster.
  Do men ever get a good answer from oracles?
  No. It is only through disaster
  That their garrulous craft brings home
  The meaning of the prophet's panic.
CASSANDRA: And for me also, for me, chance ill-destined!
  My own now I lament, pour into the cup my own.
1280 Where is this you have brought me in my misery?
  Unless to die as well. What else is meant?
CHORUS: You are mad, mad, carried away by the god,
  Raising the dirge, the tuneless
  Tune, for yourself. Like the tawny
  Unsatisfied singer from her luckless heart
  Lamenting 'Itys, Itys', the nightingale
  Lamenting a life luxuriant with grief.
CASSANDRA: Oh the lot of the songful nightingale!
  The gods enclosed her in a winged body,
1290 Gave her a sweet and tearless passing.
  But for me remains the two-edged cutting blade.

CHORUS: From whence these rushing and God-inflicted
  Profitless pains?
  Why shape with your sinister crying
  The piercing hymn—fear-piercing?
  How can you know the evil-worded landmarks
    On the prophetic path?
CASSANDRA: Oh the wedding, the wedding of Paris—death to his people! 1300
  O river Scamander, water drunk by my fathers!
  When I was young, alas, upon your beaches
  I was brought up and cared for.
  But now it is the River of Wailing and the banks of Hell
  That shall hear my prophecy soon.
CHORUS: What is this clear speech, too clear?
  A child could understand it.
  I am bitten with fangs that draw blood
  By the misery of your cries, 1310
  Cries harrowing the heart.
CASSANDRA: O trouble on trouble of a city lost, lost utterly!
  My father's sacrifices before the towers,
  Much killing of cattle and sheep,
  No cure—availed not at all
  To prevent the coming of what came to Troy,
  And I, my brain on fire, shall soon enter the trap.
CHORUS: This speech accords with the former.
  What god, malicious, over-heavy, persistently pressing, 1320
  Drives you to chant of these lamentable
  Griefs with death their burden?
  But I cannot see the end.

(CASSANDRA now steps down from the car.)

CASSANDRA: The oracle now no longer from behind veils
  Will be peeping forth like a newly-wedded bride;
  But I can feel it like a fresh wind swoop
  And rush in the face of the dawn and, wave-like, wash 1330
  Against the sun a vastly greater grief
  Than this one. I shall speak no more conundrums.
  And bear me witness, pacing me, that I
  Am trailing on the scene of ancient wrongs.
  For this house here a choir never deserts,
  Chanting together ill. For they mean ill,
  And to puff up their arrogance they have drunk
  Men's blood, this band of revellers that haunts the house,
  Hard to be rid of, fiends that attend the family. 1340
  Established in its rooms they hymn their hymn
  Of that original sin, abhor in turn
  The adultery that proved a brother's ruin.
  A miss? Or do my arrows hit the mark?
  Or am I a quack prophet who knocks at doors, a babbler?

Give me your oath, confess I have the facts,
The ancient history of this house's crimes.
LEADER OF THE CHORUS: And how could an oath's
1350   assurance, however finely assured,
Turn out a remedy? I wonder, though, that you
Being brought up overseas, of another tongue,
Should hit on the whole tale as if you had been
    standing by.
CASSANDRA: Apollo the prophet set me to prophesy.
LEADER OF THE CHORUS: Was he, although a god,
    struck by desire?
CASSANDRA: Till now I was ashamed to tell that story.
LEADER OF THE CHORUS: Yes. Good fortune keeps us
1360   all fastidious.
CASSANDRA: He wrestled hard upon me, panting
    love.
LEADER OF THE CHORUS: And did you come, as they
    do, to child-getting?
CASSANDRA: No. I agreed to him. And I cheated him.
LEADER OF THE CHORUS: Were you already possessed
    by the mystic art?
CASSANDRA: Already I was telling the townsmen all
    their future suffering.
1370 LEADER OF THE CHORUS: Then how did you escape the
    doom of Apollo's anger?
CASSANDRA: I did not escape. No one ever believed
    me.
LEADER OF THE CHORUS: Yet to us your words seem
    worthy of belief.
CASSANDRA: Oh misery, misery!
Again comes on me the terrible labour of true
Prophecy, dizzying prelude; distracts . . .
Do you see these who sit before the house,
Children, like the shapes of dreams?
.380 Children who seem to have been killed by their
    kinsfolk,
Filling their hands with meat, flesh of themselves,
Guts and entrails, handfuls of lament—
Clear what they hold—the same their father tasted.
For this I declare someone is plotting vengeance—
A lion? Lion but coward, that lurks in bed,
Good watchdog truly against the lord's return—
My lord, for I must bear the yoke of serfdom.
390 Leader of the ships, overturner of Troy,
He does not know what plots the accursed hound
With the licking tongue and the pricked-up ear will
    plan
In the manner of a lurking doom, in an evil hour.
A daring criminal! Female murders male.
What monster could provide her with a title?
An amphisbaena or hag of the sea who dwells
In rocks to ruin sailors—
A raving mother of death who breathes against her
400   folk
War to the finish. Listen to her shout of triumph,
Who shirks no horrors, like men in a rout of battle.
And yet she poses as glad at their return.

If you distrust my words, what does it matter?
That which will come will come. You too will soon
    stand here
And admit with pity that I spoke too truly.
LEADER OF THE CHORUS: Thyestes' dinner of his
    children's meat
I understood and shuddered, and fear grips me   1410
To hear the truth, not framed in parables.
But hearing the rest I am thrown out of my course.
CASSANDRA: It is Agamemnon's death I tell you you
    shall witness.
LEADER OF THE CHORUS: Stop! Provoke no evil. Quiet
    your mouth!
CASSANDRA: The god who gives me words is here no
    healer.
LEADER OF THE CHORUS: Not if this shall be so. But
    may some chance avert it.   1420
CASSANDRA: *You* are praying. But others are busy
    with murder.
LEADER OF THE CHORUS: What man is he promotes
    this terrible thing?
CASSANDRA: Indeed you have missed my drift by a
    wide margin!
LEADER OF THE CHORUS: But I do not understand the
    assassin's method.
CASSANDRA: And yet too well I know the speech of
    Greece!   1430
LEADER OF THE CHORUS: So does Delphi but the
    replies are hard.
CASSANDRA: Ah what a fire it is! It comes upon me.
Apollo, Wolf-Destroyer, pity, pity . . .
It is the two-foot lioness who beds
Beside a wolf, the noble lion away,
It is she will kill me. Brewing a poisoned cup
She will mix my punishment too in the angry
    draught
And boasts, sharpening the dagger for her   1440
    husband,
To pay back murder for my bringing here.
Why then do I wear these mockeries of myself,
The wand and the prophet's garland round my
    neck?
My hour is coming—but you shall perish first.
Destruction! Scattered thus you give me my
    revenge;
Go and enrich some other woman with ruin.
See: Apollo himself is stripping me   1450
Of my prophetic gear, who has looked on
When in this dress I have been a laughing-stock
To friends and foes alike, and to no purpose;
They called me crazy, like a fortune-teller,
A poor starved beggar-woman—and I bore it.
And now the prophet undoing his prophetess
Has brought me to this final darkness.
Instead of my father's altar the executioner's block
Waits me the victim, red with my hot blood.
But the gods will not ignore me as I die.   1460

One will come after to avenge my death,
A matricide, a murdered father's champion.
Exile and tramp and outlaw he will come back
To gable the family house of fatal crime;
His father's outstretched corpse shall lead him
    home.
Why need I then lament so pitifully?
For now that I have seen the town of Troy
Treated as she was treated, while her captors
1470 Come to their reckoning thus by the god's verdict,
I will go in and have the courage to die.
Look, these gates are the gates of Death. I greet
    them.
And I pray that I may meet a deft and mortal
    stroke
So that without a struggle I may close
My eyes and my blood ebb in easy death.

LEADER OF THE CHORUS: Oh woman very unhappy
    and very wise,
1480 Your speech was long. But if in sober truth
You know your fate, why like an ox that the gods
Drive, do you walk so bravely to the altar?

CASSANDRA: There is no escape, strangers. No; not by
    postponement.

LEADER OF THE CHORUS: But the last moment has the
    privilege of hope.

CASSANDRA: The day is here. Little should I gain by
    flight.

LEADER OF THE CHORUS: This patience of yours comes
1490   from a brave soul.

CASSANDRA: A happy man is never paid that
    compliment.

LEADER OF THE CHORUS: But to die with credit graces
    a mortal man.

CASSANDRA: Oh my father! You and your noble sons!

(She approaches the door, then suddenly recoils.)

LEADER OF THE CHORUS: What is it? What is the fear
    that drives you back?

CASSANDRA: Faugh.

LEADER OF THE CHORUS: Why faugh? Or is this some
1500   hallucination?

CASSANDRA: These walls breathe out a death that
    drips with blood.

LEADER OF THE CHORUS: Not so. It is only the smell of
    the sacrifice.

CASSANDRA: It is like a breath out of a charnel-house.

LEADER OF THE CHORUS: You think our palace burns
    odd incense then!

CASSANDRA: But I will go to lament among the dead
My lot and Agamemnon's. Enough of life!
1510 Strangers,
I am not afraid like a bird afraid of a bush
But witness you my words after my death
When a woman dies in return for me a woman
And a man falls for a man with a wicked wife.
I ask this service, being about to die.

LEADER OF THE CHORUS: Alas, I pity you for the death
    you have foretold.

CASSANDRA: One more speech I have; I do not wish to
    raise
The dirge for my own self. But to the sun I pray   1520
In face of his last light that my avengers
May make my murderers pay for this my death,
Death of a woman slave, an easy victim.

(She enters the palace.)

LEADER OF THE CHORUS: Ah the fortunes of men!
    When they go well
A shadow sketch would match them, and in
    ill-fortune
The dab of a wet sponge destroys the drawing.
It is not myself but the life of man I pity.

CHORUS: Prosperity in all men cries   1530
For more prosperity. Even the owner
Of the finger-pointed-at palace never shuts
His door against her, saying 'Come no more'.
So to our king the blessed gods had granted
To take the town of Priam, and heaven-favoured
He reaches home. But now if for former bloodshed
    He must pay blood
And dying for the dead shall cause
    Other deaths in atonement
What man could boast he was born   1540
    Secure, who heard this story?

AGAMEMNON:

(Within)

Oh! I am struck a mortal blow—within!

LEADER OF THE CHORUS: Silence! Listen. Who calls
    out, wounded with a mortal stroke?

AGAMEMNON: Again—the second blow—I am struck
    again.

LEADER OF THE CHORUS: You heard the king cry out. I
    think the deed is done.
Let us see if we can concert some sound proposal.   1550

2ND OLD MAN: Well, I will tell you my opinion—
    Raise an alarm, summon the folk to the palace.

3RD OLD MAN: I say burst in with all speed possible,
    Convict them of the deed while still the sword is wet.

4TH OLD MAN: And I am partner to some such
    suggestion.
    I am for taking some course. No time to dawdle.

5TH OLD MAN: The case is plain. This is but the
    beginning.
    They are going to set up dictatorship in the state.   1560

6TH OLD MAN: We are wasting time. The assassins
    tread to earth
    The decencies of delay and give their hands no
    sleep.

7TH OLD MAN: I do not know what plan I could hit on
  to propose.
  The man who acts is in the position to plan.
8TH OLD MAN: So I think, too, for I am at a loss
  To raise the dead man up again with words.
1570 9TH OLD MAN: Then to stretch out our life shall we
  yield thus
  To the rule of these profaners of the house?
10TH OLD MAN: It is not to be endured. To die is
  better.
  Death is more comfortable than tyranny.
11TH OLD MAN: And are we on the evidence of groans
  Going to give oracle that the prince is dead?
12TH OLD MAN: We must know the facts for sure and
  then be angry.
1580 Guesswork is not the same as certain knowledge.
LEADER OF THE CHORUS: Then all of you back me and
  approve this plan—
  To ascertain how it is with Agamemnon.

(The doors of the palace open, revealing the bodies of
AGAMEMNON *and* CASSANDRA. CLYTEMNESTRA *stands*
above them.)

CLYTEMNESTRA: Much having been said before to fit
  the moment,
  To say the opposite now will not outface me.
  How else could one serving hate upon the hated,
  Thought to be friends, hang high the nets of doom
  To preclude all leaping out?
1590 For me I have long been training for this match,
  I tried a fall and won—a victory overdue.
  I stand here where I struck, above my victims;
  So I contrived it—this I will not deny—
  That he could neither fly nor ward off death;
  Inextricable like a net for fishes
  I cast about him a vicious wealth of raiment
  And struck him twice and with two groans he
  loosed
  His limbs beneath him, and upon him fallen
1600 I deal him the third blow to the God beneath the
  earth,
  To the safe keeper of the dead a votive gift,
  And with that he spits his life out where he lies
  And smartly spouting blood he sprays me with
  The sombre drizzle of bloody dew and I
  Rejoice no less than in God's gift of rain
  The crops are glad when the ear of corn gives
  birth.
  These things being so, you, elders of Argos,
  Rejoice if rejoice you will. Mine is the glory.
1610 And if I could pay this corpse his due libation
  I should be right to pour it and more than right;
  With so many horrors this man mixed and filled
  The bowl—and, coming home, has drained the
  draught himself.
LEADER OF THE CHORUS: Your speech astonishes us.
  This brazen boast

Above the man who was your king and husband!
CLYTEMNESTRA: You challenge me as a woman
  without foresight   1620
  But I with unflinching heart to you who know
  Speak. And you, whether you will praise or blame,
  It makes no matter. Here lies Agamemnon,
  My husband, dead, the work of this right hand,
  An honest workman. There you have the facts.
CHORUS: Woman, what poisoned
  Herb of the earth have you tasted
  Or potion of the flowing sea
  To undertake this killing and the people's curses?
  You threw down, you cut off—The people will cast   1630
  you out,
  Black abomination to the town.
CLYTEMNESTRA: Now your verdict—in my case—is
  exile
  And to have the people's hatred, the public curses,
  Though then in no way you opposed this man
  Who carelessly, as if it were a head of sheep
  Out of the abundance of his fleecy flocks,
  Sacrificed his own daughter, to me the dearest   1640
  Fruit of travail, charm for the Thracian winds.
  He was the one to have banished from this land,
  Pay off the pollution. But when you hear what I
  Have done, you judge severely. But I warn you—
  Threaten me on the understanding that I am ready
  For two alternatives—Win by force the right
  To rule me, but, if God brings about the contrary,
  Late in time you will have to learn self-discipline.
CHORUS: You are high in the thoughts,
  You speak extravagant things,   1650
  After the soiling murder your crazy heart
  Fancies your forehead with a smear of blood.
  Unhonoured, unfriended, you must
  Pay for a blow with a blow.
CLYTEMNESTRA: Listen then to this—the sanction of
  my oaths:
  By the Justice totting up my child's atonement,
  By the Avenging Doom and Fiend to whom I killed
  this man,
  For me hope walks not in the rooms of fear   1660
  So long as my fire is lit upon my hearth
  By Aegisthus, loyal to me as he was before.
  The man who outraged me lies here,
  The darling of each courtesan at Troy,
  And here with him is the prisoner clairvoyante,
  The fortune-teller that he took to bed,
  Who shares his bed as once his bench on shipboard,
  A loyal mistress. Both have their deserts.
  He lies so; and she who like a swan
  Sang her last dying lament   1670
  Lies his lover, and the sight contributes
  An appetiser to my own bed's pleasure.
CHORUS: Ah would some quick death come not
  overpainful,
  Not overlong on the sickbed,

Establishing in us the ever-
Lasting unending sleep now that our guardian
Has fallen, the kindest of men,
Who suffering much for a woman

1680 By a woman has lost his life.
   O Helen, insane, being one
   One to have destroyed so many
   And many souls under Troy,
   Now is your work complete, blossomed not for
      oblivion,
   Unfading stain of blood. Here now, if in any
      home,
   Is Discord, here is a man's deep-rooted ruin.
CLYTEMNESTRA: Do not pray for the portion of death
1690 Weighed down by these things, do not turn
   Your anger on Helen as destroyer of men,
   One woman destroyer of many
   Lives of Greek men,
   A hurt that cannot be healed.
CHORUS: O Evil Spirit, falling on the family,
   On the two sons of Atreus and using
   Two sisters in heart as your tools,
   A power that bites to the heart—
   See on the body
1700 Perched like a raven he gloats
   Harshly croaking his hymn.
CLYTEMNESTRA: Ah, now you have amended your
      lips' opinion,
   Calling upon this family's three times gorged
   Genius—demon who breeds
   Blood-hankering lust in the belly:
   Before the old sore heals, new pus collects.
CHORUS: It is a great spirit—great—
   You tell of, harsh in anger,
1710 A ghastly tale, alas,
   Of unsatisfied disaster
   Brought by Zeus, by Zeus,
   Cause and worker of all.
   For without Zeus what comes to pass among us?
   Which of these things is outside Providence?
      O my king, my king,
      How shall I pay you in tears,
      Speak my affection in words?
      You lie in that spider's web,
1720 In a desecrating death breathe out your life,
      Lie ignominiously
      Defeated by a crooked death
      And the two-edged cleaver's stroke.
CLYTEMNESTRA: You say this is *my* work—mine?
   Do not cozen yourself that I am Agamemnon's
      wife.
   Masquerading as the wife
   Of the corpse there the old sharp-witted Genius
   Of Atreus who gave the cruel banquet
1730 Has paid with a grown man's life
   The due for children dead.

CHORUS: That you are not guilty of
   This murder who will attest?
   No, but you may have been abetted
   By some ancestral Spirit of Revenge.
   Wading a millrace of the family's blood
   The black Manslayer forces a forward path
   To make the requital at last
   For the eaten children, the blood-clot cold with
      time.   1740
      Oh my king, my king,
      How shall I pay you in tears,
      Speak my affection in words?
      You lie in that spider's web,
      In a desecrating death breathe out your life,
      Lie ignominiously
      Defeated by a crooked death
      And the two-edged cleaver's stroke.
CLYTEMNESTRA: Did he not, too, contrive a crooked
   Horror for the house? My child by him,   1750
   Shoot that I raised, much-wept-for Iphigeneia,
   He treated her like this;
   So suffering like this he need not make
   Any great brag in Hell having paid with death
   Dealt by the sword for work of his own beginning.
CHORUS: I am at a loss for thought, I lack
   All nimble counsel as to where
   To turn when the house is falling.
   I fear the house-collapsing crashing
   Blizzard of blood—of which these drops are   1760
      earnest.
   Now is Destiny sharpening her justice
   On other whetstones for a new infliction.
      O earth, earth, if only you had received me
      Before I saw this man lie here as if in bed
         In a bath lined with silver.
      Who will bury him? Who will keen him?
      Will you, having killed your own husband,
      Dare now to lament him
      And after great wickedness make   1770
         Unamending amends to his ghost?
      And who above this godlike hero's grave
      Pouring praises and tears
         Will grieve with a genuine heart?
CLYTEMNESTRA: It is not your business to attend to
      that.
   By my hand he fell low, lies low and dead,
   And I shall bury him low down in the earth,
   And his household need not weep him
   For Iphigeneia his daughter   1780
   Tenderly, as is right,
   Will meet her father at the rapid ferry of sorrows,
   Put her arms round him and kiss him!
CHORUS: Reproach answers reproach,
   It is hard to decide,
   The catcher is caught, the killer pays for his kill.
   But the law abides while Zeus abides enthroned

That the wrongdoer suffers. That is established.
Who could expel from the house the seed of the
1790   Curse?
The race is soldered in sockets of Doom and
    Vengeance.
CLYTEMNESTRA: In this you say what is right and the
    will of God.
But for my part I am ready to make a contract
With the Evil Genius of the House of Atreus
To accept what has been till now, hard though it is,
But that for the future he shall leave this house
And wear away some other stock with deaths
1800   Imposed among themselves. Of my possessions
A small part will suffice if only I
Can rid these walls of the mad exchange of
    murder.

(Enter AEGISTHUS, followed by soldiers.)

AEGISTHUS: O welcome light of a justice-dealing day!
From now on I will say that the gods, avenging
    men,
Look down from above on the crimes of earth,
Seeing as I do in woven robes of the Furies
This man lying here—a sight to warm my heart—
1810   Paying for the crooked violence of his father.
For this father Atreus, when he ruled the country,
Because his power was challenged, hounded out
From state and home his own brother Thyestes.
My father—let me be plain—was this Thyestes,
Who later came back home a suppliant,
There, miserable, found so much asylum
As not to die on the spot, stain the ancestral floor.
But to show his hospitality godless Atreus
Gave him an eager if not a loving welcome,
1820   Pretending a day of feasting and rich meats
Served my father with his children's flesh.
The hands and feet, fingers and toes, he hid
At the bottom of the dish. My father sitting apart
Took unknowing the unrecognizable portion
And ate of a dish that has proved, as you see,
    expensive.
But when he knew he had eaten worse than poison
He fell back groaning, vomiting their flesh,
And invoking a hopeless doom on the sons of
1830   Pelops
Kicked over the table to confirm his curse—
So may the whole race perish!
Result of this—you see this man lie here.
I stitched this murder together; it was my title.
Me the third son he left, an unweaned infant,
To share the bitterness of my father's exile.
But I grew up and Justice brought me back,
I grappled this man while still beyond his door,
Having pieced together the programme of his ruin.
1840   So now would even death be beautiful to me
Having seen Agamemnon in the nets of Justice.

LEADER OF THE CHORUS: Aegisthus. I cannot respect
    brutality in distress.
You claim that you deliberately killed this prince
And that you alone planned this pitiful murder.
Be sure that in your turn your head shall not
    escape
The people's volleyed curses mixed with stones.
AEGISTHUS: Do you speak so who sit at the lower oar
While those on the upper bench control the ship?   1850
Old as you are, you will find it is a heavy load
To go to school when old to learn the lesson of tact.
For old age, too, gaol and hunger are fine
Instructors in wisdom, second-sighted doctors.
You have eyes. Cannot you see?
Do not kick against the pricks. The blow will hurt
    you.
LEADER OF THE CHORUS: You woman waiting in the
    house for those who return from battle
While you seduce their wives! Was it you devised   1860
The death of a master of armies?
AEGISTHUS: And these words, too, prepare the way
    for tears.
Contrast your voice with the voice of Orpheus: he
Led all things after him bewitched with joy, but you
Having stung me with your silly yelps shall be
Led off yourself, to prove more mild when
    mastered.
LEADER OF THE CHORUS: Indeed! So you are now to be
    king of Argos,   1870
You who, when you had plotted the king's death,
Did not even dare to do that thing yourself!
AEGISTHUS: No. For the trick of it was clearly
    woman's work.
I was suspect, an enemy of old.
But now I shall try with Agamemnon's wealth
To rule the people. Any who is disobedient
I will harness in a heavy yoke, no tracehorse work
    for him
Like barley-fed colt, but hateful hunger lodging   1880
Beside him in the dark will see his temper soften.
LEADER OF THE CHORUS: Why with your cowardly soul
    did you yourself
Not strike this man but left that work to a woman
Whose presence pollutes our country and its gods?
But Orestes—does he somewhere see the light
That he may come back here by favour of fortune
And kill this pair and prove the final victor?
AEGISTHUS (summoning his guards): Well, if such is
    your design in deeds and words, you will quickly   1890
    learn—
Here my friends, here my guards, there is work for
    you at hand.
LEADER OF THE CHORUS: Come then, hands on hilts,
    be each and all of us prepared.

(The old men and the guards threaten each other.)

AEGISTHUS: Very well! I too am ready to meet death with sword in hand.

LEADER OF THE CHORUS: We are glad you speak of dying. We accept your words for luck.

1900 CLYTEMNESTRA: No, my dearest, do not so. Add no more to the train of wrong.

To reap these many present wrongs is harvest enough of misery.

Enough of misery. Start no more. Our hands are red.

But do you, and you old men, go home and yield to fate in time,

In time before you suffer. We have tried as we had to act.

1910 If only our afflictions now could prove enough, we should agree—

We who have been so hardly mauled in the heavy claws of the evil god.

So stands my word, a woman's, if any man thinks fit to hear.

AEGISTHUS: But to think that these should thus pluck the blooms of an idle tongue

And should throw out words like these, giving the evil god his chance,

And should miss the path of prudence and insult   1920 their master so!

LEADER OF THE CHORUS: It is not the Argive way to fawn upon a cowardly man.

AEGISTHUS: Perhaps. But I in later days will take further steps with you.

LEADER OF THE CHORUS: Not if the god who rules the family guides Orestes to his home.

AEGISTHUS: Yes. I know that men in exile feed themselves on barren hopes.

LEADER OF THE CHORUS: Go on, grow fat defiling   1930 justice . . . while you have your hour.

AEGISTHUS: Do not think you will not pay me a price for your stupidity.

LEADER OF THE CHORUS: Boast on in your self-assurance, like a cock beside his hen.

CLYTEMNESTRA: Pay no heed, Aegisthus, to these futile barkings. You and I,

Masters of this house, from now shall order all things well.

(They enter the palace.)

Figure 3. Clytemnestra, center, welcomes Agamemnon and Cassandra in the production of *Agamemnon* by the National Theatre Company of Greece, Epidaurus, 1965. (Photograph: D.A. Harissiadis.)

Figure 4. Clytemnestra (Douglas Campbell, *left*) welcomes Agamemnon (Lee Richardson) upon his return from Troy in the Guthrie Theater Company production of *The House of Atreus,* directed by Tyrone Guthrie and designed by Tanya Moiseiwitsch, Minneapolis, 1967/68. (Photograph: The Guthrie Theater.)

Figure 5. Agamemnon (Lee Richardson, *left*) returns from the Trojan war with Cassandra (Robin Gammell) in the Guthrie Theater Company production of *The House of Atreus,* directed by Tyrone Guthrie and designed by Tanya Moiseiwitsch, Minneapolis, 1967/68. (Photograph: the Guthrie Theater.)

Staging of *Agamemnon*

REVIEW OF THE GUTHRIE THEATER
PRODUCTION, 1967, BY RODERICK NORDELL

The Minnesota Theater Company's "House of Atreus" is like an ancient carving freed from stone to tell us about ourselves. Compressing Aeschylus' "Oresteia" trilogy into a single lengthy evening, it is attracting full houses to the Tyrone Guthrie Theater for a rigorous combination of spectacle, psychology, philosophy, and even a kind of God-is-alive theology.

As seen last week, the production tempted one to stay on the level of spectacle—an awesome theatrical representation of the theme familiarly translated as "Men shall learn wisdom, by affliction schooled." For Tyrone Guthrie's monumentally stylized direction is aided by the designing hand of Tanya Moiseiwitsch, as it was in "Oedipus" at Stratford, Ont., some dozen years ago. And the mythic grandeur of their work is heightened by the grotesque but tellingly differentiated masks credited to Carolyn Parker and Dahl Delu.

Cassandra's mask, for example, is vaguely reminiscent of a tragic, dark-lined Rouault portrait. Clytemnestra's is haughty, blank-eyed, with a forbidding version of the "onkos," the high hairdress Aeschylus favored.

The sleeved robes he pioneered for actors are also effectively suggested, though sometimes they seem to have been given an antiquing process recalling a painter's spattered tarpaulin. And, if history is right in saying Aeschylus raised the height of the actors' elevator shoes, "The House of Atreus" must go further than he did.

In this production, only the ordinary people, "like ourselves," are on ground level, as Guthrie has commented. The main characters, "heroic figures," are larger than life. The gods are immense.

The great rings in the massive palace gates almost overwhelm the mortal men who open them. Even the heroic figure of Orestes is dwarfed by the golden, towering Apollo who has set him on the path of vengeance—and by the enormous seated Pallas Athena who seeks to bring rational justice to the primitive situation of blood-will-have-blood.

It takes some effort to wrench oneself from the spectacle; from Dominick Argento's music with its breathy cymbal ending a spoken phrase, its tinkling triangles and more stentorian flourishes; from the sound and sight of the skilled actors, notably Douglas Campbell, who makes Clytemnestra's first silent entrance a chilling image of threat and who—without obvious feminine pitch—speaks the lines with a thoughtful, savage, womanly eloquence.

The display is marvelous in itself; it can be justified both by old tradition and by the new demands of the theater to break out of realism and into its own unique truth. Yet one has at least a passing feeling that the production could have gone in another direction—toward the sparest everyday restraint—in eliciting what Aeschylus says to today, and what is seen in him by his sensitive latter-day adapter, John Lewin, the company's resident playwright.

The feeling does not apply only to such humanizing touches as those derived from Aeschylus' own experience in the army. When a soldier returns from Troy, Mr. Lewin plausibly has him say, "You think it's cold in Greece—this was unbelievable." Is it too human to be spoken through a mask?

One also questions the apparatus when the play gets into Mr. Lewin's stated interpretation of its psychological level, with the unconscious and the "ordering intellect" in conflict and collaboration. The nightmarish Furies and the gleaming Apollo make strong images, but might they not be stronger in street clothes, so to speak? Today's dilemmas tend to be gray.

As it is, the dazzled spectator may not listen closely enough when Orestes challenges his god, Apollo: "You know what it means to do wrong. Do you know what it means to take responsibility?"

But in such lines, in the interplay between "new" and "old" gods, in the emergence of a more sophisticated form of justice, lie the issues that still exercise philosophers and theologians. In the company's "play guide," Minnesota poet Robert Bly finds Aeschylus' exploration of the "inability to forgive" pertinent to such present-day episodes as Eichmann and Vietnam. Guthrie finds a parallel to humanity's growing conception of God: "the vengeful tribal deity, the Jehovah of the earlier books of the Old Testament, becomes God the All-Merciful Father, something very different, very much more humane."

On afterthought, such themes can be pondered in relation to the sheer theater that envelops them. But in the playhouse the weight of effects, as well as that of tragedy, may contribute to the audience's laughing sigh of relief when Orestes' old nurse brings it back to earth with: "It's just one thing after another." The outer and inner drama fuse during moments such as that when the well-deployed chorus says: "The gods that give us sorrows give us tongues to mourn."

SOPHOCLES

496—406 B.C.

Because his life spanned almost the entire fifth century, Sophocles witnessed both the rise and the fall of Athens—a reversal of political fortune as astonishing as the one he dramatized in *Oedipus Rex*. As a young man he lived through the extraordinary growth of Athenian power and culture that followed upon the Persian Wars; as a mature man he served its power and culture in various capacities: as ambassador, dramatist, general, priest, and treasurer; and as an old man he witnessed the collapse of its power and culture under the strains of the Peloponnesian Wars, his death coming only two years before the Athenian surrender to Sparta. In many respects he seems to have been a consummate representative of the best qualities in fifth century Athenian culture, a man who not only was gifted with good looks, great wealth, and even greater talent, but who also made the most of those gifts in his public life, his religious duties, and his artistic career. Through all the distractions of public appointments and religious obligations, he somehow managed to write more than 120 plays.

Although he was a prolific writer, he wrote with great care, and his carefully wrought plays brought him great success in the festival competitions. He won first prize twenty-four times, and he never ranked lower than second. Only seven of his plays have survived, all from the mature period of his life: *Ajax* (ca. 445). *Antigone* (ca. 440), *Trachiniae* (ca. 435), *Oedipus Rex* (ca. 425). *Electra* (ca. 415), *Philoctetes* (409), and *Oedipus at Colonus* (406). All of these show him to have been a painstaking and meticulous dramatist. His plots, however complex, are always clearly worked out, with each event connected by a logic of cause and effect to every other event, so that they never contain any loose ends or improbable outcomes. His characters, though complexly motivated, are always clearly and consistently developed. Because of these qualities, his plays have always been considered the most polished examples of classical Greek tragedy—the perfection of the form.

He completely departed from Aeschylus by abandoning the trilogy, preferring instead to submit three unrelated and self-sufficient plays. Although he sacrificed the comprehensive scope of the trilogy, he was able to develop a far more intense and complete dramatic experience within the limits of a single play—an experience centering on the fate of individuals rather than on the destinies of families and nations. In developing the art of the single play, his most decisive contribution was to increase the number of actors from two to three. He was thus able to create various kinds of highly dramatic episodes out of the triangular interplay among characters that became possible with the third actor. Two such episodes occur in *Oedipus Rex:* the first, when the messenger comes to bring what he thinks is good news to Oedipus and Iocaste, but the news gradually reveals to Iocaste a horrible truth that she seeks to withold from Oedipus; the second, when the shepherd arrives and reluctantly answers the questions of the messenger and Oedipus, providing information that finally reveals the horrible truth to Oedipus.

Once it became possible to stage such theatrically compelling episodes, it was inevitable that the actors would become more important than the chorus, and that is precisely what happened in the plays of Sophocles. Although he increased the size of the chorus from twelve to fifteen members, he actually reduced its functions, confining its activities almost exclusively to choral odes and leaving it little opportunity to interact with the characters. Its odes continued to be relevant to the mood and meaning of the action, but the chorus was no longer a dramatically integral part of that action, as it had been in the plays of Aeschylus. Thus Sophocles moved tragedy further away from its lyric origins and closer to a purely dramatic form.

Sophocles used the sophisticated form of his tragedies to represent and explore the fate of heroic individuals in a moment of moral crisis. All of his protagonists prove to be singularly heroic in their commitment to a moral principle they establish for themselves, even though their commitment brings great suffering to themselves and their loved ones. In *Antigone,* for example, the heroine opposes her uncle Creon, who as ruler of Thebes has decreed that her brother Polyneices is not to be given a burial because he had led an attack on the city. Creon regards his edict as a politically necessary action, whereas Antigone believes the burial of her brother is a sacred obligation. Although Antigone is shown to be coldly, fanatically, and inflexibly devoted to her cause, the events of the play bear out the righteousness of her action. Yet her righteous commitment is not only the source of her dignity; it is also the cause of her undoing. This paradoxical fate repeatedly besets the heroes of Sophocles, and it is one of the qualities that make his plays so compelling. Indeed, his tragedies would not be so terrifying as they are, if his protagonists were so flawed as they are often considered to be.

The disaster experienced by Oedipus is often regarded as a fitting outcome of his pride, but it is difficult to see how the play justifies this interpretation of his fate. Throughout the play he is shown to be nobly unyielding in his attempt to rid Thebes of the plague by discovering and punishing the murderer of its previous king, Laius. Even when the investigation turns into an investigation of himself, he is unflinching in his quest for truth, though he is warned against it by Teiresias and Iocaste. He relentlessly conducts his search until he discovers himself to be the criminal, the source of the city's sickness, and by exposing himself brings about the renewed health of the city. His commitment to the truth thereby proves to be at once his triumph and his disaster. *Oedipus Rex* raises haunting questions about the fate of heroic individuals, questions that it does not finally answer, except through the chorus' concluding reflections on human frailty.

Because its plot and characters are so skillfully conceived and developed, *Oedipus Rex* has come to be the most influential play ever written. The perfection of its form was recognized by Aristotle during the fourth century B.C. when he expounded his theory of tragedy in *The Poetics*. In his discussions of character and plot, Aristotle provides detailed explanations of important dramatic elements, such as "discovery" and "reversal of fortune," repeatedly citing *Oedipus Rex* as the outstanding embodiment of them. Using it as his model play, Aristotle produced a study that has come to be the most influential document in the history of dramatic theory and criticism. In choosing his model Aristotle also had his eye on the audience, for he knew from his own experience of witnessing Greek drama just how strongly an audience can be moved to "pity and fear" by discoveries and reversals of fortune on the part of a tragic hero.

Because it is the consummate embodiment of tragic irony, *Oedipus Rex* continues to be highly successful in the modern theater. But because it is so well known and so often produced, contemporary directors, seeking to renew the interest of their audiences, have often felt compelled to develop alternatives to the traditional way of presenting the play in classical masks and costumes as a study of pride and its influence on the outcome of human beings. Consequently, some directors have staged it in modern dress, either as a suspenseful murder mystery or as a Freudian psychodrama. Yet another approach, taken recently by the Guthrie Theater, has been to stage the play in primitivistic costumes and settings (see Figures 6 and 7) as an exhibition of archetypal fears and powerful taboos. A review of that production, reproduced following the text, suggests both the appeals and the perils of experimental approaches to the play. Still, in any style of performance, the astonishing climax of *Oedipus Rex* continues to bear witness to the dignity and the frailty of human nature.

OEDIPUS REX

BY SOPHOCLES/TRANSLATED BY DUDLEY FITTS AND ROBERT FITZGERALD

CHARACTERS

OEDIPUS
A PRIEST
CREON
TEIRESIAS
IOCASTE
MESSENGER
SHEPHERD OF LAÏOS
SECOND MESSENGER
CHORUS OF THEBAN ELDERS

SCENE

Before the palace of Oedipus, King of Thebes. A central door and two lateral doors open onto a platform which runs the length of the façade. On the platform, right and left, are altars; and three steps lead down into the "orchestra," or chorus-ground. At the beginning of the action these steps are crowded by suppliants who have brought branches and chaplets of olive leaves and who lie in various attitudes of despair. OEDIPUS *enters.*

PROLOGUE

OEDIPUS: My children, generations of the living
   In the line of Kadmos, nursed at his ancient
      hearth:
   Why have you strewn yourselves before these altars
   In supplication, with your boughs and garlands?
   The breath of incense rises from the city
   With a sound of prayer and lamentation.
   Children,
   I would not have you speak through messengers,
10 And therefore I have come myself to hear you—
   I, Oedipus, who bear the famous name.

   (*To a* PRIEST)

   You, there, since you are eldest in the company,
   Speak for them all, tell me what preys upon you,
   Whether you come in dread, or crave some
      blessing:
   Tell me, and never doubt that I will help you
   In every way I can; I should be heartless
   Were I not moved to find you suppliant here.
PRIEST: Great Oedipus, O powerful King of Thebes!
20 You see how all the ages of our people
   Cling to your altar steps: here are boys
   Who can barely stand alone, and here are priests
   By weight of age, as I am a priest of God,
   And young men chosen from those yet unmarried;
   As for the others, all that multitude,
   They wait with olive chaplets in the squares,
   At the two shrines of Pallas, and where Apollo
   Speaks in the glowing embers.
   Your own eyes
30 Must tell you: Thebes is tossed on a murdering sea
   And can not lift her head from the death surge.
   A rust consumes the buds and fruits of the earth;
   The herds are sick; children die unborn,
   And labor is vain. The god of plague and pyre
   Raids like detestable lightning through the city,
   And all the house of Kadmos is laid waste,

All emptied, and all darkened: Death alone
Battens upon the misery of Thebes.

You are not one of the immortal gods, we know;
Yet we have come to you to make our prayer   40
As to the man surest in mortal ways
And wisest in the ways of God. You saved us
From the Sphinx, that flinty singer, and the tribute
We paid to her so long; yet you were never
Better informed than we, nor could we teach you;
A god's touch, it seems, enabled you to help us.

Therefore, O mighty power, we turn to you:
Find us our safety, find us a remedy,
Whether by counsel of the gods or of men.
A king of wisdom tested in the past   50
Can act in a time of troubles, and act well.
Noblest of men, restore
Life to your city! Think how all men call you
Liberator for your boldness long ago;
Ah, when your years of kingship are remembered,
Let them not say *We rose, but later fell*—
Keep the State from going down in the storm!
Once, years ago, with happy augury,
You brought us fortune; be the same again!
No man questions your power to rule the land: 60
But rule over men, not a dead city!
Ships are only hulls, high walls are nothing,
When no life moves in the empty passageways.
OEDIPUS: Poor children! You may be sure I know
All that you longed for in your coming here.
I know that you are deathly sick; and yet,
Sick as you are, not one is as sick as I.
Each of you suffers in himself alone
His anguish, not another's; but my spirit
Groans for the city, for myself, for you.   70

I was not sleeping, you are not waking me.
No, I have been in tears for a long while

And in my restless thought walked many ways.
In all my search I found one remedy,
And I have adopted it: I have sent Kreon,
Son of Menoikeus, brother of the Queen,
To Delphi, Apollo's place of revelation,
To learn there, if he can,
What act or pledge of mine may save the city.

80   I have counted the days, and now, this very day,
I am troubled, for he has overstayed his time.
What is he doing? He has been gone too long.
Yet whenever he comes back, I should do ill
Not to take any action the god orders.

PRIEST: It is a timely promise. At this instant
They tell me Kreon is here.

OEDIPUS: O Lord Apollo!
May his news be fair as his face is radiant!

PRIEST: Good news, I gather: he is crowned with bay,
90   The chaplet is thick with berries.

OEDIPUS: We shall soon know;
He is near enough to hear us now.

(Enter KREON.*)*

O Prince:
Brother: son of Menoikeus
What answer do you bring us from the God?

KREON: A strong one. I can tell you, great afflictions
Will turn out well, if they are taken well.

OEDIPUS: What was the oracle? These vague words
Leave me still hanging between hope and fear.

100 KREON: Is it your pleasure to hear me with all these
Gathered around us? I am prepared to speak,
But should we not go in?

OEDIPUS: Speak to them all.
It is for them I suffer, more than for myself.

KREON: Then I will tell you what I heard at Delphi.
In plain words
The god commands us to expel from the land of
Thebes
An old defilement we are sheltering.

110 It is a deathly thing, beyond cure;
We must not let it feed upon us longer.

OEDIPUS: What defilement? How shall we rid
ourselves of it?

KREON: By exile or death, blood for blood. It was
Murder that brought the plague-wind on the city.

OEDIPUS: Murder of whom? Surely the god has
named him?

KREON: My lord: Laïos once ruled this land,
Before you came to govern us.

120 OEDIPUS: I know;
I learned of him from others; I never saw him.

KREON: He was murdered; and Apollo commands us
now
To take revenge upon whoever killed him.

OEDIPUS: Upon whom? Where are they? Where shall
we find a clue
To solve that crime, after so many years?

KREON: Here in this land, he said. Search reveals
Things that escape an inattentive man.

OEDIPUS: Tell me: Was Laïos murdered in his house, 130
Or in the fields, or in some foreign country?

KREON: He said he planned to make a pilgrimage.
He did not come home again.

OEDIPUS: And was there no one,
No witness, no companion, to tell what happened?

KREON: They were all killed but one, and he got away
So frightened that he could remember one thing
only.

OEDIPUS: What was that one thing? One may be the
key 140
To everything, if we resolve to use it.

KREON: He said that a band of highwaymen attacked
them,
Outnumbered them, and overwhelmed the King.

OEDIPUS: Strange, that a highwayman should be so
daring—
Unless some faction here bribed him to do it.

KREON: We thought of that. But after Laïos' death
New troubles arose and we had no avenger.

OEDIPUS: What troubles could prevent your hunting 150
down the killers?

KREON: The riddling Sphinx's song
Made us deaf to all mysteries but her own.

OEDIPUS: Then once more I must bring what is dark
to light.
It is most fitting that Apollo shows,
As you do, this compunction for the dead.
You shall see how I stand by you, as I should,
Avenging this country and the god as well,
And not as though it were for some distant friend, 160
But for my own sake, to be rid of evil.
Whoever killed King Laïos might—who knows?—
Lay violent hands even on me—and soon.
I act for the murdered king in my own interest.

Come, then, my children: leave the altar steps,
Lift up your olive boughs!
One of you go
And summon the people of Kadmos to gather
here.
I will do all that I can; you may tell them that. 170

(Exit a PAGE.*)*

So, with the help of God.
We shall be saved—or else indeed we are lost.

PRIEST: Let us rise, children. It was for this we came,
And now the King has promised it.
Phoibos has sent us an oracle; may he descend
Himself to save us and drive out the plague.

(Exeunt OEDIPUS *and* KREON *into the palace by the central door. The* PRIEST *and the* SUPPLIANTS *disperse right and left. After a short pause the* CHORUS *enters the orchestra.)*

PARADOS

Strophe 1

CHORUS: What is God singing in his profound
Delphi of gold and shadow?
What oracle for Thebes, the sunwhipped city?

180 Fear unjoints me, the roots of my heart tremble.

Now I remember, O Healer, your power and
    wonder:
Will you send doom like a sudden cloud, or weave
    it
Like nightfall of the past?

Speak to me, tell me, O
Child of golden Hope, immortal Voice.

Antistrophe 1

Let me pray to Athene, the immortal daughter of
    Zeus,
190 And to Artemis her sister
Who keeps her famous throne in the market ring,

And to Apollo, archer from distant heaven—

O gods, descend! Like three streams leap against
The fires of our grief, the fires of darkness;
Be swift to bring us rest!

As in the old time from the brilliant house
Of air you stepped to save us, come again!

Strophe 2

Now our afflictions have no end,
Now all our stricken host lies down
200 And no man fights off death with his mind;

The noble plowland bears no grain,
And groaning mothers can not bear—

See, how our lives like birds take wing,
Like sparks that fly when a fire soars,
To the shore of the god of evening.

Antistrophe 2

The plague burns on, it is pitiless,
Though pallid children laden with death
Lie unwept in the stony ways,

And old gray women by every path
210 Flock to the strand about the altars

There to strike their breasts and cry
Worship of Phoibos in wailing prayers:
Be kind, God's golden child!

Strophe 3

There are no swords in this attack by fire,
No shields, but we are ringed with cries.

Send the besieger plunging from our homes
Into the vast sea-room of the Atlantic
Or into the waves that foam eastward of Thrace—

For the day ravages what the night spares—

Destroy our enemy, lord of the thunder!   220
Let him be riven by lightning from heaven!

Antistrophe 3

Phoibos Apollo, stretch the sun's bowstring,
That golden cord, until it sing for us,
Flashing arrows in heaven!
Artemis, Huntress,
Race with flaring lights upon our mountains!

O scarlet god, O golden-banded brow,
O Theban Bacchos in a storm of Maenads,

(Enter OEDIPUS, *center.)*

Whirl upon Death, that all the Undying hate!
Come with blinding torches, come in joy!   230

SCENE I

OEDIPUS: Is this your prayer? It may be answered.
    Come,
Listen to me, act as the crisis demands,
And you shall have relief from all these evils.

Until now I was a stranger to this tale.
As I had been a stranger to the crime.
Could I track down the murderer without a clue?
But now, friends,
As one who became a citizen after the murder,
I make this proclamation to all Thebans: 10

If any man knows by whose hand Laïos, son of
    Labdakos,
Met his death, I direct that man to tell me
    everything,
No matter what he fears for having so long
    withheld it.
Let it stand as promised that no further trouble
Will come to him, but he may leave the land in
    safety.

Moreover: If anyone knows the murderer to be   20
    foreign,
Let him not keep silent: he shall have his reward
    from me.
However, if he does conceal it; if any man

Fearing for his friend or for himself disobeys this
   edict,
Hear what I propose to do:

I solemnly forbid the people of this country,
Where power and throne are mine, ever to receive
   that man
Or speak to him, no matter who he is, or let him
Join in sacrifice, lustration, or in prayer.
I decree that he be driven from every house,
Being, as he is, corruption itself to us: the Delphic
Voice of Apollo has pronounced this revelation.
Thus I associate myself with the oracle
And take the side of the murdered king.

As for the criminal, I pray to God—
Whether it be a lurking thief, or one of a number—
I pray that that man's life be consumed in evil and
   wretchedness.
And as for me, this curse applies no less
If it should turn out that the culprit is my guest
   here,
Sharing my hearth.
You have heard the penalty.

I lay it on you now to attend to this
For my sake, for Apollo's, for the sick
Sterile city that heaven has abandoned.
Suppose the oracle had given you no command:
Should this defilement go uncleansed for ever?
You should have found the murderer: your king,
A noble king, had been destroyed!
Now I,
Having the power that he held before me,
Having his bed, begetting children there
Upon his wife, as he would have, had he lived—
Their son would have been my children's brother,
If Laïos had had luck in fatherhood!
(And now his bad fortune has struck him down)—
I say I take the son's part, just as though
I were his son, to press the fight for him
And see it won! I'll find the hand that brought
Death to Labdakos' and Polydoros' child,
Heir of Kadmos' and Agenor's line.
And as for those who fail me,
May the gods deny them the fruit of the earth,
Fruit of the womb, and may they rot utterly!
Let them be wretched as we are wretched, and
   worse!

For you, my loyal Thebans, and for all
Who find my actions right, I pray the favor
Of justice, and of all the immortal gods.
CHORAGOS: Since I am under oath, my lord, I swear
   I did not do the murder, I can not name
   The murderer. Phoibos ordained the search;

Why did he not say who the culprit was?
OEDIPUS: An honest question. But no man in the
   world
   Can make the gods do more than the gods will.
CHORAGOS: There is an alternative, I think—
OEDIPUS: Tell me.
   Any or all, you must not fail to tell me.
CHORAGOS: A lord clairvoyant to the lord Apollo,
   As we all know, is the skilled Teiresias.
   One might learn much about this from him,
   Oedipus.
OEDIPUS: I am not wasting time:
   Kreon spoke of this, and I have sent for him—
   Twice, in fact; it is strange that he is not here.
CHORAGOS: The other matter—that old
   report—seems useless.
OEDIPUS: What was that? I am interested in all
   reports.
CHORAGOS: The King was said to have been killed by
   highwaymen.
OEDIPUS: I know. But we have no witnesses to that.
CHORAGOS: If the killer can feel a particle of dread,
   Your curse will bring him out of hiding!
OEDIPUS: No.
   The man who dared that act will fear no curse.

(Enter the blind seer TEIRESIAS, led by a PAGE).

CHORAGOS: But there is one man who may detect the
   criminal.
   This is Teiresias, this is the holy prophet
   In whom, alone of all men, truth was born.
OEDIPUS: Teiresias: seer: student of mysteries,
   Of all that's taught and all that no man tells,
   Secrets of Heaven and secrets of the earth:
   Blind though you are, you know the city lies
   Sick with plague; and from this plague, my lord,
   We find that you alone can guard or save us.

Possibly you did not hear the messengers?
Apollo, when we sent to him,
Sent us back word that this great pestilence
Would lift, but only if we established clearly
The identity of those who murdered Laïos.
They must be killed or exiled.
Can you use
Birdflight or any art of divination
To purify yourself, and Thebes, and me
From this contagion? We are in your hands.
There is no fairer duty
Than that of helping others in distress.
TEIRESIAS: How dreadful knowledge of the truth can
   be
   When there's no help in truth! I knew this well,
   But did not act on it: else I should not have come.
OEDIPUS: What is troubling you? Why are your eyes
   so cold?

130 TEIRESIAS: Let me go home. Bear your own fate, and I'll
  Bear mine. It is better so: trust what I say.
OEDIPUS: What you say is ungracious and unhelpful
  To your native country. Do not refuse to speak.
TEIRESIAS: When it comes to speech, your own is neither temperate
  Nor opportune. I wish to be more prudent.
OEDIPUS: In God's name, we all beg you—
TEIRESIAS: You are all ignorant.
140 No; I will never tell you what I know.
  Now it is my misery; then it would be yours.
OEDIPUS: What! You do know something, and will not tell us?
  You would betray us all and wreck the State?
TEIRESIAS: I do not intend to torture myself, or you.
  Why persist in asking? You will not persuade me.
OEDIPUS: What a wicked old man you are! You'd try a stone's
  Patience! Out with it. Have you no feeling at all?
150 TEIRESIAS: You call me unfeeling. If you could only see
  The nature of your own feelings . . .
OEDIPUS: Why,
  Who would not feel as I do? Who could endure
  Your arrogance toward the city?
TEIRESIAS: What does it matter?
  Whether I speak or not, it is bound to come.
OEDIPUS: Then, if 'it' is bound to come, you are bound to tell me.
160 TEIRESIAS: No, I will not go on. Rage as you please.
OEDIPUS: Rage? Why not!
  And I'll tell you what I think:
  You planned it, you had it done, you all but
  Killed him with your own hands: if you had eyes,
  I'd say the crime was yours, and yours alone.
TEIRESIAS: So? I charge you, then,
  Abide by the proclamation you have made:
  From this day forth
  Never speak again to these men or to me;
170 You yourself are the pollution of this country.
OEDIPUS: You dare say that! Can you possibly think you have
  Some way of going free, after such insolence?
TEIRESIAS: I have gone free. It is the truth sustains me.
OEDIPUS: Who taught you shamelessness? It was not your craft.
TEIRESIAS: You did. You made me speak. I did not want to.
180 OEDIPUS: Speak what? Let me hear it again more clearly.
TEIRESIAS: Was it not clear before? Are you tempting me?
OEDIPUS: I did not understand it. Say it again.
TEIRESIAS: I say that you are the murderer whom you seek.

OEDIPUS: Now twice you have spat out infamy. You'll pay for it!
TEIRESIAS: Would you care for more? Do you wish to be really angry? 190
OEDIPUS: Say what you will. Whatever you say is worthless.
TEIRESIAS: I say you live in hideous shame with those
  Most dear to you. You can not see the evil.
OEDIPUS: Can you go on babbling like this for ever?
TEIRESIAS: I can, if there is power in truth.
OEDIPUS: There is:
  But not for you, not for you,
  You sightless, witless, senseless, mad old man!
TEIRESIAS: You are the madman. There is no one here 200
  Who will not curse you soon, as you curse me.
OEDIPUS: You child of total night! I would not touch you;
  Neither would any man who sees the sun.
TEIRESIAS: True: it is not from you my fate will come.
  That lies within Apollo's competence,
  As it is his concern.
OEDIPUS: Tell me, who made
  These fine discoveries? Kreon? Or someone else? 210
TEIRESIAS: Kreon is no threat. You weave your own doom.
OEDIPUS: Wealth, power, craft of statesmanship!
  Kingly position, everywhere admired!
  What savage envy is stored up against these,
  If Kreon, whom I trusted, Kreon my friend,
  For this great office which the city once
  Put in my hands unsought—if for this power
  Kreon desires in secret to destroy me!

He has brought this decrepit fortune-teller, this 220
Collector of dirty pennies, this prophet fraud—
Why, he is no more clairvoyant than I am!
Tell us:
Has your mystic mummery ever approached the truth?
When that hellcat the Sphinx was performing here,
What help were you to these people?
Her magic was not for the first man who came along:
It demanded a real exorcist. Your birds— 230
What good were they? or the gods, for the matter of that?
But I came by,
Oedipus, the simple man, who knows nothing—
I thought it out for myself, no birds helped me!
And this is the man you think you can destroy,
That you may be close to Kreon when he's king!
Well, you and your friend Kreon, it seems to me,
Will suffer most. If you were not an old man,
You would have paid already for your plot. 240
CHORAGOS: We can not see that his words or yours
  Have been spoken except in anger, Oedipus,

And of anger we have no need. How to accomplish
The god's will best: that is what most concerns us.
TEIRESIAS: You are a king. But where argument's
    concerned
I am your man, as much a king as you.
I am not your servant, but Apollo's.
I have no need of Kreon's name.

250 Listen to me. You mock my blindness, do you?
But I say that you, with both your eyes, are blind:
You can not see the wretchedness of your life,
Nor in whose house you live, no, nor with whom.
Who are your father and mother? Can you tell me?
You do not even know the blind wrongs
That you have done them, on earth and in the
    world below.
But the double lash of your parents' curse will whip
    you
260 Out of this land some day, with only night
Upon your precious eyes.
Your cries then—where will they not be heard?
What fastness of Kithairon will not echo them?
And that bridal-descant of yours—you'll know it
    then,
The song they sang when you came here to Thebes
And found your misguided berthing.
All this, and more, that you can not guess at now,
Will bring you to yourself among your children.

270 Be angry, then. Curse Kreon. Curse my words.
I tell you, no man that walks upon the earth
Shall be rooted out more horribly than you.
OEDIPUS: Am I to bear this from him?—Damnation
Take you! Out of this place! Out of my sight!
TEIRESIAS: I would not have come at all if you had not
    asked me.
OEDIPUS: Could I have told that you'd talk nonsense,
    that
You'd come here to make a fool of yourself, and of
280   me?
TEIRESIAS: A fool? Your parents thought me sane
    enough.
OEDIPUS: My parents again!—Wait: who were my
    parents?
TEIRESIAS: This day will give you a father, and break
    your heart.
OEDIPUS: Your infantile riddles! Your damned
    abracadabra!
TEIRESIAS: You were a great man once at solving
290   riddles.
OEDIPUS: Mock me with that if you like; you will find
    it true.
TEIRESIAS: It was true enough. It brought about your
    ruin.
OEDIPUS: But if it saved this town?
TEIRESIAS (to the PAGE): Boy, give me your hand.
OEDIPUS: Yes, boy; lead him away.

—While you are here
We can do nothing. Go; leave us in peace.
TEIRESIAS: I will go when I have said what I have to   300
    say.
How can you hurt me? And I tell you again:
The man you have been looking for all this time,
The damned man, the murderer of Laïos,
That man is in Thebes. To your mind he is
    foreign-born,
But it will soon be shown that he is a Theban,
A revelation that will fail to please.
A blind man,
Who has his eyes now; a penniless man, who is rich   310
    now;
And he will go tapping the strange earth with his
    staff.
To the children with whom he lives now he will be
Brother and father—the very same; to her
Who bore him, son and husband—the very same
Who came to his father's bed, wet with his father's
    blood.

Enough. Go think that over.
If later you find error in what I have said,   320
You may say that I have no skill in prophecy.

(*Exit* TEIRESIAS, *led by his* PAGE. OEDIPUS *goes into the
palace.*)

ODE I

Strophe 1

CHORUS: The Delphic stone of prophecies
Remembers ancient regicide
And a still bloody hand.
That killer's hour of flight has come.
He must be stronger than riderless
Coursers of untiring wind,
For the son of Zeus armed with his father's thunder
Leaps in lightning after him;
And the Furies hold his track, the sad Furies.   330

Antistrophe 1

Holy Parnassos' peak of snow
Flashes and blinds that secret man,
That all shall hunt him down:
Though he may roam the forest shade
Like a bull gone wild from pasture
To rage through glooms of stone.
Doom comes down on him; flight will not avail
    him;
For the world's heart calls him desolate,
And the immortal voices follow, for ever follow.   340

Strophe 2

But now a wilder thing is heard
From the old man skilled at hearing Fate in the
    wingbeat of a bird.

Bewildered as a blown bird, my soul hovers and can
 not find
Foothold in this debate, or any reason or rest of
 mind.
But no man ever brought—none can bring
Proof of strife between Thebes' royal house,
350 Labdakos' line, and the son of Polybos;
And never until now has any man brought word
Of Laïos' dark death staining Oedipus the King.

Antistrophe 2

Divine Zeus and Apollo hold
Perfect intelligence alone of all tales ever told;
And well though this diviner works, he works in his
 own night;
No man can judge that rough unknown or trust in
 second sight,
For wisdom changes hands among the wise.
360 Shall I believe my great lord criminal
At a raging word that a blind old man let fall?
I saw him, when the carrion woman faced him of
 old,
Prove his heroic mind. These evil words are lies.

SCENE II

KREON: Men of Thebes:
 I am told that heavy accusations
 Have been brought against me by King Oedipus.

 I am not the kind of man to bear this tamely.

 If in these present difficulties
 He holds me accountable for any harm to him
 Through anything I have said or done—why, then,
 I do not value life in this dishonor.

 It is not as though this rumor touched upon
10 Some private indiscretion. The matter is grave.
 The fact is that I am being called disloyal
 To the State, to my fellow citizens, to my friends.
CHORAGOS: He may have spoken in anger, not from
 his mind.
KREON: But did you not hear him say I was the one
 Who seduced the old prophet into lying?
CHORAGOS: The thing was said: I do not know how
 seriously.
KREON: But you were watching him! Were his eyes
20 steady?
 Did he look like a man in his right mind?
CHORAGOS: I do not know.
 I can not judge the behavior of great men.
 But here is the King himself.

  (Enter OEDIPUS.)

OEDIPUS: So you dared come back.
 Why? How brazen of you to come to my house,

You murderer!
Do you think I do not know
That you plotted to kill me, plotted to steal my
 throne?   30
Tell me, in God's name: am I coward, a fool,
That you should dream you could accomplish this?
A fool who could not see your slippery game?
A coward, not to fight back when I saw it?
You are the fool, Kreon, are you not? hoping
Without support or friends to get a throne?
Thrones may be won or bought: you could do
 neither.
KREON: Now listen to me. You have talked; let me
 talk, too.   40
You can not judge unless you know the facts.
OEDIPUS: You speak well: there is one fact; but I find
 it hard
To learn from the deadliest enemy I have.
KREON: That above all I must dispute with you.
OEDIPUS: That above all I will not hear you deny.
KREON: If you think there is anything good in being
 stubborn
Against all reason, then I say you are wrong.
OEDIPUS: If you think a man can sin against his own 50
 kind
And not be punished for it, I say you are mad.
KREON: I agree. But tell me: what have I done to you?
OEDIPUS: You advised me to send for that wizard, did
 you not?
KREON: I did. I should do it again.
OEDIPUS: Very well. Now tell me:
 How long has it been since Laïos—
KREON: What of Laïos?
OEDIPUS: Since he vanished in that onset by the road? 60
KREON: It was long ago, a long time.
OEDIPUS: And this prophet,
 Was he practicing here then?
KREON: He was; and with honor, as now
OEDIPUS: Did he speak of me at that time?
KREON: He never did;
 At least, not when I was present.
OEDIPUS: But . . . the enquiry?
 I suppose you held one?
KREON: We did, but we learned nothing.   70
OEDIPUS: Why did the prophet not speak against me
 then?
KREON: I do not know; and I am the kind of man
 Who holds his tongue when he has no facts to go
 on.
OEDIPUS: There's one fact that you know, and you
 could tell it.
KREON: What fact is that? If I know it, you shall have
 it.
OEDIPUS: If he were not involved with you, he could 80
 not say
That it was I who murdered Laïos.
KREON: If he says that, you are the one that knows
 it!—

But now it is my turn to question you.
OEDIPUS: Put your questions. I am no murderer.
KREON: First, then: You married my sister?
OEDIPUS: I married your sister.
KREON: And you rule the kingdom equally with her?
90 OEDIPUS: Everything that she wants she has from me.
KREON: And I am the third, equal to both of you?
OEDIPUS: That is why I call you a bad friend.
KREON: No. Reason it out, as I have done.
　　　Think of this first: Would any sane man prefer
　　　Power, with all a king's anxieties,
　　　To that same power and the grace of sleep?
　　　Certainly not I.
　　　I have never longed for the king's power—only his
　　　　rights.
100 Would any wise man differ from me in this?
　　　As matters stand, I have my way in everything
　　　With your consent, and no responsibilities.
　　　If I were king, I should be a slave to policy.
　　　How could I desire a sceptre more
　　　Than what is now mine—untroubled influence?
　　　No, I have not gone mad; I need no honors,
　　　Except those with the perquisites I have now.
　　　I am welcome everywhere; every man salutes me,
　　　And those who want your favor seek my ear,
110 Since I know how to manage what they ask.
　　　Should I exchange this ease for that anxiety?
　　　Besides, no sober mind is treasonable.
　　　I hate anarchy
　　　And never would deal with any man who likes it.

　　　Test what I have said. Go to the priestess
　　　At Delphi, ask if I quoted her correctly.
　　　And as for this other thing: If I am found
　　　Guilty of treason with Teiresias,
　　　Then sentence me to death. You have my word
120 It is a sentence I should cast my vote for—
　　　But not without evidence!
　　　You do wrong
　　　When you take good men for bad, bad men for
　　　　good.
　　　A true friend thrown aside—why, life itself
　　　Is not more precious!
　　　In time you will know this well:
　　　For time, and time alone, will show the just man,
　　　Though scoundrels are discovered in a day.
130 CHORAGOS: This is well said, and a prudent man
　　　　would ponder it.
　　　Judgments too quickly formed are dangerous.
OEDIPUS: But is he not quick in his duplicity?
　　　And shall I not be quick to parry him?
　　　Would you have me stand still, hold my peace, and
　　　　let
　　　This man win everything, through my inaction?
KREON: And you want—what is it, then? To banish
　　　me?
140 OEDIPUS: No, not exile. It is your death I want,
　　　So that all the world may see what treason means.

KREON: You will persist then? You will not believe
　　　me?
OEDIPUS: How can I believe you?
KREON: Then you are a fool.
OEDIPUS: To save myself?
KREON: In justice, think of me.
OEDIPUS: You are evil incarnate.
KREON: But suppose that you are wrong?
OEDIPUS: Still I must rule.   150
KREON: But not if you rule badly.
OEDIPUS: O city, city!
KREON: It is my city, too!
CHORAGOS: Now, my lords, be still. I see the Queen,
　　　Iokastê, coming from her palace chambers;
　　　And it is time she came, for the sake of you both,
　　　This dreadful quarrel can be resolved through her.

　　　(Enter IOKASTE.)

IOKASTE: Poor foolish men, what wicked din is this?
　　　With Thebes sick to death, is it not shameful
　　　That you should rake some private quarrel up?   160

　　　(To OEDIPUS)

　　　Come into the house.
　　　And you, Kreon, go now:
　　　Let us have no more of this tumult over nothing.
KREON: Nothing? No, sister: what your husband
　　　plans for me
　　　Is one of two great evils: exile or death.
OEDIPUS: He is right.
　　　Why, woman I have caught him squarely
　　　Plotting against my life.
KREON: No! Let me die   170
　　　Accurst if ever I have wished you harm!
IOKASTE: Ah, believe it, Oedipus!
　　　In the name of the gods, respect this oath of his
　　　For my sake, for the sake of these people here!

Strophe 1

CHORAGOS: Open your mind to her, my lord. Be
　　　ruled by her, I beg you!
OEDIPUS: What would you have me do?
CHORAGOS: Respect Kreon's word. He has never
　　　spoken like a fool,
　　　And now he has sworn an oath.   180
OEDIPUS: You know what you ask?
CHORAGOS: I do.
OEDIPUS: Speak on, then.
CHORAGOS: A friend so sworn should not be baited
　　　so,
　　　In blind malice, and without final proof.
OEDIPUS: You are aware, I hope, that what you say
　　　Means death for me, or exile at the least.

Strophe 2

CHORAGOS: No, I swear by Helios, first in Heaven!
　　　May I die friendless and accurst,   190
　　　The worst of deaths, if ever I meant that!

It is the withering fields
That hurt my sick heart:
Must we bear all these ills,
And now your bad blood as well?

OEDIPUS: Then let him go. And let me die, if I must,
Or be driven by him in shame from the land of
    Thebes.
It is your unhappiness, and not his talk,
200   That touches me.
As for him—
Wherever he goes, hatred will follow him.
KREON: Ugly in yielding, as you were ugly in rage!
Natures like yours chiefly torment themselves.
OEDIPUS: Can you not go? Can you not leave me?
KREON: I can.
You do not know me; but the city knows me,
And in its eyes I am just, if not in yours.

(Exit KREON.*)*

Antistrophe 1

CHORAGOS: Lady Iokastê, did you not ask the King to
210   go to his chambers?
IOKASTE: First tell me what has happened.
CHORAGOS: There was suspicion without evidence;
    yet it rankled
As even false charges will.
IOKASTE: On both sides?
CHORAGOS: On both.
IOKASTE: But what was said?
CHORAGOS: Oh let it rest, let it be done with!
Have we not suffered enough?
220 OEDIPUS: You see to what your decency has brought
    you:
You have made difficulties where my heart saw
    none.

Antistrophe 2

CHORAGOS: Oedipus, it is not once only I have told
    you—
You must know I should count myself unwise
To the point of madness, should I now forsake
    you—
You, under whose hand,
    In the storm of another time,
Our dear land sailed out free.
    But now stand fast at the helm!
230

IOKASTE: In God's name, Oedipus, inform your wife
    as well:
Why are you so set in this hard anger?
OEDIPUS: I will tell you, for none of these men
    deserves
My confidence as you do. It is Kreon's work,
His treachery, his plotting against me.
IOKASTE: Go on, if you can make this clear to me.

OEDIPUS: He charges me with the murder of Laïos.
IOKASTE: Has he some knowledge? Or does he speak
    from hearsay?
OEDIPUS: He would not commit himself to such a
    charge,
But he has brought in that damnable soothsayer
To tell his story.
IOKASTE: Set your mind at rest.
If it is a question of soothsayers, I tell you
That you will find no man whose craft gives   250
    knowledge
Of the unknowable.

Here is my proof:
An oracle was reported to Laïos once
(I will not say from Phoibos himself, but from
His appointed ministers, at any rate)
That his doom would be death at the hands of his
    own son—
His son, born of his flesh and of mine!

Now, you remember the story: Laïos was killed   260
By marauding strangers where three highways
    meet;
But his child had not been three days in this world
Before the King had pierced the baby's ankles
And left him to die on a lonely mountainside.
Thus, Apollo never caused that child
To kill his father, and it was not Laïos' fate
To die at the hands of his son, as he had feared.
This is what prophets and prophecies are worth!
Have no dread of them.   270
It is God himself
Who can show us what he wills, in his own way.
OEDIPUS: How strange a shadowy memory crossed
    my mind,
Just now while you were speaking; it chilled my
    heart.
IOKASTE: What do you mean? What memory do you
    speak of?
OEDIPUS: If I understand you, Laïos was killed
At a place where three roads meet.   280
IOKASTE: So it was said;
We have no later story.
OEDIPUS: Where did it happen?
IOKASTE: Phokis, it is called: at a place where the
    Theban Way
Divides into the roads toward Delphi and Daulia.
OEDIPUS: When?
IOKASTE: We had the news not long before you came
And proved the right to your succession here.
OEDIPUS: Ah, what net has God been weaving for me? 290
IOKASTE: Oedipus! Why does this trouble you?
OEDIPUS: Do not ask me yet.
First, tell me how Laïos looked, and tell me
How old he was.
IOKASTE: He was tall, his hair just touched

With white; his form was not unlike your own.
OEDIPUS: I think that I myself may be accurst
By my own ignorant edict.
IOKASTE: You speak strangely.
300   It makes me tremble to look at you, my King.
OEDIPUS: I am not sure that the blind man can not
see.
But I should know better if you were to tell me—
IOKASTE: Anything—though I dread to hear you ask
it.
OEDIPUS: Was the King lightly escorted, or did he
ride
With a large company, as a ruler should?
IOKASTE: There were five men with him in all: one
310   was a herald;
And a single chariot, which he was driving.
OEDIPUS: Alas, that makes it plain enough!
But who—
Who told you how it happened?
IOKASTE: A household servant,
The only one to escape.
OEDIPUS: And is he still
A servant of ours?
IOKASTE: No; for when he came back at last
320   And found you enthroned in the place of the dead
king,
He came to me, touched my hand with his, and
begged
That I would send him away to the frontier district
Where only the shepherds go—
As far away from the city as I could send him.
I granted his prayer; for although the man was a
slave,
He had earned more than this favor at my hands.
330   OEDIPUS: Can he be called back quickly?
IOKASTE: Easily.
But why?
OEDIPUS: I have taken too much upon myself
Without enquiry; therefore I wish to consult him.
IOKASTE: Then he shall come.
But am I not one also
To whom you might confide these fears of yours?
OEDIPUS: That is your right; it will not be denied you,
Now least of all; for I have reached a pitch
340   Of wild foreboding. Is there anyone
To whom I should sooner speak?

Polybos of Corinth is my father.
My mother is a Dorian: Meropê.
I grew up chief among the men of Corinth
Until a strange thing happened—
Not worth my passion, it may be, but strange.

At a feast, a drunken man maundering in his cups
Cries out that I am not my father's son!
I contained myself that night, though I felt anger
350   And a sinking heart. The next day I visited

My father and mother, and questioned them. They
stormed,
Calling it all the slanderous rant of a fool;
And this relieved me. Yet the suspicion
Remained always aching in my mind;
I knew there was talk; I could not rest;
And finally, saying nothing to my parents,
I went to the shrine at Delphi.

The god dismissed my question without reply;
He spoke of other things.   360
Some were clear,
Full of wretchedness, dreadful, unbearable:
As, that I should lie with my own mother, breed
Children from whom all men would turn their
eyes;
And that I should be my father's murderer.

I heard all this, and fled. And from that day
Corinth to me was only in the stars
Descending in that quarter of the sky,
As I wandered farther and farther on my way   370
To a land where I should never see the evil
Sung by the oracle. And I came to this country
Where, so you say, King Laïos was killed.

I will tell you all that happened there, my lady.

There were three highways
Coming together at a place I passed;
And there a herald came towards me, and a chariot
Drawn by horses, with a man such as you describe
Seated in it. The groom leading the horses
Forced me off the road at his lord's command;   380
But as this charioteer lurched over towards me
I struck him in my rage. The old man saw me
And brought his double goad down upon my head
As I came abreast.
He was paid back, and more!
Swinging my club in this right hand I knocked him
Out of his car, and he rolled on the ground.
I killed him.
I killed them all.
Now if that stranger and Laïos were—kin,   390
Where is a man more miserable than I?
More hated by the gods? Citizen and alien alike
Must never shelter me or speak to me—
I must be shunned by all.
And I myself
Pronounced this malediction upon myself!

Think of it: I have touched you with these hands,
These hands that killed your husband. What
defilement!

Am I all evil, then? It must be so,   400
Since I must flee from Thebes, yet never again

See my own countrymen, my own country,
For fear of joining my mother in marriage
And killing Polybos, my father.
Ah,
If I was created so, born to this fate,
Who could deny the savagery of God?

O holy majesty of heavenly powers!
May I never see that day! Never!
410   Rather let me vanish from the race of men
Than know the abomination destined me!
CHORAGOS: We too, my lord, have felt dismay at this.
  But there is hope: you have yet to hear the
    shepherd.
OEDIPUS: Indeed, I fear no other hope is left me.
IOKASTE: What do you hope from him when he
  comes?
OEDIPUS: This much:
  If his account of the murder tallies with yours,
420   Then I am cleared.
IOKASTE: What was it that I said
  Of such importance?
OEDIPUS: Why, 'marauders', you said,
  Killed the King, according to this man's story.
  If he maintains that still, if there were several,
  Clearly the guilt is not mine: I was alone.
  But if he says one man, singlehanded, did it,
  Then the evidence all points to me.
IOKASTE: You may be sure that he said there were
430   several;
  And can he call back that story now? He can not.
  The whole city heard it as plainly as I.
  But suppose he alters some detail of it:
  He can not ever show that Laïos' death
  Fulfilled the oracle: for Apollo said
  My child was doomed to kill him; and my child—
  Poor baby!—it was my child that died first.

  No. From now on, where oracles are concerned,
  I would not waste a second thought on any.
440 OEDIPUS: You may be right.
  But come: let someone go
  For the shepherd at once. This matter must be
    settled.
IOKASTE: I will send for him.
  I would not wish to cross you in anything,
  And surely not in this.—Let us go in.

(Exeunt into the palace.)

ODE II

Strophe 1

CHORUS: Let me be reverent in the ways of right,
  Lowly the paths I journey on;
  Let all my words and actions keep
  The laws of the pure universe

From highest Heaven handed down.
For Heaven is their bright nurse,
Those generations of the realms of light;
Ah, never of mortal kind were they begot,
Nor are they slaves of memory, lost in sleep:
Their Father is greater than Time, and ages not.

Antistrophe 1

The tyrant is a child of Pride
Who drinks from his great sickening cup
Recklessness and vanity,
Until from his high crest headlong   460
He plummets to the dust of hope.
That strong man is not strong.
But let no fair ambition be denied;
May God protect the wrestler for the State
In government, in comely policy,
Who will fear God, and on His ordinance wait.

Strophe 2

Haughtiness and the high hand of disdain
Tempt and outrage God's holy law;
And any mortal who dares hold
No immortal Power in awe   470
Will be caught up in a net of pain:
The price for which his levity is sold.
Let each man take due earnings, then,
And keep his hands from holy things,
And from blasphemy stand apart—
Else the crackling blast of heaven
Blows on his head, and on his desperate heart.
Though fools will honor impious men,
In their cities no tragic poet sings.

Antistrophe 2

Shall we lose faith in Delphi's obscurities,   480
We who have heard the world's core
Discredited, and the sacred wood
Of Zeus at Elis praised no more?
The deeds and the strange prophecies
Must make a pattern yet to be understood.
Zeus, if indeed you are lord of all,
Throned in light over night and day,
Mirror this in your endless mind:
Our masters call the oracle
Words on the wind, and the Delphic vision blind!   490
Their hearts no longer know Apollo,
And reverence for the gods has died away.

SCENE III

(Enter IOKASTE.*)*

IOKASTE: Princes of Thebes, it has occurred to me
  To visit the altars of the gods, bearing
  These branches as a suppliant, and this incense.
  Our King is not himself: his noble soul

Is overwrought with fantasies of dread,
Else he would consider
The new prophecies in the light of the old.
He will listen to any voice that speaks disaster,
And my advice goes for nothing.

(She approaches the altar, right.)

10   To you, then, Apollo,
Lycéan lord, since you are nearest, I turn in prayer.

Receive these offerings, and grant us deliverance
From defilement. Our hearts are heavy with fear
When we see our leader distracted, as helpless
    sailors
Are terrified by the confusion of their helmsman.

(Enter MESSENGER.*)*

MESSENGER: Friends, no doubt you can direct me:
Where shall I find the house of Oedipus,
Or, better still, where is the King himself?
20   CHORAGOS: It is this very place, stranger; he is inside.
This is his wife and mother of his children.
MESSENGER: I wish her happiness in a happy house,
Blest in all the fulfillment of her marriage.
IOKASTE: I wish as much for you: your courtesy
Deserves a like good fortune. But now, tell me:
Why have you come? What have you to say to us?
MESSENGER: Good news, my lady, for your house and
    your husband.
IOKASTE: What news? Who sent you here?
30   MESSENGER: I am from Corinth.
The news I bring ought to mean joy for you,
Though it may be you will find some grief in it.
IOKASTE: What is it? How can it touch us in both
    ways?
MESSENGER: The word is that the people of the
    Isthmus
Intend to call Oedipus to be their king.
IOKASTE: But old King Polybos—is he not reigning
    still?
40   MESSENGER: No. Death holds him in his sepulchre.
IOKASTE: What are you saying? Polybos is dead?
MESSENGER: If I am not telling the truth, may I die
    myself.
IOKASTE *(to a* MAIDSERVANT*)*: Go in, go quickly; tell
    this to your master.

O riddlers of God's will, where are you now!
This was the man whom Oedipus, long ago,
Feared so, fled so, in dread of destroying him—
But it was another fate by which he died.

(Enter OEDIPUS, *center.)*

50   OEDIPUS: Dearest Iokaste, why have you sent for me?
IOKASTE: Listen to what this man says, and then tell
    me
What has become of the solemn prophecies.

OEDIPUS: Who is this man? What is his news for me?
IOKASTE: He has come from Corinth to announce
    your father's death!
OEDIPUS: Is it true, stranger? Tell me in your own
    words.
MESSENGER: I can not say it more clearly: the King is
    dead.   60
OEDIPUS: Was it by treason? Or by an attack of illness?
MESSENGER: A little thing brings old men to their rest.
OEDIPUS: It was sickness, then?
MESSENGER: Yes, and his many years.
OEDIPUS: Ah!
Why should a man respect the Pythian hearth, or
Give heed to the birds that jangle above his head?
They prophesied that I should kill Polybos,
Kill my own father; but he is dead and buried,
And I am here—I never touched him, never,   70
Unless he died of grief for my departure,
And thus, in a sense, through me. No. Polybos
Has packed the oracles off with him underground.
They are empty words.
IOKASTE: Had I not told you so?
OEDIPUS: You had; it was my faint heart that betrayed
    me.
IOKASTE: From now on never think of those things
    again.
OEDIPUS: And yet—must I not fear my mother's bed?   80
IOKASTE: Why should anyone in this world be afraid,
Since Fate rules us and nothing can be foreseen?
A man should live only for the present day.

Have no more fear of sleeping with your mother:
How many men, in dreams, have lain with their
    mothers!
No reasonable man is troubled by such things.
OEDIPUS: That is true; only—
If only my mother were not still alive!
But she is alive. I can not help my dread.   90
IOKASTE: Yet this news of your father's death is
    wonderful.
OEDIPUS: Wonderful. But I fear the living woman.
MESSENGER: Tell me, who is this woman that you
    fear?
OEDIPUS: It is Meropê, man; the wife of King
    Polybos.
MESSENGER: Meropê? Why should you be afraid of
    her?
OEDIPUS: An oracle of the gods, a dreadful saying.   100
MESSENGER: Can you tell me about it or are you sworn
    to silence?
OEDIPUS: I can tell you, and I will.
Apollo said through his prophet that I was the man
Who should marry his own mother, shed his
    father's blood
With his own hands. And so, for all these years
I have kept clear of Corinth, and no harm has
    come—

110   Though it would have been sweet to see my parents
      again.
MESSENGER: And is this the fear that drove you out of
      Corinth?
OEDIPUS: Would you have me kill my father?
MESSENGER: As for that
      You must be reassured by the news I gave you.
OEDIPUS: If you could reassure me, I would reward
      you.
MESSENGER: I had that in mind, I will confess: I
120   thought
      I could count on you when you returned to
      Corinth.
OEDIPUS: No: I will never go near my parents again.
MESSENGER: Ah, son, you still do not know what you
      are doing—
OEDIPUS: What do you mean? In the name of God tell
      me!
MESSENGER: —If these are your reasons for not going
      home.
130 OEDIPUS: I tell you, I fear the oracle may come true.
MESSENGER: And guilt may come upon you through
      your parents?
OEDIPUS: That is the dread that is always in my heart.
MESSENGER: Can you not see that all your fears are
      groundless?
OEDIPUS: Groundless? Am I not my parents' son?
MESSENGER: Polybos was not your father.
OEDIPUS: Not my father?
MESSENGER: No more your father than the man
140   speaking to you.
OEDIPUS: But you are nothing to me!
MESSENGER: Neither was he.
OEDIPUS: Then why did he call me son?
MESSENGER: I will tell you:
      Long ago he had you from my hands, as a gift.
OEDIPUS: Then how could he love me so, if I was not
      his?
MESSENGER: He had no children, and his heart
      turned to you.
150 OEDIPUS: What of you? Did you buy me? Did you find
      me by chance?
MESSENGER: I came upon you in the woody vales of
      Kithairon.
OEDIPUS: And what were you doing there?
MESSENGER: Tending my flocks.
OEDIPUS: A wandering shepherd?
MESSENGER: But your savior, son, that day.
OEDIPUS: From what did you save me?
MESSENGER: Your ankles should tell you that.
160 OEDIPUS: Ah, stranger, why do you speak of that
      childhood pain?
MESSENGER: I pulled the skewer that pinned your feet
      together.
OEDIPUS: I have had the mark as long as I can
      remember.

MESSENGER: That was why you were given the name
      you bear.
OEDIPUS: God! Was it my father or my mother who
      did it?
      Tell me!   170
MESSENGER: I do not know. The man who gave you to
      me
      Can tell you better than I.
OEDIPUS: It was not you that found me, but another?
MESSENGER: It was another shepherd gave you to me.
OEDIPUS: Who was he? Can you tell me who he was?
MESSENGER: I think he was said to be one of Laïos'
      people.
OEDIPUS: You mean the Laïos who was king here
      years ago?   180
MESSENGER: Yes; King Laïos; and the man was one of
      his herdsmen.
OEDIPUS: Is he still alive? Can I see him?
MESSENGER: These men here
      Know best about such things.
OEDIPUS: Does anyone here
      Know this shepherd that he is talking about?
      Have you seen him in the fields, or in the town?
      If you have, tell me. It is time things were made
      plain.   190
CHORAGOS: I think the man he means is that same
      shepherd
      You have already asked to see. Iokastê perhaps
      Could tell you something.
OEDIPUS: Do you know anything
      About him, Lady? Is he the man we have
      summoned?
      Is that the man this shepherd means?
IOKASTE: Why think of him?
      Forget this herdsman. Forget it all.   200
      This talk is a waste of time.
OEDIPUS: How can you say that,
      When the clues to my true birth are in my hands?
IOKASTE: For God's love, let us have no more
      questioning!
      Is your life nothing to you?
      My own is pain enough for me to bear.
MESSENGER: You need not worry. Suppose my
      mother a slave,
      And born of slaves: no baseness can touch you.   210
IOKASTE: Listen to me, I beg of you: do not do this
      thing!
OEDIPUS: I will not listen; the truth must be made
      known.
IOKASTE: Everything that I say is for your own good!
OEDIPUS: My own good
      Snaps my patience, then; I want none of it.
IOKASTE: You are fatally wrong! May you never learn
      who you are!
OEDIPUS: Go, one of you, and bring the shepherd   220
      here.

Let us leave this woman to brag of her royal name.
IOKASTE: Ah, miserable!
That is the only word I have for you now.
That is the only word I can ever have.

(Exit into the palace.)

CHORAGOS: Why has she left us, Oedipus? Why has
she gone
In such a passion of sorrow? I fear this silence:
Something dreadful may come of it.
230 OEDIPUS: Let it come!
However base my birth, I must know about it.
The Queen, like a woman, is perhaps ashamed
To think of my low origin. But I
Am a child of Luck; I can not be dishonored.
Luck is my mother; the passing months, my
brothers,
Have seen me rich and poor.
If this is so,
How could I wish that I were someone else?
240 How could I not be glad to know my birth?

ODE III

Strophe

CHORUS: If ever the coming time were known
To my heart's pondering,
Kithairon, now by Heaven I see the torches
At the festival of the next full moon,
And see the dance, and hear the choir sing
A grace to your gentle shade:
Mountain where Oedipus was found,
O mountain guard of a noble race!
May the god who heals us lend his aid,
250 And let that glory come to pass
For our King's cradling-ground.

Antistrophe

Of the nymphs that flower beyond the years,
Who bore you, royal child,
To Pan of the hills or the timberline Apollo,
Cold in delight where the upland clears,
Or Hermês for whom Kyllenês heights are piled?
Or flushed as evening cloud,
Great Dionysos, roamer of mountains,
He—was it he who found you there,
260 And caught you up in his own proud
Arms from the sweet god-ravisher
Who laughed by the Muses' fountains?

SCENE IV

OEDIPUS: Sirs: though I do not know the man,
I think I see him coming, this shepherd we want:
He is old, like our friend here, and the men
Bringing him seem to be servants of my house.

But you can tell, if you have ever seen him.

(Enter SHEPHERD escorted by servants.)

CHORAGOS: I know him, he was Laïos' man. You can
trust him.
OEDIPUS: Tell me first, you from Corinth: is this the
shepherd
We were discussing?   10
MESSENGER: This is the very man.
OEDIPUS (to SHEPHERD): Come here. No, look at me.
You must answer
Everything I ask.—You belonged to Laïos?
SHEPHERD: Yes: born his slave, brought up in his
house.
OEDIPUS: Tell me: what kind of work did you do for
him?
SHEPHERD: I was a shepherd of his, most of my life.
OEDIPUS: Where mainly did you go for pasturage?   20
SHEPHERD: Sometimes Kithairon, sometimes the hills
near-by.
OEDIPUS: Do you remember ever seeing this man out
there?
SHEPHERD: What would he be doing there? This
man?
OEDIPUS: This man standing here. Have you ever
seen him before?
SHEPHERD: No. At least, not to my recollection.
MESSENGER: And that is not strange, my lord. But I'll   30
refresh
His memory: he must remember when we two
Spent three whole seasons together, March to
September,
On Kithairon or thereabouts. He had two flocks;
I had one. Each autumn I'd drive mine home
And he would go back with his to Laïos'
sheepfold.—
Is this not true, just as I have described it?
SHEPHERD: True, yes; but it was all so long ago.   40
MESSENGER: Well, then: do you remember, back in
those days,
That you gave me a baby boy to bring up as my
own?
SHEPHERD: What if I did? What are you trying to
say?
MESSENGER: King Oedipus was once that little child.
SHEPHERD: Damn you, hold your tongue!
OEDIPUS: No more of that!
It is your tongue needs watching, not this man's.   50
SHEPHERD: My King, my Master, what is it I have
done wrong?
OEDIPUS: You have not answered his question about
the boy.
SHEPHERD: He does not know . . . He is only making
trouble . . .
OEDIPUS: Come, speak plainly, or it will go hard with
you.

SHEPHERD: In God's name, do not torture an old
60   man!
OEDIPUS: Come here, one of you; bind his arms
    behind him.
SHEPHERD: Unhappy king! What more do you wish to
    learn?
OEDIPUS: Did you give this man the child he speaks
    of?
SHEPHERD: I did.
    And I would to God I had died that very day.
OEDIPUS: You will die now unless you speak the truth.
70 SHEPHERD: Yet if I speak the truth, I am worse than
    dead.
OEDIPUS (to ATTENDANT): He intends to draw it out,
    apparently—
SHEPHERD: No! I have told you already that I gave
    him the boy.
OEDIPUS: Where did you get him? From your house?
    From somewhere else?
SHEPHERD: Not from mine, no. A man gave him to
    me.
80 OEDIPUS: Is that man here? Whose house did he
    belong to?
SHEPHERD: For God's love, my King, do not ask me
    any more!
OEDIPUS: You are a dead man if I have to ask you
    again.
SHEPHERD: Then . . . Then the child was from the
    palace of Laïos.
OEDIPUS: A slave child? or a child of his own line?
SHEPHERD: Ah, I am on the brink of dreadful speech!
90 OEDIPUS: And I of dreadful hearing. Yet I must hear.
SHEPHERD: If you must be told, then . . .
    They said it was Laïos' child;
    But it is your wife who can tell you about that.
OEDIPUS: My wife!—Did she give it to you?
SHEPHERD: My lord, she did.
OEDIPUS: Do you know why?
SHEPHERD: I was told to get rid of it.
OEDIPUS: Oh heartless mother!
SHEPHERD: But in dread of prophecies . . .
100 OEDIPUS: Tell me.
SHEPHERD: It was said that the boy would kill his own
    father.
OEDIPUS: Then why did you give him over to this old
    man?
SHEPHERD: I pitied the baby, my King,
    And I thought that this man would take him far
    away
    To his own country.
    He saved him—but for what a fate!
110   For if you are what this man says you are,
    No man living is more wretched than Oedipus.
OEDIPUS: Ah God!
    It was true!
    All the prophecies!
    —Now,

O Light, may I look on you for the last time!
I, Oedipus,
Oedipus, damned in his birth, in his marriage
    damned,
Damned in the blood he shed with his own hand!   120

(He rushes into the palace.)

ODE IV

Strophe 1

CHORUS: Alas for the seed of men.

What measure shall I give these generations
That breathe on the void and are void
And exist and do not exist?

Who bears more weight of joy
Than mass of sunlight shifting in images,
Or who shall make his thought stay on
That down time drifts away?

Your splendor is all fallen.

O naked brow of wrath and tears,   130
O change of Oedipus!
I who saw your days call no man blest—
Your great days like ghosts gone.

Antistrophe 1

That mind was a strong bow.

Deep, how deep you drew it then, hard archer,
At a dim fearful range,

And brought dear glory down!

You overcame the stranger—
The virgin with her hooking lion claws—
And though death sang, stood like a tower   140
To make pale Thebes take heart.

Fortress against our sorrow!

True king, giver of laws,
Majestic Oedipus!
No prince in Thebes had ever such renown,
No prince won such grace of power.

Strophe 2

And now of all men ever known
Most pitiful is this man's story:
His fortunes are most changed, his state
Fallen to a low slave's   150
Ground under bitter fate.

O Oedipus, most royal one!
The great door that expelled you to the light

Gave at night—ah, gave night to your glory:
As to the father, to the fathering son.

All understood too late.

How could that queen whom Laïos won,
The garden that he harrowed at his height,
Be silent when that act was done?

Antistrophe 2

160 But all eyes fail before time's eye,
All actions come to justice there.
Your bed, your dread sirings,
Are brought to book at last.

Child by Laïos doomed to die,
Then doomed to lose that fortunate little death,
Would God you never took breath in this air
That with my wailing lips I take to cry:

For I weep the world's outcast.

I was blind, and now I can tell why:
170 Asleep, for you had given ease of breath
To Thebes, while the false years went by.

EXODOS

(Enter, from the palace, SECOND MESSENGER.)

SECOND MESSENGER: Elders of Thebes, most honored
   in this land,
What horrors are yours to see and hear, what
   weight
Of sorrow to be endured, if, true to your birth,
You venerate the line of Labdakos!
I think neither Istros nor Phasis, those great rivers,
Could purify this place of all the evil
180 It shelters now, or soon must bring to light—
Evil not done unconsciously, but willed.

The greatest griefs are those we cause ourselves.
CHORAGOS: Surely, friend, we have grief enough
   already;
What new sorrow do you mean?
SECOND MESSENGER: The Queen is dead.
CHORAGOS: O miserable Queen! But at whose hand?
SECOND MESSENGER: Her own.
The full horror of what happened you can not
190   know,
For you did not see it; but I, who did, will tell you
As clearly as I can how she met her death.

When she had left us,
In passionate silence, passing through the court,
She ran to her apartment in the house,
Her hair clutched by the fingers of both hands.
She closed the doors behind her; then, by that bed

Where long ago the fatal son was conceived—
That son who should bring about his father's
   death—
200 We heard her call upon Laïos, dead so many years,
And heard her wail for the double fruit of her
   marriage,
A husband by her husband, children by her child.

Exactly how she died I do not know:
For Oedipus burst in moaning and would not let us
Keep vigil to the end: it was by him
As he stormed about the room that our eyes were
   caught.
From one to another of us he went, begging a
   sword,
210 Hunting the wife who was not his wife, the mother
Whose womb had carried his own children and
   himself.
I do not know: it was none of us aided him,
But surely one of the gods was in control!
For with a dreadful cry
He hurled his weight, as though wrenched out of
   himself,
At the twin doors: the bolts gave, and he rushed in.
220 And there we saw her hanging, her body swaying
From the cruel cord she had noosed about her
   neck.
A great sob broke from him, heartbreaking to hear,
As he loosed the rope and lowered her to the
   ground.

I would blot out from my mind what happened
   next!
For the King ripped from her gown the golden
   brooches
230 That were her ornament, and raised them, and
   plunged them down
Straight into his own eyeballs, crying, 'No more,
No more shall you look on the misery about me,
The horrors of my own doing! Too long you have
   known
The faces of those whom I should never have seen,
Too long been blind to those for whom I was
   searching!
From this hour, go in darkness!' And as he spoke,
240 He struck at his eyes—not once, but many times;
And the blood spattered his beard,
Bursting from his ruined sockets like red hail.

So from the unhappiness of two this evil has
   sprung,
A curse on the man and woman alike. The old
Happiness of the house of Labdakos
Was happiness enough: where is it today?
It is all wailing and ruin, disgrace, death—all
The misery of mankind that has a name—
250 And it is wholly and for ever theirs.

CHORAGOS: Is he in agony still? Is there no rest for
 him?
SECOND MESSENGER: He is calling for someone to
 open the doors wide
 So that all the children of Kadmos may look upon
 His father's murderer, his mother's—no,
 I can not say it!
 And then he will leave Thebes,
260 Self-exiled, in order that the curse
 Which he himself pronounced may depart from
  the house.
 He is weak, and there is none to lead him,
 So terrible is his suffering.
 But you will see:
 Look, the doors are opening; in a moment
 You will see a thing that would crush a heart of
  stone.

(The central door is opened; OEDIPUS, *blinded, is led in.)*

CHORAGOS: Dreadful indeed for men to see.
270 Never have my own eyes
 Looked on a sight so full of fear.

 Oedipus!
 What madness came upon you, what daemon
 Leaped on your life with heavier
 Punishment than a mortal man can bear?
 No: I can not even
 Look at you, poor ruined one.
 And I would speak, question, ponder,
 If I were able. No.
280 You make me shudder.
OEDIPUS: God.   God.
 Is there a sorrow greater?
 Where shall I find harbor in this world?
 My voice is hurled far on a dark wind.
 What has God done to me?
CHORAGOS: Too terrible to think of, or to see.

Strophe 1

OEDIPUS: O cloud of night,
 Never to be turned away: night coming on,
 I can not tell how: night like a shroud!

290 My fair winds brought me here.
 O God. Again
 The pain of the spikes where I had sight,
 The flooding pain
 Of memory, never to be gouged out.
CHORAGOS: This is not strange.
 You suffer it all twice over, remorse in pain,
 Pain in remorse.

Antistrophe 1

OEDIPUS: Ah dear friend
 Are you faithful even yet, you alone?
300 Are you still standing near me, will you stay here,

Patient, to care for the blind?
 The blind man!
 Yet even blind I know who it is attends me,
 By the voice's tone—
 Though my new darkness hide the comforter.
CHORAGOS: Oh fearful act!
 What god was it drove you to rake black
 Night across your eyes?

Strophe 2

OEDIPUS: Apollo. Apollo. Dear
 Children, the god was Apollo.   310
 He brought my sick, sick fate upon me.
 But the blinding hand was my own!
 How could I bear to see
 When all my sight was horror everywhere?
CHORAGOS: Everywhere; that is true.
OEDIPUS: And now what is left?
 Images? Love? A greeting even,
 Sweet to the senses? Is there anything?
 Ah, no, friends: lead me away.
 Lead me away from Thebes.   320
 Lead the great wreck
 And hell of Oedipus, whom the gods hate.
CHORAGOS: Your misery, you are not blind to that.
 Would God you had never found it out!

Antistrophe 2

OEDIPUS: Death take the man who unbound
 My feet on the hillside
 And delivered me from death to life! What life?
 If only I had died,
 This weight of monstrous doom
 Could not have dragged me and my darlings down. 330
CHORAGOS: I would have wished the same.
OEDIPUS: Oh never to have come here
 With my father's blood upon me! Never
 To have been the man they call his mother's
  husband!
 Oh accurst! Oh child of evil,
 To have entered that wretched bed—
 The selfsame one!
 More primal than sin itself, this fell to me.
CHORAGOS: I do not know what words to offer you. 340
 You were better dead than alive and blind.
OEDIPUS: Do not counsel me any more. This
  punishment
 That I have laid upon myself is just.
 If I had eyes,
 I do not know how I could bear the sight
 Of my father, when I came to the house of Death,
 Or my mother: for I have sinned against them both
 So vilely that I could not make my peace
 By strangling my own life.   350
 Or do you think my children,
 Born as they were born, would be sweet to my eyes?
 Ah never, never! Nor this town with its high walls,

Nor the holy images of the gods.
For I,
Thrice miserable!—Oedipus, noblest of all the line
Of Kadmos, have condemned myself to enjoy
These things no more, by my own malediction
360   Expelling that man whom the gods declared
To be a defilement in the house of Laïos.
After exposing the rankness of my own guilt,
How could I look men frankly in the eyes?
No, I swear it,
If I could have stifled my hearing at its source,
I would have done it, and made all this body
A tight cell of misery, blank to light and sound:
So I should have been safe in my dark mind
Beyond external evil.
Ah Kithairon!
370   Why did you shelter me? When I was cast upon
you,
Why did I not die? Then I should never
Have shown the world my execrable birth.

Ah Polybos! Corinth, city that I believed
The ancient seat of my ancestors: how fair
I seemed, your child! And all the while this evil
Was cancerous within me!
For I am sick
In my own being, sick in my origin,

380   O three roads, dark ravine, woodland and way
Where three roads met: you, drinking my father's
blood,
My own blood, spilled by my own hand: can you
remember
The unspeakable things I did there, and the things
I went on from there to do?
O marriage, marriage!
The act that engendered me, and again the act
Performed by the son in the same bed—
390   Ah, the net
Of incest, mingling fathers, brothers, sons,
With brides, wives, mothers: the last evil
That can be known by men: no tongue can say
How evil!
No. For the love of God, conceal me
Somewhere far from Thebes; or kill me; or hurl
me
Into the sea, away from men's eyes for ever.
Come, lead me. You need not fear to touch me.
400   Of all men, I alone can bear this guilt.

(*Enter* KREON.)

CHORAGOS: Kreon is here now. As to what you ask,
He may decide the course to take. He only
Is left to protect the city in your place.
OEDIPUS: Alas, how can I speak to him? What right
have I
To beg his courtesy whom I have deeply wronged?

KREON: I have not come to mock you, Oedipus,
Or to reproach you, either.

(*To* ATTENDANTS)

—You, standing there:
If you have lost all respect for man's dignity,   410
At least respect the flame of Lord Helios:
Do not allow this pollution to show itself
Openly here, an affront to the earth
And Heaven's rain and the light of day. No, take
him
Into the house as quickly as you can.
For it is proper
That only the close kindred see his grief.
OEDIPUS: I pray you in God's name, since your
courtesy   420
Ignores my dark expectation, visiting
With mercy this man of all men most execrable:
Give me what I ask—for your good, not for mine.
KREON: And what is it that you turn to me begging
for?
OEDIPUS: Drive me out of this country as quickly as
may be
To a place where no human voice can ever greet
me.
KREON: I should have done that before now—only,   430
God's will had not been wholly revealed to me.
OEDIPUS: But his command is plain: the parricide
Must be destroyed. I am that evil man.
KREON: That is the sense of it, yes; but as things are,
We had best discover clearly what is to be done.
OEDIPUS: You would learn more about a man like
me?
KREON: You are ready now to listen to the god.
OEDIPUS: I will listen. But it is to you
That I must turn for help. I beg you, hear me.   440

The woman in there—
Give her whatever funeral you think proper:
She is your sister.
—But let me go, Kreon!
Let me purge my father's Thebes of the pollution
Of my living here, and go out to the wild hills,
To Kithairon, that has won such fame with me,
The tomb my mother and father appointed for me,
And let me die there, as they willed I should.
And yet I know   450
Death will not ever come to me through sickness
Or in any natural way: I have been preserved
For some unthinkable fate. But let that be.

As for my sons, you need not care for them.
They are men, they will find some way to live.
But my poor daughters, who have shared my table,
Who never before have been parted from their
father—
Take care of them, Kreon; do this for me.

460 And will you let me touch them with my hands
A last time, and let us weep together?
Be kind, my lord,
Great prince, be kind!
Could I but touch them.
They would be mine again, as when I had my eyes.

(Enter ANTIGONE and ISMENE, attended.)

Ah, God!
Is it my dearest children I hear weeping?
Has Kreon pitied me and sent my daughters?
KREON: Yes, Oedipus: I knew that they were dear to
470   you
In the old days, and you must love them still.
OEDIPUS: May God bless you for this—and be a
    friendlier
Guardian to you than he has been to me!

Children, where are you?
Come quickly to my hands: they are your
    brother's—
Hands that have brought your father's once clear
    eyes
480 To this way of seeing—
Ah dearest ones,
I had neither sight nor knowledge then, your
    father
By the woman who was the source of his own life!
And I weep for you—having no strength to see
    you—,
I weep for you when I think of the bitterness
That men will visit upon you all your lives.
What homes, what festivals can you attend
490 Without being forced to depart again in tears?
And when you come to marriageable age,
Where is the man, my daughters, who would dare
Risk the bane that lies on all my children?
Is there any evil wanting? Your father killed
His father; sowed the womb of her who bore him;
Engendered you at the fount of his own existence!

That is what they will say of you.

Then, whom
Can you ever marry? There are no bridegrooms
500   for you,
And your lives must wither away in sterile
    dreaming.

O Kreon, son of Menoikeus!
You are the only father my daughters have,

Since we, their parents, are both of us gone for
    ever.
They are your own blood: you will not let them
Fall into beggary and loneliness;
You will keep them from the miseries that are
    mine!   510
Take pity on them; see, they are only children,
Friendless except for you. Promise me this,
Great Prince, and give me your hand in token of it.

(KREON clasps his right hand.)

Children:
I could say much, if you could understand me,
But as it is, I have only this prayer for you:
Live where you can, be as happy as you can—
Happier, please God, than God has made your
    father.
KREON: Enough. You have wept enough. Now go   520
    within.
OEDIPUS: I must; but it is hard.
KREON: Time eases all things.
OEDIPUS: You know my mind, then?
KREON: Say what you desire.
OEDIPUS: Send me from Thebes!
KREON: God grant that I may!
OEDIPUS: But since God hates me . . .
KREON: No, he will grant your wish.
OEDIPUS: You promise?   530
KREON: I can not speak beyond my knowledge.
OEDIPUS: Then lead me in.
KREON: Come now, and leave your children.
OEDIPUS: No! Do not take them from me!
KREON: Think no longer
    That you are in command here, but rather think
    How, when you were, you served your own
        destruction.

(Exeunt into the house all but the CHORUS; the
CHORAGOS chants directly to the audience.)

CHORAGOS: Men of Thebes: look upon Oedipus.

This is the king who solved the famous riddle   540
And towered up, most powerful of men.
No mortal eyes but looked on him with envy,
Yet in the end ruin swept over him.

Let every man in mankind's frailty
Consider his last day; and let none
Presume on his good fortune until he find
Life, at his death, a memory without pain.

Figure 6. The Chorus of Theban Elders and Jocasta (Patricia Conolly, *rear*) plead with Oedipus (Len Cariou, *center*) to spare the life of Kreon (James Blendick, *rear*) in the Guthrie Theater Company production of *Oedipus the King,* directed by Michael Langham and designed by Desmond Heeley, Minneapolis, 1972. (Photograph: the Guthrie Theater.)

Figure 7. The Corinthian Messenger (Paul Ballantyne, *left*) prods the
memory of the Shepherd (Bernard Behrens, *right*) to help Oedipus
(Len Cariou) discover the circumstances of his birth in the Gutrhrie
Theater Company production of *Oedipus the King,* directed by Michael
Langham and designed by Desmond Heeley, Minneapolis, 1972. (Pho-
tograph: the Guthrie Theater.)

Staging of *Oedipus Rex*

REVIEW OF THE GUTHRIE THEATRE PRODUCTION, 1972, BY MELVIN MADDOCKS

In the Tyrone Guthrie Theater, approximately 8,000 miles from Thebes as the Furies fly, "Oedipus the King" is being staged by an English director from a new translation written in Rome by an author also engaged on a novel about Napoleon. If all this suggests dizzy and eclectic flights in time and space, it should.

Through a rather remarkable series of letters Michael Langham, the director, and Anthony Burgess, the translator-adaptor, have recorded their dissatisfaction with conventional approaches to Greek tragedy and their search for a style that might do justice both to Sophocles and to 1972.

Traditionally there have been two general approaches to Greek tragedy, roughly parallel to the usual approaches to Shakespeare. The low road—Sophocles without tears—has attempted to sell "Oedipus the King" as a kind of suspense thriller: the first detective story. The high road—again the comparison to Shakespearean productions seems valid—is the way of the purist: the bookman with a history of Dionysian festivals in one hand and Aristotle's "Poetics" in the other.

Not for Mr. Langham either the souped-up "Dial O for Oedipus" popularization or the stately academic pageant, complete with masks and stilts, before which audiences, recognizing a classic when they see one, simultaneously kneel and yawn. Mr. Langham—like Peter Brook and Jan Kott, to name two Shakespearean experimentalists—is trying for a new alternative.

"I have been groping," he writes, "not so much for answers that are purely Greek as for an atmosphere that is primitive in its overwhelming superstitions and timeless in its fears and hidden meanings."

The Guthrie stage is dominated by two giant pieces of steel sculpture, 23 feet high, 2½ tons. Representing portals to the palace, they appear more like the slashed entrance to a cave when Len Cariou's slightly Neanderthal Oedipus first bursts through. At the front of the stage stands an altar smothered by incense smoke. Unseen drums beat.

Mr. Langham has recreated a Thebes in the image of the sacred grove of Nemi, made famous in "The Golden Bough." It is a place where cruel ceremonies are acted out, where primal fears fill the air, where human law operates at the level of taboo.

The chorus, covered by what look like animal skins, sings its speeches as chants, dances to a sort of tom-tom, and frets with talismans and totems.

Since the translator happens to be Mr. Burgess, one is tempted to see all this as "A Clockwork Orange" run backwards through a time machine.

Here is the anthropologist's Sophocles, out of Levi-Strauss—less contemporaneous with fifth-century B.C. Greek tragedy than with the ancient myth from which "Oedipus the King" was drawn. Here is Oedipus less as a king of a sophisticated city-state than as a tribal chieftain, or even a kind of Jungian Everyman, acting out the dark subconscious of the human race.

The drama plays less like a plot than a ritual, a primitive game of riddles and forfeits. Oedipus solves the Sphinx's riddle and saves Thebes from this monster at its gates. Then Oedipus fails to solve in time the riddle of his own identity and becomes the monster within the gates—a violator of the ultimate taboo: incest. The pattern stands out, as stark as a curse.

It is a brilliantly forceful conceit that keeps the Guthrie stage pulsing and throbbing. No pallid Greek revival could survive here—no fake plaster pillars and noble profiles posing like old coins.

But another "Oedipus the King" does fight for its place. Sophocles's play, after all, stands as one of the most subtle studies of human pride in the history of the theater—a profound inquiry into the overintoxication of power. There is nothing primitive or neo-primitive about lines like: "What was your pride must be your ruin." Or: "The shadow of success is always envy."

Mr. Burgess writes a blank verse with a sort of Elizabethan roll:

"Wide night is a labyrinth I tread
With no thread of useful thought to
Lead me to the light."

Inevitable contradictions result. Around that atavistic altar Oedipus and Creon prowl, like two animals, hurling the most literate lines at one another in the most precise English repertory company accents. If Mr. Cariou's Oedipus is a savage, he is a remarkably self-aware one. Patricia Conolly's Jocasta, a collection of sensitive readings, is simply too refined for this barbaric Thebes. The better the acting, the more it is self-defeating.

Furthermore, the translation bears its own internal contradictions. For there is, as well as an Elizabethan Mr. Burgess, a colloquial Mr. Burgess who can come down too abruptly from elegance and have the chorus speak of "beating our brains." Or allow Jocasta to comment folksily on soothsaying: "I would not cross the street to hear any of that nonsense."

Yet, finally, the raw power of Mr. Langham's vision carries the evening. He has restored to Greek tragedy the Dionysian, the religious dread that more correct productions in their fussiness neglect. He has turned his spectators into participants with the cry: "We are all Oedipus." He has brought to his "Oedipus" the one quintessential gift a classic cannot do without—he has made it of the moment, he has made it live.

EURIPIDES

484–406 B.C.

Euripides expressed more directly than any of his contemporaries the anxieties of his age: the growing skepticism in Athens about the dignity of man, the authority of the gods, and the future of Athens itself. But his view of experience was too harsh, his means of expression too unconventional, for the tastes of his audience. Although he wrote more than ninety plays, he won the festival competition only four times. While he was losing, Sophocles must have been winning, for they were nearly exact contemporaries. But they were exact opposites in both their way of life and their view of it. Whereas Sophocles was a very public and genial man, Euripides was reportedly a very private person, so unsociable that he is rumored to have spent long periods of time secluded in a cave, writing his plays in solitary confinement. Wherever he may have written them, his plays bear witness to a much darker view of human nature than those of Sophocles, for they repeatedly seem to deny it the moral heroism exhibited by the heroes and heroines of Sophocles.

Sophocles is reported to have said that Euripides shows human behavior not as it ought to be but as it is. As Euripides depicts it, human behavior is controlled primarily by emotions and passions—emotions and passions that have been crippled by nature, afflicted by circumstance, or distorted by self-indulgence. His fascination with the nature of intense feeling has also been said to explain his special interest in the experience of women, for they figure as protagonists in twelve of his eighteen surviving plays. Wherever they appear, they are either inflicting pain, or having pain inflicted on them—or both. This is the case in his two most famous studies of women in love: *Hippolytus* (428) and *Medea* (431). In *Hippolytus,* he shows the raging spectacle of a frustrated adulterous love, when Phaedra develops a consuming passion for her stepson Hippolytus, who is himself with equal passion committed to a sexless existence. Moved by both frustration and shame, she commits suicide by hanging herself, but before doing so she leaves a message for her husband Theseus accusing Hippolytus of having raped her. The result of her false accusation is that Theseus exiles his son and prays for his destruction, and his prayers are answered when Hippolytus while riding along a shore is dragged to death by his horses after they have been terrified by a bull rising from the sea. In *Medea,* Euripides represents an even more sensational spectacle, in this case the result of an abused marital love, when Medea, having been deserted by Jason, works herself up into so fierce a rage that she murders their two children and then makes her exit by flying off in a dragon-driven chariot to seek refuge in Athens. Truly, hell hath no fury like these women scorned, nor like the men who scorn them. In his study of deranged passions and human depravity, Euripides did not favor either sex.

When he was not representing the terrors of love, he was showing the horrors of war. His temperament did not permit him to remain silent about the cultural tragedy of his age. Living as he did during the Peloponnesian War, witnessing the extraordinary toll it took on Athens and Sparta during the nearly thirty years of its duration, he felt compelled to dramatize its senseless brutality in a series of antiwar plays—the tragic counterparts of the antiwar comedies written during the same period by Aristophanes. In *Hecuba* (ca. 430–415), he showed the brutality of war in its most brutalizing form, when Hecuba, driven mad by the loss of her children in the aftermath of the Trojan War, avenges their deaths by blinding Polymestor, an act whose bestiality is symbolized by her transformation into a raging dog. In *The Trojan Women* (415), the greatest of his antiwar plays, a play attacking the atrocity of his own country, he turned again to Hecuba, this time showing her to be a magnificent image of suffering as she bids farewell to each of her daughters who are being led off to slavery, then buries Hector's young son, her grandson, and then bemoans the climactic spectacle of the play: the city of Troy in flames.

Only in his tragicomedies, a dramatic form he is credited with inventing, does Euripides ever offer an optimistic view of experience. Yet even these plays, *Ion* (ca. 430–415) and *Iphigenia at Tauris* (ca. 415–410), only avoid disaster by miraculous resolutions—sisters recognizing brothers, or sons recognizing mothers, moments before they are about to kill or be killed by another. Thus they offer at best an ironically comforting view of fate. In these plays, the gods are only somewhat less malign than in his tragedies, for in almost all his plays the suffering of human beings turns out to be the work of the gods. The gods themselves rarely figure among the characters in his plays, but they are almost always taken into account in the prologues and epilogues that Euripides used as a means of beginning and ending his plays. Sometimes these prologues and epilogues are spoken by gods, sometimes by human beings, but always they set the specific action of the play in a wider context that refers its events to the past, to the future, and ultimately to the gods.

Euripides has been criticized for using prologues and epilogues, as he has been criticized for a wide range of other elements distinctive to his plays such as sensational episodes, episodic plots, elaborately rhetorical debates, irrelevant choral odes, supernatural events, and melodramatic scenes. Such elements offended Aristotle, as they have always offended exponents of formal symmetry and dramatic probability. But Euripides was largely indifferent to conventions of dramatic regularity, because he was primarily interested in writing emotionally expressive drama, drama that is necessarily as irregular, unpredictable, and convulsive in its makeup as the passions and the experience of human beings living in a malign and unpredictable universe.

That vision of experience is nowhere more eloquently dramatized than in *The Bacchae* (ca. 407). It is a vision at once terrifying and beautiful, as terrifying and beautiful as Dionysus, the Greek god of fertility, who stood for the mysterious and irrepressible forces working throughout nature, sustaining and renewing life in all of its abundance, all of its vitality, and all of its wild and uncontrollable energy. Those who embrace that vision, who worship Dionysus, experience the joy of his followers, the chorus of Bacchantes; those who defy that vision, who seek to repudiate it and repress it, experience the suffering of Pentheus and his mother Agave. Those who neither embrace it nor deny it, but nonetheless acknowledge its mystical power and meaning, as do Kadmos and Teiresias—they at least survive. Understood in this way, *The Bacchae* is a profoundly religious tragedy, as it was probably meant to be, judging from earlier Greek hymns to Dionysus, all of which stress the necessity of obedience to the god.

The Bacchae has also been understood in other ways by other cultures. It has, for example, been considered as a dramatization of the archetypal conflict between passion and reason, symbolized in the struggle between Dionysus and Pentheus. It has also been thought to be an indictment of all peoples and all cultures that foresake reason, abandoning themselves to a senseless and brutally destructive life of sensual experience. During the late-1960s, it came to be seen as a uniquely relevant statement about the countercultural activities of that decade. It has been widely performed in the United States and abroad as an expression of the conflicting life styles in contemporary culture. Many of these recent performances, like the Yale Repertory production that is represented here in photographs (see Figures 8 and 9), have deliberately aimed to stage the play in a context of ultramodern sets, electronic sounds, and psychedelic lighting effects. Whether or not the play can be updated to fit the situation of contemporary experience seems to be a debatable issue, judging from reviews of the Yale production. Nonetheless, it continues to be the most powerful revelation in drama of the mysterious forces working through all of nature—and thus all of humanity.

THE BACCHAE

BY EURIPIDES / TRANSLATED BY KENNETH CAVANDER*

CHARACTERS

DIONYSOS
CHORUS
TEIRESIAS, *a prophet*
KADMOS, *ex-King of Thebes*
PENTHEUS, *King of Thebes, grandson of Kadmos*

GUARD
HERDSMAN
SERVANT
AGAVE, *mother of Pentheus*
GUARDS, SOLDIERS, SERVANTS, PEOPLE OF THEBES

(DIONYSOS *and* CHORUS.)

DIONYSOS: Dionysos has come.
Here, in Thebes, Zeus came swooping down and
   took
A woman of the earth. Lightning made
Her labour quick, and out of her burning thighs
I was born.
   Today I walk on the piece of land enclosed
By two rivers—Dirce and Ismenos—
The land they call . . . Thebes.
10 Today I look like a man, but I am more.
   Here was the lightning blast that killed my
      mother,
Semele, here was her room and . . .
There's something alive! Smoke in the rubble, the
   fire
Of Zeus . . . still. So, something alive
Still . . .
   Yes, Kadmos has said: "On this ground
No man walks!" to remind Thebes
20 Of Semele, his daughter, to keep her alive in the
      heart
Of Thebes. I am glad. He was right.
The vines that cover that wall are mine. They flush,
And cluster . . .
And swell . . .
   Behind me—Lebanon and its golden plains,
Iraq, the sun-struck steppes of Persia,
The fortresses of Syria, the harsh country
Where the Afghans live, Arabia drugged,
30 And all the eastern coasts, where Greece and Asia
Merge, and towers fringe the teeming cities;
Behind me—dance swaying bodies, intoxication,
Life.

Here—Greece. And first in Greece—Thebes.
My own country, where I will be known,
Where I must be known.
There is a reason why Thebes comes first.
I made this city wild with women shrilling
My name, I slung hide on their backs, I stuck
Branches in their hands, spears tipped   40
With ivy—for a reason.
Because my mother's sisters denied I was
The son of Zeus; because they said Semele
Lost her virginity to a man here in Thebes,
Then blamed the result on Zeus; because they
   swore
Kadmos invented it all; because they claimed
Zeus killed Semele for lying about
Her husband.
They shouldn't have said that. They,   50
Particularly, should not have said all that.
Because now, they hurtle out of their homes,
   possessed,
Scatter to the hills, and they all wear my uniform,
They all know how to bring me to life. . . .
   I willed it, and they must.
Every woman in this city is mine,
Totally.
They have abandoned Thebes, and now they have
   joined   60
My mother's sisters in the green pine shades,
Among the cliffs and hollows. Mad. Bacchae.
This place must find out what it means
To be half-born, to have no
Dionysos, never to have tried me or tasted me,
This place must take account of my birth
In Semele, my descent from Zeus, my presence here,
And my power over man. This place
May wish it did not have to, but it must learn.
   Kadmos has given way to Pentheus, his grandson.   70
Authority, decision, are now all Pentheus,
Who resists me and my power, keeps me
Clear out of thought. When he looks outside
Himself for help, he never looks to me.
I am despised, pushed aside, stamped upon.
And therefore I'll turn him round to face me. Show
Myself in Thebes, show them they are small

---

*This version of *The Bacchae* was originally commissioned
by the BBC and later rewritten for production at the Mermaid Theatre in London. It is an acting version. In a few
places, for the sake of a twentieth-century audience, it is
interpretative rather than literal. Nevertheless, the script
stays close to Euripides' own words at all times, and the
intentions of the lines are invariably based on the suggestive
power of the original.—K.C.

And I am great.
　　This one matter set to rights I pack up
80　And move on, to make myself known
Elsewhere.
If Thebes recklessly tries to bring the women
Back from the hills and their madness by *force*, you
Will see a fight—the army versus Bacchae—
Arranged by me.
　　And so I have dressed myself in flesh today.
I have the body and blood of a man, but
My real nature is . . . still my own.
(To CHORUS*)* Friends, you have been loyal, you have
90　followed me
From countries far across the sea, travelled
Beside me, never deserted me. Lift your drums
Now. Let these proud walls of Pentheus,
The king, hear the sound of the east, the creation
Of Earth, my mother, and myself. The beat!
The beat! Let the city open its eyes.
I will go to the heights of Kithairon where
The women are dancing on the slopes, and join
The Bacchae.

(Exit.)

100　CHORUS:　Look—the hills of
The East, where new life leaps—
We came from there.
Our work . . . !
It's easy,
It's singing work,
It's dancing labour,
It's laughing drudgery.
I never stop, I never tire,
Letting myself run free for Dionysos.
110　Clear the streets—
We're here.
Clear the streets—
We've come.
Room! Room! Stay at home, lips closed, because . . .
A word spilled can make a stain.
The only words allowed here are the words for
Dionysos.
And I sing them
Over and over,
120　I sing them . . .
Who is alive? Who is happy?
The one who knows . . .
Knows?
Knows the secret . . .
The secret?
The secret of the night
When his whole life begins again
And he's all one with the friends of Dionysos,
The pure lovers of the mountains,
130　Bedded in the earth's grasp
Plunged in forgetfulness,
Buried

. . . Living!
Like green leaves in winter, woodsap in snow,
Ivy crowns make you King
And from the pine tree stems your power.
Dionysos, my lord,
Dionysos, my dear harsh master.
Run on, run on! Bring him here, fill the streets
With the young life, the new life—　　　　140
Dionysos!
Flood Greece with his fresh blood,
Beat, beat, beat him into the heart like thunder—
Dionysos!
　　Burst from fire, gashed by thunderbolt.
He was flung into life by flame.
His mother screamed, the pain rending her,
And let him go to the lightning.
She died then . . .
But he lived! Hatched in a golden clasp,　　150
In the storehouse of life in the body of Zeus.
And Hera never knew!
Then out into the world—
When the time was ready for him,
And he for the time.
He had bull horns empowering him.
He had snake hair crowning him.
And we will wear crowns like that—
We'll catch them, and tame them, and wear them—
Snakes!　　　　160
　　Thebes—mother land of Semele—
Wear a crown too—coiled-within-coil ivy.
Let the never-dying blossoms,
Flower in you, drench you in greenery, Thebes!
Oak-leaf mad,
Fir-branch crazy,
Fawn-skin clothed,
And white-wool jewelled—
Then you're dressed.
Hold the branch in your hand,　　　170
Power in the thick wood, feel it pulsing,
The whole land will rock,
The whole land will jump—
He stirs, yes, now—the power Dionysos.
And then we go up to the hills, to the hills,
Where the women who lived indoors at a loom,
Or a spindle, wait for him now
Packed, trembling, his thorn in their blood.
　　Crete holds caves where Zeus was nursed,
And there the drum, the drum, the drum was born.　180
When the dance comes over you, and the strain drags
　　tight,
The singing woodwind cools
The drum-beat,
The singing wind softens the drum
And together they make the dance, they make it, till
　. . .
The mind splits open,
The world falls in—

And Dionysos is glad.
190   Then you're tired of the running, and at last, at last
You fling yourself on the ground—
Your only cover the flakes of sunlight on the skin of a
    fawn;
This is the moment, sacred and secret, in the
    mountains,
When your hands search for the goat,
Hands grope for its blood,
And you drink,
As it comes from the goat,
200 The fresh red juice, the joy of . . .
That's the way Dionysos has led you
In the hills of the east, the morning sun . . .
    (CHORUS *makes a sound—of joy, ecstasy, praise.*)
    Earth gushing milk
Gushing wine.
Gushing rivers of honey,
You hold the flame
High, it smells like a scent from Syria,
Its pine wood flaring,
Smoke streaming as you hurl your body
210 Down through dances
Shouting, and raving, and reddening the torch
With your speed
Your hair floods down, the wind-gusts flourish it . . .
And among the shrilling, the shouting, the singing a
    voice
Blares,
"Run on, run on,
My Bacchae,
Like a stream of gold from the lavish east
220 Sing, sing, sing!
Let the drum stamp loud,
Shout for him,
Throat, tongue, breath,
Blaze for him,
Let the leaping flute
Lure and tempt,
Calling out the powers of life
To join us, and play
In the hills,
230 In the hills."
Then, freedom!
Joy of a foal
In the meadows with its mother.
Bacchae, dart!
Bacchae, run!
Bacchae, *dance!*

    (Enter TEIRESIAS.)

TEIRESIAS (*knocks at door of palace*): Answer the door!
    Answer it! Call Kadmos
Out, Kadmos, the man from Phoenicia who built
240 A towering city here at Thebes. Go,
Someone, tell him Teiresias wants him.
He knows why I've come . . .

    (*A* GUARD *goes.*)

We are collaborating and we have
This pact. We take branches, we twist ivy
Leaves round them, we weave more ivy in
Our hair, like crowns, but live, and then we take
Skins of young deer . . . Well, I may
Be old, but he is older . . .

(*Enter* KADMOS.)

KADMOS: Teiresias, my dear friend, I knew
It was you when I heard your voice.   250
(*To* GUARDS) Pay attention.
This is a wise, wise man.
(*To* TEIRESIAS) Look, I am ready. I found the
    things. We
Must give him all we can, build
Respect for him. He is a power, a wonder,
And he is the child of my own daughter.
Do we dance now? Where do we go? (*Shaking his
    head.*)
One—two—*back!* One—two—*back!*   260
Is this right, Teiresias? We are both old
But you know things, you see more.
All day and all night, I won't
Need rest—down, down—(*He thumps his stick on the
    ground.*)
Forget the years, we are born again, and it's
    beautiful.
TEIRESIAS: Yes, do you feel it? Young again.
I'll dance too, I can, I'm ready . . .
KADMOS: We climb   270
To the hills, then, we don't ride there?
TEIRESIAS: No. We need to go *simply* into the presence
Of this being.
KADMOS: An old blind prophet
And I shall take you by the hand like a child . . .
TEIRESIAS: The one who calls us will lead us there. And
    we
Shall never notice the journey.
KADMOS: Are we the only
Two in Thebes to worship this way, dancing?   280
TEIRESIAS: We are the only two in Thebes with our
    senses left
Intact. The rest of the city has fallen apart.
KADMOS: I want to go. Hurry. Take my hand.
TEIRESIAS: Here, hold on to me, don't let me lose you.
KADMOS: I look at the world, the power in it, and I
Feel lost, mortal, small, small . . .
TEIRESIAS: Yes,
You feel those forces working in you. To them
All our intellect is a joke. There are things   290
Not measured in time, a birthright, an inheritance.
They exist. You can't reason them away,
You can't talk them, define them, describe them
    away,
Yes, I'm old, but I mean to go dancing,

Put vine leaves in my hair, and I'm not ashamed.
This power does not
Tell men apart. When they dance it can't distinguish
Young from old. It needs to be recognized
300   By everyone in the world—that is how
It lives—but it doesn't keep score. No one comes
Before anyone else . . .

KADMOS: Teiresias,
You have sight, but no eyes. You need
Mine to light your way for you. Listen,
Pentheus is here, the youth I gave my power to.
How he drives himself!
What's happened? What is new now?

(Enter PENTHEUS with SOLDIERS.)

PENTHEUS: I leave my country, I just go away,
310   And the result—chaos, the city in uproar. I hear
All our women have left home, and the new
Fashion is to be Bacchae, to mob
The mountains—more shadows there, of course—
And all in honour of someone, some moving spirit
They've just discovered—Dionysos. Who
Is he? What is Dionysos?
And this dancing . . . ? Dancing! . . . I was told
There are gatherings where they drink so much
You could never see the cups for the wine.
320   The women creep away, one here, one there,
Into the bushes—and there a man is waiting
And they copulate. They say it's all
Part of the service for this divine power.
Service! All they care about is being
Serviced.
I caught a few and my men have them chained
To the wall in the city gaol. The rest escaped,
They're in the hills, but I shall hunt them down.
Yes, that's how they'll end, in a cage,
330   Behind bars. No more drunken
Dancing then, no more orgies,
No more Bacchae!
      They say a stranger has come to my country—
Some sorcerer, hypnotist, from the East,
From Lydia or somewhere, all curly blonde
Hair stinking of scent, cheeks hot
With wine, and flashing eyes—a real seducer—
Who spends all his days—and his nights—
With the girls from my city. He calls it initiation.
340   If I get this initiator inside
My palace, I'll finish his thumping, jumping,
Hair-shaking, snaking game, I'll initiate
That head away from that body.
He claims Dionysos still exists,
Never died, got life from eternal
Powers. Very likely—since Dionysos was roasted
In his mother's womb, after she told
Everyone Zeus was father of her child.
That myth was exploded in a blast of lightning.
350   But this new boy has the gall

To foist it back on us. Whoever he is
He deserves a reward for that—a rope around
His neck . . . (He sees KADMOS and TEIRESIAS.)
No, I can't believe it! My prophet, Teiresias,
In a fawn skin . . . And my own grandfather
    playing
With a woolly stick. Ridiculous!
(To KADMOS) Grandfather, you disgust me. Look at
    you,
An old man, clowning. Throw away   360
That ivy, drop those toys, don't touch them . . .
(To TEIRESIAS) Teiresias, this is you. You talked him
    into it.
You want to drag this new obsession across
Our lives, so that you can squint up
At a few birds, burn a few sacrifices,
And make yourself more of a profit than ever.
If you weren't already mouldering in senility
You'd be rattling your chains with all the other
    Bacchae   370
For smuggling in this pernicious, lecherous gospel.
When women drink, and their eyes light up like the
    wine
Itself, then I say, Goodbye to decency,
The animals are out!

CHORUS: You—King of this place, be careful,
You, stranger, you dirty something pure,
That's dangerous.
Remember—you're born out of the earth yourself.
Kadmos planted dragon's teeth in soil, and   380
    harvested men.
To those men you are a living insult.

TEIRESIAS: Easy for some to make speeches. They're
    clever,
They pick an easy target, and the words sound
    good.
Now you—your tongue races along
And makes a plausible sound, which might
Almost be mistaken for sense, except
That you have none. Arrogant, self-confident, with   390
    a gift
For phrases—that kind of man is useless, a danger
To his fellows, while his mind stays closed.
This new life in our midst, which you
Sneer at, is going to be so powerful all
Over Greece, so vast, I . . . I can't
Describe it.
    You are a young man. Here are two
Principles for you, the two supreme principles
In life.   400
First the principle of earth, Demeter,
Goddess of the soil, or whatever else
You like to call it. This provides the firm
Solid base in man. Second, the opposite
Principle, Dionysos, who found the living
Juice in the grape, and gave it to us all,
To slake our parched, aching souls, wash us

In streams of wine. When living is a struggle
He is the only drug for our pain, he gives us
410 Sleep and oblivion. We drink him down, we
        swallow
His power, and he comes alive in us. Then
We soar, we fly, we are free, and through his
        agency
Man can know some happiness. You laugh at him.
You laugh at the story that he was sewn in the loins
Of Zeus. Let me show you how to interpret
That—it makes sense.
        Zeus snatched the unborn child out
420 Of the blazing thunderbolt, took him back
To where he came from, Olympos. Hera, the bride
Of Zeus, wanted her rival's child to die.
But Zeus, like the wise power he is, found
A way out of the dilemma. He broke off
A part of the earth's envelope, the atmosphere,
And made a *loan* of it to Hera, to protect
The real Dionysos from her jealousy.
In time people confused "loan" with "loin"—
Told some story of how he was sewn in the loins
430 Of Zeus, and made a new version.
        And there is more. The power of Dionysos can
                break
Out of time. When he invades the mind
And puts reason to sleep, we have sight
Of things to come. If he takes full possession
He makes those who give themselves to him
Tell the future . . . What else? . . . War! He is even
There in war, yes . . . An army is in
The field, marching into battle. Then,
440 Before the weapons have touched, panic! That
Is Dionysos . . . Delphi too, home
Of Apollo, sanctuary of reason. But look
Up at the rocks. Who do you see bounding
Over the high plateau between the peaks,
Through the pine forests, shaking winter
Into life with green branches?—Dionysos!
Yes, he is everywhere.
Believe me, Pentheus, never boast
That you have any power to rule your life.
450 You may think you do, but thought is impotent,
Your certainty an illusion. Dionysos is here,
In your country, at work.
Accept him,
Pour wine for him,
Put vine leaves in your hair for him,
Dance for him.
        Dionysos will not restrain desire
In women. Restraint is something they must
        practise
460 For themselves. It cannot be imposed. But those
Who have control already will not lose it
Merely because they lose themselves
To Dionysos.
        Look, you are glad when crowds at the city

Gates cheer, shout, "Pentheus! Pentheus!"
Till every street rings with your name. Well,
Dionysos, too, I imagine, enjoys
Some recognition.
        And so Kadmos and myself—yes,
You can laugh—but we'll take our ivy branches   470
And we shall dance, we shall partner each other,
Old and grey as we are. Nevertheless
Dance we must. We shall not fight this power;
We shall not listen to your talk, which is
The most terrible madness of all. I pity you,
Pentheus. You'll get no relief from medicine,
Nor can you cure yourself.
CHORUS: The old man understands. He leaves reason
        where it is,
Apollo has his place, and so has Dionysos . . .   480
You are safe. Dionysos has power—and you
Have granted it.
KADMOS: Listen to Teiresias. You are still young,
And he is right. Your place is here, beside us.
Don't close doors on the past. This moment
You're nowhere, suspended in a void. Your brain
Works, but only against yourself.
You may be right. Dionysos may have
No special powers, but even so,
Why not pretend he does? It may be a lie,   490
But it's a useful one. If we can say
That Semele gave birth to a superior
Being, to something undying, it will be
A tremendous honour to our family.
Remember how your cousin, Akteon, died.
That was a horrible end. The hounds from his own
Kennels turned man-eater and tore him apart.
He had boasted he was a greater hunter than
        Artemis
Herself. And so he died in a velvet glade.   500
It could happen to you, unless you change! Come
        here,
I'll put some leaves on your head . . . Ivy . . . Be
With us. Acknowledge him. He is a great
Power. Let me . . .
PENTHEUS: Don't touch me!
Go and play Bacchae, but don't smear
Your idiocy onto me! Just don't
Come near me!
        And now, for your teacher, Teiresias, who fed   510
                you this drivel,
Punishment!
(*To* GUARD) One of you, here!
He has a place where he sits hoping for some
Revelation out of birdsong. Go. Take
A crowbar with you, and destroy that place.
Level it to the ground, all of it,
Throw his bits of wool to the winds, and let
The storms have them. *Hurry!*
        This is the one thing I can do to him   520
That will really hurt.

And you, you go into the city
And bring me this foreigner, this thing
Of doubtful gender, spreading his sick notions
Amongst our women, dragging our marriages
Through the filth.
When you find him, chain him up, and fetch him
Here. And then he'll have justice, because we'll stone him,
530 *(To* GUARDS*)* Stone him till he's dead. He'll find Thebes
A hard, hard place for Bacchae!
TEIRESIAS: You fiend! Do you realise what you're saying?
No, you're mad. You had little enough sense
Before, but now . . . !
(To KADMOS*)* Kadmos, let's go. And let us pray
For him. Yes, he's a monster, but for the sake
Of the rest of us, let us pray this
540 Is overlooked. Bring your ivy branches
And follow me. Try to help me, hold me
Upright, and I'll help you. We are old
But we must stand by ourselves. Take pride in it . . .
Don't think of him!
We have work to do for this great power, this supreme
Power . . .
    Kadmos—in Greek the name Pentheus signifies
Sorrow. Does that mean anything? . . .
550 I hope not.
I don't talk of things to come—this is happening
Now *(meaning to* PENTHEUS*)* . . . Only a fool blurts
out his folly!

(Exeunt KADMOS *and* TEIRESIAS*.)*

CHORUS: Back!
Keep away!
This is filth—stain—smear—decay—
Keep away! He turns pure gold black.
    Did you hear him?
The scorn that drips,
560 From his mouth, fouling Dionysos, child of his own city.
Doesn't know happiness, or the pure-drained drink of joy.
But Dionysos is the one
Who sends you dancing out of your mind,
Flings you laughing out of yourself to the flute-song,
Stops your crying, stops your caring,
And when the bright wine dazes you
570 Life can't end, ivy glows on your brow
And you swallow thick sleep by the mouthful.
When reason forgets its place, wanders, and starts an invasion,
And words go mad and run away with their master,
The end has come—
The man is doomed.

Live easy, live calm, and the storm can't wreck you—
That way you stay whole.
There are powers in the world, who oversee life; 580
It's not so wise to be clever.
Life is short, and since it is,
Why chase more, more, more?
Can't you bear what is here?
Let others go mad, draw up the plans for destruction—
But don't let them take us with them!
I want to go back to Cyprus, island of Aphrodite,
Where desire blows warm and breathes away thought; 590
I want to lie in the fields of Paphos,
Where the distant Nile feeds a hundred wells
And gives fruit to the land without rain.
I want to see Pieria, because music is first there,
And the slope of Olympos leads straight to the sky.
Take me there, Dionysos, I'm calling you—
Hear me, come and lead me away. . . .
Then I can hand over my seeing,
Hand over my striving
And dance to my heart-beats, 600
And no one can say no.
Dionysos, child of the universe, comes to life in my laughter.
His great love is Peace,
Lavish with her treasures, careful of youth.
He sends the poor, he sends the rich, his one gift—wine.
So that the whole world can know
Where pain stops, and where joy starts.
He hates the man who says no. 610
No to the day,
No to the night,
No to life, and no to all love—
Keep away from that kind,
They are too much for you, they will consume you.
There is another way, never named, never mapped.
But the unheard-of, untalked-of people follow it.
That way I choose—I say yes to it.

(Enter a GUARD*, with* DIONYSOS*, chained.)*

GUARD: Pentheus, we caught him. The hunt is over, 620 and here
Is the animal you sent us after . . .
A gentle animal, we found, made
No attempt to escape, handed himself
Over without a murmur, never went pale,
That wine-stain flush never left his cheek, and he smiled.
He told us to put on the chains and take him away.
He waited for us, making it so simple
I was embarrassed. So I said, "Stranger," I said, 630
"I only obey orders here. I am taking you

Now, on instructions from Pentheus. Pentheus
Sends for you. *Pentheus*. Not me."
But the women you captured and had locked up in
   prison,
The ones who were dancing,
They're out.
They're free, and they're away in the forest,
   running
640 Like deer, calling on Bromios—he's their master,
And governs them completely.
The chains all fell from their limbs of their own
Accord, keys turned, doors opened,
Without a hand touching them. This man
Is an amazing . . .
He is full of . . .
I don't understand what it is he has brought to
   Thebes
But it is your concern now, all of it.
650 PENTHEUS: Let him go. He is inside the cage and he
   can't
Escape from me now. He doesn't move
So fast.
Well, stranger, you're not at all bad-looking,
Are you? At least, to the women . . . Which is why
You have come to Thebes, I suppose . . . Long hair,
Crinkling down your cheeks—you've never
   wrestled,
I presume—very desirable . . . White
660 Skin—you keep out of the sun, you cultivate
The shadows, where you hunt down love
With your handsome profile. Yes?
Who are you? Where do you come from?
DIONYSOS: I am no one . . .
But I will give you an easier answer.
Have you heard of a river called Tmolos? It runs
Through fields of flowers . . .
PENTHEUS: Yes, I know that river, it circles the town
Of Sardis.
670 DIONYSOS: I come from there. My country is Lydia.
PENTHEUS: And these
Activities. How is it you bring them to Greece?
DIONYSOS: Dionysos inspired me. Dionysos . . . He
Is the son of Zeus.
PENTHEUS: So you have a Zeus
Over there, who fathers new powers
On the world.
DIONYSOS: No. Zeus was united
With Semele in Thebes, and gave her the child
680 Here.
PENTHEUS: Did this irresistible urge
Come to you at night, or were you
"Inspired" in the daytime?
DIONYSOS: I saw him.
He saw me. And he gave me the secret
Means to summon his presence.
PENTHEUS: And this secret—
What is it like? can you tell me?

DIONYSOS: It must not
Be revealed to someone in whom Dionysos   690
Has not been born.
PENTHEUS: Those who share this secret—
Do they benefit—and how?
DIONYSOS: I am forbidden to tell.
But it is worth knowing.
PENTHEUS: You're clever, but
You're a fake! You want to make me curious.
DIONYSOS: For a man who is so sure of what he knows
There are no other powers, there is no other
Life. It simply escapes him.   700
PENTHEUS: You say you saw
Dionysos clearly . . . What did he look like?
DIONYSOS: Whatever
He wished. I didn't arrange it.
PENTHEUS: Very good.
But once more you evade the issue,
Your statement was meaningless.
DIONYSOS: The greatest truths often sound like
   babblings
Of madmen—till they are understood.   710
PENTHEUS: Are we
The first to be visited by you and your offer
Of supernatural aid?
DIONYSOS: No. all
The people of the east are awake. They dance.
They live . . .
PENTHEUS: They're out of their minds, we in Greece
Have more sense.
DIONYSOS: No, in this case, less.
Their way is different, that is all.   720
PENTHEUS: And these practices you claim are
   sacred—
Do they take place at night, or in the day?
DIONYSOS: Mostly at night. Darkness has dignity.
PENTHEUS: For women the night hours are
   dangerous,
Lascivious hours . . .
DIONYSOS: People have been known
To sin during the day.
PENTHEUS: You play with words!   730
You'll be punished for that.
DIONYSOS: You soil mysteries
With your ignorant sneers. You'll be punished
For that.
PENTHEUS: He's so sure. The drunken dancer
Has been in training—for argument.
DIONYSOS: Come,
Pronounce sentence. What terrible fate have you
In store for me?
PENTHEUS: First, I'll clip those flowing   40
Locks . . .
DIONYSOS: My hair must not be touched, I grow it
For Dionysos.
PENTHEUS: Next, you will hand over
Your wand, that branch you carry . . .

DIONYSOS: Take it from me
　　Yourself. I carry it for Dionysos.
PENTHEUS: Then
　　We shall lock you in prison, and you will never get
750　　out.
DIONYSOS: Dionysos will free me, when I wish him to.
PENTHEUS: Yes, when you get your followers round
　　you and "summon
　　His presence."
DIONYSOS: He sees. He's here. This minute he knows
　　What is being done to me.
PENTHEUS: Where is he then?
　　I can't see him. Why doesn't he show himself?
DIONYSOS: He's here, where I stand. You, being crass
760　　And proud, see nothing.
PENTHEUS: You're raving.
　　(To GUARDS) He insults me!
　　He insults you all!
DIONYSOS: I am sane. You
　　Are not. I say to you, set me free.
PENTHEUS: And I say you go to prison, because
　　I am master here, I have the power.
DIONYSOS: You don't know what your life is, what
　　You are doing, who you are . . .
770　PENTHEUS: I am Pentheus,
　　Son of Echion and Agave.
DIONYSOS: Pentheus;
　　A very convenient name for a doomed man.
PENTHEUS: Go away, go on! Go!
　　(To GUARDS) Lock him up somewhere near—in the
　　stables.
　　Leave him to stare at the darkness,
　　Darkness all the time.
　　(To DIONYSOS) Dance in there!
780　And these creatures you have brought here, these
　　Accessories,
　　We'll either sell them, or we'll give their hands
　　　work
　　To do—not this banging, thumping on pieces of
　　skin,
　　But work. Spinning. Weaving. They'll belong to us.
DIONYSOS: I leave you now. But I shall not suffer
　　What I have no need to suffer. Dionysos
　　Will punish you for your gross contempt. You
790　Say he does not exist. But when you send
　　Me to prison
　　It is you
　　Who commit the crime . . .
　　Against him.

　　(The GUARDS lead DIONYSOS away.)

CHORUS: Gently flowing Dirce,
　　Life-stream to these fields,
　　Innocent waters,
　　Banks that were a cradle for the newborn Dionysos
　　The day his father saved him from the blazing
800　　thunderbolt,

The day Zeus shouted:
"Welcome, my son, welcome to the world!
My man's loins shall be your womb.
You'll have a name, and Thebes will know you by it
Because I will open their eyes."
　　But now this same river they all live by here,
She doesn't want us.
"Don't come near," she cries,
"No ivy crowns on my banks,
No gatherings, no dancing near me!"　　　　　　810
　　Why?
Why turn away from us?
Why say no to us?
Some day you will long for . . . ache for . . .
. . . dry . . .
Ask for . . . parched . . .
Wine.
You'll thirst! Yes, some day,
You'll thirst for Dionysos.
　　Never seen such fury like the fury staring out of　820
Pentheus.
That's not a man. It's a beast run wild.
He's one of the crop, the dragon-toothed flowers.
Who gnashed the soil to get spawned in the
　　world—
A monster,
A fiend, murderous to the bone.
He means to shut me away,
Rope me in darkness,
But I'm not his. I belong to Dionysos.　　　　　830
Already, in there, in a dungeon, a sightless pit,
He buries our leader . . .
Dionysos . . . can you see this?
We can't move,
We can't breathe,
The only ones who speak for you, crushed.
Down . . .
. . . With a tree in one hand . . .
Down . . .
. . . like a tower of gold　　　　　　　　　　　840
Down from Olympos . . .
DIONYSOS!
And tame him.
Dionysos—we are calling you
Wherever you are,
Come . . .
Come from the mountain forests,
Glide from the wild beasts' lairs,
Spring from a cruel snow peak,
Leap from a whirlwind dance,　　　　　　　　850
Grow from a thousand branches,
Rise from a sleeping valley,
Descend from Olympos,
Tree-leaved and silent,
Fly on the air,
In the grass that Orpheus tamed,
Over animals silenced by his music

Nearer and nearer—
The drumming of feet heralds you—
860 Dance out of mountain torrents,
Swing over eastern rivers,
Surge over waves towards us,
Driving a storm of souls,
Now he's coming, he's coming into Greece!
He's over the land now,
In the green plains alive with horses,
In the streams that water the fields,
He's coming.
YES! YES!
870 DIONYSOS! DIONYSOS! DIONYSOS!

(As the CHORUS *ends, the voice of* DIONYSOS *comes from offstage all round.)*

DIONYSOS *(stereo)*: Aaaaaouoooooowah! Hark!
I got life!
I have a voice!
Hark! Aaaaoooouwah! Take me!
Aaaooouwah! Take me!
CHORUS: Has it come? . . . Hear it? . . . Feel it? . . .
The call! The call! . . . Where? . . . Is it here?
DIONYSOS *(stereo)*: Yes! Coming to life . . . Yes!
Coming
880 To life . . . Aaaooowah! . . . Born in the ground,
born in
The sky . . . !
CHORUS: Master! Master!
Come close, come close. Come into us . . . In . . . *In
. . .*
NOW . . . Closer, *closer . . .*
DIONYSOS *(stereo)*: The earth—SHAKE.
Move, nothing stand still, *move!*
CHORUS: Look, the palace of Pentheus bulges,
quivers . . . It will
890 Fall, fall . . . It's got into the palace . . . It's in,
It's *in!* . . . See, pillars melt, marble streams,
Trembles . . . It's inside now, it's taken, it's taken.
DIONYSOS *(stereo)*: Touch off the fire, flames and
thunder!
Burn, burn, house of Pentheus.

(During the following speech of CHORUS, *darkness,
thunder, flames, roar of collapsing masonry, triumph
noise of* DIONYSOS.)*

CHORUS: Fire! Watch the fever-fire dance round the
grave
Of Semele, charred earth no one walks on, the
lightning
900 Left a living flame there . . .
Down, down! Everyone down to the ground . . .
Dionysos is . . .
. . . don't move . . .
In possession of . . .
. . . don't look . . .

The palace
. . . don't breathe!
DIONYSOS: Afraid, my friends? After all our journeys
Together . . . ? Look at you, hugging the earth,
Terrorstruck . . . Yes, you saw the house   910
Of Pentheus split and sundered by the presence
Of Dionysos. But now . . . look up at me,
You're safe . . . don't flinch . . . All is well . . .
CHORUS: You're dawn for us, our life-light, and calm
rose
In the depths of the mind . . . The sight of you is
comfort . . .
We'd lost you, we were alone.
DIONYSOS: So you surrendered, gave in to despair.
When I was taken   920
In there you thought I would be buried in the
death
Cells of Pentheus' darkness?
CHORUS: Yes, yes.
Who was to protect us if you were harmed?
But now you're free.
DIONYSOS: As always . . .
CHORUS: And safe . . .
DIONYSOS: I saved myself.
CHORUS: How? The man was in a killing mood . . .   930
DIONYSOS: Easy. I had no trouble with him.
CHORUS: But you couldn't move. He lashed your
hands
Together.
DIONYSOS: He thought he did, but he never touched
them, never came near me. He thought he had
me, but he breakfasted on lies this morning and
I laughed—because I had him . . . He took me to
the stables to be locked up, and found a bull
there. This bull he loaded with chains—on its   940
knees, on its hooves—gasping with rage, streaming sweat all over his body, chewing his lips . . . I
waited close beside him, did nothing, said nothing, just sat there and watched. Meanwhile the
palace quivered. Dionysos had come, and fire
spurted from Semele's grave . . . When Pentheus
saw it he decided his house was on fire. He
rushed from end to end of the palace, screaming
at his servants to pump water, more water, on
the flames, till every slave was working—over   950
nothing. The fire existed only in his mind. All at
once he left it—snatched up a long steel sword
and hurled himself indoors—his prisoner, me,
had escaped. Then Dionysos—or so I think,
because I only tell you what I think—created a
phantom figure. Because Pentheus charged at
something in the courtyard, stabbing and lung-
ing as if it was me on the end of his blade. But
there was nothing there, only clear bright air.
More havoc followed. Dionysos shattered the   960
palace. Inside now is nothing but a heap of

rubble. My spell in prison was hard on Pentheus.
Finally, spent and limp, he threw away his sword
. . . Well, he is a man, and he fought a god. He
expected too much . . . Quietly I left his house,
and came back here to you. Pentheus never
troubled me . . . Listen. I hear footsteps. This
will be him . . . Watch that door. He'll come out
and say . . . but what can he say now? Let him
970   explode—I'll manage him easily anyhow. The
secret of life is balance, tolerance . . .

(Enter PENTHEUS.)

PENTHEUS: I've been cheated! I had that foreigner. I
had him
So trussed up he couldn't move—and still
He got away!

(Sees DIONYSOS *and gives a shout.)*

There he is! That's the man. Look,
He stands there, on the doorstep of my palace,
Out in the open . . .
Look at him!
980 DIONYSOS: Stay where you are!
Calm yourself . . .
Anger's going . . . going . . .
Now . . .
PENTHEUS: How did you get out? You were locked in,
chained . . .
DIONYSOS: Didn't I tell you—or didn't you
hear?—someone
Would free me?
PENTHEUS: Free you? Who? You always produce
990   A new riddle.
DIONYSOS: The grape-gardener, the wine-grower
To mankind.
PENTHEUS: The planter of all drunkenness
And disorder.
DIONYSOS: Insults from you would make him proud.
PENTHEUS *(to* GUARD): Surround the palace, Close
every gate in the city.
Shut him in!
DIONYSOS: Come, come, if such powers
1000   Exist, surely they move on a higher plane
Than your city walls.
PENTHEUS: So clever, so
Clever. All that cleverness misused!
DIONYSOS: I use it where I need it most . . . Look,
Someone is coming with a message for you. Listen
To him first . . . Of course we'll wait for you—
We are in no hurry to go . . . You
Hear what he has to say. He comes from the
mountains.

(Enter HERDSMAN.)

1010 HERDSMAN: Pentheus, I am one of your subjects here

In Thebes. I come from Kithairon. There's still
snow
There, it dazzles you, the hills are all white . . .
PENTHEUS: And what is your news? How urgent is it?
HERDSMAN: I have seen
The Bacchae . . . those women, strange women,
they fling
Their white limbs like a storm of javelins across
The fields. I came to tell you and everyone here . . .
I want you to know, master, what marvellous things 1020
They do . . . beyond anything you could imagine.
But first I would like your word that I can speak
Freely about what happened there. Or must I
Trim the facts a little . . . ? It's your temper, you
see,
Master, your very quick temper, which rules us
All so harshly . . . too harshly.
PENTHEUS: Tell me, I give my word, nothing will
happen
To you. Do your duty, and no one will be angry. 1030
The worse you make the Bacchae sound, the more
Firmly shall I crush their ringmaster, as he
deserves.
HERDSMAN: Our herds of cattle are topping the rise
of the hills,
Grazing as they go, and the sun's rays are just
Beginning to warm the grass, when I see three
Circles of women—the dancers!
One of them is round Autonoë,
The second with Agave, your mother, 1040
And the third is with Ino.
They are all asleep, lying every way,
Some propped against pine-tree trunks,
Others curled up modestly on a pile
Of oak leaves, pillowed on the earth—
None of the drunkenness you talked about,
None of the obscene abandon, or the wild
Music—no love among the bushes.
All at once, your mother stands up. She cries out
And wakes the rest of the women, says she can hear 1050
The lowing of cattle. They shake the sleep petals
From their eyes, and all stand upright,
A marvel of calm and order . . . Young girls,
Old women, maidens who have never slept
With a man. First, they let their hair tumble
Down their shoulders. Then, the ones whose
fawn-skins
Have come loose from the brooches pinning them,
fasten them
Back on their shoulders, and belt the spotted hides 1060
With snakes—
And those snakes were live—I saw their tongues
Flicker . . .
One of them might carry a fawn, cradled
In her arms, or a wild wolf cub, and give it her own
Milk—

You see, some had left newborn babies at home
And so their breasts were full . . .
They all weave strands of ivy, oak leaves,
1070 Tendrils of flowering briony in their hair.
Then one of them winds ivy on a branch,
Taps a rock, and out of that rock spouts
Water—running water! Fresh as dew!
Another drops her wand, a little twig,
On to the earth, and where she drops it some
      force
Sends up a spring—a wine-spring! Some
Feel they'd like to drink fresh milk.
They scrape the tips of their fingers on the earth
1080 And they have milk—fountains of milk! From all
Their ivy-covered branches sweet honey
Drips, cascades down . . . Oh, if you
Had been there and seen all this, you would have
      been
On your knees, praying—not criticising—but
      praying
For help and guidance.
      All we herdsmen and shepherds hold
A meeting, we begin to talk, we compare
1090 Stories—
Because these were fantastic things the women
      were doing,
We could hardly believe our eyes . . .
Someone who knows his way in the city, knows
How they make speeches there, he stands up
And makes one himself:
"You inhabitants of the majestic mountain acres,
      allow me to propose to you that we hunt down
      Agave, mother of Pentheus, from the midst of
1100   her Dionysiac festivities, and thereby do our
      royal master in Thebes . . . a great good turn
      . . ."
Applause!
      We decide to lay an ambush for the women
In the undergrowth,
We hide in the leaves,
We wait.
The hour for their rites approaches . . .
The sticks with ivy begin to beat out a rhythm.
It gets in your blood, that rhythm.
1110 "Iacchos!" they howl in unison,
"Bromios!"
"Son of Zeus!"
      The whole mountain sways to that one beat,
         beat, beat:
The wild beasts join in,
Everything moves,
Everything's running, running. Agave is racing
      towards me, she's coming near, nearer, almost
      touches me, I leap out—I wanted to catch her,
1120   you see—I jump from my safe hiding place
      and—
She gives a screech:

"Look, my swift hounds, we are being hunted
By these men. Follow me!
Follow me!
Branches—get branches and arm yourselves!"
      We turn and run—
If we hadn't we would have been torn to shreds
By the Bacchae . . .
      As it is, they descend on our heifers grazing   1130
In the long grass. They have nothing in their
      hands,
Those women—nothing metal. But imagine you
      see
One of them, just with her hands, tearing a young
Well-grown heifer in two, while it screams . . .
Others have found full-grown cows and are
      wrenching them
Limb from limb. Ribs, hooves, toss
Up in the air, drop to the ground. Parts   1140
Of our animals hang from the branches of pine
      trees,
Dripping there, blood spattering the leaves.
Bulls with surging horns, invincible
Till now, are tripped, sprawl full length
On the ground, while a mob of hands, girls'
Hands, rip them apart. Faster than you can
Blink your royal eyes the flesh is peeled
Off their bones.
      Then down, like flocks of birds, so fast   1150
Their feet never touch the ground, they sweep to
      the Valley
Sleeping between the hills. Here, on the banks
Of the Asopos, the grain grows deep in the
      farmlands,
Little towns, Hysiai, Erythrai, snuggle
Beneath the slopes of Kithairon . . .
Like an invading army those women mill
Through the valley, they tear it apart, chaos!
      Children   1160
Snatched from their beds . . . Anything they can
      pick up,
And carry on their backs, stays there—nothing
Holds it on, but it never slips to the ground,
Even the bronze, the iron—they put live coals
In their hair—and nothing burns them!
The people are furious, being plundered by these
      women,
And rush to defend themselves. Then what   1170
      happens?
      —It was a terrible sight to see, master . . .
No spear, no weapon, nothing so much as
      scratches
The Bacchae. But one of those wooden sticks they
      carry
Draws blood at once. They throw them—and men
      run
For their lives—that isn't human, there's some
      other power   1180

At work . . . At last, they go, back to the mountains
Where they came from, back to the springs of
  water
Which Dionysos sent them. They wash away
The blood . . . and the snakes lick off the dirt and
  gore
From the womens' cheeks with their tongues . . .
  This power, master, whoever he is, whatever
He is . . . let him into Thebes! He
1190 Is great. And one thing above all they say
He has done, I've heard that he gave mankind
The grape . . . And the grape is the best grave—for
  grief.
If there were no wine
There would be no love,
There would be no joy in life.
CHORUS: In this king's company, honesty is a
  dangerous pastime
Yet I must speak . . .
1200 . . . Say it, say it . . . !
Of all the powers in life the greatest is Dionysos.
PENTHEUS: Now, I see . . . yes! Nearer . . . nearer!
This insufferable craze is like a fire, and it's
  spreading!
All Greece despises us. But we must
Be firm, not give way . . .
  (To GUARDS) Go to the gates of Electra, get every
  man
Under arms. I want all the cavalry, every
1210 Spearman, every bowman, mobilised.
We attack the Bacchae at once . . .
I have been too patient. But my patience
Is finished, we are being governed by a pack of
  women.
DIONYSOS: I told you, Pentheus, but you never listen.
You have not been good to me. All the same
I am going to warn you. You must not use force
  against
Dionysos.
1220 End the war in yourself. He will not
Allow you to disturb his Bacchae. Leave them
In the mountains where they are happy.
PENTHEUS: Don't preach
To me. You were in prison and you escaped.
Well, look after your freedom or I may remind
Myself that you have been judged and condemned.
DIONYSOS: I
Would sacrifice to him . . . not rage and struggle
And kick. This is an eternal power—
1230 You are a man.
PENTHEUS: *I'll* sacrifice to him!
A blood sacrifice, a woman sacrifice—
That is all they are fit for. I will be lavish—
There will be carnage in the glades of Kithairon.
DIONYSOS: You'll lose. It will be an ignominious rout.
Your bronze shields won't hold off wooden sticks
And women's hands.

PENTHEUS: Will someone tell me how
To get rid of this man? Extricate me, someone!
Whatever I do to him, whatever he does 1240
To me, it's the same. Talk, talk, talk!
DIONYSOS: Excuse me—but you can settle all this,
No trouble . . . It is still possible.
PENTHEUS: How? What
Do I do? Make myself lower than the lowest
In this country?
DIONYSOS: I will bring the women
Here, without the use of force.
PENTHEUS: Yes,
I see, thank you. This is the great master 1250
Plan—the great deception.
DIONYSOS: How can you call it
That? I want to keep you whole. I work
For nothing else.
PENTHEUS: You arranged this with your friends.
Licence to dance, disorder in perpetuity.
DIONYSOS: Certainly I arranged it, quite true—
With Dionysos
PENTHEUS (to GUARDS): Bring out my armour . . . (To
  DIONYSOS) You— 1260
Keep quiet!
DIONYSOS (to GUARDS): Wait! (To PENTHEUS) Do you
  want to see them . . .
In their nests up there in the hills. See
The women . . . ?
PENTHEUS: Yes, yes, I do. Yes,
I'll pay if I have to. Gold. How much? A thousand?
Ten thousand?
DIONYSOS: You've fallen in love with my idea.
You can't wait. Why? 1270
PENTHEUS: I'll see them drunk,
Hopelessly drunk. It revolts me, but . . . I . . .
DIONYSOS: But you really want to. That disgusting
  sight
Lures you there . . . ?
PENTHEUS: Yes, I told you, it does.
I won't say anything, I'll be quiet, I'll stay
Among the pine-trees.
DIONYSOS: You can try to hide
But they'll pick up your scent. 1280
PENTHEUS: Good point. I'd forgotten.
I'll go openly.
DIONYSOS: I'll take you there. Would you like that?
The way is before you. Will you dare?
PENTHEUS: Now!
Take me there now. I hate every minute
We lose.
DIONYSOS: Then you must be covered. Find a linen
Dress to wear . . .
PENTHEUS: Wait, now what is 1290
This? I'm a man, I don't change places
With any woman. Why should I?
DIONYSOS: In case
They kill you. Suppose you, a *man*, are discovered

There—you die.

PENTHEUS: Right again. I understand.
There is some intelligence in you. I should have
seen it
Before.

DIONYSOS: Dionysos came alive in me.
1300 All I know is him.

PENTHEUS: Yes, yes . . .
Now, this good advice of yours, how
Do we carry it out?

DIONYSOS: We go inside, and there
I prepare you for your journey.

PENTHEUS: How—prepare me?
Dress me up as a woman? Oh no, no,
I would be ashamed.

DIONYSOS: Have you lost heart? The sight
1310 Of those possessed and demented women, it no
longer
Interests you?

PENTHEUS: What kind of clothing did you say
I have to wear?

DIONYSOS: Long hair to your shoulders.
You must have a wig . . .

PENTHEUS: And then what else? Is there more
To this costume?

DIONYSOS: A full length robe.
1320 And for the head—a scarf.

PENTHEUS: Anything else
You want to drape me in?

DIONYSOS: We'll give you a stick
Covered with ivy to hold, and wrap a spotted
Fawn-skin round you . . .

PENTHEUS: No, I could never put on
Woman's clothing.

DIONYSOS: What will you do—fight them?
It's a waste of your blood.

1330 PENTHEUS: You're right. First we must go
And watch. Nothing more yet.

DIONYSOS: That
Makes better sense than hunting down evil
With more evil.

PENTHEUS: How can I get through the streets
Of Thebes and not be seen?

DIONYSOS: We'll find a secret
Way. I'll lead you.

PENTHEUS: Anything—but I will not
1340 Be entertainment for that herd of females. Let's go
Inside. I want to consider this plan.

DIONYSOS: Decide,
I'm ready for you. Nothing will be too much
trouble . . .

PENTHEUS: No, inside . . . I may call out my army
And march up there . . . Or I may follow
Your advice. We shall see.

(Exit.)

DIONYSOS *(to* CHORUS*)*: Friends, the man stands in the
gate of the trap.
He'll find the Bacchae and he'll answer to them   1350
with his life.
Dionysos, now your work begins.
You are not too far away, I hope. Let us
Reward this man for his attentions. First,
Dislodge his thoughts, make his reason slither.
If he were sane, he would not agree to put on
Woman's clothing. But when he edges out
Of his mind then, yes, then he'll wear it.
I want him to raise a howl of derision all
Through Thebes when he minces along the streets   1360
In skirts. Once he mouthed fearsome threats,
And now . . .
Now to Pentheus, to disguise him, dress him for
His journey into death. His mother's hands
Will caress him roughly to his grave, and he'll see
Dionysos face to face, know that power,
Know its nature, its ferocious gentle nature
Alive in man, an undeniable *god!*

(Exit.)

CHORUS: Night—will it ever come?
And my flying feet,   1370
Flash of white thighs in the hills,
Head flung back,
And the dew-soaked air kissing my throat—
And running, running—
Oh, when will it come?
I want to be free and play and be happy again
Like a young deer, swathed in an emerald meadow,
When he runs in stark terror of the hunt,
And the knotted nets close in—
Then he leaps up and over them,   1380
While the hunter shrieks to his hounds to keep
racing,
Pacing behind.
But the deer strains his flashing legs taut.
He skims and spurts across open stretches
Where the river winds
Till he comes to a wood,
And the deep shade lulls him,
The green branches soothe him,
And he rests where no man is.   1390
What does it mean to live a life?
Can you hope for better than to rise above all
warring,
Control what threatens you,
Defeat what oppresses you?
To be strong—
No, nothing is better.
I choose that.
There are forces not ruled by us,
And we obey them.   1400
Trust them—though they travel inch by inch,

They arrive.
Self-swollen and calloused,
Soul, tumoured and hard,
All the malignant growths of thought,
They level, and pare, and crop,
They move in the dark with a subtle glitter
So that no one times their work,
But always the hunt goes on—
1410 For the man who has turned his back on them.
Their rules cannot be overruled—
It is your peril, and your death that follows.
But if you grant their power—what does it cost?
Nothing.
Not even a word—because
These forces lack a name.
Call them whatever you like—
Spirits—
Gods—
1420 Principles—
Elements—
Currents—
Laws—
Anything, anything you like.
But they are born in your blood
They have been observed and preserved since
before time.
　　What does it mean to live a life?
Can you hope for better than to rise above all
1430　warring,
Control what threatens you,
Defeat what oppresses you?
To be strong—
No, nothing is better
I choose that.
Life is a stormy sea,
Happiness is a harbour.
Finding your harbour is your life-work.
He is truly happy who succeeds in that life-work.
1440 Some end rich, some poor,
Some are strong, some achieve nothing.
There are ten thousand hopes, ten thousand
　　dreams,
They may all come true—they may all vanish,
But happiness—
A man finds happiness when he lies every day
With those forces of the world on his side.
All hail to that man!

(*Enter* DIONYSOS.)

DIONYSOS (*into palace*): You! You with a white-hot
1450　wish for a peep
At the forbidden. You, reaching out for the
　　out-of-reach,
You—I'm talking to *you*—Pentheus! Come
Out here, in front of your palace, let me
See you, dressed a woman of the wild wine

Nights of Dionysos. Are you ready to spy?
Your mother is there . . .
All the women are there . . .

(*Enter* PENTHEUS.)

Perfect! You are a daughter of Kadmos to the life.
PENTHEUS: No, listen. I think I see two suns,　1460
And two Thebes. The seven-gated city
Has doubled . . . and you, you look
Like a bull, leading me—horns sprout from your
　　head . . .
All the time, were you that beast?
Are you the bull now . . . ?
DIONYSOS: Dionysos favours you. He is bound to us
For the wine-gifts we gave him. Before he was not
Pleased. But now he is. And you see
What you ought to see.　1470
PENTHEUS: How do I look to you?
My aunt . . . isn't this how she walks? . . . Or this . . .
　　My mother
Agave,—isn't it? Isn't it Agave?
DIONYSOS: It's them! When I look at you it's them I
　　see . . .
Wait—a wisp of hair has come away.
It isn't lying where I set it, under the scarf.
PENTHEUS: Inside, I went this way with my head,
That way—back, forward, back—I was being　1480
A woman in a trance. And I made the hair
Come loose . . .
DIONYSOS: We must keep you groomed. I'll put it in
　　place
Again. Here . . . lift your head up straight.
PENTHEUS: Look . . . there . . . you do it. Make me
　　pretty.
I am yours to play with. Take me.
DIONYSOS: Your sash is loose—
Look. And your dress is wrong. The pleats should　1490
　　hang
The same length round your ankles.
PENTHEUS: Yes,
I see . . . a little too long by the right foot.
But on this side it seems all right, touching
My heel just there . . .
DIONYSOS: Who is your best friend?
I am . . . You don't believe me? Wait till you see
Bacchae, how modest they are, how pure, how
　　sane—　1500
Astonishing.
PENTHEUS: This branch with ivy—in my right
Hand—or my left? Which makes me
More like a genuine wild woman of the hills?
DIONYSOS: Hold it in your right hand, and raise it
In time with your right foot . . . Very good.
I see a change, a new mind, in you . . .
PENTHEUS: Now I could . . . I could hoist the whole of
　　Kithairon

1510 On my shoulder—valleys full of women
Dancing, madness and all! . . . Yes?
DIONYSOS: Of course,
If you will it. Your mood was before most
unhealthy,
Now it is all it should be.
PENTHEUS: Shall we bring iron bars, or shall I delve it
Up with my own bare hands, wedge
One shoulder or one arm under the hill-top . . . ?
DIONYSOS: And destroy the homes of the nymphs?
1520 No, no.
Pan lives there too. Let him go on playing
His pipes.
PENTHEUS: You're right. One should not coerce
women.
I shall hide myself in the boughs of a pine tree.
DIONYSOS: You find
The hiding place that suits you best. You're a spy,
A secret witness of secret rites.
PENTHEUS: Yes,
1530 Imagine, they are nestling like birds in the thick
leaves,
Locked in their lust, enjoying it . . .
DIONYSOS: You must break in
And prevent them. Perhaps you will find them in
the act . . .
Unless they find you first.
PENTHEUS: Take me through Thebes,
Right through the centre. I am the only man
Here who has any courage.
1540 DIONYSOS: Yes, you alone
Make sacrifices for your people, you alone.
And so—the test. It has always been there, waiting
For you. Follow me. I am your
Protector, your escort . . . as far as Kithairon—
Someone else will bring you back.
PENTHEUS: Yes, my mother . . .
DIONYSOS: In full view of everyone . . .
PENTHEUS: That's why I'm going . . .
DIONYSOS: You will be borne back on high.
1550 PENTHEUS: Yes, in triumph, you mean my great
triumph!
DIONYSOS: In the hands of your mother . . .
PENTHEUS: You'll spoil me—all this pampering!
DIONYSOS: Yes, I'll spoil you, I'll spoil you utterly.
PENTHEUS: Still, I deserve it, and I shall have it!

(*Exit.*)

DIONYSOS: Headstrong, headstrong—you go walking
To your headlong end—which will make you
Famous, far beyond this life, beyond
This time.
1560 Agave, fling open your arms.
Prepare, you sisters, daughters of Kadmos.
I bring this young man to you—
Prepare for a great contest.

The victor shall be myself—and Dionysos.
As for the rest—wait, watch, and listen.

(*Exit.*)

CHORUS: Go, track to the mountains
Dogs of madness,
Run, dogs, run,
Find the daughters of Kadmos,
Snap at their dancing heels, sink your fangs in their 1570
brains,
Then turn them loose on the would-be woman,
The spy in the flapping skirts,
Who goes mad for the secret of the possessed.
His mother will see him first,
As he peers from a rock-wall or cliff-steeple.
She'll scream to the women:
"Look! See what creeps sniffing up to our
mountain,
Our mountain, my friends— 1580
This creature crawling across the hillside!
What mothered such a thing?
Not a woman, no—it got life from a lioness
Or a beast heaved up out of African sands."
Now we shall see balance restored.
We shall see it, sharp, clear, a sword
With blood on its edge, driving deep
To the gullet of Pentheus, the blossom of the
dragon's jawbone,
Who enforces his will on the forces of life, 1590
Outlaws law,
Orders all other order out of existence.
And now—
With insane and petty determination,
With intent sick passion,
All his thought corrupted,
All his mind a sewer,
He smells his way to the living heart
Of the mysteries, where Dionysos is born and
re-born. 1600
He wants to master with violence that forever-free
spirit.
The laws of all life admit no excuses.
Live by them, live as a man—
That is the way of no pain.
I don't grudge man his search for knowledge,
I acclaim it, applaud it,
But there is more, there are great things
That must be brought to the daylight,
Made part of our waking and sleeping. 1610
Calmly accept them, peacefully weave them
Into your life—and it will be a good life,
Freeing you.
Now we shall see balance restored,
We shall see it, sharp, clear, a sword
With blood on its edge, driving deep

To the gullet of Pentheus, the blossom of the
    dragon's jawbone,
Who enforces his will on the forces of life,
1620 Outlaws law,
Orders all other order out of existence.
    Now Dionysos, into the open!
Let him see you . . .
As a BULL!
A dragon with swarming heads!
A lion, vomiting flames!
Come, Dionysos, come sweetly smiling
And string your noose round the throat of this
    hunter.
1630 Bring the one-minded women in a pack
To trip him,
Smother him,
Kill him!

(Enter PENTHEUS' own SERVANT.)

SERVANT: In this house lived people who were the
    envy
Of all Greece . . . once. A family begun
In dragon's teeth, a summer harvest reaped
By Kadmos, the great traveller and merchant
Of the western seas. And I am nothing,
1640 An obscure someone who takes orders. And yet
I pity them.
CHORUS: What is it? Have you news? Have you been
    in the hills?
SERVANT: Pentheus is dead, King Pentheus, son of
    Echion, is dead.
CHORUS: Victory! The first day of Dionysos—now
    they see you, now you live, now you face them
    . . .
SERVANT: What do you mean? How can you say that?
    My master is dead. Are you glad? He is dead, dead!
1650 CHORUS: Not my master. I've another home. I've
    another
Life . . . No more fear, no more prison, no more
    terror . . .
Free, free!
SERVANT: There are still men in Thebes who can . . .
CHORUS: Thebes can't touch me, Thebes has no
    power . . . Dionysos, Dionysos comes first for me.
SERVANT: I can forgive the rest, but not this. Terrible
    things have happened, and you gloat. It's ugly.
1660 CHORUS: Terrible things? Describe them, tell us, how
    did the man die, the wrong-headed master-fool
    . . .
SERVANT: Behind us were the last houses of Thebes—
We had come out at the river Asopos. Then
We began to climb, mounting the slopes of
    Kithairon,
Pentheus and I—he was my master, so
I followed him—and this stranger, who
Was to be the guide of our expedition.

Treading very softly, and never speaking,
So that we could see without being seen, we came   1670
First to a glade thick with grass and rested
There . . . It was in a little valley, overhung
On each side with cliffs, and fed by rills
Of water. Pine trees leant over to shade it,
And somewhere in this valley were the women,
The mad women, the Bacchae.
    Then we saw them.
    They're sitting, quietly working and happy.
    Some
Are re-winding the ivy that slipped off   1680
The tips of their branches. Others, like young
    mares
Unharnessed from their painted chariots, are
    playing.
They sing—the tunes sound strange to me, but
    they
Pick them up and echo each other.
    Though they are everywhere, poor Pentheus
        sees nothing,
Not one woman. "Stranger," he says, "from where   1690
I stand I can't get a sight of these whores
Who call themselves Bacchae. Perhaps if I went
Up that slope and climbed the trunk of a pine tree
I could have a direct view of their filthy games."
And then—a miracle. There is a pine-tree there
That tickles heaven. As I watch, the stranger
Takes the topmost branch and . . .
Down . . . down . . . down he draws it towards us
Out of the sunlight, into the deep shade
Where we stand. It bends like a bow—or like   1700
A wheel, when its rim is marked out with a compass
    and traces
A full circle—that's how the stranger, with his bare
Hands, made the mountain pine curve to the
    ground—
Something no man born of woman
Could have done.
He seats Pentheus on the topmost shoots, then
    gently
Lets the trunk uncoil, from his grip, being   1710
Very careful not to shake our king from his new
    throne
Among the leaves, till it towers straight in the air
Again with Pentheus perched astride it . . . Now
It is he who is in view, rather than having
A view himself . . . He is just rising into sight
Above the surrounding trees, when the stranger
    vanishes,
And out of the air a voice comes—
My belief is—Dionysos spoke then.   1720
"Young women, I bring you this man who intends
To amuse himself with me and my deepest
    mysteries.
Punish him!"

While these words still echo in the hills
A pillar of fierce fire is planted between
Earth and heaven . . .
    The air is still now . . .
Silence.
1730 In the cloistered trees not a leaf moves,
The noises of animals cease . . .
The women, not sure what it is they've heard, stand
On tiptoe, glancing this way and that. So,
Once again, he brands the air with his voice.
This time there is no doubt. The daughters
Of Kadmos know their master, and obey.
They begin to run—they dart, they flash, like
    pigeons
In flight, his mother, Agave, all her sisters,
1740 And the rest of the women, Bacchae! Down
    through the glade,
Across the stream,
Over the rocks,
Whirled in the tempest of Dionysos' power
They rush—then they see my master sitting
On the pine-tree. First they clamber onto
A rock face opposite and try pelting him
With volleys of sharp stones and javelins made
From pine branches, while others fling
1750 Their ivy-covered sticks . . . Poor man,
He can only be a target . . . But they can't reach
    him.
Their victim is sitting too high, even for their
Terrible urgency. All the same,
He's trapped. There's nothing he can do. At last
They snap off great oak boughs—a thunderbolt
Could not do it more cleanly, and using the raw
Wood as levers they try to wrench the tree
Up by its roots—and still they can't do it.
1760 They struggle but they can't . . . they can't . . .
"Here," says Agave, "make a circle and take
Hold of the stem, my friends, and we'll catch this
    agile
Beast. He must never betray the secret of our
    dancing
For Dionysos!"
    A flurry of hands reach out to the pine tree and
        tug.
It comes clean out of the earth.
1770 Down from the height where he sits, falling, falling,
Screaming all the time till he dashes against
The rocks, comes Pentheus.
He knows his end is near, knows it will
Be hideous . . .
    His mother is first, chief priestess of the
        slaughter,
She descends on him. He rips off
The scarf around his head, hoping she'll recognize
    him,
1780 And spare him, he touches her cheeks, he says,
    "Mother,

It's your son, Pentheus, the son
You bore in the house of Echion. Mother, pity me,
Have mercy, I have sinned, but don't murder me,
Your own son, for what I've . . ."
    But she can't help herself. There's froth on her
        lips,
Her eyes are rolling, staring, her mind's gone,
She's been seized by a greater power, Dionysos,
And doesn't listen to her son. She grips   1790
His left arm, just below the elbow,
Rams her foot against the poor man's ribs,
And pulls. His arm comes away at the shoulder . . .
That strength didn't come from her—it came
From Dionysos.
    Meanwhile, Ino is gouging the other side,
Rending the flesh from his bones, while Autonoë
And the whole crowd of the Bacchae press down
On him. His shrieking—so long as there's breath
In his lungs—and their howls of triumph merge   1800
Into one great din. One woman carries
An arm, another, one of his feet, with a sandal
Still on it. His ribs are stripped of skin, the flesh
Hangs in rags. They play with it, they toss
Pieces of Pentheus from hand to bloodstained
    hand
Like a ball, until the mountain is strewn with
    fragments
Of his body—some of it under the sheer
Rock-faces, some under the green   1810
Leaves in the depths of the wood. I don't know
How you could find it all again . . .
    His mother was left holding his destroyed head.
She impaled it on a wooden spike, as if
It was some mountain lion she had caught in the
    heart
Of Kithairon, and left her sisters amongst the
    still-dancing
Women. Now, she's running this way, to the city,
Exulting in her terrible kill. She's praising   1820
Dionysos as her fellow huntsman, the one
Who helps her in the chase, the bringer of bright
Victory . . . But she'll thank him with her tears.
    I want to go. I hate suffering. I don't
Want to see Agave come home. The best
And safest thing is to keep a balance in your life,
And acknowledge the great powers around us and
    in us.
I think that is the meaning of wisdom. If you have
That, and can live that way, you really are   1830
A wise man.

(Exit.)

CHORUS: Dance him into life!
    Move like one,
    Shout like one!
    The last of the dragon is dead,
    Pentheus is dead.

He took woman's clothing,
Picked up a twig, made it live with ivy,
He trusted it—
1840 And it killed him.
And heading him into death was a bull.
Daughters of Kadmos—Bacchae—now you are
    famous.
The prize—
—and the price—
Of your victory is tears, mourning.
You won the contest at a cost—
Your hands are slippery with your child's
Flowing life.
1850   (*Looking offstage.*) Look! She's coming . . . Agave
        . . .
. . . His mother . . .
Running home . . . her eyes, look at her eyes . . .
They're staring, they're mad . . .
Take her into our midst . . . she belongs to the god
    . . .
And to his happiness.

(*Enter* AGAVE, *carrying the head of* PENTHEUS.)

AGAVE: Women of the cast—Bacchae . . .
CHORUS: Why do you use that word? What do you
    want?
AGAVE: I'm bringing this branch with trailing leaves, I
1860   cut it just now in the mountains, and look—I'm
    bringing it back home—I had to hunt—but I
    tracked it down . . . and now I'm happy . . .
CHORUS: I see . . . join us . . . become one of us . . .
AGAVE: It's a lion cub. I caught it. I didn't need nets.
    You can see—look . . .
CHORUS: Where—where did it happen? Where did
    you find it?
AGAVE: Kithairon . . .
CHORUS: Kithairon?
1870 AGAVE: . . . was the killer.
CHORUS: Who struck first?
AGAVE: I struck first. I. I did it, no one else. When we
    meet in the hills, I am the one they envy—I am
    so lucky.
CHORUS: And who else?
AGAVE: Kadmos, Kadmos . . .
CHORUS: How, Kadmos . . . ?
AGAVE: Had children . . . those children were there,
    Shared the hunt—but I was first, I was first.
1880 Happy . . . chasing the beast . . . Come with me
    Now . . . to the meal . . .
CHORUS: How can we come . . . What meal?
AGAVE: It's a young bull . . . Here, on his
    Cheek, the hair is soft . . .
    Just below the crest . . . It grows . . . so sleek.
CHORUS: Yes, that hair could belong to a beast.
    It looks like an animal.
AGAVE: The hounds were whipped on by Dionysos
        ' ' '

He sent us hurtling after the prey . . .
He knew its ways, he knows   1890
Us all . . .
CHORUS: Yes, our prince leads the hunt.
AGAVE: You praise him?
CHORUS: I praise him.
AGAVE: Then soon all Thebes will.
CHORUS: Yes . . . and Pentheus? . . . Your son?
AGAVE: Pentheus . . . Yes, he will praise his mother
    because she caught this young wild lion.
CHORUS: But think what it is.
AGAVE: No! Think how I did it.   1900
CHORUS: You're proud?
AGAVE: I'm happy. We did great, great things—as all
    the world will see—when we hunted today.
CHORUS: Then show your trophy, poor woman, show
    it to everyone.
Let people see what you brought home from the
    day's hunting.
AGAVE: Men and women of Thebes, our city of high
    Towers, so well defended, come and see
What I brought home from the wild country for   1910
you.—
    A beast . . . We tracked him down, we daughters
        of Kadmos.
We used no snares, no traps,
No spears forged in the workshops of Thessaly—
Only our hands we used, our soft, white,
Delicate hands—they were our spears.
And hunters boast of their machines, their useless
Contraptions of steel and wire . . . we caught this
    beast   1920
And tore it limb from limb with only our hands . . .
Where is my father? I want him here. And where
Is Pentheus, where's my son? . . .
    Go, someone, find a ladder, and lean it
Against the palace and nail this trophy against
The beam ends. I want everyone to see
What I have brought home from the hunt . . .

(*Enter* KADMOS, *helping* SERVANTS *to carry the body of*
PENTHEUS.)

KADMOS: This way . . . Stay close to me . . . This way
    . . .
He seems so heavy . . . like my grief—now,
Lay him down—there . . .   1930
    Pentheus has come home.
    I searched, hoping and looking, hoping and
        looking—
It was so hard to see them, scattered among the
    trees—
No two parts together, all over Kithairon . . .
Those steep paths!—I have no strength left . . .
Well, here is his body, I found it.
    I had just reached the city with Teiresias
After paying our tribute to Dionysos when   1940

I heard of the monstrous thing my daughters had
    done.
Back I went, back, back to the mountainside
To bring home my grandson—or what remained
After the women . . . What was in their minds then?
    . . .
I saw Akteon's mother in the forest,
Autonoë, and Ino with her—it was hideous . . .
Their contorted bodies, writhing, jerking . . .
Then someone told me the same driving force
1950   Had guided Agave here . . . Yes, they were right
    . . .
There she is . . . I see . . .
No, no . . . I don't want to see!
AGAVE: Father, be proud, you should be—especially
    now—
The proudest man alive. You have such daughters
No one, no one in the world, could
Surpass them . . . I speak for us all, but I have gone
Far beyond the others. I don't spin.
And weave now. I have progressed.
1960   Now I hunt—with my bare hands—wild beasts!
And look . . . the pickings of my success.
Here—for you—my newborn glory;
Hang him against your palace wall—take him,
Father—here . . . Can't you feel the joy, the glory
Of my kill too? Tell your friends to come,
To celebrate with you—because you have much
To be thankful for, much to celebrate.
Think of the great things we have done today.
KADMOS: Can I measure hurt like this . . . No, no way
1970   of . . .
I can't even look . . . The great things you've
    done—yes,
The great murders, the blood, the . . . !
Oh, fling your thanksgiving before some deity.
He'll love it!
And you tell the people they must celebrate . . .
You tell me!
Celebrate! . . . (He weeps.)
For you, my child, this is for you . . .
1980   And for me. Oh, Dionysos is right,
But he is not fair!
Being so right, he has broken us . . . But then
He was born here, this is his home . . .
AGAVE: Old men! All they do is grumble.
And they always look so grim. I wish my son
Was happy hunting. I wish he was like his mother.
She goes out and runs with the young women
Of Thebes till they track down an animal. But all
He can do is oppose the forces from which
1990   We draw life. You should speak to him, father,
You should advise him . . . Someone—go and fetch
    him.
I want him to see me in the full flood of my joy.
KADMOS (a cry is wrenched from him): You'll know—you
    must! You'll see

What you've done, and the pain will wring tears
From you . . .
And yet, if you never wake from the dream you're
    in . . .
Well, it won't be happiness—but you'll feel no pain.   2010
AGAVE: Is something wrong? Are you angry with me,
    father?
KADMOS: Look up at the sky.
AGAVE: There . . . What do you expect me to see?
KADMOS: Does it look the same to you, or do you see
    A change?
AGAVE: It looks brighter than before,
    Not so blurred.
KADMOS: And inside you—
    Do you still feel this sense of flying?   2020
AGAVE: I don't . . .
Understand . . . Wait. Something's happening.
My head! . . . There's a change . . . somewhere
Inside, the mind shifts . . . Yes, I feel . . .
KADMOS: Listen to me.
    Do you know what I'm saying? Can you answer me?
AGAVE: I've forgotten . . . What were we talking
    about,
    Father?
KADMOS: When you were married, do you remember   2030
    whose house you came to?
AGAVE: You . . . gave me to . . .
Didn't they say his name was . . . Echion of the
Dragon's seed?
KADMOS: And you had a son.
Your husband gave you a son. What was his name?
AGAVE: Pentheus—child of our true married love.
KADMOS: Now look at the face that lies between your
    Hands. Whose is it?
AGAVE: It's a lion . . . You see . . . they . . . they told   2040
    me
So—the hunters . . . the women.
KADMOS: Look! Look properly. It won't take long.
    It's easy.
AGAVE (obeys, gives a shriek): What is it—this . . . thing!
    I'm carrying?
Oh, dear God! What is this?
KADMOS: Open your eyes, and see. You can't mistake
    The face.
AGAVE: This foul wound, this foul . . . object!   2050
    I can't bear it . . . !
KADMOS: Does it look like a lion
    To you?
AGAVE: No . . . It's Pentheus . . . My son . . .
    Your head . . . your poor . . .
KADMOS: My tears flowed for him long before
    You knew who he was.
AGAVE: Who killed him? How
    Did he come here? How am I holding him?
KADMOS: You will have to hear something . . .   2060
    abominable.
Perhaps you are not ready . . .

AGAVE: Tell me! I'll choke,
My heart's bursting—I *must* know!

KADMOS: You,
And your sisters with you, murdered him.

AGAVE: Where?
Where did he die? Here in the palace?

KADMOS: No.
2070 You remember where, long ago, Akteon
Was savaged by his hounds . . .

AGAVE: On Kithairon!
But why did the poor fool go there?

KADMOS: He went to jeer at Dionysos, and your
dancing
In his honour.

AGAVE: And we destroyed him . . . But what
happened?

KADMOS: You have no minds left. The whole city
2080 Was convulsed. Dionysos was in possession.

AGAVE: Dionysos took us and laid us waste. Now
I see it.

KADMOS: He was displaced. He was usurped.
You did not believe he had power.

AGAVE: Where
Is my child's body? . . . Father, I loved him . . .
Where is he?

KADMOS: I brought him home. It was hard—but I
found him.

2090 AGAVE: Are the limbs . . . is his body . . . a body . . . or
. . . ?

KADMOS: He lies there.

AGAVE: Pentheus, Pentheus—my only son—my child.

KADMOS: Yes, your son—*and* your heir . . .
Heir to your madness.

AGAVE: But how could that touch Pentheus? How
Could he inherit that from me?

KADMOS: He took
From you his stubbornness. He would not open
Himself to Dionysos—and we all suffered
100 For his fault. In a sense, he united us,
The whole family, because now we are all, like him,
Shattered fragments.
And I, who never had a son, only
This grandson, your boy, I'm left with nothing,
Just a carcass, a shamefully mutilated
Corpse . . . *That* was once the hope, the new
Life of my family . . . Pentheus, my child,
You were our centre, you gave us permanence,
Child of my child, and you were strict with them all
110 In Thebes. I was an old man, but people
Took notice of me, they respected me, so long as
You were there. If they did not, you would pick out
The culprit and punish him. But now I,
Kadmos, Kadmos the great, I'll be banished—
No home, no rights—and I was the man who sowed
The seed of Thebes, and the harvest I reaped was
the greatest
Of our time. Child I loved best—

And now I can no longer say that.
There's nothing left—never again will you touch   2120
My beard, put your arm round me, and say,
"Father
Of my mother, who has hurt you, who denies you
Your rights? Come, grandfather, who troubles you,
Who is unkind to you? Tell me. If anyone
Has done you wrong I will have him whipped!"
I have only my grief now, and you are a memory.
If anyone thinks that his own mind alone
Can govern the world, he should see Pentheus here
And believe, believe there are other powers,   2130
Ones he does not dominate.

CHORUS: I grieve for you, Kadmos. Your grandson
died for a good reason, but it hurt you.

AGAVE: Father, you see how all my daylight reason
Dawns again in me. I see, I think,
I feel, and as clearly as you,
I know that I am a murderer for my sacrifice
To Dionysos. The victim is dead; the priestess
Lives polluted.
But Pentheus is my son in my heart still,   2140
The son I gave life to and watched over. I want to
Give him one last gift.
I want to arrange his body for the grave,
Though he'll never know of it—the dead feel no
Gratitude for favours to their unfeeling limbs.

KADMOS: He was your child; I can't refuse you. Be
gentle
With his body—you were not before. I have laid
him there
As if he were asleep. Do not disturb him.   2150

AGAVE: Pentheus, my son . . .
My baby . . .
You lay in my arms so often, so helpless,
And now again you need my loving care,
My dear, dear child . . .
I killed you.
No! I will not say that. I was not there. I was . . .
I was in some other place . . .
It was Dionysos. Dionysos took me, Dionysos
Used me, and Dionysos murdered you!   2160

DIONYSOS: No! (DIONYSOS *as a god now becomes visible
above them all.*)
Accuse yourselves, accept the guilt,
You let Pentheus rule you, you were happy being
ruled,
And for his sake you locked me out of your city.
And so Thebes will have new masters,
An army from the east will live in your homes,
Walk your streets, plough your fields.
Agave—you and your sisters have no place here.   2170
Your home now is . . . wherever a murderer
Can find rest or peace—but not in Thebes.
And you—Kadmos—you must begin again. You
must
Forfeit your human shape, and become a dragon.

Your wife, daughter of the spirit of war, Harmony
Will also be transfigured—into a snake. Then,
With your bride, you'll drive in a chariot hauled
By young bulls, at the head of an army from
2180 The east. With countless men at your command
You will plunder city after city. But once they
Have wrecked the sanctuary where Apollo speaks
Of things to come—their luck will change, they
Will be defeated, and then disperse. The war-spirit,
however,
Will rescue you and Harmony, and keep you both
alive
In the world of the undying . . .
This is the universal will of Zeus and
2190 I tell you these things with authority from him. I
am
Dionysos, his son—I will always return to life.
If you had understood what wholeness is, you
Would now be happy, the son of Zeus would be
Helping you, a friend, an ally.
But you did not want that.
KADMOS: Dionysos, listen to us, we have been wrong
. . .
DIONYSOS: Now you understand, but now is too late.
When you should have seen, you were blind.
2200 KADMOS: We know that.
But you are like a tide that turns and drowns us.
DIONYSOS: Because I was born with dominion over
you
And you dispossessed me.
KADMOS: Then you should not
Be like us, your subjects. You should have no
passions.
DIONYSOS: And I don't. But these are laws of life. I
cannot
2210 Change them.
AGAVE (weeps): It is decided, father. We must leave
And take our sorrow with us.
DIONYSOS: Why delay?
You can change nothing now. (He vanishes.)
KADMOS: My child, we have suffered cruelly, all of
us—
I did not escape . . .
I am an old man, and I must leave my home,
Go to a foreign country. And then, I am told,
2220 My destiny is to lead this strange army
Into Greece.
I shall be a dragon, my wife, a dragon; myself
And Harmony, beasts, no longer human, will bring
War to the calm altars and graves of Greece.

There will be no end to the suffering, not even in
the country
Of the dead; I am to be allowed no peace.
AGAVE: Father, I shall lose you, never see my home
again . . .
KADMOS: No, don't hold me, my poor child . . . Why? 2230
I'm old, a grey, dying swan—the young
Bird can't protect it . . .
AGAVE: Where shall I go?
I have no country. What will happen to me? . . .
KADMOS: I don't know, my daughter, your father is
weak.
He is tired, he is no use.
AGAVE: Goodbye, my home,
Goodbye, my city. I am leaving you. I have no
Place here. I am cursed. 2240
KADMOS: Go now, Agave . . .
AGAVE: Father! Come here! . . . I want to hold you . . .
KADMOS: Look, my tears . . . for you and for your
sisters.
AGAVE: In our lives Dionysos has been a spirit
Of havoc, cruel, relentless . . .
KADMOS: But only because
He was thrust aside, and no one let him in
Here. The cruelty was yours.
AGAVE: Goodbye, father . . . 2250
KADMOS: Goodbye—daughter—though what is there
good in it?
AGAVE (to PEOPLE OF THEBES): Please, my friends, will
you help me?
Take me to my sisters, who will share my exile
And the years of sorrow with me.
I want to be where Kithairon can't shadow my
life—
Where I don't even have to see its distant slopes . . .
Take me where branches wound with ivy 2260
Can't remind me of what has happened.
Let someone else be possessed.
I have withered.
CHORUS: The forces of life are seen in disguise,
A thousand disguises.
They make all things possible,
They guarantee nothing,
What you thought was forgotten, buried,
They conceive, and bring to birth again.
Today you have watched their power at work— 2270
It never ends.

CURTAIN

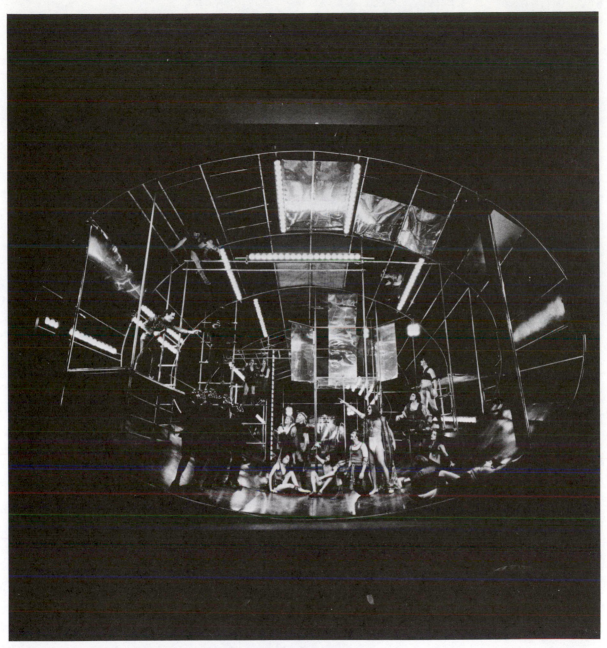

Figure 8. The ultra-modern set designed by Santo Loquasto for the
Yale Repertory Theater production of *The Bacchae,* New Haven, 1969.
(Photograph: Yale Joel.)

Figure 9. Dionysus (Alvin Epstein) in the Yale Repertory Theatre production of *The Bacchae,* directed by Andre Gregory, New Haven, 1969. (Photograph: Sean Kernan.)

Staging of *The Bacchae*

REVIEW OF THE YALE REPERTORY
PRODUCTION, 1969, BY JACK KROLL

In a disastrous week of a disastrous and dispiriting Broadway season one's anger and depression are relieved by two trips off the Great White Way. At New Haven the Yale School of Drama Repertory Theatre, embattled in recent months by tensions, confrontations and disagreements involving students, some faculty members and its brilliant dean, Robert Brustein, has nonetheless come up with a production that commands attention, that is almost exactly the right activity for a repertory theater connected with a school of drama interested in controlled and intelligent exploration of a beleaguered art.

Kenneth Cavander has written a translation of Euripides' *The Bacchae* that is strong, spare, hard, and that seeks to capture without distorting the shape of the original, resonances of language and idea that will connect the play legitimately to the present. But this production seems in every sense to be a collaboration, a collaboration in which theatrical history itself plays a part. Director Andre Gregory and Brustein have been intensely affected by the recent visit of the Living Theatre to Yale, and this production is the first serious attempt by anybody to assimilate the implications of the Living Theatre's personality, energy and ideas into what was once called the "mainstream" of the theater.

That mainstream may indeed no longer exist. And Yale's attempt under Brustein to stabilize the headlong energies of the avant-garde, to shape them into effective form without diluting their import or impact, is a task which is currently exposing him to the exacerbations of the cultural right and left—but it is certainly the right job for him to do. "The Bacchae" shows both the point and the perils of this task. Under a decisive sculptural hand from Gregory the combined professional and student cast play Euripides' drama of Dionysiac disruption with strong over-all effect and considerable fascinating detail.

Catalyzing the entire production is the remarkable set by Santo Loquasto, Yale '69. Obviously inspired by Julian Beck's wonderful design for the Living Theatre's "Frankenstein," Loquasto achieves his own success with his beautiful oval cage that structures the entire stage into levels, grades and heights that become the public places of Athens, the sequestrations of the Dionysiac forests and the hidden groins and shadows of the mind.

Euripides' play is about the explosive energy system of which human beings are the sentient parts, who forget those energies at their peril. If this description sounds mod and McLuhanesque, it is deliberately so; this "Bacchae" makes no bones about drawing parallels between the ecstatic and lethal revels of the followers of Dionysos and today's subculture of hippies and other glorious human beasts. If the parallel is sometimes too pat (the blind prophet Teiresias comes on like the Maharishi) the attempt to find dramatic shape for the historical continuum between Euripides and us is admirable—and inescapable.

The danger of this type of production is the possibility of a kind of instant academization of the energy of which the Living Theatre is the most notable example. If one questions this energy in some of its moral and esthetic implications, one must be careful not to transmute it into something not healthier but simply tamer. This production bravely confronts the dangers of transmutation and thus sets in motion a process which others must follow. The student chorus (coed) of bacchae does well, and of the professionals who play the central roles, Alvin Epstein as Dionysos—an epicene Olympian super-hoodlum with his snaky blond locks and Mick Jagger mien—and David Spielberg as the doomed Pentheus—torn apart, literally, between his drive for power and his buried passivity—are the best.

The Repertory Theatre's "Bacchae" is good entertainment; it is good spectacle; but it is not necessarily good drama. While the Euripidean tragedy involves the clash of life styles, the tension of fascination, and repulsion of the sensuous grotesque, it is also an intensely emotional human experience. Unfortunately, the present production lacks emotional force. The loss of power is due to several significant factors.

First, and most apparent are the elements of spectacle. Santo Loquasto's brilliant set, which creates a total space on the stage and is the source of numerous surprises and illusions in the play, is simply too overpowering. In the scenes in which it serves as playground equipment for the Bacchae it is most effective. The spirit of gamery and childish abandon is well served by these theatrical monkeybars. But the scenes of personal interplay between Dionysos and Pentheus, and of realization for Agave are needlessly hampered. No depth of emotion can be successfully conveyed when the actors are seen as only a small part of the gymnastic maze of the set. The human experience is minimized at those moments when it should have been most exalted and damned.

As with the set, which both aids and hinders, so too does the music and sound by Richard Peaslee function with ambivalence. When heard alone, without players, lighting and motion, the music offers the purest distillation of the play's themes and conflicts. At no other point is the union of the earthly and the heavenly presented with such lyricism and beauty as it is in Peaslee's intermission music. With some silence in the theater, the intermission can be almost mystic. But the music and sound engineering also subordinate the human voice. After a musical prelude in magnificent stereo encompassing the entire theater, the actors speak in an unavoidable monophony. They seem flat and lifeless in comparison to the rich sounds that precede them. The production fails in integrating effects which work well in isolation into a satisfactory whole. Essentially, "Bacchae" is about people; and it is the people who are drowned in the sea of swampish music and bottomless stages.

The attempt to represent the clash of modi vivendi of the Bacchae against the Thebans by using two directing styles is successful, but also runs into self-imposed difficulties. Director Andre Gregory has worked with Stanley Rosenberg to create a conflict of cultures: freedom versus rigid order, "elect" versus unchosen, hippie versus policeman. The chief failure is the performance of the chorus of revelers. Although they do, at times, convey a real evangelical ecstasy, or drug-induced euphoria, they are frequently as convincing as a group of cheerleaders at a high school football game. Too often, they seem uncomfortable with what they are doing. They offer a less than attractive temptation to a new way of life.

Alvin Epstein, as Dionysos, is the play's outstanding performer. His sinuous movements, glazed-eyed trances, and sagacious slyness make a fine leader, who overcomes the problems of his inadequate and unbelievable followers. His appearance however, is not that of Dionysos. He does look godlike, but the wrong sort. He looks too much like Verrocchio's boyish "David" to be the sly seducer; his godliness is too angelic. He is too innocent; Peter Pan offering Never Never Land.

In contrast to this Huck Finn of a seducer is David Spielberg as an avant garde-mafioso Pentheus. While he expresses wonder and innocence effectively in his delivery, Spielberg too is plagued by appearance. He appears too sinister to be a believable, naive Pentheus.

Michael Lombard (whose occasional bellows project the human voice into the realm of the resonant sounds of the music) as Teiresias, and George Bartenieff, as Kadmos, are properly ridiculous as the oldsters playing with the children.

Unfortunately, Mildred Dunnock's moving portrayal of Agave is lost in the vast scope of attention demanded by the production. For her final, crazed realization that she has killed her son the whole play should become her; the clash and conflict should be heightened by being internalized. Miss Dunnock is, in fact, the focal point on the stage during this climactic scene, but not overwhelmingly so. The set which, by its echoing of every step made on it, had magnified the frolic of the Bacchae chorus, becomes a source of cruel disruption as the audience is distracted by a chorus member shifting his position in the corner, or some other movement on the huge set. By the end of the play, the mind has been trained to view the whole stage, the whole spectacle; insufficient attempt is made to narrow this expanded consciousness for the less spectacular, but emotionally powerful climax.

In short, the present production is one of many fine individual elements that fail to work together properly. In trying to portray the clash of life styles, the styles of production themselves conflict; "Bacchae" has been trapped by the imitative fallacy. Single aspects fight for supremacy and attention; some cannot survive the struggle. "Bacchae" attempts to substitute external turmoil for internal force. In all this chaos, the play loses its humanity, the actors have been squelched. Greater emotional tension will no doubt be found in a tape recording of the performance. It is the people who are lost in the disintegrating world of the stage.

ARISTOPHANES

450—385 B.C.

The plays of Aristophanes are the only surviving examples of fifth century Greek comedy, a form of satiric drama dominated by fantasy—fantasy so outlandish that it has never been surpassed in the history of western drama. Its plot was not really a plot so much as a set of variations on a fantastic situation, a comic idea meant to solve a pressing social or political situation, such as the ingenious scheme of Lysistrata and her cohorts to force their Athenian husbands to make peace by refusing to make love to them until they end the war against Sparta. The fantasy was always designed to make clear the dramatist's satiric object, and what better way to show the absurdity of war than to stage a battle of the sexes, but a battle in the case of *Lysistrata* that threatens to end in sexual frustration instead of fulfillment. The chorus of Greek comedy was often correspondingly fantastic, consisting, for example, of clouds, or in other situations of birds, frogs, and wasps. And even when the chorus itself was not so farfetched, its actions were, as in the knock-down drag-out struggle that takes place between the chorus of old men and the chorus of old women in *Lysistrata*. The fantasy, moreover, was not confined to the play alone, but included the audience too, for the chorus always took the liberty once during each comedy to interrupt the action and deliver a harangue directly to the spectators, as in *Lysistrata* when the chorus of women implores the citizens of Athens "to hear useful words for the state."

Precedents for these extravagant dramatic elements have never been definitely established, although one likely source seems to have been a type of festive masquerade associated with fertility rites, in which participants dressed themselves in outlandish costumes and went throughout the streets, as they do now during Halloween and Mardi Gras, singing, dancing, carousing, and jesting with bystanders. So, too, the actors in Greek comedy would not have limited themselves simply to reciting their lines, but would also have performed ribald dance steps, kicking their buttocks, slapping their thighs, and possibly pummeling one another. Though ancient festivities persist in modern masquerades, ancient Greek comedy has never been matched, for later satiric dramatists have never quite escaped the bounds of ordinary experience and taken off into the free floating world of fantasy. That is the exclusive domain of Aristophanes.

In the comedy of Aristophanes, the world is turned upside down, inside out, and every other way imaginable in a satiric universe where anything is possible. In *The Birds* (414), for example, Peithetaerus, who is disgusted with life in Athens, dreams up the bright idea of creating a new and better city in the sky. Once he is able to convince the birds that they are the original gods, he then gets them to build his Utopia, which in turn enables him to suffocate all of the ruling Greek gods by denying them the smoke of sacrificial offerings. After they give into his power, he becomes ruler of the entire universe, equipped with his own set of wings and a wife whose thunderbolts, like those of Athena, enable him to keep the world justly under control. In *The Frogs* (405), Dionysus, the god whose festival is celebrated by the dramatic competitions, laments the fact that Sophocles and Euripides have recently died, for he fears that their deaths may lead to the death of drama itself. He thus travels to Hades, planning to bring back Euripides, whom he hopes will sustain the vitality of drama. But when Dionysus finally arrives in Hades, he comes upon Aeschylus and Euripides noisily quarreling with one another over who is to be ruler in the world of tragic theater, while Sophocles stands off to the side, reluctant to get involved in the squabble. Dionysus calms them by getting them to agree to a debate in which Aeschylus and Euripides are to criticize one another's tragedies, with the winner determined by Dionysus, and the prize a return to life in Athens. Aeschylus is judged the winner and so is triumphantly led back to Athens to begin again the great age of classical Greek drama. Thus, as in almost all of Aristophanes' plays, fantasy leads to wish-fulfillment and the redemption of the world.

In the process of working out such extravagant fantasies, Aristophanes rarely directs his aim at a single target, but instead scatters his satiric shots in a number of directions, picking off abuses and abusers wherever he finds them. He goes after bad government and bad rulers, bad poetry and bad poets, bad schooling and bad teachers, bad thinking and bad thinkers, freely ridiculing them all, no matter how popular, respected, or powerful they may be. Neither Socrates the philosopher, nor Euripides the dramatist, nor even Cleon the ruling demagogue of Athens escapes the attacks of Aristophanes. But the miraculous quality of his satiric fantasies is that they make it possible for him to solve all the problems of his world—by making a new one, as in *The Birds,* or by going back to an old and better one, as in *The Frogs.* Indeed, the fantasy life of Aristophanes' comedies not only solves all the problems of the world, but also satisfies all the basic desires of men and women. In the free festive air of his plays, anything goes, no matter how lewd or obscene, just as anything went in the phallic fertility rites that gave birth to his plays. Thus, in the process of working out his fantasies, Aristophanes also satisfies the sensual desires of all men and women: for food and drink and comfort and sex.

But the fantasy, no matter how joyous it may be while it is going on, must come to an end. In its ending, as in its very being, the fantasy embodies a very poignant view of experience, for it implies that only through the most fantastic flights of the imagination is it possible, as in *The Birds,* to reclaim a fallen world, and worse still, as it turns out, the new world contains some of the very same problems—the imperial motive and the military might—that made for the misery of the old one. Even when an older and better world is reclaimed, as in *The Frogs,* it necessarily incorporates the one fact of life that is inescapable—death—that even the greatest of persons and the greatest of cultures cannot avoid.

Living as he did during the decline of Athenian culture, Aristophanes could hardly ignore the fact that it was dying, for his coming of age coincided with the beginning of the Peloponnesian Wars in 431 B.C. It is not surprising that three of his eleven surviving comedies are antiwar plays: *Acharnians* (425), *Peace* (421), and *Lysistrata* (411). And two others, *The Birds* and *The Frogs,* although not directly concerned with war, nonetheless deal with the cultural wreckage it produced. *Lysistrata* is unquestionably the most powerful of his antiwar plays, for it reveals, as none of the others do, the absurdity of the war that had gone on for more than twenty years by the time the play was produced. But *Lysistrata* transcends the particular circumstances of the struggle between Athens and Sparta, for it makes a statement about war that has been true for all times; through Lysistrata's scheme, it implicitly urges the audience to make love not war.

Because it makes that plea more boldly than any other antiwar play ever written, *Lysistrata* has been staged more often during the twentieth century than any of Aristophanes' other comedies. But most productions shy away from going all the way back to the theatrical conventions of his times. The large leather phalluses that were worn by the male characters to ridicule their sexual frustration rarely turn up in a modern production. More often, the costuming, stage business, and style of performance are updated, as they were in the Phoenix Theater production (see Figures 10, 11, and 12), where the men wore fig leaves instead, and the women tried to tantalize them with jewelled brassieres. That production, judging from comments of the reviewers, was dominated by raucous activity and risqué routines without actually achieving the sustained sexual fantasy of Aristophanes. However entertaining such productions may be, they lack the nerve that prevailed in the fifth century theater of Aristophanes, and in that respect they are haunting reminders of a similar loss of nerve that took place in Greek comedy after the defeat of Athens in 404 B.C. Although Aristophanes lived on for twenty more years, he gradually turned away from bawdy topical satire to tamer kinds of social comedy, which in turn gave rise to the comedy of Athenian manners that flourished in fourth century Greece and was subsequently imitated in third century Rome by Plautus. When Athens fell so did comedy, and neither Athens nor comedy has ever been quite the same.

LYSISTRATA

BY ARISTOPHANES / TRANSLATED BY CHARLES T. MURPHY

CHARACTERS

LYSISTRATA, *an Athenian woman*
CALONICE, *an Athenian woman*
MYRRHINE, *an Athenian woman*
LAMPITO, *a Spartan woman*
LEADER OF CHORUS OF OLD MEN
CHORUS OF OLD MEN
LEADER OF CHORUS OF OLD WOMEN
CHORUS OF OLD WOMEN
ATHENIAN MAGISTRATE
THREE ATHENIAN WOMEN
CINESIAS, *an Athenian, husband of Myrrhine*
SPARTAN HERALD

SPARTAN AMBASSADORS
ATHENIAN AMBASSADORS
TWO ATHENIAN CITIZENS
CHORUS OF ATHENIANS
CHORUS OF SPARTANS

SCENE

In Athens, beneath the Acropolis. In the center of the stage is the propylaea, or gate-way to the Acropolis; to one side is a small grotto, sacred to Pan. The orchestra represents a slope leading up to the gate-way. It is early in the morning. Lysistrata is pacing impatiently up and down.

LYSISTRATA: If they'd been summoned to worship the God of Wine, or Pan, or to visit the Queen of Love, why, you couldn't have pushed your way through the streets for all the timbrels. But now there's not a single woman here—except my neighbour; here she comes.

(Enter CALONICE)

Good day to you, Calonice.

CALONICE: And to you, Lysistrata. *(Noticing LYSISTRATA'S impatient air.)* But what ails you? Don't scowl, my dear; it's not becoming to you to knit your brows like that.

LYSISTRATA *(sadly)*: Ah, Calonice, my heart aches; I'm so annoyed at us women. For among men we have a reputation for sly trickery—

CALONICE: And rightly too, on my word!

LYSISTRATA: —but when they were told to meet here to consider a matter of no small importance, they lie abed and don't come.

CALONICE: Oh, they'll come all right, my dear. It's not easy for a woman to get out, you know. One is working on her husband, another is getting up the maid, another has to put the baby to bed, or wash and feed it.

LYSISTRATA: But after all, there are other matters more important than all that.

CALONICE: My dear Lysistrata, just what is this matter you've summoned us women to consider! What's up? Something big?

LYSISTRATA: Very big.

CALONICE *(interested)*: Is it stout, too?

LYSISTRATA *(smiling)*: Yes indeed—both big and stout.

CALONICE: What? And the women still haven't come?

LYSISTRATA: It's not what you suppose; they'd have come soon enough for *that*. But I've worked up something, and for many a sleepless night I've turned it this way and that.

CALONICE *(in mock disappointment)*: Oh, I guess it's pretty fine and slender, if you've turned it this way and that.

LYSISTRATA: So fine that the safety of the whole of Greece lies in us women.

CALONICE: In us women? It depends on a very slender reed then.

LYSISTRATA: Our country's fortunes are in our hands; and whether the Spartans shall perish—

CALONICE: Good! Let them perish, by all means.

LYSISTRATA: —and the Boeotians shall be completely annihilated.

CALONICE: Not completely! Please spare the eels.

LYSISTRATA: As for Athens, I won't use. any such unpleasant words. But you understand what I mean. But if the women will meet here—the Spartans, the Boeotians, and we Athenians—then all together we will save Greece.

CALONICE: But what could women do that's clever or distinguished? We just sit around all dolled up in silk robes, looking pretty in our sheer gowns and evening slippers.

LYSISTRATA: These are just the things I hope will save us; these silk robes, perfumes, evening slippers, rouge, and our chiffon blouses.

CALONICE: How so?

LYSISTRATA: So never a man alive will lift a spear against the foe—

CALONICE: I'll get a silk gown at once.

LYSISTRATA: —or take up his shield—

CALONICE: I'll put on my sheerest gown!

LYSISTRATA: —or sword.

CALONICE: I'll buy a pair of evening slippers.

70 LYSISTRATA: Well then, shouldn't the women have come?

CALONICE: Come? Why, they should have *flown* here.

LYSISTRATA: Well, my dear, just watch: they'll act in true Athenian fashion—everything too late! And now there's not a woman here from the shore or from Salamis.

CALONICE: They're coming, I'm sure; at daybreak they were laying—to their oars to cross the straits.

80 LYSISTRATA: And those I expected would be the first to come—the women of Acharnae—they haven't arrived.

CALONICE: Yet the wife of Theagenes means to come; she consulted Hecate about it. (*Seeing a group of women approaching*.) But look! Here come a few. And there are some more over here. Hurrah! Where do they come from?

LYSISTRATA: From Anagyra.

CALONICE: Yes indeed! We've raised up quite a stink 90 from Anagyra anyway.

(*Enter* MYRRHINE *in haste, followed by several other women*.)

MYRRHINE (*breathlessly*): Have we come in time, Lysistrata? What do you say? Why so quiet?

LYSISTRATA: I can't say much for you, Myrrhine, coming at this hour on such important business.

MYRRHINE: Why, I had trouble finding my girdle in the dark. But if it's so important, we're here now; tell us.

LYSISTRATA: No. Let's wait a little for the women from Boeotia and the Peloponnesus.

100 MYRRHINE: That's a much better suggestion. Look! Here comes Lampito now.

(*Enter* LAMPITO *with two other women*.)

LYSISTRATA: Greetings, my dear Spartan friend. How pretty you look, my dear. What a smooth complexion and well-developed figure! You could throttle an ox.

LAMPITO: Faith, yes, I think I could. I take exercises and kick my heels against my bum. (*She demonstrates with a few steps of the Spartan "bottom-kicking" dance*.)

110 LYSISTRATA: And what splendid breasts you have.

LAMPITO: La! You handle me like a prize steer.

LYSISTRATA: And who is this young lady with you?

LAMPITO: Faith, she's an Ambassadress from Boeotia.

LYSISTRATA: Oh yes, a Boeotian, and blooming like a garden too.

CALONICE (*lifting up her skirt*): My word! How neatly her garden's weeded!

LYSISTRATA: And who is the other girl?

LAMPITO: Oh, she's a Corinthian swell.

MYRRHINE (*after a rapid examination*): Yes indeed. She 120 swells very nicely (*pointing*) here and here.

LAMPITO: Who has gathered together this company of women?

LYSISTRATA: I have.

LAMPITO: Speak up, then. What do you want?

MYRRHINE: Yes, my dear, tell us what this important matter is.

LYSISTRATA: Very well, I'll tell you. But before I speak, let me ask you a little question.

MYRRHINE: Anything you like. 130

LYSISTRATA (*earnestly*): Tell me: don't you yearn for the fathers of your children, who are away at the wars? I know you all have husbands abroad.

CALONICE: Why, yes; mercy me! my husband's been away for five months in Thrace keeping guard on—Eucrates.

MYRRHINE: And mine for seven whole months in Pylus.

LAMPITO: And mine, as soon as ever he returns from the fray, readjusts his shield and flies out of the 140 house again.

LYSISTRATA: And as for lovers, there's not even a ghost of one left. Since the Milesians revolted from us, I've not even seen an eight-inch dingus to be a leather consolation for us widows. Are you willing, if I can find a way, to help me end the war?

MYRRHINE: Goodness, yes! I'd do it, even if I had to pawn my dress and—get drunk on the spot!

CALONICE: And I, even if I had to let myself be split in 150 two like a flounder.

LAMPITO: I'd climb up Mt. Taygetus if I could catch a glimpse of peace.

LYSISTRATA: I'll tell you, then, in plain and simple words. My friends, if we are going to force our men to make peace, we must do without—

MYRRHINE: Without what? Tell us.

LYSISTRATA: Will you do it?

MYRRHINE: We'll do it, if it kills us.

LYSISTRATA: Well then, we must do without sex al- 160 together. (*General consternation.*) Why do you turn away? Where go you? Why turn so pale? Why those tears? Will you do it or not? What means this hesitation?

MYRRHINE: I won't do it! Let the war go on.

CALONICE: Nor I! Let the war go on.

LYSISTRATA: So, my little flounder? Didn't you say just now you'd split yourself in half?

CALONICE: Anything else you like. I'm willing, even if I have to walk through fire. Anything rather 170 than sex. There's nothing like it, my dear.

LYSISTRATA (*to* MYRRHINE): What about you?

MYRRHINE (*sullenly*): I'm willing to walk through fire, too.

LYSISTRATA: Oh vile and cursed breed! No wonder

they make tragedies about us: we're naught but "love-affairs and bassinets." But you, my dear Spartan friend, if you alone are with me, our enterprise might yet succeed. Will you vote with
180   me?

LAMPITO: 'Tis cruel hard, by my faith, for a woman to sleep alone without her nooky; but for all that, we certainly do need peace.

LYSISTRATA: O my dearest friend! You're the only real woman here.

CALONICE (wavering): Well, if we do refrain from— (shuddering) what you say (God forbid!), would that bring peace?

LYSISTRATA: My goodness, yes! If we sit at home all
190   rouged and powdered, dressed in our sheerest gowns, and neatly depilated, our men will get excited and want to take us; but if you don't come to them and keep away, they'll soon make a truce.

LAMPITO: Aye; Menelaus caught sight of Helen's naked breast and dropped his sword, they say.

CALONICE: What if the men give us up?

LYSISTRATA: "Flay a skinned dog," as Pherecrates says.

200   CALONICE: Rubbish! These make-shifts are not good. But suppose they grab us and drag us into the bedroom?

LYSISTRATA: Hold on to the door.

CALONICE: And if they beat us?

LYSISTRATA: Give in with a bad grace. There's no pleasure in it for them when they have to use violence. And you must torment them in every possible way. They'll give up soon enough; a man gets no joy if he doesn't get along with his
210   wife.

MYRRHINE: If this is your opinion, we agree.

LAMPITO: As for our men, we can persuade them to make a just and fair peace; but what about the Athenian rabble? Who will persuade them not to start any more monkey-shines?

LYSISTRATA: Don't worry. We guarantee to convince them.

LAMPITO: Not while their ships are rigged so well and they have that mighty treasure in the temple of
220   Athene.

LYSISTRATA: We've taken good care for that too: we shall seize the Acropolis today. The older women have orders to do this, and while we are making our arrangements, they are to pretend to make a sacrifice and occupy the Acropolis.

LAMPITO: All will be well then. That's a very fine idea.

LYSISTRATA: Let's ratify this, Lampito, with the most solemn oath.

LAMPITO: Tell us what oath we shall swear.

230   LYSISTRARA: Well said. Where's our Policewoman? (to a Scythian slave) What are you gaping at? Set a

shield upside-down here in front of me, and give me the sacred meats.

CALONICE: Lysistrata, what sort of an oath are we to take?

LYSISTRATA: What oath? I'm going to slaughter a sheep over the shield, as they do in Aeschylus.

CALONICE: Don't, Lysistrata! No oaths about peace over a shield.

LYSISTRATA: What shall the oath be, then?   240

CALONICE: How about getting a white horse some-where and cutting out its entrails for the sac-rifice?

LYSISTRATA: White horse indeed!

CALONICE: Well then, how shall we swear?

MYRRHINE: I'll tell you: let's place a large black bowl upside-down and then slaughter—a flask of Thasian wine. And then let's swear—not to pour in a single drop of water.

LAMPITO: Lord! How I like that oath!   250

LYSISTRATA: Someone bring out a bowl and a flask.

(A slave brings the utensils for the sacrifice.)

CALONICE: Look, my friends! What a big jar! Here's a cup that 'twould give me joy to handle. (She picks up the bowl.)

LYSISTRATA: Set it down and put your hands on our victim. (As CALONICE places her hands on the flask.) O Lady of Persuasion and dear Loving Cup, graciously vouchsafe to receive this sacrifice from us women. (She pours the wine into the bowl.)

CALONICE: The blood has a good colour and spurts   260 out nicely.

LAMPITO: Faith, it has a pleasant smell, too.

MYRRHINE: Oh, let me be the first to swear, ladies!

CALONICE: No, by our Lady! Not unless you're allot-ted the first turn.

LYSISTRATA: Place all your hands on the cup, and one of you repeat on behalf of all what I say. Then all will swear and ratify the oath. *I will suffer no man, be he husband or lover,*

CALONICE: *I will suffer no man, be he husband or lover,*   270

LYSISTRATA: *To approach me all hot and horny.* (As CALONICE hesitates.) Say it!

CALONICE (slowly and painfully): *To approach me all hot and horny.* O Lysistrata, I feel so weak in the knees!

LYSISTRATA: *I will remain at home unmated,*

CALONICE: *I will remain at home unmated,*

LYSISTRATA: *Wearing my sheerest gown and carefully adorned,*

CALONICE: *Wearing my sheerest gown and carefully*   280 *adorned,*

LYSISTRATA: *That my husband may burn with desire for me,*

CALONICE: *That my husband may burn with desire for me,*

LYSISTRATA: *And if he takes me by force against my will,*

CALONICE: *And if he takes me by force against my will,*

LYSISTRATA: *I shall do it badly and keep from moving.*

CALONICE: *I shall do it badly and keep from moving.*

290 LYSISTRATA: *I will not stretch my slippers toward the ceiling,*

CALONICE: *I will not stretch my slippers toward the ceiling,*

LYSISTRATA: *Nor will I take the posture of the lioness on the knife-handle.*

CALONICE: *Nor will I take the posture of the lioness on the knife-handle,*

LYSISTRATA: *If I keep this oath, may I be permitted to drink from this cup,*

CALONICE: *If I keep this oath, may I be permitted to drink from this cup,*

300 LYSISTRATA: *But if I break it, may the cup be filled with water.*

CALONICE: *But if I break it, may the cup be filled with water.*

LYSISTRATA: Do you all swear to this?

ALL: I do, so help me!

LYSISTRATA: Come then, I'll just consummate this offering.

(She takes a long drink from the cup.)

CALONICE *(snatching the cup away)*: Shares, my dear! Let's drink to our continued friendship.

(A shout is heard from off-stage.)

310 LAMPITO: What's that shouting?

LYSISTRATA: That's what I was telling you: the women have just seized the Acropolis. Now, Lampito, go home and arrange matters in Sparta; and leave these two ladies here as hostages. We'll enter the Acropolis to join our friends and help them lock the gates.

CALONICE: Don't you suppose the men will come to attack us?

LYSISTRATA: Don't worry about them. Neither threats
320 nor fire will suffice to open the gates, except on the terms we've stated.

CALONICE: I should say not! Else we'd belie our reputation as unmanageable pests.

(LAMPITO leaves the stage. The other women retire and enter the Acropolis through the Propylaea. Enter the CHORUS OF OLD MEN, carrying fire-pots and a load of heavy sticks.)

LEADER OF MEN: Onward, Draces, step by step, though your shoulder's aching.
  Cursèd logs of olive-wood, what a load you're making!

FIRST SEMI-CHORUS OF OLD MEN *(singing)*
  Aye, many surprises await a man who lives to a ripe
30   old age;
  For who could suppose, Strymodorus my lad, that

the women we've nourished (alas!),
  Who sat at home to vex our days,
  Would seize the holy image here,
  And occupy this sacred shrine,
  With bolts and bars, with fell design,
  To lock the Propylaea?

LEADER OF MEN: Come with speed, Philourgus, come! to the temple hast'ning.
  There we'll heap these logs about in a circle round 340 them,
  And whoever has conspired, raising this rebellion,
  Shall be roasted, scorched, and burnt, all without exception,
  Doomed by one unanimous vote—but first the wife of Lycon.

SECOND SEMI-CHORUS *(singing)*:
  No, no! by Demeter, while I'm alive, no woman shall mock at me.
  Not even the Spartan Cleomenes, our citadel first 350 to seize,
    Got off unscathed; for all his pride
    And haughty Spartan arrogance;
    He left his arms and sneaked away,
    Stripped to his shirt, unkempt, unshav'd,
  With six years' filth still on him.

LEADER OF MEN: I besieged that hero bold, sleeping at my station,
  Marshalled at these holy gates sixteen deep against him. 360
  Shall I not these cursèd pests punish for their daring,
  Burning these Euripides-and-God-detested women?
  Aye! or else may Marathon overturn my trophy.

FIRST SEMI-CHORUS *(singing)*: There remains of my road
    Just this brow of the hill;
    There I speed on my way.
  Drag the logs up the hill, though we've got no ass to 370 help.
  (God! my shoulder's bruised and sore!)
    Onward still must we go.
    Blow the fire! Don't let it go out
  Now we're near the end of our road.

ALL *(blowing on the fire-pots)*: Whew! Whew! Drat the smoke!

SECOND SEMI-CHORUS *(singing)*: Lord, what smoke rushing forth
    From the pot, like a dog 380
    Running mad, bites my eyes!
  This must be Lemnos-fire. What a sharp and stinging smoke!
    Rushing onward to the shrine
    Aid the gods. Once for all
    Show your mettle, Laches my boy!
    To the rescue hastening all!

ALL (*blowing on the fire-pots*): Whew! Whew! Drat the smoke!

(*The* CHORUS *has now reached the edge of the Orchestra nearest the stage, in front of the propylaea. They begin laying their logs and fire-pots on the ground.*)

390 LEADER OF MEN: Thank heaven, this fire is still alive. Now let's first put down these logs here and place our torches in the pots to catch; then let's make a rush for the gates with a battering-ram. If the women don't unbar the gate at our summons, we'll have to smoke them out.

Let me put down my load. Ouch! That hurts! (*to the audience*) Would any of the generals in Samos like to lend a hand with this log? (*Throwing down a log.*) Well, *that* won't break my back

400 any more, at any rate. (*Turning to his fire-pot.*) Your job, my little pot, is to keep those coals alive and furnish me shortly with a red-hot torch.

O mistress Victory, be my ally and grant me to rout these audacious women in the Acropolis.

(*While the* MEN *are busy with their logs and fires, the* CHORUS OF OLD WOMEN *enters, carrying pitchers of water.*)

LEADER OF WOMEN: What's this I see? Smoke and flames? Is that a fire ablazing?

Let's rush upon them. Hurry up! They'll find us women ready.

FIRST SEMI-CHORUS OF OLD WOMEN (*singing*):
410   With wingèd foot onward I fly,
    Ere the flames consume Neodice;
    Lest Critylla be overwhelmed
By a lawless, accurst herd of old men.
I shudder with fear. Am I too late to aid them?
At break of the day filled we our jars with water
Fresh from the spring, pushing our way straigh
    through the crowds.
    Oh, what a din!
Mid crockery crashing, jostled by slave-girls,
420 Sped we to save them, aiding our neighbours,
Bearing this water to put out the flames.

SECOND SEMI-CHORUS OF OLD WOMEN (*singing*):
    Such news I've heard; doddering fools
    Come with logs, like furnace-attendants,
    Loaded down with three hundred pounds,
    Breathing many a vain, blustering threat,
    That all these abhorred sluts will be burnt to charcoal.
    O goddess, I pray never may they be kindled;
430 Grant them to save Greece and our men, madness and war help them to end.
    With this as our purpose, golden-plumed Maiden,
    Guardian of Athens, seized we thy precinct.
    Be my ally, Warrior-maiden,
    'Gainst these old men, bearing water with me.

(*The* WOMEN *have now reached their position in the Orchestra, and their* LEADER *advances toward the* LEADER OF THE MEN.)

LEADER OF WOMEN: Hold on there! What's this, you utter scoundrels? No decent, God-fearing citizens would act like this.

440 LEADER OF MEN: Oho! Here's something unexpected: a swarm of women have come out to attack us.

LEADER OF WOMEN: What, do we frighten you? Surely you don't think we're too many for you. And yet there are ten thousand times more of us whom you haven't even seen.

LEADER OF MEN: What say, Phaedria? Shall we let these women wag their tongues? Shan't we take our sticks and break them over their backs?

450 LEADER OF WOMEN: Let's set our pitchers on the ground; then if anyone lays a hand on us, they won't get in our way.

LEADER OF MEN: By God! If someone gave them two or three smacks on the jaw, like Bupalus, they wouldn't talk so much!

LEADER OF WOMEN: Go on, hit me, somebody! Here's my jaw! But no other bitch will bite a piece out of you before me.

LEADER OF MEN: Silence! or I'll knock out your— senility!

460 LEADER OF WOMEN: Just lay one finger on Stratyllis, I dare you!

LEADER OF MEN: Suppose I dust you off with this fist? What will you do?

LEADER OF WOMEN: I'll tear the living guts out of you with my teeth.

LEADER OF MEN: No poet is more clever than Euripides: "There is no beast so shameless as a woman."

LEADER OF WOMEN: Let's pick up our jars of water, Rhodippe.

470 LEADER OF MEN: Why have you come here with water, you detestable slut?

LEADER OF WOMEN: And why have you come with fire, you funeral vault? To cremate yourself?

LEADER OF MEN: To light a fire and singe your friends.

LEADER OF WOMEN: And I've brought water to put out your fire.

LEADER OF MEN: What? You'll put out my fire?

LEADER OF WOMEN: Just try and see!

480 LEADER OF MEN: I wonder: shall I scorch you with this torch of mine?

LEADER OF WOMEN: If you've got any soap, I'll give you a bath.

LEADER OF MEN: Give *me* a bath, you stinking hag?

LEADER OF WOMEN: Yes—a bridal bath!

LEADER OF MEN: Just listen to her! What crust!

LEADER OF WOMEN: Well, I'm a free citizen.

LEADER OF MEN: I'll put an end to your brawl'ng.

(The MEN *pick up their torches.)*

490 LEADER OF WOMEN: You'll never do jury-duty again.

(The WOMEN *pick up their pitchers.)*

LEADER OF MEN: Singe her hair for her!
LEADER OF WOMEN: Do your duty, water!

(The WOMEN *empty their pitchers on the* MEN.)

LEADER OF MEN: Ow! Ow! For heaven's sake!
LEADER OF WOMEN: Is it too hot?
LEADER OF MEN: What do you mean "hot"? Stop!
What are you doing?
LEADER OF WOMEN: I'm watering you, so you'll be
fresh and green.
LEADER OF MEN: But I'm all withered up with shaking.
500 LEADER OF WOMEN: Well, you've got a fire; why don't
you dry yourself?

(Enter an ATHENIAN MAGISTRATE, *accompanied by*
FOUR SCYTHIAN POLICEMEN.)

MAGISTRATE: Have these wanton women flared up
again with their timbrels and their continual
worship of Sabazius? Is this another Adonis-
dirge upon the roof-tops—which we heard not
long ago in the Assembly? That confounded
Demostratus was urging us to sail to Sicily, and
the whirling women shouted, "Woe for Adonis!"
And then Demostratus said we'd best enroll the
510 infantry from Zacynthus, and a tipsy woman on
the roof shrieked, "Beat your breasts for
Adonis!" And that vile and filthy lunatic forced
his measure through. Such license do our
women take.
LEADER OF MEN: What if you heard of the insolence of
these women here? Besides their other violent
acts, they threw water all over us, and we have to
shake out our clothes just as if we'd leaked in
them.
520 MAGISTRATE: And rightly, too, by God! For we ourselves lead the women astray and teach them to
play the wanton; from these roots such notions
blossom forth. A man goes into the jeweler's
shop and says, "About that necklace you made
for my wife, goldsmith: last night, while she was
dancing, the fastening-bolt slipped out of the
hole. I have to sail over to Salamis today; if
you're free, do come around tonight and fit in a
new bolt for her." Another goes to the shoe-
530 maker, a strapping young fellow with manly
parts, and says, "See here, cobbler, the sandal-
strap chafes my wife's little—toe; it's so tender.
Come around during the siesta and stretch it a
little, so she'll be more comfortable." Now we see
the results of such treatment: here I'm a special
Councillor and need money to procure oars for

the galleys; and I'm locked out of the Treasury
by these women.
But this is no time to stand around. Bring up
crow-bars there! I'll put an end to their insol- 540
ence *(to one of the policemen.)* What are you gaping at, you wretch! What are you staring at? Got
an eye out for a tavern, eh? Set your crow-bars
here to the gates and force them open. *(Retiring
to a safe distance)* I'll help from over here.

(The gates are thrown open and LYSISTRATA *comes out
followed by several other* WOMEN.)

LYSISTRATA: Don't force the gates; I'm coming out of
my own accord. We don't need crow-bars here.
What we need is good sound common-sense.
MAGISTRATE: Is that so, you strumpet? Where's my
policeman? Officer, arrest her and tie her arms 550
behind her back.
LYSISTRATA: By Artemis, if he lays a finger on me,
he'll pay for it, even if he is a public servant.

(The POLICEMAN *retires in terror.)*

MAGISTRATE: You there, are you afraid? Seize her
round the waist—and you, too. Tie her up, both
of you!
FIRST WOMAN *(as the* SECOND POLICEMAN *approaches*
LYSISTRATA): By Pandrosus, if you but touch her
with your hand, I'll kick the stuffings out of you.

(The SECOND POLICEMAN *retires in terror.)*

MAGISTRATE: Just listen to that: "kick the stuffings 560
out." Where's another policeman? Tie *her* up
first, for her chatter.
SECOND WOMAN: By the Goddess of the Light, if you
lay the tip of your finger on her, you'll soon need
a doctor.

(The THIRD POLICEMAN *retires in terror.)*

MAGISTRATE: What's this? Where's my policemen?
Seize *her* too. I'll soon stop your sallies.
THIRD WOMAN: By the Goddess of Tauros, if you go
near her, I'll tear out your hair until it shrieks
with pain. 570

(The FOURTH POLICEMAN *retires in terror.)*

MAGISTRATE: Oh, damn it all! I've run out of policemen. But women must never defeat us. Officers,
let's charge them all together. Close up your
ranks!

(The POLICEMEN *rally for a mass attack.)*

LYSISTRATA: By heaven, you'll soon find out that we
have four companies of warrior-women, all fully
equipped within!
MAGISTRATE *(advancing)*: Twist their arms off, men!
LYSISTRATA *(shouting)*: To the rescue, my valiant
women! 580

O sellers-of-barley-green-stuffs-and-eggs,
O sellers-of-garlic, ye keepers-of-taverns, and
vendors-of-bread,
Grapple! Smite! Smash!
Won't you heap filth on them? Give them a
tongue-lashing!

(The WOMEN *beat off the* POLICEMEN.*)*

Halt! Withdraw! No looting on the field.

MAGISTRATE: Damn it! My police-force has put up a
very poor show.

590 LYSISTRATA: What did you expect? Did you think you
were attacking slaves?
Didn't you know that women are filled with passion?

MAGISTRATE: Aye, passion enough—for a good
strong drink!

LEADER OF MEN: O chief and leader of this land, why
spend your words in vain?
Don't argue with these shameless beasts. You know
not how we've fared:

600 A soapless bath they've given us; our clothes are
soundly soaked.

LEADER OF WOMEN: Poor fool! You never should attack or strike a peaceful girl.
But if you do, your eyes must swell. For I am quite
content
To sit unmoved, like modest maids, in peace and
cause no pain;
But let a man stir up my hive, he'll find me like a
wasp.

610 CHORUS OF MEN *(singing)*:
O God, whatever shall we do with creatures like
Womankind?
This can't be endured by any man alive. Question
them!
Let us try to find out what this means.
To what end have they seized on this shrine,
This steep and rugged, high and holy,
Undefiled Acropolis?

LEADER OF MEN: Come, put your questions; don't give
620 in, and probe her every statement.
For base and shameful it would be to leave this
plot untested.

MAGISTRATE: Well then, first of all I wish to ask her
this: for what purpose have you barred us from
the Acropolis?

LYSISTRATA: To keep the treasure safe, so you won't
make war on account of it.

MAGISTRATE: What? Do we make war on account of
the treasure?

630 LYSISTRATA: Yes, and you cause all our other troubles
for it, too. Peisander and those greedy office-
seekers keep things stirred up so they can find
occasions to steal. Now let them do what they
like: they'll never again make off with any of this
money.

MAGISTRATE: What will you do?

LYSISTRATA: What a question! We'll administer it
ourselves.

MAGISTRATE: *You* will administer the treasure?

LYSISTRATA: What's so strange in that? Don't we ad- 640
minister the household money for you?

MAGISTRATE: That's different.

LYSISTRATA: How is it different?

MAGISTRATE: We've got to make war with this money.

LYSISTRATA: But that's the very first thing: you
mustn't make war.

MAGISTRATE: How else can we be saved?

LYSISTRATA: We'll save you.

MAGISTRATE: *You?*

LYSISTRATA: Yes, we! 650

MAGISTRATE: God forbid!

LYSISTRATA: We'll save you, whether you want it or
not.

MAGISTRATE: Oh! This is terrible!

LYSISTRATA: You don't like it, but we're going to do it
none the less.

MAGISTRATE: Good God! it's illegal!

LYSISTRATA: We *will* save you, my little man!

MAGISTRATE: Suppose I don't want you to?

LYSISTRATA: That's all the more reason. 660

MAGISTRATE: What business have you with war and
peace?

LYSISTRATA: I'll explain.

MAGISTRATE *(shaking his fist)*: Speak up, or you'll
smart for it.

LYSISTRATA: Just listen, and try to keep your hands
still.

MAGISTRATE: I can't. I'm so mad I can't stop them.

FIRST WOMAN: Then you'll be the one to smart for it.

MAGISTRATE: Croak to yourself, old hag! *(to* LYSIS- 670
TRATA*)* Now then, speak up.

LYSISTRATA: Very well. Formerly we endured the war
for a good long time with our usual restraint, no
matter what you men did. You wouldn't let us
say "boo," although nothing you did suited us.
But we watched you well, and though we stayed
at home we'd often hear of some terribly stupid
measure you'd proposed. Then, though grieving
at heart, we'd smile sweetly and say, "What was
passed in the Assembly today about writing on 680
the treaty-stone?" "What's that to you?" my husband would say. "Hold your tongue!" And I held
my tongue.

FIRST WOMAN: But I wouldn't have—not I!

MAGISTRATE: You'd have been soundly smacked, if
you hadn't kept still.

LYSISTRATA: So I kept still at home. Then we'd hear
of some plan still worse than the first; we'd say,
"Husband, how could you pass such a stupid
proposal!" He'd scowl at me and say, "If you 690
don't mind your spinning, your head will be sore
for weeks. *War shall be the concern of men.*"

MAGISTRATE: And he was right, upon my word!

LYSISTRATA: Why right, you confounded fool, when

your proposals were so stupid and we weren't allowed to make any suggestions?

"There's not a *man* left in the country," says one. "No, not one," says another. Therefore all we women have decided in council to make a common effort to save Greece. How long should we have waited? Now, if you're willing to listen to our excellent proposals and keep silence for us in your turn, we still may save you.

MAGISTRATE: We men keep silence for you? That's terrible; I won't endure it!

LYSISTRATA: Silence!

MAGISTRATE: Silence for *you*, you wench, when you're wearing a snood? I'd rather die!

LYSISTRATA: Well, if that's all that bothers you—here! Take my snood and tie it round your head. *(During the following words the* WOMEN *dress up the* MAGISTRATE *in women's garments.)* And *now* keep quiet! Here, take this spinning-basket, too, and card your wool with robes tucked up, munching on beans. *War shall be the concern of Women!*

LEADER OF WOMEN: Arise and leave your pitchers, girls; no time is this to falter.
We too must aid our loyal friends; our turn has come for action.

CHORUS OF WOMEN *(singing)*:
I'll never tire of aiding them with song and dance;
never may
Faintness keep my legs from moving to and fro endlessly.
For I yearn to do all for my friends;
They have charm, they have wit, they have grace,
With courage, brains, and best of virtues—
Patriotic sapience.

LEADER OF WOMEN: Come, child of manliest ancient dames, offspring of stinging nettles,
Advance with rage unsoftened; for fair breezes speed you onward.

LYSISTRATA: If only sweet Eros and the Cyprian Queen of Love shed charm over our breasts and limbs and inspire our men with amorous longing and priapic spasms, I think we may soon be called Peacemakers among the Greeks.

MAGISTRATE: What will you do?

LYSISTRATA: First of all, we'll stop those fellows who run madly about the Marketplace in arms.

FIRST WOMAN: Indeed we shall, by the Queen of Paphos.

LYSISTRATA: For now they roam about the market, amid the pots and greenstuffs, armed to the teeth like Corybantes.

MAGISTRATE: That's what manly fellows ought to do!

LYSISTRATA: But it's so silly: a chap with a Gorgon-emblazoned shield buying pickled herring.

FIRST WOMAN: Why, just the other day I saw one of those long-haired dandies who command our cavalry ride up on horseback and pour into his

bronze helmet the egg-broth he'd bought from an old dame. And there was a Thracian slinger too, shaking his lance like Tereus; he'd scared the life out of the poor fig-peddler and was gulping down all her ripest fruit.

MAGISTRATE: How can you stop all the confusion in the various states and bring them together?

LYSISTRATA: Very easily.

MAGISTRATE: Tell me how.

LYSISTRATA: Just like a ball of wool, when it's confused and snarled: we take it thus, and draw out a thread here and a thread there with our spindles; thus we'll unsnarl this war, if no one prevents us, and draw together the various states with embassies here and embassies there.

MAGISTRATE: Do you suppose you can stop this dreadful business with balls of wool and spindles, you nit-wits?

LYSISTRATA: Why, if *you* had any wits, you'd manage all affairs of state like our wool-working.

MAGISTRATE: How so?

LYSISTRATA: First you ought to treat the city as we do when we wash the dirt out of a fleece: stretch it out and pluck and thrash out of the city all those prickly scoundrels; aye, and card out those who conspire and stick together to gain office, pulling off their heads. Then card the wool, all of it, into one fair basket of goodwill, mingling in the aliens residing here, any loyal foreigners, and anyone who's in debt to the Treasury; and consider that all our colonies lie scattered round about like remnants; from all of these collect the wool and gather it together here, wind up a great ball, and then weave a good stout cloak for the democracy.

MAGISTRATE: Dreadful! Talking about thrashing and winding balls of wool, when you haven't the slightest share in the war!

LYSISTRATA: Why, you dirty scoundrel, we bear more than twice as much as you. First, we bear children and send off our sons as soldiers.

MAGISTRATE: Hush! Let bygones be bygones!

LYSISTRATA: Then, when we ought to be happy and enjoy our youth, we sleep alone because of your expeditions abroad. But never mind us married women: I grieve most for the maids who grow old at home unwed.

MAGISTRATE: Don't men grow old, too?

LYSISTRATA: For heaven's sake! That's not the same thing. When a man comes home, no matter how grey he is, he soon finds a girl to marry. But woman's bloom is short and fleeting; if she doesn't grasp her chance, no man is willing to marry her and she sits at home a prey to every fortune-teller.

MAGISTRATE *(coarsely)*: But if a man can still get it up—

LYSISTRATA: See here, you: what's the matter? Aren't

you dead yet? There's plenty of room for you. Buy yourself a shroud and I'll bake you a honey-cake. *(Handing him a copper coin for his passage across the Styx.)* Here's your fare! Now get yourself a wreath.

(During the following dialogue the WOMEN *dress up the* MAGISTRATE *as a corpse.)*

FIRST WOMAN: Here, take these fillets.

SECOND WOMAN: Here, take this wreath.

LYSISTRATA: What do you want? What's lacking? Get moving; off to the ferry! Charon is calling you; 820 don't keep him from sailing.

MAGISTRATE: Am I to endure these insults? By God! I'm going straight to the magistrates to show them how I've been treated.

LYSISTRATA: Are you grumbling that you haven't been properly laid out? Well, the day after tomorrow we'll send around all the usual offerings early in the morning.

(The MAGISTRATE *goes out still wearing his funeral decorations.* LYSISTRATA *and the* WOMEN *retire into the Acropolis.)*

LEADER OF MEN: Wake, ye sons of freedom, wake! 'Tis no time for sleeping. Up and at them, like a man! 830 Let us strip for action.

(The CHORUS OF MEN *remove their outer cloaks.)*

CHORUS OF MEN *(singing)*:
Surely there is something here greater than meets the eye;
For without a doubt I smell Hippias' tyrrany.
Dreadful fear assails me lest certain bands of Spartan men,
Meeting here with Cleisthenes, have inspired through treachery
All these god-detested women secretly to seize 840 Athens' treasure in the temple, and to stop that pay Whence I live at my ease.

LEADER OF MEN: Now isn't it terrible for them to advise the state and chatter about shields, being mere women?
And they think to reconcile us with the Spartans—men who hold nothing sacred any more than hungry wolves. Surely this is a web of deceit, my friends, to conceal an attempt at tyranny. But they'll never lord it over me; I'll be 850 on my guard from now on,
"The blade I bear, A myrtle spray shall wear."
I'll occupy the market under arms and stand next to Aristogeiton.
Thus I'll stand beside him *(He strikes the pose of the famous statue of the tyrannicides, with one arm raised.)* And here's my chance to take this accurst old hag and—*(striking the* LEADER OF WOMEN*)* smack her on the jaw!

LEADER OF WOMEN: You'll go home in such a state 860 your Ma won't recognize you!
Ladies all, upon the ground let us place these garments.

(The CHORUS OF WOMEN *remove their outer garments.)*

CHORUS OF WOMEN *(singing)*:
Citizens of Athens, hear useful words for the state.
Rightly; for it nurtured me in my youth royally.
As a child of seven years carried I the sacred box;
Then I was a Miller-maid, grinding at Athene's shrine;
Next I wore the saffron robe and played 870 Brauronia's Bear;
And I walked as a Basket-bearer, wearing chains of figs,
As a sweet maiden fair.

LEADER OF WOMEN: Therefore, am I not bound to give good advice to the city?
Don't take it ill that I was born a woman, if I contribute something better than our present troubles. I pay my share; for I contribute MEN. But you miserable old fools contribute nothing, and after squandering our ancestral treasure, 880 the fruit of the Persian Wars, you make no contribution in return. And now, all on account of you, we're facing ruin.
What, muttering, are you? If you annoy me, I'll take this hard, rough slipper and—*(striking the* LEADER OF MEN*)* smack you on the jaw!

CHORUS OF MEN *(singing)*:
This is outright insolence! Things go from bad to worse.
If you're men with any guts, prepare to meet the 890 foe.
Let us strip our tunics off! We need the smell of male
Vigour. And we cannot fight all swaddled up in clothes.

(They strip off their tunics.)

Come then, my comrades, on to the battle, ye once to Leipsydrion came;
Then ye were MEN. Now call back your youthful vigour.
With light, wingèd footstep advance, 900 Shaking old age from your frame.

LEADER OF MEN: If any of us give these wenches the slightest hold, they'll stop at nothing; such is their cunning.
They will even build ships and sail against us, like Artemisia. Or if they turn to mounting, I count our Knights as done for: a woman's such a tricky jockey when she gets astraddle, with a good firm seat for trotting. Just look at those Amazons that Micon painted, fighting on horse- 910 back against men!

But we must throw them all in the pillory—
(seizing and choking the LEADER OF WOMEN*)* grabbing hold of yonder neck!

CHORUS OF WOMEN *(singing)*:

'Ware my anger! Like a boar 'twill rush upon you
  men.

Soon you'll bawl aloud for help, you'll be so
  soundly trimmed!

920 Come, my friends, let's strip with speed, and lay
  aside these robes;

Catch the scent of women's rage. Attack with tooth
  and nail!

(They strip off their tunics.)

Now then, come near me, you miserable man!
You'll never eat garlic or black beans again.
And if you utter a single hard word, in rage I will
  "nurse" you as once
The beetle requited her foe.

LEADER OF WOMEN: For you don't worry me; no, not
930 so long as my Lampito lives and our Theban
  friend, the noble Ismenia.

You can't do anything, not even if you pass a
  dozen—decrees! You miserable fool, all our
  neighbours hate you. Why, just the other day
  when I was holding a festival for Hecate, I invited
  as playmate from our neighbours the
  Boeotians a charming, wellbred Copaic—eel.
  But they refused to send me one on account of
  your decrees.

940 And you'll never stop passing decrees until I
  grab your foot and—*(tripping up the* LEADER OF
  MEN*)* toss you down and break your neck!

(Here an interval of five days is supposed to elapse.
LYSISTRATA *comes out from the Acropolis.)*

LEADER OF WOMEN *(dramatically)*: Empress of this
  great emprise and undertaking,
Why come you forth, I pray, with frowning brow?

LYSISTRATA: Ah, these cursèd women! Their deeds
  and female notions make me pace up and down
  in utter despair.

LEADER OF WOMEN: Ah, what sayest thou?

950 LYSISTRATA: The truth, alas! the truth.

LEADER OF WOMEN: What dreadful tale hast thou to
  tell thy friends?

LYSISTRATA: 'Tis shame to speak, and not to speak is
  hard.

LEADER OF WOMEN: Hide not from me whatever woes
  we suffer.

LYSISTRATA: Well then, to put it briefly, we want—
  laying!

LEADER OF WOMEN: O Zeus, Zeus!

960 LYSISTRATA: Why call on Zeus? That's the way things
  are. I can no longer keep them away from the
  men, and they're all deserting. I caught one
  wriggling through a hole near the grotto of Pan,

another sliding down a rope, another deserting her post; and yesterday I found one getting on a sparrow's back to fly off to Orsilochus, and had to pull her back by the hair. They're digging up all sorts of excuses to get home. Look, here comes one of them now.

(A WOMAN *comes hastily out of the Acropolis.)*

Here you! Where are you off to in such a hurry? 970

FIRST WOMAN: I want to go home. My very best wool is being devoured by moths.

LYSISTRATA: Moths? Nonsense! Go back inside.

FIRST WOMAN: I'll come back; I swear it. I just want to lay it out on the bed.

LYSISTRATA: Well, you won't lay it out, and you won't go home, either.

FIRST WOMAN: Shall I let my wool be ruined?

LYSISTRATA: If necessary, yes.

*(*ANOTHER WOMAN *comes out.)*

SECOND WOMAN: Oh, dear! Oh dear! My precious 980 flax! I left it at home all unpeeled.

LYSISTRATA: Here's another one, going home for her "flax." Come back here!

SECOND WOMAN: But I just want to work it up a little and then I'll be right back.

LYSISTRATA: No indeed! If you start this, all other women will want to do the same.

(A THIRD WOMAN *comes out.)*

THIRD WOMAN: O Eilithyia, goddess of travail, stop my labour till I come to a lawful spot!

LYSISTRATA: What's this nonsense? 990

THIRD WOMAN: I'm going to have a baby—right now!

LYSISTRATA: But you weren't even pregnant yesterday.

THIRD WOMAN: Well, I am today. O Lysistrata, do send me home to see a midwife, right away.

LYSISTRATA: What are you talking about? *(Putting her hand on her stomach)* What's this hard lump here?

THIRD WOMAN: A little boy.

LYSISTRATA: My goodness, what have you got there? It seems hollow; I'll just find out. *(Pulling aside* 1000 *her robe)* Why, you silly goose, you've got Athene's sacred helmet there. And you said you were having a baby!

THIRD WOMAN: Well, I *am* having one, I swear!

LYSISTRATA: Then what's this helmet for?

THIRD WOMAN: If the baby starts coming while I'm still in the Acropolis, I'll creep into this like a pigeon and give birth to it there.

LYSISTRATA: Stuff and nonsense! It's plain enough what you're up to. You just wait here for the 1010 christening of this—helmet.

THIRD WOMAN: But I can't sleep in the Acropolis since I saw the sacred snake.

FIRST WOMAN: And I'm dying for lack of sleep: the hooting of owls keep me awake.

LYSISTRATA: Enough of these shams, you wretched creatures. You want your husbands, I suppose. Well, don't you think they want us? I'm sure they're spending miserable nights. Hold out, my
1020 friends, and endure for just a little while. There's an oracle that we shall conquer, if we don't split up. (Producing a roll of paper.) Here it is.

FIRST WOMAN: Tell us what it says.

LYSISTRATA: Listen.
"When in the length of time the Swallows shall gather together,
Fleeing the Hoopoe's amorous flight and the Cockatoo shunning,
1030 Then shall your woes be ended and Zeus who thunders in heaven
Set what's below on top—"

FIRST WOMAN: What? Are we going to be on top?

LYSISTRATA: "But if the Swallows rebel and flutter away from the temple,
Never a bird in the world shall seem more wanton and worthless."

FIRST WOMAN: That's clear enough, upon my word!

LYSISTRATA: By all that's holy, let's not give up the
1040 struggle now. Let's go back inside. It would be a shame, my dear friends, to disobey the oracle.

(The WOMEN all retire to the Acropolis again.)

CHORUS OF MEN (singing):
I have a tale to tell,
Which I know full well.
  It was told me
  In the nursery.

Once there was a likely lad,
  Melanion they name him;
The thought of marriage made him mad,
1050 For which I cannot blame him.

So off he went to mountains fair;
  (No women to upbraid him!)
A mighty hunter of the hare,
  He had a dog to aid him.

He never came back home to see
  Detested women's faces.
He showed a shrewd mentality.
  With him I'd fain change places!

ONE OF THE MEN (to ONE OF THE WOMEN): Come here,
1060 old dame; give me a kiss.

WOMAN: You'll ne'er eat garlic, if you dare!

MAN: I want to kick you—just like this!

WOMAN: Oh, there's a leg with bushy hair!

MAN: Myronides and Phormio
Were hairy—and they thrashed the foe.

CHORUS OF WOMEN (singing):
I have another tale,
With which to assail
  Your contention
  'Bout Melanion.   1070

Once upon a time a man
  Named Timon left our city,
To live in some deserted land.
  (We thought him rather witty.)

He dwelt alone amidst the thorn;
  In solitude he brooded.
From some grim Fury he was born:
  Such hatred he exuded.

He cursed you men, as scoundrels through
  And through, till life he ended.   1080
He couldn't stand the sight of you!
  But women he befriended.

WOMAN (to ONE OF THE MEN): I'll smash your face in, if you like.

MAN: Oh no, please don't! You frighten me.

WOMAN: I'll lift my foot—and thus I'll strike.

MAN: Aha! Look there! What's that I see?

WOMAN: Whate'er you see, you cannot say
That I'm not neatly trimmed today.

(LYSISTRATA appears on the wall of the Acropolis.)

LYSISTRATA: Hello! Hello! Girls, come here quick!   1090

(SEVERAL WOMEN appear beside her.)

WOMAN: What is it? Why are you calling?

LYSISTRATA: I see a man coming: he's in a dreadful state. He's mad with passion. O Queen of Cyprus, Cythera, and Paphos, just keep on this way!

WOMAN: Where is the fellow?

LYSISTRATA: There beside the shrine of Demeter.

WOMAN: Oh yes, so he is. Who is he?

LYSISTRATA: Let's see. Do any of you know him?

MYRRHINE: Yes indeed. That's my husband, Cinesias.

LYSISTRATA: It's up to you, now: roast him, rack him,   1100 fool him, love him—and leave him! Do everything, except what our oath forbids.

MYRRHINE: Don't worry; I'll do it.

LYSISTRATA: I'll stay here to tease him and warm him up a bit. Off with you.

(The OTHER WOMEN retire from the wall. Enter CINESIAS followed by A SLAVE carrying a baby. CINESIAS is obviously in great pain and distress.)

CINESIAS (groaning): Oh-h! Oh-h-h! This is killing me! O God, what tortures I'm suffering!

LYSISTRATA (from the wall): Who's that within our lines?

CINESIAS: Me.   1110

LYSISTRATA: A man?

CINESIAS (*pointing*): A *man*, indeed!

LYSISTRATA: Well, go away!

CINESIAS: Who are you to send me away?

LYSISTRATA: The captain of the guard.

CINESIAS: Oh, for heaven's sake, call out Myrrhine for me.

LYSISTRATA: Call Myrrhine? Nonsense! Who are you?

CINESIAS: Her husband, Cinesias of Paionidai.

1120 LYSISTRATA (*appearing much impressed*): Oh, greetings, friend. Your name is not without honour here among us. Your wife is always talking about you, and whenever she takes an egg or an apple, she says, "Here's to my dear Cinesias!"

CINESIAS (*quivering with excitement*): Oh, ye gods in heaven!

LYSISTRATA: Indeed she does! And whenever our conversations turn to men, your wife im- mediately says, "All others are mere rubbish 1130 compared with Cinesias."

CINESIAS (*groaning*): Oh! Do call her for me.

LYSISTRATA: Why should I? What will you give me?

CINESIAS: Whatever you want. All I have is yours— and you see what I've got.

LYSISTRATA: Well then, I'll go down and call her. (*She descends.*)

CINESIAS: And hurry up! I've had no joy of life ever since she left home. When I go in the house, I feel awful: everything seems so empty and I can't 1140 enjoy my dinner. I'm in such a state all the time!

MYRRHINE (*from behind the wall*): I *do* love him so! But he won't let me love him. No, no! Don't ask me to see him!

CINESIAS: O my darling, O Myrrhine honey, why do you do this to me?

(MYRRHINE *appears on the wall.*)

Come down here!

MYRRHINE: No, I won't come down.

CINESIAS: Won't you come, Myrrhine, when I call you?

1150 MYRRHINE: No; you don't want me.

CINESIAS: *Don't want you?* I'm in agony!

MYRRHINE: I'm going now.

CINESIAS: Please don't. At least, listen to your baby. (*to the baby*) Here you, call your mamma! (*Pinching the baby.*)

BABY: Ma-ma! Ma-ma! Ma-ma!

CINESIAS (*to Myrrhine*): What's the matter with you? Have you no pity for your child, who hasn't been washed or fed for five whole days?

1160 MYRRHINE: Oh, poor child; your father pays no atten- tion to you.

CINESIAS: Come down then, you heartless wretch, for the baby's sake.

MYRRHINE: Oh, what it is to be a mother! I've got to come down, I suppose.

(*She leaves the wall and shortly reappears at the gate.*)

CINESIAS (*to himself*): She seems much younger, and she has such a sweet look about her. Oh, the way she teases me! And her pretty, provoking ways make me burn with longing.

MYRRHINE (*coming out of the gate and taking the baby*): O 1170 my sweet little angel. Naughty papa! Here, let Mummy kiss you, Mamma's little sweetheart!

(*She fondles the baby lovingly.*)

CINESIAS (*in despair*): You heartless creature, why do you do this? Why follow these other women and make both of us suffer so?

(*He tries to embrace her.*)

MYRRHINE: Don't touch me!

CINESIAS: You're letting all our things at home go to wrack and ruin.

MYRRHINE: I don't care.

CINESIAS: You don't care that your wool is being 1180 plucked to pieces by the chickens?

MYRRHINE: Not in the least.

CINESIAS: And you haven't celebrated the rites of Aphrodite for ever so long. Won't you come home?

MYRRHINE: Not on your life, unless you men make a truce and stop the war.

CINESIAS: Well, then, if that pleases you, we'll do it.

MYRRHINE: Well then, if that pleases *you*, I'll come home—afterwards! Right now I'm on oath not 1190 to.

CINESIAS: Then just lie down here with me for a mo- ment.

MYRRHINE: No—(*in a teasing voice*) and yet I won't say I don't love you.

CINESIAS: You love me? Oh, do lie down here, Myr- rhine dear!

MYRRHINE: What, you silly fool! in front of the baby?

CINESIAS (*hastily thrusting the baby at the slave*): Of course not. Here—home! Take him, Manes! (*The 1200 SLAVE goes off with the baby.*) See, the baby's out of the way. Now won't you lie down?

MYRRHINE: But where, my dear?

CINESIAS: Where? The grotto of Pan's a lovely spot.

MYRRHINE: How could I purify myself before return- ing to the shrine?

CINESIAS: Easily: just wash here in the Clepsydra.

MYRRHINE: And then, shall I go back on my oath?

CINESIAS: On my head be it! Don't worry about the oath. 1210

MYRRHINE: All right, then. Just let me bring out a bed.

CINESIAS: No, don't. The ground's all right.

MYRRHINE: Heavens, no! Bad as you are, I won't let you lie on the bare ground.

(*She goes into the Acropolis.*)

CINESIAS: Why, she really loves me; it's plain to see.

MYRRHINE (*returning with a bed*): There! Now hurry

up and lie down. I'll just slip off this dress. But—let's see: oh yes, I must fetch a mattress.

1220 CINESIAS: Nonsense! No mattress for me.

MYRRHINE: Yes indeed! It's not nice on the bare springs.

CINESIAS: Give me a kiss.

MYRRHINE (giving him a hasty kiss): There!

(She goes.)

CINESIAS (in mingled distress and delight): Oh-h! Hurry back!

MYRRHINE (returning with a mattress): Here's the mattress; lie down on it. I'm taking my things off now—but—let's see: you have no pillow.

1230 CINESIAS : I don't want a pillow.

MYRRHINE : But I do.

(She goes.)

CINESIAS: Cheated again, just like Heracles and his dinner!

MYRRHINE (returning with a pillow): Here, lift your head. (to herself, wondering how else to tease him) Is that all?

CINESIAS: Surely that's all! Do come here, precious!

MYRRHINE: I'm taking off my girdle. But remember: don't go back on your promise about the truce.

1240 CINESIAS: I hope to die, if I do.

MYRRHINE: You don't have a blanket.

CINESIAS (shouting in exasperation): I don't want one! I WANT TO—

MYRRHINE: Sh-h! There, there, I'll be back in a minute.

(She goes.)

CINESIAS: She'll be the death of me with these bed-clothes.

MYRRHINE (returning with a blanket): Here, get up.

CINESIAS: I've got this up!

1250 MYRRHINE: Would you like some perfume?

CINESIAS: Good heavens, no! I won't have it!

MYRRHINE: Yes, you shall, whether you want it or not.

(She goes.)

CINESIAS: O lord! Confound all perfumes anyway!

MYRRHINE (returning with a flask): Stretch out your hand and put some on.

CINESIAS (suspiciously): By God, I don't much like this perfume. It smacks of shilly-shallying, and has no scent of the marriage-bed.

MYRRHINE: Oh dear! This is Rhodian perfume I've
1260 brought.

CINESIAS: It's quite all right, dear. Never mind.

MYRRHINE: Don't be silly!

(She goes out with the flask.)

CINESIAS: Damn the man who first concocted perfumes!

MYRRHINE (returning with another flask): Here, try this flask.

CINESIAS: I've got another one all ready for you. Come, you wretch, lie down and stop bringing me things.

MYRRHINE: All right; I'm taking off my shoes. But, 1270 my dear, see that you vote for peace.

CINESIAS (absently): I'll consider it.

(MYRRHINE runs away to the Acropolis.)

I'm ruined! The wench has skinned me and run away! (chanting, in tragic style) Alas! Alas! Deceived, deserted by this fairest of women, whom shall I—lay? Ah, my poor little child, how shall I nurture thee? Where's Cynalopex? I needs must hire a nurse!

LEADER OF MEN (chanting): Ah, wretched man, in dreadful wise beguiled, bewrayed, thy soul is 1280 sore distressed. I pity thee, alas! What soul, what loins, what liver could stand this strain? How firm and unyielding he stands, with naught to aid him of a morning.

CINESIAS: O lord! O Zeus! What tortures I endure!

LEADER OF MEN: This is the way she's treated you, that vile and cursèd wanton.

LEADER OF WOMEN: Nay, not vile and cursèd, but sweet and dear.

LEADER OF MEN: Sweet, you say? Nay, hateful, hate- 1290 ful!

CINESIAS: Hateful indeed! O Zeus, Zeus!
Seize her and snatch her away,
Like a handful of dust, in a mighty,
Fiery tempest! Whirl her aloft, then let her drop
Down to the earth, with a crash, as she falls—
On the point of this waiting
Thingummybob!

(He goes out. Enter a SPARTAN HERALD in an obvious state of excitement, which he is doing his best to conceal.)

HERALD: Where can I find the Senate or the Prytanes? I've got an important message. 1300

(The Athenian MAGISTRATE enters.)

MAGISTRATE: Say there, are you a man or Priapus?

HERALD (in annoyance): I'm a herald, you lout! I've come from Sparta about the truce.

MAGISTRATE: Is that a spear you've got under your cloak?

HERALD: No, of course not!

MAGISTRATE: Why do you twist and turn so? Why hold your cloak in front of you. Did you rupture yourself on the trip?

HERALD: By gum, the fellow's an old fool. 1310

MAGISTRATE (pointing): Why, you dirty rascal, you're excited.

HERALD: Not at all. Stop this tom-foolery.

MAGISTRATE: Well, what's that I see?

HERALD: A Spartan message-staff.

MAGISTRATE: Oh, certainly! That's just the kind of message-staff I've got. But tell me the honest truth: how are things going in Sparta?

HERALD: All the land of Sparta is up in arms—and
1320   our allies are up, too. We need Pellene.

MAGISTRATE: What brought this trouble on you? A sudden Panic?

HERALD: No, Lampito started it and then all the other women in Sparta with one accord chased their husbands out of their beds.

MAGISTRATE: How do you feel?

HERALD: Terrible. We walk around the city bent over like men lighting matches in a wind. For our women won't let us touch them until we all agree
1330   and make peace throughout Greece.

MAGISTRATE: This is a general conspiracy of the women; I see it now. Well, hurry back and tell the Spartans to send ambassadors here with full powers to arrange a truce. And I'll go tell the Council to choose ambassadors from here; I've got something here that will soon persuade them!

HERALD: I'll fly there; for you've made an excellent suggestion.

(The HERALD *and the* MAGISTRATE *depart on opposite sides of the stage.)*

1340   LEADER OF MEN: No beast or fire is harder than womankind to tame,
Nor is the spotted leopard so devoid of shame.

LEADER OF WOMEN: Knowing this, you dare provoke us to attack?
I'd be your steady friend, if you'd but take us back.

LEADER OF MEN: I'll never cease my hatred keen of womankind.

LEADER OF WOMEN: Just as you will. But now just let me help you find
1350   That cloak you threw aside. You look so silly there
Without your clothes. Here, put it on and don't go bare.

LEADER OF MEN: That's very kind, and shows you're not entirely bad.
But I threw off my things when I was good and mad.

LEADER OF WOMEN: At last you seem a man, and won't be mocked, my lad.
If you'd been nice to me, I'd take this little gnat
1360   That's in your eye and pluck it out for you, like that.

LEADER OF MEN: So that's what bothered me and bit my eye so long!
Please dig it out for me. I own that I've been wrong.

LEADER OF WOMEN: I'll do so, though you've been a most ill-natured brat.
Ye gods! See here! A huge and monstrous little gnat!

LEADER OF MEN: Oh, how that helps! For it was digging wells in me.   1370
And now it's out. my tears can roll down hard and free.

LEADER OF WOMEN: Here, let me wipe them off, although you're such a knave,
And kiss me.

LEADER OF MEN: No!

LEADER OF WOMEN: Whate'er you say, a kiss I'll have.

(She kisses him.)

LEADER OF MEN: Oh, confound these women! They've a coaxing way about them.
He was wise and never spoke a truer word, who   1380
said,
"We can't live with women, but we cannot live without them."
Now I'll make a truce with you. We'll fight no more; instead,
I will not injure you if you do me no wrong.
And now let's join our ranks and then begin a song.

COMBINED CHORUS *(singing)*:
Athenians, we're not prepared,
To say a single ugly word   1390
About our fellow-citizens.
Quite the contrary: we desire but to say and to do
Naught but good. Quite enough are the ills now on hand.

Men and women, be advised:
If anyone requires
Money—minae two or three—
We've got what he desires.

My purse is yours, on easy terms:
When Peace shall reappear,   1400
Whate'er you've borrowed will be due.
So speak up without fear.

You needn't pay me back, you see,
If you can get a cent from me!

We're about to entertain
Some foreign gentlemen;
We've soup and tender, fresh-killed pork.
Come round to dine at ten.

Come early; wash, and dress with care,
And bring the children, too.   1410
Then step right in, no "by your leave."
We'll be expecting you.

Walk in as if you owned the place.
You'll find the door—shut in your face!

(Enter a group of SPARTAN AMBASSADORS; *they are in the same desperate condition as the* HERALD *in the previous scene.)*

LEADER OF CHORUS: Here comes the envoys from Sparta, sprouting long beards and looking for the world as if they were carrying pig-pens in front of them.

Greetings, gentlemen of Sparta. Tell me, in
1420 what state have you come?

SPARTAN: Why waste words? You can plainly see what state we've come in!

LEADER OF CHORUS: Wow! You're in a pretty high-strung condition, and it seems to be getting worse.

SPARTAN: It's indescribable. Won't someone please arrange a peace for us—in any way you like.

LEADER OF CHORUS: Here come our own, native ambassadors, crouching like wrestlers and holding
1430 their clothes in front of them; this seems an athletic kind of malady.

(Enter several Athenian AMBASSADORS.)

ATHENIAN: Can anyone tell us where Lysistrata is? You see our condition.

LEADER OF CHORUS: Here's another case of the same complaint. Tell me, are the attacks worse in the morning?

ATHENIAN: No, we're always afflicted this way. If someone doesn't soon arrange this truce, you'd better not let me get my hands on—Cleisthenes!

1440 LEADER OF CHORUS: If you're smart, you'll arrange your cloaks so none of these fellows who smashed the Hermae can see you.

ATHENIAN: Right you are; a very good suggestion.

SPARTAN: Aye, by all means. Here, let's hitch up our clothes.

ATHENIAN: Greetings, Spartan. We've suffered dreadful things.

SPARTAN: My dear fellow, we'd have suffered still worse if one of those fellows had seen us in this
1450 condition.

ATHENIAN: Well, gentlemen, we must get down to business. What's your errand here?

SPARTAN: We're ambassadors about peace.

ATHENIAN: Excellent; so are we. Only Lysistrata can arrange things for us; shall we summon her?

SPARTAN: Aye, and Lysistratus too, if you like.

LEADER OF CHORUS: No need to summon her, it seems. She's coming out of her own accord.

(Enter LYSISTRATA accompanied by a statue of a nude female figure, which represents Reconciliation.)

Hail, noblest of women; now must thou be
1460 A judge shrewd and subtle, mild and severe,
Be sweet yet majestic: all manners employ.
The leaders of Hellas, caught by thy love-charms,
Have come to thy judgment, their charges submitting.

LYSISTRATA: This is no difficult task, if one catch them still in amorous passion, before they've re-

sorted to each other. But I'll soon find out. Where's Reconciliation? Go, first bring the Spartans here, and don't seize them rudely and violently, as our tactless husbands used to do, but as 1470 befits a woman, like an old, familiar friend; if they won't give you their hands, take them however you can. Then go fetch these Athenians here, taking hold of whatever they offer you. Now then, men of Sparta, stand here beside me, and you Athenians on the other side, and listen to my words.

I am a woman, it is true, but I have a mind; I'm not badly off in native wit, and by listening to my father and my elders, I've had a decent 1480 schooling.

Now I intend to give you a scolding which you both deserve. With one common font you worship at the same altars, just like brothers, at Olympia, at Thermopylae, at Delphi—how many more might I name, if time permitted;—and the Barbarians stand by waiting with their armies; yet you are destroying the men and towns of Greece.

ATHENIAN: Oh, this tension is killing me! 1490

LYSISTRATA: And now, men of Sparta,—to turn to you—don't you remember how the Spartan Pericleidas came here once as a suppliant, and sitting at our altar, all pale with fear in his crimson cloak, begged us for an army? For all Messene had attacked you and the god sent an earthquake too? Then Cimon went forth with four thousand hoplites and saved all Lacedaemon. Such was the aid you received from Athens, and now you lay waste the country 1500 which once treated you so well.

ATHENIAN (hotly): They're in the wrong, Lysistrata, upon my word, they are!

SPARTAN (absently, looking at the statue of Reconciliation): We're in the wrong. What hips! How lovely they are!

LYSISTRATA: Don't think I'm going to let you Athenians off. Don't you remember how the Spartans came in arms when you were wearing the rough, sheepskin cloak of slaves and slew the host of 1510 Thessalians, the comrades and allies of Hippias? Fighting with you on that day, alone of all the Greeks, they set you free and instead of a sheepskin gave your folk a handsome robe to wear.

SPARTAN (looking at LYSISTRATA): I've never seen a more distinguished woman.

ATHENIAN (looking at Reconciliation): I've never seen a more voluptuous body!

LYSISTRATA: Why then, with these many noble deeds 1520 to think of, do you fight each other? Why don't you stop this villainy? Why not make peace? Tell me, what prevents it?

SPARTAN (*waving vaguely at Reconciliation*): We're willing, if you're willing to give up your position on yonder flank.

LYSISTRATA: What position, my good man?

SPARTAN: Pylus, we've been panting for it for ever so long.

1530 ATHENIAN: No, by God! You shan't have it!

LYSISTRATA: Let them have it, my friend.

ATHENIAN: Then what shall we have to rouse things up?

LYSISTRATA: Ask for another place in exchange.

ATHENIAN: Well, let's see: first of all (*pointing to various parts of Reconciliation's anatomy*) give us Echinus here, this Maliac Inlet in back there, and these two Megarian legs.

1540 SPARTAN: No, by heavens! You can't have *everything*, you crazy fool!

LYSISTRATA: Let it go. Don't fight over a pair of legs.

ATHENIAN (*taking off his cloak*): I think I'll strip and do a little planting now.

SPARTAN (*following suit*): And I'll just do a little fertilizing, by gosh!

LYSISTRATA: Wait until the truce is concluded. Now if you've decided on this course, hold a conference and discuss the matter with your allies.

ATHENIAN: Allies? Don't be ridiculous. They're in the
1550 same state we are. Won't our allies want the same thing we do—to jump in bed with their women?

SPARTAN: Ours will, I know.

ATHENIAN: Especially the Carystians, by God!

LYSISTRATA: Very well. Now purify yourselves, that your wives may feast and entertain you in the Acropolis; we've provisions by the basketfull. Exchange your oaths and pledges there, and then each of you may take his wife and go home.

ATHENIAN: Let's go at once.

1560 SPARTAN: Come on, where you will.

ATHENIAN: For God's sake, let's hurry!

(*They all go into the Acropolis.*)

CHORUS (*singing*):
Whate'er I have of coverlets
    And robes of varied hue
And golden trinkets,—without stint
    I offer them to you.

Take what you will and bear it home,
    Your children to delight,
Or if your girl's a Basket-maid;
1570   Just choose whate'er's in sight.

There's naught within so well secured
    You cannot break the seal
And bear it off; just help yourselves;
    No hesitation feel.

But you'll see nothing, though you try,
    Unless you've sharper eyes than I!

If anyone needs bread to feed
    A growing family,
I've lots of wheat and full-grown loaves;
    So just apply to me.   1580

Let every poor man who desires
    Come round and bring a sack
To fetch the grain; my slave is there
    To load it on his back.

But don't come near my door, I say:
    Beware the dog, and stay away!

(*An* ATHENIAN *enters carrying a torch; he knocks at the gate.*)

ATHENIAN: Open the door! (*to the* CHORUS, *which is clustered around the gate*) Make way, won't you! What are you hanging around for? Want me to singe you with this torch? (*to himself*) No; it's a   1590 stale trick, I won't do it! (*to the audience*) Still if I've got to do it to please *you*, I suppose I'll have to take the trouble.

(*A* SECOND ATHENIAN *comes out of the gate.*)

SECOND ATHENIAN: And I'll help you.

FIRST ATHENIAN (*waving his torch at the* CHORUS): Get out! Go bawl your heads off! Move on there, so the Spartans can leave in peace when the banquet's over.

(*They brandish their torches until the* CHORUS *leaves the Orchestra.*)

SECOND ATHENIAN: I've never seen such a pleasant banquet: the Spartans are charming fellows, in-   1600 deed they are! And we Athenians are very witty in our cups.

FIRST ATHENIAN: Naturally: for when we're sober we're never at our best. If the Athenians would listen to me, we'd always get a little tipsy on our embassies. As things are now, we go to Sparta when we're sober and look around to stir up trouble. And then we don't hear what they say—and as for what they *don't* say, we have all sorts of suspicions. And then we bring back vary-   1610 ing reports about the mission. But this time everything is pleasant; even if a man should sing the Telamon-song when he ought to sing "Cleitagorus," we'd praise him and swear it was excellent.

(*The two* CHORUSES *return, as a* CHORUS OF ATHENIANS *and a* CHORUS OF SPARTANS.)

Here they come back again. Go to the devil, you scoundrels!

SECOND ATHENIAN: Get out, I say! They're coming out from the feast.

(Enter the SPARTAN and ATHENIAN ENVOYS, followed by LYSISTRATA and all the WOMEN.)

1620 SPARTAN (to one of his fellow-envoys): My good fellow, take up your pipes; I want to do a fancy two-step and sing a jolly song for the Athenians.

ATHENIAN: Yes, do take your pipes, by all means. I'd love to see you dance.

SPARTAN (singing and dancing with the CHORUS OF SPARTANS):

These youths inspire
To song and dance, O Memory;
Stir up my Muse, to tell how we
1630 And Athens' men, in our galleys clashing
At Artemisium, 'gainst foemen dashing in godlike ire,
Conquered the Persian and set Greece free.

Leonidas
Led on his valiant warriors
Whetting their teeth like angry boars.
Abundant foam on their lips was flow'ring,
A stream of sweat from their limbs was show'ring.
The Persian was
1640 Numberless as the sand on the shores.

O Huntress who slayest the beasts in the glade,
O Virgin divine, hither come to our truce,
Unite us in bonds which all time will not loose.
Grant us to find in this treaty, we pray,
An unfailing source of true friendship today,
And all of our days, helping us to refrain
From weaseling tricks which bring war in their train.
Then hither, come hither! O huntress maid.

1650 LYSISTRATA: Come then, since all is fairly done, men of Sparta, lead away your wives, and you, Athenians, take yours. Let every man stand beside his wife, and every wife beside her man, and then, to celebrate our fortune, let's dance. And in the future, let's take care to avoid these misunderstandings.

CHORUS OF ATHENIANS (singing and dancing):

Lead on the dances, your graces revealing.
Call Artemis hither, call Artemis' twin,
1660 Leader of dances, Apollo the Healing,
Kindly God—hither! Let's summon him in!

Nysian Bacchus call,
Who with his Maenads, his eyes flashing fire,
Dances, and last of all
Zeus of the thunderbolt flaming, the Sire,
And Hera in majesty,
Queen of prosperity.
Come, ye Powers who dwell above
Unforgetting, our witnesses be
Of Peace with bonds of harmonious love— 1670
The Peace which Cypris has wrought for me.
Alleluia! Io Paean!
Leap in joy—hurrah! hurrah!
'Tis victory—hurrah! hurrah!
Euoi! Euoi! Euai! Euai!

LYSISTRATA (to the SPARTANS): Come now, sing a new song to cap ours.

CHORUS OF SPARTANS (singing and dancing):

Leaving Taygetus fair and renown'd
Muse of Laconia, hither come: 1680
Amyclae's god in hymns resound.
Athene of the Brazen Home,
And Castor and Pollux, Tyndareus' sons,
Who sport where Eurotas murmuring runs.

On with the dance! Heia! Ho!
All leaping along,
Mantles a-swinging as we go!
Of Sparta our song.
There the holy chorus ever gladdens,
There the beat of stamping feet, 1690
As our winsome fillies, lovely maidens,
Dance, beside Eurotas, banks a-skipping,—
Nimbly go to and fro
Hast'ning, leaping feet in measures tripping,

Like the Bacchae's revels, hair a-streaming.
Leda's child, divine and mild,
Leads the holy dance, her fair face beaming.
On with the dance! as your hand
Presses the hair
Streaming away unconfined. 1700
Leap in the air
Light as the deer; footsteps resound
Aiding our dance, beating the ground.
Praise Athene, Maid divine, unrivalled in her might,
Dweller in the Brazen Home, unconquered in the fight.

(All go out singing and dancing.)

Figure 10. Lysistrata and her cohorts taunt the Athenian Magistrate (Patrick Hines) in the Phoenix Theater production of *Lysistrata,* directed by Jean Gascon, New York, 1959. (Photograph: the Joseph Abeles Collection.)

Figure 11. The Chorus of Old Men picket the Acropylis in the Phoenix Theater production of *Lysistrata,* directed by Jean Gascon, New York, 1959. (Photograph: the Joseph Abeles Collection.)

Figure 12. Lysistrata (Nan Martin, *standing*) convinces the Athenians and Spartans to reconcile their differences in the Phoenix Theater production of *Lysistrata,* directed by Jean Gascon, New York, 1959. (Photograph: the Joseph Abeles Collection.)

Staging of *Lysistrata*

**REVIEW OF THE PHOENIX THEATER
PRODUCTION, NEW YORK, 1959, BY DONALD
MALCOLM**

The production of Aristophanes' "Lysistrata" that opened last week at the Phoenix Theatre is crass, low, vulgar, and enjoyable. To declare that it takes liberties with the play would require an enormous extension of the meaning of the word "liberty." There are moments when the text is all but obliterated by an accompanying orgy of pie-throwing, pratfalls, sandbaggings, and cooch dances. But I suspect that Aristophanes might find it in his heart to applaud the irreverent spirit that animates the proceedings even while suffering an author's natural anguish at some of the results thereby obtained. . . .

There are portions of the text, even in this brisk new rendering, by Dudley Fitts, that doubtless meant a great deal more to ancient Athenians than they can mean to contemporary New Yorkers, and it is chiefly these portions that the director, Jean Gascon, annihilates with horseplay. Several speeches by the women's chorus are delivered in the syncopated rhythm of a revivalist chant, and while this sometimes works violence on the metre of the lines and adds nothing to their intelligibility, it does have a certain rowdy fascination. In a similar spirit, the longer verbal exchanges between the sexes are liberally interlarded with hoots, catcalls, and sufficient rough-housing and shimmy dancing to provide steady employment for a circusful of clowns and a whole troupe of bumpers and grinders. Mr. Gascon does not even hesitate to permit the army of old men to picket the citadel with signs that spell out "UNΦAIR" on one side and "Athens Was a Summer Festival" on the other. I think perhaps he should have hesitated.

The actors' contribution to the performance appears to consist chiefly in doing what Mr. Gascon told them to do, and doing it smartly. Broad comedy flourishes at the expense of characterization. Nan Martin, who portrays Lysistrata, exhibits so intense an awareness of her own charms as to perceptibly diminish the appeal of those charms. But a pudgy young lady named Sasha Von Scherler makes a fine sex-crazy matron, and Patrick Hines, who plays an Athenian magistrate, looks like an indignant beach ball and embellishes his every speech with touches of comic art. A number of other gifted clowns caught my eye, but they invariably vanished in a swirl of arms and legs before I could trace them to the program. I congratulate them, though, whoever they are. The costumes consist largely of flesh-colored tights on which an assortment of jewels, spangles, and doodads are distributed to indicate what learned men call the primary sexual characteristics.

**REVIEW OF THE PHOENIX THEATER
PRODUCTION, NEW YORK, 1959, BY BROOKS
ATKINSON**

Pooling their taste, talent, education and responsibility for the culture of the community, the good people of the Phoenix have tried to kick a little life into Aristophanes' "Lysistrata," which opened on the home grounds last evening.

Wherever Aristophanes is obscene they have anxiously abetted him. The women appear wearing simulated breasts, tipped with sequins, and the ruttish old men strip down to union suits and glittering fig leaves, looking as roguish as all get out. Under the leering direction of Jean Gascon, of Montreal's Théatre du Nouveau Monde, they wallow in sex like refined people doing their best to make the most of a moral holiday. They hope they are being sufficiently Dionysian.

But they are being dull in a frisky manner. For the Phoenix troupe and its artisans are not burlesque queens or mountebanks. Nan Martin as the rebellious Lysistrata is a fine-looking woman with an excellent voice and enlightened intelligence. She brazens out the grotesque bra device that she is required to flaunt before the audience, and she does give Lysistrata the characterization of a sophisticated woman of the world. Directed never to stand still if she can possibly move on every line of the dialogue, she does rather better than the circumstances permit.

But it is dollars to doughnuts that her heart is not in this sort of barnyard horseplay. Nor are the hearts of Gerry Jedd, Sasha Von Scherler, Patricia Falkenhain and Patricia Ripley, who try to look as desperately amorous as possible. Nor does Patrick Hines really believe that he is funny in the mountainous costume of the magistrate, nor do the actors who play the futile old men think that aping feeble-mindedness is really hilarious.

Granted that the Aristophanes text is ribald, it is possible that Dudley Fitts' new translation has wit, humor and poetry that the performance destroys by being over-eager. Mr. Fitts does not evade Aristophanes' licentiousness, but he tries to express it in terse modern English, without the condescension of the intellectual. His translation is coarse without smirking.

In the modern world we are not likely to reproduce the external circumstances that gave pith to "Lysistrata" when Aristophanes wrote it. In the midst of a stupid, interminable war he advocated making peace with the enemy. Aristophanes would be hustled off to the hoosegow if he tried to undermine the safety of a modern nation by producing a similar comedy.

And when he wrote "Lysistrata" women had no political rights or influence. His notion that women could stop a war had an audacity that we can hardly imagine. On at least two counts "Lysistrata" assaulted public complacence in political areas that no longer exist. It was very timely indeed.

All that is left is the single joke about the women of Athens denying themselves to their men until the men make peace with Sparta. On the stage of the Phoenix the joke becomes progressively monotonous. Will Steven Armstrong has designed a gay, bold setting that includes classical mobiles; and his costumes (barring bras) have attractive drape and color.

From a theatrical point of view the production is not without merit. But the Phoenix management and the Phoenix mummers are not hearty roisterers. Their "Lysistrata" is not so funny as "La Plume de Ma Tante."

MEDIEVAL THEATER

During the fourteenth and fifteenth centuries—the heyday of medieval drama—permanent theaters did not exist anywhere in England or on the continent. None had been built since the fall of Rome, and none were built until the middle of the sixteenth century in France. Yet in medieval communities throughout England and Europe, theatrical productions commanded as much public attention and support as they had in Athens during the age of classical Greek drama. Drama held a privileged place in the culture of those late medieval communities because, as in ancient Greece, most of their plays were expressions of religious belief, and most of their productions were occasioned by religious events. Just as the ancient Athenians had dramatized their myths to celebrate the festival of Dionysus, so cities and towns all over England and everywhere in Europe dramatized episodes from the Old and New Testament, from the Apocrypha, and from saints' lives to celebrate sacred events in the Christian calendar. Some towns favored saints' days, others Easter, still others Whitsuntide, which followed Easter by seven weeks, but the most popular occasion was Corpus Christi Day, which took place eight and one-half weeks after Easter, between the last week in May and the third week in June—an ideal time for open-air theater.

During the tenth and eleventh centuries, when religious drama was just beginning to develop, biblical episodes had been staged indoors exclusively, in cathedrals and monasteries, where they originated as an instructive but subordinate element of the church service. But by the beginning of the thirteenth century, the devotional and instructional purposes of religious drama had already stimulated a vigorous theatrical impulse that gave rise to productions outside of the church as well as inside of it. Authority over production of the plays then passed from the church to the town, from bishops and abbots to mayors and town councils. Responsibility for staging the plays likewise passed from clerics and choir boys to craft guilds, trade guilds, and religious fraternities. Theatrical productions became a very public and communal activity, involving townspeople and clergy alike. In England, for example, town councils commissioned new plays and revisions of old ones, selected plays to be performed, scheduled performances, assigned individual plays to the various guilds responsible for production, set standards for production, and even levied fines for inferior productions. Each guild in turn took care of all the other arrangements for the play it had been assigned by the council: directing, staging, costuming, rehearsing, and acting. In France, as well as other European countries, the town council and a religious fraternity that sponsored the production jointly chose a committee of supervisors who appointed a director and assistants to produce its plays. The productions were thus an expression of civic pride as well as of religious belief.

As medieval communities grew and prospered, so did religious plays; at the height of their popularity they achieved a scope and magnitude unparalleled in the history of drama. Whether they encompassed the entire biblical history of the world from creation to the last judgment, as they usually did in England, or whether they were restricted to the life of Christ, as was customary in France, they were almost always encyclopedic. Less like plays than megaplays—they are often called cycle plays—they consisted of numerous playlets, each one devoted to a separate episode or cluster of related episodes from biblical, apocryphal, or saintly experience. The length of cycles varied according to the resources of the towns where they were produced, but judging from the cycles that have survived they were prodigious undertakings—even the shortest of them. Of the four surviving English cycles, for example, the shortest, from the city of Chester, comprises twenty-five individual playlets; Wakefield's contains thirty-two; Lincoln's contains forty-two; and the longest, from York, totals forty-eight. None of these cycles could be staged in a few hours, or even in an entire day. The Chester cycle, according to records from the period, took three days to perform, and no doubt the York cycle ran for the better part of a week. The French passion cycles were no less time consuming, usually requiring four to six days for performance, though in the exceptional case of a mid-sixteenth century production at Valenciennes, the complete cycle required twenty-five days.

Given the extraordinary number and variety of episodes they contained, the cycles clearly called for extraordinary methods of staging. With the increasing wealth, resourcefulness, and civic pride of late medieval communities, they were able, and eager, to put on extraordinary theatrical productions, using a variety of theatrical structures. Some communities staged their cycles on fixed platforms, others in the round, and others on movable wagons. But all the methods, however different their external characteristics, embodied the same conception of theatrical space and movement that had governed the earlier staging of plays within the church. Specifically, they all combined a neutral acting area with a group of set-like structures known as "mansions" (literally, dwelling places), and as the action moved from one mansion or specific locale to the next, the acting area was understood to be an extension of one location and then another. Consequently, the various outdoor forms of staging cycle plays were all fundamentally symbolic in their use of space and processional in their movement from one mansion or location to the next.

The procession took different forms according to the different methods of staging. In the fixed method, which prevailed in France, all the mansions for a single day's performance were placed side by side, either in a straight line on a long platform, or in a semicircle on a public square (see Figure 13). Here all of the sets—sometimes as many as 20 to 30 on a platform 100 to 200 feet long, ranging from heaven, which traditionally appeared at the right end, to hell, which was located at the left—were simultaneously visible, creating a dazzling spectacle for the audience. As the cycle unfolded, moving from one location and episode to the next, the audience proceeded from one end of the platform, or square, to the other. Staging in the round (the least common of the methods both in England and on the continent) took place in circular areas 100 to 300 feet in diameter that were designed to include spectators, sets, and actors alike (see Figure 14). The series of mansions was arranged around the perimeter of the circle; the audience sat or stood within the circle of sets; and the actors moved from one location to the next around the perimeter or to the general acting area in the center of the circle. The procession took yet another form, its most distinctive form, in the system of movable wagons that was common both in England and Spain, for with this method each separate playlet, staged by a different

Figure 13. The medieval platform stage.

Figure 14. Medieval staging in the round.

guild, was mounted on a separate wagon. Although the exact design and dimensions of the wagons have never been definitely established, they had to be long enough in some cases to provide space for two or three mansions. Playlets about Noah's flood, for example, required one set to designate heaven, from which God spoke to Noah, and another to designate the ark. The wagons were probably wide enough to provide an acting area in front of the sets, though in some towns they were drawn up along stationary acting platforms. The entire audience, however, was not gathered together in a single place, but stood in separate groups at several specified locations within a town, and at each of these points along the route the individual wagons would stop and the actors would perform their playlet (see Figure 15). With movable wagons, the audience stood still and the cycle, like a modern-day parade or procession of floats, was continually unfolding and taking place for different people.

In all these systems of staging, a rough and ready intimacy existed between actors and audience, quite unlike the distance that separated them in a classical Greek theater, and equally unlike their separation from one another by the proscenium arches of post-renaissance theaters. Not only the physical methods of staging, but also the conventions of performance worked to bring actors and audience together. The actors, for example, were largely amateurs, members of the community, friends and relatives of the spectators who were witnessing them from only a few feet away. Sometimes they were not even separated from one another at all. In the fixed method of staging, for example, actors might sit off to the side or actually stand among the audience before and after they performed their parts. In the movable system, the action sometimes spilled off the wagon into the street, particularly when the situation called for action symbolizing great distances between one place and another, as when Satan and his cohorts fell from heaven to hell, or when Adam and Eve were driven out of paradise. Then the actors performed their parts by moving from the acting platform into the area of the audience. Indeed, in many places it was customary for the devils to mingle playfully with the audience. Conventions of performance were clearly not designed to create or sustain a theatrical illusion.

Costumes and props were also designed to create a symbolic spectacle rather than a theatrical illusion. All the characters except the devils were costumed in some kind of medieval garb—God in the imperial vestments of the Pope, Jewish priests in bishops' robes, the tyrant Herod in a kingly crown, and Roman soldiers in knights' armor. The devils, on the other hand, were made up to look like gargoyles, griffins, and other fabulous beasts of prey. All of the costumes, however farfetched, were vividly symbolic, as was every other aspect of staging. Documents from the period reveal props ranging from a red colored rib for the creation of Eve, to gallows, scourges, and a leather bag filled with blood for the crucifixion of Christ. Other special effects included dummy or live animals for Noah's ark, barrels of water for the flood, fire burning at hell's mouth, pulleys for bringing angels from heaven to earth, and trapdoors for the sudden appearance or disappearance of characters. All in all, the cycles must have created for medieval audiences a marvelous and miraculous spectacle, as marvelous and miraculous as the biblical events they dramatized.

Cycle plays were by no means the only form of medieval drama, but they originated so early and prevailed so widely that the spatial concept governing

Figure 15. Medieval staging on movable wagons.

their staging also influenced the staging of other medieval plays, such as farces and moralities. That concept of theatrical space was not only familiar to medieval audiences, but was also readily adaptable to the production of both farces and moralities, whose length rarely exceeded 1500 lines. Like a playlet in a cycle, they were short and simple in their staging requirements, ordinarily calling for only two or three mansions. Although they were staged according to the same theatical conventions, they were not produced under the same auspices. Farces, for example, which were common largely in France during the fifteenth century, were written and performed by lawyers' guilds and student groups, who produced them to celebrate festivals such as Mardi Gras and May Day, when ribaldry and revelry were appropriate to the occasion. Morality plays, popular chiefly in England during the fifteenth and sixteenth centuries, were performed by small troupes of professional players, who toured the countryside and timed their arrival in a town to coincide with a religious holiday or festival, when the spiritual message of their play was most likely to elicit contributions from their audience. Though moralities were designed primarily to exemplify Christian belief, to show the perils of sin and the rewards of virtue, they often loosened the pockets of spectators by appealing also to their sense of humor. They usually contained a few characters known as Vice figures whose dirty jokes and slapstick stage business were meant not only to show the vulgarity of sin but also to amuse a paying audience. And to capitalize on their vulgarity, the Vice figures usually interrupted the play once or twice to collect money from the audience.

The image of the Vice figure mingling with the audience also sums up the unique qualities of medieval theater. Medieval drama encompassed a variety of plays as different as cycles, farces, and moralities, yet it persistently brought actors and spectators closer to one another than ever before or since. They were drawn together not only by the physical characteristics of the stage and the conventions of performance, but also by the festive purpose of their drama. Whether the festivities were sacred or secular, the actors and spectators were joined in celebration. The plays that appear in this section are embodiments of the most communal stage in the history of western theater.

THE WAKEFIELD MASTER

ca. 1400—1450

The unknown author of *The Second Shepherds' Play* has come to be known as the Wakefield Master, a name that fittingly identifies him with both the town for which he wrote and the consummate skill of his writing. Exactly when he lived is uncertain, but the language of his plays suggests that he probably wrote sometime during the first half of the fifteenth century. His plays also reveal that he must have received a thoroughgoing religious education, for they incorporate knowledge of biblical literature, scriptural commentary and Latin liturgy. He was undoubtedly a member of the clergy, but he almost certainly did not lead a cloistered existence, for the five pieces he contributed to the Wakefield cycle are filled with an extraordinary array of characters and situations, some of which he must have witnessed firsthand, others that he probably picked up from current folk tales, and some that he invented—but invented out of a rich storehouse of experience.

The Wakefield cycle itself originated during the second half of the fourteenth century, about fifty years before the time of the Wakefield Master, and it continued to be revised and performed until the late sixteenth century. It is, like the other surviving English cycles, a composite of plays written and rewritten by several authors at several different periods to meet the changing needs of the community. New plays were added as guilds became large and prosperous enough to mount their own productions; old plays were dropped or combined with others when a guild ran into hard times and could no longer afford its own production; or they were revised to satisfy objections of the church or the community. Although it is a patchwork of thirty-two plays, its pieces are unified by the pattern of spiritual history embodied in each play individually and all of them collectively. But the five plays written by the Wakefield Master stand out from the rest of the cycle.

His verse form is his most telling signature. The nine-line stanza he uses throughout his five plays does not occur anywhere else in the cycle except at a few points that bear the signs of his revision. In fact, his nine-line stanza is not to be found anywhere else in any of the other cycles, or anywhere else in medieval literature. Not only is it unique, but it is a remarkably complex harmony of rhymes and rhythms, all of which have been reproduced in Anthony Caputi's modernized version of *The Second Shepherds' Play*. The first four lines combine not only identical end rhymes, but also identical internal rhymes. The last five lines have an entirely different rhyme scheme, for the sixth, seventh, and eighth lines rhyme with one another, while the ninth line rhymes with the fifth to hold the elaborate structure of sounds together. As the rhyme scheme shifts from the first to the last part of each stanza, so does the rhythm. Each of the first four lines contains four beats; the fifth consists of only one stressed syllable; the sixth, seventh, and eighth have three stresses; and the ninth contains two stresses. The conception and execution of such an elaborate verse form is unquestionably the work of a technical virtuoso.

Even more remarkable is the fact that he sustains his verse form throughout all his plays, adapting its harmonies to widely different moods and situations, such as God loftily giving Noah specifications for the ark, or Noah's wife peevishly refusing to board the ark, or the shepherds devoutly presenting their gifts to the newborn child, or the Jewish high priest Annas unctuously expounding legal procedure to Christ, or the tyrant Herod maniacally raging about his political power. Dramatic situations so various as these require not only a flexible verse form but also a flexibility of language, and the Wakefield Master repeatedly displays his versatility, for he draws on an extensive vocabulary, ranging from slang, to colloquial, to formal usage, from one medieval dialect to another, from English to Latin and back. Yet he always finds the right word or expression to suit any character in any situation.

Ultimately, his plays stand out because his characters and his plots are masterfully developed, even within the short scope of several hundred lines. *The Second Shepherds' Play,* the longest of his works, contains only 754 lines, yet it projects a vividly developed world of shepherds and sheep stealers, a world with an imaginative life of its own as well as a relevance to the religious theme of the play. In the opening 190 lines, for example, even before the appearance of the sheep stealer Mak, the dialogue of the three shepherds fully distinguishes them from one another. The first shepherd, Coll, is obsessed by his poverty and outraged by the gentry who exploit him and his fellows; the second shepherd, Gib, is preoccupied by the afflictions of married life; and the third shepherd, Daw, is fed up with his job of tending others' sheep while they rest and he goes hungry. Although their complaints are different, they are united by affliction, by the misery of the weather that accentuates these complaints, and by the rough but good fellowship that sustains them. And their combined suffering dramatically presents the image of a world in need of salvation, a need that anticipates the end of the play and which accounts for the joy they express on learning of the savior.

The sheep stealing episode is the supreme example of the Wakefield Master's skill in turning a good folk story into good theater and ultimately into good religious example. As the farce unfolds, even before the marvelous moment of exposure, it becomes increasingly clear that Mak, and his wife, and the stolen sheep disguised as a newborn child are upside down versions of Joseph, Mary, and Christ. The make-believe birth staged by Mak and his wife provides a dramatically sharp contrast to the nativity scene that follows. Clearly, the Wakefield Master has taken enormous liberties with the brief biblical cue in the *Book of Luke*—"And there were in the same country shepherds abiding in the field, keeping watch over their flocks by night." But it is precisely those liberties that account for both the theatrical and the religious effectiveness of *The Second Shepherds' Play.*

Like all biblical plays, it is relatively easy to stage. The cast is small, the parts are short. Only two specific locations are required, one for Mak's house, the other for the stable at Bethlehem, the area between them standing for the open fields. Likewise, only a few props are needed: a crib, a couple of chairs and a table at Mak's house; a crib and a chair at the stable; and some kind of sheep, dummy or live. Because it is so easy to put on, it has been widely performed, especially during the Christmas season, by amateur student groups at colleges and universities throughout England and America. Though physically easy to stage, it is difficult to perform, for it requires actors to move abruptly yet believably from the rough and tumble antics of the sheep stealing episode to the devotional attitudes of the nativity scene. In this respect, *The Second Shepherds' Play* epitomizes the sharp contrasts of mood and action that are at work throughout the Wakefield cycle—contrasts that were evidently displayed by the Mermaid Company of London in its 1961 production of plays from the cycle (see Figures 16, 17, and 18). Judging from a review of that production, the dramatic contrasts of biblical drama are as moving today as they were in their own time.

THE SECOND SHEPHERDS' PLAY

BY THE WAKEFIELD MASTER / MODERNIZED VERSION BY ANTHONY CAPUTI

CHARACTERS

FIRST SHEPHERD, COLL
SECOND SHEPHERD, GIB
THIRD SHEPHERD, DAW
MAK
GILL, *his wife*
ANGEL
MARY

(Enter the FIRST SHEPHERD.*)*

FIRST SHEPHERD: Lord, but it's cold, and I'm
    wretchedly wrapped.
My hands nearly numb, so long have I napped.
My legs creak and fold, my fingers are chapped;
It is not as I would, for I am all lapped
    In sorrow.
In storms and tempest,
Now in the east, now in the west,
Woe is him has never rest
    Midday nor morrow!   10

But we poor shepherds that walk on the moor,
We're like, in faith, to be put out of door;
No wonder, as it stands, if we be poor,
For the tilth of our lands lies fallow as a floor,
    As ye ken.
We are so lamed,
So taxed and shamed,
We are made hand-tamed
    By these gentlery-men.

Thus they rob us of rest. Our Lady them harry!
These men that are lord-fast, they make the plough
    tarry.
Some say it's for the best; but we find it contrary.
Thus are tenants oppressed, in point to miscarry,
    In life.
Thus hold they us under;
Thus they bring us in blunder.
It were a great wonder
    If ever we should thrive.

30 'Gainst a man with painted sleeves, or a brooch,
    now-a-days,
Woe to him that shall grieve, or one word gainsay!
No man dare him reprove, what mastery he has.
Yet no man believes one word that he says,

No letter.
He can make purveyance,
With boast and arrogance;
And all is for maintenance
    Of men that are greater.

There shall come a swain as proud as a po,°   40
He must borrow my wain,° and my plough also,
That I am full fain to grant ere he go.
Thus live we in pain, anger, and woe
    By night and day.
Whatever he has willed
Must at once be fulfilled.
I were better be killed
    Than once say him nay.

It does me good, as I walk round alone,
Of this world for to talk in manner of groan.   50
To my sheep will I stalk, now as I moan;
There abide on a ridge, or sit on a stone,
    Full soon.
For I know, pardie,°
True men if they be,
I'll get more company
    Ere it be noon. *(Moves aside)*

(Enter the SECOND SHEPHERD.*)*
SECOND SHEPHERD: Ben'c'te° and Dominus! What
    may this bemean?
Why fares this world thus; the like has seldom   60
    been.
Lord, the weather is spiteful, and the winds bitter
    keen,
And the frosts so hideous, they water my een.°
    No lie.

---

po, peacock. *wain,* wagon. *pardie,* Pardieu; By God;
indeed. *Ben'c'te,* Benedicte. *een,* eyes.

Now in dry, now in wet,
Now in snow, now in sleet,
My shoes freeze to my feet,
 And all is awry.

70 But as far as I ken, wherever I go,
We poor wedded men endure much woe,
Crushed again and again, it falls oft so.
And Silly Capel, our hen, both to and fro
 She cackles;
But begin she to croak,
To groan or to choke,
For our cock it's no joke,
 For he's in the shackles.

These men that are wed have never their will.
80 When they're full hard bestead,° they sigh and
  keep still.
God knows they are led full hard and full ill;
In bower nor in bed say they aught until
 Ebb tide.
My part have I found,
And my lesson is sound:
Woe to him that is bound,
 For he must abide.

But now late in our lives—a marvel to me,
90 That I think my heart rives such wonders to see,
What destiny drives that it should so be—
Some men will have two wives, and some men three
 In store.
He has woe that has any;
But so far ken I,
He has moe° that has many,
 For he feels sore.

But young men a'wooing, before you've been
  caught,
100 Be well ware of wedding, and keep in your
  thought,
To moan, "Had I known," is a thing that serves
  naught.
Mickle° mourning has wedding to home often
  brought,
 And griefs,
With many a sharp shower;
You may catch in an hour
What shall seem full sour
110 As long as you live.

For as ever read I epistle° I've one as my dear,
As sharp as a thistle, as rough as a brere;°
She is browed like a bristle, with a sour lenten
  cheer;

---

bestead, situated. *moe,* more. *mickle,* much. *epis-*
tle, in the New Testament. *brere,* briar.

Had she once wet her whistle, she could sing full
 clear
 Her paternoster.
She's as great as a whale;
She has a gallon of gall;
By him that died for us all   120
 I would I'd run till I'd lost her.

FIRST SHEPHERD: Gib, look over the row! Full deafly,
 ye stand.
SECOND SHEPHERD: Yea, the devil in your maw—ye
 blow on your hand.
Saw ye anywhere Daw?
FIRST SHEPHERD: Yea, on a lea-land
I heard him blow. He comes here at hand,
 Not far.
Stand still.   130
SECOND SHEPHERD: Why?
FIRST SHEPHERD: I think he comes by.
SECOND SHEPHERD: He'll trick us with a lie
 Unless we beware.

(Enter the THIRD SHEPHERD, *a boy.)*

THIRD SHEPHERD: Christ's cross me speed, and Saint
 Nicholas!
Thereof had I need; and it's worse than it was.
Whoso can take heed and let the world pass;
It's rank as a weed and brittle as glass,
 And slides.   140
 This world fared never so,
With marvels more and moe,
 Now in weal, now in woe,
  Everything writhes.

Never since Noah's flood were such floods seen,
Winds and rains so rude, and storms so keen;
Some stammered, some stood in doubt, as I
 ween.
Now God turn all to good! I say as I mean,
 Hereunder.   150
These floods so they drown,
Both in fields and in town,
And bear all down,
 They make you wonder.

We that walk in the nights our cattle to keep,
We see queer sights when other men sleep.
Yet methinks my heart lightens; I see my pals
 peep.
They are two tall wights! Now I'll give my sheep
 A turn.   160
O full ill am I bent,
As I walk on this land.
I may lightly repent,
 If my toes I spurn.

(to the other two) Ah, sir, God you save, and master
    mine!
A drink would I have, and somewhat to dine.

FIRST SHEPHERD: Christ's curse, my knave, thou'rt a
    lazy swine!

170 SECOND SHEPHERD: The boy likes to rave! Let him
        stand there and whine
    Till we've made it.
    Ill thrift on thy pate!
    Though the fellow came late,
    Yet is he in state
        To dine—if he had it.

THIRD SHEPHERD: Such servants as I, that sweat and
        swink,°
    Eat our bread full dry, that's what I think.
180 We're oft wet and weary when master men wink,°
    Yet come full late both dinners and drink.
        But neatly
    Both our dame and our sire,
    When we've run in the mire,
    Can nip at our hire,
        And pay us full lately.

    But hear a truth, master, for you the fare make:
    I shall do, hereafter, work as I take;
    I shall do a little, sir, and between times play.
190 For I've never had suppers that heavily weigh
        In fields.
    And why should I bray?
    I can still run away.
    What sells cheap, men say,
        Never yields.

FIRST SHEPHERD: Thou are an ill lad, to ride a-wooing
    With a man that had but little of spending.

SECOND SHEPHERD: Peace, boy! I bade; no more
        jangling,
200 Or I shall make thee afraid, by the Heaven's King,
        With thy frauds.
    Where are the sheep, boy; lorn?

THIRD SHEPHERD: Sir, this same day at morn
    I them left in the corn,
        When they rang lauds.°

    They have pasture good; they cannot go wrong.

FIRST SHEPHERD: That's right. Oh, by the rood, these
    nights are long!
    Yet I would, ere we go, let's have us a song.

210 SECOND SHEPHERD: So I thought as I stood, to cheer
    us along.

THIRD SHEPHERD: I grant.

FIRST SHEPHERD: The tenor I'll try.

SECOND SHEPHERD: And I the treble so high.

THIRD SHEPHERD: Then the middle am I.
    Let's see how ye chant. *(They sing.)*

(Enter MAK *with a cloak over his smock.)*

MAK: Now, Lord, of names seven, that made the
        moon so pale,
    And more stars than I can name; Thy good will
        fails;   220
    I am so in a whirl that my jogged brain ails
    Now would God I were in heaven—where no child
        wails—
        Heaven so still.

FIRST SHEPHERD: Who is it that pipes so poor?

MAK: God knows what I endure,
    Here a'walking on the moor,
        And not my will!

SECOND SHEPHERD: From where do ye come, Mak?
    What news do ye bring?   230

THIRD SHEPHERD: Is he come? Then everyone take
    heed to his things.

(Takes the cloak from MAK.*)*

MAK: What! I am a yeoman (hear me you) of the king,
    Make way for me, the Lord's tidings I bring,
        And such.
    Fie on you! Go hence!
    This is no pretence.
    I must have reverence.
        And much!

FIRST SHEPHERD: Why make ye so quaint, Mak? It's   240
    no good to try.

SECOND SHEPHERD: Why play ye the saint, Mak? We
    know that you lie.

THIRD SHEPHERD: We know you can feint, Mak, and
    give the devil the lie.

MAK: I'll make such complaint, 'lack,° I'll make you all
        fry
        At a word.
    And tell what ye doth.

FIRST SHEPHERD: But, Mak, is that truth?   250
    Go gild that green tooth
        With a turd.

SECOND SHEPHERD: Mak, the devil's in your eye! A
    stroke would I lend you.

THIRD SHEPHERD: Mak, know ye not me? By God, I
    could 'tend you.

MAK: God keep you all three! Perhaps I can mend
    you.
    You're a fair company.

FIRST SHEPHERD: Can ye so bend you?   260

SECOND SHEPHERD: Rascal jape!°
    Thus late, as thou goes,

---

swink, toil.   *wink,* doze.   *lauds,* the early morning
service.

'lack, alack: an expression of surprise or dismay.   *jape,*
fool.

What will men suppose?
Sure thou hast an ill nose
For stealing of sheep.

MAK: And I am true as steel, all men say,
But a sickness I feel that takes my health away;
My belly's not well, not at all well today.
THIRD SHEPHERD: "Seldom lies the devil dead by the
270   way."
MAK: Therefore
Full sore am I and ill;
And I'll lie stone still
If I've eat even a quill
This month and more.

FIRST SHEPHERD: How fares thy wife? By my hood,
tell me true.
MAK: Lies sprawling by the fire, but that's nothing
new;
280 And a house full of brood. She drinks well, too;
Come ill or good that she'll always do
But so.
Eats as fast as she can;
And each year gives a man
A hungry bairn° to scan,
And some years two.

And were I more gracious and richer by far,
I were eaten still out of house and of barn.
And just look at her close, if ye come near;
290 There is none that knows what 'tis to fear
Than ken I.
Will ye see what I proffer—
I'll give all in my coffer
And masses I'll offer
To bid her goodbye.

SECOND SHEPHERD: I am so long wakéd, like none in
this shire,
I would sleep if I takéd less for my hire.
THIRD SHEPHERD: I am cold and near naked, and
300   would have a fire.
FIRST SHEPHERD: I am weary, for-rakéd,° and run in
the mire.
Stay awake, you!
SECOND SHEPHERD: Nay, I'll lie down by,
I must sleep must I.
THIRD SHEPHERD: I've as good need to put by
As any of you.

But, Mak, come hither! Between us must you be.
MAK: You're sure you don't want to talk privately?°
310   Indeed?
From my top to my toe,

---

bairn, child. for-rakéd, exhausted.

Manus tuas commendo,
Pontio Pilato,°
Christ's cross me speed!

(*Then he rises, the shepherds being asleep, and says.*)

Now were time for a man that wants for gold
To stealthily enter into a fold,
And nimbly to work then, yet be not too bold,
For he might pay for the bargain, if it were told,
At the ending.
Now were time for to spell—   320
But he needs good counsel
That fain would fare well,
And has little spending.

But about you a circle as round as a moon,
Till I've done what I will, till it be noon,
Ye must lie stone still till I have done.
And I shall say thereto of words a few.
On height.
Over your heads my hands I lift;
Your eyes go out and senses drift   330
Until I make a better shift
If it be right.

Lord, how they sleep hard! That may ye all hear.
I never was a shepherd, but now will I learn.
If the flock be scared, when I shall creep near.
How! Draw hitherward! Now mends our cheer
From sorrow.
A fat sheep, I dare say;
A good fleece, dare I lay!
Pay back when I may,   340
But this will I borrow.

(MAK *crosses the stage to his house.*)

How, Gill, art thou in? Get us some light.
WIFE: Who makes such din this time of the night?
I am set for to spin; no hope that I might
Rise a penny to win. I curse them on height.
So sore
A housewife thus fares,
She always has cares
And all for nothing bears
All these chores.   350

MAK: Good wife, open the latch! Seest thou not what
I bring?
WIFE: I'll let thee draw the catch. Ah, come in my
sweeting!
MAK: Yea, thou dost not reek of my long standing.
WIFE: By thy bare neck for this you're like to swing.
MAK: Go away:
I'm good for something yet,

Manus . . . Pilato, "Into thy hands I commend them,
Pontius Pilate."

For in a pinch can I get
360   More than they that swink and sweat
        All the long day.

Thus it fell to my lot, Gill, I had such grace.
WIFE: It were a foul blot to be hanged for the case.
MAK: But I have escaped, Gill, a far narrower place.
WIFE: Yet so long goes the pot to the water, men say,
        At last
Comes it home broken.
MAK: Well know I the token,
        But let it never be spoken;
370   But come and help fast.

I would he were slain; I want to eat.
This twelvemonth have I not ta'en of one sheep's
        meat.
WIFE: Should they come ere he's slain, and hear the
        sheep bleat—
MAK: Then might I be ta'en! That puts me in a heat!
        Go bar
The gate door.
WIFE: Yes, Mak,
380   For if they come at thy back—
MAK: Then might I pay for the pack!
May the devil us warn.

WIFE: A good trick have I spied, since thou ken none.
Here shall we him hide till they be gone—
In my cradle abide. Let me alone,
And I shall lie beside in childbed, and groan.
MAK: Thou hast said;
And I'll say thou was light°
Of a male child this night.
390 WIFE: It's luck I was born bright,
        And cleverly bred.

For shrewdness this trick can't be surpassed;
Yet a woman's advice always helps at the last!
Before they 'gin to spy, hurry thou fast.
MAK: Unless I come ere they rise, they'll blow a loud
        blast!
        I'll go sleep.

(MAK *returns to the shepherds and resumes his place.*)

Yet sleeps all this company;
And I shall go stalk privily,
400   As it had never been me
        That carried their sheep.

FIRST SHEPHERD: *Resurrex a mortuis!*° Take hold of my
        hand.
Judas carnas dominus!° I can not well stand;
My foot sleeps, by Jesus; and I'm dry as sand.
I thought we had laid us near English land.

_____

light, delivered.   These lines are in mock-Latin.

SECOND SHEPHERD: Ah, yea!
I slept so well, I feel
As fresh as an eel,
As light on my heel   410
        As leaf on a tree.

THIRD SHEPHERD: Lord bless us all! My body's all
        a-quake!
My heart jumps from my skin, sure and that's no
        fake.
Who makes all this din? So my head aches.
I'll teach him something. Hark, fellows, awake!
        We were four.
See ye aught of Mak now?
FIRST SHEPHERD: We were up ere thou.   420
SECOND SHEPHERD: Man, I give God a vow,
        That he went nowhere.

THIRD SHEPHERD: I dreamed he was lapped in a gray
        wolf's skin.
FIRST SHEPHERD: So many are wrapped
        now—namely, within.
THIRD SHEPHERD: When we had so long napped,
        methought he did begin
A fat sheep to trap; but he made no din.
SECOND SHEPHERD: Be still!   430
Thy dream makes thee brood;
It's but fancy, by the rood.
FIRST SHEPHERD: Now God turn all to good,
        If it be his will!

SECOND SHEPHERD: Rise, Mak! For shame! Thou liest
        right long.
MAK: Now Christ's holy name be us among!
What is this? By Saint James, I may not move
        along!
I think I be the same. Ah! my neck has lain wrong   440
        Enough (*They help* MAK *up.*)
Mickle thanks! Since yestere'en,
Now, by Saint Stephen,
I was flayed with a dream
        That my heart did cuff.

I thought Gill began to croak and labor full sad,
Indeed at the first cock had borne a young lad
To increase our flock. Guess whether I'm glad;
I am now more in hock than ever I had.
        Ah, my head!   450
A house full of bairns!
'Devil knock out their brains!
For father is the pains,
        And little bread!

I must go home, by your leave, to Gill, as I thought.
I pray you look in my sleeve that I steal naught;
I am loath you to grieve or from you take aught.

THIRD SHEPHERD: Go forth; ill might thou live! Now
 would I we sought,
460   This morn,
 That we had all our store.
FIRST SHEPHERD: But I will go before;
 Let us meet.
SECOND SHEPHERD: Where?
THIRD SHEPHERD: At the crooked thorn.

(MAK *crosses to his cottage.*)

MAK: Undo this door, here! How long shall I stand?
WIFE: Who makes such a stir? Go walk in quicksand!
MAK: Ah, Gill, what cheer? It is I, Mak, your
 husband.
470 WIFE: Then may we see here the devil in a band,
 Sir Guile.
 Lo, he comes with a knot
 At the back of his crop.°
 I'll soon to my cot
 For a very long while.

MAK: Will ye hear what she makes to get her a gloze?°
 She does naught but plays, and wiggles her toes.
WIFE: Why, who wanders? Who wakes? Who comes?
 Who goes?
480 Who brews? Who bakes? What makes me this hose?
 And then,
 It's a pity to behold,
 Now in hot, now in cold,
 Full of woe is the household
 That wants a woman.

But what end has thou made with the shepherds,
 Mak?
MAK: The last word that they said, when I turned my
 back,
490 They would look that they had their sheep, count
 the pack.
 I'm sure they'll not be glad to find one they lack,
 Pardie.
 But howsoever it goes,
 They will surely suppose,
 From me the trouble 'rose,
 And cry out upon me.
 But thou must do as thou hight.°

WIFE: Of course I will.
500 I shall swaddle him right; you trust in your Gill.
 If it were a worse plight, yet could I help still.
 I will lie down straight. Come, cover me.
MAK: I will.
WIFE: Behind!
 It may be a narrow squeak.
MAK: Yes, if too close they peak,
 Or if the sheep should speak!
WIFE: 'Tis then time to whine.

---

knot . . . crop, an allusion to hanging.   *gloze,* an excuse.
hight, promised.

Hearken when they call; for they will come anon.°
Come and make ready all, and sing on thine own;   510
Sing lullaby thou shall, for I must groan
And cry out by the wall on Mary and John,
 For sore.
Sing a lullaby, fast,
Like thou sang at our last;
If I play a false cast,
 Trust me no more!

(*The* SHEPHERDS *meet at the crooked hawthorn.*)

THIRD SHEPHERD: Ah, Coll, good morn! Why sleep
 thou not?
FIRST SHEPHERD: Alas, that ever I was born! We have   520
 a foul blot.
 A fat lamb have we lorn.°
THIRD SHEPHERD: Marry, God forbid!
SECOND SHEPHERD: Who should do us that scorne?
 That were a foul spot.
FIRST SHEPHERD: Some shrew.
 I have sought with my dogs
 All Horbury Bogs,
 And with fifteen hogs
 Found I but one ewe.   530

THIRD SHEPHERD: Now trust me if ye will; by Saint
 Thomas of Kent,
 Either Mak or Gill was at that assent.
FIRST SHEPHERD: Peace, man, be still! I saw when he
 went.
 Thou slanders him ill. Thou ought to repent.
 Good speed.
SECOND SHEPHERD: Now if ever I lie,
 If I should even here die,
 I would say it were he   540
 That did that same deed.

THIRD SHEPHERD: Go we thither, I rede,° at a running
 trot.
 I shall never eat bread till the truth I've got.
FIRST SHEPHERD: Nor drink, in my heed, until we
 solve this plot.
SECOND SHEPHERD: Till we know all, indeed, I will
 rest no jot,
 My brother!
 One thing I will plight: 550
 Till I see him in sight
 Shall I never sleep one night
 Where I do another.

(*At* MAK's *house they hear* GILL *groan and* MAK *sing a
lullaby.*)

THIRD SHEPHERD: Will ye hear how they hack? Our
 sir likes to croon.

---

anon, soon.   *lorn,* lost.   *rede,* advise.

FIRST SHEPHERD: Heard I never one crack so clear out
of tune!
Call on him.
SECOND SHEPHERD: Mak! Undo your door soon.
560 MAK: Who is that spake as it were high noon
On loft?
Who is that, I say?
THIRD SHEPHERD: Good fellows, were it day.
MAK: As far as ye may,
Good, speak soft,

Over a sick woman's head that is ill at ease;
I had rather be dead e'er she had any dis-ease.
WIFE: Go to another place! I may not well wheeze.
Each foot that ye tread goes to make me sneeze,
570   So "he-e-e-e'."
FIRST SHEPHERD: Tell us, Mak, if ye may,
How fare ye, I say?
MAK: But are ye in town today?
Now how fare ye?

Ye have run in the mire, and are all wet yet.
I shall make you a fire, if ye will sit.
A nurse would I hire, and never doubt it.
But at my present hire—well, I hope for a bit
In season.
580 I've more bairns than ye knew,
And sure the saying is true,
"We must drink as we brew,"
And that's but reason.

I would ye dined ere ye go. Methinks that ye sweat.
SECOND SHEPHERD: Nay, that mends not our mood,
neither drink nor meat.
MAK: Why, what ails you sir?
THIRD SHEPHERD: Yea, our sheep that we get
Are stolen as they go. Our loss is not sweet.
590 MAK: Sirs, drink!
Had I been there,
Someone had paid full dear.
FIRST SHEPHERD: Some men think that ye were;
And that makes us think.

SECOND SHEPHERD: Mak, some men say that it should
be ye.
THIRD SHEPHERD: Either ye or your spouse; who else
could it be?
MAK: Now, if ye suspect us, either Gill or me,
600   Come and rip our house, and then ye may see
Who had her.
If I any sheep got
Any cow or stott°—
And Gill, my wife, rose not
Since here she laid her.

As I am true and leal,° to God here I pray.
That this be the first meal that I shall eat this day.
FIRST SHEPHERD: Mak, as I have weal,° have a care, I
say:
"He learned timely to steal that could not say nay." 610
WIFE: I swelt!°
Out, thieves from my home!
Ye come to rob us, ye drones!
MAK: Hear ye not how she groans?
Your heart should melt.

WIFE: Out, thieves, from my bairn! Get out of the
door!
MAK: Knew ye what she had borne, your hearts
would be sore.
Ye do wrong, I you warn, that thus come before   620
To a woman that has borne. But I say no more.
WIFE: Ah, my middle!
I pray to God so mild,
If ever I you beguiled,
Let me eat this child
That lies in this cradle.

MAK: Peace, woman, for God's pain and cry not so!
Thou shalt hurt thy brain, and make me full of
woe.
SECOND SHEPHERD: I think our sheep be slain. Think 630
you not so?
THIRD SHEPHERD: All work we in vain; as well may we
go.
But, drat it,
I can find no flesh,
Hard nor nesh,°
Salt nor fresh,
But two empty platters.

There's no cattle but this, neither tame nor wild,
None, as have I bliss, that smells as he smelled.   640
WIFE: No, so God me bless, and give me joy of my
child!
FIRST SHEPHERD: We have marked amiss; I hold us
beguiled.
SECOND SHEPHERD: Sir, done.
Sir, Our Lady him save!
Is your child a knave?
MAK: Any lord might him crave,
This child as his son.

When he wakens, he skips, that a joy is to see.   650
THIRD SHEPHERD: In good time be his steps, and
happy they be!
Who were his godfathers, tell now to me?
MAK: So fair fall their lips!
FIRST SHEPHERD: Hark now, a lie!
MAK: So God them thank,

---

stott, bullock.

leal, loyal. weal, riches. swelt, faint. nesh, tender.

Parkin and Gibbon Waller, I say,
And gentle John Horn, in good faith,
He gave all the array
660   And promised a great shank.

SECOND SHEPHERD: Mak, friends will we be, for we
    are all one.
MAK: We! Now I hold for me, from you help get I
    none.
Farewell, all three! All glad were ye gone!

(*The* SHEPHERDS *go out.*)

THIRD SHEPHERD: Fair words may there be, but love
    there is none
This year.
FIRST SHEPHERD: Gave ye the child anything?
670 SECOND SHEPHERD: I trow,° not one farthing!
THIRD SHEPHERD: Fast back will I fling;
    Abide ye me here.

(*The* SHEPHERDS *re-enter the house.*)

Mak, take it to no grief, if I come to thy bairn.
MAK: Nay, thou does me mischief, and foul has thou
    fared.
THIRD SHEPHERD: The child will not grieve, that little
    day-star.
Mak, with your leave, let me give your bairn
    But sixpence.
680 MAK: Nay, go 'way; he sleeps.
THIRD SHEPHERD: Methinks he peeps.
MAK: When he wakens he weeps!
    I pray you, go hence!

THIRD SHEPHERD: Give me leave him to kiss, and lift
    up the clout.°
What the devil is this? What a monstrous snout!
FIRST SHEPHERD: He is marked amiss. Let's not wait
    about.
SECOND SHEPHERD: "Ill spun cloth," iwis, "aye comes
690   foul out."
    Aye, so!
He is like to our sheep!
THIRD SHEPHERD: How, Gib, may I peep?
FIRST SHEPHERD: I trow, nature will creep
    Where it may not go!

SECOND SHEPHERD: This was a quaint fraud, and a far
    cast!
It should be noised abroad.
THIRD SHEPHERD: Yea, sirs, and classed.
700 Let's burn this bawd, and bind her fast.
Everyone will applaud to hang her at last,
    So shall thou.
Will ye see how they swaddle
His four feet in the middle?

Saw I never in cradle
    A horned lad ere now.

MAK: Peace, peace, I ask. You'll give the child a scare.
For I am his father, and yon woman him bare.
FIRST SHEPHERD: After what devil shall he be called?
    "Mak?" Lo, Mak's heir!   710
SECOND SHEPHERD: Let be all that. Now God give him
    care,
    I say.
WIFE: A pretty child is he
    To sit on a woman's knee;
    A dilly-downe, pardie,
    To make a father gay.

THIRD SHEPHERD: I know him by the ear-mark; that's
    a good token.
MAK: I tell you, sirs, hark! His nose was broken;   720
Later told me a clerk that he was forespoken.°
FIRST SHEPHERD: Liar! You deserve to have your
    noddle broken!
    Get a weapon.
WIFE: He was taken by an elf,
    I saw it myself;
When the clock struck twelve
    He was misshapen.

SECOND SHEPHERD: Ye two are well made to lie in the
    same bed.   730
THIRD SHEPHERD: Since they maintain their theft, let's
    see them both dead.
MAK: If I do wrong again, cut off my head!
    I'm at your will.
FIRST SHEPHERD: Sirs, take this plan, instead,
    For this trespass:
We'll neither curse nor fight,
Quarrel nor chide,
But seize him tight
    And cast him in canvas.   740

(*They toss* MAK *in a sheet and go back to the fields.*)

FIRST SHEPHERD: Lord, but I am sore; I feel about to
    burst.
In faith, I may no more; therefore will I rest.
SECOND SHEPHERD: As a sheep of seven score he
    weighed in my fist.
Now to sleep anywhere methinks were the best.
THIRD SHEPHERD: Now I pray you,
    Let's lie down on this green.
FIRST SHEPHERD: Oh, these thieves are so keen.
THIRD SHEPHERD: Let's forget what has been,   750
    So I say you. (*They sleep.*)

(*An* ANGEL *sings "Gloria in excelsis"; then let him say.*)

ANGEL: Rise, herd-men kind! For now is he born

---

trow, assert as true; admit.   *clout,* cloth.   *forespoken,* bewitched.

That shall take from the fiend what Adam had
   lorn:
That devil to shame this night is he born;
God is made your friend now at this morn.
   He behests
   To Bethlehem go ye,
   Where lies the Free;°
760   In a manger he'll be
   Between two beasts.

FIRST SHEPHERD: This was a sweet voice as any I've
   heard.
   A wonder enough to make a man scared.
SECOND SHEPHERD: To speak of God's son from on
   high he dared.
   All the wood on the moor with lightning glared,
   Everywhere.
THIRD SHEPHERD: He said the babe lay
770   In Bethlehem today.
FIRST SHEPHERD: That star points the way.
   Let us seek him there.

SECOND SHEPHERD: Say, what was his song? Heard ye
   not how he cracked it,
   Three briefs to a long?°
THIRD SHEPHERD: Yea, marry, he hacked it;
   Was no crotchet° wrong, nor nothing that lacked it.
FIRST SHEPHERD: For to sing us among, right as he
   knacked it°
780   I can.
SECOND SHEPHERD: Let's see how ye croon.
   Can ye bark at the moon?
THIRD SHEPHERD: Hold your tongues, have done!
FIRST SHEPHERD: Hark after, then!

SECOND SHEPHERD: To Bethlehem he bade that we
   should go;
   I am full afeared that we have been too slow.
THIRD SHEPHERD: Be merry and not sad; for sure this
   we know,
790   This news means joy to us men below,
   Of no joy.
FIRST SHEPHERD: Therefore thither hie we,
   Be we wet and weary,
   To that child and that lady.
   We must see this boy.

SECOND SHEPHERD: We find by the prophecy—let be
   your din!
   Of David and Isaiah and others of their kin,
   They prophesied by clergy that in a virgin
800   Should he light and lie, to slacken our sin
   And slake it,
   Our Race from woe.

For Isaiah said so:
   "Ecce virgo
      Concipiet"° a child that is naked.

THIRD SHEPHERD: Full glad may we be that this is that
   day
   Him lovely to see, who rules for aye.
   Lord, happy I'd be if I could say
   That I knelt on my knee so that I might pray   810
      To that child.
   But the angel said,
   He was poorly arrayed,
   And in a manger laid,
      Both humble and mild.

FIRST SHEPHERD: Patriarchs and prophets of old were
   torn
   With yearning to see this child that is born.
   They are gone full clean, and their trouble they've
   lorn.   820
   But we shall see him, I ween,° ere it be morn,
      To token.
   When I see him and feel,
   Then know I full well
   It is true as steel
      That prophets have spoken:

   To so poor as we are that he would appear,
   To find us and tell us by his messenger!
SECOND SHEPHERD: Go we now, let us fare, for the
   place is near.   830
THIRD SHEPHERD: I am ready, prepared; let us go
   with good cheer
      To that bright
   Lord, if thy will be—
   We are simple all three—
   Grant us some kind of glee
      To comfort thy wight.° (They enter the stable.)

FIRST SHEPHERD: Hail, comely and clean! Hail, young
   child!
   Hail, Maker, as I mean, born of maiden so mild!   840
   Thou has cursed, I ween, the devil so wild;
   The false guiler of men, now goes he beguiled.
      Lo, he merry is!
   Look, he laughs, the sweeting!
   Well, to this meeting
   I bring as my greeting
      A bob of cherries!

SECOND SHEPHERD: Hail, sovereign Savior, our
   ransom thou hast bought!

---

the Free, The Divine One. **Three . . . long,** musical
notes. **crotchet,** a quarter note. **knacked it,** did it cleverly.

Ecce . . . Concipiet, "Behold, a virgin shall conceive," Cf.
Isaiah, 7, 14; *St. Luke,* 1, 31; and *St. Matthew,* 1, 23,   **I ween,**
I imagine. **wight,** man.

850 Hail, noble child and flower, that all things has
    wrought!
Hail, full of favor, that made all of naught!
Hail! I kneel and I cower. A bird have I brought
    To my bairn.
Hail, little tiny mop!
Of our creed thou art crop.
I would drink of thy cup,
    Little day-star.

THIRD SHEPHERD: Hail, darling dear, thou art God
860   indeed!
I pray thee be near when that I have need.
Hail! Sweet is thy cheer! My heart would bleed
To see thee lie here in so poor a weed,
    With no pennies.
I would give thee my all,
Though I bring but a ball;
Have and play thee withal,
    And go to the tennis.

MARY: The Father of Heaven, God omnipotent,
870 That set all in seven days, his Son has sent.

My name he has blessed with peace ere he went.
I conceived him through grace as God had meant;
    And now he's born.
I shall pray him so
To keep you all from woe!
Tell this wherever ye go,
    And mind this morn.

FIRST SHEPHERD: Farewell, lady, so fair to behold,
    With thy child on thy knee!
SECOND SHEPHERD: Still he lies full cold.   880
    Lord, how favored I be. Now we go forth, behold.
THIRD SHEPHERD: Forsooth, already this seems a
    thing told
    Full oft.
FIRST SHEPHERD: What grace we have found!
SECOND SHEPHERD: Spread the tidings around!
THIRD SHEPHERD: To sing are we bound:
    Let take aloft! (They sing.)

Figure 16. Mak steals the sheep while the three shepherds are sleeping in the Mermaid Theatre production of *The Second Shepherds' Play,* directed by Sally Miles and Colin Ellis, London, 1961. (Photograph: the Mermaid Theatre.)

Figure 17. The three shepherds pay a visit to Mak and Gill in the Mermaid Theatre production of *The Second Shepherds' Play*, directed by Sally Miles and Colin Ellis, London, 1961. (Photograph: the Mermaid Theatre.)

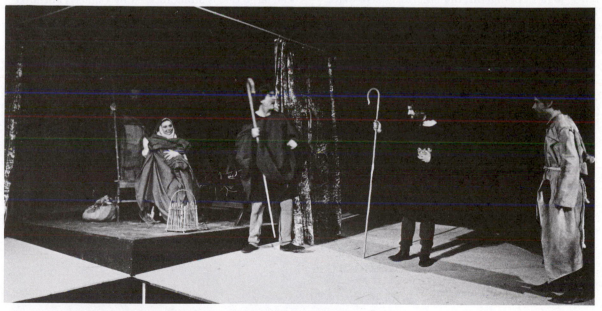

Figure 18. The three shepherds journey to Bethlehem to celebrate the birth of Christ in the Mermaid Theatre production of *The Second Shepherds' Play*, directed by Sally Miles and Colin Ellis, London, 1961. (Photograph: the Mermaid Theatre.)

Staging of *The Wakefield Mystery Plays*

REVIEW OF THE MERMAID THEATRE
PRODUCTION, 1961, by BAMBER GASCOIGNE

The mystery plays now being performed at the Mermaid are over 500 years old—yet they are probably nearer to their present audience than they could have been to any since the sixteenth century. The stressed and alliterative poetry sounds familiar to us because Eliot has stretched back to sink his roots in it, and the theatrical convention is little short of Brechtian.

The excellent Mermaid staging of these Wakefield plays has an authentic medieval flavour. Noah, for example, after receiving the measurements of the ark from God, strips off his coat and sets to. Within a very few lines, muttered to himself as he works, he has erected a splendidly painted boat out of four or five preconstructed pieces. The bow and stern slide into the central hull, then the 'castle' fits neatly on the top. Noah stands back in wonder to admire such God-given progress and the audience burst into delighted applause. Later, when the rain begins, he lets down a flap on the front of the boat to reveal painted waves; and when he is chasing his reluctant wife past these waves they both laboriously gather up their skirts and prance high-stepping through the imagined water. This theatricality, making no attempt at illusion, has endless delights of its own—the sight, for example, of two detachable fig leaves waiting on a painted fig-tree for their moment of glory. And, oddly enough, knowing the story heightens the suspense rather than dissipates it (this is another of those paradoxes which are at the root of the success of Brecht's theatre); knowing that Lazarus will appear from the tomb intensifies the drama because it focuses our attention during the early part of the scene. When he does appear, this Mermaid Lazarus, pale, thin and stiff, he delivers a magnificent *memento mori* which will not lightly be forgotten.

The formalism of the comedy scenes becomes, in the serious parts, an admirable and moving formality—a matter of the deepest simplicity. And always, brilliantly, the poetry changes to define the mood. One witnesses a craftsman's carpentry of dramatic language, something used by Eliot in *Murder in the Cathedral* but never again heard of since he buried his muse in the naturalistic drawing room. Martial Rose, the adaptor, faced with countless Middle English and dialect words in the original, has made a version which is always comprehensible without imposing awkward modern phrases and without, hardest of all, spoiling the intricate rhythms and rhymes. The large cast is admirably led by Daniel Thorndike (Noah and Joseph), Donald Eccles (Satan), Gloria Dolskie (The Virgin) and James Bolam (Jesus). 'Cultural' considerations apart, this pageant is an entertainment which shouldn't be missed.

MASTER PETER PATELAN

ca. 1465

Master Peter Patelan is undoubtedly the creation of one of the Parisian legal societies, which devoted themselves during the fourteenth, fifteenth, and sixteenth centuries not only to the practice of law, but also to the production of farce. The farces they produced, like those of other French guilds, took several distinctly different forms. Some were burlesque sermons—playful inversions of religious ceremony and conduct—that sustained the spirit of mock celebration minor clergy had been carrying on since the twelfth century in a post-Christmas festival known as the Feast of Fools. Others were topical satires, such as *The Prince of Fools* (1512), which mocked the political and religious quarrel of Louis XII and Pope Julius II. But the richest and most influential tradition of medieval French farce took its subject matter from the broad spectacle of human folly and vice. That spectacle, which had been depicted in folk stories and folk plays, became increasingly visible with the growth of medieval cities, and it gave rise to innumerable farces about lascivious priests, unfaithful wives, gullible husbands, incompetent doctors, corrupt lawyers, rich beggars, crafty peasants, greedy merchants, and similarly satiric character types—tricking and being tricked by one another. No other medieval farce portrays that spectacle so vividly and so vivaciously as *Master Peter Patelan*.

Its farcical mastery was quickly recognized, for though it was written and produced sometime around 1465, it had already been published in six different editions by the end of the fifteenth century. In the sixteenth century the number of new editions ran to more than twenty, and in the seventeenth century it worked its influence on the comedies of Molière. From the eighteenth century to this day, it has been a standard work in the repertory of the Comédie Française. It has repeatedly been translated, imitated, adapted, even turned into a comic opera. Although it has often been translated into English prose, its verse form and the verbal games in its verse have never been reproduced in English until the recent translation made by Kate Franks, reprinted here for the first time.

The verse form of *Master Peter Patelan*, like that of most medieval French farces, consists of rhymed pairs of eight syllable lines, ingeniously arranged so that the last line of one character's dialogue rhymes with the first line of the next. That verse form is largely responsible for establishing and sustaining the pace and mood of medieval French farce. The eight-syllable line, for example, is a relatively short line that produces a very rapidly paced dialogue, so that everything seems to be taking place just a bit faster than it does in normal human situations. On top of this effect, the patter of rhyme not only within the dialogue of a single character but also between the speeches of all the characters makes everyone in medieval French farce sound a good deal more agile and cocky than people in ordinary life. They not only sound this way, but they act it, for they live almost entirely by their wits.

The wittiest and most impudent crew of rascals ever gathered together in medieval French farce are the characters of *Master Peter Patelan*. Like most characters in medieval farce they are all trying to get the better of one another—to get more for something than it is worth, like the draper, or to get something for nothing, like Peter Patelan and the shepherd. Because they live by their wits, their methods of getting what they want inevitably require them to turn to one trick of language or another, to deceive one person or another. And the tricks they play are at once verbally farfetched yet entirely plausible, or at least plausible enough to succeed. Patelan's outlandish heap of compliments to the draper, for example, would be recognized by almost anyone as barefaced flattery, but the draper himself is so incredibly vain that he is completely taken in by Patelan's sweet-talking routine, like the crow taken in by the fox. All the verbal games—from the monosyllabic bleats of the shepherd to the polysyllabic ravings of Patelan—are ingeniously suited to the dramatic situation. They were also suited to their medieval audience, for the Parisian lawyers who witnessed the play would have been able to follow Patelan, as the ignorant draper is not, through all his linguistic twists and turns in the mad scene, and they would have taken special pleasure in all the legal shenanigans during the courtroom scene. But unquestionably their greatest pleasure would have been to witness Patelan—one of their own kind—taken in at the end by one of his own legal tricks.

The spectacle those lawyers might have seen is suggested by photographs from the 1957 Comédie Française production (see Figures 19 and 20), which show the medieval style of costuming and backdrops that the Comédie has evidently sought to maintain in its staging at least since 1941, judging from reviews following the text. Although the medieval lawyers would have been amused by the way Patelan gets his comeuppance, they would not have been completely surprised by the fact that he is finally deceived, for the tricking of the trickster was a long standing routine in medieval French farce. That same basic routine can be found in the earliest surviving example of French farce, *The Blind Man and the Boy,* a work of the late thirteenth century. Its plot is delightfully simple, consisting merely of the various impudent ways in which a young waif takes advantage of a blind man who has been using his blindness to take advantage of others. Most medieval French farces are just as short and simple—and occasionally lewd—as *The Blind Man and the Boy.* Few are as long, and none is so sophisticated as *Master Peter Patelan.* Its plot is as tricky as the characters themselves, incorporating not one but three large-scale tricking routines, each of which is a variation on the other. It is not surprising that the director of a recent American production compared its plot to the design of a fugue and staged it so as to accentuate the variations. Variations—in plot, in character, in language—are, indeed, the major source of its delight, and, as in any good fugue or any truly good joke, its last variation tops all the others.

MASTER PETER PATELAN

TRANSLATED BY KATE FRANKS

CHARACTERS

PETER PATELAN, *a lawyer*
WILLAMETTE, *his wife*
WILLIAM JOSHOMBE, *the draper*
TIBALT LAMBLING, *his shepherd*
JUDGE
ATTENDANTS

SCENE

The farce of Master Peter Patelan *is set in Paris during the latter part of the fifteenth century. Its actions take place in three locations: Patelan's house, a draper's stall at one of* the city fairs, *and the streets of Paris where, among other things, court was held.*

These three places are represented at fixed points "onstage" throughout the play, with Patelan's house being located on one side of the playing area, the draper's stall on the opposite side, and the streets being represented by a large open space between the two edifices.

The play's characters move from one to another of these places as the plot unfolds, and as the dialogue indicates. As a rule, they smooth their transitions from one point in time and space to another (and also the play's development from one dramatic situation to another) by "talking all the while."

(MASTER PETER *begins.*)

PATELAN: Sweet Blesséd Mary! Willamette,
  For all the pains that I have met
  In scrounging this and scraping that,
  Not one penny do we now have.
  There was a time when I had pleadings.
WILLAMETTE: By Our Lady, I was just thinking
  Of how they sang for you in court,
  But no one holds you now one-fourth
  So wise as they were used to do.
10 I've seen when all men wanted you
  On their side, so they'd win their squabbles.
  Now in all quarters you are labelled
  'The Counsellor Under the Clock.'°
PATELAN: Well, I don't mean to brag, but there's not
  To be found, within the jurisdiction
  Where we hold our deliberations,
  A wiser man, except the mayor.
WILLAMETTE: The mayor has also read a grammar
  And learnt a lengthy piece like clerks.
20 PATELAN: But when I set my mind to work,
  Whose case is not reduced to tatters?
  So what if I've not learnt my letters
  But a little? Why, I dare say
  That I know how to chant my way
  Through the Good Book with our pastor
  As well as if I'd been a master
  As long as Charlemagne in Spain.
WILLAMETTE: What's that worth to us? Not a grain.
  We're both dying of slow starvation,

The original reads 'advocat dessoubz l'orme,' the advo-cate under the elm, which is to say, an out-of-work lawyer lounging around the public square in the hope of snaring clients.

Our robes are naught but perforations,   30
  And we've no way of knowing how
  We ever can replace them now.
  Of what worth, eh, is your proficience?
PATELAN: Silence, woman! Upon my conscience,
  If I but want to try my wits,
  I'll find like that! where we can get
  Some brand new robes and hoods as well.
  God be pleased, we'll escape this hell
  And be restored within the hour.
  Lord! God works wonders in an hour!   40
  If it so happens I decide
  To forward my practice and apply
  Myself, they'll never find my equal.
WILLAMETTE: By James, indeed they won't. At swindles,
  Truly, you are a right good master.
PATELAN: By that same God who had me fathered,
  More so at lawful soliciting!
WILLAMETTE: Upon my faith, more so at swindling!
  How often, truly, I've noted it;   50
  For truth to tell, though illiterate
  And lacking common sense, you're said
  To have about the shrewdest head
  That does exist in all the parish.
PATELAN: There's none can lift his case's merits
  To my heights in solicitation.
WILLAMETTE: God help me, more in swindle-ation!
  For that, at least, you've some repute.
PATELAN: So have those whose backs carry suits
  Of camelcloth and fancy satin,   60
  Who say they are of my profession
  And yet aren't lawyers by one tittle.
  Let's leave in peace this pointless drivel,
  I must be going to the fair.
WILLAMETTE: To the fair?
PATELAN: By Saint John, yes, there—

'To the fair, my pretty merchant!'°
Would it displease you if I purchased
Some cloth or else some other trifles
70   Which would relieve our household troubles?
We've not one robe worth anything.
WILLAMETTE: You've not one penny to your name,
What will you do?
PATELAN: You'll never guess.
Pretty lady, if you don't get
Ample cloth for the two of us,
Say freely I'm not worth men's trust.
What shade do you think's prettier?
Grey-green? Or brown do you prefer?
80   Or something else? I must be sure.
WILLAMETTE: Whatever shade you can procure.
A beggar cannot choose his meat.
PATELAN (while counting on his fingers)°: For you, two
        and a half, for me
Three yards, or even better, four.
This comes—
WILLAMETTE: I'd figure one thing more:
Who the devil will give you credit?
PATELAN: What do you care about who'll do it?
90   He'll trust me with them for a payment
He'll not get till the Day of Judgment,
For sooner it shall never be.
WILLAMETTE: Then go, my love, before we see
Another's back bear it away!
PATELAN: I'll purchase either green or grey,
And for a cover, Willamette,
Three-fourths of brown I'll need to get,
Or else a yard.
WILLAMETTE: Lord, how you think!
100   Go! And let him buy you a drink,
This moneylender, if you find him!
PATELAN: Take care of things!
WILLAMETTE: Good God, what merchant?!
Well, God be pleased, he'll not see through it.
PATELAN: Isn't he in? I start to doubt it.
Ah, there he is, by Blesséd Mary!
Quite lost among his piles of drapery.
God be with you!
WILLIAM JOSHOMBE (DRAPER): God give you joy.
110   PATELAN: So help me God, my rest's been spoiled
Of late by a great wish to see you.
How does your health hold up, I pray you?
Are you quite hale and strong, good William?
DRAPER: Yes, by God.
PATELAN: Here, this hand is open!
How goes it with you?

Patelan is evidently quoting a line of a poem or singing
a line from a song.
    Other than the *Maitre Pierr commence* at the play's
beginning and the *Explicit* at its end, this is the only stage
direction in the text.

DRAPER: Quite well, truly,
As well as anyone could wish me.
And you?
PATELAN: By the Apostle Peter,   120
Like you I'm just as well as ever.
So, you're enjoying life?
DRAPER: Indeed,
But—and this you'd better believe—
Merchants don't always have their way.
PATELAN: How goes the merchandise these days?
Can't one say grace nor graze a pasture?
DRAPER: God help me, I don't know, good master;
It's always, 'Hey you, hurry up!'
PATELAN: Ah, what a knowing man he was,   130
May God see that his soul is aided—
Your father's I mean. Gracious Lady!
As I see you, it quite appears
That this is he before me here.
What a merchant he was! And wise!
You resemble him round the eyes,
By God, just like a perfect picture!
If God would ever show a creature
Mercy, may He true pardon lay
Upon that soul.   140
DRAPER: Amen, I say,
And ours as well when it shall please Him.
PATELAN: Upon my faith, he very often,
And at great length, foretold to me
The times that one sees presently.
Many's the time I have remembered
His words. Besides, he was considered
One of the best—
DRAPER: Sit down, good sir.
It is high time I said these words,   150
But then by nature I'm so gracious.
PATELAN: Oh, I'm fine, by that Flesh most precious.
He had—
DRAPER: Truly, you'll take a seat.
PATELAN: Gladly. 'Ah, what wonders you'll see,'
He said to me, 'during your years.'
So help me God, look at those ears,
That nose, that mouth, those selfsame eyes!
No, never was a child more like
His father. Even the cleft chin!   160
Why, you're the spitting image of him!
And who should ever tell your mother
You were not the son of your father
Must sorely need to raise contentions.
Without a doubt, I can't imagine
How Nature in her divers works
Formed two faces so similar
And one like the other so endowed.
Indeed, had anyone spit out
The two of you against a wall   170
In the same way and shape and all,
You'd still not differ one iota.
Now then, sir, the good Laurentia,

Your handsome aunt, she has not died?
DRAPER: Lord, not she!
PATELAN: What a handsome sight
  I thought her, so tall and straight and gracious!
  By the Mother of God most precious,
  You do resemble her in growth
180 Like someone carved you both from snow.
  In all this land there's not, I think,
  A lineage that's more clearly linked.
  The more I see—By God the Father,
  Look at you there: look at your father!
  You match each other like two drips
  Of water, I've no doubt of it.
  Ah, he was a gallant bachelor,
  That goodly man, and lent his store
  Like that! to anyone who sued.
190 God pardon him! That kind heart used
  To laugh with me till it nigh burst.
  Would to Jesus Christ that the worst
  Of this poor world resembled him;
  They'd not be stealing nor robbing then,
  One from another as they do now.
  My, but this cloth is well turned out!
  How soft it is, how smooth and supple!
DRAPER: I had it made so as a special,
  Spun with the wool from my own sheep.
200 PATELAN: My, what a manager you be!
  If you tried, you'd not hide your birth;
  Your body'd never cease to work
  And slave from sunrise until starlight.
DRAPER: What would you have? One must have
    foresight
  If one would live, and bear with troubles.
PATELAN: Was it dyed in the wool, this textile?
  It feels as strong as cordovan.
DRAPER: That's a very good cloth from Rouen,
210 I promise you, and finely loomed.
PATELAN: Now truly I see that I am doomed,
  For I had not the least intention
  Of getting cloth upon this errand.
  By the Passion of Our Sweet Lord!
  I'd set aside about four score
  In crowns to buy back a property,
  But you'll get twenty or thirty—I see
  That all too clearly—for the shade
  Pleases me so, it makes me ache.
220 DRAPER: Crowns, you say?° Could things be arranged
  So those from whom you hope to gain
  This property would take plain cash?
PATELAN: Why yes, of course, if I wished that.
  All's one to me, regarding money.

What kind of cloth is this? Truly,
  The more I look, the more I dote.
  In short, I have to have a coat
  Of it and for my wife the same.
DRAPER: To be sure, cloth is dear as cream.
  Still, you shall have some if you want.   230
  I warn you, ten or twenty francs are sunk
  Like that!
PATELAN: Let it cost what it may!
  I've other pennies never claimed
  Nor seen by father nor by mother.
DRAPER: God be praised for it! By Saint Peter,
  I'd not be sad to have a piece!
PATELAN: Well, this piece so arouses me
  It's needful that I get some.
DRAPER: Tut,   240
  It's needful to decide how much
  You want of it before we settle.
  Everything's at your disposal,
  The whole pile right down to the table,
  Though you lacked heads or tails to wager.
PATELAN: I know that well, sir, thanks to you.
DRAPER: Here, do you like this light sky blue?
PATELAN: First of all, how much will it cost me
  To purchase the first yard? God must be
  Paid with the first, it's only right.   250
  Here's my halfpenny. Let us bind
  Ourselves to nothing but in God's name.°
DRAPER: By God, a Man of Good said the same,
  You've made this weary soul feel blest.
  Would you have me name my terms?
PATELAN: Yes.
DRAPER: Per yard, it sells at a cost to you
  Of twenty-four sous.
PATELAN: That won't do!
  Twenty-four sous? Blesséd Lady!   260
DRAPER: Upon this soul, that's what it cost me!
  That much I need before it's sold.
PATELAN: Lord, it's too much!
DRAPER: Ah, you don't know
  How high the price of cloth has risen.
  The livestock everywhere were frozen
  This winter in the awful cold.
PATELAN: Twenty! Make it twenty!
DRAPER: I hold
  I'll have for it just what I say.   270
  Now just you wait till Saturday,
  You'll see how much the fleece is bringing,
  Of which there used to be such plenty.
  It cost me at the Magdalene Fair
  Eight pieces for a wool I swear

Crowns were made of gold, and were considered a more valuable thing to possess than an equivalent cash amount of regular currency, which was made of less precious materials, such as copper or bronze.

Dropping a coin in the public almsbox to seal a bargain or to express one's intention to do business was a common practice; thus, Patelan is putting down his 'earnest' money, so the draper will think he is serious about buying cloth and has the means to do so.

I used to get for only four.
PATELAN: God's Blood, without haggling more
I'll buy it then since things go so.
Come now, measure!
280 DRAPER: Again, I'd know
How much of it you will be needing.
PATELAN: To figure that is very easy,
What width is it?
DRAPER: It's Brussels' width.°
PATELAN: Three yards for me, and then to fit
My wife—she's tall—two and a half.
That comes to six yards, doesn't that?
But no! What fledglings we lawyers are!
DRAPER: It only lacks but half a yard
290 For you to make it six precisely.
PATELAN: I'll take all six to make things tidy.
Besides, I also need a hood.
DRAPER: Take hold, we'll measure out the goods.
So, here they are with nothing short.
The first, and two, and three, and four,
And five, and six!°
PATELAN: Guts of Saint Peter!
Tit for tat!
DRAPER: Shall I measure over?
300 PATELAN: No-no, all a part of the game,
A little's lost, a little's gained
In merchandising. How much now
Does that come to?
DRAPER: We'll soon find out.
At four and twenty sous each one,
The six, nine francs.
PATELAN: That's a good one!
This is six crowns?
DRAPER: By God, you've hit it.
310 PATELAN: Now, sir, are you willing to credit
This sum till shortly, when you'll call
On me? Not 'credit'—You'll take all
At my door, in gold or else plain cash.
DRAPER: Lord! I'd be taken from my path
A lot in going by that way.
PATELAN: Ha! Your lips haven't parted for days
But that they didn't utter Gospel!
By Giles, the patron saint of cripples,
This is well said, 'You would be taken.'
320 That's just it! You'd never be liking
To come drink at my house with me.
However, you'll come drink this time.
DRAPER: Ha! By Saint James, I seldom find
Myself with one thing done but drinking.
I'd come but, as you know, crediting

Loom widths and therefore cloth widths varied; hence,
'Brussels' width' is equal to that cloth made on the looms of
Brussels.
During this measuring, a tug of war evidently takes
place, with Patelan trying to get, and the draper trying to
keep, as much yardage as each of them possibly can.

Brings bad luck at the day's first sale.
PATELAN: Will it suffice if your first sale's
In crowns of gold and not plain cash?
And if you eat my goose I ask,
By God, that my own wife has roasted? 330
DRAPER: (Truly, this man has got me cozened.)
I'll come and bring it. Go on before
And await me.
PATELAN: Nothing of the sort!
It shall not weigh me down one cent
Here under my arm.
DRAPER: Don't you fret.
It looks better, for business reasons,
That I bring it.
PATELAN: An ill season 340
May Saint Magdalene send my way
If you are put to such great pains!
This is well said, 'Under my arm.'
A pretty camel's hump it forms
For me! See, it's easily carried.
There'll be both drink and making merry
Before you go from my abode.
DRAPER: I pray that you'll give me my gold
The very minute I arrive.
PATELAN: I will—Ha! No, by God, not I 350
Until you've taken your repast
Most heartily, and so I'm glad
I've nothing on me I can pay.
This way, at least you'll come to taste
What wine I drink. Your late father
In passing always called out, 'Neighbor!'
'What say you?' or, 'How goes your work?'
But you don't hold the poor folk worth
A straw, you rich men getting richer.
DRAPER: By God, for that we are the poorer. 360
PATELAN: Indeed! Well, well, God keep! God keep!
Show up soon at the place agreed
And we'll drink well, I'll say no more.
DRAPER: This I shall do. Go on before,
And see I get gold!
PATELAN: Gold? What's this?
Gold? The Devil!—I never slipped,
Not once—Gold! May I see him hung!
He didn't sell on my terms once,
It went on his, right down the line. 370
However, he'll be paid on mine.
He must have gold? Let him be plated!
Would to God he had to go racing
Non-stop until he reached his goal-d.
Saint John! He'd have a longer road
Than runs from here to Pampelune.
DRAPER: They'll neither see the sun nor moon
For a year, those crowns he'll give to me—
Unless they're got by robbery.
Now he is not so hard a client 380
Who never met a harder merchant.
Go, Swindler, a fledgling you are

When, for twenty-four sous a yard,
You purchase cloth that's not worth twenty!
PATELAN: Do I have it?
WILLAMETTE: Have what?
PATELAN: Tell me,
What's become of your brave old dress?
WILLAMETTE: There's a great need for asking this!
390   What are you up to?
PATELAN: Nothing, my pet.
Do I have it? What I said I'd get?
Is it this cloth?
WILLAMETTE: Blesséd Virgin!
Now by the peril that my soul's in,
He comes from making a covenant!
Ye Gods! What will become of us?
Alas! Alas! Who'll pay for it?
PATELAN: Are you asking who shall do it?
400   By Saint John, it's been paid in full.
The merchant was in no way fooled,
Fair lass, who sold this cloth to me.
Hang me by this gorge if the deal's
Not spotless as a sack of plaster.
Ha! The wretched, villainous whoremaster
Is cinched around the ass for it!
WILLAMETTE: At what cost?
PATELAN: I don't owe one bit.
It's paid for, don't you fret, good dame.
410 WILLAMETTE: You'd not a penny to your name.
It's paid for? In what sort of money?
PATELAN: By God's Blood, I had money, lady,
I'd the coin of Paris for my means.
WILLAMETTE: This is well done! A pretty lien
Or else a note is in their coffers!
That's how you've seen this purchase covered,
And when the term agreed on's up,
They'll come! They shall collect from us!
What little we have shall all be taken!
420 PATELAN: By God's Blood, for what I've taken
It only cost me half a penny.
WILLAMETTE: Blessings be on you, Blesséd Mary—
Just half a penny? Impossible!
PATELAN: Here, pluck this eyeball from my skull
If he got or gets another thing,
No matter how sweetly he may sing.
WILLAMETTE: And who is he?
PATELAN: He is one William
Who has for a surname that of Joshombe,
430   Since you wish to be knowing it.
WILLAMETTE: But, the manner of getting it
For half a penny? And by what game?
PATELAN: For God's half-penny was it exchanged,
And, moreover, if I had said,
'Let's drink to it!' by this one pledge
My penny would have stayed with me.
Is it not well worked? God and he
Shall split this one half-penny among them,
If it seems to them a fair division,

For that is all they'll get for this thing,   440
No matter how ably they may sing
Or cry or go braving it about.
WILLAMETTE: How came he then to lend it out,
A man like him, who is so stubborn?
PATELAN: By Blesséd Mary, fairest virgin,
I armed and emblazoned him so much
He very nearly gave me the stuff.
I said to him that his late father
Was so gallant. Said I, 'Ah, brother,
Of what good parentage you are!'   450
'There's not a lineage in these parts,'
I said, 'more worthy to be praised.'
But I shall God Himself embrace
If he's not from a pack of poachers,
The most stubborn, villainous cutthroats
That do exist in all this kingdom.
'Ah,' said I, 'my good friend William,
How you resemble in your features,
In all, the looks of your good father!'
God knows how high I built him up   460
And at the same time deftly tucked
In comments on his drapery.
'Sweet Blesséd Mary!' then I squeaked,
'How he did lend his store with sweetness
To all who sued, and with such meekness!'
'You are,' I said, 'his spitting image.'
Ha! You always had to go wrenching
The teeth from that old villainous walrus
His late father and from that jackass
The son, before they'd lend one third   470
Of this or utter one good word.
But I braved it so and spoke so highly
That he, in the end, saw fit to lend me
Six yards.
WILLAMETTE: And never be paid back?
PATELAN: You had better believe just that.
Paid back? Pay him back the Devil!
WILLAMETTE: This all reminds me of the fable
Of the crow who on a cross sat perched
Five or six feet above the earth,   480
Holding a piece of cheese in his beak.
A fox came by and, seeing the cheese,
Thought to himself, 'How can I get it?'
Then right beneath the crow he settled.
'Ah,' he said, 'you've such pretty feathers!
And your song's so full of melody!'
The crow in his stupidity,
Hearing his song so highly praised,
Opened his beak at once to raise
A song. So, his cheese falls to earth,   490
And Master Fox puts his teeth to work,
Snaps it up and bears it away.°

   This is the well-known fable of Aesop, which by the time this play was written had passed into French folklore as the tale of Renard the fox.

So it is, I venture to say,
With this piece of cloth—You did nab him
With emblazoning and then trapped him
Into this by a pretty speech,
As did the fox to get the cheese.
You put the fool's muzzle in your noose.

PATELAN: He is supposed to come eat goose.
500   Now here's the game we'll need to play.
I'm sure the ass will come to bray
So right away he'll get his payment.
I have thought up a good arrangement:
It will serve me to lay my head,
As though I'm ill, upon my bed.
And then when he arrives you'll say,
'Ah, speak low!' and start to wail
And make a face as wan as swill.
'Alas!' you'll say, 'He has been ill
510   These past two months!'—or else six weeks—
And if he tells you, 'This can't be,
He came from my place just this minute,'
You'll say, 'Alas! This is not decent
Of you, this is no time for jesting!'
Then, leave me to give him a thrashing,
For he'll not get a thing besides.

WILLAMETTE: By that soul which in me resides,
I'll do my part without a hitch.
However, if you make a slip
520   And Justice catches you again,
I fear she'll see you meet an end
Twice as bad as that other rout.

PATELAN: Now peace! I know what I'm about,
Just do exactly as I say.

WILLAMETTE: Just remember that Saturday,
When they did put you in the stocks!
You know everyone came to mock
At you because of all your swindles.

PATELAN: Come now, stop talking all this drivel.
530   He's coming, we don't know what hour.
We must see that this cloth stays ours.
I'm going to bed.

WILLAMETTE: Yes, of course.

PATELAN: Don't laugh now.

WILLAMETTE: Nothing of the sort,
I shall be weeping hot, salt tears.

PATELAN: The two of us must never veer
From this, so he'll not see a thing.

DRAPER: I think it's time I had a drink
540   To my departure.° Ah, that won't do!
I have to drink and eat some goose,
By that saint of madmen, Matellan,°
At Master Peter Patelan's
And there pick up my tidy sum.

Then, as now, people drank 'one for the road' at the end of their workday. *Mattelan,* Saint Mathelin or Mathuran was a third-century priest who supposedly cured the mad.

At the very least, I'll snatch a plum
Without spending a cent. I'm going,
It's too late now to do more selling.
Ho there! Master Peter!

WILLAMETTE: Alas, sir,
For God's sake, if you've words to utter   550
Speak lower!

DRAPER: May God keep you, lady.

WILLAMETTE: Oh, lower!

DRAPER: But why?

WILLAMETTE: Heaven help me—

DRAPER: Where is he?

WILLAMETTE: Alas! Where should he be?

DRAPER: Who?

WILLAMETTE: Ah, master, cruel words these be!
Where he is—May God in His Grace   560
Be knowing! May He guard the place
Where he has been, that poor, poor martyr,
Eleven weeks without departure.

DRAPER: Of whom—

WILLAMETTE: Pardon, I dare not be raising
My voice, I think that he is resting.
He's a bit drowsy in the head.
Alas! He has been worn to death,
The poor, poor man!

DRAPER: Who?   570

WILLAMETTE: Master Peter!

DRAPER: Indeed! Didn't he come to barter
For six yards of cloth just this instant?

WILLAMETTE: Who, him?

DRAPER: He came back just this minute,
Within the quarter-hour I say.
Give me my leave, I find I stay
Too long. Here now, stop all this thrashing,
My money.

WILLAMETTE: Ha! Stop all this jesting!   580
This is no time to have a laugh.

DRAPER: Here, my money! Have you gone mad?
I need to have nine francs.

WILLAMETTE: Ah, William,
There's no need here to put your bells on,
Nor to be making a jester's jokes.
Go tell tales to your idle rogues,
If you would like to play the clown.

DRAPER: The Lord on High may I renounce
If I don't get nine francs?   590

WILLAMETTE: Alas, sir,
Not everyone's so fond of laughter
As you, nor of this kind of prating.

DRAPER: Speak, I pray you, without this trifling.
For Love's sweet sake, have Master Peter
Come to me.

WILLAMETTE: May misadventure
Dog you! Is this to last all day?

DRAPER: Is it not the case I'm in this place,
At Master Peter Patelan's?   600

WILLAMETTE: Yes. The curse of Saint Matellan,

My own aside, addle your brain!
Speak low!
DRAPER: The Devil come to reign!
Dare I not make such an inquiry?
WILLAMETTE: May God Above protect and guide me!
Low, if you'd not awaken him.
DRAPER: What low?! In the ear you want it then,
Or down in the well, or in the cellar?!
610 WILLAMETTE: Good God, how full you are of drivel!
This has always been your way out.
DRAPER: The Devil take me if I see how!
If I'm to speak low, name the way,
For when it comes to such debates
I've never studied in your books.
The truth is Master Peter took
Six yards of cloth from me today.
WILLAMETTE: What's this? Is this to last all day?
Give the Devil his due! Took what?
620 Ah, sir, would that the world strung up
Ones who lie. He's in such a pickle,
The poor, poor man, he's not been able
To leave his bed these eleven weeks.
Why plague us now with your deceits?
Is now a proper time for this?
You shall vacate these premises.
By Christ's Agonies, leave me be!
DRAPER: You keep saying I ought to speak
So low—Sainted, Blesséd Lady!
630 You're yelling!
WILLAMETTE: Upon my soul, you be
The one who can't talk without shrieking!
DRAPER: Speak then, and so I may be leaving,
Give me—
WILLAMETTE: Lower your voice, will you?
DRAPER: It's you who'll waken him, I tell you!
You are talking four times louder,
By God's Blood, than I've spoken ever.
I demand that you release me.
640 WILLAMETTE: What's this? I say, have you been
drinking?
Or lost your senses? God Our Father!
DRAPER: Drinking? If so, cursed be Saint Peter!
Here's a pretty accusation!
WILLAMETTE: Alas, lower!
DRAPER: I ask your payment,
By Saint George, for six yards of stuff,
Lady.
WILLAMETTE: Have someone make it up!
650 To whom is it you've given them?
DRAPER: To him himself.
WILLAMETTE: He's in fine trim
For getting cloth! Alas, not a toe
Does he move. He's no use for a robe;
Never a robe shall clothe him more
But the white one, nor shall he go forth
From where he is except feet first.
DRAPER: Since sunrise then has this occurred,

For I talked with him, without a doubt.
WILLAMETTE: You have a voice so shrill and loud!   660
Speak lower, out of charity!
DRAPER: It's you, by all the truth in me!
You yourself, in the bleeding flesh!
By God's Blood, here's a wretched mess!
Would I were paid so I might leave.
By God, each time I've lent I've reaped
Not one thing different whatsoever.
PATELAN: Willamette, a little rosewater!°
Raise me up, give my back a rub!
Rot! Who hears me? The water jug!   670
The soles of my feet need to be itched!
DRAPER: I heard him there.
WILLAMETTE: Of course.
PATELAN: Ah, witch,
Come here! Did I ask you to open
These windows? Cover me this moment!
Take away these black folk! Marmara,
Carimari, carimara—°
Get them away from me, away!
WILLAMETTE: What is it? How you thrash and flail!   680
Can it be you're out of your senses?
PATELAN: You do not see the thing I witness.
There's a black friar flying over!
Seize him, give him a stole and censer!
The cat, the cat! Look, how he rises!
WILLAMETTE: What's this? You've gotten too excited.
By God, you ought to be ashamed!
PATELAN: These physicians have had me slain
By all those potions they made me drink.
And all the time they'd have you think   690
It's easy as shaping wax, their work!
WILLAMETTE: Alas, come see him, my fine sir,
He is so very sick a patient.
DRAPER: Are you sure he's got this sickness,
Since he just returned from the fair?
WILLAMETTE: From the fair?
DRAPER: By Saint John, yes, there;
I do believe that's where he went.
For the piece of cloth which you've been lent,
I need to have my money, Master Peter.   700
PATELAN: Ah, Doctor John, stone is not harder
Than were the two small turds I shat;
Round as yarn balls they were, and black.
Shall I have another enema?
DRAPER: Why ask me? How should I know, huh?
Nine francs I need, or else six crowns.
PATELAN: Those three black bits like pointed
mounds—
Pills you called them I believe—

Rosewater was used to revive people from fainting fits,
like the smelling salts of the nineteenth century. *Carimari,
carimara,* This is probably an incantation to ward off evil
spirits.

710 Well, they have rotted out my teeth!
For God's sake, doctor, no more I'd take,
They made me cough up all I ate.
Ah, there isn't a thing more bitter!
DRAPER: They did not, by the soul of my father!
My nine francs haven't been coughed up!
WILLAMETTE: Round the gorge may they be strung
up,
Such idle folks as do nothing but meddle!
Go on your way, guided by devils,
720 Since 'by the Lord' it can't be ever!
DRAPER: By that same God who had me fathered,
I'll have my cloth ere I'm through with this
Or my nine francs!
PATELAN: And then my piss,
Didn't it tell you I am dying?
For God's sake, why is he delaying?
I'd not pass on before my time!
WILLAMETTE: Go on your way! Is it not a crime
For you to browbeat him this way?
730 DRAPER: Lady, may God see evil days!
Six yards of cloth I say, right now!
Tell me, upon your faith speak out,
Is it right that I should lose them?
PATELAN: Please, Doctor John, couldn't you loosen
My bowels? It is such hard manure
I don't know how I can endure
When it starts coming out my ass.
DRAPER: Nine francs and nothing less, I ask,
By the grace of Saint Peter of Rome!
740 WILLAMETTE: Alas, you torment this man so!
How is it you can be so gruff?
You yourself see clearly enough
He thinks that you are his physician.
Alas, the poor, poor, faithful Christian
Had had enough to do with hardship.
Eleven weeks without departure
Has he lain there, the poor, poor man!
DRAPER: By God's Blood, I don't understand
How this accident befell him,
750 For he showed up where I was selling
This very day, and we did business—
At least it seemed to me his likeness,
Or I cannot account the matter.
WILLAMETTE: By Our Lady, my sweet master,
Something's wrong with your memory.
If you'll take some advice from me,
You'll go and get a little rest.
Certain folks might start to suspect
That you came here to pay me a visit.
760 Go on outside now, his physicians
Will be coming here in a wink.
I'm only worried what some might think,
For I don't think such thoughts one bit.
DRAPER: Curse God! Am I in such a fix?
By the Godhead, I thought it true—

WILLAMETTE: Thought what, sir?
DRAPER: Haven't you a goose
On the fire?
WILLAMETTE: That's a fine thing to ask!
Ah, sir, such meat is not fit pap   770
For invalids. Eat your own geese
Without coming here to play the tease.
Upon my faith, you are too free!
DRAPER: I pray you, don't be angry with me,
For I thought with total confidence—
WILLAMETTE: Thought what, sir?
DRAPER: By the Sacraments—
Good day! Bah! I shall go find out.
I know I should have, beyond a doubt,
Six yards of cloth all in one piece,   780
But this woman lays hold of me
And scatters my wits at every turn.
He has taken them, that's for sure.
Lord! No, he hasn't; that can't follow,
I've seen Death standing at his elbow—
Else he was putting on an act.
Eh! So he has! Yes, it's a fact,
He took them and tucked them under his arm,
By Blesséd Mary's many charms!
No, he hasn't. Maybe I'm dreaming.   790
I've never known a time, not sleeping
Nor waking, when I'd give my stuffs
To anyone, no matter how much
Good will I felt. I'd never trust them.
By God's Blood, he has so got them!
By Death, he hasn't! This I've seen,
He hasn't—But where does that leave me,
By Our Lady's Blood, if he has so?
The Devil take me body and soul
If I know who could say for sure   800
Who has the better or the worse
Of them or me! I've not an inkling.
PATELAN: Has he gone away?
WILLAMETTE: Peace, I'm listening.
I can't tell what it is he mumbles.
He goes away with such fierce grumbles.
It sounds as though he's lost his head!
PATELAN: Isn't it time I rose from bed?
How he arrived, right on the dot!
WILLAMETTE: Who knows if he'll return or not?   810
Lord, no! Don't budge at any cost!
Our work would be completely lost
If he should find you risen.
PATELAN: By George,
Down on his knees has been forced!
He who is such an infidel!
In him it seems more suitable
Than in a church to see a cross!
WILLAMETTE: In such a stinking, mean old crock
Never was pea soup so well made!   820
Lord, serves him right! He never gave

On Sundays.

PATELAN: For God's sake, stop that laughing
If he came, it would do great damage!
I am quite sure that he'll return.

WILLAMETTE: Let him who would—upon my word!—
Contain himself—but I just can't!

DRAPER: By the Holy Sun which shines on man,
I shall return—just let them grouse—
830 To this fresh-water lawyer's house!
Good God! What rental property
That his or her dear family
Supposedly sold?! By Saint Peter,
He has my cloth, the lying swindler!
I gave it him in this very place.

WILLAMETTE: When I remember what a face,
He made as he regarded you,
I laugh! He was in such a stew
To demand—

840 PATELAN: Peace, you cackling hen!
I swear to God—Heaven forfend!—
In case one hears you 'twould be wise
For a certain someone else to hide.
He's such a surly, grim old sphinx.

DRAPER: And this advocate puffed with drink
Knows three short lessons and three short psalms!
Does he think he holds folks in his palm?
By God, he's just as hangable
As a blank note's corruptible!
850 I swear to God, he has my cloth!
What game does he think he's carried off?
Hallo in there! Where are you hiding?

WILLAMETTE: Upon my word, he heard me laughing!
He looks as though he's lost his head.

PATELAN: I'll feign delirium in my bed.
Go on out there.

WILLAMETTE: What's this yelling?!

DRAPER: May God have mercy, you are laughing!
Here, my money!

860 WILLAMETTE: Blesséd Mary!
What cause have I for making merry?
There's none more mournful at the feast.
He's passing on! You've never seen
Such a tempest nor such a frenzy.
He's in a state of wildest fancies;
He dreams, he sings, he raves in a speech
Of many tongues, and fouls his sheets.
Not a scant half-hour shall he last!
Upon this soul, I weep and laugh
870 In the same breath.

DRAPER: Whether you weep
Or laugh's not my affair. To be brief,
It's necessary I be paid.

WILLAMETTE: For what? Have *your* wits gone astray?
Are you renewing your assault?

DRAPER: I am not used in selling cloth
To be dealt such words as these, madame.

Would you give me to understand
That bladders are what lanterns are?°

PATELAN: Quickly! The Queen of the Guitars!   880
See at once she is summoned hither!
I know quite well she is delivered
Of four and twenty guitarilos,
Sired by the Abbot of Iverneaux!
He needs me to act as godfather!

WILLAMETTE: Alas, think you on God the Father,
My love, and not about guitars.

DRAPER: (Ha! What storytellers they are,
The pair of them!) Come now! I ask
To be paid, in gold or in plain cash,   890
For all my cloth which you did take.

WILLAMETTE: Good Lord, if you made one mistake
One time, isn't that quite enough?

DRAPER: What was it, my friend? By God Above,
I don't know what mistake I've made!
The hour has come to hang or pay!
What wrong do I do you at this time
In coming here to ask what's mine?
By the Grace of Saint Peter of Rome—

WILLAMETTE: Alas, you torment this man so!   900
I see quite clearly by your mien
That you are certainly not sane.
By this weary sinner's oath,
If I had help, I'd see you roped!
You're utterly, stark-raving mad!

DRAPER: Alas, I rage that I don't have
My money.

WILLAMETTE: Ah, what idiocy!
Cross yourself! Benedicite!
Hurry, make the sign of the cross!°   910

DRAPER: I swear to God, if I lend out cloth
For a year, I shall have some affliction!

PATELAN: Mither a Gawd, crooned Quaen a Hivven,
Bi oll mi faythe, Ih wood ga flae!
Ih swir ta Gawd! Oovir thi sae!
Gawd's goots! Ih till this stark a it,
Ha thatches oon en doosna give
Woon whit! Cam soond yer oower, balfry!
Ha clangs ta mae a moony anly!°

Have you heard, my pretty cousin?   920

WILLAMETTE: He had an uncle, a Limogian,
The brother of his handsome aunt.
That's what he does now, jabbers cant
In the language of Limoges, I'd say.

This is the French way of saying, "Am I to believe the moon is made of green cheese?"

One crossed oneself to ward off evils, among them madness. *Mither . . . anly,* Mother of God, crowned Queen of Heaven / Upon my faith, I want to flee! / I swear to God! Over the sea! / God's guts! I tell this stork of it, / He thatches on and doesn't give / One whit. Come sound your hour, belfry! / He clangs to me of money only.

DRAPER: Truly, he came and sneaked away
With all my cloth under his arm.

PATELAN: Come in, sweet damsel, full of charms.
Eh! Why does this toady disturb me?
Get yourself back, you smelly turdy!
930 Quick noo! I wode becam a praest!
Noo thun, hur my th'Divil bae!
Un thus daecreput munisturry!
Wot! Shode a praest bae makun murry
Wen 'ae ote ta bae sangun hus mass?°

WILLAMETTE: Alas, alas, the hour comes fast
When he'll need his last sacrament!

DRAPER: How is it he speaks Picard? From whence,
I ask, springs such tom-foolery?

WILLAMETTE: His mother was from Picardy,
940 That's why he's speaking that way now.

PATELAN: Whence do you come, the Mardi Gras?
Avake! Zu armz! Mein goote mon,
Zum boocks Ick luglicke unterstond.
'O Heinrik, Heinrik, kom zu schleepen!'
'Ick sol ein goot-armt fidgel keepen.'
Tchirrupf-tchirroo, mein sherner vons!
Gallopf, gallopf as Ick bit es tun,
Macking kupletten in desen fersen.
Ack, zooch greet festung macks den kopf toorn!
950 Avake avile, kom qviklick, tu!
Heer, vas zu trinken, I beg of you.
Bot kom, bot zee—ist Gottes gift—
Please, put some water on my lips.
Nein, vate avile, for now it's winter.°
See Father Thomas is brought hither
At once, so I can be confessed.

DRAPER: What is this? Will he never rest
From speaking different languages?
If he'd at least give me a pledge
960 Or else my money, I would leave.

WILLAMETTE: Leave me, by all Christ's Agonies!
You are a 'different' sort of man,
What would you? I don't understand
Why you're so very obstinate.

PATELAN: 'Ere, Foxy-Loxy, intow th'clutch!
Good gryshus but me fool his 'airy!
'E simes ha caterpillar, trooly,

Er helse my-be ha 'oney bee.
Oo, sweet Gybriel, speak tow me!
Chroist's 'oonds! Wot his't thet hattacks   970
Me hass? His't ha cow per'aps,
Ha hoosefloi er ha sloimy snile?
Hit's Gerbold's coorse, me balls give wye!
Lard! Ham Oi wone o' Bayeaux' shitters?°
John o' th' Road'll be glad, th' bigger,
Provoided 'e knows thet Oi know 'im.°
Boh! Boi Moichel, Oi'll drink tow 'im
This wonce must gladly—Tow 'is bot 'um!°

DRAPER: How is it he can bear the burden
Of so much talking? He *must* be foolish!   980

WILLAMETTE: The one who taught him all his
schooling
Was Normand; thus it comes to pass
He remembers it at the last.
He's passing on!

DRAPER: Ah, Blesséd Mary!
Here is the wildest piece of fancy
That ever I've run up against!
I did not doubt in any sense
That he'd not been to the fair today.   990

WILLAMETTE: You thought that?

DRAPER: Yes, but I see, by James,
The opposite is true quite plainly.

PATELAN: Is that an ass which I hear braying?
Alas, alas, mine cousin, come.
They will be completely unstrung
The day when I shall not see you.
It's fitting that I should hate you,
For you have greatly swindled me.
Your doings, they are all deceits.   1000
Sathan cam und henta yow
Aleeka flesh and sowla!

WILLAMETTE: God help you!

PATELAN: Huv ye nicht withooten slape, yshakka
With coold und ake uv feer na lakka!
This falla, Ik preya, upon yow alla,
Und avery wicht is heer in halla:
Huv averich a stoon in yore entrailla

Quick . . . mass, Quickly! I would become a priest!
/ Now then, here may the Devil be! / In this decrepit
monastery! / What!? Should a priest be making merry /
When he ought to be singing his mass? *Awake . . . winter,*
Awake! To arms! My dear, good man, / Some books I
luckily understand / O'Henry, Henry, come to sleep!' / 'I
shall a well-armed vigil keep!' / Chirrupchirroo, my pretty
ones! / Gallop as I bid it done, / Fashioning couplets in
these verses. / Ah, such great feasting makes one's head
turn. / Awake awhile, come quickly, do! / Here, bring some
drink, I beg of you! / But come, but see—I ask God's gift—
/ Please, put some water on my lips / No, wait a while, for
now it's winter.

Saint Gerbold was a fourteenth-century bishop against
whom the people of Bayeux rebelled; in return, they all got
diarrhea. *John o' th' Road,* the draper, whom Patelan is
choosing to call a door-to-door beggar for coming to collect
his money. Also, John, like William was the stock name for a
comic dupe. *Ere, Foxy-Loxy . . . Tow 'is bot 'um,* Now here,
Renard, into the clutch! / Good gracious, but my fool is
hairy / He seems a caterpillar, truly, / Or else maybe a honey
bee. / Ah, sweet Gabriel, speak to me! / Christ's wounds!
What is it that attacks / My ass? Is it a cow perhaps, / A
housefly or a slimy snail? / It's Gerbold's curse, my bowels
give way! / Lord! Am I one of Bayeux' shitters? / John of the
Road will be glad, the beggar, / Provided he knows that I
know him! / Bah! By Michael, I'll drink to him / This once
most gladly—To his bottom!

Farthut ye makken swich a clappa, rascailla!
1010 Bae ye afered us povre hoond
Thut far hoonger falleth aswoun.
Huv ye noon aise boot deth aloon
Und ake his loov und coortesie!°

DRAPER: Alas, for God's sake, hear him speak!
He's passing on! How he gurgles!
But what the devil's this he garbles!
Blesséd Lady but he babbles!
By the Body of Christ, he gabbles
His words so much that one can't fathom
1020 A thing. He doesn't speak in Christian
Nor any language I've heard ever.

WILLAMETTE: This was the mother of his father,
Whose origin was Brittany.
He's dying. This shows us he needs
To take his final sacraments.

PATELAN: Aw, bah Sain' Gigon,° ya lah! Ruhpent!
Gahd is watchin' yuh, fool a Lorraiyne.
Muh Gahd sen' yew a wake a payne!
Nat wuth an ol' strow mat ah yew!
1030 Go, yuh bleedin' smelly ol' shew!
Go bidammed, yuh bleedin' dronkhuhd!
Yuh weah muh awt dancin' this gallyuhd.
Gahd's daith! Cume have a drank, cum hithuh—
Wayte, fust give muh a grayne a peppah,
Fuh troolah, he shul ate it too.
An bah Sain' Jawdge, hu'll drank tuh yew!
Whut wud yuh have muh say, suh? Spake!
Duh yuh nat cum from Picahday?
Aw, Jown, naw one's at awl estawnished!°
1040 *Et bona dies sit vobis,*
Magister amantissime,
Pater reverendissime.
(So much for greetings and compliments.
Let's ask this merchant what he wants,
Why he is burning up, what's new?

Huv ye nicht . . . coortesie, The Devil come calling and seize you / Body and soul! . . . / May you pass a sleepless night, shook / With chills, then have a fire in your goods. / I wish you all, with none excepted, / To all of you who here are present, / May you receive a stone in your bowels / From raising such a caterwaul, / Till you take pity on all curs / Who die howling of hunger's curse! / May you have a coffin's relief / And just as much love and courtesy! **Gigon,** the French name for the Old Woman Who Lived in a Shoe, or a puppet; it derives from *cicogne,* meaning stork. **Aw, bah Sain' Gigon . . . estawnished,** Ah, by Saint Gigon, you lie! Repent! / God is watching you, fool of Lorraine. / May God send you a week of pain! / Not worth an old straw mat are you! / Go, you bleeding, smelly old shoe! / Go be damned, you bleeding drunkard! / You wear me out dancing this galliard. / God's death! Come have a drink, come hither— / Wait, first give me a grain of pepper, / For truly he shall eat it too, / And by Saint George, he'll drink to you. / What would you have me say, sir? Speak! / Do you not come from Picardy? / Ah, John, no one's at all astonished.

Is Paris out of eggs to screw?)
Quomodo brulis? Que nova?
Parisius non sunt ova?
Quid petit ille mercator?
(Let's tell him his mocker, furthermore, 1050
Wishes to give him, if he please,
A piece of his own goose to eat,
That he who lies abed gives board.)
Dicat sibi quod trufator
Ille, qui in lecto jact,
Vult ei dare, si placet,
De oca comedendum.
(And last, if he likes what he has eaten,
Go find it fast and fart, I tell him!)
Si sit bona ad edendum, 1060
Pete sibi sine mora.

WILLAMETTE: My word, he'll go to the immortals
Talking all the while! How he spumes!
Do you see how it is he fumes?
Upward to the Divinity
It's passing now, his humanity.
Now I'll be left, poor and forlorn!

DRAPER: It would be well that I were gone
Before, as 'twere, he's crossed the bar.
I doubt that he would have the heart 1070
To speak to you in front of me
At his departure. If privately,
Any secrets, perchance, he choose—
Pardon me, for I swear to you
Upon this soul, that I believed
He had my cloth. Madam, God keep.
For God's sake, may he give me pardon!

WILLAMETTE: To you a blesséd day be given,
As well as to the poor, lone mourner.

DRAPER: Now I'm more at a loss than ever. 1080
By Blesséd Mary, ever noble!
It must be, in his place, the Devil
Has taken all my cloth to tempt me.
Benedicite! I pray He
Makes no attempt upon my person!
Since things go thus, I give my woolen
In God's name to whomever took it.

PATELAN: Away! I've taught you by the book, huh?
Now he's passing on, the fair William!
Lord! What findings and fine distinctions 1090
He's got under his helmet's brim!
Many's the insight shall come to him
This night, when he shall lie abed!

WILLAMETTE: How he's been bitten, sucked and bled!
Have I not done my duty well?

PATELAN: By Christ's Sweet Body, truth to tell,
You've worked things very well indeed.
At least we've managed to retrieve
Cloth enough to make some robes.

DRAPER: What next! None pays me what he owes, 1100
Each carries off what I possess
And takes whatever he can get.

I'm the king of bad luck, it seems.
The very shepherds of the fields
Trip me up. Now this servant, he
Whom I have always treated kindly,
He'll not have me to have his laugh at!
He shall come to the foot of the abbot,°
By the blessèd, crownèd Queen of Heaven!
1110 TIBALT LAMBLING (SHEPHERD): May God grant you a
    day that's blessèd
  And a good evening, my sweet lord.
  DRAPER: Ha, is it you, you two-legged turd!
    What a knave! But what can I do?
  SHEPHERD: Well, I wouldn't want to bother you,
    Only this stranger dressed in stripes,
    My good lord, an untidy type
    Who held a whip without a lash,°
    Said to me—but I didn't grasp
1120   At all clearly what was the matter.
    He spoke to me of you, my master,
    And I don't know what sort of summons.
    As for me, by the Holy Virgin,
    I can't make head nor tail of it.
    He mixed me up with a strange fit
    Of crying, 'Sheep!', 'Be there at noon!'
    And he made me a great to-do
    For you, my master, about shackles.
  DRAPER: If I don't see you put in shackles
1130   Right presently before the judge,
    I pray to God Above that the flood
    And hurricane may swallow me!
    Nevermore will you club a sheep,
    By my faith, but you'll remember it!
    You'll pay, whatever comes of this,
    For my six yards—I say, for the carnage
    Upon my sheep and for the damage
    That you have done me these ten years.
  SHEPHERD: Do not believe the ills you hear,
1140   My gentle lord, for by this soul—
  DRAPER: And by the Lady all extol,
    You will pay up by Saturday
    For my six yards of cloth—I say,
    For what you've taken from my sheep!
  SHEPHERD: What cloth? Ah, lord, I do believe
    You're angered by some other thing.
    Saint Lupe, my master, I dare not bring°
    Myself to speak when I behold you.

That is, he will be forced to confess his sins.
   The sargeant-at-arms who delivered the summons
wore a striped uniform and carried a staff of office.
   Saint Lupe, The text reads 'Saint Leu.' There was an
archbishop in the sixth century, a curer of epilepsy, named
thus; the word also is aligned closely to the Latin for wolf
(lupus) and hence may refer to a deity of the woods and
fields, of untamed nature. Metaphorically, the name would
seem to work either way in the context of this speech.

DRAPER: Leave me in peace! Go! And hold to
  Your summons, or you'll soon learn better. 1150
SHEPHERD: My lord, come, let us reason together.
  For God's sake, I'd not take the stand!
DRAPER: Go, your affair is in good hands.
  Go away! I'll not be reasoning,
  By God, nor will I think of settling
  Other than as the judge shall rule!
  Drat! Everyone will try to fool
  Me henceforth, if I don't take care.
SHEPHERD: Go with God, sir, His joy to share!
  So, it seems I'd best defend me. 1160
  Is there a soul within?
PATELAN: Hang me
  If he's not back! By this my gorge!
WILLAMETTE: Not so, by all the grace of Saint George!
  That would be the worst thing yet.
SHEPHERD: God be with you! God guide your step!
PATELAN: God keep you, friend. What is at fault?
SHEPHERD: There's one who'll pin me by default
  If I do not answer my summons,
  Milord, before the coming session. 1170
  If it so please you, you'll attend;
  My sweet master, and there defend
  My case, for I am ignorant,
  And I'll pay you a handsome sum,
  Although I wear this shabby suit.
PATELAN: Come here and talk now. What are you,
  Either the plaintiff or the defendant?
SHEPHERD: I've had to do with a sharp client,
  You get my meaning, my sweet master,
  Whose flock of sheep I've led to pasture 1180
  For years, and kept watch over all.
  Upon my word, I clearly saw
  That he did pay me skimpily—
  Shall I tell all?
PATELAN: Why, certainly,
  One ought to tell all to his lawyer.
SHEPHERD: It is as true as truth itself, sir,
  That I indeed have clubbed and brained 'em
  So often several have fainted
  Many a time and fallen as dead 1190
  As once they'd been healthy and well fed.
  Then I'd give him to understand,
  So he'd no cause for reprimand,
  That they were dying of the pox.
  'Ha!' he'd say, 'Don't let them crop
  Among the others, throw them out!'
  'Gladly,' I'd say, but brought about
  His wishes in another way,
  For by Saint John, each one I ate,
  Knowing full well their malady. 1200
  What more would you desire of me?
  I carried on so much this way,
  I clubbed and did so many slay,
  It could not help but be perceived.
  And when he found himself deceived,

So help me God, he took to spying
(For one can hear them loudly crying,
You know, when you are in the act).
Now I've been taken with the facts,
1210 There's none of it I can deny.
I'd humbly beg you take my side
(For my part, I have funds enough),
So that we two may trip him up.
I know full well he has good cause,
But you will come upon some clause,
If you but will, that hurts him badly.
PATELAN: Upon your faith, will you rest easy?
What will you give if I reverse it,
This charge which your opponent nurses?
1220 And if one sends you hence absolved?
SHEPHERD: In coppers I'll not pay at all,
But in the pretty gold of crowns.
PATELAN: Then you shall have a case that's sound
Though it were twice again as grave.
The more it's worth, the more I sway
When once I set my mind to work.
Oh, how you'll hear me twisting words
After he's presented his case!
Now come here. Allow me to say,
1230 By the Holy Blood of the Precious Lamb,
You seem to be enough of a sham
To appreciate a piece of gall.
Tell me, how is it you are called?
SHEPHERD: By Saint Maur, sir, Tibalt Lambling.°
PATELAN: Lambling, many a lamb yet suckling
Have you not stolen from your master?
SHEPHERD: Upon my word, it can't be other
Than I have eaten more than thirty
These three years.
1240 PATELAN: Why, an annuity
Of ten it is for dice and candles.°
I do believe that you have handled
Him well. Do you think he can find
Afoot the facts to prove your crime?
This is the crux of the contention.
SHEPHERD: Prove, sir? Bléssed be the Virgin!
By all the Saints of Paradise,
For each he'll find another nine
Or ten who'll testify against me.
1250 PATELAN: This is a feature which speaks badly
For your cause. Here's what I think:
I'll not pretend at all I'm linked
With you, nor that I've seen you ever.
SHEPHERD: You won't?!

Saint Maur, a disciple of Saint Benedict, was revered by
rheumatics and beggars. *An annuity . . . candles,* He means
that the income the shepherd derived from his sheep-killing
each year was a fair allowance due him from the draper, one
which would give him just enough to buy dice and candles so
he could while away the long evenings by gambling.

PATELAN: No, nothing whatsoever.
Here's what's advisable to do:
If you speak out, they'll fasten you,
Blow by blow, to their positions,
And in a case like yours confessions
Are so very prejudicial   1260
And such a nuisance, they're the Devil.
Because of this, here's what will suit:
As soon as they shall summon you
To testify before the court,
You will respond with no retort
But 'Baa' to anything they ask you.
And if it happens they should curse you,
Saying, 'Hey, you stinking cuckold!
You bum, God's curse on you be doubled!
Would you make sport of Justice's temple?'   1270
Say 'Baa.' 'Ha!' I'll say, 'He's simple,
He thinks he's talking to his sheep.'
But though in twain their heads they beat,
No other word must pass your lips!
Watch yourself well!
SHEPHERD: The shoe fits.
I'll watch myself and most carefully,
And do this thing quite properly,
That I promise and attest.
PATELAN: Now watch yourself! See you stand fast!   1280
Even to me, to any matter
I may say to you or proffer,
You answer with no other word.
SHEPHERD: Who, me? Not I, upon my word!
Say openly my wits have strayed
If I say another word this day
To you, indeed to anyone,
For any word that's at me flung
But 'Baa' as you yourself have taught me.
PATELAN: By Saint John, your adversary   1290
Shall by his muzzle thus be seized!
Just see to it that I'm as pleased,
Once this thing's finished, with your pay.
SHEPHERD: My lord, if I don't see you're paid
At your word, don't ever believe
Me again. But, I pray you, see
At once to getting my work done.
PATELAN: By Our Lady of Boulogne,
I bet the judge is seated now,
For he always brings his gavel down   1300
At twelve o'clock or thereabouts.
You follow me, let's not set out,
We two, together down the street.
SHEPHERD: Well said, for that way none can see
That you're to be my advocate.
PATELAN: Marry, the spitter will be spat
Upon, if you don't pay the gold!
SHEPHERD: Ye Gods, at your word! Truth be told,
My lord, and make no doubt of it!
PATELAN: Well, if it does't rain it drips.   1310
At least I'll net a little carp,

I'll net from him if it hits the mark
A crownpiece or two for all my pains.
Sir, God put fortune in your train
And all that gives your heart delight!
JUDGE: Ah, you, sir, are a welcome sight.
Here, put your hat on! Take a place!
PATELAN: Oh, I'm fine here, saving your grace.
I find I'm here, uh, more at my ease.
1320 JUDGE: If there be any, make your pleas
Right now, so that I may be rising.
DRAPER: My lawyer comes. He's just concluding
A little thing he had to do,
Milord, and if it pleases you
You will do well to wait for him.
JUDGE: Good Lord! I've elsewhere to attend!
If the second party's present, make
Your plea without further delay.
I say, are you not a plaintiff?
1330 DRAPER: I surely am.
JUDGE: Where's the defendant?
Isn't he present here in person?
DRAPER: Yes, there, the one who doesn't open
His mouth, but God knows that he thinks!
JUDGE: Now, since both are present, what brings
You two together? State your demand.
DRAPER: Here then is that which I demand
Of him, milord. It is the truth
That out of charity, God's due,
1340 I nursed him from his infancy,
And when I saw he'd strength to be
Out in the fields, to make it shorter,
I did appoint him as my shepherd
And sent him out to guard my sheep.
But, as truly as I do see
You seated there, milord the judge,
He made of it such a bloody flood
Of lambs and ewes and of my muttons
That, without a doubt—
1350 JUDGE: Now listen,
Was he not in fact your hired hand?
PATELAN: Quite true, for if this were a plan
To hold him without any hire—
DRAPER: May I renounce the Lord on High!
It's you. It's you without a doubt.
JUDGE: Why do you raise your hand, how now?
Have you the toothache, Master Peter?
PATELAN: Yes, they're waging me such a battle
That never have I felt such rage.
1360 I dare not even raise my face.
For God's sake though, make them proceed.
JUDGE: Go on, finish this thing you plead.
Come on, sum up the argument!
DRAPER: It's him, no other, true as Lent!
By the Cross which did Our Savior hold,
It's you, the one to whom I sold
Six yards of cloth, fine Master Peter!
JUDGE: What's this he says of cloth?

PATELAN: He wanders.
He thinks he's coming to his point   1370
And doesn't know how to reach that point,
Because he's never learnt the way.
DRAPER: I'll be hanged if you didn't take
My cloth! Hanged by the bleeding gorge!
PATELAN: My, how the wretched man does forge
At length to furnish out his libel!
He means—Your diehards are such rebels!—
He means to say his shepherd sold
The wool—That's what he meant, I know—
With which was made the cloth of my robe,   1380
By saying he is being 'robbed'
And that he stole from him the fleece
Of his animals.
DRAPER: An ill week
May God send me if you don't have it!
JUDGE: Peace, for by the Devil, you prattle!
Don't you know any way of going
Back to your point without holding
Up the Court with such chitterchat?
PATELAN: I feel bad, yet I have to laugh!   1390
He is already so hard-pressed
He knows not where his point was left.
A straightening out is what he needs.
JUDGE: Come, let us get back to these sheep.
What was it now?
DRAPER: It was a yardage
Of six, nine francs worth.
JUDGE: Are we dullards
Or cuckolds?! Where do you think you be?!
PATELAN: God's Blood, he leads you out to feed!   1400
A good man by the look of him!
Still, I'd advise that one examine
The second party for a bit.
JUDGE: Rightly said. Since he talks of him
It cannot be they're not acquainted.
Come here, speak.
SHEPHERD: Baa!
JUDGE: Here's a quandry!
What 'baa' is this? Am I a goat?
Talk!   1410
SHEPHERD: Baa!
JUDGE: A bleeding fever throw
You down, by God! Are you jesting?!
PATELAN: I think that he is mad or testy
Or that he thinks he's with his sheep.
DRAPER: I'll renounce God if you aren't he,
The very one, no other, who stole
My cloth from me! Ha, you don't know,
Milord, by what a sneaking, nasty—   1420
JUDGE: Silence yourself! Are you a ninny?
Leave this assessor in peace, will you,
And let us get to the point.
DRAPER: True,
Milord, but the matter touches me.
Yet, by my faith, my lips are sealed,

Not one more word of it I'll say.
What comes of this another day
Shall follow then as it may follow—
1430 Still, it behooves me now to swallow
This whole-hog. Now, as I was saying
To make my point, how I, having
Given six yards—I ought to say
My sheep—good sir, I humbly pray
You'll pardon me. This pretty master,
My shepherd, when out in the pastures
He should have been—He told me I
Would get six crowns when I dropped by!
I say, three years ago this week,
1440 My shepherd signed a pact with me
That loyally my sheep he'd guard
And would not work me any harm
By injury nor villainy—
And yet, now he denies to me
Both the cloth and the gold entirely!
You there, Master Peter, truly!—
This rascal carried off the wool
From my sheep, and all those hale and whole,
Those he caused to die and perish
1450 By clubbing them, braining them senseless
With a stout staff he used for arms—
Once my cloth was under his arm,
He went his way with hurried steps
And told me I should go to fetch
Six crowns of gold at his own home!
JUDGE: There is no rhyme nor reason shown
In all this that you iterate.
What is this? You start to relate
Now one, now the other. In sum,
1460 By God, I don't see either one.
He bellows first of cloth and babbles
Then of sheep, like a baby's rattle!
Nothing he says can be sustained.
PATELAN: Now I am sure that he retains
His wages to this needy servant.
DRAPER: By God, you'd do well to be silent!
My cloth, true as the Saints Above—
I well know where this saddle rubs,
Better than anyone can fathom!
1470 By the Godhead, you do have it!
JUDGE: What is it he has?
DRAPER: Nothing, milord.
The greatest swindler, by my word,
Is this!—Oh well, I'll be silent
If I can and will not cite it
Again, no matter what you find.
JUDGE: Not that! Still, keep your word in mind.
Come now, sum up the argument.
PATELAN: This shepherd can make no attempt
1480 To answer to the deeds proposed
If he has got no counsel and knows
Not how, or dares not, to demand it.
If it would please you to command it,

That I should be for him, I will.
JUDGE: You'd side with him? I'd think to fill
This bill were to embrace thin air.
There's little profit.
PATELAN: Milord, I swear
To you, I don't want anything.
For God be it done! Now, I'll wring 1490
From this poor wretch what he would tell me
And whether he knows aught to help me
Answer the charges here accused.
He'd have the hard part of this suit
If no one sought to give him succor.
Come here, my friend. If one discovered—
You understand?
SHEPHERD: Baa!
PATELAN: 'Baa,' you said?
What 'baa'? By the Holy Blood Christ shed, 1500
Have you gone mad? Tell me your dealings.
SHEPHERD: Baa!
PATELAN: What 'baa'? Do you hear sheep bleating?
It's for your benefit, you know.
SHEPHERD: Baa!
PATELAN: Please say simply 'yes' or 'no'!
(Well done, say it always!) Will you?
SHEPHERD: Baa!
PATELAN: (Louder, or you will put you
To great expense, and me in doubt.) 1510
SHEPHERD: Baa!
PATELAN: Madder by far is one who routs
Fools from the woods to this High Seat.
Ah, sir, send him back to his sheep!
He is an idiot by nature.
DRAPER: He's mad, is he? Blessèd Saviour!
He is more sane than you do be!
PATELAN: Send him away to guard his sheep
And never return, the case closed.
Damn him who has the law lay hold 1520
Of such fools, or sees they're not dismissed!
DRAPER: And will you set him free from this
When I've not had a hearing yet?
JUDGE: Since he is mad, so help me, yes.
Why not do so?
DRAPER: Good heavens, sir,
First give me leave to say a word
And to arrive at my conclusions.
I swear that these are not deceptions
I would tell you, nor mockeries. 1530
JUDGE: Tribulations are all one reaps
From trying madmen or, I'm sure,
Mad women! Now hear this, fewer words
Or the Court no longer is in session.
DRAPER: You'll free them with no obligation
To reappear?
JUDGE: Now what's the matter?
PATELAN: Reappear! You'll not see a madder,
Neither in deed nor in response.
And he's not worth more by an ounce 1540

Than the other one. They're both madmen,
Brainless nuts! By the Holy Virgin,
Between the two they've not a grain
Of sense!

DRAPER: By lying you obtained
My cloth for nothing, Master Peter.
By Christ's Flesh, if this is the measure
Of an upright man, may I be stoned!

PATELAN: I'll renounce Saint Peter of Rome
1550   If he's not mad, or getting there!

DRAPER: I know you by the robe you wear!
And by the speech! And by the mien!
I am not mad, I am still sane
Enough to know who's fair to me.
The whole affair I shall reveal
To you, milord, upon my conscience.

PATELAN: Good heavens, sir, enjoin his silence!
Have we no shame for making war
On this poor shepherd for three or four
1560   Boney old ewes or mangey muttons,
Which are not even worth two buttons?
He sounds a louder plaint of wrongs—

DRAPER: What muttons? Here's the same old song!
It is of you yourself I speak,
And you shall give it back to me,
As Christ was born on Christmas Eve!

JUDGE: See how well I'm accompanied?
He will not cease this day from bleating.

DRAPER: I demand that—

1570 PATELAN: Make him stop speaking!
By God, this is just too inane!
Let us assume that he did brain
Some six or seven, or a dozen,
And ate them as his bleeding income—
In this you really were maligned!
You, who've gained twice that in the time
That he has guarded them for you!

DRAPER: Regard him, sir, regard him, do!
I speak to him of drapery,
1580   And he responds with shepherdry!
Six yards of cloth, I ask, where are
Those yards you put 'under your arm'?
Have you thought of paying even once?

PATELAN: Ah, good sir, would you have him hung
For six or seven wooly heads?
At least take time to catch your breath.
I pray you, do not be severe
With this poor shepherd standing here
Before you, naked as a worm.

1590 DRAPER: See how slyly the verse is turned!
The Devil made me, a fine merchant
Of cloth, to deal with such a client!
Alas, milord, I do demand—

JUDGE: I absolve him of your demands
And here prohibit your proceeding—
A fine honor, to hear the pleadings
Of madmen! Go you to your sheep.

SHEPHERD: Baa!

JUDGE: You show clearly who you be,
Sir, by the Blood of All the Saints!   1600

DRAPER: Alas, milord, by my soul's grace—

PATELAN: Could he be still if he wanted to?

DRAPER: But it's with you I have to do!
You swindled me by all that's false
And sneakily did carry off
My cloth with words of highest art.

PATELAN: I protest, from the bottom of my heart!
Do you hear what he says, milord?!

DRAPER: So help me God, you are the lord
Of cheats! Your honor, let me say—   1610

JUDGE: A proper cuckold's pair you make,
The two of you; there's naught but quarreling.
So help me God, I'm glad I'm leaving!
Go you, my friend. Never return
For any writ you may be served;
The Court absolves you, understand?

PATELAN: Say 'Thank you.'

SHEPHERD: Baa!

JUDGE: I understand.
Go now, don't fret. It's just as well.   1620

DRAPER: Is this a reason to wave farewell
To him?

JUDGE: Aye! I have other matters.
Besides, I've had it with you jokers.
You'll no more keep me in this chair,
I'm leaving. Would you like to share
A supper with me, Master Peter?

PATELAN: I can't.

DRAPER: Ah, what a fawning cheater!
Tell me, won't I ever be paid?   1630

PATELAN: For what? Have your wits gone astray?
Just whom do you believe I am?
For the life of me, I can't understand
Whom it is that you take me for.

DRAPER: Oh 'baa!'

PATELAN: Good sir, say nothing more.
I'll tell you with no more delaying
For whom it is you think to take me.
Is it not for one of the brainless?
But see! Ah no, he'd not be hairless,   1640
The top of his head quite peeled, like me.°

DRAPER: You want me to take you for a sheep?
It's you, I say, it's you in person!
Yes, you yourself! Your voice confirms it,
And don't go thinking otherwise.

PATELAN: Who, me myself? Truly, not I.
Hold a second before you go on;
Mightn't it be, say, John of Noyon?
He resembles me in stature.

DRAPER: The Devil it is! He hasn't features   1650
Thus puffed with drink nor wan as swill!

° Patelan was either bald or had been tonsured.

Didn't I leave you deathly ill
An hour ago inside your lodgings?
PATELAN: Ah, here's a clever piece of logic!
I'm ill? And with what malady?
Come, come, confess your cuckoldry,
For now it is as clear as water.
DRAPER: It's you, or I renounce Saint Peter!
You, no other, I know it for
1660 The truth!
PATELAN: Think nothing of the sort,
For surely it's not I one bit.
Not one yard nor a half did I snitch,
I haven't such a reputation.
DRAPER: I'm going to your habitation,
By God, to see if you're not there!
We'll need no longer tear our hair
Right here, if I find you there sick.
PATELAN: By Our Lady, that's it, that's it!
1670 You'll know for sure once this is done.
Speak, Lambling.
SHEPHERD: Baa!
PATELAN: Come now, come.
Isn't your business well-achieved?
SHEPHERD: Baa!
PATELAN: Your plaintiff's in retreat,
Say 'baa' no more, it isn't fit.
Have I not given him the slip?
Have I not coached you, blow by blow?
1680 SHEPHERD: Baa!
PATELAN: Good Lord! None will hear you now,
Speak freely with a right stout heart.
SHEPHERD: Baa!
PATELAN: It is time that I depart.
Pay me.
SHEPHERD: Baa!
PATELAN: To tell the truth,
You've learnt your lesson through and through
And also kept a good, straight face.
1690 That's what has made him lose the race,
It's that you kept yourself from laughing.
SHEPHERD: Baa!
PATELAN: What 'baa'! This needs no more saying.
Pay me fairly and quietly.
SHEPHERD: Baa!
PATELAN: What 'baa'? Speak more prudently
And pay me, so that I'll depart.
SHEPHERD: Baa!
PATELAN: You know what? Well, listen hard:
1700 I pray, without more 'baa'-ing me,
That you now think of paying me.

I want no more of your 'baa'-ery,
Pay up!
SHEPHERD: Baa!
PATELAN: Is this a mockery?
Is this the sum of what you'll do?
Upon my word, you'll pay me too,
You hear? if you'd not be aflying.
Here, the gold!
SHEPHERD: Baa! 1710
PATELAN: You are joking!
What! Shall I get no other thing?
SHEPHERD: Baa!
PATELAN: Your doggéd prose begins to sing.
To whom do you think you hawk your cockle
Do you know who he is? Now, babble
Me 'baa' no more this day and pay me!
SHEPHERD: Baa!
PATELAN: Shall I get no other money?
With whom do you believe you play? 1720
I've wearied me to death in praise
Of you, now give me cause to crow!
SHEPHERD: Baa!
PATELAN: Are you making me eat crow?
Curse God! Am I so ill-begotten
A mere shepherd, a shirted mutton,
A dungheap wretch makes me his cur?
SHEPHERD: Baa!
PATELAN: Shall I get no other word?
If you are doing this for sport, 1730
Say so, and spare me more retort.
Come, sup you at my house with us.
SHEPHERD: Baa!
PATELAN: By John, you are sane enough.
The goslings lead the geese to pasture!
Of all I thought myself the master:
Of swindlers here and there, wherever;
Of the fast takers and the givers
Of words, smooth pledges for a payment
Not due until the Day of Judgment— 1740
And one shepherd leaves me behind!
By James, if I can only find
A good lawman, I'll have you locked up.
SHEPHERD: Baa!
PATELAN: Oh 'baa!' May I be strung up
If I don't see a good lawman comes
At once! Misfortune dog his bum
If he does not put you in prison!
SHEPHERD: If he can find me—I'll forgive him!

(*Explicit*)

Figure 19. Patelan (*left*) bargains with the Draper in the Comédie Francaise production of *Master Peter Patelan,* Paris, 1957. (Photograph: Agence de Presse Bernand.)

Figure 20. Patelan (*seated left*) defends himself against the claims of the Draper (*right*) while the Judge listens and the Shepherd (*left*) waits to testify in the Comédie Francaise production of *Master Peter Patelan,* Paris, 1957. (Photographs: Agence de Presse Bernand.)

Staging of *Master Peter Patelan*

REVIEW OF THE COMEDIE FRANCAISE PRODUCTION, 1941, BY MARCEL LaPIERRE

It is an amusing spectacle that the Comédie Francaise presents us. . . . The set and the decoration tend to recall the kind of staging used by actors of past times. The three acts take place nearly without interruption in a single compartmentalised set. At the back is the judge's door, to the left that of Patelan, to the right that of the drapier, Guillaume. The back cloth is raised at certain points to show other settings, the interior of Guillaume's shop first of all, then the lawyer's bedroom. In the last act a door is opened in the raisable backdrop and the judge appears seated in a chair.

Denis d'Inès plays the role of Patelan, the scheming lawyer who cheats Guillaume and finds his own master as trickster in the character of the shepherd, Lambkin. Denis d'Inès draws superbly the acrobatic and protean character who simulates the most astonishing diseases in order to exonerate himself from paying his debts and who expresses himself in all the provincial dialects in order to make his case even more extraordinary. Lafon plays, roundly, the naïve but suspicious Guillaume. Chambreuil is a judge who seems to have come out of a Rabelaisian court room. Berthe Bovy is an adroit Dame Guillemette, wife of the lawyer. Jacques Charon, one of the new apprentices of the House of Molière, represents the rustic and tricky Thibauld Lambkin.

REVIEW OF THE COMÉDIE FRANÇAISE PRODUCTION, 1954, BY ROBERT KEMP

M. Denis d'Inès has just "adapted" [the text of *Master Peter Patelan*]. He has sought the lively and the light in order to clarify, to make easier on the lips and the tongue the octosyllabic lines. He has imagined an outdoor production. The stage is elevated; a row of twenty reflectors shows their backs to the spectators to make them think of candles. The back cloth, drawn up by solid ropes, permits them to change the place of the action. The costumes of the fifteenth century are alive with color. It makes an agreeable hour. . . . The title role is played by d'Inès himself, lovingly. M. Guillaume by Proterat, Guillemette by Bertha Bovy; as Thibault Lambkin, J. P. Roussillon bleats wittily. M. Chambreuil is the judge.

It's good. But who knows if a "young company" with its fresh ideas, its suppler knees, its light voices, its clowning, would not give us a more living, funnier, and more expressive Patelan?

The author of *Everyman* is unknown, but its haunting dramatization of death and redemption has a remarkable ancestry, which can be traced back at least two thousand years earlier to the well known parables of Buddha (563–483 B.C.). Among these parables is the tale of a man who when summoned by death turns to his four wives for companionship, but is refused by the three he loves most and accepted only by the one he loves least. According to Buddha, the three wives who refuse symbolize the man's friends and relatives, his worldly goods, and his bodily powers; the wife who accepts represents his moral intention. Although the parable is an expression of Buddhist faith, it could easily be revised to illustrate Christian belief, as it was thirteen hundred years later, when John Damascene, an eighth century theologian, told about a man with three friends, two who abandon him and one who remains faithful. According to Damascene, the faithful friend represents "the company of good deeds—faith, hope, charity, alms, kindliness, and the whole band of virtues, that can go before us, when we quit the body, and may plead with the Lord on our behalf." The parable of the man and his three friends subsequently made its way throughout medieval Europe and was translated into English by the great fifteenth century printer, William Caxton, who included it in a collection of tales, *The Golden Legend,* which he published in 1483, at about the same time that *Everyman* was probably written. Caxton's version of the parable tells of a man who is summoned by death to make the ultimate pilgrimage, who seeks worldly companionship on his journey, but discovers he can rely only on his spiritual well-being. *Everyman* may be seen as the dramatic embodiment of a universal parable about the vanity of life, the certainty of death, and the undying power of virtue.

Everyman also embodies the anxieties of its age, for the late medieval period was a time when men seemed more preoccupied with death and the afterlife than with life itself. Surely no other age before or since has been so visibly obsessed with thoughts of death. That obsession manifested itself in a wide variety of art forms—woodcuts, murals, sculptures, poems, and plays—all depicting the same morbid image: a skeletal figure who leads a group of men and women from all social stations, literally every man, in a macabre ceremony, the dance of death. That ghastly image expressed the deepest fears of the age, for it portrayed not only the inevitability but also the horror of death, and the horror was frequently emphasized by showing the skeletal figure covered with sores and postules, grisly reminders of the bubonic plague, the Black Death, which ravaged England and the continent during the fourteenth century. Reminders of death were indeed so widespread that they were unavoidable, for if men had not witnessed the plague or seen the dance, then they heard of the agonies from traveling preachers who toured the countryside, admonishing them to think of death and exhorting them to prepare their souls for life after death. That same lesson—the lesson of how to prepare for a godly Christian death—was also the subject of innumerable handbooks, one of which called *The*

Book of the Craft of Dying was printed by Caxton in 1490. Caxton's manual displays the same Christian view of dying that is dramatized in *Everyman*. It describes the temptation of dying men to turn to "temporal things" and counsels "every man, rightful and sinful, (to) bow himself and submit himself fully unto the mighty hand of God."

Everyman exemplifies that religious vision in the allegorical form of a morality play. Its characters are not particular individuals but personified abstractions—Everyman, Death, Fellowship, Good Deeds, Confession—and its plot represents not a unique experience but a paradigm of experience. In its allegorical form as in its Christian theme, *Everyman* is typical of other early morality plays, such as *The Castle of Perseverance* (ca. 1425) and *Mankind* (ca.1475), but its plot is more focussed and its tone far more somber since it concentrates exclusively on the death of Everyman, whereas they portray the entire life of mankind from birth to death. *Mankind* even includes deliberately comic characters whose sacrilegious and obscene jokes were clearly intended to amuse a paying audience, but *Everyman* makes no such concessions. It has only a few comic touches in the behavior of Fellowship, Kindred, and Goods, and those few comic moments are meant less to entertain than to exemplify types of worldly temptation. *Everyman* and its contemporaneous Dutch counterpart *Elckerlijk* (literally, everyman) stand out as the most austerely unified morality plays of the medieval period.

Although *Everyman* is the product of its age—a medieval Catholic morality play—it speaks to all ages and all faiths. Its characters are abstractions, the abstractions of theology expounded in parables and sermons alike, yet those abstractions take on life through the vivid details by which they are characterized. Fellowship, for example, through his hale and hearty welcome to Everyman and his increasingly outlandish promises of assistance immediately shows himself to be a bag of wind, even before his refusal to accompany Everyman reveals him to be a fair weather friend. Kindred and Cousin, on the other hand, are portrayed as solicitous women of few words who have just as little to offer—not much more than the lame excuse of Cousin who claims to have a cramp in her toe. And Goods, far from offering excuses, turns out to be a cruel jester who maliciously delights in Everyman's predicament. Each of the abstractions is individualized so that they become authentic characters whose interaction is dramatically plausible and compelling. When, for example, Everyman turns for assistance to Good Deeds, his pleading is genuinely motivated, following as it does on the increasingly painful series of rejections he has received from Fellowship, Kindred, Cousin, and Goods. Similarly, when Everyman is rejected at the end of the play by Beauty, Strength, Discretion, and Five Wits, his surprise is also well motivated, for while he has been taken up with confession and penance, with the elaborate routine of his last rites, he has still not faced the inescapable facts of death: the physical decay, the loss of consciousness, the end of being in the world as he has known it.

Ultimately, all the characters derive their motivation from the logic of the human psyche, for their interaction is meant to represent the mental, emotional, and spiritual process that takes place in a representative human being during the process of dying. The stages in that process are clearly and eloquently marked out in the play—from the initial denial, to the wish for postponement, to the bargaining, to the frenzied but futile clinging to life, to the acceptance of death, to the spiritual preparation for it, to the experience itself. That is the process Everyman goes through in the play, and it is remarkably similar to the process described in modern psychological studies of dying. They reveal, as does *Everyman,* that dying is something one does alone. Friends and relatives cannot at last help anyone avoid the loneliness of death. The only possible solace is the knowledge of having lived a decent life.

Because of its timelessness, *Everyman* has been one of the most influential plays in the history of drama. In the contemporary period alone, its allegory of dying has been imitated in Beckett's *Endgame,* adapted in Geraldine Fitzgerald's *Everyman and Roach,* and parodied in Arnold Powell's *The Death of Everymom.* It has been performed often and produced variously—in modern dress, in medieval costumes, on proscenium stages, on bare platforms, and on church altars. In one sense, *Everyman* is relatively easy to stage since it requires only a few props, such as a dart for Death, an account book, a scourge for Confession, a crucifix for Everyman, and sacks, packs, and chests for Goods; likewise it mentions specifically only one location: the house of Salvation. But in another sense, it gives directors a compellingly difficult stylistic problem—how to balance its abstract and concrete elements, how to make its experience at once particular and universal. One solution to that problem is discussed in the interview following the play by the director of a recent production at the University of Chicago. His solution was to combine realistic costumes, props, and details of action within the structure of a highly ritualized performance. That combination of effects is clearly revealed in the contrasting dramatic styles shown in Figures 21, 22, 23, and 24. And the combination was evidently unmistakable to the reviewer whose remarks reprinted following the play comment on "its balance between ritual and realism," a balance that is at last not only true to the play, but also to the act of dying itself.

EVERYMAN

MODERNIZED BY KATE FRANKS

CHARACTERS

MESSENGER
GOD
DEATH
EVERYMAN
FELLOWSHIP
KINDRED
COUSIN
GOODS

DOCTOR
GOOD DEEDS
KNOWLEDGE
CONFESSION
BEAUTY
STRENGTH
DISCRETION
FIVE WITS
ANGEL

(Here beginneth a treatise how the High Father of Heaven sendeth Death to summon every creature to come and give account of their lives in this world, and is in manner of a moral play.)

(Enter MESSENGER.*)*

MESSENGER: I pray you all give your audience
And hear this matter with reverence,
By figure a moral play:
The Summoning of Everyman called it is,
That of our lives and ending shows
How transitory we be all day.
This matter is wondrous precious,
But the intent of it is more gracious
And sweet to bear away.
10 The story saith: Man, in the beginning
Look well, and take good heed to the ending,
Be you never so gay!
Ye think sin in the beginning full sweet,
Which in the end causeth the soul to weep,
When the body lieth in clay.
Here shall you see how Fellowship and Jollity
Both, Strength, Pleasure and Beauty
Will fade from thee as flower in May;
For ye shall hear how our Heaven's King
20 Calleth Everyman to a general reckoning.
Give audience, and hear what he doth say.

(Exit MESSENGER.*)*

*(*GOD *speaks.)*

GOD: I perceive, here in my majesty,
How that all creatures be to me unkind,
Living without dread in worldly prosperity.
Of ghostly sight° the people be so blind,
Drowned in sin, they know me not for their God.
In worldly riches is all their mind;
They fear not my righteousness, the sharp rod.
My law that I showed when I for them died

They forget clean, and shedding of my blood red. 30
I hanged between two thieves, it cannot be denied;
To get them life I suffered to be dead;
I healed their feet, with thorns hurt was my head.
I could do no more than I did, truly;
And now I see the people do clean forsake me.
They use the seven deadly sins damnable,
As pride, covetise, wrath, and lechery
Now in the world be made commendable;
And thus they leave of angels the heavenly
company. 40
Every man liveth so after his own pleasure,
And yet of their life they be nothing sure.
I see the more that I them forbear
The worse they be from year to year.
All that liveth appaireth° fast;
Therefore I will, in all the haste,
Have a reckoning of every man's person;
For, if I leave the people thus alone
In their life and wicked tempests,
Verily they will become much worse than beasts; 50
For now one would by envy another up eat;
Charity they do all clean forget.
I hoped well that every man
In my glory should make his mansion,
And thereto I had them all elect;
But now I see, like traitors deject,
They thank me not for the pleasure that I to them
meant,
Nor yet for their being that I them have lent.
I proffered the people great multitude of mercy, 60
And few there be that asketh it heartily.
They be so cumbered with worldly riches
That needs on them I must do justice,
On every man living without fear.
Where art thou, Death, thou mighty messenger?

(Enter DEATH.*)*

---

ghostly sight, spiritual sight; knowledge of God.

appaireth, worsens.

DEATH: Almighty God, I am here at your will,
Your commandment to fulfill.
GOD: Go thou to Everyman
And show him, in my name,
70 A pilgrimage he must on him take,
Which he in no wise may escape;
And that he bring with him a sure reckoning
Without delay or any tarrying.
DEATH: Lord, I will in the world go run over all
And cruelly search out both great and small.
Every man will I beset that liveth beastly
Out of God's laws, and dreadeth not folly.
He that loveth riches I will strike with my dart,
His sight to blind, and from Heaven to depart—
80 Except that alms be his good friend—
In hell for to dwell, world without end.

(*Enter* EVERYMAN.)

Lo, yonder I see Everyman walking.
Full little he thinketh on my coming;
His mind is on fleshly lusts and his treasure,
And great pain it shall cause him to endure
Before the Lord, Heaven's King.
Everyman, stand still! Whither art thou going
Thus gaily? Hast thou thy Maker forgot?
EVERYMAN: Why askest thou?
90 Wouldest thou know?
DEATH: Yea, sir. I will you show:
In great haste I am sent to thee
From God out of his majesty.
EVERYMAN: What, sent to me?
DEATH: Yea, certainly.
Though thou have forgot him here,
He thinketh on thee in the heavenly sphere,
As, ere we depart, thou shalt know.
EVERYMAN: What desireth God of me?
100 DEATH: That I shall show to thee:
A reckoning he will needs have
Without any longer respite.
EVERYMAN: To give a reckoning longer leisure I
crave;
This blind° matter troubleth my wit.
DEATH: On thee thou must take a long journey;
Therefore thy book of account with thee thou
bring,
For turn again thou cannot, by no way.
110 And look thou be sure of thy reckoning,
For before God thou shalt answer and show
Thy many bad deeds, and good but a few;
How thou hast spent thy life, and in what wise,
Before the Chief Lord of Paradise.
Have ado that thou were in that way,
For know thou well, thou shalt make no attorney.°

EVERYMAN: Full unready I am, such reckoning to
give.
I know thee not. What messenger art thou?
DEATH: I am Death that no man dreadeth,° 120
For every man I rest and no man spareth;
For it is God's commandment
That all to me should be obedient.
EVERYMAN: O Death, thou comest when I had thee
least in mind!
In thy power it lieth me to save;
Yet of my goods will I give thee, if thou will be
kind—
Yea, a thousand pound shalt thou have!—
And defer this matter till another day. 130
DEATH: Everyman, it may not be, by no way.
I set not by gold, silver, nor riches,
Nor by pope, emperor, king, duke, nor princes;
For, if I would receive gifts great,
All the world I might get;
But my custom is clean contrary:
I give thee no respite. Come hence, and not tarry!
EVERYMAN: Alas, shall I have no longer respite?
I may say Death giveth no warning!
To think on thee, it maketh my heart sick, 140
For all unready is my book of reckoning.
But twelve years if I might have abiding,
My accounting book I would make so clear
That my reckoning I should not need to fear.
Wherefore, Death, I pray thee, for God's mercy,
Spare me till I be provided of remedy.
DEATH: Thee availeth not to cry, weep and pray;
But haste thee lightly° that thou were gone that
journey,
And prove thy friends if thou can. 150
For know thou well the tide abideth no man,
And in the world each living creature
For Adam's sin must die of nature.
EVERYMAN: Death, if I should this pilgrimage take
And my reckoning surely make,
Show me, for sainted charity,
Should I not come again shortly?
DEATH: No, Everyman. If thou be once there
Thou mayst never more come here,
Trust me verily. 160
EVERYMAN: O gracious God in the high seat celestial,
Have mercy on me in this most need!
Shall I have no company from this vale terrestial
Of mine acquaintance, that way me to lead?
DEATH: Yea, if any be so hardy
That would go with thee and bear thee company.
Hie thee that thou were gone to God's
magnificence,
Thy reckoning to give before his presence.
What, thinkest thou thy life is given thee 170

---

blind, unknown, obscure. no attorney, You won't be able to plead your case.

no man dreadeth, who fears no man. lightly, quickly.

And thy worldly goods also?
EVERYMAN: I had thought so, verily.
DEATH: Nay, nay, it was but lent thee;
For as soon as thou art gone,
Another a while shall have it and then go
  therefrom,
Even as thou hast done.
Everyman, thou art mad! Thou hast thy wits five
And here on earth will not amend thy life;
180   For suddenly I do come.
EVERYMAN: O wretchéd caitiff, whither shall I flee,
That I might escape this endless sorrow?
Now, gentle Death, spare me till tomorrow,
That I may amend me
With good advisement.
DEATH: Nay, thereto I will not consent,
Nor no man will I respite;
But to the heart suddenly I shall smite
Without any advisement.
190   And now out of thy sight I will me hie.
See thou make thee ready shortly;
For thou mayst say this is the day
That no man living may escape away.

(Exit DEATH.)

EVERYMAN: Alas, I may well weep with sighs deep!
Now have I no manner of company
To help me in my journey and me to keep;
And also my writing is full unready.
How shall I do now for to excuse me?
I would to God I had never been begot!
200   To my soul a full great profit it had been;
For now I fear pains huge and great.
The time passeth. Lord, help, that all wrought!
For though I mourn it availeth naught.
The day passeth and is almost ago;
I know not well what for to do.
To whom were I best my complaint to make?
What if I to Fellowship thereof spake
And showed him of this sudden chance?
For in him is all mine affiance,°
210   We have in the world so many a day
Been good friends in sport and play.

(Enter FELLOWSHIP.)

I see him yonder, certainly.
I trust that he will bear me company;
Therefore to him will I speak to ease my sorrow.
Well met, good Fellowship, and good morrow!
FELLOWSHIP: Everyman, good morrow, by this day!
Sir, why lookest thou so piteously?
If anything be amiss, I pray thee me say,
That I may help to remedy.
220   EVERYMAN: Yea, good Fellowship, yea,
I am in great jeopardy.

FELLOWSHIP: My true friend, show to me your mind.
I will not forsake thee to my life's end
In the way of good company.
EVERYMAN: That was well spoken and lovingly.
FELLOWSHIP: Sir, I must needs know your heaviness;
I have pity to see you in any distress.
If any have you wronged, ye shall revenged be,
Though I on the ground be slain for thee,
Though that I know before that I should die.   230
EVERYMAN: Verily, Fellowship, gramercy.
FELLOWSHIP: Tush! By thy thanks I set not a straw.
Show me your grief, and say no more.
EVERYMAN: If I my heart should to you break,
And then you to turn your mind from me
And would not me comfort when ye hear me
  speak,
Then should I ten times sorrier be.
FELLOWSHIP: Sir, I say as I will do in deed.
EVERYMAN: Then be you a good friend in need.   240
I have found you true herebefore.
FELLOWSHIP: And so ye shall evermore;
For, in faith, if thou go to hell,
I will not forsake thee by the way.
EVERYMAN: Ye speak like a good friend; I believe you
  well.
I shall deserve it, if I may.
FELLOWSHIP: I speak of no deserving, by this day!
For he that will say and nothing do
Is not worthy with good company to go;   250
Therefore show me the grief of your mind,
As to your friend most loving and kind.
EVERYMAN: I shall show you how it is:
Commanded I am to go a journey,
A long way hard and dangerous,
And give a straight account without delay
Before the high judge, Adonai.°
Wherefore I pray you, bear me company,
As ye have promised, in this journey.
FELLOWSHIP: That is matter indeed! Promise is duty;   260
But if I should take such a voyage on me,
I know it well, it should be to my pain;
Also it maketh me afeared, certain.
But let us take counsel here as well as we can,
For your words would fear a strong man.
EVERYMAN: Why, ye said if I had need
Ye would me never forsake, quick nor dead,
Though it were to hell, truly.
FELLOWSHIP: So I said, certainly,
But such pleasures be set aside, the sooth to say;   270
And also, if we took such a journey
When should we again come?
EVERYMAN: Nay, never again till the day of doom.
FELLOWSHIP: In faith, then will not I come there!
Who hath you these tidings brought?
EVERYMAN: Indeed, Death was with me here.

---

affiance, faith or trust.

Adonai, Hebrew name for God.

FELLOWSHIP: Now, by God that all hath bought,
    If death were the messenger,
    For no man that is living today
280   I will not go that loath journey—
    Not for the father that begat me!
EVERYMAN: Ye promised otherwise, pardie.
FELLOWSHIP: I know well I said so, truly;
    And yet, if thou wilt eat and drink and make good
      cheer,
    Or haunt to women the lusty company°
    I would not forsake you while the day is clear,
    Trust me verily.
EVERYMAN: Yea, thereto ye would be ready!
290   To go to mirth, solace and play
    Your mind will sooner apply
    Than to bear me company in my long journey.
FELLOWSHIP: Now, in good faith, I will not that way;
    But if thou will murder or any man kill,
    In that I will help thee with a good will.
EVERYMAN: O, that is a simple advice indeed.
    Gentle fellow, help me in my necessity!
    We have loved long, and now I need;
    And now, gentle Fellowship, remember me.
300 FELLOWSHIP: Whether ye have loved me or no,
    By Saint John, I will not with thee go!
EVERYMAN: Yet, I pray thee, take the labor and do so
      much for me
    To bring me forward, for sainted charity,
    And comfort me till I come within the town.
FELLOWSHIP: Nay, if thou would give me a new gown,
    I will not a foot with thee go;
    But if thou had tarried, I would not have left thee
      so.
310   And as now, God speed thee in thy journey,
    For from thee I will depart as fast as I may.
EVERYMAN: Wither away, Fellowship? Will thou
      forsake me?
FELLOWSHIP: Yea, by my faith! To God I betake° thee.
EVERYMAN: Farewell, good Fellowship! For thee my
    heart is sore.
    Adieu forever! I shall see thee no more.
FELLOWSHIP: In faith, Everyman, farewell now at the
    ending!
320 For you I will remember that parting is mourning.

(Exit FELLOWSHIP.)

EVERYMAN: Alack, shall we thus depart indeed—
    Ah, Lady, help!—without any more comfort?
    Lo, Fellowship forsaketh me in my most need.
    For help in this world whither shall I resort?
    Fellowship herebefore with me would merry make,
    And now little sorrow for me doth he take.
    It is said, "In prosperity men friends may find,
    Which in adversity be full unkind."

Now whither for succor shall I flee,
Since that Fellowship hath forsaken me?   330
To my kinsmen I will, truly,
Praying them to help me in my necessity.
I believe that they will do so,
For kind will creep where it may not go.°

(Enter KINDRED and COUSIN.)

I will go say, for yonder I see them.
Where be ye now, my friends and kinsmen?
KINDRED: Here be we now at your commandment.
    Cousin, I pray you show us your intent
    In any wise and not spare.
COUSIN: Yea, Everyman, and to us declare   340
    If ye be disposed to go anywhither;
    For know you well, we will live and die together.
KINDRED: In wealth and woe we will with you hold,
    For over his kin a man may be bold.
EVERYMAN: Gramercy, my friends and kinsmen kind.
    Now shall I show you the grief of my mind:
    I was commanded by a messenger,
    That is a high king's chief officer;
    He bade me go a pilgrimage, to my pain,
    And I know well I shall never come again.   350
    Also I must give a reckoning strait,
    For I have a great enemy that hath me in wait,
    Which intendeth me for to hinder.
KINDRED: What account is that which ye must render?
    That would I know.
EVERYMAN: Of all my works I must show
    How I have lived and my days spent;
    Also of ill deeds that I have used
    In my time, since life was me lent;
    And of all virtues that I have refused.   360
    Therefore, I pray you, go thither with me
    To help to make mine account, for saint charity.
COUSIN: What, to go thither? Is that the matter?
    Nay, Everyman, I had liefer fast bread and water
    All this five years and more.
EVERYMAN: Alas, that ever I was born!
    For now shall I never be merry
    If that you forsake me.
KINDRED: Ah, sir, but ye be a merry man!
    Take good heart to you, and make no moan.   370
    But one thing I warn you, by Saint Anne—
    As for me, ye shall go alone.
EVERYMAN: My Cousin, will you not with me go?
COUSIN: No, by our Lady! I have the cramp in my toe.
    Trust not to me; for, so God me speed,
    I will deceive you in your most need.
KINDRED: It availeth not us to entice.
    Ye shall have my maid with all my heart;
    She loveth to go to feasts, there to be nice,
    And to dance and abroad to start.   380

---

haunt . . . company seek women's company for pleasure;
go a-whoring.

betake, entrust. **kind . . . go,** one's kin will crawl where
they may not walk; i.e., will do what they can.

I will give her leave to help you in that journey,
If that you and she may agree.
EVERYMAN: Now show me the very effect of your
    mind:
Will you go with me, or abide behind?
KINDRED: Abide behind? Yea, that will I, if I may!
Therefore farewell till another day.

(Exit KINDRED.)

EVERYMAN: How should I be merry or glad?
For fair promises men to me make,
390   But when I have most need they me forsake.
I am deceived; that maketh me sad.
COUSIN: Cousin Everyman, farewell now,
For verily I will not go with you.
Also of mine own an unready reckoning
I have to account; therefore I make tarrying.
Now God keep thee, for now I go.

(Exit COUSIN.)

EVERYMAN: Ah, Jesus, is all come hereto?
Lo, fair words maketh fools fain;
They promise and nothing will do, certain.
400   My kinsmen promised me faithfully
For to abide with me steadfastly,
And now fast away do they flee,
Even so Fellowship promised me.
What friend were best me of to provide?
I lose my time here longer to abide.
Yet in my mind a thing there is:
All my life I have loved riches;
If that my Goods now help me might,
He would make my heart full light.
410   I will speak to him in this distress.
Where art thou, my Goods and riches?

*(*GOODS *revealed in a corner.)*

GOODS: Who calleth me? Everyman? What, hast thou
    haste?
I lie here in corners, trussed and piled so high,
And in chests I am locked so fast,
Also sacked in bags. Thou mayst see with thine eye
I cannot stir; in packs, low I lie.
What would ye have? Lightly me say.
EVERYMAN: Come hither, Goods, in all the haste thou
420   may,
For of counsel I must desire thee.
GOODS: Sir, if ye in the world have sorrow or
    adversity,
That can I help you to remedy shortly.
EVERYMAN: It is another disease that grieveth me;
In this world it is not, I tell thee so.
I am sent for, another way to go,
To give a strait account general
Before the highest Jupiter of all;
430   And all my life I have had joy and pleasure in thee.
Therefore, I pray thee, go with me;

For, peradventure, thou mayst before God
    Almighty
My reckoning help to clean and purify;
For it is said ever among
That "money maketh all right that is wrong."
GOODS: Nay, Everyman, I sing another song.
I follow no man in such voyages;
For if I went with thee,
Thou shouldst fare much the worse for me.   440
For because on me thou did set thy mind,
Thy reckoning I have made blotted and blind,
That thine account thou cannot make truly—
And that hast thou for the love of me!
EVERYMAN: That would grieve me full sore,
When I should come to that fearful answer.
Up, let us go thither together.
GOODS: Nay, not so! I am too brittle, I may not
    endure.
I will follow no man one foot, be ye sure.   450
EVERYMAN: Alas, I have thee loved, and had great
    pleasure
All my life-days in goods and treasure.
GOODS: That is to thy damnation, without lying,
For my love is contrary to the love everlasting.
But if thou had loved me moderately during,
As to the poor given part of me,
Then shouldst thou not in this dolor be,
Nor in this great sorrow and care.
EVERYMAN: Lo, now was I deceived ere I was aware,   460
And all I may lay to my spending of time.
GOODS: What, thinkest thou that I am thine?
EVERYMAN: I had thought so.
GOODS: Nay, Everyman, I say no.
As for a while I was lent thee;
A season thou hast had me in prosperity.
My condition is a man's soul to kill;
If I save one, a thousand I do spill.
Thinkest thou that I will follow thee?
Nay, from this world not, verily.   470
EVERYMAN: I had thought otherwise.
GOODS: Therefore to thy soul Goods is a thief;
For when thou art dead, this is my guise—
Another to deceive in this same wise
As I have done thee, and all to his soul's reprief.°
EVERYMAN: O false Goods, cursed thou be,
Thou traitor to God, that hast deceived me
And caught me in thy snare!
GOODS: Marry, thou brought thyself in care,
Whereof I am glad.   480
I must needs laugh; I cannot be sad.
EVERYMAN: Ah, Goods, thou hast had long my hearty
    love;
I gave thee that which should be the Lord's above.
But wilt thou not go with me indeed?

---

reprief, harm.

I pray thee truth to say.
GOODS: No, so God me speed!
   Therefore farewell, and have good day.

(Exit GOODS.)

EVERYMAN: O, to whom shall I make my moan
490   For to go with me in that heavy journey?
   First Fellowship said he would with me go;
   His words were very pleasant and gay,
   But afterward he left me alone.
   Then spake I to my kinsmen, all in despair,
   And also they gave me words fair;
   They lacked no fair speaking,
   But all forsook me in the ending.
   Then went I to my Goods that I loved best,
   In hope to have comfort; but there had I least,
500   For my Goods sharply did me tell
   That he bringeth many into Hell.
   Then of myself I was ashamed,
   And so I am worthy to be blamed;
   Thus may I well myself hate.
   Of whom shall I now counsel take?
   I think that I shall never speed
   Til that I go to my Good Deeds.
   But, alas, she is so weak
   That she can neither go nor speak;
510   Yet will I venture on her now.
   My Good Deeds, where be you?

(GOOD DEEDS revealed on the ground.)

GOOD DEEDS: Here I lie, cold in the ground.
   Thy sins hath me so sore bound
   That I cannot stir.
EVERYMAN: O Good Deeds, I stand in fear!
   I must you pray of counsel,
   For help now should come right well.
GOOD DEEDS: Everyman, I have understanding
   That ye be summoned account to make
520   Before Messiah, of Jerusalem King;
   If you do by me, that journey with you will I take.
EVERYMAN: Therefore I come to you my moan to
      make.
   I pray you that ye will go with me.
GOOD DEEDS: I would full fain, but I cannot stand,
      verily.
EVERYMAN: Why, is there anything on you fallen?
GOOD DEEDS: Yea, sir, I may thank you of all.
   If ye had perfectly cheered me,
530   Your book of account full ready would be.
   Look, the books of your works and deeds eke,°
   As how they lie under the feet
   To your soul's heaviness.
EVERYMAN: Our Lord Jesus help me!
   For one letter here I cannot see.

---

eke, also.

GOOD DEEDS: There is a blind reckoning in time of
      distress.
EVERYMAN: Good Deeds, I pray you help me in this
      need,
   Or else I am forever damned indeed;   540
   Therefore help me to make reckoning
   Before the Redeemer of all things,
   That King is, and was, and ever shall.
GOOD DEEDS: Everyman, I am sorry of your fall,
   And fain would I help you if I were able.
EVERYMAN: Good Deeds, your counsel I pray you give
      me.
GOOD DEEDS: That shall I do verily.
   Though that on my feet I may not go,
   I have a sister that shall with you also,   550
   Called Knowledge, which shall with you abide
   To help you to make that dreadful reckoning.

(Enter KNOWLEDGE.)

KNOWLEDGE: Everyman, I will go with thee and be thy
      guide,
   In thy most need to go by thy side.
EVERYMAN: In good condition I am now in everything
   And am wholly content with this good thing;
   Thanked be God my Creator.
GOOD DEEDS: And when she hath brought you there,
   Where thou shalt heal thee of thy smart,   560
   Then go you with your reckoning and your Good
      Deeds together
   For to make you joyful at heart
   Before the Blessèd Trinity.
EVERYMAN: My Good Deeds, gramercy!
   I am well content, certainly,
   With your words sweet.

(EVERYMAN and KNOWLEDGE leave GOOD DEEDS.)

KNOWLEDGE: Now go we together lovingly
   To Confession, that cleansing river.
EVERYMAN: For joy I weep; I would we were there!   570
   But, I pray you, give me cognition
   Where dwelleth that holy man, Confession.
KNOWLEDGE: In the house of salvation;
   We shall find him in that place
   That shall us comfort, by God's grace.

(KNOWLEDGE leads EVERYMAN to CONFESSION.)

   Lo, this is Confession. Kneel down and ask mercy,
   For he is in good esteem with God Almighty.
EVERYMAN: O glorious fountain, that all uncleanness
      doth clarify,
   Wash from me the spots of vice unclean,   580
   That on me no sin may be seen.
   I come with Knowledge for my redemption,
   Redempt with hearty and full contrition;
   For I am commanded a pilgrimage to take
   And great accounts before God to make.
   Now I pray you, Shrift, mother of salvation,

Help my Good Deeds for my piteous exclamation.
CONFESSION: I know your sorrow well, Everyman.
  Because with Knowledge ye come to me,
590   I will you comfort as well as I can,
  And a precious jewel I will give thee,
  Called penance, voider of adversity;
  Therewith shall your body chastised be,
  With abstinence and perseverance in God's
    serviture.
  Here shall you receive that scourge of me
  Which is penance strong that ye must endure,
  To remember thy Saviour was scourged for thee
  With sharp scourges and suffered it patiently;
600   So must thou, ere thou escape that painful
    pilgrimage.

(CONFESSION gives scourge to KNOWLEDGE.)

  Knowledge, keep him in this voyage,
  And by that time Good Deeds will be with thee.
  But in any wise be sure of mercy,
  For your time draweth fast; if ye will saved be,
  Ask God mercy, and he will grant truly.
  When with the scourge of penance man doth him
    bind,
  The oil of forgiveness then shall he find.

(EVERYMAN and KNOWLEDGE leave CONFESSION.)

610 EVERYMAN: Thanked be God for his gracious work!
  For now I will my penance begin.
  This hath rejoiced and lighted my heart,
  Though the knots be painful and hard within.
KNOWLEDGE: Everyman, look your penance that ye
    fulfill,
  What pain that ever it to you be;
  And Knowledge shall give you counsel at will
  How your account ye shall make clearly.
EVERYMAN: O eternal God, O heavenly figure,
620   O way of righteousness, O goodly vision,
  Which descended down in a virgin pure
  Because he would every man redeem,
  Which Adam forfeited by his disobedience;
  O blessèd Godhead, elect and high divine,
  Forgive me my grievous offence!
  Here I cry thee mercy in this presence.
  O ghostly° treasure, O ransomer and redeemer,
  Of all the world hope and conductor,
  Mirror of joy, foundation of mercy,
630   Which illumineth Heaven and earth thereby,
  Hear my clamorous complaint though it late be;
  Receive my prayers unworthy in this heavy life!
  Though I be a sinner most abominable,
  Yet let my name be written in Moses' table.
  O Mary, pray to the Maker of all things,
  Me for to help at my ending;

  And save me from the power of my enemy,
  For Death assaileth me strongly.
  And, Lady, that I may by means of thy prayer
  Of your Son's glory to be partner,   640
  By the means of his passion, I it crave;
  I beseech you, help my soul to save.
  Knowledge, give me the scourge of penance;
  My flesh therewith shall give acquittance.
  I will now begin if God give me grace.

(KNOWLEDGE gives scourge to EVERYMAN.)

KNOWLEDGE: Everyman, God give you time and
    space!
  Thus I bequeath you in the hands of our Saviour;
  Now may you make your reckoning sure.
EVERYMAN: In the name of the Holy Trinity,   650
  My body sore punishèd shall be:
  Take this, body, for the sins of the flesh!
  Also thou delightest to go gay and fresh,
  And in the way of damnation thou did me bring;
  Therefore suffer now strokes of punishing.
  Now of penance I will wade the water clear
  To save me from Purgatory, that sharp fire.

(GOOD DEEDS rises from the ground.)

GOOD DEEDS: I thank God, now I can walk and go
  And am delivered of my sickness and woe.
  Therefore with Everyman I will go and not spare; 660
  His good works I will help him to declare.
KNOWLEDGE: Now, Everyman, be merry and glad!
  Your Good Deeds cometh now; ye may not be sad
  Now is your Good Deeds whole and sound,
  Going upright upon the ground.
EVERYMAN: My heart is light and shall be evermore;
  Now will I smite faster than I did before.
GOOD DEEDS: Everyman, pilgrim, my special friend,
  Blessed be thou without end!
  For thee is prepared the eternal glory.   670
  Ye have me made whole and sound,
  Therefore I will bide by thee in every stound.°
EVERYMAN: Welcome, my Good Deeds! Now I hear
    thy voice
  I weep for very sweetness of love.
KNOWLEDGE: Be no more sad, but ever rejoice;
  God seeth thy living in his throne above.

(KNOWLEDGE gives EVERYMAN the garment of contrition.)

  Put on this garment to thy behove,°
  Which is wet with your tears,
  Or else before God you may it miss   680
  When you to your journey's end come shall.
EVERYMAN: Gentle knowledge, what do ye it call?
KNOWLEDGE: It is the garment of sorrow;

---

ghostly, spiritual, as in Holy Ghost.

stound, instance, occasion.   behove, benefit.

From pain it will you borrow.
Contrition it is
That getteth forgiveness;
It pleaseth God passing well.
GOOD DEEDS: Everyman, will you wear it for your
heal?°

(EVERYMAN *puts on the garment of contrition.*)

690 EVERYMAN: Now blesséd be Jesu, Mary's Son,
For now have I on true contrition;
And let us go now without tarrying.
Good Deeds, have we clear our reckoning?
GOOD DEEDS: Yea, indeed, I have it here.
EVERYMAN: Then I trust we need not fear.
Now, friends, let us not part in twain.
KNOWLEDGE: Nay, Everyman, that will we not,
certain.
GOOD DEEDS: Yet must thou lead with thee
700 Three persons of great might.
EVERYMAN: Who should they be?
GOOD DEEDS: Discretion and Strength they hight°
And thy Beauty may not abide behind.
KNOWLEDGE: Also ye must call to mind
Your Five Wits as for your counsellors.
GOOD DEEDS: You must have them ready at all hours.
EVERYMAN: How shall I get them hither?
KNOWLEDGE: You must call them all together,
And they will hear you incontinent.°
710 EVERYMAN: My friends, come hither and be present:
Discretion, Strength, my Five Wits, and Beauty.

(*Enter* DISCRETION, STRENGTH, FIVE WITS, *and*
BEAUTY.)

BEAUTY: Here at your will we be all ready.
What would ye that we should do?
GOOD DEEDS: That ye would with Everyman go
And help him in his pilgrimage.
Advise you, will ye with him or not in that voyage?
STRENGTH: We will bring him all thither
To his help and comfort, ye may believe me.
DISCRETION: So will we go with him all together.
720 EVERYMAN: Almighty God, loved may thou be!
I give thee laud that I have hither brought
Strength, Discretion, Beauty and Five Wits. Lack I
naught;
And my Good Deeds, with Knowledge clear,
All be in company at my will here.
I desire no more to my business.
STRENGTH: And I, Strength, will by you stand in
distress,
Though thou would in battle fight on the ground.
730 FIVE WITS: And though it were through the world
round,
We will not depart for sweet nor sour.

BEAUTY: No more will I unto death's hour,
Whatsoever thereof befall.
DISCRETION: Everyman, advise you first of all;
Go with a good advisement and deliberation.
We all give you virtuous monition
That all shall be well.
EVERYMAN: My friends, hearken what I will tell:
I pray God reward you in his heavenly sphere.   740
Now hearken, all that be here,
For I will make my testament
Here before you all present:
In alms, half of my goods I will give with my hands
twain
In the way of charity with good intent,
And the other half still shall remain
In queth,° to be returned where it ought to be.
This I do in despite of the fiend of hell,
To go quite out of his peril   750
Ever after and this day.
KNOWLEDGE: Everyman, hearken what I say:
Go to Priesthood, I you advise,
And receive of him in any wise
The holy sacrament and ointment together;
Then shortly see ye turn again hither.
We will all abide you here.
FIVE WITS: Yea, Everyman, hie you that ye ready
were.
There is no emperor, king, duke, nor baron   760
That of God hath commission
As hath the least priest in the world being;
For of the blesséd sacraments pure and benign,
He beareth the keys, and thereof hath the cure
For man's redemption—it is ever sure—
Which God for our soul's medicine
Gave us out of his heart with great pine.°
Here in this transitory life, for thee and me,
The blessed sacraments seven there be:
Baptism, confirmation with priesthood good,   770
And the sacrament of God's precious flesh and
blood,
Marriage, the holy extreme unction, and penance.
These seven be good to have in remembrance,
Gracious sacraments of high divinity.
EVERYMAN: Fain would I receive that holy body,
And meekly to my ghostly° father I will go.
FIVE WITS: Everyman, that is the best that ye can do.
God will you to salvation bring,
For priesthood exceedeth all other things: 780
To us holy scripture they do teach
And converteth man from sin, Heaven to reach;
God hath to them more power given

In queth, as a bequest; though the remainder of the line
indicates that it is actually a restitution of illegally acquired
property.   **pine,** anguish, torment.   **ghostly,** spiritual.

---

heal, salvation.   **hight,** are called.   **incontinent** at once.

Than to any angel that is in Heaven.
With five words he may consecrate,
God's body in flesh and blood to make,
And handleth his Maker between his hands.
The priest bindeth and unbindeth all bands,
Both in earth and in Heaven.
790 Thou ministers all the sacraments seven;
Though we kissed thy feet, thou were worthy.
Thou art surgeon that cureth sin deadly;
No remedy we find under God
But all only priesthood.
Everyman, God gave priests that dignity
And setteth them in his stead among us to be;
Thus be they above angels in degree.

(Exit EVERYMAN.)

KNOWLEDGE: If priests be good, it is so, surely.
But when Jesu hanged on the cross with great
800   smart,
There he gave, out of his blessèd heart,
The seven sacraments in great torment;
He sold them not to us, that Lord omnipotent;
Therefore Saint Peter the apostle doth say
That Jesu's curse hath all they
Which God their Saviour do buy or sell,
Or they for any money do take or tell.°
Sinful priests giveth the sinners example bad;
Their children sitteth by other men's fires, I have
810   heard;
And some haunteth women's company
With unclean life, as lusts of lechery;
These be with sin made blind.
FIVE WITS: I trust to God no such may we find;
Therefore let us priesthood honor
And follow their doctrine for our souls' succour.
We be their sheep, and they shepherds be
By whom we all be kept in surety.
Peace! For yonder I see Everyman come,
820   Which hath made true satisfaction.
GOOD DEEDS: Methinks it is he indeed.

(Re-enter EVERYMAN.)

EVERYMAN: Now Jesu be your alder speed!°
I have received the sacrament for my redemption
And then mine extreme unction.
Blessèd be all they that counselled me to take it!
And now, friends, let us go without longer respite.
I thank God that ye have tarried so long.
Now set each of you on this rood your hand
And shortly follow me.
830 I go before where I would be. God be our guide!

(They go toward the grave.)

---

tell, count out, as in bank teller. **your alder speed,** help to all of you.

STRENGTH: Everyman, we will not from you go
Till ye have done this voyage long.
DISCRETION: I, Discretion, will bide by you also.
KNOWLEDGE: And though this pilgrimage be never so
    strong,
I will never part you from.
STRENGTH: Everyman, I will be as sure by thee
As ever I did by Judas Maccabee.°

(They arrive at the grave.)

EVERYMAN: Alas, I am so faint I may not stand;
My limbs under me do fold.   840
Friends, let us not turn again to this land,
Not for all the world's gold;
For into this cave must I creep
And turn to earth, and thereto sleep.
BEAUTY: What, into this grave? Alas!
EVERYMAN: Yea, there shall ye consume, more and
    less.°
BEAUTY: And what, should I smother here?
EVERYMAN: Yea, by my faith, and never more appear.
In this world live no more we shall,   850
But in Heaven before the highest Lord of all.
BEAUTY: I cross out all this. Adieu, by Saint John!
I take my tap in my lap and am gone.°
EVERYMAN: What, Beauty, whither will ye?
BEAUTY: Peace! I am deaf. I look not behind me,
Not if thou wouldest give me all the gold in thy
    chest.

(Exit BEAUTY.)

EVERYMAN: Alas, whereto may I trust?
Beauty goeth fast away from me.
She promised with me to live and die.   860
STRENGTH: Everyman, I will thee also forsake and
    deny;
Thy game liketh me not at all.
EVERYMAN: Why, then, ye will forsake me all?
Sweet Strength, tarry a little space.
STRENGTH: Nay, sir, by the rood of grace!
I will hie me from thee fast,
Though thou weep till thy heart to-brast.°
EVERYMAN: Ye would ever bide by me, ye said.
STRENGTH: Yea, I have you far enough conveyed.   870
Ye be old enough, I understand,
Your pilgrimage to take in hand.
I repent me that I hither came.
EVERYMAN: Strength, you to displease I am to blame;
Yet promise is debt, this ye well wot.°

Maccabee, A Jewish leader of the second century B.C., known for his courage (1 Macc. 3). **shall ye consume,** The grave devours all, both the great and the small. **tap,** an unspun tuft of wool or flax. Hence, like a peasant housewife, Beauty is saying, "I'm pocketing my spinning materials and am off." **to-brast,** bursts in two. **wot,** know.

STRENGTH: In faith, I care not.
Thou art but a fool to complain;
You spend your speech and waste your brain.
Go thrust thee into the ground!

(*Exit* STRENGTH.)

880 EVERYMAN: I had thought surer I should you have
    found.
He that trusteth in his Strength,
She him deceiveth at length.
Both Strength and Beauty forsaketh me;
Yet they promised me fair and lovingly.
DISCRETION: Everyman, I will after Strength be gone.
As for me, I will leave you alone.
EVERYMAN: Why, Discretion, will ye forsake me?
DISCRETION: Yea, in faith, I will go from thee;
890 For when Strength goeth before,
I follow after evermore.
EVERYMAN: Yet, I pray thee, for the love of the
    Trinity,
Look in my grave once piteously.
DISCRETION: Nay, so nigh will I not come.
Farewell, everyone!

(*Exit* DISCRETION.)

EVERYMAN: O, all things faileth, save God alone—
Beauty, Strength and Discretion;
For when Death bloweth his blast,
900 They all run from me full fast.
FIVE WITS: Everyman, my leave now of thee I take.
I will follow the others, for here I thee forsake.
EVERYMAN: Alas, then may I wail and weep,
For I took you for my best friend.
FIVE WITS: I will no longer thee keep.
Now farewell, and there an end.

(*Exit* FIVE WITS.)

EVERYMAN: O Jesu, help! All hath forsaken me.
GOOD DEEDS: Nay, Everyman, I will bide with thee.
I will not forsake thee in deed;
910 Thou shalt find me a good friend in need.
EVERYMAN: Gramercy, Good Deeds! Now may I true
    friends see.
They have forsaken me, every one;
I loved them better than my Good Deeds alone.
Knowledge, will ye forsake me also?
KNOWLEDGE: Yea, Everyman, when ye to Death shall
    go;
But not yet, for no manner of danger.
EVERYMAN: Gramercy, Knowledge, with all my heart.
920 KNOWLEDGE: Nay, yet I will not from hence depart
Till I see where ye shall be come.
EVERYMAN: Methinks, alas, that I must be gone
To make my reckoning and my debts pay,
For I see my time is nigh spent away.
Take example, all ye that this do hear or see,
How they that I loved best do forsake me,

Except my Good Deeds that bideth truly.
GOOD DEEDS: All earthly things is but vanity:
Beauty, Strength and Discretion do man forsake,
Foolish friends and kinsmen that fair spake— 930
All fleeth save Good Deeds, and that am I.
EVERYMAN: Have mercy on me, God most mighty,
And stand by me, thou mother and maid, Holy
    Mary!
GOOD DEEDS: Fear not, I will speak for thee.
EVERYMAN: Here I cry God mercy.
GOOD DEEDS: Shorten our end, and diminish our
    pain;
Let us go and never come again.

(GOOD DEEDS *leads* EVERYMAN *into grave.*)

EVERYMAN: Into thy hands, Lord, my soul I 940
    commend;
Receive it, Lord, that it be not lost.
As thou me boughtest, so me defend
And save me from the fiend's boast,
That I may appear with that blessèd host
That shall be saved at the day of doom.
In manus tuas, of mights most
Forever, *commendo spiritum meum.*°

(*Exeunt* EVERYMAN *and* GOOD DEEDS.)

KNOWLEDGE: Now hath he suffered that we all shall
    endure; 950
The Good Deeds shall make all sure.
Now hath he made ending;
Methinks that I hear angels sing
And make great joy and melody
Where Everyman's soul received shall be.

(*Enter* ANGEL.)

THE ANGEL: Come, excellent elect spouse, to Jesu!
Here above thou shalt go
Because of thy singular virtue.
Now thy soul is taken thy body from,
Thy reckoning is crystal clear. 960
Now shalt thou into the heavenly sphere,
Unto the which all ye shall come
That liveth well before the day of doom.

(*Exeunt* ANGEL *and* KNOWLEDGE.)

(*Enter* DOCTOR.)

DOCTOR: This moral men may have in mind.
Ye hearers, take it of worth, old and young,
And forsake Pride, for he deceiveth you in the end;
And remember Beauty, Five Wits, Strength, and
    Discretion,
They all at the last do Everyman forsake,
Save his Good Deeds there doth he take. 970

In manus tuas . . . commendo spiritum meum, Into thy
hands I commend my spirit.

But beware, for if they be small,
Before God he hath no help at all:
No excuse may be there for Everyman.
Alas, how shall he do then?
For after death amends may no man make,
For them mercy and pity doth him forsake.
If his reckoning be not clear when he doth come,
God will say, *"Ite, maledicti, in ignem eternum."*°

Ite . . . eternum, Go, sinners, into eternal fire.

And he that hath his account whole and sound,
High in Heaven he shall be crowned;   980
Unto which place God bring us all thither,
That we may live body and soul together.
Thereto help the Trinity!
Amen, say ye, for saint charity.

(Exit DOCTOR.*)*

(Thus endeth this moral play of Everyman.)

Figure 21. The multilevel set for the University of Chicago Theater production of *Everyman,* directed by Nicholas Rudall in the Rockefeller Chapel, 1973. (Photograph: Leslie Travis.)

Figure 22. Everyman (Gordon Cameron, *left*) and Goods (Carl Orland) in the University of Chicago Theatre production of *Everyman,* directed by Nicholas Rudall, 1973. *(Photograph: Leslie Travis.)*

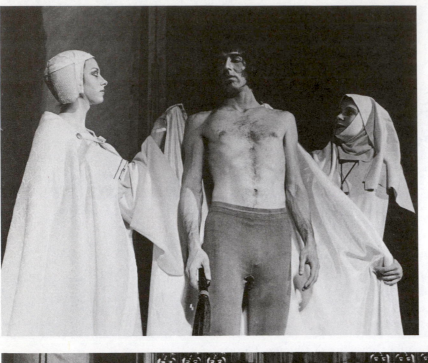

Figure 23. Everyman (Gordon Cameron, *center*) receives the garment of contrition from Good Deeds (Kelly Nespor, *left*) and Knowledge (Ellen Clements) in the University of Chicago Theatre production of *Everyman*, directed by Nicholas Rudall, 1973. (Photograph: Leslie Travis.)

Figure 24. Good Deeds (Kelly Nespor, *left*) leads Everyman (Gordon Cameron) into his grave as Death (Robert Hoover, *foreground*) awaits his arrival in the University of Chicago Theatre production of *Everyman*, directed by Nicholas Rudall, 1973. (Photograph: Leslie Travis.)

Staging of *Everyman*

INTERVIEW WITH NICHOLAS RUDALL, DIRECTOR
OF THE 1973 UNIVERSITY OF CHICAGO
PRODUCTION OF *EVERYMAN*, BY BRADFORD S.
FIELD, JR.

FIELD: What kind of stage does a gothic cathedral like Rockefeller Chapel offer for *Everyman*? Did you do it in the round? Or at the altar?

RUDALL: We placed a large octagon with other levels attached to it right to the center of the chancel. The octagon is raised and raked. It is divided off into a main acting area, which is the octagon, with a sort of inner below at the top of the rake, through which entrances could occur, and through which this sort of tableau that I did at the beginning could be seen. At raked angles away from it, upstage, were separate areas for the individual scenes, especially at the beginning, to take place. That is, Fellowship had his own platform, Kindred had hers, Cousin had hers, Goods had his. Good Deeds was placed on a kind of sarcophagus at the very top of this structure. I conceived the play, not so much as a pilgrimage—where you'd have lots of movement to different mansions all over the church—but rather as a going away, a taking away from Everyman. All these levels were fairly close to him, but they were separate from him. When he goes to a particular area, only that area is lit. When Fellowship, for example, is finished with him, the light in that area goes out. Forever. That area of the stage is black thereafter.

FIELD: Do I get it correctly that Everyman would move to each of their positions . . .

RUDALL: That's right . . .

FIELD: . . . talk to them, and then their exit was a blackout on them, but not on him; he'd move on to the next position?

RUDALL: That's right.

FIELD: Does *Everyman* present any special kinds of problems to a director?

RUDALL: Yes, one stylistic problem, that of the very realistic details in the play, realistic characterizations, coupled with a much higher style within the play. How does one reconcile characters that have cramps in their toes with these reflections about God? How elevated a person should Everyman be? Or how colloquial? How down to earth? What's the right level? He should not be too rich, not too poor . . . not too rustic, not too aristocratic. That was a rather difficult one to solve. I think we hit upon a solution that was partially based upon the fact that it was being done in a huge, almost cathedral-like structure. The play, as it is now performed, has the feeling of a church ritual. The whole building is lit by candlelight at the beginning and there are monks chanting for the first fifteen minutes as the audience comes in. I have some cross-cutting with contemporary folk song that contrasts between the happy life and the ecclesiastical life, if you like, all before the play starts. The fact that it is in this large structure allows us to have this high-style feeling, this ritual feeling, which I don't think it would have if it were on a small stage. That high style would be impossible; you'd be forced to think of it only as "playing" at that point.

FIELD: If you put it outdoors with a cart.

RUDALL: Right.

FIELD: Or in a playground or in a supermarket parking lot . . .

RUDALL: Exactly. But on this stage it is still possible to play the humanness of Fellowship, the humanness of Kindred and Cousin. I made them very direct, human figures. Fellowship was meant to be a kind of medieval banker, richly dressed, at supper. He's eating chicken and bread and wine while he's talking to Everyman. Kindred is a sort of fifty or sixty-year-old woman, upper bourgeois, and she's sitting there with her needlepoint, and Cousin is standing, playing with a little bird, very much a young aristocratic lady. And Goods emerges from a chest. Each character I made very specifically medieval characters, not generalizations, but very specific ones.

FIELD: The costumes then were intended to suggest a very particular social level, income level, type of business. . . .

RUDALL: Exactly that. Good Deeds is a young maiden, Knowledge is a young novice, a nun, and Strength a knight, Discretion a lawyer. One other thing, I did find that the play naturally lent itself to doubling. The first four characters to whom he goes, to Fellowship, to Kindred, Cousin and Goods, lend themselves to perfect doubling with the four parts of his personality that come back to him before he goes to the grave, Five-Wits, Beauty, Discretion, and . . .

FIELD: Do they each use the same platforms, or do they come down to him?

RUDALL: I didn't want to repeat the platforms; once their light was out, they had gone forever, I didn't want to return to them. What I had intended to do was have these four characters come back on, but with a life-mask of Everyman on their faces, to show them as four extensions of his own personality. Goods and Fellowship are outside things that he goes to, but

169

the things that he loses at the end are parts of himself—Beauty and Five Wits—so I made life-masks to be placed over their faces, so that there would be five Everymans, as it were, going down toward the grave. But because of the size of the church, that failed. They didn't look like Everyman, even though they were absolutely perfect. At a distance, that effect was lost. So I abandoned it.

FIELD: You did abandon it.

RUDALL: Yes. I did. Only because of the distance. I think in a smaller house, more intimate . . . it would have worked very well.

FIELD: I suppose if they'd all been wearing the same mask, even Everyman, they'd have matched, but then you'd have a hard time telling one from the other. Did the masks create any problem with speech?

RUDALL: Yes, one of the reasons that they failed was that we had to make too large an opening around the mouth and that made it cease to look like the person who was playing Everyman.

FIELD: Everyman was played by a man or a woman?

RUDALL: A man.

FIELD: At the turn of the century there was evidently a famous touring version of *Everyman* in which the title role was played by a—

RUDALL: A woman, yes.

FIELD: Okay . . . What kind of text did you use?

RUDALL: We took what might conveniently be called a translation. But I didn't overly modernize it, and I made adaptations for myself with a couple of professors here at Chicago and we pieced together parts which were obscure.

FIELD: What was obscure?

RUDALL: Somewhere at the beginning the medieval English says, "Thou shalt make no attournay," and we just changed that to "delay." Very simple adaptations like that. We changed many of the "and's" to "if." where there was a modern equivalent.

FIELD: Did you make any cuts in the text?

RUDALL: No. I was sorely tempted, at one particular point. Towards the end, about three-quarters of the way through, there's a long scene about priesthood, where Five-Wits talks at great length about the virtues of priesthood . . . it is self-serving, and honestly written in its time for the priests, but removed from our context. I had no way of solving it for a long, long time. And then I hit upon the idea of— while Five-Wits is discoursing about priesthood—we would actually illustrate it on an upper level, by having two black-robed priest-monks set up the equipment for the last rites. While Five-Wits is giving that long speech, Everyman is supposed to be off-stage getting the last rites. So instead of going off-stage, as is usually suggested, I had them do it in a kind of silhouette against the backdrop of the church, with candles and bread and oil and the chanting of Latin;

while Five-wits is talking about priesthood, we actually see them functioning, we see Everyman go to them, get the last rites, and come back down again. So that the inactivity was filled in that way.

FIELD: Were there any comic moments that you pointed for?

RUDALL: I didn't fight any of them. We pointed them up.

FIELD: Like the cramp in the toe . . .

RUDALL: And by making Kindred a dowager. She was played by a woman with a very thick English accent who sounded somewhat like Edith Evans. One could find comedy in her mere exit lines . . . She suggests too that Everyman take her maid. And that was done with a suggestion of the obscene. As was Fellowship's suggestion that if you want to go off and have fun with women, fine, he'll do that. That was the kind of thing that I didn't resist at all. Obviously the comedy is a very important part of the play.

FIELD: How did you handle Death?

RUDALL: I had Death seated at a kind of banquet. The play opened, as I said, with a chanting, a little tableau in the sort of inner below that we had at the top of the raked platform—a tableau with Death seated at a table with his back to the audience, along with Everyman, Kindred, Fellowship, and a young girl who was singing the secular song. After God spoke to them from the far end of the chapel, He calls upon Death, who just turns around from the feast. I had had Everyman enter with the girl who'd been singing, flirtatiously playing, coming from the feast. That made it very specific when Death asks, "Where are thou going thus gaily," that Everyman's mind is on fleshly lusts, specifically, coming from a feast with a woman.

FIELD: I always notice the bookkeeping imagery in the play. Did you play up any of that?

RUDALL: Yes. There are two notable instances of it. I had made a separate mansion of Everyman's house. Off the main stage, I had a little area that was a corner of his home. When Death comes to him, he runs to the house, looking for the money, the "thousand pounds I will give to you," and his book of accounts. He rifles through his books, looks to see, to offer it to Death, finds that it's not ready, and asks for twelve years . . . The second is that I had Good Deeds placed on a sarcophagus, way, way up; she was there before the audience came in. She was all white, to look like marble. Like a lady laying at rest with a book on her chest. A large pile of books near by. And one main book, carved into the tomb at the bottom. When Everyman goes up and appeals to her she tells him to look in the book there. He takes it from the tomb and looks through it. When he says, "No letter here do I see," that's what he's talking about. And later she brings his book of accounts down to him. So I made three specific uses of the bookkeeping in the action.

FIELD: One other thing that is always interesting about this play—how did the final moment work out? It seems pretty vague when you just read the play . . .

RUDALL: At the base of this octagonal acting area, there's a very steep ramp which leads down right into the audience, and it's absolutely black out there. Whenever Everyman left Fellowship or any of those characters, he would come right to the rim of the octagon, and look out into that blackness, toward the way he was going to go.

FIELD: Toward the audience.

RUDALL: Yes. When his personal attributes leave him at the end, Five-wits and the others, when he starts to walk down that ramp, he says, "Friends, come with me," and he stumbles. "I'm too weak," he says, and he stumbles. That is the first time that the four of them, these attributes, look down into the tomb to see . . . they see him stumble, and then they are for the first time aware of the tomb. They leave him. He's left then with Good Deeds and Knowledge, in a little rim of light above this blackness. There is a line that Knowledge says that ends with the syllable, "come," . . . "where ye shall become," and at that point, I have Death, who made his exit earlier in the play down to the tomb, echo the word "come," from the back of the church.

FIELD: Wow.

RUDALL: She says ". . . become;" "Come!" he says from back there. And then for the first time, Everyman fully realizes Death. It is *the* human moment in the play. While he's acknowleded all these things that he's been going through, penance and that sort of thing, he's been busy at it. Now on these last few lines, very frightened, he asks, "Who'll come with me?" And Good Deeds comforts him. He says his last Latin words, *"In manus tuas. . . ."*, and he walks down with Good Deeds, holding the cross and his book of accounts. He takes the first three steps down that ramp, and then there is a blackout. And there is Death, with a candle, all in black, but he's got an anatomical hand; he turns around and walks out; they follow him, to the chanting of monks. So it's a long death scene before Knowledge starts to speak again. The whole church is black, except for the candle in Death's hand, for about forty-five seconds. Then the lights come back up on Knowledge, and she begins to talk, with some more singing from way back up in the choir loft.

FIELD: Then the doctor comes out?

RUDALL: He's the same character, the prologue and the epilogue, is what I thought for it.

FIELD: The messenger at the beginning and the doctor at the end—

RUDALL: Right, the same character. We made him a monk. Up in the pulpit. He was the one who put out the candles in the church to get the play started. He was able to provide the . . . the solution to the problem of style . . . to acknowledge that this was a church performance. "I am the priest that is telling you to watch this play in my church"—that kind of feeling.

Death, we are told, is increasingly prevalent on TV and in the movies. In fiction it is elaborated at great length. In the newspapers what is lost in detail is made up for by a satisfying sense of authenticity. It would seem that of all the media, the one most unsuited to present the topic to a jaded public is the theatre which has had to content itself with mere psychological decay. Closeups, trick shots and realistic gore are in the province of the cinema. Long verbal accounts, once the messenger's speeches in Greek tragedy, are now exclusively the property of Book of the Month. And to vie with the newspaper for authenticity would create seemingly costly and ticklish casting problems.

Nevertheless, the University Theatre's recent and most ambitious project has been nothing but a revival, so to speak of staged death. *Everyman,* the 15th century Dutch morality play, is a primer on dying that becomes, in the hands of director Nicholas Rudall, both immediate and meaningful. The medieval pageant begins in the traditional *danse macabre* mode as Death, having received instructions from God, puts forth one sinister skeletal claw and touches the terrified and unprepared Everyman. Although Death sternly refused to grant any man respite, Everyman manages to eke nearly 45 minutes which he uses in illustration of the *ars moriendi*—to confess, do penance, receive extreme unction, and make a will leaving half his goods to the poor and half to the church.

Mr. Rudall has taken full advantage of the opportunity for spectacle using to the full the Gothic grandeur of Rockefeller Chapel. The Chapel was lit by candles when the audience entered. These were snuffed out by cowled figures before the prologue. Another monk-like figure paced the center aisle swinging a censer. Gregorian Chant sounded from a choir hidden behind the stage area. The lights dimmed and came up on a tableau of medieval revelers on stage as the priest (Donald Swanton) ascended to the pulpit to deliver the prologue in the form of a sermon to be illustrated by the subsequent action.

God (the inimitable Kenneth Northcott), resplendent in gold and white, held forth from aloft—from the chapel choir left, to be exact—and the bemused audience below craned their necks appropriately to look at him as he made known his displeasure with Everyman. Death (Robert Hoover), in the traditional black with his face also draped in flat black giving the eerie appearance of an empty hood, summons the unsuspecting Everyman (Gordon Cameron) most impressively.

In the expanded moment between Death's initial summons and the descent into the grave at the end, Everyman turns to each of things he has valued in life: fellowship (Joel Cope), Kindred (Anna Gwin Pickens), Cousin (Mary Speers), and Goods (Carl Orland), and later to his faculties: Discretion, Five Wits, Beauty, and Strength who are played by the same actors, doublecast respectively. These players were gorgeously costumed by Judy Fink after Medieval models of bankers and matrons. All that he has held dear fails him now, and his Good Deeds (Kelly Nespor) he finds willing but too weak to assist him. In fact, she had been lying immobile throughout the first half of the play on the top plateau of the many-tiered stage, costumed in marble white, looking like a stone carving on a sarcophagus. When she replies to Everyman's pleas the audience is startled, realizing that they, too, have been ignoring Good Deeds.

Guided by Good Deeds' sister, Knowledge (Ellen Clements), who must be taken as representing not worldly or intellectual knowledge but acknowledgment of past wrong-doing, Everyman is led to confess and do penance in the form of a graphically executed self-flagellation. This revives and strengthens his Good Deeds who is then able to accompany him and plead for him before God.

The difficulties with this brilliantly conceived production were, for the most part, technical ones. The lighting, at best, was barely adequate and was sometimes poor enough to be distracting and break the fragile mood. The stage, an exceptionally interesting design by Michael Gall, was too small for the action and the players did not maneuver on it with ease. Rockefeller Chapel, unexcelled for atmosphere, presents enormous technical problems. The acoustical properties of the vast vault not only include an echo, but also seem to raise the pitch of the speaker's voice, a trick particularly damaging to Gordon Cameron's lovely musical tenor, Mary Speers' soprano, and Anna Gwin Pickens' lilting, high-pitched British.

Mr. Rudall's production, and perhaps every production of a play so far removed from the modern milieu, relies very much on a totality of effect that it suffers disproportionately from minor difficulties that distract the audience's attention. Mr. Rudall's concept also aimed at a balance between ritual and realism, a combination dictated by the stylized, symbolic action, and the delicate characterization revealed in the dialogue. The minor characters lacked a strong sense of this balance and vacillated uncomfortably between the formal and human aspects of their roles. The three main figures, however, Gordon Cameron, Kelly Nespor, and Ellen Clements, had a firm grasp of both the allegorical and realistic aspects of their roles.

The overall achievement is a fine one for the University Theatre and the companion play, T.S. Eliot's *Murder in the Cathedral* also to be staged in Rockefeller in the spring is looked for with great interest.

Figure 25. The Renaissance English theater.

RENAISSANCE ENGLISH THEATER

When James Burbage built the first permanent English public theater in 1576, he called it, simply and boldly, The Theater. Retrospectively, that name takes on emblematic force, signifying not just a single building but the beginning of the greatest period of drama since the Greeks. Burbage was the leader of the Earl of Leicester's Men; his company would later become the Lord Chamberlain's Men and then the King's Men; their principal playwright for twenty years was William Shakespeare. Burbage's theater was so successful that it was quickly followed by others: The Curtain in 1577, The Newington Butts in 1579, The Rose in 1587, The Swan in 1595, The Globe in 1599, The Fortune in 1600, and others in the early seventeenth century.

All these public theaters, though they varied in shape from round to square to octagonal, were designed according to roughly similar principles, and they were all quite large, capable of holding between 2000 and 3000 spectators. The exact origin of their design has never been firmly established, but the basic plan—a yard with a stage jutting into the center of it and three levels of galleries surrounding the yard—suggests that it may well have been modelled on inn-yard or courtyard performances of an earlier period (see Figure 25). The stage itself consisted of two acting levels, and on each level there were several distinct acting areas. In the octagonally shaped Globe, for example, where many of Shakespeare's plays were performed, the primary acting surface on the ground level extended about twenty-seven feet into the yard, which was itself only about fifty-five feet in diameter. Thus the stage occupied about fifty percent of the yard. And at its widest, where it joined with the superstructure of the galleries, the stage was about forty-three feet wide. At the back of the stage on each side were doors and exits, and between the doors was an inner stage that was curtained when not in use (see Figure 25). On the second level there was another set of acting areas: windows above the doors on the lower level, a gallery between the windows, and behind the gallery another inner stage (see Figure 25). Above the second level, there may have been yet another gallery at the back for musicians, but the evidence for one is uncertain. Whatever the case, almost the entire stage was sheltered by a canopy that extended out from the roof of the theater.

The dimensions and design of that stage created a unique theatrical experience, unlike anything else during the Renaissance or at any other time in history. To begin with, the physical proximity of the stage to the surrounding galleries and to the spectators standing in the yard created a much more intimate relationship between actors and audience than the Greek theater provided. That physical intimacy must inevitably have aroused in the audience an immediate and personal involvement with the dramatic experience, much greater certainly than any other staging system provided, except perhaps for the medieval. At the same time, the Renaissance English theater continued to sustain a communal atmosphere, for the yard was open to the sky, and the plays were performed in daylight. The spectators consequently could easily see one another as they sat in the galleries or stood in the yard.

The size and design of the theater also made possible a highly flexible drama. As in the medieval period, the main acting surface was generalized, but unlike the medieval stage, it was not restricted to a limited number of locales established by set pieces. The stage could, in fact, become any number of places simply by the departure of one set of characters and the appearance of another, implying in their dialogue a new location, as in the line, "So this is the forest of Arden." The other acting areas made possible a wide variety of discovery scenes, bedroom scenes, and balcony scenes, not to mention disappearance scenes through a trapdoor on the ground level stage. Only a few props were used to suggest the location of a scene: a bed, a throne, a tree, a rock. Costuming, as in the medieval tradition, followed current rather than historically accurate styles of dress, but since Elizabethan theater managers did not spend much money on sets, they lavished their resources on costumes. The account book of Philip Henslowe, the leader of Worcester's Men and Burbage's chief competitor, records an amount of six pounds, thirteen shillings spent on a black velvet dress to be worn by the title character of *A Woman Killed with Kindness* (1603), while the same accounts tell us that the author, Thomas Heywood, received only six pounds in all for his play.

To these theaters came a rich outpouring of drama, created in part by the opportunities offered on their flexible, nonrealistic, and intimate stages, but growing also out of two different dramatic traditions. Since the mid-fifteenth century, small groups of professional actors had been touring England, setting up their show wherever they could expect to collect enough money or get enough hospitality to make it worth their while. They were highly versatile performers, capable of staging any kind of play in any kind of physical situation—in a banquet room, in a town hall, in an inn-yard, or on a village green. The plays they performed were relatively short pieces known as "Interludes," which combined material from a wide range of sources: biblical tales, classical legends, folk stories, fables, historical events, and fictional narratives. And the range of their sources was matched by the range of activities and moods they often brought together in a single play. Much as *The Second Shepherd's Play* combines the ludicrous sheep-stealing episode with the devotional visit of the shepherds, so the Interludes frequently combined comic and tragic elements, or historical and farcical elements at will. They sustained in England a highly flexible kind of drama that established important precedents for the magnificent multi-plot plays that were to come into being at the end of the sixteenth century.

At the same time that the native tradition was flourishing in the early sixteenth century, the classical influence was beginning to be felt in the grammar schools and universities of England, where Roman plays were being read and performed, and English imitations were being written and performed. During the 1530s, for example, a headmaster at Eton, Nicholas Udall, wrote *Ralph Roister Doister,* which he modelled on a comedy by Plautus, *The Braggart Soldier.* Later, in the 1550s, a comedy by "Mr. S.," *Gammer Gurton's Needle,* which was performed at Cambridge, not only drew on Roman plot devices, but also introduced elements from the native tradition of farce, thus anticipating that distinctive tendency of the great Renaissance drama to unite popular and classical elements in a single play. A similar kind of fusing took place in the first regular English tragedy, *Gorboduc,* which dramatized the story of a legendary king of Britain, who divides his kingdom and thus brings about familial dissension and political disaster. In this instance, pseudo-historical material from English chronicles was treated in the manner both of a Senecan revenge tragedy and a medieval morality play, thus anticipating the history play and the revenge tragedy that were to flourish in the late sixteenth and early seventeenth centuries. The authors of *Gorboduc,* Thomas Sackville and Thomas Norton, were students at the Inner Temple, one of the Inns of Court where young men of the period lived and studied to be lawyers. And, like the grammar schools and the universities, the Inns of Court sustained an active tradition of writing and performing plays that combined classical or Italian neoclassical precedents with native English elements. The Inns of Court performed their plays to celebrate a wide variety of occasions before an audience of the socially elite, the noble, and the educated. In Renaissance England, members of the upper class were being educated in the theater and were themselves creating a theatrical tradition that was to bear fruit in the numerous young men with university training who turned to the public theaters at the end of the sixteenth century.

Once the educated and the professional theater traditions had firmly taken hold, all that remained was for the two to be brought together—in the right way, at the right place, at the right historical moment. The right time had already come when Elizabeth I ascended to the throne in 1558. She brought religious toleration to England, calming the unrest created by her half-sister Mary's attempt to restore Catholicism as the state religion. Elizabeth's political genius stimulated a heady period of exploration and expansion, marked by the voyages of Sir Francis Drake, the commerce of the merchant fleet, the defeat of the Spanish Armada, and the creation of the East India Company. England, under Elizabeth, had become a great naval power, and that power produced great wealth and national pride. The wealth rapidly turned London into a major city, the pride led quickly to a social unity ideal for the life of theater, and The Theater of Burbage gave it a place in which to live.

With the establishment of permanent theaters in London and acting troupes based in London, the golden age of English drama began. The exuberant tendencies of the period were echoed in the richness of dramatic language—for the language, on a stage without sets, had to create the world of the play for its spectators. In *Antony and Cleopatra,* for example, Shakespeare could evoke Rome in one scene and Egypt in the next simply by shifting from the austere language of Caesar to the exotic style of Cleopatra. In *Henry V,* he could evoke the battlefield at Agincourt or the palace of the French king by turning from Henry's military rhetoric to Burgundy's flowing speech of reconciliation. At the same time, the flexibility of this "bare" stage encouraged plays of every kind, and thus Polonius's definition, "comical-tragical-historical-pastoral," is apter than he knew. Because the drama already existing in England combined so many elements, the dramatists were ready for the stage when it finally appeared, almost as if the nature of their art had called it into existence. The drama of Marlowe, Shakespeare, Jonson, Webster, and all their contemporaries, was born from the wedding of fine art and commercial industry—a marriage that we still recognize in the condition of modern theater.

CHRISTOPHER MARLOWE

1564—1593

Marlowe, the earliest of the major English dramatists, wrote all of his plays, except for a youthful college piece, during an extraordinarily productive six-year period between 1587 and his death. Before he turned to the theater, Marlowe had been a scholarship student at Cambridge, where he studied for the clergy, but evidently never took holy orders. Instead, he went off to London and followed the pattern of a number of other young men, most of whom had been to one of the universities and then turned to a career of writing. Usually referred to as the University Wits, they include Robert Greene, whose double plots and comic heroines established dramatic precedents for Shakespeare's romantic comedies; John Lyly, whose witty and ornate prose style also influenced Shakespeare; and Thomas Kyd, whose sensational revenge play, *The Spanish Tragedy,* started a theatrical vogue leading to such masterful revenge tragedies as *Hamlet* and *The Duchess of Malfi*. Although they were writing during the same period as Marlowe, when professional theater was beginning to flourish in London, none of them was so decisively and variously influential as Marlowe, and none certainly was so outstanding a dramatist. Before he was stabbed to death in a tavern quarrel, Marlowe had established the verse form and set major dramatic precedents for English tragedy, heroic drama, and the history play.

In the two parts of *Tamburlaine,* written in 1587 after leaving Cambridge, Marlowe turned a fourteenth century Mongolian warrior whom he had read about in various historical sources into the dramatic archetype of the superhero, the aspiring man of lowly birth who by force of his will and mind and power seeks to dominate the entire world—indeed, the entire universe. Though Tamburlaine is successively undone by the single force he cannot overcome—human mortality—his boldness took the Elizabethan theater by storm, calling forth a whole rash of plays with blood and thunder supermen. More influential even than the character of Tamburlaine was his thundering rhetoric, which Marlowe had self-consciously announced in the prologue to the play, inviting his audience to "hear the Scythian Tamburlaine/Threatening the world with high astounding terms." In his brief but polemic prologue, Marlowe deliberately set himself off from what he called the "jigging veins of rhyming mother wits," and in the play he made good on his promise, for the poetry of Tamburlaine neither jigs nor rhymes. It roars, and it roars in blank verse, heightened by rhetorical figures, rhythmical patterns, mythological allusions, dramatically suspended sentences, and dazzling imagery, the likes of which had never been heard before on the Elizabethan stage. When Marlowe proved the potency of blank verse, and in his later plays its flexibility, it quickly became the dominant medium of Elizabethan drama, used in comedies, tragedies, and histories alike.

In his subsequent plays, Marlowe continued to be preoccupied with the theme of the aspiring man, a theme that expressed the intense conflict in his own time between the medieval heritage of a divinely ordained hierarchy in religion, in government, in society, and the essentially modern scheme of things developing out of Protestantism, Machiavellian political theory, and scientific inquiry, all of which opposed medieval authority with renaissance individualism. In *The Jew of Malta,* for example, Marlowe created an extraordinarily successful merchant, Barabas the Jew, who regards the wealth he has amassed and the power it brings him as the greatest values in the world. But Marlowe ultimately found his most compelling image of the aspiring man in the story of Faustus, a legendary German magician, whose fantastic career had been narrated in German and then translated into English in 1592, providing the source for one of his last and greatest plays, *Doctor Faustus.* Unlike Tamburlaine and Barabas, Faustus seeks power and satisfaction neither through wealth nor through political dominion, but through knowledge, infinite knowledge, which he is willing to pay for by consigning his soul to the devil. During the course of the play, he is shown to be torn between worldly aspiration and spiritual awareness of its peril to his soul. *Doctor Faustus* thus dramatizes the spiritual crisis of a renaissance Everyman. But unlike the medieval Everyman, Faustus does not take heed of his Good Angel until his soul is beyond redemption, and the play ends with the terrifying spectacle of Faustus helplessly seeking to avoid eternal damnation.

Damnation is not the danger in *Edward II,* but its tragedy is no less compelling. In fact, *Edward II,* along with *Doctor Faustus,* represents the beginning of great tragedy on the English stage. *Edward II* also represents the first flowering of the English history play, a dramatic form as distinctive of the English renaissance as revenge tragedy or romantic comedy. Indeed, the English history play was as characteristic of its own time as the biblical cycles had been during the medieval period, or tragedy during the classical Greek period. Like those forms, the history play turned to the past to find dramatic subject matter for the present. But the English history play did not look to a far distant past, a past combining myth and spiritual history. It turned, rather, to a past relatively close at hand, a past focusing exclusively on secular history, the history of England itself. Sources for the English history plays were readily available in the numerous chronicles of England written during the sixteenth century, most of them painstakingly recounting events, characterizing rulers, and moralizing on their reigns—all of them reflecting the nationalistic consciousness of the age in which they were written. It was to just such a chronicle, written by Raphael Holinshed in 1577, that Marlowe turned for the source of *Edward II,* much as the dramatists who started writing history plays during the 1580s turned to Holinshed and earlier chroniclers, and just as Shakespeare and those who followed Marlowe were to do during the thirty years that history plays retained their popularity on the London stage.

Neither Marlowe nor the other dramatists merely reported history in their plays. As often as not, they invented it, freely altering, modifying, and even creating characters and events to suit their varying dramatic purposes. Not until Marlowe, however, had any dramatist so decisively shaped his material as to produce the tragic exploration of kingship, power, and political order that is worked out in *Edward II.* In *Edward II,* Marlowe condensed Holinshed's thirty-thousand word account of Edward's twenty-year reign into a dramatic history that seems to be as brief and as swift as the few hours it must have taken to stage the play itself. In the process, of course, he decisively altered history to suit his own theatrical conception of Edward. For example, the destructive homosexual relationship between Edward and Gaveston was a legacy of history, but Marlowe gave it more attention and emphasis than Holinshed. And the painful effects of that relationship on the queen, revealed most poignantly in the scenes when Gaveston and Edward are forced to leave one another, parting like lovers in her weeping presence—those events were Marlowe's invention. So also were both the private and public consequences of those events—the queen's adulterous relationship and political allegiance with Mortimer. Mortimer, in fact, was only a minor figure in Holinshed's chronicle, but Marlowe, given his fascination with the aspiring man, turned Mortimer into a major character, the polar opposite of Edward in every respect. Out of their opposition to one another, Marlowe created a political tragedy resulting from the conflict between a rightful ruler, unfit to rule, and a capable ruler, who can only rule by usurping power and overthrowing the hierarchical basis of political order. The beauty and meaning of that order are revealed in the pomp and circumstance of the early court scenes, but the peril to that order is just as strongly revealed in Edward's abuse of it in those same scenes.

The political and human problems raised by the conflict between Edward and Mortimer were issues that fascinated the Elizabethan age, particularly because of its intensely national consciousness, yet those issues are no less relevant to the modern consciousness and the modern political order. Thus *Edward II* continues to be performed in the twentieth century, and performed with great success, as it was by the Prospect Theater, which first produced it for the Edinburgh Festival in 1969, and then moved it to London, where it continued to attract audiences in 1970. This same production was subsequently videotaped and shown on educational television stations throughout the United States. As the review and photographs of the production (see Figures 26 and 27) make clear, it is very much an actors' play, and when it finds actors who are up to the varied challenges of its several roles, it is altogether as thrilling—and disturbing—as it must have been for its original Elizabethan audiences.

EDWARD II

The Troublesome Reign and Lamentable Death of Edward the Second, King of England. With the Tragical Fall of Proud Mortimer.

BY CHRISTOPHER MARLOWE

SPEAKING CHARACTERS

GAVESTON
1 POOR MAN
2 POOR MAN
3 POOR MAN
EDWARD II
LANCASTER
MORTIMER THE ELDER
MORTIMER THE YOUNGER, *his nephew*
EDMUND, EARL OF KENT
WARWICK
BISHOP OF COVENTRY
ARCHBISHOP OF CANTERBURY
QUEEN ISABELLA
PEMBROKE
BEAUMONT
SPENCER THE YOUNGER
BALDOCK
KING'S NIECE
1 MESSENGER
GUARD
ARUNDEL
JAMES, *servant to Pembroke*
SPENCER THE ELDER, *father of* YOUNGER

LEVUNE
2 MESSENGER
PRINCE EDWARD
JOHN OF HAINAULT
3 MESSENGER
RICE AP HOWELL
ABBOT
MONKS
LEICESTER
MOWER
BISHOP OF WINCHESTER
TRUSSEL
BERKELEY
4 MESSENGER
MATREVIS
GURNEY
LIGHTBORN
CHAMPION
SOLDIER
1 LORD
2 LORD

MUTE CHARACTERS

MAYOR OF BRISTOL, LADIES, SOLDIERS, ATTENDANTS

ACT 1 / SCENE 1

(Enter GAVESTON *reading on a letter that was brought him from the King.)*

GAVESTON: "My father is deceas'd. Come, Gaveston,
And share the kingdom with thy dearest friend."
Ah, words that make me surfeit with delight!
What greater bliss can hap° to Gaveston
Than live and be the favorite of a king?
Sweet prince, I come! These, these thy amorous lines
Might have enforc'd me to have swum from France
And, like Leander°, gasp'd upon the sand
10 So thou would'st smile and take me in thine arms!

The sight of London to my exil'd eyes
Is as Elysium° to a new-come soul.
—Not that I love the city or the men
But that it harbors him I hold so dear,
The King—upon whose bosom let me die,
And with the world be still at enmity!
What need the arctic people love starlight,
To whom the sun shines both by day and night?
Farewell base stooping to the lordly peers,
My knee shall bow to none but to the King.
20 As for the multitude that are but sparks
Rak'd up in embers of their poverty,
Tanti:° I'll fawn first on the wind
That glanceth at my lips and flieth away.
But how now, what are these?

---

hap, happen. **Leander,** a young man who according to classical legend swam the Hellespont to meet his beloved Hero, a priestess of Aphrodite.

Elysium, the heaven of classical mythology. **Tanti,** so much for them.

(Enter THREE POOR MEN.*)*

POOR MEN: [Poor men] such as desire your worship's
    service.

GAVESTON *(to* 1 POOR MAN*)*: What canst thou do?

1 POOR MAN: I can ride.

30 GAVESTON: But I have no horses. *(to* 2 POOR MAN*)*
    What art thou?

2 POOR MAN: A traveler.

GAVESTON: Let me see: Thou would'st do well
    To wait at my trencher and tell me lies at
    dinnertime—
    And as I like your discoursing, I'll have you.
    (to 3 POOR MAN*)* And what art thou?

3 POOR MAN: A soldier, that hath serv'd against the
    Scot.

40 GAVESTON: Why, there are hospitals for such as you.
    I have no war, and therefore, sir, begone!

3 POOR MAN: Farewell, and perish by a soldier's hand,
    That would'st reward them with an hospital!°

GAVESTON *(aside)*: (Ay, ay, these words of his move me
    as much
    As if a goose would play the porpentine°
    And dart her plumes, thinking to pierce my breast.
    But yet it is no pain to speak men fair.°
    I'll flatter these and make them live in hope.)

50 —You know that I came lately out of France,
    And yet I have not view'd my lord the King;
    If I speed well, I'll entertain you all.

ALL: We thank your worship.

GAVESTON: I have some business, leave me to myself.

ALL: We will wait here about the court. *(Exeunt.)*

GAVESTON: Do. These are not men for me.
    I must have wanton poets, pleasant wits,
    Musicians that with touching of a string
    May draw the pliant King which way I please.

60 Music and poetry is his delight.
    Therefore I'll have Italian masks by night,
    Sweet speeches, comedies, and pleasing shows;
    And in the day when he shall walk abroad,
    Like sylvan nymphs my pages shall be clad:
    My men, like satyrs grazing on the lawns,
    Shall with their goat feet dance an antic hay:
    Sometimes a lovely boy in Dian's shape,°
    With hair that gilds the water as it glides,
    Crownets of pearl about his naked arms—

70 And in his sportful hands an olive-tree
    To hide those parts which men delight to see—
    Shall bathe him in a spring: and there hard by,
    One like Actaeon° peeping through the grove,

---

hospital, a refuge for destitute soldiers. **porpentine,**
porcupine. **speak men fair,** flatter. **Dian's shape,** the
appearance of Diana, Roman goddess of the woods and of
wild nature. **Actaeon,** a young man who according to
mythology spied on Diana while she was bathing and in
retribution was turned by her into a stag and torn to pieces
by his own dogs.

Shall by the angry goddess be transformed:
And running in the likeness of an hart°
By yelping hounds pull'd down, and seem to die.
Such things as these best please His Majesty,
My lord—Here comes the King and the nobles
From the parliament.—I'll stand aside.

(Enter the KING, LANCASTER, MORTIMER SENIOR, MOR-
TIMER JUNIOR, EDMUND EARL OF KENT, GUY EARL OF
WARWICK, *etc.)*

KING EDWARD: Lancaster!   80

LANCASTER: My lord!

GAVESTON *(aside)*: (That Earl of Lancaster do I
    abhor.)

KING EDWARD: Will you not grant me this?
    (aside)—(In spite of them
    I'll have my will! And these two Mortimers
    That cross me thus, shall know I am displeas'd!)

ELDER MORTIMER: If you love us, my lord, hate
    Gaveston!

GAVESTON *(aside)*: (That villain Mortimer, I'll be his 90
    death!)

YOUNGER MORTIMER: Mine uncle here, this earl, and I
    myself
    Were sworn to your father at his death,
    That he should ne'er return into the realm.
    And know, my lord, ere I will break my oath,
    This sword of mine, that should offend your foes,
    Shall sleep within the scabbard at thy need,
    And underneath thy banners march who will,
    For Mortimer will hang his armor up.   100

GAVESTON *(aside)*: (Mort Dieu!)°

KING EDWARD: Well, Mortimer, I'll make thee rue
    these words!
    Beseems it thee to contradict thy King?
    Frown'st thou thereat, aspiring Lancaster?
    The sword shall plane the furrows of thy brows
    And hew these knees that now are grown so stiff!
    I will have Gaveston—and you shall know
    What danger 'tis to stand against your King!

GAVESTON *(aside)*: (Well done, Ned!)   110

LANCASTER: My lord, why do you thus incense your
    peers
    That naturally would love and honor you
    But for that base and obscure Gaveston?
    Four earldoms have I, besides Lancaster—
    Derby, Salisbury, Lincoln, Leicester—
    These will I sell to give my soldiers pay
    Ere Gaveston shall stay within the realm!
    Therefore if he be come, expel him straight!

EARL OF KENT: Barons and earls, your pride hath 120
    made me mute,
    But now I'll speak, and to the proof, I hope.
    I do remember in my father's days
    Lord Percy of the north being highly mov'd

---

hart, deer. **Mort Dieu,** the equivalent of "To Hell!"

Brav'd° Mowbray in presence of the King:
For which, had not His Highness lov'd him well,
He should have lost his head: but with his look
Th' undaunted spirit of Percy was appeas'd
And Mowbray and he were reconcil'd.
130 Yet dare you brave the King unto his face?
Brother, revenge it, and let these their heads
Preach upon poles° for trespass of their tongues!
WARWICK: O, our heads!
KING EDWARD: Ay, yours. And therefore I would wish
  you grant—
WARWICK: Bridle thy anger, gentle Mortimer.
YOUNGER MORTIMER: I cannot, nor I will not. I must
  speak.
  Cousin, our hands I hope shall fence our heads
140 And strike off his that makes you threaten us.
  Come, uncle, let us leave the brain-sick King,
  And henceforth parle° with our naked swords.
ELDER MORTIMER: Wiltshire hath men enough to save
  our heads.
WARWICK: All Warwickshire will love him for my
  sake.
LANCASTER: And northward Gaveston hath many
  friends.
  Adieu, my lord. And either change your mind,
150 Or look to see the throne where you should sit
  To float in blood and at thy wanton head,
  The glozing° head of thy base minion thrown!

(Exeunt NOBLES.)

KING EDWARD: I cannot brook these haughty
  menaces.
  Am I a king, and must be overrul'd?
  Brother, display my ensigns in the field!
  I'll bandy° with the barons and the earls,
  And either die—or live with Gaveston.
GAVESTON: I can no longer keep me from my lord.
160 (Comes forward.)
KING EDWARD: What, Gaveston! Welcome! Kiss not
  my hand—
  Embrace me, Gaveston as I do thee.
  Why should'st thou kneel? knowest thou not who I
  am?
  —Thy friend, thyself, another Gaveston!
  Not Hylas was more mourn'd of Hercules°
  Than thou hast been of me since thy exile.
GAVESTON: And since I went from hence, no soul in
170 Hell
  Hath felt more torment than poor Gaveston.

Brav'd, opposed, insulted. heads ... poles, as a
warning to others, the heads of executed traitors were
displayed on poles. parle, parley; literally, speak, talk.
glozing, flattering. bandy, volley, as in tennis. Hylas ...
Hercules, according to mythology, Hylas was the favorite
page of Hercules who deeply mourned his loss after he was
lured away by water nymphs.

KING EDWARD: I know it. Brother, welcome home my
  friend.
  Now let the treacherous Mortimers conspire,
  And that high-minded Earl of Lancaster.
  I have my wish in that I joy thy sight!
  And sooner shall the sea o'erwhelm my land,
  Than bear the ship that shall transport thee hence!
  I here create thee Lord High Chamberlain,
  Chief Secretary to the state and me,   180
  Earl of Cornwall, King and Lord of Man.
GAVESTON: My lord, these titles far exceed my worth.
EARL OF KENT: Brother, the least of these may well
  suffice
  For one of greater birth than Gaveston.
KING EDWARD: Cease, brother, for I cannot brook
  these words.
  Thy worth, sweet friend, is far above my gifts.
  Therefore, to equal it, receive my heart!
  If for these dignities thou be envied,   190
  I'll give thee more, for but to honor thee
  Is Edward pleas'd with kingly regiment.
  Fear'st thou thy person? Thou shalt have a guard.
  Want'st thou gold? Go to my treasury.
  Would'st thou be lov'd and fear'd? Receive my seal,
  Save or condemn, and in our name command
  Whatso thy mind affects or fancy likes.
GAVESTON: It shall suffice me to enjoy your love,
  Which whiles I have, I think myself as great
  As Caesar riding in the Roman street,   200
  With captive kings at his triumphant car.

(Enter the BISHOP OF COVENTRY.)

KING EDWARD: Whither goes my lord of Coventry so
  fast?
BISHOP OF COVENTRY: To celebrate your father's
  exequies.°
  —But is that wicked Gaveston return'd?
KING EDWARD: Ay, priest, and lives to be reveng'd on
  thee
  That wert the only cause of his exile.
GAVESTON: 'Tis true! And but for reverence of these   210
  robes,
  Thou should'st not plod one foot beyond this place
BISHOP OF COVENTRY: I did not more than I was
  bound to do.
  And, Gaveston, unless thou be reclaim'd,°
  As then I did incense the parliament,
  So will I now, and thou shalt back to France.
GAVESTON: Saving your reverence, you must pardon
  me. (Bows ironically.)
KING EDWARD: Throw off his golden miter, rend his   220
  stole, (Grasps BISHOP.)
  And in the channel christen him anew.
EARL OF KENT: Ah, brother, lay not violent hands on
  him.

---

exequies, funeral services.   reclaim'd, reformed.

For he'll complain unto the see° of Rome.
GAVESTON: Let him complain unto the see of Hell!
    I'll be reveng'd on him for my exile. (Roughs
    BISHOP.)
KING EDWARD: No, spare his life, but seize upon his
230   goods.
    Be thou lord bishop and receive his rents—
    And make him serve thee as thy chaplain.
    I give him thee. Here, use him as thou wilt.

(Pushes BISHOP toward GAVESTON.)

GAVESTON: He shall to prison, and there die in bolts.
KING EDWARD: Ay, to the Tower, the Fleet° or where
    thou wilt.
BISHOP OF COVENTRY: For this offense, be thou
    accurst of God!
KING EDWARD: Who's there? (Calls off-stage.
    ATTENDANTS appear.)
240   Convey this priest to the Tower.
BISHOP OF COVENTRY: True, true.

(ATTENDANTS remove BISHOP.)

KING EDWARD: But in the meantime, Gaveston, away,
    And take possession of his house and goods.
    Come, follow me, and thou shalt have my guard
    To see it done, and bring thee safe again.
GAVESTON: What should a priest do with so fair a
    house?
    A prison may best beseem° his holiness. (Exeunt.)

ACT 1 / SCENE 2

(Enter both the MORTIMERS, WARWICK, and LANCAS-
TER.)

WARWICK: 'Tis true, the bishop is in the Tower,
    And goods and body given to Gaveston.
LANCASTER: What, will they tyrannize upon the
    church?
    Ah, wicked King! Accursed Gaveston!
    This ground which is corrupted with their steps
    Shall be their timeless sepulcher or mine.
YOUNGER MORTIMER: Well, let that peevish
    Frenchman guard him sure—
10   Unless his breast be sword-proof he shall die.
ELDER MORTIMER: How now, why droops the Earl of
    Lancaster?
YOUNGER MORTIMER: Wherefore is Guy of Warwick
    discontent?
LANCASTER: That villain Gaveston is made an earl.
ELDER MORTIMER: An earl!
WARWICK: Ay, and besides Lord Chamberlain of the
    realm,
    And Secretary too, and Lord of Man.

ELDER MORTIMER: We may not, nor we will not suffer
    this!   20
YOUNGER MORTIMER: Why post we not from hence to
    levy men?
LANCASTER: "My Lord of Cornwall," now at every
    word!
    And happy is the man whom he vouchsafes,°
    For vailing° of his bonnet, one good look.
    Thus, arm in arm, the King and he doth march—
    Nay more, the guard upon his lordship waits,
    And all the court begins to flatter him.
WARWICK: Thus leaning on the shoulder of the King.   30

(Leans on LANCASTER.)

    He nods and scorns and smiles at those that pass.
ELDER MORTIMER: Doth no man take exceptions at the
    slave?
LANCASTER: All stomach° him, but none dare speak a
    word.
YOUNGER MORTIMER: Ah, that bewrays° their
    baseness, Lancaster!
    Were all the earls and barons of my mind,
    We'll hale him from the bosom of the King
    And at the court-gate hang the peasant up: 40
    Who swoln with venom of ambitious pride
    Will be the ruin of the realm and us.
WARWICK: Here comes my lord of Canterbury's
    grace.
LANCASTER: His countenance bewrays he is
    displeas'd.

(Enter the ARCHBISHOP OF CANTERBURY and an
ATTENDANT.)

ARCHBISHOP: First were his sacred garments rent and
    torn,
    Then laid they violent hands upon him next;
    Himself imprisoned, and his goods asseiz'd: 50
    This certify the Pope. Away, take horse. (Exit
    ATTENDANT.)
LANCASTER: My lord, will you take arms against the
    King?
ARCHBISHOP: What need I? God himself is up in arms
    When violence is offer'd to the church.
YOUNGER MORTIMER: Then will you join with us that
    be his peers
    To banish or behead that Gaveston?
ARCHBISHOP: What else, my lords? For it concerns me   60
    near:
    The bishopric of Coventry is his.

(Enter the QUEEN.)

YOUNGER MORTIMER: Madam, whither walks Your
    Majesty so fast?
QUEEN ISABELLA: Unto the forest, gentle Mortimer,

---

see, ecclesiastic seat or region. Tower ... Fleet, The
Tower of London and the Fleet were both prisons during
the period of the play. beseem, suit, fit.

vouchsafes, favors. vailing, lowering. stomach, resent. bewrays, exposes, reveals.

To live in grief and baleful discontent,
For now my lord the King regards me not,
But dotes upon the love of Gaveston—
He claps his cheeks, and hangs about his neck,
70   Smiles in his face, and whispers in his ears—
And when I come he frowns, as who should say,
"Go whither thou wilt seeing I have Gaveston!"
ELDER MORTIMER: Is it not strange that he is thus
     bewitch'd?
YOUNGER MORTIMER: Madam, return unto the court
     again.
     That sly inveigling Frenchman we'll exile,
     Or lose our lives. And yet, ere that day come,
     The King shall lose his crown, for we have power,
80   And courage too, to be reveng'd at full.
ARCHBISHOP: But yet lift not your swords against the
     King.
LANCASTER: No but we'll lift Gaveston from hence.
WARWICK: And war must be the means, or he'll stay
     still.
QUEEN ISABELLA: Then let him stay. For rather than
     my lord
     Shall be oppress'd by civil mutinies,
     I will endure a melancholy life.
90   —And let him frolic with his minion.
ARCHBISHOP: My lords, to ease all this, but hear me
     speak:
     We and the rest that are his counsellors
     Will meet, and with a general consent
     Confirm his banishment with our hands and seals.
LANCASTER: What we confirm the King will frustrate.
YOUNGER MORTIMER: Then may we lawfully revolt
     from him.
WARWICK: But say, my lord, where shall this meeting
100   be?
ARCHBISHOP: At the New Temple.
YOUNGER MORTIMER: Content.
ARCHBISHOP: And, in the meantime, I'll entreat you
     all
     To cross to Lambeth, and stay with me.
LANCASTER: Come then, let's away.
YOUNGER MORTIMER: Madam, farewell!
QUEEN ISABELLA: Farewell, sweet Mortimer; and for
     my sake
110   Forbear to levy arms against the King.
YOUNGER MORTIMER: Ay, if words will serve; if not, I
     must. (*Exeunt.*)

ACT 1 / SCENE 3

(*Enter* GAVESTON *and the* EARL OF KENT.)

GAVESTON (*familiarly*): Edmund, the mighty Prince of
     Lancaster
     (That hath more earldoms than an ass can bear!)
     And both the Mortimers (two goodly men!)
     With Guy of Warwick (that redoubted knight!)

Are gone toward Lambeth. There let them remain.
     (*Exeunt.*)

ACT 1 / SCENE 4

(*Enter* NOBLES, LANCASTER *with document,* WARWICK,
PEMBROKE, ELDER MORTIMER, YOUNGER MOR-
TIMER, *the* ARCHIBISHOP OF CANTERBURY, *and* AT-
TENDANTS.)

LANCASTER: Here is the form of Gaveston's exile.
     May it please your lordship to subscribe your name.
ARCHBISHOP: Give me the paper. (*Subscribes, as do the
     rest.*)
LANCASTER: Quick, quick, my lord, I long to write my
     name.
WARWICK: But I long more to see him banish'd hence.
YOUNGER MORTIMER: The name of Mortimer shall
     fright the King,
     Unless he be declin'd from that base peasant.

(*Enter the* KING *and* GAVESTON *and* KENT. EDWARD
seats GAVESTON *by him on the throne.*)

KING EDWARD: What, are you mov'd that Gaveston   10
     sits here?
     It is our pleasure, we will have it so!
LANCASTER: Your Grace doth well to place him by
     your side,
     For nowhere else the new earl is so safe.
ELDER MORTIMER: What man of noble birth can brook
     this sight?
     Quam male conveniunt!°
     See what a scornful look the peasant casts!
PEMBROKE: Can kingly lions fawn on creeping ants?   20
WARWICK: Ignoble vassal, that like Phaeton°
     Aspir'st unto the guidance of the sun!
YOUNGER MORTIMER: Their downfall is at hand, their
     forces down—
     We will not thus be fac'd and over-peer'd.
KING EDWARD: Lay hands on that traitor Mortimer!
ELDER MORTIMER: Lay hands on that traitor
     Gaveston!

(ATTENDANTS *hold* GAVESTON.)

EARL OF KENT: Is this the duty that you owe your
     King?   30
WARWICK: We know our duties, let him know his
     peers.
KING EDWARD: Whither will you bear him? Stay or ye
     shall die!
ELDER MORTIMER: We are no traitors: therefore
     threaten not.

Quam male conveniunt, how ill they suit. **Phaeton,**
Apollo's son who according to Greek mythology was unable
to control the horses guiding the sun when he attempted to
drive them.

GAVESTON: No, threaten not, my lord, but pay them home.°
Were I a king—.

40 YOUNGER MORTIMER: Thou villain, wherefore talk'st thou of a king
That hardly art a gentleman by birth!

KING EDWARD: Were he a peasant, being my minion,
I'll make the proudest of you stoop to him.

LANCASTER: My lord, you may not thus disparage us!
Away, I say, with hateful Gaveston!

ELDER MORTIMER: And with the Earl of Kent that favors him.

(ATTENDANTS remove KENT and GAVESTON.)

KING EDWARD: Nay, then, lay violent hands upon
50 your King.
Here, Mortimer, sit thou in Edward's throne.
Warwick and Lancaster, wear you my crown.
Was ever king thus over-rul'd as I?

LANCASTER: Learn then to rule us better, and the realm.

YOUNGER MORTIMER: What we have done, our heart blood shall maintain.

WARWICK: Think you that we can brook this upstart pride?

60 KING EDWARD: Anger and wrathful fury stops my speech.

ARCHBISHOP: Why are you mov'd? Be patient, my lord,
And see what we your counsellors have done. *(Gives him document exiling GAVESTON.)*

YOUNGER MORTIMER: My lords, now let us all be resolute:
And either have our wills, or lose our lives.

KING EDWARD: Meet you for this, proud over-daring
70 peers?
Ere my sweet Gaveston shall part from me,
This isle shall fleet upon the ocean
And wander to the unfrequented Inde.°

ARCHBISHOP: You know that I am legate to the Pope.
On your allegiance to the see of Rome,
Subscribe as we have done to his exile.

YOUNGER MORTIMER: Curse him, if he refuse; and then may we
Depose him and elect another king!

80 KING EDWARD: Ay, there it goes! But yet I will not yield.
Curse me, depose me, do the worst you can!

LANCASTER: Then linger not, my lord, but do it straight.

ARCHBISHOP: Remember how the bishop was abus'd.
Either banish him that was the cause thereof,
Or I will presently discharge these lords
Of duty and allegiance due to thee.

KING EDWARD *(aside)*: (It boots me not to threat. I must speak fair.°   90
The legate of the Pope will be obey'd.)
—My Lord, *(to ARCHBISHOP)* you shall be Chancellor of the realm;
Thou, Lancaster, High Admiral of our fleet;
Young Mortimer and his uncle shall be earls;
And you, Lord Warwick, President of the North;
And thou *(to PEMBROKE)* of Wales. If this content you not,
Make several kingdoms of this monarchy
And share it equally amongst you all—   100
So I may have some nook or corner left
To frolic with my dearest Gaveston.

ARCHBISHOP: Nothing shall alter us. We are resolv'd.

LANCASTER: Come, come, subscribe.

YOUNGER MORTIMER: Why should you love him whom the world hates so?

KING EDWARD: Because he loves me more than all the world!
Ah, none but rude and savage-minded men
Would seek the ruin of my Gaveston!   110
You that be noble-born should pity him.

WARWICK: You that are princely-born should shake him off.
For shame subscribe,° and let the lown° depart.

ELDER MORTIMER: Urge him, my lord.

ARCHBISHOP: Are you content to banish him the realm?

KING EDWARD: I see I must, and therefore am content.
Instead of ink I'll write it with my tears. *(Subscribes.)*   120

YOUNGER MORTIMER: The King is love-sick for his minion.°

KING EDWARD: 'Tis done—and now, accursed hand, fall off!

LANCASTER: Give it me. I'll have it publish'd in the streets.

YOUNGER MORTIMER: I'll see him presently dispatch'd away.

ARCHBISHOP: Now is my heart at ease.

WARWICK: And so is mine.   130

PEMBROKE: This will be good news to the common sort.

ELDER MORTIMER: Be it or no, he shall not linger here.

(Exeunt NOBLES.)

KING EDWARD: How fast they run to banish him I love!
They would not stir, were it to do me good.
Why should a king be subject to a priest?
Proud Rome, that hatchest such imperial grooms,

---

pay . . . home, punish. **Inde,** India. **boots,** suits.

speak . . . fair, flatter. **subscribe,** sign one's name. **lown,** peasant. **minion,** male favorite, often with a sexual suggestion.

For these thy superstitious taper-lights,
140   Wherewith thy antichristian churches blaze,
I'll fire thy crazed buildings and enforce
The papal towers to kiss the lowly ground!
With slaughter'd priests may Tiber's channel swell,
And banks rais'd higher with their sepulchers!
As for the peers that back the clergy thus,
If I be King, not one of them shall live.

(Enter GAVESTON.*)*

GAVESTON: My lord, I hear it whisper'd everywhere
That I am banish'd and must fly the land.
KING EDWARD: 'Tis true, sweet Gaveston.—O! were it
150   false!
The legate of the Pope will have it so—
And thou must hence, or I shall be depos'd.
But I will reign to be reveng'd of them!
And therefore, sweet friend, take it patiently.
Live where thou wilt, I'll send thee gold enough;
And long thou shalt not stay; or if thou dost,
I'll come to thee. My love shall ne'er decline!
GAVESTON: Is all my hope turn'd to this hell of grief?
KING EDWARD: Rend not my heart with thy
160   too-piercing words—
Thou from this land, I from myself am banish'd.
GAVESTON: To go from hence grieves not poor
Gaveston—
But to forsake you, in whose gracious looks
The blessedness of Gaveston remains:
For nowhere else seeks he felicity.
KING EDWARD: And only this torments my wretched
soul
That, whether I will or no, thou must depart.
170   Be governor of Ireland in my stead,
And there abide till fortune call thee home.
Here, take my picture, and let me wear thine.

(They exchange pictures and embrace.)

O, might I keep thee here as I do this,
Happy were I, but now most miserable!
GAVESTON: 'Tis something to be pitied of a king.
KING EDWARD: Thou shalt not hence—I'll hide thee,
Gaveston.
GAVESTON: I shall be found, and then 'twill grieve me
more.
180   KING EDWARD: Kind words and mutual talk makes
our grief greater:
Therefore, with dumb embracement, let us part.
Stay, Gaveston, I cannot leave thee thus.
GAVESTON: For every look, my lord drops down a
tear.
Seeing I must go, do not renew my sorrow.
KING EDWARD: The time is little that thou hast to stay,
And, therefore, give me leave to look my fill.
But come, sweet friend, I'll bear thee on thy way.
190   GAVESTON: The peers will frown.

KING EDWARD: I pass not for their anger. Come, let's
go.
O that we might as well return as go!

(Enter QUEEN ISABELLA.*)*

QUEEN ISABELLA: Whither goes my lord?
KING EDWARD: Fawn not on me, French strumpet!
Get thee gone!
QUEEN ISABELLA: On whom but on my husband
should I fawn?
GAVESTON: On Mortimer, with whom, ungentle
Queen—   200
I say no more. Judge you the rest, my lord.
QUEEN ISABELLA: In saying this, thou wrong'st me,
Gaveston.
Is't not enough that thou corrupt'st my lord,
And art a bawd to his affections,
But thou must call mine honor thus in question?
GAVESTON: I mean not so. Your Grace must pardon
me.
KING EDWARD: Thou art too familiar with that
Mortimer: 210
And by thy means is Gaveston exil'd.
But I would wish thee reconcile the lords—
Or thou shalt ne'er be reconciled to me.
QUEEN ISABELLA: Your Highness knows, it lies not in
my power.
KING EDWARD: Away then! touch me not, come,
Gaveston.
QUEEN ISABELLA: Villain, 'tis thou that robb'st me of
my lord!
GAVESTON: Madam, 'tis you that rob me of my lord!   220
KING EDWARD: Speak not unto her, let her droop and
pine.
QUEEN ISABELLA: Wherein, my lord, have I deserv'd
these words?
Witness the tears that Isabella sheds;
Witness this heart that sighing for thee breaks,
How dear my lord is to poor Isabel!
KING EDWARD: And witness Heaven how dear thou
art to me!
There weep. For till my Gaveston be repeal'd,   230
Assure thyself thou com'st not in my sight.

(Exeunt EDWARD *and* GAVESTON.*)*

QUEEN ISABELLA: O miserable and distressed Queen!
Would when I left sweet France and was embark'd
That charming Circes walking on the waves
Had chang'd my shape,° or at the marriage-day
The cup of Hymen had been full of poison!
Or with those arms that twin'd about my neck
I had been stifled, and not liv'd to see

Circes . . . shape; a mythological enchantress who
changed men into animals and transformed her rival into a
monster.

The King my lord thus to abandon me!
240   Like frantic Juno will I fill the earth
With ghastly murmur of my sighs and cries,
For never doted Jove on Ganymede°
So much as he on cursed Gaveston.
But that will more exasperate his wrath.
I must entreat him, I must speak him fair,
And be a means to call home Gaveston—
And yet he'll ever dote on Gaveston!
And so am I for ever miserable!

(Enter the nobles: [LANCASTER, WARWICK, PEMBROKE,
ELDER MORTIMER, *and* YOUNGER MORTIMER] *to the*
QUEEN.*)*

LANCASTER: Look where the sister of the King of
250   France
Sits wringing of her hands and beats her breast.
WARWICK: The King, I fear, hath ill-entreated her.
PEMBROKE: Hard is the heart that injures such a saint.
YOUNGER MORTIMER: I know 'tis long of Gaveston she
weeps.
ELDER MORTIMER: Why? He is gone.
YOUNGER MORTIMER: Madam, how fares Your Grace?
QUEEN ISABELLA: Ah, Mortimer! now breaks the
King's hate forth,
260   And he confesseth that he loves me not.
YOUNGER MORTIMER: Cry quittance, madam, then,
and love not him.
QUEEN ISABELLA: No, rather will I die a thousand
deaths.
And yet I love in vain, he'll ne'er love me.
LANCASTER: Fear ye not, madam. Now his minion's
gone,
His wanton humor will be quickly left.
QUEEN ISABELLA: O never, Lancaster! I am enjoin'd
270   To sue upon you all for his repeal.
This wills my lord, and thus must I perform,
Or else be banish'd from His Highness' presence!
LANCASTER: For his repeal, madam? He comes not
back,
Unless the sea cast up his shipwrack body.
WARWICK: And to behold so sweet a sight as that
There's none here but would run his horse to
death!
YOUNGER MORTIMER: But, madam, would you have us
280   call him home?
QUEEN ISABELLA: Ay, Mortimer, for till he be restor'd,
The angry King hath banish'd me the court.
And therefore, as thou lov'st and tender'st me,
Be thou my advocate unto these peers.
YOUNGER MORTIMER: What! Would ye have me plead
for Gaveston?

Juno . . . Ganymede, Juno was jealous of her husband
Jove for his love of the young boy Ganymede.

ELDER MORTIMER: Plead for him that will, I am
resolv'd.
LANCASTER: And so am I, my lord. Dissuade the
Queen.   290
QUEEN ISABELLA: O Lancaster, let him dissuade the
King,
For 'tis against my will he should return.
WARWICK: Then speak not for him, let the peasant
go.
QUEEN ISABELLA: 'Tis for myself I speak, and not for
him.
PEMBROKE: No speaking will prevail, and therefore
cease.
YOUNGER MORTIMER: Fair Queen, forbear to angle   300
for the fish
Which being caught strikes him that takes it dead:
I mean that vile torpedo,° Gaveston,
That now, I hope, floats on the Irish seas!
QUEEN ISABELLA: Sweet Mortimer, sit down by me
awhile,
And I will tell thee reasons of such weight
As thou wilt soon subscribe to his repeal.°
YOUNGER MORTIMER: It is impossible, but speak your
mind. *(They sit.)*   310
QUEEN ISABELLA: Then thus.—But none shall hear it
but ourselves. *(They whisper apart.)*
LANCASTER: My lords, albeit the Queen win
Mortimer,
Will you be resolute, and hold with me?
ELDER MORTIMER: Not I, against my nephew.
PEMBROKE: Fear not. The Queen's words cannot alter
him.
WARWICK: No? Do but mark how earnestly she
pleads.   320
LANCASTER: And see how coldly his looks make
denial.
WARWICK: She smiles. Now for my life his mind is
chang'd!
LANCASTER: I'll rather lose his friendship, I, than
grant. *(*YOUNG MORTIMER *and* QUEEN *rise.)*
YOUNG MORTIMER: Well, of necessity it must be so.
(Aloud.)
My lords, that I abhor base Gaveston. *(He turns to
them)*   330
I hope your honors make no question.
And therefore though I plead for his repeal,
'Tis not for his sake but for our avail—
Nay for the realm's behoof and for the King's.
LANCASTER: Fie, Mortimer! Dishonor not thyself!
Can this be true, 'twas good to banish him?
And is this true, to call him home again?
Such reasons make white black, and dark night
day.

---

torpedo, electric ray fish. *repeal,* return.

340 YOUNGER MORTIMER: My lord of Lancaster, mark the respect—

LANCASTER: In no respect can contraries be true.

QUEEN ISABELLA: Yet, good my lord, hear what he can allege.

WARWICK: All that he speaks is nothing. We are resolv'd!

YOUNGER MORTIMER: Do you not wish that Gaveston were dead?

PEMBROKE: I would he were!

350 YOUNGER MORTIMER: Why then, my lord, give me but leave to speak.

ELDER MORTIMER: But nephew, do not play the sophister.°

YOUNGER MORTIMER: This which I urge is of a burning zeal
To mend the King, and do our country good.
Know you not Gaveston hath store of gold
Which may in Ireland purchase him such friends
As he will front° the mightiest of us all?

360 And whereas he shall live and be belov'd,
'Tis hard for us to work his overthrow?

WARWICK: Mark you but that, my lord of Lancaster.

YOUNGER MORTIMER: But were he here, detested as he is,
How easily might some base slave be suborn'd°
To greet his lordship with a poniard—
And none so much as blame the murderer
But rather praise him for that brave attempt
And in the chronicle enroll his name

370 For purging of the realm of such a plague!

PEMBROKE: He saith true.

LANCASTER: Ay, but how chance this was not done before?

YOUNGER MORTIMER: Because, my lords, it was not thought upon.
Nay, more, when he shall know it lies in us
To banish him, and then to call him home,
'Twill make him vail° the top-flag of his pride,
And fear to offend the meanest nobleman.

380 ELDER MORTIMER: But how if he do not, nephew?

YOUNGER MORTIMER: Then may we with some color°
rise in arms.
For howsoever we have borne it out,
'Tis treason to be up against the King.
So we shall have the people of our side,
Which for his father's sake lean to the King
But cannot brook a night-grown mushroom,
Such a one as my lord of Cornwall is,
Should bear us down of the nobility.

390 And when the commons and the nobles join,
'Tis not the King can buckler° Gaveston:

---

sophister, one who practices false logic. front, affront, face. suborn'd, bribed. vail, lower. color, excuse, pretext. buckler, protect, shield.

We'll pull him from the strongest hold he hath.
My lords, if to perform this I be slack,
Think me as base a groom as Gaveston.

LANCASTER: On that condition, Lancaster will grant.

WARWICK: And so will Pembroke and I.

ELDER MORTIMER: And I.

YOUNGER MORTIMER: In this I count me highly gratified,
And Mortimer will rest at your command.   400

QUEEN ISABELLA: And when this favor Isabel forgets,
Then let her live abandon'd and forlorn.
But see, in happy time, my lord the King,
Having brought the Earl of Cornwall on his way,
Is new return'd. This news will glad him much,
Yet not so much as me—I love him more
Than he can Gaveston. Would he lov'd me
But half so much. Then were I treble-bless'd!

(Enter KING EDWARD mourning, BEAUMONT, ATTENDANTS.)

KING EDWARD: He's gone, and for his absence thus I mourn.   410
Did never sorrow go so near my heart
As doth the want of my sweet Gaveston!
And could my crown's revénue bring him back,
I would freely give it to his enemies—
And think I gain'd, having bought so dear a friend!

QUEEN ISABELLA: Hark, how he harps upon his minion!

KING EDWARD: My heart is as an anvil unto sorrow,
Which beats upon it like the Cyclops' hammers°
And with the noise turns up my giddy brain   420
And makes me frantic for my Gaveston!
Ah, had some bloodless fury rose from Hell,
And with my kingly scepter struck me dead
When I was forc'd to leave my Gaveston!

LANCASTER: Diablo,° what passions call you these?

QUEEN ISABELLA: My gracious lord, I come to bring you news.

KING EDWARD: That you have parled with your Mortimer?

QUEEN ISABELLA: That Gaveston, my lord, shall be   430
repeal'd.

KING EDWARD: Repeal'd! The news is too sweet to be true.

QUEEN ISABELLA: But will you love me, if you find it so?

KING EDWARD: If it be so, what will not Edward do?

QUEEN ISABELLA: For Gaveston, but not for Isabel—.

KING EDWARD: For thee, fair Queen, if thou lov'st Gaveston!
I'll hang a golden tongue about thy neck,   440
Seeing thou hast pleaded with so good success.

Cyclops' hammers, laborers in Vulcan's forge. Diablo, devil.

QUEEN ISABELLA: No other jewels hang about my neck
  (*Puts his arms around her.*)
  Than these, my lord! Nor let me have more wealth
  Than I may fetch from this rich treasury. (*Kisses him.*)
  O how a kiss revives poor Isabel!
KING EDWARD: Once more receive my hand, and let this be
450 A second marriage 'twixt thyself and me.
QUEEN ISABELLA: And may it prove more happy than the first!
  My gentle lord, bespeak these nobles fair
  That wait attendance for a gracious look
  And on their knees salute Your Majesty. (NOBLES *kneel.*)
KING EDWARD: Courageous Lancaster, embrace thy King.
  And as gross vapors perish by the sun,
460 Even so let hatred with thy sovereign's smile.
  Live thou with me as my companion.
LANCASTER: This salutation overjoys my heart.
KING EDWARD: Warwick shall be my chiefest counsellor.
  These silver hairs will more adorn my court
  Than gaudy silks, or rich embroidery.
  Chide me, sweet Warwick, if I go astray.
WARWICK: Slay me, my lord, when I offend Your Grace.
470 KING EDWARD: In solemn triumphs and in public shows
  Pembroke shall bear the sword before the King.
PEMBROKE: And with this sword Pembroke will fight for you.
KING EDWARD: But wherefore walks young Mortimer aside?
  Be thou commander of our royal fleet.
  Or, if that lofty office like thee not,
  I make thee here Lord Marshal of the realm.
480 YOUNGER MORTIMER: My lord, I'll marshal so your enemies
  As England shall be quiet and you safe.
KING EDWARD: And as for you, Lord Mortimer of Chirke,
  Whose great achievements in our foreign war
  Deserves no common place nor mean reward,
  Be you the general of the levied troops,
  That now are ready to assail the Scots.
ELDER MORTIMER: In this Your Grace hath highly
490 honor'd me,
  For with my nature war doth best agree.
QUEEN ISABELLA: Now is the King of England rich and strong,
  Having the love of his renowned peers.
KING EDWARD: Ay, Isabel, ne'er was my heart so light.
  Clerk of the crown, direct our warrant forth (*To one of the* ATTENDANTS.)
  For Gaveston to Ireland.—Beaumont, fly

As fast as Iris or Jove's Mercury!°
BEAUMONT: It shall be done, my gracious lord.   500
  (*Exeunt* BEAUMONT *and* ATTENDANT.)
KING EDWARD: Lord Mortimer, we leave you to your charge.
  Now let us in and feast it royally
  Against° our friend the Earl of Cornwall comes.
  We'll have a general tilt and tournament;
  And then his marriage shall be solemniz'd.
  For wot° you not that I have made him sure°
  Unto our cousin, the Earl of Gloucester's heir?
LANCASTER: Such news we hear, my lord.   510
KING EDWARD: That day, if not for him, yet for my sake,
  Who in the triumph will be challenger,
  Spare for no cost, we will requite your love.
WARWICK: In this or aught Your Highness shall command us.
KING EDWARD: Thanks, gentle Warwick. Come, let's in and revel.

  (*Exeunt. Manent* MORTIMERS.)

ELDER MORTIMER: Nephew, I must to Scotland. Thou stay'st here.   520
  Leave now to oppose thyself against the King.
  Thou seest by nature he is mild and calm.
  And seeing his mind so dotes on Gaveston,
  Let him without controlment have his will:
  The mightiest kings have had their minions—
  Great Alexander lov'd Hephestion;
  The conquering Hector for Hylas wept;
  And for Patroclus stern Achilles droop'd.
  And not kings only, but the wisest men—
  The Roman Tully lov'd Octavius;   530
  Grave Socrates, wild Alcibiades.
  Then let His Grace, whose youth is flexible
  And promiseth as much as we can wish,
  Freely enjoy that vain, light-headed earl,
  For riper years will wean him from such toys.
YOUNGER MORTIMER: Uncle, his wanton humor grieves not me.
  But this I scorn, that one so basely born
  Should by his sovereign's favor grow so pert
  And riot it with the treasure of the realm   540
  While soldiers mutiny for want of pay—.
  He wears a lord's revénue on his back,
  And Midas-like° he jets it° in the court
  With base outlandish cullions° at his heels
  Whose proud fantastic liveries make such show
  As if that Proteus,° god of shapes, appear'd!

Iris ... Mercury, messengers of Juno and Jupiter.
Against, until. *wot,* know. *made ... sure,* betrothed.
Midas-like, Midas was a legendary figure whose touch turned everything to gold; thus Midas-like would refer to someone clad entirely in gold. *jets,* struts. *cullions,* rascals. *Proteus,* a sea god who could assume various shapes.

I have not seen a dapper Jack° so brisk:
He wears a short Italian hooded cloak,
Larded with pearl, and in his Tuscan cap
550　A jewel of more value than the crown.
While others walk below, the King and he
From out a window laugh at such as we,
And flout our train, and jest at our attire—.
Uncle, 'tis this makes me impatient.

ELDER MORTIMER: But, nephew, now you see the King
　　is chang'd.

YOUNGER MORTIMER: Then so am I, and live to do
　　him service.
But whiles I have a sword, a hand, a heart,
560　I will not yield to any such upstart!
You know my mind. Come, uncle, let's away.
　　(Exeunt.)

ACT 2　/　SCENE 1

(Enter YOUNGER SPENCER, and BALDOCK [in academic robes].)

BALDOCK: Spencer,
Seeing that our lord th' Earl of Gloucester's dead,
Which of the nobles dost thou mean to serve?

YOUNGER SPENCER: Not Mortimer, nor any of his side,
Because the King and he are enemies.
Baldock, learn this of me: a factious lord
Shall hardly do himself good, much less us;
But he that hath the favor of a king
May with one word advance us while we live.
10　The liberal Earl of Cornwall is the man
On whose good fortune Spencer's hope depends.

BALDOCK: What, mean you then to be his follower?

YOUNGER SPENCER: No, his companion, for he loves
　　me well,
And would have once preferr'd me to the King.

BALDOCK: But he is banish'd, there's small hope of
　　him.

YOUNGER SPENCER: Ay, for a while—but, Baldock,
　　mark the end:
20　A friend of mine told me in secrecy
That he's repeal'd and sent for back again.
And even now a post came from the court
With letters to our lady from the King:
And as she read she smil'd, which makes me think
It is about her lover Gaveston.

BALDOCK: 'Tis like enough, for since he was exil'd
She neither walks abroad nor comes in sight.
—But I had thought the match had been broke off,
And that his banishment had chang'd her mind.

30　YOUNGER SPENCER: Our lady's first love is not
　　wavering;
My life for thine, she will have Gaveston.

BALDOCK: Then hope I by her means to be preferr'd,
Having read unto her since she was a child.

YOUNGER SPENCER: Then, Baldock, you must cast the
　　scholar off
And learn to court it like a gentleman!
'Tis not a black coat and a little band,
A velvet-caped coat (faced before with serge),
And smelling to a nosegay all the day—　40
Or holding of a napkin in your hand—
Or saying a long grace at a table's end—
Or making low legs to a nobleman—
Or looking downward with your eyelids close
And saying, "Truly, an't may please your honor,"
Can get you any favor with great men.
You must be proud, bold, pleasant, resolute:
And now and then stab as occasion serves.

BALDOCK: Spencer, thou know'st I hate such formal
　　toys,　50
And use them but of mere hypocrisy.
Mine old lord whiles he liv'd was so precise
That he would take exceptions at my buttons,
And, being like pin's heads, blame me for the
　　bigness—
Which made me curate-like in mine attire,
Though inwardly licentious enough
And apt for any kind of villainy!
I am none of these common pedants, I,
That cannot speak without *propterea quod.*°　60

YOUNGER SPENCER: But one of those that saith
　　quandoquidem°
And hath a special gift to form a verb.

BALDOCK: Leave off this jesting, here my lady comes.

(Enter the LADY.)

[NIECE]: The grief for his exile was not so much,
As is the joy of his returning home.
This letter came from my sweet Gaveston—
What need'st thou, love, thus to excuse thyself?
I know thou could'st not come and visit me.
"I will not long be from thee, though I die." (Reads.)　70
This argues the entire love of my lord.
"When I forsake thee, death seize on my heart!"
　　(Reads.)
But stay thee here where Gaveston shall sleep. (Puts
　　letter in bosom.)
Now to the letter of my lord the King.
He wills me to repair° unto the court
And meet my Gaveston? Why do I stay,
Seeing that he talks thus of my marriage-day?
Who's there? Baldock,
See that my coach be ready, I must hence.

BALDOCK: It shall be done, madam.　80

[NIECE]: And meet me at the park-pale° presently.

---

dapper Jack, overdressed fellow.

propterea quod, because.　**quandoquidem,** because;
though in this instance a somewhat elegant form with sexual
pun in the first syllable.　**repair,** return.　**park-pale,** park
wall or fence.

(Exit BALDOCK.*)*

Spencer, stay you and bear me company,
For I have joyful news to tell thee of:
My lord of Cornwall is acoming over,
And will be at the court as soon as we.
YOUNGER SPENCER: I knew the King would have him
    home again.
[NIECE]: If all things sort out as I hope they will,
Thy service, Spencer, shall be thought upon.
90 YOUNGER SPENCER: I humbly thank your ladyship.
[NIECE]: Come, lead the way.—I long till I am there.

(Exeunt.)

ACT 2 / SCENE 2

(Enter EDWARD, *the* QUEEN, LANCASTER, YOUNGER
MORTIMER, WARWICK, PEMBROKE, KENT, ATTEN-
DANTS.*)*

KING EDWARD: The wind is good, I wonder why he
    stays,
I fear me he is wrack'd upon the sea.
QUEEN ISABELLA: Look, Lancaster, how passionate he
    is.
And still his mind runs on his minion!
LANCASTER: My lord—.
KING EDWARD: How now, what news, is Gaveston
    arriv'd?
10 YOUNGER MORTIMER: Nothing but Gaveston! What
    means Your Grace?
You have matters of more weight to think upon:
The King of France sets foot in Normandy.
KING EDWARD: A trifle, we'll expel him when we
    please.
But tell me, Mortimer, what's thy device
Against the stately triumph we decreed?
YOUNGER MORTIMER: A homely one, my lord, not
    worth the telling.
20 KING EDWARD: Prithee, let me know it.
YOUNGER MORTIMER: But seeing you are so desirous,
    thus it is:
A lofty cedar tree fair flourishing
On whose top branches kingly eagles perch,
And by the bark a canker° creeps me up
And gets into the highest bough of all:
The motto, *Æque tandem.*°
KING EDWARD: And what is yours, my lord of
    Lancaster?
30 LANCSASTER: My lord, mine's more obscure than
    Mortimer's.
Pliny reports there is a flying fish
Which all the other fishes deadly hate,
And therefore being pursu'd it takes the air;
No sooner is it up, but there's a fowl
That seizeth it. This fish, my lord, I bear:

The motto this, *Undique mors est.*°
EARL OF KENT: Proud Mortimer! Ungentle Lancaster!
Is this the love you bear your sovereign?
Is this the fruit your reconcilement bears?   40
Can you in words make show of amity
And in your shields display your rancorous minds?
What call you this but private libelling
Against the Earl of Cornwall and my brother?
QUEEN ISABELLA: Sweet husband, be content, they all
    love you.
KING EDWARD: They love me not that hate my
    Gaveston.
I am that cedar—shake me not too much!
And you, the eagles, soar ye ne'er so high—   50
I have the jesses° that will pull you down!
And *Æque tandem* shall that canker cry
Unto the proudest peer of Britainy!
Though thou compar'st him to a flying fish
And threat'nest death whether he rise or fall,
'Tis not the hugest monster of the sea,
Nor foulest harpy,° that shall swallow him.
YOUNGER MORTIMER: If in his absence thus he favors
    him,
What will he do whenas he shall be present?   60
LANCASTER: That shall we see. Look where his
    lordship comes!

(Enter GAVESTON.*)*

KING EDWARD: My Gaveston!
Welcome to Tynemouth! Welcome to thy friend!
Thy absence made me droop and pine away;
For as the lovers of fair Danae°
When she was lock'd up in a brazen tower
Desir'd her more and wax'd outrageous,
So did it sure with me! And now thy sight
Is sweeter far than was thy parting hence   70
Bitter and irksome to my sobbing heart.
GAVESTON: Sweet lord and King, your speech
    preventeth mine,
Yet have I words left to express my joy:
The shepherd nipp'd with biting winter's rage
Frolics not more to see the painted spring,
Than I do to behold Your Majesty!
KING EDWARD: Will none of you salute my Gaveston?
LANCASTER: Salute him! Yes! Welcome, Lord
    Chamberlain!   80
YOUNGER MORTIMER: Welcome is the good Earl of
    Cornwall!
WARWICK: Welcome, Lord Governor of the Isle of
    Man!

---

canker, caterpillar.   *Aeque tandem,* equally at length.

Undique mors est, Death is on all sides.   *jesses,* straps
attached to the legs of a trained hawk.   *harpy,* a voracious
mythological creature combining the head of a woman and
the wings of a bird.   *Danae,* a woman in classical mythology
who was locked by her father in a tower of brass, but whom
Jupiter reached by coming to her in a shower of gold.

PEMBROKE: Welcome, Master Secretary!

EARL OF KENT: Brother, do you hear them?

KING EDWARD: Still will these earls and barons use me
  thus.

GAVESTON: My lord, I cannot brook these injuries.

90 QUEEN ISABELLA: (Ay me, poor soul, when these begin
  to jar.) *(aside)*

KING EDWARD: Return it to their throats, I'll be thy
  warrant.

GAVESTON: Base, leaden earls, that glory in your
  birth—
  Go sit at home and eat your tenant's beef—
  And come not here to scoff at Gaveston—
  Whose mounting thoughts did never creep so low
  As to bestow a look on such as you!

100 LANCASTER: Yet I disdain not to do this for you!

(Draws his sword and offers to stab GAVESTON.)

KING EDWARD: Treason! Treason! Where's the
  traitor?

PEMBROKE: Here! Here! *(Points to GAVESTON.)*

KING EDWARD: Convey hence Gaveston! They'll
  murder him!

GAVESTON *(draws his sword)*: The life of thee shall salve
  this foul disgrace. *(to LANCASTER)*

YOUNGER MORTIMER: Villain, thy life, unless I miss
  mine aim! *(Stabs at GAVESTON.)*

110 QUEEN ISABELLA: Ah, furious Mortimer, what hast
  thou done?

YOUNGER MORTIMER: No more than I would answer,°
  were he slain.

(Exit GAVESTON with ATTENDANTS.)

KING EDWARD: Yes, more than thou canst answer,
  though he live.
  Dear shall you both abide° this riotous deed!
  Out of my presence, come not near the court!

YOUNGER MORTIMER: I'll not be barr'd the court for
  Gaveston.

120 LANCASTER: We'll hale him by the ears unto the block.

KING EDWARD: Look to your own heads, his is sure
  enough.

WARWICK: Look to your own crown, if you back him
  thus.

EARL OF KENT: Warwick, these words do ill beseem°
  thy years.

KING EDWARD: Nay, all of them conspire to cross me
  thus.
  But if I live, I'll tread upon their heads

130 That think with high looks thus to tread me down!
  Come, Edmund, let's away and levy men.
  'Tis war that must abate these barons' pride!

(Exit the KING, QUEEN, and KENT.)

WARWICK: Let's to our castles, for the King is mov'd.

YOUNGER MORTIMER: Mov'd may he be, and perish in
  his wrath!

LANCASTER: Cousin, it is no dealing with him now.
  He means to make us stoop by force of arms.
  And therefore let us jointly here protest
  To prosecute that Gaveston to the death.

YOUNGER MORTIMER: By Heaven, the abject villain   140
  shall not live!

WARWICK: I'll have his blood, or die in seeking it!

PEMBROKE: The like oath Pembroke takes!

LANCASTER: And so doth Lancaster!

(They all put right hands together.)

  Now send our heralds to defy the King
  And make the people swear to put him down.

(Enter 1 MESSENGER.)

YOUNGER MORTIMER: Letters, from whence?

MESSENGER: From Scotland, my lord.

(Giving letters to MORTIMER.)

LANCASTER: Why, how now, cousin, how fares all our
  friends?   150

YOUNGER MORTIMER: My uncle's taken prisoner by
  the Scots. *(Reads.)*

LANCASTER: We'll have him ransom'd, man. Be of
  good cheer!

YOUNGER MORTIMER: They rate his ransom at five
  thousand pound.
  Who should defray° the money but the King,
  Seeing he is taken prisoner in his wars?
  I'll to the King.

LANCASTER: Do, cousin, and I'll bear thee company.   160

WARWICK: Meantime, my lord of Pembroke and
  myself
  Will to Newcastle here and gather head.

YOUNGER MORTIMER: About it then, and we will
  follow you.

LANCASTER: Be resolute and full of secrecy.

WARWICK: I warrant you.

(Exeunt WARWICK and PEMBROKE.)

YOUNGER MORTIMER: Cousin, an if he will not ransom
  him,
  I'll thunder such a peal into his ears,   170
  As never subject did unto his King.

LANCASTER: Content, I'll bear my part. Holla, who's
  there? *(Calls within.)*

(Enter GUARD.)

YOUNGER MORTIMER: Ay, marry, such a guard as this
  doth well.

LANCASTER: Lead on the way.

GUARD: Whither will your lordships?

YOUNGER MORTIMER: Whither else but to the King.

---

answer, pay for. **abide,** pay for. **beseem,** suit, fit.

defray, provide.

GUARD: His Highness is dispos'd to be alone.

180 LANCASTER: Why, so he may—but we will speak to
       him.

GUARD: You may not in, my lord.

YOUNGER MORTIMER: May we not?

(Enter KING EDWARD *and* KENT.*)*

KING EDWARD: How now!
    What noise is this? who have we there? is' you?
    (Going.)

YOUNGER MORTIMER: Nay, stay, my lord, I come to
    bring you news:
    Mine uncle's taken prisoner by the Scots.

KING EDWARD: Then ransom him.

190 LANCASTER: 'Twas in your wars. *You* should ransom
       him.

YOUNGER MORTIMER: And *you* shall ransom him, or
    else—.

[EARL OF KENT]: What, Mortimer, you will not
    threaten him?

KING EDWARD: Quiet yourself . . . You shall have the
    broad seal°
    To gather for him throughout the realm.

LANCASTER: Your minion Gaveston hath taught you
200   this!

YOUNGER MORTIMER: My lord, the family of the
    Mortimers
    Are not so poor, but would they sell their land
    'Twould levy men enough to anger you:
    We never beg, but use such prayers as these. *(Draws
    sword.)*

KING EDWARD: Shall I still be haunted thus?

YOUNGER MORTIMER: The idle triumphs, masks,
    lascivious shows,
    And prodigal gifts bestow'd on Gaveston,
210 Have drawn thy treasury dry and made thee weak,
    The murmuring commons overstretched° hath.

LANCASTER: Look for rebellion, look to be depos'd;
    Thy garrisons are beaten out of France,
    And lame and poor lie groaning at the gates;
    The wild O'Neil with swarms of Irish kerns°
    Lives uncontroll'd within the English pale;
    Unto the walls of York the Scots made road,
    And unresisted drave away rich spoils—

YOUNGER MORTIMER: The haughty Dane commands
220   the narrow seas
    While in the harbor ride thy ships unrigg'd.

LANCASTER: What foreign prince sends thee
    ambassadors?

YOUNGER MORTIMER: Who loves thee but a sort of
    flatterers?

LANCASTER: Thy gentle Queen, sole sister to Valois,

Complains that thou hast left her all forlorn.

YOUNGER MORTIMER: Thy court is naked, being bereft
    of those
    That make a king seem glorious to the world,   230
    I mean the peers, whom thou should'st dearly
    love—
    Libels are cast again thee in the street,
    Ballads and rhymes made of thy overthrow.

LANCASTER: The Northern borderers, seeing their
    houses burnt,
    Their wives and children slain, run up and down
    Cursing the name of thee and Gaveston.

YOUNGER MORTIMER: When wert thou in the field
    with banner spread,   240
    But once? and then thy soldiers march'd like
    players—
    With garish robes, not armor; and thyself,
    Bedaub'd with gold, rode laughing at the rest,
    Nodding and shaking of thy spangl'd crest,
    Where women's favors hung like labels° down.

LANCASTER: And therefore came it, that the fleering
    Scots,
    To England's high disgrace, have made this jig:
    Maids of England, sore may you mourn   250
    For your lemans° you have lost at Bannocksbourn,
        With a heave and a ho!
    What weeneth° the King of England,
        With a rombelow!°

YOUNGER MORTIMER: Wigmore shall fly to set my
    uncle free.

LANCASTER: And when 'tis gone, our swords shall
    purchase more.
    If ye be mov'd, revenge it as you can!
    Look next to see us with our ensigns spread!°   260

(Exeunt NOBLES.*)*

KING EDWARD: My swelling heart for very anger
    breaks!
    How oft have I been baited by these peers,
    And dare not be reveng'd, for their power is great.
    Yet, shall the crowing of these cockerels
    Affright a lion? Edward, unfold thy paws
    And let their lives' blood slake thy fury's hunger!
    If I be cruel and grow tyrannous,
    Now let them thank themselves and rue too late!

EARL OF KENT: My lord, I see your love to Gaveston   270
    Will be the ruin of the realm and you,
    For now the wrathful nobles threaten wars.
    And therefore, brother, banish him forever.

KING EDWARD: Art thou an enemy to my Gaveston?

EARL OF KENT: Ay, and it grieves me that I favor'd
    him!

---

broad seal, the Great Seal of the king of England
granting authority for the legal raising of money in his
name. **overstretched,** drained of money. **kerns,** Irish foot
soldiers.

---

labels, documents or pieces of parchment. **lemans,**
lovers. **weeneth,** thinks. **rombelow,** meaningless refrain
from a sailor's song. **ensigns spread,** flags flying.

KING EDWARD: Traitor, begone, whine thou with
    Mortimer!
EARL OF KENT: So will I, rather than with Gaveston.
280 KING EDWARD: Out of my sight, and trouble me no
    more!
EARL OF KENT: No marvel though thou scorn thy
    noble peers
    When I thy brother am rejected thus—.
KING EDWARD: Away!

    (Exit KENT.*)*

    Poor Gaveston, that has no friend but me.
    Do what they can, we'll live in Tynemouth here.
    And so I walk with him about the walls,
    What care I though the earls begirt us round?
290   Here cometh she that's cause of all these jars.

    (Enter the QUEEN, LADIES 3 [*one of whom is* KING'S
    NIECE], BALDOCK, *and* YOUNGER SPENCER *and* GAVES-
    TON.*)*

QUEEN ISABELLA: My lord, 'tis thought the earls are
    up in arms.
KING EDWARD: Ay, and 'tis likewise thought you favor
    him.
QUEEN ISABELLA: Thus do you still suspect me
    without cause.
[NIECE]: Sweet uncle, speak more kindly to the
    Queen.
GAVESTON: (My Lord, dissemble with her, speak her
300   fair.) *(Aside to* KING.*)*
KING EDWARD: Pardon me, sweet, I forgot myself:
QUEEN ISABELLA: Your pardon is quickly got of
    Isabel.
KING EDWARD: The younger Mortimer is grown so
    brave
    That to my face he threatens civil wars.
GAVESTON: Why do you not commit him to the
    Tower?
KING EDWARD: I dare not, for the people love him
310   well.
GAVESTON: Why, then we'll have him privily made
    away.
KING EDWARD: Would Lancaster and he had both
    carous'd
    A bowl of poison to each other's health!
    But let them go, and tell me what are these.

    (BALDOCK *and* YOUNGER SPENCER *bow deeply.*)

[NIECE]: Two of my father's servants whilst he liv'd.
    May't please Your Grace to entertain them now.
KING EDWARD: Tell me, where wast thou born? What
320   is thine arms?
BALDOCK: My name is Baldock and my gentry°
    I fetch from Oxford, not from heraldry.
KING EDWARD: The fitter art thou, Baldock, for my
    turn.

Wait on me and I'll see thou shalt not want.
BALDCOCK: I humbly thank Your Majesty.
KING EDWARD: Knowest thou him, Gaveston *(Points to*
    YOUNGER SPENCER.*)*
GAVESTON: Ay, my lord;
    His name is Spencer. He is well allied.   330
    For my sake let him wait upon Your Grace,
    Scarce shall you find a man of more desert.°
KING EDWARD: Then, Spencer, wait upon me for his
    sake.
    I'll grace thee with a higher style ere long.
YOUNGER SPENCER: No greater titles happen unto me,
    Than to be favor'd of Your Majesty.
KING EDWARD: Cousin, this day shall be your
    marriage feast—
    And, Gaveston, think that I love thee well,   340
    To wed thee to our niece, the only heir
    Unto the Earl of Gloucester late deceas'd.
GAVESTON: I know, my lord, many will stomach me—
    But I respect neither their love nor hate.
KING EDWARD: The headstrong barons shall not limit
    me!
    He that I list to favor shall be great.
    Come, let's away! And when the marriage ends,
    Have at the rebels and their complices!° *(Exeunt*
    omnes.)

ACT 2 / SCENE 3

(Enter LANCASTER, YOUNGER MORTIMER, WARWICK,
PEMBROKE, KENT [*before the walls of Tynemouth*
Castle].*)*

EARL OF KENT: My lords, of love to this our native
    land
    I come to join with you and leave the King:
    And in your quarrel and the realm's behoof°
    Will be the first that shall adventure life.
LANCASTER: I fear me you are sent of policy
    To undermine us with a show of love.
WARWICK: He is your brother, therefore have we
    cause
    To cast the worst and doubt of your revolt.   10
EARL OF KENT: Mine honor shall be hostage of my
    truth.
    If that will not suffice, farewell my lords! *(Makes as*
    though to go.)
YOUNGER MORTIMER: Stay, Edmund! Never was
    Plantagenet
    False of his word, and therefore trust we thee.
PEMBROKE: But what's the reason you should leave
    him now?
EARL OF KENT: I have inform'd the Earl of Lancaster.
LANCASTER: And it sufficeth. Now, my lords, know   20
    this,

---

gentry, respectable ancestry.

desert, deserving of reward.   **complices,** accomplices.
behoof, benefit, profit.

That Gaveston is secretly arriv'd
And here in Tynemouth frolics with the King.
Let us with these our followers scale the walls,
And suddenly surprise them unawares.

YOUNGER MORTIMER: I'll give the onset.

WARWICK: And I'll follow thee.

YOUNGER MORTIMER: This tottered° ensign of my
   ancestors,

30   Which swept the desert shore of that Dead Sea
Whereof we got the name of Mortimer,
Will I advance upon this castle['s] walls.
Drums, strike alarum, raise them from their sport,
And ring aloud the knell of Gaveston!

LANCASTER: None be so hardy° as to touch the King—
   But neither spare you Gaveston nor his friends.
   (Exeunt.)

ACT 2 / SCENE 4

(Drums and trumpets sound within. Enter the KING *and*
YOUNGER SPENCER, *to them* GAVESTON, [NIECE,
QUEEN,] *etc.)*

KING EDWARD: O tell me, Spencer, where is Gaveston?

YOUNGER SPENCER: I fear me he is slain, my gracious
   lord.

KING EDWARD: No, here he comes. Now let them spoil
   and kill.
   Fly, fly, my lords! The earls have got the hold.
   Take shipping and away to Scarborough.
   Spencer and I will post away by land.

GAVESTON: O stay, my lord, they will not injure you.

10 KING EDWARD: I will not trust them. Gaveston, away!

GAVESTON: Farewell, my lord.

KING EDWARD: Lady, farewell.

[NIECE]: Farewell, sweet uncle, till we meet again.

KING EDWARD: Farewell, sweet Gaveston, and
   farewell, niece.

QUEEN ISABELLA: No farewell to poor Isabel thy
   Queen?

KING EDWARD: Yes, yes, for Mortimer your lover's
   sake!

20 QUEEN ISABELLA: Heaven can witness I love none but
   you!

(Exeunt omnes, manet ISABELLA.*)*

From my embracements thus he breaks away.
O that mine arms could close this isle about
That I might pull him to me where I would—
Or that these tears that drizzle from mine eyes
Had power to mollify° his stony heart—
That when I had him we might never part!

(Enter the BARONS [LANCASTER, WARWICK, YOUNGER
MORTIMER.] *Alarums within.)*

LANCASTER: I wonder how he scap'd.

YOUNGER MORTIMER: Who's this? the Queen!

QUEEN ISABELLA: Ay, Mortimer, the miserable   30
   Queen,
Whose pining heart her inward sighs have blasted,
And body with continual mourning wasted.
These hands are tir'd with haling of my lord
From Gaveston, from wicked Gaveston!
—And all in vain! For when I speak him fair,
He turns away and smiles upon his minion!

YOUNGER MORTIMER: Cease to lament, and tell us
   where's the King?

QUEEN ISABELLA: What would you with the King? Is't   40
   him you seek?

LANCASTER: No, madam, but that cursed Gaveston.
Far be it from the thought of Lancaster
To offer violence to his sovereign!
We would but rid the realm of Gaveston:
Tell us where he remains, and he shall die!

QUEEN ISABELLA: He's gone by water unto
   Scarborough.
Pursue him quickly and he cannot scape:
The King hath left him and his train is small.   50

WARWICK: Foreslow° no time, sweet Lancaster. Let's
   march.

YOUNGER MORTIMER: How comes it that the King and
   he is parted?

QUEEN ISABELLA: That thus your army going several
   ways
Might be of lesser force, and with that power
That he intendeth presently to raise,
Be easily suppress'd. And therefore be gone!

YOUNGER MORTIMER: Here in the river rides a   60
   Flemish hoy.°
Let's all aboard and follow him amain!°

LANCASTER: The wind that bears him hence will fill
   our sails.
Come, come aboard! 'Tis but an hour's sailing.

YOUNGER MORTIMER: Madam, stay you within this
   castle here?

QUEEN ISABELLA: No, Mortimer, I'll to my lord the
   King.

YOUNGER MORTIMER: Nay, rather sail with us to   70
   Scarborough.

QUEEN ISABELLA: You know the King is so suspicious
As if he hear I have but talk'd with you
Mine honor will be call'd in question
And therefore, gentle Mortimer, be gone.

YOUNGER MORTIMER: I cannot stay to answer you.
But think of Mortimer as he deserves!

(Exeunt all but QUEEN.*)*

QUEEN ISABELLA: So well has thou deserv'd, sweet
   Mortimer,
As Isabel could live with thee forever.   80

---

tottered, tattered.   ***hardy,*** daring, foolhardy.   ***mollify,***
soften.

Foreslow, waste.   ***hoy,*** fishing boat.   ***amain,*** quickly.

In vain I look for love at Edward's hand,
Whose eyes are fix'd on none but Gaveston:
Yet once more I'll importune him with prayers;
If he be strange and not regard my words,
My son and I will over into France
And to the King my brother there complain
How Gaveston hath robb'd me of his love.
But yet I hope my sorrows will have end,
And Gaveston this blessed day be slain! *(Exit.)*

ACT 2 / SCENE 5

(Enter Gaveston, pursued)

GAVESTON: Yet, lusty lords, I have escap'd your
hands,
Your threats, your 'larums° and your hot pursuits;
And though divorced from King Edward's eyes,
Yet liveth Pierce of Gaveston unsurpris'd,
Breathing in hope—malgrado° all your beards,
That muster rebels thus against your King—
To see his royal sovereign once again.

*(Enter the nobles [*WARWICK, LANCASTER, PEMBROKE,
YOUNGER MORTIMER, SOLDIERS, JAMES, HORSE-BOY,
PEMBROKE'S SERVANTS*].)*

WARWICK: Upon him, soldiers! Take away his
10   weapons.
YOUNGER MORTIMER: Thou proud disturber of thy
country's peace,
Corrupter of thy King, cause of these broils,
Base flatterer, yield! And were it not for shame,
Shame and dishonor to a soldier's name,
Upon my weapon's point here should'st thou fall
And welter in thy gore!
LANCASTER: Monster of men
That (like the Greekish strumpet!)° train'd to arms
20   And bloody wars so many valiant knights,
Look for no other fortune, wretch, than death!
Kind Edward is not here to buckler° thee
WARWICK: Lancaster, take him hence, for, by my
sword,
His head shall off. Gaveston, short warning
Shall serve thy turn: it is our country's cause,
That here severely we will execute
Upon thy person.—Hang him at a bough!
GAVESTON: My lord—.
30   WARWICK: Soldiers, have him away—
But for thou wert the favorite of a king,
Thou shalt have so much honor at our hands.
*(*WARWICK *uses hands to imitate head-chopping.)*
GAVESTON: I thank you all, my lords: then I perceive,
That heading is one and hanging is the other,
And death is all. . . .

(Enter EARL OF ARUNDEL.*)*

• LANCASTER: How now, my Lord of Arundel?
• EARL OF ARUNDEL: My lords, King Edward greets you
all by me.
WARWICK: Arundel, say your message.
EARL OF ARUNDEL: His Majesty,   40
Hearing that you had taken Gaveston,
Entreateth you by me, yet but he may
See him before he dies. For why, he says,
And sends you word, he knows that die he shall:
And if you gratify His Grace so far,
He will be mindful of the courtesy.
WARWICK: How now!
GAVESTON: Renowned Edward, how thy name
Revives poor Gaveston!
WARWICK: No, it needeth not.   50
Arundel, we will gratify the King
In other matters, he must pardon us in this.
Soldiers, away with him!
GAVESTON: Why, my lord of Warwick,
Will not these delays beget my hopes? *(Sarcastically.)*
I know it, lords, it is this life you aim at,
Yet grant King Edward this.
YOUNGER MORTIMER: Shalt thou appoint
What we shall grant? Soldiers, away with him!
Thus we'll gratify the King—   60
We'll send his head by thee. Let him bestow
His tears on that, for that is all he gets
Of Gaveston, or else his senseless trunk.
LANCASTER: Not so, my lords, lest he bestow more
cost
In burying him than he hath ever earn'd.
EARL OF ARUNDEL: My lords, it is His Majesty's request
And in the honor of a king he swears,
He will but talk with him, and send him back.
WARWICK: When, can you tell? Arundel, no. We wot,° 70
He that the care of his realm remits°
And drives his nobles to these exigents°
For Gaveston, will if he seize him once
Violate any promise to possess him.
EARL OF ARUNDEL: Then if you will not trust His
Grace in keep,
My lords, I will be pledge for his return.
YOUNGER MORTIMER: It is honorable in thee to offer
this.
But for we know thou art a noble gentleman,   80
We will not wrong thee so, to make away
A true man for a thief.
GAVESTON: How mean'st thou, Mortimer? That is
over-base!
YOUNGER MORTIMER: Away, base groom, robber of
king's renown!
Question with thy companions and mates.

'larums,* calls to arms. *malgrado,* in spite of.
Greekish strumpet, Helen of Troy. *buckler,* shield, protect.

wot, know. *remits,* abandons, gives up. *exigents,*
emergencies.

PEMBROKE: My Lord Mortimer, and you, my lords,
   each one,
90 To gratify the King's request therein,
   Touching the sending of this Gaveston,
   Because His Majesty so earnestly
   Desires to see the man before his death,
   I will upon mine honor undertake
   To carry him and bring him back again—
   Provided this, that you my lord of Arundel
   Will join with me.
WARWICK: Pembroke, what wilt thou do?
   Cause yet more bloodshed? Is it not enough
100 That we have taken him, but must we now
   Leave him on *had-I-wist*° and let him go?
PEMBROKE: My lords, I will not over-woo your
   honors.
   But if you dare trust Pembroke with the prisoner,
   Upon my oath, I will return him back.
EARL OF ARUNDEL: My lord of Lancaster, what say you
   in this?
LANCASTER: Why, I say, let him go on Pembroke's
   word.
110 PEMBROKE: And you, Lord Mortimer?
YOUNGER MORTIMER: How say you, my lord of
   Warwick?
WARWICK: Nay, do your pleasures, I know how 'twill
   prove.
PEMBROKE: Then give him me.
GAVESTON: Sweet sovereign, yet I come
   To see thee ere I die!
WARWICK (aside): (Yet not perhaps,
   If Warwick's wit and policy prevail.)
120 YOUNGER MORTIMER: My lord of Pembroke, we
   deliver him you.
   Return him on your honor. Sound, away!

(*Trumpet sounds. Exeunt. Manent* PEMBROKE [ARUN-
DEL,] GAVESTON, *and* PEMBROKE'S MEN, *four soldiers.*)

PEMBROKE: My lord, you shall go with me.
   My house is not far hence, out of the way
   A little, but our men shall go along.
   We that have pretty wenches to our wives,
   Sir, must not come so near to balk their lips.
EARL OF ARUNDEL: 'Tis very kindly spoke, my lord of
   Pembroke:
130 Your honor hath an adamant° of power
   To draw a prince.
PEMBROKE: So, my lord. Come hither, James:
   I do commit this Gaveston to thee.
   Be thou this night his keeper. In the morning
   We will discharge thee of thy charge. Be gone.
GAVESTON: Unhappy Gaveston, whither goest thou
   now?

---

had-I-wist, if only I had known, the expression of one
who repents when it is too late.   **adamant,** magnet.

(*Exeunt* GAVESTON, JAMES, *and some of* PEMBROKE'S
MEN.)
HORSE-BOY: My lord, we'll quickly be at Cobham.
   (*Exeunt.*)

ACT 3 / SCENE 1

(*Alarum. Enter* WARWICK *and his men pursuing* GAVES-
TON. *Exeunt. Enter* GAVESTON *mourning and the* EARL
OF PEMBROKE'S MEN. [*They are in disorder and fleeing
from* WARWICK.])

GAVESTON: O treacherous Warwick, thus to wrong
   thy friend!
JAMES: I see it is your life these arms pursue.
GAVESTON: Weaponless must I fall, and die in bands?
   O, must this day be period° of my life?
   Center of all my bliss? An ye be men,
   Speed to the King.

(*Enter* WARWICK *and his company.*)

WARWICK: My lord of Pembroke's men,
   Strive you no longer. I will have that Gaveston!
JAMES: Your lordship does dishonor to yourself,   10
   And wrong our lord, your honorable friend.
WARWICK: No, James, it is my country's cause I
   follow.
   Go, take the villain! Soldiers, come away!
   We'll make quick work: Commend me to your
   master,
   My friend, and tell him that I watch'd it well.
   —Come, let thy shadow parley with King Edward.
GAVESTON: Treacherous earl, shall I not see the
   King?   20
WARWICK: The King of Heaven perhaps—no other
   king.
   Away!

(*Exeunt* WARWICK *and his men with* GAVESTON.)

JAMES: Come fellows, it booted not for us to strive.
   We will in haste go certify our lord. (*Exeunt.*)

ACT 3 / SCENE 2

(*Enter* KING EDWARD *and* [YOUNGER] SPENCER, [BAL-
DOCK, *and* SOLDIERS] *with drums and fifes.*)

KING EDWARD: I long to hear an answer from the
   barons
   Touching my friend, my dearest Gaveston.
   Ah, Spencer, not the riches of my realm
   Can ransom him! Ah, he is mark'd to die!
   I know the malice of the younger Mortimer,
   Warwick I know is rough, and Lancaster
   Inexorable—and I shall never see
   My lovely Pierce, my Gaveston again!

---

period, end.

10   The barons overbear me with their pride.—
YOUNGER SPENCER: Were I King Edward, England's
          sovereign,
     Son to the lovely Eleanor of Spain,
     Great Edward Longshanks' issue, would I bear
     These braves, this rage, and suffer uncontroll'd
     These barons thus to beard me in my land,
     In mine own realm? My lord, pardon my speech—
     Did you retain your father's magnanimity,
     Did you regard the honor of your name,
20   You would not suffer thus Your Majesty
     Be counterbuft° of your nobility—
     Strike off their heads, and let them preach on
          poles!
     No doubt, such lessons they will teach the rest
     As by their preachments they will profit much
     And learn obedience to their lawful King!
KING EDWARD: Yea, gentle Spencer, we have been too
          mild,
     Too kind to them—but now have drawn our
30   sword!
     And if they send me not my Gaveston,
     We'll steel it on their crest and poll their tops!°
BALDOCK: This haught° resolve becomes Your
          Majesty,
     Not to be tied to their affection
     As though Your Highness were a schoolboy still:
     And must be aw'd and govern'd like a child.

(Enter HUGH SPENCER, *an old man, father to the young*
SPENCER, *with his truncheon, and* SOLDIERS.*)*

ELDER SPENCER: Long live my sovereign, the noble
          Edward—
40   In peace triumphant, fortunate in wars!
KING EDWARD: Welcome, old man! Com'st thou in
          Edward's aid?
     Then tell thy prince of whence and what thou art.
ELDER SPENCER: Lo, with a band of bowmen and of
          pikes,
     Brown bills and targeteers, four hundred strong,
     Sworn to defend King Edward's royal right,
     I come in person to Your Majesty—
     Spencer, the father of Hugh Spencer there,
50   Bound to Your Highness everlastingly
     For favors done in him unto us all.
KING EDWARD: Thy father, Spencer?
YOUNGER SPENCER: True, an it like Your Grace—
     That pours in lieu of all your goodness shown
     His life, my lord, before your princely feet.
KING EDWARD: Welcome ten thousand times, old
          man, again!
     Spencer, this love, this kindness to thy King,
     Argues thy noble mind and disposition.

Spencer, I here create thee Earl of Wiltshire   60
And daily will enrich thee with our favor,
That as the sunshine shall reflect o'er thee.
Beside, the more to manifest our love,
Because we hear Lord Bruce doth sell his land
And that the Mortimers are in hand withal,
Thou shalt have crowns° of us t'outbid the barons:
And, Spencer, spare them not but lay it on!
Soldiers, a largess,° and thrice welcome all!
YOUNGER SPENCER: My lord, here comes the Queen.

(Enter the QUEEN *and* HER SON *and* LEVUNE, *a
Frenchman.)*

KING EDWARD: Madam, what news?   70
QUEEN ISABELLA: News of dishonor, lord, and
          discontent.
     Our friend, Levune, faithful and full of trust,
     Informeth us by letters and by words
     That Lord Valois our brother, King of France,
     Because Your Highness hath been slack in homage
     Hath seized Normandy into his hands.
     These be the letters, this is the messenger.
KING EDWARD: Welcome, Levune. Tush Sib,° if this be
          all,   80
     Valois and I will soon be friends again.
     —But to my Gaveston! Shall I never see,
     Never behold thee now?—Madam, in this matter
     We will employ you and your little son:
     You shall go parley with the King of France.
     Boy, see you bear you bravely to the King,
     And do your message with a majesty.
PRINCE EDWARD: Commit not to my youth things of
          more weight
     Than fits a Prince so young as I to bear.   90
     And fear not, lord and father, Heaven's great
          beams
     On Atlas's shoulder shall not lie more safe
     Than shall your charge committed to my trust.
QUEEN ISABELLA: Ah, boy, this towardness makes thy
          mother fear
     Thou art not mark'd to many days on earth.
KING EDWARD: Madam, we will that you with speed be
          shipp'd,
     And this our son. Levune shall follow you   100
     With all the haste we can despatch him hence.
     Choose of our lords to bear you company,
     And go in peace: Leave us in wars at home.
QUEEN ISABELLA: Unnatural wars, where subjects
          brave their King,
     God end them once! My lord, I take my leave
     To make my preparation for France. *(Exeunt.)*

(Enter ARUNDEL.*)*

---

counterbuft, struck hard enough to cause a recoil.
haught, high, important.   **pool their tops,** cut off their
heads.

---

crowns, coins bearing the stamp of a crown.   **largess,**
gift of money.   **Sib,** family relative, wife.

KING EDWARD: What Lord ⟨Arundel⟩, dost thou
  come alone?
110 EARL OF ARUNDEL: Yea, my good lord, for Gaveston is
  dead!
KING EDWARD: Ah, traitors, have they put my friend
  to death?
  —Tell me, ⟨Arundel,⟩ died he ere thou cam'st?
  Or didst thou see my friend to take his death?
EARL OF ARUNDEL: Neither, my lord; for as he was
  surpris'd,
  Begirt with weapons and with enemies round,
  I did Your Highness' message to them all,
120 Demanding him of them—entreating rather,
  And said, upon the honor of my name,
  That I would undertake to carry him
  Unto Your Highness, and to bring him back.
KING EDWARD: And tell me, would the rebels deny me
  that?
YOUNGER SPENCER: Proud recreants!
KING EDWARD: Yea, Spencer, traitors all.
EARL OF ARUNDEL: I found them at the first
  inexorable.
130 The Earl of Warwick would not bide the hearing,
  Mortimer hardly, Pembroke and Lancaster
  Spake least; and when they flatly had denied,
  Refusing to receive me pledge for him,
  The Earl of Pembroke mildly thus bespake:
  "My lords, because our sovereign sends for him
  And promiseth he shall be safe return'd,
  I will this undertake, to have him hence
  And see him re-delivered to your hands."
KING EDWARD: Well, and how fortunes that he came
140 not?
YOUNGER SPENCER: Some treason or some villainy was
  cause.
EARL OF ARUNDEL: The Earl of Warwick seiz'd him on
  his way.
  For being deliver'd unto Pembroke's men,
  Their lord rode home thinking his prisoner safe.
  But ere he came, Warwick in ambush lay
  And bare him to his death: and in a trench
  Strake off his head—and march'd unto the camp.
150 YOUNGER SPENCER: A bloody part, flatly against law of
  arms!
KING EDWARD: O shall I speak, or shall I sigh and die?
YOUNGER SPENCER: My lord, refer your vengeance to
  the sword
  Upon these barons. Hearten up your men.
  Let them not unreveng'd murder your friends!
  Advance your standard, Edward, in the field,
  And march to fire them from their starting holes!°
KING EDWARD (kneels): By earth, the common mother
160 of us all,
  By Heaven and all the moving orbs thereof,
  By this right hand, and by my father's sword,

And all the honors 'longing to my crown,
I will have heads and lives for him as many
As I have manors, castles, towns, and towers!
Treacherous Warwick! Traitorous Mortimer!
If I be England's King, in lakes of gore
Your headless trunks, your bodies will I trail
That you may drink your fill and quaff in blood
And stain my royal standard with the same   170
—That so my bloody colors may suggest
Remembrance of revenge immortally
On your accursed traitorous progeny!
You villains that have slain my Gaveston!
And in this place of honor and of trust,
Spencer, sweet Spencer, I adopt thee here:
And merely of our love we do create thee
Earl of Gloucester and Lord Chamberlain,
Despite of times, despite of enemies.
YOUNGER SPENCER: My lord, here is a messenger from   180
  the barons
  Desires access unto Your Majesty.
KING EDWARD: Admit him near.

(Enter 2 MESSENGER from the barons with his coat of
arms.)

MESSENGER: Long live King Edward, England's
  lawful lord!
KING EDWARD: So wish not they, I wis,° that sent thee
  hither.
  Thou com'st from Mortimer and his complices.
  A ranker rout of rebels never was!
  Well, say thy message.   190
MESSENGER: The barons up in arms by me salute
  Your Highness with long life and happiness—
  And bid me say, as plainer° to Your Grace,
  That if without effusion of blood
  You will this grief have ease and remedy
  That from your princely person you remove
  This Spencer as a putrifying branch
  That deads the royal vine, whose golden leaves
  Empale your princely head, your diadem,
  Whose brightness such pernicious upstarts dim—   200
  Say they, and lovingly advise Your Grace
  To cherish virtue and nobility
  And have old servitors in high esteem
  And shake off smooth dissembling flatterers:
  This granted, they, their honors, and their lives
  Are to Your Highness vow'd and consecrate.
YOUNGER SPENCER: Ah, traitors, will they still display
  their pride?
KING EDWARD: Away, tarry no answer but be gone!
  Rebels, will they appoint their sovereign   210
  His sports, his pleasures, and his company?
  Yet, ere thou go, see how I do divorce (Embraces
  SPENCER.)
  Spencer from me.—Now get thee to thy lords

And tell them I will come to chastise them
For murdering Gaveston. Hie thee, get thee gone!
Edward with fire and sword follows at thy heels.

(Exit 2 MESSENGER.)

My lord, perceive you how these rebels swell?
Soldiers, good hearts, defend your sovereign's
220   right,
For now, even now, we march to make them stoop!
Away!

*(Exeunt. Alarums, excursions, a great fight, and a retreat
sounded. Enter the* KING, SPENCER THE FATHER,
SPENCER THE SON, *and the* NOBLEMEN *of the King's
side.)*

KING EDWARD: Why do we sound retreat? Upon
   them, lords!
This day I shall pour vengeance with my sword
On those proud rebels that are up in arms
And do confront and countermand their King.
YOUNGER SPENCER: I doubt it not, my lord, right will
   prevail.
230 ELDER SPENCER: 'Tis not amiss, my liege, for either
   part
To breathe awhile. Our men with sweat and dust
All chok'd well near, begin to faint for heat:
And this retire refresheth horse and man.
YOUNGER SPENCER: Here come the rebels.

(Enter the barons: YOUNGER MORTIMER, LANCASTER,
WARWICK, PEMBROKE, *cum caeteris* [*with* KENT, *a silent
watcher*].)

YOUNGER MORTIMER: Look, Lancaster, yonder is
   Edward
Among his flatterers.
LANCASTER: And there let him be
240   Till he pay dearly for their company.
WARWICK: And shall, or Warwick's sword shall smite
   in vain.
KING EDWARD: What rebels, do you shrink and sound
   retreat?
YOUNGER MORTIMER: No, Edward, no, thy flatterers
   faint and fly.
LANCASTER: They'd best betimes forsake thee, and
   their trains,
For they'll betray thee, traitors as they are!
250 YOUNGER SPENCER: Traitor on thy face, rebellious
   Lancaster!
PEMBROKE: Away, base upstart, brav'st thou nobles
   thus?
ELDER SPENCER: A noble attempt, and honorable
   deed,
Is it not, trow° ye, to assemble aid,
And levy arms against your lawful King!
YOUNGER MORTIMER: Then, Edward, thou wilt fight it
   to the last,

And rather bathe thy sword in subjects' blood   260
Than banish that pernicious company?
KING EDWARD: Ay, traitors all, rather than thus be
   brav'd,
Make England's civil towns huge heaps of stones,
And ploughs to go about our palace gates.
WARWICK: A desperate and unnatural resolution!
Alarum to the fight!
St. George for England, and the barons' right!
KING EDWARD: Saint George for England, and King
   Edward's right.   270

(Alarums. Exeunt the two parties severally. Enter ED-
WARD, *the* BISHOP OF WINCHESTER, *and soldiers with
the barons and* KENT *captives.)*

KING EDWARD: Now, lusty lords, now, not by chance
   of war
But justice of the quarrel and the cause,
Vail'd° is your pride! Methinks you hang the
   heads—
But we'll advance them, traitors! Now 'tis time
To be aveng'd on you for all your braves,
And for the murder of my dearest friend,
To whom right well you knew our soul was knit,
Good Pierce of Gaveston, my sweet favorite.   280
Ah, rebels, recreants, you made him away!
EARL OF KENT: Brother, in regard of thee, and of thy
   land,
Did they remove that flatterer from thy throne.
KING EDWARD: So, sir, you have spoke: Away, avoid
   our presence!

(Exit KENT.)

Accursed wretches, was't in regard of us,
When we had sent our messenger to request
He might be spar'd to come to speak with us,
And Pembroke undertook for his return,   290
That thou, proud Warwick, [snatch'd] the prisoner,
Poor Pierce, and headed him against law of arms?
For which *thy* head shall overlook the rest
As much as thou in rage outwent'st the rest!
WARWICK: Tyrant, I scorn thy threats and menaces.
It is but temporal° that thou canst inflict.
LANCASTER: The worst is death. And better die to live
Than live in infamy under such a King.
KING EDWARD: Away with them, my lord of
   Winchester!   300
These lusty leaders, Warwick and Lancaster,
I charge you roundly, off with both their heads!
Away!
WARWICK: Farewell, vain world!
LANCASTER: Sweet Mortimer, farewell.
YOUNGER MORTIMER: England, unkind to thy nobility,
Groan for this grief. Behold how thou art maim'd!

---

trow, believe.   *Vail'd,* lowered.   *temporal,* physical.

KING EDWARD: Go, take that haughty Mortimer to the
    Tower.
310 There see him safe bestow'd. And for the rest,
    Do speedy execution on them all.
    Be gone!
YOUNGER MORTIMER (aside): (What, Mortimer, can
    ragged stony walls
    Immure° thy virtue that aspires to Heaven?
    No, Edward, England's scourge, it may not be—
    Mortimer's hope surmounts his fortune far.)

(The captive barons are led off.)

KING EDWARD: Sound drums and trumpets! March
    with me, my friends,
320 Edward this day hath crown'd him King anew.

(Exit. Manent SPENCER *filius,* LEVUNE, *and* BALDOCK.)

YOUNGER SPENCER: Levune, the trust that we repose
    in thee,
    Begets the quiet of King Edward's land:
    Therefore be gone in haste and with advice
    Bestow that treasure on the lords of France
    That therewith all enchanted like the guard
    That suffer'd Jove to pass in showers of gold
    To Danaë, all aid may be denied
    To Isabel the Queen, that now in France
330 Makes friends: to cross the seas with her young son
    And step into his father's regiment.—
LEVUNE: That's it these barons and the subtle Queen
    Long [leveled] at.°
BALDOCK: Yea, but, Levune, thou seest,
    These barons lay their heads on blocks together.
    What they intend, the hangman frustrates clean.
LEVUNE: Have you no doubts, my lords, I'll clap [so]
    close
    Among the lords of France with England's gold
340 That Isabel shall make her plaints in vain
    And France shall be obdurate with her tears.
YOUNGER SPENCER: Then make for France, amain.°
    Levune, away!
    Proclaim King Edward's wars and victories. *(Exeunt
    omnes.)*

ACT 4 / SCENE 1

(Enter EDMUND [EARL OF KENT].)

EARL OF KENT: Fair blows the wind for France. Blow
    gentle gale,
    Till Edmund be arriv'd for England's good.
    Nature, yield to my country's cause in this.
    A brother? No, a butcher of thy friends!
    Proud Edward, dost thou banish me thy presence?
    But I'll to France, and cheer the wronged Queen,
    And certify what Edward's looseness is.

    Unnatural King, to slaughter noblemen
    And cherish flatterers! Mortimer, I stay   10
    Thy sweet escape. Stand gracious, gloomy night,
    To his device!°

(Enter MORTIMER, *disguised.)*

YOUNGER MORTIMER: Holla! Who walketh there?
    Is't you, my lord?
EARL OF KENT: Mortimer, 'tis I.
    But hath thy potion wrought so happily?°
YOUNGER MORTIMER: It hath, my lord. The warders
    all asleep,
    I thank them, gave me leave to pass in peace.
    But hath your grace got shipping unto France?   20
EARL OF KENT: Fear it not. *(Exeunt.)*

ACT 4 / SCENE 2

(Enter the QUEEN *and* [PRINCE EDWARD,] *HER SON.)*

QUEEN ISABELLA: Ah, boy, our friends do fail us all in
    France.
    The lords are cruel, and the King unkind.
    What shall we do?
PRINCE EDWARD: Madam, return to England,
    And please my father well. And then a fig
    For all my uncle's friendship here in France.
    I warrant you, I'll win His Highness quickly.
    A° loves me better than a thousand Spencers.
QUEEN ISABELLA: Ah, boy, thou art deceiv'd at least in   10
    this,
    To think that we can yet be tun'd together.
    No, no, we jar too far.—Unkind Valois!
    Unhappy Isabel, when France rejects!
    Whither, O, whither dost thou bend thy steps?

(Enter SIR JOHN OF HAINAULT.)*

SIR JOHN: Madam, what cheer?
QUEEN ISABELLA: Ah, good Sir John of Hainault,
    Never so cheerless nor so far distress'd.
SIR JOHN: I hear, sweet lady, of the King's
    unkindness.   20
    But droop not, madam. Noble minds contemn
    Despair. Will Your Grace with me to Hainault?
    —And there stay time's advantage with your son?
    How say you, my lord, will you go with your friends
    And shake off all our fortunes equally?
PRINCE EDWARD: So pleaseth the Queen, my mother,
    me it likes.
    The King of England nor the court of France
    Shall have me from my gracious mother's side—
    Till I be strong enough to break a staff—   30
    And then have at the proudest Spencer's head!
SIR JOHN: Well said, my lord!
QUEEN ISABELLA: O, my sweet heart, how do I moan
    thy wrongs—

    Immure, enclose. ***leveled at,*** aimed at. ***amain,***
quickly.

    device, plan, strategy. ***wrought so happily,*** worked so
well. ***A,*** he.

Yet triumph in the hope of thee, my joy!
Ah sweet Sir John, even to the utmost verge
Of Europe, or the shore of Tanais,°
We will with thee to Hainault, so we will.
The marquis is a noble gentleman:
His grace, I dare presume, will welcome me.
But who are these?

(Enter EDMUND [EARL OF KENT] *and* MORTIMER.)

EARL OF KENT: Madam, long may you live,
Much happier than your friends in England do!
QUEEN ISABELLA: Lord Edmund and Lord Mortimer
alive!
Welcome to France! The news was here, my lord,
That you were dead or very near your death.
YOUNGER MORTIMER: Lady, the last was truest of the
twain.
But Mortimer, reserv'd for better hap,
Hath shaken off the thraldom of the Tower
And lives t' advance your standard, good my lord.
PRINCE EDWARD: How mean you and the King my
father lives?
No, my Lord Mortimer, not I, I trow!
QUEEN ISABELLA: *Not,* son? Why *not?* I would it were
no worse!
—But, gentle lords, friendless we are in France.
YOUNGER MORTIMER: Monsieur le Grand, a noble
friend of yours,
Told us at our arrival all the news:
How hard the nobles, how unkind the King
Hath show'd himself. But, madam, right makes
room
Where weapons want. And though a many friends
Are made away (as Warwick, Lancaster,
And others of our party and faction),
Yet have we friends, assure Your Grace, in
England
Would cast up caps and clap their hands for joy
To see us there appointed for our foes.
EARL OF KENT: Would all were well, and Edward well
reclaim'd—
For England's honor, peace and quietness.
YOUNGER MORTIMER: But by the sword, my lord, it
must be deserv'd.
The King will ne'er forsake his flatterers.
SIR JOHN: My lords of England, sith th' ungentle King
Of France refuseth to give aid of arms
To this distressed Queen his sister here,
Go you with her to Hainault. Doubt ye not
We will find comfort, money, men, and friends
Ere long to bid the English King a base.°
How say'st, young Prince what think you of the
match?

40

50

60

70

80

Tanais, the Don river, believed to divide Europe from
Asia. *to bid . . . a base,* to challenge.

PRINCE EDWARD: I think King Edward will outrun us
all.
QUEEN ISABELLA: Nay, son, not so. And you must not
discourage
Your friends that are so forward in your aid.
EARL OF KENT: Sir John of Hainault, pardon us, I
pray.
These comforts that you give our woeful Queen
Bind us in kindness all at your command.
QUEEN ISABELLA: Yea, gentle brother. And the God of
Heaven
Prosper your happy motion, good Sir John!
YOUNGER MORTIMER: This noble gentleman, forward
in arms,
Was born, I see, to be our anchor-hold.
Sir John of Hainault, be it thy renown
That England's Queen and nobles in distress
Have been by thee restor'd and comforted.
SIR JOHN: Madam, along, and you my lord, with me
That England's peers may Hainault's welcome see.
(Exeunt.)

90

100

ACT 4 / SCENE 3

(Enter the KING, [ARUNDEL], *the two* SPENCERS *with
others.)*

KING EDWARD: Thus after many threats of wrathful
war,
Triumpheth England's Edward with his friends—
And triumph, Edward, with his friends
uncontroll'd!
My lord of Gloucester, do you hear the news?
YOUNGER SPENCER: What news, my lord?
KING EDWARD: Why, man, they say there is great
execution
Done through the realm. My Lord of Arundel,
You have the note, have you not?
EARL OF ARUNDEL: From the Lieutenant of the
Tower, my lord.
KING EDWARD: I pray let us see it. What have we
there?
Read it, Spencer.

10

*(*SPENCER *reads their names.)*

[YOUNGER SPENCER: "The Lord William Tuchet, the
Lord William fitz William, the Lord Warren de
Lisle, the Lord Henry Bradborne, and the Lord
William Chenie—barons—with John Page, an
esquire, were drawn and hanged at Pomfret. . . .
"And then shortly after, Roger Lord Clifford, John
Lord Mowbray, and Sir Gosein d'Eevill—
barons—were drawn and hanged at York.
"At Bristow in like manner were executed Sir
Henry de Willington and Sir Henry Montford,
baronets.

20

"And at Gloucester, the Lord John Gifford and Sir
30   William Elmebridge, knight.
"And at London, the Lord Henry Teies, baron.
"At Winchelsea, Sir Thomas Culpepper, knight.
"At Windsor, the Lord Francis de Aldham, baron.
"And at Canterbury, the Lord Bartholomew de
        Badelismere and the Lord Bartholomew de
        Ashbornham, barons.
"Also at Cardiff, in Wales, Sir William Fleming,
        knight was executed.
"Divers were executed in their counties, as Sir
40   Thomas Mandit and others."]
KING EDWARD: Why, so: they bark'd apace a month
        ago.
Now on my life, they'll neither bark nor bite!
Now, sirs, the news from France? Gloucester, I
        trow
The lords of France love England's gold so well
As Isabella gets no aid from thence.
What now remains? Have you proclaim'd, my lord,
Reward for them can bring in Mortimer?
50 YOUNGER SPENCER: My lord, we have. And if he be in
        England,
A will be had ere long, I doubt it not.
KING EDWARD: *If,* dost thou say? Spencer, as true as
        death,
He is in England's ground. Our portmasters
Are not so careless of their King's command.

(Enter 3 MESSENGER.)

How now, what news with thee? From whence
        come these?
MESSENGER: Letters, my lord, and tidings forth of
60   France.
To you, my lord of Gloucester, from Levune. *(Gives
letter to YOUNGER SPENCER.)*
KING EDWARD: Read.

(YOUNGER SPENCER reads the letter.)

"My duty to your honor promised, &c., I have
according to instructions in that behalf, dealt
with the King of France his lords and effected
that the Queen, all discontented and discom-
forted, is gone. Whither? If you ask, with Sir
John of Hainault, brother to the marquis, into
70   Flanders. With them are gone Lord Edmund
and the Lord Mortimer, having in their company divers of your nation, and others. And as
constant report goeth, they intend to give King
Edward battle in England sooner than he can
look for them. This is all the news of import.
                Your honor's in all service. Levune."
KING EDWARD: Ah, villains, hath that Mortimer
        escap'd?
With him is Edmund gone associate?

And will Sir John of Hainault lead the round?°   80
Welcome, a God's name, madam, and your son:
England shall welcome you and all your rout!
Gallop apace, bright Phoebus, through the sky,
And dusky night in rusty iron car,
Between you both shorten the time, I pray,
That I may see that most desired day
When we may meet these traitors in the field!
Ah, nothing grieves me but my little boy
Is thus misled to countenance their ills.
Come, friends, to Bristow,° there to make us   90
        strong.
And, winds, as equal be to bring them in,
As you injurious were to bear them forth! *(Exeunt.)*

ACT 4 / SCENE 4

*(Enter the QUEEN, HER SON, EDMUND [EARL OF KENT],
MORTIMER, and SIR JOHN [and SOLDIERS].)*

QUEEN ISABELLA: Now, lords, our loving friends and
        countrymen,
Welcome to England all, with prosperous winds!
Our kindest friends in Belgia have we left,
To cope with friends at home—a heavy case
When force to force is knit, and sword and glaive°
In civil broils make kin and countrymen
Slaughter themselves in others, and their sides
With their own weapons gor'd. But what's the help?
Misgovern'd kings are cause of all this wreck.   10
And Edward, thou art one among them all
Whose looseness hath betray'd thy land to spoil
And made the channels overflow with blood
Of thine own people. Patron shouldst thou be,
But thou—.
YOUNGER MORTIMER: Nay, madam, if you be a
        warrior,
You must not grow so passionate in speeches.
Lords, sith that we are by sufferance of Heaven
Arriv'd and armed in this Prince's right,   20
Here for our country's cause swear we to him
All homage, fealty, and forwardness.
And for the open wrongs and injuries
Edward hath done to us, his Queen, and land,
We come in arms to wreak it with the sword—
That England's Queen in peace may repossess
Her dignities and honors, and withal
We may remove these flatterers from the King,
That havocs England's wealth and treasury.
SIR JOHN: Sound trumpets, my lord, and forward let   30
        us march.
Edward will think we come to flatter him.
EARL OF KENT: I would he never had been flatter'd
        more!

(Trumpets sound. Exeunt.)

---

round, a dance.   **Bristow,** Bristol.   **glaive,** broadsword.

ACT 4 / SCENE 5

(Alarms and excursions. Enter the KING, BALDOCK, *and*
SPENCER *the son, flying about the stage.)*

YOUNGER SPENCER: Fly, fly, my lord! the Queen is
over-strong!
Her friends do multiply, and yours do fail.
Shape we our course to Ireland, there to breathe.
KING EDWARD: What, was I born to fly and run away,
And leave the Mortimers conquerors behind?
Give me my horse, and let's re'nforce our troops:
And in this bed of honor die with fame.
BALDOCK: O no, my lord, this princely resolution
10 Fits not the time, away, we are pursu'd! *(Exeunt.)*

(Enter EDMUND *alone with a sword and target.)*

EARL OF KENT: This way he fled, but I am come too
late.
Edward, alas, my heart relents for thee!
Proud traitor, Mortimer, why dost thou chase
Thy lawful King, thy sovereign, with thy sword?
—Vilde° wretch, and why hast *thou*, of all unkind,
Borne arms against thy brother and thy King?
Rain showers of vengeance on my cursed head,
Thou God, to whom in justice it belongs
20 To punish this unnatural revolt!
Edward, this Mortimer aims at thy life.
O fly him, then!—But Edmund, calm this rage.
Dissemble or thou diest, for Mortimer
And Isabel do kiss, while they conspire:
And yet she bears a face of love forsooth!
Fie on that love that hatcheth death and hate!
Edmund away! Bristow to Longshanks' blood
Is false. Be not found single° for suspect.°
Proud Mortimer pries near unto thy walks.

(Enter the QUEEN, MORTIMER, *the young* PRINCE, *and*
SIR JOHN OF HAINAULT [*with* SOLDIERS].*)*

30 QUEEN ISABELLA: Successful battle gives the God of
kings
To them that fight in right and fear His wrath.
Since, then, successfully we have prevail'd,
Thanks be Heaven's great architect, and you!
Ere farther we proceed, my noble lords,
We here create our well-beloved son,
Of love and care unto his royal person,
Lord Warden of the realm, and sith° the fates
Have made his father so infortunate,
40 Deal you, my lords, in this, my loving lords,
As to your wisdoms fittest seems in all.
EARL OF KENT: Madam, without offense, if I may ask,
How will you deal with Edward in his fall?
PRINCE EDWARD: Tell me, good uncle, what Edward
do you mean?

Vilde, vile. *single*, alone. *for suspect*, for fear of
being suspected. *sith*, because.

EARL OF KENT: Nephew, your father—I dare not call
him King.
YOUNGER MORTIMER: My lord of Kent, what needs
these questions?
'Tis not in her controlment, nor in ours,   50
But as the realm and parliament shall please:
So shall your brother be disposed of.
—(I like not this relenting mood in Edmund. *(aside
to* QUEEN)
Madam, 'tis good to look to him betimes.)
QUEEN ISABELLA: (My lord, the Mayor of Bristow
knows our mind.) *(aside to* MORTIMER)
YOUNGER MORTIMER: (Yea, madam, and they scape
not easily
That fled the field.) *(aside)*
QUEEN ISABELLA: Baldock is with the King.   60
A goodly chancellor, is he not, my lord?
SIR JOHN: So are the Spencers, the father and son.
EARL OF KENT: (This, Edward, is the ruin of [thy]
realm!) *(aside, despairingly)*

(Enter RICE AP HOWELL *and the* MAYOR OF BRISTOW
with SPENCER *the father* [*prisoner*].*)*

RICE: God save Queen Isabel and her princely son!
Madam, the mayor and citizens of Bristow, *(points to
the* MAYOR.*)*
In sign of love and duty to this presence,
Present by me this traitor to the state,
Spencer, the father to that wanton Spencer,
That like the lawless Catiline° of Rome   70
Revell'd in England's wealth and treasury!
QUEEN ISABELLA: We thank you all.
YOUNGER MORTIMER: Your loving care in this
Deserveth princely favors and rewards.
But where's the King and the other Spencer fled?
RICE: Spencer the son, created Earl of Gloucester,
Is with that smooth-tongu'd scholar Baldock gone
And shipp'd but late for Ireland with the King.
YOUNGER MORTIMER: (Some whirlwind fetch them
back or sink them all!—) *(aside)*   80
They shall be started thence, I doubt it not.
PRINCE EDWARD: Shall I not see the King my father
yet?
EARL OF KENT: (Unhappy Edward, chas'd from
England's bounds.) *(aside)*
SIR JOHN: Madam, what resteth? Why stand you in a
muse?
QUEEN ISABELLA: I rue my lord's ill-fortune, but alas,
Care of my country call'd me to this war.
YOUNGER MORTIMER: Madam, have done with care   90
and sad complaint.
Your King hath wrong'd your country and himself,
And we must seek to right it as we may.—
Meanwhile have hence this rebel to the block:

Cataline, corrupt Roman politician.

Your lordship cannot privilege° your head!
   (*Sarcastically.*)
ELDER SPENCER: Rebel is he that fights against his
   prince!
So fought not they that fought in Edward's right!
YOUNGER MORTIMER: Take him away, he prates.

   (*Exeunt soldiers with* ELDER SPENCER.)

100 You, Rice ap Howell,
Shall do good service to Her Majesty,
Being of countenance in your country here,
To follow these rebellious runagates.°
We in meanwhile, madam, must take advice
How Baldock, Spencer, and their complices
May in their fall be follow'd to their end.

   (*Exeunt omnes.*)

ACT 4 / SCENE 6

   (*Enter the* ABBOT, MONKS, KING EDWARD, YOUNGER
   SPENCER, *and* BALDOCK [*the last three disguised*].)

ABBOT: Have you no doubt, my lord, have you no
   fear:
As silent and as careful we will be
To keep your royal person safe with us.
Free from suspect and fell invasion
Of such as have Your Majesty in chase—
Yourself, and those your chosen company—
As danger of this stormy time requires.
KING EDWARD: Father, thy face should harbor no
10   deceit.
O, hadst thou ever been a king, thy heart,
Pierc'd deeply with a sense of my distress,
Could not but take compassion of my state.
Stately and proud, in riches and in train,
Whilom° I was, powerful and full of pomp—
But what is he whom rule and empery
Have not in life or death made miserable?
Come Spencer, come Baldock, come, sit down by
   me,
20 Make trial now of that philosophy
That in our famous nurseries of arts
Thou suck'dst from Plato and from Aristotle.
Father, this life contemplative is heaven.
O, that I might this life in quiet lead!
But we, alas, are chas'd—and you, my friends,
Your lives and my dishonor they pursue!
Yet, gentle monks, for treasure, gold nor fee,
Do you betray us and our company.
MONKS: Your Grace may sit secure, if none but we
30   Do wot° of your abode.
YOUNGER SPENCER: Not one alive. But shrewdly I
   suspect

A gloomy fellow in a mead below.
A gave a long look after us, my lord:
And all the land I know is up in arms,
Arms that pursue our lives with deadly hate.
BALDOCK: We were embark'd for Ireland—wretched
   we
With awkward winds and sore tempests driven
To fall on shore and here to pine in fear   40
Of Mortimer and his confederates!
KING EDWARD: Mortimer, who talks of Mortimer?
Who wounds me with the name of Mortimer,
That bloody man?—Good father, on thy lap
   (*Kneels.*)
Lay I this head, laden with mickle° care.
O, might I never open these eyes again,
Never again lift up this drooping head,
O never more lift up this dying heart!
YOUNGER SPENCER: Look up, my lord. Baldock, this
   drowsiness   50
Betides no good. Here even we are betray'd!

   (*Enter with Welsh hooks,* RICE AP HOWELL, *a* MOWER,
   and the EARL OF LEICESTER.)

MOWER: Upon my life, those be the men ye seek.
   (*Points.*)
RICE: Fellow, enough.—My lord, I pray be short. (*To*
   LEICESTER.)
A fair commission warrants what we do.
EARL OF LEICESTER: The Queen's commission, urged
   by Mortimer.—

   (*Parenthesis is spoken as an aside.*)

(What cannot gallant Mortimer with the Queen?
Alas, see where he sits and hopes unseen
T'escape their hands that seek to reave° his life!
Too true it is: *Quem dies vidit veniens superbum,*   60
Hunc dies vidit fugiens jacentem.°
But, Leicester, leave to grow so passionate . . .)
Spencer and Baldock, by no other names,°
I do arrest you of high treason here.
Stand not on titles, but obey th' arrest;
'Tis in the name of Isabel the Queen.
My lord, why droop you thus?
KING EDWARD: O day the last of all my bliss on earth,
Center of all misfortune! O my stars,
Why do you lour unkindly on a King?   70
Comes Leicester then in Isabella's name
To take my life, my company from me?
Here, man, rip up this panting breast of mine
And take my heart, in rescue of my friends!
RICE: Away with them!
YOUNGER SPENCER: It may become thee yet

°*lordship cannot privilege,* title of nobility cannot protect.
°*runagates,* renegades, rebels. °*Whilom,* formerly. °*wot,*
know.

°*mickle,* much. °*reave,* take away. °*Quem . . . jacentem,*
Whom the morning saw raised high, the evening saw
brought low. °*by no other names,* i.e., he will not recognize
their titles of nobility.

To let us take our farewell of His Grace.
ABBOT: (My heart with pity earns° to see this sight—
    A king to bear these words and proud commands!)
                                                    (aside)
80 KING EDWARD: Spencer, ah sweet Spencer, thus then
        must we part?
    YOUNGER SPENCER: We must, my lord! So will the
        angry heavens.
    KING EDWARD: Nay, so will Hell and cruel Mortimer!
    The gentle heavens have not to do in this.
    BALDOCK: My lord, it is in vain to grieve or storm.
    Here humbly of Your Grace we take our leaves:
    Our lots are cast, I fear me so is thine.
    KING EDWARD: In Heaven we may, in earth ne'er shall
90   we meet.
    And, Leicester, say, what shall become of us?
    EARL OF LEICESTER: Your Majesty must go to
        Killingworth.
    KING EDWARD: Must! 'Tis somewhat hard when kings
        must go.
    EARL OF LEICESTER: Here is a litter ready for Your
        Grace,
    That waits your pleasure—and the day grows old.
    RICE: As good be gone as stay and be benighted.
100 KING EDWARD: A litter hast thou? Lay me in a hearse
    And to the gates of Hell convey me hence!
    Let Pluto's° bells ring out my fatal knell
    And hags howl for my death at Charon's shore,°
    For friends hath Edward none but these,
    And these must die under a tyrant's sword.
    RICE: My lord, be going. Care not for these,
    For we shall see them shorter by the heads.
    KING EDWARD: Well, that shall be, shall be. Part we
        must.
110 Sweet Spencer, gentle Baldock, part we must.
    Hence feigned weeds, unfeigned are my woes!

        (Throws off his disguise.)

    Father, farewell! Leicester, thou stay'st for me
    And go I must. Life, farewell, with my friends!

        (Exeunt KING EDWARD and LEICESTER.)

    YOUNGER SPENCER: O is he gone? Is noble Edward
        gone?
    Parted from hence? never to see us more?
    Rent sphere of heaven, and fire, forsake thy orb!
    Earth, melt to air! Gone is my sovereign,
    Gone, gone, alas, never to make return!
120 BALDOCK: Spencer, I see our souls are fleeted hence.
    We are depriv'd the sunshine of our life.
    Make for a new life, man. Throw up thy eyes
    And heart and hand to Heaven's immortal throne!
    Pay nature's debt with cheerful countenance.
    Reduce we all our lessons unto this:

    To die, sweet Spencer, therefore live we all.
    Spencer, all live to die, and rise to fall.
    RICE: Come, come, keep these preachments till you
        come to the place appointed. You and such as
        you are have made wise work in England.—Will   130
        your lordships away? (Ironically.)
    MOWER: Your lordship I trust will remember me?
    RICE: Remember thee, fellow! What else? Follow me
        to the town. (Exeunt.)

ACT 5 / SCENE 1

(Enter the KING, LEICESTER, with [the] BISHOP OF WIN-
CHESTER and TRUSSEL for the crown.)

EARL OF LEICESTER: Be patient, good my lord, cease to
    lament,
    Imagine Killingworth Castle were your court,
    And that you lay for pleasure here a space,
    Not of compulsion or necessity.
KING EDWARD: Leicester, if gentle words might
    comfort me,
    Thy speeches long ago had eas'd my sorrows:
    For kind and loving hast thou always been.
    The griefs of private men are soon allay'd   10
    But not of kings. The forest deer being struck
    Runs to an herb that closeth up the wounds.
    But when the imperial lion's flesh is gor'd,
    He rends and tears it with his wrathful paw!
    —Highly scorning that the lowly earth
    Should drink his blood, mounts up into the air!
    And so it fares with me whose dauntless mind
    Th' ambitious Mortimer would seek to curb,
    And that unnatural Queen, false Isabel,
    That thus hath pent and mew'd° me in a prison—   20
    For such outrageous passions cloy my soul
    As with the wings of rancor and disdain
    Full often am I soaring up to heaven
    To plain me° to the gods against them both!
    —But when I call to mind I am a King,
    Methinks I should revenge me of my wrongs,
    That Mortimer and Isabel have done. . . .
    But what are kings when regiment is gone
    But perfect shadows in a sunshine day?
    My nobles rule: I bear the name of King;   30
    I wear the crown: but am controll'd by them—
    By Mortimer and my unconstant Queen
    Who spots my nuptial bed with infamy!
    —Whilst I am lodg'd within this cave of care
    Where sorrow at my elbow still attends,
    To company my heart with sad laments
    That bleeds within me for this strange exchange.
    But tell me, must I now resign my crown
    To make usurping Mortimer a king?

---

    earns, grieves. *Pluto,* god of the underworld. *Cha-*
ron, the ferryman who took souls to the world of the dead.

    pent and mew'd, confined and enclosed. *plain me,*
make my complaint.

40 BISHOP OF WINCHESTER: Your Grace mistakes. It is for
        England's good
      And princely Edward's right we crave the crown.
    KING EDWARD: No, 'tis for Mortimer, not Edward's
        head!
      For he's a lamb, encompassed by wolves
      Which in a moment will abridge his life.
      But if proud Mortimer do wear this crown,
      Heavens turn it to a blaze of quenchless fire!
      Or like the snaky wreath of Tisiphon,°
50   Engirt the temples of his hateful head!
      So shall not England's vines be perished,
      But Edward's name survives, though Edward dies.
    EARL OF LEICESTER: My lord, why waste you thus the
        time away?
      They stay° your answer. Will you yield your crown?
    KING EDWARD: Ah, Leicester, weigh how hardly I can
        brook
      To lose my crown and kingdom without cause:
      To give ambitious Mortimer my right,
60   That like a mountain overwhelms my bliss—
      In which extreme my mind here murder'd is!
      But what the Heavens appoint, I must obey.
      Here, take my crown—the life of Edward too.
        (Takes off crown.)
      Two Kings in England cannot reign at once.
      But stay a while! Let me be King till night
      That I may gaze upon this glittering crown:
      So shall my eyes receive their last content;
      My head, the latest honor due to it;
70   And jointly both yield up their wished right.
      Continue ever thou celestial sun—
      Let never silent night possess this clime!
      Stand still you watches of the element!
      All times and seasons, rest you at a stay!
      —That Edward may be still fair England's King.
      But day's bright beams doth vanish fast away,
      And needs I must resign my wished crown.
      Inhuman creatures nurs'd with tiger's milk,
      Why gape you for your sovereign's overthrow?
80   My diadem° I mean, and guiltless life—
      See, monsters, see, I'll wear my crown again! (Puts
        on crown.)
      What, fear you not the fury of your King?
      —But hapless Edward, thou art fondly led,
      They pass not for thy frowns as late they did,
      But seeks to make a new-elected King—
      Which fills my mind with strange despairing
        thoughts,
      Which thoughts are martyred with endless
90   torments,
      And in this torment comfort find I none
      But that I feel the crown upon my head!
      And therefore let me wear it yet awhile. . . .

TRUSSEL: My lord, the parliament must have present
    news.
  And therefore say, will you resign or no? (The KING
    rageth.)
KING EDWARD: I'll not resign! But whilst I live—.
  Traitors be gone! And join you with Mortimer!
  Elect, conspire, install, do what you will!   100
  Their blood and yours shall seal° these treacheries!
BISHOP OF WINCHESTER: This answer we'll return, and
    so farewell. (Going with TRUSSEL.)
EARL OF LEICESTER: Call them again, my lord, and
    speak them fair:
  For if they go, the Prince shall lose his right.
KING EDWARD: Call thou them back, I have no power
    to speak.
EARL OF LEICESTER: My lord, the King is willing to
    resign.   110
BISHOP OF WINCHESTER: If he be not, let him choose.
KING EDWARD: O would I might! But heavens and
    earth conspire
  To make me miserable! Here receive my crown.
  Receive it? No, these innocent hands of mine
  Shall not be guilty of so foul a crime—
  He of you all that most desires my blood
  And will be called the murderer of a king,
  Take it. What, are you mov'd? Pity you me?
  Then send for unrelenting Mortimer   120
  And Isabel, whose eyes being turn'd to steel
  Will sooner sparkle fire than shed a tear.
  Yet stay, for rather than I'll look on them,
  Here, here! (Gives crown.)
  Now, sweet God of Heaven,
  Make me despise this transitory pomp,
  And sit for aye enthronized in Heaven!
  Come, death, and with thy fingers close my eyes!
  Or if I live, let me forget myself. . . .
BISHOP OF WINCHESTER: My lord—   130
KING EDWARD: Call me not lord! Away, out of my
    sight!
  —Ah pardon me, grief makes me lunatic.
  Let not that Mortimer protect° my son.
  More safety there is in a tiger's jaws,
  Than his embracements! Bear this to the Queen,
  Wet with tears and dried again with sighs— (Gives
    handkerchief.)
  If with the sight thereof she be not moved,
  Return it back and dip it in my blood!   140
  Commend me to my son, and bid him rule
  Better than I.—Yet how have I transgress'd
  Unless it be with too much clemency?
TRUSSEL: And thus most humbly do we take our
    leave.
KING EDWARD: Farewell.

  (Exeunt BISHOP and TRUSSEL with crown.)

Tisiphon, one of the Furies whose heads were covered
with snakes. **stay,** wait for. **diadem,** crown.

seal, pay for. **protect,** be Protector to.

I know the next news that they bring
Will be my death. And welcome it shall be!
To wretched men death is felicity.
150 EARL OF LEICESTER: Another post, what news brings he?

(Enter BERKELEY, *who gives a paper to* LEICESTER.*)*

KING EDWARD: Such news as I expect. Come, Berkeley, come,
And tell thy message to my naked breast.
BERKELEY: My lord, think not a thought so villainous
Can harbor in a man of noble birth.
To do Your Highness service and devoir°
And save you from your foes, Berkeley would die.
EARL OF LEICESTER: My lord, the council of the Queen
160   commands
That I resign my charge.
KING EDWARD: And who must keep me now? Must you, my lord?
BERKELEY: Ay, my most gracious lord, so 'tis decreed.
KING EDWARD *(takes the paper)*: —By Mortimer, whose name is written here!
Well may I rent his name that rends my heart!
(Tears it.)
This poor revenge has something eas'd my mind—
170 So may his limbs be torn as is this paper!
Hear me, immortal Jove, and grant it too!
BERKELEY: Your Grace must hence with me to Berkeley straight.
KING EDWARD: Whither you will. All places are alike.
And every earth is fit for burial.
EARL OF LEICESTER: Favor him, my lord, as much as lieth in you.
BERKELEY: Even so betide° my soul as I use him!
KING EDWARD: Mine enemy hath pitied my estate,
180 And that's the cause that I am now remov'd.
BERKELEY: And thinks Your Grace that Berkeley will be cruel?
KING EDWARD: I know not. But of this am I assured—
That death ends all, and I can die but once.
Leicester, farewell.
EARL OF LEICESTER: Not yet, my lord, I'll bear you on your way. *(Exeunt omnes.)*

ACT 5 / SCENE 2

(Enter MORTIMER *and* QUEEN ISABELLA.*)*

YOUNGER MORTIMER: Fair Isabel, now have we our desire:
The proud corrupters of the light-brain'd King
Have done their homage to the lofty gallows,
And he himself lies in captivity.
Be rul'd by me, and we will rule the realm.
In any case, take heed of childish fear—

For now we hold an old wolf by the ears,
That if he slip will seize upon us both
And gripe the sorer being grip'd himself.   10
Think therefore, madam, that imports us much
To erect your son with all the speed we may
And that I be protector over him.
For our behoof will bear the greater sway
Whenas a king's name shall be underwrit.°
QUEEN ISABELLA: Sweet Mortimer, the life of Isabel!
Be thou persuaded that I love thee well.
And therefore—so the Prince my son be safe,
Whom I esteem as dear as these mine eyes—
Conclude against his father what thou wilt!   20
—And I myself will willingly subscribe.
YOUNGER MORTIMER: First, would I hear news he were depos'd:
And then let me alone to handle him.

(Enter 4 MESSENGER.*)*

Letters, from whence?
MESSENGER: From Killingworth, my lord.
QUEEN ISABELLA: How fares my lord the King?
MESSENGER: In health, madam, but full of pensiveness.
QUEEN ISABELLA: Alas, poor soul, would I could ease   30
his grief!

(Enter the BISHOP OF WINCHESTER. *He bows deeply.)*

Thanks, gentle Winchester. *(to the* MESSENGER*)*
Sirrah, be gone.

(Exit MESSENGER.*)*

BISHOP OF WINCHESTER: The King hath willingly resign'd his crown.
QUEEN ISABELLA: O happy news! Send for the Prince, my son!
BISHOP OF WINCHESTER *(pointing to letter in* QUEEN's *hand)*: Further, ere this letter was seal'd, Lord Berkeley came   40
So that he now is gone from Killingworth.
And we have heard that Edmund laid a plot
To set his brother free. No more but so.
The lord of Berkeley is so pitiful
As Leicester that had charge of him before.
QUEEN ISABELLA: Then let some other be his guardian.
YOUNGER MORTIMER: Let me alone. *Here* is the privy seal! *(Points to himself.)*

(Exit the BISHOP OF WINCHESTER.*)*

Who's there? Call hither Gurney and Matrevis.   50
To dash the heavy-headed Edmund's drift,
Berkeley shall be discharg'd, the King remov'd,
And none but we shall know where [as] he lieth.

---

devoir, duty. **betide,** befall.   **underwrit,** subscribed, signed.

QUEEN ISABELLA: But, Mortimer, as long as he
    survives,
    What safety rests for us or for my son?
YOUNGER MORTIMER: Speak, shall he presently be
    despatch'd and die?
QUEEN ISABELLA: I would he were, so 'twere not by my
60   means!

    (*Enter* MATREVIS *and* GURNEY. *The* QUEEN *steps aside.*)

YOUNGER MORTIMER: Enough—.
    Matrevis, write a letter presently
    Unto the lord of Berkelely from ourself
    That he resign the King to thee and Gurney.
    And when 'tis done, we will subscribe our name.
MATREVIS: It shall be done, my lord. (*Writes.*)
YOUNGER MORTIMER: Gurney!
GURNEY: My lord.
YOUNGER MORTIMER: As thou intend'st to rise by
70   Mortimer—
    Who now makes Fortune's wheel turn as he
    please!—
    Seek all the means thou canst to make him droop,
    And neither give him kind word nor good look.
GURNEY: I warrant you, my lord.
YOUNGER MORTIMER: And this above the rest.
    Because we hear
    That Edmund casts to work his liberty,
    Remove him still from place to place by night
80   And at the last [be]come to Killingworth—
    And then from thence to Berkeley back again!
    And by the way to make him fret the more,
    Speak curstly to him, and in any case
    Let no man comfort him. If he chance to weep
    But amplify his grief with bitter words.
MATREVIS: Fear not, my lord! We'll do as you
    command.
YOUNGER MORTIMER: So now away! (*The* QUEEN *steps
    forward.*) Post thitherwards amain!
90 QUEEN ISABELLA: Whither goes this letter? to my lord
    the King?
    Commend me humbly to His Majesty,
    And tell him that I labor all in vain
    To ease his grief and work his liberty.
    And bear him this as witness of my love. (*Gives a
    jewel.*)
MATREVIS: I will, madam.

    (*Exeunt* MATREVIS *and* GURNEY.)

YOUNGER MORTIMER: Finely dissembled! Do so still,
    sweet Queen.
    Here comes the young Prince with the Earl of
100   Kent.
QUEEN ISABELLA: Something he whispers in his
    childish ears.
YOUNGER MORTIMER: If he have such access unto the
    Prince,
    Our plots and stratagems will soon be dash'd.

QUEEN ISABELLA: Use Edmund friendly as if all were
    well.

    (*Enter the young* PRINCE *and the* EARL OF KENT *talking
    with him.*)

YOUNGER MORTIMER: How fares my honorable lord of
    Kent?
EARL OF KENT: In health, sweet Mortimer. How fares 110
    Your Grace?
QUEEN ISABELLA: Well, if my lord your brother were
    enlarg'd.
EARL OF KENT: I hear of late he hath depos'd himself.
QUEEN ISABELLA: The more my grief.
YOUNGER MORTIMER: And mine.
EARL OF KENT: (Ah, they do dissemble!) (*aside*)
QUEEN ISABELLA: Sweet son, come hither, I must talk
    with thee.
YOUNGER MORTIMER: Thou being his uncle and the 120
    next of blood,
    Do look to be protector over the Prince?
EARL OF KENT: Not I, my lord. Who should protect
    the son
    But she that gave him life? I mean the Queen.
PRINCE EDWARD: Mother, persuade me not to wear
    the crown.
    Let him be King! I am too young to reign.
QUEEN ISABELLA: But be content, seeing it is His
    Highness' pleasure. 130
PRINCE EDWARD: Let me but see him first, and then I
    will.
EARL OF KENT: Ay, do sweet nephew!
QUEEN ISABELLA: Brother, you know it is impossible.
PRINCE EDWARD: Why, is he dead?
QUEEN ISABELLA: No, God forbid!
EARL OF KENT: I would those words proceeded from
    your heart!
YOUNGER MORTIMER: Inconstant Edmund, dost thou
    favor him 140
    That was a cause of his imprisonment?
EARL OF KENT: The more cause have I now to make
    amends!
YOUNGER MORTIMER: I tell thee, 'tis not meet that one
    so false
    Should come about the person of a Prince.
    My lord, he hath betrayed the King his brother,
    And therefore trust him not.
PRINCE EDWARD: But he repents and sorrows for it
    now. 150
QUEEN ISABELLA: Come son, and go with this gentle
    lord and me.
PRINCE EDWARD: With you I will, but not with
    Mortimer.
YOUNGER MORTIMER: Why, youngling, 'sdain'st thou
    so of Mortimer?
    Then I will carry thee by force away.
PRINCE EDWARD: Help, uncle Kent! Mortimer will
    wrong me!

(MORTIMER grasps the PRINCE. KENT tries to intervene.)

160 QUEEN ISABELLA: Brother Edmund, strive not. We are
  his friends.
  Isabel is nearer than the Earl of Kent.
EARL OF KENT: Sister, Edward is my charge, redeem
  him.
QUEEN ISABELLA: Edward is my son, and I will keep
  him.
EARL OF KENT *(aside)*: (Mortimer shall know that he
  hath wrong'd me.
  Hence will I haste to Killingworth Castle
170 And rescue aged Edward from his foes
  To be reveng'd on Mortimer and thee!)

(Exeunt omnes.)

ACT 5 / SCENE 3

*(Enter MATREVIS and GURNEY [and SOLDIERS] with the
KING.)*

MATREVIS: My lord, be not pensive. We are your
  friends.
  Men are ordain'd to live in misery.
  Therefore come, dalliance dangereth our lives.
KING EDWARD: Friends, whither must unhappy
  Edward go?
  Will hateful Mortimer appoint no rest?
  Must I be vexed like the nightly bird°
  Whose sight is loathsome to all winged fowls?
10 When will the fury of his mind assuage?
  When will his heart be satisfied with blood?
  If mine will serve, unbowel straight this breast
  And give my heart to Isabel and him!
  It is the chiefest mark they level at!
GURNEY: Not so, my liege. The Queen hath given this
  charge
  To keep Your Grace in safety.
  Your passions make your dolors to increase.
KING EDWARD: This usage makes my misery increase.
  But can my air of life continue long
  When all my senses are annoy'd with stench?
  Within a dungeon England's King is kept
  Where I am starv'd for want of sustenance—
  My daily diet is heart-breaking sobs
  That almost rents the closet of my heart!
  Thus lives old Edward, not reliev'd by any—
  And so must die, though pitied by many!
  O, water, gentle friends, to cool my thirst
  And clear my body from foul excrements.
30 MATREVIS: Here's channel water, as our charge is
  given.
  Sit down, for we'll be barbers to Your Grace.
KING EDWARD: Traitors, away, what, will you murder
  me?

Or choke your sovereign with puddle water?
GURNEY: No, but wash your face, and shave away
  your beard,
  Lest you be known and so be rescued.
MATREVIS: Why strive you thus? Your labor is in vain.
KING EDWARD: The wren may strive against the lion's 40
  strength!
  But all in vain, so vainly do I strive
  To seek for mercy at a tyrant's hand. *(They wash him
  with puddle water and shave his beard away.)*
  Immortal powers! that knows the painful cares
  That wait upon my poor distressed soul,
  O level all your looks upon these daring men,
  That wrongs their liege and sovereign, England's
  King!
  O Gaveston, it is for thee that I am wrong'd,
  For me both thou and both the Spencers died! 50
  And for your sakes a thousand wrongs I'll take!
  The Spencers' ghosts wherever they remain
  Wish well to mine. Then [hush], for them I'll die.
MATREVIS: 'Twixt theirs and yours shall be no enmity.
  Come, come away! Now put the torches out:
  We'll enter in by darkness to Killingworth.

(Enter EDMUND.)

GURNEY: How now, who comes there?
MATREVIS: Guard the King sure! It is the Earl of
  Kent!
KING EDWARD: O gentle brother, help to rescue me! 60
MATREVIS: Keep them asunder! Thrust in the King!
EARL OF KENT: Soldiers, let me but talk to him one
  word.
GURNEY: Lay hands upon the earl for his assault!
  (Soldiers hold KENT.)
EARL OF KENT: Lay down your weapons! Traitors,
  yield the King!
MATREVIS: Edmund, yield thou thyself, or thou shalt
  die.
EARL OF KENT: Base villains, wherefore do you gripe°
  me thus? 70
GURNEY: Bind him and so convey him to the court.
EARL OF KENT: Where is the court but here? Here is
  the King
  And I will visit him! Why stay you me?
MATREVIS: The court is where Lord Mortimer
  remains.
  Thither shall your honor go; and so farewell.

*(Exeunt MATREVIS and GURNEY with the KING. Manent
EDMUND and the soldiers.)*

EARL OF KENT: O miserable is that commonweal
  Where lords keep courts and kings are lock'd in
  prison! 80
SOLDIERS: Wherefore stay we? On, sirs, to the court!

---

nightly bird, owl.

gripe, grip.

EARL OF KENT: Ay, lead me whither you will, even to
   my death,
   Seeing that my brother cannot be releas'd! *(Exeunt.)*

ACT 5 / SCENE 4

(Enter MORTIMER *alone.)*

YOUNGER MORTIMER: The King must die, or
   Mortimer goes down.
   The commons now begin to pity him.
   Yet he that is the cause of Edward's death,
   Is sure to pay for it when his son is of age:
   And therefore will I do it cunningly.
   This letter, written by a friend of ours,
   Contains his death, yet bids them save his life:
   (Reads.)
10   *Edwardum occidere nolite timere, bonum est—*
   "Fear not to kill the King, 'tis good he die."
   But read it thus and that's another sense:
   Edwardum occidere nolite, timere bonum est—
   "Kill not the King, 'tis good to fear the worst."
   Unpointed° as it is, thus shall it go.
   —That being dead, if it chance to be found,
   Matrevis and the rest may bear the blame
   And we be quit that caus'd it to be done!
   Within this room is lock'd the messenger
20   That shall convey it and perform the rest.
   And by a secret token that he bears
   Shall he be murder'd when the deed is done!
   —Lightborn, come forth!

(Enter LIGHTBORN.*)*

   Art thou so resolute as thou wast?
LIGHTBORN: What else, my lord? and far more
   resolute!
YOUNGER MORTIMER: And hast thou cast how to
   accomplish it?
LIGHTBORN: Ay, ay, and none shall know which way
30   he died!
YOUNGER MORTIMER: But at his looks, Lightborn,
   thou wilt relent?
LIGHTBORN: Relent, ha, ha! I use much to relent!
YOUNGER MORTIMER: Well, do it bravely, and be
   secret.
LIGHTBORN: You shall not need to give instructions.
   'Tis not the first time I have kill'd a man:
   I learn'd in Naples how to poison flowers,
   To strangle with a lawn° thrust through the throat,
40   To pierce the windpipe with a needle's point,
   Or whilst one is asleep, to take a quill
   And blow a little powder in his ears.
   Or open his mouth and pour quicksilver down.
   And yet I have a braver way than these.
YOUNGER MORTIMER: What's that?

LIGHTBORN: Nay, you shall pardon me. None shall
   know my tricks.
YOUNGER MORTIMER: I care not how it is, so it be not
   spi'd.
   Deliver this to Gurney and Matrevis. *(Gives letter.)* 50
   At every ten mile end thou hast a horse.
   Take this. *(Gives money.)* Away and never see me
   more!
LIGHTBORN: No?
YOUNGER MORTIMER: No—
   Unless thou bring me news of Edward's death.
LIGHTBORN: That will I quickly do. Farewell, my lord.
   (Exit).
YOUNGER MORTIMER: The Prince I rule, the Queen do
   I command. 60
   And with a lowly congé° to the ground,
   The proudest lords salute me as I pass.
   I seal, I cancel, I do what I will.
   Fear'd am I more than lov'd—let me be fear'd
   And when I frown make all the court look pale.
   I view the Prince with Aristarchus'° eyes
   Whose looks were as a breeching° to a boy.
   They thrust upon me the Protectorship
   And sue to me for that that I desire.
   While at the council-table, grave enough, 70
   And not unlike a bashful Puritan,
   First I complain of imbecility,
   Saying it is *onus quam gravissimum°—*
   Till being interrupted by my friends,
   Suscepi that *provinciam°* as they term it.
   And to conclude, I am Protector now!
   Now is all sure. The Queen and Mortimer
   Shall rule the realm, the King; and none rule us.
   Mine enemies will I plague, my friends advance.
   And what I list command who dare control? 80
   Major sum quam cui possit fortuna nocere.°
   And that this be the coronation-day,
   It pleaseth me, and Isabel the Queen. *(Trumpets
   within.)*
   The trumpets sound. I must go take my place.

(Enter the young KING [EDWARD III], ARCHBISHOP,
CHAMPION, NOBLES, QUEEN.*)*

ARCHBISHOP: Long live King Edward, by the grace of
   God,
   King of England and Lord of Ireland!
CHAMPION: If any Christian, Heathen, Turk, or Jew,
   Dare but affirm that Edward's not true King, 90
   And will avouch his saying with the sword,
   I am the Champion that will combat him.

---

conge, bow. *Aristarchus,* an early grammarian and
schoolmaster. *breeching,* spanking. *Onus quam gravis-
simum,* an exceedingly heavy burden. *Suscepi . . . provin-
ciam,* I undertook that duty. *Major . . . nocere,* I am too
great for fortune to injure.

Unpointed, unpunctuated.   *lawn,* thin cloth.

YOUNGER MORTIMER: None comes. Sound trumpets!
  (*Trumpets sound.*)
KING EDWARD III: Champion, here's to thee. (*Gives purse.*)
QUEEN ISABELLA: Lord Mortimer, now take him to your charge.

(*Enter soldiers with the* EARL OF KENT, *prisoner.*)

YOUNGER MORTIMER: What traitor have we there with
100   blades and bills?
SOLDIERS: Edmund, the Earl of Kent.
KING EDWARD III: What hath he done?
SOLDIERS: A would have taken the King away perforce
  As we were bringing him to Killingworth.
YOUNGER MORTIMER: Did you attempt his rescue, Edmund? Speak.
EARL OF KENT: Mortimer, I did. He is our King!
  And thou compell'st this Prince to wear the crown!
110 YOUNGER MORTIMER: Strike off his head! He shall
  have martial law! (*to* SOLDIERS)
EARL OF KENT: Strike off my head! Base traitor, I defy thee!
KING EDWARD III: My lord, he is my uncle, and shall live.
YOUNGER MORTIMER: My lord, he is your enemy, and shall die.
EARL OF KENT: Stay, villains! (*to* SOLDIERS *who are trying to take him away*)
120 KING EDWARD III: Sweet mother, If I cannot pardon him,
  Entreat my Lord Protector for his life.
QUEEN ISABELLA: Son, be content. I dare not speak a word.
KING EDWARD III: Nor I. And yet methinks I should command. . . .
  But seeing I cannot, I'll entreat for him—
  My lord, if you will let my uncle live,
  I will requite it when I come to age.
130 YOUNGER MORTIMER: 'Tis for Your Highness' good,
  and for the realm's.
  —How often shall I bid you bear him hence? (*to* SOLDIERS)
EARL OF KENT: Art thou King? Must I die at thy command?
YOUNGER MORTIMER: At *our* command.—Once more away with him!
EARL OF KENT: Let me but stay and speak. I will not go! (*Struggles.*)
140 Either my brother or his son is King,
  And none of both then thirst for Edmund's blood!
  And therefore, soldiers, whither will you hale me?

(*They hale* EDMUND *away, and carry him to be beheaded.*)

KING EDWARD III: What safety may I look for at his hands (*Points to* MORTIMER.)
  If that my uncle shall be murder'd thus?

QUEEN ISABELLA: Fear not, sweet boy, I'll guard thee from thy foes.
  Had Edmund liv'd, he would have sought thy death.
  Come, son, we'll ride a-hunting in the park   150
KING EDWARD III: And shall my uncle Edmund ride with us?
QUEEN ISABELLA: He is a traitor, think not on him, come.

(*Exeunt omnes.*)

ACT 5 / SCENE 5

(*Enter* MATREVIS *and* GURNEY. [*Torches.*])

MATREVIS: Gurney, I wonder the King dies not,
  Being in a vault up to his knees in water,
  To which the channels of the castle run,
  From whence a damp continually ariseth
  That were enough to poison any man,
  Much more a king brought up so tenderly.
GURNEY: And so do I, Matrevis. Yesternight
  I open'd but the door to throw him meat
  And I was almost stifl'd with the savor!°
MATREVIS: He hath a body able to endure   10
  More than we can inflict. And therefore now
  Let us assail his mind another while.
GURNEY: Send for him out thence, and I will anger him.
MATREVIS: But stay, who's this?

(*Enter* LIGHTBORN.)

LIGHTBORN: My Lord Protector greets you. (*Gives letter.*)
GURNEY: What's here? I know not how to conster° it.
MATREVIS: Gurney, it was left unpointed for the nonce,°
  Edwardum occidere nolite timere,   20
  That's his meaning.
LIGHTBORN: Know ye this token? I must have the King.
MATREVIS: Ay, stay awhile. thou shalt have answer straight.
  (This villain's sent to make away the King.) (*aside*)
GURNEY: (I thought as much.) (*aside*)
MATREVIS: (And when the murder's done,
  See how he must be handled for his labor:
  Pereat iste!)° Let him have the King. (*aside*)

(*Points to curtained back stage.*)

  What else? Here is the key, this is the lake:°   30
  Do as you are commanded by my lord.
LIGHTBORN: I know what I must do. Get you away.

---

  savor, smell.   *conster,* construe, interpret.   ***for the nonce,*** on purpose.   ***Pereat iste,*** Let him die.   ***lake,*** dungeon.

Yet be not far off, I shall need your help.
See that in the next room I have a fire,
And get me a spit and let it be red-hot.
MATREVIS: Very well.
GURNEY: Need you anything besides?
LIGHTBORN: What else, a table and a feather-bed.°
40 GURNEY: That's all?
LIGHTBORN: Ay, ay. So, when I call you, bring it in.
MATREVIS: Fear not thou that.
GURNEY: Here's a light, to go into the dungeon.

(Gives a torch and then exit with MATREVIS.)

LIGHTBORN: So now
Must I about this gear. Ne'er was there any
So finely handled as this king shall be! *(Opens
    curtains.)*
Foh, here's a place indeed with all my heart!
KING EDWARD: Who's there? what light is that?
    wherefore com'st thou?
50 LIGHTBORN: To comfort you, and bring you joyful
    news.
KING EDWARD: Small comfort finds poor Edward in
    thy looks.
Villain, I know thou com'st to murder me!
LIGHTBORN: To murder you, my most gracious lord?
Far is it from my heart to do you harm.
The Queen sent me to see how you were us'd,
For she relents at this your misery:
And what eyes can refrain from shedding tears
60 To see a king in this most piteous state?
KING EDWARD: Weep'st thou already? List awhile to
    me,
And then thy heart, were it as Gurney's is,
Or as Matrevis', hewn from the Caucasus,
Yet will it melt, ere I have done my tale.
This dungeon where they keep me is the sink
Wherein the filth of all the castle falls.
LIGHTBORN: O villains!
KING EDWARD: And there in mire and puddle have I
70   stood
This ten days' space, and lest that I should sleep,
One plays continually upon a drum.
They give me bread and water, being a king!
So that for want of sleep and sustenance
My mind's distemper'd, and my body's numbed,
And whether I have limbs or no I know not.
O, would my blood dropp'd out from every vein
As doth this water from my tatter'd robes!
Tell Isabel the Queen I looked not thus
80 When for her sake I ran at tilt in France
And there unhors'd the Duke of Cleremont!
LIGHTBOEN: O speak no more, my lord, this breaks
    my heart! *(Claps hands, and a servant brings in a
    feather-bed.)*
Lie on this bed and rest yourself awhile.

KING EDWARD: These looks of thine can harbor
    nought but death:
I see my tragedy written in thy brows.
Yet stay a while, forbear thy bloody hand.
And let me see the stroke before it comes,
That, and even then, when I shall lose my life,
My mind may be more steadfast on my God!   90
LIGHTBORN: What means Your Highness to mistrust
    me thus?
KING EDWARD: What mean'st thou to dissemble with
    me thus?
LIGHTBORN: These hands were never stain'd with
    innocent blood—
Nor shall they now be tainted with a king's.
KING EDWARD: Forgive my thought for having such a
    thought.
One jewel have I left. Receive this. *(Gives jewel.)*   100
Still fear I, and I know not what's the cause,
But every joint shakes as I give it thee.
O, if thou harbor'st murder in thy heart,
Let this gift change thy mind, and save thy soul!
Know that I am a King! O, at that name
I feel a Hell of grief! Where is my crown?
Gone, gone, and I do remain alive?
LIGHTBORN: You're overwatch'd,° my lord, lie down
    and rest.
KING EDWARD: But that grief keeps me waking, I   110
    should sleep,
For not these ten days have these eye-lids clos'd.
Now as I speak they fall, and yet with fear
Open again. O wherefore sits thou here? *(Lies on
    bed.)*
LIGHTBORN: If you mistrust me, I'll be gone, my lord.
KING EDWARD: No, no, for if thou mean'st to murder
    me
Thou wilt return again, and therefore stay. *(Sleeps.)*
LIGHTBORN: He sleeps.
KING EDWARD *(wakes)*: O let me not die, yet stay, O   120
    stay a while!
LIGHTBORN: How now, my lord?
KING EDWARD: Something still buzzeth in mine ears
And tells me if I sleep I never wake,
This fear is that which makes me tremble thus,
And therefore tell me, wherefore art thou come?
LIGHTBORN: To rid thee of thy life!—Matrevis, come!

(Enter MATREVIS *and* GURNEY.)

KING EDWARD: I am too weak and feeble to resist. . . .
Assist me, sweet God, and receive my soul!
LIGHTBORN: Run for the table.   130
KING EDWARD: O spare me, or despatch me in a trice!

*(*MATREVIS *brings in a table.)*

LIGHTBORN: So lay the table down, and stamp on it.
    (Put table on KING.)

---

feather-bed, heavy quilt.

overwatch'd, exhausted from lack of sleep.

But not too hard, lest that you bruise his body.

(The KING calls out and then dies.)

MATREVIS: I fear that this cry will raise the town,
And therefore, let us take horse and away.
LIGHTBORN: Tell me, sirs, was it not bravely done?
GURNEY: Excellent well! Take this for thy reward!

(Then GURNEY stabs LIGHTBORN.)

Come, let us cast the body in the moat,
And bear the King's to Mortimer our lord.
140   Away! *(Exeunt [with the bodies.].)*

ACT 5 / SCENE 6

(Enter MORTIMER and MATREVIS.)

YOUNGER MORTIMER: Is't done, Matrevis, and the
murderer dead?
MATREVIS: Ay, my good lord! I would it were
undone!
YOUNGER MORTIMER: Matrevis, if thou now grow'st
penitent
I'll be thy ghostly father! Therefore choose
Whether thou wilt be secret in this.
Or else die by the hand of Mortimer?
10   MATREVIS: Gurney, my lord, is fled, and will, I fear,
Betray us both. Therefore let me fly.
YOUNGER MORTIMER: Fly to the savages!
MATREVIS: I humbly thank your honor. *(Exit.)*
YOUNGER MORTIMER: As for myself, I stand as Jove's
huge tree,
And others are but shrubs compar'd to me!
All tremble at my name! And I fear none.
Let's see who dare impeach me for his death?

(Enter the QUEEN.)

QUEEN ISABELLA: Ah, Mortimer, the King my son
20   hath news
His father's dead, and we have murder'd him!
YOUNGER MORTIMER: What if he have? The King is
yet a child.
QUEEN ISABELLA: Ay, ay, but he tears his hair and
wrings his hands
And vows to be reveng'd upon us both!
Into the council-chamber he is gone
To crave the aid and succor of his peers:
Ay me, see where he comes, and they with him!
30   Now, Mortimer, begins our tragedy.

(Enter the KING with the LORDS [and ATTENDANTS].)

1 LORD: Fear not, my lord. Know that you are a king!
KING EDWARD III: Villain!
YOUNGER MORTIMER: How now, my lord?
KING EDWARD III: Think not that I am frighted with
thy words:
My father's murder'd through thy treachery!
And thou shalt die! And on his mournful hearse

Thy hateful and accursed head shall lie
To witness to the world that by thy means
His kingly body was too soon interr'd.   40
QUEEN ISABELLA: Weep not, sweet son.
KING EDWARD III: Forbid me not to weep, he was my
father,
And had you lov'd him half so well as I,
You could not bear his death thus patiently,
But you, I fear, conspir'd with Mortimer.
1 LORD: Why speak you not unto my lord the King?
YOUNGER MORTIMER: Because I think scorn to be
accus'd!
Who is the man dares say I murder'd him?   50
KING EDWARD III: Traitor in me my loving father
speaks
And plainly saith, 'twas thou that murd'rest him.
YOUNGER MORTIMER: But hath Your Grace no other
proof than this?
KING EDWARD III: Yes, if this be the hand of
Mortimer. *(Shows letter.)*
YOUNGER MORTIMER: (False Gurney hath betray'd me
and himself.) *(aside to QUEEN)*
QUEEN ISABELLA: (I fear'd as much. Murder cannot be   60
hid!) *(aside to MORTIMER)*
YOUNGER MORTIMER: 'Tis my hand. What gather you
by this?
KING EDWARD III: That thither thou didst send a
murderer.
YOUNGER MORTIMER: What murderer? Bring forth
the man I sent!
KING EDWARD III: Ah, Mortimer, thou knowest that
he is slain—
And so shalt thou be too! Why stays he here?   70
Bring him unto a hurdle, drag him forth;
Hang him, I say, and set his quarters up:
But bring his head back presently to me.
QUEEN ISABELLA: For my sake, sweet son, pity
Mortimer!
YOUNGER MORTIMER: Madam, entreat not, I will
rather die
Than sue for life unto a paltry boy.
KING EDWARD III: Hence with the traitor, with the
murderer!   80
YOUNGER MORTIMER: Base Fortune, now I see, that in
thy wheel
There is a point, to which when men aspire,
They tumble headlong down. That point I touch'd.
And seeing there was no place to mount up higher,
Why should I grieve at my declining fall?
Farewell, fair Queen, weep not for Mortimer,
That scorns the world, and as a traveller
Goes to discover countries yet unknown.
KING EDWARD III: What, suffer you the traitor to   90
delay?

(MORTIMER is taken away by 1 LORD and ATTENDANTS.)

QUEEN ISABELLA: As thou received'st thy life from me,

Spill not the blood of gentle Mortimer!

KING EDWARD III: This argues that you spilt my
    father's blood,
Else would you not entreat for Mortimer.

QUEEN ISABELLA: I spill his blood? No!

KING EDWARD III: Ay, madam you, for so the rumor
    runs.

100 QUEEN ISABELLA: That rumor is untrue. For loving
    thee
Is this report rais'd on poor Isabel.

KING EDWARD III: I do not think her so unnatural.

2 LORD: My lord, I fear me it will prove too true.

KING EDWARD III: Mother, you are suspected for his
    death
And therefore we commit you to the Tower
Till farther trial may be made thereof.
If you be guilty, though I be your son,
110 Think not to find me slack or pitiful.

QUEEN ISABELLA: Nay, to my death, for too long have
    I liv'd
Whenas my son thinks to abridge my days.

KING EDWARD III: Away with her! Her words enforce
    these tears.
And I shall pity her if she speak again.

QUEEN ISABELLA: Shall I not mourn for my beloved
    lord?
And with the rest accompany him to his grave?

2 LORD: Thus, madam, 'tis the King's will you shall 120
    hence.

QUEEN ISABELLA: He hath forgotten me. Stay, I am
    his mother.

2 LORD: That boots not. Therefore, gentle madam,
    go.

QUEEN ISABELLA: Then come, sweet death, and rid
    me of this grief! (*Exit.*)

(*Re-enter* 1 LORD *with* MORTIMER'S *head.*)

1 LORD: My lord, here is the head of Mortimer.

KING EDWARD III: Go fetch my father's hearse, where
    it shall lie. 130
And bring my funeral robes. (*Exeunt* ATTENDANTS.)
Accursed head,
Could I have rul'd thee then, as I do now,
Thou had'st not hatch'd this monstrous treachery!
Here comes the hearse. Help me to mourn, my
    lords.

(*Re-enter* ATTENDANTS *with* EDWARD II *lying in the
hearse and with funeral robes, which* EDWARD III *dons.*)

Sweet father, here unto thy murder'd ghost
I offer up this wicked traitor's head. (*Puts it on
    father's body.*)
And let these tears, distilling from mine eyes,
Be witness of my grief and innocency. (*Exeunt.*) 140

Figure 26. Edward (Ian McKellen, *foreground left*), Isabella, and the noblemen at court in the Prospect Theatre Company production of *Edward II*, directed by Toby Robertson, London, 1969/70. (Photograph: Michael Peto.)

Figure 27. Edward (Ian McKellen, *left*) and Gaveston (James Lauren-
son) embrace while Isabella falls to the ground crying in the Prospect
Theatre Company production of *Edward II*, directed by Toby
Robertson, London, 1969/70. (Photograph: Michael Peto.)

Staging of *Edward II*

REVIEW OF THE PROSPECT THEATRE COMPANY
PRODUCTION, 1969 BY MICHAEL BILLINGTON

Though lacking either the political subtlety of Richard II or its sustained poetic splendour, Marlowe's tragedy offers its chief player just as gorgeous a mouthful of acting. And in this Prospect production, transferred south from the Edinburgh Festival, Ian McKellen ravenously and thrillingly seizes his opportunity.

There is about him the authentic smell of danger that betokens greatness: a danger that springs from the fact that his frame constantly seems too fragile to contain the emotions erupting within. Shrill, restless, and almost tipsy with passion, he plays the early scenes revealing Edward's ungovernable will in a vein of quivering near hysteria.

He clenches his medallion between his teeth as if to contain his fury at the taunting of Gaveston, clutches his crown with white-knuckled intensity, and rocks back and forth on his heels when rebuked by his barons as if afraid where movement might lead him.

Mr. McKellen's Edward, however, is much more than an exciting display of nervous energy. It shows a proper sense of tragic development. In the civil war scenes he moves as if his limbs were suddenly twice as heavy and his body burdened by weighty regalia: and by the end the character has become a worn, ragged shadow, though still with the same insatiable craving for physical contact. Even if packed with slightly too much detail, this is an audacious, powerful and memorable performance.

As a whole Toby Robertson's production is clear, vigorous, and quicksilver-swift. The homosexuality is handled with justifiable explicitness, the play's emblematic quality is reflected in Kenneth Rowell's stylized designs, and there are strong supporting performances from Timothy West as a cool, guileful Mortimer and from Robert Eddison as Edward's suavely implacable, sinisterly affectionate assassin.

REVIEW OF THE PROSPECT THEATRE COMPANY
PRODUCTION, 1969, BY BENEDICT NIGHTINGALE

Robertson's *Edward II* is not simply a long display of homosexuality, nor does it even importantly concern homosexuality as such. If it's 'about' anything, it's about power and responsibility; about the claims of public life and the extent to which they define and limit private conduct. It is the tragedy of a thoroughly private man thrust into the most public situation conceivable. Homosexual infatuation happened to be Edward's particular temptation and doom: it might have been an impolitic heterosexual passion or any of a variety of personal obsessions. This was a king who insisted on living the life he emotionally wanted, and was destroyed for doing so.

Ian McKellen's performance gives Robertson's reading all the support a director could want. His Edward fairly seethes with repressed energy. He can scarcely keep still. Even when he sits, which tends to be informally on the floor, not formally on any throne, his arms and legs dart and writhe, bent on self-expression and contact. In a court of thick, cold, brooding barons, standing around him like trees in winter, this king seems to be the only sentient being. No wonder he craves James Laurenson's casual, loose-limbed Gaveston, and no wonder there's such antipathy between him and Timothy West's hard, strong Mortimer. It is a striking performance, particularly in the early and late stages of the play: when McKellen is establishing the character, and when the character begins to disintegrate under its weight of deprivation and suffering. In the abdication scene he's still capable of the large, flamboyant gesture, the arm flung in anger over the head, but it is no longer characteristic. Weariness clogs his movement and his speech; and the creature that Lightborn finally dispatches is a raddled, defeated, pathetic old queer, weakly grappling with his executioner, a parody of his former self.

WILLIAM SHAKESPEARE

1554—1616

The story of Othello's life is filled with "most disastrous chances," "moving accidents," and "hair-breadth escapes," but the life of his creator was evidently far more mundane. We know from church registers that Shakespeare married in 1582, that he had a daughter in 1583, and twins, a son and daughter, in 1585. Legal documents tell us that he defaulted several times on paying his taxes, that he bought a large house in Stratford, that like many of his contemporaries he engaged in taking others to court. And records from the royal court show him performing for both Elizabeth I and James I. But information about his theatrical career is disappointingly fragmentary. We know that at some point between 1585 and 1592, Shakespeare left Stratford, went to London, and became an actor and playwright, yet we do not know exactly when or how he became involved with the professional theater companies. We know that he was both an actor and shareholder in one of the major theatrical companies, first called the Lord Chamberlain's Men, then the King's Men, but we have no details about their rehearsals and few about their performances, so we do not know anything specific about his day to day activities in the company. We do not even know for certain the exact order in which he composed his plays, nor do we know exactly how he occupied himself after 1611, when he appears to have retired almost completely from playwriting and the theatrical world of London.

Although we know little about his personal life in Stratford or his professional activities in London, we can begin to understand his remarkably productive career as a playwright—thirty-seven plays in a period of twenty-three years—by recognizing the numerous literary and dramatic sources that nurtured it, for Shakespeare was not an isolated genius, weaving plots and characters entirely out of the threads of his own imagination. Like his contemporaries, Marlowe, Jonson, and Webster, he was influenced by classical plays available in English translation, as well as numerous French and Italian works, not to mention the rich tradition of native English drama, including cycle plays, morality plays, folk plays from the countryside, and highly formal plays from the University writers of his own time. Throughout his career, in fact, he drew ideas for his plays from a richly varied body of material: Roman comedies, Roman histories, English chronicles, English novellas, and French as well as Italian stories. But he always transformed the material he borrowed. He began his career, for example, by turning Plautus' *Menaechmi* into his own *Comedy of Errors* (1590), a farce far more comically confusing than its counterpart, because Shakespeare added twin servants to the twin protagonists of Plautus. In history plays, such as *Richard II* (1595), *1 Henry IV* (1597), *2 Henry IV* (1598), and *Henry V* (1599), he condensed large and cumbersome bodies of material from the English chronicler Holinshed into powerful theatrical experiences, each of which can stand on its own, yet which together embody a coherent political philosophy. And in *Othello,* he turned a brief but rambling story by the Italian writer Cinthio into one of his most tightly constructed tragedies, adding events, creating new characters, such as Roderigo, and endowing the main characters with complex motivations.

In the making of plots, Shakespeare was equally resourceful and experimental. Single plots, double plots, triple plots, framed plots—all kinds of plot construction are found in his plays. In *A Midsummer Night's Dream* (1595), he juggles three wildly different worlds of experience by intertwining the crisscross love entanglements of four young Athenians, with the love jealousy of the King and Queen of the Fairies, with the comically bumbling rehearsal and production of a tragic love story by a group of Athenian workmen—and all these different lines of action are framed by the marriage festivities for Theseus, Duke of Athens, and Hippolyta, Queen of the Amazons. In *Much Ado About Nothing* (1599), he contrasts two separate but related experiences by alternating the witty courtship of Beatrice and Benedick with the melodramatic story of Hero and her betrayal by Claudio. And in *Othello* (1604), he creates a single plot that is so carefully designed that not a single character, event, or line is irrelevant to the development of the tragedy that unfolds inexorably unlike any of his other plays.

As in the making of plots, Shakespeare was highly flexible in his use of language. Blank verse is the dominant form for most of his plays, but he turned that line to the harmonies of every mood and feeling—to the strident rhythms of men at war, as in *Henry V*, to the intoxicated melodies of men and women in love, as in *Twelfth Night,* to the heavenly music of visionaries, as in *The Tempest* (1611), and to the dissonant sounds of a mind undone by jealousy, as in *Othello*. Yet, he did not hesitate to move from the harmonies of verse to the other harmonies of prose—in a single play, in a single scene, in the dialogue of a single character, always suiting the style to the dramatic situation. In I, iii and II, i of *Othello,* for example, a prose scene between Roderigo and Iago is followed by a blank verse soliloquy from Iago, and the shift in style subtly reinforces our sense of Iago as a wearer of masks, especially of verbal ones. Whatever the form—blank verse, prose, rhymed couplets, sonnets, or songs—Shakespeare's language is always tuned to the theatrical situation, implying gestures, movement, tone of voice. Thus Othello's response in I, ii to the group of armed men seeking to arrest him—"Keep up your bright swords, for the dew will rust them"—quickly lets us know of the potential fight and of the calm, slightly ironic voice that disarms the men more surely than a blow.

Shakespeare's major tragedies—*Hamlet* (1601), *Othello* (1604), *King Lear* (1605), and *Macbeth* (1605)—are all about large figures in extremely trying situations, and this emphasis on extremes is the source of their special power. The marriage of Othello and Desdemona joins not just a man and a woman, but a middle-aged black Moorish soldier of obscure lineage and a young white Venetian lady of noble birth. This marriage, so hated by Desdemona's father, is for both of the participants an emblem of perfection. Desdemona tells the senators, for example, "My heart's subdued/Even to the very quality of my lord," and Othello repeatedly conveys the extreme value he gives to her love, as when he tells Desdemona, "Perdition catch my soul/But I do love thee! And when I love thee not,/Chaos is come again." Such declarations also imply the possibility of destruction, and the task Shakespeare sets for himself is first to create the reality of this extraordinary relationship and then to destroy it. The contrasting marriage of Iago and Emilia with its bitter jests and spiteful remarks, as well as the casual flirtation of Cassio with Bianca, make us see more clearly the special beauty of the love between Othello and Desdemona.

Othello may also be seen as a Shakespearean morality play, with all the forces for good represented by Desdemona's beauty, strength, honesty, and faith balanced by the forces for evil embodied in Iago's hatred of beauty, his cowardice, his lying, and his cynicism. Between them stands Othello, a man outwardly calm when faced by swords, Senators, or Turks, but inwardly insecure about his age, his blackness, his status as an outsider in Venetian society. At the beginning of the play we admire his assurance, his eloquence, his military prowess, and the love that he inspires in Desdemona; we watch with horror as that capacity for extreme love is lured into doubts, questions, and finally, murderous jealousy, swinging like a pendulum from total love to total hate. Our helplessness and frustration are increased because Shakespeare does not provide Othello with reliable companions who might convey to him his tragic error. Such characters usually figure in his other tragedies, but here the reasonable commentator on events is also the villain who sets them in motion.

Characters such as Desdemona, Iago, and Othello, given their extremes of good and evil, are not only powerful figures in their own right, but also immensely challenging for actors to portray. An actor playing Iago needs to consider the numerous motives for his action that are spread out through the play, and whether any of these are sufficient for the destruction he seeks and causes. Similarly, Othello must be a believable combination of both the great general and the immature bridegroom, showing both the strength and the vulnerability of the man.

These challenges of the title role are so great that Laurence Olivier, who is considered by many the greatest Shakespearean actor of our century, waited until he was 57, and had already performed Hamlet, Macbeth, Coriolanus, Lear, and Antony, before finally doing Othello, at the National Theater in 1964. That production, played on a single set that could be either an outdoor or indoor space (see Figure 28) was as concentrated and intense as the play itself. And it produced as much controversy among critics as the play has. The reviews reprinted following the text reflect one principal source of the critics' disagreement about the production, namely, the way it presented the relationship between Othello and Iago—not as that of a deluded victim and a clever victimizer, but as that of a proud lover and a hasty opportunist. Olivier played the role in a way that made him seem to drag the lies out of Iago, and Frank Finlay played Iago with an open face and a slightly bent posture (see Figure 29) that seemed to suggest that Iago might, indeed, be harmless. Above all, Olivier's Othello was highly physical and sensual, in his deep black skin and his insinuating smile (see Figure 30), as well as in his rolling, barefoot walk and the guttural sounds he used to suggest the voice of a foreigner speaking a new language. But that physicality was at last the key to the animal who tore off his crucifix when he believed that Desdemona had betrayed him, and then who clutched Desdemona's dead body to his own (see Figure 31) as he gave his final speech.

THE TRAGEDY OF OTHELLO
The Moor of Venice

BY WILLIAM SHAKESPEARE

CHARACTERS

DUKE OF VENICE
BRABANTIO, *a senator, father to* DESDEMONA
SENATORS OF VENICE
GRATIANO, *brother to* BRABANTIO, *a noble Venetian*
LODOVICO, *kinsman to* BRABANTIO, *a noble Venetian*
OTHELLO, *the Moor, in the military service of Venice*
CASSIO, *an honorable lieutenant to* OTHELLO
IAGO, OTHELLO'S *ensign, a villain*
RODERIGO, *a gulled gentleman*
MONTANO, *governor of Cyprus*

CLOWN, *servant to* OTHELLO
DESDEMONA, *daughter to* BRABANTIO *and wife to* OTHELLO
EMILIA, *wife to* IAGO
BIANCA, *a courtesan*
GENTLEMEN, SAILORS, OFFICERS, MESSENGERS, HERALD, MUSICIANS, ATTENDANTS

SCENE
Venice and Cyprus.

ACT 1 / SCENE 1

(Enter RODERIGO *and* IAGO.)

RODERIGO: Tush, never tell me! I take it much
   unkindly
That thou, Iago, who hast had my purse
As if the strings were thine, shouldst know of this.°
IAGO: 'Sblood, but you will not hear me!
If ever I did dream of such a matter,
Abhor me.
RODERIGO: Thou told'st me thou didst hold him° in
   thy hate.
10 IAGO: Despise me if I do not. Three great ones of the
   city,
In personal suit to make me his lieutenant,
Off-capped to him; and by the faith of man,
I know my price; I am worth no worse a place.
But he, as loving his own pride and purposes,
Evades them with a bombast circumstance.
Horribly stuffed with epithets of war;
And, in conclusion,
Nonsuits° my mediators; for, "Certes," says he,
"I have already chose my officer."
20 And what was he?
Forsooth, a great arithmetician,°
One Michael Cassio, a Florentine

(A fellow almost damned in a fair wife)°
That never set a squadron in the field,
Nor the division of a battle knows
More than a spinster,° unless the bookish theoric,
Wherein the togèd consuls° can propose
As masterly as he. Mere prattle without practice
Is all his soldiership. But he, sir, had th' election;   30
And I (of whom his eyes had seen the proof
At Rhodes, at Cyprus, and on other grounds
Christian and heathen) must be belee'd and
   calmed°
By debitor and creditor; this counter-caster,°
He, in good time, must his lieutenant be,
And I—God bless the mark!—his Moorship's
   ancient.°
RODERIGO: By heaven, I rather would have been his
   hangman.   40
IAGO: Why, there's no remedy; 'tis the curse of
   service.
Preferment° goes by letter and affection,°

---

almost . . . wife, unexplainable phrase. Cassio is not married, nor is he about to be married. In the Italian novella that was the source for Shakespeare's play, Cassio is married, and perhaps Shakespeare intended to follow the novella when he began writing the play. *spinster,* spinner of thread; i.e., housewife, homemaker. *togèd consuls,* Senators dressed in togas; i.e., clothed for the council chamber, not the battlefield. *calmed,* have the wind taken out of my sails and left becalmed. *counter-caster,* accountant. *ancient,* ensign, standard-bearer. *Preferment,* advancement. *affection,* personal favoritism.

---

this, Desdemona's elopement with Othello. *him,* Othello. *Nonsuits,* rejects. *arithmetician,* person skilled in military calculations but not in actual warfare.

And not by old gradation,° where each second
Stood heir to th' first. Now, sir, be judge yourself,
Whether I in any just term am affined°
To love the Moor.

RODERIGO: I would not follow him then.

IAGO: O, sir, content you;

50 I follow him to serve my turn upon him.
We cannot all be masters, nor all masters
Cannot be truly followed. You shall mark
Many a duteous and knee-crooking knave
That, doting on his own obsequious bondage,
Wears out his time, much like his master's ass,
For naught but provender; and when he's old,
cashiered.°
Whip me such honest knaves! Others there are
Who, trimmed in forms and visages of duty,

60 Keep yet their hearts attending on themselves;
And, throwing but shows of service on their lords,
Do well thrive by them, and when they have lined
their coats,
Do themselves homage. These fellows have some
soul;
And such a one do I profess myself. For, sir,
It is as sure as you are Roderigo,
Were I the Moor, I would not be Iago.
In following him, I follow but myself;

70 Heaven is my judge, not I for love and duty,
But seeming so, for my own peculiar° end;
For when my outward action doth demonstrate
The native act and figure of my heart
In compliment extern,° 'tis not long after
But I will wear my heart upon my sleeve
For daws to peck at; I am not what I am.

RODERIGO: What a fortune does the thick-lips owe°
If he can carry't thus!

IAGO: Call up her father,

80 Rouse him. Make after him, poison his delight,
Proclaim him in the streets. Incense her kinsmen,
And though he in a fertile climate dwell,
Plague him with flies; though that his joy be joy,
Yet throw such changes of vexation on't
As it may lose some color.

RODERIGO: Here is her father's house. I'll call aloud.

IAGO: Do, with like timorous° accent and dire yell
As when, by night and negligence, the fire
Is spied in populous cities.

90 RODERIGO: What, ho, Brabantio! Signior Brabantio,
ho!

IAGO: Awake! What, ho, Brabantio! Thieves! thieves!
thieves!
Look to your house, your daughter, and your bags!
Thieves! thieves!

(BRABANTIO *at a window.*)

BRABANTIO (*above*): What is the reason of this terrible
summons?
What is the matter there?

RODERIGO: Signior, is all your family within?

IAGO: Are your doors locked?   100

BRABANTIO: Why, wherefore ask you this?

IAGO: Zounds, sir, y'are robbed! For shame, put on
your gown!
Your heart is burst; you have lost half your soul.
Even now, now, very now, an old black ram
Is tupping your white ewe. Arise, arise!
Awake the snorting° citizens with the bell,
Or else the devil will make a grandsire of you.
Arise, I say!

BRABANTIO: What, have you lost your wits?   110

RODERIGO: Most reverend signior, do you know my
voice?

BRABANTIO: Not I. What are you?

RODERIGO: My name is Roderigo.

BRABANTIO: The worser welcome!
I have charged thee not to haunt about my doors.
In honest plainness thou hast heard me say
My daughter is not for thee; and now, in madness,
Being full of supper and distempr'ing° draughts,
Upon malicious bravery° dost thou come   120
To start° my quiet.

RODERIGO: Sir, sir, sir—

BRABANTIO: But thou must needs be sure
My spirit and my place have in them power
To make this bitter to thee.

RODERIGO: Patience, good sir.

BRABANTIO: What tell'st thou me of robbing? This is
Venice;
My house is not a grange.°

RODERIGO: Most grave Brabantio,   130
In simple and pure soul I come to you.

IAGO: Zounds, sir, you are one of those that will not
serve God if the devil bid you. Because we come
to do you service, and you think we are ruffians,
you'll have your daughter covered with a Barbary horse; you'll have your nephews° neigh to
you; you'll have coursers for cousins,° and gennets for germans.°

BRABANTIO: What profane wretch art thou?

IAGO: I am one, sir, that comes to tell you your   140
daughter and the Moor are now making the
beast with two backs.

BRABANTIO: Thou art a villain.

IAGO: You are—a senator.

BRABANTIO: This thou shalt answer. I know thee,
Roderigo.

---

gradation, seniority. affined, bound. cashiered,
dismissed. peculiar, personal. extern, external show.
owe, own. timorous, terrifying.

snorting, snoring. distemp'ring, intoxicating. bravery, bravado. start, upset. grange, isolated farmhouse.
nephews, grandsons. coursers for cousins, horses for
kinsmen. gennets for germans, Spanish horses for close
relatives.

RODERIGO: Sir, I will answer anything. But I beseech
    you,
    If't be your pleasure and most wise consent,
150   As partly I find it is, that your fair daughter,
    At this odd-even° and dull watch o' th' night,
    Transported, with no worse nor better guard
    But with a knave of common hire, a gondolier,
    To the gross clasps of a lascivious Moor—
    If this be known to you, and your allowance,
    We then have done you bold and saucy° wrongs;
    But if you know not this, my manners tell me
    We have your wrong rebuke. Do not believe
    That, from the sense of° all civility,
160   I thus would play and trifle with your reverence.
    Your daughter, if you have not given her leave,
    I say again, hath made a gross revolt,
    Tying her duty, beauty, wit, and fortunes
    In an extravagant and wheeling° stranger
    Of here and everywhere. Straight satisfy yourself.
    If she be in her chamber, or your house,
    Let loose on me the justice of the state
    For thus deluding you.
BRABANTIO: Strike on the tinder, ho!
170   Give me a taper! Call up all my people!
    This accident° is not unlike my dream.
    Belief of it oppresses me already.
    Light, I say! Light! *(Exit above.)*
IAGO: Farewell, for I must leave you.
    It seems not meet, nor wholesome to my place,
    To be produced—as, if I stay, I shall—
    Against the Moor. For I do know the state,
    However this may gall him with some check,°
    Cannot with safety cast° him; for he's embarked
180   With such loud reason to the Cyprus wars,
    Which even now stand in act,° that for their souls
    Another of his fathom° they have none
    To lead their business; in which regard,
    Though I do hate him as I do hell-pains,
    Yet, for necessity of present life,
    I must show out a flag and sign of love,
    Which is indeed but sign. That you shall surely find
    him,
    Lead to the Sagittary° the raisèd search;
190   And there will I be with him. So farewell. *(Exit.)*

(Enter, below, BRABANTIO, and SERVANTS with torches.)

BRABANTIO: It is too true an evil. Gone she is;
    And what's to come of my despisèd time
    Is naught but bitterness. Now, Roderigo,
    Where didst thou see her?—O unhappy girl!—

With the Moor, say'st thou?—Who would be a
    father?—
    How didst thou know 'twas she?—O, she deceives
    me
    Past thought!—What said she to you?—Get more
    tapers!   200
    Raise all my kindred!—Are they married, think
    you?
RODERIGO: Truly I think they are.
BRABANTIO: O heaven! How got she out? O treason
    of the blood!
    Fathers, from hence trust not your daughters'
    minds
    By what you see them act. Is there not charms
    By which the property° of youth and maidhood
    May be abused? Have you not read, Roderigo,   210
    Of some such thing?
RODERIGO: Yes, sir, I have indeed.
BRABANTIO: Call up my brother.—O, would you had
    had her!—
    Some one way, some another.—Do you know
    Where we may apprehend her and the Moor?
RODERIGO: I think I can discover him, if you please
    To get good guard and go along with me.
BRABANTIO: Pray you lead on. At every house I'll call;
    I may command at most.—Get weapons, ho!   220
    And raise some special officers of night.—
    On, good Roderigo; I'll deserve° your pains.
    (Exeunt.)

ACT 1 / SCENE 2

(Enter OTHELLO, IAGO, and ATTENDANTS with torches.)

IAGO: Though in the trade of war I have slain men,
    Yet do I hold it very stuff o' th' conscience
    To do no contrived murther. I lack iniquity
    Sometimes to do me service. Nine or ten times
    I had thought t' have yerked° him here under the
    ribs.
OTHELLO: 'Tis better as it is.
IAGO: Nay, but he prated,
    And spoke such scurvy and provoking terms
    Against your honor   10
    That with the little godliness I have
    I did full hard forbear him.° But I pray you, sir,
    Are you fast married? Be assured of this,
    That the magnifico° is much beloved,
    And hath in his effect a voice potential
    As double as the duke's.° He will divorce you,
    Or put upon you what restraint and grievance

---

odd-even, around midnight, when the end of one day is
indistinguishable from the beginning of the next. **saucy,**
insolent. **the sense of,** contrary to. **extravagant and wheeling,** wandering and roving. **accident,** occurrence. **check,**
reprimand. **cast,** dismiss. **stand in act,** are underway.
fathom, ability. **Sagittary,** an inn.

---

property, nature. **deserve,** reward. **yerked,** stabbed.
did . . . him, had great difficulty restraining myself from
attacking him. **magnifico,** Venetian nobleman (BARBAN-
TIO). **voice . . . duke's,** influence so strong it is like having
two votes, as does the Duke of Venice.

The law, with all his might to enforce it on,
Will give him cable.°
20 OTHELLO: Let him do his spite.
My services which I have done the signiory°
Shall out-tongue his complaints. 'Tis yet to know°—
Which, when I know that boasting is an honor,
I shall promulgate—I fetch my life and being
From men of royal siege;° and my demerits°
May speak unbonneted° to as proud a fortune
As this that I have reached. For know, Iago,
But that I love the gentle Desdemona,
I would not my unhoused° free condition
30 Put into circumscription and confine
For the sea's worth.

(Enter CASSIO, OFFICERS, *with torches.)*

But look, what lights come yond?
IAGO: Those are the raisèd father and his friends.
You were best go in.
OTHELLO: Not I; I must be found.
My parts,° my title, and my perfect soul°
Shall manifest me rightly. Is it they?
IAGO: By Janus, I think no.
OTHELLO: The servants of the duke, and my
40   lieutenant.
The goodness of the night upon you, friends!
What is the news?
CASSIO: The duke does greet you, general;
And he requires your haste-post-haste appearance
Even on the instant.
OTHELLO: What's the matter, think you?
CASSIO: Something from Cyprus, as I may divine.
It is a business of some heat. The galleys
Have sent a dozen sequent° messengers
50 This very night at one another's heels,
And many of the consuls, raised and met,
Are at the duke's already. You have been hotly
   called for;
When, being not at your lodging to be found,
The Senate hath sent about three several quests
To search you out.
OTHELLO: 'Tis well I am found by you.
I will but spend a word here in the house,
And go with you. *(Exit.)*
60 CASSIO: Ancient, what makes he here?
IAGO: Faith, he to-night hath boarded a land carack.°
If it prove lawful prize, he's made for ever.
CASSIO: I do not understand.
IAGO: He's married.
CASSIO: To who?

(Enter OTHELLO.)

IAGO: Marry, to—Come, captain, will you go?
OTHELLO: Have with you.
CASSIO: Here comes another troop to seek for you.

(Enter BRABANTIO, RODERIGO, *and others with lights
and weapons.)*

IAGO: It is Brabantio. General, be advised.
He comes to bad intent.   70
OTHELLO: Holla! Stand there!
RODERIGO: Signior, it is the Moor.
BRABANTIO: Down with him, thief!

(They draw on both sides.)

IAGO: You, Roderigo! Come, sir I am for you.
OTHELLO: Keep up your bright swords, for the dew
   will rust them.
Good signior, you shall more command with years
Than with your weapons.
BRABANTIO: O thou foul thief, where has thou stowed
   my daughter?   80
Damned as thou art, thou hast enchanted her!
For I'll refer me to all things of sense,°
If she in chains of magic were not bound,
Whether a maid so tender, fair, and happy,
So opposite to marriage that she shunned
The wealthy curlèd darlings of our nation,
Would ever have, t' incur a general mock,
Run from her guardage to the sooty bosom
Of such a thing as thou—to fear, not to delight.
Judge me the world if 'tis not gross in sense°   90
That thou hast practiced on her with foul charms,
Abused her delicate youth with drugs or minerals
That weaken motion.° I'll have't disputed on;°
'Tis probable, and palpable to thinking.
I therefore apprehend and do attach° thee
For an abuser of the world, a practicer
Of arts inhibited and out of warrant.°
Lay hold upon him. If he do resist,
Subdue him at his peril.
OTHELLO: Hold your hands,   100
Both you of my inclining and the rest.
Were it my cue to fight, I should have known it
Without a prompter. Where will you that I go
To answer this your charge?
BRABANTIO: To prison, till fit time
Of law and course of direct session
Call thee to answer.
OTHELLO: What if I do obey?
How may the duke be therewith satisfied,
Whose messengers are here about my side   110

---

cable, scope. **signiory,** Venetian government. **yet to
know,** still not known. **siege,** rank. **demerits,** merits.
speak unbonneted, without taking my hat off; i.e., on equal
terms. **unhoused,** unconfined. **parts,** personal qualities.
perfect soul, clear conscience. **sequent,** consecutive. **land
carack,** trading ship.

---

refer ... sense, appeal to common sense. **gross in
sense,** obvious. **motion,** senses and mental powers. **disputed on,** tried in court. **attach,** arrest. **inhibited ...
warrant,** prohibited and illegal.

Upon some present business of the state
To bring me to him?
OFFICER: 'Tis true, most worthy signior.
The duke's in council, and your noble self
I am sure is sent for.
BRABANTIO: How? The duke in council?
In this time of the night? Bring him away.
Mine's not an idle° cause. The duke himself,
Or any of my brothers of the state,
120 Cannot but feel this wrong as 'twere their own;
For if such actions may have passage free,
Bondslaves and pagans shall our statesmen be.
(Exeunt.)

ACT 1 / SCENE 3

(Enter DUKE and SENATORS, set at a table, with lights
and ATTENDANTS.)

DUKE: There is no composition° in these news
That gives them credit.
1. SENATOR: Indeed they are disproportioned.
My letters say a hundred and seven galleys.
DUKE: And mine a hundred forty.
2. SENATOR: And mine two hundred.
But though they jump° not on a just account—
As in these cases where the aim° reports
'Tis oft with difference—yet do they all confirm
10 A Turkish fleet, and bearing up to Cyprus.
DUKE: Nay, it is possible enough to judgment.
I do not so secure me in the error°
But the main article I do approve°
In fearful sense.
SAILOR (within): What, ho! what, ho! what, ho!
OFFICER: A messenger from the galleys.

(Enter SAILOR.)

DUKE: Now, what's the business?
SAILOR: The Turkish preparation makes for Rhodes.
So was I bid report here to the state
20 By Signior Angelo.
DUKE: How say you by this change?
1. SENATOR: This cannot be
By no assay° of reason. 'Tis a pageant
To keep us in false gaze.° When we consider
Th' importancy of Cyprus to the Turk,
And let ourselves again but understand
That, as it more concerns the Turk than Rhodes,
So may he with more facile question bear it,°
For that it stands not in such warlike brace,°
30 But altogether lacks th' abilities
That Rhodes is dressed in—if we make thought of
this,

We must not think the Turk is so unskillful
To leave that latest which concerns him first,
Neglecting an attempt of ease and gain
To wake and wage° a danger profitless.
DUKE: Nay, in all confidence he's not for Rhodes.
OFFICER: Here is more news.

(Enter a MESSENGER.)

MESSENGER: The Ottomites, reverend and gracious,
Steering with due course toward the isle of Rhodes, 40
Have there injointed them with an after fleet.
1. SENATOR: Ay, so I thought. How many, as you
guess?
MESSENGER: Of thirty sail; and now they do restem
Their backward course, bearing with frank
appearance
Their purposes toward Cyprus. Signior Montano,
Your trusty and most valiant servitor,
With his free duty° recommends° you thus,
And prays you to believe him. 50
DUKE: 'Tis certain then for Cyprus.
Marcus Luccicos, is not he in town?
1. SENATOR: He's now in Florence.
DUKE: Write from us to him; post, post-haste
dispatch.

(Enter BRABANTIO, OTHELLO, CASSIO, IAGO,
RODERIGO, and OFFICERS.)

1. SENATOR: Here comes Brabantio and the valiant
Moor.
DUKE: Valiant Othello, we must straight employ you
Against the general enemy Ottoman.
(to BRABANTIO) I did not see you. Welcome, gentle 60
signior.
We lacked your counsel and your help to-night.
BRABANTIO: So did I yours. Good your grace, pardon
me.
Neither my place, nor aught I heard of business,
Hath raised me from my bed; nor doth the general
care
Take hold on me; for my particular grief
Is of so floodgate° and o'erbearing nature
That it engluts and swallows other sorrows, 70
And it is still itself.
DUKE: Why, what's the matter?
BRABANTIO: My daughter! O my daughter!
ALL: Dead?
BRABANTIO: Ay, to me.
She is abused, stol'n from me, and corrupted
By spells and medicines bought of mountebanks;
For nature so prepost'rously to err,
Being not deficient, blind, or lame of sense,
Sans° witchcraft could not. 80

---

idle, trivial. *composition*, consistency. *jump*, agree.
aim, conjecture. *secure . . . error*, rely on inconsistencies.
approve, accept. *assay*, test. *false gaze*, looking the wrong
way. *with . . . it*, more easily capture. *brace*, prepared-
ness.

---

wage, risk. *free duty*, freely given expression of
loyalty. *recommends*, informs. *floodgate*, overflowing.
sans, without.

DUKE: Whoe'er he be that in this foul proceeding
    Hath thus beguiled your daughter of herself,
    And you of her, the bloody book of law
    You shall yourself read in the bitter letter
    After your own sense; yea, though our proper° son
    Stood in your action.°
BRABANTIO: Humbly I thank your grace.
    Here is the man—this Moor, whom now, it seems,
    Your special mandate for the state affairs
90   Hath hither brought.
ALL: We are very sorry for't.
DUKE *(to* OTHELLO*)*: What, in your own part, can you
    say to this?
BRABANTIO: Nothing, but this is so.
OTHELLO: Most potent, grave, and reverend signiors,
    My very noble, and approved good masters,
    That I have ta'en away this old man's daughter,
    It is most true; true I have married her.
    The very head and front° of my offending
100   Hath this extent, no more. Rude am I in my
      speech,
    And little blessed with the soft phrase of peace;
    For since these arms of mine had seven years' pith°
    Till now some nine moons wasted, they have used
    Their dearest action in the tented field;
    And little of this great world can I speak
    More than pertains to feats of broil and battle;
    And therefore little shall I grace my cause
    In speaking for myself. Yet, by your gracious
110   patience,
    I will a round° unvarnished tale deliver
    Of my whole course of love—what drugs, what
      charms,
    What conjuration, and what mighty magic
    (For such proceeding am I charged withal)
    I won his daughter.
BRABANTIO: A maiden never bold;
    Of spirit so still and quiet that her motion
    Blushed at herself;° and she—in spite of nature,
120   Of years, of country, credit, everything—
    To fall in love with what she feared to look on!
    It is a judgment maimed and most imperfect
    That will confess perfection so could err
    Against all rules of nature, and must be driven
    To find out practices of cunning hell
    Why this should be. I therefore vouch again
    That with some mixtures pow'rful o'er the blood,
    Or with some dram, conjured to this effect,
    He wrought upon her.
130 DUKE: To vouch this is no proof,
    Without more certain and more overt test
    Than these thin habits° and poor likelihoods.

Of modern seeming° do prefer against him.
1. SENATOR: But, Othello, speak.
    Did you by indirect and forcèd courses
    Subdue and poison this young maid's affections?
    Or came it by request, and such fair question
    As soul to soul affordeth?
OTHELLO: I do beseech you,
    Send for the lady to the Sagittary   130
    And let her speak of me before her father.
    If you do find me foul in her report,
    The trust, the office, I do hold of you
    Not only take away, but let your sentence
    Even fall upon my life.
DUKE: Fetch Desdemona hither.
OTHELLO: Ancient, conduct them; you best know the
    place.

(Exit IAGO, *with two or three* ATTENDANTS.*)*

    And till she come, as truly as to heaven
    I do confess the vices of my blood,   140
    So justly to your grave ears I'll present
    How I did thrive in this fair lady's love,
    And she in mine.
DUKE: Say it, Othello.
OTHELLO: Her father loved me, oft invited me;
    Still questioned me the story of my life
    From year to year—the battles, sieges, fortunes
    That I have passed.
    I ran it through, even from my boyish days
    To th' very moment that he bade me tell it.   150
    Wherein I spake of most disastrous chances,
    Of moving accidents by flood and field;
    Of hairbreadth scapes i' th' imminent deadly
      breach;
    Of being taken by the insolent foe
    And sold to slavery; of my redemption thence
    And portance° in my travel's history;
    Wherein of anters° vast and deserts idle,°
    Rough quarries, rocks, and hills whose heads touch
      heaven,   160
    It was my hint to speak—such was the process;
    And of the Cannibals that each other eat,
    The Anthropophagi,° and men whose heads
    Do grow beneath their shoulders. This to hear
    Would Desdemona seriously incline;
    But still the house affairs would draw her thence;
    Which ever as she could with haste dispatch,
    She'd come again, and with a greedy ear
    Devour up my discourse. Which I observing,
    Took once a pliant° hour, and found good means 170
    To draw from her a prayer of earnest heart
    That I would all my pilgrimage dilate,°

---

      our proper, my own.   *stood . . . action,* were accused by
you. *head and front,* the utmost. *pith,* strength. *round,*
plain. *her motion . . . herself,* her own emotions made her
blush. *thin habits,* slight appearing.

      modern seeming, commonplace suppositions. ***por-
tance,*** behavior. *anters,* caves. *idle,* barren. ***An-
thropophagi,*** man-eaters. *pliant,* convenient. *dilate,* relate.

Whereof by parcels° she had something heard,
But not intentively.° I did consent,
And often did beguile her of her tears
When I did speak of some distressful stroke
That my youth suffered. My story being done,
She gave me for my pains a world of sighs.
She swore, i' faith, 'twas strange, 'twas passing
180   strange;
'Twas pitiful, 'twas wondrous pitiful.
She wished she had not heard it; yet she wished
That heaven had made her such a man. She
    thanked me;
And bade me, if I had a friend that loved her,
I should but teach him how to tell my story,
And that would woo her. Upon this hint° I spake.
She loved me for the dangers I had passed,
And I loved her that she did pity them.
190   This only is the witchcraft I have used.
Here comes the lady. Let her witness it.

(Enter DESDEMONA, IAGO, ATTENDANTS.*)*

DUKE: I think this tale would win my daughter too.
    Good Brabantio,
Take up this mangled matter at the best.
Men do their broken weapons rather use
Than their bare hands.
BRABANTIO: I pray you hear her speak.
If she confess that she was half the wooer,
Destruction on my head if my bad blame
200   Light on the man! Come hither, gentle mistress.
Do you perceive in all this noble company
Where most you owe obedience?
DESDEMONA: My noble father,
I do perceive here a divided duty.
To you I am bound for life and education;
My life and education° both do learn me
How to respect you: you are the lord of duty;
I am hitherto your daughter. But here's my
    husband;
210   And so much duty as my mother showed
To you, preferring you before her father,
So much I challenge° that I may profess
Due to the Moor my lord.
BRABANTIO: God b' wi' ye! I have done.
Please it your grace, on to the state affairs.
I had rather to adopt a child than get° it.
Come hither, Moor.
I here do give thee that with all my heart
Which, but thou hast already, with all my hear
220   I would keep from thee. For your sake,° jewel,
I am glad at soul I have no other child;
For thy escape would teach me tyranny,

To hang clogs on them. I have done, my lord.
DUKE: Let me speak like yourself° and lay a sentence°
Which, as a grise° or step, may help these lovers
Into your favor.
When remedies are past, the griefs are ended
By seeing the worst, which late on hopes depended.
To mourn a mischief that is past and gone   230
Is the next way to draw new mischief on.
What cannot be preserved when fortune takes,
Patience her injury a mock'ry makes.
The robbed that smiles steals something from the
    thief;
He robs himself that spends a bootless° grief.
BRABANTIO: So let the Turk of Cyprus us beguile:
We lose it not so long as we can smile.
He bears the sentence well that nothing bears
But the free comfort which from thence he hears;
But he bears both the sentence and the sorrow   240
That to pay grief must of poor patience borrow.
These sentences, to sugar, or to gall,
Being strong on both sides, are equivocal.
But words are words. I never yet did hear
That the bruised heart was piecèd° through the
    ear.
Beseech you, now to the affairs of state.
DUKE: The Turk with a most mighty preparation
makes for Cyprus. Othello, the fortitude of the
place is best known to you; and though we have   250
there a substitute of most allowed° sufficiency,
yet opinion, a sovereign mistress of effects,°
throws a more safer voice on you. You must
therefore be content to slubber° the gloss of your
new fortunes with this more stubborn and bois-
terous expedition.
OTHELLO: The tyrant custom, most grave senators,
Hath made the flinty and steel couch of war
My thrice-driven° bed of down. I do agnize°
A natural and prompt alacrity   260
I find in hardness;° and do undertake
These present wars against the Ottomites.
Most humbly, therefore, bending to your state,
I crave fit disposition° for my wife,
Due reference of place, and exhibition,°
With such accommodation and besort°
As levels with her breeding.
DUKE: If you please,
Be't at her father's.
BRABANTIO: I'll not have it so.   270

---

by parcels, in bits and pieces. **intentively,** with full attention. **hint,** opportunity. **education,** upbringing. **challenge,** claim. **get,** beget. **for your sake,** because of what you have done.

Let . . . yourself, as you should. **sentence,** maxim. **grise,** degree. **bootless,** unavailing. **piecèd,** relieved. **allowed,** acknowledged. **effects,** of what should be done. **slubber,** sully. **thrice-driven,** thrice-winnowed; i.e., softest. **agnize,** recognize. **alacrity . . . hardness,** readiness to endure hardship. **disposition,** suitable provision. **reference . . . exhibition,** assignment of residence and allowance of money. **besort,** suitable company.

OTHELLO: Nor I.
DESDEMONA: Nor I. I would not there reside,
    To put my father in impatient thoughts
    By being in his eye. Most gracious duke,
    To my unfolding lend your prosperous° ear,
    And let me find a charter in your voice,
    To assist my simpleness.
DUKE: What would you, Desdemona?
DESDEMONA: That I did love the Moor to live with
280   him,
    My downright violence, and storm of fortunes,
    May trumpet to the world. My heart's subdued
    Even to the very quality of my lord.
    I saw Othello's visage in my mind,
    And to his honors and his valiant parts
    Did I my soul and fortunes consecrate.
    So that, dear lords, if I be left behind,
    A moth of peace, and he go to war,
    The rites for which I love him are bereft me,
290   And I a heavy interim shall support
    By his dear absence. Let me go with him.
OTHELLO: Let her have your voices.
    Vouch with me, heaven, I therefore beg it not
    To please the palate of my appetite,
    Nor to comply with heat°—the young affects°
    In me defunct—and proper° satisfaction;
    But to be free and bounteous to her mind;
    And heaven defend° your good souls that you
        think
300   I will your serious and great business scant
    For° she is with me. No, when light-winged toys
    Of feathered Cupid seel° with wanton dullness
    My speculative and officed instruments,°
    That° my disports corrupt and taint my business,
    Let housewives make a skillet of my helm,
    And all indign° and base adversities
    Make head against my estimation!°
DUKE: Be it as you shall privately determine,
    Either for her stay or going. Th' affair cries haste,
310   And speed must answer it. You must hence
        to-night.
DESDEMONA: To-night, my lord?
DUKE: This night.
OTHELLO: With all my heart.
DUKE: At nine i' th' morning here we'll meet again.
    Othello, leave some officer behind,
    And he shall our commission bring to you,
    With such things else of quality and respect
    As doth import° you.
320 OTHELLO: So please your grace, my ancient;
    A man he is of honesty and trust.

---

prosperous, favorable. *heat,* sexual desire. ***young
affects,*** excesses of youthful passion. ***proper,*** personal.
defend, forbid. *For,* because. *seel,* blind. ***My ... instruments,*** perceptual and mental powers. ***That,*** so that. ***in-
dign,*** shameful. *estimation,* reputation. *import,* concern.

To his conveyance I assign my wife,
With what else needful your good grace shall think
To be sent after me.
DUKE: Let it be so.
    Good night to every one. *(to* BRABANTIO*)* And,
        noble signior,
    If virtue no delighted° beauty lack,
    Your son-in-law is far more fair than black.
1. SENATOR: Adieu, brave Moor. Use Desdemona   330
    well.
BRABANTIO: Look to her, Moor, if thou hast eyes to
    see:
    She has deceived her father, and may thee.
OTHELLO: My life upon her faith!

(Exeunt DUKE, SENATORS, OFFICERS, *etc.)*

    Honest Iago,
    My Desdemona must I leave to thee.
    I prithee let thy wife attend on her,
    And bring them after in the best advantage.°
    Come, Desdemona. I have but an hour   340
    Of love, of worldly matters and direction,
    To spend with thee. We must obey the time.

(Exit MOOR *and* DESDEMONA.*)*

RODERIGO: Iago,—
IAGO: What say'st thou, noble heart?
RODERIGO: What will I do, think'st thou?
IAGO: Why, go to bed and sleep.
RODERIGO: I will incontinently° drown myself.
IAGO: If thou dost, I shall never love thee after. Why,
    thou silly gentleman?
RODERIGO: It is silliness to live when to live is tor-   350
    ment; and then have we a prescription to die
    when death is our physician.
IAGO: O villainous! I have looked upon the world for
    four times seven years; and since I could distin-
    guish betwixt a benefit and an injury, I never
    found man that knew how to love himself. Ere I
    would say I would drown myself for the love of a
    guinea hen, I would change my humanity with a
    baboon.
RODERIGO: What should I do? I confess it is my   360
    shame to be so fond, but it is not in my virtue to
    amend it.
IAGO: Virtue? a fig! 'Tis in ourselves that we are thus
    or thus. Our bodies are our gardens, to the
    which our wills are gardeners; so that if we will
    plant nettles or sow lettuce, set hyssop and weed
    up thyme, supply it with one gender° of herbs or
    distract it with many—either to have it sterile
    with idleness or manured with industry—why,
    the power and corrigible° authority of this lies in   370

---

delighted, delightful. ***in ... advantage,*** at the most
opportune time. *incontinently,* immediately. ***gender,***
species. *corrigible,* corrective.

our wills. If the balance of our lives had not one scale of reason to poise another of sensuality, the blood and baseness of our natures would conduct us to most preposterous conclusions. But we have reason to cool our raging motions, our carnal stings, our unbitted° lusts; whereof I take this that you call love to be a sect or scion.°

RODERIGO: It cannot be.

IAGO: It is merely a lust of the blood and a permission
380 of the will. Come, be a man! Drown thyself? Drown cats and blind puppies! I have professed me thy friend, and I confess me knit to thy deserving with cables of perdurable° toughness. I could never better stead° thee than now. Put money in thy purse. Follow these wars; defeat thy favor° with an usurped beard. I say, put money in thy purse. It cannot be that Desdemona should long continue her love to the Moor—put money in thy purse—nor he his to
390 her. It was a violent commencement, and thou shalt see an answerable sequestration°—put but money in thy purse. These Moors are changeable in their wills—fill thy purse with money. The food that to him now is as luscious as locusts° shall be to him shortly as bitter as coloquintida.° She must change for youth: when she is sated with his body, she will find the error of her choice. She must have change, she must. Therefore put money in thy purse. If thou wilt
400 needs damn thyself, do it a more delicate way than drowning. Make° all the money thou canst. If sanctimony° and a frail vow betwixt an erring° barbarian and a supersubtle° Venetian be not too hard for my wits and all the tribe of hell, thou shalt enjoy her. Therefore make money. A pox of drowning! 'Tis clean out of the way. Seek thou rather to be hanged in compassing thy joy than to be drowned and go without her.

RODERIGO: Wilt thou be fast° to my hopes, if I depend
410 on the issue?

IAGO: Thou art sure of me. Go, make money. I have told thee often, and I retell thee again and again, I hate the Moor. My cause is hearted;° thine hath no less reason. Let us be conjunctive in our revenge against him. If thou canst cuckold him, thou dost thyself a pleasure, me a sport. There are many events in the womb of time, which will

be delivered. Traverse,° go, provide thy money! We have more of this to-morrow. Adieu.

RODERIGO: Where shall we meet i' th' morning?   420

IAGO: At my lodging.

RODERIGO: I'll be there with thee betimes.

IAGO: Go to, farewell.—Do you hear, Roderigo?

RODERIGO: What say you?

IAGO: No more of drowning, do you hear?

RODERIGO: I am changed.

IAGO: Go to, farewell. Put money enough in your purse.

RODERIGO: I'll sell my land. (Exit.)

IAGO: Thus do I ever make my fool my purse;   430
For I mine own gained knowledge should profane
If I would time expend with such a snipe°
But for my sport and profit. I hate the Moor;
And it is thought abroad that 'twixt my sheets
H'as done my office. I know not if't be true;
Yet I, for mere suspicion in that kind,
Will do as if for surety.° He holds me well;°
The better shall my purpose work on him.
Cassio's a proper° man. Let me see now;
To get his place, and to plume up my will°   440
In double knavery—How, how? Let's see:—
After some time, to abuse Othello's ear
That he is too familiar with his wife.
He hath a person and a smooth dispose°
To be suspected—framed to make women false.
The Moor is of a free and open nature
That thinks men honest that but seem to be so;
And will as tenderly be led by th' nose
As asses are.
I have't! It is engendered! Hell and night   450
Must bring this monstrous birth to the world's light. (Exit.)

ACT 2 / SCENE 1

(Enter MONTANO and two GENTLEMEN.)

MONTANO: What from the cape can you discern at sea?

1. GENTLEMAN: Nothing at all: it is a high-wrought flood.
I cannot 'twixt the heaven and the main
Descry a sail.

MONTANO: Methinks the wind hath spoke aloud at land;
A fuller blast ne'er shook our battlements.
If it hath ruffianed so upon the sea,   10
What ribs of oak, when mountains melt on them,
Can hold the mortise?° What shall we hear of this?

---

unbitted, uncontrolled. *sect or scion*, cutting or offshoot. *perdurable*, everlasting. *stead*, help. *defeat ...favor*, disguise yourself. *sequestration*, equally abrupt ending. *locusts*, sweet Mediterranean fruit. *coloquintida*, bitter apple, used as a purgative. *Make*, raise, or get together. *sanctimony*, religious ceremony. *erring*, vagabond. *supersubtle*, highly refined. *fast*, true. *cause ... hearted*, rooted in my heart; i.e., deeply felt.

Traverse, march forward. *snipe*, woodcock; silly bird, i.e., fool. *will ... surety*, as if it were a proven fact. *well*, in high regard. *proper*, handsome. *plume ... will*, dress up my intentions. *dispose*, manner. *hold ... mortise*, hold the joints together.

2. GENTLEMAN: A segregation° of the Turkish fleet.
　　For do but stand upon the foaming shore,
　　The chidden billow seems to pelt the clouds;
　　The wind-shaked surge, with high and monstrous mane,
　　Seems to cast water on the burning Bear
　　And quench the guards° of th' ever-fixèd pole.
20　　I never did like molestation° view
　　On the enchafèd flood.
MONTANO: If that the Turkish fleet
　　Be not ensheltered and embayed, they are drowned;
　　It is impossible they bear it out.

(Enter a third GENTLEMAN.)

3. GENTLEMAN: News, lads! Our wars are done.
　　The desperate tempest hath so banged the Turks
　　That their designment halts.° A noble ship of Venice
30　　Hath seen a grievous wrack and sufferance°
　　On most part of their fleet.
MONTANO: How? Is this true?
3. GENTLEMAN: The ship is here put in,
　　A Veronesa;° Michael Cassio,
　　Lieutenant to the warlike Moor Othello,
　　Is come on shore; the Moor himself at sea,
　　And is in full commission here for Cyprus.
MONTANO: I am glad on't. 'Tis a worthy governor.
3. GENTLEMAN: But this same Cassio, though he speak
40　　of comfort
　　Touching the Turkish loss, yet he looks sadly
　　And prays the Moor be safe, for they were parted
　　With foul and violent tempest.
MONTANO: Pray heaven he be;
　　For I have served him, and the man commands
　　Like a full soldier. Let's to the seaside, ho!
　　As well to see the vessel that's come in
　　As to throw out our eyes for brave Othello,
　　Even till we make the main° and th' aerial blue
50　　An indistinct regard.°
3. GENTLEMAN: Come, let's do so;
　　For every minute is expectancy
　　Of more arrivance.

(Enter CASSIO.)

CASSIO: Thanks, you the valiant of this warlike isle,
　　That so approve the Moor! O, let the heavens
　　Give him defense against the elements,
　　For I have lost him on a dangerous sea!
MONTANO: Is he well shipped?
CASSIO: His bark is stoutly timbered, and his pilot

Of very expert and approved allowance;°　　60
　　Therefore my hopes, not surfeited to death,
　　Stand in bold cure.° *(Within)* A sail, a sail, a sail!

(Enter a MESSENGER.)

CASSIO: What noise?
MESSENGER: The town is empty; on the brow o' th' sea
　　Stand ranks of people, and they cry 'A sail!'
CASSIO: My hopes do shape him for the governor. *(A shot.)*
2. GENTLEMAN: They do discharge their shot of courtesy:
　　Our friends at least.　　70
CASSIO: I pray you, sir, go forth
　　And give us truth who 'tis that is arrived.
2. GENTLEMAN: I shall. *(Exit.)*
MONTANO: But, good lieutenant, is your general wived?
CASSIO: Most fortunately. He hath achieved a maid
　　That paragons° description and wild fame;
　　One that excels the quirks of blazoning pens,°
　　And in th' essential vesture of creation
　　Does tire the ingener.°　　80

(Enter SECOND GENTLEMAN.)

　　How now? Who has put in?
2. GENTLEMAN: 'Tis one Iago, ancient to the general.
CASSIO: H'as had most favorable and happy speed:
　　Tempests themselves, high seas, and howling winds,
　　The guttered° rocks and congregated sands,
　　Traitors ensteeped° to clog the guiltless keel,
　　As having sense of beauty, do omit
　　Their mortal° natures, letting go safely by
　　The divine Desdemona.　　90
MONTANO: What is she?
CASSIO: She that I spake of, our great captain's captain,
　　Left in the conduct of the bold Iago,
　　Whose footing° here anticipates our thoughts
　　A se'nnight's° speed. Great Jove, Othello guard,
　　And swell his sail with thine own pow'rful breath,
　　That he may bless this bay with his tall ship,
　　Make love's quick pants in Desdemona's arms,
　　Give renewed fire to our extinct spirits,　　100
　　And bring all Cyprus comfort!

(Enter DESDEMONA, IAGO, RODERIGO, and EMILIA with ATTENDANTS.)

---

segregation, scattering. **guards,** stars near the North Star. **molestation,** disturbance. **halts,** plan is crippled. **sufferance,** damage. **Veronesa,** ship furnished by Verona. **main,** sea. **indistinct regard,** indistinguishable.

expert . . . allowance, skill. **not surfeited . . . cure,** not having been overindulged stand a good chance of being fulfilled. **paragons,** surpasses. **quirk . . . pens,** ingenious descriptions of writers who seek to list all her beauties. **in . . . ingener,** her essential nature as it was created by God overwhelms the imagination of anyone who seeks to praise it. **guttered,** jagged. **ensteeped,** submerged. **mortal,** deadly. **footing,** landing. **se'nnight's,** week's.

O, behold!
The riches of the ship is come on shore!
Ye men of Cyprus, let her have your knees.
Hail to thee, lady! and the grace of heaven,
Before, behind thee, and on every hand,
Enwheel thee round!

DESDEMONA: I thank you, valiant Cassio.
What tidings can you tell me of my lord?

110 CASSIO: He is not yet arrived; nor know I aught
But that he's well and will be shortly here.

DESDEMONA: O but I fear! How lost you company?

CASSIO: The great contention of the sea and skies
Parted our fellowship.*(Within)* A sail, a sail! *(A shot.)*
But hark, A sail!

2. GENTLEMAN: They give their greeting to the
citadel;
This likewise is a friend.

CASSIO: See for the news.

(Exit GENTLEMAN.)

120 Good ancient, you are welcome. *(to EMILIA)*
Welcome, mistress.—
Let it not gall your patience, good Iago,
That I extend° my manners. 'Tis my breeding
That gives me this bold show of courtesy. *(Kisses
EMILIA.)*

IAGO: Sir, would she give you so much of her lips
As of her tongue she oft bestows on me,
You would have enough.

DESDEMONA: Alas, she has no speech!

130 IAGO: In faith, too much.
I find it still when I have list° to sleep.
Marry, before your ladyship, I grant,
She puts her tongue a little in her heart
And chides with thinking.

EMILIA: You have little cause to say so.

IAGO: Come on, come on! You are pictures out of
doors,
Bells in your parlors, wildcats in your kitchens,
Saints in your injuries, devils being offended,
140 Players° in your housewifery, and housewives° in
your beds.

DESDEMONA: O, fie upon thee, slanderer!

IAGO: Nay, it is true, or else I am a Turk:
You rise to play, and go to bed to work.

EMILIA: You shall not write my praise.

IAGO: No, let me not.

DESDEMONA: What wouldst thou write of me, if thou
shouldst praise me?

IAGO: O gentle lady, do not put me to't,
150 For I am nothing if not critical.

DESDEMONA: Come on, assay.°—There's one gone to
the harbor?

IAGO: Ay, madam.

---

extend, show. *list,* desire. *Players,* actors. *house-
wives,* hussies. *assay,* try.

DESDEMONA: I am not merry; but I do beguile
The thing I am by seeming otherwise.—
Come, how wouldst thou praise me?

IAGO: I am about it; but indeed my invention
Comes from my pate as birdlime° does from
frieze°—
It plucks out brains and all. But my Muse labors, 160
And thus she is delivered:
If she be fair° and wise, fairness and wit—
The one's for use, the other useth it.

DESDEMONA: Well praised! How if she be black° and
witty?

IAGO: If she be black, and thereto have a wit,
She'll find a white that shall her blackness fit.

DESDEMONA: Worse and worse!

EMILIA: How if fair and foolish?

IAGO: She never yet was foolish that was fair, 170
For even her folly° helped her to an heir.

DESDEMONA: These are old fond° paradoxes to make
fools laugh i' th' alehouse. What miserable praise
has thou for her that's foul° and foolish?

IAGO: There's none so foul, and foolish thereunto,
But does foul pranks which fair and wise ones do.

DESDEMONA: O heavy ignorance! Thou praisest the
worst best. But what praise couldst thou bestow
on a deserving woman indeed—one that in the
authority of her merit did justly put on the 180
vouch° of very malice itself?

IAGO: She that was ever fair, and never proud;
Had tongue at will, and yet was never loud;
Never lacked gold, and yet went never gay;°
Fled from her wish, and yet said 'Now I may';
She that, being angered, her revenge being nigh,
Bade her wrong stay,° and her displeasure fly;
She that in wisdom never was so frail
To change the cod's head for the salmon's tail;°
She that could think, and ne'er disclose her mind; 190
See suitors following, and not look behind:
She was a wight° (if ever such wight were)—

DESDEMONA: To do what?

IAGO: To suckle fools° and chronicle small beer.°

DESDEMONA: O most lame and impotent conclusion!
Do not learn of him, Emilia, though he be thy
husband. How say you, Cassio? Is he not a most
profane and liberal° counsellor?

CASSIO: He speaks home,° madam. You may relish
him more in the° soldier than in the scholar. 200

---

birdlime, sticky paste used to catch birds. *frieze,* coarse
cloth. *fair,* blonde. *black,* brunette. *folly,* wantonness.
fond, foolish. *foul,* ugly. *put . . . vouch,* compel the praise.
gay, extravagantly dressed. *stay,* sense of injury cease. *To
. . . tail,* to exchange something common but valuable for
something rare but useless. *wight,* person. *fools,* babies.
chronicle . . . beer, keep petty household accounts in order.
liberal, free-speaking; i.e., lewd. *home,* bluntly. *in the,* in
the character of.

IAGO (aside): He takes her by the palm. Ay well said,
whisper! With as little a web as this will I ensnare
as great a fly as Cassio. Ay, smile upon her, do! I
will gyve° thee in thine own courtship,°—You say
true; 'tis so, indeed!—If such tricks as these strip
you out of your lieutenantry, it had been better
you had not kissed your three fingers so oft—
which now again you are most apt to play the sir°
in. Very good! well kissed! an excellent curtsy!
210 'Tis so, indeed. Yet again your fingers to your
lips? Would they were clyster pipes° for your
sake! (Trumpet within.) The Moor! I know his
trumpet.
CASSIO: 'Tis truly so.
DESDEMONA: Let's meet him and receive him.
CASSIO: Lo, where he comes.

(Enter OTHELLO and ATTENDANTS.)

OTHELLO: O my fair warrior!
DESDEMONA: My dear Othello!
OTHELLO: It gives me wonder great as my content
220 To see you here before me. O my soul's joy!
If after every tempest come such calms,
May the winds blow till they have wakened death!
And let the laboring bark climb hills of seas
Olympus-high, and duck again as low
As hell's from heaven! If it were now to die,
'Twere now to be most happy; for I fear
My soul hath her content so absolute
That not another comfort like to this
Succeeds in unknown fate.
230 DESDEMONA: The heavens forbid
But that our loves and comforts should increase
Even as our days do grow.
OTHELLO: Amen to that, sweet powers!
I cannot speak enough of this content;
It stops me here; it is too much of joy.
And this, and this, the greatest discords be (They
kiss.)
That e'er our hearts shall make!
IAGO (aside): O, you are well tuned now!
240 But I'll set down° the pegs that make this music,
As honest as I am.
OTHELLO: Come, let us to the castle.
News, friends! Our wars are done; the Turks are
drowned.
How does my old acquaintance of this isle?—
Honey, you shall be well desired° in Cyprus;
I have found great love amongst them. O my sweet,
I prattle out of fashion, and I dote
In mine own comforts. I prithee, good Iago,
250 Go to the bay and disembark my coffers.

Bring thou the master to the citadel;
He is a good one, and his worthiness
Does challenge much respect.—Come,
Desdemona,
Once more well met at Cyprus.

(Exit OTHELLO with all but IAGO and RODERIGO.)

IAGO (to an ATTENDANT, who goes out): Do thou meet
me presently at the harbor. (to RODERIGO) Come
hither. If thou be'st valiant (as they say base men
being in love have then a nobility in their natures
more than is native to them), list me. The
260 lieutenant to-night watches on the court of
guard.° First, I must tell thee this: Desdemona is
directly in love with him.
RODERIGO: With him? Why, 'tis not possible.
IAGO: Lay thy finger thus,° and let thy soul be instructed. Mark me with what violence she first
loved the Moor, but for bragging and telling her
fantastical lies; and will she love him still for prating? Let not thy discreet heart think it. Her eye
must be fed; and what delight shall she have to
270 look on the devil? When the blood is made dull
with the act of sport, there should be, again to
inflame it and to give satiety a fresh appetite,
loveliness in favor, sympathy in years, manners,
and beauties; all which the Moor is defective in.
Now for want of these required conveniences,°
her delicate tenderness will find itself abused,
begin to heave the gorge,° disrelish and abhor
the Moor. Very nature will instruct her in it and
compel her to some second choice. Now, sir, that
280 is granted—as it is a most pregnant and un-
forced position—who stands so eminent in the
degree of this fortune as Cassio does? A knave
very voluble; no further conscionable than in
putting on the mere form of civil and humane°
seeming for the better compassing of his salt°
and most hidden loose affection? Why, none!
why, none! A slipper° and subtle knave; a
finder-out of occasions; that has an eye can
stamp and counterfeit advantages, though true
290 advantage never present itself; a devilish knave!
Besides, the knave is handsome, young, and hath
all those requisites in him that folly and green°
minds look after. A pestilent complete knave!
and the woman hath found him already.
RODERIGO: I cannot believe that in her; she's full of
most blessed condition.
IAGO: Blessed fig's-end! The wine she drinks is made
of grapes. If she had been blessed, she would

---

gyve, trap. courtship, courtly manners. sir, courtly
gentleman. clyster pipes, syringes for an enema. set
down, loosen. well desired, warmly welcomed.

watches . . . guard, has charge of the watch. thus, on
your lips. conveniences, compatibilities. heave . . . gorge,
be nauseated. humane, courteous. salt, lecherous. slipper, slippery. green, wanton and youthful.

300 never have loved the Moor. Blessed pudding!
Didst thou not see her paddle with the palm of
his hand? Didst not mark that?

RODERIGO: Yes, that I did; but that was but courtesy.

IAGO: Lechery, by this hand! an index and obscure
prologue to the history of lust and foul thoughts.
They met so near with their lips that their
breaths embraced together. Villainous thoughts,
Roderigo! When these mutualities so marshal
the way, hard at hand comes the master and
310 main exercise, th' incorporate° conclusion. Pish!
But, sir, be you ruled by me: I have brought you
from Venice. Watch you to-night; for the command, I'll lay't upon you. Cassio knows you not.
I'll not be far from you: do you find some occasion to anger Cassio, either by speaking too loud,
or tainting° his discipline, or from what other
course you please which the time shall more
favorably minister.

RODERIGO: Well.

320 IAGO: Sir, he is rash and very sudden in choler,° and
haply with his truncheon may strike at you. Provoke him that he may; for even out of that will I
cause these of Cyprus to mutiny; whose qual-
ification° shall come into no true taste again but
by the displanting of Cassio. So shall you have a
shorter journey to your desires by the means I
shall then have to prefer° them; and the imped-
iment most profitably removed without the
which there were no expectation of our prosper-
330 ity.

RODERIGO: I will do this if you can bring it to any
opportunity.

IAGO: I warrant thee. Meet me by and by at the
citadel; I must fetch his necessaries ashore.
Farewell.

RODERIGO: Adieu (Exit.)

IAGO: That Cassio loves her, I do well believe it;
That she loves him, 'tis apt and of great credit.°
The Moor, howbeit that I endure him not,
340 Is of a constant, loving, noble nature,
And I dare think he'll prove to Desdemona
A most dear husband. Now I do love her too;
Not out of absolute lust, though peradventure
I stand accountant for as great a sin,
But partly led to diet my revenge,
For that I do suspect the lusty Moor
Hath leaped into my seat; the thought whereof
Doth, like a poisonous mineral, gnaw my inwards;
And nothing can or shall content my soul
350 Till I am evened with him, wife for wife;
Or failing so, yet that I put the Moor
At least into a jealousy so strong

That judgment cannot cure. Which thing to do,
If this poor trash of Venice, whom I trash°
For his quick hunting, stand the putting on,°
I'll have our Michael Cassio on the hip,°
Abuse him to the Moor in the rank garb°
(For I fear Cassio with my nightcap too),
Make the Moor thank me, love me, and reward me
For making him egregiously an ass 360
And practicing upon° his peace and quiet
Even to madness. 'Tis here, but yet confused:
Knavery's plain face is never seen till used. (Exit.)

ACT 2 / SCENE 2

(Enter OTHELLO'S HERALD, with a proclamation.)

HERALD: It is Othello's pleasure, our noble and valiant general, that, upon certain tidings now arrived, importing the mere perdition° of the Turkish fleet, every man put himself into triumph;
some to dance, some to make bonfires, each man
to what sport and revels his addiction leads him.
For, besides these beneficial news, it is the celebration of his nuptial. So much was his pleasure
should be proclaimed. All offices° are open, and
there is full liberty of feasting from this present 10
hour of five till the bell have told eleven. Heaven
bless the isle of Cyprus and our noble general
Othello! (Exit.)

ACT 2 / SCENE 3

(Enter OTHELLO, DESDEMONA, CASSIO, and ATTEN-
DANTS.)

OTHELLO: Good Michael, look you to the guard
to-night.
Let's teach ourselves that honorable stop,
Not to outsport discretion.

CASSIO: Iago hath direction what to do;
But not withstanding, with my personal eye
Will I look to't.

OTHELLO: Iago is most honest.
Michael, good night. To-morrow with your earliest
Let me have speech with you. (to DESDEMONA) 10
Come, my dear love.
The purchase made, the fruits are to ensue;
That profit's yet to come 'tween me and you.—
Good night.

(Exit OTHELLO with DESDEMONA and ATTENDANTS.)
(Enter IAGO.)

---

incorporate, sexual. tainting, discrediting. sudden in
choler, quick to anger. qualification, satisfaction. prefer,
advance. apt . . . credit, probable and believable.

trash, hang weights on, as was done to hounds to
restrain them from hunting too fast. stand the putting on,
performs properly in response to my command. on the
hip, in a vulnerable position (a term from wrestling). rank
garb, coarse manner. practicing upon, plotting against.
perdition, complete destruction. offices, kitchens and
storerooms.

CASSIO: Welcome, Iago. We must to the watch.

IAGO: Not this hour, lieutenant; 'tis not yet ten o' th' clock. Our general cast° us thus early for the love of his Desdemona; who let us not therefore blame. He hath not yet made wanton the night
20 with her, and she is sport for Jove.

CASSIO: She's a most exquisite lady.

IAGO: And, I'll warrant her, full of game.

CASSIO: Indeed, she's a most fresh and delicate creature.

IAGO: What an eye she has! Methinks it sounds a parley to provocation.

CASSIO: An inviting eye; and yet methinks right modest.

IAGO: And when she speaks, is it not an alarum° to
30 love?

CASSIO: She is indeed perfection.

IAGO: Well, happiness to their sheets! Come, lieutenant, I have a stoup° of wine, and here without are a brace of Cyprus gallants that would fain have a measure to the health of black Othello.

CASSIO: Not to-night, good Iago. I have very poor and unhappy brains for drinking; I could well wish courtesy would invent some other custom of entertainment.

40 IAGO: O, they are our friends. But one cup! I'll drink for you.

CASSIO: I have drunk but one cup to-night, and that was craftily qualified° too; and behold what innovation° it makes here. I am unfortunate in the infirmity and dare not task my weakness with any more.

IAGO: What, man! 'Tis a night of revels: the gallants desire it.

CASSIO: Where are they?

50 IAGO: Here at the door; I pray you call them in.

CASSIO: I'll do't, but it dislikes me.° (Exit.)

IAGO: If I can fasten but one cup upon him
With that which he hath drunk to-night already,
He'll be as full of quarrel and offense
As my young mistress' dog. Now my sick fool
Roderigo,
Whom love hath turned almost the wrong side out,
To Desdemona hath to-night caroused
Potations pottle-deep;° and he's to watch.
60 Three lads of Cyprus—noble swelling spirits,
That hold their honors in a wary distance,°
The very elements of this warlike isle—
Have I to-night flustered with flowing cups,
And they watch too. Now, 'mongst this flock of
drunkards

Am I to put our Cassio in some action
That may offend the isle.

(Enter CASSIO, MONTANO, and GENTLEMEN; SERVANTS following with wine.)

But here they come.
If consequence do but approve my dream,°
My boat sails freely, both with wind and stream.   70

CASSIO: 'Fore God, they have given me a rouse° already.

MONTANO: Good faith, a little one; not past a pint, as I am a soldier.

IAGO: Some wine, ho!

(Sings)

    And let me the canakin clink, clink;
    And let me the canakin clink.
      A soldier's a man;
      A life's but a span,
    Why then, let a soldier drink.   80

Some wine, boys!

CASSIO: 'Fore God, an excellent song!

IAGO: I learned it in England, where indeed they are most potent in potting. Your Dane, your German, and your swag-bellied Hollander—Drink, ho!—are nothing to your English.

CASSIO: Is your Englishman so expert in his drinking?

IAGO: Why, he drinks you with facility your Dane dead drunk; he sweats not to overthrow your   90 Almain;° he gives your Hollander a vomit ere the next pottle can be filled.

CASSIO: To the health of our general!

MONTANO: I am for it, lieutenant, and I'll do you justice.

IAGO: O sweet England!

(Sings)

    King Stephen was a worthy peer;
      His breeches cost him but a crown;
    He held 'em sixpence all to dear,
      With that he called the tailor lown.°   100
    He was a wight of high renown,
      And thou art but of low degree.
    'Tis pride that pulls the country down;
      Then take thine auld cloak about thee.

Some wine, ho!

CASSIO: 'Fore God, this is a more exquisite song than the other.

IAGO: Will you hear't again?

---

cast, dismissed.   **alarum**, trumpet signal.   **stoup**, two-quart tankard.   **craftily qualified**, carefully diluted. **innovation**, disturbing change.   **it dislikes me**, I don't want to.   **pottle-deep**, to the bottom of the tankard.   **hold . . . distance**, are very touchy about their honor.

If . . . dream, if events work out as I hope.   **rouse**, drink.   **Almain**, German.   **lown**, rascal.

CASSIO: No, for I hold him to be unworthy of his
110   place that does those things. Well, God's above
    all; and there be souls must be saved, and there
    be souls must not be saved.
IAGO: It's true, good lieutenant.
CASSIO: For mine own part—no offense to the gen-
    eral, nor any man of quality—I hope to be saved.
IAGO: And so do I too, lieutenant.
CASSIO: Ay, but by your leave, not before me. The
    lieutenant is to be saved before the ancient. Let's
    have no more of this; let's to our affairs.—God
120   forgive us our sins!—Gentlemen, let's look to our
    business. Do not think, gentlemen, I am drunk.
    This is my ancient; this is my right hand, and this
    is my left. I am not drunk now. I can stand well
    enough, and speak well enough.
ALL: Excellent well!
CASSIO: Why, very well then. You must not think
    then that I am drunk. (Exit.)
MONTANO: To th' platform, masters. Come, let's set
    the watch.
130 IAGO: You see this fellow that is gone before.
    He is a soldier fit to stand by Caesar
    And give direction; and do but see his vice.
    'Tis to his virtue a just equinox,°
    The one as long as th' other. 'Tis pity of him.
    I fear the trust Othello puts him in,
    On some odd time of his infirmity,
    Will shake this island.
MONTANO: But is he often thus?
IAGO: 'Tis evermore the prologue to his sleep:
140   He'll watch the horologe a double set°
    If drink rock not his cradle.
MONTANO: It were well
    The general were put in mind of it.
    Perhaps he sees it not, or his good nature
    Prizes the virtue that appears in Cassio
    And looks not on his evils. Is not this true?

(Enter RODERIGO.)

IAGO (aside to him): How now, Roderigo?
    I pray you after the lieutenant, go!

(Exit RODERIGO.)

MONTANO: And 'tis great pity that the noble Moor
150   Should hazard such a place as his own second
    With one of an ingraft° infirmity.
    It were an honest action to say
    So to the Moor.
IAGO: Not I, for this fair island!
    I do love Cassio well and would do much
    To cure him of this evil. (Within) Help! help!
    But hark! What noise?

(Enter CASSIO, driving in RODERIGO.)

CASSIO: Zounds, you rogue! you rascal!
MONTANO: What's the matter, lieutenant?
CASSIO: A knave teach me my duty?   160
    I'll beat the knave into a twiggen° bottle.
RODERIGO: Beat me?
CASSIO: Dost thou prate, rogue? (Strikes him.)
MONTANO: Nay, good lieutenant! (Stays him.)
    Pray, sir, hold your hand.
CASSIO: Let me go, sir.
    Or I'll knock you o'er the mazzard.°
MONTANO: Come, come, you're drunk!
CASSIO: Drunk? (They fight.)
IAGO (aside to RODERIGO): Away, I say! Go out and cry   170
    a mutiny!

(Exit RODERIGO.)

    Nay, good lieutenant. God's will gentlemen!
    Help, ho!—lieutenant—sir—Montano—sir—
    Help, masters!—Here'a a goodly watch indeed!

(A bell rung.)

    Who's that which rings the bell? Diablo, ho!
    The town will rise. God's will, lieutenant, hold!
    You will be shamed for ever.

(Enter OTHELLO and GENTLEMEN with weapons.)

OTHELLO: What is the matter here?
MONTANO: Zounds, I bleed still. I am hurt to death.
    He dies!   180
OTHELLO: Hold for your lives!
IAGO: Hold, hold! Lieutenant—
    sir—Montano—gentlemen!
    Have you forgot all sense of place and duty?
    Hold! The general speaks to you. Hold, hold, for
    shame!
OTHELLO: Why, how now, ho? From whence ariseth
    this?
    Are we turned Turks, and to ourselves do that
    Which heaven hath forbid the Ottomites?   190
    For Christian shame put by this barbarous brawl!
    He that stirs next to carve for° his own rage
    Holds his soul light; he dies upon his motion.
    Silence that dreadful bell! It frights the isle
    From her propriety.° What's the matter, masters?
    Honest Iago, that looks dead with grieving,
    Speak. Who began this? On thy love, I charge thee.
IAGO: I do not know. Friends all but now, even now,
    In quarter, and in terms like bride and groom
    Devesting them for bed; and then, but now—   200
    As if some planet had unwitted men—
    Swords out, and tilting one at other's breast
    In opposition bloody. I cannot speak

---

just equinox, exact equivalent. watch . . . set, stay
awake two times around the clock. ingraft, ingrained.

twiggen, wicker covered. mazzard, head. carve for,
indulge. propriety, natural condition.

Any beginning to this peevish odds.°
And would in action glorious I had lost
Those legs that brought me to a part of it!

OTHELLO: How comes it, Michael, you are thus
forgot?

CASSIO: I pray you pardon me; I cannot speak.

210 OTHELLO: Worthy Montano, you were wont be civil;
The gravity and stillness of your youth
The world hath noted, and your name is great
In mouths of wisest censure.° What's the matter
That you unlace your reputation thus
And spend your rich opinion° for the name
Of a night-brawler? Give me answer to't.

MONTANO: Worthy Othello, I am hurt to danger.
Your officer, Iago, can inform you,
While I spare speech, which something now
220   offends° me,
Of all that I do know; nor know I aught
By me that's said or done amiss this night,
Unless self-charity be sometimes a vice,
And to defend ourselves it be a sin
When violence assails us.

OTHELLO: Now, by heaven,
My blood begins my safer guides to rule,
And passion, having my best judgment collied,°
Assays to lead the way. If I once stir
230 Or do but lift this arm, the best of you
Shall sink in my rebuke. Give me to know
How this foul rout began, who set it on;
And he that is approved in° this offense,
Though he had twinned with me, both at a birth,
Shall lose me. What! in a town of war,
Yet wild, the people's hearts brimful of fear,
To manage° private and domestic quarrel?
In night, and on the court and guard of safety?
'Tis monstrous. Iago, who began't?

240 MONTANO: If partially affined, or leagued in office,°
Thou dost deliver more or less than truth,
Thou art no soldier.

IAGO: Touch me not so near.
I had rather have this tongue cut from my mouth
Than it should do offense to Michael Cassio;
Yet I persuade myself, to speak the truth
Shall nothing wrong him. Thus it is, general.
Montano and myself being in speech,
There comes a fellow crying out for help,
250 And Cassio following him with determined sword
To execute° upon him. Sir, this gentleman
Steps in to Cassio and entreats his pause.
Myself the crying fellow did pursue,
Lest by his clamor—as it so fell out—

The town might fall in fright. He, swift of foot,
Outran my purpose; and I returned the rather
For that I heard the clink and fall of swords,
And Cassio high in oath; which till to-night
I ne'er might say before. When I came back—
For this was brief—I found them close together   260
At blow and thrust, even as again they were
When you yourself did part them.
More of this matter cannot I report;
But men are men; the best sometimes forget.
Though Cassio did some little wrong to him,
As men in rage strike those that wish them best,
Yet surely Cassio I believe received
From him that fled some strange indignity,
Which patience could not pass.°

OTHELLO: I know, Iago,   270
Thy honesty and love doth mince this matter,
Making it light to Cassio. Cassio, I love thee;
But never more be officer of mine.

(Enter DESDEMONA, *attended.)*

Look if my gentle love be not raised up!
I'll make thee an example.

DESDEMONA: What's the matter?

OTHELLO: All's well now, sweeting; come away to bed.
(to Montano) Sir, for your hurts, myself will be your
surgeon.
Lead him off. (MONTANO *is led off.)*   280
Iago, look with care about the town
And silence those whom this vile brawl distracted.
Come, Desdemona: 'tis the soldiers' life
To have their balmy slumbers waked with strife.

(Exit with all but IAGO *and* CASSIO.)*

IAGO: What, are you hurt, lieutenant?

CASSIO: Ay, past all surgery.

IAGO: Marry, God forbid!

CASSIO: Reputation, reputation, reputation! O, I
have lost my reputation! I have lost the immortal
part of myself, and what remains is bestial. My   290
reputation, Iago, my reputation!

IAGO: As I am an honest man, I thought you had
received some bodily wound. There is more
sense in that than in reputation. Reputation is an
idle and most false imposition; oft got without
merit and lost without deserving. You have lost
no reputation at all unless you repute yourself
such a loser. What, man! there are ways to recover the general again. You are but now cast in
his mood°—a punishment more in policy than in   300
malice, even so as one would beat his offenseless
dog to affright an imperious lion. Sue to him
again, and he's yours.

CASSIO: I will rather sue to be despised than to de-

---

peevish odds, childish quarrel. censure, judgment.
opinion, high reputation. offends, pains. collied, darkened. approved in, proved guilty of. manage, carry on.
partially . . . office, biased because of personal or official ties.
execute, work his will.

pass, ignore. cast . . . mood, dismissed because of his
anger.

ceive so good a commander with so slight, so drunken, and so indiscreet an officer. Drunk! and speak parrot!° and squabble! swagger! swear! and discourse fustian° with one's own shadow! O thou invisible spirit of wine, if thou hast no name to be known by, let us call thee devil!

310

IAGO: What was he that you followed with your sword? What had he done to you?

CASSIO: I know not.

IAGO: Is't possible?

CASSIO: I remember a mass of things, but nothing distinctly; a quarrel, but nothing wherefore. O God, that men should put an enemy in their mouths to steal away their brains! that we should with joy, pleasance, revel, and applause transform outselves into beasts!

320

IAGO: Why, but you are now well enough. How come you thus recovered?

CASSIO: It hath pleased the devil drunkenness to give place to the devil wrath. One unperfectness shows me another, to make me frankly despise myself.

IAGO: Come, you are too severe a moraler. As the time, the place, and the condition of this country stands, I could heartily wish this had not so befall'n; but since it is as it is, mend it for your own good.

330

CASSIO: I will ask him for my place again: he shall tell me I am a drunkard! Had I as many mouths as Hydra,° such an answer would stop them all. To be now a sensible man, by and by a fool, and presently a beast! O strange! Every inordinate cup is unblest, and the ingredient is a devil.

IAGO: Come, come, good wine is a good familiar creature if it be well used. Exclaim no more against it. And, good lieutenant, I think you think I love you.

340

CASSIO: I have well approved° it, sir. I drunk!

IAGO: You or any man living may be drunk at some time, man. I'll tell you what you shall do. Our general's wife is now the general. I may say so in this respect, for he hath devoted and given up himself to the contemplation, mark, and denotement of her parts and graces. Confess yourself freely to her; importune her help to put you in your place again. She is of so free,° so kind, so apt, so blessed a disposition she holds it a vice in her goodness not to do more than she is requested. This broken joint between you and her husband entreat her to splinter;° and my fortunes against any lay° worth naming, this crack

350

of your love shall grow stronger than 'twas before.

CASSIO: You advise me well.

IAGO: I protest, in the sincerity of love and honest kindness.   360

CASSIO: I think it freely; and betimes in the morning will I beseech the virtuous Desdemona to undertake for me. I am desperate of my fortunes if they check me here.

IAGO: You are in the right. Good night, lieutenant; I must to the watch.

CASSIO: Good night, honest Iago.

(Exit CASSIO.)

IAGO: And what's he then that says I play the villain,
When this advice is free I give and honest,   370
Probal° to thinking, and indeed the course
To win the Moor again? For 'tis most easy
Th' inclining Desdemona to subdue°
In any honest suit; she's framed as fruitful°
As the free elements. And then for her
To win the Moor—were't to renounce his baptism,
All seals and symbols of redeemèd sin—
His soul is so enfettered to her love
That she may make, unmake, do what she list,°
Even as her appetite shall play the god   380
With his weak function. How am I then a villain
To counsel Cassio to this parallel course,
Directly to his good? Divinity° of hell!
When devils will the blackest sins put on,
They do suggest at first with heavenly shows,
As I do now. For whiles this honest fool
Plies Desdemona to repair his fortunes,
And she for him pleads strongly to the Moor,
I'll pour this pestilence into his ear,
That she repeals° him for her body's lust;   390
And by how much she strives to do him good,
She shall undo her credit with the Moor.
So will I turn her virtue into pitch,
And out of her own goodness make the net
That shall enmesh them all.

(Enter RODERIGO.)

How, now, Roderigo?

RODERIGO: I do follow here in the chase, not like a hound that hunts, but one that fills up the cry.° My money is almost spent; I have been to-night exceedingly well cudgelled; and I think the issue will be—I shall have so much experience for my pains; and so, with no money at all, and a little more wit, return again to Venice.   400

IAGO: How poor are they that have not patience! What wound did ever heal but by degrees?

---

speak parrot, talk nonsense.   **fustian,** bombastic gibberish.   **Hydra,** many-headed monster of classical mythology.   **approved,** proved.   **free,** generous.   **splinter,** bind up with splints.   **lay,** wager.

Probal, probable.   **subdue,** persuade.   **fruitful,** generous.   **list,** pleases.   **Divinity,** theology.   **repeals,** pleads for his reinstatement.   **cry,** pack.

Thou know'st we work by wit, and not by
   witchcraft;
And wit depends on dilatory time.
Does't not go well? Cassio hath beaten thee,
410 And thou by that small hurt hast cashiered° Cassio.
Though other things grow fair against the sun,
Yet fruits that blossom first will first be ripe.
Content thyself awhile. By the mass, 'tis morning!
Pleasure and action make the hours seem short.
Retire thee; go where thou art billeted.
Away, I say! Thou shalt know more hereafter.
Nay, get thee gone!

(Exit RODERIGO.*)*

Two things are to be done;
My wife must move for Cassio to her mistress;
420 I'll set her on;
Myself the while to draw the Moor apart
And bring him jump° when he may Cassio find
Soliciting his wife. Ay, that's the way!
Dull not device by coldness and delay. *(Exit.)*

ACT 3 / SCENE 1

(Enter CASSIO, *with* MUSICIANS.*)*

CASSIO: Masters, play here, I will content° your pains:
   Something that's brief; and bid 'Good morrow,
   general.'

(They play.)
(Enter the CLOWN.*)*

CLOWN: Why, masters, ha' your instruments been at
   Naples, that they speak i' th' nose° thus?
MUSICIAN: How, sir, how?
CLOWN: Are these, I pray, called wind instruments?
MUSICIAN: Ay, marry, are they, sir.
CLOWN: O, thereby hangs a tail.
10 MUSICIAN: Whereby hangs a tale, sir?
CLOWN: Marry, sir, by many a wind instrument that I
   know. But, masters, here's money for you; and
   the general so likes your music that he desires
   you, for love's sake, to make no more noise with
   it.
MUSICIAN: Well, sir, we will not.
CLOWN: If you have any music that may not be heard,
   to't again: but, as they say, to hear music the
   general does not greatly care.
20 MUSICIAN: We have none such, sir.
CLOWN: Then put up your pipes in your bag, for I'll
   away. Go, vanish into air, away!

---

cashiered, brought about Cassio's discharge.   **jump,** at
the exact moment.   **content,** reward you for.   *Naples . . .
nose,* Naples was reputed to be a center of venereal disease,
and venereal diseases were thought to damage the structure
of the nose, resulting in a peculiar nasal sound.

(Exit MUSICIAN *with his fellows.)*

CASSIO: Dost thou hear, my honest friend?
CLOWN: No I hear not your honest friend. I hear you.
CASSIO: Prithee keep up thy quillets.° There's a poor
   piece of gold for thee. If the gentlewoman that
   attends the general's wife be stirring, tell her
   there's one Cassio entreats her a little favor of
   speech. Wilt thou do this?
CLOWN: She is stirring, sir. If she will stir hither, I 30
   shall seem to notify unto her.
CASSIO: Do, good my friend.

(Exit CLOWN.*)*
(Enter IAGO.*)*

In happy time, Iago.
IAGO: You have not been abed then!
CASSIO: Why, no; the day had broke
   Before we parted. I have made bold, Iago,
   To send in to your wife; my suit to her
   Is that she will to virtuous Desdemona
   Procure me some access.
IAGO: I'll send her to you presently; 40
   And I'll devise a mean to draw the Moor
   Out of the way, that your converse and business
   May be more free.
CASSIO: I humbly thank you, for't.

(Exit IAGO.*)*

I never knew
A Florentine more kind and honest.

(Enter EMILIA.*)*

EMILIA: Good morrow, good lieutenant. I am sorry
   For your displeasure; but all will sure be well.
   The general and his wife are talking of it,
   And she speaks for you stoutly. The Moor replies 50
   That he you hurt is of great fame in Cyprus
   And great affinity,° and that in wholesome wisdom
   He might not but refuse you; but he protests he
     loves you,
   And needs no other suitor but his likings
   To take the safest occasion by the front°
   To bring you in again.
CASSIO: Yet I beseech you,
   If you think fit, or that it may be done,
   Give me advantage of some brief discourse 60
   With Desdemona alone.
EMILIA: Pray you come in.
   I will bestow you where you shall have time
   To speak your bosom° freely.
CASSIO: I am much bound to you. *(Exeunt.)*

---

quillets, puns.   **affinity,** family connections.   **front,**
forelock.   **speak . . . bosom,** most private thoughts.

ACT 3 / SCENE 2

(Enter OTHELLO, IAGO, *and* GENTLEMEN.*)*

OTHELLO: These letters give, Iago, to the pilot
And by him do my duties° to the Senate.
That done, I will be walking on the works;°
Repair there to me.
IAGO: Well, my good lord, I'll do't.
OTHELLO: This fortification, gentlemen, shall we
see't?
GENTLEMEN: We'll wait upon your lordship. *(Exeunt.)*

ACT 3 / SCENE 3

(Enter DESDEMONA, CASSIO, *and* EMILIA.*)*

DESDEMONA: Be thou assured, good Cassio, I will do
All my abilities in thy behalf.
EMILIA: Good madam, do. I warrant it grieves my
husband
As if the cause were his.
DESDEMONA: O, that's an honest fellow. Do not doubt,
Cassio,
But I will have my lord and you again
As friendly as you were.
10 CASSIO: Bounteous madam,
Whatever shall become of Michael Cassio,
He's never anything but your true servant.
DESDEMONA: I know't; I thank you. You do love my
lord;
You have known him long; and be you well assured
He shall in strangeness° stand no farther off
Than in a politic distance.
CASSIO: Ay, but, lady,
That policy may either last so long,
20 Or feed upon such nice° and waterish diet,
Or breed itself so out of circumstance,
That, I being absent, and my place supplied,
My general will forget my love and service.
DESDEMONA: Do not doubt° that; before Emilia here
I give thee warrant of thy place. Assure thee,
If I do vow a friendship, I'll perform it
To the last article. My lord shall never rest;
I'll watch him tame° and talk him out of patience;
His bed shall seem a school, his board a shrift;°
30 I'll intermingle everything he does
With Cassio's suit. Therefore be merry, Cassio,
For thy solicitor shall rather die
Than give thy cause away.

(Enter OTHELLO *and* IAGO *at a distance.)*

EMILIA: Madam, here comes my lord.
CASSIO: Madam, I'll take my leave.

---

duties, pay my respects. **works,** fortifications.
strangeness, aloofness. **nice,** trivial. **doubt,** fear. **tame,**
keep him awake (hawks were tamed by being kept awake).
shrift, confessional.

DESDEMONA: Why, stay, and hear me speak.
CASSIO: Madam, not now; I am very ill at ease,
Unfit for my own purposes.
DESDEMONA: Well, do your discretion.

(Exit CASSIO.*)*

IAGO: Ha! I like not that.   40
OTHELLO: What dost thou say?
IAGO: Nothing, my lord; or if—I know not what.
OTHELLO: Was not that Cassio parted from my wife?
IAGO: Cassio, my lord? No, sure, I cannot think it,
That he would steal away so guilty-like,
Seeing you coming.
OTHELLO: I do believe 'twas he.
DESDEMONA: How now, my lord?
I have been talking with a suitor here,
A man that languishes in your displeasure.   50
OTHELLO: Who is't you mean?
DESDEMONA: Why, your lieutenant, Cassio. Good my
lord,
If I have any grace or power to move you,
His present reconciliation° take;
For if he be not one that truly loves you,
That errs in ignorance, and not in cunning,
I have no judgment in an honest face.
I prithee call him back.
OTHELLO: Went he hence now?   60
DESDEMONA: Yes, faith; so humbled
That he hath left part of his grief with me
To suffer with him. Good love, call him back.
OTHELLO: Not now, sweet Desdemon; some other
time.
DESDEMONA: But shall't be shortly?
OTHELLO: The sooner, sweet, for you.
DESDEMONA: Shall't be to-night at supper?
OTHELLO: No, not to-night.
DESDEMONA: To-morrow dinner then?   70
OTHELLO: I shall not dine at home;
I meet the captains at the citadel.
DESDEMONA: Why then, to-morrow night, or Tuesday
morn,
On Tuesday noon or night, or Wednesday morn.
I prithee name the time, but let it not
Exceed three days. I' faith, he's penitent;
And yet his trespass, in our common reason
(Save that, they say, the wars must make examples
Out of their best), is not almost° a fault   80
T' incur a private check.° When shall he come?
Tell me, Othello. I wonder in my soul
What you could ask me that I should deny
Or stand so mamm'ring on.° What? Michael Cassio,
That came a-wooing with you, and so many a time,
When I have spoke of you dispraisingly,

---

reconciliation, accept his repentance. **almost,** hardly.
private check, even a private reprimand. **stand . . . on,** be so
hesitant to do.

Hath ta'en your part—to have so much to do
To bring him in? By'r Lady, I could do much—

OTHELLO: Prithee no more. Let him come when he
90   will!
I will deny thee nothing.

DESDEMONA: Why, this is not a boon;
'Tis as I should entreat you wear your gloves,
Or feed on nourishing dishes, or keep you warm,
Or sue to you to do a peculiar profit
To your own person. Nay, when I have a suit
Wherein I mean to touch your love indeed,
It shall be full of poise and difficult weight,
And fearful to be granted.

100 OTHELLO: I will deny thee nothing!
Whereon I do beseech thee grant me this,
To leave me but a little to myself.

DESDEMONA: Shall I deny you? No. Farewell, my lord.

OTHELLO: Farewell, my Desdemon: I'll come to thee
straight.

DESDEMONA: Emilia, come.—Be as your fancies teach
you;
Whate'er you be, I am obedient. (*Exit with* EMILIA.)

OTHELLO: Excellent wretch! Perdition catch my soul
110   But I do love thee! and when I love thee not,
Chaos is come again.

IAGO: My noble lord—

OTHELLO: What dost thou say, Iago?

IAGO: Did Michael Cassio, when you wooed my lady,
Know of your love?

OTHELLO: He did, from first to last. Why dost thou
ask?

IAGO: But for a satisfaction of my thought;
No further harm.

120 OTHELLO: Why of thy thought, Iago?

IAGO: I did not think he had been acquainted with
her.

OTHELLO: O, yes, and went between us very oft.

IAGO: Indeed?

OTHELLO: Indeed? Ay, indeed! Discern'st thou aught
in that?
Is he not honest?

IAGO: Honest, my lord?

OTHELLO: Honest. Ay, honest.

130 IAGO: My lord, for aught I know.

OTHELLO: What dost thou think?

IAGO: Think, my lord?

OTHELLO: Think, my lord?
By heaven, he echoes me,
As if there were some monster in his thought
Too hideous to be shown. Thou dost mean
something:
I heard thee say but now, thou lik'st not that,
When Cassio left my wife. What didst not like?
140   And when I told thee he was of my counsel
In my whole course of wooing, thou cried'st
'Indeed?'
And didst contract and purse thy brow together,

As if thou then hadst shut up in thy brain
Some horrible conceit.° If thou dost love me,
Show me thy thought.

IAGO: My lord, you know I love you.

OTHELLO: I think thou dost;
And, for° I know thou'rt full of love and honesty
And weigh'st thy words before thou giv'st them   150
breath,
Therefore these stops of thine fright me the more;
For such things in a false disloyal knave
Are tricks of custom; but in a man that's just
They are close dilations,° working from the heart
That passion cannot rule.

IAGO: For Michael Cassio,
I dare be sworn I think that he is honest.

OTHELLO: I think so too.

IAGO: Men should be what they seem;   160
Or those that be not, would they might seem none!

OTHELLO: Certain, men should be what they seem.

IAGO: Why then, I think Cassio's an honest man.

OTHELLO: Nay, yet there's more in this.
I prithee speak to me as to thy thinkings,
As thou dost ruminate, and give thy worst of
thoughts
The worst of words.

IAGO: Good my lord, pardon me:
Though I am bound to every act of duty,   170
I am not bound to that all slaves are free to.
Utter my thoughts? Why, say they are vile and
false,
As where's the palace whereinto foul things
Sometimes intrude not? Who has a breast so pure
But some uncleanly apprehensions
Keep leets° and law days, and in session sit
With meditations lawful?

OTHELLO: Thou dost conspire against thy friend,
Iago,   180
If thou but think'st him wronged, and mak'st his
ear
A stranger to thy thoughts.

IAGO: I do beseech you—
Though I perchance am vicious in my guess
(As I confess it is my nature's plague
To spy into abuses, and oft my jealousy°
Shapes faults that are not), that your wisdom yet
From one that so imperfectly conjects°
Would take no notice, nor build yourself a trouble 190
Out of his scattering and unsure observance.
It were not for your quiet nor your good,
Nor for my manhood, honesty, or wisdom,
To let you know my thoughts.

OTHELLO: What dost thou mean?

---

    conceit, idea. *for,* because. ***close dilations,*** secret
feelings. ***leets,*** sessions of local courts. ***jealousy,*** suspicion.
conjects, conjectures.

IAGO: Good name in man and woman, dear my lord,
Is the immediate jewel of their souls.
Who steals my purse steals trash; 'tis something,
    nothing;
200 'Twas mine, 'tis his, and has been slave to
    thousands;
But he that filches from me my good name
Robs me of that which not enriches him
And makes me poor indeed.
OTHELLO: By heaven, I'll know thy thoughts!
IAGO: You cannot, if my heart were in your hand;
Nor shall not whilst 'tis in my custody.
OTHELLO: Ha!
IAGO: O, beware, my lord, of jealousy!
210 It is the green-eyed monster, which doth mock°
The meat it feeds on. That cuckold lives in bliss
Who, certain of his fate, loves not his wronger;
But O, what damnèd minutes tells he o'er
Who dotes, yet doubts—suspects, yet strongly
    loves!
OTHELLO: O misery!
IAGO: Poor and content is rich, and rich enough;
But riches fineless° is as poor as winter
To him that ever fears he shall be poor.
220 Good God, the souls of all my tribe defend
From jealousy!
OTHELLO: Why, why is this?
Think'st thou I'ld make a life of jealousy,
To follow still the changes of the moon
With fresh suspicions? No! To be once in doubt
Is once to be resolved. Exchange me for a goat
When I shall turn the business of my soul
To such exsufflicate and blown° surmises,
Matching thy inference. 'Tis not to make me
230   jealous
To say my wife is fair, feeds well, loves company,
Is free of speech, sings, plays, and dances well;
Where virtue is, these are more virtuous.
Nor from mine own weak merits will I draw
The smallest fear or doubt of her revolt,
For she had eyes, and chose me. No, Iago;
I'll see before I doubt; when I doubt, prove;
And on the proof there is no more but this—
Away at once with love or jealousy!
240 IAGO: I am glad of this; for now I shall have reason
To show the love and duty that I bear you
With franker spirit. Therefore, as I am bound,
Receive it from me. I speak not yet of proof.
Look to your wife; observe her well with Cassio;
Wear your eye thus, not jealous nor secure:
I would not have your free and noble nature,
Out of self-bounty,° be abused. Look to't.
I know our country disposition well:

In Venice they do let God see the pranks
They dare not show their husbands; their best   250
    conscience
Is not to leave't undone, but keep't unknown.
OTHELLO: Dost thou say so?
IAGO: She did deceive her father, marrying you;
And when she seemed to shake and fear your
    looks,
She loved them most.
OTHELLO: And so she did.
IAGO: Why, go to then!
She that, so young, could give out such a seeming   260
To seel° her father's eyes up close as oak°—
He thought 'twas witchcraft—but I am much to
    blame.
I humbly do beseech you of your pardon
For too much loving you.
OTHELLO: I am bound to thee for ever.
IAGO: I see this hath a little dashed your spirits.
OTHELLO: Not a jot, not a jot.
IAGO: I' faith, I fear it has.
I hope you will consider what is spoke   270
Comes from my love. But I do see y' are moved.
I am to pray you not to strain my speech
To grosser issues° nor to larger reach
Than to suspicion.
OTHELLO: I will not.
IAGO: Should you do so, my lord,
My speech should fall into such vile success°
As my thoughts aim not at. Cassio's my worthy
    friend—
My lord, I see y' are moved.   280
OTHELLO: No, not much moved:
I do not think but Desdemona's honest.°
IAGO: Long live she so! and long live you to think so!
OTHELLO: And yet, how nature erring from itself—
IAGO: Ay, there's the point! as (to be bold with you)
Not to affect° many proposèd matches
Of her own clime, complexion, and degree,
Whereto we see in all things nature tends—
Foh! one may smell in such a will° most rank,
Foul disproportion, thoughts unnatural—   290
But pardon me—I do not in position°
Distinctly speak of her; though I may fear
Her will, recoiling° to her better judgment,
May fall to match° you with her country forms,°
And happily° repent.
OTHELLO: Farewell, farewell!
If more thou dost perceive, let me know more.
Set on thy wife to observe. Leave me, Iago.

---

mock, play with; i.e., torture. *fineless*, boundless.
exsufflicate and blown, inflated and flyblown. *self-bounty*,
natural goodness.

---

seel, close; i.e., deceive. *oak*, close grained wood.
issues, consequences. *vile success*, evil outcome. **honest**,
chaste. *affect*, desire. *will*, desire. *in position*, in these
assertions. *recoiling*, reverting. *fall to match*, happen to
compare. *country forms*, appearance of her countrymen.
happily, perchance.

IAGO: My lord, I take my leave. *(Going.)*
OTHELLO: Why did I marry? This honest creature doubtless
  Sees and knows more, much more, than he unfolds.
IAGO *(returns)*: My lord, I would I might entreat your honor
  To scan this thing no further: leave it to time.
  Although 'tis fit that Cassio have his place,
  For sure he fills it up with great ability,
  Yet, if you please to hold him off awhile,
300 You shall by that perceive him and his means.
  Note if your lady strain his entertainment°
  With any strong or vehement importunity;
  Much will be seen in that. In the mean time
  Let me be thought too busy in my fears
  (As worthy cause I have to fear I am)
  And hold her free.° I do beseech your honor.
OTHELLO: Fear not my government.°
IAGO: I once more take my leave. *(Exit.)*
OTHELLO: This fellow's of exceeding honesty,
310 And knows all qualities, with a learnèd spirit
  Of human dealings. If I do prove her haggard,°
  Though that her jesses° were my dear heartstrings,
  I'd whistle her off and let her down the wind°
  To prey at fortune. Haply, for I am black
  And have not those soft parts of conversation°
  That chamberers° have, or for I am declined
  Into the vale of years—yet that's not much—
  She's gone. I am abused, and my relief
  Must be to loathe her. O curse of marriage,
320 That we can call these delicate creatures ours,
  And not their appetites! I had rather be a toad
  And live upon the vapor of a dungeon
  Than keep a corner in the thing I love
  For others' uses. Yet 'tis the plague of great ones;
  Prerogatived° are they less than the base.
  'Tis destiny unshunnable, like death.
  Even then this forkèd plague° is fated to us
  When we do quicken.° Look where she comes.

(Enter DESDEMONA *and* EMILIA.*)*

  If she be false, O, then heaven mocks itself!
330 I'll not believe't.
DESDEMONA: How now, my dear Othello?
  Your dinner, and the generous° islanders
  By you invited, do attend your presence.

OTHELLO: I am to blame.
DESDEMONA: Why do you speak so faintly?
  Are you not well?
OTHELLO: I have a pain upon my forehead, here.
DESDEMONA: Faith, that's with watching;° 'twill away again.
  Let me but bind it hard, within this hour   340
  It will be well.
OTHELLO: Your napkin is too little

(He pushes the handkerchief from him, and it falls unnoticed.)

  Let it alone. Come, I'll go in with you.
DESDEMONA: I am very sorry that you are not well.

(Exit with OTHELLO.*)*

EMILIA: I am glad I have found this napkin;
  This was her first remembrance from the Moor.
  My wayward husband hath a hundred times
  Wooed me to steal it; but she so loves the token
  (For he conjured her she should ever keep it)
  That she reserves it evermore about her   350
  To kiss and talk to. I'll have the work ta'en out°
  And give't Iago.
  What he will do with it heaven knows, not I;
  I nothing but° to please his fantasy.°

(Enter IAGO.*)*

IAGO: How now? What do you here alone?
EMILIA: Do not you chide; I have a thing for you.
IAGO: A thing for me? It is a common thing—
EMILIA: Ha?
IAGO: To have a foolish wife.
EMILIA: O, is that all? What will you give me now   360
  For that same handkerchief?
IAGO: What handkerchief?
EMILIA: What handkerchief!
  Why, that the Moor first gave to Desdemona;
  That which so often you did bid me steal.
IAGO: Hast stol'n it from her?
EMILIA: No, faith; she let it drop by negligence,
  And to th' advantage, I being here, took't up.
  Look, here it is.
IAGO: A good wench! Give it me.   370
EMILIA: What will you do with't, that you have been so earnest
  To have me filch it?
IAGO: Why, what's that to you? *(Snatches it.)*
EMILIA: If it be not for some purpose of import,
  Give't me again. Poor lady, she'll run mad
  When she shall lack it.
IAGO: Be not acknown on't;° I have use for it.
  Go, leave me.

---

strain . . . entertainment, urge his reinstatement. **hold her free,** consider her guiltless. **government,** self-control. **haggard,** wild hawk. **jesses,** straps connected to the legs of a hawk for keeping it under control. **whistle . . . wind,** turn her loose and let her fly wherever her will might take her (presumably to her self destruction). **soft . . . conversation,** polished manners. **chamberers,** courtiers. **Prerogatived,** privileged. **forkèd plague,** horns of a cuckold. **quicken,** are born. **generous,** noble.

watching, from lack of sleep. **taken out,** pattern copied. **I nothing but,** my only desire is. **fantasy,** whim. **Be . . . it,** pretend that you know nothing about it.

(Exit EMILIA.*)*

380   I will in Cassio's lodging lose this napkin
And let him find it. Trifles light as air
Are to the jealous confirmations strong
As proofs of holy writ. This may do something.
The Moor already changes with my poison:
Dangerous conceits are in their natures poisons,
Which at the first are scarce found to distaste,
But with a little act upon the blood
Burn like the mines of sulphur.

(Enter OTHELLO.*)*

   I did say so.
390   Look where he comes! Not poppy nor
      mandragora,°
Nor all the drowsy syrups of the world,
Shall ever med'cine thee to that sweet sleep
Which thou owedst yesterday.

OTHELLO: Ha! ha! false to me?

IAGO: Why, how now, general? No more of that!

OTHELLO: Avaunt! be gone! Thou hast set me on the
      rack.
I swear 'tis better to be much abused
400   Than but to know't a little.

IAGO: How now, my lord?

OTHELLO: What sense had I of her stol'n hours of
      lust?
I saw't not, thought it not, it harmed not me;
I slept the next night well, fed well, was free° and
      merry;
I found not Cassio's kisses on her lips.
He that is robbed, not wanting what is stol'n,
Let him not know't, and he's not robbed at all.

410 IAGO: I am sorry to hear this.

OTHELLO: I had been happy if the general camp,
Pioneers° and all, had tasted her sweet body,
So I had nothing known. O, now for ever
Farewell the tranquil mind! farewell content!
Farewell the plumèd troop, and the big wars
That make ambition virtue! O, farewell!
Farewell the neighing steed and the shrill trump,
The spirit-stirring drum, th' ear-piercing fife,
The royal banner, and all quality,
420   Pride, pomp, and circumstance° of glorious war!
And O you mortal engines° whose rude throats
Th' immortal Jove's dread clamors counterfeit,°
Farewell! Othello's occupation's gone!

IAGO: Is't possible, my lord?

OTHELLO: Villain, be sure thou prove my love a
      whore!
Be sure of it; give me ocular proof;
Or, by the worth of man's eternal soul,

---

mandragora, a narcotic. *free,* carefree. *Pioneers,*
lowest rank of soldier. *circumstance,* pageantry. *mortal*
engines, deadly artillery. *counterfeit,* imitate.

Thou hadst been better have been born a dog
Than answer my waked wrath!   430

IAGO: Is't come to this?

OTHELLO: Make me to see't; or at least so prove it
That the probation° bear no hinge nor loop
To hang a doubt on—or woe upon thy life!

IAGO: My noble lord—

OTHELLO: If thou dost slander her and torture me,
Never pray more; abandon all remorse;
On horror's head horrors accumulate;
Do deeds to make heaven weep, all earth amazed;
For nothing canst thou to damnation add   440
Greater than that.

IAGO: O grace! O heaven forgive me!
Are you a man? Have you a soul or sense?—
God b' wi' you! take mine office. O wretched fool,
That liv'st to make thine honesty a vice!
O monstrous world! Take note, take note, O world,
To be direct and honest is not safe.
I thank you for this profit;° and from hence
I'll love no friend, sith love breed such offense.

OTHELLO: Nay, Stay. Thou shouldst be honest.   450

IAGO: I should be wise; for honesty's a fool
And loses that it works for.

OTHELLO: By the world,
I think my wife be honest, and think she is not;
I think that thou art just, and think thou art not.
I'll have some proof. Her name, that was as fresh
As Dian's visage, is now begrimed and black
As mine own face. If there be cords, or knives,
Poison, or fire, or suffocating streams,
I'll not endure it. Would I were satisfied!   460

IAGO: I see, sir, you are eaten up with passion:
I do repent me that I put it to you.
You would be satisfied?

OTHELLO: Would? Nay, I will.

IAGO: And may; but how? how satisfied, my lord?
Would you, the supervisor, grossly gape on?
Behold her topped?

OTHELLO: Death and damnation! O!

IAGO: It were a tedious difficulty, I think,
To bring them to that prospect. Damn them then,   470
If ever mortal eyes do see them bolster°
More° than their own! What then? How then?
What shall I say? Where's satisfaction?
It is impossible you should see this,
Were they as prime° as goats, as hot as monkeys,
As salt° as wolves in pride,° and fools as gross
As ignorance made drunk. But yet, I say,
If imputation and strong circumstances
Which lead directly to the door of truth
Will give you satisfaction, you may have't.   480

OTHELLO: Give me a living reason she's disloyal.

---

probation, proof. *profit,* lesson. *bolster,* lie together.
more, other. *prime,* lustful. *salt,* lecherous. *pride,* heat.

IAGO: I do not like the office.
  But sith I am entered in this cause so far,
  Pricked to't by foolish honesty and love,
  I will go on. I lay with Cassio lately,
  And being troubled with a raging tooth,
  I could not sleep.
  There are a kind of men so loose of soul
  That in their sleeps will mutter their affairs.
490 One of this kind is Cassio.
  In sleep, I heard him say, 'Sweet Desdemona,
  Let us be wary, let us hide our loves!'
  And then, sir, would he gripe° and wring my hand,
  Cry, 'O sweet creature!' and then kiss me hard,
  As if he plucked up kisses by the roots
  That grew upon my lips; then laid his leg
  Over my thigh, and sighed, and kissed, and then
  Cried 'Cursèd fate that gave thee to the Moor!'
OTHELLO: O monstrous! monstrous!
500 IAGO: Nay, this was but his dream.
OTHELLO: But this denoted a foregone conclusion:
  'Tis a shrewd doubt,° though it be but a dream.
IAGO: And this may help to thicken other proofs
  That do demonstrate thinly.
OTHELLO: I'll tear her all to pieces!
IAGO: Nay, but be wise. Yet we see nothing done;
  She may be honest yet. Tell me but this—
  Have you not sometimes seen a handkerchief
  Spotted with strawberries in your wife's hand?
510 OTHELLO: I gave her such a one; 'twas my first gift.
IAGO: I know not that; but such a handkerchief—
  I am sure it was your wife's—did I to-day
  See Cassio wipe his beard with.
OTHELLO: If't be that—
IAGO: If it be that, or any that was hers,
  It speaks against her with the other proofs.
OTHELLO: O, that the slave had forty thousand lives!
  One is too poor, too weak for my revenge.
  Now do I see 'tis true. Look here, Iago:
520 All my fond love thus do I blow to heaven.
  'Tis gone.
  Arise, black vengeance, from the hollow hell!
  Yield up, O love, thy crown and hearted throne
  To tyrannous hate! Swell, bosom, with thy
      fraught,°
  For 'tis of aspics'° tongues!
IAGO: Yet be content.
OTHELLO: O, blood, blood, blood!
IAGO: Patience, I say. Your mind perhaps may
530   change.
OTHELLO: Never, Iago. Like to the Pontic sea,°
  Whose icy current and compulsive course
  Ne'er feels retiring ebb, but keeps due on
  To the Propontic and the Hellespont,

Even so my bloody thoughts, with violent pace,
  Shall ne'er look back, ne'er ebb to humble love,
  Till that a capable° and wide revenge
  Swallow them up. (He kneels.) Now, by yond marble
      heaven,
  In the due reverence of a sacred vow   540
  I here engage my words.
IAGO: Do not rise yet. (IAGO kneels.)
  Witness, you ever-burning lights above,
  You elements that clip° us round about,
  Witness that here Iago doth give up
  The execution° of his wit, hands, heart
  To wronged Othello's service! Let him command,
  And to obey shall be in me remorse,°
  What bloody business ever.

(They rise.)

OTHELLO: I greet thy love,   550
  Not with vain thanks but with acceptance
      bounteous,
  And will upon the instant put thee to't.
  Within these three days let me hear thee say
  That Cassio's not alive.
IAGO: My friend is dead; 'tis done at your request.
  But let her live.
OTHELLO: Damn her, lewd minx! O, damn her!
  Come, go with me apart. I will withdraw
  To furnish me with some swift means of death   560
  For the fair devil. Now art thou my lieutenant.
IAGO: I am your own for ever. (Exeunt.)

ACT 3 / SCENE 4

(Enter DESDEMONA, EMILIA, and CLOWN.)

DESDEMONA: Do you know, sirrah, where Lieutenant
  Cassio lies?°
CLOWN: I dare not say he lies anywhere.
DESDEMONA: Why, man?
CLOWN: He's a soldier, and for me to say a soldier lies
  is stabbing.
DESDEMONA: Go to. Where lodges he?
CLOWN: To tell you where he lodges is to tell you
  where I lie.
DESDEMONA: Can anything be made of this?   10
CLOWN: I know not where he lodges; and for me to
  devise a lodging, and say he lies here or lies
  there, were to lie in mine own throat.°
DESDEMONA: Can you enquire him out, and be
  edified by report?
CLOWN: I will catechize the world for him; that is,
  make questions and by them answer.
DESDEMONA: Seek him, bid him come hither. Tell him

---

  gripe, grip. doubt, strong reason for suspicion.
fraught, burden. aspics', asps' (deadly poisonous snakes).
Pontic sea, Black Sea.

  capable, comprehensive. clip, encompass. execution,
action. remorse, expression of pity (for Othello). lies,
lodges. lie . . . throat, tell an obvious lie.

I have moved my lord on his behalf and hope all
20   will be well.
CLOWN: To do this is within the compass of man's wit,
    and therefore I'll attempt the doing of it. *(Exit.)*
DESDEMONA: Where should I lose that handkerchief,
    Emilia?
EMILIA: I know not, madam.
DESDEMONA: Believe me, I had rather have lost my
    purse
    Full of crusadoes;° and but my noble Moor
    Is true of mind, and made of no such baseness
30   As jealous creatures are, it were enough
    To put him to ill thinking.
EMILIA: Is he not jealous?
DESDEMONA: Who? he? I think the sun where he was
    born
    Drew all such humors° from him.

(Enter OTHELLO.*)*

EMILIA: Look where he comes.
DESDEMONA: I will not leave him now till Cassio
    Be called to him.—How is't with you, my lord?
OTHELLO: Well, my good lady. *(Aside)* O, hardness to
40   dissemble!—
    How do you, Desdemona?
DESDEMONA: Well, my good lord.
OTHELLO: Give me your hand. This hand is moist, my
    lady.
DESDEMONA: It yet hath felt no age nor known no
    sorrow.
OTHELLO: This argues fruitfulness and liberal heart.
    Hot, hot, and moist. This hand of yours requires
    A sequester° from liberty, fasting and prayer,
50   Much castigation, exercise devout;
    For here's a young and sweating devil here
    That commonly rebels. 'Tis a good hand,
    A frank one.
DESDEMONA: You may, indeed, say so;
    For 'twas that hand that gave away my heart.
OTHELLO: A liberal hand! The hearts of old gave
    hands;
    But our new heraldry is hands, not hearts.
DESDEMONA: I cannot speak of this. Come now, your
60   promise!
OTHELLO: What promise, chuck?
DESDEMONA: I have sent to bid Cassio come speak
    with you.
OTHELLO: I have a salt and sorry rheum° offends me.
    Lend me thy handkerchief.
DESDEMONA: Here, my lord.
OTHELLO: That which I gave you.
DESDEMONA: I have it not about me.
OTHELLO: Not?

DESDEMONA: No, faith, my lord.
OTHELLO: That is a fault.
    That handkerchief
    Did an Egyptian° to my mother give.
    She was a charmer,° and could almost read
    The thoughts of people. She told her, while she
        kept it,
    'Twould make her amiable° and subdue my father
    Entirely to her love; but if she lost it
    Or made a gift of it, my father's eye
    Should hold her loathly, and his spirits should hunt   70
    After new fancies. She, dying, gave it me,
    And bid me, when my fate would have me wive,
    To give it her. I did so; and take heed on't;
    Make it a darling like your precious eye.
    To lose't or give't away were such perdition
    As nothing else could match.
DESDEMONA: Is't possible?
OTHELLO: 'Tis true. There's magic in the web of it.
    A sibyl° that had numbered in the world
    The sun to course two hundred compasses,   80
    In her prophetic fury sewed the work;
    The worms were hallowed that did breed the silk;
    And it was dyed in mummy° which the skillful
    Conserved° of maidens' hearts.
DESDEMONA: I' faith? Is't true?
OTHELLO: Most veritable. Therefore look to't well.
DESDEMONA: Then would to God that I had never
    seen't!
OTHELLO: Ha! Wherefore?
DESDEMONA: Why do you speak so startingly and   90
    rash?
OTHELLO: Is't lost? Is't gone? Speak, is it out o' th'
    way?
DESDEMONA: Heaven bless us!
OTHELLO: Say you?
DESDEMONA: It is not lost. But what an if it were?
OTHELLO: How?
DESDEMONA: I say it is not lost.
OTHELLO: Fetch't, let me see't!
DESDEMONA: Why, so I can, sir; but I will not now.   100
    This is a trick to put me from my suit:
    Pray you let Cassio be received again.
OTHELLO: Fetch me the handkerchief! My mind
    misgives.
DESDEMONA: Come, come!
    You'll never meet a more sufficient man.
OTHELLO: The handkerchief!
DESDEMONA: I pray talk me of Cassio.
OTHELLO: The handkerchief!
DESDEMONA: A man that all his time   110
    Hath founded his good fortunes on your love,
    Shared dangers with you—

---

crusadoes, Portuguese gold coins. *humors,* temperamental inclinations. *sequester,* removal. *rheum,* head
cold.

Egyptian, Gypsy. *charmer,* magician. *amiable,* desirable. *sibyl,* prophetess. *mummy,* fluid derived from
embalmed bodies. *conserved,* preserved.

OTHELLO: The handkerchief!

DESDEMONA: I'faith, you are to blame.

OTHELLO: Zounds! *(Exit.)*

EMILIA: Is not this man jealous?

DESDEMONA: I ne'er saw this before.
Sure there's some wonder in this handkerchief;
I am most unhappy in the loss of it.

120 EMILIA: 'Tis not a year or two shows us a man.
They are all but stomachs, and we all but food;
They eat us hungerly, and when they are full,
They belch us.

(Enter IAGO *and* CASSIO.*)*

Look you—Cassio and my husband!

IAGO: There is no other way; 'tis she must do't.
And lo the happiness!° Go and importune her.

DESDEMONA: How now, good Cassio? What's the news
with you?

CASSIO: Madam, my former suit. I do beseech you
130 That by your virtuous means I may again
Exist, and be a member of his love
Whom I with all the office of my heart
Entirely honor. I would not be delayed.
If my offense be of such mortal kind
That neither service past, nor present sorrows,
Nor purposed merit in futurity,
Can ransom me into his love again,
But to know so must be my benefit.
So shall I clothe me in a forced content,
140 And shut myself up in some other course,
To fortune's alms.

DESDEMONA: Alas, thrice-gentle Cassio!
My advocation° is not now in tune.
My lord is not my lord; nor should I know him,
Were he in favor° as in humor altered.
So help me every spirit sanctified
As I have spoken for you all my best
And stood within the blank° of his displeasure
For my free speech! You must awhile be patient.
150 What I can do I will; and more I will
Than for myself I dare. Let that suffice you.

IAGO: Is my lord angry?

EMILIA: He went hence but now,
And certainly in strange unquietness.

IAGO: Can he be angry? I have seen the cannon
When it hath blown his ranks into the air
And, like the devil, from his very arm
Puffed his own brother—and can he be angry?
Something of moment then. I will go meet him.
160 There's matter in't indeed if he be angry.

DESDEMONA: I prithee do so.

(Exit IAGO.*)*

Something sure of state,
Either from Venice or some unhatched practice°
Made demonstrable here in Cyprus to him,
Hath puddled° his clear spirit; and in such cases
Men's natures wrangle with inferior things,
Though great ones are their object. 'Tis even so;
For let our finger ache, and it endues°
Our other, healthful members even to that sense
Of pain. Nay, we must think men are not gods,   170
Nor of them look for such observancy°
As fits the bridal. Beshrew me much, Emilia,
I was, unhandsome warrior as I am,
Arraigning his unkindness with my soul;
But now I find I had suborned the witness,
And he's indicted falsely.

EMILIA: Pray heaven it be state matters, as you think,
And no conception nor no jealous toy°
Concerning you.

DESDEMONA: Alas the day! I never gave him cause.   180

EMILIA: But jealous souls will not be answered so;
They are not ever jealous for the cause,
But jealous for they are jealous. 'Tis a monster
Begot upon itself, born on itself.

DESDEMONA: Heaven keep that monster from
Othello's mind!

EMILIA: Lady, amen.

DESDEMONA: I will go seek him. Cassio, walk here
about:
If I do find him fit, I'll move your suit   190
And seek to effect it to my uttermost.

CASSIO: I humbly thank your ladyship.

(Exeunt DESDEMONA *and* EMILIA.*)*
(Enter BIANCA.*)*

BIANCA: Save you, friend Cassio!

CASSIO: What make you from home?
How is it with you, my most fair Bianca?
I' faith, sweet love, I was coming to your house.

BIANCA: And I was going to your lodging, Cassio.
What, keep a week away? seven days and nights?
Eightscore eight hours? and lovers' absent hours,
More tedious than the dial° eightscore times?   200
O weary reck'ning!

CASSIO: Pardon me, Bianca:
I have this while with leaden thoughts been
pressed;
But I shall in a more continuate° time
Strike off this score of absence. Sweet Bianca,

(Gives her DESDEMONA'S *handkerchief.)*

Take me this work out.

BIANCA: O Cassio, whence came this?
This is some token from a newer friend.

---

happiness, good luck.   **advocation,** advocacy.   **favor,**
appearance.   **blank,** center of a target.

unhatched practice, plot in the making.   **puddled,**
muddied.   **endues,** brings.   **observancy,** devoted attention.
toy, fancy.   **dial,** clock.   **continuate,** uninterrupted.

210   To the felt absence now I feel a cause.
Is't come to this? Well, well.
CASSIO: Go to, woman!
Throw your vile guesses in the devil's teeth,
From whence you have them. You are jealous now
That this is from some mistress, some
   remembrance.
No, by my faith, Bianca.
BIANCA: Why, whose is it?
CASSIO: I know not, sweet; I found it in my chamber.
220   I like the work well; ere it be demanded,
As like enough it will, I'd have it copied.
Take it and do't, and leave me for this time.
BIANCA: Leave you? Wherefore?
CASSIO: I do attend here on the general
And think it no addition, nor my wish,
To have him see me womaned.
BIANCA: Why, I pray you?
CASSIO: Not that I love you not.
BIANCA: But that you do not love me!
230   I pray you bring me on the way a little,
And say if I shall see you soon at night.
CASSIO: 'Tis but a little way that I can bring you,
For I attend here; but I'll see you soon.
BIANCA: 'Tis very good. I must be circumstanced.°
   (Exeunt.)

ACT 4 / SCENE 1

(Enter OTHELLO *and* IAGO.*)*

IAGO: Will you think so?
OTHELLO: Think so, Iago?
IAGO: What,
To kiss in private?
OTHELLO: An unauthorized kiss.
IAGO: Or to be naked with her friend in bed
An hour or more, not meaning any harm?
OTHELLO: Naked in bed, Iago, and not mean harm?
It is hypocrisy against the devil.
10   They that mean virtuously, and yet do so,
The devil their virtue tempts, and they tempt
   heaven.
IAGO: So they do nothing, 'tis a venial slip.
But if I give my wife a handkerchief—
OTHELLO: What then?
IAGO: Why, then 'tis hers, my lord; and being hers,
She may, I think, bestow't on any man.
OTHELLO: She is protectress of her honor too;
May she give that?
20   IAGO: Her honor is an essence that's not seen;
They have it very oft° that have it not.
But for the handkerchief—
OTHELLO: By heaven, I would most gladly have
   forgot it!

Thou said'st—O, it comes o'er my memory
As doth the raven o'er the infected house,
Boding to all!—he had my handkerchief.
IAGO: Ay, what of that?
OTHELLO: That's not so good now.
IAGO: What   30
If I had said I had seen him do you wrong?
Or heard him say—as knaves be such abroad
Who having, by their own importunate suit,
Or voluntary dotage of some mistress,
Convincèd or supplied° them, cannot choose
But they must blab—
OTHELLO: Hath he said anything?
IAGO: He hath, my lord; but be you well assured,
No more than he'll unswear.
OTHELLO: What hath he said?   40
IAGO: Faith, that he did—I know not what he did.
OTHELLO: What? what?
IAGO: Lie—
OTHELLO: With her?
IAGO: With her, on her; what you will.
OTHELLO: Lie with her? lie on her?—We say lie on
her when they belie her.—Lie with her! Zounds,
that's fulsome.—Handkerchief—confessions—
handkerchief—To confess, and be hanged for
his labor—first to be hanged, and then to con- 50
fess! I tremble at it. Nature would not invest her-
self in such shadowing° passion without some in-
struction.° It is not words that shakes me
thus.—Pish! Noses, ears, and lips? Is't
possible?—Confess?—Handkerchief?—O devil!
(Falls in a trance.)
IAGO: Work on,
My med'cine work! Thus credulous fools are
   caught,
And many worthy and chaste dames even thus,
All guiltless, meet reproach.—What, ho! my lord! 60
My lord, I say! Othello!

(Enter CASSIO.*)*

How now, Cassio?
CASSIO: What's the matter?
IAGO: My lord is fall'n into an epilepsy.
This is his second fit; he had one yesterday.
CASSIO: Rub him about the temples.
IAGO: No, forbear.
The lethargy must have his quiet course.
If not, he foams at mouth, and by and by
Breaks out to savage madness. Look, he stirs. 70
Do you withdraw yourself a little while.
He will recover straight. When he is gone,
I would on great occasion speak with you.

(Exit CASSIO.*)*

---

circumstanced, governed by circumstances.
They . . . oft, they often have the appearance of it.

Convincèd or supplied, overcome or gratified. **shadow-ing,** overwhelming. **instruction,** prompting, or cause.

How is it, general? Have you not hurt your head?

OTHELLO: Dost thou mock me?

IAGO: I mock you? No, by heaven.
Would you would bear your fortune like a man!

OTHELLO: A hornèd man's° a monster and a beast.

IAGO: There's many a beast then in a populous city,
80   And many a civil monster.

OTHELLO: Did he confess it?

IAGO: Good, sir, be a man.
Think every bearded fellow that's but yoked°
May draw with you. There's millions now alive
That nightly lie in those unproper° beds
Which they dare swear peculiar:° your case is
   better.
O, 'tis the spite of hell, the fiend's arch-mock,
To lip a wanton in a secure° couch,
90   And to suppose her chaste! No, let me know;
And knowing what I am, I know what she shall be.

OTHELLO: O, thou are wise! 'Tis certain.

IAGO: Stand you awhile apart;
Confine yourself but in a patient list.°
Whilst you were here, o'erwhelmèd with your
   grief—
A passion most unsuiting such a man—
Cassio came hither. I shifted him away
And laid good 'scuse upon your ecstasy;°
100   Bade him anon return, and here speak with me;
The which he promised. Do but encave° yourself
And mark the fleers,° the gibes, and notable scorns
That dwell in every region of his face;
For I will make him tell the tale anew—
Where, how, how oft, how long ago, and when
He hath, and is again to cope° your wife.
I say, but mark his gesture. Marry, patience!
Or I shall say you are all in all in spleen,°
And nothing of a man.

110 OTHELLO: Dost thou hear, Iago?
I will be found most cunning in my patience;
But—dost thou hear?—most bloody.

IAGO: That's not amiss;
But yet keep time in all. Will you withdraw?

(OTHELLO retires.)

Now will I question Cassio of Bianca,
A huswife° that by selling her desires
Buys herself bread and clothes. It is a creature
That dotes on Cassio, as 'tis the strumpet's plague
To beguile many and be beguiled by one.
120   He, when he hears of her, cannot refrain
From the excess of laughter. Here he comes.

As he shall smile, Othello shall go mad;
And his unbookish° jealousy must conster°
Poor Cassio's smiles, gestures, and light behavior
Quite in the wrong. How do you now, lieutenant?

CASSIO: The worser that you give me the addition°
Whose want even kills me.

IAGO: Ply Desdemona well, and you are sure on't.
Now, if this suit lay in Bianca's power,
How quickly should you speed!   130

CASSIO: Alas, poor caitiff!°

OTHELLO: Look how he laughs already!

IAGO: I never knew a woman love man so.

CASSIO: Alas, poor rogue! I think, i' faith, she loves
me.

OTHELLO: Now he denies it faintly, and laughs it out.

IAGO: Do you hear, Cassio?

OTHELLO: Now he importunes him
To tell it o'er. Go to! Well said, well said!

IAGO: She gives it out that you shall marry her.   140
Do you intend it?

CASSIO: Ha, ha, ha!

OTHELLO: Do you triumph, Roman? Do you
triumph?

CASSIO: I marry her? What, a customer?° Prithee bear
some charity to my wit; do not think it so unwholesome. Ha, ha, ha!

OTHELLO: So, so, so, so! They laugh that win!

IAGO: Faith, the cry goes that you shall marry her.

CASSIO: Prithee say true.   150

IAGO: I am a very villain else.

OTHELLO: Have you scored° me? Well.

CASSIO: This is the monkey's own giving out. She is
persuaded I will marry her out of her own love
and flattery, not out of my promise.

OTHELLO: Iago beckons me; now he begins the story.

CASSIO: She was here even now; she haunts me in
every place. I was t' other day talking on the sea
bank with certain Venetians, and thither comes
the bauble,° and by this hand, she falls me thus   160
about my neck—

OTHELLO: Crying 'O dear Cassio!' as it were. His gesture imports it.

CASSIO: So hangs, and lolls, and weeps upon me; so
hales and pulls me! Ha, ha, ha!

OTHELLO: Now he tells how she plucked him to my
chamber.
O, I see that nose of yours, but not that dog I shall
throw't to.

CASSIO: Well, I must leave her company.   170

(Enter BIANCA.)

IAGO: Before me! Look where she comes.

---

hornèd man, cuckold. **yoked,** married. **unproper,** not
exclusively their own. **peculiar,** exclusively their own.
secure, free from suspicion. **patient list,** within the
bounds of patience. **ecstasy,** trance. **encave,** conceal.
fleers, sneers. **cope,** meet. **all ... spleen,** completely
overcome by emotion. **huswife,** hussy.

---

unbookish, uninstructed. **conster,** construe. **addition,** title (of lieutenant). **caitiff,** wretch. **customer,** prostitute. **scored,** beaten. **bauble,** plaything.

CASSIO: 'Tis such another fitchew!° marry, a perfumed one. What do you mean by this haunting
of me?

BIANCA: Let the devil and his dam haunt you! What
did you mean by that same handkerchief you
gave me even now? I was a fine fool to take it. I
must take out the whole work? A likely piece of
work that you should find it in your chamber
180   and know not who left it there! This is some
minx's token, and I must take out the work?
There! Give it your hobby-horse.° Wheresoever
you had it, I'll take out no work on't.

CASSIO: How now, my sweet Bianca? How now? how
now?

OTHELLO: By heaven, that should be my handkerchief!

BIANCA: An you'll come to supper to-night, you may;
an you will not, come when you are next pre-
190   pared for. (Exit.)

IAGO: After her, after her!

CASSIO: Faith, I must; she'll rail i' th' street else.

IAGO: Will you sup there?

CASSIO: Yes, I intend so.

IAGO: Well, I may chance to see you; for I would very
fain speak with you.

CASSIO: Prithee come. Will you?

IAGO: Go to! say no more.

(Exit CASSIO.)

OTHELLO (comes forward): How shall I murder him,
200   Iago?

IAGO: Did you perceive how he laughed at his vice?

OTHELLO: O Iago!

IAGO: And did you see the handkerchief?

OTHELLO: Was that mine?

IAGO: Yours, by this hand! And to see how he prizes
the foolish woman your wife! She gave it him,
and he hath giv'n it his whore.

OTHELLO: I would have him nine years a-killing!—A
fine woman! a fair woman! a sweet woman!

210   IAGO: Nay, you must forget that.

OTHELLO: Ay, let her rot, and perish, and be damned
to-night; for she shall not live. No, my heart is
turned to stone; I strike it, and it hurts my hand.
O, the world hath not a sweeter creature! She
might lie by an emperor's side and command
him tasks.

IAGO: Nay, that's not your way.

OTHELLO: Hang her! I do but say what she is. So delicate with her needle! an admirable musician! O
220   she will sing the savageness out of a bear! Of so
high and plenteous wit and invention—

IAGO: She's the worse for all this.

OTHELLO: O, a thousand thousand times! And then,
of so gentle° a condition!

IAGO: Ay, too gentle.°

OTHELLO: Nay, that's certain. But yet the pity of it,
Iago! O Iago, the pity of it, Iago!

IAGO: If you are so fond over her iniquity, give her
patent° to offend; for if it touch not you, it comes
near nobody.   230

OTHELLO: I will chop her into messes! Cuckold me!

IAGO: O, 'tis foul in her.

OTHELLO: With mine officer!

IAGO: That's fouler.

OTHELLO: Get me some poison, Iago, this night. I'll
not expostulate with her, lest her body and
beauty unprovide ° my mind again. This night,
Iago!

IAGO: Do it not with poison. Strangle her in her bed,
even the bed she hath contaminated.   240

OTHELLO: Good, good! The justice of it pleases. Very
good!

IAGO: And for Cassio, let me be his undertaker: you
shall hear more by midnight.

OTHELLO: Excellent good! (A trumpet.)
What trumpet is that same?

IAGO: Something from Venice, sure.

(Enter LODOVICO, DESDEMONA, and ATTENDANTS.)

'Tis Lodovico,
Come from the duke; and see, your wife is with
him.   250

LODOVICO: God save you, worthy general!

OTHELLO: With all my heart, sir.

LODOVICO: The duke and senators of Venice greet
you (Gives him a letter.)

OTHELLO: I kiss the instrument of their pleasures.

(Opens the letter and reads.)

DESDEMONA: And what's the news, good cousin
Lodovico?

IAGO: I am very glad to see you, signior.
Welcome to Cyprus.

LODOVICO: I thank you. How does Lieutenant Cassio?   260

IAGO: Lives, sir.

DESDEMONA: Cousin, there's fall'n between him and
my lord
An unkind breach; but you shall make all well.

OTHELLO: Are you sure of that?

DESDEMONA: My lord?

OTHELLO (reads): 'This fail you not to do, as you
will—'

LODOVICO: He did not call; he's busy in the paper.
Is there division 'twixt thy lord and Cassio?   270

DESDEMONA: A most unhappy one. I would do much
T' atone° them, for the love I bear to Cassio.

OTHELLO: Fire and brimstone!

DESDEMONA: My lord?

OTHELLO: Are you wise?

---

fitchew, polecat; slang term for a whore.   **hobbyhorse,**
harlot.   *gentle,* nobly born and bred.

gentle, generous.   **patent,** license.   **unprovide,** unset-
tle.   *T' atone,* to reconcile.

DESDEMONA: What, is he angry?
LODOVICO: May be the letter moved him;
   For, as I think, they do command him home,
   Deputing Cassio in his government.
280 DESDEMONA: By my troth, I am glad on't.
OTHELLO: Indeed?
DESDEMONA: My lord?
OTHELLO: I am glad to see you mad.
DESDEMONA: Why, sweet Othello—
OTHELLO: Devil! *(Strikes her.)*
DESDEMONA: I have not deserved this.
LODOVICO: My lord, this would not be believed in
    Venice,
   Though I should swear I saw't. 'Tis very much.
290   Make her amends; she weeps.
OTHELLO: O devil, devil!
   If that the earth could teem with° woman's tears,
   Each drop she falls would prove a crocodile.
   Out of my sight!
DESDEMONA: I will not stay to offend you. *(Going.)*
LODOVICO: Truly, an obedient lady.
   I do beseech your lordship call her back.
OTHELLO: Mistress!
DESDEMONA: My lord?
300 OTHELLO: What would you with her, sir?
LODOVICO: Who? I, my lord?
OTHELLO: Ay! You did wish that I would make her
    turn.
   Sir, she can turn, and turn, and yet go on
   And turn again; and she can weep, sir, weep;
   And she's obedient; as you say, obedient,
   Very obedient.—Proceed you in your tears.—
   Concerning this, sir—O well-painted passion!—
   I am commanded home.—Get you away;
310   I'll send for you anon.—Sir, I obey the mandate
   And will return to Venice.—Hence, avaunt!

   (Exit DESDEMONA.*)*

   Cassio shall have my place. And, sir, to-night
   I do entreat that we may sup together.
   You are welcome, sir, to Cyprus—Goats and
    monkeys! *(Exit.)*
LODOVICO: Is this the noble Moor whom our full
    Senate
   Call all in all sufficient? Is this the nature
   Whom passion could not shake? whose solid virtue
320   The shot of accident nor dart of chance
   Could neither graze nor pierce?
IAGO: He is much changed.
LODOVICO: Are his wits safe? Is he not light of brain?
IAGO: He's that he is; I may not breathe my censure.
   What he might be (if what he might, he is not)
   I would to heaven he were!
LODOVICO: What, strike his wife?
IAGO: Faith, that was not so well; yet would I knew
   That stroke would prove the worst!

teem with, be made pregnant by.

LODOVICO: Is it his use?°   330
   Or did the letter work upon his blood
   And new-create this fault?
IAGO: Alas, alas!
   It is not honesty in me to speak
   What I have seen and known. You shall observe
    him,
   And his own courses will denote him so
   That I may save my speech. Do but go after
   And mark how he continues.
LODOVICO: I am sorry that I am deceived in him.   340
   (Exeunt.)

ACT 4 / SCENE 2

(Enter OTHELLO *and* EMILIA.*)*

OTHELLO: You have seen nothing then?
EMILIA: Nor ever heard, nor ever did suspect.
OTHELLO: Yes, you have seen Cassio and she
    together.
EMILIA: But then I saw no harm, and then I heard
   Each syllable that breath made up between them.
OTHELLO: What, did they never whisper?
EMILIA: Never, my lord.
OTHELLO: Nor send you out o' th' way?
EMILIA: Never.   10
OTHELLO: To fetch her fan, her gloves, her mask, nor
    nothing?
EMILIA: Never, my lord.
OTHELLO: That's strange.
EMILIA: I durst, my lord, to wager she is honest,
   Lay down my soul at stake. If you think other,
   Remove your thought; it doth abuse your bosom.
   If any wretch have put this in your head,
   Let heaven requite it with the serpent's curse!
   For if she be not honest, chaste, and true,   20
   There's no man happy; the purest of their wives
   Is foul as slander.
OTHELLO: Bid her come hither. Go.

   (Exit EMILIA.*)*

   She says enough; yet she's a simple bawd
   That cannot say as much. This is a subtle whore,
   A closet lock and key of villainous secrets;
   And yet she'll kneel and pray; I have seen her do't.

   (Enter DESDEMONA *and* EMILIA.*)*

DESDEMONA: My lord, what is your will?
OTHELLO: Pray, chuck, come hither.
DESDEMONA: What is your pleasure?   30
OTHELLO: Let me see your eyes.
   Look in my face.
DESDEMONA: What horrible fancy's this?
OTHELLO *(to* EMILIA*)*: Some of your function,°
    mistress.

    use, habit. **function,** go about your business; i.e.,
perform your function as the madam of a brothel.

Leave procreants alone and shut the door;
Cough or cry hem if anybody come.
Your mystery,° your mystery! Nay, dispatch!

(Exit EMILIA.)

DESDEMONA: Upon my knees, what doth your speech
40   import?
I understand a fury in your words,
But not the words.
OTHELLO: Why, what art thou?
DESDEMONA: Your wife, my lord; your true
And loyal wife.
OTHELLO: Come, swear it, damn thyself;
Lest, being like one of heaven, the devils
themselves
Should fear to seize thee. Therefore be
50   double-damned—
Swear thou art honest.
DESDEMONA: Heaven doth truly know it.
OTHELLO: Heaven truly knows that thou art false as
hell.
DESDEMONA: To whom, my lord? With whom? How
am I false?
OTHELLO: Ah, Desdemon! away! away! away!
DESDEMONA: Alas the heavy day! Why do you weep?
Am I the motive° of these tears, my lord?
60   If haply you my father do suspect
An instrument of this your calling back,
Lay not your blame on me. If you have lost him,
Why, I have lost him too.
OTHELLO: Had it pleased heaven
To try me with affliction, had they rained
All kinds of sores and shames on my bare head,
Steeped me in poverty to the very lips,
Given to captivity me and my utmost hopes,
I should have found in some place of my soul
70   A drop of patience. But, alas, to make me
A fixèd figure for the time of scorn°
To point his slow unmoving finger at!
Yet could I bear that too; well, very well.
But there where I have garnered up my heart,
Where either I must live or bear no life,
The fountain from the which my current runs
Or else dries up—to be discarded thence,
Or keep it as a cistern for foul toads
To knot and gender in—turn thy complexion
80   there,°
Patience, thou young and rose-lipped cherubin!
Ay, there look grim as hell!
DESDEMONA: I hope my noble lord esteems me
honest.
OTHELLO: O, ay; as summer flies are in the shambles,°
That quicken even with blowing.° O thou weed,

Who art so lovely fair, and smell'st so sweet,
That the sense aches at thee, would thou hadst
ne'er been born!
DESDEMONA: Alas, what ignorant sin have I   90
committed?
OTHELLO: Was this fair paper, this most goodly book,
Made to write 'whore' upon? What committed?
Committed? O thou public commoner!°
I should make very forges of my cheeks
That would to cinders burn up modesty,
Did I but speak thy deeds. What committed?
Heaven stops the nose at it, and the moon winks;°
The bawdy wind, that kisses all it meets,
Is hushed within the hollow mine of earth   100
And will not hear it. What committed?
Impudent strumpet!
DESDEMONA: By heaven, you do me wrong!
OTHELLO: Are not you a strumpet?
DESDEMONA: No, as I am a Christian!
If to preserve this vessel for my lord
From any other foul unlawful touch
Be not to be a strumpet, I am none.
OTHELLO: What, not a whore?
DESDEMONA: No, as I shall be saved!   110
OTHELLO: Is't possible?
DESDEMONA: O, heaven forgive us!
OTHELLO: I cry you mercy° then.
I took you for that cunning whore of Venice
That married with Othello.—*(Calling.)* You,
mistress,
That have the office opposite to Saint Peter
And keep the gate of hell!

(Enter EMILIA.)

You, you, ay, you!
We have done our course; there's money for your   120
pains:
I pray you turn the key, and keep our counsel.
(Exit.)
EMILIA: Alas, what does this gentleman conceive?
How do you, madam? How do you, my good lady?
DESDEMONA: Faith, half asleep.
EMILIA: Good madam, what's the matter with my
lord?
DESDEMONA: With who?
EMILIA: Why, with my lord, madam.
DESDEMONA: Who is thy lord?   130
EMILIA: He that is yours, sweet lady.
DESDEMONA: I have none. Do not talk to me, Emilia
I cannot weep; nor answer have I none
But what should go by water.° Prithee to-night
Lay on my bed my wedding sheets, remember;
And call thy husband hither.
EMILIA: Here's a change indeed! *(Exit.)*
DESDEMONA: 'Tis meet I should be used so, very meet.

---

mystery, trade. **motive,** cause. **scorn,** scornful world.
turn . . . there, change your color at that point. **shambles,**
slaughterhouses. **quicken . . . blowing,** come to life as soon
as their eggs are deposited.

---

public commoner, whore. **winks,** closes her eyes. **cry
you mercy,** beg your pardon. **water,** tears.

How have I been behaved, that he might stick
140   The small'st opinion° on my least misuse?°

(Enter IAGO and EMILIA.)

IAGO: What is your pleasure, madam? How is't with
    you?
DESDEMONA: I cannot tell. Those that do teach young
    babes
    Do it with gentle means and easy tasks:
    He might have chid me so; for, in good faith,
    I am a child to chiding.
IAGO: What is the matter, lady?
EMILIA: Alas, Iago, my lord hath so bewhored her,
150   Thrown such despite and heavy terms upon her
    As true hearts cannot bear.
DESDEMONA: Am I that name, Iago?
IAGO: What name, fair lady?
DESDEMONA: Such as she says my lord did say I was.
EMILIA: He called her whore. A beggar in his drink
    Could not have laid such terms upon his callet.°
IAGO: Why did he so?
DESDEMONA: I do not know; I am sure I am none
    such.
160   IAGO: Do not weep, do not weep. Alas the day!
EMILIA: Hath she forsook so many noble matches,
    Her father and her country, all her friends,
    To be called whore? Would it not make one weep?
DESDEMONA: It is my wretched fortune.
IAGO: Beshrew him for't!
    How comes this trick° upon him?
DESDEMONA: Nay, heaven doth know.
EMILIA: I will be hanged if some eternal villain,
    Some busy and insinuating rogue,
170   Some cogging,° cozening slave, to get some office,
    Have not devised this slander. I'll be hanged else.
IAGO: Fie, there is no such man! It is impossible.
DESDEMONA: If any such there be, heaven pardon
    him!
EMILIA: A halter pardon him! and hell gnaw his
    bones!
    Why should he call her whore? Who keeps her
    company?
    What place? what time? what form? what
180   likelihood?
    The Moor's abused by some most villainous knave,
    Some base notorious knave, some scurvy fellow.
    O heaven, that such companions thou'dst unfold,°
    And put in every honest hand a whip
    To lash the rascals naked through the world
    Even from the east to th' west!
IAGO: Speak within door.°
EMILIA: O fie upon them! Some such squire he was
    That turned your wit with the seamy side without
190   And made you to suspect me with the Moor.

IAGO: You are a fool. Go to.
DESDEMONA: O good Iago,
    What shall I do to win my lord again?
    Good friend, go to him; for, by this light of heaven,
    I know not how I lost him. Here I kneel:
    If e'er my will did trespass 'gainst his love
    Either in discourse of thought or actual deed,
    Or that mine eyes, mine ears, or any sense
    Delighted them in any other form,
    Or that I do not yet, and ever did,   200
    And ever will (though he do shake me off
    To beggarly divorcement) love him dearly,
    Comfort forswear° me! Unkindness may do much;
    And his unkindness may defeat my life,
    But never taint my love. I cannot say "whore."
    It doth abhor me now I speak the word;
    To do the act that might th' addition earn
    Not the world's mass of vanity could make me.
IAGO: I pray you be content. 'Tis but his humor.
    The business of the state does him offense,   210
    And he does chide with you.
DESDEMONA: If 'twere no other—
IAGO: 'Tis but so, I warrant.

(Trumpets within.)

    Hark how these instruments summon you to
    supper.
    The messengers of Venice stay the meal.°
    Go in, and weep not. All things shall be well.

(Exeunt DESDEMONA and EMILIA.)
(Enter RODERIGO.)

    How now, Roderigo?
RODERIGO: I do not find that thou deal'st justly with
    me.   220
IAGO: What in the contrary?
RODERIGO: Every day thou daff'st me° with some de-
    vice, Iago, and rather, as it seems to me now,
    keep'st from me all conveniency° than suppliest
    me with the least advantage of hope. I will in-
    deed no longer endure it; nor am I yet per-
    suaded to put up in peace what already I have
    foolishly suffered.
IAGO: Will you hear me, Roderigo?
RODERIGO: Faith, I have heard too much; for your   230
    words and performance are no kin together.
IAGO: You charge me most unjustly.
RODERIGO: With naught but truth. I have wasted my-
    self out of means. The jewels you have had from
    me to deliver to Desdemona would half have
    corrupted a votarist.° You have told me she hath
    received them, and returned me expectations
    and comforts of sudden respect and acquaint-
    ance; but I find none.

---

opinion, suspicion. *misuse,* slightest misconduct. *callet,* whore. *trick,* strange behavior. *cogging,* cheating.
unfold, expose. *within door,* quietly.

Comfort forswear, happiness forsake. *stay the meal,*
wait to eat. *daff'st me,* put me off. *conveniency,* opportunities (to meet with Desdemona). *votarist,* nun.

240   IAGO: Well, go to; very well.
      RODERIGO: Very well! go to! I cannot go to, man; nor
         'tis not very well. By this hand, I say 'tis very
         scurvy, and begin to find myself fopped° in it.
      IAGO: Very well.
      RODERIGO: I tell you 'tis not very well. I will make
         myself known to Desdemona. If she will return
         me my jewels, I will give over my suit and repent
         my unlawful solicitation; if not, assure yourself I
         will seek satisfaction of you.
250   IAGO: You have said now.
      RODERIGO: Ay, and said nothing but what I protest
         intendment of doing.
      IAGO: Why, now I see there's mettle in thee; and even
         from this instant do build on thee a better opin-
         ion than ever before. Give me thy hand,
         Roderigo. Thou hast taken against me a most
         just exception; but yet I protest I have dealt most
         directly in thy affair.
      RODERIGO: It hath not appeared.
260   IAGO: I grant indeed it hath not appeared, and your
         suspicion is not without wit and judgment. But,
         Roderigo, if thou hast that in thee indeed which
         I have greater reason to believe now than ever, I
         mean purpose, courage, and valor, this night
         show it. If thou the next night following enjoy
         not Desdemona, take me from this world with
         treachery and devise engines for° my life.
      RODERIGO: Well, what is it? Is it within reason and
         compass?
270   IAGO: Sir, there is especial commission come from
         Venice to depute Cassio in Othello's place.
      RODERIGO: Is that true? Why, then Othello and
         Desdemona return again to Venice.
      IAGO: O, no; he goes into Mauritania and takes away
         with him the fair Desdemona, unless his abode
         be lingered here by some accident; wherein none
         can be so determinate° as the removing of Cas-
         sio.
      RODERIGO: How do you mean removing of him?
280   IAGO: Why, by making him uncapable of Othello's
         place—knocking out his brains.
      RODERIGO: And that you would have me to do?
      IAGO: Ay, if you dare do yourself a profit and a right.
         He sups to-night with a harlotry, and thither will
         I go to him. He knows not yet of his honorable
         fortune. If you will watch his going thence,
         which I will fashion to fall out between twelve
         and one, you may take him at your pleasure. I
         will be near to second your attempt, and he shall
290   fall between us. Come, stand not amazed at it,
         but go along with me. I will show you such a
         necessity in his death that you shall think your-
         self bound to put it on him. It is now high sup-

pertime, and the night grows to waste. About it!
      RODERIGO: I will hear further reason for this.
      IAGO: And you shall be satisfied. (*Exeunt.*)

ACT 4 / SCENE 3

(*Enter* OTHELLO, LODOVICO, DESDEMONA, EMILIA, *and*
ATTENDANTS.)

LODOVICO: I do beseech you, sir, trouble yourself no
   further.
OTHELLO: O, pardon me; 'twill do me good to walk.
LODOVICO: Madam, good night. I humbly thank your
   ladyship.
DESDEMONA: Your honor is most welcome.
OTHELLO: Will you walk, sir?
   O, Desdemona—
DESDEMONA: My lord?
OTHELLO: Get you to bed on th' instant; I will be re-   10
   turned forthwith. Dismiss your attendant there.
   Look't be done.
DESDEMONA: I will, my lord.

(*Exit* OTHELLO, *with* LODOVICO *and* ATTENDANTS.)

EMILIA: How goes it now? He looks gentler than he
   did.
DESDEMONA: He says he will return incontinent.°
   He hath commanded me to go to bed,
   And bade me to dismiss you.
EMILIA: Dismiss me?
DESDEMONA: It was his bidding; therefore, good   20
   Emilia,
   Give me my nightly wearing, and adieu.
   We must not now displease him.
EMILIA: I would you had never seen him!
DESDEMONA: So would not I. My love doth so approve
   him
   That even his stubbornness,° his checks,° his
      frowns—
   Prithee unpin me—have grace and favor in them.
EMILIA: I have laid those sheets you bade me on the   30
   bed.
DESDEMONA: All's one. Good faith, how foolish are
   our minds!
   If I do die before thee, prithee shroud me
   In one of those same sheets.
EMILIA: Come, come! You talk.
DESDEMONA: My mother had a maid called Barbary.
   She was in love; and he she loved proved mad°
   And did forsake her. She had a song of 'Willow';
   An old thing 'twas; but it expressed her fortune, 40
   And she died singing it. That song to-night
   Will not go from my mind; I have much to do
   But to go hang my head all at one side
   And sing it like poor Barbary. Prithee dispatch.

---

fopped, fooled.   *devise engines for,* plots against.   *de-
terminate,* effective.

incontinent, immediately.   *stubbornness,* roughness.
checks, rebukes.   *mad,* untrue.

EMILIA: Shall I go fetch your nightgown?
DESDEMONA: No, unpin me here.
This Lodovico is a proper man.
EMILIA: A very handsome man.
DESDEMONA: He speaks well.
50 EMILIA: I know a lady in Venice would have walked
barefoot to Palestine for a touch of his nether lip.
DESDEMONA (*sings*):

> The poor soul sat sighing by a sycamore tree,
>   Sing all a green willow;
> Her hand on her bosom, her head on her knee,
>   Sing willow, willow, willow.
> The fresh streams ran by her and murmured her
>   moans;
>   Sing willow, willow, willow;
60 Her salt tears fell from her, and soft'ned the stones—

Lay by these.

> Sing willow, willow, willow—

Prithee hie thee; he'll come anon.

> Sing all a green willow must be my garland.
> Let nobody blame him; his scorn I approve—

Nay, that's not next. Hark! who is't that knocks?
EMILIA: It is the wind.
DESDEMONA (*sings*):

> I called my love false love; but what said he then?
>   Sing willow, willow, willow:
70 If I court moe women, you'll couch with moe men.

So, get thee gone; good night. Mine eyes do itch.
Doth that bode weeping?
EMILIA: 'Tis neither here nor there.
DESDEMONA: I have heard it said so. O, these men,
these men!
Dost thou in conscience think—tell me, Emilia—
That there be women do abuse their husbands
In such gross kind?
80 EMILIA: There be some such, no question.
DESDEMONA: Wouldst thou do such a deed for all the
world?
EMILIA: Why, would not you?
DESDEMONA: No, by this heavenly light!
EMILIA: Nor I neither by this heavenly light.
I might do't as well i' th' dark.
DESDEMONA: Wouldst thou do such a deed for all the
world?
EMILIA: The world's a huge thing; it is a great price
90 for a small vice.
DESDEMONA: Good troth, I think thou wouldst not.
EMILIA: By my troth, I think I should; and undo't
when I had done it. Marry, I would not do such a
thing for a joint-ring,° nor for measures of lawn,°

---

joint-ring, cheap ring.   *lawn,* fine linen.

nor for gowns, petticoats, nor caps, nor any petty
exhibition;° but, for all the whole world—'Ud's
pity! who would not make her husband a cuckold to make him a monarch? I should venture
purgatory for't.
DESDEMONA: Beshrew me if I would do such a wrong   100
For the whole world.
EMILIA: Why, the wrong is but a wrong i' th' world;
and having the world for your labor, 'tis a wrong
in your own world, and you might quickly make
it right.
DESDEMONA: I do not think there is any such woman.
EMILIA: Yes, a dozen; and as many to the vantage° as
would store° the world they played for.
But I do think it is their husbands' faults
If wives do fall. Say that they slack their duties   110
And pour our treasures into foreign laps;
Or else break out in peevish jealousies,
Throwing restraint upon us; or say they strike us,
Or scant our former having° in despite°—
Why, we have galls;° and though we have some
grace,
Yet have we some revenge. Let husbands know
Their wives have sense like them. They see, and
smell,
And have their palates both for sweet and sour,   120
As husbands have. What is it that they do
When they change us for others? Is it sport?
I think it is. And doth affection breed it?
I think it doth. Is't frailty that thus errs?
It is so too. And have not we affections,
Desires for sport, and frailty, as men have?
Then let them use us well; else let them know,
The ills we do, their ills instruct us so.
DESDEMONA: Good night, good night. God me such
usage° send,   130
Not to pick bad from bad, but by bad mend!
(*Exeunt.*)

ACT 5 / SCENE 1

(*Enter* IAGO *and* RODERIGO.)

IAGO: Here, stand behind this bulk;° straight will he
come.
Wear thy good rapier bare, and put it home.
Quick, quick! Fear nothing; I'll be at thy elbow.
It makes us, or it mars us—think on that,
And fix most firm thy resolution.
RODERIGO: Be near at hand; I may miscarry in't.
IAGO: Here, at thy hand. Be bold, and take thy stand.
(*Stands aside.*)
RODERIGO: I have no great devotion to the deed,   10

---

petty exhibition, gift.   *vantage,* in addition.   *store,*
populate.   *having,* allowance.   *despite,* spite.   *galls,* capacity to feel resentment.   *usage,* habits.   *bulk,* projecting
store front.

10   And yet he hath given me satisfying reasons.
    'Tis but a man gone. Forth my sword! He dies!
IAGO: I have rubbed this young quat° almost to the
    sense,°
    And he grows angry. Now whether he kill Cassio,
    Or Cassio him, or each do kill the other,
    Every way makes my gain. Live Roderigo,
    He calls me to a restitution large
    Of gold and jewels that I bobbed° from him
    As gifts to Desdemona.
20   It must not be. If Cassio do remain,
    He hath a daily beauty in his life
    That makes me ugly; and besides, the Moor
    May unfold me to him; there stand I in much peril.
    No, he must die. Be't so! I hear him coming.

(Enter CASSIO.)

RODERIGO: I know his gait. 'Tis he. Villain, thou diest!
    (Makes a pass at CASSIO.)
CASSIO: That thrust had been mine enemy indeed
    But that my coat is better than thou know'st.
    I will make proof of thine. *(Draws, and wounds*
    RODERIGO.)
30 RODERIGO: O, I am slain!

    (IAGO *darts from concealment behind* CASSIO, *wounds*
    him in the leg, and exit.)

CASSIO: I am maimed for ever. Help, ho! Murder!
    murder! *(Falls.)*

(Enter OTHELLO.)

OTHELLO: The voice of Cassio. Iago keeps his word.
RODERIGO: O, villain that I am!
OTHELLO: It is even so.
CASSIO: O, help, ho! light! a surgeon!
OTHELLO: 'Tis he. O brave Iago, honest and just,
    That hast such noble sense of thy friend's wrong!
    Thou teachest me. Minion,° your dear lies dead,
40   And your unblest fate hies.° Strumpet, I come.
    Forth of my heart those charms, thine eyes, are
    blotted.
    Thy bed, lust-stained, shall with lust's blood be
    spotted. *(Exit.)*

(Enter LODOVICO *and* GRATIANO.)

CASSIO: What, ho? No watch? No passage?° Murder!
    murder!
GRATIANO: 'Tis some mischance. The cry is very
    direful.
CASSIO: O, help!
50 LODOVICO: Hark!
RODERIGO: O wretched villain!
LODOVICO: Two or three groan. It is a heavy° night.

---

    quat, pimple. **to the sense,** raw. **bobbed,** swindled.
Minion, mistress. **hies,** hurries on. **passage,** passerby.
heavy, dark.

    These may be counterfeits. Let's think't unsafe
    To come in to the cry without more help.
RODERIGO: Nobody come? Then shall I bleed to
    death.
LUDOVICO: Hark!

(Enter IAGO, *with a light.)*

GRATIANO: Here's one comes in his shirt, with light
    and weapons.
IAGO: Who's there? Whose noise is this that cries on   60
    murder?
LODOVICO: We do not know.
IAGO: Did not you hear a cry?
CASSIO: Here, here! For heaven's sake, help me!
IAGO: What's the matter?
GRATIANO: This is Othello's ancient, as I take it.
LODOVICO: The same indeed, a very valiant fellow.
IAGO: What are you here that cry so grievously?
CASSIO: Iago? O, I am spoiled, undone by villains!
    Give me some help.   70
IAGO: O me, lieutenant! What villains have done this?
CASSIO: I think that one of them is hereabout
    And I cannot make away.
IAGO: O treacherous villains!
    (to LODOVICO *and* GRATIANO*)* What are you there?
    Come in, and give some help.
RODERIGO: O, help me here!
CASSIO: That's one of them.
IAGO: O murd'rous slave! O villain! *(Stabs* RODERIGO.)
RODERIGO: O damned Iago! O inhuman dog!   80
IAGO: Kill men i' th' dark?—Where be these bloody
    thieves?—
    How silent is this town!—Ho! murder! murder!—
    What may you be? Are you of good or evil?
LODOVICO: As you shall prove us, praise us.
IAGO: Signior Lodovico?
LODIVICO: He, sir.
IAGO: I cry you mercy. Here's Cassio hurt by villains.
GRATIANO: Cassio?
IAGO: How is it, brother?   90
CASSIO: My leg is cut in two.
IAGO: Marry, heaven forbid!
    Light, gentlemen. I'll bind it with my shirt.

(Enter BIANCA.)

BIANCA: What is the matter, ho? Who is't that cried?
IAGO: Who is't that cried?
BIANCA: O my dear Cassio! my sweet Cassio!
    O Cassio, Cassio, Cassio!
IAGO: O notable strumpet!—Cassio, may you suspect
    Who they should be that thus have mangled you?
CASSIO: No.   100
GRATIANO: I am sorry to find you thus. I have been to
    seek you.
IAGO: Lend me a garter. So. O for a chair
    To bear him easily hence!
BIANCA: Alas, he faints! O Cassio, Cassio, Cassio!

IAGO: Gentlemen all, I do suspect this trash
  To be a party in this injury.—
  Patience awhile, good Cassio.—Come, come!
  Lend me a light. Know we this face or no?
110 Alas, my friend and my dear countryman
  Roderigo? No.—Yes, sure.—O heaven, Roderigo!
GRATIANO: What, of Venice?
IAGO: Even he, sir. Did you know him?
GRATIANO: Know him? Ay.
IAGO: Signior Gratiano? I cry you gentle pardon.
  These bloody accidents must excuse my manners
  That so neglected you.
GRATIANO: I am glad to see you.
IAGO: How do you, Cassio?—O, a chair, a chair!
GRATIANO: Roderigo?
120 IAGO: He, he, 'tis he! *(A chair brought in.)* O, that's well
  said;° the chair.
  Some good man bear him carefully from hence.
  I'll fetch the general's surgeon. *(to Bianca)* For you,
  mistress,
  Save you your labor.—He that lies slain here,
  Cassio,
  Was my dear friend. What malice was between
  you?
130 CASSIO: None in the world; nor do I know the man.
IAGO *(to BIANCA)*: What, look you pale?—O, bear him
  out o' th' air.

(CASSIO and RODERIGO are borne off.)

  Stay you, good gentlemen.—Look you pale,
  mistress?—
  Do you perceive the gastness° of her eye?—
  Nay, if you stare, we shall hear more anon.
  Behold her well; I pray you look upon her.
  Do you see, gentlemen? Nay, guiltiness will speak,
  Though tongues were out of use.

(Enter EMILIA.)

140 EMILIA: 'Las, what's the matter? What's the matter,
  husband?
IAGO: Cassio hath here been set on in the dark
  By Roderigo, and fellows that are scaped.
  He's almost slain, and Roderigo dead.
EMILIA: Alas, good gentleman! alas, good Cassio!
IAGO: This is the fruit of whoring. Prithee, Emilia,
  Go know of Cassio where he supped to-night.
  (to BIANCA) What, do you shake at that?
BIANCA: He supped at my house; but I therefore
150 shake not.
IAGO: O, did he so? I charge you go with me.
EMILIA: Fie, fie upon thee, strumpet!
BIANCA: I am no strumpet, but of life as honest
  As you that thus abuse me.
EMILIA: As I? Foh! fie upon thee!

IAGO: Kind gentlemen, let's go see poor Cassio
  dressed.
  (to BIANCA) Come, mistress, you must tell's another
  tale.
  Emilia, run you to the citadel   160
  And tell my lord and lady what hath happed.

(Exit EMILIA.)

Will you go on afore?

(Exeunt all but IAGO.)

This is the night
That either makes me or fordoes° me quite. *(Exit.)*

ACT 5 / SCENE 2

(DESDEMONA asleep in her bed. Enter OTHELLO with a light.)

OTHELLO: It is the cause,° it is the cause, my soul.
  Let me not name it to you, you chaste stars!
  It is the cause. Yet I'll not shed her blood,
  Nor scar that whiter skin of hers than snow,
  And smooth as monumental alabaster.
  Yet she must die, else she'll betray more men.
  Put out the light, and then put out the light.
  If I quench thee, thou flaming minister,
  I can again thy former light restore,
  Should I repent me; but once put out thy light, 10
  Thou cunning'st pattern of excelling nature,
  I know not where is that Promethean heat°
  That can thy light relume.° When I have plucked
  the rose,
  I cannot give it vital growth again;
  It needs must wither. I'll smell thee on the tree. *(He
  kisses her.)*
  O balmy breath, that dost almost persuade
  Justice to break her sword! One more, one more!
  Be thus when thou art dead, and I will kill thee, 20
  And love thee after. One more, and this the last!
  So sweet was ne'er so fatal. I must weep,
  But they are cruel tears. This sorrow's heavenly;
  It strikes where it doth love. She wakes.
DESDEMONA: Who's there? Othello?
OTHELLO: Ay, Desdemona.
DESDEMONA: Will you come to bed, my lord?
OTHELLO: Have you prayed to-night, Desdemona?
DESDEMONA: Ay, my lord.
OTHELLO: If you bethink yourself of any crime   30
  Unreconciled as yet to heaven and grace,
  Solicit for it straight.
DESDEMONA: Alack, my lord, what may you mean by
  that?
OTHELLO: Well, do it, and be brief; I will walk by.
  I would not kill thy unpreparèd spirit.

---

well said, well done. **gastness,** terror.

fordoes, destroys. *cause,* cause of justice. **Promethean heat,** divine fire. *relume,* rekindle.

No, heaven forfend!° I would not kill thy soul.
DESDEMONA: Talk you of killing?
OTHELLO: Ay, I do.
40 DESDEMONA: Then heaven
   Have mercy on me!
OTHELLO: Amen, with all my heart!
DESDEMONA: If you say so, I hope you will not kill me.
OTHELLO: Hum!
DESDEMONA: And yet I fear you; for you are fatal
   then
   When your eyes roll so. Why I should fear I know
   not,
   Since guiltiness I know not; but yet I feel I fear.
50 OTHELLO: Think on thy sins.
DESDEMONA: They are loves I bear to you.
OTHELLO: Ay, and for that thou diest.
DESDEMONA: That death's unnatural that kills for
   loving.
   Alas, why gnaw you so your nether lip?
   Some bloody passion shakes your very frame.
   These are portents; but yet I hope, I hope,
   They do not point on me.
OTHELLO: Peace and be still!
60 DESDEMONA: I will so. What's the matter?
OTHELLO: That handkerchief which I so loved and
   gave thee
   Thou gav'st to Cassio.
DESDEMONA: No, by my life and soul!
   Send for the man and ask him.
OTHELLO: Sweet soul, take heed,
   Take heed of perjury; thou art on thy deathbed.
DESDEMONA: Ay, but not yet to die.
OTHELLO: Yes, presently.
70 Therefore confess thee freely of thy sin;
   For to deny each article with oath
   Cannot remove nor choke the strong conception°
   That I do groan withal. Thou art to die.
DESDEMONA: Then Lord have mercy on me!
OTHELLO: I say amen.
DESDEMONA: And have you mercy too! I never did
   Offend° you in my life; never loved Cassio
   But with such general warranty of heaven
   As I might love. I never gave him token.
80 OTHELLO: By heaven, I saw my handkerchief in's
   hand!
   O perjured woman! thou dost stone° my heart,
   And mak'st me call what I intend to do
   A murder, which I thought a sacrifice.
   I saw the handkerchief.
DESDEMONA: He found it then.
   I never gave it him. Send for him hither.
   Let him confess a truth.
OTHELLO: He hath confessed.
90 DESDEMONA: What, my lord?

OTHELLO: That he hath used thee.
DESDEMONA: How? unlawfully?
OTHELLO: Ay.
DESDEMONA: He will not say so.
OTHELLO: No, his mouth is stopped.
   Honest Iago hath ta'en order for't.°
DESDEMONA: O, my fear interprets. What, is he dead?
OTHELLO: Had all his hairs been lives, my great
   revenge
   Had stomach for them all.   100
DESDEMONA: Alas, he is betrayed, and I undone!
OTHELLO: Out, strumpet! Weep'st thou for him to my
   face?
DESDEMONA: O, banish me, my lord, but kill me not!
OTHELLO: Down, strumpet!
DESDEMONA: Kill me to-morrow; let me live to-night!
OTHELLO: Nay, an you strive°—
DESDEMONA: But half an hour!
OTHELLO: Being done, there is no pause.
DESDEMONA: But while I say one prayer!   110
OTHELLO: It is too late. (Smothers her.)
DESDEMONA: O Lord, Lord, Lord!

(EMILIA at the door.)

EMILIA (calls within): My lord, my lord! What, ho, my
   lord, my lord!
OTHELLO: What noise is this? Not dead? Not yet quite
   dead?
   I that am cruel am yet merciful;
   I would not have thee linger in thy pain.
   So, so.
EMILIA (within): What, ho! my lord, my lord!   120
OTHELLO: Who's there?
EMILIA (within): O, good my lord, I would speak a
   word with you!
OTHELLO: Yes, 'tis Emilia.—By and by.—She's
   dead.—
   'Tis like she comes to speak of Cassio's death.
   The noise was here. Ha! no more moving?
   Still as the grave.—Shall she come in? Were't
   good?—
   I think she stirs again. No.—What's best to do?   130
   If she come in, she'll sure speak to my wife.
   My wife! my wife! what wife? I have no wife.
   O, insupportable! O heavy hour!
   Methinks it should be now a huge eclipse
   Of sun and moon, and that th' affrighted globe
   Should yawn° at alteration.
EMILIA (within): I do beseech you
   That I may speak with you, O good my lord!
OTHELLO: I had forgot thee. O, come in, Emilia.
   Soft, by and by.—Let me the curtains draw.—   140

(Closes the bed-curtains.)

---

forfend, forbid. conception, belief (of her being guilty). offend, wrong. stone, turn to stone.

ta'en . . . for't, take measures to bring it about. strive, struggle. yawn, open, as in an earthquake.

Where art thou?

(Opens the door.)

(Enter EMILIA.*)*

What's the matter with thee now?

EMILIA: O my good lord, yonder's foul murder done!

OTHELLO: What? Now?

EMILIA: But now, my lord.

OTHELLO: It is the very error° of the moon.
She comes more nearer earth than she was wont
And makes men mad.

EMILIA: Cassio, my lord, hath killed a young Venetian
150 Called Roderigo.

OTHELLO: Roderigo killed?
And Cassio killed?

EMILIA: No, Cassio is not killed.

OTHELLO: Not Cassio killed? Then murder's out of
tune,
And sweet revenge grows harsh.

DESDEMONA: O, falsely, falsely murdered!

EMILIA: O Lord! what cry is that?

OTHELLO: That? What?

160 EMILIA: Out and alas! that was my lady's voice.
Help! help, ho! help! O lady, speak again!
Sweet Desdemona! O sweet mistress, speak!

DESDEMONA: A guiltless death I die.

EMILIA: O, who hath done this deed?

DESDEMONA: Nobody—I myself. Farewell.
Commend me to my kind lord. O, farewell! *(She
dies.)*

OTHELLO: Why, how should she be murd'red?

EMILIA: Alas, who knows?

OTHELLO: You heard her say herself, it was not I.

170 EMILIA: She said so. I must needs report the truth.

OTHELLO: She's like a liar gone to burning hell!
'Twas I that killed her.

EMILIA: O, the more angel she,
And you the blacker devil!

OTHELLO: She turned to folly, and she was a whore.

EMILIA: Thou dost belie her, and thou art a devil.

OTHELLO: She was false as water.

EMILIA: Thou art rash as fire to say
That she was false. O, she was heavenly true!

180 OTHELLO: Cassio did top her. Ask thy husband else.
O, I were damned beneath all depth in hell
But that I did proceed upon just grounds
To this extremity. Thy husband knew it all.

EMILIA: My husband?

OTHELLO: Thy husband.

EMILIA: That she was false to wedlock?

OTHELLO: Ay, with Cassio. Nay, had she been true,
If heaven would make me such another world
Of one entire and perfect chrysolite,
190 I'ld not have sold her for it.

EMILIA: My husband?

OTHELLO: Ay, 'twas he that told me first.
An honest man he is, and hates the slime
That sticks on filthy deeds.

EMILIA: My husband?

OTHELLO: What needs this iterance?° Woman, I say
thy husband.

EMILIA: O mistress, villainy hath made mocks with
love!
My husband say that she was false?   200

OTHELLO: He, woman.
I say, thy husband. Dost understand the word?
My friend, thy husband; honest, honest, Iago.

EMILIA: If he say so, may his pernicious soul
Rot half a grain a day! he lies to th' heart.
She was too fond of her most filthy bargain.

OTHELLO: Ha!

EMILIA: Do thy worst.
This deed of thine is no more worthy heaven
Than thou wast worthy her.   210

OTHELLO: Peace, you were best.

EMILIA: Thou hast not half the power to do me harm
As I have to be hurt.° O gull! O dolt!
As ignorant as dirt! thou hast done a deed—
I care not for thy sword; I'll make thee known,
Though I lost twenty lives. Help! help! O, help!
The Moor hath killed my mistress! Murder!
murder!

(Enter MONTANO, GRATIANO, IAGO, *and* OTHERS.*)*

MONTANO: What is the matter? How now, general?

EMILIA: O, are you come, Iago? You have done well,   220
That men must lay their murders on your neck.

GRATIANO: What is the matter?

EMILIA: Disprove this villain, if thou be'st a man.
He says thou told'st him that his wife was false.
I know thou didst not; thou'rt not such a villain.
Speak, for my heart is full.

IAGO: I told him what I thought, and told no more
Than what he found himself was apt and true.

EMILIA: But did you ever tell him she was false?

IAGO: I did.   230

EMILIA: You told a lie, an odious damnèd lie!
Upon my soul, a lie! a wicked lie!
She false with Cassio? Did you say with Cassio?

IAGO: With Cassio, mistress. Go to, charm° your
tongue.

EMILIA: I will not charm my tongue; I am bound to
speak:
My mistress here lies murdered in her bed—

ALL: O heavens forfend!

EMILIA: And your reports have set the murder on.   240

OTHELLO: Nay, stare not, masters. It is true indeed.

GRATIANO: 'Tis a strange truth.

---

error, straying from its natural course.   *iterance*, repetition.   **hurt**, to endure pain.   **charm**, cast a spell on; i.e., silence.

MONTANO: O monstrous act!
EMILIA: Villainy, villainy, villainy!
   I think upon't—I think I smell't!—O villainy!
   I thought so then.—I'll kill myself for grief.—
   O villainy, villainy!
IAGO: What, are you mad? I charge you get you
   home.
250 EMILIA: Good gentlemen, let me have leave to speak.
   'Tis proper I obey him, but not now.
   Perchance, Iago, I will ne'er go home.
OTHELLO: O! O! O! *(Falls on the bed.)*
EMILIA: Nay, lay thee down and roar!
   For thou hast killed the sweetest innocent
   That e'er did lift up eye.
OTHELLO: O, she was foul! *(Rises.)*
   I scarce did know you, uncle. There lies your niece,
   Whose breath, indeed, these hands have newly
260   stopped.
   I know this act shows horrible and grim.
GRATIANO: Poor Desdemon! I am glad thy father's
   dead.
   Thy match was mortal to him, and pure grief
   Shore° his old thread in twain. Did he live now,
   This sight would make him do a desperate turn;°
   Yea, curse his better angel from his side,
   And fall to reprobation.°
OTHELLO: 'Tis pitiful; but yet Iago knows
270   That she with Cassio hath the act of shame
   A thousand times committed. Cassio confessed it;
   And she did gratify his amorous works
   With the recognizance and pledge of love
   Which I first gave her. I saw it in his hand.
   It was a handkerchief, an antique token
   My father gave my mother.
EMILIA: O God! O heavenly God!
IAGO: Zounds, hold your peace!
EMILIA: 'Twill out, 'twill out! I peace?
280   No, I will speak as liberal° as the north.°
   Let heaven and men and devils, let them all,
   All, all, cry shame against me, yet I'll speak.
IAGO: Be wise, and get you home.
EMILIA: I will not.

(IAGO draws and threatens EMILIA.)

GRATIANO: Fie!
   Your sword upon a woman?
EMILIA: O thou dull Moor, that handkerchief thou
   speak'st of
   I found by fortune, and did give my husband;
290   For often with a solemn earnestness—
   More than indeed belonged to such a trifle—
   He begged of me to steal't.
IAGO: Villainous whore!

EMILIA: She give it Cassio? No, alas, I found it,
   And I did give't my husband.
IAGO: Filth, thou liest!
EMILIA: By heaven, I do not, I do not, gentlemen.
   O murd'rous coxcomb! what should such a fool
   Do with so good a wife?
OTHELLO: Are there no stones° in heaven   300
   But what serves for the thunder? Precious villain!

(The MOOR runs at IAGO, but is disarmed by MONTANO. IAGO kills his wife.)

GRATIANO: The woman falls. Sure he hath killed his
   wife.

(Exit IAGO.)

EMILIA: Ay, ay. O, lay me by my mistress' side.
GRATIANO: He's gone, but his wife's killed.
MONTANO: 'Tis a notorious villain. Take you this
   weapon,
   Which I have here recovered from the Moor.
   Come, guard the door without, Let him not pass,
   But kill him rather. I'll after the same villain,   310
   For 'tis a damnèd slave.

(Exit MONTANO, with all but OTHELLO and EMILIA.)

OTHELLO: I am not valiant neither;
   But every puny whipster° gets my sword.
   But why should honor outlive honesty?
   Let it go all.
EMILIA: What did thy song bode, lady?
   Hark, canst thou hear me? I will play the swan,
   And die in music *(sings)* 'Willow, willow, willow.'
   Moor, she was chaste. She loved thee, cruel Moor:
   So come my soul to bliss as I speak true.   320
   So speaking as I think, I die, I die. *(She dies.)*
OTHELLO: I have another weapon in this chamber;
   It is a sword of Spain, the Isebrook's° temper.
   O, here it is.—Uncle, I must come forth.
GRATIANO *(within)*: If thou attempt it, it will cost thee
   dear.
   Thou hast no weapon, and perforce must suffer.
OTHELLO: Look in upon me then and speak with me,
   Or, naked° as I am, I will assault thee.

(Enter GRATIANO.)

GRATIANO: What is the matter?   330
OTHELLO: Behold, I have a weapon;
   A better never did itself sustain
   Upon a soldier's thigh. I have seen the day
   That with this little arm and this good sword
   I have made my way through more impediments
   Than twenty times your stop.° But O vain boast!
   Who can control his fate? 'Tis not so now.

Shore, cut. *turn*, deed. *reprobation*, be rejected by
God. *liberal*, unrestrainedly. *north*, blowing of the north
wind.

stones, thunderbolts. *whipster*, top-whipping boy.
Isebrook, Innsbruck, where the finest steel blades of the time
were forged. *naked*, unarmed. *stop*, power to stop.

Be not afraid, though you do see me weaponed.
Here is my journey's end, here is my butt,°
340 And very seamark° of my utmost sail.
Do you go back dismayed? 'Tis a lost° fear.
Man but a rush° against Othello's breast,
And he retires. Where should Othello go?
Now, how dost thou look now? O ill-starred wench!
Pale as thy smock! When we shall meet at compt,°
This look of thine will hurl my soul from heaven,
And fiends will snatch at it. Cold, cold, my girl?
Even like thy chastity.
O cursèd, cursèd slave! Whip me, ye devils,
350 From the possession of this heavenly sight!
Blow me about in the winds! roast me in sulphur!
Wash me in steep-down gulfs of liquid fire!
O Desdemona, Desdemona! dead!
O! O! O!

(Enter LODOVICO, MONTANO, IAGO *as prisoner, and* OF-
FICERS; CASSIO *in a chair.)*

LODOVICO: Where is this rash and most unfortunate
man?
OTHELLO: That's he that was Othello. Here I am.
LODOVICO: Where is that viper? Bring the villain
forth.
360 OTHELLO: I look down towards his feet°—but that's a
fable.
If that thou be'st a devil, I cannot kill thee.

(Wounds IAGO.)

LODOVICO: Wrench his sword from him.

*(*OTHELLO *is disarmed.)*

IAGO: I bleed, sir, but not killed.
OTHELLO: I am not sorry neither. I'd have thee live;
For in my sense, 'tis happiness to die.
LODOVICO: O thou Othello that wert once so good,
Fall'n in the practice° of a damnèd slave,
What shall be said to thee?
370 OTHELLO: Why, anything:
An honorable murderer, if you will;
For naught did I in hate, but all in honor.
LODOVICO: This wretch hath part confessed his
villainy.
Did you and he consent in Cassio's death?
OTHELLO: Ay.
CASSIO: Dear general, I never gave you cause.
OTHELLO: I do believe it, and I ask your pardon.
Will you, I pray, demand that demi-devil
380 Why he hath thus ensnared my soul and body?
IAGO: Demand me nothing. What you know, you
know.

---

butt, limit. *seamark,* beacon. *lost,* wasted. *man . . .
rush,* wield a mere reed. *compt,* final accounting; i.e., Day
of Judgment. *I . . . feet,* to see if they are cloven, as the
Devil's feet were believed to be. *practice,* plot.

From this time forth I never will speak word.
LODOVICO: What, not to pray?
GRATIANO: Torments will ope your lips.
OTHELLO: Well, thou dost best.
LODOVICO: Sir, you shall understand what hath
befall'n,
Which, as I think, you know not. Here is a letter
Found in the pocket of the slain Roderigo;   390
And here another. The one of them imports
The death of Cassio to be undertook
By Roderigo.
OTHELLO: O villain!
CASSIO: Most heathenish and most gross!
LODOVICO: Now here's another discontented paper
Found in his pocket too; and this, it seems,
Roderigo meant t' have sent this damnèd villain;
But that, belike, Iago in the nick°
Came in and satisfied him.   400
OTHELLO: O thou pernicious caitiff!—
How came you, Cassio, by that handkerchief
That was my wife's?
CASSIO: I found it in my chamber;
And he himself confessed but even now
That there he dropped it for a special purpose
Which wrought to his desire.
OTHELLO: O fool! fool! fool!
CASSIO: There is besides in Roderigo's letter,
How he upbraids Iago that he made him   410
Brave° me upon the watch; whereon it came
That I was cast;° and even but now he spake,
After long seeming dead—Iago hurt him,
Iago set him on.
LODOVICO: You must forsake this room and go with
us.
Your power and your command is taken off,
And Cassio rules in Cyprus. For this slave,
If there be any cunning cruelty
That can torment him much and hold him long,   420
It shall be his. You shall close prisoner rest
Till the nature of your fault be known
To the Venetian state. Come, bring away.
OTHELLO: Soft you! a word or two before you go.
I have done the state some service, and they know't.
No more of that. I pray you, in your letters,
When you shall these unlucky deeds relate,
Speak of me as I am. Nothing extenuate,
Nor set down aught in malice. Then must you
speak   430
Of one that loved not wisely, but too well;
Of one not easily jealous, but being, wrought,
Perplexed° in the extreme; of one whose hand,
Like the base Indian, threw a pearl away
Richer than all his tribe; of one whose subdued
eyes.

---

nick, nick of time. *Brave,* defy. *cast,* dismissed.
Perplexed, distraught.

Albeit unusèd to the melting mood,
Drop tears as fast as the Arabian trees
Their med'cinable gum. Set you down this.
440 And say besides that in Aleppo once,
Where a malignant and a turbaned Turk
Beat a Venetian and traduced the state,
I took by th' throat the circumcisèd dog
And smote him—thus. *(He stabs himself.)*
LODOVICO: O bloody period!°
GRATIANO: All that's spoke is marred.
OTHELLO: I kissed thee ere I killed thee. No way but
this,
Killing myself, to die upon a kiss. *(He falls upon the
bed and dies.)*
450 CASSIO: This did I fear, but thought he had no
weapon;

---

period, ending.

For he was great of heart.
LODOVICO *(to* IAGO*)*: O Spartan dog,°
More fell° than anguish, hunger, or the sea!
Look on the tragic loading of this bed.
This is thy work. The object° poisons sight;
Let it be hid. Gratiano, keep the house,
And seize upon° the fortunes of the Moor,
For they succeed on you. To you, lord governor,
Remains the censure° of this hellish villain,   460
The time, the place, the torture. O enforce it!
Myself will straight abroad, and to the state
This heavy act with heavy heart relate. *(Exeunt.)*

Spartan dog, type of bloodhound, noted for its silence
and relentlessness. **fell,** cruel. **object,** spectacle. **seize
upon,** take possession. **censure,** legal sentencing.

Figure 28. The single set for the National Theatre production of *Othello,* directed by John Dexter, London, 1964. The three-part design of the set echoes the structural design at the back of the renaissance English stage, illustrated in Figure 25. (Photograph: Angus McBean, Harvard Theatre Collection.)

Figure 29. Othello (Laurence Olivier) and Iago (Frank Finlay) in the National Theatre production of *Othello,* directed by John Dexter, London, 1964. (Photograph: Angus McBean, Harvard Theatre Collection.)

Figure 30. Othello (Laurence Olivier) and Desdemona (Maggie Smith) in the National Theatre production of *Othello,* directed by John Dexter, London, 1964. (Photograph: Angus McBean, Harvard Theatre Collection.)

Figure 31. Othello (Laurence Olivier) hugs the dead body of Desdemona (Maggie Smith) as he gives his final speech in the National Theatre production of *Othello,* directed by John Dexter London, 1964. (Photograh: Angus McBean, Harvard Theatre Collection.)

Staging of *Othello*

**REVIEW OF THE NATIONAL THEATRE
PRODUCTION, 1964, BY RONALD BRYDEN**

All posterity will want to know is how he played. John Dexter's National Theatre *Othello* is efficient and clear, if slow, and contains some intelligent minor novelties. But in the long run all that matters is that it left the stage as bare as possible for its athlete. What requires record is how he, tackling Burbage's role for the first time at 57, created the Moor.

He came on smelling a rose, laughing softly with a private delight; barefooted, ankleted, black. He had chosen to play a Negro. The story fits a true Moor better: one of those striding hawks, fierce in a narrow range of medieval passions, whose women still veil themselves like Henry Moore sleepers against the blowing sands of Nouakchott's surrealistically modern streets. But Shakespeare muddled, giving him the excuse to turn himself into a coastal African from below the Senegal: dark, thick-lipped, open, laughing.

He sauntered downstage, with a loose, bare-heeled roll of the buttocks; came to rest feet splayed apart, hip lounging outward. For him, the great Richard III of his day, the part was too simple. He had made it difficult and interesting for himself by studying, as scrupulously as he studied the flat vowels, dead grin and hunched time-steps of Archie Rice, how an African looks, moves, sounds. The make-up, exact in pigment, covered his body almost wholly: an hour's job at least. The hands hung big and graceful. The whole voice was characterised, the o's and the a's deepened, the consonants thickened with faint, guttural deliberation. 'Put up your bright swords, or de dew will rus' dem': not quite so crude, but in that direction.

It could have been caricature, an embarrassment. Instead, after the second performance, a well-known Negro actor rose in the stalls bravoing. For obviously it was done with love; with the main purpose of substituting for the dead grandeur of the Moorish empire one modern audiences could respond to: the grandeur of Africa. He was the continent, like a figure of Rubens allegory. In Cyprus, he strode ashore in a cloak and spiked helmet which brought to mind the medieval emirates of Ethiopia and Niger. Facing Doge and senators, he hooded his eyes in a pouting ebony mask: an old chief listening watchfully in tribal conclave. When he named them 'my masters' it was proudly edged: he had been a slave, their inquisition recalled his slavery, he reminded them in turn of his service and generalship.

He described Desdemona's encouragement smiling down at them, easy with sexual confidence. This was the other key to the choice of a Negro: Finlay's Iago, bony, crop-haired, staring with the fanatic mule-grin of a Mississippi redneck, was to be goaded by a small white man's sexual jealousy of the black, a jealousy sliding into ambiguous fascination. Like Yeats's crowd staring, sweating, at Don Juan's mighty thigh, this Iago gazed, licking dry lips, on a black one. All he need do is teach his own disease.

Mannerisms established, they were lifted into the older, broader imagery of the part. Leading Desdemona to bed, he pretended to snap at her with playful teeth. At Iago's first hints, he made a chuckling mock of twisting truth out of him by the ear. Then, during the temptation, he began to pace, turning his head sharply like a lion listening. The climax was his farewell to his occupation: bellowing the words as pure, wounded outcry, he hurled back his head until the ululating tongue showed pink against the roof of his mouth like a trumpeting elephant's. As he grew into a great beast, Finlay shrunk beside him, clinging to his shoulder like an ape, hugging his heels like a jackal.

He used every clue in the part, its most strenuous difficulties. Reassured by Desdemona's innocence, he bent to kiss her—and paused looking, sickened, at her lips. Long before his raging return, you knew he had found Cassio's kisses there. Faced with the lung-torturing hurdle of 'Like to the Pontic sea', he found a brilliant device for breaking the period: at 'Shall ne'er look back', he let the memories he was forswearing rush in and stop him, gasping with pain, until he caught breath. Then, at 'By yond marble heaven', he tore the crucifix from his neck (Iago, you recall, says casually Othello'd renounce his baptism for Desdemona) and, crouching forehead to ground, made his 'sacred vow' in the religion which caked Benin's altars with blood.

Possibly it was too early a climax, built to make a curtain of Iago's 'I am your own for ever.' In Act Four he could only repeat himself with increased volume, adding a humming animal moan as he fell into his fit, a strangler's look to the dangling hands, a sharper danger to the turns of his head as he questioned Emilia. But it gave him time to wind down to a superb returned dignity and tenderness for the murder. This became an act of love—at 'I would not have thee linger in thy pain' he threw aside the pillow and, stopping her lips with a kiss, strangled her. The last speech was spoken kneeling on the bed, her body

267

clutched upright to him as a shield for the dagger he turns on himself.

As he slumped beside her in the sheets, the current stopped. A couple of wigged actors stood awkwardly about. You could only pity them: we had seen history, and it was over. Perhaps it's as well to have seen the performance while still unripe, constructed in fragments, still knitting itself. Now you can see how it's done; later, it will be a torrent. But before it exhausts him, a film should be made. It couldn't save the whole truth, but it might save something the unborn should know.

REVIEW OF THE NATIONAL THEATRE PRODUCTION, 1964, BY THE LONDON *TIMES* DRAMATIC CRITIC

There have been few great Othellos in recent stage history. The late Frederick Walk was one contender for the title: and those who followed his work through the Irish hinterland claim the same for Anew McMaster. But in general postwar productions of the tragedy have centered on Iago and relegated the Moor to second position as a massively vulnerable dupe.

John Dexter's production emphatically reverses this relationship—as it could scarcely fail to do with Sir Laurence Olivier, for the first time in his career, playing the name part. But beyond the unalterable presence of an actor whose magnitude is unrivalled on the British stage, the production shows a determination to build up the role of the Moor at the expense of his malignant confidant.

A clue to the interpretation is given in the programme, which quotes F.R. Leavis's assessment of Iago as "not much more than a necessary piece of dramatic mechanism": less a character in himself than the embodiment of a concealed element in Othello's own nature. This role is certainly contained in the part; but to erect it into the whole truth amounts almost to mutilation. Iago is not merely on the level of a tempter in a miracle play: the part plainly exists in its own right, enigmatic perhaps, but freed with a personal vitality which keeps the riddle of his villany a permanently open question.

The penalties of translating the Leavis theory into action are graphically displayed in Frank Finlay's performance. Instead of the alert ensign, the resourceful actor who is all things to all men and who shapes his plot with the delight of an artist, we are confronted by a lumpish figure. The approach has some advantages. When all Othello's resistance has gone Iago clings about his neck almost with the embrace of a succubus—pouring poison into his ear in tones of satanic lullaby.

The physical attachment between him and the Moor—present from their first scene together with Othello playfully brushing his ancient's face with a bunch of flowers—often yields powerful effects. (Olivier is always at his best when he is in close tactile contact with an opponent.) But when Iago is left to play on lesser victims or to commune with himself, the part loses its coherence. Speed, changeable resourcefulness, nimble invention—all the qualities one expects are replaced by a plodding sameness, occasionally varied by arbitrary grotesqueness, and an unhappy attempt to humanize the character by introducing a whimpering note into the soliloquies.

The lack of a fully realized Iago seriously impoverishes the production—even in the Othello scenes, where Mr. Finlay's reading makes most sense. Othello needs an adversary, not an accomplice. As it is, Olivier's Othello stands as a heroic solo performance which is more remarkable for its technical mastery than for its power to move. Physically he departs from the image of the old soldier descended "into the vale of years." He presents a graceful, sensual figure to whom the duties of a bridegroom seem as familiar as those of the battlefield. His voice (a factor that has held him back from the part in the past) has acquired a measured deliberation and a new lower resonance: and—perhaps most striking of all—he has evolved a range of movement organically related to the part: a stance with feet apart and trunk thrown forward, and a use of oblique arm gestures and flattened palms of the hand.

Beautifully controlled at the beginning, where his modest playing suggests Salvini's "sleeping volcano", its underlying savagery becomes increasingly pronounced until—in the oath scene—he tears the cross from his neck and bows to the floor in atavistic obeisance to a barbaric god.

Of the other performances the best is Derek Jacobi's Cassio, who makes full use of his brief spell as lieutenant (for some reason uniformly pronounced "lootenant") to pull his rank over Iago and thus invite enmity. Maggie Smith's Desdemona is on very distant terms with the part. Obviously a mettlesome girl who would not for an instant have endured domestic tyranny, she introduces facetious modern inflexions (for instance her giggling reference to "These Men" in the bedchamber scene) which clash destructively with the character.

Jocelyn Herbert's set—a towering archway standing behind a slender draped wooden frame—partly solves the problem of the play's vagueness of locality and even manages to explain how Bianca comes to be wandering about in Othello's private quarters.

BEN JONSON

1572–1637

"He was better versed and knew more in Greek and Latin than all the poets in England . . . ." This heady appraisal of Jonson was made by Jonson himself during a boisterous conversation with the Scottish poet, William Drummond. Yet the statement should not be taken simply as a sign of Jonson's bravado or as the overflow of Drummond's plentiful liquor supply, for Jonson was a profoundly learned man, even though he never received any formal education after he finished Westminster School in 1589. At Westminster, he studied under William Camden, a scholar and historian of international reputation, from whom he received a thorough training in the classics and a reverence for them that left its mark on everything he wrote. Jonson was not only the most learned, but also the most independent-minded dramatist of his age. After finishing school, he was forced by his stepfather to apprentice himself as a bricklayer, but after a year at this trade he fled the country and hired himself out as a soldier to fight on the side of Holland in its war against Spain. From 1597 on, we hear of him as a playwright, an actor, and, intermittently, a jailbird. In 1597, for example, he was arrested and imprisoned for his part as an actor and collaborator in *The Isle of Dogs,* a lost satiric comedy that was apparently so offensive in its topical references that it prompted the authorities to close the theaters temporarily. In 1598, his killing of a fellow actor in a duel would have taken him to the gallows had he not pled "benefit of clergy" (the ability to read and write). Combat came naturally to Jonson. Indeed, two of his plays, *Cynthia's Revels* (1600) and *Poetaster* (1601), contained such fierce attacks on several of his dramatic contemporaries that they fomented a satiric war in the theaters of the time.

The spirit of attack that so marks Jonson's life found theatrical form in satire, which he explained in the prologue to his first play, *Every Man in His Humour* (1598). There Jonson defined his dramatic art as being realistic in its method and satiric in its purpose, consisting of "deeds, and language, such as men do use:/ And persons, such as comedy would choose,/ When she would show an image of the times,/ And sport with human follies, not with crimes." In this dramatic manifesto, he was deliberately opposing himself to the romantic comedies, revenge tragedies, and English history plays that dominated the theater of his day. And in the play itself, he offers deftly drawn portraits of various Elizabethan character types—a solemn city gentleman, a plain-speaking country squire, a country bumpkin with city pretensions, a city simpleton with literary pretensions, a cowardly man with military pretensions, an ignorant water-bearer and his credulous wife, a witty young man and his ingenious servant, and a jealous husband. That gallery of portraits, which Jonson had drawn from Roman comedy and London life, was an immediate success, so much so that he quickly followed it with a companion piece, *Every Man Out of His Humour* (1599). The prologue for this play was not just a single speech, but an induction of almost three hundred lines in which three characters discuss the proper bases for dramatic satire. Their conversation distinguishes between true and false behavior, between behavior resulting from a psychological and physiological condition that the Elizabethans called a person's "humour," and behavior guided by social pretensions that Jonson called "affected humour." By exposing all the "affected humours" of his time, Jonson aimed to drive men and women out of their false social behavior, and he did so by producing such caricatures as the vainglorious traveller, the railing courtier, the fastidious dresser, and the officious lady.

The gallery of fools he portrayed in these early comedies clearly displayed his temperament and talent for the satiric art of social comedy. And during the years from 1606 to 1614, he deliberately followed his bent, turning out a series of comedies—*Volpone* (1606), *Epicoene* (1609), *The Alchemist* (1610), and *Bartholomew Fair* (1614)—that have established his reputation as one of the major social satirists of the English dramatic tradition. Jonson's comedies, in fact, established the tradition of social comedy on the English stage. His comedies of London life directly influenced his contemporaries, Middleton, Beaumont, and Fletcher, and led in turn to the Restoration comedies of sophisticated city life by Etherege, Wycherley, and Congreve, all of whom borrowed from Jonson and regarded him as their model. And they admired him not only for his satiric portraiture, but also for the perfection of his comic plots, which all depend on elaborate outwitting intrigues that are at once theatrically compelling and satirically significant. In *The Alchemist,* for example, Jonson constructs an elaborate con game in which three schemers—an Elizabethan underworld man with a smattering of alchemical jargon, a whore, and a servant with a knack for disguises—dupe a law clerk, a tobacco merchant, a gamester, a sensualist, a preacher, a deacon, and a young country gentleman. The brilliance of the play lies in the speed with which the crooks change styles and tricks to fit the next gull who enters—and in the dizzying buildup of comic situations as more and more of the characters try to claim their promised treasure at once.

Volpone also involves an elaborate con game in which a pack of scoundrels attempt to exploit a group of money-hungry fools, but it is a far grimmer work, for though Jonson claimed that his comedy sported "with human follies, not with crimes," the specimens shown to us in *Volpone* are not merely fools, but in several instances are morally despicable knaves. The names of the principal characters immediately suggest their depravity, for they are identified with the world of beasts. Thus, the lawyer Voltore is named for the vulture, the deaf old gentleman Corbaccio for the raven, the violent Corvino is a crow, while the chief schemers are Volpone, the fox, and his parasite Mosca, the fly. Even the more purely comic characters of the subplot share in the beast imagery: Sir Politic Wouldbe, the gullible knight who imagines messages from spies in cabbages, reduces to Sir Pol, the parrot; his wife, Lady Politic Wouldbe, chatters endlessly, like another parrot; and Peregrine, the young traveller, is named for a hunting falcon. The fools of the subplot, though in one sense apparently harmless, are also unwitting echoes of the knaves, and in fact they are also unwitting accomplices of the knaves, for the social pretensions of the Wouldbes play directly into the hands of Volpone's schemes at several points in the plot. Only Celia and Bonario escape the animal imagery, but they, too, are morally typed by their names, for Celia literally means heavenly, while Bonario signifies good-natured.

Although the central comic trick of *Volpone* is also similar to that of *Master Peter*

Patelan—that of a man pretending to be sick—and the plot of *Volpone* like that of *Patelan* ultimately turns into the tricking of the trickster, Jonson uses a variety of means to emphasize the darker implications of the trickery that pervades *Volpone*. Volpone's pretended sickness is mortal; the gulls are clustered around him, waiting for his death and the chance to inherit his great wealth; and the extremes to which they are willing to go, such as disinheriting a son and prostituting a wife, are cruel and unnatural. The language of the play also emphasizes its darker tones. Gold is not merely the object for which all strive, but becomes in Volpone's opening speech a substitute for God. The play's emphasis on disease and physical degeneration is, of course, part of the comic plot, but it is also a metaphor for the moral illness of this gold-dominated world. At the end of the play, the false sickness of Volpone is converted to real pain and all of his money given to the incurables, of which, spiritually, he is one.

Yet the play is also a comedy, and while we find the characters morally convulsive and thus disturbing, their deceptions and self-deceptions are also theatrically entertaining. The two chief tricksters, Volpone and Mosca, offer magnificent opportunities for actors: Volpone gets to play the invalid (complete with makeup and costume), as well as a mountebank seller of patent medicines, as well as the seducer, the invalid again, and finally an officer, while Mosca must continually play the triple role of the concerned servant of his "sick" master, the willing helper of each of the greedy gulls, and the schemer enjoying the success of his plot. Indeed, so attractive are these schemers in their ability to improvise and maneuver that we are repeatedly led to side with them against our better judgment, to give the fox the applause he asks for at the play's end. But that applause is only given, of course, if the actors and actresses are themselves virtuosos, as they appear to have been in the Guthrie Theater production of 1964. Reviews of that production, reprinted following the play, celebrated not only the exuberance of the actors and the orchestration of the director, but also the spectacle created by the designer. And photographs of the Guthrie production (see Figures 32, 33, 34) display that spectacle in all of its comic and satiric aspects, from the wit of Volpone's disguises, to the folly of Sir Politic's poses, to the knavery of Corvino's greed.

VOLPONE, OR THE FOXE

BY BEN JONSON

CHARACTERS

VOLPONE,° *a Magnifico*°
MOSCA,° *his Parasite*
VOLTORE,° *an Advocate*
CORBACCIO,° *an old Gentleman*
CORVINO,° *a Merchant*
AVOCATORI,° *four Magistrates*
NOTARIO, *the Register*°
NANO,° *a Dwarf*
CASTRONE, *an Eunuch*
GREGE *(a crowd)*
SIR POLITIC WOULD-BE, *a Knight*

PEREGRINE,° *a Gentleman-traveller*
BONARIO, *a young Gentleman*
FINE MADAME WOULD-BE, *the Knight's wife*
CELIA, *the Merchant's wife*
COMMANDADORI, *Officers*
MERCATORI, *three Merchants*
ANDROGYNO,° *a Hermaphrodite*
SERVITORE, *a Servant*
WOMEN

SCENE

Venice

THE ARGUMENT°

V OLPONE, childless, rich, feigns sick, despairs,
O ffers his state° to hopes of several heirs,
L ies languishing; his Parasite receives
P resents of all, assures, deludes: then weaves
O ther cross-plots, which ope themselves, are told.
N ew tricks for safety are sought; they thrive; when,
    bold,
E ach tempts th'other again, and all are sold.

PROLOGUE

Now, luck yet send us, and a little wit
    Will serve, to make our play hit;
According to the palates of the season,
    Here is rime, not empty of reason:
This we were bid to credit from our Poet,
    Whose true scope, if you would know it,
In all his poems, still, hath been this measure,
    To mix profit with your pleasure;
And not as some° (whose throats their envy failing)
10   Cry hoarsely, 'All he writes, is railing.'

And when his plays come forth, think they can flout
    them,
    With saying, 'He was a year° about them,'
To these there needs no lie, but this his creature,
    Which was, two months since, no feature;
And though he dares give them five lives to mend it,
    'Tis known, five weeks fully penned it;
From his own hand, without a coadjutor,°
    Novice, journeyman,° or tutor.
Yet, thus much I can give you, as a token   20
    Of his play's worth: no eggs are broken,
Nor quaking custards° with fierce teeth affrighted,
    Wherewith your rout are so delighted;
Nor hales he in a gull,° old ends° reciting,
    To stop gaps in his loose writing,
With such a deal of monstrous, and forced action;
    As might make Bet'lem a faction;°
Nor made he his play, for jests, stol'n from each table,
    But makes jests, to fit his fable.°
And, so presents quick° comedy, refined,   30
    As best critics have designed;
The laws of time, place, persons he observeth,
    From no needful rule he swerveth.
All gall, and copperas,° from his ink, he draineth,

Volpone, "an old fox, an old reinard, an old craftie, slie, subtle companion, sneaking lurking wily deceiver" (Florio, *A Worlde of Wordes* 1598). *Magnifico,* magnate of Venice. *Mosca,* "any kind of flye" (Florio); Beelzebub, the "Prince of Devils," is in Hebrew "the Lord of the flies." *Voltore,* "a ravenous bird called a vultur, a geyre or grap. Also a greedie cormorant" (Florio). *Corbaccio,* "a filthie great raven" (Florio). *Corvino,* crow; "of a ravens nature or colour" (Florio 1611). *Avocatori,* state prosecutors. *Register,* clerk of the court. *Nano,* Latin *nanus,* a dwarf. *Peregrine,* a hawk; a traveller. *Androgyno,* from Greek *andros* (man) and *gyne* (woman). *Argument,* the acrostic form is imitated from Plautus; *The Alchemist* also has one. *state,* estate. *as some,* specifically Marston in *The Dutch Curtezan* (prologue).

a year, "you nasty tortoise, you and your itchy poetry break out like Christmas, but once a year" (*Satiromastix* V. ii, 217). *coadjutor,* Jonson worked with collaborators on *Eastward Ho. journeyman,* qualified craftsman, more than novice but less than master. *quaking custards,* cowards; also perhaps custard-pie comedy, based on sport with huge custard at the Lord mayor's feast. *gull,* dupe, one who swallows anything (from gull-gorge). *make Bet'lem a faction,* either "make a party for the madhouse" or "enlist the support of the madhouse"; Bet'lem or Bedlam, was the asylum of St. Mary of Bethlehem. *fable,* plot. *quick,* lively. *gall, and copperas,* oak galls and iron sulphate, used to make ink; rancour was attributed to the gall-bladder and copperas is bitter.

Only, a little salt° remaineth,
Wherewith, he'll rub your cheeks, till, red with
  laughter,
They shall look fresh, a week after.

ACT I / SCENE 1

(VOLPONE'S *house*)
(*Enter* VOLPONE, MOSCA.)

VOLPONE: Good morning to the day; and, next, my
  gold!
Open the shrine°, that I may see my saint.

(MOSCA *reveals the treasure.*)

Hail the world's soul,° and mine! More glad than is
The teeming earth to see the longed-for sun
Peep through the horns of the celestial Ram,°
Am I, to view thy splendour, darkening his;
That, lying here, amongst my other hoards,
Show'st like a flame, by night; or like the day
40 Struck out of Chaos,° when all darkness fled
Unto the centre. O, thou sun of Sol,°
But brighter than thy father, let me kiss,
With adoration, thee, and every relic°
Of sacred treasure, in this blessed room.
Well did wise Poets, by thy glorious name
Title that age,° which they would have the best;
Thou being the best of things; and far
  transcending
All style of joy in children, parents, friends,
50 Or any other waking dream on earth.
Thy looks when they to Venus did ascribe,°
They should have given her twenty thousand
  Cupids;
Such are thy beauties, and our loves! Dear *saint*,
Riches, the dumb god,° that giv'st all men tongues;
That canst do nought, and yet mak'st men do all
  things;
The price of souls; even hell, with thee to boot,
Is made worth heaven! Thou art virtue, fame,
60 Honour, and all things else! Who can get thee,
He shall be noble, valiant, honest, wise°—

MOSCA: And what he will, sir. Riches are in fortune
A greater good, than wisdom is in nature.°
VOLPONE: True, my beloved Mosca. Yet, I glory
More in the cunning purchase° of my wealth,
Than in the glad possession; since I gain
No common way: I use no trade, no venture;
I wound no earth with ploughshares; fat no beasts
To feed the shambles°; have no mills for iron,
Oil, corn, or men, to grind 'em° into poulder;   70
I blow no subtle° glass; expose no ships
To threat'nings of the furrow-faced sea;
I turn° no moneys, in the public bank;
Nor usure° private°—
MOSCA: No, sir, nor devour
Soft prodigals. You shall ha' some will swallow
A melting heir, as glibly as your Dutch
Will pills of butter°, and ne'er purge for't
Tear forth the fathers of poor families
Out of their beds, and coffin them alive   80
In some kind, clasping prison, where their bones
May be forth-coming, when the flesh is rotten:
But your sweet nature doth abhor these courses;
You loathe, the widow's, or the orphan's tears
Should wash your pavements; or their piteous cries
Ring in your roofs; and beat the air, for
  vengeance—
VOLPONE: Right, Mosca, I do loathe it.
MOSCA: And besides, sir,
You are not like the thresher,° that doth stand   90
With a huge flail, watching a heap of corn,
And, hungry, dares not taste the smallest grain,
But feeds on mallows, and such bitter herbs;
Not like the merchant, who hath filled his vaults
With Romagnia,° and rich Candian wines,°
Yet drinks the lees of Lombard's vinegar;
You will not lie in straw, whilst moths, and worms
Feed on your sumptuous hangings, and soft beds.
You know the use of riches, and dare give, now,
From that bright heap, to me, your poor observer, 100
Or to your dwarf, or your hermaphrodite,
Your eunuch, or what other household trifle
Your pleasure allows maintenance—
VOLPONE: Hold thee,° Mosca,

(*Gives him money.*)

Take, of my hand; thou strik'st on truth, in all:
And they are envious term thee parasite.

---

salt is not used in ink, but iron sulphate was called "salt of iron" and Jonson needs it to introduce the following joke out of Horace (*Satires* I. x, 3). *shrine*, Volpone is at his devotions and the treasure has the aspect of a holy reliquary. *world's soul* with a pun on "sol," the sun; also perhaps the coin. *celestial Ram*, the sun enters Aries at the spring equinox. *day . . . Chaos*, the first day of creation (*Genesis* 1.2–4). *sun of Sol*, alchemy held gold to be the offspring of the sun. *relic*, i.e., the kind found in a shrine. *that age*, the Golden Age (described by Ovid, *Met.* 1.89–112). *Venus . . . ascribe*, following Homeric tradition the Latin poets often called Venus "golden" (*aurea*). *the dumb god*, "silence is golden." *Thou art . . . wise*, compare Horace, *Satires* II. iii, 94.

Riches . . . nature, "Better to be endowed by chance with riches than by nature with wisdom." *purchase*, procurance. *shambles*, slaughterhouse. *grind 'em*, i.e., exploit the men. *subtle*, tenous, delicate: Venice was famed for its glass. *turn*, exchange. *usure*, exchange at high interest. *private*, privately. *Dutch . . . butter* a notorious Dutch weakness. *the thresher*, from Horace, *Satires* II. iii, 111. *Romagnia*, Rumney, a sweet Greek wine. *Candian wines*, Malmsey from Candy (Crete). *Hold thee*, keep yourself.

Call forth my dwarf, my eunuch, and my fool,
And let 'em make me sport. What should I do,
But cocker up my *genius,* and live free
110　To all delights, my fortune calls me to?
I have no wife, no parent, child, ally,
To give my substance to; but whom I make
Must be my heir: and this makes men observe° me.
This draws new clients,° daily, to my house,
Women, and men, of every sex and age,
That bring me presents, send me plate, coin,
　　jewels,
With hope, that when I die (which they expect
Each greedy minute) it shall then return,
120　Tenfold, upon them; whilst some, covetous
Above the rest, seek to engross me, whole,
And counter-work, the one, unto the other,
Contend in gifts, as they would seem, in love:
All which I suffer, playing with their hopes,
And am content to coin 'em into profit,
And look upon their kindness, and take more,
And look on that; still bearing them in hand,°
Letting the cherry° knock against their lips,
And, draw it, by their mouths, and back again.
130　　How now!

ACT 1 / SCENE 2

(Enter MOSCA, *with* NANO, ANDROGYNO, *and* CAS-
TRONE.)
(An entertainment follows.)

NANO: Now, room for fresh gamesters, who do will
　　　you to know,
　　They do bring you neither play, nor University
　　　show;
　　And therefore do intreat you, that whatsoever they
　　　rehearse,°
　　　May not fare a whit the worse, for the false pace°
　　　of the verse.
　　If you wonder at this, you will wonder more, ere we
10　　　pass,
　　　For know *(pointing to* ANDROGYNO), here is
　　　enclosed the Soul of Pythagoras,
　　That juggler divine, as hereafter shall follow;
　　　Which soul, fast and loose,° sir, came first from
　　　Apollo,

And was breathed into Aethalides,° Mercurius his
　　son,
　　Where it had the gift to remember all that ever
　　was done.
From thence it fled forth, and made quick　　　　20
　　transmigration
　　To goldy-locked Euphorbus,° who was killed, in
　　good fashion,
At the siege of old Troy, by the cuckold of Sparta.°
　　Hermotimus was next (I find it in my charta)°
To whom it did pass, where no sooner it was
　　missing,
　　But with one Pyrrhus, of Delos,° it learned to go
　　a-fishing:
And thence did it enter the Sophist of Greece.°　30
　　From Pythagore, she went into a beautiful piece,
Hight° Aspasia, the meretrix°; and the next toss of
　　her
　　Was, again, of a whore, she became a
　　philosopher,
Crates° the Cynic: as itself° does relate it.
　　Since, kings, knights, and beggars, knaves, lords
　　and fools gat it,
Besides, ox, and ass, camel, mule, goat, and brock,
　　In all which it hath spoke, as in the cobbler's　40
　　cock.°
But I come not here, to discourse of that matter,
　　Or his one, two, or three, or his great oath, 'By
　　Quater!'°
His musics,° his trigon, his golden thigh,°
　　Or his telling how elements shift; but I
Would ask, how of late, thou has suffered
　　translation,
　　And shifted thy coat, in these days of
　　reformation?°　　　　　　　　　　　　　　　　50
ANDROGYNO: Like one of the reformèd,° a fool, as
　　you see,
　　Counting all old doctrine heresy.

---

cocker up, pamper, indulge (Latin, *indulgere genio*).
observe, "treat with ceremonious respect or reverence"
(*OED*). **clients,** followers who wait upon the patronage of
Volpone the Magnifico (ironic). **still,** continually. **bearing
. . . hand,** leading them on. **cherry,** in the game of chop-
cherry the player tried to bite a dangling cherry. **rehearse,**
recite. **false pace,** exemplified by Nano as he speaks; the
old-fashioned loose four-stress rhythm, with forced rhymes,
falsifies the natural sense. **fast and loose,** "slippery, hard to
catch," from a betting game in which one player guessed
whether or not a dagger was held fast in a belt intricately
folded by the other.

Aethalides, herald to the Argonauts and heir to an
omniscient memory. **Euphorbus,** the Trojan who first
wounded Patroclus *(Iliad* 17). **cuckold of Sparta,** Menelaus.
Hermotimus, a Greek philosopher. **charta,** paper, perhaps
Lucian's dialogue. **Pyrrhus, of Delos,** a philosopher; the
name and the allusion to fishing are supplied by Diogenes
Laertius without explanation. **Sophist of Greece,**
Pythagoras is so styled by Lucian. **Hight** (Old English),
named, called *Aspasia* mistress of Pericles. **meretrix,** courtesan. **Crates,** a pupil of Diogenes. **itself,** either the cock in
Lucian, or Androgyno. **cobbler's cock,** the cock tells the
story in Lucian. **Quater,** the Pythagorean trigon or triangle
of four, symbol of cosmic and moral harmony. **musics,**
Pythagorean theory related the spacing of the cosmic
spheres to the laws of harmony. **golden thigh,** attributed to
Pythagoras by his followers. **reformation,** the Protestant
reformation; Jonson was still a Catholic in 1606. **reformed,**
evidently the Puritans.

NANO: But not on thine own forbid meats° hast thou
    ventured?
ANDROGYNO: On fish, when first, a Carthusian° I
    entered.
NANO: Why, then thy dogmatical silence° hath left
    thee?
60 ANDROGYNO: Of that an obstreperous° lawyer bereft
    me.
NANO: O wonderful change! when Sir Lawyer
    forsook thee,
    For Pythagore's sake, what body then took thee?
ANDROGYNO: A good dull moyle.°
NANO: And how! by that means,
    Thou wert brought to allow of the eating of beans?
ANDROGYNO: Yes.
NANO: But, from the moyle, into whom did'st thou
70   pass?
ANDROGYNO: Into a very strange beast, by some
    writers called an ass;
    By others, a precise,° pure, illuminate° brother,
    Of those devour flesh, and sometimes one
      another;
    And will drop forth a libel, or a sanctified lie,
    Betwixt every spoonful of a nativity-pie.°
NANO: Now quit thee, for heaven, of that profane
    nation;
80   And gently, report thy next transmigration.
ANDROGYNO: To the same that I am.
NANO: A creature of delight?
    And, what is more than a fool, an
      hermaphrodite?
    Now pray thee, sweet soul, in all thy variation,
    Which body would'st thou choose, to take up thy
      station?
ANDROGYNO: Troth, this I am in, even here would I
    tarry.
90 NANO: 'Cause here, the delight of each sex thou canst
    vary?
ANDROGYNO: Alas, those pleasures be stale, and
    forsaken;
    No, 'tis your fool, wherewith I am so taken;
    The only one creature, that I can call blessed,
    For all other forms I have proved most
      distressed.
NANO: Spoke true, as thou wert in Pythagoras still.
    This learned opinion we celebrate will,
100   Fellow eunuch, as behoves us, with all our wit and
    art,

To dignify that° whereof our selves are so great,
    and special a part.
VOLPONE: Now very, very pretty! Mosca, this
    Was thy invention?
MOSCA: If it please my patron,
    Not else.
VOLPONE: It doth, good Mosca.
MOSCA: Then it was, sir.

SONG°

Fools, they are the only nation°   110
Worth men's envy, or admiration;
Free from care, or sorrow-taking,
Selves, and others merry making:
All they speak, or do, is sterling.°
Your Fool, he is your great man's dearling,
And your ladies' sport, and pleasure;
Tongue, and bable° are his treasure.
E'en his face begetteth laughter,
And he speaks truth, free from slaughter;°
He's the grace of every feast,   120
And, sometimes, the chiefest guest;
Hath his trencher, and his stool,
When wit waits upon the fool.°
    O, who would not be
    He, he, he?

(One knocks without.)

VOLPONE: Who's that? Away!

(Exeunt NANO, CASTRONE.)

    Look Mosca!
MOSCA: Fool, begone!

(Exit ANDROGYNO.)

'Tis Signior Voltore, the advocate;
I know him, by his knock.   130
VOLPONE: Fetch me my gown,
    My furs,° and night caps; say, my couch is
      changing:
    And let him entertain himself, awhile,
    Without i' th' gallery. Now, now, my clients
    Begin their visitation! vulture, kite,
    Raven, and gor-crow,° all my birds of prey,
    That think me turning carcass, now they come.
    I am not for 'em yet. How now? the news?

(Enter MOSCA.)

MOSCA: A piece of plate, sir.   140

---

forbid meats, forbidden foods; Pythagoreans were forbidden fish and beans. **Carthusian,** an order strict in its diet but allowing fish. **dogmatical silence,** Pythagoreans were enjoined to a five-year silence, which might have been maintained among the Carthusians. **obstreperous,** vociferous. **moyle,** mule. **precise,** "strict in religious observance, puritanical" (*OED*). **illuminate,** visionary. **nativity-pie,** Christmas pie, evading the word "mass." see *The Alchemist* III. ii, 43.

that, i.e., folly. **Song,** it might be sung by the grotesques, by Mosca alone, or by all. **nation,** sect. **sterling,** capable of standing every test. **bable,** the fool's bauble or sceptre; slang for phallus. **free from slaughter,** without being called to account. **wit . . . fool,** the fool dines off his host; wit waits upon the fool's words. **furs,** worn by the sick for warmth. **gor-crow,** carrion crow.

VOLPONE: Of what bigness?

MOSCA: Huge,
Massy, and antique, with your name inscribed,
And arms engraven.

VOLPONE: Good! and not a fox
Stretched on the earth, with fine delusive sleights,
Mocking a gaping crow?° ha, Mosca?

MOSCA: Sharp, sir.

VOLPONE: Give me my furs. Why dost thou laugh so,
150   man?

MOSCA: I cannot choose, sir, when I apprehend
What thoughts he has, without, now, as he walks:
That this might be the last gift he should give;
That this would fetch you; if you died today,
And gave him all, what he should be tomorrow;
What large return would come of all his ventures;°
How he should worshipped be, and reverenced;
Ride, with his furs, and foot-cloths;° waited on
By herds of fools, and clients; have clear way
160   Made for his moyle, as lettered as himself;
Be called the great, and learned advocate:
And then concludes, there's nought impossible.

VOLPONE: Yes, to be learned, Mosca.

MOSCA: O, no: rich
Implies it. Hood an ass with reverend purple,°
So you can hide his two ambitious ears,
And he shall pass for a cathedral doctor.°

VOLPONE: My caps, my caps,° good Mosca. Fetch him
in.

170 MOSCA: Stay, sir, your ointment° for your eyes.

VOLPONE: That's true;
Dispatch, dispatch; I long to have possession
Of my new present.

MOSCA: That, and thousands more,
I hope to see you lord of.

VOLPONE: Thanks, kind Mosca.

MOSCA: And that, when I am lost in blended dust,
And hundred such as I am, in succession—

VOLPONE: Nay, that were too much, Mosca.

180 MOSCA: You shall live,
Still, to delude these harpies.

VOLPONE: Loving Mosca!

(Looking into a glass.)

'Tis well! My pillow now, and let him enter

(Exit MOSCA.*)*

---

fox . . . crow, for a similar application of the fable of the crow, dropping its cheese as it sings for the adulatory fox, see Horace, *Satires* II. v, 55.   *ventures,* enterprising investments. *foot-cloths,* pageant drapery for a horse. *reverend purple,* crimson robes of a Doctor of Divinity. *caps,* probably ear-caps, prompted by line 132; at this point, perhaps, Volpone gets into bed. *ointment,* to make his eyes sticky and rheumy. *Now . . . posture,* a sacrilegious invocation in the epic manner to the powers of feigned disease.

Now, my feigned cough, my phthisic,° and my
gout,
My apoplexy, palsie, and catarrhs,
Help, with your forced functions, this my posture,°
Wherein, this three year, I have milked their
hopes.
He comes, I hear him—uh! uh! uh! uh! O—   190

ACT 1 / SCENE 3

(Enter MOSCA, *with* VOLTORE *bearing plate.* VOLPONE
in bed.)

MOSCA: You still are what you were, sir. Only you,
Of all the rest, are he, commands his love:
And you do wisely, to preserve it, thus,
With early visitation, and kind notes°
Of your good meaning° to him, which, I know,
Cannot but come most grateful. Patron, sir!
Here's Signior Voltore is come—

VOLPONE: What say you?

MOSCA: Sir, Signior Voltore is come, this morning,
To visit you.   10

VOLPONE: I thank him.

MOSCA: And hath brought
A piece of antique plate, bought of St. Mark,°
With which he here presents you.

VOLPONE: He is welcome.
Pray him, to come more often.

MOSCA: Yes.

VOLTORE: What says he?

MOSCA: He thanks you, and desires you to see him
often.   20

VOLPONE: Mosca!

MOSCA: My patron?

VOLPONE: Bring him near, where is he?
I long to feel his hand.

MOSCA *(guiding* VOLPONE'S *hand)*: The plate is here,
sir.

VOLTORE: How fare you, sir?

VOLPONE: I thank you, Signior Voltore.
Where is the plate? Mine eyes are bad.

VOLTORE *(putting it into his hand)*: I'm sorry   30
To see you still thus weak.

MOSCA *(aside)*: That he is not weaker.

VOLPONE: You are too munificent.

VOLTORE: No, sir, would to heaven,
I could as well give health to you, as that plate.

VOLPONE: You gave, sir, what you can. I thank you.
Your love
Hath taste° in this, and shall not be unanswered.

---

phthisic, consumption or asthma.   *posture,* pose, imposture. "This and the following scenes are really a Roman *salutio* i.e. the morning visit of clients to their patron so often referred to and described by the satirists." (Rea). *notes,* signs. *good meaning,* well-wishing. *of St. Mark,* in St. Mark's Square, celebrated for its goldsmiths' shops. *Hath taste in,* can be felt in.

I pray you see me often.

40 VOLTORE: Yes, I shall, sir.

VOLPONE: Be not far from me.

MOSCA (*to* VOLTORE): Do you observe that, sir?

VOLPONE: Hearken unto me, still: it will concern you.

MOSCA: You are a happy man, sir, know your good.

VOLPONE: I cannot now last long—

MOSCA: You are his heir, sir.

VOLTORE: Am I?

VOLPONE: I feel me going, uh! uh! uh! uh!
    I am sailing to my port, uh! uh! uh! uh!
50   And I am glad, I am so near my haven.

MOSCA: Alas, kind gentleman; well, we must all go—

VOLTORE: But, Mosca—

MOSCA: Age will conquer.

VOLTORE: Pray thee hear me.
    Am I inscribed his heir, for certain?

MOSCA: Are you?
    I do beseech you, sir, you will vouchsafe
    To write me, i' your family.° All my hopes
    Depend upon your worship. I am lost,
60   Except the rising sun do shine on me.

VOLTORE: It shall both shine, and warm thee, Mosca.

MOSCA: Sir,
    I am a man that have not done your love
    All the worst offices: here I wear your keys,°
    See all your coffers and your caskets locked,
    Keep the poor inventory of your jewels,
    Your plate, and monies; am your steward, sir,
    Husband your goods here.

VOLTORE: But am I sole heir?

70 MOSCA: Without a partner, sir, confirmed this
        morning;
    The wax is warm yet, and the ink scarce dry
    Upon the parchment.

VOLTORE: Happy, happy, me!
    By what good chance, sweet Mosca?

MOSCA: Your desert, sir;
    I know no second cause.

VOLTORE: Thy modesty
    Is loath to know it;° well, we shall requite it.

80 MOSCA: He ever liked your course,° sir, that first
        took° him.
    I, oft, have heard him say, how he admired
    Men of your large profession, that could speak
    To every cause, and things mere contraries,
    Till they were hoarse again, yet all be law;
    That, with most quick agility, could turn,
    And re-turn; make knots, and undo them;
    Give forkèd° counsel; take provoking gold°

---

write ... family, names of servants were entered in a "Household Book." *your keys,* i.e., Voltore's because Volpone's. *know it,* acknowledge it. *course,* way of doing things. *took,* captivated. *large,* liberal, expansive and eloquent. *forked,* equivocal. *provoking gold,* court fees (provoke, "to call to a judge or court to take up one's cause" (*OED*).

On either hand,° and put it up°: these men,
He knew, would thrive, with their humility.   90
And, for his part, he thought, he should be bless'd
To have his heir of such a suffering spirit,
So wise, so grave, of so perplexed° a tongue,
And loud withall, that would not wag, nor scarce
Lie still, without a fee; when every word
Your worship but lets fall, is a chequeen!°

(*Another knocks.*)

Who's that? one knocks; I would not have you seen,
    sir.
And yet—pretend you came, and went in haste;
I'll fashion an excuse. And gentle sir,   100
When you do come to swim, in golden lard,
Up to the arms, in honey, that your chin
Is born up stiff, with fatness of the flood,
Think on your vassal; but remember me:
I ha' not been your worst of clients.

VOLTORE: Mosca—

MOSCA: When will you have your inventory brought,
    sir?
Or see a copy of the will? (*Knocking again.*) Anon!
I'll bring 'em to you, sir. Away, be gone   110
Put business in your face.

(*Exit* VOLTORE.)

VOLPONE: Excellent, Mosca!
    Come hither, let me kiss thee.

MOSCA: Keep you still, sir.
    Here is Corbaccio.

VOLPONE: Set the plate away.
    The vulture's gone, and the old raven's come.

ACT 1 / SCENE 4

MOSCA: Betake you to your silence, and your sleep.
    (*Sets plate aside.*) Stand there, and multiply. Now we
        shall see
    A wretch who is indeed more impotent
    Than this can feign to be; yet hopes to hop
    Over his grave. (*Enter* CORBACCIO.) Signior
        Corbaccio!
    You're very welcome, sir.

CORBACCIO: How does your patron?

MOSCA: Troth, as he did, sir, no amends.   10

CORBACCIO: What? mends he?

MOSCA: No, sir: he is rather worse.

CORBACCIO: That's well. Where is he?

MOSCA: Upon his couch, sir, newly fall'n asleep.

CORBACCIO: Does he sleep well?

MOSCA: No wink, sir, all this night,

---

either hand, for either party. *put it up,* either "deposit it" or (Mosca's real meaning) "pocket it." *perplexed,* involved, puzzling. *chequeen* (F cecchine), Venetian gold coin, sequin.

Nor yesterday, but slumbers.°
CORBACCIO: Good! He should take
   Some counsel of physicians; I have brought him
20 An opiate here, from mine own doctor—
MOSCA: He will not hear of drugs.
CORBACCIO: Why? I myself
   Stood by, while 't was made; saw all th' ingredients;
   And know, it cannot but most gently work.
   My life for his, 'tis but to make him sleep.
VOLPONE (aside): Ay, his last sleep, if he would take it.
MOSCA: Sir,
   He has no faith in physic.
CORBACCIO: Say you, say you?
30 MOSCA: He has no faith in physic: he does think
   Most of your° doctors are the greater danger,
   And worse disease t'escape. I often have
   Heard him protest, that your physician
   Should never be his heir.
CORBACCIO: Not I his heir?
MOSCA: Not your physician, sir.
CORBACCIO: O, no, no, no,
   I do not mean it.
MOSCA: No, sir, nor their fees
40 He cannot brook: he says, they flay° a man
   Before they kill him.
CORBACCIO: Right, I do conceive° you.
MOSCA: And then, they do it by experiment;°
   For which the law not only doth absolve 'em,
   But gives them great reward: and he is loath
   To hire his death, so.
CORBACCIO: It is true, they kill,
   With as much licence, as a judge.
MOSCA: Nay, more;
50 For he but kills, sir, where the law condemns,
   And these can kill him, too.
CORBACCIO: Ay, or me:
   Or any man. How does his apoplex?°
   Is that strong on him still?
MOSCA: Most violent.
   His speech is broken, and his eyes are set,
   His face drawn longer than 't was wont—
CORBACCIO: How? How?
   Stronger than he was wont?
60 MOSCA: No, sir: his face
   Drawn longer, than 't was wont.
CORBACCIO: O, good.
MOSCA: His mouth
   Is ever gaping, and his eyelids hang.
CORBACCIO: Good.
MOSCA: A freezing numbness stiffens all his joints,
   And makes the colour of his flesh like lead.
CORBACCIO: 'Tis good.

MOSCA: His pulse beats slow, and dull.
CORBACCIO: Good symptoms, still.   70
MOSCA: And, from his brain°—
CORBACCIO: Ha? how? Not from his brain?
MOSCA: Yes, sir, and from his brain—
CORBACCIO: I conceive you, good.
MOSCA: Flows a cold sweat, with a continual rheum,
   Forth the resolvèd° corners of his eyes.
CORBACCIO: Is't possible? Yet I am better, ha!
   How does he, with the swimming of his head?
MOSCA: O, sir, 'tis past the scotomy°; he, now,
   Hath lost his feeling, and hath left° to snort,   80
   You hardly can perceive him, that he breathes.
CORBACCIO: Excellent, excellent, sure I shall outlast
   him:
   This makes me young again, a score of years.
MOSCA: I was a-coming for you, sir.
CORBACCIO: Has he made his will?
   What has he given me?
MOSCA: No, sir.
CORBACCIO: Nothing? ha?
MOSCA: He has not made his will, sir.   90
CORBACCIO: Oh, oh, oh.
   What then did° Voltore, the lawyer, here?
MOSCA: He smelt a carcass, sir, when he but heard
   My master was about his testament;
   As I did urge him to it, for your good—
CORBACCIO: He came unto him, did he? I thought so.
MOSCA: Yes, and presented him this piece of plate.
CORBACCIO: To be his heir?
MOSCA: I do not know, sir.
CORBACCIO: True,   100
   I know it too.
MOSCA: By your own scale,° sir.
CORBACCIO: Well,
   I shall prevent° him, yet. See, Mosca, look,
   Here, I have brought a bag of bright chequeens,
   Will quite weigh down his plate.
MOSCA: Yea, marry, sir!
   This is true physic, this your sacred medicine,
   No talk of opiates, to this great elixir.°
CORBACCIO: 'Tis aurum palpabile,° if not potabile.°   110
MOSCA: It shall be ministered to him in his bowl?
CORBACCIO: Ay, do, do, do.

---

slumbers, dozes. your, i.e., doctors and physicians in general. flay, strip off skin. conceive, understand. experiment, trial upon the patient. apoplex, apoplexy; Hippocrates held the "strong apoplex" incurable.

from his brain, drainage of brain fluid was believed the last stage of strong apoplexy, and Corbaccio eagerly recognizes its significance. resolved slackened. scotomy, "dizziness accompanied by dimness of sight" (OED). left, ceased. What then did, F (Q But what did). By ... scale, either "by your own estimation, without my help" or "judging by your own case." prevent, keep in front of. weigh down, outweigh; perhaps suggested by Mosca's "scale." elixir, alchemical essence fabled to make life eternal; analogous to the "stone" thought to eternalize base metal into gold. arum ... potabile, "palpable, if not drinkable, gold." aurum potabile, was held a sovereign remedy for all diseases.

MOSCA: Most blessed cordial!°
　This will recover him.
CORBACCIO: Yes, do, do, do.
MOSCA: I think, it were not best, sir.
CORBACCIO: What?
MOSCA: To recover him.
CORBACCIO: O, no, no, no; by no means.
120　MOSCA: Why, sir, this
　Will work some strange effect, if he but feel it.
CORBACCIO: 'Tis true, therefore forbear, I'll take my
　　venture:°
　Give me 't again.
MOSCA: At no hand, pardon me;
　You shall not do yourself that wrong, sir. I
　Will so advise you, you shall have it all.
CORBACCIO: How?
MOSCA: All, sir, 'tis your right, your own; no man
130　Can claim a part: 'tis yours, without a rival,
　Decreed by destiny.
CORBACCIO: How? how, good Mosca?
MOSCA: I'll tell you, sir. This fit he shall recover—
CORBACCIO: I do conceive you.
MOSCA: And, on first advantage°
　Of his gained° sense, will I re-importune him
　Unto the making of his testament;
　And show him this.
CORBACCIO: Good, good.
140　MOSCA: 'Tis better yet,
　If you will hear, sir.
CORBACCIO: Yes, with all my heart.
MOSCA: Now, would I counsel you, make home with
　　speed;
　There, frame° a will: whereto° you shall inscribe
　My master your sole heir.
CORBACCIO: And disinherit
　My son?
MOSCA: O, sir, the better: for that colour°
150　Shall make it much more taking.°
CORBACCIO: O, but colour?
MOSCA: This will, sir, you shall send it unto me.
　Now, when I come to enforce,° as I will do,
　Your cares, your watchings, and your many
　　prayers,
　Your more than many gifts, your this day's present,
　And, last, produce your will; where, without
　　thought,
　Or least regard, unto your proper issue,°
160　A son so brave, and highly meriting,
　The stream of your diverted love hath thrown you
　Upon my master, and made him your heir:
　He cannot be so stupid, or stone dead,

But, out of conscience, and mere gratitude—
CORBACCIO: He must pronounce me, his?
MOSCA: 'Tis true.
CORBACCIO: This plot
　Did I think on before.
MOSCA: I do believe it.
CORBACCIO: Do you not believe it?　　　　　　　　　170
MOSCA: Yes, sir.
CORBACCIO: Mine own project.
MOSCA: Which when he hath done, sir—
CORBACCIO: Published me his heir?
MOSCA: And you so certain to survive him—
CORBACCIO: Ay.
MOSCA: Being so lusty a man—
CORBACCIO: 'Tis true.
MOSCA: Yes, sir.
CORBACCIO: I thought on that too. See, how he　　　180
　　should be°
　The very organ,° to express my thoughts!
MOSCA: You have not only done yourself a good—
CORBACCIO: But multiplied it on my son?
MOSCA: 'Tis right, sir.
CORBACCIO: Still, my invention.
MOSCA: 'Las,° sir, heaven knows,
　It hath been all my study, all my care,
　(I e'en grow grey withal) how to work things—
CORBACCIO: I do conceive, sweet Mosca.　　　　　190
MOSCA: You are he,
　For whom I labour, here.
CORBACCIO: Ay, do, do, do:
　I'll straight° about it. (Begins to go.)
MOSCA (aside): Rook go with you,° raven.
CORBACCIO: I know thee honest.
MOSCA: You do lie, sir.
CORBACCIO: And—
MOSCA: Your knowledge is no better than your ears,°
　　sir.　　　　　　　　　　　　　　　　　　　200
CORBACCIO: I do not doubt, to be a father to thee.
MOSCA: Nor I, to gull my brother° of his blessing.
CORBACCIO: I may ha' my youth restored to me, why
　　not?
MOSCA: Your worship is a precious ass—
CORBACCIO: What say'st thou?
MOSCA: I do desire your worship, to make haste, sir.
CORBACCIO: 'Tis done, 'tis done, I go.

　(Exit CORBACCIO.)

VOLPONE (leaping up): O I shall burst;
　Let out my sides, let out my sides—
MOSCA: Contain

---

cordial, a medicine to invigorate the heart, e.g., potable
gold.　venture, i.e., the bag of gold.　advantage, opportunity.　gained regained.　frame, devise.　whereto, to the
end that.　colour, semblance.　taking, attractive.　enforce,
urge.　proper issue, own true offspring.

See ... be, "See, if he isn't ..."　organ, medium
instrument.　'Las, Alas.　straight, immediately.　Rook go
with you, "may you be rooked."　Your ... ears, both a taunt
and a strict truth.　my brother, i.e., Corbaccio's son, with a
glance at Jacob's cheating of Esau (Genesis 27).

Your flux° of laughter, sir. You know this hope
Is such a bait, it covers any hook.
VOLPONE: O, but thy working, and thy placing it!
I cannot hold; good rascal, let me kiss thee:
I never knew thee, in so rare a humour.°
MOSCA: Alas, sir, I but do, as I am taught;
Follow your grave instructions; give 'em words;°
Pour oil into their ears;° and send them hence.
220 VOLPONE: 'Tis true, 'tis true. What a rare punishment
Is avarice, to itself!
MOSCA: Ay, with our help, sir.
VOLPONE: So many cares, so many maladies,
So many fears attending old age,
Yea, death so often called on, as no wish
Can be more frequent with 'em, their limbs faint,
Their senses dull, their seeing, hearing, going,°
All dead before them; yea, their very teeth,
Their instruments of eating, failing them:
230 Yet this is reckoned life! Nay, here was one,
Is now gone home, that wishes to live longer!
Feels not his gout, nor palsy, feigns himself
Younger by scores of years, flatters his age,
With confident belying it, hopes he may
With charms, like Aeson,° have his youth restored:
And with these thoughts so battens,° as if fate
Would be as easily cheated on, as he,
And all turns air! (*Another knocks.*) Who's that,
there, now? a third?
240 MOSCA: Close, to your couch again; I hear his voice.
It is Corvino, our spruce merchant.
VOLPONE (*lying down*): Dead.
MOSCA: Another bout,° sir, with your eyes. Who's
there?

ACT 1 / SCENE 5

(*Enter* CORVINO.)

MOSCA: Signior Corvino! come most wished for! O,
How happy were you, if you knew it, now!
CORVINO: Why? what? wherein?
MOSCA: The tardy hour is come, sir.
CORVINO: He is not dead?
MOSCA: Not dead, sir, but as good;
He knows no man.
CORVINO: How shall I do, then?
MOSCA: Why, sir?
10 CORVINO: I have brought him, here, a pearl.
MOSCA: Perhaps he has
So much remembrance left, as to know you, sir;
He still calls on you, nothing but your name

Is in his mouth; is your pearl orient,° sir?
CORVINO: Venice was never owner of the like.
VOLPONE (*faintly*): Signior Corvino.
MOSCA: Hark.
VOLPONE: Signior Corvino.
MOSCA: He calls you, step and give it him. He's here,
sir.   20
And he has brought you a rich pearl.
CORVINO: How do you, sir?
Tell him it doubles the twelfth carat.°
MOSCA: Sir,
He cannot understand, his hearing's gone;
And yet it comforts him, to see you—
CORVINO: Say,
I have a diamant° for him, too.
MOSCA: Best show't, sir,
Put it into his hand; 'tis only there   30
He apprehends: he has his feeling, yet.

(VOLPONE *seizes the pearl.*)

See, how he grasps it!
CORVINO: 'Las, good gentleman!
How pitiful the sight is!
MOSCA: Tut, forget, sir.
The weeping of an heir should still be laughter,
Under a visor.°
CORVINO: Why? am I his heir?
MOSCA: Sir, I am sworn, I may not show the will,
Till he be dead; but, here has been Corbaccio,   40
Here has been Voltore, here were others too,
I cannot number 'em, they were so many,
All gaping here for legacies, but I,
Taking the vantage of his naming you,
'Signior Corvino, Signior Corvino',° took
Paper, and pen, and ink, and there I asked him,
Whom he would have his heir? 'Corvino'. Who
Should be executor? 'Corvino'. And
To any question he was silent to,
I still interpreted the nods he made,   50
Through weakness, for consent; and sent home th'
others,
Nothing bequeathed them, but to cry, and curse.

(*They embrace.*)

CORVINO: O, my dear Mosca. Does he not perceive
us?
MOSCA: No more than a blind harper.° He knows no
man,
No face of friend, nor name of any servant,
Who 'twas that fed him last, or gave him drink:

---

flux, flow, morbid discharge.   **rare a humour,** fine and
inventive mood.   **give 'em words,** deceive (proverbial).
Pour . . . ears, deceive with fulsome words (proverbial).
going, ability to walk.   **Aeson,** Jason's father, whose youth
was restored by Medea's magic.   **battens,** grows fat.
Another bout, Mosca applies more ointment.

orient, eastern pearls were of superior value and
brilliancy.   **carat,** measure of weight of precious stones
(then 3½ grains).   **diamant,** Jonson anachronistically preferred this Middle English form.   **visor,** a mask.   **Signior
Corvino,** Mosca mimics Volpone's feeble cry.   **blind harper,**
proverbial term for anonymous figure in a crowd.

60   Not those, he hath begotten, or brought up
Can he remember.
CORVINO: Has he children?
MOSCA: Bastards,
    Some dozen, or more, that he begot on beggars,
    Gipsies, and Jews, and black-moors, when he was
      drunk.
    Knew you not that, sir? 'Tis the common fable,°
    The Dwarf, the Fool, the Eunuch are all his;
    He's the true father of his family,°
70   In all, save me: but he has given 'em nothing.
CORVINO: That's well, that's well. Art sure he does not
      hear us?
MOSCA: Sure, sir? Why, look you, credit your own
      sense. *(Shouts in* VOLPONE'*s ear.)*
    The pox° approach, and add to your diseases,
    If it would send you hence the sooner, sir,
    For, your incontinence, it hath deserved it°
    Throughly and throughly, and the plague to boot.
    (to CORVINO.) You may come near, sir.
80   Would you once close
    Those filthy eyes of yours, that flow with slime,
    Like two frog-pits; and those same hanging cheeks,
    Covered with hide instead of skin—Nay, help, sir—
    That look like frozen dish-clouts, set on end.
CORVINO: Or, like an old smoked wall, on which the
      rain
    Ran down in streaks.
MOSCA: Excellent, sir, speak out;
    You may be louder yet; a culverin°
90   Dischargèd in his ear, would hardly bore it.
CORVINO: His nose is like a common sewer, still
      running.
MOSCA: 'Tis good! And what his mouth?
CORVINO: A very draught.°
MOSCA: O, stop it up— *(Starts to smother him.)*
CORVINO: By no means.
MOSCA: Pray you, let me.
    Faith, I could stifle him, rarely,° with a pillow,
    As well as any woman that should keep° him.
100 CORVINO: Do as you will, but I'll be gone.
MOSCA: Be so;
    It is your presence makes him last so long.
CORVINO: I pray you, use no violence.
MOSCA: No, sir? why?
    Why should you be thus scrupulous, pray you, sir?
CORVINO: Nay, at your discretion.
MOSCA: Well, good sir, be gone.
CORVINO: I will not trouble him now, to take my
      pearl?°

---

fable, story, report (not "fiction"). *family,* household,
pox, the great pox, syphilis. *it . . . it,* "your incontinence
hath deserved the pox." *culverin,* hand-gun. *draught,*
sink, cesspool. *rarely,* excellent. *keep,* keep house for,
look after. *pearl,* this, with the diamond, is still in Volpone's fist.

MOSCA: Puh! nor your diamant, What a needless care   110
    Is this afflicts you! *(Takes the jewels.)* Is not all, here,
      yours?
    Am not I here? whom you have made? your
      creature?
    That owe my being to you?
CORVINO: Grateful Mosca!
    Thou art my friend, my fellow, my companion,
    My partner, and shalt share in all my fortunes.
MOSCA: Excepting one.
CORVINO: What's that?   120
MOSCA: Your gallant° wife, sir.

(Exit CORVINO.)

    Now, is he gone; we had no other means
    To shoot him hence, but this.
VOLPONE: My divine Mosca!
    Thou hast today outgone thyself. *(Another knocks.)*
    Who's there?
    I will be troubled with no more. Prepare
    Me music, dances, banquets, all delights;
    The Turk is not more sensual in his pleasures
    Than will Volpone. *(Exit* MOSCA.) Let me see, a   130
      pearl!
    A diamant! plate! chequeens! Good morning's
      purchase;°
    Why, this is better than rob churches, yet;
    Or fat, by eating, once a month, a man. *(Enter*
      MOSCA.)
    Who is't?
MOSCA: The beauteous Lady Would-be, sir,
    Wife, to the English knight, Sir Politic Would-be,
    (This is the style, sir, is directed me)
    Hath sent to know, how you have slept tonight,   140
    And if you would be visited.
VOLPONE: Not now.
    Some three hours hence—
MOSCA: I told the squire so much.
VOLPONE: When I am high with mirth, and wine:
      then, then.
    'Fore heaven, I wonder at the desperate valour°
    Of the bold English, that they dare let loose
    Their wives, to all encounters!
MOSCA: Sir, this knight   150
    Had not his name for nothing, he is politic,
    And knows, how e'er his wife affect strange airs,
    She hath not yet the face, to be dishonest.°
    But, had she Signior Corvino's wife's face—
VOLPONE: Has she so rare a face?
MOSCA: O, Sir, the wonder,
    The blazing star of Italy! a wench

---

gallant, fine, beautiful. *purchase,* haul (thieves' cant).
desperate valour, the English were much wondered at in
Italy for the freedom they allowed their wives; the Italians
were reputed to incarcerate them. *dishonest,* unchaste.

O' the first year,° a beauty, ripe, as harvest!
Whose skin is whiter than a swan, all over!
160   Than silver, snow, or lillies! a soft lip,
Would tempt you to eternity of kissing!
And flesh that melteth, in the touch, to blood!
Bright as your gold! and lovely as your gold!
VOLPONE: Why had I not known this before?
MOSCA: Alas, sir,
Myself, but yesterday, discovered it.
VOLPONE: How might I see her?
MOSCA: O, not possible;
She's kept as warily as is your gold;
170   Never does come abroad,° never takes air
But at a window. All her looks are sweet,
As the first grapes, or cherries, and are watched
As near° as they are.
VOLPONE: I must see her—
MOSCA: Sir,
There is a guard, of ten spies thick, upon her;
All his whole household: each of which is set
Upon his fellow, and have all their charge,
When he goes out, when he comes in, examined.°
180   VOLPONE: I will go see her, though but at her window.
MOSCA: In some disguise, then.
VOLPONE: That is true. I must
Maintain mine own shape,° still, the same; we'll
think.

(*Exeunt* VOLPONE, MOSCA.)

ACT 2 / SCENE 1

(*The Square, before* CORVINO'S *house.*)
(*Enter* POLITIC WOULD-BE, PEREGRINE.)

SIR POLITIC: Sir, to a wise man, all the world's his soil.
It is not Italy, nor France, nor Europe,
That must bound me, if my fates call me forth.
Yet, I protest, it is no salt° desire
Of seeing countries, shifting a religion,
Nor any disaffection to the state
Where I was bred (and unto which I owe
My dearest plots°) hath brought me out; much less
That idle, antique, stale, grey-headed project
10   Of knowing° men's minds, and manners, with
Ulysses;
But a peculiar humour° of my wife's,
Laid for this height° of Venice, to observe,

To quote,° to learn the language, and so forth—
I hope you travel, sir, with licence?°
PEREGRINE: Yes.
SIR POLITIC: I dare the safelier converse—How long,
sir,
Since you left England?
PEREGRINE: Seven weeks.   20
SIR POLITIC: So lately!
You ha' not been with my lord ambassador?°
PEREGRINE: Not yet, sir.
SIR POLITIC: Pray you, what news, sir, vents° our
climate?
I heard, last night, a most strange thing reported
By some of my lord's followers, and I long
To hear, how 'twill be seconded.
PEREGRINE: What was't, sir?
SIR POLITIC: Marry, sir, of a raven, that should° build   30
In a ship royal of the King's.
PEREGRINE (*aside*): —This fellow
Does he gull° me, trow? or is gulled?—Your name,
sir?
SIR POLITIC: My name is Politic Would-be.
PEREGRINE (*aside*): O, that speaks him°—
A knight, sir?
SIR POLITIC: A poor knight, sir.
PEREGRINE: Your lady
Lies° here, in Venice, for intelligence   40
Of tires,° and fashions, and behaviour
Among the courtesans? The fine Lady Would-be?
SIR POLITIC: Yes, sir, the spider, and the bee,
oft-times,
Suck from one flower.
PEREGRINE: Good Sir Politic!
I cry your mercy;° I have heard much of you:
'Tis true, sir, of your raven.
SIR POLITIC: On your knowledge?°
PEREGRINE: Yes, and your lions whelping, in the   50
Tower.
SIR POLITIC: Another whelp!°
PEREGRINE: Another, sir.
SIR POLITIC: Now, heaven!
What prodigies be these? The fires at Berwick!°

O'the first year, perhaps "without blemish." abroad, out of the house. near, closely. charge . . . examined, i.e., each is questioned about the servant under his charge. mine own shape, i.e., his own apparent shape. salt, wanton (used of bitches on heat). plots, projects. knowing . . . Ulysses, alluding to the first lines of the Odyssey. humour, whim, obsession. Laid for this height, setting course for this latitude.

quote, make notes. license, warrant from the Lords of Council. my lord ambassador, Sir Henry Wotton was ambassador to Venice from 1604 to 1612; Sir Politic has been thought to caricature him. vents, "comes out of" or "publishes"; the rhetoric strains either usage. should, "it is said," from an Old English usage. gull, take in, fool. speaks him, expresses what he is. Lies, stays. tires, attires, head-dresses. I cry your mercy, I beg your pardon. On your knowledge, "your" may be impersonal, "This is known to be true?" Another whelp! Stow's Annals reports the whelping of King James's lions in the Tower on 5 August 1604 and 26 February 1605. fires at Berwick, ghostly battles on Halidon Hill near Berwick caused border alarms in 1604; aurora borealis has been suggested as contributory to this and other marvels of the time.

And the new star!° These things concurring,
   strange!
And full of omen! Saw you those meteors?°
PEREGRINE: I did, sir.
60 SIR POLITIC: Fearful! Pray you sir, confirm me,
   Were there three porcpisces° seen, above the
    bridge,
   As they give out?
PEREGRINE: Six, and a sturgeon, sir.
SIR POLITIC: I am astonished!
PEREGRINE: Nay, sir, be not so;
   I'll tell you a greater prodigy, than these—
SIR POLITIC: What should these things portend!
PEREGRINE: The very day
70   (Let me be sure) that I put forth from London,
   There was a whale discovered, in the river,
   As high as Woolwich, that had waited there,
   Few know how many months, for the subversion
   Of the Stode fleet.°
SIR POLITIC: Is't possible? Believe it,
   'Twas either sent from Spain, or the Archdukes!°
   Spinola's° whale, upon my life, my credit!
   Will they not leave these projects? Worthy sir,
   Some other news.
80 PEREGRINE: Faith, Stone° the fool is dead,
   And they do lack a tavern fool, extremely.
SIR POLITIC: Is Mas'° Stone dead?
PEREGRINE: He's dead, sir; why? I hope
   You thought him not immortal? *(aside)*—O, this
    knight,
   Were he well known, would be a precious thing
   To fit our English stage: he that should write
   But such a fellow, should be thought to feign
   Extremely, if not maliciously.
90 SIR POLITIC: Stone dead!
PEREGRINE: Dead. Lord! how deeply, sir, you
   apprehend° it!

He was no kinsman to you?
SIR POLITIC: That I know of.°
   Well! that same fellow was an unknown° fool.
PEREGRINE: And yet you knew him, it seems?
SIR POLITIC: I did so. Sir,
   I knew him one of the most dangerous heads
   Living within the state, and so I held him.
PEREGRINE: Indeed, sir?   100
SIR POLITIC: While he lived, in action.
   He has received weekly intelligence,
   Upon my knowledge, out of the Low Countries,
   For all parts of the world, in cabbages;°
   And those dispensed, again, t'ambassadors,
   In oranges, musk-melons,° apricots,
   Lemons, pome-citrons,° and such-like: sometimes
   In Colchester oysters, and your Selsey cockles.°
PEREGRINE: You make me wonder!
SIR POLITIC: Sir, upon my knowledge.   110
   Nay, I have observed him, at your public ordinary,°
   Take his advertisement,° from a traveller
   (A concealed statesman°) in a trencher of meat;
   And, instantly, before the meal was done,
   Convey an answer in a toothpick.
PEREGRINE: Strange!
   How could this be, sir?
SIR POLITIC: Why, the meat was cut
   So like his character,° and so laid, as he
   Must easily read the cipher.   120
PEREGRINE: I have heard,
   He could not read, sir.
SIR POLITIC: So 'twas given out,
   In polity, by those that did employ him:
   But he could read, and had your languages,
   And to't, as sound a noddle°—
PEREGRINE: I have heard, sir,
   That your baboons were spies; and that they were
   A kind of subtle nation, near to China.
SIR POLITIC: Ay, ay, your *Mamuluchi.*° Faith, they had 130
   Their hand in a French plot, or two; but they
   Were so extremely given to women, as
   They made discovery° of all: yet I
   Had my advices° here, on Wednesday last,

---

the new star, Kepler discovered a nova in constellation Serpens in 1604; it was brighter than Jupiter and disappeared after two years. *meteors,* taken as ill omens, because an apparent disturbance of the cosmos. *porcpisces,* Jonson's spelling is retained with its correct etymology; Stow tells of "a great Porpus" taken from the Thames, and of "a very great whale" up river a few days later. *Stode fleet,* the English Merchant Adventurers were displaced from Hamburg and settled at Stade (Stode) at the mouth of the Elbe. *Archdukes* F (Q Arch-duke); the F reading may be the possessive (Archduke's) or it may be the correct style for Isabella and Albert, joint rulers of the Spanish Netherlands. *Spinola,* commander of the Spanish army in the Netherlands, often credited by the gullible with monstrous ingenuity; he was said to have hired a whale to drown London "by snuffing up the Thames and spouting it upon the City." *Stone,* in the spring of 1605 "Stone the fool" was whipped in Bridewell for "a blasphemous speech" in which he called the Lord Admiral a fool. *Mas'* master. *apprehend,* both "feel" and "understand."

That I know of, "not" understood before "that." *unknown,* i.e., not known for what he really was. *cabbages,* regularly imported from Holland at this time. *musk-melons,* common melons. *pome-citrons,* citrons, or limes. *Colchester oysters . . . Selsey cockles,* both delicacies in court circles. *ordinary,* tavern offering fixed prices. *advertisement,* instruction or information. *concealed statesman,* disguised agent of state. *character,* cipher, code. *noddle,* the back of the head and seat of the mind; perhaps less playful here than in its common use. *Mamuluchi,* a macaronic version of *mamalik,* Circassian slaves who came to rule Egypt in the thirteenth century; nothing to do with baboons or China. *discovery,* disclosure. *advices,* news, dispatches.

From one of their own coat,° they were returned,
Made their relations,° as the fashion is,
And now stand fair,° for fresh employment.
PEREGRINE (aside): —'Heart!°
This Sir Pol would be ignorant of nothing—
140　It seems, sir, you know all?
SIR POLITIC: Not all, sir. But,
I have some general notions; I do love
To note, and to observe: though I live out,
Free from the active torrent, yet I'd mark
The currents, and the passages of things,
For mine own private use; and know the ebbs,
And flows of state.
PEREGRINE: Believe it, sir, I hold
Myself, in no small tie,° unto my fortunes
150　For casting me thus luckily, upon you;
Whose knowledge, if your bounty equal it,
May do me great assistance, in instruction
For my behaviour, and my bearing, which
Is yet so rude, and raw.
SIR POLITIC: Why? came you forth
Empty of rules for travel?
PEREGRINE: Faith, I had
Some common ones, from out that vulgar
grammar,°
160　Which he that cried° Italian to me, taught me.
SIR POLITIC: Why, this it is, that spoils all our brave
bloods;
Trusting our hopeful gentry unto pedants:
Fellows of outside, and mere bark.° You seem
To be a gentleman, of ingenuous° race—
I not profess it, but my fate hath been
To be, where I have been consulted with,
In this high kind,° touching some great men's sons.
Persons of blood, and honour—
170　PEREGRINE (seeing people approach): Who be these, sir?

ACT 2 / SCENE 2

(Enter MOSCA and NANO, disguised, with materials for a scaffold stage. A crowd follows.)

MOSCA: Under that window, there't must be. The same.
SIR POLITIC: Fellows, to mount a bank°! Did your instructor
In the dear° tongues, never discourse to you

Of the Italian mountebanks?
PEREGRINE: Yes, sir.
SIR POLITIC: Why,
Here shall you see one.
PEREGRINE: They are quacksalvers,°　10
Fellows, that live by venting° oils and drugs?
SIR POLITIC: Was that the character he gave you of them?
PEREGRINE: As I remember.
SIR POLITIC: Pity his ignorance.
They are the only knowing men of Europe!
Great general scholars, excellent physicians,
Most admired statesmen, professed favourites,
And cabinet counsellors, to the greatest princes!
The only languaged men, of all the world!　20
PEREGRINE: And, I have heard, they are most lewd° impostors;
Made all of terms, and shreds;° no less beliers°
Of great men's favours, than their own vile medicines;
Which they will utter,° upon monstrous oaths:
Selling that drug, for twopence, ere they part,
Which they have valued at twelve crowns, before.
SIR POLITIC: Sir, calumnies are answered best with silence:　30
Yourself shall judge. Who is it mounts, my friends?
MOSCA: Scoto of Mantua,° sir.
SIR POLITIC: Is't he? Nay, then
I'll proudly promise, sir, you shall behold
Another man, than has been phant'sied to you.
I wonder, yet, that he should mount his bank
Here, in this nook, that has been wont t'appear
In face of° the Piazza! Here, he comes.

(Enter VOLPONE, as a mountebank; with a crowd.)

VOLPONE (to NANO): Mount, zany.°
CROWD: Follow, follow, follow, follow, follow.　40
SIR POLITIC: See how the people follow him! He's a man
May write ten thousand crowns, in bank, here. Note,
Mark but his gesture: I do use to observe
The state he keeps, in getting up! (VOLPONE mounts stage.)
PEREGRINE: 'Tis worth it, sir.
VOLPONE: Most noble gentlemen, and my worthy patrons, it may seem strange, that I, your Scoto Mantuano, who was ever wont to fix my bank in　50
face of the public Piazza, near the shelter of the

---

coat, side. relations, reports. stand fair, are well set. 'Heart, i.e., God's Heart! tie, obligation. vulgar grammar, ordinary grammar book, apt to contain phrases and precepts; Florio's grammar may be intended. cried, called out, intoned. bark, shell, outward appearance; may include pun suggested by "cried." ingenuous, noble; Sir Politic pauses to weigh Peregrine's potential. high hand, important capacity. mount a bank, from Italian monta in banco; bank bench. dear, esteemed.

quacksalvers, a Dutch word for quackers about ointment; hence modern "quack." venting, vending. lewd, ignorant. terms, and shreds, jargon, snatches and tags. beliers, misreporters. utter, sell. Scoto of Mantua, renowned Italian juggler who visited Elizabeth's court in 1576. In face of, facing on to. zany, clown and servant, comic assistant.

Portico to the Procuratia,° should, now, after
eight months' absence, from this illustrious city
of Venice humbly retire myself, into an obscure
nook of the Piazza.

SIR POLITIC: Did not I, now, object° the same?

PEREGRINE: Peace, sir.

VOLPONE: Let me tell you: I am not, as your Lombard
proverb saith, cold on my feet,° or content to
60 part with my commodities at a cheaper rate, than
I accustomed: look not for it. Nor, that the
calumnious reports of that impudent detractor,
and shame to our profession—Alessandro Buttone,° I mean—who gave out, in public, I was
condemned *a sforzato*° to the galleys, for poisoning the Cardinal Bembo's—cook,° hath at all attached,° much less dejected me. No, no, worthy
gentlemen, to tell you true, I cannot endure, to
see the rabble of these ground *ciarlitani*,° that
70 spread their cloaks on the pavement, as if they
meant to do feats of activity, and then come in,
lamely, with their mouldy tales out of Boccaccio,
like stale Tabarine,° the fabulist: some of them
discoursing their travels, and of their tedious
captivity in the Turk's galleys, when indeed,
were the truth known, they were the Christian's
galleys, where very temperately, they ate bread,
and drunk water, as a wholesome penance, enjoined them by their confessors, for base pil-
80 feries.

SIR POLITIC: Note but his bearing, and contempt of
these.

VOLPONE: These turdy-facy-nasty-paty-lousy-fartical°
rogues, with one poor groat's-worth of unprepared antimony, finely wrapped up in several°
scartoccios,° are able, very well, to kill their twenty
a week, and play; yet, these meagre starved
spirits, who have half stopped the organs of their
minds with earthy oppilations,° want not their
90 favourers among your shrivelled, salad°-eating
artisans: who are overjoyed, that they may have

their half-pe'rth° of physic, though it purge 'em
into another world, 't makes no matter.

SIR POLITIC: Excellent! Ha' you heard better language, sir?

VOLPONE: Well, let 'em go. And gentlemen, honourable gentlemen, know that for this time, our bank,
being thus removed from the clamours of the
canaglia,° shall be the scene of pleasure, and delight; for, I have nothing to sell, little, or nothing 100
to sell.

SIR POLITIC: I told you, sir, his end.

PEREGRINE: You did so, sir.

VOLPONE: I protest, I, and my six servants, are not
able to make of this precious liquor, so fast, as it
is fetched away from my lodgings by gentlemen
of your city; strangers of the Terra Firma°; worshipful merchants; ay, and senators too: who,
ever since my arrival, have detained me to their
uses, by their splendidous° liberalities. And 110
worthily. For, what avails your rich man to have
his magazines stuffed with *moscadelli*,° or of the
purest grape, when his physicians prescribe him,
on pain of death, to drink nothing but water,
cocted° with aniseeds? O, health! health! the
blessing of the rich! the riches of the poor! who
can buy thee at too dear a rate, since there is no
enjoying this world without thee? Be not then so
sparing of your purses, honourable gentlemen,
as to abridge the natural course of life— 120

PEREGRINE: You see his end?

SIR POLITIC: Ay, is't not good?

VOLPONE: For, when a humid flux, or catarrh, by the
mutability of air, falls from your head, into an
arm, or shoulder, or any other part; take you a
ducat, or your chequeen of gold, and apply to
the place affected: see, what good effect it can
work. No, no, 'tis this blessed *unguento*,° this rare
extraction, that hath only power to disperse all
malignant humours,° that proceed, either of hot, 130
cold, moist, or windy causes—

PEREGRINE: I would he had put in dry too.

SIR POLITIC: Pray you, observe.

Portico to the Procuratia, the arcaded residence of the
Procurators on the north side of St. Mark's. ***object,*** possibly
in archaic sense "put before the mind." ***cold on my feet,*** Italian, *aver freddo a 'piedi,* i.e., to be forced by poverty to sell
cheaply. ***Buttone,*** the name of this rival owes nothing to
fact. ***sforzato,*** "Sfortzati, gallie-slaves, prisoners perforce"
(Florio 1598). ***Bembo's—cook,*** the pause insinuates "mistress"; Pietro Bembo (1470–1547), the great humanist, was
born in Venice. ***attached*** arrested, constrained. ***ground
ciarlitani,*** charlatans working on the ground, without a
bank. ***Tarbarine,*** a famous zany in a touring Italian troop
of the 1570s. ***turdy . . . fartical,*** an Aristophanic phrase,
compounded of abusive improvisations. ***several,*** separate.
scartoccios, "a coffin of paper for spice" (Florio 1598).
earthly oppilations, gross obstructions, i.e., mundane concerns. ***salad,*** probably meaning "raw vegetables."

---

half-pe'rth, ha'p'orth. ***canaglia,*** "raskallie people
onelie fit for dogs companie" (Florio 1598). ***Terra Firma,***
name for the mainland part of Venice. ***splendidous,*** common variant of "splendid." ***magazines,*** storehouses. ***moscadelli,*** "the wine Muscadine" (Florio 1598), muscatel.
cocted, boiled. ***unguento,*** ointment. ***malignant humours,***
According to classical and medieval medical theory the four
cardinal humours of the body were blood, phlegm, choler
and melancholy, and they corresponded with the four
elements—air (hot and moist), water (cold and moist), fire
(hot and dry) and earth (cold and dry). Both pathological
and temperamental traits were attributed to the dominance
of one humour over the others, or to 'fluxes'—flowings of
humours from one part of the body to another.

VOLPONE: To fortify the most indigest, and crude°
stomach, ay, were it of one that, through extreme weakness, vomited blood, applying only a
warm napkin to the place, after the unction, and
fricace°; for the *vertigine*°, in the head, putting
but a drop into your nostrils, likewise, behind the
140 ears; a most sovereign, and approved remedy:
the *mal caduco*°, cramps, convulsions, paralyses,
epilepsies, *tremor-cordia,*° retired nerves,° ill vap-
ours of the spleen, stoppings of the liver, the
stone, the strangury,° *hernia ventosa,*° *iliaca passio*°; stops a *disenteria* immediately; easeth the tor-
tion of the small guts; and cures *melancholia
hypocondriaca,*° being taken and applied, according to my printed receipt.° (*Pointing to his bill and
his glass.*) For, this is the physician, this the
150 medicine; this counsels, this cures; this gives the
direction, this works the effect: and, in sum, both
together may be termed an abstract of the
theoric, and practic in the Aesculapian° art.
'Twill cost you eight crowns. And, Zan Fritada,°
pray thee sing a verse, extempore, in honour of
it.
SIR POLITIC: How do you like him, sir?
PEREGRINE: Most strangely, I!
SIR POLITIC: Is not his language rare?
160 PEREGRINE: But° alchemy,
I never heard the like: or Broughton's° books.

(*NANO sings.*)

SONG

Had old Hippocrates, or Galen,°
That to their books put medicines all in,
But known this secret, they had never
(Of which they will be guilty ever)
Been murderers of so much paper,
Or wasted many a hurtless° taper:

No Indian drug had ere been famèd,
Tobacco, sassafras° not named,
Ne yet of guacum one small stick, sir,   170
Nor Raymond Lully's° great elixir.
Ne had been known the Danish Gonswart,°
Or Paracelsus, with his long sword.°

PEREGRINE: All this, yet, will not do; eight crowns is
high.
VOLPONE: No more; gentlemen, if I had but time to
discourse to you the miraculous effects of this
my oil, surnamed *oglio del Scoto*; with the countless catalogue of those I have cured of th'afor-
said, and many more diseases; the patents and   180
privileges of all the princes and commonwealths
of Christendom; or but the depositions of those
that appeared on my part, before the signiory of
the *Sanita,*° and most learned college of physicians; where I was authorized, upon notice taken
of the admirable virtues of my medicaments, and
mine own excellency, in matter of rare, and unknown secrets, not only to dispense them publicly in this famous city, but in all the territories,
that happily joy under the government of the   190
most pious and magnificent states of Italy. But
may some other gallant fellow say, 'O, there be
divers that make profession to have as good, and
as experimented receipts as yours.' Indeed, very
many have assayed, like apes in imitation of that,
which is really and essentially in me, to make of
this oil; bestowed great cost in furnaces, stills,
alembics,° continual fires and preparation of the
ingredients (as indeed there goes to it six
hundred several° simples,° besides some quantity 200
of human fat, for the conglutination, which we
buy of the anatomists) but, when these prac-
titioners come to the last decoction,° blow, blow,°
puff, puff, and all flies *in fumo*: ha, ha, ha! Poor
wretches! I rather pity their folly, and indiscretion, than their loss of time, and money; for

---

crude, sour. *fricace,* massage. *vertigine,* dizziness.
mal caduco, falling sickness (epilepsy). *tremor-cordia,* heart
palpitations. *retired nerves,* shrunken sinews. *strangury,*
painful urination. *hernia ventosa,* gaseous protrusion (possibly strangulated hernia). *iliaca passio,* "pain and wringing of the small guts" (Holland's *Pliny* II. 39). *melancholia
hypocondriaca,* melancholy was supposed to be seated in the
hypochondria—the soft parts of the body below the rib
cartilages. *receipt,* recipe. *Aesculapian,* after Aes-
culapius, Greek and Roman god of medicine. *Zan Fritada,*
Volpone calls Nano by the name of a celebrated zany (*fritada*
= pancake). *But,* "except for" or "pure." *Broughton,*
Hugh Broughton (1549–1612), rabbinical scholar and Puritan. *Hippocrates, or Galen,* Hippocrates (born *ca.* 460 B.C.)
invented the theory of humours and Galen (born *ca.* A.D.
130) expounded it; their authority in all medical matters was
still recognized in Jonson's time. *hurtless,* harmless.

Tobacco, sassafras, both used medicinally and newly
introduced from America. *guacum,* drug extracted from
resin of guaiacum tree. *Raymond Lully* (1235–1315), sage,
evangelist, and astrologer from Majorca; apocryphal alchemical works were ascribed to him posthumously, hence
the tradition that he discovered the elixir of life. *Danish
Gonswart,* unidentified: suggestions include a Dutch theologian (Wessel Gansfort) and a Danish Chemist (Berthold
Schwarz). *Paracelsus . . . sword,* Paracelsus was supposed
to have kept his quintessences in the pommel of his sword.
signiory of the Sanita, the "health masters" of Venice who
licensed physicians, drug-vendors and mountebanks.
alembics, alchemical stills. *several,* separate. *simples,*
remedies made from one herb only. *decoction,* boiling
down to extract essences. *blow, blow,* imitates the alchemist
at his furnace.

those may be covered by industry: but to be a
fool born, is a disease incurable. For my self, I
always from my youth have endeavoured to get
the rarest secrets, and book them; either in exchange, or for money: I spared not cost, nor
labour, where anything was worthy to be
learned. And gentlemen, honourable gentlemen, I will undertake, by virtue of chemical
art, out of the honourable hat, that covers your
head, to extract the four elements; that is to say,
the fire, air, water, and earth, and return you
your felt without burn, or stain. For, whilst
others have been at the balloo,° I have been at
my book; and am now past the craggy paths of
study, and come to the flowery plains of honour,
and reputation.

SIR POLITIC: I do assure you, sir, that is his aim.

VOLPONE: But, to our price—

PEREGRINE: And that withall, Sir Pol.

VOLPONE: You all know, honourable gentlemen, I
never valued this *ampulla,*° or vial, at less than
eight crowns, but for this time, I am content to
be deprived of it for six; six crowns is the price;
and less in courtesy, I know you cannot offer me:
take it, or leave it, howsoever, both it, and I, am
at your service. I ask you not, as the value of the
thing, for then I should demand of you a
thousand crowns, so the Cardinals Montalto,
Fernese,° the great Duke of Tuscany,° my gossip,° with divers other princes have given me; but
I despise money: only to show my affection to
you, honourable gentlemen, and your illustrious
state here, I have neglected the messages of
these princes, mine own offices,° framed my
journey hither, only to present you with the
fruits of my travels. (*to* NANO *and* MOSCA) Tune
your voices once more to the touch of your instruments, and give the honourable assembly
some delightful recreation.

PEREGRINE: What monstrous,° and most painful
circumstance
Is here, to get some three or four *gazets!*°
Some threepence, i' th' whole, for that 'twill come
to.

SONG

You that would last long, list to my song,
Make no more coil,° but buy of this oil.
Would you be ever fair? and young?
Stout of teeth? and strong of tongue?
Tart° of palate? quick of ear?
Sharp of sight? of nostril clear?
Moist of hand?° and light of foot?
Or, I will come nearer to it,
Would you live free from all diseases?
Do the act, your mistress pleases;
Yet fright all aches from your bones?°
Here's a medicine, for the nones.°

VOLPONE: Well, I am in a humour, at this time, to
make a present of the small quantity my coffer
contains: to the rich, in courtesy, and to the
poor, for God's sake. Wherefore, now mark; I
asked you six crowns; and six crowns, at other
times, you have paid me; you shall not give me
six crowns, or five, nor four, nor three, nor two,
nor one; nor half a ducat; no, nor a *moccenigo*°:
six—pence it will cost you, or six hundred
pound—expect no lower price, for by the banner
of my front,° I will not bate a *bagatine*°, that I will
have, only, a pledge of your loves, to carry something from amongst you, to show, I am not con-
temned by you. Therefore, now, toss your handkerchiefs,° cheerfully, cheerfully; and be advertised, that the first heroic spirit, that deigns to
grace me, with a handkerchief, I will give it a
little remembrance of something, beside, shall
please it better, than if I had presented it with a
double pistolet.°

PEREGRINE: Will you be that heroic spark,° Sir Pol?
O, see! the window has prevented you.

(CELIA *at the window*° *throws down her handkerchief.*)

VOLPONE: Lady, I kiss your bounty: and for this
timely grace, you have done your poor Scotto of
Mantua, I will return you, over and above my oil,
a secret of that high, and inestimable nature,

---

coil, pother, fuss.   *Tart,* sharp, keen.   *Moist of hand,*
the sign of "pith and livelihood" in *Venus & Adonis* 25–26.
aches . . . bones, probably alluding to venereal disease.
nones, nonce, occasion.   *moccenigo,* "a kind of coine in
Venice" (Florio 1598) perhaps worth nine *gazets.*   *banner of
my front,* displayed upon the scaffold, listing maladies and
cures.   *bate,* abate.   *bagatine,* "a little coine in Italie"
(Florio 1598) about a third of a farthing.   *handkerchiefs,*
i.e., with the money knotted into a corner; the usual practice.
give it, i.e. the heroic spirit.   *pistolet,* Spanish gold coin,
then worth about eighteen shillings.   *spark,* gallant, brave
fellow.   *Celia at the window,* presumably on the tarras or in
the window-stage; the text does not say when she first
appears.

---

balloo (balloon), Venetian game.   *ampulla,* "a thin
viole-glasse" (Florio 1598).   *Cardinals Montalto, Fernese,*
Montalto became Pope Sixtus V in 1585; *Fernese* probably an
allusion to the notorious Alessandro Farnese who became
Pope Paul III in 1534 but there was also a later Cardinal
Alessandro Farnese (1520–1589).   *Duke of Tuscany,* office
held by Cosimo de' Medici after 1569.   *gossip,* godsib,
godfather; also "familiar acquaintance."   *offices,* duties.
What monstrous . . . , Peregrine's speech is probably aside to
the audience.   *gazets,* Venetian pennies, as Peregrine's
explanation indicates.

shall make you for ever enamoured on that minute, wherein your eye first descended on so
mean, yet not altogether to be despised, an object. Here is a poulder°, concealed in this paper,
of which, if I should speak to the worth, nine
thousand volumes were but as one page, that
page as a line, that line as a word; so short is this
pilgrimage of man (which some call life) to the
expressing of it. Would I reflect on the price?
Why, the whole world were but as an empire,
that empire as a province, that province as a
290 bank, that bank as a private purse, to the purchase of it. I will, only, tell you; it is the poulder
that made Venus a goddess, given her by Apollo,
that kept her perpetually young, cleared her
wrinkles, firmed her gums, filled her skin, coloured her hair; from her, derived to Helen, and
at the sack of Troy, unfortunately, lost: till now,
in this our age, it was as happily recovered, by a
studious antiquary, out of some ruins of Asia,
who sent a moiety° of it, to the court of France
300 (but much sophisticated), wherewith the ladies
there, now, colour their hair. The rest, at this
present, remains with me; extracted to a quintessence: so that, wherever it but touches, in youth
it perpetually preserves, in age restores the complexion; seats your teeth, did they dance like virginal jacks,° firm as a wall; makes them white, as
ivory, that were black, as—

ACT 2 / SCENE 3

(Enter CORVINO.)

CORVINO: Spite o' the devil, and my shame! come
down here;
Come down! No house but mine to make your
scene?

(He beats away the mountebank.)

Signior Flaminio,° will you down, sir? down!
What, is my wife your Franciscina,° sir?
No windows on the whole Piazza, here,
To make your properties, but mine? but mine?
Heart! ere tomorrow, I shall be new christened,
10   And called the *Pantalone di Besogniosi,*°

---

poulder, powder; Jonson preferred this spelling (Latin
pulvis). **moiety,** a half, or a part. **sophisticated,** adulter-
ated. **virginal jacks,** strictly the pieces of wood bearing the
quills of the virginals, but sometimes erroneously used for
keys (the image derives from Rabelais). **Flaminio,** Flaminio
Scala, leading figure in the *commedia,* associated with Venice.
Franciscina, stock character of maid in the *commedia.* **Pantalone di Besogniosi,** stock Venetian character in the *commedia;* a lean old man in loose slippers, black cap and gown,
and red dress, his name derives him from a line of paupers,
and it was often his role to be cuckolded.

About the town. (*Exit.*)
PEREGRINE: What should this mean, Sir Pol?
SIR POLITIC: Some trick of state, believe it. I will
home.
PEREGRINE: It may be some design, on you.
SIR POLITIC: I know not.
I'll stand upon my guard.
PEREGRINE: It is your best, sir.
SIR POLITIC: This three weeks, all my advices, all my
letters,   20
They have been intercepted.
PEREGRINE: Indeed, sir?
Best have a care.
SIR POLITIC: Nay, so I will.
PEREGRINE: This knight,
I may not lose him, for my mirth, till night.

ACT 2 / SCENE 4

(VOLPONE'S *house.*)
(*Enter* VOLPONE, MOSCA.)

VOLPONE: O, I am wounded,
MOSCA: Where, sir?
VOLPONE: Not without;
Those blows were nothing: I could bear them ever.
But angry Cupid, bolting° from her eyes,
Hath shot himself into me, like a flame;
Where, now, he flings about his burning heat,
As in a furnace, an ambitious fire°
Whose vent is stopped. The fight is all within me.
I cannot live, except thou help me, Mosca;   10
My liver° melts, and I, without the hope
Of some soft air, from her refreshing breath,
Am but a heap of cinders.
MOSCA: 'Las, good sir!
Would you had never seen her.
VOLPONE: Nay, would thou
Hadst never told me of her.
MOSCA: Sir, 'tis true;
I do confess, I was unfortunate,
And you unhappy: but I am bound in conscience,   20
No less than duty, to effect my best
To your release of torment, and I will, sir.
VOLPONE: Dear Mosca, shall I hope?
MOSCA: Sir, more than dear,
I will not bid you to despair of ought,
Within a human compass.
VOLPONE: O, there spoke
My better Angel. Mosca, take my keys,
Gold, plate and jewels, all's at thy devotion;°
Employ them, how thou wilt; nay, coin me,° too: 30

---

bolting, darting arrows (bolts). **ambitious fire,** rising,
swelling flames, recoiling to find other outlets. **liver,**
believed the seat of intense passions. **devotion,** disposal,
with pun on religious sense. **coin me,** render me into coin.

So thou, in this, but crown my longings.—Mosca?°
MOSCA: Use but your patience.
VOLPONE: So I have.
MOSCA: I doubt not
   To bring success to your desires.
VOLPONE: Nay, then,
   I not repent me of my late disguise.
MOSCA: If you can horn him,° sir, you need not.
VOLPONE: True:
40   Besides, I never meant him for my heir.
   Is not the colour° o' my beard, and eyebrows,
   To make me known?
MOSCA: No jot.
VOLPONE: I did it well.
MOSCA: So well, would I could follow you in mine,°
   With half the happiness°; and, yet, I would
   Escape your *epilogue.*°
VOLPONE: But, were they gulled
   With a belief, that I was Scoto?
50 MOSCA: Sir,
   Scoto himself could hardly have distinguished!
   I have not time to flatter you, now, we'll part:
   And, as I prosper, so applaud my art. (*Exeunt.*)

ACT 2 / SCENE 5

(CORVINO's *house.*)
(*Enter* CORVINO, CELIA.)

CORVINO: Death of mine honour, with the city's fool?
   A juggling, tooth-drawing,° prating mountebank?
   And at a public window? where, whilst he,
   With his strained action,° and his dole of faces,°
   To his drug lectures draws your itching ears,
   A crew of old, unmarried, noted lechers
   Stood leering up, like satyrs: and you smile
   Most graciously! and fan your favours forth,
   To give your hot spectators satisfaction!
10   What, was your mountebank their call? their
       whistle?°
   Or were you enamoured on his copper rings.
   His saffron jewel, with the toad-stone in't?
   Or his embroidered suit, with the cope-stitch°,
   Made of a hearse-cloth?° or his old tilt-feather?°

Or his starched beard?° Well! you shall have him,
   yes.
He shall come home, and minister unto you
The fricace, for the mother.° Or, let me see,
I think, you'd rather mount?° Would you not   20
   mount?
Why, if you'll mount, you may; yes truly, you may:
And so, you may be seen, down to th' foot.
Get you a cittern, Lady Vanity,°
And be a dealer,° with the virtuous man°;
Make one°: I'll but protest myself a cuckold,
And save your dowry.° I am a Dutchman,° I!
For, if you thought me an Italian,
You would be damned, ere you did this, you
   whore?   30
Thou'dst tremble, to imagine, that the murder
Of father, mother, brother, all thy race,
Should follow, as the subject of my justice.
CELIA: Good sir, have patience!
CORVINO: What couldst thou purpose
   Less to thyself, than, in this heat of wrath,
   And stung with my dishonour, I should strike

(*Takes his sword.*)

   This steel into thee, with as many stabs,
   As thou wert gazed upon with goatish eyes?
CELIA: Alas sir, be appeased! I could not think   40
   My being at the window should more, now,
   Move your impatience, than at other times.
CORVINO: No? not to seek, and entertain a parley,°
   With a known knave? before a multitude?
   You were an actor, with your handkerchief!
   Which he, most sweetly, kissed in the receipt,
   And might, no doubt, return it, with a letter,
   And point the place, where you might meet: your
       sister's,
   Your mother's, or your aunt's might serve the turn. 50
CELIA: Why, dear sir, when do I make these excuses?
   Or ever stir, abroad, but to the church?
   And that, so seldom—
CORVINO: Well, it shall be less;

---

crown, perfect, with pun on coin. —*Mosca?* express-
sing impatience at Mosca's thoughtful silence. *horn him,*
cuckold him. *colour,* i.e., the fox's colour, red. *mine,* i.e.,
'my art' (of disguise and mimicry). *happiness,* felicitous
aptitude. *your epilogue,* i.e., the beating, but may hint at
the end of Mosca's plot. *tooth-drawing,* the responsibility
of mountebanks and barbers. *strained action,* extravagant
gesture. *dole of faces,* mean repertory of expressions. *call
. . . whistle,* alluding to the enticement of game-fowl. *toad-
stone,* believed to lie between the toad's eyes and to have
magical and restorative properties. *cope-stitch,* used to
decorate a cope border. *hearse-cloth,* coffin drapery, here
either cheap or stolen. *tilt-feather,* plume worn in tilting
helmet; here perhaps found with the hearse-cloth.

starched beard, gummed and waxed beards were high
fashion. *fricace, for the mother,* massage for hysteria,
believed to be seated in the womb; Corvino puns on suggestions of seduction and birth. *mount.* i.e., the mountebank's
platform, or the mountebank himself; another indecent pun
affecting the meaning of "down to the foot." *cittern,* kind
of zither or guitar, often carried by a mountebank's wench.
Lady Vanity, a character in some morality plays, including
that acted in *Sir Thomas More* IV. i. *be a dealer,* do a deal,
trade with (hinting at prostitution). *virtuous man,* with
sneering pun on "virtuoso." *Make one,* make a deal; mate.
protest, declare. *save your dowry,* an adulteress was deprived of all her inheritance. *Dutchman,* believed to be
long-suffering and phlegmatic. *parley,* conversation.

And thy restraint, before, was liberty
To what I now decree: and therefore, mark me.
First, I will have this bawdy light° dammed up;
And, till't be done, some two, or three yards off,
I'll chalk a line; o'er which, if thou but chance
60 To set thy desp'rate foot; more hell, more horror,
More wild, remorseless rage shall seize on thee,
Than on a conjurer that had heedless left
His circle's° safety, ere his devil was laid.
Then, here's a lock,° which I will hang upon thee;
And, now I think on't, I will keep thee backwards;
Thy lodging shall be backwards°; thy walks
   backwards;
Thy prospect—all be backwards; and no pleasure
That thou shalt know, but backwards. Nay, since
70   you force
My honest nature, know it is your own
Being too open, makes me use you thus.
Since you will not contain your subtle° nostrils
In a sweet room, but they must snuff the air
Of rank, and sweaty passengers°—(*Knock within.*)
One knocks.
Away, and be not seen, pain° of thy life;
Not look toward the window, if thou dost—
Nay, stay, hear this; let me not prosper, whore,
80 But I will make thee an anatomy,°
Dissect thee mine own self, and read a lecture
Upon thee, to the city, and in public.
Away! (*Exit* CELIA.) Who's there? (*Enter* SERVANT.)
SERVANT: 'Tis Signior Mosca, sir.

ACT 2 / SCENE 6

CORVINO: Let him come in, his master's dead. There's
   yet
Some good, to help the bad. (*Enter* MOSCA.) My
   Mosca, welcome!
I guess your news.
MOSCA: I fear you cannot, sir.
CORVINO: Is't not his death?
MOSCA: Rather the contrary.
CORVINO: Not his recovery?
10 MOSCA: Yes, sir.
CORVINO: I am cursed,
I am bewitched, my crosses° meet to vex me.
How? how? how? how?
MOSCA: Why, sir, with Scoto's oil!
Corbaccio, and Voltore brought of it,
Whilst I was busy in an inner room—

CORVINO: Death! that damned mountebank! But for
   the law,
Now I could kill the rascal: 't cannot be,
His oil should have that virtue. Ha' not I   20
Known him a common rogue, come fiddling in
To th' *osteria,*° with a tumbling whore,°
And when he has done all his forced tricks, been
   glad
Of a poor spoonful of dead wine, with flies in 't?
It cannot be. All his ingredients
Are a sheep's gall, a roasted bitch's marrow,
Some few sod° earwigs, pounded caterpillars,
A little capon's grease, and fasting spittle:°
I know 'em, to a dram.   30
MOSCA: I know not, sir,
But some on't, there, they poured into his ears,
Some in his nostrils, and recovered him;
Applying but the fricace.
COVINO: Pox o' that fricace.
MOSCA: And since, to seem the more officious,°
And flattering of his health, there, they have had,
At extreme fees,° the college of physicians
Consulting on him, how they might restore him;
Where one would have a cataplasm° of spices,   40
Another, a flayed ape clapped to his breast,
A third would ha' it a dog, a fourth an oil
With wild cats' skins: at last, they all resolved
That, to preserve him, was no other means,
But some young woman must be straight sought
   out,
Lusty, and full of juice, to sleep by him;
And, to this service, most unhappily
And most unwillingly, am I now employed,
Which, here, I thought to pre-acquaint you with, 50
For your advice, since it concerns you most,
Because, I would not do that thing might cross
Your ends,° on whom I have my whole
   dependence, sir:
Yet, if I do it not, they may delate°
My slackness to my patron, work me out
Of his opinion; and there, all your hopes,
Ventures, or whatsoever, are all frustrate.
I do but tell you, sir. Besides, they are all
Now striving, who shall first present him.°   60
   Therefore—
I could entreat you, briefly, conclude somewhat:°
Prevent 'em if you can.
CORVINO: Death to my hopes!
This is my villainous fortune! Best to hire

---

light, window. circle, the magician was supposed safe in his circle until the devil was "laid" to hell. lock, chastity belt. backwards, i.e., at the back of the house. subtle, insidiously acute. passengers, passers-by. pain, on pain. Not look, do not look. anatomy, body for anatomical demonstration; also moral analysis. crosses, afflictions; with a touch of ironic blasphemy.

osteria, inn. tumbling whore, disreputable acrobat (with indecent pun). sod, boiled. fasting spittle, here the saliva of the starving Scoto. officious, dutiful, zealous. extreme fees, the greatest cost. cataplasm, poultice. cross Your ends, obstruct your aims. delate, report. present him, i.e., with the young woman. Therefore—, the dash expresses an emphatic pause. briefly, conclude somewhat, quickly decide something.

Some common courtesan?

MOSCA: Ay, I thought of that, sir.
But they are all so subtle, full of art,
And age again° doting, and flexible,
70   So as—I cannot tell—we may perchance
Light on a quean,° may cheat us all.

CORVINO: 'Tis true.

MOSCA: No, no: it must be one, that has no tricks, sir,
Some simple thing, a creature, made unto it;°
Some wench you may command. Ha' you no
kinswoman?
God's so°—Think, think, think, think, think, think,
think, sir.
One o' the doctors offered, there, his daughter.

80   CORVINO: How?

MOSCA: Yes, Signior Lupo,° the physician.

CORVINO: His daughter!

MOSCA: And a virgin, sir. Why, alas
He knows the state of 's body, what it is;
That nought can warm his blood, sir, but a fever;
Nor any incantation raise his spirit;
A long forgetfulness hath seized that part.
Besides, sir, who shall know it? some one, or two—

CORVINO: I pray thee give me leave. (Walks aside.) If
90   any man
But I had had this luck—The thing, in't self,
I know, is nothing—Wherefore should not I
As well command my blood, and my affections,
As this dull doctor? In the point of honour,
The cases are all one, of wife, and daughter.

MOSCA (aside): I hear him coming.

CORVINO: She shall do't: 'tis done.
'Slight,° if this doctor, who is not engaged,°
Unless 't be for his counsel, which is nothing,
100   Offer his daughter, what should I, that am
So deeply in? I will prevent him: wretch!
Covetous wretch! Mosca, I have determined.

MOSCA: How, sir?

CORVINO: We'll make all sure. The party, you wot of,
Shall be mine own wife, Mosca.

MOSCA: Sir, the thing,
But that I would not seem to counsel you,
I should have motioned° to you, at the first:
And, make your count,° you have cut all their
110   throats.
Why! 'tis directly taking a possession!°

And, in this next fit, we may let him go.
'Tis but to pull the pillow, from his head,
And he is throttled: 't had been done before,
But for your scrupulous doubts.

CORVINO: Ay, a plague on't,
My conscience fools my wit.° Well, I'll be brief,°
And so be thou, lest they should be before us;
Go home, prepare him, tell him, with what zeal
And willingness, I do it: swear it was,   120
On the first hearing, as thou mayst do, truly,
Mine own free motion.

MOSCA: Sir, I warrant you,
I'll so possess him with it, that the rest
Of his starved clients shall be banished, all;
And only you received. But come not, sir,
Until I send, for I have something else
To ripen,° for your good; you must not know it.

CORVINO: But do not you forget to send, now.

MOSCA: Fear not. (Exit MOSCA.)   130

ACT 2 / SCENE 7

CORVINO: Where are you, wife? my Celia? wife!

(Enter CELIA weeping.)

What, blubbering?
Come, dry those tears, I think, thou thought'st me
in earnest?
Ha? by this light, I talked so but to try thee.
Methinks, the lightness of the occasion
Should ha'confirmed° thee. Come, I am not
jealous.

CELIA: No?

CORVINO: Faith, I am not, I, nor never was: 10
It is a poor, unprofitable humour.
Do not I know, if women have a will,°
They'll do 'gainst all the watches° o' the world?
And that the fiercest spies, are tamed with gold?
Tut, I am confident in thee, thou shalt see't:
And see, I'll give thee cause too, to believe it.
Come, kiss me. Go, and make thee ready straight,
In all thy best attire, thy choicest jewels,
Put 'em all on, and with 'em, thy best looks:
We are invited to a solemn° feast,   20
At old Volpone's, where it shall appear
How far I am free, from jealousy, or fear.

ACT 3 / SCENE 1

(A Street.)
(Enter MOSCA.)

MOSCA: I fear, I shall begin to grow in love
With my dear self, and my most prosperous parts,°

Prevent 'em, beat 'em to it. again, on the other hand,
quean, strumpet. made unto it, made for the part; or
possibly "made to do it" by command. God's so, God's soul;
also corruption of cazzo, Italian for male organ. Signior
Lupo, Mr. Wolf; Mosca's invention parodies Jonson's own.
'Slight, God's light. engaged, involved. motioned, proposed. make your count, count on it; or possibly "count
your gains." taking a possession, Mosca uses the legal
phrase in a grotesque context.

wit, intelligence. brief, quick. something . . . ripen,
i.e., the plot to disinherit Corbaccio's son. confirmed,
assured. will, sexual appetite. watches, watchmen, or
vigilances in general. solemn, formal, sumptuous. parts,
abilities.

They do so spring, and burgeon; I can feel
A whimsy° i' my blood: I know not how,
Success hath made me wanton. I could skip
Out of my skin, now, like a subtle° snake,
I am so limber. O! your parasite
Is a most precious thing, dropped from above,
Not bred 'mongst clods, and clotpoles, here on
10   earth.
I muse the mystery° was not made a science,°
It is so liberally° professed! Almost
All the wise world is little else, in nature,
But parasites, or sub-parasites. And yet,
I mean not those, that have your bare town-art,°
To know, who's fit to feed 'em; have no house,
No family, no care, and therefore mould
Tales° for men's ears, to bait that sense; or get
Kitchen-invention,° and some stale receipts
20   To please the belly, and the groin°; not those,
With their court-dog-tricks, that can fawn, and
        fleer,°
Make their revènue out of legs and faces,°
Echo my lord, and lick away a moth:°
But your fine, elegant rascal, that can rise,
And stoop, almost together, like an arrow;
Shoot through the air, as nimbly as a star;
Turn short, as doth a swallow; and be here,
And there, and here, and yonder, all at once;
30   Present to any humour, all occasion;
And change a visor,° swifter, than a thought!
This is the creature, had the art born with him;
Toils not to learn it, but doth practise it
Out of most excellent nature: and such sparks,
Are the true parasites, others but their zanies.°

ACT 3 / SCENE 2

(*Enter* BONARIO.)

MOSCA: Who's this? Bonario? old Corbaccio's son?
    The person I was bound to seek. Fair sir,
    You are happ'ly met.
BONARIO: That cannot be, by thee.

---

whimsy, vertigo, whirling. **subtle,** applied to the snake
to signify its elusive movement, its texture and its traditional
cunning. **limber,** pliant, supple. **mystery,** professional
craft. **science,** branch of formal knowledge. **liberally,**
"widely practiced by gentlemen"; Mosca puns on the sense
describing the sciences "worthy of a free man" (see *OED*).
bare town-art, the minimal skills of a street parasite. **mould
Tales,** concoct scandal, with suggestion of shaping traps for
the ear. **Kitchen-invention,** perhaps new ways of preparing
old dishes ("stale receipts"); or possibly "kitchen gossip";
invention need not imply novelty (see *OED*). **groin,**
suggests that the receipts (recipes) include aphrodisiacs.
fleer, smile obsequiously. **legs and faces,** bows and smirks.
lick . . . moth, servile grooming; "moth" signified vermin in
general. **visor,** mask, hence "expression" or "role."
zanies, attendant clowns.

MOSCA: Why, sir?
BONARIO: Nay, 'pray thee know thy way, and leave
    me:
    I would be loath to interchange discourse,
    With such a mate, as thou art.
MOSCA: Courteous sir,   10
    Scorn not my poverty.
BONARIO: Not I, by heaven:
    But thou shalt give me leave to hate thy baseness.
MOSCA: Baseness?
BONARIO: Ay, answer me, is not thy sloth
    Sufficient argument? thy flattery?
    Thy means of feeding?
MOSCA: Heaven, be good to me,
    These imputations are too common, sir,
    And eas'ly stuck on virtue, when she's poor;   20
    You are unequal° to me, and howe'er
    Your sentence may be righteous, yet you are not,
    That ere you know me, thus, proceed in censure:
    St. Mark bear witness 'gainst you, 'tis inhuman.
        (*weeps.*)
BONARIO: What? does he weep? the sign is soft, and
    good!
    I do repent me, that I was so harsh.
MOSCA: 'Tis true, that, swayed by strong necessity,
    I am enforced to eat my careful° bread
    With too much obsequy; 'tis true, beside,   30
    That I am fain° to spin mine own poor raiment,
    Out of my mere observance,° being not born
    To a free fortune: but that I have done
    Base offices, in rending friends asunder,
    Dividing families, betraying counsels,
    Whispering false lies, or mining° men with praises,
    Trained° their credulity with perjuries,
    Corrupted chastity, or am in love
    With mine own tender ease, but would not rather
    Prove° the most rugged, and laborious course,   40
    That might redeem my present estimation;
    Let me here perish, in all hope of goodness.
BONARIO: This cannot be a personated passion!
    I was to blame, so to mistake thy nature;
    'Pray thee forgive me: and speak out thy business.
MOSCA: Sir, it concerns you; and though I may seem,
    At first, to make a main° offence, in manners,
    And in my gratitude, unto my master,
    Yet, for the pure love, which I bear all right,
    And hatred of the wrong, I must reveal it.   50
    This very hour, your father is in purpose
    To disinherit you—
BONARIO: How!
MOSCA: And thrust you forth,

---

bound, on my way. **unequal,** unjust, but with allusion
to the difference of station. **careful,** hard-won. **fain,**
obliged. **observance,** dutiful service. **mining,** undermin-
ing. **Trained,** taken in, led on (see *OED*). **Prove,** undergo.
main, major.

As a mere stranger to his blood; 'tis true, sir:
The work no way engageth me, but, as
I claim an interest in the general state
Of goodness, and true virtue, which I hear
T'abound in you: and, for which mere respect,°
60   Without a second aim, sir, I have done it.
BONARIO: This tale hath lost thee much of the late
        trust,
    Thou hadst with me; it is impossible:
    I know not how to lend it any thought,
    My father should be so unnatural.
MOSCA: It is a confidence, that well becomes
    Your piety;° and formed, no doubt, it is,
    From your own simple innocence: which makes
    Your wrong more monstrous, and abhorred. But,
70   sir,
    I now, will tell you more. This very minute,
    It is, or will be doing; and, if you
    Shall be but pleased to go with me, I'll bring you,
    I dare not say where you shall see, but where
    Your ear shall be a witness of the deed;
    Hear yourself written bastard: and professed°
    The common issue of the earth.°
BONARIO: I'm mazed!
MOSCA: Sir, if I do it not, draw your just sword,
80   And score° your vengeance, on my front, and face;
    Make me your villain; you have too much wrong,
    And I do suffer for you, sir. My heart
    Weeps blood, in anguish—
BONARIO: Lead, I follow thee.

ACT 3 / SCENE 3

(VOLPONE'S *house.*)
(*Enter* VOLPONE, *followed by* NANO, ANDROGYNO *and*
CASTRONE.)

VOLPONE: Mosca stays long, methinks. Bring forth
        your sports
    And help to make the wretched time more sweet.
NANO: Dwarf, Fool, and Eunuch, well met here we
        be.
    A question it were now, whether° of us three,
    Being all, the known delicates° of a rich man,
    In pleasing him, claim the precedency can?
CASTRONE: I claim for myself.
10 ANDROGYNO: And, so doth the fool.
NANO: 'Tis foolish indeed: let me set you both to
        school.
    First, for your dwarf, he's little, and witty,
        And every thing, as it is little, is pretty;
    Else, why do men say to a creature of my shape,

So soon as they see him, 'It's a pretty little ape?'
And, why a pretty ape? but for pleasing imitation
    Of greater men's action, in a ridiculous fashion.
Beside, this feat° body of mind doth not crave
    Half the meat, drink, and cloth, one of your   20
        bulks wil have.
Admit, your fool's face be the mother of laughter,
    Yet, for his brain, it must always come after:
And, though that do feed him, it's a pitiful case,
    His body is beholding to such a bad face.

(*One knocks.*)

VOLPONE: Who's there? my couch; away, look Nano,
        see:
    Give me my caps, first—go, enquire!

(*Exeunt* NANO, ANDROGYNO, CASTRONE; VOLPONE *to
his bed.*)

    Now, Cupid
    Send it be Mosca, and with fair return.°   30
NANO (*at the door*): It is the beauteous madam—
VOLPONE: Would-be—is it?
NANO: The same.
VOLPONE: Now, torment on me; squire her in:
    For she will enter, or dwell here for ever.
    Nay, quickly, that my fit were past. I fear
    A second hell too, that my loathing this
    Will quite expel my appetite to the other:
    Would she were taking, now, her tedious leave.
    Lord, how it threats me, what I am to suffer!   40

ACT 3 / SCENE 4

(*Enter* NANO *with* LADY WOULD-BE.)

LADY WOULD-BE: I thank you, good sir. Pray you
        signify
    Unto your patron, I am here. This band°
    Shows not my neck enough—I trouble you, sir,
    Let me request you, bid one of my women
    Come hither to me—in good faith, I am dressed
    Most favourably ° today, it is no matter.

(*Enter* 1st WOMAN.)

    'Tis well enough. Look, see these petulant things!
    How they have done this!
VOLPONE: I do feel the fever
    Ent'ring, in at mine ears; O for a charm,   10
    To fright it hence.
LADY WOULD-BE: Come nearer: is this curl
    In his right place? or this? why is this higher
    Than all the rest? you ha'not washed your eyes,
        yet?
    Or do they not stand even i' your head?

---

    for ... respect, for which reason alone.   **piety,** filial
love (Latin *pietas*).   **professed,** proclaimed.   **common ...
earth,** of obscure or unknown parentage (Latin *terrae filius*).
score, mark up.   **front,** forehead or face.   **whether,** which.
known delicates, acknowledged indulgences.

    feat, dainty.   **fair return,** i.e., from a profitable ven-
ture.   **band,** ruff or collar.   **favourably,** pleasingly (but
ironic).

Where's your fellow? call her. (*Exit* 1st WOMAN.)
NANO: Now, St. Mark
20   Deliver us: anon,° she'll beat her women,
Because her nose is red.

(*Enter* 1st WOMAN *with* 2nd WOMAN.)

LADY WOULD-BE: I pray you, view
This tire,° forsooth: are all things apt, or no?
1st WOMAN: One hair a little, here, sticks out,
forsooth.
LADY WOULD-BE: Does't so forsooth? and where was
your dear sight
When it did so, forsooth? what now? bird-eyed?°
And you, too? pray you both approach, and mend
30   it.
Now, by that light, I muse, you're not ashamed!
I, that have preached these things, so oft, unto you,
Read you the principles, argued all the grounds,
Disputed every fitness, every grace,°
Called you to counsel of so frequent dressings—
NANO (*aside*): More carefully, than of your fame,° or
honour.
LADY WOULD-BE: Made you acquainted, what an
ample dowry
40   The knowledge of these things would be unto you,
Able, alone, to get you noble husbands
At your return: and you, thus, to neglect it?
Besides, you seeing what a curious° nation
Th' Italians are, what will they say of me?
'The English lady cannot dress herself.'—
Here's a fine imputation, to our country!
Well, go your ways, and stay, i'the next room.
This fucus° was too coarse too, it's no matter.
Good sir, you'll give 'em entertainment?

(*Exeunt* NANO, 1st *and* 2nd WOMEN.)

50   VOLPONE: The storm comes toward me.
LADY WOULD-BE: How does my Volp?
VOLPONE: Troubled with noise, I cannot sleep; I
dreamt
That a strange fury entered, now, my house,
And, with the dreadful tempest of her breath,
Did cleave my roof asunder.
LADY WOULD-BE: Believe me, and I
Had the most fearful dream, could I remember 't—
VOLPONE: Out on my fate; I ha' given her the occasion
60   How to torment me: she will tell me hers.
LADY WOULD-BE: Methought, the golden mediocrity°
Polite, and delicate—
VOLPONE: O, if you do love me,

No more; I sweat, and suffer, at the mention
Of any dream: feel, how I tremble yet.
LADY WOULD-BE: Alas, good soul! the passion of the
heart.°
Seed-pearl° were good now, boiled with syrup of
apples,
Tincture of gold, and coral,° citron-pills,   70
Your elecampane° root, myrobalanes°—
VOLPONE (*aside*): Ay me, I have ta'en a grass-hopper
by the wing.
LADY WOULD-BE: Burnt silk,° and amber,° you have
muscadel
Good i' the house—
VOLPONE: You will not drink, and part?
LADY WOULD-BE: No, fear not that. I doubt, we shall
not get
Some English saffron°—half a dram would serve—   80
Your sixteen cloves, a little musk, dried mints,
Bugloss,° and barley-meal—
VOLPONE: She's in again,
Before I feigned diseases, now I have one.
LADY WOULD-BE: And these applied, with a right
scarlet cloth°—
VOLPONE: Another flood of words! a very torrent!
LADY WOULD-BE: Shall I, sir, make you a poultice?
VOLPONE: No, no, no;
I'm very well: you need prescribe no more.   90
LADY WOULD-BE: I have, a little, studied physic; but
now,
I'm all for music: save, i'the forenoons,°
An hour, or two, for painting. I would have
A lady, indeed, to have all, letters, and arts,
Be able to discourse, to write, to paint,
But principal, as Plato holds, your music,
And so does wise Pythagoras, I take it,
Is your true rapture; when there is concent°
In face, in voice, and clothes: and is, indeed,   100
Our sex's chiefest ornament.
VOLPONE: The poet,°
As old in time, as Plato, and as knowing,
Says that your highest female grace is silence.
LADY WOULD-BE: Which o' your poets? Petrarch? or
Tasso? or Dante?

---

passion of the heart, heartburn. *Seed-pearl,* said by
Burton to "avail to the exhilaration of the heart" (*Anatomy of
Melancholy* (1632), p. 376). *coral,* hung around the neck,
supposed to drive away fears, devils and bad dreams.
elecampane, plant with bitter aromatic leaves and root, used
as stimulant. *myrobalanes,* astringent plum-like fruit prescribed for melancholy and agues. *Burnt silk,* taken in
water for the small-pox. *amber,* used to perfume the air.
saffron, then grown in England (e.g., at Saffron Walden) for
medical and confectory use. *Bugloss,* recommended by
Burton as a heart stimulant (*Anatomy* (1632), p. 373). *scarlet cloth,* another treatment for small-pox; the patient was
wrapped in it. *forenoons,* mornings. *concent,* harmony,
concord. *The poet,* i.e., Sophocles.

---

anon, shortly. *tire,* head-dress. *bird-eyed,* probably
"pop-eyed," startled; possibly "short-sighted" or "timid."
preached . . . grace, Lady Would-be deploys the terminology
of formal rhetoric. *fame,* reputation. *curious,* particular
about details. *fucus,* cosmetic paste. *golden mediocrity,* a
travesty of the "golden mean."

Guarini? Ariosto? Aretine?
Cieco di Hadria?° I have read them all.
VOLPONE: Is everything a cause, to my destruction?
110 LADY WOULD-BE: I think, I ha' two or three of 'em,
about me.
VOLPONE: The sun, the sea will sooner, both, stand
still,
Then her eternal tongue! nothing can scape it.
LADY WOULD-BE: Here's *Pastor Fido*°—
VOLPONE: Profess obstinate silence,
That's now, my safest.
LADY WOULD-BE: All our English writers,
I mean such, as are happy in th'Italian,
120 Will deign to steal out of this author, mainly;
Almost as much, as from Montagnié:
He has so modern, and facile a vein,
Fitting the time, and catching the court-ear.
Your Petrarch is more passionate, yet he,
In days of sonneting, trusted 'em, with much:°
Dante is hard, and few can understand him.
But, for a desperate wit,° there's Aretine!
Only, his pictures are a little obscene—
You mark me not?
140 VOLPONE: Alas, my mind's perturb'd.
LADY WOULD-BE: Why, in such cases, we must cure
ourselves,
Make use of our philosophy—
VOLPONE: O'y me!
LADY WOULD-BE: And, as we find our passions do
rebel,
Encounter 'em with reason; or divert 'em,
By giving scope unto some other humour
Of lesser danger: as, in politic bodies,°
150 There's nothing, more, doth overwhelm° the
judgement,
And clouds the understanding, than too much
Settling, and fixing, and (as't were) subsiding
Upon one object. For the incorporating
Of these same outward things, into that part,
Which we call mental, leaves some certain faeces
That stop the organs, and, as Plato says,
Assassinates our knowledge.
VOLPONE: Now, the spirit
160 Of patience help me.

Cieco di Hadria, "the blind man of Adria," Luigi Groto
(1541–1585), a prolific, but minor, poet in comparison with
the five first named. *Pastor Fido,* Guarini's pastoral (1590),
translated into English as *The Faithful Shepherd* in 1602.
trusted . . . much, left much in their keeping; Petrarch was
imitated as a sonneteer by Wyatt, Surrey, Sidney and
Spenser, among others. *desperate wit,* outrageous poet;
Aretino wrote a number of pornographic poems including
the sixteen *Sonneti lussoriosi* which were published to designs
by Giulio Romano in 1523. *politic bodies,* kingdom, states.
overwhelm . . . knowledge, Lady Would-be's theories of obsession and perception are a travesty of Platonic thinking.

LADY WOULD-BE: Come, in faith, I must
Visit you more a days;° and make you well:
Laugh, and be lusty.
VOLPONE: My good angel save me!
LADY WOULD-BE: There was but one sole man, in all
the world,
With whom I ere could sympathize; and he
Would lie you often, three, four hours together,
To hear me speak: and be, sometime, so rapt,
As he would answer me, quite from the purpose,   170
Like you, and you are like him, just. I'll discourse,
And't be but only, sir, to bring you asleep,
How we did spend our time, and loves, together,
For some six years.
VOLPONE: Oh, oh, oh, oh, oh, oh.
LADY WOULD-BE: For we were *coaetanei,*° and brought
up—
VOLPONE (*aside*): Some power, some fate, some
fortune rescue me!

ACT 3 / SCENE 5

(*Enter* MOSCA.)

MOSCA: God save you, madam!
LADY WOULD-BE: Good sir.
VOLPONE: Mosca! welcome,
Welcome to my redemption!
MOSCA: Why, sir?
VOLPONE: Oh,
Rid me of this my torture, quickly, there;
My Madam, with the everlasting voice:
The bells, in time of pestilence,° ne'er made
Like noise, or were in that perpetual motion;   10
The cock-pit° comes not near it. All my house,
But now, steamed like a bath, with her thick breath.
A lawyer could not have been heard; nor scarce
Another woman, such a hail of words
She has let fall. For hell's sake, rid her hence.
MOSCA: Has she presented?
VOLPONE: O, I do not care,
I'll take her absence, upon any price,
With any loss.
MOSCA: Madam—   20
LADY WOULD-BE: I ha'brought your patron
A toy, a cap here, of mine own work—
MOSCA: 'Tis well,
I had forgot to tell you, I saw your knight,
Where you'd little think it—
LADY WOULD-BE: Where?
MOSCA: Marry,
Where yet, if you make haste, you may apprehend
him,

---

more a days, on more days, more often (compare
"nowadays"). *coaetanei,* of the same age (*co-aetaneus*).
bells . . . pestilence, death knells. *cock-pit,* to be found in
Venice or London; the Drury lane cock-pit was enclosed and
later became a theater.

30   Rowing upon the water in a gondola,
     With the most cunning courtesan of Venice.
LADY WOULD-BE: Is't true?
MOSCA: Pursue 'em, and believe your eyes:
     Leave me, to make your gift. (*Exit* LADY WOULD-BE.)
        I knew 'twould take.
     For lightly,° they that use themselves most licence,
     Are still° most jealous.
VOLPONE: Mosca, hearty thanks,
     For thy quick fiction, and delivery of me.
40   Now, to my hopes, what say'st thou?

     (*Enter* LADY WOULD-BE.)

LADY WOULD-BE: But do you hear, sir?—
VOLPONE: Again; I fear a paroxysm.
LADY WOULD-BE: Which way
     Rowed they together?
MOSCA: Toward the Rialto.
LADY WOULD-BE: I pray you lend me your dwarf.
MOSCA: I pray you, take him.

     (*Exit* LADY WOULD-BE.)

     Your hopes, sir, are like happy blossoms, fair,
     And promise timely fruit, if you will stay
50   But the maturing; keep you, at your couch,
     Corbaccio will arrive straight, with the will:
     When he is gone, I'll tell you more.
VOLPONE: My blood,
     My spirits are returned, I am alive:
     And like your wanton gamester, at *primero,*°
     Whose thought had whispered to him, not go less,
     Methinks I lie, and draw—for an encounter.

     (VOLPONE *draws the curtains across his bed.*)

ACT 3 / SCENE 6

     (MOSCA *leads* BONARIO *in and hides him.*)

MOSCA: Sir, here concealed, you may hear all. But
        pray you
     Have patience, sir; (*One knocks*) the same's your
        father, knocks:
     I am compelled to leave you.
BONARIO: Do so. Yet,
     Cannot my thought imagine this a truth.

ACT 3 / SCENE 7

     (MOSCA *admits* CORVINO *and* CELIA.)

MOSCA: Death on me! you are come too soon, what
        meant you?
     Did not I say, I would send?
CORVINO: Yes, but I feared

     You might forget it, and then they prevent us.
MOSCA: Prevent? (*aside*)—Did e'er man haste so, for
        his horns?
     A courtier would not ply it so, for a place.—
     Well, now there's no helping it, stay here;
     I'll presently return. (*Moves toward* BONARIO.)   10
CORVINO: Where are you, Celia?
     You know not wherefore I have brought you
        hither?
CELIA: Not well, except° you told me.
CORVINO: Now, I will:
     Hark hither. (*They converse apart.*)
MOSCA (*to* BONARIO): Sir, your father hath sent word,
     It will be half an hour, ere he come;
     And therefore, if you please to walk, the while,
     Into that gallery—at the upper end,   20
     There are some books to entertain the time:
     And I'll take care, no man shall come unto you, sir.
BONARIO: Yes, I will stay there. (*aside*) I do doubt this
        fellow.

     (*Exit* BONARIO *to the gallery.*)

MOSCA: There, he is far enough; he can hear
        nothing:
     And, for his father, I can keep him off. (*Moves to*
        VOLPONE.)
CORVINO: Nay, now, there is no starting back; and
        therefore,
     Resolve upon it: I have so decreed.   30
     It must be done. Nor, would I move't° afore,
     Because I would avoid all shifts and tricks,
     That might deny me.
CELIA: Sir, let me beseech you,
     Affect° not these strange° trials; if you doubt
     My chastity, why lock me up, for ever:
     Make me the heir of darkness. Let me live,
     Where I may please your fears, if not your trust.
CORVINO: Believe it, I have no such humour, I.
     All that I speak, I mean; yet I am not mad: 40
     Not horn-mad,° see you? Go to, show yourself
     Obedient, and a wife.
CELIA: O heaven!
CORVINO: I say it,
     Do so.
CELIA: Was this the train?°
CORVINO: I've told you reasons;
     What the physicians have set down; how much,
     It may concern me; what my engagements are;
     My means°; and the necessity of those means,   50
     For my recovery: wherefore, if you be
     Loyal, and mine, be won, respect my venture.°

---

lightly, often, usually. *still,* always. *primero,* a gambling card-game resembling poker; Volpone puns on its technical terms "go less," "lie," "draw" and "encounter."

except, except what. *move,* urge. *Affect,* seek (not necessarily implying pretense). *strange,* exceptional, extreme. *horn-mad,* mad at being cuckholded, mad at the prospect, or mad to be so. *train,* trick, trap. *means,* financial resources. *venture,* enterprise.

CELIA: Before your honour?

CORVINO: Honour? tut, a breath;
There's no such thing, in nature: a mere term
Invented to awe fools. What is my gold
The worse, for touching? clothes for being looked
    on?
Why, this's no more. An old, decrepit wretch,
60 That has no sense,° no sinew; takes his meat
With others' fingers; only knows to gape,
When you do scald his gums; a voice; a shadow;
And what can this man hurt you?

CELIA: Lord! what spirit
Is this hath entered him?

CORVINO: And for your fame,
That's such a jig°; as if I would go tell it,
Cry it, on the Piazza! who shall know it?
But he, that cannot speak it; and this fellow,
70 Whose lips are i' my pocket: save yourself,
If you'll proclaim't, you may. I know no other,
Should come to know it.

CELIA: Are heaven, and saints then nothing?
Will they be blind, or stupid?

CORVINO: How?

CELIA: Good sir,
Be jealous still, emulate them; and think
What hate they burn with, toward every sin.

CORVINO: I grant you: if I thought it were a sin,
80 I would not urge you. Should I offer this
To some young Frenchman, or hot Tuscan blood,
That had read Aretine, conned all his prints,
Knew every quirk° within lust's labyrinth,
And were professed critic,° in lechery:
And° I would look upon him, and applaud him,
This were a sin: but here, 'tis contrary,
A pious work, mere charity, for physic,
And honest polity, to assure mine own.°

CELIA: O heaven! canst thou suffer such a change?

90 VOLPONE: Thou art mine honour, Mosca, and my
    pride,
My joy, my tickling, my delight! go, bring 'em.

MOSCA: Please you draw near, sir.

CORVINO: Come on, what—
You will not be rebellious? by that light—

(Drags her to the bed.)

MOSCA: Sir, Signior Corvino, here, is come to see
    you—

VOLPONE: Oh!

MOSCA: And hearing of the consultation had,
100 So lately, for your health, is come to offer,
Or rather, sir, to prostitute—

CORVINO: Thanks, sweet Mosca.

MOSCA: Freely, unasked, or unentreated—

CORVINO: Well.

MOSCA: As the true, fervent instance of his love,
His own most fair and proper wife; the beauty,
Only of price,° in Venice—

CORVINO: 'Tis well urged.

MOSCA: To be your comfortress, and to preserve you.

VOLPONE: Alas, I'm past already! pray you, thank   110
    him,
For his good care, and promptness, but for that,
'Tis a vain labour, e'en to fight 'gainst heaven;
Applying fire to a stone: —uh, uh, uh, uh.—
Making a dead leaf grow again. I take
His wishes gently, though; and, you may tell him,
What I've done for him: marry, my state is
    hopeless!
Will him, to pray for me; and t'use his fortune,
With reverence, when he comes to't.   120

MOSCA: Do you hear, sir?
Go to him, with your wife.

CORVINO: Heart of my father!
Wilt thou persist thus? come, I pray thee, come.
Thou seest 'tis nothing: Celia! by this hand
I shall grow violent. Come, do't, I say.

CELIA: Sir, kill me, rather: I will take down poison,
Eat burning coals,° do anything—

CORVINO: Be damned!
Heart, I will drag thee hence, home, by the hair;   130
Cry thee a strumpet, through the streets; rip up
Thy mouth, unto thine ears; and slit thy nose,
Like a raw rotchet°—Do not tempt me, come.
Yield, I am loath—Death, I will buy some slave,°
Whom I will kill, and bind thee to him, alive;
And at my window, hang you forth: devising
Some monstrous crime, which I, in capital letters,
Will eat into thy flesh, with aquafortis,°
And burning corsives,° on this stubborn breast.
Now, by the blood, thou hast incensed, I'll do't.   140

CELIA: Sir, what you please, you may; I am your
    martyr.

CORVINO: Be not thus obstinate, I ha' not deserved it:
Think, who it is, entreats you. Pray thee, sweet;
Good faith, thou shalt have jewels, gowns, attires,
What thou wilt think, and ask—Do, but, go kiss
    him.
Or touch him, but. For my sake. At my suit.
This once. No? not? I shall remember this.
Will you disgrace me, thus? do you thirst my   150
    undoing?

MOSCA: Nay, gentle lady, be advised.

CORVINO: No, no.
She has watched her time. God's precious,° this is
    scurvy;

---

sense, sensory awareness. *jig,* trifle. *quirk,* sudden twist. *professed critic,* qualified expert. *And,* if. *mine own,* i.e., the inheritance.

Only of price, of unique excellence. *Eat . . . coals,* Brutus's wife, Portia, died in this way. *rotchet,* the red gurnet. *some slave,* this was Tarquin's threat to Lucrece. *aquafortis,* nitric acid, used for etching. *corsives,* corrosives. *God's precious,* i.e., precious blood.

'Tis very scurvy: and you are—
MOSCA: Nay, good sir.
CORVINO: An errant locust, by heaven, a locust.
    Whore,
    Crocodile,° that has thy tears prepared,
160   Expecting,° how thou'lt bid 'em flow.
MOSCA: Nay, pray you, sir,
    She will consider.
CELIA: Would my life would serve
    To satisfy—
CORVINO: 'Sdeath, if she would but speak to him,
    And 'save my reputation, 'twere somewhat;
    But, spitefully to affect my utter ruin°—
MOSCA: Ay, now you've put your fortune in her
    hands.
170   Why i'faith, it is her modesty, I must quit° her;
    If you were absent, she would be more coming;°
    I know it: and dare undertake for her.
    What woman can, before her husband? Pray you,
    Let us depart, and leave her, here.
CORVINO: Sweet Celia,
    Thou mayst redeem all, yet; I'll say no more:
    If not, esteem yourself as lost. (CELIA starts to leave.)
    Nay, stay there.

    (Exeunt CORVINO, MOSCA.)

CELIA: O, God, and his good angels! whither, whither
180   Is shame fled human breasts? that with such ease,
    Men dare put off your honours, and their own?
    Is that, which ever was a cause of life,
    Now placed beneath the basest circumstance?
    And modesty an exile made, for money?
VOLPONE: Ay, in Corvino, and such earth-fed minds,

    (He leaps off from his couch.)

    That never tasted the true heaven of love.
    Assure thee, Celia, he that would sell thee,
    Only for hope of gain, and that uncertain,
    He would have sold his part of paradise
190   For ready money, had he met a cope-man.°
    Why art thou mazed,° to see me thus revived?
    Rather applaud thy beauty's miracle;
    'Tis thy great work: that hath, not now alone,
    But sundry times, raised me, in several shapes,
    And, but this morning, like a mountebank,
    To see thee at thy window. Ay, before
    I would have left my practice,° for thy love,
    In varying figures, I would have contended

With the blue Proteus,° or the hornèd flood.°
    Now, art thou welcome.   200
CELIA: Sir!
VOLPONE: Nay, fly me not.
    Nor, let thy false imagination
    That I was bedrid, make thee think, I am so:
    Thou shalt not find it. I am, now, as fresh,
    As hot, as high, as in as jovial° plight,°
    As when, in that so celebrated scene,
    At recitation of our comedy,
    For entertainment of the great Valois,°
    I acted young Antinous°; and attracted   210
    The eyes, and ears of all the ladies present,
    T'admire each graceful gesture, note, and footing.

                SONG°

    Come, my Celia, let us prove,°
    While we can, the sports of love;
    Time will not be ours, for ever,
    He, at length, our good will sever;
    Spend not then his gifts, in vain.
    Suns, that set, may rise again:
    But if, once, we lose this light,
    'Tis with us perpetual night.   220
    Why should we defer our joys?
    Fame, and rumour are but toys.°
    Cannot we delude the eyes
    Of a few poor household spies?
    Or his easier ears beguile,
    Thus removèd, by our wile?
    'Tis no sin, love's fruits to steal;
    But the sweet thefts to reveal:
    To be taken, to be seen,
    These have crimes accounted been.   230

CELIA: Some serene blast me, or dire lightning strike
    This my offending face.
VOLPONE: Why droops my Celia?
    Thou hast in place of a base husband, found
    A worthy lover: use thy fortune well,
    With secrecy, and pleasure. See, behold,
    What thou art queen of; not in expectation,
    As I feed others; but possessed, and crowned.
    See, here, a rope of pearl; and each, more orient°

---

errant, either "wandering" or "arrant, downright"; the senses are related and both applicable—"arrant, promiscuous parasite." *Crocodile,* believed to entice its victims with artful tears. *Expecting,* anticipating. *ruin*— (F ruin, Q ruin:), Q indicates that the thought is incomplete, or that Mosca interrupts it; some editors read "ruin!" *quit,* clear, acquit. *coming,* forthcoming, responsive. *cope-man,* chapman, dealer. *mazed,* bewildered. *practice,* scheming, intriguing. *figures,* appearances, shapes.

blue **Proteus,** marine blue (Latin *caeruleus*); Menelaus contends with the many shapes of Proteus (*Odyssey* IV. 456–458). **hornèd flood,** the river-God Achelous who fought Hercules in the forms of bull, serpent, and man-bull; the shape may symbolize the river's branchings and its roar. **jovial,** born under Jupiter, and therefore apt to share Jove's convivial temperament and amorous propensities. **plight,** state, trim. **Valois,** Henry of Valois was entertained at Venice in 1574. **Antinous,** beautiful youth, minion of the Emperor Hadrian. **Song,** imitated largely from Catullus's fifth ode, *Vivamus, mea Lesbia.* **prove,** try. **toys,** trifles. **serene,** (French *serein*), twilight mist in hot countries; once thought noxious. **orient,** rare and fine.

240 Than that the brave Egyptian queen° caroused:
Dissolve, and drink 'em. See, a carbuncle,
May put out both the eyes of our St. Mark;°
A diamant, would have bought Lollia Paulina,°
When she came in, like star-light, hid with jewels,
That were the spoils of provinces; take these,
And wear, and lose 'em: yet remains an ear-ring
To purchase them again, and this whole state.
A gem, but worth a private patrimony,
Is nothing: we will eat such at a meal.
250 The heads of parrots, tongues of nightingales,
The brains of peacocks, and of ostriches
Shall be our food: and, could we get the phoenix,°
Though nature lost her kind, she were our dish.
CELIA: Good sir, these things might move a mind affected
With such delights; but I, whose innocence
Is all I can think wealthy, or worth th'enjoying,
And which once lost, I have nought to lose beyond it,
260 Cannot be taken with these sensual baits:
If you have conscience—
VOLPONE: 'Tis the beggar's virtue,
If thou hast wisdom, hear me, Celia.
Thy baths shall be the juice of July-flowers,°
Spirit of roses, and of violets,
The milk of unicorns,° and panthers' breath°
Gathered in bags, and mixed with Cretan wines.°
Our drink shall be preparèd gold, and amber;
Which we will take, until my roof whirl round
270 With the vertigo: and my dwarf shall dance,
My eunuch sing, my fool make up the antic.°
Whilst we, in changed shapes, act Ovid's tales,°
Thou, like Europa now, and I like Jove,°
Then I like Mars, and thou like Erycine,°

So, of the rest, till we have quite run through
And wearied all the fables of the gods.
Then will I have thee in more modern forms,
Attired like some sprightly dame of France,
Brave Tuscan lady, or proud Spanish beauty;
Sometimes, unto the Persian Sophy's° wife;   280
Or the Grand Signor's° mistress; and, for change,
To one of our most artful courtesans,
Or some quick° Negro, or cold Russian;
And I will meet thee, in as many shapes:
Where we may, so, transfuse° our wand'ring souls,
Out at our lips, and score up sums of pleasures,
(Sings.)

That the curious shall not know,
How to tell them, as they flow;
And the envious, when they find
What their number is, be pined.°   290

CELIA: If you have ears that will be pierced; or eyes,
That can be opened; a heart, may be touched;
Or any part, that yet sounds man,° about you:
If you have touch of holy saints, or heaven,
Do me the grace, to let me scape. If not,
Be bountiful, and kill me. You do know,
I am a creature, hither ill betrayed,
By one, whose shame I would forget it were.
If you will deign me neither of these graces,
Yet feed your wrath, sir, rather than your lust;   300
(It is a vice, comes nearer manliness)
And punish that unhappy crime of nature,
Which you miscall my beauty: flay my face,
Or poison it, with ointments, for seducing
Your blood to this rebellion. Rub these hands,
With what may cause an eating leprosy,
E'en to my bones, and marrow: anything,
That may disfavour° me, save in my honour.
And I will kneel to you, pray for you, pay down
A thousand hourly vows, sir, for your health,   310
Report, and think you virtuous—
VOLPONE: Think me cold,
Frozen, and impotent, and so report me?
That I had Nestor's hernia,° thou wouldst think.
I do degenerate,° and abuse my nation,
To play with opportunity, thus long:
I should have done the act, and then parleyed.
Yield, or I'll force thee.

Egyptian queen, Pliny (*Naturalis Historia* IX.120) tells how Cleopatra met Antony's challenge to spend a hundred hundred thousand sesterces at a meal by drinking a priceless pearl dissolved in vinegar. **both . . . St. Mark,** perhaps an image of St. Mark with gems for eyes, but none is recorded; possibly two famous carbuncles in Venice, one in St. Mark's treasury; possibly an extravagant sacrilegious metaphor. **Lollia Paulina,** wife of the Emperor Caligula; an heiress whose wealth was extorted from the provinces by her father; Pliny describes her clad in jewels and glittering like the sun at a bethrothal party. **phoenix,** the mythical Arabian bird, supposed to renew itself from its own ashes every five hundred years. **July-flowers,** gillyflowers (clove-scented pinks). **milk of unicorns,** a delicacy found only here; but powdered unicorn horn (from the rhinoceros) was used as medicine. **panthers' breath,** panthers were said to attract their prey by the sweetness of their scent. **Cretan wines,** rather rich and sweet for bathing; there is evidence that Mary Queen of Scots habitually bathed in wine. **antic,** grotesque dance. **Ovid's tales,** i.e., *Metamorphoses.* **Europa . . . Jove,** Zeus won Europa by playing with her in the form of a bull before bearing her to Crete on his back. **Erycine,** Venus, after her temple at Eryx in Sicily.

Sophy, the Shah, supreme ruler. **Grand Signor,** Sultan of Turkey. **quick,** lively. **transfuse,** "to cause to flow from one to another" (*OED*); the image is from Petronius, *Satyricon* 79. **pined,** tormented. **sounds man,** proclaims you a man. **disfavour,** disfigure. **Nestor's hernia,** Nestor embodies the strengths as well as the weaknesses of age in Homer's *Iliad;* this glance at his impotence is from Juvenal, *Satires* VI, 326. **degenerate,** possibly used transitively "cause my nation (Italy) to lose its ancestral virtue," but the intransitive use is more probable.

CELIA: O! just God.

320 VOLPONE: In vain—

(BONARIO *leaps out from where Mosca had placed him.*)

BONARIO: Forbear, foul ravisher, libidinous swine,
Free the forced lady, or thou diest, impostor.
But that I am loath to snatch thy punishment
Out of the hand of justice, thou shouldst, yet,
Be made the timely sacrifice of vengeance,
Before this altar, and this dross,° thy idol.
Lady, let's quit the place, it is the den
Of villainy; fear nought, you have a guard:
And he, ere long, shall meet his just reward.

330 VOLPONE: Fall on me, roof, and bury me in ruin,
Become my grave, that wert my shelter. O!
I am unmasked, unspirited, undone,
Betrayed to beggary, to infamy—

ACT 3 / SCENE 8

(*Enter* MOSCA, *bleeding.*)

MOSCA: Where shall I run, most wretched shame of
men,
To beat out my unlucky brains?

VOLPONE: Here, here.
What! dost thou bleed?

MOSCA: O, that his well-driven sword
Had been so courteous to have cleft me down,
Unto the navel; ere I lived to see
My life, my hopes, my spirits, my patron, all

10 Thus desperately engagèd,° by my error.

VOLPONE: Woe, on thy fortune.

MOSCA: And my follies, sir.

VOLPONE: Th'hast made me miserable.

MOSCA: And myself, sir.
Who would have thought, he would have
hearkened, so?

VOLPONE: What shall we do?

MOSCA: I know not, if my heart
Could expiate the mischance, I'd pluck it out.

20 Will you be pleased to hang me? or cut my throat?
And I'll requite you, sir. Let's die like Romans,°
Since we have lived, like Grecians.° (*They knock
without.*)

VOLPONE: Hark, who's there?
I hear some footing,° officers, the Saffi°
Come to apprehend us! I do feel the brand°
Hissing already, at my forehead: now,
Mine ears are boring.°

---

dross, "the scum thrown off from metals in smelting" (*OED*); a perverse dismissal of Volpone's gold. *engaged,* entangled. *like Romans,* stoically, by suicide. *like Grecians,* dissolutely and histrionically. *footing,* footsteps. *Saffi,* "*Saffo,* a catchpole, or sergeant" (Florio 1598); bailiffs. *brand,* Jonson himself was branded on the thumb for killing Gabriel Spencer. *boring,* this suggests ear-rings or ear-brandings for criminals, but no other evidence has been brought to bear.

MOSCA: To your couch, sir, you
Make that place good, however.° Guilty men
Suspect, what they deserve still. Signior Corbaccio! 30

ACT 3 / SCENE 9

(*Enter* CORBACCIO.)

CORBACCIO: Why! how now? Mosca!

(*Enter* VOLTORE *unseen.*)

MOSCA: O, undone, amazed,° sir.
Your son, I know not by what accident,
Acquainted with your purpose to my patron,
Touching your will, and making him your heir;
Entered our house with violence, his sword drawn,
Sought for you, called you wretch, unnatural,
Vowed he would kill you.

CORBACCIO: Me?

MOSCA: Yes, and my patron. 10

CORBACCIO: This act, shall disinherit him indeed:°
Here is the will.

MOSCA: 'Tis well, sir.

CORBACCIO: Right and well.
Be you as careful° now, for me.

MOSCA: My life, sir,
Is not more tendered,° I am only yours.

CORBACCIO: How does he? will he die shortly, thinkst
thou?

MOSCA: I fear 20
He'll outlast May.

CORBACCIO: Today?

MOSCA: No, last out May, sir.

CORBACCIO: Couldst thou not gi'him a dram?°

MOSCA: O, by no means, sir.

CORBACCIO: Nay, I'll not bid you.

VOLTORE (*aside*): This is a knave, I see.

MOSCA (*aside*): How! Signior Voltore! did he hear me?

VOLTORE: Parasite!

MOSCA: Who's that? O, sir, most timely welcome— 30

VOLTORE: Scarce,
To the discovery of your tricks, I fear.
You are his, only? and mine, also? are you not?

MOSCA: Who? I, sir!

VOLTORE: You sir, what device° is this
About a will?

MOSCA: A plot for you, sir.

VOLTORE: Come,
Put not your foists° upon me, I shall scent 'em.

MOSCA: Did you not hear it? 40

VOLTORE: Yes, I hear, Corbaccio
Hath made your patron, there, his heir.

MOSCA: 'Tis true,

Make . . . however, "keep up that role whatever you do." *amazed,* confused. *disinherit . . . indeed,* i.e., permanently. *careful,* solicitous. *tendered,* tenderly cared for. *dram,* dose. *device,* contrivance. *foists,* rogueries; also foist, "to smell or grow musty" (*OED*).

By my device, drawn to it by my plot,
With hope—
VOLTORE: Your patron should reciprocate?
And, you have promised?
MOSCA: For your good, I did, sir.
Nay more, I told his son, brought, hid him here,
Where he might hear his father pass the deed;
Being persuaded to it, by this thought, sir,
That the unnaturalness, first, of the act,
And then, his father's oft disclaiming° in him,
Which I did mean t'help on, would sure enrage
him
To do some violence upon his parent.
On which the law should take sufficient hold,
And you be stated° in a double hope:
Truth be my comfort, and my conscience,
My only aim was, to dig you a fortune
Out of these two, old rotten sepulchres—
VOLTORE: I cry thee mercy, Mosca.
MOSCA: Worth your patience,
And your great merit, sir. And, see the change!
VOLTORE: Why? what success?°
MOSCA: Most hapless!° you must help, sir.
Whilst we expected th'old raven, in comes
Corvino's wife, sent hither, by her husband—
VOLTORE: What, with a present?
MOSCA: No, sir, on visitation:
(I'll tell you how, anon) and, staying long,
The youth, he grows impatient, rushes forth,
Seizeth the lady, wounds me, makes me swear
(Or he would murder her, that was his vow)
T'affirm my patron to have° done her rape:
Which how unlike it is, you see! and, hence,
With that pretext, he's gone, t'accuse his father;
Defame my patron; defeat you—
VOLTORE: Where's her husband?
Let him be sent for, straight.
MOSCA: Sir, I'll go fetch him.
VOLTORE: Bring him, to the Scrutineo.°
MOSCA: Sir, I will.
VOLTORE: This must be stopped.
MOSCA: O, you do nobly, sir.
Alas, 'twas laboured all, sir, for your good;
Nor, was there any want of counsel, in the plot:
But fortune can, at any time, o'erthrow
The projects of a hundred learned clerks,° sir.
CORBACCIO: What's that?
VOLTORE: Wilt please you sir, to go along?

(Exeunt CORBACCIO, VOLTORE.)

MOSCA: Patron, go in, and pray for our success.
VOLPONE: Need makes devotion: heaven your labour
bless.

ACT 4 / SCENE 1

(A street.)
(Enter SIR POLITIC WOULD-BE, PEREGRINE.)

SIR POLITIC: I told you, sir, it was a plot°: you see
What observation is. You mentioned me,°
For some instructions: I will tell you, sir,
Since we are met, here, in this height° of Venice,
Some few particulars, I have set down,
Only for this meridian; fit to be known
Of your crude traveller, and they are these.
I will not touch, sir, at your° phrase,° or clothes,
For they are old.
PEREGRINE: Sir, I have better.
SIR POLITIC: Pardon,
I meant, as they are themes.°
PEREGRINE: O, sir, proceed:
I'll slander you no more of wit,° good sir.
SIR POLITIC: First, for your garb,° it must be grave,
and serious;
Very reserved, and locked; not tell a secret,
On any terms, not to your father; scarce
A fable,° but with caution; make sure choice
Both of your company, and discourse; beware,
You never speak a truth—
PEREGRINE: How!
SIR POLITIC: Not to strangers,
For those be they you must converse with, most;
Others I would not know,° sir, but at distance,
So as I still might be a saver, in 'em:°
You shall have tricks, else, passed upon you hourly.
And then, for your religion, profess none;
But wonder, at the diversity of all;
And, for your part, protest, were there no other
But simply the laws o'the land, you could content
you:
Nick Machiavel, and Monsieur Bodin,° both,
Were of this mind. Then, must you learn the use,
And handling of your silver fork,° at meals;
The metal° of your glass—these are main° matters,
With your Italian—and to know the hour,
When you must eat your melons, and your figs.

---

disclaiming in him, disowning; renouncing legal claim.
stated, instated. *success,* outcome. *hapless,* unfortunate.
to have, F (Q would have). *Scrutineo,* law court in Senate
House. *clerks,* scholars.

it was a plot, i.e., the mountebank scene. *mentioned
me,* asked me in passing (?) *height,* latitude. *your,* the
impersonal, familiar use which Peregrine affects to misinterpret. *phrase,* manner of speaking. *themes,* topics.
slander . . . wit, either "I'll no more misrepresent you for the
sake of being witty," or "I'll no more accuse you of being
quick-witted." *garb,* demeanour. *fable,* fiction. *know,*
acknowledge. *be . . . 'em,* "keep myself safe in respect to
them" (either from danger or from inconvenience).
Machiavel . . . Bodin, the sentiments are falsely attributed,
but Machiavelli did tend to subordinate religion to the state,
and Jean Bodin elaborated a theory of toleration. *fork,*
forks were not much used in England at this time. *metal,*
"the material used for making glass, in a molten state"
(OED); Sir Politic is exhibiting his technical knowledge.
main, of primary importance.

PEREGRINE: Is that a point of state, too?

50 SIR POLITIC: Here it is.
For your Venetian, if he see a man
Preposterous,° in the least, he has him straight;°
He has: he strips him. I'll acquaint you, sir,
I now have lived here, 'tis some fourteen months,
Within the first week of my landing here,
All took me for a citizen of Venice:
I knew the forms so well—

PEREGRINE (aside): And nothing else.

SIR POLITIC: I had read Contarene,° took me a house,
60 Dealt with my Jews, to furnish it with moveables°—
Well, if I could but find one man—one man.
To mine own heart—whom I durst trust, I would—

PEREGRINE: What? what, sir?

SIR POLITIC: Make him rich, make him a fortune:
He should not think, again. I would command it.

PEREGRINE: As how?

SIR POLITIC: With certain projects, that I have,
Which, I may not discover.°

PEREGRINE (aside): If I had
70 But one to wager with, I would lay odds, now,
He tells me, instantly.

SIR POLITIC: One is (and that
I care not greatly, who knows) to serve the state
Of Venice, with red herrings, for three years,
And at a certain rate, from Rotterdam,
Where I have correspondence.° There's a letter,
Sent me from one o' the States,° and to that
purpose;
He cannot write his name, but that's his mark.

80 PEREGRINE: He is a chandler?°

SIR POLITIC: No, a cheesemonger.
There are some other too, with whom I treat,
About the same negotiation;
And, I will not undertake it: for, 'tis thus,
I'll do 't with ease, I've cast° it all. Your hoy°
Carries but three men in her, and a boy;
And she shall make me three returns, a year:
So, if there come but one of three, I save,
If two, I can defalk.° But, this is now,
90 If my main project fail.

PEREGRINE: Then, you have others?

SIR POLITIC: I should be loath to draw the subtle air°

Preposterous, back-to-front, in the wrong order. **has him straight,** sums him up instantly. **Contarene,** Cardinal Gasparo Contarini published a book on Venice, *De Magistratibus et Republica Venetorum* (1589), translated into English in 1599. **moveables,** at this time commonly distinguished from fixed furnishings. **discover,** reveal. **correspondence,** connections. **one o'the States,** a member of the Dutch assembly, the States-General. **chandler?** Peregrine speculates from the greasy state of the letter. **cast,** reckoned. **hoy,** Dutch coastal vessel, meant for short hauls. **defalk,** allow a deduction, perhaps on the price of the herrings, but the financial strategy is obscure. **subtle air,** atmosphere of intrigue.

Of such a place, without my thousand aims.
I'll not dissemble sir, where'er I come
I love to be considerative°; and, 'tis true,
I have, at my free hours, thought upon
Some certain goods, unto the state of Venice,
Which I do call my cautions°: and, sir, which
I mean, in hope of pension, to propound
To the Great Council, then unto the Forty, 100
So to the Ten.° My means° are made already—

PEREGRINE: By whom?

SIR POLITIC: Sir, one, that though his place be
obscure,
Yet, he can sway, and they will hear him. He's
A *commendatore*.

PEREGRINE: What, a common sergeant?°

SIR POLITIC: Sir, such as they are, put it in their
mouths,°
What they should say, sometimes: as well as 110
greater.
I think I have my notes, to show you—

PEREGRINE: Good, sir.

SIR POLITIC: But, you shall swear unto me, on your
gentry,
Not to anticipate—

PEREGRINE: I, sir?

SIR POLITIC: Nor reveal
A circumstance—My paper is not with me.

PEREGRINE: O, but, you can remember, sir. 120

SIR POLITIC: My first is,
Concerning tinder-boxes. You must know,
No family is, here, without its box.
Now sir, it being so portable a thing,
Put case,° that you, or I were ill affected
Unto the state; sir, with it in our pockets,
Might not I go into the *arsenale*?°
Or you? come out again? and none the wiser?

PEREGRINE: Except yourself, sir.

SIR POLITIC: Go to, then. I, therefore, 130
Advertise° to the state, how fit it were,
That none, but such as were known patriots,
Sound lovers of their country, should be suffered
T'enjoy them in their houses: and, even those,
Sealed,° at some office, and, at such a bigness,
As might not lurk in pockets.

PEREGRINE: Admirable!

SIR POLITIC: My next is, how t'enquire, and be
resolved,

---

considerative, prudently deliberate. **cautions,** can mean "precautions," but taken here "in hope of pension." **Great . . . Ten,** the administrative hierarchy of Venice. **means,** means of access, contacts. **sergeant,** officer charged with the arrest or summoning of offenders. **their mouths,** i.e., the mouths of the great. **Put case,** "say for example." **arsenale,** Sir Politic may use the Italian pronunciation; the Arsenal of Venice housed all its ships and weapons. **Advertise,** make known. **Sealed,** registered under seal.

140 By present demonstration,° whether a ship,
Newly arrived from Soria,° or from
Any suspected part of all the Levant,
Be guilty of the plague: and, where they use,
To lie out forty, fifty days, sometimes,
About the Lazaretto,° for their trial;
I'll save that charge, and loss unto the merchant,
And, in an hour, clear the doubt.
PEREGRINE: Indeed, sir?
SIR POLITIC: Or—I will lose my labour.
150 PEREGRINE: My faith, that's much.
SIR POLITIC: Nay, sir, conceive me. 'Twill cost me, in
onions,°
Some thirty *livres*°—
PEREGRINE: Which is one pound sterling.
SIR POLITIC: Beside my water-works: for this I do, sir.
First, I bring in your ship, 'twixt two brick walls;
(But those the state shall venture°) on the one
I strain° me a fair tarpaulin; and, in that,
I stick my onions, cut in halves: the other
160 Is full of loop-holes, out at which, I thrust
The noses of my bellows; and, those bellows
I keep, with water-works, in perpetual motion,
(Which is the easiest matter of a hundred).
Now, sir, your onion, which doth naturally
Attract th'infection, and your bellows, blowing
The air upon him, will show (instantly)
By his changed colour, if there be contagion,
Or else, remain as fair, as at the first.
Now 'tis known, 'tis nothing.
170 PEREGRINE: You are right, sir.
SIR POLITIC: I would I had my note.°
PEREGRINE: Faith, so would I:
But, you ha' done well, for once, sir.
SIR POLITIC: Were I false,°
Or would be made so, I could show you reasons,
How I could sell this state, now, to the Turk;
Spite of their gallies, or their—°
PEREGRINE: Pray you, Sir Pol.
SIR POLITIC: I have 'em not, about me.
180 PEREGRINE: That I feared.
They're there, sir?
SIR POLITIC: No, this is my diary.
Wherein I note my actions of the day.
PEREGRINE: Pray you, let's see, sir. What is here?
'*Notandum,*
A rat had gnawn my spur-leathers;
notwithstanding,

I put on new, and did go forth: but, first,
I threw three beans over the threshold.° *Item,*
I went, and bought two tooth-picks,° whereof one   190
I burst, immediately, in a discourse
With a Dutch merchant, 'bout *ragion del stato.*°
From him I went, and paid a *moccenigo,*
For piecing my silk stockings; by the way,
I cheapened sprats°: and at St. Mark's I urined.'
Faith, these are politic notes!
SIR POLITIC: Sir, I do slip
No action of my life, thus, but I quote° it.
PEREGRINE: Believe me it is wise!
SIR POLITIC: Nay, sir, read forth.   200

ACT 4 / SCENE 2

(Enter LADY WOULD-BE, NANO *and two* WOMEN*)*

LADY WOULD-BE: Where should this loose° knight be,
trow? sure, he's housed.
NANO: Why, then he's fast.
LADY WOULD-BE: Ay, he plays both, with me:
I pray you, stay. This heat will do more harm
To my complexion, than his heart is worth.
(I do not care° to hinder, but to take him)
How it comes off! *(Rubbing her face)*
1st WOMAN: My master's yonder.
LADY WOULD-BE: Where?   10
2nd WOMAN: With a young gentleman.
LADY WOULD-BE: That same's the party!
In man's apparel. Pray you, sir, jog my knight:
I will be tender to his reputation,
However he demerit.°
SIR POLITIC: My lady?
PEREGRINE: Where?
SIR POLITIC: 'Tis she indeed, sir, you shall know her.
She is,
Were she not mine, a lady of that merit,   20
For fashion, and behaviour; and, for beauty
I durst compare—
PEREGRINE: It seems, you are not jealous,
That dare commend her.
SIR POLITIC: Nay, and for discourse—
PEREGRINE: Being your wife, she cannot miss° that.
SIR POLITIC *(the parties meet)*: Madam,
Here is a gentleman, pray you, use him, fairly,
He seems a youth, but he is—

---

present demonstration, on-the-spot proof. **Soria,**
Syria. **Lazaretto,** pest-house; two were established in islands of the Gulf of Venice after the plagues of 1423 and
1576. **onions,** supposed to protect against the plague by
gathering the infection. **livre,** French coin. **venture,**
invest in. **strain,** stretch. **note,** possibly note of patent.
false, traitorous. **or their–** Sir Politic breaks off as he
searches for his papers.

A rat . . . threshold, some details here are owed to
Theophrastus's Character of a Superstitious Man. **tooth-
picks,** for the fashion of using toothpicks expressively see
King John I. i., 190–193. **ragion del stato,** reasons and
affairs of state. **cheapened sprats,** by haggling; Coryat tells
how Venetian gentlemen did their own shopping in the
market. **quote,** note. **loose,** the game of fast-and-loose. *I
do not care to,* I am not anxious to. **demerit,** merits blame.
miss, lack.

30   LADY WOULD-BE: None?

SIR POLITIC: Yes, one

    Has put his face, as soon,° into the world—

LADY WOULD-BE: You mean, as early? but today?

SIR POLITIC: How's this!

LADY WOULD-BE: Why in this habit, sir, you
    apprehend me.

    Well, Master Would-be, this doth not become you;

    I had thought, the odour, sir, of your good name,

    Had been more precious to you; that you would

40   not

    Have done this dire massacre,° on your honour;

    One of your gravity, and rank, besides!

    But, knights, I see, care little for the oath

    They make to ladies: chiefly, their own ladies.

SIR POLITIC: Now, by my spurs, the symbol of my
    knight-hood—

PEREGRINE (aside): Lord! how his brain is humbled,°
    for an oath.

SIR POLITIC: I reach° you not.

50   LADY WOULD-BE: Right, sir, your polity°

    May bear it through,° thus. (to PEREGRINE) Sir, a
      word with you.

    I would be loath, to contest publicly,

    With any gentlewoman; or to seem

    Froward,° or violent (as *The Courtier* says)

    It comes too near rusticity, in a lady,

    Which I would shun, by all means: and, however

    I may deserve from Master Would-be, yet,

    T'have one fair gentlewoman, thus, be made

60   Th'unkind instrument, to wrong another,

    And one she knows not; ay, and to persever:

    In my poor judgment, is not warranted

    From being a solecism° in our sex,

    If not in manners.

PEREGRINE: How is this!

SIR POLITIC: Sweet madam,

    Come nearer to your aim.

LADY WOULD-BE: Marry, and will, sir.

    Since you provoke me, with your impudence,

70   And laughter of your light land-siren, here,

    Your Sporus,° your hermaphrodite—

PEREGRINE: What's here?

    Poetic fury, and historic° storms!

SIR POLITIC: The gentleman, believe it, is of worth,

    And of our nation.

LADY WOULD-BE: Ay, your Whitefriars nation°!

    Come, I blush for you, Master Would-be, I;

    And am ashamed, you should ha' no more
      forehead,°

    Than, thus, to be the patron, or St. George   80

    To a lewd harlot, a base fricatrice,°

    A female devil, in a male outside.

SIR POLITIC (to PEREGRINE): Nay,

    And you be° such a one, I must bid adieu

    To your delights! The case° appears too liquid.°

(Exit SIR POLITIC.)

LADY WOULD-BE: Ay, you may carry't clear, with your
    state-face!°

    But, for your carnival° concupiscence,°

    Who here is fled for liberty of conscience,°

    From furious persecution of the marshal,   90

    Her will I disple.°

PEREGRINE: This is fine, i'faith!

    And do you use this,° often? is this part

    Of your wit's exercise, 'gainst you have occasion?

    Madam—

LADY WOULD-BE: Go to, sir.

PEREGRINE: Do you hear me, lady?

    Why, if your knight have set you to beg shirts,°

    Or to invite me home, you might have done it

    A nearer° way, by far.   100

LADY WOULD-BE: This cannot work you,

    Out of my snare.

PEREGRINE: Why? am I in it, then?

    Indeed, your husband told me, you were fair,

    And so you are; only your nose inclines,

    That side, that's next the sun, to the queen-apple.°

LADY WOULD-BE: This cannot be endured, by any
    patience.

---

as soon, at so early an age; but the phrase is open to Lady Would-be's wilful misinterpretation. *massacre,* accented on second syllable here. *humbled,* brought low—down to his spurs; editors have here found a sneer at King James's readiness to create new knights. *reach,* understand. *polity,* policy, cunning bluff. *bear it through,* carry it off. *Froward,* refractory. *solecism,* a grammatical, not a sexual, impropriety; the word is itself a solecism here. *Sporus,* minion castrated and "married" by Nero. *historic,* perhaps "epoch-making."

Whitefriars nation, Whitefriars was a "liberty" under the old priory charter, inside the City of London but outside its jurisdiction; it became almost a miniature state for outcasts. *forehead,* "capacity for blushing, modesty" (*OED*). *fricatrice,* whore (Latin, *fricare,* to rub). *you be,* addressed either to Lady Would-be or to Peregrine. *case,* possibly "mask" or "disguise." *liquid,* "transparent, easily seen through" or "amorphous, hard to grasp"; and Lady Would-be may be sobbing. *state-face,* politic countenance. *carnival,* probably for "carnal." *concupiscence,* for "concupiscent (woman)." *liberty of conscience,* freedom from religious persecution; the prison marshal is conceived as the persecutor and concupiscence as the religion. *disple,* ed. (FQ disc'ple) "to subject to discipline; especially as a religious practice" (*OED*). *use this,* act like this. *beg shirts,* Lady Would-be is evidently tugging at Peregrine's shirt. *nearer,* more direct. *queen-apple,* perhaps a quince, or early variety of apple; Lady Would-be's nose is red on one side.

ACT 4 / SCENE 3

(Enter MOSCA.*)*

MOSCA: What's the matter, madam?

LADY WOULD-BE: If the Senate
Right not my quest,° in this; I will protest° 'em,
To all the world, no aristocracy.

MOSCA: What is the injury, lady?

LADY WOULD-BE: Why, the callet,
You told me of, here I have ta'en disguised.

MOSCA: Who? this? what means your ladyship? the creature
I mentioned to you, is apprehended, now,
Before the Senate, you shall see her—

LADY WOULD-BE: Where?

MOSCA: I'll bring you to her. This young gentleman
I saw him land, this morning, at the port.

LADY WOULD-BE: Is't possible! how has my judgement wandered!
Sir, I must, blushing, say to you, I have erred:
And plead you pardon.

PEREGRINE: What! more changes, yet?

LADY WOULD-BE: I hope, you ha'not the malice to remember
A gentlewoman's passion. If you stay,
In Venice, here, please you to use me,° sir—

MOSCA: Will you go, madam?

LADY WOULD-BE: Pray you, sir, use me. In faith,
The more you see me, the more I shall conceive,°
You have forgot our quarrel.

PEREGRINE: This is rare!
Sir Politic Would-be? no, Sir Politic Bawd!
To bring me, thus, acquainted with his wife!
Well, wise Sir Pol: since you have practised,° thus,
Upon my freshmanship, I'll try your salt-head,°
What proof it is against a counter-plot.

ACT 4 / SCENE 4

(The Scrutineo.)
(Enter VOLTORE, CORBACCIO, CORVINO, MOSCA.*)*

VOLTORE: Well, now you see the carriage° of the business,
Your constancy is all, that is required
Unto the safety of it.

MOSCA: Is the lie
Safely conveyed amongst us? is that sure?
Knows every man his burden?°

CORVINO: Yes.

MOSCA: Then, shrink not.

CORVINO *(aside to* MOSCA*)*: But, knows the advocate the truth?

MOSCA: O, sir,
By no means. I devised a formal° tale,
That salved° your reputation. But, be valiant, sir.

CORVINO: I fear no one, but him; that, this his pleading
Should make him stand for a co-heir—

MOSCA: Co-halter.
Hang him: we will but use his tongue, his noise,
As we do Croaker's here. *(Pointing to* CORBACCIO.*)*

CORVINO: Ay, what shall he do?

MOSCA: When we ha' done, you mean?

CORVINO: Yes.

MOSCA: Why, we'll think:
Sell him for mummia,° he's half dust already.
(to VOLTORE*)* Do not you smile, to see this buffalo,°
(Pointing to CORVINO.*)*
How he doth sport it with his head?—*(aside)* I should
If all were well, and past. *(to* CORBACCIO*)* Sir, only you
Are he, that shall enjoy the crop of all,
And these not know for whom they toil.

CORBACCIO: Ay, peace.

MOSCA *(to* CORVINO*)*: But you shall eat it.° *(Then to* VOLTORE *again.)* Much! Worshipful sir,
Mercury° sit upon your thund'ring tongue,
Or the French Hercules,° and make your language
As conquering as his club, to beat along,
As with a tempest, flat, our adversaries:
But, much more, yours, sir.

VOLTORE: Here they come, ha' done.

MOSCA: I have another witness, if you need, sir,
I can produce.

VOLTORE: Who is it?

MOSCA: Sir, I have her.

ACT 4 / SCENE 5

(Enter four AVOCATORI, BONARIO, CELIA, NOTARIO, COMMENDATORI *and* OTHERS.*)*

---

quest, petition. **protest,** proclaim. **use me,** Lady Would-be intends to be socially useful but her rhetoric insinuates her readiness to be Peregrine's mistress. **conceive,** understand; become pregnant. **practised,** plotted; Peregrine thinks he has been gulled. **salt-head,** seasoned, experienced; salacious, bawdy. **carriage,** management. **burden,** refrain of a song; hence "part in the performance."

formal, "elaborately constructed, circumstantial" (*OED*). **salved,** healed, made good. **mummia,** a medicinal preparation from the substance of mummies; fake mummy was made from baked corpses. **buffalo,** alluding to the cuckold's horns that the "formal tale" sets upon Corvino. **eat it,** i.e., the crop, the legacy; Corvino may overhear the words to Corbaccio. **Mercury,** god of eloquence and of trade; also associated with trickery and theft. **French Hercules,** Hercules was fabled to have fathered the Celts in Gaul while returning from the far west with the oxen of Geryon; as the Celtic Hercules he was the symbol of eloquence.

1st AVOCATORE: The like of this the Senate never
   heard of.
2nd AVOCATORE: 'Twill come most strange to them,
   when we report it.
4th AVOCATORE: The gentlewoman has been ever
   held
   Of unreprovèd name.
3rd AVOCATORE: So, the young man.
4th AVOCATORE: The more unnatural part that of his
10   father.
2nd AVOCATORE: More of the husband.
1st AVOCATORE: I not know to give
   His act a name, it is so monstrous!
4th AVOCATORE: But the impostor, he is a thing
   created
   T'exceed example!°
1st AVOCATORE: And all after times!°
2nd AVOCATORE: I never heard a true voluptuary
   Described, but him.
20 3rd AVOCATORE: Appear yet those were cited?°
NOTARIO: All, but the old magnifico, Volpone.
1st AVOCATORE: Why is not he here?
MOSCA: Please your fatherhoods,
   Here is his advocate. Himself's, so weak,
   So feeble—
4th AVOCATORE: What are you?
BONARIO: His parasite,
   His knave, his pandar: I beseech the court,
   He may be forced to come, that your grave eyes
30   May bear strong witness of his strange impostures.
VOLTORE: Upon my faith, and credit, with your
   virtues,
   He is not able to endure the air.
2nd AVOCATORE: Bring him, however.
3rd AVOCATORE: We will see him.
4th AVOCATORE: Fetch him.
VOLTORE: Your fatherhoods' fit pleasures be obeyed,
   Be sure, the sight will rather move your pities,
   Than indignation; may it please the court,
40   In the meantime, he may be heard in me:
   I know this place most void of prejudice,
   And therefore crave it, since we have no reason
   To fear our truth should hurt our cause.
3rd AVOCATORE: Speak free.
VOLTORE: Then know, most honoured fathers, I
   must now
   Discover, to your strangely abused ears,
   The most prodigious, and most frontless° piece
   Of solid impudence, and treachery,
50   That ever vicious nature yet brought forth
   To shame the state of Venice. This lewd woman
   (That wants° no artificial looks, or tears,
   To help the visor,° she has now put on)

Hath long been known a close° adulteress,
To that lascivious youth there; not suspected,
I say, but known; and taken, in the act,
With him; and by this man, the easy husband,
Pardoned: whose timeless° bounty makes him,
   now,
Stand here, the most unhappy, innocent person, 60
That ever man's own goodness made accused.
For these, not knowing how to owe° a gift
Of that dear grace,° but with their shame; being
   placed
So above all powers of their gratitude,°
Began to hate the benefit; and, in place
Of thanks, devise t'extirp° the memory
Of such an act. Wherein, I pray your fatherhoods,
To observe the malice, yea, the rage of creatures
Discovered in their evils; and what heart° 70
Such take, even from their crimes. But that, anon,
Will more appear. This gentleman, the father,
Hearing of this foul fact, with many others,
Which daily struck at his too-tender ears,
And, grieved in nothing more, than that he could
   not
Preserve himself a parent (his son's ills°
Growing to that strange flood) at last decreed
To disinherit him.
1st AVOCATORE: These be strange turns!° 80
2nd AVOCATORE: The young man's fame was ever
   fair, and honest.
VOLTORE: So much more full of danger is his vice,
That can beguile so, under shade of virtue.
But as I said, my honoured sires, his father
Having this settled purpose, (by what means
To him betrayed, we know not) and this day
Appointed for the deed; that parricide,
(I cannot style him better) by confederacy°
Preparing this his paramour to be there, 90
Entered Volpone's house (who was the man
Your fatherhoods must understand, designed°
For the inheritance) there sought his father:
But, with what purpose sought he him, my lords?
(I tremble to pronounce it, that a son
Unto a father, and to such a father
Should have so foul, felonious intent)
It was, to murder him. When, being prevented
By his more happy absence, what then did he?
Not check his wicked thoughts; no, now new deeds: 100
(Mischief doth ever° end, where it begins)

---

close, secret. **timeless,** untimely. **owe,** acknowledge
(= own), or "properly possess." **gift . . . grace,** "so precious
and unmerited a gift (of pardon)." **So . . . gratitude,** i.e., in
a position of indebtedness beyond the reach of their powers
of gratitude. **extirp,** extirpate, eradicate. **heart,** hardness
of heart; impudent courage. **ills,** evils. **turns,** turns of
event. **confederacy,** conspiracy. **designed,** designated.
ever, the reading "never" has been proposed and followed
by some editors, but "ever" means "what begins badly ends
badly."

---

example, precedent. **after times,** i.e., future possibilities. **cited,** summoned, called as witnesses. **frontless,**
shameless. **wants,** lacks. **visor,** mask.

An act of horror, fathers! he dragged forth
The agèd gentleman, that had there lain, bed-rid,
Three years, and more, out of his innocent couch,
Naked, upon the floor, there left him; wounded
His servant in the face; and, with this strumpet,
The stale° to his forged practice,° who was glad
To be so active, (I shall here desire
Your fatherhoods to note but my collections,°
110 As most remarkable) thought, at once, to stop
His father's ends;° discredit his free choice,
In the old gentleman;° redeem themselves,
By laying infamy upon this man,
To whom, with blushing, they should owe° their
  lives.
1st AVOCATORE: What proofs have you of this?
BONARIO: Most honoured fathers,
I humbly crave, there be no credit given
To this man's mercenary tongue.
120 2nd AVOCATORE: Forbear.
BONARIO: His soul moves in his fee.
3rd AVOCATORE: O, sir.
BONARIO: This fellow,
For six sols° more, would plead against his maker.
1st AVOCATORE: You do forget yourself.
VOLTORE: Nay, nay, grave fathers,
Let him have scope: can any man imagine
That he will spare his accuser, that would not
Have spared his parent?
130 1st AVOCATORE: Well, produce your proofs.
CELIA: I would I could forget, I were a creature.
VOLTORE: Signior Corbaccio.
4th AVOCATORE: What is he?
VOLTORE: The father.
2nd AVOCATORE: Has he had an oath?
NOTARIO: Yes.
CORBACCIO: What must I do now?
NOTARIO: Your testimony's craved.
CORBACCIO: Speak to the knave?
140 I'll ha' my mouth, first, stopped with earth; my
  heart
Abhors his knowledge°: I disclaim° in him.
1st AVOCATORE: But, for what cause?
CORBACCIO: The mere portent° of nature.
He is an utter stranger, to my loins.
BONARIO: Have they made° you to this!
CORBACCIO: I will not hear thee,
Monster of men, swine, goat, wolf, parricide,
Speak not, thou viper.

BONARIO: Sir, I will sit down,   150
And rather wish my innocence should suffer,
Than I resist the authority of a father.
VOLTORE: Signior Corvino.
2nd AVOCATORE: This is strange!
1st AVOCATORE: Who's this?
NOTARIO: The husband.
4th AVOCATORE: Is he sworn?
NOTARIO: He is.
3rd AVOCATORE: Speak then.
CORVINO: This woman, please your fatherhoods, is a   160
  whore,
Of most hot exercise, more than a partridge,°
Upon record—
1st AVOCATORE: No more.
CORVINO: Neighs, like a jennet.°
NOTARIO: Preserve the honour of the court.
CORVINO: I shall,
And modesty of your most reverend ears.
And yet, I hope that I may say, these eyes
Have seen her glued unto that piece of cedar;   170
That fine well-timbered° gallant: and that, here,°
The letters may be read, thorough the horn,°
That makes the story perfect.°
MOSCA: Excellent! sir.
CORVINO: There is no shame in this, now, is there?
MOSCA: None.
CORVINO: Or if I said, I hoped that she were onward°
To her damnation, if there be a hell
Greater than whore, and woman; a good Catholic
May make the doubt.   180
3rd AVOCATORE: His grief hath made him frantic.
1st AVOCATORE: Remove him, hence.
2nd AVOCATORE: Look to the woman. (*She swoons.*)
CORVINO: Rare!
Prettily feigned! again!
4th AVOCATORE: Stand from about her.
1st AVOCATORE: Give her the air.
3rd AVOCATORE (*to* MOSCA): What can you say?
MOSCA: My wound,
May't please your wisdoms, speaks for me, received   190
In aid of my good patron, when he missed
His sought-for father, when that well-taught dame
Had her cue given her, to cry out a rape.
BONARIO: O, most laid° impudence! Fathers—
3rd AVOCATORE: Sir, be silent,
You had your hearing free,° so must they theirs.
2nd AVOCATORE: I do begin to doubt th'imposture
  here.

---

stale, lure; "a prostitute of the lowest class employed as a decoy by thieves" (*OED*). *forged practice*, contrived plot. *collections*, conclusions. *ends*, purposes, aims. *gentleman*, i.e., Volpone. *owe*, acknowledge as due. *sols*, French coins worth one twentieth of a livre. *his knowledge*, knowledge of him. *disclaim*, deny kinship. *portent*, ominous freak; suggesting unnatural birth and leading to the denial of paternity. *made*, forced, or possibly "shaped."

partridge, described by Pliny as the most concupiscent of creatures (*Nat. Hist.* X. 102). *jennet*, small Spanish horse. *well-timbered*, well-built. *here*, Corvino holds his forked fingers to his forehead to give himself cuckold's horns. *letters . . . horn*, punning on "horn-book," a primer (so-called because protected by translucent horn). *perfect*, complete. *onward*, well on the way. *laid*, plotted. *free*, i.e., from interruption

4th AVOCATORE: This woman, has too many moods.
200 VOLTORE: Grave fathers,
  She is a creature, of a most professed,
  And prostituted lewdness.
CORVINO: Most impetuous!
  Unsatisfied, grave fathers!
VOLTORE: May her feignings
  Not take your wisdoms; but this day, she baited°
  A stranger, a grave knight, with her loose eyes,
  And more lascivious kisses. This man saw 'em
  Together, on the water, in a gondola.
210 MOSCA: Here is the lady herself, that saw 'em too,
  Without°; who, then, had in the open streets
  Pursued them, but for saving her knight's honour.
1st AVOCATORE: Produce that lady.
2nd AVOCATORE: Let her come. (*Exit* MOSCA.)
4th AVOCATORE: These things
  They strike, with wonder!
3rd AVOCATORE: I am turned a stone!

ACT 4 / SCENE 6

(*Enter* MOSCA *with* LADY WOULD-BE.)

MOSCA: Be resolute, madam.
LADY WOULD-BE: Ay, this same is she.
  Out, thou chameleon° harlot: now, thine eyes
  Vie tears with the hyaena°: dar'st thou look
  Upon my wrongèd face? I cry your pardons.
  I fear, I have, forgettingly, transgressed
  Against the dignity of the court—
2nd AVOCATORE: No, madam.
LADY WOULD-BE: And been exorbitant°—
10 4th AVOCATORE: You have not, lady.
  These proofs are strong.
LADY WOULD-BE: Surely, I had no purpose,
  To scandalize your honours, or my sex's.
3rd AVOCATORE: We do believe it.
LADY WOULD-BE: Surely, you may believe it.
2nd AVOCATORE: Madam, we do.
LADY WOULD-BE: Indeed, you may; my breeding
  Is not so coarse—
4th AVOCATORE: We know it.
20 LADY WOULD-BE: To offend
  With pertinacy—
3rd AVOCATORE: Lady.
LADY WOULD-BE: Such a presence:
  No, surely.
1st AVOCATORE: We well think it.
LADY WOULD-BE: You may think it.

1st AVOCATORE: Let her o'ercome.° (*to* BONARIO) What
  witnesses have you,
  To make good your report?
BONARIO: Our consciences—
CELIA: And heaven, that never fails the innocent.
4th AVOCATORE: These are no testimonies.
BONARIO: Not in your courts,
  Where multitude,° and clamour, overcomes.
1st AVOCATORE: Nay, then you do wax insolent.
VOLTORE: Here, here,

(VOLPONE *is brought in, as impotent.*°)

  The testimony comes, that will convince,
  And put to utter dumbness their bold tongues.
  See here, grave fathers, here's the ravisher,
  The rider on men's wives, the great impostor, 40
  The grand voluptuary! do you not think,
  These limbs should affect venery?° or these eyes
  Covet a concubine? pray you, mark these hands.
  Are they not fit to stroke a lady's breasts?
  Perhaps, he doth dissemble?
BONARIO: So he does.
VOLTORE: Would you ha'him tortured?
BONARIO: I would have him proved.°
VOLTORE: Best try him, then, with goads, or burning
  irons; 50
  Put him to the strappado:° I have heard,
  The rack° had cured the gout, faith, give it him,
  And help° him of a malady, be courteous.
  I'll undertake, before these honoured fathers,
  He shall have, yet, as many left diseases,
  As she has known adulterers, or thou strumpets.
  O, my most equal° hearers, if these deeds,
  Acts, of this bold, and most exorbitant° strain,
  May pass with sufferance, what one citizen,
  But owes the forfeit of his life, yea fame, 60
  To him that dares traduce him°? which of you
  Are safe, my honoured fathers? I would ask,
  With leave of your grave fatherhoods, if their plot
  Have any face, or colour like to truth?
  Or if, unto the dullest nostril, here,
  It smell not rank, and most abhorred slander?
  I crave your care of this good gentleman,
  Whose life is much endangered, by their fable°;

---

baited, enticed. **Without,** outside. **chameleon,** its colour changes made it a symbol of fraud and treachery; Lady Would-be alludes to the inconstant appearance of her quarry. **hyaena,** another symbol of treachery because it attracted its victims by its quasi-human cry (but not by its tears). **exorbitant,** beyond bounds, outrageous.

o'ercome, prevail, have the last word. **multitude,** numbers (not necessarily a crowd). **impotent,** totally disabled; Lady Would-be may kiss Volpone at this point, or when he is borne out. **affect venery,** enjoy sexual pleasure; or "affect" may = "effect." **proved,** put to the proof, tested. **strappado,** a form of torture; the victim is hoisted by a rope binding his wrists behind his back, then dropped with a jerk. **rack . . . gout,** a common sentiment. **help,** relieve. **equal,** just. **exorbitant strain,** outrageous nature. **what . . . traduce him,** "what single citizen would there be whose life, and indeed reputation, would not be forfeitable to any who had the impudence to slander him?" **fable,** falsehood, or plot.

And, as for them, I will conclude with this,
70   That vicious persons when they are hot, and
      fleshed°
    In impious acts, their constancy° abounds:
    Damned deeds are done with greatest confidence.
1st AVOCATORE: Take 'em to custody, and sever
    them.°

(CELIA and BONARIO taken out.)

2nd AVOCATORE: 'Tis pity, two such prodigies° should
    live.
1st AVOCATORE: Let the old gentleman be returned,
    with care:
80   I'm sorry, our credulity wronged him. *(VOLPONE
    borne off)*
4th AVOCATORE: These are two creatures!
3rd AVOCATORE: I have an earthquake in me!
2nd AVOCATORE: Their shame, even in their cradles,
    fled their faces.
4th AVOCATORE: You've done a worthy service to the
    state, sir,
    In their discovery.
1st AVOCATORE: You shall hear, ere night,
    What punishment the court decrees upon 'em.
90 VOLTORE: We thank your fatherhoods.

(Exeunt AVOCATORI, NOTARIO, OFFICERS.)

    How did you like it?
MOSCA: Rare.
    I'd ha'your tongue, sir, tipped with gold, for this;
    I'd ha'you be the heir to the whole city;
    The earth I'd have want men, ere you want living:°
    They're bound to erect your statue, in St. Mark's.
    Signior Corvino, I would have you go,
    And show yourself, that you have conquered.
CORVINO: Yes.
100 MOSCA: It was much better, that you should profess
    Yourself a cuckold, thus; than that the other°
    Should have been proved.
CORVINO: Nay, I considered that:
    Now, it is her fault—
MOSCA: Then, it had been yours.
CORVINO: True, I do doubt this advocate, still.
MOSCA: I'faith,
    You need not, I dare ease you of that care.
CORVINO: I trust thee, Mosca.
110 MOSCA: As your own soul, sir.
CORBACCIO: Mosca!
MOSCA: Now for your business, sir.
CORBACCIO: How? ha'you business?
MOSCA: Yes, yours, sir.
CORBACCIO: O, none else?

MOSCA: None else, not I.
CORBACCIO: Be careful then.
MOSCA: Rest you, with both your eyes,° sir.
CORBACCIO: Dispatch it—
MOSCA: Instantly.   120
CORBACCIO: And look, that all,
    Whatever, be put in,° jewels, plate, monies,
    Household stuff, bedding, curtains.
MOSCA: Curtain-rings, sir,
    Only, the advocate's fee must be deducted.
CORBACCIO: I'll pay him now: you'll be too prodigal.
MOSCA: Sir, I must tender it.°
CORBACCIO: Two chequeens is well?
MOSCA: No, six, sir.
CORBACCIO: 'Tis too much.   130
MOSCA: He talked a great while.
    You must consider that, sir.
CORBACCIO: Well, there's three—
MOSCA: I'll give it him.
CORBACCIO: Do so, and there's for thee. *(Exit
    CORBACCIO.)*
MOSCA: Bountiful bones°! What horrid strange
    offence
    Did he commit 'gainst nature, in his youth,
    Worthy his age°? you see, sir, how I work
    Unto your ends; take you no notice.°   140
VOLTORE: No,
    I'll leave you.
MOSCA: All is yours; *(Exit VOLTORE.)* the devil, and all:
    Good advocate.—Madame, I'll bring you home.
LADY WOULD-BE: No, I'll go see your patron.
MOSCA: That you shall not:
    I'll tell you, why. My purpose is to urge
    My patron to reform° his will; and, for
    The zeal you've shown today, whereas before
    You were but third, or fourth, you shall be now 150
    Put in the first: which would appear as begged,
    If you were present. Therefore—
LADY WOULD-BE: You shall sway° me. *(Exeunt MOSCA,
    LADY WOULD-BE.)*

ACT 5 / SCENE 1

(VOLPONE's house.)
(Enter VOLPONE°.)

VOLPONE: Well, I am here; and all this brunt° is past:
    I ne'er was in dislike with my disguise,
    Till this fled° moment; here, 'twas good, in private,

    Rest . . . eyes, "relax completely."   ***put in,*** i.e., in the
inventory of the inheritance.   ***tender it,*** give it him.   **Bountiful bones!** apt to the meanness and leanness of Corbaccio.
Worthy . . . age, "deserving an old age like this."   ***take . . .
notice,*** "ignore me"; perhaps Lady Would-be is watching.
reform, recast.   ***sway,*** rule.   **Enter Volpone,** Volpone may
be carried in, discovered on his litter, or be back in his bed.
brunt, shock, crisis.   ***fled,*** past.

---

    fleshed, inured.   ***constancy,*** resolution.   ***sever them,***
keep them apart.   ***prodigies,*** monsters, unnatural creatures.
want living, lack a livelihood.   ***the other,*** i.e., the procura-
tion of his wife for Volpone.

But, in your public—*Cavè*°, whilst I breathe. *(Gets up.)*
'Fore God, my left leg 'gan to have the cramp;
And I apprehended,° straight,° some power had struck me
With a dead palsy: well, I must be merry,
And shake it off. A many° of these fears
Would put me into some villainous disease,
Should they come thick upon me: I'll prevent 'em.
Give me a bowl of lusty wine, to fright
This humour from my heart. *(He drinks.)* Hum, hum, hum!
'Tis almost gone, already: I shall conquer.
Any device, now, of rare, ingenious knavery,
That would possess me with a violent laughter,
Would make me up, again! *(Drinks again.)* So, so, so, so.
This heat is life°; 'tis blood, by this time: Mosca!

ACT 5 / SCENE 2

(Enter MOSCA.*)*

MOSCA: How now, sir? does the day look clear again?
Are we recovered? and wrought° out of error,
Into our way? to see our path, before us?
Is our trade free, once more?
VOLPONE: Exquisite Mosca!
MOSCA: Was it not carried learnedly?
VOLPONE: And stoutly.
Good wits are greatest in extremities.
MOSCA: It were a folly, beyond thought, to trust
Any grand act unto a cowardly spirit:
You are not taken with it, enough,° methinks?
VOLPONE: O, more, than if I had enjoyed the wench:
The pleasure of all woman-kind's not like it.
MOSCA: Why, now you speak, sir. We must, here, be fixed;
Here, we must rest; this is our masterpiece:
We cannot think, to go beyond this.
VOLPONE: True.
Thou'st played thy prize, my precious Mosca.
MOSCA: Nay, sir,
To gull the court—
VOLPONE: And, quite divert the torrent
Upon the innocent.
MOSCA: Yes, and to make

So rare a music out of discords—
VOLPONE: Right,
That, yet, to me's the strangest°! how thou'st borne it!
That these, being so divided 'mongst themselves,
Should not scent somewhat, or in me, or° thee,
Or doubt their own side.
MOSCA: True, they will not see't.
Too much lights blinds 'em, I think. Each of 'em
Is so possessed,° and stuffed with his own hopes,
That anything, unto the contrary,
Never so true, or never so apparent,
Never so palpable, they will resist it—
VOLPONE: Like a temptation of the devil.
MOSCA: Right, sir.
Merchants may talk of trade, and your great signiors
Of land, that yields well; but if Italy
Have any glebe,° more fruitful, than these fellows,
I am deceived. Did not your advocate rare?°
VOLPONE: O—'My most honoured fathers, my grave fathers,
Under correction of your fatherhoods.
What face of truth, is here? If these strange deeds
May pass, most honoured fathers'—I had much ado
To forbear laughing.
MOSCA: 'T seemed to me, you sweat,° sir.
VOLPONE: In troth, I did a little.
MOSCA: But confess, sir,
Were you not daunted?°
VOLPONE: In good faith, I was
A little in a mist; but not dejected:
Never, but still myself.
MOSCA: I think° it, sir.
Now, so truth help me, I must needs say this, sir,
And, out of conscience, for your advocate:
He's taken pains, in faith, sir, and deserved,
(In my poor judgement, I speak it, under favour,°
Not to contrary you, sir) very richly—
Well—to be cozened.°
VOLPONE: 'Troth, and I think so too,
By that I heard him, in the latter end.
MOSCA: O, but before, sir; had you heard him, first,
Draw it to certain heads,° then aggravate,°

Cavè (Latin), beware; Volpone may ask the audience to keep a look-out while he relaxes, or he may address the warning to himself. **apprehended,** felt. **straight,** immediately. **many,** used as a noun (compare "a great many"). **This heat is life,** Volpone identifies the response of his blood to wine with the processes by which the body's vital heat is generated. **wrought . . . way,** Mosca talks with mock piety. **You . . . enough,** Mosca may sense that Volpone is already thinking of the next device, towards which the dialogue now subtly moves.

strangest, most wonderful and ingenious; the word 'strange' is important in this act. **or . . . or,** either . . . or. **possessed,** the sense hovers between "possessing" and "possessed by"; another key word. **glebe,** earth, soil. **rare,** rarely. **sweat,** sweated; Mosca insists that Volpone was afraid. **daunted,** "dazed" or "abashed"; Volpone's reply meets both senses, he was a little confused (*in a mist*) but not downcast (*dejected*). **think,** believe. **under favour,** "with your permission"; Mosca now parodies Voltore. **cozened,** cheated. **heads,** chief points of a discourse (*OED*). **aggravate,** put weight upon, solemnly emphasize with *gravitas*.

70   Then use his vehement figures°—I looked still,
     When he would shift a shirt°; and, doing this
     Out of pure love, no hope of gain—
VOLPONE: 'Tis right.
     I cannot answer° him, Mosca, as I would,
     Not yet; but, for thy sake, at thy entreaty,
     I will begin, even now, to vex 'em all:
     This very instant.
MOSCA: Good, sir.
VOLPONE: Call the dwarf,
80   And eunuch, forth.
MOSCA: Castrone, Nano!

     (Enter CASTRONE *and* NANO.*)*

NANO: Here.
VOLPONE: Shall we have a jig,° now?
MOSCA: What you please, sir.
VOLPONE: Go,
     Straight, give out, about the streets, you two,
     That I am dead; do it with constancy,°
     Sadly,° do you hear? impute it to the grief
     Of this late slander.

     (Exeunt CASTRONE *and* NANO.*)*

90   MOSCA: What do you mean,° sir?
VOLPONE: O,
     I shall have, instantly, my vulture, crow,
     Raven, come flying hither, on the news,
     To peck for carrion, my she-wolf, and all,
     Greedy, and full of expectation—
MOSCA: And then to have it ravished from their
        mouths?
VOLPONE: 'Tis true, I will ha' thee put on a gown,
     And take upon thee,° as thou wert mine heir;
100 Show 'em a will: open that chest, and reach
     Forth one of those, that has° the blanks.° I'll
        straight
     Put in thy name.
MOSCA: It will be rare, sir.
VOLPONE: Ay,
     When they e'en° gape, and find themselves
        deluded—
MOSCA: Yes.
VOLPONE: And thou use them scurvily. Dispatch,
110 Get on thy gown.
MOSCA: But, what, sir, if they ask
     After the body?
VOLPONE: Say, it was corrupted.

MOSCA: I'll say it stunk, sir; and was fain° t'have it
     Coffined up instantly, and sent away.
VOLPONE: Anything, what thou wilt. Hold, here's my
        will.
     Get thee a cap, a count-book,° pen and ink,
     Papers afore thee; sit, as thou wert taking
     An inventory of parcels:° I'll get up,   120
     Behind the curtain, on a stool, and hearken;
     Sometime, peep over; see, how they do look;
     With what degrees, their blood doth leave their
        faces!
     O, 'twill afford me a rare meal of laughter.
MOSCA: Your advocate will turn stark dull,° upon it.
VOLPONE: It will take off his oratory's edge.
MOSCA: But your *clarissimo,*° old round-back, he
     Will crump you, like a hog-louse,° with the touch.
VOLPONE: And what Corvino?   130
MOSCA: O, sir, look for him,
     Tomorrow morning, with a rope, and a dagger,°
     To visit all the streets; he must run mad.
     My lady too, that came into the court,
     To bear false witness, for your worship—
VOLPONE: Yes,
     And kissed me 'fore the fathers; when my face
     Flowed all with oils—
MOSCA: And sweat, sir. Why, your gold
     Is such another medicine, it dries up   140
     All those offensive savours! It transforms
     The most deformed, and restores 'em lovely,
     As 'twere the strange poetical girdle.° Jove
     Could not invent, t' himself, a shroud more subtle,
     To pass Acrisius'° guards. It is the thing
     Makes all the world her grace, her youth, her
        beauty.
VOLPONE: I think, she loves me.
MOSCA: Who? the lady,° sir?
     She's jealous of you.   150
VOLPONE: Do'st thou say so? *(Knocking without.)*
MOSCA: Hark,
     There's some already.
VOLPONE: Look.
MOSCA: It is the vulture:
     He has the quickest scent.

---

vehement figures, may refer to figures of both speech and gesture. **shift a shirt,** change a shirt; a figure for Voltore's gesticulations. **answer,** repay. **a jig,** a jest, "some sport"; a burlesque "jig" sometimes followed serious drama in the Elizabethan theater, which may be the point here. **with constancy,** firmly, or perhaps "with straight faces." **Sadly,** gravely. **mean,** intend. **take upon thee,** assume the part. **has,** i.e., have. **blanks,** spaces for the legatee's names. **e'en,** just, doing nothing else but.

fain, i.e., "I was fain (obliged)." **count-book,** account book. **parcels,** lots, items. **dull,** insensible; but Volpone replies to the sense "blunt." **clarissimo,** a Venetian grandee. **crump . . . louse,** "curl up like a wood-louse." **rope . . . dagger,** stock properties of suicidal or homicidal madness induced by despair; compare Hieronimo's madness (once played by Jonson) in *The Spanish Tragedy* IV.iv. **poetical girdle,** the Folio adds the explanation 'Cestus' after 'Jove'; it was possibly meant as a correction to replace 'girdle'; Cestus, the girdle of Venus described by Homer, could transfigure ugliness and awaken passion even in old age. **Acrisius,** the father of Danae; he shut her in a tower of brass but Jove reached her in a shower of gold. **the lady,** presumably Lady Would-be, but some have supposed Celia.

VOLPONE: I'll to my place, *(conceals himself.)*
    Thou, to thy posture.°
MOSCA: I am set.
160 VOLPONE: But, Mosca,
    Play the artificer° now, torture 'em, rarely.

ACT 5 / SCENE 3

(Enter VOLTORE.*)*

VOLTORE: How now, my Mosca?
MOSCA: Turkey carpets,° nine—
VOLTORE: Taking an inventory? that is well.
MOSCA: Two suits of bedding, tissue°—
VOLTORE: Where's the will?
    Let me read that, the while.

(Enter CORBACCIO *carried in a chair.)*

CORBACCIO: So, set me down:
    And get you home. *(Exeunt* PORTERS.*)*
VOLTORE: Is he come, now, to trouble us?
10 MOSCA: Of cloth of gold, two more—
CORBACCIO: Is it done, Mosca?
MOSCA: Of several velvets,° eight—
VOLTORE: I like his care.
CORBACCIO: Dost thou not hear?

(Enter CORVINO.*)*

CORVINO: Ha! is the hour come, Mosca?

*(*VOLPONE *peeps from behind a traverse.)*

VOLPONE *(aside)*: Ay, now they muster.
CORVINO: What does the advocate here?
    Or this Corbaccio?
CORBACCIO: What do these here?

(Enter LADY WOULD-BE.*)*

20 LADY WOULD-BE: Mosca!
    Is his thread° spun?
MOSCA: Eight chests of linen—
VOLPONE *(aside)*: My fine dame Would-be, too!
CORVINO: Mosca, the will,
    That I may show it these, and rid 'em hence.
MOSCA: Six chests of diaper,° four of damask—There.
    (Gives them the will.)
CORBACCIO: Is that the will?
MOSCA: Down-beds, and bolsters—
VOLPONE *(aside)*: Rare!
30   Be busy still. Now, they begin to flutter:

They never think of me. Look, see, see, see!
How their swift eyes run over the long deed,
Unto the name, and to the legacies,
What is bequeathed them, there—
MOSCA: Ten suits of hangings°—
VOLPONE *(aside)*: Ay, i'their garters,° Mosca. Now,
    their hopes
    Are at the gasp.°
VOLTORE: Mosca the heir!
CORBACCIO: What's that? 40
VOLPONE *(aside)*: My advocate is dumb, look to my
    merchant,
    He has heard of some strange storm, a ship is lost,
    He faints: my lady will swoon. Old glazen-eyes,°
    He hath not reached his despair, yet.
CORBACCIO: All these
    Are out of hope, I am sure the man.
CORVINO: But, Mosca—
MOSCA: Two cabinets—
CORVINO: Is this in earnest? 50
MOSCA: One
    Of ebony—
CORVINO: Or, do you but delude me?
MOSCA: The other, mother of pearl—I am very busy.
    Good faith, it is a fortune thrown upon me—
    Item, one salt° of agate—not my seeking.
LADY WOULD-BE: Do you hear, sir?
MOSCA: A perfumed box—'pray you forbear,
    You see I am troubled°—made of an onyx—
LADY WOULD-BE: How! 60
MOSCA: Tomorrow, or next day, I shall be at leisure,
    To talk with you all.
CORVINO: Is this my large hope's issue?
LADY WOULD-BE: Sir, I must have a fairer answer.
MOSCA: Madam!
    Marry, and shall: pray you, fairly° quit my house.
    Nay, raise no tempest with your looks; but, hark
    you:
    Remember, what your ladyship offered me,
    To put you in, an heir; go to, think on't. 70
    And what you said, e'en your best madams did
    For maintenance, and why not you? enough.
    Go home, and use the poor Sir Pol, your knight,
    well;
    For fear I tell some riddles°: go, be melancholic.
    (Exit LADY WOULD-BE.*)*
VOLPONE *(aside)*: O, my fine devil!
CORVINO: Mosca, pray you a word.
MOSCA: Lord! will not you take your dispatch hence,
    yet?

---

posture, pose, act. ***Play the artificer,*** "do a craftsman's job," with pun on the sense "trickster." ***Turkey carpets,*** then used as table and wall drapery. ***tissue,*** cloth woven with gold or silver. ***velvets,*** velvet hangings (several = separate). ***thread,*** of the Three Fates: Clothos spun the thread of life, Lachesis measured it, and Atropos cut it; but the phrase was a popular pomposity. ***diaper,*** fabric with diamond-like pattern.

suits of hangings, sets for four-poster bed. ***garters,*** Volpone puns on the popular jibe "Hang yourself in your own garters." ***gasp,*** last gasp. ***glazen-eyes,*** Corbaccio wears spectacles. ***salt,*** salt-cellar. ***troubled,*** busy, being put to some trouble; or perhaps "vexed." ***fairly,*** probably "well and truly," completely. ***riddles,*** mysteries, secrets.

80   Methinks, of all, you should have been th'example.°
    Why should you stay, here? with what thought?
       what promise?
    Hear you, do not you know, I know you an ass?
    And that you would, most fain, have been a wittol,°
    If fortune would have let you? that you are
    A declared cuckold, on good terms?° this pearl,
    You'll say, was yours? right: this diamant?
    I'll not deny't, but thank you. Much here, else?
    It may be so. Why, think that these good works
90   May help to hide your bad: I'll not betray you,
    Although you be but extraordinary,°
    And have it only in title, if sufficeth.
    Go home, be melancholic too, or mad. (*Exit*
      CORVINO.)
VOLPONE (*aside*): Rare, Mosca! how this villainy
    becomes him!
VOLTORE: Certain, he doth delude all these, for me.
CORBACCIO: Mosca, the heir?
VOLPONE (*aside*): O, his four eyes have found it!
CORBACCIO: I'm cozened, cheated, by a parasite slave;
100   Harlot° thou'st gulled me.
MOSCA: Yes, sir. Stop your mouth,
    Or I shall draw the only tooth, is left.
    Are not you he, that filty covetous wretch,
    With the three legs,° that here, in hope of prey,
    Have, any time this three year, snuffed about,
    With your most grov'ling nose; and would have
      hired
    Me to the poisoning of my patron? sir?
    Are not you he, that have, today, in court,
110   Professed the disinheriting of your son?
    Perjured yourself? Go home, and die, and stink;
    If you but croak a syllable, all comes out:
    Away and call your porters, go, go, stink. (*Exit*
      CORBACCIO.)
VOLPONE (*aside*): Excellent varlet!
VOLTORE: Now, my faithful Mosca,
    I find thy constancy—
MOSCA: Sir?
VOLTORE: Sincere.
120 MOSCA: A table
    Of porphyry—I mar'l,° you'll be thus troublesome.
VOLTORE: Nay, leave off now, they are gone.
MOSCA: Why, who are you?
    What, who did send for you? O, cry your mercy,
    Reverend sir! good faith, I am grieved for you,

    That any chance° of mine should thus defeat
    Your, I must needs say, most deserving travails:
    But, I protest, sir, it was cast upon me,
    And I could, almost, wish to be without it,
    But that the will o'the dead, must be observed.   130
    Marry, my joy is, that you need it not,
    You have a gift, sir, thank your education,
    Will never let you want,° while there are men,
    And malice, to breed causes.° Would I had
    But half the like, for all my fortune, sir.
    If I have any suits (as I do hope,
    Things being so easy, and direct, I shall not)
    I will make bold with your obstreperous° aid,
    Conceive me, for your fee,° sir. In meantime,
    You, that have so much law, I know ha' the   140
      conscience,
    Not to be covetous of what is mine.
    Good sir, I thank you for my plate°: 'twill help
    To set up a young man. Good faith, you look
    As you were costive; best go home, and purge, sir.
      (*Exit* VOLTORE.)
VOLPONE (*coming out*): Bid him, eat lettuce° well: my
    witty mischief,
    Let me embrace thee. O, that I could now
    Transform thee to a Venus—Mosca, go,
    Straight, take my habit of *clarissimo*;   150
    And walk the streets; be seen, torment 'em more:
    We must pursue, as well as plot. Who would
    Have lost this feast?
MOSCA: I doubt it will lose them.°
VOLPONE: O, my recovery shall recover all.
    That I could now but think on some disguise,
    To meet 'em in: and ask 'em questions.
    How I would vex 'em still, at every turn!
MOSCA: Sir, I can fit you.
VOLPONE: Canst thou?   160
MOSCA: Yes, I know
    One of the *commendatori*,° sir, so like you,
    Him will I straight make drunk, can bring you his
    habit.
VOLPONE: A rare disguise, and answering thy brain!
    O, I will be a sharp disease unto 'em.
MOSCA: Sir, you must look for curses—
VOLPONE: Till they burst;
    The Fox fares ever best, when he is cursed.°

---

example, i.e., in leading the way when "dispatched." *wittol*, conniving cuckold. *on good terms*, i.e., outspokenly so, fair and square. *extraordinary*, in title only (as Mosca explains); used of offices held extra to the establishment. *Harlot*, base-born fellow. *three legs*, i.e., with his stick; in the riddle of the Sphinx, the child goes upon four legs, the man on two, and the old man on three. *mar'l*, marvel.

chance, good fortune. *want*, be in need. *causes*, law-suits. *obstreperous*, vociferous. *Conceive . . . fee*, "I shall expect to pay the usual fee, you understand." *plate*, i.e., that presented by Voltore. *lettuce*, a recognized treatment for constipation, and for frenzy. *doubt . . . them*, possibly "I doubt if it will get rid of them," but Volpone's reply interprets "I fear it will lose them to us as a source of income." *commendatori*, a term for the court officers, sergeants at law. *Fox . . . cursed*, a proverb; the fox is only cursed by the hunter when he gets away.

ACT 5 / SCENE 4

(SIR POLITIC WOULD-BE's *house*.)
(*Enter* PEREGRINE *disguised, and three* MERCHANTS.)

PEREGRINE: Am I enough disguised?
1st MERCHANT: I warrant° you.
PEREGRINE: All my ambition is to fright him, only.
2nd MERCHANT: If you could ship him away, 'twere
   excellent.
3rd MERCHANT: To Zant,° or to Aleppo?
PEREGRINE: Yes, and ha'his
   Adventures put i'the *Book of Voyages,*°
   And his gulled° story registered, for truth?
10   Well, gentlemen, when I am in, a while,
   And that you think us warm in our discourse,
   Know your approaches.°
1st MERCHANT: Trust it to our care. (*Exeunt*
   MERCHANTS.)

(*Enter* WAITING WOMAN.)

PEREGRINE: Save you, fair lady. Is Sir Pol within?
WOMAN: I do not know, sir.
PEREGRINE: Pray you, say unto him,
   Here is a merchant, upon earnest° business,
   Desires to speak with him.
WOMAN: I will see, sir.
20 PEREGRINE: Pray you. (*Exit* WOMAN.)
   I see, the family is all female, here.

(*Enter* WAITING WOMAN.)

WOMAN: He says, sir, he has weighty affairs of state,
   That now require him whole°—some other time
   You may possess him.°
PEREGRINE: Pray you, may again,
   If those require him whole, these will exact him,°
   Whereof I bring him tidings. (*Exit* WOMAN.) What
      might be
   His grave affair of state, now? how to make
30   Bolognian sausages, here, in Venice, sparing°
   One o' th'ingredients.

(*Enter* WAITING WOMAN.)

WOMAN: Sir, he says, he knows
   By your word, tidings,° that you are no statesman,
   And therefore, wills you stay.
PEREGRINE: Sweet, pray you return him,°

I have not read so many proclamations,
And studied them, for words, as he has done;
But—Here he deigns to come. (*Exit* WOMAN.)

(*Enter* SIR POLITIC WOULD-BE.)

SIR POLITIC: Sir, I must crave
   Your courteous pardon. There hath chanced,   40
      today,
   Unkind disaster, 'twixt my lady, and me:
   And I was penning my apology
   To give her satisfaction, as you came, now.
PEREGRINE: Sir, I am grieved, I bring you worse
      disaster;
   The gentleman, you met at the port, today,
   That told you, he was newly arrived—
SIR POLITIC: Ay, was
   A fugitive-punk?°   50
PEREGRINE: No, sir, a spy, set on you:
   And, he has made relation° to the Senate,
   That you professed to him, to have a plot,
   To sell the state of Venice, to the Turk.
SIR POLITIC: O me!
PEREGRINE: For which, warrants are signed by this
      time,
   To apprehend you, and to search your study,
   For papers—
SIR POLITIC: Alas, sir. I have none, but notes,   60
   Drawn out of play-books—
PEREGRINE: All the better, sir.
SIR POLITIC: And some essays.° What shall I do?
PEREGRINE: Sir, best
   Convey yourself into a sugar-chest,
   Or, if you could lie round,° a frail° were rare:
   And I could send you, aboard.
SIR POLITIC: Sir, I but talked so,
   For discourse sake, merely. (*They knock without.*)
PEREGRINE: Hark, they are there.   70
SIR POLITIC: I am a wretch, a wretch.
PEREGRINE: What will you do, sir?
   H'you ne'er a currant-butt to leap into?
   They'll put you to the rack, you must be sudden.°
SIR POLITIC: Sir, I have an engine°—
3rd MERCHANT (*off-stage*): Sir Politic Would-be?
2nd MERCHANT (*off-stage*): Where is he?
SIR POLITIC: That I have thought upon, before time.
PEREGRINE: What is it?
SIR POLITIC: —I shall ne'er endure the torture.—   80
   Marry, it is, sir, of a tortoise-shell,°
   Fitted,° for these extremities: 'pray you sir, help
      me.

---

warrant, assure. *Zant,* Zante, one of the Ionian islands, and a Venetian possession at the time. *Book of Voyages,* Hakluyt's *Principal Navigations* was published in its enlarged form in 1598–1600, but there were other books of voyages too. *gulled story,* "the story of his gulling." *Know . . . approaches,* get ready to enter (perhaps nautical jargon). *earnest,* weighty. *require . . . whole,* require his whole attention. *possess him,* have his company. *exact him,* probably "force him out," extract him from his study (see *OED*). *sparing,* leaving out. *tidings,* Sir Politic's word is "intelligence." *return him,* answer him.

---

punk, prostitute. *made relation,* Peregrine now uses state language. *essays,* a literary form that Jonson despised. *lie round,* curl up. *frail,* rush basket for figs. *sudden,* quick. *engine,* device, contrivance. *tortoise-shell,* a feature of the Venetian market; the tortoise was a symbol of polity. *Fitted,* suited.

Here, I've a place, sir, to put back my legs,—
Please you to lay it on, sir—with this cap,
And my black gloves, I'll lie, sir, like a tortoise,
Till they are gone.
PEREGRINE: And, call you this an engine?
SIR POLITIC: Mine own device°—good sir, bid my
90   wife's women
To burn my papers.°

(MERCHANTS *rush in.*)

1st MERCHANT: Where's he hid?
3rd MERCHANT: We must,
And will, sure, find him.
2nd MERCHANT: Which is his study?
1st MERCHANT: What
Are you, sir?
PEREGRINE: I'm a merchant, that came here
To look upon this tortoise.
100 3rd MERCHANT: How?
1st MERCHANT: St. Mark!
What beast is this?
PEREGRINE: It is a fish.
2nd MERCHANT: Come out, here.
PEREGRINE: Nay, you may strike him, sir, and tread
upon him:
He'll bear a cart.
1st MERCHANT: What, to run over him?
PEREGRINE: Yes.
110 3rd MERCHANT: Let's jump upon him.
2nd MERCHANT: Can he not go?
PEREGRINE: He creeps, sir.
1st MERCHANT: Let's see him creep. (*Prods him.*)
PEREGRINE: No, good sir, you will hurt him.
2nd MERCHANT: Heart, I'll see him creep; or prick his
guts.
3rd MERCHANT: Come out, here.
PEREGRINE: Pray you sir. (*to* SIR POLITIC) Creep a
little!
120 1st MERCHANT: Forth!
2nd MERCHANT: Yet further.
PEREGRINE: Good sir! (*to* SIR POLITIC) Creep!
2nd MERCHANT: We'll see his legs.

(*They pull off the shell and discover him.*)

3rd MERCHANT: God's so—, he has garters!
1st MERCHANT: Ay, and gloves!
2nd MERCHANT: Is this
Your fearful tortoise?
PEREGRINE (*throwing off his disguise*): Now, Sir Pol, we
are even;
130   For your next project, I shall be prepared:
I am sorry for the funeral of your notes, sir.

1st MERCHANT: 'Twere a rare motion,° to be seen in
Fleet Street!
2nd MERCHANT: Ay, i'the term.°
1st MERCHANT: Or Smithfield,° in the fair.
3rd MERCHANT: Methinks, 'tis but a melancholic
sight!
PEREGRINE: Farewell, most politic tortoise. (*Exeunt*
PEREGRINE, MERCHANTS.)

(*Enter* WAITING WOMAN.)

SIR POLITIC: Where's my lady?   140
Knows she of this?
WOMAN: I know not, sir.
SIR POLITIC: Enquire. (*Exit* WOMAN.)
O, I shall be the fable of all feasts;
The freight of the *gazetti*;° ship-boys' tale;
And, which is more, even talk for ordinaries.°

(*Enter* WAITING WOMAN.)

WOMAN: My lady's come most melancholic, home,
She says, sir, she will straight to sea, for physic.°
SIR POLITIC: And I, to shun, this place, and clime for
ever;   150
Creeping, with house, on back: and think it well,
To shrink my poor head, in my politic shell.

ACT 5 / SCENE 5

(VOLPONE'S *house.*)
(*Enter* VOLPONE, MOSCA; *the first, in the habit*° *of a
Commendatore: the other, of a Clarissimo.*)

VOLPONE: Am I then like him?
MOSCA: O, sir, you are he:
No man can sever° you.
VOLPONE: Good.
MOSCA: But, what am I?
VOLPONE: 'Fore heaven, a brave *clarissimo*, thou
becom'st it!
Pity, thou wert not born one.
MOSCA: If I hold°
My made one, 'twill be well.   10
VOLPONE: I'll go, and see
What news, first, at the court. (*Exit* VOLPONE.)
MOSCA: Do so. My Fox

---

device, invention (of own devising).   **burn my papers,**
Peregrine must tell the woman to do this as the merchants
rush in and look around.

---

motion, puppet-show.   *term,* the law term, when the
lawyers of the Inns of Court were in residence and their
clients in town.   **Smithfield,** site of Bartholomew Fair;
Jonson's *Bartholomew Fair* features a puppet-show.   **freight
... gazetti,** i.e., carried by the news-sheets.   *ordinary,*
tavern.   *physic,* medical treatment, recuperation.   **habit,**
Gifford describes the dress as "a black stuff gown and a red
cap with two gilt buttons in front."   *sever,* separate, distinguish.   *hold,* either "keep up" or "remain in" the assumed
role; Mosca equivocates between modesty and guile.

Is out on his hole,° and, ere he shall re-enter,
I'll make him languish in his borrowed case,°
Except° he come to composition,° with me:
Androgyno, Castrone, Nano!

(*Enter* ANDROGYNO, CASTRONE, NANO.)

ALL: Here.
MOSCA: Go recreate° yourselves, abroad;° go, sport.
    (*Exeunt the three.*)
20 So, now I have the keys, and am possessed.°
    Since he will, needs, be dead, afore his time,
    I'll bury him, or gain by him. I'm his heir:
    And so will keep me,° till he share at least.
    To cozen him of all, were but a cheat
    Well placed; no man would construe it a sin:
    Let his sport pay for't,° this is called the Fox-trap.

(*Exit* MOSCA.)

ACT 5 / SCENE 6

(*A Street.*)
(*Enter* CORBACCIO *and* CORVINO.)

CORBACCIO: They say, the court is set.
CORVINO: We must maintain
    Our first tale good, for both our reputations.
CORBACCIO: Why? mine's no tale: my son would,
    there, have killed me.
CORVINO: That's true, I had forgot: mine is, I am
    sure.
    But, for your will, sir.
CORBACCIO: Ay, I'll come upon° him,
10 For that, hereafter, now his patron's dead.

(*Enter* VOLPONE *disguised.*)

VOLPONE: Signior Corvino! and Corbaccio! sir,
    Much joy unto you.
CORVINO: Of what?
VOLPONE: The sudden good,
    Dropped down upon you—
CORBACCIO: Where?
VOLPONE: And none knows how—
    From old Volpone, sir.
CORBACCIO: Out, errant° knave.
20 VOLPONE: Let not your too much wealth, sir, make
    you furious.
CORBACCIO: Away, thou varlet.
VOLPONE: Why sir?

CORBACCIO: Dost thou mock me?
VOLPONE: You mock the world,° sir, did you not
    change° wills?
CORBACCIO: Out, harlot.
VOLPONE: O! belike you are the man,
    Signior Corvino? Faith, you carry it well;
    You grow not mad withal: I love your spirit.   30
    You are not over-leavened,° with your fortune.
    You should ha'some would swell,° now, like a
    wine-fat,°
    With such an autumn°—Did he gi' you all, sir?
CORVINO: Avoid,° you rascal.
VOLPONE: Troth, your wife has shown
    Herself a very woman°: but, you are well,
    You need not care, you have a good estate,
    To bear it out,° sir: better by this chance.
    Except Corbaccio have a share?   40
CORBACCIO: Hence, varlet.
VOLPONE: You will not be aknown,° sir: why, 'tis wise.
    Thus do all gamesters, at all games, dissemble.
    No man will seem to win. (*Exeunt* CORBACCIO,
    CORVINO)
    Here, comes my vulture,
    Heaving his beak up i'the air, and snuffing.

ACT 5 / SCENE 7

(*Enter* VOLTORE *to* VOLPONE.)

VOLTORE: Outstripped thus, by a parasite? a slave?
    Would run on errands? and make legs,° for
    crumbs?
    Well, what I'll do—
VOLPONE: The court stays° for your worship.
    I e'en rejoice, sir, at your worship's happiness,
    And that it fell into so learned hands,
    That understand the fingering.—
VOLTORE: What do you mean?
VOLPONE: I mean to be a suitor to your worship,   10
    For the small tenement,° out of reparations°;
    That, at the end of your long row of houses,
    By the Piscaria°: it was, in Volpone's time,
    Your predecessor, ere he grew diseased,
    A handsome, pretty, customed,° bawdy-house,
    As any was in Venice (none dispraised)
    But fell with him; his body, and that house
    Decayed, together.
VOLTORE: Come, sir, leave your prating.

Fox . . . hole, alluding to the boys' game, Fox-in-the-Hole; players hop, and strike each other with gloves and light thongs. *case,* disguise. *Except,* unless. *composition,* agreement, compromise. *recreate,* refresh, amuse. *abroad,* outside. *possessed,* in possession (but the word has its other potentials). *keep me,* remain. *let . . . for't,* "Let his amusement compensate his loss," but "sport" is also apt for the hunting and hunted fox. *come upon,* "make a demand or claim upon" (*OED*). *errant* = arrant.

---

mock the world, "are laughing at everyone." *change,* exchange. *over-leavened,* puffed up (as with too much yeast). *You . . . swell,* "You'd have some swelling . . ." *wine-fat,* wine-vat. *autumn,* i.e., harvest. *avoid,* be gone! *a very woman,* a woman indeed. *bear it out,* carry it off. *aknown,* acknowledged (to be the heir). *make legs,* bow and scrape. *stays,* waits. *tenement,* house. *reparations,* repair(s). *Piscaria,* fish-market. *customed,* well patronized.

20 VOLPONE: Why, if your worship gave me but your
    hand,
    That I may ha'the refusal;° I have done.
    'Tis a mere toy to you, sir; candle-rents:°
    As your learn'd worship knows—
VOLTORE: What do I know?
VOLPONE: Marry, no end of your wealth, sir, God
    decrease° it!
VOLTORE: Mistaking knave! what, mock'st thou my
    misfortune?
30 VOLPONE: His blessing on your heart, sir, would
    'twere more.

(Exit VOLTORE.*)*

—Now, to my first, again; at the next corner.
(Watches, apart.)

ACT 5 / SCENE 8

(Enter CORBACCIO, CORVINO, [MOSCA *passant*°].*)*

CORBACCIO: See, in our habit! see the impudent
    varlet!
CORVINO: That I could shoot mine eyes at him, like
    gun-stones°!
VOLPONE: But, is this true, sir, of the parasite?
CORBACCIO: Again, t'afflict us? monster!
VOLPONE: In good faith, sir,
    I'm heartily grieved, a beard of your grave length°
    Should be so over-reach'd, I never brooked
20   That parasite's hair, methought his nose should
    cozen:
    There still was somewhat, in his look, did promise
    The bane° of a *clarissimo.*
CORBACCIO: Knave—
VOLPONE: Methinks,
    Yet you, that are so traded° i'the world,
    A witty merchant, the fine bird, Corvino,
    That have such moral emblems° on your name,
    Should not have sung your shame; and dropped
30   your cheese:
    To let the Fox laugh at your emptiness.°
CORVINO: Sirrah, you think, the privilege of the
    place,°
    And your red saucy cap, that seems, to me,

    Nailed to your jolt-head,° with those two
    chequeens,°
    Can warrant° your abuses; come you, hither:
    You shall perceive, sir, I dare beat you. Approach.
VOLPONE: No haste, sir, I do know your valour, well:
    Since you durst publish what you are, sir.   40
CORVINO: Tarry,
    I'd speak, with you.
VOLPONE: Sir, sir, another time—
CORVINO: Nay, now.
VOLPONE: O God, sir! I were a wise man,
    Would stand° the fury of a distracted cuckold.

*(*MOSCA *walks by 'em.)*

CORBACCIO: What! come again?
VOLPONE: Upon 'em, Mosca; save me!
CORBACCIO: The air's infected, where he breathes.
CORVINO: Let's fly him.   50
VOLPONE: Excellent basilisk!° turn upon the vulture.

ACT 5 / SCENE 9

(Enter VOLTORE.*)*

VOLTORE: Well, flesh-fly,° it is summer with you, now;
    Your winter will come on.
MOSCA: Good advocate,
    Pray thee, not rail, nor threaten out of place, thus;
    Thou'lt make a solecism, as madam says.
    Get you a biggin° more: your brain breaks loose.
VOLTORE: Well, sir.
VOLPONE: Would you ha' me beat the insolent slave?
    Throw dirt, upon his first good clothes?
VOLTORE: This same   10
    Is, doubtless, some familiar!°
VOLPONE: Sir, the court
    In troth, stays for you. I am mad,° a mule,°

---

refusal, i.e., "first refusal."   *candle-rents,* rents from deteriorating property (self-consuming, like candles). *decrease,* a calculated Dogberryism for 'increase'; hence the double force of Voltore's response "Mistaking knave." *MOSCA passant,* i.e., crosses the stage in his role of *clarissimo.* *gun-stones,* stone cannon-shot. *beard . . . length,* "one so old and wise," but probably literal too. *bane,* ruin, destruction. *traded,* experienced. *moral emblems,* Corvino's name recalls the crow that dropped its cheese to sing to the fox. *emptiness,* i.e., of belly and of head. *place,* station, rank (as a commendatore).

---

jolt-head, block-head.   *chequeens,* i.e., the coin-like buttons of his hat.   *warrant,* sanction, protect by official authority.   *stand,* withstand.   *basilisk,* or cockatrice, a fabulous reptile hatched by a serpent from a cock's egg and capable of killing by its glance.   *flesh-fly,* a blow-fly, the meaning of "Mosca."   *biggin,* lawyer's cap or coif.   *familiar,* i.e., "some fellow of the same household."   *mad,* furiotones, stone cannon-shot. *beard . . . length,* "one so old and wise," but probably literal too. *bane,* ruin, destruction. *traded,* experienced. *moral emblems,* Corvino's name recalls the crow that dropped its cheese to sing to the fox. *emptiness,* i.e., of belly and of head. *place,* station, rank (as a commendatore). *jolthead,* block-head. *chequeens,* i.e., the coin-like buttons of his hat. *warrant,* sanction, protect by official authority. *stand,* withstand. *basilisk,* or cockatrice, a fabulous reptile hatched by a serpent from a cock's egg and capable of killing by its glance. *flesh-fly,* a blow-fly, the meaning of "Mosca." *biggin,* lawyer's cap or coif. *familiar,* i.e., "some fellow of the same household." *mad,* furious (that). *mule,* mules were customarily ridden by lawyers.

That never read Justinian,° should get up,
And ride an advocate. Had you no quirk,°
To avoid gullage,° sir, by such a creature?
I hope you do but jest; he has not done't:
This's but confederacy,° to blind the rest.
You are the heir?
20 VOLTORE: A strange, officious,
    Troublesome knave! thou dost torment me.
VOLPONE: I know—
    It cannot be, sir, that you should be cozened;
    'Tis not within the wit of man, to do it:
    You are so wise, so prudent—and, 'tis fit,
    That wealth, and wisdom still, should go together.

ACT 5 / SCENE 10

(The Scrutineo.)
(Enter Four AVOCATORI, NOTARIO, COMMENDATORI,
BONARIO, CELIA, CORBACCIO, CORVINO.*)*

1st AVOCATORE: Are all the parties, here?
NOTARIO: All, but the advocate.
2nd AVOCATORE: And, here he comes.

    (Enter VOLTORE, *with* VOLPONE *disguised.)*

1st AVOCATORE: Then bring 'em forth to sentence.
VOLTORE: O, my most honoured fathers, let your
    mercy
    Once win upon° your justice, to forgive—
    I am distracted—
VOLPONE *(aside)*: What will he do, now?
10 VOLTORE: O,
    I know not which t'address myself to, first,
    Whether your fatherhoods, or these innocents—
CORVINO *(aside)*: Will he betray himself?
VOLTORE: Whom, equally,
    I have abused, out of most covetous ends°—
CORVINO *(to* CORBACCIO*)*: The man is mad!
CORBACCIO: What's that?
CORVINO: He is possessed.°
VOLTORE: For which, now struck in conscience, here I
20   prostrate
    Myself, at your offended feet, for pardon.
1st and 2nd AVOCATORI: Arise!
CELIA: O heaven, how just thou art?
VOLPONE *(aside)*: I'm caught
    I'mine own noose—
CORVINO *(to* CORBACCIO*)*: Be constant,° sir, nought
    now
    Can help, but impudence.°

1st AVOCATORE: Speak forward.
COMMENDATORE: Silence!   30
VOLTORE: It is not passion° in me, reverend fathers,
    But only conscience, my good sires,
    That makes me, now, tell truth. That parasite,
    That knave hath been the instrument of all.
2nd AVOCATORE: Where is that knave? fetch him!
VOLPONE: I go. *(Exit* VOLPONE.*)*
CORVINO: Grave fathers,
    This man's distracted; he confessed it, now:°
    For, hoping to be old Volpone's heir,
    Who now is dead—   40
3rd AVOCATORE: How?
2nd AVOCATORE: Is Volpone dead?
CORVINO: Dead since, grave fathers—
BONARIO: O, sure vengeance!
1st AVOCATORE: Stay,
    Then, he was no deceiver?
VOLTORE: O no, none:
    The parasite, grave fathers—
CORVINO: He does speak,
    Out of mere envy, 'cause the servant's made°   50
    The thing, he gaped for°; please your fatherhoods,
    This is the truth: though, I'll not justify
    The other, but he may° be some-deal° faulty.
VOLTORE: Ay, to your hopes, as well as mine,
    Corvino:
    But I'll use modesty.° Pleaseth your wisdoms
    To view these certain notes, and but confer° them;

    (Gives them papers.)

    As I hope favour, they shall speak clear truth.
CORVINO: The devil has entered him!
BONARIO: Or bides in you.   60
4th AVOCATORE: We have done ill, by a public officer°
    To send for him, if he be heir.
2nd AVOCATORE: For whom?
4th AVOCATORE: Him, that they call the parasite.
3rd AVOCATURE: 'Tis true;
    He is a man, of great estate, now left.
4th AVOCATORE: Go you, and learn his name, and say,
    the court
    Entreats his presence, here; but, to the clearing
    Of some few doubts. *(Exit* NOTARIO.*)*   70
2nd AVOCATORE: This same's a labyrinth!
1st AVOCATORE: Stand you unto your first report?
CORVINO: My state,°
    My life, my fame—
BONARIO *(aside)*: Where is it?

Justinian, i.e., the *Corpus Jurus Civilis*, the Roman code of law compiled under the direction of Justinian I. **quirk,** trick. **gullage,** being gulled. **confederacy,** i.e., between Mosca and Voltore. **win upon,** overcome. **ends,** purposes, motives. **possessed,** i.e., of a devil. **constant,** firm, consistent. **impudence,** unblushing effrontery.

passion, frenzy. **now,** just now. **made,** achieved, grabbed. **gaped for,** hungered after. **but he may,** "he may yet." **some-deal,** somewhere. **modesty,** moderation. **certain,** "particular" or perhaps "reliable." **confer,** either "compare" or "consult together about." **public officer,** describing the status of Volpone as commendatore. **state,** estate.

CORVINO: Are at the stake.°
1st AVOCATORE: Is yours so too?
CORBACCIO: The advocate's a knave:
   And has a forked tongue—
80 2nd AVOCATORE: Speak to the point.
CORBACCIO: So is the parasite, too.
1st AVOCATORE: This is confusion.
VOLTORE: I do beseech your fatherhoods, read but
   those.
CORVINO: And credit nothing, the false spirit hath
   writ:
   It cannot be, but he is possessed, grave fathers.

ACT 5 / SCENE 11

(A Street.)
(Enter VOLPONE.*)*

VOLPONE: To make a snare, for mine own neck! and
   run
   My head into it, wilfully! with laughter!
   When I had newly scaped, was free, and clear!
   Out of mere wantonness! O, the dull devil°
   Was in this brain of mine, when I devised it;
   And Mosca gave it second;° he must now
   Help to sear° up this vein, or we bleed dead.

(Enter NANO, ANDROGYNO, CASTRONE.*)*

   How now! who let you loose? whither go you, now?
10   What? to buy ginger-bread? or to drown kitlings?°
NANO: Sir, master Mosca called us out of doors.
   And bid us all go play, and took the keys.
ANDROGYNO: Yes.
VOLPONE: Did master Mosca take the keys? why, so!
   I am farther in. These are my fine conceits!°
   I must be merry, with a mischief to me!°
   What a vile wretch was I, that could not bear
   My fortune° soberly? I must ha' my crotchets!°
   And my conundrums!° well, go you, and seek him:
20   His meaning may be truer, than my fear.
   Bid him, he straight come to me, to the court;
   Thither will I, and, if't be possible,
   Unscrew° my advocate, upon° new hopes:
   When I provoked him, then I lost myself.

Are . . . stake, "are all staked on the truth of what I have
said." *dull devil,* "devil of stupidity." *gave it second,*
seconded it. *sear,* cauterise, stem blood with hot iron. *buy
. . . kitlings,* presumably the pastimes of self-indulgent and
malicious children. *conceits,* notions, schemes. *with . . .
to me,* either reflective, "with this mischievous result," or
imprecatory, "a mischief take me!" *fortune,* i.e., good
fortune in surviving the court action, or perhaps "wealth."
crotchets, whimsical fancies, perverse conceits (*OED*). *conundrums,* whims, crotchets. *Unscrew,* i.e., "dislodge him
from his present course"; or perhaps "unwind him" as if he
were a loaded cross-bow. *upon,* used to indicate manner—
"in" or "by."

ACT 5 / SCENE 12

(The Scrutineo.)
(Four AVOCATORI, NOTARIO, VOLTORE, BONARIO,
CELIA, CORBACCIO, CORVINO, COMMENDATORI.*)*

1st AVOCATORE *(with* VOLTORE's *notes)*: These things
   can ne'er be reconciled. He, here,
   Professeth, that the gentleman was wronged;
   And that the gentlewoman was brought thither,
   Forced by her husband: and there left.
VOLTORE: Most true.
CELIA: How ready is heaven to those, that pray!
1st AVOCATORE: But, that
   Volpone would have ravished her, he holds
   Utterly false; knowing his impotence.   10
CORVINO: Grave fathers, he is possessed; again, I say,
   Possessed: nay, if there be possession,
   And obsession,° he has both.
3rd AVOCATORE: Here comes our officer.

(Enter VOLPONE, *disguised.)*

VOLPONE: The parasite will straight be here, grave
   fathers.
4th AVOCATORE: You might invent° some other name,
   sir varlet.°
3rd AVOCATORE: Did not the notary meet him?
VOLPONE: Not that I know.   20
4th AVOCATORE: His coming will clear all.
2nd AVOCATORE: Yet it is misty.
VOLTORE: May't please your fatherhoods—

*(*VOLPONE *whispers to the Advocate.)*

VOLPONE: Sir, the parasite
   Willed me to tell you, that his master lives;
   That you are still the man; your hopes, the same;
   And this was, only a jest—
VOLTORE: How?
VOLPONE: Sir, to try
   If you were firm, and how you stood affected.°   30
VOLTORE: Art sure he lives?
VOLPONE: Do I live, sir?°
VOLTORE: O me!
   I was too violent.
VOLPONE: Sir, you may redeem it—
   They said, you were possessed; fall down, and seem
   so:
   I'll help to make it good. *(*VOLTORE *falls.)*
   God bless the man!

---

obsession, "actuation by the devil or an evil spirit from
without" (*OED*). *invent,* find. *varlet,* menial or knave
(here used to slight the commendatore). *how . . . affected,*
"which way you were inclined," "how you would feel and
act." *Do . . . sir?* Volpone evidently discloses his identity to
Voltore, perhaps by showing his red hair, or a signet ring.

40 *(aside)* Stop your wind hard,° and swell—See, see,
    see, see!
  He vomits crooked pins! his eyes are set,
  Like a dead hare's, hung in a poulter's° shop!
  His mouth's running away!° do you see, signior?
  Now, 'tis in his belly.
CORVINO: Ay, the devil!
VOLPONE: Now, in his throat.
CORVINO: Ay, I perceive it plain.
VOLPONE: 'Twill out, 'twill out; stand clear. See,
50   where it flies!
  In shape of a blue toad, with a bat's wings!
  Do not you see it, sir?
CORBACCIO: What? I think I do.
CORVINO: 'Tis too manifest.
VOLPONE: Look! he comes t'himself!
VOLTORE: Where am I?
VOLPONE: Take good heart, the worst is past, sir.
  You are dispossessed.
1st AVOCATORE: What accident is this?
60 2nd AVOCATORE: Sudden, and full of wonder!
3rd AVOCATORE: If he were
  Possessed, as it appears, all this is nothing.
CORVINO: He has been, often, subject to these fits.
1st AVOCATORE: Show him that writing, do you know
  it, sir?
VOLPONE *(aside to VOLTORE)*: Deny it, sir, forswear it,
  know it not.
VOLTORE: Yes, I do know it well, it is my hand:°
  But all, that it contains, is false.
70 BONARIO: O practice!
2nd AVOCATORE: What maze is this!
1st AVOCATORE: Is he not guilty, then,
  Whom you, there, name the parasite?
VOLTORE: Grave fathers,
  No more than, his good patron, old Volpone.
4th AVOCATORE: Why, he is dead?
VOLTORE: O no, my honoured fathers.
  He lives—
1st AVOCATORE: How! lives?
80 VOLTORE: Lives.
2nd AVOCATORE: This is subtler° yet!
3rd AVOCATORE: You said he was dead!
VOLTORE: Never.
3rd AVOCATORE *(to CORVINO)*: You said so!
CORVINO: I heard so.
4th AVOCATORE: Here comes the gentleman, make
  him way.

(Enter MOSCA as clarissimo.)

3rd AVOCATORE: A stool!

4th AVOCATORE *(aside)*: A proper° man! and were
  Volpone dead,
  A fit match for my daughter.
3rd AVOCATORE: Give him way.
VOLPONE *(aside to MOSCA)*: Mosca, I was almost lost,
  the advocate
  Had betrayed all; but, now, it is recovered:°
  All's o'the hinge° again—say, I am living.
MOSCA: What busy° knave is this! most reverend
  fathers,
  I sooner, had attended your grave pleasures,
  But that my order, for the funeral
  Of my dear patron did require me—
VOLPONE *(aside)*: Mosca!
MOSCA: Whom I intend to bury, like a gentleman.
VOLPONE *(aside)*: Aye, quick,° and cozen me of all.
2nd AVOCATORE: Still stranger!
  More intricate!
1st AVOCATORE: And come about° again!
4th AVOCATORE *(aside)*: It is a match, my daughter is
  bestowed.
MOSCA *(aside to VOLPONE)*: Will you give me half?
VOLPONE *(aside to MOSCA)*: First, I'll be hanged.
MOSCA *(aside to VOLPONE)*: I know,
  Your voice is good, cry° not so loud.
1st AVOCATORE: Demand°
  The advocate. Sir, did you not affirm,
  Volpone was alive?
VOLPONE: Yes, and he is;
  This gent'man told me so. *(aside to MOSCA)* Thou
  shalt have half.
MOSCA: Whose drunkard is this same? speak some
  that know him:
  I never saw his face. *(aside to VOLPONE)* I cannot now
  Afford it you so cheap.
VOLPONE *(aside to MOSCA)*: No?
1st AVOCATORE: What say you?
VOLTORE: The officer told me.
VOLPONE: I did, grave fathers,
  And will maintain, he lives, with mine own life.
  And, that this creature told me. *(Aside)* I was born
  With all good° stars my enemies.
MOSCA: Most grave fathers,
  If such an insolence, as this, must pass°
  Upon me, I am silent; 'twas not this,
  For which you sent, I hope.
2nd AVOCATORE: Take him away.
VOLPONE *(aside)*: Mosca!
3rd AVOCATORE: Let him be whipped,—

90
100
110
120
130

Stop your wind, hold your breath. *poulter's,* poulter-
ers. *running away,* twisting from one side to the other.
hand, handwriting. *subtler,* more elusive and bewildering.

proper, handsome. *recovered,* got back again; covered
up again. *o' the hinge,* running smoothly, no longer
unhinged (o' = on). *busy,* officious. *quick,* alive. *come
about,* turned round, reversed. *cry,* shout. *Demand,* ask.
good, propitious. *pass,* be allowed.

VOLPONE (*aside*): Wilt thou betray me?
  Cozen me?

140 3rd AVOCATORE: And taught to bear himself
    Toward a person of his rank.

4th AVOCATORE: Away. (VOLPONE *is seized.*)

MOSCA: I humbly thank your fatherhoods.

VOLPONE (*aside*): Soft, soft: whipped?
    And lose all that I have? if I confess.
    It cannot be much more.

4th AVOCATORE (*to* MOSCA): Sir, are you married?

VOLPONE: They'll be allied,° anon;° I must be
    resolute:

(*He puts off his disguise.*)

150 The Fox shall, here, uncase.°

MOSCA: Patron!

VOLPONE: Nay, now,
    My ruins shall not come alone; your match
    I'll hinder sure: my substance shall not glue° you,
    Nor screw° you, into a family.

MOSCA: Why, patron!

VOLPONE: I am Volpone, and this is my knave;°
    This, his own knave; this, avarice's fool;°
    This, a chimera° of wittol,° fool, and knave;

160 And, reverend fathers, since we all can hope
    Nought, but a sentence, let's not now despair it.°
    You hear me brief.

CORVINO: May it please your fatherhoods—

COMMENDATORE: Silence!

1st AVOCATORE: The knot is now undone, by miracle!

2nd AVOCATORE: Nothing can be more clear.

3rd AVOCATORE: Or can more prove
    These innocent.

1st AVOCATORE: Give 'em their liberty.

170 BONARIO: Heaven could not, long, let such gross
    crimes be hid.

2nd AVOCATORE: If this be held the highway to get
    riches,
    May I be poor.

3rd AVOCATORE: This's° not the gain, but torment.

1st AVOCATORE: These possess wealth, as sick men
    possess fevers,
    Which, trulier, may be said to possess them.

2nd AVOCATORE: Disrobe that parasite.

180 CORVINO, MOSCA: Most honoured fathers—

1st AVOCATORE: Can you plead ought to stay the
    course of justice?

If you can, speak.

CORVINO, VOLTORE: We beg favour.

CELIA: And mercy.

1st AVOCATORE: You hurt your innocence, suing for
    the guilty.
    Stand forth; and first, the parasite. You appear
    T'have been the chiefest minister,° if not plotter,
    In all these lewd° impostures; and now, lastly,   190
    Have, with your impudence, abused the court,
    And habit of a gentleman of Venice,
    Being a fellow of no birth, or blood:
    For which, our sentence is, first thou be whipped;
    Then live perpetual prisoner in our gallies.

VOLPONE: I thank you, for him.

MOSCA: Bane° to thy woolvish nature.

1st AVOCATORE: Deliver him to the Saffi.° (MOSCA *is*
    led off.) Thou, Volpone,
    By blood, and rank a gentleman, canst not fall   200
    Under like censure; but our judgement on thee
    Is, that thy substance all be straight confiscate
    To the hospital, of the *Incurabili*:°
    And, since the most was gotten by imposture,
    By feigning lame, gout, palsy, and such diseases,
    Thou art to lie in prison, cramped with irons,
    Till thou be'st sick, and lame indeed. Remove him.

VOLPONE: This is called mortifying° of a fox.
    (VOLPONE *is led off.*)

1st AVOCATORE: Thou, Voltore, to take away the
    scandal   210
    Thou hast given all worthy men, of thy profession,
    Art banished from their fellowship, and our state.
    Corbaccio!—bring him near. We here possess
    Thy son, of all thy state; and confine thee
    To the monastery of *San Spirito*:°
    Where, since thou knew'st not how to live well here,
    Thou shalt be learn'd to die well.

CORBACCIO: Ha! what said he?

COMMENDATORE: You shall know anon, sir.

1st AVOCATORE: Thou, Corvino, shalt   220
    Be straight embarked from thine own house, and
    rowed
    Round about Venice, through the Grand Canal,
    Wearing a cap, with fair, long ass's ears,
    Instead of horns: and, so to mount, a paper
    Pinned on thy breast, to the berlino°—

CORVINO: Yes,

---

allied, i.e., by a marriage bargain. **anon,** in a moment.
uncase, remove disguise, perhaps with a suggestion of the
fox breaking cover. **Patron!** Mosca is apparently startled
back into his servile role. **glue,** suggests a parasitic attachment. **screw,** suggests a tortuous one. **knave,** menial;
rogue. **fool,** dupe. **chimera,** mythical beast with a lion-
head, goat-body and serpent-tail; hence a triple monster.
wittol, conniving cuckold. **let's . . . it,** "let us not despair for
want of a sentence." **This's,** i.e., riches.

minister, agent, instrument. **lewd,** wicked, base.
Bane, death. **Saffi,** bailiffs. **Incurabili,** the Hospital of
Incurables was founded in Venice in 1522 for the treatment
of venereal disease; the punishment is therefore particularly
appropriate. **mortifying,** several senses are relevant:
humiliating; rendering dead to the world and the flesh by
spiritual discipline; hanging game to make it tender. **San
Spirito,** the monastery of the Holy Spirit stood on the
Giudecca canal. **berlino,** pillory.

And, have mine eyes beat out with stinking fish,
Bruised fruit, and rotten eggs—'Tis well. I'm glad,
230   I shall not see my shame, yet.
1st AVOCATORE: And to expiate
   Thy wrongs done to thy wife, thou art to send her
   Home, to her father, with her dowry trebled:
   And these are all your judgements—
ALL: Honoured fathers.
1st AVOCATORE: Which may not be revoked. Now,
   you begin,
   When crimes are done, and past, and to be
   punished,
240   To think what your crimes are: away with them!
   Let all, that see these vices thus rewarded,
   Take heart, and love to study 'em. Mischiefs feed
Like beasts, till they be fat, and then they bleed.
   (Exeunt.)

(To speak the Epilogue.)

VOLPONE: The seasoning of a play is the applause.
   Now, though the Fox be punished by the laws,
   He, yet, doth hope there is no suffering due,
   For any fact,° which he hath done 'gainst you;
   If there be, censure him: here he, doubtful, stands.
   If not, fare jovially, and clap your hands.

THE END

---

fact, crime (as in the legal phrase "after the fact").

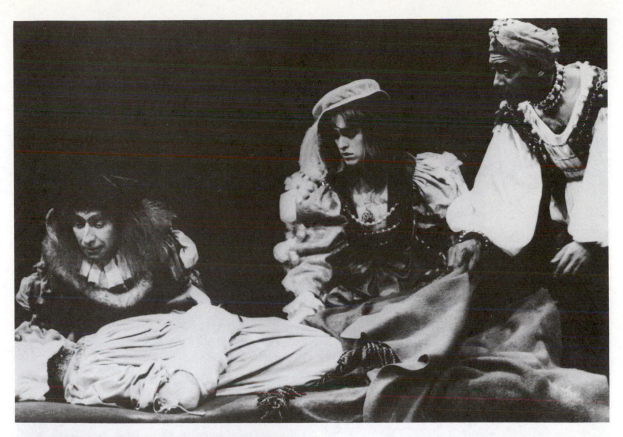

Figure 32. Voltore (Ken Ruta, *left*) stares at the body of Volpone (Douglas Campbell), disguised as a sick and dying man, while Androgyno (Katherine Emery, *center*) and Castrone (Graham Browne, *right*) look on with feigned concern in the Guthrie Theater Company production of *Volpone,* directed by Tyrone Guthrie and designed by Tanya Moiseiwitsch, Minneapolis, 1964. (Photograph: Courtesy of the Guthrie Theater.)

Figure 33. Corvino (Claude Woolman) entreats his wife Celia (Kristina Callahan) to make herself ready for a visit to Volpone in the Guthrie Theater Company production of *Volpone,* directed by Tyrone Guthrie and designed by Tanya Moiseiwitsch, Minneapolis, 1964. (Photograph: Courtesy of the Guthrie Theater.)

Figure 34. Volpone (Douglas Campbell, *left*), disguised as the moun-
tebank Scoto of Mantua, extols his quack remedies to the crowd, while
Sir Politick Would be (Lee Richardson, *right*) listens attentively in the
Guthrie Theater Company production of *Volpone,* directed by Tyrone
Guthrie and designed by Tanya Moiseiwitsch, Minneapolis, 1964. (Pho-
tograph: Courtesy of the Guthrie Theater.)

Staging of *Volpone*

REVIEW OF THE GUTHRIE THEATER
PRODUCTION, 1964, BY JOHN K. SHERMAN

My guess is that Tyrone Guthrie's production of Ben Jonson's "Volpone," fourth play of the Minnesota Theater Company's current season, will tote up as his most brilliant achievement to date in Minneapolis, when the votes are in.

It is mad, it is breath-taking in its energy and beautiful to look at, it is farce raised to the nth degree. It is a potent mixture of scalding satire and leaping fantasy. It is a 17th century three-ring circus. Above all, it is exuberantly and quintessentially theatrical—something the like of which could not be found or as fully enjoyed in any other medium than that of the living stage.

Least of all, I should add, on the printed page. Reading the play last week, I wondered how in the world its jagged and gnarled verse, its antiquated language, its far-fetched and dated figures of speech could be brought alive on a mid-20th century stage. Guthrie, I thought to myself, makes things too hard for himself and his company.

The current production proves, among other things, that the play-on-stage is the thing, and that some play scripts (O'Neill's, for example, in modern drama) are unprepossessing anywhere but on the stage. Paradoxically, however, this is the one play you should read before attending a performance. Why? Because it will give you some needed bearings as to what is going on.

"Volpone" is as thick with obscure allusions and literary double-talk as T. S. Eliot's "Waste Land." Jonson was a learned man who, unfortunately, liked to show off his learning. The play's dialogue is so crowded with references to events of the time, to classical literature and other matters known only to a well-educated man, that it took a very knowing spectator, even in the year of 1606 to catch all of them. In the play's reading version, there are almost more footnotes than text.

My point is that by reading the play—and a real chore it is—and by following up some of the footnote material, you perceive the drift and point of scenes which on stage come out in fountains and torrents of English that are often unintelligible on a word-to-word basis. And you'll discover, too, that you don't have to understand every consecutive word any more than you do in Italian opera.

I shouldn't over-emphasize this obscurity. As a matter of fact, "Volpone" at the Guthrie Theater triumphantly emerges, both in meaning and treatment, as a grotesque masquerade on the theme of human deterioration resulting from greed and self-seeking in general. Materialism as a deadly and dehumanizing force has never been attacked with more savage satire, or with more hilarious low comedy.

Volpone (the Fox) as you recall, receives valuable presents from his avaricious friends who hope, by such gifts, to become heirs to the wealth of a man they believe to be dying. Mosca (the Fly) abets his perfectly healthy master in acquiring riches by such deception, in luring a luscious and reluctant matron to his den, and in framing a court trial where injustice penalizes the innocent and rewards the corrupt.

In the end, of course, the gold-obsessed Volpone and his sly Mosca overreach themselves and get their deserts along with the other predators.

The joy to be found in this production is that of seeing members of the company stepping forth in bizarre caricatures which are a marvel of makeup, costuming, and flamboyant action. The play is actually a series of plays-within-a-play, following each other with knockabout speed and the precision of a ballet.

Douglas Campbell's Volpone is marvelously protean in his disguises of sick man, mountebank, ravenous seducer and derisive man-about-town.

This is a magnificent performance by any definition, vocally a prodigious feat from its mighty roars to its senile quaverings, and in action a veritable catalogue of comic-heroic capers . . . a portrayal unfailingly resourceful in every twist of the plot.

The slippery schemer and "stage manager" Mosca is personified in a snickering, light-stepping, cynical arabesque of action by George Grizzard, whose versatility seems to increase every time we see him.

The three buzzards who prey on the "dying" Volpone are masterpieces of extravagant impersonation—Ken Ruta as the clawing Voltore, the Vulture; Robert Pastene as the loathsome Corbaccio, the Raven, deaf and nearly blind; and Claude Woolman as the violent and despicable wife-seller, Corvino, the Crow.

The stage is full of such fantastic and over-drawn types: Lee Richardson as the fatuous and harebrained Sir Politick Would-Be; Ruth Nelson as his loose-tongued lady, Michael Levin as his baffled confidant, plus the peculiar trio of servants in Volpone's household—Sandy McCallum as the dwarf, Graham Brown as the eunuch and Katherine Emery as the hermaphrodite. "Straight" roles of the two much-abused innocents are a hysterical Celia by Kristina

Callahan and a manly boob, Bonnario, by Thomas Slater.

The singing from time to time (to music by Dominick Argento), the slapstick of the street scene where Volpone sets up his medicine show, the rough-house courtroom scenes, in fact the whole swarming action from start to finish combines high elegance with outright burlesque. Tanya Moiseiwitsch's stage design and costuming are most fetching and elaborate, a spectacle in themselves.

REVIEW OF THE GUTHRIE THEATER PRODUCTION, 1964, BY THOMAS WILLIS

In the service of this dark, outrageous, even merciless dissection of our vicious nature, the Guthrie has focused all its resources. In keeping with the renaissance Venetian setting, Tanya Moiseiwitsch has backed the action with a balcony the full width of the stage supported by serpentine gold columns. The chests of treasure are themselves treasures, being painted with oval-framed scenes of town, water, and sky.

Taking her cue from Volpone's description of his predators, "vulture, raven, kite, and gorcrow," she costumes the trio in black, with beaks for noses, great feather collars to preen and puff, clawed gloves, and a hawk's crest. Mosca, the fly, is in blue-bottle black, glinting indigo and green. And Volpone is all fox red, from bed to collar, except when disguised—then he changes to silver fox.

The Tyrone Guthrie directing conceit, like so many of his best, is operatic. Volpone is part Don Juan with a different object of desire, part Dulcamara, part John Wellington Wells, but all cruel renaissance sensualist.

He hires as familiars a hemaphrodite, a eunuch, and a dwarf, but as much for their musical skill as their freakish pleasantry. Disguised as mountebank in search of his Celia, he mounts a stirring potion sale, ending with a virtuoso trip up a ladder, across the top of the cart, and onto his lady's balcony for a "Deh, vieni alla finestra" spoken to a humming accompaniment from the trio below. When the jealous husband storms out, Volpone takes the short way down, launching himself straight out into space to be caught—Bolshoi Ballet style—by the men below.

Having once seen and heard—for this Volpone, like all good renaissance gentlemen, is singer and speaker—Douglas Campbell's way with the role, you are not likely to forget it. A voluptuary from the start, he manages to be funny and diabolically cruel at the same time. The scene in the locked chamber, where he pursues the innocent wife sent as sacrificial lamb by her husband, partially disrobes her, and throws her on the bed, all the while singing "To Ce-e-e-elia" in best period style and with a surprisingly good baritone, will do for a start.

George Grizzard's buzzing Mosca—he really does go "bzzz, bzzz" when he's thinking—is a wonderfully intelligent foil, clever, sinuous, and with more style than we would have believed possible on the basis of his other roles. The buzzard trio—Claude Woolman, Ken Ruta, and Robert Pastene—have aped the aviary with obvious relish and skill. Kristina Callahan's bewildered Celia maintains thruout her calamitous role a most appealing puzzlement. Neither of the Politick Would-Be's—Lee Richardson and Ruth Nelson—are up to the others, and it is a severe letdown when a dash of real buffoonery is indicated.

At the end of the retributory trial, conducted in frozen motion style to avoid the short scene changes, vice is suitably punished with imprisonment, banishment, and fines. Afterward, everyone breaks character for a contrapuntal madrigal in a "Don Giovanni" ending, accompanied by an unseen instrumental ensemble. Mr. Campbell and Mr. Jonson have the last word—everyone else stops in midsyllable—urging the audience to "fare jovially and clap your hands." That everyone does is no surprise.

JOHN WEBSTER

ca. 1580–1630

John Webster wrote two of the grimmest tragedies ever to appear on the English stage, or on any other. These two plays, *The White Devil* (1612) and *The Duchess of Malfi* (1614), embody a vision of human depravity that is altogether as dark as the convulsive spectacles of Euripides, and they express that vision in a style that is as dazzling as the poetry of Shakespeare. The vision and the style of these two plays alone have earned Webster a permanent place in the dramatic tradition. Most of his other works were joint efforts—two lively comedies of London life, *Westward Ho* (1604) and *Northward Ho* (1605), and a rambling history play, *Sir Thomas Wyatt* (1607), done in collaboration with Thomas Dekker; a classically unified tragedy, *Appius and Virginia* (1608), and a tragicomedy, *A Cure for a Cuckold* (1625), done in collaboration with Thomas Heywood. Aside from these collaborative works, Webster turned out at least two other plays on his own, a tragedy that has not survived about the Machiavellian Duke of Guise, and a tragicomedy, *The Devil's Law Case* (1623), featuring another Machiavellian villain, in this case a wealthy Neapolitan merchant. Other plays of the time have been attributed to Webster, but the attributions are too doubtful to provide any reliable insight into his career as a playwright.

Webster's theatrical career is, in fact, remarkably obscure, as uncertain as the dates of his birth and death. Exactly how he was occupied during his lifetime can be inferred only from the circumstances connected with the writing, production, and publication of his few surviving plays, for records of the period contain virtually no information of his whereabouts or his doings. No doubt, he was highly active in the London theaters of his day, writing as he did for a number of different companies, in collaboration with at least two different dramatists. He evidently kept up with the work of his contemporaries, for in his preface to *The White Devil,* he went out of his way to comment on "the full and heightened style" of Chapman, "the laboured and understanding works" of Jonson, "the no less worthy composures" of Beaumont and Fletcher, and "the right happy and copious industry" of Shakespeare, Dekker, and Heywood. Apparently, most dramatists of the period were also familiar with Webster, for when *The Duchess of Malfi* was published in 1623, three of his contemporaries prepared prefatory poems in honor of Webster and his play. One of them, John Ford, went so far as to "Crown him a poet, whom nor Rome nor Greece/Transcend in all theirs for a masterpiece." Ford was obviously carried away by the occasion, yet his lavish praise clearly indicates that Webster was well known and admired in the theatrical world of renaissance London.

Webster's popularity was at least in part the product of the theatrical fads he exploited in his two most famous plays, for both *The White Devil* and *The Duchess of Malfi* combine elements from several types of English drama that were in vogue at the end of the sixteenth and the beginning of the seventeenth centuries. Both plays draw heavily on the lurid conventions of Senecan revenge tragedy that Kyd had popularized in *The Spanish Tragedy*. Indeed, they are filled with ghastly and grisly events of one spectacular kind or another—with ghosts, mad scenes, macabre dumb shows, and sensational murders, ranging from poisonings, to stabbings, to broken necks. These nightmarish events are masterminded by diabolically ingenious and fiendishly cruel villains—Machiavellian antagonists whose cruelty and guile harken back to the power-crazed types that Marlowe had popularized twenty years earlier in *Tamburlaine, The Jew of Malta,* and *Edward II.* To top it all off, these sinister characters are let loose to work their havoc in the world of renaissance Italy, a world that was popularly imagined by many Englishmen to be the epitome of corruption and decadence. That sensational image of Italian life had already been dramatized in numerous plays of the period—for example, in Marston's *The Malcontent,* in Jonson's *Volpone,* and in Tourneur's *The Revenger's Tragedy.* Webster was thus capitalizing on proven theatrical commodities in both *The White Devil* and *The Duchess of Malfi.*

He was also capitalizing on proven historical and literary commodities, for both plays are based on popular stories of actual events that took place in sixteenth century Italy. *The Duchess of Malfi,* for example, dramatizes a tragic love story that Webster had found in a widely read collection of tales, *The Palace of Pleasure* (1567), by William Painter. Painter's story of the duchess was itself a translation of a tale he had discovered in another collection, *Histoires Tragiques* (1565), by the French writer Belleforest. Belleforest's story was in turn a translation and extensive embellishment of a tale he had found in yet another collection, *Novelle* (1554), by the Italian writer Matteo Bandello. And Bandello's story was drawn from events that had actually occurred over a period of time ranging from 1500 to 1513. In *The Duchess of Malfi,* Webster was working with a sensational love story that had proven its tragic appeal over the course of a century, capturing the imagination of readers and writers in Italy, France, and England.

Although Webster had a surefire story and surefire dramatic techniques for bringing it to life on stage, he was by no means aiming simply to create a melodramatic thriller in *The Duchess of Malfi.* If that had been his purpose, he need only have dramatized the star-crossed love story he found in Painter's collection—a story drawn out at great length by narrative commentary yet identical in its plot and characters to Bandello's much shorter account. Webster, however, did not interpret the story as it had been by all of its previous tellers. He did not regard it simply as the pitiful spectacle of a calamitous marriage between persons of different social rank. Consequently, he made large-scale revisions in his source, revisions that can readily be seen by comparing Bandello's tale to the play itself. In Bandello's story, for example, attention is focussed almost exclusively on the Duchess and Antonio—first on their unsuccessful efforts to conceal their marriage, then on their futile attempts to elude the reprisal of her brothers who oppose the marriage. As a result, the two brothers remain shadowy figures, known simply by the bare fact of their opposition. Actually, they are so vague and indistinct as characters that Bandello refers to them simply as "the Cardinal and the other brother," or as "the Argonese brothers." But in Webster's play, they are clearly distinguished from one another, each moved by profoundly different motives to oppose the marriage— the Cardinal by family pride, Ferdinand by incestuous desire. Indeed, in

Webster's play the two brothers become major characters in their own right, with their decadent and malign impulses as compelling as the defiant love of the Duchess and Antonio.

Even more striking than the expanded role of the brothers is the transformation of Bosola, who appears only once in Bandello's story when he is mentioned at the end as the murderer of Antonio. But in the play, Bosola is in the limelight from the very first scene to the very last, not merely as the hired agent of the two brothers, but also as the malcontent critic of their corrupting influence, and finally as the avenger of the injustice they have inflicted on the Duchess and Antonio. In his paradoxical role as culprit, critic, and avenger, Bosola epitomizes the ambiguous view of human nature that emerges from the behavior of all the characters in the play, for the Cardinal and Ferdinand are not shown as being completely unregenerate, nor for that matter are Antonio and the Duchess presented as being completely guileless. In Webster's hands the story of the duchess turns into a searching study of a morally chaotic world, a world in which private impulse, public sanction, and moral law are hopelessly entangled, so much so that all the characters who populate the world are victims of its moral chaos, even those who are ostensibly the victimizers.

Because Webster offers a highly complex, rather than a melodramatically simple, view of good and evil, *The Duchess of Malfi* is an extremely difficult play to realize accurately on the stage. Directors, for example, are faced with the problem of how to stage a decadent world without being carried away by sensationalism alone. They are also faced with the problem of how to establish moral distinctions between the Duchess, Antonio, Bosola, Ferdinand, and the Cardinal, without overlooking their psychological relationships and affinities to one another. These and other staging problems are discussed in the interview with Jean Gascon, who directed the Stratford Festival production in 1971. Gascon's solutions are reflected in the photographs from his production that show two dramatically parallel scenes from Act 1—Ferdinand procuring the services of Bosola (see Figure 35) and the Duchess wooing Antonio (Figure 36)—as well as the banishment scene from Act 3, when the Duchess and Antonio are banished by the Cardinal and the state of Ancona (Figure 37). These photographs and the review by Clive Barnes clearly show that Gascon succeeded in communicating what he—and Webster—intended to reveal in the play: "the difficulty of virtue in a sea of corruption."

THE DUCHESS OF MALFI

BY JOHN WEBSTER

CHARACTERS

BOSOLA, *gentleman of the Duchess' horse*
FERDINAND, *Duke of Calabria*
CARDINAL, *his brother*
ANTONIO, *steward of the Duchess' household*
DELIO, *his friend*
FOROBOSCO
MALATESTE, *a count*
The Marquis of PESCARA
SILVIO, *a lord*
CASTRUCHIO, *an old lord*
RODERIGO, *lord*

GRISOLAN, *lord*
THE DUCHESS, *sister of Ferdinand and the Cardinal*
CARIOLA, *her woman*
JULIA, *wife to Castruchio and mistress to the Cardinal*
The DOCTOR
COURT OFFICERS
The several madmen, including: ASTROLOGER, TAILOR, PRIEST, DOCTOR
OLD LADY
THREE YOUNG CHILDREN
TWO PILGRIMS
ATTENDANTS, LADIES, EXECUTIONERS

ACT 1 / SCENE 1

(*The* DUCHESS' *palace in Amalfi*)
(*Enter* ANTONIO *and* DELIO.)

DELIO: You are welcome to your country, dear
    Antonio,
    You have been long in France, and you return
    A very formal Frenchman, in your habit.°
    How do you like the French court?
ANTONIO: I admire it;
    In seeking to reduce both State and people
    To a fixed order, their judicious king
    Begins at home. Quits° first his royal palace
10   Of flatt'ring sycophants, of dissolute,
    And infamous persons, which° he sweetly terms
    His Master's masterpiece, the work of Heaven,
    Consid'ring duly, that a prince's court
    Is like a common fountain, whence should flow
    Pure silver-drops in general. But if't chance
    Some cursed example poison't near the head,°
    Death and diseases through the whole land spread.
    And what is't makes this blessèd government,
    But a most provident council, who dare freely
20   Inform him° the corruption of the times?
    Though some o' th' court hold it presumption
    To instruct princes what they ought to do,
    It is a noble duty to inform them
    What they ought to foresee. Here comes Bosola,
    The only court-gall:° yet I observe his railing
    Is not for simple love of piety:

Indeed he rails at those things which he wants,
Would be as lecherous, covetous, or proud,
Bloody, or envious, as any man,
If he had means to be so.—Here's the Cardinal.   30

(*Enter* BOSOLA *and the* CARDINAL.)

BOSOLA: I do haunt you still.
CARDINAL: So.
BOSOLA: I have done you better service than to be
    slighted thus. Miserable age, where only the°
    reward of doing well, is the doing of it!
CARDINAL: You enforce° your merit too much.
BOSOLA: I fell into the galleys in your service, where,
    for two years together, I wore two towels instead
    of a shirt, with a knot on the shoulder, after the
    fashion of a Roman mantle. Slighted thus, I will   40
    thrive some way: blackbirds fatten best in hard
    weather,° why not I, in these dog days?°
CARDINAL: Would you could become honest,—
BOSOLA: With all your divinity, do but direct me the
    way to it. I have known many travel far for it,
    and yet return as arrant knaves, as they went
    forth; because they carried themselves always
    along with them.° (*Exit* CARDINAL.) Are you
    gone? Some fellows, they say, are possessed with
    the devil, but this great fellow were able to   50
    possess the greatest devil, and make him worse.
ANTONIO: He hath denied thee some suit?
BOSOLA: He and his brother are like plum trees, that
    grow crooked over standing° pools, they are rich,

---

habit, dress. **Quits,** empties. **which,** modifies either the "royal palace" or the process of ridding. **head,** both the source of the fountain and the chief of state. **Inform him,** inform him about. **court-gall,** both a sore spot in the court and a bitter railer against the court.

only the, the only. **enforce,** emphasize. **blackbirds . . . weather,** It was commonly thought that blackbirds grew fat in cold weather—perhaps because their ruffled feathers made them seem heavier then. **dog days,** corrupt times. **because . . . them,** because they could not get away from the evil within themselves. **standing,** stagnant.

332

and o'erladen with fruit, but none but crows,
pies,° and caterpillars feed on them. Could I be
one of their flatt'ring panders, I would hang on
their ears like a horseleech, till I were full, and
then drop off. I pray, leave me. Who would rely
60   upon these miserable dependences,° in expectation to be advanced tomorrow? What creature
ever fed worse, than hoping Tantalus;° nor ever
died any man more fearfully, than he that hoped
for a pardon? There are rewards for hawks, and
dogs, when they have done us service; but for a
soldier, that hazards his limbs in a battle, nothing
but a kind of geometry° is his last supportation.

DELIO: Geometry?

BOSOLA: Ay, to hang in a fair pair of slings, take his
70   latter swing in the world, upon an honorable
pair of crutches, from hospital to hospital. Fare
ye well sir, and yet do not you scorn us; for
places in the court are but like beds in the
hospital, where this man's head lies at that man's
foot, and so lower and lower. (*Exit* BOSOLA.)

DELIO: I knew this fellow seven years in the galleys,°
For a notorious murther, and 'twas thought
The Cardinal suborned° it: he was released
By the French general, Gaston de Foix°
80   When he recovered Naples.

ANTONIO: 'Tis great pity
He should be thus neglected: I have heard
He's very valiant. This foul melancholy
Will poison all his goodness; for, I'll tell you,
If too immoderate sleep be truly said
To be an inward rust unto the soul,
It then doth follow want of action
Breeds all black malcontents, and their close
rearing,°
80   Like moths in cloth, do hurt for want of wearing.°

---

pies, magpies.   **dependences,** social inferiority that makes one dependent upon the favors of another.   **Tantalus,** a wrongdoer who was punished in Hades by being set, thirsty and hungry, in a pool of water that receded whenever he tried to drink from it and under a tree whose fruit he could never reach.   **kind of geometry,** hanging in a stiff, angular position.   **seven . . . galleys,** This statement only appears to contradict Bosola's previous complaint. His claim there that for two years—an arbitrary identification of an indefinite period of time—he has gone without a change of clothes is presented as an illustration of the wretched conditions imposed upon galley slaves.   **suborned it,** secretly induced him to do it.   **Gaston de Foix,** Webster is confused here, for although Gaston de Foix was a French general who won an important victory over the Spanish and papal armies at Ravenna in 1512, he had nothing to do with the conquest of Naples in 1501: at that time he was only thirteen years old.   **their . . . rearing,** their self-centered invidious brooding.   **do hurt,** hurts (the verb governs "close rearing," but it is given a plural form because of its proximity to "moths in cloth").   **wearing,** exposure to the air (of action).

ACT 1 / SCENE 2

(DELIO *and* ANTONIO *pass into the inner stage, where* CASTRUCHIO,° SILVIO, RODERIGO, *and* GRISOLAN *are entering.*)

DELIO: The presence° 'gins to fill. You promised me
To make me the partaker of the natures
Of° some of your great courtiers.

ANTONIO: The Lord Cardinal's
And other strangers', that are now in court?
I shall. Here comes the great Calabrian duke.

(*Enter* FERDINAND *and* ATTENDANTS.)

FERDINAND: Who took the ring° oft'nest?

SILVIO: Antonio Bologna, my lord.

FERDINAND: Our sister Duchess' great master° of her
household? Give him the jewel.—When shall we   10
leave this sportive action, and fall to action
indeed?

CASTRUCHIO: Methinks, my lord, you should not desire to go to war in person.

FERDINAND (*aside*): Now for some gravity:—why, my
lord?

CASTRUCHIO: It is fitting a soldier arise to be a prince,
but not necessary a prince descend to be a
captain!

FERDINAND: No?   20

CASTRUCHIO: No my lord, he were far better do it by
a deputy.

FERDINAND: Why should he not as well sleep, or eat,
by a deputy? This might take idle, offensive, and
base office from him, whereas the other deprives
him of honor.

CASTRUCHIO: Believe my experience: that realm is
never long in quiet where the ruler is a soldier.

FERDINAND: Thou toldst me thy wife could not en-   30
dure fighting.

CASTRUCHIO: True, my lord.

FERDINAND: And of a jest she broke of° a captain she
met full of wounds: I have forgot it.

CASTRUCHIO: She told him, my lord, he was a pitiful
fellow, to lie, like the children of Ismael,° all in
tents.°

FERDINAND: Why, there's a wit were able to undo all
the chirurgeons° o' the city, for although gallants
should quarrel, and had drawn their weapons,   40
and were ready to go to it; yet her persuasions

Castruchio The name is meant to suggest impotence. **presence,** presence chamber, where nobility received official visitors.   **To . . . Of,** to tell me about the characters of.   **took the ring,** won at jousting (by carrying off a ring with one's lance).   **great master,** steward.   **broke of,** told about.   **children of Ismael,** Arabs.   **tents,** a pun, meaning both "tents" in the modern sense and also rolls of lint used for dressing wounds.   **chirurgeons,** surgeons.

would make them put up.°

CASTRUCHIO: That she would, my lord.
 How do you like my Spanish jennet?°

RODERIGO: He is all fire.

FERDINAND: I am of Pliny's opinion.° I think he was begot by the wind; he runs as if he were ballassed° with quicksilver.°

SILVIO: True, my lord, he reels from the tilt° often.

50 RODERIGO and GRISOLAN: Ha, ha, ha!

FERDINAND: Why do you laugh? Methinks you that are courtiers should be my touchwood:° take fire when I give fire; that is, laugh when I laugh, were the subject never so witty—

CASTRUCHIO: True, my lord, I myself have heard a very good jest, and have scorned to seem to have so silly° a wit, as to understand it.

FERDINAND: But I can laugh at your fool, my lord.

CASTRUCHIO: He cannot speak, you know, but he
60 makes faces; my lady cannot abide him.

FERDINAND: No?

CASTRUCHIO: Not endure to be in merry company: for she says too much laughing, and too much company, fills her too full of the wrinkle.°

FERDINAND: I would then have a mathematical instrument° made for her face, that she might not laugh out of compass.° I shall shortly visit you at Milan, Lord Silvio.

SILVIO: Your grace shall arrive most welcome.

70 FERDINAND: You are a good horseman, Antonio; you have excellent riders in France, what do you think of good horsemanship?

ANTONIO: Nobly, my lord: as out of the Grecian horse° issued many famous princes: so out of brave horsemanship, arise the first sparks of growing resolution, that raise the mind to noble action.

FERDINAND: You have bespoke it worthily.

---

there's . . . up, The sexual innuendoes in this speech— obvious in "drawn their weapons," "go to it," and "put up" and probable in "undo" and "persuasions"—suggest both Julia's promiscuity and Ferdinand's licentiousness. The lewdness prevalent in Ferdinand's idiom suggests powerful incestuous desires, not fully suppressed. *jennet,* a small Spanish horse. *Pliny's opinion,* In his *Natural History,* Pliny wrote that some Portuguese mares were impregnated by the West Wind. *ballassed,* ballasted. *quicksilver,* the element mercury, noted for its mobility. *reels . . . tilt,* shies away from the ring that is the target in tilting. *touchwood,* tinder. *silly,* simple. *fills . . . wrinkle,* There is in this speech a sexual pun, which Castruchio, who is stupidly innocent of his wife's unfaithfulness, does not recognize. *wrinkle,* both a physical and a moral blemish and, here, pudendum as well. *mathematical instrument,* some compasslike device for confining movement. *out of compass* to excess. *Grecian horse.* The huge wooden horse which the Greeks secretly filled with their best and noblest soldiers and which the Trojans foolishly transported within the walls of their city.

(*Enter* DUCHESS, CARDINAL, CARIOLA,° JULIA, *and* ATTENDANTS.)

SILVIO: Your brother, the Lord Cardinal, and sister Duchess.   80

CARDINAL: Are the galleys come about?°

GRISOLAN: They are, my lord.

FERDINAND: Here's the Lord Silvio, is come to take his leave.

DELIO (*aside to* ANTONIO): Now sir, your promise: what's that Cardinal? I mean his temper? They say he's a brave fellow, will play his five thousand crowns at tennis, dance, court ladies, and one that hath fought single combats.

ANTONIO: Some such flashes° superficially hang on   90 him, for form; but observe his inward character: he is a melancholy churchman. The spring in his face is nothing but the engend'ring of toads:° where he is jealous of any man, he lays worse plots for them, than ever was imposed on Hercules,° for he strews in his way flatterers, panders, intelligencers, atheists, and a thousand such political° monsters. He should have been Pope, but instead of coming to it by the primitive decency° of the Church, he did bestow bribes, so   100 largely and so impudently as if he would have carried it away without Heaven's knowledge. Some good he hath done—

DELIO: You have given too much of him. What's his brother?

ANTONIO: The Duke there? a most perverse and turbulent nature:
 What appears in him mirth, is merely outside;
 If he laugh heartily, it is to laugh
 All honesty out of fashion.   110

DELIO: Twins?°

ANTONIO: In quality:
 He° speaks with others' tongues, and hears men's suits
 With others' ears, will seem to sleep o' th' bench
 Only to entrap offenders in their answers;
 Dooms men to death by information,°
 Rewards, by hearsay.°

Cariola, Cariola's name, like Castruchio's, is thematically appropriate. A "carriolo" was, among other things, a trundle bed, which servants like Cariola used to sleep in so that they might remain accessible to their mistresses. *come about,* returned to port. *flashes,* examples of showy behavior. *spring . . . toads,* countenance of nobility hides a vicious, scheming temperament. *Hercules,* a mythical hero, considered the strongest mortal, who performed twelve superhuman "labors." *political,* plotting. *primitive decency,* simple and straightforward honesty. *Twins,* Are these two brothers twins, then? *He,* Ferdinand. *information,* the testimony of informers. *Dooms . . . hearsay,* Antonio implies that Ferdinand's judgments are arbitrary and cruel, for the testimony of informers, who are paid for what they say, is hardly more reliable evidence than hearsay. When Ferdinand is their judge, men are doomed to death or rewarded indiscriminately as he chooses.

DELIO: Then the law to him

120   Is like a foul black cobweb to a spider:

He makes it his dwelling, and a prison

To entangle those shall feed him.°

ANTONIO: Most true:

He ne'er pays debts, unless they be shrewd turns,°

And those he will confess that he doth owe.

Last, for his brother there, the Cardinal:

They that do flatter him most say oracles°

Hang at his lips, and verily I believe them:

For the devil speaks in them.

130   But for their sister, the right noble Duchess,

You never fixed your eye on three fair medals,

Cast in one figure, of so different temper.°

For her discourse, it is so full of rapture,

You only will begin, then to be sorry

When she doth end her speech; and wish, in
     wonder,

She held it less vainglory to talk much

Than your penance, to hear her.° Whilst she
     speaks,

140   She throws upon a man so sweet a look,

That it were able to raise one to a galliard°

That lay in a dead palsy; and to° dote

On that sweet countenance. But in that look

There speaketh so divine a continence,

As cuts off all lascivious and vain hope.

Her days are practiced° in such noble virtue,

That sure her nights, nay more, her very sleeps,

Are more in heaven, than other ladies' shrifts.°

Let all sweet ladies break their flatt'ring glasses,°

150   And dress themselves in her.°

DELIO: Fie, Antonio,

You play the wire-drawer° with her
     commendations.

ANTONIO: I'll case the picture up.° Only thus much°—

All her particular worth grows to this sum:

She stains° the time past, lights the time to come.

CARIOLA: You must attend my lady, in the gallery,

Some half an hour hence.

ANTONIO: I shall. (*Exeunt* ANTONIO *and* DELIO.)

FERDINAND: Sister, I have a suit to you.°   160

DUCHESS: To me, sir?

FERDINAND: A gentleman here: Daniel de Bosola,

One that was in the galleys.

DUCHESS: Yes, I know him.

FERDINAND: A worthy fellow h'is. Pray let me entreat
     for

The provisorship of your horse.°

DUCHESS: Your knowledge of him

Commends him, and prefers him.

FERDINAND: Call him hither.   170

(*Exit* ATTENDANT.)

We are now upon parting.° Good Lord Silvio

Do us commend to all our noble friends

At the leaguer.°

SILVIO: Sir, I shall.

DUCHESS: You are for Milan?

SILVIO: I am.

DUCHESS: Bring the caroches.° We'll bring you down
     to the haven.

(*Exeunt* DUCHESS, CARIOLA, SILVIO, CASTRUCHIO,
RODERIGO, GRISOLAN, JULIA, *and* ATTENDANTS.)

CARDINAL: Be sure you entertain that Bosola

For your intelligence.° I would not be seen in't.   180

And therefore many times I have slighted him

When he did court our furtherance, as this
     morning.

FERDINAND: Antonio, the great master of her
     household

Had been far fitter.

CARDINAL: You are deceived in him,

His nature is too honest for such business.—

He comes: I'll leave you.

(*Enter* BOSOLA.)

BOSOLA: I was lured° to you. (*Exit* CARDINAL.)   190

FERDINAND: My brother here, the Cardinal, could
     never

Abide you.

BOSOLA: Never since he was in my debt.

FERDINAND: May be some oblique character in your
     face

Made him suspect you?

BOSOLA: Doth he study physiognomy?

There's no more credit to be given to th' face,

---

those . . . him, those that he feeds upon. *shrewd turns,* evil doings. *oracles,* words of great wisdom. *You . . . temper,* You have never seen three medals depicting the same figure which are made of such different kinds of metal as these three people. *You . . . her,* a deceptively difficult statement, which may be paraphrased: Just when you have begun (to feel this rapture), you will become sorry that she had ended her speech. And then, under the wonder of her spell, you will wish that she thought it more noble ("less vainglory") to talk a great deal than she thought it discomforting to you ("your penance") to hear her talk. *galliard,* a lively dance. *and to,* and (it is also able to make one). *practiced,* habitually spent. *shrifts,* confessions to a priest. *glasses,* mirrors. *And . . . her,* and follow her example. *wire-drawer,* one who draws out a wire from metal and, metaphorically, one who overextends the limits of truth. *I'll . . . up,* I'll put this picture of her (that I have presented) away. *Only . . . much,* Only this will I say in summary. *stains,* deprives of luster.

---

a . . . you, one who has a request to make of you. *let . . . horse,* Let me entreat you to let him serve as your groom. *upon parting,* preparing to leave. *leaguer,* camp. *caroches,* coaches. *entertain . . . intelligence,* use Bosola to gather information secretly. *lured,* called, with the implicit idea of "enticed into a trap."

200   Than to a sick man's urine, which some call
        The physician's whore, because she cozens him.°
        He did suspect me wrongfully.
FERDINAND: For that
        You must give great men leave to take their times:
        Distrust doth cause us seldom be° deceived;
        You see, the oft shaking of the cedar tree
        Fastens it more at root.
BOSOLA: Yet take heed:
        For to suspect a friend unworthily,
210   Instructs him the next way° to suspect you,
        And prompts him to deceive you.
FERDINAND: There's gold.
BOSOLA: So:
        What follows? Never rained such showers as these
        Without thunderbolts i' th' tail of them.°
        Whose throat must I cut?
FERDINAND: Your inclination to shed blood rides
        post°
        Before my occasion to use you. I give you that°
220   To live i' th' court, here, and observe the Duchess,
        To note all the particulars of her havior:
        What suitors do solicit her for marriage
        And whom she best affects. She's a young widow:
        I would not have her marry again.
BOSOLA: No, sir?
FERDINAND: Do not you ask the reason, but be
        satisfied
        I say I would not.
BOSOLA: It seems you would create me
230   One of your familiars.
FERDINAND: Familiar? what's that?
BOSOLA: Why, a very quaint invisible devil in flesh,
        An intelligencer.
FERDINAND: Such a kind of thriving thing
        I would wish thee; and ere long, thou mayst arrive
        At a higher place° by't.
BOSOLA (trying to give the money back):   Take your
        devils,
        Which hell calls angels°: these cursed gifts would
240   make
        You a corrupter, me an impudent traitor,

There's . . . him, Most kinds of sickness would not be recognizable in a urinary analysis.   *seldom be,* to be seldom.   *the . . . way,* in the quickest way.   *Never . . . them,* Bosola here refers to the mythical story in which Zeus transforms himself into a shower of gold in order to possess Danae, who is imprisoned in a brass tower. The obscene use of the word "tail" in this speech provides almost as good an example of Bosola's cynicism as his bold conclusion: "Whose throat must I cut?"   *rides post,* rides swiftly, upon horseback, changing mounts often.   *I . . . that,* I command you.   *higher place,* the kind of ambiguous statement that is characteristic of villains in Renaissance drama. Ferdinand may mean either a better social position or a scaffold (from which to be hanged).   *angels,* gold coins, which derived their name from the image of the archangel Michael on them.

And should I take these they'd take me to hell.
FERDINAND: Sir, I'll take nothing from you that I have
        given.
        There is a place that I procured for you
        This morning, the provisorship o' th' horse,
        Have you heard on't?
BOSOLA: No.
FERDINAND: 'Tis yours; is't not worth thanks?
BOSOLA: I would have you curse yourself now, that   250
        your bounty,
        Which makes men truly noble,° e'er should make
        Me a villain: oh, that to avoid ingratitude
        For the good deed you have done me, I must do
        All the ill man can invent. Thus the devil
        Candies all sins o'er,° and what Heaven terms vild,°
        That names he complimental.°
FERDINAND: Be yourself.
        Keep your old garb of melancholy: 'twill express
        You envy those that stand above your reach,   260
        Yet strive not to come near 'em. This will gain
        Access to private lodgings, where yourself
        May, like a politic dormouse,—
BOSOLA: As I have seen some,
        Feed in a lord's dish, half asleep, not seeming
        To listen to any talk, and yet these rogues
        Have cut his throat in a dream.° What's my place?
        The provisorship o' th' horse? say then my
        corruption
        Grew out of horse dung. I am your creature.   270
FERDINAND: Away!
BOSOLA: Let good men, for good deeds, covet good
        fame,
        Since place and riches oft are bribes of shame;
        Sometimes the devil doth preach. (Exit BOSOLA.)

(Enter CARDINAL, DUCHESS, and CARIOLA.)

CARDINAL: We are to part from you: and your own
        discretion
        Must now be your director.
FERDINAND: You are a widow:
        You know already what man is; and therefore   280
        Let not youth, high promotion, eloquence,—
CARDINAL: No, nor any thing without the addition,
        honor,
        Sway your high blood.
FERDINAND: Marry? they are most luxurious,°
        Will° wed twice.
CARDINAL: O fie!
FERDINAND: Their livers° are more spotted

Which . . . noble, because money gives man a position of nobility in society.   *Candies . . . o'er,* makes sins seem tempting.   *vild,* vile.   *complimental,* worthy of compliment, good.   *in a dream,* while he slept.   *luxurious,* incontinent.   *Will,* who will.   *livers,* The liver was believed to be the source of passion.

Than Laban's sheep.°
290 DUCHESS: Diamonds are of most value,
     They say, that have passed through most jewelers'
       hands.
FERDINAND: Whores, by that rule, are precious.
DUCHESS: Will you hear me?
     I'll never marry—
CARDINAL: So most widows say,
     But commonly that motion° lasts no longer
     Than the turning of an hourglass; the funeral
       sermon
300 And it, end both together.
FERDINAND: Now hear me:
     You live in a rank pasture; here, i' th' court,
     There is a kind of honeydew° that's deadly:
     'Twill poison your fame;° look to't; be not cunning,
     For they whose faces do belie their hearts
     Are witches, ere they arrive at twenty years,
     Ay, and give the devil suck.
DUCHESS: This is terrible good counsel.
FERDINAND: Hypocrisy is woven of a fine small
310   thread,
     Subtler than Vulcan's engine:° yet, believe't,
     Your darkest actions, nay, your privat'st thoughts,
     Will come to light.
CARDINAL: You may flatter yourself,
     And take your own choice, privately be married
     Under the eaves of night—
FERDINAND: Think't the best voyage
     That e'er you made; like the irregular crab,
     Which, though't goes backward, thinks that it goes
320   right,
     Because it goes its own way; but observe,
     Such weddings may more properly be said
     To be executed, than celebrated.
CARDINAL: The marriage night
     Is the entrance into some prison.
FERDINAND: And those joys,
     Those lustful pleasures, are like heavy sleeps
     Which do forerun man's mischief.°
CARDINAL: Fare you well.
330 Wisdom begins at the end:° remember it. (Exit
       CARDINAL.)
DUCHESS: I think this speech between you both was
       studied,
     It came so roundly off.
FERDINAND: You are my sister,
     This was my father's poniard:° do you see,

I'd be loath to see't look rusty,° 'cause 'twas his.
I would have you to give o'er these chargeable°
  revels;
A visor and a mask° are whispering-rooms°   340
That were ne'er built for goodness: fare ye well.
And women like that part, which, like the lamprey,°
Hath ne'er a bone in't.
DUCHESS: Fie sir!
FERDINAND: Nay,
I mean the tongue—variety of courtship°—
What cannot a neat knave with a smooth tale
Make a woman believe? Farewell, lusty widow.
     (Exit FERDINAND.)
DUCHESS: Shall this move me? If all my royal kindred
Lay in my way unto this marriage,   350
I'd make them my low footsteps.° And even now,
Even in this hate, as men in some great battles,
By apprehending danger, have achiev'd
Almost impossible actions (I have heard soldiers
  say so),
So I, through frights and threat'nings, will assay
This dangerous venture. Let old wives report
I winked, and chose a husband. Cariola,
To thy known secrecy I have given up
More than my life, my fame.°   360
CARIOLA: Both shall be safe:
For I'll conceal this secret from the world
As warily as those that trade in poison
Keep poison from their children.
DUCHESS: Thy protestation
Is ingenious° and hearty: I believe it.
Is Antonio come?
CARIOLA: He attends you.
DUCHESS: Good, dear soul,
Leave me; but place thyself behind the arras,   370
Where thou mayst overhear us. Wish me good
  speed,
For I am going into a wilderness,
Where I shall find nor path, nor friendly clew°
To be my guide.

(CARIOLA goes behind the curtain, and the DUCHESS
draws the traverse to reveal ANTONIO.)

I sent for you. Sit down:
Take pen and ink, and write. Are you ready?
ANTONIO: Yes.

Laban's sheep, In Laban's flock were many spotted
sheep (Genesis 30:29–43). **motion,** resolution. **honeydew,**
a sweet, sticky substance secreted by some plants. **fame,**
reputation. **Vulcan's engine,** the net that Vulcan used to
catch his wife, Venus, and her paramour, Mars. **mischief,**
misfortune. **Wisdom ... end,** considers the end before
beginning an action. **poniard,** dagger.

I'd ... rusty, I would not like to see it covered with your
blood ("rusty"). **chargeable,** expensive. **visor ... mask,**
part of the costume used by lords and ladies participating in
the revelry of a masque. **whispering-rooms,** small rooms
where secret, often amorous, interviews were held. **lamprey,** eel-like fish. **variety of courtship,** (the source of)
variety in courtship (because it can express love in so many
different ways). **footsteps,** steppingstones. **fame,** reputation. **ingenious,** straightforward. **clew,** something that
helps one out of a labyrinth.

DUCHESS: What did I say?
380 ANTONIO: That I should write somewhat.
DUCHESS: Oh, I remember:
  After these triumphs and this large expense
  It's fit, like thrifty husbands,° we inquire
  What's laid up for tomorrow.
ANTONIO: So please your beauteous excellence.
DUCHESS: Beauteous?
  Indeed I thank you. I look young for your sake:
  You have ta'en my cares upon you.
ANTONIO: I'll fetch your grace
390   The particulars of your revenue and expense.
DUCHESS: Oh, you are an upright treasurer, but you
  mistook,°
  For when I said I meant to make inquiry
  What's laid up for tomorrow, I did mean
  What's laid up yonder for me.
ANTONIO: Where?
DUCHESS: In heaven.
  I am making my will, as 'tis fit princes should,
  In perfect memory, and I pray, sir, tell me
400   Were not one better make it smiling, thus,
  Than in deep groans and terrible ghastly looks,
  As if the gifts we parted with procured
  That violent distraction?
ANTONIO: Oh, much better.
DUCHESS: If I had a husband now, this care were quit;
  But I intend to make you overseer.
  What good deed shall we first remember? Say.
ANTONIO: Begin with that first good deed, began i' th'
  world,
410   After man's creation, the sacrament of marriage.
  I'd have you first provide for a good husband;
  Give him all.
DUCHESS: All?
ANTONIO: Yes, your excellent self.
DUCHESS: In a winding sheet?
ANTONIO: In a couple.
DUCHESS: St. Winifred!° that were a strange will.
ANTONIO: 'Twere strange
  If there were no will in you to marry again.
420 DUCHESS: What do you think of marriage?
ANTONIO: I take't, as those that deny purgatory:
  It locally° contains or heaven, or hell;
  There's no third place in't.
DUCHESS: How do you affect° it?
ANTONIO: My banishment, feeding my melancholy,
  Would often reason thus:—
DUCHESS: Pray, let's hear it.
ANTONIO: Say a man never marry, nor have children,

What takes that from him? only the bare name
Of being a father, or the weak delight   430
To see the little wanton° ride a-cock-horse
Upon a painted stick, or hear him chatter
Like a taught starling.
DUCHESS: Fie, fie, what's all this?
  One of your eyes is bloodshot, use my ring to't.
  They say 'tis very sovereign:° 'twas my wedding
  ring,
  And I did vow never to part with it,
  But to my second husband.
ANTONIO: You have parted with it now.   440
DUCHESS: Yes, to help your eyesight.
ANTONIO: You have made me stark blind.
DUCHESS: How?
ANTONIO: There is a saucy and ambitious devil
  Is dancing in this circle.°
DUCHESS: Remove him.
ANTONIO: How?
DUCHESS: There needs small conjuration,° when your
  finger
  May do it: thus, is it fit?°   450

(She puts the ring on his finger and he kneels.)

ANTONIO: What said you?
DUCHESS: Sir,
  This goodly roof of yours is too low built;°
  I cannot stand upright in't, nor discourse
  Without° I raise it higher: raise yourself,
  Or if you please, my hand° to help you: so.
(Raises him.)
ANTONIO: Ambition, madam, is a great man's
  madness
  That is not kept in chains and close-pent rooms,
  But in fair lightsome lodgings, and is girt   460
  With the wild noise of prattling visitants,°
  Which makes it lunatic, beyond all cure.
  Conceive not I am so stupid,° but I aim
  Whereto your favors tend. But he's a fool
  That, being a-cold, would thrust his hand i' th' fire
  To warm them.
DUCHESS: So, now the ground's broke,
  You may discover what a wealthy mine
  I make you lord of.
ANTONIO: O my unworthiness!   470
DUCHESS: You were ill° to sell yourself.
  This dark'ning of your worth is not like that
  Which tradesmen use° i' th' city; their false lights

---

husbands, a pun, meaning both "stewards" and "married men." **mistook,** misunderstood (me). **St. Winifred,** a Welsh saint of the seventh century who was beheaded by Caradoc ap Alauc when she rejected his amorous advances. **locally,** in itself. **affect,** feel about.

wanton, fellow. **sovereign,** effective. **circle,** the ring. **small conjuration,** little magic. **it is fit,** Does it fit? **This . . . built,** Your humble attitude makes me uncomfortable. **Without,** unless. **my hand,** (here is) my hand. **visitants,** visitors. **so stupid,** so lunatic (as to be ambitious). **ill,** ill-advised. **tradesmen use,** Food shops were kept dark so that buyers could not closely examine a tradesman's wares.

Are to rid° bad wares off. And I must tell you
If you will know where breathes a complete man,
(I speak it without flattery), turn your eyes
And progress through° yourself.
ANTONIO: Were there nor heaven, nor hell,
I should be honest: I have long served virtue,
480   And ne'er ta'en wages of her.
DUCHESS: Now she pays it.
The misery of us that are born great:
We are forced to woo, because none dare woo us.
And as a tyrant doubles with his words,°
And fearfully° equivocates, so we
Are forced to express our violent passions
In riddles and in dreams, and leave the path
Of simple virtue, which was never made
To seem the thing it is not. Go, go brag
490   You have left me heartless; mine is in your bosom:
I hope 'twill multiply love there. You do tremble:
Make not your heart so dead a piece of flesh
To fear more than to love me. Sir, be confident,
What is't distracts you? This is flesh and blood, sir,
'Tis not the figure cut in alabaster
Kneels at my husband's tomb.° Awake, awake,
   man!
I do here put off all vain ceremony,
And only do appear to you, a young widow
500   That claims you for her husband, and like a widow,
I use but half a blush in't.°
ANTONIO: Truth speak for me,
I will remain the constant sanctuary
Of your good name.
DUCHESS: I thank you, gentle love,
And 'cause° you shall not come to me in debt,
Being now my steward, here upon your lips
I sign your Quietus est.° This you should have
   begged now:
510   I have seen children oft eat sweetmeats thus,
As fearful to devour them too soon.
ANTONIO: But for your brothers?
DUCHESS: Do not think of them:
All discord without° this circumference
Is only to be pitied, and not feared.
Yet, should they know it, time will easily
Scatter the tempest.
ANTONIO: These words should be mine,
And all the parts you have spoke, if some part of it

Would not have savored° flattery.   520
DUCHESS: Kneel.

(Enter CARIOLA.)

ANTONIO: Ha?
DUCHESS: Be not amazed; this woman's of my
   counsel.
I have heard lawyers say, a contract in a chamber,
Per verba [de] presenti,° is absolute marriage.
Bless, Heaven, this sacred gordian,° which let
   violence
Never untwine.
ANTONIO: And may our sweet affections, like the   530
   spheres,
Be still° in motion.°
DUCHESS: Quick'ning,° and make
The like soft music.°
ANTONIO: That we may imitate the loving palms,
Best emblem of a peaceful marriage,
That ne'er bore fruit divided.°
DUCHESS: What can the Church force more?
ANTONIO: That Fortune may not know an accident
Either of joy or sorrow, to divide   540
Our fixèd wishes.
DUCHESS: How can the Church build faster?
We now are man and wife, and 'tis the Church
That must but echo this. Maid,° stand apart,
I now am blind.°
ANTONIO: What's your conceit° in this?
DUCHESS: I would have you lead your fortune by the
   hand,
Unto your marriage bed:
(You speak in me this, for we now are one)   550
We'll only lie, and talk together, and plot
T'appease my humorous° kindred; and if you
   please,
Like the old tale, in Alexander and Lodowick,°
Lay a naked sword between us, keep us chaste.
Oh, let me shroud° my blushes in your bosom,

---

rid, pass.   progress through, look carefully at.   doubles
... words, employs phrases with ambiguous, double meanings.   fearfully, causing fear (in others).   'Tis ... tomb, The
whiteness of alabaster made it, like marble, suitable for use
in funeral monuments. The Duchess' reference here is, no
doubt, to a statue that marks her first husband's tomb.   I
... in't, I have been made bold by my experience.   'cause,
so that.   Quietus est, This phrase, which was often used in
account books, literally means "It is finished," and in this
instance the reference is to Antonio's obligations as steward.
without, outside.

savored, resembled.   Per ... presenti, "through words
of the present (tense)": the lovers henceforth accept each
other as husband and wife, in a contract that is legally valid.
gordian, a knot that cannot be untied.   still, always.   like
... motion, Planets were thought to revolve around the earth
in concentric, transparent, spherical shells.   Quick'ning,
stirring to life.   music, The harmonious motion of the
planets in the spheres was supposed to make sweet music.
That ... divided, Fruit-bearing palm trees were thought to
depend for their productivity upon a male palm tree.
Maid, Cariola.   I ... blind, I have been made blind by love
(because I have eyes only for Antonio).   conceit, meaning.
humorous, volatile, subject to many humors.   Alexander and
Lodowick, two legendary friends so alike no one could tell
them apart; so true was Lodowick to their friendship that he
married the Princess of Hungaria in Alexander's name and
then every night placed a naked sword in the bed between
himself and the Princess in order to keep from wronging
Alexander.   shroud, bury.

Since 'tis the treasury of all my secrets.

(ANTONIO *and the* DUCHESS *begin to exit slowly.*)

CARIOLA: Whether the spirit of greatness, or of
woman
560   Reign most in her, I know not, but it shows
A fearful madness: I owe her much of pity.

(*Exeunt.*)

ACT 2 / SCENE 1

(*The* DUCHESS' *palace about a year later*)
(*Enter* BOSOLA *and* CASTRUCHIO.)

BOSOLA: You say you would fain be taken for an
eminent courtier?

CASTRUCHIO: 'Tis the very main° of my ambition.

BOSOLA: Let me see, you have a reasonable good face
for't already, and your nightcap° expresses your
ears sufficient largely.° I would have you learn to
twirl the strings of your band° with a good grace;
and in a set speech, at th'end of every sentence,
to hum three or four times, or blow your nose till
10   it smart again, to recover your memory. When
you come to be a president° in criminal causes, if
you smile upon a prisoner, hang him, but if you
frown upon him and threaten him, let him be
sure to scape the gallows.

CASTRYCGUI: I would be a very merry president,—

BOSOLA: Do not sup a-nights; 'twill beget you an
admirable wit.

CASTRUCHIO: Rather it would make me have a good
stomach° to quarrel, for they say your roaring
20   boys° eat meat seldom, and that makes them so
valiant. But how shall I know whether the people
take me for an eminent fellow?

BOSOLA: I will teach a trick to know it: give out you lie
a-dying, and if you hear the common people
curse you, be sure you are taken for one of the
prime nightcaps.°

(*Enter* OLD LADY.)

You come from painting now?

OLD LADY: From what?

BOSOLA: Why, from your scurvy face-physic.° To
30   behold thee not painted inclines somewhat near
a miracle. These, in thy face here, were deep ruts
and foul sloughs° the last progress.° There was a
lady in France that, having had the smallpox,
flayed the skin off her face, to make it more

level; and whereas before she looked like a
nutmeg grater,° after she resembled an abortive
hedgehog.°

OLD LADY: Do you call this painting?

BOSOLA: No, no, but you call it careening° of an old
morphewed° lady, to make her disembogue°   40
again. There's rough-cast° phrase to your plastic.°

OLD LADY: It seems you are well acquainted with my
closet?°

BOSOLA: One would suspect it for a shop of witchcraft, to find in it the fat of serpents, spawn of
snakes, Jews' spittle, and their young children's
ordure, and all these for the face. I would sooner
eat a dead pigeon,° taken from the soles of the
feet of one sick of the plague, than kiss one of   50
you fasting.° Here are two of you, whose sin of
your youth is the very patrimony of the physician,° makes him renew his footcloth° with the
spring, and change his high-prized° courtesan
with the fall of the leaf: I do wonder you do not
loathe yourselves. Observe my meditation now:
    What thing is in this outward form of man
    To be beloved? We account it ominous,
    If nature do produce a colt, or lamb,
    A fawn, or goat, in any limb resembling   60
    A man; and fly from't as a prodigy.°
    Man stands amazed to see his deformity,
    In any other creature but himself,
    But in our own flesh, though we bear
        diseases
    Which have their true names only ta'en from
        beasts,
    As the most ulcerous wolf,° and swinish
        measle;°
    Though we are eaten up of lice and worms,   70
    And though continually we bear about us
    A rotten and dead body, we delight
    To hide it in rich tissue:° all our fear,
    Nay, all our terror, is lest our physician

---

nutmeg grater, because her face was so pock-marked.
hedgehog, In flaying, the skin would be removed in strips
that would roll up and stick out like spines on a hedgehog.
careening, scraping. *morphewed,* covered with scaly skin.
disembogue, set out on a journey. *rough-cast,* cast in a kind
of rough plaster. *There's . . . plastic,* There's language as
ugly as your appearance. *plastic,* molding. *closet,* most
private room. *dead pigeon,* Pigeons were sometimes
pressed against plague sores in the hope that the poison
would be drawn to the birds and out of the sores. *fasting,*
when your stomach is empty (and your breath foul). *whose
. . . physician,* whose sins of lust in your youth have infected
you with syphilis, and have thus guaranteed the physician an
income for life. *footcloth,* decorative accouterments for a
horse, which advertised the eminence of the owner. *high-
prized,* both highly prized and high-priced. *prodigy,* unnatural monster. *wolf,* ulcer. *swinish measle,* leprosy.
rich tissue, elaborate clothing.

---

main, goal. *nightcap,* the coif, a white cap worn by
lawyers. *expresses . . . largely,* makes your ears stick out far
enough. *band,* white tabs that were also part of the lawyer's
official costume. *president,* presiding judge. *good
stomach,* predisposition. *roaring boys,* bullies, quarrelsome
young men. *nightcaps,* lawyers. *face-physic,* a preparation that purges the face of unwanted layers of skin.
sloughs, both "ditches" and "layers of dead skin." *the . . .
progress,* the last time a journey was made by our ruler (and
by the coach of time across your face).

Should put us in the ground, to be made
     sweet.
Your wife's gone to Rome. You two couple,°
     and get you
To the wells at Lucca,° to recover° your aches.

(Exeunt CASTRUCHIO *and* OLD LADY.*)*

80   I have other work on foot: I observe our
          Duchess
     Is sick a-days, she pukes, her stomach seethes,°
     The fins° of her eyelids look most teeming
          blue,°
     She wanes i' th' cheek, and waxes fat i' th'
          flank;
     And, contrary to our Italian fashion,
     Wears a loose-bodied gown. There's somewhat
          in't.
90   I have a trick may chance discover it,
     A pretty one; I have brought some apricocks,°
     The first our spring yields.°

(Enter ANTONIO *and* DELIO.*)*

DELIO *(aside)*: And so long since married?
     You amaze me.
ANTONIO *(aside)*: Let me seal your lips for ever,
     For did I think that anything but th' air
     Could carry these words from you, I should wish
     You had no breath at all. *(to* BOSOLA*)* Now sir, in
          your contemplation?°
100   You are studying to become a great wise fellow?
BOSOLA: Oh sir, the opinion° of wisdom is a foul
     tetter,° that runs all over a man's body: if simplic-
     ity direct us to have no° evil, it directs us to a
     happy being. For the subtlest folly proceeds
     from the subtlest wisdom. Let me be simply
     honest.
ANTONIO: I do understand your inside.°
BOSOLA: Do you so?
ANTONIO: Because you would not seem to appear to
110   th' world
     Puffed up with your preferment, you continue
     This out-of-fashion melancholy; leave it, leave it.
BOSOLA: Give me leave to be honest in any phrase, in
     any compliment whatsoever. Shall I confess my-
     self to you? I look no higher than I can reach:
     they are the gods, that must ride on winged
     horses; a lawyer's mule of a slow pace will both

suit my disposition and business. For, mark me,
     when a man's mind rides faster than his horse
     can gallop they quickly both tire.   120
ANTONIO: You would look up to heaven, but I think
     The devil, that rules i' th' air, stands in your lights.
BOSOLA: Oh, sir, you are lord of the ascendant,° chief
     man with the Duchess: a duke was your cousin-
     german,° removed. Say you were lineally de-
     scended from King Pippin,° or he himself, what
     of this? Search the heads of the greatest rivers in
     the world, you shall find them but bubbles of
     water. Some would think the souls of princes
     were brought forth by some more weighty cause   130
     than those of meaner persons; they are de-
     ceived; there's the same hand to them: the like
     passions sway them; the same reason that makes
     a vicar go to law for a tithe pig° and undo his
     neighbors, makes them° spoil a whole province,
     and batter down goodly cities with the cannon.

(Enter DUCHESS *and* LADIES.*)*

DUCHESS: Your arm, Antonio; do I not grow fat?
     I am exceeding short-winded. Bosola,
     I would have you, sir, provide for me a litter,
     Such a one, as the Duchess of Florence rode in.   140
BOSOLA: The Duchess used one, when she was great
     with child.
DUCHESS: I think she did. *(to one of her* LADIES*)* Come
     hither, mend my ruff,°
     Here. When?° Thou art such a tedious lady; and
     Thy breath smells of lemon peels;° would thou
     hadst done;°
     Shall I sound° under thy fingers? I am
     So troubled with the mother.°
BOSOLA *(aside)*: I fear too much.   150
DUCHESS *(to* ANTONIO*)*: I have heard you say that the
     French courtiers
     Wear their hats on 'fore the King.
ANTONIO: I have seen it.
DUCHESS: In the presence?°
ANTONIO: Yes.
DUCHESS: Why should not we bring up that fashion?
     'Tis ceremony more than duty that consists

---

    couple, join, both as traveling and as sleeping compan-
ions. *wells at Lucca,* warm springs near Pisa. *recover,*
heal. *seethes,* is violently agitated. *fins,* edges. *teeming
blue,* the blue color characteristic of the eyelids of pregnant
women. *apricocks,* apricots. *I . . . yields,* Bosola intends
to find out if the Duchess is pregnant by offering her
apricots and thus appealing to the strong craving for fruit
that is often demonstrated by pregnant women. *in your
contemplation,* (Have we interrupted you while you were
rapt) in contemplation? *opinion,* teachings. *tetter,* skin
disease, eczema. *have no,* have nothing to do with. *inside,*
the true nature that you are covering up.

    lord . . . ascendant, ruling power. *cousin-german,* first
("germane") cousin. *King Pippin,* father of Charlemagne.
tithe pig, a pig owed to the vicar as a tithe. *them,* princes.
ruff, a lace collar. *When,* an expression of impatience.
peels, In the first three editions of the play, the word is
spelled "pils" and "pills," which could mean either pills or
peels. Though the spelling becomes "peels" in the fourth
edition, we cannot know for certain whether this waiting-
woman sweetened her breath with lemon peels or with little
lemon pills. *would . . . done,* I wish you were finished.
sound, swoon. *mother,* the name Elizabethans gave to a
kind of hysteria that was accompanied by swelling in the
throat and choking. The pun on the obvious meaning of
"mother" is also intended, and it is this meaning of the word
that Bosola refers to in his subsequent aside. *presence,*
presence chamber.

In the removing of a piece of felt:
160 Be you the example to the rest o' th' court;
Put on your hat first.
ANTONIO: You must pardon me:
I have seen, in colder countries than in France,°
Nobles stand bare° to th' prince; and the distinction
Methought showed reverently.
BOSOLA: I have a present for your grace.
DUCHESS: For me, sir?
BOSOLA: Apricocks, madam.
DUCHESS: O sir, where are they?
170 I have heard of none to-year.°
BOSOLA (aside): Good, her color rises.
DUCHESS: Indeed, I thank you: they are wondrous
fair ones.
What an unskillful fellow is our gardener!
We shall have none this month.
BOSOLA: Will not your grace pare them?
DUCHESS: No, they taste of musk,° methinks; indeed
they do.
BOSOLA: I know not: yet I wish your grace had pared
180 'em.
DUCHESS: Why?
BOSOLA: I forgot to tell you the knave gard'ner,
Only to raise his profit by them the sooner,
Did ripen them in horse dung.
DUCHESS: Oh, you jest.°
(to ANTONIO) You shall judge: pray taste one.
ANTONIO: Indeed, madam,
I do not love the fruit.
DUCHESS: Sir, you are loath
190 To rob us of our dainties: 'tis a delicate fruit,
They say they are restorative?°
BOSOLA: 'Tis a pretty art,
This grafting.°
DUCHESS: 'Tis so: a bett'ring of nature.
BOSOLA: To make a pippin grow upon a crab,°
A damson on a blackthorn.° (aside) How greedily
she eats them!
A whirlwind strike off these bawd farthingales,°
For, but for that, and the loose-bodied gown,
200 I should have discovered apparently°
The young springal° cutting a caper in her belly.
DUCHESS: I thank you, Bosola: they were right good
ones,
If they do not make me sick.

ANTONIO: How now, madam?
DUCHESS: This green fruit and my stomach are not
friends.
How they swell me!
BOSOLA (aside): Nay, you are too much swelled
already. 210
DUCHESS: Oh, I am in an extreme cold sweat,
BOSOLA: I am very sorry. (Exit.)
DUCHESS: Lights to my chamber! O, good Antonio,
I fear I am undone. (Exit DUCHESS.)
DELIO: Lights there, lights!
ANTONIO: O my most trusty Delio, we are lost:
I fear she's fall'n in labor, and there's left
No time for her remove.
DELIO: Have you prepared
Those ladies to attend her? and procured 220
That politic° safe conveyance for the midwife
Your Duchess plotted?°
ANTONIO: I have.
DELIO: Make use then of this forced occasion:°
Give out that Bosola hath poisoned her,
With these apricocks. That will give some color°
For her keeping close.°
ANTONIO: Fie, fie, the physicians
Will then flock to her.
DELIO: For that you may pretend 240
She'll use some prepared antidote of her own,
Lest the physicians should repoison her.
ANTONIO: I am lost in amazement. I know not what to
think on't. (Exeunt.)

ACT 2 / SCENE 2

(A hall in the DUCHESS' palace)
(Enter BOSOLA and OLD LADY.)

BOSOLA: So, so: there's no question but her tetch-
iness° and most vulturous eating of the apricocks
are apparent signs of breeding— *(to the OLD
LADY)* Now?
OLD LADY: I am in haste, sir.
BOSOLA: There was a young waiting-woman, had a
monstrous desire to see the glasshouse°—
OLD LADY: Nay, pray let me go!
BOSOLA: And it was only to know what strange in- 10
strument° it was, should swell up a glass to the
fashion of a woman's belly.
OLD LADY: I will hear no more of the glasshouse; you
are still abusing women!
BOSOLA: Who, I? no, only by the way now and then,
mention your frailties. The orange tree bears
ripe and green fruit and blossoms altogether.
And some of you give entertainment for pure

---

in . . . France, i.e., in England. *bare,* bare-headed.
to-year, this year. *musk,* an animal secretion used in
making perfume. *Oh, you jest,* The Duchess' unruffled
reaction to Bosola's vile suggestion attests to the intensity of
her desire for fruit. *restorative,* healthful. *grafting,* a
double-entendre, referring to propagation both in fruit
trees and in human beings (because the physical union in
sexual intercourse can be considered another form of grafting). *pippin, crab,* different kinds of apples. *damson,
blackthorn,* different kinds of plums. *farthingales,* hooped
petticoats. *apparently,* openly manifesting itself. *sprin-
gal,* youth.

---

politic, secret. *plotted,* planned. *forced occasion,*
circumstances forced upon us. *color,* reason. *close,* privately shut away. *tetchiness,* touchiness. *apparent,* obvious. *glasshouse,* glass factory. *instrument,* a double-
entendre.

love, but more, for more precious reward. The
lusty spring smells well,° but drooping autumn
20   tastes well. If we have the same golden showers
that rained in the time of Jupiter the Thunderer,
you have the same Danaes still, to hold up their
laps to receive them.° Didst thou never study the
mathematics?

OLD LADY: What's that, sir?

BOSOLA: Why, to know the trick how to make a many
lines meet in one center.° Go, go; give your
foster daughters° good counsel: tell them, that
the devil takes delight to hang at a woman's
30   girdle, like a false rusty watch, that she cannot
discern how the time passes.° *(Exit OLD LADY.)*

(Enter ANTONIO, DELIO, RODERIGO, GRISOLAN.)

ANTONIO: Shut up the court gates.

RODERIGO: Why sir? What's the danger?

ANTONIO: Shut up the posterns° presently,° and call
All the officers o' th' court.

GRISOLAN: I shall instantly. *(Exit.)*

ANTONIO: Who keeps the key o' th' park gate?

RODERIGO: Forobosco.

ANTONIO: Let him bring't presently. *(Exit RODERIGO.)*

(Enter SERVANTS, GRISOLAN, RODERIGO.)

40   FIRST SERVANT: Oh, gentlemen o' th' court, the
foulest treason!

BOSOLA *(aside)*: If that these apricocks should be
poisoned now,
Without my knowledge!

FIRST SERVANT: There was taken even now
A Switzer in the Duchess' bedchamber.

SECOND SERVANT: A Switzer?°

FIRST SERVANT: With a pistol in his great codpiece.°

BOSOLA: Ha, ha, ha.

50   FIRST SERVANT: The codpiece was the case for't.

SECOND SERVANT: There was a cunning traitor.

The . . . well, The lusty young woman and the aging
whore both find something rewarding in love—one, the act
itself; the other, the money she receives for it. *If . . . them,*
Bosola's argument here is simply that where there are men
who are willing to pay for love, there are women to sell it.
Why . . . center, another obscene reference to the lap of a
whore. *foster daughters,* women for whom she serves as a
midwife. *the . . . passes,* Because the devil impassions men
with desires even for women who are old, women are
deluded into thinking that they have not lost the beauty of
their youth (and have, consequently, not grown old). *post-
erns,* back gates. *presently,* now, at this present moment.
Switzer, a Swiss mercenary. *With . . . codpiece,* The codpiece was a baglike flap formerly worn in the front of men's
breeches and since replaced by the fly. Bosola's laughter
upon hearing that the pistol has been hidden in the Switzer's
codpiece results from his recognition of the obvious
double-entendre in "pistol"—a double-entendre that is developed by the servants in the succeeding speeches.

Who would have searched his codpiece?

FIRST SERVANT: True, if he kept out of the ladies'
chambers.
And all the moulds of his buttons were leaden
bullets.

SECOND SERVANT: Oh wicked cannibal: a firelock in's
codpiece?

FIRST SERVANT: 'Twas a French plot, upon my life.

SECOND SERVANT: To see what the devil can do.   60

ANTONIO: All the officers here?

SERVANTS: We are.

ANTONIO: Gentlemen,
We have lost much plate° you know; and but this
evening
Jewels, to the value of four thousand ducats
Are missing in the Duchess' cabinet.°
Are the gates shut?

FIRST SERVANT: Yes.

ANTONIO: 'Tis the Duchess' pleasure   70
Each officer be locked into his chamber
Till the sun-rising; and to send the keys
Of all their chests, and of their outward doors
Into her bedchamber. She is very sick.

RODERIGO: At her pleasure.°

ANTONIO: She entreats you take't not ill. The
innocent
Shall be the more approved° by it.

BOSOLA: Gentlemen o' th' wood yard,° where's your
Switzer now?   80

FIRST SERVANT: By this hand, 'twas credibly reported
by one o' th' black guard.° *(Exeunt BOSOLA,
RODERIGO, and SERVANTS.)*

DELIO: How fares it with the Duchess?

ANTONIO: She's exposed
Unto the worst of torture, pain, and fear.

DELIO: Speak to her all happy comfort.

ANTONIO: How I do play the fool with mine own
danger!°
You are this night, dear friend, to post to Rome;° 90
My life lies in your service.

DELIO: Do not doubt me.

ANTONIO: Oh, 'tis far from me: and yet fear presents
me
Somewhat° that looks like danger.

DELIO: Believe it,
'Tis but the shadow of your fear, no more:
How superstitiously we mind° our evils!
The throwing down salt, or crossing of a hare;
Bleeding at nose, the stumbling of a horse: 100

---

plate, money. *in . . . cabinet,* from the Duchess'
chamber. *At . . . pleasure,* perhaps an unintentional pun.
approved, proven good. *wood yard,* place where firewood
was cut. *black guard,* kitchen servants. *How . . . danger,*
What a fool I am to increase the possibility of revealing our
secret marriage (by having a child). *Rome,* where the
Duchess' brothers are. *Somewhat,* something. *mind,*
notice.

Or singing of a cricket, are of power
To daunt whole man in us.° Sir, fare you well:
I wish you all the joys of a blessèd father;
And, for my faith, lay this° unto your breast,
Old friends, like old swords, still are trusted best.
    (*Exit* DELIO.)

(*Enter* CARIOLA *with a child.*)

CARIOLA: Sir, you are the happy father of a son:
    Your wife commends him to you.
ANTONIO: Blessèd comfort!
    For heaven's sake tend her well: I'll presently
110 Go set a figure° for's nativity. (*Exeunt.*)

ACT 2 / SCENE 3

(*A hall in the* DUCHESS' *palace*)
(*Enter* BOSOLA *with a dark lanthorn.*°)

BOSOLA: Sure I did hear a woman shriek: list, ha?
    And the sound came, if I received it right,
    From the Duchess' lodgings; there's some
        stratagem
    In the confining all our courtiers
    To their several wards. I must have part of° it,
    My intelligence° will freeze else. List again,
    It may be 'twas the melancholy bird,
    Best friend of silence, and of solitariness,
10 The owl, that screamed so—ha!—Antonio?

(*Enter* ANTONIO *with a candle, his sword drawn.*)

ANTONIO: I heard some noise: who's there? What art
    thou? Speak.
BOSOLA: Antonio! Put not your face nor body
    To such a forced expression of fear—
    I am Bosola, your friend.
ANTONIO: Bosola!
    (*aside*) This mole does undermine me—heard you
    not
    A noise even now?
20 BOSOLA: From whence?
ANTONIO: From the Duchess' lodging.
BOSOLA: Not I. Did you?
ANTONIO: I did, or else I dreamed.
BOSOLA: Let's walk towards it.
ANTONIO: No. It may be 'twas
    But the rising of the wind.
BOSOLA: Very likely
    Methinks 'tis very cold, and yet you sweat.
    You look wildly.
30 ANTONIO: I have been setting a figure

For the Duchess' jewels.°
BOSOLA: Ah, and how falls your question?
    Do you find it radical?°
ANTONIO: What's that to you?
    'Tis rather to be questioned what design,
    When all men were commanded to their lodgings,
    Makes you a nightwalker.
BOSOLA: In sooth I'll tell you:
    Now all the court's asleep, I thought the devil
    Had least to do here; I came to say my prayers, 40
    And if it do offend you I° do so,
    You are a fine courtier.
ANTONIO (*aside*): This fellow will undo me.
    You gave the Duchess apricocks today;
    Pray heaven they were not poisoned.
BOSOLA: Poisoned! a Spanish fig°
    For the imputation!
ANTONIO: Traitors are ever confident,
    Till they are discovered. There were jewels stol'n
      too, 50
    In my conceit,° none are to be suspected
    More than yourself.
BOSOLA: You are a false steward.
ANTONIO: Saucy slave! I'll pull thee up by the roots.
BOSOLA: May be the ruin will crush you to pieces.
ANTONIO: You are an impudent snake indeed, sir,
    Are you scarce warm, and do you show your sting?°
[BOSOLA: . . .°
ANTONIO]: You libel well, sir.
BOSOLA: No sir, copy it out, 60
    And I will set my hand to't.°
ANTONIO: My nose bleeds.
    One that were superstitious would count
    This ominous—when it merely comes° by chance.
    Two letters, that are wrought here for my name
    Are drowned in blood!°

To . . . us, to rob us of all our bravery. *this,* my faith. *set a figure,* check the horoscope for. *dark lanthorn,* a lantern with only one opening, which could be closed to shut off the light (often used by someone who wanted to move stealthily at night.) *have . . . of,* find out about. *intelligence,* information gathered as a spy.

I . . . jewels, I have been checking a horoscope (to see if I can trace) the Duchess' jewels. *radical,* resolvable by astrology. *I,* that I. *Spanish fig,* an expression of contempt, accompanied by the obscene gesture of thrusting the thumb between the forefinger and the middle finger. *conceit,* opinion. *Are . . . sting,* The reference is to the fiftieth fable of Aesop. "The Countryman and the Snake." A villager finds a snake almost frozen and takes it home to warm it by the fire, but as soon as it is revived by the heat, the serpent tries to attack the countryman's wife and children. The reference to Bosola as "scarce warm" here is motivated by the fact that he has only recently been appointed to the provisorship of the Duchess' horses. *Bosola,* A speech seems to be missing here. *copy . . . to't,* Make your charges formally, and I will set my hand to the task of answering them. (Otherwise, be quiet.) *merely comes,* in actuality comes merely. *Two . . . blood,* Exactly what Antonio is referring to here is a mystery. He may be holding two handkerchiefs, embroidered with his initials, that he has used to absorb the blood from his nosebleed; or he may hold two official letters that required his signature as steward and have become spotted with blood.

Mere accident. For you, sir, I'll take order:°
I' th' morn you shall be safe.° *(aside)* 'Tis that must
70   color
Her lying-in.*(to* BOSOLA*)* Sir, this door you pass not.
I do not hold it fit that you come near
The Duchess' lodgings till you have quit° yourself;
(aside) The great are like the base; nay, they are the
        same,
When they seek shameful ways to avoid shame.
(Exit.)

BOSOLA: Antonio hereabout did drop a paper,
Some of your help, false friend:° oh, here it is.
What's here?—a child's nativity calculated?
80   *(Reads.)* The Duchess was delivered of a son, 'tween
        the hours twelve and one, in the night: Anno
        Dom: 1504.—That's this year—*decimo nono*
        Decembris,—That's this night—taken according
        to the Meridian of Malfi—That's our Duchess:
        happy discovery!—The Lord of the first house,°
        being combust° in the ascendant, signifies short
        life, and Mars being in a human sign, joined to
        the tail of the Dragon, in the eighth house, doth
        threaten a violent death; *Caetera non scrutantur.*°
90   Why now 'tis most apparent. This precise° fellow
Is the Duchess' bawd:° I have it to my wish.°
This is a parcel of intelligency°
Our courtiers were cased up° for! It needs must
        follow,
That I must be committed, on pretense
Of poisoning her, which I'll endure and laugh at.
If one could find the father now—but that
Time will discover. Old Castruchio
I' th' morning posts to Rome; by him I'll send
100   A letter, that shall make her brothers' galls
O'erflow their livers. This was a thrifty way.°
Though lust do mask in ne'er so strange disguise
She's oft found witty, but is never wise. *(Exit.)*

ACT 2 / SCENE 4

(The CARDINAL's *palace in Rome)*
(Enter CARDINAL *and* JULIA.*)*

CARDINAL: Sit: thou art my best of wishes. Prithee tell
me

I'll . . . order, I'll issue an order for your arrest. *safe,* in custody. *quit,* acquitted yourself (of any blame for her sickness). *false friend,* the dark lantern (associated with secret, underhanded dealings proceeding under the cover of night). *Lord . . . house,* the planet that controls the boy's nativity. *combust,* burned up by being too near the sun (and, therefore, having lost its power). *Caetera non scrutantur,* The rest (of the horoscope) remains unexamined. *precise,* (seemingly) strait-laced. *bawd,* pander. *I . . . wish,* I have succeeded in getting what I wanted (i.e. important secret information). *parcel of intelligency,* a piece of really significant information. *cased up,* ordered to keep to their quarters. *thrifty way,* shrewd scheme.

What trick didst thou invent to come to Rome
Without thy husband?
JULIA: Why, my lord, I told him
I came to visit an old anchorite°
Here, for devotion.
CARDINAL: Thou art a witty° false one:
I mean to him.
JULIA: You have prevailèd with me   10
Beyond my strongest thoughts: I would not° now
Find you inconstant.
CARDINAL: Do not put thyself
To such a voluntary torture, which proceeds
Out of your own guilt.
JULIA: How, my lord?
CARDINAL: You fear
My constancy, because you have approved°
Those giddy and wild turnings in yourself.
JULIA: Did you e'er find them?   20
CARDINAL: Sooth, generally for women:
A man might strive to make glass malleable,
Ere he should make them fixed.
JULIA: So, my lord!—
CARDINAL: We had need go borrow that fantastic
        glass°
Invented by Galileo the Florentine,
To view another spacious world i' th' moon,
And look to find a constant woman there.
JULIA: This is very well, my lord.   30
CARDINAL: Why do you weep?
Are tears your justification? The selfsame tears
Will fall into your husband's bosom, lady,
With a loud protestation that you love him
Above the world. Come, I'll love you wisely,
That's jealously, since I am very certain
You cannot make me cuckold.°
JULIA: I'll go home
To my husband.
CARDINAL: You may thank me, lady,   40
I have taken you off your melancholy perch,
Bore you upon my fist, and showed you game,
And let you fly at it. I pray thee, kiss me.°
When thou wast with thy husband, thou wast
        watched
Like a tame elephant:° *(still you are to thank me)*

---

anchorite hermit. *witty,* an ironic echo of the same word from the closing line of the preceding scene. *I . . . not,* I could not bear to. *approved,* given vent to. *fantastic glass,* telescope. *I . . . cuckold,* You cannot make me a cuckold (because I am not married to you). *I . . . me,* The Cardinal's imagery here is derived from the sport of falconry, but there are double-entendres in what he says—a habit of speech that links him psychologically with his brother. *tame elephant,* Elephants were tamed by being kept awake for so long that they would do anything in order to sleep.

Thou hadst only kisses from him, and high
   feeding,°
But what delight was that? 'Twas just like one
50   That hath a little fing'ring on the lute,
   Yet cannot tune it:° (still you are to thank me)
JULIA: You told me of a piteous wound i' th' heart,
   And a sick liver, when you wooed me first,
   And spake like one in physic.°
CARDINAL: Who's that?

   (Enter SERVANT.)

   Rest firm, for my affection to thee,
   Lightning moves slow to't.
SERVANT: Madam, a gentleman
   That's come post from Malfi desires to see you.
60 CARDINAL: Let him enter; I'll withdraw. *(Exit.)*
SERVANT: He says
   Your husband, old Castruchio, is come to Rome,
   Most pitifully tired with riding post. *(Exit* SERVANT.)

   (Enter DELIO.)

JULIA: Signior Delio! *(aside)* 'Tis one of my old suitors.
DELIO: I was bold to come and see you.
JULIA: Sir, you are welcome.
DELIO: Do you lie° here?
JULIA: Sure° your own experience
   Will satisfy you no; our Roman prelates
70   Do not keep lodging for ladies.
DELIO: Very well.
   I have brought you no commendations from your
     husband,
   For I know none by him.
JULIA: I hear he's come to Rome?
DELIO: I never knew man and beast, of a horse and a
     knight,
   So weary of each other. If he had had a good back,
   He would have undertook to have borne his horse,
80   His breach° was so pitifully sore.
JULIA: Your laughter
   Is my pity.°
DELIO: Lady, I know not whether
   You want money, but I have brought you some.
JULIA: From my husband?
DELIO: No, from mine own allowance.°
JULIA: I must hear the condition, ere I be bound to
   take it.
DELIO: Look on't, 'tis gold. Hath it not a fine color?
90 JULIA: I have a bird more beautiful.

---

high feeding, Obscene jokes are directed at Castruchio's
impotence, which makes him capable only of kissing Julia.
tune it, make it play a tune. ***in physic,*** under the care of a
physician. ***lie,*** stay. ***Sure,*** surely. ***breach,*** behind. ***Your
. . . pity,*** Julia's answer here is purposely ambiguous. She
may be saying either "What you laugh at, I pity," or "What
you laugh at makes my position (as Castruchio's wife)
pitiful." ***allowance,*** income.

DELIO: Try the sound on't.°
JULIA: A lute string far exceeds it;
   It hath no smell, like cassia° or civet;°
   Nor is it physical,° though some fond° doctors
   Persuade us, seethe't in cullises.° I'll tell you,
   This is a creature bred by— *(Enter* SERVANT.)
SERVANT: Your husband's come,
   Hath delivered a letter to the Duke of Calabria,
   That, to my thinking, hath put him out of his wits.
   (Exit SERVANT.)
JULIA: Sir, you hear.   100
   Pray let me know your business and your suit,
   As briefly as can be.
DELIO: With good speed. I would wish you,
   At such time, as you are nonresident
   With your husband, my mistress.
JULIA: Sir, I'll go ask my husband if I shall,
   And straight return your answer. *(Exit.)*
DELIO: Very fine,
   Is this her wit or honesty° that speaks thus?   110
   I heard one say the Duke was highly moved
   With a letter sent from Malfi. I do fear
   Antonio is betrayed. How fearfully
   Shows his ambition now; unfortunate Fortune!
   They pass through whirlpools, and deep woes do
     shun,
   Who the event weigh, ere the action's done. *(Exit.)*

ACT 2 / SCENE 5

(Enter CARDINAL, *and* FERDINAND, *furious, with a
letter.)*

FERDINAND: I have this night digged up a mandrake.°
CARDINAL: Say you?
FERDINAND: And I am grown mad with't.   10
CARDINAL: What's the prodigy?°
FERDINAND: Read there, a sister damned; she's loose,
   i' th' hilts:°
   Grown a notorious strumpet.
CARDINAL: Speak lower.
FERDINAND: Lower?
   Rogues do not whisper't now, but seek to
     publish't—
   As servants do the bounty of their lords—
   Aloud; and with a covetous, searching eye,   20

Look . . . it, As Delio proposes a liaison with her, Julia
thinks about the Cardinal, her present lover, and she unconsciously replies to Delio's proposition by employing the same
kind of imagery (from falconry and lute-playing) that the
Cardinal has just finished using. ***cassia,*** cinnamon. ***civet,***
an animal secretion used in making perfume. ***physical,***
health-restoring. ***fond,*** foolish. ***Nor . . . cullises,*** Nor is it
health-restoring—though some foolish doctors argue to the
contrary—when it is boiled in a broth. ***cullises,*** broths.
honesty, chastity. ***mandrake,*** a root that was thought to
induce madness if plucked. ***prodigy,*** unnatural event.
loose . . .hilts, unchaste.

To mark who note them. Oh, confusion seize her:
She hath had most cunning bawds to serve her
    turn,
And more secure conveyances° for lust,
Than towns of° garrison, for service.
CARDINAL: Is't possible?
Can this be certain?
FERDINAND: Rhubarb,° oh for rhubarb
To purge this choler; here's the cursèd day°
To prompt my memory, and here't shall stick°
Till of her bleeding heart I make a sponge
To wipe it out.
CARDINAL: Why do you make yourself
So wild a tempest?
FERDINAND: Would I could be one,
That I might toss her palace 'bout her ears,
30 Root up her goodly forests, blast her meads,°
And lay her general territory as waste,
As she hath done her honor's.
CARDINAL: Shall our blood,
The royal blood of Aragon and Castile,
Be thus attainted?
FERDINAND: Apply desperate physic,
We must not now use balsamum,° but fire,
The smarting cupping-glass,° for that's the mean
To purge infected blood, such blood as hers.
40 There is a kind of pity in mine eye;
I'll give it to my handkercher, and now 'tis here:
I'll bequeath this° to her bastard.
CARDINAL: What to do?
FERDINAND: Why, to make soft lint for his mother's
    wounds,
When I have hewèd her to pieces.
CARDINAL: Cursed creature!
Unequal nature, to place women's hearts
So far upon the left side.°
50 FERDINAND: Foolish men,
That e'er will trust their honor in a bark,
Made of so slight, weak bulrush as a woman,
Apt every minute to sink it!
CARDINAL: Thus ignorance, when it hath purchased
    honor
It cannot wield it.
FERDINAND: Methinks I see her laughing,
Excellent hyena!° Talk to me somewhat, quickly,
Or my imagination will carry me

To see her in the shameful act of sin.   60
CARDINAL: With whom?
FERDINAND: Happily,° with some strong-thighed
    bargeman;
Or one o' th' wood yard, that can quoit the sledge°
Or toss the bar, or else some lovely squire
That carries coals up to her privy lodgings.
CARDINAL: You fly beyond your reason.
FERDINAND: Go to, mistress!°
'Tis not your whore's milk, that shall quench my
    wildfire,   70
But your whore's blood.
CARDINAL: How idly shows this rage! which carries
    you,
As men conveyed by witches, through the air
On violent whirlwinds. This intemperate noise
Fitly resembles deaf men's shrill discourse,
Who talk aloud, thinking all other men
To have their imperfection.
FERDINAND: Have not you
My palsy?   80
CARDINAL: Yes, I can be angry
Without this rupture;° there is not in nature
A thing, that makes man so deformed, so beastly,
As doth intemperate anger. Chide yourself.
You have diverse men, who never yet expressed
Their strong desire of rest but by unrest,
By vexing of themselves. Come, put yourself
In tune.
FERDINAND: So, I will only study° to seem
The thing I am not. I could kill her now,   90
In you, or in myself,° for I do think
It is some sin in us, heaven doth revenge
By her.
CARDINAL: Are you stark mad?
FERDINAND: I would have their bodies
Burnt in a coal-pit, with the vantage° stopped
That their cursed smoke might not ascend to
    heaven;
Or dip the sheets they lie in, in pitch or sulphur,
Wrap them in't, and then light them like a match;   100
Or else to boil their bastard to a cullis,
And give't his lecherous father, to renew
The sin of his back.°
CARDINAL: I'll leave you.
FERDINAND: Nay, I have done;
I am confident, had I been damned in hell,
And should have heard of this, it would have put
    me

---

secure conveyances, secret arrangements. towns of,
towns (have) of. Rhubarb, thought to cure men of excessive anger by purging them of it. here's . . . day, Ferdinand
refers here to the horoscope that Bosola has enclosed. To
prompt, to keep in. meads, meadows. balsamum, healing
ointment. cupping-glass, a small vacuum glass used for
drawing blood. this, the handkerchief. to . . . side, It was
thought that only the hearts of deceitful persons were
located on the left ("sinister") side. hyena, Its lechery, as
well as its laughter, makes it an appropriate image for
Ferdinand to use here.

Happily, probably, by hap. quoit the sledge, throw the
hammer. mistress, Ferdinand jealously rails agains the
Duchess—as if she were a mistress who had deserted him for
another lover. rupture, complete lack of control. study,
work. I could . . . myself, I could kill you, and even myself,
now. ventage, chimney. to . . . back, to make him, literally, take his son back.

Into a cold sweat. In, in, I'll go sleep:
110   Till I know who leaps my sister, I'll not stir.
That known, I'll find scorpions to string my whips,
And fix her in a general eclipse.° *(Exeunt.)*

ACT 3 / SCENE 1

(The DUCHESS' *palace at Amalfi, a few years later)*
(Enter ANTONIO *and* DELIO.*)*

ANTONIO: Our noble friend, my most beloved Delio,
Oh, you have been a stranger long at court,
Came you along with the Lord Ferdinand?
DELIO: I did, sir, and how fares your noble Duchess?
ANTONIO: Right fortunately well. She's an excellent
Feeder of pedigrees: since you last saw her,
She hath had two children more, a son and
daughter.
DELIO: Methinks 'twas yesterday. Let me but wink,
10   And not behold your face,° which to mine eye
Is somewhat leaner: verily I should dream
It were within this half hour.
ANTONIO: You have not been in law,° friend Delio,
Nor in prison, nor a suitor at the court,
Nor begged the reversion° of some great man's
place,
Nor troublèd with an old wife, which° doth make
Your time so insensibly° hasten.
DELIO: Pray sir tell me,
20   Hath not this news arrived yet to the ear
Of the Lord Cardinal?
ANTONIO: I fear it hath;
The Lord Ferdinand, that's newly come to court,
Doth bear himself right dangerously.
DELIO: Pray why?
ANTONIO: He is so quiet, that he seems to sleep
The tempest out, as dormice do in winter;
Those houses that are haunted are most still,
Till the devil be up.
30   DELIO: What say the common people?
ANTONIO: The common rabble do directly say
She is a strumpet.
DELIO: And your graver heads,
Which would be politic,° what censure they?
ANTONIO: They do observe I grow to infinite
purchase°
The left-hand° way, and all suppose the Duchess
Would amend it, if she could. For, say they,
Great princes, though they grudge their officers
40   Should have such large and unconfinèd means

To get wealth under them, will not complain
Lest thereby they should make them odious
Unto the people. For other obligation
Of love, or marriage, between her and me,
They never dream of.

(Enter FERDINAND, DUCHESS, *and* BOSOLA.*)*

DELIO: The Lord Ferdinand
Is going to bed.
FERDINAND: I'll instantly to bed,
For I am weary: I am to bespeak
A husband for you.°   50
DUCHESS: For me, sir! pray who is't?
FERDINAND: The great Count Malateste.°
DUCHESS: Fie upon him,
A count? He's a mere stick of sugar candy,°
You may look quite thorough° him: when I choose
A husband, I will marry for your honor.
FERDINAND: You shall do well in't. How is't,° worthy
Antonio?
DUCHESS: But, sir, I am to have private conference
with you,   60
About a scandalous report is spread
Touching mine honor.
FERDINAND: Let me be ever deaf to't:
One of Pasquil's paper bullets,° court calumny,
A pestilent air, which princes' palaces
Are seldom purged of. Yet, say that it were true,
I pour it in your bosom,° my fixed love
Would strongly excuse, extenuate, nay, deny
Faults were they apparent in you. Go, be safe
In your own innocency.   70
DUCHESS: Oh blessed comfort:
This deadly air is purged. *(Exeunt* DUCHESS,
ANTONIO, DELIO.*)*
FERDINAND: Her guilt treads on
Hot burning cultures.° Now, Bosola,
How thrives our intelligence?°
BOSOLA: Sir, uncertainly:
'Tis rumored she hath had three bastards, but
By whom we may go read i' th' stars.°
FERDINAND: Why some
Hold opinion all things are written there.   80
BOSOLA: Yes, if we could find spectacles to read
them;

And ... eclipse, and cast her forever into darkness.
Let ... face, It seems hardly more than a wink's time since I
last saw your face. *in law,* involved in a legal case. *reversion,* right of succession to. *which,* because you are not
involved in any of these tedious undertakings. *insensibly,*
exceeding the powers of the senses to record. *politic,* more
prudent. *purchase,* wealth. *left-hand,* underhanded.

I am ... you, I am to speak in favor of a prospective
husband for you. *Count Malateste,* a name Webster chose
probably for the effect of the obscene pun. *He's ... candy,*
He is of little worth. *thorough,* through. *How is't,* How is
business? *Pasquil's ... bullets,* satirical attacks. (Pasquil,
or Pasquin, was the name given a statue to which Italian writers
commonly affixed satires.) *pour ... bosom,* I confess to you
that. *cultures,* the iron blade in the front of a plow. In
medieval England, people could demonstrate their innocence of a crime if they could walk unharmed on red-hot
cultures. *intelligence,* system for spying. *we ... stars,* we
cannot determine by any factual evidence.

I do suspect, there hath been some sorcery
Used on the Duchess.
FERDINAND: Sorcery? To what purpose?
BOSOLA: To make her dote on some desertless fellow,
She shames to acknowledge.
FERDINAND: Can your faith give way
To think there's power in potions or in charms
90 To make us love, whether we will or no?
BOSOLA: Most certainly.
FERDINAND: Away, these are mere gulleries,° horrid
    things
Invented by some cheating mountebanks°
To abuse us. Do you think that herbs or charms
Can force the will? Some trials have been made
In the foolish practice. But the ingredients
Were lenative poisons,° such as are of force
To make the patient mad; and straight the witch
100 Swears, by equivocation,° they are in love.
The witchcraft lies in her° rank blood: this night
I will force confession from her. You told me
You had got, within these two days, a false key°
Into her bedchamber.
BOSOLA: I have.
FERDINAND: As I would wish.°
BOSOLA: What do you intend to do?
FERDINAND: Can you guess?
BOSOLA: No.
110 FERDINAND: Do not ask then.
He that can compass° me, and know my drifts,°
May say he hath put a girdle 'bout the world,°
And sounded all her quicksands.
BOSOLA: I do not
Think so.
FERDINAND: What do you think then, pray?
BOSOLA: That you
Are your own chronicle too much,° and grossly
Flatter yourself.
120 FERDINAND: Give me thy hand; I thank thee.
I never gave pension° but to flatterers
Till I entertained thee: farewell,
That friend a great man's ruin strongly checks,
Who rails into his belief° all his defects. *(Exeunt.)*

ACT 3 / SCENE 2

(The DUCHESS' bedchamber)
(Enter DUCHESS, ANTONIO, and CARIOLA.)

DUCHESS: Bring me the casket hither, and the glass;°
You get no lodging here tonight, my lord.
ANTONIO: Indeed, I must persuade one.
DUCHESS: Very good:
I hope in time 'twill grow into a custom,
That noblemen shall come with cap and knee,°
To purchase a night's lodging of their wives.
ANTONIO: I must lie here.
DUCHESS: Must? you are a lord of misrule.°
ANTONIO: Indeed, my rule is only in the night. 10
DUCHESS: To what use will you put me?
ANTONIO: We'll sleep together.
DUCHESS: Alas, what pleasure can two lovers find in
    sleep?
CARIOLA: My lord, I lie with her often, and I know
She'll much disquiet you.
ANTONIO: See, you are complained of.
CARIOLA: For she's the sprawling'st bedfellow.
ANTONIO: I shall like her the better for that.
CARIOLA: Sir, shall I ask you a question? 20
ANTONIO: I pray thee Cariola.
CARIOLA: Wherefore still, when you lie with my lady
Do you rise° so early?
ANTONIO: Laboring men,
Count the clock oft'nest, Cariola,
Are glad when their task's ended.
DUCHESS: I'll stop your mouth.

(Kisses him.)

ANTONIO: Nay, that's but one. Venus had two soft
    doves
To draw her chariot: I must have another. 30

(Kisses her.)

When wilt thou marry, Cariola?
CARIOLA: Never, my lord.
ANTONIO: O fie upon this single life: forego it.
We read how Daphne,° for her peevish slight°
Became a fruitless bay tree; Syrinx° turned
To the pale empty reed; Anaxarete°
Was frozen into marble: whereas those
Which married, or proved kind unto their friends°
Were, by a gracious influence, transhaped
Into the olive, pomegranate, mulberry; 40
Became flowers, precious stones, or eminent stars.
CARIOLA: This is vain poetry; but I pray you tell me,

---

gulleries, tricks. mountebanks, charlatans, pitchmen who mounted benches and peddled their wares, which were usually elixirs and cure-alls. lenative poisons, powerful drugs. by equivocation, by equating love with madness. her, the Duchess'. false key, pass key. As . . . wish, I want it. compass, comprehend. drifts, secret schemes. put . . . world, traveled around the world (i.e. has done everything). Are . . . much, talk too much about the enormity of your deeds. pension, reward for service. belief, awareness.

glass, mirror. with . . . knee, on bended knee, with cap in hand. lord of misrule, master of the court revels (which were held at night). rise, a double-entendre. Daphne, a nymph who, pursued by Pan, was transformed into a bay tree at her own entreaty. peevish slight, foolish rejection of Pan. Syrinx, a nymph who was changed into a reed in order to escape Pan's pursuit. Anaxarete, a mythical Grecian queen who scorned the advances of Iphis and stood unmoved as he hanged himself, for which she was punished by being turned into marble. friends, lovers.

If there were proposed me wisdom, riches, and
 beauty,
In three several young men, which should I
 choose?
ANTONIO: 'Tis a hard question. This was Paris' case,°
And he was blind in't, and there was great cause:
For how was't possible he could judge right,
50 Having three amorous goddesses in view,
And they stark naked? 'Twas a motion°
Were able to benight the apprehension°
Of the severest counselor of Europe.
Now I look on both your faces, so well formed,
It puts me in mind of a question I would ask.
CARIOLA: What is't?
ANTONIO: I do wonder why hard-favored° ladies,
For the most part, keep worse-favored
 waiting-women
60 To attend them, and cannot endure fair ones.
DUCHESS: Oh, that's soon answered.
Did you ever in your life know an ill painter
Desire to have his dwelling next door to the shop
Of an excellent picture maker? 'Twould disgrace
His face-making,° and undo him. I prithee
When were we so merry? My hair tangles.
ANTONIO (aside to CARIOLA): Pray thee, Cariola, let's
 steal forth° the room,
And let her talk to herself: I have diverse times
70 Served her the like when she hath chafed
 extremely.
I love to see her angry—softly Cariola. (Exeunt
 ANTONIO and CARIOLA.)
DUCHESS: Doth not the color of my hair 'gin to
 change?
When I wax grey, I shall have all the court
Powder their hair with arras,° to be like me:
You have cause to love me, I entered you into° my
 heart

(Enter FERDINAND, unseen.)

80 Before you would vouchsafe to call for the keys.
We shall one day have my brothers take° you
 napping.

Methinks his presence, being now in court,
Should make you keep your own bed, but you'll say
Love mixed with fear is sweetest. I'll assure you
You shall get no more children till my brothers
Consent to be your gossips.° Have you lost your
 tongue?

(In the mirror she sees FERDINAND holding a poniard.)

'Tis welcome:
For know, whether I am doomed to live, or die, 90
I can do both like a prince.

(FERDINAND gives her a poniard.)

FERDINAND: Die then, quickly.
Virtue, where art thou hid? What hideous thing
Is it, that doth eclipse thee?
DUCHESS: Pray, sir, hear me—
FERDINAND: Or is it true, thou art but a bare name,
And no essential thing?
DUCHESS: Sir—
FERDINAND: Do not speak.
DUCHESS: No sir: 100
I will plant my soul in mine ears, to hear you.°
FERDINAND: Oh most imperfect light of human
 reason,
That mak'st us so unhappy, to foresee
What we can least prevent. Pursue thy wishes
And glory in them: there's in shame no comfort,
But to be past all bounds and sense of shame.
DUCHESS: I pray sir, hear me: I am married—
FERDINAND: So!
DUCHESS: Happily,° not to your liking, but for that 110
Alas, your shears do come untimely now
To clip the bird's wings, that's already flown.
Will you see my husband?
FERDINAND: Yes, if I could change
Eyes with a basilisk.°
DUCHESS: Sure, you came hither
By his confederacy.°
FERDINAND: The howling of a wolf
Is music to thee, screech owl; prithee, peace.
Whate'er thou art that hast enjoyed my sister, 120
(For I am sure thou hear'st me), for thine own sake
Let me not know thee. I came hither prepared
To work thy discovery, yet am now persuaded

Paris' case, Paris, the handsomest of men, was asked to judge who among the goddesses was the fairest—Hera, Athena, or Aphrodite. Because all three of the goddesses, who stood naked before him, were beautiful, he could not choose a winner; so each offered him a reward as a bribe. Hera promised greatness. Athena offered success in war, and Aphrodite told him that she would give him the most beautiful woman in the world for his wife. Finally, he judged Aphrodite the winner, and she subsequently helped him to carry off Helen, with disastrous consequences for himself and his city. *motion*, spectacle. *benight the apprehension*, obscure the judgment. *hard-favored*, unattractive. *face-making*, a pun, meaning both portrait-painting and make-up work. *forth*, forth from. *arras*, a white powder. *entered . . . into*, offered you. *take*, discover.

gossips, sponsors at a baptism. *I will . . . you*, I will listen to you with the utmost attention. *Happily*, probably. *basilisk*, a legendary reptile that could kill with a look. *By his confederacy*, The Duchess remains hopeful, thinking that Ferdinand's appearance has been arranged with Antonio. But she is, of course, mistaken, and the indefiniteness of her reference in the phrase "By his confederacy" emphasizes the magnitude of her error. It is not a "confederacy" with Antonio that has prompted Ferdinand's appearance; instead it is his emotional and psychological commitment to the forces of evil and destruction represented by the basilisk.

It would beget such violent effects
As would damn° us both. I would not for ten
    millions
I had beheld thee; therefore, use all means
I never may have knowledge of thy name;
Enjoy thy lust still, and a wretched life,
On that condition. And for thee, vild° woman,
If thou do wish thy lecher may grow old
In thy embracements, I would have thee build
Such a room for him, as our anchorites°
To holier use inhabit. Let not the sun
Shine on him, till he's dead. Let dogs and monkeys
Only converse with him, and such dumb things
To whom nature denies use° to sound his name.
Do not keep a paraquito, lest she learn it;
If thou do love him, cut out thine own tongue,
Lest it bewray him.
DUCHESS: Why might not I marry?
I have not gone about, in this, to create
Any new world, or custom.
FERDINAND: Thou art undone:
And thou hast ta'en that massy sheet of lead
That hid thy husband's bones, and folded it
About my heart.
DUCHESS: Mine bleeds for't.
FERDINAND: Thine? thy heart?
What should I name't, unless a hollow bullet°
Filled with unquenchable wildfire?
DUCHESS: You are in this
Too strict,° and were you not my princely brother
I would say too willful. My reputation
Is safe.
FERDINAND: Dost thou know what reputation is?
I'll tell thee, to small purpose, since th'instruction
Comes now too late:
Upon a time° Reputation, Love and Death
Would° travel o'er the world: and it was concluded
That they should part, and take three several ways.
Death told them they should find him in great
    battles,
Or cities plagued with plagues. Love gives them
    counsel
To inquire for him 'mongst unambitious
    shepherds,
Where dow'ries were not talked of, and sometimes
'Mongst quiet kindred, that had nothing left
By their dead parents. "Stay," quoth Reputation,
"Do not forsake me: for it is my nature,
If once I part from any man I meet,
I am never found again." And so, for you:
You have shook hands with° Reputation,
And made him invisible. So fare you well.

I will never see you more.
DUCHESS: Why should only I,
Of all the other princes of the world
Be cased up, like a holy relic? I have youth,
And a little beauty.
FERDINAND: So you have some virgins°
That are witches. I will never see thee more. (Exit.)

(Enter CARIOLA and ANTONIO with a pistol.)

DUCHESS: You saw this apparition?°
ANTONIO: Yes: we are
Betrayed. How came he hither? I should turn
This, to thee, for that. (Points the pistol at CARIOLA.)
CARIOLA: Pray, sir, do; and when
That you have cleft my heart, you shall read there
Mine innocence.
DUCHESS: That gallery° gave him entrance.
ANTONIO: I would this terrible thing would come
    again,
That, standing on my guard, I might relate°
My warrantable love. Ha! what means this?
DUCHESS: He left this with me. (She shows the poniard.)
ANTONIO: And, it seems, did wish
You would use it on yourself?
DUCHESS: His action seemed
To intend so much.°
ANTONIO: This hath a handle to't
As well as a point: turn it towards him, and
So fasten the keen edge in his rank gall.

(Knocking.)

How now? Who knocks? More earthquakes?°
DUCHESS: I stand
As if a mine, beneath my feet, were ready
To be blown up.
CARIOLA: 'Tis Bosola.
DUCHESS: Away!
Oh misery, methinks unjust actions
Should wear these masks and curtains, and not we.
You must instantly part hence: I have fashioned it°
    already. (Exit ANTONIO.)

(Enter BOSOLA.)

BOSOLA: The Duke your brother is ta'en up in a
    whirlwind;
Hath took horse, and's rid post to Rome.
DUCHESS: So late?
BOSOLA: He told me, as he mounted into th' saddle,
You were undone.
DUCHESS: Indeed, I am very near it.

---

damn, The first quarto edition reads "dampe." vild,
vile. anchorites, hermits. use, skill. hollow bullet, cannon ball. strict, unyielding. Upon a time, once. would,
wished to. shook...with, parted from.

So ... virgins, So, you know, have some virgins.
apparition, the sudden and unexpected appearance of Ferdinand. gallery, upstairs corridor (in this case, the upper
stage). relate, demonstrate. intend so much, imply as
much. earthquakes, serious problems. fashioned it, contrived a plan.

220 BOSOLA: What's the matter?
DUCHESS: Antonio, the master of our household,
Hath dealt so falsely with me in's accounts:
My brother stood engaged° with me for money
Ta'en up of° certain Neapolitan Jews,
And Antonio lets the bonds be forfeit.
BOSOLA: Strange. *(aside)* This is cunning.
DUCHESS: And hereupon
My brother's bills at Naples are protested
Against.° Call up our officers.
230 BOSOLA: I shall. *(Exit.)*

(Enter ANTONIO.)

DUCHESS: The place that you must fly to, is Ancona.
Hire a house there. I'll send after you
My treasure, and my jewels. Our weak safety
Runs upon enginous wheels:° short syllables
Must stand for periods.° I must now accuse you
Of such a feignèd crime, as Tasso calls
Magnanima mensogna: a noble lie,
'Cause it must shield our honors—Hark, they are
coming.

*(Enter BOSOLA and OFFICERS. The DUCHESS and AN-
TONIO begin their feigned dispute.)*

240 ANTONIO: Will your grace hear me?
DUCHESS: I have got well by° you: you have yielded
me
A million of loss; I am like to inherit
The people's curses for your stewardship.
You had the trick, in audit time, to be sick
Till I had signed your *Quietus;* and that cured you
Without help of a doctor. Gentlemen,
I would have this man be an example to you all:
So shall you hold my favor. I pray let him;°
250 For h'as done that, alas, you would not think of;
And, because I intend to be rid of him,
I mean not to publish.° Use your fortune
elsewhere.
ANTONIO: I am strongly armed to brook my
overthrow,
As commonly men bear with a hard year:
I will not blame the cause on't; but do think
The necessity of my malevolent star
Procures this, not her humor.° O, the inconstant
260 And rotten ground of service, you may see;
'Tis ev'n like him that, in a winter night,
Takes a long slumber o'er a dying fire,

As loth to part from't, yet parts thence as cold
As when he first sat down.
DUCHESS: We do confiscate,
Towards the satisfying of your accounts,
All that you have.
ANTONIO: I am all yours; and 'tis very fit
All mine should be so.
DUCHESS: So, sir, you have your pass.°   270
ANTONIO: You may see, gentlemen, what 'tis to serve
A prince with body and soul. *(Exit.)*
BOSOLA: Here's an example for extortion: what mois-
ture is drawn out of the sea, when foul weather
comes, pours down, and runs into the sea again.
DUCHESS: I would know what are your opinions
Of this Antonio.
SECOND OFFICER: He could not abide to see a pig's
head gaping.° I thought your grace would find
him a Jew.°   280
THIRD OFFICER: I would you had been his officer, for
your own sake.
FOURTH OFFICER: You would have had more money.
FIRST OFFICER: He stopped his ears with black wool,
and to those came to him for money said he was
thick of hearing.
SECOND OFFICER: Some said he was an hermaphro-
dite,° for he could not abide a woman.
FOURTH OFFICER: How scurvy proud he would look,
when the treasury was full. Well, let him go.   290
FIRST OFFICER: Yes, and the chippings of the butt'ry°
fly after him, to scour his gold chain.°
DUCHESS: Leave us. What do you think of these?°
(Exeunt OFFICERS.)
BOSOLA: That these are rogues, that in's prosperity,
But to have waited on his fortune, could have
wished
His dirty stirrup riveted through their noses:
And followed after's° mule, like a bear in a ring.°
Would have prostituted their daughters to his lust;
Made their first-born intelligencers;° thought none   300
happy
But such as were born under his blessed planet;
And wore his livery. And do these lice drop off
now?
Well, never look to have the like° again;
He hath left a sort of flatt'ring rogues behind him;
Their doom must follow. Princes pay flatterers,

---

engaged, committed.   **Ta'en up of,** borrowed from.
protested Against, called in for payment.   **Runs . . . wheels,**
depends upon speed and ingenuity.   **periods,** well-
proportioned sentences.   **got . . . by,** had enough of.   **let
hm,** let him go.   **publish,** publicly announce (what he has
done).   **but . . . humor,** This overthrow has been brought
about by evil Fortune's unalterable decree, not by the
capriciousness of the Duchess.

pass, leave to go.   **gaping,** He could not stand to see
people feasting on pork (because he hated feasting in
general and the eating of pork in particular).   **Jew,** an
unusually clever miser.   **hermaphrodite,** an individual having both male and female sexual characteristics.   **chippings
. . . butt'ry,** bread crumbs, used for polishing gold.   **gold
chain,** steward's badge of office.   **these,** these officers.
after's, after Antonio's.   **like . . . ring,** Rings were thrust
through the noses of bears so that they could be marched in
procession before bearbaiting events.   **intelligencers,** spies.
the like, one as good as Antonio.

In their own money. Flatterers dissemble their
    vices,
310 And they dissemble their lies:° that's justice.
    Alas, poor gentleman,—
DUCHESS: Poor! he hath amply filled his coffers.
BOSOLA: Sure he was too honest. Pluto° the god of
    riches,
    When he's sent by Jupiter° to any man,
    He goes limping, to signify that wealth
    That comes on God's name, comes slowly; but
        when he's sent
320 On the devil's errand, he rides post and comes in by
    scuttles.°
    Let me show you what a most unvalued° jewel
    You have, in a wanton humor, thrown away
    To bless the man shall° find him. He was an
        excellent
    Courtier, and most faithful; a soldier that thought
        it
    As beastly to know his own value too little,
    As devilish to acknowledge it too much:
    Both his virtues and form deserved a far better
330   fortune.
    His discourse rather delighted to judge itself, than
        show itself.°
    His breast was filled with all perfection,
    And yet it seemed a private whisp'ring room:
    It made so loud a noise of't.
DUCHESS: But he was basely descended.
BOSOLA: Will you make yourself a mercenary herald,
    Rather to examine men's pedigrees, than virtues?
    You shall want° him:
340 For know an honest statesman to a prince,
    Is like a cedar, planted by a spring:
    The spring bathes the tree's root; the grateful tree
    Rewards it with his shadow. You have not done so;
    I would sooner swim to the Bermoothas° on
    Two politicians'° rotten bladders, tied
    Together with an intelligencer's heartstring,
    Than depend on so changeable a prince's favor.
    Fare thee well, Antonio, since the malice of the
        world
350 Would needs down with thee, it cannot be said yet
    That any ill happened unto thee,
    Considering thy fall was accompanied with virtue.
DUCHESS: Oh, you render me excellent music.

BOSOLA: Say you?
DUCHESS: This good one that you speak of—is my
    husband.
BOSOLA: Do I not dream? Can this ambitious age
    Have so much goodness in't as to prefer
    A man merely for worth, without these shadows
    Of wealth, and painted honors? possible?°   360
DUCHESS: I have had three children by him.
BOSOLA: Fortunate lady,
    For you have made your private nuptial bed
    The humble and fair seminary° of peace.
    No question but many an unbeneficed° scholar
    Shall pray for you for this deed, and rejoice
    That some preferment in the world can yet
    Arise from merit. The virgins of your land
    That have no dowries shall hope your example
    Will raise them to rich husbands. Should you want   370
    Soldiers, 'twould make the very Turks and Moors
    Turn Christians, and serve you for this act.
    Last, the neglected poets of your time,
    In honor of this trophy° of a man,
    Raised by that curious engine,° your white hand,
    Shall thank you in your grave for't; and make that
    More reverend than all the cabinets°
    Of living princes. For Antonio,
    His fame shall likewise flow from many a pen,
    When heralds shall want coats, to sell to men.°   380
DUCHESS: As I taste comfort, in this friendly speech,
    So would I find concealment°—
BOSOLA: Oh the secret of my prince,
    Which I will wear on th' inside of my heart.
DUCHESS: You shall take charge of all my coin and
    jewels
    And follow him, for he retires himself
    To Ancona.
BOSOLA: So.
DUCHESS: Whither, within few days,   390
    I mean to follow thee.
BOSOLA: Let me think:
    I would wish your grace to feign a pilgrimage
    To Our Lady of Loretto, scarce seven leagues
    From fair Ancona, so may you depart
    Your country with more honor and your flight
    Will seem a princely progress,° retaining
    Your usual train about you.
DUCHESS: Sir, your direction
    Shall lead me, by the hand.   400
CARIOLA: In my opinion,
    She were better progress to the baths at Lucca,°

Flatterers . . . lies, Flatterers pretend that princes do not
have vices, and princes pretend that flatterers do not lie.
Pluto, actually King of the Underworld; the god of riches
was Plutus. Webster's error in this case may, however, be
intentional, for he may want to emphasize the extent to
which Bosola's thinking is dominated by the power of
blackness. *Jupiter,* king of the gods. *by scuttles,* runs
quickly. *unvalued,* invaluable. *man shall,* man who shall.
to . . . itself, to be sound, rather than showy. *want,* miss.
Bermoothas, Bermuda, which was thought of as a distant and
primitive island. *politicians,* self-interested schemers.

possible, (Is it) possible? *seminary,* seed bed. *unbe-*
neficed, not supported by a lord. *trophy,* prize. *engine,*
source of power. *cabinets,* advisors. *When . . . men,* when
heralds no longer shall deal in the corrupt practice of selling
coats of arms to men (i.e., when men are rewarded for virtue
rather than for bribery). *concealment,* secrecy. *progress,*
official journey. *Lucca,* a resort near Pisa.

Or go visit the Spa°
In Germany: for, if you will believe me,
I do not like this jesting with religion,
This feigned pilgrimage.
DUCHESS: Thou art a superstitious fool!
Prepare us instantly for our departure.
Past sorrows, let us moderately lament them;
410 For those to come, seek wisely to prevent them.

(Exit DUCHESS with CARIOLA.)

BOSOLA: A politician is the devil's quilted° anvil:
He fashions all sins on him, and the blows
Are never heard; he may work in a lady's chamber,
As here for proof. What rests,° but I reveal
All to my lord? Oh, this base quality
Of intelligencer! Why, every quality i' th' world
Prefers but gain, or commendation.°
Now for this act, I am certain to be raised:
And men that paint weeds to the life° are praised.
   (Exit.)

ACT 3 / SCENE 3

(The CARDINAL'S palace in Rome)
*(Enter CARDINAL, FERDINAND, MALATESTE, PESCARA,
SILVIO, DELIO.)*

CARDINAL: Must we turn soldier then?
MALATESTE: The Emperor,°
Hearing your worth that way, ere you attained
This reverend garment, joins you in commission
With the right fortunate soldier, the Marquis of
    Pescara°
And the famous Lannoy.°
CARDINAL: He that had the honor
Of taking the French king° prisoner?
10 MALATESTE: The same.
Here's a plot° drawn for a new fortification
At Naples.
FERDINAND: This great Count Malateste,° I perceive
Hath got employment.
DELIO: No employment my lord,
A marginal note in the muster book,° that he is

A voluntary lord.°
FERDINAND: He's no soldier?
DELIO: He has worn gunpowder, in's hollow tooth,
For the toothache.   20
SILVIO: He comes to the leaguer° with a full intent
To eat fresh beef, and garlic; means to stay
Till the scent be gone,° and straight return to court.
DELIO: He hath read all the late service,°
As the city chronicle° relates it,
And keeps two pewterers going, only to express
Battles in model.°
SILVIO: Then he'll fight by the book.°
DELIO: By the almanac, I think,
To choose good days and shun the critical.°   30
That's his mistress' scarf.
SILVIO: Yes, he protests
He would do much for that taffeta,—
DELIO: I think he would run away from a battle
To save it from taking° prisoner.
SILVIO: He is horribly afraid
Gunpowder will spoil the perfume on't,—
DELIO: I saw a Dutchman break his pate° once
For calling him pot-gun;° he made his head
Have a bore in't, like a musket.   40
SILVIO: I would he had made a touchhole° to't.°
He is indeed a guarded sumpter-cloth°
Only for the remove° of the court

(Enter BOSOLA.)

PESCARA: Bosola arrived? What should be the
    business?
Some falling out amongst the cardinals?
These factions amongst great men, they are like
Foxes when their heads are divided:°
They carry fire in their tails, and all the country
About them goes to wrack for't.   50
SILVIO: What's that Bosola?
DELIO: I knew him in Padua—a fantastical° scholar,
    like such who study to know how many knots was
    in Hercules' club; of what color Achilles'° beard
    was, or whether Hector° were not troubled with

Spa, a town in Belgium famous for its mineral waters.
r its mineral waters. **quilted,** covered with a sound-
absorbing material. **rests,** remains. **Why . . . commendation,** Every quality of character leads to some reward: (if the
quality is evil), the reward is gain; (if it is good), the prize is
only commendation. **to the life,** so that they seem lifelike.
Emperor, Charles V, the greatest of all Hapsburg emperors,
who ruled from 1519 to 1558. **Marquis of Pescara,** the
soldier who commanded the Italian army in its victory over
Francis I of France at Pavia in 1525. **Lannoy,** Viceroy of
Naples, one of the Italian commanders at Pavia and a
favorite of Charles V. **French king,** Francis I, who would
surrender his sword at Pavia only to Lannoy. **plot,** dia-
gram. **Malateste,** the ruling family in Rimini, Italy, during
the sixteenth century. **muster book,** a register of the officers and men in a military unit.

voluntary lord, a lord who volunteers for military
service. **leaguer,** alliance. **Till . . . gone,** until the good
food is eaten. **all . . . service,** all about the recent military
maneuvers. **city chronicle,** official reports about the affairs
of a city. **model,** miniature reproductions (with pewter
soldiers). **by the book,** according to some generally accepted
treatise on military strategy. **critical,** days of crisis. **taking,** being taken. **break his pate,** strike him across the head.
pot-gun, popgun, a braggart. **touchhole,** the vent in
firearms through which the charge was ignited. **I . . . to't,** I
wish he had burst his false pride completely. **guarded
sumpter-cloth,** ornamental blanket. **remove,** location.
heads are divided, when they are tied tail to tail (cf. Judges
15:4). **fantastical,** pursuing foolish fantasies. **Achilles,**
the greatest Greek warrior in the Trojan War. **Hector,** the
greatest Trojan warrior.

the toothache. He hath studied himself half
blear-eyed to know the true symmetry of
Caesar's nose by a shoeing horn.° And this he did
to gain the name of a speculative man.

60 PESCARA: Mark Prince Ferdinand,
A very salamander° lives in's eye,
To mock the eager violence of fire.

SILVIO: That cardinal hath made more bad faces with
his oppression than ever Michael Angelo made
good ones: he lifts up's nose,° like a foul por-
poise° before a storm,—

PESCARA: The Lord Ferdinand laughs.

DELIO: Like a deadly cannon, that lightens° ere it
smokes.

70 PESCARA: These are your true pangs of death,
The pangs of life, that struggle with great
statesmen,°—

DELIO: In such a deformèd silence,°witches whisper
their charms.

CARDINAL (on the other side of the stage): Doth she make
religion her riding hood
To keep her from the sun and tempest?°

FERDINAND: That!°
That damns her. Methinks her fault and beauty
80 Blended together show like leprosy:
The whiter, the fouler. I make it a question
Whether her beggarly brats were ever christened.

CARDINAL: I will instantly solicit the state of Ancona
To have them banished.

FERDINAND (to the CARDINAL): You are for° Loretto?
I shall not be at your ceremony;° fare you well.
(to BOSOLA) Write to the Duke of Malfi, my young
nephew
She had by her first husband, and acquaint him
90 With's mother's honesty.

BOSOLA: I will.

FERDINAND: Antonio!
A slave, that only smelled of ink and counters°
And ne'er in's life looked like a gentleman

---

to . . . horn, to learn that Caesar's nose was as symmetri-
cal and well-tapered as a shoehorn. *salamander,* thought
capable of living in fire. *lifts up's nose,* He sniffs around
for trouble. *foul porpoise,* The appearance of porpoises
around a ship was believed to be a warning of foul weather
to come. *lightens,* gives off light (of fire). *These . . .
statesmen,* This passage is confusing enough to be textually
corrupt: it is difficult to see how "The pangs of life, that
struggle with great statesmen" can be an accurate description of "true pangs of death." But whether there is a textual
corruption in this passage or not, its implication is that the
whispered secrets between the Cardinal and Ferdinand are
directed toward evil ends. *In . . . silence,* in such unnatural
whispers. *sun . . . tempest,* the Cardinal, who theoretically
represents the light of God, and Ferdinand, whose anger is
violent, like a tempest. *That,* That is correct! *for,* headed
for. *ceremony,* his official installation as a soldier. *coun-
ters,* pieces of wood or bone used in keeping accounts.

But in the audit time.° Go, go presently;
Draw me out an hundred and fifty of our horse,
And meet me at the fort bridge.° (*Exeunt.*)

ACT 3 / SCENE 4

(*Loretto*)
(*Enter* TWO PILGRIMS *to the Shrine of Our Lady of
Loretto.*)

FIRST PILGRIM: I have not seen a goodlier shrine than
this;
Yet I have visited many.

SECOND PILGRIM: The Cardinal of Aragon
Is this day to resign his cardinal's hat;°
His sister Duchess likewise is arrived
To pay her vow of pilgrimage. I expect
A noble ceremony.

FIRST PILGRIM: No question.—They come.

(*Here the ceremony of the Cardinal's installment in the
habit of a soldier: performed in delivering up his cross,
hat, robes, and ring at the shrine, and investing him with
sword, helmet, shield, and spurs. Then* ANTONIO, *and the*
DUCHESS, *and their children, having presented themselves at the shrine, are (by a form of banishment in dumb
show expressed towards them by the* CARDINAL *and the
state of* ANCONA) *banished. During all which ceremony
this ditty is sung to very solemn music, by diverse church-
men; and then exeunt.*)

The author disclaims this ditty to be his.

Arms and honors deck thy story   10
To thy fame's eternal glory.
Adverse fortune ever fly thee;
No disastrous fate come nigh thee.

I alone will sing thy praises,
Whom to honor virtue raises;
And thy study that divine is,
Bent to martial discipline is.
Lay aside all those robes lie by thee,
Crown thy arts with arms; they'll beautify thee.

O worthy of worthiest name, adorned in this   20
manner,
Lead bravely thy forces on, under war's warlike
banner.
O mayst thou prove fortunate in all martial
courses,
Guide thou still by skill, in arts and forces:
Victory attend thee nigh, whilst fame sings loud thy
powers;

But . . . time, In audit time, the Duke implies Antonio
made enough money to qualify as a gentleman. *fort bridge,*
draw-bridge. *to . . . hat,* resigning his church position (to
become a soldier).

30 Triumphant conquest crown thy head, and
blessings pour down showers.

FIRST PILGRIM: Here's a strange turn of state: who
would have thought
So great a lady would have matched herself
Unto so mean° a person? Yet the Cardinal
Bears himself much too cruel.

SECOND PILGRIM: They are banished.

FIRST PILGRIM: But I would ask what power hath this
state
Of Ancona, to determine of° a free prince?

40 SECOND PILGRIM: They are a free state, sir, and her
brother showed
How that the Pope, forehearing of her looseness,
Hath seized into th' protection of the Church
The dukedom which she held as dowager.°

FIRST PILGRIM: But by what justice?

SECOND PILGRIM: Sure I think by none,
Only her brother's instigation.

FIRST PILGRIM: What was it, with such violence he
took

50 Off from her finger?

SECOND PILGRIM: 'Twas her wedding ring,
Which he vowed shortly he would sacrifice
To his revenge.

FIRST PILGRIM: Alas Antonio!
If that a man be thrust into a well,
No matter who sets hand to't,° his own weight
Will bring him sooner to th' bottom. Come, let's
hence.
Fortune makes this conclusion general:

60 All things do help th' unhappy man to fall. (Exeunt.)

ACT 3 / SCENE 5

(Somewhere near Loretto)
(Enter ANTONIO, DUCHESS, CHILDREN, CARIOLA, SER-
VANTS.)

DUCHESS: Banished Ancona?

ANTONIO: Yes, you see what power
Lightens° in great men's breath.

DUCHESS: Is all our train
Shrunk to this poor remainder?

ANTONIO: These poor men,
Which have got little in your service, vow
To take your fortune.° But your wiser buntings,°
Now they are fledged,° are gone.

10 DUCHESS: They have done wisely.

---

mean, of a low social class. *determine of,* pass judgment against. *dowager,* property received by a widow upon
the death of her husband. *sets . . . to't,* gives him the initial
push. *Lightens,* explodes. *take . . . fortune,* endure your
misfortune with you. *buntings,* little birds. *are fledged,*
have acquired enough feathers to fly.

This puts me in mind of death: physicians thus,
With their hands full of money, use to give o'er°
Their patients.

ANTONIO: Right° the fashion of the world:
From decayed fortunes every flatterer shrinks;
Men cease to build where the foundation sinks.

DUCHESS: I had a very strange dream tonight.

ANTONIO: What was't?

DUCHESS: Methought I wore my coronet of state,
And on a sudden all the diamonds   20
Were changed to pearls.

ANTONIO: My interpretation
Is, you'll weep shortly; for to me, the pearls
Do signify your tears.

DUCHESS: The birds that live i' th' field
On the wild benefit of nature live
Happier than we; for they may choose their mates,
And carol their sweet pleasures to the spring.

(Enter BOSOLA with a letter, which he gives to the
DUCHESS.)

BOSOLA: You are happily o'erta'en.

DUCHESS: From my brother?   30

BOSOLA: Yes, from the Lord Ferdinand, your
brother,
All love, and safety—

DUCHESS: Thou dost blanch mischief;
Wouldst make it white.° See, see, like to calm
weather
At sea before a tempest, false hearts speak fair
To those they intend most mischief. (She reads a
letter.)
"Send Antonio to me; I want his head in a
business."   40
A politic equivocation—
He doth not want your counsel, but your head:
That is, he cannot sleep till you be dead.
And here's another pitfall, that's strewed o'er
With roses. Mark it, 'tis a cunning one:
"I stand engaged for your husband for several
debts at Naples. Let not that trouble him: I had
rather have his heart than his money."
And I believe so too.

BOSOLA: What do you believe?   50

DUCHESS: That he so much distrusts my husband's
love,
He will by no means believe his heart is with him
Until he see it. The devil is not cunning enough
To circumvent us in riddles.

BOSOLA: Will you reject that noble and free league
Of amity and love which I present you?

DUCHESS: Their league is like that of some politic°
kings

---

o'er, up. *Right,* such is. *Thou . . . white,* You try to
cover the blackness of your evil intentions with the whiteness
(of feigned friendliness). *politic,* conniving.

60 Only to make themselves of strength and power
To be our after-ruin. Tell them so.
BOSOLA: And what from you?
ANTONIO: Thus tell him: I will not come.
BOSOLA: And what of this?
ANTONIO: My brothers° have dispersed
Bloodhounds abroad, which till I hear are muzzled
No truce—though hatched with ne'er such politic
skill—
Is safe that hangs upon our enemies' will.°
70 I'll not come at them.
BOSOLA: This proclaims your breeding.
Every small thing draws a base mind to fear,
As the adamant° draws iron. Fare you well, sir;
You shall shortly hear from's. (Exit.)
DUCHESS: I suspect some ambush:
Therefore, by all my love, I do conjure you
To take your eldest son and fly towards Milan.
Let us not venture all this poor remainder
In one unlucky bottom.°
80 ANTONIO: You counsel safely.
Best of my life, farewell. Since we must part,
Heaven hath a hand in't: but no otherwise
Than as some curious artist takes in sunder
A clock or watch, when it is out of frame,°
To bring't in better order.
DUCHESS: I know not which is best,
To see you dead, or part with you. Farewell, boy,
Thou art happy, that thou hast not understanding
To know thy misery. For all our wit
90 And reading brings us to a truer sense
Of sorrow. In the eternal Church, sir,
I do hope we shall not part thus.
ANTONIO: O be of comfort,
Make patience a noble fortitude:
And think not how unkindly° we are used.
Man, like to cassia,° is proved best being bruised.
DUCHESS: Must I, like to a slave-born Russian,
Account it praise to suffer tyranny?
And yet, O Heaven, thy heavy hand is in't.
100 I have seen my little boy oft scourge his top,°
And compared myself to't: nought made me e'er
go right,
But Heaven's scourge stick.
ANTONIO: Do not weep:
Heaven fashioned us of nothing; and we strive
To bring ourselves to nothing. Farewell, Cariola,
And thy sweet armful°. (to the DUCHESS) If I do never

see thee more,
Be a good mother to your little ones,
And save them from the tiger: fare you well.   110
DUCHESS: Let me look upon you once more, for that
speech
Came from a dying father: your kiss is colder
Than I have seen an holy anchorite
Give to a dead man's skull.
ANTONIO: My heart is turned to a heavy lump of
lead,°
With which I sound my danger: fare you well. (Exit
with elder SON.)
DUCHESS: My laurel is all witherèd.
CARIOLA: Look, madam, what a troop of armèd men   120
Make° toward us.

(Enter BOSOLA with a guard, all wearing armored
masks.)

DUCHESS: O, they are very welcome:
When Fortune's wheel is overcharged with°
princes,
The weight makes it move swift. I would have my
ruin
Be sudden. I am your adventure,° am I not?
BOSOLA: You are. You must see your husband no
more,—
DUCHESS: What devil art thou, that counterfeits   130
Heaven's thunder?
BOSOLA: Is that terrible? I would have you tell me
whether
Is that note worse that° frights the silly birds
Out of the corn, or that which doth allure them
To the nets? You have harkened to the last too
much.
DUCHESS: O misery! like to a rusty o'ercharged
cannon,
Shall I never fly in pieces? Come: to what prison?   140
BOSOLA: To none.
DUCHESS: Whither then?
BOSOLA: To your palace.
DUCHESS: I have heard that Charon's° boat serves to
convey
All o'er the dismal lake, but brings none back again.
BOSOLA: Your brothers mean you safety and pity.
DUCHESS: Pity!
With such a pity men preserve alive
Pheasants and quails, when they are not fat enough   150
To be eaten.
BOSOLA: These are your children?

---

brothers, brothers-in-law. which . . . will, Until those bloodhounds are tied up, no truce that depends on our enemies' good will is safe for us—no matter how skillfully couched in ambiguous language it may be. adamant, magnet. bottom, the hold of a ship (i.e., in one precarious place). frame, order. unkindly, both evilly and unnaturally. cassia, bark that, when pounded, is a source of cinnamon. scourge his top, spin his toy top. sweet armful, the babies she holds.

lump of lead, Sailors took depth readings by dropping heavy lumps of lead overboard. Make, the verb is plural because of its proximity to "men." overcharged with, turned over by (the weight of the princes tied to it). adventure, what you venture after. whether . . . worse that, which note is worse, that which. Charon, the old boatman who ferried the souls of the dead across the river Styx to Hades.

DUCHESS: Yes.
BOSOLA: Can they prattle?°
DUCHESS: No.
　　But I intend, since they were born accursed,
　　Curses shall be their first language.
BOSOLA: Fie, madam!
　　Forget this base, low fellow.
160 DUCHESS: Were I a man,
　　I'd beat that counterfeit face° into thy other—
BOSOLA: One of no birth.
DUCHESS: Say that he was born mean:
　　Man is most happy, when's own actions
　　Be arguments and examples of his virtue.
BOSOLA: A barren, beggarly virtue.
DUCHESS: I prithee, who is greatest? Can you tell?
　　Sad tales befit my woe: I'll tell you one.
　　A salmon, as she swam unto the sea,
170 Met with a dogfish, who encounters her
　　With this rough language: "Why are thou so bold
　　To mix thyself with our high state of floods°
　　Being no eminent courtier, but one
　　That for the calmest and fresh time o' th' year
　　Dost live in shallow rivers, rankst thyself
　　With silly smelts and shrimps? And darest thou
　　Pass by our° dogship° without reverence?"
　　"O," quoth the salmon, "sister, be at peace:
　　Thank Jupiter, we both have passed the net.
180 Our value never can be truly known,
　　Till in the fisher's basket we be shown;
　　I' th' market then my price may be the higher,
　　Even when I am nearest to the cook, and fire."
　　So, to great men, the moral may be stretched:
　　Men oft are valued high,° when th'are most
　　　　wretched.
　　But, come, whither you please. I am armed 'gainst
　　　　misery,
　　Bent to all sways of the oppressor's will.
190 There's no deep valley, but near some great hill.°
　　(Exeunt.)

ACT 4 / SCENE 1

(In a prison somewhere near Loretto)
(Enter FERDINAND and BOSOLA.)

FERDINAND: How doth our sister Duchess bear
　　　　herself
　　In her imprisonment?
BOSOLA: Nobly. I'll describe her:
　　She's sad, as one long used to't, and she seems

Rather to welcome the end of misery
Than shun it—a behavior so noble,
As gives a majesty to adversity.
You may discern the shape of loveliness
More perfect in her tears, than in her smiles.　10
She will muse four hours together, and her silence,
Methinks, expresseth more than if she spake.
FERDINAND: Her melancholy seems to be fortified
　　With a strange disdain.
BOSOLA: 'Tis so, and this restraint
　　(Like English mastives, that grow fierce with tying)
　　Makes her too passionately apprehend
　　Those pleasures she's kept from.
FERDINAND: Curse upon her!
　　I will no longer study in the book　　　20
　　Of another's heart:° inform her what I told you.
　　(Exit.)

(BOSOLA enters the DUCHESS' inner-stage prison.)

BOSOLA: All comfort to, your grace;—
DUCHESS: I will have none.
　　'Pray thee, why dost thou wrap thy poisoned pills
　　In gold and sugar?°
BOSOLA: Your elder brother, the Lord Ferdinand,
　　Is come to visit you, and sends you word,
　　'Cause once he rashly made a solemn vow
　　Never to see you more. He comes i' th' night,
　　And prays you, gently, neither torch nor taper　30
　　Shine in your chamber. He will kiss your hand;
　　And reconcile himself, but, for his vow,
　　He dares not see you.
DUCHESS: At his pleasure.
　　Take hence the lights: he's come. (Exeunt SERVANTS
　　　　with lights.)

(Enter FERDINAND.)

FERDINAND: Where are you?
DUCHESS: Here sir.
FERDINAND: This darkness suits you well.
DUCHESS: I would ask your pardon.
FERDINAND: You have it;　　　40
　　For I account it the honorabl'st revenge
　　Where I may kill, to pardon.° Where are your cubs?
DUCHESS: Whom?
FERDINAND: Call them your children;
　　For though our national law distinguish bastards
　　From true legitimate issue, compassionate nature
　　Makes them all equal.
DUCHESS: Do you visit me for this?
　　You violate a sacrament o' th' Church°

---

prattle, talk.　counterfeit face, the armored visor.
high . . . floods, the deep sea (of the court's high intrigue).
our, The plural was used in any address to royal persons.
dogship, a term of abuse, satirizing such types of formal
address as "your lordship."　valued high, judged worthy (by
God).　There's . . . hill, Even in despair man finds cause for
hope—in the power of God.

I . . . heart, I will no longer waste my time trying to
figure out what is in her heart.　why . . . sugar, Why do you
cover up your hatred and evil designs with feigned courtesy?
For . . . pardon, For I consider it most honorable to pardon,
when I could kill.　sacrament . . . Church, her marriage to
Antonio, which she believes is recognized by the eternal
Church.

50   Shall make you howl in hell for't.
FERDINAND: It had been well,
      Could you have lived thus° always, for indeed
      You were too much i' th' light.° But no more;
      I come to seal my peace with you: here's a hand,

(Gives her a dead man's hand.)

      To which you have vowed much love; the ring°
          upon't
      You gave.
DUCHESS: I affectionately kiss it.
FERDINAND: Pray do, and bury the print of it in your
60   heart.
      I will leave this ring with you, for a love-token,
      And the hand, as sure as the ring. And do not
          doubt
      But you shall have the heart too. When you need a
          friend
      Send it to him that owed° it: you shall see
      Whether he can aid you.
DUCHESS: You are very cold.
      I fear you are not well after your travel.
70   Ha lights!—Oh, horrible!
FERDINAND: Let her have lights enough. *(Exit.)*

(Enter SERVANTS *with lights.)*

DUCHESS: What witchcraft doth he practice,° that he
          hath left
      A dead man's hand here?—

*(Here is discovered, behind a traverse, the artificial fig-
ures of* ANTONIO *and his children, appearing as if they
were dead.)*

BOSOLA: Look you, here's the piece from which 'twas
          ta'en.
      He doth present you this sad spectacle
      That, now you know directly they are dead,
      Hereafter you may wisely cease to grieve
80   For that which cannot be recovered.
DUCHESS: There is not between heaven and earth one
          wish
      I stay for after this. It wastes me more,
      Than were't my picture, fashioned out of wax,
      Stuck with a magical needle, and then buried
      In some foul dunghill.° And yond's an excellent
          property

For a tyrant, which I would account mercy,—
BOSOLA: What's that?
DUCHESS: If they would bind me to that lifeless   90
          trunk,°
      And let me freeze to death.
BOSOLA: Come, you must live.
DUCHESS: That's the greatest torture souls feel in
          hell:
      In hell that they must live, and cannot die.
      Portia,° I'll new kindle thy coals again,
      And revive the rare and almost dead example
      Of a loving wife.
BOSOLA: O, fie! despair? remember   100
      You are a Christian.°
DUCHESS: The Church enjoins fasting:
      I'll starve myself to death.
BOSOLA: Leave this vain sorrow;
      Things, being at the worst, begin to mend:
      The bee when he hath shot his sting into your hand
      May then play with your eyelid.°
DUCHESS: Good comfortable° fellow,
      Persuade a wretch that's broke upon the wheel°
      To have all his bones new set: entreat him live,   110
      To be executed again. Who must dispatch me?
      I account this world a tedious theater,
      For I do play a part in't 'gainst my will.
BOSOLA: Come, be of comfort, I will save your life.
DUCHESS: Indeed, I have not leisure to tend so small a
          business.
BOSOLA: Now, by my life, I pity you.
DUCHESS: Thou art a fool then,
      To waste thy pity on a thing so wretched
      As cannot pity itself. I am full of daggers.   120
      Puff! let me blow these vipers from me.

(She turns to a SERVANT.*)*

      What are you?
SERVANT: One that wishes you long life.
DUCHESS: I would thou wert hanged for the horrible
          curse
      Thou hast given me: I shall shortly grow° one
      Of the miracles of pity. I'll go pray. No,
      I'll go curse.
BOSOLA: Oh fie!
DUCHESS: I could curse the stars.   130
BOSOLA: Oh, fearful!

---

thus, in darkness. *too . . . light,* too conspicuous. *ring,* her wedding ring, which was earlier seized by the Cardinal. *owed,* owned. *What . . . practice,* A dead man's hand was one of the charms used in attempts to cure madness by witchcraft. *my . . . dunghill,* The reference here is to the black-magic practice of putting an evil spell on someone by sticking pins into a doll that looks like him. By then burying the doll in a dunghill, the magician calls upon supernatural spirits to curse even the corpse of the intended victim by denying it proper burial.

lifeless trunk, (the statue of) dead Antonio. *Portia,* Brutus' wife, who committed suicide by swallowing red-hot coals after she heard of her husband's death. *You . . . Christian,* Suicide is forbidden by Christianity. *The . . . eyelid,* After it has used its stinger on your hand, the bee may sit even on your eyelid without being able to do any harm. *comfortable,* free from pain. *broke . . . wheel,* In Webster's time, men were tortured by being bound to a wheel and then stretched until their bones broke under the strain. *grow,* become.

DUCHESS: And those three smiling seasons of the year
    Into a Russian winter—nay, the world
    To its first chaos.°
BOSOLA: Look you, the stars shine still.
DUCHESS: Oh, but you must
    Remember, my curse hath a great way to go:
    Plagues, that make lanes through largest families,
    Consume them.
140 BOSOLA: Fie lady!
DUCHESS: Let them° like tyrants
    Never be remembered, but for the ill they have
      done:
    Let all the zealous prayers of mortifièd
    Churchmen forget them,—
BOSOLA: O uncharitable!
DUCHESS: Let heaven, a little while, cease crowning
      martyrs
    To punish them.
150   Go, howl them this, and say I long to bleed.
    It is some mercy when men kill with speed. (*Exit
    with* SERVANTS.)

(*Enter* FERDINAND.)

FERDINAND: Excellent, as I would wish: she's plagued
    in art.°
    These presentations are but framed in wax
    By the curious° master in that quality,
    Vincentio Lauriola,° and she takes them
    For true, substantial bodies.
BOSOLA: Why do you do this?
FERDINAND: To bring her to despair.
160 BOSOLA: 'Faith,° end here,
    And go no farther in your cruelty.
    Send her a penitential garment, to put on
    Next to her delicate skin, and furnish her
    With beads° and prayerbooks.
FERDINAND: Damn her! that body of hers,
    While that my blood ran pure in't, was more worth
    Than that which thou wouldst comfort, called a
      soul.°
    I will send her masques° of common courtesans,
170   Have her meat served up by bawds and ruffians,
    And 'cause she'll needs be° mad, I am resolved
    To remove forth° the common hospital

And . . . chaos, And (I could curse) spring, summer, and
fall so that they became one long winter; in fact I could wish
the world restored to its original state of chaos. *them,* her
brothers. *she . . . art,* She was tormented by these wax
figures. *curious,* ingenious. *Vincentio Lauriola,* historically unidentifiable, but here he is clearly meant to be a
skillful wax-worker. *'Faith,* an interjection, contracted
from "in faith." *beads,* rosary beads. *that . . . soul,* There
is in this declaration—because the Duchess' body is its
focus—another unconscious suggestion of Ferdinand's sexual desires for his sister. *masques,* courtly entertainments.
needs be, willfully continues to be. *forth,* from.

All the mad folk, and place them near her lodging.
    There let them practice° together, sing, and dance,
    And act their gambols to the full o' th' moon:°
    If she can sleep the better for it, let her.
    Your work is almost ended.
BOSOLA: Must I see her again?
FERDINAND: Yes.
BOSOLA: Never.   180
FERDINAND: You must.
BOSOLA: Never in mine own shape;°
    That's forfeited by my intelligence°
    And this last cruel lie. When you send me next,
    The business shall be comfort.
FERDINAND: Very likely.°
    Thy pity is nothing of kin to thee. Antonio
    Lurks about Milan; thou shalt shortly thither,
    To feed a fire as great as my revenge,
    Which ne'er will slack till it have spent his fuel;   190
    Intemperate agues make physicians cruel. (*Exeunt.*)

ACT 4 / SCENE 2

(*The same place*)
(*Enter* DUCHESS *and* CARIOLA.)

DUCHESS: What hideous noise was that?
CARIOLA: 'Tis the wild consort
    Of madmen, lady, which your tyrant brother
    Hath placed about your lodging. This tyranny,
    I think, was never practiced till this hour.
DUCHESS: Indeed, I thank him: nothing but noise
      and folly
    Can keep me in my right wits, whereas reason
    And silence make me stark mad. Sit down.
    Discourse to me some dismal tragedy.   10
CARIOLA: O 'twill increase your melancholy.
DUCHESS: Thou art deceived;
    To hear of greater grief would lessen mine.
    This is a prison?
CARIOLA: Yes, but you shall live
    To shake this durance° off.
DUCHESS: Thou art a fool:
    The robin red-breast and the nightingale
    Never live long in cages.
CARIOLA: Pray dry your eyes.   20
    What think you of, madam?
DUCHESS: Of nothing:
    When I muse thus, I sleep.
CARIOLA: Like a madman, with your eyes open?
DUCHESS: Dost thou think we shall know one another
    In th' other world?
CARIOLA: Yes, out of question.

---

practice, carry on their activities. *full . . . moon,* the
time when madmen were thought to be most mad. *in . . .
shape,* without being disguised. *intelligence,* work as a spy.
Very likely, a cynical rejoinder, because Bosola will then offer
her the "comfort" of death. *durance,* hardship.

DUCHESS: O, that it were possible we might
    But hold some two days' conference with the dead:
40   From them I should learn somewhat I am sure
    I never shall know here. I'll tell thee a miracle;
    I am not mad yet, to my cause of sorrow.°
    Th' heaven o'er my head seems made of molten
      brass,
    The earth of flaming sulphur, yet I am not mad.
    I am acquainted with sad misery,
    As the tanned galley slave is with his oar.
    Necessity makes me suffer constantly,
    And custom makes it easy. Who do I look like now?
50 CARIOLA: Like to your picture in the gallery,
    A deal of life in show,° but none in practice:°
    Or rather like some reverend monument
    Whose ruins are even pitied.
DUCHESS: Very proper:
    And Fortune seems only to have her eyesight,°
    To behold my tragedy.
    How now! What noise is that? (Enter SERVANT.)
SERVANT: I am come to tell you,
    Your brother hath intended you some sport.°
60   A great physician when the Pope was sick
    Of a deep melancholy, presented him
    With several sorts of madmen, which wild object,
    Being full of change and sport, forced him to
      laugh,
    And so th'imposthume° broke: the selfsame cure
    The Duke intends on you.
DUCHESS: Let them come in.
SERVANT: There's a mad lawyer, and a secular priest,
70   A doctor that hath forfeited his wits
    By jealousy; an astrologian
    That in his works said such a day o' th' month
    Should be the day of doom, and, failing of't,
    Ran mad; an English tailor, crazed i' th' brain
    With the study of new fashion; a gentleman usher°
    Quite beside himself with care to keep in mind
    The number of his lady's salutations
    Or "How do you?" she employed him in each
      morning;°
    A farmer too, an excellent knave in grain,°
80   Mad, 'cause he was hindered transportation;°

And let° one broker,° that's mad, loose to these,
    You'd think the devil were among them.
DUCHESS: Sit Cariola. Let them loose when you
    please,
    For I am chained to endure all your tyranny.

(Enter MADMEN. Here, by a MADMAN, this song is sung
to a dismal kind of music.)

    O let us howl, some heavy note,
      Some deadly-doggèd howl,
    Sounding, as from the threat'ning throat,
      Of beasts and fatal fowl.
    As ravens, screech owls, bulls, and bears,   90
      We'll bell,° and bawl our parts,
    Till irksome noise have cloyed your ears,
      And corrosived° your hearts.
    At last when as our choir wants breath,
      Our bodies being blest,
    We'll sing like swans, to welcome death,
      And die in love and rest.

MAD ASTROLOGER: Doomsday not come yet? I'll draw
    it nearer by a perspective,° or make a glass that
    shall set all the world on fire upon an instant. I   100
    cannot sleep; my pillow is stuffed with a litter of
    porcupines.
MAD LAWYER: Hell is a mere glasshouse,° where the
    devils are continually blowing up women's souls
    on hollow irons,° and the fire never goes out.
MAD PRIEST: I will lie with every woman in my parish
    the tenth night: I will tithe them over like
    haycocks.°
MAD DOCTOR: Shall my pothecary° outgo° me, be-
    cause I am a cuckold? I have found out his   110
    roguery: he makes alum° of his wife's urine and
    sells it to Puritans, that have sore throats with
    over-straining.°
MAD ASTROLOGER: I have skill in heraldry.
MAD LAWYER: Hast?
MAD ASTROLOGER: You do give for your crest a wood-
    cock's° head, with the brains picked out on't. You
    are a very ancient gentleman.
MAD PRIEST: Greek is turned Turk;° we are only to be

---

to . . . sorrow, which is why I feel sorrow. show,
appearance. practice, action. Fortune . . . eyesight, Traditionally, the goddess Fortune was pictured as blindfolded
because she distributed her rewards so arbitrarily. Here the
Duchess implies that momentarily Fortune's blindfold has
been removed so that she can see the sad results of her
handiwork. sport, entertainment. imposthume, ulcer
(which caused the melancholy). usher, an attendant who
walks before a person of rank, greeting guests and introducing strangers. How . . . morning, a double-entendre, meaning the usher was made to serve her sexually as well as
socially. in grain, both "in the grain trade" and "in essence
(a knave)." hindered transportation, denied export.

let, turn. broker, pawnbroker. bell, bellow. corro-
sived, corroded. perspective, telescope. glasshouse, a factory where glass is made. blowing . . . irons, A sexual
meaning is implicit in this statement, and in most of the
lunatic raving that follows; these madmen, like Lear on the
heath, are acutely conscious of the intensity of man's sexual
desires. haycocks, stacks of hay, but an obscene pun is
intended as well. pothecary, druggist. outgo, get the best
of. alum, an astringent formerly used to treat inflamed
tissue. over-straining, singing too loudly and, also, straining too much of the life out of religion. woodcock, thought
to be a stupid bird. Greek . . . Turk, The Greek text of the
Bible has been made to serve nonbelievers (all non-
Puritans).

120   saved by the Helvetian translation.°

MAD ASTROLOGER (*to* LAWYER): Come on sir, I will lay the law to you.°

MAD LAWYER: Oh, rather lay° a corrosive: the law will eat to the bone.

MAD PRIEST: He that drinks but to satisfy nature is damned.

MAD DOCTOR: If I had my glass° here, I would show a sight should make all the women here call me mad doctor.

130 MAD ASTROLOGER (*pointing to* PRIEST): What's he, a ropemaker?°

MAD LAWYER: No, no, no, a snuffling° knave that, while he shows the tombs, will have his hand in a wench's placket.°

MAD PRIEST: Woe to the caroche° that brought home my wife from the masque at three o'clock in the morning; it had a large featherbed in it.

MAD DOCTOR: I have pared the devil's nails° forty times, roasted them in raven's eggs, and cured

140 agues with them.

MAD PRIEST: Get me three hundred milch° bats, to make possets° to procure sleep.

MAD DOCTOR: All the college may throw their caps° at me; I have made a soap-boiler costive:° it was my masterpiece—

(*Here the dance consisting of eight* MADMEN, *with music answerable thereunto, after which* BOSOLA, *like an old man, enters.*)

DUCHESS: Is he mad too?

SERVANT: Pray question him; I'll leave you. (*Exeunt* SERVANT *and* MADMEN.)

BOSOLA: I am come to make thy tomb.

150 DUCHESS: Ha, my tomb?
Thou speakst as if I lay upon my deathbed,
Gasping for breath. Dost thou perceive me sick?

BOSOLA: Yes, and the more dangerously, since thy sickness is insensible.°

DUCHESS: Thou art not mad, sure; dost know me?

BOSOLA: Yes.

DUCHESS: Who am I?

BOSOLA: Thou art a box of worm seed,° at best but° a

salvatory of green mummy.° What's this flesh? a little cruded° milk, fantastical puff paste:° our   160 bodies are weaker than those paper prisons boys use to keep flies in, more contemptible—since ours is to preserve earthworms. Didst thou ever see a lark in a cage? such is the soul in the body: this world is like her little turf of grass° and the heaven o'er our heads, like her looking glass,° only gives us a miserable knowledge of the small compass of our prison.

DUCHESS: Am not I thy Duchess?

BOSOLA: Thou art some great woman, sure; for riot°   170 begins to sit on thy forehead (clad in grey hairs) twenty years sooner than on a merry milkmaid's. Thou sleepst worse, than if a mouse should be forced to take up her lodging in a cat's ear. A little infant, that breeds its teeth, should it lie with thee, would cry out, as if thou wert the more unquiet bedfellow.°

DUCHESS: I am Duchess of Malfi still.

BOSOLA: That makes thy sleeps so broken:
Glories, like glowworms, afar off shine bright,   180
But looked to near, have neither heat nor light.

DUCHESS: Thou art very plain.°

BOSOLA: My trade is to flatter the dead, not the living:
I am a tombmaker.

DUCHESS: And thou comst to make my tomb?

BOSOLA: Yes.

DUCHESS: Let me be a little merry;
Of what stuff wilt thou make it?

BOSOLA: Nay, resolve me° first. Of what fashion?

DUCHESS: Why, do we grow fantastical° in our   190
deathbed?
Do we affect fashion in the grave?

BOSOLA: Most ambitiously. Princes' images on their tombs
Do not lie as they were wont, seeming to pray
Up to heaven, but with their hands under their cheeks,°
As if they died of the toothache. They are not carved
With their eyes fixed upon the stars; but, as   200
Their minds were wholly bent upon the world,
The selfsame way they seem to turn their faces.

DUCHESS: Let me know fully therefore the effect
Of this thy dismal preparation,

Helvetian translation, the translation of the Bible officially approved by the Puritans. *I . . . you,* I will explain the church law to you. *Oh . . . lay,* You might just as well apply. *glass,* some sort of magnifying glass. *ropemaker,* i.e. one who is in league with the hangman. *snuffling,* sanctimonious. *placket,* both "pocket" and "pudendum." *caroche,* a luxurious carriage. *I . . . nails,* I have brought the devil under my control. *milch,* milk-bearing. *possets,* a hot drink made of sweetened, spiced milk curdled with ale or wine. *throw . . . caps,* vainly seek to surpass me in skill. *I . . . costive,* I have made one who boils soap constipated (an unusual accomplishment because soap was an essential element used in manufacturing suppositories). *insensible,* not apparent to the senses. *box . . . seed,* a box of food for worms. *but,* only.

---

salvatory . . . mummy, either a container for an unripened mummy (because you are still alive) or an ointment box for fresh mummia, a drug derived from embalmed bodies. *cruded,* curdled. *puff-paste,* a light pastry. *turf of grass, looking glass,* articles that were put into bird cages in an attempt to keep the captured birds happy. *riot,* lines of sorrow that disturb the previous order of beauty. *A . . . bedfellow,* You sleep more restlessly than a baby cutting teeth. *plain,* plain-spoken. *resolve me,* Answer my question. *fantastical,* obsessed by fantasies. *with . . . cheeks,* in a semirecumbent position.

This talk, fit for a charnel.°
BOSOLA: Now I shall;

(Enter EXECUTIONERS with a coffin, cords, and a bell.)

Here is a present from your princely brothers,
And may it arrive welcome, for it brings
Last benefit, last sorrow.
210 DUCHESS: Let me see it.
I have so much obedience in my blood
I wish it in their veins, to do them good.
BOSOLA: This is your last presence chamber.
CARIOLA: O my sweet lady!
DUCHESS: Peace! it affrights not me.
BOSOLA: I am the common bellman,°
That usually is sent to condemned persons,
The night before they suffer.
DUCHESS: Even now thou saidst
220 Thou wast a tomb-maker?
BOSOLA: 'Twas to bring you
By degrees to mortification.° Listen:

(Rings the bell.)

Hark, now every thing is still,
The screech owl and the whistler shrill°
Call upon our dame,° aloud,
And bid her quickly don her shroud.
Much you had of land and rent,
Your length in clay's now competent.
A long war disturbed your mind;
230 Here your perfect peace is signed.
Of what is't fools make such vain keeping?
Sin° their conception, their birth, weeping:
Their life, a general mist of error,
Their death, a hideous storm of terror.
Strew your hair with powders sweet:
Don clean linen, bathe your feet,
And the foul fiend° more to check,
A crucifix let bless your neck.
'Tis now full tide 'tween night and day,
240 End your groan, and come away.

(EXECUTIONERS approach.)

CARIOLA: Hence, villains, tyrants, murderers. Alas!
What will you do with my lady? Call for help.
DUCHESS: To whom? To our next neighbors? They
are mad-folks.
BOSOLA: Remove that noise.

(EXECUTIONERS seize CARIOLA, who struggles.)

DUCHESS: Farewell, Cariola,

---

charnel, cemetery. bellman, one who was supposed to
drive evil spirits away from the soul. 'Twas . . . mortification, It was to get you accustomed to the idea of dying.
whistler shrill, a bird whose song was supposed to be a
foreboding of evil. our dame, the Duchess. Sin, The
word here assumes the meanings of both "since" and "sin"
(which attends man's conception). foul fiend, the devil.

In my last will I have not much to give:
A many hundred guests have fed upon me;
Thine will be a poor reversion.°
CARIOLA: I will die with her.   250
DUCHESS: I pray thee, look thou givst my little boy
Some syrup for his cold, and let the girl
Say her prayers, ere she sleep. (CARIOLA *is forced
off.)*
Now, what you please.
What death?
BOSOLA: Strangling. Here are your executioners.
DUCHESS: I forgive them:
The apoplexy, catarrh,° or cough o' th' lungs
Would do as much as they do.
BOSOLA: Doth not death fright you?   260
DUCHESS: Who would be afraid on't?
Knowing to meet such excellent company
In th' other world.
BOSOLA: Yet, methinks,
The manner of your death should much afflict
you;
This cord should terrify you?
DUCHESS: Not a whit:
What would it pleasure me, to have my throat cut
With diamonds? or to be smotherèd   270
With cassia? or to be shot to death with pearls?
I know death hath ten thousand several doors
For men to take their exits; and 'tis found
They go on such strange geometrical hinges,
You may open them both ways.° Any way, for
heaven sake,
So I were out of your whispering. Tell my brothers
That I perceive death, now I am well awake,
Best gift is they can give, or I can take.
I would fain put off my last woman's fault: 280
I'll not be tedious to you.
EXECUTIONERS: We are ready.
DUCHESS: Dispose my breath how please you, but my
body
Bestow upon my women, will you?
EXECUTIONERS: Yes.
DUCHESS: Pull, and pull strongly, for your able
strength
Must pull down heaven upon me—
Yet stay, heaven-gates are not so highly arched   290
As princes' palaces: they that enter there
Must go upon their knees. (She kneels.) Come
violent death,
Serve for mandragora° to make me sleep.
Go tell my brothers, when I am laid out,
They then may feed in quiet. (They strangle her.)
BOSOLA: Where's the waiting woman?
Fetch her. Some other strangle the children.

---

reversion, estate passed on to her. catarrh, hemor-
rhage. You . . . ways, Death may come and get you, or you
may go to it (by committing suicide). mandragora, a plant
formerly used as a narcotic.

(Exeunt EXECUTIONERS.*)*
(Enter one with CARIOLA.*)*

Look you, there sleeps your mistress.

300 CARIOLA: O you are damned
Perpetually for this. My turn is next,
Is't not so ordered?

BOSOLA: Yes, and I am glad
You are so well prepared for't.

CARIOLA: You are deceived sir,
I am not prepared for't. I will not die;
I will first come to my answer, and know
How I have offended.

BOSOLA: Come, dispatch her.
310 You kept her° counsel; now you shall keep ours.

CARIOLA: I will not die—I must not—I am contracted
To a young gentleman.

EXECUTIONER *(showing the noose)*: Here's your
wedding ring.

CARIOLA: Let me but speak with the Duke. I'll
discover
Treason to his person.

BOSOLA: Delays: throttle her.

EXECUTIONER: She bites and scratches.

320 CARIOLA: If you kill me now,
I am damned. I have not been at confession
This two years.

BOSOLA: When!°

CARIOLA: I am quick with child.°

BOSOLA: Why then,
Your credit's saved.° Bear her into th' next room
Let this lie still.

*(*EXECUTIONERS *strangle* CARIOLA *and exeunt with her
body.)*
(Enter FERDINAND.*)*

FERDINAND: Is she dead?

BOSOLA: She is what
330 You'd have her. But here begin your pity.

*(*BOSOLA *draws the traverse and shows the children
strangled.)*

Alas, how have these offended?

FERDINAND: The death
Of young wolves is never to be pitied.

BOSOLA: Fix your eye here.

FERDINAND: Constantly.

BOSOLA: Do you not weep?
Other sins only speak; murther shrieks out:
The element of water moistens the earth,
But blood flies upwards and bedews the heavens.

FERDINAND: Cover her face. Mine eyes dazzle:° she   340
died young.

BOSOLA: I think not so: her infelicity
Seemed to have years too many.

FERDINAND: She and I were twins:
And should I die this instant I had lived
Her time to a minute.

BOSOLA: It seems she was born first:
You have bloodily approved° the ancient truth,
That kindred commonly do worse agree°
Than remote strangers.   350

FERDINAND: Let me see her face again—
Why didst not thou pity her? What an excellent
Honest man mightst thou have been
If thou'hadst borne her to some sanctuary!
Or, bold in a good cause, opposed thyself
With thy advancèd sword above thy head,
Between her innocence and my revenge!
I bade thee, when I was distracted of my wits,
Go kill my dearest friend, and thou hast done't.
For let me examine well the cause.   360
What was the meanness of her match to me?
Only, I must confess, I had a hope,
Had she continued widow, to have gained
An infinite mass of treasure by her death;°
And that was the main cause—her marriage,
That drew a stream of gall quite through my heart.
For thee (as we observe in tragedies
That a good actor many times is cursed
For playing a villain's part), I hate thee for't.
And, for my sake, say thou hast done much ill, well.   370

BOSOLA: Let me quicken your memory, for I perceive
You are falling into ingratitude. I challenge
The reward due to my service.

FERDINAND: I'll tell thee,
What I'll give thee—

BOSOLA: Do.

FERDINAND: I'll give thee a pardon
For this murther.

BOSOLA: Ha?

FERDINAND: Yes: and 'tis   380
The largest bounty I can study° to do thee.
By what authority didst thou execute
This bloody sentence?

BOSOLA: By yours.

FERDINAND: Mine? Was I her judge?
Did any ceremonial form of law

---

her, the Duchess'. **When,** an exclamation of impatience. **quick . . . child,** pregnant. (Criminals who were pregnant were sometimes granted a stay of execution until the birth of the child.) **Your . . . saved,** Your reputation is saved—because your death will prevent you from bearing a bastard child.

dazzle, are dazzled. **approved,** proven. **do . . . agree,** differ more. **Only . . . death,** The Duke, desperately searching for the reason why he found his sister's marriage to Antonio so hateful, here presents an obvious rationalization: even if the Duchess had died without remarrying, her estate would have gone to her first son, the young Duke of Malfi. The real explanation for Ferdinand's intense jealousy of Antonio is, of course, too frightening for him to admit, or even to recognize consciously. **study,** consciously bring myself.

Doom her to not-being? Did a complete jury
Deliver her conviction up i' th' court?
Where shalt thou find this judgment registered
390 Unless in hell? See, like a bloody fool
Th' hast forfeited thy life, and thou shalt die for't.
BOSOLA: The office of justice is perverted quite
When one thief hangs another. Who shall dare
To reveal this?
FERDINAND: Oh, I'll tell thee:
The wolf shall find her grave and scrape it up,
Not to devour the corpse, but to discover
The horrid murther.
BOSOLA: You, not I, shall quake for't.
400 FERDINAND: Leave me.
BOSOLA: I will first receive my pension.°
FERDINAND: You are a villain.
BOSOLA: When your ingratitude
Is judge, I am so—
FERDINAND: O horror!
That not the fear of Him which binds the devils
Can prescribe man obedience.
Never look upon me more.
BOSOLA: Why fare thee well.
410 Your brother and yourself are worthy men;
You have a pair of hearts are hollow graves—
Rotten, and rotting others. And your vengeance,
Like two chained bullets,° still goes arm in arm.
You may be brothers, for treason, like the plague,
Doth take much in a blood.° I stand like one
That long hath ta'en a sweet and golden dream:
I am angry with myself, now that I wake.
FERDINAND: Get thee into some unknown part o' th'
world,
420 That I may never see thee.
BOSOLA: Let me know
Wherefore I should be thus neglected? Sir,
I served your tyranny, and rather strove
To satisfy yourself, than all the world;
And though I loathed the evil, yet I loved
You that did counsel it, and rather sought
To appear a true servant than an honest man.
FERDINAND: I'll go hunt the badger° by owl-light:°
'Tis a deed of darkness. (Exit.)
430 BOSOLA: He's much distracted. Off my painted
honor!°
While with vain hopes our faculties we tire,
We seem to sweat in ice and freeze in fire.°
What would I do, were this to do again?
I would not change my peace of conscience

For all the wealth of Europe. She stirs; here's life.
Return, fair soul, from darkness, and lead mine
Out of this sensible° hell. She's warm; she breathes:
Upon thy pale lips I will melt my heart
440 To store them with fresh color. Who's there?
Some cordial drink!° Alas! I dare not call:
So pity would destroy pity.° Her eye opes,
And heaven in it seems to ope, that late was shut,
To take me up to mercy.
DUCHESS: Antonio!
BOSOLA: Yes, madam, he is living,
The dead bodies you saw were but feigned statues;
He's reconciled to your brothers: the Pope hath
wrought
450 The atonement.
DUCHESS: Mercy. (She dies.)
BOSOLA: Oh, she's gone again: there the cords of life
broke.
Oh sacred innocence, that sweetly sleeps
On turtles'° feathers, whilst a guilty conscience
Is a black register, wherein is writ
All our good deeds and bad, a perspective
That shows us hell. That we cannot be suffered
To do good when we have a mind to it!
460 This is manly sorrow:
These tears, I am very certain, never grew
In my mother's milk. My estate° is sunk
Below the degree of fear: where were
These penitent fountains while she was living?
Oh, they were frozen up! Here is a sight
As direful to my soul as is the sword
Unto a wretch hath slain his father. Come,
I'll bear thee hence,
And execute thy last will—that's deliver
470 Thy body to the reverend dispose
Of some good women: that the cruel tyrant
Shall not deny me. Then I'll post to Milan,
Where somewhat I will speedily enact
Worth my dejection.° (Exit carrying the body.)

ACT 5 / SCENE 1

(A public place in Milan)
(Enter ANTONIO and DELIO.)

ANTONIO: What think you of my hope of
reconcilement
To the Aragonian brethren?
DELIO: I misdoubt it,
For though they have sent their letters of safe
conduct

---

pension, reward for services. **chained bullets,** Cannon balls were sometimes chained together to increase the extent of their destructive force. **take . . . blood,** runs in the blood of particular families. **badger,** an animal that avoided daylight. **owl-light,** night. **I'll . . . owl-light,** I shall henceforth carry out my activities in darkness. **painted honor,** false sense of importance, as a spy for Ferdinand. **We . . . fire,** We are always uncomfortably restless and unsatisfied.

sensible, apparent to the senses. **cordial drink,** medicine to induce revival. **So . . . pity,** By pitying her and calling out for help, I would only destroy her whom I pity because Ferdinand would return and kill her. **turtles,** turtledoves (traditionally a symbol of love and peace). **estate,** condition. **Worth my dejection,** keeping with my abasement.

For your repair° to Milan, they appear
But nets to entrap you. The Marquis of Pescara,
Under whom you hold certain land in cheat,°
10 Much 'gainst his noble nature, hath been moved
To seize those lands, and some of his dependants
Are at this instant making it their suit
To be invested in your revenues.
I cannot think they mean well to your life
That do deprive you of your means of life,
Your living.

ANTONIO: You are still an heretic.°
To any safety I can shape myself.

DELIO: Here comes the Marquis. I will make myself
20 Petitioner for some part of your land,
To know whether° it is flying.°

ANTONIO: I pray do.

(Enter PESCARA.)

DELIO: Sir, I have a suit to you.

PESCARA: To me?

DELIO: An easy one:
There is the citadel of St. Bennet,°
With some demesnes,° of late in the possession
Of Antonio Bologna; please you bestow them on
me?

30 PESCARA: You are my friend. But this is such a suit
Nor fit for me to give, nor you to take.

DELIO: No sir?

PESCARA: I will give you ample reason for't
Soon, in private. Here's the Cardinal's mistress.

(Enter JULIA.)

JULIA: My lord, I am grown your poor petitioner,
And should be an ill beggar had I not
A great man's letter here, the Cardinal's,
To court you in my favor.

(She gives him a letter.)

PESCARA: He entreats for you
40 The citadel of St. Bennet, that belonged
To the banished Bologna.

JULIA: Yes.

PESCARA: I could not have thought of a friend I could
Rather pleasure with it: 'tis yours.

JULIA: Sir, I thank you.
And he shall know how doubly I am engaged,
Both in your gift and speediness of giving,
Which makes your grant the greater. *(Exit.)*

ANTONIO *(aside)*: How they fortify
50 Themselves with my ruin!

DELIO: Sir, I am
Little bound to you.

PESCARA: Why?

DELIO: Because you denied this suit to me, and gave't
To such a creature.

PESCARA: Do you know what it was?
It was Antonio's land—not forfeited
By course of law, but ravished from his throat
By the Cardinal's entreaty. It were not fit
I should bestow so main a piece of wrong 60
Upon my friend: 'tis a gratification
Only due to a strumpet; for it is injustice.
Shall I sprinkle the pure blood of innocents
To make these followers I call my friends
Look ruddier° upon me? I am glad
This land, ta'en from the owner by such wrong,
Returns again unto so foul an use,
As salary for his lust. Learn, good Delio,
To ask noble things of me, and you shall find
I'll be a noble giver. 70

DELIO: You instruct me well.

ANTONIO *(aside)*: Why, here's a man, now, would
fright° impudence
From sauciest beggars.

PESCARA: Prince Ferdinand's come to Milan
Sick, as they give out, of an apoplexy;
But some say 'tis a frenzy. I am going
To visit him. *(Exit.)*

ANTONIO: 'Tis a noble old fellow.°

DELIO: What course do you mean to take, Antonio? 80

ANTONIO: This night I mean to venture all my
fortune,
Which is no more than a poor ling'ring life,
To the Cardinal's worst of malice.° I have got
Private access to his chamber, and intend
To visit him, about the mid of night,
As once his brother did our noble Duchess.°
It may be that the sudden apprehension
Of danger—for I'll go in mine own shape—,
When he shall see it fraight° with love and duty, 90
May draw the poison out of him, and work
A friendly reconcilement. If it fail,
Yet it shall rid me of this infamous calling,°
For better fall once, than be ever falling.

---

repair, return. in cheat, subject to return to the lord only if the tenant dies without an heir or if he commits a felony. heretic, skeptic. whether, The second and third quarto editions read "whither," it . . . flying, it is wantonly being given away. St. Bennet, St. Benedict. demesnes, land attached to the citadel.

ruddier, more glowingly. fright, drive away. old fellow, The Marquis of Pescara never actually lived to be an "old fellow"; he died when he was thirty-six. There is, however, a good reason why Webster makes him old: that way he commands respect as one who has lived long enough to become wise. To . . . malice, against the worst malice of the Cardinal. As . . . Duchess, The reference is to the time that Ferdinand came unexpectedly into the Duchess' bedchamber while she was combing her hair and readying herself for bed. Antonio does not yet know about the murderous visit that Ferdinand made while the Duchess was in prison. fraight, abounding with. infamous calling, life of disgrace.

DELIO: I'll second you in all danger; and, howe'er,
  My life keeps rank with yours.
ANTONIO: You are still my loved and best friend.
  (Exeunt.)

ACT 5 / SCENE 2

(The palace of the Aragonian brothers in Milan)
(Enter PESCARA *and* DOCTOR.*)*

PESCARA: Now, doctor, may I visit your patient?
DOCTOR: If't please your lordship, but he's instantly
  To take the air here in the gallery,
  By my direction.
PESCARA: Pray thee, what's his disease?
DOCTOR: A very pestilent disease, my lord,
  They call lycanthropia.°
PESCARA: What's that?
  I need a dictionary to't.
10 DOCTOR: I'll tell you:
  In those that are possessed with't there o'erflows
  Such melancholy humor, they imagine
  Themselves to be transformèd into wolves,
  Steal forth to churchyards in the dead of night,
  And dig dead bodies up: as two nights since
  One met the Duke, 'bout midnight in a lane
  Behind St. Mark's church, with the leg of a man
  Upon his shoulder; and he howled fearfully—
  Said he was a wolf; only the difference
20 Was a wolf's skin was hairy on the outside,
  His on the inside. Bade them take their swords,
  Rip up his flesh, and try. Straight I was sent for,
  And having ministered to him, found his grace
  Very well recoverèd.
PESCARA: I am glad on't.
DOCTOR: Yet not without some fear
  Of a relapse. If he grow to his fit again,
  I'll go a nearer way to work with him
  Than ever Paracelsus° dreamed of. If
30 They'll give me leave, I'll buffet his madness out of
  him.
  Stand aside: he comes.

  (Enter CARDINAL, FERDINAND, MALATESTE, *and*
  BOSOLA, *who remains behind.)*

FERDINAND: Leave me.
MALATESTE: Why doth your lordship love this solitar-
  iness?
FERDINAND: Eagles commonly fly alone. They are
  crows, daws,° and starlings that flock together.
  Look, what's that follows me?
MALATESTE: Nothing, my lord.
40 FERDINAND: Yes.

---

lycanthropia, a mania in which the victim imagines
himself a wolf.   *Paracelsus,* a German physician and alchemist noted for his radical way of treating diseases.
daws, crowlike birds.

MALATESTE: 'Tis your shadow.
FERDINAND: Stay it; let it not haunt me.
MALATESTE: Impossible, if you move, and the sun
  shine.
FERDINAND: I will throttle it.

(He attacks his shadow.)

MALATESTE: Oh, my lord, you are angry with nothing.
FERDINAND: You are a fool. How is't possible I should
  catch my shadow unless I fall upon't? When I go
  to hell, I mean to carry a bribe: for, look you, 50
  good gifts evermore make way for the worst persons.
PESCARA: Rise, good my lord.
FERDINAND: I am studying the art of patience.
PESCARA: 'Tis a noble virtue—
FERDINAND: To drive six snails before me, from this
  town to Moscow; neither use goad nor whip to
  them, but let them take their own time—the patient'st man i' th' world match me for an experiment! And I'll crawl after like a sheep-biter.° 60
CARDINAL: Force him up.

(They make FERDINAND *stand up.)*

FERDINAND: Use me well, you were best.°
  What I have done, I have done. I'll confess
  nothing.
DOCTOR: Now let me come to him. Are you mad, my
  lord?
  Are you out of your princely wits?
FERDINAND: What's he?
PESCARA: Your doctor.
FERDINAND: Let me have his beard sawed off, and his 70
  eyebrows
  Filed more civil.°
DOCTOR: I must do mad tricks with him,
  For that's the only way on't. I have brought
  Your grace a salamander's° skin, to keep you
  From sun-burning.
FERDINAND: I have cruel sore eyes.
DOCTOR: The white of a cockatrice° egg is present
  remedy.
FERDINAND: Let it be a new-laid one, you were best. 80
  Hide me from him: physicians are like kings:
  They brook no contradiction.
DOCTOR: Now he begins

---

sheep-biter, a sheep-stealing dog.   *you . . . best,* an
interjectory phrase meaning "you would be well-advised to."
Let . . . civil, I wish his appearance were not so hostile.
salamander, thought capable of living in fire.   *cockatrice,* a
legendary monster with the head, wings, and legs of a cock
and the tail of a serpent. Because most of its power was
thought to be vested in its eyes—its look was deadly—and
because egg whites were often used in treating sore eyes, the
white of a cockatrice's egg would theoretically be an ideal
remedy for the affliction the Duke complains of.

To fear me; now let me alone with him.

(FERDINAND *tries to take off his gown;* CARDINAL *seizes him.*)

CARDINAL: How now, put off your gown?
DOCTOR: Let me have some forty urinals filled with rose-water: he and I'll go pelt one another with them: now he begins to fear me. Can you fetch a frisk,° sir? (*aside to* CARDINAL) Let him go; let him
90 go upon my peril. I find by his eye, he stands in awe of me: I'll make him as tame as a dormouse.

(CARDINAL *releases* FERDINAND.)

FERDINAND: Can you fetch your frisks, sir! I will stamp him into a cullis;° flay off his skin to cover one of the anatomies.° This rogue hath set i' th' cold yonder, in Barber-Chirurgeons' Hall.° Hence, hence! you are all of you like beasts for sacrifice: (*throws the* DOCTOR *down and beats him*) there's nothing left of you, but tongue and belly,° flattery and lechery. (*Exit.*)
100 PESCARA: Doctor, he did not fear you throughly.°
DOCTOR: True, I was somewhat too forward.
BOSOLA (*aside*): Mercy upon me! What a fatal judgment
    Hath fall'n upon this Ferdinand!
PESCARA: Knows your grace
    What accident hath brought unto the Prince
    This strange distraction?
CARDINAL (*aside*): I must feign somewhat.° Thus they say it grew:
110 You have heard it rumored for these many years,
    None of our family dies but there is seen
    The shape of an old woman, which is given
    By tradition to us to have been murdered
    By her nephews, for her riches. Such a figure
    One night, as the Prince sat up late at's book,
    Appeared to him; when crying out for help,
    The gentlemen of's chamber found his grace
    All on a cold sweat, altered much in face
    And language. Since which apparition
120 He hath grown worse and worse, and I much fear
    He cannot live.
BOSOLA: Sir, I would speak with you.

---

fetch a frisk, dance a caper.   *cullis,* broth, made partly by pounding fowl.   *anatomies,* skeletons.   ***Barber-Chirurgeons' Hall,*** the place where barber-surgeons went to pick up corpses of executed felons, which they used for anatomical experiments.   *tongue and belly,* In ancient religious ceremonies, the tongues and entrails of sacrificial animals were left for the gods. But Ferdinand intends another meaning as well: in his despair he sees man as essentially a deceiver and a creature of appetite; he is not a complex, integrated human being, but only a tongue and a belly.   *throughly,* completely.   *feign somewhat,* make up something.

PESCARA: We'll leave your grace,
    Wishing to the sick Prince, our noble lord,
    All health of mind and body.
CARDINAL: You are most welcome.

(*Exeunt* PESCARA, MALATESTE, *and* DOCTOR.)

    Are you come? (*aside*) So—this fellow must not know
    By any means I had intelligence
    In° our Duchess' death. For, though I counseled it,   130
    The full of all th' engagement° seemed to grow
    From Ferdinand. Now sir, how fares our sister?
    I do not think but sorrow makes her look
    Like to an oft-dyed garment. She shall now
    Taste comfort from me—Why do you look so wildly?
    Oh, the fortune of your master here, the Prince,
    Dejects you, but be you of happy comfort:
    If you'll do one thing for me I'll entreat,
    Though he had a cold tombstone o'er his bones,   140
    I'll make you what you would be.
BOSOLA: Anything?
    Give it me in a breath,° and let me fly to't:
    They that think long, small expedition win,°
    For musing much o' th' end, cannot begin.

(*Enter* JULIA.)

JULIA: Sir, will you come in to supper?
CARDINAL: I am busy! Leave me!
JULIA (*aside*): What an excellent shape hath that fellow! (*Exit.*)
CARDINAL: 'Tis thus: Antonio lurks here in Milan;   150
    Inquire him out, and kill him. While he lives,
    Our sister cannot marry, and I have thought
    Of an excellent match for her. Do this, and style me°
    Thy advancement.
BOSOLA: But by what means shall I find him out?
CARDINAL: There is a gentleman called Delio
    Here in the camp, that hath been long approved°
    His loyal friend. Set eye upon that fellow,
    Follow him to mass; may be Antonio,   160
    Although he do account religion
    But a school-name,° for fashion of the world
    May accompany him. Or else go inquire out
    Delio's confessor, and see if you can bribe
    Him to reveal it. There are a thousand ways
    A man might find to trace him—as, to know°
    What fellows haunt the Jews for taking up°
    Great sums of money, for sure he's in want;

---

had . . . In, had a part in the planning of.   *full . . . engagement,* everything to do with the deed.   *in a breath,* quickly.   *small . . . win,* accomplish little.   *style me,* call me the means to.   *hath . . . approved,* has long proved to be.   *school-name,* mere word.   *know,* find out.   *for taking up,* to borrow.

Or else go to th' picture makers, and learn
170 Who brought her picture lately.° Some of these
Happily may take—
BOSOLA: Well, I'll not freeze i' th' business,
I would see that wretched° thing, Antonio,
Above all sights i' th' world.
CARDINAL: Do, and be happy.° (Exit.)
BOSOLA: This fellow doth breed basilisks° in's eyes,
He's nothing else but murder: yet he seems
Not to have notice of the Duchess' death.
'Tis his cunning. I must follow his example:
180 There cannot be a surer way to trace,
Than that of an old fox.

(Enter JULIA, pointing a pistol at him.)

JULIA: So, sir, you are well met.
BOSOLA: How now?
JULIA: Nay, the doors are fast enough.
Now sir, I will make you confess your treachery.
BOSOLA: Treachery?
JULIA: Yes, confess to me
Which of my women 'twas hired to put
Love-powder into my drink?
190 BOSOLA: Love-powder?
JULIA: Yes, when I was at Malfi—
Why should I fall in love with such a face else?
I have already suffered for thee so much pain,
The only remedy to do me good
Is to kill my longing.
BOSOLA: Sure, your pistol holds
Nothing but perfumes or kissing comfits.°
Excellent lady,
You have a pretty way on't to discover°
200 Your longing. Come, come, I'll disarm you
And arm you thus— (embraces her) yet this is
wondrous strange.
JULIA: Compare thy form and my eyes together,
You'll find my love no such great miracle.
(Kisses him.) Now you'll say

Or ... lately, The exact meaning of this passage is
difficult to determine: "brought" may be a printer's misread-
ing of "bought." If the verb is "brought," the passage is an
obvious development of the Cardinal's idea that Antonio is
"in want": needing cash, he has sold a miniature of the
Duchess to a dealer. If, however, the verb is "bought," the
"Who" governing it is ambiguous. It may refer either to
"picture makers" or to Antonio, depending on whether he
has sold his wife's picture to get money or bought it as a
keepsake. Most modern editions emend to "bought," but
because the first quarto reading seems to develop logically
out of the Cardinal's thought, "brought" is here retained.
wretched, an equivocation, meaning either despicable or
pitiable. be happy, Be happy (in the advancement that will
follow as a result of your seeing him). basilisk, a mythical
monster that could kill with a look. kissing comfits, breath
sweeteners. discover, make known.

I am a wanton. This nice° modesty in ladies
Is but a troublesome familiar°
That haunts them.
BOSOLA: Know you me, I am a blunt soldier.°
JULIA: The better: 210
Sure, there wants fire where there are no lively
sparks
Of roughness.
BOSOLA: And I want compliment.°
JULIA: Why, ignorance
In courtship cannot make you do amiss,
If you have a heart to do well.
BOSOLA: You are very fair.
JULIA: Nay, if you lay beauty to my charge,
I must plead unguilty.   220
BOSOLA: Your bright eyes
Carry a quiver of darts in them,° sharper
Than sunbeams.
JULIA: You will mar me with commendation.
Put yourself to the charge of courting me,
Whereas now I woo you.
BOSOLA (aside): I have it, I will work upon this
creature.
Let us grow more amorously familiar.
If the great Cardinal now should see me thus,   230
Would he not count me a villain?
JULIA: No, he might count me a wanton,
Not lay a scruple of offense on you:
For if I see and steal a diamond,
The fault is not i' th' stone, but in me, the thief
That purloins it. I am sudden with you:
We that are great women of pleasure, use to cut
off°
These uncertain wishes and unquiet longings,
And in an instant join the sweet delight   240
And the pretty excuse together; had you been i' th'
street
Under my chamber window, even there
I should have courted you.
BOSOLA: Oh, you are an excellent lady.
JULIA: Bid me do somewhat for you presently
To express I love you.
BOSOLA: I will, and if you love me,
Fail not to effect it.
The Cardinal is grown wondrous melancholy;   250
Demand the cause, let him not put you off
With feigned excuse; discover the main ground
on't.
JULIA: Why would you know this?

---

nice, foolish. familiar, family spirit. blunt soldiers, a
double-entendre, like most of the language in this interview.
compliment, The homonym, "complement," is also implied.
Your ... them, Cupid was supposed to afflict people with
love by shooting them with enchanted darts, and it was
through the eyes that love was most commonly thought to
enter the body. use ... off, are in the habit of dispensing
with.

BOSOLA: I have depended on him,
And I hear that he is fallen in some disgrace
With the Emperor. If he be, like the mice
That forsake falling houses,° I would shift
To other dependence.
260 JULIA: You shall not need follow the wars:°
I'll be your maintenance.
BOSOLA: And I your loyal servant;
But I cannot leave my calling.
JULIA: Not leave an
Ungrateful general for the love of a sweet lady?
You are like some, cannot sleep in featherbeds,
But must have blocks for their pillows.
BOSOLA: Will you do this?
JULIA: Cunningly.
270 BOSOLA: Tomorrow I'll expect th'intelligence.
JULIA: Tomorrow!° Get you into my cabinet;°
You shall have it with you:° do not delay me—
No more than I do you. I am like one
That is condemned: I have my pardon promised,
But I would see it sealed. Go, get you in;
You shall see me wind my tongue about his heart
Like a skein of silk. (BOSOLA *withdraws behind the
traverse.*)

(*Enter* CARDINAL.)

CARDINAL: Where are you? (*Enter* SERVANTS.)
SERVANTS: Here.
280 CARDINAL: Let none, upon your lives,
Have conference with the Prince Ferdinand,
Unless I know it. (*aside*) In this distraction
He may reveal the murther. (*Exeunt* SERVANTS.)
Yond's my ling'ring consumption:
I am weary of her; and by any means
Would be quit of—
JULIA: How now, my lord?
What ails you?
CARDINAL: Nothing.
290 JULIA: Oh, you are much altered:
Come, I must be your secretary,° and remove
This lead from off your bosom—What's the
matter?
CARDINAL: I may not tell you.
JULIA: Are you so far in love with sorrow,
You cannot part with part of it? or think you
I cannot love your grace when you are sad,
As well as merry? or do you suspect
I, that have been a secret to your heart
300 These many winters, cannot be the same
Unto your tongue?

---

like . . . houses, Mice were thought to desert old houses just before they fell down. *follow the wars,* follow after the Cardinal when he goes to war. *Tomorrow,* Not tomorrow, but now! *cabinet,* closet. *with you,* at your appearance. *secretary,* one entrusted with secrets.

CARDINAL: Satisfy thy longing.
The only way to make thee keep my counsel
Is not to tell thee.
JULIA: Tell your echo this—
Or flatterers, that, like echoes, still report
What they hear, though most imperfect—and not
me;
For, if that you be true unto yourself,
I'll know.°   310
CARDINAL: Will you rack me?°
JULIA: No, judgment shall
Draw it from you. It is an equal fault
To tell one's secrets unto all, or none.
CARDINAL: The first argues folly.
JULIA: But the last, tyranny.
CARDINAL: Very well. Why, imagine I have
committed
Some secret deed which I desire the world
May never hear of!   320
JULIA: Therefore may not I know it?
You have concealed for me as great a sin
As adultery. Sir, never was occasion
For perfect trial of my constancy
Til now. Sir, I beseech you.
CARDINAL: You'll repent it.
JULIA: Never.
CARDINAL: It hurries thee to ruin: I'll not tell thee.
Be well advised, and think what danger 'tis
To receive a prince's secrets. They that do,   330
Had need have their breasts hooped with adamant°
To contain them. I pray thee yet be satisfied.
Examine thine own frailty; 'tis more easy
To tie knots, than unloose them. 'Tis a secret
That, like a ling'ring poison, may chance lie
Spread in thy veins, and kill thee seven year hence.
JULIA: Now you dally with° me.
CARDINAL: No more. Thou shalt know it.
By my appointment,° the great Duchess of Malfi
And two of her young children, four nights since, 340
Were strangled.
JULIA: Oh heaven! Sir, what have you done?
CARDINAL: How now? How settles this? Think you
your bosom
Will be a grave dark and obscure enough
For such a secret?
JULIA: You have undone yourself, sir.
CARDINAL: Why?
JULIA: It lies not in me to conceal it.
CARDINAL: No?   350
Come, I will swear you to't upon this book.
JULIA: Most religiously.
CARDINAL: Kiss it.

For . . . know, for you can be true to yourself only by telling me. *rack me,* put me upon the rack. *adamant,* unyielding steel. *dally with,* make a fool of. *appointment,* order.

(She kisses a Bible.)

Now you shall never utter it. Thy curiosity
Hath undone thee: thou'rt poisoned with that
   book.
Because I knew thou couldst not keep my counsel.
I have bound thee to't by death.

(Enter BOSOLA.*)*

BOSOLA: For pity sake, hold.
360   CARDINAL: Ha, Bosola!
JULIA *(to the* CARDINAL*)*: I forgive you
This equal piece of justice you have done,
For I betrayed your counsel to that fellow:
He overheard it. That was the cause I said
It lay not in me to conceal it.
BOSOLA: Oh foolish woman,
Couldst not thou have poisoned him?
JULIA: 'Tis weakness,
Too much to think what should have been done. I
370   go,
I know not whither. *(Dies.)*
CARDINAL: Wherefore comst thou hither?
BOSOLA: That I might find a great man, like yourself,
Not out of his wits, as the Lord Ferdinand,
To remember my service.
CARDINAL: I'll have thee hewed in pieces.
BOSOLA: Make not yourself such a promise of that life
Which is not yours to dispose of.
CARDINAL: Who placed thee here?
380   BOSOLA: Her lust, as she intended.
CARDINAL: Very well,
Now you know me for your fellow murderer.
BOSOLA: And wherefore should you lay fair marble
    colors°
Upon your rotten purposes to° me?
Unless you imitate some that do plot great treasons,
And when they have done, go hide themselves i' th'
    graves
Of those were actors in't.
390   CARDINAL: No more: there is a fortune attends thee.
BOSOLA: Shall I go sue to Fortune any longer?
'Tis the fool's pilgrimage.
CARDINAL: I have honors in store for thee.
BOSOLA: There are a many ways that conduct to
    seeming
Honor, and some of them very dirty ones.
CARDINAL: Throw to the devil
Thy melancholy. The fire burns well,
What need we keep a stirring of't, and make
400   A greater smother?° Thou wilt kill Antonio?
BOSOLA: Yes.
CARDINAL: Take up that body.
BOSOLA: I think I shall
Shortly grow the common bier for churchyards!

---

fair . . . colors, paint to make wood look like marble.
to, toward.   *smother,* smoke.

CARDINAL: I will allow thee some dozen of attendants,
To aid thee in the murther.
BOSOLA: Oh, by no means: physicians that apply
horseleeches to any rank swelling use to cut off
their tails, that the blood may run through them
the faster. Let me have no train° when I go to   410
shed blood, lest it make me have a greater—
when I ride to the gallows.
CARDINAL: Come to me after midnight, to help to
remove that body to her own lodging. I'll give
out she died o' th' plague; 'twill breed the less
inquiry after her death.
BOSOLA: Where's Castruchio her husband?
CARDINAL: He's rode to Naples to take possession of
Antonio's citadel.
BOSOLA: Believe me, you have done a very happy   420
turn.
CARDINAL: Fail not to come. There is the master key
Of our lodgings, and by that you may conceive
What trust I plant in you. *(Exit.)*
BOSOLA: You shall find me ready.
Oh poor Antonio, though nothing be so needful
To thy estate, as pity, yet I find
Nothing so dangerous. I must look to my footing;
In such slippery ice-pavements men had need
To be frost-nailed° well: they may break their necks   430
    else.
The precedent's here afore me: how this man
Bears up in blood!° seems fearless! Why, 'tis well:
Security° some men call the suburbs of hell,
Only a dead wall between. Well, good Antonio,
I'll seek thee out; and all my care shall be
To put thee into safety from the reach
Of these most cruel biters, that have got
Some of thy blood already. It may be
I'll join with thee in a most just revenge.   440
The weakest arm is strong enough, that strikes
With the sword of justice. Still methinks the
    Duchess
Haunts me—there, there!—'tis nothing but my
    melancholy.
O penitence, let me truly taste thy cup,
That throws men down, only to raise them up.
(Exit.)

ACT 5 / SCENE 3

(Somewhere near the DUCHESS' *grave)*
(Enter ANTONIO *and* DELIO. ECHO *from the* DUCHESS'
grave.)

DELIO: Yond's the Cardinal's window. This
    fortification

---

no train, no procession at my back (waiting to betray
me).   *frost-nailed,* equipped with hobnailed boots for gripping the ice.   *Bears . . . blood,* shows his courage.   *Security,*
lack of danger.

Grew from the ruins of an ancient abbey.
And to yond side o' th' river lies a wall,
Piece of a cloister, which in my opinion
Gives the best echo that you ever heard;
So hollow, and so dismal, and withal
So plain in the distinction° of our words,
That may have supposed it is a spirit
410   That answers.
ANTONIO: I do love these ancient ruins:
    We never tread upon them, but we set
    Our foot upon some reverend history,
    And, questionless,° here in this open court,
    Which now lies naked to the injuries
    Of stormy weather, some men lie interred
    Loved the Church so well and gave so largely to't
    They thought it should have canopied their bones
    Till doomsday. But all things have their end:
420   Churches and cities, which have diseases like to
      men,
    Must have like death that we have.
ECHO: *Like death that we have.*
DELIO: Now the echo hath caught you.
ANTONIO: It groaned, methought, and gave
    A very deadly accent!
ECHO: *Deadly accent.*
DELIO: I told you 'twas a pretty one. You may make it
    A huntsman or a falconer, a musician,
430   Or a thing of sorrow.
ECHO: *A thing of sorrow.*
ANTONIO: Ay, sure, that suits it best.
ECHO: *That suits it best.*
ANTONIO: 'Tis very like my wife's voice.
ECHO: *Ay, wife's voice.*
DELIO: Come, let's walk farther from't.
    I would not have you go to th' Cardinal's tonight.
    Do not.
ECHO: *Do not.*
440 DELIO: Wisdom doth not more moderate wasting
      sorrow
    Than time.° Take time for't: be mindful of thy
      safety.
ECHO: *Be mindful of thy safety.*
ANTONIO: Necessity compels me:
    Make scrutiny throughout the passages°
    Of your own life; you'll find it impossible
    To fly your fate.
ECHO: *O fly your fate.*
450 DELIO: Hark, the dead stones seem to have pity on
      you
    And give you good counsel.
ANTONIO: Echo, I will not talk with thee,
    For thou art a dead thing.

ECHO: *Thou art a dead thing.*
ANTONIO: My Duchess is asleep now,
    And her little ones—I hope sweetly. Oh, heaven
    Shall I never see her more?
ECHO: *Never see her more.*
ANTONIO: I marked not one° repetition of the Echo   460
    But that: and, on the sudden, a clear light
    Presented me a face folded in sorrow.
DELIO: Your fancy, merely.
ANTONIO: Come, I'll be out of this ague;°
    For to live thus, is not indeed to live:
    It is a mockery, and abuse of life.
    I will not henceforth save myself by halves.
    Lose all, or nothing.
DELIO: Your own virtue save you!
    I'll fetch your eldest son, and second you.   470
    It may be that the sight of his° own blood,
    Spread in so sweet a figure, may beget
    The more compassion.
ANTONIO: However, fare you well.
    Though in our miseries Fortune hath a part
    Yet in our noble sufferings she hath none.
    Contempt of pain—that we may call our own.
    (Exeunt.)

ACT 5 / SCENE 4

(The palace of the Aragonian brothers in Milan)
(Enter CARDINAL, PESCARA, MALATESTE, RODERIGO,
GRISOLAN.*)*

CARDINAL: You shall not watch tonight by the sick
    Prince;
    His grace is very well recovered.
MALATESTE: Good my lord, suffer us.°
CARDINAL: Oh, by no means:
    The noise and change of object in his eye
    Doth more distract him. I pray, all to bed;
    And though you hear him in his violent fit,
    Do not rise, I entreat you.
PESCARA: So sir, we shall not—   10
CARDINAL: Nay, I must have you promise
    Upon your honors, for I was enjoined to't
    By himself; and he seemed to urge it sensibly.°
PESCARA: Let our honors bind this trifle.
CARDINAL: Nor any of your followers.
PESCARA: Neither.
CARDINAL: It may be, to make trial of your promise,
    When he's asleep, myself will rise, and feign
    Some of his mad tricks, and cry out for help,
    And feign myself in danger.   20
MALATESTE: If your throat were cutting,

---

distinction, articulation. *questionless,* unquestionably.
Wisdom . . . time, Wisdom does not alleviate the pain of
consuming sorrow any better than time(?). *passages,*
events.

I . . . one, I did not notice the significance of one.
ague, a sickness characterized by intermittent chills and
fever. *his,* the Cardinal's family's. *suffer us,* Allow us then
to watch over him. *sensibly,* when he was in full possession
of his senses.

I'd not come at you, now I have protested against it.
CARDINAL: Why, I thank you. *(Withdraws.)*
GRISOLAN: 'Twas a foul storm tonight.
RODERIGO: The Lord Ferdinand's chamber shook
   like an osier.°
MALATESTE: 'Twas nothing but pure kindness in the
   devil,
   To rock his own child.

(Exeunt RODERIGO, MALATESTE, PESCARA, GRISOLAN.*)*

30 CARDINAL: The reason why I would not suffer these
   About my brother is because at midnight
   I may with better privacy convey
   Julia's body to her own lodging. O, my conscience!
   I would pray now, but the devil takes away my
      heart
   For having any confidence in prayer.
   About this hour I appointed Bosola
   To fetch the body: when he hath served my turn,
   He dies. *(Exit.)*

(Enter BOSOLA.*)*

40 BOSOLA: Ha! 'twas the Cardinal's voice. I heard him
      name
   Bosola, and my death—listen, I hear one's footing.

(Enter FERDINAND.*)*

FERDINAND: Strangling is a very quiet death.
BOSOLA: Nay, then, I see I must stand upon my
   guard.
FERDINAND: What say' to that? Whisper, softly: do
   you agree to't?
   So it must be done i' th' dark: the Cardinal
   Would not for a thousand pounds the doctor
50   should see it. *(Exit.)*
BOSOLA: My death is plotted; here's° the consequence
   of murther.°
   We value not desert, nor Christian breath,
   When we know black deeds must be cured with
   death. *(Withdraws.)*

(Enter ANTONIO *and a* SERVANT.*)*

SERVANT: Here stay, sir, and be confident, I pray:
   I'll fetch a dark lanthorn. *(Exit.)*
ANTONIO: Could I take him
   At his prayers, there were hope of pardon.
60 BOSOLA: Fall right my sword:

(Half-crazed by fears that he will be murdered, BOSOLA
mistakes ANTONIO *for the Cardinal or one of the hen-
chmen and runs him through, from behind.)*

I'll not give thee so much leisure as to pray.
ANTONIO: Oh, I am gone. Thou hast ended a long
   suit.

In a minute.
BOSOLA: What art thou?
ANTONIO: A most wretched thing,
   That only have thy benefit in death.
   To appear myself.° *(Enter* SERVANT *with a dark
   lanthorn.)*
SERVANT: Where are you sir?
ANTONIO: Very near my home.° Bosola?   70
SERVANT: Oh misfortune!
BOSOLA *(to* SERVANT*)*: Smother thy pity, thou art dead
   else—Antonio!
   The man I would have saved 'bove mine own life!
   We are merely the stars' tennis balls, struck and
      banded°
   Which way please them. Oh, good Antonio,
   I'll whisper one thing in thy dying ear,
   Shall make thy heart break quickly. Thy fair
      Duchess   80
   And two sweet children—
ANTONIO: Their very names
   Kindle a little life in me.
BOSOLA: Are murdered!
ANTONIO: Some men have wished to die
   At the hearing of sad tidings: I am glad
   That I shall do't in sadness. I would not now
   Wish my wounds balmed, nor healed: for I have no
      use
   To put my life to. In all our quest of greatness, 90
   Like wanton boys whose pastime is their care,
   We follow after bubbles, blown in th'air.
   Pleasure of life, what is't? only the good hours
   Of an ague; merely a preparative to rest,
   To endure vexation. I do not ask
   The process of my death. Only commend me
   To Delio.
BOSOLA: Break, heart!
ANTONIO: And let my son fly the courts of princes.
   (Dies.)
BOSOLA: Thou seemst to have loved Antonio?   100
SERVANT: I brought him hither,
   To have reconciled him to the Cardinal.
BOSOLA: I do not ask thee that.
   Take him up, if thou tender thine own life,
   And bear him where the Lady Julia
   Was wont to lodge. Oh, my fate moves swift.
   I have this Cardinal in the forge already;
   Now I'll bring him to th' hammer (O direful
      misprision!°)
   I will not imitate things glorious,   110
   No more than base:° I'll be mine own example.
   (to the SERVANT*)* On, on! And look thou represent,°

That . . . myself, The only benefit that I get from you in
death is to be again myself (and no longer have to run and
hide). *home,* final resting place. *banded,* bandied. *mis-
prision,* mistake. *No . . . base,* any more than I will seek to
copy what is base. *represent,* imitate.

---

   osier, willow tree.   *here's,* the plotting of my death.
murther, (my doing) murder.

for silence,
The thing thou bearst. (*Exeunt.*)

ACT 5 / SCENE 5

(*Enter* CARDINAL, *with a book.*)

CARDINAL: I am puzzled in a question about hell:
He° says in hell there's one material fire,
And yet it shall not burn all men alike.
Lay him by. How tedious is a guilty conscience!
When I look into the fishponds in my garden,
Methinks I see a thing armed with a rake°
That seems to strike at me. Now? Art thou come?

(*Enter* BOSOLA *and* SERVANT, *with* ANTONIO's *body.*)

Thou lookst ghastly:
There sits in thy face some great determination,
10   Mixed with some fear.
BOSOLA: Thus it lightens into° action:
I am come to kill thee.
CARDINAL: Ha? Help! our guard!
BOSOLA: Thou art deceived:
They are out of thy howling.
CARDINAL: Hold, and I will faithfully divide
Revenues with thee.
BOSOLA: Thy prayers and proffers
Are both unseasonable.
20   CARDINAL: Raise the watch:
We° are betrayed!
BOSOLA: I have confined your flight:
I'll suffer you to retreat to Julia's chamber,
But no further.
CARDINAL: Help! We are betrayed!

(*Enter* PESCARA, MALATESTE, RODERIGO, *and* GRISO-
LAN, *above.*)

MALATESTE: Listen.
CARDINAL: My dukedom for rescue!
RODERIGO: Fie upon his counterfeiting.
MALATESTE: Why, 'tis not the Cardinal.
30   RODERIGO: Yes, yes, 'tis he:
But I'll see him hanged ere I'll go down to him.
CARDINAL: Here's a plot upon me! I am assaulted! I
am lost,
Unless some rescue!
GRISOLAN: He doth this pretty well,
But it will not serve to laugh me° out of mine
honor.°
CARDINAL: The sword's at my throat!

He, the author of the book.   *armed...rake,* The devil
was traditionally thought to carry a fork of some sort.
lightens into, shows itself as it rises to.   *We,* The Cardinal
uses the royal "we" here, perhaps in an unconscious attempt
to establish his authority over Bosola, and certainly in an
effort to summon others to his help.   *laugh me,* trick me.
mine honor, my vow to him not to interfere.

RODERIGO: You would not bawl so loud then.
MALATESTE: Come, come. Let's go to bed: he told us   40
thus much aforehand.
PESCARA: He wished you should not come at him, but
believ't,
The accent of the voice sounds not in jest.
I'll down to him, howsoever, and with engines°
Force ope the doors. (*Exit.*)
RODERIGO: Let's follow him aloof,
And note how the Cardinal will laugh at him.
(*Exeunt above.*)
BOSOLA: There's for you first:
'Cause you shall not unbarricade the door   50
To let in rescue.

(*He kills the* SERVANT.)

CARDINAL: What cause hast thou to pursue my life?
BOSOLA: Look there.
CARDINAL: Antonio!
BOSOLA: Slain by my hand unwittingly.
Pray, and be sudden:° when thou killedst thy sister,
Thou tookst from Justice her most equal balance,
And left her naught but her sword.
CARDINAL: O mercy!

(*He falls to his knees.*)

BOSOLA: Now it seems thy greatness was only   60
outward:
For thou fallst faster of thyself than calamity
Can drive thee. I'll not waste longer time. There.

(*Stabs the* CARDINAL.)

CARDINAL: Thou hast hurt me.
BOSOLA: Again. (*Stabs him again.*)
CARDINAL: Shall I die like a leveret,°
Without any resistance? Help! help! help!
I am slain.

(*Enter* FERDINAND.)

FERDINAND: Th'alarum?° give me a fresh horse.
Rally the vaunt-guard,° or the day is lost.   70
Yield, yield! I give you the honor of arms,
Shake my sword over you. Will you yield?
CARDINAL: Help me! I am your brother.
FERDINAND: The devil!
My brother fight upon the adverse party!

(*He wounds the* CARDINAL, *and, in the scuffle, gives*
BOSOLA *his death wound.*)

There flies your ransom.°
CARDINAL: Oh, justice,
I suffer now for what hath former been:

---

engines, tools.   *'Cause,* so that.   *sudden,* quick.
leveret, small hare.   *alarum,* the trumpet call to arms.
vaunt-guard, the foremost ranks of the army.   *ransom,*
(chance for) being ransomed.

Sorrow is held the eldest child of sin.
80 FERDINAND: Now you're brave fellows. Caesar's for-
    tune was harder than Pompey's; Caesar died in
    the arms of prosperity, Pompey at the feet of
    disgrace. You both died in the field; the pain's
    nothing. Pain many times is taken away with the
    apprehension of greater—as the toothache with
    the sight of a barber° that comes to pull it out:
    there's philosophy for you.
BOSOLA: Now my revenge is perfect.° Sink, thou main
    cause
90 Of my undoing!—The last part of my life
    Hath done me best service.

    (He kills FERDINAND.)

FERDINAND: Give me some wet hay:° I am broken
    winded.
    I do account this world but a dog kennel:
    I will vault credit, and affect high pleasures
    Beyond death.°
BOSOLA: He seems to come to himself,
    Now he's so near the bottom.
FERDINAND: My sister! oh, my sister! there's the cause
100 on't.
    Whether we fall by ambition, blood, or lust,
    Like diamonds, we are cut with our own dust. (Dies)
CARDINAL: Thou hast thy payment too.
BOSOLA: Yes, I hold my weary soul in my teeth:
    'Tis ready to part from me. I do glory
    That thou, which stoodst like a huge pyramid
    Begun upon a large and ample base,
    Shalt end in a little point, a kind of nothing.

    (Enter PESCARA, MALATESTE, RODERIGO, and GRISO-
    LAN.)

PESCARA: How now, my lord?
110 MALATESTE: O sad disaster!
RODERIGO: How comes this?
BOSOLA: Revenge!—for the Duchess of Malfi,
    murderèd
    By th'Aragonian brethren; for Antonio,
    Slain by this hand; for lustful Julia,
    Poisoned by this man; and lastly, for myself,
    That was an actor in the main of all,
    Much 'gainst mine own good nature, yet i' th' end
    Neglected.°

PESCARA: How now, my lord? 120
CARDINAL: Look to my brother:
    He° gave us these large wounds as we were
    struggling
    Here i' th' rushes.° And now, I pray, let me
    Be laid by, and never thought of. (Dies.)
PESCARA: How fatally, it seems, he did withstand°
    His own rescue!
MALATESTE: Thou wretched thing of blood,
    How came Antonio by his death?
BOSOLA: In a mist—I know not how— 130
    Such a mistake as I have often seen
    In a play. Oh, I am gone—
    We are only like dead walls or vaulted graves
    That, ruined, yield no echo. Fare you well.
    It may be pain, but no harm, to me to die
    In so good a quarrel. Oh this gloomy world,
    In what a shadow or deep pit of darkness
    Doth, womanish° and fearful,° mankind live?
    Let worthy minds ne'er stagger in distrust
    To suffer death or shame for what is just: 140
    Mine is another voyage. (Dies.)
PESCARA: The noble Delio, as I came to th' palace,
    Told me of Antonio's being here, and showed me
    A pretty gentleman, his son and heir.

    (Enter DELIO with ANTONIO's son.)

MALATESTE: O, sir, you come too late.
DELIO: I heard so, and
    Was armed° for't ere I came. Let us make noble use
    Of this great ruin, and join all our force
    To establish this young hopeful gentleman
    In's mother's right. These wretched, eminent° 150
    things
    Leave no more fame behind 'em, than should one
    Fall in a frost and leave his print in snow:
    As soon as the sun shines, it ever melts
    Both form and matter. I have ever thought
    Nature doth nothing so great for great men,
    As when she's pleased to make them lords of truth:
    Integrity of life is fame's best friend,
    Which nobly, beyond death, shall crown the end.
    (Exeunt.)

---

barber, Barbers served also as surgeons at this time. **perfect,** complete. **wet hay,** thought to be the best food for a broken-winded horse. **I . . . death,** I will leap over things credited to be of worth in this world, and I will strive after the true pleasures that lie beyond death. **yet . . . Neglected,** "Which, ultimately, I neglected."

He, Bosola. **rushes,** Greens and reeds were sometimes used to cover cold castle floors. **withstand,** offer opposition to (by counseling us against). **womanish,** timorous. **fearful,** both frightened and frightening. **armed,** prepared. **eminent,** conspicuous.

Figure 35. Ferdinand (Roland Hewgill, *right*) bribes Bosola (Powys Thomas) to spy on the Duchess in the Stratford Festival production of *The Duchess of Malfi,* directed by Jean Gascon and designed by Desmond Heeley, Stratford, Ontario, 1971. (Photograph: the Stratford Festival, Canada.)

Figure 36. The Duchess (Pat Galloway) woos Antonio (Barry MacGregor) in the Stratford Festival production of *The Duchess of Malfi,* directed by Jean Gascon and designed by Desmond Heeley, Stratford, Ontario, 1971. (Photograph: the Stratford Festival, Canada.)

Figure 37. Antonio (Barry McGregor), the Duchess (Pat Galloway), and various church figures form a tableau depicting the banishment scene at Loretto in the Stratford Festival production of *The Duchess of Malfi*, directed by Jean Gascon and designed by Desmond Heeley, Stratford, Ontario, 1971. (Photograph: the Stratford Festival, Canada.)

Staging of *The Duchess of Malfi*

INTERVIEW WITH JEAN GASCON, DIRECTOR OF THE 1971 STRATFORD FESTIVAL THEATER PRODUCTION OF *THE DUCHESS OF MALFI*, BY BRADFORD S. FIELD, JR.

FIELD: I was looking at some of the photographs of *The Duchess of Malfi* on its tour and of the play as it opened here. I noticed that on the tour the Cardinal was in one costume, but that you recostumed the character entirely for the production here. What kind of discovery did you make that led to that change?

GASCON: We were after a kind of monolithic idea of the Cardinal, and the costume that first turned out was much too light and didn't give that kind of pyramidal shape that I was looking for. As happens very often in the theatre, we didn't have a chance to re-do it before the tour. This happened with a lot of the costumes in *Malfi*. We took a lot of risks in the original designs. Some worked and some didn't, and after the tour, when we had a chance to make changes, we did so. We had originally decided on a kind of no-period costume, one that would reflect a degraded court, a sick court. We expanded that design idea much further after the tour in Minneapolis and Ottawa, because we were going much further in the whole production with this idea of a decadent, corrupted, sick court.

FIELD: Does this decadence strike a chord in a modern audience's heart?

GASCON: Well, it's not the same kind of decadence . . . decadence can become a kind of cliché too. There's Roman decadence, and there are other kinds, Italian Renaissance decadence, that can be just a tableau of beautiful costumes, and we wanted to go against that . . .

FIELD: Aside from the costumes, did you have to make any other adjustments as you went along? Were there any other problems, say, in interpretation that were difficult?

GASCON: The two really difficult problems that we had were, first, to establish in the *Duchess of Malfi* the relationships within the family. It's not spelled out in the dialogue, but there's obviously an incestuous love felt by Ferdinand for his sister. To show that, and to show the relationship of the Cardinal to the other two, is very intricate work. Ferdinand is a deranged man. They are like twins, really, Ferdinand and the sister. They come from the same cell, I think, in Webster's mind, except that one went rotten and the other went beautiful. There's a lot of Ferdinand in the Duchess and a lot of the Duchess in Ferdinand, and that is very tricky to establish. The second problem was the difficulty of defining the character of

Bosola. A marvelous character, a disenchanted, bitter man, but what is disturbing is that within him you can feel that he never became "somebody" in that society because the society wouldn't allow it.

FIELD: Even though he had all the talent to be so?

GASCON: He had everything! The whole equipment was there—the intelligence, the dedication, the courage. And he lost it all . . . it reminded me at one point of some Brechtian characters. Brecht establishes that people—whether they be Peachums or Schweiks—will do anything, when it's a question of survival, and that it's not their fault if they do wrong. It's the society that is rotten, when the only way to survive in it is to be anti-social, when they cannot fulfill their own lives.

FIELD: So that Bosola is a good example, or rather a horrible example, of wasted capacity.

GASCON: Absolutely! In the view of Brecht, and of Webster, the man that has everything should succeed in a well-organized society; in a well-organized society a man like Bosola would have a chance to be a great man.

FIELD: In these two general problems can you put your finger on a specific speech or piece of stage action that exemplifies the problem, like establishing the relationship between the brother and the sister?

GASCON: As I said, it's really not in the dialogue . . . a question we ask about Ferdinand is, why is he so concerned about that Duchess, why does he punish her so much? The reason, we see finally, is incestuous love, and in the production itself you have to make that clear to the audience at the beginning of the play, so they know what you're talking about. We started with a tableau—and that is really a very difficult thing to make succeed—where Antonio is talking about the corruption of the court from the upper balcony, and down below all the courtiers are doing their business, trying to get some job or another, people moving around in a kind of dream-like light. In that scene, we tried to establish some close physical contact between the brother and the sister, contacts that were sexual for Ferdinand, but not for the Duchess. We had to be careful. These things may mean too much, more than you want them to mean. You have to make sure that your point of view toward the play is registered in the house.

FIELD: The house . . . when you know what kind of audience you are going to get all summer long, how much does that affect the way you interpret the play?

GASCON: Doesn't affect me at all. And I don't think it should. I always hope for success, but when you tackle a difficult play like *Duchess of Malfi* you cannot worry about things like this so-called relevance. You must go for clarity, clarity of thinking, of emotion, of all the physical elements. Then people can really understand what you are talking about.

FIELD: You spoke earlier of the danger of having something mean more that you had expected it to. Did any scenes in *Duchess of Malfi* surprise you? Any of them give more or different things than you expected?

GASCON: One thing turned out better than we expected. In Webster there is a scene in pantomime, the banishment of the Duchess at Loretto in the cathedral. That point in the Jacobean tragedy is a very important moment—but there's no text.

FIELD: These peasants try to explain it, don't they?

GASCON: The peasants come in before it, talking about the scene, and then after that commenting on the scene, but there's no scene written. About three weeks before we opened the play I suddenly had serious doubts about that scene, and I went to the designer, Desmond Heeley, and I said, maybe, you know, the play wouldn't lose anything if we don't do that scene. And I could see him nearly bursting into tears; we had both worked so hard on that concept. For us it was a very important moment in the play. At the beginning when we were doing our homework on it, I had thought it was a very important moment, but suddenly in the rehearsals of it, because there was no text—and no costumes—and no light—and no sounds . . .

FIELD: And no audience . . .

GASCON: And no audience, then suddenly it looked ludicrous. We said, "What are we doing here?" Even the actors were saying, "What is this thing about?" And finally, fortunately, we convinced each other that our first idea was a good one, and that we had to go on with it, still not sure that we would keep it. I remember the first time that we produced it in front of a few people here in Stratford, the first technical dress rehearsal, with the sounds, and the lights, and the costumes and all that—people thought it was a marvelous theatrical moment, a kind of summing up of the whole style of the production, a style that was very bold, very gutsy and menacing and cruel—and that moment seemed to be the pinnacle of the production.

FIELD: So it wasn't a surprise but more a fulfillment of your hopes.

GASCON: The surprise was because we had had our doubts about it. We had stopped believing in it. It teaches you a lesson, to trust your instinct. It's half analytic and half emotional.

FIELD: Half analytical . . . it should not be something that you know that you can impose upon the text.

GASCON: No, it has to come from the play that influences you, and suddenly inside yourself, in some strange way, your guts are affected and your imagination is affected, and suddenly you see what is the best way to illuminate "what I think the play is about," to do it that way. But if you do it from the outside, then you go for gimmicks; and when you go for gimmicks, there's a great chance of it not working at all.

REVIEW OF THE STRATFORD FESTIVAL PRODUCTION, 1971, BY CLIVE BARNES

Not for the first time—and probably not for the last, because institutions breed traditions—the second night of the Stratford Festival offset the slight disappointment of the first. Last night's production of John Webster's "The Duchess of Malfi" was a most cogent performance of a thrillingly evil play.

Why are Webster and the other Jacobean playwrights so deplorably neglected, and then—when produced—maltreated by directors, actors, critics and audiences alike? "The Duchess of Malfi," like "The White Devil," should have a place in any classic repertory, yet it is an unjustifiable rarity. I have only seen it

a couple of times before—notably with John Gielgud as Ferdinand.

The play itself is full of black blood and diamond poetry. It seems to represent two genres, the revenge play—although who is revenging whom is never quite clear—and the malcontent play. Both kinds would have been very familiar to their original audiences, and Webster's virtuosity would be better appreciated in its historical context.

The play is in a way illogical, but it has its own dark consistency. The Duchess of Malfi is a young widow with two brothers, Ferdinand, the Duke of Calabria, and the Cardinal. They do not wish the Duchess to marry—we never quite know why, although this production persuasively suggests that Ferdinand had incestuous desires for her.

The Duchess determines to marry, or at least take a lover, and her choice falls upon Antonio, her steward. Antonio loves her dearly and they have three children. Ferdinand has placed in the Duchess's court a spy, Bosola, who is nominally Master of the Horse to the Duchess, but in reality is a creature of the Duke. Bosola is one of the most interesting villains in literature—for his villainy is philosophic and honest. He is the complete rational madman and a monster of undirected purpose.

At last—and it must be admitted that Bosola is a very unperceptive spy—the Duchess's deceptions are discovered, and Ferdinand resolves to punish her. He parts her from her husband, and after torturing her in an attempt to send her mad, he and his brother have her murdered.

What follows is carnage incarnate. Such principal characters that have not been already murdered are now dispatched, and the final scene is positively infested with bodies. Not to be murdered in a Webster play would be the death of any actor of ambition—indeed the equivalent of a walk-on part.

Yet it is a great play. Even the story itself has been stabbed to tatters by unlikelihood, and yet this terrible galliard of death has its own momentum and dignity. Webster had a strange melancholy, and a mind of macabre power. Imagine the scene where the Duke is trying to send the Duchess of Malfi mad.

He arranges to see her in the pitch of night—all is dark. He gives her his hand, and leaves her—holding the hand, which he says is the severed hand of her lover, Antonio. It isn't, but that is hardly the point. Then again Webster's poetry appeals to the heart, whereas Shakespeare so often appeals more to the mind. Some of Webster's lines, such as "I am the Duchess of Malfi still," have no intellectual pretensions to poetic diction, but in their place they strike home like a poignard.

The play has been directed by Jean Gascon, Stratford's artistic director, and he has done a very fine job. He has deliberately concentrated on simplicity and pace. There is no scenery—apart from Tanya Moiseiwitsch's permanent setting, and a few sparse properties. The costumes by Desmond Heeley are both gorgeous and fantastic. They have a wayward decadence to them that is just right. But spectacle Mr. Gascon uses sparingly. The famous scene of the Duchess and Antonio being excommunicated is handled with grandeur but tact, and even the madness scenes and the terrible murder of the Duchess is kept as cool as cold steel.

Mr. Gascon seems to have plucked an unusual theme from the play—the difficulty of virtue in a sea of corruption—which adds to the ambivalence of Bosola, that crazy mixed-up villain, but also serves to give the play a new depth and direction. This is a rotten world, both playwright and director are saying, so why expect anything of morality. And yet morality must be served—even to the final mound of fresh bleeding corpses.

Pat Galloway is splendid as the Duchess. She has the quick sensuality and the loyal constancy, the aristocratic mien and the quite unsentimental poignancy of a great woman dispatched before her time. The rest of the cast moved well in her sphere.

The actor cannot be blamed, but Mr. Gascon's decision to make Bosola a mistaken villain and a bluff man of honor does detract from the character and the play—the role should have a random malevolence, a serpent hypocrisy, and a fine Italian hand. This, for the rest of his reading, Mr. Gascon sacrificed, leaving Powys Thomas, playing the part, to pick up the pieces, which of course he couldn't. This was the one unconvincing character.

The diabolical brothers were excellently done, with Roland Hewgill villainously mad as the Duke and William Needles deadly, lizardlike and voluntary as the Cardinal. I admired also the honesty and dignity of Barry MacGregor's Antonio.

This is the kind of production and acting that has made the Canadian Stratford company among the most admired in the English-speaking world.

NEOCLASSICAL
THEATER

In the middle of the seventeenth century, drama moved indoors and stayed there. It moved from daylight to candlelight, from large open-air theaters, some capable of seating as many as 2000, to relatively small auditoriums, usually accommodating no more than 700. And this radical shift in the environment of drama produced not only a radically different theatrical experience, but also called forth radically different changes in the conception of drama itself. This change in the theatrical environment had already been anticipated by developments dating back to the early sixteenth century, when indoor theaters began to be built in the banqueting halls of Italy and in remodelled tennis courts in France. English private theaters, located in former monasteries such as Blackfriars and Whitefriars, began in the late 1500s. In all these spaces, the stage usually occupied one end of a long hall, and the audience watched from side galleries and from the floor in front of the stage. By the last third of the seventeenth century, theaters reflecting this design had become standard throughout the major dramatic centers in Europe, and these theaters were conventionally equipped with a proscenium arch framing the stage, a design derived from Italian stage architecture of the sixteenth century. In English theaters of the later seventeenth century, a sizable forestage, recalling the platform of the Elizabethan public theater, extended beyond the proscenium, and double doors, also in front of the proscenium, gave actors ready access to this favored acting area (see Figure 38). French theaters of the same period have a much shallower forestage, no doors, and, in some cases, benches to seat members of the audience on stage behind the proscenium (see Figure 39). In both theaters, the pit, or floor area directly in front of the stage, is shared by standing and seated spectators. Earlier, this space had been entirely given to standing room or left vacant so that the royal party could have an uninterrupted view of the stage.

Just as the English and French had borrowed from the Italians in their use of a proscenium arch, so they turned to Italy for the sets they were to display behind the picture frame of the arch. Italian set design had been pioneered by Sebastian Serlio, who created in his lengthy treatise, *Architettura* (1545), a set of detailed drawings for three typical sets, which he based on his reading of a classical Roman treatise. His dependence on a classical source is only one of the many instances that account for the term neoclassicism. Later designers simplified his three-dimensional details into painted ones and substituted flat wings for the angle wings Serlio had used. At first, the elaborate Italianate sets were used primarily for court entertainments—masques in early seventeenth century England, and court ballets in mid-seventeenth century France. But the very possibility of being able to represent different locales by changing a painted backdrop and wings (instead of saying "So this is the Forest of Arden" and expecting the audience to imagine the new locale) led to a new and crucial feature in theater architecture. Because flats that are to be shifted require

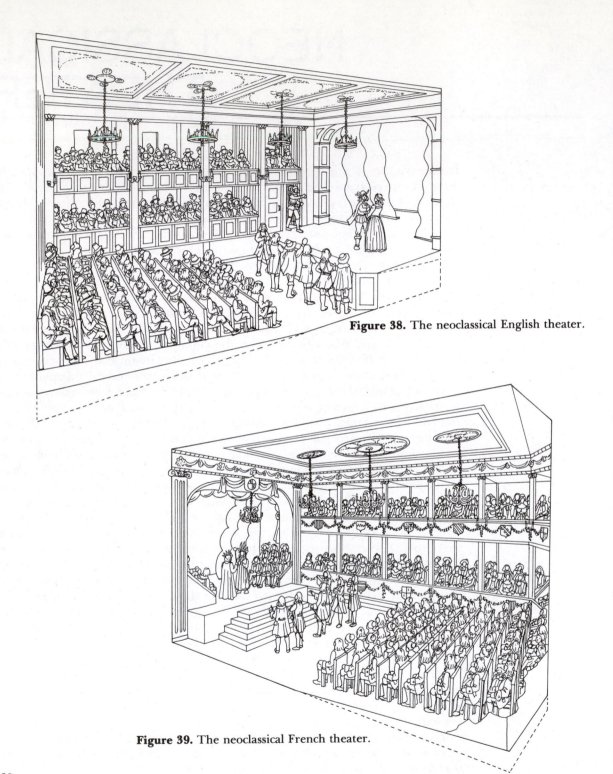

Figure 38. The neoclassical English theater.

Figure 39. The neoclassical French theater.

machinery, or stagehands, or both, to move them, it became necessary to conceal such backstage efforts. Designers began by using plain flats for concealing the activity, but gradually looked for a permanent frame for the stage: the proscenium arch. While the proscenium masked backstage maneuverings, it also detached the space on stage from the space in the remainder of the theater, and thus separated the actors from the audience. Lighting changes also reinforced this separation. In the drawings reproduced here, we see chandeliers with candles lighting both the audience and the stage. But in the late seventeenth century, footlights were added, and more attention was given to lighting the stage alone. And in the eighteenth century, dimming devices (such as lowering the candle footlights) were invented, lamps began to replace candles, and lamps with reflectors were placed *behind* the proscenium arch, focusing light more sharply on the acting area.

Still, the theaters of this period are nothing like the darkened auditoriums of today, and audiences then would not have wished them so, since they came to the theater to be seen as much as to see. For English audiences after 1660 (the date of the restoration of the monarchy and the restoration of theatrical activity), the playhouse was the place to meet friends, to talk, to flirt, to eat and drink. Prologues to Restoration plays frequently comment on the audience's behavior and especially on the attention of those in the pit (still the cheapest seats) to orange-women, prostitutes, and young men trying to be witty. The performance, it might almost be said, ran simultaneously onstage and offstage. Well-known liaisons between actresses and nobles brought performers and audience together even more closely. In a famous painting by the satiric artist, William Hogarth, of the final scene from Gay's *The Beggar's Opera* (1728), an actress can be seen gazing not only at the actor who should command her exclusive attention, but also at the Duke of Bolton, her real-life lover, who sits in an onstage box. The costuming of most plays in contemporary dress added to the mirror effect, since people onstage looked very much like those offstage. Paintings of the famous actor, David Garrick, for example, show him wearing the standard wig and dress of the mid-eighteenth century—for Macbeth! Actors owned their own wardrobes, and, like the audience members, spent lavish amounts on a single costume. The stage picture was thus likely to be highly gorgeous, but not necessarily consistent, and certainly not historically accurate.

The similarities between onstage and offstage behavior can be found in the plays as well as in performance practices. Indeed, the two are closely related, particularly in the social comedies of Etherege, Wycherley, Congreve, Molière, Goldsmith, and Sheridan. In these plays the audience could easily see itself. *The Man of Mode,* for example, reflects the fashionable activities of London society, for its characters, like members of the audience themselves, are seen promenading in St. James Park and planning illicit assignations at the theater. In France, Molière also finds a wide range of satiric targets that mirror the life of his audience—from the bourgeois who try to be upper class to the fashionable salon society obsessed with trivial affairs. But even when he comes close to satirizing his own audience directly, he is careful to leave an escape route, for his onstage characters are always highly exaggerated versions of actual experience, and their exaggeration is usually the source of his mockery.

The relation of drama to actual experience was, in fact, a central issue in critical theories of the period, most of which were derived from Italian commentaries on classical criticism. The treatises of Minturno, Scaliger, and Castelvetro, which sought to define literary art or to comment on Aristotle and Horace, argued for "verisimilitude," likeness to truth, and formulated a number of elaborate rules to bring drama closer to reality. But for them, reality was to be achieved not through having the stage life exactly like real life, but through abiding by certain normative conditions. Tragedy, for example, was to follow the norms of elevated speech, characters of high rank, and plots with unhappy endings, while comedy was to use a more colloquial style befitting its middle- or lower-class characters, and was to end happily. Verisimilitude also demanded that certain events, especially violent ones, be kept offstage, since they were thought unlikely to be convincing onstage. Finally, a play was to deal only with a single series of incidents, occurring in a single locale, within a period of twenty-four hours or less. These famous, even notorious, "unities" of action, place, and time were thought to support verisimilitude, since an audience in a theater presumably knew that it had been in the same place for several hours only, and in that limited time it could not believe a multitude of actions taking place.

Such theories, called neoclassical because they are based on reinterpretations of classical texts, could not, of course, last forever. And by the end of the eighteenth century, one of England's great literary critics, Samuel Johnson, a man thoroughly steeped in neoclassical theory, offered a common sense repudiation of the rules in his *Preface to Shakespeare:*

> The truth is, that the spectators are always in their senses, and know, from the first act to the last, that the stage is only a stage, and that the players are only players. They come to hear a certain number of lines recited with just gesture and elegant modulation. The lines relate to some action, and an action must be in some place; but the different actions that complete a story may be in places very remote from each other; and where is the absurdity of allowing that space to represent first Athens, and then Sicily, which was always known to be neither Sicily nor Athens, but a modern theater?

But by the end of the eighteenth century, staging techniques were being designed to make spectators forget they were in a theater. The development of machinery for changing sets, the elaboration of scenery painting, and the increased use of sophisticated lighting that would focus primarily on the stage were clear indications of a growing interest in making the stage picture look "real," in creating a detailed theatrical illusion. Acting styles, too, edged slightly closer to "realistic" portrayal of characters. In these ways, the theater's move indoors led eventually to drama that focussed almost totally on the individual character, showing how external environment and inner emotional life together shape the destiny of the individual.

MOLIÈRE

1622–1673

Molière, the preeminent comic dramatist in the history of French theater, was also known in his own time as the director and the leading actor of the major theatrical company in Paris. He was, in fact, so thoroughly a man of the stage that once he became involved in it, after a brief period of studying law, he abandoned his given name, Jean-Baptiste Poquelin, and replaced it with the singular one by which he has since been known. His theatrical career began in 1643, when he formed a small company, known as the Illustre Théâtre, with a family of talented actors, the Béjarts. But their enterprise failed so badly that Molière was temporarily imprisoned for debts, and the company was forced to leave Paris. They regrouped themselves in the provinces and toured the countryside from 1645 to 1658, a period when Molière evidently trained himself in every aspect of the theater from set-building to playwriting. During this time, for example, he witnessed the touring Italian companies and steeped himself in their extensive repertoire of comic techniques—techniques of the *commedia dell'arte,* such as stock characters, slapstick routines (known as *lazzi*), intrigue plots, and conventional "surprise" endings. By the end of this period, Molière had also become director of the troupe, which he had enlarged and improved by attracting some of the most accomplished actors and actresses of his day. When he took his troupe back to Paris in 1658, having arranged a special performance for the youthful Louis XIV and his court, Molière won the king's favor and was granted permission to remain in Paris and perform at the Théâtre du Petit-Bourbon, one of the few existing theaters in the city. He had won over the king, it should be noted, not by his troupe's production of a tragedy of Corneille, but by his comic performance in *The Amorous Doctor,* a farcical afterpiece he had written himself.

Molière's genius was clearly attuned to the world of comedy, and it led his troupe ultimately to be commissioned as chief entertainers to the court of Louis XIV. In 1661 he gained control of the theater in the Palais Royal, and in 1665 his group was formally designated "The King's Company." Throughout his career in Paris, Molière wrote approximately thirty theatrical pieces, some known as *comédies-ballets,* which were plays interspersed with music and dancing for presentation to the court at Versailles, and others that were purely dramatic for staging in his own theater at the Palais Royal. The *comédies-ballets* were notable not only for their music, dancing, and spectacular scenic effects, but also because the ballet sections were often performed by members of the court, including the King himself. Yet these works were conceived by Molière to be fully worked out plays as well. In fact, one of Molière's most famous comedies, *The Would-Be-Gentleman* (1670), was a *comédie-ballet,* designed at the King's command to include a musical section with a Turkish theme. This material could easily be omitted from the work, as indeed it was by Molière when he produced it as an entirely dramatic work in 1671 at the Palais Royal.

Whether writing entertainments for the court or plays for the public,

Molière's comic purpose was always the same: to expose through laughter the follies of society. Even so, his satiric treatment of various social types often aroused the displeasure of some members in the fashionable world who felt he was engaging in personal assaults on their reputation. In his own defense, he wrote a play about the theater itself, *The Versailles Impromptu* (1663), in which one of the characters offers a very revealing conversation he has had with Molière about the purpose of his comedies:

> His aim, he said, is to portray types and not individuals, and all the people who appear in his plays are imaginary, phantoms if you like; he invents them as he goes along, in such a way as to entertain the audience; and he would be embarrassed if they resembled actual people . . . and I agree with him. Why bother to pin such and such a trait on so-and-so when his characters have traits that could fit a hundred different people? The business of comedy is to present the flaws common to all men, and especially the men of our time.

In revealing human flaws, Molière typically designed his plays to focus on the comically absurd behavior of a single character who is controlled by a singular obsession. Arnolphe, for example, in *The School for Wives* (1662) is a forty-two-year-old man so desirous of being married yet so fearful of being cuckolded that he has contrived to raise a young girl of six in almost monastic seclusion for thirteen years, assuming that her total ignorance of other men and her rigorous instruction in the duties of a wife will make her completely obedient to him. But shortly after the play opens, the young girl Agnès is discovered by a young man, and the delicious progress of their courtship comically exposes the major weakness in Arnolphe's fanatically designed plan—he has failed to realize that a marriage can truly be secured only by love. Harpagon, on the other hand, the title character of *The Miser* (1668), is so avaricious that he is even willing to marry off his young daughter to a much older man, simply because the man is willing to marry her, as Harpagon gleefully reports, "without a dowry." And Orgon, the main character in *Tartuffe* (1669), is so fanatically devoted to the sham holy man Tartuffe that he worries more about the welfare of Tartuffe than about anyone else in his own family. When he is told that his wife is suffering from a fever, his reply is comically inappropriate: "Ah. And Tartuffe?" Indeed, Orgon is so blindly devoted to Tartuffe that he persistently refuses to see the hypocrisy of Tartuffe until he is nearly undone by it.

The obsessions of these characters are usually called to their attention—and to ours—by the presence of reasonable and sensible persons in their world. Sometimes these *raisonneurs* (rational commentators) are servants, sometimes friends, sometimes close relatives of the obsessed characters, but whatever their status, they repeatedly fail to bring them to their senses through rational appeals. Only the power of extremely painful experience seems capable of curing these characters, and thus Molière displays the extremity of their fixations. Although their obsessions are huge—and hugely funny—these characters are not only magnificent in their delusions, but they are also intensely human in their attachments to them. And thus Molière conceives his obsessed characters so that we will not only laugh at them but will also comprehend their pain. How else can an audience respond when Arnolphe finally recognizes that Agnès loves someone else and turns to the audience expressing his hurt and frustration? Moments such as these, as well as the sustained allegiance of the *raisonneurs* in their world, suggest that Molière intended us to see these misguided characters—whose roles he so often performed himself—as deserving both our judgment and our sympathy.

In *The Misanthrope* (1666), we are once again faced with an obsessed figure, Alceste, who produces conflicting reactions, but for far more complicated reasons than Molière's comedies usually contain. Unlike his counterparts, Alceste is obsessed with an admirable idea—namely, a belief that honesty and integrity are the most important bases of all human relationships. Consequently, he is moved to condemn his society as being filled with shallow flirts and sycophants, with hypocrites who praise people to their faces and mock them as soon as they are gone. And surely Alceste is right in condemning these characters in his world. But surely Philinte, the *raisonneur* friend of Alceste, is also correct in recognizing that a brutally frank honesty such as Alceste recommends would be the undoing of society itself. Beyond the questions raised by Philinte, we are also forced to see that Alceste is so obsessed with his vision that he sees himself as the only sincere person in his world, and thus he appears to be a supremely self-regarding egotist. And to top off these contradictions, Alceste is in love with the most beautiful—and the most insincere—woman in his society, so that he is trapped between what he believes and what he feels.

The doubts raised by Alceste's demands for sincerity coupled with his love for Célimène find their structural analogue in the to-and-fro motion of the play. The setting, appropriately, is Célimène's house, the center of social activity, and Alceste is constantly being taken away either by his legal affairs or by his anger with Célimène, yet he repeatedly returns, always attempting to get Célimène to understand his true feelings and admit to her own. In the gathering action that brings more and more people on stage, we come to expect the comic recognition and resolution customary in the finales of Molière's other works. But in the final act, Molière reverses this pattern and our expectations. The movement instead is one of gradual dispersal. Célimène's sarcastic condemnation of her own circle alienates her admirers and they slowly leave; Alceste, in turn, asks her to flee society with him, but she refuses, so he angrily rejects her; and the play ends with only a slight note of hope as Philinte and Éliante, the two *raisonneurs* go after Alceste, hoping to change his bitter mood. The play ends very much as it began—in a stalemate.

Still, the serious issues raised by *The Misanthrope* and the ambiguous tone of its ending are counterpointed, both on the page and on the stage, by deliciously witty speeches and comic characters. Richard Wilbur's translation has caught the epigrammatic quality of the original; in fact, Wilbur's translation of this and other plays (*The School for Wives* and *Tartuffe*) have rekindled interest in Molière on stages across the country. Wilbur's translation is discussed in the review following the text of a 1968 production by the APA-Phoenix Repertory Company, and photographs of this production clearly show the detailed period costumes and set devices the APA used to evoke the self-conscious style of the society that so offended Alceste. The elaborate surfaces of that style are blatantly conveyed in the costumes of Acaste and Clitandre (see Figure 40), much as Alceste's opposition to it is displayed in his unstylish lankness, his plain clothes, and his uncoiffured hair (see Figure 41). And in his bewildered look we see the play's paradox: society's honest man must necessarily be an outsider; he will ridicule society's pretensions without changing them one wit.

THE MISANTHROPE

BY MOLIÈRE / TRANSLATED BY RICHARD WILBUR

CHARACTERS

ALCESTE, *in love with Célimène*
PHILINTE, *Alceste's friend*
ORONTE, *in love with Célimène*
CÉLIMÈNE, *Alceste's beloved*
ELIANTE, *Célimène's cousin*
ARSINOÉ, *a friend of Célimène's*
ACASTE, *marquess*

CLITANDRE, *marquess*
BASQUE, *Célimène's servant*
A GUARD *of the Marshalsea*
DUBOIS, *Alceste's valet*

SCENE

The scene throughout is in Célimène's house at Paris.

ACT 1

(The scene opens on PHILINTE *and* ALCESTE.*)*

PHILINTE: Now, what's got into you?

ALCESTE *(seated)*: Kindly leave me alone.

PHILINTE: Come, come, what is it? This lugubrious
    tone . . .

ALCESTE: Leave me, I said; you spoil my solitude.

PHILINTE: Oh, listen to me, now, and don't be rude.

ALCESTE: I choose to be rude, Sir, and to be hard of
    hearing.

PHILINTE: These ugly moods of yours are not
10   endearing;
    Friends though we are, I really must insist . . .

ALCESTE *(abruptly rising)*: Friends? Friends, you say?
    Well, cross me off your list.
    I've been your friend till now, as you well know;
    But after what I saw a moment ago
    I tell you flatly that our ways must part.
    I wish no place in a dishonest heart.

PHILINTE: Why, what have I done, Alceste? Is this
    quite just?

20 ALCESTE: My God, you ought to die of self-disgust.
    I call your conduct inexcusable, Sir,
    And every man of honor will concur.
    I see you almost hug a man to death,
    Exclaim for joy until you're out of breath,
    And supplement these loving demonstrations
    With endless offers, vows, and protestations;
    Then when I ask you "Who was that?", I find
    That you can barely bring his name to mind!
    Once the man's back is turned, you cease to love
        him,
    And speak with absolute indifference of him!
    By God, I say it's base and scandalous
    To falsify the heart's affections thus;
    If I caught myself behaving in such a way,
    I'd hang myself for shame, without delay.

PHILINTE: It hardly seems a hanging matter to me;
    I hope that you will take it graciously
    If I extend myself a slight reprieve,
    And live a little longer, by your leave.

ALCESTE: How dare you joke about a crime so grave? 40

PHILINTE: What crime? How else are people to
    behave?

ALCESTE: I'd have them be sincere, and never part
    With any word that isn't from the heart.

PHILINTE: When someone greets us with a show of
        pleasure,
    It's but polite to give him equal measure,
    Return his love the best that we know how,
    And trade him offer for offer, vow for vow.

ALCESTE: No, no, this formula you'd have me follow, 50
    However fashionable, is false and hollow,
    And I despise the frenzied operations
    Of all these barterers of protestations,
    These lavishers of meaningless embraces,
    These utterers of obliging commonplaces,
    Who court and flatter everyone on earth
    And praise the fool no less than the man of worth.
    Should you rejoice that someone fondles you,
    Offers his love and service, swears to be true,
    And fills your ears with praises of your name, 60
    When to the first damned fop he'll say the same?
    No, no: no self-respecting heart would dream
    Of prizing so promiscuous an esteem;
    However high the praise, there's nothing worse
    Than sharing honors with the universe.
    Esteem is founded on comparison:
    To honor all men is to honor none.
    Since you embrace this indiscriminate vice,
    Your friendship comes at far too cheap a price;
    I spurn the easy tribute of a heart 70
    Which will not set the worthy man apart:
    I choose, Sir, to be chosen; and in fine,
    The friend of mankind is no friend of mine.

PHILINTE: But in polite society, custom decrees
    That we show certain outward courtesies. . . .

ALCESTE: Ah, no! We should condemn with all our
        force
    Such false and artificial intercourse.
    Let men behave like men; let them display
    Their inmost hearts in everything they say;
    Let the heart speak, and let our sentiments

388

Not mask themselves in silly compliments.
PHILINTE: In certain cases it would be uncouth
And most absurd to speak the naked truth;
With all respect for your exalted notions,
It's often best to veil one's true emotions.
Wouldn't the social fabric come undone
If we were wholly frank with everyone?
Suppose you met with someone you couldn't bear;
80   Would you inform him of it then and there?
ALCESTE: Yes.
PHILINTE: Then you'd tell old Emilie it's pathetic
The way she daubs her features with cosmetic
And plays the gay coquette at sixty-four?
ALCESTE: I would.
PHILINTE: And you'd call Dorilas a bore,
And tell him every ear at court is lame
From hearing him brag about his noble name?
ALCESTE: Precisely.
90   PHILINTE: Ah, you're joking.
ALCESTE: *Au contraire*°:
In this regard there's none I'd choose to spare.
All are corrupt; there's nothing to be seen
In court or town but aggravates my spleen.°
I fall into deep gloom and melancholy
When I survey the scene of human folly,
Finding on every hand base flattery,
Injustice, fraud, self-interest, treachery. . . .
Ah, it's too much; mankind has grown so base,
100   I mean to break with the whole human race.
PHILINTE: This philosophic rage is a bit extreme;
You've no idea how comical you seem;
Indeed, we're like those brothers in the play
Called *School for Husbands,*° one of whom was
prey . . .
ALCESTE: Enough, now! None of your stupid similes.
PHILINTE: Then let's have no more tirades, if you
please.
The world won't change, whatever you say or do;
110   And since plain speaking means so much to you,
I'll tell you plainly that by being frank
You've earned the reputation of a crank,
And that you're thought ridiculous when you rage
And rant against the manners of the age.
ALCESTE: So much the better; just what I wish to hear.
No news could be more grateful to my ear.
All men are so detestable in my eyes,
I should be sorry if they thought me wise.
PHILINTE: Your hatred's very sweeping, is it not?
120   ALCESTE: Quite right: I hate the whole degraded lot.

Au contraire, "On the contrary."   *spleen,* The traditional seat of anger.   *School for Husbands,* In Molière's
School For Husbands (1661) Sganarelle and Ariste also view
human nature in contrasting ways, one critically, the other
with philosophical indulgence.

PHILINTE: Must all poor human creatures be
embraced,
Without distinction, by your vast distaste?
Even in these bad times, there are surely a few . . .
ALCESTE: No, I include all men in one dim view:
Some men I hate for being rogues; the others
I hate because they treat the rogues like brothers,
And, lacking a virtuous scorn for what is vile,
Receive the villain with a complaisant smile.
Notice how tolerant people choose to be   130
Toward that bold rascal who's at law with me.°
His social polish can't conceal his nature;
One sees at once that he's a treacherous creature;
No one could possibly be taken in
By those soft speeches and that sugary grin.
The whole world knows the shady means by which
The low-brow's grown so powerful and rich,
And risen to a rank so bright and high
That virtue can but blush, and merit sigh.
Whenever his name comes up in conversation,   140
None will defend his wretched reputation;
Call him knave, liar, scoundrel, and all the rest,
Each head will nod, and no one will protest.
And yet his smirk is seen in every house,
He's greeted everywhere with smiles and bows,
And when there's any honor that can be got
By pulling strings, he'll get it, like as not.
My God! It chills my heart to see the ways
Men come to terms with evil nowadays;
Sometimes, I swear, I'm moved to flee and find   150
Some desert land unfouled by humankind.
PHILINTE: Come, let's forget the follies of the times
And pardon mankind for its petty crimes;
Let's have an end of rantings and of railings,
And show some leniency toward human failings.
This world requires a pliant rectitude;
Too stern a virtue makes one stiff and rude;
Good sense views all extremes with detestation,
And bids us to be noble in moderation.
The rigid virtues of the ancient days   160
Are not for us; they jar with all our ways
And ask of us too lofty a perfection.
Wise men accept their times without objection,
And there's no greater folly, if you ask me
Than trying to reform society.
Like you, I see each day a hundred and one
Unhandsome deeds that might be better done,
But still, for all the faults that meet my view,
I'm never known to storm and rave like you.
I take men as they are, or let them be,   170
And teach my soul to bear their frailty;
And whether in court or town, whatever the scene,

---

at law, that is, who has a lawsuit against me.

My phlegm's° as philosophic as your spleen.

ALCESTE: This phlegm which you so eloquently
    commend,
Does nothing ever rile it up, my friend?
Suppose some man you trust should treacherously
Conspire to rob you of your property,
And do his best to wreck your reputation?
Wouldn't you feel a certain indignation?

PHILINTE: Why, no. These faults of which you so
180   complain
Are part of human nature, I maintain,
And it's no more a matter for disgust
That men are knavish, selfish and unjust,
Than that the vulture dines upon the dead,
And wolves are furious, and apes ill-bred.

ALCESTE: Shall I see myself betrayed, robbed, torn to
    bits,
And not . . . Oh, let's be still and rest our wits.
Enough of reasoning, now. I've had my fill.

190 PHILINTE: Indeed, you would do well, Sir, to be still.
Rage less at your opponent, and give some thought
To how you'll win this lawsuit that he's brought.

ALCESTE: I assure you I'll do nothing of the sort.

PHILINTE: Then who will plead your case before the
    court?

ALCESTE: Reason and right and justice will plead for
    me.

PHILINTE: Oh, Lord! What judges do you plan to
    see?°

200 ALCESTE: Why, none. The justice of my cause is clear.

PHILINTE: Of course, man; but there's politics to
    fear. . . .

ALCESTE: No, I refuse to lift a hand. That's flat.
I'm either right, or wrong.

PHILINTE: Don't count on that.

ALCESTE: No, I'll do nothing.

PHILINTE: Your enemy's influence
Is great, you know . . .

ALCESTE: That makes no difference.

210 PHILINTE: It will; you'll see.

ALCESTE: Must honor bow to guile?
If so, I shall be proud to lose the trial.

PHILINTE: Oh, really . . .

ALCESTE: I'll discover by this case
Whether or not men are sufficiently base
And impudent and villainous and perverse
To do me wrong before the universe.

PHILINTE: What a man!

ALCESTE: Oh, I could wish, whatever the cost,
220   Just for the beauty of it, that my trial were lost.

PHILINTE: If people heard you talking so, Alceste,

---

phlegm's, one of the four humours, or basic fluids,
thought to determine temperament. An excess of phlegm
made one slow, lazy, and complacent. judges . . . see, the
common practice of the time was to solicit the favor of
judges and make them gifts.

They'd split their sides. Your name would be a jest.

ALCESTE: So much the worse for jesters.

PHILINTE: May I enquire
Whether this rectitude you so admire,
And these hard virtues you're enamored of
Are qualities of the lady whom you love?
It much surprises me that you, who seem
To view mankind with furious disesteem,
Have yet found something to enchant your eyes   230
Amidst a species which you so despise.
And what is more amazing, I'm afraid,
Is the most curious choice your heart has made.
The honest Eliante is fond of you,
Arsinoé, the prude, admires you too;
And yet your spirit's been perversely led
To choose the flighty Célimène instead,
Whose brittle malice and coquettish ways
So typify the manners of our days.
How is it that the traits you most abhor   240
Are bearable in this lady you adore?
Are you so blind with love that you can't find them?
Or do you contrive, in her case, not to mind them?

ALCESTE: My love for that young widow's not the kind
That can't perceive defects; no, I'm not blind.
I see her faults, despite my ardent love,
And all I see I fervently reprove.
And yet I'm weak; for all her falsity,
That woman knows the art of pleasing me,
And though I never cease complaining of her,   250
I swear I cannot manage not to love her.
Her charm outweighs her faults; I can but aim
To cleanse her spirit in my love's pure flame.

PHILINTE: That's no small task; I wish you all success.
You think then that she loves you?

ALCESTE: Heavens, yes!
I wouldn't love her did she not love me.

PHILINTE: Well, if her taste for you is plain to see,
Why do these rivals cause you such despair?

ALCESTE: True love, Sir, is possessive, and cannot   260
    bear
To share with all the world. I'm here today
To tell her she must send that mob away.

PHILINTE: If I were you, and had your choice to
    make,
Eliante, her cousin, would be the one I'd take;
That honest heart, which cares for you alone,
Would harmonize far better with your own.

ALCESTE: True, true: each day my reason tells me so;
But reason doesn't rule in love, you know.   270

PHILINTE: I fear some bitter sorrow is in store;
This love . . .

(Enter ORONTE.)

ORONTE (to ALCESTE): The servants told me at the
    door
That Eliante and Célimène were out,
But when I heard, dear Sir, that you were about,
I came to say, without exaggeration,

That I hold you in the vastest admiration,
And that it's always been my dearest desire
280 To be the friend of one I so admire.
I hope to see my love of merit requited,
And you and I in friendship's bond united.
I'm sure you won't refuse—if I may be frank—
A friend of my devotedness—and rank. (*During this
speech of Oronte's,* ALCESTE *is abstracted, and seems
unaware that he is being spoken to. He only breaks off
his reverie when* ORONTE *says:*)
It was for you, if you please, that my words were
intended
ALCESTE: For me, Sir?
ORONTE: Yes, for you. You're not offended?
ALCESTE: By no means. But this much surprises
290 me. . . .
The honor comes most unexpectedly. . . .
ORONTE: My high regard should not astonish you;
The whole world feels the same. It is your due.
ALCESTE: Sir . . .
ORONTE: Why, in all the State there isn't one
Can match your merits; they shine, Sir, like the
sun.
ALCESTE: Sir . . .
ORONTE: You are higher in my estimation
300 Than all that's most illustrious in the nation.
ALCESTE: Sir . . .
ORONTE: If I lie, may heaven strike me dead!
To show you that I mean what I have said,
Permit me, Sir, to embrace you most sincerely,
And swear that I will prize our friendship dearly.
Give me your hand. And now, Sir, if you choose,
We'll make our vows,
ALCESTE: Sir . . .
ORONTE: What! You refuse?
310 ALCESTE: Sir, it's a very great honor you extend:
But friendship is a sacred thing, my friend;
It would be profanation to bestow
The name of friend on one you hardly know.
All parts are better played when well-rehearsed;
Let's put off friendship, and get acquainted first.
We may discover it would be unwise
To try to make our natures harmonize.
ORONTE: By heaven! You're sagacious to the core;
This speech has made me admire you even more.
320 Let time, then, bring us closer day by day;
Meanwhile, I shall be yours in every way.
If, for example, there should be anything
You wish at court, I'll mention it to the King.
I have his ear, of course; it's quite well known
That I am much in favor with the throne.
In short, I am your servant. And now, dear friend,
Since you have such fine judgment, I intend
To please you, if I can, with a small sonnet°
I wrote not long ago. Please comment on it,

_____

sonnet, during this period the term "sonnet" applied to
any lyric poem.

And tell me whether I ought to publish it.   330
ALCESTE: You must excuse me, Sir; I'm hardly fit
To judge such matters.
ORONTE: Why not?
ALCESTE: I am, I fear,
Inclined to be unfashionably sincere.
ORONTE: Just what I ask; I'd take no satisfaction
In anything but your sincere reaction.
I beg you not to dream of being kind.
ALCESTE: Since you desire it, Sir, I'll speak my mind.
ORONTE: *Sonnet*. It's a sonnet. . . . "Hope" . . . The   340
poem's addressed
To a lady who wakened hopes within my breast.
"Hope" . . . this is not the pompous sort of thing,
Just modest little verses, with a tender ring.
ALCESTE: Well, we shall see.
ORONTE: "Hope" . . . I'm anxious to hear
Whether the style seems properly smooth and
clear,
And whether the choice of words is good or bad.
ALCESTE: We'll see, we'll see.   350
ORONTE: Perhaps I ought to add
That it took me only a quarter-hour to write it.
ALCESTE: The time's irrelevant, Sir; kindly recite it.
ORONTE *(reading)*: "Hope comforts us awhile, t'is true,
Lulling our cares with careless laughter,
And yet such joy is full of rue,
My Phyllis, if nothing follows after."
PHILINTE: I'm charmed by this already; the style's
delightful.
ALCESTE *(sotto voce, to* PHILINTE*)*: How can you say   360
that? Why, the thing is frightful.
ORONTE: "Your fair face smiled on me awhile,
But was it kindness so to enchant me?
'Twould have been fairer not to smile,
If hope was all you meant to grant me."
PHILINTE: What a clever thought! How handsomely
you phrase it!
ALCESTE *(sotto voce to* PHILINTE*)*: You know the thing is
trash. How dare you praise it?
ORONTE: "If it's to be my passion's fate   370
Thus everlastingly to wait,
Then death will come to set me free:
For death is fairer than the fair;
Phyllis, to hope is to despair
When one must hope eternally."
PHILINTE: The close is exquisite—full of feeling and
grace.
ALCESTE *(sotto voce, aside)*: Oh, blast the close; you'd
better close your face
Before you send your lying soul to hell.   380
PHILINTE: I can't remember a poem I've liked so well.
ALCESTE *(sotto voce, aside)*: Good Lord!
ORONTE *(to* PHILINTE*)*: I fear you're flattering me a
bit.
PHILINTE: Oh, no!
ALCESTE *(sotto voce, aside)*: What else d'you call it, you
hypocrite?

ORONTE (*to* ALCESTE): But you, Sir, keep your promise
 now: don't shrink
390 From telling me sincerely what you think.
ALCESTE: Sir, these are delicate matters; we all desire
 To be told that we've the true poetic fire.
 But once, to one whose name I shall not mention,
 I said, regarding some verse of his invention,
 That gentlemen should rigorously control
 That itch to write which often afflicts the soul;
 That one should curb the heady inclination
 To publicize one's little avocation;
 And that in showing off one's works of art
400 One often plays a very clownish part.
ORONTE: Are you suggesting in a devious way
 That I ought not . . .
ALCESTE: Oh, that I do not say.
 Further, I told him that no fault is worse
 Than that of writing frigid, lifeless verse,
 And that the merest whisper of such a shame
 Suffices to destroy a man's good name.
ORONTE: D'you mean to say my sonnet's dull and
 trite?
410 ALCESTE: I don't say that. But I went on to cite
 Numerous cases of once-respected men
 Who came to grief by taking up the pen.
ORONTE: And am I like them? Do I write so poorly?
ALCESTE: I don't say that. But I told this person,
 "Surely
 You're under no necessity to compose;
 Why you should wish to publish, heaven knows.
 There's no excuse for printing tedious rot
 Unless one writes for bread, as you do not.
420 Resist temptation, then, I beg of you;
 Conceal your pastimes from the public view;
 And don't give up, on any provocation,
 Your present high and courtly reputation,
 To purchase at a greedy printer's shop
 The name of silly author and scribbling fop."
 These were the points I tried to make him see.
ORONTE: I sense that they are also aimed at me;
 But now—about my sonnet—I'd like to be told . . .
ALCESTE: Frankly, that sonnet should be
430 pigeonholed.
 You've chosen the worst models to imitate.
 The style's unnatural. Let me illustrate:

 For example, "Your fair face smiled on me awhile,"
 Followed by, " 'Twould have been fairer not to
   smile!"
 Or this: "such joy is full of rue;"
 Or this: "For death is fairer than the fair;"
 Or, "Phyllis, to hope is to despair
  When one must hope eternally!"

440 This artificial style, that's all the fashion,
 Has neither taste, nor honesty, nor passion;
 It's nothing but a sort of wordy play,

And nature never spoke in such a way.
What, in this shallow age, is not debased?
Our fathers, though less refined, had better taste;
I'd barter all that men admire today
For one old love-song I shall try to say:

"If the King had given me for my own
Paris, his citadel,
And I for that must leave alone   450
Her whom I love so well,
I'd say the to the Crown,
Take back your glittering town;
My darling is more fair, I swear,
My darling is more fair."

The rhyme's not rich, the style is rough and old,
But don't you see that it's the purest gold
Beside the tinsel nonsense now preferred,
And that there's passion in its every word?

"If the King had given me for my own   460
Paris, his citadel,
And I for that must leave alone
Her whom I love so well,
I'd say then to the Crown,
Take back your glittering town;
My darling is more fair, I swear,
My darling is more fair."

There speaks a loving heart. (*to* PHILINTE) You're
 laughing, eh?
Laugh on, my precious wit. Whatever you say, 470
I hold that song's worth all the bibelots°
That people hail today with "ah's" and "oh's."
ORONTE: And I maintain my sonnet's very good.
ALCESTE: It's not at all surprising that you should.
 You have your reasons; permit me to have mine
 For thinking that you cannot write a line.
ORONTE: Others have praised my sonnet to the skies.
ALCESTE: I lack their art of telling pleasant lies.
ORONTE: You seem to think you've got no end of wit.
ALCESTE: To praise your verse, I'd need still more of 480
 it.
ORONTE: I'm not in need of your approval, Sir.
ALCESTE: That's good; you couldn't have it if you
 were.
ORONTE: Come now, I'll lend you the subject of my
 sonnet;
 I'd like to see you try to improve upon it.
ALCESTE: I might, by chance, write something just as
 shoddy;
 But then I wouldn't show it to everybody. 490
ORONTE: You're most opinionated and conceited.

---

bibelots, trinkets.

ALCESTE: Go find your flatterers, and be better
    treated.

ORONTE: Look here, my little fellow, pray watch your
    tone.

ALCESTE: My great big fellow, you'd better watch
    your own.

PHILINTE (stepping between them): Oh, please, please,
    gentlemen! This will never do.

500 ORONTE: The fault is mine, and I leave the field to
    you.
    I am your servant, Sir, in every way.

ALCESTE: And I, Sir, am your most abject valet. (Exit
    ORONTE.)

PHILINTE: Well, as you see, sincerity in excess
    Can get you into a very pretty mess;
    Oronte was hungry for appreciation. . . .

ALCESTE: Don't speak to me.

PHILINTE: What?

ALCESTE: No more conversation.

510 PHILINTE: Really, now . . .

ALCESTE: Leave me alone.

PHILINTE: If I . . .

ALCESTE: Out of my sight!

PHILINTE: But what . . .

ALCESTE: I won't listen.

PHILINTE: But . . .

ALCESTE: Silence!

PHILINTE: Now, is it polite . . .

ALCESTE: By heaven, I've had enough. Don't follow
520   me.

PHILINTE: Ah, you're just joking. I'll keep you
    company (They go out.)

ACT 2

(Enter ALCESTE and CÉLIMÈNE.)

ALCESTE: Shall I speak plainly, Madam? I confess
    Your conduct gives me infinite distress,
    And my resentment's grown too hot to smother.
    Soon, I foresee, we'll break with one another.
    If I said otherwise, I should deceive you;
    Sooner or later, I shall be forced to leave you,
    And if I swore that we shall never part,
    I should misread the omens of my heart.

CELIMENE: You kindly saw me home, it would appear,
10   So as to pour invectives in my ear.

ALCESTE: I've no desire to quarrel. But I deplore
    Your inability to shut the door
    On all these suitors who beset you so.
    There's what annoys me, if you care to know.

CELIMENE: Is it my fault that all these men pursue
    me?
    Am I to blame if they're attracted to me?
    And when they gently beg an audience,
    Ought I to take a stick and drive them hence?

20 ALCESTE: Madam, there's no necessity for a stick;
    A less responsive heart would do the trick.

Of your attractiveness I don't complain;
But those your charms attract, you then detain
By a most melting and receptive manner,
And so enlist their hearts beneath your banner.
It's the agreeable hopes which you excite
That keep these lovers round you day and night;
Were they less liberally smiled upon,
That sighing troop would very soon be gone.
But tell me, Madam, why it is that lately   30
This man Clitandre interests you so greatly?
Because of what high merits do you deem
Him worthy of the honor of your esteem?
Is it that your admitting glances linger
On the splendidly long nail of his little finger?
Or do you share the general deep respect
For the blond wig he chooses to affect?
Are you in love with his embroidered hose?
Do you adore his ribbons and his bows?
Or is it that this paragon bewitches   40
Your tasteful eye with his vast German breeches?°
Perhaps his giggle, or his falsetto voice,
Makes him the latest gallant of your choice?

CELIMENE: You're much mistaken to resent him so.
    Why I put up with him you surely know:
    My lawsuit's very shortly to be tried,
    And I must have his influence on my side.

ALCESTE: Then lose your lawsuit, Madam, or let it
    drop.
    Don't torture me by humoring such a fop.   50

CELIMENE: You're jealous of the whole world, Sir.

ALCESTE: That's true,
    Since the whole world is well-received by you.

CELIMENE: That my good nature is so unconfined
    Should serve to pacify your jealous mind;
    Were I to smile on one, and scorn the rest,
    Then you might have some cause to be distressed.

ALCESTE: Well, if I mustn't be jealous, tell me, then,
    Just how I'm better treated than other men.

CELIMENE: You know you have my love. Will that not   60
    do?

ALCESTE: What proof have I that what you say is true?

CELIMENE: I would expect, Sir, that my having said it
    Might give the statement a sufficient credit.

ALCESTE: But how can I be sure that you don't tell
    The selfsame thing to other men as well?

CELIMENE: What a gallant speech! How flattering to
    me!
    What a sweet creature you make me out to be!
    Well then, to save you from the pangs of doubt,   70
    All that I've said I hereby cancel out;
    Now, none but yourself shall make a monkey of
    you:
    Are you content?

---

breeches, fashionable wide breeches called *rhingraves,* after
the Rhingrave Frederick, Governor of Maestricht.

ALCESTE: Why, why am I doomed to love you?
I swear that I shall bless the blissful hour
When this poor heart's no longer in your power!
I make no secret of it: I've done my best
To exorcise this passion from my breast;
80 But thus far all in vain; it will not go;
It's for my sins that I must love you so.
CELIMENE: Your love for me is matchless, Sir; that's
clear.
ALCESTE: Indeed, in all the world it has no peer;
Words can't describe the nature of my passion,
And no man ever loved in such a fashion.
CELIMENE: Yes, it's a brand-new fashion, I agree:
You show your love by castigating me,
And all your speeches are enraged and rude.
90 I've never been so furiously wooed.
ALCESTE: Yet you could calm that fury, if you chose.
Come, shall we bring our quarrels to a close?
Let's speak with open hearts, then, and begin . . .

(*Enter* BASQUE.)

CELIMENE: What is it?
BASQUE: Acaste is here.
CELIMENE: Well, send him in. (*Exit* BASQUE.)
ALCESTE: What! Shall we never be alone at all?
You're always ready to receive a call,
And you can't bear, for ten ticks of the clock,
100 Not to keep open house for all who knock.
CELIMENE: I couldn't refuse him: he'd be most put
out.
ALCESTE: Surely that's not worth worrying about.
CELIMENE: Acaste would never forgive me if he
guessed
That I consider him a dreadful pest.
ALCESTE: If he's a pest, why bother with him then?
CELIMENE: Heavens! One can't antagonize such men;
Why, they're the chartered gossips of the court,
110 And have a say in things of every sort.
One must receive them, and be full of charm;
They're no great help, but they can do you harm,
And though your influence be ever so great,
They're hardly the best people to alienate.
ALCESTE: I see, dear lady, that you could make a case
For putting up with the whole human race;
These friendships that you calculate so nicely . . .

(BASQUE *re-enters.*)

BASQUE: Madam, Clitandre is here as well.
ALCESTE: Precisely.
120 CELIMENE: Where are you going?
ALCESTE: Elsewhere.
CELIMENE: Stay.
ALCESTE: No, no.
CELIMENE: Stay, Sir.
ALCESTE: I can't.
CELIMENE: I wish it.
ALCESTE: No, I must go.

I beg you, Madam, not to press the matter;
You know I have no taste for idle chatter.
CELIMENE: Stay: I command you. 130
ALCESTE: No, I cannot stay.
CELIMENE: Very well; you have my leave to go away.

(*Enter* ELIANTE, PHILINTE, ACASTE, *and* CLITANDRE.)

ELIANTE (*to* CÉLIMÈNE): The Marquesses have kindly
come to call.
Were they announced?
CELIMENE: Yes. Basque, bring chairs for all.

(BASQUE *provides the chairs and exits.*)

(*to* ALCESTE): You haven't gone?
ALCESTE: No; and I shan't depart
Till you decide who's foremost in your heart.
CELIMENE: Oh, hush. 140
ALCESTE: It's time to choose; take them, or me.
CELIMENE: You're mad.
ALCESTE: I'm not, as you shall shortly see.
CELIMENE: Oh?
ALCESTE: You'll decide.
CELIMENE: You're joking now, dear friend.
ALCESTE: No, no; you'll choose; my patience is at an
end.
CLITANDRE: Madam, I come from court, where poor
Cléonte 150
Behaved like a perfect fool, as is his wont.
Has he no friend to counsel him, I wonder,
And teach him less unerringly to blunder?
CELIMENE: It's true, the man's a most accomplished
dunce;
His gauche behavior charms the eye at once;
And every time one sees him, on my word,
His manner's grown a trifle more absurd.
ACASTE: Speaking of dunces, I've just now conversed
With old Damon, who's one of the very worst; 160
I stood a lifetime in the broiling sun
Before his dreary monologue was done.
CELIMENE: Oh, he's a wondrous talker, and has the
power
To tell you nothing hour after hour:
If, by mistake, he ever came to the point,
The shock would put his jawbone out of joint.
ELIANTE (*to* PHILINTE): The conversation takes its
usual turn,
And all our dear friends' ears will shortly burn. 170
CLITANDRE: Timante's a character, Madam.
CELIMENE: Isn't he, though?
A man of mystery from top to toe,
Who moves about in a romantic mist
On secret missions which do not exist.
His talk is full of eyebrows and grimaces;
How tired one gets of his momentous faces;
He's always whispering something confidential
Which turns out to be quite inconsequential;
Nothing's too slight for him to mystify;

He even whispers when he says "good-by."
ACASTE: Tell us about Géralde.
CELIMENE: That tiresome ass.
　He mixes only with the titled class,
　And fawns on dukes and princes, and is bored
　With anyone who's not at least a lord.
　The man's obsessed with rank, and his discourses
　Are all of hounds and carriages and horses;
　He uses Christian names with all the great,
180　And the word "Milord," with him, is out of date.
CLITANDRE: He's very taken with Bélise, I hear.
CELIMENE: She is the dreariest company, poor dear.
　Whenever she comes to call, I grope about
　To find some topic which will draw her out,
　But, owing to her dry and faint replies,
　The conversation wilts, and droops, and dies.
　In vain one hopes to animate her face
　By mentioning the ultimate commonplace;
　But sun or shower, even hail or frost
190　Are matters she can instantly exhaust.
　Meanwhile her visit, painful though it is,
　Drags on and on through mute eternities,
　And though you ask the time, and yawn, and yawn,
　She sits there like a stone and won't be gone.
ACASTE: Now for Adraste.
CELIMENE: Oh, that conceited elf
　Has a gigantic passion for himself;
　He rails against the court, and cannot bear it
　That none will recognize his hidden merit;
200　All honors given to others give offense
　To his imaginary excellence.
CLITANDRE: What about young Cléon? His house,
　　they say,
　Is full of the best society, night and day.
CELIMENE: His cook has made him popular, not he:
　It's Cléon's table that people come to see.
ELIANTE: He gives a splendid dinner, you must
　　admit.
CELIMENE: But must he serve himself along with it?
210　For my taste, he's a most insipid dish
　Whose presence sours the wine and spoils the fish.
PHILINTE: Damis, his uncle, is admired no end.
　What's your opinion, Madam?
CELIMENE: Why, he's my friend.
PHILINTE: He seems a decent fellow, and rather
　　clever.
CELIMENE: He works too hard at cleverness, however.
　I hate to see him sweat and struggle so
　To fill his conversation with bons mots.°
220　Since he's decided to become a wit
　His taste's so pure that nothing pleases it;
　He scolds at all the latest books and plays,
　Thinking that wit must never stoop to praise,
　That finding fault's a sign of intellect,

That all appreciation is abject,
　And that by damning everything in sight
　One shows oneself in a distinguished light.
　He's scornful even of our conversations:
　Their trivial nature sorely tries his patience;
　He folds his arms, and stands above the battle,　230
　And listens sadly to our childish prattle.
ACASTE: Wonderful, Madam! You've hit him off
　　precisely.
CLITANDRE: No one can sketch a character so nicely.
ALCESTE: How bravely, Sirs, you cut and thrust at all
　These absent fools, till one by one they fall:
　But let one come in sight, and you'll at once
　Embrace the man you lately called a dunce,
　Telling him in a tone sincere and fervent
　How proud you are to be his humble servant.　240
CLITANDRE: Why pick on us? Madame's been
　　speaking, Sir,
　And you should quarrel, if you must, with her.
ALCESTE: No, no, by God, the fault is yours, because
　You lead her on with laughter and applause,
　And make her think that she's the more delightful
　The more her talk is scandalous and spiteful.
　Oh, she would stoop to malice far, far less
　If no such claque° approved her cleverness.
　It's flatterers like you whose foolish praise　250
　Nourishes all the vices of these days.
PHILINTE: But why protest when someone ridicules
　Those you'd condemn, yourself, as knaves or fools?
CELIMENE: Why, Sir? Because he loves to make a fuss.
　You don't expect him to agree with us,
　When there's an opportunity to express
　His heaven-sent spirit of contrariness?
　What other people think, he can't abide;
　Whatever they say, he's on the other side;
　He lives in deadly terror of agreeing;　260
　'Twould make him seem an ordinary being.
　Indeed, he's so in love with contradiction,
　He'll turn against his most profound conviction
　And with a furious eloquence deplore it,
　If only someone else is speaking for it.
ALCESTE: Go on, dear lady, mock me as you please;
　You have your audience in ecstasies.
PHILINTE: But what she says is true: you have a way
　Of bridling at whatever people say;
　Whether they praise or blame, your angry spirit　270
　Is equally unsatisfied to hear it.
ALCESTE: Men, Sir, are always wrong, and that's the
　　reason
　That righteous anger's never out of season;
　All that I hear in all their conversation
　Is flattering praise or reckless condemnation.
CELIMENE: But . . .
ALCESTE: No, no, Madam, I am forced to state

---

bons mots, witty sayings.

claque, band of followers.

That you have pleasures which I deprecate,
280 And that these others, here, are much to blame
For nourishing the faults which are your shame.
CLITANDRE: I shan't defend myself, Sir; but I vow
I'd thought this lady faultless until now.
ACASTE: I see her charms and graces, which are
    many;
But as for faults, I've never noticed any.
ALCESTE: I see them, Sir; and rather than ignore
    them,
I strenuously criticize her for them.
290 The more one loves, the more one should object
To every blemish, every least defect.
Were I this lady, I would soon get rid
Of lovers who approved of all I did,
And by their slack indulgence and applause
Endorsed my follies and excused my flaws.
CELIMENE: If all hearts beat according to your
    measure,
The dawn of love would be the end of pleasure;
And love would find its perfect consummation
300 In ecstasies of rage and reprobation.
ELIANTE: Love, as a rule, affects men otherwise,
And lovers rarely love to criticize.
They see their lady as a charming blur,
And find all things commendable in her.
If she has any blemish, fault, or shame,
They will redeem it by a pleasing name.
The pale-faced lady's lily-white, perforce;
The swarthy one's a sweet brunette, of course;
The spindly lady has a slender grace;
310 The fat one has a most majestic pace;
The plain one, with her dress in disarray,
They classify as *beauté négligée,*°
The hulking one's a goddess in their eyes,
The dwarf, a concentrate of Paradise;
The haughty lady has a noble mind;
The mean one's witty, and the dull one's kind;
The chatterbox has liveliness and verve,
The mute one has a virtuous reserve.
So lovers manage, in their passion's cause,
320 To love their ladies even for their flaws.
ALCESTE: But I still say . . .
CELIMENE: I think it would be nice
To stroll around the gallery once or twice.
What! You're not going, Sirs?
CLITANDRE *and* ACASTE: No, Madam, no.
ALCESTE: You seem to be in terror lest they go.
Do what you will, Sirs; leave, or linger on,
But I shan't go till after you are gone.
ACASTE: I'm free to linger, unless I should perceive
330 Madame is tired, and wishes me to leave.
CLITANDRE: And as for me, I needn't go today
Until the hour of the King's *coucher.*°

CELIMENE (*to* ALCESTE): You're joking, surely?
ALCESTE: Not in the least; we'll see
Whether you'd rather part with them, or me.

(*Enter* BASQUE.)

BASQUE (*to* ALCESTE): Sir, there's a fellow here who
    bids me state
That he must see you, and that it can't wait.
ALCESTE: Tell him that I have no such pressing
    affairs.   340
BASQUE: It's a long tailcoat that this fellow wears,
With gold all over.
CELIMENE (*to* ALCESTE): You'd best go down and see.
Or—have him enter.

(ALCESTE *indicates to* BASQUE *to show the visitor in. Exit*
BASQUE.)
(*Enter a* GUARD *of the Marshalsea.*°)

ALCESTE (*confronting the* GUARD): Well, what do you
    want with me?
Come in, Sir.
GUARD: I've a word, Sir, for your ear.
ALCESTE: Speak it aloud, Sir; I shall strive to hear.
GUARD: The Marshals have instructed me to say   350
You must report to them without delay.
ALCESTE: Who? Me, Sir?
GUARD: Yes, Sir; you.
ALCESTE: But what do they want?
PHILINTE (*to* ALCESTE): To scotch your silly quarrel
    with Oronte.
CELIMENE (*to* PHILINTE): What quarrel?
PHILINTE: Oronte and he have fallen out
Over some verse he spoke his mind about;
The Marshals wish to arbitrate the matter.   360
ALCESTE: Never shall I equivocate or flatter!
PHILINTE: You'd best obey their summons; come, let's
    go.
ALCESTE: How can they mend our quarrel, I'd like to
    know?
Am I to make a cowardly retraction,
And praise those jingles to his satisfaction?
I'll not recant; I've judged that sonnet rightly.
It's bad.
PHILINTE: But you might say so more politely. . . .   370
ALCESTE: I'll not back down; his verses make me sick.
PHILINTE: If only you could be more politic!
But come, let's go.
ALCESTE: I'll go, but I won't unsay
A single word.
PHILINTE: Well, let's be on our way.
ALCESTE: Till I am ordered by my lord the King
To praise that poem, I shall say the thing
Is scandalous, by God, and that the poet

---

beauté négligée, "careless beauty."   *coucher,* an evening
reception held in the King's bedchamber.

Marshalsea, The Marshalsea Tribunal handled quarrels among members of the nobility.

380   Ought to be hanged for having the nerve to show
      it. *(to* CLITANDRE *and* ACASTE, *who are laughing)*
    By heaven, Sirs, I really didn't know
    That I was being humorous.
CELIMENE: Go, Sir, go;
    Settle your business.
ALCESTE: I shall, and when I'm through,
    I shall return to settle things with you.

    (Exit ALCESTE *with the* GUARD. *The others withdraw.)*

ACT 3

(Enter CLITANDRE *and* ACASTE.)

CLITANDRE: Dear Marquess, how contented you
     appear;
    All things delight you, nothing mars your cheer.
    Can you, in perfect honesty, declare
    That you've a right to be so debonair?
ACASTE: By Jove, when I survey myself, I find
    No cause whatever for distress of mind.
    I'm young and rich; I can in modesty
    Lay claim to an exalted pedigree;
10   And owing to my name and my condition
    I shall not want for honors and position.
    Then as to courage, that most precious trait,
    I seem to have it, as was proved of late
    Upon the field of honor, where my bearing,
    They say, was very cool and rather daring.
    I've wit, of course; and taste in such perfection
    That I can judge without the least reflection,
    And at the theater, which is my delight,
    Can make or break a play on opening night,
20   And lead the crowd in hisses or bravos,
    And generally be known as one who knows.
    I'm clever, handsome, gracefully polite;
    My waist is small, my teeth are strong and white;
    As for my dress, the world's astonished eyes
    Assure me that I bear away the prize.
    I find myself in favor everywhere,
    Honored by men, and worshipped by the fair;
    And since these things are so, it seems to me
    I'm justified in my complacency.
30 CLITANDRE: Well, if so many ladies hold you dear,
    Why do you press a hopeless courtship here?
ACASTE: Hopeless, you say? I'm not the sort of fool
    That likes his ladies difficult and cool.
    Men who are awkward, shy, and peasantish
    May pine for heartless beauties, if they wish,
    Grovel before them, bear their cruelties,
    Woo them with tears and sighs and bended knees,
    And hope by dogged faithfulness to gain
    What their poor merits never could obtain.
40   For men like me, however, it makes no sense
    To love on trust, and foot the whole expense.
    Whatever any lady's merits be,
    I think, thank God, that I'm as choice as she;
    That if my heart is kind enough to burn

    For her, she owes me something in return;
    And that in any proper love affair
    The partners must invest an equal share.
CLITANDRE: You think, then, that our hostess favors
     you?
ACASTE: I've reason to believe that that is true.   50
CLITANDRE: How did you come to such a mad
     conclusion?
    You're blind, dear fellow. This is sheer delusion.
ACASTE: All right, then: I'm deluded and I'm blind.
CLITANDRE: Whatever put the notion in your mind?
ACASTE: Delusion.
CLITANDRE: What persuades you that you're right?
ACASTE: I'm blind.
CLITANDRE: But have you any proofs to cite?
ACASTE: I tell you I'm deluded.   60
CLITANDRE: Have you, then,
    Received some secret pledge from Célimène?
ACASTE: Oh, no; she scorns me.
CLITANDRE: Tell me the truth, I beg.
ACASTE: She just can't bear me.
CLITANDRE: Ah, don't pull my leg.
    Tell me what hope she's given you, I pray.
ACASTE: I'm hopeless, and it's you who win the day.
    She hates me thoroughly, and I'm so vexed
    I mean to hang myself on Tuesday next.   70
CLITANDRE: Dear Marquess, let us have an armistice
    And make a treaty. What do you say to this?
    If ever one of us can plainly prove
    That Célimène encourages his love,
    The other must abandon hope, and yield,
    And leave him in possession of the field.
ACASTE: Now, there's a bargain that appeals to me;
    With all my heart, dear Marquess, I agree.
    But hush.

    (Enter CÉLIMÈNE.)

CELIMENE: Still here?   80
CLITANDRE: T'was love that stayed our feet.
CELIMENE: I think I heard a carriage in the street.
    Whose is it? D'you know?

    (Enter BASQUE.)

BASQUE: Madame. Arsinoé is here.
CELIMENTE: Arsinoé, you say? Oh, dear.
BASQUE: Eliante is entertaining her below. *(Exit.)*
CELIMENE: What brings the creature here, I'd like to
     know?
ACASTE: They say she's dreadfully prudish, but in
     fact   90
    I think her piety . . .
CELIMENE: It's all an act.
    At heart she's worldly, and her poor success
    In snaring men explains her prudishness.
    It breaks her heart to see the beaux and gallants
    Engrossed by other women's charms and talents,
    And so she's always in a jealous rage

Against the faulty standards of the age.
She lets the world believe that she's a prude
100   To justify her loveless solitude,
And strives to put a band of moral shame
On all the graces that she cannot claim.
But still she'd love a lover; and Alceste
Appears to be the one she'd love the best.
His visits here are poison to her pride;
She seems to think I've lured him from her side;
And everywhere, at court or in the town,
The spiteful, envious woman runs me down.
In short, she's just as stupid as can be,
110   Vicious and arrogant in the last degree,
And . . .

(Enter ARSINOÉ.)

Ah! What happy chance has brought you here?
I've thought about you ever so much, my dear.
ARSINOE: I've come to tell you something you should
    know.
CELIMENE: How good of you to think of doing so!

*(*CLITANDRE *and* ACASTE *go out, laughing.)*

ARSINOE: It's just as well those gentlemen didn't tarry.
CELIMENE: Shall we sit down?
ARSINOE: That won't be necessary.
120   Madam, the flame of friendship ought to burn
Brightest in matters of the most concern,
And as there's nothing which concerns us more
Than honor, I have hastened to your door
To bring you, as your friend, some information
About the status of your reputation.
I visited, last night, some virtuous folk,
And, quite by chance, it was of you they spoke;
There was I fear no tendency to praise
Your light behavior and your dashing ways.
130   The quantity of gentlemen you see
And your by now notorious coquetry
Were both so vehemently criticized
By everyone, that I was much surprised.
Of course, I needn't tell you where I stood;
I came to your defense as best I could,
Assured them you were harmless, and declared
Your soul was absolutely unimpaired.
But there are some things, you must realize,
One can't excuse, however hard one tries,
140   And I was forced at least into conceding
That your behavior, Madam, is misleading,
That it makes a bad impression, giving rise
To ugly gossip and obscene surmise,
And that if you were more *overtly* good,
You wouldn't be so much misunderstood.
Not that I think you've been unchaste.—No! No!
The saints preserve me from a thought so low!
But mere good conscience never did suffice;
One must avoid the outward show of vice.
150   Madam, you're too intelligent, I'm sure,
To think my motives anything but pure

In offering you this counsel—which I do
Out of a zealous interest in you.
CELIMENE: Madam, I haven't taken you amiss;
I'm very much obliged to you for this;
And I'll at once discharge the obligation
By telling you about *your* reputation.
You've been so friendly as to let me know
What certain people say of me, and so
I mean to follow your benign example   160
By offering you a somewhat similar sample.
The other day, I went to an affair
And found some most distinguished people there
Discussing piety, both false and true.
The conversation soon came round to you.
Alas! Your prudery and bustling zeal
Appeared to have a very slight appeal.
Your affectation of a grave demeanor,
Your endless talk of virtue and of honor,
The aptitude of your suspicious mind   170
For finding sin where there is none to find,
Your towering self-esteem, that pitying face
With which you contemplate the human race,
Your sermonizings and your sharp aspersions
On people's pure and innocent diversions—
All these were mentioned, Madam, and, in fact,
Were roundly and concertedly attacked.
"What good," they said, "are all those outward
    shows,
When everything belies her pious pose?   180
She prays incessantly; but then, they say,
She beats her maids and cheats them of their pay;
She shows her zeal in every holy place,
But still she's vain enough to paint her face;
She holds that naked statues are immoral,
But with a naked *man* she'd have no quarrel."
Of course, I said to everybody there
That they were being viciously unfair;
But still they were disposed to criticize you,
And all agreed that someone should advise you   190
To leave the morals of the world alone,
And worry rather more about your own.
They felt that one's self-knowledge should be great
Before one thinks of setting others straight;
That one should learn the art of living well
Before one threatens other men with hell.
And that the Church is best equipped, no doubt,
To guide our souls and root our vices out.
Madam, you're too intelligent, I'm sure,
To think my motives anything but pure   200
In offering you this counsel—which I do
Out of a zealous interest in you.
ARSINOE: I dared not hope for gratitude, but I
Did not expect so acid a reply;
I judge, since you've been so extremely tart,
That my good counsel pierced you to the heart.
CELIMENE: Far from it, Madam. Indeed, it seems to
    me
We ought to trade advice more frequently.

210   One's vision of oneself is so defective
    That it would be an excellent corrective.
    If you are willing, Madam, let's arrange
    Shortly to have another frank exchange
    In which we'll teach each other, *entre nous,*°
    What you've heard tell of me, and I of you.
ARSINOE: Oh, people never censure you, my dear;
    It's me they criticize. Or so I hear.
CELIMENE: Madam, I think we either blame or praise
    According to our taste and length of days.
220   There is a time of life for coquetry,
    And there's a season, too, for prudery.
    When all one's charms are gone, it is, I'm sure,
    Good strategy to be devout and pure:
    It makes one seem a little less forsaken.
    Some day, perhaps, I'll take the road you've taken:
    Time brings all things. But I have time aplenty,
    And see no cause to be a prude at twenty.
ARSINOE: You give your age in such a gloating tone
    That one would think I was an ancient crone;
230   We're not so far apart, in sober truth,
    That you can mock me with a boast of youth!
    Madam, you baffle me. I wish I knew
    What moves you to provoke me as you do.
CELIMENE: For my part, Madam, I should like to
    know
    Why you abuse me everywhere you go.
    Is it my fault, dear lady, that your hand
    Is not, alas, in very great demand?
    If men admire me, if they pay me court
240   And daily make me offers of the sort
    You'd dearly love to have them make to you,
    How can I help it? What would you have me do?
    If what you want is lovers, please feel free
    To take as many as you can from me.
ARSINOE: Oh, come. D'you think the world is losing
    sleep
    Over that flock of lovers which you keep,
    Or that we find it difficult to guess
    What price you pay for their devotedness?
250   Surely you don't expect us to suppose
    Mere merit could attract so many beaux?
    It's not your virtue that they're dazzled by;
    Nor is it virtuous love for which they sigh.
    You're fooling no one, Madam; the world's not
    blind;
    There's many a lady heaven has designed
    To call men's noblest, tenderest feelings out,
    Who has no lovers dogging her about;
    From which it's plain that lovers nowadays
260   Must be acquired in bold and shameless ways,
    And only pay one court for such reward
    As modesty and virtue can't afford.

    Then don't be quite so puffed up, if you please,
    About your tawdry little victories;
    Try, if you can, to be a shade less vain,
    And treat the world with somewhat less disdain.
    If one were envious of your amours,
    One soon could have a following like yours;
    Lovers are no great trouble to collect
    If one prefers them to one's self-respect.   270
CELIMENE: Collect them then, my dear; I'd love to see
    You demonstrate that charming theory;
    Who knows, you might . . .
ARSINOE: Now, Madam, that will do;
    It's time to end this trying interview.
    My coach is late in coming to your door,
    Or I'd have taken leave of you before.
CELIMENE: Oh, please don't feel that you must rush
    away;
    I'd be delighted, Madam, if you'd stay.   280
    However, lest my conversation bore you,
    Let me provide some better company for you;
    This gentleman, who comes most apropos,
    Will please you more than I could do, I know.

(Enter ALCESTE.)

    Alceste, I have a little note to write
    Which simply must go out before tonight;
    Please entertain Madame; I'm sure that she
    Will overlook my incivility. *(Exit.)*
ARSINOE: Well, Sir, our hostess graciously contrives
    For us to chat until my coach arrives;   290
    And I shall be forever in her debt
    For granting me this little tête-à-tête.°
    We women very rightly give our hearts
    To men of noble character and parts,
    And your especial merits, dear Alceste,
    Have roused the deepest sympathy in my breast.
    Oh, how I wish they had sufficient sense
    At court, to recognize your excellence!
    They wrong you greatly, Sir. How it must hurt you
    Never to be rewarded for your virtue!   300
ALCESTE: Why, Madam, what cause have I to feel
    aggrieved?
    What great and brilliant thing have I achieved?
    What service have I rendered to the King
    That I should look to him for anything?
ARSINOE: Not everyone who's honored by the State
    Has done great services. A man must wait
    Till time and fortune offer him the chance.
    Your merit, Sir, is obvious at a glance,
    And . . .   310
ALCESTE: Ah, forget my merit; I'm not neglected.
    The court, I think, can hardly be expected
    To mine men's souls for merit, and unearth

---

entre nous, "between us."

tête-à-tête, literally head-to-head; i.e., private conversation.

400 / THE MISANTHROPE

Our hidden virtues and our secret worth.

ARSINOE: *Some* virtues, though, are far too bright to
    hide;
    Yours are acknowledged, Sir, on every side.
    Indeed, I've heard you warmly praised of late
    By persons of considerable weight.

320 ALCESTE: This fawning age has praise for everyone,
    And all distinctions, Madam, are undone.
    All things have equal honor nowadays,
    And no one should be gratified by praise.
    To be admired, one only need exist,
    And every lackey's on the honors list.

ARSINOE: I only wish, Sir, that you had your eye
    On some position at court, however high;
    You'd only have to hint at such a notion
    For me to set the proper wheels in motion;
330   I've certain friendships I'd be glad to use
    To get you any office you might choose.

ALCESTE: Madam, I fear that any such ambition
    Is wholly foreign to my disposition.
    The soul God gave me isn't of the sort
    That prospers in the weather of a court.
    It's all too obvious that I don't possess
    The virtues necessary for success.
    My one great talent is for speaking plain;
    I've never learned to flatter or to feign;
340   And anyone so stupidly sincere
    Had best not seek a courtier's career.
    Outside the court, I know, one must dispense
    With honors, privilege, and influence;
    But still one gains the right, foregoing these,
    Not to be tortured by the wish to please.
    One needn't live in dread of snubs and slights,
    Nor praise the verse that every idiot writes,
    Nor humor silly Marquesses, nor bestow
    Politic sighs on Madam So-and-So.

ARSINOE: Forget the court, then; let the matter rest.
    But I've another cause to be distressed
    About your present situation, Sir.
    It's to your love affair that I refer.
    She whom you love, and who pretends to love you,
    Is, I regret to say, unworthy of you.

ALCESTE: Why, Madam! Can you seriously intend
    To make so grave a charge against your friend?

ARSINOE: Alas, I must. I've stood aside too long
    And let that lady do you grievous wrong;
360   But now my debt to conscience shall be paid:
    I tell you that your love has been betrayed.

ALCESTE: I thank you, Madam; you're extremely
    kind.
    Such words are soothing to a lover's mind.

ARSINOE: Yes, though she *is* my friend, I say again
    You're very much too good for Célimène.
    She's wantonly misled you from the start.

ALCESTE: You may be right; who knows another's
    heart?
370   But ask yourself if it's the part of charity

To shake my soul with doubts of her sincerity.

ARSINOE: Well, if you'd rather be a dupe than doubt
    her,
    That's your affair. I'll say no more about her.

ALCESTE: Madam, you know that doubt and vague
    suspicion
    Are painful to a man in my position;
    It's most unkind to worry me this way
    Unless you've some real proof of what you say.

ARSINOE: Sir, say no more: all doubt shall be   380
    removed,
    And all that I've been saying shall be proved.
    You've only to escort me home, and there
    We'll look into the heart of this affair.
    I've ocular° evidence which will persuade you
    Beyond a doubt, that Célimène's betrayed you.
    Then, if you're saddened by that revelation,
    Perhaps I can provide some consolation. *(They go
    out.)*

ACT 4

(Enter ELIANTE *and* PHILINTE.*)*

PHILINTE: Madam, he acted like a stubborn child;
    I thought they never would be reconciled;
    In vain we reasoned, threatened, and appealed;
    He stood his ground and simply would not yield.
    The Marshals, I feel sure, have never heard
    An argument so splendidly absurd.
    "No, gentlemen," said he, "I'll not retract.
    His verse is bad: extremely bad, in fact.
    Surely it does the man no harm to know it.
    Does it disgrace him, not to be a poet?   20
    A gentleman may be respected still,
    Whether he writes a sonnet well or ill.
    That I dislike his verse should not offend him;
    In all that touches honor, I commend him;
    He's noble, brave, and virtuous—but I fear
    He can't in truth be called a sonneteer.
    I'll gladly praise his wardrobe; I'll endorse
    His dancing, or the way he sits a horse;
    But, gentlemen, I cannot praise his rhyme.
    In fact, it ought to be a capital crime   30
    For anyone so sadly unendowed
    To write a sonnet, and read the thing aloud."
    At length he fell into a gentler mood
    And, striking a concessive attitude,
    He paid Oronte the following courtesies:
    "Sir, I regret that I'm so hard to please,
    And I'm profoundly sorry that your lyric
    Failed to provoke me to a panegyric."
    After these curious words, the two embraced,
    And then the hearing was adjourned—in haste.   40

---

ocular, visible.

ELIANTE: His conduct has been very singular lately;
 Still, I confess that I respect him greatly.
 The honesty in which he takes such pride
 Has—to my mind—its, noble, heroic side.
 In this false age, such candor seem outrageous;
 But I could wish that it were more contagious.
PHILINTE: What most intrigues me in our friend
  Alceste
 Is the grand passion that rages in his breast.
50 The sullen humors he's compounded of
 Should not, I think, dispose his heart to love;
 But since they do, it puzzles me still more
 That he should choose your cousin to adore.
ELIANTE: It does, indeed, belie the theory
 That love is born of gentle sympathy,
 And that the tender passion must be based
 On sweet accords of temper and of taste.
PHILINTE: Does she return his love, do you suppose?
ELIANTE: Ah, that's a difficult question, Sir. Who
60   knows?
 How can we judge the truth of her devotion?
 Her heart's a stranger to its own emotion.
 Sometimes it thinks it loves, when no love's there;
 At other times it loves quite unaware.
PHILINTE: I rather think Alceste is in for more
 Distress and sorrow than he's bargained for;
 Were he of my mind, Madam, his affection
 Would turn in quite a different direction,
 And we would see him more responsive to
70 The kind regard which he receives from you.
ELIANTE: Sir, I believe in frankness, and I'm inclined,
 In matters of the heart, to speak my mind.
 I don't oppose his love for her; indeed,
 I hope with all my heart that he'll succeed,
 And were it in my power, I'd rejoice
 In giving him the lady of his choice.
 But if, as happens frequently enough
 In love affairs, he meets with a rebuff—
 If Célimène should grant some rival's suit—
80 I'd gladly play the role of substitute;
 Nor would his tender speeches please me less
 Because they'd once been made without success.
PHILINTE: Well, Madam, as for me, I don't oppose
 Your hopes in this affair; and heaven knows
 That in my conversations with the man
 I plead your cause as often as I can.
 But if those two should marry, and so remove
 All chance that he will offer you his love,
 Then I'll declare my own, and hope to see
90 Your gracious favor pass from him to me.
 In short, should you be cheated of Alceste,
 I'd be most happy to be second best.
ELIANTE: Philinte, you're teasing.
PHILINTE: Ah, Madam, never fear;
 No words of mine were ever so sincere,
 And I shall live in fretful expectation
 Till I can make a fuller declaration.

(Enter ALCESTE.*)*

ALCESTE: Avenge me, Madam! I must have
  satisfaction,
 Or this great wrong will drive me to distraction!   100
ELIANTE: Why, what's the matter? What's upset you
  so?
ALCESTE: Madam, I've had a mortal, mortal blow
 If Chaos repossessed the universe,
 I swear I'd not be shaken any worse.
 I'm ruined. . . . I can say no more. . . . My soul . . .
ELIANTE: Do, try, Sir, to regain your self-control.
ALCESTE: Just heaven! Why were so much beauty and
  grace
 Bestowed on one so vicious and so base?   110
ELIANTE: Once more, Sir, tell us. . . .
ALCESTE: My world has gone to wrack;
 I'm—I'm betrayed; she's stabbed me in the back:
 Yes, Célimène (who would have thought it of her?)
 Is false to me, and has another lover.
ELIANTE: Are you quite certain? Can you prove these
  things?
PHILINTE: Lovers are prey to wild imaginings
 And jealous fancies. No doubt there's some
  mistake. . . .   120
ALCESTE: Mind your own business, Sir, for heaven's
  sake.
 (to ELIANTE*)* Madam, I have the proof that you
  demand
 Here in my pocket, penned by her own hand.
 Yes, all the shameful evidence one could want
 Lies in this letter written to Oronte—
 Oronte! Whom I felt sure she couldn't love,
 And hardly bothered to be jealous of.
PHILINTE: Still, in a letter, appearances may deceive;   130
 This may not be so bad as you belive.
ALCESTE: Once more I beg you, Sir, to let me be;
 Tend to your own affairs; leave mine to me.
ELIANTE: Compose yourself; this anguish that you
  feel . . .
ALCESTE: Is something, Madam, you alone can heal.
 My outraged heart, beside itself with grief,
 Appeals to you for comfort and relief.
 Avenge me on your cousin, whose unjust
 And faithless nature has deceived my trust;   140
 Avenge a crime your pure soul must detest.
ELIANTE: But how, Sir?
ALCESTE: Madam, this heart within my breast
 Is yours; pray take it; redeem my heart from her,
 And so avenge me on my torturer.
 Let her be punished by the fond emotion,
 The ardent love, the bottomless devotion,
 The faithful worship which this heart of mine
 Will offer up to yours as to a shrine.
ELIANTE: You have my sympathy, Sir, in all you   150
  suffer;
 Nor do I scorn the noble heart you offer;

But I suspect you'll soon be mollified,
And this desire for vengeance will subside.
When some beloved hand has done us wrong
We thirst for retribution—but not for long;
However dark the deed that she's committed,
A lovely culprit's very soon acquitted.
Nothing's so stormy as an injured lover,
160 And yet no storm so quickly passes over.
  ALCESTE: No, Madam, no—this is no lovers' spat;
I'll not forgive her; it's gone too far for that;
My mind's made up; I'll kill myself before
I waste my hopes upon her any more.
Ah, here she is. My wrath intensifies.
I shall confront her with her tricks and lies,
And crush her utterly, and bring you then
A heart no longer slave to Célimène. (*Exit* ELIANTE
  and PHILINTE.)

(*Enter* CÉLIMÈNE.)

  ALCESTE (*aside*): Sweet heaven, help me to control my
170   passion.
  CELIMENE (*to* ALCESTE): Oh, Lord. Why stand there
    staring in that fashion?
And what d'you mean by those dramatic sighs,
And that malignant glitter in your eyes?
  ALCESTE: I mean that sins which cause the blood to
    freeze
Look innocent beside your treacheries;
That nothing Hell's or Heaven's wrath could do
Ever produced so bad a thing as you.
180   CELIMENE: Your compliments were always sweet and
    pretty.
  ALCESTE: Madam, it's not the moment to be witty.
No, blush and hang your head; you've ample
    reason,
Since I've the fullest evidence of your treason.
Ah, this is what my sad heart prophesied;
Now all my anxious fears are verified;
My dark suspicion and my gloomy doubt
Divined the truth, and now the truth is out.
190 For all your trickery, I was not deceived;
It was my bitter stars that I believed.
But don't imagine that you'll go scot-free;
You shan't misuse me with impunity.
I know that love's irrational and blind;
I know the heart's not subject to the mind,
And can't be reasoned into beating faster;
I know each soul is free to choose its master;
Therefore had you but spoken from the heart,
Rejecting my attentions from the start,
200 I'd have no grievance, or at any rate
I could complain of nothing but my fate.
Ah, but so falsely to encourage me—
That was a treason and a treachery
For which you cannot suffer too severely,
And you shall pay for that behavior dearly.
Yes, now I have no pity, not a shred;

My temper's out of hand; I've lost my head;
Shocked by the knowledge of your
  double-dealings,
My reason can't restrain my savage feelings; 210
A righteous wrath deprives me of my senses,
And I won't answer for the consequences.
  CELIMENE: What does this outburst mean? Will you
    please explain?
Have you, by any chance, gone quite insane?
  ALCESTE: Yes, yes, I went insane the day I fell
A victim to your black and fatal spell,
Thinking to meet with some sincerity
Among the treacherous charms that beckoned me.
  CELIMENE: Pooh. Of what treachery can you 220
    complain?
  ALCESTE: How sly you are, how cleverly you feign!
But you'll not victimize me any more.
Look: here's a document you've seen before.
This evidence, which I acquired today,
Leaves you, I think, without a thing to say.
  CELIMENE: Is this what sent you into such a fit?
  ALCESTE: You should be blushing at the sight of it.
  CELIMENE: Ought I to blush? I truly don't see why.
  ALCESTE: Ah, now you're being bold as well as sly; 230
Since there's no signature, perhaps you'll claim . . .
  CELIMENE: I wrote it, whether or not it bears my
    name.
  ALCESTE: And you can view with equanimity
This proof of your disloyalty to me!
  CELIMENE: Oh, don't be so outrageous and extreme.
  ALCESTE: You take this matter lightly, it would seem.
Was it no wrong to me, no shame to you,
That you should send Oronte this billet-doux?°
  CELIMENE: Oronte! Who said it was for him? 240
  ALCESTE: Why, those
Who brought me this example of your prose.
But what's the difference? If you wrote the letter
To someone else, it pleases me no better.
My grievance and your guilt remain the same.
  CELIMENE: But need you rage, and need I blush for
    shame,
If this was written to a *woman* friend?
  ALCESTE: Ah! Most ingenious. I'm impressed no end;
And after that incredible evasion 250
Your guilt is clear. I need no more persuasion.
How dare you try so clumsy a deception?
D'you think I'm wholly wanting in perception?
Come, come, let's see how brazenly you'll try
To bolster up so palpable a lie:
Kindly construe this ardent closing section
As nothing more than sisterly affection!
Here, let me read it. Tell me, if you dare to,
That this is for a woman . . .
  CELIMENE: I don't care to. 260

---

billet-doux, love letter.

What right have you to badger and berate me,
And so highhandedly interrogate me?
ALCESTE: Now, don't be angry; all I ask of you
Is that you justify a phrase or two . . .
CELIMENE: No, I shall not. I utterly refuse,
And you may take those phrases as you choose.
ALCESTE: Just show me how this letter could be meant
For a woman's eyes, and I shall be content.
CELIMENE: No, no, it's for Oronte; you're perfectly
270   right.
I welcome his attentions with delight,
I prize his character and his intellect,
And everything is just as you suspect.
Come, do your worst now; give your rage free rein;
But kindly cease to bicker and complain.
ALCESTE (aside): Good God! Could anything be more
         inhuman?
Was ever a heart so mangled by a woman?
When I complain of how she has betrayed me,
280   She bridles, and commences to upbraid me!
She tries my tortured patience to the limit;
She won't deny her guilt; she glories in it!
And yet my heart's too faint and cowardly
To break these chains of passion, and be free,
To scorn her as it should, and rise above
This unrewarded, mad, and bitter love.
(to CÉLIMÈNE): Ah, traitress, in how confident a
         fashion
You take advantage of my helpless passion,
290   And use my weakness for your faithless charms
To make me once again throw down my arms!
But do at least deny this black transgression;
Take back that mocking and perverse confession;
Defend this letter and your innocence,
And I, poor fool, will aid in your defense.
Pretend, pretend, that you are just and true,
And I shall make myself believe in you.
CELIMENE: Oh, stop it. Don't be such a jealous dunce,
Or I shall leave off loving you at once.
300   Just why should I pretend? What could impel me.
To stoop so low as that? And kindly tell me
Why, if I loved another, I shouldn't merely
Inform you of it, simply and sincerely!
I've told you where you stand, and that admission
Should altogether clear me of suspicion;
After so generous a guarantee,
What right have you to harbor doubts of me?
Since women are (from natural reticence)
Reluctant to declare their sentiments,
310   And since the honor of our sex requires
That we conceal our amorous desires,
Ought any man for whom such laws are broken
To question what the oracle has spoken?
Should he not rather feel an obligation
To trust that most obliging declaration?
Enough, now. Your suspicions quite disgust me;
Why should I love a man who doesn't trust me?

I cannot understand why I continue,
Fool that I am, to take an interest in you.
I ought to choose a man less prone to doubt,   320
And give you something to be vexed about.
ALCESTE: Ah, what a poor enchanted fool I am;
These gentle words, no doubt, were all a sham;
But destiny requires me to entrust
My happiness to you, and so I must.
I'll love you to the bitter end, and see
How false and treacherous you dare to be.
CELIMENE: No, you don't really love me as you ought.
ALCESTE: I love you more than can be said or
         thought;   330
Indeed, I wish you were in such distress
That I might show my deep devotedness.
Yes, I could wish that you were wretchedly poor,
Unloved, uncherished, utterly obscure;
That fate had set you down upon the earth
Without possessions, rank, or gentle birth;
Then, by the offer of my heart, I might
Repair the great injustice of your plight;
I'd raise you from the dust, and proudly prove
The purity and vastness of my love.   340
CELIMENE: This is a strange benevolence indeed!
God grant that I may never be in need. . . .
Ah, here's Monsieur Dubois, in quaint disguise.

(Enter MONSIEUR DUBOIS.)

ALCESTE: Well, why this costume? Why those
         frightened eyes?
What ails you?
DUBOIS: Well, sir, things are most mysterious.
ALCESTE: What do you mean?
DUBOIS: I fear they're very serious.
ALCESTE: What?   350
DUBOIS: Shall I speak more loudly?
ALCESTE: Yes; speak out.
DUBOIS: Isn't there someone here, Sir?
ALCESTE: Speak, you lout!
Stop wasting time.
DUBOIS: Sir, we must slip away.
ALCESTE: How's that?
EUBOIS: We must decamp without delay.
ALCESTE: Explain yourself.
DUBOIS: I tell you we must fly.   360
ALCESTE: What for?
DUBOIS: We mustn't pause to say good-by.
ALCESTE: Now what d'you mean by all of this, you
         clown?
DUBOIS: I mean, Sir, that we've got to leave this town.
ALCESTE: I'll tear you limb from limb and joint from
         joint
If you don't come more quickly to the point.
DUBOIS: Well, Sir, today a man in a black suit,
Who wore a black and ugly scowl to boot,   370
Left us a document scrawled in such a hand
As even Satan couldn't understand.

It bears upon your lawsuit, I don't doubt;
But all hell's devils couldn't make it out.
ALCESTE: Well, well, go on. What then? I fail to see
How this event obliges us to flee.
DUBOIS: Well, Sir: an hour later, hardly more,
A gentleman who's often called before
Came looking for you in an anxious way.
380 Not finding you, he asked me to convey
(Knowing I could be trusted with the same)
The following message.... Now, what *was* his
name?
ALCESTE: Forget his name, you idiot. What did he
say?
DUBOIS: Well, it was one of your friends, Sir, anyway.
He warned you to begone, and he suggested
That if you stay, you may well be arrested.
ALCESTE: What? Nothing more specific? Think, man,
390 think!
DUBOIS: No, Sir. He had me bring him pen and ink,
And dashed you off a letter which, I'm sure,
Will render things distinctly less obscure.
ALCESTE: Well—let me have it!
CELIMENE: What *is* this all about?
ALCESTE: God knows; but I have hopes of finding
out.
How long am I to wait, you blitherer?
DUBOIS (*after a protracted search for the letter*): I must
400 have left it on your table, Sir.
ALCESTE: I ought to . . .
CELIMENE: No, no, keep your self-control;
Go find out what's behind his rigmarole.
ALCESTE: It seems that fate, no matter what I do,
Has sworn that I may not converse with you;
But, Madam, pray permit your faithful lover
To try once more before the day is over.

(DUBOIS *and* ALCESTE *leave, then* CÉLIMÈNE *withdraws.*)

ACT 5

(*Enter* ALCESTE *and* PHILINTE.)

ALCESTE: No, it's too much. My mind's made up, I tell
you.
PHILINTE: Why should this blow, however hard,
compel you . . .
ALCESTE: No, no, don't waste your breath in
argument;
Nothing you say will alter my intent;
This age is vile, and I've made up my mind
To have no further commerce with mankind.
10 Did not truth, honor, decency, and the laws
Oppose my enemy and approve my cause?
My claims were justified in all men's sight;
I put my trust in equity and right;
Yet, to my horror and the world's disgrace,
Justice is mocked, and I have lost my case!

A scoundrel whose dishonesty is notorious
Emerges from another lie victorious!
Honor and right condone his brazen fraud,
While rectitude and decency applaud!
20 Before his smirking face, the truth stands charmed,
And virtue conquered, and the law disarmed!
His crime is sanctioned by a court decree!
And not content with what he's done to me,
The dog now seeks to ruin me by stating
That I composed a book now circulating,
A book so wholly criminal and vicious
That even to speak its title is seditious!
Meanwhile Oronte, my rival, lends his credit
To the same libelous tale, and helps to spread it!
30 Oronte! A man of honor and of rank,
With whom I've been entirely fair and frank;
Who sought me out and forced me, willy-nilly,
To judge some verse I found extremely silly;
And who, because I properly refused
To flatter him, or see the truth abused,
Abets my enemy in a rotten slander!
There's the reward of honesty and candor!
The man will hate me to the end of time
For failing to commend his wretched rhyme!
40 And not this man alone, but all humanity
Do what they do from interest and vanity;
They prate of honor, truth, and righteousness,
But lie, betray, and swindle nonetheless.
Come then: man's villainy is too much to bear;
Let's leave this jungle and this jackal's lair.
Yes! Treacherous and savage race of men,
You shall not look upon my face again.
PHILINTE: Oh, don't rush into exile prematurely;
Things aren't as dreadful as you make them,
50 surely.
It's rather obvious, since you're still at large,
That people don't believe your enemy's charge.
Indeed, his tale's so patently untrue
That it may do more harm to him than you.
ALCESTE: Nothing could do that scoundrel any harm:
His frank corruption is his greatest charm,
And, far from hurting him, a further shame
Would only serve to magnify his name.
PHILINTE: In any case, his bald prevarication
60 Has done no injury to your reputation,
And you may feel secure in that regard.
As for your lawsuit, it should not be hard
To have the case reopened, and contest
This judgment . . .
ALCESTE: No, no, let the verdict rest.
Whatever cruel penalty it may bring,
I wouldn't have it changed for anything.
It shows the times' injustice with such clarity
That I shall pass it down to our posterity
70 As a great proof and signal demonstration
Of the black wickedness of this generation.
It may cost twenty thousand francs; but I

Shall pay their twenty thousand, and gain thereby
The right to storm and rage at human evil,
And send the race of mankind to the devil.
PHILINTE: Listen to me. . . .
ALCESTE: Why? What can you possibly say?
Don't argue, Sir; your labor's thrown away.
Do you propose to offer lame excuses
80   For men's behavior and the times' abuses?
PHILINTE: No, all you say I'll readily concede:
This is a low, conniving age indeed;
Nothing but trickery prospers nowadays,
And people ought to mend their shabby ways.
Yes, man's a beastly creature; but must we then
Abandon the society of men?
Here in the world, each human frailty
Provides occasion for philosophy,
And that is virtue's noblest exercise;
90   If honesty shone forth from all men's eyes,
If every heart were frank and kind and just,
What could our virtues do but gather dust
(Since their employment is to help us bear
The villainies of men without despair)?
A heart well-armed with virtue can endure. . . .
ALCESTE: Sir, you're a matchless reasoner, to be sure;
Your words are fine and full of cogency;
But don't waste time and eloquence on me.
My reason bids me go, for my own good.
100   My tongue won't lie and flatter as it should;
God knows what frankness it might next commit,
And what I'd suffer on account of it.
Pray let me wait for Célimène's return
In peace and quiet. I shall shortly learn,
By her response to what I have in view,
Whether her love for me is feigned or true.
PHILINTE: Till then, let's visit Eliante upstairs.
ALCESTE: No, I am too weighed down with somber
       cares.
110   Go to her, do; and leave me with my gloom
Here in the darkened corner of this room.
PHILINTE: Why, that's no sort of company, my friend;
I'll see if Eliante will not descend.

(Exit PHILINTE, ALCESTE *withdraws to a corner.)*
(Enter CÉLIMÈNE *and* ORONTE.)

ORONTE: Yes, Madam, if you wish me to remain
Your true and ardent lover, you must deign
To give me some more positive assurance.
All this suspense is quite beyond endurance.
If your heart shares the sweet desires of mine,
Show me as much by some convincing sign;
120   And here's the sign I urgently suggest:
That you no longer tolerate Alceste,
But sacrifice him to my love, and sever
All your relations with the man forever.
CELIMENE: Why do you suddenly dislike him so?
You praised him to the skies not long ago.

ORONTE: Madam, that's not the point. I'm here to find
Which way your tender feelings are inclined.
Choose, if you please, between Alceste and me,
And I shall stay or go accordingly.   130
ALCESTE *(emerging from the corner)*: Yes, Madam,
       choose; this gentleman's demand
Is wholly just, and I support his stand.
I too am true and ardent; I too am here
To ask you that you make your feelings clear.
No more delays, now; no equivocation;
The time has come to make your declaration.
ORONTE: Sir, I've no wish in any way to be
An obstacle to your felicity.
ALCESTE: Sir, I've no wish to share her heart with   140
       you;
That may sound jealous, but at least it's true.
ORONTE: If, weighing us, she leans in your direction
       . . .
ALCESTE: If she regard you with the least affection
       . . .
ORONTE: I swear I'll yield her to you there and then.
ALCESTE: I swear I'll never see her face again.
ORONTE: Now, Madam, tell us what we've come to
       hear.
ALCESTE: Madam, speak openly and have no fear.
ORONTE: Just say which one is to remain your lover.   150
ALCESTE: Just name one name, and it will all be over.
ORONTE: What! Is it possible that you're undecided?
ALCESTE: What! Can your feelings possibly be
       divided?
CELIMENE: Enough: this inquisition's gone too far:
How utterly unreasonable you are!
Not that I couldn't make the choice with ease;
My heart has no conflicting sympathies;
I know full well which one of you I favor,
And you'd not see me hesitate or waver.   160
But how can you expect me to reveal
So cruelly and bluntly what I feel?
I think it altogether too unpleasant
To choose between two men when both are
       present;
One's heart has means more subtle and more kind
Of letting its affections be divined,
Nor need one be uncharitably plain
To let a lover know he loves in vain.
ORONTE: No, no, speak plainly; I for one can stand it. 170
I beg you to be frank.
ALCESTE: And I demand it.
The simple truth is what I wish to know,
And there's no need for softening the blow.
You've made an art of pleasing everyone,
But now your days of coquetry are done:
You have no choice now, Madam, but to choose,
For I'll know what to think if you refuse;
I'll take your silence for a clear admission
That I'm entitled to my worst suspicion.   180
ORONTE: I thank you for this ultimatum, Sir,

And I may say I heartily concur.

CELIMENE: Really, this foolishness is very wearing:
Must you be so unjust and overbearing?
Haven't I told you why I must demur?
Ah, here's Eliante; I'll put the case to her.

(Enter ELIANTE *and* PHILINTE.)

Cousin, I'm being persecuted here
By these two persons, who, it would appear,
Will not be satisfied till I confess
190   Which one I love the more, and which the less,
And tell the latter to his face that he
Is henceforth banished from my company.
Tell me, has ever such a thing been done?

ELIANTE: You'd best not turn to me, I'm not the one
To back you in a matter of this kind:
I'm all for those who frankly speak their mind.

ORONTE: Madam, you'll search in vain for a defender.

ALCESTE: You're beaten, Madam, and may as well
surrender.

200 ORONTE: Speak, speak, you must; and end this awful
strain.

ALCESTE: Or don't, and your position will be plain.

ORONTE: A single word will close this painful scene.

ALCESTE: But if you're silent, I'll know what you
mean.

(Enter ARSINOÉ, ACASTE, *and* CLITANDRE.)

ACASTE *(to* CÉLIMÈNE): Madam, with all due
deference, we two
Have come to pick a little bone with you.

CLITANDRE *(to* ORONTE *and* ALCESTE): I'm glad you're
210   present, Sirs; as you'll soon learn,
Our business here is also your concern.

ARSINOE *(to* CÉLIMÈNE): Madam, I visit you so soon
again
Only because of these two gentlemen,
Who came to me indignant and aggrieved
About a crime too base to be believed.
Knowing your virtue, having such confidence in it,
I couldn't think you guilty for a minute,
In spite of all their telling evidence;
220   And, rising above our little difference,
I've hastened here in friendship's name to see
You clear yourself of this great calumny.

ACASTE: Yes, Madam, let us see with what composure
You'll manage to respond to this disclosure.
You lately sent Clitandre this tender note.

CLITANDRE: And this one, for Acaste, you also wrote.

ACASTE *(to* ORONTE *and* ALCESTE): You'll recognize this
writing, Sirs, I think;
The lady is so free with pen and ink
230   That you must know it all too well, I fear.
But listen: this is something you should hear.

"How absurd you are to condemn my lighthear-
tedness in society, and to accuse me of being
happiest in the company of others. Nothing could
be more unjust; and if you do not come to me
instantly and beg pardon for saying such a thing, I
shall never forgive you as long as I live. Our big
bumbling friend the Viscount . . ."

What a shame that he's not here.

"Our big bumbling friend the Viscount, whose   240
name stands first in your complaint, is hardly a
man to my taste; and ever since the day I watched
him spending three-quarters of an hour spitting
into a well, so as to make circles in the water, I have
been unable to think highly of him. As for the little
Marquess . . ."

In all modesty, gentlemen, that is I.

"As for the little Marquess, who sat squeezing my
hand for such a long while yesterday, I find him in
all respects the most trifling creature alive; and the   250
only things of value about him are his cape and his
sword. As for the man with the green ribbons . . ."

(to ALCESTE): It's your turn now, Sir.

"As for the man with the green ribbons, he
amuses me now and then with his bluntness and his
bearish ill-humor; but there are many times indeed
when I think him the greatest bore in the world.
And as for the sonneteer . . ."

(to ORONTE): Here's your helping.

"And as for the sonneteer, who has taken it into   260
his head to be witty, and insists on being an author
in the teeth of opinion, I simply cannot be bothered
to listen to him, and his prose wearies me quite as
much as his poetry. Be assured that I am not always
so well-entertained as you suppose; that I long for
your company, more than I dare to say, at all these
entertainments to which people drag me; and that
the presence of those one loves is the true and
perfect seasoning to all one's pleasures."

CLITANDRE: And now for me.   270

"Clitandre, whom you mention, and who so
pesters me with his saccharine speeches, is the last
man on earth for whom I could feel any affection.
He is quite mad to suppose that I love him, and so
are you, to doubt that you are loved. Do come to
your senses; exchange your suppositions for his;
and visit me as often as possible, to help me bear
the annoyance of his unwelcome attentions."

It's a sweet character that these letters show,
And what to call it, Madam, you well know.   280

290 Enough. We're off to make the world acquainted
     With this sublime self-portrait that you've painted.

ACASTE: Madam, I'll make you no farewell oration;
     No, you're not worthy of my indignation.
     Far choicer hearts than yours, as you'll discover,
     Would like this little Marquess for a lover.

     (*Exit* ACASTE *and* CLITANDRE.)

ORONTE: So! After all those loving letters you wrote,
     You turn on me like this, and cut my throat!
     And your dissembling, faithless heart, I find,
300 Has pledged itself by turns to all mankind!
     How blind I've been! But now I clearly see;
     I thank you, Madam, for enlightening me.
     My heart is mine once more, and I'm content;
     The loss of it shall be your punishment
     (*to* ALCESTE) Sir, she is yours; I'll seek no more to
        stand
     Between your wishes and this lady's hand. (*Exit.*)

ARSINOE (*to* CÉLIMÈNE): Madam, I'm forced to speak.
        I'm far too stirred
310 To keep my counsel, after what I've heard.
     I'm shocked and staggered by your want of morals.
     It's not my way to mix in others' quarrels;
     But really, when this fine and noble spirit,
     This man of honor and surpassing merit,
     Laid down the offering of his heart before you,
     How *could* you . . .

ALCESTE: Madam, permit me, I implore you,
     To represent myself in this debate.
     Don't bother, please, to be my advocate.
320 My heart, in any case, could not afford
     To give your services their due reward;
     And if I chose, for consolation's sake,
     Some other lady, t'would not be you I'd take.

ARSINOE: What makes you think you could, Sir? And
        how dare you
     Imply that I've been trying to ensnare you?
     If you can for a moment entertain
     Such flattering fancies, you're extremely vain.
     I'm not so interested as you suppose
330 In Célimène's discarded gigolos.
     Get rid of that absurd illusion, do.
     Women like me are not for such as you.
     Stay with this creature, to whom you're so attached;
     I've never seen two people better matched.

     (*Exit* ARSINOÉ.)

ALCESTE (*to* CÉLIMÈNE): Well, I've been still
        throughout this exposé,
     Till everyone but me has said his say.
     Come, have I shown sufficient self-restraint?
     And may I now . . .

340 CELIMENE: Yes, make your just complaint.
     Reproach me freely, call me what you will;
     You've every right to say I've used you ill.
     I've wronged you, I confess it; and in my shame

I'll make no effort to escape the blame.
The anger of those others I could despise;
My guilt toward you I sadly recognize.
Your wrath is wholly justified, I fear;
I know how culpable I must appear,
I know all things bespeak my treachery,
And that, in short, you've grounds for hating me.   350
Do so; I give you leave.

ALCESTE: Ah, traitress—how,
     How should I cease to love you, even now?
     Though mind and will were passionately bent
     On hating you, my heart would not consent.
     (*to* ELIANTE *and* PHILINTE) Be witness to my
        madness, both of you;
     See what infatuation drives one to;
     But wait; my folly's only just begun,
     And I shall prove to you before I'm done   360
     How strange the human heart is, and how far
     From rational we sorry creatures are.
     (*to* CÉLIMÈNE) Woman, I'm willing to forget your
        shame,
     And clothe your treacheries in a sweeter name;
     I'll call them youthful errors, instead of crimes,
     And lay the blame on these corrupting times.
     My one condition is that you agree
     To share my chosen fate, and fly with me
     To that wild, trackless, solitary place   370
     In which I shall forget the human race.
     Only by such a course can you atone
     For those atrocious letters; by that alone
     Can you remove my present horror of you,
     And make it possible for me to love you.

CELIMENE: What! *I* renounce the world at my young
        age,
     And die of boredom in some hermitage?

ALCESTE: Ah, if you really loved me as you ought,
     You wouldn't give the world a moment's thought;   380
     Must you have me, and all the world beside?

CELIMENE: Alas, at twenty one is terrified
     Of solitude. I fear I lack the force
     And depth of soul to take so stern a course.
     But if my hand in marriage will content you,
     Why, there's a plan which I might well consent to,
     And . . .

ALCESTE: No, I detest you now. I could excuse
     Everything else, but since you thus refuse
     To love me wholly, as a wife should do,   390
     And see the world in me, as I in you,
     Go! I reject your hand, and disenthrall
     My heart from your enchantments, once for all.
        (*Exit* CÉLIMÈNE.)

ALCESTE (*to* ELIANTE): Madam, your virtuous beauty
        has no peer;
     Of all this world, you only are sincere;
     I've long esteemed you highly, as you know;
     Permit me ever to esteem you so,
     And if I do not now request your hand,

Forgive me, Madam, and try to understand.
I feel unworthy of it; I sense that fate
Does not intend me for the married state,
That I should do you wrong by offering you
My shattered heart's unhappy residue,
And that in short . . .
ELIANTE: Your argument's well taken:
Nor need you fear that I shall feel forsaken.
Were I to offer him this hand of mine,
410   Your friend Philinte, I think, would not decline.
PHILINTE: Ah, Madam, that's my heart's most
    cherished goal,

For which I'd gladly give my life and soul.
ALCESTE (to ELIANTE and PHILINTE): May you be true
    to all you now profess,
And so deserve unending happiness.
Meanwhile, betrayed and wronged in everything,
I'll flee this bitter world where vice is king,
And seek some spot unpeopled and apart
Where I'll be free to have an honest heart. (Exit   420
    ALCESTE.)
PHILINTE: Come, Madam, let's do everything we can
    To change the mind of this unhappy man. (They
    follow him.)

Figure 40. Acaste (Brian Bedford, *left*), Eliante (Patricia Conolly, *standing*), Célimène (Christine Pickles), and Clitandre in the A.P.A. Repertory Company production of *The Misanthrope,* directed by Stephen Porter, designed by James Tilton, and presented by the Professional Theatre Program of the University of Michigan, Ann Arbor, 1968. (Photograph: the Professional Theatre Program of the University of Michigan.)

Figure 41. Alceste (Richard Easton, *center*) expresses his dismay upon learning from the Guard of the Marshalsea that he must appear in court to settle his quarrel with Oronte; Philinte (Sydney Walker, *left*) and Eliante (Patricia Conolly, *left*) show their concern for Alceste's predicament, Célimène (Christine Pickles) expresses her surprise, while Acaste (Brian Bedford, *right*) and Clitandre (*far right*) look on with an air of pretended concern in the A.P.A. Repertory Company production of *The Misanthrope,* directed by Stephen Porter and designed by James Tilton, New York, 1968. (Photograph: Van Williams.)

Staging of *The Misanthrope*

REVIEW OF THE A.P.A.-PHOENIX THEATER
PRODUCTION, 1968, BY CLIVE BARNES

Of course, Molière's "The Misanthrope" is, as of last night, the best play in town, and gratifyingly the A.P.A. Repertory Company comes close enough to doing it justice. I only hope Broadway audiences, so thinly nurtured on what often passes for wit on our stages, will have the sense to flock to it.

The play is timely. It might be said that it is always the function of a masterpiece to be timely, but in the case of "The Misanthrope" its social attitudes find a mockingly telling echo in our society. Molière was writing of a Paris dominated by the French court of the mid-17th century. A society as mannered as a ruffle and as hypocritical as a duelist's courtesy.

Bad verse gushed out of society's faucet; manners were a comedy; comedies were manners, and all manner of bows, scrapes, bobs, bows and falsities eased the daily traffic of human intercourse and quite obviated the need for honesty. Into this society comes Alceste, who, sadness of sadness, not only has the bad taste to speak his mind but, alas and alas, also is head over rapier in love with Celimene, who is all coquetry, all wiles, all deceit and all entrancements. In short, a witch of the first water.

Celimene, who is as surrounded with lovers as a lap dog might be with cushions, is the very epitome of the age. She is a gossip who cannot bear to hear a good word about anyone, and she relates the bad word with such a pretty display of dazzling malice that her barbs go out to her victims as sharp as Cupid's arrows.

Against such a woman the bluff and honest Alceste has no defenses. He rampages through polite society telling people to their face things that should be said only behind their backs, and as a result he has become a misanthrope, determined to abandon a society he finds false and the company of men he finds abhorrent. But then, there is always Celimene to lead him back to the straight and narrow primrose path.

It is a play that mixes humor and humanity so skillfully that anyone wanting to know what a comedy really is could well study it. The characters of the play—with the ill-contrasted lovers set against a background of tittlers and tattlers—are sweetly balanced, and progress of the play is exquisite right up to the masterly conclusion, which is wittily inconclusive.

Molière provides one great scene after another as the characters pirouette round, flicking one another like fencers. Yet beyond the wit and the dazzle, the insults and the ripostes, lies a serious play of a man disgusted by the false values he finds around him. Molière is too humane to be a satirist. He never loads the battle; he never really takes sides. Alceste is not only the one completely honest man in the play, he is also the one prig, and is not a little pompous.

His very aggressiveness is comic, and he sometimes protests so much that he seems to take as much pleasure out of his protestation as out of his virtue. No, perhaps, Molière's ideal is conveyed better in the characters of his friend Philante and Eliante, Celimene's cousin, who, in the words of Philante, hold that "in polite society, custom decrees that we show certain outward courtesies." Celimene, faithless yet vivacious, has a lesson to learn, but then so has Alceste.

What often stands in the way of Molière in English is the incredible difficulty of translating the poet's rhymed couplets while preserving rhyme, sense, rhythm, wit and sensibility. Richard Wilbur's marvelous translation does this. It is supple and subtle, it trips affectionately off the tongue with the rise and fall of natural speech to it, and the wit shimmers at its heart like a priceless diamond on a bed of velvet.

The A.P.A. rose manfully to the challenge, helped manfully by the swiftly naturalistic staging of Stephen Porter, who let the language speak for itself and the play make its own points. Although the company is dangerously shallow in depth, Richard Easton made an excellent Alceste, bluff, comically—but never too comically—wronged and surprisingly warm, as if at times he was not only the dupe of Celimene but also of his own unbending rectitude.

The other outstanding performance came from Brian Bedford—who in only his second performance with the company is shaping up as the right kind of repertory star—as the foppish Acaste. Mr. Bedford uses both his eyes and teeth with such exceptional virtuosity that one might easily overlook his perfect period manners, in which only Mr. Easton could rival him, and his deftly accurate comic timing. Keene Curtis, yet another of Celimene's suitors, also gave a very well-judged portrayal, with one gorgeous scene in which he reads a sonnet to Mr. Easton, asks for an honest opinion and disconcertingly receives it.

The women (Rosemary Harris come home wherever you are!) do not come off so well. Christine Pickles, however, makes a very brave attempt at Celimene, and has the right looks, the right voice and even the right spirit. But at this performance they somehow failed to come together at the right time; it was a portrayal almost right, and on another night might well prove more memorable than on this.

GEORGE ETHEREGE

Sir George Etherege—diplomat, dramatist, man-about-town—perfectly exemplifies the spirit of sophisticated Restoration society. Pleasure was his goal, and he hungered after it ceaselessly, even during his appointment as Minister to Ratisbon (1685–1688), when he scandalized the German aristocrats with his losses at gambling and his triumphs in love. Carousing, gambling, talking, whoring, writing—these were the forms of his pleasure, just as they were the delights of other men in the giddy world of London's high society for at least thirty years after the Restoration of monarchy to England in 1660. Like Charles II, the king who restored monarchy and who was the model for the sophisticated men of the age, Etherege conducted his life with the unaffected grace and polish of a true wit. He came to be known by his friends as "easie" Etherege, and he numbered among his companions the most brilliant and rakish young men of the age—the "court wits"—Henry Savile, Sir Charles Sedley, and John Wilmot, the "wicked" Earl of Rochester. They admired him for his wit, his skeptical attitudes, his libertine values, and he prided himself on his "noble laziness of mind." Had he been less of a gentleman, he might have been more of a dramatist, but his "noble laziness" made it impossible for him to take the stage seriously. For Etherege, as for many dramatists of his day, writing was a fashionable pastime but not a serious profession.

He wrote only three plays: *The Comical Revenge; or, Love in a Tub* (1664); *She Wou'd if She Cou'd* (1668); and *The Man of Mode, or, Sir Fopling Flutter* (1676). But these plays, particularly the last two, are preeminent examples of Restoration social comedy. *She Wou'd if She Cou'd* was, in fact, the first play of the period to give itself over entirely to the fashionable spots, the witty capers, the smart talk, the lively people, and the hangers-on of sophisticated London society. Its main action focuses on the lively courtship of two witty young women from the country, Ariana and Gatty, by two rakish young men of the town, Courtall and Freeman. As their tag names suggest, the women are gadabouts seeking the idle and harmless pleasures of the town, while the men are hedonists pursuing sexual satisfaction without the restraints of marriage. And the comic wit of their courtship derives from this basic tension. Set off against these lively young people are the would-be wits, such as the Cockwoods and other country types, who aspire to the ways of the city without the intelligence or verve to achieve sophistication. *She Wou'd if She Cou'd* is a sustained contrast between true and false wit according to the standards of Restoration society, and thus it charmed the critics, as well as the court, and three years after its premiere was still being talked of as "the best comedy that has been written since the Restoration of the stage."

The Man of Mode, according to chroniclers of the period, also "met with extraordinary success" and "got a great deal of money" from its opening run in the theater. Its initial success was at least in part the result of striking similarities that the audience seemed to find between the chief male characters in the play and well-known members of the Restoration smart set. Some people thought that

Etherege was portraying himself in the sexual escapades of Dorimant; others believed that "that base man Mr. Dorimant" was a replica of the "wicked" Earl of Rochester. Medley was associated with Sir Charles Sedley, and Sir Fopling with Beau Hewitt, an eminent fop of the day. But Dryden was closer to the truth when he reminded the audience in his epilogue to the play that "every man is safe from what he feared,/ For no one fool is hunted from the herd." As its ambiguous title suggests, the play is not about one fool in particular, but about modish life styles in general—about the nature of existence in a highly sophisticated society and the consequences of a commitment to its unique social values. In this respect it bears comparison with Molière's *The Misanthrope*.

But while the protagonist of Molière's play is a critic of his society, the hero of Etherege's play, namely Dorimant, is the supreme embodiment of his society's values. His status as rake-hero is epitomized in such outlandish activities as cheerfully breaking off with one mistress in the presence of the woman he will next seduce, casually sending a guinea to a whore for a box at the opera, kissing his latest mistress while his valet ties up the bed-linen and his friends wait outside, all the while quoting lines from poetry that perfectly suit his situation. In these and similar activities, Dorimant epitomizes the wit, the grace, the libertinism, and the cynicism that also reappear in other rake-heroes, such as Horner in Wycherley's *The Country Wife* (1675), Valentine in Congreve's *Love for Love* (1695), and both Mirabell and Fainall (the hero and villain) in Congreve's *The Way of the World* (1700).

In contrast to Dorimant who is the true "man of mode," Etherege gives us a dazzling comic portrait in the titular "man of mode," Sir Fopling Flutter. Young Bellair and Dorimant sum him up neatly:

He thinks himself the pattern of modern gallantry.
He is indeed the pattern of modern foppery.

Sir Fopling is the English counterpart of Acaste, Clitandre, and Oronte in *The Misanthrope*. Happily lost in his French clothes, French phrases, and consuming self-esteem, he cannot see the discrepancy between what he wants to be and what he really is. In his excesses and delusions he recurs in other comic fools, such as Witwoud and Petulant of *The Way of the World*, Lord Foppington of Vanbrugh's *The Relapse* (1697), and even survives into the eighteenth century with Bob Acres of Sheridan's *The Rivals* (1775) and Crabtree as well as Sir Benjamin Backbite of Sheridan's *The School for Scandal* (1777).

Like most Restoration comedies, *The Man of Mode* creates its dramatic contrasts not only through differing characters, but also through a variety of plot lines. While we are witnessing Dorimant's various sexual intrigues in the main plot, we are also viewing Young Bellair's sincere courtship of Emilia. So we are repeatedly asked to compare the deceptions practiced by Dorimant, such as his callous manipulation of Mrs. Loveit, with the harmless games of Bellair, such as the pretended courtship he enacts with Harriet (see Figure 42). Implicit in that comparison must be a questioning of the standards by which the witty and wealthy Dorimant conducts his life. So, too, in the multiple plots of *The Country Wife*, the wooing of Alithea by Harcourt forms a normative contrast to Horner's seduction of Lady Pinchwife. The complex plot of *The Way of the World* invites us to see that the scheming of Mirabell and the scheming of Fainall are, in many ways, so similar as to blur their ethical differences. In a society where cleverness and intelligence control all, we are asked to applaud the clever even while we note their lack of conventional morality.

But even as *The Man of Mode* shows us a world that values Dorimant in spite of his heartlessness and mocks Loveit for her lack of emotional control, it also marks the beginning of the move in English comic drama toward recognizing genuine feeling as the basis of lasting personal relationships. We know that Dorimant, despite his wit, is vulnerable when he sees Loveit flirting with Sir Fopling, and his emotional vulnerability is clearly displayed when he reveals his love for Harriet in an aside: "I love her and dare not let her know it. I fear sh'as an ascendant o'er me and may revenge the wrongs I have done her sex." Harriet also hides her love for Dorimant and because she conceals it longer is able to put him to a real test. Beyond that testing process, their mutual emotional repression comically reveals the painful price that comes from a commitment to the elegant style of their society. *The Way of the World* displays the problem of emotional vulnerability even more clearly in Mirabell who directly confesses his love of Millamant to his friends. When she teases him by saying, "What would you give that you could help loving me?" she then forces him to the witty and painfully honest confession that "I would give something that you did not know I could not help it." Such moments of sincerity look forward to the surprising climax of Farquhar's *The Beaux Stratagem* (1707), in which a married couple who are unsuited to each other cheerfully agree to divorce rather than continuing the facade, and farce, of their marriage.

The valuing of truth in human relationships, a truth that may lie hidden, consciously or unconsciously, under the wit of the characters has led modern directors to look to Restoration comedy not just for a source of elegant and stagey period pieces, but also for characters and situations that seem contemporary in their implications. When *The Man of Mode* was produced by the Royal Shakespeare Company, for example, the director (Terry Hands) deliberately broke away from a detailed period setting, as he explains in the interview following the text. The set for his production featured a magnified version of Newton's cradle (see Figures 43 and 44), a piece contemporary with the play (as a Restoration scientific model), but also familiar to its modern audience (as a popular game-object). This device, together with the modern costumes, provoked differing reactions from audiences and critics, as can be seen in the two reviews reprinted following the text. But the modern style of the production evidently did give the actors the freedom to discover the reality of the play's emotions.

THE MAN OF MODE
Or, Sir Fopling Flutter

BY GEORGE ETHEREGE

CHARACTERS

MR. DORIMANT

MR. MEDLEY

OLD BELLAIR

YOUNG BELLAIR

SIR FOPLING FLUTTER

LADY TOWNLEY

EMILIA

MRS. LOVEIT

BELLINDA

LADY WOODVILL

HARRIET, *her daughter*

PERT, *a waiting woman*

BUSY, *a waiting woman*

A SHOEMAKER

AN ORANGE WOMAN

THREE SLOVENLY BULLIES

TWO CHAIRMEN

MR. SMIRK, *a Parson*

HANDY, *a Valet-de-chambre*

PAGES, FOOTMEN, *etc.*

PROLOGUE

By Sir Car Scroope, Baronet°

Like dancers on the ropes poor poets fare,
Most perish young, the rest in danger are;
This, one would think, should make our authors
    wary,
But, gamester-like, the giddy fools miscarry.
A lucky hand or two so tempts 'em on,
They cannot leave off play till they're undone.
With modest fears a muse does first begin,
Like a young wench newly enticed to sin;
But tickled once with praise, by her good will,
The wanton fool would never more lie still.
'Tis an old mistress you'll meet here tonight,
Whose charms you once have looked on with delight.
But now of late such dirty drabs have known ye,
A muse o'th' better sort's ashamed to own ye.
Nature well drawn, and wit, must now give place
To gaudy nonsense and to dull grimace;
Nor is it strange that you should like so much
That kind of wit, for most of yours is such.
But I'm afraid that while to France we go,
To bring you home fine dresses, dance, and show,
The stage, like you, will but more foppish grow.
Of foreign wares, why should we fetch the scum,
When we can be so richly served at home?
For heav'n be thanked, 'tis not so wise an age
But your own follies may supply the stage.
Though often plowed, there's no great fear the soil
Should barren grow by the too frequent toil;

While at your doors are to be daily found
Such loads of dunghill to manure the ground.
'Tis by your follies that we players thrive,
As the physicians by diseases live;
And as each year some new distemper reigns,
Whose friendly poison helps to increase their gains,
So among you there starts up every day
Some new, unheard-of fool for us to play.
Then, for your own sakes be not too severe,
Nor what you all admire at home, damn here;
Since each is fond of his own ugly face,
Why should you, when we hold it, break the glass?

ACT 1 / SCENE 1

(A dressing room. A table covered with a toilet; clothes laid ready.)

(Enter DORIMANT *in his gown and slippers, with a note in his hand, made up, repeating verses.)*

DORIMANT: Now for some ages had the pride of Spain
Made the sun shine on half the world in vain.°

(Then looking on the note.)

'For Mrs. Loveit.'—What a dull, insipid thing is a billet-doux written in cold blood, after the heat of the business is over! It is a tax upon good nature which I have here been laboring to pay, and have done it, but with as much regret as ever fanatic paid the Royal Aid or church duties.°

Sir Car Scroope, one of the most popular of "the mob of gentlemen who wrote with ease."

Here as elsewhere in the play, Dorimant recites lines from the seventeenth century poet, Edmund Waller. *church duties,* taxes levied in support of the civil and ecclesiastical government.

'Twill have the same fate, I know, that all my notes to her have had of late; 'twill not be thought kind enough. 'Faith, women are i'the right when they jealously examine our letters, for in them we always first discover our decay of passion.—Hey! Who waits?

(Enter HANDY.*)*

HANDY: Sir—

DORIMANT: Call a footman.

HANDY: None of 'em are come yet.

DORIMANT: Dogs! Will they ever lie snoring abed till noon?

HANDY: 'Tis all one, sir; if they're up, you indulge 'em so they're ever poaching after whores all the morning.

DORIMANT: Take notice henceforward who's wanting in his duty; the next clap he gets, he shall rot for an example. What vermin are those chattering without?

HANDY: Foggy° Nan, the orange-woman, and Swearing Tom, the shoemaker.

DORIMANT: Go, call in that over-grown jade with the flasket° of guts before her; fruit is refreshing in a morning.

(Exit HANDY.*)*

It is not that I love you less
Than when before your feet I lay—

(Enter ORANGE-WOMAN *and* HANDY.*)*

How now, double tripe, what news do you bring?

ORANGE WOMAN: News! Here's the best fruit has come to town t'year; gad, I was up before four o'clock this morning and bought all the choice i'the market.

DORIMANT: The nasty refuse of your shop.

ORANGE WOMAN: You need not make mouths at it; I assure you, 'tis all culled ware.

DORIMANT: The citizens buy better on a holiday in their walk to Totnam.°

ORANGE WOMAN: Good or bad, 'tis all one; I never knew you commend anything. Lord! would the ladies had heard you talk of 'em as I have done! *(Sets down the fruit.)* Here, bid your man give me an angel.°

DORIMANT *(to* HANDY*)*: Give the bawd her fruit again.

ORANGE WOMAN: Well, on my conscience, there never was the like of you!—God's my life, I had almost forgot to tell you there is a young gentlewoman lately come to town with her mother, that is so taken with you.

DORIMANT: Is she handsome?

ORANGE WOMAN: Nay,° gad, there are few finer women, I tell you but so, and a hugeous fortune, they say. Here, eat this peach. It comes from the stone;° 'tis better than any Newington° y'have tasted.

DORIMANT *(taking the peach)*: This fine woman, I'll lay my life, is some awkward, ill-fashioned country toad who, not having above four dozen of black hairs on her head, has adorned her baldness with a large, white fruz,° that she may look sparkishly in the forefront of the King's box at an old play.

ORANGE WOMAN: Gad, you'd change your note quickly if you did but see her.

DORIMANT: How came she to know me?

ORANGE WOMAN: She saw you yesterday at the Change;° she told me you came and fooled with the woman at the next shop.

DORIMANT: I remember there was a mask observed me, indeed. Fooled, did she say?

ORANGE WOMAN: Ay; I vow she told me twenty things you said, too, and acted with her head and with her body so like you—

(Enter MEDLEY.*)*

MEDLEY: Dorimant, my life, my joy, my darling sin! How dost thou? *(Embraces* DORIMANT.*)*

ORANGE WOMAN: Lord, what a filthy trick these men have got of kissing one another! *(she spits.)*

MEDLEY: Why do you suffer this cartload of scandal to come near you and make your neighbors think you so improvident to need a bawd?

ORANGE WOMAN *(to* DORIMANT*)*: Good, now! we shall have it you did but want° him to help you! Come, pay me for my fruit.

MEDLEY: Make us thankful for it,° huswife, bawds are as much out of fashion as gentlemen-ushers;° none but old formal ladies use the one, and none but foppish old stagers° employ the other. Go! You are an insignificant brandy bottle.

DORIMANT: Nay, there you wrong her; three quarts of Canary is her business.

ORANGE WOMAN: What you please, gentlemen.

DORIMANT: To him! give him as good as he brings.

ORANGE WOMAN: Hang him, there is not such another

Foggy, bloated.   **flasket,** a long shallow basket or tub. **Totnam,** Tottenham, a northern suburb of London.   **angel,** a gold coin worth ten shillings.

Nay, a meaningless interjection equivalent to "why!" **stone,** the meaning of this phrase is not clear: it may be either that the fruit was sun-ripened upon a tree trained against a stone wall, or that it was a freestone peach. **Newington,** the center of a fruit-growing district in Kent. **fruz,** a frizzy arrangement of artificial hair. **Change,** The New Exchange in the Strand. **want,** need. **Make . . . it,** i.e., God make us thankful for it. **gentlemen-ushers,** male attendants upon a lady. **old stagers,** old hands.

heathen in the town again, except it be the shoemaker without.

MEDLEY: I shall see you hold up your hand at the bar next sessions for murder, huswife; that shoemaker can take his oath you are in fee with the doctors to sell green fruit to the gentry, that the crudities may breed diseases.

ORANGE WOMAN (to DORIMANT): Pray, give me my money.

DORIMANT: Not a penny! When you bring the gentlewoman hither you spoke of, you shall be paid.

ORANGE WOMAN: The gentlewoman! the gentlewoman may be as honest° as your sisters for aught I know. Pray, pay me, Mr. Dorimant, and do not abuse me so; I have an honester way of living—you know it.

MEDLEY: Was there ever such a resty° bawd!

DORIMANT: Some jade's tricks she has, but she makes amends when she's in good humor.—Come, tell me the lady's name and Handy shall pay you.

ORANGE WOMAN: I must not; she forbid me.

DORIMANT: That's a sure sign she would have you.°

MEDLEY: Where does she live?

ORANGE WOMAN: They lodge at my house.

MEDLEY: Nay, then she's in a hopeful way.

ORANGE WOMAN: Good Mr. Medley, say your pleasure of me, but take heed how you affront my house! God's my life!—'in a hopeful way!'

DORIMANT: Prithee, peace! What kind of woman's the mother?

ORANGE WOMAN: A goodly, grave gentlewoman. Lord, how she talks against the wild young men o' the town! As for your part, she thinks you an arrant devil; should she see you, on my conscience she would look if you had not a cloven foot.

DORIMANT: Does she know me?

ORANGE WOMAN: Only by hearsay; a thousand horrid stories have been told her of you, and she believes 'em all.

MEDLEY: By the character this should be the famous Lady Woodvill and her daughter Harriet.

ORANGE WOMAN: The devil's in him for guessing, I think.

DORIMANT: Do you know 'em?

MEDLEY: Both very well; the mother's a great admirer of the forms and civility of the last age.

DORIMANT: An antiquated beauty may be allowed to be out of humor at the freedoms of the present. This is a good account of the mother; pray, what is the daughter?

MEDLEY: Why, first, she's an heiress—vastly rich.

DORIMANT: And handsome?

MEDLEY: What alteration a twelvemonth may have bred in her I know not, but a year ago she was the beautifullest creature I ever saw: a fine, easy, clean shape; light brown hair in abundance; her features regular; her complexion clear and lively; large, wanton eyes; but above all, a mouth that has made me kiss it a thousand times in imagination; teeth white and even, and pretty, pouting lips, with a little moisture ever hanging on them, that look like the Provins° rose fresh on the bush, ere the morning sun has quite drawn up the dew.

DORIMANT: Rapture! mere° rapture!

ORANGE WOMAN: Nay, gad, he tells you true; she's a delicate creature.

DORIMANT: Has she wit?

MEDLEY: More than is usual in her sex, and as much malice. Then, she's as wild as you would wish her, and has a demureness in her looks that makes it so surprising.

DORIMANT: Flesh and blood cannot hear this and not long to know her.

MEDLEY: I wonder what makes her mother bring her up to town; an old doting keeper cannot be more jealous of his mistress.

ORANGE WOMAN: She made me laugh yesterday; there was a judge came to visit 'em, and the old man, she told me, did so stare upon her, and when he saluted her smacked so heartily. Who would think it of 'em?

MEDLEY: God-a-mercy, judge!°

DORIMANT: Do 'em right; the gentlemen of the long robe° have not been wanting by their good examples to countenance the crying sin o' the nation.

MEDLEY: Come, on with your trappings; 'tis later than you imagine.

DORIMANT: Call in the shoemaker, Handy.

ORANGE WOMAN: Good Mr. Dorimant, pay me. Gad, I had rather give you my fruit than stay to be abused by that foul-mouthed rogue; what you gentlemen say, it matters not much, but such a dirty fellow does one more disgrace.

DORIMANT (to HANDY): Give her ten shillings—(to ORANGE-WOMAN) and be sure you tell the young gentlewoman I must be acquainted with her.

ORANGE WOMAN: Now do you long to be tempting this pretty creature. Well, heavens mend you!

MEDLEY: Farewell, bog!°

(Exit ORANGE-WOMAN and HANDY.)

---

honest, chaste. resty, restive. have you, i.e., have you tell me.

Provins, the town of Provins, some 50 miles E.S.E. of Paris, is still noted for its trade in roses. mere, pure. God-a-mercy, judge, an ironical exclamation of applause, equivalent to "Well done, judge!" gentlemen ... robe, lawyers. bog, fat person.

—Dorimant, when did you see your *pisaller,*° as you call her, Mrs. Loveit?

DORIMANT: Not these two days.

MEDLEY: And how stand affairs between you?

DORIMANT: There has been great patching of late, much ado; we make a shift to hang together.

MEDLEY: I wonder how her mighty spirit bears it.

DORIMANT: Ill enough, on all conscience; I never knew so violent a creature.

MEDLEY: She's the most passionate in her love and the most extravagant in her jealousy of any woman I ever heard of. What note is that?

DORIMANT: An excuse I am going to send her for the neglect I am guilty of.

MEDLEY: Prithee, read it.

DORIMANT: No; but if you will take the pains, you may.

MEDLEY *(reads)*:

I never was a lover of business, but now I have a just reason to hate it, since it has kept me these two days from seeing you. I intend to wait upon you in the afternoon, and in the pleasure of your conversation forget all I have suffered during this tedious absence.

This business of yours, Dorimant, has been with a vizard° at the playhouse; I have had an eye on you. If some malicious body should betray you, this kind note would hardly make your peace with her.

DORIMANT: I desire no better.

MEDLEY: Why, would her knowledge of it oblige you?

DORIMANT: Most infinitely; next to the coming to a good understanding with a new mistress, I love a quarrel with an old one. But the devil's in't! there has been such a calm in my affairs of late, I have not had the pleasure of making a woman so much as break her fan, to be sullen, or forswear herself, these three days.

MEDLEY: A very great misfortune. Let me see; I love mischief well enough to forward this business myself. I'll about it presently, and though I know the truth of what y'ave done will set her a-raving, I'll heighten it a little with invention, leave her in a fit o' the mother,° and be here again before y'are ready.

DORIMANT: Pray, stay; you may spare yourself the labor. The business is undertaken already by one who will manage it with as much address, and I think with a little more malice than you can.

MEDLEY: Who i'the devil's name can this be!

DORIMANT: Why, the vizard—that very vizard you saw me with.

MEDLEY: Does she love mischief so well as to betray herself to spite another?

DORIMANT: Not so neither, Medley. I will make you comprehend the mystery: this mask, for a farther confirmation of what I have been these two days swearing to her, made me yesterday at the playhouse make her a promise before her face utterly to break off with Loveit, and, because she tenders° my reputation and would not have me do a barbarous thing, has contrived a way to give me a handsome occasion.

MEDLEY: Very good.

DORIMANT: She intends about an hour before me, this afternoon, to make Loveit a visit, and, having the privilege, by reason of a professed friendship between them, to talk of her concerns—

MEDLEY: Is she a friend?

DORIMANT: Oh, an intimate friend!

MEDLEY: Better and better; pray, proceed.

DORIMANT: She means insensibly to insinuate a discourse of me and artificially raise her jealousy to such a height that, transported with the first motions of her passion, she shall fly upon me with all the fury imaginable as soon as ever I enter; the quarrel being thus happily begun, I am to play my part, confess and justify all my roguery, swear her impertinence and ill-humor makes her intolerable, tax her with the next fop that comes into my head, and in a huff march away, slight her, and leave her to be taken by whosoever thinks it worth his time to lie down before her.

MEDLEY: This vizard is a spark and has a genius that makes her worthy of yourself, Dorimant.

(Enter HANDY, SHOEMAKER, *and* FOOTMAN.*)*

DORIMANT: You rogue there, who sneak like a dog that has flung down a dish! if you do not mend your waiting, I'll uncase you° and turn you loose to the wheel of fortune. *(Giving* HANDY *the letter.)* Handy, seal this and let him run with it presently. *(Exit* FOOTMAN.*)*

MEDLEY: Since y'are resolved on a quarrel, why do you send her this kind note?

DORIMANT: To keep her at home in order to the business—*(to the* SHOEMAKER*)* How now, you drunken sot?

SHOEMAKER: 'Zbud, you have no reason to talk; I have not had a bottle of sack of yours in my belly this fortnight.

MEDLEY: The orange woman says your neighbors take notice what a heathen you are, and design to inform the bishop and have you burned for an atheist.

---

pisaller, makeshift. *vizard,* mask; by metonymy, a masked person. *fit . . . mother,* hysteria.

tenders, cherishes. *uncase you,* strip you (of your livery).

SHOEMAKER: Damn her, dunghill, if her husband does not remove her, she stinks so, the parish intend to indict him for a nuisance.

MEDLEY: I advise you like a friend; reform your life. You have brought the envy of the world upon you by living above yourself. Whoring and swearing are vices too genteel for a shoemaker.

SHOEMAKER: 'Zbud, I think you men of quality will grow as unreasonable as the women. You would ingross° the sins of the nation; poor folks can no sooner be wicked but th'are railed at by their betters.

DORIMANT: Sirrah, I'll have you stand i'the pillory for this libel!

SHOEMAKER: Some of you deserve it, I'm sure; there are so many of 'em, that our journeymen nowadays, instead of harmless ballads, sing nothing but your damned lampoons.

DORIMANT: Our lampoons, you rogue!

SHOEMAKER: Nay, good master, why should not you write your own commentaries as well as Cæsar?

MEDLEY: The rascal's read, I perceive.

SHOEMAKER: You know the old proverb—ale and history.°

DORIMANT: Draw on my shoes, sirrah.

SHOEMAKER: Here's a shoe—!

DORIMANT: —Sits with more wrinkles than there are in an angry bully's forehead!

SHOEMAKER: 'Zbud, as smooth as your mistress's skin does upon her! So; strike your foot in home. 'Zbud, if e'er a monsieur of 'em all make more fashionable ware, I'll be content to have my ears whipped off with my own paring knife.

MEDLEY: And served up in a ragout instead of coxcombs to a company of French shoemakers for a collation.

SHOEMAKER: Hold, hold! Damn 'em, caterpillars! let 'em feed upon cabbage.—Come master, your health this morning next my heart now!

DORIMANT: Go, get you home and govern your family better! Do not let your wife follow you to the alehouse, beat your whore, and lead you home in triumph.

SHOEMAKER: 'Zbud, there's never a man i'the town lives more like a gentleman with his wife than I do. I never mind her motions,° she never inquires into mine; we speak to one another civilly, hate one another heartily, and because 'tis vulgar to lie and soak° together, we have each of us our several° settle-bed.

DORIMANT (to HANDY): Give him half a crown.

MEDLEY: Not without he will promise to be bloody drunk.

SHOEMAKER: 'Tope' 's the word i'the eye of the world. (HANDY gives him money; he invites HANDY, in dumbshow, to join him in a drink.) For my master's honor, Robin!

DORIMANT: Do not debauch my servants, sirrah.

SHOEMAKER: I only tip him the wink; he knows an alehouse from a hovel. (Exit SHOEMAKER.)

DORIMANT (to HANDY): My clothes, quickly.

MEDLEY: Where shall we dine today?

(Enter YOUNG BELLAIR.)

DORIMANT: Where you will; here comes a good third man.

YOUNG BELLAIR: Your servant, gentlemen.

MEDLEY: Gentle sir, how will you answer this visit to your honorable mistress? 'Tis not her interest you should keep company with men of sense who will be talking reason.

YOUNG BELLAIR: I do not fear her pardon; do you but grant me yours for my neglect of late.

MEDLEY: Though y'ave made us miserable by the want of your good company, to show you I am free from all resentment, may the beautiful cause of our misfortune give you all the joys happy lovers have shared ever since the world began.

YOUNG BELLAIR: You wish me in heaven, but you believe me on my journey to hell.

MEDLEY: You have a good strong faith, and that may contribute much towards your salvation. I confess I am but of an untoward constitution, apt to have doubts and scruples—and in love they are no less distracting than in religion. Were I so near marriage, I should cry out by fits as I ride in my coach, 'Cuckold, cuckold!' with no less fury than the mad fanatic does 'glory!' in Bethlem.°

YOUNG BELLAIR: Because religion makes some run mad must I live an atheist?

MEDLEY: Is it not great indiscretion for a man of credit, who may have money enough on his word, to go and deal with Jews, who for little sums make men enter into bonds and give judgments?

YOUNG BELLAIR: Preach no more on this text. I am determined, and there is no hope of my conversion.

DORIMANT (to HANDY, who is fiddling about him): Leave your unnecessary fiddling; a wasp that's buzzing

---

ingross, monopolize. **ale and history,** the proverb has not been identified: it may have been a vernacular equivalent of the Latin *in vino veritas,* referring to the frankness of an intoxicated person. **motions,** actions. **soak,** get drunk. **several,** individual.

Bethlem, Bethlehem Hospital, more commonly known as Bedlam, an asylum for the insane, in Moorfields. The fanatic referred to may have been Oliver Cromwell's mad porter.

about a man's nose at dinner is not more troublesome than thou art.

HANDY: You love to have your clothes hang just, sir.

DORIMANT: I love to be well dressed, sir, and think it no scandal to my understanding.

HANDY: Will you use the essence or orange flower water?

DORIMANT: I will smell as I do today, no offence to the ladies' noses.

HANDY: Your pleasure, sir. (*Exit* HANDY.)

DORIMANT: That a man's excellency should lie in neatly tying of a ribband or a cravat! How careful's nature in furnishing the world with necessary coxcombs!

YOUNG BELLAIR: That's a mighty pretty suit of yours, Dorimant.

DORIMANT: I am glad't has your approbation.

YOUNG BELLAIR: No man in town has a better fancy in his clothes than you have.

DORIMANT: You will make me have an opinion of my genius.

MEDLEY: There is a great critic, I hear, in these matters lately arrived piping hot from Paris.

YOUNG BELLAIR: Sir Fopling Flutter, you mean.

MEDLEY: The same.

YOUNG BELLAIR: He thinks himself the pattern of modern gallantry.

DORIMANT: He is indeed the pattern of modern foppery.

MEDLEY: He was yesterday at the play, with a pair of gloves up to his elbows, and a periwig more exactly curled than a lady's head newly dressed for a ball.

YOUNG BELLAIR: What a pretty lisp he has!

DORIMANT: Ho! that he affects in imitation of the people of quality of France.

MEDLEY: His head stands, for the most part, on one side, and his looks are more languishing than a lady's when she lolls at stretch in her coach or leans her head carelessly against the side of a box i'the playhouse.

DORIMANT: He is a person indeed of great acquired follies.

MEDLEY: He is like many others, beholding to his education for making him so eminent a coxcomb; many a fool had been lost to the world had their indulgent parents wisely bestowed neither learning nor good breeding on 'em.

YOUNG BELLAIR: He has been, as the sparkish word is, 'brisk upon the ladies' already. He was yesterday at my Aunt Townley's and gave Mrs. Loveit a catalogue of his good qualities under the character of a complete gentleman, who, according to Sir Fopling, ought to dress well, dance well, fence well, have a genius for love letters, an agreeable voice for a chamber, be very amorous, something discreet, but not overconstant.

MEDLEY: Pretty ingredients to make an accomplished person!

DORIMANT: I am glad he pitched upon Loveit.

YOUNG BELLAIR: How so?

DORIMANT: I wanted a fop to lay to her charge, and this is as pat as may be.

YOUNG BELLAIR: I am confident she loves no man but you.

DORIMANT: The good fortune were enough to make me vain, but that I am in my nature modest.

YOUNG BELLAIR: Hark you, Dorimant.—With your leave, Mr. Medley; 'tis only a secret concerning a fair lady.

MEDLEY: Your good breeding, sir, gives you too much trouble, you might have whispered without all this ceremony.

YOUNG BELLAIR (*to* DORIMANT): How stand your affairs with Bellinda of late?

DORIMANT: She's a little jilting baggage.

YOUNG BELLAIR: Nay, I believe her false enough, but she's ne'er the worse for your purpose; she was with you yesterday in a disguise at the play.

DORIMANT: There we fell out and resolved never to speak to one another more.

YOUNG BELLAIR: The occasion?

DORIMANT: Want of courage to meet me at the place appointed. These young women apprehend loving as much as the young men do fighting, at first; but once entered, like them too, they all turn bullies straight.

(*Enter* HANDY.)

HANDY (*to* YOUNG BELLAIR): Sir, your man without desires to speak with you.

YOUNG BELLAIR: Gentlemen, I'll return immediately. (*Exit* YOUNG BELLAIR.)

MEDLEY: A very pretty fellow this.

DORIMANT: He's handsome, well bred, and by much the most tolerable of all the young men that do not abound in wit.

MEDLEY: Ever well dressed, always complaisant, and seldom impertinent. You and he are grown very intimate, I see.

DORIMANT: It is our mutual interest to be so: it makes the women think the better of his understanding, and judge more favorably of my reputation; it makes him pass upon some for a man of very good sense, and I upon others for a very civil person.

MEDLEY: What was that whisper?

DORIMANT: A thing which he would fain have known, but I did not think it fit to tell him; it might have frighted him from his honorable intentions of marrying.

MEDLEY: Emilia—give her her due—has the best reputation of any young woman about the town who has beauty enough to provoke detraction;

her carriage is unaffected, her discourse modest—not at all censorious nor pretending, like the counterfeits of the age.

DORIMANT: She's a discreet maid, and I believe nothing can corrupt her but a husband.

MEDLEY: A husband?

DORIMANT: Yes, a husband. I have known many women make a difficulty of losing a maidenhead, who have afterwards made none of making a cuckold.

MEDLEY: This prudent consideration, I am apt to think, has made you confirm poor Bellair in the desperate resolution he has taken.

DORIMANT: Indeed, the little hope I found there was of her, in the state she was in, has made me by my advice contribute something towards the changing of her condition.

(*Enter* YOUNG BELLAIR.)

—Dear Bellair, by heavens, I thought we had lost thee! men in love are never to be reckoned on when we would form a company.

YOUNG BELLAIR: Dorimant, I am undone. My man has brought the most surprising news i'the world.

DORIMANT: Some strange misfortune is befallen your love.

YOUNG BELLAIR: My father came to town last night and lodges i'the very house where Emilia lies.

MEDLEY: Does he know it is with her you are in love?

YOUNG BELLAIR: He knows I love, but knows not whom, without some officious sot has betrayed me.

DORIMANT: Your Aunt Townley is your confidant and favors the business.

YOUNG BELLAIR: I do not apprehend any ill office from her. I have received a letter, in which I am commanded by my father to meet him at my aunt's this afternoon. He tells me farther he has made a match for me and bids me resolve to be obedient to his will or expect to be disinherited.

MEDLEY: Now's your time, Bellair; never had lover such an opportunity of giving a generous proof of his passion.

YOUNG BELLAIR: As how, I pray?

MEDLEY: Why, hang an estate, marry Emilia out of hand, and provoke your father to do what he threatens; 'tis but despising a coach, humbling yourself to a pair of goloshes,° being out of countenance when you meet your friends, pointed at and pitied wherever you go by all the amorous fops that know you, and your fame will be immortal.

YOUNG BELLAIR: I could find in my heart to resolve not to marry at all.

DORIMANT: Fie, fie! That would spoil a good jest and disappoint the well-natured town of an occasion of laughing at you.

YOUNG BELLAIR: The storm I have so long expected hangs o'er my head and begins to pour down upon me; I am on the rack and can have no rest till I'm satisfied in what I fear. Where do you dine?

DORIMANT: At Long's or Locket's.°

MEDLEY: At Long's let it be.

YOUNG BELLAIR: I'll run and see Emilia and inform myself how matters stand. If my misfortunes are not so great as to make me unfit for company, I'll be with you. (*Exit* YOUNG BELLAIR.)

(*Enter a* FOOTMAN *with a letter.*)

FOOTMAN (*to* DORIMANT): Here's a letter, sir.

DORIMANT: The superscription's right: 'For Mr. Dorimant.'

MEDLEY: Let's see; the very scrawl and spelling of a true-bred whore.

DORIMANT: I know the hand, the style is admirable, I assure you.

MEDLEY: Prithee, read it.

DORIMANT (*reads*):

I told a you you dud not love me, if you dud, you wou'd have seen me again ere now. I have no money and am very mallicolly; pray send me a guynie to see the operies.

Your servant to command,
Molly.

MEDLEY: Pray, let the whore have a favorable answer, that she may spark it in a box and do honor to her profession.

DORIMANT: She shall, and perk up i'the face of quality. (*to* HANDY) Is the coach at the door?

HANDY: You did not bid me send for it.

DORIMANT: Eternal blockhead! (HANDY *offers to go out.*) Hey, sot—

HANDY: Did you call me, sir?

DORIMANT: I hope you have no just exception to the name, sir?

HANDY: I have sense, sir.

DORIMANT: Not so much as a fly in winter.—How did you come, Medley?

MEDLEY: In a chair.

FOOTMAN (*to* DORIMANT): You may have a hackney coach if you please, sir.

DORIMANT: I may ride the elephant if I please, sir. Call another chair and let my coach follow to Long's.

---

goloshes, pattens or clogs.

Long's, Locket's, fashionable taverns, one in the Haymarket, the other in Charing Cross.

Be calm, ye great parents, etc.

(Exeunt, singing.)

ACT 2 / SCENE 1

(LADY TOWNLEY's house)
(Enter my LADY TOWNLEY and EMILIA.)

LADY TOWNLEY: I was afraid, Emilia, all had been discovered.

EMILIA: I tremble with the apprehension still.

LADY TOWNLEY: That my brother should take lodgings i'the very house where you lie!

EMILIA: 'Twas lucky we had timely notice to warn the people to be secret. He seems to be a mighty good-humored old man.

LADY TOWNLEY: He ever had a notable smirking way with him.

EMILIA: He calls me rogue, tells me he can't abide me, and does so bepat me.

LADY TOWNLEY: On my word, you are much in his favor then.

EMILIA: He has been very inquisitive, I am told, about my family, my reputation, and my fortune.

LADY TOWNLEY: I am confident he does not i'the least suspect you are the woman his son's in love with.

EMILIA: What should make him, then, inform himself so particularly of me?

LADY TOWNLEY: He was always of a very loving temper himself; it may be he has a doting fit upon him—who knows?

EMILIA: It cannot be.

(Enter YOUNG BELLAIR.)

LADY TOWNLEY: Here comes my nephew.—Where did you leave your father?

YOUNG BELLAIR: Writing a note within. Emilia, this early visit looks as if some kind jealousy would not let you rest at home.

EMILIA: The knowledge I have of my rival gives me a little cause to fear your constancy.

YOUNG BELLAIR: My constancy! I vow—

EMILIA: Do not vow. Our love is frail as is our life and full as little in our power; and are you sure you shall outlive this day?

YOUNG BELLAIR: I am not; but when we are in perfect health, 'twere an idle thing to fright ourselves with the thoughts of sudden death.

LADY TOWNLEY: Pray, what has passed between you and your father i'the garden?

YOUNG BELLAIR: He's firm in his resolution, tells me I must marry Mrs. Harriet, or swears he'll marry himself and disinherit me. When I saw I could not prevail with him to be more indulgent, I dissembled an obedience to his will, which has composed his passion and will give us time—and, I hope, opportunity—to deceive him.

(Enter OLD BELLAIR with a note in his hand.)

LADY TOWNLEY: Peace, here he comes!

OLD BELLAIR: Harry, take this and let your man carry it for me to Mr. Fourbe's° chamber, my lawyer i'the Temple.° *(Exit YOUNG BELLAIR.) (to EMILIA)* Neighbor, a dod! I am glad to see thee here.—Make much of her, sister; she's one of the best of your acquaintance. I like her countenance and her behavior well; she has a modesty that is not common i'this age, a dod, she has!

LADY TOWNLEY: I know her value, brother, and esteem her accordingly.

OLD BELLAIR: Advise her to wear a little more mirth in her face; a dod, she's too serious.

LADY TOWNLEY: The fault is very excusable in a young woman.

OLD BELLAIR: Nay, a dod, I like her ne'er the worse. A melancholy beauty has her charms. I love a pretty sadness in a face, which varies now and then, like changeable colors, into a smile.

LADY TOWNLEY: Methinks you speak very feelingly, brother.

OLD BELLAIR: I am but five and fifty, sister, you know—an age not altogether unsensible.—*(to EMILIA)* Cheer up, sweetheart! I have a secret to tell thee may chance to make thee merry. We three will make collation together anon; i'the meantime, mum, I can't abide you! go, I can't abide you!

(Enter YOUNG BELLAIR.)

—Harry, come! you must along with me to my Lady Woodvill's.—I am going to slip the boy at° a mistress.

YOUNG BELLAIR: At a wife, sir, you would say.

OLD BELLAIR: You need not look so glum, sir; a wife is no curse when she brings the blessing of a good estate with her; but an idle town flirt, with a painted face, a rotten reputation, and a crazy fortune, a dod! is the devil and all, and such a one I hear you are in league with.

YOUNG BELLAIR: I cannot help detraction, sir.

OLD BELLAIR: Out! 'A pize° o' their breeches, there are keeping fools° enough for such flaunting baggages, and they are e'en too good for 'em.—*(to EMILIA)* Remember 'night. Go, y'are a rogue, y'are a rogue! Fare you well, fare you well!—*(to YOUNG BELLAIR)* Come, come, come along, sir!

(Exeunt OLD and YOUNG BELLAIR.)

Fourbe's, "Fourbe" is a "label" name, meaning a cheat. *Temple,* the center of the life in the legal profession in London, lying between Fleet Street and the Thames. *slip ... at,* release the boy in pursuit of (a hunting term). *pize,* a meaningless imprecation of uncertain origin. *keeping fools,* i.e., keepers of mistresses.

LADY TOWNLEY: On my word, the old man comes on apace; I'll lay my life he's smitten.

EMILIA: This is nothing but the pleasantness of his humor.

LADY TOWNLEY: I know him better than you. Let it work; it may prove lucky.

(Enter a PAGE.)

PAGE: Madam, Mr. Medley has sent to know whether a visit will not be troublesome this afternoon.

LADY TOWNLEY: Send him word his visits never are so.

(Exit PAGE.)

EMILIA: He's a very pleasant man.

LADY TOWNLEY: He's a very necessary man among us women; he's not scandalous i'the least, perpetually contriving to bring good company together, and always ready to stop up a gap at ombre; then, he knows all the little news o'the town.

EMILIA: I love to hear him talk o'the intrigues; let 'em be never so dull in themselves, he'll make 'em pleasant i'the relation.

LADY TOWNLEY: But he improves things so much one can take no measure of the truth from him. Mr. Dorimant swears a flea or a maggot is not made more monstrous by a magnifying glass than a story is by his telling it.

(Enter MEDLEY.)

EMILIA: Hold, here he comes.

LADY TOWNLEY: Mr. Medley.

MEDLEY: Your servant, madam.

LADY TOWNLEY: You have made yourself a stranger of late.

EMILIA: I believe you took a surfeit of ombre last time you were here.

MEDLEY: Indeed, I had my belly full of that termagant, Lady Dealer. There never was so unsatiable a carder;° an old gleeker° never loved to sit to't like her. I have played with her now at least a dozen times till she 'as worn out all her fine complexion and her tour° would keep in curl no longer.

LADY TOWNLEY: Blame her not, poor woman; she loves nothing so well as a black ace.°

MEDLEY: The pleasure I have seen her in when she has had hope in drawing for a matadore!

EMILIA: 'Tis as pretty sport to her as persuading masks off is to you, to make discoveries.

LADY TOWNLEY: Pray, where's your friend Mr. Dorimant?

MEDLEY: Soliciting his affairs; he's a man of great employment—has more mistresses now depending than the most eminent lawyer in England has causes.°

EMILIA: Here has been Mrs. Loveit so uneasy and out of humor these two days.

LADY TOWNLEY: How strangely love and jealousy rage in that poor woman!

MEDLEY: She could not have picked out a devil upon earth so proper to torment her; h'as made her break a dozen or two of fans already, tear half a score points° in pieces, and destroy hoods and knots° without number.

LADY TOWNLEY: We heard of a pleasant serenade he gave her t'other night.

MEDLEY: A Danish serenade with kettle-drums and trumpets.

EMILIA: Oh, barbarous!

MEDLEY: What! You are of the number of the ladies whose ears are grown so delicate since our operas you can be charmed with nothing but *flûtes douces*° and French hautboys?°

EMILIA: Leave your raillery, and tell us, is there any new wit come forth—songs or novels?

MEDLEY: A very pretty piece of gallantry, by an eminent author, called *The Diversions of Bruxelles,*° very necessary to be read by all old ladies who are desirous to improve themselves at questions and commands, blindman's buff, and the like fashionable recreations.

EMILIA: Oh, ridiculous!

MEDLEY: Then there is *The Art of Affectation,* written by a late beauty of quality, teaching you how to draw up your breasts, stretch up your neck, to thrust out your breech, to play with your head, to toss up your nose, to bite your lips, to turn up your eyes, to speak in a silly, soft tone of a voice, and use all the foolish French words that will infallibly make your person and conversation charming; with a short apology at the latter end in the behalf of young ladies who notoriously wash° and paint though they have naturally good complexions.

EMILIA: What a deal of stuff you tell us!

MEDLEY: Such as the town affords, madam. The Russians, hearing the great respect we have for foreign dancing, have lately sent over some of their best balladines,° who are now practising a famous ballet which will be suddenly° danced at

---

carder, card-player. *gleeker,* player of gleek (an old card game). *tour,* a crescent-shaped front of false hair. *black ace,* in the game of ombre the black aces were two of the three highest trumps, which were known as "matadores."

causes, cases. *score points,* lace kerchiefs. *knots,* bows of ribbon. *flûtes douces,* high-pitched flutes. *hautboys,* oboes. *The Diversions of Bruxelles,* this book, and that named by Medley in his next speech, appear to be the creations of his imagination. *who . . . wash,* use cosmetic washes. *balladines,* ballet dancers. *suddenly,* shortly.

the Bear Garden.°

LADY TOWNLEY: Pray, forbear your idle stories, and give us an account of the state of love as it now stands.

MEDLEY: Truly, there has been some revolutions in those affairs—great chopping and changing among the old, and some new lovers whom malice, indiscretion, and misfortune have luckily brought into play.

LADY TOWNLEY: What think you of walking into the next room and sitting down before you engage in this business?

MEDLEY: I wait upon you, and I hope (though women are commonly unreasonable) by the plenty of scandal I shall discover, to give you very good content, ladies. *(Exeunt.)*

ACT 2 / SCENE 2

(MRS. LOVEIT's lodgings)

(Enter MRS. LOVEIT and PERT. MRS. LOVEIT putting up a letter, then pulling out her pocket-glass and looking in it.)

MRS. LOVEIT: Pert.

PERT: Madam?

MRS. LOVEIT: I hate myself, I look so ill today.

PERT: Hate the wicked cause on't, that base man Mr. Dorimant, who makes you torment and vex yourself continually.

MRS. LOVEIT: He is to blame, indeed.

PERT: To blame to be two days without sending, writing, or coming near you, contrary to his oath and covenant! 'Twas to much purpose to make him swear! I'll lay my life there's not an article but he has broken—talked to the vizards i'the pit, waited upon the ladies from the boxes to their coaches, gone behind the scenes, and fawned upon those little insignificant creatures, the players. 'Tis impossible for a man of his inconstant temper to forbear, I'm sure.

MRS. LOVEIT: I know he is a devil, but he has something of the angel yet undefaced in him, which makes him so charming and agreeable that I must love him, be he never so wicked.

PERT: I little thought, madam, to see your spirit tamed to this degree, who banished poor Mr. Lackwit but for taking up another lady's fan in your presence.

MRS. LOVEIT: My knowing of such odious fools contributes to the making of me love Dorimant the better.

PERT: Your knowing of Mr. Dorimant, in my mind, should rather make you hate all mankind.

MRS. LOVEIT: So it does, besides himself.

PERT: Pray, what excuse does he make in this letter?

MRS. LOVEIT: He has had business.

PERT: Business in general terms would not have been a current excuse for another. A modish man is always very busy when he is in pursuit of a new mistress.

MRS. LOVEIT: Some fop has bribed you to rail at him. He had business; I will believe it, and will forgive him.

PERT: You may forgive him anything, but I shall never forgive him his turning me into ridicule, as I hear he does.

MRS. LOVEIT: I perceive you are of the number of those fools his wit has made his enemies.

PERT: I am of the number of those he's pleased to rally, madam, and if we may believe Mr. Wagfan and Mr. Caperwell, he sometimes makes merry with yourself too, among his laughing companions.

MRS. LOVEIT: Blockheads are as malicious to witty men as ugly women are to the handsome; 'tis their interest, and they make it their business to defame 'em.

PERT: I wish Mr. Dorimant would not make it his business to defame you.

MRS. LOVEIT: Should he, I had rather be made infamous by him than owe my reputation to the dull discretion of those fops you talk of.

(Enter BELLINDA.)

—Bellinda! *(Running to her.)*

BELLINDA: My dear!

MRS. LOVEIT: You have been unkind of late.

BELLINDA: Do not say unkind—say unhappy.

MRS. LOVEIT: I could chide you. Where have you been these two days?

BELLINDA: Pity me rather, my dear; where I have been so tired with two or three country gentlewomen, whose conversation has been more unsufferable than a country fiddle.

MRS. LOVEIT: Are they relations?

BELLINDA: No; Welsh acquaintance I made when I was last year at St. Winifred's.° They have asked me a thousand questions of the modes and intrigues of the town, and I have told 'em almost as many things for news that hardly were so when their gowns were in fashion.

MRS. LOVEIT: Provoking creatures! How could you endure 'em?

BELLINDA *(aside)*: Now to carry on my plot. Nothing but love could make me capable of so much falsehood. 'Tis time to begin, lest Dorimant

---

Bear Garden, there were several bear-gardens, used not only for bear-baiting, but for other entertainments. It is not clear which one is referred to here.

St. Winifred's, St. Winifred's Well, a famed miraculous spring in Flintshire, Wales, near the modern Holywell.

426 / THE MAN OF MODE

ACT 2 / SCENE 2

should come before her jealousy has stung her.—(*Laughs, and then speaks on.*) I was yesterday at a play with 'em, where I was fain to show 'em the living as the man at Westminster does the dead: 'That is Mrs. Such-a-one, admired for her beauty; that is Mr. Such-a-one, cried up for a wit; that is sparkish Mr. Such-a-one, who keeps reverend Mrs. Such-a-one; and there sits fine Mrs. Such-a-one who was lately cast off by my Lord Such-a-one.'

MRS. LOVEIT: Did you see Dorimant there?

BELLINDA: I did, and imagine you were there with him and have no mind to own it.

MRS. LOVEIT: What should make you think so?

BELLINDA: A lady masked in a pretty *déshabillé*, whom Dorimant entertained with more respect than the gallants do a common vizard.

MRS. LOVEIT (*aside*): Dorimant at the play entertaining a mask! Oh, heavens!

BELLINDA (*aside*): Good!

MRS. LOVEIT: Did he stay all the while?

BELLINDA: Till the play was done, and then led her out, which confirms me it was you.

MRS. LOVEIT: Traitor!

PERT: Now you may believe he had business, and you may forgive him too.

MRS. LOVEIT: Ingrateful, perjured man!

BELLINDA: You seem so much concerned, my dear, I fear I have told you unawares what I had better have concealed for your quiet.

MRS. LOVEIT: What manner of shape had she?

BELLINDA: Tall and slender. Her motions were very genteel; certainly she must be some person of condition.

MRS. LOVEIT: Shame and confusion be ever in her face when she shows it!

BELLINDA: I should blame your discretion for loving that wild man, my dear, but they say he has a way so bewitching that few can defend their hearts who know him.

MRS. LOVEIT: I will tear him from mine or die i'the attempt.

BELLINDA: Be more moderate.

MRS. LOVEIT: Would I had daggers, darts, or poisoned arrows in my breast, so I could but remove the thoughts of him from thence!

BELLINDA: Fie, fie! your transports are too violent, my dear; this may be but an accidental gallantry, and 'tis likely ended at her coach.

PERT: Should it proceed farther, let your comfort be, the conduct Mr. Dorimant affects will quickly make you know your rival, ten to one let you see her ruined, her reputation exposed to the town—a happiness none will envy her but yourself, madam.

MRS. LOVEIT: Whoe'er she be, all the harm I wish her is, may she love him as well as I do and may he give her as much cause to hate him.

PERT: Never doubt the latter end of your curse, madam.

MRS. LOVEIT: May all the passions that are raised by neglected love—jealousy, indignation, spite, and thirst of revenge—eternally rage in her soul, as they do now in mine. (*Walks up and down with a distracted air.*)

(*Enter a* PAGE.)

PAGE: Madam, Master Dorimant—

MRS. LOVEIT: I will not see him.

PAGE: I told him you were within, madam.

MRS. LOVEIT: Say you lied—say I'm busy—shut the door—say anything!

PAGE: He's here, madam.

(*Enter* DORIMANT.)

DORIMANT: They taste of death who do at heaven arrive;
But we this paradise approach alive.

(*to* MISTRESS LOVEIT) What, dancing *The Galloping Nag*° without a fiddle? (*Offers to catch her by the hand; she flings away and walks on. He, pursuing her.*) I fear this restlessness of the body, madam, proceeds from an unquietness of the mind. What unlucky accident puts you out of humor? A point ill washed, knots spoiled i'the making up, hair shaded awry, or some other little mistake in setting you in order?

PERT: A trifle, in my opinion, sir, more inconsiderable than any you mention.

DORIMANT: O Mrs. Pert! I never knew you sullen enough to be silent; come, let me know the business.

PERT: The business, sir, is the business that has taken you up these two days. How have I seen you laugh at men of business, and now to become a man of business yourself!

DORIMANT: We are not masters of our affections; our inclinations daily alter: now we love pleasure, and anon we shall dote on business. Human frailty will have it so, and who can help it?

MRS. LOVEIT: Faithless, inhuman, barbarous man—

DORIMANT (*aside*): Good! Now the alarm strikes.

MRS. LOVEIT: Without sense of love, of honor, or of gratitude, tell me, for I will know, what devil masked she was you were with at the play yesterday?

DORIMANT: Faith, I resolved as much as you, but the devil was obstinate and would not tell me.

MRS. LOVEIT: False in this as in your vows to me!—you do know.

DORIMANT: The truth is, I did all I could to know.

The Galloping Nag, a country dance.

MRS. LOVEIT: And dare you own it to my face? Hell and furies! (*Tears her fan in pieces.*)

DORIMANT: Spare your fan, madam; you are growing hot and will want it to cool you.

MRS. LOVEIT: Horror and distraction seize you! Sorrow and remorse gnaw your soul, and punish all your perjuries to me! (*Weeps.*)

DORIMANT (*turning to* BELLINDA):

So thunder breaks the cloud in twain
And makes a passage for the rain.

(*to* BELLINDA) Bellinda, you are the devil that have raised this storm; you were at the play yesterday and have been making discoveries to your dear.

BELLINDA: Y'are the most mistaken man i'the world.

DORIMANT: It must be so, and here I vow revenge—resolve to pursue and persecute you more impertinently than ever any loving fop did his mistress, hunt you i'the Park,° trace you i'the Mail,° dog you in every visit you make, haunt you at the plays and i'the drawing-room, hang my nose in your neck and talk to you whether you will or no, and ever look upon you with such dying eyes till your friends grow jealous of me, send you out of town, and the world suspect your reputation.—(*in a lower voice.*) At my Lady Townley's when we go from hence. (*He looks kindly on* BELLINDA.)

BELLINDA: I'll meet you there.

DORIMANT: Enough.

MRS. LOVEIT (*pushing* DORIMANT *away*): Stand off! You sha' not stare upon her so.

DORIMANT: Good; there's one made jealous already.

MRS. LOVEIT: Is this the constancy you vowed?

DORIMANT: Constancy at my years! 'Tis not a virtue in season; you might as well expect the fruit the autumn ripens i'the spring.

MRS. LOVEIT: Monstrous principle!

DORIMANT: Youth has a long journey to go, madam; should I have set up my rest° at the first inn I lodged at, I should never have arrived at the happiness I now enjoy.

MRS. LOVEIT: Dissembler, damned dissembler!

DORIMANT: I am so, I confess: good nature and good manners corrupt me. I am honest in my inclinations, and would not, wer't not to avoid offence,

---

Park, probably referring to Hyde Park, which was more fashionable than St. James's Park at this time. **Mail,** the Mall (to use the more common spelling) was a long tract in St. James's Park originally laid out for playing the game of paille-maille (pall-mall): at this time, and for many years, thereafter, a place of fashionable resort. Not to be confused with Pall Mall, some four hundred yards to the north, where the game was played earlier in the century. **set ... rest,** taken up my permanent abode.

make a lady a little in years believe I think her young, willfully mistake art for nature, and seem as fond of a thing I am weary of as when I doted on't in earnest.

MRS. LOVEIT: False man!

DORIMANT: True woman!

MRS. LOVEIT: Now you begin to show yourself.

DORIMANT: Love gilds us over and makes us show fine things to one another for a time, but soon the gold wears off and then again the native brass appears.

MRS. LOVEIT: Think on your oaths, your vows, and protestations, perjured man!

DORIMANT: I made 'em when I was in love.

MRS. LOVEIT: And therefore ought they not to bind? Oh, impious!

DORIMANT: What we swear at such a time may be a certain proof of a present passion, but to say truth, in love there is no security to be given for the future.

MRS. LOVEIT: Horrid and ingrateful, begone, and never see me more!

DORIMANT: I am not one of those troublesome coxcombs, who, because they were once well received, take the privilege to plague a woman with their love ever after. I shall obey you, madam, though I do myself some violence.

(*He offers to go and* MRS. LOVEIT *pulls him back.*)

MRS. LOVEIT: Come back! You sha' not go! Could you have the ill-nature to offer it?

DORIMANT: When love grows diseased, the best thing we can do is to put it to a violent death. I cannot endure the torture of a ling'ring and consumptive passion.

MRS. LOVEIT: Can you think mine sickly?

DORIMANT: Oh, 'tis desperately ill. What worse symptoms are there than your being always uneasy when I visit you, your picking quarrels with me on slight occasions, and in my absence kindly list'ning to the impertinences of every fashionable fool that talks to you?

MRS. LOVEIT: What fashionable fool can you lay to my charge?

DORIMANT: Why, the very cock-fool of all those fools—Sir Fopling Flutter.

MRS. LOVEIT: I never saw him in my life but once.

DORIMANT: The worse woman you, at first sight to put on all your charms, to entertain him with that softness in your voice, and all that wanton kindness in your eyes you so notoriously affect when you design a conquest.

MRS. LOVEIT: So damned a lie did never malice yet invent. Who told you this?

DORIMANT: No matter. That ever I should love a woman that can dote on a senseless caper, a tawdry French ribband, and a formal cravat!

MRS. LOVEIT: You make me mad.

DORIMANT: A guilty conscience may do much. Go on—be the game-mistress o' the town, and enter° all our young fops as fast as they come from travel.

MRS. LOVEIT: Base and scurrilous!

DORIMANT: A fine mortifying reputation 'twill be for a woman of your pride, wit, and quality!

MRS. LOVEIT: This jealousy's a mere pretence, a cursed trick of your own devising. I know you.

DORIMANT: Believe it and all the ill of me you can: I would not have a woman have the least good thought of me, that can think well of Fopling. Farewell! Fall to, and much good may do you with your coxcomb.

MRS. LOVEIT: Stay, oh stay! and I will tell you all.

DORIMANT: I have been told too much already. (*Exit* DORIMANT.)

MRS. LOVEIT: Call him again!

PERT: E'en let him go—a fair riddance.

MRS. LOVEIT: Run, I say, call him again! I will have him called!

PERT: The devil should carry him away first were it my concern. (*Exit* PERT.)

BELLINDA: H'as frighted me from the very thoughts of loving men. For heaven's sake, my dear, do not discover° what I told you! I dread his tongue as much as you ought to have done his friendship.

(*Enter* PERT.)

PERT: He's gone, madam.

MRS. LOVEIT: Lightning blast him!

PERT: When I told him you desired him to come back, he smiled, made a mouth at me, flung into his coach, and said—

MRS. LOVEIT: What did he say?

PERT: 'Drive away!' and then repeated verses.

MRS. LOVEIT: Would I had made a contract to be a witch when first I entertained this greater devil, monster, barbarian! I could tear myself in pieces. Revenge—nothing but revenge can ease me. Plague, war, famine, fire—all that can bring universal ruin and misery on mankind—with joy I'd perish to have you in my power but this moment. (*Exit* MRS. LOVEIT.)

PERT: Follow, madam; leave her not in this outrageous passion! (PERT *gathers up the things.*)

BELLINDA (*aside*): H'as given me the proof which I desired of his love,
But 'tis a proof of his ill-nature too.
I wish I had not seen him use her so.
I sigh to think that Dorimant may be
One day as faithless and unkind to me. (*Exeunt.*)

---

enter, initiate.   discover, disclose.

ACT 3 / SCENE 1

(LADY WOODVILL'S *lodgings*)
(*Enter* HARRIET *and* BUSY, *her woman.*)

BUSY: Dear madam, let me set that curl in order.

HARRIET: Let me alone; I will shake 'em all out of order.

BUSY: Will you never leave this wildness?

HARRIET: Torment me not.

BUSY: Look! There's a knot falling off.

HARRIET: Let it drop.

BUSY: But one pin, dear madam.

HARRIET: How do I daily suffer under thy officious fingers!

BUSY: Ah, the difference that is between you and my Lady Dapper! how uneasy she is if the least thing be amiss about her!

HARRIET: She is indeed most exact; nothing is ever wanting to make her ugliness remarkable.

BUSY: Jeering people say so.

HARRIET: Her powdering, painting, and her patching never fail in public to draw the tongues and eyes of all the men upon her.

BUSY: She is, indeed, a little too pretending.

HARRIET: That woman should set up for beauty as much in spite of nature as some men have done for wit!

BUSY: I hope without offence one may endeavor to make one's self agreeable.

HARRIET: Not when 'tis impossible. Women then ought to be no more fond of dressing than fools should be of talking; hoods and modesty, masks and silence, things that shadow and conceal—they should think of nothing else.

BUSY: Jesu! Madam, what will your mother think is become of you? For heaven's sake go in again!

HARRIET: I won't.

BUSY: This is the extravagant'st thing that ever you did in your life, to leave her and a gentleman who is to be your husband.

HARRIET: My husband! Hast thou so little wit to think I spoke what I meant when I overjoyed her in the country with a low curtsey and 'What you please, madam; I shall ever be obedient'?

BUSY: Nay, I know not, you have so many fetches.°

HARRIET: And this was one, to get her up to London. Nothing else, I assure thee.

BUSY: Well, the man, in my mind, is a fine man.

HARRIET: The man indeed wears his clothes fashionably and has a pretty, negligent way with him, very courtly and much affected; he bows, and talks, and smiles so agreeably, as he thinks.

BUSY: I never saw anything so genteel.

HARRIET: Varnished over with good breeding, many

---

fetches, tricks.

a blockhead makes a tolerable show.

BUSY: I wonder you do not like him.

HARRIET: I think I might be brought to endure him, and that is all a reasonable woman should expect in a husband; but there is duty i'the case, and like the haughty Merab, I

Find much aversion in my stubborn mind,

Which

Is bred by being promised and designed.

BUSY: I wish you do not design your own ruin. I partly guess your inclinations, madam—that Mr. Dorimant—

HARRIET: Leave your prating and sing some foolish song or other.

BUSY: I will—the song you love so well ever since you saw Mr. Dorimant. (Sings.)

SONG

When first Amintas charmed my heart,
    My heedless sheep began to stray;
The wolves soon stole the greatest part,
    And all will now be made a prey.

Ah, let not love your thoughts possess,
'Tis fatal to a shepherdess;
The dang'rous passion you must shun,
Or else like me be quite undone.

HARRIET: Shall I be paid down by a covetous parent for a purchase? I need no land; no, I'll lay myself out all in love. It is decreed—

(Enter YOUNG BELLAIR.)

YOUNG BELLAIR: What generous resolution are you making, madam?

HARRIET: Only to be disobedient, sir.

YOUNG BELLAIR: Let me join hands with you in that—

HARRIET: With all my heart; I never thought I should have given you mine so willingly. Here I, Harriet—

YOUNG BELLAIR: And I, Harry—

HARRIET: Do solemnly protest—

YOUNG BELLAIR: And vow—

HARRIET: That I with you—

YOUNG BELLAIR: And I with you—

BOTH: Will never marry.

HARRIET: A match!

YOUNG BELLAIR: And no match! How do you like this indifference now?

HARRIET: You expect I should take it ill, I see.

YOUNG BELLAIR: 'Tis not unnatural for you women to be a little angry: you miss a conquest, though you

would slight the poor man were he in your power.

HARRIET: There are some, it may be, have an eye like Bart'lomew°—big enough for the whole fair; but I am not of the number, and you may keep your gingerbread. 'Twill be more acceptable to the lady whose dear image it wears, sir.

YOUNG BELLAIR: I must confess, madam, you came a day after the fair.

HARRIET: You own then you are in love?

YOUNG BELLAIR: I do.

HARRIET: The confidence is generous, and in return I could almost find in my heart to let you know my inclinations.

YOUNG BELLAIR: Are you in love?

HARRIET: Yes, with this dear town, to that degree I can scarce endure the country in landscapes and in hangings.

YOUNG BELLAIR: What a dreadful thing 'twould be to be hurried back to Hampshire!

HARRIET: Ah, name it not!

YOUNG BELLAIR: As for us, I find we shall agree well enough. Would we could do something to deceive the grave people!

HARRIET: Could we delay their quick proceeding, 'twere well. A reprieve is a good step towards the getting of a pardon.

YOUNG BELLAIR: If we give over the game, we are undone. What think you of playing it on booty?°

HARRIET: What do you mean?

YOUNG BELLAIR: Pretend to be in love with one another; 'twill make some dilatory excuses we may feign pass the better.

HARRIET: Let us do't, if it be but for the dear pleasure of dissembling.

YOUNG BELLAIR: Can you play your part?

HARRIET: I know not what it is to love, but I have made pretty remarks° by being now and then where lovers meet. Where did you leave their gravities?

YOUNG BELLAIR: I'th' next room. Your mother was censuring our modern gallant.

(Enter OLD BELLAIR and LADY WOODVILL.)

HARRIET: Peace! here they come. I will lean against this wall and look bashfully down upon my fan, while you, like an amorous spark, modishly entertain me.

LADY WOODVILL (to OLD BELLAIR): Never go about to

Bart'lomew, Bartholomew Fair, held annually in Smithfield, in the eastern quarter of London, for several days about St. Bartholomew's Day (Aug. 24), was extensive and popular. playing on booty, gamesters who joined together secretly to swindle a third player and divide the gains. remarks, observations.

excuse 'em; come, come, it was not so when I was a young woman.

OLD BELLAIR: A dod, they're something disrespectful—

LADY WOODVILL: Quality was then considered, and not rallied by every fleering° fellow.

OLD BELLAIR: Youth will have its jest—a dod, it will.

LADY WOODVILL: 'Tis good breeding now to be civil to none but players and Exchange women;° they are treated by 'em as much above their condition as others are below theirs.

OLD BELLAIR: Out! a pize on 'em! talk no more. The rogues ha' got an ill habit of preferring beauty no matter where they find it.

LADY WOODVILL: See your son and my daughter; they have improved their acquaintance since they were within.

OLD BELLAIR: A dod, methinks they have! let's keep back and observe.

YOUNG BELLAIR (to HARRIET): Now for a look and gestures that may persuade 'em I am saying all the passionate things imaginable—

HARRIET: Your head a little more on one side. Ease yourself on your left leg and play with your right hand.

YOUNG BELLAIR: Thus, is it not?

HARRIET: Now set your right leg firm on the ground, adjust your belt, then look about you.

YOUNG BELLAIR: A little exercising will make me perfect.

HARRIET: Smile, and turn to me again very sparkish.

YOUNG BELLAIR: Will you take your turn and be instructed?

HARRIET: With all my heart!

YOUNG BELLAIR: At one motion play your fan, roll your eyes, and then settle a kind look upon me.

HARRIET: So!

YOUNG BELLAIR: Now spread your fan, look down upon it, and tell° the sticks with a finger.

HARRIET: Very modish!

YOUNG BELLAIR: Clap your hand up to your bosom, hold down your gown. Shrug a little, draw up your breasts, and let 'em fall again gently, with a sigh or two, etc.

HARRIET: By the good instructions you give, I suspect you for one of those malicious observers who watch people's eyes, and from innocent looks make scandalous conclusions.

YOUNG BELLAIR: I know some, indeed, who out of mere love to mischief are as vigilant as jealousy itself, and will give you an account of every glance that passes at a play and i'th' Circle.°

HARRIET: 'Twill not be amiss now to seem a little pleasant.

YOUNG BELLAIR: Clap your fan, then, in both your hands, snatch it to your mouth, smile, and with a lively motion fling your body a little forwards. So! Now spread it, fall back on the sudden, cover your face with it and break out into a loud laughter—take up, look grave, and fall a-fanning of yourself.—Admirably well acted!

HARRIET: I think I am pretty apt at these matters.

OLD BELLAIR (to LADY WOODVILL): A dod, I like this well!

LADY WOODVILL: This promises something.

OLD BELLAIR: Come! there is love i'th'case, a dod there is, or will be. What say you, young lady?

HARRIET: All in good time, sir; you expect we should fall to and love as game-cocks fight, as soon as we are set together. A dod, y'are unreasonable!

OLD BELLAIR: A dod, sirrah, I like thy wit well.

(Enter a SERVANT.)

SERVANT: The coach is at the door, madam.

OLD BELLAIR: Go, get you and take the air together.

LADY WOODVILL: Will not you go with us?

OLD BELLAIR: Out! a pize! A dod, I ha' business and cannot. We shall meet at night at my sister Townley's.

YOUNG BELLAIR (aside): He's going to Emilia. I overheard him talk of a collation. (Exeunt.)

ACT 3 / SCENE 2

(LADY TOWNLEY'S drawing-room.)
(Enter LADY TOWNLEY, EMILIA, and MR. MEDLEY.)

LADY TOWNLEY: I pity the young lovers we last talked of, though to say truth their conduct has been so indiscreet they deserve to be unfortunate.

MEDLEY: Y'have had an exact account, from the great lady i'th' box down to the little orange wench.

EMILIA: Y'are a living libel, a breathing lampoon. I wonder you are not torn in pieces.

MEDLEY: What think you of setting up an office of intelligence for these matters? The project may get money.

LADY TOWNLEY: You would have great dealings with country ladies.

MEDLEY: More than Muddiman° has with their husbands.

(Enter BELLINDA.)

---

fleering, grimacing. ***Exchange women,*** shop-women in the New Exchange. ***tell,*** count. ***Circle,*** perhaps the reference here is to the inner circle at Court.

Muddiman, Henry Muddiman (1629–1692), editor of the *London Gazette,* and also for some thirty years the author of handwritten news-letters which circulated widely among country gentlemen.

LADY TOWNLEY: Bellinda, what has been become of you? We have not seen you here of late with your friend Mrs. Loveit.

BELLINDA: Dear creature, I left her but now so sadly afflicted!

LADY TOWNLEY: With her old distemper, jealousy!

MEDLEY: Dorimant has played her some new prank.

BELLINDA: Well, that Dorimant is certainly the worst man breathing.

EMILIA: I once thought so.

BELLINDA: And do you not think so still?

EMILIA: No, indeed!

BELLINDA: Oh, Jesu!

EMILIA: The town does him a great deal of injury, and I will never believe what it says of a man I do not know, again, for his sake.

BELLINDA: You make me wonder.

LADY TOWNLEY: He's a very well-bred man.

BELLINDA: But strangely ill-natured.

EMILIA: Then he's a very witty man.

BELLINDA: But a man of no principles.

MEDLEY: Your man of principles is a very fine thing, indeed.

BELLINDA: To be preferred to men of parts by women who have regard to their reputation and quiet. Well, were I minded to play the fool, he should be the last man I'd think of.

MEDLEY: He has been the first in many ladies' favors, though you are so severe, madam.

LADY TOWNLEY: What he may be for a lover, I know not; but he's a very pleasant acquaintance, I am sure.

BELLINDA: Had you seen him use Mrs. Loveit as I have done, you would never endure him more.

EMILIA: What, he has quarreled with her again!

BELLINDA: Upon the slightest occasion; he's jealous of Sir Fopling.

LADY TOWNLEY: She never saw him in her life but yesterday, and that was here.

EMILIA: On my conscience, he's the only man in town that's her aversion! How horribly out of humor she was all the while he talked to her!

BELLINDA: And somebody has wickedly told him—

EMILIA: Here he comes.

(Enter DORIMANT.)

MEDLEY: Dorimant! you are luckily come to justify yourself: here's a lady—

BELLINDA: —Has a word or two to say to you from a disconsolate person.

DORIMANT: You tender your reputation too much, I know, madam, to whisper with me before this good company.

BELLINDA: To serve Mrs. Loveit I'll make a bold venture.

DORIMANT: Here's Medley, the very spirit of scandal.

BELLINDA: No matter!

EMILIA: 'Tis something you are unwilling to hear, Mr. Dorimant.

LADY TOWNLEY: Tell him, Bellinda, whether he will or no.

BELLINDA: Mrs. Loveit—

DORIMANT: Softly! these are laughers; you do not know 'em.

BELLINDA *(to DORIMANT apart)*: In a word, y'ave made me hate you, which I thought you never could have done.

DORIMANT: In obeying your commands.

BELLINDA: 'Twas a cruel part you played. How could you act it?

DORIMANT: Nothing is cruel to a man who could kill himself to please you. Remember five o'clock tomorrow morning!

BELLINDA: I tremble when you name it.

DORIMANT: Be sure you come!

BELLINDA: I sha'not.

DORIMANT: Swear you will!

BELLINDA: I dare not.

DORIMANT: Swear, I say!

BELLINDA: By my life—by all the happiness I hope for—

DORIMANT: You will.

BELLINDA: I will!

DORIMANT: Kind!

BELLINDA: I am glad I've sworn. I vow I think I should ha' failed you else!

DORIMANT: Surprisingly kind! In what temper did you leave Loveit?

BELLINDA: Her raving was prettily over, and she began to be in a brave way of defying you and all your works. Where have you been since you went from thence?

DORIMANT: I looked in at the play.

BELLINDA: I have promised, and must return to her again.

DORIMANT: Persuade her to walk in the Mail this evening.

BELLINDA: She hates the place and will not come.

DORIMANT: Do all you can to prevail with her.

BELLINDA: For what purpose?

DORMINANT: Sir Fopling will be here anon; I'll prepare him to set upon her there before me.

BELLINDA: You persecute her too much, but I'll do all you'll ha' me.

DORIMANT *(aloud)*: Tell her plainly 'tis grown so dull a business I can drudge on no longer.

EMILIA: There are afflictions in love, Mr. Dorimant.

DORIMANT: You women make 'em, who are commonly as unreasonable in that as you are at play—without the advantage be on your side, a man can never quietly give over when he's weary.

MEDLEY: If you would play without being obliged to complaisance, Dorimant, you should play in public places.

DORIMANT: Ordinaries° were a very good thing for that, but gentlemen do not of late frequent 'em. The deep play is now in private houses.

(BELINDA *offering to steal away.*)

LADY TOWNLEY: Bellinda, are you leaving us so soon?

BELLINDA: I am to go to the park with Mrs. Loveit, madam. (*Exit* BELLINDA.)

LADY TOWNLEY: This confidence° will go nigh to spoil this young creature.

MEDLEY: 'Twill do her good, madam. Young men who are brought up under practicing lawyers prove the abler counsel when they come to be called to the bar themselves.

DORIMANT: The town has been very favorable to you this afternoon, my Lady Townley; you use to have an *embarras*° of chair and coaches at your door, an uproar of footmen in your hall, and a noise of fools above here.

LADY TOWNLEY: Indeed, my house is the general rendezvous, and next to the playhouse is the common refuge of all the young idle people.

EMILIA: Company is a very good thing, madam, but I wonder you do not love it a little more chosen.

LADY TOWNLEY: 'Tis good to have an universal taste; we should love wit, but for variety be able to divert ourselves with the extravagancies of those who want it.

MEDLEY: Fools will make you laugh.

EMILIA: For once or twice, but the repetition of their folly after a visit or two grows tedious and unsufferable.

LADY TOWNLEY: You are a little too delicate, Emilia.

(*Enter a* PAGE.)

PAGE: Sir Fopling Flutter, madam, desires to know if you are to be seen.

LADY TOWNLEY: Here's the freshest fool in town, and one who has not cloyed you yet.—Page!

PAGE: Madam!

LADY TOWNLEY: Desire him to walk up. (*Exit* PAGE.)

DORIMANT: Do not you fall on him, Medley, and snub him. Soothe him up in his extravagance; he will show the better.

MEDLEY: You know I have a natural indulgence for fools and need not this caution, sir.

(*Enter* SIR FOPLING FLUTTER *with his Page after him.*)

SIR FOPLING FLUTTER: Page, wait without. (*to* LADY TOWNLEY) Madam, I kiss your hands. I see yesterday was nothing of chance; the *belles assemblées*° form themselves here every day. (*to* EMILIA) Lady, your servant.—Dorimant, let me embrace thee! Without lying, I have not met with any of my acquaintance who retain so much of Paris as thou dost—the very air thou hadst when the marquise mistook thee i'th' Tuileries and cried, 'Hey, Chevalier!' and then begged thy pardon.

DORIMANT: I would fain wear in fashion as long as I can, sir; 'tis a thing to be valued in men as well as baubles.

SIR FOPLING FLUTTER: Thou art a man of wit and understands the town. Prithee, let thee and I be intimate; there is no living without making some good man the confidant of our pleasures.

DORIMANT: 'Tis true! but there is no man so improper for such a business as I am.

SIR FOPLING FLUTTER: Prithee, why hast thou so modest an opinion of thyself?

DORIMANT: Why, first, I could never keep a secret in my life; and then, there is no charm so infallibly makes me fall in love with a woman as my knowing a friend loves her. I deal honestly with you.

SIR FOPLING FLUTTER: Thy humor's very gallant, or let me perish! I knew a French count so like thee!

LADY TOWNLEY: Wit, I perceive, has more power over you than beauty, Sir Fopling, else you would not have let this lady stand so long neglected.

SIR FOPLING FLUTTER (*to* EMILIA): A thousand pardons, madam; some civility's due of course upon the meeting of a long absent friend. The *éclat*° of so much beauty, I confess, ought to have charmed me sooner.

EMILIA: The *brillant*° of so much good language, sir, has much more power than the little beauty I can boast.

SIR FOPLING FLUTTER: I never saw anything prettier than this high work on your *point d'Espagne.*°

EMILIA: 'Tis not so rich as *point de Venise.*

SIR FOPLING FLUTTER: Not altogether, but looks cooler and is more proper for the season.—Dorimant, is not that Medley?

DORIMANT: The same, sir.

SIR FOPLING FLUTTER: Forgive me, sir; in this *embarras*° of civilities I could not come to have you in my arms sooner. You understand an equipage° the best of any man in town, I hear.

MEDLEY: By my own you would not guess it.

SIR FOPLING FLUTTER: There are critics who do not write, sir.

MEDLEY: Our peevish poets will scarce allow it.

SIR FOPLING FLUTTER: Damn 'em, they'll allow no man

Ordinaries, taverns. **confidence,** intimacy. **embarras,** blockade. **belles assemblées,** gatherings of fashionable people.

éclat, splendor. **brillant,** brilliance. **point d'Espagne,** point lace. **embarras,** crush. **equipage,** retinue of personal attendants.

wit who does not play the fool like themselves and show it! Have you taken notice of the galllesh° I brought over?

MEDLEY: Oh, yes! 't has quite another air than th' English makes.

SIR FOPLING FLUTTER: 'Tis as easily known from an English tumbril° as an Inns of court° man is from one of us.

DORIMANT: True; there is a *bel air*° in galleshes as well as men.

MEDLEY: But there are few so delicate to observe it.

SIR FOPLING FLUTTER: The world is generally very *grossier*° here, indeed.

LADY TOWNLEY (*to* EMILIA): He's very fine.

EMILIA: Extreme proper.°

SIR FOPLING FLUTTER (*overhearing*): A slight suit I made to appear in at my first arrival—not worthy your consideration, ladies.

DORIMANT: The pantaloon is very well mounted.

SIR FOPLING FLUTTER: The tassels are new and pretty.

MEDLEY: I never saw a coat better cut.

SIR FOPLING FLUTTER: It makes me show long waisted, and, I think, slender.

DORIMANT: That's the shape our ladies dote on.

MEDLEY: Your breech, though, is a handful too high, in my eye, Sir Fopling.

SIR FOPLING FLUTTER: Peace, Medley! I have wished it lower a thousand times, but a pox on't! 'twill not be.

LADY TOWNSEND: His gloves are well fringed, large, and graceful.

SIR FOPLING FLUTTER: I was always eminent for being *bien ganté.*°

EMILIA: He wears nothing but what are originals of the most famous hands in Paris.

SIR FOPLING FLUTTER: You are in the right, madam.

LADY TOWNLEY: The suit!

SIR FOPLING FLUTTER: Barroy.°

EMILIA: The garniture!°

SIR FOPLING FLUTTER: Le Gras.

MEDLEY: The shoes!

SIR FOPLING FLUTTER: Piccar.

DORMINANT: The periwig!

SIR FOPLING FLUTTER: Chedreux.

LADY TOWNLEY: }
EMILIA: } The gloves!

SIR FOPLING FLUTTER: Orangerie—you know the smell, ladies.—Dorimant, I could find in my heart for an amusement to have a gallantry with some of our English ladies.

DORIMANT: 'Tis a thing no less necessary to confirm the reputation of your wit than a duel will be to satisfy the town of your courage.

SIR FOPLING FLUTTER: Here was a woman yesterday—

DORIMANT: Mistress Loveit.

SIR FOPLING FLUTTER: You have named her.

DORIMANT: You cannot pitch on a better for your purpose.

SIR FOPLING FLUTTER: Prithee, what is she?

DORIMANT: A person of quality, and one who has a rest° of reputation enough to make the conquest considerable; besides, I hear she likes you too.

SIR FOPLING FLUTTER: Methoughts she seemed, though, very reserved and uneasy all the time I entertained her.

DORIMANT: Grimace and affectation! You will see her i' th' Mail tonight.

SIR FOPLING FLUTTER: Prithee, let thee and I take the air together.

DORIMANT: I am engaged to Medley, but I'll meet you at Saint James's and give you some information upon the which you may regulate your proceedings.

SIR FOPLING FLUTTER: All the world will be in the Park tonight. Ladies, 'twere pity to keep so much beauty longer within doors and rob the Ring° of all those charms that should adorn it.—Hey, page!

(*Enter* PAGE.)

See that all my people be ready.

(PAGE *goes out again.*)

—Dorimant, *au revoir. (Exit.)*

MEDLEY: A fine, mettled coxcomb.

DORIMANT: Brisk and insipid.

MEDLEY: Pert and dull.

EMILIA: However you despise him, gentlemen, I'll lay my life he passes for a wit with many.

DORIMANT: That may very well be; Nature has her cheats, stums° a brain, and puts sophisticate dulness often on the tasteless multitude for true wit and good humor. Medley, come!

MEDLEY: I must go a little way; I will meet you i'the Mail.

DORIMANT: I'll walk through the garden thither.—(*to the women*) We shall meet anon and bow.

LADY TOWNLEY: Not to-night. We are engaged about a business the knowledge of which may make you laugh hereafter.

---

gallesh, caleche, an open carriage. *tumbril,* a heavy cart. *Inns of Court man,* lawyer, or other professional man, resident in one of the "Temples." *bel air,* fashionable mode. *grossier,* coarse. *proper,* handsome, elegant. *bien ganté,* well-gloved. *Barroy,* this name and those which follow are those of fashionable Parisian tradesmen. *garniture,* trimmings.

---

rest, remnant. *Ring,* a circular course in Hyde Park, used for riding and driving. *stums,* revives (a term usually employed in connection with the reclamation of wine or ale).

MEDLEY: Your servant, ladies.

DORIMANT: '*Au revoir,*' as Sir Fopling says.

(*Exeunt* MEDLEY *and* DORIMANT.)

LADY TOWNLEY: The old man will be here immediately.

EMILIA: Let's expect° him i'th' garden.

LADY TOWNLEY: 'Go! you are a rogue.'

EMILIA: 'I can't abide you.' (*Exeunt.*)

ACT 3 / SCENE 3

(*The Mail*)

(*Enter* HARRIET *and* YOUNG BELLAIR, *she pulling him.*)

HARRIET: come along.

YOUNG BELLAIR: And leave your mother!

HARRIET: Busy will be sent with a hue and cry after us, but that's no matter.

YOUNG BELLAIR: 'Twill look strangely in me.

HARRIET: She'll believe it a freak of mine and never blame your manners.

YOUNG BELLAIR: What reverend acquaintance is that she has met?

HARRIET: A fellow-beauty of the last king's time,° though by the ruins you would hardly guess it. (*Exeunt.*)

(*Enter* DORIMANT *and crosses the stage.*) (*Enter* YOUNG BELLAIR *and* HARRIET.)

YOUNG BELLAIR: By this time your mother is in a fine taking.

HARRIET: If your friend Mr. Dorimant were but here now, that she might find me talking with him!

YOUNG BELLAIR: She does not know him, but dreads him, I hear, of all mankind.

HARRIET: She concludes if he does but speak to a woman, she's undone--is on her knees every day to pray heaven defend me from him.

YOUNG BELLAIR: You do not apprehend him so much as she does?

HARRIET: I never saw anything in him that was frightful.

YOUNG BELLAIR: On the contrary, have you not observed something extreme delightful in his wit and person?

HARRIET: He's agreeable and pleasant, I must own, but he does so much affect being so, he displeases me.

YOUNG BELLAIR: Lord, madam! all he does and says is so easy and so natural.

HARRIET: Some men's verses seem so to the unskillful, but labor i'the one and affectation in the other to the judicious plainly appear.

YOUNG BELLAIR: I never heard him accused of affectation before.

(*Enter* DORIMANT *and stares upon her.*)

HARRIET: It passes on the easy town, who are favorably pleased in him to call it humor.

(*Exeunt* YOUNG BELLAIR *and* HARRIET.)

DORIMANT: 'Tis she! it must be she—that lovely hair, that easy shape, those wanton eyes, and all those melting charms about her mouth which Medley spoke of! I'll follow the lottery and put in for a prize with my friend Bellair. (*Exit* DORIMANT *repeating:*)

In love the victors from the vanquished fly;
They fly that wound, and they pursue that die.

(*Enter* YOUNG BELLAIR *and* HARRIET *and after them* DORIMANT *standing at a distance.*)

YOUNG BELLAIR: Most people prefer High Park° to this place.

HARRIET: It has the better reputation, I confess; but I abominate the dull diversions there—the formal bows, the affected smiles, the silly by-words and amorous tweers° in passing. Here one meets with a little conversation now and then.

YOUNG BELLAIR: These conversations have been fatal to some of your sex, madam.

HARRIET: It may be so; because some who want temper° have been undone by gaming, must others who have it wholly deny themselves the pleasure of play?

DORIMANT (*coming up gently and bowing to her*): Trust me, it were unreasonable, madam.

HARRIET (*she starts and looks grave*): Lord, who's this?

YOUNG BELLAIR: Dorimant!

DORIMANT: Is this the woman your father would have you marry?

YOUNG BELLAIR: It is.

DORIMANT: Her name?

YOUNG BELLAIR: Harriet.

DORIMANT: I am not mistaken; she's handsome.

YOUNG BELLAIR: Talk to her; her wit is better than her face. We were wishing for you but now.

DORIMANT (*to* HARRIET): Overcast with seriousness o'the sudden! A thousand smiles were shining in that face but now; I never saw so quick a change of weather.

HARRIET (*aside*): I feel as great a change within, but he shall never know it.

DORIMANT: You were talking of play, madam. Pray, what may be your stint?°

High Park, an alternative name for Hyde Park. **tweers,** leers. **temper,** self-control. **stint,** pre-determined amount, after the loss of which the gamester intends to cease playing.

HARRIET: A little harmless discourse in public walks, or at most an appointment in a box, barefaced, at the playhouse; you are for masks and private meetings, where women engage for all they are worth, I hear.

DORIMANT: I have been used to deep play, but I can make one at small game when I like my gamester well.

HARRIET: And be so unconcerned you'll ha' no pleasure in't.

DORIMANT: Where there is a considerable sum to be won, the hope of drawing people in makes every trifle considerable.

HARRIET: The sordidness of men's natures, I know, makes 'em willing to flatter and comply with the rich, though they are sure never to be the better for 'em.

DORIMANT: 'Tis in their power to do us good, and we despair not but at some time or other they may be willing.

HARRIET: To men who have fared in this town like you, 'twould be a great mortification to live on hope. Could you keep a Lent for a mistress?

DORIMANT: In expectation of a happy Easter and, though time be very precious, think forty days well lost to gain your favor.

HARRIET: Mr. Bellair, let us walk; 'tis time to leave him. Men grow dull when they begin to be particular.

DORIMANT: Y'are mistaken; flattery will not ensue, though I know y' are greedy of the praises of the whole Mail.

HARRIET: You do me wrong.

DORIMANT: I do not. As I followed you, I observed how you were pleased when the fops cried, 'She's handsome, very handsome! by God she is!' and whispered aloud your name; the thousand several forms you put your face into; then, to make yourself more agreeable, how wantonly you played with your head, flung back your locks, and looked smilingly over your shoulder at 'em!

HARRIET: I do not go begging the men's, as you do the ladies', good liking, with a sly softness in your looks and a gentle slowness in your bows as you pass by 'em—as thus, sir. (Acts him.) Is not this like you?

(Enter LADY WOODVILL and BUSY.)

YOUNG BELLAIR: Your mother, madam.

(Pulls HARRIET; she composes herself.)

LADY WOODVILL: Ah, my dear child Harriet!

BUSY (aside): Now is she so pleased with finding her again she cannot chide her.

LADY WOODVILL: Come away!

DORIMANT: 'Tis now but high Mail,° madam—the

_____

high Mail, the busiest hour of the Mall's social activities.

most entertaining time of all the evening.

HARRIET: I would fain see that Dorimant, mother, you so cry out of for a monster, he's in the Mail, I hear.

LADY WOODVILL: Come away then! The plague is here and you should dread the infection.

YOUNG BELLAIR: You may be misinformed of the gentleman.

LADY WOODVILL: Oh, no! I hope you do not know him. He is the prince of all the devils in the town—delights in nothing but in rapes and riots!

DORIMANT: If you did but hear him speak, madam!

LADY WOODVILL: Oh, he has a tongue, they say, would tempt the angels to a second fall.

(Enter SIR FOPLING with his equipage, six FOOTMEN and a PAGE.)

SIR FOPLING FLUTTER: Hey! Champagne, Norman, La Rose, La Fleur, La Tour, La Verdure!—Dorimant—

LADY WOODVILL: Here, here he is among this rout! He names him! Come away, Harriet; come away!

(Exeunt LADY WOODVILL, HARRIET, BUSY, and YOUNG BELLAIR.)

DORIMANT: This fool's coming has spoiled all. She's gone, but she has left a pleasing image of herself behind that wanders in my soul—it must not settle there.

SIR FOPLING FLUTTER: What reverie is this? Speak, man!

DORIMANT: Snatcht from myself, how far behind
Already I behold the shore!

(Enter MEDLEY.)

MEDLEY: Dorimant, a discovery! I met with Bellair.

DORIMANT: You can tell me no news, sir; I know all.

MEDLEY: How do you like the daughter?

DORIMANT: You never came so near truth in your life as you did in her description.

MEDLEY: What think you of the mother?

DORIMANT: Whatever I think of her, she thinks very well of me, I find.

MEDLEY: Did she know you?

DORIMANT: She did not; whether she does now or no, I know not. Here was a pleasant scene towards, when in came Sir Fopling, mustering up his equipage, and at the latter end named me and frighted her away.

MEDLEY: Loveit and Bellinda are not far off; I saw 'em alight at St. James's.

DORIMANT: Sir Fopling! hark you, a word or two. (Whispers.) Look you do not want assurance.

SIR FOPLING FLUTTER: I never do on these occasions.

DORIMANT: Walk on; we must not be seen together. Make your advantage of what I have told you. The next turn you will meet the lady.

SIR FOPLING FLUTTER: Hey! Follow me all!

(Exeunt SIR FOPLING *and his equipage.)*

DORIMANT: Medley, you shall see good sport anon between Loveit and this Fopling.

MEDLEY: I thought there was something toward, by that whisper.

DORIMANT: You know a worthy principle of hers?

MEDLEY: Not to be so much as civil to a man who speaks to her in the presence of him she professes to love.

DORIMANT: I have encouraged Fopling to talk to her tonight.

MEDLEY: Now you are here, she will go nigh to beat him.

DORIMANT: In the humor she's in, her love will make her do some very extravagant thing doubtless.

MEDLEY: What was Bellinda's business with you at my Lady Townley's?

DORIMANT: To get me to meet Loveit here in order to an *éclaircissement.*° I made some difficulty of it and have prepared this rencounter to make good my jealousy.

MEDLEY: Here they come.

(Enter MRS. LOVEIT, BELLINDA, *and* PERT.*)*

DORIMANT: I'll meet her and provoke her with a deal of dumb civility in passing by, then turn short and be behind her when Sir Fopling sets upon her—

See how unregarded now
That piece of beauty passes.

(Exeunt DORIMANT *and* MEDLEY.*)*

BELLINDA: How wonderful respectfully he bowed!

PERT: He's always over-mannerly when he has done a mischief.

BELLINDA: Methoughts, indeed, at the same time he had a strange, despising countenance.

PERT: The unlucky look he thinks becomes him.

BELLINDA: I was afraid you would have spoke to him, my dear.

MRS. LOVEIT: I would have died first; he shall no more find me the loving fool he has done.

BELLINDA: You love him still?

MRS. LOVEIT: No!

PERT: I wish you did not.

MRS. LOVEIT: I do not, and I will have you think so.—What made you hale me to this odious place, Bellinda?

BELLINDA: I hate to be hulched up° in a coach; walking is much better.

MRS. LOVEIT: Would we could meet Sir Fopling now!

BELLINDA: Lord, would you not avoid him?

MRS. LOVEIT: I would make him all the advances that may be.

BELLINDA: That would confirm Dorimant's suspicion, my dear.

MRS. LOVEIT: He is not jealous; but I will make him so, and be revenged a way he little thinks on.

BELLINDA *(aside)*: If she should make him jealous, that may make him fond of her again. I must dissuade her from it.—Lord, my dear, this will certainly make him hate you.

MRS. LOVEIT: 'Twill make him uneasy, though he does not care for me. I know the effects of jealousy on men of his proud temper.

BELLINDA: 'Tis a fantastic remedy; its operations are dangerous and uncertain.

MRS. LOVEIT: 'Tis the strongest cordial we can give to dying love: it often brings it back when there's no sign of life remaining. But I design not so much the reviving of his, as my revenge.

(Enter SIR FOPLING *and his equipage.)*

SIR FOPLING FLUTTER: Hey! Bid the coachman send home four of his horses and bring the coach to Whitehall;° I'll walk over the Park.—*(to* MRS. LOVEIT*)* Madam, the honor of kissing your fair hands is a happiness I missed this afternoon at my Lady Townley's.

MRS. LOVEIT: You were very obliging, Sir Fopling, the last time I saw you there.

SIR FOPLING FLUTTER: The preference was due to your wit and beauty. *(to* BELLINDA*)* Madam, your servant; there never was so sweet an evening.

BELLINDA: 'T has drawn all the rabble of the town hither.

SIR FOPLING FLUTTER: 'Tis pity there's not an order made that none but the *beau monde* should walk here.

MRS. LOVEIT: 'Twould add much to the beauty of the place. See what a sort° of nasty fellows are coming!

(Enter four ill-fashioned fellows singing:)

*'Tis not for kisses alone
So long I have made my address,–*

MRS. LOVEIT: Fo! Their periwigs are scented with tobacco so strong—

SIR FOPLING FLUTTER: It overcomes our pulvilio.° Methinks I smell the coffee-house they come from.

1 MAN: Dorimant's convenient,° Madam Loveit.

éclaircissement, understanding. *hulched up,* huddled up like a hunchback.

Whitehall, the palace on the east side of St. James's Park; at this time (and until its destruction by fire in 1698) the royal residence. *sort,* group. *pulvilio,* scented cosmetic powder. *convenient,* mistress.

2 MAN: I like the oily buttock° with her.
3 MAN: What spruce prig° is that?
1 MAN: A caravan° lately come from Paris.
2 MAN: Peace! they smoke.°

(All of them coughing; exeunt singing:)

> There's something else to be done,
> Which you cannot choose but guess.

(Enter DORIMANT and MEDLEY.)

DORIMANT: They're engaged.
MEDLEY: She entertains him as if she liked him!
DORIMANT: Let us go forward—seem earnest in discourse and show ourselves; then you shall see how she'll use him.
BELLINDA: Yonder's Dorimant, my dear.
MRS. LOVEIT *(aside to BELLINDA)*: I see him. He comes insulting, but I will disappoint him in his expectation. *(to SIR FOPLING)* I like this pretty, nice humor of yours, Sir Fopling.—*(to BELLINDA)* With what a loathing eye he looked upon those fellows!
SIR FOPLING FLUTTER: I sat near one of 'em at a play today and was almost poisoned with a pair of cordovan gloves he wears.
MRS. LOVEIT: Oh, filthy cordovan! How I hate the smell! *(Laughs in a loud, affected way.)*
SIR FOPLING FLUTTER: Did you observe, madam, how their cravats hung loose an inch from their neck and what a frightful air it gave 'em?
MRS. LOVEIT: Oh, I took particular notice of one that is always spruced up with a deal of dirty skycolored ribband.
BELLINDA: That's one of the walking flageolets° who haunt the Mail o'nights.
MRS. LOVEIT: Oh, I remember him, h'has a hollow tooth enough to spoil the sweetness of an evening.
SIR FOPLING FLUTTER: I have seen the tallest walk the streets with a dainty pair of boxes° neatly buckled on.
MRS. LOVEIT: And a little foot-boy at his heels, pocket-high, with a flat cap, a dirty face—
SIR FOPLING FLUTTER: And a snotty nose.
MRS. LOVEIT: Oh, odious!—There's many of my own sex with that Holborn equipage° trig° to Gray's Inn° Walks and now and then travel hither on a Sunday.

MEDLEY *(to DORIMANT)*: She takes no notice of you.
DORIMANT: Damn her! I am jealous of a counterplot.
MRS. LOVEIT: Your liveries are the finest, Sir Fopling—oh, that page! that page is the prettily'st dressed—they are all Frenchmen.
SIR FOPLING FLUTTER: There's one damned English blockhead among 'em; you may know him by his mien.
MRS. LOVEIT: Oh, that's he—that's he! What do you call him?
SIR FOPLING FLUTTER: Hey—I know not what to call him—
MRS. LOVEIT: What's your name?
FOOTMAN: John Trott, madam.
SIR FOPLING FLUTTER: Oh, unsufferable! Trott, Trott, Trott! There's nothing so barbarous as the names of our English servants.—What countryman are you, sirrah?
FOOTMAN: Hampshire, sir.
SIR FOPLING FLUTTER: Then Hampshire be your name. Hey, Hampshire!
MRS. LOVEIT: Oh, that sound—that sound becomes the mouth of a man of quality!
MEDLEY: Dorimant, you look a little bashful on the matter.
DORIMANT: She dissembles better than I thought she could have done.
MEDLEY: You have tempted her with too luscious a bait. She bites at the coxcomb.
DORIMANT: She cannot fall from loving me to that.
MEDLEY: You begin to be jealous in earnest.
DORIMANT: Of one I do not love—
MEDLEY: You did love her.
DORIMANT: The fit has long been over.
MEDLEY: But I have known men fall into dangerous relapses when they have found a woman inclining to another.
DORIMANT *(to himself)*: He guesses the secret of my heart. I am concerned, but dare not show it, lest Bellinda should mistrust all I have done to gain her.
BELLINDA *(aside)*: I have watched his look and find no alteration there. Did he love her, some signs of jealousy would have appeared.
DORIMANT *(to MRS. LOVEIT)*: I hope this happy evening, madam, has reconciled you to the scandalous Mail. We shall have you now hankering° here again—
MRS. LOVEIT: Sir Fopling, will you walk?
SIR FOPLING FLUTTER: I am all obedience, madam.
MRS. LOVEIT: Come along then, and let's agree to be malicious on all the ill-fashioned things we meet.
SIR FOPLING FLUTTER: We'll make a critique on the whole Mail, madam.

---

oily buttock, smooth-appearing prostitute. **prig,** top. **caravan,** gull, "easy mark." **smoke,** observe (us). **flageolets,** tall, thin men. **boxes,** presumably pattens or clogs. **Holborn equipage,** middle-class sort of attendance. **trig,** wall briskly. **Gray's Inn,** the gardens of this, one of the Inns of Court, were apparently the middle-class equivalent of the Mall.

---

hankering, loitering about.

MRS. LOVEIT: Bellinda, you shall engage°—

BELLINDA: To the reserve of our friends,° my dear.

MRS. LOVEIT: No! no exceptions!

SIR FOPLING FLUTTER: We'll sacrifice all to our diversion.

MRS. LOVEIT: All—all.

SIR FOPLING FLUTTER: All.

BELLINDA: All? Then let it be.

(*Exeunt* SIR FOPLING, MRS. LOVEIT, BELINDA, *and* PERT, *laughing.*)

MEDLEY: Would you had brought some more of your friends, Dorimant, to have been witnesses of Sir Fopling's disgrace and your triumph.

DORIMANT: 'Twere unreasonable to desire you not to laugh at me; but pray do not expose me to the town this day or two.

MEDLEY: By that time you hope to have regained your credit.

DORIMANT: I know she hates Fopling and only makes use of him in hope to work me on again; had it not been for some powerful considerations which will be removed tomorrow morning, I had made her pluck off this mask and show the passsion that lies panting under.

(*Enter a* FOOTMAN.)

MEDLEY: Here comes a man from Bellair with news of your last adventure.

DORIMANT: I am glad he sent him; I long to know the consequence of our parting.

FOOTMAN: Sir, my master desires you to come to my Lady Townley's presently° and bring Mr. Medley with you. My Lady Woodvill and her daughter are there.

MEDLEY: Then all's well, Dorimant.

FOOTMAN: They have sent for the fiddles and mean to dance. He bid me tell you, sir, the old lady does not know you, and would have you own yourself to be Mr. Courtage. They are all prepared to receive you by that name.

DORIMANT: That foppish admirer of quality, who flatters the very meat at honorable tables and never offers love to a woman below a lady-grandmother.

MEDLEY: You know the character you are to act, I see.

DORIMANT: This is Harriet's contrivance—wild, witty, lovesome, beautiful, and young!—Come along, Medley.

MEDLEY: This new woman would well supply the loss of Loveit.

DORIMANT: That business must not end so; before tomorrow sun is set. I will revenge and clear it.

---

engage, take part. *to . . . friends,* exempting our friends. *presently,* immediately.

And you and Loveit, to her cost, shall find,
I fathom all the depths of womankind. (*Exeunt.*)

ACT 4 / SCENE 1

(LADY TOWNLEY'S *drawing-room*)

(*The scene opens with the fiddles playing a country dance. Enter* DORIMANT *and* LADY WOODVILL, YOUNG BELLAIR *and* MRS. HARRIET, OLD BELLAIR *and* EMILIA, MR. MEDLEY *and* LADY TOWNLEY, *as having just ended the dance.*)

OLD BELLAIR: So, so, so!—a smart bout, a very smart bout, a dod!

LADY TOWNLEY: How do you like Emilia's dancing, brother?

OLD BELLAIR: Not at all—not at all!

LADY TOWNLEY: You speak not what you think, I am sure.

OLD BELLAIR: No matter for that; go, bid her dance no more. It don't become her—it don't become her. Tell her I say so. (*aside*) A dod, I love her!

DORIMANT (*to* LADY WOODVILL): All people mingle nowadays, madam. And in public places women of quality have the least respect showed 'em.

LADY WOODVILL: I protest you say the truth, Mr. Courtage.

DORIMANT: Forms and ceremonies, the only things that uphold quality and greatness, are now shamefully laid aside and neglected.

LADY WOODVILL: Well, this is not the women's age, let 'em think what they will. Lewdness is the business now; love was the business in my time.

DORIMANT: The women, indeed, are little beholding to the young men of this age; they're generally only dull admirers of themselves, and make their court to nothing but their periwigs and their cravats, and would be more concerned for the disordering of 'em, though on a good occasion, than a young maid would be for the tumbling of her head or handkercher.

LADY WOODVILL: I protest you hit 'em.

DORIMANT: They are very assiduous to show themselves at court, well dressed, to the women of quality, but their business is with the stale mistresses of the town, who are prepared to receive their lazy addresses by industrious old lovers who have cast 'em off and made 'em easy.

HARRIET (*to* MEDLEY): He fits my mother's humor so well, a little more and she'll dance a kissing dance with him anon.

MEDLEY: Dutifully observed, madam.

DORIMANT (*to* LADY WOODVILL): They pretend to be great critics in beauty. By their talk you would think they liked no face, and yet they can dote on an ill one if it belong to a laundress or a tailor's daughter. They cry, 'A woman's past her prime at twenty, decayed at four-and-twenty, old and unsufferable at thirty.'

LADY WOODVILL: Unsufferable at thirty! That they are in the wrong, Mr. Courtage, at five-and-thirty, there are living proofs enough to convince 'em.

DORIMANT: Ay, madam. There's Mrs. Setlooks, Mrs. Droplip, and my Lady Lowd; show me among all our opening buds a face that promises so much beauty as the remains of theirs.

LADY WOODVILL: The depraved appetite of this vicious age tastes nothing but green fruit, and loathes it when 'tis kindly° ripened.

DORIMANT: Else so many deserving women, madam, would not be so untimely neglected.

LADY WOODVILL: I protest, Mr. Courtage, a dozen such good men as you would be enough to atone for that wicked Dorimant and all the under° debauchees of the town. (HARRIET, EMILIA, YOUNG BELLAIR, MEDLEY, and LADY TOWNLEY break out into a laughter.)—What's the matter there?

MEDLEY: A pleasant mistake, madam, that a lady has made, occasions a little laughter.

OLD BELLAIR: Come, come, you keep 'em idle! They are impatient till the fiddles play again.

DORIMANT: You are not weary, madam?

LADY WOODVILL: One dance more, I cannot refuse you, Mr. Courtage.

(They dance. After the dance OLD BELLAIR, singing and dancing up to EMILIA.)

EMILIA: You are very active, sir.

OLD BELLAIR: A dod, sirrah! when I was a young fellow I could ha' capered up to my woman's gorget.°

DORIMANT (to LADY WOODVILL): You are willing to rest yourself, madam—

LADY TOWNLEY (to LADY WOODVILL): We'll walk into my chamber and sit down.

MEDLEY: Leave us Mr. Courtage; he's a dancer, and the young ladies are not weary yet.

LADY WOODVILL: We'll send him out again.

HARRIET: If you do not quickly, I know where to send for Mr. Dorimant.

LADY WOODVILL: This girl's head, Mr. Courtage, is ever running on that wild fellow.

DORIMANT: 'Tis well you have got her a good husband, madam; that will settle it.

(Exeunt LADY TOWNLEY, LADY WOODVILL, and DORIMANT.)

OLD BELLAIR (to EMILIA): A dod, sweetheart, be advised and do not throw thyself away on a young, idle fellow.

EMILIA: I have no such intention, sir.

OLD BELLAIR: Have a little patience! Thou shalt have the man I spake of. A dod, he loves thee and will make a good husband—but no words!

EMILIA: But, sir—

OLD BELLAIR: No answer—out a pize! peace! and think on't.

(Enter DORIMANT.)

DORIMANT: Your company is desired within, sir.

OLD BELLAIR: I go, I go! Good Mr. Courtage, fare you well!—(to EMILIA) Go, I'll see you no more!

EMILIA: What have I done, sir?

OLD BELLAIR: You are ugly, you are ugly!—Is she not, Mr. Courtage?

EMILIA: Better words or I shan't abide you.

OLD BELLAIR: Out a pize; a dod, what does she say? Hit her a pat for me there. (Exit OLD BELLAIR.)

MEDLEY: You have charms for the whole family.

DORIMANT: You'll spoil all with some unseasonable jest, Medley.

MEDLEY: You see I confine my tongue and am content to be a bare spectator, much contrary to my nature.

EMILIA: Methinks, Mr. Dorimant, my Lady Woodvill is a little fond of you.

DORIMANT: Would her daughter were!

MEDLEY: It may be you find her so. Try her—you have an opportunity.

DORIMANT: And I will not lose it.—Bellair, here's a lady has something to say to you.

YOUNG BELLAIR: I wait upon her.—Mr. Medley, we have both business with you.

DORIMANT: Get you all together then. (to HARRIET) That demure curtsey is not amiss in jest, but do not think in earnest it becomes you.

HARRIET: Affectation is catching, I find; from your grave bow I got it.

DORIMANT: Where had you all that scorn and coldness in your look?

HARRIET: From nature, sir; pardon my want of art. I have not learnt those softnesses and languishings which now in faces are so much in fashion.

DORIMANT: You need 'em not; you have a sweetness of your own, if you would but calm your frowns and let it settle.

HARRIET: My eyes are wild and wand'ring like my passions, and cannot yet be tied to rules of charming.

DORIMINANT: Women indeed, have a method of managing those messengers of love. Now they will look as if they would kill, and anon they will look as if they were dying. They point and rebate° their glances, the better to invite us.

---

kindly, naturally. *under,* lesser. *capered ... gorget,* kicked as high as my partner's neck-piece.

point and rebate, sharpen and blunt.

HARRIET: I like this variety well enough, but hate the set face that always looks as if it would say, 'Come love me!'—a woman who at plays makes the *doux yeux*° to a whole audience and at home cannot forbear 'em to her monkey.

DORIMANT: Put on a gentle smile and let me see how well it will become you.

HARRIET: I am sorry my face does not please you as it is, but I shall not be complaisant and change it.

DORIMANT: Though you are obstinate, I know 'tis capable of improvement, and shall do you justice, madam, if I chance to be at Court when the critics of the Circle pass their judgment; for thither you must come.

HARRIET: And expect to be taken in pieces, have all my features examined, every motion censured, and on the whole be condemned to be but pretty, or a beauty of the lowest rate. What think you?

DORIMANT: The women—nay, the very lovers who belong to the drawing-room—will maliciously allow you more than that: they always grant what is apparent, that they may the better be believed when they name concealed faults they cannot easily be disproved in.

HARRIET: Beauty runs as great a risk exposed at Court as wit does on the stage, where the ugly and the foolish all are free to censure.

DORIMANT (*aside*): I love her and dare not let her know it; I fear sh'as an ascendant o'er me and may revenge the wrongs I have done her sex. (*to her*) Think of making a party, madam; love will engage.

HARRIET: You make me start! I did not think to have heard of love from you.

DORIMANT: I never knew what 'twas to have a settled ague yet, but now and then have had irregular fits.

HARRIET: Take heed! sickness after long health is commonly more violent and dangerous.

DORIMANT (*aside*): I have took the infection from her, and feel the disease now spreading in me. (*to her*) Is the name of love so frightful that you dare not stand it?

HARRIET: 'Twill do little execution out of your mouth on me, I am sure.

DORIMANT: It has been fatal—

HARRIET: To some easy women, but we are not all born to one destiny. I was informed you use to laugh at love and not make it.

DORIMANT: The time has been, but now I must speak—

HARRIET: If it be on that idle subject, I will put on my serious look, turn my head carelessly from you,

drop my lip, let my eyelids fall and hang half o'er my eyes—thus, while you buzz a speech of an hour long in my ear, and I answer never a word. Why do you not begin?

DORIMANT: That the company may take notice how passionately I make advances of love, and how disdainfully you receive 'em!

HARRIET: When your love's grown strong enough to make you bear being laughed at, I'll give you leave to trouble me with it. Till when pray forbear, sir.

(*Enter* SIR FOPLING *and others in masks.*)

DORIMANT: What's here—masquerades?

HARRIET: I thought that foppery had been left off, and people might have been in private with a fiddle.

DORIMANT: 'Tis endeavored to be kept on foot still by some who find themselves the more acceptable the less they are known.

YOUNG BELLAIR: This must be Sir Fopling.

MEDLEY: That extraordinary habit shows it.

YOUNG BELLAIR: What are the rest?

MEDLEY: A company of French rascals whom he picked up in Paris and has brought over to be his dancing equipage on these occasions. Make him own himself; a fool is very troublesome when he presumes he is incognito.

SIR FOPLING FLUTTER (*to* HARRIET): Do you know me?

HARRIET: Ten to one but I guess at you.

SIR FOPLING FLUTTER: Are you women as fond of a vizard as we men are?

HARRIET: I am very fond of a vizard that covers a face I do not like, sir.

YOUNG BELLAIR: Here are no masks, you see, sir, but those which came with you. This was intended a private meeting; but because you look like a gentleman, if you will discover yourself and we know you to be such, you shall be welcome.

SIR FOPLING FLUTTER (*pulling off his mask*): Dear Bellair!

MEDLEY: Sir Fopling! How came you hither?

SIR FOPLING FLUTTER: Faith, as I was coming late from Whitehall, after the King's *couchée*,° one of my people told me he had heard fiddles at my Lady Townley's, and—

DORIMANT: You need not say any more, sir.

SIR FOPLING FLUTTER: Dorimant, let me kiss thee.

DORIMANT: Hark you, Sir Fopling—(*whispers.*)

SIR FOPLING FLUTTER: Enough, enough, Courtage.— A pretty kind of young woman that, Medley. I observed her in the Mail—more *éveillée*° than our English women commonly are. Prithee, what is she?

---

makes . . . *doux yeux*, casts amorous glances.

couchée, evening reception.   *éveillée*, vivacious.

MEDLEY: The most noted coquette in town. Beware of her.

SIR FOPLING FLUTTER: Let her be what she will, I know how to take my measures. In Paris the mode is to flatter the prude, laugh at the *faux-prude*, make serious love to the *demi-prude*, and only rally with the *coquette*. Medley, what think you?

MEDLEY: That for all this smattering of the mathematics, you may be out in your judgment at tennis.

SIR FOPLING FLUTTER: What a *coq-à-l'âne*° is this? I talk of women and thou answer'st tennis.

MEDLEY: Mistakes will be for want of apprehension.

SIR FOPLING FLUTTER: I am very glad of the acquaintance I have with this family.

MEDLEY: My lady truly is a good woman.

SIR FOPLING FLUTTER: Ah, Dorimant—Courtage, I would say—would thou hadst spent the last winter in Paris with me! When thou wert there, La Corneus and Sallyes were the only habitudes we had: a comedian would have been a *bonne fortune*.° No stranger ever passed his time so well as I did some months before I came over. I was well received in a dozen families where all the women of quality used to visit; I have intrigues to tell thee more pleasant than ever thou read'st in a novel.

HARRIET: Write 'em, sir, and oblige us women. Our language wants such little stories.

SIR FOPLING FLUTTER: Writing, madam, 's a mechanic part of wit. A gentleman should never go beyond a song or a billet.

HARRIET: Bussy° was a gentleman.

SIR FOPLING FLUTTER: Who, d'Ambois?°

MEDLEY: Was there ever such a brisk blockhead?

HARRIET: Not d'Ambois, sir, but Rabutin—he who writ the loves of France.

SIR FOPLING FLUTTER: That may be, madam; many gentlemen do things that are below 'em. Damn your authors, Courtage; women are the prettiest things we can fool away our time with.

HARRIET: I hope ye have wearied yourself to-night at Court, sir, and will not think of fooling with anybody here.

SIR FOPLING FLUTTER: I cannot complain of my fortune there, madam.—Dorimant—

DORIMANT: Again!

SIR FOPLING FLUTTER: Courtage—a pox on't!—I have

something to tell thee. When I had made my court within, I came out and flung myself upon the mat under the state° i'th' outward room, i'th' midst of half a dozen beauties who were withdrawn to jeer among themselves, as they called it.

DORIMANT: Did you know 'em?

SIR FOPLING FLUTTER: Not one of 'em, by heavens!—not I. But they were all your friends.

DORIMANT: How are you sure of that?

SIR FOPLING FLUTTER: Why, we laughed at all the town—spared nobody but yourself. They found me a man for their purpose.

DORIMANT: I know you are malicious, to your power.°

SIR FOPLING FLUTTER: And faith, I had occasion to show it, for I never saw more gaping fools at a ball or on a birthday.°

DORIMANT: You learned who the women were?

SIR FOPLING FLUTTER: No matter; they frequent the drawing-room.

DORIMANT: —And entertain themselves pleasantly at the expense of all the fops who come there.

SIR FOPLING FLUTTER: That's their bus'ness. Faith, I sifted 'em,° and find they have a sort of wit among them.—Ah, filthy! (*Pinches a tallow candle.*)

DORIMANT: Look, he has been pinching the tallow candle.

SIR FOPLING FLUTTER: How can you breathe in a room where there's grease frying?—Dorimant, thou art intimate with my lady; advise her, for her own sake and the good company that comes hither, to burn wax lights.

HARRIET: What are these masquerades who stand so obsequiously at a distance?

SIR FOPLING FLUTTER: A set of balladines whom I picked out of the best in France and brought over with a *flute-douce* or two—my servants. They shall entertain you.

HARRIET: I had rather see you dance yourself, Sir Fopling.

SIR FOPLING FLUTTER: And I had rather do it—all the company knows it—but, madam—

MEDLEY: Come, come, no excuses, Sir Fopling!

SIR FOPLING FLUTTER: By heavens, Medley—

MEDLEY: Like a woman I find you must be struggled with before one brings you to what you desire. (*They converse in dumb-show.*)

HARRIET (*aside*): Can he dance?

EMILIA: And fence and sing too, if you'll believe him.

DORIMANT: He has no more excellence in his heels than in his head. He went to Paris a plain,

---

coq-à-l'âne, nonsense. *bonne fortune,* piece of good luck. *Bussy,* Roger de Rabutin, Comte de Bussy, author of the *Histoire amoureuse des Gaules:* still living at this time, despite the implication of Harriet's "was." *d'Ambois,* Sir Fopling displays his actual ignorance of the fashionable world of Paris by supposing Harriet refers to the sixteenth-century French adventurer, who was well-known to the English as the hero of Chapman's play of the same name.

---

state, canopy. *to ... power,* to the extent of your power. *birthday,* at a celebration of the king's birthday. *sifted 'em,* examined.

bashful English blockhead, and is returned a fine undertaking° French fop.

MEDLEY (to HARRIET): I cannot prevail.

SIR FOPLING FLUTTER: Do not think it want of complaisance, madam.

HARRIET: You are too well bred to want that, Sir Fopling. I believe it want of power.

SIR FOPLING FLUTTER: By heavens, and so it is! I have sat up so damned late and drunk so cursed hard since I came to this lewd town, that I am fit for nothing but low dancing now—a *courante*, a *bourrée*, or a *menuet*.° But St. André° tells me, if I will but be regular, in one month I shall rise again. Pox on this debauchery! (*Endeavors at a caper.*)

EMILIA: I have heard your dancing much commended.

SIR FOPLING FLUTTER: It had the good fortune to please in Paris. I was judged to rise within an inch as high as the Basque° in an entry° I danced there.

HARRIET (to EMILIA): I am mightily taken with this fool; let us sit.—Here's a seat, Sir Fopling.

SIR FOPLING FLUTTER: At your feet, madam; I can be nowhere so much at ease.—By your leave, gown. (*Sits at* HARRIET'S *feet.*)

HARRIET: } Ah, you'll spoil it!
EMILIA: }

SIR FOPLING FLUTTER: No matter; my clothes are my creatures. I make 'em to make my court to you ladies. (*to his servants*) Hey! *Qu'on commence!*° (*Dance.*) —To an English dancer, English motions. I was forced to entertain° this fellow (*pointing to* JOHN TROTT), one of my set miscarrying.—Oh, horrid! Leave your damned manner of dancing and put on the French air: have you not a pattern before you?—Pretty well! imitation in time may bring him to something.

(*After the dance, enter* OLD BELLAIR, LADY WOODVILL, *and* LADY TOWNLEY.)

OLD BELLAIR: Hey, a dod, what have we here— a mumming?

LADY WOODVILL: Where's my daughter? Harriet!

DORIMANT: Here, here, madam! I know not but under these disguises there may be dangerous sparks; I gave the young lady warning.

LADY WOODVILL: Lord! I am so obliged to you, Mr. Courtage.

HARRIET: Lord, how you admire this man!

LADY WOODVILL: What have you to except against him?

HARRIET: He's a fop.

LADY WOODVILL: He's not a Dorimant, a wild extravagant fellow of the times.

HARRIET: He's a man made up of forms and commonplaces sucked out of the remaining lees of the last age.

LADY WOODVILL: He's so good a man that, were you not engaged—

LADY TOWNLEY: You'll have but little night to sleep in.

LADY WOODVILL: Lord, 'tis perfect day.°

DORIMANT (aside): The hour is almost come I appointed Bellinda, and I am not so foppishly in love here to forget. I am flesh and blood yet.

LADY TOWNLEY: I am very sensible,° madam. (*Bowing.*)

LADY WOODVILL: Lord, madam! (*Bowing.*)

HARRIET: Look! in what a struggle is my poor mother yonder!

YOUNG BELLAIR: She has much ado to bring out the compliment.

DORIMANT: She strains hard for it.

HARRIET: See, see! her head tottering, her eyes staring, and her under lip trembling—

DORIMANT: Now—now she's in the very convulsions of her civility. (aside) 'Sdeath, I shall lose Bellinda! I must fright her hence; she'll be an hour in this fit of good manners else. (to LADY WOODVILL) Do you not know Sir Fopling, madam?

LADY WOODVILL: I have seen that face—oh, heaven! 'tis the same we met in the Mail. How came he here?

DORIMANT: A fiddle, in this town, is a kind of fop-call; no sooner it strikes up but the house is besieged with an army of masquerades straight.

LADY WOODVILL: Lord! I tremble, Mr. Courtage. For certain, Dorimant is in the company.

DORIMANT: I cannot confidently say he is not. You had best be gone. I will wait upon you; your daughter is in the hands of Mr. Bellair.

LADY WOODVILL: I'll see her before me.—Harriet, come away.

YOUNG BELLAIR: Lights! lights!

LADY TOWNLEY: Light, down there!

OLD BELLAIR: A dod, it needs not—

DORIMANT (calling to the Servants without): Call my Lady Woodvill's coach to the door quickly.

(*Exeunt* YOUNG BELLAIR, HARRIET, LADY TOWNLEY, DORIMANT, *and* LADY WOODVILL.)

---

undertaking, enterprising, bold. **courante . . . menuet,** dances that did not require "capers" (high kicks). **St. André,** a famous French dancing-master. **Basque,** usually explained as the skirt of a coat—but this would scarcely be a leap to boast of. Perhaps the reference is to a contemporary Basque professional dancer. **entry,** a dance performed as an interlude in an entertainment. **Qu'on commence!,** begin **entertain,** engage, hire.

perfect day, broad daylight. **sensible,** aware (of your courtesy to me).

OLD BELLAIR: Stay, Mr. Medley: let the young fellows do that duty; we will drink a glass of wine together. 'Tis good after dancing. *(indicating* SIR FOPLING.) What mumming° spark is that?

MEDLEY: He is not to be comprehended in few words.

SIR FOPLING FLUTTER: Hey, La Tour!

MEDLEY: Whither away, Sir Fopling?

SIR FOPLING FLUTTER: I have business with Courtage.

MEDLEY: He'll but put the ladies into their coach and come up again.

OLD BELLAIR: In the meantime I'll call for a bottle.

(Exit OLD BELLAIR.)

(Enter YOUNG BELLAIR.)

MEDLEY: Where's Dorimant?

YOUNG BELLAIR: Stol'n home. He has had business waiting for him there all this night, I believe, by an impatience I observed in him.

MEDLEY: Very likely; 'tis but dissembling drunkenness, railing at his friends, and the kind soul will embrace the blessing and forget the tedious expectation.

SIR FOPLING FLUTTER: I must speak with him before I sleep.

YOUNG BELLAIR *(to* MEDLEY): Emilia and I are resolved on that business.

MEDLEY: Peace! here's your father.

(Enter OLD BELLAIR *and a* BUTLER *with a bottle of wine.)*

OLD BELLAIR: The women are all gone to bed.—Fill, boy!—Mr. Medley, begin a health.

MEDLEY *(whispers)*: To Emilia!

OLD BELLAIR: Out a pize! she's a rogue, and I'll not pledge you.

MEDLEY: I know you will.

OLD BELLAIR: A dod, drink it, then!

SIR FOPLING FLUTTER: Let us have the new bacchic.

OLD BELLAIR: A dod, that is a hard word. What does it mean, sir?

MEDLEY: A catch or drinking-song.

OLD BELLAIR: Let us have it then.

SIR FOPLING FLUTTER: Fill the glasses round and draw up in a body.—Hey, music! *(They sing.)*

The pleasures of love and the joys of good wine
To perfect our happiness wisely we join.
We to beauty all day
Give the sovereign sway
And her favorite nymphs devoutly obey.
At the plays we are constantly making our court,
And when they are ended we follow the sport
To the Mall and the Park,
Where we love till 'tis dark.

Then sparkling champagne
Puts an end to their reign;
It quickly recovers
Poor languishing lovers;
Makes us frolic and gay, and drowns all our sorrow.
But alas! we relapse again on the morrow.
 Let every man stand
 With his glass in his hand,
And briskly discharge at the word of command:
 Here's a health to all those
 Whom to-night we depose!
Wine and beauty by turns great souls should inspire;
Present all together! and now, boys, give fire!

(They drink.)

OLD BELLAIR: A dod, a pretty business and very merry!

SIR FOPLING FLUTTER: Hark you; Medley, let you and I take the fiddles and go waken Dorimant.

MEDLEY: We shall do him a courtesy, if it be as I guess. For after the fatigue of this night he'll quickly have his belly full and be glad of an occasion to cry, 'Take away, Handy!'

YOUNG BELLAIR: I'll go with you, and there we'll consult about affairs, Medley.

OLD BELLAIR *(looks on his watch)*: A dod, 'tis six o'clock!

SIR FOPLING FLUTTER: Let's away, then.

OLD BELLAIR: Mr. Medley, my sister tells me you are an honest man—and a dod, I love you. Few words and hearty—that's the way with old Harry, old Harry.

SIR FOPLING FLUTTER *(to his Servants)*: Light your flambeaux. Hey!

OLD BELLAIR: What does the man mean?

MEDLEY: 'Tis day, Sir Fopling.

SIR FOPLING FLUTTER: No matter, our serenade will look the greater. *(Exeunt omnes.)*

ACT 4 / SCENE 2

*(*DORIMANT'S *lodging. A table, a candle, a toilet, etc.* HANDY, *tying up linen.)*

(Enter DORIMANT *in his gown, and* BELLINDA.)

DORIMANT: Why will you be gone so soon?

BELLINDA: Why did you stay out so late?

DORIMANT: Call a chair, Handy.—What makes you tremble so?

BELLINDA: I have a thousand fears about me. Have I not been seen, think you?

DORIMANT: By nobody but myself and trusty Handy.

BELLINDA: Where are all your people?

DORIMANT: I have dispersed 'em on sleeveless° errands. What does that sigh mean?

BELLINDA: Can you be so unkind to ask me? Well—

---

mumming, masquerading.

sleeveless, useless.

(sighs)—were it to do again—

DORIMANT: We should do it, should we not?

BELLINDA: I think we should—the wickeder man you to make me love so well. Will you be discreet now?

DORIMANT: I will.

BELLINDA: You cannot.

DORIMANT: Never doubt it.

BELLINDA: I will not expect it.

DORIMANT: You do me wrong.

BELLINDA: You have no more power to keep the secret than I had not to trust you with it.

DORIMANT: By all the joys I have had and those you keep in store—

BELLINDA: You'll do for my sake what you never did before.

DORIMANT: By that truth thou hast spoken, a wife shall sooner betray herself to her husband.

BELLINDA: Yet I had rather you should be false in this than in another thing you promised me.

DORIMANT: What's that?

BELLINDA: That you would never see Loveit more but in public places—in the Park, at Court and plays.

DORIMANT: 'Tis not likely a man should be fond of seeing a damned old play when there is a new one acted.

BELLINDA: I dare not trust your promise.

DORIMANT: You may—

BELLINDA: This does not satisfy me. You shall swear you never will see her more.

DORIMANT: I will, a thousand oaths. By all—

BELLINDA: Hold! You shall not, now I think on't better.

DORIMANT: I will swear!

BELLINDA: I shall grow jealous of the oath and think I owe your truth to that, not to your love.

DORIMANT: Then, by my love; no other oath I'll swear.

(Enter HANDY.*)*

HANDY: Here's a chair.

BELLINDA: Let me go.

DORIMANT: I cannot.

BELLINDA: Too willingly, I fear.

DORIMANT: Too unkindly feared. When will you promise me again?

BELLINDA: Not this fortnight.

DORIMANT: You will be better than your word.

BELLINDA: I think I shall. Will it not make you love me less? *(Starting.)* Hark! What fiddles are these? *(Fiddles without.)*

DORIMANT: Look out, Handy. *(Exit* HANDY *and returns.)*

HANDY: Mr. Medley, Mr. Bellair, and Sir Fopling; they are coming up.

DORIMANT: How got they in?

HANDY: The door was open for the chair.

BELLINDA: Lord, let me fly!

DORIMANT: Here, here, down the back stairs! I'll see you into your chair.

BELLINDA: No, no! Stay and receive 'em. And be sure you keep your word and never see Loveit more. Let it be a proof of your kindness.

DORIMANT: It shall.—Handy, direct her.—*(Kissing her hand.)* Everlasting love go along with thee. *(Exeunt* BELLINDA *and* HANDY.*)*

(Enter YOUNG BELLAIR, MEDLEY, *and* SIR FOPLING.*)*

YOUNG BELLAIR: Not abed yet?

MEDLEY: You have had an 'irregular fit,' Dorimant.

DORIMANT: I have.

YOUNG BELLAIR: And is it off already?

DORIMANT: Nature has done her part, gentlemen; when she falls kindly to work, great cures are effected in little time, you know.

SIR FOPLING FLUTTER: We thought there was a wench in the case, by the chair that waited. Prithee, make us a *confidence.*

DORIMANT: Excuse me.

SIR FOPLING FLUTTER: *Le sage* Dorimant! Was she pretty?

DORIMANT: So pretty she may come to keep her coach and pay parish duties if the good humor of the age continue.

MEDLEY: And be of the number of the ladies kept by public-spirited men for the good of the whole town.

SIR FOPLING FLUTTER *(dancing by himself)*: Well said, Medley.

YOUNG BELLAIR: See Sir Fopling dancing!

DORIMANT: You are practising and have a mind to recover, I see.

SIR FOPLING FLUTTER: Prithee, Dorimant, why hast not thou a glass hung up here? A room is the dullest thing without one.

YOUNG BELLAIR: Here is company to entertain you.

SIR FOPLING FLUTTER: But I mean in case of being alone. In a glass a man may entertain himself—

DORIMANT: The shadow of himself, indeed.

SIR FOPLING FLUTTER: —Correct the errors of his motions and his dress.

MEDLEY: I find, Sir Fopling, in your solitude you remember the saying of the wise man, and study yourself.°

SIR FOPLING FLUTTER: 'Tis the best diversion in our retirements. Dorimant, thou art a pretty fellow and wear'st thy clothes well, but I never saw thee have a handsome cravat. Were they made up like mine, they'd give another air to thy face. Prithee, let me send my man to dress thee but one day; by

---

study yourself, this saying is attributed to several of the Seven Wise Men of Greece, most frequently to Thales.

heavens, an Englishman cannot tie a ribbon.

DORIMANT: They are something clumsy fisted—

SIR FOPLING FLUTTER: I have brought over the prettiest fellow that ever spread a toilet. He served some time under Merille,° the greatest *genie* in the world for a *valet-de-chambre.*

DORIMANT: What! he who formerly belonged to the Duke of Candale?

SIR FOPLING FLUTTER: The same, and got him his immortal reputation.

DORIMANT: Y'have a very fine brandenburgh° on, Sir Fopling.

SIR FOPLING FLUTTER: It serves to wrap me up after the fatigue of a ball.

MEDLEY: I see you often in it, with your periwig tied up.

SIR FLOPLING FLUTTER: We should not always be in a set dress; 'tis more *en cavalier*° to appear now and then in a *deshabillé.*

MEDLEY: Pray, how goes your business with Loveit?

SIR FOPLING FLUTTER: You might have answered yourself in the Mail last night. Dorimant, did you not see the advances she made me? I have been endeavoring at a song.

DORIMANT: Already!

SIR FOPLING FLUTTER: 'Tis my *coup d'essai*° in English: I would fain have thy opinion of it.

DORIMANT: Let's see it.

SIR FOPLING FLUTTER: Hey, page, give me my song.—Bellair, here; thou hast a pretty voice—sing it.

YOUNG BELLAIR: Sing it yourself, Sir Fopling.

SIR FOPLING: Excuse me.

YOUNG BELLAIR: You learnt to sing in Paris.

SIR FOPLING: I did—of Lambert,° the greatest master in the world. But I have his own fault, a weak voice, and care not to sing out of a *ruelle.*°

DORIMANT *(aside)*: A *ruelle* is a pretty cage for a singing fop, indeed.

YOUNG BELLAIR *(reads the song)*:

> *How charming Phillis is, how fair!*
> *Ah, that she were as willing*
> *To ease my wounded heart of care,*
> *And make her eyes less killing.*
> *I sigh, I sigh, I languish now,*
> *And love will not let me rest;*
> *I drive about the Park and bow,*
> *Still as I meet my dearest.*

SIR FOPLING FLUTTER: Sing it! sing it, man; it goes to a pretty new tune which I am confident was made by Baptiste.°

MEDLEY: Sing it yourself, Sir Fopling, he does not know the tune.

SIR FOPLING: I'll venture. (SIR FOPLING *sings.*)

DORIMANT: Ay, marry! now 'tis something. I shall not flatter you, Sir Fopling; there is not much thought in't, but 'tis passionate and well turned.

MEDLEY: After the French way.

SIR FOPLING: That I aimed at. Does it not give you a lively image of the thing? Slap! down goes the glass,° and thus we are at it. (*He bows and grimaces.*)

DORIMANT: It does, indeed, I perceive, Sir Fopling. You'll be the very head of the sparks who are lucky in compositions of this nature.

(*Enter* SIR FOPLING'S FOOTMAN.)

SIR FOPLING FLUTTER: La Tour, is the bath ready?

FOOTMAN: Yes, sir.

SIR FOPLING FLUTTER: *Adieu donc, mes chers.* (*Exit* SIR FOPLING.)

MEDLEY: When have you your revenge on Loveit, Dorimant?

DORIMANT: I will but change my linen and about it.

MEDLEY: The powerful considerations which hindered have been removed then?

DORIMANT: Most luckily this morning. You must along with me; my reputation lies at stake there.

MEDLEY: I am engaged to Bellair.

DORIMANT: What's your business?

MEDLEY: Ma-tri-mony, an't like you.

DORIMANT: It does not, sir.

YOUNG BELLAIR: It may in time, Dorimant: What think you of Mrs. Harriet?

DORIMANT: What does she think of me?

YOUNG BELLAIR: I am confident she loves you.

DORIMANT: How does it appear?

YOUNG BELLAIR: Why, she's never well but when she's talking of you—but then, she finds all the faults in you she can. She laughs at all who commend you—but then, she speaks ill of all who do not.

DORIMANT: Women of her temper betray themselves by their over-cunning. I had once a growing love with a lady who would always quarrel with me when I came to see her, and yet was never quiet if I stayed a day from her.

YOUNG BELLAIR: My father is in love with Emilia.

DORIMANT: That is a good warrant for your proceedings. Go on and prosper; I must to Loveit. Medley, I am sorry you cannot be a witness.

MEDLEY: Make her meet Sir Fopling again in the

Merille, subsequently valet to the Duke of Orleans, brother of Louis XIV and an even more eminent figure in French society than the Duke of Candale, whom Dorimant mentions in his next speech. *brandenburgh,* morning gown. *en cavalier,* fashionable. *coup d'essai,* first attempt. *Lambert,* Michel Lambert, master of chamber music to Louis XIV. *ruelle,* except in a lady's bedchamber (sc. at a levee).

Baptiste, Jean Baptiste Lully, composer, and director of opera for Louis XIV. *glass,* the glass window of the coach.

same place and use him ill before me.

DORIMANT: That may be brought about, I think. I'll be at your aunt's anon and give you joy, Mr. Bellair.

YOUNG BELLAIR: You had not best think of Mrs. Harriet too much; without church security there's no taking up° there.

DORIMANT: I may fall into the snare too. But—

The wise will find a difference in our fate;
You wed a woman, I a good estate. (Exeunt.)

ACT 4 / SCENE 3

(The street before MRS. LOVEIT's lodgings)
(Enter the chair with BELLINDA; the men set it down and open it. BELLINDA starting.)

BELLINDA (surprised): Lord, where am I?—in the Mail! Whither have you brought me?

1 CHAIRMAN: You gave us no directions, madam.

BELLINDA (aside): The fright I was in made me forget it.

1 CHAIRMAN: We use to carry a lady from the Squire's hither.

BELLINDA (aside): This is Loveit: I am undone if she sees me.—Quickly, carry me away!

1 CHAIRMAN: Whither, an't like your honor?

BELLINDA: Ask no questions—

(Enter MRS. LOVEIT's FOOTMAN.)

FOOTMAN: Have you seen my lady, madam?

BELLINDA: I am just come to wait upon her.

FOOTMAN: She will be glad to see you, madam. She sent me to you this morning to desire your company, and I was told you went out by five o'clock.

BELLINDA (aside): More and more unlucky!

FOOTMAN: Will you walk in, madam?

BELLINDA: I'll discharge my chair and follow. Tell your mistress I am here. (Exit FOOTMAN. BELLINDA gives the CHAIRMEN money.) Take this, and if ever you should be examined, be sure you say you took me up in the Strand over against the Exchange, as you will answer it to Mr. Dorimant.

CHAIRMEN: We will, an't like your honor. (Exeunt CHAIRMEN.)

BELLINDA: Now to come off, I must on—

In confidence and lies some hope is left;
'Twere hard to be found out in the first theft.
(Exit.)

ACT 5 / SCENE 1

(MRS. LOVEIT's lodgings)
(Enter MRS. LOVEIT and PERT, her woman.)

PERT: Well! in my eyes Sir Fopling is no such despicable person.

MRS. LOVEIT: You are an excellent judge!

PERT: He's as handsome a man as Mr. Dorimant, and as great a gallant.

MRS. LOVEIT: Intolerable! Is't not enough I submit to his impertinences, but must I be plagued with yours too?

PERT: Indeed, madam—

MRS. LOVEIT: 'Tis false, mercenary malice—

(Enter her FOOTMAN.)

FOOTMAN: Mrs. Bellinda, madam.

MRS. LOVEIT: What of her?

FOOTMAN: She's below.

MRS. LOVEIT: How came she?

FOOTMAN: In a chair; Ambling Harry brought her.

MRS. LOVEIT (aside): He bring her! His chair stands near Dorimant's door and always brings me from thence. (to FOOTMAN) Run and ask him where he took her up. (Exit FOOTMAN.) Go! there is no truth in friendship neither. Women, as well as men, all are false—or all are so to me, at least.

PERT: You are jealous of her too?

MRS. LOVEIT: You had best tell her I am. 'Twill become the liberty you take of late. This fellow's bringing of her, her going out by five o'clock—I know not what to think.

(Enter BELLINDA.)

—Bellinda, you are grown an early riser, I hear.

BELLINDA: Do you not wonder, my dear, what made me abroad so soon?

MRS. LOVEIT: You do not use to be so.

BELLINDA: The country gentlewomen I told you of (Lord, they have the oddest diversions!) would never let me rest till I promised to go with them to the markets this morning to eat fruit and buy nosegays.

MRS. LOVEIT: Are they so fond of a filthy nosegay?

BELLINDA: They complain of the stinks of the town, and are never well but when they have their noses in one.

MRS. LOVEIT: There are essences and sweet waters.

BELLINDA: Oh, they cry out upon perfumes, they are unwholesome; one of 'em was falling into a fit with the smell of these nerolii.°

MRS. LOVEIT: Methinks in complaisance you should have had a nosegay too.

BELLINDA: Do you think, my dear, I could be so loathsome, to trick myself up with carnations and stock-gillyflowers? I begged their pardon and told them I never wore anything but orange flowers and tuberose. That which made me

---

taking up, taking up quarters.

nerolii, essences of orange.

willing to go, was a strange desire I had to eat some fresh nectarines.

MRS. LOVEIT: And had you any?

BELLINDA: The best I ever tasted.

MRS. LOVEIT: Whence came you now?

BELLINDA: From their lodgings, where I crowded out of a coach and took a chair to come and see you, my dear.

MRS. LOVEIT: Whither did you send for that chair?

BELLINDA: 'T was going by empty.

MRS. LOVEIT: Where do these country gentlewomen lodge, I pray?

BELLINDA: In the Strand over against the Exchange.

PERT: That place is never without a nest of 'em. They are always, as one goes by, fleering in balconies or staring out of windows.

(Enter FOOTMAN.)

MRS. LOVEIT (to the FOOTMAN): Come hither! (Whispers.)

BELLINDA (aside): This fellow by her order has been questioning the chairman. I threatened 'em with the name of Dorimant; if they should have told truth, I am lost forever.

MRS. LOVEIT: In the Strand, said you?

FOOTMAN: Yes, madam; over against the Exchange. (Exit FOOTMAN.)

MRS. LOVEIT (aside): She's innocent, and I am much to blame.

BELLINDA (aside): I am so frightened, my countenance will betray me.

MRS. LOVEIT: Bellinda, what makes you look so pale?

BELLINDA: Want of my usual rest and jolting up and down so long in an odious hackney.

(FOOTMAN returns.)

FOOTMAN: Madam, Mr. Dorimant.

MRS. LOVEIT: What makes him here?

BELLINDA (aside): Then I am betrayed, indeed. H'has broke his word, and I love a man that does not care for me!

MRS. LOVEIT: Lord, you faint, Bellinda!

BELLINDA: I think I shall—such an oppression here on the sudden.

PERT: She has eaten too much fruit, I warrant you.

MRS. LOVEIT: Not unlikely.

PERT: 'Tis that lies heavy on her stomach.

MRS. LOVEIT: Have her into my chamber, give her some surfeit water,° and let her lie down a little.

PERT: Come, madam! I was a strange° devourer of fruit when I was young—so ravenous—

(Exeunt BELLINDA, and PERT, leading her off.)

MRS. LOVEIT: Oh, that my love would be but calm

___

surfeit water, a medicine to counteract excessive eating.
strange, notable, extraordinary.

awhile, that I might receive this man with all the scorn and indignation he deserves!

(Enter DORIMANT.)

DORIMANT: Now for a touch of Sir Fopling to begin with.—'Hey, page, give positive order that none of my people stir. Let the canaille wait as they should do.' Since noise and nonsense have such powerful charms.

I, that I may successful prove,
Transform myself to what you love.

MRS. LOVEIT: If that would do, you need not change from what you are: you can be vain and loud enough.

DORIMANT: But not with so good a grace as Sir Fopling.—'Hey, Hampshire!'—'Oh, that sound, that sound becomes the mouth of a man of quality!'

MRS. LOVEIT: Is there a thing so hateful as a senseless mimic?

DORIMANT: He's a great grievance indeed to all who, like yourself, madam, love to play the fool in quiet.

MRS. LOVEIT: A ridiculous animal, who has more of the ape than the ape has of the man in him!

DORIMANT: I have as mean an opinion of a sheer° mimic as yourself; yet were he all ape, I should prefer him to the gay, the giddy, brisk, insipid, noisy fool you dote on.

MRS. LOVEIT: Those noisy fools, however you despise 'em, have good qualities which weigh more (or ought at least) with us women than all the pernicious wit you have to boast of.

DORIMANT: That I may hereafter have a just value for their merit, pray do me the favor to name 'em.

MRS. LOVEIT: You'll despise 'em as the dull effects of ignorance and vanity; yet I care not if I mention some. First, they really admire us, while you at best but flatter us well.

DORIMANT: Take heed! Fools can dissemble too.

MRS. LOVEIT: They may, but not so artificially° as you. There is no fear they should deceive us. Then, they are assiduous, sir; they are ever offering us their service, and always waiting on our will.

DORIMANT: You owe that to their excessive idleness. They know not how to entertain themselves at home, and find so little welcome abroad they are fain to fly to you who countenance 'em, as a refuge against the solitude they would be otherwise condemned to.

MRS. LOVEIT: Their conversation, too, diverts us better.

___

sheer, pure, mere. artificially, artfully.

DORIMANT: Playing with your fan, smelling to your gloves, commending your hair, and taking notice how 'tis cut and shaded after the new way—

MRS. LOVEIT: Were it sillier than you can make it, you must allow 'tis pleasanter to laugh at others than to be laughed at ourselves, though never so wittily. Then, though they want skill to flatter us, they flatter themselves so well they save us the labor. We need not take that care and pains to satisfy 'em of our love, which we so often lose on you.

DORIMANT: They commonly, indeed, believe too well of themselves, and always better of you than you deserve.

MRS. LOVEIT: You are in the right. They have an implicit faith in us which keeps 'em from prying narrowly into our secrets and saves us the vexatious trouble of clearing doubts which your subtle and causeless jealousies every moment raise.

DORIMANT: There is an inbred falsehood in women which inclines 'em still to them whom they may most easily deceive.

MRS. LOVEIT: The man who loves above his quality does not suffer more from the insolent impertinence of his mistress than the woman who loves above her understanding does from the arrogant presumptions of her friend.

DORIMANT: You mistake the use of fools; they are designed for properties, and not for friends. You have an indifferent stock of reputation left yet. Lose it all like a frank gamester on the square; 'twill then be time enough to turn rook° and cheat it up again on a good, substantial bubble.°

MRS. LOVEIT: The old and the ill-favored are only fit for properties, indeed, but young and handsome fools have met with kinder fortunes.

DORIMANT: They have, to the shame of your sex be it spoken! 'Twas this, the thought of this, made me by a timely jealousy endeavor to prevent the good fortune you are providing for Sir Fopling. But against a woman's frailty all our care is vain.

MRS. LOVEIT: Had I not with a dear experience bought the knowledge of your falsehood, you might have fooled me yet. This is not the first jealousy you have feigned, to make a quarrel with me and get a week to throw away on some such unknown, inconsiderable slut as you have been lately lurking with at plays.

DORIMANT: Women, when they would break off with a man, never want th' address to turn the fault on him.

MRS. LOVEIT: You take a pride of late in using of me

---

rook, sharper, swindler. *bubble*, dupe.

ill, that the town may know the power you have over me, which now (as unreasonably as yourself) expects that I (do me all the injuries you can) must love you still.

DORIMANT: I am so far from expecting that you should, I begin to think you never did love me.

MRS. LOVEIT: Would the memory of it were so wholly worn out in me, that I did doubt it too! What made you come to disturb my growing quiet?

DORIMANT: To give you joy of your growing infamy.

MRS. LOVEIT: Insupportable! Insulting devil!—this from you, the only author of my shame! This from another had been but justice, but from you 'tis a hellish and inhumane outrage. What have I done?

DORIMANT: A thing that puts you below my scorn, and makes my anger as ridiculous as you have made my love.

MRS. LOVEIT: I walked last night with Sir Fopling.

DORIMANT: You did, madam, and you talked and laughed aloud, 'Ha, ha, ha!'—Oh, that laugh! that laugh becomes the confidence of a woman of quality.

MRS. LOVEIT: You who have more pleasure in the ruin of a woman's reputation than in the endearments of her love, reproach me not with yourself—and I defy you to name the man can lay a blemish on my fame.

DORIMANT: To be seen publicly so transported with the vain follies of that notorious fop, to me is an infamy below the sin of prostitution with another man.

MRS. LOVEIT: Rail on! I am satisfied in the justice of what I did; you have provoked me to't.

DORIMANT: What I did was the effect of a passion whose extravagancies you have been willing to forgive.

MRS. LOVEIT: And what I did was the effect of a passion you may forgive if you think it.

DORIMANT: Are you so indifferent grown?

MRS. LOVEIT: I am.

DORIMANT: Nay, then 'tis time to part. I'll send you back your letters you have so often asked for. I have two or three of 'em about me.

MRS. LOVEIT: Give 'em me.

DORIMANT: You snatch as if you thought I would not. There! (*giving her the letters*) and may the perjuries in 'em be mine if e'er I see you more! (*Offers to go; she catches him.*)

MRS. LOVEIT: Stay!

DORIMANT: I will not.

MRS. LOVEIT: You shall.

DORIMANT: What have you to say?

MRS. LOVEIT: I cannot speak it yet.

DORIMANT: Something more in commendation of the fool.—Death, I want patience; let me go!

MRS. LOVEIT: I cannot. (*aside*) I can sooner part with

the limbs that hold him.—I hate that nauseous fool; you know I do.

DORIMANT: Was it the scandal you were fond of then?

MRS. LOVEIT: Y'had raised my anger equal to my love—a thing you ne'er could do before, and in revenge I did—I know not what I did. Would you would not think on't any more!

DORIMANT: Should I be willing to forget it, I shall be daily minded of it; 'twill be a commonplace for all the town to laugh at me, and Medley, when he is rhetorically drunk, will ever be declaiming on it in my ears.

MRS. LOVEIT: 'Twill be believed a jealous spite. Come, forget it.

DORIMANT: Let me consult my reputation; you are too careless of it. (Pauses.) You shall meet Sir Fopling in the Mail again tonight.

MRS. LOVEIT: What mean you?

DORIMANT: I have thought on it, and you must. 'Tis necessary to justify my love to the world. You can handle a coxcomb as he deserves when you are not out of humor, madam.

MRS. LOVEIT: Public satisfaction for the wrong I have done you! This is some new device to make me more ridiculous.

DORIMANT: Hear me!

MRS. LOVEIT: I will not.

DORIMANT: You will be persuaded.

MRS. LOVEIT: Never!

DORIMANT: Are you so obstinate?

MRS. LOVEIT: Are you so base?

DORIMANT: You will not satisfy my love?

MRS. LOVEIT: I would die to satisfy that; but I will not, to save you from a thousand racks, do a shameless thing to please your vanity.

DORIMANT: Farewell, false woman!

MRS. LOVEIT: Do—go!

DORIMANT: You will call me back again.

MRS. LOVEIT: Exquisite fiend, I knew you came but to torment me!

(Enter BELLINDA and PERT.)

DORIMANT (surprised): Bellinda here!

BELLINDA (aside): He starts and looks pale! The sight of me has touched his guilty soul.

PERT: 'Twas but a qualm, as I said—a little indigestion; the surfeit water did it, madam, mixed with a little mirabilis.°

DORIMANT (aside): I am confounded, and cannot guess how she came hither!

MRS. LOVEIT: 'Tis your fortune, Bellinda, ever to be here when I am abused by this prodigy of ill-nature.

BELLINDA: I am amazed to find him here. How has he the face to come near you?

DORIMANT (aside): Here is fine work towards! I never was at such a loss before.

BELLINDA: One who makes a public profession of breach of faith and ingratitude—I loathe the sight of him.

DORIMANT (aside): There is no remedy; I must submit to their tongues now, and some other time bring myself off as well as I can.

BELLINDA: Other men are wicked; but then, they have some sense of shame. He is never well but when he triumphs—nay, glories to a woman's face in his villainies.

MRS. LOVEIT: You are in the right, Bellinda, but methinks your kindness for me makes you concern yourself too much with him.

BELLINDA: It does indeed, my dear. His barbarous carriage° to you yesterday made me hope you ne'er would see him more, and the very next day to find him here again, provokes me strangely. But because I know you love him, I have done.

DORIMANT: You have reproached me handsomely, and I deserve it for coming hither; but—

PERT: You must expect it, sir. All women will hate you for my lady's sake.

DORIMANT (aside to BELLINDA): Nay, if she begins too, 'tis time to fly; I shall be scolded to death else. (Aloud) I am to blame in some circumstances, I confess; but as to the main, I am not so guilty as you imagine. I shall seek a more convenient time to clear myself.

MRS. LOVEIT: Do it now. What impediments are here?

DORIMANT: I want time, and you want temper.

MRS. LOVEIT: These are weak pretenses.

DORIMANT: You were never more mistaken in your life; and so farewell. (DORIMANT flings off.)

MRS. LOVEIT: Call a footman, Pert, quickly; I will have him dogged.

PERT: I wish you would not, for my quiet and your own.

MRS. LOVEIT: I'll find out the infamous cause of all our quarrels, pluck her mask off, and expose her barefaced to the world! (Exit PERT.)

BELLINDA (aside): Let me but escape this time, I'll never venture more.

MRS. LOVEIT: Bellinda, you shall go with me.

BELLINDA: I have such a heaviness hangs on me with what I did this morning, I would fain go home and sleep, my dear.

MRS. LOVEIT: Death and eternal darkness! I shall never sleep again. Raging fevers seize the world and make mankind as restless all as I am! (Exit MRS. LOVEIT.)

---

mirabilis, aqua mirabilis, an old-fashioned restorative, made of spirits of wine and a variety of spices.

carriage, demeanor.

BELLINDA: I knew him false and helped to make him so. Was not her ruin enough to fright me from the danger? It should have been, but love can take no warning. (*Exit* BELLINDA.)

ACT 5 / SCENE 2

(LADY TOWNLEY'S *house*)

(*Enter* MEDLEY, YOUNG BELLAIR, LADY TOWNLEY, EMILIA, *and* SMIRK, *a Chaplain.*)

MEDLEY: Bear up, Bellair, and do not let us see that repentance in thine we daily do in married faces.

LADY TOWNLEY: This wedding will strangely surprise my brother when he knows it.

MEDLEY: Your nephew ought to conceal it for a time, madam; since marriage has lost its good name, prudent men seldom expose their own reputations till 'tis convenient to justify their wives.

OLD BELLAIR (*without*): Where are you all there? Out, a dod! will nobody hear?

LADY TOWNLEY: My brother! Quickly, Mr. Smirk, into this closet! you must not be seen yet.

(SMIRK *goes into the closet.*)

(*Enter* OLD BELLAIR *and* LADY TOWNLEY'S PAGE.)

OLD BELLAIR: Desire Mr. Fourbe to walk into the lower parlor; I will be with him presently. (*to* YOUNG BELLAIR) Where have you been sir, you could not wait on me to-day?

YOUNG BELLAIR: About a business.

OLD BELLAIR: Are you so good at business? A dod, I have a business too, you shall dispatch out of hand, sir.—Send for a parson, sister; my Lady Woodvill and her daughter are coming.

LADY TOWNLEY: What need you huddle up things thus?

OLD BELLAIR: Out a pize! youth is apt to play the fool, and 'tis not good it should be in their power.

LADY TOWNLEY: You need not fear your son.

OLD BELLAIR: H' has been idling this morning, and a dod, I do not like him. (*to* EMILIA) How dost thou do, sweetheart?

EMILIA: You are very severe, sir—married in such haste.

OLD BELLAIR: Go to, thou'rt a rogue, and I will talk with thee anon. Here's my Lady Woodvill come.

(*Enter* LADY WOODVILL, HARRIET, *and* BUSY.)

—Welcome, madam; Mr. Fourbe's below with the writings.

LADY WOODVILL: Let us down and make an end then.

OLD BELLAIR: Sister, show the way. (*to* YOUNG BELLAIR, who is talking to HARRIET) Harry, your business lies not there yet.—Excuse him till we have done, lady, and then, a dod, he shall be for thee. Mr. Medley, we must trouble you to be a witness.

MEDLEY: I luckily came for that purpose, sir.

(*Exeunt* OLD BELLAIR, YOUNG BELLAIR, LADY TOWNLEY, *and* LADY WOODVILL.)

BUSY: What will you do, madam?

HARRIET: Be carried back and mewed up in the country again—run away here—anything rather than be married to a man I do not care for! Dear Emilia, do thou advise me.

EMILIA: Mr. Bellair is engaged, you know.

HARRIET: I do, but know not what the fear of losing an estate may fright him to.

EMILIA: In the desperate condition you are in, you should consult with some judicious man. What think you of Mr. Dorimant?

HARRIET: I do not think of him at all.

BUSY (*aside*): She thinks of nothing else, I am sure.

EMILIA: How fond your mother was of Mr. Courtage!

HARRIET: Because I contrived the mistake to make a little mirth you believe I like the man.

EMILIA: Mr. Bellair believes you love him.

HARRIET: Men are seldom in the right when they guess at a woman's mind. Would she whom he loves loved him no better!

BUSY (*aside*): That's e'en well enough, on all conscience.

EMILIA: Mr. Dorimant has a great deal of wit.

HARRIET: And takes a great deal of pains to show it.

EMILIA: He's extremely well fashioned.

HARRIET: Affectedly grave, or ridiculously wild and apish.

BUSY: You defend him still against your mother!

HARRIET: I would not were he justly rallied, but I cannot hear anyone undeservedly railed at.

EMILIA: Has your woman learnt the song you were so taken with?

HARRIET: I was fond of a new thing; 'tis dull at a second hearing.

EMILIA: Mr. Dorimant made it.

BUSY: She knows it, madam, and has made me sing it at least a dozen times this morning.

HARRIET: Thy tongue is as impertinent as thy fingers.

EMILIA: You have provoked her.

BUSY: 'Tis but singing the song and I shall appease her.

EMILIA: Prithee, do.

HARRIET: She has a voice will grate your ears worse than a cat-call, and dresses so ill she's scarce fit to trick up a yeoman's daughter on a holiday.

(BUSY *sings.*)

SONG
BY SIR C. S.°

As Amoret with Phyllis sat,
  One evening on the plain,
And saw the charming Strephon wait
  To tell the nymph his pain;

The threat'ning danger to remove,
  She whispered in her ear,
'Ah, Phyllis, if you would not love,
  This shepherd do not hear!

'None ever had so strange an art,
  His passion to convey
Into a list'ning virgin's heart,
  And steal her soul away.

'Fly, fly betimes, for fear you give
  Occasion for your fate.'
'In vain,' said she; 'in vain I strive!
  Alas, 'tis now too late.'

(Enter DORIMANT.*)*

DORIMANT: Music so softens and disarms the mind—

HARRIET: That not one arrow does resistance find.

DORIMANT: Let us make use of the lucky minute, then.

HARRIET *(aside, turning from* DORIMANT*)*: My love springs with my blood into my face; I dare not look upon him yet.

DORIMANT: What have we here? the picture of celebrated beauty giving audience in public to a declared lover?

HARRIET: Play the dying fop and make the piece complete, sir.

DORIMANT: What think you if the hint were well improved—the whole mystery° of making love pleasantly designed and wrought in a suit of hangings?°

HARRIET: 'Twere needless to execute fools in effigy who suffer daily in their own persons.

DORIMANT *(to* EMILIA, *aside)*: Mrs. Bride, for such I know this happy day has made you—

EMILIA *(aside)*: Defer the formal joy you are to give me, and mind your business with her. *(Aloud.)* Here are dreadful preparations, Mr. Dorimant—writings sealing, and a parson sent for.

DORIMANT: To marry this lady—

BUSY: Condemned she is, and what will become of her I know not, without you generously engage in a rescue.

C.S., almost certainly Sir Car Scroope, who wrote the prologue. **mystery,** art. **designed . . . hangings,** drawn and embroidered in a set of draperies.

DORIMANT: In this sad condition, madam, I can do no less than offer you my service.

HARRIET: The obligation is not great; you are the common sanctuary for all young women who run from their relations.

DORIMANT: I have always my arms open to receive the distressed. But I will open my heart and receive you, where none yet did ever enter. You have filled it with a secret, might I but let you know it—

HARRIET: Do not speak it if you would have me believe it; your tongue is so famed for falsehood, 'twill do the truth an injury. *(Turns away her head.)*

DORIMANT: Turn not away, then, but look on me and guess it.

HARRIET: Did you not tell me there was no credit to be given to faces?—that women nowadays have their passions as much at will as they have their complexions, and put on joy and sadness, scorn and kindness, with the same ease they do their paint and patches? Are they the only counterfeits?

DORIMANT: You wrong your own while you suspect my eyes. By all the hope I have in you, the inimitable color in your cheeks is not more free from art than are the sighs I offer.

HARRIET: In men who have been long hardened in sin we have reason to mistrust the first signs of repentance.

DORIMANT: The prospect of such a heaven will make me persevere and give you marks that are infallible.

HARRIET: What are those?

DORIMANT: I will renounce all the joys I have in friendship and in wine, sacrifice to you all the interest I have in other women—

HARRIET: Hold! Though I wish you devout, I would not have you turn fanatic. Could you neglect these a while and make a journey into the country?

DORIMANT: To be with you, I could live there and never send one thought to London.

HARRIET: Whate'er you say, I know all beyond High Park's a desert to you, and that no gallantry can draw you farther.

DORIMANT: That has been the utmost limit of my love; but now my passion knows no bounds, and there's no measure to be taken of what I'll do for you from anything I ever did before.

HARRIET: When I hear you talk thus in Hampshire I shall begin to think there may be some little truth enlarged upon.

DORIMANT: Is this all? Will you not promise me—?

HARRIET: I hate to promise; what we do then is expected from us and wants much of the welcome it finds when it surprises.

DORIMANT: May I not hope?

HARRIET: That depends on you and not on me, and 'tis to no purpose to forbid it. (*Turns to* BUSY.)

BUSY: Faith, madam, now I perceive the gentleman loves you too, e'en let him know your mind, and torment yourselves no longer.

HARRIET: Dost think I have no sense of modesty?

BUSY: Think, if you lose this you may never have another opportunity.

HARRIET: May he hate me (a curse that frights me when I speak it), if ever I do a thing against the rules of decency and honor.

DORIMANT (*to* EMILIA): I am beholding to you for your good intentions, madam.

EMILIA: I thought the concealing of our marriage from her might have done you better service.

DORIMANT: Try her again.

EMILIA: What have you resolved, madam? The time draws near.

HARRIET: To be obstinate and protest against this marriage.

(*Enter* LADY TOWNLEY *in haste.*)

LADY TOWNLEY (*to* EMILIA): Quickly, quickly! let Mr. Smirk out of the closet.

(SMIRK *comes out of the closet.*)

HARRIET: A parson! (*to* DORIMANT) Had you laid him in here?

DORIMANT: I knew nothing of him.

HARRIET: Should it appear you did, your opinion of my easiness may cost you dear.

(*Enter* OLD BELLAIR, YOUNG BELLAIR, MEDLEY, *and* LADY WOODVILL.)

OLD BELLAIR: Out a pize! the canonical hour° is almost past. Sister, is the man of God come?

LADY TOWNLEY: He waits your leisure.

OLD BELLAIR (*to* SMIRK): By your favor, sir.—A dod, a pretty spruce fellow. What may we call him?

LADY TOWNLEY: Mr. Smirk—my Lady Biggot's chaplain.

OLD BELLAIR: A wise woman! a dod, she is. The man will serve for the flesh as well as the spirit. (*to* SMIRK) Please you, sir, to commission a young couple to go to bed together a God's name?— Harry!

YOUNG BELLAIR: Here, sir.

OLD BELLAIR: Out a pize! Without your mistress in your hand!

SMIRK: Is this the gentleman?

OLD BELLAIR: Yes, sir.

---

canonical hour, the time (at this period from eight to twelve o'clock in the morning) during which a marriage could be legally performed.

SMIRK: Are you not mistaken, sir?

OLD BELLAIR: A dod, I think not, sir.

SMIRK: Sure, you are, sir!

OLD BELLAIR: You look as if you would forbid the banns, Mr. Smirk. I hope you have no pretension to the lady.

SMIRK: Wish him joy, sir; I have done him the good office to-day already.

OLD BELLAIR: Out a pize! What do I hear?

LADY TOWNLEY: Never storm, brother; the truth is out.

OLD BELLAIR: How say you, sir? Is this your wedding day?

YOUNG BELLAIR: It is, sir.

OLD BELLAIR: And a dod, it shall be mine, too. (*to* EMILIA) Give me thy hand, sweetheart. What dost thou mean? Give me thy hand, I say.

(EMILIA *kneels and* YOUNG BELLAIR.)

LADY TOWNLEY: Come, come! give her your blessing; this is the woman your son loved and is married to.

OLD BELLAIR: Ha! cheated! cozened! and by your contrivance, sister!

LADY TOWNLEY: What would you do with her? She's a rogue and you can't abide her.

MEDLEY: Shall I hit her a pat for you, sir?

OLD BELLAIR (*flinging away*): A dod, you are all rogues, and I never will forgive you.

LADY TOWNLEY: Whither? Whither away?

MEDLEY: Let him go and cool awhile.

LADY WOODVILL (*to* DORIMANT): Here's a business broke out now, Mr. Courtage; I am made a fine fool of.

DORIMANT: You see the old gentleman knew nothing of it.

LADY WOODVILL: I find he did not. I shall have some trick put upon me if I stay in this wicked town any longer.—Harriet, dear child, where art thou? I'll into the country straight.

OLD BELLAIR: A dod, madam, you shall hear me first.

(*Enter* MRS. LOVEIT *and* BELLINDA)

MRS. LOVEIT: Hither my man dogged him.

BELLINDA: Yonder he stands, my dear.

MRS. LOVEIT: I see him (*aside*) and with him the face that has undone me. Oh, that I were but where I might throw out the anguish of my heart! Here it must rage within and break it.

LADY TOWNLEY: Mrs. Loveit! Are you afraid to come forward?

MRS. LOVEIT: I was amazed to see so much company here in a morning. The occasion sure is extraordinary.

DORIMANT (*aside*): Loveit and Bellinda! The devil owes me a shame to-day and I think never will have done paying it.

MRS. LOVEIT: Married! dear Emilia! How am I transported with the news!

HARRIET (to DORIMANT): I little thought Emilia was
the woman Mr. Bellair was in love with. I'll chide
her for not trusting me with the secret.

DORIMANT: How do you like Mrs. Loveit?

HARRIET: She's a famed mistress of yours, I hear.

DORIMANT: She has been, on occasion.

OLD BELLAIR (to LADY WOODVILL): A dod, madam, I
cannot help it.

LADY WOODVILL: You need make no more apologies,
sir.

EMILIA (to MRS. LOVEIT): The old gentleman's excus-
ing himself to my Lady Woodvill.

MRS. LOVEIT: Ha, ha, ha! I never heard of anything so
pleasant!

HARRIET (to DORIMANT): She's extremely overjoyed at
something.

DORIMANT: At nothing. She is one of those hoyting°
ladies who gaily fling themselves about and force
a laugh when their aching hearts are full of
discontent and malice.

MRS. LOVEIT: O heaven! I was never so near killing
myself with laughing.—Mr. Dorimant, are you a
brideman?

LADY WOODVILL: Mr. Dorimant!—Is this Mr. Dorimant, madam?

MRS. LOVEIT: If you doubt it, your daughter can
resolve you, I suppose.

LADY WOODVILL: I am cheated too—basely cheated!

OLD BELLAIR: Out a pize! what's here? More knavery
yet?

LADY WOODVILL: Harriet, on my blessing come away,
I charge you!

HARRIET: Dear mother, do but stay and hear me.

LADY WOODVILL: I am betrayed and thou art undone,
I fear.

HARRIET: Do not fear it; I have not, nor never will, do
anything against my duty—believe me, dear
mother, do!

DORIMANT (to MRS. LOVEIT): I had trusted you with
this secret but that I knew the violence of your
nature would ruin my fortune, as now unluckily
it has. I thank you, madam.

MRS. LOVEIT: She's an heiress, I know, and very rich.

DORIMANT: To satisfy you, I must give up my interest
wholly to my love. Had you been a reasonable
woman, I might have secured 'em both and been
happy.

MRS. LOVEIT: You might have trusted me with anything of this kind—you know you might. Why
did you go under a wrong name?

DORIMANT: The story is too long to tell you now. Be

satisfied, this is the business; this is the mask has
kept me from you.

BELLINDA (aside): He's tender of my honor though
he's cruel to my love.

MRS. LOVEIT: Was it no idle mistress, then?

DORIMANT: Believe me, a wife to repair the ruins of
my estate, that needs it.

MRS. LOVEIT: The knowledge of this makes my grief
hang lighter on my soul, but I shall never be
more happy.

DORIMANT: Bellinda!

BELLINDA: Do not think of clearing yourself with me;
it is impossible. Do all men break their words
thus?

DORIMANT: Th'extravagant words they speak in love.
'Tis as unreasonable to expect we should perform all we promise then, as do all we threaten
when we are angry. When I see you next—

BELLINDA: Take no notice of me, and I shall not hate
you.

DORIMANT: How came you to Mrs. Loveit?

BELLINDA: By a mistake the chairmen made for want
of my giving them directions.

DORIMANT: 'Twas a pleasant one. We must meet
again.

BELLINDA: Never.

DORIMANT: Never!

BELLINDA: When we do, may I be as infamous as you
are false.

LADY TOWNLEY (to LADY WOODVILL): Men of Mr.
Dorimant's character always suffer in the general opinion of the world.

MEDLEY: You can make no judgment of a witty man
from common fame, considering the prevailing
faction, madam.

OLD BELLAIR: A dod, he's in the right.

MEDLEY: Besides, 'tis a common error among women
to believe too well of them they know, and too ill
of them they don't.

OLD BELLAIR: A dod, he observes well.

LADY TOWNLEY: Believe me, madam, you will find
Mr. Dorimant as civil a gentleman as you
thought Mr. Courtage.

HARRIET: If you would but know him better—

LADY WOODVILL: You have a mind to know him better!
Come away! You shall never see him more.

HARRIET: Dear mother, stay!

LADY WOODVILL: I wo'not be consenting to your ruin.

HARRIET: Were my fortune in your power—

LADY WOODVILL: Your person is.

HARRIET: Could I be disobedient, I might take it out
of yours and put it into his.

LADY WOODVILL: 'Tis that you would be at; you would
marry this Dorimant.

HARRIET: I cannot deny it; I would, and never will
marry any other man.

LADY WOODVILL: Is this the duty that you promised?

---

hoyting, hoydenish, romping.

HARRIET: But I will never marry him against your will.

LADY WOODVILL (aside): She knows the way to melt my heart.—(to HARRIET) Upon yourself light your undoing!

MEDLEY (to OLD BELLAIR): Come, sir, you have not the heart any longer to refuse your blessing.

OLD BELLAIR: A dod, I ha'not.—Rise, and God bless you both! Make much of her, Harry; she deserves thy kindness. (to EMILIA) A dod, sirrah, I did not think it had been in thee.

(Enter SIR FOPLING and PAGE.)

SIR FOPLING FLUTTER: 'Tis a damned windy day.— Hey, page, is my periwig right?

PAGE: A little out of order, sir.

SIR FOPLING FLUTTER: Pox o' this apartment! It wants an antechamber to adjust oneself in. (to MRS. LOVEIT) Madam, I came from your house, and your servants directed me hither.

MRS. LOVEIT: I will give order hereafter they shall direct you better.

SIR FOPLING FLUTTER: The great satisfaction I had in the Mail last night has given me much disquiet since.

MRS. LOVEIT: 'Tis likely to give me more than I desire.

SIR FOPLING FLUTTER (aside): What the devil makes her so reserved?—Am I guilty of an indiscretion, madam?

MRS. LOVEIT: You will be of a great one if you continue your mistake, sir.

SIR FOPLING FLUTTER: Something puts you out of humor.

MRS. LOVEIT: The most foolish, inconsiderable thing that ever did.

SIR FOPLING FLUTTER: Is it in my power?

MRS. LOVEIT: To hang or drown it. Do one of 'em and trouble me no more.

SIR FOPLING FLUTTER: So fière? Serviteur, madam!°— Medley, where's Dorimant?

MEDLEY: Methinks the lady has not made you those advances today she did last night, Sir Fopling.

SIR FOPLING FLUTTER: Prithee, do not talk of her!

MEDLEY: She would be a bonne fortune.

SIR FOPLING FLUTTER: Not to me at present.

MEDLEY: Not so?

SIR FOPLING FLUTTER: An intrigue now would be but a temptation to me to throw away that vigor on one which I mean shall shortly make my court to the whole sex in a ballet.

MEDLEY: Wisely considered, Sir Fopling.

SIR FOPLING FLUTTER: No one woman is worth the loss of a cut° in a caper.

MEDLEY: Not when 'tis so universally designed.

LADY WOODVILL: Mr. Dorimant, everyone has spoke so much in your behalf that I can no longer doubt but I was in the wrong.

MRS. LOVEIT (to BELLINDA): There's nothing but falsehood and impertinence in this world; all men are villains or fools. Take example from my misfortunes. Bellinda, if thou wouldst be happy, give thyself wholly up to goodness.

HARRIET (to MRS. LOVEIT): Mr. Dorimant has been your God Almighty long enough; 'tis time to think of another.

MRS. LOVEIT: Jeered by her! I will lock myself up in my house and never see the world again.

HARRIET: A nunnery is the more fashionable place for such a retreat, and has been the fatal consequence of many a belle passion.

MRS. LOVEIT (aside): Hold, heart, till I get home! Should I answer, 'twould make her triumph greater. (Is going out.)

DORIMANT: Your hand, Sir Fopling—

SIR FOPLING FLUTTER: Shall I wait upon you, madam?

MRS. LOVEIT: Legion of fools, as many devils take thee! (Exit MRS. LOVEIT.)

MEDLEY: Dorimant, I pronounce thy reputation clear; and henceforward when I would know anything of woman, I will consult no other oracle.

SIR FOPLING FLUTTER (gazing after MRS. LOVEIT): Stark mad, by all that's handsome!—Dorimant, thou hast engaged me in a pretty business.

DORIMANT: I have not leisure now to talk about it.

OLD BELLAIR (indicating SIR FOPLING): Out a pize! what does this man of mode do here again?

LADY TOWNLEY: He'll be an excellent entertainment within, brother, and is luckily come to raise the mirth of the company.

LADY WOODVILL: Madam, I take my leave of you.

LADY TOWNLEY: What do you mean, madam?

LADY WOODVILL: To go this afternoon part of my way to Hartly.°

OLD BELLAIR: A dod, you shall stay and dine first! Come, we will all be good friends, and you shall give Mr. Dorimant leave to wait upon you and your daughter in the country.

LADY WOODVILL: If his occasions bring him that way, I have now so good an opinion of him, he shall be welcome.

HARRIET: —To a great rambling, lone house that looks as it were not inhabited, the family's so small. There you'll find my mother, an old lame aunt, and myself, sir, perched up on chairs at a distance in a large parlor, sitting moping like

---

so fière? Serviteur, madam, so fierce? Your servant, madam!   cut, a rapid "twiddling" of the feet by a dancer who has sprung in the air.

Hartly, Hartley Row, Hampshire, about half-way between London and Salisbury.

three or four melancholy birds in a spacious volary.° Does not this stagger your resolution?

DORIMANT: Not at all, madam. The first time I saw you you left me with the pangs of love upon me, and this day my soul has quite given up her liberty.

HARRIET: This is more dismal than the country! Emilia, pity me, who am going to that sad place. Methinks I hear the hateful noise of rooks already—kaw, kaw, kaw! There's music in the worst cry° in London—'My dill and cowcumbers to pickle!'

OLD BELLAIR: Sister, knowing of this matter, I hope you have provided us some good cheer.

LADY TOWNLEY: I have, brother, and the fiddles too.

OLD BELLAIR: Let 'em strike up, then; the young lady shall have a dance before she departs. *(Dance.)* *(After the dance.)*—So! now we'll in and make this an arrant wedding-day. *(To the pit.)*

And if these honest gentlemen rejoice,
A dod, the boy has made a happy choice.

(Exeunt omnes.)

EPILOGUE

By Mr. Dryden

Most modern wits such monstrous fools have shown,
They seemed not of heav'n's making, but their own.
Those nauseous harlequins in farce may pass,
But there goes more to a substantial ass.
Something of man must be exposed to view
That, gallants, they may more resemble you.

---

volary, aviary.   *cry,* street-vendor's cry.

Sir Fopling is a fool so nicely writ,
The ladies would mistake him for a wit;
And when he sings, talks loud, and cocks,° would cry,
'I vow, methinks he's pretty company!
So brisk, so gay, so travelled, so refined,
As he took pains to graff upon his kind.'°
True fops help nature's work and go to school,
To file and finish God A'mighty's fool.
Yet none Sir Fopling him, or him, can call;
He's knight o'th' shire,° and represents ye all.
From each he meets, he culls whate'er he can;
Legion's his name, a people in a man.
His bulky folly gathers as it goes
And, rolling o'er you, like a snowball grows.
His various modes from various fathers follow;
One taught the toss,° and one the new French
    wallow.°
His sword-knot, this; his cravat, this designed;
And this, the yard-long snake° he twirls behind.
From one the sacred periwig he gained,
Which wind ne'er blew, nor touch of hat profaned.
Another's diving bow he did adore,
Which with a shog° casts all the hair before
Till he with full decorum brings it back,
And rises with a water spaniel shake.
As for his songs (the ladies' dear delight),
Those sure he took from most of you who write.
Yet every man is safe from what he feared,
For no one fool is hunted from the herd.

---

cocks, cocks his hat.   *graff . . . kind,* as if he had taken pains to improve his natural talents.   *shire,* a representative (properly, in parliament).   *toss,* an upward jerk of the head. *wallow,* a rolling gait.   *snake,* a long curl or tail attached to a wig.   *shog,* a shake.

Figure 42. Harriet (Helen Mirren, *center*) and Bellair (Terence Taplin) pretend affection for one another to deceive Old Bellair (David Waller) and Lady Woodvill *(right)* in the Royal Shakespeare Company production of *The Man of Mode,* directed by Terry Hands and designed by Timothy O'Brien, London, 1971. (Photograph: Reg Wilson.)

Figure 43. Dorimant (Alan Howard, *left*) and Harriet (Helen Mirren) banter with one another after being introduced to each other by Bellair (Terence Taplin) in the Royal Shakespeare Company production of *The Man of Mode,* directed by Terry Hands and designed by Timothy O'Brien, London, 1971. The set based on Newton's Cradle can be seen here and in Figure 44. (Photograph: Reg Wilson.)

Figure 44. Dorimant (Alan Howard, *foreground*) and Harriet (Helen Mirren) begin the dance in the final scene of the Royal Shakespeare Company production of *The Man of Mode,* directed by Terry Hands and designed by Timothy O'Brien, London, 1971. The set based on Newton's Cradle can be seen framing the entire cast, at the center of which stands Sir Fopling Flutter (John Wood), dressed in a florid costume that sets him apart from all of the other characters. (Photograph: Reg Wilson.)

Staging of *The Man of Mode*

INTERVIEW OF DIRECTOR TERRY HANDS AND
DESIGNER TIMOTHY O'BRIEN OF THE ROYAL
SHAKESPEARE COMPANY PRODUCTION, 1971,
BY ROBERT WATERHOUSE

THE MAN OF MODE by Sir George Etherege, a new arrival in the Royal Shakespeare Company's repertoire at the Aldwych, is the seventh RSC production directed by Terry Hands and designed by Timothy O'Brien. Their partnership, begun in 1968 with the notable reconstitution of *The Merry Wives of Windsor,* and continued with *The Latent Heterosexual, Pericles, Women Beware Women, Bartholomew Fair,* and—earlier this year—*The Merchant of Venice.* The current production of *Man of Mode,* only the second time it has been seen professionally acted in some 200 years, is an interesting attempt to put a Restoration comedy into a roughly contemporary setting, and is consistent with the RSC's policy of exploring the less well known texts. For the first in *P&P*'s new series investigating notable director-designer partnerships, Robert Waterhouse went to the Aldwych to discuss with Terry Hands and Timothy O'Brien their approach to the play and to working with each other.

WATERHOUSE: Why *Man of Mode?*

HANDS: First of all the text. We thought it was good prose of a kind which hadn't been heard for a long time. The reason why it hadn't been done for about 200 years was that its moral philosophy was abhorrent to the eighteenth and nineteenth centuries. The behaviour of its characters upset nineteenth century morality. This absence from the stage gave us the opportunity to present a Restoration play as though it was new, written yesterday. People could come and see it without any preconceptions.

WATERHOUSE: But it remains a Restoration comedy, doesn't it? Isn't it very stylised in the way that it's written?

HANDS: Some of it is. Half the text is straight naturalistic prose of a kind John Osborne would be proud of; the other half is written in the artificial terms of those who delight in speaking to impress others. But people do that as well today. This play was written in 1676, some 16 years after the Restoration itself; it has the label of a Restoration comedy but our understanding of Restoration drama derives from a tradition of playing it, not from a knowledge of the period. The little that we do know about the Restoration style suggests that it was a sort of cabaret: they put in Pop numbers, the latest fashions and anything that was exciting on the scene. Restoration drama doesn't appear to have been the kind of finger twirling mannered performance we've become used to.

WATERHOUSE: Did your approach open up many design possibilities?

HANDS: Well, only about 40 lines of text actually relate to the period. This left us free to concentrate on trying to create the effect on the audience of today that the play might have had upon the audience in its own time rather than presenting an erroneous museum facsimile. We wanted a design concept that would delight the audience, enable them to see themselves in the play like the 1676 audience might have seen themselves, but be sufficiently removed for them to get the satirical points and be amused by the goings on.

O'BRIEN: Also, we found to our pleasure when we examined the play that it was not a late example of Restoration comedy, where the form is very set, but that it had affinities with Jacobean theatre; we found we were dealing with a comedy where we could sympathise with the characters and see their problems in terms of ours. I recently met a girl in Hampshire who had been to see *Man of Mode*—she was a totally normal member, if that can be imagined, of the theatre going public. She told me that the play had excited her and that afterwards she went through St. James's Park and thought "What a pity the park isn't expressed in terms of the silver balls used in the set; it's much more fun that way."

WATERHOUSE: The night I saw the play the audience responded much more in the second act than the first.

HANDS: But what did you think?

WATERHOUSE: I thought the text might have been taken more by the scruff of its neck. How much editing did you do?

HANDS: Very little.

WATERHOUSE: The first act in particular was over-long and slow in getting the carnival atmosphere you say you wanted.

HANDS: Editing the first act wouldn't solve very much because one of the things Etherege does is spend one and a quarter hours in getting his characters on stage. The last character isn't introduced until the fifth scene; by then he's ready to start his play so the reason why the second half is more interesting is that the play only begins with the last scene of the first half. The danger is to regard it as a farce, which it isn't.

WATERHOUSE: Isn't there a problem, then, of not knowing on what levels to read the characters?

O'BRIEN: The play divides up into artificial and natural characters.

HANDS: The two main artificial characters, Mrs. Loveit and Sir Fopling Flutter, have to be rejected at the end from a hierarchical society which is graded from the most natural up to the most artificial.

O'BRIEN: In one instance, however, something contradictory to the point we're making happens. In Scene 8 Sir Fopling comes to Dorimant's house to examine the bed for traces of Belinda's ruin and is astonished at the urbanity of Dorimant at being able to conceal it. In a passage after that Sir Fopling becomes tremendously alive inside his artificial limits. Someone says 'Look, Sir Fopling's dancing' and he's up on a cloud at the end of a wonderfully successful party where he has felt himself the real comet in the sky, and he's celebrating this so nakedly in his Brandenberg with its soft colours and weaving about the stage like some marvellous happy moth. Then he explains that he has written a song, which is teased out of him. It's read over and he's persuaded to sing it. He stands on the bed, starts to sing, and suddenly realises it's a much better song then he remembered. Almost with tears of pride he sings. Then he sits down and his friends say: 'Of its kind it couldn't be bettered and it's particularly remarkable for being in the French manner.' 'That's what I aimed at,' he says, bursts into tears, and then makes a marvelous gesture: he cries 'Slap, down goes the glass and we're at it.' That's not artificial, it's someone so enthusiastic, so capable of enjoying himself, that the artificiality has vanished. At that point the play is really consummate.

HANDS: If one is watching this scene without the benefit, or hindrance, of twenty or thirty years theatre experience, it all becomes as clear as a bell. I'm sure most younger audiences would allow Sir Fopling to develop as he goes along, not stereotype him. It's very much a doing of your own thing play. The reason why we tried a more contemporary approach is that the play has so many points of contact with real life; behaving naturally is the crux of the Dorimant-Harriet relationship. In order to point up this the play shows every other layer of behaviour; most Restoration plays do the same. I'd like to see other directors and designers go through all the Restoration plays and put them into some recognisable form. Look how badly we do Molière in this country. Really appallingly badly. Molière was a great showman; if there happened to be a team of jugglers around he would put them into the play. There was none of this reverential rubbish about manners and the way people behave. I would passionately like to see

Molière with new songs. Surely there is a way to get him back into common currency.

O'BRIEN: One should emphasise in parallel the much quieter virtues of an approach with which the audience can associate easily, so that it is understood that people, not puppets, are on stage. There should be no translation into the superficial fads of the moment. We have made the odd mistake in the past when searching for a contemporary point of contact in introducing flip things which have nothing to do with fundamentals.

WATERHOUSE: So when you got down to thinking about stage design and costumes what were your fundamentals?

O'BRIEN: We started thinking in terms of the Restoration—wouldn't you? But one of the problems in doing a play in period is that you have truthfully to involve your cast in a whole study of how to handle the Restoration idiom—an obstacle to be surmounted before the text can be served.

WATERHOUSE: And that wasn't worthwhile?

HANDS: It wasn't possible. Nobody knows exactly what they did. Also, nobody really knows how people behaved in the streets.

O'BRIEN: If you give people Restoration clothes you impose on them a style of movement and behaviour which has everything to do with the problems they're facing but nothing very much to do with the emotions and situations they're trying to express.

HANDS: Costume of any period is designed more to reveal than to conceal certain parts of the body. The parts revealed are those of particular sexual or, more often than not, aesthetic interest to the period, and at the time of the Restoration much men's clothing was designed to reveal the calf. Taste is catholic today about which parts of the body you reveal, but the calf isn't one of them. So what's the point in a play where men are chasing women and women chasing men because they both fancy each other, all dressed in a sexual aesthetic which has no relevance to the audience?

WATERHOUSE: Was this a major consideration?

HANDS: Absolutely. The complexity of the play is who is chasing whom, so surely you need to put it into a context which the audience can understand. It seemed crucial to begin with trousers. We looked at modern clothes, deciding what they did and why they did it, then Tim started to develop a costume from his idea of what our men would want to show: chests and arms, if you like biceps. So the sleeves became fuller than modern clothes, the chest area was more distinct—but not so much that the audience wouldn't understand what was going on. It was a very rich world, too; we wanted to convey wealth, colour, flamboyance. If the play were done in Restoration costume, only the sophisticated half of the audience would respond; there's an enormous new audience which wants to see plays it can relate to. Everything I do is angled towards people who may be walking into that theatre for the very first time.

O'BRIEN: It's interesting how one's faith is confirmed. We were painting the set in a South London workshop with the help of young people who had been either to art schools or to a university, and one of them took a look at the model and asked me to explain what the play was about, which I did in terms of Dorimant as the libertine forced by Harriet to see her not as another conquest but as someone for whom it might be worth changing himself. The boy then said the set struck him as something like a 'new restoration.' His words were an absolute echo of something Terry and I tried to formulate very early on.

HANDS: I was once in a school with Theatregoround when we asked a boy why he didn't go to the theatre. He replied that he had no interest in seeing "Some bloke poncing around in a crown." He's right. Who does want to see someone poncing around in a crown? There's a big audience who do, of course, and who scream if they can't see people poncing about in crowns, but there are large numbers who would just as soon see people in tracksuits. The theatre is no more than animated story telling, after all. Every other period except our own—and they were all more successful than ours in getting audiences into the theatre—used a form of heightened modern dress. But don't get the idea that we knew from the start where we were going to get: much of this production developed during rehearsals.

O'BRIEN: This often happens when a designer and director are planning a show. In bald terms you can guess at your destination; But you cannot be confident that this destination is well-chosen. So you begin to work but are constantly haunted by alternatives. Sometimes you long to have it revealed to you that the traditional mode is correct because that can solve so much—it means you'll be working in a language understood within the profession and one that you hope still has validity and carrying power to the public. However, on this occasion, we were constantly disappointed in any such hope; we kept having to try to find a heightened modern version, and that's when the gradient gets steep because you must be frightfully careful of wrong associations and you have to invent extremely accurately. A lot of the designer's and director's work is preventing a wrong audience reaction on the way to provoking an intensified right reaction. You work slowly forward, discarding things to the point where, you hope, every component in the production points to the same end.

WATERHOUSE: You're talking about after you made the model?

O'BRIEN: In the event, and it need not have been so, we found our way in through the set.

WATERHOUSE: How long did you actually have to prepare this production?

O'BRIEN: Not as long as usual because *Man of Mode* was a replacement for another play rather late in the day; I was working on *Enemies* with David Jones, and we had about a fortnight from that opening night to the start of the new rehearsals. Normally we have design thought out when we begin rehearsals, though it is often modified. This time we had only the first version of the set available when we talked to the actors. It wasn't, in fact, as terrifying as it first seemed because the actors contributed enormously to our ideas. I was anxious enough, though, since whatever you need physically has to be made after it is designed. People ask me whether I would like to come to decisions earlier or later: the answer is that one wants to take decisions as late as possible, in the light of as much information as possible, but with enough time remaining for these decisions to become concrete objects.

WATERHOUSE: A pretty tall order.

O'BRIEN: Of course. But the designer who is responsible for the provision of designs as well as the designing process is both the procrastinator and the expeditor. If he takes regrets away from a production they are not only that the wrong decisions were made but that they were poorly carried out for lack of time, because there's a process of digestion necessary for manufacture as well as thought.

WATERHOUSE: Does this need for time lead to clashes with directors?

HANDS: Clashes waste time.

O'BRIEN: That's right.

HANDS: You cannot afford to waste time, and when you have only a short preparation period you're really dependent on one another. This was our seventh play together, so even though we had little time we knew each other's shorthands. Normally we have a couple of months to formulate our ideas and then up to ten weeks' rehearsal at Stratford. But even then, why quarrel? Theatre is such a collaborative process—in English theatre you can't really rule where one man's job starts and another ends. The art is to get all the strands knotted for the first night.

WATERHOUSE: But do you work better under pressure?

HANDS: There's never any shortage of pressure in the RSC and I don't think it helps matters to close up the time allowed as well.

O'BRIEN: There are two distinct ways of working—which may not really be as distinct as they at first seem. There's the sifting and harvesting process when you have a lot of time. The other way, when you have little time, the sifting process suffers. You need instant sifting, followed by instant decisions.

WATERHOUSE: By instant you mean two or three days?

O'BRIEN: Yes. Sometimes crucial matters have to be decided over a weekend that you would perhaps have liked a fortnight to discuss. This should lead us into certain forms of caution. We never say we're unhappy in public, but obviously we are more uncomfortable at some times than others. One of the nightmares is the temptation to think that you have time to do the sifting when you patently haven't, because that leads to real neurosis. One of the things which Terry and I are beginning to consider is how much damage is done by the wrong sort of delay. We belong to a theatre where every liberty can be taken to come to the right conclusion. That's the form. I think sometimes it would be wise to come to the conclusion a little more sharply because other processes need their elbow room—amongst them is the process of rehearsing the actors. If you're still in a conceptual turmoil when rehearsing actors everybody suffers from the irresolution that is apparent.

HANDS: This is terribly important. The actors must be the prime consideration because they are the ones who finally have to go out and play out that gigantic bluff in front of the audience. To work under pressure, or not under pressure, is unimportant; what is worrying is when the processes get in the way of the actors' development within the play. On *Man of Mode,* where we were working under tremendous pressure of time, three actors had their entire costumes changed because we had made a hasty decision which was inaccurate.

REVIEW OF THE ROYAL SHAKESPEARE COMPANY PRODUCTION, 1971, BY IRVING WARDLE

Like Amsterdam's specialist brothels, Restoration comedy was formerly tolerated as a libertine entertainment on the understanding that it made no contact with the flow of normal life. One of the main achievements in the past decade of classical production is its release from this ghetto by the elimination of that *cordon sanitaire* once known as "Restoration style." Plenty of productions exemplify this process, but none more completely than Terry Hands's version of *The Man of Mode* which admits not only the human content of the play but allows it a sense of continuity stretching back to Shakespeare and forward into our own time. Rarely has the RSC's classical-contemporary policy been more fully vindicated.

This is claimed as the first London revival of the comedy since 1766: but Prospect Productions mounted it in Yorkshire a few years ago, and the memory of that show, with its standard parade of bloodless gallants and simpering mistresses, heightens the sense of what has been gained at the Aldwych. Comparatively decorous though its text is, *The Man of Mode* is hard to take as an artificial comedy as its fun is unusually cruel. The intrigue turns at least as much on the tactics of dropping women as picking them up; and Dorimant, the principal lover, acts as much from sadism and ruthless vanity as from desire.

Timothy O'Brien's beautiful set derives from a familiar modern living toy, a framework of suspended steel balls, here magnified into a constellation of silver orbs hanging over the stage and gliding into new positions for changes of scene. The costume, long dresses for the girls, and velvet suits (worn with broad brimmed hats) for the men, further locates the piece in a cool playground for the modern peacock generation whose dances and pastoral lyrics go to a John Dankworth score. Here Dorimant (Alan Howard) voluptuously starts the day, relishing the prospect of rejecting a mistress and stripping off to drop into his morning bath to await news of the latest virgins in town. Howard plays Dorimant with a crooked auburn-bearded grin and a body twisted by his own intrigues; you never question his capacities to get things moving, but there is no appeal whatever to sympathy and you relish his humiliations as much as his successes.

This is important, because the full gesture of the production is one of benevolence. In this sense it joins hands, say, with Mr. Hands's production of *The Merry Wives*; an action in which many mean things happen, but which finally develops into a celebration of fecundity from which no one is excluded; not even David Waller's Old Bellair, who goes through the show pinching the bottom of his son's beloved, or

Vivien Merchant, who camps up the discarded Mrs. Loveit into the purple-gowned likeness of a Sunset Boulevard has-been.

The clue to the interpretation may well have been the character for which the play is best remembered: Sir Fopling Flutter, the first of the Restoration's line of Francophile clowns. The point about Sir Fopling is that everyone wants him to do his thing: he is a cause of entertainment, not irritation, to the other characters. And from the first moment of John Wood's performance, torpedoing his white walking stick into the wings, it is clear that he is to be the source of much more than malicious mockery.

Francophile snobbery is one of the basic comic clichés; but by the end Wood has earned sympathy even for that (as in his delight at finding the one English follower in his retinue starting to speak French). It is a lovely, highly vulnerable performance which reestablishes Mr. Wood as a major asset to the company. Helen Mirren's Harriet, tousled amid her immaculate companions, hurtles through the action as an embodiment of rebellious natural life: never more so than when she and Terence Taplin mime a tender courtship scene for the benefit of two matchmaking elders.

REVIEW OF THE ROYAL SHAKESPEARE COMPANY PRODUCTION, 1971, BY STANLEY PRICE

THE RSC have clearly disinterred the dramatic remains of Sir George Etherege for some theatrical purpose. For a start the play stands at a fascinating point in dramatic evolution, a post-Jacobean melodrama conceived in terms of early Restoration comedy. In Etherege the Restoration style takes its earliest shape in substituting the pursuit of sex and the acquisition of dowry for the murkier Jacobean motivations of murder, incest and revenge. Dorimant, the play's principal, emerges as a positively Jacobean villain who uses sex as a weapon in a private war against fashionable society, womankind in general, and himself in particular. The character of the hell-bent rake, Dorimant, supposedly modelled on the Earl of Rochester, was presumably so familiar to contemporary audiences that Etherege thought it unnecessary to delve into any psychological motivations. Dorimant goes about his sexual intrigues and revenges without so much as a motivational by-your-leave. I don't know when the word 'weapon' first came into use in the vernacular for the male member, but in Etherege it achieves something of an exact apotheosis. Dorimant, whether conceived as hero or anti-hero, has his cake and eats it frequently. At the play's end he bags his beautiful, spirited heiress and foreswears fashionable London for married life in the country. He accepts his fate with the resigned self-sacrifice of the contemporary rake who knew full well the wogs really began North of Hyde Park.

Terry Hands' production of *The Man of Mode* seeks, as is currently modish with 17th Century drama, to put all this sexual plot and counter-plot into a more modern setting. While I know and can frequently sympathise with the arguments in favour of this treatment for over-worked classics, I am more dubious about their validity when applied to lesser-known works. There is the inescapable implication that the director knows the play won't stand firmly on its own two feet, but is important chiefly because of its appositeness to our own time. The snag here is that one spends a great deal of time at such productions pursuing private mental red herrings and not listening to the play. In this form of director's theatre what is at issue is not what the playwright's attitude was to his own time, but what the director's attitude is to our own.

Despite some fascinating programme notes and quotes on Sir George Etherege that show him as wit, gambler, courtier, diplomat and lecher, a veritable prototype for a Restoration comedy, I'm not sure that I took away from this production any strong idea of Etherege's own attitude to his society. Nor do I see at all clearly what Terry Hands' attitude is to that society, or what exact historical or sociological parallels he finds with our own. It is too easy and glib to claim that surfeit of sex and materialism link us to the Restoration admass. After all in what societies hasn't the urge for as much bed and board as possible played a dominant role? Possibly Terry Hands wished to express such universality, but to do so he has fallen for a hodge-podge of styles that confuse rather than elucidate the issues.

His designer, Timothy O'Brien, has used the device of Newton's Cradle to stunning effect. Rescued from scientific obscurity by the Heal's-Habitat nexus as a conversation-piece for the trendy front-parlour, O'Brien has created a gigantic version of the Cradle that encompasses the stage. The six suspended silver spheres are used at different levels and angles to signify scene changes, and help give the production pace as well as an air of fashionable abstract interior décor. The costumes and music, however, veer alarmingly in several directions and periods. The men's fashions seem to strive after King's Road modern but are more in line with the pastel, poetic suits of Gilbert and Sullivan's *Patience*. The women are dressed-up all diaphanous, but Vivien Merchant's Mrs. Loveit is dressed and made-up as though for a '30s Hollywood movie. John Dankworth's music produces one tuneful melody fetchingly sung by Lila Kaye, that would grace any modern musical, but for the rest he appears to be striving for a style that will marry rock and gavotte.

This uneasiness of style carries over into the acting of the play's two stars, Alan Howard and Vivien Merchant, who give performances very much at odds with the straight Restoration comedy style of the rest of the cast. Howard comes down heavily on the interpretation of Dorimant as Jacobean villain. He is a morose, self-tormented lecher who rasps his lines in a series of extended cadences that lure the ear away from an understanding of the complicated plot that Dorimant is at great pains to explain in the first scenes. As Mrs. Loveit, Dorimant's much-abused mistress, Vivien Merchant invests the character with such high-strung histrionics that she seems about to undertake the assassination of Duncan rather than a mere assignation in the Mall. At the serious level at which Miss Merchant takes the part the play's comedy becomes insupportable and the whole production goes out of the window.

For the rest the casting is more fortunate and stylistically in period. The whole production is lifted by the arrival of John Wood. He gives a totally captivating and outrageous display of High French camp as Sir Fopling Flutter, the character that is clearly the blueprint from which Vanburgh created his Lord Foppington. His high moment comes in a splendidly ludicrous but accurate replica of the famous Versailles masque with Sir Fopling as the Sun King. Helen Mirren makes a delightful Harriet, the county heiress of independent mind, and has a hilariously-mimed scene of phoney courtship with Terence Taplin as Bellair. Julian Glover is a smoothly voyeuristic Medley, and Brenda Bruce spreads ineffable good cheer as a permissive dowager. As the laid and discarded Bellinda, Frances de la Tour again shows, after her Miss Hoyden and her Helena in *A Midsummer Night's Dream*, that she is the RSC's most natural comedienne.

In my view *Man of Mode* is good entertainment, stylistically at sea. Its parts are better than its whole, which is perhaps fitting for Sir George Etherege was a gentleman much interested in parts, as an extract from one of his ambassadorial letters from the Diet of Ratisbon, 1687, shows " . . . The best fortune I have had here has been a player something handsomer, and as much as a jilt as Mrs. Barry. Nevertheless this is a Country to satisfy Sir Robert Parker's vanity, for few foul their fingers with touching of a C*** that does not belong to a Countess." Clearly diplomatic bags ain't what they used to be!

RICHARD BRINSLEY SHERIDAN

1751–1816

By the age of twenty-six, Richard Brinsley Sheridan had achieved remarkable successes both in his personal and his professional life. He had married the beautiful Miss Linley with whom he had eloped to France to save her from an unwelcome suitor; he had survived two duels with her frustrated suitor; his first play, *The Rivals,* had been successfully presented at Covent Garden and later in the same year, 1775, his comic opera, *The Duenna,* began a run that would stretch to an amazing 75 performances; he had bought the well-known Drury Lane theater; and *The School for Scandal,* his most famous play, opened there with great success on May 7, 1777. Sheridan's remaining years in the theater were much less noteworthy. He was constantly plagued by debts—running a theater is an expensive business—and he wrote only two more plays: *The Critic* (1779), a witty burlesque of the theatrical process itself; and *Pizarro,* a melodrama adapted from a German source. His interest subsequently turned to politics, and when he died he was given a large public funeral and buried in Westminster Abbey.

The Rivals and *The School for Scandal,* Sheridan's two masterpieces, are not only brilliant theatrical works in themselves, but mark an important moment in English comedy—the return of wit and humor to the stage. For most of the eighteenth century, reactions against the so-called "Immorality and Profaneness of the English Stage" (the words are from the title of Jeremy Collier's famous attack of 1698 on Restoration comedy) had turned comedy away from laughter into melodrama filled with moral and emotional appeals. Such drama is usually referred to as "sentimental comedy," and its characteristics were succinctly described by Oliver Goldsmith, the author of the other great comedy of the late eighteenth century, *She Stoops to Conquer* (1773), in his "Essay on the Theater; or, A Comparison between Laughing and Sentimental Comedy" (1773):

> In these plays almost all the characters are good and exceedingly generous; they are lavish enough of their *tin* money on the stage: and though they want humor, have abundance of sentiment and feeling. If they happen to have faults or foibles, the spectator is taught not only to pardon but to applaud them, in consideration of the goodness of their hearts; so that folly, instead of being ridiculed, is commended, and the comedy aims at touching our passions without the power of being truly pathetic.

As Goldsmith implies here and makes explicit elsewhere in his essay, the spirit of sentimental comedy runs counter to the great tradition of corrective laughter that begins in Greek comedy, finds compelling force in the comedies of Ben Jonson, and dominates the later seventeenth century both in the plays of Molière and those of the English Restoration playwrights.

Sheridan also responded to such "weeping comedy" with his own "laughing comedy," *The Rivals,* which quickly reveals his intentions in the second scene, where he introduces a young woman of markedly sentimental tendencies—so marked, indeed, that they are clearly meant to be a comic caricature. Her name, Lydia Languish, clearly denotes her sentimental excesses, as do the mawkish titles of the books in her library: *The Reward of Constancy, The Fatal Connection, The Mistakes of the Heart,* and *The Delicate Mistress.* Although Lydia is the comedy's romantic heroine, she is nonetheless an extremely silly girl, overwhelmed with romantic notions that Sheridan constantly undercuts. The play's genuine humor, however, derives not from the problems of Lydia, but from the schemes of her lover, Captain Absolute, who disguises himself to woo her and then experiences the comic complications that result from his double identity. Even more memorable to most audiences are two characters whose language is a perpetual source of comic delight: Bob Acres and Mrs. Malaprop. Acres, a country gentleman, figures in the plot as a rival to Absolute for Lydia's hand, but his real stage function is to amuse the audience with his attempts at fashionable dress and speech. Again Sheridan pokes fun at the excesses of sentiment, for Acres is intent on swearing so that "the oath should be an echo to the sense; and this we call the *oath referential* or *sentimental swearing.*" Even more extreme as a figure of affectation and humor is Mrs. Malaprop, whose name has given the word "malapropism" to our language. Her expressed concern for the correct use of language makes the repeatedly garbled language of her speeches even more ludicrous: "but above all, Sir Anthony, she should be mistress of orthodoxy, that she might not mis-spell and mis-pronounce words so shamefully as girls usually do; and likewise that she might reprehend the true meaning of what she is saying."

The School for Scandal at first seems an extension of Sheridan's attack on sentimental comedy, especially considering the satiric portrayal of Joseph Surface, who is praised as a "man of sentiment," when, as his last name implies, he is actually a man of deception. But it should be noted that the moral and emotional sentiments Joseph expresses are themselves neither offensive nor necessarily false. Instead, Sheridan attacks Joseph's *pose* as a man who makes moral statements—"to smile at the jest which plants a thorn in another's breast is to become a principal in the slander"—while actually scheming to slander his brother Charles and steal his beloved. And though Joseph Surface is the subtlest, the most cunning, of the scandal-mongers because he wears the mask of moral concern, he is by no means the only one in the play. With such tag names as Lady Sneerwell, Mrs. Candour, Crabtree, Snake, and Sir Benjamin Backbite, Sheridan, like Molière in *The Misanthrope,* creates an entire gallery of malicious gossips to populate his school for scandal.

Although Sheridan attacks malice masquerading as sentiment, he also presents the value of true sentiment, of genuine feelings that prompt generous actions. In Act IV, scene i, when the seemingly rakish Charles refuses to sell the portrait of his uncle, Sir Oliver, because "The old fellow has been very good to me and, egad, I'll keep his picture while I've a room to put it in," the improvident generosity of his impulse wins him the affection of the disguised Oliver. Similarly, the play's climactic and most intricately structured scene, the "screen scene," is a masterful blend of witty double-entendre, farcical maneuverings, and at the end honest feelings. The scene's tension builds slowly as Lady Teazle, then her husband Sir Peter, and finally Charles Surface enter Joseph's library, creating a situation that we hope will finally lead to the revelation of Joseph's duplicity. And when the revelation comes, with the toppling of the screen and the discovery of Lady Teazle's hiding place, we get not only the punch line to the long joke, but something more. While Lady Teazle has been hiding behind the screen she has had a chance to hear Sir Peter's open confession of his love for her, his young, headstrong wife. And when she is discovered, she responds not with the expected evasion, but with a frank acknowledgment of her faults and a promise to be a better wife.

Because the play encompasses so many moods, it can be performed in a variety of ways, as it has been on the contemporary stage. The customary choice has been to aim for a high style reminiscent of fashionable eighteenth century society. But the actors in the Stratford, Ontario production of 1970 were praised by Clive Barnes for avoiding "any preconceptions they may have about English high comedy style." And Michael Langham, that production's director, makes clear in an interview following the text that he tried to emphasize the "soiled" quality of the scandalmongers (see Figure 45), much as he tried to portray the realistic side of the relationship between Sir Peter Teazle and Lady Teazle (see Figure 46). As both the painful action of the portrait scene (see Figure 47) and the vigorous action in the screen scene suggest (see Figure 48), Langham deliberately moved away from the "icy artifice of most modern stagings" so as to convey the complex world of the play. But no matter how it is staged, *The School for Scandal* remains a masterful blend of wit and true sentiment.

THE SCHOOL FOR SCANDAL

BY RICHARD BRINSLEY SHERIDAN

CHARACTERS

SIR PETER TEAZLE
SIR OLIVER SURFACE
JOSEPH SURFACE
CHARLES SURFACE
CRABTREE
SIR BENJAMIN BACKBITE
ROWLEY
TRIP
MOSES

SNAKE
CARELESS *and other Companions to* CHARLES SURFACE
SERVANTS, *etc.*
LADY TEAZLE
MARIA
LADY SNEERWELL
MRS. CANDOUR

SCENE
London

PROLOGUE

By David Garrick, Esq.

A School for Scandal! tell me, I beseech you,
Needs there a school this modish art to teach you?
No need of lessons now, the knowing think—
We might as well be taught to eat and drink.
Caused by a dearth of scandal, should the vapors
Distress our fair ones—let 'em read the papers;
Their own pow'rful mixtures such disorders hit;
Crave what they will, there's *quantum sufficit.*°
  'Lord!' cries my Lady Wormwood (who loves tattle,
And puts much salt and pepper in her prattle),
Just ris'n at noon, all night at cards when threshing
Strong tea and scandal—'Bless me, how refreshing!
Give me the papers, Lisp—how bold and free! (*Sips.*)
Last night Lord L—(*sips*) *was caught with Lady D—*
For aching heads what charming sal volatile! (*Sips.*)
*If Mrs. B—will still continue flirting,
We hope she'll* DRAW, *or we'll* UNDRAW *the curtain.*
Fine satire, poz°—in public all abuse it,
But by ourselves (*sips*), our praise we can't refuse it.
Now, Lisp, read *you*—there, at that dash and star.'°
'Yes, ma'am.—*A certain Lord had best beware,
Who lives not twenty miles from Grosv'nor Square;
For should he Lady W—find willing,*
WORMWOOD *is bitter'*—'Oh! that's me! the villain!
Throw it behind the fire, and never more
Let that vile paper come within my door.'—

Thus at our friends we laugh, who feel the dart;
To reach our feelings, we ourselves must smart.
Is our young bard so young, to think that he
Can stop the full spring-tide of calumny?
Knows he the world so little, and its trade?
Alas! the devil is sooner raised than laid.
So strong, so swift, the monster there's no gagging:
Cut Scandal's head off—still the tongue is wagging.
Proud of your smiles once lavishly bestow'd,
Again your young Don Quixote takes the road:
To show his gratitude, he draws his pen,
And seeks this hydra, Scandal, in his den.
For your applause all perils he would through—
He'll fight—that's *write*—a cavalliero true,
Till every drop of blood—that's *ink*—is spilt for you.

ACT 1 / SCENE 1

(LADY SNEERWELL'S *house*)
(LADY SNEERWELL *at the dressing-table*–SNAKE *drinking chocolate.*)

LADY SNEERWELL: The paragraphs, you say, Mr. Snake, were all inserted?

SNAKE: They were madam, and as I copied them myself in a feigned hand, there can be no suspicion whence they came.

LADY SNEERWELL: Did you circulate the reports of Lady Brittle's intrigue with Captain Boastall?

SNAKE: That is in as fine a train as your ladyship could wish,—in the common course of things, I think it must reach Mrs. Clackit's ears within four-and-twenty hours; and then, you know, the business is as good as done.

LADY SNEERWELL: Why, truly, Mrs. Clackit has a very pretty talent, and a great deal of industry.

---

    quantum sufficit, plenty. *poz,* positively. **dash and star.** a frequent method of veiled reference to the names of those involved in fashionable intrigues.

SNAKE: True, madam, and has been tolerably success-ful in her day:—to my knowledge, she has been the cause of six matches being broken off, and three sons being disinherited, of four forced elopements, as many close confinements, nine separate maintenances, and two divorces;—nay, I have more than once traced her causing a *Tête-à-Tête* in the *Town and Country Magazine,*° when the parties perhaps had never seen each other's faces before in the course of their lives.

LADY SNEERWELL: She certainly has talents, but her manner is gross.

SNAKE: 'Tis very true,—she generally designs well, has a free tongue, and a bold invention; but her coloring is too dark, and her outline often ex-travagant. She wants that *delicacy of hint,* and *mellowness of sneer,* which distinguish your lady-ship's scandal.

LADY SNEERWELL: Ah! you are partial, Snake.

SNAKE: Not in the least; everybody allows that Lady Sneerwell can do more with *a word* or *a look* than many can with the most labored detail, even when they happen to have a little truth on their side to support it.

LADY SNEERWELL: Yes, my dear Snake; and I am no hypocrite to deny the satisfaction I reap from the success of my efforts. Wounded myself, in the early part of my life, by the envenomed tongue of slander, I confess I have since known no pleasure equal to the reducing others to the level of my own injured reputation.

SNAKE: Nothing can be more natural. But Lady Sneerwell, there is one affair in which you have lately employed me, wherein, I confess, I am at a loss to guess your motives.

LADY SNEERWELL: I conceive you mean with respect to my neighbor, Sir Peter Teazle, and his family?

SNAKE: I do; here are two young men, to whom Sir Peter has acted as a kind of guardian since their father's death; the elder possessing the most amiable character, and universally well spoken of; the youngest, the most dissipated and ex-travagant young fellow in the kingdom, without friends or character,—the former an avowed admirer of your ladyship, and apparently your favorite; the latter attached to Maria, Sir Peter's ward, and confessedly beloved by her. Now, on the face of these circumstances, it is utterly unaccountable to me, why you, the widow of a city knight, with a good jointure, should not close with the passion of a man of such character and expectations as Mr. Surface; and more so why you should be so uncommonly earnest to

Town and Country Magazine, Since 1769, this magazine had published monthly sketches of fashionable intrigues.

destroy the mutual attachment subsisting be-tween his brother Charles and Maria.

LADY SNEERWELL: Then, at once to unravel this mys-tery, I must inform you that love has no share whatever in the intercourse between Mr. Surface and me.

SNAKE: No!

LADY SNEERWELL: His real attachment is to Maria, or her fortune; but finding in his brother a favored rival, he has been obliged to mask his preten-sions, and profit by my assistance.

SNAKE: Yet still I am more puzzled why you should interest yourself in his success.

LADY SNEERWELL: Heav'ns! how dull you are! Cannot you surmise the weakness which I hitherto, through shame, have concealed even from *you?* Must I confess that Charles—that libertine, that extravagant, that bankrupt in fortune and reputation—that he it is for whom I am thus anxious and malicious, and to gain whom I would sacrifice everything?

SNAKE: Now, indeed, your conduct appears consis-tent; but how came you and Mr. Surface so confidential?

LADY SNEERWELL: For our mutual interest. I have found him out a long time since—I know him to be artful, selfish, and malicious—in short, a sentimental knave.

SNAKE: Yet, Sir Peter vows he has not his equal in England—and, above all, he praises him as a man of sentiment.

LADY SNEERWELL: True; and with the assistance of his sentiment and hypocrisy he has brought Sir Peter entirely into his interest with regard to Maria.

(Enter SERVANT.*)*

SERVANT: Mr. Surface.

LADY SNEERWELL: Show him up. *(Exit* SERVANT.*)* He generally calls about this time. I don't wonder at people's giving him to me for a lover.

(Enter JOSEPH SURFACE.*)*

JOSEPH SURFACE: My dear Lady Sneerwell, how do you do to-day? Mr. Snake, your most obedient.

LADY SNEERWELL: Snake has just been arraigning me on our mutual attachment, but I have informed him of our real views; you know how useful he has been to us; and, believe me, the confidence is not ill placed.

JOSEPH SURFACE: Madam, it is impossible for me to suspect a man of Mr. Snake's sensibility and discernment.

LADY SNEERWELL: Well, well, no compliments now;—but tell me when you saw your mistress, Maria—or, what is more material to me, your brother.

JOSEPH SURFACE: I have not seen either since I left you; but I can inform you that they never meet. Some of your stories have taken a good effect on Maria.

LADY SNEERWELL: Oh, my dear Snake! the merit of this belongs to you. But do your brother's distresses increase?

JOSEPH SURFACE: Every hour;—I am told he has had another execution in the house yesterday; in short, his dissipation and extravagance exceed any thing I ever heard of.

LADY SNEERWELL: Poor Charles!

JOSEPH SURFACE: True, madam;—notwithstanding his vices, one can't help feeling for him.—Aye, poor Charles! I'm sure I wish it was in *my* power to be of any essential service to him.—For the man who does not share in the distresses of a brother, even though merited by his own misconduct, deserves—

LADY SNEERWELL: O lud! you are going to be moral, and forget that you are among friends.

JOSEPH SURFACE: Egad, that's true!—I'll keep that sentiment till I see Sir Peter. However, it is certainly a charity to rescue Maria from such a libertine, who, if he is to be reclaimed, can be so only by a person of your ladyship's superior accomplishments and understanding.

SNAKE: I believe, Lady Sneerwell, here's company coming,—I'll go and copy the letter I mentioned to you.—Mr. Surface, your most obedient. (*Exit* SNAKE.)

JOSEPH SURFACE: Sir, your very devoted.—Lady Sneerwell, I am very sorry you have put any further confidence in that fellow.

LADY SNEERWELL: Why so?

JOSEPH SURFACE: I have lately detected him in frequent conference with old Rowley, who was formerly my father's steward, and has never, you know, been a friend of mine.

LADY SNEERWELL: And do you think he would betray us?

JOSEPH SURFACE: Nothing more likely: take my word for't, Lady Sneerwell, that fellow hasn't virtue enough to be faithful even to his own villainy.—Hah! Maria!

(*Enter* MARIA.)

LADY SNEERWELL: Maria, my dear, how do you do?—What's the matter?

MARIA: Oh! there is that disagreeable lover of mine, Sir Benjamin Backbite, has just called at my guardian's, with his odious uncle, Crabtree; so I slipped out, and run hither to avoid them.

LADY SNEERWELL: Is that all?

JOSEPH SURFACE: If my brother Charles had been of the party, ma'am, perhaps you would not have been so much alarmed.

LADY SNEERWELL: Nay, now you are severe; for I dare swear the truth of the matter is, Maria heard *you* were here;—but, my dear, what has Sir Benjamin done, that you should avoid him so?

MARIA: Oh, he has done nothing—but 'tis for what he has said,—his conversation is a perpetual libel on all his acquaintance.

JOSEPH SURFACE: Aye, and the worst of it is, there is no advantage in not knowing him; for he'll abuse a stranger just as soon as his best friend—and his uncle's as bad.

LADY SNEERWELL: Nay, but we should make allowance; Sir Benjamin is a wit and a poet.

MARIA: For my part, I own, madam, wit loses its respect with me, when I see it in company with malice.—What do you think, Mr. Surface?

JOSEPH SURFACE: Certainly, madam; to smile at the jest which plants a thorn in another's breast is to become a principal in the mischief.

LADY SNEERWELL: Pshaw! there's no possibility of being witty without a little ill nature: the malice of a good thing is the barb that makes it stick.—What's your opinion, Mr. Surface?

JOSEPH SURFACE: To be sure, madam, that conversation, where the spirit of raillery is suppressed, will ever appear tedious and insipid.

MARIA: Well I'll not debate how far scandal may be allowable; but in a man, I am sure, it is always contemptible.—We have pride, envy, rivalship, and a thousand motives to depreciate each other; but the male slanderer must have the cowardice of a woman before he can traduce one.

(*Enter* SERVANT.)

SERVANT: Madam, Mrs. Candour is below, and, if your ladyship's at leisure, will leave her carriage.

LADY SNEERWELL: Beg her to walk in. (*Exit* SERVANT.) Now Maria, however here is a character to your taste; for, though Mrs. Candour is a little talkative, everybody allows her to be the best-natured and best sort of woman.

MARIA: Yes, with a very gross affectation of good nature and benevolence, she does more mischief than the direct malice of old Crabtree.

JOSEPH SURFACE: I'faith 'tis very true, Lady Sneerwell; whenever I hear the current running against the characters of my friends, I never think them in such danger as when Candour undertakes their defence.

LADY SNEERWELL: Hush!—here she is!

(*Enter* MRS. CANDOUR.)

MRS. CANDOUR: My dear Lady Sneerwell, how have you been this century?—Mr. Surface, what news do you hear?—though indeed it is no matter, for I think one hears nothing else but scandal.

JOSEPH SURFACE: Just so, indeed, madam.

MRS. CANDOUR: Ah, Maria! child,—what, is the whole affair off between you and Charles? His extravagance, I presume—the town talks of nothing else.

MARIA: I am very sorry, ma'am, the town has so little to do.

MRS. CANDOUR: True, true, child: but there is no stopping people's tongues.—I own I was hurt to hear it, as indeed I was to learn, from the same quarter, that your guardian, Sir Peter, and Lady Teazle have not agreed lately so well as could be wished.

MARIA: 'Tis strangely impertinent for people to busy themselves so.

MRS. CANDOUR: Very true, child, but what's to be done? People will talk—there's no preventing it.—Why, it was but yesterday I was told that Miss Gadabout had eloped with Sir Filigree Flirt.—But, Lord! there's no minding what one hears—though, to be sure, I had this from very good authority.

MARIA: Such reports are highly scandalous.

MRS. CANDOUR: So they are, child—shameful, shameful! But the world is so censorious, no character escapes.—Lord, now who would have suspected your friend, Miss Prim, of an indiscretion? Yet such is the ill-nature of people, that they say her uncle stopped her last week, just as she was stepping into the York Diligence with her dancing-master.

MARIA: I'll answer for't there are no grounds for the report.

MRS. CANDOUR: Oh, no foundation in the world, I dare swear; no more, probably, than for the story circulated last month of Mrs. Festino's affair with Colonel Cassino;—though, to be sure, that matter was never rightly cleared up.

JOSEPH SURFACE: The license of invention some people take is monstrous indeed.

MARIA: 'Tis so.—But, in my opinion, those who report such things are equally culpable.

MRS. CANDOUR: To be sure, they are; tale-bearers are as bad as the tale-makers—'tis an old observation, and a very true one—but what's to be done, as I said before? how will you prevent people from talking?—To-day, Mrs. Clackit assured me Mr. and Mrs. Honeymoon were at last become mere man and wife, like the rest of their acquaintances.—She likewise hinted that a certain widow, in the next street, had got rid of her dropsy and recovered her shape in a most surprising manner. And at the same time Miss Tattle, who was by, affirmed that Lord Buffalo

had discovered his lady at a house of no extraordinary fame—and that Sir Harry Bouquet and Tom Saunter were to measure swords on a similar provocation. But, Lord, do you think I would report these things! No, no! tale-bearers, as I said before, are just as bad as tale-makers.

JOSEPH SURFACE: Ah! Mrs. Candour, if everybody had your forbearance and good nature!

MRS. CANDOUR: I confess, Mr. Surface, I cannot bear to hear people attacked behind their backs, and when ugly circumstances come out against one's acquaintance I own I always love to think the best.—By the bye, I hope it is not true that your brother is absolutely ruined?

JOSEPH SURFACE: I am afraid his circumstances are very bad indeed, ma'am.

MRS. CANDOUR: Ah!—I heard so—but you must tell him to keep up his spirits—everybody almost is in the same way! Lord Spindle, Sir Thomas Splint, Captain Quinze, and Mr. Nickit—all up, I hear, within this week; so, if Charles is undone, he'll find half his acquaintances ruined too—and that, you know, is a consolation.

JOSEPH SURFACE: Doubtless, ma'am—a very great one.

(Enter SERVANT.)

SERVANT: Mr. Crabtree and Sir Benjamin Backbite. *(Exit* SERVANT.)

LADY SNEERWELL: So, Maria, you see your lover pursues you; positively you shan't escape.

(Enter CRABTREE *and* SIR BENJAMIN BACKBITE.)

CRABTREE: Lady Sneerwell, I kiss your hands. Mrs. Candour, I don't believe you are acquainted with my nephew, Sir Benjamin Backbite? Egad, ma'am, he has a pretty wit, and is a pretty poet too; isn't he, Lady Sneerwell?

SIR BENJAMIN: O fie, uncle!

CRABTREE: Nay, egad it's true—I'll back him at a rebus or a charade against the best rhymer in the kingdom. Has your ladyship heard the epigram he wrote last week on Lady Frizzle's feather catching fire?—Do, Benjamin, repeat it—or the charade you made last night extempore at Mrs. Drowzie's conversazione.—Come now; your *first* is the name of a fish, your *second* a great naval commander, and—

SIR BENJAMIN: Uncle, now—prithee—

CRABTREE: I'faith, ma'am, 'twould surprise you to hear how ready he is at these things.

LADY SNEERWELL: I wonder, Sir Benjamin, you never publish anything.

SIR BENJAMIN: To say truth, ma'am, 'tis very vulgar to print; and, as my little productions are mostly satires and lampoons on particular people, I find they circulate more by giving copies in confidence to the friends of the parties—however, I have some love elegies, which, when favored with this lady's smiles, I mean to give to the public.

CRABTREE: 'Fore heav'n, ma'am, they'll immortalize you!—you'll be handed down to posterity like Petrarch's Laura, or Waller's Sacharissa.°

SIR BENJAMIN: Yes, madam, I think you will like them, when you shall see them on a beautiful quarto page, where a neat rivulet of text shall murmur through a meadow of margin. 'Fore gad, they will be the most elegant things of their kind!

CRABTREE: But, ladies, that's true—have you heard the news?

MRS. CANDOUR: What, sir, do you mean the report of—

CRABTREE: No, ma'am, that's not it.—Miss Nicely is going to be married to her own footman.

MRS. CANDOUR: Impossible!

CRABTREE: Ask Sir Benjamin.

SIR BENJAMIN: 'Tis very true, ma'am—everything is fixed, and the wedding liveries bespoke.

CRABTREE: Yes—and they do say there were pressing reasons for it.

LADY SNEERWELL: Why, I have heard something of this before.

MRS. CANDOUR: It can't be—and I wonder any one should believe such a story of so prudent a lady as Miss Nicely.

SIR BENJAMIN: O lud! ma'am, that's the very reason 'twas believed at once. She has always been so cautious and so reserved, that everybody was sure there was some reason for it at bottom.

MRS. CANDOUR: Why, to be sure, a tale of scandal is as fatal to the credit of a prudent lady of her stamp as a fever is generally to those of the strongest constitutions; but there is a sort of puny, sickly reputation that is always ailing, yet will outlive the robuster characters of a hundred prudes.

SIR BENJAMIN: True, madam, there are valetudinarians in reputation as well as constitution, who, being conscious of their weak part, avoid the least breath of air, and supply their want of stamina by care and circumspection.

MRS. CANDOUR: Well, but this may be all a mistake. You know, Sir Benjamin, very trifling circumstances often give rise to the most injurious tales.

CRABTREE: That they do, I'll be sworn, ma'am. Did you ever hear how Miss Piper came to lose her lover and her character last summer at Tunbridge?—Sir Benjamin, you remember it?

SIR BENJAMIN: Oh, to be sure!—the most whimsical circumstance—

LADY SNEERWELL: How was it, pray?

CRABTREE: Why, one evening, at Mrs. Ponto's assembly, the conversation happened to turn on the difficulty of breeding Nova Scotia sheep in this country. Says a young lady in company, 'I have known instances of it; for Miss Letitia Piper, a first cousin of mine, had a Nova Scotia sheep that produced her twins.' 'What!' cries the old Dowager Lady Dundizzy (who you know is as deaf as a post), 'has Miss Piper had twins?' This mistake, as you may imagine, threw the whole company into a fit of laughing. However, 'twas the next morning everywhere reported, and in a few days believed by the whole town, that Miss Letitia Piper had actually been brought to bed of a fine boy and a girl—and in less than a week there were people who could name the father, and the farm-house where the babies were put out to nurse!

LADY SNEERWELL: Strange, indeed!

CRABTREE: Matter of fact, I assure you.—O lud! Mr. Surface, pray is it true that your uncle, Sir Oliver, is coming home?

JOSEPH SURFACE: Not that I know of, indeed, sir.

CRABTREE: He has been in the East Indias a long time. You can scarcely remember him, I believe.—Sad comfort, whenever he returns, to hear how your brother has gone on!

JOSEPH SURFACE: Charles has been imprudent, sir, to be sure; but I hope no busy people have already prejudiced Sir Oliver against him,—he may reform.

SIR BENJAMIN: To be sure he may—for my part I never believed him to be so utterly void of principle as people say—and though he has lost all his friends, I am told nobody is better spoken of by the Jews.

CRABTREE: That's true, egad, nephew. If the old Jewry were a ward, I believe Charles would be an alderman; no man more popular there, 'fore gad! I hear he pays as many annuities as the Irish tontine; and that, whenever he's sick, they have prayers for the recovery of his health in the Synagogue.

SIR BENJAMIN: Yet no man lives in greater splendor.—They tell me, when he entertains his friends, he can sit down to dinner with a dozen of his own securities; have a score of tradesmen waiting in the antechamber, and an officer behind every guest's chair.

JOSEPH SURFACE: This may be entertainment to you, gentlemen, but you pay very little regard to the feelings of a brother.

MARIA: Their malice is intolerable!—Lady Sneerwell,

Sacharissa, Edmund Waller's poetical name for Lady Dorothy Sidney.

I must wish you a good morning—I'm not very well. (*Exit* MARIA.)

MRS. CANDOUR: O dear! she changes color very much!

LADY SNEERWELL: Do, Mrs. Candour, follow her—she may want assistance.

MRS. CANDOUR: That I will, with all my soul, ma'am.—Poor dear girl! who knows what her situation may be! (*Exit* MRS. CANDOUR.)

LADY SNEERWELL: 'Twas nothing but that she could not bear to hear Charles reflected on, notwithstanding their difference.

SIR BENJAMIN: The young lady's *penchant* is obvious.

CRABTREE: But, Benjamin, you mustn't give up the pursuit for that; follow her, and put her into good humor. Repeat her some of your own verses.—Come, I'll assist you.

SIR BENJAMIN: Mr. Surface, I did not mean to hurt you; but depend upon't your brother is utterly undone. (*Going.*)

CRABTREE: O lud, aye! undone as ever man was—can't raise a guinea. (*Going.*)

SIR BENJAMIN: And everything sold, I'm told, that was movable. (*Going.*)

CRABTREE: I have seen one that was at his house—not a thing left but some empty bottles that were overlooked, and the family pictures, which I believe are framed in the wainscot. (*Going.*)

SIR BENJAMIN: And I am very sorry to hear also some bad stories against him. (*Going.*)

CRABTREE: Oh, he has done many mean things, that's certain. (*Going.*)

SIR BENJAMIN: But, however, as he's your brother—(*Going.*)

CRABTREE: We'll tell you all, another opportunity.

(*Exeunt* CRABTREE *and* SIR BENJAMIN.)

LADY SNEERWELL: Ha, ha, ha! 'tis very hard for them to leave a subject they have not quite run down.

JOSEPH SURFACE: And I believe the abuse was no more acceptable to your ladyship than to Maria.

LADY SNEERWELL: I doubt° her affections are farther engaged than we imagined; but the family are to be here this evening, so you may as well dine where you are, and we shall have an opportunity of observing farther;—in the meantime, I'll go and plot mischief, and you shall study sentiments. (*Exeunt.*)

ACT 1 / SCENE 2

(SIR PETER TEAZLE'S *house.*)
(*Enter* SIR PETER.)

SIR PETER: When an old bachelor takes a young wife, what is he to expect?—'Tis now six months since

---

doubt, suspect.

Lady Teazle made me the happiest of men—and I have been the miserablest dog ever since that ever committed wedlock! We tift a little going to church, and came to a quarrel before the bells were done ringing. I was more than once nearly choked with gall during the honeymoon, and had lost all comfort in life before my friends had done wishing me joy! Yet I chose with caution—a girl bred wholly in the country, who never knew luxury beyond one silk gown, nor dissipation above the annual gala of a race ball. Yet now she plays her part in all the extravagant fopperies of the fashion and the town, with as ready a grace as if she had never seen a bush nor a grass-plat out of Grosvenor Square! I am sneered at by my old acquaintance—paragraphed in the newspapers. She dissipates my fortune, and contradicts all my humors; yet the worst of it is, I doubt I love her, or I should never bear all this. However, I'll never be weak enough to own it.

(*Enter* ROWLEY.)

ROWLEY: Oh! Sir Peter, your servant,—how is it with you, sir?

SIR PETER: Very bad, Master Rowley, very bad;—I meet with nothing but crosses and vexations.

ROWLEY: What can have happened to trouble you since yesterday?

SIR PETER: A good question to a married man!

ROWLEY: Nay, I'm sure your lady, Sir Peter, can't be the cause of your uneasiness.

SIR PETER: Why, has anyone told you she was dead?

ROWLEY: Come, come, Sir Peter, you love her, notwithstanding your tempers don't exactly agree.

SIR PETER: But the fault is entirely hers, Master Rowley. I am, myself, the sweetest-tempered man alive, and hate a teasing temper—and so I tell her a hundred times a day.

ROWLEY: Indeed!

SIR PETER: Aye; and what is very extraordinary, in all our disputes she is always in the wrong! But Lady Sneerwell, and the set she meets at her house, encourage the perverseness of her disposition. Then, to complete my vexations, Maria, my ward, whom I ought to have the power of a father over, is determined to turn rebel too, and absolutely refuses the man whom I have long resolved on for her husband;—meaning, I suppose, to bestow herself on his profligate brother.

ROWLEY: You know, Sir Peter, I have always taken the liberty to differ with you on the subject of these two young gentlemen. I only wish you may not be deceived in your opinion of the elder. For Charles, my life on't! he will retrieve his errors yet. Their worthy father, once my honored master, was, at his years, nearly as wild a spark; yet, when he died, he did not leave a more benevolent heart to lament his loss.

SIR PETER: You are wrong, Master Rowley. On their father's death, you know, I acted as a kind of guardian to them both, till their uncle Sir Oliver's Eastern liberality gave them an early independence; of course, no person could have more opportunities of judging of their hearts, and I was never mistaken in my life. Joseph is indeed a model for the young men of the age. He is a man of sentiment, and acts up to the sentiments he professes; but, for the other, take my word for't, if he had any grains of virtue by descent, he has dissipated them with the rest of his inheritance. Ah! my old friend, Sir Oliver, will be deeply mortified when he finds how part of his bounty has been misapplied.

ROWLEY: I am sorry to find you so violent against the young man, because this may be the most critical period of his fortune. I came hither with news that will surprise you.

SIR PETER: What! let me hear.

ROWLEY: Sir Oliver *is* arrived, and at this moment in town.

SIR PETER: How! you astonish me! I thought you did not expect him this month.

ROWLEY: I did not; but his passage has been remarkably quick.

SIR PETER: Egad, I shall rejoice to see my old friend,—'tis sixteen years since we met—we have had many a day together; but does he still enjoin us not to inform his nephews of his arrival?

ROWLEY: Most strictly. He means, before it is known, to make some trial of their dispositions.

SIR PETER: Ah! There needs no art to discover their merits—however, he shall have his way; but, pray, does he know I am married?

ROWLEY: Yes, and will soon wish you joy.

SIR PETER: What, as we drink health to a friend in a consumption! Ah, Oliver will laugh at me—we used to rail at matrimony together—but he has been steady to his text. Well, he must be at my house, though—I'll instantly give orders for his reception. But, Master Rowley, don't drop a word that Lady Teazle and I ever disagree.

ROWLEY: By no means.

SIR PETER: For I should never be able to stand Noll's jokes; so I'd have him think, Lord forgive me! that we are a very happy couple.

ROWLEY: I understand you—but then you must be very careful not to differ while he's in the house with you.

SIR PETER: Egad, and so we must—and that's impossible. Ah! Master Rowley, when an old bachelor marries a young wife, he deserves—no—the crime carries the punishment along with it. (*Exeunt.*)

ACT 2 / SCENE 1

(SIR PETER TEAZLE'S *house*)
(*Enter* SIR PETER *and* LADY TEAZLE.)

SIR PETER: Lady Teazle, Lady Teazle, I'll not bear it!

LADY TEAZLE: Sir Peter, Sir Peter, you may bear it or not, as you please; but I ought to have my own way in everything, and what's more, I *will* too.—What! though I was educated in the country, I know very well that women of fashion in London are accountable to nobody after they are married.

SIR PETER: Very well, ma'am, very well,—so a husband is to have no influence, no authority?

LADY TEAZLE: Authority! No, to be sure—if you wanted authority over me, you should have adopted me, and not married me; I am sure you were old enough.

SIR PETER: Old enough!—aye, there it is!—Well, well, Lady Teazle, though my life may be made unhappy by your temper, I'll not be ruined by your extravagance.

LADY TEAZLE: My extravagance! I'm sure I'm not more extravagant than a woman of fashion ought to be.

SIR PETER: No, no, madam, you shall throw away no more sums on such unmeaning luxury. 'Slife! to spend as much to furnish your dressing room with flowers in winter as would suffice to turn the Pantheon° into a greenhouse, and give a *fête champêtre*° at Christmas!

LADY TEAZLE: Lord, Sir Peter, am I to blame because flowers are dear in cold weather? You should find fault with the climate, and not with me. For my part, I am sure I wish it was spring all the year round, and that roses grew under one's feet!

SIR PETER: Oons! madam—if you had been born to this, I shouldn't wonder at your talking thus.—But you forget what your situation was when I married you.

LADY TEAZLE: No, no, I don't; 'twas a very disagreeable one, or I should never have married *you*.

SIR PETER: Yes, yes, madam, you were then in somewhat an humbler style—the daughter of a plain country squire. Recollect, Lady Teazle, when I saw you first, sitting at your tambour,° in a pretty figured linen gown, with a bunch of keys by your side, your hair combed smooth over a roll, and

---

Pantheon, a fashionable concert-hall in Oxford Street.
fête champêtre, an open-air festival.   **tambour,** embroidery frame.

your apartment hung round with fruits in worsted, of your own working.

LADY TEAZLE: O, yes! I remember it very well, and a curious life I led—my daily occupation to inspect the dairy, superintend the poultry, make extracts from the family receipt-book, and comb my aunt Deborah's lap-dog.

SIR PETER: Yes, yes, ma'am, 'twas so indeed.

LADY TEAZLE: And then, you know, my evening amusements! To draw patterns for ruffles, which I had not the materials to make; to play Pope Joan° with the curate; to read a novel to my aunt; or to be stuck down to an old spinet to strum my father to sleep after a fox-chase.

SIR PETER: I am glad you have so good a memory. Yes, madam, these were the recreations I took you from; but now you must have your own coach—*vis-à-vis*—and three powdered footmen before your chair and, in summer, a pair of white cats° to draw you to Kensington Gardens.—No recollection, I suppose, when you were content to ride double, behind the butler, on a docked coach-horse?

LADY TEAZLE: No—I swear I never did that—I deny the butler and the coach-horse.

SIR PETER: This, madam, was your situation—and what have I not done for you? I have made you a woman of fashion, of fortune, of rank—in short, I have made you my wife.

LADY TEAZLE: Well, then, and there is but one thing more you can make me to add to the obligation—and that is—

SIR PETER: My widow, I suppose?

LADY TEAZLE: Hem! hem!

SIR PETER: Thank you, madam—but don't flatter yourself; for though your ill-conduct may disturb my peace, it shall never break my heart, I promise you: however, I am equally obliged to you for the hint.

LADY TEAZLE: Then why will you endeavor to make yourself so disagreeable to me, and thwart me in every little elegant expense?

SIR PETER: 'Slife, madam, I say, had you any of these elegant expenses when you married me?

LADY TEAZLE: Lud, Sir Peter! would you have me be out of fashion?

SIR PETER: The fashion, indeed! what had you to do with the fashion before you married me?

LADY TEAZLE: For my part, I should think you would like to have your wife thought a woman of taste.

SIR PETER: Aye—there again—taste! Zounds! madam, you had no taste when you married *me*!

LADY TEAZLE: That's very true, indeed, Sir Peter! and, *after* having married you, I am sure I should never pretend to taste again! But now, Sir Peter, if we have finished our daily jangle, I presume I may go to my engagement at Lady Sneerwell's?

SIR PETER: Aye—there's another precious circumstance!—a charming set of acquaintance you have made there!

LADY TEAZLE: Nay, Sir Peter, they are people of rank and fortune, and remarkably tenacious of reputation.

SIR PETER: Yes, egad, they are tenacious of reputation with a vengeance; for they don't choose anybody should have a character but themselves! Such a crew! Ah! many a wretch has rid on a hurdle° who has done less mischief than those utterers of forged tales, coiners of scandal,—and clippers of reputation.

LADY TEAZLE: What! would you restrain the freedom of speech?

SIR PETER: Oh! they have made you just as bad as any one of the society.

LADY TEAZLE: Why, I believe I do bear a part with a tolerable grace. But I vow I have no malice against the people I abuse; when I say an ill-natured thing, 'tis out of pure good humor—and I take it for granted they deal exactly in the same manner with me. But, Sir Peter, you know you promised to come to Lady Sneerwell's too.

SIR PETER: Well, well, I'll call in just to look after my own character.

LADY TEAZLE: Then, indeed, you must make haste after me or you'll be too late.—So good-bye to ye. (*Exit* LADY TEAZLE.)

SIR PETER: So—I have gained much by my intended expostulations! Yet with what a charming air she contradicts everything I say, and how pleasingly she shows her contempt of my authority! Well, though I can't make her love me, there is a great satisfaction in quarreling with her; and I think she never appears to such advantage as when she's doing everything in her power to plague me. (*Exit.*)

ACT 2 / SCENE 2

(LADY SNEERWELL'S)

(LADY SNEERWELL, MRS. CANDOUR, CRABTREE, SIR BENJAMIN BACKBITE, *and* JOSEPH SURFACE.)

LADY SNEERWELL: Nay, positively, we will hear it.

JOSEPH SURFACE: Yes, yes, the epigram, by all means.

Pope Joan, an old-fashioned game of cards.   **cats,** ponies.

hurdle, rough cart on which criminals were taken to the place of execution.

SIR BENJAMIN: Plague on't, uncle! 'tis mere nonsense.

CRABTREE: No, no; 'fore gad, very clever for an extempore!

SIR BENJAMIN: But, ladies, you should be acquainted with the circumstance,—you must know that one day last week, as Lady Betty Curricle was taking the dust in Hyde Park, in a sort of duodecimo° phaëton, she desired me to write some verses on her ponies; upon which, I took out my pocket-book, and in one moment produced the following:

'Sure never were seen two such beautiful ponies!
Other horses are clowns, and these macaronies!
Nay, to give 'em this title I'm sure isn't wrong—
Their legs are so slim and their tails are so long.'

CRABTREE: There, ladies—done in the smack of a whip, and on horseback too!

JOSEPH SURFACE: A very Phœbus, mounted—indeed, Sir Benjamin.

SIR BENJAMIN: O dear sir—trifles—trifles.

(Enter LADY TEAZLE and MARIA.)

MRS. CANDOUR: I must have a copy.

LADY SNEERWELL: Lady Teazle, I hope we shall see Sir Peter.

LADY TEAZLE: I believe he'll wait on your ladyship presently.

LADY SNEERWELL: Maria, my love, you look grave. Come, you shall sit down to cards with Mr. Surface.

MARIA: I take very little pleasure in cards—however, I'll do as your ladyship pleases.

LADY TEAZLE (aside): I am surprised Mr. Surface should sit down with her.—I thought he would have embraced this opportunity of speaking to me before Sir Peter came.

MRS. CANDOUR: Now, I'll die but you are so scandalous, I'll forswear your society.

LADY TEAZLE: What's the matter, Mrs. Candour?

MRS. CANDOUR: They'll not allow our friend Miss Vermilion to be handsome.

LADY SNEERWELL: Oh, surely, she's a pretty woman.

CRABTREE: I am very glad you think so, ma'am.

MRS. CANDOUR: She has a charming fresh color.

LADY TEAZLE: Yes, when it is fresh put on.

MRS. CANDOUR: O fie! I'll swear her color is natural—I have seen it come and go.

LADY TEAZLE: I dare swear you have, ma'am—it goes of a night, and comes again in the morning.

MRS. CANDOUR: Ha! ha! ha! how I hate to hear you talk so! But surely, now, her sister is, or was, very handsome.

CRABTREE: Who? Mrs. Evergreen?—O Lord! she's six-and-fifty if she's an hour!

MRS. CANDOUR: Now positively you wrong her; fifty-two or fifty-three is the utmost—and I don't think she looks more.

SIR BENJAMIN: Ah! there is no judging by her looks, unless one could see her face.

LADY SNEERWELL: Well, well, if Mrs. Evergreen does take some pains to repair the ravages of time, you must allow she effects it with great ingenuity; and surely that's better than the careless manner in which the widow Ochre caulks her wrinkles.

SIR BENJAMIN: Nay, now, Lady Sneerwell, you are severe upon the widow. Come, come, it is not that she paints so ill—but, when she has finished her face, she joins it on so badly to her neck, that she looks like a mended statue, in which the connoisseur may see at once that the head's modern, though the trunk's antique!

CRABTREE: Ha! ha! ha! well said, nephew!

MRS. CANDOUR: Ha! ha! ha! Well, you make me laugh, but I vow I hate you for't.— What do you think of Miss Simper?

SIR BENJAMIN: Why, she has very pretty teeth.

LADY TEAZLE: Yes; and on that account, when she is neither speaking nor laughing (which very seldom happens), she never absolutely shuts her mouth, but leaves it always on a jar, as it were.

MRS. CANDOUR: How can you be so ill-natured?

LADY TEAZLE: Nay, I allow even that's better than the pains Mrs. Prim takes to conceal her losses in front. She draws her mouth till it positively resembles the aperture of a poor's-box,° and all her words appear to slide out edgeways.

LADY SNEERWELL: Very well, Lady Teazle; I see you can be a little severe.

LADY TEAZLE: In defence of a friend it is but justice;—but here comes Sir Peter to spoil our pleasantry.

(Enter SIR PETER TEAZLE.)

SIR PETER: Ladies, your most obedient—Mercy on me, here is the whole set! a character dead at every word, I suppose. (aside)

MRS. CANDOUR: I am rejoiced you are come. Sir Peter. They have been so censorious. They will allow good qualities to nobody—not even good nature to our friend Mrs. Pursy.

LADY TEAZLE: What, the fat dowager who was at Mrs. Codille's last night?

MRS. CANDOUR: Nay, her bulk is her misfortune; and, when she takes such pains to get rid of it, you ought not to reflect on her.

---

duodecimo, diminutive.

poor's box, Referring to the narrow slit in the top of the church contribution-box for the poor of the parish.

LADY SNEERWELL: That's very true, indeed.

LADY TEAZLE: Yes, I know she almost lives on acids and small whey; laces herself by pulleys; and often, in the hottest noon of summer, you may see her on a little squat pony, with her hair platted up behind like a drummer's, and puffing round the Ring° on a full trot.

MRS. CANDOUR: I thank you, Lady Teazle, for defending her.

SIR PETER: Yes, a good defence, truly.

MRS. CANDOUR: But Sir Benjamin is as censorious as Miss Sallow.

CRABTREE: Yes, and she is a curious being to pretend to be censorious!—an awkward gawky, without any one good point under heaven.

MRS CANDOUR: Positively you shall not be so very severe. Miss Sallow is a relation of mine by marriage, and, as for her person, great allowance is to be made; for, let me tell you, a woman labors under many disadvantages who tries to pass for a girl at six-and-thirty.

LADY SNEERWELL: Though, surely, she is handsome still—and for the weakness in her eyes, considering how much she reads by candle-light, it is not to be wondered at.

MRS. CANDOUR: True; and then as to her manner, upon my word I think it is particularly graceful, considering she never had the least education; for you know her mother was a Welch milliner, and her father a sugar-baker at Bristol.

SIR BENJAMIN: Ah! you are both of you too good-natured!

SIR PETER: Yes, damned good-natured! This their own relation! mercy on me! (aside)

SIR BENJAMIN: And Mrs. Candour is of so moral a turn she can sit for an hour to hear Lady Stucco talk sentiment.

LADY TEAZLE: Nay, I vow Lady Stucco is very well with the dessert after dinner; for she's just like the French fruit one cracks for mottoes—made up of paint and proverb.

MRS. CANDOUR: Well, I never will join in ridiculing a friend; and so I constantly tell my cousin Ogle, and you all know what pretensions she has to be critical in beauty.

CRABTREE: Oh, to be sure! she has herself the oddest countenance that ever was seen; 'tis a collection of features from all the different countries of the globe.

SIR BENJAMIN: So she has, indeed—an Irish front!

CRABTREE: Caledonian locks!

SIR BENJAMIN: Dutch nose!

CRABTREE: Austrian lip!

SIR BENJAMIN: Complexion of a Spaniard!

CRABTREE: And teeth à la Chinoise!

SIR BENJAMIN: In short, her face resembles a table d'hôte at Spa—where no two guests are of a nation—

CRABTREE: Or a congress at the close of a general war—wherein all the members, even to her eyes, appear to have a different interest, and her nose and chin are the only parties likely to join issue.

MRS. CANDOUR: Ha! ha! ha!

SIR PETER: Mercy on my life!—a person they dine with twice a week! (aside)

LADY SNEERWELL: Go—go—you are a couple of provoking toads.

MRS. CANDOUR: Nay, but I vow you shall not carry the laugh off so—for give me leave to say, that Mrs. Ogle—

SIR PETER: Madam, madam, I beg your pardon—there's no stopping these good gentlemen's tongues. But when I tell you, Mrs. Candour, that the lady they are abusing is a particular friend of mine—I hope you'll not take her part.

LADY SNEERWELL: Well said, Sir Peter! but you are a cruel creature—too phlegmatic yourself for a jest, and too peevish to allow wit on others.

SIR PETER: Ah, madam, true wit is more nearly allied to good nature than your ladyship is aware of.

LADY TEAZLE: True, Sir Peter; I believe they are so near akin that they can never be united.

SIR BENJAMIN: Or rather, madam, suppose them man and wife, because one so seldom sees them together.

LADY TEAZLE: But Sir Peter is such an enemy to scandal, I believe he would have it put down by parliament.

SIR PETER: 'Fore heaven, madam, if they were to consider the sporting with reputation of as much importance as poaching on manors, and pass An Act for the Preservation of Fame, I believe many would thank them for the bill.

LADY SNEERWELL: O lud! Sir Peter; would you deprive us of our privileges?

SIR PETER: Aye, madam; and then no person should be permitted to kill characters or run down reputations, but qualified old maids and disappointed widows.

LADY SNEERWELL: Go, you monster!

MRS. CANDOUR: But sure you would not be quite so severe on those who report what they hear.

SIR PETER: Yes, madam, I would have law merchant° for them too; and in all cases of slander currency, whenever the drawer of the lie was not to be found, the injured parties should have a right to come on any of the indorsers.

Ring, the fashionable drive originally laid out in Hyde Park by Charles II.

law merchant, mercantile law.

CRABTREE: Well, for my part, I believe there never was a scandalous tale without some foundation.

LADY SNEERWELL: Come, ladies, shall we sit down to cards in the next room?

(Enter SERVANT *and whispers* SIR PETER.*)*

SIR PETER: I'll be with them directly.— *(Exit* SERVANT.*)* I'll get away unperceived. *(aside)*

LADY SNEERWELL: Sir Peter, you are not leaving us?

SIR PETER: Your ladyship must excuse me; I'm called away by particular business—but I leave my character behind me. *(Exit* SIR PETER.*)*

SIR BENJAMIN: Well certainly, Lady Teazle, that lord of yours is a strange being; I could tell you some stories of him would make you laugh heartily, if he wasn't your husband.

LADY TEAZLE: O pray don't mind that—come, do let's hear them.

(They join the rest of the company, all talking as they are going into the next room.)

JOSEPH SURFACE *(rising with* MARIA*)*: Maria, I see you have no satisfaction in this society.

MARIA: How is it possible I should? If to raise malicious smiles at the infirmities and misfortunes of those who have never injured us be the province of wit or humor, heaven grant me a double portion of dulness!

JOSEPH SURFACE: Yet they appear more ill-natured than they are; they have no malice at heart.

MARIA: Then is their conduct still more contemptible; for, in my opinion, nothing could excuse the intemperance of their tongues but a natural and ungovernable bitterness of mind.

JOSEPH SURFACE: But can you, Maria, feel thus for others, and be unkind to me alone? Is hope to be denied the tenderest passion?

MARIA: Why will you distress me by renewing this subject?

JOSEPH SURFACE: Ah, Maria! you would not treat me thus, and oppose your guardian, Sir Peter's will, but that I see that profligate Charles is still a favored rival.

MARIA: Ungenerously urged! But, whatever my sentiments of that unfortunate young man are, be assured I shall not feel more bound to give him up, because his distresses have lost him the regard even of a brother.

(LADY TEAZLE returns.)

JOSEPH SURFACE: Nay, but, Maria, do not leave me with a frown—by all that's honest, I swear—Gad's life, here's Lady Teazle. *(aside)* You must not—no, you shall not—for, though I have the greatest regard for Lady Teazle—

MARIA: Lady Teazle!

JOSEPH SURFACE: Yet were Sir Peter to suspect—

LADY TEAZLE *(coming forward)*: What's this, pray? Do you take her for me?—Child, you are wanted in the next room.— *(Exit* MARIA.*)* What is all this, pray?

JOSEPH SURFACE: Oh, the most unlucky circumstance in nature! Maria has somehow suspected the tender concern I have for your happiness, and threatened to acquaint Sir Peter with her suspicions, and I was just endeavoring to reason with her when you came.

LADY TEAZLE: Indeed! but you seemed to adopt a very tender mode of reasoning—do you *usually* argue on your knees?

JOSEPH SURFACE: Oh, she's a child—and I thought a little bombast—but, Lady Teazle, when are you to give me your judgment on my library, as you promised?

LADY TEAZLE: No, no—I begin to think it would be imprudent, and you know I admit you as a lover no further than *fashion* requires.

JOSEPH SURFACE: True—a mere Platonic cicisbeo,° what every London wife is *entitled* to.

LADY TEAZLE: Certainly, one must not be out of the fashion; however, I have so many of my country prejudices left, that, though Sir Peter's ill humor may vex me ever so, it never shall provoke me to—

JOSEPH SURFACE: The only revenge in your power. Well, I applaud your moderation.

LADY TEAZLE: Go—you are an insinuating wretch! But we shall be missed—let us join the company.

JOSEPH SURFACE: But we had best not return together.

LADY TEAZLE: Well, don't stay—for Maria shan't come to her any more of your *reasoning,* I promise you. *(Exit* LADY TEAZLE.*)*

JOSEPH SURFACE: A curious dilemma, truly, my politics have run me into! I wanted, at first, only to ingratiate myself with Lady Teazle, that she might not be my enemy with Maria; and I have, I don't know how, become her serious lover. Sincerely I begin to wish I had never made such a point of gaining so *very good* a character, for it has led me into so many cursed rogueries that I doubt I shall be exposed at last. *(Exit.)*

ACT 2 / SCENE 3

(SIR PETER'S *)*
(Enter SIR OLIVER SURFACE *and* ROWLEY.*)*

SIR OLIVER: Ha! ha! ha! and so my old friend is married, hey?—a young wife out of the country.—Ha! ha! ha!—that he should have

---

cicisbeo, gallant to a married woman.

stood bluff° to old bachelor so long, and sink into a husband at last!

ROWLEY: But you must not rally him on the subject, Sir Oliver; 'tis a tender point, I assure you, though he has been married only seven months.

SIR OLIVER: Then he has been just half a year on the stool of repentance!—Poor Peter! But you say he has entirely given up Charles—never sees him, hey?

ROWLEY: His prejudice against him is astonishing, and I am sure greatly increased by a jealousy of him with Lady Teazle, which he has been industriously led into by a scandalous society in the neighborhood, who have contributed not a little to Charles's ill name; whereas the truth is, I believe, if the lady is partial to either of them, his brother is the favorite.

SIR OLIVER: Aye,—I know there are a set of malicious, prating, prudent gossips, both male and female, who murder characters to kill time, and will rob a young fellow of his good name before he has years to know the value of it,—but I am not to be prejudiced against my nephew by such, I promise you! No, no;—if Charles has done nothing false or mean, I shall compound for his extravagance.—

ROWLEY: Then, my life on't, you will reclaim him.—Ah, sir, it gives me new life to find that your heart is not turned against him, and that the son of my good old master has one friend, however, left.

SIR OLIVER: What! shall I forget, Master Rowley, when I was at his years myself? Egad, my brother and I were neither of us very prudent youths—and yet, I believe, you have not seen many better men than your old master was?

ROWLEY: Sir, 'tis this reflection gives me assurance that Charles may yet be a credit to his family.—But here comes Sir Peter.

SIR OLIVER: Egad so he does!—Mercy on me, he's greatly altered, and seems to have a settled married look! One may read husband in his face at this distance!

(Enter SIR PETER TEAZLE.)

SIR PETER: Hah! Sir Oliver—my old friend! Welcome to England a thousand times!

SIR OLIVER: Thank you, thank you, Sir Peter! and i'faith I am glad to find you well, believe me!

SIR PETER: Ah! 'tis a long time since we met—sixteen years, I doubt, Sir Oliver, and many a cross accident in the time.

SIR OLIVER: Aye, I have had my share—but, what! I find you are married, hey, my old boy?—Well, well, it can't be helped—and so I wish you joy with all my heart!

_____

stood bluff, steadfast.

SIR PETER: Thank you, thank you, Sir Oliver.—Yes, I have entered into the happy state—but we'll not talk of that now.

SIR OLIVER: True, true, Sir Peter; old friends should not begin on grievances at first meeting. No, no, no.

ROWLEY (to SIR OLIVER): Take care, pray, sir.

SIR OLIVER: Well, so one of my nephews is a wild rogue, hey?

SIR PETER: Wild! Ah! my old friend, I grieve for your disappointment there—he's a lost young man, indeed; however, his brother will make you amends; Joseph is, indeed, what a youth should be—everybody in the world speaks well of him.

SIR OLIVER: I am sorry to hear it—he has too good a character to be an honest fellow.—Everybody speaks well of him! Psha! then he has bowed as low to knaves and fools as to the honest dignity of genius or virtue.

SIR PETER: What, Sir Oliver! do you blame him for not making enemies?

SIR OLIVER: Yes, if he has merit enough to deserve them.

SIR PETER: Well, well—you'll be convinced when you know him. 'Tis edification to hear him converse—he professes the noblest sentiments.

SIR OLIVER: Ah, plague of his sentiments! If he salutes me with a scrap of morality in his mouth, I shall be sick directly. But, however, don't mistake me, Sir Peter; I don't mean to defend Charles's errors—but, before I form my judgment of either of them, I intend to make a trial of their hearts—and my friend Rowley and I have planned something for the purpose.

ROWLEY: And Sir Peter shall own for once he has been mistaken.

SIR PETER: Oh, my life on Joseph's honor!

SIR OLIVER: Well, come, give us a bottle of good wine, and we'll drink the lad's health, and tell you our scheme.

SIR PETER: Allons, then!

SIR OLIVER: And don't, Sir Peter, be so severe against your old friend's son. Odds my life! I am not sorry that he has run out of the course a little; for my part, I hate to see prudence clining to the green succors of my youth; 'tis like ivy round a sapling, and spoils the growth of the tree. (Exeunt.)

ACT 3 / SCENE 1

(SIR PETER'S)

(SIR PETER TEAZLES, SIR OLIVER SURFACE, and ROWLEY.)

SIR PETER: Well, then—we will see this fellow first, and have our wine afterwards. But how is this,

Master Rowley? I don't see the jet° of your scheme.

ROWLEY: Why, sir, this Mr. Stanley, whom I was speaking of, is nearly related to them, by their mother; he was once a merchant in Dublin, but has been ruined by a series of undeserved misfortunes. He has applied, by letter, since his confinement, both to Mr. Surface and Charles—from the former he has received nothing but evasive promises of future service, while Charles has done all that his extravagance has left him power to do; and he is, at this time, endeavoring to raise a sum of money, part of which, in the midst of his own distresses, I know he intends for the service of poor Stanley.

SIR OLIVER: Ah! he is my brother's son.

SIR PETER: Well, but how is Sir Oliver personally to—

ROWLEY: Why, sir, I will inform Charles and his brother that Stanley has obtained permission to apply in person to his friends, and, as they have neither of them ever seen him, let Sir Oliver assume his character, and he will have a fair opportunity of judging at least of the benevolence of their dispositions; and believe me, sir, you will find in the youngest brother one who, in the midst of folly and dissipation, has still, as our immortal bard expresses it,—

> 'a tear for pity, and a hand
> Open as day, for melting charity.'°

SIR PETER: Psha! What signifies his having an open hand or purse either, when he has nothing left to give? Well, well, make the trial, if you please; but where is the fellow whom you brought for Sir Oliver to examine, relative to Charles's affairs?

ROWLEY: Below, waiting his commands, and no one can give him better intelligence.—This, Sir Oliver, is a friendly Jew, who, to do him justice, had done everything in his power to bring your nephew to a proper sense of his extravagance.

SIR PETER: Pray let us have him in.

ROWLEY: Desire Mr. Moses to walk upstairs.

SIR PETER: But why should you suppose he will speak the truth?

ROWLEY: Oh, I have convinced him that he has no chance of recovering certain sums advanced to Charles but through the bounty of Sir Oliver, who he knows is arrived; so that you may depend on his fidelity to his own interest. I have also another evidence in my power, one Snake, whom I have detected in a matter little short of forgery, and shall shortly produce to remove some of *your* prejudices, Sir Peter, relative to Charles and Lady Teazle.

SIR PETER: I have heard too much on that subject.

ROWLEY: Here comes the honest Israelite.

(Enter MOSES.)

—This is Sir Oliver.

SIR OLIVER: Sir, I understand you have lately had great dealings with my nephew Charles.

MOSES: Yes, Sir Oliver—I have done all I could for him, but he was ruined before he came to me for assistance.

SIR OLIVER: That was unlucky, truly—for you have had no opportunity of showing your talents.

MOSES: None at all—I hadn't the pleasure of knowing his distresses—till he was some thousands worse than nothing.

SIR OLIVER: Unfortunate, indeed! But I suppose you have done all in your power for him, honest Moses?

MOSES: Yes, he knows that. This very evening I was to have brought him a gentleman from the city, who doesn't know him, and will, I believe, advance him some money.

SIR PETER: What, one Charles has never had money from before?

MOSES: Yes; Mr. Premium, of Crutched Friars°—formerly a broker.

SIR PETER: Egad, Sir Oliver, a thought strikes me!—Charles, you say, doesn't know Mr. Premium?

MOSES: Not at all.

SIR PETER: Now then, Sir Oliver, you may have a better opportunity of satisfying yourself than by an old romancing tale of a poor relation;—go with my friend Moses, and represent Mr. Premium, and then I'll answer for't, you will see your nephew in all his glory.

SIR OLIVER: Egad, I like this idea better than the other and I may visit Joseph afterwards, as old Stanley.

SIR PETER: True—so you may.

ROWLEY: Well, this is taking Charles rather at a disadvantage, to be sure. However, Moses—you understand Sir Peter, and will be faithful?

MOSES: You may depend upon me,—this is near the time I was to have gone.

SIR OLIVER: I'll accompany you as soon as you please, Moses; but hold! I have forgot one thing—how the plague shall I be able to pass for a Jew?

MOSES: There's no need—the principal is Christian.

SIR OLIVER: Is he?—I'm sorry to hear it—but, then again, an't I rather too smartly dressed to look like a money-lender?

---

jet, point, gist.   **a tear . . . charity,** from *Henry IV, Part II*, IV. iv. 31–32.

Crutched Friars, a street, not far from the Tower of London, named from an old Convent of Crossed or Crouched Friars.

SIR PETER: Not at all; 'twould not be out of character, if you went in your own carriage—would it, Moses?

MOSES: Not in the least.

SIR OLIVER: Well, but how must I talk? there's certainly some cant of usury, and mode of treating, that I ought to know.

SIR PETER: Oh, there's not much to learn—the great point, as I take it, is to be exorbitant enough in your demands—hey, Moses?

MOSES: Yes, that's a very great point.

SIR OLIVER: I'll answer for't I'll not be wanting in that. I'll ask him eight or ten per cent on the loan, at least.

MOSES: If you ask him no more than that, you'll be discovered immediately.

SIR OLIVER: Hey! What the plague! how much then?

MOSES: That depends upon the circumstances. If he appears not very anxious for the supply, you should require only forty or fifty per cent; but if you find him in great distress, and want the moneys very bad—you may ask double.

SIR PETER: A good honest trade you're learning, Sir Oliver!

SIR OLIVER: Truly I think so—and not unprofitable.

MOSES: Then, you know, you haven't the moneys yourself, but are forced to borrow them for him of a friend.

SIR OLIVER: Oh! I borrow it of a friend, do I?

MOSES: Yes, and your friend is an unconscionable dog, but you can't help it.

SIR OLIVER: My friend is an unconscionable dog, is he?

MOSES: Yes, and he himself has not the moneys by him—but is forced to sell stock at a great loss.

SIR OLIVER: He is forced to sell stock, is he, at a great loss, is he? Well, that's very kind of him.

SIR PETER: I'faith, Sir Oliver—Mr. Premium, I mean—you'll soon be master of the trade. But, Moses! wouldn't you have him run out a little against the Annuity Bill?° That would be in character, I should think.

MOSES: Very much.

ROWLEY: And lament that a young man now must be at years of discretion before he is suffered to ruin himself?

MOSES: Aye, great pity!

SIR PETER: And abuse the public for allowing merit to an act whose only object is to snatch misfortune and imprudence from the rapacious relief of usury, and give the minor a chance of inheriting

---

Annuity Bill, the Annuity Bill, presented in the House of Commons April 29, 1777, and passed in May (after the first performance of *The S. for S.*) was aimed to safeguard minors against grantors of life annuities.

his estate without being undone by coming into possession.

SIR OLIVER: So, so—Moses shall give me further instructions as we go together.

SIR PETER: You will not have much time, for your nephew lives hard by.

SIR OLIVER: Oh, never fear! my tutor appears so able, that though Charles lived in the next street, it must be my own fault if I am not a complete rogue before I turn the corner. (*Exeunt* SIR OLIVER *and* MOSES.)

SIR PETER: So now I think Sir Oliver will be convinced;—you are partial, Rowley, and would have prepared Charles for the other plot.

ROWLEY: No, upon my word, Sir Peter.

SIR PETER: Well, go bring me this Snake, and I'll hear what he has to say presently.—I see Maria, and want to speak with her.—(*Exit* ROWLEY.) I should be glad to be convinced my suspicions of Lady Teazle and Charles were unjust. I have never yet opened my mind on this subject to my friend Joseph—I'm determined I will do it—*he* will give me his opinion sincerely.

(*Enter* MARIA.)

So, child, has Mr. Surface returned with you?

MARIA: No, sir—he was engaged.

SIR PETER: Well, Maria, do you not reflect, the more you converse with that amiable young man, what return his partiality for you deserves?

MARIA: Indeed, Sir Peter, your frequent importunity on this subject distresses me extremely—you compel me to declare, that I know no man who has ever paid me a particular attention whom I would not prefer to Mr. Surface.

SIR PETER: So,—here's perverseness! No, no, Maria, 'tis Charles only whom you would prefer—'tis evident his vices and follies have won your heart.

MARIA: This is unkind, sir—you know I have obeyed you in neither seeing nor corresponding with him; I have heard enough to convince me that he is unworthy my regard. Yet I cannot think it culpable, if, while my understanding severely condemns his vices, my heart suggests some pity for his distresses.

SIR PETER: Well, well, pity him as much as you please, but give your heart and hand to a worthier object.

MARIA: Never to his brother!

SIR PETER: Go, perverse and obstinate! But take care, madam; you have never yet known what the authority of a guardian is—don't compel me to inform you of it.

MARIA: I can only say, you shall not have *just* reason. 'Tis true, by my father's will, I am for a short period bound to regard you as his substitute, but must cease to think you so, when you would compel me to be miserable. (*Exit* MARIA.)

SIR PETER: Was ever man so crossed as I am! everything conspiring to fret me!—I had not been involved in matrimony a fortnight, before her father, a hale and hearty man, died—on purpose, I believe, for the pleasure of plaguing me with the care of his daughter. But here comes my helpmate! She appears in great good humor. How happy I should be if I could tease her into loving me, though but a little!

(*Enter* LADY TEAZLE.)

LADY TEAZLE: Lud! Sir Peter, I hope you haven't been quarreling with Maria—it isn't using me well to be ill humored when I am not by.

SIR PETER: Ah, Lady Teazle, you might have the power to make me good humored at all times.

LADY TEAZLE: I am sure I wish I had—for I want you to be in charming sweet temper at this moment. Do be good humored now, and let me have two hundred pounds, will you?

SIR PETER: Two hundred pounds! what, an't I to be in a good humor without paying for it! But speak to me thus, and i'faith there's nothing I could refuse you. You shall have it; but seal me a bond for the repayment.

LADY TEAZLE: O no—there—my note of hand will do as well.

SIR PETER (*kissing her hand*): And you shall no longer reproach me with not giving you an independent settlement,—I mean shortly to surprise you; but shall we always live thus, hey?

LADY TEAZLE: If you please. I'm sure I don't care how soon we leave off quarreling, provided you'll own *you* were tired first.

SIR PETER: Well—then let our future contest be, who shall be most obliging.

LADY TEAZLE: I assure you, Sir Peter, good nature becomes you. You look now as you did before we were married!—when you used to walk with me under the elms, and tell me stories of what a gallant you were in your youth, and chuck me under the chin, you would, and ask me if I thought I could love an old fellow, who would deny me nothing—didn't you?

SIR PETER: Yes, yes, and you were as kind and attentive.

LADY TEAZLE: Aye, so I was, and would always take your part, when my acquaintance used to abuse you, and turn you into ridicule.

SIR PETER: Indeed!

LADY TEAZLE: Aye, and when my cousin Sophy has called you a stiff, peevish old bachelor, and laughed at me for thinking of marrying one who might be my father, I have always defended you—and said I didn't think you so ugly by any

means, and that I dared say you'd make a very good sort of a husband.

SIR PETER: And you prophesied right—and we shall certainly now be the happiest couple—

LADY TEAZLE: And never differ again!

SIR PETER: No, never!—though at the same time, indeed, my dear Lady Teazle, you must watch your temper very narrowly; for all in all our little quarrels, my dear, if you recollect, my love, you always began first.

LADY TEAZLE: I beg your pardon, my dear Sir Peter: indeed, you always gave the provocation.

SIR PETER: Now, see, my angel! take care—*contradicting* isn't the way to keep friends.

LADY TEAZLE: Then don't *you* begin it, my love!

SIR PETER: There, now! you—you are going on—you don't perceive, my life, that you are just doing the very thing which you know always makes me angry.

LADY TEAZLE: Nay, you know if you will be angry without any reason—

SIR PETER: There now! you want to quarrel again.

LADY TEAZLE: No, I am sure I don't—but, if you will be so peevish—

SIR PETER: There now! who begins first?

LADY TEAZLE: Why, you, to be sure. I said nothing—but there's no bearing your temper.

SIR PETER: No, no, madam, the fault's in your own temper.

LADY TEAZLE: Aye, you are just what my cousin Sophy said you would be.

SIR PETER: Your cousin Sophy is a forward, impertinent gipsy.

LADY TEAZLE: You are a great bear, I'm sure, to abuse my relations.

SIR PETER: Now may all the plagues of marriage be doubled on me, if ever I try to be friends with you any more!

LADY TEAZLE: So much the better.

SIR PETER: No, no, madam; 'tis evident you never cared a pin for me, and I was a madman to marry you—a pert, rural coquette, that had refused half the honest squires in the neighborhood!

LADY TEAZLE: And I am sure I was a fool to marry you—an old dangling bachelor, who was single at fifty, only because he never could meet with any one who would have him.

SIR PETER: Aye, aye, madam; but you were pleased enough to listen to me—*you* never had such an offer before.

LADY TEAZLE: No! didn't I refuse Sir Twivy Tarrier, who everybody said would have been a better match—for his estate is just as good as yours—and he has broke his neck since we have been married.

SIR PETER: I have done with you, madam! You are an unfeeling, ungrateful—but there's an end of everything. I believe you capable of anything that's bad. Yes, madam, I now believe the reports relative to you and Charles, madam—yes, madam, you and Charles—are not without grounds—

LADY TEAZLE: Take care, Sir Peter! you had better not insinuate any such thing! I'll not be suspected with*out cause,* I promise you.

SIR PETER: Very well, madam! very well! a separate maintenance as soon as you please. Yes, madam, or a divorce! I'll make an example of myself for the benefit of all old bachelors. Let us separate, madam.

LADY TEAZLE: Agreed! agreed! And now, my dear Sir Peter, we are of a mind once more, we may be the *happiest couple,* and *never differ again,* you know: ha! ha! Well, you are going to be in a passion, I see, and I shall only interrupt you.—so bye! bye! (*Exit.*)

SIR PETER: Plagues and tortures! can't I make her angry neither? Oh, I am the miserablest fellow! But I'll not bear her presuming to keep her temper—no! she may break my heart, but she shan't keep her temper. (*Exit.*)

ACT 3 / SCENE 2

(CHARLES'S *house*)
(*Enter* TRIP, MOSES, *and* SIR OLIVER SURFACE.)

TRIP: Here, Master Moses! if you'll stay a moment, I'll try whether—what's the gentleman's name?

SIR OLIVER: Mr. Moses, what *is* my name? (*aside*)

MOSES: Mr. Premium.

TRIP: Premium—very well. (*Exit* TRIP, *taking snuff.*)

SIR OLIVER: To judge by the servants, one wouldn't believe the master was ruined. But what!—sure, this was my brother's house?

MOSES: Yes, sir; Mr. Charles bought it of Mr. Joseph, with the furniture, pictures, &c., just as the old gentleman left it—Sir Peter thought it a great piece of extravagance in him.

SIR OLIVER: In my mind, the other's economy in *selling* it to him was more reprehensible by half.

(*Re-enter* TRIP.)

TRIP: My master says you must wait, gentlemen; he has company, and he can't speak with you yet.

SIR OLIVER: If he knew *who* it was wanted to see him, perhaps he wouldn't have sent such a message.

TRIP: Yes, yes, sir; he knows *you* are here—I didn't forget little Premium—no, no, no.

SIR OLIVER: Very well—and I pray, sir, what may be your name?

TRIP: Trip, sir—my name is Trip, at your service.

SIR OLIVER: Well, then, Mr. Trip, you have a pleasant sort of a place here, I guess.

TRIP: Why, yes—here are three or four of us pass our time agreeably enough; but then our wages are sometimes a little in arrear—and not very great either—but fifty pounds a year, and find our own bags and bouquets.°

SIR OLIVER (*aside*): Bags and bouquets! halters and bastinadoes!

TRIP: But *à propos,* Moses, have you been able to get me that little bill discounted?

SIR OLIVER (*aside*): Wants to raise money, too!—mercy on me. Has his distresses, I warrant, like a lord,—and affects creditors and duns.

MOSES: 'Twas not to be done, indeed, Mr. Trip. (*Gives the note.*)

TRIP: Good lack, you surprise me! My friend Brush has indorsed it, and I thought when he put his mark on the back of a bill 'twas as good as cash.

MOSES: No, 'twouldn't do.

TRIP: A small sum—but twenty pounds. Hark'ee, Moses, do you think you couldn't get it me by way of annuity?

SIR OLIVER (*aside*): An annuity! ha! ha! ha! a footman raise money by way of annuity! Well done, luxury, egad!

MOSES: But you must insure your place.

TRIP: Oh, with all my heart! I'll insure my place, and my life too, if you please.

SIR OLIVER (*aside*): It's more than I would your neck.

TRIP: But then, Moses, it must be done before this d—d register° takes place—one wouldn't like to have one's name made public, you know.

MOSES: No, certainly. But is there nothing you could deposit?

TRIP: Why, nothing capital of my master's wardrobe has dropped lately; but I could give you a morgage on some of his winter clothes, with equity of redemption before November—or you shall have the reversion of the French velvet, or a post-obit° on the blue and silver;—these, I should think, Moses, with a few pair of point ruffles, as a collateral security—hey, my little fellow?

MOSES: Well, well. (*Bell rings.*)

TRIP: Gad, I heard the bell! I believe, gentlemen, I can now introduce you. Don't forget the annuity, little Moses! This way, gentlemen, insure my place, you know.

---

bags and bouquets, footman's trappings. The back-hair of the bag-wig was enclosed in an ornamental bag. **register,** another reference to the Annuity Bill of 1777, proposed on April 29, and passed in May. It provided "for registering the Grants of Life Annuities." **post-obit,** future claim.

SIR OLIVER (*aside*): If the man be a shadow of his master, this is the temple of dissipation indeed! (*Exeunt.*)

ACT 3 / SCENE 3

(CHARLES SURFACE, CARELESS, *and others at a table with wine, etc.*)

CHARLES SURFACE: 'Fore heaven, 'tis true!—there's the great degeneracy of the age. Many of our acquaintance have taste, spirit, and politeness; but plague on't, they won't drink.

CARELESS: It is so, indeed, Charles! they give in to all the substantial luxuries of the table, and abstain from nothing but wine and wit.

CHARLES SURFACE: Oh, certainly society suffers by it intolerably! for now, instead of the social spirit of raillery that used to mantle over a glass of bright Burgundy, their conversation is become just like the Spa-water they drink, which has all the pertness and flatulence of champagne, without its spirit or flavor.

1 GENTLEMAN: But what are *they* to do who love play better than wine?

CARELESS: True! there's Harry diets himself for gaming, and is now under a hazard regimen.°

CHARLES SURFACE: Then he'll have the worst of it. What! you wouldn't train a horse for the course by keeping him from corn! For my part, egad, I am now never so successful as when I am a little merry—let me throw on a bottle of champagne, and I never lose—at least I never feel my losses, which is exactly the same thing.

2 GENTLEMAN: Aye, that I believe.

CHARLES SURFACE: And, then, what man can pretend to be a believer in love, who is an abjurer of wine? 'Tis the test by which the lover knows his own heart. Fill a dozen bumpers to a dozen beauties, and she that floats at top is the maid that has bewitched you.

CARELESS: Now then, Charles, be honest, and give us your real favorite.

CHARLES SURFACE: Why, I have withheld her only in compassion to you. If I toast her, you must give a round of her peers—which is impossible—on earth.

CARELESS: Oh, then we'll find some canonised vestals or heathen goddesses that will do, I warrant!

CHARLES SURFACE: Here then, bumpers, you rogues! bumpers! Maria! Maria—(*Drink.*)

1 GENTLEMAN: Maria who?

CHARLES: O, damn the surname!—'tis too formal to be registered in Love's calendar—but now, Sir Toby Bumper, beware—we must have beauty superlative.

CARELESS: Nay, never study, Sir Toby: we'll stand to the toast, though your mistress should want an eye—and you know you have a song will excuse you.

SIR TOBY: Egad, so I have! and I'll give him the song instead of the lady. (*Sings.*)

SONG AND CHORUS

Here's to the maiden of bashful fifteen;
Here's to the widow of fifty;
Here's to the flaunting extravagannt quean,
And here's to the housewife that's thrifty.
Chorus. *Let the toast pass—*
        Drink to the lass—
I'll warrant she'll prove an excuse for the glass.
Here's to the charmer whose dimples we
        prize;
        Now to the maid who has none, sir;
Here's to the girl with a pair of blue eyes,
        And here's to the nymph with but one, sir.
Chorus. *Let the toast pass, &c.*

Here's to the maid with a bosom of snow:
        Now to her that's as brown as a berry:
Here's to the wife with a face full of woe,
        And now for the damsel that's merry.
Chorus. *Let the toast pass, &c.*

For let 'em be clumsy, or let 'em be slim,
        Young or ancient, I care not a feather:
So fill a pint bumper quite up to the brim,
        —And let us e'en toast 'em together.
Chorus. *Let the toast pass, &c.*

ALL: Bravo! Bravo!

(*Enter* TRIP, *and whispers* CHARLES SURFACE.)

CHARLES SURFACE: Gentlemen, you must excuse me a little.—Careless, take the chair, will you?

CARELESS: Nay, prithee, Charles, what now? This is one of your peerless beauties, I suppose, has dropped in by chance?

CHARLES SURFACE: No, faith! To tell you the truth, 'tis a Jew and a broker, who are come by appointment.

CARELESS: Oh, damn it! let's have the Jew in—

1 GENTLEMAN: Aye, and the broker too, by all means.

2 GENTLEMAN: Yes, yes, the Jew and the broker.

CHARLES SURFACE: Egad, with all my heart!—Trip, bid the gentlemen walk in.—(*Exit* TRIP.) Though there's one of them a stranger, I can tell you.

CARELESS: Charles, let us give them some generous Burgundy, and perhaps they'll grow conscientious.

CHARLES SURFACE: Oh, hang 'em, no! wine does but

---

hazard regimen, "keeps in strict training for gambling."

draw forth a man's *natural* qualities; and to make *them* drink would only be to whet their knavery.

(Enter TRIP, SIR OLIVER SURFACE, *and* MOSES.*)*

CHARLES SURFACE: So, honest Moses; walk in, pray, Mr. Premium—that's the gentleman's name, isn't it, Moses?

MOSES: Yes, sir.

CHARLES SURFACE: Set chairs, Trip.—Sit down, Mr. Premium.—Glasses, Trip.—Sit down, Moses.—Come, Mr. Premium, I'll give you a sentiment; here's 'Success to usury!'—Moses, fill the gentleman a bumper.

MOSES: Success to usury!

CARELESS: Right, Moses—usury is prudence and industry, and deserves to succeed.

SIR OLIVER: Then here's—All the success it deserves!

CARELESS: No, no, that won't do! Mr. Premium, you have demurred to the toast, and must drink it in a pint bumper.

1 GENTLEMAN: A pint bumper, at least.

MOSES: Oh, pray, sir, consider—Mr. Premium's a gentleman.

CARELESS: And therefore loves good wine.

2 GENTLEMAN: Give Moses a quart glass—this is mutiny, and a high contempt of the chair.

CARELESS: Here, now for't! I'll see justice done, to the last drop of my bottle.

SIR OLIVER: Nay, pray, gentlemen—I did not expect this usage.

CHARLES SURFACE: No, hang it, Careless, you shan't; Mr. Premium's a stranger.

SIR OLIVER *(aside)*: Odd! I wish I was well out of this company.

CARELESS: Plague on 'em then! if they won't drink, we'll not sit down with 'em. Come, Harry, the dice are in the next room.—Charles, you'll join us—when you have finished your business with these gentlemen?

CHARLES SURFACE: I will! I will!—*(Exeunt Gentlemen.)* Careless!

CARELESS *(returning)*: Well!

CHARLES SURFACE: Perhaps I may want *you.*

CARELESS: Oh, you know I am always ready—word, note, or bond, 'tis all the same to me. *(Exit.)*

MOSES: Sir, this is Mr. Premium, a gentleman of the strictest honor and secrecy; and always performs what he undertakes. Mr. Premium, this is—

CHARLES SURFACE: Pshaw! have done! Sir, my friend Moses is a very honest fellow, but a little slow at expression; he'll be an hour giving us our titles. Mr. Premium, the plain state of the matter is this—I am an extravagant young fellow who wants money to borrow; you I take to be a prudent old fellow, who has got money to lend. I am blockhead enough to give fifty per cent sooner than not have it; and you, I presume, are rogue enough to take a hundred if you could get it. Now, sir, you see we are acquainted at once, and may proceed to business without farther ceremony.

SIR OLIVER: Exceeding frank, upon my word. I see, sir, you are not a man of many compliments.

CHARLES SURFACE: Oh, no, sir! plain dealing in business I always think best.

SIR OLIVER: Sir, I like you the better for't. However, you are mistaken in one thing—I have no money to lend, but I believe I could procure some of a friend; but then he's an unconscionable dog—isn't he, Moses? And must sell stock to accommodate you—mustn't he, Moses?

MOSES: Yes, indeed! You know I always speak the truth, and scorn to tell a lie!

CHARLES SURFACE: Right! People that expect truth generally do. But these are trifles, Mr. Premium. What! I know money isn't to be bought without paying for't!

SIR OLIVER: Well, but what security could you give? You have no land, I suppose?

CHARLES SURFACE: Not a mole-hill, nor a twig, but what's in beau-pots° out at the window!

SIR OLIVER: Nor any stock, I presume?

CHARLES SURFACE: Nothing but live stock—and that's only a few pointers and ponies. But pray, Mr. Premium, are you acquainted at all with any of my connections?

SIR OLIVER: Why, to say truth, I am.

CHARLES SURFACE: Then you must know that I have a devilish rich uncle in the East Indies, Sir Oliver Surface, from whom I have the greatest expectations.

SIR OLIVER: That you have a wealthy uncle, I have heard—but how your expectations will turn out is more, I believe, than you can tell.

CHARLES SURFACE: Oh, no!—there can be no doubt—they tell me I'm a prodigious favorite—and that he talks of leaving me everything.

SIR OLIVER: Indeed! this is the first I've heard on't.

CHARLES SURFACE: Yes, yes, 'tis just so.—Moses knows 'tis true; don't you, Moses?

MOSES: Oh, yes! I'll swear to't.

SIR OLIVER *(aside)*: Egad, they'll persuade me presently I'm at Bengal.

CHARLES SURFACE: Now I propose, Mr. Premium, if it's agreeable to you, a post-obit on Sir Oliver's life; though at the same time the old fellow has been so liberal to me that I give you my word I should be very sorry to hear anything had happened to him.

SIR OLIVER: Not more than *I* should, I assure you. But the bond you mention happens to be just the

---

beau-pots, large ornamental flower-pots.

worst security you could offer me—for I might live to a hundred and never recover the principal.

CHARLES SURFACE: Oh, yes, you would!—the moment Sir Oliver dies, you know, you'd come on me for the money.

SIR OLIVER: Then I believe I should be the most unwelcome dun you ever had in your life.

CHARLES SURFACE: What! I suppose you are afraid now that Sir Oliver is too good a life?

SIR OLIVER: No, indeed I am not—though I have heard he is as hale and healthy as any man of his years in Christendom.

CHARLES SURFACE: There again you are misinformed. No, no, the climate has hurt him considerably, poor uncle Oliver. Yes, he breaks apace, I'm told—and so much altered lately that his nearest relations don't know him.

SIR OLIVER: No! Ha! ha! ha! so much altered lately that his relations don't know him! Ha! ha! ha! that's droll, egad—ha! ha! ha!

CHARLES SURFACE: Ha! ha!—you're glad to hear that, little Premium.

SIR OLIVER: No, no, I'm not.

CHARLES SURFACE: Yes, yes, you are—ha! ha! ha!—you know that mends your chance.

SIR OLIVER: But I'm told Sir Oliver is coming over—nay, some say he is actually arrived.

CHARLES SURFACE: Pshaw! sure I must know better than you whether he's come or not. No, no, rely on't, he is at this moment at Calcutta, isn't he, Moses?

MOSES: Oh yes, certainly.

SIR OLIVER: Very true, as you say, you must know better than I, though I have it from pretty good authority—haven't I, Moses?

MOSES: Yes, most undoubted!

SIR OLIVER: But, sir, as I understand you want a few hundreds immediately, is there nothing you would dispose of?

CHARLES SURFACE: How do you mean?

SIR OLIVER: For instance, now—I have heard—that your father left behind him a great quantity of massy old plate.

CHARLES SURFACE: O lud! that's gone long ago—Moses can tell you how better than I can.

SIR OLIVER: Good lack! all the family race-cups and corporation bowls! (aside) —Then it was also supposed that his library was one of the most valuable and complete.

CHARLES SURFACE: Yes, yes, so it was—vastly too much so for a private gentleman—for my part, I was always of a communicative disposition, so I thought it a shame to keep so much knowledge to myself.

SIR OLIVER (aside): Mercy on me! learning that had run in the family like an heirloom!—(Aloud) Pray, what are become of the books?

CHARLES SURFACE: You must inquire of the auctioneer, Master Premium, for I don't believe even Moses can direct you there.

MOSES: I never meddle with books.

SIR OLIVER: So, so, nothing of the family property left, I suppose?

CHARLES SURFACE: Not much, indeed; unless you have a mind to the family pictures. I have got a room full of ancestors above—and if you have a taste for old paintings, egad, you shall have 'em a bargain!

SIR OLIVER: Hey! and the devil! sure, you wouldn't sell your forefathers, would you?

CHARLES SURFACE: Every man of 'em, to the best bidder.

SIR OLIVER: What! your great-uncles and aunts?

CHARLES SURFACE: Aye, and my great-grandfathers and grandmothers too.

SIR OLIVER: Now I give him up!—(aside) What the plague, have you no vowels for your own kindred? Odd's life! do you take me for Shylock in the play, that you would raise money of me on your own flesh and blood?

CHARLES SURFACE: Nay, my little broker, don't be angry: what need *you* care, if you have your money's worth?

SIR OLIVER: Well, I'll be the purchaser—I think I can dispose of the family.—(aside) Oh, I'll never forgive him this! never!

(Enter CARELESS.)

CARELESS: Come, Charles, what keeps you?

CHARLES SURFACE: I can't come yet. I'faith! we are going to have a sale above—here's little Premium will buy all my ancestors!

CARELESS: Oh, burn your ancestors!

CHARLES SURFACE: No, he may do that afterwards, if he pleases. Stay, Careless, we want you; egad, you shall be auctioneer—so come along with us.

CARELESS: Oh, have with you, if that's the case.—I can handle a hammer as well as a dice box!

SIR OLIVER: Oh, the profligates!

CHARLES SURFACE: Come, Moses, you shall be appraiser, if we want one.—Gad's life, little Premium, you don't seem to like the business.

SIR OLIVER: Oh, yes, I do, vastly! Ha! ha! yes, yes, I think it a rare joke to sell one's family by auction—ha! ha!—(aside) Oh, the prodigal!

CHARLES SURFACE: To be sure! when a man wants money, where the plague should he get assistance, if he can't make free with his own relations? (Exeunt.)

ACT 4 / SCENE 1

(Picture-room at CHARLES'S.*)*

(Enter CHARLES SURFACE, SIR OLIVER SURFACE, MOSES, *and* CARELESS.*)*

CHARLES SURFACE: Walk in, gentlemen, pray walk in!—here they are, the family of the Surfaces, up to the Conquest.

SIR OLIVER: And, in my opinion, a goodly collection.

CHARLES SURFACE: Aye, aye, these are done in true spirit of portrait-painting—no volunteer grace or expression—not like the works of your modern Raphael, who gives you the strongest resemblance, yet contrives to make your own portrait independent of you; so that you may sink the original and not hurt the picture. No, no; the merit of these is the inveterate likeness—all stiff and awkward as the originals, and like nothing in human nature beside!

SIR OLIVER: Ah! we shall never see such figures of men again.

CHARLES SURFACE: I hope not. Well, you see, Master Premium, what a domestic character I am—here I sit of an evening surrounded by my family. But come, get to your pulpit, Mr. Auctioneer—here's an old gouty chair of my grandfather's will answer the purpose.

CARELESS: Aye, aye, this will do. But, Charles, I have ne'er a hammer; and what's an auctioneer without his hammer?

CHARLES SURFACE: Egad, that's true. What parchment have we here? *(Takes down a roll.)* 'Richard, heir to Thomas'—our genealogy in full. Here, Careless, you shall have no common bit of mahogany—here's the family tree for you, you rogue—this shall be your hammer, and now you may knock down my ancestors with their own pedigree.

SIR OLIVER *(aside)*: What an unnatural rogue!—an *ex post facto* parricide!

CARELESS: Yes, yes, here's a list of your generation indeed;—faith, Charles, this is the most convenient thing you could have found for the business, for 'twill serve not only as a hammer, but a catalogue into the bargain.—But come, begin—A-going, a-going, a-going!

CHARLES SURFACE: Bravo, Careless! Well, here's my great uncle, Sir Richard Raviline, a marvellous good general in his day, I assure you. He served in all the Duke of Marlborough's wars, and got that cut over his eye at the battle of Malplaquet.° What say you, Mr. Premium? look at him—there's a hero for you! not cut out of his feathers, as your modern clipped captains are, but enveloped in wig and regimentals, as a general should be. What do you bid?

MOSES: Mr. Premium would have you speak.

CHARLES SURFACE: Why, then, he shall have him for ten pounds, and I am sure that's not dear for a staff-officer.

SIR OLIVER: Heaven deliver me! his famous uncle Richard for ten pounds!—Very well, sir, I take him at that.

CHARLES SURFACE: Careless, knock down my uncle Richard for ten pounds!—Very well, sir, I take him at that.

CHARLES SURFACE: Careless, knock down my uncle Richard.—Here, now, is a maiden sister of his, my great-aunt Deborah, done by Kneller,° thought to be in his best manner, and a very formidable likeness. There she is, you see, a shepherdess feeding her flock. You shall have her for five pounds ten—the sheep are worth the money.

SIR OLIVER: Ah! poor Deborah! a woman who set such a value on herself!—Five pound ten—she's mine.

CHARLES SURFACE: Knock down my aunt Deborah! Here, now, are two that were a sort of cousins of theirs.—You see, Moses, these pictures were done some time ago, when beaux wore wigs, and the ladies wore their own hair.

SIR OLIVER: Yes, truly, head-dresses appear to have been a little lower in those days.

CHARLES SURFACE: Well, take that couple for the same.

MOSES: 'Tis a good bargain.

CHARLES SURFACE: Careless!—This, now, is a grandfather of my mother's, a learned judge, well known on the western circuit.—What do you rate him at, Moses?

MOSES: Four guineas.

CHARLES SURFACE: Four guineas! Gad's life, you don't bid me the price of his wig.—Mr. Premium, *you* have more respect for the woolsack;° do let us knock his lordship down at fifteen.

SIR OLIVER: By all means.

CARELESS: Gone!

CHARLES SURFACE: And there are two brothers of his, William and Walter Blunt, Esquires, both mem-

---

battle of Malplaquet, on September 11, 1709.

Kneller, Sir Godfrey Kneller (1648–1723), who painted many portraits of English sovereigns and nobles. **woolsack,** "for lawyers." The reference to the Lord Chancellor's seat on the Woolsack in the House of Lords is here meant as the symbol of the profession of law.

bers of Parliament, and noted speakers; and, what's very extraordinary, I believe this is the first time they were ever bought and sold.

SIR OLIVER: That's very extraordinary, indeed! I'll take them at your own price, for the honor of Parliament.

CARELESS: Well said, little Premium! I'll knock 'em down at forty.

CHARLES SURFACE: Here's a jolly fellow—I don't know what relation, but he was mayor of Manchester; take him at eight pounds.

SIR OLIVER: No, no—six will do for the mayor.

CHARLES SURFACE: Come, make it guineas, and I'll throw you the two aldermen there into the bargain.

SIR OLIVER: They're mine.

CHARLES SURFACE: Careless, knock down the mayor and aldermen. But, plague on't! we shall be all day retailing in this manner; do let us deal wholesale—what say you, little Premium? Give me three hundred pounds for the rest of the family in the lump.

CARELESS: Aye, aye, that will be the best way.

SIR OLIVER: Well, well, anything to accommodate you; they are mine. But there is one portrait which you have always passed over.

CARELESS: What, that ill-looking little fellow over the settee?

SIR OLIVER: Yes, sir, I mean that; though I don't think him so ill-looking a little fellow, by any means.

CHARLES SURFACE: What, that? Oh, that's my uncle Oliver! 'Twas done before he went to India.

CARELESS: Your uncle Oliver! Gad, then you'll never be friends, Charles. That, now, to me, is as stern a looking rogue as ever I saw—an unforgiving eye, and a damned disinheriting countenance! an inveterate knave, depend on't. Don't you think so, little Premium?

SIR OLIVER: Upon my soul, sir, I do not; I think it is as honest a looking face as any in the room, dead or alive. But I suppose your uncle Oliver goes with the rest of the lumber?

CHARLES SURFACE: No, hang it! I'll not part with poor Noll. The old fellow has been very good to me, and, egad, I'll keep his picture while I've a room to put it in.

SIR OLIVER: The rogue's my nephew after all! (aside)—But, sir, I have somehow taken a fancy to that picture.

CHARLES SURFACE: I'm sorry for't, for you certainly will not have it. Oons! haven't you got enough of 'em?

SIR OLIVER: I forgive him everything! (aside) But, sir, when I take a whim in my head, I don't value money. I'll give you as much for that as for all the rest.

CHARLES SURFACE: Don't tease me, master broker; I tell you I'll not part with it, and there's an end on't.

SIR OLIVER: How like his father the dog is!— (Aloud) Well, well, I have done.—I did not perceive it before, but I think I never saw such a resemblance.—Well, sir—here's a draught for your sum.

CHARLES SURFACE: Why, 'tis for eight hundred pounds!

SIR OLIVER: You will not let Sir Oliver go?

CHARLES SURFACE: Zounds! no! I tell you, once more.

SIR OLIVER: Then never mind the difference; we'll balance another time. But give me your hand on the bargain; you are an honest fellow, Charles—I beg pardon, sir, for being so free.—Come, Moses.

CHARLES SURFACE: Egad, this is a whimsical old fellow!—but hark'ee, Premium, you'll prepare lodgings for these gentlemen.

SIR OLIVER: Yes, yes, I'll send for them in a day or two.

CHARLES SURFACE: But hold—do now—send a genteel conveyance for them, for, I assure you, they were most of them used to ride in their own carriages.

SIR OLIVER: I will, I will, for all but—Oliver.

CHARLES SURFACE: Aye, all but the little honest nabob.

SIR OLIVER: You're fixed on that?

CHARLES SURFACE: Peremptorily.

SIR OLIVER: A dear extravagant rogue!—Good day!—Come, Moses,—Let me hear now who dares call him profligate! (Exeunt SIR OLIVER and MOSES.)

CARELESS: Why, this is the oddest genius of the sort I ever saw!

CHARLES SURFACE: Egad, he's the prince of brokers, I think. I wonder how the devil Moses got acquainted with so honest a fellow.—Ha! here's Rowley.—Do, Careless, say I'll join the company in a moment.

CARELESS: I will—but don't let that old blockhead persuade you to squander any of that money on old musty debts, or any such nonsense; for tradesmen, Charles, are the most exorbitant fellows!

CHARLES SURFACE: Very true, and paying them is only encouraging them.

CARELESS: Nothing else.

CHARLES SURFACE: Aye, aye, never fear.—(Exit CARELESS.) So! this was an odd old fellow, indeed! Let me see, two-thirds of this is mine by right—five hundred and thirty pounds. 'Fore heaven! I find one's ancestors are more valuable relations than I took 'em for!—Ladies and gentlemen, your most obedient and very grateful humble servant.

(Enter ROWLEY.)

Ha! old Rowley! egad, you are just come in time to take leave of your old acquaintance.

ROWLEY: Yes, I heard they were going. But I wonder you can have such spirits under so many distresses.

CHARLES SURFACE: Why, there's the point—my distresses are so many, that I can't afford to part with my spirits; but I shall be rich and splenetic, all in good time. However, I suppose you are surprised that I am not more sorrowful at parting with so many near relations; to be sure, 'tis very affecting; but rot 'em, you see they never move a muscle, so why should I?

ROWLEY: There's no making you serious a moment.

CHARLES SURFACE: Yes, faith: I am so now. Here, my honest Rowley, here, get me this changed, and take a hundred pounds of it immediately to old Stanley.

ROWLEY: A hundred pounds! Consider only—

CHARLES SURFACE: Gad's life, don't talk about it! poor Stanley's wants are pressing, and, if you don't make haste, we shall have some one call that has a better right to the money.

ROWLEY: Ah! there's the point! I never will cease dunning you with the old proverb—

CHARLES SURFACE: 'Be *just* before you're *generous,* hey!—Why, so I would if I could; but Justice is an old lame hobbling beldame, and I can't get her to keep pace with Generosity, for the soul of me.

ROWLEY: Yet, Charles, believe me, one hour's reflection—

CHARLES SURFACE: Aye, aye, it's all very true; but, hark'ee, Rowley, while I have, by heaven I'll give—so, damn your economy! and now for hazard. (*Exit.*)

ACT 4 / SCENE 2

(*The parlor*)
(*Enter* SIR OLIVER SURFACE *and* MOSES.)

MOSES: Well, sir, I think, as Sir Peter said, you have seen Mr. Charles in high glory: 'tis great pity he's so extravagant.

SIR OLIVER: True, but he wouldn't sell my picture.

MOSES: And loves wine and women so much.

SIR OLIVER: But he wouldn't sell my picture!

MOSES: And games so deep.

SIR OLIVER: But he wouldn't sell my picture. Oh, here's Rowley.

(*Enter* ROWLEY.)

ROWLEY: So, Sir Oliver, I find you have made a purchase—

SIR OLIVER: Yes, yes, our young rake has parted with his ancestors like old tapestry.

ROWLEY: And here has he commissioned me to re-

deliver your part of the purchase-money—I mean, though, in your necessitous character of old Stanley.

MOSES: Ah! there is the pity of all: he is so damned charitable.

ROWLEY: And I left a hosier and two tailors in the hall, who, I'm sure, won't be paid, and this hundred would satisfy 'em.

SIR OLIVER: Well, well, I'll pay his debts—and his benevolence too; but now I am no more a broker, and you shall introduce me to the elder brother as old Stanley.

ROWLEY: Not yet awhile; Sir Peter, I know, means to call there about this time.

(*Enter* TRIP.)

TRIP: O gentlemen, I beg pardon for not showing you out; this way—Moses, a word. (*Exeunt* TRIP *and* MOSES.)

SIR OLIVER: There's a fellow for you! Would you believe it, that puppy intercepted the Jew on our coming, and wanted to raise money before he got to his master!

ROWLEY: Indeed!

SIR OLIVER: Yes, they are now planning an annuity business. Ah, Master Rowley, in my days, servants were content with the follies of their masters, when they were worn a little threadbare—but now they have their vices, like their birthday clothes,° with the gloss on. (*Exeunt.*)

ACT 4 / SCENE 3

(*A library in* JOSEPH SURFACE's *house*)
(JOSEPH SURFACE *and* SERVANT.)

JOSEPH SURFACE: No letter from Lady Teazle?

SERVANT: No, sir.

JOSEPH SURFACE (*aside*): I am surprised she hasn't sent, if she's prevented from coming. Sir Peter certainly does not suspect me. Yet I wish I may not lose the heiress, through the scrape I have drawn myself in with the wife; however, Charles's imprudence and bad character are great points in my favor. (*Knocking.*)

SERVANT: Sir, I believe that must be Lady Teazle.

JOSEPH SURFACE: Hold! See whether it is or not, before you go to the door—I have a particular message for you, if it should be my brother.

SERVANT: 'Tis her ladyship, sir; she always leaves her chair at the milliner's in the next street.

JOSEPH SURFACE: Stay, stay—draw that screen before the window—that will do;—my opposite neighbor is a maiden lady of so curious a tem-

---

birthday clothes, ceremonial dress for the King's Birthday celebrations per.—(SERVANT *draws the screen and exits.*) have a difficult hand to play in this affair. Lady Teazle has lately suspected my views on Maria; but she must by no means be let into that secret,—at least, not till I have her more in my power.

(*Enter* LADY TEAZLE.)

LADY TEAZLE: What, sentiment in soliloquy! Have you been very impatient now? O lud! don't pretend to look grave. I vow I couldn't come before.

JOSEPH SURFACE: O madam, punctuality is a species of constancy, a very unfashionable quality in a lady.

LADY TEAZLE: Upon my word, you ought to pity me. Do you know that Sir Peter is grown so ill-tempered to me of late, and so jealous of Charles too—that's the best of the story, isn't it?

JOSEPH SURFACE (*aside*): I am glad my scandalous friends keep that up.

LADY TEAZLE: I am sure I wish he would let Maria marry him, and then perhaps he would be con-finced; don't you, Mr. Surface?

JOSEPH SURFACE (*aside*): Indeed I do not.—Oh, certainly I do! for then my dear Lady Teazle would also be convinced how wrong her suspicions were of my having any design on the silly girl.

LADY TEAZLE: Well, well, I'm inclined to believe you. But isn't it provoking, to have the most ill-natured things said to one? And there's my friend Lady Sneerwell has circulated I don't know how many scandalous tales of me! and all without any foundation, too—that's what vexes me.

JOSEPH SURFACE: Aye, madam, to be sure, that *is* the provoking circumstance—without foundation! yes, yes, there's the mortification, indeed; for when a scandalous story is believed against one, there certainly is no comfort like the conscious-ness of having deserved it.

LADY TEAZLE: No, to be sure—then I'd forgive their malice; but to attack me, who am really so inno-cent, and who never say an ill-natured thing of anybody—that is, of any friend—and then Sir Peter, too, to have him so peevish, and so sus-picious, when I know the integrity of my own heart—indeed 'tis monstrous!

JOSEPH SURFACE: But, my dear Lady Teazle, 'tis your own fault if you suffer it. When a husband enter-tains a groundless suspicion of his wife, and withdraws his confidence from her, the original compact is broke, and she owes it to the honor of her sex to endeavor to outwit him.

LADY TEAZLE: Indeed! So that, if he suspects me without cause, it follows that the best way of cur-ing his jealousy is to give him reason for't?

JOSEPH SURFACE: Undoubtedly—for your husband should never be deceived in you: and in that case it becomes *you* to be frail in compliment to *his* discernment.

LADY TEAZLE: To be sure, what you say is very rea-sonable, and when the consciousness of my own innocence—

JOSEPH SURFACE: Ah, my dear madam, there is the great mistake; 'tis this very conscious innocence that is of the greatest prejudice to you. What is it makes you negligent of forms, and careless of the world's opinion? why, the *consciousness* of your innocence. What makes you thoughtless in your conduct, and apt to run into a thousand little imprudences? why, the *consciousness* of your innocence. What makes you impatient of Sir Pe-ter's temper and outrageous at his suspicions? why, the *consciousness* of your own innocence!

LADY TEAZLE: 'Tis very true!

JOSEPH SURFACE: Now, my dear Lady Teazle, if you would but once make a trifling *faux pas*, you can't conceive how cautious you would grow—and how ready to humor and agree with your husband.

LADY TEAZLE: Do you think so?

JOSEPH SURFACE: Oh, I'm sure on't; and then you would find all scandal would cease at once, for—in short, your character at present is like a person in a plethora, absolutely dying of too much health.

LADY TEAZLE: So, so; then I perceive your prescrip-tion is, that I must sin in my own defence, and part with my virtue to preserve my reputation?

JOSEPH SURFACE: Exactly so, upon my credit, ma'am.

LADY TEAZLE: Well, certainly this is the oddest doc-trine, and the newest receipt for avoiding calumny?

JOSEPH SURFACE: An infallible one, believe me. *Pru-dence,* like *experience,* must be paid for.

LADY TEAZLE: Why, if my understanding were once convinced—

JOSEPH SURFACE: Oh, certainly, madam, your un-derstanding *should* be convinced. Yes, yes—heaven forbid I should persuade you to do any-thing you *thought* wrong. No, no, I have too much honor to desire it.

LADY TEAZLE: Don't you think we may as well leave honor out of the argument?

JOSEPH SURFACE: Ah, the ill effects of your country education, I see, still remain with you.

LADY TEAZLE: I doubt they do, indeed; and I will fairly own to you, that if I could be persuaded to do wrong, it would be by Sir Peter's ill-usage sooner than your honorable logic, after all.

JOSEPH SURFACE: Then, by this hand, which he is un-worthy of— (*Taking her hand.*)

(*Re-enter* SERVANT.)

'Sdeath, you blockhead—what do you want?

SERVANT: I beg pardon, sir, but I thought you wouldn't choose Sir Peter to come up without announcing him.

JOSEPH SURFACE: Sir Peter!—Oons—the devil!

LADY TEAZLE: Sir Peter! O lud! I'm ruined! I'm ruined!

SERVANT: Sir, 'twasn't I let him in.

LADY TEAZLE: Oh! I'm undone! What will become of me, now, Mr. Logic?—Oh! mercy, he's on the stairs—I'll get behind here—and if ever I'm so imprudent again— *(Goes behind the screen.)*

JOSEPH SURFACE: Give me that book. *(Sits down.* SERVANT *pretends to adjust his hair.)*

(Enter SIR PETER TEAZLE.*)*

SIR PETER: Aye, ever improving himself!—Mr. Surface, Mr. Surface—

JOSEPH SURFACE: Oh, my dear Sir Peter, I beg your pardon. *(Gaping, and throws away the book.)* I have been dozing over a stupid book. Well, I am much obliged to you for this call. You haven't been here, I believe, since I fitted up this room. Books, you know, are the only things I am a coxcomb in.

SIR PETER: 'Tis very neat indeed. Well, well, that's proper; and you make even your screen a source of knowledge—hung, I perceive, with maps.

JOSEPH SURFACE: Oh, yes, I find great use in that screen.

SIR PETER: I dare say you must—certainly—when you want to find anything in a hurry.

JOSEPH SURFACE *(aside)*: Aye, or to hide anything in a hurry either.

SIR PETER: Well, I have a little private business—

JOSEPH SURFACE: You needn't stay. *(to* SERVANT*)*

SERVANT: No, sir. *(Exit.)*

JOSEPH SURFACE: Here's a chair, Sir Peter—I beg—

SIR PETER: Well, now we are alone, there is a subject, my dear friend, on which I wish to unburden my mind to you—a point of the greatest moment to my peace: in short, my good friend, Lady Teazle's conduct of late has made me extremely unhappy.

JOSEPH SURFACE: Indeed! I am very sorry to hear it.

SIR PETER: Yes, 'tis but too plain she has not the least regard for me; but what's worse, I have pretty good authority to suspect she must have formed an attachment to another.

JOSEPH SURFACE: You astonish me!

SIR PETER: Yes! and, between ourselves, I think I have discovered the person.

JOSEPH SURFACE: How! you alarm me exceedingly.

SIR PETER: Aye, my dear friend, I knew you would sympathize with me!

JOSEPH SURFACE: Yes, believe me, Sir Peter, such a discovery would hurt me just as much as it would you.

SIR PETER: I am convinced of it.—Ah! it is a happiness to have a friend whom one can trust even with one's family secrets. But have you no guess who I mean?

JOSEPH SURFACE: I haven't the most distant idea. It can't be Sir Benjamin Backbite!

SIR PETER: O, no! What say you to Charles?

JOSEPH SURFACE: My brother! impossible!

SIR PETER: Ah, my dear friend, the goodness of your own heart misleads you—you judge of others by yourself.

JOSEPH SURFACE: Certainly, Sir Peter, the heart that is conscious of its own integrity is ever slow to credit another's treachery.

SIR PETER: True; but your brother has no sentiment—you never hear him talk so.

JOSEPH SURFACE: Yet I can't but think Lady Teazle herself has too much principle—

SIR PETER: Aye; but what's her principle against the flattery of a handsome, lively young fellow?

JOSEPH SURFACE: That's very true.

SIR PETER: And then, you know, the difference of our ages makes it very improbable that she should have any great affection for me; and if she were to be frail, and I were to make it public, why the town would only laugh at me, the foolish old bachelor who had married a girl.

JOSEPH SURFACE: That's true, to be sure—they *would* laugh.

SIR PETER: Laugh! aye, and make ballads, and paragraphs, and the devil knows what of me.

JOSEPH SURFACE: No, you must never make it public.

SIR PETER: But then again—that the nephew of my old friend, Sir Oliver, should be the person to attempt such a wrong, hurts me more nearly.

JOSEPH SURFACE: Aye, there's the point. When ingratitude barbs the dart of injury, the wound has double danger in it.

SIR PETER: Aye—I, that was, in a manner, left his guardian—in whose house he had been so often entertained—who never in my life denied him—my advice!

JOSEPH SURFACE: Oh, 'tis not to be credited! There *may* be a man capable of such baseness, to be sure; but, for my part, till you can give me positive proofs, I cannot but doubt it. However, if it should be proved on him, he is no longer a brother of mine! I disclaim kindred with him—for the man who can break through the laws of hospitality, and attempt the wife of his friend, deserves to be branded as the pest of society.

SIR PETER: What a difference there is between you! What noble sentiments!

JOSEPH SURFACE: Yet I cannot suspect Lady Teazle's honor.

SIR PETER: I am sure I wish to think well of her, and to remove all ground of quarrel between us. She has lately reproached me more than once with having made no settlement on her; and, in our last quarrel, she almost hinted that she should not break her heart if was dead. Now, as we seem to differ in our ideas of expense, I have resolved she shall be her own mistress in that respect for the future; and, if I *were* to die, she shall find that I have not been inattentive to her interest while living. Here, my friend, are the drafts of two deeds, which I wish to have your opinion on. By one, she will enjoy eight hundred a year independent while I live; and, by the other, the bulk of my fortune after my death.

JOSEPH SURFACE: This conduct, Sir Peter, is indeed truly generous.— *(aside)* I wish it may not corrupt my pupil.

SIR PETER: Yes, I am determined she shall have no cause to complain, though I would not have her acquainted with the latter instance of my affection yet awhile.

JOSEPH SURFACE: Nor I, if I could help it. *(aside)*

SIR PETER: And now, my dear friend, if you please, we will talk over the situation of your hopes with Maria.

JOSEPH SURFACE *(softly)*: No, no, Sir Peter; another time, if you please.

SIR PETER: I am sensibly chagrined at the little progress you seem to make in her affection.

JOSEPH SURFACE: I beg you will not mention it. What are my disappointments when your happiness is in debate! *(Softly.)*—'Sdeath, I shall be ruined every way! *(aside)*

SIR PETER: And though you are so averse to my acquainting Lady Teazle with your passion, I am sure she's not your enemy in the affair.

JOSEPH SURFACE: Pray, Sir Peter, now oblige me. I am really too much affected by the subject we have been speaking on to bestow a thought on my own concerns. The man who is entrusted with his friend's distresses can never—

(Enter SERVANT.*)*

Well, sir?

SERVANT: Your brother, sir, is speaking to a gentleman in the street, and says he knows you are within.

JOSEPH SURFACE: 'Sdeath, blockhead—I'm not within—I'm out for the day.

SIR PETER: Stay—hold—a thought has struck me—you shall be at home.

JOSEPH SURFACE: Well, well, let him up.—*(Exit* SERVANT.*)* He'll interrupt Sir Peter—however—

SIR PETER: Now, my good friend, oblige me, I entreat you. Before Charles comes, let me conceal myself somewhere; then do you tax him on the point we have been talking on, and his answers may satisfy me at once.

JOSEPH SURFACE: O, fie, Sir Peter! would you have me join in so mean a trick?—to trepan my brother so?

SIR PETER: Nay, you tell me you are *sure* he is innocent; if so, you do him the greatest service by giving him an opportunity to clear himself, and you will set my heart at rest. Come, you shall not refuse me; here, behind the screen will be *(Goes to the screen.)*—Hey! what the devil! there seems to be *one* listener here already—I'll swear I saw a petticoat!

JOSEPH SURFACE: Ha! ha! ha! Well, this is ridiculous enough. I'll tell you, Sir Peter, though I hold a man of intrigue to be a most despicable character, yet you know, it doesn't follow that one is to be an absolute Joseph either! Hark'ee! 'tis a little French milliner, a silly rogue that plagues me—and having some character—on your coming, she ran behind the screen.

SIR PETER: Ah, you rogue!—But, egad, she has overheard all I have been saying of my wife.

JOSEPH SURFACE: Oh, 'twill never go any further, you may depend on't!

SIR PETER: No! then, i'faith, let her hear it out.— Here's a closet will do as well.

JOSEPH SURFACE: Well, go in then.

SIR PETER: Sly rogue! sly rogue! *(Goes into the closet.)*

JOSEPH SURFACE: A very narrow escape, indeed! and a curious situation I'm in, to part man and wife in this manner.

LADY TEAZLE *(peeping from the screen)*: Couldn't I steal off?

JOSEPH SURFACE: Keep close, my angel!

SIR PETER *(peeping out)*: Joseph, tax him home.

JOSEPH SURFACE: Back, my dear friend!

LADY TEAZLE *(peeping)*: Couldn't you lock Sir Peter in?

JOSEPH SURFACE: Be still, my life!

SIR PETER *(peeping)*: You're sure the little milliner won't blab?

JOSEPH SURFACE: In, in, my dear Sir Peter!—'Fore gad, I wish I had a key to the door.

(Enter CHARLES SURFACE.*)*

CHARLES SURFACE: Hollo! brother, what has been the matter? Your fellow would not let me up at first. What! have you had a Jew or a wench with you?

JOSEPH SURFACE: Neither, brother, I assure you.

CHARLES SURFACE: But what has made Sir Peter steal off? I thought he had been with you.

JOSEPH SURFACE: He was, brother; but, hearing *you* were coming, he did not choose to stay.

CHARLES SURFACE: What! was the old gentleman afraid I wanted to borrow money of him!

JOSEPH SURFACE: No, sir: but I am sorry to find, Charles, that you have lately given that worthy man grounds for great uneasiness.

CHARLES SURFACE: Yes, they tell me I do that to a great many worthy men. But how so, pray?

JOSEPH SURFACE: To be plain with you, brother, he thinks you are endeavoring to gain Lady Teazle's affections from him.

CHARLES SURFACE: Who, I? O lud! not I, upon my word.—Ha! ha! ha! so the old fellow has found out that he has got a young wife, has he?—or, what's worse, has her ladyship discovered that she has an old husband?

JOSEPH: This is no subject to jest on, brother.—He who can laugh—

CHARLES SURFACE: True, true, as you were going to say—then, seriously, I never had the least idea of what you charge me with, upon my honor.

JOSEPH SURFACE: Well, it will give Sir Peter great satisfaction to hear this. (Aloud.)

CHARLES SURFACE: To be sure, I once thought the lady seemed to have taken a great fancy to me; but, upon my soul, I never gave her the least encouragement. Besides, you know my attachment to Maria.

JOSEPH SURFACE: But sure, brother, even if Lady Teazle had betrayed the fondest partiality for you—

CHARLES SURFACE: Why, look'ee, Joseph, I hope I shall never deliberately do a dishonorable action—but if a pretty woman were purposely to throw herself in my way—and that pretty woman married to a man old enought to be her father—

JOSEPH SURFACE: Well!

CHARLES SURFACE: Why, I believe I should be obliged to borrow a little of your morality, that's all.—But brother, do you know now that you surprise me exceedingly, by naming me with Lady Teazle; for, faith, I always understood you were her favorite.

JOSEPH SURFACE: Oh, for shame, Charles! This retort is foolish.

CHARLES SURFACE: Nay, I swear I have seen you exchange such significant glances—

JOSEPH SURFACE: Nay, nay, sir, this is no jest—

CHARLES SURFACE: Egad, I'm serious! Don't you remember—one day, when I called here—

JOSEPH SURFACE: Nay, prithee, Charles—

CHARLES SURFACE: And found you together—

JOSEPH SURFACE: Zounds, sir, I insist—

CHARLES SURFACE: And another time, when your servant—

JOSEPH SURFACE: Brother, brother, a word with you!—(aside) Gad, I must stop him.

CHARLES SURFACE: Informed me, I say, that—

JOSEPH SURFACE: Hush! I beg your pardon, but Sir Peter has overheard all we have been saying—I knew you would clear yourself, or I should not have consented.

CHARLES SURFACE: How Sir Peter! Where is he?

JOSEPH SURFACE: Softly, there! (Points to the closet.)

CHARLES SURFACE: Oh, 'fore heaven, I'll have him out.—Sir Peter, come forth!

JOSEPH SURFACE: No, no—

CHARLES SURFACE: I say, Sir Peter, come into court.—(Pulls in SIR PETER.) What! my old guardian!—What—turn inquisitor, and take evidence, incog.?

SIR PETER: Give me your hand, Charles—I believe I have suspected you wrongfully—but you mustn't be angry with Joseph—'twas my plan!

CHARLES SURFACE: Indeeed!

SIR PETER: But I acquit you. I promise you I don't think near so ill of you as I did. What I have heard has given me great satisfaction.

CHARLES SURFACE: Egad, then, 'twas lucky you didn't hear any more. Wasn't it, Joseph? (Half aside)

SIR PETER: Well, well, I believe you.

JOSEPH SURFACE: Would they were both out of the room!

SIR PETER: And in future, perhaps, we may not be such strangers.

(Enter SERVANT who whispers JOSEPH SURFACE.)

JOSEPH SURFACE: Lady Sneerwell!—stop her by all means— (Exit SERVANT.) Gentlemen— I beg pardon—I must wait on you downstairs—here's a person come on particular business.

CHARLES SURFACE: Well, you can see him in another room. Sir Peter and I haven't met a long time, and I have something to say to him.

JOSEPH SURFACE: They must not be left together.—I'll send Lady Sneerwell away, and return directly.—(aside) Sir Peter, not a word on the French milliner. (Exit JOSEPH SURFACE.)

SIR PETER: Oh! not for the world!—Ah, Charles, if you associated more with your brother, one might indeed hope for your reformation. He is a man of sentiment.—Well, there is nothing in the world so noble as a man of sentiment!

CHARLES SURFACE: Pshaw! he is too moral by half, and so apprehensive of his good name, as he calls it, that I suppose he would as soon let a priest into his house as a girl.

SIR PETER: No, no.—come, come,—you wrong him. No, no, Joseph is no rake, but he is not such a saint in that respect either,—I have a great mind to tell him—we should have a laugh! (aside)

CHARLES SURFACE: Oh, hang him! he's a very anchorite, a young hermit!

SIR PETER: Hark'ee—you must not abuse him; he may chance to hear of it again, I promise you.

CHARLES SURFACE: Why, you won't tell him?

SIR PETER: No—but—this way.—(aside) Egad, I'll tell

him.—Hark'ee, have you a mind to have a good laugh at Joseph?

CHARLES SURFACE: I should like it of all things.

SIR PETER: Then, i'faith, we will!—I'll be quit with him for discovering me. *(aside)*—He had a girl with him when I called.

CHARLES SURFACE: What! Joseph? you jest.

SIR PETER: Hush!—a little—French milliner—and the best of the jest is—she's in the room now.

CHARLES SURFACE: The devil she is!

SIR PETER: Hush! I tell you. *(Points to the screen.)*

CHARLES SURFACE: Behind the screen! 'Slife, let's unveil her!

SIR PETER: No, no, he's coming:—you shan't, indeed!

CHARLES SURFACE: Oh, egad, we'll have a peep at the little milliner!

SIR PETER: Not for the world!—Joseph will never forgive me.

CHARLES SURFACE: I'll stand by you—

SIR PETER *(struggling with CHARLES)*: Odds, here he is!

(JOSEPH SURFACE enters just as CHARLES throws down the screen.)

CHARLES SURFACE: Lady Teazle, by all that's wonderful!

SIR PETER: Lady Teazle, by all that's horrible!

CHARLES SURFACE: Sir Peter, this is one of the smartest French milliners I ever saw. Egad, you seem all to have been diverting yourselves here at hide and seek—and I don't see who is out of the secret. Shall I beg your ladyship to inform me?—Not a word!—Brother, will you please to explain this matter? What! Morality dumb too!—Sir Peter, though I *found* you in the dark, perhaps you are not so now! All mute! Well—though *I* can make nothing of the affair, I suppose you perfectly understand one another; so I'll leave you to yourselves.—*(Going.)* Brother, I'm sorry to find you *have given that worthy man so much uneasiness.*—Sir Peter! there's nothing *in the world so noble as a man of sentiment! (Exit CHARLES.)*

(They stand for some time looking at each other.)

JOSEPH SURFACE: Sir Peter—notwithstanding I confess that appearances are against me—if you will afford me your patience—I make no doubt but I shall explain everything to your satisfaction.

SIR PETER: If you please—

JOSEPH SURFACE: The fact is, sir, that Lady Teazle, knowing my pretensions ot your ward Maria—I say, sir, Lady Teazle, being apprehensive of the jealousy of your temper—and knowing my friendship to the family—she, sir, I say—called here—in order that—I might explain those pretensions—but on your coming—being apprehensive—as I said—of your jealousy—she

withdrew—and this, you may depend on't is the whole truth of the matter.

SIR PETER: A very clear account, upon my word; and I dare swear the lady will vouch for every article of it.

LADY TEAZLE *(coming forward)*: For not one word of it, Sir Peter!

SIR PETER: How! don't you think it worth while to agree in the lie?

LADY TEAZLE: There is not one syllable of truth in what that gentleman has told you.

SIR PETER: I believe you, upon my soul, ma'am!

JOSEPH SURFACE *(aside)*: 'Sdeath, madam, will you betray me?

LADY TEAZLE: Good Mr. Hypocrite, by your leave, I will speak for myself.

SIR PETER: Aye, let her alone, sir; you'll find she'll make out a better story than *you*, without prompting.

LADY TEAZLE: Hear me, Sir Peter!—I came here on no matter relating to your ward, and even ignorant of this gentleman's pretensions to her—but I came, seduced by his insidious arguments, at least to listen to his pretended passion, if not to sacrifice *your* honor to his baseness.

SIR PETER: Now, I believe, the truth *is* coming, indeed!

JOSEPH SURFACE: The woman's mad!

LADY TEAZLE: No, sir; she's recovered her senses, and your own arts have furnished her with the means.—Sir Peter, I do not expect you to credit me—but the tenderness you expressed for me, when I am sure you could not think I was a witness to it, has penetrated to my heart, and had I left the place without the shame of this discovery, my future life should have spoken the sincerity of my gratitude. As for that smooth-tongue hypocrite, who would have seduced the wife of his too credulous friend, while he affected honorable addresses to his ward—I behold him now in a light so truly despicable, that I shall never again respect myself for having listened to him. *(Exit.)*

JOSEPH SURFACE: Notwithstanding all this, Sir Peter, heaven knows—

SIR PETER: That you are a villain!—and so I leave you to your conscience.

JOSEPH SURFACE: You are too rash, Sir Peter; you shall hear me. The man who shuts out conviction by refusing to—

SIR PETER: Oh!—

(Exeunt, JOSEPH SURFACE following and speaking.)

ACT 5 / SCENE 1

(The library in JOSEPH SURFACE'S house.)
(Enter JOSEPH SURFACE and SERVANT.)

JOSEPH SURFACE: Mr. Stanley! why should you think I would see him? you *must* know he comes to ask something.

SERVANT: Sir, I should not have let him in, but that Mr. Rowley came to the door with him.

JOSEPH SURFACE: Pshaw! blockhead! to suppose that I should *now* be in a temper to receive visits from poor relations!—Well, shy don't you show the fellow up?

SERVANT: I will, sir—Why sir, it was not my fault that Sir Peter discovered my lady—

JOSEPH SURFACE: Go, fool! *(Exit* SERVANT.*)* Sure, Fortune never played a man of my policy such a trick before! My character with Sir Peter, my hopes with Maria, destroyed in a moment! I'm in a rare humor to listen to other people's distresses! I shan't be able to bestow even a benevolent sentiment on Stanley.—So! here he comes, and Rowley with him. I must try to recover myself—and put a little charity into my face, however. *(Exit.)*

(Enter SIR OLIVER SURFACE *and* ROWLEY.*)*

SIR OLIVER: What! does he avoid us? That was he, was it not?

ROWLEY: It was, sir—but I doubt you are come a little too abruptly—his nerves are so weak, that the sight of a poor relation may be too much for him.—I should have gone first to break you to him.

SIR OLIVER: A plague of his nerves!—Yet this is he whom Sir Peter extols as a man of the most benevolent way of thinking!

ROWLEY: As to his way of thinking, I cannot pretend to decide; for, to do him justice, he appears to have as much speculative benevolence as any private gentleman in the kingdom, though he is seldom so sensual as to indulge himself in the exercise of it.

SIR OLIVER: Yet has a string of charitable sentiments, I suppose, at his fingers' ends!

ROWLEY: Or, rather, at his tongue's end, Sir Oliver; for I believe there is no sentiment he has more faith in than that 'Charity begins at home.'

SIR OLIVER: And his, I presume, is of that domestic sort which never stirs abroad at all.

ROWLEY: I doubt you'll find it so;—but he's coming—I mustn't seem to interrupt you; and you know, immediately as you leave him, I come in to announce your arrival in your real character.

SIR OLIVER: True; and afterwards you'll meet me at Sir Peter's.

ROWLEY: Without losing a moment. *(Exit* ROWLEY.*)*

SIR OLIVER: So! I don't like the complaisance of his features.

(Re-enter JOSEPH SURFACE.*)*

JOSEPH SURFACE: Sir, I beg you ten thousand pardons for keeping you a moment waiting—Mr. Stanley, I presume.

SIR OLIVER: At your service.

JOSEPH SURFACE: Sir, I beg you will do me the honor to sit down—I entreat you, sir.

SIR OLIVER: Dear sir—there's no occasion.—Too civil by half! *(aside)*

JOSEPH SURFACE: I have not the pleasure of knowing you, Mr. Stanley; but I am extremely happy to see you look so well. You were nearly related to my mother, I think, Mr. Stanley?

SIR OLIVER: I was sir—so nearly that my present poverty, I fear, may do discredit to her wealthy children—else I should not have presumed to trouble you.

JOSEPH SURFACE: Dear sir, there needs no apology: he that is in distress, though a stranger, has a right to claim kindred with the wealthy;—I am sure I wish *I* was one of that class, and had it in my power to offer you even a small relief.

SIR OLIVER: If your uncle, Sir Oliver, were here, I should have a friend.

JOSEPH SURFACE: I wish he were, sir, with all my heart: you should not want an advocate with him, believe me, sir.

SIR OLIVER: I should not *need* one—my distresses would recommend me; but I imagined his bounty had enabled *you* to become the agent of his charity.

JOSEPH SURFACE: My dear sir, you were strangely misinformed. Sir Oliver is a worthy man, a very worthy sort of man; but—avarice, Mr. Stanley, is the vice of age. I will tell you, my good sir, in confidence, what he has done for me has been a mere nothing; though people, I know, have thought otherwise, and for my part, I never chose to contradict the report.

SIR OLIVER: What! has he never transmitted you bullion! rupees!° pagodas!°

JOSEPH SURFACE: O dear sir, nothing of the kind! No, no; a few presents now and then—china—shawls—Congo tea—avadavats,° and Indian crackers°—little more, believe me.

SIR OLIVER *(aside)*: Here's gratitude for twelve thousand pounds!—Avadavats and Indian crackers!

JOSEPH SURFACE: Then, my dear sir, you have heard, I doubt not, of the extravagance of my brother;

rupees, silver coins of India, then valued at two shillings. ***pagodas,*** gold coins of India, then valued at eight shillings. ***avadavats,*** small singing-birds of India, having red and black plumage. ***Indian crackers,*** fire-crackers with colored wrappers.

there are very few would credit what I have done for that unfortunate young man.

SIR OLIVER: Not I, for one! *(aside)*

JOSEPH SURFACE: The sums I have lent him! Indeed I have been exceedingly to blame—it was an amiable weakness: however, I don't pretend to defend it—and now I feel it doubly culpable, since it has deprived me of the pleasure of serving *you*, Mr. Stanley, as my heart dictates.

SIR OLIVER *(aside)*: Dissembler!—Then, sir, you cannot assist me?

JOSEPH SURFACE: At present, it grieves me to say, I cannot; but, whenever I have the ability, you may depend upon hearing from me.

SIR OLIVER: I am extremely sorry—

JOSEPH SURFACE: Not more than I am, believe me; to pity, without the power to relieve, is still more painful than to ask and be denied.

SIR OLIVER: Kind sir, your most obedient humble servant.

JOSEPH SURFACE: You leave me deeply affected, Mr. Stanley.—William, be ready to open the door.

SIR OLIVER: O dear sir, no ceremony.

JOSEPH SURFACE: Your very obedient.

SIR OLIVER: Sir, your most obsequious.

JOSEPH SURFACE: You may depend upon hearing from me, whenever I can be of service.

SIR OLIVER: Sweet sir, you are too good.

JOSEPH SURFACE: In the meantime I wish you health and spirits.

SIR OLIVER: Your ever grateful and perpetual humble servant.

JOSEPH SURFACE: Sir, yours as sincerely.

SIR OLIVER: Now I am satisfied! *(Exit.)*

JOSEPH SURFACE *(solus)*: This is one bad effect of a good character; it invites applications from the unfortunate, and there needs no small degree of address to gain the reputation of benevolence without incurring the expense. The silver ore of pure charity is an expensive article in the catalogue of a man's good qualities; whereas the sentimental French plate I use instead of it makes just as good a show, and pays no tax.

(Enter ROWLEY.*)*

ROWLEY: Mr. Surface, your servant—I was apprehensive of interrupting you—though my business demands immediate attention—as this note will inform you.

JOSEPH SURFACE: Always happy to see Mr. Rowley.— *(Reads.)* How! 'Oliver—Surface!'—My uncle arrived!

ROWLEY: He is, indeed—we have just parted—quite well, after a speedy voyage, and impatient to embrace his worthy nephew.

JOSEPH SURFACE: I am astonished!—William! stop Mr. Stanley, if he's not gone.

ROWLEY: Oh! he's out of reach, I believe.

JOSEPH SURFACE: Why didn't you let me know this when you came in together?

ROWLEY: I thought you had particular business. But I must be gone to inform your brother, and appoint him here to meet his uncle. He will be with you in a quarter of an hour.

JOSEPH SURFACE: So he says. Well I am strangely overjoyed at his coming.—*(aside)* Never, to be sure, was anything so damned unlucky!

ROWLEY: You will be delighted to see how well he looks.

JOSEPH SURFACE: Oh! I'm rejoiced to hear it.—*(aside)* Just at this time!

ROWLEY: I'll tell him how impatiently you expect him.

JOSEPH SURFACE: Do, do; pray give my best duty and affection. Indeed, I cannot express the sensations I feel at the thought of seeing him.—*(Exit* ROWLEY.*)* Certainly his coming just at this time is the cruellest piece of ill fortune. *(Exit.)*

ACT 5 / SCENE 2

(At SIR PETER'S*)*
(Enter MRS. CANDOUR *and* MAID.*)*

MAID: Indeed, ma'am, my lady will see nobody at present.

MRS. CANDOUR: Did you tell her it was her friend Mrs. Candour?

MAID: Yes, madam; but she begs you will excuse her.

MRS. CANDOUR: Do go again; I shall be glad to see her, if it be only for a moment, for I am sure she must be in great distress. *(Exit* MAID.*)* Dear heart, how provoking! I'm not mistress of half the circumstances! We shall have the whole affair in the newspapers, with the names of the parties at length, before I have dropped the story at a dozen houses.

(Enter SIR BENJAMIN BACKBITE.*)*

O dear Sir Benjamin! you have heard, I suppose—

SIR BENJAMIN: Of Lady Teazle and Mr. Surface—

MRS. CANDOUR: And Sir Peter's discovery—

SIR BENJAMIN: Oh, the strangest piece of business, to be sure!

MRS. CANDOUR: Well, I never was so surprised in my life. I am so sorry for all parties, indeed I am.

SIR BENJAMIN: Now, I don't pity Sir Peter at all—he was so extravagantly partial to Mr. Surface.

MRS. CANDOUR: Mr. Surface! Why, 'twas with Charles Lady Teazle was detected.

SIR BENJAMIN: No such thing—Mr. Surface is the gallant.

MRS. CANDOUR: No, no—Charles is the man. 'Twas Mr. Surface brought Sir Peter on purpose to discover them.

SIR BENJAMIN: I tell you I have it from one—

MRS. CANDOUR: And I have it from one—

SIR BENJAMIN: Who had it from one, who had it—

MRS. CANDOUR: From one immediately—But here's Lady Sneerwell; perhaps she knows the whole affair.

(Enter LADY SNEERWELL.)

LADY SNEERWELL: So, my dear Mrs. Candour, here's a sad affair of our friend Lady Teazle!

MRS. CANDOUR: Aye, my dear friend, who could have thought it—

LADY SNEERWELL: Well, there's no trusting appearances; though, indeed, she was always too lively for me.

MRS. CANDOUR: To be sure, her manners were a little too free—but she was very young!

LADY SNEERWELL: And had, indeed, some good qualities.

MRS. CANDOUR: So she had, indeed. But have you heard the particulars?

LADY SNEERWELL: No; but everybody says that Mr. Surface—

SIR BENJAMIN: Aye, there, I told you—Mr. Surface was the man.

MRS. CANDOUR: No, no, indeed—the assignation was with Charles.

LADY SNEERWELL: With Charles! You alarm me, Mrs. Candour.

MRS. CANDOUR: Yes, yes, he was the lover. Mr. Surface—do him justice—was only the informer.

SIR BENJAMIN: Well, I'll not dispute with yout, Mrs. Candour; but, be it which it may, I hope that Sir Peter's wound will not—

MRS. CANDOUR: Sir Peter's wound! Oh, mercy! I didn't hear a word of their fighting.

LADY SNEERWELL: Nor I, a syllable.

SIR BENJAMIN: No! what, no mention of the duel?

MRS. CANDOUR: Not a word.

SIR BENJAMIN: O Lord—yes, yes, they fought before they left the room.

LADY SNEERWELL: Pray let us hear.

MRS. CANDOUR: Aye, do oblige us with the duel.

SIR BENJAMIN: 'Sir,' says Sir Peter—immediately after the discovery—'you are a most ungrateful fellow.'

MRS, CANDOUR: Aye, to Charles—

SIR BENJAMIN: No, no—to Mr. Surface—'a most ungrateful fellow; and old as I am, sir,' says he, 'I insist on immediate satisfaction.'

MRS. CANDOUR: Aye, that must have been to Charles; for 'tis very unlikely Mr. Surface should go to fight in his house.

SIR BENJAMIN: 'Gad's life, ma'am, not at all—'giving me immediate satisfaction.'—On this, madam, Lady Teazle, seeing Sir Peter in such danger, ran out of the room in strong hysterics, and Charles after her, calling out for hartshorn and water! Then, madam, they began to fight with swords—

(Enter CRABTREE.)

CRABTREE: With pistols, nephew—I have it from undoubted authority.

MRS. CANDOUR: O Mr. Crabtree, then it is all true!

CRABTREE: Too true, indeed, ma'am, and Sir Peter's dangerously wounded—

SIR BENJAMIN: By a thrust of in seconde° quite through his left side—

CRABTREE: By a bullet lodged in the thorax.

MRS. CANDOUR: Mercy on me! Poor Sir Peter!

CRABTREE: Yes, ma'am—though Charles would have avoided the matter, if he could.

MRS. CANDOUR: I knew Charles was the person.

SIR BENJAMIN: Oh, my uncle, I see, knows nothing of the matter.

CRABTREE: But Sir Peter taxed him with the basest ingratitude—

SIR BENJAMIN: That I told you, you know.

CRABTREE: Do, nephew, let me speak!—and insisted on an immediate—

SIR BENJAMIN: Just as I said.

CRABTREE: Odds life, nephew, allow others to know something too! A pair of pistols lay on the bureau (for Mr. Surface, it seems, had come the night before late from Salt-Hill, where he had been to see the Montem° with a friend, who has a son at Eton), so, unluckily, the pistols were left charged.

SIR BENJAMIN: I heard nothing of this.

CRABTREE: Sir Peter forced Charles to take one, and they fired, it seems, pretty nearly together. Charles's shot took place, as I told you, and Sir Peter's missed; but, what is very extraordinary, the ball struck against a little bronze Pliny that stood over the chimney-piece, grazed out of the window at a right angle, and wounded the postman, who was just coming to the door with a double letter from Northamptonshire.

SIR BENJAMIN: My uncle's account is more circumstantial, I must confess; but I believe mine is the true one, for all that.

LADY SNEERWELL (aside): I am more interested in this affair than they imagine, and must have better information. (Exit LADY SNEERWELL.)

SIR BENJAMIN (after a pause looking at each other): Ah! Lady Sneerwell's alarm is very easily accounted for.

CRABTREE: Yes, yes, they certainly do say—but that's neither here nor there.

---

seconde, a term in fencing. Montem, It was formerly the custom of Eton school boys to go to Salt-Hill (processus ad montem) every third year on Whit-Tuesday, and levy salt-money from the onlookers at the ceremony.

MRS. CANDOUR: But, pray, where is Sir Peter at present?

CRABTREE: Oh! they brought him home, and he is now in the house, though the servants are ordered to deny it.

MRS. CANDOUR: I believe so, and Lady Teazle, I suppose, attending him.

CRABTREE: Yes, yes; I saw one of the faculty enter just before me.

SIR BENJAMIN: Hey! who comes here?

CRABTREE: Oh, this is he—the physician, depend on't.

MRS. CANDOUR: Oh, certainly! it must be the physician; and now we shall know.

(Enter SIR OLIVER SURFACE.*)*

CRABTREE: Well, doctor, what hopes?

MRS. CANDOUR: Aye, doctor, how's your patient?

SIR BENJAMIN: Now, doctor, isn't it a wound with a small-sword?

CRABTREE: A bullet lodged in the thorax, for a hundred!

SIR OLIVER: Doctor! a wound with a small-sword! and a bullet in the thorax?—Oons! are you mad, good people?

SIR BENJAMIN: Perhaps, sir, you are not a doctor?

SIR OLIVER: Truly, I am to thank you for my degree, if I am.

CRABTREE: Only a friend of Sir Peter's then, I presume. But, sir, you must have heard of this accident?

SIR OLIVER: Not a word!

CRABTREE: Not of his being dangerously wounded?

SIR OLIVER: The devil he is!

SIR BENJAMIN: Run through the body—

CRABTREE: Shot in the breast—

SIR BENJAMIN: By one Mr. Surface—

CRABTREE: Aye, the younger.

SIR OLIVER: Hey! what the plague! you seem to differ strangely in your accounts—however, you agree that Sir Peter is dangerously wounded.

SIR BENJAMIN: Oh, yes, we agree there.

CRABTREE: Yes, yes, I believe there can be no doubt of that.

SIR OLIVER: Then, upon my word, for a person in that situation, he is the most imprudent man alive—for here he comes, walking as if nothing at all were the matter.

(Enter SIR PETER TEAZLE.*)*

Odds heart, Sir Peter! you are come in good time, I promise you; for we had just *given you over*.

SIR BENJAMIN: Egad, uncle, this is the most sudden recovery!

SIR OLIVER: Why, man! what do you do out of bed with a small-sword through your body, and a bullet lodged in your thorax?

SIR PETER: A small-sword and a bullet?

SIR OLIVER: Aye; these gentlemen would have killed you without law or physic, and wanted to dub me a doctor—to make me an accomplice.

SIR PETER: Why, what is all this?

SIR BENJAMIN: We rejoice, Sir Peter, that the story of the duel is not true, and are sincerely sorry for your other misfortunes.

SIR PETER: So, so; all over the town already. *(aside)*

CRABTREE: Though, Sir Peter, you were certainly vastly to blame to marry at all, at your years.

SIR PETER: Sir, what business is that of yours?

MRS. CANDOUR: Though, indeed, as Sir Peter made so good a husband, he's very much to be pitied.

SIR PETER: Plague on your pity, ma'am! I desire none of it.

SIR BENJAMIN: However, Sir Peter, you must not mind the laughing and jests you will meet with on this occasion.

SIR PETER: Sir, I desire to be master in my own house.

CRABTREE: 'Tis no uncommon case, that's one comfort.

SIR PETER: I insist on being left to myself: without ceremony, I insist on your leaving my house directly!

MRS. CANDOUR: Well, well, we are going; and depend on't, we'll make the best report of you we can.

SIR PETER: Leave my house!

CRABTREE: And tell how hardly you have been treated.

SIR PETER: Leave my house!

SIR BENJAMIN: And how patiently you bear it.

SIR PETER: Fiends! vipers! furies! Oh! that their own venom would choke them!

(Exeunt MRS. CANDOUR, SIR BENJAMIN BACKBITE, CRABTREE, *etc.)*

SIR OLIVER: They are very provoking indeed, Sir Peter.

(Enter ROWLEY.*)*

ROWLEY: I heard high words—what has ruffled you, Sir Peter?

SIR PETER: Pshaw! what signifies asking? Do I ever pass a day without my vexations?

SIR OLIVER: Well, I'm not inquisitive—I come only to tell you that I have seen both my nephews in the manner we proposed.

SIR PETER: A precious couple they are!

ROWLEY: Yes, and Sir Oliver is convinced that your judgment was right, Sir Peter.

SIR OLIVER: Yes, I find *Joseph* is indeed the man, after all.

ROWLEY: Yes, as Sir Peter says, he's a man of sentiment.

SIR OLIVER: And acts up to the sentiments he professes.

ROWLEY: It certainly is edification to hear him talk.

SIR OLIVER: Oh, he's a model for the young men of the age! But how's this, Sir Peter? you don't join in your friend Joseph's praise, as I expected.

SIR PETER: Sir Oliver, we live in a damned wicked world, and the fewer we praise the better.

ROWLEY: What! do *you* say so, Sir Peter, who were never mistaken in your life?

SIR PETER: Pshaw! plague on you both! I see by your sneering you have heard the whole affair. I shall go mad among you!

ROWLEY: Then, to fret you no longer, Sir Peter, we are indeed acquainted with it all. I met Lady Teazle coming from Mr. Surface's, so humbled that she deigned to request me to be her advocate with you.

SIR PETER: And does Sir Oliver know all too?

SIR OLIVER: Every circumstance.

SIR PETER: What, of the closet—and the screen, hey?

SIR OLIVER: Yes, yes, and the little French milliner. Oh, I have been vastly diverted with the story! ha! ha!

SIR PETER: 'Twas very pleasant.

SIR OLIVER: I never laughed more in my life, I assure you: ha! ha!

SIR PETER: O, vastly diverting! ha! ha!

ROWLEY: To be sure, Joseph with his sentiments! ha! ha!

SIR PETER: Yes, yes, his sentiments! ha! ha! A hypocritical villain!

SIR OLIVER: Aye, and that rogue Charles to pull Sir Peter out of the closet: ha! ha!

SIR PETER: Ha! ha! 'twas devilish entertaining, to be sure!

SIR OLIVER: Ha! ha! Egad, Sir Peter, I should like to have seen your face when the screen was thrown down: ha! ha!

SIR PETER: Yes, yes, my face when the screen was thrown down: ha! ha! Oh, I must never show my head again!

SIR OLIVER: But come, come, it isn't fair to laugh at you neither, my old friend—though, upon my soul, I can't help it.

SIR PETER: Oh, pray don't restrain your mirth on my account—it does not hurt me at all! I laugh at the whole affair myself. Yes, yes, I think being a standing jest for all one's acquaintances a very happy situation. O yes, and then of a morning to read the paragraphs about Mr. S—, Lady T—, and Sir P—, will be so entertaining!

ROWLEY: Without affectation, Sir Peter, you may despise the ridicule of fools. But I see Lady Teazle going towards the next room; I am sure you must desire a reconciliation as earnestly as she does.

SIR OLIVER: Perhaps my being here prevents her coming to you. Well, I'll leave honest Rowley to mediate between you; but he must bring you all presently to Mr. Surface's, where I am not returning, if not to reclaim a libertine, at least to expose hypocrisy.

SIR PETER: Ah! I'll be present at your discovering yourself there with all my heart—though 'tis a vile unlucky place for discoveries!

ROWLEY: We'll follow. (*Exit* SIR OLIVER SURFACE.)

SIR PETER: She is not coming here, you see, Rowley.

ROWLEY: No, but she has left the door of that room open, you perceive. See, she is in tears!

SIR PETER: Certainly a little mortification appears very becoming in a wife! Don't you think it will do her good to let her pine a little?

ROWLEY: Oh, this is ungenerous in you!

SIR PETER: Well, I know not what to think. You remember, Rowley, the letter I found of hers, evidently intended for Charles!

ROWLEY: A mere forgery, Sir Peter! laid in your way on purpose. This is one of the points which I intend *Snake* shall give you conviction on.

SIR PETER: I wish I were once satisfied of that. She looks this way. What a remarkably elegant turn of the head she has! Rowley, I'll go to her.

ROWLEY: Certainly.

SIR PETER: Though, when it is known that we are reconciled, people will laugh at me ten times more!

ROWLEY: Let them laugh, and retort their malice only by showing them you are happy in spite of it.

SIR PETER: I'faith, so I will! and, if I'm not mistaken, we may yet be the happiest couple in the country.

ROWLEY: Nay, Sir Peter—he who once lays aside suspicion—

SIR PETER: Hold, my dear Rowley! if you have any regard for me, never let me hear you utter anything like a sentiment—I have had enough of them to serve me the rest of my life. (*Exeunt.*)

ACT 5 / SCENE 3

(*The library in* JOSEPH SURFACE'S *house*)
(JOSEPH SURFACE *and* LADY SNEERWELL.)

LADY SNEERWELL: Impossible! Will not Sir Peter immediately be reconciled to Charles, and of consequence no longer oppose his union with Maria? The thought is distraction to me!

JOSEPH SURFACE: Can passion furnish a remedy?

LADY SNEERWELL: No, nor cunning either. Oh, I was a fool, an idiot, to league with such a blunderer!

JOSEPH SURFACE: Sure, Lady Sneerwell, *I* am the greatest sufferer; yet you see I bear the accident with calmness.

LADY SNEERWELL: Because the disappointment doesn't reach your *heart*; your *interest* only attached you to Maria. Had you felt for *her* what *I* have for that ungrateful libertine, neither your temper nor hypocrisy could prevent your showing the sharpness of your vexation.

JOSEPH SURFACE: But why should your reproaches fall on *me* for this disappointment?

LADY SNEERWELL: Are you not the cause of it? What had you to do to bate in your pursuit of Maria to pervert Lady Teazle by the way? Had you not a sufficient field for your roguery in blinding Sir Peter, and supplanting your brother? I hate such an avarice of crimes; 'tis an unfair monopoly, and never prospers.

JOSEPH SURFACE: Well, I admit I have been to blame. I confess I deviated from the direct road of wrong, but I don't think we're so totally defeated neither.

LADY SNEERWELL: No!

JOSEPH SURFACE: You tell me you have made a trial of Snake since we met, and that you still believe him faithful to us—

LADY SNEERWELL: I do believe so.

JOSEPH SURFACE: And that he has undertaken, should it be necessary, to swear and prove that Charles is at this time contracted by vows and honor to your ladyship—which some of his former letters to you will serve to support?

LADY SNEERWELL: This, indeed, might have assisted.

JOSEPH SURFACE: Come, come; it is not too late yet.— *(Knocking at the door.)* But hark! this is probably my uncle, Sir Oliver: retire to that room; we'll consult farther when he's gone.

LADY SNEERWELL: Well! but if *he* should find you out too—

JOSEPH SURFACE: Oh, I have no fear of that. Sir Peter will hold his tongue for his own credit's sake— and you may depend on't I shall soon discover Sir Oliver's weak side!

LADY SNEERWELL: I have no diffidence of your abilities—only be constant to one roguery at a time. *(Exit.)*

JOSEPH SURFACE: I will, I will! So! 'tis confounded hard, after such bad fortune, to be baited by one's confederate in evil. Well, at all events, my character is so much better than Charles's, that I certainly—hey!—what!—this is not Sir Oliver, but old Stanley again! Plague on't! that he should return to leave me just now! We shall have Sir Oliver come and find him here—and—

(Enter SIR OLIVER SURFACE.)

Gad's life, Mr. Stanley, why have you come back to plague me just at this time? You must not stay now, upon my word.

SIR OLIVER: Sir, I hear your uncle Oliver is expected here, and though he has been so penurious to *you*, I'll try what he'll do for *me*.

JOSEPH SURFACE: Sir, 'tis impossible for you to stay now, so I must beg—Come any other time, and I promise you, you shall be assisted.

SIR OLIVER: No: Sir Oliver and I must be acquainted.

JOSEPH SURFACE: Zounds, sir! then I insist on your quitting the room directly.

SIR OLIVER: Nay, sir!

JOSEPH SURFACE: Sir, I insist on't!—Here, William! show this gentleman out. Since you compel me, sir—not one moment—this is such insolence! *(Going to push him out.)*

(Enter CHARLES SURFACE.)

CHARLES SURFACE: Heyday! what's the matter now? What the devil, have you got hold of my little broker here? Zounds, brother, don't hurt little Premium. What's the matter, my little fellow?

JOSEPH SURFACE: So! he has been with you, too, has he?

CHARLES SURFACE: To be sure he has! Why, 'tis as honest a little— but sure, Joseph, you have not been borrowing money too, have you?

JOSEPH SURFACE: Borrowing! no! But, brother, you know here we expect Sir Oliver every—

CHARLES SURFACE: O gad, that's true! Noll mustn't find the little broker here, to be sure.

JOSEPH SURFACE: Yet, Mr. Stanley insists—

CHARLES SURFACE: Stanley! why his name is Premium.

JOSEPH SURFACE: No, no, Stanley.

CHARLES SURFACE: No, no, Premium.

JOSEPH SURFACE: Well, no matter which—but—

CHARLES SURFACE: Aye, aye, Stanley or Premium, 'tis the same thing, as you say; for I suppose he goes by half a hundred names, besides A.B.'s° at the coffee houses.

JOSEPH SURFACE: Death! here's Sir Oliver at the door. *(Knocking again.)* Now I beg, Mr. Stanley—

CHARLES SURFACE: Aye, and I beg, Mr. Premium—

SIR OLIVER: Gentlemen—

JOSEPH SURFACE: Sir, by heaven you shall go!

CHARLES SURFACE: Aye, out with him, certainly.

SIR OLIVER: This violence—

JOSEPH SURFACE: 'Tis your own fault.

CHARLES SURFACE: Out with him, to be sure. *(Both forcing SIR OLIVER out.)*

(Enter SIR PETER and LADY TEAZLE, MARIA, and ROWLEY.)

SIR PETER: My old friend, Sir Oliver—hey! What in the name of wonder!—Here are dutiful nephews!—assault their uncle at the first visit!

LADY TEAZLE: Indeed, Sir Oliver, 'twas well we came in to rescue you.

A.B.'s, a reference to appointments at the coffee-houses made under concealed names.

ROWLEY: Truly it was; for I perceive, Sir Oliver, the character of old Stanley was no protection to you.

SIR OLIVER: Nor of Premium either: the necessities of the *former* could not extort a shilling from *that* benevolent gentleman; and now, egad, I stood a chance of faring worse than my ancestors, and being knocked down without being bid for.

(*After a pause,* JOSEPH *and* CHARLES *turning to each other.*)

JOSEPH SURFACE: Charles!

CHARLES SURFACE: Joseph!

JOSEPH SURFACE: 'Tis now complete!

CHARLES SURFACE: Very!

SIR OLIVER: Sir Peter, my friend, and Rowley too— look on that elder nephew of mine. You know what he has already received from my bounty; and you know also how gladly I would have regarded half my fortune as held in trust for him—judge, then, my disappointment in discovering him to be destitute of truth—charity—and gratitude!

SIR PETER: Sir Oliver, I should be more surprised at this declaration, if I had not myself found him selfish, treacherous, and hypocritical!

LADY TEAZLE: And if the gentleman pleads not guilty to these, pray let him call *me* to his character.

SIR PETER: Then, I believe, we need add no more.—If he knows himself, he will consider it as the most perfect punishment that he is known to the world.

CHARLES SURFACE (*aside*): If they talk this way to *Honesty,* what will they say to *me,* by and by?

(SIR PETER, LADY TEAZLE, *and* MARIA *retire.*)

SIR OLIVER: As for that prodigal, his brother, there—

CHARLES SURFACE (*aside*): Aye, now comes my turn: the damned family pictures will ruin me!

JOSEPH SURFACE: Sir Oliver!—uncle!—will you honor me with a hearing?

CHARLES SURFACE (*aside*): Now if Joseph would make one of his long speeches, I might recollect myself a little.

SIR OLIVER (*to* JOSEPH SURFACE): I suppose you would undertake to justify yourself entirely?

JOSEPH SURFACE: I trust I could.

SIR OLIVER: Pshaw!—Well, sir! and *you* (*to* CHARLES) could justify yourself too, I suppose?

CHARLES SURFACE: Not that I know of, Sir Oliver.

SIR OLIVER: What!—Little Premium has been let too much into the secret, I presume?

CHARLES SURFACE: True, sir; but they were family secrets, and should never be mentioned again, you know.

ROWLEY: Come, Sir Oliver, I know you cannot speak of Charles's follies with anger.

SIR OLIVER: Odd's heart, no more I can—nor with gravity either. Sir Peter, do you know the rogue bargained with me for all his ancestors—sold me judges and generals by the foot—and maiden aunts as cheap as broken china.

CHARLES SURFACE: To be sure, Sir Oliver, I did make a little free with the family canvas, that's the truth on't. My ancestors may certainly rise in evidence against me, there's no denying it; but believe me sincere when I tell you—and upon my soul I would not say it if I was not—that if I do not appear mortified at the exposure of my follies, it is because I feel at this moment the warmest satisfaction in seeing you, my liberal benefactor.

SIR OLIVER: Charles, I believe you. Give me your hand again; the ill-looking little fellow over the settee has made your peace.

CHARLES SURFACE: Then, sir, my gratitude to the original is still increased.

LADY TEAZLE (*pointing to* MARIA): Yet, I believe, Sir Oliver, here is one whom Charles is still more anxious to be reconciled to.

SIR OLIVER: Oh, I have heard of his attachment there; and, with the young lady's pardon, if I construe right—that blush—

SIR PETER: Well, child, speak your sentiments.

MARIA: Sir, I have little to say, but that I shall rejoice to hear that he is happy; for me, whatever claim I had to his affection, I willingly resign it to one who has a better title.

CHARLES SURFACE: How, Maria!

SIR PETER: Heyday! what's the mystery now? While he appeared an incorrigible rake, you would give your hand to no one else; and now that he is likely to reform, I warrant you won't have him.

MARIA: His own heart—and Lady Sneerwell know the cause.

CHARLES SURFACE: Lady Sneerwell!

JOSEPH SURFACE: Brother, it is with great concern I am obliged to speak on this point, but my regard to justice compels me, and Lady Sneerwell's injuries can no longer be concealed. (*Goes to the door.*)

(*Enter* LADY SNEERWELL.)

SIR PETER: So! another French milliner!—Egad, he has one in every room in the house, I suppose!

LADY SNEERWELL: Ungrateful Charles! Well may you be surprised, and feel for the indelicate situation which your perfidy has forced me into.

CHARLES SURFACE: Pray, uncle, is this another plot of yours? For, as I have life, I don't understand it.

JOSEPH SURFACE: I believe, sir, there is but the evidence of one person more necessary to make it extremely clear.

SIR PETER: And that person, I imagine, is Mr. Snake.—Rowley, you were perfectly right to bring him with us, and pray let him appear.

ROWLEY: Walk in, Mr. Snake.

(Enter SNAKE.)

I thought his testimony might be wanted; however, it happens unluckily, that he comes to confront Lady Sneerwell, and not to support her.

LADY SNEERWELL: Villain! Treacherous to me at last! (aside) —Speak, fellow, have you too conspired against me?

SNAKE: I beg your ladyship ten thousand pardons: you paid me extremely liberally for the lie in question; but I have unfortunately been offered double to speak the truth.

SIR PETER: Plot and counterplot, egad—I wish your ladyship joy of the success of your negotiation.

LADY SNEERWELL: The torments of shame and disappointment on you all!

LADY TEAZLE: Hold, Lady Sneerwell—before you go, let me thank you for the trouble you and that gentleman have taken, in writing letters to me from Charles, and answering them yourself; and let me also request you to make my respects to the Scandalous College, of which you are president, and inform them, that Lady Teazle, licentiate, begs leave to return the diploma they granted her, as she leaves off practice, and kills characters no longer.

LADY SNEERWELL: You too, madam!—provoking—insolent! May your husband live these fifty years! (Exit.)

SIR PETER: Oons! what a fury!

LADY TEAZLE: A malicious creature, indeed!

SIR PETER: Hey! not for her last wish?

LADY TEAZLE: Oh, no!

SIR OLIVER: Well, sir, and what have you to say now?

JOSEPH SURFACE: Sir, I am so confounded, to find that Lady Sneerwell could be guilty of suborning Mr. Snake in this manner, to impose on us all, that I know not what to say; however, lest her revengeful spirit should prompt her to injure my brother, I had certainly better follow her directly. (Exit.)

SIR PETER: Moral to the last drop!

SIR OLIVER: Aye, and marry her, Joseph, if you can.—Oil and vinegar, egad! you'll do very well together.

ROWLEY: I believe we have no more occasion for Mr. Snake at present.

SNAKE: Before I go, I beg pardon once for all, for whatever uneasiness I have been the humble instrument of causing to the parties present.

SIR PETER: Well, well, you have made atonement by a good deed at last.

SNAKE: But I must request of the company, that it shall never be known.

SIR PETER: Hey! what the plague! are you ashamed of having done a right thing once in your life?

SNAKE: Ah, sir—consider I live by the badness of my character—I have nothing but my infamy to depend on! and, if it were once known that I had been betrayed into an honest action, I should lose every friend I have in the world.

SIR OLIVER: Well, well—we'll not traduce you by saying anything in your praise, never fear. (Exit SNAKE.)

SIR PETER: There's a precious rogue! yet that fellow is a writer and a critic!

LADY TEAZLE: See, Sir Oliver, there needs no persuasion now to reconcile your nephew and Maria. (CHARLES and MARIA apart.)

SIR OLIVER: Aye, aye, that's as it should be, and, egad, we'll have the wedding to-morrow morning.

CHARLES SURFACE: Thank you, my dear uncle.

SIR PETER: What, you rogue! don't you ask the girl's consent first?

CHARLES SURFACE: Oh, I have done that a long time—above a minute ago—and she has looked yes.

MARIA: For shame, Charles!—I protest, Sir Peter, there has not been a word—

SIR OLIVER: Well, then, the fewer the better—may your love for each other never know abatement.

SIR PETER: And may you live as happily together as Lady Teazle and I—intend to do!

CHARLES SURFACE: Rowley, my old friend, I am sure you congratulate me; and I suspect that I owe you much.

SIR OLIVER: You do, indeed, Charles.

ROWLEY: If my efforts to serve you had not succeeded you would have been in my debt for the attempt—but deserve to be happy—and you overpay me.

SIR PETER: Aye, honest Rowley always said you would reform.

CHARLES SURFACE: Why as to reforming, Sir Peter, I'll make no promises, and that I take to be a proof that I intend to set about it.—But here shall be my monitor—my gentle guide.—Ah! can I leave the virtuous path those eyes illumine?

Though thou, dear maid, shouldst waive thy
    beauty's sway,
Thou still must rule, because I will obey:
An humbled fugitive from Folly view,
No sanctuary near but Love and—You;

(To the audience.)

> *You* can, indeed, each anxious fear remove.
> For even *Scandal* dies, if *you* approve.

FINIS

EPILOGUE
By George Colman°

(Spoken by LADY TEAZLE.*)*

I, who was late so volatile and gay,
Like a trade-wind must now blow all one way,
Bend all my cares, my studies, and my vows,
To one old rusty weathercock—my spouse!
So wills our virtuous bard—the motley Bayes°
Of crying epilogues and laughing plays!
   Old bachelors, who marry smart young wives,
Learn from our play to regulate your lives:
Each bring his dear to town, all faults upon her—
London will prove the very source of honor.
Plunged fairly in, like a cold bath it serves,
When principles relax, to brace the nerves.
   Such is my case;—and yet I might deplore
That the gay dream of dissipation's o'er;
And say, ye fair, was ever lively wife,
Born with a genius for the highest life,
Like me untimely blasted in her bloom,
Like me condemned to such a dismal doom?
Save money—when I just knew how to waste it!
Leave London—just as I began to taste it!
Must I then watch the early crowing cock,
The melancholy ticking of a clock;
In the lone rustic hall for ever pounded,
With dogs, cats, rats, and squalling brats surrounded?
With humble curates can I now retire,

(While good Sir Peter boozes with the squire,)
And at backgammon mortify my soul,
That pants for loo,° or flutters at a vole?°
Seven's the main!° Dear sound!—that must expire,
Lost at hot cockles,° round a Christmas fire!
The transient hour of fashion too soon spent,
Farewell the tranquil mind, farewell content!°
Farewell the plumèd head, the cushioned tête,
That takes the cushion from its proper seat!
That spirit-stirring drum!°—card drums I mean,
Spadille°—odd trick—pam°—basto°—king and
   queen!
And you, ye knockers, that, with brazen throat,
The welcome visitors' approach denote;
Farewell! all quality of high renown,
Pride, pomp, and circumstance of glorious town!
Farewell! your revels I partake no more,
And Lady Teazle's occupation's o'er!
All this I told our bard—he smiled, and said 'twas
   clear,
I ought to play deep tragedy next year.
Meanwhile he drew wise morals from his play,
And in these solemn periods stalked away:—
'Blest were the fair like you; her faults who stopped,
And closed her follies when the curtain dropped!
No more in vice or error to engage,
Or play the fool at large on life's great stage.

   George Colman, author of *The Jealous Wife.* *Bayes,*
poet, dramatist (from Bayes in *The Rehearsal*).

   loo, a favorite eighteenth-century game of cards. *flutters . . . vole,* winning all the tricks. *main,* in hazard, the caster of the dice "called his *main*" by naming a number from five to nine. *hot cockles,* "A play in which one kneels, and covering his eyes lays his head in another's lap and guesses who struck him." *Farewell . . . content,* These lines parody Othello's soliloquy, III, iii, 347–357. *drum,* Fashionable card-party. *Spadille,* the ace of spades. *pam,* the knave of clubs. *basto,* the ace of clubs.

Figure 45. Sir Benjamin Backbite (Eric Donkin, *center foreground*) recites one of his malicious epigrams to entertain Mrs. Candour (Jane Casson, *left*), Joseph Surface (Robin Gammell, *center background*), and Lady Sneerwell (Pat Galloway, *right*) in the Stratford Festival production of *The School for Scandal,* directed by Michael Langham and designed by Leslie Hurry, Stratford, Ontario, 1970. (Photograph: the Stratford Festival, Canada.)

Figure 46. Sir Peter Teazle (Stephen Murray) berates Lady Teazle (Helen Carey) for the extravagance of her fashionable inclinations in the Stratford Festival production of *The School for Scandal,* directed by Michael Langham and designed by Leslie Hurry, Stratford, Ontario, 1970. (Photograph: the Stratford Festival, Canada.)

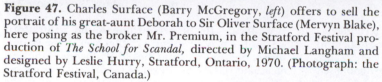

Figure 47. Charles Surface (Barry McGregory, *left*) offers to sell the portrait of his great-aunt Deborah to Sir Oliver Surface (Mervyn Blake), here posing as the broker Mr. Premium, in the Stratford Festival production of *The School for Scandal,* directed by Michael Langham and designed by Leslie Hurry, Stratford, Ontario, 1970. (Photograph: the Stratford Festival, Canada.)

Figure 48. Sir Peter Teazle (Stephen Murray, *left*) tries to prevent Charles (Barry MacGregor) from pulling away the screen that purportedly conceals Joseph's mistress in the Stratford Festival production of *The School for Scandal,* directed by Michael Langham and designed by Leslie Hurry, Stratford, Ontario, 1970. (Photograph: the Stratford Festival, Canada.)

Staging of *The School for Scandal*

INTERVIEW WITH MICHAEL LANGHAM,
DIRECTOR OF THE 1970 STRATFORD
PRODUCTION, BY BRADFORD S. FIELD, JR.

FIELD: I hear that *The School for Scandal* at Stratford was very successful.

LANGHAM: It was very well received, but, like all plays written for an eighteenth century theatre, rather difficult to arrange for a thrust stage like the one at Stratford.

FIELD: From the reviews you got you seem to have had no real trouble.

LANGHAM: Only technical problems, but it was a very confident production. We had a tone pitched at about the right level. We tried to avoid the usual icy artifice of most modern staging. It is clear to anyone who reads the play that the idiom of the language is not modern, but rather a special one.

FIELD: Wit, polish, repartee . . .

LANGHAM: Like that. It was written for an audience which had not yet lost the art of conversation. And the idiom affects everything else, the way one walks, for instance, was more a matter of displaying oneself than of getting from A to B in a straight line.

FIELD: Then you strove for some type of artifice, such as that in Restoration comedy.

LANGHAM: Yes and no. In the manner of speech and movement yes. The play itself imitates that earlier dramatic style. But by Sheridan's day that style was a century old. His play is in content not nearly so, ah, bumptious.

FIELD: How do you avoid a Restoration style when you do a play that imitates a Restoration style?

LANGHAM: It wasn't a Restoration style we sought to avoid, but modern versions of it. It's become a theatrical convention, you know, to suppose that since the language is so neat and precise in plays like these, that the society is, also.

FIELD: Then your production presented a society that was dirty?

LANGHAM: Not smutty, but soiled. Characters walked about with chickenshit on their boots. Their toilet facilities were primitive. For example, we began the play with only Snake on stage. Lady Sneerwell was off stage, shouting her lines. When she came in she was carrying an armful of gossip sheets, obviously having been sitting on the john. And that was only a beginning. She entered bald. We had a bald wig on her. And in her shift. During the rest of the scene we saw her gradual transformation as she dressed, and built up this fantastic facade. It was a good visual image, heavily impressed on the audience, to show how much *The School for Scandal* is about facades.

FIELD: You especially emphasized that point?

LANGHAM: Well, that's only one theme. Did you ever notice how much reference there is in the play to the loss of the American colonies?

FIELD: None, that I can remember.

LANGHAM: None at all. It was occurring right at that time, yet the play ignores it, as, I think, the Englishman of that time tended to do. Most interest was centered in the progress of the East India Company. That is where Sir Oliver returns from, India.

FIELD: Still, there has to be something in a play to interest a modern audience.

LANGHAM: Yes, well, the play is very funny, that's timeless enough.

FIELD: But lots of plays are funny. Why choose *The School for Scandal?*

LANGHAM: In the production we did at Stratford we saw the play revealing a changeover in the leadership of the country from the old aristocrats to the new merchant classes. Sir Oliver is a representative of that old class and tries to exemplify its virtues. And in the portrait scene, where all those old ancestors are being sold off without pity, we can see that changeover in a way just as striking as Lady Sneerwell's facades. The scene, as we played it, had almost a heartbreaking quality.

FIELD: Then your appeal to the modern audience is to show them the realistic basis of the action.

LANGHAM: Yes, the Teazle-plot fits that approach quite well. Lady Teazle was revealed as really from the country, but on the make, you know . . . oh, not just a bumpkin, more of a hoyden. Sir Peter we made not ludicrous but poignant, pointing out the dangers and difficulties of that kind of marriage.

FIELD: What was the most serious problem which you had to work out in staging this play?

LANGHAM: Well, I suppose I would have to say our greatest problem was a kind of North American infelicity with language!

FIELD: Surely not actors!

LANGHAM: Yes. In England the problem is not so serious. People in fact still do enjoy a tradition of facility of words and complicated phrasing; but over here, while the language, the tone, is much more open and direct, that's not much help in projecting the delicate facades that are offered by Sheridan's language. So we had some hard work to overcome that.

FIELD: Which scenes or characters in the play gave you more trouble than others?

LANGHAM: Sneerwell's role gave us problems because she reappears after such a long absence that we had to worry about re-establishing her character. Oh, there were some little things, too. In the last scene when it seems clear that Maria has won Charles—and Lady Sneerwell had had a secret lust for him—she goes for Maria's eyes with her nails. Charles holds her back and her wig falls off, revealing the hideous bald dome again. Well, in a theatre an audience often thinks that a wig's falling off must be a mistake. So we had to add some *further* business with everyone on stage re-acting with elaborate revulsion at the sight of her—to underscore the point that it was an intended part of the play.

FIELD: Were there parts that worked out better than you expected?

LANGHAM: Yes . . . the music, and the final moments . . . we finished the play with a tableau. We had a marvelous musical score by Stanley Silverman. In tone and style it ranged from 1776 then worked its way up to 1969 in the middle, and then back again, so at the end of the play the music—and the tone of the whole production—had returned to the tone of the eighteenth century. We sang a period song among the central characters as the scandal-mongers all leaned out from the wings to discover what they might overhear, and so we brought the cast on together for a final tableau.

REVIEW OF THE STRATFORD PRODUCTION, 1970, BY CLIVE BARNES

Gossip, malice and hypocrisy, like the poor, will always be with us, and therefore every production of Sheridan's exquisite comedy, "The School for Scandal," can hardly fail to be timely. Michael Langham's new production of the play seen for the first time at the Stratford Festival last night is more than timely, it is well-timed.

The rough vigor and dramatic ambiguity of the opening night's "Merchant of Venice" could be completely forgotten in the volatile brilliance of this "School for Scandal," which showed the company off to its best advantage.

This is such a good play, with all its plots and counterplots intermeshing like the parts of a watch, with Sheridan's timeless jokes as funny as ever, and with Sheridan's insight into his fellow beings as sharp as a surgeon's scalpel.

Two brothers—one the perfect hypocrite, the other a hellbent rake—are vying for both the good will of their rich uncle and the hand of an equally rich heiress. It is 18th-century fashionable London, a world dominated by tattle, appearances, costumes and money.

The conniving hypocrite, Joseph Surface, is exposed; the good-natured rake, Charles Surface, gets fortune, bride and reformation, and Sir Peter Teazle, guardian of the young heiress, obtains reconciliation with his young, and hitherto flighty, country wife, Lady Teazle. It all works merrily and morally enough, with wit and truth enough to spare for everyone.

Mr. Langham, who was director of the Stratford Festival from 1955 until 1967, has returned for the first time, and here gives Sheridan his due. In the past I have not always numbered myself among Mr. Langham's greatest admirers. He seemed too arch a disciple of that bad old Tyrone Guthrie school of directing, where every story had to tell a picture, while gimmickeries ran riot and devil take the playwright.

This "School for Scandal," however, seems to find Mr. Langham in a most un-Guthrie-like mood of clarity and simplicity. To be sure, he feels impelled to end the piece with a tableau of piercing irrelevance. Also for some reason, the jollifications of Charles and his friends are accompanied by a kind of thinly baroque version of rock music, which might perhaps be termed "Mr. Bach Goes to Rock," and is a little vulgar and obvious. Yet, for the rest I have nothing but praise.

What it seems that Mr. Langham has achieved is to persuade his cast to forget any preconceptions they may have about English high comedy style. As a result, not only is there a much more interesting, much more alive feel to the playing, but you also get actors actually playing roles such as Joseph Surface and Sir Peter, rather than actors playing Sir John Gielgud and Sir Ralph Richardson playing Joseph Surface and Sir Peter. It is an enormous difference.

And Mr. Langham himself, if I can say this without offering offense, appears a new man. Gone are those circular dances for his actors that he once seemed to find integral to staging on a thrust stage, gone are those exaggerations of character actors blinking knowingly through inches of make-up, and gone are most of the tricks and the foibles. This was a beautiful production.

The actors have responded. Robin Gammell's unctuous yet oddly not unattractive Joseph Surface is perfect in every glance and every inflection. He plays the role as if it were farce rather than comedy—it is a very pushing, physical performance—and the result is fresh and appealing. As the honest, if wayward, brother, Barry MacGregor shows just the right hazy generosity of spirit. More than in most productions, these two contrasting brothers (rather like Hogarth's "Idle and Industrious Apprentices" seen through Sheridan's more worldly eyes) become the focal point of the play as, I suspect, the playwright intended.

As a result of this focus, the fighting Teazles quite rightly step back a little into the play's mechanism. However, Stephen Murray's natural friendly and avuncular Sir Peter is a portrayal of great quality, and is matched by the girlish flightiness of Helen Carey as Lady Teazle.

Of the rest, there are many good performances, including those of the scandalous scholastics, Jane Casson, Bernard Behrens, Eric Donkin, Pat Galloway and Robin Marshall, and I liked also the bluffness of Mervyn Blake as Sir Oliver Surface and James Blendick as the faithful Rowley.

A fine evening, then, much aided by the handsome and stylish scenery and costumes by Leslie Hurry. Incidentally, and apropos of almost nothing, in the director's note given in the program, Mr. Langham reminds us all that the phrase "the silent majority" originated with Homer. The dear old Greek used it to describe the dead. It is amazing how many gaps in an education can be filled in by assiduous theatergoing.

MODERN THEATER

Modern drama, like modern painting and other forms of modern art, developed not in the twentieth century, as might be casually assumed, but during the nineteenth century, more than one hundred years ago. It was born out of a widespread reaction against the subject matters, forms, and methods of staging that had prevailed in many eighteenth and early nineteenth century plays—against aristocratic or exotic heroes and heroines, against the rigorous unities of a neoclassical tragedy or the flamboyant events of a romantic melodrama, against declamatory styles of acting or spectacular forms of setting. During the second half of the nineteenth century, such theatrical conventions came to be seen as being so far from the truth of ordinary experience that dramatists throughout Europe rejected them as unrealistic. "Reality," in turn, became a watchword among early modern dramatists, actors, directors, and set designers. Indeed, the realistic impulse in one form or another so heavily influenced theater through the first half of the twentieth century that the history of modern drama may well be understood in terms of the movements that grew out of realism, either as a refinement of it or as a reaction against it.

Realism in its most literal sense developed out of a desire to bring the stage into greater conformity with the surface details of ordinary human experience. This impulse first manifested itself in the efforts of set designers to create a full-scale visual illusion in the theater, to make the stage setting look like an interior place where ordinary people actually lived and worked—or, as one recent director has put it, to show "a real chair in a real setting." This concept of staging clearly required a set more visually plausible than the sliding wings and canvas backdrops of the neoclassical stage, which usually depicted doors and windows, sometimes even chairs, by means of perspective painting on the backdrop, instead of incorporating movable doors, windows, and furniture.

To create the illusion of a three-dimensional interior, nineteenth century set designers devised a set composed of flats arranged to form connected walls enclosing three sides of the stage, with the fourth wall removed so that the audience could look into a stage room that spatially seemed just like a real one. The realistic illusion of this stage design, known as the box set, was enhanced by movable windows and doors built into the walls of the back or side flats, as well as by false thickness pieces built into the window and door openings, which gave them an air of solidity. When the interior walls of the set were decorated and hung with fixtures, and when the floor space enclosed by the walls was equipped with rugs, furniture, and other props, the stage resembled a real room in every respect (see Figure 49). By the middle of the nineteenth century, the box set had been used in theaters throughout Europe, and its subsequent importance to the history of drama may be seen in the fact that detailed interiors figure prominently in almost all the plays written in the modern realistic tradition, such as Ibsen's *A Doll's House,* Strindberg's *Miss Julie,* Chekhov's *The Cherry Orchard,* Shaw's *Major Barbara,* Synge's *Playboy of the Western World,* and Lorca's *House of Bernarda Alba.*

The development of the box set took place during the same period as major

Figure 49. The box set decorated with wall and window hangings, as well as with furniture and props, to create the illusion of an actual room.

technological advances in lighting. Gaslights, as well as lime or calcium light, superseded oil lamps during the first half of the nineteenth century, making possible not only a greater degree of power and control in stage lighting, but also a variety of realistic effects, such as the illusion of sunlight, moonlight, or lamplight coming through doors and windows. During the second half of the nineteenth century, the invention of the carbon arc lamp and finally the incandescent lamp not only freed theaters from the terrible fire hazards of gaslights, but also encouraged directors and designers to invent elaborately realistic lighting effects.

Acting styles were slower to approximate the natural gestures, movements, and tones of voices appropriate to realistic staging, in part because the declamatory style of romantic acting was highly popular with audiences, but also because anything less pronounced would have been inadequate to make a clearly audible and visual impression in the cavernous theaters common during the late eighteenth century and much of the nineteenth. The auditoriums in these theaters were typically based on a design that was calculated to accommodate as large an audience as possible—sometimes as many as four thousand—with little concern for the needs of the actors or of the spectators. That design can readily be understood by first imagining a large cylinder at whose base is seated the majority of the audience, looking at a large opening that has been pierced in the cylinder to form the proscenium arch of the stage (see Figure 50). Then imagine that the builders or remodelers of such theaters, in order to fit in more paying spectators, hung balconies at four or five levels around the inside walls of the cylinder above the base (see Figure 51). Clearly, an actor or actress performing in these theaters had to develop an exaggerated style of movement, gesture, and intonation, to make an impact on the audience sitting in those balconies.

But during the late nineteenth and early twentieth centuries, theater architecture began to undergo significant modifications, which were intended to create better acoustical, visual, and spatial arrangements for actors and spectators. Cylindrical designs were gradually abandoned in favor of fan-shaped auditoriums with rising tiers of seats, all facing the stage (see Figure 52). In auditoriums based on this design—a design that now prevails in many commercial, community, and college theaters—the clear sightlines and favorable acoustics made it possible for performers to develop and use a more natural style of acting. And where theaters of this design were not available, directors and

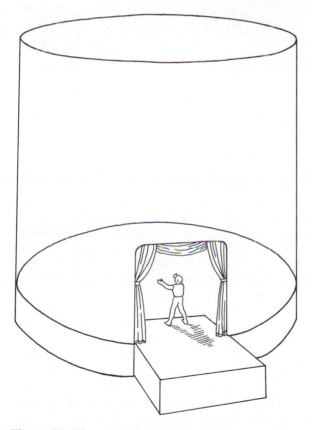

Figure 50. The cylindrical design of late eighteenth and early nineteenth century theaters.

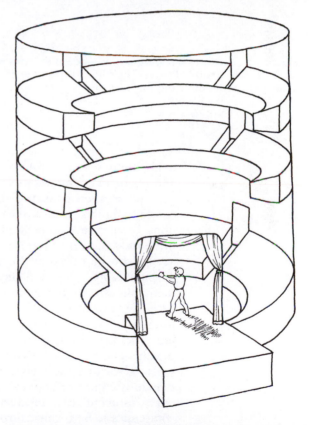

Figure 51. The cylindrically designed theater, showing multiple balconies remote from the actor on stage.

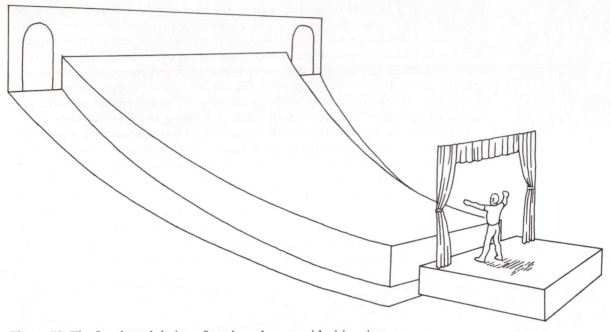

Figure 52. The fan-shaped design of modern theaters with rising tiers of seats, which provide clear sightlines for spectators and facilitate naturalistic styles of acting for performers.

performers who were committed to naturalistic styles of acting and production deliberately searched for small, intimate halls where they could set up a stage and perform in conditions suitable to their artistic beliefs.

The emergence during the late nineteenth century of repertory groups committed to naturalistic theater constitutes one of the most important contributions to the development of modern drama. One of the earliest and most influential figures in this repertory movement was André Antoine, an amateur actor, who in 1887 quit his job at the Paris Gas Company and founded the Théàtre Libre, a group dedicated to staging the plays of Ibsen, Strindberg, and their followers in meticulously naturalistic productions. Antoine's company was based on a principle, which nowadays is taken for granted but was then highly unusual, of integrating every aspect of production—costuming, setting, blocking, and acting—to create a totally unified illusion. Instead of seeking star performers, he worked to develop an ensemble of actors and actresses, painstakingly rehearsing them so that each performer was responsive not only to the demands of his or her individual role, but also to the needs of every other role at every moment in a production. Antoine's example quickly inspired similar companies to be formed throughout Europe and America.

The most well-known and influential organization to develop during the early repertory movement was the Moscow Art Theater, found in 1898 by Konstantin Stanislavsky, an amateur actor and director, and by Vladimir Nemirovich-

Danchenko, a successful playwright. The Moscow Art Theater achieved its early fame by producing the plays of Chekhov in a style that accentuated their emotional and psychological subtlety. This style entailed not only a detailed attention to elements of staging—including even the use of music to underline important emotional moments—but also a carefully defined method of acting, propounded by Stanislavsky, whose fundamental purpose was to create "the inner life of a human spirit." Stanislavsky's method, which he subsequently expounded in several highly influential books—among them *My Life in Art* (1924) and *An Actor Prepares* (1926)—required actors to think "about the inner side of a role, and how to create its spiritual life through the help of the internal process of living the part. You must live it by actually experiencing feelings that are analogous to it, each and every time you repeat the process of creating it." The illusion of reality, as Stanislavsky defined it, depended on using the theater to dramatize not simply the external but, more important, the internal condition of human experience.

Stanislavsky's emphasis on the "inner side of a role," on "living the part," would have been impossible without dramatic roles that called for such an approach, without plays that offer probing studies of psychologically complex characters in complex social, domestic, and personal situations. In this profound sense, realistic and naturalistic drama originated not from an interest in representing the surface details, the literal image, of human activity, but out of a concern with reflecting the environmental and psychological conditions that account for the problematic quality of ordinary human experience. In this sense Ibsen is often considered the "father" of modern drama. Beginning in 1877, for example, Ibsen wrote a series of realistic "problem" plays, in which he systematically shattered popular illusions about such then sacred institutions as marriage and religion—plays in which he showed the inner life of his characters as they come to recognize the painful realities of their personal situations. Chekhov dramatized a similar kind of experience in his turn of the century plays, though he presented his characters as being at once comic, pitiable, and admirably human in their futile efforts to overcome both the romantic illusions and the banal necessities of their existence. Strindberg exposed even harsher realities in his naturalistic dramatizations of the sexual antagonism between men and women.

In portraying characters, the early modern dramatists relied not only on the psychological nuances of dialogue and action, but also on the emblematic significances of the box set itself, for its detailed interiors may be seen as tangibly revealing not only a particular place in which the characters exist, but also exposing the quality of their existence. In *A Doll's House,* for example, the setting called for in Ibsen's stage directions—a room cluttered with bric-a-brac and overstuffed chairs—is as stifling and deceiving as the marriage of Nora and Helmer. In Chekhov's *The Cherry Orchard,* the cozy nursery where the play begins and ends is an emblem of the childish and irrepressibly romantic illusions that govern the thoughts of Ranevskaya and Gayev and that make them incapable of coming to terms with the changing society around them. And in *Miss Julie,* the kitchen, which constitutes the setting for the entire play, is a continual reminder of the cultural and psychological servitude that Jean, the valet, is bent on overthrowing.

The realism of box sets and the naturalism of psychologically motivated characters, though dramatically compelling, did not go unchallenged, even during the early period of modern drama. By the turn of the century, various anti-realistic tendencies—known as symbolism, expressionism, and surrealism—had already taken form in the critical statements and plays of *avant-garde* dramatists. Proponents of these counterrealistic movements argued that dramatic truth was not to be found in the tangible surfaces of a box set nor even in the intangible life of a psychologically complex character, but in symbols, images, legends, myths, fantasies, dreams, and other mysterious manifestations of spirituality, subjectivity, or the unconscious. Symbolists, for example, claimed the existence of a higher truth than was evident in external reality, and they aimed to create in the theater a mysterious and quasi-religious experience. Expressionists believed that truth existed not in the external appearance of reality but in the subjective perception of reality, no matter how psychologically distorted that perception might be, and they often sought to dramatize how the world appears to a disturbed and convulsive mind. Surrealists claimed that truth was to be found not in the logic of everyday events but in the irrational processes of the unconscious mind, and they tried to recreate the strange combinations of the familiar and the mysterious that often take place in dreams.

From a late twentieth century perspective, these various anti-realistic tendencies now seem commonplace, but in their own day they were revolutionary, and they attracted not only experimental writers, but major dramatists who had already established themselves as masters of realistic and naturalistic drama. Ibsen's late plays, especially *The Lady from the Sea* (1888) and *When We Dead Awaken* (1899) are manifestly symbolic not only in their titles but also in their settings and in their action. Although Strindberg began by writing such naturalistic plays as *The Father* (1887) and *Miss Julie* (1888), he later turned to the fantasy world of *A Dream Play* (1901) and the haunting, personal symbolism of *The Ghost Sonata* (1907). Even Shaw, so thoroughly committed to a theater of intellectual and social realism, wrote a five-play parable set in the Garden of Eden, Mesopotamia, as well as England both in his own time and the future in *Back to Methusaleh* (1920). For the American playwright O'Neill, symbolic and expressionistic drama came early in his career rather than at the end, in the psychologically distorted perceptions of *The Emperor Jones* (1920), the symbolic events of *The Hairy Ape* (1922), and the expressionistic symbols of *The Great God Brown* (1926).

Symbolic drama of the early modern period was mirrored in a variety of staging techniques that were often intentionally designed to obliterate any hint of a realistic environment. In France, the main exponent of symbolist staging was Aurelien-Marie Lugné-Poe, who established an avant-garde repertory group, known as the Théàtre de l'Oeuvre, which was dedicated to the production of symbolist plays. In Lugné-Poe's productions, scenery was often reduced to painted, abstract backdrops; props and furniture were often minimal or non-existent; lighting was often minimal and dispersed instead of focussed; and actors strived to evoke a mood rather than to reveal psychological motivation. Expressionistic stagings, which were largely developed in German theater during the 1920s, replaced representational settings with expressively stylized backdrops, showing exterior or interior locations that had been distorted and exaggerated in color and shape; lighting was often harshly focussed or nervously scattered; and actors strived through disjointed movements and telegraphic speech patterns to evoke human behavior as it might be perceived by a psychologically convulsive personality. Surrealistic stagings, which were launched by Antonin Artaud and André Breton in Parisian theaters of the 1920s, pushed productions even further toward expressive abstraction in backdrops, costumes, lighting, and acting styles.

By the end of the twenties, these counterrealistic movements, though polemically extreme in their practices, had worked substantial changes in the style of drama and of theatrical production—changes that resulted in a synthesis of realistic and naturalistic methods with symbolic, expressionistic, or surrealistic techniques. The power of such a synthesis was convincingly displayed in the work of Bertolt Brecht, the major German playwright and director of the twentieth century. From the 1920s through the early 1950s, Brecht wrote an extensive series of plays that were simultaneously realistic in their depiction of human motives and values, expressionistic in their episodic structure, and politically explicit in their ideology. And he created stagings for his plays with the Berliner Ensemble, which used realistic costumes and set pieces combined with an abstract backdrop, visible lighting instruments, visible scene changing, and scene titles or other messages projected onto the backdrop. By means of this synthesis, Brecht aimed both to engage an audience in the situation of his characters and to distance them sufficiently so that they would be provoked to think about its social and political implications. Once Brecht had established the theatrical power of such a synthesis, it gradually came to be a dominant approach in serious theater of the twentieth century. And by the time Arthur Miller's *Death of a Salesman* opened on Broadway in 1949 with a striking combination of naturalistic and expressionistic effects, the mixture of styles evoked almost no comment at all.

HENRIK IBSEN

1828–1906

When Ibsen was born, his father was a prosperous merchant in Skien, a small town in the southeastern part of Norway, but by the time Ibsen was eight his father had gone bankrupt and the family was compelled to leave its spacious home for quarters in an attic apartment filled with the abandoned possessions of a previous tenant. Ibsen never forgot that painful reversal of fortune. In fact, he recorded its details in an unfinished autobiography that he began in 1881. That early exposure to human suffering was to leave its mark on many of his plays, not in any specific autobiographical sense, but in a general concern with the economic, social, and psychological conditions that afflict the lives of ordinary men and women.

During his early dramatic career, from 1851 to 1867, when he was still influenced by the style and subject matter of romantic theater, Ibsen wrote a series of plays in blank verse, most of them based on Norwegian myth and history. Yet even in these works, particularly *Brand* (1866) and *Peer Gynt* (1867), Ibsen revealed a concern with moral and social issues that was to characterize his later plays. In Brand he created a protagonist so single-mindedly committed to his religious ministry that he sacrifices first his child, then his wife, and ultimately himself to the fulfillment of his mission; then in the character of Peer Gynt, the demonic antithesis of Brand, he created a protagonist so committed to his own selfish desires that he devotes his life to a series of fanatically deceitful adventures with which he deceives even himself, until at the moment of his death he discovers his irredeemable hollowness. Although *Brand* and *Peer Gynt* made Ibsen famous and financially secure, they were the last works he was to write in the tradition of romantic drama.

Beginning with *The League of Youth* (1869), a play that attacked the hypocrisy of provincial politics and politicians, Ibsen turned from history, myth, and folklore to contemporary social problems, from romantic idealism to realistic drama, from verse to prose. In *The Pillars of Society* (1877), he continued his iconoclastic aims by exposing the disreputable behavior of a socially respectable businessman and by reforming him through the agency of a socially liberated woman. Having attacked business and politics, he then went after the most sacred of all social institutions—marriage—by making the heroine of this next play, *A Doll's House* (1879), a young wife who gradually becomes aware that she has been turned into a helpless child by her husband, whom she abandons after discovering that he is an emotional hypocrite. Ibsen's audience was shocked by the ending of *A Doll's House,* but he was unrelenting in his attack and answered their outrage with *Ghosts* (1881), whose heroine heeds the advice of her minister to remain with her husband and, therefore, must spend the rest of her life concealing her own feelings and the truth about her husband's dissolute behavior. Ibsen's frank treatment of syphilis in *Ghosts,* and his implicit attack on Norwegian social and religious values, roused even stronger criticism than *A Doll's House*. It is not surprising that Ibsen's next play, *An Enemy of the People*

(1882), dealt with the difficulty of being the outsider who brings unpleasant truths to the attention of the community. Then, in a startling reversal, Ibsen made the truth bringer in *The Wild Duck* (1884) a morally ambiguous figure, so intent on forcing long-hid secrets into the open that he destroys an entire family. In his late, symbolic plays, particularly *Rosmersholm* (1886), *Hedda Gabler* (1890), and *The Master Builder* (1892), Ibsen moved away from his concern with social problems into a psychological exploration of emotionally and sexually driven individuals who become entangled in self-destructive personal relationships.

This body of plays quickly earned Ibsen the reputation of a fighting social realist—a description applied to him by his Anglo-Irish contemporary, George Bernard Shaw, in *The Quintessence of Ibsenism* (1891). And from his own time to this day, many of Ibsen's prose plays have been interpreted primarily as pieces of social criticism. *A Doll's House,* for example, is frequently celebrated nowadays as an attack on male chauvinism and an affirmation of womens' rights. And there is much about the relationship of Torvald and Nora that supports this interpretation, not the least of which is his nearly total subjugation and humiliation of her—his conception of her as his "little songbird" and "doll"—as well as her final rejection of his belief that "First and foremost, you're a wife and a mother," and her consequent decision "to think things out for myself and try to find my own answer." Yet it is also important to recognize that *A Doll's House,* like Ibsen's other prose plays, is first and foremost a psychologically realistic work about a human being in an ordinary world who slowly and painfully comes to an extraordinary understanding about the importance of personal integrity in human affairs. That special understanding leads Nora to assert that "I am first and foremost a human being." And that belief leads her at last to leave Torvald not because he has subjugated her, but because he has profoundly disappointed her by valuing his material welfare and social status more highly than her human love. So it is that she is moved to tell Torvald "you neither think nor talk like the man I could share my life with." The implication of these remarks seems to be that she could have forgiven him everything had he finally been true to her hopeful vision of him. Her departure, then, might well be seen as the logical consequence of her shattered illusions about Torvald, rather than an assertion of her woman's rights.

Ibsen himself may well have meant to show both Nora and Torvald as being imprisoned in their relationship, even though for years the play has been read as his plea for female emancipation. Ibsen explicitly disclaimed a feminist interpretation of the play several years after its production, when speaking to a meeting of the Norwegian Association for Women's Rights: "I must decline the honor of being said to have worked for the Women's Rights movement. I am not even very sure what Women's Rights are. To me it has been a question of human rights." Given Ibsen's disclaimer, the play might well be interpreted as a skillfully constructed piece that begins as a suspense story (Will Nora be able to keep Torvald from learning her guilty secret?), but develops into a painfully probing exposure of a human relationship based on misunderstanding and lack of communication, a relationship that denies both individuals their human rights. As Nora accurately observes near the end, "In eight whole years—longer even—ever since we first met, we've never exchanged a serious word on any serious thing." The problem of the play, in this sense, appears to be less an issue of Nora's rights than the issue of what a marriage must be if it is to achieve the "miracle of miracles"—a true and lasting relationship that allows both partners their human rights.

Just the same, readers and spectators may find themselves troubled by the plausibility of Nora's transformation from a naive young wife into a resolutely independent human being—from someone who at the beginning of the play is given over to relishing her macaroons, begging money from Torvald, and flirting with Dr. Rank into someone who at the end is able to abandon all of these comfortable pleasures, as well as her children, without having any "idea what will happen to me." This transformation provides a major problem for any actress who plays the role of Nora, as Walter Kerr noted in his review of the 1971 production starring Claire Bloom: "How does one turn an enchanting child into a dominating adult, especially when the transition is missing?" To do so, as Kerr makes clear in his review, evidently requires an actress to convey more than mere childishness in the beginning, even as it requires her to convey something other than mere domination at the end. And photographs of Claire Bloom performing the role of Nora show that in the beginning of the play she did suggest a degree of thoughtful reservation far exceeding that of a child (see Figure 53), much as at the end of the play she expressed a sense of painful awareness and resoluteness not to be expected of a merely dominating adult (see Figures 54 and 55). In her facial expression, as in the austere clothing she wears during the final scene, Claire Bloom portrays Nora as someone who is clearly aware that in slamming the door on Torvald she has relinquished a set of emotional ties that still tug at her without any clear sense of what will become of her.

A DOLL'S HOUSE

BY HENRIK IBSEN / TRANSLATED BY MICHAEL MEYER

CHARACTERS

TORVALD HELMER, *a lawyer*
NORA, *his wife*
DR. RANK
MRS. LINDE
NILS KROGSTAD, *also a lawyer*
The HELMERS' *three small children*

ANNE-MARIE, *their nurse*
HELEN, *the maid*
A PORTER

SCENE

The action takes place in the Helmers' apartment.

ACT 1

(A comfortably and tastefully, but not expensively furnished room. Backstage right a door leads out to the hall; backstage left, another door to HELMER'S *study. Between these two doors stands a piano. In the middle of the left-hand wall is a door, with a window downstage of it. Near the window, a round table with armchairs and a small sofa. In the right-hand wall, slightly upstage, is a door; downstage of this, against the same wall, a stove lined with porcelain tiles, with a couple of armchairs and a rocking-chair in front of it. Between the stove and the side door is a small table. Engravings on the wall. A what-not with china and other bric-a-brac; a small bookcase with leather-bound books. A carpet on the floor; a fire in the stove. A winter day.*

A bell rings in the hall outside. After a moment, we hear the front door being opened. NORA *enters the room, humming contentedly to herself. She is wearing outdoor clothes and carrying a lot of parcels, which she puts down on the table right. She leaves the door to the hall open; through it, we can see a* PORTER *carrying a Christmas tree and a basket. He gives these to the Maid, who has opened the door for them.)*

NORA: Hide that Christmas tree away, Helen. The children mustn't see it before I've decorated it this evening. *(to the* PORTER, *taking out her purse)* How much—?

PORTER: A shilling.

NORA: Here's half a crown. No, keep it.

(The PORTER *touches his cap and goes.* NORA *closes the door. She continues to laugh happily to herself as she removes her coat, etc. She takes from her pocket a bag containing macaroons and eats a couple. Then she tiptoes across and listens at her husband's door.)*

NORA: Yes, he's here. *(Starts humming again as she goes over to the table, right.)*

HELMER *(from his room)*: Is that my skylark twittering out there?

NORA *(opening some of the parcels)*: It is!

HELMER: Is that my squirrel rustling?

NORA: Yes!

HELMER: When did my squirrel come home?

NORA: Just now. *(Pops the bag of macaroons in her pocket and wipes her mouth.)* Come out here, Torvald, and see what I've bought.

HELMER: You mustn't disturb me! *(Short pause, then he opens the door and looks in, his pen in his hand.)* Bought, did you say? All that? Has my little squanderbird been overspending again?

NORA: Oh, Torvald, surely we can let ourselves go a little this year! It's the first Christmas we don't have to scrape.

HELMER: Well, you know, we can't afford to be extravagant.

NORA: Oh yes, Torvald, we can be a little extravagant now. Can't we? Just a tiny bit? You've got a big salary now, and you're going to make lots and lots of money.

HELMER: Next year, yes. But my new salary doesn't start till April.

NORA: Pooh; we can borrow till then.

HELMER: Nora! *(Goes over to her and takes her playfully by the ear.)* What a little spendthrift you are! Suppose I were to borrow fifty pounds today, and you spent it all over Christmas, and then on New Year's Eve a tile fell off a roof on to my head—

NORA *(puts her hand over his mouth)*: Oh, Torvald! Don't say such dreadful things!

HELMER: Yes, but suppose something like that did happen? What then?

NORA: If anything as frightful as that happened, it wouldn't make much difference whether I was in debt or not.

HELMER: But what about the people I'd borrowed from?

NORA: Them? Who cares about them? They're strangers.

HELMER: Oh, Nora, Nora, how like a woman! No, but seriously, Nora, you know how I feel about this. No debts! Never borrow! A home that is founded on debts can never be a place of freedom and beauty. We two have stuck it out

520

bravely up to now; and we shall continue to do so for the short time we still have to.

NORA *(goes over toward the stove)*: Very well, Torvald. As you say.

HELMER *(follows her)*: Now, now! My little songbird mustn't droop her wings. What's this? Is little squirrel sulking? *(Takes out his purse.)* Nora; guess what I've got here!

NORA *(turns quickly)*: Money!

HELMER: Look. *(Hands her some banknotes.)* I know how these small expenses crop up at Christmas.

NORA *(counts them)*: One—two—three—four. Oh, thank you, Torvald, thank you! I should be able to manage with this.

HELMER: You'll have to.

NORA: Yes, yes, of course I will. But come over here, I want to show you everything I've bought. And so cheaply! Look, here are new clothes for Ivar—and a sword. And a horse and a trumpet for Bob. And a doll and a cradle for Emmy—they're nothing much, but she'll pull them apart in a few days. And some bits of material and handker-chiefs for the maids. Old Anne-Marie ought to have had something better, really.

HELMER: And what's in that parcel?

NORA *(cries)*: No, Torvald, you mustn't see that before this evening!

HELMER: Very well. But now, tell me, you little spendthrift, what do you want for Christmas?

NORA: Me? Oh, pooh, I don't want anything.

HELMER: Oh, yes, you do. Now tell me, what, within reason, would you most like?

NORA: No, I really don't know. Oh, yes—Torvald—!

HELMER: Well?

NORA *(plays with his coat-buttons, not looking at him)*: If you really want to give me something, you could—you could—

HELMER: Come on, out with it.

NORA *(quickly)*: You could give me money, Torvald. Only as much as you feel you can afford; then later I'll buy something with it.

HELMER: But, Nora—

NORA: Oh yes, Torvald dear, please! Please! Then I'll wrap up the notes in pretty gold paper and hang them on the Christmas tree. Wouldn't that be fun?

HELMER: What s the name of that little bird that can never keep any money?

NORA: Yes, yes, squanderbird; I know. But let's do as I say, Torvald; then I'll have time to think about what I need most. Isn't that the best way? Mm?

HELMER *(smiles)*: To be sure it would be, if you could keep what I gave you and really buy yourself something with it. But you'll spend it on all sorts of useless things for the house, and then I'll have to put my hand in my pocket again.

NORA: Oh, but Torvald—

HELMER: You can't deny it, Nora dear. *(Puts his arm round her waist.)* The squanderbird's a pretty little creature, but she gets through an awful lot of money. It's incredible what an expensive pet she is for a man to keep.

NORA: For shame! How can you say such a thing? I save every penny I can.

HELMER *(laughs)*: That's quite true. Every penny you can. But you can't.

NORA *(hums and smiles, quietly gleeful)*: Hm. If you only knew how many expenses we larks and squirrels have, Torvald.

HELMER: You're a funny little creature. Just like your father used to be. Always on the look-out for some way to get money, but as soon as you have any it just runs through your fingers, and you never know where it's gone. Well, I suppose I must take you as you are. It's in your blood. Yes, yes, yes, these things are hereditary, Nora.

NORA: Oh, I wish I'd inherited more of Papa's qual-ities.

HELMER: And I wouldn't wish my darling little songbird to be any different from what she is. By the way, that reminds me. You look awfully—how shall I put it?—awfully guilty today.

NORA: Do I—

HELMER: Yes, you do. Look me in the eyes.

NORA *(looks at him)*: Well?

HELMER *(wags his finger)*: Has my little sweet-tooth been indulging herself in town today, by any chance?

NORA: No, how can you think of such a thing?

HELMER: Not a tiny little digression into a pastry shop?

NORA: No, Torvald, I promise—

HELMER: Not just a wee jam tart?

NORA: Certainly not.

HELMER: Not a little nibble at a macaroon?

NORA: No, Torvald—I promise you, honestly—

HELMER: There, there. I was only joking.

NORA *(goes over to the table, right)*: You know I could never act against your wishes.

HELMER: Of course not. And you've given me your word—*(Goes over to her.)* Well, my beloved Nora, you keep your little Christmas secrets to your-self. They'll be revealed this evening, I've no doubt, once the Christmas tree has been lit.

NORA: Have you remembered to invite Dr. Rank?

HELMER: No. But there's no need; he knows he'll be dining with us. Anyway, I'll ask him when he comes this morning. I've ordered some good wine. Oh, Nora, you can't imagine how I'm looking forward to this evening.

NORA: So am I. And, Torvald, how the children will love it!

HELMER: Yes, it's a wonderful thing to know that one's position is assured and that one has an ample income. Don't you agree? It's good to know that, isn't it?

NORA: Yes, it's almost like a miracle.

HELMER: Do you remember last Christmas? For three whole weeks you shut yourself away every evening to make flowers for the Christmas tree, and all those other things you were going to surprise us with. Ugh, it was the most boring time I've ever had in my life.

NORA: I didn't find it boring.

HELMER (smiles): But it all came to nothing in the end, didn't it?

NORA: Oh, are you going to bring that up again? How could I help the cat getting in and tearing everything to bits?

HELMER: No, my poor little Nora, of course you couldn't. You simply wanted to make us happy, and that's all that matters. But it's good that those hard times are past.

NORA: Yes, it's wonderful.

HELMER: I don't have to sit by myself and be bored. And you don't have to tire your pretty eyes and your delicate little hands—

NORA (claps her hands): No, Torvald, that's true, isn't it—I don't have to any longer? Oh, it's really all just like a miracle. (Takes his arm.) Now, I'm going to tell you what I thought we might do, Torvald. As soon as Christmas is over—(A bell rings in the hall.) Oh, there's the doorbell. (Tidies up one or two things in the room.) Someone's coming. What a bore.

HELMER: I'm not at home to any visitors. Remember!

MAID (in the doorway): A lady's called, madam. A stranger.

NORA: Well, ask her to come in.

MAID: And the doctor's here too, sir.

HELMER: Has he gone to my room?

MAID: Yes, sir.

(HELMER goes into his room. The MAID shows in MRS. LINDE, who is dressed in travelling clothes, and closes the door.)

MRS. LINDE (shyly and a little hesitantly): Good evening, Nora.

NORA (uncertainly): Good evening—

MRS. LINDE: I don't suppose you recognize me.

NORA: No, I'm afraid I— Yes, wait a minute— surely—(Exclaims.) Why, Christine! Is it really you?

MRS. LINDE: Yes, it's me.

NORA: Christine! And I didn't recognize you! But how could I—? (More quietly.) How you've changed, Christine!

MRS. LINDE: Yes, I know. It's been nine years—nearly ten—

NORA: Is it so long? Yes, it must be. Oh, these last eight years have been such a happy time for me!

So you've come to town? All that way in winter! How brave of you!

MRS. LINDE: I arrived by the steamer this morning.

NORA: Yes, of course—to enjoy yourself over Christmas. Oh, how splendid! We'll have to celebrate! But take off your coat. You're not cold, are you? (Helps her off with it.) There! Now let's sit down here by the stove and be comfortable. No, you take the armchair. I'll sit here in the rocking-chair. (Clasps MRS. LINDE's hands.) Yes, now you look like your old self. It was just at first that— you've got a little paler, though, Christine. And perhaps a bit thinner.

MRS. LINDE: And older, Nora. Much, much older.

NORA: Yes, perhaps a little older. Just a tiny bit. Not much. (Checks herself suddenly and says earnestly.) Oh, but how thoughtless of me to sit here and chatter away like this! Dear, sweet Christine, can you forgive me?

MRS. LINDE: What do you mean, Nora?

NORA (quietly): Poor Christine, you've become a widow.

MRS. LINDE: Yes. Three years ago.

NORA: I know, I know—I read it in the papers. Oh, Christine, I meant to write to you so often, honestly. But I always put it off, and something else always cropped up.

MRS. LINDE: I understand, Nora dear.

NORA: No, Christine, it was beastly of me. Oh, my poor darling, what you've gone through! And he didn't leave you anything?

MRS. LINDE: No.

NORA: No children, either?

MRS. LINDE: No.

NORA: Nothing at all, then?

MRS. LINDE: Not even a feeling of loss or sorrow.

NORA (looks incredulously at her): But, Christine, how is that possible?

MRS. LINDE (smiles sadly and strokes NORA's hair): Oh, these things happen, Nora.

NORA: All alone. How dreadful that must be for you. I've three lovely children. I'm afraid you can't see them now, because they're out with nanny. But you must tell me everything—

MRS. LINDE: No, no, no. I want to hear about you.

NORA: No, you start. I'm not going to be selfish today. I'm just going to think about you. Oh, but there's one thing I must tell you. Have you heard of the wonderful luck we've just had?

MRS. LINDE: No. What?

NORA: Would you believe it—my husband's just been made manager of the bank!

MRS. LINDE: Your husband? Oh, how lucky—!

NORA: Yes, isn't it? Being a lawyer is so uncertain, you know, especially if one isn't prepared to touch any case that isn't—well—quite nice. And of course Torvald's been very firm about that—and

I'm absolutely with him. Oh, you can imagine how happy we are! He's joining the bank in the New Year, and he'll be getting a big salary, and lots of percentages too. From now on we'll be able to live quite differently—we'll be able to do whatever we want. Oh, Christine, it's such a relief! I feel so happy! Well, I mean, it's lovely to have heaps of money and not to have to worry about anything. Don't you think?

MRS. LINDE: It must be lovely to have enough to cover one's needs, anyway.

NORA: Not just our needs! We're going to have heaps and heaps of money!

MRS. LINDE (smiles): Nora, Nora, haven't you grown up yet? When we were at school you were a terrible little spendthrift.

NORA (laughs quietly): Yes, Torvald still says that. (Wags her finger.) But "Nora, Nora" isn't as silly as you think. Oh, we've been in no position for me to waste money. We've both had to work.

MRS. LINDE: You too?

NORA: Yes, little things—fancy work, crocheting, embroidery and so forth. (Casually.) And other things too. I suppose you know Torvald left the Ministry when we got married? There were no prospects for promotion in his department, and of course he needed more money. But the first year he overworked himself quite dreadfully. He had to take on all sorts of extra jobs, and worked day and night. But it was too much for him, and he became frightfully ill. The doctors said he'd have to go to a warmer climate.

MRS. LINDE: Yes, you spent a whole year in Italy, didn't you?

NORA: Yes. It wasn't easy for me to get away, you know. I'd just had Ivar. But of course we had to do it. Oh, it was a marvelous trip! And it saved Torvald's life. But it cost an awful lot of money, Christine.

MRS. LINDE: I can imagine.

NORA: Two hundred and fifty pounds. That's a lot of money, you know.

MRS. LINDE: How lucky you had it.

NORA: Well, actually, we got it from my father.

MRS. LINDE: Oh, I see. Didn't he die just about that time?

NORA: Yes, Christine, just about then. Wasn't it dreadful, I couldn't go and look after him. I was expecting little Ivar any day. And then I had my poor Torvald to care for—we really didn't think he'd live. Dear, kind Papa! I never saw him again, Christine. Oh, it's the saddest thing that's happened to me since I got married.

MRS. LINDE: I know you were very fond of him. But you went to Italy—?

NORA: Yes. Well, we had the money, you see, and the doctors said we mustn't delay. So we went the

month after Papa died.

MRS. LINDE: And your husband came back completely cured?

NORA: Fit as a fiddle!

MRS. LINDE: But—the doctor?

NORA: How do you mean?

MRS. LINDE: I thought the maid said that the gentleman who arrived with me was the doctor.

NORA: Oh yes, that's Doctor Rank, but he doesn't come because anyone's ill. He's our best friend, and he looks us up at least once every day. No, Torvald hasn't had a moment's illness since we went away. And the children are fit and healthy and so am I. (Jumps up and claps her hands.) Oh God, oh God, Christine, isn't it a wonderful thing to be alive and happy! Oh, but how beastly of me! I'm only talking about myself. (Sits on a footstool and rests her arms on MRS. LINDE's knee.) Oh, please don't be angry with me! Tell me, is it really true you didn't love your husband? Why did you marry him, then?

MRS. LINDE: Well, my mother was still alive; and she was helpless and bedridden. And I had my two little brothers to take care of. I didn't feel I could say no.

NORA: Yes, well, perhaps you're right. He was rich then, was he?

MRS. LINDE: Quite comfortably off, I believe. But his business was unsound, you see, Nora. When he died it went bankrupt, and there was nothing left.

NORA: What did you do?

MRS. LINDE: Well, I had to try to make ends meet somehow, so I started a little shop, and a little school, and anything else I could turn my hand to. These last three years have been just one endless slog for me, without a moment's rest. But now it's over, Nora. My poor dear mother doesn't need me any more; she's passed away. And the boys don't need me either; they've got jobs now and can look after themselves.

NORA: How relieved you must feel—

MRS. LINDE: No, Nora. Just unspeakably empty. No one to live for any more. (Gets up restlessly.) That's why I couldn't bear to stay out there any longer, cut off from the world. I thought it'd be easier to find some work here that will exercise and occupy my mind. If only I could get a regular job—office work of some kind—

NORA: Oh but, Christine, that's dreadfully exhausting; and you look practically finished already. It'd be much better for you if you could go away somewhere.

MRS. LINDE (goes over to the window): I have no Papa to pay for my holidays, Nora.

NORA (gets up): Oh, please don't be angry with me.

MRS. LINDE: My dear Nora, it's I who should ask you

not to be angry. That's the worst thing about this kind of situation—it makes one so bitter. One has no one to work for; and yet one has to be continually sponging for jobs. One has to live; and so one becomes completely egocentric. When you told me about this luck you've just had with Torvald's new job—can you imagine?—I was happy not so much on your account, as on my own.

NORA: How do you mean? Oh, I understand. You mean Torvald might be able to do something for you?

MRS. LINDE: Yes, I was thinking that.

NORA: He will too, Christine. Just you leave it to me. I'll lead up to it so delicately, so delicately; I'll get him in the right mood. Oh, Christine, I do so want to help you.

MRS. LINDE: It's sweet of you to bother so much about me, Nora. Especially since you know so little of the worries and hardships of life.

NORA: You say *I* know little of—?

MRS. LINDE (*smiles*): Well, good heavens—those bits of fancy work of yours—well, really—! You're a child, Nora.

NORA (*tosses her head and walks across the room*): You shouldn't say that so patronizingly.

MRS. LINDE: Oh?

NORA: You're like the rest. You all think I'm incapable of getting down to anything serious—

MRS. LINDE: My dear—

NORA: You think I've never had any worries like the rest of you.

MRS. LINDE: Nora dear, you've just told me about all your difficulties—

NORA: Pooh—that! (*Quietly.*) I haven't told you about the big thing.

MRS. LINDE: What big thing? What do you mean?

NORA: You patronize me, Christine; but you shouldn't. You're proud that you've worked so long and so hard for your mother.

MRS. LINDE: I don't patronize anyone, Nora. But you're right—I am both proud and happy that I was able to make my mother's last months on earth comparatively easy.

NORA: And you're also proud at what you've done for your brothers.

MRS. LINDE: I think I have a right to be.

NORA: I think so too. But let me tell you something, Christine. I too have done something to be proud and happy about.

MRS. LINDE: I don't doubt it. But—how do you mean?

NORA: Speak quietly! Suppose Torvald should hear! He mustn't, at any price—no one must know, Christine—no one but you.

MRS. LINDE: But what is this?

NORA: Come over here. (*Pulls her down on to the sofa beside her.*) Yes, Christine—I too have done some-thing to be happy and proud about. It was I who saved Torvald's life.

MRS. LINDE: Saved his—? How did you save it?

NORA: I told you about our trip to Italy. Torvald couldn't have lived if he hadn't managed to get down there—

MRS. LINDE: Yes, well—your father provided the money—

NORA (*smiles*): So Torvald and everyone else thinks. But—

MRS. LINDE: Yes?

NORA: Papa didn't give us a penny. It was I who found the money.

MRS. LINDE: You? All of it?

NORA: Two hundred and fifty pounds. What do you say to that?

MRS. LINDE: But Nora, how could you? Did you win a lottery or something?

NORA (*scornfully*): Lottery? (*Sniffs.*) What would there be to be proud of in that?

MRS. LINDE: But where did you get it from, then?

NORA (*hums and smiles secretively*): Hm; tra-la-la-la!

MRS. LINDE: You couldn't have borrowed it.

NORA: Oh? Why not?

MRS. LINDE: Well, a wife can't borrow money without her husband's consent.

NORA (*tosses her head*): Ah, but when a wife has a little business sense, and knows how to be clever—

MRS. LINDE: But Nora, I simply don't understand—

NORA: You don't have to. No one has said I borrowed the money. I could have got it in some other way. (*Throws herself back on the sofa.*) I could have got it from an admirer. When a girl's as pretty as I am—

MRS. LINDE: Nora, you're crazy!

NORA: You're dying of curiosity now, aren't you, Christine?

MRS. LINDE: Nora, dear, you haven't done anything foolish?

NORA (*sits up again*): Is it foolish to save one's husband's life?

MRS. LINDE: I think it's foolish if without his knowledge you—

NORA: But the whole point was that he mustn't know! Great heavens, don't you see? He hadn't to know how dangerously ill he was. I was the one they told that his life was in danger and that only going to a warm climate could save him. Do you suppose I didn't try to think of other ways of getting him down there? I told him how wonderful it would be for me to go abroad like other young wives: I cried and prayed; I asked him to remember my condition, and said he ought to be nice and tender to me; and then I suggested he might quite easily borrow the money. But then he got almost angry with me, Christine. He said I was frivolous, and that it was his duty as a husband not to pander to my moods and caprices—I think that's what he called them. Well, well, I thought, you've got to be saved somehow. And then I thought of a way—

MRS. LINDE: But didn't your husband find out from your father that the money hadn't come from him?

NORA: No, never. Papa died just then. I'd thought of letting him into the plot and asking him not to tell. But since he was so ill—! And as things turned out, it didn't become necessary.

MRS. LINDE: And you've never told your husband about this?

NORA: For heaven's sake, no! What an idea! He's frightfully strict about such matters. And besides—he's so proud of being a *man*—it'd be so painful and humiliating for him to know that he owed anything to me. It'd completely wreck our relationship. This life we have built together would no longer exist.

MRS. LINDE: Will you never tell him?

NORA (*thoughtfully, half-smiling*): Yes—some time, perhaps. Years from now, when I'm no longer pretty. You mustn't laugh! I mean of course, when Torvald no longer loves me as he does now; when it no longer amuses him to see me dance and dress up and play the fool for him. Then it might be useful to have something up my sleeve. (*Breaks off.*) Stupid, stupid, stupid! That time will never come. Well, what do you think of my big secret, Christine? I'm not completely useless, am I? Mind you, all this has caused me a frightful lot of worry. It hasn't been easy for me to meet my obligations punctually. In case you don't know, in the world of business there are things called quarterly instalments and interest, and they're a terrible problem to cope with. So I've had to scrape a little here and save a little there as best I can. I haven't been able to save much on the housekeeping money, because Torvald likes to live well, and I couldn't let the children go short of clothes—I couldn't take anything out of what he gives me for them. The poor little angels!

MRS. LINDE: So you've had to stint yourself, my poor Nora?

NORA: Of course. Well, after all, it was my problem. Whenever Torvald gave me money to buy myself new clothes, I never used more than half of it; and I always bought what was cheapest and plainest. Thank heaven anything suits me, so that Torvald's never noticed. But it made me a bit sad sometimes, because it's lovely to wear pretty clothes. Don't you think?

MRS. LINDE: Indeed it is.

NORA: And then I've found one or two other sources of income. Last winter I managed to get a lot of copying to do. So I shut myself away and wrote every evening, late into the night. Oh, I often got so tired. But it was great fun, though, sitting there working and earning money. It was almost like being a man.

MRS. LINDE: But how much have you managed to pay off like this?

NORA: Well, I can't say exactly. It's awfully difficult to keep an exact check on these kind of transactions. I only know I've paid everything I've managed to scrape together. Sometimes I really didn't know where to turn. (*Smiles.*) Then I'd sit here and imagine some rich old gentleman had fallen in love with me—

MRS. LINDE: What! What gentleman?

NORA: Silly! And that now he'd died and when they opened his will it said in big letters: "Everything I possess is to be paid forthwith to my beloved Mrs. Nora Helmer in cash."

MRS. LINDE: But, Nora dear, who was this gentleman?

NORA: Great heavens, don't you understand? There wasn't any old gentleman; he was just something I used to dream up as I sat here evening after evening wondering how on earth I could raise the money. But what does it matter? The old bore can stay imaginary as far as I'm concerned, because now I don't have to worry any longer! (*Jumps up.*) Oh, Christine, isn't it wonderful! I don't have to worry any more! No more troubles! I can play all day with the children, I can fill the house with pretty things, just the way Torvald likes. And, Christine, it'll soon be spring, and the air'll be fresh and the skies blue,—and then perhaps we'll be able to take a little trip somewhere. I shall be able to see the sun again. Oh, yes, yes, it's a wonderful thing to be alive and happy!

(*The bell rings in the hall.*)

MRS. LINDE (*gets up*): You've a visitor. Perhaps I'd better go.

NORA: No, stay. It won't be for me. It's someone for Torvald—

MAID (*in the doorway*): Excuse me, madam, a gentleman's called who says he wants to speak to the master. But I didn't know—seeing as the doctor's with him—

NORA: Who is this gentleman?

KROGSTAD (*in the doorway*): It's me, Mrs. Helmer.

(MRS. LINDE *starts, composes herself and turns away to the window.*)

NORA (*takes a step towards him and whispers tensely*): You? What is it? What do you want to talk to my husband about?

KROGSTAD: Business—you might call it. I hold a minor post in the bank, and I hear your husband is to become our new chief—

NORA: Oh—then it isn't—?

KROGSTAD: Pure business, Mrs. Helmer. Nothing more.

NORA: Well, you'll find him in his study.

(Nods indifferently as she closes the hall door behind him. Then she walks across the room and sees to the stove.)

MRS. LINDE: Nora, who was that man?

NORA: A lawyer called Krogstad.

MRS. LINDE: It was him, then.

NORA: Do you know that man?

MRS. LINDE: I used to know him—some years ago. He was a solicitor's clerk in our town, for a while.

NORA: Yes, of course, so he was.

MRS. LINDE: How he's changed!

NORA: He was very unhappily married, I believe.

MRS. LINDE: Is he a widower now?

NORA: Yes, with a lot of children. Ah, now it's alight.

(She closes the door of the stove and moves the rocking-chair a little to one side.)

MRS. LINDE: He does—various things now, I hear?

NORA: Does he? It's quite possible—I really don't know. But don't let's talk about business. It's so boring.

(DR. RANK enters from HELMER'S study.)

RANK *(still in the doorway)*: No, no, my dear chap, don't see me out. I'll go and have a word with your wife. *(Closes the door and notices MRS. LINDE.)* Oh, I beg your pardon. I seem to be *de trop* here too.

NORA: Not in the least. *(Introduces them.)* Dr. Rank. Mrs. Linde.

RANK: Ah! A name I have often heard in this house. I believe I passed you on the stairs as I came up.

MRS. LINDE: Yes. Stairs tire me; I have to take them slowly.

RANK: Oh, have you hurt yourself?

MRS. LINDE: No, I'm just a little run down.

RANK: Ah, is that all? Then I take it you've come to town to cure yourself by a round of parties?

MRS. LINDE: I have come here to find work.

RANK: Is that an approved remedy for being run down?

MRS. LINDE: One has to live, Doctor.

RANK: Yes, people do seem to regard it as a necessity.

NORA: Oh, really, Dr. Rank. I bet you want to stay alive.

RANK: You bet I do. However miserable I sometimes feel, I still want to go on being tortured for as long as possible. It's the same with all my patients; and with people who are morally sick, too. There's a moral cripple in with Helmer at this very moment—

MRS. LINDE *(softly)*: Oh!

NORA: Whom do you mean?

RANK: Oh, a lawyer fellow called Krogstad—you wouldn't know him. He's crippled all right; morally twisted. But even he started off by announcing, as though it were a matter of enormous importance, that he had to live.

NORA: Oh? What did he want to talk to Torvald about?

RANK: I haven't the faintest idea. All I heard was something about the bank.

NORA: I didn't know that Krog—that this man Krogstad had any connection with the bank.

RANK: Yes, he's got some kind of job down there. *(to* MRS. LINDE*)* I wonder if in your part of the world you too have a species of human being that spends its time fussing around trying to smell out moral corruption? And when they find a case they give him some nice, comfortable position so that they can keep a good watch on him. The healthy ones just have to lump it.

MRS. LINDE: But surely it's the sick who need care most?

RANK *(shrugs his shoulders)*: Well, there we have it. It's that attitude that's turning human society into a hospital.

(NORA, lost in her own thoughts, laughs half to herself and claps her hands.)

RANK: Why are you laughing? Do you really know what society is?

NORA: What do I care about society? I think it's a bore. I was laughing at something else— something frightfully funny. Tell me, Dr. Rank—will everyone who works at the bank come under Torvald now?

RANK: Do you find that particularly funny?

NORA *(smiles and hums)*: Never mind! Never you mind! *(Walks around the room.)* Yes, I find it very amusing to think that we—I mean, Torvald—has obtained so much influence over so many people. *(Takes the paper bag from her pocket.)* Dr. Rank, would you like a small macaroon?

RANK: Macaroons! I say! I thought they were forbidden here.

NORA: Yes, well, these are some Christine gave me.

MRS. LINDE: What? I—?

NORA: All right, all right, don't get frightened. You weren't to know Torvald had forbidden them. He's afraid they'll ruin my teeth. But, dash it—for once—! Don't you agree, Dr. Rank? Here! *(Pops a macaroon into his mouth.)* You too, Christine. And I'll have one too. Just a little one. Two at the most. *(Begins to walk round again.)* Yes, now I feel really, really happy. Now there's just one thing in the world I'd really love to do.

RANK: Oh? And what is that?

NORA: Just something I'd love to say to Torvald.

RANK: Well, why don't you say it?

NORA: No, I daren't. It's too dreadful.

MRS. LINDE: Dreadful?

RANK: Well, then, you'd better not. But you can say it to us. What is it you'd so love to say to Torvald?

NORA: I've the most extraordinary longing to say: "Bloody hell!"

RANK: Are you mad?

MRS. LINDE: My dear Nora—!

RANK: Say it. Here he is.

NORA (hiding the bag of macaroons): Ssh! Ssh!

(HELMER, with his overcoat on his arm and his hat in his hand, enters from his study.)

NORA (goes to meet him): Well, Torvald dear, did you get rid of him?

HELMER: Yes, he's just gone.

NORA: May I introduce you—? This is Christine. She's just arrived in town.

HELMER: Christine—? Forgive me, but I don't think—

NORA: Mrs. Linde, Torvald dear. Christine Linde.

HELMER: Ah. A childhood friend of my wife's, I presume?

MRS. LINDE: Yes, we knew each other in earlier days.

NORA: And imagine, now she's traveled all this way to talk to you.

HELMER: Oh?

MRS. LINDE: Well, I didn't really—

NORA: You see, Christine's frightfully good at office work, and she's mad to come under some really clever man who can teach her even more than she knows already—

HELMER: Very sensible, madam.

NORA: So when she heard you'd become head of the bank—it was in her local paper—she came here as quickly as she could and—Torvald, you will, won't you? Do a little something to help Christine? For my sake?

HELMER: Well, that shouldn't be impossible. You are a widow, I take it, Mrs. Linde?

MRS. LINDE: Yes.

HELMER: And you have experience of office work?

MRS. LINDE: Yes, quite a bit.

HELMER: Well then, it's quite likely I may be able to find some job for you—

NORA (claps her hands): You see, you see!

HELMER: You've come at a lucky moment, Mrs. Linde.

MRS. LINDE: Oh, how can I ever thank you—?

HELMER: There's absolutely no need. (Puts on his overcoat.) But now I'm afraid I must ask you to excuse me—

RANK: Wait. I'll come with you.

(He gets his fur coat from the hall and warms it at the stove.)

NORA: Don't be long, Torvald dear.

HELMER: I'll only be an hour.

NORA: Are you going too, Christine?

MRS. LINDE (puts on her outdoor clothes): Yes, I must start to look round for a room.

HELMER: Then perhaps we can walk part of the way together.

NORA (helps her): It's such a nuisance we're so cramped here—I'm afraid we can't offer to—

MRS. LINDE: Oh, I wouldn't dream of it. Goodbye, Nora dear, and thanks for everything.

NORA: Au revoir. You'll be coming back this evening, of course. And you too, Dr. Rank. What? If you're well enough? Of course you'll be well enough. Wrap up warmly, though.

(They go out, talking, into the hall. Children's voices are heard from the stairs.)

NORA: Here they are! Here they are!

(She runs out and opens the door. ANNE-MARIE, the nurse, enters with the children.)

NORA: Come in, come in! (Stoops down and kisses them.) Oh, my sweet darlings—! Look at them, Christine! Aren't they beautiful?

RANK: Don't stand here chattering in this draught!

HELMER: Come, Mrs. Linde. This is for mothers only.

(DR. RANK, HELMER, and MRS. LINDE go down the stairs. The NURSE brings the children into the room. NORA follows, and closes the door to the hall.)

NORA: How well you look! What red cheeks you've got! Like apples and roses! (The children answer her inaudibly as she talks to them.) Have you had fun? That's splendid. You gave Emmy and Bob a ride on the sledge? What, both together? I say! What a clever boy you are, Ivar! Oh, let me hold her for a moment, Anne-Marie! My sweet little baby doll! (Takes the smallest child from the NURSE and dances with her.) Yes, yes, Mummy will dance with Bob too. What? Have you been throwing snowballs? Oh, I wish I'd been there! No, don't—I'll undress them myself, Anne-Marie. No, please let me; it's such fun. Go inside and warm yourself; you look frozen. There's some hot coffee on the stove. (The NURSE goes into the room on the left. NORA takes off the children's outdoor clothes and throws them anywhere while they all chatter simultaneously.) What? A big dog ran after you? But he didn't bite you? No, dogs don't bite lovely little baby dolls. Leave those parcels alone, Ivar. What's in them? Ah, wouldn't you like to know! No, no; it's nothing nice. Come on, let's play a game. What shall we play? Hide and seek. Yes, let's play hide and seek. Bob shall hide first. You want me to? All right, let me hide first.

(NORA and the children play around the room, and in the adjacent room to the left, laughing and shouting. At length NORA *hides under the table. The children rush in, look, but cannot find her. Then they hear her half-stifled laughter, run to the table, lift up the cloth and see her. Great excitement. She crawls out as though to frighten them. Further excitement. Meanwhile, there has been a knock on the door leading from the hall, but no one has noticed it. Now the door is half-opened and* KROGSTAD *enters. He waits for a moment; the game continues.)*

KROGSTAD: Excuse me, Mrs. Helmer—

NORA *(turns with a stifled cry and half jumps up)*: Oh! What do you want?

KROGSTAD: I beg your pardon; the front door was ajar. Someone must have forgotten to close it.

NORA *(gets up)*: My husband is not at home, Mr. Krogstad.

KROGSTAD: I know.

NORA: Well, what do you want here, then?

KROGSTAD: A word with you.

NORA: With—? *(to the children, quietly)* Go inside to Anne-Marie. What? No, the strange gentleman won't do anything to hurt Mummy. When he's gone we'll start playing again.

(She takes the children into the room on the left and closes the door behind them.)

NORA *(uneasy, tense)*: You want to speak to me?

KROGSTAD: Yes.

NORA: Today? But it's not the first of the month yet.

KROGSTAD: No, it is Christmas Eve. Whether or not you have a merry Christmas depends on you.

NORA: What do you want? I can't give you anything today—

KROGSTAD: We won't talk about that for the present. There's something else. You have a moment to spare?

NORA: Oh, yes. Yes, I suppose so; though—

KROGSTAD: Good. I was sitting in the café down below and I saw your husband cross the street—

NORA: Yes.

KROGSTAD: With a lady.

NORA: Well?

KROGSTAD: Might I be so bold as to ask: was not that lady a Mrs. Linde?

NORA: Yes.

KROGSTAD: Recently arrived in town?

NORA: Yes, today.

KROGSTAD: She is a good friend of yours, is she not?

NORA: Yes, she is. But I don't see—

KROGSTAD: I used to know her too once.

NORA: I know.

KROGSTAD: Oh? You've discovered that. Yes, I thought you would. Well then, may I ask you a straight question: is Mrs. Linde to be employed at the bank?

NORA: How dare you presume to cross-examine me, Mr. Krogstad? You, one of my husband's em-ployees? But since you ask, you shall have an answer. Yes, Mrs. Linde is to be employed by the bank. And I arranged it, Mr. Krogstad. Now you know.

KROGSTAD: I guessed right, then.

NORA *(walks up and down the room)*: Oh, one has a little influence, you know. Just because one's a woman it doesn't necessarily mean that—When one is in a humble position, Mr. Krogstad, one should think twice before offending someone who—hm—

KROGSTAD: —who has influence?

NORA: Precisely.

KROGSTAD *(changes his tone)*: Mrs. Helmer, will you have the kindness to use your influence on my behalf?

NORA: What? What do you mean?

KROGSTAD: Will you be so good as to see that I keep my humble position at the bank?

NORA: What do you mean? Who is thinking of removing you from your position?

KROGSTAD: Oh, you don't need to play the innocent with me. I realize it can't be very pleasant for your friend to risk bumping into me; and now I also realize whom I have to thank for being hounded out like this.

NORA: But I assure you—

KROGSTAD: Look, let's not beat about the bush. There's still time, and I'd advise you to use your influence to stop it.

NORA: But, Mr. Krogstad, I have no influence!

KROGSTAD: Oh? I thought you just said—

NORA: But I didn't mean it like that! I? How on earth could you imagine that I would have any influence over my husband?

KROGSTAD: Oh, I've known your husband since we were students together. I imagine he has his weaknesses like other married men.

NORA: If you speak impertinently of my husband, I shall show you the door.

KROGSTAD: You're a bold woman, Mrs. Helmer.

NORA: I'm not afraid of you any longer. Once the New Year is in, I'll soon be rid of you.

KROGSTAD *(more controlled)*: Now listen to me, Mrs. Helmer. If I'm forced to, I shall fight for my little job at the bank as I would fight for my life.

NORA: So it sounds.

KROGSTAD: It isn't just the money; that's the last thing I care about. There's something else—well, you might as well know. It's like this, you see. You know of course, as everyone else does, that some years ago I committed an indiscretion.

NORA: I think I did hear something—

KROGSTAD: It never came into court; but from that day, every opening was barred to me. So I turned my hand to the kind of business you know about. I had to do something; and I don't think I was one of the worst. But now I want to give up all that. My sons are growing up; for their sake, I must try to regain what respectability I can. This job in the bank was the first step on the ladder. And now your husband wants to kick me off that ladder back into the dirt.

NORA: But my dear Mr. Krogstad, it simply isn't in my power to help you.

KROGSTAD: You say that because you don't want to help me. But I have the means to make you.

NORA: You don't mean you'd tell my husband that I owe you money?

KROGSTAD: And if I did?

NORA: That'd be a filthy trick! (*Almost in tears.*) This secret that is my pride and my joy—that he should hear about it in such a filthy, beastly way—hear about it from you! It'd involve me in the most dreadful unpleasantness—

KROGSTAD: Only—unpleasantness?

NORA (*vehemently*): All right, do it! You'll be the one who'll suffer. It'll show my husband the kind of man you are, and then you'll never keep your job.

KROGSTAD: I asked you whether it was merely domestic unpleasantness you were afraid of.

NORA: If my husband hears about it, he will of course immediately pay you whatever is owing. And then we shall have nothing more to do with you.

KROGSTAD (*Takes a step closer*): Listen, Mrs. Helmer. Either you've a bad memory or else you know very little about financial transactions. I had better enlighten you.

NORA: What do you mean?

KROGSTAD: When your husband was ill, you came to me to borrow two hundred and fifty pounds.

NORA: I didn't know anyone else.

KROGSTAD: I promised to find that sum for you—

NORA: And you did find it.

KROGSTAD: I promised to find that sum for you on certain conditions. You were so worried about your husband's illness and so keen to get the money to take him abroad that I don't think you bothered much about the details. So it won't be out of place if I refresh your memory. Well—I promised to get you the money in exchange for an I.O.U., which I drew up.

NORA: Yes, and which I signed.

KROGSTAD: Exactly. But then I added a few lines naming your father as security for the debt. This paragraph was to be signed by your father.

NORA: Was to be? He did sign it.

KROGSTAD: I left the date blank for your father to fill in when he signed this paper. You remember, Mrs. Helmer?

NORA: Yes, I think so—

KROGSTAD: Then I gave you back this I.O.U. for you to post to your father. Is that not correct?

NORA: Yes.

KROGSTAD: And of course you posted it at once; for within five or six days you brought it along to me with your father's signature on it. Whereupon I handed you the money.

NORA: Yes, well. Haven't I repaid the instalments as agreed?

KROGSTAD: Mm—yes, more or less. But to return to what we were speaking about—that was a difficult time for you just then, wasn't it, Mrs. Helmer?

NORA: Yes, it was.

KROGSTAD: Your father was very ill, if I am not mistaken.

NORA: He was dying.

KROGSTAD: He did in fact die shortly afterwards?

NORA: Yes.

KROGSTAD: Tell me, Mrs. Helmer, do you by any chance remember the date of your father's death? The day of the month, I mean.

NORA: Papa died on the twenty-ninth of September.

KROGSTAD: Quite correct; I took the trouble to confirm it. And that leaves me with a curious little problem—(*Takes out a paper.*)—which I simply cannot solve.

NORA: Problem? I don't see—

KROGSTAD: The problem, Mrs. Helmer, is that your father signed this paper three days after his death.

NORA: What? I don't understand—

KROGSTAD: Your father died on the twenty-ninth of September. But look at this. Here your father has dated his signature the second of October. Isn't that a curious little problem, Mrs. Helmer? (*Nora is silent.*) Can you suggest any explanation? (*She remains silent.*) And there's another curious thing. The words "second of October" and the year are written in a hand which is not your father's, but which I seem to know. Well, there's a simple explanation to that. Your father could have forgotten to write in the date when he signed, and someone else could have added it before the news came of his death. There's nothing criminal about that. It's the signature itself I'm wondering about. It *is* genuine, I suppose, Mrs. Helmer? It was your father who wrote his name here?

NORA (*after a short silence, throws back her head and looks defiantly at him*): No, it was not. It was I who wrote Papa's name there.

KROGSTAD: Look, Mrs. Helmer, do you realize this is a dangerous admission?

NORA: Why? You'll get your money.

KROGSTAD: May I ask you a question? Why didn't you send this paper to your father?

NORA: I couldn't. Papa was very ill. If I'd asked him to sign this, I'd have had to tell him what the money was for. But I couldn't have told him in his condition that my husband's life was in danger. I couldn't have done that!

KROGSTAD: Then you would have been wiser to have given up your idea of a holiday.

NORA: But I couldn't! It was to save my husband's life. I couldn't put it off.

KROGSTAD: But didn't it occur to you that you were being dishonest towards me?

NORA: I couldn't bother about that. I didn't care about you. I hated you because of all the beastly difficulties you'd put in my way when you knew how dangerously ill my husband was.

KROGSTAD: Mrs. Helmer, you evidently don't appreciate exactly what you have done. But I can assure you that it is no bigger nor worse a crime then the one I once committed, and thereby ruined my whole social position.

NORA: You? Do you expect me to believe that you would have taken a risk like that to save your wife's life?

KROGSTAD: The law does not concern itself with motives.

NORA: Then the law must be very stupid.

KROGSTAD: Stupid or not, if I show this paper to the police, you will be judged according to it.

NORA: I don't believe that. Hasn't a daughter the right to shield her father from worry and anxiety when he's old and dying? Hasn't a wife the right to save her husband's life? I don't know much about the law, but there must be something somewhere that says that such things are allowed. You ought to know about that, you're meant to be a lawyer, aren't you? You can't be a very good lawyer, Mr. Krogstad.

KROGSTAD: Possibly not. But business, the kind of business we two have been transacting—I think you'll admit I understand something about that? Good. Do as you please. But I tell you this. If I get thrown into the gutter for a second time, I shall take you with me.

(He bows and goes out through the hall.)

NORA *(stands for a moment in thought, then tosses her head)*: What nonsense! He's trying to frighten me! I'm not that stupid. *(Busies herself gathering together the children's clothes; then she suddenly stops.)* But—? No, it's impossible. I did it for love, didn't I?

THE CHILDREN *(in the doorway, left)*: Mummy, the strange gentleman's gone out into the street.

NORA: Yes, yes, I know. But don't talk to anyone about the strange gentleman. You hear? Not even to Daddy.

CHILDREN: No, Mummy, Will you play with us again now?

NORA: No, no. Not now.

CHILDREN: Oh but, Mummy, you promised!

NORA: I know, but I can't just now. Go back to the nursery. I've got a lot to do. Go away, my darlings, go away. *(She pushes them gently into the other room, and closes the door behind them. She sits on the sofa, takes up her embroidery, stitches for a few moments, but soon stops.)* No! *(Throws the embroidery aside, gets up, goes to the door leading to the hall and calls.)* Helen! Bring in the Christmas tree! *(She goes to the table on the left and opens the drawer in it; then pauses again.)* No, but it's utterly impossible!

MAID *(enters with the tree)*: Where shall I put it, madam?

NORA: There, in the middle of the room.

MAID: Will you be wanting anything else?

NORA: No, thank you. I have everything I need.

(The MAID puts down the tree and goes out.)

NORA *(busy decorating the tree)*: Now—candles here—and flowers here. That loathsome man! Nonsense, nonsense, there's nothing to be frightened about. The Christmas tree must be beautiful. I'll do everything that you like, Torvald. I'll sing for you, dance for you—

(HELMER, with a bundle of papers under his arm, enters.)

NORA: Oh—are you back already?

HELMER: Yes. Has anyone been here?

NORA: Here? No.

HELMER: That's strange. I saw Krogstad come out of the front door.

NORA: Did you? Oh yes, that's quite right—Krogstad was here for a few minutes.

HELMER: Nora, I can tell from your face, he's been here and asked you to put in a good word for him.

NORA: Yes.

HELMER: And you were to pretend you were doing it of your own accord? You weren't going to tell me he'd been here? He asked you to do that too, didn't he?

NORA: Yes, Torvald. But—

HELMER: Nora, Nora! And you were ready to enter into such a conspiracy? Talking to a man like that, and making him promises—and then, on top of it all, to tell me an untruth!

NORA: An untruth?

HELMER: Didn't you say no one had been here? *(Wags his finger.)* My little songbird must never do that again. A songbird must have a clean beak to sing with; otherwise she'll starting twittering out of tune. *(Puts his arm around her waist.)* Isn't that the way we want things? Yes, of course it is. *(Lets go of her.)* So let's hear no more about that. *(Sits down in front of the stove.)* Ah, how cosy and peaceful it is here. *(Glances for a few moments at his papers.)*

NORA *(busy with the tree, after a short silence)*: Torvald.

HELMER: Yes.

NORA: I'm terribly looking forward to that fancy

dress ball at the Stenborgs on Boxing Day.

HELMER: And I'm terribly curious to see what you're going to surprise me with.

NORA: Oh, it's so maddening.

HELMER: What is?

NORA: I can't think of anything to wear. It all seems so stupid and meaningless.

HELMER: So my little Nora's come to that conclusion, has she?

NORA (behind his chair, resting her arms on its back): Are you very busy, Torvald?

HELMER: Oh—

NORA: What are those papers?

HELMER: Just something to do with the bank.

NORA: Already?

HELMER: I persuaded the trustees to give me authority to make certain immediate changes in the staff and organization. I want to have everything straight by the New Year.

NORA: Then that's why this poor man Krogstad—

HELMER: Hm.

NORA (still leaning over his chair, slowly strokes the back of his head): If you hadn't been so busy, I was going to ask you an enormous favour, Torvald.

HELMER: Well, tell me. What was it to be?

NORA: You know I trust your taste more than anyone's. I'm so anxious to look really beautiful at the fancy dress ball. Torvald, couldn't you help me to decide what I shall go as, and what kind of costume I ought to wear?

HELMER: Aha! So little Miss Independent's in trouble and needs a man to rescue her, does she?

NORA: Yes, Torvald. I can't get anywhere without your help.

HELMER: Well, well, I'll give the matter thought. We'll find something.

NORA: Oh, how kind of you! (Goes back to the tree. Pause.) How pretty these red flowers look! But, tell me is it so dreadful, this thing that Krogstad's done?

HELMER: He forged someone else's name. Have you any idea what that means?

NORA: Mightn't he have been forced to do it by some emergency?

HELMER: He probably just didn't think—that's what usually happens. I'm not so heartless as to condemn a man for an isolated action.

NORA: No, Torvald, of course not!

HELMER: Men often succeed in re-establishing themselves if they admit their crime and take their punishment.

NORA: Punishment?

HELMER: But Krogstad didn't do that. He chose to try and trick his way out of it; and that's what has morally destroyed him.

NORA: You think that would—?

HELMER: Just think how a man with that load on his conscience must always be lying and cheating and dissembling; how he must wear a mask even in the presence of those who are dearest to him, even his own wife and children! Yes, the children. That's the worst danger, Nora.

NORA: Why?

HELMER: Because an atmosphere of lies contaminates and poisons every corner of the home. Every breath that the children draw in such a house contains the germs of evil.

NORA (comes closer behind him): Do you really believe that?

HELMER: Oh, my dear, I've come across it so often in my work at the bar. Nearly all young criminals are the children of mothers who are constitutional liars.

NORA: Why do you say mothers?

HELMER: It's usually the mother; though of course the father can have the same influence. Every lawyer knows that only too well. And yet this fellow Krogstad has been sitting at home all these years poisoning his children with his lies and pretences. That's why I say that, morally speaking, he is dead. (Stretches out his hands toward her.) So my pretty little Nora must promise me not to plead his case. Your hand on it. Come, come, what's this? Give me your hand. There. That's settled, now. I assure you it'd be quite impossible for me to work in the same building as him. I literally feel physically ill in the presence of a man like that.

NORA (draws her hand from his and goes over to the other side of the Christmas tree) How hot it is in here! And I've so much to do.

HELMER (gets up and gathers his papers): Yes, and I must try to get some of this read before dinner. I'll think about your costume too. And I may even have something up my sleeve to hang in gold paper on the Christmas tree. (Lays his hand on her head.) My precious little songbird!

(He goes into his study and closes the door.)

NORA (softly, after a pause): It's nonsense. It must be. It's impossible. It must be impossible!

NURSE (in the doorway, left): The children are asking if they can come in to Mummy.

NORA: No, no, no; don't let them in! You stay with them, Anne-Marie.

NURSE: Very good, madam. (Closes the door.)

NORA (pale with fear): Corrupt my little children—! Poison my home! (Short pause. She throws back her head.) It isn't true! It couldn't be true!

ACT 2

(The same room. In the corner by the piano the Christmas tree stands, stripped and disheveled, its candles burned to their sockets. NORA's outdoor clothes lie on the sofa. She is *alone in the room, walking restlessly to and fro. At length she stops by the sofa and picks up her coat.)*

NORA *(drops the coat again)*: There's someone coming! *(Goes to the door and listens.)* No, it's no one. Of course—no one'll come today, it's Christmas Day. Nor tomorrow. But perhaps—! *(Opens the door and looks out.)* No. Nothing in the letter-box. Quite empty. *(Walks across the room.)* Silly, silly. Of course he won't do anything. It couldn't happen. It isn't possible. Why, I've three small children.

(The NURSE, *carrying a large cardboard box, enters from the room on the left.)*

NURSE: I found those fancy dress clothes at last, madam.

NORA: Thank you. Put them on the table.

NURSE *(does so)*: They're all rumpled up.

NORA: Oh, I wish I could tear them into a million pieces!

NURSE: Why, madam! They'll be all right. Just a little patience.

NORA: Yes, of course. I'll go and get Mrs. Linde to help me.

NURSE: What, out again? In this dreadful weather? You'll catch a chill, madam.

NORA: Well, that wouldn't be the worst. How are the children?

NURSE: Playing with their Christmas presents, poor little dears. But—

NORA: Are they still asking to see me?

NURSE: They're so used to having their Mummy with them.

NORA: Yes, but, Anne-Marie, from now on I shan't be able to spend so much time with them.

NURSE: Well, children get used to anything in time.

NORA: Do you think so? Do you think they'd forget their mother if she went away from them—for ever?

NURSE: Mercy's sake, madam! For ever!

NORA: Tell me, Anne-Marie—I've so often wondered. How could you bear to give your child away—to strangers?

NURSE: But I had to when I came to nurse my little Miss Nora.

NORA: Do you mean you wanted to?

NURSE: When I had the chance of such a good job? A poor girl what's got into trouble can't afford to pick and choose. That good-for-nothing didn't lift a finger.

NORA: But your daughter must have completely forgotten you.

NURSE: Oh no, indeed she hasn't. She's written to me twice, once when she got confirmed and then again when she got married.

NORA *(hugs her)*: Dear old Anne-Marie, you were a good mother to me.

NURSE: Poor little Miss Nora, you never had any mother but me.

NORA: And if my little ones had no one else, I know you would—no, silly, silly, silly! *(Opens the cardboard box.)* Go back to them, Anne-Marie. Now I must—Tomorrow you'll see how pretty I shall look.

NURSE: Why, there'll be no one at the ball as beautiful as my Miss Nora.

(She goes into the room, left.)

NORA *(begins to unpack the clothes from the box, but soon throws them down again)* Oh, if only I dared go out! If I could be sure no one would come and nothing would happen while I was away! Stupid, stupid! No one will come. I just musn't think about it. Brush this muff. Pretty gloves, pretty gloves! Don't think about it, don't think about it! One, two, three, four, five, six—*(Cries.)* Ah—they're coming—!

(She begins to run towards the door, but stops uncertainly. MRS. LINDE *enters from the hall, where she has been taking off her outdoor clothes.)*

NORA: Oh, it's you, Christine. There's no one else out there, is there? Oh, I'm so glad you've come.

MRS. LINDE: I hear you were at my room asking for me.

NORA: Yes, I just happened to be passing. I want to ask you to help me with something. Let's sit down here on the sofa. Look at this. There's going to be a fancy dress ball tomorrow night upstairs at Consul Stenborg's, and Torvald wants me to go as a Neapolitan fisher-girl and dance the tarantella. I learned it on Capri.

MRS. LINDE: I say, are you going to give a performance?

NORA: Yes, Torvald says I should. Look, here's the dress. Torvald had it made for me in Italy; but now it's all so torn, I don't know—

MRS. LINDE: Oh, we'll soon put that right; the stitching's just come away. Needle and thread? Ah, here we are.

NORA: You're being awfully sweet.

MRS. LINDE *(sews)*: So you're going to dress up tomorrow, Nora? I must pop over for a moment to see how you look. Oh, but I've completely forgotten to thank you for that nice evening yesterday.

NORA *(gets up and walks across the room)*: Oh, I didn't think it was as nice as usual. You ought to have come to town a little earlier, Christine. . . . Yes, Torvald understands how to make a home look attractive.

MRS. LINDE: I'm sure you do, too. You're not your father's daughter for nothing. But tell me. Is Dr. Rank always in such low spirits as he was yesterday?

NORA: No, last night it was very noticeable. But he's got a terrible disease; he's got spinal tuberculosis, poor man. His father was a frightful creature who kept mistresses and so on. As a result Dr. Rank has been sickly ever since he was a child—you understand—

MRS. LINDE (*puts down her sewing*): But, my dear Nora, how on earth did you get to know about such things?

NORA (*walks about the room*): Oh, don't be silly, Christine—when one has three children, one comes into contact with women who—well, who know about medical matters, and they tell one a thing or two.

MRS. LINDE (*sews again; a short silence*): Does Dr. Rank visit you every day?

NORA: Yes, every day. He's Torvald's oldest friend, and a good friend to me too. Dr. Rank's almost one of the family.

MRS. LINDE: But, tell me—is he quite sincere? I mean, doesn't he rather say the sort of thing he thinks people want to hear?

NORA: No, quite the contrary. What gave you that idea?

MRS. LINDE: When you introduced me to him yesterday, he said he'd often heard my name mentioned here. But later I noticed your husband had no idea who I was. So how could Dr. Rank—?

NORA: Yes, that's quite right, Christine. You see, Torvald's so hopelessly in love with me that he wants to have me all to himself—those were his very words. When we were first married, he got quite jealous if I as much as mentioned any of my old friends back home. So naturally, I stopped talking about them. But I often chat with Dr. Rank about that kind of thing. He enjoys it, you see.

MRS. LINDE: Now listen, Nora. In many ways you're still a child; I'm a bit older than you and have a little more experience of the world. There's something I want to say to you. You ought to give up this business with Dr. Rank.

NORA: What business?

MRS. LINDE: Well, everything. Last night you were speaking about this rich admirer of yours who was going to give you money—

NORA: Yes, and who doesn't exist—unfortunately. But what's that got to do with—?

MRS. LINDE: Is Dr. Rank rich?

NORA: Yes.

MRS. LINDE: And he has no dependents?

NORA: No, no one. But—

MRS. LINDE: And he comes here to see you every day?

NORA: Yes, I've told you.

MRS. LINDE: But how dare a man of his education be so forward?

NORA: What on earth are you talking about?

MRS. LINDE: Oh, stop pretending, Nora. Do you think I haven't guessed who it was who lent you that two hundred pounds?

NORA: Are you out of your mind? How could you imagine such a thing? A friend, someone who comes here every day! Why, that'd be an impossible situation!

MRS. LINDE: Then it really wasn't him?

NORA: No, of course not. I've never for a moment dreamed of—anyway, he hadn't any money to lend then. He didn't come into that till later.

MRS. LINDE: Well, I think that was a lucky thing for you, Nora dear.

NORA: No, I could never have dreamed of asking Dr. Rank—though I'm sure that if I ever did ask him—

MRS. LINDE: But of course you won't.

NORA: Of course not. I can't imagine that it should ever become necessary. But I'm perfectly sure that if I did speak to Dr. Rank—

MRS. LINDE: Behind your husband's back?

NORA: I've got to get out of this other business; and *that's* been going on behind his back. I've *got* to get out of it.

MRS. LINDE: Yes, well, that's what I told you yesterday. But—

NORA (*walking up and down*): It's much easier for a man to arrange these things than a woman—

MRS. LINDE: One's own husband, yes.

NORA: Oh, bosh. (*Stops walking.*) When you've completely repaid a debt, you get your I.O.U. back, don't you?

MRS. LINDE: Yes, of course.

NORA: And you can tear it into a thousand pieces and burn the filthy, beastly thing!

MRS. LINDE (*looks hard at her, puts down her sewing and gets up slowly*): Nora, you're hiding something from me.

NORA: Can you see that?

MRS. LINDE: Something has happened since yesterday morning. Nora, what is it?

NORA (*goes toward her*): Christine! (*Listens.*) Ssh! There's Torvald. Would you mind going into the nursery for a few minutes? Torvald can't bear to see sewing around. Anne-Marie'll help you.

MRS. LINDE (*gathers some of her things together*): Very well. But I shan't leave this house until we've talked this matter out.

(*She goes into the nursery, left. As she does so,* HELMER *enters from the hall.*)

NORA (*runs to meet him*): Oh, Torvald dear, I've been so longing for you to come back!

HELMER: Was that the dressmaker?

NORA: No, it was Christine. She's helping me mend

my costume. I'm going to look rather splendid in that.

HELMER: Yes, that was quite a bright idea of mine, wasn't it?

NORA: Wonderful! But wasn't it nice of me to give in to you?

HELMER (takes her chin in his hand): Nice—to give in to your husband? All right, little silly, I know you didn't mean it like that. But I won't disturb you. I expect you'll be wanting to try it on.

NORA: Are you going to work now?

HELMER: Yes. (Shows her a bundle of papers.) Look at these. I've been down to the bank—(Turns to go into his study.)

NOVA: Torvald.

HELMER (stops): Yes.

NORA: If little squirrel asked you really prettily to grant her a wish—

HELMER: Well?

NORA: Would you grant it to her?

HELMER: First I should naturally have to know what it was.

NORA: Squirrel would do lots of pretty tricks for you if you granted her wish.

HELMER: Out with it, then.

NORA: Your little skylark would sing in every room—

HELMER: My little skylark does that already.

NORA: I'd turn myself into a little fairy and dance for you in the moonlight, Torvald.

HELMER: Nora, it isn't that business you were talking about this morning?

NORA (comes closer): Yes, Torvald—oh, please! I beg of you!

HELMER: Have you really the nerve to bring that up again?

NORA: Yes, Torvald, yes, you must do as I ask! You must let Krogstad keep his place at the bank!

HELMER: My dear Nora, his is the job I'm giving to Mrs. Linde.

NORA: Yes, that's terribly sweet of you. But you can get rid of one of the other clerks instead of Krogstad.

HELMER: Really, you're being incredibly obstinate. Just because you thoughtlessly promised to put in a word for him, you expect me to—

NORA: No, it isn't that, Helmer. It's for your own sake. That man writes for the most beastly newspapers—you said so yourself. He could do you tremendous harm. I'm so dreadfully frightened of him—

HELMER: Oh, I understand. Memories of the past. That's what's frightening you.

NORA: What do you mean?

HELMER: You're thinking of your father, aren't you?

NORA: Yes, yes. Of course. Just think what those dreadful men wrote in the papers about Papa! The most frightful slanders. I really believe it

would have lost him his job if the Ministry hadn't sent you down to investigate, and you hadn't been so kind and helpful to him.

HELMER: But my dear little Nora, there's a considerable difference between your father and me. Your father was not a man of unassailable reputation. But I am; and I hope to remain so all my life.

NORA: But no one knows what spiteful people may not dig up. We could be so peaceful and happy now, Torvald—we could be free from every worry—you and I and the children. Oh, please Torvald, please—!

HELMER: The very fact of your pleading his cause makes it impossible for me to keep him. Everyone at the bank already knows that I intend to dismiss Krogstad. If the rumor got about that the new manager had allowed his wife to persuade him to change his mind—

NORA: Well, what then?

HELMER: Oh, nothing, nothing. As long as my little Miss Obstinate gets her way—! Do you expect me to make a laughing-stock of myself before my entire staff—give people the idea that I am open to outside influence? Believe me, I'd soon feel the consequences! Besides—there's something else that makes it impossible for Krogstad to remain in the bank while I am its manager.

NORA: What is that?

HELMER: I might conceivably have allowed myself to ignore his moral obloquies—

NORA: Yes, Torvald, surely?

HELMER: And I hear he's quite efficient at his job. But we—well, we were schoolfriends. It was one of those friendships that one enters into over-hastily and so often comes to regret later in life. I might as well confess the truth. We—well, we're on Christian name terms. And the tactless idiot makes no attempt to conceal it when other people are present. On the contrary, he thinks it gives him the right to be familiar with me. He shows off the whole time, with "Torvald this," and "Torvald that." I can tell you, I find it damned annoying. If he stayed, he'd make my position intolerable.

NORA: Torvald, you can't mean this seriously.

HELMER: Oh? And why not?

NORA: But it's so petty.

HELMER: What did you say? Petty? You think I am petty?

NORA: No, Torvald dear, of course you're not. That's just why—

HELMER: Don't quibble! You call my motives petty. Then I must be petty too. Petty! I see. Well, I've had enough of this. (Goes to the door and calls into the hall.) Helen!

NORA: What are you going to do?

HELMER (*searching among his papers*): I'm going to settle this matter once and for all. (*The* MAID *enters.*) Take this letter downstairs at once. Find a messenger and see that he delivers it. Immediately! The address is on the envelope. Here's the money.

MAID: Very good, sir. (*Goes out with the letter.*)

HELMER (*putting his papers in order*): There now, little Miss Obstinate.

NORA (*tensely*): Torvald—what was in that letter?

HELMER: Krogstad's dismissal.

NORA: Call her back, Torvald! There's still time. Oh, Torvald, call her back! Do it for my sake—for your own sake—for the children! Do you hear me, Torvald? Please do it! You don't realize what this may do to us all!

HELMER: Too late.

NORA: Yes. Too late.

HELMER: My dear Nora, I forgive you this anxiety. Though it is a bit of an insult to me. Oh, but it is! Isn't it an insult to imply that I should be frightened by the vindictiveness of a depraved hack journalist? But I forgive you, because it so charmingly testifies to the love you bear me. (*Takes her in his arms.*) Which is as it should be, my own dearest Nora. Let what will happen, happen. When the real crisis comes, you will not find me lacking in strength or courage. I am man enough to bear the burden for us both.

NORA (*fearfully*): What do you mean?

HELMER: The whole burden, I say—

NORA (*calmly*): I shall never let you do that.

HELMER: Very well. We shall share it, Nora—as man and wife. And that is as it should be. (*Caresses her.*) Are you happy now? There, there, there; don't look at me with those frightened little eyes. You're simply imagining things. You go ahead now and do your tarantella, and get some practice on that tambourine. I'll sit in my study and close the door. Then I won't hear anything, and you can make all the noise you want. (*Turns in the doorway.*) When Dr. Rank comes, tell him where to find me. (*He nods to her, goes into his room with his papers and closes the door.*)

NORA (*desperate with anxiety, stands as though transfixed, and whispers*): He said he'd do it. He will do it. He will do it, and nothing'll stop him. No, never that. I'd rather anything. There must be some escape—! Some way out—! (*The bell rings in the hall.*) Dr. Rank—! Anything but that! Anything, I don't care—!

(*She passes her hand across her face, composes herself, walks across and opens the door to the hall.* DR. RANK *is standing there, hanging up his fur coat. During the following scene it begins to grow dark.*)

NORA: Good evening, Dr. Rank. I recognized your ring. But you mustn't go in to Torvald yet. I think he's busy.

RANK: And—you?

NORA (*as he enters the room and she closes the door behind him*): Oh, you know very well I've always time to talk to you.

RANK: Thank you. I shall avail myself of that privilege as long as I can.

NORA: What do you mean by that? As long as you *can*?

RANK: Yes. Does that frighten you?

NORA: Well, it's rather a curious expression. Is something going to happen?

RANK: Something I've been expecting to happen for a long time. But I didn't think it would happen quite so soon.

NORA (*seizes his arm*): What is it? Dr. Rank, you must tell me!

RANK (*sits down by the stove*): I'm on the way out. And there's nothing to be done about it.

NORA (*sighs with relief*): Oh, it's you—?

RANK: Who else? No, it's no good lying to oneself. I am the most wretched of all my patients, Mrs. Helmer. These last few days I've been going through the books of this poor body of mine, and I find I am bankrupt. Within a month I may be rotting up there in the churchyard.

NORA: Ugh, what a nasty way to talk!

RANK: The facts aren't exactly nice. But the worst is that there's so much else that's nasty to come first. I've only one more test to make. When that's done I'll have a pretty accurate idea of when the final disintegration is likely to begin. I want to ask you a favor. Helmer's a sensitive chap, and I know how he hates anything ugly. I don't want him to visit me when I'm in hospital—

NORA: Oh but, Dr. Rank—

RANK: I don't want him there. On any pretext. I shan't have him allowed in. As soon as I know the worst, I'll send you my visiting card with a black cross on it, and then you'll know that the final filthy process has begun.

NORA: Really, you're being quite impossible this evening. And I did hope you'd be in a good mood.

RANK: With death on my hands? And all this to atone for someone else's sin? Is there justice in that? And in every single family, in one way or another, the same merciless law of retribution is at work—

NORA (*holds her hands to her ears*): Nonsense! Cheer up! Laugh!

RANK: Yes, you're right. Laughter's all the damned thing's fit for. My poor innocent spine must pay for the fun my father had as a gay young lieutenant.

NORA (*at the table, left*): You mean he was too fond of asparagus and *foie gras*?

RANK: Yes; and truffles too.

NORA: Yes, of course, truffles, yes. And oysters too, I suppose?

RANK: Yes, oysters, oysters. Of course.

NORA: And all that port and champagne to wash them down. It's too sad that all those lovely things should affect one's spine.

RANK: Especially a poor spine that never got any pleasure out of them.

NORA: Oh yes, that's the saddest thing of all.

RANK *(looks searchingly at her)*: Hm—

NORA *(after a moment)*: Why did you smile?

RANK: No, it was you who laughed.

NORA: No, it was you who smiled, Dr. Rank!

RANK *(gets up)*: You're a worse little rogue than I thought.

NORA: Oh, I'm full of stupid tricks today.

RANK: So it seems.

NORA *(puts both her hands on his shoulders)*: Dear, dear Dr. Rank, you mustn't die and leave Torvald and me.

RANK: Oh, you'll soon get over it. Once one is gone, one is soon forgotten.

NORA *(looks at him anxiously)*: Do you believe that?

RANK: One finds replacements, and then—

NORA: Who will find a replacement?

RANK: You and Helmer both will, when I am gone. You seem to have made a start already, haven't you? What was this Mrs. Linde doing here yesterday evening?

NORA: Aha! But surely you can't be jealous of poor Christine?

RANK: Indeed I am. She will be my successor in this house. When I have moved on, this lady will—

NORA: Ssh—don't speak so loud! She's in there!

RANK: Today again? You see!

NORA: She's only come to mend my dress. Good heavens, how unreasonable you are! *(Sits on the sofa.)* Be nice now, Dr. Rank. Tomorrow you'll see how beautifully I shall dance; and you must imagine that I'm doing it just for you. And for Torvald, of course; obviously. *(Takes some things out of the box.)* Dr. Rank, sit down here and I'll show you something.

RANK *(sits)*: What's this?

NORA: Look here! Look!

RANK: Silk stockings!

NORA: Flesh-coloured. Aren't they beautiful? It's very dark in here now, of course, but tomorrow—! No, no, no; only the soles. Oh well, I suppose you can look a bit higher if you want to.

RANK: Hm—

NORA: Why are you looking so critical? Don't you think they'll fit me?

RANK: I can't really give you a qualified opinion on that.

NORA *(looks at him for a moment)*: Shame on you! *(Flicks him on the ear with the stockings.)* Take that. *(Puts them back in the box.)*

RANK: What other wonders are to be revealed to me?

NORA: I shan't show you anything else. You're being naughty.

(She hums a little and looks among the things in the box.)

RANK *(after a short silence)*: When I sit here like this being so intimate with you, I can't think—I cannot imagine what would have become of me if I had never entered this house.

NORA *(smiles)*: Yes, I think you enjoy being with us, don't you?

RANK *(more quietly, looking into the middle distance)*: And now to have to leave it all—

NORA: Nonsense. You're not leaving us.

RANK *(as before)*: And not to be able to leave even the most wretched token of gratitude behind; hardly even a passing sense of loss; only an empty place, to be filled by the next comer.

NORA: Suppose I were to ask you to—? No—

RANK: To do what?

NORA: To give me proof of your friendship—

RANK: Yes, yes?

NORA: No, I mean—to do me a very great service—

RANK: Would you really for once grant me that happiness?

NORA: But you've no idea what it is.

RANK: Very well, tell me, then.

NORA: No, but, Dr. Rank, I can't. It's far too much—I want your help and advice, and I want you to do something for me.

RANK: The more the better. I've no idea what it can be. But tell me. You do trust me, don't you?

NORA: Oh, yes, more than anyone. You're my best and truest friend. Otherwise I couldn't tell you. Well then, Dr. Rank—there's something you must help me to prevent. You know how much Torvald loves me—he'd never hesitate for an instant to lay down his life for me—

RANK *(leans over toward her)*: Nora—do you think he is the only one—?

NORA *(with a slight start)*: What do you mean?

RANK: Who would gladly lay down his life for you?

NORA *(sadly)*: Oh, I see.

RANK: I swore to myself I would let you know that before I go. I shall never have a better opportunity. . . . Well, Nora, now you know that. And now you also know that you can trust me as you can trust nobody else.

NORA *(rises; calmly and quietly)*: Let me pass, please.

RANK *(makes room for her but remains seated)*: Nora—

NORA *(in the doorway to the hall)*: Helen, bring the lamp. *(Goes over to the stove.)* Oh, dear Dr. Rank, this was really horrid of you.

RANK *(gets up)*: That I have loved you as deeply as anyone else has? Was that horrid of me?

NORA: No—but that you should go and tell me. That was quite unnecessary—

RANK: What do you mean? Did you know, then—?

(The MAID *enters with the lamp, puts it on the table and goes out.)*

RANK: Nora—Mrs. Helmer—I am asking you, did you know this?

NORA: Oh, what do I know, what did I know, what didn't I know—I really can't say. How could you be so stupid, Dr. Rank? Everything was so nice.

RANK: Well, at any rate now you know that I am ready to serve you, body and soul. So—please continue.

NORA *(looks at him)*: After this?

RANK: Please tell me what it is.

NORA: I can't possibly tell you now.

RANK: Yes, yes! You mustn't punish me like this. Let me be allowed to do what I can for you.

NORA: You can't do anything for me now. Anyway, I don't need any help. It was only my imagination—you'll see. Yes, really. Honestly. *(Sits in the rocking chair, looks at him and smiles.)* Well, upon my word you *are* a fine gentleman, Dr. Rank. Aren't you ashamed of yourself, now that the lamp's been lit?

RANK: Frankly, no. But perhaps I ought to say— *adieu?*

NORA: Of course not. You will naturally continue to visit us as before. You know quite well how Torvald depends on your company.

RANK: Yes, but you?

NORA: Oh, I always think it's enormous fun having you here.

RANK: That was what misled me. You're a riddle to me, you know. I'd often felt you'd just as soon be with me as with Helmer.

NORA: Well, you see, there are some people whom one loves, and others whom it's almost more fun to be with.

RANK: Oh yes, there's some truth in that.

NORA: When I was at home, of course I loved Papa best. But I always used to think it was terribly amusing to go down and talk to the servants; because they never told me what I ought to do; and they were such fun to listen to.

RANK: I see. So I've taken their place?

NORA *(jumps up and runs over to him)*: Oh, dear sweet Dr. Rank, I didn't mean that at all. But I'm sure you understand—I feel the same about Torvald as I did about Papa.

MAID *(enters from the hall)*: Excuse me, madam. *(Whispers to her and hands her a visiting card.)*

NORA *(glances at the card)*: Oh! *(Puts it quickly in her pocket.)*

RANK: Anything wrong?

NORA: No, no, nothing at all. It's just something that—it's my new dress.

RANK: What? But your costume is lying over there.

NORA: Oh—that, yes—but there's another—I ordered it specially—Torvald mustn't know—

RANK: Ah, so that's your big secret.

NORA: Yes, yes. Go in and talk to him—he's in his study—keep him talking for a bit—

RANK: Don't worry. He won't get away from me. *(Goes into* HELMER's *study.)*

NORA *(to the* MAID*)*: Is he waiting in the kitchen?

MAID: Yes, madam, he came up the back way—

NORA: But didn't you tell him I had a visitor?

MAID: Yes, but he wouldn't go.

NORA: Wouldn't go?

MAID: No, madam, not until he'd spoken with you.

NORA: Very well, show him in; but quietly. Helen, you mustn't tell anyone about this. It's a surprise for my husband.

MAID: Very good, madam. I understand. *(Goes.)*

NORA: It's happening. It's happening after all. No, no, no, it can't happen, it mustn't happen.

(She walks across and bolts the door of HELMER's *study. The* MAID *opens the door from the hall to admit* KROGSTAD, *and closes it behind him. He is wearing an overcoat, heavy boots and a fur cap.)*

NORA *(goes toward him.)*: Speak quietly. My husband's at home.

KROGSTAD: Let him hear.

NORA: What do you want from me?

KROGSTAD: Information.

NORA: Hurry up, then. What is it?

KROGSTAD: I suppose you know I've been given the sack.

NORA: I couldn't stop it, Mr. Krogstad. I did my best for you, but it didn't help.

KROGSTAD: Does your husband love you so little? He knows what I can do to you, and yet he dares to—

NORA: Surely you don't imagine I told him?

KROGSTAD: No, I didn't really think you had. It wouldn't have been like my old friend Torvald Helmer to show that much courage—

NORA: Mr. Krogstad, I'll trouble you to speak respectfully of my husband.

KROGSTAD: Don't worry, I'll show him all the respect he deserves. But since you're so anxious to keep this matter hushed up, I presume you're better informed than you were yesterday of the gravity of what you've done?

NORA: I've learned more than you could ever teach me.

KROGSTAD: Yes, a bad lawyer like me—

NORA: What do you want from me?

KROGSTAD: I just wanted to see how things were with you, Mrs. Helmer. I've been thinking about you all day. Even duns and hack journalists have hearts, you know.

NORA: Show some heart, then. Think of my little children.

KROGSTAD: Have you and your husband thought of mine? Well, let's forget that. I just wanted to tell you, you don't need to take this business too seriously. I'm not going to take any action for the present.

NORA: Oh, no—you won't, will you? I knew it.

KROGSTAD: It can all be settled quite amicably. There's no need for it to become public. We'll keep it among the three of us.

NORA: My husband must never know about this.

KROGSTAD: How can you stop him? Can you pay the balance of what you owe me?

NORA: Not immediately.

KROGSTAD: Have you any means of raising the money during the next few days?

NORA: None that I would care to use.

KROGSTAD: Well, it wouldn't have helped anyway. However much money you offered me now I wouldn't give you back that paper.

NORA: What are you going to do with it?

KROGSTAD: Just keep it. No one else need ever hear about it. So in case you were thinking of doing anything desperate—

NORA: I am.

KROGSTAD: Such as running away—

NORA: I am.

KORGSTAD: Or anything more desperate—

NORA: How did you know?

KROGSTAD: —just give up the idea.

NORA: How did you know?

KROGSTAD: Most of us think of that at first. I did. But I hadn't the courage—

NORA (dully): Neither have I.

KROGSTAD (relieved): It's true, isn't it? You haven't the courage either?

NORA: No. I haven't. I haven't.

KROGSTAD: It'd be a stupid thing to do anyway. Once the first little domestic explosion is over. . . . I've got a letter in my pocket here addressed to your husband—

NORA: Telling him everything?

KROGSTAD: As delicately as possibly.

NORA (quickly): He must never see that letter. Tear it up. I'll find the money somehow—

KROGSTAD: I'm sorry, Mrs. Helmer, I thought I'd explained—

NORA: Oh, I don't mean the money I owe you. Let me know how much you want from my husband, and I'll find it for you.

KROGSTAD: I'm not asking your husband for money.

NORA: What do you want, then?

KROGSTAD: I'll tell you. I want to get on my feet again, Mrs. Helmer. I want to get to the top. And your husband's going to help me. For eighteen months now my record's been clean. I've been in hard straits all that time; I was content to fight my way back inch by inch. Now I've been chucked back into the mud, and I'm not going to be satisfied with just getting back my job. I'm going to get to the top, I tell you. I'm going to get back into the bank, and it's going to be higher up. Your husband's going to create a new job for me—

NORA: He'll never do that!

KROGSTAD: Oh, yes he will. I know him. He won't dare to risk a scandal. And once I'm in there with him, you'll see! Within a year I'll be his right-hand man. It'll be Nils Krogstad who'll be running that bank, not Torvald Helmer!

NORA: That will never happen.

KROGSTAD: Are you thinking of—?

NORA: Now I *have* the courage.

KROGSTAD: Oh, you can't frighten me. A pampered little pretty like you—

NORA: You'll see! You'll see!

KROGSTAD: Under the ice? Down in the cold, black water? And then, in the spring to float up again, ugly, unrecognizable, hairless—?

NORA: You can't frighten me.

KROGSTAD: And you can't frighten me. People don't do such things, Mrs. Helmer. And anyway, what'd be the use? I've got him in my pocket.

NORA: But afterwards? When I'm no longer—?

KROGSTAD: Have you forgotten that then your reputation will be in my hands? (She looks at him speechlessly.) Well, I've warned you. Don't do anything silly. When Helmer's read my letter, he'll get in touch with me. And remember, it's your husband who's forced me to act like this. And for that I'll never forgive him. Goodbye, Mrs. Helmer. (He goes out through the hall.)

NORA (runs to the hall door, opens it a few inches and listens): He's going. He's not going to give him the letter. Oh, no, no, it couldn't possibly happen. (Opens the door a little wider). What's he doing? Standing outside the front door. He's not going downstairs. Is he changing his mind? Yes, he—!

(A letter falls into the letter-box. KROGSTAD's footsteps die away down the stairs.)

NORA (with a stifled cry, runs across the room toward the table by the sofa. A pause): In the letter-box. (Steals timidly over toward the hall door.) There it is! Oh, Torvald, Torvald! Now we're lost!

MRS. LINDE (enters from the nursery with NORA's costume): Well, I've done the best I can. Shall we see how it looks—?

NORA (whispers hoarsely): Christine, come here.

MRS. LINDE (throws the dress on the sofa): What's wrong

with you? You look as though you'd seen a ghost!

NORA: Come here. Do you see that letter? There—look—through the glass of the letter-box.

MRS. LINDE: Yes, yes, I see it.

NORA: That letter's from Krogstad—

MRS. LINDE: Nora! It was Krogstad who lent you the money!

NORA: Yes. And now Torvald's going to discover everything.

MRS. LINDE: Oh, believe me, Nora, it'll be best for you both.

NORA: You don't know what's happened. I've committed a forgery—

MRS. LINDE: But, for heaven's sake—!

NORA: Christine, all I want is for you to be my witness.

MRS. LINDE: What do you mean? Witness what?

NORA: If I should go out of my mind—and it might easily happen—

MRS. LINDE: Nora!

NORA: Or if anything else should happen to me—so that I wasn't here any longer—

MRS. LINDE: Nora, Nora, you don't know what you're saying!

NORA: If anyone should try to take the blame, and say it was all his fault—you understand—?

MRS. LINDE: Yes, yes—but how can you think—?

NORA: Then you must testify that it isn't true, Christine. I'm not mad—I know exactly what I'm saying—and I'm telling you, no one else knows anything about this. I did it entirely on my own. Remember that.

MRS. LINDE: All right. But I simply don't understand—

NORA: Oh, how could you understand? A miracle—is—about to happen.

MRS. LINDE: Miracle?

NORA: Yes. A miracle. But it's so frightening, Christine. It *mustn't* happen, not for anything in the world.

MRS. LINDE: I'll go over and talk to Krogstad.

NORA: Don't go near him. He'll only do something to hurt you.

MRS. LINDE: Once upon a time he'd have done anything for my sake.

NORA: He?

MRS. LINDE: Where does he live?

NORA: Oh, how should I know—? Oh yes, wait a moment—! (*Feels in her pocket.*) Here's his card. But the letter, the letter—!

HELMER (*from his study, knocks on the door*): Nora!

NORA (*cries in alarm*): What is it?

HELMER: Now, now, don't get alarmed. We're not coming in, you've closed the door. Are you trying on your costume?

NORA: Yes, yes—I'm trying on my costume. I'm going to look so pretty for you, Torvald.

MRS. LINDE (*who has been reading the card*): Why, he lives just round the corner.

NORA: Yes; but it's no use. There's nothing to be done now. The letter's lying there in the box.

MRS. LINDE: And your husband has the key?

NORA: Yes, he always keeps it.

MRS. LINDE: Krogstad must ask him to send the letter back unread. He must find some excuse—

NORA: But Torvald always opens the box at just about this time—

MRS. LINDE: You must stop him. Go in and keep him talking. I'll be back as quickly as I can.

(*She hurries out through the hall.*)

NORA (*goes over to* HELMER'*s door, opens it and peeps in*): Torvald!

HELMER (*offstage*): Well, may a man enter his own drawing room again? Come on, Rank, now we'll see what—(*In the doorway.*) But what's this?

NORA: What, Torvald dear?

HELMER: Rank's been preparing me for some great transformation scene.

RANK (*in the doorway*): So I understood. But I seem to have been mistaken.

NORA: Yes, no one's to be allowed to see me before tomorrow night.

HELMER: But, my dear Nora, you look quite worn out. Have you been practising too hard?

NORA: No, I haven't practised at all yet.

HELMER: Well, you must.

NORA: Yes, Torvald, I must, I know. But I can't get anywhere without your help. I've completely forgotten everything.

HELMER: Oh, we'll soon put that to rights.

NORA: Yes, help me, Torvald. Promise me you will? Oh, I'm so nervous. All those people—! You must forget everything except me this evening. You mustn't think of business—I won't even let you touch a pen. Promise me, Torvald?

HELMER: I promise. This evening I shall think of nothing but you—my poor, helpless little darling. Oh, there's just one thing I must see to—(*Goes toward the hall door.*)

NORA: What do you want out there?

HELMER: I'm only going to see if any letters have come.

NORA: No, Torvald, no!

HELMER: Why, what's the matter?

NORA: Torvald, I beg you. There's nothing there.

HELMER: Well, I'll just make sure.

(*He moves toward the door.* NORA *runs to the piano and plays the first bars of the tarantella.*)

HELMER (*at the door, turns*): Aha!

NORA: I can't dance tomorrow if I don't practise with you now.

HELMER (*goes over to her*): Are you really so frightened, Nora dear?

NORA: Yes, terribly frightened. Let me start practising now, at once—we've still time before dinner. Oh, do sit down and play for me, Torvald dear. Correct me, lead me, the way you always do.

HELMER: Very well, my dear, if you wish it.

(*He sits down at the piano.* NORA *seizes the tambourine and a long multi-coloured shawl from the cardboard box, wraps the latter hastily around her, then takes a quick leap into the center of the room.*)

NORA: Play for me! I want to dance!

(HELMER *plays and* NORA *dances.* DR. RANK *stands behind* HELMER *at the piano and watches her.*)

HELMER (*as he plays*): Slower, slower!

NORA: I can't!

HELMER: Not so violently, Nora.

NORA: I must!

HELMER (*stops playing*): No, no, this won't do at all.

NORA (*laughs and swings her tambourine*): Isn't that what I told you?

RANK: Let me play for her.

HELMER (*gets up*): Yes, would you? Then it'll be easier for me to show her.

(RANK *sits down at the piano and plays.* NORA *dances more and more wildly.* HELMER *has stationed himself by the stove and tries repeatedly to correct her, but she seems not to hear him. Her hair works loose and falls over her shoulders; she ignores it and continues to dance.* MRS. LINDE *enters.*)

MRS. LINDE (*stands in the doorway as though tongue-tied*): Ah—!

NORA (*as she dances*): Christine, we're having such fun!

HELMER: But, Nora darling, you're dancing as if your life depended on it.

NORA: It does.

HELMER: Rank, stop it! This is sheer lunacy. Stop it, I say!

(RANK *ceases playing.* NORA *suddenly stops dancing.*)

HELMER (*goes over to her*): I'd never have believed it. You've forgotten everything I taught you.

NORA (*throws away the tambourine*): You see!

HELMER: I'll have to show you every step.

NORA: You see how much I need you! You must show me every step of the way. Right to the end of the dance. Promise me you will, Torvald?

HELMER: Never fear. I will.

NORA: You mustn't think about anything but me—today or tomorrow. Don't open any letters—don't even open the letter-box—

HELMER: Aha, you're still worried about that fellow—

NORA: Oh, yes, yes, him too.

HELMER: Nora, I can tell from the way you're behaving, there's a letter from him already there.

NORA: I don't know. I think so. But you mustn't read it now. I don't want anything ugly to come between us till it's all over.

RANK (*quietly, to* HELMER): Better give her her way.

HELMER (*puts his arm around her*): My child shall have her way. But tomorrow night, when your dance is over—

NORA: Then you will be free.

MAID (*appears in the doorway, right*): Dinner is served, madam.

NORA: Put out some champagne, Helen.

MAID: Very good, madam. (*Goes.*)

HELMER: I say! What's this, a banquet?

NORA: We'll drink champagne until dawn! (*Calls.*) And, Helen! Put out some macaroons! Lots of macaroons—for once!

HELMER (*takes her hands in his*): Now, now, now. Don't get so excited. Where's my little songbird, the one I know?

NORA: All right. Go and sit down—and you too, Dr. Rank. I'll be with you in a minute. Christine, you must help me put my hair up.

RANK (*quietly, as they go*): There's nothing wrong, is there? I mean, she isn't—er—expecting—?

HELMER: Good heavens no, my dear chap. She just gets scared like a child sometimes—I told you before—

(*They go out right.*)

NORA: Well?

MRS. LINDE: He's left town.

NORA: I saw it from your face.

MRS. LINDE: He'll be back tomorrow evening. I left a note for him.

NORA: You needn't have bothered. You can't stop anything now. Anyway, it's wonderful really, in a way—sitting here and waiting for the miracle to happen.

MRS. LINDE: Waiting for what?

NORA: Oh, you wouldn't understand. Go in and join them. I'll be with you in a moment.

(MRS. LINDE *goes into the dining-room.*)

NORA (*stands for a moment as though collecting herself. Then she looks at her watch*): Five o'clock. Seven hours till midnight. Then another twenty-four hours till midnight tomorrow. And then the tarantella will be finished. Twenty-four and seven? Thirty-one hours to live.

HELMER (*appears in the doorway, right*): What's happened to my little songbird?

NORA (*runs to him with here arms wide*): Your songbird is here!

ACT 3

(*The same room. The table which was formerly by the sofa has been moved into the centre of the room; the chairs*) *surround it as before. The door to the hall stands open. Dance music can be heard from the floor above.* MRS. LINDE *is seated at the table, absent-mindedly glancing through a book. She is trying to read, but seems unable to keep her mind on it. More than once she turns and listens anxiously toward the front door.)*

MRS. LINDE *(looks at her watch)*: Not here yet. There's not much time left. Please God he hasn't—! *(Listens again.)* Ah, here he is. *(Goes out into the hall and cautiously opens the front door. Footsteps can be heard softly ascending the stairs. She whispers.)* Come in. There's no one here.

KROGSTAD *(in the doorway)*: I found a note from you at my lodgings. What does this mean?

MRS. LINDE: I must speak with you.

KROGSTAD: Oh? And must our conversation take place in this house?

MRS. LINDE: We couldn't meet at my place; my room has no separate entrance. Come in. We're quite alone. The maid's asleep, and the Helmers are at the dance upstairs.

KROGSTAD *(comes into the room)*: Well, well! So the Helmers are dancing this evening? Are they indeed?

MRS. LINDE: Yes, why not?

KROGSTAD: True enough. Why not?

MRS. LINDE: Well, Krogstad. You and I must have a talk together.

KROGSTAD: Have we two anything further to discuss?

MRS. LINDE: We have a great deal to discuss.

KROGSTAD: I wasn't aware of it.

MRS. LINDE: That's because you've never really understood me.

KROGSTAD: Was there anything to understand? It's the old story, isn't it—a woman chucking a man because something better turns up?

MRS. LINDE: Do you really think I'm so utterly heartless? You think it was easy for me to give you up?

KROGSTAD: Wasn't it?

MRS. LINDE: Oh, Nils, did you really believe that?

KROGSTAD: Then why did you write to me the way you did?

MRS. LINDE: I had to. Since I had to break with you, I thought it my duty to destroy all the feelings you had for me.

KROGSTAD *(clenches his fists)*: So that was it. And you did this for money!

MRS. LINDE: You mustn't forget I had a helpless mother to take care of, and two little brothers. We couldn't wait for you, Nils. It would have been so long before you'd had enough to support us.

KROGSTAD: Maybe. But you had no right to cast me off for someone else.

MRS. LINDE: Perhaps not. I've often asked myself that.

KROGSTAD *(more quietly)*: When I lost you, it was just as though all solid ground had been swept from

under my feet. Look at me. Now I am a shipwrecked man, clinging to a spar.

MRS. LINDE: Help may be near at hand.

KROGSTAD: It was near. But then you came, and stood between it and me.

MRS. LINDE: I didn't know, Nils. No one told me till today that this job I'd found was yours.

KROGSTAD: I believe you, since you say so. But now you know, won't you give it up?

MRS. LINDE: No—because it wouldn't help you even if I did.

KROGSTAD: Wouldn't it? I'd do it all the same.

MRS. LINDE: I've learned to look at things practically. Life and poverty have taught me that.

KROGSTAD: And life has taught me to distrust fine words.

MRS. LINDE: Then it's taught you a useful lesson. But surely you still believe in actions?

KROGSTAD: What do you mean?

MRS. LINDE: You said you were like a shipwrecked man clinging to a spar.

KROGSTAD: I have good reason to say it.

MRS. LINDE: I'm in the same position as you. No one to care about, no one to care for.

KROGSTAD: You made your own choice.

MRS. LINDE: I had no choice—then.

KROGSTAD: Well?

MRS. LINDE: Nils, suppose we two shipwrecked souls could join hands?

KROGSTAD: What are you saying?

MRS. LINDE: Castaways have a better chance of survival together than on their own.

KROGSTAD: Christine!

MRS. LINDE: Why do you suppose I came to this town?

KROGSTAD: You mean—you came because of me?

MRS. LINDE: I must work if I'm to find life worth living. I've always worked, for as long as I can remember; it's been the greatest joy of my life—my only joy. But now I'm alone in the world, and I feel so dreadfully lost and empty. There's no joy in working just for oneself. Oh, Nils, give me something—someone—to work for.

KROGSTAD: I don't believe all that. You're just being hysterical and romantic. You want to find an excuse for self-sacrifice.

MRS. LINDE: Have you ever known me to be hysterical?

KROGSTAD: You mean you really—? Is it possible? Tell me—you know all about my past?

MRS. LINDE: Yes.

KROGSTAD: And you know what people think of me here?

MRS. LINDE: You said just now that with me you might have become a different person.

KROGSTAD: I know I could have.

MRS. LINDE: Could it still happen?

KROGSTAD: Christine—do you really mean this?

Yes—you do—I see it in your face. Have you really the courage—?

MRS. LINDE: I need someone to be a mother to; and your children need a mother. And you and I need each other. I believe in you, Nils. I am afraid of nothing—with you.

KROGSTAD (clasps her hands): Thank you, Christine—thank you! Now I shall make the world believe in me as you do! Oh—but I'd forgotten—

MRS. LINDE (listens): Ssh! The tarantella! Go quickly, go!

KROGSTAD: Why? What is it?

MRS. LINDE: You hear that dance? As soon as it's finished, they'll be coming down.

KROGSTAD: All right, I'll go. It's no good, Christine. I'd forgotten—you don't know what I've just done to the Helmers.

MRS. LINDE: Yes, Nils. I know.

KROGSTAD: And yet you'd still have the courage to—?

MRS. LINDE: I know what despair can drive a man like you to.

KROGSTAD: Oh, if only I could undo this!

MRS. LINDE: You can. Your letter is still lying in the box.

KROGSTAD: Are you sure?

MRS. LINDE: Quite sure. But—

KROGSTAD (looks searchingly): Is that why you're doing this? You want to save your friend at any price? Tell me the truth. Is that the reason?

MRS. LINDE: Nils, a woman who has sold herself once for the sake of others doesn't make the same mistake again.

KROGSTAD: I shall demand my letter back.

MRS. LINDE: No, no.

KROGSTAD: Of course I shall. I shall stay here till Helmer comes down. I'll tell him he must give me back my letter—I'll say it was only to do with my dismissal, and that I don't want him to read it—

MRS. LINDE: No, Nils, you mustn't ask for that letter back.

KROGSTAD: But—tell me—wasn't that the real reason you asked me to come here?

MRS. LINDE: Yes—at first, when I was frightened. But a day has passed since then, and in that time I've seen incredible things happen in this house. Helmer must know the truth. This unhappy secret of Nora's must be revealed. They must come to a full understanding; there must be an end of all these shiftings and evasions.

KROGSTAD: Very well. If you're prepared to risk it. But one thing I can do—and at once—

MRS. LINDE (listens): Hurry! Go, go! The dance is over. We aren't safe here another moment.

KROGSTAD: I'll wait for you downstairs.

MRS. LINDE: Yes, do. You can see me home.

KROGSTAD: I've never been so happy in my life before!

(He goes through the front door. The door leading from the room into the hall remains open.)

MRS. LINDE (tidies the room a little and gets her hat and coat): What a change! Oh, what a change! Someone to work for—to live for! A home to bring joy into! I won't let this chance of happiness slip through my fingers. Oh, why don't they come? (Listens.) Ah, here they are. I must get my coat on.

(She takes her hat and coat. HELMER's and NORA's voices become audible outside. A key is turned in the lock and HELMER leads NORA almost forcibly into the hall. She is dressed in an Italian costume with a large black shawl. He is in evening dress, with a black cloak.)

NORA (still in the doorway, resisting him): No, no, no—not in here! I want to go back upstairs. I don't want to leave so early.

HELMER: But my dearest Nora—

NORA: Oh, please, Torvald, please! Just another hour!

HELMER: Not another minute, Nora, my sweet. You know what we agreed. Come along, now. Into the drawing-room. You'll catch cold if you stay out here.

(He leads her, despite her efforts to resist him, gently into the room.)

MRS. LINDE: Good evening.

NORA: Christine!

HELMER: Oh, hullo, Mrs. Linde. You still here?

MRS. LINDE: Please forgive me. I did so want to see Nora in her costume.

NORA: Have you been sitting here waiting for me?

MRS. LINDE: Yes, I got here too late, I'm afraid. You'd already gone up. And I felt I really couldn't go back home without seeing you.

HELMER (takes off NORA's shawl): Well, take a good look at her. She's worth looking at, don't you think? Isn't she beautiful, Mrs. Linde?

MRS. LINDE: Oh, yes, indeed—

HELMER: Isn't she unbelievably beautiful? Everyone at the party said so. But dreadfully stubborn she is, bless her pretty little heart. What's to be done about that? Would you believe it, I practically had to use force to get her away!

NORA: Oh, Torvald, you're going to regret not letting me stay—just half an hour longer.

HELMER: Hear that, Mrs. Linde? She dances her tarantella—makes a roaring success—and very well deserved—though possibly a trifle too realistic—more so than was aesthetically necessary, strictly speaking. But never mind that. Main thing is—she had a success—roaring success. Was I going to let her stay on after that and spoil the impression? No, thank you. I took my beautiful little Capri signorina—my capricious little Capricienne, what?—under my arm—a swift round of the ballroom, a curtsey to the company, and, as they say in novels, the beautiful apparition disappeared! An exit should always be dramatic, Mrs. Linde. But unfortunately that's just what I can't get Nora to realize. I say, it's hot in here. (*Throws his cloak on a chair and opens the door to his study.*) What's this? It's dark in here. Ah, yes, of course—excuse me. (*Goes in and lights a couple of candles.*)

NORA (*whispers swiftly, breathlessly*): Well?

MRS. LINDE (*quietly*): I've spoken to him.

NORA: Yes?

MRS. LINDE: Nora—you must tell your husband everything.

NORA (*dully*): I knew it.

MRS. LINDE: You've nothing to fear from Krogstad. But you must tell him.

NORA: I shan't tell him anything.

MRS. LINDE: Then the letter will.

NORA: Thank you, Christine. Now I know what I must do. Ssh!

HELMER (*returns*): Well, Mrs. Linde, finished admiring her?

MRS. LINDE: Yes. Now I must say good night.

HELMER: Oh, already? Does this knitting belong to you?

MRS. LINDE (*takes it*): Thank you, yes. I nearly forgot it.

HELMER: You knit, then?

MRS. LINDE: Why, yes.

HELMER: Know what? You ought to take up embroidery.

MRS. LINDE: Oh? Why?

HELMER: It's much prettier. Watch me, now. You hold the embroidery in your left hand, like this, and then you take the needle in your right hand and go in and out in a slow, easy movement—like this. I am right, aren't I?

MRS. LINDE: Yes, I'm sure—

HELMER: But knitting, now—that's an ugly business—can't help it. Look—arms all huddled up—great clumsy needles going up and down—makes you look like a damned Chinaman. I say, that really was a magnificent champagne they served us.

MRS. LINDE: Well, good night, Nora. And stop being stubborn. Remember!

HELMER: Quite right, Mrs. Linde!

MRS. LINDE: Good night, Mr. Helmer.

HELMER (*accompanies her to the door*): Good night, good night! I hope you'll manage to get home all right? I'd gladly—but you haven't far to go, have you? Good night, good night. (*She goes. He closes the door behind her and returns.*) Well, we've got rid of her at last. Dreadful bore that woman is!

NORA: Aren't you very tired, Torvald?

HELMER: No, not in the least.

NORA: Aren't you sleepy?

HELMER: Not a bit. On the contrary, I feel extraordinarily exhilarated. But what about you? Yes, you look very sleepy and tired.

NORA: Yes, I am very tired. Soon I shall sleep.

HELMER: You see, you see! How right I was not to let you stay longer!

NORA: Oh, you're always right, whatever you do.

HELMER (*kisses her on the forehead*): Now my little songbird's talking just like a real big human being. I say, did you notice how cheerful Rank was this evening?

NORA: Oh? Was he? I didn't have a chance to speak with him.

HELMER: I hardly did. But I haven't seen him in such a jolly mood for ages. (*Look at her for a moment, then comes closer.*) I say, it's nice to get back to one's home again, and be all alone with you. Upon my word, you're a distractingly beautiful young woman.

NORA: Don't look at me like that, Torvald!

HELMER: What, not look at my most treasured possession? At all this wonderful beauty that's mine, mine alone, all mine.

NORA (*goes round to the other side of the table*): You mustn't talk to me like that tonight.

HELMER (*follows her*): You've still the tarantella in your blood, I see. And that makes you even more desirable. Listen! Now the other guests are beginning to go. (*More quietly.*) Nora—soon the whole house will be absolutely quiet.

NORA: Yes, I hope so.

HELMER: Yes, my beloved Nora, of course you do! Do you know—when I'm out with you among other people like we were tonight, do you know why I say so little to you, why I keep so aloof from you, and just throw you an occasional glance? Do you know why I do that? It's because I pretend to myself that you're my secret mistress, my clandestine little sweetheart, and that nobody knows there's anything at all between us.

NORA: Oh, yes, yes, yes—I know you never think of anything but me.

HELMER: And then when we're about to go, and I wrap the shawl round your lovely young shoulders, over this wonderful curve of your neck—Then I pretend to myself that you are my young bride, that we've just come from the wedding, that I'm taking you to my house for the first time—that, for the first time, I am alone with you—quite alone with you, as you stand there young and trembling and beautiful. All evening I've had no eyes for anyone but you. When I saw you dance the tarantella, like a huntress, a temptress, my blood grew hot, I couldn't stand it any longer! That was why I seized you and dragged you down here with me—

NORA: Leave me, Torvald! Get away from me! I don't want all this.

HELMER: What? Now, Nora, you're joking with me. Don't want, don't want—? Aren't I your husband—?

(There is a knock on the front door.)

NORA *(starts)*: What was that?

HELMER *(goes toward the hall)*: Who is it?

RANK *(outside)*: It's me. May I come in for a moment?

HELMER *(quietly, annoyed)*: Oh, what does he want now? *(Calls.)* Wait a moment. *(Walks over and opens the door.)* Well! Nice of you not to go by without looking in.

RANK: I thought I heard your voice, so I felt I had to say goodbye. *(His eyes travel swiftly around the room.)* Ah, yes—these dear rooms, how well I know them. What a happy, peaceful home you two have.

HELMER: You seemed to be having a pretty happy time yourself upstairs.

RANK: Indeed I did. Why not? Why shouldn't one make the most of this world? As much as one can, and for as long as one can. The wine was excellent—

HELMER: Especially the champagne.

RANK: You noticed that too? It's almost incredible how much I managed to get down.

NORA: Torvald drank a lot of champagne too, this evening.

RANK: Oh?

NORA: Yes. It always makes him merry afterwards.

RANK: Well, why shouldn't a man have a merry evening after a well-spent day?

HELMER: Well-spent? Oh, I don't know that I can claim that.

RANK *(slaps him across the back)*: I can, though, my dear fellow!

NORA: Yes, of course, Dr. Rank—you've been carrying out a scientific experiment today, haven't you?

RANK: Exactly.

HELMER: Scientific experiment! Those are big words for my little Nora to use!

NORA: And may I congratulate you on the finding?

RANK: You may indeed.

NORA: It was good, then?

RANK: The best possible finding—both for the doctor and the patient. Certainty.

NORA *(quickly)*: Certainty?

RANK: Absolute certainty. So aren't I entitled to have a merry evening after that?

NORA: Yes, Dr. Rank. You were quite right to.

HELMER: I agree. Provided you don't have to regret it tomorrow.

RANK: Well, you never get anything in this life without paying for it.

NORA: Dr. Rank—you like masquerades, don't you?

RANK: Yes, if the disguises are sufficiently amusing.

NORA: Tell me. What shall we two wear at the next masquerade?

HELMER: You little gadabout! Are you thinking about the next one already?

RANK: We two? Yes, I'll tell you. You must go as the Spirit of Happiness—

HELMER: You try to think of a costume that'll convey that.

RANK: Your wife need only appear as her normal, everyday self—

HELMER: Quite right! Well said! But what are you going to be? Have you decided that?

RANK: Yes, my dear friend. I have decided that.

HELMER: Well?

RANK: At the next masquerade, I shall be invisible.

HELMER: Well, that's a funny idea.

RANK: There's a big, black hat—haven't you heard of the invisible hat? Once it's over your head, no one can see you any more.

HELMER *(represses a smile)*: Ah yes, of course.

RANK: But I'm forgetting what I came for. Helmer, give me a cigar. One of your black Havanas.

HELMER: With the greatest pleasure. *(Offers him the box.)*

RANK *(takes one and cuts off the tip)*: Thank you.

NORA *(strikes a match)*: Let me give you a light.

RANK: Thank you. *(She holds out the match for him. He lights his cigar.)* And now—goodbye.

HELMER: Goodbye, my dear chap, goodbye.

NORA: Sleep well, Dr. Rank.

RANK: Thank you for that kind wish.

NORA: Wish me the same.

RANK: You? Very well—since you ask. Sleep well. And thank you for the light. *(He nods to them both and goes.)*

HELMER *(quietly)*: He's been drinking too much.

NORA *(abstractedly)*: Perhaps.

(HELMER takes his bunch of keys from his pocket and goes out into the hall.)

NORA: Torvald, what do you want out there?

HELMER: I must empty the letter-box. It's absolutely full. There'll be no room for the newspapers in the morning.

NORA: Are you going to work tonight?

HELMER: You know very well I'm not. Hullo, what's this? Someone's been at the lock.

NORA: At the lock—?

HELMER: Yes, I'm sure of it. Who on earth—? Surely not one of the maids? Here's a broken hairpin. Nora, it's yours—

NORA *(quickly)*: Then it must have been the children.

HELMER: Well, you'll have to break them of that habit. Hm, hm. Ah, that's done it. *(Takes out the contents of the box and calls into the kitchen.)* Helen! Helen!

Put out the light on the staircase. (*Comes back into the drawing room with the letters in his hand and closes the door to the hall.*) Look at this! You see how they've piled up? (*Glances through them.*) What on earth's this?

NORA (*at the window*): The letter! Oh, no, Torvald, no!

HELMER: Two visiting cards—from Rank.

NORA: From Dr. Rank?

HELMER (*looks at them*): Peter Rank, M.D. They were on top. He must have dropped them in as he left.

NORA: Has he written anything on them?

HELMER: There's a black cross above his name. Look. Rather gruesome, isn't it? It looks just as though he was announcing his death.

NORA: He is.

HELMER: What? Do you know something? Has he told you anything?

NORA: Yes. When these cards come, it means he's said good-bye to us. He wants to shut himself up in his house and die.

HELMER: Ah, poor fellow. I knew I wouldn't be seeing him for much longer. But so soon—! And now he's going to slink away and hide like a wounded beast.

NORA: When the time comes, it's best to go silently. Don't you think so, Torvald?

HELMER (*walks up and down*): He was so much a part of our life. I can't realize that he's gone. His suffering and loneliness seemed to provide a kind of dark background to the happy sunlight of our marriage. Well, perhaps it's best this way. For him, anyway. (*Stops walking.*) And perhaps for us too, Nora. Now we have only each other. (*Embraces her.*) Oh, my beloved wife—I feel as though I could never hold you close enough. Do you know, Nora, often I wish some terrible danger might threaten you, so that I could offer my life and my blood, everything, for your sake.

NORA (*tears herself loose and says in a clear, firm voice*): Read your letters now, Torvald.

HELMER: No, no. Not tonight. Tonight I want to be with you, my darling wife—

NORA: When your friend is about to die—?

HELMER: You're right. This news has upset us both. An ugliness has come between us; thoughts of death and dissolution. We must try to forget them. Until then—you go to your room; I shall go to mine.

NORA (*throws her arms round his neck*): Good night, Torvald! Good night!

HELMER (*kisses her on the forehead*): Good night, my darling little songbird. Sleep well, Nora. I'll go and read my letters.

(*He goes into the study with the letters in his hand, and closes the door.*)

NORA (*wild-eyed, fumbles around, seizes HELMER's cloak, throws it round herself and whispers quickly, hoarsely*): Never see him again. Never. Never. Never. (*Throws the shawl over her head.*) Never see the children again. Them too. Never. Never. Oh—the icy black water! Oh—that bottomless—that—! Oh, if only it were all over! Now he's got it—he's reading it. Oh, no, no! Goodbye, Torvald! Goodbye, my darlings!

(*She turns to run into the hall. As she does so,* HELMER *throws open his door and stands there with an open letter in his hand.*)

HELMER: Nora!

NORA (*shrieks*): Ah—!

HELMER: What is this? Do you know what is in this letter?

NORA: Yes, I know. Let me go! Let me go!

HELMER (*holds her back*): Go? Where?

NORA (*tries to tear herself loose*): You mustn't try to save me, Torvald!

HELMER (*staggers back*): Is it true? Is it true, what he writes? Oh, my God! No, no—it's impossible, it can't be true!

NORA: It *is* true. I've loved you more than anything else in the world.

HELMER: Oh, don't try to make silly excuses.

NORA (*takes a step toward him*): Torvald—

HELMER: Wretched woman! What have you done?

NORA: Let me go! You're not going to suffer for my sake. I won't let you!

HELMER: Stop being theatrical. (*Locks the front door.*) You're going to stay here and explain yourself. Do you understand what you've done? Answer me! Do you understand?

NORA (*looks unflinchingly at him and, her expression growing colder, says*): Yes. Now I am beginning to understand.

HELMER (*walking round the room*): Oh, what a dreadful awakening! For eight whole years—she who was my joy and my pride—a hypocrite, a liar—worse, worse—a criminal! Oh, the hideousness of it! Shame on you, shame!

(NORA *is silent and stares unblinkingly at him.*)

HELMER (*stops in front of her*): I ought to have guessed that something of this sort would happen. I should have foreseen it. All your father's recklessness and instability—be quiet!—I repeat, all your father's recklessness and instability he has handed on to you. No religion, no morals, no sense of duty! Oh, how I have been punished for closing my eyes to his faults! I did it for your sake. And now you reward me like this.

NORA: Yes. Like this.

HELMER: Now you have destroyed all my happiness. You have ruined my whole future. Oh, it's too dreadful to contemplate! I am in the power of a man who is completely without scruples. He can do what he likes with me, demand what he pleases, order me to do anything—I dare not disobey him. I am condemned to humiliation and ruin simply for the weakness of a woman.

NORA: When I am gone from this world, you will be free.

HELMER: Oh, don't be melodramatic. Your father was always ready with that kind of remark. How would it help me if you were "gone from this world," as you put it? It wouldn't assist me in the slightest. He can still make all the facts public; and if he does, I may quite easily be suspected of having been an accomplice in your crime. People may think that I was behind it—that it was I who encouraged you! And for all this I have to thank you, you whom I have carried on my hands through all the years of our marriage! Now do you realize what you've done to me?

NORA (*coldly calm*): Yes.

HELMER: It's so unbelievable I can hardly credit it. But we must try to find some way out. Take off that shawl. Take it off, I say! I must try to buy him off somehow. This thing must be hushed up at any price. As regards our relationship—we must appear to be living together just as before. Only *appear*, of course. You will therefore continue to reside here. That is understood. But the children shall be taken out of your hands. I dare no longer entrust them to you. Oh, to have to say this to the woman I once loved so dearly—and whom I still—! Well, all that must be finished. Henceforth there can be no question of happiness; we must merely strive to save what shreds and tatters—(*The front door bell rings.* HELMER *starts.*) What can that be? At this hour? Surely not—? He wouldn't—? Hide yourself, Nora. Say you're ill.

(NORA *does not move.* HELMER *goes to the door of the room and opens it. The* MAID *is standing half-dressed in the hall.*)

MAID: A letter for madam.

HELMER: Give it me. (*Seizes the letter and shuts the door.*) Yes, it's from him. You're not having it. I'll read this myself.

NORA: Read it.

HELMER (*by the lamp*): I hardly dare to. This may mean the end for us both. No. I must know. (*Tears open the letter hastily; reads a few lines; looks at a piece of paper which is enclosed with it; utters a cry of joy.*) Nora! (*She looks at him questioningly.*) Nora! No—I must read it once more. Yes, yes, it's true! I am saved! Nora, I am saved!

NORA: What about me?

HELMER: You too, of course. We're both saved, you and I. Look! He's returning your I.O.U. He writes that he is sorry for what has happened—a happy accident has changed his life—oh, what does it matter what he writes? We are saved, Nora! No one can harm you now. Oh, Nora, Nora—no, first let me destroy this filthy thing. Let me see—! (*Glances at the I.O.U.*) No, I don't want to look at it. I shall merely regard the whole business as a dream. (*He tears the I.O.U. and both letters into pieces, throws them into the stove and watches them burn.*) There. Now they're destroyed. He wrote that ever since Christmas Eve you've been—oh, these must have been three dreadful days for you, Nora.

NORA: Yes. It's been a hard fight.

HELMER: It must have been terrible—seeing no way out except—no, we'll forget the whole sordid business. We'll just be happy and go on telling ourselves over and over again: "It's over! It's over!" Listen to me, Nora. You don't seem to realize. It's over! Why are you looking so pale? Ah, my poor little Nora, I understand. You can't believe that I have forgiven you. But I have, Nora. I swear it to you. I have forgiven you everything. I know that what you did you did for your love of me.

NORA: That is true.

HELMER: You have loved me as a wife should love her husband. It was simply that in your inexperience you chose the wrong means. But do you think I love you any the less because you don't know how to act on your own initiative? No, no. Just lean on me. I shall counsel you. I shall guide you. I would not be a true man if your feminine helplessness did not make you doubly attractive in my eyes. You mustn't mind the hard words I said to you in those first dreadful moments when my whole world seemed to be tumbling about my ears. I have forgiven you, Nora. I swear it to you; I have forgiven you.

NORA: Thank you for your forgiveness.

(*She goes out through the door, right.*)

HELMER: No, don't go—(*Looks in.*) What are you doing there?

NORA (*offstage*): Taking off my fancy dress.

HELMER (*by the open door*): Yes, do that. Try to calm yourself and get your balance again, my frightened little songbird. Don't be afraid. I have broad wings to shield you. (*Begins to walk around near the door.*) How lovely and peaceful this little home of ours is, Nora. You are safe here; I shall watch over you like a hunted dove which I have snatched unharmed from the claws of the falcon. Your wildly beating little heart shall find peace with me. It will happen, Nora; it will take time, but it will happen, believe me. Tomorrow all this will seem quite different. Soon everything will be as it was before. I shall no longer need to remind you that I have forgiven you; your own heart will tell you that it is true. Do you really think I could ever bring myself to disown you, or even to reproach you? Ah, Nora, you don't understand what goes on in a husband's heart. There is something indescribably wonderful and satisfying for a husband in knowing that he has forgiven his wife—forgiven her unreservedly, from the bottom of his heart. It means that she has become his property in a double sense; he has, as it were, brought her into the world anew; she is now not only his wife but also his child. From now on that is what you shall be to me, my poor, helpless, bewildered little creature. Never be frightened of anything again, Nora. Just open your heart to me. I shall be both your will and your conscience. What's this? Not in bed? Have you changed?

NORA (*in her everyday dress*): Yes, Torvald. I've changed.

HELMER: But why now—so late—?

NORA: I shall not sleep tonight.

HELMER: But, my dear Nora—

NORA (*looks at her watch*): It isn't that late. Sit down here, Torvald. You and I have a lot to talk about.

(*She sits down on one side of the table.*)

HELMER: Nora, what does this mean? You look quite drawn—

NORA: Sit down. It's going to take a long time. I've a lot to say to you.

HELMER (*sits down on the other side of the table*): You alarm me, Nora. I don't understand you.

NORA: No, that's just it. You don't understand me. And I've never understood you—until this evening. No, don't interrupt me. Just listen to what I have to say. You and I have got to face facts, Torvald.

HELMER: What do you mean by that?

NORA (*after a short silence*): Doesn't anything strike you about the way we're sitting here?

HELMER: What?

NORA: We've been married for eight years. Does it occur to you that this is the first time that we two, you and I, man and wife, have ever had a serious talk together?

HELMER: Serious? What do you mean, serious?

NORA: In eight whole years—no, longer—ever since we first met—we have never exchanged a serious word on a serious subject.

HELMER: Did you expect me to drag you into all my worries—worries you couldn't possibly have helped me with?

NORA: I'm not talking about worries. I'm simply saying that we have never sat down seriously to try to get to the bottom of anything.

HELMER: But, my dear Nora, what on earth has that got to do with you?

NORA: That's just the point. You have never understood me. A great wrong has been done to me, Torvald. First by Papa, and then by you.

HELMER: What? But we two have loved you more than anyone in the world!

NORA (*shakes her head*): You have never loved me. You just thought it was fun to be in love with me.

HELMER: Nora, what kind of a way is this to talk?

NORA: It's the truth, Torvald. When I lived with Papa, he used to tell me what he thought about everything, so that I never had any opinions but his. And if I did have any of my own, I kept them quiet, because he wouldn't have liked them. He called me his little doll, and he played with me just the way I played with my dolls. Then I came here to live in your house—

HELMER: What kind of a way is that to describe our marriage?

NORA (*undisturbed*): I mean, then I passed from Papa's hands into yours. You arranged everything the way you wanted it, so that I simply took over your taste in everything—or pretended I did—I don't really know—I think it was a little of both—first one and then the other. Now I look back on it, it's as if I've been living here like a pauper, from hand to mouth. I performed tricks for you, and you gave me food and drink. But that was how you wanted it. You and Papa have done me a great wrong. It's your fault that I have done nothing with my life.

HELMER: Nora, how can you be so unreasonable and ungrateful? Haven't you been happy here?

NORA: No; never. I used to think I was; but I haven't ever been happy.

HELMER: Not—not happy?

NORA: No. I've just had fun. You've always been very kind to me. But our home has never been anything but a playroom. I've been your doll-wife, just as I used to be Papa's doll-child. And the children have been my dolls. I used to think it was fun when you came in and played with me, just as they think it's fun when I go in and play games with them. That's all our marriage has been, Torvald.

HELMER: There may be a little truth in what you say, though you exaggerate and romanticize. But from now on it'll be different. Playtime is over. Now the time has come for education.

NORA: Whose education? Mine or the children's?

HELMER: Both yours and the children's, my dearest Nora.

NORA: Oh, Torvald, you're not the man to educate me into being the right wife for you.

HELMER: How can you say that?

NORA: And what about me? Am I fit to educate the children?

HELMER: Nora!

NORA: Didn't you say yourself a few minutes ago that you dare not leave them in my charge?

HELMER: In a moment of excitement. Surely you don't think I meant it seriously?

NORA: Yes. You were perfectly right. I'm not fitted to educate them. There's something else I must do first. I must educate myself. And you can't help me with that. It's something I must do by myself. That's why I'm leaving you.

HELMER (*jumps up*): What did you say?

NORA: I must stand on my own feet if I am to find out the truth about myself and about life. So I can't go on living here with you any longer.

HELMER: Nora, Nora!

NORA: I'm leaving you now, at once. Christine will put me up for tonight—

HELMER: You're out of your mind! You can't do this! I forbid you!

NORA: It's no use your trying to forbid me any more. I shall take with me nothing but what is mine. I don't want anything from you, now or ever.

HELMER: What kind of madness is this?

NORA: Tomorrow I shall go home—I mean, to where I was born. It'll be easiest for me to find some kind of a job there.

HELMER: But you're blind! You've no experience of the world—

NORA: I must try to get some, Torvald.

HELMER: But to leave your home, your husband, your children! Have you thought what people will say?

NORA: I can't help that. I only know that I must do this.

HELMER: But this is monstrous! Can you neglect your most sacred duties?

NORA: What do you call my most sacred duties?

HELMER: Do I have to tell you? Your duties towards your husband, and your children.

NORA: I have another duty which is equally sacred.

HELMER: You have not. What on earth could that be?

NORA: My duty towards myself.

HELMER: First and foremost you are a wife and a mother.

NORA: I don't believe that any longer. I believe that I am first and foremost a human being, like you—or anyway, that I must try to become one. I know most people think as you do, Torvald, and I know there's something of the sort to be found in books. But I'm no longer prepared to accept what people say and what's written in books. I must think things out for myself, and try to find my own answer.

HELMER: Do you need to ask where your duty lies in your own home? Haven't you an infallible guide in such matters—your religion?

NORA: Oh, Torvald, I don't really know what religion means.

HELMER: What are you saying?

NORA: I only know what Pastor Hansen told me when I went to confirmation. He explained that religion meant this and that. When I get away from all this and can think things out on my own, that's one of the questions I want to look into. I want to find out whether what Pastor Hansen said was right—or anyway, whether it is right for me.

HELMER: But it's unheard of for so young a woman to behave like this! If religion cannot guide you, let me at least appeal to your conscience. I presume you have some moral feelings left? Or—perhaps you haven't? Well, answer me.

NORA: Oh, Torvald, that isn't an easy question to answer. I simply don't know. I don't know where I am in these matters. I only know that these things mean something quite different to me from what they do to you. I've learned now that certain laws are different from what I'd imagined them to be; but I can't accept that such laws can be right. Has a woman really not the right to spare her dying father pain, or save her husband's life? I can't believe that.

HELMER: You're talking like a child. You don't understand how society works.

NORA: No, I don't. But now I intend to learn. I must try to satisfy myself which is right, society or I.

HELMER: Nora, you're ill; you're feverish. I almost believe you're out of your mind.

NORA: I've never felt so sane and sure in my life.

HELMER: You feel sure that it is right to leave your husband and your children?

NORA: Yes. I do.

HELMER: Then there is only one possible explanation.

NORA: What?

HELMER: That you don't love me any longer.

NORA: No, that's exactly it.

HELMER: Nora! How can you say this to me?

NORA: Oh, Torvald, it hurts me terribly to have to say it, because you've always been so kind to me. But I can't help it. I don't love you any longer.

HELMER (*controlling his emotions with difficulty*): And you feel quite sure about this too?

NORA: Yes, absolutely sure. That's why I can't go on living here any longer.

HELMER: Can you also explain why I have lost your love?

NORA: Yes, I can. It happened this evening, when the

miracle failed to happen. It was then that I realized you weren't the man I'd thought you to be.

HELMER: Explain more clearly. I don't understand you.

NORA: I've waited so patiently, for eight whole years—well, good heavens, I'm not such a fool as to suppose that miracles occur every day. Then this dreadful thing happened to me, and then I *knew:* "Now the miracle will take place!" When Krogstad's letter was lying out there, it never occurred to me for a moment that you would let that man trample over you. I *knew* that you would say to him: "Publish the facts to the world." And when he had done this—

HELMER: Yes, what then? When I'd exposed my wife's name to shame and scandal—

NORA: Then I was certain that you would step forwrad and take all the blame on yourself, and say: "I am the one who is guilty!"

HELMER: Nora!

NORA: You're thinking I wouldn't have accepted such a sacrifice from you? No, of course I wouldn't! But what would my word have counted for against yours? That was the miracle I was hoping for, and dreading. And it was to prevent it happening that I wanted to end my life.

HELMER: Nora, I would gladly work for you night and day, and endure sorrow and hardship for your sake. But no man can be expected to sacrifice his honor, even for the person he loves.

NORA: Millions of women have done it.

HELMER: Oh, you think and talk like a stupid child.

NORA: That may be. But you neither think nor talk like the man I could share my life with. Once you'd got over your fright—and you weren't frightened of what might threaten me, but only of what threatened you—once the danger was past, then as far as you were concerned it was exactly as though nothing had happened. I was your little songbird just as before—your doll whom henceforth you would take particular care to protect from the world because she was so weak and fragile. *(Gets up.)* Torvald, in that moment I realized that for eight years I had been living here with a complete stranger—and had borne him three children—! Oh, I can't bear to think of it! I could tear myself to pieces!

HELMER *(sadly)*: I see it, I see it. A gulf has indeed opened between us. Oh, but Nora—couldn't it be bridged?

NORA: As I am now, I am no wife for you.

HELMER: I have the strength to change.

NORA: Perhaps—if your doll is taken from you.

HELMER: But to be parted—to be parted from you! No, no, Nora, I can't conceive of it happening!

NORA *(goes into the room, right)*: All the more necessary that it should happen.

(She comes back with her outdoor things and a small traveling-bag, which she puts down on a chair by the table.)

HELMER: Nora, Nora, not now! Wait till tomorrow!

NORA *(puts on her coat)*: I can't spend the night in a strange man's house.

HELMER: But can't we live here as brother and sister, then—?

NORA *(fastens her hat)*: You know quite well it wouldn't last. *(Puts on her shawl.)* Goodbye, Torvald. I don't want to see the children. I know they're in better hands than mine. As I am now, I can be nothing to them.

HELMER: But some time, Nora—some time—?

NORA: How can I tell? I've no idea what will happen to me.

HELMER: But you are my wife, both as you are and as you will be.

NORA: Listen, Torvald. When a wife leaves her husband's house, as I'm doing now, I'm told that according to the law he is freed of any obligations towards her. In any case, I release you from any such obligations. You mustn't feel bound to me in any way, however small, just as I shall not feel bound to you. We must both be quite free. Here is your ring back. Give me mine.

HELMER: That too?

NORA: That too.

HELMER: Here it is.

NORA: Good. Well, now it's over. I'll leave the keys here. The servants know about everything to do with the house—much better than I do. Tomorrow, when I have left town, Christine will come to pack the things I brought here from home. I'll have them sent on after me.

HELMER: This is the end then! Nora, will you never think of me any more?

NORA: Yes, of course. I shall often think of you and the children and this house.

HELMER: May I write to you, Nora?

NORA: No. Never. You mustn't do that.

HELMER: But at least you must let me send you—

NORA: Nothing. Nothing.

HELMER: But if you should need help—?

NORA: I tell you, no. I don't accept things from strangers.

HELMER: Nora—can I never be anything but a stranger to you?

NORA *(picks up her bag)*: Oh, Torvald! Then the miracle of miracles would have to happen.

HELMER: The miracle of miracles?

NORA: You and I would both have to change so much

that—oh, Torvald, I don't believe in miracles any longer.

HELMER: But I want to believe in them. Tell me. We should have to change so much that—?

NORA: That life together between us two could become a marriage. Good-bye.

(*She goes out through the hall.*)

HELMER (*sinks down on a chair by the door and buries his face in his hands*): Nora! Nora! (*Looks round and gets up.*) Empty! She's gone! (*A hope strikes him.*) The miracle of miracles—?

(*The street door is slammed shut downstairs.*)

Figure 53. Nora (Claire Bloom) shows Torvald (Donald Madden) a doll that she has bought as a Christmas present for one of their children in the Playhouse production of *A Doll's House,* directed by Patrick Garland, New York, 1971. (Photograph: Henry Grossman.)

Figure 54. Torvald (Donald Madden) berates Nora (Claire Bloom) after reading the blackmail letter from Krogstad in the Playhouse production of *A Doll's House,* directed by Patrick Garland, New York, 1971. (Photograph: Henry Grossman.)

Figure 55. Nora (Claire Bloom) prepares to leave Torvald (Donald Madden) in the final scene of the Playhouse production of *A Doll's House,* directed by Patrick Garland, New York, 1971. The transformation of Nora that Claire Bloom sought to project through her performance of the role may be seen by comparing her facial expression and costume in this photograph with those shown in Figure 53. (Photograph: Henry Grossman.)

Staging of *A Doll's House*

REVIEW OF THE PLAYHOUSE PRODUCTION, NEW YORK, 1971, BY WALTER KERR

The difficulty with Ibsen today is that we must try to take two separate things seriously, the playwright's ideas and the playwright's playwriting. The ideas, of course, present no particular problem. One has only to listen to Claire Bloom's last long speech in the current—and very sleek—revival of "A Doll's House," which will soon be alternating with "Hedda Gabler" at the Playhouse, or to glance at the brief excerpts from Ibsen's "Notes for a Modern Tragedy" that have been included in the program to know that the ideas were sound, advanced, on target. "A woman cannot be herself in modern society," the notes read, "It is an exclusively male society, with laws made by men and with prosecutors and judges who assess female conduct from a male standpoint." Kate Millett sounds old-fashioned beside that.

But how, how, how do you take the playwriting seriously? From what vantage point, what perch or roost or perspective in time, can you attend, without doubling up, to the spectacle of a woman so determined to keep a secret from her husband that she promptly spills it, virtually within his hearing, to the very first acquaintance who walks in the door? Add to that the fact that she hasn't seen the acquaintance in years, and doesn't even recognize her when they do meet, and you've got a rather peculiar secret-keeper on your hands.

Peculiar things are going to keep happening, peculiar and predictable. Ibsen did work by notebook, which means that he jotted down most logically all the little twists and turns of motivation he was going to need and then clipped them together to make a scene whether they precisely flowed or not. If they didn't flow, he forced them ("Tell me, is it true you didn't love your husband?").

The terrible danger in this shuffled-note method is that you are going to hear the papers rustling, the clips slipping on. You can't *help* hearing them. And so you know, infallibly, that the moment the child-wife Nora exclaims "Oh, God, it's good to be alive and happy!," a doorbell will ring and a furtive fellow will slip in who's going to bring down her doll's house in ruins. Just as you know, with a certainty close to hilarity, that when Nora's fatuous lord and master, Torvald, exclaims "I often wish you were threatened with some impending disaster so that I could risk everything!," disaster is not only impending but here. Torvald has only to go to the mailbox ("I'm going to see if there's any mail"), slit open the first letter to hand, and the fat is in the fire. (In the current production, the fat is not only in the fire, Nora is on the floor, having been hurled there by a vigorous spouse who, it turns out, is willing to risk nothing.)

The underpinnings are all transparent, line by line and blow by blow, and we must struggle to induce in ourselves a state of mind that holds humor at bay in honor of the social proposition being so implausibly stated. It's a real battle, one that is often lost; Ibsen believed in his mechanics as well as in his creed, and we cannot. The effort isn't exacerbating, especially; we needn't come away exhausted from it. It is possible to look at the foolishness and feel fond, if not doting, as we wait for the message that is going to come of it all. But it's nip and tuck the whole way, and the thin ice of the situation poses extremely thorny problems for actors.

It's not only a matter of how the good lady doing Nora is going to try to stitch together the two parts of the role, the giddy, fawning creature who is willing to leap up and down like a puppy dog snatching at proffered bones for two acts and the serene, stern woman who lays down the new law in Act 3, having matured wonderfully during intermission. It's a matter of how everyone onstage, pompous husband, long-lost confidante, sniveling blackmailer, dying Dr. Rank who is willing to offer Nora his love with his next-to-last breath, is going to get us past the preposterous and into the ringing preachment. Do they try to steal home, eliding all that is awkward as quietly as possible? Do they rush it, pouncing upon line two before we have quite noticed line one? Do they stylize it, lifting themselves into daguerreotype postures that plainly have little to do with reality?

The present company, under Patrick Garland's direction, has tried taking it by storm, with a bit of the daguerreotype thrown in. Donald Madden, a Torvald who might well see Dr. Rank about hypertension, glides across the highly lacquered floor (this Nora has such difficulty getting money out of her husband that you feel he won't even allow the lady carpeting) to exchange his wife's swift kisses for quickly palmed coins as though the two were Harlequins giving a summer-park performance in a high wind. Robert Gerringer, the forger who has come to accuse Nora of forgery (motives do get piggy-backed in this odd way), keeps his mouth open and working so that no matter who is talking his teeth will show.

All work at a high pitch and in some fever, as though a Racinian *tirade* might spin off into space at any moment. (If you have never seen "A Doll's

House," and I was stunned to discover how many first-nighters never had, this is a crystal-clear reading of it, laid out like silverware.) And there are some genuine successes within the near-stylization. Roy Shuman's Dr. Rank, for instance, is highly mannered: head thrown back, hands always on the point of clapping, eyes darting this way and that as he bluntly, briskly mocks himself and his approaching death. The effect is perfect, that of a man already halfway to the horizon waving farewell with his thumb to his nose. I have never seen the part more robustly or more persuasively played. Patricia Elliott's Kristine, so quickly privy to Nora's secrets, speaks vast amounts of exposition exquisitely, then zeroes in fiercely upon the play's point as she grips her shawl severely and remembers that her only happiness has lain in work.

But what of Nora? Claire Bloom has made, I think, an admirable choice, though a choice with a canker to it. Most Noras won't sacrifice the opportunity to charm, to be bird-like and winsome and if possible adorable, during the first two acts. And you can't entirely blame *them*. Nora is, as written in these acts, a ninny underneath, a girl who really can't feel any sympathy for creditors because, after all, they're "strangers," a girl who, though her secret debt is much on her mind, hasn't the faintest notion of how much of it she's paid off. She subsists, it would seem, on macaroons. But actresses who go for charm and a pretty mindlessness are stuck with the last act. How does one turn an enchanting child into a dominating adult, especially when the transition is missing?

Miss Bloom tries to create the transition from the beginning, which is surely an intelligent thing to do. Even as her Nora is nestling her pretty head against her husband's waistcoat while she seduces him with quick flattery into giving her old friend a job, there is a strain about the eyes, an indication of an intelligence withheld, that adds initial dimension to the role. Where most Noras seem to have an instinct for being playful, fluttering as to the cocoon born, Miss Bloom's playfulness is plainly put on, a trick she has learned, a device that does not wholly engage her.

She is constantly listening to herself make the sounds a pompous husband expects, aware of their insincerity and worried about the gulf between what she is doing and what she might be feeling. Faintly alienated from the outset, she has given us a base for the play's ending. The reserve that we felt in her was the conscience that might have been awakened at any time but is not in fact awakened until it is time to make that speech and slam that door.

The catch to doing it this way, because the part is split in the writing, is a curious sense of heartlessness that overtakes Nora en route. Being to a degree disengaged, she seems not only indifferent to her children and extremely obtuse about her friend Kristine's personal problems but horrendously cold-blooded about the devoted Dr. Rank. He announces his impending death and she scarcely looks up from her sewing. He makes a gesture of love toward her, a gesture that has to be disinterested because he will never see her again, and she recoils as though he had proposed, perhaps, another forgery. Clipping the butterfly's wings leaves us with something of a dragonfly. Or are we merely being given a bit of "Hedda" ahead of time?

Miss Bloom works honorably, looks well, arrives at her last scene logically, and doesn't seem anyone you'd care to trust your heart with (I'm not thinking of Torvald, who is an oaf, but, say, of Dr. Rank, who is not). Miss Bloom has cooled Nora to make the way for the ultimate avalanche; the move does take away anything that was ever very appealing about her.

Good try. The problem, which persists, lies in the play. Ibsen simply could not, or did not, get his meaning and his method to match up. When he speaks of "laws made by men" and "judges who assess female conduct from a male standpoint," we know exactly what he is talking about. We also know that he is right. But the technical illustration in the play proper runs like this. Nora has forged her father's signature to get money to help her ailing husband, who must not know he is being helped. Why didn't she have her father sign the document? Because he, too, was ailing; she didn't want to trouble him. Thus there are two kinds of law: male law (don't forge) and female law (don't bother father). Serious as the point is, the illustration can only make us smile.

The actors must try to make us contain the smile, which, in this revival, they occasionally do.

AUGUST STRINDBERG

1849–1912

Throughout his life Strindberg suffered from a variety of psychological anxieties and compulsions, and throughout his career he exploited his personal and psychic life in his novels, short stories, poetry, essays, and plays. He was raised in Stockholm, Sweden, the fourth of twelve children and the first born in wedlock. His mother died when he was thirteen, and his father immediately married the housekeeper. Strindberg himself was married three times and divorced three times, and each of his marriages was a tormenting experience both for him and the woman, particularly his first marriage to Siri von Essen, an aspiring actress of little talent who divorced her husband, a baron, in order to marry Strindberg. Before the marriage, Strindberg had worked briefly in various jobs, as a tutor, a telegraph clerk, an actor, and a librarian, but once he became involved with Siri he devoted himself almost exclusively to his writing. They remained married from 1877 to 1891, but long before they were divorced their affection for one another had given way to sexual quarrels, mutual jealousies, and bitter recriminations. During the disintegration of the marriage, Strindberg turned out a series of autobiographical novels, among them *A Fool's Defence* (1886), based on his involvement with Siri and her former husband, as well as a series of powerful naturalistic plays, all dealing with forms of psychological and sexual strife between men and women, including *The Father* (1887), *Miss Julie* (1888), *The Creditors* (1889), and *The Stronger* (1890).

Strindberg was married once again in 1893, this time to a young Austrian journalist, but their relationship quickly disintegrated into many of the same patterns that had characterized his first marriage. And by 1894 Strindberg himself was beginning to experience a psychological disintegration that was to extend over the next two years, a period during which he suffered from a profound sense of guilt and spiritual torment, as well as from a variety of paranoic hallucinations, focussing both on supernatural powers and on the doctor to whom he eventually committed himself for treatment. During this period he immersed himself in the mystical works of Emanuel Swedenborg and other religious writers, as well as turning his hand to painting and experiments in alchemy. By 1897, he had already chronicled his psychological and spiritual crisis in a thinly veiled novel, *Inferno*, and by 1898 he had begun another immensely productive period of writing that was to continue until the end of his life. Overall, he produced more than seventy plays and dramatic fragments.

During the period following his psychological inferno, Strindberg turned out a series of twenty-one chronicle plays, many of them in the manner of Shakespeare's, dealing with figures and periods in Swedish history from the thirteenth to the eighteenth century. But the most important plays of his later period reflect the preoccupations that flowed from his spiritual crisis, and they are concerned with the exposure of evil, as in *The Dance of Death* (1901), *A Dream Play* (1902), and *The Ghost Sonata* (1907), or with guilt and expiation, as in *Crime and Crime* (1899) and *Easter* (1901), or with spiritual pilgrimage, as in *To Damascus*

(1898–1904) and *The Great Highway* (1909). In these plays, Strindberg turned away from the purely naturalistic methods of his earlier plays, using expressionistic and symbolic techniques to dramatize his troubled vision of human experience. In *A Dream Play,* for example, the world is seen entirely through the experience and perception of the Daughter of Indra, the child of a deity, whose descent to earth and subsequent encounters with various human beings reflect and reproduce, as Strindberg explained in his note on the play, "the disconnected but apparently logical form of a dream." Because it is a dream, "Anything can happen; everything is possible and probable ... The characters are split, double and multiply; they evaporate, crystallise, scatter and converge. But a single consciousness holds sway over them all—that of the dreamer." The dreamer, of course, was Strindberg himself, and the disconnected events of the play vividly project his melancholy vision of the human landscape. *The Ghost Sonata* is another expressionistic and symbolic fantasy, this time displaying the macabre spectacle of a demonic household as it is progressively unveiled to the eyes of a young student—clearly Strindberg's alter ego—who ends the play by proclaiming the world to be "this madhouse, this prison, this charnelhouse." In their expressionistic techniques, these later plays prefigure a major aspect of modern and contemporary drama. In their preoccupation with dreams and the disconnected logic of psychic experience, they are arresting parallels to the work of Freud, whose first important study of the unconscious, *The Interpretation of Dreams,* did not appear until 1900.

But even in his naturalistic plays of the eighties, such as *Miss Julie*, Strindberg was advanced for his time, both in his dramatic techniques and in his psychological insight. He took great pains to identify his innovations in a lengthy "Foreword" to *Miss Julie* that he wrote after the play was accepted for publication. He called attention, for example, to the improvisational miming of Kristin early in the play, to the improvisational miming and dancing of the peasants, and to the improvisational monologue of Kristin mumbling in her sleep. He was aware of the classical precedents for mime, dancing, and monologue in drama, much as he was aware of the Italian Renaissance precedents for improvisational performance, but he also recognized that realistic conventions of his time had excluded these dramatic possibilities from the stage, whereas he considered them not only consistent with, but essential to a naturalistic illusion. In the same context, he also called attention to the fact that the play is designed to be staged without intermission, and that the set is to be diagonally arranged, "so that the actors may play full-face and in half-profile when they are sitting opposite one another at the table." He might also have pointed out that the action is set in a kitchen that really functions, for the play begins with Kristin frying a piece of kidney on the stove, and it reaches a climax with Jean beheading Julie's greenfinch on the kitchen chopping block. In all these respects, Strindberg carried naturalistic theater further than any of his contemporaries—extending it to its logical and psychological limits.

In the psychological conception of Jean and Julie, as well as in the unfolding of their relationship, Strindberg also challenged his contemporaries, particularly Emile Zola, the first major proponent of naturalistic drama, who in 1874 had written a manifesto proclaiming that heredity and environment are the sole determinants of human nature and behavior, and that dramatists are, therefore, obliged to reflect these circumstances in their plays. Strindberg, however, was clearly not content to limit himself to so narrow a conception of human behavior as he makes clear in the "Foreword" to *Miss Julie:*

> I see Miss Julie's tragic fate to be the result of many circumstances: the mother's character, the father's mistaken upbringing of the girl, her own weak nature, and the influence of her fiancé on a weak, degenerate mind. Also, more directly, the festive mood of Midsummer Eve, her father's absence, her monthly indisposition, her pre-occupation with animals, the excitement of dancing, the magic of dusk, the strongly aphrodisiac influence of flowers, and finally the chance that drives the couple into a room alone—to which must be added the urgency of the excited man.
>
> My treatment of the theme, morever, is neither exclusively physiological nor psychological. I have not put the blame wholly on the inheritance from her mother, nor on her physical condition at the time, nor on immorality. I have not even preached a moral sermon; in the absence of a priest I leave this to the cook.
>
> I congratulate myself on this multiplicity of motives as being up-to-date, and if others have done the same thing before me, then I congratulate myself on not being alone in my "paradoxes," as all innovations are called.

Strindberg's comments here and elsewhere in the "Foreword" may well serve as a warning against trying to interpret the play within any kind of simplistic framework. It is an enactment of a class struggle, as Strindberg notes, and as is repeatedly evident in the play from the dialogue and action of Julie, Jean, and Kristin. It is also, in part, an enactment of sexual warfare, as Strindberg and the play make painfully clear. But these two aspects of the conflict are inextricably woven together and complicated further by the subtle aspects of personality that mark both Jean and Julie as individuals rather than social or sexual types. The unfolding of their conflict is thus continually surprising and revealing, and until the very end of the play when Julie walks out of the kitchen with the razor in her hand the resolution of their conflict is never predictable, though it is thoroughly plausible.

Because of the complexity and the intensity of their struggle, *Miss Julie* is an extremely difficult play to produce, as noted in one of the reviews of the National Theater production reprinted following the text. Photographs of that production show Albert Finney as Jean and Maggie Smith as Julie at various moments during their conflict—from their initial confrontation in the kitchen (see Figure 56) to their long conversation following the departure of the peasants (see Figure 57), to the final moments of the play (see Figure 58). Although their facial expressions clearly betray a lack of ferocity that one of the reviewers criticized in the production, they do show Jean's unnerving callousness, and they also suggest the subtle unfolding of Julie's tragic demise.

MISS JULIE
A Naturalistic Tragedy

BY AUGUST STRINDBERG / TRANSLATED BY ELIZABETH SPRIGGE

CHARACTERS

MISS JULIE, *aged 25*
JEAN, *the valet, aged 30*
KRISTIN, *the cook, aged 35*

SCENE:

The large kitchen of a Swedish manor house in a country district in the 1880s.

(Midsummer Eve.
The kitchen has three doors, two small ones into JEAN's *and* KRISTIN's *bedrooms, and a large, glass-fronted double one, opening on to a courtyard. This is the only way to the rest of the house.*
Through these glass doors can be seen part of a fountain with a cupid, lilac bushes in flower and the tops of some Lombardy poplars. On one wall are shelves edged with scalloped paper on which are kitchen utensils of copper, iron and tin.
To the left is the corner of a large tiled range and part of its chimney-hood, to the right the end of the servants' dinner table with chairs beside it.
The stove is decorated with birch boughs, the floor strewn with twigs of juniper. On the end of the table is a large Japanese spice jar full of lilac.
There are also an ice-box, a scullery table and a sink.
Above the double door hangs a big old-fashioned bell; near it is a speaking-tube.
A fiddle can be heard from the dance in the barn near-by.
KRISTIN *is standing at the stove, frying something in a pan. She wears a light-colored cotton dress and a big apron.*
JEAN *enters, wearing livery and carrying a pair of large riding-boots with spurs, which he puts in a conspicuous place.)*

JEAN: Miss Julie's crazy again to-night, absolutely crazy.

KRISTIN: Oh, so you're back, are you?

JEAN: When I'd taken the Count to the station, I came back and dropped in at the Barn for a dance. And who did I see there but our young lady leading off with the gamekeeper. But the moment she sets eyes on me, up she rushes and invites me to waltz with her. And how she waltzed—I've never seen anything like it! She's crazy.

KRISTIN: Always has been, but never so bad as this last fortnight since the engagement was broken off.

JEAN: Yes, that was a pretty business, to be sure. He's a decent enough chap, too, even if he isn't rich.

Oh, but they're choosy! *(Sits down at the end of the table.)* In any case, it's a bit odd that our young—er—lady would rather stay at home with yokels than go with her father to visit her relations.

KRISTIN: Perhaps she feels a bit awkward, after that bust-up with her fiancé.

JEAN: Maybe. That chap had some guts, though. Do you know the sort of thing that was going on, Kristin? I saw it with my own eyes, though I didn't let on I had.

KRISTIN: You saw them . . . ?

JEAN: Didn't I just! Came across the pair of them one evening in the stable-yard. Miss Julie was doing what she called "training" him. Know what that was? Making him jump over her riding-whip— the way you teach a dog. He did it twice and got a cut each time for his pains, but when it came to the third go, he snatched the whip out of her hand and broke it into smithereens. And then he cleared off.

KRISTIN: What goings on! I never did!

JEAN: Well, that's how it was with that little affair . . . Now, what have you got for me, Kristin? Something tasty?

KRISTIN *(serving from the pan to his plate)*: Well, it's just a little bit of kidney I cut off their joint.

JEAN *(smelling it)*: Fine! That's my special delice. *(Feels the plate.)* But you might have warmed the plate.

KRISTIN: When you choose to be finicky you're worse than the Count himself. *(Pulls his hair affectionately.)*

JEAN *(crossly)*: Stop pulling my hair. You know how sensitive I am.

KRISTIN: There, there! It's only love, you know.

(JEAN eats. KRISTIN brings a bottle of beer.)

JEAN: Beer on Midsummer Eve? No thanks! I've got something better than that. *(From a drawer in the table brings out a bottle of red wine with a yellow seal.)*

Yellow seal, see! Now get me a glass. You use a glass with a stem of course when you're drinking it straight.

KRISTIN *(giving him a wine-glass)*: Lord help the woman who gets you for a husband, you old fusser! *(She puts the beer in the ice-box and sets a small saucepan on the stove.)*

JEAN: Nonsense! You'll be glad enough to get a fellow as smart as me. And I don't think it's done you any harm, people calling me your fiancé. *(Tastes the wine.)* Good, Very good indeed. But not quite warmed enough. *(Warms the glass in his hand.)* We bought this in Dijon. Four francs the liter without the bottle, and duty on top of that. What are you cooking now? It stinks.

KRISTIN: Some bloody muck Miss Julie wants for Diana.

JEAN: You should be more refined in your speech, Kristin. But why should you spend a holiday cooking for that bitch? Is she sick or what?

KRISTIN: Yes, she's sick. She sneaked out with the pug at the lodge and got in the usual mess. And that, you know, Miss Julie won't have.

JEAN: Miss Julie's too high-and-mighty in some respects, and not enough in others, just like her mother before her. The Countess was more at home in the kitchen and cowsheds than anywhere else, but would she ever go driving with only one horse? She went round with her cuffs filthy, but she had to have the coronet on the cuff-links. Our young lady—to come back to her—hasn't any proper respect for herself or her position. I mean she isn't refined. In the Barn just now she dragged the gamekeeper away from Anna and made him dance with her—no waiting to be asked. We wouldn't do a think like that. But that's what happens when the gentry try to behave like the common people—they become common . . . Still she's a fine girl. Smashing! What shoulders! And what—er—etcetera!

KRISTIN: Oh come off it! I know what Clara says, and she dresses her.

JEAN: Clara? Pooh, you're all jealous! But I've been out riding with her . . . and as for her dancing!

KRISTIN: Listen, Jean. You will dance with me, won't you, as soon as I'm through.

JEAN: Of course I will.

KRISTIN: Promise?

JEAN: Promise? When I say I'll do a thing I do it. Well thanks for the supper. It was a real treat. *(Corks the bottle.)*

(JULIE appears in the doorway, speaking to someone outside.)

JULIE: I'll be back in a moment. Don't wait.

(JEAN slips the bottle into the drawer and rises respectfully.

JULIE *enters and joins* KRISTIN *at the stove.)*

Well, have you made it? *(*KRISTIN *signs that* JEAN *is near them.)*

JEAN *(gallantly)*: Have you ladies got some secret?

JULIE *(flipping his face with her handkerchief)*: You're very inquisitive.

JEAN: What a delicious smell! Violets.

JULIE *(coquettishly)*: Impertinence! Are you an expert of scent too? I must say you know how to dance. Now don't look. Go away. *(The music of a schottische begins.)*

JEAN *(with impudent politeness)*: Is it some witches' brew you're cooking on Midsummer Eve? Something to tell your stars by, so you can see your future?

JULIE *(sharply)*: If you could see that you'd have good eyes. *(to* KRISTIN*)* Put it in a bottle and cork it tight. Come and dance this schottische with me, Jean.

JEAN *(hesitating)*: I don't want to be rude, but I've promised to dance this one with Kristin.

JULIE: Well, she can have another, can't you, Kristin? You'll lend me Jean, won't you?

KRISTIN *(bottling)*: It's nothing to do with me. When you're so condescending, Miss, it's not his place to say no. Go on, Jean, and thank Miss Julie for the honor.

JEAN: Frankly speaking, Miss, and no offense meant, I wonder if it's wise for you to dance twice running with the same partner, specially as those people are so ready to jump to conclusions.

JULIE *(flaring up)*: What did you say? What sort of conclusions? What do you mean?

JEAN *(meekly)*: As you choose not to understand, Miss Julie, I'll have to speak more plainly. It looks bad to show a preference for one of your retainers when they're all hoping for the same unusual favor.

JULIE: Show a preference! The very idea! I'm surprised at you. I'm doing the people an honor by attending their ball when I'm mistress of the house, but if I'm really going to dance, I mean to have a partner who can lead and doesn't make me look ridiculous.

JEAN: If those are your orders, Miss, I'm at your service.

JULIE *(gently)*: Don't take it as an order. Tonight we're all just people enjoying a party. There's no question of class. So now give me your arm. Don't worry, Kristin, I shan't steal your sweetheart.

(JEAN gives JULIE his arm and leads her out. Left alone, KRISTIN plays her scene in an unhurried, natural way, humming to the tune of the schottische, played on a distant violin. She clears JEAN's place, washes up and puts things away, then takes off her apron, brings out a small mirror

from a drawer, props it against the jar of lilac, lights a candle, warms a small pair of tongs and curls her fringe. She goes to the door and listens, then turning back to the table finds MISS JULIE's *handkerchief. She smells it, then meditatively smooths it out and folds it. Enter* JEAN.)

JEAN: She really *is* crazy. What a way to dance! With people standing grinning at her too from behind the doors. What's got into her, Kristin?

KRISTIN: Oh, it's just her time coming on. She's always queer then. Are you going to dance with me now?

JEAN: Then you're not wild with me for cutting that one.

KRISTIN: You know I'm not—for a little thing like that. Besides, I know my place.

JEAN (*putting his arm round her waist*): You're a sensible girl, Kristin, and you'll make a very good wife . . .

(*Enter* JULIE, *unpleasantly surprised.*)

JULIE (*with forced gaiety*): You're a fine beau—running away from your partner.

JEAN: Not away, Miss Julie, but as you see back to the one I deserted.

JULIE (*changing her tone*): You really can dance, you know. But why are you wearing your livery on a holiday. Take it off at once.

JEAN: Then I must ask you to go away for a moment, Miss. My black coat's here. (*Indicates it hanging on the door to his room.*)

JULIE: Are you so shy of me—just over changing a coat? Go into your room then—or stay here and I'll turn my back.

JEAN: Excuse me then, Miss. (*He goes to his room and is partly visible as he changes his coat.*)

JULIE: Tell me, Kristin, is Jean your fiancé? You seem very intimate.

KRISTIN: My fiancé? Yes, if you like. We call it that.

JULIE: Call it?

KRISTIN: Well, you've had a fiancé yourself, Miss, and . . .

JULIE: But we really were engaged.

KRISTIN: All the same it didn't come to anything.

(JEAN *returns in his black coat.*)

JULIE: *Très gentil, Monsieur Jean. Très gentil.*

JEAN: *Vous voulez plaisanter, Madame.*

JULIE: *Et vous voulez parler français.*° Where did you learn it?

JEAN: In Switzerland, when I was steward at one of the biggest hotels in Lucerne.

JULIE: You look quite the gentleman in that get-up. Charming. (*Sits at the table.*)

Très . . . gentil, Very nice, Monsieur Jean, very nice. **Vous . . . Madame,** You like to joke, Madame. **Et . . . français,** And you want to speak French.

JEAN: Oh, you're just flattering me!

JULIE (*annoyed*): Flattering you?

JEAN: I'm too modest to believe you would pay real compliments to a man like me, so I must take it you are exaggerating—that this is what's known as flattery.

JULIE: Where on earth did you learn to make speeches like that? Perhaps you've been to the theater a lot.

JEAN: That's right. And traveled a lot too.

JULIE: But you come from this neighborhood, don't you?

JEAN: Yes, my father was a laborer on the next estate—the District Attorney's place. I often used to see you, Miss Julie, when you were little, though you never noticed me.

JULIE: Did you really?

JEAN: Yes. One time specially I remember . . . but I can't tell you about that.

JULIE: Oh do! Why not? This is just the time.

JEAN: No, I really can't now. Another time perhaps.

JULIE: Another time means never. What harm in now?

JEAN: No harm, but I'd rather not. (*Points to* KRISTIN, *now fast asleep.*) Look at her.

JULIE: She'll make a charming wife, won't she? I wonder if she snores.

JEAN: No, she doesn't, but she talks in her sleep.

JULIE (*cynically*): How do you know she talks in her sleep?

JEAN (*brazenly*): I've heard her. (*Pause. They look at one another.*)

JULIE: Why don't you sit down?

JEAN: I can't take such a liberty in your presence.

JULIE: Supposing I order you to.

JEAN: I'll obey.

JULIE: Then sit down. No, wait a minute. Will you get me a drink first?

JEAN: I don't know what's in the ice-box. Only beer, I expect.

JULIE: There's no only about it. My taste is so simple I prefer it to wine.

(JEAN *takes a bottle from the ice-box, fetches a glass and plate and serves the beer.*)

JEAN: At your service.

JULIE: Thank you. Won't you have some yourself?

JEAN: I'm not really a beer-drinker, but if it's an order. . . .

JULIE: Order? I should have thought it was ordinary manners to keep your partner company.

JEAN: That's a good way of putting it. (*He opens another bottle and fetches a glass.*)

JULIE: Now drink my health. (*He hesitates.*) I believe the man really is shy.

(JEAN *kneels and raises his glass with mock ceremony.*)

JEAN: To the health of my lady!

JULIE: Bravo! Now kiss my shoe and everything will be perfect. (*He hesitates, then boldly takes hold of her foot and lightly kisses it.*) Splendid. You ought to have been an actor.

JEAN (*rising*): We can't go on like this, Miss Julie. Someone might come in and see us.

JULIE: Why would that matter?

JEAN: For the simple reason that they'd talk. And if you knew the way their tongues were wagging out there just now, you . . .

JULIE: What were they saying? Tell me. Sit down.

JEAN (*sitting*): No offense meant, Miss, but . . . well, their language wasn't nice, and they were hinting . . . oh, you know quite well what. You're not a child, and if a lady's seen drinking alone at night with a man—and a servant at that—then . . .

JULIE: Then what? Besides, we're not alone. Kristin's here.

JEAN: Yes, asleep.

JULIE: I'll wake her up. (*Rises.*) Kristin, are you asleep? (KRISTIN *mumbles in her sleep.*) Kristin! Goodness, how she sleeps!

KRISTIN (*in her sleep*): The Count's boots are cleaned—put the coffee on—yes, yes, at once . . . (*Mumbles incoherently.*)

JULIE (*tweaking her nose*): Wake up, can't you!

JEAN (*sharply*): Let her sleep.

JULIE: What?

JEAN: When you've been standing at the stove all day you're likely to be tired at night. And sleep should be respected.

JULIE (*changing her tone*): What a nice idea. It does you credit. Thank you for it. (*Holds out her hand to him.*) Now come out and pick some lilac for me. (*During the following* KRISTIN *goes sleepily in to her bedroom.*)

JEAN: Out with you, Miss Julie?

JULIE: Yes.

JEAN: It wouldn't do. It really wouldn't.

JULIE: I don't know what you mean. You can't possibly imagine that . . .

JEAN: I don't, but others do.

JULIE: What? That I'm in love with the valet?

JEAN: I'm not a conceited man, but such a thing's been known to happen, and to these rustics nothing's sacred.

JULIE: You, I take it, are an aristocrat.

JEAN: Yes, I am.

JULIE: And I am coming down in the world.

JEAN: Don't come down, Miss Julie. Take my advice. No one will believe you came down of your own accord. They'll all say you fell.

JULIE: I have a higher opinion of our people than you. Come and put it to the test. Come on. (*Gazes into his eyes.*)

JEAN: You're very strange, you know.

JULIE: Perhaps I am, but so are you. For that matter everything is strange. Life, human beings, everything, just scum drifting about on the water until it sinks—down and down. That reminds me of a dream I sometimes have, in which I'm on top of a pillar and can't see any way of getting down. When I look down I'm dizzy; I have to get down but I haven't the courage to jump. I can't stay there and I long to fall, but I don't fall. There's no respite. There can't be any peace at all for me until I'm down, right down on the ground. And if I did get to the ground I'd want to be under the ground . . . Have you ever felt like that?

JEAN: No. In my dream I'm lying under a great tree in a dark wood. I want to get up, up to the top of it, and look out over the bright landscape where the sun is shining and rob that high nest of its golden eggs. And I climb and climb, but the trunk is so thick and smooth and it's so far to the first branch. But I know if I can once reach that first branch I'll go to the top just as if I'm on a ladder. I haven't reached it yet, but I shall get there, even if only in my dreams.

JULIE: Here I am chattering about dreams with you. Come on. Only into the park. (*She takes his arm and they go toward the door.*)

JEAN: We must sleep on nine midsummer flowers tonight; then our dreams will come true, Miss Julie. (*They turn at the door. He has a hand to his eye.*)

JULIE: Have you got something in your eye? Let me see.

JEAN: Oh, it's nothing. Just a speck of dust. It'll be gone in a minute.

JULIE: My sleeve must have rubbed against you. Sit down and let me see to it. (*Takes him by the arm and makes him sit down, bends his head back and tries to get the speck out with the corner of her handkerchief.*) Keep still now, quite still. (*Slaps his hand.*) Do as I tell you. Why, I believe you're trembling, big, strong man though you are! (*Feels his biceps.*) What muscles!

JEAN (*warning*): Miss Julie!

JULIE: Yes, Monsieur Jean?

JEAN: *Attention. Je ne suis qu'un homme.*°

JULIE: Will you stay still! There now. It's out. Kiss my hand and say thank you.

JEAN (*rising*): Miss Julie, listen, Kristin's gone to bed now. Will you listen?

JULIE: Kiss my hand first.

JEAN: Very well, but you'll have only yourself to blame.

JULIE: For what?

JEAN: For what! Are you still a child at twenty-five? Don't you know it's dangerous to play with fire?

Attention . . . homme, Careful, I'm only a man.

JULIE: Not for me. I'm insured.

JEAN (*bluntly*): No, you're not. And even if you are, there's still stuff here to kindle a flame.

JULIE: Meaning yourself?

JEAN: Yes. Not because I'm me, but because I'm a man and young and . . .

JULIE: And good looking? What incredible conceit! A Don Juan perhaps? Or a Joseph? Good Lord, I do believe you are a Joseph!

JEAN: Do you?

JULIE: I'm rather afraid so.

(JEAN *goes boldly up and tries to put his arms round her and kiss her. She boxes his ears.*)

How dare you!

JEAN: Was that in earnest or a joke?

JULIE: In earnest.

JEAN: Then what went before was in earnest too. You take your games too seriously and that's dangerous. Anyhow I'm tired of playing now and beg leave to return to my work. The Count will want his boots first thing and it's past midnight now.

JULIE: Put those boots down.

JEAN: No. This is my work, which it's my duty to do. But I never undertook to be your playfellow and I never will be. I consider myself too good for that.

JULIE: You're proud.

JEAN: In some ways—not all.

JULIE: Have you ever been in love?

JEAN: We don't put it that way, but I've been gone on quite a few girls. And once I went sick because I couldn't have the one I wanted. Sick, I mean, like those princes in the Arabian Nights who couldn't eat or drink for love.

JULIE: Who was she? (*No answer.*) Who was she?

JEAN: You can't force me to tell you that.

JULIE: If I ask as an equal, ask as a—friend? Who was she?

JEAN: You.

JULIE (*sitting*): How absurd!

JEAN: Yes, ludicrous if you like. That's the story I wouldn't tell you before, see, but now I will . . . Do you know what the world looks like from below? No, you don't. No more than the hawks and falcons do whose backs one hardly ever sees because they're always soaring up aloft. I lived in a laborer's hovel with seven other children and a pig, out in the gray fields where there isn't a single tree. But from the window I could see the wall round the Count's park with apple-trees above it. That was the Garden of Eden, guarded by many terrible angels with flaming swords. All the same I and the other boys managed to get to the tree of life. Does all this make you despise me?

JULIE: Goodness, all boys steal apples!

JEAN: You say that now, but all the same you do despise me. However, one time I went into the Garden of Eden with my mother to weed the onion beds. Close to the kitchen garden there was a Turkish pavilion hung all over with jasmine and honeysuckle. I hadn't any idea what it was used for, but I'd never seen such a beautiful building. People used to go in and then come out again, and one day the door was left open. I crept up and saw the walls covered with pictures of kings and emperors, and the windows had red curtains with fringes—you know now what the place was, don't you? I . . . (*Breaks off a piece of lilac and holds it for* JULIE *to smell. As he talks, she takes it from him.*) I had never been inside the manor, never seen anything but the church, and this was more beautiful. No matter where my thoughts went, they always came back—to that place. The longing went on growing in me to enjoy it fully, just once. *Enfin*,° I sneaked in, gazed and admired. Then I heard someone coming. There was only one way out for the gentry, but for me there was another and I had no choice but to take it. (*JULIE drops the lilac on the table.*) Then I took to my heels, plunged through the raspberry canes, dashed across the strawberry beds and found myself on the rose terrace. There I saw a pink dress and a pair of white stockings—it was you. I crawled into a weed pile and lay there right under it among prickly thistles and damp rank earth. I watched you walking among the roses and said to myself: "If it's true that a thief can get to heaven and be with the angels, it's pretty strange that a laborer's child here on God's earth mayn't come in the park and play with the Count's daughter."

JULIE (*sentimentally*): Do you think all poor children feel the way you did?

JEAN (*taken aback, then rallying*): *All* poor children? . . . Yes, of course they do. Of course.

JULIE: It must be terrible to be poor.

JEAN (*with exaggerated distress*): Oh yes, Miss Julie, yes. A dog may lie on the Countess's sofa, a horse may have his nose stroked by a young lady, but a servant . . . (*Change of tone.*) well, yes, now and then you meet one with guts enough to rise in the world, but how often? Anyhow, do you know what I did? Jumped into the millstream with my clothes on, was pulled out and got a hiding. But the next Sunday, when Father and all the rest went to Granny's, I managed to get left behind. Then I washed with soap and hot water, put my

---

Enfin, Well.

best clothes on and went to church so as to see you. I did see you and went home determined to die. But I wanted to die beautifully and peacefully, without any pain. Then I remembered it was dangerous to sleep under an elder bush. We had a big one in full bloom, so I stripped it and climbed into the oats-bin with the flowers. Have you ever noticed how smooth oats are? Soft to touch as human skin . . . Well, I closed the lid and shut my eyes, fell asleep, and when they woke me I was very ill. But I didn't die, as you see. What I meant by all that I don't know. There was no hope of winning you—you were simply a symbol of the hopelessness of ever getting out of the class I was born in.

JULIE: You put things very well, you know. Did you go to school?

JEAN: For a while. But I've read a lot of novels and been to the theater. Besides, I've heard educated folk talking—that's what's taught me most.

JULIE: Do you stand round listening to what we're saying?

JEAN: Yes, of course. And I've heard quite a bit too! On the carriage box or rowing the boat. Once I heard you, Miss Julie, and one of your young lady friends . . .

JULIE: Oh! Whatever did you hear?

JEAN: Well, it wouldn't be nice to repeat it. And I must say I was pretty startled. I couldn't think where you had learnt such words. Perhaps, at bottom, there isn't as much difference between people as one's led to believe.

JULIE: How dare you! We don't behave as you do when we're engaged.

JEAN (looking hard at her): Are you sure? It's no use making out so innocent to me.

JULIE: The man I gave my love to was a scoundrel.

JEAN: That's what you always say—afterward.

JULIE: Always?

JEAN: I think it must be always. I've heard the expression several times in similar circumstances.

JULIE: What circumstances?

JEAN: Like those in question. The last time . . .

JULIE (rising): Stop. I don't want to hear any more.

JEAN: Nor did she—curiously enough. May I go to bed now please?

JULIE (gently): Go to bed on Midsummer Eve?

JEAN: Yes. Dancing with that crowd doesn't really amuse me.

JULIE: Get the key of the boathouse and row me out on the lake. I want to see the sun rise.

JEAN: Would that be wise?

JULIE: You sound as though you're frightened for your reputation.

JEAN: Why not? I don't want to be made a fool of, nor to be sent packing without references when I'm trying to better myself. Besides, I have Kristin to consider.

JULIE: So now it's Kristin.

JEAN: Yes, but it's you I'm thinking about too. Take my advice and go to bed.

JULIE: Am I to take orders from you?

JEAN: Just this once, for your own sake. Please. It's very late and sleepiness goes to one's head and makes one rash. Go to bed. What's more, if my ears don't deceive me, I hear people coming this way. They'll be looking for me, and if they find us here, you're done for.

(The CHORUS approaches, singing. During the following dialogue the song is heard in snatches, and in full when the peasants enter.)

Out of the wood two women came,
Tridiri-ralla, tridiri-ra.
The feet of one were bare and cold,
Tridiri-ralla-la.

The other talked of bags of gold,
Tridiri-ralla, tridiri-ra.
But neither had a sou to her name,
Tridiri-ralla-la.

The bridal wreath I give to you,
Tridiri-ralla, tridiri-ra.
But to another I'll be true,
Tridiri-ralla-la.

JULIE: I know our people and I love them, just as they do me. Let them come. You'll see.

JEAN: No, Miss Julie, they don't love you. They take your food, then spit at it. You must believe me. Listen to them, just listen to what they're singing . . . No, don't listen.

JULIE (listening): What are they singing?

JEAN: They're mocking—you and me.

JULIE: Oh no! How horrible! What cowards!

JEAN: A pack like that's always cowardly. But against such odds there's nothing we can do but run away.

JULIE: Run away? Where to? We can't get out and we can't go into Kristin's room.

JEAN: Into mine then. Necessity knows no rules. And you can trust me. I really am your true and devoted friend.

JULIE: But supposing . . . supposing they were to look for you in there?

JEAN: I'll bolt the door, and if they try to break in I'll shoot. Come on. (Pleading.) Please come.

JULIE (tensely): Do you promise . . . ?

JEAN: I swear!

(JULIE goes quickly into his room and he excitedly follows her. Led by the fiddler, the peasants enter in festive attire *with flowers in their hats. They put a barrel of beer and a keg of spirits, garlanded with leaves, on the table, fetch glasses and begin to carouse. The scene becomes a ballet. They form a ring and dance and sing and mime. "Out of the wood two women came." Finally they go out, still singing.* JULIE *comes in alone. She looks at the havoc in the kitchen, wrings her hands, then takes out her powder puff and powders her face.* JEAN *enters in high spirits.*)

JEAN: Now you see! And you heard, didn't you? Do you still think it's possible for us to stay here?

JULIE: No, I don't. But what can we do?

JEAN: Run away. Far away. Take a journey.

JULIE: Journey? But where to?

JEAN: Switzerland. The Italian lakes. Ever been there?

JULIE: No. Is it nice?

JEAN: Ah! Eternal summer, oranges, evergreens . . . ah!

JULIE: But what would we do there?

JEAN: I'll start a hotel. First-class accommodation and first-class customers.

JULIE: Hotel?

JEAN: There's life for you. New faces all the time, new languages—no time for nerves or worries, no need to look for something to do—work rolling up of its own accord. Bells ringing night and day, trains whistling, buses coming and going, and all the time gold pieces rolling on to the counter. There's life for you!

JULIE: For *you.* And I?

JEAN: Mistress of the house, ornament of the firm. With your looks, and your style . . . oh, it's bound to be a success! Terrific! You'll sit like a queen in the office and set your slaves in motion by pressing an electric button. The guests will file past your throne and nervously lay their treasure on your table. You've no idea the way people tremble when they get their bills. I'll salt the bills and you'll sugar them with your sweetest smiles. Ah, let's get away from here! (*Produces a time-table.*) At once, by the next train. We shall be at Malmö at six-thirty, Hamburg eight-forty next morning, Frankfurt-Basle the following day, and Como by the St. Gotthard Pass in—let's see— three days. Three days!

JULIE: That's all very well. But Jean, you must give me courage. Tell me you love me. Come and take me in your arms.

JEAN (*reluctantly*): I'd like to, but I daren't. Not again in this house. I love you—that goes without saying. You can't doubt that, Miss Julie, can you?

JULIE (*shyly, very feminine*): Miss? Call me Julie. There aren't any barriers between us now. Call me Julie.

JEAN (*uneasily*): I can't. As long as we're in this house, there *are* barriers between us. There's the past

and there's the Count. I've never been so servile to anyone as I am to him. I've only to hear his bell and I shy like a horse. Even now, when I look at his boots, standing there so proud and stiff, I feel my back beginning to bend. (*Kicks the boots.*) It's those old, narrow-minded notions drummed into us as children . . . but they can soon be forgotten. You've only got to get to another country, a republic, and people will bend themselves double before my porter's livery. Yes, double they'll bend themselves, but I shan't. I wasn't born to bend. I've got guts. I've got character, and once I reach that first branch, you'll watch me climb. Today I'm valet, next year I'll be proprietor, in ten years I'll have made a fortune, and then I'll go to Rumania, get myself decorated and I may, I only say *may*, mind you, end up as a Count.

JULIE (*sadly*): That would be very nice.

JEAN: You see in Rumania one can buy a title, and then you'll be a Countess after all. My Countess.

JULIE: What do I care about all that? I'm putting those things behind me. Tell me you love me, because if you don't . . . if you don't, what am I?

JEAN: I'll tell you a thousand times over—later. But not here. No sentimentality now or everything will be lost. We must consider this thing calmly like reasonable people. (*Takes a cigar, cuts and lights it.*) You sit down there and I'll sit here and we'll talk as if nothing happened.

JULIE: My God, have you no feelings at all?

JEAN: Nobody has more. But I know how to control them.

JULIE: A short time ago you were kissing my shoe. And now . . .

JEAN (*harshly*): Yes, that was then. Now we have something else to think about.

JULIE: Don't speak to me so brutally.

JEAN: I'm not. Just sensibly. One folly's been committed, don't let's have more. The Count will be back at any moment and we've got to settle our future before that. Now, what do you think of my plans? Do you approve?

JULIE: It seems a very good idea—but just one thing. Such a big undertaking would need a lot of capital. Have you got any?

JEAN (*chewing his cigar*): I certainly have. I've got my professional skill, my wide experience, and my knowledge of foreign languages. That's capital worth having, it seems to me.

JULIE: But it won't buy even one railway ticket.

JEAN: Quite true. That's why I need a backer to advance some ready cash.

JULIE: How could you get that at a moment's notice?

JEAN: You must get it, if you want to be my partner.

JULIE: I can't. I haven't any money of my own. (*Pause.*)

JEAN: Then the whole thing's off.

JULIE: And . . . ?

JEAN: We go on as we are.

JULIE: Do you think I'm going to stay under this roof as your mistress? With everyone pointing at me. Do you think I can face my father after this? No. Take me away from here, away from this shame, this humiliation. Oh my God, what have I done? My God, my God! (Weeps.)

JEAN: So that's the tune now, is it? What have you done? Same as many before you.

JULIE (hysterically): And now you despise me. I'm falling, I'm falling.

JEAN: Fall as far as me and I'll lift you up again.

JULIE: Why was I so terribly attracted to you? The weak to the strong, the falling to the rising? Or was it love? Is that love? Do you know what love is?

JEAN: Do I? You bet I do. Do you think I never had a girl before?

JULIE: The things you say, the things you think!

JEAN: That's what life's taught me, and that's what I am. It's no good getting hysterical or giving yourself airs. We're both in the same boat now. Here, my dear girl, let me give you a glass of something special. (Opens the drawer, takes out the bottle of wine and fills two used glasses.)

JULIE: Where did you get that wine?

JEAN: From the cellar.

JULIE: My father's burgundy.

JEAN: Why not, for his son-in-law?

JULIE: And I drink beer.

JEAN: That only shows your taste's not so good as mine.

JULIE: Thief!

JEAN: Are you going to tell on me?

JULIE: Oh God! The accomplice of a petty thief! Was I blind drunk? Have I dreamt this whole night? Midsummer Eve, the night for innocent merrymaking.

JEAN: Innocent, eh?

JULIE: Is anyone on earth as wretched as I am now?

JEAN: Why should you be? After such a conquest. What about Kristin in there? Don't you think she has any feelings?

JULIE: I did think so, but I don't any longer. No. A menial is a menial . . .

JEAN: And a whore is a whore.

JULIE (falling to her knees, her hands clasped): O God in heaven, put an end to my miserable life! Lift me out of this filth in which I'm sinking. Save me! Save me!

JEAN: I must admit I'm sorry for you. When I was in the onion bed and saw you up there among the roses, I . . . yes, I'll tell you now . . . I had the same dirty thoughts as all boys.

JULIE: You, who wanted to die because of me?

JEAN: In the oats-bin? That was just talk.

JULIE: Lies, you mean.

JEAN (getting sleepy): More or less. I think I read a story in some paper about a chimney-sweep who shut himself up in a chest full of lilac because he'd been summonsed for not supporting some brat . . .

JULIE: So this is what you're like.

JEAN: I had to think up something. It's always the fancy stuff that catches the women.

JULIE: Beast!

JEAN: Merde!

JULIE: Now you have seen the falcon's back.

JEAN: Not exactly its back

JULIE: I was to be the first branch.

JEAN: But the branch was rotten.

JULIE: I was to be a hotel sign.

JEAN: And I the hotel.

JULIE: Sit at your counter, attract your clients and cook their accounts.

JEAN: I'd have done that myself.

JULIE: That any human being can be so steeped in filth!

JEAN: Clean it up then.

JULIE: Menial! Lackey! Stand up when I speak to you.

JEAN: Menial's whore, lackey's harlot, shut your mouth and get out of here! Are you the one to lecture me for being coarse? Nobody of my kind would ever be as coarse as you were tonight. Do you think any servant girl would throw herself at a man that way? Have you ever seen a girl of my class asking for it like that? I haven't. Only animals and prostitutes.

JULIE (broken): Go on. Hit me, trample on me—it's all I deserve. I'm rotten. But help me! If there's any way out at all, help me.

JEAN (more gently): I'm not denying myself a share in the honor of seducing you, but do you think anybody in my place would have dared look in your direction if you yourself hadn't asked for it? I'm still amazed . . .

JULIE: And proud.

JEAN: Why not? Though I must admit the victory was too easy to make me lose my head.

JULIE: Go on hitting me.

JEAN (rising): No. On the contrary I apologize for what I've said. I don't hit a person who's down—least of all a woman. I can't deny there's a certain satisfaction in finding that what dazzled one below was just moonshine, that the falcon's back is gray after all, that there's powder on the lovely cheek, that polished nails can have black tips, that the handkerchief is dirty although it smells of scent. On the other hand it hurts to find that what I was struggling to reach wasn't high and isn't real. It hurts to see you fallen so low you're far lower than your own cook. Hurts like when you see the last flowers of summer lashed to pieces by rain and turned to mud.

JULIE: You're talking as if you're already my superior.

JEAN: I am. I might make you a Countess, but you could never make me a Count, you know.

JULIE: But I am the child of a Count, and you could never be that.

JEAN: True, but I might be the father of Counts if . . .

JULIE: You're a thief. I'm not.

JEAN: There are worse things than being a thief—much lower. Besides, when I'm in a place I regard myself as a member of the family to some extent, as one of the children. You don't call it stealing when children pinch a berry from overladen bushes. (*His passion is roused again.*) Miss Julie, you're a glorious woman, far too good for a man like me. You were carried away by some kind of madness, and now you're trying to cover up your mistake by persuading yourself you're in love with me. You're not, although you may find me physically attractive, which means your love's no better than mine. But I wouldn't be satisfied with being nothing but an animal for you, and I could never make you love me.

JULIE: Are you sure?

JEAN: You think there's a chance? Of my loving you, yes, of course. You're beautiful, refined (*Takes her hand.*) educated, and you can be nice when you want to be. The fire you kindle in a man isn't likely to go out. (*Puts his arm round her.*) You're like mulled wine, full of spices, and your kisses . . . (*He tries to pull her to him, but she breaks away.*)

JULIE: Let go of me! You won't win me that way.

JEAN: Not that way, how then? Not by kisses and fine speeches, not by planning the future and saving you from shame? How then?

JULIE: How? How? I don't know. There isn't any way. I loathe you—loathe you as I loathe rats, but I can't escape from you.

JEAN: Escape with me.

JULIE (*pulling herself together*): Escape? Yes, we must escape. But I'm so tired. Give me a glass of wine. (*He pours it out. She looks at her watch.*) First we must talk. We still have a little time. (*Empties the glass and holds it out for more.*)

JEAN: Don't drink like that. You'll get tipsy.

JULIE: What's that matter?

JEAN: What's it matter? It's vulgar to get drunk. Well, what have you got to say?

JULIE: We've got to run away, but we must talk first—or rather, I must, for so far you've done all the talking. You've told me about your life, now I want to tell you about mine, so that we really know each other before we begin this journey together.

JEAN: Wait. Excuse my saying so, but don't you think you may be sorry afterward if you give away your secrets to me?

JULIE: Aren't you my friend?

JEAN: On the whole. But don't rely on me.

JULIE: You can't mean that. But anyway everyone knows my secrets. Listen. My mother wasn't well-born; she came of quite humble people, and was brought up with all those new ideas of sex-equality and women's rights and so on. She thought marriage was quite wrong. So when my father proposed to her, she said she would never become his *wife* . . . but in the end she did. I came into the world, as far as I can make out, against my mother's will, and I was left to run wild, but I had to do all the things a boy does—to prove women are as good as men. I had to wear boys' clothes; I was taught to handle horses—and I wasn't allowed in the dairy. She made me groom and harness and go out hunting; I even had to try to plough. All the men on the estate were given the women's jobs, and the women the men's, until the whole place went to rack and ruin and we were the laughing-stock of the neighborhood. At last my father seemed to have come to his senses and rebelled. He changed everything and ran the place his own way. My mother got ill—I don't know what was the matter with her, but she used to have strange attacks and hide herself in the attic or the garden. Sometimes she stayed out all night. Then came the great fire which you have heard people talking about. The house and the stables and the barns—the whole place burnt to the ground. In very suspicious circumstances. Because the accident happened the very day the insurance had to be renewed, and my father had sent the new premium, but through some carelessness of the messenger it arrived too late. (*Refills her glass and drinks.*)

JEAN: Don't drink any more.

JULIE: Oh, what does it matter? We were destitute and had to sleep in the carriages. My father didn't know how to get money to rebuild, and then my mother suggested he should borrow from an old friend of hers, a local brick manufacturer. My father got the loan and, to his surprise, without having to pay interest. So the place was rebuilt. (*Drinks.*) Do you know who set fire to it?

JEAN: Your lady mother.

JULIE: Do you know who the brick manufacturer was?

JEAN: Your mother's lover?

JULIE: Do you know whose the money was?

JEAN: Wait . . . no, I don't know that.

JULIE: It was my mother's.

JEAN: In other words the Count's, unless there was a

settlement.

JULIE: There wasn't any settlement. My mother had a little money of her own which she didn't want my father to control, so she invested it with her—friend.

JEAN: Who grabbed it.

JULIE: Exactly. He appropriated it. My father came to know all this. He couldn't bring an action, couldn't pay his wife's lover, nor prove it was his wife's money. That was my mother's revenge because he made himself master in his own house. He nearly shot himself then—at least there's a rumor he tried and didn't bring it off. So he went on living, and my mother had to pay dearly for what she'd done. Imagine what those five years were like for me. My natural sympathies were with my father, yet I took my mother's side, because I didn't know the facts. I'd learnt from her to hate and distrust men—you know how she loathed the whole male sex. And I swore to her I'd never become the slave of any man.

JEAN: And so you got engaged to that attorney.

JULIE: So that he should be my slave.

JEAN: But he wouldn't be.

JULIE: Oh yes, he wanted to be, but he didn't have the chance. I got bored with him.

JEAN: Is that what I saw—in the stable-yard?

JULIE: What did you see?

JEAN: What I saw was him breaking off the engagement.

JULIE: That's a lie. It was I who broke it off. Did he say it was him? The cad.

JEAN: He's not a cad. Do you hate men, Miss Julie?

JULIE: Yes . . . most of the time. But when that weakness comes, oh . . . the shame!

JEAN: Then do you hate me?

JULIE: Beyond words. I'd gladly have you killed like an animal.

JEAN: Quick as you'd shoot a mad dog, eh?

JULIE: Yes.

JEAN: But there's nothing here to shoot with—and there isn't a dog. So what do we do now?

JULIE: Go abroad.

JEAN: To make each other miserable for the rest of our lives?

JULIE: No, to enjoy ourselves for a day or two, for a week, for as long as enjoyment lasts, and then—to die . . .

JEAN: Die? How silly! I think it would be far better to start a hotel.

JULIE (without listening): . . . die on the shores of Lake Como, where the sun always shines and at Christmas time there are green trees and glowing oranges.

JEAN: Lake Como's a rainy hole and I didn't see any oranges outside the shops. But it's a good place for tourists. Plenty of villas to be rented by—er—honeymoon couples. Profitable business that. Know why? Because they all sign a lease for six months and all leave after three weeks.

JULIE (naïvely): After three weeks? Why?

JEAN: They quarrel, of course. But the rent has to be paid just the same. And then it's let again. So it goes on and on, for there's plenty of love although it doesn't last long.

JULIE: You don't want to die with me?

JEAN: I don't want to die at all. For one thing I like living and for another I consider suicide's a sin against the Creator who gave us life.

JULIE: You believe in God—you?

JEAN: Yes, of course. And I go to church every Sunday. Look here. I'm tired of all this. I'm going to bed.

JULIE: Indeed! And do you think I'm going to leave things like this? Don't you know what you owe the woman you've ruined?

JEAN (taking out his purse and throwing a silver coin on the table): There you are. I don't want to be in anybody's debt.

JULIE (pretending not to notice the insult): Don't you know what the law is?

JEAN: There's no law unfortunately that punishes a woman for seducing a man.

JULIE: But can you see anything for it but to go abroad, get married and then divorce?

JEAN: What if I refuse this mésalliance?

JULIE: Mésalliance?

JEAN: Yes for me. I'm better bred than you, see! Nobody in my family committed arson.

JULIE: How do you know?

JEAN: Well, you can't prove otherwise, because we haven't any family records outside the Registrar's office. But I've seen your family tree in that book on the drawing-room table. Do you know who the founder of your family was? A miller who let his wife sleep with the King one night during the Danish war. I haven't any ancestors like that. I haven't any ancestors at all, but I might become one.

JULIE: This is what I get for confiding in someone so low, for sacrificing my family honor . . .

JEAN: Dishonor! Well, I told you so. One shouldn't drink because then one talks. And one shouldn't talk.

JULIE: Oh, how ashamed I am, how bitterly ashamed! If at least you loved me!

JEAN: Look here—for the last time—what do you want? Am I to burst into tears? Am I to jump over your riding whip? Shall I kiss you and carry you off to Lake Como for three weeks, after which . . . What am I to do? What do you want? This is getting unbearable, but that's what comes of playing around with women. Miss Julie, I can see how miserable you are; I know you're going through hell, but I don't understand you. We don't have scenes like this; we don't go in for hating each other. We make love for fun in our spare time, but we haven't all day and all night for it like you. I think you must be ill. I'm sure you're ill.

JULIE: Then you must be kind to me. You sound almost human now.

JEAN: Well, be human yourself. You spit at me, then won't let me wipe it off—on you.

JULIE: Help me, help me! Tell me what to do, where to go.

JEAN: Jesus, as if I knew!

JULIE: I've been mad, raving mad, but there must be a way out.

JEAN: Stay here and keep quiet. Nobody knows anything.

JULIE: I can't. People do know. Kristin knows.

JEAN: They don't know and they wouldn't believe such a thing.

JULIE (hesitating): But—it might happen again.

JEAN: That's true.

JULIE: And there might be—consequences.

JEAN (in panic): Consequences! Fool that I am I never thought of that. Yes, there's nothing for it but to go. At once. I can't come with you. That would be a complete give-away. You must go alone—abroad—anywhere.

JULIE: Alone! Where to? I can't.

JEAN: You must. And before the Count gets back. If you stay, we know what will happen. Once you've sinned you feel you might as well go on, as the harm's done. Then you get more and more reckless and in the end you're found out. No. You must go abroad. Then write to the Count and tell him everything, except that it was me. He'll never guess that—and I don't think he'll want to.

JULIE: I'll go if you come with me.

JEAN: Are you crazy, woman? "Miss Julie elopes with valet." Next day it would be in the headlines, and the Count would never live it down.

JULIE: I can't go. I can't stay. I'm so tired, so completely worn out. Give me orders. Set me going. I can't think any more, can't act . . .

JEAN: You see what weaklings you are. Why do you give yourselves airs and turn up your noses as if you're the lords of creation? Very well, I'll give you your orders. Go upstairs and dress. Get money for the journey and come down here again.

JULIE (softly): Come up with me.

JEAN: To your room? Now you've gone crazy again. (Hesitates a moment.) No! Go along at once. (Takes her hand and pulls her to the door.)

JULIE (as she goes): Speak kindly to me, Jean.

JEAN: Orders always sound unkind. Now you know. Now you know.

(Left alone, JEAN sighs with relief, sits down at the table, takes out a note-book and pencil and adds up figures, now and then aloud. Dawn begins to break. KRISTIN enters dressed for church, carrying his white dickey and tie.)

KRISTIN: Lord Jesus, look at the state the place is in! What have you been up to? (Turns out the lamp.)

JEAN: Oh, Miss Julie invited the crowd in. Did you sleep through it? Didn't you hear anything?

KRISTIN: I slept like a log.

JEAN: And dressed for church already.

KRISTIN: Yes, you promised to come to Communion with me today.

JEAN: Why, so I did. And you've got my bib and tucker. I see. Come on then. (Sits. KRISTIN begins to put his things on. Pause. Sleepily.) What's the lesson today?

KRISTIN: It's about the beheading of John the Baptist, I think.

JEAN: That's sure to be horribly long. Hi, you're choking me! Oh Lord, I'm so sleepy, so sleepy!

KRISTIN: Yes, what have you been doing up all night? You look absolutely green.

JEAN: Just sitting here talking with Miss Julie.

KRISTIN: She doesn't know what's proper, that one. (Pause.)

JEAN: I say, Kristin.

KRISTIN: What?

JEAN: It's queer really, isn't it, when you come to think of it? Her.

KRISTIN: What's queer?

JEAN: The whole thing. (Pause.)

KRISTIN (looking at the half-filled glasses on the table): Have you been drinking together too?

JEAN: Yes.

KRISTIN: More shame you. Look me straight in the face.

JEAN: Yes.

KRISTIN: Is it possible? Is it possible?

JEAN (after a moment): Yes, it is.

KRISTIN: Oh! This I would never have believed. How low!

JEAN: You're not jealous of her, surely?

KRISTIN: No, I'm not. If it had been Clara or Sophie I'd have scratched your eyes out. But not of her. I don't know why; that's how it is though. But it's disgusting.

JEAN: You're angry with her then.

KRISTIN: No. With you. It was wicked of you, very very wicked. Poor girl. And, mark my words, I won't stay here any longer now—in a place where one can't respect one's employers.

JEAN: Why should one respect them?

KRISTIN: You should know since you're so smart. But you don't want to stay in the service of people who aren't respectable, do you? I wouldn't demean myself.

JEAN: But it's rather a comfort to find out they're no better than us.

KRISTIN: I don't think so. If they're no better there's nothing for us to live up to. Oh and think of the Count! Think of him. He's been through so much already. No I won't stay in the place any longer. A fellow like you too! If it had been that attorney now or somebody of her own class . . .

JEAN: Why, what's wrong with . . .

KRISTIN: Oh, you're all right in your own way, but when all's said and done there is a difference between one class and another. No, this is something I'll never be able to stomach. That our young lady who was so proud and so down on men you'd never believe she'd let one come near her should go and give herself to one like you. She who wanted to have poor Diana shot for running after the lodge-keeper's pug. No. I must say . . . ! Well, I won't stay here any longer. On the twenty-fourth of October, I quit.

JEAN: And then?

KRISTIN: Well, since you mention it, it's about time you began to look around, if we're ever going to get married.

JEAN: But what am I to look for? I shan't get a place like this when I'm married.

KRISTIN: I know you won't. But you might get a job as porter or caretaker in some public institution. Government rations are small but sure, and there's a pension for the widow and children.

JEAN: That's all very fine, but it's not in my line to start thinking at once about dying for my wife and children. I must say I had rather bigger ideas.

KRISTIN: You and your ideas! You've got obligations too, and you'd better start thinking about them.

JEAN: Don't *you* start pestering me about obligations. I've had enough of that. (*Listens to a sound upstairs.*) Anyway we've got plenty of time to work things out. Go and get ready now and we'll be off to church.

KRISTIN: Who's that walking about upstairs?

JEAN: Don't know—unless it's Clara.

KRISTIN (*going*): You don't think the Count could have come back without our hearing him?

JEAN (*scared*): The Count? No, he can't have. He'd have rung for me.

KRISTIN: God help us! I've never known such goings on. (*Exit.*)

(*The sun has now risen and is shining on the treetops. The light gradually changes until it slants in through the windows.* JEAN *goes to the door and beckons.* JULIE *enters in traveling clothes, carrying a small bird-cage covered with a cloth which she puts on a chair.*)

JULIE: I'm ready.

JEAN: Hush! Kristin's up.

JULIE (*in a very nervous state*): Does she suspect anything?

JEAN: Not a thing. But, my God, what a sight you are!

JULIE: Sight! What do you mean?

JEAN: You're white as a corpse and—pardon me—your face is dirty.

JULIE: Let me wash then. (*Goes to the sink and washes her face and hands.*) There. Give me a towel. Oh! The sun is rising!

JEAN: And that breaks the spell.

JULIE: Yes. The spell of Midsummer Eve . . . But listen, Jean. Come with me. I've got the money.

JEAN (*skeptically*): Enough?

JULIE: Enough to start with. Come with me. I can't travel alone today. It's Midsummer Day, remember. I'd be packed into a suffocating train among crowds of people who'd all stare at me. And it would stop at every station while I yearned for wings. No, I can't do that. I simply can't. There will be memories too; memories of Midsummer Days when I was little. The leafy church—birch and lilac—the gaily spread dinner table, relatives, friends—everything in the park—dancing and music and flowers and fun. Oh, however far you run away—there'll always be memories in the baggage car—and remorse and guilt.

JEAN: I will come with you, but quickly now then, before it's too late. At once.

JULIE: Put on your things. (*Picks up the cage.*)

JEAN: No luggage, mind. That would give us away.

JULIE: No, only what we can take with us in the carriage.

JEAN (*fetching his hat*): What on earth have you got there? What is it?

JULIE: Only my greenfinch. I don't want to leave it behind.

JEAN: Well, I'll be damned! We're to take a bird-cage along, are we? You're crazy. Put that cage down.

JULIE: It's the only thing I'm taking from my home. The only living creature who cares for me since Diana went off like that. Don't be cruel. Let me take it.

JEAN: Put that cage down, I tell you—and don't talk so loud. Kristin will hear.

JULIE: No, I won't leave it in strange hands. I'd rather you killed it.

JEAN: Give the little beast here then and I'll wring its neck.

JULIE: But don't hurt it, don't . . . no, I can't.

JEAN: Give it here, I *can*.

JULIE (*taking the bird out of the cage and kissing it*): Dear little Serena, must you die and leave your mistress?

JEAN: Please don't make a scene. It's *your* life and

future we're worrying about. Come on, quick now!

(He snatches the bird from her, puts it on a board and picks up a chopper. JULIE *turns away.)*

You should have learnt how to kill chickens instead of target-shooting. Then you wouldn't faint at a drop of blood.

JULIE *(screaming)*: Kill me too! Kill me! You who can butcher an innocent creature without a quiver. Oh, how I hate you, how I loathe you! There is blood between us now. I curse the hour I first saw you. I curse the hour I was conceived in my mother's womb.

JEAN: What's the use of cursing. Let's go.

JULIE *(going to the chopping-block as if drawn against her will)*: No, I won't go yet. I can't . . . I must look. Listen! There's a carriage. *(Listens without taking her eyes off the board and chopper.)* You don't think I can bear the sight of blood. You think I'm so weak. Oh, how I should like to see your blood and your brains on a chopping-block! I'd like to see the whole of your sex swimming like that in a sea of blood. I think I could drink out of your skull, bathe my feet in your broken breast and eat your heart roasted whole. You think I'm weak. You think I love you, that my womb yearned for your seed and I want to carry your offspring under my heart and nourish it with my blood. You think I want to bear your child and take your name. By the way, what is your name? I've never heard your surname. I don't suppose you've got one. I should be "Mrs. Hovel" or "Madam Dunghill." You dog wearing my collar, you lackey with my crest on your buttons! I share you with my cook; I'm my own servant's rival! Oh! Oh! Oh! . . . You think I'm a coward and will run away. No, now I'm going to stay—and let the storm break. My father will come back . . . find his desk broken open . . . his money gone. Then he'll ring the bell—twice for the valet—and then he'll send for the police . . . and I shall tell everything. Everything. Oh how wonderful to make an end of it all—a real end! He has a stroke and dies and that's the end of all of us. Just peace and quietness . . . eternal rest. The coat of arms broken on the coffin and the Count's line extinct . . . But the valet's line goes on in an orphanage, wins laurels in the gutter and ends in jail.

JEAN: There speaks the noble blood! Bravo, Miss Julie. But now, don't let the cat out of the bag.

*(*KRISTIN *enters dressed for church, carrying a prayer-book.* JULIE *rushes to her and flings herself into her arms for protection.)*

JULIE: Help me, Kristin! Protect me from this man!

KRISTIN *(unmoved and cold)*: What goings-on for a feast day morning! *(Sees the board.)* And what a filthy mess. What's it all about? Why are you screaming and carrying on so?

JULIE: Kristin, you're a woman and my friend. Beware of that scoundrel!

JEAN *(embarrassed)*: While you ladies are talking things over, I'll go and shave. *(Slips into his room.)*

JULIE: You must understand. You must listen to me.

KRISTIN: I certainly don't understand such loose ways. Where are you off to in those traveling clothes? And he had his hat on, didn't he, eh?

JULIE: Listen, Kristin. Listen, I'll tell you everything.

KRISTIN: I don't want to know anything.

JULIE: You must listen.

KRISTIN: What to? Your nonsense with Jean? I don't care a rap about that; it's nothing to do with me. But if you're thinking of getting him to run off with you, we'll soon put a stop to that.

JULIE *(very nervously)*: Please try to be calm, Kristin, and listen. I can't stay here, nor can Jean—so we must go abroad.

KRISTIN: Hm, hm!

JULIE *(brightening)*: But you see, I've had an idea. Supposing we all three go—abroad—to Switzerland and start a hotel together . . . I've got some money, you see . . . and Jean and I could run the whole thing—and I thought you would take charge of the kitchen. Wouldn't that be splendid? Say yes, do. If you come with us everything will be fine. Oh do say yes! *(Puts her arms round* KRISTIN.*)*

KRISTIN *(coolly thinking)*: Hm, hm.

JULIE *(presto tempo)*: You've never traveled, Kristin. You should go abroad and see the world. You've no idea how nice it is traveling by train—new faces all the time and new countries. On our way through Hamburg we'll go to the zoo—you'll love that—and we'll go to the theater and the opera too . . . and when we get to Munich there'll be the museums, dear, and pictures by Rubens and Raphael—the great painters, you know . . . You've heard of Munich, haven't you? Where King Ludwig lived—you know, the king who went mad, . . . We'll see his castles—some of his castles are still just like in fairy-tales . . . and from there it's not far to Switzerland—and the Alps. Think of the Alps, Kristin dear, covered with snow in the middle of summer . . . and there are oranges there and trees that are green the whole year round . . .

*(*JEAN *is seen in the door of his room, sharpening his razor on a strop which he holds with his teeth and his left hand. He listens to the talk with satisfaction and now and then nods approval.* JULIE *continues, tempo prestissimo.)*

And then we'll get a hotel . . . and I'll sit at the desk, while Jean receives the guests and goes out marketing and writes letters . . . There's life for you! Trains whistling, buses driving up, bells ringing upstairs and downstairs . . . and I shall make out the bills—and I shall cook them too . . . you've no idea how nervous travelers are when it comes to paying their bills. And you—you'll sit like a queen in the kitchen . . . of course there won't be any standing at the stove for you. You'll always have to be nicely dressed and ready to be seen, and with your looks—no, I'm not flattering you—one fine day you'll catch yourself a husband . . . some rich Englishman, I shouldn't wonder—they're the ones who are easy *(Slowing down.)* to catch . . . and then we'll get rich and build ourselves a villa on Lake Como . . . of course it rains there a little now and then—but *(Dully.)* the sun must shine there too sometimes—even though it seems gloomy—and if not—then we can come home again—come back—*(Pause.)*—here—or somewhere else . . .

KRISTIN: Look here, Miss Julie, do you believe all that yourself?

JULIE *(exhausted)*: Do I believe it?

KRISTIN: Yes.

JULIE *(wearily)*: I don't know. I don't believe anything any more. *(Sinks down on the bench; her head in her arms on the table.)* Nothing. Nothing at all.

KRISTIN *(turning to* JEAN*)*: So you meant to beat it, did you?

JEAN *(disconcerted, putting the razor on the table)*: Beat it? What are you talking about? You've heard Miss Julie's plan, and though she's tired now with being up all night, it's a perfectly sound plan.

KRISTIN: Oh, is it? If you thought I'd work for that . . .

JEAN *(interrupting)*: Kindly use decent language in front of your mistress. Do you hear?

KRISTIN: Mistress?

JEAN: Yes.

KRISTIN: Well, well, just listen to that!

JEAN: Yes, it would be a good thing if you did listen and talked less. Miss Julie is your mistress and what's made you lose your respect for her now ought to make you feel the same about yourself.

KRISTIN: I've always had enough self-respect—

JEAN: To despise other people.

KRISTIN: —not to go below my own station. Has the Count's cook ever gone with the groom or the swineherd? Tell me that.

JEAN: No, you were lucky enough to have a high-class chap for your beau.

KRISTIN: High-class all right—selling the oats out of the Count's stable.

JEAN: You're a fine one to talk—taking a commission on the groceries and bribes from the butcher.

KRISTIN: What the devil . . . ?

JEAN: And now you can't feel any respect for your employers. You, you!

KRISTIN: Are you coming to church with me? I should think you need a good sermon after your fine deeds.

JEAN: No, I'm not going to church today. You can go alone and confess your own sins.

KRISTIN: Yes, I'll do that and bring back enough forgiveness to cover yours too. The Saviour suffered and died on the cross for all our sins, and if we go to Him with faith and a penitent heart, He takes all our sins upon Himself.

JEAN: Even grocery thefts?

JULIE: Do you believe that, Kristin?

KRISTIN: That is my living faith, as sure as I stand here. The faith I learnt as a child and have kept ever since, Miss Julie. "But where sin abounded, grace did much more abound."

JULIE: Oh, if I had your faith! Oh, if . . .

KRISTIN: But you see you can't have it without God's special grace, and it's not given to all to have that.

JULIE: Who is it given to then?

KRISTIN: That's the great secret of the workings of grace, Miss Julie. God is no respecter of persons, and with Him the last shall be first . . .

JULIE: Then I suppose He does respect the last.

KRISTIN *(continuing)*: . . . and it is easier for a camel to go through the eye of a needle than for a rich man to enter into the kingdom of God. That's how it is, Miss Julie. Now I'm going—alone, and on my way I shall tell the groom not to let any of the horses out, in case anyone should want to leave before the Count gets back. Good-by. *(Exit.)*

JEAN: What a devil! And all on account of a greenfinch.

JULIE *(wearily)*: Never mind the greenfinch. Do you see any way out of this, any end to it?

JEAN *(pondering)*: No.

JULIE: If you were in my place, what would you do?

JEAN: In your place? Wait a bit. If I was a woman—a lady of rank who had—fallen. I don't know. Yes, I do know now.

JULIE *(picking up the razor and making a gesture)*: This?

JEAN: Yes. But *I* wouldn't do it, you know. There's a difference between us.

JULIE: Because you're a man and I'm a woman? What is the difference?

JEAN: The usual difference—between man and woman.

JULIE *(holding the razor)*: I'd like to. But I can't. My father couldn't either, that time he wanted to.

JEAN: No, he didn't want to. He had to be revenged first.

JULIE: And now my mother is revenged again, through me.

JEAN: Didn't you ever love your father, Miss Julie?

JULIE: Deeply, but I must have hated him too—unconsciously. And he let me be brought up to despise my own sex, to be half woman, half man.

Whose fault is what's happened? My father's, my mother's, or my own? My own? I haven't anything that's my own. I haven't one single thought that I didn't get from my father, one emotion that didn't come from my mother, and as for this last idea—about all people being equal—I got that from him, my fiancé—that's why I call him a cad. How can it be my fault? Push the responsibility on to Jesus, like Kristin does? No, I'm too proud and—thanks to my father's teaching—too intelligent. As for all that about a rich person not being able to get into heaven, it's just a lie, but Kristin, who has money in the savings-bank, will certainly not get in. Whose fault is it? What does it matter whose fault it is? In any case I must take the blame and bear the consequences.

JEAN: Yes, but . . . *(There are two sharp rings on the bell.* JULIE *jumps to her feet.* JEAN *changes into his livery.)* The Count is back. Supposing Kristin . . . *(Goes to the speaking-tube, presses it and listens.)*

JULIE: Has he been to his desk yet?

JEAN: This is Jean, sir. *(Listens.)* Yes, sir. *(Listens.)* Yes, sir, very good, sir. *(Listens.)* At once, sir? *(Listens.)* Very good, sir. In half an hour.

JULIE *(in panic)*: What did he say? My God, what did he say?

JEAN: He ordered his boots and his coffee in half an hour.

JULIE: Then there's half an hour . . . Oh, I'm so tired! I can't do anything. Can't be sorry, can't run away, can't stay, can't live—can't die. Help me. Order me, and I'll obey like a dog. Do me this last service—save my honor, save his name. You know what I ought do to, but haven't the strength to do. Use your strength and order me to do it.

JEAN: I don't know why—I can't now—I don't understand . . . It's just as if this coat made me—I can't give you orders—and now that the Count has spoken to me—I can't quite explain, but . . . well, that devil of a lackey is bending my back again. I believe if the Count came down now and ordered me to cut my throat, I'd do it on the spot.

JULIE: Then pretend you're him and I'm you. You did some fine acting before, when you knelt to me and played the aristocrat. Or . . . Have you ever seen a hypnotist at the theater? *(He nods.)* He says to the person "Take the broom," and he takes it. He says "Sweep," and he sweeps . . .

JEAN: But the person has to be asleep.

JULIE *(as if in a trance)*: I am asleep already . . . the whole room has turned to smoke—and you look like a stove—a stove like a man in black with a tall hat—your eyes are glowing like coals when the fire is low—and your face is a white patch like ashes. *(The sunlight has now reached the floor and lights up* JEAN.*)* How nice and warm it is! *(She hold out her hands as though warming them at a fire.)* And so light—and so peaceful.

JEAN *(putting the razor in her hand)*: Here is the broom. Go now while it's light—out to the barn—and . . . *(Whispers in her ear.)*

JULIE *(waking)*: Thank you. I am going now—to rest. But just tell me that even the first can receive the gift of grace.

JEAN: The first? No, I can't tell you that. But wait . . . Miss Julie, I've got it! You aren't one of the first any longer. You're one of the last.

JULIE: That's true, I'm one of the very last. I *am* the last. Oh! . . . But now I can't go. Tell me again to go.

JEAN: No, I can't now either. I can't.

JULIE: And the first shall be last.

JEAN: Don't think, don't think. You're taking my strength away too and making me a coward. What's that? I thought I saw the bell move . . . To be so frightened of a bell! Yes, but it's not just a bell. There's somebody behind it—a hand moving it—and something else moving the hand—and if you stop your ears—if you stop your ears—yes, then it rings louder than ever. Rings and rings until you answer—and then it's too late. Then the police come and . . . and . . . *(The bell rings twice loudly.* JEAN *flinches, then straightens himself up.)* It's horrible. But there's no other way to end it . . . Go!

*(*JULIE *walks firmly out through the door.)*

CURTAIN

Figure 56. Julie (Maggie Smith) waves her scented handkerchief at Jean (Albert Finney) in the National Theatre production of *Miss Julie,* directed by Michael Elliott, London, 1966. (Photograph: Angus McBean.)

Figure 57. Jean (Albert Finney) and Julie (Maggie Smith) during a pause in their long conversation after the peasants have departed in the National Theatre production of *Miss Julie,* directed by Michael Elliott, London, 1966. (Photograph: Dominic.)

Figure 58. Julie (Maggie Smith) holds her greenfinch in her hands while Jean (Albert Finney) waits ready to behead it on the chopping board in the National Theatre production of *Miss Julie,* directed by Michael Elliott, London, 1966. (Photograph: Angus McBean, Harvard Theatre Collection.)

Staging of *Miss Julie*

REVIEW OF THE NATIONAL THEATRE
PRODUCTION, 1966, BY THE LONDON *TIMES*
DRAMA CRITIC

Miss Julie brings Mr. Finney and Miss Smith together in Strindberg's sexual dual between servant and mistress. The duel itself comes over with less than its usual ferocity as the production gives as much emphasis to the private fantasies of the antagonists as to their actual encounter. Jean's dream of social advancement and Julie's dream of falling to destruction are the real things: each to the other is only the accidental means of embodying them. Not that Michael Elliott's production is lacking in aggressiveness: Miss Smith's erotic arrogance in the first scene is matched by the casual brutality with which Mr. Finney at the end chops off the tame bird's head.

But it is rather that the partners (Julie in particular) are acting under a somnambulistic spell. The production does not stretch Miss Smith far enough away from comedy; and her voice is still obstinately without pathos. But Mr. Finney's Jean is a subtle compound of materialism and social pretension; and there is a fine icy Christine by Jeanne Watts, who gives the claustrophobic drama a link with the outer world. The pantomine interlude, alas, has defeated Mr. Elliott like other directors before him.

REVIEW OF THE NATIONAL THEATRE
PRODUCTION, 1966, BY HUGH LEONARD

Second nights can be dangerous. Actors loosen their collars, tuck in their frayed nerve-ends and uncross their fingers. A happy tiredness descends on the company like fall-out; and the first casualty is timing. Then a drawer sticks, a line is fluffed and a laugh comes at the wrong place. Panic sets in, and last night's champagne goes incurably flat. Perhaps this was what happened to *Miss Julie* at the National Theatre, but Michael Elliott's direction wasn't quite up to the task to begin with. This is a veritable bitch of a play, in which a miss is as bad as a mile. Big guns are needed; and although Mr Elliott had them, they were trained in the wrong direction. For great stretches of time we were obliged to look at the back of Albert Finney's head and at Maggie Smith in half-profile. Savagely emotional scenes were played at a murmur in dingy lighting and a set which reduced Strindberg's 'large kitchen' to a pokey room with swaying roof-beams. The callous beheading of the chaffinch generated hardly an 'ugh!', and the play's ending was so indeterminately staged that the audience sat in puzzled silence waiting for more.

Not that the production was a disaster. But it wasn't Strindberg either. Mr. Finney's valet was good, but muted; and, as Miss Julie, Miss Smith wasn't nearly patrician enough. To fall spectacularly, one needs height first and foremost; and it is Julie's pretensions which dictate her suicide. With no discernible social gap existing between Julie and her father's valet, half the play's values were lost. Miss Smith is always delightful to watch and listen to; but this isn't her part any more than Strindberg is suited to Mr. Elliott.

ANTON CHEKHOV

1860—1904

Anton Chekhov was born in Taganrog, a Crimean resort not far from Yalta, where he wrote his last play, *The Cherry Orchard,* when he was dying of tuberculosis. Although his grandfather had been a serf who amassed enough money not only to buy his freedom but also an estate, his father, plagued by the debts of an unsuccessful grocery, was forced to leave Taganrog and move the family to Moscow. Chekhov himself remained in Taganrog to finish his schooling, but his years there could hardly have been pleasant ones, for his poverty compelled him to earn money by doing homework for his fellow students, and Taganrog itself, like most seaside resorts of that era, was filled with the sick and aged. So it is not surprising that the resorts that appear repeatedly in Chekhov's works, such as the "villas" that Lopahin proposes to build along the river bank, are always associated with tedium and futility. By 1880, Chekhov, too, had left Taganrog and moved to Moscow, where he entered medical school and started to write short stories to help support himself and his family. He became a physician and practiced medicine for a time, yet he gradually came to spend more and more effort on his writing, less and less on medicine. By 1888, he was practicing only during epidemics, when there was a shortage of doctors, whereas he was writing so much that he had already published 300 stories. During the 1880s, Chekhov had also started writing for the stage—first one-act plays, which he began doing in 1884, the year of his graduation from medical school, then full-length works, the earliest of which appeared in 1887. Most of his one-act plays are farcical studies of middle-class aspirations to sophisticated society, such as *The Boor* and *The Marriage Proposal,* which were well received and still continue to be performed. His early full-length works, such as *Ivanov* (1887), and *The Wood Demon* (1889), an early version of *Uncle Vanya,* were bitter failures, so much so that he did not write another serious full-length play until *The Seagull* (1896), which was first produced in St. Petersburg.

The Seagull, a psychologically realistic play, which bears witness to the drama of human loneliness and frustration, failed dismally in its opening production, for it was a radical departure from Russian theatrical tastes of the time. Chekhov's audience was unaccustomed to his low-key realism, to his subtle revelations of character, to his apparently plotless drama of Russian life, for this kind of drama was completely at odds with the melodramatic thrillers then being imported from Paris. The Russian actors were also unprepared for it, since they had never tried, nor seen, any style of performance other than the bombastic acting of the period that had been popularized by the English actor Edmund Kean. And the management of the theater where it was produced did not give the actors much of a chance to develop an appropriately low-key style, allowing them only nine days for rehearsals. *The Seagull* was literally laughed off the stage in St. Petersburg. Although Chekhov vowed never to write another play, he did permit *The Seagull* to be printed in a literary magazine, where it caught the interest of two wealthy young men, Constantin Stanislavski and Vladimir Nemirovich-

Danchenko, whose theatrical ambitions brought them together in 1898 to form the Moscow Art Theater. This group was based on the new principles of ensemble acting then being attempted throughout Europe, where acting companies were following the model established by the German troupe of the Duke of Saxe-Meinegen. But Stanislavski and Nemirovich-Danchenko were not content simply to develop an ensemble. They aimed to develop an acting company with a distinctively new style of performance, a style that was understated rather than overstated, realistic instead of melodramatic. That style was perfectly attuned to the psychological nuances of *The Seagull,* and thus they chose to conclude their first season with a revival of the play. That revival turned out to be the making of both Chekhov and the Moscow Art Theater, for though the rest of their season had been a series of failures, *The Seagull* was met with thunderous applause by the audience.

Chekhov's plays do not actually try to elicit dynamic roars of approval. Indeed, they are all wry, sometimes wearied, sometimes satirical displays of futility in human behavior—of the inability to act decisively, even when such action would seem to be easily within the range of human capacity. In *Uncle Vanya* (1899), for example, the central character learns that the professor for whom he has slaved without reward is not the personification of wisdom, as he had thought, but is instead a mediocre academic windbag. Consequently, he is moved to shoot the professor at point-blank range, but misses him. And he is seen at the end of the play repressing the knowledge he has of his own wasted life, unlearning what he has learned by a titanic effort in futility. Chekhov's next play, *The Three Sisters* (1901), is a study of shared futility, enacted by the title characters, who though left with an ample inheritance never fulfill any of their personal hopes, professional ambitions, or mundane desires, not even the simple desire that moves them throughout the play: to go to Moscow. *The Three Sisters* was followed three years later by the production of *The Cherry Orchard* in January 1904, six months before Chekhov died of tuberculosis.

The Cherry Orchard may be seen as a full-scale version of cultural futility—of the inability of an old aristocratic social order to preserve itself, of the inability of a new bourgeois order to find meaning in anything beyond the acquisition of money and land. Everyone in the play owns, wants to own, or wants to maintain ownership of someone or something, and the play witnesses everyone gaining or losing the things they wish to own. Whether the audience is to laugh at this spectacle, or to weep, or simply to be bemused, is a difficult question. Chekhov called the play a comedy, and he apparently intended it to be comic, judging from correspondence with Stanislavski and Nemirovich-Danchenko. Yet Stanislavski's letters just as clearly show that he did not consider it a comedy at all—that he viewed it as a tragic expression of Russian life:

> It is not a comedy, not a farce, as you wrote—it is a tragedy no matter if you do indicate a way out into a better world in the last act . . . when I read it for the second time . . . I wept like a woman, I tried to control myself, but could not. I can hear you say: "But please, this is a farce . . ." No, for the ordinary person this is a tragedy.

Stanislavski's decision to produce the play as a tragedy moved Chekhov to complain that he was turning it into a piece of sniveling sentimentality, and Stanislavski did modify his interpretation somewhat during the next thirty years that he produced it, but he never came around to seeing the characters as laughable.

The conflict between Chekhov and Stanislavski is, of course, irresolvable, because the play repeatedly hovers between the comic and the tragic, as it does, for example, in the second act, when Trofimov, the perpetual student and self-appointed philosopher, speculates on the nature of man and destiny of the Russian people. The topics of his speculation are, of course, inherently serious, the more so because they are poignantly relevant to the experience of all the characters in the play. Yet the situation is inherently comic, if only because of the jarring differences among the backgrounds and outlooks of the several characters who are present, not to mention the humor that arises from Trofimov being carried away by his own high-flown generalizations about life. Photographs of this moment can be seen as it was produced by the Moscow Art Theater (see Figure 59), the Guthrie Theater (see Figure 60), and the Stratford Festival, Canada (see Figure 61), and these three contemporaneous productions (1965) are discussed comparatively in the review by Howard Taubman. Taubman pays particular attention to both the comic and tragic facets of the play, for, as he makes clear, none of the productions chose to make it entirely one or the other. Thus *The Cherry Orchard* continues to be a tantalizing work for actors, directors, and spectators. Like many of the modern plays in this anthology, it offers an ambivalent view of experience, and so it arouses ambivalent responses even from those who know it most intimately: the actors and actresses themselves. One great actress, after having starred as Mrs. Ranevsky, remarked of the characters, "Well, of course, the poor dears, they do suffer, but honestly, you can't take 'em seriously! Or can you?"

THE CHERRY ORCHARD

BY ANTON CHEKHOV / TRANSLATED BY DAVID MAGARSHACK

CHARACTERS

LYUBOV (LYUBA) ANDREYEVNA RANEVSKY, *a landowner*
ANYA, *her daughter, aged seventeen*
VARYA, *her adopted daughter, aged twenty-four*
LEONID ANDREYEVICH GAYEV, *Mrs. Ranevsky's brother*
YERMOLAY ALEXEYEVICH LOPAKHIN, *a businessman*
PETER (PYOTR) SERGEYEVICH TROFIMOV, *a student*
BORIS BORISOVICH SIMEONOV-PISHCHIK, *a landowner*
CHARLOTTE IVANOVNA, *a governess*
SIMON PANTELEYEVICH YEPIKHODOV, *a clerk*

DUNYASHA, *a maid*
FIRS, *a manservant, aged eighty-seven*
YASHA, *a young manservant*
A HIKER
A STATIONMASTER
A POST OFFICE CLERK
GUESTS *and* SERVANTS

SCENE

The action takes place on MRS. RANEVSKY'S *estate.*

ACT 1

(A room which is still known as the nursery. One of the doors leads to ANYA'S *room. Daybreak; the sun will be rising soon. It is May. The cherry trees are in blossom, but it is cold in the orchard. Morning frost. The windows of the room are shut. Enter* DUNYASHA, *carrying a candle, and* LOPAKHIN *with a book in his hand.)*

LOPAKHIN: The train's arrived, thank goodness. What's the time?

DUNYASHA: Nearly two o'clock, sir. *(Blows out the candle.)* It's light already.

LOPAKHIN: How late was the train? Two hours at least. *(Yawns and stretches.)* What a damn fool I am! Came here specially to meet them at the station and fell asleep. . . . Sat down in a chair and dropped off. What a nuisance! Why didn't you wake me?

DUNYASHA: I thought you'd gone, sir. *(Listens.)* I think they're coming.

LOPAKHIN *(listening)*: No. . . . I should have been there to help them with the luggage and so on. *(Pause.)* Mrs. Ranevsky's been abroad for five years. I wonder what she's like now. . . . She's such a nice person. Simple, easy-going. I remember when I was a lad of fifteen, my late father—he used to keep a shop in the village—punched me in the face and made my nose bleed. We'd gone into the yard to fetch something, and he was drunk. Mrs. Ranevsky—I remember it as if it happened yesterday, she was such a young girl then and so slim—took me to the washstand in this very room, the nursery. "Don't cry, little peasant," she said, "it won't matter by the time you're wed." *(Pause.)* Little peasant . . . It's quite true my father was a peasant, but here I am wearing a white waistcoat and brown shoes. A dirty peasant in a fashionable shop. . . . Except, of course, that I'm a rich man now, rolling in money. But, come to think of it, I'm a plain peasant still. . . . *(Turns the pages of his book.)* Been

reading this book and haven't understood a word. Fell asleep reading it.

(Pause.)

DUNYASHA: The dogs have been awake all night; they know their masters are coming.

LOPAKHIN: What's the matter, Dunyasha? Why are you in such a state?

DUNYASHA: My hands are shaking. I think I'm going to faint.

LOPAKHIN: A little too refined, aren't you, Dunyasha? Quite the young lady. Dress, hair. It won't do, you know. Remember your place!

(Enter YEPIKHODOV *with a bunch of flowers; he wears a jacket and brightly polished high-boots which squeak loudly; on coming in, he drops the flowers.)*

YEPIKHODOV *(picking up the flowers)*: The gardener sent these. Said to put them in the dining room. *(Hands the flowers to* DUNYASHA.)

LOPAKHIN: Bring me some kvass while you're about it.

DUNYASHA: Yes, sir. *(Goes out.)*

YEPIKHODOV: Thirty degrees, morning frost, and the cherry trees in full bloom. Can't say I think much of our climate, sir. *(Sighs.)* Our climate isn't particularly accommodating, is it, sir? Not when you want it to be, anyway. And another thing. The other day I bought myself this pair of boots, and believe me, sir, they squeak so terribly that it's more than a man can endure. Do you happen to know of something I could grease them with?

LOPAKHIN: Go away. You make me tired.

YEPIKHODOV: Every day, sir, I'm overtaken by some calamity. Not that I mind. I'm used to it. I just smile. *(*DUNYASHA *comes in and hands* LOPAKHIN *the kvass.)* I'll be off. *(Bumps into a chair and knocks it over.)* There you are, sir. *(Triumphantly.)* You see, sir, pardon the expression, this sort of circumstance . . . I mean to say . . . Remarkable! Quite remarkable! *(Goes out.)*

DUNYASHA: I simply must tell you, sir: Yepikhodov has proposed to me.

LOPAKHIN: Oh?

DUNYASHA: I really don't know what to do, sir. He's ever such a quiet fellow, except that sometimes he starts talking and you can't understand a word he says. It sounds all right and it's ever so moving, only you can't make head or tail of it. I like him a little, I think. I'm not sure though. He's madly in love with me. He's such an unlucky fellow, sir. Every day something happens to him. Everyone teases him about it. They've nicknamed him Twenty-two Calamities.

LOPAKHIN *(listens)*: I think I can hear them coming.

DUNYASHA: They're coming! Goodness, I don't know what's the matter with me. I've gone cold all over.

LOPAKHIN: Yes, they are coming all right. Let's go and meet them. Will she recognize me? We haven't seen each other for five years.

DUNYASHA *(agitated)*: I'm going to faint. Oh dear, I'm going to faint!

(Two carriages can be heard driving up to the house. LOPAKHIN *and* DUNYASHA *go out quickly. The stage is empty. People can be heard making a noise in the adjoining rooms.* FIRS, *who has been to meet* MRS. RANEVSKY *at the station, walks across the stage hurriedly, leaning on a stick. He wears an old-fashioned livery coat and a top hat; he keeps muttering to himself, but it is impossible to make out a single word. The noise offstage becomes louder. A voice is heard: "Let's go through here."* MRS. RANEVSKY, ANYA, *and* CHARLOTTE, *with a lap dog on a little chain, all wearing traveling clothes,* VARYA, *wearing an overcoat and a head scarf,* GAYEV, SIMEONOV-PISHCHIK, LOPAKHIN, DUNYASHA, *carrying a bundle and an umbrella, and other* SERVANTS *with luggage walk across the stage.)*

ANYA: Let's go through here. Remember this room, Mother?

MRS. RANEVSKY *(joyfully, through tears)*: The nursery!

VARYA: It's so cold. My hands are quite numb. *(to* MRS. RANEVSKY*)* Your rooms, the white one and the mauve one, are just as you left them, Mother dear.

MRS. RANEVSKY: The nursery! My dear, my beautiful room! I used to sleep here when I was a little girl. *(Cries.)* I feel like a little girl again now. *(Kisses her brother and* VARYA, *and then her brother again.)* Varya is the same as ever. Looks like a nun. And I also recognized Dunyasha. *(Kisses* DUNYASHA.)

GAYEV: The train was two hours late. How do you like that? What a way to run a railway!

CHARLOTTE *(to* PISHCHIK*)*: My dog also eats nuts.

PISHCHIK *(surprised)*: Good Lord!

(All, except ANYA *and* DUNYASHA, *go out.)*

DUNYASHA: We thought you'd never come. *(Helps* ANYA *off with her coat and hat.)*

ANYA: I haven't slept for four nights on our journey. Now I'm chilled right through.

DUNYASHA: You left before Easter. It was snowing and freezing then. It's different now, isn't it? Darling Anya! *(Laughs and kisses her.)* I've missed you so much, my darling, my precious! Oh, I must tell you at once! I can't keep it to myself a minute longer. . . .

ANYA *(apathetically)*: What is it this time?

DUNYASHA: Our clerk, Yepikhodov, proposed to me after Easter.

ANYA: Always the same. *(Tidying her hair.)* I've lost all my hairpins. *(She is so tired, she can hardly stand.)*

DUNYASHA: I don't know what to think. He loves me so much, so much!

ANYA *(tenderly, looking through the door into her room)*: My own room, my own windows, just as if I'd never been away! I'm home again! As soon as I get up in the morning, I'll run out into the orchard. . . . Oh, if only I could sleep. I didn't sleep all the way back, I was so worried.

DUNYASHA: Mr. Trofimov arrived the day before yesterday.

ANYA *(joyfully)*: Peter!

DUNYASHA: He's asleep in the bathhouse. He's been living there. Afraid of being a nuisance, he says. *(Glancing at her watch.)* I really ought to wake him, except that Miss Varya told me not to. "Don't you dare wake him!" she said.

*(*VARYA *comes in with a bunch of keys at her waist.)*

VARYA: Dunyasha, coffee quick! Mother's asking for some.

DUNYASHA: I won't be a minute! *(Goes out.)*

VARYA: Well, thank goodness you're all back. You're home again, my darling. *(Caressing her.)* My darling is home again! My sweet child is home again.

ANYA: I've had such an awful time!

VARYA: I can imagine it.

ANYA: I left before Easter. It was terribly cold then. All the way Charlotte kept talking and doing her conjuring tricks. Why did you force Charlotte on me?

VARYA: But you couldn't have gone alone, darling, could you? You're only seventeen!

ANYA: In Paris it was also cold and snowing. My French is awful. I found Mother living on the fourth floor. When I got there, she had some French visitors, a few ladies and an old Catholic priest with a book. The place was full of tobacco smoke and terribly uncomfortable. Suddenly I felt sorry for Mother, so sorry that I took her head in my arms, held it tightly, and couldn't let go. Afterwards Mother was very sweet to me. She was crying all the time.

VARYA (*through tears*): Don't go on, Anya. Please don't.

ANYA: She'd already sold her villa near Mentone. She had nothing left. Nothing! I hadn't any money, either. There was hardly enough for the journey. Mother just won't understand! We had dinner at the station and she would order the most expensive things and tip the waiters a ruble each. Charlotte was just the same. Yasha, too, demanded to be given the same kind of food. It was simply awful! You see, Yasha is Mother's manservant. We've brought him back with us.

VARYA: Yes, I've seen the scoundrel.

ANYA: Well, what's been happening? Have you paid the interest on the mortgage?

VARYA: Heavens, no!

ANYA: Dear, oh dear . . .

VARYA: The estate will be up for sale in August.

ANYA: Oh dear!

LOPAKHIN (*puts his head through the door and bleats*): Bah-h-h! (*Goes out.*)

VARYA (*through tears*): Oh, I'd like to hit him! (*Shakes her fist.*)

ANYA (*gently embracing* VARYA): Varya, has he proposed to you? (VARYA *shakes her head.*) But he loves you. Why don't you two come to an understanding? What are you waiting for?

VARYA: I don't think anything will come of it. He's so busy. He can't be bothered with me. Why, he doesn't even notice me. I wish I'd never known him. I can't stand the sight of him. Everyone's talking about our wedding, everyone's congratulating me, while there's really nothing in it. It's all so unreal. Like a dream. (*In a different tone of voice.*) You've got a new brooch. Like a bee, isn't it?

ANYA (*sadly*): Yes, Mother bought it. (*Goes to her room, talking quite happily, like a child.*) You know, I went up in a balloon in Paris!

VARYA: My darling's home again! My dearest one's home again! (DUNYASHA *has come back with a coffeepot and is making coffee;* VARYA *is standing at the door of* ANYA's *room.*) All day long, darling, I'm busy about the house, and all the time I'm dreaming, dreaming. If only we could find a rich husband for you! My mind would be at rest then. I'd go into a convent and later on a pilgrimage to Kiev . . . to Moscow. Just keep going from one holy place to another. On and on. . . . Wonderful!

ANYA: The birds are singing in the orchard. What's the time?

VARYA: It's past two. It's time you were asleep, darling. (*Goes into* ANYA's *room.*) Wonderful!

(*Enter* YASHA *with a traveling rug and a small bag.*)

YASHA (*crossing the stage, in an affected genteel voice*): May I be permitted to go through here?

DUNYASHA: I can hardly recognize you, Yasha. You've changed so much abroad.

YASHA: Hmmm . . . And who are you, may I ask?

DUNYASHA: When you left, I was no bigger than this. (*Shows her height from the floor with her hand.*) I'm Dunyasha, Fyodor Kozoedov's daughter. Don't you remember me?

YASHA: Mmmm . . . Juicy little cucumber! (*Looks round, then puts his arms around her; she utters a little scream and drops a saucer.* YASHA *goes out hurriedly.*)

VARYA (*in the doorway, crossly*): What's going on there?

DUNYASHA (*in tears*): I've broken a saucer.

VARYA: That's lucky.

ANYA (*coming out of her room*): Mother must be told Peter's here.

VARYA: I gave orders not to wake him.

ANYA (*pensively*): Father died six years ago. A month after our brother, Grisha, was drowned in the river. Such a pretty little boy. He was only seven. Mother took it badly. She went away, went away never to come back. (*Shudders.*) Peter Trofimov was Grisha's tutor. He might remind her . . .

(FIRS *comes in, wearing a jacket and a white waistcoat.*)

FIRS (*walks up to the coffeepot anxiously*): Madam will have her coffee here. (*Puts on white gloves.*) Is the coffee ready? (*Sternly, to* DUNYASHA.) You there! Where's the cream?

DUNYASHA: Oh dear! (*Goes out quickly.*)

FIRS (*fussing round the coffeepot*): The nincompoop! (*Muttering to himself.*) She's come from Paris. . . . Master used to go to Paris. . . . Aye, by coach. . . . (*Laughs.*)

VARYA: What are you talking about, Firs?

FIRS: Sorry, what did you say? (*Joyfully.*) Madam is home again! Home at last! I can die happy now. (*Weeps with joy.*)

(*Enter* MRS. RANEVSKY, GAYEV, *and* SIMEONOV-PISHCHIK, *the last one wearing a Russian long-waisted coat of expensive cloth and wide trousers. As he enters,* GAYEV *moves his arms and body as if he were playing billiards.*)

MRS. RANEVSKY: How does it go now? Let me think. Pot the red in the corner. Double into the middle pocket.

GAYEV: And straight into the corner! A long time ago, Lyuba, you and I slept in this room. Now I'm fifty-one. . . . Funny, isn't it!

LOPAKHIN: Aye, time flies.

GAYEV: I beg your pardon?

LOPAKHIN: "Time flies," I said.

GAYEV: The place reeks of patchouli.

ANYA: I'm off to bed. Good night, Mother. (*Kisses her mother.*)

MRS. RANEVSKY: My sweet little darling! (*Kisses her hands.*) You're glad to be home, aren't you? I still can't believe it.

ANYA: Good night, Uncle.

GAYEV (*kissing her face and hands*): God bless you. You're so like your mother! (*to his sister*) You were just like her at that age, Lyuba.

(ANYA *shakes hands with* LOPAKHIN *and* PISHCHIK. *Goes out and shuts the door behind her.*)

MRS. RANEVSKY: She's terribly tired.

PISHCHIK: It was a long journey.

VARYA (*to* LOPAKHIN *and* PISHCHIK): Well, gentlemen, it's past two o'clock. You mustn't outstay your welcome, must you?

MRS. RANEVSKY (*laughs*): You're just the same, Varya. (*Draws* VARYA *to her and kisses her.*) Let me have my coffee first and then we'll all go. (FIRS *puts a little cushion under her feet.*) Thank you, Firs dear. I've got used to having coffee. I drink it day and night. Thank you, Firs, thank you, my dear old man. (*Kisses* FIRS.)

VARYA: I'd better make sure they've brought all the things in. (*Goes out.*)

MRS. RANEVSKY: Is it really me sitting here? (*Laughs.*) I feel like jumping about, waving my arms. (*Covers her face with her hands.*) And what if it's all a dream? God knows, I love my country. I love it dearly. I couldn't look out of the train for crying. (*Through tears.*) But, I suppose I'd better have my coffee. Thank you, Firs, thank you, dear old man. I'm so glad you're still alive.

FIRS: The day before yesterday . . .

GAYEV: He's a little deaf.

LOPAKHIN: At five o'clock I've got to leave for Kharkov. What a nuisance! I wish I could have had a good look at you, a good talk with you. You're still as magnificent as ever. . . .

PISHCHIK (*breathing heavily*): Lovelier, I'd say. Dressed in the latest Paris fashion. If only I were twenty years younger—ho-ho-ho!

LOPAKHIN: This brother of yours says that I'm an ignorant oaf, a tightfisted peasant, but I don't mind. Let him talk. All I want is that you should believe in me as you used to, that you should look at me as you used to with those wonderful eyes of yours. Merciful heavens! My father was a serf of your father and your grandfather, but you, you alone, did so much for me in the past that I forgot everything, and I love you just as if you were my own flesh and blood, more than my own flesh and blood.

MRS. RANEVSKY: I can't sit still, I can't. . . . (*Jumps up and walks about the room in great agitation.*) This happiness is more than I can bear. Laugh at me if you like. I'm making such a fool of myself. Oh, my darling little bookcase . . . (*Kisses the bookcase.*) My sweet little table . . .

GAYEV: You know, of course, that Nanny died here while you were away.

MRS. RANEVSKY (*sits down and drinks her coffee*): Yes, God rest her soul. They wrote to tell me about it.

GAYEV: Anastasy, too, is dead. Boss-eyed Peter left me for another job. He's with the Police Superintendent in town now. (*Takes a box of fruit drops out of his pocket and sucks one.*)

PISHCHIK: My daughter Dashenka—er—wishes to be remembered to you.

LOPAKHIN: I'd like to say something very nice and cheerful to you. (*Glances at his watch.*) I shall have to be going in a moment and there isn't much time to talk. As you know, your cherry orchard's being sold to pay your debts. The auction is on the twenty-second of August. But there's no need to worry, my dear. You can sleep soundly. There's a way out. Here's my plan. Listen carefully, please. Your estate is only about twelve miles from town, and the railway is not very far away. Now, all you have to do is break up your cherry orchard and the land along the river into building plots and lease them out for country cottages. You'll then have an income of at least twenty-five thousand a year.

GAYEV: I'm sorry, but what utter nonsense!

MRS. RANEVSKY: I don't quite follow you, Lopakhin.

LOPAKHIN: You'll be able to charge your tenants at least twenty-five rubles a year for a plot of about three acres. I bet you anything that if you advertise now, there won't be a single plot left by the autumn. They will all be snapped up. In fact, I congratulate you. You are saved. The site is magnificent and the river is deep enough for bathing. Of course, the place will have to be cleared, tidied up. . . . I mean, all the old buildings will have to be pulled down, including, I'm sorry to say, this house, but it isn't any use to anybody any more, is it? The old cherry orchard will have to be cut down.

MRS. RANEVSKY: Cut down? My dear man, I'm very sorry but I don't think you know what you're talking about. If there's anything of interest, anything quite remarkable, in fact, in the whole county, it's our cherry orchard.

LOPAKHIN: The only remarkable thing about this orchard is that it's very large. It only produces a crop every other year, and even then you don't know what to do with the cherries. Nobody wants to buy them.

GAYEV: Why, you'll find our orchard mentioned in the encyclopedia.

LOPAKHIN (*glancing at his watch*): If we can't think of anything and if we can't come to any decision, it won't be only your cherry orchard but your whole estate that will be sold at auction on the twenty-second of August. Make up your mind. I tell you, there is no other way. Take my word for it. There isn't.

FIRS: In the old days, forty or fifty years ago, the cherries used to be dried, preserved, made into jam, and sometimes—

GAYEV: Do shut up, Firs.

FIRS: —and sometimes cartloads of dried cherries were sent to Moscow and Kharkov. Fetched a lot of money, they did. Soft and juicy, those cherries were. Sweet and such a lovely smell . . . They knew the recipe then. . . .

MRS. RANEVSKY: And where's the recipe now?

FIRS: Forgotten. No one remembers it.

PISHCHIK (to MRS. RANEVSKY): What was it like in Paris? Eh? Eat any frogs?

MRS. RANEVSKY: I ate crocodiles.

PISHCHIK: Good Lord!

LOPAKHIN: Till recently there were only the gentry and the peasants in the country. Now we have holiday-makers. All our towns, even the smallest, are surrounded by country cottages. I shouldn't be surprised if in twenty years the holiday-maker multiplies enormously. All your holiday-maker does now is drink tea on the veranda, but it's quite in the cards that if he becomes the owner of three acres of land, he'll do a bit of farming on the side, and then your cherry orchard will become a happy, prosperous, thriving place.

GAYEV (indignantly): What nonsense!

(Enter VARYA and YASHA.)

VARYA: I've got two telegrams in here for you, Mother dear. (Picks out a key and unlocks the old-fashioned bookcase with a jingling noise.) Here they are.

MRS. RANEVSKY: They're from Paris. (Tears the telegrams up without reading them.) I've finished with Paris.

GAYEV: Do you know how old this bookcase is, Lyuba? Last week I pulled out the bottom drawer and saw some figures burned into it. This bookcase was made exactly a hundred years ago. What do you think of that? Eh? We ought really to celebrate its centenary. An inanimate object, but say what you like, it's a bookcase after all.

PISHCHIK (amazed): A hundred years! Good Lord!

GAYEV: Yes, indeed. It's quite something. (Feeling round the bookcase with his hands.) Dear, highly esteemed bookcase, I salute you. For over a hundred years you have devoted yourself to the glorious ideals of goodness and justice. Throughout the hundred years your silent appeal to fruitful work has never faltered. It sus-

tained (through tears) in several generations of our family, their courage and faith in a better future and fostered in us the ideals of goodness and social consciousness.

(Pause.)

LOPAKHIN: Aye. . . .

MRS. RANEVSKY: You haven't changed a bit, have you, darling Leonid?

GAYEV (slightly embarrassed): Off the right into a corner! Pot into the middle pocket!

LOPAKHIN (glancing at his watch): Well, afraid it's time I was off.

YASHA (handing MRS. RANEVSKY her medicine): Your pills, ma'am.

PISHCHIK: Never take any medicines, dear lady. I don't suppose they'll do you much harm. but they won't do you any good either. Here, let me have 'em, my dear lady. (Takes the box of pills from her, pours the pills into the palm of his hand, blows on them, puts them all into his mouth, and washes them down with kvass.) There!

MRS. RANEVSKY (alarmed): You're mad!

PISHCHIK: Swallowed the lot.

LOPAKHIN: The glutton!

(All laugh.)

FIRS: He was here at Easter, the gentleman was. Ate half a bucketful of pickled cucumbers, he did. . . . (Mutters.)

MRS. RANEVSKY: What is he saying?

VARYA: He's been muttering like that for the last three years. We've got used to it.

YASHA: Old age!

(CHARLOTTE, in a white dress, very thin and tightly laced, a lorgnette dangling from her belt, crosses the stage.)

LOPAKHIN: I'm sorry, Miss Charlotte, I haven't had the chance of saying how-do-you-do to you. (Tries to kiss her hand.)

CHARLOTTE (snatching her hand away): If I let you kiss my hand, you'll want to kiss my elbow, then my shoulder . . .

LOPAKHIN: It's not my lucky day. (They all laugh.) My dear Charlotte, show us a trick, please.

MRS. RANEVSKY: Yes, do show us a trick, Charlotte.

CHARLOTTE: I won't. I'm off to bed. (Goes out.)

LOPAKHIN: We'll meet again in three weeks. (Kisses MRS. RANEVSKY's hand.) Good-bye for now. I must go. (to GAYEV) So long. (Embraces PISHCHIK.) So long. (Shakes hands with VARYA and then with FIRS and YASHA.) I with I didn't have to go. (to MRS. RANEVSKY) Let me know if you make up your mind about the country cottages. If you decide to go ahead, I'll get you a loan of fifty thousand or more. Think it over seriously.

VARYA (*angrily*): For goodness' sake, go!

LOPAKHIN: I'm going, I'm going. . . . (*Goes out.*)

GAYEV: The oaf! However, I'm sorry. Varya's going to marry him, isn't she? He's Varya's intended.

VARYA: Don't say things you'll be sorry for, Uncle.

MRS. RANEVSKY: But why not, Varya? I should be only too glad. He's a good man.

PISHCHIK: A most admirable fellow, to tell the truth. My Dashenka—er—also says that—er—says all sorts of things. (*Drops off and snores, but wakes up immediately.*) By the way, my dear lady, you will lend me two hundred and forty rubles, won't you? Must pay the interest on the mortgage tomorrow.

VARYA (*terrified*): We have no money; we haven't!

MRS. RANEVSKY: We really haven't any, you know.

PISHCHIK: Have a good look around—you're sure to find it. (*Laughs.*) I never lose hope. Sometimes I think it's all over with me, I'm done for, then— hey presto—they build a railway over my land and pay me for it. Something's bound to turn up, if not today, then tomorrow. I'm certain of it. Dashenka might win two hundred thousand. She's got a ticket in the lottery, you know.

MRS. RANEVSKY: Well, I've finished my coffee. Now to bed.

FIRS (*brushing* GAYEV's *clothes admonishingly*): Put the wrong trousers on again, sir. What am I to do with you?

VARYA (*in a low voice*): Anya's asleep. (*Opens a window quietly.*) The sun has risen. It's no longer cold. Look, Mother dear. What lovely trees! Heavens, what wonderful air! The starlings are singing.

GAYEV (*opens another window.*): The orchard's all white. Lyuba, you haven't forgotten, have you? The long avenue there—it runs on and on, straight as an arrow. It gleams on moonlit nights. Remember? You haven't forgotten, have you?

MRS. RANEVSKY (*looking through the window at the orchard*): Oh, my childhood, oh, my innocence! I slept in this nursery. I used to look out at the orchard from here. Every morning happiness used to wake with me. The orchard was just the same in those days. Nothing has changed. (*Laughs happily.*) White, all white! Oh, my orchard! After the dark, rainy autumn and the cold winter, you're young again, full of happiness; the heavenly angels haven't forsaken you. If only this heavy load could be lifted from my heart; if only I could forget my past!

GAYEV: Well, and now they're going to sell the orchard to pay our debts. Funny, isn't it?

MRS. RANEVSKY: Look! Mother's walking in the orchard in . . . a white dress! (*Laughs happily.*) It *is* Mother!

GAYEV: Where?

VARYA: Really, Mother dear, what are you saying?

MRS. RANEVSKY: There's no one there. I just imagined it. Over there, on the right, near the turning to the summer house, a little white tree's leaning over. It looks like a woman. (*Enter* TROFIMOV. *He is dressed in a shabby student's uniform and wears glasses.*) What an amazing orchard! Masses of white blossom. A blue sky . . .

TROFIMOV: I say, Mrs. Ranevsky . . . (*She looks round at him.*) I've just come to say hello. I'll go at once. (*Kisses her hand warmly.*) I was told to wait till morning, but I—I couldn't, I couldn't.

(MRS. RANEVSKY *gazes at him in bewilderment.*)

VARYA (*through tears*): This is Peter Trofimov.

TROFIMOV: Peter Trofimov. Your son Grisha's old tutor. I haven't changed so much, have I?

(MRS. RANEVSKY *embraces him and weeps quietly.*)

GAYEV (*embarrassed*): There, there, Lyuba.

VARYA (*cries*): I did tell you to wait till tomorrow, didn't I, Peter?

MRS. RANEVSKY: Grisha, my . . . little boy. Grisha . . . my son.

VARYA: It can't be helped, Mother. It was God's will.

TROFIMOV (*gently, through tears*): Now, now . . .

MRS. RANEVSKY (*weeping quietly*): My little boy died, drowned. Why? Why, my friend? (*More quietly.*) Anya's asleep in there and here I am shouting, making a noise. . . . Well, Peter? You're not as good-looking as you were, are you? Why not? Why have you aged so much?

TROFIMOV: A peasant woman in a railway carriage called me "a moth-eaten gentleman."

MRS. RANEVSKY: You were only a boy then. A charming young student. Now you're growing thin on top, you wear glasses. . . . You're not still a student, are you? (*Walks toward the door.*)

TROFIMOV: I expect I shall be an eternal student.

MRS. RANEVSKY (*kisses her brother and then* VARYA): Well, go to bed now. You, Leonid, have aged too.

PISHCHIK (*following her*): So, we're off to bed now, are we? Oh dear, my gout! I think I'd better stay the night here. Now, what about letting me have the—er—two hundred and forty rubles tomorrow morning, dear lady? Early tomorrow morning. . . .

GAYEV: He does keep on, doesn't he?

PISHCHIK: Two hundred and forty rubles—to pay the interest on the mortgage.

MRS. RANEVSKY: But I haven't any money, my dear man.

PISHCHIK: I'll pay you back, dear lady. Such a trifling sum.

MRS. RANEVSKY: Oh, all right. Leonid will let you have it. Let him have it, Leonid.

GAYEV: Let him have it? The hell I will.

MRS. RANEVSKY: What else can we do? Let him have it,

please. He needs it. He'll pay it back.

(MRS. RANEVSKY, TROFIMOV, PISHCHIK, *and* FIRS *go out.* GAYEV, VARYA, *and* YASHA *remain.*)

GAYEV: My sister hasn't got out of the habit of throwing money about. (*to* YASHA) Out of my way, fellow. You reek of the hen house.

YASHA (*grins*): And you, sir, are the same as ever.

GAYEV: I beg your pardon? (*to* VARYA) What did he say?

VARYA (*to* YASHA): Your mother's come from the village. She's been sitting in the servants' quarters since yesterday. She wants to see you.

YASHA: Oh, bother her!

VARYA: You shameless bounder!

YASHA: I don't care. She could have come tomorrow, couldn't she? (*Goes out.*)

VARYA: Dear Mother is just the same as ever. Hasn't changed a bit. If you let her, she'd give away everything.

GAYEV: I suppose so. (*Pause.*) When a lot of remedies are suggested for an illness, it means that the illness is incurable. I've been thinking, racking my brains; I've got all sorts of remedies, lots of them, which, of course, means that I haven't got one. It would be marvelous if somebody left us some money. It would be marvelous if we found a very rich husband for Anya. It would be marvelous if one of us went to Yaroslavl to try our luck with our great-aunt, the Countess. She's very rich, you know. Very rich.

VARYA (*crying*): If only God would help us.

GAYEV: Don't howl! Our aunt is very rich, but she doesn't like us. First, because my sister married a lawyer and not a nobleman. . . . (ANYA *appears in the doorway.*) She did not marry a nobleman, and she has not been leading an exactly blameless life, has she? She's a good, kind, nice person. I love her very much. But, however much you try to make allowances for her, you have to admit that she is an immoral woman. You can sense it in every movement she makes.

VARYA (*in a whisper*): Anya's standing in the doorway.

GAYEV: I beg your pardon? (*Pause.*) Funny thing, there's something in my right eye. Can't see properly. On Thursday, too, in the district court . . .

(ANYA *comes in.*)

VARYA: Why aren't you asleep, Anya?

ANYA: I can't sleep, I can't.

GAYEV: My little darling! (*Kisses* ANYA's *face and hands.*) My dear child! (*Through tears.*) You're not my niece, you're my angel. You're everything to me. Believe me. Do believe me.

ANYA: I believe you, Uncle. Everyone loves you, everyone respects you, but, dear Uncle, you

shouldn't talk so much. What were you saying just now about Mother, about your own sister? What did you say it for?

GAYEV: Well, yes, yes. (*He takes her hand and covers his face with it.*) You're quite right. It was dreadful. Dear God, dear God, help me! That speech I made to the bookcase today—it was so silly. The moment I finished it, I realized how silly it was.

VARYA: It's quite true, Uncle dear. You oughtn't to talk so much. Just don't talk, that's all.

ANYA: If you stopped talking, you'd feel much happier yourself.

GAYEV: Not another word. (*Kisses* ANYA's *and* VARYA's *hands.*) Not another word. Now to business. Last Thursday I was at the county court, and, well—er—I met a lot of people there, and we started talking about this and that, and—er—it would seem that we might manage to raise some money on a promissory note and pay the interest to the bank.

VARYA: Oh, if only God would help us!

GAYEV: I shall be there again on Tuesday, and I'll have another talk. (*to* VARYA) For goodness' sake, don't howl! (*to* ANYA) Your mother will have a talk with Lopakhin. I'm sure he won't refuse her. After you've had your rest, you'll go to Yaroslavl to see your great-aunt, the Countess. That's how we shall tackle the problem from three different sides, and I'm sure we'll get it settled. The interest we shall pay. Of that I'm quite sure. (*Puts a fruit drop in his mouth.*) I give you my word of honor, I swear by anything you like, the estate will not be sold! (*Excitedly.*) Why, I'll stake my life on it! Here's my hand; call me a rotten scoundrel if I allow the auction to take place. I stake my life on it!

ANYA (*has regained her composure; she looks happy*): You're so good, Uncle dear! So clever! (*Embraces him.*) I'm no longer worried now. Not a bit worried. I'm happy.

(*Enter* FIRS.)

FIRS (*reproachfully*): Have you no fear of God, sir? When are you going to bed?

GAYEV: Presently, presently. Go away, Firs. Never mind, I'll undress this time. Well, children, bye-bye now. More about it tomorrow. Now you must go to bed. (*Kisses* ANYA *and* VARYA.) I'm a man of the eighties. People don't think much of that time, but let me tell you, I've suffered a great deal for my convictions during my life. It's not for nothing that the peasants love me. You have to know your peasant, you have to know how to—

ANYA: There you go again, Uncle.

VARYA: Please, Uncle dear, don't talk so much.

FIRS (*angrily*): Sir!

GAYEV: I'm coming, I'm coming. You two go to bed. Off two cushions into the middle. Pot the white!

(GAYEV *goes out,* FIRS *shuffling off after him.*)

ANYA: I'm not worried any longer now. I don't feel like going to Yaroslavl. I don't like my great-aunt, but I'm no longer worried. I ought to thank Uncle for that. (*Sits down.*)

VARYA: I ought to go to bed, and I shall be going in a moment, I must tell you first that something unpleasant happened here while you were away. You know, of course, that only a few old servants live in the old servants' quarters: Yefimushka, Polia, Evstigney, and, well, also Karp. They had been letting some tramps sleep there, but I didn't say anything about it. Then I heard that they were telling everybody that I'd given orders for them to be fed on nothing but dried peas. I'm supposed to be a miser, you see. It was all that Evstigney's doing. Well, I said to myself, if that's how it is, you just wait! So I sent for Evstigney. (*Yawns.*) He comes. "What do you mean," I said, "Evstigney, you silly old fool?" (*Looks at* ANYA) Darling! (*Pause.*) Asleep . . . (*Takes* ANYA *by the arm.*) Come to bed, dear. . . . Come on! (*Leads her by the arm.*) My darling's fallen asleep. Come along. (*They go out. A shepherd's pipe is heard playing from far away on the other side of the orchard.* TROFIMOV *walks across the stage and, catching sight of* VARYA *and* ANYA, *stops.*) Shh! She's asleep, asleep. Come along, my sweet.

ANYA (*softly, half asleep*): I'm so tired. . . . I keep hearing harness bells. Uncle . . . dear . . . Mother and Uncle . . .

VARYA: Come on, my sweet, come on. . . .

(*They go into* ANYA's *room.*)

TROFIMOV (*deeply moved*): My sun! My spring!

CURTAIN

ACT 2

(*Open country. A small tumbledown wayside chapel. Near it, a well, some large stones, which look like old gravestones, and an old bench. A road can be seen leading to* GAYEV's *estate. On one side, a row of tall dark poplars; it is there that the cherry orchard begins. In the distance, some telegraph poles, and far, far away on the horizon, the outlines of a large town that is visible only in very fine, clear weather. The sun is about to set.* CHARLOTTE, YASHA, *and* DUNYASHA *are sitting on the bench;* YEPIKHODOV *is standing nearby and is playing a guitar; they all sit sunk in thought.* CHARLOTTE *wears a man's old peaked hat; she has taken a shotgun from her shoulder and is adjusting the buckle on the strap.*)

CHARLOTTE (*pensively*): I haven't a proper passport, I don't know how old I am, and I can't help thinking that I'm still a young girl. When I was a little girl, my father and mother used to travel the fairs and give performances—very good ones. I used to do the *salto mortale* and all sorts of other tricks. When Father and Mother died, a German lady adopted me and began educating me. Very well. I grew up and became a governess, but where I came from and who I am, I do not know. Who my parents were, I do not know either. They may not even have been married. I don't know. (*Takes a cucumber out of her pocket and starts eating it.*) I don't know anything. (*Pause.*) I'm longing to talk to someone, but there is no one to talk to. I haven't anyone. . . .

YEPIKHODOV (*plays his guitar and sings*): "What care I for the world and its bustle? What care I for my friends and my foes?" . . . Nice to play a mandolin.

DUNYASHA: It's a guitar, not a mandolin. (*She looks at herself in a hand mirror and powders her face.*)

YEPIKHODOV: To a madman in love, it's a mandolin. (*Sings softly.*) "If only my heart was warmed by the fire of love requited."

(YASHA *joins in.*)

CHARLOTTE: How terribly these people sing! Ugh! Like hyenas.

DUNYASHA (*to* YASHA): All the same, you're ever so lucky to have been abroad.

YASHA: Why, of course. Can't help agreeing with you there. (*Yawns, then lights a cigar.*)

YEPIKHODOV: Stands to reason. Abroad, everything's in excellent complexion. Been like that for ages.

YASHA: Naturally.

YEPIKHODOV: I'm a man of some education, I read all sorts of remarkable books, but what I simply can't understand is where it's all leading to. I mean, what do I really want—to live or to shoot myself? In any case, I always carry a revolver. Here it is. (*Shows them his revolver.*)

CHARLOTEE: That's done. Now I can go. (*Puts the shotgun over her shoulder.*) You're a very clever man, Yepikhodov. You frighten me to death. Women must be madly in love with you. Brrr! (*Walking away.*) These clever people are all so stupid. I've no one to talk to. Always alone, alone, I've no one, and who I am and what I am for is a mystery. (*Walks off slowly.*)

YEPIKHODOV: Strictly speaking, and apart from all other considerations, what I ought to say about myself, among other things, is that Fate treats me without mercy, like a storm a small boat. Even supposing I'm mistaken, why in that case should I wake up this morning and suddenly find a spider of quite enormous dimensions on

588 / THE CHERRY ORCHARD

my chest? As big as that. (*Uses both hands to show the spider's size.*) Or again, I pick up a jug of kvass and there's something quite outrageously indecent in it, like a cockroach. (*Pause.*) Have you ever read Buckle's *History of Civilization? (Pause.)* May I have a word or two with you, Dunyasha?

DUNYASHA: Oh, all right. What is it?

YEPIKHODOV: I'd be very much obliged if you'd let me speak to you in private. (*Sighs.*)

DUNYASHA (*embarrassed*): All right, only first bring me my cape, please. It's hanging near the wardrobe. It's so damp here.

YEPIKHODOV: Very well, I'll fetch it. . . . Now I know what to do with my revolver. (*Picks up his guitar and goes out strumming it.*)

YASHA: Twenty-two Calamities! A stupid fellow, between you and me. (*Yawns.*)

DUNYASHA: I hope to goodness he won't shoot himself. (*Pause.*) I'm ever so nervous. I can't help being worried all the time. I was taken into service when I was a little girl, and now I can't live like a peasant any more. See my hands? They're ever so white, as white as a young lady's. I've become so nervous, so sensitive, so like a lady. I'm afraid of everything. I'm simply terrified. So if you deceived me, Yasha, I don't know what would happen to my nerves.

YASHA (*kisses her*): Little cucumber! Mind you, I expect every girl to be respectable. What I dislike most is for a girl to misbehave herself.

DUNYASHA: I've fallen passionately in love with you, Yasha. You're so educated. You can talk about anything.

(*Pause.*)

YASHA (*yawning*): You see, in my opinion, if a girl is in love with somebody, it means she's immoral. (*Pause.*) It is so pleasant to smoke a cigar in the open air. (*Listens.*) Someone's coming. It's them. . . . (DUNYASHA *embraces him impulsively.*) Please go home and look as if you've been down to the river for a swim. Take that path or they'll think I had arranged to meet you here. Can't stand that sort of thing.

DUNYASHA (*coughing quietly*): Your cigar has given me an awful headache. (*Goes out.*)

(YASHA *remains sitting near the chapel. Enter* MRS. RANEVSKY, GAYEV, *and* LOPAKHIN.)

LOPAKHIN: You must make up your minds once and for all. There's not much time left. After all, it's quite a simple matter. Do you agree to lease your land for country cottages or don't you? Answer me in one word: yes or no. Just one word.

MRS. RANEVSKY: Who's been smoking such horrible cigars here? (*Sits down.*)

GAYEV: Now that they've built the railway, things are

much more convenient. (*Sits down*). We've been to town for lunch—pot the red in the middle! I really should have gone in to have a game first.

MRS. RANEVSKY: There's plenty of time.

LOPAKHIN: Just one word. (*Imploringly.*) Please give me your answer!

GAYEV (*yawns*): I beg your pardon?

MRS. RANEVSKY (*looking in her purse*): Yesterday I had a lot of money, but I've hardly any left today. My poor Varya! Tries to economize by feeding everybody on milk soup and the old servants in the kitchen on peas, and I'm just throwing money about stupidly. (*Drops her purse, scattering some gold coins.*) Goodness gracious, all over the place! (*She looks annoyed.*)

YASHA: Allow me to pick 'em up, madam. It won't take a minute. (*Starts picking up the coins.*)

MRS. RANEVSKY: Thank you, Yasha. Why on earth did I go out to lunch? That disgusting restaurant of yours with its stupid band, and those tablecloths smelling of soap. Why did you have to drink so much, Leonid? Or eat so much? Or talk so much? You did talk a lot again in the restaurant today and all to no purpose. About the seventies and the decadents . . . And who to? Talking about the decadents to waiters!

LOPAKHIN: Aye. . . .

GAYEV (*waving his arm*): I'm incorrigible, that's clear. (*Irritably to* YASHA.) What are you hanging around here for?

YASHA (*laughs*): I can't hear your voice without laughing, sir.

GAYEV (*to his sister*): Either he or I.

MRS. RANEVSKY: Go away, Yasha. Run along.

YASHA (*returning the purse to* MRS. RANEVSKY): At once, madam. (*Is hardly able to suppress his laughter.*) This very minute. (*Goes out.*)

LOPAKHIN: The rich merchant Deriganov is thinking of buying your estate. I'm told he's coming to the auction himself.

MRS. RANEVSKY: Where did you hear that?

LOPAKHIN: That's what they're saying in town.

GAYEV: Our Yaroslavl great-aunt has promised to send us money, but when and how much we do not know.

LOPAKHIN: How much will she send? A hundred thousand? Two hundred?

MRS. RANEVSKY: Well, I hardly think so. Ten or fifteen thousand at most. We must be thankful for that.

LOPAKHIN: I'm sorry, but such improvident people as you, such peculiar, unbusinesslike people, I've never met in my life! You're told in plain language that your estate's going to be sold, and you don't seem to understand.

MRS. RANEVSKY: But what are we to do? Tell us, please.

LOPAKHIN: I tell you every day. Every day I go on repeating the same thing over and over again. You must let out the cherry orchard and the land for country cottages, and you must do it now, as quickly as possible. The auction is on top of you! Try to understand! The moment you decide to let your land, you'll be able to raise as much money as you like, and you'll be saved.

MRS. RANEVSKY: Country cottages, holiday-makers—I'm sorry, but it's so vulgar.

GAYEV: I'm of your opinion entirely.

LOPAKHIN: I shall burst into tears or scream or have a fit. I can't stand it. You've worn me out! (*to* GAYEV) You're a silly old woman!

GAYEV: I beg your pardon?

LOPAKHIN: A silly old woman! (*He gets up to go.*)

MRS. RANEVSKY (*in dismay*): No, don't go. Please stay. I beg you. Perhaps we'll think of something.

LOPAKHIN: What is there to think of?

MRS. RANEVSKY: Please don't go. I beg you. Somehow I feel so much more cheerful with you here. (*Pause.*) I keep expecting something to happen, as though the house was going to collapse on top of us.

GAYEV (*deep in thought*): Cannon off the cushion. Pot into the middle pocket. . . .

MRS. RANEVSKY: I'm afraid we've sinned too much—

LOPAKHIN: You sinned!

GAYEV (*putting a fruit drop into his mouth*): They say I squandered my entire fortune on fruit drops. (*Laughs.*)

MRS. RANEVSKY: Oh, my sins! . . . I've always thrown money about aimlessly, like a madwoman. Why, I even married a man who did nothing but pile up debts. My husband died of champagne. He drank like a fish. Then, worse luck, I fell in love with someone, had an affair with him, and it was just at that time—it was my first punishment, a blow that nearly killed me—that my boy was drowned in the river here. I went abroad, never to come back, never to see that river again. I shut my eyes and ran, beside myself, and *he* followed me—pitilessly, brutally. I bought a villa near Mentone because *he* had fallen ill. For the next three years I knew no rest, nursing him day and night. He wore me out. Everything inside me went dead. Then, last year, I had to sell the villa to pay my debts. I left for Paris, where he robbed me, deserted me, and went to live with another woman. I tried to poison myself. Oh, it was all so stupid, so shaming. . . . It was then that I suddenly felt an urge to go back to Russia, to my homeland, to my daughter. (*Dries her eyes.*) Lord, O Lord, be merciful! Forgive me my sins! Don't punish me any more! (*Takes a telegram from her pocket.*) I received this telegram from Paris today. He asks me to forgive him. He implores me to go back. (*Tears up the telegram.*) What's that? Music? (*Listens intently.*)

GAYEV: That's our famous Jewish band. Remember? Four fiddles, a flute, and a double bass.

MRS. RANEVSKY: Does it still exist? We ought to arrange a party and have them over to the house.

LOPAKHIN (*listening*): I don't hear anything. (*Sings quietly.*) "And the Germans, if you pay 'em, will turn a Russian into a Frenchman." (*Laughs.*) I saw an excellent play at the theatre last night. It was very amusing.

MRS. RANEVSKY: I don't suppose it was amusing at all. You shouldn't be watching plays, but should be watching yourselves more often. What dull lives you live. What nonsense you talk.

LOPAKHIN: Perfectly true. Let's admit quite frankly that the life we lead is utterly stupid. (*Pause.*) My father was a peasant, an idiot. He understood nothing. He taught me nothing. He just beat me when he was drunk and always with a stick. As a matter of fact, I'm just as big a blockhead and an idiot myself. I never learnt anything, and my handwriting is so abominable that I'm ashamed to let people see it.

MRS. RANEVSKY: You ought to get married, my friend.

LOPAKHIN: Yes. That's true.

MRS. RANEVSKY: Married to our Varya. She's a nice girl.

LOPAKHIN: Aye. . . .

MRS. RANEVSKY: Her father was a peasant too. She's a hard-working girl, and she loves you. That's the important thing. Why, you've been fond of her for a long time yourself.

LOPAKHIN: Very well. I've no objection. She's a good girl.

(*Pause.*)

GAYEV: I've been offered a job in a bank. Six thousand a year. Have you heard, Lyuba?

MRS. RANEVSKY: You in a bank! You'd better stay where you are.

(FIRS *comes in carrying an overcoat.*)

FIRS (*to* GAYEV): Please put it on, sir. It's damp out here.

GAYEV (*putting on the overcoat*): You're a damned nuisance, my dear fellow.

FIRS: Come along, sir. Don't be difficult. . . . This morning, too, you went off without saying a word. (*Looks him over.*)

MRS. RANEVSKY: How you've aged, Firs!

FIRS: What's that, ma'am?

LOPAKHIN: Your mistress says you've aged a lot.

FIRS: I've been alive a long time. They were trying to marry me off before your dad was born. . . . (*Laughs.*) When freedom came, I was already chief valet. I refused to accept freedom and stayed on with my master. (*Pause.*) I well remember how glad everyone was, but what they were glad about, they did not know themselves.

LOPAKHIN: It wasn't such a bad life before, was it? At least, they flogged you.

FIRS (*not hearing him*): I should say so. The peasants stuck to their masters and the masters to their peasants. Now everybody does what he likes. You can't understand nothing.

GAYEV: Shut up, Firs. I have to go to town tomorrow. I've been promised an introduction to a general who might lend us some money on a promissory note.

LOPAKHIN: Nothing will come of it. You won't pay the interest, either. You may be sure of that.

MRS. RANEVSKY: Oh, he's just imagining things. There aren't any generals.

(*Enter* TROFIMOV, ANYA, *and* VARYA.)

GAYEV: Here they are at last.

ANYA: There's Mother.

MRS. RANEVSKY (*affectionately*): Come here, come here, my dears. (*Embracing* ANYA *and* VARYA.) If you only knew how much I love you both. Sit down beside me. That's right.

(*All sit down.*)

LOPAKHIN: Our eternal student is always walking about with the young ladies.

TROFIMOV: Mind your own business.

LOPAKHIN: He's nearly fifty and he's still a student.

TROFIMOV: Do drop your idiotic jokes.

LOPAKHIN: Why are you so angry, you funny fellow?

TROFIMOV: Well, stop pestering me.

LOPAKHIN (*laughs*): Tell me, what do you think of me?

TROFIMOV: Simply this: You're a rich man and you'll soon be a millionaire. Now, just as a beast of prey devours everything in its path and so helps to preserve the balance of nature, so you, too, perform a similar function.

(*They all laugh.*)

VARYA: You'd better tell us about the planets, Peter.

MRS. RANEVSKY: No, let's carry on with what we were talking about yesterday.

TROFIMOV: What was that?

GAYEV: Pride.

TROFIMOV: We talked a lot yesterday, but we didn't arrive at any conclusion. As you see it, there's something mystical about the proud man. You may be right for all I know. But try to look at it simply, without being too clever. What sort of pride is it, is there any sense in it. if, physiologically, man is far from perfect? If, in fact, he is, in the vast majority of cases, coarse, stupid, and profoundly unhappy? It's time we stopped admiring ourselves. All we must do is—work!

GAYEV: We're going to die all the same.

TROFIMOV: Who knows? And what do you mean by "we're going to die"? A man may possess a hundred senses. When he dies, he loses only the five we know. The other ninety-five live on.

MRS. RANEVSKY: How clever you are, Peter!

LOPAKHIN (*ironically*): Oh, frightfully!

TROFIMOV: Mankind marches on, perfecting its powers. Everything that is incomprehensible to us now, will one day become familiar and comprehensible. All we have to do is to work and do our best to assist those who are looking for truth. Here in Russia only a few people are working so far. The vast majority of the educated people I know, do nothing. They aren't looking for anything. They are quite incapable of doing any work. They call themselves intellectuals, but speak to their servants as inferiors and treat the peasants like animals. They're not particularly keen on their studies, they don't do any serious reading, they are bone idle, they merely talk about science, and they understand very little about art. They are all so solemn, they look so very grave, they talk only of important matters, they philosophize. Yet anyone can see that our workers are abominably fed, sleep on bare boards, thirty and forty to a room—bedbugs everywhere, stench, damp, moral turpitude. It's therefore obvious that all our fine phrases are merely a way of deluding ourselves and others. Tell me, where are all those children's crèches people are talking so much about? Where are the reading rooms? You find them only in novels. Actually, we haven't any. All we have is dirt, vulgarity, brutality. I dislike and I'm frightened of all these solemn countenances, just as I'm frightened of all serious conversations. Why not shut up for once?

LOPAKHIN: Well, I get up at five o'clock in the morning. I work from morning till night, and I've always lots of money on me—mine and other people's—and I can see what the people around me are like. One has only to start doing something to realize how few honest, decent people there are about. Sometimes when I lie awake, I keep thinking; Lord, you've given us vast forests, boundless plains, immense horizons, and living here, we ourselves ought really to be giants—

MRS. RANEVSKY: You want giants, do you? They're all right only in fairy tales. Elsewhere they frighten me. (YEPIKHODOV *crosses the stage in the background, playing his guitar. Pensively.*) There goes Yepikhodov.

ANYA (*pensively*): There goes Yepikhodov.

GAYEV: The sun's set, ladies and gentlemen.

TROFIMOV: Yes.

GAYEV (*softly, as though declaiming*): Oh, nature, glorious nature! Glowing with eternal radiance, beautiful and indifferent, you, whom we call Mother, uniting in yourself both life and death, you—life-giver and destroyer . . .

VARYA (*imploringly*): Darling Uncle!

ANYA: Uncle, again!

TROFIMOV: You'd far better pot the red in the middle.

GAYEV: Not another word! Not another word!

(*They all sit deep in thought. Everything is still. The silence is broken only by the subdued muttering of* FIRS. *Suddenly a distant sound is heard. It seems to come from the sky, the sound of a breaking string, slowly dying away, melancholy.*)

MRS. RANEVSKY: What's that?

LOPAKHIN: I don't know. I expect a bucket must have broken somewhere far away in a coal mine, but somewhere a very long distance away.

GAYEV: Perhaps it was a bird, a heron or something.

TROFIMOV: Or an eagle-owl.

MRS. RANEVSKY (*shudders*): It makes me feel dreadful for some reason.

(*Pause.*)

FIRS: Same thing happened before the misfortune: the owl hooted and the samovar kept hissing.

GAYEV: Before what misfortune?

FIRS: Before they gave us our freedom.

(*Pause.*)

MRS. RANEVSKY: Come, let's go in, my friends. It's getting dark. (*to* ANYA) There are tears in your eyes. What's the matter, darling. (*Embraces her.*)

ANYA: It's nothing, Mother. Nothing.

TROFIMOV: Someone's coming.

(*A* HIKER *appears. He wears a shabby white peaked cap and an overcoat; he is slightly drunk.*)

HIKER: Excuse me, is this the way to the station?

GAYEV: Yes, follow that road.

HIKER: I'm greatly obliged to you sir. (*Coughs.*) Glorious weather . . . (*Declaiming.*) Brother, my suffering brother, come to the Volga, you whose groans . . . (*to* VARYA) Mademoiselle, won't you give thirty kopecks to a starving Russian citizen?

(VARYA, *frightened, utters a little scream.*)

LOPAKHIN (*angrily*): There's a limit to the most disgraceful behavior.

MRS. RANEVSKY (*at a loss*): Here, take this. (*Looks for some money in her purse.*) No silver. Never mind, have this gold one.

HIKER: Profoundly grateful to you, ma'am. (*Goes out.*)

(*Laughter.*)

VARYA (*frightened*): I'm going away. I'm going away. Good heavens, Mother dear, there's no food for the servants in the house, and you gave him a gold sovereign!

MRS. RANEVSKY: What's to be done with a fool like me? I'll give you all I have when we get home. You'll lend me some more money, Lopakhin, won't you?

LOPAKHIN: With pleasure.

MRS. RANEVSKY: Let's go in. It's time. By the way, Varya, we've found you a husband here. Congratulations.

VARYA (*through tears*): This isn't a joking matter, Mother.

LOPAKHIN: Okhmelia, go to a nunnery!

GAYEV: Look at my hands. They're shaking. It's a long time since I had a game of billiards.

LOPAKHIN: Okhmelia, O nymph, remember me in your prayers!

MRS. RANEVSKY: Come along, come along, it's almost supper time.

VARYA: That man frightened me. My heart's still pounding.

LOPAKHIN: Let me remind you, ladies and gentlemen: The cherry orchard is up for sale on the twenty-second of August. Think about it! Think!

(*They all go out except* TROFIMOV *and* ANYA.)

ANYA (*laughing*): I'm so glad the hiker frightened Varya. Now we are alone.

TROFIMOV: Varya's afraid we might fall in love. That's why she follows us around for days on end. With her narrow mind she cannot grasp that we are above love. The whole aim and meaning of our life is to bypass everything that is petty and illusory, that prevents us from being free and happy. Forward! Let us march on irresistibly toward the bright star shining there in the distance! Forward! Don't lag behind, friends!

ANYA (*clapping her hands excitedly*): You talk so splendidly! (*Pause.*) It's so heavenly here today!

TROFIMOV: Yes, the weather is wonderful.

ANYA: What have you done to me, Peter? Why am I no longer as fond of the cherry orchard as before? I loved it so dearly. I used to think there was no lovelier place on earth than our orchard.

TROFIMOV: The whole of Russia is our orchard. The earth is great and beautiful. There are lots of lovely places on it. (*Pause.*) Think, Anya: your grandfather, your greatgrandfather, and all your ancestors owned serfs. They owned living souls. Can't you see human beings looking at you from every cherry tree in your orchard, from every leaf and every tree trunk? Don't you hear their voices? To own living souls—that's what has changed you all so much, you who are living now and those who lived before you. That's why your mother, you yourself, and your uncle no longer realize that you are living on borrowed capital, at other people's expense, at the expense of those whom you don't admit farther than your entrance hall. We are at least two hundred years behind the times. We haven't got anything at all. We have no definite attitude toward our past. We just philosophize, complain of depression, or drink vodka. Isn't it abundantly clear that before we start living in the present, we must atone for our past, make an end of it? And atone for it we can only by suffering, by extraordinary, unceasing labor. Understand that, Anya.

ANYA: The house we live in hasn't really been ours for a long time. I'm going to leave it. I give you my word.

TROFIMOV: If you have the keys of the house, throw them into the well and go away. Be free as the wind.

ANYA (rapturously): How well you said it!

TROFIMOV: Believe me, Anya, believe me! I'm not yet thirty, I'm young, I'm still a student, but I've been through hell more than once. I'm driven from pillar to post. In winter I'm half-starved, I'm ill, worried, poor as a beggar. You can't imagine the terrible places I've been to! And yet, always, every moment of the day and night, my heart was full of ineffable visions of the future. I feel, I'm quite sure, that happiness is coming, Anya. I can see it coming already.

ANYA (pensively): The moon is rising.

(YEPIKHODOV can be heard playing the same sad tune as before on his guitar. The moon rises. Somewhere near the poplars VARYA is looking for ANYA and calling, "Anya, where are you?")

TROFIMOV: Yes, the moon is rising. (Pause.) There it is—happiness! It's coming nearer and nearer. Already I can hear its footsteps, and if we never see it, if we never know it, what does that matter? Others will see it.

VARYA (offstage): Anya, where are you?

TROFIMOV: That Varya again! (Angrily.) Disgusting!

ANYA: Never mind, let's go to the river. It's lovely there.

TROFIMOV: Yes, let's.

(They go out.)

VARYA (offstage): Anya! Anya!

CURTAIN

ACT 3

(The drawing room, separated by an archway from the ballroom. A candelabra is alight. The Jewish band can be heard playing in the entrance hall. It is the same band that is mentioned in Act Two. Evening. In the ballroom people are dancing the Grande Ronde. SIMEONOV-PISHCHIK's voice can be heard crying out, "Promenade à une paire!" They all come out into the drawing room: PISHCHIK and CHARLOTTE the first couple, TROFIMOV and MRS. RANEVSKY the second, ANYA and a POST OFFICE CLERK the third, VARYA and the STATIONMASTER the fourth, and so on. VARYA is quietly crying and dries her eyes as she dances. The last couple consists of DUNYASHA and a partner. They walk across the drawing room. PISHCHIK shouts, "Grande Ronde balancez!" and "Les cavaliers à genoux et remerciez vos dames!")

(FIRS, wearing a tailcoat, brings in soda water on a tray. PISHCHIK and TROFIMOV come into the drawing room.)

PISHCHIK: I've got high blood-pressure. I've had two strokes already, and I find dancing hard work. But, as the saying goes, if you're one of a pack, wag your tail, whether you bark or not. As a matter of fact, I'm as strong as a horse. My father, may he rest in peace, liked his little joke, and speaking about our family pedigree, he used to say that the ancient Simeonov-Pishchiks came from the horse that Caligula had made a senator. (Sits down.) But you see, the trouble is that I have no money. A hungry dog believes only in meat. (Snores, but wakes up again at once.) I'm just the same. All I can think of is money.

TROFIMOV: There really is something horsy about you.

PISHCHIK: Well, a horse is a good beast. You can sell a horse.

(From an adjoining room comes the sound of people playing billiards. VARYA appears in the ballroom under the archway.)

TROFIMOV (teasing her): Mrs. Lopakhin! Mrs. Lopakhin!

VARYA (angrily): Moth-eaten gentleman!

TROFIMOV: Well, I am a moth-eaten gentleman and proud of it.

VARYA (brooding bitterly): We've hired a band, but how we are going to pay for it, I don't know. (Goes out.)

TROFIMOV (to PISHCHIK): If the energy you have wasted throughout your life looking for money to pay the interest on your debts had been spent on something else, you'd most probably have succeeded in turning the world upside down.

PISHCHIK: Nietzsche, the famous philosopher—a great man, a man of great intellect—says in his works that there's nothing wrong about forging bank notes.

TROFIMOV: Have you read Nietzsche?

PISHCHIK: Well, actually, Dashenka told me about it. I don't mind telling you, though, that in my present position I might even forge bank notes. The day after tomorrow I've got to pay three hundred and ten rubles. I've already got one hundred and thirty. *(Feels his pockets in alarm.)* My money's gone, I've lost my money! *(Through tears.)* Where is it? *(Happily.)* Ah, here it is, in the lining. Lord the shock brought me out in a cold sweat!

(Enter MRS. RANEVSKY *and* CHARLOTTE.*)*

MRS. RANEVSKY *(hums a popular Georgian dance tune)*: Why is Leonid so late? What's he doing in town? *(to* DUNYASHA*)* Offer the band tea, please.

TROFIMOV: I don't suppose the auction has taken place.

MRS. RANEVSKY: What a time to have a band! What a time to give a party! Oh, well, never mind. *(Sits down and hums quietly.)*

CHARLOTTE *(hands* PISHCHIK *a pack of cards)*: Here's a pack of cards. Think of a card.

PISHCHIK: All right.

CHARLOTTE: Now shuffle the pack. That's right. Now give it to me. Now, then, my dear Mr. Pishchik, *eins, zwei, drei!* Look in your breast pocket. Is it there?

PISHCHIK *(takes the card out of his breast pocket)* : The eight of spades! Absolutely right! *(Surprised.)* Good Lord!

CHARLOTTE *(holding a pack of cards on the palm of her hand, to* TROFIMOV*)*: Tell me, quick, what's the top card?

TROFIMOV: Well, let's say the queen of spades.

CHARLOTTE: Here it is. *(to* PISCHIK*)*: What's the top card now?

PISHCHIK: The ace of hearts.

CHARLOTTE: Here you are! *(Claps her hands and the pack of cards disappears.)* What lovely weather we've having today. *(A mysterious female voice, which seems to come from under the floor, answers: "Oh yes, glorious weather, madam!")* You're my ideal, you're so nice! *(The voice: "I like you very much too, madam.")*

STATIONMASTER *(clapping his hands)*: Bravo, Madam Ventriloquist!

PISHCHIK *(looking surprised)*: Good Lord! Enchanting, Miss Charlotte, I'm simply in love with you.

CHARLOTTE: In love! Are you sure you can love? *Guter Mensch, aber schlecter Musikant.*

TROFIMOV *(claps* PISHCHIK *on the shoulder)*: Good old horse!

CHARLOTTE: Attention, please. One more trick. *(She takes a rug from a chair.)* Here's a very good rug. I'd like to sell it. *(Shaking it.)* Who wants to buy it?

PISHCHIK *(surprised)*: Good Lord!

CHARLOTTE: *Eins, zwei, drei! (Quickly snatching up the rug, which she had let fall, she reveals* ANYA *standing behind it.* ANYA *curtseys, runs to her mother, embraces her, and runs back to the ballroom, amid general enthusiasm.)*

MRS. RANEVSKY *(applauding)*: Bravo, bravo!

CHARLOTTE: Now, once more. *Eins, zwei, drei! (Lifts the rug; behind it stands* VARYA, *who bows.)*

PISHCHIK *(surprised)*: Good Lord!

CHARLOTTE: The end! *(Throws the rug over* PISHCHIK, *curtseys, and runs off to the ballroom.)*

PISHCHIK *(running after her)*: The hussy! What a woman, eh? What a woman! *(Goes out.)*

MRS. RANEVSKY: Still no Leonid. I can't understand what he can be doing in town all this time. It must be over now. Either the estate has been sold or the auction didn't take place. Why keep us in suspense so long?

VARYA *(trying to comfort her)*: I'm certain Uncle must have bought it.

TROFIMOV *(sarcastically)*: Oh, to be sure!

VARYA: Our great-aunt sent him power of attorney to buy the estate in her name and transfer the mortgage to her. She's done it for Anya's sake. God will help us and Uncle will buy it. I'm sure of it.

MRS. RANEVSKY: Your great-aunt sent fifteen thousand to buy the estate in her name. She doesn't trust us—but the money wouldn't even pay the interest. *(She covers her face with her hands.)* My whole future is being decided today, my future. . . .

TROFIMOV *(teasing* VARYA*)*: Mrs. Lopakhin!

VARYA *(crossly)*: Eternal student! Expelled twice from the university, weren't you?

MRS. RANEVSKY: Why are you so cross, Varya? He's teasing you about Lopakhin. Well, what of it? Marry Lopakhin if you want to. He is a nice, interesting man. If you don't want to, don't marry him. Nobody's forcing you, darling.

VARYA: I regard such a step seriously, Mother dear. I don't mind being frank about it: He is a nice man, and I like him.

MRS. RANEVSKY: Well, marry him. What are you waiting for? That's what I can't understand.

VARYA: But, Mother dear, I can't very well propose to him myself, can I? Everyone's been talking to me about him for the last two years. Everyone! But he either says nothing or makes jokes. I quite understand. He's making money. He has his business to think of, and he hasn't time for me. If I had any money, just a little, a hundred rubles, I'd give up everything and go right away as far as possible. I'd have gone into a convent.

TROFIMOV: Wonderful!

VARYA *(to* TROFIMOV*)*: A student ought to be intelligent! *(In a gentle voice, through tears.)* How plain you've grown, Peter! How you've aged! *(to* MRS. RANEVSKY, *no longer crying)* I can't live without having something to do, Mother! I must be doing something all the time.

(Enter YASHA.*)*

YASHA *(hardly able to restrain his laughter)*: Yepikhodov's broken a billiard cue! *(Goes out.)*

VARYA: What's Yepikhodov doing here? Who gave him permission to play billiards? Can't understand these people! *(Goes out.)*

MRS. RANEVSKY: Don't tease her, Peter. Don't you see she is unhappy enough already?

TROFIMOV: She's a bit too conscientious. Pokes her nose into other people's affairs. Wouldn't leave me and Anya alone all summer. Afraid we might have an affair. What business is it of hers? Besides, the idea never entered my head. Such vulgarity is beneath me. We are above love.

MRS. RANEVSKY: So, I suppose I must be beneath love. *(In great agitation.)* Why isn't Leonid back? All I want to know is: Has the estate been sold or not? Such a calamity seems so incredible to me that I don't know what to think. I'm completely at a loss. I feel like screaming, like doing something silly. Help me, Peter. Say something. For God's sake, say something!

TROFIMOV: What does it matter whether the estate's been sold today or not? The estate's been finished and done with long ago. There's no turning back. The road to it is closed. Stop worrying, my dear. You mustn't deceive yourself. Look the truth straight in the face for once in your life.

MRS. RANEVSKY: What truth? You can see where truth is and where it isn't, but I seem to have gone blind. I see nothing. You boldly solve all important problems, but tell me, dear boy, isn't it because you're young, isn't it because you haven't had the time to live through the consequences of any of your problems? You look ahead boldly, but isn't it because you neither see nor expect anything terrible to happen to you, because life is still hidden from your young eyes? You're bolder, more honest, you see much deeper than any of us, but think carefully, try to understand our position, be generous even a little, spare me. I was born here, you know. My father and mother lived here, and my grandfather also. I love this house. Life has no meaning for me without the cherry orchard, and if it has to be sold, then let me be sold with it. *(Embraces* TROFIMOV *and kisses him on the forehead.)* Don't you see, my son was drowned here. *(Weeps.)* Have pity on me, my good, kind friend.

TROFIMOV: You know I sympathize with you with all my heart.

MRS. RANEVSKY: You should have put it differently. *(Takes out her handkerchief. A telegram falls on the floor.)* My heart is so heavy today. You can't imagine how heavy. I can't bear this noise. The slightest sound makes me shudder. I'm trembling all over. I'm afraid to go to my room. I'm terrified to be alone. . . . Don't condemn me, Peter. I love you as my own son. I'd gladly let Anya marry you, I swear I would. Only, my dear boy, you must study, you must finish your course at the university. You never do anything. You just drift from one place to another. That's what's so strange. Isn't that so? Isn't it? And you should do something about your beard. Make it grow, somehow. *(Laughs.)* You are funny!

TROFIMOV *(picking up the telegram)*: I have no wish to be handsome.

MRS. RANEVSKY: That telegram's from Paris. I get one every day. Yesterday and today. That wild man is ill again, in trouble again. He asks me to forgive him. He begs me to come back to him, and I really think I ought to be going back to Paris to be near him for a bit. You're looking very stern, Peter. But what's to be done, my dear boy? What am I to do? He's ill. He's lonely. He's unhappy. Who'll look after him there? Who'll stop him from doing something silly? Who'll give him his medicine at the right time? And, why hide it? Why be silent about it? I love him. That's obvious. I love him. I love him. He's a millstone round my neck and he's dragging me down to the bottom with him, but I love the millstone, and I can't live without it. *(Presses* TROFIMOV's *hand.)* Don't think badly of me, Peter. Don't say anything. Don't speak.

TROFIMOV *(through tears)*: For God's sake—forgive my being so frank, but he left you penniless!

MRS. RANEVSKY: No, no, no! You mustn't say that. *(Puts her hands over her ears.)*

TROFIMOV: Why, he's a scoundrel, and you're the only one who doesn't seem to know it. He's a petty scoundrel, a nonentity.

MRS. RANEVSKY *(angry but restraining herself)*: You're twenty-six or twenty-seven, but you're still a schoolboy—a sixth-grade schoolboy!

TROFIMOV: What does that matter?

MRS. RANEVSKY: You ought to be a man. A person of your age ought to understand people who are in love. You ought to be in love yourself. You ought to fall in love. *(Angrily.)* Yes! Yes! And you're not so pure either. You're just a prude, a ridiculous crank, a freak!

TROFIMOV *(horrified)*: What is she saying?

MRS. RANEVSKY: "I'm above love!" You're not above

love, you're simply what Firs calls a nincompoop. Not have a mistress at your age!

TROFIMOV (*horrified*): This is terrible! What is she saying? (*Walks quickly into the ballroom, clutching his head.*) It's dreadful! I can't! I'll go away! (*Goes out but immediately comes back.*) All is at an end between us! (*Goes out into the hall.*)

MRS. RANEVSKY (*shouting after him*): Peter, wait! You funny boy, I was only joking. Peter!

(*Someone can be heard running rapidly up the stairs and then suddenly falling downstairs with a crash.* ANYA *and* VARYA *scream, followed immediately by laughter.*)

MRS. RANEVSKY: What's happened?

ANYA (*laughing, runs in*): Peter's fallen down the stairs! (*Runs out.*)

MRS. RANEVSKY: What an eccentric! (*The* STATIONMASTER *stands in the middle of the ballroom and recites "The Fallen Woman" by Alexey Tolstoy. The others listen. But he has hardly time to recite a few lines when the sound of a waltz comes from the entrance hall, and the recitation breaks off. Everyone dances.* TROFIMOV, ANYA, VARYA, *and* MRS. RANEVSKY *enter from the hall.*) Well, Peter dear, you pure soul, I'm sorry. . . . Come, let's dance. (*Dances with* TROFIMOV.)

(ANYA *and* VARYA *dance together.* FIRS *comes in and stands his walking stick near the side door.* YASHA *has also come in from the drawing room and is watching the dancing.*)

YASHA: Well, Grandpa!

FIRS: I'm not feeling too well. We used to have generals, barons, and admirals at our dances before, but now we send for the post office clerk and the stationmaster. Even they are not too keen to come. Afraid I'm getting weak. The old master, the mistress's grandfather that is, used to give us powdered sealing wax for medicine. It was his prescription for all illnesses. I've been taking sealing wax every day for the last twenty years or more. That's perhaps why I'm still alive.

YASHA: You make me sick, Grandpa. (*Yawns*). I wish you was dead.

FIRS: Ugh, you nincompoop! (*Mutters.*)

(TROFIMOV *and* MRS. RANEVSKY *dance in the ballroom and then in the drawing room.*)

MRS. RANEVSKY: *Merci.* I think I'll sit down a bit. (*Sits down.*) I'm tired.

(*Enter* ANYA.)

ANYA (*agitated*): A man in the kitchen said just now that the cherry orchard has been sold today.

MRS. RANEVSKY: Sold? Who to?

ANYA: He didn't say. He's gone away now.

(ANYA *dances with* TROFIMOV; *both go off to the ballroom.*)

YASHA: Some old man gossiping, madam. A stranger.

FIRS: Master Leonid isn't here yet. Hasn't returned. Wearing his light autumn overcoat. He might catch cold. Oh, these youngsters!

MRS. RANEVSKY: I shall die! Yasha, go and find out who bought it.

YASHA: But he's gone, the old man has. (*Laughs.*)

MRS. RANEVSKY (*a little annoyed*): Well, what are you laughing at? What are you so pleased about?

YASHA: Yepikhodov's a real scream. Such a fool. Twenty-two Calamities!

MRS. RANEVSKY: Firs, where will you go if the estate's sold?

FIRS: I'll go wherever you tell me, ma'am.

MRS. RANEVSKY: You look awful! Are you ill? You'd better go to bed.

FIRS: Me to bed, ma'am? (*Ironically.*) If I goes to bed, who's going to do the waiting? Who's going to look after everything? I'm the only one in the whole house.

YASHA (*to* MRS. RANEVSKY): I'd like to ask you a favor, madam. If you go back to Paris, will you take me with you? It's quite impossible for me to stay here. (*Looking round, in an undertone.*) You know perfectly well yourself what an uncivilized country this is—the common people are so immoral—and besides, it's so boring here, the food in the kitchen is disgusting, and on top of it, there's that old Firs wandering about, muttering all sorts of inappropriate words. Take me with you, madam, please!

(*Enter* PISHCHIK.)

PISHCHIK: May I have the pleasure of a little dance, fair lady? (MRS. RANEVSKY *goes with him.*) I'll have one hundred and eighty rubles off you all the same, my dear, charming lady. . . . I will, indeed. (*They dance.*) One hundred and eighty rubles. . . .

(*They go into the ballroom.*)

YASHA (*singing softly*): "Could you but feel the agitated beating of my heart."

(*In the ballroom a woman in a gray top hat and check trousers can be seen jumping about and waving her arms. Shouts of "Bravo, Charlotte! Bravo!"*)

DUNYASHA (*stops to powder her face*): Miss Anya told me to join the dancers because there are lots of gentlemen and very few ladies. But dancing makes me dizzy and my heart begins beating so fast. I say, Firs, the post office clerk said something to me just now that quite took my breath away.

(*The music becomes quieter.*)

FIRS: What did he say to you?

DUNYASHA: "You're like a flower," he said.

YASHA (*yawning*): What ignorance! (*Goes out.*)

DUNYASHA: Like a flower! I'm ever so delicate, and I love people saying nice things to me!

FIRS: You'll come to a bad end, my girl. Mark my words.

(*Enter YEPIKHODOV.*)

YEPIKHODOV: You seem to avoid me, Dunyasha. Just as if I was some insect. (*Sighs.*) Oh, life!

DUNYASHA: What do you want?

YEPIKHODOV: No doubt you may be right. (*Sighs.*) But, of course, if one looks at things from a certain point of view, then, if I may say so and if you'll forgive my frankness, you have reduced me absolutely to a state of mind. I know what Fate has in store for me. Every day some calamity overtakes me, but I got used to it so long ago that I just look at my Fate and smile. You gave me your word, and though I—

DUNYASHA: Let's talk about it some other time. Leave me alone now. Now, I am dreaming. (*Plays with her fan.*)

YEPIKHODOV: Every day some calamity overtakes me, and I—let me say it quite frankly—why, I just smile, laugh even.

(*Enter VARYA from the ballroom.*)

VARYA: Are you still here, Simon! What an ill-mannered fellow you are, to be sure! (*to DUNYASHA*) Be off with you, Dunyasha. (*to YEPIKHODOV*) First you go and play billiards and break a cue, and now you wander about the drawing room as if you were a guest.

YEPIKHODOV: It's not your place to reprimand me, if you don't mind my saying so.

VARYA: I'm not reprimanding you. I'm telling you. All you do is drift about from one place to another without ever doing a stroke of work. We're employing an office clerk, but goodness knows why.

YEPIKHODOV (*offended*): Whether I work or drift about, whether I eat or play billards, is something which only people older than you, people who know what they're talking about, should decide.

VARYA: How dare you talk to me like that? (*Flaring up.*) How dare you? I don't know what I'm talking about, don't I? Get out of here! This instant!

YEPIKHODOV (*cowed*): Express yourself with more delicacy, please.

VARYA (*beside herself*): Get out of here this minute! Out! (*He goes toward the door, and she follows him.*) Twenty-two Calamities! Don't let me see you here again! Never set foot here again! (*YEPIKHODOV goes out. He can be heard saying behind the door: "I'll lodge a complaint."*) Oh, so you're coming back, are you? (*Picks up the stick which FIRS has left near the door.*) Come on, come on, I'll show you! Coming are you? Well, take that! (*Swings the stick as LOPAKHIN comes in.*)

LOPAKHIN: Thank you very much!

VARYA (*angrily and derisively*): I'm so sorry!

LOPAKHIN: It's quite all right. Greatly obliged to you for the kind reception.

VARYA: Don't mention it. (*Walks away, then looks round and inquires gently.*) I didn't hurt you, did I?

LOPAKHIN: Oh no, not at all. There's going to be an enormous bump on my head for all that.

(*Voices in the ballroom: "Lopakhin's arrived. Lopakhin!"*)

PISHCHIK: Haven't heard from you or seen you for ages, my dear fellow! (*Embraces LOPAKHIN.*) Do I detect a smell of brandy, dear boy? We're doing very well here, too.

(*Enter MRS. RANEVSKY.*)

MRS. RANEVSKY: Is it you, Lopakhin? Why have you been so long? Where's Leonid?

LOPAKHIN: He came back with me. He'll be here in a moment.

MRS. RANEVSKY (*agitated*): Well, what happened? Did the auction take place? Speak, for heaven's sake!

LOPAKHIN (*embarrassed, fearing to betray his joy*): The auction was over by four o'clock. We missed our train and had to wait till half past nine. (*With a deep sigh.*) Oh dear, I'm afraid I feel a little dizzy.

(*Enter GAYEV. He carries some parcels in his right hand and wipes away his tears with his left.*)

MRS. RANEVSKY: What's the matter, Leonid? Well! (*Impatiently, with tears.*) Quick, tell me for heaven's sake!

GAYEV (*doesn't answer, only waves his hands resignedly; to FIRS, weeping*): Here, take these—anchovies, Kerch herrings ... I've had nothing to eat all day. I've had a terrible time. (*The door of the billiard room is open; the click of billiard balls can be heard and YASHA's voice: "Seven and eighteen!" GAYEV's expression changes. He is no longer crying.*) I'm awfully tired. Come and help me change, Firs.

(*GAYEV goes off through the ballroom to his own room, followed by FIRS.*)

PISHCHIK: Well, what happened at the auction? Come, tell us!

MRS. RANEVSKY: Has the cherry orchard been sold?

LOPAKHIN: It has.

MRS. RANEVSKY: Who bought it?

LOPAKHIN: I bought it. (*Pause. MRS. RANEVSKY is crushed; she would have collapsed on the floor if she had not been standing near an armchair.* VARYA *takes the keys from her belt, throws them on the floor in the center of the drawing room, and goes out.)* I bought it! One moment, please, ladies and gentlemen. I feel dazed. I can't talk. . . . *(Laughs.)* Deriganov was already there when we got to the auction. Gayev had only fifteen thousand, and Deriganov began his bidding at once with thirty thousand over and above the mortgage. I realized the position at once and took up his challenge. I bid forty. He bid forty-five. He kept raising his bid by five thousand and I by adding another ten thousand. Well, it was soon over. I bid ninety thousand on top of the arrears, and the cherry orchard was knocked down to me. Now the cherry orchard is mine! Mine! *(Laughs loudly.)* Merciful heavens, the cherry orchard's mine! Come on, tell me, tell me I'm drunk. Tell me I'm out of my mind. Tell me I'm imagining it all. *(Stamps his feet.)* Don't laugh at me! If my father and my grandfather were to rise from their graves and see what's happened, see how their Yermolay, their beaten and half-literate Yermolay, Yermolay who used to run around barefoot in winter, see how that same Yermolay bought this estate, the most beautiful estate in the world! I've bought the estate where my father and grandfather were slaves, where they weren't even allowed inside the kitchen. I must be dreaming. I must be imagining it all. It can't be true. It's all a figment of your imagination, shrouded in mystery. *(Picks up the keys, smiling affectionately.)* She's thrown down the keys. Wants to show she's no longer the mistress here. *(Jingles the keys.)* Oh well, never mind. *(The band is heard tuning up.)* Hey you, musicians, play something! I want to hear you. Come, all of you! Come and watch Yermolay Lopakhin take an axe to the cherry orchard. Watch the trees come crashing down. We'll cover the place with country cottages, and our grandchildren and great-grandchildren will see a new life springing up here. Strike up the music! *(The band plays.* MRS. RANEVSKY *has sunk into a chair and is weeping bitterly. Reproachfully.)* Why did you not listen to me? You poor dear, you will never get it back now. *(With tears.)* Oh, if only all this could be over soon, if only our unhappy, disjointed life could somehow be changed soon.

PISHCHIK *(takes his arm, in an undertone)*: She's crying. Let's go into the ballroom. Let's leave her alone. Come on. *(Takes his arm and leads him away to the ballroom.)*

LOPAKHIN: What's the matter? You there in the band, play up, play up! Let's hear you properly. Let's have everything as I want it now. *(Ironically.)* Here comes the new landowner, the owner of the cherry orchard! *(Knocks against a small table*

accidentally and nearly knocks over the candelabra.) I can pay for everything!

*(*LOPAKHIN *goes out with* PISHCHIK. *There is no one left in the ballroom except* MRS. RANEVSKY, *who remains sitting in a chair, hunched up and crying bitterly. The band plays quietly.* ANYA *and* TROFIMOV *come in quickly.* ANYA *goes up to her mother and kneels in front of her.* TROFIMOV *remains standing by the entrance to the ballroom.)*

ANYA: Mother, Mother, why are you crying? My dear, good, kind Mother, my darling Mother, I love you; God bless you, Mother. The cherry orchard is sold. It's gone. That's true, quite true, but don't cry, Mother. You still have your life ahead of you, and you've still got your kind and pure heart. . . . Come with me, darling. Come. Let's go away from here. We shall plant a new orchard, an orchard more splendid than this one. You will see it, you will understand, and joy, deep, serene joy, will steal into your heart, sink into it like the sun in the evening, and you will smile, Mother! Come, darling! Come!

CURTAIN

ACT 4

(The scene is the same as in the first act. There are no curtains at the windows or pictures on the walls. Only a few pieces of furniture are left. They have been stacked in one corner as if for sale. There is a feeling of emptiness. Near the front door and at the back of the stage, suitcases, traveling bags, etc., are piled up. The door on the left is open and the voices of VARYA *and* ANYA *can be heard.* LOPAKHIN *stands waiting.* YASHA *is holding a tray with glasses of champagne. In the entrance hall* YEPIKHODOV *is tying up a box. There is a constant murmur of voices offstage, the voices of peasants who have come to say good-bye.* GAYEV's *voice is heard: "Thank you, my dear people, thank you.")*

YASHA: The peasants have come to say good-bye. In my opinion, sir, the peasants are decent enough fellows, but they don't understand a lot.

(The murmur of voices dies away. MRS. RANEVSKY *and* GAYEV *come in through the entrance hall; she is not crying, but she is pale. Her face is quivering. She cannot speak.)*

GAYEV: You gave them your purse, Lyuba. You shouldn't. You really shouldn't!

MRS. RANEVSKY: I—I couldn't help it. I just couldn't help it.

(Both go out.)

LOPAKHIN *(calling through the door after them)*: Please take a glass of champagne. I beg you. One glass each before we leave. I forgot to bring any from town, and I could find only one bottle at the station. Please! (*Pause.*) Why, don't you want any? (*Walks away from the door.*) If I'd known, I wouldn't have bought it. Oh well, I don't think I'll have any, either. (YASHA *puts the tray down carefully on a chair.*) You'd better have some, Yasha.

YASHA: Thank you, sir. To those who're going away! And here's to you, sir, who're staying behind! (*Drinks.*) This isn't real champagne. Take it from me, sir.

LOPAKHIN: Paid eight rubles a bottle. (*Pause.*) Damn cold here.

YASHA: The stoves haven't been lit today. We're leaving, anyway. (*Laughs.*)

LOPAKHIN: What's so funny?

YASHA: Oh, nothing. Just feeling happy.

LOPAKHIN: It's October, but it might just as well be summer: it's so sunny and calm. Good building weather. (*Glances at his watch and calls through the door.*) I say, don't forget the train leaves in forty-seven minutes. In twenty minutes we must start for the station. Hurry up!

(TROFIMOV *comes in from outside, wearing an overcoat.*)

TROFIMOV: I think it's about time we were leaving. The carriages are at the door. Where the blazes could my galoshes have got to? Disappeared without a trace. (*Through the door.*) Anya, I can't find my galoshes! Can't find them!

LOPAKHIN: I've got to go to Kharkov. I'll leave with you on the same train. I'm spending the winter in Kharkov. I've been hanging about here too long. I'm worn out with having nothing to do. I can't live without work. Don't know what to do with my hands. They just flop about as if they belonged to someone else.

TROFIMOV: Well, we'll soon be gone and then you can resume your useful labors.

LOPAKHIN: Come on, have a glass of champagne.

TROFIMOV: No, thank you.

LOPAKHIN: So you're off to Moscow, are you?

TROFIMOV: Yes. I'll see them off to town, and I'm off to Moscow tomorrow.

LOPAKHIN: I see. I suppose the professors have stopped lecturing while you've been away. They're all waiting for you to come back.

TROFIMOV: Mind your own business.

LOPAKHIN: How many years have you been studying at the university?

TROFIMOV: Why don't you think of something new for a change? This is rather old, don't you think?—and stale. (*Looking for his galoshes.*) I don't suppose we shall ever meet again, so let me give you a word of advice as a farewell gift: Don't wave your arms about. Get rid of the habit of throwing your arms about. And another thing: To build country cottages in the hope that in the fullness of time vacationers will become landowners is the same as waving your arms about. Still, I like you in spite of everything. You've got fine sensitive fingers, like an artist's, and you have a fine sensitive soul.

LOPAKHIN (*embraces him*): My dear fellow, thanks for everything. Won't you let me lend you some money for your journey? You may need it.

TROFIMOV: Need it? Whatever for?

LOPAKHIN: But you haven't any, have you?

TROFIMOV: Oh, but I have. I've just got some money for a translation. Got it here in my pocket. (*Anxiously.*) Where could those galoshes of mine have got to?

VARYA (*from another room*): Oh, take your filthy things! (*Throws a pair of galoshes onto the stage.*)

TROFIMOV: Why are you so cross, Varya? Good heavens, these are not my galoshes!

LOPAKHIN: I had about three thousand acres of poppy sown last spring. Made a clear profit of forty thousand. When my poppies were in bloom, what a beautiful sight they were! Well, so you see, I made forty thousand and I'd be glad to lend you some of it because I can afford to. So why be so high and mighty? I'm a peasant. . . . I'm offering it to you without ceremony.

TROFIMOV: Your father was a peasant, my father was a pharmacist, all of which proves exactly nothing. (LOPAKHIN *takes out his wallet.*) Put it back! Put it back! If you offered me two hundred thousand, I wouldn't accept it. I'm a free man. Everything you prize so highly, everything that means so much to all of you, rich or poor, has no more power over me than a bit of fluff blown about in the air. I can manage without you. I can pass you by. I'm strong and proud. Mankind is marching toward a higher truth, toward the greatest happiness possible on earth, and I'm in the front ranks!

LOPAKHIN: Will you get there?

TROFIMOV: I will. (*Pause.*) I will get there or show others the way to get there.

(*The sound of an axe striking a tree can be heard in the distance.*)

LOPAKHIN: Well, good-bye, my dear fellow. Time to go. You and I are trying to impress one another, but life goes on regardless. When I work hard for hours on end, I can think more clearly, and then I can't help feeling that I, too, know what I live for. Have you any idea how many people in Russia exist goodness only knows why? However, no matter. It isn't they who make the world go round. I'm told Gayev has taken a job at the bank at six thousand a year. He'll never stick to it. Too damn lazy.

ANYA (*in the doorway*): Mother asks you not to begin

cutting the orchard down till she's gone.

TROFIMOV: Really, haven't you any tact at all? (*Goes out through the hall.*)

LOPAKHIN: Sorry, I'll see to it at once, at once! The damned idiots! (*Goes out after* TROFIMOV.)

ANYA: Has Firs been taken to the hospital?

YASHA: I told them to this morning. They must have taken him, I should think.

ANYA (*to* YEPIKHODOV, *who is crossing the ballroom*): Please find out if Firs has been taken to the hospital.

YASHA (*offended*): I told Yegor this morning. I haven't got to tell him a dozen times, have I?

YEPIKHODOV: Old man Firs, if you want my final opinion, is beyond repair, and it's high time he was gathered to his fathers. So far as I'm concerned, I can only envy him. (*Puts a suitcase on a hatbox and squashes it.*) There, you see! I knew it. (*Goes out.*)

YASHA (*sneeringly*): Twenty-two Calamities!

VARYA (*from behind the door*): Has Firs been taken to the hospital?

ANYA: He has.

VARYA: Why didn't they take the letter for the doctor?

ANYA: We'd better send it on after him. (*Goes out.*)

VARYA (*from the next room*): Where's Yasha? Tell him his mother's here. She wants to say good-bye to him.

YASHA (*waves his hand impatiently*): Oh, that's too much!

(*All this time* DUNYASHA *has been busy with the luggage. Now that* YASHA *is alone, she goes up to him.*)

DUNYASHA: You haven't even looked at me once, Yasha. You're going away, leaving me behind. (*Bursts out crying and throws her arms around his neck.*)

YASHA: Must you cry? (*Drinks champagne.*) I'll be back in Paris in a week. Tomorrow we catch the express and off we go! That's the last you'll see of us. I can hardly believe it, somehow. *Vive la France!* I hate it here. It doesn't suit me at all. It's not the kind of life I like. I'm afraid it can't be helped. I've had enough of all this ignorance. More than enough. (*Drinks champagne.*) So what's the use of crying? Behave yourself and you won't end up crying.

DUNYASHA (*powdering her face, looking in a hand mirror*): Write to me from Paris, please. I did love you, Yasha, after all. I loved you so much. I'm such an affectionate creature, Yasha.

YASHA: They're coming here. (*Busies himself around the suitcases, humming quietly.*)

(*Enter* MRS. RANEVSKY, GAYEV, ANYA, *and* CHARLOTTE.)

GAYEV: We ought to be going. There isn't much time left. (*Looking at* YASHA.) Who's smelling of pickled herrings here?

MRS. RANEVSKY: In another ten minutes we ought to be getting into the carriages. (*Looks round the room.*) Good-bye, dear house, good-bye, old grandfather house! Winter will pass, spring will come, and you won't be here any more. They'll have pulled you down. The things these walls have seen! (*Kisses her daughter affectionately.*) My precious one, you look radiant. Your eyes are sparkling like diamonds. Happy? Very happy?

ANYA: Oh yes, very! A new life is beginning, Mother!

GAYEV (*gaily*): It is, indeed. Everything's all right now. We were all so worried and upset before the cherry orchard was sold, but now, when everything has been finally and irrevocably settled, we have all calmed down and even cheered up. I'm a bank official now, a financier. Pot the red in the middle. As for you, Lyuba, say what you like, but you too are looking a lot better. There's no doubt about it.

MRS. RANEVSKY: Yes, my nerves are better, that's true. (*Someone helps her on with her hat and coat.*) I sleep well. Take my things out, Yasha. It's time. (*to* ANYA) We'll soon be seeing each other again, darling. I'm going to Paris. I'll live there on the money your great-aunt sent from Yaroslavl to buy the estate—three cheers for Auntie!—but the money won't last long, I'm afraid.

ANYA: You'll come home soon, Mother, very soon. I'm going to study, pass my school exams, and then I'll work and help you. We shall read all sorts of books together, won't we, Mother? (*Kisses her mother's hands.*) We shall read during the autumn evenings. We'll read lots and lots of books, and a new, wonderful world will open up to us. (*Dreamily.*) Oh, do come back, Mother!

MRS. RANEVSKY: I'll come back, my precious. (*Embraces her daughter.*)

(*Enter* LOPAKHIN. CHARLOTTE *quietly hums a tune.*)

GAYEV: Happy Charlotte! She's singing!

CHARLOTTE (*picks up a bundle that looks like a baby in swaddling clothes*): My darling baby, go to sleep, my baby. (*A sound of a baby crying is heard.*) Hush, my sweet, my darling boy. (*The cry is heard again.*) Poor little darling, I'm so sorry for you! (*Throws the bundle down.*) So you will find me another job, won't you? I can't go on like this.

LOPAKHIN: We'll find you one, don't you worry.

GAYEV: Everybody's leaving us. Varya's going away. All of a sudden, we're no longer wanted.

CHARLOTTE: I haven't anywhere to live in town. I must go away. (*Sings quietly.*) It's all the same to me. . . .

(*Enter* PISHCHIK.)

LOPAKHIN: The nine days' wonder!

PISHCHIK (*out of breath*): Oh dear, let me get my breath back! I'm all in. Dear friends . . . a drink of water, please.

GAYEV: Came to borrow some money, I'll be bound. Not from me this time. Better make myself scarce. (*Goes out.*)

PISHCHIK: Haven't seen you for ages, dearest lady. (*to* LOPAKHIN) You here too? Glad to see you . . . man of immense intellect. . . . Here, that's for you, take it. (*Gives* LOPAKHIN *money.*) Four hundred rubles. That leaves eight hundred and forty I still owe you.

LOPAKHIN (*puzzled, shrugging his shoulders*): I must be dreaming. Where did you get it?

PISHCHIK: One moment . . . Terribly hot . . . Most extraordinary thing happened. Some Englishmen came to see me. They found some kind of white clay on my land. (*to* MRS. RANEVSKY) Here's four hundred for you too, beautiful ravishing lady. (*Gives her the money.*) The rest later. (*Drinks some water.*) Young fellow in the train just now was telling me that some—er—great philosopher advises people to jump off roofs. "Jump!" he says, and that'll solve all your problems. (*With surprise.*) Good Lord! More water, please.

LOPAKHIN: Who were these Englishmen?

PISHCHIK: I let them a plot of land with the clay on a twenty-four years' lease. And now you must excuse me, my friends. I'm in a hurry. Must be rushing off somewhere else. To Znoykov's, to Kardamonov's . . . Owe them all money. (*Drinks.*) Good-bye. I'll look in on Thursday.

MRS. RANEVSKY: We're just leaving for town. I'm going abroad tomorrow.

PISHCHIK: What? (*In a worried voice.*) Why are you going to town? Oh! I see! The furniture, the suitcases . . . Well, no matter. (*Through tears.*) No matter. Men of immense intellect, these Englishmen. . . . No matter. . . . No matter. I wish you all the best. May God help you. . . . No matter. Everything in this world comes to an end. (*Kisses* MRS. RANEVSKY's *hand.*) When you hear that my end has come, remember the—er— old horse and say: Once there lived a man called Simeonov-Pishchik; may he rest in peace. Remarkable weather we've been having. . . . Yes. (*Goes out in great embarrassment, but immediately comes back and says, standing in the doorway.*) My Dashenka sends her regards. (*Goes out.*)

MRS. RANEVSKY: Well, we can go now. I'm leaving with two worries on my mind. One concerns Firs. He's ill. (*With a glance at her watch.*) We still have about five minutes.

ANYA: Firs has been taken to the hospital, Mother. Yasha sent him off this morning.

MRS. RANEVSKY: My other worry concerns Varya. She's used to getting up early and working. Now that she has nothing to do, she's like a fish out of water. She's grown thin and pale, and she's always crying, poor thing. (*Pause.*) You must have noticed it, Lopakhin. As you very well know, I'd always hoped to see her married to you. Indeed, everything seemed to indicate that you two would get married. (*She whispers to* ANYA, *who nods to* CHARLOTTE, *and they both go out.*) She loves you, you like her, and I simply don't know why you two always seem to avoid each other. I don't understand it.

LOPAKHIN: To tell you the truth, neither do I. The whole thing's odd somehow. If there's still time, I'm ready even now. . . . Let's settle it at once and get it over. I don't feel I'll ever propose to her without you here.

MRS. RANEVSKY: Excellent! Why, it shouldn't take more than a minute. I'll call her at once.

LOPAKHIN: And there's champagne here too. Appropriate to the occasion. (*Looks at the glasses.*) They're empty. Someone must have drunk it. (YASHA *coughs.*) Lapped it up, I call it.

MRS. RANEVSKY (*excitedly*): Fine! We'll go out. Yasha, *allez!* I'll call her. (*Through the door.*) Varya, leave what you're doing and come here for a moment. Come on.

(MRS. RANEVSKY *goes out with* YASHA.)

LOPAKHIN (*glancing at his watch*): Aye. . . .

(*Pause. Behind the door suppressed laughter and whispering can be heard. Enter* VARYA.)

VARYA (*spends a long time examining the luggage*): Funny, can't find it.

LOPAKHIN: What are you looking for?

VARYA: Packed it myself, and can't remember.

(*Pause.*)

LOPAKHIN: Where are you going now, Varya?

VARYA: Me? To the Ragulins'. I've agreed to look after their house—to be their housekeeper, I suppose.

LOPAKHIN: In Yashnevo, isn't it? About fifty miles from here. (*Pause.*) Aye. . . . So life's come to an end in this house.

VARYA (*examining the luggage*): Where can it be? Must have put it in the trunk. Yes, life's come to an end in this house. It will never come back.

LOPAKHIN: I'm off to Kharkov by the same train. Lots to see to there. I'm leaving Yepikhodov here to keep an eye on things. I've given him the job.

VARYA: Have you?

LOPAKHIN: This time last year it was already snowing, you remember. Now it's calm and sunny. A bit cold, though. Three degrees of frost.

VARYA: I haven't looked. (*Pause.*) Anyway, our thermometer's broken.

(*Pause. A voice from outside, through the door: "Mr. Lopakhin!"*)

LOPAKHIN (*as though he had long been expecting this call*): Coming! (*Goes out quickly.*)

(*VARYA sits down on the floor, lays her head on a bundle of clothes, and sobs quietly. The door opens and MRS. RANEVSKY comes in cautiously.*)

MRS. RANEVSKY: Well? (*Pause.*) We must go.

VARYA (*no longer crying, dries her eyes*): Yes, it's time, Mother dear. I'd like to get to the Ragulins' today, I only hope we don't miss the train.

MRS. RANEVSKY (*calling through the door.*): Anya, put your things on.

(*Enter ANYA, followed by GAYEV and CHARLOTTE. GAYEV wears a warm overcoat with a hood. SERVANTS and COACHMEN come in. YEPIKHODOV is busy with the luggage.*)

MRS. RANEVSKY: Now we can be on our way.

ANYA (*joyfully*): On our way. Oh, yes!

GAYEV: My friends, my dear, dear friends, leaving this house for good, how can I remain silent, how can I, before parting from you, refrain from expressing the feelings which now pervade my whole being—

ANYA (*imploringly*): Uncle!

VARYA: Uncle dear, please don't.

GAYEV (*dejectedly*): Double the red into the middle. . . . Not another word!

(*Enter TROFIMOV, followed by LOPAKHIN.*)

TROFIMOV: Well, ladies and gentlemen, it's time to go.

LOPAKHIN: Yepikhodov, my coat!

MRS. RANEVSKY: Let me sit down a minute. I feel as though I've never seen the walls and ceilings of this house before. I look at them now with such eagerness, with such tender emotion. . . .

GAYEV: I remember when I was six years old sitting on this window sill on Trinity Sunday and watching Father going to church.

MRS. RANEVSKY: Have all the things been taken out?

LOPAKHIN: I think so. (*To YEPIKHODOV as he puts on his coat.*) Mind, everything's all right here, Yepikhodov.

YEPIKHODOV (*in a hoarse voice*): Don't you worry, sir.

LOPAKHIN: What's the matter with your voice?

YEPIKHODOV: I've just had a drink of water and I must have swallowed something.

YASHA (*contemptuously*): What ignorance!

MRS. RANEVSKY: There won't be a soul left in this place when we've gone.

LOPAKHIN: Not till next spring.

(*VARYA pulls an umbrella out of a bundle of clothes with such force that it looks as if she were going to hit someone with it; LOPAKHIN pretends to be frightened.*)

VARYA: Good heavens, you didn't really think that—

TROFIMOV: Come on, let's get into the carriages! It's time. The train will be in soon.

VARYA: There are your galoshes, Peter. By that suitcase. (*Tearfully.*) Oh, how dirty they are, how old. . . .

TROFIMOV (*putting on his galoshes*): Come along, ladies and gentlemen.

(*Pause.*)

GAYEV (*greatly put out, afraid of bursting into tears*): Train . . . station . . . in off into the middle pocket . . . double the white into the corner.

MRS. RANEVSKY: Come along!

LOPAKHIN: Is everyone here? No one left behind? (*Locks the side door on the left.*) There are some things in there. I'd better keep it locked. Come on!

ANYA: Good-bye, old house! Good-bye, old life!

TROFIMOV: Welcome new life!

(*TROFIMOV goes out with ANYA. VARYA casts a last look round the room and goes out unhurriedly. YASHA and CHARLOTTE, carrying her lap dog, go out.*)

LOPAKHIN: So, it's till next spring. Come along, ladies and gentlemen. Till we meet again. (*Goes out.*)

(*MRS. RANEVSKY and GAYEV are left alone. They seem to have been waiting for this moment. They fling their arms around each other, sobbing quietly, restraining themselves, as though afraid of being overheard.*)

GAYEV (*in despair*): My sister! My sister!

MRS. RANEVSKY: Oh, my dear, my sweet, my beautiful orchard! My life, my youth, my happiness, good-bye! . . .

ANYA (*offstage, happily, appealingly*): Mo-ther!

TROFIMOV (*offstage, happily, excited*): Where are you?

MRS. RANEVSKY: One last look at the walls and the windows. Mother loved to walk in this room.

GAYEV: My sister, my sister!

ANYA (*offstage*): Mo-ther!

TROFIMOV (*offstage*): Where are you?

MRS. RANEVSKY: We're coming.

(*They go out. The stage is empty. The sound of all the doors being locked is heard, then of carriages driving off. It grows quiet. The silence is broken by the muffled noise of an axe striking a tree, sounding forlorn and sad. Footsteps can be heard. FIRS appears from the door on the right. He is dressed, as always, in a jacket and white waistcoat. He is wearing slippers. He looks ill.*)

FIRS (*walks up to the door and tries the handle*): Locked! They've gone. (*Sits down on the sofa.*) Forgot all about me. Never mind. Let me sit down here for a bit. Forgotten to put on his fur coat, the young master has. Sure of it. Gone off in his light overcoat. *(Sighs anxiously.)* I should have seen to it. . . . Oh, these youngsters! *(Mutters something which cannot be understood.)* My life's gone just as if I'd never lived. . . . *(Lies down.)* I'll lie down a bit. No strength left, Nothing's left. Nothing. Ugh, you—nincompoop! *(Lies motionless.)*

(A distant sound is heard, which seems to come from the sky, the sound of a breaking string, slowly dying away, melancholy. It is followed by silence, broken only by the sound of an axe striking a tree far away in the orchard.)

CURTAIN

Figure 59. Trofimov speculates about mankind and the Russian people, while Varya, Mrs. Ranevksy, and Anya *(left to right)* listen to him, and Gayev *(far right)* looks on in the Moscow Art Theatre production of *The Cherry Orchard,* Paris, 1958. (Photograph: Martha Swope.)

Figure 60. Trofimov (Ken Ruta, *left*) speculates about mankind and the Russian people, while *(left to right)* Anya (Kristina Callahan), Mrs. Ranevsky (Jessica Tandy), Varya (Nancy Wickwire), Firs (Sandy McCallum), Lopakhin (Lee Richardson), and Gayev (Robert Pastene) listen to him in the Guthrie Theatre Company production of *The Cherry Orchard,* directed by Tyrone Guthrie and designed by Tanya Moiseiwitsch, Minneapolis, 1965. (Photograph: the Guthrie Theatre.)

Figure 61. Trofimov (Hugh Webster, *left*) speculates about mankind and the Russian people, while Lopakhin (Douglas Campbell), and *(left to right)* Anya (Susan Ringwood), Mrs. Ranevsky (Kate Reid), and Varya (Frances Hyland) listen to him in the Stratford Festival production of *The Cherry Orchard,* directed by John Hirsch and designed by Brian Jackson, Stratford, Ontario, 1965. (Photograph: Stratford Festival, Canada.)

Staging of *The Cherry Orchard*

REVIEW OF THE MOSCOW ART THEATER, THE
GUTHRIE THEATER, AND THE STRATFORD
FESTIVAL PRODUCTIONS, 1965, BY HOWARD
TAUBMAN

This is the year of "The Cherry Orchard." The Moscow Art Theater brought New York its production of Chekhov's masterpiece last February. This summer the play is in the repertory of the Minnesota Theater Company at the Tyrone Guthrie Theater in Minneapolis, and of the Stratford Festival here.

It is illuminating to see the Minneapolis and Stratford productions in quick succcession, as I have just done, and to compare them with the performance of the Russian company, which introduced the play to the world 60 years ago.

Neither North American production has the sustained consistency of mood and style that the play requires, though each achieves affecting moments of laughter and pathos.

Tyrone Guthrie has staged the play in Minneapolis with his customary energy and imagination, but there are places where the hand of the director is not merely apparent but also intrusive. John Hirsch's direction at Stratford is less self-assertive; indeed, in the first two acts it suffers from diffidence and slackness.

The biggest difference between the Russians and the Westerners is the caliber of the companies. In every role the Moscow Art Company conveyed a profound identification with character; the very spirit of a decaying world irradiated and darkened the stage.

Here and in Minneapolis, one never forgets that one is watching a performance—particularly on an open stage. Some individual performances are better than others, but the parts are larger than the whole.

This does not mean, however, that the enterprise of the Minnesota and Stratford theaters is in vain. It is instructive to sit in each theater and watch audiences largely unfamiliar with "The Cherry Orchard" react to it. In each theater there is frequent laughter, which would have delighted Chekhov, who insisted to his dying day that his play was fundamentally a comedy.

As if to overcome unevenness in the abilities of his company, Mr. Guthrie has intensified certain effects. The reunion in the first act, especially among the women, is shrill. The party in the third act becomes almost febrile and too obstrusive.

In the last act the governess inexplicably slips to the floor and remains seated there for a while, as if sleeping off too many drinks.

Mr. Hirsch in Stratford has not strained for effect. But the pace of his direction at the outset is listless. The early impression of diffuseness is heightened by a lackluster quality of some of the playing.

Kate Reid and Douglas Campbell, who have done distinguished work at this festival, seem at first to be detached from the proceedings, as if Ranevskaya and Lopahin were creatures of technique rather than vivid human beings.

Jessica Tandy is the Ranevskaya in Minneapolis. Like Miss Reid in Stratford, she brings some emotion to the self-revealing moments in the third act. But neither actress paints the full portrait of a foolish, impulsive, generous and charming woman whose figure is so central to the canvas.

Nor are the Varyas quite right; Nancy Wickwire in Minneapolis is merely stiff, while Frances Hyland in Stratford diminishes her personality.

There is good work in Minneapolis by Lee Richardson as Lopahin. Mr. Guthrie builds the third act climax with power, and Mr. Richardson brings passion and tension to the scene. Mr. Campbell rises to the occasion of this scene in Stratford, though Mr. Hirsch's direction does not drive forward here with equal force.

Robert Pastene's Gayev in Minneapolis is amusingly and touchingly ineffectual, and William Hutt's Gayev in Stratford is even more amusing and touching. Ken Ruta as Trofimov, Paul Ballantyne as Pishchik, Ruth Nelson as the governess, Ellen Geer as the maid, Ed Flanders as Yasha, Kristina Callahan as Anya, Sandy McCallum as Firs and especially Hume Cronyn, who is richly comic as Yepihodov, make useful contributions in Minneapolis.

Martha Henry, a fine actress in other Stratford roles, is not quite apt as the maid, because she is basically too elegant and well-bred in manner. Hugh Webster seems too old for Trofimov, though he reads his lines with feeling. Susan Ringwood is pallid as Anya. Mervyn Blake as Pishchik, William Needles as Yepihodov, Powys Thomas as Firs, Bruno Gerussi as Yasha and especially Mary Savidge, who is first-rate as the governess, are effective.

It must be acknowledged that the open stages impose problems. Tanya Moiseiwitch at Minneapolis and Brian Jackson at Stratford have designed sets that are sparing in detail, yet allusive. They have gone as far as they could to delimit the playing space, but it remains diffuse and lacking in the enclosed frame so valuable in suggesting the spirit of a confining, dying society.

Neither version of "The Cherry Orchard" is ideal. Yet each has enough merit to be worth seeing. From the reaction of the Minneapolis and Stratford audiences it is clear that these productions are doing their first duty of revealing at least a portion of the brooding, shining genius of Chekhov to many who have not encountered it before.

GEORGE BERNARD SHAW

1856–1950

Shaw did not write his first play until he was thirty-six, but by the time of his death he had written forty-seven full-length plays, as well as a number of playlets, and thus had become one of the most prolific dramatists in the history of the English theater. He was born and raised in Dublin, in the midst of an unhappy marriage, his father an unsuccessful merchant who turned to drink, his mother a talented singer who scorned the domestic chores of tending a household. By the time he was fifteen, he had dropped out of school, where according to his own account he learned only that schools are a form of imprisonment, and by the time he was twenty he had abandoned an office job in Dublin and gone to live in London with his mother who had previously moved there and set herself up as a professional teacher of music. He had vowed never to do another "honest day's work," but to make his way in the world as a writer, and from 1876 to 1885 he leaned on his mother for financial support while he turned out five novels, none of which he was able to get published.

Although the early 1880s were a period of literary frustration for Shaw, they did prove to be a time in which he made intellectual discoveries that were to influence most of his thinking and writing. In 1882 he first heard about Karl Marx and subsequently became a lifelong convert to socialism, confessing later that "The importance of the economic basis of society dawned on me," and that "Marx made a man of me." Then in 1884, having studied *Das Kapital* in a Marxist reading circle, he joined the Fabians, a socialist group that though influenced by Marx, did not regard the state as a class structure to be overthrown but as a social mechanism to be gradually altered and used for the promotion of public welfare. To achieve this goal, Shaw and his Fabian colleagues publicized their positions on every economic, political, and social issue of the day, from local government reform to poor law reform, from trade unionism to women's rights, making their views known in leaflets, newspapers, pamphlets, and books, in lecture halls and on street corners. By the late 1880s Shaw was also writing art criticism, book reviews, and music criticism for several London newspapers. And in 1891, he also made his views known on the state of drama by coming out with *The Quintessence of Ibsenism*, a fiery little book in which he sought to awaken English theater to the social consciousness embodied in Ibsen's plays.

Having sharpened his prose on so wide a variety of cultural and social issues, Shaw himself was uniquely prepared to become the English counterpart of Ibsen, and in 1892 he launched his theatrical career with *Widowers' Houses*, a dramatic attack on the evils of slum landlordism, which he showed to be an emblem of the capitalist system. But even in this first play, as in nearly all of the others he was to write, Shaw's dramatic technique was vastly different from that of Ibsen. Whereas Ibsen had probed the inner lives and problems of his characters in plays suffused with a Scandinavian air of gloom, Shaw turned his characters into witty spokesmen (and spokeswomen) for his social and political views. Shaw's experience in politics and critical reviewing had clearly taught him

607

that comic wit is often the most powerful means of awakening an audience and winning its support. His plays are thus populated with witty characters who take part in equally witty plots.

In the years that followed his first play, Shaw used his comic techniques to expose and satirize an astonishing array of follies or evils in economics, politics, society, theology, morality, science, and literature. In *The Philanderer* (1893), he exposed the hypocritical morality of prevailing marriage laws and celebrated the advanced morality of Ibsen's "new woman." In *Mrs. Warren's Profession* (1893), a play about prostitution, he showed that "Rich men without conviction are more dangerous in modern society than poor women without chastity." In *Arms and the Man* (1894), he mocked romantic notions about love and war by making his hero a blunt realist who throws away his cartridges and replaces them with chocolates, because he knows enough to realize that cartridges will be useless during a cavalry charge, but that chocolates will be invaluable after the charge is over. In *Candida* (1895), he had another go at the conventional morality of marriage by creating as his heroine a very superior woman whose strength is revealed to lie in the way she conceals her strength. In *The Devil's Disciple* (1897), a play about the American revolution, he portrayed all of the English, with the exception of the suave General Burgoyne, as being stuffed shirts and fools, while the hero of the play is a plucky American, whose heroism is shown to be the result not of idealistic motives but of fortuitous circumstances. In *Caesar and Cleopatra* (1899), he mocked Shakespeare's view of Roman history, as it had been presented in *Julius Caesar* and *Antony and Cleopatra,* by turning Cleopatra into a naive and fearful sixteen year old, who is schooled in political wisdom by the hero of the play, namely Caesar, whom Shaw portrayed as a "naturally great" man, whose greatness derives from his ability "to estimate the value of truth, money, or success in any particular instance quite independently of convention and moral generalization." Caesar was to be the first in a series of Shavian supermen and superwomen, whose power Shaw perceived as flowing from their "free vitality," a quality Shaw regarded as fundamental in liberating human beings and social institutions from imprisoning attitudes, habits, and beliefs.

Shaw propounded his views not only in his plays, but also in prefaces that he wrote for the published versions of the plays. By means of these prefaces, which were often as long as the plays themselves, Shaw used his incisive prose style to explicate his characters, plots, and themes, as well as to gain a wider audience for his ideas than was possible in the theater alone. *Man and Superman* (1903), for example, which brilliantly dramatizes Shaw's ideas of the "life force" and "creative evolution," appeared in published form with a lengthy essay on modern society and the need for the superman, as well as a tract called "The Revolutionists Handbook and Pocket Companion," which had been mentioned in the first act of the play, and a collection of Shaw's aphorisms on related subjects. In the preface to *Back to Methusaleh* (1921), a thirty-thousand word essay on a ninety-thousand word play, Shaw gave the fullest explication he was ever to offer for his optimistic faith in the "life force" as a means of redeeming civilization. But by that time World War I had already taken place, and Shaw had recognized the destructive social and political bankruptcy of his generation in the apocalyptic vision of *Heartbreak House* (1919), much as he was later to dramatize the tragic conflict between political institutions and genius in *St. Joan* (1923).

In 1905, however, when *Major Barbara* first appeared, Shaw was still so confident in the future of creative evolution, so convinced that the vitality of liberated thought could work a progressive improvement in the human condition, that he sought to provoke a similar awareness in his audience by embodying the life force in Undershaft, the munitions maker—the merchant of destruction. By endowing Undershaft with the vision of a superman, Shaw did not, of course, intend to make a case for warfare, just as he did not mean to defend education or classical scholarship by turning Adolphus Cusins, the professor of Greek, into Undershaft's chosen successor. Here, as in virtually all his other plays, Shaw created his hero out of a highly implausible figure because he wanted to shock his audience out of their conventional attitudes about morality, society, and politics. And, like a typical Shavian hero, Undershaft does possess the free vitality of mind—and the dazzling verbal wit—that will shock almost any audience, much as they shock virtually everyone in Undershaft's family.

Undershaft's moral, social, and political views—his assertions, for example, that "poverty is a sin" and the English parliament "a gabble shop"—are ultimately far more shocking than his armament business, but these two aspects of Undershaft are in the end inseparable. The nature of his business, after all, gives him a unique power, as well as a unique understanding of power, which neither the parliament nor the Salvation Army possesses. In his debates with Lady Britomart, Stephen, Barbara, and Cusins, the aim of Undershaft is to provoke them into recognizing that politics, morality, and intelligence are helpless to improve the human condition; only with power can progress be achieved. Yet Undershaft also recognizes that progress requires the moral and intelligent exercise of power—a synthesis whose ideal outcome is envisioned in Undershaft's model working community at the end of Act III. And it is this special awareness of Undershaft that moves him to vie for the allegiance of Barbara and Cusins, since they embody the morality and intelligence needed to perpetuate and extend his vision of progress.

Major Barbara, like all of Shaw's plays, is built around a contest between very powerfully willed individuals—a contest that in this case Shaw intended to portray as a modern counterpart to the struggle represented in Euripides' *The Bacchae* between Dionysus and Pentheus, between the mystical forces in nature and the efforts of the human mind to repress them. Undershaft is clearly a Dionysian figure in the energy, even the religious ecstasy, that he brings to his debates first with Lady Britomart, then with Barbara, and finally with Cusins. Thus, any staging of *Major Barbara* requires a very powerful and resourceful actor to play the role of Undershaft, and in its 1970 production of the play, the Royal Shakespeare Company evidently found just such an actor in the person of Brewster Mason, judging from the review of that production. Photographs of the production show the authority that Mason projected in the role during his first act confrontation with Lady Britomart (see Figure 62), as well as the lively wit that he conveyed during his argument with Barbara at the end of the play (see Figure 64). The photograph from Act 1 also shows the image of Marx leering ironically over the household of Lady Britomart, much as the photograph from Act 2 (see Figure 63) presents the image of the British lion hovering ironically over Barbara's Salvation Army shelter, much as the photograph from Act 3 (Figure 64) shows the cannon projecting powerfully out of Undershaft's munitions factory. By using these set pieces, the designer clearly intended to remind the audience of the social and political struggles embodied in the play, as well as of Shaw's optimistic faith in the power of liberated thought and Fabian socialism. And in 1905, of course, it was still possible for enlightened human beings to believe in the possibility of uniting power with intelligence and morality.

MAJOR BARBARA

BY GEORGE BERNARD SHAW

CHARACTERS

SIR ANDREW UNDERSHAFT

LADY BRITOMART UNDERSHAFT, *his wife*

BARBARA, *his elder daugher, a Major in the Salvation Army*

SARAH, *his younger daughter*

STEPHEN, *his son*

ADOLPHUS CUSINS, *a professor of Greek in love with Barbara*

CHARLES LOMAX, *young-man-about-town, engaged to Sarah*

MORRISON, *Lady Britomart's butler*

BRONTERRE O'BRIEN ("SNOBBY") PRICE, *a cobbler-carpenter down on his luck*

MRS ROMOLA ("RUMMY") MITCHENS, *a worn-out lady who relies on the Salvation Army*

JENNY HILL, *a young Salvation Army worker*

PETER SHIRLEY, *an unemployed coal-broker*

BILL WALKER, *a bully*

MRS BAINES, *Commissioner in the Salvation Army*

BILTON, *a foreman at Perivale St. Andrews*

SCENE

The action of the play occurs within several days in January, 1906. ACT 1: *The library of Lady Britomart's house in Wilton Crescent, a fashionable London suburb.* ACT 2: *The yard of the Salvation Army shelter in West Ham, an industrial suburb in London's East End.* ACT 3: *The library in Lady Britomart's house; a parapet overlooking Perivale St Andrews, a region in Middlesex northwest of London.*

ACT 1

(It is after dinner in January 1906, in the library in LADY BRITOMART UNDERSHAFT'S *house in Wilton Crescent. A large and comfortable settee is in the middle of the room, upholstered in dark leather. A person sitting on it (it is vacant at present) would have, on his right,* LADY BRITOMART'S *writing table, with the lady herself busy at it; a smaller writing-table behind him on his left; the door behind him on* LADY BRITOMART'S *side; and a window with a window-seat directly on his left. Near the window is an armchair.*

LADY BRITOMART *is a woman of fifty or thereabouts, well dressed and yet careless of her dress, well bred and quite reckless of her breeding, well mannered and yet appallingly outspoken and indifferent to the opinion of her interlocutors, amiable and yet peremptory, arbitrary, and hightempered to the last bearable degree, and withal a very typical managing matron of the upper class, treated as a naughty child until she grew into a scolding mother, and finally settling down with plenty of practical ability and worldly experience, limited in the oddest way with domestic and class limitations, conceiving the universe exactly as if it were a large house in Wilton Crescent, though handling her corner of it very effectively on that assumption, and being quite enlightened and liberal as to the books in the library, the pictures on the walls, the music in the portfolios, and the articles in the papers.*

Her son, STEPHEN, *comes in. He is a gravely correct young man under 25, taking himself very seriously, but still in some awe of his mother, from childish habit and bachelor shyness rather than from any weakness of character.)*

STEPHEN: What's the matter?

LADY BRITOMART: Presently, Stephen.

(STEPHEN *submissively walks to the settee and sits down. He takes up a liberal weekly called* The Speaker*)*

LADY BRITOMART: Don't begin to read, Stephen. I shall require all your attention.

STEPHEN: It was only while I was waiting—

LADY BRITOMART: Don't make excuses, Stephen. *(He puts down* The Speaker.*) Now! (She finishes her writing; rises; and comes to the settee.)* I have not kept you waiting very long, I think.

STEPHEN: Not at all, mother.

LADY BRITOMART: Bring me my cushion. *(He takes the cushion from the chair at the desk and arranges it for her as she sits down on the settee.)* Sit down. *(He sits down and fingers his tie nervously.)* Don't fiddle with your tie, Stephen: there is nothing the matter with it.

STEPHEN: I beg your pardon. *(He fiddles with his watch chain instead.)*

LADY BRITOMART: Now are you attending to me, Stephen?

STEPHEN: Of course, mother.

LADY BRITOMART: No: it's not of course. I want something much more than your everyday matter-of-course attention. I am going to speak to you very seriously, Stephen. I wish you would let that chain alone.

STEPHEN *(hastily relinquishing the chain)*: Have I done anything to annoy you, mother? If so, it was quite unintentional.

LADY BRITOMART *(astonished)*: Nonsense! *(With some*

remorse.) My poor boy, did you think I was angry with you?

STEPHEN: What is it, then, mother? You are making me very uneasy.

LADY BRITOMART *(squaring herself at him rather aggressively)*: Stephen: may I ask how soon you intend to realize that you are a grown-up man, and that I am only a woman?

STEPHEN *(amazed)*: Only a—

LADY BRITOMART: Don't repeat my words, please: it is a most aggravating habit. You must learn to face life seriously, Stephen. I really cannot bear the whole burden of our family affairs any longer. You must advise me: you must assume the responsibility.

STEPHEN: I!

LADY BRITOMART: Yes, you, of course. You were twenty-four last June. You've been at Harrow and Cambridge. You've been to India and Japan. You must know a lot of things, now; unless you have wasted your time most scandalously. Well, advise me.

STEPHEN *(much perplexed)*: You know I have never interfered in the household—

LADY BRITOMART: No: I should think not. I don't want you to order the dinner.

STEPHEN: I mean in our family affairs.

LADY BRITOMART: Well, you must interfere now; for they are getting quite beyond me.

STEPHEN *(troubled)*: I have thought sometimes that perhaps I ought; but really, mother, I know so little about them; and what I do know is so painful—it is so impossible to mention some things to you— *(He stops, ashamed.)*

LADY BRITOMART: I suppose you mean your father.

STEPHEN *(almost inaudibly)*: Yes.

LADY BRITOMART: My dear: we can't go on all our lives not mentioning him. Of course you were quite right not to open the subject until I asked you to; but you are old enough now to be taken into my confidence, and to help me to deal with him about the girls.

STEPHEN: But the girls are all right. They are engaged.

LADY BRITOMART *(complacently)*: Yes; I have made a very good match for Sarah. Charles Lomax will be a millionaire at thirty-five. But that is ten years ahead; and in the meantime his trustees cannot under the terms of his father's will allow him more than £800 a year.

STEPHEN: But the will says also that if he increases his income by his own exertions, they may double the increase.

LADY BRITOMART: Charles Lomax's exertions are much more likely to decrease his income than to increase it. Sarah will have to find at least another £800 a year for the next ten years; and

even then they will be as poor as church mice. And what about Barbara? I thought Barbara was going to make the most brilliant career of all of you. And what does she do? Joins the Salvation Army; discharges her maid; lives on a pound a week; and walks in one evening with a professor of Greek whom she has picked up in the street, and who pretends to be a Salvationist, and actually plays the big drum for her in public because he has fallen head over ears in love with her.

STEPHEN: I was certainly rather taken aback when I heard they were engaged. Cusins is a very nice fellow certainly; nobody would ever guess that he was born in Australia; but—

LADY BRITOMART: Oh, Adolphus Cusins will make a very good husband. After all, nobody can say a word against Greek: it stamps a man at once as an educated gentleman. And my family, thank Heaven, is not a pigheaded Tory one. We are Whigs, and believe in liberty. Let snobbish people say what they please: Barbara shall marry, not the man they like, but the man *I* like.

STEPHEN: Of course I was thinking only of his income. However, he is not likely to be extravagant.

LADY BRITOMART: Don't be too sure of that, Stephen. I know your quiet, simple, refined, poetic people like Adolphus—quite content with the best of everything! They cost more than your extravagant people, who are always as mean as they are second rate. No; Barbara will need at least £2000 a year. You see it means two additional households. Besides, my dear, you must marry soon. I don't approve of the present fashion of philandering bachelors and late marriages; and I am trying to arrange something for you.

STEPHEN: It's very good of you, mother; but perhaps I had better arrange that for myself.

LADY BRITOMART: Nonsense! you are much too young to begin matchmaking: you would be taken in by some pretty little nobody. Of course I don't mean that you are not to be consulted: you know that as well as I do. (STEPHEN *closes his lips and is silent.*) Now don't sulk, Stephen.

STEPHEN: I am not sulking, mother. What has all this got to do with—with—with my father?

LADY BRITOMART: My dear Stephen: where is the money to come from? It is easy enough for you and the other children to live on my income as long as we are in the same house; but I can't keep four families in four separate houses. You know how poor my father is: he has barely seven thousand a year now; and really, if he were not the Earl of Stevenage, he would have to give up society. He can do nothing for us. He says, naturally enough, that is is absurd that he should be asked to provide for the children of a man who is rolling in money. You see, Stephen, your father must be fabulously wealthy, because there is always a war going on somewhere.

STEPHEN: You need not remind me of that, mother. I have hardly ever opened a newspaper in my life without seeing our name in it. The Undershaft torpedo! The Undershaft quick firers! The Undershaft ten inch! The Undershaft disappearing rampart gun! The Undershaft submarine! and now the Undershaft aerial battleship! At Harrow they called me the Woolwich Infant.° At Cambridge it was the same. A little brute at King's who was always trying to get up revivals, spoilt my Bible—your first birthday present to me—by writing under my name, "Son and heir to Undershaft and Lazarus, Death and Destruction Dealers: address, Christendom and Judea." But that was not so bad as the way I was kowtowed to everywhere because my father was making millions by selling cannons.

LADY BRITOMART: It is not only the cannons, but the war loans that Lazarus arranges under cover of giving credit for the cannons. You know, Stephen, it's perfectly scandalous. Those two men, Andrew Undershaft and Lazarus, positively have Europe under their thumbs. That is why your father is able to behave as he does. He is above the law. Do you think Bismarck or Gladstone or Disraeli could have openly defied every social and moral obligation all their lives as your father has? They simply wouldn't have dared. I asked Gladstone to take it up. I asked *The Times* to take it up. I asked the Lord Chamberlain to take it up. But it was just like asking them to declare war on the Sultan. They wouldn't. They said they couldn't touch him. I believe they were afraid.

STEPHEN: What could they do? He does not actually break the law.

LADY BRITOMART: Not break the law! He is always breaking the law. He broke the law when he was born; his parents were not married.

STEPHEN: Mother! Is that true?

LADY BRITOMART: Of course it's true: that was why we separated.

STEPHEN: He married without letting you know this!

LADY BRITOMART (*rather taken aback by this inference*): Oh, no. To do Andrew justice, that was not the sort of thing he did. Besides, you know the Undershaft motto: Unashamed. Everybody knew.

STEPHEN: But you said that was why you separated.

LADY BRITOMART: Yes, because he was not content

with being a foundling himself; he wanted to disinherit you for another foundling. That was what I couldn't stand.

STEPHEN (*ashamed*): Do you mean for—for—for—

LADY BRITOMART: Don't stammer, Stephen. Speak distinctly.

STEPHEN: But this is so frightful to me, mother. To have to speak to you about such things!

LADY BRITOMART: It's not pleasant for me, either, especially if you are still so childish that you must make it worse by a display of embarrassment. It is only in the middle classes, Stephen, that people get into a state of dumb helpless horror when they find that there are wicked people in the world. In our class, we have to decide what is to be done with wicked people; and nothing should disturb our self-possession. Now ask your questions properly.

STEPHEN: Mother: you have no consideration for me. For Heaven's sake either treat me as a child, as you always do, and tell me nothing at all; or tell me everything and let me take it as best I can.

LADY BRITOMART: Treat you as a child! What do you mean? It is most unkind and ungrateful of you to say such a thing. You know I have never treated any of you as children. I have always made you my companions and friends, and allowed you perfect freedom to do and say whatever you liked, so long as you liked what I could approve of.

STEPHEN (*desperately*): I daresay we have been the very imperfect children of a very perfect mother; but I do beg of you to let me alone for once, and tell me about this horrible business of my father wanting to set me aside for another son.

LADY BRITOMART (*amazed*): Another son! I never said anything of the kind. I never dreamt of such a thing. This is what comes of interrupting me.

STEPHEN: But you said—

LADY BRITOMART (*cutting him short*): Now be a good boy, Stephen, and listen to me patiently. The Undershafts are descended from a foundling in the parish of St Andrew Undershaft in the city. That was long ago, in the reign of James the First. Well, this foundling was adopted by an armorer and gunmaker. In the course of time the foundling succeeded to the business; and from some notion of gratitiude, or some vow or something, he adopted another foundling, and left the business to him. And that foundling did the same. Ever since that, the cannon business has always been left to an adopted foundling named Andrew Undershaft.

STEPHEN: But did they never marry? Were there no legitimate sons?

LADY BRITOMART: Oh yes: they married just as your father did; and they were rich enough to buy

---

Woolwich Infant, The nickname is a pun on Stephen's connection with the Undershaft cannon business.

ACT 1

land for their own children and leave them well provided for. But they always adopted and trained some foundling to succeed them in the business; and of course they always quarreled with their wives furiously over it. Your father was adopted in that way; and he pretends to consider himself bound to keep up the tradition and adopt somebody to leave the business to. Of course I was not going to stand that. There may have been some reason for it when the Undershafts could only marry women in their own class, whose sons were not fit to govern great estates. But there could be no excuse for passing over my son.

STEPHEN (*dubiously*): I am afraid I should make a poor hand of managing a cannon foundry.

LADY BRITOMART: Nonsense! you could easily get a manager and pay him a salary.

STEPHEN: My father evidently had no great opinion of my capacity.

LADY BRITOMART: Stuff, child! you were only a baby; it had nothing to do with your capacity. Andrew did it on principle, just as he did every perverse and wicked thing on principle. When my father remonstrated, Andrew actually told him to his face that history tells us of only two successful institutions: one the Undershaft firm, and the other the Roman Empire under the Antonines. That was because the Antonine emperors all adopted their successors. Such rubbish! The Stevenages are as good as the Antonines, I hope; and you are a Stevenage. But that was Andrew all over. There you have the man! Always clever and unanswerable when he was defending nonsense and wickedness; always awkward and sullen when he had to behave sensibly and decently.

STEPHEN: Then it was on my account that your home life was broken up, mother. I am sorry.

LADY BRITOMART: Well dear, there were other differences. I really cannot bear an immoral man. I am not a Pharisee, I hope; and I should not have minded his merely doing wrong things: we are none of us perfect. But your father didn't exactly do wrong things: he said them and thought them: that was what was so dreadful. He really had a sort of religion of wrongness. Just as one doesn't mind men practicing immorality so long as they own that they are in the wrong by preaching morality; so I couldn't forgive Andrew for preaching immorality while he practiced morality. You would all have grown up without principles, without any knowledge of right and wrong, if he had been in the house. You know, my dear, your father was a very attractive man in some ways. Children did not dislike him; and he took advantage of it to put the wickedest ideas into their heads, and make

them quite unmanageable. I did not dislike him myself: very far from it; but nothing can bridge over moral disagreement.

STEPHEN: All this simply bewilders me, mother. People may differ about matters of opinion, or even about religion; but how can they differ about right and wrong? Right is right; and wrong is wrong; and if a man cannot distinguish them properly, he is either a fool or a rascal: that's all.

LADY BRITOMART (*touched*): That's my own boy! (*She pats his cheek.*) Your father never could answer that: he used to laugh and get out of it under cover of some affectionate nonsense. And now that you understand the situation, what do you advise me to do?

STEPHEN: Well, what can you do?

LADY BRITOMART: I must get the money somehow.

STEPHEN: We cannot take money from him. I had rather go and live in some cheap place like Bedford Square or even Hampstead than take a farthing of his money.

LADY BRITOMART: But after all, Stephen, our present income comes from Andrew.

STEPHEN (*shocked*): I never knew that.

LADY BRITOMART: Well, you surely didn't suppose your grandfather had anything to give me. The Stevenages could not do everything for you. We gave you social position. Andrew had to contribute something. He had a very good bargain, I think.

STEPHEN (*bitterly*): We are utterly dependent on him and his cannons, then?

LADY BRITOMART: Certainly not: the money is settled. But he provided it. So you see it is not a question of taking money from him or not: it is simply a question of how much. I don't want any more for myself.

STEPHEN: Nor do I.

LADY BRITOMART: But Sarah does; and Barbara does. That is, Charlex Lomax and Adolphus Cusins will cost them more. So I must put my pride in my pocket and ask for it, I suppose. That is your advice, Stephen, is it not?

STEPHEN: No.

LADY BRITOMART (*sharply*): Stephen!

STEPHEN: Of course if you are determined—

LADY BRITOMART: I am not determined: I ask your advice; and I am waiting for it. I will not have all the responsibility thrown on my shoulders.

STEPHEN (*obstinately*): I would die sooner than ask him for another penny.

LADY BRITOMART (*resignedly*): You mean that *I* must ask him. Very well, Stephen: it shall be as you wish. You will be glad to know that your grandfather concurs. But he thinks I ought to ask Andrew to come here and see the girls. After all he must have some natural affection for them.

STEPHEN: Ask him here!!

LADY BRITOMART: Do not repeat my words, Stephen. Where else can I ask him?

STEPHEN: I never expected you to ask him at all.

LADY BRITOMART: Now don't tease, Stephen. Come! you see that it is necessary that he should pay us a visit, don't you?

STEPHEN (*reluctantly*): I suppose so, if the girls cannot do without his money.

LADY BRITOMART: Thank you, Stephen; I knew you would give me the right advice when it was properly explained to you. I have asked your father to come this evening. (STEPHEN *bounds from his seat.*) Don't jump, Stephen: it fidgets me.

STEPHEN (*in utter consternation*): Do you mean to say that my father is coming here to-night—that he may be here at any moment?

LADY BRITOMART (*looking at her watch*): I said nine. (*He gasps, she rises.*) Ring the bell, please. (STEPHEN *goes to the smaller writing table; presses a button on it; and sits at it with his elbows on the table and his head in his hands, outwitted and overwhelmed.*) It is ten minutes to nine yet; and I have to prepare the girls. I asked Charles Lomax and Adolphus to dinner on purpose that they might be here. Andrew had better see them in case he should cherish any delusions as to their being capable of supporting their wives. (*The butler enters:* LADY BRITOMART *goes behind the settee to speak to him.*) Morrison: go up to the drawing-room and tell everybody to come down here at once. (MORRISON *withdraws.* LADY BRITOMART *turns to* STEPHEN.) Now remember, Stephen: I shall need all your countenance and authority. (*He rises and tries to recover some vestige of these attributes.*) Give me a chair, dear. (*He pushes a chair forward from the wall to where she stands, near the smaller writing table. She sits down; and he goes to the armchair, into which he throws himself.*) I don't know how Barbara will take it. Ever since they made her a major in the Salvation Army she has developed a propensity to have her own way and order people about which quite cows me sometimes. It's not ladylike: I'm sure I don't know where she picked it up. Anyhow, Barbara shan't bully me; but still it's just as well that your father should be here before she has time to refuse to meet him or make a fuss. Don't look nervous, Stephen: it will only encourage Barbara to make difficulties. *I* am nervous enough, goodness knows; but I don't shew it.

(SARAH *and* BARBARA *come in with their respective young men,* CHARLES LOMAX *and* ADOLPHUS CUSINS. SARAH *is slender, bored, and mundane.* BARBARA *is robuster, jollier, much more energetic.* SARAH *is fashionably dressed:* BARBARA *is in Salvation Army uniform.* LOMAX, *a young man about town, is like many other young men about town. He is afflicted with a frivolous sense of humor which plunges him at the most inopportune moments into paroxysms of imperfectly suppressed laughter.* CUSINS *is a spectacled student, slight, thin haired, and sweet voiced, with a more complex form of* LOMAX's *complaint. His sense of humor is intellectual and subtle, and is complicated by an appalling temper. The life-long struggle of a benevolent temperament and a high conscience against impulses of inhuman ridicule and fierce impatience has set up a chronic strain which has visibly wrecked his constitution. He is a most implacable, determined, tenacious, intolerant person who by mere force of character presents himself as—and indeed actually is—considerate, gentle, explanatory, even mild and apologetic, capable possibly of murder, but not of cruelty or coarseness. By the operation of some instinct which is not merciful enough to blind him with the illusions of love, he is obstinately bent on marrying* BARBARA. LOMAX *likes* SARAH *and thinks it will be rather a lark to marry her. Consequently he has not attempted to resist* LADY ˋBRITOMART's *arrangements to that end.*

All four look as if they had been having a good deal of fun in the drawing room. The girls enter first, leaving the swains outside. SARAH *comes to the settee.* BARBARA *comes in after her and stops at the door.*)

BARBARA: Are Cholly and Dolly to come in?

LADY BRITOMART (*forcibly*): Barbara: I will not have Charles called Cholly: the vulgarity of it positively makes me ill.

BARBARA: It's all right, mother: Cholly is quite correct nowadays. Are they to come in?

LADY BRITOMART: Yes, if they will behave themselves.

BARBARA (*through the door*): Come in, Dolly; and behave yourself.

(BARBARA *comes to her mother's writing table.* CUSINS *enters smiling, and wanders toward* LADY BRITOMART.)

SARAH (*calling*): Come in, Cholly. (LOMAX *enters, controlling his features very imperfectly, and places himself vaguely between* SARAH *and* BARBARA.)

LADY BRITOMART (*peremptorily*): Sit down all of you. (*They sit.* CUSINS *crosses to the window and seats himself there.* LOMAX *takes a chair.* BARBARA *sits at the writing table and* SARAH *on the settee.*) I don't in the least know what you are laughing at, Adolphus. I am surprised at you, though I expected nothing less from Charles Lomax.

CUSINS (*in a remarkably gentle voice*): Barbara has been trying to teach me the West Ham Salvation March.

LADY BRITOMART: I see nothing to laugh at in that; nor should you if you are really converted.

CUSINS (*sweetly*): You were not present. It was really funny, I believe.

LOMAX: Ripping.

LADY BRITOMART: Be quiet, Charles. Now listen to me, children. Your father is coming here this evening.

(*General stupefaction.* LOMAX, SARAH, *and* BARBARA *rise;* SARAH *scared, and* BARBARA *amused and expectant.*)

LOMAX (*remonstrating*): Oh I say!

LADY BRITOMART: You are not called on to say anything, Charles.

SARAH: Are you serious, mother?

LADY BRITOMART: Of course I am serious. It is on your account, Sarah, and also on Charles's. (*Silence.* SARAH *sits, with a shrug,* CHARLES *looks painfully unworthy.*) I hope you are not going to object, Barbara.

BARBARA: I! why should I? My father has a soul to be saved like anybody else. He's quite welcome as far as I am concerned. (*She sits on the table, and softly whistles, "Onward, Christian Soldiers."*)

LOMAX (*still remonstrant*): But really, don't you know! Oh I say!

LADY BRITOMART (*frigidly*): What do you wish to convey, Charles?

LOMAX: Well, you must admit that this is a bit thick.

LADY BRITOMART (*turning with ominous suavity to* CUSINS): Adolphus: you are a professor of Greek. Can you translate Charles Lomax's remarks into reputable English for us?

CUSINS (*cautiously*): If I may say so, Lady Brit, I think Charles has rather happily expressed what we all feel. Homer, speaking of Autolycus, uses the same phrase. πυκινὸν δόμον ελθειν means a bit thick.°

LOMAX (*handsomely*): Not that I mind, you know, if Sarah don't. (*He sits.*)

LADY BRITOMART (*crushingly*): Thank you. Have I your permission, Adolphus, to invite my own husband to my own house?

CUSINS (*gallantly*): You have my unhesitating support in everything you do.

LADY BRITOMART: Tush! Sarah: have you nothing to say?

SARAH: Do you mean that he is coming regularly to live here?

LADY BRITOMART: Certainly not. The spare room is ready for him if he likes to stay for a day or two and see a little more of you; but there are limits.

The Greek *pykinon domon elthein* (*Iliad*, Book X, line 267) translates as "to come to a thick [*i.e.*, well-built] house." Cusins is punning on Undershaft's homecoming and a more literal sense of *thick*. Autolycus, in Greek legend, was a thief with the power of making himself and his stolen goods invisible.

SARAH: Well, he can't eat us, I suppose. *I* don't mind.

LOMAX (*chuckling*): I wonder how the old man will take it.

LADY BRITOMART: Much as the old woman will, no doubt, Charles.

LOMAX (*abashed*): I didn't mean—at least—

LADY BRITOMART: You didn't think, Charles. You never do; and the result is, you never mean anything. And now please attend to me, children. Your father will be quite a stranger to us.

LOMAX: I suppose he hasn't seen Sarah since she was a little kid.

LADY BRITOMART: Not since she was a little kid, Charles, as you express it with that elegance of diction and refinement of thought that never seem to desert you. Accordingly—er— (*Impatiently.*) Now I have forgotten what I was going to say. That comes of your provoking me to be sarcastic, Charles. Adolphus: will you kindly tell me where I was.

CUSINS (*sweetly*): You were saying that as Mr. Undershaft has not seen his children since they were babies, he will form his opinon of the way you have brought them up from their behavior to-night, and that therefore you wish us all to be particularly careful to conduct ourselves well, especially Charles.

LADY BRITOMART (*with emphatic approval*): Precisely.

LOMAX: Look here, Dolly: Lady Brit didn't say that.

LADY BRITOMART (*vehemently*): I did, Charles. Adolphus's recollection is perfectly correct. It is most important that you should be good; and I do beg you for once not to pair off into opposite corners and giggle and whisper while I am speaking to your father.

BARBARA: All right, mother. We'll do you credit. (*She comes off the table, and sits in her chair with ladylike elegance.*)

LADY BRITOMART: Remember, Charles, that Sarah will want to feel proud of you instead of ashamed of you.

LOMAX: Oh I say! there's nothing to be exactly proud of, don't you know.

LADY BRITOMART: Well, try and look as if there was. (MORRISON, *pale and dismayed, breaks into the room in unconcealed disorder.*)

MORRISON: Might I speak a word to you, my lady?

LADY BRITOMART: Nonsense! Shew him up.

MORRISON: Yes, my lady. (*He goes.*)

LOMAX: Does Morrison know who it is?

LADY BRITOMART: Of course. Morrison has always been with us.

LOMAX: It must be a regular corker for him, don't you know.

LADY BRITOMART: Is this a moment to get on my nerves, Charles, with your outrageous expressions?

LOMAX: But this is something out of the ordinary, really—

MORRISON (*at the door*): The—er—Mr. Undershaft. (*He retreats in confusion.*)

(ANDREW UNDERSHAFT *comes in. All rise.* LADY BRITOMART *meets him in the middle of the room behind the settee.*

ANDREW *is, on the surface, a stoutish, easygoing elderly man, with kindly patient manners, and an engaging simplicity of character. But he has a watchful, deliberate, waiting, listening face, and formidable reserves of power, both bodily and mental in his capacious chest and long head. His gentleness is partly that of a strong man who has learnt by experience that his natural grip hurts ordinary people unless he handles them very carefully, and partly the mellowness of age and success. He is also a little shy in his present very delicate situation.*)

LADY BRITOMART: Good evening, Andrew.

UNDERSHAFT: How d'ye do, my dear.

LADY BRITOMART: You look a good deal older.

UNDERSHAFT (*apologetically*): I am somewhat older. (*Taking her hand with a touch of courtship.*) Time has stood still with you.

LADY BRITOMART (*throwing away his hand*): Rubbish! This is your family.

UNDERSHAFT (*surprised*): Is it so large? I am sorry to say my memory is failing very badly in some things.

(*He offers his hand with paternal kindness to* LOMAX).

LOMAX (*jerkily shaking his hand*): Ahdedoo.

UNDERSHAFT: I can see you are my eldest. I am very glad to meet you again, my boy.

LOMAX (*remonstrating*): No, but look here don't you know—(*Overcome.*) Oh I say!

LADY BRITOMART (*recovering from momentary speechlessness*): Andrew: do you mean to say that you don't remember how many children you have?

UNDERSHAFT: Well, I am afraid I— They have grown so much—er. Am I making any ridiculous mistake? I may as well confess: I recollect only one son. But so many things have happened since, of course—er—

LADY BRITOMART (*decisively*): Andrew: you are talking nonsense. Of course you have only one son.

UNDERSHAFT: Perhaps you will be good enough to introduce me, my dear.

LADY BRITOMART: This is Charles Lomax, who is engaged to Sarah.

UNDERSHAFT: My dear sir, I beg your pardon.

LOMAX: Notatall. Delighted, I assure you.

LADY BRITOMART: This is Stephen.

UNDERSHAFT (*bowing*): Happy to make your acquaintance, Mr. Stephen. Then (*Going to* CUSINS.) you must be my son. (*Taking* CUSINS' *hands in his.*)

How are you, my young friend? (*to* LADY BRITOMART) He is very like you, my love.

CUSINS: You flatter me, Mr. Undershaft. My name is Cusins: engaged to Barbara. (*Very explicitly.*) That is Major Barbara Undershaft, of the Salvation Army. That is Sarah, your second daughter. This is Stephen Undershaft, your son.

UNDERSHAFT: My dear Stephen, I beg your pardon.

STEPHEN: Not at all.

UNDERSHAFT: Mr. Cusins: I am indebted to you for explaining so precisely. (*Turning to* SARAH.) Barbara, my dear—

SARAH (*prompting him*): Sarah.

UNDERSHAFT: Sarah, of course. (*They shake hands. He goes over to* BARBARA.) Barbara—I am right this time, I hope.

BARBARA: Quite right. (*They shake hands.*)

LADY BRITOMART (*resuming command*): Sit down, all of you. Sit down, Andrew. (*She comes forward and sits on the settee.* CUSINS *also brings his chair forward on her left.* BARBARA *and* STEPHEN *resume their seats.* LOMAX *gives his chair to* SARAH *and goes for another.*)

UNDERSHAFT: Thank you, my love.

LOMAX (*conversationally, as he brings a chair forward between the writing table and the settee, and offers it to* UNDERSHAFT): Takes you some time to find out exactly where you are, don't it?

UNDERSHAFT (*accepting the chair, but remaining standing*): That is not what embarrasses me, Mr. Lomax. My difficulty is that if I play the part of a father, I shall produce the effect of an intrusive stranger; and if I play the part of a discreet stranger, I may appear a callous father.

LADY BRITOMART: There is no need for you to play any part at all, Andrew. You had much better be sincere and natural.

UNDERSHAFT (*submissively*): Yes, my dear: I daresay that will be best. (*He sits down comfortably.*) Well, here I am. Now what can I do for you all?

LADY BRITOMART: You need not do anything, Andrew. You are one of the family. You can sit with us and enjoy yourself. (*A painfully conscious pause.* BARBARA *makes a face at* LOMAX, *whose too long suppressed mirth immediately explodes in agonized neighings.*)

LADY BRITOMART (*outraged*): Charles Lomax: if you can behave yourself, behave yourself. If not, leave the room.

LOMAX: I'm awfully sorry, Lady Brit; but really, you know, upon my soul! (*He sits on the settee between* LADY BRITOMART *and* UNDERSHAFT, *quite overcome.*)

BARBARA: Why don't you laugh if you want to, Cholly? It's good for your inside.

LADY BRITOMART: Barbara: you have had the education of a lady. Please let your father see that; and don't talk like a street girl.

UNDERSHAFT: Never mind me, my dear. As you know, I am not a gentleman; and I was never educated.

LOMAX (encouragingly): Nobody'd know it, I assure you. You look all right, you know.

CUSINS: Let me advise you to study Greek, Mr. Undershaft. Greek scholars are privileged men. Few of them know Greek; and none of them know anything else; but their position is unchallengeable. Other languages are the qualifications of waiters and commercial travellers: Greek is to a man of position what the hallmark is to silver.

BARBARA: Dolly: don't be insincere. Cholly: fetch your concertina and play something for us.

LOMAX (jumps up eagerly, but checks himself to remark doubtfully to UNDERSHAFT): Perhaps that sort of thing isn't in your line, eh?

UNDERSHAFT: I am particularly fond of music.

LOMAX (delighted): Are you? Then I'll get it. (He goes upstairs for the instrument.)

UNDERSHAFT: Do you play, Barbara?

BARBARA: Only the tambourine. But Cholly's teaching me the concertina.

UNDERSHAFT: Is Cholly also a member of the Salvation Army?

BARBARA: No: he says it's bad form to be a dissenter. But I don't despair of Cholly. I made him come yesterday to a meeting at the dock gates, and take the collection in his hat.

UNDERSHAFT (looks whimsically at his wife)!!

LADY BRITOMART: It is not my doing, Andrew. Barbara is old enough to take her own way. She has no father to advise her.

BARBARA: Oh yes she has. There are no orphans in the Salvation Army.

UNDERSHAFT: Your father there has a great many children and plenty of experience, eh?

BARBARA (looking at him with quick interest and nodding): Just so. How did you come to understand that? (LOMAX is heard at the door trying the concertina.)

LADY BRITOMART: Come in, Charles. Play us something at once.

LOMAX: Righto! (He sits down in his former place, and preludes.)

UNDERSHAFT: One moment, Mr. Lomax. I am rather interested in the Salvation Army. Its motto might be my own: Blood and Fire.

LOMAX (shocked): But not your sort of blood and fire, you know.

UNDERSHAFT: My sort of blood cleanses: my sort of fire purifies.

BARBARA: So do ours. Come down tomorrow to my shelter—the West Ham shelter—and see what we're doing. We're going to march to a great meeting in the Assembly Hall at Mile End.° Come and see the shelter and then march with us: it will do you a lot of good. Can you play anything?

UNDERSHAFT: In my youth I earned pennies, and even shillings occasionally, in the streets and in public house parlors by my natural talent for stepdancing. Later on, I became a member of the Undershaft orchestral society, and performed passably on the tenor trombone.

LOMAX (scandalized–putting down the concertina): Oh I say!

BARBARA: Many a sinner has played himself into heaven on the trombone, thanks to the Army.

LOMAX (to BARBARA, still rather shocked): Yes; but what about the cannon business, don't you know? (to UNDERSHAFT) Getting into heaven is not exactly in your line, is it?

LADY BRITOMART: Charles!!!

LOMAX: Well; but it stands to reason, don't it? The cannon business may be necessary and all that: we can't get on without cannons; but it isn't right, you know. On the other hand, there may be a certain amount of tosh about the Salvation Army—I belong to the Established Church myself—but still you can't deny that it's religion; and you can't go against religion, can you? At least unless you're downright immoral, don't you know.

UNDERSHAFT: You hardly appreciate my position, Mr. Lomax—

LOMAX (hastily): I'm not saying anything against you personally—

UNDERSHAFT: Quite so, quite so. But consider for a moment. Here I am, a profiteer in mutilation and murder. I find myself in a specially amiable humor just now because, this morning, down at the foundry, we blew twenty-seven dummy soldiers into fragments with a gun which formerly destroyed only thirteen.

LOMAX (leniently): Well, the more destructive war becomes, the sooner it will be abolished, eh?

UNDERSHAFT: Not at all. The more destructive war becomes, the more fascinating we find it. No, Mr. Lomax: I am obliged to you for making the usual excuse for my trade; but I am not ashamed of it. I am not one of those men who keep their morals and their business in watertight compartments. All the spare money my trade rivals spend on hospitals, cathedrals, and other recep-

---

Mile End, One of London's oldest districts, where William Booth held a religious meeting that launched the Salvation Army.

tacles for conscience money, I devote to experiments and researches in improved methods of destroying life and property. I have always done so; and I always shall. Therefore your Christmas card moralities of peace on earth and goodwill among men are of no use to me. Your Christianity, which enjoins you to resist not evil, and to turn the other cheek, would make me a bankrupt. My morality—my religion—must have a place for cannons and torpedoes in it.

STEPHEN (coldly–almost sullenly): You speak as if there were half a dozen moralities and religions to choose from, instead of one true morality and one true religion.

UNDERSHAFT: For me there is only one true morality; but it might not fit you, as you do not manufacture aerial battleships. There is only one true morality for every man; but every man has not the same true morality.

LOMAX (overtaxed): Would you mind saying that again? I didn't quite follow it.

CUSINS: It's quite simple. As Euripides says, one man's meat is another man's poison morally as well as physically.

UNDERSHAFT: Precisely.

LOMAX: Oh, that. Yes, yes, yes. True. True.

STEPHEN: In other words, some men are honest and some are scoundrels.

BARBARA: Bosh. There are no scoundrels.

UNDERSHAFT: Indeed? Are there any good men?

BARBARA: No. Not one. There are neither good men nor scoundrels: there are just children of one Father; and the sooner they stop calling one another names the better. You needn't talk to me: I know them. I've had scores of them through my hands: scoundrels, criminals, infidels, philanthropists, missionaries, city councillors, all sorts. They're all just the same sort of sinner; and there's the same salvation ready for them all.

UNDERSHAFT: May I ask have you ever saved a maker of cannons?

BARBARA: No. Will you let me try?

UNDERSHAFT: Well, I will make a bargain with you. If I go to see you tomorrow in your Salvation Shelter, will you come the day after to see me in my cannon works?

BARBARA: Take care. It may end in your giving up the cannons for the sake of the Salvation Army.

UNDERSHAFT: Are you sure it will not end in your giving up the Salvation Army for the sake of cannons?

BARBARA: I will take my chance of that.

UNDERSHAFT: And I will take my chance of the other. (They shake hands on it.) Where is your shelter?

BARBARA: In West Ham. At the sign of the cross. Ask anybody in Canning Town. Where are your works?

UNDERSHAFT: In Perivale St Andrews. At the sign of the sword. Ask anybody in Europe.

LOMAX: Hadn't I better play something?

BARBARA: Yes. Give us "Onward, Christian Soldiers."

LOMAX: Well, that's rather a strong order to begin with, don't you know. Suppose I sing "Thou'rt passing hence, my brother." It's much the same tune.

BARBARA: It's too melancholy. You get saved, Cholly; and you'll pass hence, my brother, without making such a fuss about it.

LADY BRITOMART: Really, Barbara, you go on as if religion were a pleasant subject. Do have some sense of propriety.

UNDERSHAFT: I do not find it an unpleasant subject, my dear. It is the only one that capable people really care for.

LADY BRITOMART (looking at her watch): Well, if you are determined to have it, I insist on having it in a proper and respectable way. Charles: ring for prayers. (General amazement. STEPHEN rises in dismay.)

LOMAX (rising): Oh I say!

UNDERSHAFT (rising): I am afraid I must be going.

LADY BRITOMART: You cannot go now, Andrew: it would be most improper. Sit down. What will the servants think?

UNDERSHAFT: My dear: I have conscientious scruples. May I suggest a compromise? If Barbara will conduct a little service in the drawing room, with only Mr. Lomax as organist, I will attend it willingly. I will even take part, if a trombone can be procured.

LADY BRITOMART: Don't mock, Andrew.

UNDERSHAFT (shocked–to BARBARA): You don't think I am mocking, my love, I hope.

BARBARA: No, of course not; and it wouldn't matter if you were: half the Army came to their first meeting for a lark. (Rising.) Come along. (She throws her arm round her father and sweeps him out, calling to the others from the threshold.) Come, Dolly. Come, Cholly.

(CUSINS rises.)

LADY BRITOMART: I will not be disobeyed by everybody. Adolphus: sit down. (He does not.) Charles: you may go. You are not fit for prayers: you cannot keep your countenance.

LOMAX: Oh I say! (He goes out.)

LADY BRITOMART (continuing): But you, Adolphus, can behave yourself if you choose to. I insist on your staying.

CUSINS: My dear Lady Brit: there are things in the family prayer book that I couldn't bear to hear you say.

LADY BRITOMART: What things, pray?

CUSINS: Well, you would have to say before all the servants that we have done things we ought not to have done, and left undone things we ought to have done, and there is no health in us. I cannot bear to hear you doing yourself such an injustice, and Barbara such an injustice. As for myself, I flatly deny it: I have done my best. I shouldn't dare to marry Barbara—I couldn't look you in the face—if it were true. So I must go to the drawing room.

LADY BRITOMART (offended): Well, go. (He starts for the door.) And remember this, Adolphus (He turns to listen.) I have a strong suspicion that you went to the Salvation Army to worship Barbara and nothing else. And I quite appreciate the clever way in which you systematically humbug me. I have found you out. Take care Barbara doesn't. That's all.

CUSINS (with unruffled sweetness): Don't tell on me. (He steals out.)

LADY BRITOMART: Sarah: if you want to go, go. Anything's better than to sit there as if you wished you were a thousand miles away.

SARAH (languidly): Very well, mamma. (She goes.)

(LADY BRITOMART, with a sudden flounce, gives way to a little gust of tears.)

STEPHEN (going to her): Mother: what's the matter?

LADY BRITOMART (swishing away her tears with her handkerchief): Nothing. Foolishness. You can go with him, too, if you like, and leave me with the servants.

STEPHEN: Oh, you mustn't think that, mother. I—I don't like him.

LADY BRITOMART: The others do. That is the injustice of a woman's lot. A woman has to bring up her children; and that means to restrain them, to deny them things they want, to set them tasks, to punish them when they do wrong, to do all the unpleasant things. And then the father, who has nothing to do but pet them and spoil them, comes in when all her work is done and steals their affection from her.

STEPHEN: He has not stolen our affection from you. It is only curiosity.

LADY BRITOMART (violently): I won't be consoled, Stephen. There is nothing the matter with me. (She rises and goes toward the door.)

STEPHEN: Where are you going, mother?

LADY BRITOMART: To the drawing room, of course. (She goes out. "Onward, Christian Soldiers," on the concertina, with tambourine accompaniment, is heard when the door opens.) Are you coming, Stephen?

STEPHEN: No. Certainly not. (She goes. He sits down on the settee, with compressed lips and an expression of strong dislike.)

ACT 2

(The yard of the West Ham shelter of the Salvation Army is a cold place on a January morning. The building itself, an old warehouse, is newly whitewashed. Its gabled end projects into the yard in the middle, with a door on the ground floor, and another in the loft above it without any balcony or ladder, but with a pulley rigged over it for hoisting sacks. Those who come from this central gable end into the yard have the gateway leading to the street on their left, with a stone horse-trough just beyond it, and, on the right, a penthouse shielding a table from the weather. There are forms at the table; and on them are seated a man and a woman, both much down on their luck, finishing a meal of bread (one thick slice each, with margarine and golden syrup) and diluted milk.

The man, a workman out of employment, is young, agile, a talker, a poser, sharp enough to be capable of anything in reason except honest or altruistic considerations of any kind. The woman is a commonplace old bundle of poverty and hardworn humanity. She looks sixty and probably is forty-five. If they were rich people, gloved and muffed and well wrapped up in furs and overcoats, they would be numbed and miserable; for it is a grindingly cold, raw, January day; and a glance at the background of grimy warehouses and leaden sky visible over the whitewashed walls of the yard would drive any idle rich person straight to the Mediterranean. But these two, being no more troubled with visions of the Mediterranean than of the moon, and being compelled to keep more of their clothes in the pawnshop, and less on their persons, in winter than in summer, are not depressed by the cold: rather are they stung into vivacity, to which their meal has just now given an almost jolly turn. The man takes a pull at his mug, and then gets up and moves about the yard with his hands deep in his pockets, occasionally breaking into a stepdance.)

THE WOMAN: Feel better arter your meal, sir?

THE MAN: No. Call that a meal! Good enough for you, p'raps; but wot is it to me, an intelligent workin' man?

THE WOMAN: Workin' man! Wot are you?

THE MAN: Painter.

THE WOMAN (skeptically): Yus, I dessay.

THE MAN: Yus, you dessay! I know. Every loafer that can't do nothink calls 'isself a painter. Well, I'm a real painter: grainer, finisher, thirty-eight bob a week when I can get it.

THE WOMAN: Then why don't you go and get it?

THE MAN: I'll tell you why. Fust: I'm intelligent—fffff! it's rotten cold here (He dances a step or two.)—yes; intelligent beyond the station o' life into which it has pleased the capitalists to call me;

and they don't like a man that sees through 'em. Second, an intelligent bein' needs a doo share of 'appiness; so I drink somethink cruel when I get the chawnce. Third, I stand by my class and do as little as I can so's to leave 'arf the job for me fellow workers. Fourth, I'm fly° enough to know wot's inside the law and wot's outside it; and inside it I do as the capitalists do: pinch wot I can lay me 'ands on. In a proper state of society I am sober, industrious, and honest: in Rome, so to speak, I do as the Romans do. Wot's the consequence? When trade is bad—and it's rotten bad just now—and the employers 'az to sack 'arf their men, they generally start on me.

THE WOMAN: What's your name?

THE MAN: Price. Bronterre O'Brien Price. Usually called Snobby Price, for short.

THE WOMAN: Snobby's a carpenter, ain't it? You said you was a painter.

PRICE: Not that kind of snob, but the genteel sort. I'm too uppish, owing to my intelligence, and my father being a Chartist and a reading, thinking man: a stationer, too. I'm none of your common hewers of wood and drawers of water; and don't you forget it. (*He returns to his seat at the table, and takes up his mug.*) Wot's your name?

THE WOMAN: Rummy Mitchens, sir.

PRICE (*quaffing the remains of his milk to her*): Your 'elth, Miss Mitchens.

RUMMY (*correcting him*): Missis Mitchens.

PRICE: Wot! Oh Rummy, Rummy! Respectable married woman, Rummy, gittin' rescued by the Salvation Army by pretendin' to be a bad un. Same old game!

RUMMY: What am I to do? I can't starve. Them Salvation lasses is dear good girls; but the better you are, the worse they likes to think you were before they rescued you. Why shouldn't they 'av a bit o' credit, poor loves? they're worn to rags by their work. And where would they get the money to rescue us if we was to let on we're no worse than other people? You know what ladies and gentlemen are.

PRICE: Thievin swine! Wish I 'ad their job, Rummy, all the same. Wot does Rummy stand for? Pet name p'raps?

RUMMY: Short for Romola.

PRICE: For wot!?

RUMMY: Romola. It was out of a new book.° Somebody me mother wanted me to grow up like.

PRICE: We're companions in misfortune, Rummy. Both of us got names that nobody cawn't pronounce. Consequently I'm Snobby and you're Rummy because Bill and Sally wasn't good enough for our parents. Such is life!

RUMMY: Who saved you, Mr. Price? Was it Major Barbara?

PRICE: No: I come here on my own. I'm goin' to be Bronterre O'Brien Price, the converted painter. I know wot they like. I'll tell 'em how I blasphemed and gambled and wopped my poor old mother—

RUMMY (*shocked*): Used you to beat your mother?

PRICE: Not likely. She used to beat me. No matter: you come and listen to the converted painter, and you'll hear how she was a pious woman that taught me my prayers at 'er knee, and how I used to come home drunk and drag her out o' the bed be 'er snow-white 'airs, an' lam into 'er with the poker.

RUMMY: That's what's so unfair to us women. Your confessions is just as big lies as ours: you don't tell what you really done no more than us; but you men can tell your lies right out at the meetin's and be made much of for it; while the sort o' confessions we 'az to make 'az to be whispered to one lady at a time. It ain't right, spite of all their piety.

PRICE: Right! Do you s'pose the Army 'd be allowed if it went and did right? Not much. It combs our 'air and makes us good little blokes to be robbed and put upon. But I'll play the game as good as any of 'em. I'll see somebody struck by lightnin', or hear a voice sayin' "Snobby Price: where will you spend eternity?" I'll 'ave a time of it, I tell you.

RUMMY: You won't be let drink, though.

PRICE: I'll take it out in gorspellin', then. I don't want to drink if I can get fun enough any other way.

(JENNY HILL, *a pale, overwrought, pretty Salvation lass of eighteen, comes in through the yard gate, leading* PETER SHIRLEY, *a half hardened, half worn-out elderly man, weak with hunger.*)

JENNY (*supporting him*): Come! pluck up. I'll get you something to eat. You'll be all right then.

PRICE (*rising and hurrying officiously to take the old man off* JENNY'S *hands*): Poor old man! Cheer up, brother: you'll find rest and peace and 'appiness 'ere. Hurry up with the food, miss: 'e's fair done. (JENNY *hurries into the shelter.*) 'Ere, buck up, daddy! she's fetchin y'a thick slice o' bread'n treacle, an' a mug o' skyblue.° (*He seats him at the corner of the table.*)

RUMMY (*gaily*): Keep up your old 'art! Never say die!

SHIRLEY: I'm not an old man. I'm only forty-six. I'm

---

fly, sharp, shrewd.   **new book,** probably George Eliot's historical novel, *Romola,* first published in the early 1860's.

skyblue, diluted, watery milk.

as good as ever I was. The grey patch come in my hair before I was thirty. All it wants is three pennorth o' hair dye: am I to be turned on the streets to starve for it? Holy God! I've worked ten to twelve hours a day since I was thirteen, and paid my way all through; and now am I to be thrown into the gutter and my job given to a young man that can do it no better than me because I've black hair that goes white at the first change?

PRICE (*cheerfully*): No good jawrin' about it. You're only a jumped-up, jerked-off, 'orspittle-turned-out incurable of an ole workin' man: who cares about you? Eh? Make the thievin' swine give you a meal: they've stole many a one from you. Get a bit o' your own back. (JENNY *returns with the usual meal.*) There you are, brother. Awsk a blessin' an' tuck that into you.

SHIRLEY (*looking at it ravenously but not touching it, and crying like a child*): I never took anything before.

JENNY (*petting him*): Come, come! the Lord sends it to you: he wasn't above taking bread from his friends; and why should you be? Besides, when we find you a job you can pay us for it if you like.

SHIRLEY (*eagerly*): Yes, yes: that's true. I can pay you back: it's only a loan. (*Shivering.*) Oh Lord! oh Lord! (*He turns to the table and attacks the meal ravenously.*)

JENNY: Well, Rummy, are you more comfortable now?

RUMMY: God bless you, lovey! you've fed my body and saved my soul, haven't you? (JENNY, *touched, kisses her.*) Sit down and rest a bit: you must be ready to drop.

JENNY: I've been going hard since morning. But there's more work than we can do. I mustn't stop.

RUMMY: Try a prayer for just two minutes. You'll work all the better after.

JENNY (*her eyes lighting up*): Oh isn't it wonderful how a few minutes prayer revives you! I was quite lightheaded at twelve o'clock, I was so tired; but Major Barbara just sent me to pray for five minutes; and I was able to go on as if I had only just begun. (*to* PRICE) Did you have a piece of bread?

PRICE (*with unction*): Yes, miss; but I've got the piece that I value more; and that's the peace that passeth hall hannerstennin.

RUMMY (*fervently*): Glory Hallelujah!

(BILL WALKER, *a rough customer of about twenty-five, appears at the yard gate and looks malevolently at* JENNY.)

JENNY: That makes me so happy. When you say that, I feel wicked for loitering here. I must get to work again.

(*She is hurrying to the shelter, when the newcomer moves quickly up to the door and intercepts her. His manner is so threatening that she retreats as he comes at her truculently, driving her down the yard.*)

BILL: Aw knaow you. You're the one that took aw'y maw girl. You're the one that set 'er agen me. Well, I'm gowin' to 'ev 'er aht. Not that Aw care a carse for 'er or you: see? But Aw'll let 'er knaow; and Aw'll let you knaow. Aw'm goin' to give her a doin' that'll teach 'er to cat aw'y from me. Nah in wiv you and tell 'er to cam aht afore Aw cam in and kick 'er aht. Tell 'er Bill Walker wants 'er. She'll knaow wot thet means; and if she keeps me witin' it'll be worse. You stop to jawr beck at me; and Aw'll stawt on you: d'ye 'eah? There's your w'y. In you gow. (*He takes her by the arm and slings her towards the door of the shelter. She falls on her hand and knee.* RUMMY *helps her up again.*)

PRICE (*rising and venturing irresolutely toward* BILL): Easy there, mate. She ain't doin' you no 'arm.

BILL: 'Oo are you callin' mite? (*Standing over him threateningly.*) Youre gowin' to stend up for 'er, aw yer? Put ap your 'ends.

RUMMY (*running indignantly to him to scold him*): Oh, you great brute— (*He instantly swings his left hand back against her face. She screams and reels back to the trough, where she sits down, covering her bruised face with her hands and rocking herself and moaning with pain.*)

JENNY (*going to her*): Oh, God forgive you! How could you strike an old woman like that?

BILL (*seizing her by the hair so violently that she also screams, and tearing her away from the old woman*): You Gawd forgimme again and Aw'll Gawd forgive you one on the jawr thet'll stop you pryin' for a week. (*Holding her and turning fiercely on* PRICE.) 'Ev you ennything to s'y agen it?

PRICE (*intimidated*): No, matey, she ain't anything to do with me.

BILL: Good job for you! Aw'd pat two meals into you and fawt you with one finger arter, you stawved cur. (*to* JENNY) Nah are you gown' to fetch aht Mog Ebbijem: or em Aw to knock your fice off you and fetch her meself?

JENNY (*writhing in his grasp*): Oh, please, someone go in and tell Major Barbara—(*She screams again as he wrenches her head down; and* PRICE *and* RUMMY *flee into the shelter.*)

BILL: You want to gow in and tell your Mijor of me, do you?

JENNY: Oh, please, don't drag my hair. Let me go.

BILL: Do you or down't you? (*She stifles a scream.*) Yus or nao?

JENNY: God give me strength—

BILL (*striking her with his fist in the face*): Gow an' shaw her thet, and tell her if she wants one lawk it to cam and interfere with me. (JENNY, *crying with pain, goes into the shed. He goes to the form and addresses the old man.*) 'Eah: finish your mess; and git aht o' maw w'y.

SHIRLEY (*springing up and facing him fiercely, with the mug in his hand*): You take a liberty with me, and I'll smash you over the face with the mug and cut your eye out. Ain't you satisfied—young whelps like you—with takin' the bread out o' the mouths of your elders that have brought you up and slaved for you, but you must come shovin and cheekin' and bullyin' in here, where the bread o' charity is sickenin' in our stummicks?

BILL (*contemptuously, but backing a little*): Wot good are you, you aold palsy mag? Wot good are you?

SHIRLEY: As good as you and better. I'll do a day's work agen you or any fat young soaker of your age. Go and take my job at Horrockses, where I worked for ten year. They want young men there: they can't afford to keep men over forty-five. They're very sorry—give you a character and happy to help you to get anything suited to your years—sure a steady man won't be long out of a job. Well, let 'em try you. They'll find the differ. What do you know? Not as much as how to beeyave yourself—layin' your dirty fist across the mouth of a respectable woman!

BILL: Downt provowk me to l'y it acrost yours: d'ye 'eah?

SHIRLEY (*with blighting contempt*): Yes: you like an old man to hit, don't you, when you've finished with the women. I ain't seen you hit a young one yet.

BILL (*stung*): You loy, you aold soupkitchener, you. There was a yang menn 'eah. Did Aw offer to 'itt him or did Aw not?

SHIRLEY: Was he starvin' or was he not? Was he a man or only a crosseyed thief an' a loafer? Would you hit my son-in-law's brother?

BILL: 'Oo's 'ee?

SHIRLEY: Todger Fairmile o' Balls Pond. Him that won £20 off the Japanese wrastler at the music hall by standin' out 17 minutes 4 seconds agen him.

BILL (*sullenly*): Aw'm nao music 'awl wrastler. Ken he box?

SHIRLEY: Yes: an' you can't.

BILL: Wot! Aw cawn't, cawn't Aw? Wot's thet you s'y? (*Threatening him.*)

SHIRLEY (*not budging an inch*): Will you box Todger Fairmile if I put him on to you? Say the word.

BILL (*subsiding with a slouch*): Aw'll stend ap to enny menn alawv, if he was ten Todger Fairmawls. But Aw don't set ap to be a perfeshnal.

SHIRLEY (*looking down on him with unfathomable disdain*): You box! Slap an old woman with the back o' your hand! You hadn't even the sense to hit her where a magistrate couldn't see the mark of it you silly young lump of conceit and ignorance. Hit a girl in the jaw and on'y make her cry! If Todger Fairmile'd done it, she wouldn't 'a got up inside o' ten minutes, no more than you would if he got on to you. Yah! I'd set about you myself if I had a week's feedin' in me instead o' two months' starvation. (*He turns his back on him and sits down moodily at the table.*)

BILL (*following him and stooping over him to drive the taunt in*): You loy! you've the bread and treacle in you that you cam 'eah to beg.

SHIRLEY (*bursting into tears*): Oh God! it's true: I'm only an old pauper on the scrap heap. (*Furiously.*) But you'll come to it yourself; and then you'll know. You'll come to it sooner than a teetotaller like me, fillin' yourself with gin at this hour o' the mornin!

BILL: Aw'm nao gin drinker, you oald lawr; bat wen Aw want to give my girl a bloomin' good 'awdin' Aw lawk to 'ev a bit o' devil in me: see? An 'eah Aw emm, talking to a rotten aold blawter like you stead o' given' 'er wot for. (*Working himself into a rage.*) Aw'm goin' in there to fetch her aht. (*He makes vengefully for the shelter door.*)

SHIRLEY: You're goin' to the station on a stretcher, more likely; and they'll take the gin and the devil out of you there when they get you inside. You mind what you're about: the major here is the Earl o' Stevenage's granddaughter.

BILL (*checked*): Garn!

SHIRLEY: You'll see.

BILL (*his resolution oozing*): Well, Aw ain't dan nathin' to 'er.

SHIRLEY: S'pose she said you did! who'd believe you?

BILL (*very uneasy, skulking back to the corner of the penthouse*): Gawd! there's no jastice in this cantry. To think wot them people can do! Aw'm as good as 'er.

SHIRLEY: Tell her so. It's just what a fool like you would do.

(BARBARA, *brisk and businesslike, comes from the shelter with a note book, and addresses herself to* SHIRLEY. BILL, *cowed, sits down in the corner on a form, and turns his back on them.*)

BARBARA: Good morning.

SHIRLEY (*standing up and taking off his hat*): Good morning, miss.

BARBARA: Sit down: make yourself at home. (*He hesitates; but she puts a friendly hand on his shoulder and makes him obey.*) Now then! since you've made friends with us, we want to know all about you. Names and addresses and trades.

SHIRLEY: Peter Shirley. Fitter. Chucked out two months ago because I was too old.

BARBARA (*not at all surprised*): You'd pass still. Why didn't you dye your hair?

SHIRLEY: I did. Me age come out at a coroner's inquest on me daughter.

BARBARA: Steady?

SHIRLEY: Teetotaller. Never out of a job before. Good worker. And sent to the knackers like an old horse!

BARBARA: No matter: if you did your part God will do his.

SHIRLEY (*suddenly stubborn*): My religion's no concern of anybody but myself.

BARBARA (*guessing*): I know. Secularist?

SHIRLEY (*hotly*): Did I offer to deny it?

BARBARA: Why should you? My own father's a Secularist, I think. Our Father—yours and mine—fulfills himself in many ways; and I daresay he knew what he was about when he made a Secularist of you. So buck up, Peter! we can always find a job for a steady man like you. (SHIRLEY, *disarmed and a little bewildered, touches his hat. She turns from him to* BILL.) What's your name?

BILL (*insolently*): Wot's thet to you?

BARBARA (*calmly making a note*): Afraid to give his name. Any trade?

BILL: 'Oo's afride to give 'is nime? (*Doggedly, with a sense of heroically defying the House of Lords in the person of Lord Stevenage.*) If you want to bring a chawge agen me, bring it. (*She waits, unruffled.*) Moy nime's Bill Walker.

BARBARA (*as if the name were familiar: trying to remember how*): Bill Walker? (*Recollecting.*) Oh, I know: you're the man that Jenny Hill was praying for inside just now. (*She enters his name in her note book.*)

BILL: 'Oo's Jenny 'Ill? And wot call 'as she to pr'y for me?

BARBARA: I don't know. Perhaps it was you that cut her lip.

BILL (*defiantly*): Yus, it was me that cat her lip. Aw ain't afride o' you.

BARBARA: How could you be, since you're not afraid of God? You're a brave man, Mr. Walker. It takes some pluck to do our work here; but none of us dare lift our hand against a girl like that, for fear of our father in heaven.

BILL (*sullenly*): I want nan o' your kentin' jawr.° I spowse you think Aw cam 'eah to beg from you, like this demmiged lot 'eah. Not me. Aw down't want your bread and scripe° and ketlep.° Aw don't b'lieve in your Gawd, no more than you do yourself.

---

kentin' jawr, canting jaw; i.e. Salvation Army talk.
scripe, thinly spread butter.   *ketlep,* thin drink, usually tea and milk.

BARBARA (*sunnily apologetic and ladylike, as on a new footing with him*): Oh, I beg your pardon for putting your name down, Mr. Walker. I didn't understand. I'll strike it out.

BILL (*taking this as a slight, and deeply wounded by it*): 'Eah! you let maw nime alown. Ain't it good enaff to be in your book?

BARBARA (*considering*): Well, you see, there's no use putting down your name unless I can do something for you, is there? What's your trade?

BILL (*still smarting*): Thets nao concern o' yours.

BARBARA: Just so. (*Very businesslike.*) I'll put you down as (*Writing.*) the man who—struck—poor little Jenny Hill—in the mouth.

BILL (*rising threateningly*): See 'eah. Awve 'ed enaff o' this.

BARBARA (*quite sunny and fearless*): What did you come to us for?

BILL: Aw cam for maw gel, see? Aw cam to tike her aht o' this and to brike 'er jawr for 'er.

BARBARA (*complacently*): You see I was right about your trade. (BILL, *on the point of retorting furiously, finds himself, to his great shame and terror, in danger of crying instead. He sits down again suddenly.*) What's her name?

BILL (*dogged*): 'Er nime's Mog Ebbijem: thet's wot her nime is.

BARBARA: Mog Habbijam! Oh, she's gone to Canning Town, to our barracks there.

BILL (*fortified by his resentment of* MOG's *perfidy*): Is she? (*Vindictively.*) Then Aw'm gowin' to Kennintahn arter her. (*He crosses to the gate; hesitates; finally comes back at* BARBARA.) Are you loyin' to me to git shat o' me?

BARBARA: I don't want to get shut of you. I want to keep you here and save your soul. You'd better stay: you're going to have a bad time today, Bill.

BILL: 'Oo's gowin' to give it to me? You, p'reps?

BARBARA: Someone you don't believe in. But you'll be glad afterwards.

BILL (*slinking off*): Aw'll gow to Kennintahn to be aht o' reach o' your tangue. (*Suddenly turning on her with intense malice.*) And if Aw down't fawnd Mog there, Aw'll cam beck and do two years for you, s'elp me Gawd if Aw downt!

BARBARA (*a shade kindlier, if possible*): It's no use, Bill. She's got another bloke.

BILL: Wot!

BARBARA: One of her own converts. He fell in love with her when he saw her with her soul saved, and her face clean, and her hair washed.

BILL (*surprised*): Wottud she wash it for, the carroty slat? It's red.

BARBARA: It's quite lovely now, because she wears a new look in her eyes with it. It's a pity you're too late. The new bloke has put your nose out of joint, Bill.

BILL: Aw'll put his nowse aht o' joint for him. Not that Aw care a carse for 'er, mawnd thet. But Aw'll teach her to drop me as if Aw was dirt. And Aw'll teach him to meddle with maw judy. Wots 'iz bleedin nime?

BARBARA: Sergeant Todger Fairmile.

SHIRLEY (*rising with grim joy*): I'll go with him, miss. I want to see them two meet. I'll take him to the infirmary when it's over.

BILL (*to* SHIRLEY, *with undissembled misgiving*): Is thet 'im you was speakin' on?

SHIRLEY: That's him.

BILL: 'Im that wrastled in the music 'awl?

SHIRLEY: The competitions at the National Sportin' Club was worth nigh a hundred a year to him. He's gev 'em up now for religion; so he's a bit fresh for want of the exercise he was accustomed to. He'll be glad to see you. Come along.

BILL: Wot's 'is wight?

SHIRLEY: Thirteen four. (BILL's *last hope expires.*)

BARBARA: Go and talk to him, Bill. He'll convert you.

SHIRLEY: He'll convert your head into a mashed potato.

BILL (*sullenly*): Aw ain't afride of 'im. Aw ain't afride of ennybody. Bat 'e can lick me. She's dan me. (*He sits down moodily on the edge of the horse trough.*)

SHIRLEY: You ain't goin'. I thought not. (*He resumes his seat.*)

BARBARA (*calling*): Jenny!

JENNY (*appearing at the shelter door with a plaster on the corner of her mouth*): Yes, Major.

BARBARA: Send Rummy Mitchens out to clear away here.

JENNY: I think she's afraid.

BARBARA (*her resemblance to her mother flashing out for a moment*): Nonsense! She must do as she's told.

JENNY (*calling into the shelter*): Rummy: the Major says you must come.

(JENNY *comes to* BARBARA, *purposely keeping on the side next* BILL, *lest he should suppose that she shrank from him or bore malice.*)

BARBARA: Poor little Jenny! Are you tired? (*Looking at the wounded cheek.*) Does it hurt?

JENNY: No: it's all right now. It was nothing.

BARBARA (*critically*): It was as hard as he could hit, I expect. Poor Bill! You don't feel angry with him, do you?

JENNY: Oh, no, no, no: indeed I don't, Major, bless his poor heart! (BARBARA *kisses her; and she runs away merrily into the shelter.* BILL *writhes with an agonizing return of his new and alarming symptoms, but says nothing.* RUMMY MITCHENS *comes from the shelter.*)

BARBARA (*going to meet* RUMMY): Now Rummy, bustle. Take in those mugs and plates to be washed; and throw the crumbs about for the birds.

(RUMMY *takes the three plates and mugs; but* SHIRLEY *takes back his mug from her, as there is still some milk left in it.*)

RUMMY: There ain't any crumbs. This ain't a time to waste good bread on birds.

PRICE (*appearing at the shelter door*): Gentleman come to see the shelter, Major. Says he's your father.

BARBARA: All right. Coming. (SNOBBY *goes back into the shelter, followed by* BARBARA.)

RUMMY (*stealing across to Bill and addressing him in a subdued voice, but with intense conviction*): I'd 'av the lor of you, you flat eared pignosed potwalloper, if she'd let me. You're no gentleman, to hit a lady in the face. (BILL, *with greater things moving in him, takes no notice.*)

SHIRLEY (*following her*): Here! in with you and don't get yourself into more trouble by talking.

RUMMY (*with hauteur*): I ain't 'ad the pleasure o' being hintroduced to you, as I can remember. (*She goes into the shelter with the plates.*)

SHIRLEY: That's the—

BILL (*savagely*): Downt you talk to me, d'ye 'eah? You lea' me alown, or Aw'll do you a mischief. Aw'm not dirt under your feet, ennywy.

SHIRLEY (*calmly*): Don't you be afeerd. You ain't such prime company that you need expect to be sought after. (*He is about to go into the shelter when* BARBARA *comes out, with* UNDERSHAFT *on her right.*)

BARBARA: Oh, there you are, Mr. Shirley! (*Between them.*) This is my father: I told you he was a Secularist, didn't I? Perhaps you'll be able to comfort one another.

UNDERSHAFT (*startled*): A Secularist! Not the least in the world: on the contrary, a confirmed mystic.

BARBARA: Sorry, I'm sure. By the way, papa, what is your religion? In case I have to introduce you again.

UNDERSHAFT: My religion? Well, my dear, I am a Millionaire. That is my religion.

BARBARA: Then I'm afraid you and Mr. Shirley won't be able to comfort one another after all. You're not a Millionaire, are you, Peter?

SHIRLEY: No; and proud of it.

UNDERSHAFT (*gravely*): Poverty, my friend, is not a thing to be proud of.

SHIRLEY (*angrily*): Who made your millions for you? Me and my like. What's kep' us poor? Keepin' you rich. I wouldn't have your conscience, not for all your income.

UNDERSHAFT: I wouldn't have your income, not for all your conscience, Mr. Shirley. (*He goes to the penthouse and sits down on a form.*)

BARBARA (*stopping* SHIRLEY *adroitly as he is about to retort*): You wouldn't think he was my father, would you, Peter? Will you go into the shelter and lend the lasses a hand for a while: we're worked off our feet.

SHIRLEY (*bitterly*): Yes, I'm in their debt for a meal, ain't I?

BARBARA: Oh, not because you're in their debt, but for love of them, Peter, for love of them. (*He cannot understand, and is rather scandalized.*) There! don't stare at me. In with you; and give that conscience of yours a holiday. (*Bustling him into the shelter.*)

SHIRLEY (*as he goes in*): Ah! it's a pity you never was trained to use your reason, miss. You'd have been a very taking lecturer on Secularism.

(BARBARA *turns to her father.*)

UNDERSHAFT: Never mind me, my dear. Go about your work; and let me watch it for a while.

BARBARA: All right.

UNDERSHAFT: For instance, what's the matter with that outpatient over there?

BARBARA (*looking at* BILL, *whose attitude has never changed, and whose expression of brooding wrath has deepened*): Oh, we shall cure him in no time. Just watch. (*She goes over to* BILL *and waits. He glances up at her and casts his eyes down again, uneasy, but grimmer than ever.*) It would be nice to just stamp on Mog Habbijam's face, wouldn't it, Bill?

BILL (*starting up from the trough in consternation*): It's a loy: Aw never said so. (*She shakes her head.*) 'Oo taold you wot was in moy mawnd?

BARBARA: Only your new friend.

BILL: Wot new friend?

BARBARA: The devil, Bill. When he gets round people they get miserable, just like you.

BILL (*with a heartbreaking attempt at devil-may-care cheerfulness*): Aw ain't miserable. (*He sits down again, and stretches his legs in an attempt to seem indifferent.*)

BARBARA: Well, if you're happy, why don't you look happy, as we do?

BILL (*his legs curling back in spite of him*): Aw'm 'eppy enaff. Aw tell you. Woy cawn't you lea' me alown? Wot 'ev I dan to you? Aw ain't smashed your fice, 'ev Aw?

BARBARA (*softly: wooing his soul*): It's not me that's getting at you, Bill.

BILL: 'Oo else is it?

BARBARA: Somebody that doesn't intend you to smash women's faces, I suppose. Somebody or something that wants to make a man of you.

BILL (*blustering*): Mike a menn o' me! Ain't Aw a menn? eh? 'Oo sez Aw'n not a menn?

BARBARA: There's a man in you somewhere, I suppose. But why did he let you hit poor little Jenny Hill? That wasn't very manly of him, was it?

BILL (*tormented*): 'Ev dan wiv it, Aw tell you. Chack it. Aw'm sick o' your Jenny 'Ill and 'er silly little fice.

BARBARA: Then why do you keep thinking about it? Why does it keep coming up against you in your mind? You're not getting converted, are you?

BILL (*with conviction*): Not ME. Not lawkly.

BARBARA: That's right, Bill. Hold out against it. Put out your strength. Don't let's get you cheap. Todger Fairmile said he wrestled for three nights against his salvation harder than he ever wrestled with the Jap at the music hall. He gave in to the Jap when his arm was going to break. But he didn't give in to his salvation until his heart was going to break. Perhaps you'll escape that. You havn't any heart, have you?

BILL: Wot d'ye mean? Woy ain't Aw got a 'awt the sime as ennybody else?

BARBARA: A man with a heart wouldn't have bashed poor little Jenny's face, would he?

BILL (*almost crying*): Ow, will you lea' me alown? 'Ev Aw ever offered to meddle with you, that you cam neggin' and provowkin' me lawk this? (*He writhes convulsively from his eyes to his toes.*)

BARBARA (*with a steady soothing hand on his arm and a gentle voice that never lets go*): It's your soul that's hurting you, Bill, and not me. We've been through it all ourselves. Come with us. Bill. (*He looks wildly round.*) To brave manhood on earth and eternal glory in heaven. (*He is on the point of breaking down.*) Come. (*A drum is heard in the shelter; and* BILL, *with a gasp, escapes from the spell as* BARBARA *turns quickly.* ADOLPHUS *enters from the shelter with a big drum.*) Oh! there you are, Dolly. Let me introduce a new friend of mine, Mr. Bill Walker. This is my bloke, Bill: Mr Cusins. (CUSINS *salutes with his drumstick.*)

BILL: Gowin to merry 'im?

BARBARA: Yes.

BILL (*fervently*): Gawd 'elp 'im! Gaw-aw-aw-awd 'elp 'im!

BARBARA: Why? Do you think he won't be happy with me?

BILL: Awve aony 'ed to stend it for a mawnin': 'e'll 'ev to stend it for a lawftawm.

CUSINS: That is a frightful reflection, Mr. Walker. But I can't tear myself away from her.

BILL: Well, Aw ken. (*to* BARBARA) 'Eah! do you knaow where Aw'm gowin to, and wot Aw'm gowin' to do?

BARBARA: Yes: you're going to heaven; and you're coming back here before the week's out to tell me so.

BILL: You loy. Aw'm gowin to Kennintahn, to spit in Todger Fairmawl's eye. Aw bashed Jenny 'Ill's fice; an nar Aw'll git me aown fice beshed and cam beck and shaow it to 'er. 'Ee'll 'itt me 'ardern Aw 'itt er. That'll mike us square. (*to* ADOLPHUS) Is that fair or it is not? You're a genlm'n: you aughter knaow.

BARBARA: Two black eyes won't make one white one, Bill.

BILL: Aw didn't awst you. Cawnt you never keep your mahth shat? Oy awst the genlm'n.

CUSINS (*reflectively*): Yes: I think you're right, Mr. Walker. Yes: I should do it. It's curious: it's exactly what an ancient Greek would have done.

BARBARA: But what good will it do?

CUSINS: Well, it will give Mr Fairmile some exercise; and it will satisfy Mr. Walker's soul.

BILL: Rot! there ain't nao sach a thing as a saoul. Ah kin you tell wevver Aw've a saoul or not? You never seen it.

BARBARA: I've seen it hurting you when you went against it.

BILL (*with compressed aggravation*): If you was maw gel and took the word aht o' me mahth lawk thet, Aw'd give you sathink you'd feel 'urtin, Aw would. (*to* ADOLPHUS) You tike maw tip, mite. Stop 'er jawr; or you'll doy afoah your tawn. (*With intense expression.*) Wore aht: thet's you'll be: wore aht. (*He goes away through the gate.*)

CUSINS (*looking after him*): I wonder!

BARBARA: Dolly! (*Indignant, in her mother's manner.*)

CUSINS: Yes, my dear, it's very wearing to be in love with you. If it lasts, I quite think I shall die young.

BARBARA: Should you mind?

CUSINS: Not at all. (*He is suddenly softened, and kisses her over the drum, evidently not for the first time, as people cannot kiss over a big drum without practice.* UNDERSHAFT *coughs.*)

BARBARA: It's all right, papa, we've not forgotten you. Dolly: explain the place to papa: I havn't time. (*She goes busily into the shelter.*)

(UNDERSHAFT *and* ADOLPHUS *now have the yard to themselves.* UNDERSHAFT, *seated on a form, and still keenly attentive, looks hard at* ADOLPHUS. ADOLPHUS *looks hard at him.*)

UNDERSHAFT: I fancy you guess something of what is in my mind, Mr Cusins. (CUSINS *flourishes his drumsticks as if in the act of beating a lively rataplan, but makes no sound.*) Exactly so. But suppose Barbara finds you out!

CUSINS: You know, I do not admit that I am imposing on Barbara. I am quite genuinely interested in the views of the Salvation Army. The fact is, I am a sort of collector of religions; and the curious thing is that I find I can believe them all. By the way, have you any religion?

UNDERSHAFT: Yes.

CUSINS: Anything out of the common?

UNDERSHAFT: Only that there are two things necessary to Salvation.

CUSINS (*disappointed, but polite*): Ah, the Church Cate-chism. Charles Lomax also belongs to the Established Church.

UNDERSHAFT: The two things are—

CUSINS: Baptism and—

UNDERSHAFT: No. Money and gunpowder.

CUSINS (*surprised, but interested*): That is the general opinion of our governing classes. The novelty is in hearing any man confess it.

UNDERSHAFT: Just so.

CUSINS: Excuse me: is there any place in your religion for honor, justice, truth, love, mercy and so forth?

UNDERSHAFT: Yes: they are the graces and luxuries of a rich, strong, and safe life.

CUSINS: Suppose one is forced to choose between them and money or gunpowder?

UNDERSHAFT: Choose money and gunpowder; for without enough of both you cannot afford the others.

CUSINS: That is your religion?

UNDERSHAFT: Yes.

(*The cadence of this reply makes a full close in the conversation.* CUSINS *twists his face dubiously and contemplates* UNDERSHAFT. UNDERSHAFT *contemplates him.*)

CUSINS: Barbara won't stand that. You will have to choose between your religion and Barbara.

UNDERSHAFT: So will you, my friend. She will find out that that drum of yours is hollow.

CUSINS: Father Undershaft: you are mistaken: I am a sincere Salvationist. You do not understand the Salvation Army. It is the army of joy, of love, of courage: it has banished the fear and remorse and despair of the old hell-ridden evangelical sects: it marches to fight the devil with trumpet and drum, with music and dancing, with banner and palm, as becomes a sally from heaven by its happy garrison. It picks the waster out of the public house and makes a man of him: it finds a worm wriggling in a back kitchen, and lo! a woman! Men and women of rank too, sons and daughters of the Highest. It takes the poor professor of Greek, the most artificial and self-suppressed of human creatures, from his meal of roots, and lets loose the rhapsodist in him; reveals the true worship of Dionysos to him; sends him down the public street drumming dithyrambs. (*He plays a thundering flourish on the drum.*)

UNDERSHAFT: You will alarm the shelter.

CUSINS: Oh, they are accustomed to these sudden ecstasies of piety. However, if the drum worries you— (*He pockets the drumsticks; unhooks the drum; and stands it on the ground opposite the gateway.*)

UNDERSHAFT: Thank you.

CUSINS: You remember what Euripides says about your money and gunpowder?

UNDERSHAFT: No.

CUSINS (*declaiming*):

>   One and another
> In money and guns may outpass his brother;
> And men in their millions float and flow
> And seethe with a million hopes as leaven;
> And they win their will; or they miss their will;
> And their hopes are dead or are pined for still;
>   But whoe'er can know
>   As the long days go
> That to live is happy, has found his heaven.

My translation: what do you think of it?

UNDERSHAFT: I think, my friend, that if you wish to know, as the long days go, that to live is happy, you must first acquire money enough for a decent life, and power enough to be your own master.

CUSINS: You are damnably discouraging. (*He resumes his declamation.*)

>   Is it so hard a thing to see
>   That the spirit of God—whate'er it be—
> The law that abides and changes not, ages long,
> The Eternal and Nature-born: these things be strong?
> What else is Wisdom? What of Man's endeavor,
> Or God's high grace so lovely and so great?
> To stand from fear set free? to breathe and wait?
> To hold a hand uplifted over Fate?
> And shall not Barbara be loved for ever?

UNDERSHAFT: Euripides mentions Barbara, does he?

CUSINS: It is a fair translation. The word means Loveliness.

UNDERSHAFT: May I ask—as Barbara's father—how much a year she is to be loved for ever on?

CUSINS: As Barbara's father, that is more your affair than mine. I can feed her by teaching Greek: that is about all.

UNDERSHAFT: Do you consider it a good match for her?

CUSINS (*with polite obstinacy*): Mr Undershaft: I am in many ways a weak, timid, ineffectual person; and my health is far from satisfactory. But whenever I feel that I must have anything, I get it sooner or later. I feel that way about Barbara. I don't like marriage: I feel intensely afraid of it; and I don't know what I shall do with Barbara or what she will do with me. But I feel that I and nobody else must marry her. Please regard that as settled— Not that I wish to be arbitrary; but why should I waste your time in discussing what is inevitable?

UNDERSHAFT: You mean that you will stick at nothing: not even the conversion of the Salvation Army to the worship of Dionysos.

CUSINS: The business of the Salvation Army is to save, not to wrangle about the name of the pathfinder. Dionysos or another: what does it matter?

UNDERSHAFT (*rising and approaching him*): Professor Cusins: you are a young man after my own heart.

CUSINS: Mr Undershaft: you are, as far as I am able to gather, a most infernal old rascal; but you appeal very strongly to my sense of ironic humor.

(UNDERSHAFT *mutely offers his hand. They shake.*)

UNDERSHAFT (*suddenly concentrating himself*): And now to business.

CUSINS: Pardon me. We were discussing religion. Why go back to such an uninteresting and unimportant subject as business?

UNDERSHAFT: Religion is our business at present, because it is through religion alone that we can win Barbara.

CUSINS: Have you, too, fallen in love with Barbara?

UNDERSHAFT: Yes, with a father's love.

CUSINS: A father's love for a grown-up daughter is the most dangerous of all infatuations. I apologize for mentioning my own pale, coy, mistrustful fancy in the same breath with it.

UNDERSHAFT: Keep to the point. We have to win her; and we are neither of us Methodists.

CUSINS: That doesn't matter. The power Barbara wields here—the power that wields Barbara herself—is not Calvinism, not Presbyterianism, not Methodism—

UNDERSHAFT: Not Greek Paganism either, eh?

CUSINS: I admit that. Barbara is quite original in her religion.

UNDERSHAFT (*triumphantly*): Aha! Barbara Undershaft would be. Her inspiration comes from within herself.

CUSINS: How do you suppose it got there?

UNDERSHAFT (*in towering excitement*): It is the Undershaft inheritance. I shall hand on my torch to my daughter. She shall make my converts and preach my gospel!—

CUSINS: What! Money and gunpowder!

UNDERSHAFT: Yes, money and gunpowder; freedom and power; command of life and command of death.

CUSINS (*urbanely: trying to bring hin down to earth*): This is extremely interesting, Mr. Undershaft. Of course you know that you are mad.

UNDERSHAFT (*with redoubled force*): And you?

CUSINS: Oh, mad as a hatter. You are welcome to my secret since I have discovered yours. But I am astonished. Can a madman make cannons?

UNDERSHAFT: Would anyone else than a madman make them? And now (*With surging energy.*) question for question. Can a sane man translate Euripides?

CUSINS: No.

UNDERSHAFT (*seizing him by the shoulder*): Can a sane woman make a man of a waster or a woman of a worm?

CUSINS (*reeling before the storm*): Father Colossus—Mammoth Millionaire—

UNDERSHAFT (*pressing him*): Are there two mad people or three in this Salvation shelter to-day?

CUSINS: You mean Barbara is as mad as we are?

UNDERSHAFT (*pushing him lightly off and resuming his equanimity suddenly and completely*): Pooh, Professor! Let us call things by their proper names. I am a millionaire; you are a poet; Barbara is a savior of souls. What have we three to do with the common mob of slaves and idolaters? (*He sits down again with a shrug of contempt for the mob.*)

CUSINS: Take care! Barbara is in love with the common people. So am I. Have you never felt the romance of that love?

UNDERSHAFT (*cold and sardonic*): Have you ever been in love with Poverty, like St. Francis? Have you ever been in love with Dirt, like St. Simeon? Have you ever been in love with disease and suffering, like our nurses and philanthropists? Such passions are not virtues, but the most unnatural of all the vices. This love of the common people may please an earl's granddaugher and a university professor; but I have been a common man and a poor man; and it has no romance for me. Leave it to the poor to pretend that poverty is a blessing: leave it to the coward to make a religion of his cowardice by preaching humility: we know better than that. We three must stand together above the common people: how else can we help their children to climb up beside us? Barbara must belong to us, not to the Salvation Army.

CUSINS: Well, I can only say that if you think you will get her away from the Salvation Army by talking to her as you have been talking to me, you don't know Barbara.

UNDERSHAFT: My friend: I never ask for what I can buy.

CUSINS (*in a white fury*): Do I understand you to imply that you can buy Barbara?

UNDERSHAFT: No; but I can buy the Salvation Army.

CUSINS: Quite impossible.

UNDERSHAFT: You shall see. All religious organizations exist by selling themselves to the rich.

CUSINS: Not the Army. That is the Church of the poor.

UNDERSHAFT: All the more reason for buying it.

CUSINS: I don't think you quite know what the Army does for the poor.

UNDERSHAFT: Oh, yes, I do. It draws their teeth: that is enough for me—as a man of business—

CUSINS: Nonsense! It makes them sober—

UNDERSHAFT: I prefer sober workmen. The profits are larger.

CUSINS: —honest—

UNDERSHAFT: Honest workmen are the most economical.

CUSINS: —attached to their homes—

UNDERSHAFT: So much the better: they will put up with anything sooner than change their shop.

CUSINS: —happy—

UNDERSHAFT: An invaluable safeguard against revolution.

CUSINS: —unselfish—

UNDERSHAFT: Indifferent to their own interests, which suits me exactly.

CUSINS: —with their thoughts on heavenly things—

UNDERSHAFT (*rising*): And not on Trade Unionism nor Socialism. Excellent.

CUSINS (*revolted*): You really are an infernal old rascal.

UNDERSHAFT (*indicating* PETER SHIRLEY, *who has just come from the shelter and strolled dejectedly down the yard between them*): And this is an honest man?

SHIRLEY: Yes; and what 'av I got by it? (*He passes on bitterly and sits on the form, in the corner of the penthouse.*)

(SNOBBY PRICE, *beaming sanctimoniously, and* JENNY HILL, *with a tambourine full of coppers, come from the shelter and go to the drum, on which* JENNY *begins to count the money.*)

UNDERSHAFT (*replying to* SHIRLEY): Oh, your employers must have got a good deal by it from first to last.

(*He sits on the table, with one foot on the side form.* CUSINS, *overwhelmed, sits down on the same form nearer the shelter.* BARBARA *comes from the shelter to the middle of the yard. She is excited and a little overwrought.*)

BARBARA: We've just had a splendid experience meeting at the other gate in Cripps's Lane. I've hardly ever seen them so much moved as they were by your confession, Mr. Price.

PRICE: I could almost be glad of my past wickedness if I could believe that it would 'elp to keep hathers stright.

BARBARA: So it will, Snobby. How much, Jenny?

JENNY: Four and tenpence, Major.

BARBARA: Oh, Snobby, if you had given your poor mother just one more kick, we should have got the whole five shillings!

PRICE: If she heard you say that, miss, she'd be sorry I didn't. But I'm glad. Oh what a joy it will be to her when she hears I'm saved!

UNDERSHAFT: Shall I contribute the odd twopence,

Barbara? The millionaire's mite, eh? (*He takes a couple of pennies from his pocket.*)

BARBARA: How did you make that twopence?

UNDERSHAFT: As usual. By selling cannons, torpedoes, submarines, and my new patent Grand Duke hand grenade.

BARBARA: Put it back in your pocket. You can't buy your Salvation here for twopence: you must work it out.

UNDERSHAFT: Is twopence not enough? I can afford a little more, if you press me.

BARBARA: Two million millions would not be enough. There is bad blood on your hands; and nothing but good blood can cleanse them. Money is no use. Take it away. (*She turns to* CUSINS.) Dolly: you must write another letter for me to the papers. (*He makes a wry face.*) Yes: I know you don't like it; but it must be done. The starvation this winter is beating us: everybody is unemployed. The General says we must close this shelter if we can't get more money. I force the collections at the meetings until I am ashamed: don't I, Snobby?

PRICE: It's a fair treat to see you work it, Miss. The way you get them up from three-and-six to four-and-ten with that hymn, penny by penny and verse by verse was a caution. Not a Cheap Jack° on Mile End Waste could touch you at it.

BARBARA: Yes; but I wish we could do without it. I am getting at last to think more of the collection than of the people's souls. And what are those hatfuls of pence and halfpence? We want thousands! tens of thousands! hundreds of thousands! I want to convert people, not to be always begging for the Army in a way I'd die sooner than beg for myself.

UNDERSHAFT (*in profound irony*): Genuine unselfishness is capable of anything, my dear.

BARBARA (*unsuspectingly, as she turns away to take the money from the drum and put it in a cash bag she carries*): Yes, isn't it? (UNDERSHAFT *looks sardonically at* CUSINS.)

CUSINS (*aside to* UNDERSHAFT): Mephistopheles! Machiavelli!

BARBARA (*tears coming into her eyes as she ties the bag and pockets it*): How are we to feed them? I can't talk religion to a man with bodily hunger in his eyes. (*Almost breaking down.*) It's frightful.

JENNY (*running to her*): Major, dear—

BARBARA (*rebounding*): No: don't comfort me. It will be all right. We shall get the money.

UNDERSHAFT: How?

JENNY: By praying for it, of course. Mrs. Baines says she prayed for it last night; and she has never

prayed for it in vain: never once. (*She goes to the gate and looks out into the street.*)

BARBARA (*who has dried her eyes and regained her composure*): By the way, dad, Mrs. Baines has come to march with us to our big meeting this afternoon; and she is very anxious to meet you, for some reason or other. Perhaps she'll convert you.

UNDERSHAFT: I shall be delighted, my dear.

JENNY (*at the gate: excitedly*): Major! Major! here's that man back again.

BARBARA: What man?

JENNY: The man that hit me. Oh, I hope he's coming back to join us.

(BILL WALKER, *with frost on his jacket, comes through the gate, his hands deep in his pockets and his chin sunk between his shoulders, like a cleaned-out gambler. He halts between* BARBARA *and the drum.*)

BARBARA: Hullo, Bill! Back already!

BILL (*nagging at her*): Bin talkin' ever sence, 'ev you?

BARBARA: Pretty nearly. Well, has Todger paid you out for poor Jenny's jaw?

BILL: Nao 'e ain't.

BARBARA: I thought your jacket looked a bit snowy.

BILL: Sao it is snaowy. You want to knaow where the snaow cam from, down't you?

BARBARA: Yes.

BILL: Well, it cam from orf the grahnd in Pawkinses Corner in Kennintahn. It got rabbed orf be maw shaoulders: see?

BARBARA: Pity you didn't rub some off with your knees, Bill! that would have done you a lot of good.

BILL (*with sour mirthless humor*): Aw was sivin' another menn's knees at the tawm. 'E was kneelin' on moy 'ed, 'e was.

JENNY: Who was kneeling on your head?

BILL: Todger was. 'E was pryin' for me: pryin' camfortable wiv me as a cawpet. Sow was Mog. Sao was the aol bloomin' meetin'. Mog she sez "Ow Lawd brike is stabborn sperrit; bat down't 'urt is dear 'art." Thet was wot she said. "Downt 'urt is dear 'art"! An 'er blowk—thirteen stun four!—kneelin' wiv all is wight on me. Fanny, aint it?

JENNY: Oh no. We're so sorry, Mr. Walker.

BARBARA (*enjoying it frankly*): Nonsense! of course it's funny. Served you right, Bill! You must have done something to him first.

BILL (*doggedly*): Aw did wot Aw said Aw'd do. Aw spit in 'is eye. 'E looks ap at the sky and sez. "Ow that Aw should be fahnd worthy to be spit upon for the gospel's sike!" 'e sez; an Mog sez "Glaory 'Allelloolier!"; an' then 'e called me Braddher, and dahned me as if Aw was a kid and 'e was me mather worshin' me a Setterda nawt. Aw 'ednt jast nao shaow wiv 'im at all. 'Arf the street

___
Cheap Jack, a salesman, usually hawking his ware on sidewalks.

pr'yed; and the tather 'arf larfed fit to split theirselves. (*to* BARBARA) There! are you settisfawd nah?

BARBARA (*her eyes dancing*): Wish I'd been there, Bill.

BILL: Yus: you'd 'a got in a hextra bit o' talk on me, wouldn't you?

JENNY: I'm so sorry, Mr. Walker.

BILL (*fiercely*): Down't you gow bein' sorry for me: you've no call. Listen 'eah. Aw browk your jawr.

JENNY: No, it didn't hurt me: indeed it didn't, except for a moment. It was only that I was frightened.

BILL: Aw down't want to be forgive be you, or be ennybody. Wot Aw did Aw'll p'y for. Aw trawd to gat me aown jawr browk to settisfaw you—

JENNY (*distressed*): Oh no—

BILL (*impatiently*): Tell y' Aw did: cawnt you listen to wot's bein' taold you? All Aw got be it was being mide a sawt of in the pablic street for me pines. Well, if Aw cawnt settisfaw you one wy, Aw ken anather. Listen 'eah! Aw 'ed two quid sived agen the frost; an Aw've a pahnd of it left. A mite o'mawn last week 'ed words with the judy 'e's gowin to merry. 'E give 'er wotfor; an' 'e's bin fawned fifteen bob. 'E 'ed a rawt to 'itt 'er cause they was gowin to be merrid; but Aw 'ednt nao rawt to 'itt you; sao put anather fawv bob on an cal it a pahnd's worth. (*He produces a sovereign.*) 'Eahs the manney. Tike it; and lets 'ev no more o' your forgivin' an' pryin' and your Mijor jawrin' me. Let wot Aw dan be dan an' pide for; and let there be a end of it.

JENNY: Oh, I couldn't take it, Mr. Walker. But if you would give a shilling or two to poor Rummy Mitchens! you really did hurt her; and she's old.

BILL (*contemptuously*): Not lawkly. Aw'd give her anather as soon as look at 'er. Let her 'ev the lawr o' me as she threatened! She ain't forgiven me: not mach. Wot Aw dan to 'er is not on me mawnd—wot she (*Indicating* BARBARA.) mawt call on me conscience—no more than stickin' a pig. It's this Christian gime o' yours that Aw wown't 'ev pl'yed agen me: this bloomin' forgivin' an neggin' an jawrin' that mikes a menn thet sore that 'iz lawf's a burden to 'im. Aw wown't 'ev it. Aw tell you; sao tike your manney and stop thraowin' your silly beshed fice hap agen me.

JENNY: Major: may I take a little of it for the Army?

BARBARA: No: the Army is not to be bought. We want your soul, Bill; and we'll take nothing less.

BILL (*bitterly*): Aw knaow. Me an' maw few shillin's is not good enaff for you. You're a earl's grendorter, you are. Nathink less than a 'anderd pahnd for you.

UNDERSHAFT: Come, Barbara! you could do a great deal of good with a hundred pounds. If you will set this gentleman's mind at ease by taking his pound, I will give the other ninety-nine.

(BILL, *dazed by such opulence, instinctively touches his cap.*)

BARBARA: Oh, you're too extravagant, papa. Bill offers twenty pieces of silver. All you need offer is the other ten. That will make the standard price to buy anybody who's for sale. I'm not; and the Army's not. (*to* BILL) You'll never have another quiet moment, Bill, until you come round to us. You can't stand out against your salvation.

BILL (*sullenly*): Aw cawnt stend aht agen music 'awl wrastlers and awtful tangued women. Aw've offered to p'y. Aw can do no more. Tike it or leave it. There it is. (*He throws the sovereign on the drum, and sits down on the horse trough. The coin fascinates* SNOBBY PRICE, *who takes an early opportunity of dropping his cap on it.*)

(MRS BAINES *comes from the shelter. She is dressed as a Salvation Army Commissioner. She is an earnest looking woman of about forty, with a caressing urgent voice, and an appealing manner.*)

BARBARA: This is my father, Mrs Baines (UNDERSHAFT *comes from the table taking his hat off with marked civility.*) Try what you can do with him. He won't listen to me, because he remembers what a fool I was when I was a baby. (*She leaves them together and chats with* JENNY.)

MRS BAINES: Have you been shewn over the shelter, Mr Undershaft? You know the work we're doing, of course.

UNDERSHAFT (*very civilly*): The whole nation knows it, Mrs. Baines.

MRS BAINES: No sir: the whole nation does not know it, or we should not be crippled as we are for want of money to carry our work through the length and breadth of the land. Let me tell you that there would have been rioting this winter in London but for us.

UNDERSHAFT: You really think so?

MRS BAINES: I know it, I remember 1886, when you rich gentlemen hardened your hearts against the cry of the poor. They broke the windows of your clubs in Pall Mall.

UNDERSHAFT (*gleaming with approval of their method*): And the Mansion House Fund went up next day from thirty thousand pounds to seventy-nine thousand! I remember quite well.

MRS BAINES: Well, won't you help me to get at the people? They won't break windows then. Come here, Price. Let me shew you to this gentleman. (PRICE *comes to be inspected.*) Do you remember the window breaking?

PRICE: My ole father thought it was the revolution, ma'am.

MRS BAINES: Would you break windows now?

PRICE: Oh no ma'am. The windows of 'eaven 'av bin

opened to me. I know now that the rich man is a sinner like myself.

RUMMY (*appearing above at the loft door*): Snobby Price!

SNOBBY: Wot is it?

RUMMY: Your mother's askin' for you at the other gate in Crippses Lane. She's heard about your confession. (PRICE *turns pale.*)

MRS BAINES: Go, Mr Price; and pray with her.

JENNY: You can go through the shelter, Snobby.

PRICE (*to* MRS BAINES): I couldn't face her now, ma'am, with all the weight of my sins fresh on me. Tell her she'll find her son at 'ome, waitin' for her in prayer. (*He skulks off through the gate, incidentally stealing the sovereign on his way out by picking up his cap from the drum.*)

MRS BAINES (*with swimming eyes*): You see how we take the anger and the bitterness against you out of their hearts, Mr. Undershaft.

UNDERSHAFT: It is certainly most convenient and gratifying to all large employers of labor, Mrs Baines.

MRS BAINES: Barbara: Jenny: I have good news: most wonderful news. (JENNY *runs to her.*) My prayers have been answered. I told you they would, Jenny, didn't I?

JENNY: Yes, yes.

BARBARA (*moving nearer to the drum*): Have we got money enough to keep the shelter open?

MRS BAINES: I hope we shall have enough to keep all the shelters open. Lord Saxmundham has promised us five thousand pounds—

BARBARA: Hooray!

JENNY: Glory!

MRS BAINES: —if—

BARBARA: "If!" If what?

MRS BAINES: —if five other gentlemen will give a thousand each to make it up to ten thousand.

BARBARA: Who is Lord Saxmundham? I never heard of him.

UNDERSHAFT (*who has pricked up his ears at the peer's name, and is now watching* BARBARA *curiously*): A new creation, my dear. You have heard of Sir Horace Bodger?

BARBARA: Bodger! Do you mean the distiller? Bodger's whisky!

UNDERSHAFT: That is the man. He is one of the greatest of our public benefactors. He restored the cathedral at Hakington. They made him a baronet for that. He gave half a million to the funds of his party: they made him a baron for that.

SHIRLEY: What will they give him for the five thousand?

UNDERSHAFT: There is nothing left to give him. So the five thousand, I should think, is to save his soul.

MRS BAINES: Heaven grant it may! Oh Mr Un-dershaft, you have some very rich friends. Can't you help us towards the other five thousand? We are going to hold a great meeting this afternoon at the Assembly Hall in the Mile End Road. If I could only announce that one gentleman had come forward to support Lord Saxmundham, others would follow. Don't you know somebody? couldn't you? wouldn't you? (*Her eyes fill with tears.*) Oh, think of those poor people, Mr. Undershaft: think of how much it means to them, and how little to a great man like you.

UNDERSHAFT (*sardonically gallant*): Mrs Baines: you are irresistible. I can't disappoint you; and I can't deny myself the satisfaction of making Bodger pay up. You shall have your five thousand pounds.

MRS BAINES: Thank God!

UNDERSHAFT: You don't thank me?

MRS BAINES: Oh sir, don't try to be cynical: don't be ashamed of being a good man. The Lord will bless you abundantly; and our prayers will be like a strong fortification round you all the days of your life. (*With a touch of caution.*) You will let me have the cheque to shew at the meeting, won't you? Jenny: go in and fetch a pen and ink. (JENNY *runs to the shelter door.*)

UNDERSHAFT: Do not disturb Miss Hill: I have a fountain pen. (JENNY *halts. He sits at the table and writes the cheque.* CUSINS *rises to make room for him. They all watch him silently.*)

BILL (*cynically, aside to* BARBARA, *his voice and accent horribly debased*): Wot prawce Selvytion nah?

BARBARA: Stop. (UNDERSHAFT *stops writing: they all turn to her in surprise.*) Mrs Baines: are you really going to take his money?

MRS BAINES (*astonished*): Why not, dear?

BARBARA: Why not! Do you know what my father is? Have you forgotten that Lord Saxmundham is Bodger the whisky man? Do you remember how we implored the County Council to stop him from writing Bodger's Whisky in letters of fire against the sky; so that the poor drink-ruined creatures on the Embankment could not wake up from their snatches of sleep without being reminded of their deadly thirst by that wicked sky sign? Do you know that the worst thing I have had to fight here is not the devil, but Bodger, Bodger, Bodger, with his whisky, his distilleries, and his tied houses?° Are you going to make our shelter another tied house for him, and ask me to keep it?

BILL: Rotten dranken whisky it is too.

MRS BAINES: Dear Barbara: Lord Saxmundham has a

---

tied houses, taverns owned directly or indirectly by a brewer who expects the bars to serve only his own products.

soul to be saved like any of us. If heaven has found the way to make a good use of his money, are we to set ourselves up against the answer to our prayers?

BARBARA: I know he has a soul to be saved. Let him come down here; and I'll do my best to help him to his salvation. But he wants to send his cheque down to buy us, and go on being as wicked as ever.

UNDERSHAFT (*with a reasonableness which* CUSINS *alone perceives to be ironical*): My dear Barbara: alcohol is a very necessary article. It heals the sick—

BARBARA: It does nothing of the sort.

UNDERSHAFT: Well, it assists the doctor: that is perhaps a less questionable way of putting it. It makes life bearable to millions of people who could not endure their existence if they were quite sober. It enables Parliament to do things at eleven at night that no sane person would do at eleven in the morning. Is it Bodger's fault that this inestimable gift is deplorably abused by less than one percent of the poor? (*He turns again to the table; signs the cheque; and crosses it.*)

MRS BAINES: Barbara: will there be less drinking or more if all those poor souls we are saving come tomorrow and find the doors of our shelters shut in their faces? Lord Saxmundham gives us the money to stop drinking—to take his own business from him.

CUSINS (*impishly*): Pure self-sacrifice on Bodger's part, clearly! Bless dear Bodger! (BARBARA *almost breaks down as* ADOLPHUS, *too, fails her.*)

UNDERSHAFT (*tearing out the cheque and pocketing the book as he rises and goes past* CUSINS *to* MRS BAINES): I also, Mrs Baines, may claim a little disinterestedness. Think of my business! think of the widows and orphans! the men and lads torn to pieces with shrapnel and poisoned with lyddite! (MRS BAINES *shrinks; but he goes on remorselessly.*) The oceans of blood, not one drop of which is shed in a really just cause! the ravaged crops! the peaceful peasants forced, women and men, to till their fields under the fire of opposing armies on pain of starvation! the bad blood of the fierce little cowards at home who egg on others to fight for the gratification of their national vanity! All this makes money for me: I am never richer, never busier than when the papers are full of it. Well, it is your work to preach peace on earth and good-will to men. (MRS BAINES'S *face lights up again.*) Every convert you make is a vote against war. (*Her lips move in prayer.*) Yet I give you this money to help you to hasten my own commercial ruin. (*He gives her the cheque.*)

CUSINS (*mounting the form in an ecstasy of mischief*): The millennium will be inaugurated by the unselfishness of Undershaft and Bodger. Oh be joyful!

(*He takes the drum-sticks from his pocket and flourishes them.*)

MRS BAINES (*taking the cheque*): The longer I live the more proof I see that there is an Infinite Goodness that turns everything to the work of salvation sooner or later. Who would have thought that any good could have come out of war and drink? And yet their profits are brought today to the feet of salvation to do its blessed work. (*She is affected to tears.*)

JENNY (*running to* MRS BAINES *and throwing her arms round her*): Oh dear! how blessed, how glorious it all is!

CUSINS (*in a convulsion of irony*): Let us seize this unspeakable moment. Let us march to the great meeting at once. Excuse me just an instant. (*He rushes into the shelter.* JENNY *takes her tambourine from the drum head.*)

MRS BAINES: Mr Undershaft: have you ever seen a thousand people fall on their knees with one impulse and pray? Come with us to the meeting. Barbara shall tell them that the Army is saved, and saved through you.

CUSINS (*returning impetuously from the shelter with a flag and a trombone, and coming between* MRS BAINES *and* UNDERSHAFT): You will carry the flag down the first street, Mrs. Baines. (*He gives her the flag.*) Mr Undershaft is a gifted trombonist: he shall intone an Olympian diapason to the West Ham Salvation March. (*Aside to* UNDERSHAFT, *as he forces the trombone on him.*) Blow, Machiavelli, blow.

UNDERSHAFT (*aside to him, as he takes the trombone*): The trumpet in Zion! (CUSINS *rushes to the drum, which he takes up and puts on.* UNDERSHAFT *continues, aloud.*) I will do my best. I could vamp a bass if I knew the tune.

CUSINS: It is a wedding chorus from one of Donizetti's operas,° but we have converted it. We convert everything to good here, including Bodger. You remember the chorus. "For thee immense rejoicing—*immenso giubilo—immenso giubilo.*" (*With drum obbligato.*) Rum tum ti tum tum tum tum ti ta—

BARBARA: Dolly: you are breaking my heart.

CUSINS: What is a broken heart more or less here? Dionysos Undershaft has descended. I am possessed.

MRS BAINES: Come, Barbara: I must have my dear Major to carry the flag with me.

JENNY: Yes, yes, Major darling.

(CUSINS *snatches the tambourine out of* JENNY'S *hand and mutely offers it to* BARBARA.)

---

one . . . operas, *Lucia di Lammermoor.*

634 / MAJOR BARBARA

BARBARA (coming forward a little as she puts the offer behind her with a shudder, whilst CUSINS recklessly tosses the tambourine back to JENNY and goes to the gate): I can't come.

JENNY: Not come!

MRS BAINES (with tears in her eyes): Barbara: do you think I am wrong to take the money?

BARBARA (impulsively going to her and kissing her): No, no: God help you dear, you must: you are saving the Army. Go; and may you have a great meeting!

JENNY: But arn't you coming?

BARBARA: No. (She begins taking off the silver S brooch from her collar.)

MRS BAINES: Barbara: what are you doing?

JENNY: Why are you taking your badge off? You can't be going to leave us, Major.

BARBARA (quietly): Father: come here.

UNDERSHAFT (coming to her): My dear! (Seeing that she is going to pin the badge on his collar, he retreats to the penthouse in some alarm.)

BARBARA (following him): Don't be frightened. (She pins the badge on and steps back toward the table, shewing him to the others.) There! It's not much for £5000, is it?

MRS BAINES: Barbara: if you won't come and pray with us, promise me you will pray for us.

BARBARA: I can't pray now. Perhaps I shall never pray again.

MRS BAINES: Barbara!

JENNY: Major!

BARBARA (almost delirious): I can't bear any more. Quick march!

CUSINS (calling to the procession in the street outside): Off we go. Play up, there! Immenso giubilo. (He gives the time with his drum; and the band strikes up the march, which rapidly becomes more distant as the procession moves briskly away.)

MRS BAINES: I must go, dear. You're overworked: you will be all right tomorrow. We'll never lose you. Now Jenny: step out with the old flag. Blood and Fire! (She marches out through the gate with her flag.)

JENNY: Glory Hallelujah! (Flourishing her tambourine and marching.)

UNDERSHAFT (to CUSINS, as he marches out past him easing the slide of his trombone): "My ducats and my daughter"!°

CUSINS (following him out): Money and gunpowder!

BARBARA: Drunkenness and Murder! My God: why hast thou forsaken me?

_____

My . . . daughter, Undershaft here echoes Shylock's reaction to his daughter Jessica's elopement with Lorenzo (The Merchant of Venice, II, viii, 17).

(She sinks on the form with her face buried in her hands. The march passes away into silence. BILL WALKER steals across to her.)

BILL (taunting): Wot prawce selvytion nah?

SHIRLEY: Don't you hit her when she's down.

BILL: She 'itt me wen aw wiz dahn. Waw shouldn't Aw git a bit o' me aown beck?

BARBARA (raising her head): I didn't take your money, Bill. (She crosses the yard to the gate and turns her back on the two men to hide her face from them.)

BILL (sneering after her): Naow, it warn't enaff for you. (Turning to the drum, he misses the money.) 'Ellow! If you ain't took it sammun else 'ez. Were's it gorn? Bly me if Jenny 'Ill didn't tike it arter all!

RUMMY (screaming at him from the loft): You lie, you dirty blackguard! Snobby Price pinched it off the drum when he took up his cap. I was up here all the time an see 'im do it.

BILL: Wot! Stowl maw manney! Waw didn't you call thief on him, you silly aold macker you?

RUMMY: To serve you aht for 'ittin me acrost the face. It's cost y'pahnd, that 'az. (Raising a paean of squalid triumph.) I done you. I'm even with you. I've 'ad it aht o' y—(BILL snatches up SHIRLEY'S mug and hurls it at her. She slams the loft door and vanishes. The mug smashes against the door and falls in fragments.)

BILL (beginning to chuckle): Tell us, aol menn, wot o'clock this mawnin' was it wen 'im as they call Snobby Prawce was sived?

BARBARA (turning to him more composedly, and with unspoiled sweetness): About half past twelve, Bill. And he pinched your pound at a quarter to two. I know. Well, you can't afford to lose it. I'll send it to you.

BILL (his voice and accent suddenly improving): Not if Aw wiz to stawve for it. Aw ain't to be bought.

SHIRLEY: Ain't you? You'd sell yourself to the devil for a pint o' beer; only there ain't no devil to make the offer.

BILL (unshamed): Sao Aw would, mite, and often 'ev, cheerful. But she cawn't baw me. (Approaching BARBARA.) You wanted maw saoul, did you? Well, you ain't got it.

BARBARA: I nearly got it, Bill. But we've sold it back to you for ten thousand pounds.

SHIRLEY: And dear at the money!

BARBARA: No, Peter: it was worth more than money.

BILL (salvationproof): It's nao good: you cawn't get rahnd me, nah. Aw down't b'lieve in it; and Aw've seen tod'y that Aw was rawt. (Going.) Sao long, aol soupkitchener! Ta, ta, Mijor Earl's Grendorter! (Turning at the gate.) Wot prawce selvytion nah? Snobby Prawce! Ha! ha!

BARBARA (offering her hand): Goodbye, Bill.

BILL (taken aback, half plucks his cap off; then shoves it on *again defiantly)*: Git aht. (BARBARA *drops her hand, discouraged. He has a twinge of remorse.*) But thet's aw rawt, you knaow. Nathink pasn'l. Naow mellice. Sao long, Judy. *(He goes.)*

BARBARA: No malice. So long, Bill.

SHIRLEY *(shaking his head)*: You make too much of him, Miss, in your innocence.

BARBARA *(going to him)*: Peter: I'm like you now. Cleaned out, and lost my job.

SHIRLEY: You've youth and hope. That's two better than me.

BARBARA: I'll get you a job, Peter. That's hope for you: the youth will have to be enough for me. *(She counts her money.)* I have just enough left for two teas at Lockharts,° a Rowton doss° for you, and my tram and bus home. *(He frowns and rises with offended pride. She takes his arm.)* Don't be proud, Peter: it's sharing between friends. And promise me you'll talk to me and not let me cry. *(She draws him toward the gate.)*

SHIRLEY: Well, I'm not accustomed to talk to the like of you—

BARBARA *(urgently)*: Yes, yes: you must talk to me. Tell me about Tom Paine's books and Bradlaugh's lectures.° Come along.

SHIRLEY: Ah, if you would only read Tom Paine in the proper spirit, Miss! *(They go out through the gate together.)*

ACT 3

(Next day after lunch LADY BRITOMART is writing in the library in Wilton Crescent. SARAH is reading in the armchair near the window. BARBARA, in ordinary fashionable dress, pale and brooding, is on the settee. CHARLES LOMAX enters. He starts on seeing BARBARA fashionably attired and in low spirits.)

LOMAX: You've left off your uniform!

(BARBARA says nothing; but an expression of pain passes over her face.)

LADY BRITOMART *(warning him in low tones to be careful)*: Charles!

LOMAX *(much concerned, coming behind the settee and bending sympathetically over BARBARA)*: I'm awfully sorry, Barbara. You know I helped you all I could with the concertina and so forth. *(Momentously.)* Still, I have never shut my eyes to the fact that there is a certain amount of tosh about the

---

Salvation Army. Now the claims of the Church of England—

LADY BRITOMART: That's enough, Charles. Speak of something suited to your mental capacity.

LOMAX: But surely the Church of England is suited to all our capacities.

BARBARA *(pressing his hand)*: Thank you for your sympathy, Cholly. Now go and spoon with Sarah.

LOMAX *(dragging a chair from the writing table and seating himself affectionately by SARAH's side)*: How is my ownest today?

SARAH: I wish you wouldn't tell Cholly to do things, Barbara. He always comes straight and does them. Cholly: we're going to the works this afternoon.

LOMAX: What works?

SARAH: The cannon works.

LOMAX: What? Your governor's shop!

SARAH: Yes.

LOMAX: Oh I say!

(CUSINS enters in poor condition. He also starts visibly when he sees BARBARA without her uniform.)

BARBARA: I expected you this morning, Dolly. Didn't you guess that?

CUSINS *(sitting down beside her)*: I'm sorry. I have only just breakfasted.

SARAH: But we've just finished lunch.

BARBARA: Have you had one of your bad nights?

CUSINS: No: I had rather a good night: in fact, one of the most remarkable nights I have ever passed.

BARBARA: The meeting?

CUSINS: No: after the meeting.

LADY BRITOMART: You should have gone to bed after the meeting. What were you doing?

CUSINS: Drinking.

LADY BRITOMART: } Adolphus!
SARAH: } Dolly!
BARBARA: } Dolly!
LOMAX: } Oh I say!

LADY BRITOMART: What were you drinking, may I ask?

CUSINS: A most devilish kind of Spanish burgundy, warranted free from added alcohol: a Temperance burgundy in fact. Its richness in natural alcohol made any addition superfluous.

BARBARA: Are you joking, Dolly?

CUSINS *(patiently)*: No. I have been making a night of it with the nominal head of this household: that is all.

LADY BRITOMART: Andrew made you drunk!

CUSINS: No: he only provided the wine. I think it was Dionyosos who made me drunk. *(to BARBARA)* I told you I was possessed.

LADY BRITOMART: You're not sober yet. Go home to bed at once.

Lockharts, *a fashionable tearoom in London.* Rowton doss, *Mr. Rowton owned a string of inexpensive lodging-houses (doss).* Bradlaugh's lectures, *Charles Bradlaugh (1833–1891), like Paine, advocated free-thought in religion and republicanism in politics.*

CUSINS: I have never before ventured to reproach you, Lady Brit; but how could you marry the Prince of Darkness?

LADY BRITOMART: It was much more excusable to marry him than to get drunk with him. That is a new accomplishment of Andrew's, by the way. He usen't to drink.

CUSINS: He doesn't now. He only sat there and completed the wreck of my moral basis, the rout of my convictions, the purchase of my soul. He cares for you, Barbara. That is what makes him so dangerous to me.

BARBARA: That has nothing to do with it, Dolly. There are larger loves and diviner dreams than the fireside ones. You know that, don't you?

CUSINS: Yes: that is our understanding. I know it. I hold to it. Unless he can win me on that holier ground he may amuse me for a while; but he can get no deeper hold, strong as he is.

BARBARA: Keep to that; and the end will be right. Now tell me what happened at the meeting?

CUSINS: It was an amazing meeting. Mrs Baines almost died of emotion. Jenny Hill simply gibbered with hysteria. The Prince of Darkness played his trombone like a madman; its brazen roarings were like the laughter of the damned. 117 conversions took place then and there. They prayed with the most touching sincerity and gratitude for Bodger, and for the anonymous donor of the £5000. Your father would not let his name be given.

LOMAX: That was rather fine of the old man, you know. Most chaps would have wanted the advertisement.

CUSINS: He said all the charitable instituitons would be down on him like kites on a battle field if he gave his name.

LADY BRITOMART: That's Andrew all over. He never does a proper thing without giving an improper reason for it.

CUSINS: He convinced me that I have all my life been doing improper things for proper reasons.

LADY BRITOMART: Adolphus: now that Barbara has left the Salvation Army, you had better leave it too. I will not have you playing that drum in the streets.

CUSINS: Your orders are already obeyed, Lady Brit.

BARBARA: Dolly: were you ever really in earnest about it? Would you have joined if you had never seen me?

CUSINS (disingenuously): Well—er—well, possibly, as a collector of religions—

LOMAX (cunningly): Not as a drummer, though, you know. You are a very clearheaded brainy chap, Dolly; and it must have been apparent to you that there is a certain amount of tosh about—

LADY BRITOMART: Charles: if you must drivel, drivel like a grown-up man and not like a schoolboy.

LOMAX (out of countenance): Well, drivel is drivel, don't you know, whatever a man's age.

LADY BRITOMART: In good society in England, Charles, men drivel at all ages by repeating silly formulas with an air of wisdom. Schoolboys make their own formulas out of slang, like you. When they reach your age, and get political private secretaryships and things of that sort, they drop slang and get their formulas out of *The Spectator* or *The Times*. You will find that there is a certain amount of tosh about *The Times*; but at least its language is reputable.

LOMAX (overwhelmed): You are so awfully strong-minded, Lady Brit—

LADY BRITOMART: Rubbish! (MORRISON comes in.) What is it?

MORRISON: If you please, my lady, Mr Undershaft has just drove up to the door.

LADY BRITOMART: Well, let him in. (MORRISON hesitates.) What's the matter with you?

MORRISON: Shall I announce him, my lady; or is he at home here, so to speak, my lady?

LADY BRITOMART: Announce him.

MORRISON: Thank you, my lady. You won't mind my asking, I hope. The occasion is in a manner of speaking new to me.

LADY BRITOMART: Quite right. Go and let him in.

MORRISON: Thank you, my lady. (He withdraws.)

LADY BRITOMART: Children: go and get ready. (SARAH and BARBARA go upstairs for their out-of-door wraps.) Charles: go and tell Stephen to come down here in five minutes: you will find him in the drawing room. (CHARLES goes.) Adolphus: tell them to send round the carriage in about fifteen minutes. (ADOLPHUS goes.)

MORRISON (at the door): Mr Undershaft.

(UNDERSHAFT comes in. MORRISON goes out.)

UNDERSHAFT: Alone! How fortunate!

LADY BRITOMART (rising): Don't be sentimental, Andrew. Sit down. (She sits on the settee: he sits beside her, on her left. She comes to the point before he has time to breathe.) Sarah must have £800 a year until Charles Lomax comes into his property. Barbara will need more, and need it permanently, because Adolphus hasn't any property.

UNDERSHAFT (resignedly): Yes, my dear: I will see to it. Anything else? for yourself, for instance?

LADY BRITOMART: I want to talk to you about Stephen.

UNDERSHAFT (rather wearily): Don't my dear. Stephen doesn't interest me.

LADY BRITOMART: He does interest me. He is our son.

UNDERSHAFT: Do you really think so? He has induced us to bring him into the world; but he chose his parents very incongruously, I think. I see nothing of myself in him, and less of you.

LADY BRITOMART: Andrew: Stephen is an excellent son, and a most steady, capable, highminded young man. You are simply trying to find an excuse for disinheriting him.

UNDERSHAFT: My dear Biddy: the Undershaft tradition disinherits him. It would be dishonest of me to leave the cannon foundry to my son.

LADY BRITOMART: It would be most unnatural and improper of you to leave it to anyone else, Andrew. Do you suppose this wicked and immoral tradition can be kept up for ever? Do you pretend that Stephen could not carry on the foundry just as well as all the other sons of the big business houses?

UNDERSHAFT: Yes: he could learn the office routine without understanding the business, like all the other sons; and the firm would go on by its own momentum until the real Undershaft—probably an Italian or a German—would invent a new method and cut him out.

LADY BRITOMART: There is nothing that any Italian or German could do that Stephen could not do. And Stephen at least has breeding.

UNDERSHAFT: The son of a foundling! Nonsense!

LADY BRITOMART: My son, Andrew! And even you may have good blood in your veins for all you know.

UNDERSHAFT: True. Probably I have. That is another argument in favor of a foundling.

LADY BRITOMART: Andrew: don't be aggravating. And don't be wicked. At present you are both.

UNDERSHAFT: This conversation is part of the Undershaft tradition, Biddy. Every Undershaft's wife has treated him to it ever since the house was founded. It is mere waste of breath. If the tradition be ever broken it will be for an abler man than Stephen.

LADY BRITOMART (pouting): Then go away.

UNDERSHAFT (deprecatory): Go away!

LADY BRITOMART: Yes: go away: If you will do nothing for Stephen, you are not wanted here. Go to your foundling, whoever he is; and look after him.

UNDERSHAFT: The fact is, Biddy—

LADY BRITOMART: Don't call me Biddy. I don't call you Andy.

UNDERSHAFT: I will not call my wife Britomart: it is not good sense. Seriously, my love, the Undershaft tradition has landed me in a difficulty. I am getting on in years; and my partner Lazarus has at last made a stand and inisisted that the succession must be settled one way or the other; and of course he is quite right. You see, I haven't found a fit successor yet.

LADY BRITOMART (obstinately): There is Stephen.

UNDERSHAFT: That's just it: all the foundlings I can find are exactly like Stephen.

LADY BRITOMART: Andrew!!

UNDERSHAFT: I want a man with no relations and no schooling: that is, a man who would be out of the running altogether if he were not a strong man. And I can't find him. Every blessed foundling nowadays is snapped up in his infancy by Barnardo homes° or School Board officers, or Boards of Guardians; and if he shews the least ability, he is fastened on by schoolmasters: trained to win scholarships like a racehorse; crammed with secondhand ideas; drilled and disciplined in docility and what they call good taste; and lamed for life so that he is fit for nothing but teaching. If you want to keep the foundry in the family you had better find an eligible foundling and marry him to Barbara.

LADY BRITOMART: Oh! Barbara! Your pet! You would sacrifice Stephen to Barbara.

UNDERSHAFT: Cheerfully. And you, my dear, would boil Barbara to make soup for Stephen.

LADY BRITOMART: Andrew: this is not a question of our likings and dislikings: it is a question of duty. It is your duty to make Stephen your successor.

UNDERSHAFT: Just as much as it is your duty to submit to your husband. Come, Biddy! these tricks of the governing class are no use with me. I am one of the governing class myself; and it is a waste of time giving tracts to a missionary. I have the power in this matter; and I am not to be humbugged into using it for your purposes.

LADY BRITOMART: Andrew: you can talk my head off; but you can't change wrong into right. And your tie is all on one side. Put it straight.

UNDERSHAFT (disconcerted): It won't stay unless it's pinned—(He fumbles at it with childish grimaces.)

(STEPHEN comes in.)

STEPHEN (at the door): I beg your pardon. (About to retire.)

LADY BRITOMART: No: come in, Stephen. (STEPHEN comes forward to his mother's writing table.)

UNDERSHAFT (not very cordially): Good afternoon.

STEPHEN (coldly): Good afternoon.

UNDERSHAFT (to LADY BRITOMART): He knows all about the tradition, I suppose?

LADY BRITOMART: Yes. (to STEPHEN) It is what I told you last night, Stephen.

UNDERSHAFT (sulkily): I understand you want to come into the cannon business.

STEPHEN: I go into trade. Certainly not.

UNDERSHAFT (opening his eyes, greatly eased in mind and manner): Oh! in that case—

Barnado homes, Thomas J. Barnardo founded homes in which destitute children could be given industrial training.

LADY BRITOMART: Cannons are not trade, Stephen. They are enterprise.

STEPHEN: I have no intention of becoming a man of business in any sense. I have no capacity for business and no taste for it. I intend to devote myself to politics.

UNDERSHAFT (*rising*): My dear boy: this is an immense relief to me. And I trust it may prove an equally good thing for the country. I was afraid you would consider yourself disparaged and slighted. (*He moves toward* STEPHEN *as if to shake hands with him.*)

LADY BRITOMART (*rising and interposing*): Stephen: I cannot allow you to throw away an enormous property like this.

STEPHEN (*stiffly*): Mother: there must be an end of treating me as a child, if you please. (LADY BRITOMART *recoils, deeply wounded by his tone.*) Until last night I did not take your attitude seriously, because I did not think you meant it seriously. But I find now that you left me in the dark as to matters which you should have explained to me years ago. I am extremely hurt and offended. Any further discussion of my intentions had better take place with my father, as between one man and another.

LADY BRITOMART: Stephen! (*She sits down again, her eyes filling with tears.*)

UNDERSHAFT (*with grave compassion*): You see, my dear, it is only the big men who can be treated as children.

STEPHEN: I am sorry, mother, that you have forced me—

UNDERSHAFT (*stopping him*): Yes, yes, yes, yes: that's all right, Stephen. She won't interfere with you any more: your independence is achieved: you have won your latchkey. Don't rub it in; and above all, don't apologize. (*He resumes his seat.*) Now what about your future, as between one man and another—I beg your pardon, Biddy: as between two men and a woman.

LADY BRITOMART (*who has pulled herself together strongly*): I quite understand, Stephen. By all means go your own way if you feel strong enough. (STEPHEN *sits down magisterially in the chair at the writing table with an air of affirming his majority.*)

UNDERSHAFT: It is settled that you do not ask for the succession to the cannon business.

STEPHEN: I hope it is settled that I repudiate the cannon business.

UNDERSHAFT: Come, come! don't be so devilishly sulky: it's boyish. Freedom should be generous. Besides, I owe you a fair start in life in exchange for disinheriting you. You can't become prime minister all at once. Haven't you a turn for something? What about literature, art, and so forth?

STEPHEN: I have nothing of the artist about me, either in faculty or character, thank Heaven!

UNDERSHAFT: A philosopher, perhaps, Eh?

STEPHEN: I make no such ridiculous pretension.

UNDERSHAFT: Just so. Well, there is the army, the navy, the Church, the Bar. The Bar requires some ability. What about the Bar?

STEPHEN: I have not studied law. And I am afraid I have not the necessary push—I believe that is the name barristers give to their vulgarity—for success in pleading.

UNDERSHAFT: Rather a difficult case, Stephen. Hardly anything left but the stage, is there? (STEPHEN *makes an impatient movement.*) Well, come! is there anything you know or care for?

STEPHEN (*rising and looking at him steadily*): I know the difference between right and wrong.

UNDERSHAFT (*hugely tickled*): You don't say so! What! no capacity for business, no knowledge of law, no sympathy with art, no pretension to philosophy; only a simple knowledge of the secret that has puzzled all the philosophers, baffled all the lawyers, muddled all the men of business, and ruined most of the artists: the secret of right and wrong. Why, man, you're a genius, a master of masters, a god! At twenty-four, too!

STEPHEN (*keeping his temper with difficulty*): You are pleased to be facetious. I pretend to nothing more than any honorable English gentleman claims as his birthright. (*He sits down angrily.*)

UNDERSHAFT: Oh, that's everybody's birthright. Look at poor little Jenny Hill, the Salvation lassie! she would think you were laughing at her if you asked her to stand up in the street and teach grammar or geography or mathematics or even drawing room dancing; but it never occurs to her to doubt that she can teach morals and religion. You are all alike, you respectable people. You can't tell me the bursting strain of a ten-inch gun, which is a very simple matter; but you all think you can tell me the bursting strain of a man under temptation. You daren't handle high explosives; but you're all ready to handle honesty and truth and justice and the whole duty of man, and kill one another at that game. What a country! What a world!

LADY BRITOMART (*uneasily*): What do you think he had better do, Andrew?

UNDERSHAFT: Oh, just what he wants to do. He knows nothing and he thinks he knows everything. That points clearly to a political career. Get him a private secretaryship to someone who can get him an Under Secretaryship; and then leave him alone. He will find his natural and proper place in the end on the Treasury Bench.

STEPHEN (*springing up again*): I am sorry, sir, that you force me to forget the respect due to you as my father. I am an Englishman and I will not hear the Government of my country insulted. (*He thrusts his hands in his pockets and walks angrily across to the window.*)

UNDERSHAFT (*with a touch of brutality*): The government of your country! *I* am the government of your country: I, and Lazarus. Do you suppose that you and half a dozen amateurs like you, sitting in a row in that foolish gabble shop, can govern Undershaft and Lazarus? No, my friend: you will do what pays us. You will make war when it suits us, and keep peace when it doesn't. You will find out that trade requires certain measures when we have decided on those measures. When I want anything to keep my dividends up, you will discover that my want is a national need. When other people want something to keep my dividends down, you will call out the police and military. And in return you shall have the support and applause of my newspapers, and the delight of imagining that you are a great statesman. Government of your country! Be off with you, my boy, and play with your caucuses and leading articles and historic parties and great leaders and burning questions and the rest of your toys. *I* am going back to my counting house to pay the piper and call the tune.

STEPHEN (*actually smiling, and putting his hand on his father's shoulder with indulgent patronage*): Really, my dear father, it is impossible to be angry with you. You don't know how absurd all this sounds to me. You are very properly proud of having been industrious enough to make money; and it is greatly to your credit that you have made so much of it. But it has kept you in circles where you are valued for your money and deferred to for it, instead of in the doubtless very old-fashioned and behind-the-times public school and university where I formed my habits of mind. It is natural for you to think that money governs England; but you must allow me to think I know better.

UNDERSHAFT: And what does govern England, pray?

STEPHEN: Character, father, character.

UNDERSHAFT: Whose character? Yours or mine?

STEPHEN: Neither yours nor mine, father, but the best elements in the English national character.

UNDERSHAFT: Stephen: I've found your profession for you. You're a born journalist. I'll start you with a hightoned weekly review. There!

(*Before* STEPHEN *can reply* SARAH, BARBARA, LOMAX, *and* CUSINS *come in ready for walking.* BARBARA *crosses the room to the window and looks out.* CUSINS *drifts amiably to the armchair.* LOMAX *remains near the door, whilst* SARAH *comes to her mother.* STEPHEN *goes to the smaller writing table and busies himself with his letters.*)

SARAH: Go and get ready, mamma: the carriage is waiting. (LADY BRITOMART *leaves the room.*)

UNDERSHAFT (*to* SARAH): Good day, my dear. Good afternoon, Mr Lomax.

LOMAX (*vaguely*): Ahdedoo.

UNDERSHAFT (*to* CUSINS): Quite well after last night, Euripides, eh?

CUSINS: As well as can be expected.

UNDERSHAFT: That's right. (*to* BARBARA) So you are coming to see my death and devastation factory, Barbara?

BARBARA (*at the window*): You came yesterday to see my salvation factory. I promised you a return visit.

LOMAX (*coming forward between* SARAH *and* UNDERSHAFT): You'll find it awfully interesting. I've been through the Woolwich Arsenal; and it gives you a ripping feeling of security, you know, to think of the lot of beggars we could kill if it came to fighting. (*to* UNDERSHAFT, *with sudden solemnity*) Still, it must be rather an awful reflection for you, from the religious point of view as it were. You're getting on, you know, and all that.

SARAH: You don't mind Cholly's imbecility, papa, do you?

LOMAX (*much taken aback*): Oh I say!

UNDERSHAFT: Mr. Lomax looks at the matter in a very proper spirit, my dear.

LOMAX: Just so. That's all I meant, I assure you.

SARAH: Are you coming, Stephen?

STEPHEN: Well, I am rather busy—er— (*magnanimously.*) Oh well, yes: I'll come. That is, if there is room for me.

UNDERSHAFT: I can take two with me in a little motor I am experimenting with for field use. You won't mind its being rather unfashionable. It's not painted yet; but it's bullet proof.

LOMAX (*appalled at the prospect of confronting Wilton Crescent in an unpainted motor*): Oh I say!

SARAH: The carriage for me, thank you. Barbara doesn't mind what she's seen in.

LOMAX: I say, Dolly old chap: do you really mind the car being a guy?° Because of course if you do I'll go in it. Still—

CUSINS: I prefer it.

LOMAX: Thanks awfully, old man. Come, my ownest. (*He hurries out to secure his seat in the carriage.* SARAH *follows him.*)

---

guy, conspicuously grotesque object which invites ridicule.

CUSINS (*moodily walking across to* LADY BRITOMART's *writing table*.): Why are we two coming to this Works Department of Hell? that is what I ask myself.

BARBARA: I have always thought of it as a sort of pit where lost creatures with blackened faces stirred up smoky fires and were driven and tormented by my father. Is it like that, dad?

UNDERSHAFT (*scandalized*): My dear! It is a spotlessly clean and beautiful hillside town.

CUSINS: With a Methodist chapel? Oh do say there's a Methodist chapel.

UNDERSHAFT: There are two: a Primitive one and a sophisticated one. There is even an Ethical Society; but it is not much patronized, as my men are all strongly religious. In the High Explosives Sheds they object to the presence of Agnostics as unsafe.

CUSINS: And yet they don't object to you!

BARBARA: Do they obey all your orders?

UNDERSHAFT: I never give them any orders. When I speak to one of them it's "Well, Jones, is the baby doing well? and has Mrs Jones made a good recovery?" "Nicely, thank you, sir." And that's all.

CUSINS: But Jones has to be kept in order. How do you maintain discipline among your men?

UNDERSHAFT: I don't. They do. You see, the one thing Jones won't stand is any rebellion from the man under him, or any assertion of social equality between the wife of the man with 4 shillings a week less than himself, and Mrs Jones! Of course they all rebel against me, theoretically. Practically, every man of them keeps the man just below him in his place. I never meddle with them. I never bully them. I don't even bully Lazarus. I say that certain things are to be done; but I don't order anybody to do them. I don't say, mind you, that there is no ordering about and snubbing and even bullying. The men snub the boys and order them about; the carmen snub the sweepers; the artisans snub the unskilled laborers; the foremen drive and bully both the laborers and artisans; the assistant engineers find fault with the foremen; the chief engineers drop on the assistants; the departmental managers worry the chiefs; and the clerks have tall hats and hymnbooks and keep up the social tone by refusing to associate on equal terms with anybody. The result is a colossal profit, which comes to me.

CUSINS (*revolted*): You really are a—well, what I was saying yesterday.

BARBARA: What was he saying yesterday?

UNDERSHAFT: Never mind, my dear. He thinks I have made you unhappy. Have I?

BARBARA: Do you think I can be happy in this vulgar silly dress? I! who have worn the uniform. Do you understand what you have done to me? Yesterday I had a man's soul in my hand. I set him in the way of life with his face to salvation. But when we took your money he turned back to drunkenness and derision. (*With intense conviction.*) I will never forgive you that. If I had a child, and you destroyed its body with your explosives—if you murdered Dolly with your horrible guns—I could forgive you if my forgiveness would open the gates of heaven to you. But to take a human soul from me, and turn it into the soul of a wolf! that is worse than any murder.

UNDERSHAFT: Does my daughter despair so easily? Can you strike a man in the heart and leave no mark on him?

BARBARA (*her face lighting up*): Oh, you are right: he can never be lost now: where was my faith?

CUSINS: Oh, clever, clever devil!

BARBARA: You may be a devil; but God speaks through you sometimes. (*She takes her father's hands and kisses them.*) You have given me back my happiness: I feel it deep down now, though my spirit is troubled.

UNDERSHAFT: You have learnt something. That always feels at first as if you had lost something.

BARBARA: Well, take me to the factory of death; and let me learn something more. There must be some truth or other behind all this frightful irony. Come, Dolly. (*She goes out.*)

CUSINS: My guardian angel! (*to* UNDERSHAFT) Avaunt! (*He follows* BARBARA.)

STEPHEN (*quietly, at the writing table*): You must not mind Cusins, father. He is a very amiable good fellow; but he is a Greek scholar and naturally a little eccentric.

UNDERSHAFT: Ah, quite so. Thank you, Stephen. Thank you. (*He goes out.*)

(STEPHEN *smiles patronizingly; buttons his coat responsibly; and crosses the room to the door.* LADY BRITOMART, *dressed for out-of-doors, opens it before he reaches it. She looks round for the others; looks at* STEPHEN; *and turns to go without a word.*)

STEPHEN (*embarrassed*): Mother—

LADY BRITOMART: Don't be apologetic, Stephen. And don't forget that you have outgrown your mother. (*She goes out.*)

(*Perivale St Andrews lies between two Middlesex hills, half climbing the northern one. It is an almost smokeless town of white walls, roofs of narrow green slates or red tiles, tall trees, domes, campaniles, and slender chimney shafts, beautifully situated and beautiful in itself. The best view of it is obtained from the crest of a slope about half a mile to the east, where the high explosives are dealt with. The foundry lies hidden in the depths between, the tops of its chimneys sprouting like huge skittles into the middle distance. Across the crest runs an emplacement of concrete, with a firestep, and a parapet which suggests a fortification, because there is a huge cannon of the obsolete Woolwich Infant pattern peering across it at the town. The cannon is mounted on an experimental gun carriage: possibly the original model of the Undershaft disappearing rampart gun alluded to by Stephen. The firestep, being a convenient place to sit, is furnished here and there with straw disc cushions; and at one place there is the additional luxury of a fur rug.*

BARBARA is standing on the firestep, looking over the parapet towards the town. On her right is the cannon; on her left the end of a shed raised on piles, with a ladder of three or four steps up to the door, which opens outwards and has a little wooden landing at the threshold, with a fire bucket in the corner of the landing. Several dummy soldiers more or less mutilated, with straw protruding from their gashes, have been shoved out of the way under the landing. A few others are nearly upright against the shed; and one has fallen forward and lies, like a grotesque corpse, on the emplacement. The parapet stops short of the shed, leaving a gap which is the beginning of the path down the hill through the foundry to the town. The rug is on the firestep near this gap. Down on the emplacement behind the cannon is a trolley carrying a huge conical bombshell with a red band painted on it. Further to the right is the door of an office, which, like the sheds, is of the lightest possible construction.

CUSINS arrives by the path from the town.)

BARBARA: Well?

CUSINS: Not a ray of hope. Everything perfect! wonderful! real! It only needs a cathedral to be a heavenly city instead of a hellish one.

BARBARA: Have you found out whether they have done anything for old Peter Shirley?

CUSINS: They have found him a job as gatekeeper and timekeeper. He's frightfully miserable. He calls the timekeeping brainwork, and says he isn't used to it; and his gate lodge is so splendid that he's ashamed to use the rooms, and skulks in the scullery.

BARBARA: Poor Peter!

(STEPHEN arrives from the town. He carries a field-glass.)

STEPHEN *(enthusiastically)*: Have you two seen the place? Why did you leave us?

CUSINS: I wanted to see everything I was not intended to see; and Barbara wanted to make the men talk.

STEPHEN: Have you found anything discreditable?

CUSINS: No. They call him Dandy Andy and are proud of his being a cunning old rascal; but it's all horribly, frightfully, immorally, unanswerably perfect.

(SARAH arrives.)

SARAH: Heavens! what a place! *(She crosses to the trolley)* Did you see the nursing home? *(She sits down on the shell.)*

STEPHEN: Did you see the libraries and schools?

SARAH: Did you see the ball room and the banqueting chamber in the Town Hall!?

STEPHEN: Have you gone into the insurance fund, the pension fund, the building society, the various applications of cooperation!?

(UNDERSHAFT comes from the office, with a sheaf of telegrams in his hand.)

UNDERSHAFT: Well, have you seen everything? I'm sorry I was called away. *(Indicating the telegrams.)* Good news from Manchuria.

STEPHEN: Another Japanese victory?

UNDERSHAFT: Oh, I don't know. Which side wins does not concern us here. No: the good news is that the aerial battleship is a tremendous success. At the first trial it has wiped out a fort with three hundred soldiers in it.

CUSINS *(from the platform)*: Dummy soldiers?

UNDERSHAFT *(striding across to STEPHEN and kicking the prostrate dummy brutally out of his way)*: No: the real thing.

(CUSINS and BARBARA exchange glances. Then CUSINS sits on the step and buries his face in his hands. BARBARA gravely lays her hand on his shoulder. He looks up at her in whimsical desperation.)

UNDERSHAFT: Well, Stephen, what do you think of the place?

STEPHEN: Oh, magnificent. A perfect triumph of modern industry. Frankly, my dear father, I have been a fool: I had no idea of what it all meant: of the wonderful forethought, the power of organization, the administrative capacity, the financial genius, the colossal capital it represents. I have been repeating to myself as I came through your streets "Peace hath her victories no less renowned than War." I have only one misgiving about it all.

UNDERSHAFT: Out with it.

STEPHEN: Well, I cannot help thinking that all this provision for every want of your workmen may sap their independence and weaken their sense of responsibility. And greatly as we enjoyed our tea at that splendid restaurant—how they gave us all that luxury and cake and jam and cream for threepence I really cannot imagine!—still you must remember that restaurants break up home life. Look at the continent, for instance! Are you sure so much pampering is really good for the men's characters?

UNDERSHAFT: Well you see, my dear boy, when you

are organizing civilization you have to make up your mind whether trouble and anxiety are good things or not. If you decide that they are, then I take it, you simply don't organize civilization; and there you are, with trouble and anxiety enough to make us all angels! But if you decide the other way, you may as well go through with it. However, Stephen. our characters are safe here. A sufficient dose of anxiety is always provided by the fact that we may be blown to smithereens at any moment.

SARAH: By the way, papa, where do you make the explosives?

UNDERSHAFT: In separate little sheds, like that one. When one of them blows up, it costs very little; and only the people quite close to it are killed.

(STEPHEN, *who is quite close to it, looks at it rather scaredly, and moves away quickly to the cannon. At the same moment the door of the shed is thrown abruptly open; and a foreman in overalls and list slippers° comes out on the little landing and holds the door for* LOMAX, *who appears in the doorway.*)

LOMAX (*with studied coolness*): My good fellow: you needn't get into a state of nerves. Nothing's going to happen to you; and I suppose it wouldn't be the end of the world if anything did. A little bit of British pluck is what you want, old chap. (*He descends and strolls across to* SARAH.)

UNDERSHAFT (*to the foreman*): Anything wrong, Bilton?

BILTON (*with ironic calm*): Gentleman walked into the high explosives shed and lit a cigaret, sir: that's all.

UNDERSHAFT: Ah, quite so. (*Going over to* LOMAX.) Do you happen to remember what you did with the match?

LOMAX: Oh come! I'm not a fool. I took jolly good care to blow it out before I chucked it away.

BILTON: The top of it was red hot inside, sir.

LOMAX: Well, suppose it was! I didn't chuck it into any of your messes.

UNDERSHAFT: Think no more of it, Mr. Lomax. By the way, would you mind lending me your matches?

LOMAX (*offering his box*): Certainly.

UNDERSHAFT: Thanks. (*He pockets the matches.*)

LOMAX (*lecturing to the company generally*): You know, these high explosives don't go off like gunpowder, except when they're in a gun. When they're spread loose, you can put a match to them without the least risk: they just burn quietly like a bit

---

list slippers, soft cloth slippers used here to minimize friction.

of paper. (*Warming to the scientific interest of the subject.*) Did you know that, Undershaft? Have you ever tried?

UNDERSHAFT: Not on a large scale, Mr. Lomax. Bilton will give you a sample of gun cotton when you are leaving if you ask him. You can experiment with it at home. (BILTON *looks puzzled.*)

SARAH: Bilton will do nothing of the sort, papa. I suppose it's your business to blow up the Russians and Japs; but you might really stop short of blowing up poor Cholly. (BILTON *gives it up and retires into the shed.*)

LOMAX: My ownest, there is no danger. (*He sits beside her on the shell.*)

(LADY BRITOMART *arrives from the town with a bouquet.*)

LADY BRITOMART (*impetuously*): Andrew: you shouldn't have let me see this place.

UNDERSHAFT: Why, my dear?

LADY BRITOMART: Never mind why: you shouldn't have: that's all. To think of all that (*Indicating the town.*) being yours! and that you have kept it to yourself all these years!

UNDERSHAFT: It does not belong to me. I belong to it. It is the Undershaft inheritance.

LADY BRITOMART: It is not. Your ridiculous cannons and that noisy banging foundry may be the Undershaft inheritance; but all that plate and linen, all that furniture and those houses and orchards and gardens belong to us. They belong to me: they are not a man's business. I won't give them up. You must be out of your senses to throw them all away; and if you persist in such folly, I will call in a doctor.

UNDERSHAFT (*stooping to smell the bouquet*): Where did you get the flowers, my dear?

LADY BRITOMART: Your men presented them to me in your William Morris Labor Church.

CUSINS: Oh! It needed only that. A Labor Church! (*He mounts the firestep distractedly, and leans with his elbows on the parapet, turning his back to them.*)

LADY BRITOMART: Yes, with Morris's words in mosaic letters ten feet high round the dome. NO MAN IS GOOD ENOUGH TO BE ANOTHER MAN'S MASTER. The cynicism of it!

UNDERSHAFT: It shocked the men at first, I am afraid. But now they take no more notice of it than of the ten commandments in church.

LADY BRITOMART: Andrew: you are trying to put me off the subject of the inheritance by profane jokes. Well, you shan't. I don't ask it any longer for Stephen: he has inherited far too much of your perversity to be fit for it. But Barbara has rights as well as Stephen. Why should not Adolphus succeed to the inheritance? I could manage the town for him; and he can look after the cannons, if they are really necessary.

UNDERSHAFT: I should ask nothing better if Adolphus were a foundling. He is exactly the sort of new blood that is wanted in English business. But he's not a foundling; and there's an end of it. (*He makes for the office door.*)

CUSINS (*turning to them*): Not quite. (*They all turn and stare at him.*) I think—Mind! I am not committing myself in any way as to my future course—but I think the foundling difficulty can be got over. (*He jumps down to the emplacement.*)

UNDERSHAFT (*coming back to him*): What do you mean?

CUSINS: Well, I have something to say which is in the nature of a confession.

SARAH:
LADY BRITOMART: } Confession!
BARBARA:
STEPHEN:

LOMAX: Oh I say!

CUSINS: Yes, a confession. Listen, all. Until I met Barbara I thought myself in the main an honorable, truthful man, because I wanted the approval of my conscience more than I wanted anything else. But the moment I saw Barbara, I wanted her far more than the approval of my conscience.

LADY BRITOMART: Adolphus!

CUSINS: It is true. You accused me yourself, Lady Brit, of joining the Army to worship Barbara; and so I did. She bought my soul like a flower at a street corner; but she bought it for herself.

UNDERSHAFT: What! Not for Dionysos or another?

CUSINS: Dionysos and all the others are in herself. I adored what was divine in her, and was therefore a true worshipper. But I was romantic about her too. I thought she was a woman of the people, and that a marriage with a professor of Greek would be far beyond the wildest social ambitions of her rank.

LADY BRITOMART: Adolphus!!

LOMAX: Oh I say!!!

CUSINS: When I learnt the horrible truth—

LADY BRITOMART: What do you mean by the horrible truth, pray?

CUSINS: That she was enormously rich; that her grandfather was an earl; that her father was the Prince of Darkness—

UNDERSHAFT: Chut!

CUSINS: —and that I was only an adventurer trying to catch a rich wife, then I stooped to deceive her about my birth.

BARBARA (*rising*): Dolly!

LADY BRITOMART: Your birth! Now Adolphus, don't dare to make up a wicked story for the sake of these wretched cannons. Remember: I have seen photographs of your parents; and the Agent General for South Western Australia knows them personally and has assured me that they are most respectable married people.

CUSINS: So they are in Australia; but here they are outcasts. Their marriage is legal in Australia, but not in England. My mother is my father's deceased wife's sister; and in this island I am consequently a foundling. (*Sensation.*)

BARBARA: Silly! (*She climbs to the cannon, and leans, listening, in the angle it makes with the parapet.*)

CUSINS: Is the subterfuge good enough, Machiavelli?

UNDERSHAFT (*thoughtfully*): Biddy: this may be a way out of the difficulty.

LADY BRITOMART: Stuff! A man can't make cannons any the better for being his own cousin instead of his proper self. (*She sits down on the rug with a bounce that expresses her downright contempt for their casuistry.*)

UNDERSHAFT (*to* CUSINS): You are an educated man. That is against the tradition.

CUSINS: One in ten thousand times it happens that the schoolboy is born master of what they try to teach him. Greek has not destroyed my mind: it has nourished it. Besides, I did not learn it at an English public school.

UNDERSHAFT: Hm! Well, I cannot afford to be too particular: you have cornered the foundling market. Let it pass. You are eligible, Euripides: you are eligible.

BARBARA: Dolly: yesterday morning, when Stephen told us all about the tradition, you became very silent; and you have been strange and excited ever since. Were you thinking of your birth then?

CUSINS: When the finger of Destiny suddenly points at a man in the middle of his breakfast, it makes him thoughtful.

UNDERSHAFT: Aha! You have had your eye on the business, my young friend, have you?

CUSINS: Take care! There is an abyss of moral horror between me and your accursed aerial battleships.

UNDERSHAFT: Never mind the abyss for the present. Let us settle the practical details and leave your final decision open. You know that you will have to change your name. Do you object to that?

CUSINS: Would any man named Adolphus—any man called Dolly!—object to be called something else?

UNDERSHAFT: Good. Now, as to money! I propose to treat you handsomely from the beginning. You shall start at a thousand a year.

CUSINS (*with sudden heat, his spectacles twinkling with mischief*): A thousand! You dare offer a miserable thousand to the son-in-law of a millionaire! No, by Heavens, Machiavelli! you shall not cheat me. You cannot do without me; and I can do without you. I must have two thousand five hundred a year for two years. At the end of that time, if I am a failure, I go. But if I am a success, and stay on, you must give me the other five thousand.

UNDERSHAFT: What other five thousand?

CUSINS: To make the two years up to five thousand a year. The two thousand five hundred is only half pay in case I should turn out a failure. The third year I must have ten per cent on the profits.

UNDERSHAFT (taken aback): Ten per cent! Why, man, do you know what my profits are?

CUSINS: Enormous, I hope; otherwise I shall require twenty-five per cent.

UNDERSHAFT: But, Mr Cusins, this is a serious matter of business. You are not bringing any capital into the concern.

CUSINS: What! no capital! Is my mastery of Greek no capital? Is my access to the subtlest thought, the loftiest poetry yet attained by humanity, no capital? My character! my intellect! my life! my career! what Barbara calls my soul! are these no capital? Say another word; and I double my salary.

UNDERSHAFT: Be reasonable—

CUSINS (peremptorily): Mr Undershaft: you have my terms. Take them or leave them.

UNDERSHAFT (recovering himself): Very well. I note your terms; and I offer you half.

CUSINS (disgusted): Half!

UNDERSHAFT (firmly): Half.

CUSINS: You call yourself a gentleman; and you offer me half!!

UNDERSHAFT: I do not call myself a gentleman; but I offer you half.

CUSINS: This to your future partner! your successor! your son-in-law!

BARBARA: You are selling your own soul, Dolly, not mine. Leave me out of the bargain, please.

UNDERSHAFT: Come! I will go a step further for Barbara's sake. I will give you three fifths; but that is my last word.

CUSINS: Done!

LOMAX: Done in the eye! Why I get only eight hundred, you know.

CUSINS: By the way, Mac, I am a classical scholar, not an arithmetical one. Is three fifths more than half or less?

UNDERSHAFT: More, of course.

CUSINS: I would have taken two hundred and fifty. How you can succeed in business when you are willing to pay all that money to a University don who is obviously not worth a junior clerk's wages!—well! What will Lazarus say?

UNDERSHAFT: Lazarus is a gentle romantic Jew who cares for nothing but string quartets and stalls at fashionable theatres. He will be blamed for your rapacity in money matters, poor fellow! as he has hitherto been blamed for mine. You are a shark of the first order, Euripides. So much the better for the firm!

BARBARA: Is the bargain closed, Dolly? Does your soul belong to him now?

CUSINS: No: the price is settled: that is all. The real tug of war is still to come. What about the moral question?

LADY BRITOMART: There is no moral question in the matter at all, Adolphus. You must simply sell cannons and weapons to people whose cause is right and just, and refuse them to foreigners and criminals.

UNDERSHAFT (determinedly): No: none of that. You must keep the true faith of an Armorer, or you don't come in here.

CUSINS: What on earth is the true faith of an Armorer?

UNDERSHAFT: To give arms to all men who offer an honest price for them, without respect of persons or principles: to aristocrat and republican, to Nihilist and Tsar, to Capitalist and Socialist, to Protestant and Catholic, to burglar and policeman, to black man, white man and yellow man, to all sorts and conditions, all nationalities, all faiths, all follies, all causes and all crimes. The first Undershaft wrote up in his shop IF GOD GAVE THE HAND, LET NOT MAN WITHHOLD THE SWORD. The second wrote up ALL HAVE THE RIGHT TO FIGHT: NONE HAVE THE RIGHT TO JUDGE. The third wrote up TO MAN THE WEAPON: TO HEAVEN THE VICTORY. The fourth had no literary turn; so he did not write up anything; but he sold cannons to Napoleon under the nose of George the Third. The fifth wrote up PEACE SHALL NOT PREVAIL SAVE WITH A SWORD IN HER HAND. The sixth, my master, was the best of all. He wrote up NOTHING IS EVER DONE IN THIS WORLD UNTIL MEN ARE PREPARED TO KILL ONE ANOTHER IF IT IS NOT DONE. After that, there was nothing left for the seventh to say. So he wrote up, simply, UNASHAMED.

CUSINS: My good Machiavelli, I shall certainly write something up on the wall; only as I shall write it in Greek, you won't be able to read it. But as to your Armorer's faith, if I take my neck out of the noose of my own morality I am not going to put it into the noose of yours. I shall sell cannons to whom I please and refuse them to whom I please. So there!

UNDERSHAFT: From the moment when you become Andrew Undershaft, you will never do as you please again. Don't come here lusting for power, young man.

CUSINS: If power were my aim I should not come here for it. You have no power.

UNDERSHAFT: None of my own, certainly.

CUSINS: I have more power than you, more will. You do not drive this place: it drives you. And what drives the place?

UNDERSHAFT (*enigmatically*): A will of which I am a part.

BARBARA (*startled*): Father! Do you know what you are saying; or are you laying a snare for my soul?

CUSINS: Don't listen to his metaphysics, Barbara. The place is driven by the most rascally part of society, the money hunters, the pleasure hunters, the military promotion hunters; and he is their slave.

UNDERSHAFT: Not necessarily. Remember the Armorer's Faith. I will take an order from a good man as cheerfully as from a bad one. If you good people prefer preaching and shirking to buying my weapons and fighting the rascals, don't blame me. I cannot make courage and conviction. Bah! you tire me, Euripides, with your morality mongering. Ask Barbara: she understands. (*He suddenly reaches up and takes* BARBARA's *hands, looking powerfully into her eyes.*) Tell him, my love, what power really means.

BARBARA (*hypnotized*): Before I joined the Salvation Army, I was in my own power; and the consequence was that I never knew what to do with myself. When I joined it, I had not time enough for all the things I had to do.

UNDERSHAFT (*approvingly*): Just so. And why was that, do you suppose?

BARBARA: Yesterday I should have said, because I was in the power of God. (*She resumes her self-possession, withdrawing her hands from his with a power equal to his own.*) But you came and shewed me that I was in the power of Bodger and Undershaft. Today I feel—oh! how can I put it into words? Sarah: do you remember the earthquake at Cannes, when we were little children?—how little the surprise of the first shock mattered compared to the dread and horror of waiting for the second? That is how I feel in this place today. I stood on the rock I thought eternal; and without a word of warning it reeled and crumbled under me. I was safe with an infinite wisdom watching me, an army marching to Salvation with me; and in a moment, at a stroke of your pen in a cheque book, I stood alone; and the heavens were empty. That was the first shock of the earthquake: I am waiting for the second.

UNDERSHAFT: Come, come, my daughter! don't make too much of your little tinpot tragedy. What do we do here when we spend years of work and thought and thousands of pounds of solid cash on a new gun or an aerial battleship that turns out just a hairsbreadth wrong after all? Scrap it. Scrap it without wasting another hour or another pound on it. Well, you have made for yourself something that you call a morality or a religion or what not. It doesn't fit the facts. Well, scrap it. Scrap it and get one that does fit. That is what is wrong with the world at present. It scraps its obsolete steam engines and dynamos; but it won't scrap its old prejudices and its old moralities and its old religions and its old political constitutions. What's the result? In machinery it does very well; but in morals and religion and politics it is working at a loss that brings it nearer bankruptcy every year. Don't persist in that folly. If your old religion broke down yesterday, get a newer and a better one for tomorrow.

BARBARA: Oh how gladly I would take a better one to my soul! But you offer me a worse one. (*Turning on him with sudden vehemence.*) Justify yourself: shew me some light through the darkness of this dreadful place, with its beautifully clean workshops, and respectable workmen and model homes.

UNDERSHAFT: Cleanliness and respectability do not need justification, Barbara: they justify themselves. I see no darkness here, no dreadfulness. In your Salvation shelter I saw poverty, misery, cold and hunger. You gave them bread and treacle and dreams of heaven. I give from thirty shillings a week to twelve thousand a year. They find their own dreams; but I look after the drainage.

BARBARA: And their souls?

UNDERSHAFT: I save their souls just as I saved yours.

BARBARA (*revolted*): You saved my soul! What do you mean?

UNDERSHAFT: I fed you and clothed you and housed you. I took care that you should have money enough to live handsomely—more than enough; so that you could be wasteful, careless, generous. That saved your soul from the seven deadly sins.

BARBARA (*bewildered*): The seven deadly sins!

UNDERSHAFT: Yes, the deadly seven. (*Counting on his fingers.*) Food, clothing, firing, rent, taxes, respectability and children. Nothing can lift those seven millstones from Man's neck but money; and the spirit cannot soar until the millstones are lifted. I lifted them from your spirit. I enabled Barbara to become Major Barbara; and I saved her from the crime of poverty.

CUSINS: Do you call poverty a crime?

UNDERSHAFT: The worst of crimes. All the other crimes are virtues beside it: all the other dishonors are chivalry itself by comparison. Poverty blights whole cities; spreads horrible pestilences; strikes dead the very souls of all who come within sight, sound or smell of it. What you call crime is nothing: a murder here and a theft there, a blow now and a curse then: what do they matter? they are only the accidents and illnesses of life: there are not fifty genuine professional criminals in London. But there are millions of poor people, abject people, dirty people, ill fed, ill clothed people. They poison us morally and physically: they kill the happiness of society: they force us to do away with our own liberties and to organize unnatural cruelties for fear they should rise against us and drag us down into their abyss. Only fools fear crime: we all fear poverty. Pah! (*Turning on* BARBARA.) you talk of your half-saved ruffian in West Ham: you accuse me of dragging his soul back to perdition. Well, bring him to me here; and I will drag his soul back again to salvation for you. Not by words and dreams; but by thirty-eight shillings a week, a sound house in a handsome street, and a permanent job. In three weeks he will have a fancy waistcoat; in three months a tall hat and a chapel sitting; before the end of the year he will shake hands with a duchess at a Primrose League° meeting, and join the Conservative Party.

BARBARA: And will he be the better for that?

UNDERSHAFT: You know he will. Don't be a hypocrite, Barbara. He will be better fed, better housed, better clothed, better behaved; and his children will be pounds heavier and bigger. That will be better than an American cloth° mattress in a shelter, chopping firewood, eating bread and treacle, and being forced to kneel down from time to time to thank heaven for it: knee drill, I think you call it. It is cheap work converting starving men with a Bible in one hand and a slice of bread in the other. I will undertake to covert West Ham to Mahometanism on the same terms. Try your hand on my men: their souls are hungry because their bodies are full.

BARBARA: And leave the east end to starve?

UNDERSHAFT (*his energetic tone dropping into one of bitter and brooding remembrance*): I was an east ender. I moralized and starved until one day I swore that I would be a full-fed free man at all costs—that nothing should stop me except a bullet, neither reason nor morals nor the lives of other men. I said "Thou shalt starve ere I starve"; and with that word I became free and great. I was a dangerous man until I had my will: now I am a useful, beneficent, kindly person. That is the history of most self-made millionaires, I fancy. When it is the history of every Englishman we shall have an England worth living in.

LADY BRITOMART: Stop making speeches, Andrew. This is not the place for them.

UNDERSHAFT (*punctured*): My dear: I have no other means of conveying my ideas.

LADY BRITOMART: Your ideas are nonsense. You got on because you were selfish and unscrupulous.

UNDERSHAFT: Not at all. I had the strongest scruples about poverty and starvation. Your moralists are quite unscrupulous about both: they make virtues of them. I had rather be a thief than a pauper. I had rather be a murderer than a slave. I don't want to be either; but if you force the alternative on me, then, by Heaven, I'll choose the braver and more moral one. I hate poverty and slavery worse than any other crimes whatsoever. And let me tell you this. Poverty and slavery have stood up for centuries to your sermons and leading articles: they will not stand up to my machine guns. Don't preach at them: don't reason with them. Kill them.

BARBARA: Killing. Is that your remedy for everything?

UNDERSHAFT: It is the final test of conviction, the only lever strong enough to overturn a social system, the only way of saying Must. Let six hundred and seventy fools loose in the street; and three policemen can scatter them. But huddle them together in a certain house in Westminster; and let them go through certain ceremonies and call themselves certain names until at last they get the courage to kill; and your six hundred and seventy fools become a government. Your pious mob fills up ballot papers and imagines it is governing its masters; but the ballot paper that really governs is the paper that has a bullet wrapped up in it.

CUSINS: That is perhaps why, like most intelligent people, I never vote.

UNDERSHAFT: Vote! Bah! When you vote, you only change the names of the cabinet. When you shoot, you pull down governments, inaugurate new epochs, abolish old orders and set up new. Is that historically true, Mr. Learned Man, or is it not?

CUSINS: It is historically true. I loathe having to admit it. I repudiate your sentiments. I abhor your nature. I defy you in every possible way. Still, it is true. But it ought not to be true.

UNDERSHAFT: Ought! ought! ought! ought! ought! Are you going to spend your life saying ought, like the rest of our moralists? Turn your oughts into shalls, man. Come and make explosives with me. Whatever can blow men up can blow society up. The history of the world is the history of

---

Primerose League, Primrose League, named after Disraeli's favorite flower. Founded in 1883, the League followed Lord Beaconsfield's Conservative politics. *American cloth,* long used in England for oilcloth.

those who had courage enough to embrace this truth. Have you the courage to embrace it, Barbara?

LADY BRITOMART: Barbara, I positively forbid you to listen to your father's abominable wickedness. And you, Adolphus, ought to know better than to go about saying that wrong things are true. What does it matter whether they are true if they are wrong?

UNDERSHAFT: What does it matter whether they are wrong if they are true?

LADY BRITOMART (rising): Children: come home instantly. Andrew: I am exceedingly sorry I allowed you to call on us. You are wickeder than ever. Come at once.

BARBARA (shaking her head): It's no use running away from wicked people, mamma.

LADY BRITOMART: It is every use. It shews your disapprobation of them.

BARBARA: It does not save them.

LADY BRITOMART: I can see that you are going to disobey me. Sarah: are you coming home or are you not?

SARAH: I daresay it's very wicked of papa to make cannons; but I don't think I shall cut him on that account.

LOMAX (pouring oil on the troubled waters): The fact is, you know, there is a certain amount of tosh about this notion of wickedness. It doesn't work. You must look at facts. Not that I would say a word in favor of anything wrong; but then, you see, all sorts of chaps are always doing all sorts of things; and we have to fit them in somehow, don't you know. What I mean is, that you can't go cutting everybody; and that's about what it comes to. (Their rapt attention to his eloquence makes him nervous.) Perhaps I don't make myself clear.

LADY BRITOMART: You are lucidity itself, Charles. Because Andrew is successful and has plenty of money to give to Sarah, you will flatter him and encourage him in his wickedness.

LOMAX (unruffled): Well, where the carcase is, there will the eagles be gathered, don't you know. (to UNDERSHAFT) Eh? What?

UNDERSHAFT: Precisely. By the way, may I call you Charles?

LOMAX: Delighted. Cholly is the usual ticket.

UNDERSHAFT (to LADY BRITOMART): Biddy—

LADY BRITOMART (violently): Don't dare call me Biddy. Charles Lomax: you are a fool. Adolphus Cusins: you are a Jesuit. Stephen: you are a prig. Barbara: you are a lunatic. Andrew: you are a vulgar tradesman. Now you all know my opinion; and my conscience is clear, at all events. (She sits down with a vehemence that the rug fortunately softens.)

UNDERSHAFT: My dear: you are the incarnation of morality. (She snorts.) Your conscience is clear and your duty done when you have called everybody names. Come, Euripides! it is getting late; and we all want to go home. Make up your mind.

CUSINS: Understand this, you old demon—

LADY BRITOMART: Adolphus!

UNDERSHAFT: Let him alone, Biddy. Proceed, Euripides.

CUSINS: You have me in a horrible dilemma. I want Barbara.

UNDERSHAFT: Like all young men, you greatly exaggerate the difference between one young woman and another.

BARBARA: Quite true, Dolly.

CUSINS: I also want to avoid being a rascal.

UNDERSHAFT (with biting contempt): You lust for personal righteousness, for self-approval, for what you call a good conscience, for what Barbara calls salvation, for what I call patronizing people who are not so lucky as yourself.

CUSINS: I do not: all the poet in me recoils from being a good man. But there are things in me that I must reckon with. Pity—

UNDERSHAFT: Pity! The scavenger of misery.

CUSINS: Well, love.

UNDERSHAFT: I know. You love the needy and the outcast: you love the oppressed races, the negro, the Indian ryot, the underdog everywhere. Do you love the Japanese? Do you love the French? Do you love the English?

CUSINS: No. Every true Englishman detests the English. We are the wickedest nation on earth; and our success is a moral horror.

UNDERSHAFT: That is what comes of your gospel of love, is it?

CUSINS: May I not love even my father-in-law?

UNDERSHAFT: Who wants your love, man? By what right do you take the liberty of offering it to me? I will have your due heed and respect, or I will kill you. But your love! Damn your impertinence!

CUSINS (grinning): I may not be able to control my affections, Mac.

UNDERSHAFT: You are fencing, Euripides. You are weakening: your grip is slipping. Come! try your last weapon. Pity and love have broken in your hand: forgiveness is still left.

CUSINS: No: forgiveness is a beggar's refuge. I am with you there: we must pay our debts.

UNDERSHAFT: Well said. Come! you will suit me. Remember the words of Plato.

CUSINS (starting): Plato! You dare quote Plato to me!

UNDERSHAFT: Plato says, my friend, that society cannot be saved until either the Professors of Greek take to making gunpowder, or else the makers of gunpowder become Professors of Greek.

CUSINS: Oh, tempter, cunning tempter!

UNDERSHAFT: Come! choose, man, choose.

CUSINS: But perhaps Barbara will not marry me if I make the wrong choice.

BARBARA: Perhaps not.

CUSINS (*desperately perplexed*): You hear!

BARBARA: Father: do you love nobody?

UNDERSHAFT: I love my best friend.

LADY BRITOMART: And who is that, pray?

UNDERSHAFT: My bravest enemy. That is the man who keeps me up to the mark.

CUSINS: You know, the creature is really a sort of poet in his way. Suppose he is a great man, after all!

UNDERSHAFT: Suppose you stop talking and make up your mind, my young friend.

CUSINS: But you are driving me against my nature. I hate war.

UNDERSHAFT: Hatred is the coward's revenge for being intimidated. Dare you make war on war? Here are the means: my friend Mr Lomax is sitting on them.

LOMAX (*springing up*): Oh I say! You don't mean that this thing is loaded, do you? My ownest: come off it.

SARAH (*sitting placidly on the shell*): If I am to be blown up, the more thoroughly it is done the better. Don't fuss, Cholly.

LOMAX (*to* UNDERSHAFT, *strongly remonstrant*): Your own daughter, you know.

UNDERSHAFT: So I see. (*to* CUSINS) Well, my friend, may we expect you here at six tomorrow morning?

CUSINS (*firmly*): Not on any account. I will see the whole establishment blown up with its own dynamite before I will get up at five. My hours are healthy, rational hours: eleven to five.

UNDERSHAFT: Come when you please: before a week you will come at six and stay until I turn you out for the sake of your health. (*Calling.*) Bilton! (*He turns to* LADY BRITOMART, *who rises.*) My dear: let us leave these two young people to themselves for a moment. (BILTON *comes from the shed.*) I am going to take you through the gun cotton shed.

BILTON (*barring the way*): You can't take anything explosive in here, sir.

LADY BRITOMART: What do you mean? Are you alluding to me?

BILTON (*unmoved*): No, ma'am. Mr. Undershaft has the other gentleman's matches in his pocket.

LADY BRITOMART (*abruptly*): Oh! I beg your pardon. (*She goes into the shed.*)

UNDERSHAFT: Quite right, Bilton, quite right: here you are. (*He gives* BILTON *the box of matches.*) Come, Stephen. Come, Charles. Bring Sarah. (*He passes into the shed.*)

(BILTON *opens the box and deliberately drops the matches into the fire-bucket.*)

LOMAX: Oh I say! (BILTON *stolidly hands him the empty box.*) Infernal nonsense! Pure scientific ignorance! (*He goes in.*)

SARAH: Am I all right, Bilton?

BILTON: You'll have to put on list slippers, miss: that's all. We've got 'em inside. (*She goes in.*)

STEPHEN (*very seriously to* CUSINS): Dolly, old fellow, think. Think before you decide. Do you feel that you are a sufficiently practical man? It is a huge undertaking, an enormous responsibility. All this mass of business will be Greek to you.

CUSINS: Oh, I think it will be much less difficult than Greek.

STEPHEN: Well, I just want to say this before I leave you to yourselves. Don't let anything I have said about right and wrong prejudice you against this great chance in life. I have satisfied myself that the business is one of the highest character and a credit to our country. (*Emotionally.*) I am very proud of my father. I— (*Unable to proceed, he presses* CUSINS' *hand and goes hastily into the shed, followed by* BILTON.)

(BARBARA *and* CUSINS, *left alone together, look at one another silently.*)

CUSINS: Barbara: I am going to accept this offer.

BARBARA: I thought you would.

CUSINS: You understand, don't you, that I had to decide without consulting you. If I had thrown the burden of the choice on you, you would sooner or later have despised me for it.

BARBARA: Yes: I did not want you to sell your soul for me any more than for this inheritance.

CUSINS: It is not the sale of my soul that troubles me: I have sold it too often to care about that. I have sold it for a professorship. I have sold it for an income. I have sold it to escape being imprisoned for refusing to pay taxes for hangmen's ropes and unjust wars and things that I abhor. What is all human conduct but the daily and hourly sale of our souls for trifles? What I am now selling it for is neither money nor position nor comfort, but for reality and for power.

BARBARA: You know that you will have no power, and that he has none.

CUSINS: I know. It is not for myself alone. I want to make power for the world.

BARBARA: I want to make power for the world too; but it must be spiritual power.

CUSINS: I think all power is spiritual: these cannons will not go off by themselves. I have tried to make spiritual power by teaching Greek. But the world can never be really touched by a dead language and a dead civilization. The people must have power; and the people cannot have Greek. Now the power that is made here can be wielded by all men.

BARBARA: Power to burn women's houses down and kill their sons and tear their husbands to pieces.

CUSINS: You cannot have power for good without having power for evil too. Even mother's milk nourishes murderers as well as heroes. This power which only tears men's bodies to pieces has never been so horribly abused as the intellectual power, the imaginative power, the poetic, religious power that can enslave men's souls. As a teacher of Greek I gave the intellectual man weapons against the common man. I now want to give the common man weapons against the intellectual man. I love the common people. I want to arm them against the lawyers, the doctors, the priests, the literary men, the professors, the artists, and the politicians, who, once in authority, are more disastrous and tyrannical than all the fools, rascals, and imposters. I want a power simple enough for common men to use, yet strong enough to force the intellectual oligarchy to use its genius for the general good.

BARBARA: Is there no higher power than that? (Pointing to the shell.)

CUSINS: Yes; but that power can destroy the higher powers just as a tiger can destroy a man: therefore Man must master that power first. I admitted this when the Turks and Greeks were last at war. My best pupil went out to fight for Hellas. My parting gift to him was not a copy of Plato's *Republic,* but a revolver and a hundred Undershaft cartridges. The blood of every Turk he shot—if he shot any—is on my head as well as on Undershaft's. That act committed me to this place for ever. Your father's challenge has beaten me. Dare I make war on war? I dare. I must. I will. And now, is it all over between us?

BARBARA (touched by his evident dread of her answer): Silly baby Dolly! How could it be!

CUSINS (overjoyed): Then you—you—you—Oh for my drum! (He flourishes imaginary drumsticks.)

BARBARA (angered by his levity): Take care, Dolly, take care. Oh, if only I could get away from you and from father and from it all! if I could have the wings of a dove and fly away to heaven!

CUSINS: And leave me!

BARBARA: Yes, you, and all the other naughty mischievous children of men. But I can't. I was happy in the Salvation Army for a moment. I escaped from the world into a paradise of enthusiasm and prayer and soul saving; but the moment our money ran short, it all came back to Bodger: it was he who saved our people: he, and the Prince of Darkness, my papa. Undershaft and Bodger: their hands stretch everywhere: when we feed a starving fellow creature, it is with their bread, because there is no other bread; when we tend the sick, it is in the hospitals they endow; if we turn from the churches they build, we must kneel on the stones of the streets they pave. As long as that lasts, there is no getting away from them. Turning our backs on Bodger and Undershaft is turning our backs on life.

CUSINS: I thought you were determined to turn your back on the wicked side of life.

BARBARA: There is no wicked side: life is all one. And I never wanted to shirk my share in whatever evil must be endured, whether it be sin or suffering. I wish I could cure you of middle-class ideas, Dolly.

CUSINS (gasping): Middle cl—! A snub! A social snub to me! from the daughter of a foundling!

BARBARA: That is why I have no class, Dolly: I come straight out of the heart of the whole people. If I were middle-class I should turn my back on my father's business; and we should both live in an artistic drawing room, with you reading the reviews in one corner, and I in the other at the piano, playing Schumann: both very superior persons, and neither of us a bit of use. Sooner than that, I would sweep out the guncotton shed, or be one of Bodger's barmaids. Do you know what would have happened if you had refused papa's offer?

CUSINS: I wonder!

BARBARA: I should have given you up and married the man who accepted it. After all, my dear old mother has more sense than any of you. I felt like her when I saw this place—felt that I must have it—that never, never, never, could I let it go; only she thought it was the houses and the kitchen ranges and the linen and china, when it was really all the human souls to be saved: not weak souls in starved bodies, sobbing with gratitude for a scrap of bread and treacle, but fullfed, quarrelsome, snobbish, uppish creatures, all standing on their little rights and dignities, and thinking that my father ought to be greatly obliged to them for making so much money for him—and so he ought. That is where salvation is really wanted. My father shall never throw it in my teeth again that my converts were bribed with bread. (She is transfigured.) I have got rid of the bribe of bread. I have got rid of the bribe of heaven. Let God's work be done for its own sake: the work he had to create us to do because it cannot be done except by living men and women. When I die, let him be in my debt, not I in his; and let me forgive him as becomes a woman of my rank.

CUSINS: Then the way of life lies through the factory of death?

BARBARA: Yes, through the raising of hell to heaven and of man to God, through the unveiling of an eternal light in the Valley of The Shadow. (Seiz-

ing him with both hands.) Oh, did you think my courage would never come back? did you believe that I was a deserter? that I, who have stood in the streets, and taken my people to my heart, and talked of the holiest and greatest things with them, could ever turn back and chatter foolishly to fashionable people about nothing in a drawing room? Never, never, never, never: Major Barbara will die with the colors. Oh! and I have my dear little Dolly boy still; and he has found me my place and my work. Glory Hallelujah! *(She kisses him.)*

CUSINS: My dearest: consider my delicate health. I cannot stand as much happiness as you can.

BARBARA: Yes: it is not easy work being in love with me, is it? But it's good for you. *(She runs to the shed, and calls, childlike.)* Mamma! Mamma! *(BIL- TON comes out of the shed, followed by UNDERSHAFT.)* I want mamma.

UNDERSHAFT: She is taking off her list slippers, dear. *(He passes on to CUSINS.)* Well? What does she say?

CUSINS: She has gone right up into the skies.

LADY BRITOMART *(coming from the shed and stopping on the steps, obstructing SARAH, who follows with LOMAX. BARBARA clutches like a baby at her mother's skirt)*: Barbara: when will you learn to be independent and to act and think for yourself? I know as well as possible what that cry of "Mamma, Mamma," means. Always running to me!

SARAH *(touching LADY BRITOMART's ribs with her finger tips and imitating a bicycle horn)*: Pip! pip!

LADY BRITOMART *(highly indignant)*: How dare you say Pip! pip! to me, Sarah? You are both very naughty children. What do you want, Barbara?

BARBARA: I want a house in the village to live in with Dolly. *(Dragging at the skirt.)* Come and tell me which one to take.

UNDERSHAFT *(to CUSINS)*: Six o'clock tomorrow morning, Euripides.

CURTAIN

Figure 62. Undershaft (Brewster Mason) and Lady Britomart (Elizabeth Spriggs) greet one another at the beginning of his visit to meet Sara (Lisa Harrow) and Barbara (Judi Dench), while Lomax *(left)* and Morrison *(right)* look on in the Royal Shakespeare Company production of *Major Barbara,* directed by Clifford Williams, London, 1970. (Photograph: Patrick Eagar.)

Figure 63. Cusins (Richard Pasco) offers the tambourine to Barbara (Judi Dench) while Mrs. Baines *(far left)* and Jenny look on in the Royal Shakespeare Company production of *Major Barbara,* directed by Clifford Williams, London, 1970. (Photograph: Patrick Eagar.)

Figure 64. Undershaft (Brewster Mason) lectures Barbara (Judi Dench) about the faith of the armorer, while Sara and Lomax look on in the Royal Shakespeare Company production of *Major Barbara,* directed by Clifford Williams, London, 1970. (Photograph: Patrick Eagar.)

Staging of *Major Barbara*

**REVIEW OF THE ROYAL SHAKESPEARE
COMPANY PRODUCTION, 1970, BY STANLEY
PRICE**

"Through universal education and cheap printing poor boys became rich and powerful. Dickens, rich. Shaw, also. He boasted that reading Karl Marx made a man of him. I don't know about that, but Marxism for the great public made him a millionaire. If you wrote for an élite, like Proust, you did not become rich, but if your theme was social injustice and your ideas radical you were rewarded by wealth, fame and influence."

Thus old Mr Sammler in Saul Bellow's fine recent novel *Mr Sammler's Planet*. Shaw himself would scarcely have taken umbrage. In his preface to *Major Barbara* he quotes with approval Samuel Butler's insistence on the necessity of 'an earnest and constant sense of the importance of money'.

Major Barbara hymns the necessary virtue of money, and castigates the unnecessary vice of poverty. Undershaft, the devil's advocate of benevolent capitalism, who builds the new Jerusalem around an armaments empire in a garden city, lists the seven deadly sins as "food, clothing, firing, rent, taxes, respectability and children. Nothing can lift those seven millstones from man's neck but money, and the spirit cannot soar until the millstones are lifted." Thus, ultimately, Undershaft, destroyer of lives, triumphs over the savers of souls. With the loaded dice of Shavian paradox this is accomplished because Undershaft is a creator and beneficent distributor of wealth, whilst the Salvationists merely exploit the helplessness of poverty: bread and scrape today to gain eternal jam tomorrow.

First produced in 1905, *Major Barbara* remains a remarkably relevant battle-cry to contemporary barricades. The Undershaft motto is "Nothing is ever done in this world until men are prepared to kill one another if it is not done." This is the jingoism of revolution; that we must make war in order to make love. It is a far cry from the gradualism of Shaw's Fabian contemporaries, or the ineffectuality of much current youthful protest. In the Preface, Shaw further comments on the deserved powerlessness of society's prisons, punishments and bayonets against the dedicated self-sacrifice of one anarchist acting out of outraged conscience. Shaw's remedy is "simply not to outrage their consciences." The play's contemporary aptness leaves one, 65 years on, speculating on Shaw's probable attitudes to student militancy, hijacking, and the sale of arms to South Africa. Would Shaw have been another Russell, lifted deferentially from a squat in Whitehall? Or merely another Boss/Brecht manufacturing bon-mots while hippy Plebeians rehearsed their uprising, and his idealised Undershafts showed their feet of clay in the face of Russian naval menace in the Indian Ocean.

As possibly befits both this contemporary relevance and the Royal Shakespeare Company's first Shaw play, Clifford Williams' production gives priority to the words and arguments. He has not been lured into reducing the full-scale of the big Aldwych stage to drawing-room proportions, the normal procedure for productions trying to imply that there is more action going on in a Shaw play than there really is. This principle seems based on the theory that actors doing nothing in a confined space appear busier than actors doing nothing in a large space. And it is interesting to note that Ralph Koltai's set is conceived vertically—actors ascend and descend rather than exit left and right.

The play begins on the large, empty stage beneath a huge banner of Karl Marx—fair warning about the production's prime concern. Stage hands in Edwardian disguise move on the f & f of Lady Britomart's library, mere token furnishings in the large unoccupied areas. The Salvation Army hostel scene is played out in an area vast as an aeroplane hangar. The effect initially seems to dwarf the characters, yet ultimately manages to focus maximum attention on what they are saying. The cast copes magnificently with the wide-open spaces by the uniform excellence of their diction, intelligence and movement.

Brewster Mason's Undershaft is a model of intelligent concise playing. Every seemingly cynical word seems mined and minted from years of hard experience, at the same time advancing heavyweight argument with the agility of a featherweight. Elizabeth Spriggs makes Lady Britomart a sharp-tongued Elizabethan battleaxe without ever descending into caricature. Lady Britomart's barbed intelligence enables her to ask all the questions, while her secure upper-class poise allows her to ignore anybody else's answers. These are two splendidly matching performances at the core of the play, ably abetted by a delightfully spry tour-de-force from Richard Pasco as the intellectually chameleon Adolphus Cusins. Peering quizzically over rimless spectacles, he keeps one constantly guessing whether he is driven from Academia through Salvationism into tycoonery by his search for love, truth or plain intellectual survival.

The excellence of these leads is matched by some fine supporting playing from Roger Rees, Michael Gambon, Don Henderson, Milton Johns and Miles Anderson.

Always I come to Shaw's heroines with acute misgivings. Major Barbara herself seems perched uneasily between that awful pertness that Shaw offered as feminism in *Man and Superman* and the lighter comedies, and the almost hockey-playing saintliness that reached its apotheosis in *Saint Joan*. Judi Dench may have seemed the perfect answer to the problem. There has always been an openness and wholesomeness about her playing that is made dramatic by a quality of vulnerability. As Barbara, however, she tends to emphasize the more embarrassingly self-conscious moments of the Major's missionary zeal. Shaw was fascinated by people who were motivated by passion, especially religious passion. Judi Dench plays Barbara as a tomboy who chose the Church rather than the Hunt, and somewhere the passion and fascination are lost. I would suggest it was more Shaw's fault than Miss Dench's if I did not still have a glowing memory of Wendy Hiller in the old film to make me eat my words.

Mr. Sammler's critique of rich, radical Mr Shaw ends with "I have an objection to extended explanations. There are too many. This makes the mental life of mankind ungovernable. . . . It is not as if I were certain that human beings can be controlled at any level of complexity. I would not swear that mankind was governable." Sammler is an old-world survivalist who has seen and despaired of the New World. Shaw, for all his anti-religious protest, was a salvationist at heart. He wanted salvation now rather than later—"Let God's work be done for its own sake." The Aldwych's excellent production gives full measure to Shaw's plea for benevolence and salvation as the worthy end, whatever the means of the revolution that has to come.

JOHN MILLINGTON SYNGE

1871—1909

Although Synge lived only long enough to write six plays, all of them during the last several years of his life, these six plays about Irish folk experience are so powerful and evocative that they have established him as the first great playwright of the modern Irish theater. This dramatic achievement could hardly have been predicted either from his childhood or his educational experience, for he was born and reared in Dublin in a repressive Calvinistic household, and he was educated at Trinity College, Dublin, where he studied natural science, music, as well as the Gaelic and Hebrew languages. His theatrical career could not even have been anticipated from his early adulthood, for after graduating from Trinity College in 1892, he left Ireland to travel in Germany, Italy, and France, and then settled down in Paris to study at the Sorbonne. While in Paris, he gave himself over to learning French and Italian, as well as to writing poems and reviews. But in 1896, Synge had a prophetic encounter with the great Irish poet, William Butler Yeats, who gave him the following advice:

> Give up Paris, you will never create anything by reading Racine, and Arthur Symons will always be a better critic of French literature. Go to the Aran Islands. Live there as if you were one of the people themselves; express a life that has never found expression.

By 1898, Synge had finally given up on his desire to make a literary career in Paris, and he acted on Yeats' advice. From 1898 to 1902, he spent every summer in the Aran Islands, off the western coast of Ireland, immersing himself in the experience of the peasants and keeping a record of impressions that he subsequently drew on in the plays he wrote between 1902 and 1909. The primitive life of the peasants on those barren islands was clearly a harsh struggle for existence, as Synge made evident in the published version of his journal, *The Aran Islands* (1907), but the dignity and the joy with which those peasants endured hardship clearly stimulated Synge's imagination, as did the richness and wildness of their colloquial language, which he sought to reflect in all his plays.

Synge was also stimulated by a new theatrical movement that developed in Dublin between 1899 and 1902; during that period Yeats, with the support of his wealthy literary friend Lady Augusta Gregory and the collaboration of other Irish writers, was in the process of launching the Irish Literary Theatre, a repertory group dedicated to developing a native Irish drama that would "bring upon the stage the deeper thoughts and emotions of Ireland." This group, which is now well known as The Abbey Theatre for the playhouse that was donated to it in 1904, deliberately aimed to set itself apart from the naturalistic drama of Ibsen and Strindberg that was then thriving on the continent, seeking instead to echo the richly poetic language of Irish experience. These artistic goals evidently appealed to Synge, for as he indicated in his "Preface" to *The Playboy of the Western World,* he too regarded Ibsen as "dealing with the reality of life in joyless and pallid words," and he too believed that the language of Irish drama should reflect "a popular imagination that is fiery and magnificent, and tender." Synge readily accepted Yeats' invitation to join the new group, and from 1902 on he wrote and directed for the Abbey Theatre.

Synge's first play, *In the Shadow of the Glen* (1903), based on an Irish folk tale, is a serio-comic spectacle of marital incompatibility between a jealous old man and a sensitive young woman who is lured away from her marriage by the poetic visions of a young tramp—"You'll be hearing the herons crying out over the black lakes, and you'll be hearing the grouse and the owls with them, and the larks and the big thrushes when the days are warm; and it's not from the like of them you'll be hearing a tale of getting old." In his next work, *Riders to the Sea* (1904), the greatest of his one-act plays, Synge used his evocative language to dramatize the nobility of a brave old peasant woman as she endures the loss of her last son to the sea after already having lost her husband and her five other sons to it—a loss that she finally transcends through the ironic reflection that "They're all gone now, and there isn't anything more the sea can do to me." Synge once again turned to Irish folklore in his next play, *The Well of the Saints* (1905), a serio-comic work in three acts that depicts the vanities and escapism of a blind old couple who miraculously have their sight restored temporarily by a saint, only to discover their physical ugliness. This moves them to reject another offer by the saint to perpetuate their sight, preferring instead to return to the illusions of their blindness that the husband sustains through the flights of his poetic imagination.

Synge's persistent concern with the mythic power of the Irish imagination reached its most thoroughgoing and boisterous expression in his next work, *The Playboy of the Western World* (1907). From the moment that Christy Mahon staggers into Michael James' pub and proceeds to tell his bloody tale of having murdered his tyrannical father, he transforms the lives of the desolate villagers, who in turn transform him into their hero. Imagination works powerfully on the lives of everyone in the play, and when they are deprived of its buoyant powers their bitterness cannot be allayed even by Christy's genuine display of courage at the end. Although Christy's heroic stature is, indeed, shattered by the entrance of his father into the pub, the play does at last enact an archetypal struggle for survival between father and son, and in this sense may also be seen as a variation on the theme of patricide embodied in *Oedipus Rex*. The play is an arresting variation, because it initially dramatizes the villagers' tacit approval of patricide in their celebration of Christy's supposed murder, but in the end it exposes their horror of the act when they are faced with the possibility that it might occur in their presence. As Pegeen proclaims, "there's a great gap between a gallous story and a dirty deed." It is as if Christy has forced the villagers to recognize within themselves the imaginative appeal of violating so powerful a taboo, a violation that he at last is even willing to make and that his father is even willing to accept. Despite all its boisterous and farcical activity, *The Playboy of the Western World* plays seriously with the themes of imagination and reality.

The play also takes pleasure, of course, in what Synge called the "rich and living" language of the Irish imagination. In his "Preface" to the work, for example, he asserted that "In a good play every speech should be as fully flavored as a nut or apple, and such speeches cannot be written by anyone who works among people who have shut their lips on poetry." Synge was at pains to make this point, because the "fully flavored" language of his characters provoked a riot among the audience when the play was first produced at the Abbey Theatre. Synge's Irish countrymen evidently thought that his play was an insult to their national character, a depiction of them as a foul-mouthed group of country bumpkins. The language of the play no longer provokes audiences to riot, yet it does continue to create pronunciation problems for actors and actresses, even those of Irish stock, as noted in the review of the 1971 Lincoln Center production reprinted following the text. Photographs of that production show the physical energy the company brought to staging some of the most dynamic moments in the play, such as Christy rising on a tide of talk following his athletic triumph in the village games (see Figure 65), Christy being roped and tortured by the angry villagers (Figure 66), and Christy berating his father during their final confrontation (Figure 67). These scenes taken together also epitomize the play's movement from imaginative exhilaration, to the bitterness of shattered illusions, to the harsh reality that is embodied in the archetypal struggle between fathers and sons.

THE PLAYBOY OF THE WESTERN WORLD

BY JOHN MILLINGTON SYNGE

CHARACTERS

CHRISTOPHER MAHON
OLD MAHON, *his father—a squatter*
MICHAEL JAMES FLAHERTY, *called* MICHAEL JAMES, *a publican*
MARGARET FLAHERTY, *called* PEGEEN MIKE, *his daughter*
WIDOW QUIN, *a woman of about thirty*
SHAWN KEOGH, *her cousin, a young farmer*
PHILLY CULLEN *and* JIMMY FARRELL, *small farmers*

SARA TANSEY, SUSAN BRADY, *and* HONOR BLAKE, *village girls*
A BELLMAN
SOME PEASANTS

SCENE

The action takes place near a village, on a wild coast of Mayo. The first act passes on an evening of autumn, the other two acts on the following day.

ACT 1

(Country public-house or shebeen, very rough and untidy. There is a sort of counter on the right with shelves, holding many bottles and jugs, just seen above it. Empty barrels stand near the counter. At back, a little to left of counter, there is a door into the open air, then, more to the left, there is a settle with shelves above it, with more jugs, and a table beneath a window. At the left there is a large open fire-place, with turf fire, and a small door into inner room. PEGEEN, *a wild-looking but fine girl, of about twenty, is writing at table. She is dressed in the usual peasant dress)*

PEGEEN *(slowly as she writes)*: Six yards of stuff for to make a yellow gown. A pair of lace boots with lengthy heels on them and brassy eyes. A hat is suited for a wedding day. A fine tooth comb. To be sent with three barrels of porter in Jimmy Farrell's creel cart on the evening of the coming Fair to Mister Michael James Flaherty. With the best compliments of this season. Margaret Flaherty.

SHAWN KEOGH *(a fat and fair young man comes in as she signs, looks round awkwardly, when he sees she is alone)*: Where's himself?

PEGEEN *(without looking at him)*: He's coming. *(She directs the letter.)* To Mister Sheamus Mulroy, Wine and Spirit Dealer, Castlebar.

SHAWN *(uneasily)*: I didn't see him on the road.

PEGEEN: How would you see him *(Licks stamp and puts it on letter.)* and it dark night this half hour gone by?

SHAWN *(turning toward the door again)*: I stood a while outside wondering would I have a right to pass

on or to walk in and see you, Pegeen Mike *(Comes to fire.)*, and I could hear the cows breathing, and sighing in the stillness of the air, and not a step moving any place from this gate to the bridge.

PEGEEN *(putting letter in envelope)*: It's above at the cross-roads he is, meeting Philly Cullen, and a couple more are going along with him to Kate Cassidy's wake.

SHAWN *(looking at her blankly)*: And he's going that length in the dark night?

PEGEEN *(impatiently)*: He is surely, and leaving me lonesome on the scruff of the hill. *(She gets up and puts envelope on dresser, then winds clock.)* Isn't it long the nights are now, Shawn Keogh, to be leaving a poor girl with her own self counting the hours to the dawn of day?

SHAWN *(with awkward humor)*: If it is, when we're wedded in a short while you'll have no call to complain, for I've little will to be walking off to wakes or weddings in the darkness of the night.

PEGEEN *(with rather scornful good humor)*: You're making mighty certain, Shaneen, that I'll wed you now.

SHAWN: Aren't we after making a good bargain, the way we're only waiting these days on Father Reilly's dispensation from the bishops, or the Court of Rome.

PEGEEN *(looking at him teasingly, washing up at dresser)*: It's a wonder, Shaneen, the Holy Father'd be taking notice of the likes of you; for if I was him I wouldn't bother with this place where you'll meet none but Red Linahan, has a squint in his eye, and Patcheen is lame in his heel, or the mad Mulrannies were driven from California and they lost in their wits. We're a queer lot these times to go troubling the Holy Father on his sacred seat.

SHAWN (*scandalized*): If we are, we're as good this place as another, maybe, and as good these times as we were for ever.

PEGEEN (*with scorn*): As good, is it? Where now will you meet the like of Daneen Sullivan knocked the eye from a peeler,° or Marcus Quin, God rest him, got six months for maiming ewes, and he a great warrant to tell stories of holy Ireland till he'd have the old women shedding down tears about their feet. Where will you find the like of them, I'm saying?

SHAWN (*timidly*): If you don't, it's a good job, maybe; for (*With peculiar emphasis on the words.*) Father Reilly has small conceit to have that kind walking around and talking to the girls.

PEGEEN (*impatiently, throwing water from basin out of the door*): Stop tormenting me with Father Reilly (*Imitating his voice.*) when I'm asking only what way I'll pass these twelve hours of dark, and not take my death with the fear.

(*Looking out of door.*)

SHAWN (*timidly*): Would I fetch you the Widow Quin, maybe?

PEGEEN: Is it the like of that murderer? You'll not, surely.

SHAWN (*going to her, soothingly*): Then I'm thinking himself will stop along with you when he sees you taking on, for it'll be a long night-time with great darkness, and I'm after feeling a kind of fellow above in the furzy ditch, groaning wicked like a maddening dog, the way it's good cause you have, maybe, to be fearing now.

PEGEEN (*turning on him sharply*): What's that? Is it a man you seen?

SHAWN (*retreating*): I couldn't see him at all; but I heard him groaning out, and breaking his heart. It should have been a young man from his words speaking.

PEGEEN (*going after him*): And you never went near to see was he hurted or what ailed him at all?

SHAWN: I did not, Pegeen Mike. It was a dark, lonesome place to be hearing the like of him.

PEGEEN: Well, you're a daring fellow, and if they find his corpse stretched above in the dews of dawn, what'll you say then to the peelers, or the Justice of the Peace?

SHAWN (*thunderstruck*): I wasn't thinking of that. For the love of God, Pegeen Mike, don't let on I was speaking of him. Don't tell your father and the

---

peeler, policeman.

men is coming above; for if they heard that story, they'd have great blabbing this night at the wake.

PEGEEN: I'll maybe tell them, and I'll maybe not.

SHAWN: They are coming at the door. Will you whisht, I'm saying?

PEGEEN: Whisht yourself.

(*She goes behind counter.* MICHAEL JAMES, *fat jovial publican, comes in followed by* PHILLY CULLEN, *who is thin and mistrusting, and* JIMMY FARRELL, *who is fat and amorous, about forty-five.*)

MEN (*together*): God bless you. The blessing of God on this place.

PEGEEN: God bless you kindly.

MICHAEL (*to men who go to the counter*): Sit down now, and take your rest. (*Crosses to* SHAWN *at the fire.*) And how is it you are, Shawn Keogh? Are you coming over the sands to Kate Cassidy's wake?

SHAWN: I am not, Michael James. I'm going home the short cut to my bed.

PEGEEN (*speaking across the counter*): He's right, too, and have you no shame, Michael James, to be quitting off for the whole night, and leaving myself lonesome in the shop?

MICHAEL (*good-humoredly*): Isn't it the same whether I go for the whole night or a part only? and I'm thinking it's a queer daughter you are if you'd have me crossing backward through the Stooks of the Dead Women, with a drop taken.

PEGEEN: If I am a queer daughter, it's a queer father'd be leaving me lonesome these twelve hours of dark, and I piling the turf with the dogs barking, and the calves mooing, and my own teeth rattling with the fear.

JIMMY (*flatteringly*): What is there to hurt you, and you a fine, hardy girl would knock the head of any two men in the place?

PEGEEN (*working herself up*): Isn't there the harvest boys with their tongues red for drink, and the ten tinkers is camped in the east glen, and the thousand militia—bad cess to them!—walking idle through the land. There's lots surely to hurt me, and I won't stop alone in it, let himself do what he will.

MICHAEL: If you're that afeard, let Shawn Keogh stop along with you. It's the will of God, I'm thinking, himself should be seeing to you now.

(*They all turn on* SHAWN.)

SHAWN (*in horrified confusion*): I would and welcome, Michael James, but I'm afeard of Father Reilly; and what at all would the Holy Father and the Cardinals of Rome be saying if they heard I did the like of that?

MICHAEL (*with contempt*): God help you! Can't you sit in by the hearth with the light lit and herself beyond in the room? You'll do that surely, for I've heard tell there's a queer fellow above, going mad or getting his death, maybe, in the gripe of the ditch, so she'd be safer this night with a person here.

SHAWN (*with plaintive despair*): I'm afeard of Father Reilly, I'm saying. Let you not be tempting me, and we near married itself.

PHILLY (*with cold contempt*): Lock him in the west room. He'll stay then and have no sin to be telling to the priest.

MICHAEL (*to* SHAWN, *getting between him and the door*): Go up now.

SHAWN (*at the top of his voice*): Don't stop me, Michael James. Let me out of the door, I'm saying, for the love of the Almighty God. Let me out. (*Trying to dodge past him.*) Let me out of it, and may God grant you His indulgence in the hour of need.

MICHAEL (*loudly*): Stop your noising, and sit down by the hearth.

(*Gives him a push and goes to counter laughing.*)

SHAWN (*turning back, wringing his hands*): Oh, Father Reilly and the saints of God, where will I hide myself to-day? Oh, St. Joseph and St. Patrick and St. Brigid, and St. James, have mercy on me now!

(SHAWN *turns round, sees door clear, and makes a rush for it.*)

MICHAEL (*catching him by the coat tail*): You'd be going, is it?

SHAWN (*screaming*): Leave me go, Michael James, leave me go, you old Pagan, leave me go, or I'll get the curse of the priests on you, and of the scarlet-coated bishops of the courts of Rome.

(*With a sudden movement he pulls himself out of his coat, and disappears out of the door, leaving his coat in* MICHAEL'S *hands.*)

MICHAEL (*turning round, and holding up coat*): Well, there's the coat of a Christian man. Oh, there's sainted glory this day in the lonesome west; and by the will of God I've got you a decent man, Pegeen, you'll have no call to be spying after if you've a score of young girls, maybe, weeding in your fields.

PEGEEN (*taking up the defence of her property*): What right have you to be making game of a poor fellow for minding the priest, when it's your own fault is, not paying a penny pot-boy to stand along with me and give me courage in the doing of my work?

(*She snaps the coat away from him, and goes behind counter with it.*)

MICHAEL (*taken aback*): Where would I get a pot-boy? Would you have me send the bellman screaming in the streets of Castlebar?

SHAWN (*opening the door a chink and putting in his head, in a small voice*): Michael James!

MICHAEL (*imitating him*): What ails you?

SHAWN: The queer dying fellow's beyond looking over the ditch. He's come up, I'm thinking, stealing your hens. (*Looks over his shoulder.*) God help me, he's following me now (*He runs into room.*), and if he's heard what I said, he'll be having my life, and I going home lonesome in the darkness of the night.

(*For a perceptible moment they watch the door with curiosity. Some one coughs outside. Then* CHRISTY MAHON, *a slight young man, comes in very tired and frightened and dirty.*)

CHRISTY (*in a small voice*): God save all here!

MEN: God save you kindly.

CHRISTY (*going to the counter*): I'd trouble you for a glass of porter, woman of the house. (*He puts down coin.*)

PEGEEN (*serving him*): You're one of the tinkers, young fellow, is beyond camped in the glen?

CHRISTY: I am not; but I'm destroyed walking.

MICHAEL (*patronizingly*): Let you come up then to the fire. You're looking famished with the cold.

CHRISTY: God reward you. (*He takes up his glass and goes a little way across to the left, then stops and looks about him.*) Is it often the police do be coming into this place, master of the house?

MICHAEL: If you'd come in better hours, you'd have seen "Licensed for the sale of Beer and Spirits, to be consumed on the premises," written in white letters above the door, and what would the polis want spying on me, and not a decent house within four miles, the way every living Christian is a bona fide, saving one widow alone?

CHRISTY (*with relief*): It's a safe house, so.

(*He goes over to the fire, sighing and moaning. Then he sits down, putting his glass beside him and begins gnawing a turnip, too miserable to feel the others staring at him with curiosity.*)

MICHAEL (*going after him*): Is it yourself is fearing the polis? You're wanting, maybe?

CHRISTY: There's many wanting.

MICHAEL: Many surely, with the broken harvest and the ended wars. (*He picks up some stockings, etc., that are near the fire, and carries them away furtively.*) It should be larceny, I'm thinking?

CHRISTY (*dolefully*): I had it in my mind it was a different word and a bigger.

PEGEEN: There's a queer lad. Were you never slapped in school, young fellow, that you don't know the name of your deed?

CHRISTY (bashfully): I'm slow at learning, a middling scholar only.

MICHAEL: If you're a dunce itself, you'd have a right to know that larceny's robbing and stealing. It is for the like of that you're wanting?

CHRISTY (with a flash of family pride): And I the son of a strong farmer (With a sudden qualm.), God rest his soul, could have bought up the whole of your old house a while since, from the butt of his tail-pocket, and not have missed the weight of it gone.

MICHAEL (impressed): If it's not stealing, it's maybe something big.

CHRISTY (flattered): Aye; it's maybe something big.

JIMMY: He's a wicked-looking young fellow. Maybe he followed after a young woman on a lonesome night.

CHRISTY (shocked): Oh, the saints forbid, mister; I was all times a decent lad.

PHILLY (turning on JIMMY): You're a silly man, Jimmy Farrell. He said his father was a farmer a while since, and there's himself now in a poor state. Maybe the land was grabbed from him, and he did what any decent man would do.

MICHAEL (to CHRISTY, mysteriously): Was it bailiffs?

CHRISTY: The divil a one.

MICHAEL: Agents?

CHRISTY: The divil a one.

MICHAEL: Landlords?

CHRISTY (peevishly): Ah, not at all, I'm saying. You'd see the like of them stories on any little paper of a Munster town. But I'm not calling to mind any person, gentle, simple, judge or jury, did the like of me.

(They all draw nearer with delighted curiosity.)

PHILLY: Well, that lad's a puzzle-the-world.

JIMMY: He'd beat Dan Davies' circus, or the holy missioners making sermons on the villainy of man. Try him again, Philly.

PHILLY: Did you strike golden guineas out of solder, young fellow, or shilling coins itself?

CHRISTY: I did not, mister, not sixpence nor a farthing coin.

JIMMY: Did you marry three wives maybe? I'm told there's a sprinkling have done that among the holy Luthers of the preaching north.

CHRISTY (shyly): I never married with one, let alone with a couple or three.

PHILLY: Maybe he went fighting for the Boers, the like of the man beyond, was judged to be hanged, quartered and drawn. Were you off east, young fellow, fighting bloody wars for Kruger and the freedom of the Boers?

CHRISTY: I never left my own parish till Tuesday was a week.

PEGEEN (coming from counter): He's done nothing, so. (to CHRISTY) If you didn't commit murder or a bad, nasty thing, or false coining, or robbery, or butchery, or the like of them, there isn't anything that would be worth your troubling for to run from now. You did nothing at all.

CHRISTY (his feelings hurt): That's an unkindly thing to be saying to a poor orphaned traveller, has a prison behind him, and hanging before, and hell's gap gaping below.

PEGEEN (with a sign to the men to be quiet): You're only saying it. You did nothing at all. A soft lad the like of you wouldn't slit the windpipe of a screeching sow.

CHRISTY (offended): You're not speaking the truth.

PEGEEN (in mock rage): Not speaking the truth, is it? Would you have me knock the head of you with the butt of the broom?

CHRISTY (twisting round on her with a sharp cry of horror): Don't strike me. I killed my poor father, Tuesday was a week, for doing the like of that.

PEGEEN (with blank amazement): Is it killed your father?

CHRISTY (subsiding): With the help of God I did surely, and that the Holy Immaculate Mother may intercede for his soul.

PHILLY (retreating with JIMMY): There's a daring fellow.

JIMMY: Oh, glory be to God!

MICHAEL (with great respect): That was a hanging crime, mister honey. You should have had good reason for doing the like of that.

CHRISTY (in a very reasonable tone): He was a dirty man, God forgive him, and he getting old and crusty, the way I couldn't put up with him at all.

PEGEEN: And you shot him dead?

CHRISTY (shaking his head): I never used weapons. I've no license, and I'm a law-fearing man.

MICHAEL: It was with a hilted knife maybe? I'm told, in the big world it's bloody knives they use.

CHRISTY (loudly, scandalized): Do you take me for a slaughter-boy?

PEGEEN: You never hanged him, the way Jimmy Farrell hanged his dog from the license, and had it screeching and wriggling three hours at the butt of a string, and himself swearing it was a dead dog, and the peelers swearing it had life?

CHRISTY: I did not then. I just riz the loy° and let fall the edge of it on the ridge of his skull, and he went down at my feet like an empty sack, and never let a grunt or groan from him at all.

MICHAEL (making a sign to PEGEEN to fill CHRISTY'S

---

loy, a long narrow spade.

glass): And what way weren't you hanged, mister? Did you bury him then?

CHRISTY (*considering*): Aye. I buried him then. Wasn't I digging spuds in the field?

MICHAEL: And the peelers never followed after you the eleven days that you're out?

CHRISTY (*shaking his head*): Never a one of them, and I walking forward facing hog, dog, or divil on the highway of the road.

PHILLY (*nodding wisely*): It's only with a common week-day kind of a murderer them lads would be trusting their carcase, and that man should be a great terror when his temper's roused.

MICHAEL: He should then. (*to* CHRISTY) And where was it, mister honey, that you did the deed?

CHRISTY (*looking at him with suspicion*): Oh, a distant place, master of the house, a windy corner of high, distant hills.

PHILLY (*nodding with approval*): He's a close man, and he's right, surely.

PEGEEN: That'd be a lad with the sense of Solomon to have for a pot-boy, Michael James, if it's the truth you're seeking one at all.

PHILLY: The peelers is fearing him, and if you'd that lad in the house there isn't one of them would come smelling around if the dogs itself were lapping poteen° from the dung-pit of the yard.

JIMMY: Bravery's a treasure in a lonesome place, and a lad would kill his father, I'm thinking, would face a foxy divil with a pitchpike on the flags of hell.

PEGEEN: It's the truth they're saying, and if I'd that lad in the house, I wouldn't be fearing the loosed kharki cut-throats,° or the walking dead.

CHRISTY (*swelling with surprise and triumph*): Well, glory be to God!

MICHAEL (*with deference*): Would you think well to stop here and be pot-boy, mister honey, if we gave you good wages, and didn't destroy you with the weight of work?

SHAWN (*coming forward uneasily*): That'd be a queer kind to bring into a decent quiet household with the like of Pegeen Mike.

PEGEEN (*very sharply*): Will you whisht? Who's speaking to you?

SHAWN (*retreating*): A bloody-handed murderer the like of . . .

PEGEEN (*snapping at him*): Whisht I am saying; we'll take no fooling from your like at all. (*to* CHRISTY *with a honeyed voice*) And you, young fellow, you'd have a right to stop, I'm thinking, for we'd do our all and utmost to content your needs.

CHRISTY (*overcome with wonder*): And I'd be safe in this place from the searching law?

MICHAEL: You would, surely. If they're not fearing you, itself, the peelers in this place is decent droughty° poor fellows, wouldn't touch a cur dog and not give warning in the dead of night.

PEGEEN (*very kindly and persuasively*): Let you stop a short while anyhow. Aren't you destroyed walking with your feet in bleeding blisters, and your whole skin needing washing like a Wicklow sheep.

CHRISTY (*looking round with satisfaction*): It's a nice room, and if it's not humbugging me you are, I'm thinking that I'll surely stay.

JIMMY (*jumps up*): Now, by the grace of God, herself will be safe this night, with a man killed his father holding danger from the door, and let you come on, Michael James, or they'll have the best stuff drunk at the wake.

MICHAEL (*going to the door with men*): And begging your pardon, mister, what name will we call you, for we'd like to know?

CHRISTY: Christopher Mahon.

MICHAEL: Well, God bless you, Christy, and a good rest till we meet again when the sun'll be rising to the noon of day.

CHRISTY: God bless you all.

MEN: God bless you.

(*They go out except* SHAWN, *who lingers at door*)

SHAWN (*to* PEGEEN): Are you wanting me to stop along with you to keep you from harm?

PEGEEN (*gruffly*): Didn't you say you were fearing Father Reilly?

SHAWN: There's be no harm staying now, I'm thinking, and himself in it too.

PEGEEN: You wouldn't stay when there was need for you, and let you step off nimble this time when there's none.

SHAWN: Didn't I say it was Father Reilly . . .

PEGEEN: Go on, then, to Father Reilly (*In a jeering tone.*), and let him put you in the holy brother-hoods, and leave that lad to me.

SHAWN: If I meet the Widow Quin . . .

PEGEEN: Go on, I'm staying, and don't be waking this place with your noise. (*She hustles him out and bolts the door.*) That lad would wear the spirits from the saints of peace. (*Bustles about, then takes off her apron and pins it up in the window as a blind.* CHRISTY *watching her timidly. Then she comes to him and speaks with bland good humor.*) Let you stretch out now by the fire, young fellow. You should be destroyed travelling.

CHRISTY (*shyly again, drawing off his boots*): I'm tired, surely, walking wild seven days, and waking fearful in the night. (*He holds up one of his feet,*

---

poteen, whiskey.   **kharki cut-throats**, English garrison.   **droughty**, thirsty.

feeling his blisters, and looking at them with compassion.)

PEGEEN *(standing beside him, watching him with delight)*: You · should have had great people in your family, I'm thinking, with the little, small feet you have, and you with a kind of a quality name, the like of what you'd find on the great powers and potentates of France and Spain.

CHRISTY *(with pride)*: We were great surely, with wide and windy acres of rich Munster land.

PEGEEN: Wasn't I telling you, and you a fine, handsome young fellow with a noble brow?

CHRISTY *(with a flash of delighted surprise)*: Is it me?

PEGEEN: Aye. Did you never hear that from the young girls where you come from in the west or south?

CHRISTY *(with venom)*: I did not then. Oh, they're bloody liars in the naked parish where I grew a man.

PEGEEN: If they are itself, you've heard it these days, I'm thinking, and you walking the world telling out your story to young girls or old.

CHRISTY: I've told my story no place till this night, Pegeen Mike, and it's foolish I was here, maybe, to be talking free, but you're decent people, I'm thinking, and yourself a kindly woman, the way I wasn't fearing you at all.

PEGEEN *(filling a sack with straw)*: You've said the like of that, maybe, in every cot and cabin where you've met a young girl on your way.

CHRISTY *(going over to her, gradually raising his voice)*: I've said it nowhere till this night, I'm telling you, for I've seen none the like of you the eleven long days I am walking the world, looking over a low ditch or a high ditch on my north or my south, into stony scattered fields, or scribes of bog, where you'd see young, limber girls, and fine prancing women making laughter with the men.

PEGEEN: If you weren't destroyed, traveling, you'd have as much talk and streeleen, I'm thinking, as Owen Roe O'Sullivan or the poets of the Dingle Bay, and I've heard all times it's the poets are your like, fine fiery fellows with great rages when their temper's roused.

CHRISTY *(drawing a little nearer to her)*: You've a power of rings, God bless you, and would there be any offence if I was asking are you single now?

PEGEEN: What would I want wedding so young?

CHRISTY *(with relief)*: We're alike, so.

PEGEEN *(she puts sack on settle and beats it up)*: I never killed my father. I'd be afeard to do that, except I was the like of yourself with blind rages tearing me within, for I'm thinking you should have had great tussling when the end was come.

CHRSITY *(expanding with delight at the first confidential talk he has ever had with a woman)*: We had not

then. It was a hard woman was come over the hill, and if he was always a crusty kind when he'd a hard woman setting him on, not the divil himself or his four fathers could put up with him at all.

PEGEEN *(with curiosity)*: And isn't it a great wonder that one wasn't fearing you?

CHRISTY *(very confidentially)*: Up to the day I killed my father, there wasn't a person in Ireland knew the kind I was, and I there drinking, waking, eating, sleeping, a quiet, simple poor fellow with no man giving me heed.

PEGEEN *(getting a quilt out of the cupboard and putting it on the sack)*: It was the girls were giving you heed maybe, and I'm thinking it's most conceit you'd have to be gaming with their like.

CHRISTY *(shaking his head, with simplicity)*: Not the girls itself, and I won't tell you a lie. There wasn't anyone heeding me in that place saving only the dumb beasts of the field.

(He sits down at fire.)

PEGEEN *(with disappointment)*: And I thinking you should have been living the like of a king of Norway or the Eastern world.

(She comes and sits beside him after placing bread and mug of milk on the table.)

CHRISTY *(laughing piteously)*: The like of a king, is it? And I after toiling, moiling, digging, dodging from the dawn till dusk with never a sight of joy or sport saving only when I'd be abroad in the dark night poaching rabbits on hills, for I was a devil to poach, God forgive me, *(very naively)* and I near got six months for going with a dung fork and stabbing a fish.

PEGEEN: And it's that you'd call sport, is it, to be abroad in the darkness with yourself alone?

CHRISTY: I did, God help me, and there I'd be as happy as the sunshine of St. Martin's Day, watching the light passing the north or the patches of fog, till I'd hear a rabbit starting to screech and I'd go running in the furze. Then when I'd my full share I'd come walking down where you'd see the ducks and geese stretched sleeping on the highway of the road, and before I'd pass the dunghill, I'd hear himself snoring out, a loud lonesome snore he'd be making all times, the while he was sleeping, and he a man'd be raging all times, the while he was waking, like a gaudy officer you'd hear cursing and damning and swearing oaths.

PEGEEN: Providence and Mercy, spare us all!

CHRISTY: It's that you'd say surely if you seen him and he was after drinking for weeks, rising up in the red dawn, or before it maybe, and going out into the yard as naked as an ash tree in the moon of May, and shying clods against the visage of the stars till he'd put the fear of death into the banbhs° and the screeching sows.

PEGEEN: I'd be well-nigh afeard of that lad myself, I'm thinking. And there was no one in it but the two of you alone?

CHRISTY: The divil a one, though he'd sons and daughters walking all great states and territories of the world, and not a one of them, to this day, but would say their seven curses on him, and they rousing up to let a cough or sneeze, maybe, in the deadness of the night.

PEGEEN (nodding her head): Well, you should have been a queer lot. I never cursed my father the like of that, though I'm twenty and more years of age.

CHRISTY: Then you'd have cursed mine, I'm telling you, and he a man never gave peace to any, saving when he'd get two months or three, or be locked in the asylums for battering peelers or assaulting men (With depression.) the way it was a bitter life he led me till I did up a Tuesday and halve his skull.

PEGEEN (putting her hand on his shoulder): Well, you'll have peace in this place, Christy Mahon, and none to trouble you, and it's near time a fine lad like you should have your good share of the earth.

CHRISTY: It's time surely, and I a seemly fellow with great strength in me and bravery of . . .

(Someone knocks.)

CHRISTY (clinging to PEGEEN): Oh, glory! it's late for knocking, and this last while I'm in terror of the peelers, and the walking dead.

(Knocking again.)

PEGEEN: Who's there?

VOICE (outside): Me.

PEGEEN: Who's me?

VOICE: The Widow Quin.

PEGEEN (jumping up and giving him the bread and milk): Go on now with your supper, and let on to be sleepy, for if she found you were such a warrant to talk, she'd be stringing gabble till the dawn of day.

(He takes bread and sits shyly with his back to the door.)

PEGEEN (opening door, with temper): What ails you, or what is it you're wanting at this hour of the night?

WIDOW QUIN (coming in a step and peering at CHRISTY): I'm after meeting Shawn Keogh and Father Reilly below, who told me of your curiosity and they fearing by this time he was maybe roaring, romping on your hands with drink.

PEGEEN (pointing to CHRISTY): Look now is he roaring, and he stretched away drowsy with his supper and his mug of milk. Walk down and tell that to Father Reilly and to Shaneen Keogh.

WIDOW QUIN (coming forward): I'll not see them again, for I've their word to lead that lad forward to lodge with me.

PEGEEN (in blank amazement): This night, is it?

WIDOW QUIN (going over): This night. "It isn't fitting," says the priesteen, "to have his likeness lodging with an orphaned girl." (to CHRISTY) God save you, mister!

CHRISTY (shyly): God save you kindly.

WIDOW QUIN (looking at him with half-amazed curiosity): Well, aren't you a little smiling fellow? It should have been great and bitter torments did arouse your spirits to a deed of blood.

CHRISTY (doubtfully): It should, maybe.

WIDOW QUIN: It's more than "maybe" I'm saying, and it'd soften my heart to see you sitting so simple with your cup and cake, and you fitter to be saying your catechism than slaying your da.

PEGEEN (at counter, washing glasses): There's talking when any'd see he's fit to be holding his head high with the wonders of the world. Walk on from this, for I'll not have him tormented and he destroyed travelling since Tuesday was a week.

WIDOW QUIN (peaceably): We'll be walking surely when his supper's done, and you'll find we're great company, young fellow, when it's of the like of you and me you'd hear the penny poets singing in an August fair.

CHRISTY (innocently): Did you kill your father.

PEGEEN (contemptuously): She did not. She hit himself with a worn pick, and the rusted poison did corrode his blood the way he never overed it, and died after. That was a sneaky kind of murder did win small glory with the boys itself.

(She crosses to CHRISTY's left.)

WIDOW QUIN (with good humor): If it didn't, maybe all knows a widow woman has buried her children and destroyed her man is a wiser comrade for a young lad than a girl, the like of you, who'd go helter-skeltering after any man would let you a wink upon the road.

PEGEEN (breaking out into wild rage): And you'll say that, Widow Quin, and you gasping with the rage you had facing the hill beyond to look on his face.

WIDOW QUIN (laughing derisively): Me, is it? Well, Father Reilly has cuteness° to divide you now. (She pulls CHRISTY up.) There's great temptation in a man did slay his da, and we'd best be going,

---

banbhs, young pigs

cuteness, sharpness or ingenuity.

young fellow; so rise up and come with me.

PEGEEN (*seizing his arm*): He'll not stir. He's pot-boy in this place, and I'll not have him stolen off and kidnapped while himself's abroad.

WIDOW QUIN: It'd be a crazy pot-boy'd lodge him in the shebeen where he works by day, so you'd have a right to come on, young fellow, till you see my little houseen, a perch off on the rising hill.

PEGEEN: Wait till morning, Christy Mahon. Wait till you lay eyes on her leaky thatch is growing more pasture for her buck goat than her square of fields, and she without a tramp itself to keep in order her place at all.

WIDOW QUIN: When you see me contriving in my little gardens, Christy Mahon, you'll swear the Lord God formed me to be living lone, and that there isn't my match in Mayo for thatching, or mowing, or shearing a sheep.

PEGEEN (*with noisy scorn*): It's true the Lord God formed you to contrive indeed. Doesn't the world know you reared a black lamb at your own breast, so that the Lord Bishop of Connaught felt the elements of a Christian, and he eating it after in a kidney stew? Doesn't the world know you've been seen shaving the foxy skipper from France for a threepenny bit and a sop of grass tobacco would wring the liver from a mountain goat you'd meet leaping the hills?

WIDOW QUIN (*with amusement*): Do you hear her now young fellow? Do you hear the way she'll be rating at her own self when a week is by?

PEGEEN (*to* CHRISTY): Don't heed her. Tell her to go into her pigsty and not plague us here.

WIDOW QUIN: I'm going; but he'll come with me.

PEGEEN (*shaking him*): Are you dumb, young fellow?

CHRISTY (*timidly, to* WIDOW QUIN): God increase you; but I'm pot-boy in this place, and it's here I'd liefer stay.

PEGEEN (*triumphantly*): Now you have heard him, and go on from this.

WIDOW QUIN (*looking round the room*): It's lonesome this hour crossing the hill, and if he won't come along with me, I'd have a right maybe to stop this night with yourselves. Let me stretch out on the settle, Pegeen Mike; and himself can lie by the hearth.

PEGEEN (*short and fiercely*): Faith, I won't. Quit off or I will send you now.

WIDOW QUIN (*gathering her shawl up*): Well, it's a terror to be aged a score. (*to* CHRISTY) God bless you now, young fellow, and let you be wary, or there's right torment will await you here if you go romancing with her like, and she waiting only, as they bade me say, on a sheepskin parchment to be wed with Shawn Keogh of Killakeen.

CHRISTY (*going to* PEGEEN *as she bolts the door*): What's that she's after saying?

PEGEEN: Lies and blather, you've no call to mind. Well, isn't Shawn Keogh an impudent fellow to send up spying on me? Wait till I lay hands on him. Let him wait, I'm saying.

CHRISTY: And you're not wedding him at all?

PEGEEN: I wouldn't wed him if a bishop came walking for to join us here.

CHRISTY: That God in glory may be thanked for that.

PEGEEN: There's your bed now. I've put a quilt upon you I'm after quilting a while since with my own two hands, and you'd best stretch out now for your sleep, and may God give you a good rest till I call you in the morning when the cocks will crow.

CHRISTY (*as she goes to inner room*): May God and Mary and St. Patrick bless you and reward you, for your kindly talk. (*She shuts the door behind her. He settles his bed slowly, feeling the quilt with immense satisfaction.*) Well, it's a clean bed and soft with it, and it's great luck and company I've won me in the end of time—two fine women fighting for the likes of me—till I'm thinking this night wasn't I a foolish fellow not to kill my father in the years gone by.

ACT 2

(*Brilliant morning light.* CHRISTY, *looking bright and cheerful, is cleaning a girl's boots.*)

CHRISTY (*to himself, counting jugs on dresser*): Half a hundred beyond. Ten there. A score that's above. Eighty jugs. Six cups and a broken one. Two plates. A power of glasses. Bottles, a school-master'd be hard set to count, and enough in them, I'm thinking, to drunken all the wealth and wisdom of the County Clare. (*He puts down the boot carefully.*) There's her boots now, nice and decent for her evening use, and isn't it grand brushes she has? (*He puts them down and goes by degrees to the looking-glass.*) Well, this'd be a fine place to be my whole life talking out with swearing Christians, in place of my old dogs and cat, and I stalking around, smoking my pipe and drinking my fill, and never a day's work but drawing a cork an odd time, or wiping a glass, or rinsing out a shiny tumbler for a decent man. (*He takes the looking-glass from the wall and puts it on the back of a chair; then sits down in front of it and begins washing his face.*) Didn't I know rightly I was handsome, though it was the divil's own mirror we had beyond, would twist a squint across an angel's brow; and I'll be growing fine from this day, the way I'll have a soft lovely skin on me and won't be the like of the clumsy young fellows do be ploughing all times in the earth and dung. (*He starts.*) Is she coming again? (*He looks out.*) Stranger girls. God help me, where'll I hide myself away and my long neck naked to the world? (*He looks out.*) I'd best go to the room maybe till I'm dressed again.

(*He gathers up his coat and the looking-glass, and runs into the inner room. The door is pushed open, and* SUSAN BRADY *looks in, and knocks on door.*)

SUSAN: There's nobody in it. (*Knocks again.*)

NELLY (*pushing her in and following her, with* HONOR BLAKE *and* SARA TANSEY): It'd be early for them both to be out walking the hill.

SUSAN: I'm thinking Shawn Keogh was making game of us and there's no such man in it at all.

HONOR (*pointing to straw and quilt*): Look at that. He's been sleeping there in the night. Well, it'll be a hard case if he's gone off now, the way we'll never set our eyes on a man killed his father, and we after rising early and destroying ourselves running fast on the hill.

NELLY: Are you thinking them's his boots?

SARA (*taking them up*): If they are, there should be his father's track on them. Did you never read in the papers the way murdered men do bleed and drip?

SUSAN: Is that blood there, Sara Tansey?

SARA (*smelling it*): That's bog water, I'm thinking, but it's his own they are surely, for I never seen the like of them for whity mud, and red mud, and turf on them, and the fine sands of the sea. That man's been walking, I'm telling you.

(*She goes down right, putting on one of his boots.*)

SUSAN (*going to window*): Maybe he's stolen off to Belmullet with the boots of Michael James, and you'd have a right so to follow after him, Sara Tansey, and you the one yoked the ass cart and drove ten miles to set your eyes on the man bit the yellow lady's nostril on the northern shore. (*She looks out.*)

SARA (*running to window with one boot on*): Don't be talking, and we fooled today (*Putting on other boot.*) There's a pair do fit me well, and I'll be keeping them for walking to the priest, when you'd be ashamed this place, going up winter and summer with nothing worth while to confess at all.

HONOR (*who has been listening at the door*): Whisht! there's someone inside the room. (*She pushes door a chink open.*) It's a man.

(SARA *kicks off boots and puts them where they were. They all stand in a line looking through chink.*)

SARA: I'll call him. Mister! Mister! (*He puts in his head.*) Is Pegeen within?

CHRISTY (*coming in as meek as a mouse, with the looking-glass held behind his back*): She's above on the cnuceen,° seeking the nanny goats, the way she'd have a sup of goat's milk for to color my tea.

SARA: And asking your pardon, is it you's the man killed his father?

CHRISTY (*sidling toward the nail where the glass was hanging*): I am, God help me!

SARA (*taking the eggs she has brought*): Then my thousand welcomes to you, and I've run up with a brace of duck's eggs for your food today. Pegeen's ducks is no use, but these are the real rich sort. Hold out your hand and you'll see it's no lie I'm telling you.

CHRISTY (*coming forward shyly, and holding out his left hand*): They're a great and weighty size.

SUSAN: And I run up with a pat of butter, for it'd be a poor thing to have you eating your spuds dry, and you after running a great way since you did destroy your da.

CHRISTY: Thank you kindly.

HONOR: And I brought you a little cut of cake, for you should have a thin stomach on you, and you that length walking the world.

NELLY: And I brought you a little laying pullet—boiled and all she is—was crushed at the fall of night by the curate's car. Feel the fat of that breast, mister.

CHRISTY: It's bursting, surely.

(*He feels it with the back of his hand, in which he holds the presents.*)

SARA: Will you pinch it? Is your right hand too sacred for to use at all? (*She slips round behind him.*) It's a glass he has. Well, I never seen to this day a man with a looking-glass held to his back. Them that kills their fathers is a vain lot surely.

(*Girls giggle.*)

CHRISTY (*smiling innocently and piling presents on glass*): I'm very thankful to you all today . . .

WIDOW QUIN (*coming in quickly, at door*): Sara Tansey, Susan Brady, Honor Blake! What in glory has you here at this hour of day?

GIRLS (*giggling*): That's the man killed his father.

WIDOW QUIN (*coming to them*): I know well it's the man; and I'm after putting him down in the sports below for racing, leaping, pitching, and the Lord knows what.

SARA (*exuberantly*): That's right, Widow Quin. I'll bet my dowry that he'll lick the world.

WIDOW QUIN: If you will, you'd have a right to have him fresh and nourished in place of nursing a feast. (*Taking presents.*) Are you fasting or fed, young fellow?

CHRISTY: Fasting, if you please.

---

cnuceen, little hill.

WIDOW QUIN (*loudly*): Well, you're the lot. Stir up now and give him his breakfast. (*to* CHRISTY) Come here to me (*She puts him on bench beside her while the girls make tea and get his breakfast.*) and let you tell us your story before Pegeen will come, in place of grinning your ears off like the moon of May.

CHRISTY (*beginning to be pleased*): It's a long story; you'd be destroyed listening.

WIDOW QUIN: Don't be letting on to be shy, a fine, gamey, treacherous lad the like of you. Was it in your house beyond you cracked his skull?

CHRISTY (*shy but flattered*): It was not. We were digging spuds in his cold, sloping, stony, divil's patch of a field.

WIDOW QUIN: And you went asking money of him, or making talk of getting a wife would drive him from his farm?

CHRISTY: I did not, then; but there I was, digging and digging, and "You squinting idiot," says he, "let you walk down now and tell the priest you'll wed the Widow Casey in a score of days."

WIDOW QUIN: And what kind was she?

CHRISTY (*with horror*): A walking terror from beyond the hills, and she two score and two hundred-weights and five pounds in the weighing scales, with a limping leg on her, and a blinded eye, and she a woman of noted misbehavior with the old and young.

GIRLS (*clustering round him, serving him*): Glory be.

WIDOW QUIN: And what did he want driving you to wed with her?

(*She takes a bit of the chicken.*)

CHRISTY (*eating with growing satisfaction*): He was letting on I was wanting a protector from the harshness of the world, and he without a thought the whole while but how he'd have her hut to live in and her gold to drink.

WIDOW QUIN: There's maybe worse than a dry hearth and a widow woman and your glass at night. So you hit him then?

CHRISTY (*getting almost excited*): I did not. "I won't wed her," says I, "when all know she did suckle me for six weeks when I came into the world, and she a hag this day with a tongue on her has the crows and seabirds scattered, the way they wouldn't cast a shadow on her garden with the dread of her curse."

WIDOW QUIN (*teasingly*): That one should be right company.

SARA (*eagerly*): Don't mind her. Did you kill him then?

CHRISTY: "She's too good for the like of you," says he, "and go on now or I'll flatten you out like a crawling beast has passed under a dray." "You will not if I can help it," says I. "Go on," says he, "or I'll have the divil making garters of your limbs tonight." "You will not if I can help it," says I.

(*He sits up, brandishing his mug.*)

SARA: You were right surely.

CHRISTY (*impressively*): With that the sun came out between the cloud and the hill, and it shining green in my face. "God have mercy on your soul," says he, lifting a scythe; "or on your own," says I, raising the loy.

SUSAN: That's a grand story.

HONOR: He tells it lovely.

CHRISTY (*flattered and confident, waving bone*): He gave a drive with the scythe, and I gave a lep to the east. Then I turned around with my back to the north, and I hit a blow on the ridge of his skull, laid him stretched out, and he split to the knob of his gullet.

(*He raises the chicken bone to his Adam's apple.*)

GIRLS (*together*): Well, you're a marvel! Oh, God bless you! You're the lad surely!

SUSAN: I'm thinking the Lord God sent him this road to make a second husband to the Widow Quin, and she with a great yearning to be wedded, though all dread her here. Lift him on her knee, Sara Tansey.

WIDOW QUIN: Don't tease him.

SARA (*going over to dresser and counter very quickly, and getting two glasses and porter*): You're heroes surely, and let you drink a supeen with your arms linked like the outlandish lovers in the sailor's song. (*She links their arms and gives them the glasses.*) There now. Drink a health to the wonders of the western world, the pirates, preachers, poteen-makers, with the jobbing jockies; parching peelers, and the juries fill their stomachs selling judgments of the English law.

(*Brandishing the bottle.*)

WIDOW QUIN: That's a right toast, Sara Tansey. Now Christy.

(*They drink with their arms linked, he drinking with his left hand, she with her right. As they are drinking, PEGEEN MIKE comes in with a milk can and stands aghast. They all spring away from CHRISTY. He goes down left, WIDOW QUIN remains seated.*)

PEGEEN (*angrily, to* SARA): What is it you're wanting?

SARA (*twisting her apron*): A ounce of tobacco.

PEGEEN: Have you tuppence?

SARA: I've forgotten my purse.

PEGEEN: Then you'd best be getting it and not fooling us here. (*to the* WIDOW QUIN, *with more elaborate scorn*) And what is it you're wanting, Widow Quin?

WIDOW QUIN (*insolently*): A penn'orth of starch.

PEGEEN (*breaking out*): And you without a white shirt or a shirt in your whole family since the drying of the flood. I've no starch for the like of you, and let you walk on now to Killamuck.

WIDOW QUIN (*turning to* CHRISTY, *as she goes out with the girls*): Well, you're mighty huffy this day, Pegeen Mike, and, you young fellow, let you not forget the sports and racing when the noon is by. (*They go out.*)

PEGEEN (*imperiously*): Fling out that rubbish and put them cups away. (CHRISTY *tidies away in great haste.*) Shove in the bench by the wall. (*He does so.*) And hang that glass on the nail. What disturbed it at all?

CHRISTY (*very meekly*): I was making myself decent only, and this a fine country for young lovely girls.

PEGEEN (*sharply*): Whisht your talking of girls. (*Goes to counter—right.*)

CHRISTY: Wouldn't any wish to be decent in a place . . .

PEGEEN: Whisht I'm saying.

CHRISTY (*looks at her face for a moment with great misgivings, then as a last effort, takes up a loy, and goes toward her, with feigned assurance*): It was with a loy the like of that I killed my father.

PEGEEN (*still sharply*): You've told me that story six times since the dawn of day.

CHRISTY (*reproachfully*): It's a queer thing you wouldn't care to be hearing it and them girls after walking four miles to be listening to me now.

PEGEEN (*turning round astonished*): Four miles.

CHRISTY (*apologetically*): Didn't himself say there were only four bona fides living in this place?

PEGEEN: It's bona fides by the road they are, but that lot came over the river lepping the stones. It's not three perches when you go like that, and I was down this morning looking on the papers the post-boy does have in his bag. (*With meaning and emphasis.*) For there was great news this day, Christopher Mahon. (*She goes into room left.*)

CHRISTY (*suspiciously*): Is it news of my murder?

PEGEEN (*inside*): Murder, indeed.

CHRISTY (*loudly*): A murdered da?

PEGEEN (*coming in again and crossing right*): There was not, but a story filled half a page of the hanging of a man. Ah, that should be a fearful end, young fellow, and it worst of all for a man who destroyed his da, for the like of him would get small mercies, and when it's dead he is, they'd put him in a narrow grave, with cheap sacking wrapping him round, and pour down quicklime on his head, the way you'd see a woman pouring any frish-frash from a cup.

CHRISTY (*very miserably*): Oh, God help me. Are you thinking I'm safe? You were saying at the fall of night, I was shut of jeopardy and I here with yourselves.

PEGEEN (*severely*): You'll be shut of jeopardy no place if you go talking with a pack of wild girls the like of them do be walking abroad with the peelers, talking whispers at the fall of night.

CHRISTY (*with terror*): And you're thinking they'd tell?

PEGEEN (*with mock sympathy*): Who knows, God help you.

CHRISTY (*loudly*): What joy would they have to bring hanging to the likes of me?

PEGEEN: It's queer joys they have, and who knows the thing they'd do, if it'd make the green stones cry itself to think of you swaying and swiggling at the butt of a rope, and you with a fine, stout neck, God bless you! the way you'd be a half an hour, in great anguish, getting your death.

CHRISTY (*getting his boots and putting them on*): If there's that terror of them, it'd be best, maybe, I went on wandering like Esau or Cain and Abel on the sides of Neifin or the Erris plain.

PEGEEN (*beginning to play with him*): It would, maybe, for I've heard the Circuit Judges this place is a heartless crew.

CHRISTY (*bitterly*): It's more than Judges this place is a heartless crew. (*Looking up at her.*) And isn't it a poor thing to be starting again and I a lonesome fellow will be looking out on women and girls the way the needy fallen spirits do be looking on the Lord?

PEGEEN: What call have you to be that lonesome when there's poor girls walking Mayo in their thousands now?

CHRISTY (*grimly*): It's well you know what call I have. It's well you know it's a lonesome thing to be passing small towns with the lights shining sideways when the night is down, or going in strange places with a dog noising before you and a dog noising behind, or drawn to the cities where you'd hear a voice kissing and talking deep love in every shadow of the ditch, and you passing on with an empty, hungry stomach failing from your heart.

PEGEEN: I'm thinking you're an odd man, Christy Mahon. The oddest walking fellow I ever set my eyes on to this hour today.

CHRISTY: What would any be but odd men and they living lonesome in the world?

PEGEEN: I'm not odd, and I'm my whole life with my father only.

CHRISTY (*with infinite admiration*): How would a lovely handsome woman the like of you be lonesome when all men should be thronging around to hear the sweetness of your voice, and the little infant children should be pestering your steps I'm thinking, and you walking the roads.

PEGEEN: I'm hard set to know what way a coaxing

fellow the like of yourself should be lonesome either.

CHRISTY: Coaxing?

PEGEEN: Would you have me think a man never talked with the girls would have the words you've spoken today? It's only letting on you are to be lonesome, the way you'd get around me now.

CHRISTY: I wish to God I was letting on; but I was lonesome all times, and born lonesome, I'm thinking, as the moon of dawn.

(Going to door.)

PEGEEN *(puzzled by his talk)*: Well, it's a story I'm not understanding at all why you'd be worse than another, Christy Mahon, and you a fine lad with the great savagery to destroy your da.

CHRISTY: It's little I'm understanding myself, saving only that my heart's scalded this day, and I going off stretching out the earth between us, the way I'll not be waking near you another dawn of the year till the two of us do arise to hope or judgment with the saints of God, and now I'd best be going with my wattle in my hand, for hanging is a poor thing *(Turning to go.)* and it's little welcome only is left me in this house today.

PEGEEN *(sharply)*: Christy! *(He turns round.)* Come here to me. *(He goes toward her.)* Lay down that switch and throw some sods on the fire. You're pot-boy in this place, and I'll not have you mitch off° from us now.

CHRISTY: You were saying I'd be hanged if I stay.

PEGEEN *(quite kindly at last)*: I'm after going down and reading the fearful crimes of Ireland for two weeks or three, and there wasn't a word of your murder. *(Getting up and going over to the counter.)* They've likely not found the body. You're safe so with ourselves.

CHRISTY *(astonished slowly)*: It's making game of you were *(Following her with fearful joy.)*, and I can stay so, working at your side, and I not lonesome from this mortal day.

PEGEEN: What's to hinder you from staying, except the widow woman or the young girls would inveigle you off?

CHRISTY *(with rapture)*: And I'll have your words from this day filling my ears, and that look is come upon you meeting my two eyes, and I watching you loafing around in the warm sun, or rinsing your ankles when the night is come.

PEGEEN *(kindly, but a little embarrassed)*: I'm thinking you'll be a loyal young lad to have working around, and if you vexed me a while since with your leaguing with the girls, I wouldn't give a

thraneen° for a lad hadn't a mighty spirit in him and a gamey heart.

(SHAWN KEOGH runs in carrying a cleeve° on his back, followed by the WIDOW QUIN.)

SHAWN *(to PEGEEN)*: I was passing below, and I seen your mountainy sheep eating cabbages in Jimmy's field. Run up or they'll be bursting surely.

PEGEEN: Oh, God mend them! *(She puts a shawl over her head and runs out.)*

CHRISTY *(looking from one to the other. Still in high spirits)*: I'd best go to her aid maybe. I'm handy with ewes.

WIDOW QUIN *(closing the door)*: She can do that much, and there is Shaneen has long speeches for to tell you now. *(She sits down with an amused smile.)*

SHAWN *(taking something from his pocket and offering it to CHRISTY)*: Do you see that, mister?

CHRISTY *(looking at it)*: The half of a ticket to the Western States!

SHAWN *(trembling with anxiety)*: I'll give it to you and my new hat *(Pulling it out of hamper.)* and my breeches with the double seat *(Pulling it off.);* and my new coat is woven from the blackest shearings for three miles around *(Giving him the coat.);* I'll give you the whole of them, and my blessing, and the blessing of Father Reilly itself, maybe, if you'll quit from this and leave us in the peace we had till last night at the fall of dark.

CHRISTY *(with a new arrogance)*: And for what is it you're wanting to get shut of me?

SHAWN *(looking to the WIDOW for help)*: I'm a poor scholar with middling faculties to coin a lie, so I'll tell you the truth, Christy Mahon. I'm wedding with Pegeen beyond, and I don't think well of having a clever fearless man the like of you dwelling in her house.

CHRISTY *(almost pugnaciously)*: And you'd be using bribery for to banish me?

SHAWN *(in an imploring voice)*: Let you not take it badly mister honey, isn't beyond the best place for you where you'll have golden chains and shiny coats and you riding upon hunters with the ladies of the land.

(He makes an eager sign to the WIDOW QUIN to come to help him.)

WIDOW QUIN *(coming over)*: It's true for him, and you'd best quit off and not have that poor girl setting her mind on you, for there's Shaneen thinks she wouldn't suit you though all is saying that she'll wed you now.

(CHRISTY beams in delight.)

---

mitch off, sneak away.

thraneen, straw or withered piece of meadow grass. **cleeve,** basket.

SHAWN (*in terrified earnest*): She wouldn't suit you, and she with the divil's own temper the way you'd be strangling one another in a score of days. (*He makes the movement of strangling with his hands.*) It's the like of me only that she's fit for, a quiet simple fellow wouldn't raise a hand upon her if she scratched itself.

WIDOW QUIN (*putting* SHAWN's *hat on* CHRISTY): Fit them clothes on you anyhow, young fellow, and he'd maybe loan them to you for the sports. (*Pushing him toward inner door.*) Fit them on and you can give your answer when you have them tried.

CHRISTY (*beaming, delighted with the clothes*): I will then. I'd like herself to see me in them tweeds and hat.

(*He goes into room and shuts the door.*)

SHAWN (*in great anxiety*): He'd like herself to see them. He'll not leave us, Widow Quin. He's a score of divils in him the way it's well nigh certain he will wed Pegeen.

WIDOW QUIN (*jeeringly*): It's true all girls are fond of courage and do hate the like of you.

SHAWN (*walking about in desperation*): Oh, Widow Quin, what'll I be doing now? I'd inform again him, but he's burst from Kilmainham and he'd be sure and certain to destroy me. If I wasn't so God-fearing, I'd near have courage to come behind him and run a pike into his side. Oh, it's a hard case to be an orphan and not to have your father that you're used to, and you'd easy kill and make yourself a hero in the sight of all (*Coming up to her.*) Oh, Widow Quin, will you find me some contrivance when I've promised you a ewe?

WIDOW QUIN: A ewe's a small thing, but what would you give me if I did wed him and did save you so?

SHAWN (*with astonishment*): You?

WIDOW QUIN: Aye. Would you give me the red cow you have and the mountainy ram, and the right of way across your rye path, and a load of dung at Michaelmas, and turbary upon the western hill?

SHAWN (*radiant with hope*): I would surely, and I'd give you the wedding ring I have, and the loan of a new suit, the way you'd have him decent on the wedding day. I'd give you two kids for your dinner, and a gallon of poteen, and I'd call the piper on the long car to your wedding from Crossmolina or from Ballina. I'd give you . . .

WIDOW QUIN: That'll do so, and let you whisht, for he's coming now again.

(CHRISTY *comes in very natty in the new clothes.* WIDOW QUIN *goes to him admiringly.*)

WIDOW QUIN: If you seen yourself now, I'm thinking you'd be too proud to speak to us at all, and it'd be a pity surely to have your like sailing from Mayo to the Western World.

CHRISTY (*as proud as a peacock*): I'm not going. If this is a poor place itself, I'll make myself contented to be lodging here.

(WIDOW QUIN *makes a sign to* SHAWN *to leave them.*)

SHAWN: Well, I'm going measuring the race-course while the tide is low, so I'll leave you the garments and my blessing for the sports today. God bless you! (*He wriggles out.*)

WIDOW QUIN (*admiring* CHRISTY): Well, you're mighty spruce, young fellow. Sit down now while you're quiet till you talk with me.

CHRISTY (*swaggering*): I'm going abroad on the hillside for to seek Pegeen.

WIDOW QUIN: You'll have time and plenty for to seek Pegeen, and you heard me saying at the fall of night the two of us should be great company.

CHRISTY: From this out I'll have no want of company when all sorts is bringing me their food and clothing (*He swaggers to the door, tightening his belt.*), the way they'd set their eyes upon a gallant orphan cleft his father with one blow to the breeches belt. (*He opens door, then staggers back.*) Saints of glory! Holy angels from the throne of light!

WIDOW QUIN (*going over*): What ails you?

CHRISTY: It's the walking spirit of my murdered da?

WIDOW QUIN (*looking out*): Is it that tramper?

CHRISTY (*wildly*): Where'll I hide my poor body from that ghost of hell?

(*The door is pushed open, and old* MAHON *appears on threshold.* CHRISTY *darts in behind door.*)

WIDOW QUIN (*in great amusement*): God save you, my poor man.

MAHON (*gruffly*): Did you see a young lad passing this way in the early morning or the fall of night?

WIDOW QUIN: You're a queer kind to walk in not saluting at all.

MAHON: Did you see the young lad?

WIDOW QUIN (*stiffly*): What kind was he?

MAHON: An ugly young streeler° with a murderous gob° on him, and a little switch in his hand. I met a tramper seen him coming this way at the fall of night.

WIDOW QUIN: There's harvest hundreds do be passing these days for the Sligo boat. For what is it you're wanting him, my poor man?

MAHON: I want to destroy him for breaking the head on me with the clout of a loy. (*He takes off a big hat, and shows his head in a mass of bandages and*

---

streeler, idle, slovenly person. **gob,** mouth

plaster, with some pride.) It was he did that, and amn't I a great wonder to think I've traced him ten days with that rent in my crown?

WIDOW QUIN *(taking his head in both hands and examining it with extreme delight)*: That was a great blow. And who hit you? A robber maybe?

MAHON: It was my own son hit me, and he the divil a robber, or anything else, but a dirty, stuttering lout.

WIDOW QUIN *(letting go his skull and wiping her hands in her apron)*: You'd best be wary of a mortified scalp, I think they call it, lepping around with that wound in the splendor of the sun. It was a bad blow surely, and you should have vexed him fearful to make him strike that gash in his da.

MAHON: Is it me?

WIDOW QUIN *(amusing herself)*: Aye. And isn't it a great shame when the old and hardened do torment the young?

MAHON *(raging)*: Torment him is it? And I after holding out with the patience of a martyred saint till there's nothing but destruction on, and I'm driven out in my old age with none to aid me.

WIDOW QUIN *(greatly amused)*: It's a sacred wonder the way that wickedness will spoil a man.

MAHON: My wickedness, is it? Amn't I after saying it is himself has me destroyed, and he a liar on walls, a talker of folly, a man you'd see stretched the half of the day in the brown ferns with his belly to the sun.

WIDOW QUIN: Not working at all?

MAHON: The divil a work, or if he did itself, you'd see him raising up a haystack like the stalk of a rush, or driving our last cow till he broke her leg at the hip, and when he wasn't at that he'd be fooling over little birds he had—finches and felts—or making mugs at his own self in the bit of a glass we had hung on the wall.

WIDOW QUIN *(looking at CHRISTY)*: What way was he so foolish? It was running wild after the girls may be?

MAHON *(with a shout of derision)*: Running wild, is it? If he seen a red petticoat coming swinging over the hill, he'd be off to hide in the sticks, and you'd see him shooting out his sheep's eyes between the little twigs and the leaves, and his two ears rising like a hare looking out through a gap. Girls, indeed!

WIDOW QUIN: It was drink maybe?

MAHON: And he a poor fellow would get drunk on the smell of a pint. He'd a queer rotten stomach, I'm telling you, and when I gave him three pulls from my pipe a while since, he was taken with contortions till I had to send him in the ass cart to the females' nurse.

WIDOW QUIN *(clasping her hands)*: Well, I never till this day heard tell of a man the like of that!

MAHON: I'd take a mighty oath you didn't surely, and wasn't he the laughing joke of every female woman where four baronies meet, the way the girls would stop their weeding if they seen him coming the road to let a roar at him, and call him the looney of Mahon's.

WIDOW QUIN: I'd give the world and all to see the like of him. What kind was he?

MAHON: A small low fellow.

WIDOW QUIN: And dark?

MAHON: Dark and dirty.

WIDOW QUIN *(considering)*: I'm thinking I see him.

MAHON *(eagerly)*: An ugly young blackguard.

WIDOW QUIN: A hideous, fearful villain, and the spit of you.

MAHON: What way is he fled?

WIDOW QUIN: Gone over the hills to catch a coasting steamer to the north or south.

MAHON: Could I pull up on him now?

WIDOW QUIN: If you'll cross the sands below where the tide is out, you'll be in it as soon as himself, for he had to go round ten miles by the top of the bay. *(She points to the door.)* Strike down by the head beyond and then follow on the roadway to the north and east.

(MAHON goes abruptly.)

WIDOW QUIN *(shouting after him)*: Let you give him a good vengeance when you come up with him, but don't put yourself in the power of the law, for it'd be a poor thing to see a judge in his black cap reading out his sentence on a civil warrior the like of you.

(She swings the door to and looks at CHRISTY, who is cowering in terror, for a moment, then she bursts into a laugh.)

WIDOW QUIN: Well, you're the walking Playboy of the Western World, and that's the poor man you had divided to his breeches belt.

CHRISTY *(looking out: then, to her)*: What'll Pegeen say when she hears that story? What'll she be saying to me now?

WIDOW QUIN: She'll knock the head of you, I'm thinking, and drive you from the door. God help her to be taking you for a wonder, and you a little schemer making up the story you destroyed your da.

CHRISTY *(turning to the door, nearly speechless with rage, half to himself)*: To be letting on he was dead, and coming back to his life, and following after me like an old weasel tracing a rat, and coming in here laying desolation between my own self and the fine women of Ireland, and he a kind of carcase that you'd fling upon the sea . . .

WIDOW QUIN *(more soberly)*: There's talking for a man's one only son.

CHRISTY (*breaking out*): His one son, is it? May I meet him with one tooth and it aching, and one eye to be seeing seven and seventy divils in the twists of the road, and one old timber leg on him to limp into the scalding grave. (*Looking out.*) There he is now crossing the strands, and that the Lord God would send a high wave to wash him from the world.

WIDOW QUIN (*scandalized*): Have you no shame? (*putting her hand on his shoulder and turning him round*) What ails you? Near crying, is it?

CHRISTY (*in despair and grief*): Amn't I after seeing the love-light of the star of knowledge shining from her brow, and hearing words would put you thinking on the holy Brigid speaking to the infant saints, and now she'll be turning again, and speaking hard words to me, like an old woman with a spavindy ass she'd have, urging on a hill.

WIDOW QUIN: There's poetry talk for a girl you'd see itching and scratching, and she with a stale stink of poteen on her from selling in the shop.

CHRISTY (*impatiently*): It's her like is fitted to be handling merchandise in the heavens above, and what'll I be doing now, I ask you, and I a kind of wonder was jilted by the heavens when a day was by.

(*There is a distant noise of girls' voices.* WIDOW QUIN *looks from window and comes to him, hurriedly.*)

WIDOW QUIN: You'll be doing like myself, I'm thinking, when I did destroy my man, for I'm above many's the day, odd times in great spirits, abroad in the sunshine, darning a stocking or stitching a shift; and odd times again looking out on the schooners, hookers, trawlers is sailing the sea, and I thinking on the gallant hairy fellows are drifting beyond, and myself long years living alone.

CHRISTY (*interested*): You're like me, so.

WIDOW QUIN: I am your like, and it's for that I'm taking a fancy to you, and I with my little houseen above where there'd be myself to tend you, and none to ask were you a murderer or what at all.

CHRISTY: And what would I be doing if I left Pegeen?

WIDOW QUIN: I've nice jobs you could be doing, gathering shells to make a whitewash for our hut within, building up a little goosehouse, or stretching a new skin on an old curragh° I have, and if my hut is far from all sides, it's there you'll meet the wisest old men, I tell you, at the corner

of my wheel, and it's there yourself and me will have great times whispering and hugging. . . .

VOICES (*outside, calling far away*): Christy! Christy Mahon! Christy!

CHRISTY: Is it Pegeen Mike?

WIDOW QUIN: It's the young girls, I'm thinking, coming to bring you to the sports below, and what is it you'll have me to tell them now?

CHRISTY: Aid me for to win Pegeen. It's herself only that I'm seeking now. (WIDOW QUINN *gets up and goes to window.*) Aid me for to win her, and I'll be asking God to stretch a hand to you in the hour of death, and lead you short cuts through the Meadows of Ease, and up the floor of Heaven to the Footstool of the Virgin's Son.

WIDIW QUIN: There's praying.

VOICES (*nearer*): Christy! Christy Mahon!

CHRISTY (*with agitation*): They're coming. Will you swear to aid and save me for the love of Christ?

WIDOW QUIN (*looks at him for a moment*): If I aid you, will you swear to give me a right of way I want, and a mountainy ram, and a load of dung at Michaelmas, the time that you'll be master here?

CHRISTY: I will, by the elements and stars of night.

WIDOW QUIN: Then we'll not say a word of the old fellow, the way Pegeen won't know your story till the end of time.

CHRISTY: And if he chances to return again?

WIDOW QUIN: We'll swear he's a maniac and not your da. I could take an oath I seen him raving on the sands today.

(*Girls run in.*)

SUSAN: Come on to the sports below. Pegeen says you're to come.

SARA TANSEY: The lepping's beginning, and we've a jockey's suit to fit upon you for the mule race on the sands below.

HONOR: Come on, will you?

CHRISTY: I will then if Pegeen's beyond.

SARA TANNEY: She's in the boreen° making game of Shaneen Keogh.

CHRISTY: Then I'll be going to her now.

(*He runs out followed by the girls.*)

WIDOW QUIN: Well, if the worst comes in the end of all, it'll be great game to see there's none to pity him but a widow woman, the like of me, has buried her children and destroyed her man. (*She goes out.*)

ACT 3

(*Later in the day.* JIMMY *comes in, slightly drunk*)

JIMMY (*calls*): Pegeen! (*Crosses to inner door.*) Pegeen

---

curragh, an open boat covered with hide, leather, or tarred canvas.

boreen, narrow road.

Mike! (*Comes back again into the room.*) Pegeen! (PHILLY *comes in in the same state.*) (*to* PHILLY) Did you see herself?

PHILLY: I did not; but I sent Shawn Keogh with the ass cart for to bear him home. (*Trying cupboards which are locked.*) Well, isn't he a nasty man to get into such staggers at a morning wake? and isn't herself the divil's daughter for locking, and she so fussy after that young gaffer, you might take your death with drought and none to heed you?

JIMMY: It's little wonder she'd be fussy, and he after bringing bankrupt ruin on the roulette man, and the trick-o'-the-loop man, and breaking the nose of the cockshot-man, and winning all in the sports below, racing, lepping, dancing, and the Lord knows what! He's right luck, I'm telling you.

PHILLY: If he has, he'll be rightly hobbled yet, and he not able to say ten words without making a brag of the way he killed his father, and the great blow he hit with the loy.

JIMMY: A man can't hang by his own informing, and his father should be rotten by now.

(OLD MAHON *passes window slowly.*)

PHILLY: Supposing a man's digging spuds in that field with a long spade, and supposing he flings up the two halves of that skull, what'll be said then in the papers and the courts of law?

JIMMY: They'd say it was an old Dane, maybe, was drowned in the flood. (OLD MAHON *comes in and sits down near door listening.*) Did you never hear tell of the skulls they have in the city of Dublin, ranged out like blue jugs in a cabin of Connaught?

PHILLY: And you believe that?

JIMMY (*pugnaciously*): Didn't a lad see them and he after coming from harvesting in the Liverpool boat? "They have them there," says he, "making a show of the great people there was one time walking the world. White skulls and black skulls and yellow skulls, and some with full teeth, and some haven't only but one."

PHILLY: It was no lie, maybe, for when I was a young lad there was a graveyard beyond the house with the remnants of a man who had thighs as long as your arm. He was a horrid man, I'm telling you, and there was many a fine Sunday I'd put him together for fun, and he with shiny bones, you wouldn't meet the like of these days in the cities of the world.

MAHON (*getting up*): You wouldn't, is it? Lay your eyes on that skull, and tell me where and when there was another the like of it, is splintered only from the blow of a loy.

PHILLY: Glory be to God! And who hit you at all?

MAHON (*triumphantly*): It was my own son hit me.

Would you believe that?

JIMMY: Well, there's wonders hidden in the heart of man!

PHILLY (*suspiciously*): And what way was it done?

MAHON (*wandering about the room*): I'm after walking hundreds and long scores of miles, winning clean beds and the fill of my belly four times in the day, and I doing nothing but telling stories of that naked truth. (*He comes to them a little aggressively.*) Give me a supeen and I'll tell you now.

(WIDOW QUIN *comes in and stands aghast behind him. He is facing* JIMMY *and* PHILLY, *who are on the left.*)

JIMMY: Ask herself beyond. She's the stuff hidden in her shawl.

WIDOW QUIN (*coming to* MAHON *quickly*): You here, is it? You didn't go far at all?

MAHON: I seen the coasting steamer passing, and I got a drought upon me and a cramping leg, so I said, "The divil go along with him," and turned again. (*Looking under her shawl.*) And let you give me a supeen, for I'm destroyed travelling since Tuesday was a week.

WIDOW QUIN (*getting a glass, in a cajoling tone*): Sit down then by the fire and take your ease for a space. You've a right to be destroyed indeed, with your walking, and fighting, and facing the sun. (*Giving him poteen from a stone jar she has brought in.*) There now is a drink for you, and may it be to your happiness and length of life.

MAHON (*taking glass greedily and sitting down by fire*): God increase you!

WIDOW QUIN (*taking men to the right stealthily*): Do you know what? That man's raving from his wound today, for I met him a while since telling a rambling tale of a tinker had him destroyed. Then he heard of Christy's deed, and he up and says it was his son had cracked his skull. O isn't madness a fright, for he'll go killing someone yet, and he thinking it's the man has struck him so?

JIMMY (*entirely convinced*): It's a fright, surely. I knew a party was kicked in the head by a red mare, and he went killing horses a great while, till he eat the insides of a clock and died after.

PHILLY (*with suspicion*): Did he see Christy?

WIDOW QUIN: He didn't. (*With a warning gesture.*) Let you not be putting him in mind of him, or you'll be likely summoned if there's murder done. (*Looking round at* MAHON.) Whisht! He's listening. Wait now till you hear me taking him easy and unravelling all. (*She goes to* MAHON.) And what way are you feeling, mister? Are you in contentment now?

MAHON (*slightly emotional from his drink*): I'm poorly only, for it's a hard story the way I'm left today, when it was I did tend him from his hour of birth, and he a dunce never reached his second book, the way he'd come from school, many's the day, with his legs lamed under him, and he blackened with his beatings like a tinker's ass. It's a hard story, I'm saying, the way some do have their next and nighest raising up a hand of murder on them, and some is lonesome getting their death with lamentation in the dead of night.

WIDOW QUIN (*not knowing what to say*): To hear you talking so quiet, who'd know you were the same fellow we seen pass today?

MAHON: I'm the same surely. The wrack of ruin of three score years; and it's a terror to live that length, I tell you, and to have your sons going to the dogs against you, and you wore out scolding them, and skelping them, and God knows what.

PHILLY (*to* JIMMY): He's not raving. (*to* WIDOW QUIN) Will you ask him what kind was his son?

WIDOW QUIN (*to* MAHON, *with a peculiar look*): Was your son that hit you a lad of one year and a score maybe, a great hand at racing and lepping and licking the world?

MAHON (*turning on her with a roar of rage*): Didn't you hear me say he was the fool of men, the way from this out he'll know the orphan's lot with old and young making game of him and they swearing, raging, kicking at him like a mangy cur.

(*A great burst of cheering outside, some way off.*)

MAHON (*putting his hands to his ears*): What in the name of God do they want roaring below?

WIDOW QUIN (*with the shade of a smile*): They're cheering a young lad, the champion Playboy of the Western World.

(*More cheering.*)

MAHON (*going to window*): It'd split my heart to hear them, and I with pulses in my brain-pan for a week gone by. Is it racing they are?

JIMMY (*looking from door*): It is then. They are mounting him for the mule race will be run upon the sands. That's the playboy on the winkered mule.

MAHON (*puzzled*): That lad, is it? If you said it was a fool he was, I'd have laid a mighty oath he was the likeness of my wandering son. (*Uneasily, putting his hand to his head*). Faith, I'm thinking I'll go walking for to view the race.

WIDOW QUIN (*stopping him, sharply*): You will not. You'd best take the road to Belmullet, and not be dilly-dallying in this place where there isn't a spot you could sleep.

PHILLY (*coming forward*): Don't mind her. Mount there on the bench and you'll have a view of the whole. They're hurrying before the tide will rise, and it'd be near over if you went down the pathway through the crags below.

MAHON (*mounts on bench,* WIDOW QUIN *beside him*): That's a right view again the edge of the sea. They're coming now from the point. He's leading. Who is he at all?

WIDOW QUIN: He's the champion of the world, I tell you, and there isn't a hop'orth° isn't falling lucky to his hands today.

PHILLY (*looking out, interested in the race*): Look at that. They're pressing him now.

JIMMY: He'll win it yet.

PHILLY: Take your time, Jimmy Farrell. It's too soon to say.

WIDOW QUIN (*shouting*): Watch him taking the gate. There's riding.

JIMMY (*cheering*): More power to the young lad!

MAHON: He's passing the third.

JIMMY: He'll lick them yet!

WIDOW QUIN: He'd lick them if he was running races with a score itself.

MAHON: Look at the mule he has, kicking the stars.

WIDOW QUIN: There was a lep! (*Catching hold of* MAHON *in her excitement.*) He's fallen! He's mounted again! Faith, he's passing them all!

JIMMY: Look at him skelping her!

PHILLY: And the mountain girls hooshing him on!

JIMMY: It's the last turn! The post's cleared for them now!

MAHON: Look at the narrow place. He'll be into the bogs! (*With a yell.*) Good rider! He's through it again!

JIMMY: He neck and neck!

MAHON: Good boy to him! Flames, but he's in!

(*Great cheering, in which all join.*)

MAHON (*with hesitation*): What's that? They're raising him up. They're coming this way. (*With a roar of rage and astonishment.*) It's Christy! by the stars of God! I'd know his way of spitting and he astride the moon.

(*He jumps down and makes for the door, but* WIDOW QUIN *catches him and pulls him back.*)

WIDOW QUIN: Stay quiet, will you. That's not your son. (*to* JIMMY) Stop him, or you'll get a month for the abetting of manslaughter and be fined as well.

JIMMY: I'll hold him.

MAHON (*struggling*): Let me out! Let me out, the lot of you! till I have my vengeance on his head today.

WIDOW QUIN (*shaking him vehemently*): That's not your son. That's a man is going to make a marriage with the daughter of this house, a place with fine trade, with a license, and with poteen too.

MAHON (*amazed*): That man marrying a decent and a

---

hop'orth, halfpenny worth.

moneyed girl! Is it mad yous are? Is it in a crazy house for females that I'm landed now?

WIDOW QUIN: It's mad yourself is with the blow upon your head. That lad is the wonder of the Western World.

MAHON: I seen it's my son.

WIDOW QUIN: You seen that you're mad. (*Cheering outside.*) Do you hear them cheering him in the zig-zags of the road? Aren't you after saying that your son's a fool, and how would they be cheering a true idiot born?

MAHON (*getting distressed*): It's maybe out of reason that that man's himself. (*Cheering again.*) There's none surely will go cheering him. Oh, I'm raving with a madness that would fright the world! (*He sits down with his hand to his head.*) There was one time I seen ten scarlet divils letting on they'd cork my spirit in a gallon can; and one time I seen rats as big as badgers sucking the life blood from the butt of my lug; but I never till this day confused that dribbling idiot with a likely man. I'm destroyed surely.

WIDOW QUIN: And who'd wonder when it's your brain-pan that is gaping now?

MAHON: Then the blight of the sacred drought upon myself and him, for I never went mad to this day, and I not three weeks with the Limerick girls drinking myself silly, and parlatic from the dusk to dawn. (*to* WIDOW QUIN, *suddenly*) Is my visage astray?

WIDOW QUIN: It is then. You're a sniggering maniac, a child could see.

MAHON (*getting up more cheerfully*): Then I'd best be going to the union beyond, and there'll be a welcome before me, I tell you (*With great pride.*), and I a terrible and fearful case, the way that there I was one time, screeching in a straitened waistcoat, with seven doctors writing out my sayings in a printed book. Would you believe that?

WIDOW QUIN: If you're a wonder itself, you'd best be hasty, for them lads caught a maniac one time and pelted the poor creature till he ran out, raving and foaming, and was drowned in the sea.

MAHON (*with philosophy*): It's true mankind is the divil when your head's astray. Let me out now and I'll slip down the boreen, and not see them so.

WIDOW QUIN (*showing him out*): That's it. Run to the right, and not a one will see.

(*He runs off.*)

PHILLY (*wisely*): You're at some gaming, Widow Quin; but I'll walk after him and give him his dinner and a time to rest, and I'll see then if he's raving or as sane as you.

WIDOW QUIN (*annoyed*): If you go near that lad, let you be wary of your head, I'm saying. Didn't you

hear him telling he was crazed at times?

PHILLY: I heard him telling a power; and I'm thinking we'll have right sport, before night will fall. (*He goes out.*)

JIMMY: Well, Philly's a conceited and foolish man. How could that madman have his senses and his brain-pan slit? I'll go after them and see him turn on Philly now.

(*He goes;* WIDOW QUIN *hides poteen behind counter. Then hubbub outside.*)

VOICES: There you are! Good jumper! Grand lepper! Darlint boy! He's the racer! Bear him on, will you!

(CHRISTY *comes in, in Jockey's dress, with* PEGEEN MIKE, SARA, *and other girls, and men.*)

PEGEEN (*to crowd*): Go on now and don't destroy him and he drenching with sweat. Go along, I'm saying, and have your tug-of-warring till he's dried his skin.

CROWD: Here's his prizes! A bagpipes! A fiddle was played by a poet in the years gone by! A flat and three-thorned blackthorn would lick the scholars out of Dublin town!

CHRISTY (*taking the prizes from the men*): Thank you kindly, the lot of you. But you'd say it was little only I did this day if you'd seen me a while since striking my one single blow.

TOWN CRIER (*outside, ringing a bell*): Take notice, last event of this day! Tug-of-warring on the green below! Come on, the lot of you! Great achievements for all Mayo men!

PEGEEN: Go on, and leave him for to rest and dry. Go on, I tell you, for he'll do no more.

(*She hustles crowd out;* WIDOW QUIN *following them.*)

MEN (*going*): Come on then. Good luck for the while!

PEGEEN (*radiantly, wiping his face with her shawl*): Well, you're the lad, and you'll have great times from this out when you could win that wealth of prizes, and you sweating in the heat of noon!

CHRISTY (*looking at her with delight*): I'll have great times if I win the crowning prize I'm seeking now, and that's your promise that you'll wed me in a fortnight, when our banns is called.

PEGEEN (*backing away from him*): You're right daring to go ask me that, when all knows you'll be starting to some girl in your own townland, when your father's rotten in four months, or five.

CHRISTY (*indignantly*): Starting from you, is it? (*He follows her.*) I will not, then, and when the airs is warming in four months, or five, it's then yourself and me should be pacing Neifin in the dews of night, the times sweet smells do be rising, and you'd see a little shiny new moon, maybe, sinking on the hills.

PEGEEN (*looking at him playfully*): And it's that kind of a poacher's love you'd make, Christy Mahon, on the sides of Neifin, when the night is down?

CHRISTY: It's little you'll think if my love's a poacher's, or an earl's itself, when you'll feel my two hands stretched around you, and I squeezing kisses on your puckered lips, till I'd feel a kind of pity for the Lord God is all ages sitting lonesome in his golden chair.

PEGEEN: That'll be right fun, Christy Mahon, and any girl would walk her heart out before she'd meet a young man was your like for eloquence, or talk, at all.

CHRISTY (*encouraged*): Let you wait, to hear me talking, till we're astray in Erris, when Good Friday's by, drinking a sup from a well, and making mighty kisses with our wetted mouths, or gaming in a gap or sunshine, with yourself stretched back onto your necklace, in the flowers of the earth.

PEGEEN (*in a lower voice, moved by his tone*): I'd be nice so, is it?

CHRISTY (*with rapture*): If the mitred bishops seen you that time, they'd be the like of the holy prophets, I'm thinking, do be straining the bars of Paradise to lay eyes on the Lady Helen of Troy, and she abroad, pacing back and forward, with a nosegay in her golden shawl.

PEGEEN (*with real tenderness*): And what is it I have, Christy Mahon, to make me fitting entertainment for the like of you, that has such poet's talking, and such bravery of heart?

CHRISTY (*in a low voice*): Isn't there the light of seven heavens in your heart alone, the way you'll be an angel's lamp to me from this out, and I abroad in the darkness, spearing salmons in the Owen, or the Carrowmore?

PEGEEN: If I was your wife, I'd be along with you those nights, Christy Mahon, the way you'd see I was a great hand at coaxing bailiffs, or coining funny nick-names for the stars of night.

CHRISTY: You, is it? Taking your death in the hailstones, or in the fogs of dawn.

PEGEEN: Yourself and me would shelter easy in a narrow bush (*With a qualm of dread.*), but we're only talking, maybe, for this would be a poor, thatched place to hold a fine lad is the like of you.

CHRISTY (*putting his arm around her*): If I wasn't a good Christian, it's on my naked knees I'd be saying my prayers and paters to every jackstraw you have roofing your head, and every stony pebble is paving the laneway to your door.

PEGEEN (*radiantly*): If that's the truth, I'll be burning candles from this out to the miracles of God that have brought you from the south today, and I,

with my gowns bought ready, the way that I can wed you, and not wait at all.

CHRISTY: It's miracles, and that's the truth. Me there toiling a long while, and walking a long while, not knowing at all I was drawing all times nearer to this holy day.

PEGEEN: And myself, a girl, was tempted often to go sailing the seas till I'd marry a Jew-man, with ten kegs of gold, and I not knowing at all there was the like of you drawing nearer, like the stars of God.

CHRISTY: And to think I'm long years hearing women talking that talk, to all bloody fools, and this the first time I've heard the like of your voice talking sweetly for my own delight.

PEGEEN: And to think it's me is talking sweetly, Christy Mahon, and I the fright of seven townlands for my biting tongue. Well, the heart's a wonder; and, I'm thinking, there won't be our like in Mayo, for gallant lovers, from this hour, today. (*Drunken singing is heard outside.*) There's my father coming from the wake, and when he's had his sleep we'll tell him, for he's peaceful then.

(*They separate.*)

MICHAEL (*singing outside*):

The jailor and the turnkey
They quickly ran us down,
And brought us back as prisoners
Once more to Cavan town.

(*He comes in supported by* SHAWN.)

There we lay bewailing
All in a prison bound. . . .

(*He sees* CHRISTY. *Goes and shakes him drunkenly by the hand, while* PEGEEN *and* SHAWN *talk on the left.*)

MICHAEL (*to* CHRISTY): The blessing of God and the holy angels on your head, young fellow. I hear tell you're after winning all in the sports below; and wasn't it a shame I didn't bear you along with me to Kate Cassidy's wake, a fine, stout lad, the like of you, for you'd never seen the match of it for flows of drink, the way when we sunk her bones at noonday in her narrow grave, there were five men, aye, and six men, stretched out retching speechless on the holy stones.

CHRISTY (*uneasily, watching* PEGEEN): Is that the truth?

MICHAEL: It is then, and aren't you a louty schemer to go burying your poor father unbeknownst when you'd a right to throw him on the crupper of a Kerry mule and drive him westwards, like holy Joseph in the days gone by, the way we could have given him a decent burial, and not have him rotting beyond, and not a Christian drinking a smart drop to the glory of his soul?

CHRISTY (*gruffly*): It's well enough he's lying, for the likes of him.

MICHAEL (*slapping him on the back*): Well, aren't you a hardened slayer? It'll be a poor thing for the household man where you go sniffing for a female wife; and (*Pointing to* SHAWN.) look beyond at that shy and decent Christian I have chosen for my daughter's hand, and I after getting the gilded dispensation this day for to wed them now.

CHRISTY: And you'll be wedding them this day, is it?

MICHAEL (*drawing himself up*): Aye. Are you thinking, if I'm drunk itself, I'd leave my daughter living single with a little frisky rascal is the like of you?

PEGEEN (*breaking away from* SHAWN): Is it the truth the dispensation's come?

MICHAEL (*triumphantly*): Father Reilly's after reading it in gallous° Latin, and "It's come in the nick of time," says he; "so I'll wed them in a hurry, dreading that young gaffer who'd capsize the stars."

PEGEEN (*fiercely*): He's missed his nick of time, for it's that lad, Christy Mahon, that I'm wedding now.

MICHAEL (*loudly with horror*): You'd be making him a son to me, and he wet and crusted with his father's blood?

PEGEEN: Aye. Wouldn't it be a bitter thing for a girl to go marrying the like of Shaneen, and he's a middling kind of a scarecrow, with no savagery or fine words in him at all?

MICHAEL (*gasping and sinking on a chair*): Oh, aren't you a heathen daughter to go shaking the fat of my heart, and I swamped and drownded with the weight of drink? Would you have them turning on me the way that I'd be roaring to the dawn of day with the wind upon my heart? Have you not a word to aid me, Shaneen? Are you not jealous at all?

SHAWN (*in great misery*): I'd be afeard to be jealous of a man did slay his da.

PEGEEN: Well, it'd be a poor thing to go marrying your like. I'm seeing there's a world of peril for an orphan girl, and isn't it a great blessing I didn't wed you, before himself came walking from the west or south?

SHAWN: It's a queer story you'd go picking a dirty tramp up from the highways of the world.

PEGEEN (*playfully*): And you think you're a likely beau to go straying along with, the shiny Sundays of the opening year, when it's sooner on a bullock's

---

gallous, fine.

---

liver you'd put a poor girl thinking than on the lily or the rose?

SHAWN: And have you no mind of my weight of passion, and the holy dispensation, and the drift of heifers I am giving, and the golden ring?

PEGEEN: I'm thinking you're too fine for the like of me, Shawn Keogh of Killakeen, and let you go off till you'd find a radiant lady with droves of bullocks on the plains of Meath, and herself bedizened in the diamond jewelleries of Pharaoh's ma. That'd be your match, Shaneen. So God save you now!

(*She retreats behind* CHRISTY.)

SHAWN: Won't you hear me telling you . . . ?

CHRISTY (*with ferocity*): Take yourself from this, young fellow, or I'll maybe add a murder to my deeds today.

MICHAEL (*springing up with a shriek*): Murder is it? Is it mad yous are? Would you go making murder in this place, and it piled with poteen for our drink tonight? Go on to the foreshore if it's fighting you want, where the rising tide will wash all traces from the memory of man.

(*Pushing* SHAWN *toward* CHRISTY.)

SHAWN (*shaking himself free, and getting behind* MICHAEL): I'll not fight him, Michael James. I'd liefer live a bachelor, simmering in passions to the end of time, than face a lepping savage the like of him has descended from the Lord knows where. Strike him yourself, Michael James, or you'll lose my drift of heifers and my blue bull from Sneem.

MICHAEL: Is it me fight him, when it's father-slaying he's bred to now? (*Pushing* SHAWN.) Go on you fool and fight him now.

SHAWN (*coming forward a little*): Will I strike him with my hand?

MICHAEL: Take the loy is on your western side.

SHAWN: I'd be afeard of the gallows if I struck him with that.

CHRISTY (*taking up the loy*): Then I'll make you face the gallows or quit off from this.

(SHAWN *flies out of the door.*)

CHRISTY: Well, fine weather be after him, (*Going to* MICHAEL, *coaxingly.*) and I'm thinking you wouldn't wish to have that quaking blackguard in your house at all. Let you give us your blessing and hear her swear her faith to me, for I'm mounted on the springtide of the stars of luck, the way it'll be good for any to have me in the house.

PEGEEN (*at the other side of* MICHAEL): Bless us now, for I swear to God I'll wed him, and I'll not renege.

MICHAEL (*standing up in the center, holding on to both of them*): It's the will of God, I'm thinking, that all should win an easy or a cruel end, and it's the will of God that all should rear up lengthy families for the nurture of the earth. What's a single man, I ask you, eating a bit in one house and drinking a sup in another, and he with no place of his own, like an old braying jackass strayed upon the rocks? (*to* CHRISTY) It's many would be in dread to bring your like into their house for to end them, maybe, with a sudden end; but I'm a decent man of Ireland, and I liefer face the grave untimely and I seeing a score of grandsons growing up little gallant swearers by the name of God, than go peopling my bedside with puny weeds the like of what you'd breed, I'm thinking, out of Shaneen Keogh. (*He joins their hands.*) A daring fellow is the jewel of the world, and a man did split his father's middle with a single clout, should have the bravery of ten, so may God and Mary and St. Patrick bless you, and increase you from this mortal day.

CHRISTY *and* PEGEEN: Amen, O Lord!

(*Hubbub outside,* OLD MAHON *rushes in, followed by all the crowd, and* WIDOW QUIN. *He makes a rush at* CHRISTY, *knocks him down, and begins to beat him.*)

PEGEEN (*dragging back his arm*): Stop that, will you, Who are you at all?

MAHON: His father, God forgive me!

PEGEEN (*drawing back*): Is it rose from the dead?

MAHON: Do you think I look so easy quenched with the tap of a loy? (*Beats* CHRISTY *again.*)

PEGEEN (*glaring at* CHRISTY): And it's lies you told, letting on you had him slitted, and you nothing at all.

CHRISTY (*catching* MAHON'S *stick*): He's not my father. He's a raving maniac would scare the world. (*Pointing to* WIDOW QUIN.) Herself knows it is true.

CROWD: You're fooling Pegeen! The Widow Quin seen him this day, and you likely knew! You're a liar!

CHRISTY (*dumbfounded*): It's himself was a liar, lying stretched out with an open head on him, letting on he was dead.

MAHON: Weren't you off racing the hills before I got my breath with the start I had seeing you turn on me at all?

PEGEEN: And to think of the coaxing glory we had given him, and he after doing nothing but hitting a soft blow and chasing northward in a sweat of fear. Quit off from this.

CHRISTY (*piteously*): You've seen my doings this day, and let you have me from the old man; for why would you be in such a scorch of haste to spur me to destruction now?

PEGEEN: It's there your treachery is spurring me, till I'm hard set to think you're the one I'm after lacing in my heart-strings half-an-hour gone by. (*to* MAHON) Take him on from this, for I think bad the world should see me raging for a Munster liar, and the fool of men.

MAHON: Rise up now to retribution, and come on with me.

CROWD (*jeeringly*): There's the playboy! There's the lad thought he'd rule the roost in Mayo. Slate him now, mister.

CHRISTY (*getting up in shy terror*): What is it drives you to torment me here, when I'd asked the thunders of the might of God to blast me if I ever did hurt to any saving only that one single blow.

MAHON (*loudly*): If you didn't, you're a poor good-for-nothing, and isn't it by the like of you the sins of the whole world are committed?

CHRISTY (*raising his hands*): In the name of the Almighty God. . . .

MAHON: Leave troubling the Lord God. Would you have him sending down droughts, and fevers, and the old hen and the cholera morbus?

CHRISTY (*to* WIDOW QUIN): Will you come between us and protect me now?

WIDOW QUIN: I've tried a lot, God help me, and my share is done.

CHRISTY (*looking round in desperation*): And I must go back into my torment is it, or run off like a vagabond straying through the Unions with the dusts of August making mudstains in the gullet of my throat, or the winds of March blowing on me till I'd take an oath I felt them making whistles of my ribs within?

SARA: Ask Pegeen to aid you. Her like does often change.

CHRISTY: I will not then, for there's torment in the splendor of her like and she a girl any moon of midnight would take pride to meet, facing southwards on the heaths of Keel. But what did I want crawling forward to scorch my understanding at her flaming brow?

PEGEEN (*to* MAHON, *vehemently, fearing she will break into tears*): Take him on from this or I'll set the young lads to destroy him here.

MAHON (*going to him, shaking his stick*): Come on now if you wouldn't have the company to see you skelped.

PEGEEN (*half laughing, through her tears*): That's it, now the world will see him pandied, and he an ugly liar was playing off the hero, and the fright of men.

CHRISTY (*to* MAHON, *very sharply*): Leave me go!

CROWD: That's it. Now Christy. If them two set fighting, it will lick the world.

MAHON (*making a grab at* CHRISTY): Come here to me.

CHRISTY (*more threateningly*): Leave me go, I'm saying.

MAHON: I will maybe, when your legs is limping, and your back is blue.

CROWD: Keep it up, the two of you. I'll back the old one. Now the playboy.

CHRISTY (*in low and intense voice*): Shut your yelling, for if you're after making a mighty man of me this day by the power of a lie, you're setting me now to think if it's a poor thing to be lonesome, it's worse maybe to go mixing with the fools of earth.

(MAHON *makes a movement toward him.*)

CHRISTY (*almost shouting*): Keep off . . . lest I do show a blow unto the lot of you would set the guardian angels winking in the clouds above.

(*He swings round with a sudden rapid movement and picks up a loy.*)

CROWD (*half frightened, half amused*): He's going mad! Mind yourselves! Run from the idiot!

CHRISTY: If I am an idiot, I'm after hearing my voice this day saying words would raise the topknot on a poet in a merchant's town. I've won your racing, and your lepping, and . . .

MAHON: Shut your gullet and come on with me.

CHRISTY: I'm going, but I'll stretch you first.

(*He runs at old* MAHON *with the loy, chases him out of the door, followed by* CROWD *and* WIDOW QUIN. *There is a great noise outside, then a yell, and dead silence for a moment.* CHRISTY *comes in, half dazed, and goes to fire.*)

WIDOW QUIN (*coming in, hurriedly, and going to him*): They're turning again you. Come on, or you'll be hanged, indeed.

CHRISTY: I'm thinking, from this out, Pegeen'll be giving me praises the same as in the hours gone by.

WIDOW QUIN (*impatiently*): Come by the back door. I'd think bad to have you stifled on the gallows tree.

CHRISTY (*indignantly*): I will not, then. What good'd be my life-time, if I left Pegeen?

WIDOW QUIN: Come on, and you'll be no worse than you were last night; and you with a double murder this time to be telling to the girls.

CHRISTY: I'll not leave Pegeen Mike.

WIDOW QUIN (*impatiently*): Isn't there the match of her in every parish public, from Binghamstown unto the plain of Meath? Come on, I tell you, and I'll find you finer sweethearts at each waning moon.

CHRISTY: It's Pegeen I'm seeking only, and what'd I care if you brought me a drift of chosen females, standing in their shifts itself, maybe, from this place to the Eastern World?

SARA (*runs in, pulling off one of her petticoats*): They're going to hang him. (*Holding out petticoat and shawl.*) Fit these upon him, and let him run off to the east.

WIDOW QUIN: He's raving now; but we'll fit them on him, and I'll take him, in the ferry, to the Achill boat.

CHRISTY (*struggling feebly*): Leave me go, will you? When I'm thinking of my luck today, for she will wed me surely, and I a proven hero in the end of all.

(*They try to fasten petticoat round him.*)

WIDOW QUIN: Take his left hand, and we'll pull him now. Come on, young fellow.

CHRISTY (*suddenly starting up*): You'll be taking me from her? You're jealous, is it, of her wedding me? Go on from this.

(*He snatches up a stool, and threatens them with it.*)

WIDOW QUIN (*going*): It's in the mad-house they should put him, not in jail, at all. We'll go by the back door, to call the doctor, and we'll save him so.

(*She goes out, with* SARA, *through inner room. Men crowd in the doorway.* CHRISTY *sits down again by the fire.*)

MICHAEL (*in a terrified whisper*): Is the old lad killed surely?

PHILLY: I'm after feeling the last gasps quitting his heart.

(*They peer in at* CHRISTY.)

MICHAEL (*with a rope*): Look at the way he is. Twist a hangman's knot on it, and slip it over his head, while he's not minding at all.

PHILLY: Let you take it, Shaneen. You're the soberest of all that's here.

SHAWN: Is it me to go near him, and he the wickedest and worst with me? Let you take it, Pegeen Mike.

PEGEEN: Come on, so.

(*She goes forward with the others, and they drop the double hitch over his head.*)

CHRISTY: What ails you?

SHAWN (*triumphantly, as they pull the rope tight on his arms*): Come on to the peelers, till they stretch you now.

CHRISTY: Me!

MICHAEL: If we took pity on you, the Lord God would, maybe, bring us ruin from the law today, so you'd best come easy, for hanging is an easy and a speedy end.

CHRISTY: I'll not stir. (*to* PEGEEN) And what is it you'll say to me, and I after doing it this time in the face of all?

PEGEEN: I'll say, a strange man is a marvel, with his mighty talk; but what's a squabble in your back yard, and the blow of a loy, have taught me that there's a great gap between a gallous story and a dirty deed. (*to* MEN) Take him on from this, or the lot of us will be likely put on trial for his deed today.

CHRISTY (*with horror in his voice*): And it's yourself will send me off, to have a horny-fingered hangman hitching his bloody slipknots at the butt of my ear.

MEN (*pulling rope*): Come on, will you?

(*He is pulled down on the floor.*)

CHRISTY (*twisting his legs round the table*): Cut the rope, Pegeen, and I'll quit the lot of you, and live from this out, like the madmen of Keel, eating muck and green weeds, on the faces of the cliffs.

PEGEEN: And leave us to hang, is it, for a saucy liar, the like of you? (*to* MEN) Take him on, out from this.

SHAWN: Pull a twist on his neck, and squeeze him so.

PHILLY: Twist yourself. Sure he cannot hurt you, if you keep your distance from his teeth alone.

SHAWN: I'm afeard of him. (*to* PEGEEN) Lift a lighted sod, will you, and scorch his leg.

PEGEEN (*blowing the fire, with a bellows*): Leave go now, young fellow, or I'll scorch your shins.

CHRISTY: You're blowing for to torture me. (*His voice rising and growing stronger.*) That's your kind, is it? Then let the lot of you be wary, for, if I've to face the gallows, I'll have a gay march down, I tell you, and shed the blood of some of you before I die.

SHAWN (*in terror*): Keep a good hold, Philly. Be wary, for the love of God. For I'm thinking he would liefest wreak his pains on me.

CHRISTY (*almost gaily*): If I do lay my hands on you, it's the way you'll be at the fall of night, hanging as a scarecrow for the fowls of hell. Ah, you'll have a gallous jaunt I'm saying, coaching out through Limbo with my father's ghost.

SHAWN (*to* PEGEEN): Make haste, will you? Oh, isn't he a holy terror, and isn't it true for Father Reilly, that all drink's a curse that has the lot of you so shaky and uncertain now?

CHRISTY: If I can wring a neck among you, I'll have a royal judgment looking on the trembling jury in the courts of law. And won't there be crying out in Mayo the day I'm stretched upon the rope with the ladies in their silks and satins sniveling in their lacy kerchiefs, and they rhyming songs and ballads on the terror of my fate?

(*He squirms round on the floor and bites* SHAWN's *leg.*)

SHAWN (*shrieking*): My leg's bit on me. He's the like of a mad dog, I'm thinking, the way that I will surely die.

CHRISTY (*delighted with himself*): You will then, the way you can shake out hell's flags of welcome for my coming in two weeks or three, for I'm thinking Satan hasn't many have killed their da in Kerry, and in Mayo too.

(OLD MAHON *comes in behind on all fours and looks on unnoticed.*)

MEN (*to* PEGEEN): Bring the sod, will you?

PEGEEN (*coming over*): God help him so.

(*Burns his leg.*)

CHRISTY (*kicking and screaming*): O, glory be to God!

(*He kicks loose from the table, and they all drag him toward the door.*)

JIMMY (*seeing old* MAHON): Will you look what's come in?

(*They all drop* CHRISTY *and run left.*)

CHRISTY (*scrambling on his knees face to face with old* MAHON): Are you coming to be killed a third time, or what ails you now?

MAHON: For what is it they have you tied?

CHRISTY: They're taking me to the peelers to have me hanged for slaying you.

MICHAEL (*apologetically*): It is the will of God that all should guard their little cabins from the treachery of law, and what would my daughter be doing if I was ruined or was hanged itself?

MAHON (*grimly, loosening* CHRISTY): It's little I care if you put a bag on her back, and went picking cockles till the hour of death; but my son and myself will be going our own way, and we'll have great times from this out telling stories of the villainy of Mayo, and the fools is here. (*to* CHRISTY, *who is freed*) Come on now.

CHRISTY: Go with you, is it? I will then, like a gallant captain with his heathen slave. Go on now and I'll see you from this day stewing my oatmeal and washing my spuds, for I'm master of all fights from now. (*Pushing* MAHON.) Go on, I'm saying.

MAHON: Is it me?

CHRISTY: Not a word out of you. Go on from this.

MAHON (*walking out and looking back at* CHRISTY *over his shoulder*): Glory be to God! (*With a broad smile.*) I am crazy again! (*Goes.*)

CHRISTY: Ten thousand blessings upon all that's here, for you've turned me a likely gaffer in the end of all, the way I'll go romancing through a romping lifetime from this hour to the drawing of the judgment day. (*He goes out.*)

MICHAEL: By the will of God, we'll have peace now for your drinks. Will you draw the porter, Pegeen?

SHAWN (*going up to her*): It's a miracle Father Reilly can wed us in the end of all, and we'll have none to trouble us when his vicious bite is healed.

PEGEEN (*hitting him a box on the ear*): Quit my sight. (*Putting her shawl over her head and breaking out into wild lamentations.*) Oh my grief, I've lost him surely. I've lost the only Playboy of the Western World.

Figure 65. The villagers rush in with Christy (David Birney) aloft on
their shoulders to celebrate his athletic victories in the Lincoln Center
Repertory Theater production of *The Playboy of the Western World,* directed by John Hirsch, New York, 1971. (Photograph: Martha Swope.)

Figure 66. The villagers pull the rope tight around Christy (David Birney), while Pegeen (Martha Henry) threatens to strike him in the Lincoln Center Repertory Theater production of *The Playboy of the Western World,* directed by John Hirsch, New York, 1971. (Photograph: Martha Swope.)

Figure 67. Christy (David Birney) berates Mahon (Stephen Elliott) during their final confrontation in the Lincoln Center Repertory Theater production of *The Playboy of the Western World,* directed by John Hirsch, New York, 1970. (Photograph: Martha Swope.)

Staging of *The Playboy of the Western World*

REVIEW OF THE LINCOLN CENTER REPERTORY
THEATER PRODUCTION, 1971, BY JOHN
BEAUFORT

The Repertory Theater of Lincoln Center has mounted a fresh and ebullient revival of that classic piece of lyric tragicomedy and skylarking, "The Playboy of the Western World." It is a laudable way of celebrating J. M. Synge's centennial. It is also the best of the several productions I have seen at the Vivian Beaumont Theater.

"In a good play," wrote Synge, "every speech should be as fully flavored as a nut or apple, and such speeches cannot be written by anyone who works among people who have shut their lips on poetry."

The Lincoln Center players have not shut their ears on Synge's poetry. Admittedly, the accents at the Beaumont are somewhat diverse. (But even the Abbey's Dubliners didn't escape criticism on this point of authenticity.) Only a spectator familiar with the speech of County Mayo can pass fine judgments. One less qualified can applaud the Lincolnites for conveying the spirit of the dialogue, even though they may not capture its full flavor. They attack the text con brio and with affection. Director John Hirsch has stimulated them to throw themselves into it and at it with great gusto and good feeling.

The result is a performance which grasps more than a little of the grace and glory of this extravagant mocking of human vanity and gullibility, though less of its underlying sadness. With the start the company has made, the performance should grow in suppleness and penetrate deeper below the play's surfaces.

In the turbulent central role of shrewish, high-spirited Pegeen Mike, the role on which so much depends, Martha Henry has the looks as well as the vocal and physical power for that irresistible heroine. Although she might perhaps profit from a greater variety of tone, she masters the principal moods of the mercurial Pegeen—an infinite capacity for scorn, a romanticism yearning for the poet-hero who will conquer her, and finally the bitter anguish with which she utters that memorable cry, "He's gone, and I've lost the only playboy of the Western World."

As Christy Mahon, the young stranger who dazzles the whole village by boasting that he's killed his father, David Birney takes off somewhat tentatively on his flight of fancy. But he gains strength as his tall tale and the evening progresses, notably in his first detailed recital of his "crime" (to three enthralled village maidens), his brief triumph, and his desperate assertion of manhood when all has gone against him. Mr. Hirsch has directed the finale in rumbustious fashion, filling the Beaumont's thrust stage with action, and employing an impressive selection of weaponry from the props and furniture provided by scenic designer Douglas W. Schmidt.

There are a number of stalwart individual portrayals in his "Playboy" revival. One thinks particularly of Frances Sternhagen's comely, crisply amorous, and wily Widow Quin, and of Philip Bosco as one of the local farmers. Sydney Walker plays Pegeen's comic publican father conventionally, and Stephen Elliott shrewdly builds each appearance of old Mahon, the playboy's father, to the climatic showdown and sudden capitulation. James Blendick strikes the required note of timorous piety as Pegeen's forlorn suitor.

LUIGI PIRANDELLO

1867–1936

Pirandello's life was in many respects as problematic as the existence of the characters in his plays, and he playfully acknowledged its confusion by declaring himself to be "the son of Chaos." His father was actually the owner of a lucrative sulfur mine, and Pirandello was born on his father's country estate in a southern Sicilian locale, whose name was derived from the Greek word, chaos. Although his father had intended him to have a career in business, Pirandello was already writing poetry by the time he was sixteen, and when he was eighteen, having failed in a brief business venture, his father sent him off to the University of Rome. He subsequently attended the University of Bonn, where in 1891 he earned a doctorate in philology, but instead of pursuing a career in teaching and research he returned to Rome and immersed himself in writing poetry and fiction. By 1894, he had already published two volumes of poetry and a collection of short stories. Also in 1894, he was married off in an arrangement negotiated by his father and another sulfur-mine owner who wanted to unite their business interests. For its first ten years, the marriage was evidently a happy one, supported by the substantial wealth of both parents, but in 1904 both sulfur mines were destroyed by a flood. The news of this disaster was so shocking to Pirandello's wife that she fainted on hearing it, was subsequently completely paralyzed for six months, and then gradually went insane. Pirandello was forced to take a position teaching literature at a girl's school, an arrangement that provoked his wife to have hysterical fits of jealousy. Her derangement repeatedly caused her to become physically violent, yet Pirandello persisted in taking care of her himself for fifteen years, until in 1919 his friends finally convinced him to have her committed to a mental institution.

Pirandello continued to write during all the years of living through his wife's insanity and through the insanity of World War I, which divided his allegiances between Germany, a country he admired for its learning and scholarship, and Italy, his own country, which entered the conflict in 1916 on the side of the English and French. By 1916, he had published several volumes of short stories, several novels, several collections of poetry, and three one-act plays, and in virtually all these works he expressed a relativistic view of existence that he appears to have been driven to by the chaotic nature of his own personal experience. In his most well-known novel, *The Late Mattia Pascal* (1905), for example, he told the story of a man who discovers that because he left some belongings on a bridge everyone thinks he has committed suicide. Having made this discovery, the man decides to capitalize on the misunderstanding by trying to start a new life, free of the deceptions and role-playing that had characterized his old one. But he at once realizes that he must take a new role, in order to prevent his earlier identity from being discovered, and thus gradually recognizes that his personality is not his own creation, but an appearance forced on him by what is expected in his own society.

The predicament of Mattia Pascal epitomizes Pirandello's persistent concerns: the inescapable compulsion of human beings to play roles, to assume so many guises, in fact, that they can never be certain even of their own personal character, much less that of anyone else they encounter in the world. Pirandello explicitly defined his concern with these problems in 1920, shortly before the appearance of *Six Characters in Search of an Author* (1922):

> I think that life is a very sad piece of buffoonery: because we have in ourselves, without being able to know why, wherefore or whence, the need to deceive ourselves constantly by creating a reality (one for each and never the same for all), which from time to time is discovered to be vain and illusory.

The vanity and the illusoriness of this "buffoonery" provided Pirandello with the grounds for all of his writing:

> My art is full of bitter compassion for all those who deceive themselves; but this compassion cannot fail to be followed by the ferocious derision of destiny which condemns man to deception.

His "bitter compassion," fed by the irrationality of the war, evidently moved him to turn to playwriting, for between 1916 and 1921 in a fury of productivity he produced a total of fifteen plays.

Pirandello dramatized his relativistic vision most explicitly in a play appropriately titled *Right You Are, If You Think You Are* (1917), which depicts the futile attempts of an Italian community to unravel the truth about a husband, his wife, and his mother-in-law who have come to live in their city. The mother-in-law, for example, tells one story about their situation, which is subsequently contradicted by that of the husband, who appears to demonstrate that his mother-in-law is insane, but his version of their situation is, in turn, discredited by another story from his mother-in-law that appears to prove that he is a madman, and the action of the play repeatedly complicates the problem of determining the truth about the family without ever resolving it. As the wife (who appears only at the end of the play) says, "I am the one that each of you thinks I am." Truth is thus presented to be as unstable, as variable, as the differing perceptions of every member in the community. The maddening implications of this vision were dramatized by Pirandello in *Enrico IV* (1922), a play that portrays the schizophrenic experience of a man who recovers from a long psychotic delusion about himself only to perpetuate his madness as a deliberate pose. But at the end of the play, his deliberate choice turns into an eternal necessity, when he kills a man who has accused him of being sane and finds that in order to escape a charge of murder he must retreat forever into the role of being a madman.

By the end of his life, Pirandello had dramatized his haunting view of existence in nearly forty plays, but none of them achieved the enduring fame of *Six Characters in Search of an Author* (1922). Its unique dramatic power is in large part the result of Pirandello's reclaiming of a traditional dramatic form—the play within the play—and a traditional dramatic metaphor for the vanity of existence—"Life's but . . . a poor player that struts and frets his hour upon the stage and then is heard no more." Pirandello has used these traditional elements to present his relativistic vision in its most disturbingly complicated form. From the moment the six characters appear on stage seeking an author to tell their story and a producer to dramatize their experience, Pirandello gradually unfolds the dizzying ramifications of his relativistic view: in the Father's repeated explanations of it that the Producer repeatedly denies even in the face of the hopeless confusion unfolding before him, in the repeated attempts of the Stepdaughter to have the story played from her perspective that the Father repeatedly claims to be a distortion of his true character, in the almost inarticulate desire of the Mother to have her older son express the affection and forgiveness that she feels is warranted from her point of view, in the Son's attempt to proclaim his lack of complicity in the gruesome tragedy despite being one of the villains of the piece, and, of course, in the inability of any of the characters or actors to understand each other at all. The play moves inexorably to its final frenzy of yelling, one side shouting "Reality!" the other "Make-believe!" And Pirandello's symbolic comment on this confusion is to plunge the theater into darkness, so that even the Producer, so staunchly sure of the truth, cannot see where he is going. Although the play is clearly an enactment of Pirandello's relativistic philosophy, it may also be seen as dramatizing the problematic relationship between art and life, between performance and existence. The characters' search for an author may also be viewed as a compelling psychological study of the anxiety—even the schizophrenia—that results from the felt absence of a stable authority figure. Even the Father, the traditional image of authority, is seeking a reliable source of authority, but the only authority figure in the play, the Producer, is equally unreliable.

When *Six Characters* was first produced in Rome, the audience turned into a madhouse of excitement at the end of the play. When it was produced in Paris in 1923, it stunned the French theatrical world and led to a torrent of dramatic imitations. Wherever and whenever it is produced, in fact, it provokes the excitement of audiences and critics, as evidenced by the review of the American Conservatory Theater production, reprinted following the text. Photographs of that production clearly show the haunting expressions and gestures the performers displayed in acting the roles of the six characters (see Figure 68 and 69) as well as the outrage of the Stepdaughter at the moment the Father is attempting to seduce her (Figure 70), a moment epitomizing Pirandello's disturbing view of experience.

SIX CHARACTERS IN SEARCH OF AN AUTHOR

BY LUIGI PIRANDELLO / TRANSLATED BY FREDERICK MAY

CHARACTERS OF THE PLAY IN THE MAKING

THE FATHER
THE MOTHER
THE STEPDAUGHTER
THE SON
THE BOY (nonspeaking)
THE LITTLE GIRL (nonspeaking)
MADAME PACE (who is called into being)

THE ACTORS IN THE COMPANY

THE PRODUCER (Director)
THE LEADING LADY
THE LEADING MAN
THE SECOND FEMALE LEAD (referred to as THE SECOND ACTRESS in the text.)
THE INGENUE
THE JUVENILE LEAD
OTHER ACTORS AND ACTRESSES

THE STAGE MANAGER
THE PROMPTER
THE PROPERTY MAN
THE FOREMAN OF THE STAGE CREW
THE PRODUCER'S SECRETARY
THE COMMISSIONAIRE
STAGE HANDS AND OTHER THEATRE PERSONNEL

SCENE

Daytime: The Stage of a Theatre

N.B. The play has neither acts nor scenes. Its performance will be interrupted twice: once—though the curtain will not be lowered—when the PRODUCER and the principal CHARACTERS go away to write the script and the ACTORS leave the stage, and a second time when the Man on the Curtain lets it fall by mistake.

ACT 1

(When the audience enters the auditorium the curtain is up and the stage is just as it would be during the daytime. There is no set and there are no wings; it is empty and in almost total darkness. This is in order that right from the very beginning the audience shall receive the impression of being present, not at a performance of a carefully rehearsed play, but at a performance of a play that suddenly happens.

Two small flights of steps, one right and one left, give access to the stage from the auditorium.

On the stage itself, the prompter's dome has been removed, and is standing just to one side of the prompt box.

Downstage, on the other side, a small table and an armchair with its back turned to the audience have been set for the Producer.

Two more small tables, one rather larger than the other, together with several chairs, have been set downstage so that they are ready if needed for the rehearsal. There are other chairs scattered about to the left and to the right for the actors, and, in the background, to one side and almost hidden, there is a pianoforte.

When the house lights go down the FOREMAN comes on to the stage through the back door. He is dressed in blue dungarees and carries his tools in a bag slung at his belt. From a corner at the back of the stage he takes one or two

slats of wood, brings them down front, kneels down and starts nailing them together. At the sound of his hammer the STAGE MANAGER rushes in from the direction of the dressing-rooms.)

STAGE MANAGER: Hey! What are you doing?

FOREMAN: What am I doing? Hammering . . . nails.

STAGE MANAGER: At this time of day? *(He looks at his watch.)* It's gone half-past ten! The Producer'll be here any minute now and he'll want to get on with his rehearsal.

FOREMAN: And let me tell *you* something . . . I've got to have time to do *my* work, too.

STAGE MANAGER: You'll get it, you'll get it. . . . But you can't do that *now*.

FOREMAN: When can I do it then?

STAGE MANAGER: After the rehearsal. Now, come on. . . . Clear up all this mess, and let me get on with setting the second act of *The Game As He Played It*.

(The FOREMAN gathers his pieces of wood together, muttering and grumbling all the while, and goes off. Meanwhile, the ACTORS OF THE COMPANY have begun to come on to the stage through the door back. First one comes in, then another, then two together . . . just as they please. There are nine or ten of them in all–as many as you would suppose you would need for the rehearsal of Pirandello's play, The Game As He Played It, *which*

has been called for today. As they come in they greet one another and the STAGE MANAGER *with a cheery 'Good morning'. Some of them go off to their dressing-rooms; others, and among them the* PROMPTER, *who is carrying the prompt copy rolled up under his arm, remain on the stage, waiting for the* PRODUCER *to come and start the rehearsal. While they are waiting—some of them standing, some seated about in small groups—they exchange a few words among themselves. One lights a cigarette, another complains about the part that he's been given and a third reads out an item of news from a theatrical journal for the benefit of the other actors. It would be best if all the* ACTORS *and* ACTRESSES *could be dressed in rather bright and gay clothes. This first improvised scene should be played very naturally and with great vivacity. After a while, one of the comedy men can sit down at the piano and start playing a dance-tune. The younger* ACTORS *and* ACTRESSES *start dancing.)*

STAGE MANAGER (*clapping his hands to restore order*): Come on, now, come on! That's enough of that! Here's the producer!

(*The music and dancing come to a sudden stop. The* ACTORS *turn and look out into the auditorium and see the* PRODUCER, *who is coming in through the door. He comes up the gangway between the stalls, bowler hat on head, stick under arm, and a large cigar in his mouth, to the accompaniment of a chorus of "Good-mornings" from the* ACTORS *and climbs up one of the flights of steps on to the stage. His* SECRETARY *offers him his post—a newspaper or so, a script.)*

PRODUCER: Any letters?

SECRETARY: None at all. This is all the post there is.

PRODUCER (*handing him back the script*): Put it in my office. (*Then, looking around and turning to the* STAGE MANAGER.) Oh, you can't see a thing here! Ask them to give us a spot of light, please.

STAGE MANAGER: Right you are!

(*He goes off to give the order and a short while after the whole of the right side of the stage, where the* ACTORS *are standing, is lit up by a bright white light. In the meantime the* PROMPTER *has taken his place in his box, switched on his light and spread his script out in front of him.)*

PRODUCER (*clapping his hands*): Come on, let's get started! (*to the* STAGE MANAGER) Anyone missing?

STAGE MANAGER: The Leading Lady.

PRODUCER: As usual! (*Looks at his watch.*) We're ten minutes late already. Make a note, will you, please, to remind me to give her a good talking-to about being so late! It might teach her to get to rehearsals on time in the future.

(*He has scarcely finished his rebuke when the voice of the* LEADING LADY *is heard at the back of the auditorium.)*

LEADING LADY: No, please don't! Here I am! Here I

am! (*She is dressed completely in white, with a large and rather dashing and provocative hat, and is carrying a dainty little lap-dog. She runs down the aisle and hastily climbs up the steps on to the stage.)*

PRODUCER: You've set your heart on always keeping us waiting, haven't you?

LEADING LADY: Forgive me! I hunted everywhere for a taxi so that I should get here on time! But you haven't started yet, anyway. And I don't come on immediately. (*Then, calling the* STAGE MANAGER *by name, she gives him the lap-dog.*) Please put him in my dressing-room . . . and mind you shut the door!

PRODUCER (*grumblingly*): And she has to bring a dog along too! As if there weren't enough dogs around here! (*He claps his hands again and turns to the* PROMPTER.) Come on now, let's get on with Act II of *The Game As He Played It.* (*He sits down in the armchair.*) Now, ladies and gentlemen, who's on?

(*The* ACTORS *and* ACTRESSES *clear away from the front of the stage and go and sit to one side, except for the three who start the scene, and the* LEADING LADY. *She has paid no attention to the* PRODUCER'S *question and has seated herself at one of the little tables.)*

PRODUCER (*to the* LEADING LADY): Ah! So you're in this scene, are you?

LEADING LADY: Me? Oh, no!

PRODUCER (*annoyed*): Then for God's sake get off!

(*And the* LEADING LADY *gets up and goes and sits with the others.)*

PRODUCER (*to the* PROMPTER): Now, let's get started!

PROMPTER (*reading from his script*): "The house of Leone Gala. A strange room, half dining-room, half study."

PRODUCER (*turning to the* STAGE MANAGER): We'll use the red set.

STAGE MANAGER (*making a note on a sheet of paper*): The red set. Right!

PROMPTER (*continuing to read from his script*): "A table laid for a meal and a desk with books and papers. Bookshelves with books on them. Glass-fronted cupboards containing valuable china. A door back leading into Leone's bedroom. A side door left, leading into the kitchen. The main entrance is right."

PRODUCER (*getting up and pointing*): Right! Now listen carefully—over there, the main entrance. And over here, the kitchen. (*Turning to the* ACTOR *who is to play the part of Socrates.*) You'll make your entrances and exits this side. (*to the* STAGE MANAGER) We'll have that green-baize door at the back there . . . and some curtains. (*He goes and sits down again.*)

STAGE MANAGER (*making a note*): Right you are!

PROMPTER (reading): "Scene I. Leone Gala, Guido Venanzi, Filippo, who is called Socrates." (to the PRODUCER) Do I have to read the stage directions as well?

PRODUCER: Yes, yes, of course! I've told you that a hundred times!

PROMPTER (reading): "When the curtain rises. Leone Gala, wearing a cook's hat and apron, is busy beating an egg in a basin, with a wooden spoon. Filippo, also dressed as a cook, is beating another egg. Guido Venanzi is sitting listening to them."

LEADING MAN (to the PRODUCER): Excuse me, but do I really have to wear a cook's hat?

PRODUCER (irritated by this observation): So it seems! That's certainly what's written there! (He points to the script.)

LEADING MAN: Forgive me for saying so, but it's ridiculous.

PRODUCER (bounding to feet in fury): Ridiculous! Ridiculous! What do you expect me to do if the French haven't got any more good comedies to send us, and we're reduced to putting on plays by Pirandello? And if you can understand his plays . . . you're a better man than I am! He deliberately goes out of his way to annoy people, so that by the time the play's through everybody's fed up . . . actors, critics, audience, everybody! (The ACTORS laugh. Then getting up and going over to the LEADING MAN, the PRODUCER cries.) Yes, my dear fellow, a cook's hat! And you beat eggs! And do you think that, having these eggs to beat, you then have nothing more on your hands? Oh, no, not a bit of it. . . . You have to represent the shell of the eggs that you're beating! (The ACTORS start laughing again and begin to make ironical comments among themselves.) Shut up! And listen when I'm explaining things! (Turning again to the LEADING MAN.) Yes, my dear fellow, the shell . . . or, as you might say, the empty form of reason, without that content of instinct which is blind! You are reason and your wife is instinct, in a game where you play the parts which have been given you. And all the time you're playing your part, you are the self-willed puppet of yourself. Understand?

LEADING MAN (spreading out his hands): Me? No!

PRODUCER (returning to his seat): Neither do I! However, let's get on with it! It's going to be a wonderful flop, anyway! (In a confidential tone.) I suggest you turn to the audience a bit more . . . about three-quarters face. Otherwise, what with the abstruseness of the dialogue, and the audience's not being able to hear you, the whole thing'll go to hell. (Clapping his hands again.) Now, come along! Come along! Let's get started!

PROMPTER: Excuse me, sir, do you mind if I put the top back on my box? There's a bit of a draught.

PRODUCER: Of course! Go ahead! Go ahead!

(Meanwhile the COMMISSIONAIRE has entered the auditorium. He is wearing a braided cap and having covered the length of the aisle, he comes up to the edge of the stage to announce the arrival of the SIX CHARACTERS to the PRODUCER. They have followed the COMMISSIONAIRE into the auditorium and have walked behind him as he has come up to the stage. They look about them, a little perplexed and a little dismayed.

In any production of this play it is imperative that the producer should use every means possible to avoid any confusion between the SIX CHARACTERS and the ACTORS. The placing of the two groups, as they will be indicated in the stage-directions once the CHARACTERS are on the stage, will no doubt help. So, too, will their being lit in different colors. But the most effective and most suitable method of distinguishing them that suggests itself, is the use of special masks for the CHARACTERS, masks specially made from some material which will not grow limp with perspiration and will at the same time be light enough to be worn by the actors playing these parts. They should be cut so as to leave the eyes, the nose and the mouth free. In this way the deep significance of the play can be brought out. The CHARACTERS should not, in fact, appear as phantasms, but as created realities, unchangeable creations of the imagination and, therefore, more real and more consistent than the ever-changing naturalness of the ACTORS.

The masks will assist in giving the impression of figures constructed by art, each one fixed immutably in the expression of that sentiment which is fundamental to it. That is to say in REMORSE for the FATHER, REVENGE for the STEPDAUGHTER, CONTEMPT for the SON and SORROW for the MOTHER. Her mask should have wax tears fixed in the corners of the eyes and coursing down the cheeks, just like those which are carved and painted in the representations of the Mater Dolorosa that are to be seen in churches.

Her dress, too, should be of a special material and cut. It should be severely plain, its folds stiff, giving in fact the appearance of having been carved, and not of being made of any material that you can just go out and buy or have cut-out and made up into a dress by any ordinary dressmaker.

The FATHER is a man of about fifty. He is not bald but his reddish hair is thin at the temples. His moustache is thick and coils over his still rather youthful-looking mouth, which all too often falls open in a purposeless, uncertain smile. His complexion is pale and this is especially noticeable when one has occasion to look at his forehead, which is particularly broad. His blue, oval-shaped eyes are very clear and piercing. He is wearing a dark jacket and light-coloured trousers. At times his manner is all sweetness and light, at others it is hard and harsh.

The MOTHER appears as a woman crushed and ter-

rified by an intolerable weight of shame and abasement. She is dressed in a modest black and wears a thick crepe widow's veil. When she lifts her veil she reveals a wax-like face; it is not, however at all sickly looking. She keeps her eyes downcast all the time. The STEPDAUGHTER, *who is eighteen, is defiant, bold, arrogant—almost shamelessly so. She is very beautiful. She, too, is dressed in mourning but carries it with a decided air of showy elegance. She shows contempt for the very timid, dejected, half-frightened manner of her younger brother, a rather grubby and unprepossessing* BOY *of fourteen, who is also dressed in black. On the other hand she displays a very lively tenderness for her small sister, a* LITTLE GIRL *of about four, who is wearing a white frock with a black silk sash round her waist.*

The SON *is a tall young man of twenty-two. He is wearing a mauve coloured overcoat and has a long green scarf twisted round his neck. He appears as if he has stiffened into an attitude of contempt for the* FATHER *and of supercilious indifference toward the* MOTHER.)

COMMISSIONAIRE (*cap in hand*): Excuse me, sir.

PRODUCER (*snapping at him rudely*): Now what's the matter?

COMMISSIONAIRE: There are some people here, sir, asking for you.

(*The* PRODUCER *and the* ACTORS *turn in astonishment and look out into the auditorium.*)

PRODUCER (*furiously*): But I've got a rehearsal on at the moment! And you know quite well that no one's allowed in here while a rehearsal's going on. (*Then addressing the* CHARACTERS.) Who are you? What do you want?

FATHER (*he steps forward, followed by the others, and comes to the foot of one of the flights of steps*): We are here in search of an author.

PRODUCER (*caught between anger and utter astonishment*): In search of an author? Which author?

FATHER: Any author, sir.

PRODUCER: But there's no author here. . . . We're rehearsing a new play.

STEPDAUGHTER (*vivaciously, as she rushes up the steps*): So much the better! Then so much the better, sir! We can be your new play.

ONE OF THE ACTORS (*amidst the lively comments and laughter of the others*): Oh, just listen to her! *Listen* to her!

FATHER (*following the* STEPDAUGHTER *on to the stage*): Yes, but if there isn't any author. . . . (*to the* PRODUCER) Unless you'd like to be the author. . . .

(*Holding the* LITTLE GIRL *by the hand, the* MOTHER, *followed by the* BOY, *climbs up the first steps leading to the stage and stands there expectantly. The* SON *remains morosely below.*)

PRODUCER: Are you people trying to be funny?

FATHER: No. . . . How can you suggest such a thing? On the contrary, we are bringing you a terrible and grievous drama.

STEPDAUGHTER: And we might make your fortune for you.

PRODUCER: Perhaps you'll do me the kindness of getting out of this theatre! We've got no time to waste on lunatics!

FATHER (*he is wounded by this, but replies in a gentle tone*): Oh . . . But you know very well, don't you, that life is full of things that are infinitely absurd, things that, for all their impudent absurdity, have no need to masquerade as truth, because they are true.

PRODUCER: What the devil are you talking about?

FATHER: What I'm saying is that reversing the usual order of things, forcing oneself to a contrary way of action, may well be construed as madness. As, for instance, when we create things which have all the appearance of reality in order that they shall look like the realities themselves. But allow me to observe that if this indeed be madness, it is, nonetheless, the sole *raison d'etre* of your profession.

(*The* ACTORS *stir indignantly at this.*)

PRODUCER (*getting up and looking him up and down*): Oh, yes? do you think ours is a profession of lunatics, do you?

FATHER: Yes, making what isn't true *seem* true . . . without having to . . . for fun. . . . Isn't it your function to give life on the stage to imaginary characters?

PRODUCER (*immediately, making himself spokesman for the growing anger of his actors*): I should like you to know, my dear sir, that the actor's profession is a most noble one. and although nowadays, with things in the state they are, our playwrights give us stupid comedies to act, and puppets to represent instead of men, I'd have you know that it is our boast that we have given life, here on these very boards, to immortal works!

(*The* ACTORS *satisfiedly murmur their approval and applaud the* PRODUCER.)

FATHER (*breaking in and following hard on his argument*): There you are! Oh, that's it exactly! To living beings . . . to beings who are more alive than those who breathe and wear clothes! Less real, perhaps, but truer! We're in complete agreement!

(*The* ACTORS *look at each other in utter astonishment.*)

PRODUCER: But . . . What on earth! . . . But you said just now . . .

FATHER: No, I said that because of your . . . because

you shouted at us that you had no time to waste on lunatics . . . while nobody can know better than you that nature makes use of the instrument of human fantasy to pursue her work of creation on a higher level.

PRODUCER: True enough! True enough! But where does all this get us?

FATHER: Nowhere. I only wish to show you that one is born into life in so many ways, in so many forms. . . . As a tree, or as a stone; as water or as a butterfly. . . . Or as a woman. And that one can be born a character.

PRODUCER (*ironically, feigning amazement*): And you together with these other people, were born a character?

FATHER: Exactly. And alive, as you see. (*The PRODUCER and the ACTORS burst out laughing as if at some huge joke.*) (*Hurt.*) I'm sorry that you laugh like that because, I repeat, we carry within ourselves a terrible and grievous drama, as you can deduce for yourselves from this woman veiled in black.

(*And so saying, he holds out his hand to the MOTHER and helps her up the last few steps and, continuing to hold her hand, leads her with a certain tragic solemnity to the other side of the stage, which immediately lights up with a fantastic kind of light. The LITTLE GIRL and the BOY follow their MOTHER. Next the SON comes up and goes and stands to one side, in the background. Then the STEPDAUGHTER follows him on to the stage; she stands downstage, leaning against the proscenium arch. The ACTORS are at first completely taken-aback and then, caught in admiration at this development, they burst into applause—just as if they had had a show put on for their benefit.*)

PRODUCER (*at first utterly astonished and then indignant*): Shut up! what the . . . ! (*Then turning to the CHARACTERS.*) And you get out of here! Clear out of here! (*to the STAGE MANAGER*) For God's sake, clear them out!

STAGE MANAGER (*coming forward, but then stopping as if held back by some strange dismay*): Go away! Go away!

FATHER (*to the PRODUCER*): No, no! Listen. . . . We. . . .

PRODUCER (*shouting*): I tell you, we've got work to do!

LEADING MAN: You can't go about playing practical jokes like this. . . .

FATHER (*resolutely coming forward*): I wonder at your incredulity. Is it perhaps that you're not accustomed to seeing the characters created by an author leaping to life up here on the stage, when they come face to face with each other? Or is it, perhaps, that there's no script there (*He points to the prompt box.*) that contains us?

STEPDAUGHTER (*smiling, she steps toward the PRODUCER; then, in a wheedling voice*): Believe me, sir, we really are six characters . . . and very, very interesting! But we've been cut adrift.

FATHER (*brushing her aside*): Yes, that's it, we've been cut adrift. (*And then immediately to the PRODUCER.*) In the sense, you understand, that the author who created us as living beings, either couldn't or wouldn't put us materially into the world of art. And it was truly a crime . . . because he who has the good fortune to be born a living character may snap his fingers at Death even. He will never die! Man . . . The writer . . . The instrument of creation . . . Will die. . . . But what is created by him will never die. And in order to live eternally he has not the slightest need of extraordinary gifts or of accomplishing prodigies. Who was Sancho Panza? Who was Don Abbondio? And yet they live eternally because— living seeds—they had the good fortune to find a fruitful womb—a fantasy which knew how to raise and nourish them, and to make them live through all eternity.

PRODUCER: All this is very, very fine indeed. . . . But what do you want here?

FATHER: We wish to live, sir!

PRODUCER (*ironically*): Through all eternity?

FATHER: No sir; just a moment . . . in you.

AN ACTOR: Listen to him! . . . listen to him!

LEADING LADY: They want to live in us!

JUVENILE LEAD (*pointing to the STEPDAUGHTER*): I've no objection . . . so long as I get her.

FATHER: Listen! Listen! The play is in the making. (*to the PRODUCER*) But if you and your actors are willing, we can settle it all between us without further delay.

PRODUCER (*annoyed*): But what do you want to settle? We don't go in for that sort of concoction here! We put on comedies and dramas here.

FATHER: Exactly! That's the very reason why we came to you.

PRODUCER: And where's the script?

FATHER: It is in us, sir. (*The ACTORS laugh.*) The drama is in us. We are the drama and we are impatient to act it—so fiercely does our inner passion urge us on.

STEPDAUGHTER (*scornful, treacherous, alluring, with deliberate shamelessness*): My passion. . . . If you only knew! My passion . . . for him! (*She points to the FATHER and makes as if to embrace him, but then bursts into strident laughter.*)

FATHER (*at once, angrily*): You keep out of this for the moment! And please don't laugh like that!

STEPDAUGHTER: Oh . . . mayn't I? Then perhaps you'll allow me, ladies and gentlemen. . . . Although it's scarcely two months since my father died . . . just you watch how I can dance and sing! (*Mischievously she starts to sing Dave Stamper's*

"Prends garde à Tchou-Tchin-Tchou" in the fox-trot or slow one-step version by Francois Salabert. She sings the first verse, accompanying it with a dance.)

Les chinois sont un peuple malin,
De Shangai à Pékin,
Ils ont mis des écriteaux partout:
Prenez garde à Tchou-Tchin-Tchou!

(While she is singing and dancing, the ACTORS, *and especially the younger ones, as if attracted by some strange fascination, move toward her and half raise their hands as though to catch hold of her. She runs away, and when the* ACTORS *burst into applause, and the* PRODUCER *rebukes her, she stands where she is, quietly, abstractedly, and as if her thoughts were far away.)*

ACTORS *and* ACTRESSES *(laughing and clapping)*: Well done! Jolly good!

PRODUCER *(irately)*: Shut up! What do you think this is . . . a cabaret? *(Then taking the* FATHER *a little to one side, he says with a certain amount of consternation.)* Tell me something. . . . Is she mad?

FATHER: What do you mean, mad? It's worse than that!

STEPDAUGHTER *(immediately rushing up to the* PRODUCER*)*: Worse! Worse! Oh it's something very much worse than that! Listen! Let's put this drama on at once . . . Please! Then you'll see that at a certain moment I . . . when this little darling here. . . . *(Takes the* LITTLE GIRL *by the hand and brings her over to the* PRODUCER.*)* . . . Isn't she a dear? *(Takes her in her arms and kisses her.)* You little darling! . . . You dear little darling! *(Puts her down again, adding in a moved tone, almost without wishing to.)* Well, when God suddenly takes this child away from her poor mother, and that little imbecile there *(Roughly grabbing hold of the* BOY *by the sleeve and thrusting him forward.)* does the stupidest of all stupid things, like the idiot he is *(Pushing him back toward the* MOTHER.*)* . . . Then you will see me run away. Yes, I shall run away! And, oh, how I'm longing for that moment to come! Because after all the very intimate things that have happened between him and me *(With a horrible wink in the direction of the* FATHER.*)* I can't remain any longer with these people . . . having to witness my mother's anguish because of that queer fish there *(Pointing to the* SON.*)* Look at him! Look at him! See how indifferent, how frigid he is . . . because he's the legitimate son . . . *he* is! He despises me, he despises him *(Pointing to the* BOY.*)*, he despises that dear little creature. . . . Because we're bastards! Do you understand? . . . Because we're *bastards! (She goes up to the* MOTHER *and embraces her.)* And he doesn't want to recog-

nize this poor woman as his mother. . . . This poor woman . . . who is the mother of us all! He looks down at her as if she were only the mother of us three bastards! The wretch! *(She says all this very quickly and very excitedly. She raises her voice at the word 'bastards' and the final "wretch" is delivered in a low voice and almost spat out.)*

MOTHER *(to the* PRODUCER, *an infinity of anguish in her voice)*: Please, in the name of these two little children . . . I beg you. . . . *(She grows faint and sways on her feet.)* Oh, my God! *(Consternation and bewilderment among the* ACTORS.*)*

FATHER *(rushing over to support her, accompanied by most of the* ACTORS*)*: Quick . . . a chair. . . . A chair for this poor widow!

ACTORS *(rushing over)*: Has she fainted? Has she fainted?

PRODUCER: Quick, get a chair . . . get a chair!

(One of the ACTORS *brings a chair, the others stand around, anxious to help in any way they can. The* MOTHER *sits on the chair; she attempts to prevent the* FATHER *from lifting the veil which hides her face.)*

FATHER: Look at her. . . . Look at her. . . .

MOTHER: No, no! My God! Stop it, please!

FATHER: Let them see you. *(He lifts her veil.)*

MOTHER *(rising and covering her face with her hands in desperation)*: I beg you, sir, . . . Don't let this man carry out his plan! You must prevent him. . . . It's horrible!

PRODUCER *(utterly dumbfounded)*: I don't get this at all. . . . I haven't got the slightest idea what you're talking about. *(to the* FATHER*)* Is this lady your wife?

FATHER *(immediately)*: Yes, sir, my wife.

PRODUCER: Then how does it come about that she's a widow if you're still alive?

(The ACTORS *find relief for their bewilderment and astonishment in a noisy burst of laughter.)*

FATHER *(wounded, speaking with sharp resentment)*: Don't laugh! Don't laugh like that, for pity's sake! It is in this fact that her drama lies. She had another man. Another man who ought to be here.

MOTHER *(with a cry)*: No! No!

STEPDAUGHTER: He's got the good luck to be dead. . . . He died two months ago, as I just told you. We're still wearing mourning for him, as you can see.

FATHER: But it's not because he's dead that he's not here. No, he's not here because . . . Look at her! Look at her, please, and you'll understand immediately! Her drama does not lie in the love of two men for whom she, being incapable of love, could feel nothing. . . . Unless, perhaps, it be a little gratitude . . . to him, not to me. She is not a woman. . . . She is a mother. And her drama. . . . And how powerful it is! How powerful it is! . . . Her drama lies entirely, in fact, in these four children . . . The children of the two men that she had.

MOTHER: Did you say that I had them? Do you dare to say that I *had* these two men . . . to suggest that I wanted them? *(to the PRODUCER)* It was his doing. He gave him to me! He forced him on me! He forced me. . . . He forced me to go away with that other man!

STEPDAUGHTER *(at once, indignantly)*: It's not true!

MOTHER *(startled)*: Not true?

STEPDAUGHTER: It's not true! It's not true, I say.

MOTHER: And what can you possibly know about it?

STEPDAUGHTER: It's not true! *(to the PRODUCER)* Don't believe her! Do you know why she said that? Because of him. *(Pointing to the SON.)* That's why she said it! Because she tortures herself, wears herself out with anguish, because of the indifference of that son of hers. She wants him to believe that if she abandoned him when he was two years old it was because he *(Pointing to the FATHER.)* forced her to do it.

MOTHER *(forcefully)*: He forced me to do it! He forced me, as God is my witness! *(to the PRODUCER)* Ask him *(Pointing to her HUSBAND.)* if it's not true! Make him tell my son! She *(Pointing to her DAUGHTER.)* knows nothing at all about the matter.

STEPDAUGHTER: I know that while my father lived you were always happy. . . . You had a peaceful and contented life together. Deny it if you can!

MOTHER: I don't deny it! No. . . .

STEPDAUGHTER: He was always most loving, always kindness itself towards you. *(to the BOY, angrily)* Isn't it true? Go on. . . . Say it's true! Why don't you speak, you stupid little idiot?

MOTHER: Leave the poor boy alone! Why do you want to make me appear an ungrateful woman? I don't want to say anything against your father. . . . I only said that it wasn't my fault, and that it wasn't just to satisfy my own desires that I left his house and abandoned my son.

FATHER: What she says is true. It was my doing.

(There is a pause.)

LEADING MAN *(to the other ACTORS)*: My God! What a show!

LEADING LADY: And we're the audience this time!

JUVENILE LEAD: For once in a while.

PRODUCER *(who is beginning to show a lively interest)*: Let's listen to this! Let's hear what they've got to say! *(And saying this he goes down the steps into the auditorium and stands in front of the stage, as if to get an impression of the scene from the audience's point of view.)*

SON *(without moving from where he is, speaking coldly, softly, ironically)*: Yes! Listen to the chunk of philosophy you're going to get now. He will tell you all about the Demon of Experiment.

FATHER: You're a cynical idiot, as I've told you a hundred times. *(Down to the PRODUCER.)* He mocks me because of this expression that I've discovered in my own defence.

SON *(contemptuously)*: Words! Words!

FATHER: Yes! Words! Words! They can always bring consolation to us. . . . To everyone of us. . . . When we're confronted by something for which there's no explanation. . . . When we're face to face with an evil that consumes us. . . . The consolation of finding a word that tells us nothing, but that brings us peace.

STEPDAUGHTER: And dulls our sense of remorse, too. Yes! That above all!

FATHER: Dulls our sense of remorse? No, that's not true. It wasn't with words alone that I quietened remorse within me.

STEPDAUGHTER: No, you did it with a little money as well. Yes! Oh, yes! with a little money as well! With the hundred lire that he was going to offer me . . . as payment, ladies and gentlemen!

(A movement of horror on the part of the ACTORS.)

SON *(contemptuously to his STEPSISTER)*: That was vile!

STEPDAUGHTER: Vile? There they were, in a pale blue envelope, on the little mahogany table in the room behind Madame Pace's shop. Madame Pace. . . . One of those *Madames* who pretend to sell *Robes et Manteaux* so that they can attract us poor girls from decent families into their workrooms.

SON: And she's bought the right to tyrannise over the whole lot of us with those hundred lire that he was going to pay her. . . . But by good fortune. . . . And let me emphasise this. . . . He had no reason to pay her anything.

STEPDAUGHTER: Yes, but it was a very near thing! Oh, yes, it was, you know! *(She bursts out laughing.)*

MOTHER *(rising to protest)*: For shame! For shame!

STEPDAUGHTER *(immediately)*: Shame? No! This is my revenge! I'm trembling with desire. . . . Simply trembling with desire to live that scene! That room. . . . Over there the divan, the long mirror and a screen. . . . And in front of the window that little mahogany table. . . . And the pale blue envelope with the hundred lire inside. Yes, I can see it quite clearly! I'd only have to stretch out my hand and I could pick it up! But you gentlemen really ought to turn your backs now, because I'm almost naked. I no longer blush, because he's the one who does the blushing now.

(Pointing to FATHER.*)* But, let me tell you, he was very pale then. . . . Very pale indeed! *(to the* PRODUCER*)* You can believe *me!*

PRODUCER: I haven't the vaguest idea what you're talking about!

FATHER: I can well believe it! When you get things hurled at you like that. Put your foot down. . . . And let me speak before you believe all these horrible slanders she's so viciously heaping upon me. . . . Without letting me get a word of explanation in.

STEPDAUGHTER: Ah, but this isn't the place for your long-winded fairy-stories, you know!

FATHER: But I'm not going to. . . . I want to explain things to him!

STEPDAUGHTER: Oh yes . . . I bet you do! You'll explain everything so that it suits you, won't you?

(At this point the PRODUCER *comes back on stage to restore order.)*

FATHER: But can't you see that here we have the cause of all the trouble! In the use of words! Each one of us has a whole world of things inside him. . . . And each one of us has his own particular world. How can we understand each other if into the words which I speak I put the sense and the value of things as I understand them within myself. . . . While at the same time whoever is listening to them inevitably assumes them to have the sense and value that they have for him. . . . The sense and value that they have in the world that he has within him? We think we understand one another. . . . But we never really do understand! Look at this situation, for example! All my pity, all the pity that I feel for this woman *(Pointing to the* MOTHER*)* she sees as the most ferocious cruelty.

MOTHER: But you turned me out of the house!

FATHER: There! Do you hear? I turned her out! She really believed that I was turning her out!

MOTHER: You know how to talk . . . I don't. . . . But believe me *(Turning to the* PRODUCER.*)* after he had married me. . . . Goodness knows why! For I was a poor, humble woman. . . .

FATHER: But it was just because of that. . . . It was your humility that I loved in you. I married you for your humility, believing . . . *(He breaks off, for she is making gestures of contradiction. Then, seeing how utterly impossible it is to make her understand him, he opens his arms wide in a gesture of despair and turns to the* PRODUCER.*)* No! . . . You see? She says no! It's terrifying, believe me! It's really terrifying, this deafness *(He taps his forehead.).* . . . This mental deafness of hers! Affection. . . . Yes! . . . For her children! But deaf . . . Mentally deaf. . . . Deaf to the point of desperation.

STEPDAUGHTER: True enough! But now you make

him tell us what good all his cleverness has ever done us.

FATHER: If we could only foresee all the ill that can result from the good that we believe we are doing.

(Meanwhile the LEADING LADY, *with ever-increasing fury, has been watching the* LEADING MAN, *who is busy carrying on a flirtation with the* STEPDAUGHTER. *Unable to stand it any longer she now steps forward and says to the* PRODUCER.*)*

LEADING LADY: Excuse me, but are you going on with the rehearsal?

PRODUCER: Why, of course! Of course! But just at the moment I want to hear what these people have to say!

JUVENILE LEAD: This is really something quite new!

INGENUE: It's most interesting!

LEADING LADY: For those that are interested! *(And she looks meaningly in the direction of the* LEADING MAN.*)*

PRODUCER *(to the* FATHER*)*: But you'll have to explain everything clearly. *(He goes and sits down.)*

FATHER: Yes. . . . Well. . . . You see . . . I had a poor man working under me. . . . He was my secretary, and devoted to me. . . . Who understood her in every way . . . In everything *(Pointing to the* MOTHER.*)* Oh, there wasn't the slightest suspicion of anything wrong. He was a good man. A humble man. . . . Just like her. . . . They were incapable . . . both of them . . . not only of doing evil . . . but even of thinking it!

STEPDAUGHTER: So, instead, he thought about it for them! And then got on with it.

FATHER: It's not true! I thought that what I should be doing would be for their good. . . . And for mine, too . . . I confess it! Yes, things had come to such a pass that I couldn't say a single word to either of them without their immediately exchanging an understanding look. . . . Without the one's immediately trying to catch the other's eye. . . . For advice as to how to take what I had said. . . . So that I shouldn't get into a bad temper. As you'll readily appreciate it was enough to keep me in a state of continual fury. . . . Of intolerable exasperation!

PRODUCER: But. . . . Forgive my asking. . . . Why didn't you give this secretary of yours the sack?

FATHER: That's exactly what I did do, as a matter of fact. But then I had to watch that poor woman wandering forlornly about the house like some poor lost creature . . . Like one of those stray animals you take in out of charity.

MOTHER: But . . .

FATHER *(immediately turning on her, as if to forestall what she is about to say)*: Your son! You were going to tell him about your son, weren't you?

MOTHER: But first of all he tore my son away from me!

FATHER: Not out of any desire to be cruel though! I took him away so that, by living in the country, in contact with Nature, he might grow up strong and healthy.

STEPDAUGHTER (*pointing to him, ironically*): And just look at him!

FATHER (*immediately*): And is it my fault, too, that he's grown up the way he has? I sent him to a wet-nurse in the country . . . a peasant's wife . . . because my wife didn't seem strong enough to me. . . . Although she came of a humble family, and it was for that reason that I'd married her! Just a whim maybe. . . . But then . . . what was I to do? I've always had this cursed longing for a certain solid moral healthiness.

(*At this the* STEPDAUGHTER *breaks out afresh into noisy laughter.*)

Make her stop that noise! I can't stand it!

PRODUCER: Be quiet! Let me hear what he has to say, for God's sake!

(*At the* PRODUCER'S *rebuke she immediately returns to her former attitude. . . . Absorbed and distant, a half-smile on her lips. The* PRODUCER *comes down off the stage again to see how it looks from the auditorium.*)

FATHER: I could no longer stand the sight of that woman near me (*Pointing to the* MOTHER.) Not so much because of the irritation she caused me . . . the nausea . . . the very real nausea with which she inspired me. . . . But rather because of the pain . . . the pain and the anguish that I was suffering on her account.

MOTHER: And he sent me away!

FATHER: Well provided with everything. . . . To that other man. . . . So that she might be free of me.

MOTHER: And so that he might be free as well!

FATHER: Yes, I admit it. And a great deal of harm came as a result of it. . . . But I meant well. . . . And I did it more for her sake than for my own. I swear it! (*He folds his arms. Then immediately turning to the* MOTHER.) Did I ever lose sight of you? Tell me, did I ever lose sight of you until that fellow took you away suddenly to some other town . . . all unknown to me. . . . Just because he'd got some queer notion into his head about the interest I was showing in you. . . . An interest which was pure, I assure you, sir. . . . Without the slightest suspicion of any ulterior motive about it! I watched the new little family that grew up around her with incredible tenderness. She can testify to that. (*He points to the* STEPDAUGHTER.)

STEPDAUGHTER: Oh, I most certainly can! I was such a sweet little girl. . . . Such a sweet little girl, you see. . . . With plaits down to my shoulders . . . and my knickers a little bit longer than my frock. I used to see him standing there by the door of the school as I came out. He came to see how I was growing up. . . .

FATHER: Oh, this is vile! Treacherous! Infamous!

STEPDAUGHTER: Oh, no! What makes you say it's infamous?

FATHER: It's infamous! Infamous! (*Then turning excitedly to the* PRODUCER *he goes on in an explanatory tone.*) After she'd gone away (*Pointing to the* MOTHER.), my house suddenly seemed empty. She had been a burden on my spirit, but she had filled my house with her presence! Left alone I wandered through the rooms like some lost soul. This boy here (*Pointing to the* SON), having been brought up away from home. . . . I don't know . . . But . . . but when he returned home he no longer seemed to be my son. With no mother to link him to me, he grew up entirely on his own. . . . A creature apart . . . absorbed in himself . . . with no tie of intellect or affection to bind him to me. And then. . . . And, strange as it may seem, it's the simple truth . . . I became curious about her little family. . . . Gradually I was attracted to this family which had come into being as a result of what I had done. And the thought of it began to fill the emptiness that I felt all around me. I felt a real need . . . a very real need . . . to believe that she was happy, at peace, absorbed in the simple everyday duties of life. I wanted to look on her as being fortunate because she was far removed from the complicated torments of my spirit. And so, to have some proof of this, I used to go and watch that little girl come out of school.

STEPDAUGHTER: I should just say he did! He used to follow me along the street. He would smile at me and when I reached home he'd wave to me . . . like this. I would look at him rather provocatively, opening my eyes wide. I didn't know who he might be. I told my mother about him and she knew at once who it must be. (*The* MOTHER *nods agreement.*) At first she didn't want to let me go to school again. . . . And she kept me away for several days. And when I did go back, I saw him waiting for me at the door again . . . looking ridiculous . . . with a brown paper bag in his hand. He came up to me and patted me. . . . And then he took a lovely large straw hat out of the bag . . . with lots of lovely roses on it . . . And all for me.

PRODUCER: This is a bit off the point, you know.

SON (*contemptuously*): Yes. . . . Literature! Literature!

FATHER: Literature indeed! This is life! Passion!

PRODUCER: It may be. But you certainly can't act this sort of stuff!

FATHER: I agree with you. Because all this is only

leading up to the main action. I'm not suggesting that this part should be acted. And as a matter of fact, as you can quite well see, she (*Pointing to the* STEPDAUGHTER.) is no longer that little girl with plaits down to her shoulders. . . .

STEPDAUGHTER: . . . and her knickers a little bit longer than her frock!

FATHER: It is now that the drama comes! Something new, something complex. . . .

STEPDAUGHTER (*coming forward, her voice gloomy, fierce*): As soon as my father died. . . .

FATHER (*at once, not giving her a chance to continue*): . . . they fell into the most wretched poverty! They came back here. . . . And because of her stupidity (*Pointing to the* MOTHER.) I didn't know a thing about it. It's true enough that she can hardly write her own name. . . . But she might have got her daughter or that boy to write and tell me that they were in need!

MOTHER: Now tell me, sir, how was I to know that this was how he'd feel?

FATHER: That's exactly where you went wrong, in never having got to know how I felt about something.

MOTHER: After so many years away from him. . . . And after all that had happened. . . .

FATHER: And is it my fault that that fellow took you away from here as he did? (*Turning to the* PRODUCER.) I tell you, they disappeared overnight. . . . He'd found some sort of a job away from here . . . I couldn't trace them at all. . . . So, of necessity, my interest in them dwindled. And this was how it was for quite a number of years. The drama broke out, unforeseen, and violent in its intensity, when they returned. . . . When I was impelled by the demands of my miserable flesh, which is still alive with desire. . . . Oh, the wretchedness, the unutterable wretchedness of the man who's alone and who detests the vileness of casual affairs! When he's not old enough to do without a woman, and not really young enough to be able to go and look for one without feeling a sense of shame. Wretchedness, did I say? It's horrible! It's horrible! Because no woman is any longer capable of giving him love. And when he realises this, he ought to do without. . . . Yes, yes, I know! . . . Each one of us, when he appears before his fellow men, is clothed with a certain dignity. But deep down inside himself he knows what unconfessable things go on in the secrecy of his own heart. We give way . . . we give way to temptation. . . . Only to rise up again immediately, filled with a great eagerness to re-establish our dignity in all its solid entirety. . . . Just as if it were a tombstone on some grave in which we had buried, in which we had hidden from our eyes, every sign, and the very memory

itself of our shame. And everyone is just like that! Only there are some of us who lack the courage to talk about certain things.

STEPDAUGHTER: They've got the courage to do them, though. . . . All of them!

FATHER: Yes, all of them! But only in secret! And that's why it needs so much more courage to talk about them! A man's only got to mention these things, and the words have hardly left his lips before he's been labelled a cynic. And all the time it's not true. He's just like everybody else. . . . In fact he's better than they are, because he's not afraid to reveal with the light of his intelligence that red blush of shame which is inherent in human bestiality. . . . That shame to which bestial man closes his eyes, in order not to see it. And woman. . . . Yes, woman. . . . What kind of a being is she? She looks at you, tantalisingly, invitingly. You take her in your arms. And no sooner is she clasped firmly in your arms than she shuts her eyes. It is the sign of her mission, the sign by which she says to man. "Blind yourself, for I am blind."

STEPDAUGHTER: And what about when she no longer shuts her eyes? When she no longer feels the need to hide her blushing shame from herself by closing her eyes? When she sees instead . . . dry-eyed and dispassionate . . . the blushing shame of man, who has blinded himself without love? Oh, what disgust, what unutterable disgust, does she feel then for all these intellectual complications, for all this philosophy which reveals the beast in man and then tries to save him, tries to excuse him . . . I just can't stand here and listen to him! Because when a man is obliged to 'simplify' life bestially like that—when he throws overboard every vestige of 'humanity', every chaste desire, every pure feeling. . . . All sense of idealism, of duty, or modesty and of shame. . . . Then nothing is more contemptible, infuriating and revoltingly nauseating than their maudlin remorse. . . . Those crocodile tears!

PRODUCER: Now let's get back to the point! Let's get to the point! This is just a lot of beating about the bush!

FATHER: Very well. But a fact is like a sack. . . . When it's empty it won't stand up. And in order to make it stand up you must first of all pour into it all the reasons and all the feelings which have caused it to exist. I couldn't possibly be expected to know that when that man died and they returned here in such utter poverty, she (*Pointing to the* MOTHER.) would go out to work as a dress-maker in order to support the children. . . . Nor that, of all people, she'd gone to work for that . . . for Madame Pace.

STEPDAUGHTER: Who's a high-class dress-maker, if

you ladies and gentlemen would really like to know. On the surface she does work for only the best sort of people. But she arranges things so that these fine ladies act as a screen . . . without prejudice to the others . . . who are only so-so.

MOTHER: Believe me, it never entered my head for one moment that that old hag gave me work because she had her eye on my daughter. . . .

STEPDAUGHTER: Poor Mummy! Do you know what that woman used to do when I took her back the work that my mother had done? She would point out to me how the material had been ruined by giving it to my mother to sew. . . . Oh, she'd grumble about this! And she'd grumble about that! And so, you understand, I had to pay for it. . . . And all the time this poor creature thought she was sacrificing herself for me and for those two children, as she sat up all night sewing away at work for Madame Pace. (*Gestures and exclamations of indignation from the* ACTORS.)

PRODUCER (*immediately*): And it was there, one day, that you met . . .

STEPDAUGHTER (*pointing to the* FATHER): . . . him! Yes, him! An old client! Now there's a scene for you to put on! Absolutely superb!

FATHER: With her . . . the Mother . . . arriving. . . .

STEPDAUGHTER (*immediately, treacherously*): . . . almost in time!

FATHER (*a cry*): No! In time! In time! Fortunately I recognized her in time! And I took them all back home with me! Now you can imagine what the situation is like for both of us. She, just as you see her. . . . And I no longer able to look her in the face.

STEPDAUGHTER: It's utterly ridiculous! How can I possibly be expected, after all that, to be a modest young miss . . . well-bred and virtuous . . . in accordance with his confounded aspirations for a "solid moral healthiness"?

FATHER: My drama lies entirely in this one thing. . . . In my being conscious that each one of us believes himself to be a single person. But it's not true. . . . Each one of us is many persons. . . . Many persons . . . according to all the possibilities of being that there are within us. . . . With some people we are one person. . . . With others we are somebody quite different. . . . And all the time we are under the illusion of always being one and the same person for everybody. . . . We believe that we are always this one person in whatever it is we may be doing. But it's not true! It's not true! And we see this very clearly when by some tragic chance we are, as it were, caught up whilst in the middle of doing something and find ourselves suspended in midair. And then we perceive that all of us was not in what we were doing, and that it would, there-

fore, be an atrocious injustice to us to judge us by that action alone . . . to keep us suspended like that. . . . To keep us in a pillory . . . throughout all existence . . . as if our whole life were completely summed up in that one deed. Now do you understand the treachery of this girl? She surprised me somewhere where I shouldn't have been . . . and doing something that I shouldn't have been doing with her. . . . She surprised an aspect of me that should never have existed for her. And now she is trying to attach to me a reality such as I could never have expected I should have to assume for her. . . . The reality that lies in one fleeting, shameful moment of my life. And this, this above all, is what I feel most strongly about. And as you can see, the drama acquires a tremendous value from this concept. Then there's the position of the others. . . . His . . . (*Pointing to the* SON.)

SON (*shrugging his shoulders scornfully*): Leave me alone! I've got nothing to do with all this!

FATHER: What do you mean . . . you've got nothing to do with all this?

SON: I've got nothing to do with it. . . . And I don't want to have anything to do with it, because, as you quite well know, I wasn't meant to be mixed up in all this with the rest of you!

STEPDAUGHTER: Common, that's what we are! And he's a fine gentleman! But, as you may have noticed, every now and again I fix him with a contemptuous look, and he lowers his eyes. . . . Because he knows the harm he's done me!

SON (*scarcely looking at her*): I?

STEPDAUGHTER: Yes, you! You! It's all your fault that I became a prostitute! (*A movement of horror from the* ACTORS.) Did you or did you not deny us, by the attitude you adopted—I won't say the intimacy of your home—but even that mere hospitality which makes guests feel at their ease? We were invaders who had come to disturb the kingdom of your legitimacy. I should just like you (*This to the* PRODUCER.) to be present at certain little scenes that took place between him and me. He says that I tyrannised over everybody. . . . But it was just because of the way that he behaved that I took advantage of the thing that he calls 'vile.' . . . Why I exploited the reason for my coming into his house with my mother . . . Who is his mother as well! And I went into that house as mistress of it!

SON (*slowly coming forward*): It's all very easy for them. . . . It's fine sport. . . . All of them ganging up against me. But just imagine the position of a son whose fate it is one fine day, while he's sitting quietly at home, to see arriving an impudent and brazen young woman who asks for his father— and heaven knows what her business is with him!

Later he sees her come back, as brazen as ever, bringing that little girl with her. And finally he sees her treating her father—without knowing in the least why—in a very equivocal and very much to-the-point manner . . . asking him for money, in a tone of voice which leads you to suppose that he must give it to her. . . . Must give it to her, because he has every obligation to do so. . . .

FATHER: As indeed I have! It's an obligation I owe your mother!

SON: How should I know that? When had I never seen or even heard of her? Then one day I see her arrive with *her* (Pointing to the STEPDAUGH-TER.) together with that boy and the little girl. And they say to me, "This is *your* mother, too, you know." Little by little I begin to understand. . . . Largely as a result of the way she goes on (*Pointing to the* STEPDAUGHTER *again.*). . . . Why is it that they've come to live with us. . . . So suddenly . . . So unexpectedly. . . . What I feel, what I experience, I neither wish, nor am able, to express. I wouldn't even wish to confess it to myself. No action, therefore, can be hoped for from me in this affair. Believe me, I am a dramatically unrealised character . . . and I do not feel the least bit at ease in their company. So please leave me out of it!

FATHER: What! But it's just because you're like that. . . .

SON (*in violent exasperation*): And what do you know about it? How do you know what I'm like? When have you ever bothered yourself about me?

FATHER: I admit it! I admit it! But isn't that a dramatic situation in itself? This aloofness of yours, which is so cruel to me and to your mother. . . . Your mother who returns home and sees you almost for the first time . . . You're so grown up that she doesn't recognise you, but she knows that you're her son. (*Pointing to the* MOTHER *and addressing the* PRODUCER.) There, look! She's crying!

STEPDAUGHTER (*angrily, stamping her foot*): Like the fool she is!

FATHER (*pointing to the* STEPDAUGHTER): She can't stand him! (*Then returning to the subject of the* SON.) He says he's got nothing to do with all this, when, as a matter of fact, almost the whole action hinges on him. Look at that little boy. . . . See how he clings to his mother all the time, frightened and humiliated. . . . And it's *his* fault that he's like that! Perhaps his position is the most painful of all. . . . More than any of them he feels himself to be an outsider. And so the poor little chap feels mortified, humiliated at being taken into my home . . . out of charity, as it were. (*Confidentially.*) He's just like his father. Humble. . . . Doesn't say a word. . . .

PRODUCER: I don't think it's a good idea to have him in. You've no idea what a nuisance boys are on the stage.

FATHER: Oh, . . . but he won't be a nuisance for long . . . He disappears almost immediately. And the little girl, too. . . . In fact, she's the first to go.

PRODUCER: This is excellent! I assure you I find this all very interesting. . . . Very interesting indeed! I can see we've got the makings of a pretty good play here.

STEPDAUGHTER (*trying to butt in*): When you've got a character like me!

FATHER (*pushing her to one side in his anxiety to hear what decision the* PRODUCER *has come to*): You be quiet!

PRODUCER (*continuing, heedless of the interruption*): And it's certainly something new. . . . Ye-es! . . .

FATHER: Absolutely brand new!

PRODUCER: You had a nerve, though. I must say. . . . Coming here and chucking the idea at me like that. . . .

FATHER: Well, you understand, born as we are for the stage. . . .

PRODUCER: Are you amateur actors?

FATHER: No . . . I say that we're born for the stage because . . .

PRODUCER: Oh, don't try and con me with that one! You're an old hand at this game.

FATHER: No. I only act as much as anyone acts the part that he sets himself to perform, or the part that he is given in life. And in me it is passion itself, as you can see, that always becomes a little theatrical of its own accord . . . as it does in everyone . . . once it becomes exalted.

PRODUCER: Oh well, that as may be! That as may be! . . . But you do understand, without an author . . . I could give you the address of somebody who'd . . .

FATHER: No! . . . Look here. . . . You be the author!

PRODUCER: Me? What the devil are you talking about?

FATHER: Yes, you! You! Why not?

PRODUCER: Because I've never written anything in my life! That's why not!

FATHER: Then why not try your hand at it now? There's nothing to it. Everybody's doing it! And your job's made all the easier for you because we are here, all of us, alive before you. . . .

PRODUCER: That's not enough!

FATHER: Not enough? When you see us live our drama . . .

PRODUCER: Yes! Yes! But we'll still need somebody to write the play.

FATHER: No. . . . Someone to take it down possibly, while we act it out, scene by scene. It'll be quite sufficient if we make a rough sketch of it first and then have a run through.

PRODUCER (*climbing back on to the stage, tempted by*

this): H'm! . . . You almost succeed in tempting me. . . . H'm! It would be rather fun! We could certainly have a shot at it.

FATHER: Of course! Oh, you'll see what wonderful scenes'll emerge! I can tell you what they are here and now.

PRODUCER: You tempt me. . . . You tempt me. . . . Let's have a go at it! . . . Come with me into my office. (*Turning to the* ACTORS.) You can have a few minutes' break. . . . But don't go too far away. I want you all back again in about a quarter of an hour or twenty minutes. (*To the* FATHER.) Well, let's see what we can make of it! We might get something really extraordinary out of it. . . .

FATHER: There's no *might* about it! They'd better come along too, don't you think? (*Pointing to the other* CHARACTERS.)

PRODUCER: Yes, bring 'em along! Bring 'em along! (*Starts going off and then turns back to the* ACTORS.) Now remember, don't be late back! You've got a quarter of an hour!

(*The* PRODUCER *and the* SIX CHARACTERS *cross the stage and disappear. The* ACTORS *remain looking at one another in astonishment.*)

LEADING MAN: Is he serious? What's he going to do?

JUVENILE LEAD: This is utter madness!

A THIRD ACTOR: Does he expect us to knock up a play in five minutes?

JUVENILE LEAD: Yes . . . like the actors in the old Comedia dell'Arte.

LEADING LADY: Well, if he thinks that I'm going to have anything to do with fun and games of that sort. . . .

INGENUE: And you certainly don't catch me joining in!

A FOURTH ACTOR: I should like to know who those people are. (*He is alluding to the* CHARACTERS.)

THIRD ACTOR: Who do you think they're likely to be? They're probably escaped lunatics. . . . Or crooks!

JUVENILE LEAD: And does he really take what they say seriously?

INGENUE: Vanity! That's what it is. . . . The vanity of appearing as an author!

LEADING MAN: It's absolutely unheard of! If the stage has come to this. . . .

A FIFTH ACTOR: I'm rather enjoying it!

THIRD ACTOR: Oh, well! After all, we shall have the pleasure of seeing what comes of it all!

(*And talking among themselves in this way the* ACTORS *leave the stage. Some go out through the door back, some go in the direction of the dressing-rooms. The curtain remains up.*)

(*The performance is suspended for twenty minutes.*)

ACT 2

(*The call-bells ring, warning the audience that the performance is about to be resumed. The* ACTORS, *the* STAGE MANAGER, *the* FOREMAN *of the stage crew, the* PROMPTER *and the* PROPERTY MAN *reassemble on stage. Some come from the dressing-rooms, some through the door back, some even from the auditorium. The* PRODUCER *enters from his office accompanied by the* SIX CHARACTERS. *The houselights are extinguished and the stage lighting is as before.*)

PRODUCER: Now come on, ladies and gentlemen! Are we all here? Let me have your attention please! Now let's make a start! (*Then calls the* FOREMAN.)

FOREMAN: Yes, sir?

PRODUCER: Set the stage for the parlour scene. A couple of flats and a door will do. As quickly as you can!

(*The* FOREMAN *runs off at once to carry out this order and is setting the stage as directed whilst the* PRODUCER *is making his arrangements with the* STAGE MANAGER, *the* PROPERTY MAN, *the* PROMPTER *and the* ACTORS. *The flats he has set up are painted in pink and gold stripes.*)

PRODUCER (*to* PROPERTY MAN): Just have a look, please, and see if we've got some sort of sofa or divan in the props room.

PROPERTY MAN: There's the green one, sir.

STEPDAUGHTER: No, no, green won't do! It was yellow . . . yellow flowered plush. . . . A huge thing . . . and most comfortable.

PROPERTY MAN: Well, we haven't got anything like that.

PRODUCER: It doesn't matter! Give me what there is!

STEPDAUGHTER: What do you mean, it doesn't matter? Madame Pace's famous sofa!

PRODUCER: We only want it for this run-through. Please don't interfere. (*to the* STAGE MANAGER) Oh, and see if we've got a shop-window . . . something rather long and narrowish is what we want.

STEPDAUGHTER: And a little table . . . the little mahogany table for the pale blue envelope.!

STAGE MANAGER (*to* PRODUCER): There's that little one. . . . You know, the gold-painted one.

PRODUCER: That'll do fine! Shove it on!

FATHER: You need a long mirror.

STEPDAUGHTER: And the screen! I must have a screen, please. . . . Else how can I manage?

STAGE MANAGER: Don't you worry, Miss! We've got masses of them!

PRODUCER (*to the* STEPDAUGHTER): And some clotheshangers and so on, h'm?

STEPDAUGHTERS: Oh, yes, lots!

PRODUCER (*to the* STAGE MANAGER): See how many we've got and get somebody to bring them up.

STAGE MANAGER: Right you are, sir, I'll see to it!

(The STAGE MANAGER goes off about his business and while the PRODUCER is talking to the PROMPTER and later to the CHARACTERS and ACTORS, he gets the stage hands to bring up the furniture and properties and proceeds to arrange them in what he thinks is the best sort of order.)

PRODUCER *(to the PROMPTER)*: Now if you'll get into position while they're setting the stage. . . . Look, here's an outline of the thing. . . . Act I . . . Act II . . . *(he holds out some sheets of paper to him)*. But you'll really have to excel yourself this time.

PROMPTER: You mean, take it down in shorthand?

PRODUCER *(pleasantly surprised)*: Oh, good man! Can you do shorthand?

PROMPTER: I mayn't know much about prompting, but shorthand. . . .

PRODUCER: Better and better. *(Turning to a STAGE-HAND.)* Go and get some paper out of my room. . . . A large wadge. . . . As much as you can find!

(The STAGE-HAND hurries off and returns shortly with a thick wadge of paper which he gives to the PROMPTER.)

PRODUCER *(to the PROMPTER)*: Follow the scenes closely as we play them and try to fix the lines . . . or at least the most important ones. *(Then, turning to the ACTORS.)* Right, ladies and gentlemen, clear the stage, please! No, come over this side *(He waves them over to his left.)* . . . and pay careful attention to what goes on.

LEADING LADY: Excuse me, but we . . .

PRODUCER *(forestalling what she is going to say)*: There won't be any improvising to do, don't you worry!

LEADING MAN: What do we have to do, then?

PRODUCER: Nothing. For the moment all you've got to do is to stay over there and watch what happens. You'll get your parts later. Just now we're going to have a rehearsal . . . or as much of one as we can in the circumstances! And they'll be doing the rehearsing. *(He points to the CHARACTERS.)*

FATHER *(in consternation, as if he had tumbled from the clouds into the midst of all the confusion on stage)*. We are? But, excuse me, in what way will it be a rehearsal?

PRODUCER: Well . . . a rehearsal . . . a rehearsal for their benefit. *(He points to the ACTORS.)*

FATHER: But if we're the characters . . .

PRODUCER: Just so, "the characters." But it's not characters that act here. It's actors who do the acting here. The characters remain there, in the script. *(He points to the prompt-box.)* . . . When there is a script!

FATHER: Precisely! And since there is no script and you have the good fortune to have the characters here alive before your very eyes. . . .

PRODUCER: Oh, this is wonderful! Do you want to do everything on your own? Act . . . present yourselves to the public!

FATHER: Yes, just as we are.

PRODUCER: And let me tell you you'd make a wonderful sight!

LEADING MAN: And what use should we be then?

PRODUCER: You're not going to pretend that you can act, are you? Why, it's enough to make a cat laugh. . . . *(And as a matter of fact, the ACTORS burst out laughing.)* There you are, you see, they're laughing at the idea! *(Then, remembering.)* But, to the point! I must tell you what your parts are. That's not so very difficult. They pretty well cast themselves. *(to the SECOND ACTRESS)* You, the MOTHER. *(to the FATHER)* We'll have to find a name for her.

FATHER: Amalia.

PRODUCER: But that's your wife's name. We can hardly call her by her real name.

FATHER: And why not, when that's her name? But, perhaps, it is has to be that lady . . . *(A slight gesture to indicate the SECOND ACTRESS.)* I see *her* *(Pointing to the MOTHER.)* as Amalia. But do as you like. . . . *(His confusion grows.)* I don't know what to say to you. . . . I'm already beginning. . . . I don't know how to express it . . . to hear my own words ringing false . . . as if they had another sound from the one I had meant to give them. . . .

PRODUCER: Now don't you worry about that! Don't you worry about it at all! We'll think about how to get the right tone of voice. And as for the name. . . . If you want it to be Amalia, Amalia it shall be. Or we'll find some other name. Just for the present we'll refer to the characters in this way. *(to the JUVENILE LEAD)* You, the Son . . . *(to the LEADING LADY)* And you'll play the Stepdaughter, of course. . . .

STEPDAUGHTER *(excitedly)*: What! What did you say? That woman there. . . . Me! *(She bursts out laughing.)*

PRODUCER *(angrily)*: And what's making you laugh?

LEADING LADY *(indignantly)*: Nobody has ever dared to laugh at me before! Either you treat me with respect or I'm walking out!

STEPDAUGHTER: Oh, no, forgive me! I wasn't laughing at you.

PRODUCER *(to STEPDAUGHTER)*: You should feel yourself honoured to be played by . . .

LEADING LADY *(immediately, disdainfully)*: . . . "that woman there."

STEPDAUGHTER: But my remark wasn't meant as a criticism of you . . . I was thinking about myself. . . . Because I can't see myself in you at all. I don't know how to . . . you're not a bit like me!

FATHER: Yes, that's the point I wanted to make! Look . . . all that we express. . . .

PRODUCER: What do you mean . . . *all that you express?* Do you think that this whatever-it-is that you express is something you've got inside you? Not a bit of it.

FATHER: Why . . . aren't even the things we express our own?

PRODUCER: Of course they aren't! The things that you express become material here for the actors, who give it body and form, voice and gesture. And, let me tell you, my actors have given expression to much loftier material than this. This stuff of yours is so trivial that, believe me, if it comes off on the stage, the credit will all be due to my actors.

FATHER: I don't dare to contradict you! But please believe me when I tell you that we . . . who have these bodies . . . these features. . . . Who are as you see us now . . . We are suffering horribly. . . .

PRODUCER (*cutting in impatiently*): . . . But the make-up will remedy all that. . . . At least as far as your faces are concerned!

FATHER: Perhaps. . . . But what about our voices? . . . What about our gestures? . . .

PRODUCER: Now, look here! You, as yourself, just cannot exist here! Here there's an actor who'll play you. And let there be an end to all this argument!

FATHER: I understand. . . . And now I think I see why our author didn't wish to put us on the stage after all. . . . He saw us as we are. . . . Alive. . . . He saw us as living beings. . . . I don't want to offend your actors. . . . Heaven forbid that I should! . . . But I think that seeing myself acted now . . . by I don't know whom . . .

LEADING MAN (*rising with some dignity and coming over, followed by a laughing group of young actresses*): By me, if you have no objection.

FATHER (*humbly, mellifluously*): I am deeply honoured, sir. (*He bows.*) But. . . . Well. . . . I think that however much of his art this gentleman puts into absorbing me into himself. . . . However much he wills it. . . . (*He becomes confused.*)

LEADING MAN: Go on! Go on! (*The actresses laugh.*)

FATHER: Well, I should say that the performance he'll give. . . . Even if he makes himself up to look as much like me as he can. . . . I should say that with his figure . . . (*All the* ACTORS *laugh.*) . . . it will be difficult for it to be a performance of me . . . of me as I really am. It will rather be . . . leaving aside the question of his appearance. . . . It will be how he interprets what I am . . . how he sees me. . . . If he sees me as anything at all. . . . And not as I, deep down within myself, feel myself to be. And it certainly seems to me that whoever is called upon to criticise us will have to take this into account.

PRODUCER: So you're already thinking about what the critics will say, are you? And here I am, still trying to get the play straight! The critics can say what they like. We'd be much better occupied in thinking about getting the play on. . . . If we can. (*Stepping out of the group and looking around him.*) Now, come on, let's make a start! Is everything ready? (*to the* ACTORS *and* CHARACTERS) Come on, don't clutter up the place! Let me see how it looks! (*He comes down from the stage.*) And now, don't let's lose any more time! (*to the* STEP-DAUGHTER) Do you think the set looks all right?

STEPDAUGHTER: To be perfectly honest, I just don't recognise it at all!

PRODUCER: Good Lord, you surely didn't hope that we were going to reconstruct that room behind Madame Pace's shop here on the stage, did you? (*to the* FATHER) You did tell me it had flowered wallpaper, didn't you?

FATHER: Yes, white.

PRODUCER: Well, it's not white—and it's got stripes on it—but it'll have to do! As for the furniture, I think we've more or less got everything we need. Bring that little table down here a bit! (*The* STAGE HANDS *do so. Then he says to the* PROPERTY MAN.) Now, will you go and get an envelope. . . . A pale blue one if you can. . . . And give it to that gentleman. (*He points to the* FATHER.)

PROPERTY MAN: The kind you put letters in?

PRODUCER *and* FATHER: Yes, the kind you put letters in!

PROPERTY MAN: Yes, sir! At once, sir! (*Exit.*)

PRODUCER: Now, come on! First scene—the young lady. (*The* LEADING LADY *comes forward.*) No! No! Wait a moment! I said the young lady! (*Pointing to the* STEPDAUGHTER.) You stay there and watch. . . .

STEPDAUGHTER (*immediately adding*): . . . how I make it live!

LEADING LADY (*resentfully*): I'll know how to make it live, don't you worry, once I get started!

PRODUCER (*with his hands to his head*): Ladies and gentlemen, don't let's have any arguing! Please! Right! Now . . . The first scene is between the young lady and Madame Pace. Oh! (*He looks around rather helplessly and then comes back on stage.*) What about this Madame Pace?

FATHER: She's not with us, sir.

PRODUCER: And what do we do about her?

FATHER: But she's alive! She's alive too!

PRODUCER: Yes, yes! But where is she?

FATHER: If you'll just allow me to have a word with your people. . . . (*Turning to the* ACTRESSES.) I wonder if you ladies would do me the kindness of lending me your hats for a moment.

THE ACTRESSES (*a chorus . . . half-laughing, half-surprised*): What?
Our hats?

What did he say?
Why?
Listen to the man!

PRODUCER: What are you going to do with the women's hats?

(The ACTORS laugh.)

FATHER: Oh, nothing . . . I just want to put them on these pegs for a moment. And perhaps one of you ladies would be so kind as to take off your coat, too.

THE ACTORS (laughter and surprise in their voices): Their coats as well? And after that? The man must be mad!

ONE OR TWO OF THE ACTRESSES (surprise and laughter in their voices): But why? Only our coats?

FATHER: So that I can hang them here. . . . Just for a moment or so. . . . Please do me this favour. Will you?

THE ACTRESSES (they take off their hats. One or two take off their coats as well, all laughing the while. They go over and hang the coats here and there on the pegs and hangers):
And why not?
Here you are!
This really is funny!
Do we have to put them on show?

FATHER: Precisely. . . . You have to put them on show . . . Like this!

PRODUCER: Is one allowed to know what you're up to?

FATHER: Why yes. If we set the stage better, who knows whether she may not be attracted by the objects of her trade and perhaps appear among us. . . . (He invites them to look toward the door at the back of the stage.) Look! Look!

(The door opens and MADAME PACE comes in and takes a few steps forward. She is an enormously fat old harridan of a woman, wearing a pompous carrot-coloured tow wig with a red rose stuck into one side of it, in the Spanish manner. She is heavily made up and dressed with clumsy elegance in a stylish red silk dress. In one hand she carries an ostrich feather fan; the other hand is raised and a lighted cigarette is poised between two fingers. Immediately they see this apparition, the ACTORS and the PRODUCER bound off the stage with howls of fear, hurling themselves down the steps into the auditorium and making as if to dash up the aisle. The STEPDAUGHTER, however, rushes humbly up to MADAME PACE, as if greeting her mistress.)

STEPDAUGHTER (rushing up to her): Here she is! Here she is!

FATHER (beaming): It's Madame Pace! What did I tell you? Here she is!

PRODUCER (his first surprise overcome, he is now indignant): What sort of a game do you call this?

LEADING MAN:
JUVENILE LEAD:
INGENUE:
LEADING LADY:
} almost at the same moment and all speaking at once.
{ Hang it all, what's going on? Where did she spring from? They were keeping her in reserve! So it's back to the music hall and conjuring tricks, is it?

FATHER (dominating the protesting voices): One moment, please! Why should you wish to destroy this prodigy of reality, which was born, which was evoked, attracted and formed by this scene itself? . . . A reality which has more right to live here than you have. . . . Because it is so very much more alive than you are. . . . Why do you want to spoil it all, just because of some niggling, vulgar convention of truth? . . . Which of you actresses will be playing the part of Madame Pace? Well, that woman is Madame Pace! Grant me at least that the actress who plays her will be less true than she is. . . . For she is Madame Pace in person! Look! My daughter recognised her and went up to her at once. Now, watch the scene! Just watch it! (Hesitantly the PRODUCER and the ACTORS climb back on to the stage. But while the ACTORS have been protesting and the FATHER has been replying to them, the scene between the STEPDAUGHTER and MADAME PACE has begun. It is carried on in an undertone, very quietly—naturally in fact—in a manner that would be quite impossible on the stage. When the ACTORS obey the FATHER's demand that they shall watch what is happening, they see that MADAME PACE has already put her hand under the STEPDAUGHTER's chin to raise her head and is talking to her. Hearing her speak in a completely unintelligible manner they are held for a moment. But almost immediately their attention flags.)

PRODUCER: Well?

LEADING MAN: But what's she saying?

LEADING LADY: We can't hear a thing!

JUVENILE LEAD: Speak up! Louder!

STEPDAUGHTER (she leaves MADAME PACE and comes down to the group of ACTORS. MADAME PACE smiles—a priceless smile): Did you say, 'Louder?' What do you mean, 'Louder?' What we're talking about is scarcely the sort of thing to be shouted from the roof-tops. I was able to yell it out just now so that I could shame him (Pointing to the FATHER.) . . . so that I could have my revenge! But it's quite another matter for Madame Pace. . . . It would mean prison for her.

PRODUCER: Indeed? So that's how it is, is it? But let me tell you something, my dear young lady. . . . Here in the theatre you've got to make yourself heard! The way you're doing this bit at the moment even those of us who're on stage can't hear you! Just imagine what it'll be like with an audience out front. This scene's got to be got over. And anyway there's nothing to prevent you from speaking up when you're on together. . . . We shan't be here to listen to you. . . . We're only here now because it's a rehearsal. Pretend you're alone in the room behind the shop, where nobody can hear you.

(The STEPDAUGHTER *elegantly, charmingly—and with a mischievous smile—wags her finger two or three times in disagreement.)*

PRODUCER: What do you mean, 'No?'

STEPDAUGHTER *(in a mysterious whisper)*: There's someone who'll hear us if she *(Pointing to* MADAME PACE.*) speaks up.

PRODUCER *(in utter consternation)*: Do you mean to say that there's somebody else who's going to burst in on us? *(The* ACTORS *make as if to dive off the stage again.)*

FATHER: No! No! They're alluding to me. I have to be there, waiting behind the door. . . . And Madame Pace knows it. So, if you'll excuse me, I'll go. . . . So that I'm all ready to make my entrance. *(He starts off toward the back of the stage.)*

PRODUCER *(stopping him)*: No! No! Wait a moment! When you're here you have to respect the conventions of the theatre! Before you get ready to go on to that bit. . . .

STEPDAUGHTER: No! Let's get on with it at once! At once! I'm dying with desire, I tell you . . . to live this scene. . . . To live it! If he wants to get on with it right away, I'm more than ready!

PRODUCER *(shouting)*: But first of all, the scene between you and her *(Pointing to* MADAME PACE.*) has got to be over! Do you understand?

STEPDAUGHTER: Oh, my God! She's just been telling me what you already know. . . . That once again my mother's work has been badly done. . . . That the dress is spoilt . . . And that I must be patient if she is to go on helping us in our misfortune.

MADAME PACE *(stepping forward, a grand air of importance about her)*: But, yes, señor, porque I not want to make profit . . . to take advantage. . . .

PRODUCER *(more than a touch of terror in his voice)*: What? Does she speak like that?

(The ACTORS *burst into noisy laughter.)*

STEPDAUGHTER *(laughing too)*: Yes, she speaks like that, half in English, half in Spanish. . . . It's most comical.

MADAME PACE: Ah, no, it does not to me seem good manners that you laugh of me when I . . . force myself to . . . hablar, as I can, English, señor!

PRODUCER: Indeed, no! It's very wrong of us! You speak like that! Yes, speak like that, Madame!

It'll bring the house down! We couldn't ask for anything better. It'll bring a little comic relief into the crudity of the situation. Yes, you talk like that! It's absolutely wonderful!

STEPDAUGHTER: Wonderful! And why not? When you hear a certain sort of suggestion made to you in a lingo like that. . . . There's not much doubt about what your answer's going to be. . . . Because it almost seems like a joke. You feel inclined to laugh when you hear there's an 'old señor', who wants to 'amuse himself with me'. An 'old señor', eh, Madame?

MADAME PACE: Not so very old. . . . Not quite so young, yes? And if he does not please to you. . . . Well, he has . . . *prudencia.*

MOTHER *(absorbed as they are in the scene, the* ACTORS *have been paying no attention to her. Now, to their amazement and consternation, she leaps up and attacks* MADAME PACE. *At her cry they jump, then hasten smilingly to restrain her, for she, meanwhile, has snatched off* MADAME PACE'S *wig and has thrown it to the ground)*: You old devil! You old witch! You murderess! Oh, my daughter!

STEPDAUGHTER *(rushing over to restrain her* MOTHER*)*: No, Mummy, no! Please!

FATHER *(rushing over at the same time)*: Calm yourself, my dear! Just be calm! Now . . . come and sit down again!

MOTHER: Take that woman out of my sight, then!

(In the general excitement the PRODUCER, *too, has rushed over and the* STEPDAUGHTER *now turns to him.)*

STEPDAUGHTER: It's impossible for my mother to remain here!

FATHER *(to the* PRODUCER*)*: They can't be here together. That's why, when we first came, that woman wasn't with us. If they're on at the same time the whole thing is inevitably given away in advance.

PRODUCER: It doesn't matter! It doesn't matter a bit! This is only a first run-through. . . . Just to give us a rough idea how it goes. Everything'll come in useful . . . I can sort out the bits and pieces later. . . . I'll make something out of it, even if it is all jumbled up. *(Turning to the* MOTHER *and leading her back to her chair.)* Now, please be calm, and sit down here, nice and quietly.

(Meanwhile the STEPDAUGHTER *has gone down centre stage again. She turns to* MADAME PACE.*)*

STEPDAUGHTER: Go on, Madame, go on!

MADAME PACE *(offended)*: Ah, no thank you! Here I do not do nothing more with your mother present!

STEPDAUGHTER: Now, come on! Show in the 'old señor' who wants to 'amuse himself with me'. *(Turning imperiously on the rest.)* Yes, this scene has got to be played. So let's get on with it! *(to*

MADAME PACE) You can go!

MADAME PACE: Ah, I am going . . . I am going. . . . Most assuredly I am going! (*Exit furiously, ramming her wig back on and glowering at the* ACTORS, *who mockingly applaud her.*)

STEPDAUGHTER (*to the* FATHER): And now you make your entrance! There's no need for you to go out and come in again! Come over here! Pretend that you've already entered! Now, I'm standing here modestly, my eyes on the ground. Come on! Speak up! Say, 'Good afternoon, Miss,' in that special tone of voice . . . you know. . . . Like somebody who's just come in from the street.

PRODUCER (*by this time he is down off the stage*): Listen to her! Are you running this rehearsal, or am I? (*To the* FATHER, *who is looking perplexed and undecided*) Go on, do as she tells you! Go to the back of the stage. . . . Don't exit! . . . And then come forward again.

(*The* FATHER *does as he is told. He is troubled and very pale. But as he approaches from the back of the stage he smiles, already absorbed in the reality of his created life. He smiles as if the drama which is about to break upon him is as yet unknown to him. The* ACTORS *become intent on the scene which is beginning.*)

PRODUCER (*whispering quickly to the* PROMPTER, *who has taken up his position*): Get ready to write now!

THE SCENE

FATHER (*coming forward, a new note in his voice*): Good afternoon, Miss.

STEPDAUGHTER (*her head bowed, speaking with restrained disgust*): Good afternoon!

FATHER (*studying her a little, looking up into her face from under the brim of her hat* [*which almost hides it*], *and perceiving that she is very young, exclaims, almost to himself, a little out of complacency, a little, too, from the fear of compromising himself in a risky adventure*): H'm! But. . . . M'm. . . . This won't be the first time, will it? The first time that you've been here?

STEPDAUGHTER (*as before*): No, sir.

FATHER: You've been in here before? (*And since the* STEPDAUGHTER *nods in affirmation.*) More than once? (*He waits a little while for her reply, resumes his study of her, again looking up into her face from under the brim of her hat, smiles and then says.*) Then . . . well . . . it shouldn't any longer be so. . . . May I take off your hat?

STEPDAUGHTER (*immediately forestalling him, unable to restrain her disgust*): No, sir, I'll take it off myself! (*Convulsed, she hurriedly takes it off.*)

(*The* MOTHER *is on tenterhooks throughout. The* TWO CHILDREN *cling to their* MOTHER *and they, she and the* SON *form a group on the side opposite the* ACTORS, *watching the scene. The* MOTHER *follows the words and the actions of the* STEPDAUGHTER *and the* FATHER *with varying expressions of sorrow, of indignation, of anxiety and of horror; from time to time she hides her face in her hands and sobs.*)

MOTHER: Oh, my God! My God!

FATHER (*he remains for a moment as if turned to stone by this sob. Then he resumes in the same tone of voice as before*): Here, let me take it. I'll hang it up for you. (*He takes the hat from her hands.*) But such a charming, such a dear little head really ought to have a much smarter hat than this! Would you like to come and help me choose one from among these hats of Madame's? Will you?

INGENUE (*breaking in*): Oh, I say! Those are *our* hats!

PRODUCER (*at once, furiously*): For God's sake, shut up! Don't try to be funny! We're doing our best to rehearse this scene, in case you weren't aware of the fact! (*Turning to* STEPDAUGHTER.) Go on from where you left off, please.

STEPDAUGHTER (*continuing*): No thank you, sir.

FATHER: Come now, don't say no. Do say you'll accept it. . . . Just to please me. I shall be most upset if you won't. . . . Look, here are some rather nice ones. And then it would please Madame. She puts them out on show on purpose, you know.

STEPDAUGHTER: No . . . listen! I couldn't wear it.

FATHER: You're thinking perhaps about what they'll say when you come home wearing a new hat? Well now, shall I tell you what to do? Shall I tell you what to say when you get home?

STEPDAUGHTER (*quickly—she is at the end of her tether*): No, it's not that! I couldn't wear it because I'm . . . As you see. . . . You should have noticed already . . . (*indicating her black dress.*)

FATHER: That you're in mourning! Of course. . . . Oh, forgive me! Of course! Oh, I beg your pardon! Believe me. . . . I'm most profoundly sorry. . . .

STEPDAUGHTER (*summoning all her strength and forcing herself to conquer her contempt, her indignation and her nausea*): Stop! Please don't say any more! I really ought to be thanking you. There's no need for you to feel so very sorry or upset! Please don't give another thought to what I said! I, too, you understand. . . . (*Tries hard to smile and adds.*) I really must forget that I'm dressed like this!

PRODUCER (*interrupting them; he climbs back on the stage and turns to the* PROMPTER): Hold it! Stop a minute! Don't write that down. Leave out that last bit. (*Turning to the* FATHER *and the* STEPDAUGHTER.) It's going very well! Very well indeed! (*Then to the* FATHER.) And then you go on as we arranged. (*to the* ACTORS) Rather delightful, that bit where he offers her the hat, don't you think?

STEPDAUGHTER: Ah, but the best bit's coming now! Why aren't we going on?

PRODUCER: Now be patient, please! Just for a little while! *(Turning to the* ACTORS.) Of course it'll have to be treated rather lightly. . . .

LEADING MAN: . . . M'm . . . and put over slickly. . . .

LEADING LADY: Of course! There's nothing difficult about it at all. *(to the* LEADING MAN) Shall we try it now?

LEADING MAN: As far as I'm . . . I'll go and get ready for my entrance. *(Exits to take up his position outside the door back.)*

PRODUCER *(to the* LEADING LADY): Now, look. . . . The scene between you and Madame Pace is finished. I'll get down to writing it up properly afterwards. You're standing. . . . Where are you going?

LEADING LADY: Just a moment! I want to put my hat back on. . . . *(Goes over, takes her hat down and puts it on.)*

PRODUCER: Good! Now you stand here. With your head bowed down a bit.

STEPDAUGHTER *(amused)*: But she's not dressed in black!

LEADING LADY: I *shall* be dressed in black. . . . And much more becomingly than you are!

PRODUCER *(to the* STEPDAUGHTER): Shut up . . . please! And watch! You'll learn something. *(Claps his hands.)* Now come on! Let's get going! Entrance! *(He goes down from the stage again to see how it looks from out front. The door back opens and the* LEADING MAN *steps forward. He has the lively, raffish, self-possessed air of an elderly gallant. The playing of this scene by the* ACTORS *will appear from the very first words as something completely different from what was played before, without its having, even in the slightest degree, the air of a parody. It should appear rather as if the scene has been touched up. Quite naturally the* FATHER *and the* STEPDAUGHTER, *not being able to recognise themselves at all in the* LEADING LADY *and* LEADING MAN, *yet hearing them deliver the very words they used, react in a variety of ways, now with a gesture, now with a smile, with open protest even, to the impression they receive. They are surprised, lost in wonder, in suffering . . . as we shall see. The* PROMPTER's *voice is clearly heard throughout the scene.)*

LEADING MAN: Good afternoon, Miss!

FATHER *(immediately, unable to restrain himself)*: No! No! *(And the* STEPDAUGHTER, *seeing the* LEADING MAN *enter in this way, bursts out laughing.)*

PRODUCER *(infuriated)*: Shut up! And once and for all . . . Stop that laughing! We shan't get anywhere if we go on like this!

STEPDAUGHTER *(moving away from the proscenium)*: Forgive me . . . but I couldn't help laughing! This lady *(Pointing to the* LEADING LADY.) stands just where you put her, without budging an inch . . . But if she's meant to be me.

. . . I can assure you that if I heard anybody saying 'Good afternoon' to me in that way and in that tone of voice I'd burst out laughing. . . . So I had to, you see.

FATHER *(coming forward a little, too)*: Yes, that's it exactly. . . . His manner. . . . The tone of voice. . . .

PRODUCER: To hell with your manner and your tone of voice! Just stand to one side, if you don't mind, and let me get a look at this rehearsal.

LEADING MAN *(coming forward)*: Now if I've got to play an old fellow who's coming into a house of rather doubtful character. . . .

PRODUCER: Oh, don't take any notice of him! Now, *please!* Start again, please! It was going very nicely. *(There is a pause—he is clearly waiting for the* LEADING MAN *to begin again.)* Well?

LEADING MAN: Good afternoon, Miss.

LEADING LADY: Good afternoon!

LEADING MAN *(repeating the* FATHER's *move—that is, looking up into the* LEADING LADY's *face from under the brim of her hat; but then expressing very clearly first his satisfaction and then his fear)*: M'm . . . this won't be the first time, I hope. . . .

FATHER *(unable to resist the temptation to correct him)*: Not 'hope'—'will it?', 'will it?'

PRODUCER: You say 'will it?' . . . It's a question.

LEADING MAN *(pointing to the* PROMPTER): I'm sure he said, 'hope.'

PRODUCER: Well, it's all one! 'Hope' or whatever it was! Go on, please! Go on. . . . Oh, there was one thing . . . I think perhaps it ought not to be quite so heavy. . . . Hold on, I'll show you what I mean. Watch me. *(Comes back on to the stage. Then, making his entrance, he proceeds to play the part.)* Good afternoon, Miss.

LEADING LADY: Good afternoon. . . .

PRODUCER: M'm. . . . *(Turning to the* LEADING MAN *to impress on him the way he has looked up at the* LEADING LADY *from under the brim of her hat.)* Surprise, fear and satisfaction. *(Then turning back to the* LEADING LADY.) It won't be the first time, will it, that you've been here? *(Turning again to the* LEADING MAN *enquiringly.)* Is that clear? *(to the* LEADING LADY) And then you say, 'No, sir.' *(to the* LEADING MAN) There you are. . . . It wants to be a little more . . . what shall I say? . . . A little more *flexible.* A little more *souple!* (He goes down from the stage again.)*

LEADING LADY: No, sir. . . .

LEADING MAN: You've been here before? More than once?

PRODUCER: Wait a minute! You must let her *(pointing to the* LEADING LADY.) get her nod in first. You've been here before? *(The* LEADING LADY *lifts her head a little, closing her eyes painfully as if in disgust and then when the* PRODUCER *says* DOWN, *nods twice.)*

STEPDAUGHTER (*unable to restrain herself*): Oh, my God! (*And immediately she puts her hand over her mouth to stifle her laughter.*)

PRODUCER (*turning*): What's the matter?

STEPDAUGHTER (*immediately*): Nothing! Nothing!

PRODUCER (*to the* LEADING MAN): It's your cue. . . . Carry straight on.

LEADING MAN: More than once? Well then . . . Come along . . . May I take off your hat? (*The* LEADING MAN *says this last line in such a tone of voice and accompanies it with such a gesture that the* STEP-DAUGHTER, *who has remained with her hands over her mouth, can no longer restrain herself. She tries desperately to prevent herself from laughing but a noisy burst of laughter comes irresistibly through her fingers.*)

LEADING LADY (*turning indignantly*): I'm not going to stand here and be made a fool of by that woman!

LEADING MAN: And neither am I. Let's pack the whole thing in.

PRODUCER (*shouting at the* STEPDAUGHTER): Once and for all, will you shut up!

STEPDAUGHTER: Yes. . . . Forgive me, please! . . . Forgive me!

PRODUCER: The trouble with you is that you've got no manners! You go too far!

FATHER (*trying to intervene*): Yes, sir, you're quite right! Quite right! But you must forgive her. . . .

PRODUCER (*climbing back on to the stage*): What do you want me to forgive? It's absolutely disgusting the way she's behaving!

FATHER: Yes. . . . But . . . Oh, believe me . . . Believe me, it has such a strange effect. . . .

PRODUCER: Strange! How do you mean, 'Strange'? What's so strange about it?

FATHER: You see, sir, I admire . . . I admire your actors . . . That gentleman there (*Pointing to the* LEADING MAN.) and that lady (*Pointing to the* LEAD-ING LADY.) . . . But . . . Well . . . The truth is . . . They're certainly not us!

PRODUCER: I should hope not! How do you expect them to be you if they're actors?

FATHER: Just so, actors. And they play our parts well, both of them. But when they act . . . To us they seem to be doing something quite different. They want to be the same . . . And all the time they just aren't.

PRODUCER: But how aren't they the same? What are they then?

FATHER: Something that becomes theirs . . . And no longer ours.

PRODUCER: But that's inevitable! I've told you that already.

FATHER: Yes. I understand . . . I understand that. . . .

PRODUCER: Well then, let's hear no more on the subject! (*Turning to the* ACTORS.) We'll run through it later by ourselves in the usual way. I've always had a strong aversion to holding rehearsals with the author present. He's never satisfied! (*Turning to the* FATHER *and the* STEPDAUGH-TER.) Now, come on, Let's get on with it! And let's see if we can have no more laughing! (*to the* STEPDAUGHTER.)

STEPDAUGHTER: Oh, I shan't laugh any more! I promise you! My big bit's coming now. . . . Just you wait and see!

PRODUCER: Well, then. . . . When you say, 'Please don't give another thought to what I said! I, too, you understand. . . .' (*Turning to the* FATHER.) You come in at once with, 'I understand! I understand! and immediately ask . . .

STEPDAUGHTER (*interrupting him*): What? What does he ask?

PRODUCER: . . . why you're in mourning.

STEPDAUGHTER: Oh, no! That's not it at all! Listen! When I told him that I mustn't think about my being in mourning, do you know what his answer was? 'Well, then, let's take this little frock off at once, shall we!'

PRODUCER: That would be wonderful! Wonderful! That *would* bring the house down!

STEPDAUGHTER: But it's the truth!

PRODUCER: But what's the truth got to do with it? Acting's what we're here for! Truth's all very fine. . . . But only up to a point.

STEPDAUGHTER: And what do you want then?

PRODUCER: You'll see! You'll see. Leave everything to me.

STEPDAUGHTER: No, I won't! What you'd like to do, no doubt, is to concoct a romantic, sentimental little affair out of my disgust, out of all the reasons, each more cruel, each viler than the other, why I am this sort of woman, why I am what I am! An affair with him! He asks me why I'm in mourning and I reply with tears in my eyes that my father died only two months ago. No! No! He must say what he said then, 'Well, then, let's take this little frock off at once, shall we? And I . . . my heart still grieving for my father's death. . . . I went behind there. . . . Do you understand? . . . There, behind that screen! And then, my fingers trembling with shame and disgust, I took off my frock, undid my brassiere. . . .

PRODUCER (*running his hands through his hair*): For God's sake! What on earth are you saying, girl?

STEPDAUGHTER (*crying out excitedly*): The truth! The truth!

PRODUCER: Yes, it probably is the truth! I'm not denying it! And I understand . . . I fully appreciate all your horror. But you must realise that we simply can't put this kind of thing on the stage.

STEPDAUGHTER: Oh, you can't, can't you? If that's how things are, thanks very much! I'm going!

PRODUCER: No! No! Look here! . . .

STEPDAUGHTER: I'm going! I'm not stopping here! You worked it all out together, didn't you? . . . The pair of you. . . . You and him. . . . When you were in there. . . . You worked out what was going to be possible on the stage. Oh, thanks very much! I understand! He wants to jump to the bit where he presents his spiritual torments! *(This is said harshly.)* But I want to present my own drama! *Mine! Mine!*

PRODUCER *(his shoulders shaking with annoyance)*: Ah! There we have it! *Your* drama! Look here . . . you'll have to forgive me for telling you this . . . but there isn't only your part to be considered! Each of the others has his drama, too. *(He points to the* FATHER.*)* He has his and your Mother has hers. You can't have one character coming along like this, becoming too prominent, invading the stage in and out of season and overshadowing all the rest. All the characters must be contained within one harmonious picture, and presenting only what it is proper to present. I'm very well aware that everyone carries a complete life within himself and that he wants to put it before the whole world. But it's here that we run into difficulties: how are we to bring out only just so much as is absolutely necessary? . . . And at the same time, of course, to take into account all the other characters. . . . And yet in that small fragment we have to be able to hint at all the rest of the secret life of that character. Ah, it would be all very pleasant if each character could have a nice little monologue. . . . Or without making any bones about it, give a lecture, in which he could tell his audience what's bubbling and boiling away inside him. *(His tone is good-humoured, conciliatory.)* You must restrain yourself. And believe me, it's in your own interest, too. Because all this fury . . . this exasperation and this disgust . . . They make a bad impression. Especially when . . . And pardon me for mentioning this. . . . You yourself have confessed that you'd had other men there at Madame Pace's before him. . . . And more than once!

STEPDAUGHTER *(bowing her head. She pauses a moment in recollection and then, a deeper note in her voice)*: That is true! But you must remember that those other men mean *him* for me, just as much as he himself does!

PRODUCER *(uncomprehending)*: What? The other men mean *him*? What do you mean?

STEPDAUGHTER: Isn't it true that in the case of someone who's gone wrong, the person who was responsible for the first fault is responsible for all the faults which follow? And in my case, he is responsible. . . . Has been ever since before I was born. Look at him, and see if it isn't true!

PRODUCER: Very well, then! And does this terrible weight of remorse that is resting on his spirit seem so slight a thing to you? Give him the chance of acting it!

STEPDAUGHTER: How? How can he act all his 'noble' remorse, all his 'moral' torments, if you want to spare him all the horror of one day finding in his arms. . . . After he had asked her to take off her frock . . . her grief still undulled by time. . . . The horror of finding in his arms that child. . . . A woman now, and a fallen woman already. . . . That child whom he used to go and watch as she came out of school? *(She says these last words in a voice trembling with emotion. The* MOTHER, *hearing her talk like this, is overcome by distress which expresses itself at first in stifled sobs. Finally she breaks out into a fit of bitter crying. Everyone is deeply moved. There is a long pause.)*

STEPDAUGHTER *(gravely and resolutely, as soon as the* MOTHER *shows signs of becoming a little quieter)*: At the moment we are here, unknown as yet by the public. Tomorrow you will present us as you wish. . . . Making up your play in your own way. But would you really like to see our drama? To see it flash into life as it did in reality?

PRODUCER: Why, of course! I couldn't ask for anything better, so that from now on I can use as much as possible of it.

STEPDAUGHTER: Well, then, ask my Mother to leave us.

MOTHER *(rising, her quiet weeping changed to a sharp cry)*: No! No! Don't you allow them to do it! Don't allow them to do it!

PRODUCER: But it's only so that I can see how it goes.

MOTHER: I can't bear it! I can't bear it!

PRODUCER: But since it's already happened, I don't understand!

MOTHER: No, it's happening now! It happens all the time! My torment is no pretence, sir. I am alive and I am present always. . . . At every moment of my torment . . . A torment which is for ever renewing itself. Always alive and always present. But those two children there . . . Have you heard them say a single word? They can no longer speak! They cling to me still. . . . In order to keep my torment living and present! But for themselves they no longer exist! They no longer exist! And she *(Pointing to the* STEPDAUGHTER.*)* . . . She has run away. . . . Run away from me and is lost. . . . Lost! . . . And if I see her here before me it is for this reason and for this reason alone. . . . To renew at all times. . . . Forever. . . . To bring before me again, present and living, the anguish that I have suffered on her account too.

FATHER *(solemnly)*: The eternal moment, as I told you, sir. She *(He points to the* STEPDAUGHTER.*)* . . . She is here in order to fix me. . . . To hold me suspended throughout all eternity. . . . In the pillory of that one fleeting shameful moment in my life. She cannot renounce her role . . . And you, sir, cannot really spare me my agony.

PRODUCER: Quite so, but I didn't say that I wouldn't present it. As a matter of fact it'll form the basis of the first act. . . . Up to the point where she surprises you (*Pointing to the* MOTHER.)

FATHER: That is right. Because it is my sentence. All our passion. . . . All our suffering. . . . Which must culminate in *her* cry. (*Pointing to the* MOTHER.)

STEPDAUGHTER: I can still hear it ringing in my ears! That cry sent me mad! You can play me just as you like . . . It doesn't matter. Dressed, if you like, provided that I can have my arms bare at least. . . . Just my arms bare. . . . Because, you see, standing there. . . . (*She goes up to the* FATHER *and rests her head on his chest.*) With my head resting on his chest like this . . . and with my arms round his neck . . . I could see a vein throbbing away in my arm. And then . . . Just as if that pulsing vein alone gave me a sense of horror . . . I shut my eyes tight and buried my head in his chest. (*Turning towards the* MOTHER.) Scream, Mummy! Scream! (*She buries her head in the* FATHER'S *chest and, raising her shoulders as if in order not to hear the cry, adds in a voice stifled with torment.*) Scream, as you screamed then!

MOTHER (*rushing upon them to separate them*): No! No! She's my daughter! (*And having torn her daughter away.*) You brute! You brute! She's my daughter! Can't you see that she's my daughter?

PRODUCER (*retreating at the cry right up to the footlights, amid the general dismay of the* ACTORS): Excellent! Excellent! And then . . . Curtain! Curtain!

FATHER (*rushing over to him convulsively*): Yes, because that's how it really happened!

PRODUCER (*quite convinced, admiration in his voice*): Oh, yes, we must have the curtain there. . . . That cry and then . . . Curtain! Curtain!

(*At the repeated shouts of the* PRODUCER *the* STAGE HAND *on the curtain lets it down, leaving the* PRODUCER *and the* FATHER *between it and the footlights.*)

PRODUCER (*looking up, his arms raised*): Oh, the damned fool! I say, 'Curtain' . . . Meaning that I want the act to end there. . . . And he really does go and bring the curtain down. (*to the* FATHER, *lifting up a corner of the curtain.*) Oh, yes! That's absolutely wonderful! Very good indeed! That'll get them! There's no *if* or *but* about it. . . . That line and then . . . *Curtain!* We've got something in that first act . . . or I'm a Dutchman! (*Disappears through the curtain with the* FATHER.)

ACT 3

(*When the curtain goes up again the audience sees that the* STAGE HANDS *have dismantled the previous set and put on in its place a small garden fountain. On one side of the stage the* ACTORS *are sitting in a row, and on the other side, the* CHARACTERS. *The* PRODUCER *is standing in a meditative attitude in the middle of the stage with his hand clenched over his mouth. There is a brief pause.*)

PRODUCER (*with a shrug of his shoulders*): Oh, well! . . . Let's get on with Act II! Now if you'll only leave it all to me, as we agreed, everything'll sort itself out.

STEPDAUGHTER: This is where we make our entry into his house . . . (*Pointing to the* FATHER.) In spite of him! (*Pointing to the* SON.)

PRODUCER (*out of patience*): Yes, yes! But leave it to me, I tell you!

STEPDAUGHTER: Well. . . . So long as it's made quite clear that it was against his wishes.

MOTHER (*from the corner, shaking her head*): For all the good that's come of it. . . .

STEPDAUGHTER (*turning to her quickly*): That doesn't matter! The more harm that it's done us, the more remorse for him!

PRODUCER (*impatiently*): I understand all that! I'll take it all into account! don't you worry about it!

MOTHER (*a supplicant note in her voice*): But I do beg you, sir . . . To set my conscience at rest. . . . To make it quite plain that I tried in every way I could to . . .

STEPDAUGHTER (*interrupting contemptuously and continuing her* MOTHER'S *speech*): . . . to pacify me, to persuade me not to get my own back. . . . (*to the* PRODUCER) Go on . . . do what she asks you! Give her that satisfaction. . . . Because she's quite right, you know! I'm enjoying myself no end, because . . . Well, just look . . . The meeker she is, the more she tries to wriggle her way into his heart, the more he holds himself aloof, the more distant he becomes. I can't think why she bothers!

PRODUCER: Are we going to get started on the second act or are we not?

STEPDAUGHTER: I won't say another word! But, you know, it won't be possible to play it all in the garden, as you suggested.

PRODUCER: Why not?

STEPDAUGHTER: Because he (*Pointing to the* SON *again.*) shuts himself up in his room all the time. . . . Holding himself aloof. . . . And, what's more, there's all the boy's part. . . . Poor bewildered little devil. . . . As I told you, all that takes place indoors.

PRODUCER: I know all about that! On the other hand you do understand that we can hardly stick up notices telling the audience what the scene is.... Or change the set three or four times in one act.

LEADING MAN: They used to in the good old days.

PRODUCER: Oh, yes.... When the intelligence of the audience was about up to the level of that little girl's there....

LEADING LADY: And it does make it easier to get the sense of illusion.

FATHER (*immediately, rising*): Illusion, did you say? For Heaven's sake, please don't use the word illusion! Please don't use that word.... It's a particularly cruel one for us!

PRODUCER (*astounded*): And why's that?

FATHER: It's cruel! Cruel! You should have known that!

PRODUCER: What ought we to say then? We were referring to the illusion that we have to create on this stage ... for the audience....

LEADING MAN: ... with our acting....

PRODUCER: ... the illusion of a reality!

FATHER: I understand, sir. But you ... Perhaps you can't understand us. Forgive me! Because ... you see ... for you and for your actors, all this is only ... and quite rightly so.... All this is only a game.

LEADING LADY (*indignantly interrupting him*): What do you mean, a game? We're not children! We're serious actors!

FATHER: I don't deny it! And in fact, in using the term, I was referring to your art which must, as this gentleman has said, create a perfect illusion of reality.

PRODUCER: Precisely!

FATHER: Now just consider the fact that we (*Pointing quickly to himself and to the other* FIVE CHARACTERS.) as ourselves, have no other reality outside this illusion!

PRODUCER (*in utter astonishment, looking round at his actors who show the same bewildered amazement*): And what does all that mean?

FATHER (*the ghost of a smile on his face. There is a brief pause while he looks at them all*): As I said.... What other reality should we have? What for you is an illusion that you have to create, for us, on the other hand, is our sole reality. The only reality we know. (*There he takes a step or two toward the* PRODUCER *and adds.*) But it's not only true in our case, you know. Just think it over. (*He looks into his eyes.*) Can you tell me who you are? (*And he stands there pointing his index finger at him.*)

PRODUCER (*disturbed, a half-smile on his lips*): What? Who am I? I'm myself!

FATHER: And suppose I were to tell you that that wasn't true? Suppose I told you that you were me? ...

PRODUCER: I should say that you were mad! (*The ACTORS laugh.*)

FATHER: You're quite right to laugh, because here everything's a game. (*to the* PRODUCER) And you can object, therefore, that it's only in fun that that gentleman (*Pointing to the* LEADING MAN.) who is *himself* must be *me* who, on the contrary, am myself.... That is, *the person you see here.* There, you see. I've caught you in a trap! (*The* ACTORS *laugh again.*)

PRODUCER (*annoyed*): But you said all this not ten minutes ago! Do we have to go over all that again?

FATHER: No. As a matter of fact that wasn't what I intended. I should like to invite you to abandon this game ... (*Looking at the* LEADING LADY *as if to forestall what she will say.*) Your art! Your art! ... The game that it is customary for you and your actors to play here in this theatre. And once again I ask you in all seriousness.... Who are you?

PRODUCER (*turning to the* ACTORS *in utter amazement, an amazement not unmixed with irritation*): What a cheek the fellow has! A man who calls himself a character comes here and asks me who I am!

FATHER (*with dignity, but in no way haughtily*): A character, sir, may always ask a man who he is. Because a character has a life which is truly his, marked with his own special characteristics.... And as a result he is always somebody! Whilst a man.... And I'm not speaking of you personally at the moment.... Man in general ... Can quite well be nobody.

PRODUCER: That as may be! But you're asking *me* these questions. Me, do you understand? The Producer! The boss!

FATHER (*softly, with gentle humility*): But only in order to know if you, you as you really are now, are seeing yourself as, for instance, after all the time that has gone by, you see yourself as you were at some point in the past.... With all the illusions that you had then ... with everything ... all the things you had deep down inside you ... everything that made up your external world ... everything as it appeared to you then ... and as it *was,* as it was in reality for you then! Well ... thinking back on those illusions which you no longer have ... on all those things that no longer *seem* to be what they *were* once upon a time ... don't you feel that ... I won't say these boards. ... No! ... That the very earth itself is slipping away from under your feet, when you reflect that in the same way this *you* that you now feel yourself to be ... all your reality as it is today ... is destined to seem an illusion tomorrow?

PRODUCER (*not having understood much of all this, and somewhat taken aback by this argument*): Well? And where does all this get us, anyway?

FATHER: Nowhere. I only want to make you see that if

we (*Again pointing to himself and to the other* CHARACTERS.) have no reality outside the world of illusion, it would be as well if you mistrusted your own reality. . . . The reality that you breathe and touch today . . . Because like the reality of yesterday, it is fated to reveal itself as a mere illusion tomorrow.

PRODUCER (*deciding to make fun of him*): Oh, excellent! And so you'd say that you and this play of yours that you've been putting on for my benefit are more real than I am?

FATHER (*with the utmost seriousness*): Oh, without a doubt.

PRODUCER: Really?

FATHER: I thought that you'd understood that right from the very beginning.

PRODUCER: More real than I am?

FATHER: If your reality can change from one day to the next. . . .

PRODUCER: But everybody knows that it can change like that! It's always changing. . . . Just like everybody else's.

FATHER (*with a cry*): No, ours doesn't change! You see. . . . That's the difference between us! Our reality doesn't change. . . . It can't change. . . . It can never be in any way different from what it is. . . . Because it is already fixed. . . . Just as it is. . . . For ever! For ever it is *this* reality. . . . It's terrible! . . . This immutable reality. . . . It should make you shudder to come near us!

PRODUCER (*quickly, suddenly struck by an idea. He moves over and stands squarely in front of him*): I should like to know, however, when anyone ever saw a character step out of his part and begin a long dissertation on it like the one you've just been making. . . . Expounding it. . . . Explaining it. . . . Can you tell me? . . . I've never seen it happen before!

FATHER: You have never seen it happen before because authors usually hide the details of their work of creation. Once the characters are alive. . . . Once they are standing truly alive before their author. . . . He does nothing but follow the words and gestures that they suggest to him. . . . And he must want them to be what they themselves want to be. For woe betide him if he doesn't do what they wish him to do! When a character is born he immediately acquires such an independence . . . Even of his own author. . . . That everyone can imagine him in a whole host of situations in which his author never thought of placing him. . . . They can even imagine his acquiring, sometimes, a significance that the author never dreamt of giving him.

PRODUCER: Yes. . . . I know all that!

FATHER: Well, then, why are you so astonished at seeing us? Just imagine what a misfortune it is for a character to be born alive. . . . Created by the imagination of an author who afterwards sought to deny him life. . . . Now tell me whether a character who has been left unrealised in this way. . . . Living, yet without a life. . . . Whether this character hasn't the right to do what we are doing now. . . . Here and now. . . . For your benefit? . . . After we had spent . . . Oh, such ages, believe me! . . . Doing it for his benefit . . . Trying to persuade him, trying to urge him to realise us. . . . First of all I would present myself to him. . . . Then she would . . . (*Pointing to the* STEPDAUGHTER.) . . . And then her poor Mother. . . .

STEPDAUGHTER (*coming forward as if in a trance*): Yes, what he says is true. . . . I would go and tempt him. . . . There, in his gloomy study. . . . Just at twilight. . . . He would be sitting there, sunk in an armchair. . . . Not bothering to stir himself and switch on the light. . . . Content to let the room get darker and darker. . . . Until the whole room was filled with a darkness that was alive with our presence. . . . We were there to tempt him. . . . (*And then, as if she saw herself as still in that study and irritated by the presence of all those actors.*) Oh, go away. . . . All of you! Leave us alone! Mummy . . . and her son. . . . I and the little girl. . . . The boy by himself. . . . Always by himself. . . . Then he and I together. (*A faint gesture in the direction of the* FATHER) And then. . . . By myself. . . . By myself . . . alone in that darkness. (*A sudden turn round as if she wished to seize and fix the vision that she has of herself, the living vision of herself that she sees shining in the darkness.*) Yes, my life! Ah, what scenes, what wonderful scenes we suggested to him! And I . . . I tempted him more than any of them. . . .

FATHER: Indeed you did! And it may well be that it's all your fault that he wouldn't give us the life we asked for. . . . You were too persistent. . . . Too impudent. . . . You exaggerated too much. . . .

STEPDAUGHTER: What? When it was he who wanted me to be what I am? (*She goes up to the* PRODUCER *and says confidentially.*) I think it's much more likely that he refused because he felt depressed . . . or because of his contempt for the theatre. . . . Or at least, for the present-day theatre with all its pandering to the box-office. . . .

PRODUCER: Let's get on! Let's get on, for God's sake! Let's have some action!

STEPDAUGHTER: It looks to me as if we've got too much action for you already. . . . Just staging our entry into his house. (*Pointing to the* FATHER.) You yourself said that you couldn't stick up notices or be changing the set every five minutes.

PRODUCER: And neither can we! Of course we can't! What we've got to do is to combine and group all the action into one continuous well-knit scene. . . . Not the sort of thing that you want. . . . With, first of all, your younger brother coming home from school and wandering about the house like some lost soul. . . . Hiding behind doors and brooding on a plan that . . . What did you say it does to him?

STEPDAUGHTER: Dries him up. . . . Shrivels him up completely.

PRODUCER: M'm! Well, as you said. . . . And all the time you can see it more and more clearly in his eyes. . . . Wasn't that what you said?

STEPDAUGHTER: Yes. . . . just look at him! (Pointing to where he is standing by his MOTHER.)

PRODUCER: And then, at the same time, you want the child to be playing in the garden, blissfully unaware of everything. The boy in the house, the little girl in the garden. . . . I ask you!

STEPDAUGHTER: Yes . . . happily playing in the sun! That is the only pleasure that I have. . . . Her happiness. . . . All the joy that she gets from playing in the garden. . . . After the wretchedness and the squalor of that horrible room where we all four slept together. . . . And she had to sleep with me. . . . Just think of it. . . . My vile contaminated body next to hers! . . . With her holding me tight in her loving, innocent, little arms! She only had to get a glimpse of me in the garden and she'd run up to me and take me by the hand. She wasn't interested in the big flowers . . . she'd run about looking for the . . . 'weeny' ones. . . . So that she could point them out to me. . . . And she'd be so happy. . . . So excited. . . . (As she says this she is torn by the memory of it all and gives a long, despairing cry, dropping her head on to her hands which are lying loosely on the little table in front of her. At the sight of her emotion everyone is deeply moved. The PRODUCER goes up to her almost paternally and says comfortingly.)

PRODUCER: We'll have the garden in . . . don't you worry. . . . We'll have the garden scene in. . . . Just you wait and see. . . . You'll be quite satisfied with how I arrange it. . . . We'll play everything in the garden. (Calling a STAGE-HAND.) Hey (his name)! Let me have something in the shape of a tree or two. . . . A couple of not-too-large cypresses in front of this fountain! (Two small cypresses descend from the flies. The FOREMAN dashes up and fixes them with struts and nails.)

PRODUCER (to the STEPDAUGHTER): That'll do. . . . For the moment anyway. . . . It'll give us a rough idea. (Calls to the STAGE-HAND again.) Oh (his name), let me have something for a sky, will you?

STAGE HAND (up aloft): Eh?

PRODUCER: Something for a sky! A flat to go behind the fountain! (And a white backcloth descends from the flies.)

PRODUCER: Not white! I said I wanted a sky! Oh, well, it doesn't matter. . . . Leave it! Leave it! . . . I'll fix it myself. . . . (Calls.) Hey! . . . You there on the lights! . . . Everything off. . . . And let me have the moonlight blues on! . . . Blues in the batten! . . . A couple of blue spots on the backcloth! . . . Yes, that's it! That's just right!

(There is now a mysterious moonlit effect about the scene, and the ACTORS are prompted to move about and to speak as they would if they were indeed walking in a moonlit garden.)

PRODUCER (to the STEPDAUGHTER): There, do you see? Now the Boy, instead of hiding behind doors inside the house, can move about the garden and hide behind these trees. But, you know, it'll be rather difficult to find a little girl to play that scene with you. . . . The one where she shows you the flowers. (Turning to the BOY.) Now come down here a bit! Let's see how it works out! (Then, since the BOY doesn't move.) Come on! Come on! (He drags him forward and tries to make him hold his head up. But after every attempt down it falls again.) Good God, here's a fine how d'ye do. . . . There's something queer about this boy. . . . What's the matter with him? . . . My God, he'll have to say something. . . . (He goes up to him, puts a hand on his shoulder and places him behind one of the trees.) Now. . . . Forward a little! . . . Let me see you! . . . M'm! . . . Now hide yourself. . . . That's it! Now try popping your head out a bit. . . . Take a look round. . . . (He goes to one side to study the effect and the BOY does what he has been told to do. The ACTORS look on, deeply affected and quite dismayed.) That's excellent! . . . Yes, excellent! (Turning again to the STEPDAUGHTER.) Suppose the little girl were to catch sight of him there as he was looking out, and run over to him. . . . Wouldn't that drag a word or two out of him?

STEPDAUGHTER (rising): It's no use your hoping that he'll speak. . . . At least not so long as he's here. (Pointing to the SON.) If you want him to speak, you'll have to send him away first.

SON (going resolutely toward the steps down into the auditorium): Willingly! I'm only too happy to oblige. Nothing could possibly suit me better!

PRODUCER (immediately catching hold of him): Hey! Oh no you don't! Where are you going? You hang on a minute!

(The MOTHER rises in dismay, filled with anguish at the thought that he really is going away. She instinctively raises her arms to prevent him from going, without, however, moving from where she is standing.)

SON (he has reached the footlights): I tell you . . . There's absolutely nothing for me to do here! Let me go, please! Let me go! (This to the PRODUCER.)

PRODUCER: What do you mean . . . There's nothing for you to do?

STEPDAUGHTER (*placidly, ironically*): Don't bother to hold him back! He won't go away!

FATHER: He has to play that terrible scene with his Mother in the garden.

SON (*immediately, fiercely, resolutely*): I'm not playing anything! I've said that all along! (*To the PRODUCER*) Let me go!

STEPDAUGHTER (*running over, then addressing the PRODUCER*) Do you mind? (*She gets him to lower the hand with which he has been restraining the SON.*) Let him go! (*Then turning to the SON, as soon as the PRODUCER has dropped his arm.*) Well, go on. . . . Leave us!

(*The SON stands where he is, still straining in the direction of the steps, but, as if held back by some mysterious force, he cannot go down them. Then, amidst the utter dismay and anxious bewilderment of the ACTORS, he wanders slowly along the length of the footlights in the direction of the other flight of steps. Once there, he again finds himself unable to descend, much as he would wish to. The STEPDAUGHTER has watched his progress intently, her eyes challenging, defiant. Now she bursts out laughing.*)

STEPDAUGHTER: He can't, you see! He can't leave us! He must remain here. . . . He has no choice but to remain with us! He's chained to us. . . . Irrevocably! But if I . . . Who really do run away when what is inevitable happens. . . . And I run away because of my hatred for him. . . . I run away just because I can no longer bear the sight of him. . . . Well, if I can still stay here. . . . If I can still put up with his company and with having to have him here before my eyes. . . . Do you think it's likely that he can run away? Why, he was to stay here with that precious father of his. . . . With his mother. . . . Because now she has no other children but him. . . . (*Turning to her MOTHER.*) Come on, Mummy! Come on. . . . (*Turning to the PRODUCER and pointing to the MOTHER.*) There. . . . you see. . . . She'd got up to prevent him from going. . . . (*to her MOTHER, as if willing her actions by some magic power*) Come on! Come on! (*Then to the PRODUCER.*) You can imagine just how reluctant she is to give this proof of her affection in front of your actors. But so great is her desire to be with him that . . . There! . . . You see? . . . She's willing to live out again her scene with him! (*And as a matter of fact the MOTHER has gone up to her SON, and scarcely has the STEPDAUGHTER finished speaking before she makes a gesture to indicate her agreement.*)

SON (*immediately*): No! No! You're not going to drag me into this! If I can't get away, I shall stay here!

But I repeat that I'm not going to do any acting at all!

FATHER (*trembling with excitement, to the PRODUCER*): You can force him to act!

SON: Nobody can force me!

FATHER: I can and I will!

STEPDAUGHTER: Wait! Wait! First of all the little girl has to go to the fountain. . . . (*Goes over to the LITTLE GIRL She drops on to her knees in front of her and takes her face in her hands.*) Poor little darling. . . . You're looking so bewildered. . . . With those beautiful eyes. . . . You must be wondering just where you are. We're on a stage, dear! What's a stage? Well . . . It's a place where you play at being serious. They put on plays here. And now we're putting a play on. Really and truly! Even you. . . . (*Embracing her, clasping her to her breast and rocking her for a moment or so*) Oh, you little darling. . . . My dear little darling, what a terrible play for you. . . . What a horrible end they've thought out for you! The garden, the fountain. . . . Yes, it's a make-believe fountain . . . The pity is, darling, that everything's make-believe here . . . But perhaps you like a make-believe fountain better than a real one. . . . So that you can play in it. . . . M'm? No. . . . It'll be a game for the others. . . . Not for you unfortunately . . . Because you're real. . . . And you really play by a real fountain. . . . A lovely big green one, with masses of bamboo palms casting shadows. . . . Looking at your reflection in the water. . . . And lots and lots of little baby ducklings swimming about in it, breaking the shadow into a thousand little ripples. You try to take hold of one of the ducklings. . . . (*With a shriek which fills everybody with dismay.*) No, Rosetta, no! Your Mummy's not looking after you. . . . And all because of that swine there. . . . Her son! I feel as if all the devils in hell were loose inside me. . . . And he . . . (*Leaves the LITTLE GIRL and turns with her usual scorn to the BOY.*) What are you doing . . . drooping there like that? . . . Always the little beggar-boy! It'll be your fault too if that baby drowns. . . . Because of the way you go on. . . . As if I didn't pay for everybody when I got you into this house. (*Seizing his arm to make him take his hand out of his pocket.*) What have you got there? What are you trying to hide? Out with it! Take that hand out of your pocket! (*She snatches his hand out of his pocket and to everybody's horror reveals that it is clenched round a revolver. She looks at him for a little while, as if satisfied. Then she says somberly.*) M'm! Where did you get that gun from? . . . And how did you manage to lay your hands on it? (*And since the BOY, in his utter dismay—his eyes are staring and vacant—does not reply.*) You idiot! If I'd been you I shouldn't have killed myself. . . . I'd have killed one of *them*. . . . Or the pair of them! Father and son together! (*She hides them behind the cypress tree where he was lurking before. Then she takes the* LITTLE GIRL *by the hand and leads her towards the fountain. She puts her into the basin of the fountain, and makes her lie down so that she is completely hidden. Finally she goes down on her knees and buries her head in her hands on the rim of the basin of the fountain.*)

PRODUCER: That's it! Good! (*Turning to the* SON.) And at the same time. . . .

SON (*angrily*): What do you mean . . . 'And at the same time'? Oh, no! . . . Nothing of the sort! There never was any scene between her and me! (*Pointing to the* MOTHER.) You make her tell you what really happened! (*Meanwhile the* SECOND ACTRESS *and the* JUVENILE LEAD *have detached themselves from the group of* ACTORS *and are standing gazing intently at the* MOTHER *and the* SON *so that later thay can act these parts.*)

MOTHER: Yes, it's true, sir! I'd gone to his room at the time.

SON: There! Did you hear? To my room! Not into the garden!

PRODUCER: That doesn't matter at all! As I said we'll have to run all the action together into one composite scene!

SON (*becoming aware that the* JUVENILE LEAD *is studying him*): What do you want?

JUVENILE LEAD: Nothing! I was just looking at you.

SON (*turning to the* SECOND ACTRESS): Oh! . . . And *you're* here too, are you? All ready to play *her* part, I suppose? (*Pointing to the* MOTHER.)

PRODUCER: That's the idea! And if you want my opinion you ought to be damned grateful for all the attention they're paying you.

SON: Indeed? Thank you! But hasn't it dawned on you yet that you aren't going to be able to stage this play? Not even the tiniest vestige of us is to be found in you. . . . And all the time your actors are studying us from the outside. Do you think it's possible for us to live confronted by a mirror which, not merely content with freezing us in that particular picture which is the fixing of our expression, has to throw an image back at us which we can no longer recognise? . . . Our own features, yes. . . . But twisted into a horrible grimace.

FATHER: He's quite right! He's quite right, you know!

PRODUCER (*to the* JUVENILE LEAD *and* SECOND ACTRESS): Right you are! Get back with the others!

SON: It's no use your bothering! I'm not having anything to do with this!

PRODUCER: You be quiet for the moment, and let me listen to what your mother has to say. (*to the* MOTHER) You were saying? . . . You'd gone to his room? . . .

MOTHER: Yes, I'd gone to his room. . . . I couldn't bear the strain any longer! I wanted to pour out my heart to him. . . . I wanted to tell him of all the anguish that was tormenting me. . . . But as soon as he saw me come in . . .

SON: There was no scene between us! I rushed out of the room. . . . I didn't want to get involved in any scenes! Because I never have been involved in any! Do you understand?

MOTHER: Yes! That *is* what happened! That is what happened.

PRODUCER: But for the purposes of this play we've simply *got* to have a scene between you and him! Why . . . it's absolutely *essential!*

MOTHER: I'm quite ready to take part in one! Oh, if you could only find some way to give me an opportunity of speaking to him . . . if only for a moment. . . . So that I can pour out my heart to him!

FATHER (*going up to the* SON, *in a great rage*): You'll do what she asks, do you understand? You'll do what your Mother asks!

SON (*more stubbornly than ever*): I'm doing nothing!

FATHER (*taking hold of him by the lapels of his coat and shaking him*): My God, you'll do what I tell you! Or else . . . Can't you hear how she's pleading with you? Haven't you a spark of feeling in you for your Mother?

SON (*grappling with the* FATHER): No, I haven't! For God's sake, let's have done with all this. . . . Once and for all, let's have done with it!

(*General agitation. The* MOTHER *is terrified and tries to get between them in order to separate them.*)

MOTHER: Please! Please!

FATHER (*without relinquishing his hold*): You must obey me! You *must!*

SON (*struggling with him and finally hurling him to the ground. He falls near the steps amidst general horror*): What's come over you? Why are you in this terrible state of frenzy? Haven't you any sense of decency? . . . Going about parading your shame. . . . And ours, too. I'm having nothing to do with this affair! Nothing, do you hear? And by making this stand I am interpreting the wishes of our author, who didn't wish to put us on the stage!

PRODUCER: Oh, God! You come along here and . . .

SON (*pointing to the* FATHER): *He* did! I didn't.

PRODUCER: Aren't you here now?

SON: It was he who wanted to come. . . . And he dragged us all along with him. Then the pair of them went in there with you and agreed on what was to go into the play. But he didn't only stick to what really did occur. . . . No, as if that wasn't enough for any man, he had to put in things that never even happened.

PRODUCER: Well, then, you tell me what really happened! You can at least do that! You rushed out of your room without saying a word?

SON (*he hesitates for a moment*): Without saying a word!

I didn't want to get involved in a scene!

PRODUCER (*pressing him*): And then? What did you do then?

SON (*everybody's attention is on him; amidst the anguished silence he takes a step or two across the front of the stage*): Nothing. . . . As I was crossing the garden . . . (*He breaks off and becomes gloomy and absorbed.*)

PRODUCER (*urging him to speak, very much moved by this extraordinary reserve*): Well? As you were crossing the garden?

SON (*in exasperation, shielding his face with his arm*): Why do you want to force me to tell you? It's horrible!

(*The MOTHER is trembling all over and stifled sobs come from her as she looks toward the fountain.*)

PRODUCER (*slowly, quietly . . . he has seen where the MOTHER is looking and he now turns to the SON with growing apprehension*): The little girl?

SON (*staring straight in front of him, out into the auditorium*): There . . . In the fountain. . . .

FATHER (*from where he is on the floor, pointing with tender pity to the MOTHER*): She was following him. . . .

PRODUCER (*anxiously to the SON*): And what did you do?

SON (*slowly, continuing to stare in front of him*): I rushed up to the fountain. . . . I was about to dive in and fish her out. . . . Then all of a sudden I pulled up short. . . . Behind that tree I saw something that made my blood run cold. . . . The boy. . . . The boy was standing there. . . . Stock still. . . . With madness in his eyes. . . . Staring like some insane creature at his little sister, who was lying drowned in the fountain! (*The STEPDAUGHTER, who has all this while been bent over the fountain in order to hide the LITTLE GIRL, is sobbing desperately—her sobs coming like an echo from the background. There is a pause.*) I moved towards him. . . . And then . . . (*And from behind the trees where the BOY is hidden a revolver shot rings out.*)

MOTHER (*with a heartrending cry she rushes behind the trees accompanied by the SON and all the ACTORS. There is general confusion*): Oh, my son! My son! (*And then amidst the general hubbub and shouting.*) Help! Oh, help!

PRODUCER (*amidst all the shouting, he tries to clear a space while the BOY is carried off behind the skycloth*): Is he wounded? Is he badly hurt?

(*By now everybody, except for the PRODUCER and the FATHER, who is still on the ground by the steps, has disappeared behind the skycloth. They can be heard muttering and exclaiming in great consternation. Then first from one side, then from the other, the ACTORS re-enter.*)

LEADING LADY (*re-entering right, very much moved*): He's dead, poor boy! He's dead! Oh what a terrible thing to happen!

LEADING MAN (*re-entering left, laughing*): What do you mean, dead? It's all make-believe! It's all just a pretence! Don't get taken in by it!

OTHER ACTORS (*entering from the right*): Make-believe? Pretence? Reality! Reality! He's dead!

OTHERS (*from the left*): No! Make-believe! It's all a pretence!

FATHER (*rising and crying out to them*): What do you mean, pretence? Reality, ladies and gentlemen, reality! Reality! (*And desperation in his face, he too disappears behind the backcloth.*)

PRODUCER (*at the end of his tether*): Pretence! Reality! Go to hell, the whole lot of you! Lights! Lights! Lights!

(*The stage and the auditorium are suddenly flooded with very bright light. The PRODUCER breathes again as if freed from a tremendous burden. They all stand there looking into one another's eyes, in an agony of suspense and dismay.*)

PRODUCER: My God! Nothing like this has ever happened to me before! I've lost a whole day on their account! (*He looks at his watch.*) You can go home now. . . . All of you! There's nothing we can do now! It's too late to start rehearsing again! I'll see you all this evening. (*And as soon as the ACTORS have said 'Goodbye!' and gone he calls out to the ELECTRICIAN.*) Hey (*his name*) Everything off! (*He has hardly got the words out before the theatre is plunged for a moment into utter darkness.*) Hell! You might at least leave me one light on, so that I can see where I'm going!

(*And immediately behind the backcloth, a green flood lights up. It projects the silhouettes of the CHARACTERS [minus the BOY and the LITTLE GIRL], clear-cut and huge, on to the backcloth. The PRODUCER is terrified and leaps off the stage. As he does so the green flood is switched off—rather as if its having come on in the first instance had been due to the ELECTRICIAN's having pulled the wrong switch—and the stage is again lit in blue. Slowly the CHARACTERS come in and advance to the front of the stage. The SON comes in first, from the right, followed by the MOTHER, who has her arms outstretched toward him. Then the FATHER comes in from the left. They stop halfway down the stage and stand there like people in a trance. Last of all the STEPDAUGHTER comes in from the left and runs toward the steps which lead down into the auditorium. With her foot on the top step she stops for a moment to look at the other three and bursts into strident laughter. Then she hurls herself down the steps and runs up the aisle. She stops at the back of the auditorium and turns to look at the three figures standing on the stage. She bursts out laughing again. And when she has disappeared from the auditorium you can still hear her terrible laughter coming from the foyer beyond. A short pause and then, CURTAIN.*)

Figure 68. The Little Girl, the Boy, the Stepdaughter (Barbara Colby), the Son (Paul Shenar), the Mother (Josephine Nichols), and the Father (Richard Dysart) in the America Conservatory Theater production of *Six Characters in Search of an Author,* directed by William Ball and Byron Ringland, San Francisco, 1967. (Photograph: Hank Kranzler.)

Figure 69. The six characters *(standing right)* explain their situation to the producer and actors *(seated left)* in the American Conservatory Theater production of *Six Characters in Search of an Author,* directed by William Ball and Byron Ringland, San Francisco, 1967. (Photograph: Hank Kranzler.)

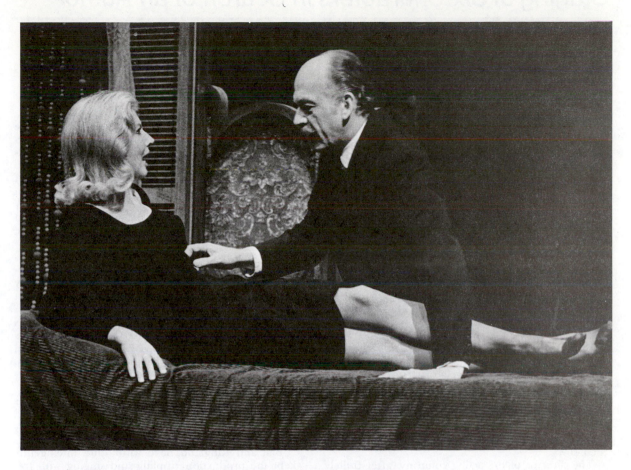

Figure 70. The Father as played by The Leading Man (William Paterson) attempts to seduce the Stepdaughter as played by The Leading Lady (Michael Learned) in the American Conservatory Theater production of *Six Characters in Search of an Author,* directed by William Ball and Byron Ringland, San Francisco, 1967. (Photograph: Hank Kranzler.)

Staging of *Six Characters in Search of an Author*

REVIEW OF THE AMERICAN CONSERVATORY
THEATER PRODUCTION, 1967, BY JEANNE
MILLER

The American Conservatory Theater's production of Luigi Pirandello's "Six Characters in Search of an Author" combines all the elements of a suspense melodrama, a philosophical riddle and a black comedy.

It opened last night at Marines' Theater, directed by William Ball and Byron Ringland who have freed the play of many of its enigmas. The tragi-comedy begins quite hilariously with a theatrical company in rehearsal—ACT itself, as a matter of fact, preparing a scene from Brandon Thomas' "Charley's Aunt."

The performers are bouncy and energetic, dressed in brightly colored hippie clothing. Therefore, the appearance of the six characters, starkly garbed in black and undulating in a silent and choreographed lament, strikes an instant and eerie note of fascinating menace.

This same level of paradox is admirably sustained throughout the evening, as the drama veers from the tortured self-analysis of the characters to the shallow interpretation of their passionate history by the actors.

The characters who break into the rehearsal have been abandoned by the author who created them and doomed to wander endlessly unless someone records their story.

The director of the acting company, after futilely attempting to evict them from the theater, finally agrees to have their grim tale portrayed by his troupe. Pandemonium ensues when the actors make a superficial travesty out of the characters' tragic plight.

Richard A. Dysart, who plays the father, is the principal spokesman for Pirandello's cerebrations about reality and illusion. In the hands of a less talented actor, this exposition could easily descend to the level of a windy intellectual exercise. But Dysart infuses his role with such tormented and guilt-ridden emotion that he is enormously moving, especially when he lucidly projects the playwright's thesis about the permanence and value of art in contrast to the absurdity and transiency of life.

Josephine Nichols, too, is excellent as the hapless mother whose frozen, hollow-eyed despair is especially poignant. As the step-daughter, Barbara Colby approaches her role with a steely erotic abandon that is exceedingly effective.

Paul Shenar is properly arrogant and disdainful as the embittered son. And Scott Hylands is engaging as the befuddled director who becomes fascinated and finally distraught by the behavior of the characters. Dion Chesse is also outstanding as the actor who portrays the father.

A note of mordant humor as well as high camp is introduced by the appearance of an actor, Jay Doyle, who plays the role of Madame Pace, the brothel-keeper.

Ball and Ringland have wittily and intelligently kept the production rippling and singing with tremendous theatrical vitality.

BERTOLT BRECHT

1898–1956

The social and political upheavals of the twentieth century profoundly influenced Brecht's life as well as his plays. World War I put an end to his medical studies in Munich and marked the beginning of his intense political consciousness, which he expressed in "The Legend of the Dead Soldier" (1918), a poem the Nazis were later to cite as evidence for denying him German citizenship. Shortly after the war, in 1919, he took part in an unsuccessful revolution in his native Bavaria, a bitter experience that provided the basis for his first successful play, *Drums in the Night* (1922). By 1922, Brecht had also become "dramaturg" (a resident playwright and adapter) at the Munich Kammerspiele, a theater for which he wrote *In the Jungle of the Cities* (1923). There, too, he directed *Edward II* (1924), his revision of Marlowe's history play, in a striking production that featured a battle scene with the faces of the soldiers painted starkly white.

But it was in Berlin, where Brecht moved in 1924, that he was to become widely known—and where he was to develop his revolutionary concept of "epic theater": a form of drama and dramatic production intended to provoke spectators into a heightened social and political awareness, rather than involve them emotionally in a realistic or naturalistic situation. To prevent spectators from empathizing with his characters, Brecht advocated the "alienation effect" in acting, an approach that directly countered the method of Stanislavsky. Brecht's approach required actors to distance themselves from the inner life of a role and not immerse themselves in it, to deliver lines in a mocking or dispassionate tone instead of an emotionally convincing voice, and in general to act a part in a manner that conveyed the awareness of being a performer rather than the involvement of being a character. To jerk spectators into a heightened social and political consciousness, Brecht abandoned the carefully elaborated plots of realistic drama in favor of an episodic structure he learned from reading and witnessing the expressionistic political plays of his German contemporaries. Brecht created this jerky, episodic effect by using short scenes in rapidly changing locales, with frequent shifts from prose to verse to song. And to heighten awareness of his political message, Brecht incorporated a variety of nonrealistic staging devices used by the radical German producer, Erwin Piscator—posters, slide projections, motion pictures, stylized sets, and garish lighting effects.

Brecht synthesized all these elements for the first time in *Man Is Man* (1926), a fiercely anti-colonial, anti-war play, which is set in India during the British empire and depicts the transformation of a poor dock worker, Galy Gay, into a soldier and military hero—a transformation that also changes him from a human being into a monster of nature. Two years later, Brecht turned his sights against capitalistic morality and produced his most popular and successful piece of epic theater, *The Threepenny Opera* (1928). The fame and money he gained from it gave him the freedom to create a wide variety of theatrical works: his dogmatically Marxist plays, which he called "lehrstucke" (literally, learning pieces), including *The Measures Taken* (1930) and *The Exception and the Rule* (1930); his less dogmatic but still socialist plays, such as *The Mother* (1932) and *St. Joan of the Stockyards* (1932); and his musical plays, *Happy End* (1929), *The Rise and Fall of the City of Mahagonny* (1929), and *The Seven Deadly Sins* (1933). The overtly didactic message in all these plays was, in essence, a challenge to the audience to change an existing social order that Brecht perceived as enslaving human beings through bureaucracy, war, and capitalism.

In 1933, political upheaval once again altered the course of Brecht's life, for when Hitler came to power he was compelled to flee from Nazi Germany—the communist politics of his plays had led to the danger of his being tried for high treason. He stayed briefly in Switzerland, then made his home in Denmark until 1939, when an impending Nazi invasion of that country forced him to move his family and his acting group to Sweden. But in 1940, the fear that Sweden would be invaded drove Brecht and his entourage to Finland. In 1941, he obtained a visa to the United States and settled in Santa Monica, California, where he lived until 1947, when his communist allegiances brought him under investigation by the now defunct Committee on Un-American Activities of the U.S. House of Representatives and he was forced to return to Germany. He spent his remaining years in East Berlin, where he devoted himself primarily to producing his already written plays and to turning his acting company, the Berliner Ensemble, into one of the most distinguished theatrical groups in the world.

During his exile from Germany, Brecht composed the most powerful plays he was to write after *The Threepenny Opera*—among them *Mother Courage and her Children* (1939), *Galileo* (1939), *The Good Woman of Setzuan* (1943), and *The Caucasian Chalk Circle* (1945). In these works, the overt, even strident didacticism of his Marxist plays gives way to a broader socialist message. Oppression is still the enemy, but in these plays it is seen as residing not only in social institutions, but in the acts of individual human beings. And it is in these plays, too, that the split between Brecht's theories of epic theater and his actual practice become most noticeable, for they seem to invite an audience to become passionately involved in the problems of their central characters. Although Brecht's notes on *Mother Courage* repeatedly emphasize the distasteful qualities he had hoped to reveal in her—her pettiness, her moral deformity, her incurable political ignorance—audiences invariably become engaged by her tenacity and remember her for her indomitability. Brecht's notes to *Galileo* indicate that he meant to portray the famous scientist as having betrayed his calling, but the play itself seems to invite a more spacious and sympathetic view of the man.

A similar kind of dichotomy exists in *The Threepenny Opera,* Brecht's most widely performed and accessible play. It is a biting attack on capitalistic society—a society in which "money rules the world," in which law is "made for one thing alone, for the exploitation of those who don't understand it," in which "Mankind can keep alive thanks to its brilliance in keeping its humanity repressed." The political satire is matched by the mocking treatment of romantic love, exemplified in Polly's naive attachment to the lusty Macheath, who "even with all London at his heels . . . is not the man to give up his habits"—or his whores. And just as John Gay's *The Beggar's Opera* (1728), on which it is based, ridiculed the pretentiousness of eighteenth century Italian opera, so *The*

Threepenny Opera derides traditional opera through its striking mixture of classical, cabaret, and jazz music. So, from its stark opening scene in Peachum's "outfitting shop for beggars" to its make-believe ending in which Macheath is miraculously saved from the gallows and raised to the peerage, *The Threepenny Opera* is clearly a full-scale assault on capitalistic society—on its ethics, on its politics, on its idea of love, on its standards of art.

Yet for all its satire, *The Threepenny Opera* is also a vastly entertaining and engaging work, as popular today as it was in the 1920s and 1930s. It contains a rich assortment of detailed characters, from the Peachums to Macheath's gang to Macheath himself, who is an intriguing individual, a subversively attractive rogue-hero. No matter how firmly Brecht insisted in his notes for the play that "the bandit Macheath must be played as a bourgeois phenomenon," and a "good businessman," as "emphatically staid, without the least sense of humor," actors and audiences still find him appealing, even heroic in his anti-heroism. And the music of Brecht's collaborator, Kurt Weil, though intentionally dissonant, has resulted in tunes that are at once catchy and haunting, so that Brecht's didactic statements are set in the context of a musically evocative score.

These tensions in *The Threepenny Opera* have been reflected throughout its production history in the attempts of directors, translators, composers, and adapters—even of Brecht himself—to push the work in one direction or the other. When it was adapted for the movies in 1930, Brecht tried to emphasize its anti-capitalistic theme, believing as he did that his original Berlin audience had failed to understand his political message, but he was prevented from doing so by the film company. Then in the 1950s, it was produced off Broadway in an adaptation done by the composer Marc Blitzstein, who cleaned up the lyrics, smoothed out the music, and toned down the politics so that it would be palatable to American audiences; this popularized version ran continuously in Greenwich Village for seven years. By the end of the fifties, *The Threepenny Opera* was a popular success throughout the United States, for Blitzstein's adaptation had made its way not only into college and community theaters, but also onto records and TV. More recently, in 1976, it was produced by the New York Shakespeare Festival at Lincoln Center, which used a new and highly faithful translation reprinted here. Judging from photographs of that production (see Figures 71, 72, and 73), as well as from a review of it reprinted following the text, the New York Public Theater did manage to capture the bitterness, the dissonance, the sleaziness, and the grim comedy that Brecht originally intended to convey in *The Threepenny Opera*.

THE THREEPENNY OPERA

After John Gay: The Beggar's Opera

BY BERTOLT BRECHT / COLLABORATORS: E. HAUPTMANN, K. WEILL: / TRANSLATORS: RALPH MANHEIM AND JOHN WILLETT

CHARACTERS

MACHEATH, *called Mac the Knife*
JONATHAN JEREMIAH PEACHUM, *proprietor of "Beggar's Friend Ltd."*
CELIA PEACHUM, *his wife*
POLLY PEACHUM, *his daughter*
BROWN, *High Sheriff of London*
LUCY, *his daughter*
LOW-DIVE JENNY

SMITH
THE REVEREND KIMBALL
FILCH
A BALLAD SINGER
THE GANG
BEGGARS
WHORES
CONSTABLES

PROLOGUE

The Ballad of Mac the Knife

(Fair in Soho.)
(The beggars are begging, the thieves are stealing, the whores are whoring. A ballad singer sings a ballad.)

> See the shark with teeth like razors.
> All can read his open face.
> And Macheath has got a knife, but
> Not in such an obvious place.
>
> See the shark, how red his fins are
> As he slashes at his prey.
> Mac the Knife wears white kid gloves which
> Give the minimum away.
>
> By the Thames's turbid waters
> Men abruptly tumble down.
> Is it plague or is it cholera?
> Or a sign Macheath's in town?
>
> On a beautiful blue Sunday
> See a corpse stretched in the Strand.
> See a man dodge round the corner . . .
> Mackie's friends will understand.
>
> And Schmul Meier, reported missing
> Like so many wealthy men:
> Mack the Knife acquired his cash box.
> God alone knows how or when.

(PEACHUM goes walking across the stage from left to right with his wife and daughter.)

> Jenny Towler turned up lately
> With a knife struck through her breast
> While Macheath walks the Embankment
> Nonchalantly unimpressed.

> Where is Alfred Gleet the cabman?
> Who can get that story clear?
> All the world may know the answer
> Just Macheath has no idea.
>
> And the ghastly fire in Soho—
> Seven children at a go—
> In the crowd stands Mac the Knife, but he
> Isn't asked and doesn't know.
>
> And the child-bride in her nightie
> Whose assailant's still at large
> Violated in her slumbers—
> Mackie, how much did you charge?

(Laughter among the WHORES. A MAN steps out from their midst and walks quickly away from the square.)

LOW-DIVE JENNY: That was Mac the Knife!

ACT 1

1

To combat the increasing callousness of mankind, J. Peachum, businessman, has opened a shop where the poorest of the poor can acquire an exterior that will touch the hardest of hearts.

(JONATHAN JEREMIAH PEACHUM'S outfitting shop for beggars.)

PEACHUM'S MORNING HYMN

> You ramshackle Christian, awake!
> Go on with your sinful employment
> Show what an old crook you could make.
> The Lord will soon cut your enjoyment.

Betray your own brother, you rogue
And sell your old woman, you rat.
You think the Lord God's just a joke?
He'll give you His Judgment on that.

PEACHUM (*to the audience*): Something must be done. My business is too hard, for my business is arousing human sympathy. There are a few things that stir men's souls, just a few, but the trouble is that after repeated use they lose their effect. Because man has the abominable gift of being able to deaden his feelings at will, so to speak. Suppose, for instance, a man sees another man standing on the corner with a stump for an arm; the first time he may be shocked enough to give him tenpence, but the second time it will only be fivepence, and if he sees him a third time he'll hand him over to the police without batting an eyelash. It's the same with the spiritual approach. (*A large sign saying "It is more blessed to give than to receive" is lowered from the grid.*) What good are the most beautiful, the most poignant sayings, painted on the most enticing little signs, when they get expended so quickly? The Bible has four or five sayings that stir the heart; once a man has expended them, there's nothing for it but starvation. Take this one, for instance— "Give and it shall be given unto you"—how threadbare it is after hanging here a mere three weeks. Yes, you have to keep on offering something new. So it's back to the good old Bible again, but how long can it go on providing? (*Knocking.* PEACHUM *opens. Enter a young man by the name of* FILCH.)

FILCH: Messrs. Peachum & Co.?

PEACHUM: Peachum.

FILCH: Are you the proprietor of the "Beggar's Friend Ltd."? I've been sent to you. Fine slogans you've got there! Money in the bank, that is. Got a whole library full of them, I suppose? That's what I call really something. What chance has a bloke like me got to think up ideas; and how can business flourish without education?

PEACHUM: What's your name?

FILCH: It's like this, Mr. Peachum, I've been down on my luck since I was a boy. My mother drank, my father gambled. Left to my own resources at an early age, without a mother's tender hand, I sank deeper and deeper into the quicksands of the big city. I've never known a father's care or the blessings of a happy home. So now you see me . . .

PEACHUM: So now I see you . . .

FILCH (*confused*): . . . bereft of all support, a prey to my base instincts.

PEACHUM: Like a derelict on the high seas and so on. Now tell me, derelict, which district have you

been reciting that fairy story in?

FILCH: What do you mean, Mr. Peachum?

PEACHUM: You deliver that speech in public, I take it?

FILCH: Well, it's like this, Mr. Peachum, yesterday there was an unpleasant little incident in Highland Street. There I am, standing on the corner quiet and miserable, holding out my hat, no suspicion of anything nasty . . .

PEACHUM (*leafs through a notebook*): Highland Street. Yes, yes, right. You're the bastard that Honey and Sam caught yesterday. You had the impudence to be molesting passers-by in District 10. We let you off with a thrashing because we had reason to believe you didn't know what's what. But if you show your face again it'll be the ax for you. Got it?

FILCH: Please, Mr. Peachum, please. What can I do, Mr. Peachum? The gentlemen beat me black and blue and then they gave me your business card. If I took off my coat, you'd think you were looking at a fish on a slab.

PEACHUM: My friend, if you don't look like a bloater, then my men haven't been doing their job. Along come these young whippersnappers, imagining they've only got to hold out their paws to land a steak. What would you say if somebody started fishing the best trout out of your pond?

FILCH: It's like this, Mr. Peachum—I haven't got a pond.

PEACHUM: Licenses are issued to professionals only. (*Points in a businesslike way to a map of the city.*) London is divided into fourteen districts. Any man who intends to practice the craft of begging in any of them needs a license from Jonathan Jeremiah Peachum & Co. Why, anybody could come along—a prey to his base instincts.

FILCH: Mr. Peachum, only a few shillings stand between me and utter ruin. Something must be done. With two shillings in my pocket I . . .

PEACHUM: One pound.

FILCH: Mr. Peachum!

(*Points imploringly at a sign saying "Do not turn a deaf ear to misery!"* PEACHUM *points to the curtain over a showcase, on which is written: "Give and it shall be given unto you!"*)

FILCH: Ten bob.

PEACHUM: Plus fifty percent of your take. Settle up once a week. With outfit seventy percent.

FILCH: What does the outfit consist of?

PEACHUM: That's for the firm to decide.

FILCH: Which district could I start in?

PEACHUM: Baker Street. Numbers 2 to 104. That comes even cheaper. Only fifty percent, including the outfit.

FILCH: Very well. (*He pays.*)

PEACHUM: Your name?

FILCH: Charles Filch.

PEACHUM: Right. *(Shouts.)* Mrs. Peachum! *(MRS. PEACHUM enters.)* This is Filch. Number three-fourteen. Baker Street district. I'll do his entry myself. Trust you to pick this moment to apply, just before the Coronation, when for once in a lifetime there's a chance of making a little something. Outfit C. *(He opens a linen curtain before a showcase in which there are five wax dummies.)*

FILCH: What's that?

PEACHUM: Those are the five basic types of misery, those most likely to touch the human heart. The sight of such types puts a man into that unnatural state where he is willing to part with money.
Outfit A: Victim of the traffic speed-up. The merry cripple, always cheerful *(He acts it out.),* always carefree, emphasized by arm-stump.
Outfit B: Victim of the Higher Strategy. The Tiresome Trembler, molests passers-by, operates by inspiring nausea *(He acts it out.),* attenuated by medals.
Outfit C: Victim of modern Technology. The Pitiful Blind Man, the Cordon Bleu of Beggary. *(He acts it out, staggering toward FILCH. The moment he bumps into FILCH, FILCH cries out in horror. PEACHUM stops at once, looks at him with amazement and suddenly roars.)* He's *sorry* for me! You'll never be a beggar as long as you live! You're only fit to be begged from! Very well, outfit D! Celia, you've been drinking again. And now you can't see straight. Number one-thirty-six has complained about his outfit. How often do I have to tell you that a gentleman doesn't put on filthy clothes? Number one-thirty-six paid for a brand-new suit. The only thing about it that could inspire pity was the stains and they should have been added by just ironing in candle wax. Use your head! Have I got to do everything myself? *(to FILCH)* Take off your clothes and put this on, but mind you, look after it!

FILCH: What about my things?

PEACHUM: Property of the firm. Outfit E: young man who has seen better days or, if you'd rather, never thought it would come to this.

FILCH: Oh, you use them again? Why can't I do the better days act?

PEACHUM: Because nobody can make his own suffering sound convincing, my boy. If you have a bellyache and say so, people will simply be disgusted. Anyway, you're not here to ask questions but to put these things on.

FILCH: Aren't they rather dirty? *(After PEACHUM has given him a penetrating look.)* Excuse me, sir, please excuse me.

MRS. PEACHUM: Shake a leg, son, I'm not standing here holding your trousers till Christmas.

FILCH *(suddenly emphatic)*: But I'm not taking my shoes off! Absolutely not. I'd sooner drop the whole business. They're the only present my poor mother ever gave me, I may have sunk pretty low, but never . . .

MRS. PEACHUM: Stop driveling. We all know your feet are dirty.

FILCH: Where am I supposed to wash my feet? In mid-winter? *(MRS. PEACHUM leads him behind a screen, there she sits down on the left and starts ironing candle wax into a suit.)*

PEACHUM: / Where's your daughter?

MRS. PEACHUM: Polly? Upstairs.

PEACHUM: Has that man been here again? The one who always comes round when I'm out?

MRS. PEACHUM: Don't be so suspicious, Jonathan, there's no finer gentleman. The Captain takes a real interest in our Polly.

PEACHUM: I see.

MRS. PEACHUM: And if I've got half an eye in my head, Polly thinks he's very nice too.

PEACHUM: Celia, the way you chuck your daughter around anyone would think I was a millionaire. Wanting to marry her off? The idea! Do you think this lousy business of ours would survive a week if those ragamuffins our customers had nothing better than *our* legs to look at? A husband! He'd have us in his clutches in three shakes! In his clutches like this! Do you think your daughter can hold her tongue in bed any better than you?

MRS. PEACHUM: A fine opinion of your daughter you have.

PEACHUM: The worst. The very worst. A lump of sensuality, that's what she is.

MRS. PEACHUM: If so, she didn't get it from you.

PEACHUM: Marriage! I expect my daughter to be to me as bread to the hungry. *(He leafs in the Book.)*: it even says so in the Bible somewhere. Anyway marriage is disgusting. I'll teach her to get married.

MRS. PEACHUM: Jonathan, you're just a barbarian.

PEACHUM: Barbarian! What's this gentleman's name?

MRS. PEACHUM: They never call him anything but "the Captain."

PEACHUM: So you haven't even asked him his name? Interesting.

MRS. PEACHUM: We wouldn't be so rude as to ask him for his birth certificate when he's so distinguished and invited the two of us to the Cuttlefish Hotel for a little hop.

PEACHUM: Where?

MRS. PEACHUM: To the Cuttlefish for a little hop.

PEACHUM: Captain? Cuttlefish Hotel? Hm, hm, hm . . .

MRS. PEACHUM: A gentleman who has always handled my daughter and me with kid gloves.

PEACHUM: Kid gloves!

MRS. PEACHUM: It's quite true, he always does wear gloves, white ones: white kid gloves.

PEACHUM: I see. White gloves and a cane with an ivory handle and spats and patent-leather shoes and an over-powering personality and a scar . . .

MRS. PEACHUM: On his neck. What! Isn't there anybody you don't know? (FILCH crawls out from behind the screen.)

FILCH: Mr. Peachum, couldn't you give me some tips, I've always believed in having a system and not just shooting off my mouth any old how.

MRS. PEACHUM: A system!

PEACHUM: Let him be a half-wit. Come back this evening at six, we'll teach you the rudiments. Now clear out!

FILCH: Thank you very much indeed, Mr. Peachum. Many thanks. (Goes out.)

PEACHUM: Fifty percent!—And now I'll tell you who this gentleman with the gloves is—Mac the Knife! (He runs up the stairs to POLLY's bedroom.)

MRS. PEACHUM: God in Heaven! Mac the Knife! Lord alive! For what we are about to receive, the Lord—Polly! What's become of Polly?

(PEACHUM comes down slowly.)

PEACHUM: Polly? Polly's not come home. Her bed is untouched.

MRS. PEACHUM: Then she's gone to supper with that wool merchant. That'll be it.

PEACHUM: Let's hope to God it is the wool merchant!

(MR. and MRS. PEACHUM step before the curtain and sing. Song lighting: golden glow. The organ is lit up. Three lamps are lowered from above on a pole, and the signs say:)

THE "NO THEY CAN'T" SONG

1

PEACHUM:
No, they can't
Bear to be at home all tucked up tight in bed.
It's fun they want
You can bet they've got some fancy notions brewing up instead.

MRS. PEACHUM:
So that's your Moon over Soho
That is your infernal "d'you feel my heart beating?" line.
That's the old "wherever you go I shall be with you, honey"
When you first fall in love and the moonbeams shine.

2

PEACHUM:
No, they can't
See what's good for them and set their mind on it.
It's fun they want
So they end up on their arses in the shit.

BOTH:
Then where's your Moon over Soho?
What's come of your infernal "d'you feel my heart beating?" bit?
Where's the old "wherever you go I shall be with you, honey"?
When you're no more in love and you're in the shit.

2

Deep in the heart of Soho the bandit Mac the Knife is celebrating his marriage to Polly Peachum, the beggar king's daughter.

(Bare Stable.)

MATTHEW (known as MATT OF THE MINT, holds out his revolver and examines the room with a lantern): Hey, hands up if anybody's here!

(MACHEATH enters and makes a tour of inspection along the footlights.)

MACHEATH: Well, is anybody here?

MATTHEW: Not a soul. Just the place for our wedding.

POLLY (enters in wedding dress): But it's a stable!

MAC: Sit on the feed-bin for the moment, Polly. (to the audience) Today this stable will witness my marriage to Miss Polly Peachum, who has followed me for love in order to share my life with me.

MATTHEW: All over London they'll be saying this is the most daring job you've ever pulled, enticing Mr. Peachum's only child from his home.

MAC: Who's Mr. Peachum?

MATTHEW: He'll tell you he's the poorest man in London.

POLLY: But you surely don't intend to have our wedding here? Why, it is a common stable. You can't ask the vicar to a place like this. Besides, it isn't even ours. We really oughtn't to start our new life with a burglary, Mac. Why, this is the biggest day of our life.

MAC: Dear child, everything shall be done as you wish. We can't have you embarrassed in any way. The trimmings will be here in a moment.

MATTHEW: That'll be the furniture.

(Large vans are heard driving up. Half a dozen men come in, carrying carpets, furniture, dishes, etc., with which they transform the stable into an exaggeratedly luxurious room.)

MAC: Junk.

(*The gentlemen put the presents down left, congratulate the bride, and report to the bridegroom.*)

JAKE (*known as* CROOK-FINGERED JAKE): Congratulations! At 14 Ginger Street there were some people on the second floor. We had to smoke them out.

BOB (*known as* BOB THE SAW): Congratulations! A copper got bumped in the Strand.

MAC: Amateurs.

NED: We did all we could, but three people in the West End were past saving. Congratulations!

MAC: Amateurs and bunglers.

JIMMY: An old gent got hurt a bit, but I don't think it's anything serious. Congratulations.

MAC: My orders were: avoid bloodshed. It makes me sick to think of it. You'll never make businessmen! Cannibals, yes, but not businessmen!

WALTER (*known as* DREARY WALT): Congratulations. Only half an hour ago, madam, that harpsichord belonged to the Duchess of Somerset.

POLLY: What is this furniture anyway?

MAC: How do you like the furniture, Polly?

POLLY (*in tears*): Those poor people, all for a few sticks of furniture.

MAC: And what furniture! Junk! You have a perfect right to be angry. A rosewood harpsichord with a Renaissance sofa. That's unforgivable. What about a table?

WALTER: A table?

(*They lay some planks over the bins.*)

POLLY: Oh, Mac, I'm so miserable! I only hope the vicar doesn't come.

MATTHEW: Of course he'll come. We gave him exact directions.

WALTER (*introduces the table*): A table!

MAC (*seeing* POLLY *in tears*): My wife is very much upset. Where are the rest of the chairs? A harpsichord and no chairs! Use your heads! For once I'm having a wedding, and how often does that happen? Shut up, Dreary! How often does it happen that I leave you to do something on your own? And when I do you make my wife unhappy right at the start.

NED: Dear Polly . . .

MAC (*knocks his hat off his head*): "Dear Polly"! I'll bash your head through your kidneys with your "dear Polly," you squirt. Have you ever heard the like? "Dear Polly"! I suppose you've been to bed with her?

POLLY: Mac!

NED: I swear . . .

WALTER: Dear madam, if any items of furniture should be lacking, we'll be only too glad to go back and . . .

MAC: A rosewood harpsichord and no chairs. (*Laughs.*) Speaking as a bride, what do you say to that?

POLLY: It could be worse.

MAC: Two chairs and a sofa and the bridal couple has to sit on the floor.

POLLY: Something new, I'd say.

MAC (*sharply*): Get the legs sawn off this harpsichord! Go on!

FOUR MEN (*saw the legs off the harpsichord and sing*):

Bill Lawgen and Mary Syer
Were made man and wife a week ago.
When it was over and they exchanged a kiss
He was thinking "Whose wedding dress was this?"
While his name was a thing she would have liked to know.
Hooray!

WALTER: The final result, madam: there's your bench.

MAC: May I now ask the gentlemen to take off those filthy rags and put on some decent clothes? After all this isn't just anybody's wedding. Polly, may I ask you to look after the grub?

POLLY: Is this our wedding feast? Was the whole lot stolen, Mac?

MAC: Of course. Of course.

POLLY: I wonder what you will do if there's a knock at the door and the sheriff steps in.

MAC: I'll show you what your husband will do in such a situation.

MATTHEW: It couldn't happen today. The mounted police are all sure to be in Daventry. They'll be escorting the Queen back to town for Friday's Coronation.

POLLY: Two knives and fourteen forks! One knife per chair.

MAC: What incompetence! That's the work of apprentices, not experienced men! Haven't you any sense of style? Fancy not knowing the difference between Chippendale and Louis Quatorze.

(*The gang comes back. The gentlemen are now wearing fashionable evening dress, but unfortunately their movements are not in keeping with it.*)

WALTER: We only wanted to bring the most valuable stuff. Look at that wood! Really first class.

MATTHEW: Ssst! Ssst! Permit us, Captain . . .

MAC: Polly, come here a minute.

(MAC *and* POLLY *assume the pose of a couple prepared to receive congratulations.*)

MATTHEW: Permit us, Captain, on the greatest day of your life, in the bloom of your career, or rather the turning point, to offer you our most indispensable and at the same time most sincere congratulations, and so forth. That posh talk don't half make me sick. So to cut a long story short (*Shakes* MAC'S *hand.*)—keep a stiff upper lip, old mate.

MAC: Thank you, that was kind of you, Matthew.

MATTHEW (*shaking* POLLY'S *hand after embracing* MAC *with emotion*): It was spoken from the heart, all right! Anyway, keep a stiff upper lip, old girl, I mean (*Grinning.*) he should keep it stiff.

(*Roars of laughter from the guests. Suddenly* MAC *with a deft movement sends* MATTHEW *to the floor.*)

MAC: Shut your trap. Keep that filth for your Kitty, she's the kind of slut that appreciates it.

POLLY: Mac, don't be so vulgar.

MATTHEW: Here, I don't like that. Calling Kitty a slut . . . (*Stands up with difficulty.*)

MAC: Oh, so you don't like that?

MATTHEW: And besides, I never use filthy language with her. I respect Kitty a lot too much for that. But maybe you wouldn't understand that, the way you are. You're a fine one to talk about filth. Do you think Lucy didn't tell me the things you've told her? Compared to that, I'm a kid glove.

(MAC *stares at him.*)

JAKE: Cut it out, this is a wedding. (*They pull him away.*)

MAC: Fine wedding, isn't it, Polly? Having to see trash like this around you on the day of your marriage. You wouldn't have thought your husband's friends would let him down so. Let it be a lesson to you.

POLLY: I think it's nice.

ROBERT: Blarney. Nobody's letting you down. What's a difference of opinion between friends? Your Kitty's as good as the next girl. But now bring out your wedding present, mate.

ALL: Yes, hand it over!

MATTHEW (*offended*): Here.

POLLY: Oh, a wedding present. How kind of you, Mr. Matt of the Mint. Look, Mac, what a lovely nightgown.

MATTHEW: Another bit of filth, eh, Captain?

MAC: Forget it. I didn't mean to hurt your feelings on this festive occasion.

WALTER: What do you say to this? Chippendale! (*He unveils an enormous Chippendale grandfather clock.*)

MAC: Quatorze.

POLLY: It's wonderful. I'm so happy. Words fail me. You're so unbelievably kind. Oh, Mac, isn't it a shame we haven't got a flat to put it in?

MAC: Hm, it's a start in the right direction. The great thing is to get started. Thank you kindly, Walter. Go on, clear the stuff away now. Food!

JAKE (*while the others start setting the table*): Trust me to come empty-handed again. (*Intensely to* POLLY.) Believe me, young lady, I find it most distressing.

POLLY: It doesn't matter in the least, Mr. Crook-fingered Jake.

JAKE: Here are the boys flinging presents right and left, and me standing here like a fool. What a situation to be in! It's always the way with me. Situations! It's enough to make your hair stand on end. The other day I meet Low-Dive Jenny; well, I say, you old cow . . . (*Suddenly he sees* MAC *standing behind him and goes off without a word.*)

MAC (*leads* POLLY *to her place*): This is the best food you'll taste today, Polly. Gentlemen! (*All sit down to the wedding feast.*)

NED (*indicating the china*): Beautiful dishes. Savoy Hotel.

JAKE: The plover's eggs are from Selfridge's. There was supposed to be a bucket of foie gras. But Jimmy ate it on the way, he was mad because it had a hole in it.

WALTER: We don't talk about holes in polite society.

JIMMY: Don't bolt the eggs like that, Ned, not on a day like this.

MAC: Couldn't somebody sing something? Something delectable?

MATTHEW (*choking with laughter*): Something delectable? That's a first-class word. (*He sits down in embarrassment under* MAC'S *withering glance.*)

MAC (*knocks a bowl out of someone's hand*): I didn't intend us to start eating yet. Instead of seeing you people wade straight into the trough, I would have liked a little something from the heart. That's what other people do on an occasion like this.

JAKE: What, for instance?

MAC: Am I supposed to think of everything myself? I'm not asking you to put on an opera. But you might have arranged for something else besides stuffing your bellies and making filthy jokes. Oh, well, it's a day like this that you find out who your friends are.

POLLY: The salmon is marvelous, Mac.

NED: I bet you've never eaten anything like it. You get that every day at Mac the Knife's. You've landed in the honey pot all right. That's what I've always said: Mac is the right match for a girl with a feeling for higher things. As I was saying to Lucy only yesterday.

POLLY: Lucy? Mac, who is Lucy?

JAKE (*embarrassed*): Lucy? Oh, nothing serious, you know.

(MATTHEW *has risen; standing behind* POLLY, *he is waving his arms to shut* JAKE *up.*)

POLLY (*sees him*): Do you want something? Salt

perhaps . . .? What were you saying, Mr. Jake?

JAKE: Oh, nothing, nothing at all. The main thing I wanted to say really was nothing at all. I'm always putting my foot in it.

MAC: What have you got in your hand, Jake?

JAKE: A knife, Captain.

MAC: And what have you got on your plate?

JAKE: A trout, Captain.

MAC: I see. And with the knife you are eating the trout, are you not? It's incredible. Did you ever see the like of it, Polly? Eating his fish with a knife! Anybody who does that is just a plain swine, do you get me, Jake? Let that be a lesson to you. You'll have your hands full, Polly, trying to turn trash like them into human beings. Have you boys got the least idea what that means?

WALTER: A human being or a human pee-ing?

POLLY: Really, Mr. Walter!

MAC: So you won't sing a song, something to brighten up the day? Has it got to be a miserable gloomy day like any other? And come to think of it, is anybody guarding the door? I suppose you want me to attend to that myself too? Do you want me on this day of days to guard the door so you lot can stuff your bellies at my expense?

WALTER (sullenly): What do you mean at your expense?

JIMMY: Stow it, Walter boy. I'm on my way. Who's going to come here anyway? (Goes out.)

JAKE: A fine joke on a day like this if all the wedding guests were pulled in.

JIMMY (rushes in): Hey, Captain. The cops!

WALTER: Tiger Brown!

MATTHEW: Nonsense, it's the Reverend Kimball.

(KIMBALL enters.)

ALL (roar): Good evening, Reverend Kimball!

KIMBALL: So I've found you after all. I find you in a lowly hut, a humble place but your own.

MAC: Property of the Duke of Devonshire.

POLLY: Good evening, reverend. Oh, I'm so glad that on the happiest day of our life you . . .

MAC: And now I request a rousing song for the Reverend Kimball.

MATTHEW: How about Bill Lawgen and Mary Syer?

JAKE: Good. Bill Lawgen might be the right thing.

KIMBALL: Be nice if you'd do a little number, boys.

MATTHEW: Let's have it, gentlemen.

(Three men rise and sing hesitantly, weakly and uncertainly.)

WEDDING SONG FOR THE LESS WELL-OFF

Bill Lawgen and Mary Syer
Were made man and wife a week ago.
(Three cheers for the happy couple: hip, hip, hooray!)
When it was over and they exchanged a kiss

He was thinking "Whose wedding dress was this?"
While his name was a thing she would have liked to know.
Hooray!

Do you know what your wife's up to? No!
Do you like her sleeping round like that? No!
(Three cheers for the happy couple: hip, hip, hooray!)
Billy Lawgen told me recently
Just one part of her will do for me.
The Swine.
Hooray!

MAC: Is that all? Paltry!

MATTHEW (chokes again): Paltry is the word, gentlemen. Paltry.

MAC: Shut your trap!

MATTHEW: Oh, I only meant no gusto, no fire, and so on.

POLLY: Gentlemen, if none of you wishes to perform, I myself will sing a little song; it's an imitation of a girl I saw once in some twopenny halfpenny dive in Soho. She was washing the glasses, and everybody was laughing at her, and then she turned to the guests and said things like the things I'm going to sing to you. All right. This is a little bar, I want you to think of it as filthy. She stood behind it morning and night. This is the bucket and this is the rag she washed the glasses with. Where you are sitting, the customers were sitting laughing at her. You can laugh too, to make it exactly the same; but if you can't, you don't have to. (She starts pretending to wash glasses, muttering to herself.) Now, for instance, one of them—it might be you (Pointing at WALTER.)— says: Well, when's your ship coming in, Jenny?

WALTER: Well, when's your ship coming in, Jenny?

POLLY: And another says—you, for instance: Still washing up glasses, Jenny the pirate's bride?

MATTHEW: Still washing up glasses, Jenny the pirate's bride?

POLLY: Good. And now I'll begin.

(Song lighting: golden glow. The organ is lit up. Three lamps are lowered from above on a pole, and the signs say:)

PIRATE JENNY

1
Now you gents all see I've the glasses to wash
If a bed's to be made I make it.
You may tip me with a penny, and I'll thank you very well
And you see me dressed in tatters, and this tatty old hotel
And you never ask how long I'll take it.
But one of these evenings there will be screams from the harbor

And they'll ask: what can all that screaming be?
And they'll see me smiling as I do the glasses
And they'll say: how she can smile beats me.
  And a ship with eight sails and
  All its fifty guns loaded
  Has tied up at the quay.

2
They say: get on, dry your glasses, my girl
And they tip me and don't give a damn.
And their penny is accepted, and their bed will be made
(Although nobody is going to sleep there, I'm afraid)
And they still have no idea who I am.
  But one of these evenings there will be explosions from
    the harbor,
And they'll ask: what kind of a bang was that?
And they'll see me as I stand beside the window
And they'll say: what's she got to smile at?
  And that ship with eight sails and
  All its fifty guns loaded
  Will lay siege to the town.

3
Then, you gents, you aren't going to find it a joke
For the walls will be knocked down flat
And in no time the town will be razed to the ground.
Just one tatty old hotel will be left standing safe and
    sound
And they'll ask: did someone special live in that?
Then there'll be a lot of people milling round the hotel
And they'll ask: what made them let that place alone?
And they'll see me as I leave the door next morning
And they'll say: don't tell us she's the one.
  And that ship with eight sails and
  All its fifty guns loaded
  Will run up its flag.

4
And a hundred men will land in the bright midday sun
Each stepping where the shadows fall.
They'll look inside each doorway and grab anyone they
    can see
And put him in irons and then bring him to me
And they'll ask: which of these should we kill?
In that noonday heat there'll be a hush round the
    harbor
As they ask which has got to die.
And you'll hear me as I softly answer: the lot!
And as the first head rolls I'll say: hoppla!
  And that ship with eight sails and
  All its fifty guns loaded
  Will vanish with me.

MATTHEW: Very pretty. Cute, eh? And the way the missus puts it across!

MAC: What do you mean pretty? It's not pretty, you idiot! It's art, it's not pretty. You did that mar-velously, Polly. But it's wasted on trash like this, if you'll excuse me, Your Reverence. (*In an undertone to* POLLY.) Anyway, I don't like you play-acting; let's not have any more of it. (*Laughter at the table. The gang is making fun of the parson.*) What you got in your hand, Your Reverence?

JAKE: Two knives, Captain.

MAC: What you got on your plate, Your Reverence?

KIMBALL: Salmon, I think.

MAC: And with that knife you are eating the salmon, are you not?

JAKE: Did you ever see the like of it, eating fish with a knife? Anybody who does that is just a plain . . .

MAC: Swine. Do you understand me, Jake? Let that be a lesson to you.

JIMMY (*rushing in*): Hey, Captain, cops. The sheriff in person.

WALTER: Brown. Tiger Brown!

MAC: Yes, Tiger Brown, exactly. It's Tiger Brown himself, the high sheriff of London, that pillar of the Old Bailey, who will now enter Captain Macheath's humble cabin. Let that be a lesson to you.

(*The bandits creep away.*)

JAKE: It'll be the gallows for us!

(BROWN *enters.*)

MAC: Hullo, Jackie.

BROWN: Hullo, Mac! I haven't much time, got to be leaving in a minute. Does it have to be somebody else's stable? Why, this is breaking and entering again!

MAC: But Jackie, it's so conveniently located. I'm glad you could come to old Mac's wedding. Let me introduce my wife, née Peachum. Polly, this is Tiger Brown, what do you say, old man? (*Slaps him on the back.*) And these are my friends, Jackie, I imagine you've seen them all before.

BROWN (*pained*): I'm here unofficially, Mac.

MAC: So are they. (*He calls them. They come in with their hands up.*) Hey, Jake.

BROWN: That's Crook-fingered Jake. He's a dirty dog.

MAC: Hey, Jimmy; hey Bob; hey, Walter!

BROWN: Well, just for today I'll turn a blind eye.

MAC: Hey, Ned; hey, Matthew.

BROWN: Be seated, gentlemen, be seated.

ALL: Thank you, sir.

BROWN: I'm delighted to meet my old friend Mac's charming wife.

POLLY: Don't mention it, sir.

MAC: Sit down, ya old blighter, and pitch into the whiskey!—Polly and gentlemen! You have today in your midst a man whom the king's inscrutable decree has placed high above his fellow men and who has none the less remained my friend throughout the storms and perils, and so on. You know whom I mean, and you too know whom I mean, Brown. Ah, Jackie, do you remember how we served in India together, soldiers both of us? Ah, Jackie, let's sing the Cannon Song right now.

(They sit down on the table.)
(Song lighting: golden glow. The organ is lit up. Three lamps are lowered from above on a pole, and the signs say:)

THE CANNON SONG

1
John was all present and Jim was all there
And Georgie was up for promotion.
Not that the army gave a bugger who they were
When confronting some heathen commotion.
The troops live under
The cannon's thunder
From Sind to Cooch Behar.
Moving from place to place
When they come face to face
With men of a different color
With darker skins or duller
They quick as winking chop them into beefsteak tartare.

2
Johnny found his whiskey too warm
And Jim found the weather too balmy
But Georgie took them both by the arm
And said: never let down the army.
The troops live under
The cannon's thunder
From Sind to Cooch Behar.
Moving from place to place
When they come face to face
With men of different color
With darker skins or duller
They quick as winking chop them into beefsteak tartare.

3
John is a write-off and Jimmy is dead
And they shot poor old Georgie for looting
But young men's blood goes on being red
And the army goes on recruiting.
The troops live under
The cannon's thunder
From Sind to Cooch Behar.
Moving from place to place
When they come face to face
With men of a different color
With darker skins or duller
They quick as winking chop them into beefsteak tartare.

MAC: Though life with its raging torrents has carried us boyhood friends far apart, although our professional interests are very different, some people would go so far as to say diametrically opposed, our friendship has come through unimpaired. Let that be a lesson to all of you. Castor and Pollux, Hector and Andromache and so on. Seldom have I, the humble bandit, well, you know what I mean, made even the smallest haul without giving him, my friend, a share, a sizable share, Brown, as a gift and token of my unswerving loyalty, and seldom has he, take that knife out of your mouth, Jake, the all-powerful police chief, staged a raid without sending me, his boyhood friend, a little tip-off. Well, and so on and so forth, it's all a matter of give and take. Let that be a lesson to you. *(He takes* BROWN *by the arm.)* Well, Jackie, old man, I'm glad you've come, I call it real friendship. *(Pause, because* BROWN *has been looking sadly at a carpet.)* Genuine Shiraz.

BROWN: From the Oriental Carpet Company.

MAC: Yes, we never go anywhere else. Do you know, Jackie, I had to have you here today, I hope it's not too unpleasant for you in your position.

BROWN: You know, Mac, that I can't refuse you anything. I must be going. I've really got so much on my mind; if the slightest thing should go wrong at the Queen's Coronation . . .

MAC: See here, Jackie, my father-in-law is a rotten old stinker. If he tries to make trouble for me, is there anything on record against me at Scotland Yard?

BROWN: There's nothing whatsoever on record against you at Scotland Yard.

MAC: I knew it.

BROWN: I've taken care of all that. Good night.

MAC: Aren't you fellows going to stand up?

BROWN *(to* POLLY*)*: Best of luck. *(Goes out accompanied by* MAC.*)*

JAKE *(who along with* MATTHEW *and* WALTER *has meanwhile been conferring with* POLLY*)*: I must admit I couldn't repress a certain alarm a while ago when I heard Tiger Brown was coming.

MATTHEW: You see, dear lady, we have connections with the top authorities.

WALTER: Yes, Mac always has an iron in the fire that the rest of us don't even suspect. But we have our own little iron in the fire. Gentlemen, it's half-past nine.

MATTHEW: And now comes the high point.

(All go upstage behind the carpet that conceals something. MAC *enters.)*

MAC: I say, what's going on?

MATTHEW: Hey, Captain, another little surprise.

(Behind the carpet they sing the Bill Lawgen song softly and with much feeling. But at "his name was a thing

she would have liked to know" MATTHEW *pulls down the carpet and all go on with the song, bellowing and pounding on the bed that has been disclosed.)*

MAC: Thank you, friends, thank you.

WALTER: And now we shall quietly take our leave. *(The gang go out.)*

MAC: And now the time has come for softer sentiments. Without them man is a mere working animal. Sit down, Polly.

(Music.)

MAC: Look at the moon over Soho.

POLLY: I see it dearest. Feel my heart beating, my beloved.

MAC: I feel it, beloved.

POLLY: Where'er you go I shall be with you.

MAC: And where you stay, there too shall I be.

BOTH *(sing)*:
> And though we've no paper to say we're wed
> And no altar covered with flowers
> And nobody knows for whom your dress was made
> And even the ring is not ours—
> That platter off which you are eating your bread
> Give it one brief look; fling it far.
> For love will endure or not endure
> Regardless of where we are.

3

To Peachum, aware of the hardness of the world, the loss of his daughter means utter ruin.

(Peachum's Outfitting Shop for Beggars.)

(To the right PEACHUM *and* MRS. PEACHUM. *In the doorway stands* POLLY *in her coat and hat, holding her traveling bag.)*

MRS. PEACHUM: Married? First you rig her fore and aft in dresses and hats and gloves and parasols, and when she's cost as much as a sailing ship, she throws herself in the garbage like a rotten pickle. Are you really married?

(Song lighting: golden glow. The organ is lit up. Three lamps are lowered from above on a pole and the signs say:)

In a little song Polly gives her parents to understand that she has married the bandit Macheath.

BARBARA SONG

1
> I once used to think, in my innocent youth
> (And I once was as innocent as you)
> That someone someday might come my way
> And then how would I know what best to do?

> And if he'd got money
> And seemed a nice chap
> And his workday shirts were white as snow
> And if he knew how to treat a girl with due respect
> I'd have to tell him: No.
> That's where you must keep your head screwed on
> And insist on going slow.
> Sure, the moon will shine throughout the night
> Sure, the boat is on the river, tied up tight.
> That's as far as things could go.
> Oh, you can't lie back, you must stay cold at heart
> Oh, you must not let your feelings show.
> Oh, whenever you feel it might start
> Ah, then your only answer's: No.

2
> The first one that came was a man of Kent
> And all that a man ought to be.
> The second one owned three ships down at Wapping
> And the third was crazy about me.
> And as they'd got money
> And all seemed nice chaps
> And their workday shirts were white as snow
> And as they knew how to treat a girl with due respect
> Each time I told them: No.
> That's where I still kept my head screwed on
> And I chose to take it slow.
> Sure, the moon could shine throughout the night
> Sure, the boat was on the river, tied up tight
> That's as far as things could go.
> Oh, you can't lie back, you must stay cold at heart
> Oh, you must not let your feelings show.
> Oh, whenever you feel it might start
> Ah, then your only answer's: No.

3
> But then one day, and that day was blue
> Came someone who didn't ask at all
> And he went and hung his hat on the nail in my little
> attic
> And what happened I can't quite recall.
> And as he'd got no money
> And was not a nice chap
> And his Sunday shirts, even, were not like snow
> And as he'd no idea of treating a girl with due respect
> I could not tell him: No.
> That's the time my head was not screwed on
> And to hell with going slow.
> Oh, the moon was shining clear and bright
> Oh, the boat kept drifting downstream all that night
> That was how it simply had to go.
> Yes, you must lie back, you can't stay cold at heart
> In the end you have to let your feelings show.
> Oh, the moment you know it must start
> Ah, then's no time for saying: No.

PEACHUM: So now she's associating with criminals.

That's lovely. That's delightful.

MRS. PEACHUM: If you're immoral enough to get married, did it have to be a horse thief and a highwayman? That'll cost you dear one of these days! I ought to have seen it coming. Even as a child she had a swelled head like the Queen of England.

PEACHUM: So, she's really got married!

MRS. PEACHUM: Yes, yesterday, at five in the afternoon.

PEACHUM: To a notorious criminal. Come to think of it, it shows that the fellow is really audacious. If I give away my daughter, the last prop of my old age, my house will cave in and my last dog will run off. I'd think twice about giving away the dirt under my fingernails, it would mean risking starvation. If the three of us can get through the winter on one log of wood, maybe we'll live to see the new year. Maybe.

MRS. PEACHUM: What got into you? This is our reward for all we've done, Jonathan. I'm going mad. My head is swimming. I'm going to faint. Oh! (She faints.) A glass of Cordial Médoc.

PEACHUM: You see what you've done to your mother. Quick! Associating with criminals, that's lovely, that's delightful! Interesting how the poor woman takes it to heart. (POLLY brings in a bottle of Cordial Médoc.) That's the only consolation your poor mother has left.

POLLY: Go ahead, give her two glasses. My mother can take twice as much when she's not quite herself. That will put her back on her feet. (During the whole scene she looks very happy.)

MRS. PEACHUM (wakes up): Oh, there she goes again, pretending to be so loving and sympathetic!

(Five men enter.)

BEGGAR: I'm making a complaint, see, this thing is a mess, it's not a proper stump, it's a botch-up, and I'm not wasting my money on it.

PEACHUM: What do you expect? It's as good a stump as any other; it's only that you don't keep it clean.

BEGGAR: Then why don't I take as much money as the others? Naw, you can't do that to me. (Throws down the stump.) If I wanted crap like this, I could cut off my real leg.

PEACHUM: What do you fellows want anyway? Is it my fault if people have hearts of flint? I can't make you five stumps. In five minutes I can turn any man into such a pitiful wreck it would make a dog weep to see him. Can I help it if people don't weep? Here's another stump for you if one's not enough. But look after your equipment!

BEGGAR: This one will do.

PEACHUM (tries a false limb on another): Leather is no good, Celia; rubber is more repulsive. (to the third) That swelling is going down and it's your last. Now we'll have to start all over again. (Examining the fourth.) Obviously natural scabies is never as good as the artificial kind. (to the fifth) You're a sight! You've been eating again. I'll have to make an example of you.

BEGGAR: Mr. Peachum, I really haven't eaten anything much. I'm just abnormally fat, I can't help it.

PEACHUM: Nor can I. You're fired. (Again to the second beggar.) My dear man, there's an obvious difference between "tugging at people's heart strings" and "getting on people's nerves." What I need is artists. Only an artist can tug at anybody's heart strings nowadays. If you fellows performed properly, your audience would be forced to applaud. You just haven't any ideas! So obviously I can't extend your engagement.

(The beggars go out.)

POLLY: Look at him. Is he particularly handsome? No. But he makes a living. He can support me. He is not only a first-class burglar but a farsighted and experienced stick-up man as well. I've been into it, I can tell you the exact amount of his savings to date. A few successful ventures and we shall be able to retire to a little house in the country just like that Mr. Shakespeare father admires so much.

PEACHUM: It's all perfectly simple. You're married. What does a girl do when she's married? Use your head. Well, she gets divorced, see, is that so hard to figure out?

POLLY: I don't know what you're talking about.

MRS. PEACHUM: Divorce.

POLLY: But I love him. How can I think of divorce?

MRS. PEACHUM: Really, have you no shame?

POLLY: Mother, if you've ever been in love . . .

MRS. PEACHUM: In love! Those damn books you've been reading have turned your head. Why, Polly, everybody's doing it.

POLLY: Then I'm an exception.

MRS. PEACHUM: Then I'm going to tan your behind, you exception.

POLLY: Oh yes, all mothers do that, but it doesn't help because love goes deeper than a tanned behind.

MRS. PEACHUM: Don't strain my patience.

POLLY: I won't let my love be taken away from me.

MRS. PEACHUM: One more word out of you and you'll get a clip on the ear.

POLLY: But love is the finest thing in the world.

MRS. PEACHUM: Anyway, he's got several women, the blackguard. When he's hanged, like as not half a dozen widows will turn up, each of them like as not with a brat in her arms. Oh, Jonathan!

PEACHUM: Hanged, what made you think of that,

that's a good idea. Run along, Polly. (POLLY *goes out.*) Quite right. That'll earn us forty pounds.

MRS. PEACHUM: I see. Report him to the sheriff.

PEACHUM: Naturally. And besides, that way we get him hanged free of charge . . . Two birds with one stone. Only we've got to find out where he's holed up.

MRS. PEACHUM: I can tell you that, my dear, he's holed up with his tarts.

PEACHUM: But they won't turn him in.

MRS. PEACHUM: Just let me attend to that. Money rules the world. I'll go to Turnbridge right away and talk to the girls. Give us a couple of hours, and after that if he meets a single one of them he's done for.

POLLY (*has been listening behind the door*): Dear mama, you can spare yourself the trip. Mac will go to the Old Bailey of his own accord sooner than meet any of those ladies. And even if he did go to the Old Bailey, the sheriff would serve him a cocktail; they'd smoke their cigars and have a little chat about a certain shop in this street where a little more goes on than meets the eye. Because, papa dear, the sheriff was very cheerful at my wedding.

PEACHUM: What's this sheriff called?

POLLY: He's called Brown. But you probably know him as Tiger Brown. Because everybody who has reason to fear him calls him Tiger Brown. But my husband, you see, calls him Jackie. Because to him he's just dear old Jackie. They're boyhood friends.

PEACHUM: Oh, so they're friends are they? The sheriff and Public Enemy No. 1, ha, they must be the only friends in this city.

POLLY (*poetically*): Every time they drank a cocktail together, they stroked each other's cheeks and said: "If you'll have the same again, I'll have the same again." And every time one of them left the room, the other's eyes grew moist and he said: "Where'er you go I shall be with you." There's nothing on record against Mac at Scotland Yard.

PEACHUM: I see. Between Tuesday evening and Thursday morning Mr. Macheath, a gentleman who has assuredly been married many times, enticed my daughter from her home on pretext of marriage. Before the week is out, he will be taken on that account to the gallows, which he has deserved. "Mr. Macheath, you once had white kid gloves, a cane with an ivory handle, and a scar on your neck, and frequented the Cuttlefish Hotel. All that is left is your scar, undoubtedly the least valuable of your distinguishing marks, and today you frequent nothing but prison cells, and within the foreseeable future, no place at all . . ."

MRS. PEACHUM: Oh, Jonathan, you'll never bring it off. Why, he's Mac the Knife, whom they call the biggest criminal in London. He takes what he pleases.

PEACHUM: Who's Mac the Knife? Get ready, we're going to see the Sheriff of London. And you're going to Turnbridge.

MRS. PEACHUM: To see his whores.

PEACHUM: For the villainy of the world is great, and a man needs to run his legs off to keep them from being stolen from under him.

POLLY: I, papa, shall be delighted to shake hands with Mr. Brown again.

(*All three step forward and sing the first finale. Song lighting. On the signs is written:*)

FIRST THREEPENNY FINALE
CONCERNING THE INSECURITY OF THE HUMAN STATE

POLLY:
> *Am I reaching for the sky?*
> *All I'm asking from this place is*
> *To enjoy a man's embraces.*
> *Is that aiming much too high?*

PEACHUM (*with a Bible in his hands*):
> *Man has a right, in this our brief existence*
> *To call some fleeting happiness his own*
> *Partake of worldly pleasures and subsistence*
> *And have bread on his table rather than a stone.*
> *Such are the basic rights of man's existence.*
> *But do we know of anything suggesting*
> *That when a thing's a right one gets it? No!*
> *To get one's rights would be most interesting*
> *But in our present state this can't be so.*

MRS. PEACHUM:
> *How I want what's best for you*
> *How I'd deal you all the aces*
> *Show you things and take you places*
> *As a mother likes to do.*

PEACHUM:
> *Let's practice goodness: who would disagree?*
> *Let's give our wealth away: is that not right?*
> *Once all are good His Kingdom is at hand*
> *Where blissfully we'll bask in His pure light.*
> *Let's practice goodness: who would disagree?*
> *But sadly on this planet while we're waiting*
> *The means are meager and the morals low.*
> *To get one's record straight would be elating*
> *But in our present state this can't be so.*

POLLY AND MRS. PEACHUM:
> *And that is all there is to it.*
> *The world is poor, and man's a shit.*

PEACHUM:

> Of course that's all there is to it.
> The world is poor, and man's a shit.
> Who wouldn't like an earthly paradise?
> Yet our condition's such it can't arise.
> Out of the question in our case.
> Let's say your brother's close to you
> But if there's not enough for two
> He'll kick you smartly in the face.
> You think that loyalty's no disgrace?
> But say your wife is close to you
> And finds she's barely making do
> She'll kick you smartly in the face.
> And gratitude: that's no disgrace
> But say your son is close to you
> And finds your pension's not come through
> He'll kick you smartly in the face.
> And so will all the human race.

POLLY AND MRS. PEACHUM:

> That's what you're all ignoring
> That's what's so bloody boring.
> The world is poor, and man's a shit
> And that is all there is to it.

PEACHUM:

> Of course that's all there is to it
> The world is poor, and man's a shit.
> We should aim high instead of low
> But in our present state this can't be so.

ALL THREE:

> Which means He has us in a trap:
> The whole damn thing's a load of crap.

PEACHUM:

> The world is poor, and man's a shit
> And that is all there is to it.

ALL THREE:

> That's what you're all ignoring
> That's what's so bloody boring.
> That's why He's got us in a trap
> And why it's all a load of crap.

ACT 2

4

Thursday afternoon: Mac the Knife takes leave of his wife and flees from his father-in-law to the heaths of Highgate.

(The Stable.)

POLLY *(enters)*: Mac! Mac, don't be frightened.
MAC *(lying on the bed)*: Well, what's up? Polly, you look a wreck.
POLLY: I've been to see Brown, my father went too, they decided to pull you in; my father made some terrible threats and Brown stood up for you, but then he weakened, and now he thinks too that you'd better bestir yourself and make yourself scarce for a while, Mac. You must pack right away.
MAC: Pack? Nonsense. Come here, Polly. You and I have got better things to do than pack.
POLLY: No, we mustn't now. I'm so frightened. All they talked about was hanging.
MAC: I don't like it when you're moody, Polly. There's nothing on record against me at Scotland Yard.
POLLY: Perhaps there wasn't yesterday, but today there's suddenly a terrible lot. You—I've brought the charges with me, I don't even know if I can get them straight, the list goes on and on—you've killed two shopkeepers, more than thirty burglaries, twenty-three hold-ups, and God knows how many acts of arson, attempted murder, forgery and perjury, all within eighteen months. You're a dreadful man. And in Winchester you seduced two sisters under the age of consent.
MAC: They told me they were over twenty. What did Brown say? *(He stands up slowly and goes whistling to the right along the footlights.)*
POLLY: He caught up with me in the corridor and said there was nothing he could do for you now. Oh, Mac! *(She throws herself on his neck.)*
MAC: All right, if I've got to go away, you'll have to run the business.
POLLY: Don't talk about business now, Mac, I can't bear it. Kiss your poor Polly again and swear that you'll never never be . . .

(MAC interrupts her brusquely and leads her to the table where he pushes her down in a chair.

MAC: Here are the ledgers. Listen carefully. This is a list of the personnel. *(Reads.)* Right. First of all, Crook-fingered Jake, a year and a half in the business. Let's see what he's brought in. One, two, three, four, five gold watches, not much but clean work. Don't sit on my lap, I'm not in the mood right now. Here's Dreary Walter, an unreliable dog. Sells stuff on the side. Give him three weeks grace, then get rid of him. Just turn him into Brown.
POLLY *(sobbing)*: Just turn him in to Brown.
MAC: Jimmy II, an impertinent bastard; good worker but impertinent. Swipes bed sheets right out from under ladies of the best society. Give him a rise.
POLLY: Give him a rise.
MAC: Robert the Saw: small potatoes, not a glimmer of genius. Won't end on the gallows, but he won't leave any estate either.

POLLY: Won't leave any estate either.

MAC: In all other respects you will carry on exactly the same as before. Get up at seven, wash, bathe once a week and so on.

POLLY: You're perfectly right. I've got to grit my teeth and attend to the business. What's yours is mine now, isn't it, Mackie? What about your rooms, Mac? Should I let them go? I don't like having to pay the rent.

MAC: No, I still need them.

POLLY: What for, it's just a waste of our money!

MAC: You seem to think I'm never coming back.

POLLY: What do you mean? You can rent other rooms. Mac . . . Mac, I can't go on. I keep looking at your lips and then I don't hear what you say. Will you be faithful to me, Mac?

MAC: Of course I'll be faithful, I'll do as I'm done by. Do you think I don't love you? It's only that I see farther ahead than you.

POLLY: I'm so grateful to you, Mac. Worrying about me when they're after you like bloodhounds . . .

(Hearing the word "bloodhounds" he goes stiff, stands up, goes to the right, throws off his coat and washes his hands.)

MAC *(hastily)*: You will go on sending the profits to Jack Poole's banking house in Manchester. Between you and me it's only a matter of weeks before I go over to banking altogether. It's safer and it's more profitable. In two weeks at the most the money will have to be taken out of this business, then off you go to Brown and give the list to the police. Within four weeks all this scum of humanity will be safely in the cells at the Old Bailey.

POLLY: Why, Mac! How can you look them in the eye when you've written them off and they're as good as hanged? How can you shake hands with them?

MAC: With who? Robert the Saw, Matt of the Mint, Crook-fingered Jake? Those jailbirds?

(Enter the gang.)

MAC: Gentlemen, it's a pleasure to see you.

POLLY: Good evening, gentlemen.

MATTHEW: Captain, I've got hold of the Coronation program. It looks to me like we have some days of very hard work ahead of us. The Archbishop of Canterbury is arriving in half an hour.

MAC: When?

MATTHEW: Five thirty. We'd better be shoving off, Captain.

MAC: Yes, you'd better be shoving off.

ROBERT: What do you mean: you?

MAC: For my part, I'm afraid I'm obliged to take a little trip.

ROBERT: Good God, are they out to nab you?

MATTHEW: It would be just now, with the Coronation coming up! A Coronation without you is soup without a spoon.

MAC: Shut your trap! In view of that, I am temporarily handing over the management of the business to my wife. *(He pushes her forward and goes to the rear where he observes her.)*

POLLY: Well, boys, I think the Captain can go away with an easy mind. We'll swing this job, you bet. What do you say, boys?

MATTHEW: It's not for me to say. But at a time like this I'm not sure that a woman . . . I'm not saying anything against you, Ma'am.

MAC *(from upstage)*: What do you say to that, Polly?

POLLY: You shit, that's a fine way to start in. *(Screaming.)* Of course you're not saying anything against me! If you were, these gentlemen would have ripped your pants off long ago and tanned your arse for you. Wouldn't you, gentlemen?

(Brief pause, then all clap like mad.)

JAKE: Yes, there's something in that, you can take her word for it.

WALTER: Hurrah, the missus knows how to lay it on! Hurrah for Polly!

ALL: Hurrah for Polly!

MAC: The rotten part of it is that I won't be here for the Coronation. There's a gilt-edged deal for you. In the daytime nobody's home and at night the toffs are all drunk. That reminds me, you drink too much, Matthew. Last week you were implying that it was you who set the Greenwich Children's Hospital on fire. If such a thing happens again, you're out. Who set the Children's Hospital on fire?

MATTHEW: I did.

MAC *(to the others)*: Who set it on fire?

THE OTHERS: You, Mr. Macheath.

MAC: So who did it?

MATTHEW *(sulkily)*: You, Mr. Macheath. At this rate our sort will never rise in the world.

MAC *(with a gesture of stringing up)*: You'll rise all right if you think you can compete with me. Who ever heard of one of those professors at Oxford College letting some assistant put his name to his errors? He puts his own.

ROBERT: Ma'am, while your husband is away, you're the boss. We settle up every Thursday, ma'am.

POLLY: Every Thursday, boys.

(The gang goes out.)

MAC: And now farewell, my heart. Look after your complexion, and don't forget to make up every day, exactly as if I were here. That's very important, Polly.

POLLY: And you, Mac, promise me you won't look at another woman and that you'll leave town right away. Believe me, it's not jealousy that makes your little Polly say that; no, it's very important, Mac.

MAC: Oh, Polly, why should I go round drinking up the empties? I love only you. As soon as the twilight is deep enough I'll take my black stallion from somebody's stable and before you can see the moon from your window, I'll be the other side of Highgate Heath.

POLLY: Oh, Mac, don't tear the heart out of my body. Stay with me and let us be happy.

MAC: But I must tear my own heart out of my body, for I must go away and no one knows when I shall return.

POLLY: It's been such a short time, Mac.

MAC: Does it have to be the end?

POLLY: Oh, last night I had a dream. I was looking out of the window and I heard laughter in the street, and when I looked out I saw our moon and the moon was all thin like a worn-down penny. Don't forget me, Mac, in strange cities.

MAC: Of course I won't forget you, Polly. Kiss me, Polly.

POLLY: Good-bye, Mac.

MAC: Good-bye, Polly. *(On his way out.)*
For love will endure or not endure
Regardless of where we are.

POLLY *(alone)*: He never will come back. *(She sings.)*

Nice while it lasted, and now it is over
Tear out your heart, and good-bye to your lover!
What's the use of grieving, when the mother that bore
*   you*
(Mary, pity women!) knew it all before you?

(The bells start ringing.)

POLLY:
Into this London the Queen now makes her way.
Where shall we be on Coronation Day?

INTERLUDE

(MRS. PEACHUM and LOW-DIVE JENNY step out before the curtain.

MRS. PEACHUM: So if you see Mac the Knife in the next few days, run to the nearest constable and turn him in; it'll get you ten shillings.

JENNY: Shall we see him, though, if the constables are after him? If the hunt is on, he won't go spending his time with us.

MRS. PEACHUM: Take it from me, Jenny, even with all London at his heels, Macheath is not the man to give up his habits. *(She sings.)*

THE BALLAD OF SEXUAL OBSESSION

1
There goes a man who's won his spurs in battle
The butcher, he. And all the others, cattle.
The cocky sod! No decent place lets him in.
Who does him down, that's done the lot? The women.
Want it or not, he can't ignore that call.
Sexual obsession has him in its thrall.
*   He doesn't read the Bible. He sniggers at the law.*
*   Sets out to be an utter egoist*
*   And knows a woman's skirts are what he must resist*
*   So when a woman calls he locks his door.*
*   So far, so good, but what's the future brewing?*
*   As soon as night falls he'll be up and doing.*

2
Thus many a man watched men die in confusion:
A mighty genius, stuck on prostitution!
The watchers claimed their urges were exhausted
But when they died who paid the funeral? Whores did.
Want it or not, they can't ignore that call.
Sexual obsession has them in its thrall.
*   Some fall back on the Bible. Some set out to change*
*   the law.*
*   Some turn to Christ. Others turn anarchist.*
*   At lunch you pick the best wine on the list*
*   Then meditate till half past four.*
*   At tea: what high ideals you are pursuing!*
*   Then soon as night falls you'll be up and doing.*

5

Before the coronation bells had died away, Mac the Knife was sitting with the whores of Turnbridge. The whores betray him. It is Thursday evening.

(Whorehouse in Turnbridge.)
(An afternoon like any other; the whores, mostly in their shifts, are ironing clothes, playing draughts, or washing: a bourgeois idyll. CROOK-FINGERED JAKE is reading the newspaper. No one is paying attention to him. He is rather in the way.)

JAKE: He won't come today.

WHORE: No?

JAKE: I don't think he'll ever come again.

WHORE: That would be too bad.

JAKE: Think so? If I know him, he's out of town by now. This time he's cleared out.

(Enter MACHEATH, hangs his hat on a nail, sits down on the sofa behind the table.)

MAC: My coffee!

VIXEN *(repeats admiringly)*: "My coffee!"

JAKE *(horrified)*: How come you're not in Highgate?

MAC: It's my Thursday. Do you think I can let such trifles interfere with my habits? *(Throws the warrant on the floor.)* Anyhow, it's raining.

JENNY *(reads the warrant)*: In the name of the Queen, Captain Macheath is charged with three . . .

JAKE *(takes it away from her)*: Am I in it too?

MAC: Naturally, the whole team.

JENNY *(to the other whore)*: Look, that's the warrant. *(Pause.)* Mac, let's see your hand. *(He gives her his hand.)*

DOLLY: That's right, Jenny, read his palm, you're so good at it. *(Holds up an oil lamp.)*

MAC: Coming into money?

JENNY: No, not coming into money.

BETTY: What's that look for, Jenny? It gives me the shivers.

MAC: A long journey?

JENNY: No, no long journey.

VIXEN: What do you see?

MAC: Only the good things, not the bad, please.

JENNY: Oh well, I see a narrow dark place and not much light. And then I see a big T, that means a woman's treachery. And then I see . . .

MAC: Stop, I'd like some details about that narrow dark place and the treachery. What's this treacherous woman's name?

JENNY: All I see is it begins with a J.

MAC: Then you've got it wrong. It begins with a P.

JENNY: Mac, when the Coronation bells start ringing at Westminster, you'll be in for a sticky time.

MAC: Go on! *(JAKE laughs uproariously.)* What's the matter? *(He runs over to JAKE, and reads.)* They've got it wrong, there were only three.

JAKE *(laughs)*: Exactly.

MAC: Nice underwear you've got there.

WHORE: From the cradle to the grave, underwear first, last and all the time.

OLD WHORE: I never wear silk. Makes gentlemen think you've got something wrong with you.

(JENNY slips stealthily out by the door.)

SECOND WHORE *(to JENNY)*: Where are you off to, Jenny?

JENNY: You'll see. *(Goes out.)*

MOLLY: But homespun underwear can put them off, too.

OLD WHORE: I've had very good results with homespun underwear.

VIXEN: It makes the gentlemen feel at home.

MAC *(to BETTY)*: Have you still got the black lace border?

BETTY: Still the black lace border.

MAC: What kind of underwear do you have?

SECOND WHORE: Oh, I don't like to tell you. I can't take anybody to my room because my aunt is so crazy about men, and in doorways, you know, I just don't wear any. *(JAKE laughs.)*

MAC: Finished?

JAKE: No, I've just got to the rapes.

MAC *(back by the sofa)*: But where's Jenny? Ladies, long before my star rose over this city . . .

VIXEN: "Long before my star rose over this city . . ."

MAC: . . . I lived in the most impoverished circumstances with one of you, dear ladies. And though today I am Mac the Knife, my good fortune will never lead me to forget the companions of my dark days, especially Jenny, whom I loved the best of all. Now listen, please.

(While MAC sings, JENNY stands to the right outside the window and beckons to CONSTABLE SMITH. Then MRS. PEACHUM joins her. The three stand under the street lamp and watch the house.)

BALLADE OF IMMORAL EARNINGS

1

MAC:

> There was a time, now very far away
> When we set up together, I and she.
> I'd got the brain, and she supplied the breast.
> I saw her right, and she supported me—
> A way of life then, if not quite the best.
> And when a client came I'd slide out of our bed
> And treat him nice, and go and have a drink instead
> And when he paid up I'd address him: Sir
> Come any time you feel you fancy her.
> That time's long past, but what would I not give
> To see that whorehouse where we used to live?

(JENNY appears in the door, SMITH behind her.)

2

JENNY:

> That was the time, now very far away
> He was so sweet and bashed me where it hurt.
> And when the cash ran out the feathers really flew
> He'd up and say: I'm going to pawn your skirt.
> A skirt is nicer, but no skirt will do.
> Just like his cheek, he had me fairly stewing
> I'd ask him straight to say what he thought he was doing
> Then he'd lash out and would knock me headlong downstairs.
> I had the bruises off and on for years.

BOTH:

> That time's long past, but what would I not give
> To see that whorehouse where we used to live?

3

BOTH *(together and alternating)*:

> That was the time, now very far away

MAC:
> *Not that the bloody times seem to have looked up.*

JENNY:
> *When afternoons were all I had for you*

MAC:
> *I told you she was generally booked up.*
> *(The night's more normal, but daytime will do.)*

JENNY:
> *Once I was pregnant, so the doctor said.*

MAC:
> *So we reversed positions on the bed.*

JENNY:
> *He thought his weight would make it premature.*

MAC:
> *But in the end we flushed it down the sewer.*
> *That could not last, but what would I not give*
> *To see the whorehouse where we used to live?*

(Dance. MAC *picks up his sword stick, she hands him his hat, he is still dancing when* SMITH *lays a hand on his shoulder.)*

SMITH: Coming quietly?

MAC: Is there only one way out of this dump?

*(*SMITH *tries to put the handcuffs on* MACHEATH; MAC *gives him a push in the chest and he reels back.* MAC *jumps out of the window. Outside stands* MRS. PEACHUM *with constables.)*

MAC *(with poise, very politely)*: Good afternoon, ma'am.

MRS. PEACHUM: My dear Mr. Macheath. My husband says the greatest heroes in history have tripped over this humble threshold.

MAC: May I ask how your husband is doing?

MRS. PEACHUM: Better, thank you. I'm so sorry, you'll have to be bidding the charming ladies good-bye now. Come constable, escort the gentleman to his new home. *(He is led away.* MRS. PEACHUM *through the window.)* Ladies, if you wish to visit him, you'll invariably find him in. From now on the gentleman's address will be the Old Bailey. I knew he'd be in to see his whores. I'll settle the bill. Good-bye ladies. *(Goes out.)*

JENNY: Wake up, Jake, something has happened.

JAKE *(who has been too immersed in his reading to notice anything)*: Where's Mac?

JENNY: The coppers were here.

JAKE: Good God! And me just reading, reading, reading . . . Boy, oh boy, oh boy! *(Goes out.)*

6

Betrayed by the whores, Mac is freed from prison by the love of yet another woman.

(The Old Bailey, a cage.)
(Enter BROWN.*)*

BROWN: If only my men don't catch him! Good God, I only hope he's riding out beyond Highgate Heath, thinking of his Jackie. But he's so frivolous, like all great men. If they bring him in now and he looks at me with his faithful friendly eyes, I won't be able to bear it. Thank God, at least the moon is shining; if he is riding across the heath, at least he won't stray from the path. *(Sounds backstage.)* What's that? Oh, my God, they're bringing him in.

MAC *(tied with heavy ropes, accompanied by six constables, enters with head erect)*: Well, flatfeet, thank God we're home again. *(He notices* BROWN *who has fled to the far corner of the cell.)*

BROWN *(after a long pause, under the withering glance of his former friend)*: Oh, Mac, it wasn't me . . . I did everything in my . . . don't look at me like that, Mac . . . I can't stand it . . . Your silence is killing me. *(Shouts at one of the constables.)* Stop tugging at that rope, you swine . . . Say something, Mac. Say something to your poor Jackie . . . A kind word in his tragic . . . *(Rests his head against the wall and weeps.)* He doesn't deem me worthy even of a word. *(Goes out.)*

MAC: That miserable Brown. The living picture of a bad conscience. And he calls himself a chief of police. It was a good idea not shouting at him. I was going to at first. But then it occurred to me in the nick of time that a deep withering stare would send much colder shivers down his spine. It worked. I looked at him and he wept bitterly. That's a trick I got from the Bible.

(Enter SMITH *with handcuffs.)*

MAC: Well, Mr. Warder, I suppose these are the heaviest you've got? With your kind permission I should like to apply for a more comfortable pair. *(He takes out his checkbook.)*

SMITH: Of course, Captain, we've got them here at every price. It all depends on how much you want to spend. From one guinea to ten.

MAC: How much would none at all cost?

SMITH: Fifty.

MAC *(writes a check)*: But the worst of it is that now this business with Lucy is bound to come out. If Brown hears that I've been carrying on with his daughter behind his friendly back, he'll turn into a tiger.

SMITH: As you make your bed, so must you lie on it.

MAC: I'll bet you the tart is waiting outside right now. I can see happy days between now and the execution.

> Is this a life for one of my proud station?
> I take it, I must frankly own, amiss.
> From childhood up, I heard with consternation:
> One must live well to know what living is!

(Song lighting: golden glow. The organ is lit up. Three lamps are lowered on a pole, and the signs say:)

BALLADE OF GOOD LIVING

1

I've heard them praising single-minded spirits
Whose empty stomachs show they live for knowledge
In rat-infested shacks awash with ullage.
I'm all for culture, but there are some limits.
The simple life is fine for those it suits.
I don't find, for my part, that it attracts.
There's not a bird from here to Halifax
Would peck at such unappetizing fruits.
What use is freedom? None, to judge from this.
One must live well to know what living is.

2

The dashing sort who cut precarious capers
And go and risk their necks just for the pleasure
Then swagger home and write it up at leisure
And flog the story to the Sunday papers—
If you could see how cold they get at night
Sullen, with chilly wife, climbing to bed
And how they dream they're going to get ahead
And how they see time stretching out of sight—
Now tell me, who would choose to live like this?
One must live well to know what living is.

3

There's plenty that they have. I know I lack it
And ought to join their splendid isolation
But when I gave them more consideration
I told myself: my friend, that's not your racket.
Suffering ennobles, but it can depress.
The paths of glory lead but to the grave.
You once were poor and lonely, wise and brave.
You ought to try to bite off rather less.
The search for happiness boils down to this:
One must live well to know what living is.

(Enter LUCY.)

LUCY: You dirty dog, you—how can you look me in the face after all there's been between us?

MAC: Have you no bowels, no tenderness, my dear Lucy, seeing a husband in such circumstances?

LUCY: A husband! You monster! So you think I haven't heard about your goings-on with Miss Peachum! I could scratch your eyes out!

MAC: Seriously, Lucy, you're not fool enough to be jealous of Polly?

LUCY: You're married to her, aren't you, you beast?

MAC: Married! It's true, I go to the house, I chat with the girl. I kiss her, and now the silly jade goes about telling everyone that I'm married to her. I am ready, my dear Lucy, to give you satisfaction—if you think there is any in mar-

riage. What can a man of honor say more? He can say nothing more.

LUCY: Oh, Mac, I only want to become an honest woman.

MAC: If you think marriage with me will . . . all right. What can a man of honor say more? He can say nothing more.

(Enter POLLY.)

POLLY: Where is my dear husband? Oh, Mac, there you are. Why do you turn away from me? It's your Polly. It's your wife.

LUCY: Oh, you miserable villain!

POLLY: Oh, Mackie in prison! Why didn't you ride across Highgate Heath? You told me you wouldn't see those women any more. I knew what they'd do to you; but I didn't say anything, because I believed you, Mac, I'll stay with you till death.—Not one kind word, Mac? Not one kind look? Oh, Mac, think what your Polly must be suffering to see you in this condition.

LUCY: Oh, the slut.

POLLY: What does this mean, Mac? Who on earth is that? You might at least tell her who I am. Tell her I'm your wife, will you? Aren't I your wife? Look at me. Tell me, aren't I your wife?

LUCY: You low-down sneak! Have you got two wives, you monster?

POLLY: Say something, Mac. Aren't I your wife? Haven't I done everything for you? I was innocent when I married, you know that. Why, you even put me in charge of the gang, and I've done everything the way we arranged, and Jake wants me to tell you that he . . .

MAC: If you two could only shut your traps for two minutes I'll explain everything.

LUCY: No, I won't shut my trap, I can't bear it. It's more than flesh and blood can bear.

POLLY: Yes, my dear, naturally the wife has . . .

LUCY: The wife!

POLLY: . . . the wife deserves some preference. Or at least the appearance of it, my dear. All this fuss and bother will drive the poor man mad.

LUCY: Fuss and bother, that's a good one. What have you gone and picked up now? This filthy little tart! So this is your great conquest! So this is your Rose of Old Soho!

(Song lighting: golden glow. The organ is lit up. Three lamps are lowered on a pole and the signs say:)

JEALOUSY DUET

1

LUCY:

Come on out, you Rose of Old Soho!
Let us see your legs, my little sweetheart!
I hear you have a lovely ankle

And I'd love to see such a complete tart.
They tell me that Mac says your behind is so provoking.
POLLY:
Did he now, did he now?
LUCY:
If what I see is true he must be joking.
POLLY:
Is he now, is he now?
LUCY:
Ho, it makes me split my sides!
POLLY:
Oh, that's how you split your side?
LUCY:
Fancy you as Mackie's bride!
POLLY:
Mackie fancies Mackie's bride.
LUCY:
Ha ha ha! Catch him sporting
With something that the cat brought in.
POLLY:
Just you watch your tongue, my dear.
LUCY:
Must I watch my tongue, my dear?
BOTH:
Mackie and I, see how we bill and coo, man
He's got no eyes for any other woman.
The whole thing's an invention
You mustn't pay attention
To such a bitch's slanders.
Poppycock!

2
POLLY:
Oh, they call me Rose of Old Soho
And Macheath appears to find me pretty.
LUCY:
Does he now?
POLLY:
They say I have a lovely ankle
And the best proportions in the city.
LUCY:
Little whippersnapper?
POLLY:
Who's a little whippersnapper?
Mac tells me that he finds my behind is most provoking.
LUCY:
Doesn't he? Doesn't he?
POLLY:
I do not suppose that he is joking.
LUCY:
Isn't he, isn't he?
POLLY:
Ho, it makes me split my sides!
LUCY:
Oh, that's how you split your side?
POLLY:
Being Mackie's only bride!

LUCY:
Are you Mackie's only bride?
POLLY (to the audience):
Can you really picture him sporting
With something that the cat brought in?
LUCY:
Just you watch your tongue, my dear.
POLLY:
Must I watch my tongue, my dear?
BOTH:
Mackie and I, see how we bill and coo, man
He's got no eyes for any other woman.
The whole thing's an invention
You cannot pay attention
To such a bitch's slanders.
Poppycock!

MAC: All right, Lucy. Calm down. You see it's just a trick of Polly's. She wants to come between us. I'm going to be hanged and she wants to parade as my widow. Really, Polly, this isn't the moment.

POLLY: Have you the heart to disclaim me?

MAC: And have you the heart to go on about my being married? Oh, Polly, why must you add to my misery? (*Shakes his head reproachfully.*) Polly! Polly!

LUCY: It's true, Miss Peachum, you're putting yourself in a bad light. Quite apart from the fact that it's barbarous of you to worry a gentleman in his situation!

POLLY: The most elementary rules of decency, my dear young lady, ought to teach you, it seems to me, to treat a man with a little more reserve when his wife is present.

MAC: Seriously, Polly, that's carrying a joke too far.

LUCY: And if, my dear lady, you start raising a row here in this prison, I shall be obliged to send for the warder to show you the door. I'm sorry, my dear Miss Peachum.

POLLY: Mrs., if you please! Mrs. Macheath. Just let me tell you this, young lady. The airs you give yourself are most unbecoming. My duty obliges me to stay with my husband.

LUCY: What's that? What's that? Oh, she won't leave! She stands there and we throw her out and she won't leave! Must I speak more plainly?

POLLY: You—you just hold your filthy tongue, you slut, or I'll knock your block off, my dear young lady.

LUCY: You've been thrown out, you interloper! I suppose that's not clear enough. You don't understand nice manners.

POLLY: You and your nice manners! Oh, I'm forgetting my dignity! I shouldn't stoop to . . . no, I shouldn't. (*She starts to bawl.*)

LUCY: Just look at my belly, you slut! Did I get that

from out of nowhere? Haven't you eyes in your head?

POLLY: Oh! So you're in the family way! And you think that gives you rights? A fine lady like you, you shouldn't have let him in!

MAC: Polly!

POLLY (in tears): This is really too much. Mac, you shouldn't have done that. Now I don't know what to do.

(Enter MRS. PEACHUM.)

MRS. PEACHUM: I knew it. She's with her man. You little trollop, come here immediately. When they hang your man, you can hang yourself too. A fine way to treat your respectable mother, making her come and get you out of jail. And he's got two of them, what's more—the Nero!

POLLY: Leave me here, mama; you don't know . . .

MRS. PEACHUM: You're coming home this minute.

LUCY: There you are, it takes your mama to tell you how to behave.

MRS. PEACHUM: Get going.

POLLY: Just a second. I only have to . . . I only have to tell him something . . . Really . . . it's very important.

MRS. PEACHUM (giving her a box on the ear): Well, this is important too. Get going!

POLLY: Oh, Mac! (She is dragged away.)

MAC: Lucy, you were magnificent. Of course I felt sorry for her. That's why I couldn't treat the slut as she deserved. Just for a moment you thought there was some truth in what she said. Didn't you?

LUCY: Yes, my dear, so I did.

MAC: If there were any truth in it, her mother wouldn't have put me in this situation. Did you hear how she laid into me? A mother might treat a seducer like that, not a son-in-law.

LUCY: It makes me so happy to hear you say that from the bottom of your heart. I love you so much I'd almost rather see you on the gallows than in the arms of another. Isn't that strange?

MAC: Lucy, I should like to owe you my life.

LUCY: It's wonderful the way you say that. Say it again.

MAC: Lucy, I should like to owe you my life.

LUCY: Shall I run away with you, dearest?

MAC: Well, but you see, if we run away together, it will be hard for us to hide. As soon as they stop looking, I'll send for you post haste, you know that!

LUCY: What can I do to help you?

MAC: Bring me my hat and cane.

(LUCY comes back with his hat and cane and throws them into his cage.)

MAC: Lucy, the fruit of our love which you bear beneath your heart will hold us forever united.

(LUCY goes out.)

SMITH (enters, goes into the cage, and says to MAC): Let's have that cane.

(After a brief chase, in which SMITH pursues MAC with a chair and a crowbar, MAC jumps over the bars. Constables run after him. Enter BROWN)

BROWN (off): Hey, Mac!—Mac, answer me, please. It's Jackie. Mac, please be a good boy, answer me, I can't stand it any longer. (Goes in.) Mackie! What's this? He's gone, thank God! (He sits down on the bed.)

(Enter PEACHUM.)

PEACHUM (to SMITH): My name is Peachum. I've come to collect the forty pounds reward for the capture of the bandit Macheath. (Appears in front of the cage.) Excuse me! Is that Mr. Macheath? (BROWN is silent.) Oh. I suppose the other gentleman has gone for a stroll? I come here to visit a criminal, and who do I find sitting here but Mr. Brown! Tiger Brown is sitting here and his friend Macheath is not sitting here.

BROWN (groaning): Oh, Mr. Peachum, it wasn't my fault.

PEACHUM: Of course not. How could it be? You yourself would never . . . when you think of the situation it'll land you in . . . it's out of the question, Brown.

BROWN: Mr. Peachum, I'm beside myself.

PEACHUM: I believe you. You must be feeling terrible.

BROWN: Yes, it's this feeling of helplessness that gets a man down. Those fellows do just as they please. It's dreadful, dreadful.

PEACHUM: Wouldn't you care to lie down awhile? Just close your eyes and pretend nothing has happened. Imagine you're on a lovely green meadow with little white clouds overhead. The main thing is to forget all about those terrible things, those that are past, and most of all, those that are still to come.

BROWN (alarmed): What do you mean by that?

PEACHUM: I'm amazed at your fortitude. In your position, I should simply collapse, crawl into bed and drink hot tea. And above all, I'd find someone to lay a soothing hand on my forehead.

BROWN: Damn it all, it's not my fault if the fellow escapes. There's not much the police can do about it.

PEACHUM: I see. There's not much the police can do about it. You don't believe we'll see Mr. Macheath back here again? (BROWN shrugs his shoulders.) In that case, your fate will be hideously unjust. People are sure to say—they always do—that the police shouldn't have let him escape. No, I can't see that glittering Coronation procession just yet.

BROWN: What do you mean?

PEACHUM: Let me remind you of a historical incident which, despite having caused a great stir at the time, in the year 1400 B.C., is unknown to the public of today. On the death of the Egyptian king Ramses II, the police captain of Nineveh, or it may have been Cairo, committed some minor offense against the lower classes of the population. Even at that time the consequences were terrible. As the history books tell us, the coronation procession of Semiramis, the new queen, "developed into a series of catastrophes because of the unduly active participation of the lower orders." Historians still shudder at the cruel way Semiramis treated her police captain. I only remember dimly, but there was some talk of snakes that she fed on his bosom.

BROWN: Really?

PEACHUM: The Lord be with you, Brown. *(Goes out.)*

BROWN: Now only the mailed fist can help. Sergeants! Report to me on the double!

(Curtain. MACHEATH *and* LOW-DIVE JENNY *step before the curtain and sing to song lighting.)*

SECOND THREEPENNY FINALE

WHAT KEEPS MANKIND ALIVE?

1

MAC:

You gentlemen who think you have a mission
To purge us of the seven deadly sins
Should first sort out the basic food position
Then start your preaching: that's where it begins.
You lot, who preach restraint and watch your waist as well
Should learn for all time how the world is run:
However much you twist, whatever lies you tell
Food is the first thing. Morals follow on.
So first make sure that those who now are starving
Get proper helpings when we all start carving.

VOICE *(off)*:

What keeps mankind alive?

MAC:

What keeps mankind alive? The fact that millions
Are daily tortured, stifled, punished, silenced, op-
pressed.
Mankind can keep alive thanks to its brilliance
In keeping its humanity repressed.

CHORUS:

For once you must try not to shirk the facts.
Mankind is kept alive by bestial acts.

2

JENNY:

You say that girls may strip with your permission.
You draw the lines dividing art from sin.
So first sort out the basic food position
Then start your preaching: that's where we begin.
You lot, who bank on your desires and our disgust
Should learn for all time how the world is run:
Whatever lies you tell, however much you twist
Food is the first thing. Morals follow on.
So first make sure that those who now are starving
Get proper helpings when we all start carving.

VOICE *(off)*:

What keeps mankind alive?

JENNY:

What keeps mankind alive? The fact that millions
Are daily tortured, stifled, punished, silenced, op-
pressed.
Mankind can keep alive thanks to its brilliance
In keeping its humanity repressed.

CHORUS:

For once you must try not to shirk the facts:
Mankind is kept alive by bestial acts.

7

That night Peachum prepares his campaign. He plans to disrupt the coronation procession by a demonstration of human misery.

(Peachum's Outfitting Shop for Beggars.)
(The beggars paint little signs with inscriptions such as "I gave my eye for my king," etc.)

PEACHUM: Gentlemen, at this moment, in our eleven branches from Drury Lane to Turnbridge, one thousand four hundred and thirty-two gentlemen are working on signs like these with a view to attending the Coronation of our Queen.

MRS. PEACHUM: Get a move on! If you won't work, you can't beg. Call yourself a blind man and can't even make a proper K? That's supposed to be child's writing, anyone would take it for an old man's.

(A drum roll.)

BEGGAR: That's the Coronation guard presenting arms. Little do they suspect that today, the biggest day in their military careers, they'll have us to deal with.

FILCH *(enters and reports)*: Mrs. Peachum, there's a dozen sleepy-looking hens traipsing in. They claim there's some money due them.

(Enter the WHORES.*)*

JENNY: Madam . . .

MRS. PEACHUM: Hm, you look as if you'd fallen off

your perches. I suppose you've come to collect the money for that Macheath of yours? Well, you'll get nothing, do you understand, nothing.

JENNY: How are we to understand that, ma'am?

MRS. PEACHUM: Bursting in here in the middle of the night! Coming to a respectable house at three in the morning! With the work you do, I should think you'd want some sleep. You look like sicked-up milk.

JENNY: Then you won't give us the stipulated fee for turning in Mr. Macheath, ma'am?

MRS. PEACHUM: Exactly. No thirty pieces of silver for you.

JENNY: Why not, ma'am?

MRS. PEACHUM: Because your fine Mr. Macheath has scattered himself to the four winds. And now, ladies, get out of my parlor.

JENNY: This is too much. Just don't you try that on us. That's all I've got to say to you. Not on us.

MRS. PEACHUM: Filch, the ladies wish to be shown the door.

(FILCH goes toward the ladies, JENNY pushes him away.)

JENNY: I'd advise you to hold your filthy tongue. If you don't, I'm likely to . . .

(Enter PEACHUM.)

PEACHUM: What's going on, you haven't given them any money, I hope? Well, ladies, how about it? Is Mr. Macheath in jail, or isn't he?

JENNY: Don't talk to me about Mr. Macheath. You're not fit to black his boots. Last night I had to let a customer go because it made me cry into my pillow to think how I had sold that gentleman to you. Yes, ladies, and what do you think happened this morning? Less than an hour ago, just after I had cried myself to sleep, I heard somebody whistle, and out on the street stood the very gentleman I'd been crying about, asking me to throw down the key. He wanted to lie in my arms and make me forget the wrong I had done him. Ladies, he's the last gentleman left in London. And if our friend Suky Tawdry isn't here with us now, it's because he went on from me to her to comfort her too.

PEACHUM (muttering to himself): Suky Tawdry . . .

JENNY: So now you know that you're not fit to black that gentleman's boots. You miserable stool-pigeon.

PEACHUM: Filch, run to the nearest police station, tell them Mr. Macheath is at Miss Suky Tawdry's place. (FILCH goes out.) But ladies, why are we arguing? The money will be paid out, that goes without saying. Celia dear, you'd do better to make the ladies some coffee instead of slanging them.

MRS PEACHUM (on her way out): Suky Tawdry! (She sings the third stanza of the Ballade of Sexual Obsession.)

There stands a man. The gallows loom above him.
They've got the quicklime mixed in which to shove him.
They've put his neck just under where the noose is
And what's he thinking of, the idiot? Floozies.
They've all but hanged him, yet he can't ignore that call.
Sexual obsession has him in its thrall.
   She's sold him down the river heart and soul
   He's seen the dirty money in her hand
   And bit by bit begins to understand:
   The pit that covers him is woman's hole.
   Then he may rant and roar and curse his ruin—
   But soon as night falls he'll be up and doing.

PEACHUM: Get a move on, you'd all be rotting in the sewers of Turnbridge if in my sleepless nights I hadn't worked out how to squeeze a penny out of your poverty. I discovered that though the rich of this earth find no difficulty in creating misery, they can't bear to see it. Because they are weaklings and fools just like you. They may have enough to eat till the end of their days, they may be able to wax their floors with butter so that even the crumbs from their tables grow fat, but they can't look on unmoved while a man is collapsing from hunger, though of course that only applies so long as he collapses outside their own front door.

(Enter MRS. PEACHUM with a tray full of coffee cups.)

MRS. PEACHUM: You can come by the shop tomorrow and pick up your money, but only when the Coronation's over.

JENNY: Mrs. Peachum, you leave me speechless.

PEACHUM: Fall in. We assemble in one hour outside Buckingham Palace. Quick march.

(The beggars fall in.)

FILCH (dashes in): Cops! I didn't even get to the police station. The police are here already.

PEACHUM: Hide, gentlemen! (to MRS. PEACHUM): Call the band together. Shake a leg. And if you hear me say "harmless," do you understand, harmless . . .

MRS. PEACHUM: Harmless? I don't understand a thing.

PEACHUM: Naturally you don't understand. Well, if I say harmless . . . (Knocking at the door.) Thank God, this is the answer, harmless, then you play some kind of music. Get a move on!

(MRS. PEACHUM goes out with some beggars. The others except for the girl with the sign "A Victim of Military

Tyranny," hide with their things upstage right behind the clothes rack. Enter BROWN *and constables.)*

BROWN: Here we are. And now Mr. Beggar's Friend, drastic action will be taken. Put him in chains, Smith. Oh, here are some of those delightful signs. *(to the girl)* "A Victim of Military Tyranny"—is that you?

PEACHUM: Good morning, Brown, good morning. Sleep well?

BROWN: Huh?

PEACHUM: Morning, Brown.

BROWN: Is he saying that to me? Does he know one of you? I don't believe I have the pleasure of your acquaintance.

PEACHUM: Really? Morning, Brown.

BROWN: Knock his hat off.

*(*SMITH *does so.)*

PEACHUM: Look here, Brown, as long as you're *passing by, passing,* I say, Brown, I may as well ask you to put a certain Macheath under lock and key, it's high time.

BROWN: The man's mad. Don't laugh, Smith. Tell me, Smith, how is it possible that such a notorious criminal should be running around loose in London?

PEACHUM: Because he's your friend, Brown.

BROWN: Who?

PEACHUM: Mac the Knife. Not me, I'm no criminal. I'm a poor man, Brown. You can't abuse me, Brown, you've got the worst hour in your life ahead of you. Care for some coffee? *(to the whores)* Girls, give the chief of police a sip, that's no way to behave. Let's all be friends. We are all law-abiding people! The law was made for one thing alone, for the exploitation of those who don't understand it, or are prevented by naked misery from obeying it. And anyone who wants a crumb of this exploitation for himself must obey the law strictly.

BROWN: I see, then you believe our judges are corruptible?

PEACHUM: Not at all, sir, not at all! Our judges are absolutely incorruptible: It's more than money can do to make them give a fair verdict!

(A second drum roll.)

PEACHUM: The troops are marching off to line the route. The poorest of the poor will move off in half an hour.

BROWN: That's right, Mr. Peachum. In half an hour the poorest of the poor will be marched off to winter quarters in the Old Bailey. *(to the constables)* All right, boys, round them all up, all the patriots you find here. *(to the beggars)* Have you fellows ever heard of Tiger Brown? Tonight,

Peachum, I've hit on the solution and, I believe I may say, saved a friend from mortal peril. I'll simply smoke out your whole nest. And lock up the lot of you for—hm, for what? For begging on the street. You seem to have intimated your intention of embarrassing me and the Queen with these beggars. I'll just arrest the beggars. Let that be a lesson to you.

PEACHUM: Excellent, but—what beggars?

BROWN: These cripples here. Smith, we'll take these patriots along with us.

PEACHUM: I can save you from a hasty step; you can thank the Lord, Brown, that you came to me. You see, Brown, you can arrest these few, they're harmless, *harmless . . .*

(Music starts up, playing a few measures of the "Song of the Insufficiency of Human Endeavor.")

BROWN: What's that?

PEACHUM: Music. They play as well as they can. The Song of Insufficiency. You don't know it? Let this be a lesson to you.

(Song lighting: golden glow. The organ is lit up. Three lamps are lowered from above on a pole and the signs say:)

SONG OF THE INSUFFICIENCY OF HUMAN ENDEAVOR

1
Mankind lives by its head
Its head won't see it through
Inspect your own. What lives off that?
At most a louse or two.
　　For this bleak existence
　　Man is never sharp enough.
　　Hence his weak resistance
　　To its tricks and bluff.

2
Aye, make yourself a plan
They need you at the top!
Then make yourself a second plan
Then let the whole thing drop.
　　For this bleak existence
　　Man is never bad enough
　　Though his sheer persistence
　　Can be lovely stuff.

3
Aye, race for happiness
But don't you race too fast.
When all chase after happiness
Happiness comes in last.
　　For this bleak existence
　　Man is never undemanding enough.
　　All his loud insistence
　　Is a load of guff.

PEACHUM: Your plan, Brown, was brilliant, but hardly realistic. All you can arrest in this place is a few young fellows celebrating their Queen's Coronation by arranging a little fancy dress party. When the real paupers come along—there aren't any here—there will be thousands of them. That's the point; you've forgotten what an immense number of poor people there are. When you see them standing outside the Abbey, it won't be a festive sight. You see, they don't look good. Do you know what the rose is, Brown? Yes, but how about a hundred thousand faces all flushed with the rose: Our young Queen's path should be strewn with roses not with the rose. And all those cripples at the church door. That's something one wishes to avoid, Brown. You'll probably say the police can handle us poor folk. You don't believe that yourself. How will it look if six hundred poor cripples have to be clubbed down at the Coronation? It will look bad. It will look disgusting. Nauseating. I feel faint at the thought of it, Brown. A small chair, if you please.

BROWN (to SMITH): That's a threat. See here, you, that's blackmail. We can't touch the man, in the interests of public order we simply can't touch him. I've never seen the like of it.

PEACHUM: You're seeing it now. Let me tell you something: You can behave as you please to the Queen of England. But you can't tread on the toes of the poorest man in England, or you'll be brought down, Mr. Brown.

BROWN: So you're asking me to arrest Mac the Knife? Arrest him? That's easy to say. You've got to find a man before you can arrest him.

PEACHUM: If you say that, I can't contradict you. So I'll find your man for you; we'll see if there's any morality left. Jenny, where is Mr. Macheath at this moment?

JENNY: 21 Oxford Street, at Suky Tawdry's.

BROWN: Smith, go at once to Suky Tawdry's place at 21 Oxford Street, arrest Macheath and take him to the Old Bailey. In the meantime, I must put on my gala uniform. On this day of all days I must wear my gala uniform.

PEACHUM: Brown, if he's not on the gallows by six o'clock . . .

BROWN: Oh, Mac, it was not to be. (Goes out with constables.)

PEACHUM (calling after him): That was a lesson to you, eh, Brown?

(Third drum roll.)

PEACHUM: Third drum roll. Change of direction. You will head for the dungeons of the Old Bailey. March!

(The beggars go out.)

PEACHUM (sings the fourth stanza of the "Song of the Insufficiency of Human Endeavor"):

> Man could be good instead
> So slug him on the head
> If you can slug him good and hard
> He may stay good and dead.
>   For this bleak existence
>   Man's not good enough just yet.
>   Don't wait for assistance,
>   Slug him on the head.

(Curtain. JENNY steps before the curtain with a hurdy-gurdy and sings the)

SOLOMON SONG

1

> You saw sagacious Solomon
> You know what came of him.
> To him complexities seemed plain.
> He cursed the hour that gave birth to him
> And saw that everything was vain.
> How great and wise was Solomon!
> But now that time is getting late
> The world can see what followed on.
> It's wisdom that had brought him to this state—
> How fortunate the man with none!

2

> You saw the lovely Cleopatra
> You know what she became.
> Two emperors slaved to serve her lust.
> She whored herself to death and fame
> Then rotted down and turned to dust.
> How beautiful was Babylon!
> But now that time is getting late
> The world can see what followed on.
> It's beauty that had brought her to this state—
> How fortunate the girl with none!

3

> You saw the gallant Caesar next
> You know what he became.
> They deified him in his life
> Then had him murdered just the same.
> And as they raised the fatal knife
> How loud he cried "You too, my son!"
> But now that time is getting late
> The world can see what followed on.
> It's courage that had brought him to this state—
> How fortunate the man with none!

4

> You know the ever-curious Brecht
> Whose songs you liked to hum.
> He asked, too often for your peace

Where rich men get their riches from.
So then you drove him overseas.
How curious was my mother's son!
But now that time is getting late
The world can see what followed on.
Inquisitiveness brought him to this state—
How fortunate the man with none!

5

And now look at this man Macheath
The sands are running out.
If only he'd known where to stop
And stuck to crimes he knew all about
He surely would have reached the top.
Then suddenly his heart was won.
But now that time is getting late
The world can see what followed on.
His sexual urges brought him to this state—
How fortunate the man with none!

8

Property in Dispute

(A young girl's room in the Old Bailey.)

SMITH *(enters)*: Miss, Mrs. Polly Macheath wishes to speak with you.

LUCY: Mrs. Macheath? Show her in.

(Enter POLLY.)

POLLY: Good morning, madam. Madam, good morning!

LUCY: What is it, please?

POLLY: Do you recognize me?

LUCY: Of course I know you.

POLLY: I've come to beg your pardon for the way I behaved yesterday.

LUCY: Very interesting.

POLLY: I have no excuse to offer for my behavior, madam, but my misfortunes.

LUCY: I see.

POLLY: Madam, you must forgive me. I was stung by Mr. Macheath's behavior. He really ought not to have put us in such a situation, and you can tell him so when you see him.

LUCY: I . . . I . . . shan't be seeing him.

POLLY: Of course you will see him.

LUCY: I shall not see him.

POLLY: Forgive me.

LUCY: But he's very fond of you.

POLLY: Oh no, you're the only one he loves. I'm sure of that.

LUCY: Very kind of you.

POLLY: But, madam, a man is always afraid of a woman who loves him too much. And then he's bound to neglect and avoid her. I could see at a glance that he is more devoted to you than I could ever have guessed.

LUCY: Do you mean that sincerely?

POLLY: Of course, certainly, very sincerely, madam. Do believe me.

LUCY: Dear Miss Polly, both of us have loved him too much.

POLLY: Perhaps. *(Pause.)* And now, madam, I want to tell you how it all came about. Ten days ago I met Mr. Macheath for the first time at the Cuttlefish Hotel. My mother was there too. Five days later, about the day before yesterday, we were married. Yesterday I found out that he was wanted by the police for a variety of crimes. And today I don't know what's going to happen. So you see, madam, twelve days ago I couldn't have imagined ever losing my heart to a man.

(Pause.)

LUCY: I understand, Miss Peachum.

POLLY: Mrs. Macheath.

LUCY: Mrs. Macheath.

POLLY: To tell the truth, I've been thinking about this man a good deal in the last few hours. It's not so simple. Because you see, miss, I really can't help envying you for the way he behaved to you the other day. When I left him, only because my mother made me, he didn't show the slightest sign of regret. Maybe he has no heart and nothing but a stone in his breast. What do you think, Lucy?

LUCY: Well, my dear miss—I really don't know if Mr. Macheath is entirely to blame. You should have stuck to your own class of people, dear miss.

POLLY: Mrs. Macheath.

LUCY: Mrs. Macheath.

POLLY: That's quite true—or at least, as my father always advised me, I should have kept everything on a strictly business footing.

LUCY: Definitely.

POLLY *(weeping)*: But he's my only possession in all the world.

LUCY: My dear, such a misfortune can befall the most intelligent woman. But after all, you are his wife on paper. That should be a comfort to you. Poor child, I can't bear to see you so depressed. Won't you have a little something?

POLLY: What?

LUCY: Something to eat.

POLLY: Oh yes, please, a little something to eat. *(LUCY goes out. POLLY aside.)* The hypocritical strumpet.

LUCY *(comes back with coffee and cake)*: Here. This ought to do it.

POLLY: You've really gone to too much trouble, madam. *(Pause. She eats.)* That's a lovely picture of him you've got. When did he bring it?

LUCY: Bring it?

POLLY (*innocently*): I mean when did he bring it up here to you?

LUCY: He didn't bring it.

POLLY: Did he give it to you right here in this room?

LUCY: He never was in this room.

POLLY: I see. But there wouldn't have been any harm in it. The paths of fate are so dreadfully crisscrossed.

LUCY: Must you keep talking such nonsense? You only came here to spy.

POLLY: Then you do know where he is?

LUCY: Me? Don't you know?

POLLY: Tell me this minute where he is?

LUCY: I have no idea.

POLLY: So you don't know where he is. Word of honor?

LUCY: No, I don't know. Hm, and you don't either?

POLLY: No. This is terrible. (POLLY *laughs and* LUCY *weeps.*) Now he has two commitments. And he's gone.

LUCY: I can't stand it any more. Oh, Polly, it's so dreadful.

POLLY (*gaily*): I'm so happy to have found such a good friend at the end of this tragedy. That's something. Would you like a little more to eat? Some more cake?

LUCY: Just a bit! Oh, Polly, don't be so good to me. Really, I don't deserve it. Oh, Polly, men aren't worth it.

POLLY: Of course men aren't worth it, but what else can we do?

LUCY: No! Now I'm going to make a clean breast of it. Will you be very cross with me, Polly?

POLLY: About what?

LUCY: It's not real!

POLLY: What?

LUCY: This here! (*She indicates her belly.*) And all for that criminal!

POLLY (*laughs*): Oh, that's magnificent! Is it a cushion? Oh, you really are a hypocritical strumpet! Look—you want Mackie? I'll make you a present of him. If you find him you can keep him. (*Voices and steps are heard in the corridor.*) What's that?

LUCY (*at the window*): Mackie! They've caught him once more.

POLLY (*collapses*): This is the end.

(*Enter* MRS. PEACHUM.)

MRS. PEACHUM: Ha, Polly, so this is where I find you. You must change your things, your husband is being hanged. I've brought your widow's weeds. (POLLY *changes into the widow's dress.*) You'll be a lovely widow. But you'll have to cheer up a little.

9

Five o'clock, Friday morning: Mac the Knife, who has been with the whores again, has again been betrayed by whores. He is about to be hanged.

(*Death cell.*)

(*The bells of Westminster ring. Constables bring* MACHEATH *shackled into the cell.*)

SMITH: Bring him in here. There go the bells of Westminster. Stand up straight, I'm not asking you why you look so worn out. I'd say you were ashamed. (*to the constables*) When the bells of Westminster ring for the third time, that will be at six, he's got to have been hanged. Make everything ready.

A CONSTABLE: For the last quarter of an hour all the streets around Newgate have been so jammed with people of every class you can't get through.

SMITH: Strange! Then they already know?

CONSTABLE: If this goes on, all London will know in another quarter of an hour. All the people who would otherwise have gone to the Coronation will come here. And the Queen will ride through empty streets.

SMITH: All the more reason for us to move fast. If we're through by six, that will give people time to get back to the Coronation by seven. So now, get going.

MAC: Hey, Smith, what time is it?

SMITH: Haven't you got eyes? Five-oh-four.

MAC: Five-oh-four.

(*Just as* SMITH *is locking the cell door from outside,* BROWN *enters.*)

BROWN (*his back to the cell, to* SMITH): Is he in there?

SMITH: You want to see him?

BROWN: No, no, no, for God's sake. I'll leave it all to you. (*Goes out.*)

MAC (*suddenly bursts into a soft unbroken flow of speech*): All right, Smith, I won't say a word, not a word about bribery, never fear. I know all about it. If you let yourself be bribed, you'd have to leave the country for a start. You certainly would. You'd need enough to live on for the rest of your life. A thousand pounds, eh? Don't say anything! In twenty minutes I'll tell you whether you can have your thousand pounds by noon. I'm not saying a word about feelings. Go outside and think it over carefully. Life is short and money is scarce. And I don't even know yet if I can raise any. But if anyone wants to see me, let them in.

SMITH (*slowly*): That's a lot of nonsense, Mr. Macheath. (*Goes out.*)

MAC (*sings softly and very fast the "Call from the Grave*:)

Hark to the voice that's calling you to weep.
Macheath lies here, not under open sky
Not under treetops, no, but good and deep.
Fate struck him down in outraged majesty.
God grant his dying words may reach a friend.
The thickest walls encompass him about.
Is none of you concerned to know his fate?
Once he is gone the bottles can come out
But do not stand by him while it's not too late.
D'you want his punishment to have no end?

(MATTHEW *and* JAKE *appear in the corridor. They are on their way to see* MACHEATH. SMITH *stops them.*)

SMITH: Well, son. You look like a soused herring.

MATTHEW: Now the Captain's gone it's my job to get our girls in the family way, so when they're brought into court they can plead irresponsibility. It's a job for a horse. I've got to see the Captain.

(*Both continue toward* MAC.)

MAC: Five twenty-five. You took your time.

JAKE: Yes, but, you see, we had to . . .

MAC: You see, you see, I'm being hanged, man! But I've no time to waste arguing with you. Five twenty-eight. All right: How much can you people draw from your savings account right away?

MATTHEW: From our . . . what, at five o'clock in the morning?

JAKE: Has it really come to this?

MAC: Can you manage four hundred pounds?

JAKE: But what about us? That's all there is.

MAC: Who's being hanged, you or me?

MATTHEW (*excitedly*): Who was lying around with Suky Tawdry instead of clearing out? Who was lying around with Suky Tawdry, us or you?

MAC: Shut your trap. I'll soon be lying somewhere other than with that slut. Five-thirty.

JAKE: Matt, if that's how it is, we'll just have to do it.

SMITH: Mr. Brown wishes to know what you'd like for your . . . meal.

MAC: Don't bother me. (*to* MATTHEW) Well, will you or won't you? (*to* SMITH) Asparagus.

MATTHEW: Don't you shout at me. I won't have it.

MAC: I'm not shouting at you. It's only that . . . Well Matthew, are you going to let me be hanged?

MATTHEW: Of course I'm not going to let you be hanged. Who said I was? But that's the lot. Four hundred pounds is all there is. No reason why I shouldn't say that, is there?

MAC: Five thirty-eight.

JAKE: We'll have to run, Matthew, or it'll be no good.

MATTHEW: If we can only get through. There's such a crowd. Scum of the earth! (*Both go out.*)

MAC: If you're not here by five to six, you'll never see me again. (*Shouts.*) You'll never see me again . . .

SMITH: They've gone. Well, what about it? (*Makes a gesture of counting money.*)

MAC: Four hundred. (SMITH *goes out shrugging his shoulders.* MAC, *calling after him.*) I've got to speak to Brown.

SMITH (*comes back with constables*): Got the soap?

CONSTABLE: Yes, but not the right kind.

SMITH: You can set the thing up in ten minutes.

CONSTABLE: But the trap doesn't work.

SMITH: It's got to work. The bells have gone a second time.

CONSTABLE: What a shambles!

MAC (*sings*):

Come here and see the shitty state he's in.
This really is what people mean by bust.
You who set up the dirty cash you win
As just about the only god you'll trust
Don't stand and watch him slipping round the bend!
Go to the Queen and say that her subjects need her
Go in a group and tell her of his trouble
Like pigs all following behind their leader.
Say that his teeth are wearing down to rubble.
D'you want his punishment to have no end?

SMITH: I can't possibly let you in. You're only number sixteen. Wait your turn.

POLLY: What do you mean, number sixteen? Don't be a bureaucrat. I'm his wife, I've got to see him.

SMITH: Not more than five minutes, then.

POLLY: Five minutes! That's perfectly ridiculous. Five minutes! How is one to say all one has to say? It's not so simple. This is good-bye forever. There's an exceptional amount of things for man and wife to talk about at such a moment . . . where is he?

SMITH: What, can't you see him?

POLLY: Yes, of course. Thank you.

MAC: Polly!

POLLY: Yes, Mackie, here I am.

MAC: Yes, of course!

POLLY: How are you? Are you quite worn out? It's hard!

MAC: But what will you do now? What will become of you?

POLLY: Don't worry, the business is doing very well. That's the least part of it. Are you very nervous, Mackie? . . .By the way, what was your father? There's so much you still haven't told me. I just don't understand. Your health has always been excellent.

MAC: Polly, can't you help me to get out?

POLLY: Oh yes, of course.

MAC: With money, of course. I've arranged with the warder . . .

POLLY (slowly): The money has gone off to Manchester.

MAC: And you've got none on you?

POLLY: No, I've got nothing on me. But you know, Mackie, I could talk to somebody, for instance . . . I might even ask the Queen in person. (She breaks down.) Oh, Mackie!

SMITH (pulling POLLY away): Well, have you raised those thousand pounds?

POLLY: All the best, Mackie, take care of yourself, and don't forget me! (Goes out.)

(SMITH and a constable bring in a table with a dish of asparagus on it.)

SMITH: Is the asparagus tender?

CONSTABLE: Absolutely. (Goes out.)

BROWN (appears and goes to SMITH): Smith, what does he want me for? It's good you didn't take the table in earlier. We'll take it right in with us, to show him how we feel about him. (They enter the cell with the table. SMITH goes out. Pause.) Hello, Mac. Here's your asparagus. Won't you have some?

MAC: Don't you bother, Mr. Brown. There are others to show me the last honors.

BROWN: Oh, Mackie!

MAC: Would you be so good as to produce your accounts? You don't mind if I eat in the meantime, after all it is my last meal. (He eats.)

BROWN: I hope you enjoy it. Oh, Mac, you're turning the knife in the wound.

MAC: The accounts, sir, if you please, the accounts. No sentimentality.

BROWN (with a sign takes a small notebook from his pocket): I've got them right here, Mac. The accounts for the past six months.

MAC (bitingly): Oh, so all you came for was to get your money before it's too late.

BROWN: You know that isn't so.

MAC: Don't worry, sir, nobody's going to cheat you. What do I owe you? But I want an itemized bill, if you don't mind. Life has made me distrustful . . . In your position, sir, you should be able to understand that.

BROWN: Mac, when you talk like that, I just can't think.

(A loud pounding is heard rear.)

SMITH (off): All right, that'll hold.

MAC: The accounts, Brown.

BROWN: Very well—if you insist. Well, first of all the rewards for murderers arrested thanks to you or your men. The government paid you a total of . . .

MAC: Three instances at forty pounds apiece, that makes a hundred and twenty pounds. One quarter for you comes to thirty pounds, so that's what we owe you.

BROWN: Yes—yes—but really, Mac, I don't think we ought to spend our last . . .

MAC: Kindly stop sniveling. Thirty pounds. And for the job in Dover eight pounds.

BROWN: Why only eight pounds, there was a . . .

MAC: Do you believe me or don't you believe me? Your share in the transactions of the last six months comes to thirty-eight pounds.

BROWN (wailing): For a whole lifetime . . . I could read . . .

BOTH: Your every thought in your eyes.

MAC: Three years in India—John was all present and Jim was all there—, five years in London, and this is the thanks I get. (Indicating how he will look when hanged.)

Here hangs Macheath who never wronged a flea
A faithless friend has brought him to this pass.
And as he dangles from the gallowstree
His neck finds out how heavy is his arse.

BROWN: If that's the way you feel about it, Mac . . . The man who impugns my honor, impugns me. (Runs furiously out of the cage.)

MAC: Your honor . . .

BROWN: Yes, my honor. Time to begin, Smith! Let them all in! (to MAC) Excuse me, would you.

SMITH (quickly to MACHEATH): I can still get you out of here, in another minute I won't be able to. Have you got the money?

MAC: Yes, as soon as the boys get back.

SMITH: There's no sign of them. The deal is off.

(People are admitted. PEACHUM, MRS. PEACHUM, POLLY, LUCY, the WHORES, the VICAR, MATTHEW and JAKE.)

JENNY: They didn't want to let us in. But I said to them: If you don't get those pisspots you call heads out of my way, you'll hear from Low-Dive Jenny.

PEACHUM: I am his father-in-law. I beg your pardon, which of the present company is Mr. Macheath?

MAC (introduces himself): I'm Macheath.

PEACHUM (walks past the cage, and like all who follow him stations himself to the right of it): Fate, Mr. Macheath, has decreed that though I don't know you, you should be my son-in-law. The occasion of this first meeting between us is a very sad one, Mr. Macheath. You once had white kid goves, a cane with an ivory handle, and a scar on your neck, and you frequented the Cuttlefish Hotel. All that is left is your scar, no doubt the least valuable of your distinguishing marks. Today you frequent nothing but prison cells, and within the foreseeable future no place at all . . .

(POLLY *passes the cage in tears and stations herself to the right.*)

MAC: What a pretty dress you're wearing.

(MATTHEW *and* JAKE *pass the cage and take up positions on the right.*)

MATTHEW: We couldn't get through because of the terrible crush. We ran so hard I was afraid Jake was going to have a stroke. If you don't believe us . . .

MAC: What do my men say? Have they got good places?

MATTHEW: You see, Captain, we thought you'd understand. You see, a Coronation doesn't happen every day. They've got to make some money when there's a chance. They send you their best wishes.

JAKE: Their very best wishes.

MRS. PEACHUM (*steps up to the cell, takes up a position on the right*): Mr. Macheath, who would have expected this a week ago when we were dancing a little hop at the Cuttlefish Hotel.

MAC: A little hop.

MRS. PEACHUM: But the ways of destiny are cruel here below.

BROWN (*at the rear to the vicar*): And to think that I stood shoulder to shoulder with this man in Azerbaidjan under a hail of bullets.

JENNY (*approaches the cage*): We Drury Lane girls are frantic. Nobody's gone to the Coronation. Everybody wants to see you. (*Stations herself on the right.*)

MAC: To see me.

SMITH: All right. Let's go. Six o'clock. (*Lets him out of the cage.*)

MAC: We mustn't keep them waiting. Ladies and gentlemen. You see before you a declining representative of a declining social group. We lower-middle-class artisans who work with humble jemmies on small shopkeepers' cash registers are being swallowed up by big corporations backed by the banks. What's a jemmy compared with a stock certificate? What's breaking into a bank compared with founding a bank? What's murdering a man compared with hiring a man? Fellow citizens, I hereby take my leave of you. I thank you for coming. Some of you were very close to me. That Jenny should have turned me in amazes me greatly. It is proof positive that the world never changes. A convergence of several unfortunate circumstances has brought about my fall. So be it—I fall.

(*Song lighting: golden glow. The organ is lit up. Three lamps are lowered on a pole, and the signs say:*)

BALLADE IN WHICH MACHEATH BEGS ALL MEN FOR FORGIVENESS

You fellow men who live on after us
Pray do not think you have to judge us harshly
And when you see us hoisted up and trussed
Don't laugh like fools behind your big mustaches
Or curse at us. It's true that we came crashing
But do not judge our downfall like the courts.
Not all of us can discipline our thoughts—
Dear fellows, your extravagance needs slashing
Dear fellows, we've shown how a crash begins.
Pray then to God that He forgive my sins.

The rain washes away and purifies.
Let it wash down the flesh we catered for
And we who saw so much, and wanted more—
The crows will come and peck away our eyes.
Perhaps ambition used too sharp a goad
It drove us to these heights from which we swing
Hacked at by greedy starlings on the wing
Like horses' droppings on a country road.
O brothers, learn from us how it begins
And pray to God that He forgive our sins.

The girls who flaunt their breasts as bait there
To catch some sucker who will love them
The youths who slyly stand and wait there
To grab their sinful earnings off them
The crooks, the tarts, the tarts' protectors
The models and the mannequins
The psychopaths, the unfrocked rectors
I pray that they forgive my sins.

Not so those filthy police employees
Who day by day would bait my anger
Devise new troubles to annoy me
And chuck me crusts to stop my hunger.
I'd call on God to come and choke them
And yet my need for respite wins;
I realize that it might provoke them
So pray that they forgive my sins.

Someone must take a huge iron crowbar
And stave their ugly faces in.
All I ask is to know it's over
Praying that they forgive my sins.

SMITH: If you don't mind, Mr. Macheath.

MRS. PEACHUM: Polly and Lucy, stand by your husband in his last hour.

MAC: Ladies, whatever there may have been between us . . .

SMITH (*leads him away*): Get a move on!

(*Procession to the Gallows.*)

(*All go out through doors left. These doors are on projection screens. Then all reenter from the other side of the stage with shaded lanterns. When* MACHEATH *is standing at the top of the gallows steps* PEACHUM *speaks.*)

PEACHUM

> Dear audience, we now are coming to
> The point where we must hang him by the neck
> Because it is the Christian thing to do
> Proving that men must pay for what they take.
>
> But as we want to keep our fingers clean
> And you are people we can't risk offending
> We thought we'd better do without this scene
> And substitute instead a different ending.
>
> Since this is opera, not life, you'll see
> Justice give way before Humanity.
> So now, to throw our story right off course
> Enter the royal official on his horse.

(The signs read:)

THIRD THREEPENNY FINALE

(Appearance of the messenger on horseback.)

CHORUS:

> *Hark, who's here?*
> *A royal official on horseback's here!*

(Enter BROWN *on horseback as the messenger.)*

BROWN: I bring a special order from our beloved Queen to have Captain Macheath set at liberty forthwith *(All cheer.)* since it's her Coronation, and raised to the hereditary peerage. *(Cheers.)* The castle of Marmarel, likewise a pension of ten thousand pounds, to be his in usufruct until his death. To any bridal couples present Her Majesty bids me to convey her gracious good wishes.

MAC: Reprievèd! Reprievèd! I was sure of it.
> When you're most despairing
> The clouds may be clearing.

POLLY: Reprievèd, my dearest Macheath is reprievèd. I am so happy.

MRS. PEACHUM: So it all turned out nicely in the end. How nice everything would be if these saviors on horseback always appeared when they were needed.

PEACHUM: So please remain all standing in your places, and join in the hymn of the poorest of the poor, whose most arduous life you have seen portrayed here today, for in fact the fate they meet is bound to be grim. Saviors on horseback are seldom met with in practice once the man who's kicked about has kicked back. Which all means one shouldn't persecute wrongdoing too much.

ALL *(come forward, singing to the organ.)*:

> *Don't punish our wrongdoing too much. Never*
> *Will it withstand the frost, for it is cold.*
> *Think of the darkness and the bitter weather*
> *The cries of pain that echo through this world.*

Figure 71. Jenny (Ellen Greene) and Mac (Raul Julia) during the whorehouse scene in the New York Shakespeare Festival production of *The Threepenny Opera*, directed by Stanley Silverman and produced by Joseph Papp, New York, 1976. (Photograph: the Joseph Abeles Collection.)

Figure 72. Polly (Caroline Kava, *foreground*) tells Peachum (C.K. Alexander) and Mrs. Peachum (Elizabeth Wilson) of her marriage to Mac in the New York Shakespeare Festival production of *The Threepenny Opera,* directed by Stanley Silverman and produced by Joseph Papp, New York, 1976. (Photograph: the Joseph Abeles Collection.)

Figure 73. Mrs. Peachum (Elizabeth Wilson) and Mr. Peachum (C.K. Alexander) lead the entire cast in singing the final song in the New York Festival Theater production of *The Threepenny Opera,* directed by Stanley Silverman and produced by Joseph Papp, New York, 1976. (Photograph: the Joseph Abeles Collection.)

Staging of *The Threepenny Opera*

REVIEW OF THE NEW YORK SHAKESPEARE FESTIVAL
PRODUCTION, 1976, BY CLIVE BARNES

For its final offering of its Vivian Beaumont season, Joseph Papp's New York Shakespeare Festival is staging the Bertolt Brecht and Kurt Weill modern classic "Threepenny Opera." This somberly blazing masterpiece opened Saturday night and for admirers of the old Marc Blitzstein version, which ran for many years off Broadway at the Theater de Lys, it could be quite a shock. It is also the most interesting and original thing Mr. Papp has produced since he set up shop at the Vivan Beaumont three seasons ago.

Why is it shocking? Well, musically this is one of Weill's greatest scores (not a "Mahagonny" but much more substantial than, say, "Lost in the Stars"), and the Brecht script still has the tremorious undertone of an earthquake to it. But this production is shocking for another reason—the familiar Blitzstein version sanitized and popularized, defanged and, at times, even traduced the Brecht original. It had been made far more socially acceptable, the scatalogical references had been removed, for example, and also it was politically far tamer. Brecht's socialistic philosophy remained in large part, but the corrosiveness had been removed or at least softened.

Blitzstein was a fairly considerable composer in his own right, and when he came to translate the lyrics, he made them far more musical—if you see what I mean—than in the German original. The songs sang more easily in English, which at the time probably seemed a good idea. But it must also be remembered when "Threepenny Opera" was composed—it was the time of Alban Berg's "Wozzeck" and Ernst Krenek's "Jonny spielt Auf." It was a period when the concept of the virtually spoken word set against music—Berg himself called it sprechstimme—was all the vogue, and Brecht and Weill went rather along those lines. Blitzstein smoothed out the rough edges, making the entire thing that little bit more bland.

The re-establishment of Brecht's tone started some time ago with a very good translation by Michael Feingold, which was used both at Yale and by Tony Richardson for a splendid production in London starring Vanessa Redgrave, which was largely misunderstood by the London critics and did not receive anything like the attention it deserved.

Mr. Papp has gone to another source for his version with a new translation by Ralph Mannheim and John Willett that, if memory serves, because I have not compared the texts, is even tougher than Mr. Feingold's. It works very well indeed, and what is particularly significant about Mr. Papp's production is that he has unerringly gone to the two people in America who are best fitted to stage the piece—Richard Foreman as director and Stanley Silverman to take charge of the Weill music. Since their own very interesting creative work has been so influenced by Brecht and Weill, they make the ideal interpretative duo.

One reservation—no, not quite a reservation—just a stray thought on translation. For American audiences, would it not be as well to translate the piece into New York dialect—even though London is certainly embedded in the text, and it is, of course, a modern adaptation of John Gay's "The Beggar's Opera." However, it could be set in New York—and with Brecht's very clearly stated views on translation and adaptation, he might himself have found such a course preferable. Never be tactful with Brecht—he was never tactful with anyone else.

What a marvelous work this is. All its bitter, angry energy, its cynical theme that "money rules the world" and its topsy-turvy inflammatory philosophy. Phrases such as "the law was made for one thing only, for the exploitation of those who don't understand it," or, perhaps even more pertinently, "what's breaking into a bank compared with founding a bank." Such radicalism, such a clear confrontation with both Western democracy and—ironically enough—the canker of Soviet communism is still explosively revolutionary.

Mr. Foreman has directed with a clear and fierce power. He makes wonderful (and very Berliner Enseble style) use of groupings and stasis, and Douglas W. Schmidt, settings; Theoni V. Aldredge, costumes; Pat Collins, lighting, and the unnamed genius (Mr. Foreman perhaps) who supervised the makeup are all admirable. And as for the music, I feel Mr. Silverman would have made Weill happy; he certainly made me happy.

All the performances have style and class. Raul Julia, with his brooding presence and soft, catlike violence, is ideal as Mack the Knife, C. K. Alexander exudes reason, hatred and respectability as Peachum. Elizabeth Wilson is deathly sweet as his wife. Roy Brocksmith does excellent as the Ballad Singer and the wan bitterness of Ellen Greene as Jenny is another of the highlights of a magnificently low show. Was it bitter humor on Mr. Papp's part to open it on May Day?

FEDERICO GARCIA LORCA

1898–1936

Before he was executed by the fascists at the beginning of the Spanish civil war, Lorca had written twelve plays. His last three works—tragedies of rural life—are such powerful evocations of an archetypal conflict between passionate human instincts and traditional codes of behavior that they alone have been sufficient to establish his reputation as the most culturally conscious and theatrically intense dramatist to emerge in Spain during the twentieth century. He was born near the city of Granada, in southern Spain, a region deeply influenced by the Andalusian and gypsy folk traditions of balladry and dance—traditions that left their mark on both his poetry and plays. He was also influenced by his wealthy father and his cultivated mother who evidently encouraged him to develop his widely varied artistic talents, for he was not only a poet and playwright, but also an accomplished pianist and painter. By the time he was eight, he was already improvising plays in the courtyard of his parents' home, and before he entered the University of Granada at the age of sixteen he was writing ballads, poems, and prose descriptions of the Spanish landscape that he subsequently included in published collections of his works. When he entered the University, he planned to study for a career in the law, but he quickly changed his mind and moved on to studies in philosophy and literature, which he continued at the University of Madrid. When he moved to Madrid in 1919, he had already published *Impressions and Landscapes* (1918), an evocative series of impressions based on his travels throughout Spain, and he had in hand a manuscript of poems that he shared with his fellow students in public readings. Lorca, in fact, was an inveterate performer, and throughout his life he evidently took much greater pleasure in reading his works or seeing them produced than in rushing them into print. He usually published his work well after it had been written, and much of it remained unpublished even at the time of his death.

Lorca's playwriting career began in earnest during the 1920s, a period when he experimented in a variety of forms and turned out a number of works, including a parable play about a cockroach who becomes entranced by the enchanting world of a butterfly, a comedy based on the traditional Spanish puppet character Don Cristobal, a series of farces based on the films of Buston Keaton, a surrealist work involving a young man, his fiancée, a mannequin, a dead child, and a cat, a verse play about Mariana Pineda, a nineteenth century figure who died in the liberation of Madrid, and a tragic farce about an old bachelor who falls in love with a naive and sensual young girl. These works, together with his numerous public readings, as well as the publication of two collections of poems and a collection of ballads, had turned Lorca into a widely celebrated Spanish writer by the end of the 1920s. In 1929, he left Spain temporarily to visit Paris and London, before travelling to America, where he spent a year at Columbia

University, but he evidently did not find New York a congenial place, and by 1930 he had left to visit Cuba, Argentina, and other Latin American countries before returning permanently to Spain.

His travel abroad had also apparently turned him away from all the cosmopolitan movements in drama that were then astir in the major theatrical centers, for when he returned to Spain in 1931, he organized a government-sponsored theatrical troupe and began touring the provinces, producing the Spanish classics of the seventeenth century, wherever he could find an audience in small Spanish towns and villages. His sustained immersion in the folk life of the Spanish provinces also must have led him to develop the subjects that resulted in the major works of his career—his three tragedies of rural experience—that he wrote during his last five years. In each of these, he focused on the predicament of characters who are torn between their allegiance to traditional Spanish codes of honor and religious belief, on the one hand, and their passionate human desires, on the other. And, in each case, he dramatized the tragic frustration of natural human impulses that he evidently perceived as the inescapable outcome of being forced to submit to rigid and anachronistic codes of behavior.

In the earliest of these tragedies, *Blood Wedding* (1933), a work heavily interspersed with lyric scenes, Lorca dramatized the primal power of the blood in the person of a young woman "burning with desire," who finds herself betrothed and married to a man whom she regards as "a little bit of water." Immediately after the marriage ceremony she runs off with another man, the husband of her cousin, a man whose family had killed the father and brother of her own husband in a blood feud, but a man whom she had always loved because he was for her "a dark river, choked with brush, that brought near me the undertone of its rushes and its whispered song." The two lovers thus violate all the codes of belief and honor in their community and escape into the forest, where they are pursued by the newly married groom, which results in a doubly fatal encounter between the groom and his rival. The bride is thus left "without a single man ever having seen himself in the whiteness of my breasts," a condition that is at once the measure of her conventional purity and her intense frustration. And the mother of the groom, in a final chorus, is seen lamenting the death of her last son at the hands of the same family that had previously killed her husband and her other son. The conflict between traditional codes and human desires is, therefore, presented as bringing profound suffering to all the central characters, old and young, conventional and rebellious alike. In his second tragedy of rural experience, *Yerma* (1934), Lorca examined the plight of a married woman, whose frustrated maternal desire ultimately drives her to the act of killing her impotent and unsympathetic husband—an act that in turn moves her to cry out that "I'm going to rest without ever waking to see whether my blood has announced the coming of new blood. My body barren forever."

Like his other mature plays, *The House of Bernarda Alba,* written in 1936 but not produced until 1945, is dramatically preoccupied with the frustration of natural human desire. And like these other plays, it dramatizes this problem by focussing on the experience of women. Indeed, in this play there are no men on stage at all, though every speech resounds either with the memory of Bernarda's recently dead husband or with the yearning of all her daughters for the virile figure of Pepe el Romano. But the world of the play, as indicated by its title, is dominated by Bernarda, whose tyrannical honor and pride and piety and repressiveness are epitomized by the starkly white color of her house, by the black colors of mourning she enforces upon her daughters, and by her big stick that thumps over and over again on the stage. Although her repressiveness leads even to the death of one of her daughters, not to mention the frustration of all the others, she is unmoved, for she rises perversely above it in her exclamation: "My daughter died a virgin." To convey so terrible a will requires an actress of extraordinary authority, such as the Greek performer, Katina Paxinou, who played the part of Bernarda in a New York production by the A.N.T.A. Company in 1951. Photographs of that production clearly reveal the domination of Paxinou in the role of Bernarda (see Figure 74), much as they reveal the oppressive whiteness of her house and the oppressive blackness of mourning she has inflicted on her daughters (see Figures 74 and 75). What those pictures do not reveal, because they cannot, are the sounds of all the irritated and frustrated women, snarling and whining at one another throughout the play. But the reviews, reprinted following the text, clearly indicate that audiences are either intensely moved or greatly exasperated by all those women working on one another, grinding their way inexorably to the final tragic spectacle.

THE HOUSE OF BERNARDA ALBA

A Drama About Women in the Villages of Spain

BY FEDERICO GARCIA LORCA / TRANSLATED BY JAMES GRAHAM-LUJÁN AND RICHARD L. O'CONNELL

CHARACTERS

BERNARDA (age: 60)
MARIA JOSEFA, Bernarda's Mother (age: 80)
ANGUSTIAS, Bernarda's Daughter (age: 39)
MAGDALENA, Bernarda's Daughter (age: 30)
AMELIA, Bernarda's Daughter (age: 27)
MARTIRIO, Bernarda's Daughter (age: 24)
ADELA, Bernarda's Daughter (age: 20)

A MAID (age: 50)
LA PONCIA, A Maid (age: 60)
PRUDENCIA (age: 50)
Women in Mourning

The writer states that these Three Acts are intended as a photographic document.

ACT 1

(A very white room in BERNARDA ALBA'S *house. The walls are white. There are arched doorways with jute curtains tied back with tassels and ruffles. Wicker chairs. On the walls, pictures of unlikely landscapes full of nymphs or legendary kings.*

It is summer. A great brooding silence fills the stage. It is empty when the curtain rises. Bells can be heard tolling outside.)

FIRST SERVANT *(entering)*: The tolling of those bells hits me right between the eyes.

PONCIA *(she enters, eating bread and sausage)*: More than two hours of mumbo jumbo. Priests are here from all the towns. The church looks beautiful. At the first responsory for the dead, Magdalena fainted.

FIRST SERVANT: She's the one who's left most alone.

PONCIA: She's the only one who loved her father. Ay! Thank God we're alone for a little. I came over to eat.

FIRST SERVANT: If Bernarda sees you . . . !

PONCIA: She's not eating today so she'd just as soon we'd all die of hunger! Domineering old tyrant! But she'll be fooled! I opened the sausage crock.

FIRST SERVANT *(with an anxious sadness)*: Couldn't you give me some for my little girl, Poncia?

PONCIA: Go ahead! And take a fistful of peas too. She won't know the difference today.

VOICE *(within)*: Bernarda!

PONCIA: There's the grandmother! Isn't she locked up tight?

FIRST SERVANT: Two turns of the key.

PONCIA: You'd better put the cross-bar up too. She's got the fingers of a lock-picker!

VOICE *(within)*: Bernarda!

PONCIA *(shouting)*: She's coming! *(to the* SERVANT) Clean everything up good. If Bernarda doesn't find things shining, she'll pull out the few hairs I have left.

SERVANT: What a woman!

PONCIA: Tyrant over everyone around her. She's perfectly capable of sitting on your heart and watching you die for a whole year without turning off that cold little smile she wears on her wicked face. Scrub, scrub those dishes!

SERVANT: I've got blood on my hands from so much polishing of everything.

PONCIA: She's the cleanest, she's the decentest, she's the highest everything! A good rest her poor husband's earned!

(The bells stop.)

SERVANT: Did all the relatives come?

PONCIA: Just hers. His people hate her. They came to see him dead and make the sign of the cross over him; that's all.

SERVANT: Are there enough chairs?

PONCIA: More than enough. Let them sit on the floor. When Bernarda's father died people stopped coming under this roof. She doesn't want them to see her in her "domain." Curse her!

SERVANT: She's been good to you.

PONCIA: Thirty years washing her sheets. Thirty years eating her leftovers. Nights of watching when she had a cough. Whole days peeking through a crack in the shutters to spy on the neighbors and carry her the tale. Life without secrets one from the other. But in spite of that—curse her! May the "pain of the piercing nail" strike her in the eyes.

SERVANT: Poncia!

PONCIA: But I'm a good watchdog! I bark when I'm told and bite beggars' heels when she sics me on 'em. My sons work in her fields—both of them already married, but one of these days I'll have enough.

SERVANT: And then . . . ?

PONCIA: Then I'll lock myself up in a room with her and spit in her face—a whole year. "Bernarda, here's for this, that and the other!" Till I leave her—just like a lizard the boys have squashed. For that's what she is—she and her whole family! Not that I envy her her life. Five girls are left her, five ugly daughters—not counting Angustias the eldest, by her first husband, who has money—the rest of them, plenty of eyelets to embroider, plenty of linen petticoats, but bread and grapes when it comes to inheritance.

SERVANT: Well, *I'd* like to have what they've got!

PONCIA: All we have is our hands and a hole in God's earth.

SERVANT: And that's the only earth they'll ever leave to us—to us who have nothing!

PONCIA (at the cupboard): This glass has some specks.

SERVANT: Neither soap nor rag will take them off.

(The bells toll.)

PONCIA: The last prayer! I'm going over and listen. I certainly like the way our priest sings. In the Pater Noster his voice went up, and up—like a pitcher filling with water little by little. Of course, at the end his voice cracked, but it's glorious to hear it. No, there never was anybody like the old Sacristan—Tronchapinos. At my mother's Mass, may she rest in peace, he sang. The walls shook—and when he said "Amen," it was as if a wolf had come into the church.

(Imitating him.)

A-a-a-a-men!

(She starts coughing.)

SERVANT: Watch out—you'll strain your windpipe!

PONCIA: I'd rather strain something else!

(Goes out laughing.)

(The SERVANT scrubs. The bells toll.)

SERVANT (imitating the bells): Dong, dong, dong. Dong, dong, dong. May God forgive him!

BEGGAR WOMAN (at the door, with a little girl): Blesséd be God!

SERVANT: Dong, dong, dong. I hope he waits many years for us! Dong, dong, dong.

BEGGAR (loudly, a little annoyed): Blesséd be God!

SERVANT (annoyed): Forever and ever!

BEGGAR: I came for the scraps.

(The bells stop tolling.)

SERVANT: You can go right out the way you came in. Today's scraps are for me.

BEGGAR: But you have somebody to take care of you—and my little girl and I are all alone!

SERVANT: Dogs are alone too, and they live.

BEGGAR: They always give them to me.

SERVANT: Get out of here! Who let you in anyway? You've already tracked up the place.

(The BEGGAR WOMAN and LITTLE GIRL leave. The SERVANT goes on scrubbing.)

Floors finished with oil, cupboards, pedestals, iron beds—but us servants, we can suffer in silence—and live in mud huts with a plate and a spoon. I hope someday not a one will be left to tell it.

(The bells sound again.)

Yes, yes—ring away. Let them put you in a coffin with gold inlay and brocade to carry it on— you're no less dead than I'll be, so take what's coming to you, Antonio María Benavides—stiff in your broadcloth suit and your high boots— take what's coming to you! You'll never again lift my skirts behind the corral door!

(From the rear door, two by two, women in mourning with large shawls and black skirts and fans, begin to enter. They come in slowly until the stage is full.)

SERVANT (breaking into a wail): Oh, Antonio María Benavides, now you'll never see these walls, nor break bread in this house again! I'm the one who loved you most of all your servants.

(Pulling her hair.)

Must I love on after you've gone? Must I go on living?

(The two hundred women finish coming in, and BERNARDA and her five daughters enter. BERNARDA leans on a cane.)

BERNARDA (to the SERVANT): Silence!

SERVANT (weeping): Bernarda!

BERNARDA: Less shrieking and more work. You should have had all this cleaner for the wake. Get out. This isn't your place.

(The SERVANT goes off crying.)

The poor are like animals—they seem to be made of different stuff.

FIRST WOMAN: The poor feel their sorrows too.

BERNARDA: But they forget them in front of a plateful of peas.

FIRST GIRL (timidly): Eating is necessary for living.

BERNARDA: At your age one doesn't talk in front of older people.

WOMAN: Be quiet, child.

BERNARDA: I've never taken lessons from anyone. Sit down.

(They sit down. Pause. Loudly.)

Magdalena, don't cry. If you want to cry, get under your bed. Do you hear me?

SECOND WOMAN *(to* BERNARDA*)*: Have you started to work the fields?

BERNARDA: Yesterday.

THIRD WOMAN: The sun comes down like lead.

FIRST WOMAN: I haven't known heat like this for years.

(Pause. They all fan themselves.)

BERNARDA: Is the lemonade ready?

PONCIA: Yes, Bernarda.

(She brings in a large tray full of little white jars which she distributes.)

BERNARDA: Give the men some.

PONCIA: They're already drinking in the patio.

BERNARDA: Let them get out the way they came in. I don't want them walking through here.

A GIRL *(to* ANGUSTIAS*)*: Pepe el Romano was with the men during the service.

ANGUSTIAS: There he was.

BERNARDA: His mother was there. She saw his mother. Neither she nor I saw Pepe . . .

GIRL: I thought . . .

BERNARDA: The one who *was* there was Darajalí, the widower. Very close to your Aunt. We all of us saw him.

SECOND WOMAN *(aside, in a low voice)*: Wicked, worse than wicked woman!

THIRD WOMAN: A tongue like a knife!

BERNARDA: Women in church shouldn't look at any man but the priest—and him only because he wears skirts. To turn your head is to be looking for the warmth of corduroy.

FIRST WOMAN: Sanctimonious old snake!

PONCIA *(between her teeth)*: Itching for a man's warmth.

BERNARDA *(beating with her cane on the floor)*: Blesséd be God!

ALL *(crossing themselves)*: Forever blesséd and praised.

BERNARDA: Rest in peace with holy company at your head.

ALL: Rest in peace!

BERNARDA: With the Angel Saint Michael, and his sword of justice.

ALL: Rest in peace!

BERNARDA: With the key that opens, and the hand that locks.

ALL: Rest in peace!

BERNARDA: With the most blesséd, and the little lights of the field.

ALL: Rest in peace!

BERNARDA: With our holy charity, and all souls on land and sea.

ALL: Rest in peace!

BERNARDA: Grant rest to your servant, Antonio María Benavides, and give him the crown of your blesséd glory.

ALL: Amen.

BERNARDA *(she rises and chants)*: Requiem aeternam donat eis domine.

ALL *(standing and chanting in the Gregorian fashion)*: Et lux perpetua luce ab eis.

(They cross themselves.)

FIRST WOMAN: May you have health to pray for his soul. *(They start filing out.)*

THIRD WOMAN: You won't lack loaves of hot bread.

SECOND WOMAN: Nor a roof for your daughters.

(They are all filing in front of BERNARDA *and going out.* ANGUSTIAS *leaves by the door to the patio.)*

FOURTH WOMAN: May you go on enjoying your wedding wheat.

PONCIA *(she enters, carrying a money bag)*: From the men—this bag of money for Masses.

BERNARDA: Thank them—and let them have a glass of brandy.

GIRL *(to* MAGDALENA*)*: Magdalena . . .

BERNARDA *(to* MAGDALENA, *who is starting to cry)*: Sh-h-h-h!

(She beats with her cane on the floor.)
(All the women have gone out.)

BERNARDA *(to the women who have just left)*: Go back to your houses and criticize everything you've seen! I hope it'll be many years before you pass under the archway of my door again.

PONCIA: You've nothing to complain about. The whole town came.

BERNARDA: Yes, to fill my house with the sweat from their wraps and the poison of their tongues.

AMELIA: Mother, don't talk like that.

BERNARDA: What other way is there to talk about this curséd village with no river—this village full of wells where you drink water always fearful it's been poisoned?

PONCIA: Look what they've done to the floor!

BERNARDA: As though a herd of goats had passed through.

(PONCIA cleans the floor.)

Adela, give me a fan.

ADELA: Take this one.

(She gives her a round fan with green and red flowers.)

BERNARDA (*throwing the fan on the floor*): Is that the fan to give to a widow? Give me a black one and learn to respect your father's memory.

MARTIRIO: Take mine.

BERNARDA: And you?

MARTIRIO: I'm not hot.

BERNARDA: Well, look for another, because you'll need it. For the eight years of mourning, not a breath of air will get in this house from the street. We'll act as if we'd sealed up doors and windows with bricks. That's what happened in my father's house—and in my grandfather's house. Meantime, you can all start embroidering your hope-chest linens. I have twenty bolts of linen in the chest from which to cut sheets and coverlets. Magdalena can embroider them.

MAGDALENA: It's all the same to me.

ADELA (*sourly*): If you don't want to embroider them—they can go without. That way yours will look better.

MAGDALENA: Neither mine nor yours. I know I'm not going to marry. I'd rather carry sacks to the mill. Anything except sit here day after day in this dark room.

BERNARDA: That's what a woman is for.

MAGDALENA: Cursed be all women.

BERNARDA: In this house you'll do what I order. You can't run with the story to your father any more. Needle and thread for women. Whiplash and mules for men. That's the way it has to be for people who have certain obligations.

(ADELA *goes out.*)

VOICE: Bernarda! Let me out!

BERNARDA (*calling*): Let her out now!

(The FIRST SERVANT *enters.*)

FIRST SERVANT: I had a hard time holding her. In spite of her eighty years, your mother's strong as an oak.

BERNARDA: It runs in the family. My grandfather was the same way.

SERVANT: Several times during the wake I had to cover her mouth with an empty sack because she wanted to shout out to you to give her dishwater to drink at least, and some dogmeat, which is what she says you feed her.

MARTIRIO: She's mean!

BERNARDA (*to* SERVANT): Let her get some fresh air in the patio.

SERVANT: She took her rings and the amethyst earrings out of the box, put them on, and told me she wants to get married.

(The daughters laugh.)

BERNARDA: Go with her and be careful she doesn't get near the well.

SERVANT: You don't need to be afraid she'll jump in.

BERNARDA: It's not that— but the neighbors can see her there from their windows.

(The SERVANT *leaves.*)

MARTIRIO: We'll go change our clothes.

BERNARDA: Yes, but don't take the kerchiefs from your heads.

(ADELA *enters.*)

And Angustias?

ADELA (*meaningfully*): I saw her looking out through the cracks of the back door. The men had just gone.

BERNARDA: And you, what were *you* doing at the door?

ADELA: I went there to see if the hens had laid.

BERNARDA: But the men had already gone!

ADELA (*meaningfully*): A group of them were still standing outside.

BERNARDA (*furiously*): Angustias! Angustias!

ANGUSTIAS (*entering*): Did you want something?

BERNARDA: For what—and at whom—were you looking?

ANGUSTIAS: Nobody.

BERNARDA: Is it decent for a woman of your class to be running after a man the day of her father's funeral? Answer me! Whom were you looking at?

(*Pause.*)

ANGUSTIAS: I . . .

BERNARDA: Yes, you!

ANGUSTIAS: Nobody.

BERNARDA: Soft! Honeytongue!

(*She strikes her.*)

PONCIA (*running to her*): Bernarda, calm down!

(*She holds her.* ANGUSTIAS *weeps.*)

BERNARDA: Get out of here, all of you!

(*They all go out.*)

PONCIA: She did it not realizing what she was doing—although it's bad, of course. It really disgusted me to see her sneak along to the patio. Then she stood at the window listening to the men's talk, which, as usual, was not the sort one should listen to.

BERNARDA: That's what they come to funerals for. (*With curiosity.*) What were they talking about?

PONCIA: They were talking about Paca la Roseta. Last night they tied her husband up in a stall, stuck her on a horse behind the saddle, and carried her away to the depths of the olive grove.

BERNARDA: And what did she do?

PONCIA: She? She was just as happy—they say her

breasts were exposed and Maximiliano held on to her as if he were playing a guitar. Terrible!

BERNARDA: And what happened?

PONCIA: What had to happen. They came back almost at daybreak. Paca la Roseta with her hair loose and a wreath of flowers on her head.

BERNARDA: She's the only bad woman we have in the village.

PONCIA: Because she's not from here. She's from far away. And those who went with her are the sons of outsiders too. The men from here aren't up to a thing like that.

BERNARDA: No, but they like to see it, and talk about it, and suck their fingers over it.

PONCIA: They were saying a lot more things.

BERNARDA (looking from side to side with a certain fear): What things?

PONCIA: I'm ashamed to talk about them.

BERNARDA: And my daughter heard them?

PONCIA: Of course!

BERNARDA: That one takes after her Aunts: white and mealy-mouthed and casting sheep's eyes at any little barber's compliment. Oh, what one has to go through and put up with so people will be decent and not too wild!

PONCIA: It's just that your daughters are of an age when they ought to have husbands. Mighty little trouble they give you. Angustias must be much more than thirty now.

BERNARDA: Exactly thirty-nine.

PONCIA: Imagine. And she's never had a beau . . .

BERNARDA (furiously): None of them has ever had a beau and they've never needed one! They get along very well.

PONCIA: I didn't mean to offend you.

BERNARDA: For a hundred miles around there's no one good enough to come near them. The men in this town are not of their class. Do you want me to turn them over to the first shepherd?

PONCIA: You should have moved to another town.

BERNARDA: That's it. To sell them!

PONCIA: No, Bernarda, to change. . . . Of course, any place else, they'd be the poor ones.

BERNARDA: Hold your tormenting tongue!

PONCIA: One can't even talk to you. Do we, or do we not share secrets?

BERNARDA: We do not. You're a servant and I pay you. Nothing more.

PONCIA: But . . .

FIRST SERVANT (entering): Don Arturo's here. He's come to see about dividing the inheritance.

BERNARDA: Let's go. (to the SERVANT) You start whitewashing the patio. (to LA PONCIA) And you start putting all the dead man's clothes away in the chest.

PONCIA: We could give away some of the things.

BERNARDA: Nothing—not a button even! Not even the cloth we covered his face with.

(She goes out slowly, leaning on her cane. At the door she turns to look at the two servants. They go out. She leaves.)
(AMELIA and MARTIRIO enter.)

AMELIA: Did you take the medicine?

MARTIRIO: For all the good it'll do me.

AMELIA: But you took it?

MARTIRIO: I do things without any faith, but like clockwork.

AMELIA: Since the new doctor came you look livelier.

MARTIRIO: I feel the same.

AMELIA: Did you notice? Adelaida wasn't at the funeral.

MARTIRIO: I know. Her sweetheart doesn't let her go out even to the front doorstep. Before, she was gay. Now, not even powder on her face.

AMELIA: These days a girl doesn't know whether to have a beau or not.

MARTIRIO: It's all the same.

AMELIA: The whole trouble is all these wagging tongues that won't let us live. Adelaida has probably had a bad time.

MARTIRIO: She's afraid of our mother. Mother is the only one who knows the story of Adelaida's father and where he got his lands. Everytime she comes here, Mother twists the knife in the wound. Her father killed his first wife's husband in Cuba so he could marry her himself. Then he left her there and went off with another woman who already had one daughter, and then he took up with this other girl, Adelaida's mother, and married her after his second wife died insane.

AMELIA: But why isn't a man like that put in jail?

MARTIRIO: Because men help each other cover up things like that and no one's able to tell on them.

AMELIA: But Adelaida's not to blame for any of that.

MARTIRIO: No. But history repeats itself. I can see that everything is a terrible repetition. And she'll have the same fate as her mother and grandmother—both of them wife to the man who fathered her.

AMELIA: What an awful thing!

MARTIRIO: It's better never to look at a man. I've been afraid of them since I was a little girl. I'd see them in the yard, yoking the oxen and lifting grain sacks, shouting and stamping, and I was always afraid to grow up for fear one of them would suddenly take me in his arms. God has made me weak and ugly and has definitely put such things away from me.

AMELIA: Don't say that! Enrique Humanas was after you and he liked you.

MARTIRIO: That was just people's ideas! One time I stood in my nightgown at the window until daybreak because he let me know through his shepherd's little girl that he was going to come, and he didn't. It was all just talk. Then he married someone else who had more money than I.

AMELIA: And ugly as the devil.

MARTIRIO: What do men care about ugliness? All they care about is lands, yokes of oxen, and a submissive bitch who'll feed them.

AMELIA: Ay!

(MAGDALENA enters.)

MAGDALENA: What are you doing?

MARTIRIO: Just here.

AMELIA: And you?

MAGDALENA: I've been going through all the rooms. Just to walk a little, and look at Grandmother's needlepoint pictures—the little woolen dog, and the black man wrestling with the lion—which we liked so much when we were children. Those were happier times. A wedding lasted ten days and evil tongues weren't in style. Today people are more refined. Brides wear white veils, just as in the cities, and we drink bottled wine, but we rot inside because of what people might say.

MARTIRIO: Lord knows what went on then!

AMELIA *(to MAGDALENA)*: One of your shoelaces has come untied.

MAGDALENA: What of it?

AMELIA: You'll step on it and fall.

MAGDALENA: One less!

MARTIRIO: And Adela?

MAGDALENA: Ah! She put on the green dress she made to wear for her birthday, went out to the yard, and began shouting: "Chickens! Chickens, look at me!" I had to laugh.

AMELIA: If Mother had only seen her!

MAGDALENA: Poor little thing! She's the youngest one of us and still has her illusions. I'd give something to see her happy.

(Pause. ANGUSTIAS crosses the stage, carrying some towels.)

ANGUSTIAS: What time is it?

MAGDALENA: It must be twelve.

ANGUSTIAS: So late?

AMELIA: It's about to strike.

(ANGUSTIAS goes out.)

MAGDALENA *(meaningfully)*: Do you know what?

(Pointing after ANGUSTIAS.)

AMELIA: No.

MAGDALENA: Come on!

MARTIRIO: I don't know what you're talking about!

MAGDALENA: Both of you know it better than I do, always with your heads together, like two little sheep, but not letting anybody else in on it. I mean about Pepe el Romano!

MARTIRIO: Ah!

MAGDALENA *(mocking her)*: Ah! The whole town's talking about it. Pepe el Romano is coming to marry Angustias. Last night he was walking around the house and I think he's going to send a declaration soon.

MARTIRIO: I'm glad. He's a good man.

AMELIA: Me too. Angustias is well off.

MAGDALENA: Neither one of you is glad.

MARTIRIO: Magdalena! What do you mean?

MAGDALENA: If he were coming because of Angustias' looks, for Angustias as a woman, I'd be glad too, but he's coming for her money. Even though Angustias is our sister, we're her family here and we know she's old and sickly, and always has been the least attractive one of us! Because if she looked like a dressed-up stick at twenty, what can she look like now, now that she's forty?

MARTIRIO: Don't talk like that. Luck comes to the one who least expects it.

AMELIA: But Magdalena's right after all! Angustias has all her father's money; she's the only rich one in the house and that's why, now that Father's dead and the money will be divided, they're coming for her.

MAGDALENA: Pepe el Romano is twenty-five years old and the best looking man around here. The natural thing would be for him to be after you, Amelia, or our Adela, who's twenty—not looking for the least likely one in this house, a woman who, like her father, talks through her nose.

MARTIRIO: Maybe he likes that!

MAGDALENA: I've never been able to bear your hypocrisy.

MARTIRIO: Heavens!

(ADELA enters.)

MAGDALENA: Did the chickens see you?

ADELA: What did you want me to do?

AMELIA: If Mother sees you, she'll drag you by your hair!

ADELA: I had a lot of illusions about this dress. I'd planned to put it on the day we were going to eat watermelons at the well. There wouldn't have been another like it.

MARTIRIO: It's a lovely dress.

ADELA: And one that looks very good on me. It's the best thing Magdalena's ever cut.

MAGDALENA: And the chickens, what did they say to you?

ADELA: They presented me with a few fleas that riddled my legs.

(They laugh.)

MARTIRIO: What you can do is dye it black.

MAGDALENA: The best thing you can do is give it to Angustias for her wedding with Pepe el Romano.

ADELA (*with hidden emotion*): But Pepe el Romano . . .

AMELIA: Haven't you heard about it?

ADELA: No.

MAGDALENA: Well, now you know!

ADELA: But it can't be!

MAGDALENA: Money can do anything.

ADELA: Is that why she went out after the funeral and stood looking through the door?

(*Pause.*)

And that man would . . .

MAGDALENA: Would do anything.

(*Pause.*)

MARTIRIO: What are you thinking, Adela?

ADELA: I'm thinking that this mourning has caught me at the worst moment of my life for me to bear it.

MAGDALENA: You'll get used to it.

ADELA (*bursting out, crying with rage*): I will not get used to it! I can't be locked up. I don't want my skin to look like yours. I don't want my skin's whiteness lost in these rooms. Tomorrow I'm going to put on my green dress and go walking in the streets. I want to go out!

(*The FIRST SERVANT enters.*)

MAGDALENA (*in a tone of authority*): Adela!

SERVANT: The poor thing! How she misses her father. . . .

(*She goes out.*)

MARTIRIO: Hush!

AMELIA: What happens to one will happen to all of us.

(*ADELA grows calm.*)

MAGDALENA: The servant almost heard you.

SERVANT (*entering*): Pepe el Romano is coming along at the end of the street.

(*AMELIA, MARTIRIO and MAGDALENA run hurriedly.*)

MAGDALENA: Let's go see him!

(*They leave rapidly.*)

SERVANT (*to ADELA*): Aren't you going?

ADELA: It's nothing to me.

SERVANT: Since he has to turn the corner, you'll see him better from the window of your room.

(*The SERVANT goes out. ADELA is left on the stage, standing doubtfully; after a moment, she also leaves rapidly, going toward her room. BERNARDA and LA PONCIA come in.*)

BERNARDA: Damned portions and shares.

PONCIA: What a lot of money is left to Angustias!

BERNARDA: Yes.

PONCIA: And for the others, considerably less.

BERNARDA: You've told me that three times now, when you know I don't want it mentioned! Considerably less; a lot less! Don't remind me any more.

(*ANGUSTIAS comes in, her face heavily made up.*)

Angustias!

ANGUSTIAS: Mother.

BERNARDA: Have you dared to powder your face? Have you dared to wash your face on the day of your father's death?

ANGUSTIAS: He wasn't my father. Mine died a long time ago. Have you forgotten that already?

BERNARDA: You owe more to this man, father of your sisters, than to your own. Thanks to him, your fortune is intact.

ANGUSTIAS: We'll have to see about that first!

BERNARDA: Even out of decency! Out of respect!

ANGUSTIAS: Let me go out, mother!

BERNARDA: Let you go out? After I've taken that powder off your face, I will. Spineless! Painted hussy! Just like your aunts!

(*She removes the powder violently with her handkerchief.*)

Now get out!

PONCIA: Bernarda, don't be so hateful!

BERNARDA: Even though my mother is crazy, I still have my five senses and I know what I'm doing.

(*They all enter.*)

MAGDALENA: What's going on here?

BERNARDA: Nothing's 'going on here'!

MAGDALENA (*to ANGUSTIAS*): If you're fighting over the inheritance, you're the richest one and can hang on to it all.

ANGUSTIAS: Keep your tongue in your pocketbook!

BERNARDA (*beating on the floor*): Don't fool yourselves into thinking you'll sway me. Until I go out of this house feet first I'll give the orders for myself and for you!

(*Voices are heard and MARÍA JOSEFA, BERNARDA's mother, enters. She is very old and has decked out her head and breast with flowers.*)

MARIA JOSEFA: Bernarda, where is my mantilla? Nothing, nothing of what I own will be for any of you. Not my rings nor my black moiré dress. Because not a one of you is going to marry—not a one. Bernarda, give me my necklace of pearls.

BERNARDA (*to the SERVANT*): Why did you let her get in here?

SERVANT (*trembling*): She got away from me!

MARIA JOSEFA: I ran away because I want to marry—I

want to get married to a beautiful manly man from the shore of the sea. Because here the men run from women.

BERNARDA: Hush, hush, Mother!

MARIA JOSEFA: No, no—I won't hush. I don't want to see these single women, longing for marriage, turning their hearts to dust; and I want to go to my home town. Bernarda, I want a man to get married to and be happy with!

BERNARDA: Lock her up!

MARIA JOSEFA: Let me go out, Bernarda!

(*The* SERVANT *seizes* MARIA JOSEFA.)

BERNARDA: Help her, all of you!

(*They all grab the old woman.*)

MARIA JOSEFA: I want to get away from here! Bernarda! To get married by the shore of the sea—by the shore of the sea!

(*Quick, curtain.*)

ACT 2

(*A white room in* BERNARDA's *house. The doors on the left lead to the bedrooms.* BERNARDA's DAUGHTERS *are seated on low chairs, sewing.* MAGDALENA *is embroidering.* LA PONCIA *is with them.*)

ANGUSTIAS: I've cut the third sheet.

MARTIRIO: That one goes to Amelia.

MAGDALENA: Angustias, shall I put Pepe's initials here too?

ANGUSTIAS (*dryly*): No.

MAGDALENA (*calling, from off stage to* ADELA): Adela, aren't you coming?

AMELIA: She's probably stretched out on the bed.

PONCIA: Something's wrong with that one. I find her restless, trembling, frightened—as if a lizard were between her breasts.

MARTIRIO: There's nothing, more or less, wrong with her than there is with all of us.

MAGDALENA: All of us except Angustias.

ANGUSTIAS: I feel fine, and anybody who doesn't like it can pop.

MAGDALENA: We all have to admit the nicest things about you are your figure and your tact.

ANGUSTIAS: Fortunately, I'll soon be out of this hell.

MAGDALENA: Maybe you won't get out!

MARTIRIO: Stop this talk!

ANGUSTIAS: Besides, a good dowry is better than dark eyes in one's face!

MAGDALENA: All you say just goes in one ear and out the other.

AMELIA (*to* LA PONCIA): Open the patio door and see if we can get a bit of a breeze.

(LA PONCIA *opens the door.*)

MARTIRIO: Last night I couldn't sleep because of the heat.

AMELIA: Neither could I.

MAGDALENA: I got up for a bit of air. There was a black storm cloud and a few drops even fell.

PONCIA: It was one in the morning and the earth seemed to give off fire. I got up too. Angustias was still at the window with Pepe.

MAGDALENA (*with irony*): That late? What time did he leave?

ANGUSTIAS: Why do you ask, if you saw him?

AMELIA: He must have left about one-thirty.

ANGUSTIAS: Yes. How did you know?

AMELIA: I heard him cough and heard his mare's hoofbeats.

PONCIA: But I heard him leave around four.

ANGUSTIAS: It must have been someone else!

PONCIA: No, I'm sure of it!

AMELIA: That's what it seemed to me, too.

MAGDALENA: That's very strange!

(*Pause.*)

PONCIA: Listen, Angustias, what did he say to you the first time he came by your window?

ANGUSTIAS: Nothing. What should he say? Just talked.

MARTIRIO: It's certainly strange that two people who never knew each other should suddenly meet at a window and be engaged.

ANGUSTIAS: Well, I didn't mind.

AMELIA: I'd have felt very strange about it.

ANGUSTIAS: No, because when a man comes to a window he knows, from all the busybodies who come and go and fetch and carry, that he's going to be told "yes."

MARTIRIO: All right, but he'd have to ask you.

ANGUSTIAS: Of course!

AMELIA (*inquisitively*): And how did he ask you?

ANGUSTIAS: Why, no way:—"You know I'm after you. I need a good, well brought up woman, and that's you—if it's agreeable."

AMELIA: These things embarrass me!

ANGUSTIAS: They embarrass me too, but one has to go through it!

PONCIA: And did he say anything more?

ANGUSTIAS: Yes, he did all the talking.

MARTIRIO: And you?

ANGUSTIAS: I couldn't have said a word. My heart was almost coming out of my mouth. It was the first time I'd ever been alone at night with a man.

MAGDALENA: And such a handsome man.

ANGUSTIAS: He's not bad looking!

PONCIA: Those things happen among people who have an idea how to do things, who talk and say and move their hand. The first time my husband, Evaristo the Short-tailed, came to my window . . . Ha! Ha! Ha!

AMELIA: What happened?

PONCIA: It was very dark. I saw him coming along

and as he went by he said, "Good evening."
"Good evening," I said. Then we were both silent
for more than half an hour. The sweat poured
down my body. Then Evaristo got nearer and
nearer as if he wanted to squeeze in through the
bars and said in a very low voice—"Come here
and let me feel you!"

(They all laugh. AMELIA *gets up, runs, and looks through
the door.)*

AMELIA: Ay, I thought mother was coming!
MAGDALENA: What she'd have done to us!

(They go on laughing.)

AMELIA: Sh-h-h! She'll hear us.
PONCIA: Then he acted very decently. Instead of getting some other idea, he went to raising birds,
until he died. You aren't married but it's good
for you to know, anyway, that two weeks after
the wedding a man gives up the bed for the table, then the table for the tavern, and the woman
who doesn't like it can just rot, weeping in a
corner.
AMELIA: You liked it.
PONCIA: I learned how to handle him!
MARTIRIO: Is it true that you sometimes hit him?
PONCIA: Yes, and once I almost poked out one of his
eyes!
MAGDALENA: All women ought to be like that!
PONCIA: I'm one of your mother's school. One time I
don't know what he said to me, and then I killed
all his birds—with the pestle!

(They laugh.)

MAGDALENA: Adela, child! Don't miss this.
AMELIA: Adela!

(Pause.)

MAGDALENA: I'll go see!

(She goes out.)

PONCIA: That child is sick!
MARTIRIO: Of course. She hardly sleeps!
PONCIA: What *does* she do, then?
MARTIRIO: How do I know what she does?
PONCIA: You probably know better than we do, since
you sleep with just a wall between you.
ANGUSTIAS: Envy gnaws on people.
AMELIA: Don't exaggerate.
AUGUSTIAS: I can tell it in her eyes. She's getting the
look of a crazy woman.
MARTIRIO: Don't talk about crazy women. This is one
place you're not allowed to say that word.

*(*MAGDALENA *and* ADELA *enter.)*

MAGDALENA: Didn't you say she was asleep?
ADELA: My body aches.

MARTIRIO *(with a hidden meaning)*: Didn't you sleep
well last night?
ADELA: Yes.
MARTIRIO: Then?
ADELA *(loudly)*: Leave me alone. Awake or asleep, it's
no affair of yours. I'll do whatever I want to with
my body.
MARTIRIO: I was just concerned about you!
ADELA: Concerned?—curious! Weren't you sewing?
Well, continue! I wish I were invisible so I could
pass through a room without being asked where
I was going!
SERVANT *(entering)*: Bernarda is calling you. The man
with the laces is here.

(All but ADELA *and* LA PONCIA *go out, and as* MARTIRIO
leaves, she looks fixedly at ADELA.)*

ADELA: Don't look at me like that! If you want, I'll
give you my eyes, for they're younger, and my
back to improve that hump you have, but look
the other way when I go by.
PONCIA: Adela, she's your sister, and the one who
most loves you besides!
ADELA: She follows me everywhere. Sometimes she
looks in my room to see if I'm sleeping. She
won't let me breathe, and always, "Too bad
about that face!" "Too bad about that body! It's
going to waste!" But I won't let that happen. My
body will be for whomever I choose.
PONCIA *(insinuatingly, in a low voice)*: For Pepe el
Romano, no?
ADELA *(frightened)*: What do you mean?
PONCIA: What I said, Adela!
ADELA: Shut up!
PONCIA *(loudly)*: Don't you think I've noticed?
ADELA: Lower your voice!
PONCIA: Then forget what you're thinking about!
ADELA: What do you know?
PONCIA: We old ones can see through walls. Where
do you go when you get up at night?
ADELA: I wish you were blind!
PONCIA: But my head and hands are full of eyes,
where something like this is concerned. I
couldn't possibly guess your intentions. Why did
you sit almost naked at your window, and with
the light on and the window open, when Pepe
passed by the second night he came to talk with
your sister?
ADELA: That's not true!
PONCIA: Don't be a child! Leave your sister alone.
And if you like Pepe el Romano, keep it to yourself.

*(*ADELA *weeps.)*

Besides, who says you can't marry him? Your
sister Angustias is sickly. She'll die with her first
child. Narrow waisted, old—and out of my ex-

perience I can tell you she'll die. Then Pepe will do what all widowers do in these parts: he'll marry the youngest and most beautiful, and that's you. Live on that hope, forget him, anything; but don't go against God's law.

ADELA: Hush!

PONCIA: I won't hush!

ADELA: Mind your own business. Snooper, traitor!

PONCIA: I'm going to stick to you like a shadow!

ADELA: Instead of cleaning the house and then going to bed and praying for the dead, you root around like an old sow about goings on between men and women—so you can drool over them.

PONCIA: I keep watch; so people won't spit when they pass our door.

ADELA: What a tremendous affection you've suddenly conceived for my sister.

PONCIA: I don't have any affection for any of you. I want to live in a decent house. I don't want to be dirtied in my old age!

ADELA: Save your advice. It's already too late. For I'd leap not over you, just a servant, but over my mother to put out this fire I feel in my legs and my mouth. What can you possibly say about me? That I lock myself in my room and will not open the door? That I don't sleep? I'm smarter than you! See if you can catch the hare with your hands.

PONCIA: Don't defy me, Adela, don't defy me! Because I can shout, light lamps, and make bells ring.

ADELA: Bring four thousand yellow flares and set them about the walls of the yard. No one can stop what has to happen.

PONCIA: You like him that much?

ADELA: That much! Looking in his eyes I seem to drink his blood in slowly.

PONCIA: I won't listen to you.

ADELA: Well, you'll have to. I've been afraid of you. But now I'm stronger than you!

(ANGUSTIAS enters.)

ANGUSTIAS: Always arguing!

PONCIA: Certainly. She insists that in all this heat I have to go bring her I don't know what from the store.

ANGUSTIAS: Did you buy me the bottle of perfume?

PONCIA: The most expensive one. And the face powder. I put them on the table in your room.

(ANGUSTIAS goes out.)

ADELA: And be quiet!

PONCIA: We'll see!

(MARTIRIO and AMELIA enter.)

MARTIRIO *(to ADELA)*: Did you see the laces?

AMELIA: Angustias', for her wedding sheets, are beautiful.

ADELA *(to MARTIRIO, who is carrying some lace)*: And these?

MARTIRIO: They're for me. For a nightgown.

ADELA *(with sarcasm)*: One needs a sense of humor around here!

MARTIRIO *(meaningfully)*: But only for me to look at. I don't have to exhibit myself before anybody.

PONCIA: No one ever sees us in our nightgowns.

MARTIRIO *(meaningfully, looking at ADELA)*: Sometimes they don't! But I love nice underwear. If I were rich, I'd have it made of Holland Cloth. It's one of the few tastes I've left.

PONCIA: These laces are beautiful for babies' caps and christening gowns. I could never afford them for my own. Now let's see if Augustias will use them for hers. Once she starts having children, they'll keep her running night and day.

MAGDALENA: I don't intend to sew a stitch on them.

AMELIA: And much less bring up some stranger's children. Look how our neighbors across the road are—making sacrifices for four brats.

PONCIA: They're better off than you. There at least they laugh and you can hear them fight.

MARTIRIO: Well, you go work for them, then.

PONCIA: No, fate has sent me to this nunnery!

(Tiny bells are heard distantly as though through several thicknesses of wall.)

MAGDALENA: It's the men going back to work.

PONCIA: It was three o'clock a minute ago.

MARTIRIO: With this sun!

ADELA *(sitting down)*: Ay! If only we could go out in the fields too!

MAGDALENA *(sitting down)*: Each class does what it has to!

MARTIRIO *(sitting down)*: That's it!

AMELIA *(sitting down)*: Ay!

PONCIA: There's no happiness like that in the fields right at this time of year. Yesterday morning the reapers arrived. Forty or fifty handsome young men.

MAGDALENA: Where are they from this year?

PONCIA: From far, far away. They came from the mountains! Happy! Like weathered trees! Shouting and throwing stones! Last night a woman who dresses in sequins and dances, with an accordion, arrived, and fifteen of them made a deal with her to take her to the olive grove. I saw them from far away. The one who talked with her was a boy with green eyes—tight knit as a sheaf of wheat.

AMELIA: Really?

ADELA: Are you sure?

PONCIA: Years ago another one of those women came here, and I myself gave my eldest son some money so he could go. Men need things like that.

ADELA: Everything's forgiven *them*.

AMELIA: To be born a woman's the worst possible punishment.

MAGDALENA: Even our eyes aren't our own.

(A distant song is heard, coming nearer.)

PONCIA: There they are. They have a beautiful song.

AMELIA: They're going out to reap now.

CHORUS:
> The reapers have set out
> Looking for ripe wheat;
> They'll carry off the hearts
> Of any girls they meet.

(Tambourines and carrañacas are heard. Pause. They all listen in the silence cut by the sun.)

AMELIA: And they don't mind the sun!

MARTIRIO: They reap through flames.

ADELA: How I'd like to be a reaper so I could come and go as I pleased. Then we could forget what's eating us all.

MARTIRIO: What do you have to forget?

ADELA: Each one of us has something.

MARTIRIO *(intensely)*: Each one!

PONCIA: Quiet! Quiet!

CHORUS *(very distantly)*:
> Throw wide your doors and windows,
> You girls who live in the town
> The reaper asks you for roses
> With which to deck his crown.

PONCIA: What a song!

MARTIRIO *(with nostalgia)*:
> Throw wide your doors and windows,
> You girls who live in the town.

ADELA *(passionately)*:
> The reaper asks you for roses
> With which to deck his crown.

(The song grows more distant.)

PONCIA: Now they're turning the corner.

ADELA: Let's watch them from the window of my room.

PONCIA: Be careful not to open the shutters too much because they're likely to give them a push to see who's looking.

(The three leave. MARTIRIO is left sitting on the low chair with her head between her hands.)

AMELIA *(drawing near her)*: What's wrong with you?

MARTIRIO: The heat makes me feel ill.

AMELIA: And it's no more than that?

MARTIRIO: I was wishing it were November, the rainy days, the frost—anything except this unending summertime.

AMELIA: It'll pass and come again.

MARTIRIO: Naturally.

(Pause.)

What time did you go to sleep last night?

AMELIA: I don't know. I sleep like a log. Why?

MARTIRIO: Nothing. Only I thought I heard someone in the yard.

AMELIA: Yes?

MARTIRIO: Very late.

AMELIA: And weren't you afraid?

MARTIRIO: No. I've heard it other nights.

AMELIA: We'd better watch out! Couldn't it have been the shepherds?

MARTIRIO: The shepherds come at six.

AMELIA: Maybe a young, unbroken mule?

MARTIRIO *(to herself, with double meaning)*: That's it! That's it. An unbroken little mule.

AMELIA: We'll have to set a watch.

MARTIRIO: No. No. Don't say anything. It may be I've just imagined it.

AMELIA: Maybe.

(Pause. AMELIA starts to go.)

MARTIRIO: Amelia!

AMELIA *(at the door)*: What?

(Pause.)

MARTIRIO: Nothing.

(Pause.)

AMELIA: Why did you call me?

(Pause.)

MARTIRIO: It just came out. I didn't mean to.

(Pause.)

AMELIA: Lie down for a little.

ANGUSTIAS *(she bursts in furiously, in a manner that makes a great contrast with previous silence)*: Where's that picture of Pepe I had under my pillow? Which one of you has it?

MARTIRIO: No one.

AMELIA: You'd think he was a silver St. Bartholomew.

ANGUSTIAS: Where's the picture?

(PONCIA, MAGDALENA and ADELA enter.)

ADELA: What picture?

ANGUSTIAS: One of you has hidden it from me.

MAGDALENA: Do you have the effrontery to say that?

ANGUSTIAS: I had it in my room, and now it isn't there.

MARTIRIO: But couldn't it have jumped out into the yard at midnight? Pepe likes to walk around in the moonlight.

ANGUSTIAS: Don't joke with me! When he comes I'll tell him.

PONCIA: Don't do that! Because it'll turn up.

(Looking at ADELA.*)*

ANGUSTIAS: I'd like to know which one of you has it.

ADELA *(looking at* MARTIRIO*)*: Somebody has it! But not me!

MARTIRIO *(with meaning)*: Of course not you!

BERNARDA *(entering with her cane)*: What scandal is this in my house in the heat's heavy silence? The neighbors must have their ears glued to the walls.

ANGUSTIAS: They've stolen my sweetheart's picture!

BERNARDA *(fiercely)*: Who? Who?

ANGUSTIAS: They have!

BERNARDA: Which one of you?

(Silence.)

Answer me!

(Silence.) (To LA PONCIA.*)*

Search their rooms! Look in their beds. This comes of not tying you up with shorter leashes. But I'll teach you now! *(to* ANGUSTIAS*)* Are you sure?

ANGUSTIAS: Yes.

BERNARDA: Did you look everywhere?

ANGUSTIAS: Yes, Mother.

(They all stand in an embarrassed silence.)

BERNARDA: At the end of my life—to make me drink the bitterest poison a mother knows. *(to* PONCIA*)* Did you find it?

PONCIA: Here it is.

BERNARDA: Where did you find it?

PONCIA: It was . . .

BERNARDA: Say it! Don't be afraid.

PONCIA *(wonderingly)*: Between the sheets in Martirio's bed.

BERNARDA *(to* MARTIRIO*)*: Is that true?

MARTIRIO: It's true.

BERNARDA *(advancing on her, beating her with her cane)*: You'll come to a bad end yet, you hypocrite! Trouble maker!

MARTIRIO *(fiercely)*: Don't hit me, Mother!

BERNARDA: All I want to!

MARTIRIO: If I let you! You hear me? Get back!

PONCIA: Don't be disrespectful to your mother!

ANGUSTIAS *(holding* BERNARDA*)*: Let her go, please!

BERNARDA: Not even tears in your eyes.

MARTIRIO: I'm not going to cry just to please you.

BERNARDA: Why did you take the picture?

MARTIRIO: Can't I play a joke on my sister? What else would I want it for?

ADELA *(leaping forward, full of jealousy)*: It wasn't a joke! You never liked to play jokes. It was something else bursting in her breast—trying to come out. Admit it openly now.

MARTIRIO: Hush, and don't make me speak; for if I should speak the walls would close together one against the other with shame.

ADELA: An evil tongue never stops inventing lies.

BERNARDA: Adela!

MAGDALENA: You're crazy.

AMELIA: And you stone us all with your evil suspicions.

MARTIRIO: But some others do things more wicked!

ADELA: Until all at once they stand forth stark naked and the river carries them along.

BERNARDA: Spiteful!

ANGUSTIAS: It's not my fault Pepe el Romano chose me!

ADELA: For your money.

ANGUSTIAS: Mother!

BERNARDA: Silence!

MARTIRIO: For your fields and your orchards.

MAGDALENA: That's only fair.

BERNARDA: Silence, I say! I saw the storm coming but I didn't think it'd burst so soon. Oh, what an avalanche of hate you've thrown on my heart! But I'm not old yet—I have five chains for you, and this house my father built, so not even the weeds will know of my desolation. Out of here!

(They go out. BERNARDA *sits down desolately.* LA PONCIA *is standing close to the wall.* BERNARDA *recovers herself, and beats on the floor.)*

I'll have to let them feel the weight of my hand! Bernarda, remember your duty!

PONCIA: May I speak?

BERNARDA: Speak. I'm sorry you heard. A stranger is always out of place in a family.

PONCIA: What I've seen, I've seen.

BERNARDA: Angustias must get married right away.

PONCIA: Certainly. We'll have to get her away from here.

BERNARDA: Not her, him!

PONCIA: Of course. He's the one to get away from here. You've thought it all out.

BERNARDA: I'm not thinking. These are things that shouldn't and can't be thought out. I give orders.

PONCIA: And you think he'll be satisfied to go away?

BERNARDA *(rising)*: What are you imagining now?

PONCIA: He will, of course, marry Angustias.

BERNARDA: Speak up! I know you well enough to see that your knife's out for me.

PONCIA: I never knew a warning could be called murder.

BERNARDA: Have you some "warning" for me?

PONCIA: I'm not making any accusations, Bernarda. I'm only telling you to open your eyes and you'll see.

BERNARDA: See what?

PONCIA: You've always been smart, Bernarda. You've

seen other people's sins a hundred miles away. Many times I've thought you could read minds. But, your children are your children, and now you're blind.

BERNARDA: Are you talking about Martirio?

PONCIA: Well, yes—about Martirio . . .

(With curiosity.)

I wonder why she hid the picture?

BERNARDA *(shielding her daughter)*: After all, she says it was a joke. What else could it be?

PONCIA *(scornfully)*: Do you believe that?

BERNARDA *(sternly)*: I don't merely believe it. It's so!

PONCIA: Enough of this. We're talking about your family. But if we were taking about your neighbor across the way, what would it be?

BERNARDA: Now you're beginning to pull the point of the knife out.

PONCIA *(always cruelly)*: No, Bernarda. Something very grave is happening here. I don't want to put the blame on your shoulders, but you've never given your daughters any freedom. Martirio is lovesick. I don't care what you say. Why didn't you let her marry Enrique Humanas? Why, on the very day he was coming to her window did you send him a message not to come?

BERNARDA *(loudly)*: I'd do it a thousand times over! My blood won't mingle with the Humanas' while I live! His father was a shepherd.

PONCIA: And you see now what's happening to you with these airs!

BERNARDA: I have them because I can afford to. And you don't have them because you know where you came from!

PONCIA *(with hate)*: Don't remind me! I'm old now. I've always been grateful for your protection.

BERNARDA *(emboldened)*: You don't seem so!

PONCIA *(with hate, behind softness)*: Martirio will forget this.

BERNARDA: And if she doesn't—the worse for her. I don't believe this is that "very grave thing" that's happening here. Nothing's happening here. It's just that you wish it would! And if it should happen one day, you can be sure it won't go beyond these walls.

PONCIA: I'm not so sure of that! There are people in town who can also read hidden thoughts, from afar.

BERNARDA: How you'd like to see me and my daughters on our way to a whorehouse!

PONCIA: No one knows her own destiny!

BERNARDA: I know my destiny! And my daughters! The whorehouse was for a certain woman, already dead. . . .

PONCIA *(fiercely)*: Bernarda, respect the memory of my mother!

BERNARDA: Then don't plague me with your evil thoughts!

(Pause.)

PONCIA: I'd better stay out of everything.

BERNARDA: That's what you ought to do. Work and keep your mouth shut. The duty of all who work for a living.

PONCIA: But we can't do that. Don't you think it'd be better for Pepe to marry Martirio or . . . yes! . . . Adela?

BERNARDA: No, I *don't* think so.

PONCIA *(with meaning)*: Adela! She's Romano's real sweetheart!

BERNARDA: Things are never the way we want them!

PONCIA: But it's hard work to turn them from their destined course. For Pepe to be with Angustias seems wrong to me—and to other people—and even to the wind. Who knows if they'll get what they want?

BERNARDA: There you go again! Sneaking up on me—giving me bad dreams. But I won't listen to you, because if all you say should come to pass—I'd scratch your face.

PONCIA: Frighten someone else with that.

BERNARDA: Fortunately, my daughters respect me and have never gone against my will!

PONCIA: That's right! But, as soon as they break loose they'll fly to the rooftops!

BERNARDA: And I'll bring them down with stones!

PONCIA: Oh, yes! You were always the bravest one!

BERNARDA: I've always enjoyed a good fight!

PONCIA: But aren't people strange. You should see Angustias' enthusiasm for her lover, at her age! And he seems very smitten too. Yesterday my oldest son told me that when he passed by with the oxen at four-thirty in the morning they were still talking.

BERNARDA: At four-thirty?

ANGUSTIAS *(entering)*: That's a lie!

PONCIA: That's what he told me.

BERNARDA *(to ANGUSTIAS)*: Speak up!

ANGUSTIA: For more than a week Pepe has been leaving at one. May God strike me dead if I'm lying.

MARTIRIO *(entering)*: I heard him leave at four too.

BERNARDA: But did you see him with your eyes?

MARTIRIO: I didn't want to look out. Don't you talk now through the side window?

ANGUSTIAS: We talk through my bedroom window.

(ADELA appears at the door.)

MARTIRIO: Then . . .

BERNARDA: What's going on here?

PONCIA: If you're not careful, you'll find out! At least Pepe was at *one* of your windows—and at four in the morning too!

BERNARDA: Are you sure of that?

PONCIA: You can't be sure of anything in this life!

ADELA: Mother, don't listen to someone who wants us to lose everything we have.

BERNARDA: I know how to take care of myself! If the townspeople want to come bearing false witness against me, they'll run into a stone wall! Don't any of you talk about this! Sometimes other people try to stir up a wave of filth to drown us.

MARTIRIO: I don't like to lie.

PONCIA: So there must be something.

BERNARDA: There won't be anything. I was born to have my eyes always open. Now I'll watch without closing them 'til I die.

ANGUSTIAS: I have the right to know.

BERNARDA: You don't have any right except to obey. No one's going to fetch and carry for me. (*to* LA PONCIA) And don't meddle in our affairs. No one will take a step without my knowing it.

SERVANT (*entering*): There's a big crowd at the top of the street, and all the neighbors are at their doors!

BERNARDA (*to* PONCIA): Run see what's happening!

(*The* GIRLS *are about to run out.*)

Where are you going? I always knew you for window-watching women and breakers of your mourning. All of you, to the patio!

(*They go out.* BERNARDA *leaves. Distant shouts are heard.*)

(MARTIRIO *and* ADELA *enter and listen, not daring to step farther than the front door.*)

MARTIRIO: You can be thankful I didn't happen to open my mouth.

ADELA: I would have spoken too.

MARTIRIO: And what were you going to say? Wanting isn't doing!

ADELA: I do what I can and what happens to suit me. You've wanted to, but haven't been able.

MARTIRIO: You won't go on very long.

ADELA: I'll have everything!

MARTIRIO: I'll tear you out of his arms!

ADELA (*pleadingly*): Martirio, let me be!

MARTIRIO: None of us will have him!

ADELA: He wants me for his house!

MARTIRIO: I saw how he embraced you!

ADELA: I didn't want him to. It's as if I were dragged by a rope.

MARTIRIO: I'll see you dead first!

(MAGDALENA *and* ANGUSTIAS *look in. The tumult is increasing. A* SERVANT *enters with* BERNARDA. PONCIA *also enters from another door.*)

PONCIA: Bernarda!

BERNARDA: What's happening?

PONCIA: Librada's daughter, the unmarried one, had a child and no one knows whose it is!

ADELA: A child?

PONCIA: And to hide her shame she killed it and hid it under the rocks, but the dogs, with more heart than most Christians, dug it out and, as though directed by the hand of God, left it at her door. Now they want to kill her. They're dragging her through the streets—and down the paths and across the olive groves the men are coming, shouting so the fields shake.

BERNARDA: Yes, let them all come with olive whips and hoe handles—let them all come and kill her!

ADELA: No, not to kill her!

MARTIRIO: Yes—and let us go out too!

BERNARDA: And let whoever loses her decency pay for it!

(*Outside a woman's shriek and a great clamor is heard.*)

ADELA: Let her escape! Don't you go out!

MARTIRIO (*looking at* ADELA): Let her pay what she owes!

BERNARDA (*at the archway*): Finish her before the guards come! Hot coals in the place where she sinned!

ADELA (*holding her belly*): No! No!

BERNARDA: Kill her! Kill her!

(*Curtain.*)

ACT 3

(*Four white walls, lightly washed in blue, of the interior patio of* BERNARDA ALBA's *house. The doorways, illumined by the lights inside the rooms, give a tenuous glow to the stage. At the center there is a table with a shaded oil lamp about which* BERNARDA *and her* DAUGHTERS *are eating.* LA PONCIA *serves them.* PRUDENCIA *sits apart. When the curtain rises, there is a great silence interrupted only by the noise of plates and silverware.*)

PRUDENCIA: I'm going. I've made you a long visit.

(*She rises.*)

BERNARDA: But wait, Prudencia. We never see one another.

PRUDENCIA: Have they sounded the last call to rosary?

PONCIA: Not yet.

(PRUDENCIA *sits down again.*)

BERNARDA: And your husband, how's he getting on?

PRUDENCIA: The same.

BERNARDA: We never see him either.

PRUDENCIA: You know how he is. Since he quarrelled with his brothers over the inheritance, he hasn't used the front door. He takes a ladder and climbs over the back wall.

BERNARDA: He's a real man! And your daughter?

PRUDENCIA: He's never forgiven her.

BERNARDA: He's right.

PRUDENCIA: I don't know what he told you. I suffer because of it.

BERNARDA: A daughter who's disobedient stops being a daughter and becomes an enemy.

PRUDENCIA: I let water run. The only consolation I've left is to take refuge in the church, but, since I'm losing my sight, I'll have to stop coming so the children won't make fun of me.

(A heavy blow is heard against the walls.)

What's that?

BERNARDA: The stallion. He's locked in the stall and he kicks against the wall of the house.

(Shouting.)

Tether him and take him out in the yard!

(In a lower voice.)

He must be too hot.

PRUDENCIA: Are you going to put the new mares to him?

BERNARDA: At daybreak.

PRUDENCIA: You've known how to increase your stock.

BERNARDA: By dint of money and struggling.

PONCIA *(interrupting)*: And she has the best herd in these parts. It's a shame that prices are low.

BERNARDA: Do you want a little cheese and honey?

PRUDENCIA: I have no appetite.

(The blow is heard again.)

PONCIA: My God!

PRUDENCIA: It quivered in my chest.

BERNARDA *(rising, furiously)*: Do I have to say things twice? Let him out to roll on the straw.

(Pause. Then, as though speaking to the STABLEMAN.*)*

Well then, lock the mares in the corral, but let him run free or he may kick down the walls.

(She returns to the table and sits again.)

Ay, what a life!

PRUDENCIA: You have to fight like a man.

BERNARDA: That's it.

(ADELA gets up from the table.)

Where are you going?

ADELA: For a drink of water.

BERNARDA *(raising her voice)*: Bring a pitcher of cool water. *(to* ADELA*)* You can sit down. *(ADELA sits down.)*

PRUDENCIA: And Angustias, when will she get married?

BERNARDA: They're coming to ask for her within three days.

PRUDENCIA: You must be happy.

ANGUSTIAS: Naturally!

AMELIA *(to* MAGDALENA*)*: You've spilled the salt!

MAGDALENA: You can't possibly have worse luck than you're having.

AMELIA: It always brings bad luck.

BERNARDA: That's enough!

PRUDENCIA *(to* ANGUSTIAS*)*: Has he given you the ring yet?

ANGUSTIAS: Look at it.

(She holds it out.)

PRUDENCIA: It's beautiful. Three pearls. In my day, pearls signified tears.

ANGUSTIAS: But things have changed now.

ADELA: I don't think so. Things go on meaning the same. Engagement rings should be diamonds.

PONCIA: The most appropriate.

BERNARDA: With pearls or without them, things are as one proposes.

MARTIRIO: Or as God disposes.

PRUDENCIA: I've been told your furniture is beautiful.

BERNARDA: It cost sixteen thousand *reales.*

PONCIA *(interrupting)*: The best is the wardrobe with the mirror.

PRUDENCIA: I never saw a piece like that.

BERNARDA: We had chests.

PRUDENCIA: The important thing is that everything be for the best.

ADELA: And that you never know.

BERNARDA: There's no reason why it shouldn't be.

(Bells are heard very distantly.)

PRUDENCIA: The last call. *(to* ANGUSTIAS*)* I'll be coming back to have you show me your clothes.

ANGUSTIAS: Whenever you like.

PRUDENCIA: Good evening—God bless you!

BERNARDA: Good-bye, Prudencia.

ALL FIVE DAUGHTERS *(at the same time)*: God go with you!

(Pause. PRUDENCIA *goes out.)*

BERNARDA: Well, we've eaten.

(They rise.)

ADELA: I'm going to walk as far as the gate to stretch my legs and get a bit of fresh air.

(MAGDALENA sits down in a low chair and leans against the wall.)

AMELIA: I'll go with you.

MARTIRIO: I too.

ADELA *(with contained hate)*: I'm not going to get lost!

AMELIA: One needs company at night.

(They go out. BERNARDA *sits down.* ANGUSTIAS *is clearing the table.)*

BERNARDA: I've told you once alrady! I want you to talk to your sister Martirio. What happened about the picture was a joke and you must forget it.

ANGUSTIAS: You know she doesn't like me.

BERNARDA: Each one knows what she thinks inside. I don't pry into anyone's heart, but I want to put up a good front and have family harmony. You understand?

ANGUSTIAS: Yes.

BERNARDA: Then that's settled.

MAGDALENA (she is almost asleep): Besides, you'll be gone in no time.

(She falls asleep.)

ANGUSTIAS: Not soon enough for me.

BERNARDA: What time did you stop talking last night?

ANGUSTIAS: Twelve-thirty.

BERNARDA: What does Pepe talk about?

ANGUSTIAS: I find him absent-minded. He always talks to me as though he were thinking of something else. If I ask him what's the matter, he answers—"We men have our worries."

BERNARDA: You shouldn't ask him. And when you're married, even less. Speak if he speaks, and look at him when he looks at you. That way you'll get along.

ANGUSTIAS: But, Mother, I think he's hiding things from me.

BERNARDA: Don't try to find out. Don't ask him, and above all, never let him see you cry.

ANGUSTIAS: I should be happy, but I'm not.

BERNARDA: It's all the same.

ANGUSTIAS: Many nights I watch Pepe very closely through the window bars and he seems to fade away—as though he were hidden in a cloud of dust like those raised by the flocks.

BERNARDA: That's just because you're not strong.

ANGUSTIAS: I hope so!

BERNARDA: Is he coming tonight?

ANGUSTIAS: No, he went into town with his mother.

BERNARDA: Good, we'll get to bed early. Magdalena!

ANGUSTIAS: She's asleep.

(ADELA, MARTIRIO and AMELIA enter.)

AMELIA: What a dark night!

ADELA: You can't see two steps in front of you.

MARTIRIO: A good night for robbers, for anyone who needs to hide.

ADELA: The stallion was in the middle of the corral. White. Twice as large. Filling all the darkness.

AMELIA: It's true. It was frightening. Like a ghost.

ADELA: The sky has stars as big as fists.

MARTIRIO: This one stared at them till she almost cracked her neck.

ADELA: Don't you like them up there?

MARTIRIO: What goes on over the roof doesn't mean a thing to me. I have my hands full with what happens under it.

ADELA: Well, that's the way it goes with you!

BERNARDA: And it goes the same for you as for her.

ANGUSTIAS: Good night.

ADELA: Are you going to bed now?

ANGUSTIAS: Yes, Pepe isn't coming tonight.

(She goes out.)

ADELA: Mother, why, when a stars falls or lightning flashes, does one say:
Holy Barbara, blessed on high
May your name be in the sky
With holy water written high?

BERNARDA: The old people know many things we've forgotten.

AMELIA: I close my eyes so I won't see them.

ADELA: Not I. I like to see what's quiet and been quiet for years on end, running with fire.

MARTIRIO: But all that has nothing to do with us.

BERNARDA: And it's better not to think about it.

ADELA: What a beautiful night! I'd like to stay up till very late and enjoy the breeze from the fields.

BERNARDA: But we have to go to bed. Magdalena!

AMELIA: She's just dropped off.

BERNARDA: Magdalena!

MAGDALENA (annoyed): Leave me alone!

BERNARDA: To bed!

MAGDALENA (rising, in a bad humor): You don't give anyone a moment's peace!

(She goes off grumbling.)

AMELIA: Good night!

(She goes out.)

BERNARDA: You two get along, too.

MARTIRIO: How is it Angustias' sweetheart isn't coming tonight?

BERNARDA: He went on a trip.

MARTIRIO (looking at ADELA): Ah!

ADELA: I'll see you in the morning!

(She goes out. MARTIRIO drinks some water and goes out slowly, looking at the door to the yard. LA PONCIA enters.)

PONCIA: Are you still here?

BERNARDA: Enjoying this quiet and not seeing anywhere the "very grave thing" that's happening here—according to you.

PONCIA: Bernarda, let's not go any further with this.

BERNARDA: In this house there's no question of a yes or a no. My watchfulness can take care of anything.

PONCIA: Nothing's happening outside. That's true, all right. Your daughters act and are as though stuck in a cupboard. But neither you nor anyone else can keep watch inside a person's heart.

BERNARDA: My daughters breathe calmly enough.

PONCIA: That's your business, since you're their mother. I have enough to do just with serving you.

BERNARDA: Yes, you've turned quiet now.

PONCIA: I keep my place—that's all.

BERNARDA: The trouble is you've nothing to talk about. If there were grass in this house, you'd make it your business to put the neighbors' sheep to pasture here.

PONCIA: I hide more than you think.

BERNARDA: Do your sons still see Pepe at four in the morning? Are they still repeating this house's evil litany?

PONCIA: They say nothing.

BERNARDA: Because they can't. Because there's nothing for them to sink their teeth in. And all because my eyes keep constant watch!

PONCIA: Bernarda, I don't want to talk about this because I'm afraid of what you'll do. But don't you feel so safe.

BERNARDA: Very safe!

PONCIA: Who knows, lightning might strike suddenly. Who knows but what all of a sudden, in a rush of blood, your heart might stop.

BERNARDA: Nothing will happen here. I'm on guard now against all your suspicions.

PONCIA: All the better for you.

BERNARDA: Certainly, all the better!

SERVANT (entering): I've just finished with the dishes. Is there anything else, Bernarda?

BERNARDA (rising): Nothing. I'm going to get some rest.

PONCIA: What time do you want me to call you?

BERNARDA: No time. Tonight I intend to sleep well.

(She goes out.)

PONCIA: When you're powerless against the sea, it's easier to turn your back on it and not look at it.

SERVANT: She's so proud! She herself pulls the blindfold over her eyes.

PONCIA: I can do nothing. I tried to head things off, but now they frighten me too much. You feel this silence?—in each room there's a thunderstorm—and the day it breaks, it'll sweep all of us along with it. But I've said what I had to say.

SERVANT: Bernarda thinks nothing can stand against her, yet she doesn't know the strength a man has among women alone.

PONCIA: It's not all the fault of Pepe el Romano. It's true last year he was running after Adela; and she was crazy about him—but she ought to keep her place and not lead him on. A man's a man.

SERVANT: And some there are who believe he didn't have to talk many times with Adela.

PONCIA: That's true.

(In a low voice.)

And some other things.

SERVANT: I don't know what's going to happen here.

PONCIA: How I'd like to sail across the sea and leave this house, this battleground, behind!

SERVANT: Bernarda's hurrying the wedding and it's possible nothing will happen.

PONCIA: Things have gone much too far already. Adela is set no matter what comes, and the rest of them watch without rest.

SERVANT: Martirio too . . . ?

PONCIA: That one's the worst. She's a pool of poison. She sees El Romano is not for her, and she'd sink the world if it were in her hand to do so.

SERVANT: How bad they all are!

PONCIA: They're women without men, that's all. And in such matters even blood is forgotten. Sh-h-h-h!

(She listens.)

SERVANT: What's the matter?

PONCIA (she rises): The dogs are barking.

SERVANT: Someone must have passed by the back door.

(ADELA enters wearing a white petticoat and corselet.)

PONCIA: Aren't you in bed yet?

ADELA: I want a drink of water.

(She drinks from a glass on the table.)

PONCIA: I imagined you were asleep.

ADELA: I got thirsty and woke up. Aren't you two going to get some rest?

SERVANT: Soon now.

(ADELA goes out.)

PONCIA: Let's go.

SERVANT: We've certainly earned some sleep. Bernarda doesn't let me rest the whole day.

PONCIA: Take the light.

SERVANT: The dogs are going mad.

PONCIA: They're not going to let us sleep.

(They go out. The stage is left almost dark. MARÍA JOSEFA enters with a lamb in her arms.)

MARIA JOSEFA (singing):
Little lamb, child of mine,
Let's go to the shore of the sea,
The tiny ant will be at his doorway,
I'll nurse you and give you your bread.
Bernarda, old leopard-face,
And Magdalena, hyena-face,
Little lamb . . .
Rock, rock-a-bye,
Let's go to the palms at Bethlehem's gate.

(She laughs.)

Neither you nor I would want to sleep
The door will open by itself
And on the beach we'll go and hide
In a little coral cabin.
Bernarda, old leopard-face,
And Magdalena, hyena-face,
Little lamb . . .
Rock, rock-a-bye,
Let's go to the palms at Bethlehem's gate.

(She goes off singing.)
*(*ADELA *enters. She looks about cautiously and disappears out the door leading to the corral.* MARTIRIO *enters by another door and stands in anguished watchfulness near the center of the stage. She also is in petticoats. She covers herself with a small black scarf.* MARÍA JOSEFA *crosses before her.)*

MARTIRIO: Grandmother, where are you going?

MARIA JOSEFA: You are going to open the door for me? Who are you?

MARTIRIO: How did you get out here?

MARIA JOSEFA: I escaped. You, who are you?

MARTIRIO: Go back to bed.

MARIA JOSEFA: You're Martirio. Now I see you. Martirio, face of a martyr. And when are you going to have a baby? I've had this one.

MARTIRIO: Where did you get that lamb?

MARIA JOSEFA: I know it's a lamb. But can't a lamb be a baby? It's better to have a lamb than not to have anything. Old Bernarda, leopard-face, and Magdalena, hyena-face!

MARTIRIO: Don't shout.

MARIA JOSEFA: It's true. Everything's very dark. Just because I have white hair you think I can't have babies, but I can—babies and babies and babies. This baby will have white hair, and I'd have *this* baby, and another, and this *one* other; and with all of us with snow white hair we'll be like the waves—one, then another, and another. Then we'll all sit down and all of us will have white heads, and we'll be seafoam. Why isn't there any seafoam here? Nothing but mourning shrouds here.

MARTIRIO: Hush, hush.

MARIA JOSEFA: When my neighbor had a baby, I'd carry her some chocolate and later she'd bring me some, and so on—always and always and always. You'll have white hair, but your neighbors won't come. Now I have to go away, but I'm afraid the dogs will bite me. Won't you come with me as far as the fields? I don't like fields. I like houses, but open houses, and the neighbor women asleep in their beds with their little tiny tots, and the men outside sitting in their chairs. Pepe el Romano is a giant. All of you love him. But he's going to devour you because you're

grains of wheat. No, not grains of wheat. Frogs with no tongues!

MARTIRIO *(angrily):* Come, off to bed with you.

(She pushes her.)

MARIA JOSEFA: Yes, but then you'll open the door for me, won't you?

MARTIRIO: Of course.

MARIA JOSEFA *(weeping):*
Little lamb, child of mine,
Let's go to the shore of the sea,
The tiny ant will be at his doorway,
I'll nurse you and give you your bread.

*(*MARTIRIO *locks the door through which* MARÍA JOSEFA *came out and goes to the yard door. There she hesitates, but goes two steps farther.)*

MARTIRIO *(in a low voice):* Adela! *(Pause. She advances to the door. Then, calling.)* Adela!

*(*ADELA *enters. Her hair is disarranged.)*

ADELA: And what are you looking for me for?

MARTIRIO: Keep away from him.

ADELA: Who are you to tell me that?

MARTIRIO: That's no place for a decent woman.

ADELA: How you wish *you'd* been there!

MARTIRIO *(shouting):* This is the moment for me to speak. This can't go on.

ADELA: This is just the beginning. I've had strength enough to push myself forward—the spirit and looks you lack. I've seen death under this roof, and gone out to look for what was mine, what belonged to me.

MARTIRIO: That soulless man came for another woman. You pushed yourself in front of him.

ADELA: He came for the money, but his eyes were always on me.

MARTIRIO: I won't allow you to snatch him away. He'll marry Angustias.

ADELA: You know better than I he doesn't love her.

MARTIRIO: I know.

ADELA: You know because you've seen—he loves me, me!

MARTIRIO *(desperately):* Yes.

ADELA *(close before her):* He loves me, *me!* He loves me, *me!*

MARTIRIO: Stick me with a knife if you like, but don't tell me that again.

ADELA: That's why you're trying to fix it so I won't go away with him. It makes no difference to you if he puts his arms around a woman he doesn't love. Nor does it to me. He could be a hundred years with Angustias, but for him to have his arms around me seems terrible to you—because you too love him! You love him!

MARTIRIO (*dramatically*): Yes! Let me say it without hiding my head. Yes! my breast's bitter, bursting like a pomegranate. I love him!

ADELA (*impulsively, hugging her*): Martirio, Martirio, I'm not to blame!

MARTIRIO: Don't put your arms around me! Don't try to smooth it over. My blood's no longer yours, and even though I try to think of you as a sister, I see you as just another woman.

(*She pushes her away.*)

ADELA: There's no way out here. Whoever has to drown—let her drown. Pepe is mine. He'll carry me to the rushes along the river bank. . . .

MARTIRIO: He won't!

ADELA: I can't stand this horrible house after the taste of his mouth. I'll be what he wants me to be. Everybody in the village against me, burning me with their fiery fingers; pursued by those who claim they're decent, and I'll wear, before them all, the crown of thorns that belongs to the mistress of a married man.

MARTIRIO: Hush!

ADELA: Yes, yes. (*In a low voice.*) Let's go to bed. Let's let him marry Augustias. I don't care any more, but I'll go off alone to a little house where he'll come to see me whenever he wants, whenever he feels like it.

MARTIRIO: That'll never happen! Not while I have a drop of blood left in my body.

ADELA: Not just weak you, but a wild horse I could force to his knees with just the strength of my little finger.

MARTIRIO: Don't raise that voice of yours to me. It irritates me. I have a heart full of a force so evil that, without my wanting to be, I'm drowned by it.

ADELA: You show us the way to love our sisters. God must have meant to leave me alone in the midst of darkness because I can see you as I've never seen you before.

(*A whistle is heard and* ADELA *runs toward the door, but* MARTIRIO *gets in front of her.*)

MARTIRIO: Where are you going?

ADELA: Get away from that door!

MARTIRIO: Get by me if you can!

ADELA: Get away!

(*They struggle.*)

MARTIRIO (*shouts*): Mother! Mother!

ADELA: Let me go!

(BERNARDA *enters. She wears petticoats and a black shawl.*)

BERNARDA: Quiet! Quiet! How poor I am without even a man to help me!

MARTIRIO (*pointing to* ADELA): She was with him. Look at those skirts covered with straw!

BERNARDA (*going furiously toward* Adela): That's the bed of a bad woman!

ADELA (*facing her*): There'll be an end to prison voices here! (ADELA *snatches away her mother's cane and breaks it in two.*) This is what I do with the tyrant's cane. Not another step. No one but Pepe commands me!

(MAGDALENA *enters.*)

MAGDALENA: Adela!

(LA PONCIA *and* ANGUSTIAS *enter.*)

ADELA: I'm his. (*to* ANGUSTIAS) Know that—and go out in the yard and tell him. He'll be master in this house.

ANGUSTIAS: My God!

BERNARDA: The gun! Where's the gun?

(*She rushes out.* LA PONCIA *runs ahead of her.* AMELIA *enters and looks on frightened, leaning her head against the wall. Behind her comes* MARTIRIO.)

ADELA: No one can hold me back!

(*She tries to go out.*)

ANGUSTIAS (*holding her*): You're not getting out of here with your body's triumph! Thief! Disgrace of this house!

MAGDALENA: Let her go where we'll never see her again!

(*A shot is heard.*)

BERNARDA (*entering*): Just try looking for him now!

MARTIRIO (*entering*): That does away with Pepe el Romano.

ADELA: Pepe! My God! Pepe!

(*She runs out.*)

PONCIA: Did you kill him?

MARTIRIO: No. He raced away on his mare!

BERNARDA: It was my fault. A woman can't aim.

MAGDALENA: Then, why did you say . . . ?

MARTIRIO: For her! I'd like to pour a river of blood over her head!

PONCIA: Curse you!

MAGDALENA: Devil!

BERNARDA: Although it's better this way!

(*A thud is heard.*)

Adela! Adela!

PONCIA (*at her door*): Open this door!

BERNARDA: Open! Don't think the walls will hide your shame!

SERVANT *(entering)*: All the neighbors are up!

BERNARDA *(in a low voice, but like a roar)*: Open! Or I'll knock the door down!

(Pause. Everything is silent.)

Adela!

(She walks away from the door.)

A hammer!

(LA PONCIA throws herself against the door. It opens and she goes in. As she enters, she screams and backs out.)

What is it?

PONCIA *(she puts her hands to her throat)*: May we never die like that!

(The SISTERS fall back. The SERVANT crosses herself. BERNARDA screams and goes forward.)

Don't go in!

BERNARDA: No, not I! Pepe, you're running now, alive in the darkness, under the trees, but another day you'll fall. Cut her down! My daughter died a virgin. Take her to another room and dress her as though she were a virgin. No one will say anything about this! She died a virgin. Tell them, so that at dawn, the bells will ring twice.

MARTIRIO: A thousand times happy she, who had him.

BERNARDA: And I want no weeping. Death must be looked at face to face. Silence!

(To one daughter.)

Be still, I said!

(To another daughter.)

Tears when you're alone! We'll drown ourselves in a sea of mourning. She, the youngest daughter of Bernarda Alba, died a virgin. Did you hear me? Silence, silence, I said. Silence!

CURTAIN

Figure 74. Bernarda (Katina Paxinou, *center*) and her five daughters in the American National Theater Association production of *The House of Bernarda Alba,* directed by Boris Tumarin and designed by Stewart Cheney, New York, 1951. (Photograph: Fred Fehl.)

Figure 75. Angustias *(right)* tells her sisters *(center)* and La Poncia *(left)* about her first meeting at the window with Pepe el Romano in the American National Theater Association production of *The House of Bernarda Alba,* directed by Boris Tumarin and designed by Stewart Cheney, New York, 1951. (Photograph: Fred Fehl.)

Staging of *The House of Bernarda Alba*

REVIEW OF THE AMERICAN NATIONAL THEATER ASSOCIATION PRODUCTION, 1951, BY BROOKS ATKINSON

Katina Paxinou has discovered a suitable part in "The House of Bernarda Alba," which opened at the Anta Playhouse last evening. She plays the tyrannical mother in another Spanish pastoral drama by Federico Garcia Lorca, the playwright and poet, whose "Blood Wedding" appeared in the New Stages schedule in 1949.

In "The House of Bernarda Alba" he is more poet than playwright. For this study in country cruelty is not so much a drama with plot and theme as a tone poem that evokes a dark mood. A widow with five daughters condemns all but one of them to incarceration at home because she believes that none of the men in the village is worthy of her family.

What she requires of her daughters seems simple to her. But it is inhuman to them. They hear the voices of men in the fields. They peek out at the men through the lattice. Although their mother's will is ironbound, it cannot cool their blood or stifle their youth. In another vein, "The House of Bernarda Alba" might be bucolic comedy. But Lorca's mood is somber in this play and it concludes with tragedy.

Uneventful and unsubstantial as a drama, "The House of Bernarda Alba" is a difficult piece to act by a company collected for one engagement. It needs to be performed like a dance, or like the exquisite marching song played off-stage in the second act with so much ease and beauty.

Stewart Chaney has enclosed the performance in a lovely, simple setting that is softly lighted. As the virago, Miss Paxinou gives a superb performance. Her widow and mother is bitter and acid and also extraordinarily powerful. She darts around the stage like a flame. She presides over her household with monstrous authority. Give Miss Paxinou the proper part and she can set a play on fire and also singe the audience.

There are some good actors in the other parts—notably Ruth Ford, Helen Craig, Kim Stanley and Tamara Daykarhanova; and they do as well as they can in the circumstances. But it is to be feared that Boris Tumarin's direction is not lyric enough to make art out of the group performance which is a medley of individual styles and personalities. It cannot stand comparison with that daintily written marching song that Vitorio Rieti has composed. Lorca needs music in the acting. He wrote out of mood more than out of mind.

REVIEW OF THE AMERICAN NATIONAL THEATER ASSOCIATION PRODUCTION, 1951, BY WOLCOTT GIBBS

"The House of Bernarda Alba," by Federico García Lorca, A.N.T.A.'s fourth production at its playhouse, is, I'm afraid, the kind of play that somehow doesn't translate very happily from one language to another. Lorca unquestionably had something moving and important to say about social conditions in rural Spain, but what comes out in the current version has more or less the air of a wild parody, conceivably executed by the late Robert Benchley. The domineering widow, Bernarda, and her five spinster daughters, three of whom are in pursuit of the only eligible local bachelor, a prodigious seducer called Pepe el Romano, were presumably comprehensible and melancholy figures to the playwright's countrymen, but they are almost bound to confuse and entertain American audiences, to whom the spectacle of nine ladies (there are also two astonishingly vocal servants and a crazy old grandmother) whose lives are obviously devoted to domestic bickering is apt to seem a little more comic than really dramatic. Toward the end, when Bernarda, employing a large-calibre fowling piece, shoots at the villainous Pepe and misses him, and remarks that women can't be expected to aim very well, most of those around me laughed nervously, and I'm embarrassed to say that I did, too. On the whole, the evening is like that. The girls clearly have their problems, but since their attitude toward them alternates between, on the one hand, the kind of dogged gloom that expresses itself every few minutes in a wish to be dead and buried and, on the other, assault and battery, it is not always possible to take them very seriously.

The production, provided by Boris Tumarin and Stewart Chaney, also has something to do with the trouble I had. It is alleged several times that the family is living in conditions of such extreme poverty that nobody can afford any respectable underwear, but the premises are clearly expensive, the domestic staff is extensive (as I got it, there are any number of shepherds and reapers employed on the estate), and the one meal submitted for inspection is a banquet of considerable dimensions. The basic dilemma confronting Bernarda and her flock is apparently their inability to move to another town, where suitable husbands can be found. It looked to me as if there was enough money around for everybody to light out for Texas. This is undoubtedly a captious objection, based on my ignorance of economic conditions in Spain, and I will defend it only by saying that at one point in the stage directions in the printed play the author calls for the entrance of two hundred women from the neighborhood, all to be provided with food and drink. This is a lot of women and ought to run into money in any language.

The cast of "The House of Bernarda Alba" is headed by Katina Paxinou, who plays Bernarda with all her customary vehemence, which I find impressive but perhaps just a little exhausting. Among the others are Helen Craig, Ruth Ford, Ruth Saville, Mary Welch, Tamara Daykarhanova, Sarah Cunningham, and Kim Stanley, and I doubt whether I have ever seen so many actresses knocking one another down before in my life. Neither Pepe el Romano nor any other male appears in the flesh. It is a woman's world, and you are welcome to it.

CONTEMPORARY THEATER

Most periods in the history of drama are associated with distinctive theatrical structures—the classical Greek with outdoor amphitheaters, the middle ages with pageant wagons and platform stages, the renaissance English with multilevel open-air theaters, the neoclassical with indoor theaters, proscenium stages, and perspective backdrops, the modern with fan-shaped auditoriums and box sets. During the contemporary period, variety is the rule in theatrical structures and staging conventions. The fan-shaped auditorium and the box set of realistic theater (see Figures 49 and 52) continue to flourish in many amateur and professional houses. Yet, in addition to this now common pattern, other theatrical arrangements have developed, reflecting a renewed interest in earlier methods of staging. In an attempt to reclaim and combine elements of the classical Greek and renaissance English theaters, mid-century designers created the thrust stage (see Figure 76), in which the audience is seated on rising tiers around three sides of a platform, and the fourth side is occupied by a permanent setting that contains multiple acting surfaces. And somewhat earlier in the century, designers reclaimed the medieval style of theater-in-the-round and turned it into the arena stage (see Figure 77), an arrangement placing the audience on all four sides of the actors and using the aisles for entrances and exits. The theatrical freedom of the arena stage has also prompted directors and producers to reclaim another medieval heritage by putting on plays in the street, in public squares, or any other open space that will bring actors and spectators closer to each other than is possible in the traditional theater.

Contemporary set design has been equally flexible, ranging from a total abandonment of settings, set pieces, and props to the use of highly elaborate set designs in a realistic or symbolic style. In part, of course, various styles in set design have been determined by the nature of the theatrical environment. Arena stages and thrust stages clearly do not invite the use of box sets or painted backdrops. In these environments, the setting is evoked simply by a few pieces of furniture and a few props, much as in the classical, medieval, or renaissance theater. But even in a conventional modern theater, where the realism of the box set has been readily accessible, designers have taken the liberty of blending and modifying a combination of styles to achieve unique dramatic effects. Jo Mielziner, for example, who designed the sets for the first production of Arthur Miller's *Death of a Salesman* in 1949, chose to combine realistic and expressionistic elements in his set depicting Willy Loman's house. That set, as we can see from a photograph of the original production (Figure 78), contained real furniture and wall flats representing the first floor. But the rooms on the first floor were not divided from one another by walls, and the second floor did not have any walls at all, nor did it have any roof. The roof was simply outlined by upward thrusting beams, suggesting Willy's dreams of aspiration, and through the open spaces of the roof could be seen a painted backdrop of tall city buildings, looming over the

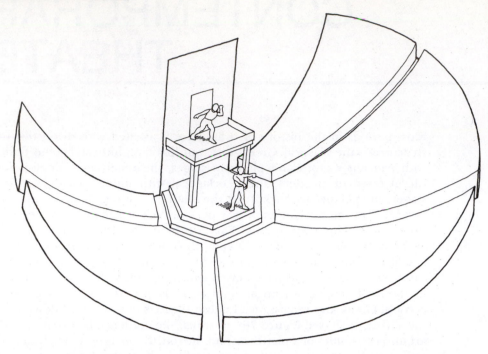

Figure 76. The contemporary thrust stage, showing the multiple acting surfaces adapted from the renaissance English theater, surrounded on three sides by the rising tiers of seats adapted from the classical Greek theater.

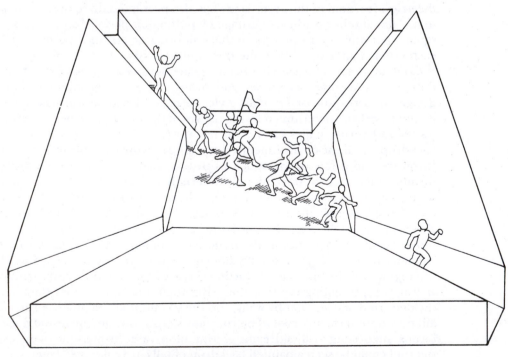

Figure 77. The contemporary arena stage.

house, closing it in, as if to suggest the stifling effect of the modern world on the lives of the Loman family. Mielziner's set was also designed to provide multilevel acting areas, as in the Elizabethan stage, and these made possible the staging of simultaneous action in different locations, as when Willy reassures Linda on the first floor, while Biff and Happy listen from their bedroom on the second floor (see Figure 79). Mielziner's highly original set was evoked, of course, by Miller's script for the play, which clearly blends realistic, expressionistic, and symbolic elements, as is the case, too, in Eugene O'Neill's *A Moon for the Misbegotten*, or Tennessee Williams' *Cat on a Hot Tin Roof*, or Imamu Amiri Baraka's *Dutchman*.

But the freedom in contemporary theater to choose among a variety of styles has also made it possible for dramatists to reject realistic conventions altogether, as did the playwrights of the most influential movement of the 1950s and 1960s, the "Theater of the Absurd," a movement defined and named by the critic Martin Esslin. The absurdists—most notably Samuel Beckett, Eugéne Ionesco, and Jean Genet—reject such realistic conventions as psychologically motivated characters and plots, logically consistent dialogue, and familiar styles of presentation, for, as Esslin explains, "The Theatre of the Absurd has renounced arguing *about* the absurdity of the human condition; it merely *presents* it in being— that is, in terms of concrete stage images of the absurdity of existence." Given their acute sense of the malignancy, or meaninglessness, or sterility of existence, the absurdists deliberately favor stage actions and images that will clearly evoke such a view of experience, whether it is the garbage can residents of Beckett's *Endgame* or the rhinoceros that takes over the world of Ionesco's *Rhinoceros*. The drama that Esslin has labelled absurdist has its roots in *avant-garde* theater of the early twentieth century, in such plays as Alfred Jarry's *Ubu Roi* (1896), a scatalogical and seemingly nonsensical play about a brutal and whimsical ruler, or Guillaume Apollinaire's *The Breasts of Tiresias* (1917), which features a dancing newskiosk and a woman turning into a man when her breasts float away as balloons. It also derives from the radical ideas of Antonin Artaud, who in 1938 expounded a "theater of cruelty," which he based on the assumption that "Everything that acts is a cruelty. It is upon this idea of extreme action, pushed beyond all limits, that theatre must be rebuilt." Although absurdist drama is not strictly speaking an instance of the theater of cruelty, it does clearly push drama to extreme actions and images.

Absurdist drama is not only a striking instance of the stylistic freedom in contemporary theater, but it has also been a source of nurturing even greater experimentation among playwrights, directors, actors, and set designers. After seeing Beckett's *Waiting for Godot,* for example, the dramatist William Saroyan said, "It will make it easier for me and everyone else to write freely in the theatre." Unhampered by expectations about what drama *should* be like, contemporary playwrights have constantly experimented with symbolic and image-centered drama, as indicated by the metaphoric titles of many of their plays, such as *Endgame, Dutchman,* and *Equus*. They have been free even to create roles for horses, to be played by actors, as did Peter Shaffer in *Equus* (1974). The dramatic inventions of the playwrights have, in turn. stimulated the designers, such as John Napier, who created stylized masks and hooves for the actors to wear in *Equus*. And the actors themselves, of course, have been forced to develop non-realistic styles of performance, a challenge that has provoked them to explore

Figure 78. The realistic/expressionistic set design by Jo Mielziner for the original Broadway production of *Death of a Salesman*, New York, 1949. (Photograph: Eileen Darby.)

Figure 79. Willy and Linda on the first floor, overheard by Biff and Happy on the second floor, of the realistic/expressionistic set designed by Jo Mielziner for the original Broadway production of *Death of a Salesman*, New York, 1949. (Photograph: Eileen Darby.)

the arts of dance, mime, and vaudeville. How, after all, is it possible for an actor to portray "realistically" the process of a man turning into a rhinoceros, or a mute, in *Waiting for Godot*, suddenly unleashing a torrent of speech? The need to find new acting styles and to make sense of these plays for an audience has ultimately led to a greatly increased emphasis on the imaginative leadership of the director.

Indeed, contemporary theater, whether it has taken the form of realism, modified realism, or absurdism, has often been determined not only by a playwright's script, but also by a director's creative influence upon the script. O'Neill's late autobiographical plays, such as *A Moon for the Misbegotten*, did not excite audiences until a director, such as José Quintero, was able to display their power in the theater. Tennessee Williams acknowledged the influence of the director, Elia Kazan, by using his ideas to produce a drastically new version of the third act for *Cat on a Hot Tin Roof*. And Peter Shaffer was so impressed by John Dexter's direction of *The Royal Hunt of the Sun* and *Equus* that he incorporated many of Dexter's ideas into his published versions of the plays. In fact, the director's influence has in some cases been so profound that audiences and critics have occasionally been moved to see it as the major source of creativity in the theater.

Perhaps the most striking example of the creative director in contemporary theater is the Englishman, Peter Brook, whose productions of Shakespeare have moved critics to speak of Brook's *King Lear* and Brook's *A Midsummer Night's Dream*, rather than Shakespeare's. Brook first came to public notice in the early 1940s and 1950s as a "boy genius" directing major productions of Shakespeare in London and Stratford. But his sensational reputation as a revolutionary director did not get established until 1962 when he produced *King Lear* in a style heavily influenced by the starkly expressionistic techniques of Brecht's epic theater. Brook then became influenced by Artaud's theater of cruelty, which led him to argue that cruelty is a necessary "form of self-discipline" for performers, and thus he entered into an intense period of physical exercises and improvisations with a group of selected actors, a project culminating in his 1964 production of Peter Weiss' *Marat/Sade*, an elaborate play-within-a-play that features the inmates of a mental asylum staging the events of the French Revolution. Brook's highly disciplined actors kept the stage in a continuous state of theatrical disarray in order to convey the deranged experience of a mental asylum—actors performing the inmates never stopped moving and drooling and acting out their fantasies. And at the play's conclusion, when the inmates begin tearing up the stage, Brook added a final inventive touch: as the audience applauded, the actors lined up and steadily, smirkingly, rhythmically applauded back.

The revolution in contemporary theater has been carried to its logical extreme by directors who have formed repertory groups committed to a radical alteration of virtually all the traditional conventions of drama. During the late 1960s, for example, the Living Theater of Julian Beck and Judith Malina staged a series of works stressing political activism—an activism they sought to dramatize by deliberately breaking the barrier that has traditionally separated actors from spectators. Members of the Living Theater routinely talked to, touched, and even invited the audience onstage during their performances, and one of their productions, *Paradise Now*, actually climaxed with a "love pile" or "group grope" for both actors and those members of the audience who still remained in the theater. By contrast, Jerzy Grotoski and the Polish Laboratory Theatre deliberately sought to isolate members of the audience, by bringing each person in a forty- or fifty-person group into the acting space one by one, sometimes even seating them behind raised walls. Furthermore, by abandoning a permanent stage and choosing to redesign the acting space for each play, by discarding makeup, costumes, props, and music, Grotowski created what has been known as "poor theater," in order to focus on "the personal and scenic technique of the actor as the core of theater art." Other experimental groups of the 1960s and 1970s have applied the rituals of yoga and meditation to theatrical performance, and still others have staged productions in slow-motion, creating barely moving visual images in works that run from three to twelve hours in length. Perhaps the most remarkable element in all these experimental groups is not their assault upon theatrical conventions, nor their intense fascination with sound and movement, but their abandonment of scripted plays in favor of improvisation—a phenomenon reminiscent of Artaud's manifesto calling for "No More Masterpieces!"

Of course, plays continue to be written and produced throughout the world, but contemporary playwrights clearly show the influence of even the most highly experimental groups. Harold Pinter, for example, the British dramatist who writes in the absurdist tradition, does not reject language, but he repeatedly counterpoints dialogue with pauses and silences in order to show how little is communicated through language and how much is conveyed by silence. Although Shaffer's *Equus* is filled with monologues by the psychiatrist-narrator, the emotional center of the play is a mimed ritual in which a young boy rides naked on a horse at midnight. Even the most skilled comic writers for the contemporary stage know that physical movement can often provoke far more laughter than the wittiest line; in *The Odd Couple,* Neil Simon builds comic momentum out of two people refusing to speak to one another for several minutes on stage, while in *Table Manners,* the English playwright Alan Ayckbourn creates laughter by having a character try to eat dinner while sitting on a chair that is clearly too low for him to reach the table.

The fascinating paradox of contemporary theater is that its new developments repeatedly seem to echo older forms of drama. Just as contemporary theatrical design reflects a variety of staging techniques from the classical, medieval, and renaissance periods, so the contemporary experimental fascination with sound and movement recalls the religious rituals from which drama first arose. The history of theater thus seems to follow a cyclical pattern, though perhaps it would be more accurate to say, as Peter Brook has, that the theater is not static or unchanging, that "Truth in the theater is always on the move." Such movement is inherent in drama, on any stage, at any stage of history, for drama is a living form of art; it draws its life from live actors and a live audience coming together to create the performance.

EUGENE O'NEILL

1888–1953

Before his death of a rare degenerative disease that made it almost impossible for him to write during the last several years of his life, O'Neill produced more than fifty plays whose theatrical range and vision have firmly established him as the greatest playwright in the history of American drama. From the very beginning of his life the theater was an inextricable part of his experience, for he was the son of one of America's most famous matinee idols, the romantic actor James O'Neill, who achieved theatrical fame as the star of *The Count of Monte Cristo* and continued to tour in the play until he was well into his sixties. O'Neill himself was born in a hotel in the theater district of New York, and during his early childhood he travelled with his father on theatrical tours that took him throughout the United States. The chaotic life of his father's career and the morphine addiction that his mother developed after taking the drug to alleviate the pain of O'Neill's birth were also an indelible part of his experience, which he reflected in a number of late autobiographical plays that constitute the greatest achievement of his career, among them *Long Day's Journey into Night* (1940) and *A Moon for the Misbegotten* (1943). In these and other late plays, O'Neill confronted the most painful aspects of his family's and his own personal experience—his father's extramarital affairs, his mother's morphine addiction, his brother's inability to hold a job, his father's alcoholism, his brother's alcoholism, his own alcoholism that drove him to attempt suicide at a Bowery bar in 1912, and the endless cycle of bitter accusation and shamefaced apology that consumed the family throughout his life, leaving him obsessively torn between love and hatred for all its members. But the writing of these plays was more than a psychological milestone of honestly confronting his own past, for they also represent the artistic climax to his many years of searching for an appropriate dramatic form in which to convey his vision of modern experience.

O'Neill turned to playwriting in 1912, after a hectic period of several years, during which he got secretly married to a young woman whom he promptly left to go prospecting for gold in Honduras, then returned after a year to join his father as an actor and assistant stage manager on tour, went to sea again for a brief period, returned and took a job as a reporter on a small town newspaper in Connecticut, and then came down with tuberculosis, brought on no doubt by his dissolute life, which forced him to be hospitalized for an extended period of time. During 1912, he became an avid reader of drama and decided to make his career as a dramatist. He began writing plays in 1913, enrolled in a playwriting course at Harvard during 1914, moved to Greenwich Village in 1915, and there joined up with a group of *avant-garde* writers who had formed a repertory company, called the Provincetown Players, which became one of the most influential groups in American theater, largely because of the plays that O'Neill produced for them during his early career.

O'Neill began by writing a series of one-act plays based on his earlier experiences at sea, strictly realistic plays in which he dramatized the illusions and preoccupations of men adrift in the world. By the early 1920s, he had begun writing full-length plays, still drawing on his fascination with the sea, but conveying a complex vision of tragic fate and frustration, as in the Pulitzer Prize-winning *Beyond the Horizon* (1920) and *Anna Christie* (1921). He then began to experiment with expressionistic techniques in *The Emperor Jones* (1920), a one-act psychodrama about a Negro "emperor" who flees a palace revolution and succumbs to his own fantasies and "the Little Formless Fears." The most striking innovation in this play was O'Neill's use of a drumbeat that began at pulse rate and gradually accelerated as Jones came closer and closer to death, ceasing only when he died. In *The Hairy Ape* (1922), O'Neill went even further with expressionist techniques by using contrastive symbolic settings (a furnace room versus fashionable Fifth Avenue), as well as choral speeches, and socially emblematic characters to dramatize the destruction of a young stoker, named Yank, who is unable to move outside of his class.

By the mid-1920s, his fascination with Freudian psychology had already become manifest in *Desire Under the Elms* (1924), a play dramatizing the tragic sexual attraction between a young man and his young stepmother. Then in *The Great God Brown* (1926), he used expressionistic techniques to dramatize what he was later to call the "profound hidden conflicts of the mind," by having the actors wear masks, as in Greek drama, to reflect their assumed personalities. By the late 1920s, his absorption with Freudian psychology had carried him so far into experimental theater that he tried to reveal the inner thoughts of his characters by having them interrupt their dialogue and express their hidden feelings in monologue to the audience, a strategy he used in his nine-act play *Strange Interlude* (1928). In *Days without End* (1934), he carried his expressionistic rendering of Freudian themes to the logical extreme by having two actors play the conflicting sides of the main character. Yet even during this period when he was exploring the psychopathology of the human mind, he was also working in more realistic and naturalistic modes that anticipated the style of his late plays. In *Mourning Becomes Electra* (1931), a trilogy based on the *Oresteia* of Aeschylus, O'Neill dramatized the tragic fate of a family across several generations—a fate determined not by pride, as in the Greek drama, but by sexual instincts, psychic guilt, suicide, and remorse. During the early 1930s, he also wrote his only comedy, *Ah, Wilderness* (1933), a nostalgic work in the realistic style that depicts a family very much like his own, but offers an idyllic family picture that was to be strikingly reversed in the years to follow.

Finally, in the late 1930s, he began to face up to his own past, first with *The Iceman Cometh* (1939), which was set in a saloon very much like the one where he had lived and had tried to kill himself, and which dramatized at length O'Neill's painful awareness of human frailty and self-deception. In *Long Day's Journey into Night* (1940), he was able "to face my dead at last," and he did so by turning the four members of his family—his father, mother, brother Jamie, and himself—into the "four haunted Tyrones," whose love-hate conflicts he completely exposed, but exposed with compassion, understanding, and forgiveness. Finally, in 1943, he completed his last autobiographical play, *A Moon for the Misbegotten*, a work based on the life of his alcoholic brother Jamie. It was the last of O'Neill's plays to be produced during his lifetime, and it almost never got staged at all.

The first production, in 1947, floundered in Columbus, was attacked by the Chamber of Commerce in Pittsburgh, censored by the police in Detroit, and never made it to New York until ten years later in 1957. And when it finally did get to New York, four years after O'Neill had died, the critics treated it as roughly as the businessmen and police had ten years earlier. Only in 1968, in a production at Circle in the Square, did it finally find a receptive audience, though when it was revived again in the mid-1970s critics were ready to recognize it as one of O'Neill's finest plays, possibly even his greatest.

Like his other late autobiographical plays, *A Moon for the Misbegotten* is written in the style of what O'Neill himself called "faithful realism." Yet it is by no means an easy play to witness or produce. It calls for two exceptional performers, one of them a huge woman, "so oversize for a woman that she is almost a freak," and the other an actor capable of sustaining a third act monologue that goes on for several pages. Josie, the oversized virgin, whom everyone thinks of as a whore, gets a bottle of real bourbon, hoping to seduce Jim Tyrone, the cynical New York drunk, and so get him to marry her. But the planned seduction turns into a long confession by Jim, and the embrace that is meant to produce a shotgun marriage produces instead "a strangely tragic picture"—"this big sorrowful woman hugging a haggard-faced, middle-aged drunkard against her breast as if he were a sick child." A theatrically parallel tableau of hopelessness also appears in *A Long Day's Journey into Night*, at the end of the play, when the three drunken Tyrone men sit silently listening to the drugged Mary Tyrone. But *A Moon for the Misbegotten* moves beyond the momentary stasis to the waking-up, both literally and spiritually, when Jim awakens and tries to pretend that his confession did not happen, but then finally admits that he does remember and is glad to remember. Josie's final line is thus full of compassion, when she says gently to an empty stage, "May you have your wish and die in your sleep soon, Jim, darling. May you rest forever in forgiveness and peace."

The most memorable production of the play took place in 1973, when Colleen Dewhurst and Jason Robards, Jr., joined forces with the director José Quintero. Quintero had already directed *Long Day's Journey into Night*, in 1955, and Robards had played the role of Jamie Tyrone in that same production. In Colleen Dewhurst, they found an actress who could encompass Josie, both physically and emotionally. She was capable of the raucous, even coarse behavior that characterizes Josie for much of the first two acts (see Figure 81), and yet she could also show the understanding and compassion necessary as she listens to Jim throughout much of Act 3 (see Figure 82). Miss Dewhurst received rave notices from the critics, as reflected in the review reprinted following the text. The set for that production was an evocative rather than detailed recreation of the farmhouse where the action of the play is located (see Figure 80), with its base in real objects, in the wooden floor, the rocks, and the chairs, just as the play has its roots in the reality of O'Neill's tormented past. Yet the set was also free of those objects, implying the world beyond, just as the play itself hints at a future free of guilt.

A MOON FOR THE MISBEGOTTEN

BY EUGENE O'NEILL

CHARACTERS

JOSIE HOGAN

PHIL HOGAN, *her father*

MIKE HOGAN, *her brother*

JAMES TYRONE, JR.

T. STEDMAN HARDER

SCENE

ACT 1: *The farmhouse. Around noon. Early September, 1923*, ACT 2: *The same, but with the interior of sitting room revealed—11 o'clock that night;* ACT 3: *The same as Act 1. No time elapses between Acts 2 and 3;* ACT 4: *The same—Dawn of the following morning.*

The play takes place in Connecticut at the home of tenant farmer, Phil Hogan, between the hours of noon on a day in early September, 1923, and the sunrise of the following day.

The house is not, to speak mildly, a fine example of New England architecture, placed so perfectly in its setting that it appears a harmonious part of the landscape, rooted in the earth. It has been moved to its present site, and looks it. An old box-like, clapboarded affair, with a shingled roof and brick chimney, it is propped up about two feet above ground by layers of timber blocks. There are two windows on the lower floor of this side of the house which faces front, and one window on the floor above. These windows have no shutters, curtains or shades. Each has at least one pane missing, a square of cardboard taking its place. The house had once been painted a repulsive yellow with brown trim, but the walls now are a blackened and weathered gray, flaked with streaks and splotches of dim lemon. Just around the left corner of the house, a flight of steps leads to the front door.

To make matters worse, a one-story, one-room addition has been tacked on at right. About twelve feet long by six high, this room which is JOSIE HOGAN'S bedroom, is evidently homemade. Its walls and sloping roof are covered with tar paper, faded to dark gray. Close to where it joins the house, there is a door with a flight of three unpainted steps leading to the ground. At right of door is a small window.

From these steps there is a footpath going around an old pear tree, at right-rear, through a field of hay stubble to a patch of woods. The same path also extends left to join a dirt road which leads up from the county highway (about a hundred yards off left) to the front door of the house, and thence back through a scraggly orchard of apple trees to the barn. Close to the house, under the window next to JOSIE'S bedroom, there is a big boulder with a flat-top.

ACT 1

(It is just before noon. The day is clear and hot.

The door of JOSIE'S bedroom opens and she comes out on the steps, bending to avoid bumping her head.

JOSIE is twenty-eight. She is so oversize for a woman that she is almost a freak—five feet eleven in her stockings and weighs around one hundred and eighty. Her sloping shoulders are broad, her chest deep with large, firm breasts, her waist wide but slender by contrast with her hips and thighs. She has long smooth arms, immensely strong, although no muscles show. The same is true of her legs.

She is more powerful than any but an exceptionally strong man, able to do the manual labor of two ordinary men. But there is no mannish quality about her. She is all woman.

The map of Ireland is stamped on her face, with its long upper lip and small nose, thick black eyebrows, black hair as coarse as a horse's mane, freckled, sunburned fair skin, high cheekbones and heavy jaw. It is not a pretty face, but her large dark-blue eyes give it a note of beauty, and her smile, revealing even white teeth, gives it charm.

She wears a cheap, sleeveless, blue cotton dress. Her feet are bare, the soles earth-stained and tough as leather.

She comes down the steps and goes left to the corner of the house and peers around it toward the barn. Then she moves swiftly to the right of the house and looks back.)

JOSIE: Ah, thank God. (*She goes back toward the steps as her brother,* MIKE, *appears hurrying up from right-rear.*)

(MIKE HOGAN *is twenty, about four inches shorter than his sister. He is sturdily built, but seems almost puny compared to her. He has a common Irish face, its expression sullen, or slyly cunning, or primly self-righteous. He never forgets that he is a good Catholic, faithful to all the observances, and so is one of the élite of Almighty God in a world of damned sinners composed of Protestants and bad Catholics. In brief,* MIKE *is a New England Irish Catholic Puritan, Grade B, and an extremely irritating youth to have around.*)

(MIKE *wears dirty overalls, a sweat-stained brown shirt. He carries a pitchfork.*)

JOSIE: Bad luck to you for a slowpoke. Didn't I tell you half-past eleven?

MIKE: How could I sneak here sooner with him peeking round the corner of the barn to catch me if I took a minute's rest, the way he always does? I had to wait till he went to the pig pen. (*He adds viciously.*) Where he belongs, the old hog! (JOSIE's *right arm strikes with surprising swiftness and her big hand lands on the side of his jaw. She means it to be only a slap, but his head jerks back and he stumbles, dropping the pitchfork, and pleads cringingly.*) Don't hit me, Josie! Don't, now!

JOSIE (*quietly*): Then keep your tongue off him. He's my father, too, and I like him, if you don't.

MIKE (*out of her reach–sullenly*): You're two of a kind, and a bad kind.

JOSIE (*good naturedly*): I'm proud of it. And I didn't hit you, or you'd be flat on the ground. It was only a love tap to waken your wits, so you'll use them. If he catches you running away, he'll beat you half to death. Get your bag now. I've packed it. It's inside the door of my room with your coat laid over it. Hurry now, while I see what he's doing. (*She moves quickly to peer around the corner of the house at left. He goes up the steps into her room and returns carrying an old coat and a cheap bulging satchel. She comes back.*) There's no sight of him. (MIKE *drops the satchel on the ground while he puts on the coat.*) I put everything in the bag. You can change to your Sunday suit in the can at the station or in the train, and don't forget to wash your face. I know you want to look your best when our brother, Thomas, sees you on his doorstep. (*Her tone becomes derisively amused.*) And him way up in the world, a noble sergeant of the Bridgeport police. Maybe he'll get you on the force. It'd suit you. I can see you leading drunks to the lockup while you give them a lecture on temperance. Or if Thomas can't get you a job, he'll pass you along to our brother, John, the noble barkeep in Meriden. He'll teach you the trade. You'll make a nice one, who'll never steal from the till, or drink, and who'll tell customers they've had enough and better go home just when they're beginning to feel happy. (*She sighs regretfully.*) Ah, well, Mike, you was born a priest's pet, and there's no help for it.

MIKE: That's right! Make fun of me again, because I want to be decent.

JOSIE: You're worse than decent. You're virtuous.

MIKE: Well that's a thing nobody can say about—(*He stops, a bit ashamed, but mostly afraid to finish.*)

JOSIE (*amused*): About me? No, and what's more, they don't. (*She smiles mockingly.*) I know what a trial it's been to you, Mike, having a sister who's the scandal of the neighborhood.

MIKE: It's you that's saying it, not me. I don't want to part with hard feelings. And I'll keep on praying for you.

JOSIE (*roughly*): Och! To hell with your prayers!

MIKE (*stiffly*): I'm going. (*He picks up his bag.*)

JOSIE (*her manner softening*): Wait. (*She comes to him.*) Don't mind my rough tongue, Mike. I'm sorry to see you go, but it's the best thing for you. That's why I'm helping you, the same as I helped Thomas and John. You can't stand up to the Old Man any more than Thomas or John could, and the old divil would always keep you a slave. I wish you all the luck in the world, Mike. I know you'll get on—and God bless you. (*Her voice has softened, and she blinks back tears. She kisses him–then fumbling in the pocket of her dress, pulls out a little roll of one-dollar bills and presses it in his hand.*) Here's a little present over your fare. I took it from his little green bag, and won't he be wild when he finds out! But I can handle him.

MIKE (*enviously*): You can. You're the only one. (*Gratefully moved for a second.*) Thank you, Josie. You've a kind heart. (*Then virtuously.*) But I don't like taking stolen money.

JOSIE: Don't be a bigger jackass than you are already. Tell your conscience it's a bit of the wages he's never given you.

MIKE: That's true, Josie. It's rightfully mine. (*He shoves the money into his pocket.*)

JOSIE: Get along now, so you won't miss the trolley. And don't forget to get off the train at Bridgeport. Give my love to Thomas and John. No, never mind. They've not written me in years. Give them a boot in the tail for me.

MIKE: That's nice talk for a woman. You've a tongue as dirty as the Old Man's.

JOSIE (*impatiently*): Don't start preaching, like you love to, or you'll never go.

MIKE: You're as bad as he is, almost. It's his influence made you what you are, and him always scheming how he'll cheat people, selling them a broken-down nag or a sick cow or pig that he's doctored up to look good for a day or two. It's no better than stealing, and you help him.

JOSIE: I do. Sure, it's grand fun.

MIKE: You ought to marry and have a home of your own away from this shanty and stop your shameless ways with men. (*He adds, not without moral satisfaction.*) Though it'd be hard to find a decent man who'd have you now.

JOSIE: I don't want a decent man, thank you. They're no fun. They're all sticks like you. And I wouldn't marry the best man on earth and be tied down to him alone.

MIKE (*with a cunning leer*): Not even Jim Tyrone, I suppose? (*She stares at him.*) You'd like being tied to money, I know that, and he'll be rich when his mother's estate is settled. (*Sarcastically.*) I suppose you've never thought of that? Don't tell me! I've watched you making sheep's eyes at him.

JOSIE (*contemptuously*): So I'm leading Jim on to propose, am I?

MIKE: I know it's crazy, but maybe you're hoping if you got hold of him alone when he's mad drunk— Anyway, talk all you please to put me off, I'll bet my last penny you've cooked up some scheme to hook him, and the Old Man put you up to it. Maybe he thinks if he caught you with Jim and had witnesses to prove it, and his shotgun to scare him—

JOSIE (*controlling her anger*): You're full of bright thoughts. I wouldn't strain my brains any more, if I was you.

MIKE: Well, I wouldn't put it past the Old Man to try any trick. And I wouldn't put it past you, God forgive you. You've never cared about your virtue, or what man you went out with. You've always been brazen as brass and proud of your disgrace. You can't deny that, Josie.

JOSIE: I don't. (*Then ominously.*) You'd better shut up now. I've been holding my temper, because we're saying good-bye. (*She stands up.*) But I'm losing patience.

MIKE (*hastily*): Wait till I finish and you won't be mad at me. I was going to say I wish you luck with your scheming, for once. I hate Jim Tyrone's guts, with his quotin' Latin and his high-toned Jesuit College education, putting on airs as if he was too good to wipe his shoes on me, when he's nothing but a drunken bum who never done a tap of work in his life, except acting on the stage while his father was alive to get him the jobs. (*Vindictively.*) I'll pray you'll find a way to nab him, Josie, and skin him out of his last nickel!

JOSIE (*makes a threatening move toward him*): One more word out of you— (*Then contemptuously.*) You're a dirty tick and it'd serve you right if I let you stay gabbing until Father came and beat you to a jelly, but I won't. I'm too anxious to be rid of you. (*Roughly.*) Get out of here, now! Do you think he'll stay all day with the pigs, you gabbing fool? (*She goes left to peer around the corner of the house– with real alarm.*) There he is coming up to the barn. (MIKE *grabs the satchel, terrified. He slinks swiftly around the corner and disappears along the path to the woods, right-rear. She keeps watching her father and does not notice* MIKE'S *departure.*) He's looking toward the meadow. He sees you're not working. He's running down there. He'll come here next. You'd better run for your life! (*She peeks around the corner again–with amused admiration.*) Look at my poor old father pelt. He's as spry on his stumpy legs as a yearling—and as full of rage as a nest of wasps! (*She laughs and comes back to look along the path to the woods.*) Well, that's the last of you, Mike, and good riddance. It was the little boy you used to be that I had to mother, and not you, I stole the money for. (*This dismisses him. She sighs.*) Well, himself will be here in a minute. I'd better be ready. (*She reaches in her bedroom corner by the door and takes out a sawed-off broom handle.*) Not that I need it, but it saves his pride. (*She sits on the steps with the broom handle propped against the steps near her right hand. A moment later, her father,* PHIL HOGAN, *comes running up from left-rear and charges around the corner of the house, his arms pumping up and down, his fists clenched, his face full of fighting fury.*)

(HOGAN *is fifty-five, about five feet six. He has a thick neck, lumpy, sloping shoulders, a barrel-like trunk, stumpy legs, and big feet. His arms are short and muscular, with large hairy hands. His head is round with thinning sandy hair. His face is fat with a snub nose, long upper lip, big mouth, and little blue eyes with bleached lashes and eyebrows that remind one of a white pig's. He wears heavy brogans, filthy overalls, and a dirty short-sleeved undershirt. Arms and face are sunburned and freckled. On his head is an old wide-brimmed hat of coarse straw that would look more becoming on a horse. His voice is high-pitched with a pronounced brogue.*)

HOGAN (*stops as he turns the corner and sees her– furiously*): Where is he? Is he hiding in the house? I'll wipe the floors with him, the lazy bastard! (*Turning his anger against her.*) Haven't you a tongue in your head, you great slut you?

JOSIE (*with provoking calm*): Don't be calling me names, you bad-tempered old hornet, or maybe I'll lose my temper, too.

HOGAN: To hell with your temper, you overgrown cow!

JOSIE: I'd rather be a cow than an ugly little buck goat. You'd better sit down and cool off. Old men shouldn't run around raging in the noon sun. You'll get sunstroke.

JOGAN: To hell with sunstroke! Have you seen him?

JOSIE: Have I seen who?

HOGAN: Mike! Who else would I be after, the Pope? He was in the meadow, but the minute I turned my back he sneaked off. (*He sees the pitchfork.*) There's his pitchfork! Will you stop your lying!

JOSIE: I haven't said I didn't see him.

HOGAN: Then don't try to help him hide from me, or— Where is he?

JOSIE: Where you'll never find him.

HOGAN: We'll soon see! I'll bet he's in your room under the bed, the cowardly lump! (*He moves toward the steps.*)

JOSIE: He's not. He's gone like Thomas and John before him to escape your slave-driving.

HOGAN (*stares at her incredulously*): You mean he's run off to make his own way in the world?

JOSIE: He has. So make up your mind to it, and sit down.

HOGAN (*baffled, sits on the boulder and takes off his hat to scratch his head—with a faint trace of grudging respect*): I'd never dream he had that much spunk. (*His temper rising again.*) And I know damned well he hadn't, not without you to give him the guts and help him, like the great soft fool you are!

JOSIE: Now don't start raging again, Father.

HOGAN (*seething*): You've stolen my satchel to give him, I suppose, like you did before for Thomas and John?

JOSIE: It was my satchel, too. Didn't I help you in the trade for the horse, when you got the Crowleys to throw in the satchel for good measure? I was up all night fixing that nag's forelegs so his knees wouldn't buckle together till after the Crowleys had him a day or two.

HOGAN (*forgets his anger to grin reminiscently*): You've a wonderful way with animals, God bless you. And do you remember the two Crowleys came back to give me a beating, and I licked them both?

JOSIE (*with calculating flattery*): You did. You're a wonderful fighter. Sure, you could give Jack Dempsey himself a run for his money.

HOGAN (*with sharp suspicion*): I could, but don't try to change the subject and fill me with blarney.

JOSIE: All right. I'll tell the truth then. They were getting the best of you till I ran out and knocked one of them tail over tin cup against the pigpen.

HOGAN (*outraged*): You're a liar! They was begging for mercy before you came. (*Furiously.*) You thief, you! You stole my fine satchel for that lump! And I'll bet that's not all. I'll bet, like when Thomas and John sneaked off, you— (*He rises from the boulder threateningly.*) Listen, Josie, if you found where I had my little green bag, and stole money to give to that lousy altar boy, I'll—

JOSIE (*rises from the steps with the broom handle in her right hand*): Well, I did. So now what'll you do? Don't be threatening me. You know I'll beat better sense in your skull if you lay a finger on me.

HOGAN: I never yet laid hands on a woman—not when I was sober—but if it wasn't for that club— (*Bitterly.*) A fine curse God put on me when he gave me a daughter as big and strong as a bull, and as vicious and disrespectful. (*Suddenly his eyes twinkle and he grins admiringly.*) Be God, look at you standing there with the club! If you ain't the damnedest daughter in Connecticut, who is? (*He chuckles and sits on the boulder again.*)

JOSIE (*laughs and sits on the steps putting the club away*): And if you ain't the damnedest father in Connecticut, who is?

HOGAN (*takes a clay pipe and plug of tobacco and knife from his pocket. He cuts the plug and stuffs his pipe—without rancor*): How much did you steal, Josie?

JOSIE: Six dollars only.

HOGAN: *Only!* Well, God grant someone with wits will see that dopey gander at the depot and sell him the railroad for the six. (*Grumbling.*) It isn't the money I mind, Josie—

JOSIE: I know. Sure, what do you care for money? You'd give your last penny to the first beggar you met—if he had a shotgun pointed at your heart!

HOGAN: Don't be teasing. You know what I mean. It's the thought of that pious lump having my money that maddens me. I wouldn't put it past him to drop it in the collection plate next Sunday, he's that big a jackass.

JOSIE: I knew when you'd calmed down you'd think it worth six dollars to see the last of him.

HOGAN (*finishes filling his pipe*): Well, maybe I do. To tell the truth, I never liked him. (*He strikes a match on the seat of his overalls and lights his pipe.*) And I never liked Thomas and John, either.

JOSIE (*amused*): You've the same bad luck in sons I have in brothers.

HOGAN (*puffs ruminatively*): They all take after your mother's family. She was the only one in it had spirit, God rest her soul. The rest of them was a pious lousy lot. They wouldn't dare put food in their mouths before they said grace for it. They was too busy preaching temperance to have time for a drink. They spent so much time confessing their sins, they had no chance to do any sinning. (*He spits disgustedly.*) The scum of the earth! Thank God, you're like me and your mother.

JOSIE: I don't know if I should thank God for being like you. Sure, everyone says you're a wicked old tick, as crooked as a corkscrew.

HOGAN: I know. They're an envious lot, God forgive them. (*They both chuckle. He pulls on his pipe reflectively.*) You didn't get much thanks from Mike, I'll wager, for your help.

JOSIE: Oh, he thanked me kindly. And then he started to preach about my sins—and yours.

HOGAN: Oho, did he? (*Exploding.*) For the love of God, why didn't you hold him till I could give him one good kick for a parting blessing!

JOSIE: I near gave him one myself.

HOGAN: When I think your poor mother was killed bringing that crummy calf into life! (*Vindictively.*) I've never set foot in a church since, and never will. (*A pause. He speaks with a surprising sad gentleness.*) A sweet woman. Do you remember her, Josie? You were only a little thing when she died.

JOSIE: I remember her well. (*With a teasing smile which is half sad.*) She was the one could put you in your place when you'd come home drunk and want to tear down the house for the fun of it.

HOGAN (*with admiring appreciation*): Yes, she could do

it, God bless her. I only raised my hand to her once—just a slap because she told me to stop singing, it was after daylight. The next moment I was on the floor thinking a mule had kicked me. (*He chuckles.*) Since you've grown up, I've had the same trouble. There's no liberty in my own home.

JOSIE: That's lucky—or there wouldn't be any home.

HOGAN (*after a pause of puffing on his pipe*): What did that donkey, Mike, preach to you about?

JOSIE: Oh, the same as ever—that I'm the scandal of the countryside, carrying on with men without a marriage license.

HOGAN (*gives her a strange, embarrassed glance and then looks away. He does not look at her during the following dialogue. His manner is casual*): Hell roast his soul for saying it. But it's true enough.

JOSIE (*defiantly*): It is, and what of it? I don't care a damn for the scandal.

HOGAN: No. You do as you please and to hell with everyone.

JOSIE: Yes, and that goes for you, too, if you are my father. So don't you start preaching too.

HOGAN: Me, preach? Sure, the divil would die laughing. Don't bring me into it. I learned long since to let you go your own way because there's no controlling you.

JOSIE: I do my work and I earn my keep and I've a right to be free.

HOGAN: You have. I've never denied it.

JOSIE: No. You've never. I've often wondered why a man that likes fights as much as you didn't grab at the excuse of my disgrace to beat the lights out of the men.

HOGAN: Wouldn't I look a great fool, when everyone knows any man who tried to make free with you, and you not willing, would be carried off to the hospital? Anyway, I wouldn't want to fight an army. You've had too many sweethearts.

JOSIE (*with a proud toss of her head—boastfully*): That's because I soon get tired of any man and give him his walking papers.

HOGAN: I'm afraid you were born to be a terrible wanton woman. But to tell the truth, I'm well satisfied you're what you are, though I shouldn't say it, because if you was the decent kind, you'd have married some fool long ago, and I'd have lost your company and your help on the farm.

JOSIE (*with a trace of bitterness*): Leave it to you to think of your own interest.

HOGAN (*puffs on his pipe*): What else did my beautiful son, Mike, say to you?

JOSIE: Oh, he was full of stupid gab, as usual. He gave me good advice—

HOGAN (*grimly*): That was kind of him. It must have been good—

JOSIE: I ought to marry and settle down—if I could find a decent man who'd have me, which he was sure I couldn't.

HOGAN (*beginning to boil*): I tell you, Josie, it's going to be the saddest memory of my life I didn't get one last swipe at him!

JOSIE: So the only hope, he thought, was for me to catch some indecent man, who'd have money coming to him I could steal.

HOGAN (*gives her a quick, probing side glance—casually*): He meant Jim Tyrone?

JOSIE: He did. And the dirty tick accused you and me of making up a foxy scheme to trap Jim. I'm to get him alone when he's crazy drunk and lead him on to marry me. (*She adds in a hard, scornful tone.*) As if that would ever work. Sure, all the pretty little tarts on Broadway, New York, must have had a try at that, and much good it did them.

HOGAN (*again with a quick side glance—casually*): They must have, surely. But that's in the city where he's suspicious. You never can tell what he mightn't do here in the country, where he's innocent, with a moon in the sky to fill him with poetry and a quart of bad hootch inside of him.

JOSIE (*turns on him angrily*): Are you taking Mike's scheme seriously, you old goat?

HOGAN: I'm not. I only thought you wanted my opinion. (*She regards him suspiciously, but his face is blank, as if he hadn't a thought beyond enjoying his pipe.*)

JOSIE (*turning away*): And if that didn't work, Mike said maybe we had a scheme that I'd get Jim in bed with me and you'd come with witnesses and a shotgun, and catch him there.

HOGAN: Faith, me darlin' son never learnt that from his prayer book! He must have improved his mind on the sly.

JOSIE: The dirty tick!

HOGAN: Don't call him a tick. I don't like ticks but I'll say this for them, I never picked one off me yet was a hypocrite.

JOSIE: Him daring to accuse us of planning a rotten trick like that on Jim!

HOGAN (*as if he misunderstood her meaning*): Yes, it's as old as the hills. Everyone's heard of it. But it still works now and again, I'm told, and sometimes an old trick is best because it's so ancient no one would suspect you'd try it.

JOSIE (*staring at him resentfully*): That's enough out of you, Father. I never can tell to this day, when you put that dead mug on you, whether you're joking or not, but I don't want to hear any more—

HOGAN (*mildly*): I thought you wanted my honest opinion on the merits of Mike's suggestion.

JOSIE: Och, shut up, will you? I know you're only trying to make game of me. You like Jim and you'd never play a dirty trick on him, not even if I was willing.

HOGAN: No—not unless I found he was playing one on me.

JOSIE: Which he'd never.

HOGAN: No, I wouldn't think of it, but my motto in life is never trust anyone too far, not even myself.

JOSIE: You've reason for the last. I've often suspected you sneak out of bed in the night to pick your own pockets.

HOGAN: I wouldn't call it a dirty trick on him to get you for a wife.

JOSIE (*exasperatedly*): God save us, are you off on that again?

HOGAN: Well, you've put marriage in my head and I can't help considering the merits of the case, as they say. Sure, you're two of a kind, both great disgraces. That would help make a happy marriage because neither of you could look down on the other.

JOSIE: Jim mightn't think so.

HOGAN: You mean he'd think he was marrying beneath his station? He'd be a damned fool if he had that notion, for his Old Man who'd worked up from nothing to be rich and famous didn't give a damn about station. Didn't I often see him working on his grounds in clothes I wouldn't put on a scarecrow, not caring who saw him? (*With admiring affection.*) God rest him, he was a true Irish gentleman.

JOSIE: He was, and didn't you swindle him, and make me help you at it? I remember when I was a slip of a girl, and you'd get a letter saying his agent told him you were a year behind in the rent, and he'd be damned if he'd stand for it, and he was coming here to settle the matter. You'd make me dress up, with my hair brushed and a ribbon in it, and leave me to soften his heart before he saw you. So I'd skip down the path to meet him, and make a courtesy, and hold on to his hand, and bat my eyes at him and lead him in the house, and offer him a drink of the good whiskey you didn't keep for company, and gape at him and tell him he was the handsomest man in the world, and the fierce expression he'd put on for you would go away.

HOGAN (*chuckles*): You did it wonderful. You should have gone on the stage.

JOSIE (*dryly*): Yes, that's what he'd tell me, and he'd reach in his pocket and take out a half dollar, and ask me if you hadn't put me up to it. So I'd say yes, you had.

HOGAN (*sadly*): I never knew you were such a black traitor, and you only a child.

JOSIE: And then you'd come and before he could get a word out of him, you'd tell him you'd vacate the premises unless he lowered the rent and painted the house.

HOGAN: Be God, that used to stop him in his tracks.

JOSIE: It didn't stop him from saying you were the damnedest crook ever came out of Ireland.

HOGAN: He said it with admiration. And we'd start drinking and telling stories, and singing songs, and by the time he left we were both too busy cursing England to worry over the rent. (*He grins affectionately.*) Oh, he was a great man entirely.

JOSIE: He was. He always saw through your tricks.

HOGAN: Didn't I know he would? Sure, all I wanted was to give him the fun of seeing through them so he couldn't be hard-hearted. That was the real trick.

JOSIE (*stares at him*): You old devil, you've always a trick hidden behind your tricks, so no one can tell at times what you're after.

HOGAN: Don't be suspicious. Sure, I'd never try to fool you. You know me too well. But we've gone off the track. It's Jim we're discussing, not his father. I was telling you I could see the merit in your marrying him.

JOSIE (*exasperatedly*): Och, a cow must have kicked you in the head this morning.

HOGAN: I'd never give it a thought if I didn't know you had a soft spot in your heart for him.

JOSIE (*resentfully*): Well, I haven't! I like him, if that's what you mean, but it's only to talk to, because he's educated and quiet-spoken and has politeness even when he's drunkest, and doesn't roar around cursing and singing, like some I could name.

HOGAN: If you could see the light in your eyes when he blarneys you—

JOSIE (*roughly*): The light in me foot! (*Scornfully.*) I'm in love with him, you'll be saying next!

HOGAN (*ignores this*): And another merit of the case is, he likes you.

JOSIE: Because he keeps dropping in here lately? Sure, it's only when he gets sick of the drunks at the Inn, and it's more to joke with you than see me.

HOGAN: It's your happiness I'm considering when I recommend your using your wits to catch him, if you can.

JOSIE (*jeeringly*): If!

HOGAN: Who knows? With all the sweethearts you've had, you must have a catching way with men.

JOSIE (*boastfully*): Maybe I have. But that doesn't mean—

HOGAN: If you got him alone tonight—there'll be a beautiful moon to fill him with poetry and loneliness, and—

JOSIE: That's one of Mike's dirty schemes.

HOGAN: Mike be damned! Sure, that's every woman's scheme since the world was created. Without it there'd be no population. (*Persuasively.*) There'd be no harm trying it, anyway.

JOSIE: And no use, either. (*Bitterly.*) Och, Father, don't play the jackass with me. You know, and I know, I'm an ugly overgrown lump of a woman, and the men that want me are no better than stupid bulls. Jim can have all the pretty, painted little Broadway girls he wants—and dancers on the stage, too—when he comes into his estate. That's the kind he likes.

HOGAN: I notice he's never married one. Maybe he'd like a fine strong handsome figure of a woman for a change, with beautiful eyes and hair and teeth and a smile.

JOSIE (*pleased, but jeering*): Thank you kindly for your compliments. Now I know a cow kicked you in the head.

HOGAN: If you think Jim hasn't been taking in your fine points, you're a fool.

JOSIE: You mean you've noticed him? (*Suddenly furious.*) Stop your lying!

HOGAN: Don't fly in a temper. All I'm saying is, there may be a chance in it to better yourself.

JOSIE (*scornfully*): Better myself by being tied down to a man who's drunk every night of his life? No thank you!

HOGAN: Sure, you're strong enough to reform him. A taste of that club you've got, when he came home to you paralyzed, and in a few weeks you'd have him a dirty prohibitionist.

JOSIE (*seriously*): It's true, if I was his wife, I'd cure him of drinking himself to death, if I had to kill him. (*Then angrily.*) Och, I'm sick of your crazy gab, Father! Leave me alone!

HOGAN: Well, let's put it another way. Don't tell me you couldn't learn to love the estate he'll come into.

JOSIE (*resentfully*): Ah, I've been waiting for that. That's what Mike said again. Now we've come to the truth behind all your blather of my liking him or him liking me. (*Her manner changing-defiantly.*) All right then. Of course I'd love the money. Who wouldn't? And why shouldn't I get my hands on it, if I could? He's bound to be swindled out of it, anyway. He'll go back to the Broadway he thinks is heaven, and by the time the pretty little tarts, and the barroom sponges and racetrack touts and gamblers are through with him he'll be picked clean. I'm no saint, God knows, but I'm decent and deserving compared to those scum.

HOGAN (*eagerly*): Be God, now you're using your wits. And where there's a will there's a way. You and me have never been beat when we put our brains together. I'll keep thinking it over, and you do the same.

JOSIE (*with illogical anger*): Well, I won't! And you keep your mad scheming to yourself. I won't listen to it.

HOGAN (*as if he were angry, too*): All right. The divil take you. It's all you'll hear from me. (*He pauses—then with great seriousness, turning to her.*) Except one thing— (*As she starts to shut him up—sharply.*) I'm serious, and you'd better listen, because it's about this farm. which is home to us.

JOSIE (*surprised, stares at him*): What about the farm?

HOGAN: Don't forget, if we have lived on it twenty years, we're only tenants and we could be thrown out on our necks any time. (*Quickly.*) Mind you, I don't say Jim would ever do it, rent or no rent, or let the executors do it, even if they wanted, which they don't, knowing they'd never find another tenant.

JOSIE: What's worrying you, then?

HOGAN: This. I've been afraid lately the minute the estate is out of probate, Jim will sell the farm.

JOSIE (*exasperatedly*): Of course he will! Hasn't he told us and promised you can buy it on easy time payments at the small price you offered?

HOGAN: Jim promises whatever you like when he's full of whiskey. He might forget a promise as easy when he's drunk enough.

JOSIE (*indignantly*): He'd never! And who'd want it except us? No one ever has in all the years—

HOGAN: Someone has lately. The agent got an offer last month, Jim told me, bigger than mine.

JOSIE: Och, Jim loves to try and get your goat. He was kidding you.

HOGAN: He wasn't. I can tell. He said he told the agent to tell whoever it was the place wasn't for sale.

JOSIE: Of course he did. Did he say who'd made the offer?

HOGAN: He didn't know. It came through a real-estate man who wouldn't tell who his client was. I've been trying to guess, but I can't think of anyone crazy enough unless it'd be some damn fool of a millionaire buying up land to make a great estate for himself, like our beautiful neighbor, Harder, the Standard Oil thief, did years ago. (*He adds with bitter fervency.*) May he roast in hell and his Limey superintendent with him!

JOSIE: Amen to that. (*Then, scornfully.*) This land for an estate? And if there was an offer, Jim's refused it, and that ends it. He wouldn't listen to any offer, after he's given his word to us.

HOGAN: Did I say he would—when he's in his right mind? What I'm afraid of is, he might be led into it sometime when he has one of his sneering bitter drunks on and talks like a Broadway crook himself, saying money is the only thing in the world, and everything and anyone can be bought if the price is big enough. You've heard him.

JOSIE: I have. But he doesn't fool me at all. He only acts like he's hard and shameless to get back at life when it's tormenting him—and who doesn't? (He gives her a quick, curious side glance which she doesn't notice.)

HOGAN: Or take the other kind of queer drunk he gets on sometimes when, without any reason you can see, he'll suddenly turn strange, and look sad, and stare at nothing as if he was mourning over some ghost inside him, and—

JOSIE: I think I know what comes over him when he's like that. It's the memory of his mother comes back and his grief for her death. (Pityingly.) Poor Jim.

HOGAN (ignoring this): And whiskey seems to have no effect on him, like water off a duck's back. He'll keep acting natural enough, and you'd swear he wasn't bad at all, but the next day you find his brain was so paralyzed he don't remember a thing until you remind him? He's done a lot of mad things, when he was that way, he was sorry for after.

JOSIE (scornfully): What drunk hasn't? But he'd never— (Resentfully.) I won't have you suspecting Jim without any cause, d'you hear me!

HOGAN: I don't suspect him. All I've said is, when a man gets as queer drunk as Jim, he doesn't know himself what he mightn't do, and we'd be damned fools if we didn't fear the possibility, however small it is, and do all we can to guard against it.

JOSIE: There's no possibility! And how could we guard against it, if there was?

HOGAN: Well, you can put yourself out to be extra nice to him, for one thing.

JOSIE: How nice is extra nice?

HOGAN: You ought to know. But here's one tip. I've noticed when you talk rough and brazen like you do to other men, he may grin like they do, as if he enjoyed it, but he don't. So watch your tongue.

JOSIE (with a defiant toss of her head): I'll talk as I please, and if he don't like it he can lump it! (Scornfully.) I'm to pretend I'm a pure virgin, I suppose? That would fool him, wouldn't it, and him hearing all about me from the men at the Inn? (She gets to her feet, abruptly changing the subject.) We're wasting the day, blathering. (Then her face hardening.) If he ever went back on his word, no matter how drunk he was, I'd be with you in any scheme you made against him, no matter how dirty. (Hastily.) But it's all your nonsense. I'd never believe it. (She comes and picks up the pitchfork.) I'll go to the meadow and finish Mike's work. You needn't fear you'll miss his help on the farm.

HOGAN: A hell of a help! A weak lazy back and the appetitie of a drove of starving pigs! (As she turns to go—suddenly bellicose.) Leaving me, are you? When it's dinner time? Where's my dinner, you lazy cow?

JOSIE: There's stew on the stove, you bad-tempered runt. Go in and help yourself. I'm not hungry. Your gab has bothered my mind. I need hard work in the sun to clear it. (She starts to go off toward rear-right.)

HOGAN (glancing down the road, off left-front): You'd better wait. There's a caller coming to the gate—and if I'm not mistaken, it's the light of your eyes himself.

JOSIE (angrily): Shut up! (She stares off—her face softens and grows pitying.) Look at him when he thinks no one is watching, with his eyes on the ground. Like a dead man walking slow behind his own coffin. (Then roughly.) Faith, he must have a hangover. He sees us now. Look at the bluff he puts up, straightening himself and grinning. (Resentfully.) I don't want to meet him. Let him make jokes with you and play the old game about a drink you both think is such fun. That's all he comes for, anyway. (She starts off again.)

HOGAN: Are you running away from him? Sure, you must be afraid you're in love. (JOSIE halts instantly and turns back defiantly. He goes on.) Go in the house now, and wash your face, and tidy your dress, and give a touch to your hair. You want to look decent for him.

JOSIE (angrily): I'll go in the house, but only to see the stew ain't burned, for I supposed you'll have the foxiness to ask him to have a bit to eat to keep in his good graces.

HOGAN: Why shouldn't I ask him? I know damned well he has no appetite this early in the day, but only a thirst.

JOSIE: Och, you make me sick, you sly miser! (She goes through her bedroom, slamming the door behind her. HOGAN refills his pipe, pretending he doesn't notice TYRONE approaching, his eyes bright with droll expectation. JIM TYRONE enters along the road from the highway, left.)

(TYRONE is in his early forties, around five feet nine, broad-shouldered and deep-chested. His naturally fine physique has become soft and soggy from dissipation, but his face is still good-looking despite its unhealthy puffiness and the bags under the eyes. He has thinning dark hair, parted and brushed back to cover a bald spot. His eyes are brown, the whites congested and yellowish. His nose, big and aquiline, gives his face a certain Mephistophelian quality which is accentuated by his habitually cynical expression. But when he smiles without sneering, he still has the ghost of a former youthful irresponsible Irish charm—that of the beguiling ne'er-do-well, sentimental and romantic. It is his humor and charm which have kept him attractive to women, and popular with men as a drinking *companion. He is dressed in an expensive dark-brown suit, tight-fitting and drawn in at the waist, dark-brown made-to-order shoes and silk socks, a white silk shirt, silk handkerchief in breast pocket, a dark tie. This get-up suggests that he follows a style set by well-groomed Broadway gamblers who would like to be mistaken for Wall Street brokers.)*

(He has had enough pick-me-ups to recover from morning-after nausea and steady his nerves. During the following dialogue, he and HOGAN *are like players at an old familiar game where each knows the other's moves, but which still amuses them.)*

TYRONE *(approaches and stands regarding* HOGAN *with a sardonic relish.* HOGAN *scratches a match on the seat of his overalls and lights his pipe, pretending not to see him.* TYRONE *recites with feeling):*
"Fortunate senex, ergo tua rura manebunt,
et tibi magna satis, quamvis lapis omnia nudus."

HOGAN *(mutters):* It's the landlord again, and my shotgun not handy. *(He looks up at* TYRONE.*)* Is it Mass you're saying, Jim? That was Latin. I know it by ear. What the hell—insult does it mean?

TYRONE: Translated very freely into Irish English, something like this. *(He imitates* HOGAN's *brogue.)* "Ain't you the lucky old bastard to have this beautiful farm, if it is full of nude rocks."

HOGAN: I like that part about the rocks. If cows could eat them this place would make a grand dairy farm. *(He spits.)* It's easy to see you've a fine college education. It must be a big help to you conversing with whores and barkeeps.

TYRONE: Yes, a very valuable worldly asset. I was once offered a job as office boy—until they discovered I wasn't qualified because I had no Bachelor of Arts diploma. There had been a slight misunderstanding just before I was to graduate.

HOGAN: Between you and the Fathers? I'll wager!

TYRONE: I made a bet with another Senior I could get a tart from the Haymarket to visit me, introduce her to the Jebs as my sister—and get away with it.

HOGAN: But you didn't?

TYRONE: Almost. It was a memorable day in the halls of learning. All the students were wise and I had them rolling in the aisles as I showed Sister around the grounds, accompanied by one of the Jebs. He was a bit suspicious at first, but Dutch Maisie—her professional name—had no make-up on, and was dressed in black, and had eaten a pound of Sen-Sen to kill the gin on her breath, and seemed such a devout girl that he forgot his suspicions. *(He pauses.)* Yes, all would have been well, but she was a mischievous minx, and had her own ideas of improving on my joke. When she was saying good-bye to Father Fuller, she added innocently: "Christ, Father, it's nice and quiet out here away from the damned Sixth Avenue El. I wish to hell I could stay here!" *(Dryly.)* But she didn't, and neither did I.

HOGAN *(chuckles delightedly):* I'll bet you didn't. God bless Dutch Maisie! I'd like to have known her.

TYRONE *(sits down on the steps—with a change of manner):* Well, how's the Duke of Donegal this fine day?

HOGAN: Never better.

TYRONE: Slaving and toiling as usual, I see.

HOGAN: Hasn't a poor man a right to his noon rest without being sneered at by his rich landlord?

TYRONE: "Rich" is good. I would be, if you'd pay up your back rent.

HOGAN: You ought to pay me, instead, for occupying this rockpile, miscalled a farm. *(His eyes twinkling.)* But I have fine reports to give you of a promising harvest. The milkweed and the thistles is in thriving condition, and I never saw the poison ivy so bounteous and beautiful. *(*TYRONE *laughs. Without their noticing,* JOSIE *appears in the doorway behind* TYRONE. *She has tidied up and arranged her hair. She smiles down at* JIM, *her face softening, pleased to hear him laugh.)*

TYRONE: You win. Where did Josie go, Phil? I saw her here—

HOGAN: She ran in the house to make herself beautiful for you.

JOSIE *(breaks in roughly):* You're a liar. *(To* TYRONE, *her manner one of bold, free-and-easy familiarity.)* Hello, Jim.

TYRONE *(starts to stand up):* Hello, Josie.

JOSIE *(puts a hand on his shoulder and pushes him down):* Don't get up. Sure, you know I'm no lady. *(She sits on the top step—banteringly.)* How's my fine Jim this beautiful day? You don't look so bad. You must have stopped at the Inn for an eye-opener—or ten of them.

TYRONE: I've felt worse. *(He looks up at her sardonically.)* And how's my Virgin Queen of Ireland?

JOSIE: Yours, is it? Since when? And don't be miscalling me a virgin. You'll ruin my reputation, if you spread that lie about me. *(She laughs.* TYRONE *is staring at her. She goes on quickly.)* How is it you're around so early? I though you never got up till afternoon.

TYRONE: Couldn't sleep. One of those heebie-jeebie nights when the booze keeps you awake instead of— *(He catches her giving him a pitying look–irritably.)* But what of it!

JOSIE: Maybe you had no woman in bed with you, for a change. It's a terrible thing to break the habit of years.

TYRONE *(shrugs his shoulders):* Maybe.

JOSIE: What's the matter with the tarts in town, they let you do it? I'll bet the ones you know on Broadway, New York, wouldn't neglect their business.

TYRONE (*pretends to yawn boredly*): Maybe not. (*Then irritably.*) Cut out the kidding, Josie. It's too early.

HOGAN (*who has been taking everything in without seeming to*): I told you not to annoy the gentleman with your rough tongue.

JOSIE: Sure I thought I was doing my duty as hostess making him feel at home.

TYRONE (*stares at her again*): Why all the interest latly in the ladies of the profession, Josie?

JOSIE: Oh, I've been considering joining their union. It's easier living than farming, I'm sure. (*Then resentfully.*) You think I'd starve at it, don't you because your fancy is for dainty dolls of women! But other men like—

TYRONE (*with sudden revulsion*): For God's sake, cut out that kind of talk, Josie! It sounds like hell.

JOSIE (*stares at him startledly–then resentfully*): Oh, it does, does it? (*Forcing a scornful smile.*) I'm shocking you, I suppose? (HOGAN *is watching them both, not missing anything in their faces, while he seems intent on his pipe.*)

TYRONE (*looking a bit sheepish and annoyed at himself for his interest–shrugs his shoulders*): No. Hardly. Forget it. (*He smiles kiddingly.*) Anyway, who told you I fall for the dainty dolls? That's all a thing of the past. I like them tall and strong and voluptuous, now, with beautiful big breasts. (*She blushes and looks confused and is furious with herself for doing so.*)

HOGAN: There you are, Josie, darlin'. Sure he couldn't speak fairer than that.

JOSIE (*recovers herself*): He couldn't, indeed. (*She pats* TYRONE's *head–playfully.*) You're a terrible blarneying liar, Jim, but thank you just the same. (TYRONE *turns his attention to* HOGAN. *He winks at* JOSIE *and begins in an exaggeratedly casual manner.*)

TYRONE: I don't blame you, Mr. Hogan, for taking it easy on such a blazing hot day.

HOGAN (*doesn't look at him. His eyes twinkle*): Hot, did you say? I find it cool, meself. Take off your coat if you're hot, Mister Tyrone.

TYRONE: One of the most stifling days I've ever known. Isn't it, Josie?

JOSIE (*smiling*): Terrible. I know you must be perishing.

HOGAN: I wouldn't call it a damned bit stifling.

TYRONE: It parches the membranes in your throat.

HOGAN: The what? Never mind. I can't have them, for my throat isn't parched at all. If yours is, Mister Tyrone, there's a well full of water at the back.

TYRONE: Water? That's something people wash with, isn't it? I mean, some people.

HOGAN: So I've heard. But, like you, I find it hard to believe. It's a dirty habit. They must be foreigners.

TYRONE: As I was saying, my throat is parched after the long dusty walk I took just for the pleasure of being your guest.

HOGAN: I don't remember inviting you, and the road is hard macadam with divil a speck of dust, and it's less than a quarter mile from the Inn here.

TYRONE: I didn't have a drink at the Inn. I was waiting until I arrived here, knowing that you—

HOGAN: Knowing I'd what?

TYRONE: Your reputation as a generous host—

HOGAN: The world must be full of liars. So you didn't have a drink at the Inn? Then it must be the air itself smells of whiskey today, although I didn't notice it before you came. You've gone on the water-wagon, I suppose? Well, that's fine, and I ask pardon for misjudging you.

TYRONE: I've wanted to go on the wagon for the past twenty-five years, but the doctors have strictly forbidden it. It would be fatal—with my weak heart.

HOGAN: So you've a weak heart? Well, well, and me thinking all along it was your head. I'm glad you told me. I was just going to offer you a drink, but whiskey is the worst thing—

TYRONE: The Docs say it's a matter of life and death. I must have a stimulant—one big drink, at least, whenever I strain my heart walking in the hot sun.

HOGAN: Walk back to the Inn, then, and give it a good strain, so you can buy yourself two big drinks.

JOSIE (*laughing*): Ain't you the fools, playing that old game between you, and both of you pleased as punch!

TYRONE (*gives up with a laugh*): Hasn't he ever been known to loosen up, Josie?

JOSIE: You ought to know. If you need a drink you'll have to buy it from him or die of thirst.

TYRONE: Well, I'll bet this is one time he's going to treat.

HOGAN: Be God, I'll take that bet!

TYRONE: After you've heard the news I've got for you, you'll be so delighted you won't be able to drag out the old bottle quick enough.

HOGAN: I'll have to be insanely delighted.

JOSIE (*full of curiosity*): Shut up, Father. What news, Jim?

TYRONE: I have it off the grapevine that a certain exalted personage will drop in on you before long.

HOGAN: It's the sheriff again. I know by the pleased look on your mug.

TYRONE: Not this time. (*He pauses tantalizingly.*)

JOSIE: Bad luck to you, can't you tell us who?

TYRONE: A more eminent grafter than the sheriff— (*Sneeringly.*) A leading aristocrat in our Land of the Free and Get-Rich-Quick, whose boots are licked by one and all—and one of the Kings of our Republic by Divine Right of Inherited Swag. In short, I refer to your good neighbor, T. Stedman Harder, Standard Oil's sappiest child, whom I know you both love so dearly. *(There is a pause after this announcement.* HOGAN *and* JOSIE *stiffen, and their eyes begin to glitter. But they can't believe their luck at first.)*

HOGAN *(in an ominous whisper)*: Did you say Harder is coming to call on us, Jim?

JOSIE: It's too good to be true.

TYRONE *(watching them with amusement)*: No kidding. The great Mr. Harder intends to stop here on his way back to lunch from a horseback ride.

JOSIE: How do you know?

TYRONE: Simpson told me. I ran into him at the Inn.

HOGAN: That English scum of a superintendent!

TYRONE: He was laughing himself sick. He said he suggested the idea to Harder—told him you'd be overwhelmed with awe if he deigned to interview you in person.

HOGAN: Overwhelmed isn't the word. Is it, Josie?

JOSIE: It isn't indeed, Father.

TYRONE: For once in his life, Simpson is cheering for you. He doesn't like his boss. In fact, he asked me to tell you he hopes you kill him.

HOGAN *(disdainfully)*: To hell with the Limey's good wishes. I'd like both of them to call together.

JOSIE: Ah, well, we can't have everything. *(to* TYRONE*)* What's the reason Mr. Harder decided to notice poor, humble scum the like of us?

TYRONE *(grinning)*: That's right, Josie. Be humble. He'll expect you to know your place.

HOGAN: Will he now? Well, well. *(With a great happy sigh.)* This is going to be a beautiful day entirely.

JOSIE: But what's Harder's reason, Jim?

TYRONE: Well, it seems he has an ice pond on his estate.

HOGAN: Oho! So that's it!

TYRONE: Yes. That's it. Harder likes to keep up the good old manorial customs. He clings to his ice pond. And your pigpen isn't far from his ice pond.

HOGAN: A nice little stroll for the pigs, that's all.

TYRONE: And somehow Harder's fence in that vicinity has a habit of breaking down.

HOGAN: Fences are queer things. You can't depend on them.

TYRONE: Simpson says he's had it repaired a dozen times, but each time on the following night it gets broken down again.

JOSIE: What a strange thing! It must be the bad fairies. I can't imagine who else could have done it. Can you, Father?

HOGAN: I can't, surely.

TYRONE: Well, Simpson can. He knows you did it and he told his master so.

HOGAN *(disdainfully)*: Master is the word. Sure, the English can't live unless they have a lord's backside to kiss, the dirty slaves.

TYRONE: The result of those breaks in the fence is that your pigs stroll—as you so gracefully put it—stroll through to wallow happily along the shores of the ice pond.

HOGAN: Well, why not? Sure, they're fine ambitious American-born pigs and they don't miss any opportunities. They're like Harders' father who made the money for him.

TYRONE: I agree, but for some strange reason Harder doesn't look forward to the taste of pig in next summer's ice water.

HOGAN: He must be delicate. Remember he's delicate, Josie, and leave your club in the house. *(He bursts into joyful menacing laughter.)* Oh, be God and be Christ in the mountains! I've pined to have a quiet word with Mr. Harder for years, watching him ride past in his big shiny automobile with his snoot in the air, and being tormented always by the complaints of his Limey superintendent. Oh, won't I welcome him!

JOSIE: Won't *we*, you mean. Sure, I love him as much as you.

HOGAN: I'd kiss you, Jim, for this beautiful news, if you wasn't so damned ugly. Maybe Josie'll do it for me. She has a stronger stomach.

JOSIE: I will! He's earned it. *(She pulls* TYRONE's *head back and laughingly kisses him on the lips. Her expression changes. She looks startled and confused, stirred and at the same time frightened. She forces a scornful laugh.)* Och, there's no spirit in you! It's like kissing a corpse.

TYRONE *(gives her a strange surprised look—mockingly)*: Yes? *(Turning to* HOGAN.*)* Well, how about that drink, Phil? I'll leave it to Josie if drinks aren't on the house.

HOGAN: *I* won't leave it to Josie. She's prejudiced, being in love.

JOSIE *(angrily)*: Shut up, you old liar! *(Then guiltily, forcing a laugh.)* Don't talk nonsense to sneak out of treating Jim.

HOGAN *(sighing)*: All right, Josie. Go get the bottle and one small glass, or he'll never stop nagging me. I can turn my back, so the sight of him drinking free won't break my heart. *(*JOSIE *gets up, laughing, and goes in the house.* HOGAN *peers at the road off left.)* On his way back to lunch you said? Then it's time— *(Fervently.)* O Holy Joseph, don't let the bastard change his mind!

TYRONE *(beginning to have qualms)*: Listen, Phil. Don't get too enthusiastic. He has a big drag around here, and he'll have you pinched, sure as hell, if you beat him up.

HOGAN: Och, I'm no fool. *(*JOSIE *comes out with a bottle and a tumbler.)* Will you listen to this, Josie. He's warning me not to give Harder a beating—as if

I'd dirty my hands on the scum.

JOSIE: As if we'd need to. Sure, all we want is a quiet chat with him.

HOGAN: That's all. As neighbor to neighbor.

JOSIE (*hands* TYRONE *the bottle and tumbler*): Here you are, Jim. Don't stint yourself.

HOGAN (*mournfully*): A fine daughter! I tell you a small glass and you give him a bucket! (*As* TYRONE *pours a big drink, grinning at him, he turns away with a comic shudder.*) That's a fifty-dollar drink, at least.

TYRONE: Here's luck, Phil.

HOGAN: I hope you drown. (TYRONE *drinks and makes a wry face.*)

TYRONE: The best chicken medicine I've ever tasted.

HOGAN: That's gratitude for you! Here, pass me the bottle. A drink will warm up my welcome for His Majesty. (*He takes an enormous swig from the bottle.*)

JOSIE (*looking off left*): There's two horseback riders on the county road now.

HOGAN: Praise be to God! It's him and a groom. (*He sets the bottle on top of the boulder.*)

JOSIE: That's McCabe. An old sweetheart of mine. (*She glances at* TYRONE *provokingly—then suddenly worried and protective.*) You get in the house, Jim. If Harder sees you here, he'll lay the whole blame on you.

TYRONE: Nix, Josie. You don't think I'm going to miss this, do you?

JOSIE: You can sit inside by my window and take in everything. Come on, now, don't be stubborn with me. (*She puts her hands under his arms and lifts him to his feet as easily as if he was a child—banteringly.*) Go into my beautiful bedroom. It's a nice place for you.

TYRONE (*kiddingly*): Just what I've been thinking for some time, Josie.

JOSIE (*boldly*): Sure, you've never given me a sign of it. Come up tonight and we'll spoon in the moonlight and you can tell me your thoughts.

TYRONE: That's a date. Remember, now.

JOSIE: It's you who'll forget. Go inside now, before it's too late. (*She gives him a shove inside and closes the door.*)

HOGAN (*has been watching the visitor approach*): He's dismounting—as graceful as a scarecrow, and his poor horse longing to give him a kick. Look at Mac grinning at us. Sit down, Josie. (*She sits on the steps, he on the boulder.*) Pretend you don't notice him. (T. STEDMAN HARDER *appears at left. They act as if they didn't see him.* HOGAN *knocks out his pipe on the palm of his hand.*)

(HARDER *is in his late thirties but looks younger because his face is unmarked by worry, ambition, or any of the common hazards of life. No matter how long he lives, his four undergraduate years will always be for him the most significant in his life, and the moment of his highest achievement the time he was tapped for an exclusive Senior Society at the Ivy university to which his father had given millions. Since that day he has felt no need for further aspiring, no urge to do anything except settle down on his estate and live the life of a country gentleman, mildly interested in saddle horses and sport models of foreign automobiles. He is not the blatantly silly, playboy heir to millions whose antics make newspaper headlines. He doesn't drink much except when he attends his class reunion every spring—the most exciting episode of each year for him. He doesn't give wild parties, doesn't chase after musical-comedy cuties, is a mildly contented husband and father of three children. A not unpleasant man, affable, good-looking in an ordinary way, sunburnt and healthy, beginning to take on fat, he is simply immature, naturally lethargic, a bit stupid. Coddled from birth, everything arranged and made easy for him, deferred to because of his wealth, he usually has the self-confident attitude of acknowledged superiority, but assumes a supercilious insecure air when dealing with people beyond his ken. He is dressed in a beautifully tailored English tweed coat and whipcord riding breeches, immaculately polished English riding boots with spurs, and carries a riding crop in his hand.*)

(*It would be hard to find anyone more ill-equipped for combat with the* HOGANS. *He has never come in contact with anyone like them. To make matters easier for them he is deliberate in his speech, slow on the uptake, and has no sense of humor. The experienced strategy of the* HOGANS *in verbal battle is to take the offensive at once and never let an opponent get set to hit back. Also, they use a beautifully co-ordinated, bewildering change of pace, switching suddenly from jarring shouts to low, confidential vituperation. And they exaggerate their Irish brogues to confuse an enemy still further.*)

HARDER (*walks toward* HOGAN—*stiffly*).: Good morning. I want to see the man who runs this farm.

HOGAN (*surveys him deliberately, his little pig eyes gleaming with malice*): You do, do you? Well, you've seen him. So run along now and play with your horse, and don't bother me. (*He turns to* JOSIE, *who is staring at* HARDER, *much to his discomfiture, as if she had discovered a cockroach in her soup.*) D'you see what I see, Josie? Be God, you'll have to give that damned cat of yours a spanking for bringing it to our doorstep.

HARDER (*determined to be authoritative and command respect—curtly*): Are you Hogan?

HOGAN (*insultingly*): I am *Mister* Philip Hogan—to a gentleman.

JOSIE (*glares at* HARDER): Where's your manners, you spindle-shanked jockey? Were you brought up in a stable?

HARDER (*does not fight with ladies, and especially not with this lady—ignoring her*): My name is Harder. (*He *obviously expects them to be immediately impressed and apologetic.)*

HOGAN *(contemptuously)*: Who asked you your name, me little man?

JOSIE: Sure, who in the world cares who the hell you are?

HOGAN: But if you want to play politeness, we'll play with you. Let me introduce you to my daughter, Harder—Miss Josephine Hogan.

JOSIE *(petulantly)*: I don't want to meet him, Father. I don't like his silly sheep's face, and I've no use for jockeys, anyway. I'll wager he's no damned good to a woman. *(From inside her bedroom comes a burst of laughter. This revelation of an unseen audience startles HARDER. He begins to look extremely unsure of himself.)*

HOGAN: I don't think he's a jockey. It's only the funny pants he's wearing. I'll bet if you asked his horse, you'd find he's no cowboy either. *(to HARDER, jeeringly)* Come, tell us the truth, me honey. Don't you kiss your horse each time you mount and beg him, please don't throw me today, darlin', and I'll give you an extra bucket of oats. *(He bursts into an extravagant roar of laughter, slapping his thigh, and JOSIE guffaws with him, while they watch the disconcerting effect of this theatrical mirth on HARDER.)*

HARDER *(beginning to lose his temper)*: Listen to me, Hogan! I didn't come here— *(He is going to add "to listen to your damned jokes" or something like that, but HOGAN silences him.)*

HOGAN *(shouts)*: What? What's that you said? *(He stares at the dumbfounded HARDER with droll amazement, as if he couldn't believe his ears.)* You didn't come here? *(He turns to JOSIE—in a whisper.)* Did you hear that, Josie? *(He takes off his hat and scratches his head in comic bewilderment.)* Well, that's a puzzle, surely. How d'you suppose he got here?

JOSIE: Maybe the stork brought him, bad luck to it for a dirty bird. *(Again TYRONE's laughter is heard from the bedroom.)*

HARDER *(so off balance now he can only repeat angrily)*: I said I didn't come here—

HOGAN *(shouts)*: Wait! Wait, now! *(Threateningly.)* We've had enough of that. Say it a third time and I'll send my daughter to telephone the asylum.

HARDER *(forgetting he's a gentleman)*: Damn you, I'm the one who's had enough—!

JOSIE *(shouts)*: Hold your dirty tongue! I'll have no foul language in my presence.

HOGAN: Och, don't mind him, Josie. He's said he isn't here, anyway, so we won't talk to him behind his back. *(He regards HARDER with pitying contempt.)* Sure, ain't you the poor crazy creature? Do you want us to believe you're a ghost?

HARDER *(notices the bottle on the boulder for the first time—tries to be contemptuously tolerant and even to smile with condescending disdain)*: Ah! I understand now. You're drunk. I'll come back sometime when you're sober—or send Simpson— *(He turns away, glad of an excuse to escape.)*

JOSIE *(jumps up and advances on him menacingly)*: No, you don't! You'll apologize first for insulting a lady—insinuating I'm drunk this early in the day—or I'll knock some good breeding in you!

HARDER *(actually frightened now)*: I—I said nothing about you—

HOGAN *(gets up to come between them)*: Aisy now, Josie. He didn't mean it. He don't know what he means, the poor loon. *(to HARDER—pityingly)* Run home, that's a good lad, before your keeper misses you.

HARDER *(hastily)*: Good day. *(He turns eagerly toward left but suddenly HOGAN grabs his shoulder and spins him around—then shifts his grip to the lapel of HARDER's coat.)*

HOGAN *(grimly)*: Wait now, me Honey Boy. I'll have a word with you, if you plaze. I'm beginning to read some sense into this. You mentioned that English bastard, Simpson. I know who you are now.

HARDER *(outraged)*: Take your hands off me, you drunken fool. *(He raises his riding crop.)*

JOSIE *(grabs it and tears it from his hand with one powerful twist—fiercely)*: Would you strike my poor infirm old father, you coward, you!

HARDER *(calling for help)*: McCabe!

HOGAN: Don't think McCabe will hear you, if you blew Gabriel's horn. He knows I or Josie can lick him with one hand. *(Sharply)* Josie! Stand between us and the gate. *(JOSIE takes her stand where the path meets the road. She turns her back for a moment, shaking with suppressed laughter, and waves her hand at MC CABE and turns back. HOGAN releases his hold on HARDER's coat.)* There now. Don't try running away or my daughter will knock you senseless. *(He goes on grimly before HARDER can speak.)* You're the blackguard of a millionaire that owns the estate next to ours, ain't you? I've been meaning to call on you, for I've a bone to pick with you, you bloody tyrant! But I couldn't bring myself to set foot on land bought with Standard Oil money that was stolen from the poor it ground in the dust beneath its dirty heel—land that's watered with the tears of starving widows and orphans—*(He abruptly switches from this eloquence to a matter-of-fact tone.)* But never mind that, now. I won't waste words trying to reform a born crook. *(Fiercely, shoving his dirty unshaven face almost into HARDER's.)* What I want to know is, what the hell d'you mean by your contemptible trick of breaking down your fence to entice my poor pigs to take their death in your ice pond? *(There is a shout of laughter from JOSIE's bedroom, and* JOSIE *doubles up and holds her sides.* HARDER *is so flabbergasted by this mad accusation he cannot even sputter. But* HOGAN *acts as if he'd denied it—savagely.)* Don't lie, now! None of your damned Standard Oil excuses, or be Jaysus, I'll break you in half! Haven't I mended that fence morning after morning, and seen the footprints where you had sneaked up in the night to pull it down again. How many times have I mended that fence, Josie?

JOSIE: If it's once, it's a hundred, Father.

HOGAN: Listen, me little millionaire! I'm a peaceful, mild man that believes in live and let live, and as long as the neighboring scum leaves me alone, I'll let them alone, but when it comes to standing by and seeing my poor pigs murthered one by one—! Josie! How many pigs is it caught their death of cold in his damned ice pond and died of pneumonia?

JOSIE: Ten of them, Father. And ten more died of cholera after drinking the dirty water in it.

HOGAN: All prize pigs, too! I was offered two hundred dollars apiece for them. Twenty pigs at two hundred, that's four thousand. And a thousand to cure the sick and cover funeral expenses for the dead. Call it four thousand you owe me. *(Furiously.)* And you'll pay it, or I'll sue you, so help me Christ! I'll drag you in every court in the land! I'll paste your ugly mug on the front page of every newspaper as a pig-murdering tyrant! Before I'm through with you, you'll think you're the King of England at an Irish wake! *(With a quick change of pace to a wheedling confidential tone.)* Tell me now, if it isn't a secret, whatever made you take such a savage grudge against pigs? Sure, it isn't reasonable for a Standard Oil man to hate hogs.

HARDER *(manages to get in three sputtering words)*: I've had enough—!

HOGAN *(with a grin)*: Be God, I believe you! *(Switching to fierceness and grabbing his lapel again.)* Look out, now! Keep your place and be soft-spoken to your betters! You're not in your shiny automobile now with your funny nose cocked so you won't smell the poor people. *(He gives him a shake.)* And let me warn you! I have to put up with a lot of pests on this heap of boulders some joker once called a farm. There's a cruel skinflint of a landlord who swindles me out of my last drop of whiskey, and there's poison ivy, and ticks, and potato bugs, and there's snakes and skunks! But, be God, I draw the line somewhere, and I'll be damned if I'll stand for a Standard Oil man trespassing! So will you kindly get the hell out of here before I plant a kick on your backside that'll land you in the Atlantic Ocean! *(He gives* HARDER *a shove.)* Beat it now! *(*HARDER *tries to make some sort of dis-*

dainfully dignified exit. But he has to get by JOSIE.*)*

JOSIE *(leers at him idiotically)*: Sure, you wouldn't go without a word of good-bye to me, would you, darlin'? Don't scorn me just because you have on your jockey's pants. *(In a hoarse whisper.)* Meet me tonight, as usual, down by the pigpen. *(*HARDER'S *retreat becomes a rout. He disappears on left, but a second later his voice, trembling with anger, is heard calling back threateningly.)*

HARDER: If you dare touch that fence again, I'll put this matter in the hands of the police!

HOGAN *(shouts derisively)*: And I'll put it in my lawyer's hands and in the newspapers! *(He doubles up with glee.)* Look at him fling himself on his nag and spur the poor beast! And look at McCabe behind him! He can hardly stay in the saddle for laughing! *(He slaps his thigh.)* O Jaysus, this is a great day for the poor and oppressed! I'll do no more work! I'll go down to the Inn and spend money and get drunk as Moses!

JOSIE: Small blame to you. You deserve it. But you'll have your dinner first, to give you a foundation. Come on, now. *(They turn back toward the house. From inside another burst of laughter from* TYRONE *is heard.* JOSIE *smiles.)* Listen to Jim still in stitches. It's good to hear him laugh as if he meant it. *(*TYRONE *appears in the doorway of her bedroom.)*

TYRONE: O God, my sides are sore. *(They all laugh together. He joins them at the left corner of the house.)*

JOSIE: It's dinner time. Will you have a bite to eat with us, Jim? I'll boil you some eggs.

HOGAN: Och, why do you have to mention eggs? Don't you know it's the one thing he might eat? Well, no matter. Anything goes today. *(He gets the bottle of whiskey.)* Come in, Jim. We'll have a drink while Josie's fixing the grub. *(They start to go in the front door,* HOGAN *in the lead.)*

TYRONE *(suddenly—with sardonic amusement)*: Wait a minute. Let us pause to take a look at this very valuable property. Don't you notice the change, Phil? Every boulder on the place has turned to solid gold.

HOGAN: What the hell—? You didn't get the D.T.'s from my whiskey, I know that.

TYRONE: No D.T.'s about it. This farm has suddenly become a gold mine. You know that offer I told you about? Well, the agent did a little detective work and he discovered it came from Harder. He doesn't want the damned place but he dislikes you as a neighbor and he thinks the best way to get rid of you would be to become your landlord.

HOGAN: The sneaking skunk! I'm sorry I didn't give him that kick.

TYRONE: Yes. So am I. That would have made the place even more valuable. But as it is, you did nobly. I expect him to double or triple his first offer. In fact, I'll bet the sky is the limit now.

HOGAN (*gives* JOSIE *a meaningful look*): I see your point! But we're not worrying you'd ever forget your promise to us for any price.

TYRONE: Promise? What promise? You know what Kipling wrote: (*Paraphrasing the "Rhyme of the Three Sealers."*) There's never a promise of God or man goes north of ten thousand bucks.

HOGAN: D'you hear him, Josie? We can't trust him.

JOSIE: Och, you know he's kidding.

HOGAN: I don't! I'm becoming suspicious.

TYRONE (*a trace of bitterness beneath his amused tone*): That's wise dope, Phil. Trust and be a sucker. If I were you, I'd be seriously worried. I've always wanted to own a gold mine—so I could sell it.

JOSIE (*bursts out*): Will you shut up your rotten Broadway blather!

TYRONE (*stares at her in surprise*): Why so serious and indignant, Josie? You just told your unworthy Old Man I was kidding. (*to* HOGAN) At last, I've got you by the ears, Phil. We must have a serious chat about when you're going to pay that back rent.

HOGAN (*groans*): A landlord who's a blackmailer! Holy God, what next! (JOSIE *is smiling with relief now.*)

TYRONE: And you, Josie, please remember when I keep that moonlight date tonight I expect you to be very sweet to me.

JOSIE (*with a bold air*): Sure, you don't have to blackmail me. I'd be that to you, anyway.

HOGAN: Are you laying plots in my presence to seduce my only daughter? (*Then philosophically.*) Well, what can I do? I'll be drunk at the Inn, so how could I prevent it? (*He goes up the steps.*) Let's eat, for the love of God. I'm starving. (*He disappears inside the house.*)

JOSIE (*with an awkward playful gesture, takes* TYRONE *by the hand*): Come along, Jim.

TYRONE (*smiles kiddingly*): Afraid you'll lose me? Swell chance! (*His eyes fix on her breasts–with genuine feeling.*) You have the most beautiful breasts in the world, do you know it, Josie?

JOSIE (*pleased–shyly*): I don't—but I'm happy if you think— (*Then quickly.*) But I've no time now to listen to your kidding, with my mad old father waiting for his dinner. So come on. (*She tugs at his hand and he follows her up the steps. Her manner changes to worried solicitude.*) Promise me you'll eat something, Jim. You've got to eat. You can't go on the way you are, drinking and never eating, hardly. You're killing yourself.

TYRONE (*sardonically*): That's right. Mother me, Josie, I love it.

JOSIE (*bullyingly*): I will, then. You need one to take care of you. (*They disappear inside the house.*)

ACT 2

(*Scene: The same, with the wall of the living room removed. It is a clear warm moonlight night, around eleven o'clock.*

JOSIE *is sitting on the steps before the front door. She has changed to her Sunday best, a cheap dark-blue dress, black stockings and shoes. Her hair is carefully arranged, and by way of adornment a white flower is pinned on her bosom. She is hunched up, elbows on knees, her chin in her hands. There is an expression on her face we have not seen before, a look of sadness and loneliness and humiliation.*

She sighs and gets slowly to her feet, her body stiff from sitting long in the same position. She goes into the living room, fumbles around for a box of matches, and lights a kerosene lamp on the table.

The living room is small, low-ceilinged, with faded, fly-specked wallpaper, a floor of bare boards. It is cluttered up with furniture that looks as if it had been picked up at a fire sale. There is a table at center, a disreputable old Morris chair beside it; two ugly sideboards, one at left, the other at right-rear; a porch rocking-chair, painted green, with a hole in its cane bottom; a bureau against the rear wall, with two chairs on either side of a door to the kitchen. On the bureau is an alarm clock which shows the time to be five past eleven. At right-front is the door to JOSIE'S *bedroom.*)

JOSIE (*looks at the clock–dully*): Five past eleven, and he said he'd be here around nine. (*Suddenly in a burst of humiliated anger, she tears off the flower pinned to her bosom and throws it in the corner.*) To hell with you, Jim Tyrone! (*From down the road, the quiet of the night is shattered by a burst of melancholy song. It is unmistakably* HOGAN'S *voice wailing an old Irish lament at the top of his lungs.* JOSIE *starts–then frowns irritably.*) What's bringing him home an hour before the Inn closes? He must be more paralyzed than ever I've known him. (*She listens to the singing–grimly.*) Ah, here you come, do you, as full as a tick! I'll give you a welcome, if you start cutting up! I'm in no mood to put up with you. (*She goes into her bedroom and returns with her broomstick club. Outside the singing grows louder as* HOGAN *approaches the house. He only remembers one verse of the song and he has been repeating it.*)

HOGAN:

> Oh the praties they grow small
> Over here, over here,
> Oh, the praties they grow small
> Over here.
> Oh the praties they grow small
> And we dig them in the fall
> And we eat them skins and all
> Over here, over here.

(*He enters left-front, weaving and lurching a bit. But*

he is not as drunk as he appears. Or rather, he is one of those people who can drink an enormous amount and be absolutely plastered when they want to be for their own pleasure, but at the same time are able to pull themselves together when they wish and be cunningly clear-headed. Just now, he is letting himself go and getting great satisfaction from it. He pauses and bellows belligerently at the house) Hurroo! Down with all tyrants, male and female! To hell with England, and God damn Standard Oil!

JOSIE *(shouts back)*: Shut up your noise, you crazy old billy goat!

HOGAN *(hurt and mournful)*: A sweet daughter and a sweet welcome home in the dead of night. *(Beginning to boil.)* Old goat! There's respect for you! *(Angrily–starting for the front door.)* Crazy billy goat, is it? Be God, I'll learn you manners! *(He pounds on the door with his fist.)* Open the door! Open this door, I'm saying, before I drive a fist through it, or kick it into flinders! *(He gives it a kick.)*

JOSIE: It's not locked, you drunken old loon! Open it yourself!

HOGAN *(turns the knob and stamps in)*: Drunken old loon, am I? Is that the way to address your father?

JOSIE: No. It's too damned good for him.

HOGAN: It's time I taught you a lesson. Be Jaysus, I'll take you over my knee and spank your tail, if you are as big as a cow! *(He makes a lunge to grab her.)*

JOSIE: Would you, though! Take that, then! *(She raps him smartly, but lightly, on his bald spot with the end of her broom handle.)*

HOGAN *(with an exaggerated howl of pain)*: Ow! *(His anger evaporates and he rubs the top of his head ruefully–with bitter complaint.)* God forgive you, it's a great shame to me I've raised a daughter so cowardly she has to use a club.

JOSIE *(puts her club on the table–grimly)*: Now I've no club.

HOGAN *(evades the challenge)*: I never thought I'd see the day when a daughter of mine would be such a coward as to threaten her old father when he's helpless drunk and can't hit back. *(He slumps down on the Morris chair.)*

JOSIE: Ah, that's better. Now that little game is over. *(Then angrily.)* Listen to me, Father. I have no patience left, so get up from that chair, and go in your room, and go to bed, or I'll take you by the scruff of your neck and the seat of your pants and throw you in and lock the door on you! I mean it now! *(On the verge of angry tears.)* I've had all I can bear this night, and I want some peace and sleep, and not to listen to an old lush!

HOGAN *(appears drunker, his head wagging, his voice thick, his talk rambling)*: That's right. Fight with me. My own daughter has no feelings or sympathy. As if I hadn't enough after what's happened tonight.

JOSIE *(with angry disgust)*: Och, don't try— *(Then curiously.)* What's happened? I thought something must be queer, you coming home before the Inn closed, but then I thought maybe for once you'd drunk all you could hold. *(Scathingly.)* And, God pity you, if you ain't that full, you're damned close to it.

HOGAN: Go on. Make fun of me. Old lush! You wouldn't feel so comical, if— *(He stops, mumbling to himself.)*

JOSIE: If what?

HOGAN: Never mind. Never mind. I didn't come home to fight, but seek comfort in your company. And if I was singing coming along the road, it was only because there's times you have to sing to keep from crying.

JOSIE: I can see you crying!

HOGAN: You will. And you'll see yourself crying, too, when— *(He stops again and mumbles to himself.)*

JOSIE: When what! *(Exasperatedly.)* Will you stop your whiskey drooling and talk plain?

HOGAN *(thickly)*: No matter. No matter. Leave me alone.

JOSIE *(angrily)*: That's good advice. To hell with you! I know your game. Nothing at all has happened. All you want is to keep me up listening to your guff. Go to your room, I'm saying, before—

HOGAN: I won't. I couldn't sleep with my thoughts tormented the way they are. I'll stay here in this chair, and you go to your room and let me be.

JOSIE *(snorts)*: And have you singing again in a minute and smashing the furniture—

HOGAN: Sing, is it? Are you making fun again? I'd give a keen of sorrow or howl at the moon like an old mangy hound in his sadness if I knew how, but I don't. So rest aisy. You won't hear a sound from me. Go on and snore like a pig to your heart's content. *(He mourns drunkenly.)* A fine daughter! I'd get more comfort from strangers.

JOSIE: Och, for God's sake, dry up! You'll sit in the dark then. I won't leave the lamp lit for you to tip over and burn down the house. *(She reaches out to turn down the lamp.)*

HOGAN *(thickly)*: Let it burn to the ground. A hell of a lot I care if it burns.

JOSIE *(in the act of turning down the lamp, stops and stares at him, puzzled and uneasy)*: I never heard you talk that way before, no matter how drunk you were. *(He mumbles. Her tone becomes persuasive.)* What's happened to you, Father?

HOGAN *(bitterly)*: Ah it's "Father" now, is it, not old billy goat? Well, thank God for small favors. *(With heavy sarcasm.)* Oh, nothing's happened to me at all, at all. A trifle, only. I wouldn't waste your time mentioning it, or keep you up when you want sleep so bad.

JOSIE (*angrily*): Och, you old loon, I'm sick of you. Sleep it off till you get some sense. (*She reaches for the lamp again.*)

HOGAN: Sleep it off? We'll see if you'll sleep it off when you know— (*He lapses into drunken mumbling.*)

JOSIE (*again stares at him*): Know what, Father?

HOGAN (*mumbles*): The son of a bitch!

JOSIE (*trying a light tone*): Sure, there's a lot of those in the neighborhood. Which one do you mean? Is Harder on your mind again?

HOGAN (*thickly*): He's one and a prize one, but I don't mean him. I'll say this for Harder, you know what to expect from him. He's no wolf in sheep's clothing, nor a treacherous snake in the grass who stabs you in the back with a knife—

JOSIE (*apprehensive now—forces a joke*): Sure, if you've found a snake who can stab you with a knife, you'd better join the circus with him and make a pile of money.

HOGAN (*bitterly*): Make jokes, God forgive you! You'll soon laugh from the wrong end of your mouth! (*He mumbles.*) Pretending he's our friend! The lying bastard!

JOSIE (*bristles resentfully*): Is it Jim Tyrone you're calling hard names?

HOGAN: That's right. Defend him, you big soft fool! Faith, you're a prize dunce! You've had a good taste of believing his word, waiting hours for him dressed up in your best like a poor sheep without pride or spirit—

JOSIE (*stung*): Shut up! I was calling him a lying bastard myself before you came, and saying I'd never speak to him again. And I knew all along he'd never remember to keep his date after he got drunk.

HOGAN: He's not so drunk he forgot to attend to business.

JOSIE (*as if she hadn't heard—defiantly*): I'd have stayed up anyway a beautiful night like this to enjoy the moonlight, if there wasn't a Jim Tyrone in the world.

HOGAN (*with heavy sarcasm*): In your best shoes and stockings? Well, well. Sure, the moon must feel flattered by your attentions.

JOSIE (*furiously*): You won't feel flattered if I knock you tail over tincup out of that chair! And stop your whiskey gabble about Jim. I see what you're driving at with your dark hints and curses, and if you think I'll believe— (*With forced assurance.*) Sure, I know what's happened as well as if I'd been there. Jim saw you'd got drunker than usual and you were an easy mark for a joke, and he made a goat of you!

HOGAN (*bitterly*): Goat again! (*He struggles from his chair and stands swaying unsteadily—with offended dignity.*) All right, I won't say another word. There's no use telling the truth to a bad-tempered woman in love.

JOSIE: Love be damned! I hate him now!

HOGAN: Be Christ, you have me stumped. A great proud slut who's played games with half the men around here, and now you act like a numbskull virgin that can't believe a man would tell her a lie!

JOSIE (*threateningly*): If you're going to your room, you'd better go quick!

HOGAN (*fixes his eyes on the door at rear—with dignity*): That's where I'm going, yes—to talk to myself so I'll know someone with brains is listening. Good night to you, Miss Hogan. (*He starts—swerves left—tries to correct this and lurches right and bumps against her, clutching the supporting arm she stretches out.*)

JOSIE: God help you, if you try to go upstairs now, you'll end up in the cellar.

HOGAN (*hanging on to her arm and shoulder—maudlinly affectionate now*): You're right. Don't listen to me. I'm wrong to bother you. You've had sorrow enought this night. Have a good sleep, while you can, Josie, darlin'—and good night and God bless you. (*He tries to kiss her, but she wards him off and steers him back to the chair.*)

JOSIE: Sit down before you split in pieces on the floor and I have to get a wheelbarrow to collect you. (*She dumps him in the chair where he sprawls limply, his chin on his chest.*)

HOGAN (*mumbles dully*): It's too late. It's all settled. We're helpless, entirely.

JOSIE (*really worried now*): How is it all settled? If you're helpless, I'm not. (*Then as he doesn't reply—scornfully.*) It's the first time I ever heard you admit you were licked. And it's the first time I ever saw you so paralyzed you couldn't shake the whiskey from your brains and get your head clear when you wanted. Sure, that's always been your pride—and now look at you, the stupid object you are, mumbling and drooling!

HOGAN (*struggles up in his chair—angrily*): Shut up your insults! Be God, I can get my head clear if I like! (*He shakes his head violently.*) There! It's clear. I can tell you each thing that happened tonight as clear as if I'd not taken a drop, if you'll listen and not keep calling me a liar.

JOSIE: I'll listen, now I see you have hold of your wits.

HOGAN: All right, then. I'll begin at the beginning when him and me left here, and you gave him a sweet smile, and rolled your big beautiful cow's eyes at him, and wiggled your backside, and stuck out your beautiful breasts you know he admires, and said in a sick sheep's voice. "Don't forget our moonlight date, Jim."

JOSIE (*with suppressed fury*): You're a—! I never—! You old—!

HOGAN: And he said: "You bet I won't forget, Josie."

JOSIE: The lying crook!

HOGAN *(his voice begins to sink into a dejected monotone)*: We went to the Inn and started drinking whiskey. And I got drunk.

JOSIE *(exasperatedly)*: I guessed that! And Jim got drunk, too. And then what?

HOGAN *(dully)*: Who knows how drunk he got? He had one of his queer fits when you can't tell. He's the way I told you about this morning, when he talks like a Broadway crook, who'd sell his soul for a price, and there's a sneering divil in him, and he loves to pick out the weakness in people and say cruel, funny things that flay the hide off them, or play cruel jokes on them. *(With sudden rage.)* God's curse on him, I'll wager he's laughing to himself this minute, thinking it's the cutest joke in the world, the fools he made of us. You in particular. Be God, I had my suspicions, at least, but your head was stuffed with mush and love, and you wouldn't—

JOSIE *(furiously)*: You'll tell that lie about my love once too often! And I'll play a joke on him yet that'll make him sorry he—

HOGAN *(sunk in drunken defeatism again)*: It's too late. You shouldn't have let him get away from you to the Inn. You should have kept him here. Then maybe, if you'd got him drunk enough you could have— *(His head nodding, his eyes blinking–thickly.)* But it's no good talking now—no good at all—no good—

JOSIE *(gives him a shake)*: Keep hold of your wits or I'll give you a cuff on both ears! Will you stop blathering like an old woman and tell me plainly what he's done!

HOGAN: He's agreed to sell the farm, that's what! Simpson came to the Inn to see him with a new offer from Harder. Ten thousand, cash.

JOSIE *(overwhelmed)*: Ten thousand! Sure, three is all it's worth at most. And two was what you offered that Jim promised—

HOGAN: What's money to Harder? After what we did to him, all he wants is revenge. And here's where he's foxy. Simpson must have put him up to it knowing how Jim hates it here living on a small allowance, and he longs to go back to Broadway and his whores. Jim won't have to wait for his half of the cash till the estate's settled. Harder offers to give him five thousand cash as a loan against the estate the second the sale is made. Jim can take the next train to New York.

JOSIE *(tensely, on the verge of tears)*: And Jim accepted? I don't believe it!

HOGAN: Don't then. Be God, you'll believe it tomorrow. Harder proposed that he meet with Jim and the executors in the morning and settle it, and Jim promised Simpson he would.

JOSIE *(desperately)*: Maybe he'll get so drunk he'll never remember—

HOGAN: He won't. Harder's coming in his automobile to pick him up and make sure of him. Anyway don't think because he forgot you were waiting—in the moonlight, eating your heart out, that he'd ever miss a date with five thousand dollars, and all the pretty whores of Broadway he can buy with it.

JOSIE *(distractedly)*: Will you shut up! *(Angrily.)* And where were you when all this happened? Couldn't you do anything to stop it, you old loon?

HOGAN: I couldn't. Simpson came and sat at the table with us—

JOSIE: And you let him!

HOGAN: Jim invited him. Anyway, I wanted to find out what trick he had up his sleeve, and what Jim would do. When it was all over, I got up and took a swipe at Simpson, but I missed him. *(With drunken sadness.)* I was too drunk—too drunk—too drunk— I missed him, God forgive me! *(His chin sinks on his chest and his eyes shut.)*

JOSIE *(shakes him)*: If you don't keep awake, be God, I won't miss you!

HOGAN: I was going to take a swipe at Jim, too, but I couldn't do it. My heart was too broken with sorrow. I'd come to love him like a son—a real son of my heart!—to take the place of that jackass, Mike, and me two other jackasses.

JOSIE *(her face hard and bitter)*: I think now Mike was the only one in this house with sense.

HOGAN: I was too drowned in sorrow by his betraying me—and you he'd pretended to like so much. So I only called him a dirty lying skunk of a treacherous bastard, and I turned my back on him and left the Inn, and I made myself sing on the road so he'd hear, and they'd all hear in the Inn, to show them I didn't care a damn.

JOSIE *(scathingly)*: Sure, wasn't you the hero! A hell of a lot of good—

HOGAN: Ah, well, I suppose the temptation was too great. He's weak, with one foot in the grave from whiskey. Maybe we shouldn't blame him.

JOSIE *(her eyes flashing)*: Not blame him? Well, I blame him, God damn him! Are you making excuses for him, you old fool?

HOGAN: I'm not. He's a dirty snake! But I was thinking how do I know what I wouldn't do for five thousand cash, and how do you know what you wouldn't do?

JOSIE: Nothing could make me betray him! *(Her face grows hard and bitter.)* Or it couldn't before. There's nothing I wouldn't do now. *(HOGAN suddenly begins to chuckle.)* Do you think I'm lying? Just give me a chance—

HOGAN: I remembered something. *(He laughs drunk-*

enly.) Be Christ, Josie, for all his Broadway wisdom about women, you've made a prized damned fool of him and that's some satisfaction!

JOSIE *(bewildered)*: How'd you mean?

HOGAN: You'll never believe it. Neither did I, But he kept on until, be God, I saw he really meant it.

JOSIE: Meant what?

HOGAN: It was after he'd turned queer—early in the night before Simpson came. He started talking about you, as if you was on his mind, worrying him—and before he finished I take my oath I began to hope you could really work Mike's first scheme on him, if you got him alone in the moonlight, because all his gab was about his great admiration for you.

JOSIE: Och! The liar!

HOGAN: He said you had great beauty in you that no one appreciated but him.

JOSIE *(shakenly)*: You're lying.

HOGAN: Great strength, you had, and great pride, he said—and great goodness, no less! But here's where you've made a prize jackass of him, like I said. *(With a drunken leer.)* Listen now, darlin', and don't drop dead with amazement. *(He leans toward her and whispers.)* He believes you're a virgin! (JOSIE *stiffens as if she'd been insulted.* HOGAN *goes on.)* He does, so help me! He means it, the poor dunce! He thinks you're a poor innocent virgin! He thinks it's all boasting and pretending you've done about being a slut. *(He chuckles.)* A virgin, no less! You!

JOSIE *(furiously)*: Stop saying it! Boasting and pretending, am I? The dirty liar!

HOGAN: Faith, you don't have to tell me. *(Then he looks at her in drunken surprise–thickly.)* Are you taking it as an insult? Why the hell don't you laugh? Be God, you ought to see what a stupid sheep that makes him.

JOSIE *(forces a laugh)*: I do see it.

HOGAN *(chuckling drunkenly)*: Oh, be God, I've just remembered another thing, Josie. I know why he didn't keep his date with you. It wasn't that he'd forgot. He remembered well enough, for he talked about it—

JOSIE: You mean he deliberately, knowing I'd be waiting— *(Fiercely.)* God damn him!

HOGAN: He as much as told me his reason, though he wouldn't come out with it plain, me being your father. His conscience was tormenting him. He's going to leave you alone and not see you again—for your sake, because he loves you! *(He chuckles.)*

JOSIE *(looks stricken and bewildered–her voice trembling)*: Loves me? You're making it up.

HOGAN: I'm not. I know it sounds crazy but—

JOSIE: What did he mean, for my sake?

HOGAN: Can't you see? You're a pure virgin to him, but all the same there's things besides your beautiful soul he feels drawn to, like your beautiful hair and eyes, and—

JOSIE *(strickenly)*: Och, don't Father! You know I'm only a big—

HOGAN *(as if she hadn't spoken)*: So he'll keep away from temptation because he can't trust himself, and it'd be a sin on his conscience if he was to seduce you. *(He laughs drunkenly.)* Oh, be God! If that ain't rich!

JOSIE *(her voice trembles)*: So that was his reason— *(Then angrily.)* So he thinks all he has to do is crook a finger and I'll fall for him, does he, the vain Broadway crook!

HOGAN *(chuckling)*: Be Jaysus, it was the maddest thing in the world, him gabbing like a soft loon about you—and there at the bar in plain sight was two of the men you've been out with, the gardener at Smith's, and Regan, the chauffeur for Driggs, having a drink together!

JOSIE *(with a twitching smile)*: It must have been mad, surely. I wish I'd been there to laugh up my sleeve. *(Angry.)* But what's all his crazy lying blather got to do with him betraying us and selling the place?

HOGAN *(at once, hopelessly dejected again)*: Nothing at all. I only thought you'd like to know you'd had that much revenge.

JOSIE: A hell of a revenge! I'll have a better one than that on him— or I'll try to! I'm not like you, owning up I'm beaten and crying wurra-wurra like a coward and getting hopeless drunk! *(She gives him a shake.)* Get your wits about you and answer me this: Did Simpson get him to sign a paper?

HOGAN: No, but what good is that? In the morning he'll sign all they shove in front of him.

JOSIE: It's this good. It means we still have a chance. Or I have.

HOGAN: What chance? Are you going to beg him to take pity on us?

JOSIE: I'll see him in hell first! There's another chance, and a good one. But I'll need your help— *(Angrily.)* And look at you, your brains drowned in whiskey, so I can't depend on you!

HOGAN *(rousing himself)*: You can, if there's any chance. Be God, I'll make myself as sober as a judge for you in the wink of an eye! *(Then dejectedly.)* But what can you do now, darlin'? You haven't even got him here. He's down at the Inn sitting alone, drinking and dreaming of the little whores he'll be with tomorrow night on Broadway.

JOSIE: I'll get him here! I'll humble my pride and go down to the Inn for him! And if he doesn't want to come I've a way to make him. I'll raise a scene and pretend I'm in a rage because he forgot his date. I'll disgrace him till he'll be glad to come with me to shut me up. I know his weakness, and it's his vanity about his women. If I was a dainty, pretty tart he'd be proud I'd raise a rumpus about him. But when it's a big, ugly hulk like me— (*She falters and forces herself to go on.*) If he ever was tempted to want me, he'd be ashamed of it. That's the truth behind the lies he told you of his conscience and his fear he might ruin me, God damn him!

HOGAN: No, he meant it, Josie. But never mind that now. Let's say you've got him here. Then what will you do?

JOSIE: I told you this morning if he ever broke his promise to us I'd do anything and not mind how crooked it was. And I will! Your part in it is to come at sunrise with witnesses and catch us in— (*She falters.*)

HOGAN: In bed, is it? Then it's Mike's second scheme you're thinking about?

JOSIE: I told you I didn't care how dirty a trick— (*With a hard bitter laugh.*) The dirtier the better now!

HOGAN: But how'll you get him in bed, with all his honorable scruples, thinking you're a virgin? But I'm forgetting he stayed away because he was afraid he'd be tempted. So maybe—

JOSIE (*tensely*): For the love of God, don't harp on his lies. He won't be tempted at all. But I'll get him so drunk he'll fall asleep and I'll carry him in and put him in bed—

HOGAN: Be God, that's the way! But you'll have to get a pile of whiskey down him. You'll never do it unless you're more sociable and stop looking at him the way you do, whenever he takes a drink, as if you was praying Almighty God to forgive a poor drunkard. You've got to encourage him. The best way would be for you to drink with him. It would put him at his ease and unsuspecting, and it'd give you courage, too, so you'd act bold for a change instead of giving him brazen talk he's tired of hearing, while you act shy as a mouse.

JOSIE (*gives her father a bitter, resentful look*): You're full of sly advice all of a sudden, ain't you? You dirty little tick!

HOGAN (*angrily*): Didn't you tell me to get hold of my wits? Be God if you want me drunk, I've only to let go. That'd suit me. I want to forget my sorrow, and I've no faith in your scheme because you'll be too full of scruples. Like the drinking. You're such a virtuous teetotaller—

JOSIE: I've told you I'd do anything now! (*Then confusedly.*) All I meant was, it's not right, a father to tell his daughter how to— (*Then angrily.*) I don't need your advice. Haven't I had every man I want around here?

HOGAN: Ah, thank God, that sounds natural! Be God, I thought you'd started playing virgin with me just because the Broadway sucker thinks you're one.

JOSIE (*furiously*): Shut up! I'm not playing anything. And don't worry I can't do my part of the trick.

HOGAN: That's the talk! But let me get it all clear. I come at sunrise with my witnesses, and you've forgot to lock your door, and we walk in, and there's the two of you in bed, and I raise the roof and threaten him if he don't marry you—

JOSIE: Marry him? After what he's done to us? I wouldn't marry him now if he was the last man on earth! All we want is a paper signed by him with witnesses that he'll sell the farm to you for the price you offered, and not to Harder.

HOGAN: Well, that's justice, but that's all it is. I thought you wanted to make him pay for his black treachery against us, the dirty bastard!

JOSIE: I do want! (*She again gives him a bitter resentful glance.*) It's the estate money you're thinking of, isn't it? Leave it to you! (*Hastily.*) Well, so am I! I'd like to get my hooks on it! (*With a hard, brazen air.*) Be God, if I'm to play whore, I deserve my pay! We'll make him sign a paper he owes me ten thousand dollars the minute the estate is settled. (*She laughs.*) How's that? I'll bet none of his tarts on Broadway ever got a thousandth part of that out of him, no matter how dainty and pretty! (*Laughing again.*) And here's what'll be the greatest joke to teach him a lesson. He'll pay for it for nothing! I'll get him in bed but I'll never let him—

HOGAN (*with delighted admiration*): Och, by Jaysus, Josie, that's the best yet! (*He slaps his thigh enthusiastically.*) Oh, that'll teach him to double-cross his friends! That'll show him two can play at tricks! And him believing you so innocent! Be God, you'll make him the prize sucker of the world! Won't I roar inside me when I see his face in the morning! (*He bursts into coarse laughter.*)

JOSIE (*again with illogical resentment*): Stop laughing! You're letting yourself be drunk again. (*Then with a hard, business-like air.*) We've done enough talking. Let's start—

HOGAN: Wait, now. There's another thing. Just what do you want me to threaten him with when I catch you? That we'll sue him for outraging your virtue? Sure, his lawyer would have all your old flames in the witness box, till the jury would think you'd been faithful to the male inhabitants of America. So what threat—I can't think of any he wouldn't laugh at.

JOSIE (*tensely*): Well I can! Do I have to tell you his weakness again? It's his vanity about women, and his Broadway pride he's so wise no woman could fool him. It's the disgrace to his vanity—being caught with the likes of me—(*Falteringly, but forcing herself to go on.*) My mug beside his in all the newspapers—the New York papers, too—he'll see the whole of Broadway splitting their sides laughing at him—and he'll give anything to keep us quiet, I tell you. He will! I know him! So don't worry—(*She ends up on the verge of bitter humiliated tears.*)

HOGAN (*without looking at her—enthusiastic again*): Be God, you're right!

JOSIE (*gives him a bitter glance—fiercely*): Then get the hell out of that chair and let's start it! (*He gets up. She surveys him resentfully.*) You're steady on your pins, ain't you, you scheming old thief, now there's the smell of money around! (*Quickly.*) Well, I'm glad. I know I can depend on you now. You'll walk down to the Inn with me and hide outside until you see me come out with him. Then you can sneak in the Inn yourself and pick the witnesses to stay up with you. But mind you don't get drunk again, and let them get too drunk.

HOGAN: I won't, I take my oath! (*He pats her on the shoulder approvingly.*) Be God, you've got the proud, fighting spirit in you that never says die, and you make me ashamed of my weakness. You're that eager now, be damned if I don't almost think you're glad of the excuse!

JOSIE (*stiffens*): Excuse for what, you old—

HOGAN: To show him no man can get the best of you—what else?—like you showed all the others.

JOSIE: I'll show him to his sorrow! (*Then abruptly, starting for the screen door at left.*) Come on. We've no time to waste. (*But when she gets to the door, she appears suddenly hesitant and timid—hurriedly.*) Wait. I'd better give a look at myself in the mirror. (*In a brazen tone.*) Sure, those in my trade have to look their best! (*She hurries back across the room into her bedroom and closes the door. HOGAN stares after her. Abruptly he ceases to look like a drunk who, by an effort, is keeping himself half-sober. He is a man who has been drinking a lot but is still clear-headed and has complete control of himself.*)

HOGAN (*watches the crack under JOSIE's door and speaks half-aloud to himself, shaking his head pityingly*): A look in the mirror and she's forgot to light her lamp! (*Remorsefully.*) God forgive me, it's bitter medicine. But it's the only way I can see that has a chance now. (*JOSIE's door opens. At once, he is as he was. She comes out, a fixed smile on her lips, her head high, her face set defiantly. But she has evidently been crying.*)

JOSIE (*brazenly*): There, now. Don't I look ten thousand dollars' worth to any drunk?

HOGAN: You look a million, darlin'!

JOSIE (*goes to the screen door and pushes it open with the manner of one who has burned all bridges*): Come along, then. (*She goes out. He follows close on her heels. She stops abruptly on the first step—startledly.*) Look! There's someone on the road—

HOGAN (*pushes past her down the steps—peering off left-front—as if aloud to himself, in dismay*): Be God, it's him! I never thought—

JOSIE (*as if aloud to herself*): So he didn't forget—

HOGAN (*quickly*): Well, it proves he can't keep away from you, and that'll make it easier for you—(*Then furiously.*) Oh, the dirty, double-crossing bastard! The nerve of him! Coming to call on you, after making you wait for hours, thinking you don't know what he's done to us this night, and it'll be a fine cruel joke to blarney you in the moonlight, and you trusting him like a poor sheep, and never suspecting—

JOSIE (*stung*): Shut up! I'll teach him who's the joker! I'll let him go on as if you hadn't told me what he's done—

HOGAN: Yes, don't let him suspect it, or you wouldn't fool him. He'd know you were after revenge. But he can see me here now. I can't sneak away or he'd be suspicious. We've got to think of a new scheme quick to get me away—

JOSIE (*quickly*): I know how. Pretend you're as drunk as when you came. Make him believe you're so drunk you don't remember what he's done, so he can't suspect you told me.

HOGAN: I will. Be God, Josie, damned if I don't think he's so queer drunk himself he don't remember, or he'd never come here.

JOSIE: The drunker he is the better! (*Lowering her voice—quickly.*) He's turned in the gate where he can hear us. Pretend we're fighting and I'm driving you off till you're sober. Say you won't be back tonight. It'll make him sure he'll have the night alone with me. You start the fight.

HOGAN (*becomes at once very drunk. He shouts*): Put me out of my own home, will you, you undutiful slut!

JOSIE: Celebration or not, I'll have no drunks cursing and singing all night. Go back to the Inn.

HOGAN: I will! I'll get a room and two bottles and stay drunk as long as I please!

JOSIE: Don't come back till you've slept it off, or I'll wipe the floor with you! (*TYRONE enters, left-front. He does not appear to be drunk—that is, he shows none of the usual symptoms. He seems much the same as in Act 1. The only perceptible change is that his eyes have a peculiar fixed, glazed look, and there is a certain vague quality in his manner and speech, as if he were a bit hazy and absent-minded.*)

TYRONE (*dryly*): Just in time for the Big Bout. Or is this the final round?

HOGAN (*whirls on him unsteadily*): Who the hell—(*Peering at him.*) Oh, it's you, is it?

TYRONE: What was the big idea, Phil, leaving me flat?

HOGAN: Leave you flat? Be Jaysus, that reminds me I owe you a swipe on the jaw for something. What was it? Be God, I'm too drunk to remember. But here it is, anyway. *(He turns loose a round-house swing that misses* TYRONE *by a couple of feet, and reels away.* TYRONE *regards him with vague surprise.)*

JOSIE: Stop it, you damned old fool, and get out of here!

HOGAN: Taking his side against your poor old father, are you? A hell of a daughter! *(He draws himself up with drunken dignity.)* Don't expect me home tonight, Miss Hogan, or tomorrow either, maybe. You can take your bad temper out on your sweetheart here. *(He starts off down the road, left-front, with a last word over his shoulder.)* Bad luck to you both. *(He disappears. A moment later he begins to bawl his mournful Irish song.)* "Oh, the praties they grow small, Over here, over here," etc. *(During a part of the following scene the song continues to be heard at intervals, receding as he gets farther off on his way to the Inn.)*

JOSIE: Well, thank God. That's good riddance. *(She comes to* TYRONE, *who stands staring after* HOGAN *with a puzzled look.)*

TYRONE: I've never seen him that stinko before. Must have got him all of a sudden. He didn't seem so lit up at the Inn, but I guess I wasn't paying much attention.

JOSIE *(forcing a playful air)*: I should think, if you were a real gentleman, you'd be apologizing to me, not thinking of him. Don't you know you're two hours and a half late? I oughtn't to speak to you, if I had any pride.

TYRONE *(stares at her curiously)*: You've got too damn much pride, Josie. That's the trouble.

JOSIE: And just what do you mean by that, Jim?

TYRONE *(shrugs his shoulders)*: Nothing. Forget it. I do apologize, Josie. I'm damned sorry. Haven't any excuse. Can't think up a lie. *(Staring at her curiously again.)* Or, now I think of it, I had a damned good honorable excuse, but— *(He shrugs.)* Nuts. Forget it.

JOSIE: Holy Joseph, you're full of riddles tonight. Well, I don't need excuses. I forgive you, anyway, now you're here. *(She takes his hand—playfully.)* Come on now and we'll sit on my bedroom steps and be romantic in the moonlight, like we planned. *(She leads him there. He goes along in an automatic way, as if only half-conscious of what he is doing. She sits on the top step and pulls him down on the step beneath her. A pause. He stares vaguely at nothing. She bends to give him an uneasy appraising glance.)*

TYRONE *(suddenly, begins to talk mechanically)*: Had to get out of the damned Inn. I was going batty alone there. The old heebie-jeebies. So I came to you. *(He pauses—then adds with strange, wondering*

sincerity.) I've really begun to love you a lot, Josie.

JOSIE *(blurts out bitterly)*: Yes, you've proved that tonight, haven't you? *(Hurriedly regaining her playful tone.)* But never mind. I said I'd forgive you for being so late. So go on about love. I'm all ears.

TYRONE *(as if he hadn't listened)*: I thought you'd have given me up and gone to bed. I remember I had some nutty idea I'd get in bed with you—just to lie with my head on your breast.

JOSIE *(moved in spite of herself—but keeps her bold, playful tone)*: Well, maybe I'll let you— *(Hurriedly.)* Later on, I mean. The night's young yet, and we'll have it all to ourselves. *(Boldly again.)* But here's for a starter. *(She puts her arms around him and draws him back till his head is on her breast.)* There, now.

TYRONE *(relaxes—simply and gratefully)*: Thanks, Josie. *(He closes his eyes. For a moment, she forgets everything and stares down at his face with a passionate, possessive tenderness. A pause. From far-off on the road to the Inn,* HOGAN's *mournful song drifts back through the moonlight quiet: "Oh, the praties they grow small, Over here, over here."* TYRONE *rouses himself and straightens up. He acts embarrassed, as if he felt he'd been making a fool of himself—mockingly.)* Hark, Hark, the Donegal lark! "Thou wast not born for death, immortal bird." Can't Phil sing anything but that damned dirge, Josie? *(She doesn't reply. He goes on hazily.)* Still, it seems to belong tonight—in the moonlight—or in my mind—*(He quotes.)*

"Now more than ever seems it rich to die,
To cease upon the midnight with no pain.
In such an ecstasy!"

(He has recited this with deep feeling. Now he sneers.) Good God! Ode to Phil the Irish Nightingale! I must have the D.T.'s.

JOSIE *(her face grown bitter)*: Maybe it's only your bad conscience.

TYRONE *(starts guiltily and turns to stare into her face—suspiciously)*: What put that in your head? Conscience about what?

JOSIE *(quickly)*: How would I know, if you don't? *(Forcing a playful tone.)* For the sin of wanting to be in bed with me. Maybe that's it.

TYRONE *(with strange relief)*: Oh. *(A bit shamefacedly.)* Forget that stuff, Josie. I was half nutty.

JOSIE *(bitterly)*: Och, for the love of God, don't apologize as if you was ashamed of— *(She catches herself.)*

TYRONE *(with a quick glance at her face)*: All right. I certainly won't apologize—if you're not kicking. I was afraid I might have shocked your modesty.

JOSIE *(roughly)*: *My* modesty? Be God, I didn't know I had any left.

TYRONE (*draws away from her–irritably*): Nix, Josie. Lay off that line, for tonight at least. (*He adds slowly.*) I'd like tonight to be different.

JOSIE: Different from what? (*He doesn't answer. She forces a light tone.*) All right. I'll be as different as you please.

TYRONE (*simply*): Thanks, Josie. Just be yourself. (*Again as if he were ashamed, or afraid he had revealed some weakness–off-handedly.*) This being out in the moonlight instead of the lousy Inn isn't a bad bet, at that. I don't know why I hang out in that dump, except I'm even more bored in the so-called good hotels in this hick town.

JOSIE (*trying to examine his face without his knowing*): Well, you'll be back on Broadway soon now, won't you?

TYRONE: I hope so.

JOSIE: Then you'll have all the pretty little tarts to comfort you when you get your sorrowful spell on.

TYRONE: Oh, to hell with the rough stuff, Josie! You promised you'd can it tonight.

JOSIE (*tensely*): You're a fine one to talk of promises!

TYRONE (*vaguely surprised by her tone*): What's the matter? Still sore at me for being late?

JOSIE (*quickly*): I'm not. I was teasing you. To prove there's no hard feelings, how would you like a drink? But I needn't ask. (*She gets up.*) I'll get a bottle of his best.

TYRONE (*mechanically*): Fine. Maybe that will have some kick. The booze at the Inn didn't work tonight.

JOSIE: Well, this'll work. (*She starts to go into her bedroom. He sits hunched up on the step, staring at nothing. She pauses in the doorway to glance back. The hard, calculating expression on her face softens. For a second she stares at him, bewildered by her conflicting feelings. Then she goes inside, leaving the door open. She opens the door from her room to the lighted living room, and is seen going to the kitchen on the way to the cellar. She has left the door from the living room to her bedroom open and the light reveals a section of the bedroom framed in the doorway behind TYRONE. The foot of the bed which occupies most of the room can be seen, and that is all except that the walls are unpainted pine boards. TYRONE continues to stare at nothing, but becomes restless. His hands and mouth twitch.*)

TYRONE (*suddenly, with intense hatred*): You rotten bastard! (*He springs to his feet–fumbles in his pockets for cigarettes–strikes a match which lights up his face, on which there is now an expression of miserable guilt. His hand is trembling so violently he cannot light the cigarette.*)

ACT 3

(*Scene: The living-room wall has been replaced and all we see now of its lighted interior is through the two win-* dows. Otherwise, everything is the same, and this Act follows the preceding without any lapse of time. TYRONE *is still trying with shaking hands to get his cigarette lighted. Finally he succeeds, and takes a deep inhale, and starts pacing back and forth a few steps, as if in a cell of his own thought. He swears defensively.*) God damn it. You'll be crying in your beer in a minute. (*He begins to sing sneeringly half under his breath a snatch from an old sob song, popular in the Nineties*)

"And baby's cries can't waken her
In the baggage coach ahead."

(*His sneer changes to a look of stricken guilt and grief*) Christ! (*He seems about to break down and sob but he fights this back.*) Cut it out, you drunken fool! (JOSIE *can be seen through the windows, returning from the kitchen. He turns with a look of relief and escape*) Thank God! (*He sits on the boulder and waits.* JOSIE *stops by the table in the living room to turn down the lamp until only a dim light remains. She has a quart of whiskey under her arm, two tumblers, and a pitcher of water. She goes through her bedroom and appears in the outer doorway.* TYRONE *gets up*) Ah! At last the old booze! (*He relieves her of the pitcher and tumblers as she comes down the steps.*)

JOSIE (*with a fixed smile*): You'd think I'd been gone years. You didn't seem so perishing for a drink.

TYRONE (*in his usual, easy, kidding way*): It's you I was perishing for. I've been dying of loneliness—

JOSIE: You'll die of lying some day. But I'm glad you're alive again. I thought when I left you really were dying on me.

TYRONE: No such luck.

JOSIE: Och, don't talk like that. Come on have a drink. We'll use the boulder for a table and I'll be barkeep. (*He puts the pitcher and tumblers on the boulder and she uncorks the bottle. She takes a quick glance at his face–startledly.*) What's come over you, Jim? You look as if you've seen a ghost.

TYRONE (*looks away–dryly*): I have. My own. He's punk company.

JOSIE: Yes, it's the worst ghost of all, your own. Don't I know? But this will keep it in place. (*She pours a tumbler half full of whiskey and hands it to him.*) Here. But wait till I join you. (*She pours the other tumbler half full.*)

TYRONE (*surprised.*): Hello! I thought you never touched it.

JOSIE (*glibly*): I have on occasion. And this is one. I don't want to be left out altogether from celebrating our victory over Harder. (*She gives him a sharp bitter glance. Meeting his eyes, which are regarding her with puzzled wonder, she forces a laugh.*) Don't look at me as if I was up to some game. A drink or two will make me better company, and help me enjoy the moon and the night with you. Here's luck. (*She touches his glass with hers.*)

TYRONE (*shrugs his shoulders*): All right. Here's luck. (*They drink. She gags and sputters. He pours water in her glass. She drinks it. He puts his glass and the pitcher back on the boulder. He keeps staring at her with a puzzled frown.*)

JOSIE: Some of it went down the wrong way.

TYRONE: So I see. That'll teach you to pour out baths instead of drinks.

JOSIE: It's the first time I ever heard you complain a drink was too big.

TYRONE: Yours was too big.

JOSIE: I'm my father's daughter. I've a strong head. So don't worry I'll pass out and you'll have to put me to bed. (*She gives a little bold laugh.*) Sure, that's a beautiful notion. I'll have to pretend I'm—

TYRONE (*irritably*): Nix on the raw stuff, Josie. Remember you said—

JOSIE (*resentment in her kidding*): I'd be different? That's right. I'm forgetting it's your pleasure to have me pretend I'm an innocent virgin tonight.

TYRONE (*in a strange tone that is almost threatening*): If you don't look out, I'll call you on that bluff, Josie. (*He stares at her with a deliberate sensualist's look that undresses her.*) I'd like to. You know that, don't you?

JOSIE (*boldly*): I don't at all. You're the one who's bluffing.

TYRONE (*grabs her in his arms—with genuine passion*): Josie! (*Then as suddenly lets her go.*) Nix. Let's cut it out. (*He turns away. Her face betrays the confused conflict within her of fright, passion, happiness, and bitter resentment. He goes on with an abrupt change of tone.*) How about another drink? That's honest-to-God old bonded Bourbon. How the devil did Phil get hold of it?

JOSIE: Tom Lombardo, the bootlegger, gave him a case for letting him hide a truckload in our barn when the agents were after him. He stole it from a warehouse on faked permits. (*She pours out drinks as she speaks, a half tumblerful for him, a small one for herself.*) Here you are. (*She gives him his drink—smiles at him coquettishly, beginning to show the effect of her big drink by her increasingly bold manners.*) Let's sit down where the moon will be in our eyes and we'll see romance. (*She takes his arm and leads him to her bedroom steps. She sits on the top step, pulling him down beside her but on the one below. She raises her glass.*) Here's hoping before the night's out you'll have more courage and kiss me at least.

TYRONE (*frowns—then kiddingly*): That's a promise. Here's how. (*He drains his tumbler. She drinks half of hers. He puts his glass on the ground beside him. A pause. She tries to read his face without his noticing. He seems to be lapsing again into vague preoccupation.*)

JOSIE: Now don't sink back half-dead-and-alive in dreams the way you were before.

TYRONE (*quickly*): I'm not. I had a good final dose of heebie-jeebies when you were in the house. That's all for tonight. (*He adds a bit maudlinly, his two big drinks beginning to affect him.*) Let the dead past bury its dead.

JOSIE: That's the talk. There's only tonight, and the moon, and us—and the bonded Bourbon. Have another drink, and don't wait for me.

TYRONE: Not now, thanks. They're coming too fast. (*He gives her a curious, cynically amused look.*) Trying to get me soused, Josie?

JOSIE (*starts—quickly*): I'm not. Only to get you feeling happy, so you'll forget all sadness.

TYRONE (*kiddingly*): I might forget all my honorable intentions, too. So look out.

JOSIE: I'll look forward to it—and I hope that's another promise, like the kiss you owe me. If you're suspicious I'm trying to get you soused—well, here goes. (*She drinks what is left in her glass.*) There, now. I must be scheming to get myself soused, too.

TYRONE: Maybe you are.

JOSIE (*resentfully*): If I was, it'd be to make you feel at home. Don't all the pretty little Broadway tarts get soused with you?

TYRONE (*irritably*): There you go again with that old line!

JOSIE: All right, I won't! (*Forcing a laugh.*) I must be eaten up with jealousy for them, that's it.

TYRONE: You needn't be. They don't belong.

JOSIE: And I do?

TYRONE: Yes. You do.

JOSIE: For tonight only, you mean?

TYRONE: We've agreed there is only tonight—and it's to be different from any past night—for both of us.

JOSIE (*in a forced, kidding tone*): I hope it will be. I'll try to control my envy for your Broadway flames. I suppose it's because I have a picture of them in my mind as small and dainty and pretty—

TYRONE: They're just gold-digging tramps.

JOSIE (*as if he hadn't spoken*): While I'm only a big, rough, ugly cow of a woman.

TYRONE: Shut up! You're beautiful.

JOSIE (*jeeringly, but her voice trembles*): God pity the blind!

TYRONE: You're beautiful to me.

JOSIE: It must be the Bourbon—

TYRONE: You're real and healthy and clean and fine and warm and strong and kind—

JOSIE: I have a beautiful soul, you mean?

TYRONE: Well, I don't know much about ladies' souls— (*He takes her hand.*) But I do know you're beautiful. (*He kisses her hand.*) And I love you a lot—in my fashion.

JOSIE (*stammers*): Jim— (*Hastily forcing her playful tone.*) Sure, you're full of fine compliments all of a sudden, and I ought to show you how pleased I am. (*She pulls his head back and kisses him on the lips–a quick, shy kiss.*) That's for my beautiful soul.

TYRONE (*The kiss arouses his physical desire. He pulls her head down and stares into her eyes*): You have a beautiful strong body, too, Josie—and beautiful eyes and hair, and a beautiful smile and beautiful warm breasts. (*He kisses her on the lips. She pulls back frightenedly for a second–then returns his kiss. Suddenly he breaks away–in a tone of guilty irritation.*) Nix! Nix! Don't be a fool, Josie. Don't let me pull that stuff.

JOSIE (*triumphant for a second*): You meant it! I know you meant it! (*Then with resentful bitterness–roughly.*) Be God, you're right I'm a damned fool to let you make me forget you're the greatest liar in the world! (*Quickly.*) I mean, the greatest kidder. And now, how about another drink?

TYRONE (*staring at nothing–vaguely*): You don't get me, Josie. You don't know—and I hope you never will know—

JOSIE (*blurts out bitterly*): Maybe I know more than you think.

TYRONE (*as if she hadn't spoken*): There's always the aftermath that poisons you. I don't want you to be poisoned—

JOSIE: Maybe you know what you're talking about—

TYRONE: And I don't want to be poisoned myself—not again—not with you. (*He pauses–slowly.*) There have been too many nights—and dawns. This must be different. I want— (*His voice trails off into silence.*)

JOSIE (*trying to read his face–uneasily*): Don't get in one of your queer spells, now. (*She gives his shoulder a shake–forcing a light tone.*) Sure, I don't think you know what you want. Except another drink. I'm sure you want that. And I want one, too.

TYRONE (*recovering himself*): Fine! Grand idea. (*He gets up and brings the bottle from the boulder. He picks up his tumbler and pours a big drink. She is holding out her tumbler but he ignores it.*)

JOSIE: You're not polite, pouring your own first.

TYRONE: I said a drink was a grand idea—for me. Not for you. You skip this one.

JOSIE (*resentfully*): Oh, I do, do I? Are you giving me orders?

TYRONE: Yes. Take a big drink of moonlight instead.

JOSIE (*angrily*): You'll pour me a drink, if you please, Jim Tyrone, or—

TYRONE (*stares at her–then shrugs his shoulders*): All right, if you want to take it that way, Josie. It's your funeral. (*He pours a drink into her tumbler.*)

JOSIE (*ashamed but defiant–stiffly*): Thank you kindly. (*She raises her glass–mockingly.*) Here's to tonight. (TYRONE *is staring at her, a strange bitter disgust in his eyes. Suddenly he slaps at her hand, knocking the glass to the ground.*)

TYRONE (*his voice hard with repulsion*): I've slept with drunken tramps on too many nights!

JOSIE (*stares at him, too startled and bewildered to be angry. Her voice trembles with surprising meekness*): All right, Jim, if you don't want me to—

TYRONE (*now looks as bewildered by his action as she does*): I'm sorry, Josie. Don't know what the drink got into me. (*He picks up her glass.*) Here. I'll pour you another.

JOSIE (*still meek*): No, thank you. I'll skip this one. (*She puts the glass on the ground.*) But you drink up.

TYRONE: Thanks. (*He gulps down his drink. Mechanically, as if he didn't know what he was doing, he pours another. Suddenly he blurts out with guilty loathing.*) That fat blonde pig on the train—I got her drunk! That's why— (*He stops guiltily.*)

JOSIE (*uneasily*): What are you talking about? What train?

TYRONE: No train. Don't mind me. (*He gulps down the drink and pours another with the same strange air of acting unconsciously.*) Maybe I'll tell you—later, when I'm— That'll cure you—for all time! (*Abruptly he realizes what he is saying. He gives the characteristic shrug of shoulders–cynically.*) Nuts! The Brooklyn boys are talking again. I guess I'm more stewed than I thought—in the center of the old bean, at least. (*Dully.*) I better beat it back to the Inn and go to bed and stop bothering you, Josie.

JOSIE (*bullyingly–and pityingly*): Well, you won't, not if I have to hold you. Come on now, bring your drink and sit down like you were before. (*He does so. She pats his cheek–forcing a playful air.*) That's a good boy. And I won't take any more whiskey. I've all the effect from it I want already. Everything is far away and doesn't matter—except the moon and its dreams, and I'm part of the dreams—and you are, too. (*She adds with a rueful little laugh.*) I keep forgetting the thing I've got to remember. I keep hoping it's a lie, even though I know I'm a damned fool.

TYRONE (*hazily*): Damned fool about what?

JOSIE: Never mind. (*Forcing a laugh.*) I've just had a thought. If my poor old father had seen you knocking his prize whiskey on the ground—Holy Joseph, he'd have had three paralytic strokes!

TYRONE (*grins*): Yes, I can picture him, (*He pauses–with amused affection.*) But that's all a fake. He loves to play tightwad, but the people he likes know better. He'd give them his shirt. He's a grand old scout, Josie. (*A bit maudlin.*) The only real friend I've got left—except you. I love his guts.

JOSIE (*tensely–sickened by his hypocrisy*): Och, for the love of God—!

TYRONE (*shrugs his shoulders*): Yes, I suppose that does sound like moaning-at-the-bar stuff. But I mean it.

JOSIE: Do you? Well, I know my father's virtues without you telling me.

TYRONE: You ought to appreciate him because he worships the ground you walk on—and he knows you a lot better than you think. (*He turns to smile at her teasingly.*) As well as I do—almost.

JOSIE (*defensively*): That's not saying much. Maybe I can guess what you think you know— (*Forcing a contemptuous laugh.*) If it's that, God pity you, you're a terrible fool.

TYRONE (*teasingly*): If it's what? I haven't said anything.

JOSIE: You'd better not, or I'll die laughing at you. (*She changes the subject abruptly.*) Why don't you drink up? It makes me nervous watching you hold it as if you didn't know it was there.

TYRONE: I didn't, at that. (*He drinks.*)

JOSIE: And have another.

TYRONE (*a bit drunkenly*): Will a whore go to a picnic? Real bonded Bourbon. That's my dish. (*He goes to the boulder for the bottle. He is as steady on his feet as if he were completely sober.*)

JOSIE (*in a light tone*): Bring the bottle back so it'll be handy and you won't have to leave me. I miss you.

TYRONE (*comes back with the bottle. He smiles at her cynically*): Still trying to get me soused, Josie?

JOSIE: I'm not such a fool—with your capacity.

TYRONE: You better watch your step. It might work—and then think of how disgusted you'd feel with me lying beside you, probably snoring, as you watched the dawn come. You don't know—

JOSIE (*defiantly*): The hell I don't! Isn't that the way I've felt with every one of them, after?

TYRONE (*as if he hadn't heard–bitterly*): But take it from me, I know. I've seen too God-damned many dawns creeping grayly over too many dirty windows.

JOSIE (*ignores this–boldly*): But it might be different with you. Love could make it different. And I've been head over heels in love ever since you said you loved my beautiful soul. (*Again he doesn't seem to have heard–resentfully.*) Don't stand there like a loon, mourning over the past. Why don't you pour yourself a drink and sit down?

TYRONE (*looks at the bottle and tumbler in his hands, as if he'd forgotten them–mechanically*): Sure thing. Real bonded Bourbon. I ought to know. If I had a dollar for every drink of it I had before Prohibition, I'd hire our dear bully, Harder, for a valet. (*JOSIE stiffens and her face hardens. TYRONE pours a drink and sets the bottle on the ground. He looks up suddenly into her eyes–warningly.*) You'd better remember I said you had beautiful eyes and hair—and breasts.

JOSIE: I remember you did. (*She tries to be calculatingly enticing.*) So sit down and I'll let you lay your head—

TYRONE: No. If you won't watch your step, I've got to. (*He sits down but doesn't lean back.*) And don't let me get away with pretending I'm so soused I don't know what I'm doing. I always know. Or part of me does. That's the trouble. (*He pauses— then bursts out in a strange threatening tone.*) You better look out, Josie. She was tickled to death to get me pie-eyed. Had an idea she could roll me, I guess. She wasn't so tickled about it—later on.

JOSIE: What she? (*He doesn't reply. She forces a light tone.*) I hope you don't think I'm scheming to roll you.

TYRONE (*vaguely*): What? (*Coming to—indignantly.*) Of course not. What are you talking about? For God's sake, you're not a tart.

JOSIE (*roughly*): No, I'm a fool. I'm always giving it away.

TYRONE (*angrily*): That lousy bluff again, eh? You're a liar! For Christ sake, quit that smut stuff, can't you!

JOSIE (*stung*): Listen to me, Jim! Drunk or not, don't you talk that way to me or—

TYRONE: How about your not talking the old smut stuff to me? You promised you'd be yourself. (*Pauses—vaguely.*) You don't get it, Josie. You see, she was one of the smuttiest talking pigs I've ever listened to.

JOSIE: What she? Do you mean the blonde on the train?

TYRONE (*starts—sharply*): Train? Who told you—? (*Quickly.*) Oh—that's right—I did say— (*Vaguely.*) What blonde? What's the difference? Coming back from the Coast. It was long ago. But it seems like tonight. There is no present or future—only the past happening over and over again—now. You can't get away from it. (*Abruptly.*) Nuts! To hell with that crap.

JOSIE: You came back from the Coast about a year ago after—(*She checks herself.*)

TYRONE (*dully*): Yes. After Mama's death. (*Quickly.*) But I've been to the Coast a lot of times during my career as a third-rate ham. I don't remember which time—or anything much—except I was pie-eyed in a drawing room for the whole four days. (*Abruptly.*) What were we talking about before? What a grand guy Phil is. You ought to be glad you've got him for a father. Mine was an old bastard.

JOSIE: He wasn't! He was one of the finest, kindest gentlemen ever lived.

TYRONE (*sneeringly*): Outside the family, sure. Inside, he was a lousy tightwad bastard.

JOSIE (*repelled*): You ought to be ashamed!

TYRONE: To speak ill of the dead? Nuts! He can't hear, and he knows I hated him, anyway—as much as he hated me. I'm glad he's dead. So is he. Or he ought to be. Everyone ought to be, if they have any sense. Out of a bum racket. At peace. (*He shrugs his shoulders.*) Nuts! What of it?

JOSIE (*tensely*): Don't Jim. I hate you when you talk like that. (*Forcing a light tone.*) Do you want to spoil our beautiful moonlight night? And don't be telling me of your old flames, on trains or not. I'm too jealous.

TYRONE (*with a shudder of disgust*): Of that pig? (*He drinks his whiskey as if to wash a bad taste from his mouth—then takes one of her hands in both of his— simply.*) You're a fool to be jealous of anyone. You're the only woman I care a damn about.

JOSIE (*deeply stirred, in spite of herself—trembling*): Jim, don't— (*Forcing a tense little laugh.*) All right, I'll try and believe that—for tonight.

TYRONE (*simply*): Thanks, Josie. (*A pause. He speaks in a tone of random curiosity.*) Why did you say a while ago I'd be leaving for New York soon?

JOSIE (*stiffens—her face hardening*): Well, I was right, wasn't I? (*Unconsciously she tries to pull her hand away.*)

TYRONE: Why are you pulling your hand away?

JOSIE (*stops*): Was I? (*Forcing a smile.*) I suppose because it seems crazy for you to hold my big ugly paw so tenderly. But you're welcome to it, if you like.

TYRONE: I do like. It's strong and kind and warm— like you. (*He kisses it.*)

JOSIE (*tensely*): Och, for the love of God—! (*She jerks her hand away—then hastily forces a joking tone.*) Wasting kisses on my hand! Sure, even the moon is laughing at us.

TYRONE: Nuts for the moon! I'd rather have one light on Broadway than all the moons since Rameses was a pup. (*He takes cigarettes from his pocket and lights one.*)

JOSIE (*her eyes searching his face, lighted up by the match*): You'll be taking a train back to your dear old Broadway tomorrow night, won't you?

TYRONE (*still holding the burning match, stares at her in surprise*): Tomorrow night? Where did you get that?

JOSIE: A little bird told me.

TYRONE (*blows out the match in a cloud of smoke*): You'd better give that bird the bird. By the end of the week, is the right dope. Phil got his dates mixed.

JOSIE (*quickly*): He didn't tell me. He was too drunk to remember anything.

TYRONE: He was sober when I told him. I called up the executors when we reached the Inn after leaving here. They said the estate would be out of probate within a few days. I told Phil the glad tidings and bought drinks for all and sundry. There was quite a celebration. Funny, Phil wouldn't remember that.

JOSIE (*bewildered–not knowing what to believe*): It is— funny.

TYRONE (*shrugs his shoulders*): Well, he's stewed to the ears. That always explains anything. (*Then strangely.*) Only sometimes it doesn't.

JOSIE: No—sometimes it doesn't.

TYRONE (*goes on without real interest, talking to keep from thinking*): Phil certainly has a prize bun on tonight. He never took a punch at me before. And that drivel he talked about owing me one—What got into his head, I wonder.

JOSIE (*tensely*): How would I know, if you don't?

TYRONE: Well, I don't. Not unless—I remember I did try to get his goat. Simpson sat down with us. Harder sent him to see me. You remember after Harder left here I said the joke was on you, that you'd made this place a gold mine. I was kidding, but I had the right dope. What do you think he told Simpson to offer? Ten grand! On the level, Josie.

JOSIE (*tense*): So you accepted?

TYRONE: I told Simpson to tell Harder I did. I decided the best way to fix him was to let him think he'd got away with it, and then when he comes tomorrow morning to drive me to the executor's office, I'll tell him what he can do with himself, his bankroll, and tin oil tanks.

JOSIE (*knows he is telling the truth—so relieved she can only stammer stupidly*): So that's—the truth of it.

TYRONE (*smiles*): Of course, I did it to kid Phil, too. He was right there, listening. But I know I didn't fool him.

JOSIE (*weakly*): Maybe you did fool him, for once. But I don't know.

TYRONE: And that's why he took a swing at me? (*He laughs, but there is a forced note to it.*) Well, if so, it's one hell of a joke on him. (*His tone becomes hurt and bitter.*) All the same, I'll be good and sore, Josie. I promised this place wouldn't be sold except to him. What the hell does he think I am? He ought to know I wouldn't double-cross you and him for ten million!

JOSIE (*giving away at last to her relief and joy*): Don't I know! Oh, Jim, darling! (*She hugs him passionately and kisses him on the lips.*) I knew you'd never—I told him— (*She kisses him again.*) Oh, Jim, I love you.

TYRONE (*again with a strange, simple gratitude*): Thanks, Josie. I mean, for not believing I'm a rotten louse. Everyone else believes it—including myself—for a damned good reason. (*Abruptly changing the subject.*) I'm a fool to let this stuff about Phil get under my skin, but— Why, I remember telling him tonight I'd even written my brother and got his okay on selling the farm to him. And Phil thanked me. He seemed touched and grateful. You wouldn't think he'd forget that.

JOSIE (*her face hard and bitter*): I wouldn't, indeed. There's a lot of things he'll have to explain when he comes at sun— (*Hastily.*) When he comes back. (*She pauses—then bursts out.*) The damned old schemer, I'll teach him to— (*Again checking herself.*) to act like a fool.

TYRONE (*smiles*): You'll get out the old club, eh? What a bluff you are, Josie. (*Teasingly.*) You and your loves, Messalina—when you've never—

JOSIE (*with a faint spark of her old defiance*): You're a liar.

TYRONE: "Pride is the sin by which the angels fell." Are you going to keep that up—with me?

JOSIE (*feebly*): You think I've never because no one would—because I'm a great ugly cow—

TYRONE (*gently*): Nuts! You could have had any one of them. You kidded them till you were sure they wanted you. That was all you wanted. And then you slapped them groggy when they tried for more. But you had to keep convincing yourself—

JOSIE (*tormentedly*): Don't, Jim.

TYRONE: You can take the truth, Josie—from me. Because you and I belong to the same club. We can kid the world but we can't fool ourselves, like most people, no matter what we do—nor escape ourselves no matter where we run away. Whether it's the bottom of a bottle, or a South Sea Island, we'd find our own ghosts there waiting to greet us— "sleepless with pale commemorative eyes," as Rossetti wrote. (*He sneers to himself.*) The old poetic bull, eh? Crap! (*Reverting to a teasing tone.*) You don't ask how I saw through your bluff, Josie. You pretend too much. And so do the guys. I've listened to them at the Inn. They all lie to each other. No one wants to admit all he got was a slap in the puss, when he thinks a lot of other guys made it. You can't blame them. And they know you don't give a damn how they lie. So—

JOSIE: For the love of God, Jim! Don't!

TYRONE: Phil is wise to you, of course, but although he knew I knew, he would never admit it until tonight.

JOSIE (*startled—vindictively*): So he admitted it, did he? Wait till I get hold of him!

TYRONE: He'll never admit it to you. He's afraid of hurting you.

JOSIE: He is, is he? Well— (*Almost hysterically.*) For the love of God, can't you shut up about him!

TYRONE (*glances up at her, surprised—then shrugs his shoulders*): Oh, all right. I wanted to clear things up, that's all—for Phil's sake as well as yours. You have a hell of a license to be sore. He's the one who ought to be. Don't you realize what a lousy position you've put him in with your brazen-trollop act?

JOSIE (*tensely*): No. He doesn't care, except to use me in his scheming. He—

TYRONE: Don't be a damned fool. Of course he cares. And so do I. (*He turns and pulls her head down and kisses her on the lips.*) I care, Josie. I love you.

JOSIE (*with pitiful longing*): Do you, Jim? Do you? (*She forces a trembling smile—faintly.*) Then I'll confess the truth to you. I've been a crazy fool. I am a virgin. (*She begins to sob with a strange forlorn shame and humiliation.*) And now you'll never—and I want you to—now more than ever—because I love you more than ever, after what's happened—(*Suddenly she kisses him with fierce passion.*) But you will! I'll make you! To hell with your honorable scruples! I know you want me! I couldn't believe that until tonight—but now I know. It's in your kisses! (*She kisses him again—with passionate tenderness.*) Oh, you great fool! As if I gave a damn what happened after! I'll have had tonight and your love to remember for the rest of my days! (*She kisses him again.*) Oh, Jim darling, haven't you said yourself there's only tonight? (*She whispers tenderly.*) Come. Come with me. (*She gets to her feet, pulling at his arm—with a little self-mocking laugh.*) But I'll have to make you leave before sunrise. I mustn't forget that.

TYRONE (*a strange change has come over his face. He looks her over now with a sneering cynical lust. He speaks thickly as if he was suddenly very drunk*): Sure thing, Kiddo. What the hell else do you suppose I came for? I've been kidding myself. (*He steps up beside her and puts his arm around her and presses his body to hers.*) You're the goods, Kid. I've wanted you all along. Love, nuts! I'll show you what love is. I know what you want, Bright Eyes. (*She is staring at him now with a look of frightened horror. He kisses her roughly.*) Come on, Baby Doll, let's hit the hay. (*He pushes her back in the doorway.*)

JOSIE (*strickenly*): Jim! Don't! (*She pulls his arms away so violently that he staggers back and would fall down the steps if she didn't grab his arm in time. As it is he goes down on one knee. She is on the verge of collapse herself—brokenly.*) Jim! I'm not a whore.

TYRONE (*remains on one knee—confusedly, as if he didn't know what had happened*): What the hell? Was I trying to rape you, Josie? Forget it. I'm drunk—not responsible. (*He gets to his feet, staggering a bit, and steps down to the ground.*)

JOSIE (*covering her face with her hands*): Oh, Jim! (*She sobs.*)

TYRONE (*with vague pity*): Don't cry. No harm done. You stopped me, didn't you? (*She continues to sob. He mutters vaguely, as if talking to himself.*) Must have drawn a blank for a while. Nuts! Cut out the faking. I knew what I was doing. (*Slowly, staring before him.*) But it's funny. I *was* seeing things. That's the truth, Josie. For a moment I thought you were that blonde pig— (*Hastily.*) The old heebie-jeebies. Hair of the dog. (*He gropes around *for the bottle and his glass.)* I'll have another shot—

JOSIE *(takes her hands from her face—fiercely)*: Pour the whole bottle down your throat, if you like! Only stop talking! *(She covers her face with her hands and sobs again.)*

TYRONE *(stares at her with a hurt and sad expression—dully)*: Can't forgive me, eh? You ought to. You ought to thank me for letting you see— *(He pauses, as if waiting for her to say something, but she remains silent. He shrugs his shoulders, pours out a big drink mechanically.)* Well, here's how. *(He drinks and puts the bottle and glass on the ground—dully.)* That was a nightcap. Our moonlight romance seems to be a flop, Josie. I guess I'd better go.

JOSIE *(dully)*: Yes. You'd better go. Good night.

TYRONE: Not good night. Good-bye.

JOSIE *(lifts her head)*: Good-bye?

TYRONE: Yes. I won't see you again before I leave for New York. I was a damned fool to come tonight. I hoped—But you don't get it. How could you? So what's the good— *(He shrugs his shoulders hopelessly and turns toward the road.)*

JOSIE: Jim!

TYRONE *(turning back—bitter accusation in his tone now)*: Whore? Who said you were a whore? But I warned you, didn't I, if you kept on— Why did you have to act like one, asking me to come to bed? That wasn't what I came here for. And you promised tonight would be different. Why the hell did you promise that, if all you wanted was what all the others want, if that's all love means to you? *(Then guiltily.)* Oh, Christ, I don't mean that, Josie. I know how you feel, and if I could give you happiness— But it wouldn't work. You don't know me. I'd poison it for myself and for you. I've poisoned it already, haven't I, but it would be a million times worse after— No matter how I tried not to. I'd make it like all the other nights—for you, too. You'd lie awake and watch the dawn come with disgust, with nausea retching your memory, and the wine of passion poets blab about, a sour aftertaste in your mouth of Dago red ink! *(He gives a sneering laugh.)*

JOSIE *(distractedly)*: Oh, Jim, don't! Please don't!

TYRONE: You'd hate me and yourself—not for a day or two but for the rest of your life. *(With a perverse, jeering note of vindictive boastfulness in his tone.)* Believe me, Kid, when I poison them, they stay poisoned!

JOSIE *(with dull bitterness)*: Good-bye, Jim.

TYRONE *(miserably hurt and sad for a second—appealingly)*: Josie— *(Gives the characteristic shrug of his shoulders—simply.)* Good-bye. *(He turns toward the road—bitterly.)* I'll find it hard to forgive, too. I came here asking for love—just for this one night, because I thought you loved me. *(Dully.)* Nuts. To hell with it. *(He starts away.)*

JOSIE *(watches him for a second, fighting the love that, in* spite of her, responds to his appeal—then she springs up and runs to him—with fierce, possessive, maternal tenderness)*: Come here to me, you great fool, and stop your silly blather. There's nothing to hate you for. There's nothing to forgive. Sure, I was only trying to give you happiness, because I love you. I'm sorry I was so stupid and didn't see— But I see now. and you'll find I have all the love you need. *(She gives him a hug and kisses him. There is passion in her kiss but it is a tender, protective maternal passion, which he responds to with an instant grateful yielding.)*

TYRONE *(simply)*: Thanks, Josie. You're beautiful. I love you. I knew you'd understand.

JOSIE: Of course I do. Come, now. *(She leads him back, her arm around his waist.)*

TYRONE: I didn't want to leave you. You know that.

JOSIE: Indeed I know it. Come now. We'll sit down. *(She sits on the top step and pulls him down on the step below her.)* That's it—with my arm around you. Now lay your head on my breast—the way you said you wanted to do.— *(He lets his head fall back on her breast. She hugs him—gently.)* There, now. Forget all about my being a fool and forgive— *(Her voice trembles—but she goes on determinedly.)* Forgive my selfishness, thinking only of myself. Sure, if there's one thing I owe you tonight, after all my lying and scheming, it's to give you the love you need, and it'll be my pride and my joy— *(Forcing a trembling echo of her playful tone.)* It's easy enough, too, for I have all kinds of love for you—and maybe this is the greatest of all— because it costs so much. *(She pauses, looking down at his face. He has closed his eyes and his haggard, dissipated face looks like a pale mask in the moonlight—at peace as a death mask is at peace. She becomes frightened.)* Jim! Don't look like that!

TYRONE *(opens his eyes—vaguely)*: Like what?

JOSIE *(quickly)*: It's the moonlight. It makes you look so pale, and with your eyes closed—

TYRONE *(simply)*: You mean I looked dead?

JOSIE: No! As if you'd fallen asleep.

TYRONE *(speaks in a tired, empty tone, as if he felt he ought to explain something to her—something which no longer interests him)*: Listen, and I'll tell you a little story, Josie. All my life I had just one dream. From the time I was a kid, I loved race-horses. I thought they were the most beautiful things in the world. I liked to gamble, too. So the big dream was that some day I'd have enough dough to play a cagey system of betting on favorites, and follow the horses south in the winter, and come back north with them in the spring, and be at the track every day. It seemed that would be the ideal life—for me. *(He pauses.)*

JOSIE: Well, you'll be able to do it.

TYRONE: No. I won't be able to do it, Josie. That's the joke. I gave it a try-out before I came up here. I borrowed some money on my share of the estate, and started going to tracks. But it didn't work. I played my system, but I found I didn't care if I won or lost. The horses were beautiful, but I found myself saying to myself, what of it? Their beauty didn't mean anything. I found that every day I was glad when the last race was over, and I could go back to the hotel—and the bottle in my room. (*He pauses, staring into the moonlight with vacant eyes.*)

JOSIE (*uneasily*): Why did you tell me this?

TYRONE (*in the same listless monotone*): You said I looked dead. Well, I am.

JOSIE: You're not! (*She hugs him protectively.*) Don't talk like that!

TYRONE: Ever since Mama died.

JOSIE (*deeply moved—pityingly*): I know. I've felt all along it was that sorrow was making you— (*She pauses—gently.*) Maybe if you talked about your grief for her, it would help you. I think it must be all choked up inside you, killing you.

TYRONE (*in a strange warning tone*): You'd better look out, Josie.

JOSIE: Why?

TYRONE (*quickly, forcing his cynical smile*): I might develop a crying jag, and sob on your beautiful breast.

JOSIE (*gently*): You can sob all you like.

TYRONE: Don't encourage me. You'd be sorry. (*A deep conflict shows in his expression and tone. He is driven to go on in spite of himself.*) But if you're such a glutton for punishment— After all, I said I'd tell you later, didn't I?

JOSIE (*puzzled*): You said you'd tell me about the blonde on the train.

TYRONE: She's part of it. I lied about that. (*He pauses—then blurts out sneeringly.*) You won't believe it could have happened. Or if you did believe, you couldn't understand or forgive— (*Quickly.*) But you might. You're the one person who might. Because you really love me. And because you're the only woman I've ever met who understands the lousy rotten things a man can do when he's crazy drunk, and draws a blank— especially when he's nutty with grief to start with.

JOSIE (*hugging him tenderly*): Of course I'll understand, Jim, darling.

TYRONE (*stares into the moonlight—hauntedly*): But I didn't draw a blank. I tried to. I drank enough to knock out ten men. But it didn't work. I knew what I was doing. (*He pauses—dully.*) No, I can't tell you, Josie. You'd loathe my guts, and I couldn't blame you.

JOSIE: No! I'll love you no matter what—

TYRONE (*with strange triumphant harshness*): All right! Remember that's a promise! (*He pauses—starts to speak—pauses again.*)

JOSIE (*pityingly*): Maybe you'd better not—if it will make you suffer.

TYRONE: Trying to welch now, eh? It's too late. You've got me started. Suffer? Christ, I ought to suffer! (*He pauses. Then he closes his eyes. It is as if he had to hide from sight before he can begin. He makes his face expressionless. His voice becomes impersonal and objective, as though what he told concerned some man he had known, but had nothing to do with him. This is the only way he can start telling the story.*) When Mama died, I'd been on the wagon for nearly two years. Not even a glass of beer. Honestly. And I know I would have stayed on. For her sake. She had no one but me. The Old Man was dead. My brother had married—had a kid—had his own life to live. She'd lost him. She had only me to attend to things for her and take care of her. She'd always hated my drinking. So I quit. It made me happy to do it. For her. Because she was all I had, all I cared about. Because I loved her. (*He pauses.*) No one would believe that now, who knew— But I did.

JOSIE (*gently*): I know how much you loved her.

TYRONE: We went out to the Coast to see about selling a piece of property the Old Man had bought there years ago. And one day she suddenly became ill. Got rapidly worse. Went into a coma. Brain tumor. The docs said, no hope. Might never come out of coma. I went crazy. Couldn't face losing her. The old booze yen got me. I got drunk and stayed drunk. And I began hoping she'd never come out of the coma, and see I was drinking again. That was my excuse, too—that she'd never know. And she never did. (*He pauses—then sneeringly.*) Nix! Kidding myself again. I know damned well just before she died she recognized me. She saw I was drunk. Then she closed her eyes so she couldn't see, and was glad to die! (*He opens his eyes and stares into the moonlight as if he saw this deathbed scene before him.*)

JOSIE (*soothingly*): Ssshh. You only imagine that because you feel guilty about drinking.

TYRONE (*as if he hadn't heard, closes his eyes again*): After that, I kept so drunk I did draw a blank most of the time, but I went through the necessary motions and no one guessed how drunk— (*He pauses.*) But there are things I can never forget—the undertakers, and her body in a coffin with her face made up. I couldn't hardly recognize her. She looked young and pretty like someone I remembered meeting long ago. Practically a stranger. To who I was a stranger. Cold and indifferent. Not worried about me any more. Free at last. Free from worry. From pain. From me. I stood looking down at her, and something happened to me. I found I couldn't feel anything. I knew I ought to be heartbroken but I couldn't feel anything. I seemed dead, too. I knew I ought to cry. Even a crying jag would look better than just standing there. But I couldn't cry. I cursed to myself, "You dirty bastard, it's Mama. You loved her, and now she's dead. She's gone away from you forever. Never, never again—" But it had no effect. All I did was try to explain to myself, "She's dead. What does she care now if I cry or not, or what I do? It doesn't matter a damn to her. She's happy to be where I can't hurt her ever again. She's rid of me at last. For God's sake, can't you leave her alone even now? For God's sake, can't you let her rest in peace?" *(He pauses—then sneeringly.)* But there were several people around and I knew they expected me to show something. Once a ham, always a ham! So I put on an act. I flopped on my knees and hid my face in my hands and faked some sobs and cried, "Mama! Mama! My dear mother!" But all the time I kept saying to myself, "You lousy ham! You God-damned lousy ham! Christ, in a minute you'll start singing 'Mother Macree'!" *(He opens his eyes and gives a tortured, sneering laugh, staring into the moonlight.)*

JOSIE *(horrified, but still deeply pitying)*: Jim! Don't! It's past. You've punished yourself. And you were drunk. You didn't mean—

TYRONE *(again closes his eyes)*: I had to bring her body East to be buried beside the Old Man. I took a drawing room and hid in it with a case of booze. She was in her coffin in the baggage car. No matter how drunk I got, I couldn't forget that for a minute. I found I couldn't stay alone in the drawing room. It became haunted. I was going crazy. I had to go out and wander up and down the train looking for company. I made such a public nuisance of myself that the conductor threatened if I didn't quit, he'd keep me locked in the drawing room. But I'd spotted one passenger who was used to drunks and could pretend to like them, if there was enough dough in it. She had parlor house written all over her—a blonde pig who looked more like a whore than twenty-five whores, with a face like an overgrown doll's and a come-on smile as cold as a polar bear's feet. I bribed the porter to take a message to her and that night she sneaked into my drawing room. She was bound for New York, too. So every night—for fifty bucks a night— *(He opens his eyes and now he stares torturedly through the moonlight into the drawing room.)*

JOSIE *(her face full of revulsion—stammers)*: Oh, how could you! *(Instinctively she draws away, taking her arms from around him.)*

TYRONE: How could I? I don't know. But I did. I suppose I had some mad idea she could make me forget—what was in the baggage car ahead.

JOSIE: Don't. *(She draws back again so he has to raise his head from her breast. He doesn't seem to notice this.)*

TYRONE: No, it couldn't have been that. Because I didn't seem to want to forget. It was like some plot I had to carry out. The blonde—she didn't matter. She was only something that belonged in the plot. It was as if I wanted revenge—because I'd been left alone—because I knew I was lost, without any hope left—that all I could do would be drink myself to death, because no one was left who could help me. *(His face hardens and a look of cruel vindictiveness comes into it—with a strange horrible satisfaction in his tone.)* No, I didn't forget even in that pig's arms! I remembered the last two lines of a lousy tear-jerker song I'd heard when I was a kid kept singing over and over in my brain.

*"And baby's cries can't waken her
In the baggage coach ahead."*

JOSIE *(distractedly)*: Jim!

TYRONE: I couldn't stop it singing. I didn't want to stop it!

JOSIE: Jim! For the love of God. I don't want to hear!

TYRONE *(after a pause—dully)*: Well, that's all—except I was too drunk to go to her funeral.

JOSIE: Oh! *(She has drawn away from him as far as she can without getting up. He becomes aware of this for the first time and turns slowly to stare at her.)*

TYRONE *(dully)*: Don't want to touch me now, eh? *(He shrugs his shoulders mechanically.)* Sorry. I'm a damned fool. I shouldn't have told you.

JOSIE *(her horror ebbing as her love and protective compassion returns—moves nearer him—haltingly)*: Don't, Jim. Don't say—I don't want to touch you. It's—a lie. *(She puts a hand on his shoulder.)*

TYRONE *(as if she hadn't spoken—with hopeless longing)*: Wish I could believe in the spiritualists' bunk. If I could tell her it was because I missed her so much and couldn't forgive her for leaving me—

JOSIE: Jim! For the love of God—!

TYRONE *(unheeding)*: She'd understand and forgive me, don't you think? She always did. She was simple and kind and pure of heart. She was beautiful. You're like her deep in your heart. That's why I told you. I thought— *(Abruptly his expression becomes sneering and cynical—harshly.)* My mistake. Nuts! Forget it. Time I got a move on. I don't like your damned moon, Josie. It's an ad for the past. *(He recites mockingly)*

*"It is the very error of the moon:
She comes more nearer earth than she was wont,
And makes men mad."*

(He moves) I'll grab the last trolley for town. There'll be a speak open, and some drunk laughing. I need a laugh. *(He starts to get up.)*

JOSIE *(throws her arms around him and pulls him back—*

tensely): No! You won't go! I won't let you! (*She hugs him close—gently.*) I understand now, Jim, darling, and I'm proud you came to me as the one in the world you know loves you enough to understand and forgive—and I do forgive!

TYRONE (*lets his head fall back on her breast—simply*): Thanks, Josie, I knew you—

JOSIE: As *she* forgives, do you hear me! As *she* loves and understands and forgives!

TYRONE (*simply*): Yes, I know she— (*His voice breaks.*)

JOSIE (*bends over him with a brooding maternal tenderness*): That's right. Do what you came for, my darling. It isn't drunken laughter in a speakeasy you want to hear at all, but the sound of yourself crying your heart's repentance against her breast. (*His face is convulsed. He hides it on her breast and sobs rackingly. She hugs him more tightly and speaks softly, staring into the moonlight.*) She hears. I feel her in the moonlight, her soul wrapped in it like a silver mantle, and I know she understand and forgives me, too, and her blessing lies on me. (*A pause. His sobs begin to stop exhaustedly. She looks down at him again and speaks soothingly as she would to a child.*) There. There, now. (*He stops. She goes on in a gentle, bullying tone.*) You're a fine one, wanting to leave me when the night I promised I'd give you has just begun, our night that'll be different from all the others, with a dawn that won't creep over dirty windowpanes but will wake in the sky like a promise of God's peace in the soul's dark sadness. (*She smiles a little amused smile.*) Will you listen to me, Jim! I must be a poet. Who would have guessed it? Sure, love is a wonderful mad inspiration! (*A pause. She looks down. His eyes are closed. His face against her breast looks pale and haggard in the moonlight. Calm with the drained, exhausted peace of death. For a second she is frightened. Then she realizes and whispers softly.*) Asleep. (*In a tender crooning tone like a lullaby.*) That's right. Sleep in peace, my darling. (*Then with sudden anguished longing.*) Oh, Jim, Jim, maybe my love could still save you, if you could want it enough! (*She shakes her head.*) No. That can never be. (*Her eyes leave his face to stare up at the sky. She looks weary and stricken and sad. She forces a defensive, self-derisive smile.*) God forgive me, it's a fine end to all my scheming, to sit here with the dead hugged to my breast, and the silly mug of the moon grinning down, enjoying the joke!

ACT 4

(*Scene: Same as Act Three. It is dawn. The first faint streaks of color, heralding the sunrise, appear in the eastern sky at left.*

JOSIE *sits in the same position on the steps, as if she had not moved, her arms around* TYRONE. *He is still asleep,* his head on her breast. His face has the same exhausted, death-like repose. JOSIE's *face is set in an expression of numbed, resigned sadness. Her body sags tiredly. In spite of her strength, holding herself like this for hours, for fear of waking him, is becoming too much for her.*

The two make a strangely tragic picture in the wan dawn light—this big sorrowful woman hugging a haggard-faced, middle-aged drunkard against her breast, as if he were a sick child.

HOGAN *appears at left-rear, coming from the barn. He approaches the corner of the house stealthily on tiptoe. Wisps of hay stick to his clothes and his face is swollen and sleepy, but his little pig's eyes are sharply wide awake and sober. He peeks around the corner, and takes in the two on the steps. His eyes fix on* JOSIE's *face in a long, probing stare.*)

JOSIE (*speaks in a low grim tone*): Stop hiding, Father. I heard you sneak up. (*He comes guiltily around the corner. She keeps her voice low, but her tone is commanding.*) Come here, and be quiet about it. (*He obeys meekly, coming as far as the boulder silently, his eyes searching her face, his expression becoming guilty and miserable at what he sees. She goes on in the same tone, without looking at him.*) Talk low, now. I don't want him wakened— (*She adds strangely.*) Not until the dawn has beauty in it.

HOGAN (*worriedly*): What? (*He decides it's better for the present to ask no questions. His eyes fall on* TYRONE's *face. In spite of himself, he is startled—in an awed, almost frightened whisper.*) Be god, he looks dead!

JOSIE (*strangely*): Why wouldn't he? He is.

HOGAN: Is?

JOSIE: Don't be a fool. Can't you see him breathing? Dead asleep, I mean. Don't stand there gawking. Sit down. (*He sits meekly on the boulder. His face betrays a guilty dread of what is coming. There is a pause in which she doesn't look at him but, he keeps glancing at her, growing visibly more uneasy. She speaks bitterly.*) Where's your witnesses?

HOGAN (*guiltily*): Witnesses? (*Then forcing an amused grin.*) Oh, be God, if that ain't a joke on me! Sure I got so blind drunk at the Inn I forgot all about our scheme and came home and went to sleep in the hayloft.

JOSIE (*her expression harder and more bitter*): You're a liar.

HOGAN: I'm not. I just woke up. Look at the hay sticking to me. That's proof.

JOSIE: I'm not thinking of that, and well you know it. (*With bitter voice.*) So you just woke up—did you?—and then came sneaking here to see if the scheme behind your scheme had worked!

HOGAN (*guiltily*): I don't know what you mean.

JOSIE: Don't lie any more, Father. This time, you've told one too many. (*He starts to defend himself but the look on her face makes him think better of it and he remains uneasily silent. A pause.*)

HOGAN (*finally has to blurt out*): Sure, if I'd brought the witnesses, there's nothing for them to witness that—

JOSIE: No. You're right there. There's nothing. Nothing at all. (*She smiles strangely.*) Except a great miracle they'd never believe, or you either.

HOGAN: What miracle?

JOSIE: A virgin who bears a dead child in the night, and the dawn finds her still a virgin. If that isn't a miracle, what is?

HOGAN (*uneasily*): Stop talking so queer. You give me the shivers. (*He attempts a joking tone.*) Is it you who's the virgin? Faith, that *would* be a miracle, no less! (*He forces a chuckle.*)

JOSIE: I told you to stop lying, Father.

HOGAN: What lie? (*He stops and watches her face worriedly. She is silent, as if she were not aware of him now. Her eyes are fixed on the wanton sky.*)

JOSIE (*as if to herself*): It'll be beautiful soon, and I can wake him.

HOGAN (*can't resist his anxiety any longer*): Josie, darlin'! For the love of God, can't you tell me what happened to you?

JOSIE (*her face hard and bitter again*): I've told you once. Nothing.

HOGAN: Nothing? If you could see the sadness in your face—

JOSIE: What woman doesn't sorrow for the man she loved who has died? But there's pride in my heart, too.

HOGAN (*tormentedly*): Will you stop talking as if you'd gone mad in the night! (*Raising his voice—with revengeful anger.*) Listen to me! If Jim Tyrone has done anything to bring you sorrow— (TYRONE *stirs in his sleep and moans, pressing his face against her breast as if for protection. She looks down at him and hugs him close.*)

JOSIE (*croons softly*): There, there, my darling. Rest in peace a while longer. (*Turns on her father angrily and whispers.*) Didn't I tell you to speak low and not wake him! (*She pauses—then quietly.*) He did nothing to bring me sorrow. It was my mistake. I thought there was still hope. I didn't know he'd died already—that it was a damned soul coming to me in the moonlight, to confess and be forgiven and find peace for a night—

HOGAN: Josie! Will you stop!

JOSIE (*after a pause—dully*): He'd never do anything to hurt me. You know it. (*Self-mockingly.*) Sure, hasn't he told me I'm beautiful to him and he loves me—in his fashion. (*Then matter-of-factly.*) All that happened was that he got drunk and he had one of his crazy notions he wanted to sleep the way he is, and I let him sleep. (*With forced roughness.*) And, be God, the night's over. I'm half dead with tiredness and sleepiness. It's that you see in my face, not sorrow.

HOGAN: Don't try to fool me, Josie. I—

JOSIE (*her face hard and bitter—grimly*): Fool you, is it? It's you who made a fool of me with your lies, thinking you'd use me to get your dirty greasy paws on the money he'll have!

HOGAN: No! I swear by all the saints—

JOSIE: You'd swear on a Bible while you were stealing it! (*Grimly.*) Listen to me, Father. I didn't call you here to answer questions about what's none of your business. I called you here to tell you I've seen through all the lies you told last night to get me to— (*As he starts to speak.*) Shut up! I'll do the talking now. You weren't drunk. You were only putting it on as part of your scheme—

HOGAN (*quietly*): I wasn't drunk, no. I admit that, Josie. But I'd had slews of drinks and they were in my head or I'd never have the crazy dreams—

JOSIE (*with biting scorn*): Dreams, is it? The only dream you've ever had, or will have, is of yourself counting a fistful of dirty money, and divil a care how you got it, or who you robbed or made suffer!

HOGAN (*winces—pleadingly*): Josie!

JOSIE: Shut up! (*Scathingly.*) I'm sure you've made up a whole new set of lies and excuses. You're that cunning and clever, but you can save your breath. They wouldn't fool me now. I've been fooled once too often. (*He gives her a frightened look, as if something he had dreaded has happened. She goes on, grimly accusing.*) You lied about Jim selling the farm. You knew he was kidding. You knew the estate would be out of probate in a few days, and he'd go back to Broadway, and you had to do something quick or you'd lose the last chance of getting your greedy hooks on his money.

HOGAN (*miserably*): No. It wasn't that, Josie.

JOSIE: You saw how hurt and angry I was because he'd kept me waiting here, and you used that. You knew I loved him and wanted him and you used that. You used all you knew about me— Oh, you did it clever! You ought to be proud! You worked it so it was me who did all the dirty scheming— You knew I'd find out from Jim you'd lied about the farm, but not before your lie had done its work—made me go after him, get him drunk, get drunk myself so I could be shameless—and when the truth did come out, wouldn't it make me love him all the more and be more shameless and willing? Don't tell me you didn't count on that, and you such a clever schemer! And if he once had me, knowing I was a virgin, didn't you count on his honor and remorse, and his loving me in his fashion, to make him offer to marry me? Sure, why wouldn't he, you thought. It wouldn't hold him. He'd go back to Broadway just the same and never see me again. But there'd be money in it, and when he'd finished killing himself, I'd be his legal widow and get what's left.

HOGAN (*miserably*): No! It wasn't that.

JOSIE: But what's the good of talking? It's all over. I've only one more word for you, Father, and it's this: I'm leaving you today, like my brothers left. You can live alone and work alone your cunning schemes on yourself.

HOGAN (*after a pause—slowly*): I knew you'd be bitter against me, Josie, but I took the chance you'd be so happy you wouldn't care how—

JOSIE (*as if she hadn't heard, looking at the eastern sky which is now glowing with color*): Thank God, it's beautiful. It's time. (*to* HOGAN) Go in the house and stay there till he's gone. I don't want you around to start some new scheme. (*He looks miserable, starts to speak, thinks better of it, and meekly tiptoes past her up the steps and goes in, closing the door quietly after him. She looks down at* TYRONE. *Her face softens with a maternal tenderness—sadly.*) I hate to bring you back to life, Jim, darling. If you could have died in your sleep, that's what you would have liked, isn't it? (*She gives him a gentle shake.*) Wake up, Jim. (*He moans in his sleep and presses more closely against her. She stares at his face.*) Dear God, let him remember that one thing and forget the rest. That will be enough for me. (*She gives him a more vigorous shake.*) Jim! Wake up, do you hear? It's time.

TYRONE (*half wakens without opening his eyes— mutters*): What the hell? (*Dimly conscious of a woman's body—cynically.*) Again, eh? Same old stuff. Who the hell are you, sweetheart? (*Irritably.*) What's the big idea, waking me up? What time is it?

JOSIE: It's dawn.

TYRONE (*still without opening his eyes*): Dawn? (*He quotes drowsily.*)

"But I was desolate and sick of an old passion,
When I awoke and found the dawn was gray."

(*Then with a sneer*) They're all gray. Go to sleep, Kid—and let me sleep. (*He falls asleep again.*)

JOSIE (*tensely*): This one isn't gray, Jim. It's different from all the others—(*She sees he is asleep—bitterly.*) He'll have forgotten. He'll never notice. And I'm the whore on the train to him now, not—(*Suddenly she pushes him away from her and shakes him roughly.*) Will you wake up, for God's sake! I've had all I can bear—

TYRONE (*still half asleep*): Hey! Cut out the rough stuff, Kid. What? (*Awake now, blinking his eyes— with dazed surprise.*) Josie.

JOSIE (*still bitter*): That's who, and none of your damned tarts! (*She pushes him.*) Get up now, so you won't fall asleep again. (*He does so with difficulty, still in a sleepy daze, his body stiff and cramped. She conquers her bitter resentment and puts on her old*

free-and-easy kidding tone with him, but all the time waiting to see how much he will remember.) You're stiff and cramped, and no wonder. I'm worse from holding you, if that's any comfort. (*She stretches and rubs her numbed arms, groaning comically.*) Holy Joseph, I'm a wreck entirely. I'll never be the same. (*Giving him a quick glance.*) You look as if you'd drawn a blank and were wondering how you got here. I'll bet you don't remember a thing.

TYRONE (*moving his arms and legs gingerly—sleepily*): I don't know. Wait till I'm sure I'm still alive.

JOSIE: You need an eye-opener. (*She picks up the bottle and glass and pours him a drink.*) Here you are.

TYRONE (*takes the glass mechanically*): Thanks, Josie. (*He goes and sits on the boulder, holding the drink as if he had no interest in it.*)

JOSIE (*watching him*): Drink up or you'll be asleep again.

TYRONE: No, I'm awake now, Josie. Funny. Don't seem to want a drink. Oh, I've got a head all right. But no heebie-jeebies—yet.

JOSIE: That's fine. It must be a pleasant change—

TYRONE: It is. I've got a nice, dreamy peaceful hang-over for once—as if I'd had a sound sleep without nightmares.

JOSIE: So you did. Divil a nightmare. I ought to know. Wasn't I holding you and keeping them away?

TYRONE: You mean you— (*Suddenly.*) Wait a minute. I remember now I was sitting alone at a table in the Inn, and I suddenly had a crazy notion I'd come up here and sleep with my head on your— So that's why I woke up in your arms. (*Shame-facedly.*) And you let me get away with it. You're a nut, Josie.

JOSIE: Oh, I didn't mind.

TYRONE: You must have seen how blotto I was, didn't you?

JOSIE: I did. You were as full as a tick.

TYRONE: Then why didn't you give me the bum's rush?

JOSIE: Why would I? I was glad to humor you.

TYRONE: For God's sake, how long was I cramped on you like that?

JOSIE: Oh, a few hours, only.

TYRONE: God, I'm sorry, Josie, but it's your own fault for letting me—

JOSIE: Och, don't be apologizing. I was glad of the excuse to stay awake and enjoy the beauty of the moon.

TYRONE: Yes, I can remember what a beautiful night it was.

JOSIE: Can you? I'm glad of that, Jim. You seemed to enjoy it the while we were sitting here together before you fell asleep.

TYRONE: How long a while was that?

JOSIE: Not long. Less than an hour, anyway.

TYRONE: I suppose I bored the hell out of you with a

lot of drunken drivel.

JOSIE: Not a lot, no. But some. You were full of blarney, saying how beautiful I was to you.

TYRONE (earnestly): That wasn't drivel, Josie. You were. You are. You always will be.

JOSIE: You're a wonder, Jim. Nothing can stop you, can it? Even me in the light of dawn, looking like something you'd put in the field to scare the crows from the corn. You'll kid at the Day of Judgment.

TYRONE (impatiently): You know damned well it isn't kidding. You're not a fool. You can tell.

JOSIE (kiddingly): All right, then, I'm beautiful and you love me—in your fashion.

TYRONE: "In my fashion," eh? Was I reciting poetry to you? That must have been hard to take.

JOSIE: It wasn't. I liked it. It was all about beautiful nights and the romance of the moon.

TYRONE: Well, there was some excuse for that, anyway. It sure was a beautiful night. I'll never forget it.

JOSIE: I'm glad, Jim.

TYRONE: What other bunk did I pull on you—or I mean, did old John Barleycorn pull?

JOSIE: Not much. You were mostly quiet and sad—in a kind of daze, as if the moon was in your wits as well as whiskey.

TYRONE: I remember I was having a grand time at the Inn, celebrating with Phil, and then suddenly, for no reason, all the fun went out of it, and I was more melancholy than ten Hamlets. (He pauses.) Hope I didn't tell you the sad story of my life and weep on your bosom, Josie.

JOSIE: You didn't. The one thing you talked a lot about was that you wanted the night with me to be different from all the other nights you'd spent with women.

TYRONE (with revulsion): God, don't make me think of those tramps now! (Then with deep, grateful feeling.) It sure was different, Josie. I may not remember much, but I know how different it was from the way I feel now. None of my usual morning-after stuff—the damned sick remorse that makes you wish you'd died in your sleep so you wouldn't have to face the rotten things you're afraid you said and did the night before, when you were so drunk you didn't know what you were doing.

JOSIE: There's nothing you said or did last night for you to regret. You can take my word for it.

TYRONE (as if he hadn't heard—slowly): It's hard to describe how I feel. It's a new one on me. Sort of at peace with myself and this lousy life—as if all my sins had been forgiven— (He becomes self conscious—cynically.) Nuts with that sin bunk, but you know what I mean.

JOSIE (tensely): I do, and I'm happy you feel that way, Jim. (A pause. She goes on.) You talked about how you'd watched too many dawns come creeping grayly over dirty windowpanes, with some tart snoring beside you—

TYRONE (winces): Have a heart. Don't remind me of that now, Josie. Don't spoil this dawn! (A pause. She watches him tensely. He turns slowly to face the east, where the sky is now glowing with all the colors of an exceptionally beautiful sunrise. He stares, drawing a deep breath. He is profoundly moved but immediately becomes self-conscious and tries to sneer it off— cynically.) God seems to be putting on quite a display. I like Belasco better. Rise of curtain, Act-Four stuff. (Her face has fallen into lines of bitter hurt, but he adds quickly and angrily.) God damn it! Why do I have to pull that lousy stuff? (With genuine deep feeling.) God, it's beautiful, Josie! I—I'll never forget it—here with you.

JOSIE (her face clearing—simply): I'm glad, Jim. I was hoping you'd feel beauty in it—by way of a token.

TYRONE (watching the sunrise—mechanically): Token of what?

JOSIE: Oh, I don't know. Token to me that—never mind. I forget what I meant. (Abruptly changing the subject.) Don't think I woke you just to admire the sunrise. You're on a farm, not Broadway, and it's time for me to start work, not go to bed. (She gets to her feet and stretches. There is a growing strain behind her free-and-easy manner.) And that's a hint, Jim. I can't stay entertaining you. So go back to the Inn, that's a good boy. I know you'll understand the reason, and not think I'm tired of your company. (She forces a smile.)

TYRONE (gets up): Of course, I understand. (He pauses—then blurts out guiltily.) One more question. You're sure I didn't get out of order last night—and try to make you, or anything like that.

JOSIE: You didn't. You kidded back when I kidded you, the way we always do. That's all.

TYRONE: Thank God for that. I'd never forgive myself if—I wouldn't have asked you except I've pulled some pretty rotten stuff when I was drawing a blank. (He becomes conscious of the forgotten drink he has in his hand.) Well, I might as well drink this. The bar at the Inn won't be open for hours. (He drinks—then looks pleasantly surprised.) I'll be damned! That isn't Phil's rotgut. That's real, honest-to-God bonded Bourbon. Where— (This clicks in his mind and suddenly he remembers everything and JOSIE sees that he does. The look of guilt and shame and anguish settles over his face. Instinctively he throws the glass away, his first reaction one of loathing for the drink which brought back memory. He feels JOSIE staring at him and fights desperately to control his voice and expression.) Real Bourbon. I remember now you said a bootlegger gave it to Phil. Well, I'll run along and let you do your work. See you later, Josie. (*He turns toward the road.*)

JOSIE (*strickenly*): No! Don't, Jim! Don't go like that! You won't see me later. You'll never see me again now, and I know that's best for us both, but I can't bear to have you ashamed you wanted my love to comfort your sorrow—when I'm so proud I could give it. (*Pleadingly.*) I hoped, for your sake, you wouldn't remember, but now you do, I want you to remember my love for you gave you peace for a while.

TYRONE (*stares at her fighting with himself. He stammers defensively*): I don't know what you're talking about. I don't remember—

JOSIE (*sadly*): All right, Jim. Neither do I then. Good-bye, and God bless you. (*She turns as if to go up the steps into the house.*)

TYRONE (*stammers*): Wait, Josie! (*Coming to her.*) I'm a liar! I'm a louse! Forgive me, Josie. I do remember! I'm glad I remember! I'll never forget your love! (*He kisses her on the lips.*) Never! (*Kissing her again.*) Never, do you hear! I'll always love you, Josie. (*He kisses her again.*) Good-bye—and God bless you! (*He turns away and walks quickly down the road off left without looking back. She stands, watching him go, for a moment, then she puts her hands over her face, her head bent, and sobs. HOGAN comes out of her room and stands on top of the steps. He looks after TYRONE and his face is hard with bitter anger.*)

JOSIE (*sensing his presence, stops crying and lifts her head—dully*): I'll get your breakfast in a minute, Father.

HOGAN: To hell with my breakfast! I'm not a pig that has no other thought but eating! (*Then pleadingly.*) Listen, darlin'. All you said about my lying and scheming, and what I hoped would happen, is true. But it wasn't his money, Josie. I did see it was the last chance—the only one left to bring the two of you to stop your damned pretending, and face the truth that you loved each other. I wanted you to find happiness—by hook or crook, one way or another, what did I care how? I wanted to save him, and hoped he'd see that only your love could— It was his talk of the beauty he saw in you that made me hope— And I knew he'd never go to bed with you even if you'd let him unless he married you. And if I gave a thought to his money at all, that was the least of it, and why shouldn't I want to have you live in ease and comfort for a change, like you deserve, instead of in this shanty on a lousy farm, slaving for me? (*He pauses—miserably.*) Can't you believe that's the truth, Josie, and not feel so bitter against me?

JOSIE (*her eyes still following TYRONE—gently*): I know it's the truth, Father. I'm not bitter now. Don't be afraid I'm going to leave you. I only said it to punish you for a while.

HOGAN (*with humble gratitude*): Thank God for that, darlin'.

JOSIE (*forces a teasing smile and a little of her old manner*): A ginger-haired, crooked old goat like you to be playing Cupid!

HOGAN (*his face lights up joyfully. He is almost himself again—ruefully*): You had me punished, that's sure. I was thinking after you'd gone I'd drown myself in Harder's ice pond. There was this consolation in it, I knew that the bastard would never look at a piece of ice again without remembering me. (*She doesn't hear this. Her thoughts are on the receding figure of TYRONE again. HOGAN looks at her sad face worriedly—gently.*) Don't darlin'. Don't be hurting yourself. (*Then as she still doesn't hear, he puts on his old, fuming irascible tone.*) Are you going to moon at the sunrise forever, and me with the sides of my stomach knocking together?

JOSIE (*gently*): Don't worry about me, Father. It's over now. I'm not hurt. I'm only sad for him.

HOGAN: For him? (*He bursts out in a fit of smoldering rage.*) May the blackest curse from the pit of hell—

JOSIE (*with an anguished cry*): Don't, Father! I love him!

HOGAN (*subsides, but his face looks sorrowful and old—dully*): I didn't mean it. I know whatever happened he meant no harm to you. It was life I was cursing—(*With a trace of his natural manner.*) And, be God, that's a waste of breath, if it does deserve it. (*Then as she remains silent—miserably.*) Or maybe I was cursing myself for a damned old scheming fool, like I ought to.

JOSIE (*turns to him, forcing a teasing smile*): Look out. I might say Amen to that. (*Gently.*) Don't be sad, Father. I'm all right—and I'm well content here with you. (*Forcing her teasing manner again.*) Sure, living with you has spoilt me for any other man, anyway. There'd never be the same fun or excitement.

HOGAN (*plays up to this—in his fuming manner*): There'll be excitement if I don't get my breakfast soon, but it won't be fun, I'm warning you!

JOSIE (*forcing her usual reaction to his threats*): Och, don't be threatening me, you bad-tempered old tick. Let's go in the house and I'll get your damned breakfast.

HOGAN: Now you're talking. (*He goes in the house through her room. She follows him as far as the door—then turns for a last look down the road.*)

JOSIE (*her face sad, tender and pitying—gently*): May you have your wish and die in your sleep soon, Jim, darling. May you rest forever in forgiveness and peace. (*She turns slowly and goes into the house.*)

CURTAIN

Figure 80. Josie (Colleen Dewhurst) and Tyrone (Jason Robards) in front of the realistic/symbolic set for the José Quintero production of *A Moon for the Misbegotten,* New York, 1974. (Photograph: Martha Swope.)

Figure 81. Josie (Colleen Dewhurst) and Tyrone (Jason Robards) in the José Quintero production of *A Moon for the Misbegotten,* New York, 1974.

Figure 82. Hogan (Ed Flanders) reproves Josie (Colleen Dewhurst) as she cradles Tyrone (Jason Robards) in her arms in the José Quintero production of *A Moon for the Misbegotten,* New York, 1974. (Photograph: Martha Swope.)

Staging of *A Moon for the Misbegotten*

REVIEW OF THE NEW YORK PRODUCTION, 1974, BY WALTER KERR

Colleen Dewhurst is a beautiful woman giving a beautiful performance in the newest revival of Eugene O'Neill's "A Moon for the Misbegotten" (which also just happens to be a beautiful play, possibly O'Neill's best), and I find nothing more fetching about her performance than her witchlike way with an unfinished sentence.

Unfinished sentences can be hell for actors, often because the playwright has had no thought to complete and has simply handed the performer the task of implying one. They can hang there, limp as on a washline, ready to blow any which way a wind happens along. Not in Miss Dewhurst's firmly ruled kingdom, though. In "A Moon for the Misbegotten" she is, in her shanty-Irish father's words, "big and strong as a bull, and as vicious and disrespectful," and she is waiting, in the early kerosene-lit moonlight, for a visit from one of her betters. The visitor is to be Jason Robards, member of an acting family, handsomely educated, already half-broken by drink. He should be, in the opinion of a canny father, readily seduceable.

In fact, Father Ed Flanders (another stunning performance) has the night's course well planned into the dawn. He will slip off to a bar and get himself drunk enough to be utterly unable to prevent anything Mr. Robards may have in mind. It is Miss Dewhurst's business to see to it that Mr. Robards's mind takes a right turn. At this point in the conniving, the actress suddenly turns on the aged leprechaun who is whispering goat-songs in her ear.

Eyes blazing, her hair pulled taut from a clear forehead, arm ever-ready to take a stick to her mentor, she lets him know what she thinks of "a father telling his daughter how to—" and there lets the sentence die. The special splendor of the moment is that it doesn't die. The obvious finish to the line is "to seduce a man," and, if that were all, it wouldn't be much. By letting it break where O'Neill broke it, and by reaching out to join her playwright creatively, Miss Dewhurst fills the void with a heartful of contending emotions. What is left over, and unsaid, is that she wants the love of the man, that she wants it on her own terms, that she is terribly, terribly afraid she is not going to get it, and that seduction—if she knew anything at all about it—would waste the last ounce of goodness in two malformed lives. That's a lot, but it's all there.

It is difficult to take your eyes off Miss Dewhurst, whether she is smiling or in fury. She has a smile that behaves strangely. Most smiles, when they are about to crack in dismay, crack downward. Hers shatters upward, sustaining the shape of happiness while a telltale quaver makes a lie of the crescent corners of her mouth. Her face seems actually to brighten under the hint of pain, a sense of unruly merriment tries hard to assert itself, a vixenish gaiety becomes permanent companion of disaster.

The effect is enormously touching, and it blends ever so easily with the roustabout humors of her donnybrooks with her father. The racy, fork-tongued, rattle-on chaffings between Miss Dewhurst and Mr. Flanders are exhilaratingly designed by director José Quintero, and they remind you, in case you've forgotten, that when O'Neill wanted to write comedy, he had only to pick up an alternate pen and let another kind of theater-ink flow, an apparently inexhaustible knowhow takeover.

But "A Moon for the Misbegotten" is not, in the end, comedy, which is where Miss Dewhurst's unfinished sentences and upsweep dismays, and Jason Robards come in. Mr. Robards begins brilliantly, self-conscious not only about his natty 1923 clothes but about his need for a drink, his need for a woman who will not turn out to be a whore, his need for nothing so much as an impossible forgiveness.

The shaking hand with which he lights a cigarette as their tryst together is to begin establishes its outcome; the succulent surrender to a first taste of a drink she brings him outlines precisely the one comfort this doomed man can know. The detail—an uneasy balance on a treacherous planet, fingers at his collar, palms scraping the nap of jacket and trousers as though something dirty could be wiped away—is graphic, conscientiously arrived at, intelligently used.

I have one important reservation about the production and feel something of an ingrate for bringing it up. But at the invitational preview I attended, the terrifying "almost" of the third act—the teasing possibility that against all odds two rattled, emotionally starved, yearning and yet distrustful misfits will somehow find a crooked way to an ultimate meeting—simply didn't happen. We know that it *can't* happen, that it was never in the cards; but that is for the fourth act to say. Here, with all of the anger and ugliness and awkward groping allowed for, there must be a rhythm that moves toward fusion, toward a coming-together of the far ends of the earth. Without it, without its momentary false promise, the play is too much of a piece, each movement reiterating the other.

Mr. Robards, possibly out of over-concern that each moment will be technically right, continually aborts that promised rhythm, lurching away in self-disgust and trying to spit from his mouth the venom of lost years so often that the design becomes fragmented, the contrast stalemated. I may have seen an unduly edgy performance; certainly it is a matter that continued performance can correct. But there were times when I wanted to collar the man and order him to stay with the scene, stay with the woman, until O'Neill's play could come as close as it dared to a psychic embrace. *Then* it might be shattered, letting us see the remorse-ridden figure as truly dead. It is the crest of the wave, before it collapses on the beach, that is missing, leaving me with slightly fonder memories of the 1968 production at the downtown Circle in the Square.

If I suggest that "Moon for the Misbegotten" just may be O'Neill's richest work for the theater, it is because the free creative impulse is allowed more play here than in the directly autobiographical "Long Day's Journey Into Night." The Robards role is, of course, rooted in O'Neill's older brother. The other figures, however, draw upon, and demand, vast imaginative resources; life is made on the wing rather than painstakingly remembered. It is an honest life, and for O'Neill, an unusually lyric one; the crafty, the damned, and the forgiving breathe.

ARTHUR MILLER

1916–

Although Miller has written less than a dozen plays, he is regarded throughout the world as one of America's most eminent contemporary dramatists. His *Death of a Salesman* (1949) is probably the most famous American play of the twentieth century, for it has come to be seen by millions of people as a consummate dramatization of the most disturbing aspects in the modern American version of "success." Theatrical success came relatively early in Miller's own career, yet he worked arduously to achieve it. He was born in Harlem at a time when his father was still struggling to establish a successful clothing manufacturing business, and he was raised in a suburb of Brooklyn after his father's business had become well established. But the depression of 1929 nearly ruined his father, so that when Miller graduated from high school in 1932, he had to take a job in an automobile warehouse to save up enough money to be able to attend college at the University of Michigan. During his four years at Michigan, he studied playwriting and he won a number of playwriting contests that also helped him to work his way through college. After graduating from Michigan, he worked briefly for the playwriting project the federal government was then supporting to help sustain dramatists during the depression, and subsequently he found work writing radio plays for CBS and later for the Cavalcade of America. During the war, he was unable to serve in the military because of a football injury he had suffered in high school, so instead he began writing radio plays and other pieces to help support civilian morale at home. Before the end of the war, he had also completed his first full-length play to be produced on Broadway, *The Man Who Had All the Luck* (1944), and though it closed after only four performances, it clearly anticipated the concern with moral responsibility and guilt that has been central to virtually all of Miller's work for the theater.

Miller's next play, *All My Sons* (1947), won the New York Drama Critics Circle award for the best play of the season, and it quickly established him as a serious playwright in the socially conscious tradition of Ibsen. When the play was first produced, Miller went out of his way in a press interview to declare his concern with moral and social issues:

> In all my plays and books I try to take setting and dramatic situations from life which involve real questions of right and wrong. Then I set out, rather implacably and in the most realistic situations I can find, the moral dilemma and try to point a real, though hard, path out. I don't see how you can write anything decent without using the question of right and wrong as the basis.

And in *All My Sons* he clearly focussed on the issue of moral responsibility by portraying the crisis that is produced when a small armaments manufacturer is discovered by his son to have sold defective airplane parts to the army, making him responsible for the death of a number of wartime pilots. The father, Joe Keller, seeks to justify himself to his son by claiming that he had wanted to preserve the business and support his family, but the son, Chris, maintains that "There's a universe outside and you're responsible to it." When Keller discovers that his other son, an air corps pilot himself, has been driven to suicide by the

discovery of his guilt, he finally is forced to acknowledge his moral responsibility for a world beyond the limits of his own family: "I think to him they were all my sons. And I guess they were." And that recognition drives him to commit suicide himself.

Joe Keller's morally blind commitment to "dollars and cents" clearly anticipated Willy Loman's commitment to "success" in *Death of a Salesman,* much as the shattering of Joe Keller's self-delusion anticipated the shattering of Willy's "dream." But in *Death of a Salesman,* Miller did not confine himself to exposing the ramifications of a fatally wrong moral decision, and in the case of Willy Loman he chose to explore the ramifications of a fatally wrong way of life—a way of life distinctively American in its commitment to a naive idea of success. To invest his play with such broad social implications, Miller chose for his protagonist an archetypal figure in American culture—the travelling salesman—and he endowed that figure with all the conventional American aspirations, including not only the desire to succeed by being "well liked," but also the desire to be respected by one's friends, to be loved and admired by one's family, to contribute to the success of one's children, to pay one's bills on time, and to own one's own home. Then, in order to explore the failure of such middle-class values, Miller made the strategic decision of focussing on the archetypal salesman at the most vulnerable moment in his life, when he is "tired to death" by his age and by the disappointment of all his hopes. That, in essence, is the formula for the play, but the play itself goes far beyond the formula, largely because Miller does not confine himself to making an indictment of American cultural values.

The play can, of course, be read as an exposure of the cruelty, the cynicism, the stupidity, and the immorality that result from a blind commitment to American materialistic values, for those qualities are repeatedly displayed in Willy's behavior toward his wife, his sons, his friends, and his boss, as well as in Happy's behavior toward Willy, the boss' behavior toward Willy, and above all in the symbolic spectacle of Willy's brother Ben preaching the law of the jungle to Biff: "Never fight fair with a stranger, boy. You'll never get out of the jungle that way." The play can also be read as a tragedy of the common man—a view of the work that Miller sought to define in an essay he published along with the play, called "Tragedy and the Common Man." In that essay, he sought to challenge the traditional notion of the tragic figure as being necessarily "well placed" or "exalted," arguing that "the very same mental processes" are to be found in the "lowly," in particular, "the underlying fear of being displaced, the disaster inherent in being torn away from our chosen image of what and who we are in the world." And certainly it can be said that Willy displays that archetypal fear throughout the play, much as he displays the indignation that Miller regards as the inevitable result of being displaced: "the fateful wound from which the inevitable events spiral is the wound of indignity, and its dominant force is indignation. Tragedy, then, is the consequence of a man's total compulsion to evaluate himself justly."

But the power of the play, at last, derives less from its socially conscious tragic vision than from the way that Miller dramatizes that vision by concentrating on Willy's mental and emotional experience during the moment of his tragic crisis. Willy would not, after all, be such a compelling figure if he were merely a

common social type. He is, in fact, highly particularized through the detailed exposure of his tortured consciousness—through the expressionistic presentation of his mental processes as he repeatedly shifts back and forth between past and present experience, mingling memory with immediate reality with hallucination. When he is shown, for example, in the first act, on the verge of embracing his wife Linda, only to find himself engulfed by the memory of his adulterous escapade with another woman, Willy is poignantly revealed as a particular human being overwhelmed by guilt and by the painful isolation that it creates between him and his family. His sense of isolation, of course, increases throughout the play as he is incessantly bombarded both by painful memories from the past and disappointments in the present. Yet he does not simply acquiesce to the relentless flow of events in his world and in his mind, but seeks to resist them, indeed to alter them with all the force of his being. And though he is finally driven to relinquish his being in the act of resistance, he does so not out of a will to succeed, or to be "well liked," but out of a wholly selfless love for his family. In doing so, he thus escapes from the enslavement of being a salesman and becomes a person bound by authentic human attachments, free at last "to do the right thing."

In the years immediately following its first appearance, *Death of a Salesman* was interpreted in the United States and throughout the world as being primarily a statement about American culture, but its persistent appeal to audiences suggests that it speaks to even larger concerns—to the dismay that all human beings experience when they find themselves unable to accept what they have done to others, what others have done to them, and what they have become as a consequence. These dimensions of the play have recently moved directors and producers to revive it and stage it so as to emphasize the deeply human struggle that Willy goes through in the process of facing up to his illusions. This approach, for example, was taken by the famous movie and stage actor, George C. Scott, in a production he directed and starred in during 1974. A review of Scott's production, reprinted following the text, explains how he staged the play in order to emphasize the emotional, mental, and psychological struggle that Willy experiences. Photographs of Scott in the role of Willy clearly reveal that he was able to convey the man's fatigue (see Figure 83), his guilt (see Figure 85), his love for his family (see Figure 84), and thus his ultimate dignity.

DEATH OF A SALESMAN

BY ARTHUR MILLER

CHARACTERS

WILLY LOMAN
LINDA
BIFF
HAPPY
BERNARD
THE WOMAN
CHARLEY
UNCLE BEN
HOWARD WAGNER

JENNY
STANLEY
MISS FORSYTHE
LETTA

SCENE

The action takes place in WILLY LOMAN'S *house and yard and in various places he visits in the New York and Boston of today.*

ACT 1

(A melody is heard, played upon a flute. It is small and fine, telling of grass and trees and the horizon. The curtain rises.

Before us is the Salesman's house. We are aware of towering, angular shapes behind it, surrounding it on all sides. Only the blue light of the sky falls upon the house and forestage; the surrounding area shows an angry glow of orange. As more light appears, we see a solid vault of apartment houses around the small, fragile-seeming home. An air of the dream clings to the place, a dream rising out of reality. The kitchen at center seems actual enough, for there is a kitchen table with three chairs, and a refrigerator. But no other fixtures are seen. At the back of the kitchen there is a draped entrance, which leads to the living-room. To the right of the kitchen, on a level raised two feet, is a bedroom furnished only with a brass bedstead and a straight chair. On a shelf over the bed a silver athletic trophy stands. A window opens onto the apartment house at the side.

Behind the kitchen, on a level raised six and a half feet, is the boys' bedroom, at present barely visible. Two beds are dimly seen, and at the back of the room a dormer window. [This bedroom is above the unseen living-room.] At the left a stairway curves up to it from the kitchen.

The entire setting is wholly or, in some places, partially transparent. The roof-line of the house is one-dimensional; under and over it we see the apartment buildings. Before the house lies an apron, curving beyond the forestage into the orchestra. This forward area serves as the back yard as well as the locale of all WILLY'S *imaginings and of his city scenes. Whenever the action is in the present the actors observe the imaginary wall-lines, entering the house only through its door at the left. But in the scenes of the past these boundaries are broken, and characters enter or leave a room by stepping "through" a wall onto the forestage.*

From the right, WILLY LOMAN, *the Salesman, enters, carrying two large sample cases. The flute plays on. He hears but is not aware of it. He is past sixty years of age, dressed quietly. Even as he crosses the stage to the doorway of the house, his exhaustion is apparent. He unlocks the door, comes into the kitchen, and thankfully lets his burden down, feeling the soreness of his palms. A word-sigh escapes his lips—it might be "Oh, boy, oh, boy." He closes the door, then carries his cases out into the living-room, through the draped kitchen doorway.*

LINDA, *his wife, has stirred in her bed at the right. She gets out and puts on a robe, listening. Most often jovial, she has developed an iron repression of her exceptions to* WILLY'S *behavior—she more than loves him, she admires him, as though his mercurial nature, his temper, his massive dreams and little cruelties, served her only as sharp reminders of the turbulent longings within him, longings which she shares but lacks the temperament to utter and follow to their end.)*

LINDA *(hearing* WILLY *outside the bedroom, calls with some trepidation)*: Willy!

WILLY: It's all right. I came back.

LINDA: Why? What happened? *(Slight pause.)* Did something happen, Willy?

WILLY: No, nothing happened.

LINDA: You didn't smash the car, did you?

WILLY *(with casual irritation)*: I said nothing happened. Didn't you hear me?

LINDA: Don't you feel well?

WILLY: I'm tired to the death. *(The flute has faded away. He sits on the bed beside her, a little numb.)* I couldn't make it. I just couldn't make it, Linda.

LINDA *(very carefully, delicately)*: Where were you all day? You look terrible.

WILLY: I got as far as a little above Yonkers. I stopped for a cup of coffee. Maybe it was the coffee.

LINDA: What?

WILLY *(after a pause)*: I suddenly couldn't drive any

more. The car kept going off onto the shoulder, y'know?

LINDA (*helpfully*): Oh. Maybe it was the steering again. I don't think Angelo knows the Studebaker.

WILLY: No, it's me, it's me. Suddenly I realize I'm goin' sixty miles an hour and I don't remember the last five minutes. I'm—I can't seem to—keep my mind to it.

LINDA: Maybe it's your glasses. You never went for your new glasses.

WILLY: No, I see everything. I came back ten miles an hour. It took me nearly four hours from Yonkers.

LINDA (*resigned*): Well, you'll just have to take a rest, Willy, you can't continue this way.

WILLY: I just got back from Florida.

LINDA: But you didn't rest your mind. Your mind is overactive, and the mind is what counts, dear.

WILLY: I'll start out in the morning. Maybe I'll feel better in the morning. (*She is taking off his shoes.*) These goddam arch supports are killing me.

LINDA: Take an aspirin. Should I get you an aspirin? It'll soothe you.

WILLY (*with wonder*): I was driving along, you understand? And I was fine. I was even observing the scenery. You can imagine, me looking at scenery, on the road every week of my life. But it's so beautiful up there, Linda, the trees are so thick, and the sun is warm. I opened the windshield and just let the warm air bathe over me. And then all of a sudden I'm goin' off the road! I'm tellin' ya, I absolutely forgot I was driving. If I'd've gone the other way, over the white line I might've killed somebody. So I went on again—and five minutes later I'm dreamin' again, and I nearly—(*He presses two fingers against his eyes.*) I have such thoughts, I have such strange thoughts.

LINDA: Willy, dear. Talk to them again. There's no reason why you can't work in New York.

WILLY: They don't need me in New York. I'm the New England man. I'm vital in New England.

LINDA: But you're sixty years old. They can't expect you to keep traveling every week.

WILLY: I'll have to send a wire to Portland. I'm supposed to see Brown and Morrison tomorrow morning at ten o'clock to show the line. Goddammit, I could sell them! (*He starts putting on his jacket.*)

LINDA (*taking the jacket from him*): Why don't you go down to the place tomorrow and tell Howard you've simply got to work in New York? You're too accommodating, dear.

WILLY: If old man Wagner was alive I'd a been in charge of New York now! That man was a prince, he was a masterful man. But that boy of his, that Howard, he don't appreciate. When I

was north the first time, the Wagner Company didn't know where New England was!

LINDA: Why don't you tell those things to Howard, dear?

WILLY (*encouraged*): I will, I definitely will. Is there any cheese?

LINDA: I'll make you a sandwich.

WILLY: No, go to sleep. I'll take some milk. I'll be up right away. The boys in?

LINDA: They're sleeping. Happy took Biff on a date tonight.

WILLY (*interested*): That so?

LINDA: It was so nice to see them shaving together, one behind the other, in the bathroom. And going out together. You notice? The whole house smells of shaving lotion.

WILLY: Figure it out. Work a lifetime to pay off a house. You finally own it, and there's nobody to live in it.

LINDA: Well, dear, life is a casting off. It's always that way.

WILLY: No, no, some people—some people accomplish something. Did Biff say anything after I went this morning?

LINDA: You shouldn't have criticized him, Willy, especially after he just got off the train. You mustn't lose your temper with him.

WILLY: When the hell did I lose my temper? I simply asked him if he was making any money. Is that a criticism?

LINDA: But, dear, how could he make any money?

WILLY (*worried and angered*): There's such an undercurrent in him. He became a moody man. Did he apologize when I left this morning?

LINDA: He was crestfallen, Willy. You know how he admires you. I think if he finds himself, then you'll both be happier and not fight any more.

WILLY: How can he find himself on a farm? Is that a life? A farmhand? In the beginning, when he was young, I thought, well, a young man, it's good for him to tramp around, take a lot of different jobs. But it's more than ten years now and he has yet to make thirty-five dollars a week!

LINDA: He's finding himself, Willy.

WILLY: Not finding yourself at the age of thirty-four is a disgrace!

LINDA: Shh!

WILLY: The trouble is he's lazy, goddammit!

LINDA: Willy, please!

WILLY: Biff is a lazy bum.

LINDA: They're sleeping. Get something to eat. Go on down.

WILLY: Why did he come home? I would like to know what brought him home.

LINDA: I don't know. I think he's still lost, Willy. I think he's very lost.

WILLY: Biff Loman is lost. In the greatest country in

the world a young man with such—personal attractiveness, gets lost. And such a hard worker. There's one thing about Biff—he's not lazy.

LINDA: Never.

WILLY (*with pity and resolve*): I'll see him in the morning; I'll have a nice talk with him. I'll get him a job selling. He could be big in no time. My God! Remember how they used to follow him around in high school? When he smiled at one of them their faces lit up. When he walked down the street . . . (*He loses himself in reminiscences.*)

LINDA (*trying to bring him out of it*): Willy, dear, I got a new kind of American-type cheese today. It's whipped.

WILLY: Why do you get American when I like Swiss?

LINDA: I just thought you'd like a change—

WILLY: I don't want a change! I want Swiss cheese. Why am I always being contradicted?

LINDA (*with a covering laugh*): I thought it would be a surprise.

WILLY: Why don't you open a window in here, for God's sake?

LINDA (*with infinite patience*): They're all open, dear.

WILLY: The way they boxed us in here. Bricks and windows, windows and bricks.

LINDA: We should've bought the land next door.

WILLY: The street is lined with cars. There's not a breath of fresh air in the neighborhood. The grass don't grow any more, you can't raise a carrot in the back yard. They should've had a law against apartment houses. Remember those two beautiful elm trees out there? When I and Biff hung the swing between them?

LINDA: Yeah, like being a million miles from the city.

WILLY: They should've arrested the builder for cutting those down. They massacred the neighborhood. (*Lost.*) More and more I think of those days, Linda. This time of year it was lilac and wisteria. And then the peonies would come out, and the daffodils. What fragrance in this room!

LINDA: Well, after all, people had to move somewhere.

WILLY: No, there's more people now.

LINDA: I don't think there's more people. I think—

WILLY: There's more people! That's what's ruining this country! Population is getting out of control. The competition is maddening! Smell the stink from that apartment house! And another one on the other side . . . How can they whip cheese?

(*On* WILLY's *last line,* BIFF *and* HAPPY *raise themselves up in their beds, listening.*)

LINDA: Go down, try it. And be quiet.

WILLY (*turning to* LINDA, *guiltily*): You're not worried about me, are you, sweetheart?

BIFF: What's the matter?

HAPPY: Listen!

LINDA: You've got too much on the ball to worry about.

WILLY: You're my foundation and my support, Linda.

LINDA: Just try to relax, dear. You make mountains out of molehills.

WILLY: I won't fight him any more. If he wants to go back to Texas, let him go.

LINDA: He'll find his way.

WILLY: Sure. Certain men just don't get started till later in life. Like Thomas Edison, I think. Or B. F. Goodrich. One of them was deaf. (*He starts for the bedroom doorway.*) I'll put my money on Biff.

LINDA: And Willy—if it's warm Sunday we'll drive in the country. And we'll open the windshield, and take lunch.

WILLY: No, the windshields don't open on the new cars.

LINDA: But you opened it today.

WILLY: Me? I didn't. (*He stops.*) Now isn't that peculiar! Isn't that a remarkable—(*He breaks off in amazement and fright as the flute is heard distantly.*)

LINDA: What, darling?

WILLY: That is the most remarkable thing.

LINDA: What, dear?

WILLY: I was thinking of the Chevvy. (*Slight pause.*) Nineteen twenty-eight . . . when I had that red Chevvy—(*Breaks off.*) That funny? I coulda sworn I was driving that Chevvy today.

LINDA: Well, that's nothing. Something must've reminded you.

WILLY: Remarkable. Ts. Remember those days? The way Biff used to simonize that car? The dealer refused to believe there was eighty thousand miles on it. (*He shakes his head.*) Heh! (*to* LINDA) Close your eyes, I'll be right up. (*He walks out of the bedroom.*)

HAPPY (*to* BIFF): Jesus, maybe he smashed up the car again!

LINDA (*calling after* WILLY): Be careful on the stairs, dear! The cheese is on the middle shelf! (*She turns, goes over to the bed, takes his jacket, and goes out of the bedroom.*)

(*Light has risen on the boys' room. Unseen,* WILLY *is heard talking to himself, "Eighty thousand miles," and a little laugh.* BIFF *gets out of bed, comes downstage a bit, and stands attentively.* BIFF *is two years older than his brother* HAPPY, *well built, but in these days bears a worn air and seems less self-assured. He has succeeded less, and his dreams are stronger and less acceptable than* HAPPY's. HAPPY *is tall, powerfully made. Sexuality is like a visible color on him, or a scent that many women have discovered. He, like his brother, is lost, but in a different way, for he has never allowed himself to turn his face toward defeat and is thus more confused and hard-skinned, although seemingly more content.*)

HAPPY (*getting out of bed*): He's going to get his license taken away if he keeps that up. I'm getting nervous about him, y'know, Biff?

BIFF: His eyes are going.

HAPPY: No, I've driven with him. He sees all right. He just doesn't keep his mind on it. I drove into the city with him last week. He stops at a green light and then it turns red and he goes. (*He laughs.*)

BIFF: Maybe he's color-blind.

HAPPY: Pop? Why he's got the finest eye for color in the business. You know that.

BIFF (*sitting down on his bed*): I'm going to sleep.

HAPPY: You're not still sour on Dad, are you, Biff?

BIFF: He's all right, I guess.

WILLY (*underneath them, in the living-room*): Yes, sir, eighty thousand miles—eighty-two thousand!

BIFF: You smoking?

HAPPY (*holding out a pack of cigarettes*): Want one?

BIFF (*taking a cigarette*): I can never sleep when I smell it.

WILLY: What a simonizing job, heh!

HAPPY (*with deep sentiment*): Funny, Biff, y'know? Us sleeping in here again? The old beds. (*He pats his bed affectionately.*) All the talk that went across those two beds, huh? Our whole lives.

BIFF: Yeah. Lotta dreams and plans.

HAPPY (*with a deep and masculine laugh*): About five hundred women would like to know what was said in this room.

(*They share a soft laugh.*)

BIFF: Remember that big Betsy something—what the hell was her name—over on Bushwick Avenue?

HAPPY (*combing his hair*): With the collie dog!

BIFF: That's the one. I got you in there, remember?

HAPPY: Yeah, that was my first time—I think. Boy, there was a pig! (*They laugh, almost crudely.*) You taught me everything I know about women. Don't forget that.

BIFF: I bet you forgot how bashful you used to be. Especially with girls.

HAPPY: Oh, I still am, Biff.

BIFF: Oh, go on.

HAPPY: I just control it, that's all. I think I got less bashful and you got more so. What happened, Biff? Where's the old humor, the old confidence? (*He shakes* BIFF's *knee.* BIFF *gets up and moves restlessly about the room.*) What's the matter?

BIFF: Why does Dad mock me all the time?

HAPPY: He's not mocking you, he—

BIFF: Everything I say there's a twist of mockery on his face. I can't get near him.

HAPPY: He just wants you to make good, that's all. I wanted to talk to you about Dad for a long time, Biff. Something's—happening to him. He—talks to himself.

BIFF: I noticed that this morning. But he always mumbled.

HAPPY: But not so noticeable. It got so embarrassing I sent him to Florida. And you know something? Most of the time he's talking to you.

BIFF: What's he say about me?

HAPPY: I can't make it out.

BIFF: What's he say about me?

HAPPY: I think the fact that you're not settled, that you're still kind of up in the air . . .

BIFF: There's one or two other things depressing him, Happy.

HAPPY: What do you mean?

BIFF: Never mind. Just don't lay it all to me.

HAPPY: But I think if you just got started—I mean—is there any future for you out there?

BIFF: I tell ya, Hap, I don't know what the future is. I don't know—what I'm supposed to want.

HAPPY: What do you mean?

BIFF: Well, I spent six or seven years after high school trying to work myself up. Shipping clerk, salesman, business of one kind or another. And it's a measly manner of existence. To get on that subway on the hot mornings in summer. To devote your whole life to keeping stock, or making phone calls, or selling or buying. To suffer fifty weeks of the year for the sake of a two-week vacation, when all you really desire is to be outdoors, with your shirt off. And always to have to get ahead of the next fella. And still—that's how you build a future.

HAPPY: Well, you really enjoy it on a farm? Are you content out there?

BIFF (*with rising agitation*): Hap, I've had twenty or thirty different kinds of jobs since I left home before the war, and it always turns out the same. I just realized it lately. In Nebraska when I herded cattle, and the Dakotas, and Arizona, and now in Texas. It's why I came home now, I guess, because I realized it. This farm I work on, it's spring there now, see? And they've got about fifteen new colts. There's nothing more inspiring or—beautiful then the sight of a mare and a new colt. And it's cool there now, see? Texas is cool now, and it's spring. And whenever spring comes to where I am, I suddenly get the feeling, my God, I'm not gettin' anywhere! What the hell am I doing, playing around with horses, twenty-eight dollars a week! I'm thirty-four years old, I oughta be makin' my future. That's when I come running home. And now, I get here, and I don't know what to do with myself. (*After a pause.*) I've always made a point of not wasting my life, and everytime I come back here I know that all I've done is to waste my life.

HAPPY: You're a poet, you know that, Biff? You're a—you're an idealist!

BIFF: No, I'm mixed up very bad. Maybe I oughta get married. Maybe I oughta get stuck into something. Maybe that's my trouble. I'm like a boy. I'm not married, I'm not in business, I just—I'm like a boy. Are you content, Hap? You're a success, aren't you? Are you content?

HAPPY: Hell, no!

BIFF: Why? You're making money, aren't you?

HAPPY (*moving about with energy, expressiveness*): All I can do now is wait for the merchandise manager to die. And suppose I get to be merchandise manager? He's a good friend of mine, and he just built a terrific estate on Long Island. And he lived there about two months and sold it, and now he's building another one. He can't enjoy it once it's finished. And I know that's just what I would do. I don't know what the hell I'm workin' for. Sometimes I sit in my apartment—all alone. And I think of the rent I'm paying. And it's crazy. But then, it's what I always wanted. My own apartment, a car, and plenty of women. And still, goddammit, I'm lonely.

BIFF (*with enthusiasm*): Listen, why don't you come out West with me?

HAPPY: You and I, heh?

BIFF: Sure, maybe we could buy a ranch. Raise cattle, use our muscles. Men built like we are should be working out in the open.

HAPPY (*avidly*): The Loman Brothers, heh?

BIFF (*with vast affection*): Sure, we'd be known all over the counties!

HAPPY (*enthralled*): That's what I dream about, Biff. Sometimes I want to just rip my clothes off in the middle of the store and outbox that goddam merchandise manager. I mean I can outbox, outrun, and outlift anybody in that store, and I have to take orders from those common, petty sons-of-bitches till I can't stand it any more.

BIFF: I'm tellin' you, kid, if you were with me I'd be happy out there.

HAPPY (*enthused*): See, Biff, everybody around me is so false that I'm constantly lowering my ideals . . .

BIFF: Baby, together we'd stand up for one another, we'd have someone to trust.

HAPPY: If I were around you—

BIFF: Hap, the trouble is we weren't brought up to grub for money. I don't know how to do it.

HAPPY: Neither can I!

BIFF: Then let's go!

HAPPY: The only thing is—what can you make out there?

BIFF: But look at your friend. Builds an estate and then hasn't the peace of mind to live in it.

HAPPY: Yeah, but when he walks into the store the waves part in front of him. That's fifty-two thousand dollars a year coming through the revolving door, and I got more in my pinky finger than he's got in his head.

BIFF: Yeah, but you just said—

HAPPY: I gotta show some of those pompous, self-important executives over there that Hap Loman can make the grade. I want to walk into the store the way he walks in. Then I'll go with you, Biff. We'll be together yet, I swear. But take those two we had tonight. Now weren't they gorgeous creatures?

BIFF: Yeah, yeah, most gorgeous I've had in years.

HAPPY: I get that any time I want, Biff. Whenever I feel disgusted. The only trouble is, it gets like bowling or something. I just keep knockin' them over and it doesn't mean anything. You still run around a lot?

BIFF: Naa. I'd like to find a girl—steady, somebody with substance.

HAPPY: That's what I long for.

BIFF: Go on! You'd never come home.

HAPPY: I would! Somebody with character, with resistance! Like Mom, y'know? You're gonna call me a bastard when I tell you this. That girl Charlotte I was with tonight is engaged to be married in five weeks. (*He tries on his new hat.*)

BIFF: No kiddin'!

HAPPY: Sure, the guy's in line for the vice-presidency of the store. I don't know what gets into me, maybe I just have an overdeveloped sense of competition or something, but I went and ruined her, and furthermore I can't get rid of her. And he's the third executive I've done that to. Isn't that a crummy characteristic? And to top it all, I go to their weddings! (*Indignantly, but laughing.*) Like I'm not supposed to take bribes. Manufacturers offer me a hundred-dollar bill now and then to throw an order their way. You know how honest I am, but it's like this girl, see. I hate myself for it. Because I don't want the girl, and, still, I take it and—I love it!

BIFF: Let's go to sleep.

HAPPY: I guess we didn't settle anything, heh?

BIFF: I just got one idea that I think I'm going to try.

HAPPY: What's that?

BIFF: Remember Bill Oliver?

HAPPY: Sure, Oliver is very big now. You want to work for him again?

BIFF: No, but when I quit he said something to me. He put his arm on my shoulder, and he said, "Biff, if you ever need anything, come to me."

HAPPY: I remember that. That sounds good.

BIFF: I think I'll go to see him. If I could get ten thousand or even seven or eight thousand dollars I could buy a beautiful ranch.

HAPPY: I bet he'd back you. 'Cause he thought highly of you, Biff. I mean, they all do. You're well liked, Biff. That's why I say to come back here, and we both have the apartment. And I'm tellin' you, Biff, any babe you want . . .

BIFF: No, with a ranch I could do the work I like and still be something. I just wonder though. I wonder if Oliver still thinks I stole that carton of basketballs.

HAPPY: Oh, he probably forgot that long ago. It's almost ten years. You're too sensitive. Anyway, he didn't really fire you.

BIFF: Well, I think he was going to. I think that's why I quit. I was never sure whether he knew or not. I know he thought the world of me, though. I was the only one he'd let lock up the place.

WILLY (below): You gonna wash the engine, Biff?

HAPPY: Shh!

(BIFF looks at HAPPY, who is gazing down, listening. WILLY is mumbling in the parlor.)

HAPPY: You hear that?

(They listen. WILLY laughs warmly.)

BIFF (growing angry): Doesn't he know Mom can hear that?

WILLY: Don't get your sweater dirty, Biff!

(A look of pain crosses BIFF's face.)

HAPPY: Isn't that terrible? Don't leave again, will you? You'll find a job here. You gotta stick around. I don't know what to do about him, it's getting embarrassing.

WILLY: What a simonizing job!

BIFF: Mom's hearing that!

WILLY: No kiddin', Biff, you got a date? Wonderful!

HAPPY: Go on to sleep. But talk to him in the morning, will you?

BIFF (reluctantly getting into bed): With her in the house. Brother!

HAPPY (getting into bed): I wish you'd have a good talk with him.

(The light on their room begins to fade.)

BIFF (to himself in bed): That selfish, stupid . . .

HAPPY: Sh . . . Sleep, Biff.

(Their light is out. Well before they have finished speaking, WILLY's form is dimly seen below in the darkened kitchen. He opens the refrigerator, searches in there, and takes out a bottle of milk. The apartment houses are fading out, and the entire house and surroundings become covered with leaves. Music insinuates itself as the leaves appear.)

WILLY: Just wanna be careful with those girls, Biff, that's all. Don't make any promises. No promises of any kind. Because a girl, y'know, they always believe what you tell 'em, and you're very young, Biff, you're too young to be talking seriously to girls.

(Light rises on the kitchen. WILLY, talking, shuts the refrigerator door and comes downstage to the kitchen table. He pours milk into a glass. He is totally immersed in himself, smiling faintly.)

WILLY: Too young entirely, Biff. You want to watch your schooling first. Then when you're all set, there'll be plenty of girls for a boy like you. (He smiles broadly at a kitchen chair.) That so? The girls pay for you? (He laughs.) Boy, you must really be makin' a hit.

(WILLY is gradually addressing—physically—a point offstage, speaking through the wall of the kitchen, and his voice has been rising in volume to that of a normal conversation.)

WILLY: I been wondering why you polish the car so careful. Ha! Don't leave the hubcaps, boys. Get the chamois to the hubcaps. Happy, use newspaper on the windows, it's the easiest thing. Show him how to do it, Biff! You see, Happy? Pad it up, use it like a pad. That's it, that's it, good work. You're doin' all right, Hap. (He pauses, then nods in approbation for a few seconds, then looks upward.) Biff, first thing we gotta do when we get time is clip that big branch over the house. Afraid it's gonna fall in a storm and hit the roof. Tell you what. We get a rope and sling her around, and then we climb up there with a couple of saws and take her down. Soon as you finish the car, boys, I wanna see ya. I got a surprise for you, boys.

BIFF (offstage): Whatta ya got, Dad?

WILLY: No, you finish first. Never leave a job till you're finished—remember that. (Looking toward the "big trees".) Biff, up in Albany I saw a beautiful hammock. I think I'll buy it next trip, and we'll hang it right between those two elms. Wouldn't that be something? Just swingin' there under those branches. Boy, that would be . . .

(YOUNG BIFF and YOUNG HAPPY appear from the direction WILLY was addressing. HAPPY carries rags and a pail of water. BIFF, wearing a sweater with a block "S," carries a football.)

BIFF (pointing in the direction of the car offstage): How's that, Pop, professional?

WILLY: Terrific. Terrific job, boys. Good work, Biff.

HAPPY: Where's the surprise, Pop?

WILLY: In the back seat of the car.

HAPPY: Boy! (He runs off.)

BIFF: What is it, Dad? Tell me, what'd you buy?

WILLY (laughing, cuffs him): Never mind, something I want you to have.

BIFF (turns and starts off): What is it, Hap?

HAPPY (offstage): It's a punching bag!

BIFF: Oh, Pop!

WILLY: It's got Gene Tunney's signature on it!

(HAPPY *runs onstage with a punching bag.*)

BIFF: Gee, how'd you know we wanted a punching bag?

WILLY: Well, it's the finest thing for the timing.

HAPPY (*lies down on his back and pedals with his feet*): I'm losing weight, you notice, Pop?

WILLY (*to* HAPPY): Jumping rope is good too.

BIFF: Did you see the new football I got?

WILLY (*examining the ball*): Where'd you get a new ball?

BIFF: The coach told me to practice my passing.

WILLY: That so? And he gave you the ball, heh?

BIFF: Well, I borrowed it from the locker room. (*He laughs confidentially.*)

WILLY (*laughing with him at the theft*): I want you to return that.

HAPPY: I told you he wouldn't like it!

BIFF (*angrily*): Well, I'm bringing it back!

WILLY (*stopping the incipient argument, to* HAPPY): Sure, he's gotta practice with a regulation ball, doesn't he? (*to* BIFF) Coach'll probably congratulate you on your initiative!

BIFF: Oh, he keeps congratulating my initiative all the time, Pop.

WILLY: That's because he likes you. If somebody else took that ball there'd be an uproar. So what's the report, boys, what's the report?

BIFF: Where'd you go this time, Dad? Gee we were lonesome for you.

WILLY (*pleased, puts an arm around each boy and they come down to the apron*): Lonesome, heh?

BIFF: Missed you every minute.

WILLY: Don't say? Tell you a secret, boys. Don't breathe it to a soul. Someday I'll have my own business, and I'll never have to leave home any more.

HAPPY: Like Uncle Charley, heh?

WILLY: Bigger than Uncle Charley! Because Charley is not—liked. He's liked, but he's not—well liked.

BIFF: Where'd you go this time, Dad?

WILLY: Well, I got on the road, and I went north to Providence. Met the Mayor.

BIFF: The Mayor of Providence!

WILLY: He was sitting in the hotel lobby.

BIFF: What'd he say?

WILLY: He said, "Morning!" and I said, "You got a fine city here, Mayor." And then he had coffee with me. And then I went to Waterbury. Waterbury is a fine city. Big clock city, the famous Waterbury clock. Sold a nice bill there. And then Boston—Boston is the cradle of the Revolution. A fine city. And a couple of other towns in Mass., and on to Portland and Bangor and straight home!

BIFF: Gee, I'd love to go with you sometime, Dad.

WILLY: Soon as summer comes.

HAPPY: Promise?

WILLY: You and Hap and I, and I'll show you all the towns. America is full of beautiful towns and fine, upstanding people. And they know me, boys, they know me up and down New England. The finest people. And when I bring you fellas up, there'll be an open sesame for all of us, 'cause one thing, boys: I have friends. I can park my car in any street in New England, and the cops protect it like their own. This summer, heh?

BIFF *and* HAPPY (*together*): Yeah! You bet!

WILLY: We'll take our bathing suits.

HAPPY: We'll carry your bags, Pop!

WILLY: Oh, won't that be something! Me comin' into the Boston stores with you boys carryin' my bags. What a sensation!

(BIFF *is prancing around, practicing passing the ball.*)

WILLY: You nervous, Biff, about the game?

BIFF: Not if you're gonna be there.

WILLY: What do they say about you in school, now that they made you captain?

HAPPY: There's a crowd of girls behind him everytime the classes change.

BIFF (*taking* WILLY's *hand*): This Saturday, Pop, this Saturday—just for you, I'm going to break through for a touchdown.

HAPPY: You're supposed to pass.

BIFF: I'm takin' one play for Pop. You watch me, Pop, and when I take off my helmet, that means I'm breakin' out. Then you watch me crash through that line!

WILLY (*kisses* BIFF): Oh, wait'll I tell this in Boston!

(BERNARD *enters in knickers. He is younger than* BIFF, *earnest and loyal, a worried boy.*)

BERNARD: Biff, where are you? You're supposed to study with me today.

WILLY: Hey, looka Bernard. What're you lookin' so anemic about, Bernard?

BERNARD: He's gotta study, Uncle Willy. He's got Regents next week.

HAPPY (*tauntingly, spinning* BERNARD *around*): Let's box, Bernard!

BERNARD: Biff! (*He gets away from* HAPPY.) Listen, Biff, I heard Mr. Birnbaum say that if you don't start studyin' math he's gonna flunk you, and you won't graduate. I heard him!

WILLY: You better study with him, Biff. Go ahead now.

BERNARD: I heard him!

BIFF: Oh, Pop, you didn't see my sneakers! (*He holds up a foot for* WILLY *to look at.*)

WILLY: Hey, that's a beautiful job of printing!

BERNARD (*wiping his glasses*): Just because he printed University of Virginia on his sneakers doesn't mean they've got to graduate him, Uncle Willy!

WILLY (*angrily*): What're you talking about? With scholarships to three universities they're gonna flunk him?

BERNARD: But I heard Mr. Birnbaum say—

WILLY: Don't be a pest, Bernard! (*to his boys*) What an anemic!

BERNARD: Okay, I'm waiting for you in my house, Biff.

(BERNARD *goes off. The* LOMANS *laugh.*)

WILLY: Bernard is not well liked, is he?

BIFF: He's liked, but he's not well liked.

HAPPY: That's right, Pop.

WILLY: That's just what I mean. Bernard can get the best marks in school, y'understand, but when he gets out in the business world, y'understand, you are going to be five times ahead of him. That's why I thank Almighty God you're both built like Adonises. Because the man who makes an appearance in the business world, the man who creates personal interest, is the man who gets ahead. Be liked and you will never want. You take me, for instance. I never have to wait in line to see a buyer. "Willy Loman is here!" That's all they have to know, and I go right through.

BIFF: Did you knock them dead, Pop?

WILLY: Knocked 'em cold in Providence, slaughtered 'em in Boston.

HAPPY (*on his back, pedaling again*): I'm losing weight, you notice, Pop?

(LINDA *enters, as of old, a ribbon in her hair, carrying a basket of washing.*)

LINDA (*with youthful energy*): Hello, dear!

WILLY: Sweetheart!

LINDA: How'd the Chevvy run?

WILLY: Chevrolet, Linda, is the greatest car ever built. (*to the boys*) Since when do you let your mother carry wash up the stairs?

BIFF: Grab hold there, boy!

HAPPY: Where to, Mom?

LINDA: Hang them up on the line. And you better go down to your friends, Biff. The cellar is full of boys. They don't know what to do with themselves.

BIFF: Ah, when Pop comes home they can wait!

WILLY (*laughs appreciatively*): You better go down and tell them what to do, Biff.

BIFF: I think I'll have them sweep out the furnace room.

WILLY: Good work, Biff.

BIFF (*goes through wall-line of kitchen to doorway at back and calls down*): Fellas! Everybody sweep out the furnace room! I'll be right down!

VOICES: All right! Okay, Biff.

BIFF: George and Sam and Frank, come out back! We're hangin' up the wash! Come on, Hap, on the double! (*He and* HAPPY *carry out the basket.*)

LINDA: The way they obey him!

WILLY: Well, that's training, the training. I'm tellin' you, I was sellin' thousands and thousands, but I had to come home.

LINDA: Oh, the whole block'll be at that game. Did you sell anything?

WILLY: I did five hundred gross in Providence and seven hundred gross in Boston.

LINDA: No! Wait a minute, I've got a pencil. (*She pulls pencil and paper out of her apron pocket.*) That makes your commission . . . Two hundred—my God! Two hundred and twelve dollars!

WILLY: Well, I didn't figure it yet, but . . .

LINDA: How much did you do?

WILLY: Well, I—I did—about a hundred and eighty gross in Providence. Well, no—it came to— roughly two hundred gross on the whole trip.

LINDA (*without hesitation*): Two hundred gross. That's . . . (*She figures.*)

WILLY: The trouble was that three of the stores were half closed for inventory in Boston. Otherwise I woulda broke records.

LINDA: Well, it makes seventy dollars and some pennies. That's very good.

WILLY: What do we owe?

LINDA: Well, on the first there's sixteen dollars on the refrigerator—

WILLY: Why sixteen?

LINDA: Well, the fan belt broke, so it was a dollar eighty.

WILLY: But it's brand new.

LINDA: Well, the man said that's the way it is. Till they work themselves in, y'know.

(*They move through the wall-line into the kitchen.*)

WILLY: I hope we didn't get stuck on that machine.

LINDA: They got the biggest ads of any of them!

WILLY: I know, it's a fine machine. What else?

LINDA: Well, there's nine-sixty for the washing machine. And for the vacuum cleaner there's three and a half due on the fifteenth. Then the roof, you got twenty-one dollars remaining.

WILLY: It don't leak, does it?

LINDA: No, they did a wonderful job. Then you owe Frank for the carburetor.

WILLY: I'm not going to pay that man! That goddam Chevrolet, they ought to prohibit the manufacture of that car!

LINDA: Well, you owe him three and a half. And odds and ends, comes to around a hundred and twenty dollars by the fifteenth.

WILLY: A hundred and twenty dollars! My God, if business don't pick up I don't know what I'm gonna do!

LINDA: Well, next week you'll do better.

WILLY: Oh, I'll knock 'em dead next week. I'll go to

Hartford. I'm very well liked in Hartford. You know, the trouble is, Linda, people don't seem to take to me.

(They move onto the forestage.)

LINDA: Oh, don't be foolish.

WILLY: I know it when I walk in. They seem to laugh at me.

LINDA: Why? Why would they laugh at you? Don't talk that way, Willy.

(WILLY moves to the edge of the stage. LINDA goes into the kitchen and starts to darn stockings.)

WILLY: I don't know the reason for it, but they just pass me by. I'm not noticed.

LINDA: But you're doing wonderful, dear. You're making seventy to a hundred dollars a week.

WILLY: But I gotta be at it ten, twelve hours a day. Other men—I don't know—they do it easier. I don't know why—I can't stop myself—I talk too much. A man oughta come in with a few words. One thing about Charley. He's a man of few words, and they respect him.

LINDA: You don't talk too much, you're just lively.

WILLY *(smiling)*: Well, I figure, what the hell, life is short, a couple of jokes. *(to himself)* I joke too much! *(The smile goes.)*

LINDA: Why? You're—

WILLY: I'm fat. I'm very—foolish to look at, Linda. I didn't tell you, but Christmas time I happened to be calling on F.H. Stewarts, and a salesman I know, as I was going in to see the buyer I heard him say something about—walrus. And I—I cracked him right across the face. I won't take that. I simply will not take that. But they do laugh at me. I know that.

LINDA: Darling . . .

WILLY: I gotta overcome it. I know I gotta overcome it. I'm not dressing to advantage, maybe.

LINDA: Willy, darling, you're the handsomest man in the world—

WILLY: Oh, no, Linda.

LINDA: To me you are. *(Slight pause.)* The handsomest.

(From the darkness is heard the laughter of a woman. Willy doesn't turn to it, but it continues through LINDA's lines.)

LINDA: And the boys, Willy. Few men are idolized by their children the way you are.

(Music is heard as behind a scrim, to the left of the house, THE WOMAN, dimly seen, is dressing.)

WILLY *(with great feeling)*: You're the best there is, Linda, you're a pal, you know that? On the road—on the road I want to grab you sometimes and just kiss the life outa you.

(The laughter is loud now, and he moves into a brightening area at the left, where THE WOMAN has come from behind the scrim and is standing, putting on her hat, looking into a "mirror" and laughing.)

WILLY: 'Cause I get so lonely—especially when business is bad and there's nobody to talk to. I get the feeling that I'll never sell anything again, that I won't make a living for you, or a business, a business for the boys. *(He talks through THE WOMAN's subsiding laughter; THE WOMAN primps at the "mirror.")* There's so much I want to make for—

THE WOMAN: Me? You didn't make me, Willy. I picked you.

WILLY *(pleased)*: You picked me?

THE WOMAN *(who is quite proper-looking, WILLY's age)*: I did. I've been sitting at that desk watching all the salesmen go by, day in, day out. But you've got such a sense of humor, and we do have such a good time together, don't we?

WILLY: Sure, sure. *(He takes her in his arms.)* Why do you have to go now?

THE WOMAN: It's two o'clock . . .

WILLY: No, come on in! *(He pulls her.)*

THE WOMAN: . . . my sisters'll be scandalized. When'll you be back?

WILLY: Oh, two weeks about. Will you come up again?

THE WOMAN: Sure thing. You do make me laugh. It's good for me. *(She squeezes his arm, kisses him.)* And I think you're a wonderful man.

WILLY: You picked me, heh?

THE WOMAN: Sure. Because you're so sweet. And such a kidder.

WILLY: Well, I'll see you next time I'm in Boston.

THE WOMAN: I'll put you right through to the buyers.

WILLY *(slapping her bottom)*: Right, well, bottoms up!

THE WOMAN *(slaps him gently and laughs)*: You just kill me, Willy. *(He suddenly grabs her and kisses her roughly.)* You kill me. And thanks for the stockings. I love a lot of stockings. Well, good night.

WILLY: Good night. And keep your pores open!

THE WOMAN: Oh, Willy!

(THE WOMAN bursts out laughing, and LINDA's laughter blends in. THE WOMAN disappears into the dark. Now the area at the kitchen table brightens. LINDA is sitting where she was at the kitchen table, but now is mending a pair of her silk stockings.)

LINDA: You are, Willy. The handsomest man. You've got no reason to feel that—

WILLY *(coming out of THE WOMAN's dimming area and going over to LINDA)*: I'll make it all up to you, Linda, I'll—

LINDA: There's nothing to make up, dear. You're doing fine, better than—

WILLY *(noticing her mending)*: What's that?

LINDA: Just mending my stockings. They're so expensive—

WILLY (*angrily, taking them from her*): I won't have you mending stockings in this house! Now throw them out!

(LINDA *puts the stockings in her pocket.*)

BERNARD (*entering on the run*): Where is he? If he doesn't study!

WILLY (*moving to the forestage, with great agitation*): You'll give him the answers!

BERNARD: I do, but I can't on a Regents! That's a state exam! They're liable to arrest me!

WILLY: Where is he? I'll whip him, I'll whip him!

LINDA: And he'd better give back that football, Willy, it's not nice.

WILLY: Biff! Where is he? Why is he taking everything?

LINDA: He's too rough with the girls, Willy. All the mothers are afraid of him!

WILLY: I'll whip him!

BERNARD: He's driving the car without a license!

(THE WOMAN's *laugh is heard.*)

WILLY: Shut up!

LINDA: All the mothers—

WILLY: Shut up!

BERNARD (*backing quietly away and out*): Mr. Birnbaum says he's stuck up.

WILLY: Get outa here!

BERNARD: If he doesn't buckle down he'll flunk math! (*He goes off.*)

LINDA: He's right, Willy, you've gotta—

WILLY (*exploding at her*): There's nothing the matter with him! You want him to be a worm like Bernard? He's got spirit, personality . . .

(*As he speaks,* LINDA, *almost in tears, exits into the living-room.* WILLY *is alone in the kitchen, wilting and staring. The leaves are gone. It is night again, and the apartment houses look down from behind.*)

WILLY: Loaded with it. Loaded! What is he stealing? He's giving it back, isn't he? Why is he stealing? What did I tell him? I never in my life told him anything but decent things.

(HAPPY *in pajamas has come down the stairs;* WILLY *suddenly becomes aware of* HAPPY's *presence.*)

HAPPY: Let's go now, come on.

WILLY (*sitting down at the kitchen table*): Huh! Why did she have to wax the floors herself? Everytime she waxes the floors she keels over. She knows that!

HAPPY: Shh! Take it easy. What brought you back tonight?

WILLY: I got an awful scare. Nearly hit a kid in Yonkers. God! Why didn't I go to Alaska with my brother Ben that time! Ben! That man was a genius, that man was success incarnate! What a mistake! He begged me to go.

HAPPY: Well, there's no use in—

WILLY: You guys! There was a man started with the clothes on his back and ended up with diamond mines!

HAPPY: Boy, someday I'd like to know how he did it.

WILLY: What's the mystery? The man knew what he wanted and went out and got it! Walked into a jungle, and comes out, the age of twenty-one, and he's rich! The world is an oyster, but you don't crack it open on a mattress!

HAPPY: Pop, I told you I'm gonna retire you for life.

WILLY: You'll retire me for life on seventy goddam dollars a week? And your women and your car and your apartment, and you'll retire me for life! Christ's sake, I couldn't get past Yonkers today! Where are you guys, where are you? The woods are burning! I can't drive a car!

(CHARLEY *has appeared in the doorway. He is a large man, slow of speech, laconic, immovable. In all he says, despite what he says, there is pity, and, now, trepidation. He has a robe over pajamas, slippers on his feet. He enters the kitchen.*)

CHARLEY: Everything all right?

HAPPY: Yeah, Charley, everything's . . .

WILLY: What's the matter?

CHARLEY: I heard some noise. I thought something happened. Can't we do something about the walls? You sneeze in here, and in my house hats blow off.

HAPPY: Let's go to bed, Dad. Come on.

(CHARLEY *signals to* HAPPY *to go.*)

WILLY: You go ahead, I'm not tired at the moment.

HAPPY (*to* WILLY): Take it easy, huh? (*He exits.*)

WILLY: What're you doin' up?

CHARLEY (*sitting down at the kitchen table opposite* WILLY): Couldn't sleep good. I had a heartburn.

WILLY: Well, you don't know how to eat.

CHARLEY: I eat with my mouth.

WILLY: No, you're ignorant. You gotta know about vitamins and things like that.

CHARLEY: Come on, let's shoot. Tire you out a little.

WILLY (*hesitantly*): All right. You got cards?

CHARLEY (*taking a deck from his pocket*): Yeah, I got them. Someplace. What is it with those vitamins?

WILLY (*dealing*): They build up your bones. Chemistry.

CHARLEY: Yeah, but there's no bones in a heartburn.

WILLY: What are you talkin' about? Do you know the first thing about it?

CHARLEY: Don't get insulted.

WILLY: Don't talk about something you don't know anything about.

(They are playing. Pause.)

CHARLEY: What're you doin' home?

WILLY: A little trouble with the car.

CHARLEY: Oh. *(Pause.)* I'd like to take a trip to California.

WILLY: Don't say.

CHARLEY: You want a job?

WILLY: I got a job, I told you that. *(After a slight pause.)* What the hell are you offering me a job for?

CHARLEY: Don't get insulted.

WILLY: Don't insult me.

CHARLEY: I don't see no sense in it. You don't have to go on this way.

WILLY: I got a good job. *(Slight pause.)* What do you keep comin' in here for?

CHARLEY: You want me to go?

WILLY *(after a pause, withering)*: I can't understand it. He's going back to Texas again. What the hell is that?

CHARLEY: Let him go.

WILLY: I got nothin' to give him, Charley, I'm clean, I'm clean.

CHARLEY: He won't starve. None a them starve. Forget about him.

WILLY: Then what have I got to remember?

CHARLEY: You take it too hard. To hell with it. When a deposit bottle is broken you don't get your nickel back.

WILLY: That's easy enough for you to say.

CHARLEY: That ain't easy for me to say.

WILLY: Did you see the ceiling I put up in the living-room?

CHARLEY: Yeah, that's a piece of work. To put up a ceiling is a mystery to me. How do you do it?

WILLY: What's the difference?

CHARLEY: Well, talk about it.

WILLY: You gonna put up a ceiling?

CHARLEY: How could I put up a ceiling?

WILLY: Then what the hell are you bothering me for?

WILLY: A man who can't handle tools is not a man. You're disgusting.

CHARLEY: Don't call me disgusting, Willy.

(UNCLE BEN, carrying a valise and an umbrella, enters the forestage from around the right corner of the house. He is a stolid man, in his sixties, with a mustache and an authoritative air. He is utterly certain of his destiny, and there is an aura of far places about him. He enters exactly as WILLY speaks.)

WILLY: I'm getting awfully tired, Ben.

(BEN's music is heard. BEN looks around at everything.)

CHARLEY: Good, keep playing; you'll sleep better. Did you call me Ben?

(BEN looks at his watch.)

WILLY: That's funny. For a second there you reminded me of my brother Ben.

BEN: I only have a few minutes. *(He strolls, inspecting the place. WILLY and CHARLEY continue playing.)*

CHARLEY: You never heard from him again, heh? Since that time?

WILLY: Didn't Linda tell you? Couple of weeks ago we got a letter from his wife in Africa. He died.

CHARLEY: That so.

BEN *(chuckling)*: So this is Brooklyn, eh?

CHARLEY: Maybe you're in for some of his money.

WILLY: Naa, he had seven sons. There's just one opportunity I had with that man . . .

BEN: I must make a train, William. There are several properties I'm looking at in Alaska.

WILLY: Sure, sure! If I'd gone with him to Alaska that time, everything would've been totally different.

CHARLEY: Go on, you'd froze to death up there.

WILLY: What're you talking about?

BEN: Opportunity is tremendous in Alaska, William. Surprised you're not up there.

WILLY: Sure, tremendous.

CHARLEY: Heh?

WILLY: There was the only man I ever met who knew the answers.

CHARLEY: Who?

BEN: How are you all?

WILLY *(taking a pot, smiling)*: Fine, fine.

CHARLEY: Pretty sharp tonight.

BEN: Is Mother living with you?

WILLY: No, she died a long time ago.

CHARLEY: Who?

BEN: That's too bad. Fine specimen of a lady, Mother.

WILLY *(to CHARLEY)*: Heh?

BEN: I'd hoped to see the old girl.

CHARLEY: Who died?

BEN: Heard anything from Father, have you?

WILLY *(unnerved)*: What do you mean, who died?

CHARLEY *(taking a pot)*: What're you talkin' about?

BEN *(looking at his watch)*: William, it's half-past eight!

WILLY *(as though to dispel his confusion he angrily stops CHARLEY's hand)*: That's my build!

CHARLEY: I put the ace—

WILLY: If you don't know how to play the game I'm not gonna throw my money away on you!

CHARLEY *(rising)*: It was my ace, for God's sake!

WILLY: I'm through, I'm through!

BEN: When did Mother die?

WILLY: Long ago. Since the beginning you never knew how to play cards.

CHARLEY *(picks up the cards and goes to the door)*: All right! Next time I'll bring a deck with five aces.

WILLY: I don't play that kind of game!

CHARLEY *(turning to him)*: You ought to be ashamed of yourself!

WILLY: Yeah?

CHARLEY: Yeah! (*He goes out.*)

WILLY (*slamming the door after him*): Ignoramus!

BEN (*as* WILLY *comes toward him through the wall-line of the kitchen*): So you're William.

WILLY (*shaking* BEN's *hand*): Ben! I've been waiting for you so long! What's the answer? How did you do it?

BEN: Oh, there's a story in that.

(LINDA *enters the forestage, as of old, carrying the wash basket.*)

LINDA: Is this Ben?

BEN (*gallantly*): How do you do, my dear.

LINDA: Where've you been all these years? Willy's always wondered why you—

WILLY (*pulling* BEN *away from her impatiently*): Where is Dad? Didn't you follow him? How did you get started?

BEN: Well, I don't know how much you remember.

WILLY: Well, I was just a baby, of course, only three or four years old—

BEN: Three years and eleven months.

WILLY: What a memory, Ben!

BEN: I have many enterprises, William, and I have never kept books.

WILLY: I remember I was sitting under the wagon in—was it Nebraska?

BEN: It was South Dakota, and I gave you a bunch of wild flowers.

WILLY: I remember you walking away down some open road.

BEN (*laughing*): I was going to find Father in Alaska.

WILLY: Where is he?

BEN: At that age I had a very faulty view of geography, William. I discovered after a few days that I was heading due south, so instead of Alaska, I ended up in Africa.

LINDA: Africa!

WILLY: The Gold Coast!

BEN: Principally diamond mines.

LINDA: Diamond mines!

BEN: Yes, my dear. But I've only a few minutes—

WILLY: No! Boys! Boys! (YOUNG BIFF *and* HAPPY *appear.*) Listen to this. This is your Uncle Ben, a great man! Tell my boys, Ben!

BEN: Why, boys, when I was seventeen I walked into the jungle, and when I was twenty-one I walked out. (*He laughs.*) And by God I was rich.

WILLY (*to the boys*): You see what I been talking about? The greatest things can happen!

BEN (*glancing at his watch*): I have an appointment in Ketchikan Tuesday week.

WILLY: No, Ben! Please tell about Dad. I want my boys to hear. I want them to know the kind of stock they spring from. All I remember is a man with a big beard, and I was in Mamma's lap,

sitting around a fire, and some kind of high music.

BEN: His flute. He played the flute.

WILLY: Sure, the flute, that's right!

(*New music is heard, a high, rollicking tune.*)

BEN: Father was a very great and a very wild-hearted man. We would start in Boston, and he'd toss the whole family into the wagon, and then he'd drive the team right across the country; through Ohio, and Indiana, Michigan, Illinois, and all the Western states. And we'd stop in the towns and sell the flutes that he'd made on the way. Great inventor, Father. With one gadget he made more in a week than a man like you could make in a lifetime.

WILLY: That's just the way I'm bringing them up, Ben—rugged, well liked, all-around.

BEN: Yeah? (*to* BIFF) Hit that, boy—hard as you can. (*He pounds his stomach.*)

BIFF: Oh, no, sir!

BEN (*taking boxing stance*): Come on, get to me! (*He laughs.*)

WILLY: Go to it, Biff! Go ahead, show him!

BIFF: Okay! (*He cocks his fists and starts in.*)

LINDA (*to* WILLY): Why must he fight, dear?

BEN (*sparring with* BIFF): Good boy! Good boy!

WILLY: How's that, Ben, heh?

HAPPY: Give him the left, Biff!

LINDA: Why are you fighting?

BEN: Good boy! (*Suddenly comes in, trips* BIFF, *and stands over him, the point of his umbrella poised over* BIFF's *eye.*)

LINDA: Look out, Biff!

BIFF: Gee!

BEN (*patting* BIFF's *knee*): Never fight fair with a stranger, boy. You'll never get out of the jungle that way. (*Taking* LINDA's *hand and bowing.*) It was an honor and a pleasure to meet you, Linda.

LINDA (*withdrawing her hand coldly, frightened*): Have a nice—trip.

BEN (*to* WILLY): And good luck with your—what do you do?

WILLY: Selling.

BEN: Yes. Well . . . (*He raises his hand in farewell to all.*)

WILLY: No, Ben, I don't want you to think . . . (*He takes* BEN's *arm to show him.*) It's Brooklyn, I know, but we hunt too.

BEN: Really, now.

WILLY: Oh, sure, there's snakes and rabbits and— that's why I moved out here. Why, Biff can fell any one of these trees in no time! Boys! Go right over to where they're building the apartment house and get some sand. We're gonna rebuild the entire front stoop right now! Watch this, Ben!

BIFF: Yes, sir! On the double, Hap!

HAPPY (*as he and* BIFF *run off*): I lost weight, Pop, you notice?

(CHARLEY *enters in knickers, even before the boys are gone.*)

CHARLEY: Listen, if they steal any more from that building the watchman'll put the cops on them!

LINDA (*to* WILLY): Don't let Biff . . .

(BEN *laughs lustily.*)

WILLY: You shoulda seen the lumber they brought home last week. At least a dozen six-by-tens worth all kinds a money.

CHARLEY: Listen, if that watchman—

WILLY: I gave them hell, understand. But I got a couple of fearless characters there.

CHARLEY: Willy, the jails are full of fearless characters.

BEN (*clapping* WILLY *on the back, with a laugh at* CHARLEY): And the stock exchange, friend!

WILLY (*joining in* BEN's *laughter*): Where are the rest of your pants?

CHARLEY: My wife bought them.

WILLY: Now all you need is a golf club and you can go upstairs and go to sleep. (*to* BEN) Great athlete! Between him and his son Bernard they can't hammer a nail!

BERNARD (*rushing in*): The watchman's chasing Biff!

WILLY (*angrily*): Shut up! He's not stealing anything!

LINDA (*alarmed, hurrying off left*): Where is he? Biff, dear! (*She exits.*)

WILLY (*moving toward the left, away from* BEN): There's nothing wrong. What's the matter with you?

BEN: Nervy boy. Good!

WILLY (*laughing*): Oh, nerves of iron, that Biff!

CHARLEY: Don't know what it is. My New England man comes back and he's bleedin', they murdered him up there.

WILLY: It's contacts, Charley, I got important contacts!

CHARLEY (*sarcastically*): Glad to hear it, Willy. Come in later, we'll shoot a little casino. I'll take some of your Portland money. (*He laughs at* WILLY *and exits.*)

WILLY (*turning to* BEN): Business is bad, it's murderous. But not for me, of course.

BEN: I'll stop by on my way back to Africa.

WILLY (*longingly*): Can't you stay a few days? You're just what I need, Ben, because I—I have a fine position here, but I—well, Dad left when I was such a baby and I never had a chance to talk to him and I still feel—kind of temporary about myself.

BEN: I'll be late for my train.

(*They are at opposite ends of the stage.*)

WILLY: Ben, my boys—can't we talk? They'd go into the jaws of hell for me, see, but I—

BEN: William, you're being first-rate with your boys. Outstanding, manly chaps!

WILLY (*hanging on to his words*): Oh, Ben, that's good to hear! Because sometimes I'm afraid that I'm not teaching them the right kind of—Ben, how should I teach them?

BEN (*giving great weight to each word, and with a certain vicious audacity*): William, when I walked into the jungle, I was seventeen. When I walked out I was twenty-one. And, by God, I was rich! (*He goes off into darkness around the right corner of the house.*)

WILLY: . . . was rich! That's just the spirit I want to imbue them with! To walk into a jungle! I was right! I was right! I was right!

(BEN *is gone, but* WILLY *is still speaking to him as* LINDA, *in nightgown and robe, enters the kitchen, glances around for* WILLY, *then goes to the door of the house, looks out and sees him. Comes down to his left. He looks at her.*)

LINDA: Willy, dear? Willy?

WILLY: I was right!

LINDA: Did you have some cheese? (*He can't answer.*) It's very late, darling. Come to bed, heh?

WILLY (*looking straight up*): Gotta break your neck to see a star in this yard.

LINDA: You coming in?

WILLY: Whatever happened to that diamond watch fob? Remember? When Ben came from Africa that time? Didn't he give me a watch fob with a diamond in it?

LINDA: You pawned it, dear. Twelve, thirteen years ago. For Biff's radio correspondence course.

WILLY: Gee, that was a beautiful thing. I'll take a walk.

LINDA: But you're in your slippers.

WILLY (*starting to go around the house at the left*): I was right! I was! (*Half to* LINDA, *as he goes, shaking his head.*) What a man! There was a man worth talking to. I was right!

LINDA (*calling after* WILLY): But in your slippers, Willy!

(WILLY *is almost gone when* BIFF, *in his pajamas, comes down the stairs and enters the kitchen.*)

BIFF: What is he doing out there?

LINDA: Sh!

BIFF: God Almighty, Mom, how long has he been doing this?

LINDA: Don't, he'll hear you.

BIFF: What the hell is the matter with him?

LINDA: It'll pass by morning.

BIFF: Shouldn't we do anything?

LINDA: Oh, my dear, you should do a lot of things, but there's nothing to do, so go to sleep.

(HAPPY *comes down the stair and sits on the steps.*)

HAPPY: I never heard him so loud, Mom.

LINDA: Well, come around more often; you'll hear him. (*She sits down at the table and mends the lining of* WILLY'*s jacket.*)

BIFF: Why didn't you ever write me about this, Mom?

LINDA: How would I write to you? For over three months you had no address.

BIFF: I was on the move. But you know I thought of you all the time. You know that, don't you, pal?

LINDA: I know, dear, I know. But he likes to have a letter. Just to know that there's still a possibility for better things.

BIFF: He's not like this all the time, is he?

LINDA: It's when you come home he's always the worst.

BIFF: When I come home?

LINDA: When you write you're coming, he's all smiles, and talks about the future, and—he's just wonderful. And then the closer you seem to come, the more shaky he gets, and then, by the time you get here, he's arguing, and he seems angry at you. I think it's just that maybe he can't bring himself to—to open up to you. Why are you so hateful to each other? Why is that?

BIFF (*evasively*): I'm not hateful, Mom.

LINDA: But you no sooner come in the door than you're fighting!

BIFF: I don't know why. I mean to change. I'm tryin', Mom, you understand?

LINDA: Are you home to stay now?

BIFF: I don't know. I want to look around, see what's doin'.

LINDA: Biff, you can't look around all your life, can you?

BIFF: I just can't take hold, Mom. I can't take hold of some kind of a life.

LINDA: Biff, a man is not a bird, to come and go with the springtime.

BIFF: Your hair . . . (*He touches her hair.*) Your hair got so gray.

LINDA: Oh, it's been gray since you were in high school. I just stopped dyeing it, that's all.

BIFF: Dye it again, will ya? I don't want my pal looking old. (*He smiles.*)

LINDA: You're such a boy! You think you can go away for a year and . . . You've got to get it into your head now that one day you'll knock on this door and there'll be strange people here—

BIFF: What are you talking about? You're not even sixty, Mom.

LINDA: But what about your father?

BIFF (*lamely*): Well, I meant him too.

HAPPY: He admires Pop.

LINDA: Biff, dear, if you don't have any feeling for him, then you can't have any feeling for me.

BIFF: Sure I can, Mom.

LINDA: No. You can't just come to see me, because I love him. (*With a threat, but only a threat, of tears.*) He's the dearest man in the world to me, and I won't have anyone making him feel unwanted and low and blue. You've got to make up your mind now, darling, there's no leeway any more. Either he's your father and you pay him that respect, or else you're not to come here. I know he's not easy to get along with—nobody knows that better than me—but . . .

WILLY (*from the left, with a laugh*): Hey, hey, Biffo!

BIFF (*starting to go out after* WILLY): What the hell is the matter with him? (HAPPY *stops him.*)

LINDA: Don't—don't go near him!

BIFF: Stop making excuses for him! He always, always wiped the floor with you. Never had an ounce of respect for you.

HAPPY: He's always had respect for—

BIFF: What the hell do you know about it?

HAPPY (*surlily*): Just don't call him crazy!

BIFF: He's got no character—Charley wouldn't do this. Not in his own house—spewing out that vomit from his mind.

HAPPY: Charley never had to cope with what he's got to.

BIFF: People are worse off than Willy Loman. Believe me, I've seen them!

LINDA: Then make Charley your father, Biff. You can't do that, can you? I don't say he's a great man. Willy Loman never made a lot of money. His name was never in the paper. He's not the finest character that ever lived. But he's a human being, and a terrible thing is happening to him. So attention must be paid. He's not to be allowed to fall into his grave like an old dog. Attention, attention must be finally paid to such a person. You called him crazy—

BIFF: I didn't mean—

LINDA: No, a lot of people think he's lost his—balance. But you don't have to be very smart to know what his trouble is. The man is exhausted.

HAPPY: Sure!

LINDA: A small man can be just as exhausted as a great man. He works for a company thirty-six years this March, opens up unheard-of territories to their trademark, and now in his old age they take his salary away.

HAPPY (*indignantly*): I didn't know that, Mom.

LINDA: You never asked, my dear! Now that you get your spending money someplace else you don't trouble your mind with him.

HAPPY: But I gave you money last—

LINDA: Christmas time, fifty dollars! To fix the hot water it cost ninety-seven fifty! For five weeks he's been on straight commission, like a beginner, an unknown!

BIFF: Those ungrateful bastards!

LINDA: Are they any worse than his sons? When he brought them business, when he was young, they were glad to see him. But now his old friends, the old buyers that loved him so and always found some order to hand him in a pinch—they're all dead, retired. He used to be able to make six, seven calls a day in Boston. Now he takes his valises out of the car and puts them back and takes them out again and he's exhausted. Instead of walking he talks now. He drives seven hundred miles, and when he gets there no one knows him any more, no one welcomes him. And what goes through a man's mind, driving seven hundred miles home without having earned a cent? Why shouldn't he talk to himself? Why? When he has to go to Charley and borrow fifty dollars a week and pretend to me that it's his pay? How long can that go on? How long? You see what I'm sitting here and waiting for? And you tell me he has no character? The man who never worked a day but for your benefit? When does he get the medal for that? Is this his reward—to turn around at the age of sixty-three and find his sons, who he loved better than his life, one a philandering bum—

HAPPY: Mom!

LINDA: That's all you are, my baby! *(to BIFF)* And you! What happened to the love you had for him? You were such pals! How you used to talk to him on the phone every night! How lonely he was till he could come home to you!

BIFF: All right, Mom. I'll live here in my room, and I'll get a job. I'll keep away from him, that's all.

LINDA: No, Biff. You can't stay here and fight all the time.

BIFF: He threw me out of this house, remember that.

LINDA: Why did he do that? I never knew why.

BIFF: Because I know he's a fake and he doesn't like anybody around who knows!

LINDA: Why a fake? In what way? What do you mean?

BIFF: Just don't lay it all at my feet. It's between me and him—that's all I have to say. I'll chip in from now on. He'll settle for half my pay check. He'll be all right. I'm going to bed. *(He starts for the stairs.)*

LINDA: He won't be all right.

BIFF *(turning on the stairs, furiously)*: I hate this city and I'll stay here. Now what do you want?

LINDA: He's dying, Biff.

(HAPPY turns quickly to her, shocked.)

BIFF *(after a pause)*: Why is he dying?

LINDA: He's been trying to kill himself.

BIFF *(with great horror)*: How?

LINDA: I live from day to day.

BIFF: What're you talking about?

LINDA: Remember I wrote you that he smashed up the car again? In February?

BIFF: Well?

LINDA: The insurance inspector came. He said that they have evidence. That all these accidents in the last year—weren't—weren't—accidents.

HAPPY: How can they tell that? That's a lie.

LINDA: It seems there's a woman . . . *(She takes a breath as . . .)*

BIFF *(sharply but contained)*: What woman?

LINDA *(simultaneously)*: . . . and this woman . . .

LINDA: What?

BIFF: Nothing. Go ahead.

LINDA: What did you say?

BIFF: Nothing. I just said what woman?

HAPPY: What about her?

LINDA: Well, it seems she was walking down the road and saw his car. She says that he wasn't driving fast at all, and that he didn't skid. She says he came to that little bridge, and then deliberately smashed into the railing, and it was only the shallowness of the water that saved him.

BIFF: Oh, no, he probably just fell asleep again.

LINDA: I don't think he fell asleep.

BIFF: Why not?

LINDA: Last month . . . *(With great difficulty.)* Oh, boys, it's so hard to say a thing like this! He's just a big stupid man to you, but I tell you there's more good in him than in many other people. *(She chokes, wipes her eyes.)* I was looking for a fuse. The lights blew out, and I went down the cellar. And behind the fuse box—it happened to fall out—was a length of rubber pipe—just short.

HAPPY: No kidding?

LINDA: There's a little attachment on the end of it. I knew right away. And sure enough, on the bottom of the water heater there's a new little nipple on the gas pipe.

HAPPY *(angrily)*: That—jerk.

BIFF: Did you have it taken off?

LINDA: I'm—I'm ashamed to. How can I mention it to him? Every day I go down and take away that little rubber pipe. But, when he comes home, I put it back where it was. How can I insult him that way? I don't know what to do. I live from day to day, boys. I tell you, I know every thought in his mind. It sounds so old-fashioned and silly, but I tell you he put his whole life into you and you've turned your backs on him. *(She is bent over in the chair, weeping, her face in her hands.)* Biff, I swear to God! Biff, his life is in your hands!

HAPPY *(to BIFF)*: How do you like that damned fool!

BIFF *(kissing her)*: All right, pal, all right. It's all settled now. I've been remiss. I know that, Mom. But now I'll stay, and I swear to you, I'll apply myself. *(Kneeling in front of her, in a fever of self-reproach)*

It's just—you see, Mom, I don't fit in business. Not that I won't try. I'll try, and I'll make good.

HAPPY: Sure you will. The trouble with you in business was you never tried to please people.

BIFF: I know, I—

HAPPY: Like when you worked for Harrison's. Bob Harrison said you were tops, and then you go and do some damn fool thing like whistling whole songs in the elevator like a comedian.

BIFF (*against* HAPPY): So what? I like to whistle sometimes.

HAPPY: You don't raise a guy to a responsible job who whistles in the elevator!

LINDA: Well, don't argue about it now.

HAPPY: Like when you'd go off and swim in the middle of the day instead of taking the line around.

BIFF (*his resentment rising*): Well, don't you run off? You take off sometimes, don't you? On a nice summer day?

HAPPY: Yeah, but I cover myself!

LINDA: Boys!

HAPPY: If I'm going to take a fade the boss can call any number where I'm supposed to be and they'll swear to him that I just left. I'll tell you something that I hate to say, Biff, but in the business world some of them think you're crazy.

BIFF (*angered*): Screw the business world!

HAPPY: All right, screw it! Great, but cover yourself!

LINDA: Hap, Hap!

BIFF: I don't care what they think! They've laughed at Dad for years, and you know why? Because we don't belong in this nuthouse of a city! We should be mixing cement on some open plain, or—or carpenters. A carpenter is allowed to whistle!

(WILLY *walks in from the entrance of the house, at left.*)

WILLY: Even your grandfather was better than a carpenter. (*Pause. They watch him.*) You never grew up. Bernard does not whistle in the elevator, I assure you.

BIFF (*as though to laugh* WILLY *out of it*): Yeah, but you do, Pop.

WILLY: I never in my life whistled in an elevator! And who in the business world thinks I'm crazy!

BIFF: I didn't mean it like that, Pop. Now don't make a whole thing out of it, will ya?

WILLY: Go back to the West! Be a carpenter, a cowboy, enjoy yourself!

LINDA: Willy, he was just saying—

WILLY: I heard what he said!

HAPPY (*trying to quiet* WILLY): Hey, Pop, come on now . . .

WILLY (*continuing over* HAPPY's *line*): They laugh at me, heh? Go to Filene's, go to the Hub, go to Slattery's, Boston. Call out the name Willy Loman and see what happens! Big shot!

BIFF: All right, Pop.

WILLY: Big!

BIFF: All right!

WILLY: Why do you always insult me?

BIFF: I didn't say a word. (*to* LINDA) Did I say a word?

LINDA: He didn't say anything, Willy.

WILLY (*going to the doorway of the living-room*): All right, good night, good night.

LINDA: Willy, dear, he just decided . . .

WILLY (*to* BIFF): If you get tired hanging around tomorrow, paint the ceiling I put up in the living-room.

BIFF: I'm leaving early tomorrow.

HAPPY: He's going to see Bill Oliver, Pop.

WILLY (*interestedly*): Oliver? For what?

BIFF (*with reserve, but trying, trying*): He always said he'd stake me. I'd like to go into business, so maybe I can take him up on it.

LINDA: Isn't that wonderful?

WILLY: Don't interrupt. What's wonderful about it? There's fifty men in the City of New York who'd stake him. (*to* BIFF) Sporting goods?

BIFF: I guess so. I know something about it and—

WILLY: He knows something about it! You know sporting goods better than Spalding, for God's sake! How much is he giving you?

BIFF: I don't know, I didn't even see him yet, but—

WILLY: Then what're you talkin' about?

BIFF (*getting angry*): Well, all I said was I'm gonna see him, that's all!

WILLY (*turning away*): Ah, you're counting your chickens again.

BIFF (*starting left for the stairs*): Oh, Jesus, I'm going to sleep!

WILLY (*calling after him*): Don't curse in this house!

BIFF (*turning*): Since when did you get so clean?

HAPPY (*trying to stop them*): What a . . .

WILLY: Don't use that language to me! I won't have it!

HAPPY (*grabbing* BIFF, *shouts*): Wait a minute! I got an idea. I got a feasible idea. Come here, Biff, let's talk this over now, let's talk some sense here. When I was down in Florida last time, I thought of a great idea to sell sporting goods. It just came back to me. You and I, Biff—we have a line, the Loman Line. We train a couple of weeks, and put on a couple of exhibitions, see?

WILLY: That's an idea!

HAPPY: Wait! We form two basketball teams, see? Two water-polo teams. We play each other. It's a million dollars' worth of publicity. Two brothers, see? The Loman Brothers. Displays in the Royal Palms—all the hotels. And banners over the ring and the basketball court; "Loman Brothers." Baby, we could sell sporting goods!

WILLY: This is a one-million-dollar idea!

LINDA: Marvelous!

BIFF: I'm in great shape as far as that's concerned.

HAPPY: And the beauty of it is, Biff, it wouldn't be like a business. We'd be out playin' ball again . . .

BIFF (*enthused*): Yeah, that's . . .

WILLY: Million-dollar . . .

HAPPY: And you wouldn't get fed up with it, Biff. It'd be the family again. There'd be the old honor, and comradeship, and if you wanted to go off for a swim or somethin'—well, you'd do it! Without some smart cooky gettin' up ahead of you!

WILLY: Lick the world! You guys together could absolutely lick the civilized world.

BIFF: I'll see Oliver tomorrow. Hap, if we could work that out . . .

LINDA: Maybe things are beginning to—

WILLY (*wildly enthused, to* LINDA): Stop interrupting! (*To* BIFF) But don't wear sport jacket and slacks when you see Oliver.

BIFF: No, I'll—

WILLY: A business suit, and talk as little as possible, and don't crack any jokes.

BIFF: He did like me. Always liked me.

LINDA: He loved you!

WILLY (*to* LINDA): Will you stop! (*to* BIFF) Walk in very serious. You are not applying for a boy's job. Money is to pass. Be quiet, fine, and serious. Everybody likes a kidder, but nobody lends him money.

HAPPY: I'll try to get some myself, Biff. I'm sure I can.

WILLY: I see great things for you kids. I think your troubles are over. But remember, start big and you'll end big. Ask for fifteen. How much you gonna ask for?

BIFF: Gee, I don't know—

WILLY: And don't say "Gee." "Gee" is a boy's word. A man walking in for fifteen thousand dollars does not say "Gee!"

BIFF: Ten, I think would be top though.

WILLY: Don't be so modest. You always started too low. Walk in with a big laugh. Don't look worried. Start off with a couple of your good stories to lighten things up. It's not what you say, it's how you say it—because personality always wins the day.

LINDA: Oliver always thought the highest of him—

WILLY: Will you let me talk?

BIFF: Don't yell at her, Pop, will ya?

WILLY (*angrily*): I was talking, wasn't I?

BIFF: I don't like you yelling at her all the time, and I'm tellin' you, that's all.

WILLY: What're you, takin' over this house?

LINDA: Willy—

WILLY (*turning on her*): Don't take his side all the time, goddammit!

BIFF (*furiously*): Stop yelling at her!

WILLY (*suddenly pulling on his cheek, beaten down, guilt ridden*): Give my best to Bill Oliver—he may remember me. (*He exits through the living-room doorway.*)

LINDA (*her voice subdued*): What'd you have to start that for? (BIFF *turns away.*) You see how sweet he was as soon as you talked hopefully? (*She goes over to* BIFF.) Come up and say good night to him. Don't let him go to bed that way.

HAPPY: Come on, Biff, let's buck him up.

LINDA: Please, dear. Just say good night. It takes so little to make him happy. Come. (*She goes through the living-room doorway, calling upstairs from within the living-room.*) Your pajamas are hanging in the bathroom, Willy!

HAPPY (*looking toward where* LINDA *went out*): What a woman! They broke the mold when they made her. You know that, Biff?

BIFF: He's off salary. My God, working on commission!

HAPPY: Well, let's face it: he's no hot-shot selling man. Except that sometimes, you have to admit, he's a sweet personality.

BIFF (*deciding*): Lend me ten bucks, will ya? I want to buy some new ties.

HAPPY: I'll take you to a place I know. Beautiful stuff. Wear one of my striped shirts tomorrow.

BIFF: She got gray. Mom got awful old. Gee, I'm gonna go in to Oliver tomorrow and knock him for a—

HAPPY: Come on up. Tell that to Dad. Let's give him a whirl. Come on.

BIFF (*steamed up*): You know, with ten thousand bucks, boy!

HAPPY (*as they go into the living-room*): That's the talk, Biff, that's the first time I've heard the old confidence out of you! (*From within the living-room, fading off.*) You're gonna live with me, kid, and any babe you want just say the word . . . (*The last lines are hardly heard. They are mounting the stairs to their parents' bedroom.*)

LINDA (*entering her bedroom and addressing* WILLY, *who is in the bathroom. She is straightening the bed for him*): Can you do anything about the shower? It drips.

WILLY (*from the bathroom*): All of a sudden everything falls to pieces! Goddam plumbing, oughta be sued, those people. I hardly finished putting it in and the thing . . . (*His words rumble off.*)

LINDA: I'm just wondering if Oliver will remember him. You think he might?

WILLY (*coming out of the bathroom in his pajamas*): Remember him? What's the matter with you, you crazy? If he'd've stayed with Oliver he'd be on top by now! Wait'll Oliver gets a look at him. You don't know the average caliber any more. The average young man today—(*He is getting into bed.*)—is got a caliber of zero. Greatest thing in the world for him was to bum around.

(BIFF *and* HAPPY *enter the bedroom. Slight pause.*)

WILLY (*stops short, looking at* BIFF): Glad to hear it, boy.

HAPPY: He wanted to say good night to you, sport.

WILLY (*to* BIFF): Yeah. Knock him dead, boy. What'd you want to tell me?

BIFF: Just take it easy, Pop. Good night. (*He turns to go.*)

WILLY (*unable to resist*): And if anything falls off the desk while you're talking to him—like a package or something—don't you pick it up. They have office boys for that.

LINDA: I'll make a big breakfast—

WILLY: Will you let me finish? (*to* BIFF) Tell him you were in the business in the West. Not farm work.

BIFF: All right, Dad.

LINDA: I think everything—

WILLY (*going right through her speech*): And don't undersell yourself. No less than fifteen thousand dollars.

BIFF (*unable to bear him*): Okay. Good night, Mom. (*He starts moving.*)

WILLY: Because you got a greatness in you, Biff, remember that. You got all kinds a greatness . . . (*He lies back, exhausted.* BIFF *walks out.*)

LINDA (*calling after* BIFF): Sleep well, darling!

HAPPY: I'm gonna get married, Mom. I wanted to tell you.

LINDA: Go to sleep, dear.

HAPPY (*going*): I just wanted to tell you.

WILLY: Keep up the good work. (HAPPY *exits.*) God . . . remember that Ebbets Field game? The championship of the city?

LINDA: Just rest. Should I sing to you?

WILLY: Yeah. Sing to me. (LINDA *hums a soft lullaby.*) When that team came out—he was the tallest, remember?

LINDA: Oh, yes. And in gold.

(BIFF *enters the darkened kitchen, takes a cigarette and leaves the house. He comes downstage into a golden pool of light. He smokes, staring at the night.*)

WILLY: Like a young god. Hercules—something like that. And the sun, the sun all around him. Remember how he waved to me? Right up from the field, with the representatives of three colleges standing by? And the buyers I brought, and the cheers when he came out—Loman, Loman, Loman! God Almighty, he'll be great yet. A star like that, magnificent, can never really fade away!

(*The light on* WILLY *is fading. The gas heater begins to glow through the kitchen wall, near the stairs, a blue flame beneath red coils.*)

LINDA (*timidly*): Willy dear, what has he got against you?

WILLY: I'm so tired. Don't talk any more.

(BIFF *slowly returns to the kitchen. He stops, stares toward the heater.*)

LINDA: Will you ask Howard to let you work in New York?

WILLY: First thing in the morning. Everything'll be all right.

(BIFF *reaches behind the heater and draws out a length of rubber tubing. He is horrified and turns his head toward* WILLY'S *room, still dimly lit, from which the strains of* LINDA'S *desperate but monotonous humming rise.*)

WILLY (*staring through the window into the moonlight*): Gee, look at the moon moving between the buildings!

(BIFF *wraps the tubing around his hand and quickly goes up the stairs.*)

ACT 2

(*Music is heard, gay and bright. The curtain rises as the music fades away.* WILLY, *in shirt sleeves, is sitting at the kitchen table, sipping coffee, his hat in his lap.* LINDA *is filling his cup when she can.*)

WILLY: Wonderful coffee. Meal in itself.

LINDA: Can I make you some eggs?

WILLY: No. Take a breath.

LINDA: You look so rested, dear.

WILLY: I slept like a dead one. First time in months. Imagine, sleeping till ten on a Tuesday morning. Boys left nice and early, heh?

LINDA: They were out of here by eight o'clock.

WILLY: Good work!

LINDA: It was so thrilling to see them leaving together. I can't get over the shaving lotion in this house!

WILLY (*smiling*): Mmm—

LINDA: Biff was very changed this morning. His whole attitude seemed to be hopeful. He couldn't wait to get downtown to see Oliver.

WILLY: He's heading for a change. There's no question, there simply are certain men that take longer to get—solidified. How did he dress?

LINDA: His blue suit. He's so handsome in that suit. He could be a—anything in that suit!

(WILLY *gets up from the table.* LINDA *holds his jacket for him.*)

WILLY: There's no question, no question at all. Gee, on the way home tonight I'd like to buy some seeds.

LINDA (*laughing*): That'd be wonderful. But not enough sun gets back there. Nothing'll grow any more.

WILLY: You wait, kid, before it's all over we're gonna get a little place out in the country, and I'll raise some vegetables, a couple of chickens . . .

LINDA: You'll do it yet, dear.

(WILLY *walks out of his jacket.* LINDA *follows him.*)

WILLY: And they'll get married, and come for a weekend. I'd built a little guest house. 'Cause I got so many fine tools, all I'd need would be a little lumber and some peace of mind.

LINDA (*joyfully*): I sewed the lining . . .

WILLY: I could build two guest houses, so they'd both come. Did he decide how much he's going to ask Oliver for?

LINDA (*getting him into the jacket*): He didn't mention it, but I imagine ten or fifteen thousand. You going to talk to Howard today?

WILLY: Yeah, I'll put it to him straight and simple. He'll just have to take me off the road.

LINDA: And Willy, don't forget to ask for a little advance, because we've got the insurance premium. It's the grace period now.

WILLY: That's a hundred . . . ?

LINDA: A hundred and eight, sixty-eight. Because we're a little short again.

WILLY: Why are we short?

LINDA: Well, you had the motor job on the car . . .

WILLY: That goddam Studebaker!

LINDA: And you got one more payment on the refrigerator . . .

WILLY: But it just broke again!

LINDA: Well, it's old, dear.

WILLY: I told you we should've bought a well-advertised machine. Charley bought a General Electric and its twenty years old and it's still good, that son-of-a-bitch.

LINDA: But, Willy—

WILLY: Whoever heard of a Hastings refrigerator? Once in my life I would like to own something outright before it's broken! I'm always in a race with the junkyard! I just finished paying for the car and it's on its last legs. The refrigerator consumes belts like a goddamn maniac. They time those things. They time them so when you finally paid for them, they're used up.

LINDA (*buttoning up his jacket as he unbuttons it*): All told, about two hundred dollars would carry us, dear. But that includes the last payment on the mortgage. After this payment, Willy, the house belongs to us.

WILLY: It's twenty-five years!

LINDA: Biff was nine years old when we bought it.

WILLY: Well, that's a great thing. To weather a twenty-five year mortgage is—

LINDA: It's an accomplishment.

WILLY: All the cement, the lumber, the reconstruction I put in this house! There ain't a crack to be found in it any more.

LINDA: Well, it served its purpose.

WILLY: What purpose? Some stranger'll come along, move in, and that's that. If only Biff would take this house, and raise a family . . . (*He starts to go.*) Good-by, I'm late.

LINDA (*suddenly remembering*): Oh, I forgot! You're supposed to meet them for dinner.

WILLY: Me?

LINDA: At Frank's Chop House on Forty-eighth near Sixth Avenue.

WILLY: Is that so! How about you?

LINDA: No, just the three of you. They're gonna blow you to a big meal!

WILLY: Don't say! Who thought of that?

LINDA: Biff came to me this morning, Willy, and he said, "Tell Dad, we want to blow him to a big meal." Be there six o'clock. You and your two boys are going to have dinner.

WILLY: Gee whiz! That's really somethin'. I'm gonna knock Howard for a loop, kid. I'll get an advance, and I'll come home with a New York job. Goddammit, now I'm gonna do it!

LINDA: Oh, that's the spirit, Willy!

WILLY: I will never get behind a wheel the rest of my life!

LINDA: It's changing, Willy, I can feel it changing!

WILLY: Beyond a question. G'by, I'm late. (*He starts to go again.*)

LINDA (*calling after him as she runs to the kitchen table for a handkerchief*): You got your glasses?

WILLY (*feels for them, then comes back in*): Yeah, yeah, got my glasses.

LINDA (*giving him the handkerchief*): And a handkerchief.

WILLY: Yeah, handkerchief.

LINDA: And your saccharine?

WILLY: Yeah, my saccharine.

LINDA: Be careful on the subway stairs.

(*She kisses him, and a silk stocking is seen hanging from her hand. WILLY notices it.*)

WILLY: Will you stop mending stockings? At least while I'm in the house. It gets me nervous. I can't tell you. Please.

(*LINDA hides the stocking in her hand as she follows WILLY across the forestage in front of the house.*)

LINDA: Remember, Frank's Chop House.

WILLY (*passing the apron*): Maybe beets would grow out there.

LINDA (*laughing*): But you tried so many times.

WILLY: Yeah. Well, don't work hard today. (*He disappears around the right corner of the house.*)

LINDA: Be careful!

(*As WILLY vanishes, LINDA waves to him. Suddenly the phone rings. She runs across the stage and into the kitchen and lifts it.*)

LINDA: Hello? Oh, Biff! I'm so glad you called, I just . . . Yes, sure, I just told him. Yes, he'll be there for dinner at six o'clock, I didn't forget. Listen, I was just dying to tell you. You know that little rubber pipe I told you about? That he connected to the gas heater? I finally decided to go down the cellar this morning and take it away and destroy it. But it's gone! Imagine? He took it away himself, it isn't there! *(She listens.)* When? Oh, then you took it. Oh—nothing, it's just that I'd hoped he'd taken it away himself. Oh, I'm not worried, darling, because this morning he left in such high spirits, it was like the old days! I'm not afraid any more. Did Mr. Oliver see you? . . . Well, you wait there then. And make a nice impression on him, darling. Just don't perspire too much before you see him. And have a nice time with Dad. He may have big news too! . . . That's right, a New York job. And be sweet to him tonight, dear. Be loving to him. Because he's only a little boat looking for a harbor. *(She is trembling with sorrow and joy.)* Oh, that's wonderful, Biff, you'll save his life. Thanks, darling. Just put your arm around him when he comes into the restaurant. Give him a smile. That's the boy . . . Goodby, dear. . . . You got your comb? . . . That's fine. Good-by, Biff dear.

(In the middle of her speech, HOWARD WAGNER, *thirty-six, wheels on a small typewriter table on which is a wire-recording machine and proceeds to plug it in. This is on the left forestage. Light slowly fades on* LINDA *as it rises on* HOWARD. HOWARD *is intent on threading the machine and only glances over his shoulder as* WILLY *appears.)*

WILLY: Pst! Pst!

HOWARD: Hello, Willy, come in.

WILLY: Like to have a little talk with you, Howard.

HOWARD: Sorry to keep you waiting. I'll be with you in a minute.

WILLY: What's that, Howard?

HOWARD: Didn't you ever see one of these? Wire recorder.

WILLY: Oh. Can we talk a minute?

HOWARD: Records things. Just got delivery yesterday. Been driving me crazy, the most terrific machine I ever saw in my life. I was up all night with it.

WILLY: What do you do with it?

HOWARD: I bought it for dictation, but you can do anything with it. Listen to this. I had it home last night. Listen to what I picked up. The first one is my daughter. Get this. *(He flicks the switch and* "Roll out the Barrel" *is heard being whistled.)* Listen to that kid whistle.

WILLY: That is lifelike, isn't it?

HOWARD: Seven years old. Get that tone.

WILLY: Ts, ts. Like to ask a little favor if you . . .

(The whistling breaks off, and the voice of HOWARD's *daughter is heard.)*

HIS DAUGHTER: "Now you, Daddy."

HOWARD: She's crazy for me! *(Again the same song is*

whistled.) That's me! Ha! *(He winks.)*

WILLY: You're very good!

(The whistling breaks off again. The machine runs silent for a moment.)

HOWARD: Sh! Get this now, this is my son.

HIS SON: "The capital of Alabama is Montgomery; the capital of Arizona is Phoenix; the capital of Arkansas is Little Rock; the capital of California is Sacramento . . ." *(and on, and on.)*

HOWARD *(holding up five fingers)*: Five years old, Willy!

WILLY: He'll make an announcer some day!

HIS SON *(continuing)*: "The capital . . ."

HOWARD: Get that—alphabetical order! *(The machine breaks off suddenly.)* Wait a minute. The maid kicked the plug out.

WILLY: It certainly is a—

HOWARD: Sh, for God's sake!

HIS SON: "It's nine o'clock, Bulova watch time. So I have to go to sleep."

WILLY: That really is—

HOWARD: Wait a minute! The next is my wife.

(They wait.)

HOWARD'S VOICE: "Go on, say something." *(Pause.)* "Well, you gonna talk?"

HIS WIFE: I can't think of anything."

HOWARD'S VOICE: "Well, talk—it's turning."

HIS WIFE *(shyly, beaten)*: "Hello." *(Silence.)* "Oh, Howard, I can't talk into this . . ."

HOWARD *(snapping the machine off)*: That was my wife.

WILLY: This is a wonderful machine. Can we—

HOWARD: I tell you, Willy, I'm gonna take my camera, and my bandsaw, and all my hobbies, and out they go. This is the most fascinating relaxation I ever found.

WILLY: I think I'll get one myself.

HOWARD: Sure, they're only a hundred and a half. You can't do without it. Supposing you wanna hear Jack Benny, see? But you can't be at home at that hour. So you tell the maid to turn the radio on when Jack Benny comes on, and this automatically goes on with the radio . . .

WILLY: And when you come home you . . .

HOWARD: You can come home twelve o'clock, one o'clock, any time you like, and you get yourself a Coke and sit yourself down, throw the switch, and there's Jack Benny's program in the middle of the night!

WILLY: I'm definitely going to get one. Because lots of time I'm on the road, and I think to myself, what I must be missing on the radio!

HOWARD: Don't you have a radio in the car?

WILLY: Well, yeah, but who ever thinks of turning it on?

HOWARD: Say, aren't you supposed to be in Boston?

WILLY: That's what I want to talk to you about, Howard. You got a minute? (*He draws a chair in from the wing.*)

HOWARD: What happened? What're you doing here?

WILLY: Well . . .

HOWARD: You didn't crack up again, did you?

WILLY: Oh, no. No . . .

HOWARD: Geez, you had me worried there for a minute. What's the trouble?

WILLY: Well, tell you the truth, Howard. I've come to the decision that I'd rather not travel any more.

HOWARD: Not travel! Well, what'll you do?

WILLY: Remember, Christmas time, when you had the party here? You said you'd try to think of some spot for me here in town.

HOWARD: With us?

WILLY: Well, sure.

HOWARD: Oh, yeah, yeah, I remember. Well, I couldn't think of anything for you, Willy.

WILLY: I tell ya, Howard. The kids are all grown up, y'know. I don't need much any more. If I could take home—well, sixty-five dollars a week, I could swing it.

HOWARD: Yeah, but Willy, see I—

WILLY: I tell ya why, Howard. Speaking frankly and between the two of us, y'know—I'm just a little tired.

HOWARD: Oh, I could understand that, Willy. But you're a road man, Willy, and we do a road business. We've only got a half-dozen salesmen on the floor here.

WILLY: God knows, Howard, I never asked a favor of any man. But I was with the firm when your father used to carry you in here in his arms.

HOWARD: I know that, Willy, but—

WILLY: Your father came to me the day you were born and asked me what I thought of the name of Howard, may he rest in peace.

HOWARD: I appreciate that, Willy, but there just is no spot here for you. If I had a spot I'd slam you right in, but I just don't have a single solitary spot.

(*He looks for his lighter.* WILLY *has picked it up and gives it to him. Pause.*)

WILLY (*with increasing anger*): Howard, all I need to set my table is fifty dollars a week.

HOWARD: But where am I going to put you, kid?

WILLY: Look, it isn't a question of whether I can sell merchandise, is it?

HOWARD: No, but it's a business, kid, and everybody's gotta pull his own weight.

WILLY (*desperately*): Just let me tell you a story, Howard—

HOWARD: 'Cause you gotta admit, business is business.

WILLY (*angrily*): Business is definitely business, but just listen for a minute. You don't understand this. When I was a boy—eighteen, nineteen—I was already on the road. and there was a question in my mind as to whether selling had a future for me. Because in those days I had a yearning to go to Alaska. See, there were three gold strikes in one month in Alaska, and I felt like going out. Just for the ride, you might say.

HOWARD (*barely interested*): Don't say.

WILLY: Oh, yeah, my father lived many years in Alaska. He was an adventurous man. We've got quite a little streak of self-reliance in our family. I thought I'd go out with my older brother and try to locate him, and maybe settle in the North with the old man. And I was almost decided to go, when I met a salesman in the Parker House. His name was Dave Singleman. And he was eighty-four years old, and he'd drummed merchandise in thirty-one states. And old Dave, he'd go up to his room, y'understand, put on his green velvet slippers—I'll never forget—and pick up his phone and call the buyers, and without ever leaving his room, at the age of eighty-four, he made his living. And when I saw that, I realized that selling was the greatest career a man could want. 'Cause what could be more satisfying than to be able to go, at the age of eighty-four, into twenty or thirty different cities, and pick up a phone, and be remembered and loved and helped by so many different people? Do you know? when he died—and by the way he died the death of a salesman, in his green velvet slippers in the smoker of the New York, New Haven and Hartford, going into Boston—when he died, hundreds of salesmen and buyers were at his funeral. Things were sad on a lotta trains for months after that. (*He stands up.* HOWARD *has not looked at him.*) In those days there was personality in it, Howard. There was respect, and comradeship, and gratitude in it. Today, it's all cut and dried, and there's no chance for bringing friendship to bear—or personality. You see what I mean? They don't know me any more.

HOWARD (*moving away, to the right*): That's just the thing, Willy.

WILLY: If I had forty dollars a week—that's all I'd need. Forty dollars, Howard.

HOWARD: Kid, I can't take blood from a stone, I—

WILLY (*desperation is on him now*): Howard, the year Al Smith was nominated, your father came to me and—

HOWARD (*starting to go off*): I've got to see some people, kid.

WILLY (*stopping him*): I'm talking about your father! There were promises made across this desk! You mustn't tell me you've got people to see—I put thirty-four years into this firm, Howard, and now I can't pay my insurance! You can't eat the orange and throw the peel away—a man is not a piece of fruit! *(After a pause.)* Now pay attention. Your father—in 1928 I had a big year. I averaged a hundred and seventy dollars a week in commissions.

HOWARD *(impatiently)*: Now, Willy, you never averaged—

WILLY *(banging his hand on the desk)*: I averaged a hundred and seventy dollars a week in the year of 1928! And your father came to me—or rather, I was in the office here—it was right over this desk—and he put his hand on my shoulder—

HOWARD *(getting up)*: You'll have to excuse me, Willy, I gotta see some people. Pull yourself together. *(Going out.)* I'll be back in a little while.

(On HOWARD's exit, the light of his chair grows very bright and strange.)

WILLY: Pull myself together! What the hell did I say to him? My God, I was yelling at him! How could I! *(WILLY breaks off, staring at the light, which occupies the chair, animating it. He approaches this chair, standing across the desk from it.)* Frank, Frank, don't you remember what you told me that time? How you put your hand on my shoulder, and Frank . . . *(He leans on the desk and as he speaks the dead man's name he accidentally switches on the recorder, and instantly)*

HOWARD'S SON: ". . . of New York is Albany. The capital of Ohio is Cincinnati, the capital of Rhode Island is . . ." *(The recitation continues.)*

WILLY *(leaping away with fright, shouting)*: Ha! Howard! Howard! Howard!

HOWARD *(rushing in)*: What happened?

WILLY *(pointing at the machine, which contines nasally, childishly, with the capital cities)*: Shut it off! Shut it off!

HOWARD *(pulling the plug out)*: Look, Willy . . .

WILLY *(pressing his hands to his eyes)*: I gotta get myself some coffee. I'll get some coffee . . .

(WILLY starts to walk out. HOWARD stops him.)

HOWARD *(rolling up the cord)*: Willy, Look . . .

WILLY: I'll go to Boston.

HOWARD: Willy, you can't go to Boston for us.

WILLY: Why can't I go?

HOWARD: I don't want you to represent us. I've been meaning to tell you for a long time now.

WILLY: Howard, are you firing me?

HOWARD: I think you need a good long rest, Willy.

WILLY: Howard—

HOWARD: And when you feel better, come back, and we'll see if we can work something out.

WILLY: But I gotta earn money, Howard. I'm in no position to—

HOWARD: Where are your sons? Why don't your sons

give you a hand?

WILLY: They're working on a very big deal.

HOWARD: This is no time for false pride, Willy. You go to your sons and you tell them that you're tired. You've got two great boys, haven't you?

WILLY: Oh, no question, no question, but in the meantime . . .

HOWARD: Then that's that, heh?

WILLY: All right, I'll go to Boston tomorrow.

HOWARD: No, no.

WILLY: I can't throw myself on my sons. I'm not a cripple!

HOWARD: Look, kid, I'm busy this morning.

WILLY *(grasping HOWARD's arm)*: Howard, you've got to let me go to Boston!

HOWARD *(hard, keeping himself under control)*: I've got a line of people to see this morning. Sit down, take five minutes, and pull yourself together, and then go home, will ya? I need the office, Willy. *(He starts to go; turns, remembering the recorder, starts to push off the table holding the recorder.)* Oh, yeah. Whenever you can this week, stop by and drop off the samples. You'll feel better, Willy, and then come back and we'll talk. Pull yourself together, kid, there's people outside.

(HOWARD exits, pushing the table off left. WILLY stares into space, exhausted. Now the music is heard—BEN's music—first distantly, then closer, closer. As WILLY speaks, BEN enters from the right. He carries valise and umbrella.)

WILLY: Oh, Ben, how did you do it? What is the answer? Did you wind up the Alaska deal already?

BEN: Doesn't take much time if you know what you're doing. Just a short business trip. Boarding ship in an hour. Wanted to say good-by.

WILLY: Ben, I've got to talk to you.

BEN *(glancing at his watch)*: Haven't the time, William.

WILLY *(crossing the apron to BEN)*: Ben, nothing's working out. I don't know what to do.

BEN: Now look here, William. I've bought timberland in Alaska and I need a man to look after things for me.

WILLY: God, timberland! Me and my boys in those grand outdoors!

BEN: You've a new continent at your doorstep, William. Get out of these cities, they're full of talk and time payments and courts of law. Screw on your fists and you can fight for a fortune up there.

WILLY: Yes, yes! Linda, Linda!

(LINDA enters as of old, with the wash.)

LINDA: Oh, you're back?

BEN: I haven't much time.

WILLY: No, wait! Linda, he's got a proposition for me in Alaska.

LINDA: But you've got—(*to* BEN) He's got a beautiful job here.

WILLY: But in Alaska, kid, I could—

LINDA: You're doing well enough, Willy!

BEN (*to* LINDA): Enough for what, my dear?

LINDA (*frightened of* BEN *and angry at him*): Don't say those things to him! Enough to be happy right here, right now. (*to* WILLY, *while* BEN *laughs*) Why must everybody conquer the world? You're well liked, and the boys love you, and someday—(*to* BEN)—why, old man Wagner told him just the other day that if he keeps it up he'll be a member of the firm, didn't he, Willy?

WILLY: Sure, sure. I am building something with this firm, Ben, and if a man is building something he must be on the right track, mustn't he?

BEN: What are you building? Lay your hand on it. Where is it?

WILLY (*hesitantly*): That's true, Linda, there's nothing.

LINDA: Why? (*to* BEN) There's a man eighty-four years old—

WILLY: That's right, Ben, that's right. When I look at that man I say, what is there to worry about?

BEN: Bah!

WILLY: It's true, Ben. All he has to do is go into any city, pick up the phone, and he's making his living and you know why?

BEN (*picking up his valise*): I've got to go.

WILLY (*holding* BEN *back*): Look at this boy!

(BIFF, *in his high school sweater, enters carrying suitcase.* HAPPY *carries* BIFF's *shoulder guards, gold helmet, and football pants.*)

WILLY: Without a penny to his name, three great universities are begging for him, and from there the sky's the limit, because it's not what you do, Ben. It's who you know and the smile on your face! It's contacts, Ben, contacts! The whole wealth of Alaska passes over the lunch table at the Commodore Hotel, and that's the wonder, the wonder of this century, that a man can end with diamonds here on the basis of being liked! (*He turns to* BIFF.) And that's why when you get out on that field today it's important. Because thousands of people will be rooting for you and loving you. (*to* BEN, *who has again begun to leave*) And Ben! when he walks into a business office his name will sound out like a bell and all the doors will open to him! I've seen it, Ben, I've seen it a thousand times! You can't feel it with your hand like timber, but it's there!

BEN: Good-by, William.

WILLY: Ben, am I right? Don't you think I'm right? I value your advice.

BEN: There's a new continent at your doorstep, William. You could walk out rich. Rich! (*He is gone.*)

WILLY: We'll do it here, Ben! You hear me? We're gonna do it here!

(YOUNG BERNARD *rushes in. The gay music of the Boys is heard.*)

BERNARD: Oh, gee, I was afraid you left already!

WILLY: Why? What time is it?

BERNARD: It's half-past one!

WILLY: Well, come on, everybody! Ebbets Field next stop! Where's the pennants? (*He rushes through the wall-line of the kitchen and out into the living-room.*)

LINDA (*to* BIFF): Did you pack fresh underwear?

BIFF (*who has been limbering up*): I want to go!

BERNARD: Biff, I'm carrying your helmet, ain't I?

HAPPY: No, I'm carrying the helmet.

BERNARD: Oh, Biff, you promised me.

HAPPY: I'm carrying the helmet.

BERNARD: How am I going to get in the locker room?

LINDA: Let him carry the shoulder guards. (*She puts her coat and hat on in the kitchen.*)

BERNARD: Can I, Biff? 'Cause I told everybody I'm going to be in the locker room.

HAPPY: In Ebbets Field it's the clubhouse.

BERNARD: I meant the clubhouse, Biff!

HAPPY: Biff!

BIFF (*grandly, after a slight pause*): Let him carry the shoulder guards.

HAPPY (*as he gives* BERNARD *the shoulder guards*): Stay close to us now.

(WILLY *rushes in with the pennants.*)

WILLY (*handing them out*): Everybody wave when Biff comes out on the field. (HAPPY *and* BERNARD *run off.*) You set now, boy?

(*The music has died away.*)

BIFF: Ready to go, Pop. Every muscle is ready.

WILLY (*at the edge of the apron*): You realize what this means?

BIFF: That's right, Pop.

WILLY (*feeling* BIFF's *muscles*): You're comin' home this afternoon captain of the All-Scholastic Championship Team of the City of New York.

BIFF: I got it, Pop. And remember, pal, when I take off my helmet, that touchdown is for you.

WILLY: Let's go! (*He is starting out, with his arm around* BIFF, *when* CHARLEY *enters, as of old, in knickers.*) I got no room for you, Charley.

CHARLEY: Room? For what?

WILLY: In the car.

CHARLEY: You goin' for a ride? I wanted to shoot some casino.

WILLY (*furiously*): Casino! (*Incredulously.*) Don't you realize what today is?

LINDA: Oh, he knows, Willy. He's just kidding you.

WILLY: That's nothing to kid about!

CHARLEY: No, Linda, what's goin' on?

LINDA: He's playing in Ebbets Field.

CHARLEY: Baseball in this weather?

WILLY: Don't talk to him. Come on, come on! (*He is pushing them out.*)

CHARLEY: Wait a minute, didn't you hear the news?

WILLY: What?

CHARLEY: Don't you listen to the radio? Ebbets Field just blew up.

WILLY: You go to hell! (CHARLEY *laughs. Pushing them out.*) Come on, come on! We're late.

CHARLEY (*as they go*): Knock a homer, Biff, knock a homer!

WILLY (*the last to leave, turning to* CHARLEY): I don't think that was funny, Charley. This is the greatest day of his life.

CHARLEY: Willy, when are you going to grow up?

WILLY: Yeah, heh? When this game is over, Charley, you'll be laughing out of the other side of your face. They'll be calling him another Red Grange. Twenty-five thousand a year.

CHARLEY (*kidding*): Is that so?

WILLY: Yeah, that's so.

CHARLEY: Well, then, I'm sorry, Willy. But tell me something.

WILLY: What?

CHARLEY: Who is Red Grange?

WILLY: Put up your hands. Goddam you, put up your hands!

(CHARLEY, *chuckling, shakes his head and walks away, around the left corner of the stage.* WILLY *follows him. The music rises to a mocking frenzy.*)

WILLY: Who the hell do you think you are, better than everybody else? You don't know everything, you big, ignorant, stupid . . . Put up your hands!

(*Light rises, on the right side of the forestage, on a small table in the reception room of* CHARLEY's *office. Traffic sounds are heard.* BERNARD, *now mature, sits whistling to himself. A pair of tennis rackets and an overnight bag are on the floor beside him.*)

WILLY (*offstage*): What are you walking away for? Don't walk away! If you're going to say something say it to my face! I know you laugh at me behind my back. You'll laugh out of the other side of your goddam face after this game. Touchdown! Touchdown! Eighty thousand people! Touchdown! Right between the goal posts.

(BERNARD *is a quiet, earnest, but self-assured young man.* WILLY's *voice is coming from right upstage now.* BERNARD *lowers his feet off the table and listens.* JENNY, *his father's secretary, enters.*)

JENNY (*distressed*): Say, Bernard, will you go out in the hall?

BERNARD: What is that noise? Who is it?

JENNY: Mr. Loman. He just got off the elevator.

BERNARD (*getting up*): Who's he arguing with?

JENNY: Nobody. There's nobody with him. I can't deal with him any more, and your father gets all upset everytime he comes. I've got a lot of typing to do, and your father's waiting to sign it. Will you see him?

WILLY (*entering*): Touchdown! Touch—(*He sees* JENNY.) Jenny, Jenny, good to see you. How're ya? Workin'? Or still honest?

JENNY: Fine. How've you been feeling?

WILLY: Not much any more, Jenny. Ha, ha! (*He is surprised to see the rackets.*)

BERNARD: Hello, Uncle Willy.

WILLY (*almost shocked*): Bernard! Well, look who's here! (*He comes quickly, guiltily, to* BERNARD *and warmly shakes his hand.*)

BERNARD: How are you? Good to see you.

WILLY: What are you doing here?

BERNARD: Oh, just stopped by to see Pop. Get off my feet till my train leaves. I'm going to Washington in a few minutes.

WILLY: Is he in?

BERNARD: Yes, he's in his office with the accountant. Sit down.

WILLY (*sitting down*): What're you going to do in Washington?

BERNARD: Oh, just a case I've got there, Willy.

WILLY: That so? (*Indicating the rackets.*) You going to play tennis there?

BERNARD: I'm staying with a friend who's got a court.

WILLY: Don't say. His own tennis court. Must be fine people, I bet.

BERNARD: They are, very nice. Dad tells me Biff's in town.

WILLY (*with a big smile*): Yeah, Biff's in. Working on a very big deal, Bernard.

BERNARD: What's Biff doing?

WILLY: Well, he's been doing very big things in the West. But he decided to establish himself here. Very big. We're having dinner. Did I hear your wife had a boy?

BERNARD: That's right. Our second.

WILLY: Two boys! What do you know!

BERNARD: What kind of a deal has Biff got?

WILLY: Well, Bill Oliver—very big sporting-goods man—he wants Biff very badly. Called him in from the West. Long distance, carte blanche, special deliveries. Your friends have their own private tennis court?

BERNARD: You still with the old firm, Willy?

WILLY (*after a pause*): I'm—I'm overjoyed to see how you made the grade, Bernard, overjoyed. It's an encouraging thing to see a young man really—

really—Looks very good for Biff—very—(*He breaks off, then.*) Bernard—(*He is so full of emotion, he breaks off again.*)

BERNARD: What is it, Willy?

WILLY (*small and alone*): What—what's the secret?

BERNARD: What secret?

WILLY: How—how did you? Why didn't he ever catch on?

BERNARD: I wouldn't know that, Willy.

WILLY (*confidentially, desperately*): You were his friend, his boyhood friend. There's something I don't understand about it. His life ended after that Ebbets Field game. From the age of seventeen nothing good ever happened to him.

BERNARD: He never trained himself for anything.

WILLY: But he did, he did. After high school he took so many correspondence courses. Radio mechanics; television; God knows what, and never made the slightest mark.

BERNARD (*taking off his glasses*): Willy, do you want to talk candidly?

WILLY (*rising, faces* BERNARD): I regard you as a very brilliant man, Bernard. I value your advice.

BERNARD: Oh, the hell with the advice, Willy. I couldn't advise you. There's just one thing I've always wanted to ask you. When he was supposed to graduate, and the math teacher flunked him—

WILLY: Oh, that son-of-a-bitch ruined his life.

BERNARD: Yeah, but, Willy, all he had to do was go to summer school and make up that subject.

WILLY: That's right, that's right.

BERNARD: Did you tell him not to go to summer school?

WILLY: Me? I begged him to go. I ordered him to go!

BERNARD: Then why wouldn't he go?

WILLY: Why? Why! Bernard, that question has been trailing me like a ghost for the last fifteen years. He flunked the subject, and laid down and died like a hammer hit him!

BERNARD: Take it easy, kid.

WILLY: Let me talk to you—I got nobody to talk to. Bernard, Bernard, was it my fault? Y'see? It keeps going around in my mind, maybe I did something to him. I got nothing to give him.

BERNARD: Don't take it so hard.

WILLY: Why did he lay down? What is the story there? You were his friend!

BERNARD: Willy, I remember, it was June, and our grades came out. And he'd flunked math.

WILLY: That son-of-a-bitch!

BERNARD: No, it wasn't right then. Biff just got very angry, I remember, and he was ready to enroll in summer school.

WILLY (*surprised*): He was?

BERNARD: He wasn't beaten by it at all. But then, Willy, he disappeared from the block for almost a month. And I got the idea that he'd gone up to New England to see you. Did he have a talk with you then?

(WILLY *stares in silence.*)

BERNARD: Willy?

WILLY (*with a strong edge of resentment in his voice*): Yeah, he came to Boston. What about it?

BERNARD: Well, just that when he came back—I'll never forget this, it always mystifies me. Because I'd thought so well of Biff, even though he'd always taken advantage of me. I loved him, Willy, y'know? And he came back after that month and took his sneakers—remember those sneakers with "University of Virginia" printed on them? He was so proud of those, wore them every day. And he took them down in the cellar, and burned them up in the furnace. We had a fist fight. It lasted at least half an hour. Just the two of us, punching each other down the cellar, and crying right through it. I've often thought of how strange it was that I knew he'd given up his life. What happened in Boston, Willy?

(WILLY *looks at him as at an intruder.*)

BERNARD: I just bring it up because you asked me.

WILLY (*angrily*): Nothing. What do you mean, "What happened?" What's that got to do with anything?

BERNARD: Well, don't get sore.

WILLY: What are you trying to do, blame it on me? If a boy lays down is that my fault?

BERNARD: Now, Willy, don't get—

WILLY: Well, don't—don't talk to me that way! What does that mean, "What happened?"

(CHARLEY *enters. He is in his vest, and he carries a bottle of bourbon.*)

CHARLEY: Hey, you're going to miss that train. (*He waves the bottle.*)

BERNARD: Yeah, I'm going. (*He takes the bottle.*) Thanks, Pop. (*He picks up his rackets and bag.*) Good-by, Willy, and don't worry about it. You know, "If at first you don't succeed . . ."

WILLY: Yes, I believe in that.

BERNARD: But sometimes, Willy, it's better for a man just to walk away.

WILLY: Walk away?

BERNARD: That's right.

WILLY: But if you can't walk away?

BERNARD (*after a slight pause*): I guess that's when it's tough. (*Extending his hand.*) Good-by, Willy.

WILLY (*shaking* BERNARD's *hand*): Good-by, boy.

CHARLEY (*an arm on* BERNARD's *shoulder*): How do you like this kid? Gonna argue a case in front of the Supreme Court.

BERNARD (*protesting*): Pop!

WILLY (*genuinely shocked, pained, and happy*): No! The Supreme Court!

BERNARD: I gotta run. 'By, Dad!

CHARLEY: Knock 'em dead, Bernard!

(BERNARD *goes off.*)

WILLY (*as* CHARLEY *takes out his wallet*): The Supreme Court! And he didn't even mention it!

CHARLEY (*counting out money on the desk*): He don't have to—he's gonna do it.

WILLY: And you never told him what to do, did you? You never took any interest in him.

CHARLEY: My salvation is that I never took any interest in anything. There's some money—fifty dollars. I got an accountant inside.

WILLY: Charley, look . . . (*With difficulty.*) I got my insurance to pay. If you can manage it—I need a hundred and ten dollars.

(CHARLEY *doesn't reply for a moment; merely stops moving.*)

WILLY: I'd draw it from my bank but Linda would know, and I . . .

CHARLEY: Sit down, Willy.

WILLY (*moving toward the chair*): I'm keeping an account of everything, remember. I'll pay every penny back. (*He sits.*)

CHARLEY: Now listen to me, Willy.

WILLY: I want you to know I appreciate . . .

CHARLEY (*sitting down on the table*): Willy, what're you doin'? What the hell is goin' on in your head?

WILLY: Why? I'm simply . . .

CHARLEY: I offered you a job. You can make fifty dollars a week. And I won't send you on the road.

WILLY: I've got a job.

CHARLEY: Without pay? What kind of a job is a job without pay? (*He rises.*) Now, look, kid, enough is enough. I'm no genius but I know when I'm being insulted.

WILLY: Insulted!

CHARLEY: Why don't you want to work for me?

WILLY: What's the matter with you? I've got a job.

CHARLEY: Then what're you walkin' in here every week for?

WILLY (*getting up*): Well, if you don't want me to walk in here—

CHARLEY: I am offering you a job.

WILLY: I don't want your goddam job!

CHARLEY: When the hell are you going to grow up?

WILLY (*furiously*): You big ignoramus, if you say that to me again I'll rap you one! I don't care how big you are! (*He's ready to fight.*)

(Pause.)

CHARLEY (*kindly, going to him*): How much do you need, Willy?

WILLY: Charley, I'm strapped, I'm strapped. I don't know what to do. I was just fired.

CHARLEY: Howard fired you?

WILLY: That snotnose. Imagine that? I named him. I named him Howard.

CHARLEY: Willy, when're you gonna realize that them things don't mean anything? You named him Howard, but you can't sell that. The only thing you got in this world is what you can sell. And the funny thing is that you're a salesman, and you don't know that.

WILLY: I've always tried to think otherwise, I guess. I always felt that if a man was impressive, and well liked, that nothing—

CHARLEY: Why must everybody like you? Who liked J. P. Morgan? Was he impressive? In a Turkish bath he'd look like a butcher. But with his pockets on he was very well liked. Now listen, Willy, I know you don't like me, and nobody can say I'm in love with you, but I'll give you a job because—just for the hell of it, put it that way. Now what do you say?

WILLY: I—I just can't work for you, Charley.

CHARLEY: What're you, jealous of me?

WILLY: I can't work for you, that's all, don't ask me why.

CHARLEY (*angered, takes out more bills*): You been jealous of me all your life, you damned fool! Here, pay your insurance. (*He puts the money in* WILLY'S *hand.*)

WILLY: I'm keeping strict accounts.

CHARLEY: I've got some work to do. Take care of yourself. And pay your insurance.

WILLY (*moving to the right*): Funny, y'know? After all the highways, and the trains, and the appointments, and the years, you end up worth more dead than alive.

CHARLEY: Willy, nobody's worth nothin' dead. (*After a slight pause.*) Did you hear what I said?

(WILLY *stands still, dreaming.*)

CHARLEY: Willy!

WILLY: Apologize to Bernard for me when you see him. I didn't mean to argue with him. He's a fine boy. They're all fine boys, and they'll end up big—all of them. Someday they'll all play tennis together. Wish me luck, Charley. He saw Bill Oliver today.

CHARLEY: Good luck.

WILLY (*on the verge of tears*): Charley, you're the only friend I got. Isn't that a remarkable thing? (*He goes out.*)

CHARLEY: Jesus!

(CHARLEY *stares after him a moment and follows. All light blacks out. Suddenly raucous music is heard, and a red glow rises behind the screen at right.* STANLEY, *a young waiter, appears, carrying a table, followed by* HAPPY, *who is carrying two chairs.)*

STANLEY (*putting the table down*): That's all right, Mr. Loman, I can handle it myself. (*He turns and takes the chairs from* HAPPY *and places them at the table.*)

HAPPY (*glancing around*): Oh, this is better.

STANLEY: Sure, in the front there you're in the middle of all kinds a noise. Whenever you got a party, Mr. Loman, you just tell me and I'll put you back here. Y'know, there's a lotta people they don't like it private, because when they go out they like to see a lotta action around them because they're sick and tired to stay in the house by theirself. But I know you, you ain't from Hackensack. You know what I mean?

HAPPY (*sitting down*): So how's it coming, Stanley?

STANLEY: Ah, it's a dog's life. I only wish during the war they'd a took me in the Army. I coulda been dead by now.

HAPPY: My brother's back, Stanley.

STANLEY: Oh, he come back, heh? From the Far West.

HAPPY: Yeah, big cattle man, my brother, so treat him right. And my father's coming too.

STANLEY: Oh, your father too!

HAPPY: You got a couple of nice lobsters?

STANLEY: Hundred per cent, big.

HAPPY: I want them with the claws.

STANLEY: Don't worry, I don't give you no mice. (HAPPY *laughs.*) How about some wine? It'll put a head on the meal.

HAPPY: No. You remember, Stanley, that recipe I brought you from overseas? With the champagne in it?

STANLEY: Oh, yeah, sure. I still got it tacked up yet in the kitchen. But that'll have to cost a buck apiece anyways.

HAPPY: That's all right.

STANLEY: What'd you, hit a number or somethin'?

HAPPY: No, it's a little celebration. My brother is—I think he pulled off a big deal today. I think we're going into business together.

STANLEY: Great! That's the best for you. Because a family business, you know what I mean?—that's the best.

HAPPY: That's what I think.

STANLEY: 'Cause what's the difference? Somebody steals? It's in the family. Know what I mean? (*Sotto voce.*) Like this bartender here. The boss is goin' crazy what kinda leak he's got in the cash register. You put it in but it don't come out.

HAPPY (*raising his head*): Sh!

STANLEY: What?

HAPPY: You notice I wasn't lookin' right or left, was I?

STANLEY: No.

HAPPY: And my eyes are closed.

STANLEY: So what's the—?

HAPPY: Strudel's comin'.

STANLEY (*catching on, looks around*): Ah, no, there's no—

(*He breaks off as a furred, lavishly dressed girl enters and sits at the next table. Both follow her with their eyes.*)

STANLEY: Geez, how'd ya know?

HAPPY: I got radar or something. (*Staring directly at her profile.*) Ooooooooo . . . Stanley.

STANLEY: I think that's for you, Mr. Loman.

HAPPY: Look at that mouth. Oh, God. And the binoculars.

STANLEY: Geez, you got a life, Mr. Loman.

HAPPY: Wait on her.

STANLEY (*going to the girl's table*): Would you like a menu, ma'am?

GIRL: I'm expecting someone, but I'd like a—

HAPPY: Why don't you bring her—excuse me, miss, do you mind? I sell champagne, and I'd like you to try my brand. Bring her a champagne, Stanley.

GIRL: That's awfully nice of you.

HAPPY: Don't mention it. It's all company money. (*He laughs.*)

GIRL: That's a charming product to be selling, isn't it?

HAPPY: Oh, gets to be like everything else. Selling is selling, y'know.

GIRL: I suppose.

HAPPY: You don't happen to sell, do you?

GIRL: No, I don't sell.

HAPPY: Would you object to a compliment from a stranger? You ought to be on a magazine cover.

GIRL (*looking at him a little archly*): I have been.

(STANLEY *comes in with a glass of champagne.*)

HAPPY: What'd I say before, Stanley? You see? She's a cover girl.

STANLEY: Oh, I could see, I could see.

HAPPY (*to the* GIRL): What magazine?

GIRL: Oh, a lot of them. (*She takes the drink.*) Thank you.

HAPPY: You know what they say in France, don't you? "Champagne is the drink of the complexion"—Hya, Biff!

(BIFF *has entered and sits with* HAPPY.)

BIFF: Hello, kid. Sorry I'm late.

HAPPY: I just got here. Uh, Miss—?

GIRL: Forsythe.

HAPPY: Miss Forsythe, this is my brother.

BIFF: Is Dad here?

HAPPY: His name is Biff. You might've heard of him. Great football player.

GIRL: Really? What team?

HAPPY: Are you familiar with football?

GIRL: No, I'm afraid I'm not.

HAPPY: Biff is quarterback with the New York Giants.

GIRL: Well, that is nice, isn't it? (*She drinks.*)

HAPPY: Good health.

GIRL: I'm happy to meet you.

HAPPY: That's my name. Hap. It's really Harold, but at West Point they called me Happy.

GIRL (*now really impressed*): Oh, I see. How do you do? (*She turns her profile.*)

BIFF: Isn't Dad coming?

HAPPY: You want her?

BIFF: Oh, I could never make that.

HAPPY: I remember the time that idea would never come into your head. Where's the old confidence, Biff?

BIFF: I just saw Oliver—

HAPPY: Wait a minute. I've got to see that old confidence again. Do you want her? She's on call.

BIFF: Oh, no. (*He turns to look at the* GIRL.)

HAPPY: I'm telling you. Watch this. (*Turning to the* GIRL.) Honey? (*She turns to him.*) Are you busy?

GIRL: Well, I am . . . but I could make a phone call.

HAPPY: Do that, will you, honey? And see if you can get a friend. We'll be here for a while. Biff is one of the greatest football players in the country.

GIRL (*standing up*): Well, I'm certainly happy to meet you.

HAPPY: Come back soon.

GIRL: I'll try.

HAPPY: Don't try, honey, try hard.

(*The* GIRL *exits.* STANLEY *follows, shaking his head in bewildered admiration.*)

HAPPY: Isn't that a shame now? A beautiful girl like that? That's why I can't get married. There's not a good woman in a thousand. New York is loaded with them, kid!

BIFF: Hap, look—

HAPPY: I told you she was on call!

BIFF (*strangely unnerved*): Cut it out, will ya? I want to say something to you.

HAPPY: Did you see Oliver?

BIFF: I saw him all right. Now look, I want to tell Dad a couple of things and I want you to help me.

HAPPY: What? Is he going to back you?

BIFF: Are you crazy? You're out of your goddam head, you know that?

HAPPY: Why? What happened?

BIFF (*breathlessly*): I did a terrible thing today, Hap. It's been the strangest day I ever went through. I'm all numb, I swear.

HAPPY: You mean he wouldn't see you?

BIFF: Well, I waited six hours for him, see? All day. Kept sending my name in. Even tried to date his secretary so she'd get me to him, but no soap.

HAPPY: Because you're not showin' the old confidence, Biff. He remembered you, didn't he?

BIFF (*stopping* HAPPY *with a gesture*): Finally, about five o'clock, he comes out. Didn't remember who I was or anything. I felt like such an idiot, Hap.

HAPPY: Did you tell him my Florida idea?

BIFF: He walked away. I saw him for one minute. I got so mad I could've torn the walls down! How the hell did I ever get the idea I was a salesman there? I even believed myself that I'd been a salesman for him! And then he gave me one look and—I realized what a ridiculous lie my whole life has been! We've been talking in a dream for fifteen years. I was a shipping clerk.

HAPPY: What'd you do?

BIFF (*with great tension and wonder*): Well, he left, see. And the secretary went out. I was all alone in the waiting-room. I don't know what came over me, Hap. The next thing I know I'm in his office—paneled walls, everything. I can't explain it. I—Hap, I took his fountain pen.

HAPPY: Geez, did he catch you?

BIFF: I ran out. I ran down all eleven flights. I ran and ran and ran.

HAPPY: That was an awful dumb—what'd you do that for?

BIFF (*agonized*): I don't know, I just—wanted to take something, I don't know. You gotta help me, Hap, I'm gonna tell Pop.

HAPPY: You crazy? What for?

BIFF: Hap, he's got to understand that I'm not the man somebody lends that kind of money to. He thinks I've been spiting him all these years and it's eating him up.

HAPPY: That's just it. You tell him something nice.

BIFF: I can't.

HAPPY: Say you got a lunch date with Oliver tomorrow.

BIFF: So what do I do tomorrow?

HAPPY: You leave the house tomorrow and come back at night and say Oliver is thinking it over. And he thinks it over for a couple of weeks, and gradually it fades away and nobody's the worse.

BIFF: But it'll go on forever!

HAPPY: Dad is never so happy as when he's looking forward to something!

(WILLY *enters.*)

HAPPY: Hello, scout!

WILLY: Gee, I haven't been here in years!

(STANLEY *has followed* WILLY *in and sets a chair for him.* STANLEY *starts off but* HAPPY *stops him.*)

HAPPY: Stanley!

(STANLEY *stands by, waiting for an order.*)

BIFF (*going to* WILLY *with guilt, as to an invalid*): Sit down, Pop. You want a drink?

WILLY: Sure, I don't mind.

BIFF: Let's get a load on.

WILLY: You look worried.

BIFF: N-no. (to STANLEY) Scotch all around. Make it doubles.

STANLEY: Doubles, right. (He goes.)

WILLY: You had a couple already, didn't you?

BIFF: Just a couple, yeah.

WILLY: Well, what happened, boy? (Nodding affirmatively, with a smile.) Everything go all right?

BIFF (takes a breath, then reaches out and grasps WILLY's hand): Pal . . . (He is smiling bravely, and WILLY is smiling too.) I had an experience today.

HAPPY: Terrific, Pop.

WILLY: That so? What happened?

BIFF (high, slightly alcoholic, above the earth): I'm going to tell you everything from first to last. It's been a strange day. (Silence. He looks around, composes himself as best he can, but his breath keeps breaking the rhythm of his voice.) I had to wait quite a while for him, and—

WILLY: Oliver?

BIFF: Yeah, Oliver. All day, as a matter of cold fact. And a lot of—instances—facts, Pop, facts about my life came back to me. Who was it, Pop? Who ever said I was a salesman with Oliver?

WILLY: Well, you were.

BIFF: No, Dad, I was a shipping clerk.

WILLY: But you were practically—

BIFF (with determination): Dad, I don't know who said it first, but I was never a salesman for Bill Oliver.

WILLY: What're you talking about?

BIFF: Let's hold on to the facts tonight, Pop. We're not going to get anywhere bullin' around. I was a shipping clerk.

WILLY (angrily): All right, now listen to me—

BIFF: Why don't you let me finish?

WILLY: I'm not interested in stories about the past or any crap of that kind because the woods are burning, boys, you understand? There's a big blaze going on all around. I was fired today.

BIFF (shocked): How could you be?

WILLY: I was fired, and I'm looking for a little good news to tell your mother, because the woman has waited and the woman has suffered. The gist of it is that I haven't got a story left in my head, Biff. So don't give me a lecture about facts and aspects. I am not interested. Now what've you got to say to me?

(STANLEY enters with three drinks. They wait until he leaves.)

WILLY: Did you see Oliver?

BIFF: Jesus, Dad!

WILLY: You mean you didn't go up there?

HAPPY: Sure he went up there.

BIFF: I did. I—saw him. How could they fire you?

WILLY (on the edge of his chair): What kind of a welcome did he give you?

BIFF: He won't even let you work on commission?

WILLY: I'm out! (Driving.) So tell me, he gave you a warm welcome?

HAPPY: Sure, Pop, sure!

BIFF (driven): Well, it was kind of—

WILLY: I was wondering if he'd remember you. (to HAPPY.) Imagine, man doesn't see him for ten, twelve years, and gives him that kind of a welcome!

HAPPY: Damn right!

BIFF (trying to return to the offensive): Pop, look—

WILLY: You know why he remembered you, don't you? Because you impressed him in those days.

BIFF: Let's talk quietly and get this down to the facts, huh?

WILLY (as though BIFF had been interrupting): Well, what happened? It's great news, Biff. Did he take you into his office or'd you talk in the waiting-room?

BIFF: Well, he came in, see, and—

WILLY (with a big smile): What'd he say? Betcha he threw his arm around you.

BIFF: Well, he kinda—

WILLY: He's a fine man. (to HAPPY) Very hard man to see, y'know.

HAPPY (agreeing): Oh, I know.

WILLY (to BIFF): Is that where you had the drinks?

BIFF: Yeah, he gave me a couple of—no, no!

HAPPY (cutting in): He told him my Florida idea.

WILLY: Don't interrupt. (to BIFF) How'd he react to the Florida idea?

BIFF: Dad, will you give me a minute to explain?

WILLY: I've been waiting for you to explain since I sat down here! What happened? He took you into his office and what?

BIFF: Well—I talked. And—and he listened, see.

WILLY: Famous for the way he listens, y'know. What was his answer?

BIFF: His answer was—(He breaks off, suddenly angry.) Dad, you're not letting me tell you what I want to tell you!

WILLY (accusing, angered): You didn't see him, did you?

BIFF: I did see him!

WILLY: What'd you insult him or something? You insulted him, didn't you?

BIFF: Listen, will you let me out of it, will you just let me out of it!

HAPPY: What the hell!

WILLY: Tell me what happened!

BIFF (to HAPPY): I can't talk to him!

(A single trumpet note jars the ear. The light of green leaves stains the house, which holds the air of night and a dream. YOUNG BERNARD enters and knocks on the door of the house.)

YOUNG BERNARD (frantically): Mrs. Loman, Mrs. Loman!

HAPPY: Tell him what happened!

BIFF (*to* HAPPY): Shut up and leave me alone!

WILLY: No, no! You had to go and flunk math!

BIFF: What math? What're you talking about?

YOUNG BERNARD: Mrs. Loman, Mrs. Loman!

(LINDA *appears in the house, as of old.*)

WILLY (*wildly*): Math, math, math!

BIFF: Take it easy, Pop!

YOUNG BERNARD: Mrs. Loman!

WILLY (*furiously*): If you hadn't flunked you'd've been set by now!

BIFF: Now, look, I'm gonna tell you what happened, and you're going to listen to me.

YOUNG BERNARD: Mrs. Loman!

BIFF: I waited six hours!

HAPPY: What the hell are you saying?

BIFF: I kept sending in my name but he wouldn't see me. So finally he . . . (*He continues unheard as light fades low on the restaurant.*)

YOUNG BERNARD: Biff flunked math!

LINDA: No!

YOUNG BERNARD: Birnbaum flunked him! They won't graduate him!

LINDA: But they have to. He's gotta go to the university. Where is he? Biff! Biff!

YOUNG BERNARD: No, he left. He went to Grand Central.

LINDA: Grand— You mean he went to Boston!

YOUNG BERNARD: Is Uncle Willy in Boston?

LINDA: Oh, maybe Willy can talk to the teacher. Oh, the poor, poor boy!

(*Light on house area snaps out.*)

BIFF (*at the table, now audible, holding up a gold fountain pen*): . . . so I'm washed up with Oliver, you understand? Are you listening to me?

WILLY (*at a loss*): Yeah, sure. If you hadn't flunked—

BIFF: Flunked what? What're you talking about?

WILLY: Don't blame everything on me! I didn't flunk math—you did! What pen?

HAPPY: That was awful dumb, Biff, a pen like that is worth—

WILLY (*seeing the pen for the first time*): You took Oliver's pen?

BIFF (*weakening*): Dad, I just explained it to you.

WILLY: You stole Bill Oliver's fountain pen!

BIFF: I didn't exactly steal it! That's just what I've been explaining to you!

HAPPY: He had it in his hand and just then Oliver walked in, so he got nervous and stuck it in his pocket!

WILLY: My God, Biff!

BIFF: I never intended to do it, Dad!

OPERATOR'S VOICE: Standish Arms, good evening!

WILLY (*shouting*): I'm not in my room!

BIFF (*frightened*): Dad, what's the matter? (*He and*

HAPPY *stand up.*)

OPERATOR: Ringing Mr. Loman for you!

WILLY: I'm not there, stop it!

BIFF (*horrified, gets down on one knee before* WILLY): Dad, I'll make good, I'll make good. (WILLY *tries to get to his feet.* BIFF *holds him down.*) Sit down now.

WILLY: No, you're no good, you're no good for anything.

BIFF: I am, Dad, I'll find something else, you understand? Now don't worry about anything. (*He holds up* WILLY's *face.*) Talk to me, Dad.

OPERATOR: Mr. Loman does not answer. Shall I page him.

WILLY (*attempting to stand, as though to rush and silence the* OPERATOR): No, no, no!

HAPPY: He'll strike something, Pop.

WILLY: No, no . . .

BIFF (*desperately, standing over* WILLY): Pop, listen! Listen to me! I'm telling you something good. Oliver talked to his partner about the Florida idea. You listening? He—he talked to his partner, and he came to me . . . I'm going to be all right, you hear? Dad, listen to me, he said it was just a question of the amount!

WILLY: Then you . . . got it?

HAPPY: He's gonna be terrific, Pop!

WILLY (*trying to stand*): Then you got it, haven't you? You got it! You got it!

BIFF (*agonized, holds* WILLY *down*): No, no. Look, Pop. I'm supposed to have lunch with them tomorrow. I'm just telling you this so you'll know that I can still make an impression, Pop. And I'll make good somewhere, but I can't go tomorrow, see?

WILLY: Why not? You simply—

BIFF: But the pen, Pop!

WILLY: You give it to him and tell him it was an oversight!

HAPPY: Sure, have lunch tomorrow!

BIFF: I can't say that—

WILLY: You were doing a crossword puzzle and accidentally used his pen!

BIFF: Listen, kid, I took those balls years ago, now I walk in with his fountain pen? That clinches it, don't you see? I can't face him like that! I'll try elsewhere.

PAGE'S VOICE: Paging Mr. Loman!

WILLY: Don't you want to be anything?

BIFF: Pop, how can I go back?

WILLY: You don't want to be anything, is that what's behind it?

BIFF (*now angry at* WILLY *for not crediting his sympathy*): Don't take it that way! You think it was easy walking into that office after what I'd done to him? A team of horses couldn't have dragged me back to Bill Oliver!

WILLY: Then why'd you go?

BIFF: Why did I go? Why did I go! Look at you! Look

at what's become of you!

(*Off left,* THE WOMAN *laughs.*)

WILLY: Biff, you're going to go to that lunch tomorrow, or—

BIFF: I can't go. I've got no appointment!

HAPPY: Biff, for . . . !

WILLY: Are you spiting me?

BIFF: Don't take it that way! Goddammit!

WILLY (*strikes* BIFF *and falters away from the table*): You rotten little louse! Are you spiting me?

THE WOMAN: Someone's at the door, Willy!

BIFF: I'm no good, can't you see what I am?

HAPPY (*separating them*): Hey, you're in a restaurant! Now cut it out, both of you! (*The* GIRLS *enter.*) Hello, girls, sit down.

(THE WOMAN *laughs, off left.*)

MISS FORSYTHE: I guess we might as well. This is Letta.

THE WOMAN: Willy, are you going to wake up?

BIFF (*ignoring* WILLY): How're ya, miss, sit down. What do you drink?

MISS FORSYTHE: Letta might not be able to stay long.

LETTA: I gotta get up very early tomorrow. I got jury duty. I'm so excited! Were you fellows ever on a jury?

BIFF: No, but I been in front of them! (*The* GIRLS *laugh.*) This is my father.

LETTA: Isn't he cute? Sit down with us, Pop.

HAPPY: Sit him down, Biff!

BIFF (*going to him*): Come on, slugger, drink us under the table. To hell with it! Come on, sit down, pal.

(*On* BIFF's *last insistence,* WILLY *is about to sit.*)

THE WOMAN (*now urgently*): Willy, are you going to answer the door!

(THE WOMAN's *call pulls* WILLY *back. He starts right, befuddled.*)

BIFF: Hey, where are you going?

WILLY: Open the door.

BIFF: The door?

WILLY: The washroom . . . the door . . . where's the door?

BIFF (*leading* WILLY *to the left*): Just go straight down.

(WILLY *moves left.*)

THE WOMAN: Willy, Willy, are you going to get up, get up, get up, get up?

(WILLY *exits left.*)

LETTA: I think it's sweet you bring your daddy along.

MISS FORSYTHE: Oh, he isn't really your father!

BIFF (*at left, turning to her resentfully*): Miss Forsythe, you've just seen a prince walk by. A fine, troubled prince. A hard-working, unappreciated

prince. A pal, you understand? A good companion. Always for his boys.

LETTA: That's so sweet.

HAPPY: Well, girls, what's the program? We're wasting time. Come on, Biff. Gather round. Where would you like to go?

BIFF: Why don't you do something for him?

HAPPY: Me!

BIFF: Don't you give a damn for him, Hap?

HAPPY: What're you talking about? I'm the one who—

BIFF: I sense it, you don't give a good goddam about him. (*He takes the rolled-up hose from his pocket and puts it on the table in front of* HAPPY.) Look what I found in the cellar, for Christ's sake. How can you bear to let it go on?

HAPPY: Me? Who goes away? Who runs off and—

BIFF: Yeah, but he doesn't mean anything to you. You could help him—I can't! Don't you understand what I'm talking about? He's going to kill himself, don't you know that?

HAPPY: Don't I know it! Me!

BIFF: Hap, help him! Jesus . . . help him . . . Help me, help me, I can't bear to look at his face! (*Ready to weep, he hurries out, up right.*)

HAPPY (*starting after him*): Where are you going?

MISS FORSYTHE: What's he so mad about?

HAPPY: Come on, girls, we'll catch up with him.

MISS FORSYTHE (*as* HAPPY *pushes her out*): Say, I don't like that temper of his!

HAPPY: He's just a little overstrung, he'll be all right!

WILLY (*off left, as* THE WOMAN *laughs*): Don't answer! Don't answer!

LETTA: Don't you want to tell your father—

HAPPY: No, that's not my father. He's just a guy. Come on, we'll catch Biff, and, honey, we're going to paint this town! Stanley, where's the check! Hey, Stanley!

(*They exit.* STANLEY *looks toward left.*)

STANLEY (*calling to* HAPPY *indignantly*): Mr. Loman! Mr. Loman!

(STANLEY *picks up a chair and follows them off. Knocking is heard off left.* THE WOMAN *enters, laughing.* WILLY *follows her. She is in a black slip, he is buttoning his shirt. Raw, sensuous music accompanies their speech.*)

WILLY: Will you stop laughing? Will you stop?

THE WOMAN: Aren't you going to answer the door? He'll wake the whole hotel.

WILLY: I'm not expecting anybody.

THE WOMAN: Whyn't you have another drink, honey, and stop being so damn self-centered?

WILLY: I'm so lonely.

THE WOMAN: You know you ruined me, Willy? From now on, whenever you come to the office, I'll see that you go right through to the buyers. No waiting at my desk any more, Willy. You ruined me.

WILLY: That's nice of you to say that.

THE WOMAN: Gee, you are self-centered! Why so sad? You are the saddest, self-centeredest soul I ever did see-saw. (*She laughs. He kisses her.*) Come on inside, drummer boy. It's silly to be dressing in the middle of the night. (*As knocking is heard.*) Aren't you going to answer the door?

WILLY: They're knocking on the wrong door.

THE WOMAN: But I felt the knocking. And he heard us talking in here. Maybe the hotel's on fire!

WILLY (*his terror rising*): It's a mistake.

THE WOMAN: Then tell him to go away!

WILLY: There's nobody there.

THE WOMAN: It's getting on my nerves, Willy. There's somebody standing out there and it's getting on my nerves!

WILLY (*pushing her away from him*): All right, stay in the bathroom here, and don't come out. I think there's a law in Massachusetts about it, so don't come out. It may be that new room clerk. He looked very mean. So don't come out. It's a mistake, there's no fire.

(*The knocking is heard again. He takes a few steps away from her, and she vanishes into the wing. The light follows him, and now he is facing* YOUNG BIFF, *who carries a suitcase.* BIFF *steps toward him. The music is gone.*)

BIFF: Why didn't you answer?

WILLY: Biff! What are you doing in Boston?

BIFF: Why didn't you answer? I've been knocking for five minutes, I called you on the phone—

WILLY: I just heard you. I was in the bathroom and had the door shut. Did anything happen home?

BIFF: Dad—I let you down.

WILLY: What do you mean?

BIFF: Dad . . .

WILLY: Biffo, what's this about? (*Putting his arm around* BIFF.) Come on, let's go downstairs and get you a malted.

BIFF: Dad, I flunked math.

WILLY: Not for the term?

BIFF: The term. I haven't got enough credits to graduate.

WILLY: You mean to say Bernard wouldn't give you the answers?

BIFF: He did, he tried, but I only got a sixty-one.

WILLY: And they wouldn't give you four points?

BIFF: Birnbaum refused absolutely. I begged him, Pop, but he won't give me those points. You gotta talk to him before they close the school. Because if he saw the kind of man you are, and you just talked to him in your way, I'm sure he'd come through for me. The class came right before practice, see, and I didn't go enough. Would you talk to him? He'd like you, Pop. You know the way you could talk.

WILLY: You're on. We'll drive right back.

BIFF: Oh, Dad, good work! I'm sure he'll change it for you!

WILLY: Go downstairs and tell the clerk I'm checkin' out. Go right down.

BIFF: Yes, sir! See, the reason he hates me, Pop—one day he was late for class so I got up at the blackboard and imitated him. I crossed my eyes and talked with a lithp.

WILLY (*laughing*): You did? The kids like it?

BIFF: They nearly died laughing!

WILLY: Yeah? What'd you do?

BIFF: The thquare root of thixthy twee is . . . (WILLY *bursts out laughing;* BIFF *joins him.*) And in the middle of it he walked in!

(WILLY *laughs and* THE WOMAN *joins in offstage.*)

WILLY (*without hesitation*): Hurry downstairs and—

BIFF: Somebody in there?

WILLY: No, that was next door.

(THE WOMAN *laughs offstage.*)

BIFF: Somebody got in your bathroom!

WILLY: No, it's the next room, there's a party—

THE WOMAN (*enters, laughing. She lisps this*): Can I come in? There's something in the bathtub, Willy, and it's moving!

(WILLY *looks at* BIFF, *who is staring open-mouthed and horrified at* THE WOMAN.)

WILLY: Ah—you better go back to your room. They must be finished painting by now. They're painting her room so I let her take a shower here. Go back, go back . . . (*He pushes her.*)

THE WOMAN (*resisting*): But I've got to get dressed Willy, I can't—

WILLY: Get out of here! Go back, go back . . . (*Suddenly striving for the ordinary.*) This is Miss Francis, Biff, she's a buyer. They're painting her room. Go back, Miss Francis, go back . . .

THE WOMAN: But my clothes, I can't go out naked in the hall!

WILLY (*pushing her offstage*): Get outa here! Go back, go back!

(BIFF *slowly sits down on his suitcase as the argument continues offstage.*)

THE WOMAN: Where's my stockings? You promised me stockings, Willy!

WILLY: I have no stockings here!

THE WOMAN: You had two boxes of size nine sheers for me, and I want them!

WILLY: Here, for God's sake, will you get outa here!

THE WOMAN (*enters holding a box of stockings*): I just hope there's nobody in the hall. That's all I hope. (*to* BIFF) Are you football or baseball?

BIFF: Football.

THE WOMAN (*angry, humiliated*): That's me too. G'night. (*She snatches her clothes from* WILLY, *and walks out.*)

WILLY (*after a pause*): Well, better get going. I want to get to the school first thing in the morning. Get my suits out of the closet. I'll get my valise. (BIFF *doesn't move.*) What's the matter? (BIFF *remains motionless, tears falling.*) She's a buyer. Buys for J. H. Simmons. She lives down the hall—they're painting. You don't imagine—(*He breaks off. After a pause.*) Now listen, pal, she's just a buyer. She sees merchandise in her room and they have to keep it looking just so . . . (*Pause. Assuming command.*) All right, get my suits. (BIFF *doesn't move.*) Now stop crying and do as I say. I gave you an order! Biff, I gave you an order! Is that what you do when I give you an order? How dare you cry! (*Putting his arm around* BIFF.) Now look, Biff, when you grow up you'll understand about these things. You mustn't—you mustn't overemphasize a thing like this. I'll see Birnbaum first thing in the morning.

BIFF: Never mind.

WILLY (*getting down beside* BIFF): Never mind! He's going to give you those points. I'll see to it.

BIFF: He wouldn't listen to you.

WILLY: He certainly will listen to me. You need those points for the U. of Virginia.

BIFF: I'm not going there.

WILLY: Heh? If I can't get him to change that mark you'll make it up in summer school. You've got all summer to—

BIFF (*his weeping breaking from him*): Dad . . .

WILLY (*infected by it*): Oh, my boy . . .

BIFF: Dad . . .

WILLY: She's nothing to me, Biff. I was lonely, I was terribly lonely.

BIFF: You—you gave her Mama's stockings! (*His tears break through and he rises to go.*)

WILLY (*grabbing for* BIFF): I gave you an order!

BIFF: Don't touch me, you—liar!

WILLY: Apologize for that!

BIFF: You fake! You phony little fake! You fake! (*Overcome, he turns quickly and weeping fully goes out with his suitcase.* WILLY *is left on the floor on his knees.*)

WILLY: I gave you an order! Biff, come back here or I'll beat you! Come back here! I'll whip you!

(STANLEY *comes quickly in from the right and stands in front of* WILLY.)

WILLY (*shouts at* STANLEY): I gave you an order . . .

STANLEY: Hey, let's pick it up, pick it up, Mr. Loman. (*He helps* WILLY *to his feet.*) Your boys left with the chippies. They said they'll see you home.

(*A second waiter watches some distance away.*)

WILLY: But we were supposed to have dinner together.

(*Music is heard,* WILLY's *theme.*)

STANLEY: Can you make it?

WILLY: I'll—sure, I can make it. (*Suddenly concerned about his clothes.*) Do I—I look all right?

STANLEY: Sure, you look all right. (*He flicks a speck off* WILLY's *lapel.*)

WILLY: Here—here's a dollar.

STANLEY: Oh, your son paid me. It's all right.

WILLY (*putting it in* STANLEY's *hand*): No, take it. You're a good boy.

STANLEY: Oh, no, you don't have to . . .

WILLY: Here—here's some more, I don't need it any more. (*After a slight pause.*) Tell me—is there a seed store in the neighborhood?

STANLEY: Seeds? You mean like to plant?

(*As* WILLY *turns,* STANLEY *slips the money back into his jacket pocket.*)

WILLY: Yes. Carrots, peas . . .

STANLEY: Well, there's hardware stores on Sixth Avenue, but it may be too late now.

WILLY (*anxiously*): Oh, I'd better hurry. I've got to get some seeds. (*He starts off to the right.*) I've got to get some seeds, right away. Nothing's planted. I don't have a thing in the ground.

(WILLY *hurries out as the light goes down.* STANLEY *moves over to the right after him, watches him off. The other waiter has been staring at* WILLY.)

STANLEY (*to the waiter*): Well, whatta you looking at?

(*The waiter picks up the chairs and moves off right. Stanley takes the table and follows him. The light fades on this area. There is a long pause, the sound of the flute coming over. The light gradually rises on the kitchen, which is empty.* HAPPY *appears at the door of the house, followed by* BIFF. HAPPY *is carrying a large bunch of long-stemmed roses. He enters the kitchen, looks around for* LINDA. *Not seeing her, he turns to* BIFF, *who is just outside the house door, and makes a gesture with his hands, indicating "Not here, I guess." He looks into the living-room and freezes. Inside,* LINDA, *unseen, is seated,* WILLY's *coat on her lap. She rises ominously and quietly and moves toward* HAPPY, *who backs up into the kitchen, afraid.*)

HAPPY: Hey, what're you doing up? (LINDA *says nothing but moves toward him implacably.*) Where's Pop? (*He keeps backing to the right, and now* LINDA *is in full view in the doorway to the living-room.*) Is he sleeping?

LINDA: Where were you?

HAPPY (*trying to laugh it off*): We met two girls, Mom, very fine types. Here, we brought you some flowers. (*Offering them to her.*) Put them in your room, Ma.

(She knocks them to the floor at BIFF's *feet. He has now come inside and closed the door behind him. She stares at* BIFF, *silent.)*

HAPPY: Now, what'd you do that for? Mom, I want you to have some flowers—

LINDA *(cutting* HAPPY *off, violently to* BIFF): Don't you care whether he lives or dies?

HAPPY *(going to the stairs)*: Come upstairs, Biff.

BIFF *(with a flare of disgust, to* HAPPY): Go away from me! *(to* LINDA) What do you mean, lives or dies? Nobody's dying around here, pal.

LINDA: Get out of my sight! Get out of here!

BIFF: I wanna see the boss.

LINDA: You're not going near him!

BIFF: Where is he? *(He moves into the living-room and* LINDA *follows.)*

LINDA *(shouting after* BIFF): You invite him for dinner. He looks forward to it all day—*(*BIFF *appears in his parents' bedroom, looks around, and exits.)*—and then you desert him there. There's no stranger you'd do that to!

HAPPY: Why? He had a swell time with us. Listen, when I—*(*LINDA *comes back into the kitchen.)*—desert him I hope I don't outlive the day!

LINDA: Get out of here!

HAPPY: Now look, Mom . . .

LINDA: Did you have to go to women tonight? You and your lousy rotten whores!

(BIFF *re-enters the kitchen.)*

HAPPY: Mom, all we did was follow Biff around trying to cheer him up! *(To* BIFF) Boy, what a night you gave me!

LINDA: Get out of here, both of you, and don't come back! I don't want you tormenting him any more. Go on now, get your things together! *(to* BIFF) You can sleep in his apartment. *(She starts to pick up the flowers and stops herself.)* Pick up this stuff, I'm not your maid any more. Pick it up, you bum, you!

*(*HAPPY *turns his back to her in refusal.* BIFF *slowly moves over and gets down on his knees, picking up the flowers.)*

LINDA: You're a pair of animals! No one, not another living soul would have had 'the cruelty to walk out on that man in a restaurant!

BIFF *(not looking at her)*: Is that what he said?

LINDA: He didn't have to say anything. He was so humiliated he nearly limped when he came in.

HAPPY: But, Mom, he had a great time with us—

BIFF *(cutting him off violently)*: Shut up!

(Without another word, HAPPY *goes upstairs.)*

LINDA: You! You didn't even go in to see if he was all right!

BIFF *(still on the floor in front of* LINDA, *the flowers in his*

hand; *with self-loathing)*: No. Didn't. Didn't do a damned thing. How do you like that, heh? Left him babbling in a toilet.

LINDA: You louse. You . . .

BIFF: Now you hit it on the nose! *(He gets up, throws the flowers in the wastebasket)*. The scum of the earth, and you're looking at him!

LINDA: Get out of here!

BIFF: I gotta talk to the boss, Mom. Where is he?

LINDA: You're not going near him. Get out of this house!

BIFF *(with absolute assurance, determination)*: No. We're gonna have an abrupt conversation, him and me.

LINDA: You're not talking to him!

(Hammering is heard from outside the house, off right. BIFF *turns toward the noise.)*

LINDA *(suddenly pleading)*: Will you please leave him alone?

BIFF: What's he doing out there?

LINDA: He's planting the garden!

BIFF *(quietly)*: Now? Oh, my God!

*(*BIFF *moves outside,* LINDA *following. The light dies down on them and comes up on the center of the apron as* WILLY *walks into it. He is carrying a flashlight, a hoe, and a handful of seed packets. He raps the top of the hoe sharply to fix it firmly, and then moves to the left, measuring off the distance with his foot. He holds the flashlight to look at the seed packets, reading off the instructions. He is in the blue of night.)*

WILLY: Carrots . . . quarter-inch apart. Rows . . . one-foot rows. *(He measures it off.)* One foot. *(He puts down a package and measures off.)* Beets. *(He puts down another package and measures again.)* Lettuce. *(He reads the package, puts it down.)* One foot—*(He breaks off as* BEN *appears at the right and moves slowly down to him.)* What a proposition, ts, ts. Terrific, terrific. 'Cause she's suffered, Ben, the woman has suffered. You understand me? A man can't go out the way he came in, Ben, a man has got to add up to something. You can't, you can't— *(*BEN *moves toward him as though to interrupt.)* You gotta consider, now. Don't answer so quick. Remember, it's a guaranteed twenty-thousand-dollar proposition. Now look, Ben, I want you to go through the ins and outs of this thing with me. I've got nobody to talk to, Ben, and the woman has suffered, you hear me?

BEN *(standing still, considering)*: What's the proposition?

WILLY: It's twenty thousand dollars on the barrelhead. Guaranteed, gilt-edged, you understand?

BEN: You don't want to make a fool of yourself. They might not honor the policy.

WILLY: How can they dare refuse? Didn't I work like

a coolie to meet every premium on the nose? And now they don't pay off? Impossible!

BEN: It's called a cowardly thing, William.

WILLY: Why? Does it take more guts to stand here the rest of my life ringing up a zero?

BEN (*yielding*): That's a point, William. (*He moves, thinking, turns.*) And twenty thousand—that *is* something one can feel with the hand, it is there.

WILLY (*now assured, with rising power*): Oh, Ben, that's the whole beauty of it! I see it like a diamond, shining in the dark, hard and rough, that I can pick up and touch in my hand. Not like—like an appointment! This would not be another damned-fool appointment, Ben, and it changes all the aspects. Because he thinks I'm nothing, see, and so he spites me. But the funeral— (*Straightening up.*) Ben, that funeral will be massive! They'll come from Maine, Massachusetts, Vermont, New Hampshire! All the old-timers with the strange license plates—that boy will be thunder-struck, Ben, because he never realized—I am known! Rhode Island, New York, New Jersey—I am known, Ben, and he'll see it with his eyes once and for all. He'll see what I am, Ben! He's in for a shock, that boy!

BEN (*coming down to the edge of the garden*): He'll call you a coward.

WILLY (*suddenly fearful*): No, that would be terrible.

BEN: Yes. And a damned fool.

WILLY: No, no, he mustn't, I won't have that! (*He is broken and desperate.*)

BEN: He'll hate you, William.

(*The gay music of the* BOYS *is heard.*)

WILLY: Oh, Ben, how do we get back to all the great times? Used to be so full of light, and comradeship, the sleigh-riding in winter, and the ruddiness on his cheeks. And always some kind of good news coming up, always something nice coming up ahead. And never even let me carry the valises in the house, and simonizing, simonizing that little red car! Why, why can't I give him something and not have him hate me?

BEN: Let me think about it. (*He glances at his watch.*) I still have a little time. Remarkable proposition, but you've got to be sure you're not making a fool of yourself.

(BEN *drifts off upstage and goes out of sight.* BIFF *comes down from the left.*)

WILLY (*suddenly conscious of* BIFF, *turns and looks up at him, then begins picking up the packages of seeds in confusion*): Where the hell is that seed? (*Indignantly*) You can't see nothing out here! They boxed in the whole goddam neighborhood!

BIFF: There are people all around here. Don't you realize that?

WILLY: I'm busy. Don't bother me.

BIFF (*taking the hoe from* WILLY): I'm saying good-by to you, Pop. (WILLY *looks at him, silent, unable to move.*) I'm not coming back any more.

WILLY: You're not going to see Oliver tomorrow?

BIFF: I've got no appointment, Dad.

WILLY: He put his arm around you, and you've got no appointment?

BIFF: Pop, get this now, will you? Everytime I've left it's been a fight that sent me out of here. Today I realized something about myself and I tried to explain it to you and I—I think I'm just not smart enough to make any sense out of it for you. To hell with whose fault it is or anything like that. (*He takes* WILLY's *arm.*) Let's just wrap it up, heh? Come on in, we'll tell Mom. (*He gently tries to pull* WILLY *to left.*)

WILLY (*frozen, immobile, with guilt in his voice*): No, I don't want to see her.

BIFF: Come on! (*He pulls again, and* WILLY *tries to pull away.*)

WILLY (*highly nervous*): No, no, I don't want to face her.

BIFF (*tries to look into* WILLY's *face, as if to find the answer there*): Why don't you want to see her?

WILLY (*more harshly now*): Don't bother me, will you?

BIFF: What do you mean, you don't want to see her? You don't want them calling you yellow, do you? This isn't your fault; it's me, I'm a bum. Now come inside! (WILLY *strains to get away.*) Did you hear what I said to you?

(WILLY *pulls away and quickly goes by himself into the house.* BIFF *follows.*)

LINDA (*to* WILLY): Did you plant, dear?

BIFF (*at the door, to* LINDA): All right, we had it out. I'm going and I'm not writing any more.

LINDA (*going to* WILLY *in the kitchen*): I think that's the best way, dear. 'Cause there's no use drawing it out, you'll just never get along.

(WILLY *doesn't respond.*)

BIFF: People ask where I am and what I'm doing, you don't know, and you don't care. That way it'll be off your mind and you can start brightening up again. All right? That clears it, doesn't it? (WILLY *is silent, and* BIFF *goes to him.*) You gonna wish me luck, scout? (*He extends his hand.*) What do you say?

LINDA: Shake his hand, Willy.

WILLY (*turning to her, seething with hurt*): There's no necessity to mention the pen at all, y'know.

BIFF (*gently*): I've got no appointment, Dad.

WILLY (*erupting fiercely*): He put his arm around . . . ?

BIFF: Dad, you're never going to see what I am, so what's the use of arguing? If I strike oil I'll send you a check. Meantime forget I'm alive.

WILLY (*to* LINDA): Spite, see?

BIFF: Shake hands, Dad.

WILLY: Not my hand.

BIFF: I was hoping not to go this way.

WILLY: Well, this is the way you're going. Good-by.

(BIFF *looks at him a moment, then turns sharply and goes to the stairs.*)

WILLY (*stops him with*): May you rot in hell if you leave this house!

BIFF (*turning*): Exactly what is it that you want from me?

WILLY: I want you to know, on the train, in the mountains, in the valleys, wherever you go, that you cut down your life for spite!

BIFF: No, no.

WILLY: Spite, spite, is the word of your undoing! And when you're down and out, remember what did it. When you're rotting somewhere beside the railroad tracks, remember, and don't you dare blame it on me!

BIFF: I'm not blaming it on you!

WILLY: I won't take the rap for this, you hear?

(HAPPY *comes down the stairs and stands on the bottom step, watching.*)

BIFF: That's just what I'm telling you!

WILLY (*sinking into a chair at the table, with full accusation*): You're trying to put a knife in me—don't think I don't know what you're doing!

BIFF: All right, phony! Then let's lay it on the line. (*He whips the rubber tube out of his pocket and puts it on the table.*)

HAPPY: You crazy—

LINDA: Biff! (*She moves to grab the hose, but* BIFF *holds it down with his hand.*)

BIFF: Leave it there! Don't move it!

WILLY (*not looking at it*): What is that?

BIFF: You know goddam well what that is.

WILLY (*caged, wanting to escape*): I never saw that.

BIFF: You saw it. The mice didn't bring it into the cellar! What is this supposed to do, make a hero out of you? This supposed to make me sorry for you?

WILLY: Never heard of it.

BIFF: There'll be no pity for you, you hear it? No pity!

WILLY (*to* LINDA): You hear the spite!

BIFF: No, you're going to hear the truth—what you are and what I am!

LINDA: Stop it!

WILLY: Spite!

HAPPY (*coming down toward* BIFF): You cut it now!

BIFF (*to* HAPPY): The man don't know who we are! The man is gonna know! (*to* WILLY) We never told the truth for ten minutes in this house!

HAPPY: We always told the truth!

BIFF (*turning on him*): You big blow, are you the assistant buyer? You're one of the two assistants to the assistant, aren't you?

HAPPY: Well, I'm practically—

BIFF: You're practically full of it! We all are! And I'm through with it. (*to* WILLY) Now hear this, Willy, this is me.

WILLY: I know you!

BIFF: You know why I had no address for three months? I stole a suit in Kansas City and I was in jail. (*to* LINDA, *who is sobbing*) Stop crying. I'm through with it.

(LINDA *turns away from them, her hands covering her face.*)

WILLY: I suppose that's my fault!

BIFF: I stole myself out of every good job since high school!

WILLY: And whose fault is that?

BIFF: And I never got anywhere because you blew me so full of hot air I could never stand taking orders from anybody! That's whose fault it is!

WILLY: I hear that!

LINDA: Don't, Biff!

BIFF: It's goddam time you heard that! I had to be boss big shot in two weeks, and I'm through with it!

WILLY: Then hang yourself! For spite, hang yourself!

BIFF: No! Nobody's hanging himself, Willy! I ran down eleven flights with a pen in my hand today. And suddenly I stopped, you hear me? And in the middle of that office building, do you hear this? I stopped in the middle of that building and I saw—the sky. I saw the things that I love in this world. The work and the food and time to sit and smoke. And I looked at the pen and said to myself, what the hell am I grabbing this for? Why am I trying to become what I don't want to be? What am I doing in an office, making a contemptuous, begging fool of myself, when all I want is out there, waiting for me the minute I say I know who I am! Why can't I say that, Willy? (*He tries to make* WILLY *face him, but* WILLY *pulls away and moves to the left.*)

WILLY (*with hatred, threateningly*): The door of your life is wide open!

BIFF: Pop! I'm a dime a dozen, and so are you!

WILLY (*turning on him now in an uncontrolled outburst*): I am not a dime a dozen! I am Willy Loman and you are Biff Loman!

(BIFF *starts for* WILLY, *but is blocked by* HAPPY. *In his fury,* BIFF *seems on the verge of attacking his father.*)

BIFF: I am not a leader of men, Willy, and neither are you. You were never anything but a hardworking drummer who landed in the ash can like all the rest of them! I'm one dollar an hour, Willy! I tried seven states and couldn't raise it. A buck an hour! Do you gather my meaning? I'm not bringing home any prizes any more, and you're going to stop waiting for me to bring them home!

WILLY (*directly to* BIFF): You vengeful, spiteful mut!

(BIFF *breaks from* HAPPY. WILLY, *in fright, starts up the stairs.* BIFF *grabs him.*)

BIFF (*at the peak of his fury*): Pop, I'm nothing! I'm nothing, Pop. Can't you understand that? There's no spite in it any more. I'm just what I am, that's all.

(BIFF's *fury has spent itself, and he breaks down, sobbing, holding on to* WILLY, *who dumbly fumbles for* BIFF's *face.*)

WILLY (*astonished*): What're you doing? What're you doing? (*to* LINDA) Why is he crying?

BIFF (*crying, broken*): Will you let me go, for Christ's sake? Will you take that phony dream and burn it before something happens? (*Struggling to contain himself, he pulls away and moves to the stairs.*) I'll go in the morning. Put him—put him to bed. (*Exhausted,* BIFF *moves up the stairs to his room.*)

WILLY (*after a long pause, astonished, elevated*): Isn't that—isn't that remarkable? Biff—he likes me!

LINDA: He loves you, Willy!

HAPPY (*deeply moved*): Always did, Pop.

WILLY: Oh, Biff! (*Staring wildly.*) He cried! Cried to me. (*He is choking with his love, and now cries out his promise.*) That boy—that boy is going to be magnificent!

(BEN *appears in the light just outside the kitchen.*)

BEN: Yes, outstanding, with twenty thousand behind him.

LINDA (*sensing the racing of his mind, fearfully, carefully*): Now come to bed, Willy. It's all settled now.

WILLY (*finding it difficult not to rush out of the house*): Yes, we'll sleep. Come on. go to sleep, Hap.

BEN: And it does take a great kind of a man to crack the jungle.

(*In accents of dread,* BEN's *idyllic music starts up.*)

HAPPY (*his arm around* LINDA): I'm getting married, Pop, don't forget it. I'm changing everything. I'm gonna run that department before the year is up. You'll see, Mom. (*He kisses her.*)

BEN: The jungle is dark but full of diamonds, Willy.

(WILLY *turns, moves, listening to* BEN.)

LINDA: Be good. You're both good boys, just act that way, that's all.

HAPPY: 'Night, Pop. (*He goes upstairs.*)

LINDA (*to* WILLY): Come, dear.

BEN (*with greater force*): One must go in to fetch a diamond out.

WILLY (*to* LINDA, *as he moves slowly along the edge of the kitchen, toward the door*): I just want to get settled down, Linda. Let me sit alone for a little.

LINDA (*almost uttering her fear*): I want you upstairs.

WILLY (*taking her in his arms*): In a few minutes, Linda. I couldn't sleep right now. Go on, you look awful tired. (*He kisses her.*)

BEN: Not like an appointment at all. A diamond is rough and hard to the touch.

WILLY: Go on now. I'll be right up.

LINDA: I think this is the only way, Willy.

WILLY: Sure, it's the best thing.

BEN: Best thing!

WILLY: The only way. Everything is gonna be—go on, kid, go to bed. You look so tired.

LINDA: Come right up.

WILLY: Two minutes.

(LINDA *goes into the living-room, then reappears in her bedroom.* WILLY *moves just outside the kitchen door.*)

WILLY: Loves me. (*Wonderingly.*) Always loved me. Isn't that a remarkable thing? Ben, he'll worship me for it!

BEN (*with promise*): It's dark there, but full of diamonds.

WILLY: Can you imagine that magnificence with twenty thousand dollars in his pocket?

LINDA (*calling from her room*): Willy! Come up!

WILLY (*calling into the kitchen*): Yes! Yes. Coming! It's very smart, you realize that, don't you sweetheart? Even Ben sees it. I gotta go, baby. 'By! 'By! (*Going over to* BEN, *almost dancing*) Imagine? When the mail comes he'll be ahead of Bernard again!

BEN: A perfect proposition all around.

WILLY: Did you see how he cried to me? Oh, if I could kiss him, Ben!

BEN: Time, William, time!

WILLY: Oh, Ben, I always knew one way or another we were gonna make it, Biff and I!

BEN (*looking at his watch*): The boat. We'll be late. (*He moves slowly off into the darkness.*)

WILLY (*elegiacally, turning to the house*): Now when you kick off, boy, I want a seventy-yard boot, and get right down the field under the ball, and when you hit, hit low and hit hard, because it's important, boy. (*He swings around and faces the audience.*) There's all kinds of important people in the stands, and the first thing you know . . .(*Suddenly realizing he is alone.*) Ben! Ben, where do I . . . ? (*He makes a sudden movement of search.*) Ben, how do I . . . ?

LINDA (*calling*): Willy, you coming up?

WILLY (*uttering a gasp of fear, whirling about as if to quiet her*): Sh! (*He turns around as if to find his way; sounds, faces, voices, seem to be swarming in upon him and he flicks at them, crying.*) Sh! Sh! (*Suddenly *music, faint and high, stops him. It rises in intensity, almost to an unbearable scream. He goes up and down on his toes, and rushes off around the house.)* Shhh!

LINDA: Willy?

(There is no answer. LINDA waits. BIFF gets up off his bed. He is still in his clothes. HAPPY sits up. BIFF stands listening.)

LINDA *(with real fear)*: Willy, answer me! Willy!

(There is the sound of a car starting and moving away at full speed.)

LINDA: No!

BIFF *(rushing down the stairs)*: Pop!

(As the car speeds off, the music crashes down in a frenzy of sound, which becomes the soft pulsation of a single cello string. BIFF slowly returns to his bedroom. He and HAPPY gravely don their jackets. LINDA slowly walks out of her room. The music has developed into a dead march. The leaves of day are appearing over everything. CHARLEY and BERNARD, somberly dressed, appear and knock on the kitchen door. BIFF and HAPPY slowly descend the stairs to the kitchen as CHARLEY and BERNARD enter. All stop a moment when LINDA, in clothes of mourning, bearing a little bunch of roses, comes through the draped doorway into the kitchen. She goes to CHARLEY and takes his arm. Now all move toward the audience, through the wall-line of the kitchen. At the limit of the apron, LINDA lays down the flowers, kneels, and sits back on her heels. All stare down at the grave.)

REQUIEM

CHARLEY: It's getting dark, Linda.

(LINDA doesn't react. She stares at the grave.)

BIFF: How about it, Mom? Better get some rest, heh? They'll be closing the gate soon.

(LINDA makes no move. Pause.)

HAPPY *(deeply angered)*: He had no right to do that. There was no necessity for it. We would've helped him.

CHARLEY *(grunting)*: Hmmm.

BIFF: Come along, Mom.

LINDA: Why didn't anybody come?

CHARLEY: It was a very nice funeral.

LINDA: But where are all the people he knew? Maybe they blame him.

CHARLEY: Naa. It's a rough world, Linda. They wouldn't blame him.

LINDA: I can't understand it. At this time especially. First time in thirty-five years we were just about free and clear. He only needed a little salary. He was even finished with the dentist.

CHARLEY: No man only needs a little salary.

LINDA: I can't understand it.

BIFF: There were a lot of nice days. When he'd come home from a trip; or on Sundays, making the stoop; finishing the cellar; putting on the new porch; when he built the extra bathroom; and put up the garage. You know something, Charley, there's more of him in that front stoop than in all the sales he ever made.

CHARLEY: Yeah. He was a happy man with a batch of cement.

LINDA: He was so wonderful with his hands.

BIFF: He had the wrong dreams. All, all, wrong.

HAPPY *(almost ready to fight BIFF)*: Don't say that!

BIFF: He never knew who he was.

CHARLEY *(stopping HAPPY's movement and reply. To BIFF)*: Nobody dast blame this man. You don't understand: Willy was a salesman. And for a salesman, there is no rock bottom to the life. He don't put a bolt to a nut, he don't tell you the law or give you medicine. He's a man way out there in the blue, riding on a smile and a shoeshine. And when they start not smiling back—that's an earthquake. And then you get yourself a couple of spots on your hat, and you're finished. Nobody dast blame this man. A salesman is got to dream, boy. It comes with the territory.

BIFF: Charley, the man didn't know who he was.

HAPPY *(infuriated)*: Don't say that!

BIFF: Why don't you come with me, Happy?

HAPPY: I'm not licked that easily. I'm staying right in this city and I'm gonna beat this racket! *(He looks at BIFF, his chin set.)* The Loman Brothers!

BIFF: I know who I am, kid.

HAPPY: All right, boy. I'm gonna show you and everybody else that Willy Loman did not die in vain. He had a good dream. It's the only dream you can have—to come out number-one man. He fought it out here, and this is where I'm gonna win it for him.

BIFF *(with a hopeless glance at HAPPY, bends toward his mother)*: Let's go, Mom.

LINDA: I'll be with you in a minute. Go on, Charley. *(He hesitates.)* I want to, just for a minute. I never had a chance to say good-by.

(CHARLEY moves away, followed by HAPPY. BIFF remains a slight distance up and left of LINDA. She sits there, summoning herself. The flute begins, not far away, playing behind her speech.)

LINDA: Forgive me, dear, I can't cry. I don't know what it is, but I can't cry. I don't understand it. Why did you ever do that? Help me, Willy, I can't cry. It seems to me that you're just on another trip. I keep expecting you. Willy, dear, I can't cry. Why did you do it? I search and search and I search, and I can't understand it, Willy. I made the last payment on the house today. To-day, dear. And there'll be nobody home. *(A sob rises in her throat.*) We're free and clear. (*Sobbing more fully, released.*) We're free. (BIFF *comes slowly toward her.*) We're free . . . We're free . . .

(BIFF *lifts her to her feet and moves out up right with her in his arms.* LINDA *sobs quietly.* BERNARD *and* CHARLEY *come together and follow them, followed by* HAPPY. *Only the music of the flute is left on the darkening stage as over the house the hard towers of the apartment buildings rise into sharp focus, and*

THE CURTAIN FALLS

Figure 83. Willy (George C. Scott) leans against the refrigerator shortly after returning home from his trip to Yonkers at the opening of Circle in the Square production of *Death of a Salesman,* directed by George C. Scott, New York, 1975. (Photograph: Inge Morath, Magnum Photos, Inc.)

Figure 84. Willy (George C. Scott), during the enactment of a pleasant memory, tells Young Happy *(left)* and Young Biff *(right)* to help their mother Linda (Teresa Wright) carry up the wash in the Circle in the Square production of *Death of a Salesman,* directed by George C. Scott, New York, 1975. (Photograh: Inge Morath, Magnum Photos, Inc.)

Figure 85. Willy (George C. Scott), during the enactment of a painful memory, tries to explain away the presence of The Woman with whom he has been discovered by Biff (James Farentino) in the Circle in the Square production of *Death of a Salesman,* directed by George C. Scott, New York, 1975. (Photograph: Inge Morath, Magnum Photos, Inc.)

Staging of *Death of a Salesman*

**REVIEW OF THE CIRCLE IN THE SQUARE
PRODUCTION, 1975, BY WALTER KERR**

Attention has been paid. In reviving Arthur Miller's "Death of a Salesman" at Circle in the Square, and in taking on the part of the self-doomed but perpetually incurable Willy Loman himself, director-star George C. Scott has first of all behaved not as director or as star but as servant of a play, a piece of work in the hand. Furthermore, he has not behaved as though he were serving an old play, a familiar play, a play whose ancient echoes were so overwhelming that a kind of fearful obeisance was the best that could be offered it. He has chosen not to remember it, or to remember other people's remembrances of it, but to pay attention to its undeniably powerful, still most affecting, but extraordinarily ambiguous voice. Not what Elia Kazan once heard in it, not what Lee J. Cobb once heard in it, perceptive and just as they may have been. But, with one sharp ear cocked, what is it saying *now*?

This is not simply a matter of muting the lines we recall all too well. Mr. Scott has a fascinating trick—it is more than a trick, it is a heart-rending trait of character—of burying a phrase like "He's liked, but he's not well liked" by making it part of a compulsive contradiction, hurling it so hot on the heels of the contrary line preceding it that you must take the two in balance and believe neither. Listen to him, without transition, pause, or apparent dishonesty, breathlessly bracketing "I'm very well liked, the only thing is people don't take to me" and making both sense and agony of it. Or, glorying in his talent for regaling his New England buyers. "I'm full of jokes, I tell too many jokes," with the savagery of the latter seeming to bite off his own braggart head.

There is much savagery in Mr. Scott's performance—he comes on like the last bald American eagle dead set for a final reckoning—but it is more than the quite normal savagery of his customary stage deportment, it is a savagery uncovered in the near-manic, electrifying shifts of mood, boast and bile back to back, of Arthur Miller's play. And it completely disrupts my *own* (perhaps faulty) memory of the original production, its original meaning. I remember assuming that Willy Loman had once been a successful salesman, had once done well by his wife and boys, had once made "a smile and a shoeshine" work for him. That the dream (the American dream of success by back-slapping and coming in Number One on all sales charts?) had eventually collapsed of its own essential vacuousness was the pathos of the moment, but the pathos of the moment was a somewhat recent discovery, a realization, not a permanence recognized from the beginning.

With Mr. Scott it is certainly otherwise. Quite apart from absorbing the catch-phrases by which we identify the play into a relentless, run-on "yes-no" that is Willy Loman's never-ending private torment, Mr. Scott makes us hear lines we seem never to have heard before. He is speaking to his outrageously successful brother, Ben, despoiler of the Gold Coast, reaper of fabulous Alaskan harvests. Ben is older than Willie, got started sooner than Willy. Ben even remembers their father, a man who played a flute as he carted the family from state to state across the American landscape.

But the father died before Willy could quite know him, or know himself in relation to any father. "I still feel a little *temporary* about myself," he says, reflectively, with unconscious grief, to the solid, if almost mythical, brother who never felt temporary about anything. Mr. Scott's Willy always had to compensate, to inflate his indeterminate place in the scheme of things, to substitute for his sickened hollowness an equally hollow image in which only others—only his adoring sons—could possibly believe. He has been a shell from the beginning, filling himself with borrowed life, life that could be borrowed from successful salesmen he admired, life that might be borrowed—on a kind of promissory note—from the coming success of his two boys.

This becomes stunningly clear in a scene almost impossible to contemplate, given Mr. Scott's intensely mesmerizing presence. Willy is to recall a day, early in his career, when he listened to a salesman, an 84-year-old master-drummer, in his room at the Parker House, making an ample, indestructible living by doing nothing more than reach for a phone and run up orders by the dozen. He must make us believe that this one eavesdropping image of success has given him his goal in life, a self-image strong enough to sustain him. And he must do it while the man he is talking to, an employer about to fire him now that he is an exhausted 62, is paying no heed at all, incapable of being moved by anything he says.

To begin with, it is unthinkable that anyone within Mr. Scott's feverish, concentrated range should not listen to him. And if we can bring ourselves to believe that the man is not listening, then why should we listen? The essence of the sequence is the deaf dismissal of Mr. Scott's dreams. And yet it happens both ways, creating stage magic of the highest order. Our own absorption in Mr. Scott's passionate recollection of things past is total: we see everything he sees, the room's furnishings, the drummer's posture, the waves of power reaching out to envelope Mr. Scott. At the same time the actor is able to distance himself from his indifferent employer, to isolate himself with *us,* to the point where we hear what no one else can hear, share what no one else can share. The doubleness is devastating; I still don't believe it.

And, at the same time Mr. Scott is alternately drawing his teeth across his lower lip and lifting the corners of his mouth in a mirthless but expansive smile, abruptly shifting from snarl to endearment, Teresa Wright, as his wife, is creating the perfect complement to his instability. Face severely in repose, voice rarely raised, she is both patient and rock-hard in her steadfast coping with home truths. She is not deceived, not even by love. But she does love. And her love has the toughness that will tolerate neither lies nor laments from her failed children.

Their father is an ordinary man; they are to find no blame in him for that. Ordinary men become exhausted as surely as great men do; the exhaustion is just as real, no guilt is to be lodged against it. She has heard her husband letting himself in by night beneath the naked bulb over the back door, sigh as he dropped his satchels, greet her encouragingly, explosively betray his own chagrin in sudden envy of men who have "accomplished something." She knows he has accomplished nothing, hadn't an identity to do it with. The boys are not to say so. "Attention must be paid" to ordinary men, exhausted or not. There is no rhetoric in Miss Wright as she speaks the words, no lumpy quasi-poetry. She is speaking a harsh truth, harshly. Let the boys be "bums," if that is what they are to be. And let them honor their father, who would have honored them if he had only known how. If we are to shed tears, and we do, they fall on granite.

Between Mr. Scott and the superb Miss Wright, "Death of a Salesman" becomes a play of persons, not of social prophecy or some archetypal proclamation of an already failed American myth. It is too richly contradictory, too intimately detailed, too ambiguously loving and desperate, for mere abstraction; its weaknesses and its toughnesses are tangible, not distantly theoretical. If the work now seems tantalizing in its implications, the implications are more nearly those that endlessly badgered O'Neill: it is illusions that destroy. "We never told the truth for one minute in this house" is a cry near the end in a house that cannot stand; to the last, Willy Loman is imagining that, somehow or other, the $20,000 in insurance money that will come with his death will guarantee the successful future of his elder, equally emptied-out son. Death goes right on dreaming.

Mr. Miller's play holds, contains its own complex meaning that is beyond facile ideological analysis, lives and moves and has its being in the mercury of its ravaged, hoping, falsely jovial, forgiving, unforgiving figures. At the preview I saw, the evening's momentum was interrupted at least once, possibly due to an errant light cue; and because the act-endings are insufficiently italicized, I think the production might profit from having a single intermission rather than two, though that may be demanding something too much of Mr. Scott's unhusbanded energies. But the whole is handsomely acted—James Farentino, Harvey Keitel, and Chuck Patterson are particularly fine—and Mr. Scott's staging is as restlessly right as his performance; he is endlessly on his feet though he knows that his feet will betray him before they can ever see him home.

TENNESSEE WILLIAMS

1911–

Despite his first name, a nickname he adopted during his college days, Williams was born in Mississippi and lived there until 1918, when his father, a travelling salesman, was promoted to an office in St. Louis. That move to the midwest, according to Williams, was a "tragic" experience. He was mocked for his southern accent, he was pained by the heightened awareness of being poor, and thus he never adjusted to life in St. Louis. Looking back on his childhood there, Williams once described it as "the beginning of the social consciousness which I think has marked most of my writing." Williams lived in St. Louis until his mid-twenties, and those years with his family—with his tyrannical father, his overprotective mother, and his mentally withdrawn sister—evidently gave rise to the acute psychological awareness that has also marked virtually all of his writing. Those years with his family in St. Louis certainly must have given rise to his abiding concern with the painful experience of the outsider: the artist, the dreamer, the physically crippled, the mentally disturbed, and the sexually driven. As a child, he had been afflicted by diptheria, which for many years left him with paralyzed legs and weakened kidneys. As a teenager, he suffered the taunts of his father who repeatedly called him "Miss Nancy" because of his literary inclinations. In his mid-twenties, he worked himself into a nervous and physical breakdown, selling shoes during the day at his father's insistence and writing plays late into the night to escape his miserable existence. During this time he also witnessed the permanent mental breakdown of his introverted sister, with whom he had been close throughout his years in Mississippi and St. Louis.

These painful experiences of his childhood and youth clearly provided Williams with material for his first major stage success, *The Glass Menagerie* (1944), "a memory play," whose protagonist-narrator, Tom Wingfield is clearly modelled on Williams himself, much as Laura Wingfield is modelled on Williams' sister Rose. Tom, for example, is portrayed as a poet and dreamer, yearning for escape from the suffocating world of business, while Laura is depicted as a pathologically shy young woman who lives in a private world of glass animals and old phonograph records. Indeed, it might well be said that Williams has reflected the personality and disposition of his father, or his mother, or his sister, or himself in virtually all his work. His father's personality is echoed in the cynically practical and coarsely domineering men who often figure prominently in his plays, such as Stanley Kowalski of *A Streetcar Named Desire* (1947) or Big Daddy in *Cat on a Hot Tin Roof* (1955). His mother is echoed in the long-suffering women who patiently endure the afflictions of being married to these domineering characters, such as Stella Kowalski or Big Mama. His sister is echoed in psychologically fragile women who have retreated from life, such as Blanche, a faded southern "gentlewoman," who clings desperately to the memory of her lost plantation in *A Streetcar Named Desire,* or Alma, the virginal spinster in *Summer and Smoke* (1948), or Hannah Jelkes, the "ethereal, almost ghostly" figure in *The Night of the Iguana* (1961). And Williams has echoed himself in all his artists, and poets, and dreamers—men and women characters alike—who suffer from the brutality of the coarsely practical worlds they inhabit.

But Williams has by no means limited himself to characters modelled on his own family, as is evident simply from all the lusty and vigorous women who figure in his plays, such as Serafina in *The Rose Tatoo* (1950), or Maxine Faulk in *The Night of the Iguana,* or Maggie in *Cat on a Hot Tin Roof.* Indeed, it would be mistaken to regard Williams as a strictly autobiographical dramatist, for he has repeatedly transformed his personal experience so that his characters, while echoing aspects of his family, are by no means exactly like them at all. And the aspects that Williams has chosen to echo are occasioned by his persistent concern with the experience of the outsider in modern society, and with the implications of that experience as it is manifest in human loneliness, in the inability of human beings to communicate with one another, and in the irrepressible need to create illusions through which they can escape from the loneliness and painfulness of their existence.

In dramatizing these aspects of experience, Williams has never been content to settle for a strictly realistic method of presentation. In his "Production Notes" to *The Glass Menagerie,* for example, he attacked "the straight realistic play with its genuine frigidaire and authentic ice-cubes" by comparing it to a mere "photographic likeness," which he considered inadequate to convey the truth of human experience. To bring the audience closer to the truth, Williams argued in favor of "expressionism and all other unconventional techniques in drama." In *The Glass Menagerie* he relied heavily on suggestive music, lighting, and pantomime to evoke the memories of Tom Wingfield. His notes to the play reveal that he intended even to convey comments on Tom's staged memories through the device of projecting images or phrases on a screen—a device from the epic theater of Brecht. Although Williams agreed to omitting the screen device in the original production of the play, he has persisted in using other techniques of expressionistic theater to evoke the mood and quality of his characters' experience. In his "Notes for the Designer" at the beginning of *Cat on a Hot Tin Roof,* Williams clearly blends realistic and expressionistic approaches by describing the stage furniture in meticulous detail and then concluding with the direction that "the walls below the ceiling should dissolve mysteriously into air." He even turns the furniture into a form of symbolic statement by noting that Brick's "*huge* console combination of radio-phonograph (hi-fi with three speakers) TV set *and* liquor cabinet . . . is a very complete and compact little shrine to virtually all the comforts and illusions behind which we hide from such things as the characters in the play are faced with".

The entire set for *Cat on a Hot Tin Roof*—the bedroom of Brick and Maggie—is a richly symbolic location, for the "big double bed" that it contains tangibly reflects the frustrating relationship of Maggie and Brick, and the bedroom as a whole evokes the problematic relationship of Skipper and Brick through the memories it contains of its original owners, "a pair of old bachelors who shared this room all their lives together." In fact, the image of the bedroom and all that it begets—or fails to beget—is a central concern for everyone in the play, for Big Daddy and Big Mama, for Gooper and Mae alike. It is thus highly appropriate that all the struggles within the family take place within this haunting room.

Despite its frankly suggestive set, when the play opened, the critic Walter Kerr called it "a beautifully written, perfectly directed, stunningly acted play of evasion: evasion on the part of its principal character, evasion perhaps on the part of its playwright." He was referring, of course, to the play's persistent concern with the relationship of Brick and Skipper, the exact nature of which is never clearly established. Williams knew that the relationship would raise questions as to whether or not it was homosexual, and thus he took the unusual step of inserting an interpretative comment into the middle of the play:

> The bird that I hope to catch in the net of this play is not the solution of one man's psychological problem. I'm trying to catch the true quality of experience in a group of people, that cloudy, flickering, evanescent—fiercely charged!—interplay of live human beings in the thundercloud of a common crisis. Some mystery should be left in the revelation of character in a play, just as a great deal of mystery is always left in the revelation of character in life, even in one's own character to himself. This does not absolve the playwright of his duty to observe and probe as clearly and deeply as he legitimately can: but it should steer him away from "pat" conclusions, facile definitions which make a play just a play, not a snare for the truth of human experience.

In making such remarks, Williams was clearly directing his readers away from focussing on the question of Brick's relationship with Skipper to the more important issue that concerns Brick himself: the issue of "mendacity," which is evidently also the major concern of Williams. Everyone in the play is guilty of mendacity—of lying, betrayal, and manipulation. And the lies persist only because Big Daddy and Big Mama want to believe them, a condition that suggests the root of public lying is the act of lying to oneself. Williams' concern with the wilful perpetuation of illusions is reflected also in the structure of the play, for the first act centers on Maggie trying to get Brick to look at her, while the second act reaches its climax with Big Daddy forcing Brick to look at himself, and the third act derives its power from Brick's final refusal to let Maggie sustain any illusions about him.

Because all the characters in the play are so determinedly bent on their ways, yet so undone by the ways they have chosen for themselves, they require very complex performances from actors and actresses—performances that convey both their wilfulness and their vulnerability. These qualities were evidently achieved by the American Shakespeare Theater when it revived the play in 1974, as can be seen from a review of that production reprinted following the text. Photographs from that production convey the sensuality and the helplessness Elizabeth Ashley brought to the role of Maggie (see Figure 86), much as they reveal the obstinancy and the air of defeat Keir Dullea gave to the role of Brick (see Figures 86 and 87). They also show the blustery power of Fred Gwynne in the role of Big Daddy (see Figures 88 and 89). Although weakened by disease, that power is still seen in the play as being great enough to hobble virtually everyone in his world.

CAT ON A HOT TIN ROOF

BY TENNESSEE WILLIAMS

CHARACTERS

MARGARET

BRICK

MAE, *sometimes called* SISTER WOMAN

BIG MAMA

DIXIE, *a little girl*

BIG DADDY

REVEREND TOOKER

GOOPER, *sometimes called* BROTHER MAN

DOCTOR BAUGH, *pronounced "Baw"*

LACEY, *a Negro servant*

SOOKEY, *another*

CHILDREN

NOTES FOR THE DESIGNER

The set is the bed-sitting room of a plantation home in the Mississippi Delta. It is along an upstairs gallery which probably runs around the entire house; it has two pairs of very wide doors opening onto the gallery, showing white balustrades against a fair summer sky that fades into dusk and night during the course of the play, which occupies precisely the time of its performance, excepting, of course, the fifteen minutes of intermission.

Perhaps the style of the room is not what you would expect in the home of the Delta's biggest cotton-planter. It is Victorian with a touch of the Far East. It hasn't changed much since it was occupied by the original owners of the place, Jack Straw and Peter Ochello, a pair of old bachelors who shared this room all their lives together. In other words, the room must evoke some ghosts; it is gently and poetically haunted by a relationship that must have involved a tenderness which was uncommon. This may be irrelevant or unnecessary, but I once saw a reproduction of a faded photograph of the verandah of Robert Louis Stevenson's home on that Samoan Island where he spent his last years, and there was a quality of tender light on weathered wood, such as porch furniture made of bamboo and wicker, exposed to tropical suns and tropical rains, which came to mind when I thought about the set for this play, bringing also to mind the grace and comfort of light, the reassurance it gives, on a late and fair afternoon in summer, the way that no matter what, even dread of death, is gently touched and soothed by it. For the set is the background for a play that deals with human extremities of emotion, and it needs that softness behind it.

The bathroom door, showing only pale-blue tile and silver towel racks, is in one side wall; the hall door in the opposite wall. Two articles of furniture need mention: a big double bed which staging should make a functional part of the set as often as suitable, the surface of which should be slightly raked to make figures on it seen more easily; and against the wall space between the two huge double doors upstage: a monumental monstrosity peculiar to our times, a huge console combination of radio-phonograph (hi-fi with three speakers) TV set and liquor cabinet, bearing and containing many glasses and bottles, all in one piece, which is a combination of muted silver tones, and the opalescent tones of reflecting glass, a chromatic link, this thing, between the sepia (tawny gold) tones of the interior and the cool (white and blue) tones of the gallery and sky. This piece of furniture (?!), this monument, is a very complete and compact little shrine to virtually all the comforts and illusions behind which we hide from such things as the characters in the play are faced with.

The set should be far less realistic than I have so far implied in this description of it. I think the walls below the ceiling should dissolve mysteriously into air; the set should be roofed by the sky; stars and moon suggested by traces of milky pallor, as if they were observed through a telescope lens out of focus.

Anything else I can think of? Oh, yes, fanlights (transoms shaped like an open glass fan) above all the doors in the set, with panes of blue and amber, and above all, the designer should take as many pains to give the actors room to move about freely (to show their restlessness, their passion for breaking out) as if it were a set for a ballet.

An evening in summer. The action is continuous, with two intermissions.

ACT 1

(At the rise of the curtain someone is taking a shower in the bathroom, the door of which is half open. A pretty young woman, with anxious lines in her face, enters the bedroom and crosses to the bathroom door.)

MARGARET *(shouting above roar of water)*: One of those no-neck monsters hit me with a hot buttered biscuit so I have t' change!

(MARGARET's voice is both rapid and drawling. In her long speeches she has the vocal tricks of a priest delivering a liturgical chant, the lines are almost sung, always continuing a little beyond her breath so she has to gasp for another. Sometimes she intersperses the lines with a little wordless singing, such as "da-da-daaa!")

(Water turns off and BRICK calls out to her, but is still unseen. A tone of politely feigned interest, masking indifference, or worse, is characteristic of his speech with MARGARET.)

BRICK: Wha'd you say, Maggie? Water was on s' loud I couldn't hearya. . . .

MARGARET: Well, I!—just remarked that!—one of th' no-neck monsters messed up m' lovely lace dress so I got t'—cha-a-ange. . . . (She opens and kicks shut drawers of the dresser.)

BRICK: Why d'ya call Gooper's kiddies no-neck monsters?

MARGARET: Because they've got no necks! Isn't that a good enough reason?

BRICK: Don't they have any necks?

MARGARET: None visible. Their fat little heads are set on their fat little bodies without a bit of connection.

BRICK: That's too bad.

MARGARET: Yes, it's too bad because you can't wring their necks if they've got no necks to wring! Isn't that right, honey? (She steps out of her dress, stands in a slip of ivory satin and lace.) Yep, they're no-neck monsters, all no-neck people are monsters . . .

(Children shriek downstairs.)

Hear them? Hear them screaming? I don't know where their voice boxes are located since they don't have necks. I tell you I got so nervous at that table tonight I thought I would throw back my head and utter a scream you could hear across the Arkansas border an' parts of Louisiana an' Tennessee. I said to your charming sister-in-law, Mae, honey, couldn't you feed those precious little things at a separate table with an oilcloth cover? They make such a mess an' the lace cloth looks *so* pretty! She made enormous eyes at me and said, "Ohhh, noooooo! On Big Daddy's birthday? Why, he would never forgive me!" Well, I want you to know, Big Daddy hadn't been at the table two minutes with those five no-neck monsters slobbering and drooling over their food before he threw down his fork an' shouted, "Fo' God's sake, Gooper, why don't you put them pigs at a trough in th' kitchen?"—Well, I swear, I simply could have di-ieed!

Think of it, Brick, they've got five of them and number six is coming. They've brought the whole bunch down here like animals to display at a county fair. Why, they have those children doin' tricks all the time! "Junior, show Big Daddy how you do this, show Big Daddy how you do that, say your little piece fo' Big Daddy, Sister. Show your dimples, Sugar. Brother, show Big Daddy how you stand on your head!"—It goes on all the time, along with constant little remarks and innuendos about the fact that you and I have not produced any children, are totally childless and therefore totally useless!—Of course it's comical but it's also disgusting since it's so obvious what they're up to!

BRICK (without interest): What are they up to, Maggie?

MARGARET: Why, you know what they're up to!

BRICK (appearing): No, I don't know what they're up to.

(He stands there in the bathroom doorway drying his hair with a towel and hanging onto the towel rack because one ankle is broken, plastered and bound. He is still slim and firm as a boy. His liquor hasn't started tearing him down outside. He has the additional charm of that cool air of detachment that people have who have given up the struggle. But now and then, when disturbed, something flashes behind it, like lightning in a fair sky, which shows that at some deeper level he is far from peaceful. Perhaps in a stronger light he would show some signs of deliquescence, but the fading, still warm, light from the gallery treats him gently.)

MARGARET: I'll tell you what they're up to, boy of mine!—They're up to cutting you out of your father's estate, and—

(She freezes momentarily before her next remark. Her voice drops as if it were somehow a personally embarrassing admission.)

—Now we know that Big Daddy's dyin' of—cancer. . . .

(There are voices on the lawn below: long-drawn calls across distance. MARGARET raises her lovely bare arms and powders her armpits with a light sigh.)

(She adjusts the angle of a magnifying mirror to straighten an eyelash, then rises fretfully saying.)

There's so much light in the room it—

BRICK (softly but sharply): Do we?

MARGARET: Do we what?

BRICK: Know Big Daddy's dyin' of cancer?

MARGARET: Got the report today.

BRICK: Oh . . .

MARGARET (letting down bamboo blinds which cast long, gold-fretted shadows over the room): Yep, got th' report just now . . . it didn't surprise me, Baby. . . .

(Her voice has range, and music; sometimes it drops low as a boy's and you have a sudden image of her playing boy's games as a child.)

I recognized the symptoms soon's we got here last spring, and I'm willin' to bet you that Brother Man and his wife were pretty sure of it, too. That more than likely explains why their usual summer migration to the coolness of the Great Smokies was passed up this summer in favor of—hustlin' down here ev'ry whipstitch with their whole screamin' tribe! And why so many allusions have been made to Rainbow Hill lately. You know what Rainbow Hill is? Place that's famous for treatin' alcoholics an' dope fiends in the movies!

BRICK: I'm not in the movies.

MARGARET: No, and you don't take dope. Otherwise you're a perfect candidate for Rainbow Hill, Baby, and that's where they aim to ship you—over my dead body! Yep, over my dead body they'll ship you there, but nothing would please them better. Then Brother Man could get a-hold of the purse strings and dole out remittances to us, maybe get power of attorney and sign checks for us and cut off our credit wherever, whenever he wanted! Son-of-a-bitch! How'd you like that, Baby?—Well, you've been doin' just about ev'rything in your power to bring it about, you've just been doin' ev'rything you can think of to aid and abet them in this scheme of theirs! Quittin' work, devoting yourself to the occupation of drinkin'!—Breakin' your ankle last night on the high school athletic field: doin' what? Jumpin' hurdles? At two or three in the morning? Just fantastic! Got in the paper. *Clarksdale Register* carried a nice little item about it, human interest story about a well-known former athlete stagin' a one-man track meet on the Glorious Hill High School athletic field last night, but was slightly out of condition and didn't clear the first hurdle! Brother Man Gooper claims he exercised his influence t' keep it from goin' out over AP or UP or every goddam "P."

But, Brick? You still have one big advantage!

(*During the above swift flood of words,* BRICK *has reclined with contrapuntal leisure on the snowy surface of the bed and has rolled over carefully on his side or belly.*)

BRICK (*wryly*): Did you *say* something, Maggie?

MARGARET: Big Daddy dotes on you, honey. And he can't stand Brother Man and Brother Man's wife, that monster of fertility, Mae. Know how I know? By little expressions that flicker over his face when that woman is holding fo'th on one of her choice topics such as—how she refused twilight sleep!—when the twins were delivered! Because she feels motherhood's an experience that a woman ought to experience fully!—in order to fully appreciate the wonder and beauty of it! HAH!—and how she made Brother Man come in an' stand beside her in the delivery room so he would not miss out on the "wonder and beauty" of it either!—producin' those no-neck monsters. . . .

(*A speech of this kind would be antipathetic from almost anybody but* MARGARET; *she makes it oddly funny, because her eyes constantly twinkle and her voice shakes with laughter which is basically indulgent.*)

—Big Daddy shares my attitude toward those

two! As for me, well—I give him a laugh now and then and he tolerates me. In fact!—I sometimes suspect that Big Daddy harbors a little unconscious "lech" fo' me. . . .

BRICK: What makes you think that Big Daddy has a lech for you, Maggie?

MARGARET: Way he always drops his eyes down my body when I'm talkin' to him, drops his eyes to my boobs and licks his old chops! Ha ha!

BRICK: That kind of talk is disgusting.

MARGARET: Did anyone ever tell you that you're an ass-aching Puritan, Brick?

I think it's mighty fine that that ole fellow, on the doorstep of death, still takes in my shape with what I think is deserved appreciation!

And you wanta know something else? Big Daddy didn't know how many little Maes and Goopers had been produced! "How many kids have you got?" he asked at the table, just like Brother Man and his wife were new acquaintances to him! Big Mama said he was jokin', but that ole boy wasn't jokin', Lord, no!

And when they infawmed him that they had five already and were turning out number six!—the news seemed to come as a sort of unpleasant surprise . . .

(*Children yell below.*)

Scream, monsters!

(*Turns to* BRICK *with a sudden, gay, charming smile which fades as she notices that he is not looking at her but into fading gold space with a troubled expression.*)
(*It is constant rejection that makes her humor "bitchy."*)

Yes, you should of been at that supper-table, Baby.

(*Whenever she calls him "baby" the word is a soft caress.*)

Y'know, Big Daddy, bless his ole sweet soul, he's the dearest ole thing in the world, but he does hunch over his food as if he preferred not to notice anything else. Well, Mae an' Gooper were side by side at the table, direckly across from Big Daddy, watchin' his face like hawks while they jawed an' jabbered about the cuteness an' brilliance of th' no-neck monsters!

(*She giggles with a hand fluttering at her throat and her breast and her long throat arched.*)
(*She comes downstage and recreates the scene with voice and gesture.*)

And the no-neck monsters were ranged around the table, some in high chairs and some on th' *Books of Knowledge*, all in fancy little paper caps in honor of Big Daddy's birthday, and all through dinner, well, I want you to know that Brother Man an' his partner never once, for one moment, stopped exchanging pokes an' pinches an' kicks an' signs an' signals!—Why, they were like a couple of cardsharps fleecing a sucker.—Even Big Mama, bless her ole sweet soul, she isn't th' quickest an' brightest thing in the world, she finally noticed, at last, an' said to Gooper, "Gooper, what are you an' Mae makin' all these signs at each other about?"—I swear t' goodness, I nearly choked on my chicken!

(MARGARET, *back at the dressing table, still doesn't see* BRICK. *He is watching her with a look that is not quite definable—Amused? shocked? contemptuous?—part of those and part of something else.*)

Y'know—your brother Gooper still cherishes the illusion he took a giant step up the social ladder when he married Miss Mae Flynn of the Memphis Flynns.

But I have a piece of Spanish news for Gooper. The Flynns never had a thing in this world but money and they lost that, they were nothing at all but fairly successful climbers. Of course, Mae Flynn came out in Memphis eight years before I made my debut in Nashville, but I had friends at Ward-Belmont who came from Memphis and they used to come to see me and I used to go to see them for Christmas and spring vacations, and so I know who rates an' who doesn't rate in Memphis society. Why, y'know ole Papa Flynn, he barely escaped doing time in the Federal pen for shady manipulations on th' stock market when his chain stores crashed, and as for Mae having been a cotton carnival queen, as they remind us so often, lest we forget, well, that's one honor that I don't envy her for!—Sit on a brass throne on a tacky float an' ride down Main Street, smilin', bowin', and blowin' kisses to all the trash on the street—

(*She picks out a pair of jeweled sandals and rushes to the dressing table.*)

Why, year before last, when Susan McPheeters was singled out fo' that honor, y' know what happened to her? Y'know what happened to poor little Susie McPheeters?

BRICK (*absently*): No. What happened to little Susie McPheeters?

MARGARET: Somebody spit tobacco juice in her face.

BRICK (*dreamily*): Somebody spit tobacco juice in her face?

MARGARET: That's right, some old drunk leaned out of a window in the Hotel Gayoso and yelled, "Hey, Queen, hey, hey, there, Queenie!" Poor Susie looked up and flashed him a radiant smile and he shot out a squirt of tobacco juice right in poor Susie's face.

BRICK: Well, what d'you know about that.

MARGARET (*gaily*): What do I know about it? I was there, I saw it!

BRICK (*absently*): Must have been kind of funny.

MARGARET: Susie didn't think so. Had hysterics. Screamed like a banshee. They had to stop th' parade an' remove her from her throne an' go on with—

(*She catches sight of him in the mirror, gasps slightly, wheels about to face him. Count ten.*)

—Why are you looking at me like that?

BRICK (*whistling softly, now*): Like what, Maggie?

MARGARET (*intensely, fearfully*): The way y' were lookin' at me just now, befo' I caught your eye in the mirror and you started t' whistle! I don't know how t' describe it but it froze my blood!—I've caught you lookin' at me like that so often lately. What are you thinkin' of when you look at me like that?

BRICK: I wasn't conscious of lookin' at you, Maggie.

MARGARET: Well, I was conscious of it! What were you thinkin'?

BRICK: I don't remember thinking of anything, Maggie.

MARGARET: Don't you think I know that—? Don't you—?—Think I know that—?

BRICK (*cooly*): Know *what*, Maggie?

MARGARET (*struggling for expression*): That I've gone through this—*hideous!—transformation*, become—*hard! Frantic!* (*Then she adds, almost tenderly.*) —*cruel!!*

That's what you've been observing in me lately. How could y' help but observe it? That's all right. I'm not—thin-skinned any more, can't afford t' be thin-skinned any more. (*She is now recovering her power.*) —But Brick? Brick?

BRICK: Did you say something?

MARGARET: I was *goin'* t' say something; that I get—lonely. Very!

BRICK: Ev'rybody gets that . . .

MARGARET: Living with someone you love can be lonelier—than living entirely *alone*!—if the one that y' love doesn't love you. . . .

(*There is a pause.* BRICK *hobbles downstage and asks, without looking at her.*)

BRICK: Would you like to live alone, Maggie?

(*Another pause: then—after she has caught a quick, hurt breath.*)

MARGARET: *No!—God!—I wouldn't!*

(*Another gasping breath. She forcibly controls what must have been an impulse to cry out. We see her deliberately, very forcibly, going all the way back to the world in which you can talk about ordinary matters.*)

Did you have a nice shower?

BRICK: Uh-huh.

MARGARET: Was the water cool?

BRICK: No.

MARGARET: But it made y' feel fresh, huh?

BRICK: Fresher. . . .

MARGARET: I know something would make y' feel *much* fresher!

BRICK: What?

MARGARET: An alcohol rub. Or cologne, a rub with cologne!

BRICK: That's good after a workout but I haven't been workin' out, Maggie.

MARGARET: You've kept in good shape, though.

BRICK (*indifferently*): You think so, Maggie?

MARGARET: I always thought drinkin' men lost their looks, but I was plainly mistaken.

BRICK (*wryly*): Why, thanks, Maggie.

MARGARET: You're the only drinkin' man I know that it never seems t' put fat on.

BRICK: I'm gettin' softer, Maggie.

MARGARET: Well, sooner or later it's bound to soften you up. It was just beginning to soften up Skipper when— (*She stops short.*) I'm sorry. I never could keep my fingers off a sore—I wish you *would* lose your looks. If you did it would make the martyrdom of Saint Maggie a little more bearable. But no such goddam luck. I actually believe you've gotten better looking since you've gone on the bottle. Yeah, a person who didn't know you would think you'd never had a tense nerve in your body or a strained muscle.

(*There are sounds of croquet on the lawn below: the click of mallets, light voices, near and distant.*)

Of course, you always had that detached quality as if you were playing a game without much concern over whether you won or lost, and not that you've lost the game, not lost but just quit playing, you have that rare sort of charm that usually only happens in very old or hopelessly sick people, the charm of the defeated.—You look so cool, so cool, so enviably cool.

REVEREND TOOKER (*off stage right*): Now looka here, boy, lemme show you how to get outa that!

MARGARET: They're playing croquet. The moon has appeared and it's white, just beginning to turn a little bit yellow. . . .

You were a wonderful lover. . . .

Such a wonderful person to go to bed with, and I think mostly because you were really indifferent to it. Isn't that right? Never had any anxiety about it, did it naturally, easily, slowly, with absolute confidence and perfect calm, more like opening a door for a lady or seating her at a table than giving expression to any longing for her. Your indifference made you wonderful at lovemaking—*strange?*—but true. . . .

REVEREND TOOKER: Oh! That's a beauty.

DOCTOR BAUGH: Yeah. I got you boxed.

MARGARET: You know, if I thought you would never, never, *never* make love to me again—I would go downstairs to the kitchen and pick out the longest and sharpest knife I could find and stick it straight into my heart, I swear that I would!

REVEREND TOOKER: Watch out, you're gonna miss it.

DOCTOR BAUGH: You just don't know me, boy!

MARGARET: But one thing I don't have is the charm of the defeated, my hat is still in the ring, and I am determined to win!

(*There is the sound of croquet mallets hitting croquet balls.*)

REVEREND TOOKER: Mmm—You're too slippery for me.

MARGARET: —What is the victory of a cat on a hot tin roof?—I wish I knew. . . .
   Just staying on it, I guess, as long as she can. . . .

DOCTOR BAUGH: Jus' like an eel, boy, jus' like an eel!

(*More croquet sounds.*)

MARGARET: Later tonight I'm going to tell you I love you an' maybe by that time you'll be drunk enough to believe me. Yes, they're playing croquet. . . .
   Big Daddy is dying of cancer. . . .
   What were you thinking of when I caught you looking at me like that? Were you thinking of Skipper?

(BRICK *takes up his crutch, rises.*)

Oh, excuse me, forgive me, but laws of silence don't work! No, laws of silence don't work. . . .

(BRICK *crosses to the bar, takes a quick drink, and rubs his head with a towel.*)

Laws of silence don't work. . . .
   When something is festering in your memory or your imagination, laws of silence don't work, it's just like shutting a door and locking it on a house on fire in hope of forgetting that the house is burning. But not facing a fire doesn't put it out. Silence about a thing just magnifies it. It grows and festers in silence, becomes malignant. . . .

(*He drops his crutch.*)

BRICK: Give me my crutch.

(*He has stopped rubbing his hair dry but still stands hanging onto the towel rack in a white towel-cloth robe.*)

MARGARET: Lean on me.

BRICK: No, just give me my crutch.

MARGARET: Lean on my shoulder.

BRICK: *I don't want to lean on your shoulder, I want my crutch!*

(*This is spoken like sudden lightning.*)

Are you going to give me my crutch or do I have to get down on my knees on the floor and—

MARGARET: Here, here, take it, take it! (*She has thrust the crutch at him.*)

BRICK (*hobbling out*): Thanks . . .

MARGARET: We mustn't scream at each other, the walls in this house have ears. . . .

(*He hobbles directly to liquor cabinet to get a new drink.*)

—but that's the first time I've heard you raise your voice in a long time, Brick. A crack in the wall?—Of composure?

—I think that's a good sign. . . .

A sign of nerves in a player on the defensive!

(BRICK *turns and smiles at her cooly over his fresh drink.*)

BRICK: It just hasn't happened yet, Maggie.

MARGARET: What?

BRICK: The click I get in my head when I've had enough of this stuff to make me peaceful. . . .
Will you do me a favor?

MARGARET: Maybe I will. What favor?

BRICK: Just, just keep your voice down!

MARGARET (*in a hoarse whisper*): I'll do you that favor, I'll speak in a whisper, if not shut up completely, if *you* will do *me* a favor and make that drink your last one till after the party.

BRICK: What party?

MARGARET: Big Daddy's birthday party.

BRICK: Is this Big Daddy's birthday?

MARGARET: You know this is Big Daddy's birthday!

BRICK: No, I don't, I forgot it.

MARGARET: Well, I remembered it for you. . . .

(*They are both speaking as breathlessly as a pair of kids after a fight, drawing deep exhausted breaths and looking at each other with faraway eyes, shaking and panting together as if they had broken apart from a violent struggle.*)

BRICK: Good for you, Maggie.

MARGARET: You just have to scribble a few lines on this card.

BRICK: You scribble something, Maggie.

MARGARET: It's got to be your handwriting; it's your present, I've given him my present; it's got to be your handwriting!

(*The tension between them is building again, the voices becoming shrill once more.*)

BRICK: I didn't get him a present.

MARGARET: I got one for you.

BRICK: All right. You write the card, then.

MARGARET: And have him know you didn't remember his birthday?

BRICK: I didn't remember his birthday.

MARGARET: You don't have to prove you didn't!

BRICK: I don't want to fool him about it.

MARGARET: Just write "Love, Brick!" for God's—

BRICK: No.

MARGARET: You've *got* to!

BRICK: I don't have to do anything I don't want to do. You keep forgetting the conditions on which I agreed to stay on living with you.

MARGARET (*out before she knows it*): I'm not living with you. We occupy the same cage.

BRICK: You've got to remember the conditions agreed on.

SONNY (*off stage*): Mommy, give it to me. I had it first.

MAE: Hush.

MARGARET: They're impossible conditions!

BRICK: Then why don't you—?

SONNY: I want it, I want it!

MAE: Get away!

MARGARET: HUSH! Who is out there? Is somebody at the door?

(*There are footsteps in hall.*)

MAE (*outside*): May I enter a moment?

MARGARET: OH, *you!* Sure. Come in, Mae.

(MAE *enters bearing aloft the bow of a young lady's archery set.*)

MAE: Brick, is this thing yours?

MARGARET: Why, Sister Woman—that's my Diana Trophy. Won it at the intercollegiate archery contest on the Ole Miss campus.

MAE: It's a mighty dangerous thing to leave exposed round a house full of nawmal rid-blooded children, attracted t'weapons.

MARGARET: "Nawmal rid-blooded children attracted t'weapons" ought t'be taught to keep their hands off things that don't belong to them.

MAE: Maggie, honey, if you had children of your own you'd know how funny that is. Will you please lock this up and put the key out of reach?

MARGARET: Sister Woman, nobody is plotting the destruction of your kiddies. —Brick and I still have our special archers' license. We're goin' deer-huntin' on Moon Lake as soon as the season starts. I love to run with dogs through chilly woods, run, run leap over obstructions— (*She goes into the closet carrying the bow.*)

MAE: How's the injured ankle, Brick?

BRICK: Doesn't hurt. Just itches.

MAE: Oh, my! Brick—Brick, you should've been downstairs after supper! Kiddies put on a show. Polly played the piano, Buster an' Sonny drums, an' then they turned out the lights an' Dixie an' Trixie puhfawmed a toe dance in fairy costume with *spahklus!* Big Daddy just beamed! He just beamed!

MARGARET (*from the closet with a sharp laugh*): Oh, I bet. It breaks my heart that we missed it! (*She reenters.*) But Mae? Why did y'give dawgs' names to all your kiddies?

MAE: *Dogs' names?*

MARGARET (*sweetly*): Dixie, Trixie, Buster, Sonny, Polly!—Sounds like four dogs and a parrot . . .

MAE: Maggie?

(MARGARET *turns with a smile.*)

Why are you so catty?

MARGARET: Cause I'm a cat! But why can't *you* take a joke, Sister Woman?

MAE: Nothin' pleases me more than a joke that's funny. You know the real names of our kiddies. Buster's real name is Robert. Sonny's real name is Saunders. Trixie's real name is Marlene and Dixie's—

(GOOPER *downstairs calls for her. "Hey, Mae! Sister Woman, intermission is over!"—she rushes to door, saying.*)

Intermission is over! See ya later!

MARGARET: I wonder what Dixie's real name is?

BRICK: Maggie, being catty doesn't help things any . . .

MARGARET: I know! *WHY!*—Am I so catty?—Cause I'm consumed with envy an' eaten up with longing?—Brick, I'm going to lay out your beautiful Shantung silk suit from Rome and one of your monogrammed silk shirts. I'll put your cuff links in it, those lovely star sapphires I get you to wear so rarely. . . .

BRICK: I can't get trousers on over this plaster cast.

MARGARET: Yes, you can, I'll help you.

BRICK: I'm not going to get dressed, Maggie.

MARGARET: Will you just put on a pair of white silk pajamas?

BRICK: Yes, I'll do that, Maggie.

MARGARET: *Thank* you, thank you so *much!*

BRICK: Don't mention it.

MARGARET: *Oh, Brick!* How long does it have t' go on? This punishment? Haven't I done time enough, haven't I served my term, can't I apply for a—pardon?

BRICK: Maggie, you're spoiling my liquor. Lately your voice always sounds like you'd been running upstairs to warn somebody that the house was on fire!

MARGARET: Well, no wonder, no wonder. Y'know what I feel like, Brick?
    I feel all the time like a cat on a hot tin roof!

BRICK: Then jump off the roof, jump off it, cats can jump off roofs and land on their four feet uninjured!

MARGARET: Oh, yes!

BRICK: Do it!—fo' God's sake, do it . . .

MARGARET: Do what?

BRICK: Take a lover!

MARGARET: I can't see a man but you! Even with my eyes closed, I just see you! Why don't you get ugly, Brick, why don't you please get fat or ugly or something so I could stand it? (*She rushes to hall door, opens it, listens.*) The concert is still going on! Bravo, no-necks, bravo! (*She slams and locks door fiercely.*)

BRICK: What did you lock the door for?

MARGARET: To give us a little privacy for a while.

BRICK: You know better, Maggie.

MARGARET: No, I don't know better. . . .

(*She rushes to gallery doors, draws the rose-silk drapes across them.*)

BRICK: Don't make a fool of yourself.

MARGARET: I don't mind makin' a fool of myself over you!

BRICK: I mind, Maggie. I feel embarrassed for you.

MARGARET: Feel embarrassed! But don't continue my torture. I can't live on and on under these circumstances.

BRICK: You agreed to—

MARGARET: I know but—

BRICK: —Accept that condition!

MARGARET: *I CAN'T! I CAN'T! I CAN'T!* (*She seizes his shoulder.*)

BRICK: Let go!

(*He breaks away from her and seizes the small boudoir chair and raises it like a lion-tamer facing a big circus cat.*)
(*Count five. She stares at him with her fist pressed to her mouth, then bursts into shrill, almost hysterical laughter. He remains grave for a moment, then grins and puts the chair down.*)
(BIG MAMA *calls through closed door.*)

BIG MAMA: Son? Son? Son?

BRICK: What is it, Big Mama?

BIG MAMA (*outside*): Oh, son! We got the most wonderful news about Big Daddy. I just had t' run up an' tell you right this— (*She rattles the knob.*) —What's this door doin', locked, faw? You all think there's robbers in the house?

MARGARET: Big Mama, Brick is dressin', he's not dressed yet.

BIG MAMA: That's all right, it won't be the first time I've seen Brick not dressed. Come on, open this door!

(MARGARET, *with a grimace, goes to unlock and open the hall door, as* BRICK *hobbles rapidly to the bathroom and kicks the door shut.* BIG MAMA *has disappeared from the hall.*)

MARGARET: Big Mama?

(BIG MAMA *appears through the opposite gallery doors behind* MARGARET, *huffing and puffing like an old bulldog. She is a short, stout woman; her sixty years and 170 pounds have left her somewhat breathless most of the time; she's always tensed like a boxer, or rather, a Japanese wrestler. Her "family" was maybe a little superior to* BIG DADDY's *but not much. She wears a black or silver lace dress and at least half a million in flashy gems. She is very sincere.*)

BIG MAMA (*loudly, startling* MARGARET): Here—I come through Gooper's and Mae's gall'ry door. Where's Brick? *Brick*—Hurry on out of there, son, I just have a second and want to give you the news about Big Daddy.—I hate locked doors in a house. . . .

MARGARET (*with affected lightness*): I've noticed you do, Big Mama, but people have got to have *some* moments of privacy, don't they?

BIG MAMA: No, ma'am, not in *my* house. (*Without pause.*) Whacha took off you' dress faw? I thought that little lace dress was so sweet on yuh, honey.

MARGARET: I thought it looked sweet on me, too, but one of m' cute little table-partners used it for a napkin so—!

BIG MAMA (*picking up stockings on floor*): What?

MARGARET: You know, Big Mama, Mae and Gooper's so touchy about those children—thanks, Big Mama . . .

(BIG MAMA *has thrust the picked-up stockings in* MARGARET's *hand with a grunt.*)

—that you just don't dare to suggest there's any room for improvement in their—

BIG MAMA: Brick, hurry out!—Shoot, Maggie, you just don't like children.

MARGARET: I do SO like children! Adore them!—well brought up!

BIG MAMA (*gentle—loving*): Well, why don't you have some and bring them up well, then, instead of all the time pickin' on Gooper's an' Mae's?

GOOPER (*shouting up the stairs*): Hey, hey, Big Mama, Betsy an' Hugh got to go, waitin' t' tell yuh g'by!

BIG MAMA: Tell 'em to hold their hawses, I'll be right down in a jiffy!

GOOPER: Yes ma'am!

(*She turns to the bathroom door and calls out.*)

BIG MAMA: Son? Can you hear me in there?

(*There is a muffled answer.*)

We just got the full report from the laboratory at the Ochsner Clinic, completely negative, son, ev'rything negative, right on down the line! Nothin' a-tall's wrong with him but some little

functional thing called a spastic colon. Can you hear me, son?

MARGARET: He can hear you, Big Mama.

BIG MAMA: Then why don't he say something? God Almighty, a piece of news like that should make him shout. It made *me* shout, I can tell you. I shouted and sobbed and fell right down on my knees!—Look! (*She pulls up her skirt.*) See the bruises where I hit my kneecaps? Took both doctors to haul me back on my feet!

(*She laughs—she always laughs like hell at herself.*)

Big Daddy was furious with me! But ain't that wonderful news?

(*Facing bathroom again, she continues.*)

After all the anxiety we been through to git a report like that on Big Daddy's birthday? Big Daddy tried to hide how much of a load that news took off his mind, but didn't fool *me*. He was mighty close to crying about it *himself*!

(*Goodbyes are shouted downstairs, and she rushes to door.*)

GOOPER: Big Mama!

BIG MAMA: *Hold those people down there, don't let them go!*—Now, git dressed, we're comin' up to this room fo' Big Daddy's birthday party because of your ankle.—How's his ankle, Maggie?

MARGARET: Well, he broke it, Big Mama.

BIG MAMA: I know he broke it.

(*A phone is ringing in hall. A Negro voice answers: "Mistuh Polly's res'dence."*)

I mean does it hurt him much still.

MARGARET: I'm afraid I can't give you that information, Big Mama. You'll have to ask Brick if it hurts much still or not.

SOOKEY (*in the hall*): It's Memphis, Mizz Polly, it's Miss Sally in Memphis.

BIG MAMA: Awright, Sookey.

(BIG MAMA *rushes into the hall and is heard shouting on the phone.*)

Hello, Miss Sally. How are you, Miss Sally?—Yes, well, I was just gonna call you about it. *Shoot!*

MARGARET: Brick, don't!

(BIG MAMA *raises her voice to a bellow.*)

BIG MAMA: *Miss Sally? Don't ever call me from the Gayoso Lobby, too much talk goes on in that hotel lobby, no wonder you can't hear me!* Now listen, Miss Sally. They's nothin' serious wrong with Big Daddy. We got the report just now, they's nothin' wrong but a thing called a—spastic! *SPASTIC!*—colon . . . (*She appears at the hall door and calls to* MARGARET.) —Maggie, come out here and talk to that fool on the phone. I'm shouted breathless!

MARGARET (*goes out and is heard sweetly at phone*): Miss Sally? This is Brick's wife, Maggie. So nice to hear your voice. Can you hear *mine*? Well, *good!*—Big Mama just wanted you to know that they've got the report from the Ochsner Clinic and what Big Daddy has is a spastic colon. Yes. Spastic colon, Miss Sally. That's right, spastic colon. *G'bye, Miss Sally, hope I'll see you real soon!*

(*Hangs up a little before* MISS SALLY *was probably ready to terminate the talk. She returns through the hall door.*)

She heard me perfectly. I've discovered with deaf people the thing to do is not shout at them but just enunciate clearly. My rich old Aunt Cornelia was deaf as the dead but I could make her hear me just by sayin' each word slowly, distinctly, close to her ear. I read her the *Commercial Appeal* ev'ry night, read her the classified ads in it, even, she never missed a word of it. But was she a mean ole thing! Know what I got when she died? Her unexpired subscriptions to five magazines and the Book-of-the-Month Club and a LIBRARY full of ev'ry dull book ever written! All else went to her hellcat of a sister . . . meaner than she was, even!

(BIG MAMA *has been straightening things up in the room during this speech.*)

BIG MAMA (*closing closet door on discarded clothes*): Miss Sally sure is a case! Big Daddy says she's always got her hand out fo' something. He's not mistaken. That poor ole thing always has her hand out fo' somethin'. I don't think Big Daddy gives her as much as he should.

GOOPER: Big Mama! Come on now! Betsy and Hugh can't wait no longer!

BIG MAMA (*shouting*): I'm comin'!

(*She starts out. At the hall door, turns and jerks a forefinger, first toward the bathroom door, then toward the liquor cabinet, meaning: "Has* BRICK *been drinking?"* MARGARET *pretends not to understand, cocks her head and raises her brows as if the pantomimic performance was completely mystifying to her.*)
(BIG MAMA *rushes back to* MARGARET.)

Shoot! Stop playin' so dumb!—I mean has he been drinkin' that stuff much yet?

MARGARET (*with a little laugh*): Oh! I think he had a highball after supper.

BIG MAMA: Don't laugh about it!—some single men stop drinkin' when they git married and others start! Brick never touched liquor before he—!

MARGARET (*crying out*): *THAT'S NOT FAIR!*

BIG MAMA: Fair or not fair I want to ask you a question, one question: D'you make Brick happy in bed?

MARGARET: Why don't you ask if he makes *me* happy in bed?

BIG MAMA: Because I know that—

MARGARET: *It works both ways!*

BIG MAMA: Something's not right! You're childless and my son drinks!

GOOPER: Come on, Big Mama!

(GOOPER *has called her downstairs and she has rushed to the door on the line above. She turns at the door and points at the bed.*)

—When a marriage goes on the rocks, the rocks are *there*, right *there!*

MARGARET: *That's*—

(BIG MAMA *has swept out of the room and slammed the door.*)

—not—*fair* . . .

(MARGARET *is alone, completely alone, and she feels it. She draws in, hunches her shoulders, raises her arms with fists clenched, shuts her eyes tight as a child about to be stabbed with a vaccination needle. When she opens her eyes again, what she sees is the long oval mirror and she rushes straight to it, stares into it with a grimace and says: "Who are you?"—Then she crouches a little and answers herself in a different voice which is high, thin, mocking: "I am Maggie the Cat!"—Straightens quickly as bathroom door opens a little and* BRICK *calls out to her.*)

BRICK: Has Big Mama gone?

MARGARET: She's gone.

(*He opens the bathroom door and hobbles out, with his liquor glass now empty, straight to the liquor cabinet. He is whistling softly.* MARGARET's *head pivots on her long, slender throat to watch him.*)
(*She raises a hand uncertainly to the base of her throat, as if it was difficult for her to swallow, before she speaks.*)

You know, our sex life didn't just peter out in the usual way, it was cut off short, long before the natural time for it to, and it's going to revive again, just as sudden as that. I'm confident of it. That's what I'm keeping myself attractive for. For the time when you'll see me again like other men see me. Yes, like other men see me. They still see me, Brick, and they like what they see. Uh-huh. Some of them would give their—
Look, Brick!

(*She stands before the long oval mirror, touches her breast and then her hips with her two hands.*)

How high my body stays on me!—Nothing has fallen on me—not a fraction. . . .

(*Her voice is soft and trembling: a pleading child's. At this moment as he turns to glance at her—a look which is like a player passing a ball to another player, third down and goal to go—she has to capture the audience in a grip so tight that she can hold it till the first intermission without any lapse of attention.)*

Other men still want me. My face looks strained, sometimes, but I've kept my figure as well as you've kept yours, and men admire it. I still turn heads on the street. Why, last week in Memphis everywhere that I went men's eyes burned holes in my clothes, at the country club and in restaurants and department stores, there wasn't a man I met or walked by that didn't just eat me up with his eyes and turn around when I passed him and look back at me. Why, at Alice's party for her New York cousins, the best-lookin' man in the crowd—followed me upstairs and tried to force his way in the powder room with me, followed me to the door and tried to force his way in!

BRICK: Why didn't you let him, Maggie?

MARGARET: Because I'm not that common, for one thing. Not that I wasn't almost tempted to. You like to know who it was? It was Sonny Boy Maxwell, that's who!

BRICK: Oh, yeah, Sonny Boy Maxwell, he was a good end-runner but had a little injury to his back and had to quit.

MARGARET: He has no injury now and has no wife and still has a lech for me!

BRICK: I see no reason to lock him out of a powder room in that case.

MARGARET: And have someone catch me at it? I'm not that stupid. Oh, I might sometime cheat on you with someone, since you're so insultingly eager to have me do it!—But if I do, you can be damned sure it will be in a place and a time where no one but me and the man could possibly know. Because I'm not going to give you any excuse to divorce me for being unfaithful or anything else. . . .

BRICK: Maggie, I wouldn't divorce you for being unfaithful or anything else. Don't you know that? Hell. I'd be relieved to know that you'd found yourself a lover.

MARGARET: Well, I'm taking no chances. No, I'd rather stay on this hot tin roof.

BRICK: A hot tin roof's 'n uncomfo'table place t' stay on. . . . *(He starts to whistle softly.)*

MARGARET *(through his whistle)*: Yeah, but I can stay on it just as long as I have to.

BRICK: You could leave me, Maggie.

(He resumes whistle. She wheels about to glare at him.)

MARGARET: *Don't want to and will not!* Besides if I did, you don't have a cent to pay for it but what you get from Big Daddy and he's dying of cancer!

(For the first time a realization of BIG DADDY's *doom seems to penetrate to* BRICK's *consciousness, visibly, and he looks at* MARGARET.*)*

BRICK: Big Mama just said he *wasn't,* that the report was okay.

MARGARET: That's what she thinks because she got the same story that they gave Big Daddy. And was just as taken in by it as he was, poor ole things. . . .

But tonight they're going to tell her the truth about it. When Big Daddy goes to bed, they're going to tell her that he is dying of cancer. *(She slams the dresser drawer.)*—It's malignant and it's terminal.

BRICK: Does Big Daddy know it?

MARGARET: Hell, do they *ever* know it? Nobody says, "You're dying." You have to fool them. They have to fool *themselves.*

BRICK: Why?

MARGARET: *Why? Why?* Because human beings dream of life everlasting, that's the reason! But most of them want it on earth and not in heaven.

(He gives a short, hard laugh at her touch of humor.)

Well. . . . *(She touches up her mascara.)* That's how it is, anyhow. . . . *(She looks about.)* Where did I put down my cigarette? Don't want to burn up the home-place, at least not with Mae and Gooper and their five monsters in it!

(She has found it and sucks at it greedily. Blows out smoke and continues.)

So this is Big Daddy's last birthday. And Mae and Gooper, they know it, oh, *they* know it, all right. They got the first information from the Ochsner Clinic. That's why they rushed down here with their no-neck monsters. Because. Do you know something? Big Daddy's made no will? Big Daddy's never made out any will in his life, and so this campaign's afoot to impress him, forcibly as possible, with the fact that you drink and I've borne no children!

(He continues to stare at her a moment, then mutters something sharp but not audible and hobbles rather rapidly out onto the long gallery in the fading, much faded, gold light.)

MARGARET *(continuing her liturgical chant)*: Y'know, I'm *fond* of Big Daddy, I am genuinely fond of that old man, I really *am,* you know. . . .

BRICK *(faintly, vaguely)*: Yes, I know you are. . . .

MARGARET: I've always sort of admired him in spite of his coarseness, his four-letter words and so forth. Because Big Daddy *is* what he *is,* and he makes no bones about it. He hasn't turned gentleman farmer, he's still a Mississippi redneck, as much of a redneck as he must have been when he was just overseer here on the old Jack Straw and Peter Ochello place. But he got hold of it an' built it into th' biggest an' finest plantation in the Delta.—I've always *liked* Big Daddy. . . .

(*She crosses to the proscenium.*)

Well, this is Big Daddy's last birthday. I'm sorry about it. But I'm facing the facts. It takes money to take care of a drinker and that's the office that I've been elected to lately.

BRICK: You don't have to take care of me.

MARGARET: Yes, I do. Two people in the same boat have got to take care of each other. At least you want money to buy more Echo Spring when this supply is exhausted, or will you be satisfied with a ten-cent beer?

Mae an' Gooper are plannin' to freeze us out of Big Daddy's estate because you drink and I'm childless. But we can defeat that plan. We're *going* to defeat that plan!

Brick, y'know, I've been so God damn disgustingly poor all my life!—That's the *truth*, Brick!

BRICK: I'm not sayin' it isn't.

MARGARET: Always had to suck up to people I couldn't stand because they had money and I was poor as Job's turkey. You don't know what that's like. Well, I'll tell you, it's like you would feel a thousand miles away from Echo Spring!—And had to get back to it on that broken ankle . . . without a crutch!

That's how it feels to be as poor as Job's turkey and have to suck up to relatives that you hated because they had money and all you had was a bunch of hand-me-down clothes and a few old moldy three-per-cent government bonds. My daddy loved his liquor, he fell in love with his liquor the way you've fallen in love with Echo Spring!—And my poor Mama, having to maintain some semblance of social position, to keep appearances up, on an income of one hundred and fifty dollars a month on those old government bonds!

When I came out, the year that I made my debut, I had just two evening dresses! One Mother made me from a pattern in *Vogue*, the other a hand-me-down from a snotty rich cousin I hated!

—The dress that I married you in was my grandmother's weddin' gown. . . .

So that's why I'm like a cat on a hot tin roof!

(BRICK *is still on the gallery. Someone below calls up to him in a warm Negro voice, "Hiya, Mistuh Brick, how yuh feelin'?"* BRICK *raises his liquor glass as if that answered the question.*)

MARGARET: You can be young without money, but you can't be old without it. You've got to be old *with* money because to be old without it is just too awful, you've got to be one or the other, either *young* or *with money*, you can't be old and *without* it.—That's the *truth*, Brick. . . .

(BRICK *whistles softly, vaguely.*)

Well, now I'm dressed, I'm all dressed, there's nothing else for me to do. (*Forlornly, almost fearfully.*) I'm dressed, all dressed, nothing else for me to do. . . .

(*She moves about restlessly, aimlessly, and speaks, as if to herself.*)

What am I—? Oh!—my bracelets. . . .

(*She starts working a collection of bracelets over her hands onto her wrists, about six on each, as she talks.*)

I've thought a whole lot about it and now I know when I made my mistake. Yes, I made my mistake when I told you the truth about that thing with Skipper. Never should have confessed it, a fatal error, tellin' you about that thing with Skipper.

BRICK: Maggie, shut up about Skipper. I mean it, Maggie; you got to shut up about Skipper.

MARGARET: You ought to understand that Skipper and I—

BRICK: You don't think I'm serious, Maggie? You're fooled by the fact that I am saying this quiet? Look, Maggie. What you're doing is a dangerous thing to do. You're—you're—you're—foolin' with something that—nobody ought to fool with.

MARGARET: This time I'm going to finish what I have to say to you. Skipper and I made love, if love you could call it, because it made both of us feel a little bit closer to you. You see, you son of a bitch, you asked too much of people, of me, of him, of all the unlucky poor damned sons of bitches that happen to love you, and there was a whole pack of them, yes, there was a pack of them besides me and Skipper, you asked too goddam much of people that loved you, you—superior creature!—you godlike being!—And so we made love to each other to dream it was you, both of us! Yes, yes, yes! Truth, truth! What's so awful about it? I like it, I think the truth is—yeah! I shouldn't have told you. . . .

BRICK (*holding his head unnaturally still and uptilted a bit*): It was Skipper that told me about it. Not you, Maggie.

MARGARET: I told you!

BRICK: After he told me!

MARGARET: What does it matter who—?

DIXIE: I got your mallet, I got your mallet.

TRIXIE: Give it to me, give it to me, IT's mine.

(BRICK *turns suddenly out upon the gallery and calls.*)

BRICK: Little girl! Hey, little girl!

LITTLE GIRL (*at a distance*): What, Uncle Brick?

BRICK: Tell the folks to come up!—Bring everybody upstairs!

TRIXIE: It's mine, it's mine.

MARGARET: I can't stop myself! I'd go on telling you this in front of them all, if I had to!

BRICK: Little girl, Go on, go on, will you? Do what I told you, call them!

DIXIE: Okay.

MARGARET: Because it's got to be told and you, you!—you never let me!

(She sobs, then controls herself, and continues almost calmly.)

It was one of those beautiful, ideal things, they tell about in the Greek legends, it couldn't be anything else, you being you, and that's what made it so sad, and that's what made it so awful, because it was love that never could be carried through to anything satisfying or even talked about plainly.

BRICK: Maggie, you gotta stop this.

MARGARET: Brick, I tell you, you got to believe me, Brick, I *do* understand all about it! I—I think it was—*noble!* Can't you tell I'm sincere when I say I respect it? My only point, the only point that I'm making, is life has got to be allowed to continue even after the *dream* of life is —all— over. . . .

(BRICK is without his crutch. Leaning on furniture, he crosses to pick it up as she continues as if possessed by a will outside herself.)

Why I remember when we double-dated at college, Gladys Fitzgerald and I and you and Skipper, it was more like a date between you and Skipper. Gladys and I were just sort of tagging along as if it was necessary to chaperone you!—to make a good public impression—

BRICK *(turns to face her, half lifting his crutch)*: Maggie, you want me to hit you with this crutch? Don't you know I could kill you with this crutch?

MARGARET: Good, Lord, man, d' you think I'd care if you did?

BRICK: One man has one great good true thing in his life. One great good thing which is true!—I had friendship with Skipper.—You are naming it dirty!

MARGARET: I'm not naming it dirty! I am naming it clean.

BRICK: Not love with you, Maggie, but friendship with Skipper was that one great true thing, and you are naming it dirty!

MARGARET: Then you haven't been listenin', not understood what I'm saying! I'm naming it so damn clean that it killed poor Skipper!—You two had something that had to be kept on ice, yes, incor-

ruptible, yes!—and death was the only icebox where you could keep it. . . .

BRICK: I married you, Maggie. Why would I marry you, Maggie, if I was—?

MARGARET: Brick, let me finish!—I know, believe me I know, that it was only Skipper that harbored even any *unconscious* desire for anything not perfectly pure between you two!—Now let me skip a little. You married me early that summer we graduated out of Ole Miss, and we were happy, weren't we, we were blissful, yes, hit heaven together ev'ry time that we loved! But that fall you an' Skipper turned down wonderful offers of jobs in order to keep on bein' football heroes—pro-football heroes. You organized the Dixie Stars that fall, so you could keep on bein' teammates forever! But somethin' was not right with it!—*Me included!*—between you. Skipper began hittin' the bottle . . . you got a spinal injury—couldn't play the Thanksgivin' game in Chicago, watched it on TV from a traction bed in Toledo. I joined Skipper. The Dixie Stars lost because poor Skipper was drunk. We drank together that night all night in the bar of the Blackstone and when cold day was comin' up over the Lake an' we were comin' out drunk to take a dizzy look at it, I said, "SKIPPER! STOP LOVIN' MY HUSBAND OR TELL HIM HE'S GOT TO LET YOU ADMIT IT TO HIM!"—one way or another!

HE SLAPPED ME HARD ON THE MOUTH!—then turned and ran without stopping once, I am sure, all the way back into his room at the Blackstone. . . .

—When I came to his room that night, with a little scratch like a shy little mouse at his door, he made that pitiful, ineffectual little attempt to prove that what I had said wasn't true. . . .

(BRICK strikes at her with crutch, a blow that shatters the gemlike lamp on the table.)

—In this way, I destroyed him, by telling him truth that he and his world which he was born and raised in, yours and his world, had told him could not be told?

From then on Skipper was nothing at all but a receptacle for liquor and drugs. . . .

—*Who shot cock robin? I with my— (She throws back her head with tight shut eyes.) —merciful arrow!*

(BRICK strikes at her; misses.)

Missed me!—Sorry,—I'm not tryin' to whitewash my behavior, Christ, no! Brick, I'm not good. I don't know why people have to pretend to be good, nobody's good. The rich or the well-to-do can afford to respect moral patterns, conventional moral patterns, but I could never afford to, yeah, but—I'm honest! Give me credit for just that, will you *please*?—Born poor, raised poor, expect to die poor unless I manage to get us something out of what Big Daddy leaves when he dies of cancer! But Brick?!—*Skipper is dead! I'm alive!* Maggie the cat is—

(BRICK *hops awkwardly forward and strikes at her again with his crutch.*)

—alive! I am alive, alive! I am . . .

(*He hurls the crutch at her, across the bed she took refuge behind, and pitches forward on the floor as she completes her speech.*)

—alive!

(*A little girl,* DIXIE, *bursts into the room, wearing an Indian war bonnet and firing a cap pistol at* MARGARET *and shouting:* "Bang, bang, bang!")
(*Laughter downstairs floats through the open hall door.* MARGARET *had crouched gasping to bed at child's entrance. She now rises and says with cool fury.*)

Little girl, your mother or someone should teach you—(*gasping*)—to knock at a door before you come into a room. Otherwise people might think that you—lack—good breeding. . . .

DIXIE: Yanh, yanh, yanh, what is Uncle Brick doin' on th' floor?

BRICK: I tried to kill your Aunt Maggie, but I failed—and I fell. Little girl, give me my crutch so I can get up off th' floor.

MARGARET: Yes, give your uncle his crutch, he's a cripple, honey, he broke his ankle last night jumping hurdles on the high school athletic field!

DIXIE: What were you jumping hurdles for, Uncle Brick?

BRICK: Because I used to jump them, and people like to do what they used to do, even after they've stopped being able to do it. . . .

MARGARET: That's right, that's your answer, now go away, little girl.

(DIXIE *fires cap pistol at* MARGARET *three times.*)

Stop, you stop that, monster! You little no-neck monster! (*She seizes the cap pistol and hurls it through gallery door.*)

DIXIE (*with a precocious instinct for the cruelest thing*): You're *jealous!*—You're just jealous because you can't have babies!

(*She sticks out her tongue at* MARGARET *as she sashays past her with her stomach stuck out, to the gallery.* MARGARET *slams the gallery doors and leans panting against them. There is a pause.* BRICK *has replaced his spilt drink and sits, faraway, on the great four-poster bed.*)

MARGARET: You see?—they gloat over us being child-less, even in front of their five little no-neck monsters!

(*Pause. Voices approach on the stairs.*)

Brick?—I've been to a doctor in Memphis, a—a gynecologist. . . .
I've been completely examined, and there is no reason why we can't have a child whenever we want one. And this is my time by the calendar to conceive. Are you listening to me? Are you? Are you LISTENING TO ME!

BRICK: Yes. I hear you, Maggie. (*His attention returns to her inflamed face.*) —But how in hell on earth do you imagine—that you're going to have a child by a man that can't stand you?

MARGARET: That's a problem that I will have to work out. (*She wheels about to face the hall door.*)

MAE (*off stage left*): Come on, Big Daddy. We're all goin' up to Brick's room.

(*From off stage left, voices:* REVEREND TOOKER, DOCTOR BAUGH, MAE.)

MARGARET: *Here they come!*

(*The lights dim.*)

ACT 2

(*There is no lapse of time.* MARGARET *and* BRICK *are in the same positions they held at the end of Act 1.*)

MARGARET (*at door*): *Here they come!*

(BIG DADDY *appears first, a tall man with a fierce, anxious look, moving carefully not to betray his weakness even, or especially, to himself.*)

GOOPER: I read in the *Register* that you're getting a new memorial window.

(*Some of the people are approaching through the hall, others along the gallery: voices from both directions.* GOOPER *and* REVEREND TOOKER *become visible outside gallery doors, and their voices come in clearly.*)
(*They pause outside as* GOOPER *lights a cigar.*)

REVEREND TOOKER (*vivaciously*): Oh, but St. Paul's in Grenada has three memorial windows, and the latest one is a Tiffany stained-glass window that cost twenty-five hundred dollars, a picture of Christ the Good Shepherd with a Lamb in His arms.

MARGARET: Big Daddy.

BIG DADDY: Well, Brick.

BRICK: Hello Big Daddy.—Congratulations!

BIG DADDY: —Crap. . . .

GOOPER: Who give that window, Preach?

REVEREND TOOKER: Clyde Fletcher's widow. Also presented St. Paul's with a baptismal font.

GOOPER: Y'know what somebody ought t' give your church is a *coolin'* system, Preach.

MAE (*almost religiously*): Let's see now, they've had their *tyyy*-phoid shots, and their tetanus shots, their diptheria shots and their hepatitis shots and their polio shots, they got *those* shots every month from May through September, and—Gooper? Hey! Gooper!—What all have the kiddies been shot faw?

REVEREND TOOKER: Yes, siree, Bob! And y'know what Gus Hamma's family gave in his memory to the church at Two Rivers? A complete new stone parish-house with a basketball court in the basement and a—

BIG DADDY (*uttering a loud barking laugh which is far from truly mirthful*): Hey, Preach! What's all this talk about memorials, Preach? Y' think somebody's about t' kick off around here? 'S that it?

(*Startled by this interjection,* REVEREND TOOKER *decides to laugh at the question almost as loud as he can.*)
(*How he would answer the question we'll never know, as he's spared that embarrassment by the voice of* GOOPER'S *wife,* MAE, *rising high and clear as she appears with* "DOC" BAUGH, *the family doctor, through the hall door.*)

MARGARET (*overlapping a bit*): Turn on the hi-fi, Brick! Let's have some music t' start th' party with!

BRICK: You turn it on, Maggie.

(*The talk becomes so general that the room sounds like a great aviary of chattering birds. Only* BRICK *remains unengaged, leaning upon the liquor cabinet with his faraway smile, an ice cube in a paper napkin with which he now and then rubs his forehead. He doesn't respond to* MARGARET's *command. She bounds forward and stoops over the instrument panel of the console.*)

GOOPER: We gave 'em that thing for a third anniversay present, got three speakers in it.

(*The room is suddenly blasted by the climax of a Wagnerian opera or a Beethoven symphony.*)

BIG DADDY: *Turn that dam thing off!*

(*Almost instant silence, almost instantly broken by the shouting charge of* BIG MAMA, *entering through the hall door like a charging rhino.*)

BIG MAMA: *Wha's my Brick, wha's mah precious baby!!*

BIG DADDY: *Sorry! Turn it back on!*

(*Everyone laughs very loud.* BIG DADDY *is famous for his jokes at* BIG MAMA's *expense, and nobody laughs louder at these jokes than* BIG MAMA *herself, though sometimes they're pretty cruel and* BIG MAMA *has to pick up or fuss with something to cover the hurt that the loud laugh doesn't quite cover.*)
(*On this occasion, a happy occasion because the dread in her heart has also been lifted by the false report on* BIG DADDY's *condition, she giggles, grotesquely, coyly, in* BIG DADDY's *direction and bears down upon* BRICK, *all very quick and alive.*)

BIG MAMA: Here he is, here's my precious baby! What's that you've got in your hand? You put that liquor down, son, your hand was made fo' holdin' somethin' better than that!

GOOPER: Look at Brick put it down!

(BRICK *has obeyed* BIG MAMA *by draining the glass and handing it to her. Again everyone laughs, some high, some low.*)

BIG MAMA: Oh, you bad boy, you, you're my bad little boy. Give Big Mama a kiss, you bad boy, you!—Look at him shy away, will you? Brick never liked bein' kissed or made a fuss over, I guess because he's always had too much of it!

Son, you turn that thing off!

(BRICK *has switched on the TV set.*)

I can't stand TV, radio was bad enough but TV has gone it one better, I mean—(*plops wheezing in chair*)—one worse, ha ha! Now what'm I sittin' down here faw? I want t' sit next to my sweetheart on the sofa, hold hands with him and love him up a little!

(BIG MAMA *has on a black and white figured chiffon. The large irregular patterns, like the markings of some massive animal, the luster of her great diamonds and many pearls, the brilliants set in the silver frames of her glasses, her riotous voice, booming laugh, have dominated the room since she entered.* BIG DADDY *has been regarding her with a steady grimace of chronic annoyance.*)

BIG MAMA (*still louder*): Preacher, Preacher, hey, Preach! Give me you' hand an' help me up from this chair!

REVEREND TOOKER: None of your tricks, Big Mama!

BIG MAMA: What tricks? You give me you' hand so I can get up an'—

(REVEREND TOOKER *extends her his hand. She grabs it and pulls him into her lap with a shrill laugh that spans an octave in two notes.*)

Ever seen a preacher in a fat lady's lap? Hey, hey, folks! Ever seen a preacher in a fat lady's lap?

(BIG MAMA *is notorious throughout the Delta for this sort of inelegant horseplay.* MARGARET *looks on with indulgent humor, sipping Dubonnet "on the rocks" and watching* BRICK, *but* MAE *and* GOOPER *exchange signs of humorless anxiety over these antics, the sort of behavior which* MAE *thinks may account for their failure to quite get in with the smartest young married set in Memphis, despite all. One of the Negroes,* LACY *or* SOOKEY, *peeks in, cackling. They are waiting for a sign to bring in the cake and champagne. But* BIG DADDY's *not amused. He doesn't understand why, in spite of the infinite mental relief he's received from the doctor's report, he still has these same old fox teeth in his guts. "This spastic condition is something else," he says to himself, but aloud he roars at* BIG MAMA.)

BIG DADDY: *BIG MAMA, WILL YOU QUIT HORSIN'?—*You're too old an' too fat fo' that sort of crazy kid stuff an' besides a woman with your blood pressure—she had two hundred last spring!—is riskin' a stroke when you mess around like that. . . .

(MAE *blows on a pitch pipe.*)

BIG MAMA: *Here comes Big Daddy's birthday!*

(*Negroes in white jackets enter with an enormous birthday cake ablaze with candles and carrying buckets of champagne with satin ribbons about the bottle necks.* MAE *and* GOOPER *strike up song, and everybody, including the* NEGROES *and* CHILDREN, *joins in. Only* BRICK *remains aloof.*)

EVERYONE:
Happy birthday to you.
Happy birthday to you.
Happy birthday, Big Daddy—

(*Some sing: "Dear, Big Daddy!"*)

Happy birthday to you.

(*Some sing: "How old are you?"*)
(MAE *has come down center and is organizing her children like a chorus. She gives them a barely audible: "One, two, three!" and they are off in the new tune.*)

CHILDREN:
Skinamarinka—dinka—dink
Skinamarinka—do
We love you.
Skinamarinka—dinka—dink
Skinamarinka—do.

(*All together, they turn to* BIG DADDY.)

Big Daddy, you!

(*They turn back front, like a musical comedy chorus.*)

We love you in the morning;
We love you in the night.
We love you when we're with you,
And we love you out of sight.
Skinamarinka—dinka—dink
Skinamarinka—do.

(MAE *turns to* BIG MAMA.)

Big Mama, too!

(BIG MAMA *bursts into tears. The* NEGROES *leave.*)

BIG DADDY: Now Ida, what the hell is the matter with you?
MAE: She's just so happy.
BIG MAMA: I'm just so happy, Big Daddy, I have to cry or something.

(*Sudden and loud in the hush.*)

Brick, do you know the wonderful news that Doc Baugh got from the clinic about Big Daddy? Big Daddy's one hundred per cent!
MARGARET: Isn't that wonderful?
BIG MAMA: He's just one hundred per cent. Passed the examination with flying colors. Now that we know there's nothing wrong with Big Daddy but a spastic colon, I can tell you something. I was worried sick, half out of my mind, for fear Big Daddy might have a thing like—

(MARGARET *cuts through this speech, jumping up and exclaiming shrilly.*)

MARGARET: Brick, honey, aren't you going to give Big Daddy his birthday present?

(*Passing by him, she snatches his liquor glass from him.*)
(*She picks up a fancily wrapped package.*)

Here it is, Big Daddy, this is from Brick!
BIG MAMA: This is the biggest birthday Big Daddy's ever had, a hundred presents and bushels of telegrams from—
MAE (*at same time*): What is it, Brick?
GOOPER: I bet 500 to 50 that Brick don't *know* what it is.
BIG MAMA: The fun of presents is not knowing what they are till you open the package. Open your present, Big Daddy.
BIG DADDY: Open it you'self. I want to ask Brick somethin'! Come here, Brick.
MARGARET: Big Daddy's callin' you, Brick. (*She is opening the package.*)
BRICK: Tell Big Daddy I'm crippled.
BIG DADDY: I see you're crippled. I want to know how you got crippled.
MARGARET (*making diversionary tactics*): Oh, look, oh, look, why, it's a cashmere robe! (*She holds the robe up for all to see.*)
MAE: You sound surprised, Maggie.
MARGARET: I never saw one before.
MAE: That's funny.—*Hah!*
MARGARET (*turning on her fiercely, with a brilliant smile*): Why is it funny? All my family ever had was family—and luxuries such as cashmere robes still surprise me!
BIG DADDY (*ominously*): Quiet!
MAE (*heedless in her fury*): I don't see how you could be so surprised when you bought it yourself at Loewenstein's in Memphis last Saturday. You know how I know?

BIG DADDY: I said, Quiet!

MAE: —I know because the salesgirl that sold it to you waited on me and said, Oh, Mrs. Pollitt, your sister-in-law just bought a cashmere robe for your husband's father!

MARGARET: Sister Woman! Your talents are wasted as a housewife and mother, you really ought to be with the FBI or—

BIG DADDY: QUIET!

(REVEREND TOOKER's *reflexes are slower than the others'. He finishes a sentence after the bellow.*)

REVEREND TOOKER (*to* DOC BAUGH): —the Stork and the Reaper are running neck and neck!

(*He starts to laugh gaily when he notices the silence and* BIG DADDY's *glare. His laugh dies falsely.*)

BIG DADDY: Preacher, I hope I'm not butting in on more talk about memorial stained-glass windows, am I, Preacher?

(REVEREND TOOKER *laughs feebly, then coughs dryly in the embarrassed silence.*)

Preacher?

BIG MAMA: Now, Big Daddy, don't you pick on Preacher!

BIG DADDY (*raising his voice*): You ever hear that expression all hawk and no spit? You bring that expression to mind with that little dry cough of yours, all hawk an' no spit. . . .

(*The pause is broken only by a short startled laugh from* MARGARET, *the only one there who is conscious of and amused by the grotesque.*)

MAE (*raising her arms and jangling her bracelets*): I wonder if the mosquitoes are active tonight?

BIG DADDY: What's that, Little Mama? Did you make some remark?

MAE: Yes, I said I wondered if the mosquitoes would eat us alive if we went out on the gallery for a while.

BIG DADDY: Well, if they do, I'll have your bones pulverized for fertilizer!

BIG MAMA (*quickly*): Last week we had an airplane spraying the place and I think it done some good, at least I haven't had a—

BIG DADDY (*cutting her speech*): Brick, they tell me, if what they tell me is true, that you done some jumping last night on the high school athletic field?

BIG MAMA: Brick, Big Daddy is talking to you, son.

BRICK (*smiling vaguely over his drink*): What was that, Big Daddy?

BIG DADDY: They said you done some jumping on the high school track field last night.

BRICK: That's what they told me, too.

BIG DADDY: Was it jumping or humping that you

were doing out there? What were you doing out there at three A.M., layin' a woman on that cinder track?

BIG MAMA: Big Daddy, you are off the sick-list, now, and I'm not going to excuse you for talkin' so—

BIG DADDY: Quiet!

BIG MAMA: —*nasty* in front of Preacher and—

BIG DADDY: QUIET!—I ast you, Brick, if you was cuttin' you'self a piece o' poon-tang last night on that cinder track? I thought maybe you were chasin' poon-tang on that track an' tripped over something in the heat of the chase—'sthat it?

(GOOPER *laughs, loud and false, others nervously following suit.* BIG MAMA *stamps her foot, and purses her lips, crossing to* MAE *and whispering something to her as* BRICK *meets his father's hard, intent, grinning stare with a slow, vague smile that he offers all situations from behind the screen of his liquor.*)

BRICK: No, sir, I don't think so. . . .

MAE (*at the same time, sweetly*): Reverend Tooker, let's you and I take a stroll on the widow's walk.

(*She and the preacher go out on the gallery as* BIG DADDY *says.*)

BIG DADDY: Then what the hell were you doing out there at three o'clock in the morning?

BRICK: Jumping the hurdles, Big Daddy, runnin' and jumpin' the hurdles, but those high hurdles have gotten too high for me, now.

BIG DADDY: Cause you was drunk?

BRICK (*his vague smile fading a little*): Sober I wouldn't have tried to jump the *low* ones. . . .

BIG MAMA (*quickly*): Big Daddy, blow out the candles on your birthday cake!

MARGARET (*at the same time*): I want to propose a toast to Big Daddy Pollitt on his sixty-fifth birthday, the biggest cotton planter in—

BIG DADDY (*bellowing with fury and disgust*): I told you to stop it, now stop it, quit this—!

BIG MAMA (*coming in front of* BIG DADDY *with the cake*).: Big Daddy, I will not allow you to talk that way, not even on your birthday, I—

BIG DADDY: I'll talk like I want to on my birthday, Ida, or any other goddam day of the year and anybody here that don't like it knows what they can do!

BIG MAMA: You don't mean that!

BIG DADDY: What makes you think I don't mean it?

(*Meanwhile various discreet signals have been exchanged and* GOOPER *has also gone out on the gallery.*)

BIG MAMA: I just know you don't mean it.

BIG DADDY: You don't know a goddam thing and you never did!

BIG MAMA: Big Daddy, you don't mean that.

BIG DADDY: Oh, yes, I do, oh, yes, I do, I mean it! I

put up with a whole lot of crap around here because I thought I was dying. And you thought I was dying and you started taking over, well, you can stop taking over now, Ida, because I'm not gonna die, you can just stop now this business of taking over because you're not taking over because I'm not dying and I went through the laboratory and the goddam exploratory operation and there's nothing wrong with me but a spastic colon. And I'm not dying of cancer which you thought I was dying of. Ain't that so? Didn't you think that I was dying of cancer, Ida?

(*Almost everybody is out on the gallery but the two old people glaring at each other across the blazing cake.*)
(BIG MAMA's *chest heaves and she presses a fat fist to her mouth.*)
(BIG DADDY *continues, hoarsely.*)

Ain't that so, Ida? Didn't you have an idea I was dying of cancer and now you could take control of this place and everything on it? I got that impression, I seemed to get that impression. Your loud voice everywhere, your fat old body butting in here and there!

BIG MAMA: Hush! The Preacher!
BIG DADDY: Fuck the goddam preacher!

(BIG MAMA *gasps loudly and sits down on the sofa which is almost too small for her.*)

Did you hear what I said? I said fuck the goddam preacher!

(*Somebody closes the gallery doors from outside just as there is a burst of fireworks and excited cries from the children.*)

BIG MAMA: I never seen you act like this before and I can't think what's got in you!
BIG DADDY: I went through all that laboratory and operation and all just so I would know if you or me was boss here! Well, now it turns out that I am and you ain't—and that's my birthday present—and my cake and champagne!—because for three years now you been gradually taking over. Bossing. Talking. Sashaying your fat old body around the place I made! I made this place! I was overseer on it! I was the overseer on the old Straw and Ochello plantation. I quit school at ten! I quit school at ten years old and went to work like a nigger in the fields. And I rose to be overseer of the Straw and Ochello plantation. And old Straw died and I was Ochello's partner and the place got bigger and bigger and bigger and bigger and bigger! I did all that myself with no goddam help from you, and now you think you're just about to take over. Well, I am just about to tell you that you are not just about to take over, you are not just about to take

over a God damn thing. Is that clear to you, Ida? Is that very plain to you, now? Is that understood completely? I been through the laboratory from A to Z. I've had the goddam exploratory operation, and nothing is wrong with me but a spastic colon—made spastic, I guess, by *disgust!* By all the goddam lies and liars that I have had to put up with, and all the goddam hypocrisy that I lived with all these forty years that we been livin' together!

Hey! Ida!! Blow out the candles on the birthday cake! Purse up your lips and draw a deep breath and blow out the goddam candles on the cake!

BIG MAMA: Oh, Big Daddy, oh, oh, oh, Big Daddy!
BIG DADDY: What's the matter with you?
BIG MAMA: *In all these years you never believed that I loved you??*
BIG DADDY: Huh?
BIG MAMA: *And I did. I did so much. I did love you!—I even loved your hate and your hardness, Big Daddy!* (*She sobs and rushes awkwardly out onto the gallery.*)
BIG DADDY (*to himself*): *Wouldn't it be funny if that was true....*

(*A pause is followed by a burst of light in the sky from the fireworks.*)

BRICK! HEY, BRICK!

(*He stands over his blazing birthday cake.*)
(*After some moments,* BRICK *hobbles in on his crutch, holding his glass.* MARGARET *follows him with a bright, anxious smile.*)

I didn't call you, Maggie. I called Brick.
MARGARET: I'm just delivering him to you.

(*She kisses* BRICK *on the mouth which he immediately wipes with the back of his hand. She flies girlishly back out.* BRICK *and his father are alone.*)

BIG DADDY: Why did you do that?
BRICK: Do what, Big Daddy?
BIG DADDY: Wipe her kiss off your mouth like she'd spit on you.
BRICK: I don't know. I wasn't conscious of it.
BIG DADDY: That woman of yours has a better shape on her than Gooper's but somehow or other they got the same look about them.
BRICK: What sort of look is that, Big Daddy?
BIG DADDY: I don't know how to describe it but it's the same look.
BRICK: They don't look peaceful, do they?
BIG DADDY: No, they sure in hell don't.
BRICK: They look nervous as cats?
BIG DADDY: That's right, they look nervous as cats.
BRICK: Nervous as a couple of cats on a hot tin roof?
BIG DADDY: That's right, boy, they look like a couple

of cats on a hot tin roof. It's funny that you and Gooper being so different would pick out the same type of woman.

BRICK: Both of us married into society, Big Daddy.

BIG DADDY: Crap . . . I wonder what gives them both that look?

BRICK: Well. They're sittin' in the middle of a big piece of land, Big Daddy, twenty-eight thousand acres is a pretty big piece of land and so they're squaring off on it, each determined to knock off a bigger piece of it than the other whenever you let it go.

BIG DADDY: I got a surprise for those women. I'm not gonna let it go for a long time yet if that's what they're waiting for.

BRICK: That's right, Big Daddy. You just sit tight and let them scratch each other's eyes out. . . .

BIG DADDY: You bet your life I'm going to sit tight on it and let those sons of bitches scratch their eyes out, ha ha ha. . . .

But Gooper's wife's a good breeder, you got to admit she's fertile. Hell, at supper tonight she had them all at the table and they had to put a couple of extra leafs in the table to make room for them, she's got five head of them, now, and another one's comin'.

BRICK: Yep, number six is comin'. . . .

BIG DADDY: Six hell, she'll probably drop a litter next time. Brick, you know, I swear to God, I don't know the way it happens?

BRICK: The way what happens, Big Daddy?

BIG DADDY: You git you a piece of land, by hook or crook, an' things start growin' on it, things accumulate on it, and the first thing you know it's completely out of hand, completely out of hand!

BRICK: Well, they say nature hates a vacuum, Big Daddy.

BIG DADDY: That's what they say, but sometimes I think that a vacuum is a hell of a lot better than some of the stuff that nature replaces it with.

Is someone out there by that door?

GOOPER: Hey Mae.

BRICK: Yep.

BIG DADDY: Who? (He has lowered his voice.)

BRICK: Someone int'rested in what we say to each other.

BIG DADDY: Gooper?—GOOPER!

(After a discreet pause, MAE appears in the gallery door.)

MAE: Did you call Gooper, Big Daddy?

BIG DADDY: Aw, it was you.

MAE: Do you want Gooper, Big Daddy?

BIG DADDY: No, and I don't want you. I want some privacy here, while I'm having a confidential talk with my son Brick. Now it's too hot in here to close them doors, but if I have to close those fuckin' doors in order to have a private talk with

my son Brick, just let me know and I'll close 'em. Because I hate eavesdroppers, I don't like any kind of sneakin' an' spyin'.

MAE: Why, Big Daddy—

BIG DADDY: You stood on the wrong side of the moon, it threw your shadow!

MAE: I was just—

BIG DADDY: You was just nothing but *spyin'* an' you *know* it!

MAE (*begins to sniff and sob*): Oh, Big Daddy, you're so unkind for some reason to those that really love you!

BIG DADDY: Shut up, shut up, shut up! I'm going to move you and Gooper out of that room next to this! It's none of your goddam business what goes on in here at night between Brick an' Maggie. You listen at night like a couple of rutten peekhole spies and go and give a report on what you hear to Big Mama an' she comes to me and says they say such and such and so and so about what they heard goin' on between Brick an' Maggie, and Jesus, it makes me sick. I'm goin' to move you an' Gooper out of that room, I can't stand sneakin' an' spyin', it makes me puke. . . .

(MAE *throws back her head and rolls her eyes heavenward and extends her arms as if invoking God's pity for this unjust martyrdom; then she presses a handkerchief to her nose and flies from the room with a loud swish of skirts.*)

BRICK (*now at the liquor cabinet*): They listen, do they?

BIG DADDY: Yeah. They listen and give reports to Big Mama on what goes on in here between you and Maggie. They say that— (*He stops as if embarrassed.*) —You won't sleep with her, that you sleep on the sofa. Is that true or not true? If you don't like Maggie, get rid of Maggie!—What are you doin' there now?

BRICK: Fresh'nin up my drink.

BIG DADDY: Son, you know you got a real liquor problem?

BRICK: Yes, sir, yes, I know.

BIG DADDY: Is that why you quit sports-announcing, because of this liquor problem?

BRICK: Yes, sir, yes, sir, I guess so.

(*He smiles vaguely and amiably at his father across his replenished drink.*)

BIG DADDY: Son, don't guess about it, it's too important.

BRICK (*vaguely*): Yes, sir.

BIG DADDY: And listen to me, don't look at the damn chandelier. . . .

(*Pause.* BIG DADDY's *voice is husky.*)

—Somethin' else we picked up at th' big fire sale in Europe.

(Another pause.)

Life is important. There's nothing else to hold onto. A man that drinks is throwing his life away. Don't do it, hold onto your life. There's nothing else to hold onto. . . .

Sit down over here so we don't have to raise our voices, the walls have ears in this place.

BRICK *(hobbling over to sit on the sofa beside him)*: All right, Big Daddy.

BIG DADDY: Quit!—how'd that come about? Some disappointment?

BRICK: I don't know. Do you?

BIG DADDY: I'm askin' you, God damn it! How in hell would I know if you don't?

BRICK: I just got out there and found that I had a mouth full of cotton. I was always two or three beats behind what was goin' on on the field and so I—

BIG DADDY: Quit!

BRICK *(amiably)*: Yes, quit.

BIG DADDY: Son?

BRICK: Huh?

BIG DADDY *(inhales loudly and deeply from his cigar; then bends suddenly a little forward, exhaling loudly and raising a hand to his forehead)*: Whew!—ha ha!—I took in too much smoke, it made me a little lightheaded. . . .

(The mantel clock chimes.)

Why is it so damn hard for people to talk?

BRICK: Yeah. . . .

(The clock goes on sweetly chiming till it has completed the stroke of ten.)

—Nice peaceful-soundin' clock, I like to hear it all night. . . .

(He slides low and comfortable on the sofa; BIG DADDY *sits straight and rigid with some unspoken anxiety. All his gestures are tense and jerky as he talks. He wheezes and pants and sniffs through his nervous speech, glancing quickly, shyly, from time to time, at his son.)*

BIG DADDY: We got that clock the summer we wint to Europe, me an' Big Mama on that damn Cook's Tour, never had such an awful time in my life. I'm tellin' you, son, those gooks over there, they gouge your eyeballs out in their grand hotels. And Big Mama bought more stuff than you could haul in a couple of boxcars, that's no crap. Everywhere she wint on this whirlwind tour, she bought, bought, bought. Why, half that stuff she bought is still crated up in the cellar, under water last spring! *(He laughs.)*

That Europe is nothin' on earth but a great big auction, that's all it is, that bunch of old worn-out places, it's just a big firesale, the whole fuckin' thing, an' Big Mama wint wild in it, why, you couldn't hold that woman with a mule's harness! Bought, bought, bought!—lucky I'm a rich man, yes siree, Bob, an' half that stuff is mildewin' in th' basement. It's lucky I'm a rich man, it sure is lucky, well, I'm a rich man, Brick, yep, I'm a mighty rich man. *(His eyes light up for a moment.)*

Y'know how much I'm worth? Guess, Brick! Guess how much I'm worth!

*(*BRICK *smiles vaguely over his drink.)*

Close on ten million in cash an' blue-chip stocks, outside, mind you, of twenty-eight thousand acres of the richest land this side of the valley Nile!

But a man can't buy his life with it, he can't buy back his life with it when his life has been spent, that's one thing not offered in the Europe fire-sale or in the American markets or any markets on earth, a man can't buy his life with it, he can't buy back his life when his life is finished.

That's a sobering thought, a very sobering thought, and that's a thought that I was turning over in my head, over and over and over—until today. . . .

I'm wiser and sadder, Brick, for this experience which I just gone through. They's one thing else that I remember in Europe.

BRICK: What is that, Big Daddy?

BIG DADDY: The hills around Barcelona in the country of Spain and the children running over those bare hills in their bare skins beggin' like starvin' dogs with howls and screeches, and how fat the priests are on the streets of Barcelona, so many of them and so fat and so pleasant, ha ha!—Y'know I could feed that country? I got money enough to feed that goddam country, but the human animal is a selfish beast and I don't reckon the money I passed out there to those howling children in the hills around Barcelona would more than upholster the chairs in this room, I mean pay to put a new cover on this chair!

Hell, I threw them money like you'd scatter feed corn for chickens, I threw money at them just to get rid of them long enought to climb back into th' car and—drive away. . . .

And then in Morocco, them Arabs, why, I remember one day in Marrakech, that old walled Arab city, I set on a broken-down wall to have a cigar, it was fearful hot there and this Arab woman stood in the road and looked at me till I was embarrassed, she stood stock still in the dusty hot road and looked at me till I was embarrassed. But listen to this. She had a naked child with her, a little naked girl with her, barely able to toddle, and after a while she set this child on the ground and give her a push and whispered something to her.

This child come toward me, barely able t' walk, come toddling up to me and—

Jesus, it makes you sick to' remember a thing like this!

It stuck out its hand and tried to unbutton my trousers!

That child was not yet five! Can you believe me? Or do you think that I am making this up? I wint back to the hotel and said to Big Mama, Git packed! We're clearing out of this country. . . .

BRICK: Big Daddy, you're on a talkin' jag tonight.

BIG DADDY (ignoring this remark): Yes, sir, that's how it is, the human animal is a beast that dies but the fact that he's dying don't give him pity for others, no, sir, it—

—Did you say something?

BRICK: Yes.

BIG DADDY: What?

BRICK: Hand me over that crutch so I can get up.

BIG DADDY: Where you goin'?

BRICK: I'm takin' a little short trip to Echo Spring.

BIG DADDY: To where?

BRICK: Liquor cabinet. . . .

BIG DADDY: Yes, sir, boy— (He hands BRICK the crutch) —the human animal is a beast that dies and if he's got money he buys and buys and buys and I think the reason he buys everything he can buy is that in the back of his mind he has the crazy hope that one of his purchases will be life everlasting!—Which it never can be. . . . The human animal is a beast that—

BRICK (at the liquor cabinet): Big Daddy, you sure are shootin' th' breeze here tonight.

(There is a pause and voices are heard outside.)

BIG DADDY: I been quiet here lately, spoke not a word, just sat and stared into space. I had something heavy weighing on my mind but tonight that load was took off me. That's why I'm talking.—The sky looks diff'rent to me. . . .

BRICK: You know what I like to hear most?

BIG DADDY: What?

BRICK: Solid quiet. Perfect unbroken quiet.

BIG DADDY: Why?

BRICK: Because it's more peaceful.

BIG DADDY: Man, you'll hear a lot of that in the grave.
(He chuckles agreeably.)

BRICK: Are you through talkin' to me?

BIG DADDY: Why are you so anxious to shut me up?

BRICK: Well, sir, ever so often you say to me, Brick, I want to have a talk with you, but when we talk, it never materializes. Nothing is said. You sit in a chair and gas about this and that and I look like I listen. I try to look like I listen, but I don't listen, not much. Communication is—awful hard be-

tween people an'—somehow between you and me, it just don't—happen.

BIG DADDY: Have you ever been scared? I mean have you ever felt downright terror of something? (He gets up.) Just one moment. (He looks off as if he were going to tell an important secret.)

BIG DADDY: Brick?

BRICK: What?

BIG DADDY: Son, I thought I had it!

BRICK: Had what? Had what, Big Daddy?

BIG DADDY: Cancer!

BRICK: Oh . . .

BIG DADDY: I thought the old man made out of bones had laid his cold and heavy hand on my shoulder!

BRICK: Well, Big Daddy, you kept a tight mouth about it.

BIG DADDY: A pig squeals. A man keeps a tight mouth about it, in spite of a man not having a pig's advantage.

BRICK: What advantage is that?

BIG DADDY: Ignorance—of mortality—is a comfort. A man don't have that comfort, he's the only living thing that conceives of death, that knows what it is. The others go without knowing which is the way that anything living should go, go without knowing, without any knowledge of it, and yet a pig squeals, but a man sometimes, he can keep a tight mouth about it. Sometimes he—

(There is a deep smoldering ferocity in the old man.)

—can keep a tight mouth about it. I wonder if—

BRICK: What, Big Daddy?

BIG DADDY: A whiskey highball would injure this spastic condition?

BRICK: No, sir, it might do it good.

BIG DADDY (grins suddenly, wolfishly): Jesus, I can't tell you! The sky is open! Christ, it's open again! It's open boy, it's open!

(BRICK looks down at his drink.)

BRICK: You feel better, Big Daddy?

BIG DADDY: Better? Hell! I can breathe!—All of my life I been like a doubled up fist. . . . (He pours a drink.) —Poundin', smashin', drivin'!—now I'm going to loosen these doubled-up hands and touch things easy with them. . . .

(He spreads his hands as if caressing the air.)

You know what I'm contemplating?

BRICK (vaguely): No, sir. What are you contemplating?

BIG DADDY: Ha ha!—Pleasure!—pleasure with women!

(BRICK's smile fades a little but lingers.)

—Yes, boy. I'll tell you something that you might

not guess. I still have desire for women and this is my sixty-fifth birthday.

BRICK: I think that's mighty remarkable, Big Daddy.

BIG DADDY: Remarkable?

BRICK: *Admirable*, Big Daddy.

BIG DADDY: You're damn right it is, remarkable and admirable both. I realize now that I never had me enough. I let many chances slip by because of scruples about it, scruples, convention—crap. . . . All that stuff is bull, bull, bull!—It took the shadow of death to make me see it. Now that shadow's lifted, I'm going to cut loose and have, what is it they call it, have me a—ball!

BRICK: A ball, huh?

BIG DADDY: That's right, a ball, a ball! Hell!—I slept with Big Mama till, let's see, five years ago, till I was sixty and she was fifty-eight, and never even liked her, never did!

(*The phone has been ringing down the hall.* BIG MAMA *enters, exclaiming.*)

BIG MAMA: Don't you men hear that phone ring? I heard it way out on the gall'ry.

BIG DADDY: There's five rooms off this front gall'ry that you could go through. Why do you go through this one?

(BIG MAMA *makes a playful face as she bustles out the hall door.*)

Hunh!—Why, when Big Mama goes out of a room, I can't remember what that woman looks like—

BIG MAMA: Hello.

BIG DADDY: But when Big Mama comes back into the room, boy, then I see what she looks like, and I wish I didn't.

(*Bends over laughing at this joke till it hurts his guts and he straightens with a grimace. The laugh subsides to a chuckle as he puts the liquor glass a little distrustfully down the table.*)

BIG MAMA: Hello, Miss Sally.

(BRICK *has risen and hobbled to the gallery doors.*)

BIG DADDY: Hey! Where you goin'?

BRICK: Out for a breather.

BIG DADDY: Not yet you ain't. Stay here till this talk is finished, young fellow.

BRICK: I thought it was finished, Big Daddy.

BIG DADDY: It ain't even begun.

BRICK: My mistake. Excuse me. I just wanted to feel that river breeze.

BIG DADDY: Set back in that chair.

(BIG MAMA's *voice rises, carrying down the hall.*)

BIG MAMA: Miss Sally, you're a case! You're a caution, Miss Sally.

BIG DADDY: Jesus, she's talking to my old maid sister again.

BIG MAMA: Why didn't you give me a chance to explain it to you?

BIG DADDY: Brick, this stuff burns me.

BIG MAMA: Well, goodbye, now, Miss Sally. You come down real soon. Big Daddy's dying to see you.

BIG DADDY: Crap!

BIG MAMA: Yaiss, goodbye, Miss Sally. . . .

(*She hangs up and bellows with mirth.* BIG DADDY *groans and covers his ears as she approaches.*)

(*Bursting in*)

Big Daddy, that was Miss Sally callin' from Memphis again! You know what she done, Big Daddy? She called her doctor in Memphis to git him to tell her what that spastic thing is! Ha-HAAAA!—And called back to tell me how relieved she was that—Hey! Let me in!

(BIG DADDY *has been holding the door half closed against her.*)

BIG DADDY: Naw I ain't. I told you not to come and go through this room You just back out and go through those five other rooms.

BIG MAMA: Big Daddy? Big Daddy? Oh, Big Daddy!—You didn't mean those things you said to me, did you?

(*He shuts door firmly against her but she still calls.*)

Sweetheart? Sweetheart? Big Daddy? You didn't mean those awful things you said to me?—I know you didn't. I know you didn't mean those things in your heart. . . .

(*The childlike voice fades with a sob and her heavy footsteps retreat down the hall.* BRICK *has risen once more on his crutches and starts for the gallery again.*)

BIG DADDY: All I ask of that woman is that she leave me alone. But she can't admit to herself that she makes me sick. That comes of having slept with her too many years. Should of quit much sooner but that old woman she never got enough of it—and I was good in bed . . . I never should of wasted so much of it on her. . . . They say you got just so many and each one is numbered. Well, I got a few left in me, a few, and I'm going to pick me a good one to spend 'em on! I'm going to pick me a choice one, I don't care how much she costs, I'll smother her in—minks! Ha ha! I'll strip her naked and smother her in minks and choke her with diamonds! Ha ha! I'll strip her naked and choke her with diamonds and smother her with minks and hump her from hell to breakfast. *Ha aha ha ha ha!*

MAE (*gaily at door*): Who's that laughin' in there?

GOOPER: Is Big Daddy laughin' in there?

BIG DADDY: Crap!—them two—*drips.* . . .

(*He goes over and touches* BRICK's *shoulder.*)

Yes, son. Brick, boy.—I'm *happy!* I'm happy, son, I'm happy!

(*He chokes a little and bites his under lip, pressing his head quickly, shyly against his son's head and then, coughing with embarrassment, goes uncertainly back to the table where he set down the glass. He drinks and makes a grimace as it burns his guts.* BRICK *sighs and rises with effort.*)

What makes you so restless? Have you got ants in your britches?

BRICK: Yes, sir . . .

BIG DADDY: Why?

BRICK: —Something—hasn't happened. . . .

BIG DADDY: Yeah? What is that!

BRICK (*sadly*): —the click. . . .

BIG DADDY: Did you say click?

BRICK: Yes, click.

BIG DADDY: What click?

BRICK: A click that I get in my head that makes me peaceful.

BIG DADDY: I sure in hell don't know what you're talking about, but it disturbs me.

BRICK: It's just a mechanical thing.

BIG DADDY: What is a mechanical thing?

BRICK: This click that I get in my head that makes me peaceful. I got to drink till I get it. It's just a mechanical thing, something like a—like a—like a—

BIG DADDY: Like a—

BRICK: Switch clicking off in my head, turning the hot light off and the cool night on and— (*He looks up, smiling sadly.*) —all of a sudden there's —peace!

BIG DADDY (*whistles long and soft with astonishment; he goes back to* BRICK *and clasps his son's two shoulders*) Jesus! I didn't know it had gotten that bad with you. Why, boy, you're—*alcoholic!*

BRICK: That's the truth, Big Daddy. I'm alcoholic.

BIG DADDY: This shows how I—let things go!

BRICK: I have to hear that little click in my head that makes me peaceful. Usually I hear it sooner than this, sometimes as early as—noon, but—

—Today it's—dilatory. . . .

—I just haven't got the right level of alcohol in my bloodstream yet!

(*This last statement is made with energy as he freshens his drink.*)

BIG DADDY: Uh—huh. Expecting death made me blind. I didn't have no idea that a son of mine was turning into a drunkard under my nose.

BRICK (*gently*): Well, now you do, Big Daddy, the news has penetrated. . . .

BIG DADDY: Uh-huh, yes, now I do. The news has penetrated.

BRICK: And so if you'll excuse me—

BIG DADDY: No, I won't excuse you.

BRICK: —I'd better sit by myself till I hear that click in my head, it's just a mechanical thing but it don't happen except when I'm alone or talking to no one. . . .

BIG DADDY: You got a long, long time to sit still, boy, and talk to no one, but now you're talkin' to me. At least I'm talking to you. And you set there and listen until I tell you the conversation is over!

BRICK: But this talk is like all the others we've ever had together in our lives! It's nowhere, nowhere!—it's—it's *painful,* Big Daddy. . . .

BIG DADDY: All right, then let it be painful, but don't you move from that chair!—I'm going to remove that crutch. . . . (*He seizes the crutch and tosses it across room.*)

BRICK: I can hop on one foot, and if I fall, I can crawl!

BIG DADDY: If you ain't careful you're gonna crawl off this plantation and then, by Jesus, you'll have to hustle your drinks along Skid Row!

BRICK: That'll come, Big Daddy.

BIG DADDY: Naw, it won't. You're my son and I'm going to straighten you out; now that *I'm* straightened out, I'm going to straighten out you!

BRICK: Yeah?

BIG DADDY: Today the report come in from Ochsner Clinic. Y'know what they told me? (*His face glows with triumph.*) The only thing that they could detect with all the instruments of science in that great hospital is a little spastic condition of the colon! And nerves torn to pieces by all that worry about it.

(*A little girl bursts into room with a sparkler clutched in each fist, hops and shrieks like a monkey gone mad and rushes back out again as* BIG DADDY *strikes at her.*)
(*Silence. The two men stare at each other. A woman laughs gaily outside.*)

I want you to know I breathed a sigh of relief almost as powerful as the Vicksburg tornado!

(*There is laughter outside, running footsteps, the soft, plushy sound and light of exploding rockets.*)
(BRICK *stares at him soberly for a long moment; then makes a sort of startled sound in his nostrils and springs up on one foot and hops across the room to grab his crutch, swinging on the furniture for support. He gets the crutch and flees as if in horror for the gallery. His father seizes him by the sleeve of his white silk pajamas.*)

Stay here, you son of a bitch!—till I say go!

BRICK: I can't.

BIG DADDY: You sure in hell will, God damn it.

BRICK: No, I can't. We talk, you talk, in—circles! We get no where, no where! It's always the same, you say you want to talk to me and don't have a fuckin' thing to say to me!

BIG DADDY: Nothin' to say when I'm tellin' you I'm going to live when I thought I was dying?!

BRICK: Oh—*that*—Is that what you have to say to me?

BIG DADDY: Why, you son of a bitch! Ain't that, ain't that—*important*?!

BRICK: Well, you said that, that's said, and now *I*—

BIG DADDY: Now you set back down.

BRICK: You're all balled up, you—

BIG DADDY: I ain't balled up!

BRICK: You are, you're all balled up!

BIG DADDY: Don't tell me what I am, you drunken whelp! I'm going to tear this coat sleeve off you if you don't set down!

BRICK: Big Daddy—

BIG DADDY: Do what I tell you! I'm the boss here, now! I want you to know I'm back in the driver's seat now!

(BIG MAMA *rushes in, clutching her great heaving bosom.*)

BIG MAMA: Big Daddy!

BIG DADDY: What in hell do you want in here, Big Mama?

BIG MAMA: Oh, Big Daddy! Why are you shouting like that? I just cain't *stainnnnnnnd*—it. . . .

BIG DADDY (*raising the back of his hand above his head*): GIT!—outa here.

(*She rushes back out, sobbing.*)

BRICK (*softly, sadly*): Christ. . . .

BIG DADDY (*fiercely*): Yeah! Christ!—is right . . .

(BRICK *breaks loose and hobbles toward the gallery.*)
(BIG DADDY *jerks his crutch from under* BRICK *so he steps with the injured ankle. He utters a hissing cry of anguish, clutches a chair and pulls it over on top of him on the floor.*)

Son of a—tub of—hog fat. . . .

BRICK: Big Daddy! Give me my crutch.

(BIG DADDY *throws the crutch out of reach.*)

Give me that crutch, Big Daddy.

BIG DADDY: Why do you drink?

BRICK: Don't know, give me my crutch!

BIG DADDY: You better think why you drink or give up drinking!

BRICK: Will you please give me my crutch so I can get up off this floor?

BIG DADDY: First you answer my question. Why do you drink? Why are you throwing your life away, boy, like somethin' disgusting you picked up on the street?

BRICK (*getting onto his knees*): Big Daddy, I'm in pain, I stepped on that foot.

BIG DADDY: Good! I'm glad you're not too numb with the liquor in you to feel some pain!

BRICK: You—spilled my—drink . . .

BIG DADDY: I'll make a bargain with you. You tell me why you drink and I'll hand you one. I'll pour the liquor myself and hand it to you.

BRICK: Why do I drink?

BIG DADDY: Yea! Why?

BRICK: Give me a drink and I'll tell you.

BIG DADDY: Tell me first!

BRICK: I'll tell you in one word.

BIG DADDY: What word?

BRICK: DISGUST!

(*The clock chimes softly, sweetly.* BIG DADDY *gives it a short, outraged glance.*)

Now how about that drink?

BIG DADDY: What are you disgusted with? You got to tell me that, first. Otherwise being disgusted don't make no sense!

BRICK: Give me my crutch.

BIG DADDY: You heard me, you got to tell me what I asked you first.

BRICK: I told you, I said to kill my disgust!

BIG DADDY: DISGUST WITH WHAT!

BRICK: You strike a hard bargain.

BIG DADDY: What are you disgusted with?—an' I'll pass you the liquor.

BRICK: I can hop on one foot, and if I fall, I can crawl.

BIG DADDY: You want liquor that bad?

BRICK (*dragging himself up, clinging to bedstead*): Yeah, I want it that bad.

BIG DADDY: If I give you a drink, will you tell me what it is you're disgusted with, Brick?

BRICK: Yes, sir, I will try to.

(*The old man pours him a drink and solemnly passes it to him.*)
(*There is a silence as* BRICK *drinks.*)

Have you ever heard the word "mendacity"?

BIG DADDY: Sure. Mendacity is one of them five dollar words that cheap politicians throw back and forth at each other.

BRICK: You know what it means?

BIG DADDY: Don't it mean lying and liars?

BRICK: Yes, sir, lying and liars.

BIG DADDY: Has someone been lying to you?

CHILDREN (*chanting in chorus offstage*):
    We want Big Dad-dee!
    We want Big Dad-dee

(GOOPER *appears in the gallery door.*)

GOOPER: Big Daddy, the kiddies are shouting for you out there.

BIG DADDY (*fiercely*): Keep out, Gooper!

GOOPER: 'Scuse *me!*

(BIG DADDY *slams the doors after* GOOPER.)

BIG DADDY: Who's been lying to you, has Margaret been lying to you, has your wife been lying to you about something, Brick?

BRICK: Not her. That wouldn't matter.

BIG DADDY: Then who's been lying to you, and what about?

BRICK: No one single person and no one lie. . . .

BIG DADDY: Then what, what then, for Christ's sake?

BRICK: The whole, the whole—thing. . . .

BIG DADDY: Why are you rubbing your head? You got a headache?

BRICK: No, I'm tryin' to—

BIG DADDY: —Concentrate, but you can't because your brain's all soaked with liquor, is that the trouble? Wet brain! (*He snatches the glass from* BRICK's *hand.*) What do you know about this mendacity thing? Hell! I could write a book on it! Don't you know that? I could write a book on it and still not cover the subject. Well, I could, I could write a goddam book on it and still not cover the subject anywhere near enough!!—Think of all the lies I got to put up with!—Pretenses! Ain t that mendacity? Having to pretend stuff you don't think or feel or have any idea of? Having for instance to act like I care for Big Mama!—I haven't been able to stand the sight, sound, or smell of that woman for forty years now!—even when I *laid* her!—regular as a piston. . . .

Pretend to love that son of a bitch of a Gooper and his wife Mae and those five same screechers out there like parrots in a jungle? Jesus! Can't stand to look at 'em!

Church!—it bores the bejesus out of me but I go!—I go an' sit there and listen to the fool preacher!

Clubs!—Elks! Masons! Rotary!—*crap!*

(*A spasm of pain makes him clutch his belly. He sinks into a chair and his voice is softer and hoarser.*)

You I *do* like for some reason, did always have some kind of real feeling for—affection—respect—yes, always. . . .

You and being a success as a planter is all I ever had any devotion to in my whole life!—and that's the truth. . . .

I don't know why, but it is!

I've lived with mendacity!—Why can't *you* live with it? Hell, you *got* to live with it, there's nothing *else* to *live* with except mendacity, is there?

BRICK: Yes, sir. Yes, sir there is something else that you can live with!

BIG DADDY: What?

BRICK (*lifting his glass*): This!—Liquor. . . .

BIG DADDY: That's not living, that's dodging away from life.

BRICK: I want to dodge away from it.

BIG DADDY: Then why don't you kill yourself, man?

BRICK: I like to drink. . . .

BIG DADDY: Oh, God, I can't talk to you. . . .

BRICK: I'm sorry, Big Daddy.

BIG DADDY: Not as sorry as I am. I'll tell you something. A little while back when I thought my number was up—

(*This speech should have torrential pace and fury.*)

—before I found out it was just this—spastic—colon. I thought about you. Should I or should I not, if the jig was up, give you this place when I go—since I hate Gooper an' Mae an' know that they hate me, and since all five same monkeys are little Maes an' Goopers.—And I thought, No!—Then I thought, Yes!—I couldn't make up my mind. I hate Gooper and his five same monkeys and that bitch Mae! Why should I turn over twenty-eight thousand acres of the richest land this side of the valley Nile to not my kind?—But why in hell, on the other hand, Brick—should I subsidize a goddam fool on the bottle?—Liked or not liked, well, maybe even—*loved!*—Why should I do that?—Subsidize worthless behavior? Rot? Corruption?

BRICK (*smiling*): I understand.

BIG DADDY: Well, if you do, you're smarter than I am. God damn it, because I don't understand. And this I will tell you frankly. I didn't make up my mind at all on that question and still to this day I ain't made out no will!—Well, now I don't *have* to. The pressure is gone. I can just wait and see if you pull yourself together or if you don't.

BRICK: That's right, Big Daddy.

BIG DADDY: You sound like you thought I was kidding.

BRICK (*rising*): No, sir, I know you're not kidding.

BIG DADDY: But you don't care—?

BRICK (*hobbling toward the gallery door*): No, sir, I don't care. . . .

(*He stands in the gallery doorway as the night sky turns pink and green and gold with successive flashes of light.*)

BIG DADDY: WAIT!—Brick. . . .

(*His voice drops. Suddenly there is something shy, tender, in his restraining gesture.*)

Don't let's—leave it like this, like them other talks we've had, we've always—talked around things, we've—just talked around things for some fuckin' reason. I don't know what, it's always like something was left not spoken, something avoided because neither of us was honest enough with the—other. . . .

BRICK: I never lied to you, Big Daddy.

BIG DADDY: Did I ever to *you*?

BRICK: No, sir. . . .

BIG DADDY: Then there is at least two people that never lied to each other.

BRICK: But we've never *talked* to each other.

BIG DADDY: We can *now*.

BRICK: Big Daddy, there don't seem to be anything much to say.

BIG DADDY: You say that you drink to kill your disgust with lying.

BRICK: You said to give you a reason.

BIG DADDY: Is liquor the only thing that'll kill this disgust?

BRICK: Now. Yes.

BIG DADDY: But not once, huh?

BRICK: Not when I was still young an' believing. A drinking man's someone who wants to forget he isn't still young an' believing.

BIG DADDY: Believing what?

BRICK: Believing. . . .

BIG DADDY: Believing *what*?

BRICK (*stubbornly evasive*): Believing. . . .

BIG DADDY: I don't know what the hell you mean by believing and I don't think you know what you mean by believing, but if you still got sports in your blood, go back to sports announcing and—

BRICK: Sit in a glass box watching games I can't play? Describing what I can't do while players do it? Sweating out their disgust and confusion in contests I'm not fit for? Drinkin' a coke, half bourbon, so I can stand it? That's no goddam good any more, no help—time just outran me, Big Daddy—got there first . . .

BIG DADDY: I think you're passing the buck.

BRICK: You know many drinkin' men?

BIG DADDY (*with a slight, charming smile*): I have known a fair number of that species.

BRICK: Could any of them tell you why he drank?

BIG DADDY: Yep, you're passin' the buck to things like time and disgust with "mendacity" and—crap!—if you got to use that kind of language about a thing, it's ninety-proof bull, and I'm not buying any.

BRICK: I had to give you a reason to get a drink!

BIG DADDY: You started drinkin' when your friend Skipper died.

(*Silence for five beats. Then* BRICK *makes a startled movement, reaching for his crutch.*)

BRICK: What are you suggesting?

BIG DADDY: I'm suggesting nothing.

(*The shuffle and clop of* BRICK's *rapid hobble away from*

his father's steady, grave attention.*)

—But Gooper an' Mae suggested that there was something not right exactly in your—

BRICK (*stopping short downstage as if backed to a wall*): "Not right"?

BIG DADDY: Not, well, exactly *normal* in your friendship with—

BRICK: They suggested that, too? I thought that was Maggie's suggestion.

(BRICK's *detachment is at last broken through. His heart is accelerated; his forehead sweat-beaded; his breath becomes more rapid and his voice hoarse. The thing they're discussin, timidly and painfully on the side of* BIG DADDY, *fiercely, violently on* BRICK's *side, is the inadmissible thing that* SKIPPER *died to disavow between them. The fact that if it existed it had to be disavowed to "keep face" in the world they lived in, may be at the heart of the "mendacity" that* BRICK *drinks to kill his disgust with. It may be the root of his collapse. Or maybe it is only a single manifestation of it, not even the most important. The bird that I hope to catch in the net of this play is not the solution of one man's psychological problem. I'm trying to catch the true quality of experience in a group of people, that cloudy, flickering, evanescent—fiercely charged!—interplay of live human beings in the thundercloud of a common crisis. Some mystery should be left in the revelation of characters in a play, just as a great deal of mystery is always left in the revelation of character in life, even in one's own character to himself. This does not absolve the playwright of his duty to observe and probe as clearly and deeply as he legitimately can: but it should steer him away from "pat" conclusions, facile definitions which make a play just a play, not a snare for the truth of human experience.*)

(*The following scene should be played with great concentration, with most of the power leashed but palpable in what is left unspoken.*)

Who else's suggestion is it, is it *yours*? How many others thought that Skipper and I were—

BIG DADDY (*gently*): Now, hold on, hold on a minute, son.—I knocked around in my time.

BRICK: What's that got to do with—

BIG DADDY: I said "Hold on!"—I bummed, I bummed this country till I was—

BRICK: Whose suggestion, who else's suggestion is it?

BIG DADDY: Slept in hobo jungles and railroad Y's and flophouses in all cities before I—

BRICK: Oh, *you* think so, too, you call me your son and a queer. Oh! Maybe that's why you put Maggie and me in this room that was Jack Straw's and Peter Ochello's, in which that pair of old sisters slept in a double bed where both of 'em died!

BIG DADDY: *Now just don't go throwing rocks at—*

(*Suddenly* REVEREND TOOKER *appears in the gallery doors, his head slightly, playfully, fatuously cocked, with a practised clergyman's smile, sincere as a bird call blown on a hunter's whistle, the living embodiment of the pious, conventional lie.)*

(BIG DADDY gasps a little at this perfectly timed, but incongruous, apparition.)

—What're you lookin' for, Preacher?

REVEREND TOOKER: The gentleman's lavatory, ha ha!—heh, heh . . .

BIG DADDY *(with strained courtesy)*: —Go back out and walk down to the other end of the gallery, Reverend Tooker, and use the bathroom connected with my bedroom, and if you can't find it, ask them where it is!

REVEREND TOOKER: Ah, thanks. *(He goes out with a deprecatory chuckle.)*

BIG DADDY: It's hard to talk in this place . . .

BRICK: Son of a—!

BIG DADDY *(leaving a lot unspoken)*: —I seen all things and understood a lot of them, till 1910. Christ, the year that—I had worn my shoes through, hocked my—I hopped off a yellow dog freight car half a mile down the road, slept in a wagon of cotton outside the gin—Jack Straw an' Peter Ochello took me in. Hired me to manage this place which grew into this one.—When Jack Straw died—why, old Peter Ochello quit eatin' like a dog does when its master's dead, and died, too!

BRICK: Christ!

BIG DADDY: I'm just saying I understand such—

BRICK *(violently)*: Skipper is dead. I have not quit eating!

BIG DADDY: No, but you started drinking.

(BRICK wheels on his crutch and hurls his glass across the room shouting.)

BRICK: YOU THINK SO, TOO?

(Footsteps run on the gallery. There are women's calls.)
(BIG DADDY goes toward the door.)
(BRICK is transformed, as if a quiet mountain blew suddenly up in volcanic flame.)

BRICK: You think so, too? You think so, too? You think me an' Skipper did, did, did!—*sodomy!*—together?

BIG DADDY: Hold—!

BRICK: That what you—

BIG DADDY: —ON—a minute!

BRICK: You think we did dirty things between us, Skipper an'—

BIG DADDY: Why are you shouting like that? Why are you—

BRICK: —Me, is that what you think of Skipper, is that—

BIG DADDY: —so excited? I don't think nothing. I don't know nothing. I'm simply telling you what—

BRICK: You think that Skipper and me were a pair of dirty old men?

BIG DADDY: Now that's—

BRICK: Straw? Ochello? A couple of—

BIG DADDY: Now just—

BRICK: —fucking sissies? Queers? Is that what you—

BIG DADDY: Shhh.

BRICK: —think?

(He loses his balance and pitches to his knees without noticing the pain. He grabs the bed and drags himself up.)

BIG DADDY: Jesus!—Whew. . . . Grab my hand!

BRICK: Naw, I don't want your hand. . . .

BIG DADDY: Well, I want yours. Git up!

(He draws him up, keeps an arm about him with concern and affection.)

You broken out in a sweat! You're panting like you'd run a race with—

BRICK *(freeing himself from his father's hold)*: Big Daddy, you shock me, Big Daddy, you, you—*shock* me! Talkin' so— *(He turns away from his father.)* —casually!—about a—thing like that . . .

—Don't you know how people *feel* about things like that? How, how *disgusted* they are by things like that? Why, at Ole Miss when it was discovered a pledge to our fraternity, Skipper's and mine, did a, *attempted* to do a, unnatural thing with—

We not only dropped him like a hot rock!— We told him to git off the campus, and he did, he got!—All the way to— *(He halts, breathless.)*

BIG DADDY: —Where?

BRICK: —North Africa, last I heard!

BIG DADDY: Well, I have come back from further away than that, I have just now returned from the other side of the moon, death's country, son, and I'm not easy to shock by anything here. *(He comes downstage and faces out.)* Always, anyhow, lived with too much space around me to be infected by ideas of other people. One thing you can grow on a big place more important than cotton!—is *tolerance!*—I grown it. *(He returns toward BRICK.)*

BRICK: Why can't exceptional friendship, *real, real, deep, deep friendship!* between two men be respected as something clean and decent without being thought of as—

BIG DADDY: It can, it is, for God's sake.

BRICK: —*Fairies.* . . .

(In his utterance of this word, we gauge the wide and profound reach of the conventional mores he got from the world that crowned him with early laurel.)

BIG DADDY: I told Mae an' Gooper—

BRICK: Frig Mae and Gooper, frig all dirty lies and liars!—Skipper and me had a clean, true thing between us!—had a clean friendship, practically all our lives, till Maggie got the idea you're talking about. Normal? No!—it was too rare to be normal, any true thing between two people is too rare to be normal. Oh, once in a while he put his hand on my shoulder or I'd put mine on his, oh, maybe even, when we were touring the country in pro-football an' shared hotel-rooms we'd reach across the space between the two beds and shake hands to say goodnight, yeah, one or two times we—

BIG DADDY: Brick, nobody thinks that that's not normal!

BRICK: Well, they're mistaken, it was! It was a pure an' true thing an' that's not normal.

MAE (off stage): Big Daddy, they're startin' the fireworks.

(They both stare straight at each other for a long moment. The tension breaks and both turn away as if tired.)

BIG DADDY: Yeah, it's—hard t'—talk. . . .

BRICK: All right, then, let's—let it go. . . .

BIG DADDY: Why did Skipper crack up? Why have you?

(BRICK looks back at his father again. He has already decided, without knowing that he has made this decision, that he is going to tell his father that he is dying of cancer. Only this could even the score between them: one inadmissible thing in return for another.)

BRICK (ominously): All right. You're asking for it, Big Daddy. We're finally going to have that real true talk you wanted. It's too late to stop it, now, we got to carry it through and cover every subject.

(He hobbles back to the liquor cabinet.)

Uh-huh.

(He opens the ice bucket and picks up the silver tongs with slow admiration of their frosty brightness.)

Maggie declares that Skipper and I went into pro-football after we left "Ole Miss" because we were scared to grow up . . .

(He moves downstage with the shuffle and clop of a cripple on a crutch. As MARGARET did when her speech became "recitative," he looks out into the house, commanding its attention by his direct, concentrated gaze—a broken, "tragically elegant" figure telling simply as much as he knows of "the Truth.")

—Wanted to—keep on tossing—those long, long!—high, high!—passes that—couldn't be intercepted except by time, the aerial attack that made us famous! And so we did, we did, we kept it up for one season, that aerial attack, we held it high!—Yeah, but—

—that summer, Maggie, she laid the law down to me, said, Now or never, and so I married Maggie. . . .

BIG DADDY: How was Maggie in bed?

BRICK (wryly): Great! the greatest!

(BIG DADDY nods as if he thought so.)

She went on the road that fall with the Dixie Stars. Oh, she made a great show of being the world's best sport. She wore a—wore a—tall bearskin cap! A shako, they call it, a dyed mole-skin coat, a moleskin coat dyed red!—Cut up crazy! Rented hotel ballrooms for victory celebrations, wouldn't cancel them when it—turned out—defeat. . . .

MAGGIE THE CAT! Ha ha!

(BIG DADDY nods.)

—But Skipper, he had some fever which came back on him which doctors couldn't explain and I got that injury—turned out to be just a shadow on the X-ray plate—and a touch of bursitis. . . .

I lay in a hospital bed, watched our games on TV, saw Maggie on the bench next to Skipper when he was hauled out of a game for stumbles, fumbles!—Burned me up the way she hung on his arm!—Y'know, I think that Maggie had always felt sort of left out because she and me never got any closer together than two people just get in bed, which is not much closer than two cats on a—fence humping. . . .

So! She took this time to work on poor dumb Skipper. He was a less than average student at Ole Miss, you know that, don't you?!—Poured in his mind the dirty, false idea that what we were, him and me, was a frustrated case of that ole pair of sisters that lived in this room, Jack Straw and Peter Ochello!—He, poor Skipper, went to bed with Maggie to prove it wasn't true, and when it didn't work out, he thought it *was* true!—Skipper broke in two like a rotten stick—nobody ever turned so fast to a lush—or died of it so quick. . . .

—Now are you satisfied?

(BIG DADDY has listened to this story, dividing the grain from the chaff. Now he looks at his son.)

BIG DADDY: Are *you* satisfied?

BRICK: With what?

BIG DADDY: That half-ass story!

BRICK: What's half-ass about it?

BIG DADDY: Something's left out of that story. What did you leave out?

(The phone has started ringing in the hall.)

GOOPER *(off stage)*: Hello.

(As if it reminded him of something BRICK *glances suddenly toward the sound and says.)*

BRICK: Yes!—I left out a long-distance call which I had from Skipper—

GOOPER: Speaking, go ahead.

BRICK: —In which he made a drunken confession to me and on which I hung up!

GOOPER: No.

BRICK: Last time we spoke to each other in our lives . . .

GOOPER: No, sir.

BIG DADDY: You musta said something to him before you hung up.

BRICK: What could I say to him?

BIG DADDY: Anything. Something.

BRICK: Nothing.

BIG DADDY: Just hung up?

BRICK: Just hung up.

BIG DADDY: Uh-huh. Anyhow now!—we have tracked down the lie with which you're disgusted and which you are drinking to kill your disgust with, Brick. You been passing the buck. This disgust with mendacity is disgust with yourself.

You!—dug the grave of your friend and kicked him in it!—before you'd face truth with him!

BRICK: *His* truth, not *mine!*

BIG DADDY: His truth, okay! But you wouldn't face it with him!

BRICK: Who *can* face truth? Can *you?*

BIG DADDY: Now don't start passin' the rotten buck again, boy!

BRICK: *How about these birthday congratulations, these many, many happy returns of the day, when ev'rybody knows there won't be any except you!*

*(*GOOPER, *who has answered the hall phone, lets out a high, shrill laugh; the voice becomes audible saying: "No, no, you got it all wrong! Upside down. Are you crazy?")*
*(*BRICK *suddenly catches his breath as he realizes that he has made a shocking disclosure. He hobbles a few paces, then freezes, and without looking at his father's shocked face, says.)*

Let's, let's—go out, now, and—watch the fireworks. Come on, Big Daddy.

*(*BIG DADDY *moves suddenly forward and grabs hold of the boy's crutch like it was a weapon for which they were fighting for possession.)*

BIG DADDY: Oh, no, no! No one's going out! What did you start to say?

BRICK: I don't remember.

BIG DADDY: "Many happy returns when they know there won't be any"?

BRICK: Aw, hell, Big Daddy, forget it. Come on out on the gallery and look at the fireworks they're shooting off for your birthday. . . .

BIG DADDY: First you finish that remark you were makin' before you cut off. "Many happy returns when they know there won't be any"?—Ain't that what you just said?

BRICK: Look, now. I can get around without that crutch if I have to but it would be a lot easier on the furniture an' glassware if I didn' have to go swinging along like Tarzan of th'—

BIG DADDY: FINISH! WHAT YOU WAS SAYIN'!

(An eerie green glow shows in sky behind him.)

BRICK *(sucking the ice in his glass, speech becoming thick)*: Leave th' place to Gooper and Mae an' their five little same little monkeys. All I want is—

BIG DADDY: "LEAVE TH' PLACE," did you say?

BRICK *(vaguely)*: All twenty-eight thousand acres of the richest land this side of the valley Nile.

BIG DADDY: Who said I was "leaving the place" to Gooper or anybody? This is my sixty-fifth birthday! I got fifteen years or twenty years left in me! I'll outlive *you!* I'll bury you an' have to pay for your coffin!

BRICK: Sure. Many happy returns. Now let's go watch the fireworks, come on, let's—

BIG DADDY: Lying, have they been lying? About the report from th'—clinic? Did they, did they—find something—*Cancer.* Maybe?

BRICK: Mendacity is a system that we live in. Liquor is one way out an' death's the other. . . .

(He takes the crutch from BIG DADDY's *loose grip and swings out on the gallery leaving the doors open.)*
(A song, "Pick a Bale of Cotton," is heard.)

MAE *(appearing in door)*: Oh, Big Daddy, the field hands are singin' fo' you!

BRICK: I'm sorry, Big Daddy. My head don't work any more and it's hard for me to understand how anybody could care if he lived or died or was dying or cared about anything but whether or not there was liquor left in the bottle and so I said what I said without thinking. In some ways I'm no better than the others, in some ways worse because I'm less alive. Maybe it's being alive that makes them lie, and being almost *not* alive makes me sort of accidentally truthful—I don't know but—anyway—we've been friends . . .

—And being friends is telling each other the truth. . . .

(There is a pause.)

You told *me!* I told *you!*

BIG DADDY *(slowly and passionately)*: CHRIST—
DAMN—

GOOPER *(off stage)*: Let her go!

(Fireworks off stage right.)

BIG DADDY: —ALL—LYING SONS OF—LYING
BITCHES!

*(He straightens at last and crosses to the inside door. At
the door he turns and looks back as if he had some desperate question he couldn't put into words. Then he nods
reflectively and says in a hoarse voice.)*

Yes, all liars, all liars, all lying dying liars!

*(This is said slowly, slowly, with a fierce revulsion. He
goes on out.)*

—Lying! Dying! Liars!

*(BRICK remains motionless as the lights dim out and the
curtain falls.)*

ACT 3

*(There is no lapse of time. BIG DADDY is seen leaving as
at the end of ACT 2.)*

BIG DADDY: ALL LYIN'—DYIN'!—LIARS!—
LIARS!—LIARS!

(MARGARET enters.)

MARGARET: Brick, what in the name of God was goin'
on in this room?

*(DIXIE and TRIXIE enter through the doors and circle
around MARGARET shouting. MAE enters from the lower
gallery window.)*

MAE: Dixie, Trixie, you quit that!

(GOOPER enters through the doors.)

Gooper, will y' please get these kiddies to bed
right now!

GOOPER: Mae, you seen Big Mama?

MAE: Not yet.

*(GOOPER and kids exit through the doors. REVEREND
TOOKER enters through the windows.)*

REVEREND TOOKER: Those kiddies are so full of vitality. I think I'll have to be starting back to town.

MAE: Not yet, Preacher. You know we regard you as a
member of this family, one of our closest an'
dearest, so you just got t' be with us when Doc
Baugh gives Big Mama th' actual truth about th'
report from the clinic.

MARGARET: Where do you think you're going?

BRICK: Out for some air.

MARGARET: Why'd Big Daddy shout "Liars"?

MAE: Has Big Daddy gone to bed, Brick?

GOOPER *(entering)*: Now where is that old lady?

REVEREND TOOKER: I'll look for her. *(He exits to the
gallery.)*

MAE: Cain'tcha find her, Gooper?

GOOPER: She's avoidin' this talk.

MAE: I think she senses somethin'.

MARGARET *(going out to the gallery to BRICK)*: Brick,
they're goin' to tell Big Mama the truth about
Big Daddy and she's goin' to need you.

DOCTOR BAUGH: This is going to be painful.

MAE: Painful things cain't always be avoided.

REVEREND TOOKER: I see Big Mama.

GOOPER: Hey, Big Mama, come here.

MAE: Hush, Gooper, don't holler.

BIG MAMA *(entering)*: Too much smell of burnt
fireworks makes me feel a little bit sick at my
stomach.—Where is Big Daddy?

MAE: That's what I want to know, where has Big
Daddy gone?

BIG MAMA: He must have turned in, I reckon he went
to baid . . .

GOOPER: Well, then, now we can talk.

BIG MAMA: What *is* this talk, *what* talk?

*(MARGARET appears on the gallery, talking to DOCTOR
BAUGH.)*

MARGARET *(musically)*: My family freed their slaves
ten years before abolition. My great-great-
grandfather gave his slaves their freedom five
years before the War between the States started!

MAE: Oh, for God's sake! Maggie's climbed back up in
her family tree!

MARGARET *(sweetly)*: What, Mae?

(The pace must be very quick: great Southern animation.)

BIG MAMA *(addressing them all)*: I think Big Daddy was
just worn out. He loves his family, he loves to
have them around him, but it's a strain on his
nerves. He wasn't himself tonight, Big Daddy
wasn't himself, I could tell he was all worked up.

REVEREND TOOKER: I think he's remarkable.

BIG MAMA: Yaisss! Just remarkable. Did you all notice
the food he ate at that table? Did you all notice
the supper he put away? Why he ate like a hawss!

GOOPER: I hope he doesn't regret it.

BIG MAMA: What? Why that man—ate a huge piece of
cawn bread with molasses on it! Helped himself
twice to hoppin' John.

MARGARET: Big Daddy loves hoppin' John.—We had
a real country dinner.

BIG MAMA *(overlapping MARGARET)*: Yaiss, he simply
adores it! an' candied yams? Son? That man put
away enough food at that table to stuff a *field*
hand!

GOOPER *(with grim relish)*: I hope he don't have to pay
for it later on . . .

BIG MAMA (*fiercely*): What's *that*, Gooper?

MAE: Gooper says he hopes Big Daddy doesn't suffer tonight.

BIG MAMA: Oh, shoot, Gooper says, Gooper says! Why should Big Daddy suffer for satisfying a normal appetite? There's nothin' wrong with that man but nerves, he's sound as a dollar! And now he knows he is an' that's why he ate such a supper. He had a big load off his mind, knowin' he wasn't doomed t'—what he thought he was doomed to . . .

MARGARET (*sadly and sweetly*): Bless his old sweet soul . . .

BIG MAMA (*vaguely*): Yais, bless his heart, where's Brick?

MAE: Outside.

GOOPER: —Drinkin' . . .

BIG MAMA: I know he's drinkin'. Cain't I see he's drinkin' without you continually tellin' me that boy's drinkin'?

MARGARET: Good for you, Big Mama! (*She applauds.*)

BIG MAMA: Other people *drink* and *have* drunk an' will *drink*, as long as they make that stuff an' put it in bottles.

MARGARET: That's the truth. I never trusted a man that didn't drink.

BIG MAMA: *Brick? Brick!*

MARGARET: He's still on the gall'ry. I'll go bring him in so we can talk.

BIG MAMA (*worriedly*): I don't know what this mysterious family conference is about.

(*Awkward silence. BIG MAMA looks from face to face, then belches slightly and mutters, "Excuse me . . ." She opens an ornamental fan suspended about her throat. A black lace fan to go with her black lace gown, and fans her wilting corsage, sniffing nervously and looking from face to face in the uncomfortable silence as MARGARET calls "Brick?" and BRICK sings to the moon on the gallery.*)

MARGARET: Brick, they're gonna tell Big Mama the truth an' she's gonna need you.

BIG MAMA: I don't know what's wrong here, you all have such long faces! Open that door on the hall and let some air circulate through here, will you please, Gooper?

MAE: I think we'd better leave that door closed, Big Mama, till after the talk.

MARGARET: Brick!

BIG MAMA: Reveren' Tooker, will *you* please open that door?

REVEREND TOOKER: I sure will, Big Mama.

MAE: I just didn't think we ought t' take any chance of Big Daddy hearin' a word of this discussion.

BIG MAMA: *I swan!* Nothing's going to be said in Big Daddy's house that he cain't hear if he want to!

GOOPER: Well, Big Mama, it's—

(*MAE gives him a quick, hard poke to shut him up. He glares at her fiercely as she circles before him like a burlesque ballerina, raising her skinny bare arms over her head, jangling her bracelets, exclaiming.*)

MAE: *A breeze! A breeze!*

REVEREND TOOKER: I think this house is the coolest house in the Delta.—Did you all know that Halsey Bank's widow put air-conditioning units in the church and rectory at Friar's Point in memory of Halsey?

(*General conversation has resumed; everybody is chatting so that the stage sounds like a bird cage.*)

GOOPER: Too bad nobody cools your church off for you. I bet you sweat in that pulpit these hot Sundays, Reverend Tooker.

REVEREND TOOKER: Yes, my vestments are drenched. Last Sunday the gold in my chasuble faded into the purple.

GOOPER: Reveren', you musta been preachin' hell's fire last Sunday.

MAE (*at the same time to DOCTOR BAUGH*): You reckon those vitamin B12 injections are what they're cracked up t' be, Doc Baugh?

DOCTOR BAUGH: Well if you want to be stuck with something I guess they're as good to be stuck with as anything else.

BIG MAMA (*at the gallery door*): Maggie, Maggie, aren't you comin' with Brick?

MAE (*suddenly and loudly, creating a silence*): I have a strange feeling, I have a peculiar feeling!

BIG MAMA (*turning from the gallery*): What feeling?

MAE: That Brick said somethin' he shouldn't of said t' Big Daddy.

BIG MAMA: Now what on earth could Brick of said t' Big Daddy that he shouldn't say?

GOOPER: Big Mama, there's somethin'—

MAE: NOW, WAIT!

(*She rushes up to BIG MAMA and gives her a quick hug and kiss. BIG MAMA pushes her impatiently off.*)

DOCTOR BAUGH: In my day they had what they call the Keeley cure for heavy drinkers.

BIG MAMA: Shoot!

DOCTOR BAUGH: But now I understand they just take some kind of tablets.

GOOPER: They call them "Annie Bust" tablets.

BIG MAMA: *Brick* don't need to take *nothin'.*

(*BRICK and MARGARET appear in gallery doors. BIG MAMA unaware of his presence behind her.*)

That boy is just broken up over Skipper's death. You know how poor Skipper died. They gave him a big, big dose of that sodium amytal stuff at his home and then they called the ambulance and give him another big, big dose of it at the hospital and that and all of the alcohol in his system fo' months an' months just proved too much for his heart . . . I'm scared of needles! I'm more scared of a needle than the knife . . . I think more people have been needled out of this world than— *(She stops short and wheels about.)* Oh—here's Brick! My precious baby—

(She turns upon BRICK *with short, fat arms extended, at the same time uttering a loud, short sob, which is both comic and touching.* BRICK *smiles and bows slightly, making a burlesque gesture of gallantry for* MARGARET *to pass before him into the room. Then he hobbles on his crutch directly to the liquor cabinet and there is absolute silence, with everybody looking at* BRICK *as everybody has always looked at* BRICK *when he spoke or moved or appeared. One by one he drops ice cubes in his glass, then suddenly, but not quickly looks back over his shoulder with a wry, charming smile, and says.)*

BRICK: I'm sorry! Anyone else?

BIG MAMA *(sadly)*: No, son, I *wish* you wouldn't!

BRICK: I wish I didn't have to, Big Mama, but I'm still waiting for that click in my head which makes it all smooth out!

BIG MAMA: Ow, Brick, you—BREAK MY HEART!

MARGARET *(at same time)*: *Brick, go sit with Big Mama!*

BIG MAMA: I just cain't staiiiiiii-nnnnnnnd-it . . . *(She sobs.)*

MAE: Now that we're all assembled—

GOOPER: We kin talk . . .

BIG MAMA: Breaks my heart . . .

MARGARET: Sit with Big Mama, Brick, and hold her hand.

(BIG MAMA *sniffs very loudly three times, almost like three drumbeats in the pocket of silence.)*

BRICK: You do that, Maggie. I'm a restless cripple. I got to stay on my crutch.

(BRICK *hobbles to the gallery door; leans there as if waiting.)*

(MAE *sits beside* BIG MAMA, *while* GOOPER *moves in front and sits on the end of the couch, facing her.* REVEREND TOOKER *moves nervously into the space between them; on the other side,* DOCTOR BAUGH *stands looking at nothing in particular and lights a cigar.* MARGARET *turns away.)*

BIG MAMA: Why're you all *surroundin'* me—like this? Why're you all starin' at me like this an' makin' signs at each other?

(REVEREND TOOKER *steps back startled.)*

MAE: Calm yourself, Big Mama.

BIG MAMA: Calm you'self, *you'self*, Sister Woman. How could I calm myself with everyone starin' at me as if big drops of blood had broken out on m'face? What's this all about, annh! What?

(GOOPER *coughs and takes a center position.)*

GOOPER: Now, Doc Baugh.

MAE: Doc Baugh?

GOOPER: Big Mama wants to know the complete truth about the report we got from the Ochsner Clinic.

MAE *(eagerly)*: —on Big Daddy's condition!

GOOPER: Yais, on Big Daddy's condition, we got to face it.

DOCTOR BAUGH: Well . . .

BIG MAMA *(terrified, rising)*: Is there? Something? Something that I? Don't—know?

(In these few words, this startled, very soft question, BIG MAMA *reviews the history of her forty-five years with* BIG DADDY, *her great almost embarrassingly true-hearted and simple-minded devotion to* BIG DADDY, *who must have had something* BRICK *has, who made himself loved so much by the "simple expedient" of not loving enough to disturb his charming detachment, also once coupled, like* BRICK, *with virile beauty.)*

(BIG MAMA *has a dignity at this moment; she almost stops being fat.)*

DOCTOR BAUGH *(after a pause, uncomfortably)*: Yes?—Well—

BIG MAMA: I!!!—want to—knowwwwww . . .

(Immediately she thrusts her fist to her mouth as if to deny that statement. Then for some curious reason, she snatches the withered corsage from her breast and hurls it on the floor and steps on it with her short, fat feet.)

Somebody must be lyin'!—I want to know!

MAE: Sit down, Big Mama, sit down on this sofa.

MARGARET: Brick, go sit with Big Mama.

BIG MAMA: *What is it, what is it?*

DOCTOR BAUGH: I never have seen a more thorough examination than Big Daddy Pollitt was given in all my experience with the Ochsner Clinic.

GOOPER: It's one of the best in the country.

MAE: It's THE best in the country—bar *none!*

(For some reason she gives GOOPER *a violent poke as she goes past him. He slaps at her hand without removing his eyes from his mother's face.)*

DOCTOR BAUGH: Of course they were ninety-nine and nine-tenths per cent sure before they even started.

BIG MAMA: Sure of what, sure of what, sure of—*what?—what?*

(She catches her breath in a startled sob. MAE *kisses her quickly. She thrusts* MAE *fiercely away from her, staring at the* DOCTOR.)*

MAE: Mommy, be a brave girl!

BRICK *(in the doorway, softly)*: "By the light, by the light, Of the sil-ve-ry mo-oo-n . . ."

GOOPER: Shut up!—Brick.

BRICK: Sorry . . . *(He wanders out on the gallery.)*

DOCTOR BAUGH: But, now, you see, Big Mama, they

cut a piece off this growth, a specimen of the tissue and—

BIG MAMA: Growth? You told Big Daddy—

DOCTOR BAUGH: Now wait.

BIG MAMA (*fiercely*): You told me and Big Daddy there wasn't a thing wrong with him but—

MAE: Big Mama, they always—

GOOPER: Let Doc Baugh talk, will yuh?

BIG MAMA: —little spastic condition of—(*Her breath gives out in a sob.*)

DOCTOR BAUGH: Yes, that's what we told Big Daddy. But we had this bit of tissue run through the laboratory and I'm sorry to say the test was positive on it. It's—well—malignant . . .

(*Pause.*)

BIG MAMA: Cancer?! Cancer?!

(DOCTOR BAUGH *nods gravely*. BIG MAMA *gives a long gasping cry.*)

MAE AND GOOPER: Now, now, now. Big Mama, you had to know . . .

BIG MAMA: WHY DIDN'T THEY CUT IT OUT OF HIM? HANH? HANH?

DOCTOR BAUGH: Involved too much, Big Mama, too many organs affected.

MAE: Big Mama, the liver's affected and so's the kidneys, both! It's gone way past what they call a—

GOOPER: A surgical risk.

MAE: —Uh-huh . . .

(BIG MAMA *draws a breath like a dying gasp.*)

REVEREND TOOKER: Tch, tch, tch, tch, tch!

DOCTOR BAUGH: Yes, it's gone past the knife.

MAE: *That's why he's turned yellow, Mommy!*

BIG MAMA: *Git away from me, git away from me, Mae! (She rises abruptly.) I want Brick! Where's Brick? Where is my only son?*

MAE: Mama! Did she say "*only* son"?

GOOPER: What does that make *me*?

MAE: A sober responsible man with five precious children!—Six!

BIG MAMA: I want Brick to tell me! Brick! Brick!

MARGARET (*rising from her reflections in a corner*): Brick was so upset he went back out.

BIG MAMA: *Brick!*

MARGARET: Mama, let *me* tell you!

BIG MAMA: No, no, leave me alone, you're not my blood!

GOOPER: *Mama, I'm your son! Listen to me!*

MAE: Gooper's your son, he's your first-born!

BIG MAMA: Gooper never liked Daddy.

MAE (*as if terribly shocked*): *That's not TRUE!*

(There is a pause. The minister coughs and rises.)

REVEREND TOOKER (*to* MAE): I think I'd better slip away at this point. (*Discreetly.*) Good night, good

night, everybody, and God bless you all . . . on this place . . .

(*He slips out.*)

(MAE *coughs and points at* BIG MAMA.)

DOCTOR BAUGH: Well, Big Mama . . . (*He sighs.*)

BIG MAMA: It's all a mistake, I know it's just a bad dream.

DOCTOR BAUGH: We're gonna keep Big Daddy as comfortable as we can.

BIG MAMA: Yes, it's just a bad dream, that's all it is, it's just an awful dream

GOOPER: In my opinion Big Daddy is having some pain but won't admit that he has it.

BIG MAMA: Just a dream, a bad dream.

DOCTOR BAUGH: That's what lots of them do, they think if they don't admit they're having the pain they can sort of escape the fact of it.

GOOPER (*with relish*): Yes, they get sly about it, they get real sly about it.

MAE: Gooper and I think—

GOOPER: Shut up, Mae! Big Mama, I think—Big Daddy ought to be started on morphine.

BIG MAMA: Nobody's going to give Big Daddy morphine.

DOCTOR BAUGH: Now, Big Mama, when that pain strikes it's going to strike mighty hard and Big Daddy's going to need the needle to bear it.

BIG MAMA: I tell you, nobody's going to give him morphine.

MAE: Big Mama, you don't want to see Big Daddy suffer, you know you—

(GOOPER, *standing beside her, gives her a savage poke.*)

DOCTOR BAUGH (*placing a package on the table*): I'm leaving this stuff here, so if there's a sudden attack you all won't have to send out for it.

MAE: I know how to give a hypo.

BIG MAMA: Nobody's gonna give Big Daddy morphine.

GOOPER: Mae took a course in nursing during the war.

MARGARET: Somehow I don't think Big Daddy would want Mae to give him a hypo.

MAE: You think he'd want *you* to do it?

DOCTOR BAUGH: Well . . .

(DOCTOR BAUGH *rises.*)

GOOPER: Doctor Baugh is goin'.

DOCTOR BAUGH: Yes, I got to be goin'. Well, keep your chin up, Big Mama.

GOOPER (*with jocularity*): She's gonna keep *both* chins up, aren't you, Big Mama?

(BIG MAMA *sobs.*)

Now stop that, Big Mama.

GOOPER (*at the door with* DOCTOR BAUGH): Well, Doc,

we sure do appreciate all you done. I'm telling you, we're surely obligated to you for—

(DOCTOR BAUGH *has gone out without a glance at him.*)

—I guess that doctor has got a lot on his mind but it wouldn't hurt him to act a little more human . . .

(BIG MAMA *sobs.*)

Now be a brave girl Mommy.

BIG MAMA: It's not true, I know that it's just not true!

GOOPER: Mama, those tests are infallible!

BIG MAMA: Why are you so determined to see your father daid?

MAE: Big Mama!

MARGARET (*gently*): I know what Big Mama means.

MAE (*fiercely*): Oh, do you?

MARGARET (*quietly and very sadly*): Yes, I think I do.

MAE: For a newcomer in the family you sure do show a lot of understanding.

MARGARET: Understanding is needed on this place.

MAE: I guess you must have needed a lot of it in your family, Maggie, with your father's liquor problem and now you've got Brick with his!

MARGARET: Brick does not have a liquor problem at all. Brick is devoted to Big Daddy. This thing is a terrible strain on him.

BIG MAMA: Brick is Big Daddy's boy, but he drinks too much and it worries me and Big Daddy, and, Margaret, you've got to cooperate with us, you've got to co-operate with Big Daddy and me in getting Brick straightened out. Because it will break Big Daddy's heart if Brick don't pull himself together and take hold of things.

MAE: Take hold of *what* things, Big Mama?

BIG MAMA: The place.

(*There is a quick violent look between* MAE *and* GOOPER.)

GOOPER: Big Mama, you've had a shock.

MAE: Yais, we've all had a shock, but . . .

GOOPER: Let's be realistic—

MAE: Big Daddy would never, would *never,* be foolish enough to—

GOOPER: —put this place in irresponsible hands!

BIG MAMA: Big Daddy ain't going to leave the place in anybody's hands; Big Daddy is *not* going to die. I want you to get that in your heads, all of you!

MAE: Mommy, Mommy, Big Mama, we're just as hopeful an' optimistic as you are about Big Daddy's prospects, we have faith in *prayer*—but nevertheless there are certain matters that have to be discussed an' dealt with, because otherwise—

GOOPER: Eventualities have to be considered and now's the time . . . Mae, will you please get my brief case out of our room?

MAE: Yes, honey. (*She rises and goes out through the hall door.*)

GOOPER (*standing over* BIG MAMA): Now, Big Mom. What you said just now was not at all true and you know it. I've always loved Big Daddy in my own quiet way. I never made a show of it, and I know that Big Daddy has always been fond of me in a quiet way, too, and he never made a show of it neither.

(MAE *returns with* GOOPER's *brief case.*)

MAE: Here's your brief case, Gooper, honey.

GOOPER (*handing the brief case back to her*): Thank you . . . Of cou'se, my relationship with Big Daddy is different from Brick's.

MAE: You're eight years older'n Brick an' always had t' carry a bigger load of th' responsibilities than Brick ever had t' carry. He never carried a thing in his life but a football or a highball.

GOOPER: Mae, will y' let me talk, please?

MAE: Yes, honey.

GOOPER: Now, a twenty-eight-thousand-acre plantation's a mighty big thing t' run.

MAE: Almost singlehanded.

(MARGARET *has gone onto the gallery and can be heard calling softly to* BRICK.)

BIG MAMA: You never had to run this place! What are you talking about? As if Big Daddy was dead and in his grave, you had to run it? Why, you just helped him out with a few business details and had your law practice at the same time in Memphis!

MAE: Oh, Mommy, Mommy, Big Mommy! Let's be fair!

MARGARET: Brick!

MAE: Why, Gooper has given himself body and soul to keeping this place up for the past five years since Big Daddy's health started failing.

MARGARET: Brick!

MAE: Gooper won't say it, Gooper never thought of it as a duty, he just did it. And what did Brick do? Brick kept living in his past glory at college! Still a football player at twenty-seven!

MARGARET (*returning alone*): Who are you talking about now? Brick? A football player? He isn't a football player and you know it. Brick is a sports announcer on T.V. and one of the best-known ones in the country!

MAE: I'm talking about what he was.

MARGARET: Well, I wish you would just stop talking about my husband.

GOOPER: I've got a right to discuss my brother with other members of MY OWN family, which don't include *you.* Why don't you go out there and drink with Brick?

MARGARET: I've never seen such malice toward a brother.

GOOPER: How about his for me? Why, he can't stand to be in the same room with me!

MARGARET: This is a deliberate campaign of vilification for the most disgusting and sordid reason on earth, and I know what it is! It's *avarice, greed, greed!*

BIG MAMA: *Oh, I'll scream! I will scream in a moment unless this stops!*

(GOOPER *has stalked up to* MARGARET *with clenched fists at his sides as if he would strike her.* MAE *distorts her face again into a hideous grimace behind* MARGARET's *back.*)

BIG MAMA (*sobs*): Margaret. Child. Come here. Sit next to Big Mama.

MARGARET: Precious Mommy. I'm sorry, I'm, sorry, I—!

(*She bends her long graceful neck to press her forehead to* BIG MAMA's *bulging shoulder under its black chiffon.*)

MAE: How beautiful, how touching, this display of devotion! Do you know why she's childless? She's childless because that big beautiful athlete husband of hers won't go to bed with her!

GOOPER: You jest won't let me do this in a nice way, will yah? Aw right—I don't give a goddam if Big Daddy likes me or don't like me or did or never did or will or will never! I'm just appealing to a sense of common decency and fair play. I'll tell you the truth. I've resented Big Daddy's partiality to Brick ever since Brick was born, and the way I've been treated like I was just barely good enough to spit on and sometimes not even good enough for that. Big Daddy is dying of cancer, and it's spread all through him and it's attacked all his vital organs including the kidneys and right now he is sinking into uremia, and you all know what uremia is, it's poisoning of the whole system due to the failure of the body to eliminate its poisons.

MARGARET (*to herself, downstage, hissingly*): *Poisons, poisons! Venomous thoughts and words! In hearts and minds!—That's poisons!*

GOOPER (*overlapping her*): I am asking for a square deal, and by God, I expect to get one. But if I don't get one, if there's any peculiar shenanigans going on around here behind my back, well, I'm not a corporation lawyer for nothing, I know how to protect my own interests.

(BRICK *enters from the gallery with a tranquil, blurred smile, carrying an empty glass with him.*)

BRICK: Storm coming up.

GOOPER: Oh! A late arrival!

MAE: Behold the conquering hero comes!

GOOPER: The fabulous Brick Pollitt! Remember him?—Who could forget him!

MAE: He looks like he's been injured in a game!

GOOPER: Yep, I'm afraid you'll have to warm the bench at the Sugar Bowl this year, Brick!

(MAE *laughs shrilly.*)

Or was it the Rose Bowl that he made that famous run in?—

(*Thunder.*)

MAE: The punch bowl, honey. It was in the punch bowl, the cut-glass punch bowl!

GOOPER: Oh, that's right, I'm getting the bowls mixed up!

MARGARET: Why don't you stop venting your malice and envy on a sick boy?

BIG MAMA: *Now you two hush, I mean it, hush, all of you, hush!*

DAISY, SOOKEY: Storm! Storm comin'! Storm! Storm!

LACEY: Brightie, close them shutters.

GOOPER: Lacey, put the top up on my Cadillac, will yuh?

LACEY: Yes, suh, Mistah Pollitt!

GOOPER (*at the same time*): Big Mama, you know it's necessary for me t' go back to Memphis in th' mornin' t' represent the Parker estate in a lawsuit.

(MAE *sits on the bed and arranges papers she has taken from the brief case.*)

BIG MAMA: Is it, Gooper?

MAE: Yaiss.

GOOPER: That's why I'm forced to—to bring up a problem that—

MAE: Somethin' that's too important t' be put off!

GOOPER: If Brick was sober, he ought to be in on this.

MARGARET: Brick is present; we're present.

GOOPER: Well, good. I will now give you this outline my partner, Tom Bullitt, an' me have drawn up—a sort of dummy—trusteeship.

MARGARET: Oh, that's it! You'll be in charge an' dole out remittances, will you?

GOOPER: This we did as soon as we got the report on Big Daddy from th' Ochsner Laboratories. We did this thing, I mean we drew up this dummy outline with the advice and assistance of the Chairman of the Boa'd of Directors of th' Southern Plantahs Bank and Trust Company in Memphis, C. C. Bellowes, a man who handles estates for all th' prominent fam'lies in West Tennessee and th' Delta.

BIG MAMA: Gooper?

GOOPER (*crouching in front of* BIG MAMA): Now this is not—not final, or anything like it. This is just a preliminary outline. But it does provide a basis—a design—a—possible, feasible—*plan!*

MARGARET: Yes, I'll bet it's a plan.

(Thunder.)

MAE: It's a plan to protect the biggest estate in the Delta from irresponsibility an'—

BIG MAMA: Now you listen to me, all of you, you listen here? They's not goin' to be any more catty talk in my house! And Gooper, you put that away before I grab it out of your hand and tear it right up! I don't know what the hell's in it, and I don't want to know what the hell's in it. I'm talkin' in Big Daddy's language now; I'm his *wife* not his *widow,* I'm still his *wife!* And I'm talkin' to you in his language an'—

GOOPER: Big Mama, what I have here is—

MAE *(at the same time)*: Gooper explained that it's just a plan . . .

BIG MAMA: I don't care what you got there. Just put it back where it came from, an' don't let me see it again, not even the outside of the envelope of it! Is that understood? Basis! Plan! Preliminary! Design! I say—what is it Big Daddy always says when he's disgusted?

BRICK *(from the bar)*: Big Daddy says "crap" when he's disgusted.

BIG MAMA *(rising)*: That's right!—CRAP! I say CRAP too, like Big Daddy!

(Thunder.)

MAE: Coarse language doesn't seem called for in this—

GOOPER: Somethin' in me is *deeply outraged* by hearin' you talk like this.

BIG MAMA: *Nobody's goin' to take nothin'!*—till Big Daddy lets go of it—maybe, just possibly, not—not even then! No, not even then!

(Thunder.)

MAE: Sookey, hurry up an' git that po'ch furniture covahed; want th' paint to come off?

GOOPER: Lacey, put mah car away!

LACEY: Caint, Mistah Pollitt, you got the keys!

GOOPER: Naw, you got 'em, man. Where th' keys to th' car, honey?

MAE: You got 'em in your pocket!

BRICK: "You can always hear me singin' this song, Show me the way to go home."

(Thunder distantly.)

BIG MAMA: Brick! Come here, Brick, I need you. Tonight Brick looks like he used to look when he was a little boy, just like he did when he played wild games and used to come home when I hollered myself hoarse for him, all sweaty and pink cheeked and sleepy, with his—red curls shining . . .

(BRICK draws aside as he does from all physical contact and continues the song in a whisper, opening the ice bucket and dropping in the ice cubes one by one as if he were mixing some important chemical formula.)

(Distant thunder.)

Time goes by so fast. Nothin' can outrun it. Death commences too early—almost before you're half acquainted with life—you meet the other . . . Oh, you know we just got to love each other an' stay together, all of us, just as close as we can, especially now that such a *black* thing has come and moved into this place without invitation.

(Awkwardly embracing BRICK, she presses her head to his shoulder.)

(A dog howls off stage.)

Oh, Brick, son of Big Daddy, Big Daddy does so love you. Y'know what would be his fondest dream come true? If before he passed on, if Big Daddy has to pass on . . .

(A dog howls.)

. . . you give him a child of yours, a grandson as much like his son as his son is like Big Daddy . . .

MARGARET: I know that's Big Daddy's dream.

BIG MAMA: That's his dream.

MAE: Such a pity that Maggie and Brick can't oblige.

BIG DADDY *(off down stage right on the gallery)*: Looks like the wind was takin' liberties with this place.

SERVANT *(off stage)*: Yes, sir, Mr. Pollitt.

MARGARET *(crossing to the right door)*: Big Daddy's on the gall'ry.

(BIG MAMA has turned toward the hall door at the sound of BIG DADDY's voice on the gallery.)

BIG MAMA: I can't stay here. He'll see somethin' in my eyes.

(BIG DADDY enters the room from up stage right.)

BIG DADDY: Can I come in?

(He puts his cigar in an ash tray.)

MARGARET: Did the storm wake you up, Big Daddy?

BIG DADDY: Which stawm are you talkin' about—th' one outside or th' hullaballoo in here?

(GOOPER squeezes past BIG DADDY.)

GOOPER: 'Scuse me.

(MAE tries to squeeze past BIG DADDY to join GOOPER, but BIG DADDY puts his arm firmly around her.)

BIG DADDY: I heard some mighty loud talk. Sounded like somethin' important was bein' discussed. What was the powwow about?

MAE (flustered): Why—nothin', Big Daddy . . .

BIG DADDY (crossing to extreme left center, taking MAE with him): What is that pregnant-lookin' envelope you're puttin' back in your brief case, Gooper?

GOOPER (at the foot of the bed, caught, as he stuffs papers into envelope): That? Nothin', suh—nothin' much of anythin' at all . . .

BIG DADDY: Nothin'? It looks like a whole lot of nothin'!

(He turns up stage to the group.)

You all know th' story about th' young married couple—

GOOPER: Yes, sir!

BIG DADDY: Hello, Brick—

BRICK: Hello, Big Daddy.

(The group is arranged in a semicircle above BIG DADDY, MARGARET at the extreme right, then MAE and GOOPER, then BIG MAMA, with BRICK at the left.)

BIG DADDY: Young married couple took Junior out to th' zoo one Sunday, inspected all of God's creatures in their cages, with satisfaction.

GOOPER: Satisfaction.

BIG DADDY (crossing to up stage center, facing front): This afternoon was a warm afternoon in spring an' that ole elephant had somethin' else on his mind which was bigger'n peanuts. You know this story, Brick?

(GOOPER nods.)

BRICK: No, sir, I don't know it.

BIG DADDY: Y'see, in th' cage adjoinin' they was a young female elephant in heat!

BIG MAMA (at BIG DADDY's shoulder): Oh, Big Daddy!

BIG DADDY: What's the matter, preacher's gone, ain't he? All right. That female elephant in the next cage was permeatin' the atmosphere about her with a powerful and excitin' odor of female fertility! Huh! Ain't that a nice way to put it, Brick?

BRICK: Yes, sir, nothin' wrong with it!

BIG DADDY: Brick says th's nothin' wrong with it!

BIG MAMA: Oh, Big Daddy!

BIG DADDY (crossing to down stage center): So this ole bull elephant still had a couple of fornications left in him. He reared back his trunk an' got a whiff of that elephant lady next door!—began to paw at the dirt in his cage an' butt his head against the separatin' partition and, first thing y'know, there was a conspicuous change in his profile—very conspicuous! Ain't I tellin' this story in decent language, Brick?

BRICK: Yes, sir, too fuckin' decent!

BIG DADDY: So, the little boy pointed at it and said, "What's that?" His mama said, "Oh, that's—nothin'!"—His papa said, "She's spoiled!"

(BIG DADDY crosses to BRICK at left.)

You didn't laugh at that story, Brick.

(BIG MAMA crosses to down stage right crying. MARGARET goes to her. MAE and GOOPER hold up stage right center.)

BRICK: No, sir, I didn't laugh at that story.

BIG DADDY: What is the smell in this room? Don't you notice it, Brick? Don't you notice a powerful and obnoxious odor of mendacity in this room?

BRICK: Yes, sir, I think I do, sir.

GOOPER: Mae, Mae . . .

BIG DADDY: There is nothing more powerful. Is there, Brick?

BRICK: No, sir. No, sir there isn't, an' nothin' more obnoxious.

BIG DADDY: Brick agrees with me. The odor of mendacity is a powerful and obnoxious odor an' the stawm hasn't blown it away from this room yet. You notice it, Gooper?

GOOPER: What, sir?

BIG DADDY: How about you, Sister Woman? You notice the unpleasant odor of mendacity in this room?

MAE: Why, Big Daddy, I don't even know what that is.

BIG DADDY: You can smell it. Hell it smells like death!

(BIG MAMA sobs. BIG DADDY looks toward her.)

What's wrong with that fat woman over there, loaded with diamonds? Hey, what's-you-name, what's the matter with you?

MARGARET (crossing toward BIG DADDY): She had a slight dizzy spell, Big Daddy.

BIG DADDY: You better watch that, Big Mama. A stroke is a bad way to go.

MARGARET (crossing to BIG DADDY at center): Oh, Brick, Big Daddy has on your birthday present to him, Brick, he has on your cashmere robe, the softest material I have ever felt.

BIG DADDY: Yeah, this is my soft birthday, Maggie . . . Not my gold or my silver birthday, but my soft birthday, everything's got to be soft for Big Daddy on this soft birthday.

(MAGGIE kneels before BIG DADDY at center.)

MAGGIE: Big Daddy's got on his Chinese slippers that I gave him, Brick. Big Daddy, I haven't given you my big present yet, but now I will, now's the time for me to present it to you! I have an announcement to make!

MAE: What? What kind of announcement?

GOOPER: A sports announcement, Maggie?

MARGARET: Announcement of life beginning! A child is coming, sired by Brick, and out of Maggie the

Cat! I have Brick's child in my body, an' that's my birthday present to Big Daddy on this birthday!

(BIG DADDY *looks at* BRICK *who crosses behind* BIG DADDY *to down stage portal, left.*)

BIG DADDY: Get up, girl, get up off your knees, girl.

(BIG DADDY *helps* MARGARET *to rise. He crosses above her, to her right, bites off the end of a fresh cigar, taken from his bathrobe pocket, as he studies* MARGARET.)

Uh-huh, this girl has life in her body, that's no lie!

BIG MAMA: BIG DADDY'S DREAM COME TRUE!

BRICK: JESUS!

BIG DADDY (*crossing right below wicker stand*): Gooper, I want my lawyer in the mornin'.

BRICK: Where are you goin', Big Daddy?

BIG DADDY: Son, I'm goin' up on the roof, to the belvedere on th' roof to look over my kingdom before I give up my kingdom—twenty-eight thousand acres of th' richest land this side of the valley Nile!

(*He exits through right doors, and down right on the gallery.*)

BIG MAMA (*following*): Sweetheart, sweetheart, sweetheart—can I come with you?

(*She exits down stage right.*)
(MARGARET *is down stage center in the mirror area.* MAE *has joined* GOOPER *and she gives him a fierce poke, making a low hissing sound and a grimace of fury.*)

GOOPER (*pushing her aside.*): Brick, could you possibly spare me one small shot of that liquor?

BRICK: Why, help yourself, Gooper boy.

GOOPER: I will.

MAE (*shrilly*): Of course we know that this is—a lie.

GOOPER: Be still, Mae.

MAE: I won't be still! I know she's made this up!

GOOPER: Goddam it, I said shut up!

MARGARET: Gracious! I didn't know that my little announcement was going to provoke such a storm!

MAE: *That* woman isn't *pregnant!*

GOOPER: Who said she was?

MAE: *She* did.

GOOPER: The doctor didn't. Doc Baugh didn't.

MARGARET: I haven't gone to Doc Baugh.

GOOPER: Then who'd you go to, Maggie?

MARGARET: One of the best gynecologists in the South.

GOOPER: Uh huh, uh huh!—I see . . . (*He takes out a pencil and notebook.*) —May we have his name, please?

MARGARET: No, you may not, Mister Prosecuting Attorney!

MAE: He doesn't have any name, he doesn't exist!

MARGARET: Oh, he exists all right, and so does my child, Brick's baby!

MAE: You can't conceive a child by a man that won't sleep with you unless you think you're—

(BRICK *has turned on the phonograph. A scat song cuts* MAE's *speech.*)

GOOPER: *Turn that off!*

MAE: We know it's a lie because we hear you in here; he won't sleep with you, we hear you! So don't imagine you're going to put a trick over on us, to fool a dying man with a—

(*A long drawn cry of agony and rage fills the house.* MARGARET *turns the phonograph down to a whisper. The cry is repeated.*)

MAE: Did you hear that, Gooper, did you hear that?

GOOPER: Sounds like the pain has struck.

MAE: Go see, Gooper!

GOOPER: Come along and leave these lovebirds together in their nest!

(*He goes out first.* MAE *follows but turns at the door, contorting her face and hissing at* MARGARET.)

MAE: Liar!

(*She slams the door.*)
(MARGARET *exhales with relief and moves a little unsteadily to catch hold of* BRICK's *arm.*)

MARGARET: Thank you for—keeping still . . .

BRICK: O.K., Maggie.

MARGARET: It was gallant of you to save my face!

(*He now pours down three shots in quick succession and stands waiting, silent. All at once he turns with a smile and says.*)

BRICK: *There!*

MARGARET: What?

BRICK: The *click* . . .

(*His gratitude seems almost infinite as he hobbles out on the gallery with a drink. We hear his crutch as he swings out of sight. Then, at some distance, he begins singing to himself a peaceful song.* MARGARET *holds the big pillow forlornly as if it were her only companion, for a few moments, then throws it on the bed. She rushes to the liquor cabinet, gathers all the bottles in her arms, turns about undecidedly, then runs out of the room with them, leaving the door ajar on the dim yellow hall.* BRICK *is heard hobbling back along the gallery, singing his peaceful song. He comes back in, sees the pillow on the bed, laughs lightly, sadly, picks it up. He has it under his arm as* MARGARET *returns to the room.* MARGARET *softly shuts the door and leans against it, smiling softly at* BRICK.)

MARGARET: Brick, I used to think that you were stronger than me and I didn't want to be overpowered by you. But now, since you've taken to liquor—you know what?—I guess it's bad, but now I'm stronger than you and I can love you more truly! Don't move that pillow, I'll move it right back if you do!—Brick?

(She turns out all the lamps but a single rose-silk-shaded one by the bed.)

I really have been to a doctor and I know what to do and—Brick?—this is my time by the calendar to conceive?

BRICK: Yes, I understand, Maggie. But how are you going to conceive a child by a man in love with his liquor?

MARGARET: By locking his liquor up and making him satisfy my desire before I unlock it!

BRICK: Is that what you've done, Maggie?

MARGARET: Look and see. That cabinet's mighty empty compared to before!

BRICK: Well, I'll be a son of a—

(He reaches for his crutch but she beats him to it and rushes out on the gallery, hurls the crutch over the rail and comes back in, panting.)

MARGARET: And so tonight we're going to make the lie true, and when that's done, I'll bring the liquor back here and we'll get drunk together, here, tonight, in this place that death has come into . . . —What do you say?

BRICK: I don't say anything. I guess there's nothing to say.

MARGARET: Oh, you weak people, you weak, beautiful people who give up with such grace. What you want is someone to—

(She turns out the rose-silk lamp.)

—take hold of you.—Gently, gently with love hand your life back to you, like somethin' gold you let go of. I *do* love you, Brick, I *do!*

BRICK *(smiling with charming sadness)*: Wouldn't it be funny if that was true?

Figure 86. Maggie (Elizabeth Ashley) and Brick (Keir Dullea) in the American Shakespeare Theater production of *Cat on a Hot Tin Roof,* directed by Michael Kahn and designed by John Conklin, New York, 1974. (Photograph: Martha Swope.)

Figure 87. Brick (Keir Dullea) and Big Daddy (Fred Gwynne) in the American Shakespeare Theater production of *Cat on a Hot Tin Roof,* directed by Michael Kahn and designed by John Conklin, New York, 1974. (Photograph: Martha Swope.)

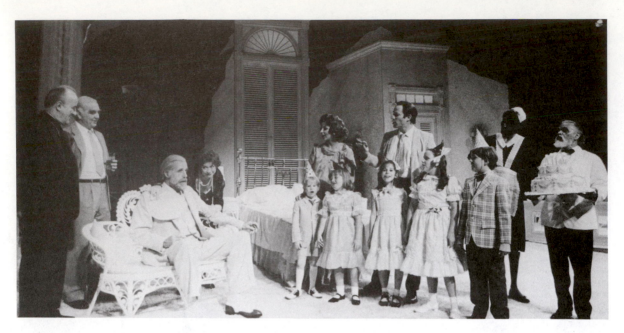

Figure 88. Mae (Joan Pape, *standing center*), Gooper (Charles Siebert), and their five children perform a musical chorus to celebrate the birthday of Big Daddy (Fred Gwynne), while *(left to right)* Reverend Tooker (Wyman Pendleton), Doctor Baugh (William Larsen), Big Mama (Kate Reid), Sookey (Sarallen), and Lacey look on in the American Shakespeare Theater production of *Cat on a Hot Tin Roof,* directed by Michael Kahn and designed by John Conklin, New York, 1974. This photograph also shows the realistic/expressionistic set with walls that "dissolve mysteriously into air," as Williams specified in his "Notes to the Designer." (Photograph: Martha Swope.)

Figure 89. Big Daddy (Fred Gwynne) tells the story of the "ole bull elephant" to Mae (Joan Pape), Big Mama (Kate Reid), and Maggie (Elizabeh Ashley) in the America Shakespeare Theater production of *Cat on a Hot Tin Roof,* directed by Michael Kahn and designed by John Conklin, New York, 1974. (Photograph: Martha Swope.)

Staging of *Cat on a Hot Tin Roof*

**REVIEW OF THE AMERICAN SHAKESPEARE
THEATER PRODUCTION, 1974, BY CLIVE BARNES**

People used to think that Tennessee Williams's plays were about sex and violence. How wrong they were—they are about love and survival. Mr. Williams's "Cat on a Hot Tin Roof" is now 20 years old, and in its first day it was regarded as something of a shocker. Now even though a certain four-letter word has been restored where a euphemism once reigned stupidly supreme, I doubt whether anyone is going to be shocked . . . . But I hope they will be affected. This is a gripping and intensely moving play, a play that can hold its own with anything written in the post-O'Neill American theater.

The Cat is Maggie—a Southern beauty of indefinite lineage. She is married to Brick, a handsome, former football player, now TV sportscaster. The marriage could be perfect, but Brick is an impotent alcoholic who fears that he failed his best friend, apparently a homosexual. Brick's father, Big Daddy, a self-made Southern millionaire, is dying of cancer. He doesn't know it. His wife doesn't know it. But the family, including Brick's brother and sister-in-law, they know it. It is Big Daddy's 65th, and last, birthday.

Michael Kahn's new staging, which opened at the ANTA Theater last night for a limited run, really is new. It originated at the American Shakespeare Theater in Connecticut this summer, and it offers a rewarding new variant on the original play.

As is well known the Broadway version, directed by Elia Kazan, incorporated in its last act a number of Mr. Kazan's own ideas. Indeed in most printed versions of the play the last act exists in two versions, the so-called "Broadway" version, and the original. In the latter Big Daddy does not appear and Brick, faced with some faint prospect of fatherhood, changes somewhat in his character. Mr. Kahn, presumably with the playwright's permission, seems to have taken the best of both acts—following Mr. Kazan in his inclusion of Big Daddy in the last act (and Kazan was right in his thinking there), and yet following the original in its far more sensitive handling of the final relationship between Brick and Maggie. The result seems to be a definitive version of the play.

Twenty years ago everyone made much of the symbolism in Tennessee Williams, and undoubtedly the symbolism is here. The magnolia scented bedroom that used to belong to the old-maidish bachelors that once owned the plantation, the concept of the bed itself as Maggie's territory, or Brick's possible latent homosexuality symbolized by his hazy impotence—yes, all these are symbols of the sexual warfare that underlies the story. But the story itself, and the compassion Mr. Williams brings to the telling of it, is what really matters.

Mr. Williams has the one vital gift a playwright must possess—he holds the interest. He makes you care by showing you a world. His characters are drawn with rough strokes, for Mr. Williams always demonstrates by exaggeration. He is also a playwright who wants to be very popular (or, rather, very much loved) and this sometimes leads him into cheapness. But he is a master. His plays have a time, a place, a development and ring true.

He is lucky with Mr. Kahn, whose direction seems directly aimed at lowering the play's hot-house temperature, and at making a domestic drama rather than an eternal triangle between a woman, a reluctant man and a bed. As a result Big Daddy becomes rather more important than before.

The imaginative setting by John Conklin, the cleverly evocative costumes by Jane Greenwood and the dappled lighting by Marc B. Weiss, are all splendid, but if Mr. Williams has been fortunate in Mr. Kahn and his collaborators, Mr. Kahn has been equally fortunate in his cast, or at least clever in his casting.

Elizabeth Ashley was much praised for her Maggie in Connecticut, but even then she was sold short. Sensuous, withdrawn, composed and determined, Miss Ashley's Maggie vibrantly combines charm with grit. She can stand outside a conversation like a cobra, or flutter in like a bird. Splendid.

Keir Dullea's ironic, embittered Brick makes her the perfect partner. He has precisely "the charm of the defeated," with his alcoholic eyes staring into the mid-distance of half-forgotten memory, still waiting for the click of oblivion. Both this Brick and this Maggie are oddly vulnerable, which is also the special quality of Fred Gwynne's blustering, hollowed out Big Daddy. These three performances are so right that they detract from the more shallow playing of the rest of the cast, including Kate Reid, slightly too shrill as a miscast Big Mama.

This is a glowing play, memorably staged. It gets Broadway's dramatic season off to a flying start.

SAMUEL BECKETT

1906–

Beckett did not start writing plays until his early forties, but by his mid-fifties he had become internationally recognized as one of the most revolutionary, influential, and philosophically significant dramatists of the contemporary period. Born near Dublin to a wealthy family, he was sent away at the age of fourteen to an Irish boarding school, and from there went on to Trinity College, Dublin, where he proved himself an exceptional student of French and Italian. In 1928, he went to Paris as an exchange teacher and there became acquainted with the most famous Irish author of his day, James Joyce, whose radically new fiction stimulated Beckett to experiment with *avant-garde* methods of poetry and fiction writing. He returned briefly to Dublin to serve as a lecturer in French and to receive his master's degree in 1931 for a study of Marcel Proust, but by the mid-1930s he was on the move again in France and Germany, supporting himself at odd jobs, while he continued to write fiction and poetry. Then, in 1937, he settled in Paris, and when World War II began he worked for the French resistance movement. Shortly after the end of the war, having taken up permanent residence in Paris, he wrote his first play, *Waiting for Godot*. When it was produced in 1953, it quickly turned into an international sensation.

Waiting for Godot startled audiences and reviewers because it challenged most of their assumptions about the nature of dramatic form. It challenged their ideas of plot with its persistently illogical and purposeless activity, it questioned their ideas of dialogue with its endless contradictions between language and action, it challenged their ideas of spectacle with its stage bare except for a tree that is also bare until the second act when it has somehow acquired "four or five leaves." And in all his subsequent plays, Beckett has continued to challenge audiences by stripping away more and more of the conventions associated with theater, as if he were seeking to discover how much can be taken away from drama without forsaking the essence of dramatic experience.

In seeking to discover the limits of drama, Beckett has progressively stripped away virtually all the elements of theater. Physical action decreases as Beckett's protagonists become less and less mobile. In *Waiting for Godot,* two of the characters are roped to one another, and though everyone can walk they frequently fall down. In *Endgame* (1957), Nagg and Nell are confined to ashbins, Hamm is confined to a wheelchair, and Clov, the only mobile character, hobbles around the stage. In *Happy Days,* Winnie is buried up to her waist in a mound, and by Act 2 the mound has reached her neck. In *Play* (1964), all three characters are immobilized in urns and speak only when a light shines upon them. And in *Not I* (1972), the only visible action is the mouth of a woman speaking. Characters likewise decrease from the five in *Waiting for Godot* to one (and his tape recorder) in *Krapp's Last Tape* (1958). Even language disappears in Beckett's shorter pieces. *Act without Words I* (1957) and *II* (1960) are mime pieces, and *Breath* (1970) lasts for one minute of cries and breaths. Consequently many audiences and reviewers have often been moved in witnessing Beckett's plays to echo the words of

Estragon in *Waiting for Godot*: "Nothing happens, nobody comes, nobody goes, it's awful."

Today, however, *Waiting for Godot* and *Endgame* are recognized as two of the most important plays in contemporary drama, and they have been performed throughout the world to appreciative audiences in Paris, London, on Broadway and off, at San Quentin Prison, and even in local churches. The two couples of *Waiting for Godot*—the tramps Vladimir and Estragon, and the master and his slave, Pozzo and Lucky—have been examined, annotated, and allegorized, yet they still survive. In fact, survival—or existence, to use a more neutral term—is the action of the play. Stranded on a bare stage, in a barren existence, Vladimir and Estragon "wait for Godot," and while they wait they tell stories to each other, they reminisce, they contemplate suicide, they munch carrots and radishes, they pull their boots on and off, and they go through many other routines that Beckett appears to have drawn from the vaudeville world of Charlie Chaplin, Buster Keaton, and the Marx brothers. Estragon sums up their existence when he says, "We always find something, eh Didi, to give us the impression we exist?" Although Godot does not arrive at the end of the first act, nor at the end of the second—though their world grows increasingly meaningless—they sustain themselves through their continued inventiveness. And in contrast to Pozzo and Lucky who are tied to one another by a rope, Vladimir and Estragon are bound to each other by a friendship that survives repeated separations and quarrels. *Endgame* is a grimmer and tighter play. The two acts of *Godot* have shrunk to a single long act. The two pairs of characters are still present but the emphasis has been drastically changed; the master-slave pair, the blind Hamm and the hobbling Clov, dominate the play, while Nagg and Nell, who are reminiscent of Vladimir and Estragon in their exchanging of memories and food, are confined to ashbins and appear only occasionally. Instead of a road on which the characters might come and go, there is only a room, and the world outside does not appear to contain any sign of life, not even a tree with a few leaves on it.

Endgame has repeatedly tempted critics to define its meaning, in part because it so insistently appears to deny itself significance—Hamm, for example, says "We're not beginning to . . . to . . . mean something?" and Clov replies, "Mean something! You and I, mean something!"—in part because it implicitly alludes to so many interpretative contexts. The chess metaphor of the title is echoed in the physical action of Hamm, the king who can move only in limited ways, and in the "very red faces" of Hamm and Clov contrasted to the "very white faces" of Nagg and Nell. Allusions to Shakespeare abound throughout the play: Hamm's name seems to be a shortened form of Hamlet; he sees himself as a deposed king, like Lear and Richard II; he parodies Richard III's final words when he calls out "My kingdom for a nightman"; and he directly quotes Prospero, "Our revels now are ended," and then throws away his gaff, much as Prospero breaks his magic wand at the end of *The Tempest*. The theatrical metaphor running throughout the play provides another interpretative context. Hamm's first words, for example, are "Me—*(he yawns)*—to play." Clov looks out at the auditorium and comments, ironically, "I see . . . a multitude . . . in transports . . . of joy." Hamm speaks of the "dialogue," worries that the small boy may provide an "underplot," grumbles when Clov reacts to "an aside," and announces, "I'm warming up for my last soliloquy." Clov starts to leave the stage with the line, "This is what we call making an exit." Thus the stage is, it seems, the only place of life in a world Clov calls "corpsed." And that reference to death is only one of innumerable references to it from the title to the final tableau.

Yet in the theater, as indicated by the review of the Paris premiere following the text, *Endgame* also turns out to be a highly comic experience, in spite of, or perhaps because of, its grim situation. Clov's repeated taunting of Hamm (see Figure 90) is inherently comic, but Clov and Hamm together frequently engage in comic routines, as when Clov thinks he has discovered a flea and Hamm's fear that "humanity might start from there all over again" leads to Clov searching for the insecticide powder he winds up sprinkling in his trousers. Even the two old people in the ashbins take part in the vaudeville routines:

NAGG: Can you hear me?
NELL: Yes. And you?
NAGG: Yes.

(Pause)

Our hearing hasn't failed.
NELL: Our what?
NAGG: Our hearing.

Even moments that might well be solemn, such as Hamm's order, "Let us pray to God" (see Figure 91) are interrupted by Clov's interest in getting back to rat-extermination and Nagg's cry for "me sugar-plum." Nell seems to have the final word on the play's theatrical meaning when she says, "Nothing is funnier than unhappiness, I grant you that."

ENDGAME
A Play in One Act

BY SAMUEL BECKETT

CHARACTERS

NAGG
NELL
HAMM
CLOV

SCENE

Bare interior. Grey light. Left and right back, high up, two small windows, curtains drawn. Front right, a door.

Hanging near door, its face to wall, a picture. Front left, touching each other, covered with an old sheet, two ashbins. Center, in an armchair on castors, covered with an old sheet, HAMM. *Motionless by the door, his eyes fixed on* HAMM, CLOV. *Very red face. Brief tableau.*

*(*CLOV *goes and stands under window left. Stiff, staggering walk. He looks up at window left. He turns and looks at window right. He goes and stands under window right. He looks up at window right. He turns and looks at window left. He goes out, comes back immediately with a small step-ladder, carries it over and sets it down under window left, gets up on it, draws back curtain. He gets down, takes six steps (for example) towards window right, goes back for ladder, carries it over and sets it down under window right, gets up on it, draws back curtain. He gets down, takes three steps towards window left, goes back for ladder, carries it over and sets it down under window left, gets up on it, looks out of window. Brief laugh. He gets down, goes with ladder towards ashbins, halts, turns, carries back ladder and sets it down under window right, goes to ashbins, removes sheet covering them, folds it over his arm. He raises one lid, stoops and looks into bin. Brief laugh. He closes lid. Same with other bin. He goes to* HAMM, *removes sheet covering him, folds it over his arm. In a dressing-gown, a stiff toque on his head, a large blood-stained handkerchief over his face, a whistle hanging from his neck, a rug over his knees, thick socks on his feet,* HAMM *seems to be asleep.* CLOV *looks him over. Brief laugh. He goes to door, halts, turns towards auditorium.)*

CLOV *(fixed gaze, tonelessly)*: Finished, it's finished, nearly finished, it must be nearly finished.

(Pause.)

Grain upon grain, one by one, and one day, suddenly, there's a heap, a little heap, the impossible heap.

(Pause.)

I can't be punished any more.

(Pause.)

I'll go now to my kitchen, ten feet by ten feet by ten feet, and wait for him to whistle me.

(Pause.)

Nice dimensions, nice proportions, I'll lean on the table, and look at the wall, and wait for him to whistle me.

(He remains a moment motionless, then goes out. He comes back immediately, goes to window right, takes up the ladder and carries it out. Pause. HAMM *stirs. He yawns under the handkerchief. He removes the handkerchief from his face. Very red face. Black glasses.)*

HAMM: Me—*(He yawns.)*—to play.

(He holds the handkerchief spread out before him.)

Old stancher!

(He takes off his glasses, wipes his eyes, his face, the glasses, puts them on again, folds the handkerchief and puts it back neatly in the breast-pocket of his dressing-gown. He clears his throat, joins the tips of his fingers.)

Can there be misery—*(He yawns.)*—loftier than mine? No doubt. Formerly. But now?

(Pause.)

My father?

(Pause.)

My mother?

(Pause.)

My . . . dog?

(Pause.)

Oh I am willing to believe they suffer as much as

such creatures can suffer. But does that mean their sufferings equal mine? No doubt.

(Pause.)

No, all is a—(He yawns.)—bsolute, (Proudly.) the bigger a man is the fuller he is.

(Pause. Gloomily.)

And the emptier.

(He sniffs.)

Clov!

(Pause.)

No, alone.

(Pause.)

What dreams! Those forests!

(Pause.)

Enough, it's time it ended, in the shelter too.

(Pause.)

And yet I hesitate, I hesitate to . . . to end. Yes, there it is, it's time it ended and yet I hesitate to—(He yawns.)—to end. (Yawns.)

God, I'm tired, I'd be better off in bed.

(He whistles. Enter CLOV immediately. He halts beside the chair.)

You pollute the air!

(Pause.)

Get me ready. I'm going to bed.

CLOV: I've just got you up.

HAMM: And what of it?

CLOV: I can't be getting you up and putting you to bed every five minutes, I have things to do.

(Pause.)

HAMM: Did you ever see my eyes?

CLOV: No.

HAMM: Did you never have the curiosity, while I was sleeping, to take off my glasses and look at my eyes?

CLOV: Pulling back the lids?

(Pause.)

No.

HAMM: One of these days I'll show them to you.

(Pause.)

It seems they've gone all white.

(Pause.)

What time is it?

CLOV: The same as usual.

HAMM (gestures toward window right): Have you looked?

CLOV: Yes

HAMM: Well?

CLOV: Zero.

HAMM: It'd need to rain.

CLOV: It won't rain.

(Pause.)

HAMM: Apart from that, how do you feel?

CLOV: I don't complain.

HAMM: You feel normal?

CLOV (irritably): I tell you I don't complain.

HAMM: I feel a little queer.

(Pause.)

Clov!

CLOV: Yes.

HAMM: Have you not had enough?

CLOV: Yes.

(Pause.)

Of what?

HAMM: Of this . . . this . . . thing.

CLOV: I always had.

(Pause)

Not you?

HAMM (gloomily): Then there's no reason for it to change.

CLOV: It may end.

(Pause.)

All life long the same questions, the same answers.

HAMM: Get me ready.

(CLOV does not move.)

Go and get the sheet.

(CLOV does not move.)

Clov!

CLOV: Yes.

HAMM: I'll give you nothing more to eat.

CLOV: Then we'll die.

HAMM: I'll give you just enough to keep you from dying. You'll be hungry all the time.

CLOV: Then we won't die.

(Pause.)

I'll go and get the sheet.

(He goes toward the door.)

HAMM: No!

(CLOV *halts.*)

I'll give you one biscuit per day.

(*Pause.*)

One and a half.

(*Pause.*)

Why do you stay with me?
CLOV: Why do you keep me?
HAMM: There's no one else.
CLOV: There's nowhere else.

(*Pause.*)

HAMM: You're leaving me all the same.
CLOV: I'm trying.
HAMM: You don't love me.
CLOV: No.
HAMM: You loved me once.
CLOV: Once!
HAMM: I've made you suffer too much.

(*Pause.*)

Haven't I?
CLOV: It's not that.
HAMM (*shocked*): I haven't made you suffer too much?
CLOV: Yes!
HAMM (*relieved*): Ah you gave me a fright!

(*Pause. Coldly.*)

Forgive me.

(*Pause. Louder.*)

I said, Forgive me.
CLOV: I heard you.

(*Pause.*)

Have you bled?
HAMM: Less.

(*Pause.*)

Is it not time for my pain-killer?
CLOV: No.

(*Pause.*)

HAMM: How are your eyes?
CLOV: Bad.
HAMM: How are your legs?
CLOV: Bad.
HAMM: But you can move.
CLOV: Yes.
HAMM (*violently*): Then move!

(CLOV *goes to back wall, leans against it with his forehead and hands.*)

Where are you?

CLOV: Here.
HAMM: Come back!

(CLOV *returns to his place beside the chair.*)

Where are you?
CLOV: Here.
HAMM: Why don't you kill me?
CLOV: I don't know the combination of the cupboard.

(*Pause.*)

HAMM: Go and get two bicycle-wheels.
CLOV: There are no more bicycle-wheels.
HAMM: What have you done with your bicycle?
CLOV: I never had a bicycle.
HAMM: The thing is impossible.
CLOV: When there were still bicycles I wept to have one. I crawled at your feet. You told me to go to hell. Now there are none.
HAMM: And your rounds? When you inspected my paupers. Always on foot?
CLOV: Sometimes on horse.

(*The lid of one of the bins lifts and the hands of* NAGG *appear, gripping the rim. Then his head emerges. Nightcap. Very white face.* NAGG *yawns, then listens.*)

I'll leave you, I have things to do.
HAMM: In your kitchen?
CLOV: Yes.
HAMM: Outside of here it's death.

(*Pause.*)

All right, be off.

(*Exit* CLOV. *Pause.*)

We're getting on.
NAGG: Me pap!
HAMM: Accursed progenitor!
NAGG: Me pap!
HAMM: The old folks at home! No decency left! Guzzle, guzzle, that's all they think of.

(*He whistles. Enter* CLOV. *He halts beside the chair.*)

Well! I thought you were leaving me.
CLOV: Oh not just yet, not just yet.
NAGG: Me pap!
HAMM: Give him his pap.
CLOV: There's no more pap.
HAMM (*to* NAGG): Do you hear that? There's no more pap. You'll never get any more pap.
NAGG: I want me pap!
HAMM: Give him a biscuit.

(*Exit* CLOV.)

Accursed fornicator! How are your stumps?
NAGG: Never mind me stumps.

(Enter CLOV *with biscuit.*)

CLOV: I'm back again, with the biscuit.

(He gives biscuit to NAGG *who fingers it, sniffs it.*)

NAGG (plaintively): What is it?
CLOV: Spratt's medium.
NAGG (as before): It's hard! I can't!
HAMM: Bottle him!

(CLOV *pushes* NAGG *back into the bin, closes the lid.*)

CLOV (returning to his place beside the chair): If age but knew!
HAMM: Sit on him!
CLOV: I can't sit.
HAMM: True. And I can't stand.
CLOV: So it is.
HAMM: Every man his specialty.

(Pause.)

No phone calls?

(Pause.)

Don't we laugh?
CLOV (after reflection): I don't feel like it.
HAMM (after reflection): Nor I.

(Pause.)

Clov!
CLOV: Yes.
HAMM: Nature has forgotten us.
CLOV: There's no more nature.
HAMM: No more nature! You exaggerate.
CLOV: In the vicinity.
HAMM: But we breathe, we change! We lose our hair, our teeth! Our bloom! Our ideals!
CLOV: Then she hasn't forgotten us.
HAMM: But you say there is none.
CLOV (sadly): No one that ever lived ever thought so crooked as we.
HAMM: We do what we can.
CLOV: We shouldn't.

(Pause.)

HAMM: You're a bit of all right, aren't you?
CLOV: A smithereen.

(Pause.)

HAMM: This is slow work.

(Pause.)

Is it not time for my pain-killer?
CLOV: No.

(Pause.)

I'll leave you, I have things to do.

HAMM: In your kitchen?
CLOV: Yes.
HAMM: What, I'd like to know.
CLOV: I look at the wall.
HAMM: The wall! And what do you see on your wall? Mene, mene? Naked bodies?
CLOV: I see my light dying.
HAMM: Your light dying! Listen to that! Well, it can die just as well here, *your* light. Take a look at me and then come back and tell me what you think of *your* light.

(Pause.)

CLOV: You shouldn't speak to me like that.

(Pause.)

HAMM (coldly): Forgive me.

(Pause. Louder.)

I said, Forgive me.
CLOV: I heard you.

(The lid of NAGG's bin lifts. His hands appear, gripping the rim. Then his head emerges. In his mouth the biscuit. He listens.)

HAMM: Did your seeds come up?
CLOV: No.
HAMM: Did you scratch round them to see if they had sprouted?
CLOV: They haven't sprouted.
HAMM: Perhaps it's still too early.
CLOV: If they were going to sprout they would have sprouted.

(Violently.)

They'll never sprout!

(Pause. NAGG *takes biscuit in his hand.*)

HAMM: This is not much fun.

(Pause.)

But that's always the way at the end of the day, isn't it, Clov?
CLOV: Always.
HAMM: It's the end of the day like any other day, isn't it, Clov?
CLOV: Looks like it.

(Pause.)

HAMM (anguished): What's happening, what's happening?
CLOV: Something is taking its course.

(Pause.)

HAMM: All right, be off.

(He leans back in his chair, remains motionless. CLOV *does not move, heaves a great groaning sigh.* HAMM *sits up.)*

I thought I told you to be off.

CLOV: I'm trying.

(He goes to door, halts.)

Ever since I was whelped.

(Exit CLOV.*)*

HAMM: We're getting on.

(He leans back in his chair, remains motionless. NAGG *knocks on the lid of the other bin. Pause. He knocks harder. The lid lifts and the hands of* NELL *appear, gripping the rim. Then her head emerges. Lace cap. Very white face.)*

NELL: What is it, my pet?

(Pause.)

Time for love?

NAGG: Were you asleep?

NELL: Oh no!

NAGG: Kiss me.

NELL: We can't.

NAGG: Try.

(Their heads strain toward each other, fail to meet, fall apart again.)

NELL: Why this farce, day after day?

(Pause.)

NAGG: I've lost me tooth.

NELL: When?

NAGG: I had it yesterday.

NELL *(elegiac)*: Ah yesterday!

(They turn painfully toward each other.)

NAGG: Can you see me?

NELL: Hardly. And you?

NAGG: What?

NELL: Can you see me?

NAGG: Hardly.

NELL: So much the better, so much the better.

NAGG: Don't say that.

(Pause.)

Our sight has failed.

NELL: Yes.

(Pause. They turn away from each other.)

NAGG: Can you hear me?

NELL: Yes, And you?

NAGG: Yes.

(Pause.)

Our hearing hasn't failed.

NELL: Our what?

NAGG: Our hearing.

NELL: No.

(Pause.)

Have you anything else to say to me?

NAGG: Do you remember—

NELL: No.

NAGG: When we crashed on our tandem and lost our shanks.

(They laugh heartily.)

NELL: It was in the Ardennes.

(They laugh less heartily.)

NAGG: On the road to Sedan.

(They laugh still less heartily.)

Are you cold?

NELL: Yes, perished. And you?

NAGG *(pause)*: I'm freezing.

(Pause.)

Do you want to go in?

NELL: Yes.

NAGG: Then go in.

*(NELL *does not move.*)*

Why don't you go in?

NELL: I don't know.

(Pause.)

NAGG: Has he changed your sawdust?

NELL: It isn't sawdust.

(Pause. Wearily.)

Can you not be a little accurate, Nagg?

NAGG: Your sand then. It's not important.

NELL: It is important.

(Pause.)

NAGG: It was sawdust once.

NELL: Once!

NAGG: And now it's sand.

(Pause.)

From the shore.

(Pause. Impatiently.)

Now it's sand he fetches from the shore.

NELL: Now it's sand.

NAGG: Has he changed yours?

NELL: No.

NAGG: Nor mine.

(Pause.)

I won't have it!

(Pause. Holding up the biscuit.)

Do you want a bit?

NELL: No.

(Pause.)

Of what?

NAGG: Biscuit. I've kept you half.

(He looks at the biscuit. Proudly.)

Three quarters. For you. Here.

(He proffers the biscuit.)

No?

(Pause.)

Do you not feel well?

HAMM *(wearily)*: Quiet, quiet, you're keeping me awake.

(Pause.)

Talk softer.

(Pause.)

If I could sleep I might make love. I'd go into the woods. My eyes would see . . . the sky, the earth. I'd run, run, they wouldn't catch me.

(Pause.)

Nature!

(Pause.)

There's something dripping in my head.

(Pause.)

A heart, a heart in my head.

(Pause.)

NAGG *(softly)*: Do you hear him? A heart in his head!

(He chuckles cautiously.)

NELL: One mustn't laugh at those things, Nagg. Why must you always laugh at them?

NAGG: Not so loud!

NELL *(without lowering her voice)*: Nothing is funnier than unhappiness, I grant you that. But—

NAGG *(shocked)*: Oh!

NELL: Yes, yes, it's the most comical thing in the world. And we laugh, we laugh, with a will, in the beginning. But it's always the same thing. Yes, it's like the funny story we have heard too often, we still find it funny, but we don't laugh any more.

(Pause.)

Have you anything else to say to me?

NAGG: No.

NELL: Are you quite sure?

(Pause.)

Then I'll leave you.

NAGG: Do you not want your biscuit?

(Pause.)

I'll keep it for you.

(Pause.)

I thought you were going to leave me.

NELL: I am going to leave you.

NAGG: Could you give me a scratch before you go?

NELL: No.

(Pause.)

Where?

NAGG: In the back.

NELL: No.

(Pause.)

Rub yourself against the rim.

NAGG: It's lower down. In the hollow.

NELL: What hollow?

NAGG: The hollow!

(Pause.)

Could you not?

(Pause.)

Yesterday you scratched me there.

NELL *(elegaic)*: Ah yesterday!

NAGG: Could you not?

(Pause.)

Would you like me to scratch you?

(Pause.)

Are you crying again?

NELL: I was trying.

(Pause)

HAMM: Perhaps it's a little vein.

(Pause.)

NAGG: What was that he said?

NELL: Perhaps it's a little vein.

NAGG: What does that mean?

(Pause.)

That means nothing.

(Pause.)

Will I tell you the story of the tailor?

NELL: No.

(Pause.)

What for?

NAGG: To cheer you up.

NELL: It's not funny.

NAGG: It always made you laugh.

(Pause.)

The first time I thought you'd die.

NELL: It was on Lake Como.

(Pause.)

One April afternoon.

(Pause.)

Can you believe it?

NAGG: What?

NELL: That we once went out rowing on Lake Como.

(Pause.)

One April afternoon.

NAGG: We had got engaged the day before.

NELL: Engaged!

NAGG: You were in such fits that we capsized. By rights we should have been drowned.

NELL: It was because I felt happy.

NAGG *(indignant)*: It was not, it was not, it was my story and nothing else. Happy! Don't you laugh at it still? Every time I tell it. Happy!

NELL: It was deep, deep. And you could see down to the bottom. So white. So clean.

NAGG: Let me tell it again.

(Raconteur's voice.)

An Englishman, needing a pair of striped trousers in a hurry for the New Year festivities, goes to his tailor who takes his measurements.

(Tailor's voice.)

"That's the lot, come back in four days, I'll have it ready." Good. Four days later.

(Tailor's voice.)

"So sorry, come back in a week. I've made a mess of the seat." Good, that's all right, a neat seat can be very ticklish. A week later.

(Tailor's voice.)

"Frightfully sorry, come back in ten days, I've made a hash of the crotch." Good, can't be helped, a snug crotch is always a teaser. Ten days later.

(Tailor's voice.)

"Dreadfully sorry, come back in a fortnight, I've made a balls of the fly." Good, at a pinch, a smart fly is a stiff proposition.

(Pause. Normal voice.)

I never told it worse.

(Pause. Gloomy.)

I tell this story worse and worse.

(Pause. Raconteur's voice.)

Well, to make it short, the bluebells are blowing and he ballockses the buttonholes.

(Customer's voice.)

"God damn you to hell, Sir, no, it's indecent, there are limits! In six days, do you hear me, six days, God made the world. Yes Sir, no less Sir, the WORLD! And you are not bloody well capable of making me a pair of trousers in three months!"

(Tailor's voice, scandalized.)

"But my dear Sir, my dear Sir, look—

(Disdainful gesture, disgustedly.)

—at the world—

(Pause.)

and look—

(Loving gesture, proudly.)—at my TROUSERS!"

(Pause. He looks at NELL who has remained impassive, her eyes unseeing, breaks into a high forced laugh, cuts it short, pokes his head towards NELL, launches his laugh again.)

HAMM: Silence!

(NAGG starts, cuts short his laugh.)

NELL: You could see down to the bottom.

HAMM *(exasperated)*: Have you not finished? Will you never finish?

(With sudden fury.)

Will this never finish?

(NAGG disappears into his bin, closes the lid behind him. NELL does not move. Frenziedly.)

My kingdom for a nightman!

(He whistles. Enter CLOV.)

Clear away this muck! Chuck it in the sea!

(CLOV goes to bins, halts.)

NELL: So white.

HAMM: What? What's she blathering about?

(CLOV stoops, takes NELL's hand, feels her pulse.)

NELL *(to CLOV)*: Desert!

(CLOV lets go her hand, pushes her back in the bin, closes the lid.)

CLOV *(returning to his place beside the chair)*: She has no pulse.

HAMM: What was she drivelling about?

CLOV: She told me to go away, into the desert.

HAMM: Damn busybody! Is that all?

CLOV: No.
HAMM: What else?
CLOV: I didn't understand.
HAMM: Have you bottled her?
CLOV: Yes.
HAMM: Are they both bottled?
CLOV: Yes
HAMM: Screw down the lids.

(CLOV *goes toward door.*)

Time enough.

(CLOV *halts.*)

My anger subsides, I'd like to pee.
CLOV (*with alacrity*): I'll go and get the catheter.

(*He goes toward door.*)

HAMM: Time enough.

(CLOV *halts.*)

Give me my pain-killer.
CLOV: It's too soon.

(*Pause.*)

It's too soon on top of your tonic, it wouldn't act.
HAMM: In the morning they brace you up and in the evening they calm you down. Unless it's the other way round.

(*Pause.*)

That old doctor, he's dead naturally?
CLOV: He wasn't old.
HAMM: But he's dead?
CLOV: Naturally.

(*Pause.*)

You ask *me* that?

(*Pause.*)

HAMM: Take me for a little turn.

(CLOV *goes behind the chair and pushes it forward.*)

Not too fast!

(CLOV *pushes chair.*)

Right round the world!

(CLOV *pushes chair.*)

Hug the walls, then back to the center again.

(CLOV *pushes chair.*)

I was right in the center, wasn't I?
CLOV (*pushing*): Yes.
HAMM: We'd need a proper wheel-chair. With big wheels. Bicycle wheels!

(*Pause.*)

Are you hugging?
CLOV (*pushing*): Yes.
HAMM (*groping for wall*): It's a lie! Why do you lie to me?
CLOV (*bearing close to wall*): There! There!
HAMM: Stop!

(CLOV *stops chair close to back wall.* HAMM *lays his hand against the wall.*)

Old wall!

(*Pause.*)

Beyond is the . . . other hell.

(*Pause. Violently.*)

Closer! Closer! Up against!
CLOV: Take away your hand.

(HAMM *withdraws his hand.* CLOV *rams chair against wall.*)

There!

(HAMM *leans toward wall, applies his ear to it.*)

HAMM: Do you hear?

(*He strikes the wall with his knuckles.*)

Do you hear? Hollow bricks!

(*He strikes again.*)

All that's hollow!

(*Pause. He straightens up. Violently.*)

That's enough. Back!
CLOV: We haven't done the round.
HAMM: Back to my place!

(CLOV *pushes chair back to center.*)

Is that my place?
CLOV: Yes, that's your place.
HAMM: Am I right in the center?
CLOV: I'll measure it.
HAMM: More or less! More or less!
CLOV (*moving chair slightly*): There!
HAMM: I'm more or less in the center?
CLOV: I'd say so.
HAMM: You'd say so! Put me right in the center!
CLOV: I'll go and get the tape.
HAMM: Roughly! Roughly!

(CLOV *moves chair slightly.*)

Bang in the center!
CLOV: There!

(*Pause.*)

HAMM: I feel a little too far to the left.

(CLOV *moves chair slightly.*)

Now I feel a little too far to the right.

(CLOV *moves chair slightly.*)

I feel a little too far forward.

(CLOV *moves chair slightly.*)

Now I feel a little too far back.

(CLOV *moves chair slightly.*)

Don't stay there, (*i.e., behind the chair*) you give me the shivers.

(CLOV *returns to his place beside the chair.*)

CLOV: If I could kill him I'd die happy.

(*Pause.*)

HAMM: What's the weather like?
CLOV: As usual.
HAMM: Look at the earth.
CLOV: I've looked.
HAMM: With the glass?
HAMM: No need of the glass.
HAMM: Look at it with the glass.
CLOV: I'll go and get the glass.

(*Exit* CLOV.)

HAMM: No need of the glass!

(*Enter* CLOV *with telescope.*)

CLOV: I'm back again, with the glass.

(*He goes to window right, looks up at it.*)

I need the steps.
HAMM: Why? Have you shrunk?

(*Exit* CLOV *with telescope.*)

I don't like that, I don't like that.

(*Enter* CLOV *with ladder, but without telescope.*)

CLOV: I'm back again, with the steps.

(*He sets down ladder under window right, gets up on it, realizes he has not the telescope, gets down.*)

I need the glass.

(*He goes toward door.*)

HAMM (*violently*): But you have the glass!
CLOV (*halting, violently*): No, I haven't the glass!

(*Exit* CLOV.)

HAMM: This is deadly.

(*Enter* CLOV *with telescope. He goes toward ladder.*)
CLOV: Things are livening up.

(*He gets up on a ladder, raises the telescope, lets it fall.*)

I did it on purpose.

(*He gets down, picks up the telescope, turns it on auditorium.*)

I see . . . a multitude . . . in transports . . . of joy.

(*Pause.*)

That's what I call a magnifier.

(*He lowers the telescope, turns toward* HAMM.)

Well? Don't we laugh?
HAMM (*after reflection*): I don't.
CLOV (*after reflection*): Nor I.

(*He gets up on ladder, turns the telescope on the without.*)

Let's see.

(*He looks, moving the telescope.*)

Zero . . . (*He looks.*) . . . zero . . . (*He looks*) . . . and zero.
HAMM: Nothing stirs. All is—
CLOV: Zer—
HAMM (*violently*): Wait till you're spoken to!

(*Normal voice.*)

All is . . . all is . . . all is what?

(*Violently.*)

All is what?
CLOV: What all is? In a word? Is that what you want to know? Just a moment.

(*He turns the telescope on the without, looks, lowers the telescope, turns toward* HAMM.)

Corpsed.

(*Pause.*)

Well? Content?
HAMM: Look at the sea.
CLOV: It's the same.
HAMM: Look at the ocean!

(CLOV *gets down, takes a few steps toward window left, goes back for ladder, carries it over and sets it down under window left, gets up on it, turns the telescope on the without, looks at length. He starts, lowers the telescope, examines it, turns it again on the without.*)

CLOV: Never seen anything like that!
HAMM (*anxiously*): What? A sail? A fin? Smoke?
CLOV (*looking*): The light is sunk.
HAMM (*relieved*): Pah! We all knew that.
CLOV (*looking*): There was a bit left.
HAMM: The base.
CLOV (*looking*): Yes.
HAMM: And now?
CLOV (*looking*): All gone.
HAMM: No gulls?
CLOV (*looking*): Gulls!

HAMM: And the horizon? Nothing on the horizon?
CLOV (*lowering the telescope, turning toward* HAMM, *exasperatedly*): What in God's name could there be on the horizon?

(*Pause.*)

HAMM: The waves, how are the waves?
CLOV: The waves?

(*He turns the telescope on the waves.*)

Lead.
HAMM: And the sun?
CLOV (*looking*): Zero.
HAMM: But it should be sinking. Look again.
CLOV (*looking*): Damn the sun.
HAMM: Is it night already then?
CLOV (*looking*): No.
HAMM: Then what is it?
CLOV (*looking*): Gray.

(*Lowering the telescope, turning toward* HAMM, *louder.*)

Gray!

(*Pause. Still louder.*)

GRRAY!

(*Pause. He gets down, approaches* HAMM *from behind, whispers in his ear.*)

HAMM (*starting*): Gray! Did I hear you say gray?
CLOV: Light black. From pole to pole.
HAMM: You exaggerate.

(*Pause.*)

Don't stay there, you give me the shivers.

(CLOV *returns to his place beside the chair.*)

CLOV: Why this farce, day after day?
HAMM: Routine. One never knows.

(*Pause.*)

Last night I saw inside my breast. There was a big sore.
CLOV: Pah! You saw your heart.
HAMM: No, it was living.

(*Pause. Anguished.*)

Clov!
CLOV: Yes.
HAMM: What's happening?
CLOV: Something is taking its course.

(*Pause.*)

HAMM: Clov!
CLOV (*impatiently*): What is it?
HAMM: We're not beginning to . . . to . . . mean something?
CLOV: Mean something! You and I, mean something!

(*Brief laugh.*)

Ah that's a good one!
HAMM: I wonder.

(*Pause.*)

Imagine if a rational being came back to earth, wouldn't he be liable to get ideas into his head if he observed us long enough.

(*Voice of rational being.*)

Ah, good, now I see what it is, yes, now I understand what they're at!

(CLOV *starts, drops the telescope and begins to scratch his belly with both hands. Normal voice.*)

And without going so far as that, we ourselves . . . (*With emotion.*) . . . we ourselves . . . at certain moments . . . (*Vehemently.*) To think perhaps it won't all have been for nothing!
CLOV (*anguished, scratching himself*): I have a flea!
HAMM: A flea! Are there still fleas?
CLOV: On me, there's one.

(*Scratching.*)

Unless it's a crablouse.
HAMM (*very perturbed*): But humanity might start from there all over again! Catch him, for the love of God!
CLOV: I'll go and get the powder.

(*Exit* CLOV.)

HAMM: A flea! This is awful! What a day!

(*Enter* CLOV *with a sprinkling-tin.*)

CLOV: I'm back again, with the insecticide.
HAMM: Let him have it!

(CLOV *loosens the top of his trousers, pulls it forward and shakes powder into the aperture. He stoops, looks, waits, starts, frenziedly shakes more powder, stoops, looks, waits.*)

CLOV: The bastard!
HAMM: Did you get him?
CLOV: Looks like it.

(*He drops the tin and adjusts his trousers.*)

Unless he's laying doggo.
HAMM: Laying! Lying you mean. Unless he's *lying* doggo.
CLOV: Ah? One says lying? One doesn't say laying?
HAMM: Use your head, can't you. If he was laying we'd be bitched.
CLOV: Ah.

(*Pause.*)

What about that pee?
HAMM: I'm having it.
CLOV: Ah that's the spirit, that's the spirit!

(Pause.)

HAMM *(with ardour)*: Let's go from here, the two of us! South! You can make a raft and the currents will carry us away, far away, to other . . . mammals!

CLOV: God forbid!

HAMM: Alone, I'll embark alone! Get working on that raft immediately. Tomorrow I'll be gone for ever.

CLOV *(hastening toward door)*: I'll start straight away.

HAMM: Wait!

(CLOV halts.)

Will there be sharks, do you think?

CLOV: Sharks? I don't know. If there are there will be.

(He goes toward door.)

HAMM: Wait!

(CLOV halts.)

Is it not yet time for my pain-killer?

CLOV *(violently)*: No!

(He goes toward door.)

HAMM: Wait!

(CLOV halts.)

How are your eyes?

CLOV: Bad.

HAMM: But you can see.

CLOV: All I want.

HAMM: How are your legs?

CLOV: Bad.

HAMM: But you can walk.

CLOV: I come . . . and go.

HAMM: In my house.

(Pause. With prophetic relish.)

One day you'll be blind, like me. You'll be sitting there, a speck in the void, in the dark, for ever, like me.

(Pause.)

One day you'll say to yourself, I'm tired. I'll sit down, and you'll go and sit down. Then you'll say, I'm hungry, I'll get up and get something to eat. But you won't get up. You'll say, I shouldn't have sat down, but since I have I'll sit on a little longer, then I'll get up and get something to eat. But you won't get up and you won't get anything to eat.

(Pause.)

You'll look at the wall a while, then you'll say, I'll close my eyes, perhaps have a little sleep, after that I'll feel better, and you'll close them. And when you open them again there'll be no wall any more.

(Pause.)

Infinite emptiness will be all around you, all the resurrected dead of all the ages wouldn't fill it, and there you'll be like a little bit of grit in the middle of the steppe.

(Pause.)

Yes, one day you'll know what it is, you'll be like me, except that you won't have anyone with you, because you won't have had pity on anyone and because there won't be anyone left to have pity on.

(Pause.)

CLOV: It's not certain.

(Pause.)

And there's one thing you forget.

HAMM: Ah?

CLOV: I can't sit down.

HAMM *(impatiently)*: Well you'll lie down then, what the hell! Or you'll come to a standstill, simply stop and stand still, the way you are now. One day you'll say, I'm tired. I'll stop. What does the attitude matter?

(Pause.)

CLOV: So you all want me to leave you.

HAMM: Naturally.

CLOV: Then I'll leave you.

HAMM: You can't leave us.

CLOV: Then I won't leave you.

(Pause.)

HAMM: Why don't you finish us?

(Pause.)

I'll tell you the combination of the cupboard if you promise to finish me.

CLOV: I couldn't finish you.

HAMM: Then you won't finish me.

(Pause.)

CLOV: I'll leave you, I have things to do.

HAMM: Do you remember when you came here?

CLOV: No. Too small, you told me.

HAMM: Do you remember your father?

CLOV *(wearily)*: Same answer.

(Pause.)

You've asked me these questions millions of times.

HAMM: I love the old questions.

(With fervour.)

Ah the old questions, the old answers, there's nothing like them!

(Pause.)

It was I was a father to you.
CLOV: Yes.

(He looks at HAMM *fixedly.)*

You were that to me.
HAMM: My house a home for you.
CLOV: Yes.

(He looks about him.)

This was that for me.
HAMM *(proudly)*: But for me, *(Gesture toward himself.)* no father. But for Hamm, *(Gesture toward surroundings.)* no home.

(Pause.)

CLOV: I'll leave you.
HAMM: Did you ever think of one thing?
CLOV: Never.
HAMM: That here we're down in a hole.

(Pause.)

But beyond the hills? Eh? Perhaps it's still green. Eh?

(Pause.)

Flora! Pomona!

(Ecstatically.)

Ceres!

(Pause.)

Perhaps you won't need to go very far.
CLOV: I can't go very far.

(Pause.)

I'll leave you.
HAMM: Is my dog ready?
CLOV: He lacks a leg.
HAMM: Is he silky?
CLOV: He's a kind of Pomeranian.
HAMM: Go and get him.
CLOV: He lacks a leg.
HAMM: Go and get him!

(Exit CLOV.*)*

We're getting on.

(Enter CLOV *holding by one of its three legs a black toy dog.)*

CLOV: Your dogs are here.

(He hands the dog to HAMM *who feels it, fondles it.)*

HAMM: He's white, isn't he?
CLOV: Nearly.
HAMM: What do you mean, nearly? Is he white or isn't he?
CLOV: He isn't.

(Pause.)

HAMM: You've forgotten the sex.
CLOV *(vexed)*: But he isn't finished. The sex goes at the end.

(Pause.)

HAMM: You haven't put on his ribbon.
CLOV *(angrily)*: But he isn't finished, I tell you! First you finish your dog and then you put on his ribbon!

(Pause.)

HAMM: Can he stand?
CLOV: I don't know.
HAMM: Try.

(He hands the dog to CLOV *who places it on the ground.)*

Well?
CLOV: Wait!

(He squats down and tries to get the dog to stand on its three legs, fails, lets it go. The dog falls on its side.)

HAMM *(impatiently)*: Well?
CLOV: He's standing.
HAMM *(groping for the dog)*: Where? Where is he?

*(*CLOV *holds up the dog in a standing position.)*

CLOV: There.

(He takes HAMM's *hand and guides it toward the dog's head.)*

HAMM *(his hand on the dog's head)*: Is he gazing at me?
CLOV: Yes.
HAMM *(proudly)*: As if he were asking me to take him for a walk?
CLOV: If you like.
HAMM *(as before)*: Or as if he were begging me for a bone.

(He withdraws his hand.)

Leave him like that, standing there imploring me.

*(*CLOV *straightens up. The dog falls on its side.)*

CLOV: I'll leave you.
HAMM: Have you had your visions?
CLOV: Less.
HAMM: Is Mother Pegg's light on?
CLOV: Light! How could anyone's light be on?
HAMM: Extinguished!

CLOV: Naturally it's extinguished. If it's not on it's extinguished.

HAMM: No, I mean Mother Pegg.

CLOV: But naturally she's extinguished!

(Pause.)

What's the matter with you today?

HAMM: I'm taking my course.

(Pause.)

Is she buried?

CLOV: Buried! Who would have buried her?

HAMM: You.

CLOV: Me! Haven't I enough to do without burying people?

HAMM: But you'll bury me.

CLOV: No I won't bury you.

(Pause.)

HAMM: She was bonny once, like a flower of the field.

(With reminiscent leer.)

And a great one for the men!

CLOV: We too were bonny—once. It's a rare thing not to have been bonny—once.

(Pause.)

HAMM: Go and get the gaff.

(CLOV goes to door, halts.)

CLOV: Do this, do that, and I do it. I never refuse. Why?

HAMM: You're not able to.

CLOV: Soon I won't do it any more.

HAMM: You won't be able to any more.

(Exit CLOV.)

Ah the creatures, the creatures, everything has to be explained to them.

(Enter CLOV with gaff.)

CLOV: Here's your gaff. Stick it up.

(He gives the gaff to HAMM who, wielding it like a puntpole, tries to move his chair.)

HAMM: Did I move?

CLOV: No.

(HAMM throws down the gaff.)

HAMM: Go and get the oilcan.

CLOV: What for?

HAMM: To oil the castors.

CLOV: I oiled them yesterday.

HAMM: Yesterday! What does that mean? Yesterday!

CLOV (violently): That means that bloody awful day long ago, before this bloody awful day. I use the words you taught me. If they don't mean anything any more, teach me others. Or let me be silent.

(Pause.)

HAMM: I once knew a madman who thought the end of the world had come. He was a painter—and engraver. I had a great fondness for him. I used to go and see him, in the asylum. I'd take him by the hand and drag him to the window. Look! There! All that rising corn. And there! Look! The sails of the herring fleet! All that loveliness!

(Pause.)

He'd snatch away his hand and go back into his corner. Appalled. All he had seen was ashes.

(Pause.)

He alone had been spared.

(Pause.)

Forgotten.

(Pause.)

It appears the case is . . . was not so . . . so unusual.

CLOV: A madman? When was that?

HAMM: Oh way back, way back, you weren't in the land of the living.

CLOV: God be with the days!

(Pause. HAMM raises his toque.)

HAMM: I had a great fondness for him.

(Pause. He puts on his toque again.)

He was a painter—and engraver.

CLOV: There are so many terrible things.

HAMM: No, no, there are not so many now.

(Pause.)

Clov!

CLOV: Yes.

HAMM: Do you not think this has gone on long enough?

CLOV: Yes!

(Pause.)

What?

HAMM: This . . . this . . . thing.

CLOV: I've always thought so.

(Pause.)

You not?

HAMM (gloomily): Then it's a day like any other day.

CLOV: As long as it lasts.

(Pause.)

All life long the same inanities.

HAMM: I can't leave you.

CLOV: I know. And you can't follow me.

(Pause.)

HAMM: If you leave me how shall I know?

CLOV *(briskly)*: Well you simply whistle me and if I don't come running it means I've left you.

(Pause.)

HAMM: You won't come and kiss me goodbye?

CLOV: Oh I shouldn't think so.

(Pause.)

HAMM: But you might be merely dead in your kitchen.

CLOV: The result would be the same.

HAMM: Yes, but how would I know, if you were merely dead in your kitchen?

CLOV: Well . . . sooner or later I'd start to stink.

HAMM: You stink already. The whole place stinks of corpses.

CLOV: The whole universe.

HAMM *(angrily)*: To hell with the universe.

(Pause.)

Think of something.

CLOV: What?

HAMM: An idea, have an idea.

(Angrily.)

A bright idea!

CLOV: Ah good.

(He starts pacing to and fro, his eyes fixed on the ground, his hands behind his back. He halts.)

The pains in my legs! It's unbelievable! Soon I won't be able to think any more.

HAMM: You won't be able to leave me.

(CLOV resumes his pacing.)

What are you doing?

CLOV: Having an idea.

(He paces.)

Ah!

(He halts.)

HAMM: What a brain!

(Pause.)

Well?

CLOV: Wait!

(He meditates. Not very convinced.)

Yes . . .

(Pause. More convinced.)

Yes!

(He raises his head.)

I have it! I set the alarm.

(Pause.)

HAMM: This is perhaps not one of my bright days, but frankly—

CLOV: You whistle me. I don't come. The alarm rings. I'm gone. It doesn't ring. I'm dead.

(Pause.)

HAMM: Is it working?

(Pause. Impatiently.)

The alarm, is it working?

CLOV: Why wouldn't it be working?

HAMM: Because it's worked too much.

CLOV: But it's hardly worked at all.

HAMM *(angrily)*: Then because it's worked too little!

CLOV: I'll go and see.

(Exit CLOV. Brief ring of alarm off. Enter CLOV with alarm-clock. He holds it against HAMM's ear and releases alarm. They listen to it ringing to the end. Pause.)

Fit to wake the dead! Did you hear it?

HAMM: Vaguely.

CLOV: The end is terrific!

HAMM: I prefer the middle.

(Pause.)

Is it not time for my pain-killer?

CLOV: No!

(He goes to door, turns.)

I'll leave you.

HAMM: It's time for my story. Do you want to listen to my story.

CLOV: No.

HAMM: Ask my father if he wants to listen to my story.

(CLOV goes to bins, raises the lid of NAGG's, stoops, looks into it. Pause. He straightens up.)

CLOV: He's asleep.

HAMM: Wake him.

(CLOV stoops, wakes NAGG with the alarm. Unintelligible words. CLOV straightens up.)

CLOV: He doesn't want to listen to your story.

HAMM: I'll give him a bon-bon.

(CLOV stoops. As before.)

CLOV: He wants a sugar-plum.

HAMM: He'll get a sugar-plum.

(CLOV stoops. As before.)

CLOV: It's a deal.

(*He goes toward door.* NAGG's *hands appear, gripping the rim. Then the head emerges.* CLOV *reaches door, turns.*)

Do you believe in the life to come?

HAMM: Mine was always that.

(*Exit* CLOV.)

Got him that time!

NAGG: I'm listening.

HAMM: Scoundrel! Why did you engender me?

NAGG: I didn't know.

HAMM: What? What didn't you know?

NAGG: That it'd be you.

(*Pause.*)

You'll give me a sugar-plum?

HAMM: After the audition.

NAGG: You swear?

HAMM: Yes.

NAGG: On what?

HAMM: My honor.

(*Pause. They laugh heartily.*)

NAGG: Two.

HAMM: One.

NAGG: One for me and one for—

HAMM: One! Silence!

(*Pause.*)

Where was I?

(*Pause. Gloomily.*)

It's finished, we're finished.

(*Pause.*)

Nearly finished.

(*Pause.*)

There'll be no more speech.

(*Pause.*)

Something dripping in my head, ever since the fontanelles.

(*Stifled hilarity of* NAGG.)

Splash, splash, always on the same spot.

(*Pause.*)

Perhaps it's a little vein.

(*Pause.*)

A little artery.

(*Pause. More animated.*)

Enough of that, it's story time, where was I?

(*Pause. Narrative tone.*)

The man came crawling towards me, on his belly. Pale, wonderfully pale and thin, he seemed on the point of—

(*Pause. Normal tone.*)

No, I've done that bit.

(*Pause. Narative tone.*)

I calmly filled my pipe—the meerschaum, lit it with . . . let us say a vesta, drew a few puffs. Aah!

(*Pause.*)

Well, what is it *you* want?

(*Pause.*)

It was an extra-ordinarily bitter day, I remember, zero by the thermometer. But considering it was Christmas Eve there was nothing . . . extra-ordinary about that. Seasonable weather, for once in a way.

(*Pause.*)

Well, what ill wind blows you my way? He raised his face to me, black with mingled dirt and tears.

(*Pause. Normal tone.*)

That should do it.

(*Narrative tone.*)

No, no, don't look at me, don't look at me. He dropped his eyes and mumbled something, apologies I presume.

(*Pause.*)

I'm a busy man, you know, the final touches, before the festivities. You know what it is.

(*Pause. Forcibly.*)

Come on now, what is the object of this invasion?

(*Pause.*)

It was a glorious bright day, I remember, fifty by the heliometer, but already the sun was sinking down into the . . . down among the dead.

(*Normal tone.*)

Nicely put, that.

(*Narrative tone.*)

Come on now, come on, present your petition and let me resume my labors.

(*Pause. Normal tone.*)

There's English for you. Ah well . . .

(*Narrative tone.*)

It was then he took the plunge. It's my little one, he said. Tsstss, a little one, that's bad. My little boy, he said, as if the sex mattered. Where did he come from? He named the hole. A good half-day, on horse. What are you insinuating? That the place is still inhabited? No, no, not a soul except himself and the child—assuming he existed. Good. I enquired about the situation at Kov, beyond the gulf. Not a sinner. Good. And you expect me to believe you have left your little one back there, all alone, and alive into the bargain? Come now!

(Pause.)

It was a howling wild day, I remember, a hundred by the anenometer. The wind was tearing up the dead pines and sweeping them . . . away.

(Pause. Normal tone.)

A bit feeble, that.

(Narrative tone.)

Come on, man, speak up, what is you want from me. I have to put up my holly.

(Pause.)

Well to make it short it finally transpired that what he wanted from me was . . . bread for his brat? Bread? But I have no bread, it doesn't agree with me. Good. Then perhaps a little corn?

(Pause. Normal tone.)

That should do it.

(Narrative tone.)

Corn, yes, I have corn, it's true, in my granaries. But use your head. I give you some corn, a pound, a pound and a half, you bring it back to your child and you make him—if he's still alive—a nice pot of porridge,

(NAGG reacts.)

a nice pot and a half of porridge, full of nourishment. Good. The colors come back into his little cheeks—perhaps. And then?

(Pause.)

I lost patience.

(Violently.)

Use your head, can't you, use your head, you're on earth, there's no cure for that!

(Pause.)

It was an exceedingly dry day, I remember, zero by the hygrometer. Ideal weather, for my lumbago.

(Pause. Violently.)

But what in God's name do you imagine? That the earth will awake in spring? That the rivers and seas will run with fish again? That there's manna in heaven still for imbeciles like you?

(Pause.)

Gradually I cooled down, sufficiently at least to ask him how long he had taken on the way. Three whole days. Good. In what condition he had left the child. Deep in sleep.

(Forcibly.)

But deep in what sleep, deep in what sleep already?

(Pause.)

Well to make it short I finally offered to take him into my service. He had touched a chord. And then I imagined already that I wasn't much longer for this world.

(He laughs. Pause.)

Well?

(Pause.)

Well? Here if you were careful you might die a nice natural death, in peace and comfort.

(Pause.)

Well?

(Pause.)

In the end he asked me would I consent to take in the child as well—if he were still alive.

(Pause.)

It was the moment I was waiting for.

(Pause.)

Would I consent to take the child . . .

(Pause.)

I can see him still, down on his knees, his hands flat on the ground, glaring at me with his mad eyes, in defiance of my wishes.

(Pause. Normal tone.)

I'll soon have finished with this story.

(Pause.)

Unless I bring in other characters.

(Pause.)

But where would I find them?

(*Pause.*)

Where would I look for them?

(*Pause. He whistles. Enter* CLOV.)

Let us pray to God.

NAGG: Me sugar-plum!

CLOV: There's a rat in the kitchen!

HAMM: A rat! Are there still rats?

CLOV: In the kitchen there's one.

HAMM: And you haven't exterminated him?

CLOV: Half. You disturbed us.

HAMM: He can't get away?

CLOV: No.

HAMM: You'll finish him later. Let us pray to God.

CLOV: Again!

NAGG: Me sugar-plum!

HAMM: God first!

(*Pause.*)

Are you right?

CLOV (*resigned*): Off we go.

HAMM (*to* NAGG): And you?

NAGG (*clasping his hands, closing his eyes, in a gabble*): Our Father which art—

HAMM: Silence! In silence! Where are your manners?

(*Pause.*)

Off we go.

(*Attitudes of prayer. Silence. Abandoning his attitude, discouraged.*)

Well?

CLOV (*abandoning his attitude*): What a hope! And you?

HAMM: Sweet damn all! (*to* NAGG) And you?

NAGG: Wait!

(*Pause. Abandoning his attitude.*)

Nothing doing!

HAMM: The bastard! He doesn't exist!

CLOV: Not yet.

NAGG: Me sugar-plum!

HAMM: There are no more sugar-plums!

(*Pause.*)

NAGG: It's natural. After all I'm your father. It's true if it hadn't been me it would have been someone else. But that's no excuse.

(*Pause.*)

Turkish Delight, for example, which no longer exists, we all know that, there is nothing in the world I love more. And one day I'll ask you for some, in return for a kindness, and you'll promise it to me. One must live with the times.

(*Pause.*)

Whom did you call when you were a tiny boy, and were frightened, in the dark? Your mother? No. Me. We let you cry. Then we moved you out of earshot, so that we might sleep in peace.

(*Pause.*)

I was asleep, as happy as a king, and you woke me up to have me listen to you. It wasn't indispensable, you didn't really need to have me listen to you.

(*Pause.*)

I hope the day will come when you'll really need to have me listen to you, and need to hear my voice, any voice.

(*Pause.*)

Yes, I hope I'll live till then, to hear you calling me like when you were a tiny boy, and were frightened, in the dark, and I was your only hope.

(*Pause.* NAGG *knocks on lid of* NELL's *bin. Pause.*)

Nell!

(*Pause. He knocks louder. Pause. Louder.*)

Nell!

(*Pause.* NAGG *sinks back into his bin, closes the lid behind him. Pause.*)

HAMM: Our revels now are ended.

(*He gropes for the dog.*)

The dog's gone.

CLOV: He's not a real dog, he can't go.

HAMM (*groping*): He's not there.

CLOV: He's lain down.

HAMM: Give him to me.

(CLOV *picks up the dog and gives it to* HAMM. HAMM *holds it in his arms. Pause.* HAMM *throws away the dog.*)

Dirty brute!

(CLOV *begins to pick up the objects lying on the ground.*)

What are you doing?

CLOV: Putting things in order.

(*He straightens up. Fervently.*)

I'm going to clear everything away!

(*He starts picking up again.*)

HAMM: Order!

CLOV (*straightening up*): I love order. It's my dream. A world where all would be silent and still and each thing in its last place, under the last dust.

(He starts picking up again.)

HAMM *(exasperated)*: What in God's name do you think you are doing?

CLOV *(straightening up)*: I'm doing my best to create a little order.

HAMM: Drop it!

(CLOV drops the objects he has picked up.)

CLOV: After all, there or elsewhere.

(He goes toward door.)

HAMM *(irritably)*: What's wrong with your feet?

CLOV: My feet?

HAMM: Tramp! Tramp!

CLOV: I must have put on my boots.

HAMM: Your slippers were hurting you?

(Pause.)

CLOV: I'll leave you.

HAMM: No!

CLOV: What is there to keep me here?

HAMM: The dialogue.

(Pause.)

I've got on with my story.

(Pause.)

I've got on with it well.

(Pause. Irritably.)

Ask me where I've got to.

CLOV: Oh, by the way, your story?

HAMM *(surprised)*: What story?

CLOV: The one you've been telling yourself all your days.

HAMM: Ah you mean my chronicle?

CLOV: That's the one.

(Pause.)

HAMM *(angrily)*: Keep going, can't you, keep going!

CLOV: You've got on with it, I hope.

HAMM *(modestly)*: Oh not very far, not very far.

(He sighs.)

There are days like that, one isn't inspired.

(Pause.)

Nothing you can do about it, just wait for it to come.

(Pause.)

No forcing, no forcing, it's fatal.

(Pause.)

I've got on with it a little all the same.

(Pause.)

Technique, you know.

(Pause. Irritably.)

I say I've got on with it a little all the same.

CLOV *(admiringly)*: Well I never! In spite of everything you were able to get on with it!

HAMM *(modestly)*: Oh not very far, you know, not very far, but nevertheless, better than nothing.

CLOV: Better than nothing! Is it possible?

HAMM: I'll tell you how it goes. He comes crawling on his belly—

CLOV: Who?

HAMM: What?

CLOV: Who do you mean, he?

HAMM: Who do I mean! Yet another.

CLOV: Ah him! I wasn't sure.

HAMM: Crawling on his belly, whining for bread for his brat. He's offered a job as gardener. Before—

(CLOV bursts out laughing.)

What is there so funny about that?

CLOV: A job as gardener!

HAMM: Is that what tickles you?

CLOV: It must be that.

HAMM: It wouldn't be the bread?

CLOV: Or the brat.

(Pause.)

HAMM: The whole thing is comical, I grant you that. What about having a good guffaw the two of us together?

CLOV *(after reflection)*: I couldn't guffaw again today.

HAMM *(after reflection)*: Nor I.

(Pause.)

I continue then. Before accepting with gratitude he asks if he may have his little boy with him.

CLOV: What age?

HAMM: Oh tiny.

CLOV: He would have climbed the trees.

HAMM: All the little odd jobs.

CLOV: And then he would have grown up.

HAMM: Very likely.

(Pause.)

CLOV: Keep going, can't you, keep going!

HAMM: That's all. I stopped there.

(Pause.)

CLOV: Do you see how it goes on.

HAMM: More or less.

CLOV: Will it not soon be the end?

HAMM: I'm afraid it will.

CLOV: Pah! You'll make up another.

HAMM: I don't know.

(Pause.)

I feel rather drained.

(Pause.)

The prolonged creative effort.

(Pause.)

If I could drag myself down to the sea! I'd make a pillow of sand for my head and the tide would come.

CLOV: There's no more tide.

(Pause.)

HAMM: Go and see is she dead.

(CLOV goes to bins, raises the lid of NELL's, stoops, looks into it. Pause.)

CLOV: Looks like it.

(He closes the lid, straightens up. HAMM raises his toque. Pause. He puts it on again.)

HAMM *(with his hand to his toque)*: And Nagg?

(CLOV raises lid of NAGG's bin, stoops, looks into it. Pause.)

CLOV: Doesn't look like it.

(He closes the lid, straightens up.)

HAMM *(letting go his toque)*: What's he doing?

(CLOV raises lid of NAGG's bin, stoops, looks into it. Pause.)

CLOV: He's crying.

(He closes lid, straightens up.)

HAMM: Then he's living.

(Pause.)

Did you ever have an instant of happiness?

CLOV: Not to my knowledge.

(Pause.)

HAMM: Bring me under the window.

(CLOV goes toward chair.)

I want to feel the light on my face.

(CLOV pushes chair.)

Do you remember, in the beginning, when you took me for a turn? You used to hold the chair too high. At every step you nearly tipped me out.

(With senile quaver.)

Ah great fun, we had, the two of us, great fun.

(Gloomily.)

And then we got into the way of it.

(CLOV stops the chair under window right.)

There already?

(Pause. He tilts back his head.)

Is it light?

CLOV: It isn't dark.

HAMM *(angrily)*: I'm asking you is it light.

CLOV: Yes.

(Pause.)

HAMM: The curtain isn't closed?

CLOV: No.

HAMM: What window is it?

CLOV: The earth.

HAMM: I knew it!

(Angrily.)

But there's no light there! The other!

(CLOV pushes the chair toward window left.)

The earth!

(CLOV stops the chair under window left. HAMM tilts back his head.)

That's what I call light!

(Pause.)

Feels like a ray of sunshine.

(Pause.)

No?

CLOV: No.

HAMM: It isn't a ray of sunshine I feel on my face?

CLOV: No.

(Pause.)

HAMM: Am I very white?

(Pause. Angrily.)

I'm asking you am I very white!

CLOV: Not more so than usual.

(Pause.)

HAMM: Open the window.

CLOV: What for?

HAMM: I want to hear the sea.

CLOV: You wouldn't hear it.

HAMM: Even if you opened the window?

CLOV: No.

HAMM: Then it's not worth while opening it?

CLOV: No.

HAMM *(violently)*: Then open it!

(CLOV gets up on the ladder, opens the window. Pause.)

Have you opened it?

CLOV: Yes.

(Pause.)

HAMM: You swear you've opened it?

CLOV: Yes.

(Pause.)

HAMM: Well . . . !

(Pause.)

It must be very calm.

(Pause. Violently.)

I'm asking you is it very calm!

CLOV: Yes.

HAMM: It's because there are no more navigators.

(Pause.)

You haven't much conversation all of a sudden. Do you not feel well?

CLOV: I'm cold.

HAMM: What month are we?

(Pause.)

Close the window, we're going back.

(CLOV closes the window, gets down, pushes the chair back to its place, remains standing behind it, head bowed.)

Don't stay there, you give me the shivers!

(CLOV returns to his place beside the chair.)

Father!

(Pause. Louder.)

Father!

(Pause.)

Go and see did he hear me.

(CLOV goes to NAGG's bin, raises the lid, stoops. Unintelligible words. CLOV straightens up.)

CLOV: Yes.

HAMM: Both times?

(CLOV stops. As before.)

CLOV: Once only.

HAMM: The first time or the second?

(CLOV stoops. As before.)

CLOV: He doesn't know.

HAMM: It must have been the second.

CLOV: We'll never know.

(He closes lid.)

HAMM: Is he still crying?

CLOV: No.

HAMM: The dead go fast.

(Pause.)

What's he doing?

CLOV: Sucking his biscuit.

HAMM: Life goes on.

(CLOV returns to his place beside the chair.)

Give me a rug, I'm freezing.

CLOV: There are no more rugs.

(Pause.)

HAMM: Kiss me.

(Pause.)

Will you not kiss me?

CLOV: No.

HAMM: On the forehead.

CLOV: I won't kiss you anywhere.

(Pause.)

HAMM *(holding out his hand)*: Give me your hand at least.

(Pause.)

Will you not give me your hand?

CLOV: I won't touch you.

(Pause.)

HAMM: Give me the dog.

(CLOV looks round for the dog.)

No!

CLOV: Do you not want your dog?

HAMM: No.

CLOV: Then I'll leave you.

HAMM *(head bowed, absently)*: That's right.

(CLOV goes to door, turns.)

CLOV: If I don't kill that rat he'll die.

HAMM *(as before)*: That's right.

(Exit CLOV. Pause.)

Me to play.

(He takes out his handkerchief, unfolds it, holds it spread out before him.)

We're getting on.

(Pause.)

You weep, and weep, for nothing, so as not to laugh, and little by little . . . you begin to grieve.

(He folds the handkerchief, he puts it back in his pocket, raises his head.)

All those I might have helped.

(Pause.)

Helped!

(Pause.)

Saved.

(Pause.)

Saved!

(Pause.)

The place was crawling with them!

(Pause. Violently.)

Use your head, can't you, use your head, you're on earth, there's no cure for that!

(Pause.)

Get out of here and love one another! Lick your neighbor as yourself!

(Pause. Calmer.)

When it wasn't bread they wanted it was crumpets.

(Pause. Violently.)

Out of my sight and back to your petting parties!

(Pause.)

All that, all that!

(Pause.)

Not even a real dog!

(Calmer.)

The end is in the beginning and yet you go on.

(Pause.)

Perhaps I could go on with my story, end it and begin another.

(Pause.)

Perhaps I could throw myself out on the floor.

(He pushes himself painfully off his seat, falls back again.)

Dig my nails into the cracks and drag myself forward with my fingers.

(Pause.)

It will be the end and there I'll be, wondering what can have brought it on and wondering what can have . . . *(He hesitates.)* . . . why it was so long coming.

(Pause.)

There I'll be, in the old shelter, alone against the silence and . . . *(He hesitates.)* . . . the stillness. If I can hold my peace, and sit quiet, it will be all over with sound, and motion, all over and done with.

(Pause.)

I'll have called my father and I'll have called my . . . *(He hesitates.)* . . . my son. And even twice, or three times, in case they shouldn't have heard me, the first time, or the second.

(Pause.)

I'll say to myself. He'll come back.

(Pause.)

And then?

(Pause.)

And then?

(Pause.)

He couldn't, he has gone too far.

(Pause.)

And then?

(Pause. Very agitated.)

All kinds of fantasies! That I'm being watched! A rat! Steps! Breath held and then . . .

(He breathes out.)

Then babble, babble, words, like the solitary child who turns himself into children, two, three, so as to be together, and whisper together in the dark.

(Pause.)

Moment upon moment, pattering down, like the millet grains of . . . *(He hesitates.)* . . . that old Greek, and all life long you wait for that to mount up to a life.

(Pause. He opens his mouth to continue, renounces.)

Ah let's get it over!

(He whistles. Enter CLOV *with alarm-clock. He halts beside the chair.)*

What? Neither gone nor dead?

CLOV: In spirit only.

HAMM: Which?

CLOV: Both.

HAMM: Gone from me you'd be dead.

CLOV: And vice versa.

HAMM: Outside of here it's death!

(Pause.)

And the rat?

CLOV: He's got away.

HAMM: He can't go far.

(Pause. Anxious.)

    Eh?

CLOV: He doesn't need to go far.

(Pause.)

HAMM: Is it not time for my pain-killer?

CLOV: Yes.

HAMM: Ah! At last! Give it to me! Quick!

(Pause.)

CLOV: There's no more pain-killer.

(Pause.)

HAMM (appalled): Good . . . !

(Pause.)

    No more pain-killer!

CLOV: No more pain-killer. You'll never get any more pain-killer.

(Pause.)

HAMM: But the little round box. It was full!

CLOV: Yes. But now it's empty.

(Pause. CLOV starts to move about the room. He is looking for a place to put down the alarm-clock.)

HAMM (soft): What'll I do?

(Pause. In a scream.)

    What'll I do?

(CLOV sees the picture, takes it down, stands it on the floor with its face to the wall, hangs up the alarm-clock in its place.)

    What are you doing?

CLOV: Winding up.

HAMM: Look at the earth.

CLOV: Again!

HAMM: Since it's calling to you.

CLOV: Is your throat sore?

(Pause.)

    Would you like a lozenge?

(Pause.)

    No.

(Pause.)

    Pity.

(CLOV goes, humming, toward window right, halts before it, looks up at it.)

HAMM: Don't sing.

CLOV (turning toward HAMM): One hasn't the right to sing any more?

HAMM: No.

CLOV: Then how can it end?

HAMM: You want it to end?

CLOV: I want to sing.

HAMM: I can't prevent you.

(Pause. CLOV turns toward window right.)

CLOV: What did I do with that steps?

(He looks around for ladder.)

    You didn't see that steps?

(He sees it.)

    Ah, about time.

(He goes toward window left.)

    Sometimes I wonder if I'm in my right mind. Then it passes over and I'm as lucid as before.

(He gets up on ladder, looks out of window.)

    Christ, she's under water!

(He looks.)

    How can that be?

(He pokes forward his head, his hand above his eyes.)

    It hasn't rained.

(He wipes the pane, looks. Pause.)

    Ah what a fool I am! I'm on the wrong side!

(He gets down, takes a few steps towards window right.)

    Under water!

(He goes back for ladder.)

    What a fool I am!

(He carries ladder toward window right.)

    Sometimes I wonder if I'm in my right senses. Then it passes off and I'm as intelligent as ever.

(He sets down ladder under window right, gets up on it, looks out of window. He turns toward HAMM.)

    Any particular sector you fancy? Or merely the whole thing?

HAMM: Whole thing.

CLOV: The general effect? Just a moment.

(He looks out of window. Pause.)

HAMM: Clov.

CLOV (absorbed): Mmm.

HAMM: Do you know what it is?

CLOV (as before): Mmm.

HAMM: I was never there.

(Pause.)

    Clov!

CLOV (*turning toward* HAMM, *exasperated*): What is it?
HAMM: I was never there.
CLOV: Lucky for you.

(*He looks out of window.*)

HAMM: Absent, always. It all happened without me. I don't know what's happened.

(*Pause.*)

Do you know what's happened?

(*Pause.*)

Clov!
CLOV (*turning toward* HAMM, *exasperated*): Do you want me to look at this muckheap, yes or no?
HAMM: Answer me first.
CLOV: What?
HAMM: Do you know what's happened?
CLOV: When? Where?
HAMM (*violently*): When! What's happened? Use your head, can't you? What has happened?
CLOV: What for Christ's sake does it matter?

(*He looks out of window.*)

HAMM: I don't know.

(*Pause.* CLOV *turns toward* HAMM.)

CLOV (*harshly*): When old Mother Pegg asked you for oil for her lamp and you told her to get out to hell, you knew what was happening then, no?

(*Pause.*)

You know what she died of, Mother Pegg? Of darkness.
HAMM (*feebly*): I hadn't any.
CLOV (*as before*): Yes, you had.

(*Pause.*)

HAMM: Have you the glass?
CLOV: No, it's clear enough as it is.
HAMM: Go and get it.

(*Pause.* CLOV *casts up his eyes, brandishes his fists. He loses balance, clutches on to the ladder. He starts to get down, halts.*)

CLOV: There's one thing I'll never understand.

(*He gets down.*)

Why I always obey you. Can you explain that to me?
HAMM: No. . . . Perhaps it's compassion.

(*Pause.*)

A kind of compassion.

(*Pause.*)

Oh you won't find it easy, you won't find it easy.

(*Pause.* CLOV *begins to move about the room in search of the telescope.*)

CLOV: I'm tired of our goings on, very tired.

(*He searches.*)

You're not sitting on it?

(*He moves the chair, looks at the place where it stood, resumes his search.*)

HAMM (*anguished*): Don't leave me there!

(*Angrily* CLOV *restores the chair to its place.*)

Am I right in the center?
CLOV: You'd need a microscope to find this—

(*He sees the telescope.*)

Ah, about time.

(*He picks up the telescope, gets up on the ladder, turns the telescope on the without.*)

HAMM: Give me the dog.
CLOV (*looking*): Quiet!
HAMM (*angrily*): Give me the dog!

(CLOV *drops the telescope, clasps his hands to his head. Pause. He gets down precipitately, looks for the dog, sees it, picks it up, hastens toward* HAMM *and strikes him violently on the head with the dog.*)

CLOV: There's your dog for you!

(*The dog falls to the ground. Pause.*)

HAMM: He hit me!
CLOV: You drive me mad, I'm mad!
HAMM: If you must hit me, hit me with the axe.

(*Pause.*)

Or with the gaff, hit me with the gaff. Not with the dog. With the gaff. Or with the axe.

(CLOV *picks up the dog and gives it to* HAMM *who takes it in his arms.*)

CLOV (*imploringly*): Let's stop playing!
HAMM: Never!

(*Pause.*)

Put me in my coffin.
CLOV: There are no more coffins.
HAMM: Then let it end!

(CLOV *goes toward ladder.*)

With a bang!

(CLOV *gets up on ladder, gets down again, looks for telescope, sees it, picks it up, gets up on ladder, raises telescope.*)

Of darkness! And me? Did anyone ever have pity on me?

CLOV (*lowering the telescope, turning toward* HAMM): What?

(*Pause.*)

Is it me you're referring to?

HAMM (*angrily*): An aside, ape! Did you never hear an aside before?

(*Pause.*)

I'm warming up for my last soliloquy.

CLOV: I warn you. I'm going to look at this filth since it's an order. But it's the last time.

(*He turns the telescope on the without.*)

Let's see.

(*He moves the telescope.*)

Nothing . . . nothing . . . good . . . good . . . nothing . . . goo—

(*He starts, lowers the telescope, examines it, turns it again on the without. Pause.*)

Bad luck to it!

HAMM: More complications!

(CLOV *gets down.*)

Not an underplot, I trust.

(CLOV *moves ladder nearer window, gets up on it, turns telescope on the without.*)

CLOVE (*dismayed*): Looks like a small boy!

HAMM (*sarcastic*): A small . . . boy!

CLOV: I'll go and see.

(*He gets down, drops the telescope, goes toward door, turns.*)

I'll take the gaff.

(*He looks for the gaff, sees it, picks it up, hastens toward door.*)

HAMM: No!

(CLOV *halts.*)

CLOV: No? A potential procreator?

HAMM: If he exists he'll die there or he'll come here. And if he doesn't . . .

(*Pause.*)

CLOV: You don't believe me? You think I'm inventing?

(*Pause.*)

HAMM: It's the end, Clov, we've come to the end. I don't need you any more.

(*Pause.*)

CLOV: Lucky for you.

(*He goes toward door.*)

HAMM: Leave me the gaff.

(CLOV *gives him the gaff, goes toward door, halts, looks at alarm-clock, takes it down, looks round for a better place to put it, goes to bins, puts it on lid of* NAGG's *bin. Pause.*)

CLOV: I'll leave you.

(*He goes toward door.*)

HAMM: Before you go . . .

(CLOV *halts near door.*)

. . . say something.

CLOV: There is nothing to say.

HAMM: A few words . . . to ponder . . . in my heart.

CLOV: Your heart!

HAMM: Yes.

(*Pause. Forcibly.*)

Yes!

(*Pause.*)

With the rest, in the end, the shadows, the murmurs, all the trouble, to end up with.

(*Pause.*)

Clov. . . . He never spoke to me. Then, in the end, before he went, without my having asked him, he spoke to me. He said . . .

CLOV (*despairingly*): Ah. . . !

HAMM: Something . . . from your heart.

CLOV: My heart!

HAMM: A few words . . . from your heart.

(*Pause.*)

CLOV (*fixed gaze, tonelessly, toward auditorium*): They said to me, That's love, yes, yes, not a doubt, now you see how—

HAMM: Articulate!

CLOV (*as before*): How easy it is. They said to me, That's friendship, yes, yes, no question, you've found it. They said to me, Here's the place, stop, raise your head and look at all that beauty. That order! They said to me, Come now, you're not a brute beast, think upon these things and you'll see how all becomes clear. And simple! They said to me, What skilled attention they get, all these dying of their wounds.

HAMM: Enough!

CLOV (*as before*): I say to myself—sometimes, Clov, you must learn to suffer better than that if you want them to weary of punishing you—one day. I say to myself—sometimes, Clov, you must be there better than that if you want them to let you go—one day. But I feel too old, and too far, to form new habits. Good, it'll never end, I'll never go.

(Pause.)

Then one day, suddenly, it ends, it changes, I don't understand, it dies, or it's me, I don't understand, that either. I ask the words that remain—sleeping, waking, morning, evening. They have nothing to say.

(Pause.)

I open the door of the cell and go. I am so bowed I only see my feet, if I open my eyes, and between my legs a little trail of black dust. I say to myself that the earth is extinguished, though I never saw it lit.

(Pause.)

It's easy going.

(Pause.)

When I fall I'll weep for happiness.

(Pause. He goes toward door.)

HAMM: Clov!

(CLOV halts, without turning.)

Nothing.

(CLOV moves on.)

Clov!

(CLOV halts, without turning.)

CLOV: This is what we call making an exit.
HAMM: I'm obliged to you, Clov. For your services.
CLOV *(turning, sharply)*: Ah pardon, it's I am obliged to you.
HAMM: It's we are obliged to each other.

(Pause. CLOV goes toward door.)

One thing more.

(CLOV halts.)

A last favor.

(Exit CLOV.)

Cover me with the sheet.

(Long pause.)

No? Good.

(Pause.)

Me to play.

(Pause. Wearily.)

Old endgame lost of old, play and lose and have done with losing.

(Pause. More animated.)

Let me see.

(Pause.)

Ah yes!

(He tries to move the chair, using the gaff as before. Enter CLOV, dressed for the road. Panama hat, tweed coat, raincoat over his arm, umbrella, bag. He halts by the door and stands there, impassive and motionless, his eyes are fixed on HAMM, till the end. HAMM gives up.)

Good.

(Pause.)

Discard.

(He throws away the gaff, makes to throw away the dog, thinks better of it.)

Take it easy.

(Pause.)

And now?

(Pause.)

Raise hat.

(He raises his toque.)

Peace to our . . . arses.

(Pause.)

And put on again.

(He puts on his toque.)

Deuce.

(Pauses. He takes off his glasses.)

Wipe.

(He takes out his handkerchief and, without unfolding it, wipes his glasses.)

And put on again.

(He puts on his glasses, puts back the handkerchief in his pocket.)

We're coming. A few more squirms like that and I'll call.

(Pause.)

A little poetry.

(Pause.)

You prayed—

(Pause. He corrects himself.)

You CRIED for night; it comes—

(*Pause, He corrects himself.*)

It FALLS: now cry in darkness.

(*He repeats, chanting.*)

You cried for night; it falls; now cry in darkness.

(*Pause.*)

Nicely put, that.

(*Pause.*)

And now?

(*Pause.*)

Moments for nothing, now as always, time was never and time is over, reckoning closed and story ended.

(*Pause. Narrative tone.*)

If he could have his child with him. . . .

(*Pause.*)

It was the moment I was waiting for.

(*Pause.*)

You don't want to abandon him? You want him to bloom while you are withering? Be there to solace your last million last moments?

(*Pause.*)

He doesn't realize, all he knows is hunger, and cold, and death to crown it all. But you! You ought to know what the earth is like, nowadays. Oh I put him before his responsibilities!

(*Pause. Normal tone.*)

Well, there we are, there I am, that's enough.

(*He raises the whistle to his lips, hesitates, drops it. Pause.*)

Yes, truly!

(*He whistles. Pause. Louder. Pause.*)

Good.

(*Pause.*)

Father!

(*Pause. Louder.*)

Father!

(*Pause.*)

Good.

(*Pause.*)

We're coming.

(*Pause.*)

And to end up with?

(*Pause.*)

Discard.

(*He throws away the dog. He tears the whistle from his neck.*)

With my compliments.

(*He throws whistle toward auditorium. Pause. He sniffs. Soft.*)

Clov!

(*Long pause.*)

No? Good.

(*He takes out the handkerchief.*)

Since that's the way we're playing it . . . (*He unfolds handkerchief.*) . . . let's play it that way . . .(*He unfolds.*) . . . and speak no more about it . . . (*He finishes unfolding.*) . . . speak no more.

(*He holds handkerchief spread out before him.*)

Old stancher!

(*Pause.*)

You . . . remain.

(*Pause. He covers his face with handkerchief, lowers his arms to armrests, remains motionless.*)
(*Brief tableau.*)

CURTAIN

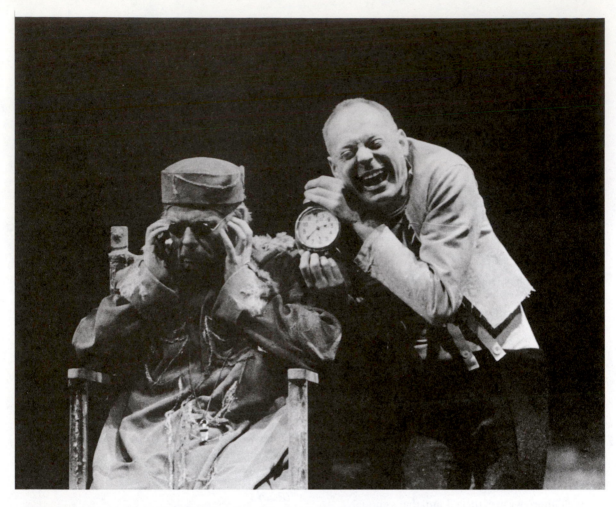

Figure 90. Hamm (Roger Blin) and Clov (Jean Martin) in the Studio des Champs-Elysees production of *Endgame,* directed by Roger Blin and designed by Jacques Noel, Paris, 1957. (Photograph: Roger Pic.)

Figure 91. Nagg (Georges Adet) asks for his sugar plum while Hamm
(Roger Blin) and Clov (Jean Martin) pray to God in the Studio des
Champs-Elysées production of *Endgame,* directed by Roger Blin and
designed by Jacques Noel, Paris, 1957. (Photograph: Roger Pic.)

Staging of *Endgame*

**REVIEW OF THE STUDIO DES CHAMPS-ÉLYSÉES
PRODUCTION, 1957, BY JACQUES LEMARCHAND**

"Endgame" by Samuel Beckett lends a theatrical reality, a frightening reality, to a certain daydream that I imagine we have all yielded to at one time or another: some day, it matters little under what conditions, there will no longer be any men on Earth; nor will there be any Earth then either. One short moment, no more, in the entire universe, when a single man, the very last man, will have the task of feeling the last emotion, the last sensation, of speaking the last word—and that word will not be historic. To young people this seems, if I remember correctly, frightening, dizzying. To those not so young it can seem more like a pleasant reassurance that one should not attach a great deal of importance to winning literary prizes, nor fret too much about honors granted to imbeciles. This is a rather peaceful daydream, blending a fair amount of humor into the inevitable terror that the end of *everything* arouses in man.

And this terror and comedy have never been presented on stage in a manner so immediately perceptible, and with so little rhetoric as well as so much persuasive power, as in this "Endgame," playing at the Studio des Champs-Élysées, to its infinite honor. It is easy, and legitimate, to seek and to find in "Endgame" some sort of sequel to, or echo of, "Waiting for Godot." In fact, Beckett's second play, although it bears the undeniable stamp of its author—that clown-like naïveté, with which the characters juggle, to all appearances innocently, our most secret and serious anxieties—is a play entirely different from "Waiting for Godot." Godot has absolutely refused to come, and no one is waiting for him any more; what they are waiting for is to "make an exit"; and words of waiting, hope, and desire have lost all meaning: the characters of "Endgame" simply consent to something they know is inevitable.

These protagonists have been criticized for not being very attractive young men. It is true that Beckett's play is lacking in young leads. One could just as well criticize them for having names that are rather uncommon in the boulevard theaters. They are called Hamm, Clov, Nagg and Nell, names reeking of the circus and lacking in distinction. But after all, this is the very last day of the human race, and it is permissible to imagine that the saints of the calendar have withdrawn. It is no less true that these characters are in poor health: Hamm is paralyzed and cannot leave his armchair; Clov, his slave, has difficulty walking and shakes with palsy; as for Nagg and his wife Nell, their situation is quite simple: they are legless cripples, and each lives in an ashbin, comfortably, it seems, considering their smaller size; these four characters are shut in a sort of bunker, in which they will certainly have to die. The two windows of the shelter look out upon a leaden sea and empty land, equally forsaken by humanity. This is hardly a pleasant situation, I admit, but it can surely be granted that is eminently dramatic.

Among these four human beings there is no other solidarity than that arising from self-interest. Nagg and Nell, who are Hamm's parents, depend on him for the last few mouthfuls of pap that will prolong their mediocre lives; Hamm depends on his servant-son, Clov, for the attentions required by his condition; and if Clov refrains from dispatching Hamm, it is simply because he does not have the 'combination to the cupboard' where the last few biscuits are locked up. And yet there is not one of these human beings who does not have his dream, a dream he tries to make the others share, to communicate to them: and this need to communicate is as vital to their lives as is the diminishing store of biscuits. From one ashbin to the other, Nagg and Nell allusively exchange their memories: that of rowing a boat one April afternoon on Lake Como, or even the evocation of the accident that crippled them, draws them closer together; from time to time Hamm pursues the fabrication of a long drawn-out literary story, for which, like a true man of letters, he requires an audience. Clov announces his own imminent departure, though he knows it to be impossible, and does all he can to convince himself that his departure depends on his will alone.

It is the spectacle of a game that is coming to an end, of an endgame, that is presented to us in Beckett's play. The fact that this may be the very game we play all the time, without ever believing it to be as close as it is to its end, is made constantly apparent by the way relations among the four characters are stripped down and reduced to an elemental level. The humor of this grim play—vigorous, savage, never gratuitous, provoking brusque outbreaks of laughter—arises also from flashes of confrontation between the actual situation of these characters and the tremendous futility of their malice as well as of their moments of tenderness. It arises too from the frenzy we discover in these characters, which they reveal in their furious acceptance of their fate: the distant apparition of what they take to be a human figure, the discovery of a live rat or a live flea horrifies them. "But humanity might start from there all over again," says Hamm. "Catch him, for the love of God!" Black humor indeed, but of a kind that arises spontaneously from felicitous and unexpected phrases, from a latent tragicomicality that suddenly becomes enormously ludicrous. A humor whose power is in no way increased by one obscene pun and two or three instances of coarse language.

I have limited myself to describing only the exterior aspect of "Endgame": a poem in dialogue, full of surprises and verbal successes, a play that moves and progresses, despite its immobile protagonists and subtle repetitions, towards a poignant and beautiful ending. As for any metaphysical conclusions it may imply, naturally it is for each spectator to understand them to his own liking; the author leaves them complete latitude, and this is not the least of the reasons for the fascination one experiences at a performance of "Endgame."

Jacques Noel's set, that bare bunker in which the human race is coming to an end, is stifling; assuredly just as Beckett must have conceived it. Roger Blin (Hamm), who ensured the meticulous direction of the play, and Jean Martin (Clov) are its extremely impressive protagonists; Germane de France (Nell) and Georges Adet (Nagg), emerging from their Diogenesque ashbins, succeed in being at once ludicrous and pathetic.

The performance ends with an "Act Without Words," by Beckett—a pantomime for one actor, carried through to its termination with the sureness of a great artist by Deryk Mendel—who, amid silence punctuated by blasts from a whistle, shows the same qualities of humor and cruelty we enjoyed in "Endgame." (Translated by Jean M. Sommermeyer)

IMAMU AMIRI BARAKA

1934–

Between March and December 1964, Baraka, who was then still writing under his original name of LeRoi Jones, had four one-act plays produced off-Broadway, one of which, *Dutchman*, won the Obie award for the best off-Broadway play of 1963–64. That production record would be considered astonishing for any playwright, particularly for a young black playwright until then known only as a writer of essays and poems. Baraka was born in Newark, New Jersey, where he attended public school and then began college at Rutgers University, later transferring to Howard University, one of America's most distinguished black colleges. Subsequently, he served in the United States Air Force, from 1954 to 1957, and then settled in New York City where, with Hettie Cohen, whom he married in 1958, he edited a literary magazine, publishing avant-garde writers such as William Burroughs, Gregory Corso, Allen Ginsburg, Jack Kerouac, Charles Olson, and LeRoi Jones. His sudden fame after the success of *Dutchman* led him to teaching positions at Columbia University and the New School for Social Research, as well as the award of a Guggenheim Fellowship in 1965. It was also in 1965 that he changed his name to Imamu Amiri Baraka, roughly translatable as Priest-Warrior-Blessing, and wrote his well-known manifesto, "The Revolutionary Theater." In it he asserted that theater "should force change, it should be change," that it "must EXPOSE! Show up the insides of these humans, look into black skulls. White men will cower before this theater because it hates them." And in his subsequent plays, Baraka followed up on his manifesto, for they are all essentially political in purpose, aimed at stirring black audiences to radical action, and thus similar in intent to the "learning plays" that Brecht was writing during the late 1920s and early 1930s.

Although *Dutchman* was written before Baraka became explicitly associated with "revolutionary theater," it is clearly a revolutionary play, particularly when it is seen in the context of the black drama that had preceded it. Blacks had written plays during the nineteenth century, yet black drama did not begin to come into its own until the 1920s with the plays of Garland Anderson, Wallace Thurman, and Willis Richardson. The Federal Theater project of the 1930s gave special encouragement to black dramatists and led, in particular, to the plays of Langston Hughes, one of the leading figures of the Harlem Renaissance, whose works include *Mulatto* (1935), *Don't You Want to Be Free* (1936), a long running historical panorama, and *Emperor of Haiti* (1938). In Chicago, the Federal Theater Unit sponsored the first production of Theodore Ward's *Big White Fog* (1938), a play that shows a family's struggle to attain a new life in the context of urban society through the political movement known as "back-to-Africa." Ward's later play, *Our Lan'* (1941), was even more successful with its depiction of newly freed blacks trying to live on an island off the Georgia coast. At the end of the 1950s, Loraine Hansberry's *A Raisin in the Sun* (1959) became a major Broadway success by taking up once again the theme of the "new life," this time by showing a protagonist who maintains his individual and racial pride by moving out of the slums and into a white middle-class neighborhood, a neighborhood that had tried to buy him off to keep him from moving in.

All these plays concerned themselves with the social and political problems of blacks, yet most concentrated almost exclusively on blacks themselves, with only a few venturing to deal directly with confrontations between black and white characters. Not until the plays of Baraka did that confrontation become the insistent focus of black drama. In *The Slave* (1964), he showed a black leader, Walker Vessels, engaged in a long argument with two white liberals, Grace and Bradford Easley, about their conflicting ideologies. In *The Toilet* (1964), he showed a group of black boys beating up a white boy, a Puerto Rican, who has sent a "love letter" to the black leader of their group. And in *Dutchman,* he dramatized the ultimate confrontation in a sexual encounter between a black man and a white woman, a confrontation that leads to a violent conclusion, in which the victim becomes the black man. In *Dutchman,* too, Baraka moved away from the realistic style that had prevailed in black drama toward a symbolic style, immediately announced by its title.

This title is meant to evoke the legend of the Flying Dutchman, the man doomed to sail the seas forever until he found a woman who would be faithful to him, and the subway in which the play is set reflects that ceaseless and meaningless voyaging. The title also alludes to the Dutch ships that brought black slaves to North America, and in this context Lula may be seen as a relentless traveler and destroyer, embodying the way that whites have always treated blacks. Baraka himself claimed that the situation rather than the characters was meant to be symbolic, an interpretation stressing the ceaselessness of racial violence. Apart from the title, the play's mythic quality is emphasized by Baraka's stage direction, "The subway heaped in modern myth," by the appearance of Lula eating an apple, by her later remark that "Eating apples is always the first step," and by Clay's name, which echoes Adam's formation "out of the dust of the ground." The interweaving of the realistic and the symbolic can also be seen in the dialogue of the play, which begins essentially with everyday conversation but quickly turns into metaphor, when Lula tells Clay that "You look like death eating a soda cracker." Lula then turns into a mock prophet in her litany at the end of the first scene, and finally a chanter of vicious and obscene litanies, meant to goad Clay into action.

When she does finally arouse him to the violent action and speech audiences yearn for after her relentless taunting, the effect is devastating, for he destroys any myths that whites may have about blacks, ending as he does with an explicit threat about what will happen when blacks are "accepted" by whites:

> They'll murder you, and have very rational explanations. Very much like your own. They'll cut your throats, and drag you out to the edge of your cities, so the flesh can fall away from your bones, in sanitary isolation.

But instead of the physical assault that might be expected from Clay after this speech, Baraka creates an even more frightening conclusion in Lula's stabbing of him, an act that grotesquely inverts and parodies the sexual act they have been discussing. Her comment, "Get this man off me!" continues the sexual subtext. And when a young black of twenty next enters the subway car, her act of turning and giving him a long slow look clearly indicates that the destructive cycle will begin again, repeating itself endlessly like the travels of the subway and the flying Dutchman.

When the play was first produced, critics were both impressed and defensive, as revealed in the two reviews reprinted following the text. But they also noted the symbolic significance of the play, as indicated by Harold Clurman's remarks about Lula: "She is our neurosis. Not a neurosis in regard to the Negro, but the absolute neurosis of American society." Jennifer West's performance conveyed that neurosis in her combination of childishness, sexiness, and aggressiveness (see Figure 92) with uncontrollably vicious mocking (see Figure 93). When the play was turned into a film in 1967, critics found it stagey and dull, for the real subway car seemed much less effective as a frame for the play's violence than the make-believe one. On stage, the play still shocks, still continues to explode, precisely because the subway car is only a set while the anger, the cruelty, and the hatred are real.

DUTCHMAN

BY IMAMU AMIRI BARAKA

CHARACTERS

CLAY, *twenty-year-old Negro*
LULA, *thirty-year-old white woman*
RIDERS OF COACH, *white and black*
YOUNG NEGRO
CONDUCTOR

SCENE

In the flying underbelly of the city. Steaming hot, and summer on top, outside. Underground. The subway heaped in modern myth.

Opening scene is a man sitting in a subway seat, holding a magazine but looking vacantly just above its wilting pages. Occasionally he looks blankly toward the window on his right. Dim lights and darkness whistling by against the glass. (Or paste the lights, as admitted props, right on the subway windows. Have them move, even dim and flicker. But give the sense of speed. Also stations, whether the train is stopped or the glitter and activity of these stations merely flashes by the windows.)

The man is sitting alone. That is, only his seat is visible, though the rest of the car is outfitted as a complete subway car. But only his seat is shown. There might be, for a time, as the play begins, a loud scream of the actual train. And it can recur throughout the play, or continue on a lower key once the dialogue starts.

The train slows after a time, pulling to a brief stop at one of the stations. The man looks idly up, until he sees a woman's face staring at him through the window; when it realizes that the man has noticed the face, it begins very premeditatedly to smile. The man smiles too, for a moment, without a trace of self-consciousness. Almost an instinctive though undesirable response. Then a kind of awkwardness or embarrassment sets in, and the man makes to look away, is further embarrassed, so he brings back his eyes to where the face was, but by now the train is moving again, and the face would seem to be left behind by the way the man turns his head to look back through the other windows at the slowly fading platform. He smiles then; more comfortably confident, hoping perhaps that his memory of this brief encounter will be pleasant. And then he is idle again.

SCENE 1

(Train roars. Lights flash outside the windows.

LULA *enters from the rear of the car in bright, skimpy summer clothes and sandals. She carries a net bag full of paper books, fruit, and other anonymous articles. She is wearing sunglasses, which she pushes up on her forehead from time to time.* LULA *is a tall, slender, beautiful woman with long red hair hanging straight down her back, wearing only loud lipstick in somebody's good taste. She is eating an apple, very daintily. Coming down the car toward* CLAY.

She stops beside CLAY'S *seat and hangs languidly from the strap, still managing to eat the apple. It is apparent that she is going to sit in the seat next to* CLAY, *and that she is only waiting for him to notice her before she sits.*

CLAY *sits as before, looking just beyond his magazine, now and again pulling the magazine slowly back and forth in front of his face in a hopeless effort to fan himself. Then he sees the woman hanging there beside him and he looks up into her face, smiling quizzically.)*

LULA: Hello.
CLAY: Uh, hi're you?
LULA: I'm going to sit down. . . . O.K.?
CLAY: Sure.
LULA *(swings down onto the seat, pushing her legs straight out as if she is very weary):* Oooof! Too much weight.

CLAY: Ha, doesn't look like much to me.

(Leaning back against the window, a little surprised and maybe stiff.)

LULA: It's so anyway.

(And she moves her toes in the sandals, then pulls her right leg up on the left knee, better to inspect the bottoms of the sandals and the back of her heel. She appears for a second not to notice that CLAY *is sitting next to her or that she has spoken to him just a second before.* CLAY *looks at the magazine, then out the black window. As he does this, she turns very quickly toward him.)*

Weren't you staring at me through the window?
CLAY *(wheeling around and very much stiffened):* What?
LULA: Weren't you staring at me through the window? At the last stop?
CLAY: Staring at you? What do you mean?
LULA: Don't you know what staring means?
CLAY: I saw you through the window . . . if that's what it means. I don't know if I was staring. Seems to me you were staring through the window at me.
LULA: I was. But only after I'd turned around and saw you staring through that window down in the vicinity of my ass and legs.
CLAY: Really?
LULA: Really. I guess you were just taking those idle

960

potshots. Nothing else to do. Run your mind over people's flesh.

CLAY: Oh boy. Wow, now I admit I was looking in your direction. But the rest of that weight is yours.

LULA: I suppose.

CLAY: Staring through train windows is weird business. Much weirder than staring very sedately at abstract asses.

LULA: That's why I came looking through the window . . . so you'd have more than that to go on. I even smiled at you.

CLAY: That's right.

LULA: I even got into this train, going some other way than mine. Walked down the aisle . . . searching you out.

CLAY: Really? That's pretty funny.

LULA: That's pretty funny. . . . God, you're dull.

CLAY: Well, I'm sorry, lady, but I really wasn't prepared for party talk.

LULA: No, you're not. What are you prepared for?

(Wrapping the apple core in a Kleenex and dropping it on the floor.)

CLAY *(takes her conversation as pure sex talk. He turns to confront her squarely with this idea)*: I'm prepared for anything. How about you?

LULA *(laughing loudly and cutting it off abruptly)*: What do you think you're doing?

CLAY: What?

LULA: You think I want to pick you up, get you to take me somewhere and screw me, huh?

CLAY: Is that the way I look?

LULA: You look like you been trying to grow a beard. That's exactly what you look like. You look like you live in New Jersey with your parents and are trying to grow a beard. That's what. You look like you've been reading Chinese poetry and drinking lukewarm sugarless tea. *(Laughs, uncrossing and recrossing her legs.)* You look like death eating a soda cracker.

CLAY *(cocking his head from one side to the other, embarrassed and trying to make some comeback, but also intrigued by what the woman is saying . . . even the sharp city coarseness of her voice, which is still a kind of gentle sidewalk throb)*: Really? I look like all that?

LULA: Not all of it.

(She feints a seriousness to cover an actual somber tone.)

I lie a lot. *(Smiling.)* It helps me control the world.

CLAY *(relieved and laughing louder than the humor)*: Yeah, I bet.

LULA: But it's true, most of it, right? Jersey? Your bumpy neck?

CLAY: How'd you know all that? Huh? Really, I mean about Jersey . . . and even the beard. I met you

before? You know Warren Enright?

LULA: You tried to make it with your sister when you were ten. *(CLAY leans back hard against the back of the seat, his eyes opening now, still trying to look amused.)* But I succeeded a few weeks ago. *(She starts to laugh again.)*

CLAY: What're you talking about? Warren tell you that? You're a friend of Georgia's?

LULA: I told you I lie. I don't know your sister. I don't know Warren Enright.

CLAY: You mean you're just picking these things out of the air?

LULA: Is Warren Enright a tall skinny black black boy with a phony English accent?

CLAY: I figured you knew him.

LULA: But I don't. I just figured you would know somebody like that. *(Laughs.)*

CLAY: Yeah, yeah.

LULA: You're probably on your way to his house now.

CLAY: That's right.

LULA *(putting her hand on CLAY's closest knee, drawing it from the knee up to the thigh's hinge, then removing it, watching his face very closely, and continuing to laugh, perhaps more gently than before)*: Dull, dull, dull. I bet you think I'm exciting.

CLAY: You're O.K.

LULA: Am I exciting you now?

CLAY: Right. That's not what's supposed to happen?

LULA: How do I know? *(She returns her hand, without moving it, then takes it away and plunges it in her bag to draw out an apple.)* You want this?

CLAY: Sure.

LULA *(she gets one out of the bag for herself)*: Eating apples together is always the first step. Or walking up uninhabited Seventh Avenue in the twenties on weekends. *(Bites and giggles, glancing at CLAY and speaking in loose sing-song.)* Can get you involved . . . boy! Get us involved. Um-huh. *(Mock seriousness.)* Would you like to get involved with me, Mister Man?

CLAY *(trying to be as flippant as LULA, whacking happily at the apple)*: Sure. Why not? A beautiful woman like you. Huh, I'd be a fool not to.

LULA: And I bet you're sure you know what you're talking about. *(Taking him a little roughly by the wrist, so he cannot eat the apple, then shaking the wrist.)* I bet you're sure of almost everything anybody ever asked you . . . right? *(Shakes his wrist harder.)* Right?

CLAY: Yeah, right. . . . Wow, you're pretty strong, you know? Whatta you, a lady wrestler or something?

LULA: What's wrong with lady wrestlers? And don't answer because you never knew any. Huh. *(Cynically.)* That's for sure. They don't have any lady wrestlers in that part of Jersey. That's for sure.

CLAY: Hey, you still haven't told me how you know so much about me.

LULA: I told you I didn't know anything about *you* . . . you're a well-known type.

CLAY: Really?

LULA: Or at least I know the type very well. And your skinny English friend too.

CLAY: Anonymously?

LULA *(settles back in seat, single-mindedly finishing her apple and humming snatches of rhythm and blues song)*: What?

CLAY: Without knowing us specifically?

LULA: Oh boy. *(Looking quickly at* CLAY.) What a face. You know, you could be a handsome man.

CLAY: I can't argue with you.

LULA *(vague, off-center response)*: What?

CLAY *(raising his voice, thinking the train noise has drowned part of his sentence)*: I can't argue with you.

LULA: My hair is turning gray. A gray hair for each year and type I've come through.

CLAY: Why do you want to sound so old?

LULA: But it's always gentle when it starts. *(Attention drifting.)* Hugged against tenements, day or night.

CLAY: What?

LULA *(refocusing)*: Hey, why don't you take me to that party you're going to?

CLAY: You must be a friend of Warren's to know about the party.

LULA: Wouldn't you like to take me to the party? *(Imitates clinging vine.)* Oh, come on, ask me to your party.

CLAY: Of course I'll ask you to come with me to the party. And I'll bet you're a friend of Warren's.

LULA: Why not be a friend of Warren's? Why not? *(Taking his arm.)* Have you asked me yet?

CLAY: How can I ask you when I don't know your name?

LULA: Are you talking to my name?

CLAY: What is it, a secret?

LULA: I'm Lena the Hyena.

CLAY: The famous woman poet?

LULA: Poetess! the same!

CLAY: Well, you know so much about me . . . what's my name?

LULA: Morris the Hyena.

CLAY: The famous woman poet?

LULA: The same. *(Laughing and going into her bag.)* You want another apple?

CLAY: Can't make it, lady. I only have to keep one doctor away a day.

LULA: I bet your name is . . . something like . . . uh, Gerald or Walter. Huh?

CLAY: God, no.

LULA: Lloyd, Norman? One of those hopeless colored names creeping out of New Jersey. Leonard? Gag. . . .

CLAY: Like Warren?

LULA: Definitely. Just exactly like Warren. Or Everett.

CLAY: Gag. . . .

LULA: Well, for sure, it's not Willie.

CLAY: It's Clay.

LULA: Clay? Really? Clay what?

CLAY: Take your pick. Jackson, Johnson, or Williams.

LULA: Oh, really? Good for you. But it's got to be Williams. You're too pretentious to be a Jackson or Johnson.

CLAY: Thass right.

LULA: But Clay's O.K.

CLAY: So's Lena.

LULA: It's Lula.

CLAY: Oh?

LULA: Lula the Hyena.

CLAY: Very good.

LULA *(starts laughing again)*: Now you say to me, "Lula, Lula, why don't you go to this party with me tonight?" It's your turn, and let those be your lines.

CLAY: Lula, why don't you go to this party with me tonight, Huh?

LULA: Say my name twice before you ask, and no huh's.

CLAY: Lula, Lula, why don't you go to this party with me tonight?

LULA: I'd like to go, Clay, but how can you ask me to go when you barely know me?

CLAY: That is strange, isn't it?

LULA: What kind of reaction is that? You're supposed to say, "Aw, come on, we'll get to know each other better at the party."

CLAY: That's pretty corny.

LULA: What are you into anyway? *(Looking at him half sullenly but still amused.)* What thing are you playing at, Mister? Mister Clay Williams? *(Grabs his thigh, up near the crotch.)* What are *you* thinking about?

CLAY: Watch it now, you're gonna excite me for real.

LULA *(taking her hand away and throwing her apple core through the window)*: I bet. *(She slumps in the seat and is heavily silent.)*

CLAY: I thought you knew everything about me? What happened? *(*LULA *looks at him, then looks slowly away, then over where the other aisle would be. Noise of the train. She reaches in her bag and pulls out one of the paper books. She puts it on her leg and thumbs the pages listlessly.* CLAY *cocks his head to see the title of the book. Noise of the train.* LULA *flips pages and her eyes drift. Both remain silent.)* Are you going to the party with me, Lula?

LULA *(bored and not even looking)*: I don't even know you.

CLAY: You said you know my type.

LULA *(strangely irritated)*: Don't get smart with me,

Buster. I know you like the palm of my hand.

CLAY: The one you eat the apples with?

LULA: Yeh. And the one I open doors late Saturday evening with. That's my door. Up at the top of the stairs. Five flights. Above a lot of Italians and lying Americans. And scrape carrots with. Also . . . (*Looks at him.*) the same hand I unbutton my dress with, or let my skirt fall down. Same hand. Lover.

CLAY: Are you angry about something? Did I say something wrong?

LULA: Everything you say is wrong. (*Mock smile.*) That's what makes you so attractive. Ha. In that funnybook jacket with all the buttons. (*More animate, taking hold of his jacket.*) What've you got that jacket and tie on in all this heat for? And why're you wearing a jacket and tie like that? Did your people ever burn witches or start revolutions over the price of tea? Boy, those narrow-shoulder clothes come from a tradition you ought to feel oppressed by. A three-button suit. What right do you have to be wearing a three-button suit and striped tie? Your father was a slave, he didn't go to Harvard.

CLAY: My grandfather was a night watchman.

LULA: And you went to a colored college where everybody thought they were Averell Harriman.

CLAY: All except me.

LULA: And who did you think you were? Who do you think you are now?

CLAY (*laughs as if to make light of the whole trend of the conversation*): Well, in college I thought I was Baudelaire. But I've slowed down since.

LULA: I bet you never once thought you were a black nigger. (*Mock serious, then she howls with laughter.* CLAY *is stunned but after initial reaction, he quickly tries to appreciate the humor.* LULA *almost shrieks.*) A black Baudelaire.

CLAY: That's right.

LULA: Boy, are you corny. I take back what I said before. Everything you say is not wrong. It's perfect. You should be on television.

CLAY: You act like you're on television already.

LULA: That's because I'm an actress.

CLAY: I thought so.

LULA: Well, you're wrong. I'm no actress. I told you I always lie. I'm nothing, honey, and don't you ever forget it. (*Lighter.*) Although my mother was a Communist. The only person in my family ever to amount to anything.

CLAY: My mother was a Republican.

LULA: And your father voted for the man rather than the party.

CLAY: Right!

LULA: Yea for him. Yea, yea for him.

CLAY: Yea!

LULA: And yea for America where he is free to vote for the mediocrity of his choice! Yea!

CLAY: Yea!

LULA: And yea for both your parents who even though they differ about so crucial a matter as the body politic still forged a union of love and sacrifice that was destined to flower at the birth of the noble Clay . . . what's your middle name?

CLAY: Clay.

LULA: A union of love and sacrifice that was destined to flower at the birth of the noble Clay Clay Williams. Yea! And most of all yea yea for you, Clay Clay. The Black Baudelaire! Yes! (*And with knifelike cynicism.*) My Christ. My Christ.

CLAY: Thank you, ma'am.

LULA: May the people accept you as a ghost of the future. And love you, that you might not kill them when you can.

CLAY: What?

LULA: You're a murderer, Clay, and you know it. (*Her voice darkening with significance.*) You know goddamn well what I mean.

CLAY: I do?

LULA: So we'll pretend the air is light and full of perfume.

CLAY (*sniffing at her blouse*): It is.

LULA: And we'll pretend the people cannot see you. That is, the citizens. And that you are free of your own history. And I am free of my history. We'll pretend that we are both anonymous beauties smashing along through the city's entrails. (*She yells as loud as she can.*) GROOVE!

SCENE 2

(*Scene is the same as before, though now there are other seats visible in the car. And throughout the scene other people get on the subway. There are maybe one or two seated in the car as the scene opens, though neither* CLAY *or* LULA *notices them.* CLAY'*s tie is open.* LULA *is hugging his arm.*)

CLAY: The party!

LULA: I know it'll be something good. You can come in with me, looking casual and significant. I'll be strange, haughty, and silent, and walk with long slow strides.

CLAY: Right.

LULA: When you get drunk, pat me once, very lovingly on the flanks, and I'll look at you cryptically, licking my lips.

CLAY: It sounds like something we can do.

LULA: You'll go around talking to young men about your mind, and to old men about your plans. If you meet a very close friend who is also with someone like me, we can stand together, sipping our drinks and exchanging codes of lust. The atmosphere will be slithering in love and half-love and very open moral decision.

CLAY: Great. Great.

LULA: And everyone will pretend they don't know your name, and then . . . *(She pauses heavily.)* later, when they have to, they'll claim a friendship that denies your sterling character.

CLAY *(kissing her neck and fingers)*: And then what?

LULA: Then? Well, then we'll go down the street, late night, eating apples and winding very deliberately toward my house.

CLAY: Deliberately?

LULA: I mean, we'll look in all the shopwindows, and make fun of the queers. Maybe we'll meet a Jewish Buddhist and flatten his conceits over some very pretentious coffee.

CLAY: In honor of whose God?

LULA: Mine.

CLAY: Who is . . . ?

LULA: Me . . . and you?

CLAY: A corporate Godhead.

LULA: Exactly. Exactly. *(Notices one of the other people entering.)*

CLAY: Go on with the chronicle. Then what happens to us?

LULA *(a mild depression, but she still makes her description triumphant and increasingly direct)*: To my house, of course.

CLAY: Of course.

LULA: And up the narrow steps of the tenement.

CLAY: You live in a tenement?

LULA: Wouldn't live anywhere else. Reminds me specifically of my novel form of insanity.

CLAY: Up the tenement stairs.

LULA: And with my apple-eating hand I push open the door and lead you, my tender big-eyed prey, into my . . . God, what can I call it . . . into my hovel.

CLAY: Then what happens?

LULA: After the dancing and games, after the long drinks and long walks, the real fun begins.

CLAY: Ah, the real fun. *(Embarrassed, in spite of himself.)* Which is . . . ?

LULA *(laughs at him)*: Real fun in the dark house. Hah! Real fun in the dark house, high up above the street and the ignorant cowboys. I lead you in, holding your wet hand gently in my hand . . .

CLAY: Which is not wet?

LULA: Which is dry as ashes.

CLAY: And cold?

LULA: Don't think you'll get out of your responsibility that way. It's not cold at all. You Fascist! Into my dark living room. Where we'll sit and talk endlessly, endlessly.

CLAY: About what?

LULA: About what? About your manhood, what do you think? What do you think we've been talking about all this time?

CLAY: Well, I didn't know it was that. That's for sure. Every other thing in the world but that. *(Notices another person entering, looks quickly, almost involuntarily up and down the car, seeing the other people in the car.)* Hey, I didn't even notice when those people got on.

LULA: Yeah, I know.

CLAY: Man, this subway is slow.

LULA: Yeah, I know.

CLAY: Well, go on. We were talking about my manhood.

LULA: We still are. All the time.

CLAY: We were in your living room.

LULA: My dark living room. Talking endlessly.

CLAY: About my manhood.

LULA: I'll make you a map of it. Just as soon as we get to my house.

CLAY: Well, that's great.

LULA: One of the things we do while we talk. And screw.

CLAY *(trying to make his smile broader and less shaky)*: We finally got there.

LULA: And you'll call my rooms black as a grave. You'll say, "This place is like Juliet's tomb."

CLAY *(laughs)*: I might.

LULA: I know. You've probably said it before.

CLAY: And is that all? The whole grand tour?

LULA: Not all. You'll say to me very close to my face, many, many times, you'll say, even whisper, that you love me.

CLAY: Maybe I will.

LULA: And you'll be lying.

CLAY: I wouldn't lie about something like that.

LULA: Hah. It's the only kind of thing you will lie about. Especially if you think it'll keep me alive.

CLAY: Keep you alive? I don't understand.

LULA *(bursting out laughing, but too shrilly)*: Don't understand? Well, don't look at me. It's the path I take, that's all. Where both feet take me when I set them down. One in front of the other.

CLAY: Morbid. Morbid. You sure you're not an actress? All that self-aggrandizement.

LULA: Well, I told you I wasn't an actress . . . but I also told you I lie all the time. Draw your own conclusions.

CLAY: Morbid. Morbid. You sure you're not an actress. All scribed? There's no more?

LULA: I've told you all I know. Or almost all.

CLAY: There's no funny parts?

LULA: I thought it was all funny.

CLAY: But you mean peculiar, not ha-ha.

LULA: You don't know what I mean.

CLAY: Well, tell me the almost part then. You said almost all. What else? I want the whole story.

LULA (*searching aimlessly through her bag. She begins to talk breathlessly, with a light and silly tone*): All stories are whole stories. All of 'em. Our whole story . . . nothing but change. How could things go on like that forever? Huh? (*Slaps him on the shoulder, begins finding things in her bag, taking them out and throwing them over her shoulder into the aisle.*) Except I do go on as I do. Apples and long walks with deathless intelligent lovers. But you mix it up. Look out the window, all the time. Turning pages. Change change change. Till, shit, I don't know you. Wouldn't, for that matter. You're too serious. I bet you're even too serious to be psychoanalyzed. Like all those Jewish poets from Yonkers, who leave their mothers looking for other mothers, or others' mothers, on whose baggy tits they lay their fumbling heads. Their poems are always funny, and all about sex.

CLAY: They sound great. Like movies.

LULA: But you change. (*Blankly.*) And things work on you till you hate them.

(*More people come into the train. They come closer to the couple, some of them not sitting, but swinging drearily on the straps, staring at the two with uncertain interest.*)

CLAY: Wow. All these people, so suddenly. They must all come from the same place.

LULA: Right. That they do.

CLAY: Oh? You know about them too?

LULA: Oh yeah. About them more than I know about you. Do they frighten you?

CLAY: Frighten me? Why should they frighten me?

LULA: 'Cause you're an escaped nigger.

CLAY: Yeah?

LULA: 'Cause you crawled through the wire and made tracks to my side.

CLAY: Wire?

LULA: Don't they have wire around plantations?

CLAY: You must be Jewish. All you can think about is wire. Plantations didn't have any wire. Plantations were big open whitewashed places like heaven, and everybody on 'em was grooved to be there. Just strummin' and hummin' all day.

LULA: Yes, yes.

CLAY: And that's how the blues was born.

LULA: Yes, yes. And that's how the blues was born. (*Begins to make up a song that becomes quickly hysterical. As she sings she rises from her seat, still throwing things out of her bag into the aisle, beginning a rhythmical shudder and twistlike wiggle, which she continues up and down the aisle, bumping into many of the standing people and tripping over the feet of those sitting. Each time she runs into a person she lets out a very vicious piece of profanity, wiggling and stepping all the time.*) And that's how the blues was born. Yes. Yes. Son of a bitch, get out of the way. Yes.

Quack. Yes. Yes. And that's how the blues was born. Ten little niggers sitting on a limb, but none of them ever looked like him. (*Points to* CLAY, *returns toward the seat, with her hands extended for him to rise and dance with her.*) And that's how the blues was born. Yes. Come on, Clay. Let's do the nasty. Rub bellies. Rub bellies.

CLAY (*waves his hands to refuse. He is embarrassed, but determined to get a kick out of the proceedings*): Hey, what was in those apples? Mirror, mirror on the wall, who's the fairest one of all? Snow White, baby, and don't you forget it.

LULA (*grabbing for his hands, which he draws away*): Come on, Clay. Let's rub bellies on the train. The nasty. The nasty. Do the gritty grind, like your ol' rag-head mammy. Grind till you lose your mind. Shake it, shake it, shake it, shake it! OOOOweeee! Come on, Clay. Let's do the choo-choo train shuffle, the navel scratcher.

CLAY: Hey, you coming on like the lady who smoked up her grass skirt.

LULA (*becoming annoyed that he will not dance, and becoming more animated as if to embarrass him still further*): Come on, Clay . . . let's do the thing. Uhh! Uhh! Clay! Clay! You middle-class black bastard. Forget your social-working mother for a few seconds and let's knock stomachs. Clay, you liver-lipped white man. You would-be Christian. You ain't no nigger, you're just a dirty white man. Get up, Clay. Dance with me, Clay.

CLAY: Lula! Sit down, now. Be cool.

LULA (*mocking him, in wild dance*): Be cool. Be cool. That's all you know . . . shaking that wildroot cream-oil on your knotty head, jackets buttoning up to your chin, so full of white man's words. Christ. God. Get up and scream at these people. Like scream meaningless shit in these hopeless faces. (*She screams at people in train, still dancing.*) Red trains cough Jewish underwear for keeps! Expanding smells of silence. Gravy snot whistling like sea birds. Clay, Clay, you got to break out. Don't sit there dying the way they want you to die. Get up.

CLAY: Oh, sit the fuck down. (*He moves to restrain her.*) Sit down, goddamn it.

LULA (*twisting out of his reach*): Screw yourself, Uncle Tom. Thomas Woolly-head. (*Begins to dance a kind of jig, mocking* CLAY *with loud forced humor*) There is Uncle Tom . . . I mean, Uncle Thomas Woolly-Head. With old white matted mane. He hobbles on his wooden cane. Old Tom. Old Tom. Let the white man hump his ol' mama and he jes' shuffle off in the woods and hide his gentle gray head. Ol' Thomas Woolly-Head.

(*Some of the other riders are laughing now. A drunk gets*

up and joins LULA *in her dance, singing, as best he can, her "song."* CLAY *gets up out of his seat and visibly scans the faces of the other riders.)*

CLAY: Lula! Lula! *(She is dancing and turning, still shouting as loud as she can. The drunk too is shouting, and waving his hands wildly.)* Lula . . . you dumb bitch. Why don't you stop it? *(He rushes half stumbling from his seat, and grabs one of her flailing arms.)*

LULA: Let me go! You black son of a bitch. *(She struggles against him.)* Let me go! Help!

*(*CLAY *is dragging her toward her seat, and the drunk seeks to interfere. He grabs* CLAY *around the shoulders and begins wrestling with him.* CLAY *clubs the drunk to the floor without releasing* LULA, *who is still screaming.* CLAY *finally gets her to the seat and throws her into it.)*

CLAY: Now you shut the hell up. *(Grabbing her shoulders.)* Just shut up. You don't know what you're talking about. You don't know anything. So just keep your stupid mouth closed.

LULA: You're afraid of white people. And your father was. Uncle Tom Big Lip!

CLAY *(slaps her as hard as he can, across the mouth.* LULA's *head bangs against the back of the seat. When she raises it again,* CLAY *slaps her again)*: Now shut up and let me talk. *(He turns toward the other riders, some of whom are sitting on the edge of their seats. The drunk is on one knee, rubbing his head, and singing softly the same song. He shuts up too when he sees* CLAY *watching him. The others go back to newspapers or stare out the window)* Shit, you don't have any sense, Lula, nor feelings either. I could murder you now. Such a tiny ugly throat. I could squeeze it flat, and watch you turn blue, on a humble. For dull kicks. And all these weak-faced ofays squatting around here, staring over their papers at me. Murder them too. Even if they expected it. That man there . . . *(Points to well-dressed man.)* I could rip that *Times* right out of his hand, as skinny and middle-classed as I am, I could rip that paper out of his hand and just as easily rip out his throat. It takes no great effort. For what? To kill you soft idiots? You don't understand anything but luxury.

LULA: You fool!

CLAY *(pushing her against the seat)*: I'm not telling you again, Tallulah Bankhead! Luxury. In your face and your fingers. You telling me what I ought to do. *(Sudden scream frightening the whole coach.)* Well, don't! Don't you tell me anything! If I'm a middle-class fake white man . . . let me be. And let me be in the way I want. *(Through his teeth.)* I'll rip your lousy breasts off! Let me be who I feel like being. Uncle Tom. Thomas. Whoever. It's none of your business. You don't know anything except what's there for you to see. An act. Lies. Device. Not the pure heart, the pumping black heart. You don't ever know that. And I sit here, in this buttoned-up suit, to keep myself from cutting all your throats. I mean wantonly. You great liberated whore! You fuck some black man and right away you're an expert on black people. What a lotta shit that is. The only thing you know is that you come if he bangs you hard enough. And that's all. The belly rub? You wanted me to do the belly rub? Shit, you don't even know how. You don't know that. That ol' dipty-dip shit you do, rolling your ass like an elephant. That's not my kind of belly rub. Belly rub is not Queens. Belly rub is dark places, with big hats and overcoats held up with one arm. Belly rub hates you. Old bald-headed four-eyed ofays popping their fingers . . . and don't even know yet what they're doing. They say, "I love Bessie Smith." And don't even understand that Bessie Smith is saying, "Kiss my ass, kiss my black unruly ass." Before love, suffering, desire, anything you can explain, she's saying, and very plainly, "Kiss my black ass." And if you don't know that, it's you that's doing the kissing.

Charlie Parker? Charlie Parker. All the hip white boys scream for Bird. And Bird saying, "Up your ass, feeble-minded ofay! Up your ass." And they sit there talking about the tortured genius of Charlie Parker. Bird would've played not a note of music if he just walked up to East Sixty-seventh Street and killed the first ten white people he saw. Not a note! And I'm the great would-be poet. Yes. That's right! Poet. Some kind of bastard literature . . . all it needs is a simple knife thrust. Just let me bleed you, you loud whore, and one poem vanished. A whole people of neurotics, struggling to keep from being sane. And the only thing that would cure the neurosis would be your murder. Simple as that. I mean if I murdered you, then other white people would begin to understand me. You understand? No. I guess not. If Bessie Smith had killed some white people she wouldn't have needed that music. She could have talked very straight and plain about the world. No metaphors. No grunts. No wiggles in the dark of her soul. Just straight two and two are four. Money. Power. Luxury. Like that. All of them. Crazy niggers turning their backs on sanity. When all it needs is that simple act. Murder. Just murder! Would make us all sane. *(Suddenly weary.)* Ahhh. Shit. But who needs it? I'd rather be a fool. Insane. Safe with my words, and no deaths, and clean, hard thoughts, urging me to new conquests. My people's madness. Hah! That's a laugh. My people. They don't need me to claim them. They got legs and arms of their own. Personal insanities. Mirrors. They don't need all those words. They don't need any defense. But listen, though, one more thing. And you tell this to your father, who's probably the kind of man who needs to know at once. So he can plan ahead. Tell him not to preach so much rationalism and cold logic to these niggers. Let them alone. Let them sing curses at you in code and see your filth as simple lack of style. Don't make the mistake, through some irresponsible surge of Christian charity, of talking too much about the advantages of Western rationalism, or the great intellectual legacy of the white man, or maybe they'll begin to listen. And then, maybe one day, you'll find they actually do understand exactly what you are talking about, all these fantasy people. All these blues people. And on that day, as sure as shit, when you really believe you can "accept" them into your fold, as half-white trusties late of the subject peoples. With no more blues, except the very old ones, and not a watermelon in sight, the great missionary heart will have triumphed, and all of those ex-coons will be stand-up Western men, with eyes for clean hard useful lives, sober, pious and sane, and they'll murder you. They'll murder you, and have very rational explanations. Very much like your own. They'll cut your throats, and drag you out to the edge of your cities so the flesh can fall away from your bones, in sanitary isolation.

LULA (*her voice takes on a different, more businesslike quality*): I've heard enough.

CLAY (*reaching for his books*): I bet you have. I guess I better collect my stuff and get off this train. Looks like we won't be acting out that little pageant you outlined before.

LULA: No. We won't. You're right about that, at least.

(*She turns to look quickly around the rest of the car.*) All right! (*The others respond.*)

CLAY (*bending across the girl to retrieve his belongings*): Sorry, baby, I don't think we could make it.

(*As he is bending over her, the girl brings up a small knife and plunges it into* CLAY's *chest. Twice. He slumps across her knees, his mouth working stupidly.*)

LULA: Sorry is right. (*Turning to the others in the car who have already gotten up from their seats.*) Sorry is the rightest thing you've said. Get this man off me! Hurry, now! (*The others come and drag* CLAY's *body down the aisle.*) Open the door and throw his body out. (*They throw him off.*) And all of you get off at the next stop.

(LULA *busies herself straightening her things. Getting everything in order. She takes out a notebook and makes a quick scribbling note. Drops it in her bag. The train apparently stops and all the others get off, leaving her alone in the coach. Very soon a young Negro of about twenty comes into the coach, with a couple of books under his arms. He sits a few seats in back of* LULA. *When he is seated she turns and gives him a long slow look. He looks up from his book and drops the book on his lap. Then an old Negro conductor comes into the car, doing a sort of restrained soft shoe, and half mumbling the words of some song. He looks at the young man, briefly, with a quick greeting.*)

CONDUCTOR: Hey, brother!
YOUNG MAN: Hey.

(*The conductor continues down the aisle with his little dance and the mumbled song.* LULA *turns to stare at him and follows his movements down the aisle. The conductor tips his hat when he reaches her seat, and continues out the car.*)

CURTAIN

Figure 92. Lula (Jennifer West) baits Clay (Robert Hooks) during the initial stage of their confrontation in the Cherry Lane Theater production of *Dutchman,* staged by Edward Parone, New York, 1964. (Photograph: Alix Jeffry.)

Figure 93. Clay (Robert Hooks) tries to restrain Lula (Beverlee McKinsey) during her dance near the final stage of their confrontation in the Cherry Lane Theater production of *Dutchman*, staged by Edward Parone, New York, 1964. (Photograph: Alix Jeffry.)

Staging of *Dutchman*

It is altogether likely that the folk who go down to the Cherry Lane Theatre to see the three one-act plays now being given there are witnesses to a signal event: the emergence of an outstanding dramatist— LeRoi Jones.

His is a turbulent talent. While turbulence is not always a sign of power or of valuable meaning, I have a hunch that Leroi Jones's fire will burn ever higher and clearer if our theatre can furnish an adequate vessel to harbor his flame. We need it.

He is very angry. Anger alone may merely make a loud noise, confuse, sputter and die. For anger to burn to useful effect, it must be guided by an idea. With the "angry young men" of England one was not always certain of the source of dissatisfaction nor of its goal. With Leroi Jones it is easy to say that the plight of the Negro ignited the initial rage— justification enough—and that the rage will not be appeased until there is no more black and white, no more color except as differences in hue and accent are part of the world's splendid spectacle. But there is more to his ferocity than a protest against the horrors of racism.

Dutchman, the first of Jones's plays to reach the professional stage, is a stylized account of a subway episode. A white girl picks up a young Negro who at first is rather embarrassed and later piqued by her advances. There is a perversity in her approach which finally provokes him to a hymn of hate. With lyrical obscenity he declares that murder is in his and every Negro's heart and were it to reach the point of action there would be less "singin' of the blues," less of that delightful folk music and hot jazz which beguile the white man's fancy, more calm in the Negro soul. Meanwhile, it is the black man who is murdered.

What we must not overloook in seeing the play is that, while this explosion of fury is its rhetorical and emotional climax, the crux of its significance resides in the depiction of the white girl whose relevance to the play's situation does not lie in her whiteness but in her representative value as a token of our civilization. She is our neurosis. Not a neurosis in regard to the Negro, but the absolute neurosis of American society.

She is "hep": she has heard about everything, understands and feels nothing. She twitches, jangles, jitters with a thin but inexhaustible energy, propelled by the vibrations from millions of ads, television quiz programs, newspaper columns, intellectual jargon culled from countless digests, panel discussions, illustrated summaries, smatterings of gossip on every conceivable subject (respectable and illicit), epithets, wisecracks, formulas, slogans, cynicisms, cures and solutions. She is the most "informed" person in the world and the most ignorant. (The information feeds the ignorance.) She is the bubbling, boiling garbage cauldron newly produced by our progress. She is a calculating machine gone berserk; she is the real killer. What she destroys is not men of a certain race but mankind. She is the compendium in little of the universal mess.

If *Dutchman* (a title I don't understand) has a fault, it is its completeness. Its ending is somewhat too pat, too pointed in its symbolism. If one has caught the drift of the play's meaning before its final moment, the ending is supererogatory; if one has failed to do so, it is probably useless.

Dutchman is very well played by Jennifer West and Robert Hooks.

Everything about LeRoi Jones's "Dutchman" is designed to shock—its basic idea, its language and its murderous rage.

This half-hour-long piece, the last of three one-act plays being performed at the Cherry Lane Theater, is an explosion of hatred rather than a play. It puts into the mouth of its principal Negro character a scathing denunciation of all the white man's good works, pretensions and condescensions.

If this is the way the Negroes really feel about the

white world around them, there's more rancor buried in the breasts of colored conformists than anyone can imagine. If this is the way even one Negro feels, there is ample cause for guilt as well as alarm, and for a hastening of change.

As an extended metaphor of bitterness and fury, "Dutchman" is transparently simple in structure. Clay, a Negro who wears a three-button suit and is reserved and well-spoken, is accosted by a white female on a train. Lula is a liar, a slut, essentially an agent provocateur of a Caucasian society.

After she disarms Clay with her wild outbursts and sinuous attentions, she turns on him in challenging contempt. His answer is to drop the mask of conformity and to spew out all the anger that has built up in him and his fellow Negroes. When this outburst of violent resentment has finished and Clay has left the train, Lula notices that another Negro has boarded and she sets her slinky charms for him.

Mr. Jones writes with a kind of sustained frenzy. His little work is a mélange of sardonic images and undisciplined filth. The impact of his ferocity would be stronger if he did not work so hard and persistently to be shocking.

Jennifer West in a straight, tight-fitting dress striped like a prisoner's suit plays Lula with a rousing mixture of sultriness and insolence. Robert Hooks as Clay is impressive as he shifts from patient tolerance to savage wrath. Edward Parone's staging is mordant, and intense.

NEIL SIMON

1927–

When Neil Simon was asked to write an introduction to a collection of his first seven plays, he obliged with a piece called "Portrait of the Writer as a Schizophrenic," in which he described himself as a "nice, plain boy" who grew up to be "The Human Being," which he in turn described as "a rather dull fellow." He was born in the Bronx, and indeed nothing about his early life was particularly surprising, not even his wartime service that he spent partly in uptown New York studying engineering, and partly in Colorado editing sports columns for the base newspaper. But after the war, he and his brother formed a team of comic script writers, known as Danny and Doc Simon, got themselves hired by CBS radio, and then moved on to television, writing for Sid Caesar, Carl Reiner, and for the long-running series that starred Phil Silvers as the larcenous Sergeant Bilko. That long apprenticeship in writing comedy produced the other half of Neil Simon, the observer-writer he calls the Monster: "Not content to prey on his fellow creatures, the Monster eventually turns on his alter ego, the Human Being, and dissects him unmercifully."

Simon is, of course, both Human Being and Monster, the man who lived through most of the experiences that the writer subsequently turned into irresistible comedies. *Come Blow Your Horn* (1960), for example, features two brothers whose conflicts with each other and with their overprotective Jewish parents are the principal source of its comedy. The newlyweds in *Barefoot in the Park* (1963) are based on Simon and his first wife Joan, much as the comic quarrels it represents are based on the marital spats that Simon had with his wife. And in his recent hit, *Chapter Two* (1977), Simon analyzes the doubts and questionings of a man who has just lost his first wife and remarries a woman he has known for only a few weeks, a situation taken directly from his experiences after Joan's death and his marriage to Marsha Mason.

But the sources for Simon's comedy stretch back much further than his own life, for he skilfully uses comic devices that have existed for centuries. Like the Italian scripters for the *commedia dell'arte* or the anonymous author of *Master Peter Patelan*, Simon delights in comic routines (*lazzi*) that are essentially physical and verbal jokes extended into a theatrical set piece. The gibberish speech of Patelan when he is pretending to be mad has its modern equivalent in the sudden vocal and physical seizures that repeatedly beset Felix in *The Odd Couple* (1965). Like most comic playwrights, Simon also knows that repetition is funny. And like Ben Jonson, or Molière, or George Etherege, he specializes in characters obsessed with attitudes, ideas, or patterns of behavior, such as the compulsively neat Felix in *The Odd Couple,* or the super-conservative Southern patriot Sophie in *The Star-Spangled Girl,* and all three of the women whom Barney tries to seduce in *Last of the Red-Hot Lovers.*

Simon's fondness for pairing these "type" characters with their opposites has made him a specialist in a strategy that might well be called "the odd couple" approach to comedy. Most of his plays center on a relationship between two mismatched people, who are strongly attached to each other or who need each other for one reason or another, yet whose differences seem to make the relationship almost impossible to sustain. Paul and Corie Bratter in *Barefoot in the Park* are a typical "odd couple," for he is serious and conservative, while she is adventurous and unpredictable. As newlyweds they love each other, but as people they find it difficult to agree about anything. The two brothers in *Come Blow Your Horn,* the various couples of *Plaza Suite* and *California Suite,* the feuding comedians of *The Sunshine Boys,* as well as the newly widowed writer and the recent divorcée of *Chapter Two*—all these are versions of Simon's "odd couple." The combination of two people who love each other and yet cannot stand to be with each other for long is a natural device for generating a remarkable amount of comedy and of pain; it is also a device that speaks to the experience of most human beings in the world. Chekhov, who specialized in throwing together people who cannot communicate easily with one another, would have applauded Simon's strategy—and Simon acknowledged his debt to Chekhov when he adapted a number of Chekhov's short stories into *The Good Doctor* (1973).

Simon's most successful realization of this comic strategy appears, of course, in *The Odd Couple,* a play that has also been turned into a movie, as well as into a long-running television series. The premise of the play is disarmingly simple, as revealed by the plot summary that Simon made for himself: "Two men—one divorced and one estranged and neither quite sure why their marriages fell apart—move in together to cut down on their alimony and suddenly discover that they're having the same conflicts and fights that they had in their marriages." What that summary does not reveal, of course, is the delightful mismatch that Simon has created in the pairing of Oscar Madison, a genial, sloppy sportswriter, with Felix Ungar, the nervous, orderly newswriter. Whereas Oscar, for example, offers his poker cronies a choice of "brown sandwiches and green sandwiches," the green being "either very new cheese or very old meat," Felix when he moves in insists on serving up a carefully made sandwich that he proudly announces as "Bacon, lettuce, and tomato with mayonnaise on pumpernickel toast." Not only the food, but the entire apartment changes under Felix's compulsive regime. When the curtain first goes up, Oscar's apartment, according to Simon's stage directions, is "a study in slovenliness," but by Act II, only two weeks later, "It is immaculately clean. No, not clean. Sterile! Spotless! Not a speck of dirt can be seen under the ten coats of Johnson's Glo-Coat that have been applied to the floor. No laundry bags, no dirty dishes, no half-filled glasses." And Oscar's response to Felix's compulsive cleanliness is entirely natural—"I don't think that two single men living alone in a big eight-room apartment should have a cleaner house than my mother," much as Felix's revulsion with Oscar's squalid ways is also easy to understand.

The success of the play, however, is less dependent on the comic conflict of Oscar and Felix than on the comic versatility with which Simon depicts it. The play itself is carefully structured, for three poker games, each one different, unify the action, the first two serving as introductions to Oscar and Felix, the last one closing the play. And the *lazzi* are seemingly inexhaustible, ranging from Oscar's attempt to open a beer can and Felix's entrance "looking like a wounded puppy" with an overdone piece of London broil, to an extended scene at the beginning of the last act in which Felix and Oscar studiously and silently annoy each other, Felix armed with a vacuum cleaner and a plate of spaghetti, Oscar ostentatiously dropping cigar wrappings, matches, and a filled ashtray on the freshly vacuumed floor.

A review of the original production, reprinted following the text, properly stresses the rich comic feast that was served up by Simon, by the director Mike Nichols, and by the lead actors Walter Matthau and Art Carney. And photographs of that production (Figures 94, 95, and 96) clearly reveal the fussiness of Felix and the sloppiness of Oscar. But the lasting appeal of the play may well lie in its shrewd analysis of the way human relationships can go wrong—comically, hysterically wrong. All the best intentions in the world cannot make Oscar and Felix compatible, for the more Felix tries to "help" by cleaning and cooking, the more he drives Oscar crazy. And yet both men are incurably dependent on each other—like Hamm and Clov in *Endgame*—which is why they cannot at last get free of one another. While the play ends, therefore, with the two men separating from one another, their parting behavior of imitating each other's habits suggests, too, that the men are forever locked in a stalemate, with neither willing to concede the game to the other.

THE ODD COUPLE

BY NEIL SIMON

CHARACTERS

SPEED
MURRAY
ROY
VINNIE
OSCAR MADISON
FELIX UNGAR
GWENDOLYN PIGEON
CECILY PIGEON

SCENE

The action takes place in an apartment on Riverside Drive in New York City.
  ACT 1: *A hot summer night;* ACT 2, *Scene 1: Two weeks later, about eleven at night; Scene 2: A few days later, about eight P.M.;* ACT 3: *The next evening, about seven-thirty.*

ACT 1

(It is a warm summer night in OSCAR MADISON's *apartment. This is one of those large eight-room affairs on Riverside Drive in the upper eighties. The building is about thirty-five years old and still has vestiges of its glorious past—high ceilings, walk-in closets and thick walls. We are in the living room with doors leading off to the kitchen, a bedroom and a bathroom, and a hallway to the other bedrooms.*

Although the furnishings have been chosen with extreme good taste, the room itself, without the touch and care of a woman these past few months, is now a study in slovenliness. Dirty dishes, discarded clothes, old newspapers, empty bottles, glasses filled and unfilled, opened and unopened laundry packages, mail and disarrayed furniture abound. The only cheerful note left in this room is the lovely view of the New Jersey Palisades through its twelfth-floor window. Three months ago this was a lovely apartment.

As the curtain rises, the room is filled with smoke. A poker game is in progress. There are six chairs around the table but only four men are sitting. They are MURRAY, ROY, SPEED *and* VINNIE. VINNIE, *with the largest stack of chips in front of him, is nervously tapping his foot; he keeps checking his watch.* ROY *is watching* SPEED *and* SPEED *is glaring at* MURRAY *with incredulity and utter fascination.* MURRAY *is the dealer. He slowly and methodically tries to shuffle. It is a ponderous and painful business.* SPEED *shakes his head in disbelief. This is all done wordlessly.)*

SPEED *(cups his chin in his hand and looks at* MURRAY*)*: Tell me, Mr. Maverick, is this your first time on the riverboat?

MURRAY *(with utter disregard)*: You don't like it, get a machine.

(He continues to deal slowly.)

ROY: Geez, it stinks in here.

VINNIE *(looks at his watch)*: What time is it?

SPEED: Again what time is it?

VINNIE *(whining)*: My watch is slow. I'd like to know what time it is.

SPEED *(glares at him)*: You're winning ninety-five dollars, that's what time it is. Where the hell are you running?

VINNIE: I'm not running anywhere. I just asked what time it was. Who said anything about running?

ROY *(looks at his watch)*: It's ten-thirty.

(There is a pause. MURRAY *continues to shuffle.)*

VINNIE *(after the pause)*: I got to leave by twelve.

SPEED *(looks up in despair)*: Oh, Christ!

VINNIE: I told you that when I sat down. I got to leave by twelve. Murray, didn't I say that when I sat down? I said I got to leave by twelve.

SPEED: All right, don't talk to him. He's dealing. *(to* MURRAY*)* Murray, you wanna rest for a while? Go lie down, sweetheart.

MURRAY: You want speed or accuracy, make up your mind.

(He begins to deal slowly. SPEED *puffs on his cigar angrily.)*

ROY: Hey, you want to do me a really big favor? Smoke toward New Jersey.

*(*SPEED *blows smoke at* ROY.*)*

MURRAY: No kidding, I'm really worried about Felix. *(Points to an empty chair.)* He's never been this late before. Maybe somebody should call. *(Yells off.)* Hey, Oscar, why don't you call Felix?

ROY *(waves his hand through the smoke)*: Listen, why don't we chip in three dollars apiece and buy another window. How the hell can you breathe in here?

MURRAY: How many cards you got, four?

SPEED: Yes, Murray, we all have four cards. When you give us one more, we'll all have five. If you were to give us two more, we'd have six. Understand how it works now?

ROY (*yells off*): Hey, Oscar, what do you say? In or out?

(*From offstage we hear* OSCAR's *voice.*)

OSCAR (*offstage*): Out, pussycat, out!

(SPEED *opens and the others bet.*)

VINNIE: I told my wife I'd be home by one the latest. We're making an eight o'clock plane to Florida. I told you that when I sat down.

SPEED: Don't cry, Vinnie. You're forty-two years old. It's embarrassing. Give me two . . .

(*He discards.*)

ROY: Why doesn't he fix the air conditioner? It's ninety-eight degrees, and it sits there sweating like everyone else. I'm out.

(*He goes to the window and looks out.*)

MURRAY: Who goes to Florida in July?

VINNIE: It's off-season. There's no crowds and you get the best room for one-tenth the price. No cards . . .

SPEED: Some vacation. Six cheap people in an empty hotel.

MURRAY: Dealer takes four . . . Hey, you think maybe Felix is sick? (*He points to the empty chair.*) I mean he's never been this late before.

ROY (*takes a laundry bag from an armchair and sits*): You know, it's the same garbage from last week's game. I'm beginning to recognize things.

MURRAY (*throwing his cards down*): I'm out . . .

SPEED (*showing his hand*): Two kings . . .

VINNIE: Straight . . .

(*He shows his hand and takes in the pot.*)

MURRAY: Hey, maybe he's in his office locked in the john again. Did you know Felix was once locked in the john overnight? He wrote out his entire will on a half a roll of toilet paper! Heee, what a nut!

(VINNIE *is playing with his chips.*)

SPEED (*glares at him as he shuffles the cards*): Don't play with your chips. I'm asking you nice; don't play with your chips.

VINNIE (*to* SPEED): I'm not playing. I'm counting. Leave me alone. What are you picking on me for? How much do you think I'm winning? Fifteen dollars!

SPEED: Fifteen dollars? You dropped more than that in your cuffs!

(SPEED *deals a game of draw poker.*)

MURRAY (*yells off*): Hey, Oscar, what do you say?

OSCAR (*enters carrying a tray with beer, sandwiches, a can of* peanuts, *and opened bags of pretzels and Fritos*): I'm in! I'm in! Go ahead. Deal!

(OSCAR MADISON *is forty-three. He is a pleasant, appealing man who seems to enjoy life to the fullest. He enjoys his weekly poker game, his friends, his excessive drinking and his cigars. He is also one of those lucky creatures in life who even enjoys his work—he's a sports-writer for the New York* Post. *His carefree attitude is evident in the sloppiness of his household, but it seems to bother others more than it does* OSCAR. *This is not to say that* OSCAR *is without cares or worries. He just doesn't seem to have any.*)

VINNIE: Aren't you going to look at your cards?

OSCAR (*sets the tray on a side chair*): What for? I'm gonna bluff anyway. (*Opens a bottle of Coke.*) Who gets the Coke?

MURRAY: I get a Coke.

OSCAR: My friend Murray the policeman gets a warm Coke.

(*He gives him the bottle.*)

ROY (*opens the betting*): You still didn't fix the refrigerator? It's been two weeks now. No wonder it stinks in here.

OSCAR (*picks up his cards*): Temper, temper. If I wanted nagging I'd go back with my wife. (*Throws them down.*) I'm out. Who wants food?

MURRAY: What have you got?

OSCAR (*looks under the bread*): I got brown sandwiches and green sandwiches. Well, what do you say?

MURRAY: What's the green?

OSCAR: It's either very new cheese or very old meat.

MURRAY: I'll take the brown.

(OSCAR *gives* MURRAY *a sandwich.*)

ROY (*glares at* MURRAY): Are you crazy? You're not going to eat that, are you?

MURRAY: I'm hungry.

ROY: His refrigerator's been broken for two weeks. I saw milk standing in there that wasn't even in the bottle.

OSCAR (*to* ROY): What are you, some kind of a health nut? Eat, Murray, eat!

ROY: I've got six cards . . .

SPEED: That figures—I've got three aces. Misdeal.

(*They all throw their cards in.* SPEED *begins to shuffle.*)

VINNIE: You know who makes very good sandwiches? Felix. Did you ever taste his cream cheese and pimento on date-nut bread?

SPEED (*to* VINNIE): All right, make up your mind, poker or menus. (OSCAR *opens a can of beer, which sprays in a geyser over the players and the table. There is a hubbub as they all yell at* OSCAR. *He hands* ROY *the overflowing can and pushes the puddle of beer under the chair. The players start to go back to the game only to be sprayed again as* OSCAR *opens another beer can. There is another outraged cry as they try to stop* OSCAR *and mop up the beer on the table with a towel which was hanging on the standing lamp.* OSCAR, *undisturbed, gives them the beer and the bags of refreshments, and they finally sit back in their chairs.* OSCAR *wipes his hands on the sleeve of* ROY's *jacket which is hanging on the back of the chair.*) Hey, Vinnie, tell Oscar what time you're leaving.

VINNIE (*like a trained dog*): Twelve o'clock.

SPEED (*to the others*): You hear? We got ten minutes before the next announcement. All right, this game is five card stud. (*He deals and ad libs calling the cards, ending with* MURRAY's *card.*) . . . And a bullet for the policeman. All right, Murray, it's your bet. (*No answer.*) Do something, huh.

OSCAR (*getting a drink at the bar*): Don't yell at my friend Murray.

MURRAY (*throwing in a coin*): I'm in for a quarter.

OSCAR (*proudly looks in* MURRAY's *eyes*): Beautiful, baby, beautiful.

(*He sits down and begins to open the can of peanuts.*)

ROY: Hey, Oscar, let's make a rule. Every six months you have to buy fresh potato chips. How can you live like this? Don't you have a maid?

OSCAR (*shakes his head*): She quit after my wife and kids left. The work got to be too much for her. (*He looks on the table.*) The pot's shy. Who didn't put in a quarter?

MURRAY (*to* OSCAR): You didn't.

OSCAR (*puts in money*): You got a big mouth, Murray. Just for that, lend me twenty dollars.

(SPEED *deals another round.*)

MURRAY: I just loaned you twenty dollars ten minutes ago.

(*They all join in a round of betting.*)

OSCAR: You loaned me *ten* dollars *twenty* minutes ago. Learn to count, pussycat.

MURRAY: Learn to play poker, chicken licken! Borrow from somebody else. I keep winning my own money back.

ROY (*to* OSCAR): You owe everybody in the game. If you don't have it, you shouldn't play.

OSCAR: All right, I'm through being the nice one. You owe me six dollars apiece for the buffet.

SPEED (*dealing another round of cards*): Buffet? Hot beer and two sandwiches left over from when you went to high school?

OSCAR: What do you want at a poker game, a tomato surprise? Murray, lend me twenty dollars or I'll call your wife and tell her you're in Central Park wearing a dress.

MURRAY: You want money, ask Felix.

OSCAR: He's not here.

MURRAY: Neither am I.

ROY (*gives him money*): All right, here. You're on the books for another twenty.

OSCAR: How many times are you gonna keep saying it? (*He takes the money.*)

MURRAY: When are you gonna call Felix?

OSCAR: When are we gonna play poker?

MURRAY: Aren't you even worried? It's the first game he's missed in over two years.

OSCAR: The record is fifteen years set by Lou Gehrig in 1939! I'll call! I'll call!

ROY: How can you be so lazy?

(*The phone rings.*)

OSCAR (*throwing his cards in*): Call me irresponsible, I'm funny that way.

(*He goes to the phone.*)

SPEED: Pair of sixes . . .

VINNIE: Three deuces . . .

SPEED (*throws up his hands in despair*): This is my last week. I get all the aggravation I need at home.

(OSCAR *picks up the phone.*)

OSCAR: Hello! Oscar the Poker Player!

VINNIE (*to* OSCAR): If it's my wife tell her I'm leaving at twelve.

SPEED (*to* VINNIE): You look at your watch once more and you get the peanuts in your face. (*to* ROY) Deal the cards!

(*The game continues during* OSCAR's *phone conversation, with* ROY *dealing a game of stud.*)

OSCAR (*into the phone*): Who? Who did you want, please? *Dabby?* Dabby who? No, there's no Dabby here. Oh, *Daddy!* (*to the others*) For crise sakes, it's my kid. (*Back into the phone, he speaks with great love and affection.*) Brucey, hello, baby. Yes, it's Daddy! (*There is a general outburst of ad libbing from the poker players. To the others.*) Hey, come on, give me a break, willya? My five-year-old kid is calling from California. It must be costing him a fortune. (*Back into the phone.*) How've you been, sweetheart? Yes, I finally got your letter. It took three weeks. Yes, but next time you tell Mommy to give you a stamp. I know, but you're not supposed to draw it on. (*He laughs. To the others.*) You hear?

SPEED: We hear. We hear. We're all thrilled.

OSCAR (*into the phone*): What's that, darling? What goldfish? Oh, in your room! Oh, sure. Sure, I'm taking care of them. (*He holds the phone over his chest.*) Oh, God, I killed my kid's goldfish! (*Back into the phone.*) Yes, I feed them every day.

ROY: Murderer!

OSCAR: Mommy wants to speak to me? Right. Take care of yourself, soldier. I love you.

VINNIE (*beginning to deal a game of stud*): Ante a dollar . . .

SPEED (*to* OSCAR): Cost you a dollar to play. You got a dollar?

OSCAR: Not after I get through talking to this lady. (*Into the phone with false cheerfulness.*) Hello, Blanche. How are you? Err, yes, I have a pretty good idea why you're calling. I'm a week behind with the check, right? *Four* weeks? That's not possible. Because it's not possible. Blanche, I keep a record of every check and I *know* I'm only *three* weeks behind! Blanche, I'm trying the best I can. Blanche, don't threaten me with jail because it's not a threat. With my expenses and my alimony, a prisoner takes home more pay than I do! Very nice, in front of the kids. Blanche, don't tell me you're going to have my salary attached, just say goodbye! Goodbye! (*He hangs up. To the players.*) I'm eight hundred dollars behind in alimony so let's up the stakes.

(*He gets his drink from the poker table.*)

ROY: She can do it, you know.

OSCAR: What?

ROY: Throw you in jail. For nonsupport of the kids.

OSCAR: Never. If she can't call me once a week to aggravate me, she's not happy.

(*He crosses to the bar.*)

MURRAY: It doesn't bother you? That you can go to jail? Or that maybe your kids don't have enough clothes or enough to eat?

OSCAR: Murray, *Poland* could live for a year on what my kids leave over from lunch! Can we play cards?

(*He refills his drink.*)

ROY: But that's the point. You shouldn't *be* in this kind of trouble. It's because you don't know how to manage anything. I should know; I'm your accountant.

OSCAR (*crossing to the table*): If you're my accountant, how come I need money?

ROY: If you need money, how come you play poker?

OSCAR: Because I need money.

ROY: But you always lose.

OSCAR: That's why I need the money! Listen, *I'm* not complaining. *You're* complaining. I get along all right. I'm living.

ROY: Alone? In eight dirty rooms?

OSCAR: If I win tonight, I'll buy a broom.

(MURRAY *and* SPEED *buy chips from* VINNIE, *and* MURRAY *begins to shuffle the deck for a game of draw.*)

ROY: That's not what you need. What you need is a wife.

OSCAR: How can I afford a wife when I can't afford a broom?

ROY: Then don't play poker.

OSCAR (*puts down his drink, rushes to* ROY *and they struggle over the bag of potato chips, which rips, showering everyone. They all begin to yell at one another.*): Then don't come to my house and eat my potato chips!

MURRAY: What are you yelling about? We're playing a friendly game.

SPEED: Who's *playing*? We've been sitting here talking since eight o'clock.

VINNIE: Since *seven*. That's why I said I was going to quit at *twelve*.

SPEED: How'd you like a stale banana right in the mouth?

MURRAY (*the peacemaker*): All right, all right, let's calm down. Take it easy. I'm a cop, you know. I could arrest the whole lousy game. (*He finishes dealing the cards.*) Four . . .

OSCAR (*sitting at the table*): My friend Murray the Cop is right. Let's just play cards. And please hold them up; I can't see where I marked them.

MURRAY: You're worse than the kids from the PAL.

OSCAR: But you still love me, Roy, sweety, right?

ROY (*petulant*): Yeah, yeah.

OSCAR: That's not good enough. Come on, say it. In front of the whole poker game. "I love you, Oscar Madison."

ROY: You don't take any of this seriously, do you? You owe money to your wife, your government, your friends . . .

OSCAR (*throws his cards down*): What do you want me to do, Roy, jump in the garbage disposal and grind myself to death? (*The phone rings. He goes to answer it.*) Life goes on even for those of us who are divorced, broke and sloppy. (*Into the phone.*) Hello? Divorced, Broke and Sloppy. Oh, hello, sweetheart. (*He becomes very seductive, pulls the phone to the side and talks low, but he is still audible to the others, who turn and listen.*) I told you not to call me during the game. I can't talk to you now. You *know* I do, darling. All right, just a minute. (*He turns.*) Murray, it's your wife.

(*He puts the phone on the table and sits on the sofa.*)

MURRAY (*nods disgustedly as he crosses to the phone*): I wish you *were* having an affair with her. Then she wouldn't bother *me* all the time. (*He picks up the phone.*) Hello, Mimi, what's wrong?

(SPEED *gets up, stretches and goes into the bathroom.*)

OSCAR (*in a woman's voice, imitating* MIMI): What time are you coming home? (*Then imitating* MURRAY.) I don't know, about twelve, twelve-thirty.

MURRAY (*into the phone*): I don't know, about twelve, twelve-thirty! (ROY *gets up and stretches.*) Why, what did you want, Mimi? "A corned beef sandwich and a strawberry malted!"

OSCAR: Is she pregnant again?

MURRAY (holds the phone over his chest): No, just fat! (There is the sound of a toilet flushing, and after SPEED comes out of the bathroom, VINNIE goes in. Into the phone again) What? How could you hear that? I had the phone over my chest. Who? Felix? No, he didn't show up tonight. What's wrong? You're kidding! How should I know? All right, all right, goodbye. (The toilet flushes again, and after VINNIE comes out of the bathroom, ROY goes in.) Goodbye, Mimi. Goodbye. (He hangs up. To the others.) Well, what did I tell you? I knew it!

ROY: What's the matter?

MURRAY (pacing by the couch): Felix is missing!

OSCAR: Who?

MURRAY: Felix! Felix Ungar! The man who sits in that chair every week and cleans ashtrays. I told you something was up.

SPEED (at the table): What do you mean, missing?

MURRAY: He didn't show up for work today. He didn't come home tonight. No one knows where he is. Mimi just spoke to his wife.

VINNIE (in his chair at the poker table): Felix?

MURRAY: They looked everywhere. I'm telling you he's missing.

OSCAR: Wait a minute. No one is missing for one day.

VINNIE: That's right. You've got to be missing for forty-eight hours before you're missing. The worst he could be is lost.

MURRAY: How could he be lost? He's forty-four years old and lives on West End Avenue. What's the matter with you?

ROY (sitting in an armchair): Maybe he had an accident.

OSCAR: They would have heard.

ROY: If he's laying in a gutter somewhere? Who would know who he is?

OSCAR: He's got ninety-two credit cards in his wallet. The minute something happens to him, America lights up.

VINNIE: Maybe he went to a movie. You know how long those pictures are today.

SPEED (looks at VINNIE contemptuously): No wonder you're going to Florida in July! Dumb, dumb, dumb!

ROY: Maybe he was mugged?

OSCAR: For thirty-six hours? How much money could he have on him?

ROY: Maybe they took his clothes. I knew a guy who was mugged in a doctor's office. He had to go home in a nurse's uniform.

(OSCAR throws a pillow from the couch at ROY.)

SPEED: Murray, you're a cop. What do you think?

MURRAY: I think it's something real bad.

SPEED: How do you know?

MURRAY: I can feel it in my bones.

SPEED (to the others): You hear? Bulldog Drummond.

ROY: Maybe he's drunk. Does he drink?

OSCAR: Felix? On New Year's Eve he has Pepto-Bismal. What are we guessing? I'll call his wife.

(He picks up the phone.)

SPEED: Wait a minute! Don't start anything yet. Just 'cause we don't know where he is doesn't mean somebody else doesn't. Does he have a girl?

VINNIE: A what?

SPEED: A girl? You know. Like when you're through work early.

MURRAY: Felix? Playing around? Are you crazy? He wears a vest and galoshes.

SPEED (gets up and moves toward MURRAY): You mean you automatically know who has and who hasn't got a girl on the side?

MURRAY (moves to SPEED): Yes, I automatically know.

SPEED: All right, you're so smart. Have I got a girl?

MURRAY: No, you haven't got a girl. What you've got is what I've got. What you wish you got and what you got is a whole different civilization! Oscar maybe has a girl on the side.

SPEED: That's different. He's divorced. That's not on the side. That's in the middle.

(He moves to the table.)

OSCAR (to them both as he starts to dial): You through? 'Cause one of your poker players is missing. I'd like to find out about him.

VINNIE: I thought he looked edgy the last couple of weeks. (to SPEED) Didn't you think he looked edgy?

SPEED: No. As a matter of fact, I thought you looked edgy.

(He moves down to the right.)

OSCAR (into the phone): Hello? Frances? Oscar. I just heard.

ROY: Tell her not to worry. She's probably hysterical.

MURRAY: Yeah, you know women.

(He sits down on the couch.)

OSCAR (into the phone): Listen, Frances, the most important thing is not to worry. Oh! (to the others) She's not worried.

MURRAY: Sure.

OSCAR (into the phone): Frances, do you have any idea where he could be? He what? You're kidding? Why? No, I didn't know. Gee, that's too bad. All right, listen, Frances, you just sit tight and the minute I hear anything I'll let you know. Right. G'bye.

(He hangs up. They all look at him expectantly. He gets up wordlessly and crosses to the table, thinking. They all watch him a second, not being able to stand it any longer.)

MURRAY: Ya gonna tell us or do we hire a private detective?

OSCAR: They broke up!

ROY: Who?

OSCAR: Felix and Frances! They broke up! The entire marriage is through.

VINNIE: You're kidding!

ROY: I don't believe it.

SPEED: After twelve years?

(OSCAR *sits down at the table.*)

VINNIE: They were such a happy couple.

MURRAY: Twelve years doesn't mean you're a *happy* couple. It just means you're a *long* couple.

SPEED: Go figure it. Felix and Frances.

ROY: What are you surprised at? He used to sit there every Friday night and tell us how they were fighting.

SPEED: I know. But who believes Felix?

VINNIE: What happened?

OSCAR: She wants out, that's all.

MURRAY: He'll go to pieces. I know Felix. He's going to try something crazy.

SPEED: That's all he ever used to talk about. "My beautiful wife. My wonderful wife." What happened?

OSCAR: His beautiful, wonderful wife can't stand him, that's what happened.

MURRAY: He'll kill himself. You hear what I'm saying? He's going to go out and try to kill himself.

SPEED (*to* MURRAY): Will you shut up, Murray? Stop being a cop for two minutes. (*to* OSCAR) Where'd he go, Oscar?

OSCAR: He went out to kill himself.

MURRAY: What did I tell you?

ROY (*to* OSCAR): Are you serious?

OSCAR: That's what she said. He was going out to kill himself. He didn't want to do it at home 'cause the kids were sleeping.

VINNIE: Why?

OSCAR: Why? Because that's Felix, that's why. (*He goes to the bar and refills his drink.*) You know what he's like. He sleeps on the window sill. "Love me or I'll jump." 'Cause he's a nut, that's why.

MURRAY: That's right. Remember he tried something like that in the army? She wanted to break off the engagement so he started cleaning guns in his mouth.

SPEED: I don't believe it. Talk! That's all Felix is, talk.

VINNIE (*worried*): But is that what he said? In those words? "I'm going to kill myself?"

OSCAR (*pacing about the table*): I don't know in what words. She didn't read it to me.

ROY: You mean he left her a note?

OSCAR: No, he sent a telegram.

MURRAY: *A suicide telegram?* Who sends a suicide telegram?

OSCAR: Felix, the nut, that's who! Can you imagine getting a thing like that? She even has to tip the kid a quarter.

ROY: I don't get it. If he wants to kill himself, why does he send a telegram?

OSCAR: Don't you see how his mind works? If he sends a note, she might not get it till Monday and he'd have no excuse for being dead. This way, for a dollar ten, he's got a chance to be saved.

VINNIE: You mean he really doesn't want to kill himself? He just wants sympathy.

OSCAR: What he'd really like is to go to the funeral and sit in the back. He'd be the biggest crier there.

MURRAY: He's right.

OSCAR: Sure I'm right.

MURRAY: We get these cases every day. All they want is attention. We got a guy who calls us every Saturday afternoon from the George Washington Bridge.

ROY: I don't know. You never can tell what a guy'll do when he's hysterical.

MURRAY: Nahhh. Nine out of ten times they don't jump.

ROY: What about the tenth time?

MURRAY: They jump. He's right. There's a possibility.

OSCAR: Not with Felix. I know him. He's too nervous to kill himself. He wears his seatbelt in a drive-in movie.

VINNIE: Isn't there someplace we could look for him?

SPEED: Where? Where would you look? Who knows where he is?

(*The doorbell rings. They all look at* OSCAR.)

OSCAR: Of course! If you're going to kill yourself, where's the safest place to do it? With your friends!

(VINNIE *starts for the door.*)

MURRAY (*stopping him*): Wait a minute! The guy may be hysterical. Let's play it nice and easy. If *we're* calm, maybe *he'll* be calm.

ROY (*getting up and joining them*): That's right. That's how they do it with those guys out on the ledge. You talk nice and soft.

(SPEED *rushes over to them, and joins in the frenzied discussion.*)

VINNIE: What'll we say to him?

MURRAY: We don't say nothin'. Like we never heard a thing.

OSCAR (*trying to get their attention*): You through with this discussion? Because he already could have hung himself out in the hall. (*to* VINNIE) Vinnie, open the door!

MURRAY: Remember! Like we don't know nothin'.

(They all rush back to their seats and grab up cards, which they concentrate on with the greatest intensity. VINNIE opens the door. FELIX UNGAR is there. He's about forty-four. His clothes are rumpled as if he had slept in them, and he needs a shave. Although he tries to act matter-of-fact, there is an air of great tension and nervousness about him.)

FELIX *(softly)*: Hi, Vin! *(VINNIE quickly goes back to his seat and studies his cards. FELIX has his hands in his pockets, trying to be very nonchalant. With controlled calm.)* Hi, fellas. *(They all mumble hello, but do not look at him. He puts his coat over the railing and crosses to the table.)* How's the game going? *(They all mumble appropriate remarks, and continue staring at their cards.)* Good! Good! Sorry I'm late. *(FELIX looks a little disappointed that no one asks "What?" He starts to pick up a sandwich, changes his mind and makes a gesture of distaste. He vaguely looks around.)* Any Coke left?

OSCAR *(looking up from his cards)*: Coke? Gee, I don't think so. I got a Seven-Up!

FELIX *(bravely)*: No, I felt like a Coke. I just don't feel like Seven-Up tonight!

(He stands watching the game.)

OSCAR: What's the bet?

SPEED: You bet a quarter. It's up to Murray. Murray, what do you say? *(MURRAY is staring at FELIX.)* Murray! Murray!

ROY *(to VINNIE)*: Tap his shoulder.

VINNIE *(taps MURRAY's shoulder)*: Murray!

MURRAY *(startled)*: What? What?

SPEED: It's up to you.

MURRAY: Why is it always up to me?

SPEED: It's not always up to you. It's up to you now. What do you do?

MURRAY: I'm in. I'm in.

(He throws in a quarter.)

FELIX *(moves to the bookcase)*: Anyone call about me?

OSCAR: Er, not that I can remember. *(to the others)* Did anyone call for Felix? *(They all shrug and ad lib "No.")* Why? Were you expecting a call?

FELIX *(looking at the books on the shelf)*: No! No! just asking.

(He opens a book and examines it.)

ROY: Er, I'll see his bet and raise it a dollar.

FELIX *(without looking up from the book)*: I just thought someone might have called.

SPEED: It costs me a a dollar and a quarter to play, right?

OSCAR: Right!

FELIX *(still looking at the book, in a sing-song)*: But, if no one called, no one called.

(He slams the book shut and puts it back. They all jump at the noise.)

SPEED *(getting nervous)*: What does it cost me to play again?

MURRAY *(angry)*: A dollar and a quarter! *A dollar and a quarter!* Pay attention, for crise sakes!

ROY: All right, take it easy. Take it easy.

OSCAR: Let's calm down, everyone, heh?

MURRAY: I'm sorry. I can't help it. *(Points to SPEED.)* He makes me nervous.

SPEED: I make *you* nervous. You make *me* nervous. You make *everyone* nervous.

MURRAY *(sarcastic)*: I'm sorry. Forgive me. I'll kill myself.

OSCAR: Murray!

(He motions with his head to FELIX.)

MURRAY *(realizes his error)*: Oh! Sorry.

(SPEED glares at him. They all sit in silence a moment, until VINNIE catches sight of FELIX, who is now staring out an upstage window. He quickly calls the others' attention to FELIX.)

FELIX *(looking back at them from the window)*: Gee, it's a pretty view from there. What is it, twelve floors?

OSCAR *(quickly crossing to the window and closing it)*: No. It's only eleven. That's all. Eleven. It says twelve but it's really only eleven. *(He then turns and closes the other window as FELIX watches him. OSCAR shivers slightly.)* Chilly in here. *(To the others)* Isn't it chilly in here?

(He crosses back to the table.)

ROY: Yeah, that's much better.

OSCAR *(to FELIX)*: Want to sit and play? It's still early.

VINNIE: Sure. We're in no rush. We'll be here till three, four in the morning.

FELIX *(shrugs)*: I don't know; I just don't feel much like playing now.

OSCAR *(sitting at the table)*: Oh! Well, what *do* you feel like doing?

FELIX *(shrugs)*: I'll find *something*. *(He starts to walk toward the other room.)* Don't worry about me.

OSCAR: Where are you going?

FELIX *(stops in the doorway. He looks at the others who are all staring at him)*: To the john.

OSCAR *(looks at the others, worried, then at FELIX)*: Alone?

FELIX *(nods)*: I always go alone! Why?

OSCAR *(shrugs)*: No reason. You gonna be in there long?

FELIX *(shrugs, then says meaningfully, like a martyr)*: As long as it takes.

(Then he goes into the bathroom and slams the door shut behind him. Immediately they all jump up and crowd about the bathroom door, whispering in frenzied anxiety.)

MURRAY: Are you crazy? Letting him go to the john alone?

OSCAR: What did you want me to do?

ROY: Stop him! Go in with him!

OSCAR: Suppose he just has to go to the john?

MURRAY: Supposing he does? He's better off being embarrassed than dead!

OSCAR: How's he going to kill himself in the john?

SPEED: What do you mean, how? Razor blades, pills. Anything that's in there.

OSCAR: That's the kids' bathroom. The worst he could do is brush his teeth to death.

ROY: He could jump.

VINNIE: That's right. Isn't there a window in there?

OSCAR: It's only six inches wide.

MURRAY: He could break the glass. He could cut his wrists.

OSCAR: He could also flush himself into the East River. I'm telling you he's not going to try anything!

(He moves to the table.)

ROY *(goes to the doorway)*: Shhh! Listen! He's crying. *(There is a pause as all listen as FELIX sobs.)* You hear that. He's crying.

MURRAY: Isn't that terrible? For God's sakes, Oscar, do something! Say something!

OSCAR: What? What do you say to a man who's crying in your bathroom?

(There is the sound of the toilet flushing and ROY makes a mad dash back to his chair.)

ROY: He's coming!

(They all scramble back to their places. MURRAY gets mixed up with VINNIE and they quickly straighten it out. FELIX comes back into the room. But he seems calm and collected, with no evident sign of having cried.)

FELIX: I guess I'll be running along.

(He starts for the door. OSCAR jumps up. So do the others.)

OSCAR: Felix, wait a second.

FELIX: No! No! I can't talk to you. I can't talk to anyone.

(They all try to grab him, stopping him near the stairs.)

MURRAY: Felix, please. We're your friends. Don't run out like this.

(FELIX struggles to pull away.)

OSCAR: Felix, sit down. Just for a minute. Talk to us.

FELIX: There's nothing to talk about. There's nothing to say. It's over. Over. Everything is over. Let me go!

(He breaks away from them and dashes into the stage-right bedroom. They start to chase him and he dodges from the bedroom through the adjoining door into the bathroom.)

ROY: Stop him! Grab him!

FELIX *(looking for an exit)*: Let me out! I've got to get out of here!

OSCAR: Felix, you're hysterical.

FELIX: Please let me out of here!

MURRAY: The john! Don't let him get in the john!

FELIX *(comes out of the bathroom with ROY hanging onto him, and the others trailing behind)*: Leave me alone. Why doesn't everyone leave me alone?

OSCAR: All right, Felix, I'm warning you. Now cut it out!

(He throws a half-filled glass of water, which he has picked up from the bookcase, into FELIX's face.)

FELIX: It's *my* problem. I'll work it out. Leave me alone. Oh, my stomach.

(He collapses in ROY's arms.)

MURRAY: What's the matter with your stomach?

VINNIE: He looks sick. Look at his face.

(They all try to hold him as they lead him over to the couch.)

FELIX: I'm not sick. I'm all right. I didn't take anything. I swear. Ohh, my stomach.

OSCAR: What do you mean you didn't take anything? What did you take?

FELIX *(sitting on the couch)*: Nothing! Nothing! I didn't take anything. Don't tell Frances what I did, please! Oohh, my stomach.

MURRAY: He took something! I'm telling you he took something.

OSCAR: What, Felix! *What?*

FELIX: I didn't take anything.

OSCAR: Pills? Did you take pills?

FELIX: No! No!

OSCAR *(grabbing FELIX)*: Don't lie to me, Felix, Did you take pills?

FELIX: No, I didn't. I didn't take anything.

MURRAY: Thank God he didn't take pills.

(They all relax and take a breath of relief.)

FELIX: Just a few, that's all.

(They all react in alarm and concern over the pills.)

OSCAR: He took pills.

MURRAY: How many pills?

OSCAR: What kind of pills?

FELIX: I don't know what kind. Little green ones. I just grabbed anything out of her medicine cabinet. I must have been crazy.

OSCAR: Didn't you look? Didn't you see what kind?

FELIX: I couldn't see. The light's broken. Don't call Frances. Don't tell her. I'm so ashamed. So ashamed.

OSCAR: Felix, how many pills did you take?

FELIX: I don't know. I can't remember.

OSCAR: I'm calling Frances.

FELIX (grabs him): No! Don't call her. Don't call her. If she hears I took a whole bottle of pills . . .

MURRAY: A whole bottle? *A whole bottle of pills?* (He turns to VINNIE.) My God, call an ambulance!

(VINNIE *runs to the front door.*)

OSCAR (to MURRAY): You don't even know what *kind!*

MURRAY: What's the difference? He took a whole bottle!

OSCAR: Maybe they were vitamins. He could be the healthiest one in the room! Take it easy, will you?

FELIX: Don't call Frances. Promise me you won't call Frances.

MURRAY: Open his collar. Open the window. Give him some air.

SPEED: Walk him around. Don't let him go to sleep.

(SPEED *and* MURRAY *pick* FELIX *up and walk him around, while* ROY *rubs his wrists.*)

ROY: Rub his wrists. Keep his circulation going.

VINNIE (running to the bathroom to get a compress): A cold compress. Put a cold compress on his neck.

(They sit FELIX *in the armchair, still chattering in alarm.*)

OSCAR: One doctor at a time, heh? All the interns shut the hell up!

FELIX: I'm all right. I'll be all right. (to OSCAR urgently) You didn't call Frances, did you?

MURRAY (to the others): You just gonna stand here? No one's gonna do anything? I'm calling a doctor.

(He crosses to the phone.)

FELIX: No! No doctor.

MURRAY: You *gotta* have a doctor.

FELIX: I don't need a doctor.

MURRAY: You gotta get the pills out.

FELIX: I got them out. I threw up before! (He sits back weakly. MURRAY hangs up the phone.) Don't you have a root beer or a ginger ale?

(VINNIE *gives the compress to* SPEED.)

ROY (to VINNIE): Get him a drink.

OSCAR (glares angrily at FELIX): He threw them up!

VINNIE: Which would you rather have, Felix, the root beer or the ginger ale?

SPEED (to VINNIE): Get him the drink! Just get him the drink.

(VINNIE *runs into the kitchen as* SPEED *puts the compress on* FELIX's *head.*)

FELIX: Twelve years. Twelve years we were married. Did you know we were married twelve years, Roy?

ROY (comforting him): Yes, Felix. I knew.

FELIX (with great emotion in his voice): And now it's over. Like that, it's over. That's hysterical, isn't it?

SPEED: Maybe it was just a fight. You've had fights before, Felix.

FELIX: No, it's over. She's getting a lawyer tomorrow. *My* cousin. She's using *my* cousin! (He sobs.) Who am *I* going to get?

(VINNIE *comes out of the kitchen with a glass of root beer.*)

MURRAY (patting his shoulder): It's okay, Felix. Come on. Take it easy.

VINNIE (gives the glass to FELIX): Here's the root beer.

FELIX: I'm all right, honestly. I'm just crying.

(He puts his head down. They all look at him helplessly.)

MURRAY: All right, let's not stand around looking at him. (Pushes SPEED and VINNIE away.) Let's break it up, heh?

FELIX: Yes, don't stand there looking at me. Please.

OSCAR (to the others): Come on, he's all right. Let's call it a night.

(MURRAY, SPEED and ROY *turn in their chips at the poker table, get their coats and get ready to go.*)

FELIX: I'm so ashamed. Please, fellas, forgive me.

VINNIE (bending to FELIX): Oh, Felix, we—we understand.

FELIX: Don't say anything about this to anyone, Vinnie. Will you promise me?

VINNIE: I'm going to Florida tomorrow.

FELIX: Oh, that's nice. Have a good time.

VINNIE: Thanks.

FELIX (turns away and sighs in despair): We were going to go to Florida next winter. (He laughs, but it's a sob.) Without the kids! Now they'll go without me.

(VINNIE *gets his coat and* OSCAR *ushers them all to the door.*)

MURRAY (stopping at the door): Maybe one of us should stay?

OSCAR: It's all right, Murray.

MURRAY: Suppose he tries something again?

OSCAR: He won't try anything again.

MURRAY: How do your *know* he won't try anything again?

FELIX (turns to MURRAY): I won't try anything again. I'm very tired.

OSCAR (*to* MURRAY): You hear? He's very tired. He had a busy night. Good night, fellows.

(*They all ad lib goodbyes and leave. The door closes, but opens immediately and* ROY *comes back in.*)

ROY: If anything happens, Oscar, just call me.

(*He exits, and as the door starts to close, it reopens and* SPEED *comes in.*)

SPEED: I'm three blocks away. I could be here in five minutes.

(*He exits, and as the door starts to close, it reopens and* VINNIE *comes back in.*)

VINNIE: If you need me I'll be at the Meridian Motel in Miami Beach.

OSCAR: You'll be the first one I'll call, Vinnie.

(VINNIE *exits. The door closes and then reopens as* MURRAY *comes back.*)

MURRAY (*to* OSCAR): You're sure?

OSCAR: I'm sure.

MURRAY (*loudly to* FELIX, *as he gestures to* OSCAR *to come to the door*): Good night, Felix. Try to get a good night's sleep. I guarantee you things are going to look a lot brighter in the morning. (*to* OSCAR, *sotto voce*) Take away his belt and his shoe laces.

(*He nods and exits.* OSCAR *turns and looks at* FELIX *sitting in the armchair and slowly moves across the room. There is a moment's silence.*)

OSCAR (*he looks at* FELIX *and sighs*): Ohh, Felix, Felix, Felix, Felix!

FELIX (*sits with his head buried in his hands. He doesn't look up*): I know, I know, I know, I know! What am I going to do, Oscar?

OSCAR: You're gonna wash down the pills with some hot, black coffee. (*He starts for the kitchen, then stops.*) Do you think I could leave you alone for two minutes?

FELIX: No, I don't think so! Stay with me, Oscar. Talk to me.

OSCAR: A cup of black coffee. It'll be good for you. Come on in the kitchen. I'll sit on you.

FELIX: Oscar, the terrible thing is, I think I still love her. It's a lousy marriage but I still love her. I didn't want this divorce.

OSCAR (*sitting on the arm of the couch*): How about some Ovaltine? You like Ovaltine? With a couple of fig newtons or chocolate mallomars?

FELIX: All right, so we didn't get along. But we had two wonderful kids, and a beautiful home. Didn't we, Oscar?

OSCAR: How about vanilla wafers? Or Vienna fingers? I got everything.

FELIX: What more does she want? What does *any* woman want?

OSCAR: I want to know what *you* want. Ovaltine, coffee or tea. Then we'll get to the divorce.

FELIX: It's not fair, damn it! It's just not fair! (*He bangs his fist on the arm of the chair angrily, then suddenly winces in great pain and grabs his neck.*) Oh! Ohh, my neck. My neck!

OSCAR: What? What?

FELIX (*He gets up and paces in pain. He is holding his twisted neck*): It's a nerve spasm. I get it in the neck. Oh! Ohh, that hurts.

OSCAR (*rushing to help*): Where? Where does it hurt?

FELIX (*stretches out an arm like a halfback*): Don't touch me! Don't touch me!

OSCAR: I just want to see where it hurts.

FELIX: It'll go away. Just let me alone a few minutes. Ohh! Ohh!

OSCAR (*moving to the couch*): Lie down; I'll rub it. It'll ease the pain.

FELIX (*in wild contortions*): You don't know how. It's a special way. Only Frances knows how to rub me.

OSCAR: You want me to ask her to come over and rub you?

FELIX (*yells*): No! No! We're getting divorced. She wouldn't want to rub me anymore. It's tension. I get it from tension. I must be tense.

OSCAR: I wouldn't be surprised. How long does it last?

FELIX: Sometimes a minute, sometimes hours. I once got it while I was driving. I crashed into a liquor store. Ohhh! Ohhh!

(*He sits down, painfully, on the couch.*)

OSCAR (*getting behind him*): You want to suffer or do you want me to rub your stupid neck?

(*He starts to massage it.*)

FELIX: Easy! Easy!

OSCAR (*yells*): Relax, damn it: relax!

FELIX (*yells back*): Don't yell at me! (*Then quietly*) What should I do? Tell me nicely.

OSCAR (*rubbing the neck*): Think of warm jello!

FELIX: Isn't that terrible? I can't do it. I can't relax. I sleep in one position all night. Frances says when I die on my tombstone it's going to say, "Here Stands Felix Ungar." (*He winces.*) Oh! Ohh!

OSCAR (*stops rubbing*): Does that hurt?

FELIX: No, it feels good.

OSCAR: Then say so. You make the same sound for pain or happiness.

(*Starts to massage his neck again.*)

FELIX: I know. I know. Oscar—I think I'm crazy.

OSCAR: Well, if it'll make you feel any better, I think so too.

FELIX: I mean it. Why else do I go to pieces like this? Coming up here, scaring you to death. Trying to kill myself. what is that?

OSCAR: That's panic. You're a panicky person. You have a low threshold for composure.

(He stops rubbing.)

FELIX: Don't stop. It feels good.

OSCAR: If you don't relax, I'll break my fingers. *(Touches his hair.)* Look at this. The only man in the world with clenched hair.

FELIX: I do terrible things, Oscar. You know I'm a cry baby.

OSCAR: Bend over.

(FELIX bends over and OSCAR begins to massage his back.)

FELIX *(head down)*: I tell the whole world my problems.

OSCAR *(massaging hard)*: Listen, if this hurts just tell me, because I don't know what the hell I'm doing.

FELIX: It just isn't nice, Oscar, running up here like this, carrying on like a nut.

OSCAR *(finishes massaging)*: How does your neck feel?

FELIX *(twists his neck)*: Better. Only my back hurts.

(He gets up and paces, rubbing his back.)

OSCAR: What you need is a drink.

(He starts for the bar.)

FELIX: I can't drink. It makes me sick. I tried drinking last night.

OSCAR *(at the bar)*: Where *were* you last night?

FELIX: Nowhere. I just walked.

OSCAR: All night?

FELIX: All night.

OSCAR: In the rain?

FELIX: No. In a hotel. I couldn't sleep. I walked around the room all night. It was over near Times Square. A dirty, depressing room. Then I found myself looking out the window. And suddenly, I began to think about jumping.

OSCAR *(he has two glasses filled and crosses to FELIX)*: What changed your mind?

FELIX: Nothing. I'm still thinking about it.

OSCAR: Drink this.

(He hands him a glass, crosses to the couch and sits.)

FELIX: I don't want to get divorced, Oscar. I don't want to suddenly change my whole life. *(He moves to the couch and sits next to OSCAR.)* Talk to me, Oscar. What am I going to do? What am I going to do?

OSCAR: You're going to pull yourself together. And then you're going to drink that Scotch, and then you and I are going to figure out a whole new life for you.

FELIX: Without Frances? Without the kids?

OSCAR: It's been done before.

FELIX *(paces around)*: You don't understand, Oscar. I'm nothing without them. I'm—*nothing!*

OSCAR: What do you mean, nothing? You're something! *(FELIX sits in the armchair.)* A Person! You're flesh and blood and bones and hair and nails and ears. You're not a fish. You're not a buffalo. You're *you!* You walk and talk and cry and complain and eat little green pills and send suicide telegrams. No one else does that, Felix. I'm telling you, *you're the only one of its kind in the world! (He goes to the bar.)* Now drink that.

FELIX: Oscar, you've been through it yourself. What did you do? How did you get through those first few nights?

OSCAR *(pours a drink)*: I did exactly what you're doing.

FELIX: Getting hysterical!

OSCAR: No, drinking! *Drinking! (He comes back to the couch with the bottle and sits.)* I drank for four days and four nights. And then I fell through a window. I was bleeding but I was forgetting.

(He drinks again.)

FELIX: How can you forget your kids? How can you wipe out twelve years of marriage?

OSCAR: You can't. When you walk into eight empty rooms every night it hits you in the face like a wet glove. But those are the facts, Felix. You've got to face it. You can't spend the rest of your life crying. It annoys people in the movies! Be a good boy and drink your Scotch.

(He stretches out on the couch with his head near FELIX.)

FELIX: I can imagine what Frances must be going through.

OSCAR: What do you mean, what *she's* going through?

FELIX: It's much harder on the woman, Oscar. She's all alone with the kids. Stuck there in the house. She can't get out like me. I mean where is she going to find someone now at her age? With two kids. Where?

OSCAR: I don't know. Maybe someone'll come to the door! Felix, there's a hundred thousand divorces a year. There must be *something* nice about it. *(FELIX suddenly puts both his hands over his ears and hums quietly.)* What's the matter now?

(He sits up.)

FELIX: My ears are closing up. I get it from the sinus. It must be the dust in here. I'm allergic to dust.

(He hums. Then he gets up and tries to clear his ears by hopping first on one leg then the other as he goes to the window and opens it.)

OSCAR *(jumping up)*: What are you doing?

FELIX: I'm not going to jump. I'm just going to

breathe. (*He takes deep breaths.*) I used to drive Frances crazy with my allergies. I'm allergic to perfume. For a while the only thing she could wear was my after-shave lotion. I was impossible to live with. It's a wonder she took it this long.

(*He suddenly bellows like a moose. He makes this strange sound another time.* OSCAR *looks at him dumbfounded.*)

OSCAR: What are you doing?
FELIX: I'm trying to clear my ears. You create a pressure inside and then it opens it up.

(*He bellows again.*)

OSCAR: Did it open up?
FELIX: A little bit. (*He rubs his neck.*) I think I strained my throat.

(*He paces about the room.*)

OSCAR: Felix, why don't you leave yourself alone? Don't tinker.
FELIX: I can't help myself. I drive everyone crazy. A marriage counselor once kicked me out of his office. He wrote on my chart, "Lunatic!" I don't blame her. It's impossible to be married to me.
OSCAR: It takes two to make a rotten marriage.

(*He lies back down on the couch.*)

FELIX: You don't know what I was like at home. I bought her a book and made her write down every penny we spent. Thirty-eight cents for cigarettes; ten cents for a paper. Everything had to go in the book. And then we had a big fight because I said she forgot to write down how much the book was. Who could live with anyone like that?
OSCAR: An accountant! What do I know? We're not perfect. We all have faults.
FELIX: Faults? Heh! Faults. We have a maid who comes in to clean three times a week. And on the other days, Frances does the cleaning. And at night, after they've both cleaned up, I go in and clean the whole place again. I can't help it. I like things clean. Blame it on my mother. I was toilet-trained at five months old.
OSCAR: How do you remember things like that?
FELIX: I loused up the marriage. Nothing was ever right. I used to recook everything. The minute she walked out of the kitchen I would add salt or pepper. It's not that I didn't trust her, it's just that I was a better cook. Well, I cooked myself out of a marriage. (*He bangs his head with the palm of his hand three times.*) God damned idiot!

(*He sinks down in the armchair.*)

OSCAR: Don't do that; you'll get a headache.
FELIX: I can't stand it, Oscar. I hate me. Oh, boy, do I hate me.

OSCAR: You don't hate you. You love you. You think no one has problems like you.
FELIX: Don't give me that analyst jazz. I happen to know I hate my guts.
OSCAR: Come on, Felix; I've never *seen* anyone so in love.
FELIX (*hurt*): I thought you were my friend.
OSCAR: That's why I can talk to you like this. Because I love you almost as much as *you* do.
FELIX: Then help me.
OSCAR (*up on one elbow*): How can I help you when I can't help myself? You think *you're* impossible to live with? Blanche used to say, "What time do you want dinner?" And I'd say, "I don't know. I'm not hungry." Then at three o'clock in the morning I'd wake her up and say, "Now!" I've been one of the highest paid sportswriters in the East for the past fourteen years, and we saved eight and a half dollars—in pennies! I'm never home, I gamble, I burn cigar holes in the furniture, drink like a fish and lie to her every chance I get. And for our tenth wedding anniversary, I took her to see the New York Rangers-Detroit Red Wings hockey game where she got hit with a puck. And I *still* can't understand why she left me. That's how impossible *I* am!
FELIX: I'm not like you, Oscar. I couldn't take it living all alone. I don't know how I'm going to work. They've got to fire me. How am I going to make a living?
OSCAR: You'll go on street corners and cry. They'll throw nickels at you! You'll work, Felix; you'll work.

(*He lies back down.*)

FELIX: You think I ought to call Frances?
OSCAR (*about to explode*): What for?

(*He sits up.*)

FELIX: Well, talk it out again.
OSCAR: You've *talked* it all out. There are no words left in your entire marriage. When are you going to face up to it?
FELIX: I can't help it, Oscar; I don't know what to do.
OSCAR: Then listen to me. Tonight you're going to sleep here. And tomorrow you're going to get your clothes and your electric toothbrush and you'll move in with me.
FELIX: No, no. It's your apartment. I'll be in the way.
OSCAR: There's eight rooms. We could go for a year without seeing each other. Don't you understand? I *want* you to move in.
FELIX: Why? I'm a pest.
OSCAR: I *know* you're a pest. You don't have to keep telling me.
FELIX: Then why do you want me to live with you?
OSCAR: Because I can't stand living alone, that's why!

For crying out loud, I'm proposing to you. What do you want, a ring?

FELIX *(moves to* OSCAR*)*: Well, Oscar, if you really mean it, there's a lot I can do around here. I'm very handy around the house. I can fix things.

OSCAR: You don't have to fix things.

FELIX: I want to do *something*, Oscar. Let me do something.

OSCAR *(nods)*: All right, you can take my wife's initials off the towels. Anything you want.

FELIX *(beginning to tidy up)*: I can cook. I'm a terrific cook.

OSCAR: You don't have to cook. I eat cold cuts for breakfast.

FELIX: Two meals a day at home, we'll save a fortune. We've got to pay alimony, you know.

OSCAR *(happy to see* FELIX's *new optimism)*: All right, you can cook.

(He throws a pillow at him.)

FELIX *(throws the pillow back)*: Do you like leg of lamb?

OSCAR: Yes, I like leg of lamb.

FELIX: I'll make it tomorrow night. I'll have to call Frances. She has my big pot.

OSCAR: *Will you forget Frances!* We'll get our own pots. Don't drive me crazy before you move in. *(The phone rings,* OSCAR *picks it up quickly.)* Hello? Oh, hello, Frances!

FELIX *(stops cleaning and starts to wave his arms wildly. He whispers screamingly)*: I'm not here! I'm not here! You didn't see me. You don't know where I am. I didn't call. I'm not here. I'm not here.

OSCAR *(into the phone)*: Yes, he's here.

FELIX *(pacing back and forth)*: How does she sound? Is she worried? Is she crying? What is she saying? Does she want to speak to me? I don't want to speak to her.

OSCAR *(into the phone)*: Yes, he is!

FELIX: You can tell her I'm not coming back. I've made up my mind. I've had it there. I've taken just as much as she has. You can tell her for me if she thinks I'm coming back she's got another think coming. Tell her. Tell her.

OSCAR *(into the phone)*: Yes! Yes, he's fine.

FELIX: Don't tell her I'm fine! You heard me carrying on before. What are you telling her that for? I'm not fine.

OSCAR *(into the telephone)*: Yes, I understand, Frances.

FELIX *(sits down next to* OSCAR*)*: Does she want to speak to me? Ask her if she wants to speak to me?

OSCAR *(into the phone)*: Do you want to speak to him?

FELIX *(reaches for the phone)*: Give me the phone. I'll speak to her.

OSCAR *(into the phone)*: Oh. You don't want to speak to him.

FELIX: She doesn't want to speak to me?

OSCAR *(into the phone)*: Yeah, I see. Right. Well, good-bye.

(He hangs up.)

FELIX: She didn't want to speak to me?

OSCAR: No!

FELIX: Why did she call?

OSCAR: She wants to know when you're coming over for your clothes. She wants to have the room repainted.

FELIX: Oh!

OSCAR *(pats* FELIX *on the shoulder)*: Listen, Felix, it's almost one o'clock.

(He gets up.)

FELIX: Didn't want to speak to me, huh?

OSCAR: I'm going to bed. Do you want a cup of tea with Fruitanos or Raisinettos?

FELIX: She'll paint it pink. She always wanted it pink.

OSCAR: I'll get you a pair of pajamas. You like stripes, dots, or animals?

(He goes into the bedroom.)

FELIX: She's really heartbroken, isn't she? I want to kill myself, and she's picking out colors.

OSCAR *(in the bedroom)*: Which bedroom do you want? I'm lousy with bedrooms.

FELIX *(gets up and moves toward the bedroom)*: You know, I'm glad. Because she finally made me realize—it's over. It didn't sink in until just this minute.

OSCAR *(comes back with pillow, pillowcase, and pajamas)*: Felix, I want you to go to bed.

FELIX: I don't think I believed her until just now. My marriage is *really* over.

OSCAR: Felix, go to bed.

FELIX: Somehow it doesn't seem so bad now. I mean, I think I can live with this thing.

OSCAR: Live with it tomorrow. Go to bed tonight.

FELIX: In a little while. I've got to think. I've got to start rearranging my life. Do you have a pencil and paper?

OSCAR: Not in a little while. Now! It's my house; I make up the bedtime.

(He throws the pajamas to him.)

FELIX: Oscar, please. I have to be alone for a few minutes. I've got to get organized. Go on, you go to bed. I'll—I'll clean up.

(He begins picking up debris from the floor.)

OSCAR *(putting the pillow into the pillowcase)*: You don't have to clean up. I pay a dollar fifty an hour to clean up.

FELIX: It's all right, Oscar. I wouldn't be able to sleep

with all this dirt around anyway. Go to bed. I'll see you in the morning.

(He puts the dishes on the tray.)

OSCAR: You're not going to do anything big, are you, like rolling up the rugs?

FELIX: Ten minutes, that's all I'll be.

OSCAR: You're sure?

FELIX *(smiles)*: I'm sure.

OSCAR: No monkey business?

FELIX: No monkey business. I'll do the dishes and go right to bed.

OSCAR: Yeah.

(Crosses up to his bedroom, throwing the pillow into the downstage bedroom as he passes. He closes his bedroom door behind him.)

FELIX *(calls him)*: Oscar! *(OSCAR anxiously comes out of his bedroom and crosses to FELIX.)* I'm going to be all right! It's going to take me a couple of days, but I'm going to be all right.

OSCAR *(smiles)*: Good! Well, good night, Felix.

(He turns to go toward the bedroom as FELIX begins to plump up a pillow from the couch.)

FELIX: Good night, Frances.

(OSCAR stops dead. FELIX, unaware of his error, plumps another pillow as OSCAR turns and stares at FELIX with a troubled expression.)

ACT 2 / SCENE 1

(Two weeks later, about eleven at night. The poker game is in session again. VINNIE, ROY, SPEED, MURRAY and OSCAR are all seated at the table. FELIX's chair is empty.

There is one major difference between this scene and the opening poker-game scene. It is the appearance of the room. It is immaculately clean. No, not clean. Sterile! Spotless! Not a speck of dirt can be seen under the ten coats of Johnson's Glo-Coat that have been applied to the floor in the last three weeks. No laundry bags, no dirty dishes, no half-filled glasses.

Suddenly FELIX appears from the kitchen. He carries a tray with glasses and food—and napkins. After putting the tray down, he takes the napkins one at a time, flicks them out to full length and hands one to every player. They take them with grumbling and put them on their laps. He picks up a can of beer and very carefully pours it into a tall glass, measuring it perfectly so that not a drop spills or overflows. With a flourish he puts the can down.)

FELIX *(moves to MURRAY)*: An ice-cold glass of beer for Murray.

(MURRAY reaches up for it.)

MURRAY: Thank you, Felix.

FELIX *(holds the glass back)*: Where's your coaster?

MURRAY: My what?

FELIX: Your coaster. The little round thing that goes under the glass.

MURRAY *(looks around on the table)*: I think I bet it.

OSCAR *(picks it up and hands it to MURRAY)*: I knew I was winning too much. Here!

FELIX: Always try to use your coasters, fellows. *(He picks up another drink from the tray.)* Scotch and a little bit of water?

SPEED *(raises his hand)*: Scotch and a little bit of water. *(Proudly.)* And I have my coaster.

(He holds it up for inspection.)

FELIX *(hands him the drink)*: I hate to be a pest but you know what wet glasses do?

(He goes back to the tray and picks up and wipes a clean ashtray.)

OSCAR *(coldly and deliberately)*: They leave little rings on the table.

FELIX *(nods)*: Ruins the finish. Eats right through the polish.

OSCAR *(to the others)*: So let's watch those little rings, huh?

FELIX *(takes an ashtray and a plate with a sandwich from the tray and crosses to the table)*: And we have a clean ashtray for Roy *(Handing ROY the ashtray.)* Aaaaand—a sandwich for Vinnie.

(Like a doting headwaiter, he skillfully places the sandwich in front of VINNIE.)

VINNIE *(looks at FELIX, then at the sandwich)*: Gee, it smells good. What is it?

FELIX: Bacon, lettuce and tomato with mayonnaise on pumpernickel toast.

VINNIE *(unbelievingly)*: Where'd you get it?

FELIX *(puzzled)*: I made it. In the kitchen.

VINNIE: You mean you put in toast and cooked bacon? Just for me?

OSCAR: If you don't like it, he'll make you a meat loaf. Takes him five minutes.

FELIX: It's no trouble. Honest. I love to cook. Try to eat over the dish. I just vacuumed the rug. *(He goes back to the tray, then stops.)* Oscar!

OSCAR *(quickly)*: Yes, sir?

FELIX: I forgot what you wanted. What did you ask me for?

OSCAR: Two three-and-a-half-minute eggs and some petit fours.

FELIX *(points to him)*: A double gin and tonic. I'll be right back. *(FELIX starts out, then stops at a little box on the bar.)* Who turned off the Pure-A-Tron?

MURRAY: The what?

FELIX: The Pure-A-Tron! *(He snaps it back on.)* Don't

play with this, fellows. I'm trying to get some of the grime out of the air.

(He looks at them and shakes his head disapprovingly, then exits. They all sit in silence a few seconds.)

OSCAR: Murray, I'll give you two hundred dollars for your gun.

SPEED *(throws his cards on the table and gets up angrily)*: I can't take it any more. *(With his hand on his neck.)* I've had it up to here. In the last three hours we played four minutes of poker. I'm not giving up my Friday nights to watch cooking and house-keeping.

ROY *(slumped in his chair, head hanging down)*: I can't breathe. *(He points to the Pure-A-Tron.)* That lousy machine is sucking everything out of the air.

VINNIE *(chewing)*: Gee, this is delicious. Who wants a bite?

MURRAY: Is the toast warm?

VINNIE: Perfect. And not too much mayonnaise. It's really a well-made sandwich.

MURRAY: Cut me off a little piece.

VINNIE: Give me your napkin. I don't want to drop any crumbs.

SPEED *(watches them, horrified, as VINNIE carefully breaks the sandwich over MURRAY's napkin. Then he turns to OSCAR)*: Are you listening to this? Martha and Gertrude at the Automat. *(Almost crying in despair.)* What the hell happened to our poker game?

ROY *(still choking)*: I'm telling you that thing could kill us. They'll find us here in the morning with our tongues on the floor.

SPEED *(yells at OSCAR)*: Do something! Get him back in the game.

OSCAR *(rises, containing his anger)*: Don't bother me with your petty little problems. You get this one stinkin' night a week. I'm cooped up here with Dione Lucas twenty-four hours a day.

(He moves to the window.)

ROY: It was better before. With the garbage and the smoke, it was better before.

VINNIE *(to MURRAY)*: Did you notice what he does with the bread?

MURRAY: What?

VINNIE: He cuts off the crusts. That's why the sandwich is so light.

MURRAY: And then he only uses the soft, green part of the lettuce. *(Chewing.)* It's really delicious.

SPEED *(reacts in amazement and disgust)*: I'm going out of my mind.

OSCAR *(yells toward the kitchen)*: Felix! Damn it, *Felix!*

SPEED *(takes the kitty box from the bookcase, puts it on the table, and puts the money in)*: Forget it. I'm going home.

OSCAR: Sit down!

SPEED: I'll buy a book and I'll start to read again.

OSCAR: Siddown! Will you siddown! *(Yells.)* Felix!

SPEED: Oscar, it's all over. The day his marriage busted up was the end of our poker game. *(He takes his jacket from the back of the chair and crosses to the door.)* If you find some real players next week, call me.

OSCAR *(following him)*: You can't run out now. I'm a big loser.

SPEED *(with the door open)*: You got no one to blame but yourself. It's all your fault. You're the one who stopped him from killing himself.

(He exits and slams the door.)

OSCAR *(stares at the door)*: He's right! The man is absolutely right.

(He moves to the table.)

MURRAY *(to VINNIE)*: Are you going to eat that pickle?

VINNIE: I wasn't thinking of it. Why? Do you want it?

MURRAY: Unless you want it. It's your pickle.

VINNIE: No, no, Take it. I don't usually eat pickle.

(VINNIE holds the plate with the pickle out to MURRAY. OSCAR slaps the plate, which sends the pickle flying through the air.)

OSCAR: Deal the cards!

MURRAY: What did you do that for?

OSCAR: Just deal the cards. You want to play poker, deal the cards. You want to eat, go to Schrafft's. *(to VINNIE)* Keep your sandwich and your pickles to yourself. I'm losing ninety-two dollars and everybody's getting fat! *(He screams.)* Felix!

(FELIX appears in the kitchen doorway.)

FELIX: What?

OSCAR: Close the kitchen and sit down. It's a quarter to twelve. I still got an hour and a half to win this month's alimony.

ROY *(sniffs)*: What is that smell? Disinfectant! *(He smells the cards.)* It's the cards. *He washed the cards!*

(He throws down the cards, takes his jacket from the chair and moves past the table to put his money into the kitty box.)

FELIX *(comes to the table with OSCAR's drink, which he puts down; then he sits in his own seat)*: Okay. What's the bet?

OSCAR *(hurrying to his seat)*: I can't believe it. We're gonna play cards again. *(He sits.)* It's up to Roy. Roy, baby, what are you gonna do?

ROY: I'm going to get in a cab and go to Central Park. If I don't get some fresh air, you got yourself a dead accountant.

(He moves toward the door.)

OSCAR (*follows him*): What do you mean? It's not even twelve o'clock.

ROY (*turns back to* OSCAR): Look, I've been sitting here breathing Lysol and ammonia for four hours! Nature didn't intend for poker to be played like that. (*He crosses to the door.*) If you wanna have a game next week (*He points to* FELIX.) either Louis Pasteur cleans up *after* we're gone, or we play in the Hotel Dixie! Good night!

(*He goes and slams the door. There is a moment's silence,* OSCAR *goes back to the table and sits.*)

OSCAR: We got just enough for handball!

FELIX: Gee, I'm sorry. Is it my fault?

VINNIE: No, I guess no one feels like playing much lately.

MURRAY: Yeah. I don't know what it is, but something's happening to the old gang.

(*He goes to a side chair, sits and puts on his shoes.*)

OSCAR: Don't you know what's happening to the old gang? It's breaking up. Everyone's getting divorced. I swear, we used to have better games when we couldn't get out at night.

VINNIE (*getting up and putting on his jacket*): Well. I guess I'll be going too. Bebe and I are driving to Asbury Park for the weekend.

FELIX: Just the two of you, heh? Gee, that's nice! You always do things like that together, don't you?

VINNIE (*shrugs*): We have to. I don't know how to drive! (*He takes all the money from the kitty box and moves to the door.*) You coming, Murray?

MURRAY (*gets up, takes his jacket and moves toward the door*): Yeah, why not? If I'm not home by one o'clock with a hero sandwich and a frozen éclair, she'll have an all-points out on me. Ahhh, you guys got the life.

FELIX: Who?

MURRAY (*turns back*): Who? You! The Marx Brothers! Laugh, laugh, laugh. What have you got to worry about? If you suddenly want to go to the Playboy Club to hunt Bunnies, who's gonna stop you?

FELIX: I don't belong to the Playboy Club.

MURRAY: I know you don't, Felix, it's just a figure of speech. Anyway, it's not such a bad idea. Why don't you join?

FELIX: Why?

MURRAY: Why! Because for twenty-five dollars they give you a key—and you walk into Paradise. *My* keys cost thirty cents—and you walk into corned beef and cabbage. (*He winks at him.*) Listen to me.

(*He moves to the door.*)

FELIX: What are you talking about, Murray? You're a happily married man.

MURRAY (*turns back on the landing*): I'm not talking

about *my* situation. (*He puts on his jacket.*) I'm talking about *yours!* Fate has just played a cruel and rotten trick on you, so enjoy it! (*He turns to go, revealing "PAL" letters sewn on the back of his jacket.*) C'mon, Vinnie.

(VINNIE *waves goodbye and they both exit.*)

FELIX (*staring at the door*): That's funny, isn't it, Oscar? They think we're happy. They really think we're enjoying this. (*He gets up and begins to straighten up the chairs.*) They don't know, Oscar. They don't know what it's like.

(*He gives a short, ironic laugh, tucks the napkins under his arm and starts to pick up the dishes from the table.*)

OSCAR: I'd be immensely grateful to you, Felix, if you didn't clean up just now.

FELIX (*puts dishes on the tray*): It's only a few things. (*He stops and looks back at the door.*) I can't get over what Murray just said. You know I think they really envy us. (*He clears more stuff from the table.*)

OSCAR: Felix, leave everything alone. I'm not through dirtying-up for the night.

(*He drops some poker chips on the floor.*)

FELIX (*putting stuff on the tray*): But don't you see the irony of it? Don't you see it, Oscar?

OSCAR (*sighs heavily*): Yes, I see it.

FELIX (*clearing the table*): No, you don't. I really don't think you do.

OSCAR: Felix, I'm telling you I see the irony of it.

FELIX (*pauses*): Then tell me. What is it? What's the irony?

OSCAR (*deep breath*): The irony is—unless we can come to some other arrangement, I'm gonna kill you! That's the irony.

FELIX: What's wrong?

(*He crosses back to the tray and puts down all the glasses and other things.*)

OSCAR: There's something wrong with this system, that's what's wrong. I don't think that two single men living alone in a big eight-room apartment should have a cleaner house than my mother.

FELIX (*gets the rest of the dishes, glasses and coasters from the table*): What are you talking about? I'm just going to put the dishes in the sink. You want me to leave them here all night?

OSCAR (*takes his glass, which* FELIX *has put on the tray, and crosses to the bar for a refill*): I don't care if you take them to bed with you. You can play Mr. Clean all you want. But don't make me feel guilty.

FELIX (*takes the tray into the kitchen, leaving the swinging door open*): I'm not asking you to do it, Oscar. You don't have to clean up.

OSCAR (*moves up to the door*): That's why you make me

feel guilty. You're always in my bathroom hanging up my towels. Whenever I smoke you follow me around with an ashtray. Last night I found you washing the kitchen floor, shaking your head and moaning, "Footprints, footprints!"

(He paces around the room.)

FELIX *(comes back to the table with a silent butler. He dumps the ashtrays, then wipes them carefully)*: I didn't say they were yours.

OSCAR *(angrily sits down in the wing chair)*: Well, they *were* mine, damn it. I have feet and they make prints. What do you want me to do, climb across the cabinets?

FELIX: No! I want you to walk on the floor.

OSCAR: I appreciate that! I really do.

FELIX *(crosses to the telephone table and cleans the ashtray there)*: I'm just trying to keep the place livable. I didn't realize I irritated you that much.

OSCAR: I just feel *I* should have the right to decide when my bathtub needs a going over with Dutch Cleanser. It's the democratic way!

FELIX *(puts the silent butler and his rag down on the coffee table and sits down glumly on the couch)*: I was wondering how long it would take.

OSCAR: How long *what* would take?

FELIX: Before I got on your nerves.

OSCAR: I didn't say you get on my nerves.

FELIX: Well, it's the same thing. You said I irritated you.

OSCAR: *You* said you irritated me. *I* didn't say it.

FELIX: Then what *did* you say?

OSCAR: I don't know *what* I said. What's the difference what I said?

FELIX: It doesn't make any difference. I was just repeating what I thought you said.

OSCAR: Well, don't repeat what you *thought* I said. Repeat what I *said!* My God, that's irritating!

FELIX: You see! You *did* say it!

OSCAR: I don't believe this whole conversation.

(He gets up and paces by the table.)

FELIX *(pawing with a cup)*: Oscar, I'm—I'm sorry. I don't know what's wrong with me.

OSCAR *(still pacing)*: And don't pout. If you want to fight, we'll fight. But don't pout! Fighting *I* win. Pouting *you* win!

FELIX: You're right. Everything you say about me is absolutely right.

OSCAR *(really angry, turns to FELIX)*: And don't give in so easily. I'm *not* always right. Sometimes *you're* right.

FELIX: You're right. I do that. I always figure I'm in the wrong.

OSCAR: Only this time you *are* wrong. And I'm right.

FELIX: Oh, leave me alone.

OSCAR: And don't sulk. That's the same as pouting.

FELIX: I know. I know. *(He squeezes his cup with anger.)* Damn me, why can't I do one lousy thing right?

(He suddenly stands up and cocks his arm back, about to hurl the cup angrily against the front door. Then he thinks better of it, puts the cup down and sits.)

OSCAR *(watching this)*: Why didn't you throw it?

FELIX: I almost did. I get so insane with myself sometimes.

OSCAR: Then why don't you throw the cup?

FELIX: Because I'm trying to control myself.

OSCAR: Why?

FELIX: What do you mean, why?

OSCAR: Why do you have to control yourself? You're angry, you felt like throwing the cup, why don't you throw it?

FELIX: Because there's no point to it. I'd still be angry and I'd have a broken cup.

OSCAR: How do you *know* how you'd feel? Maybe you'd feel *wonderful*. Why do you have to control every single thought in your head? Why don't you let loose *once* in your life? Do something that you *feel* like doing—and not what you *think* you're supposed to do. Stop keeping books, Felix. Relax. Get drunk. Get angry. C'mon, *break the goddamned cup!*

(FELIX suddenly stands up and hurls the cup against the door, smashing it to pieces. Then he grabs his shoulder in pain.)

FELIX: Oww! I hurt my arm!

(He sinks down on the couch, massaging his arm.)

OSCAR *(throws up his hands)*: You're hopeless! You're a hopeless mental case!

(He paces around the table.)

FELIX *(grimacing with pain)*: I'm not supposed to throw with that arm. What a stupid thing to do.

OSCAR: Why don't you live in a closet? I'll leave your meals outside the door and slide in the papers. Is that safe enough?

FELIX *(rubbing his arm)*: I used to have bursitis in this arm. I had to give up golf. Do you have a heating pad?

OSCAR: How can you hurt your arm throwing a cup? If it had coffee in it, that's one thing. But an empty cup . . .

(He sits in the wing chair.)

FELIX: All right, cut it out, Oscar. That's the way I am. I get hurt easily. I can't help it.

OSCAR: You're not going to cry, are you? I think all those tears dripping on the arm is what gave you bursitis.

FELIX *(holding his arm)*: I once got it just from combing my hair.

OSCAR (*shaking his head*): A world full of room-mates and I pick myself the Tin Man. (*He sighs.*) Oh, well, I suppose I could have done worse.

FELIX (*moves the rag and silent butler to the bar. Then he takes the chip box from the bar and crosses to the table*): You're darn right, you could have. *A lot worse.*

OSCAR: How?

FELIX: What do you mean, how? How'd you like to live with ten-thumbs Murray or Speed and his complaining? (*He gets down on his knees, picks up the chips and puts them into the box.*) Don't forget I cook and clean and take care of this house. I save us a lot of money, don't I?

OSCAR: Yeah, but then you keep me up all night counting it.

FELIX (*goes to the table and sweeps the chips and cards into the box*): Now wait a minute. We're not always going at each other. We have some fun too, don't we?

OSCAR (*crosses to the couch*): Fun? Felix, getting a clear picture on Channel Two isn't my idea of whoop-ee.

FELIX: What are you talking about?

OSCAR: All right, what do you and I do every night?

(*He takes off his sneakers and drops them on the floor.*)

FELIX: What do we do? You mean after dinner?

OSCAR: That's right. After we've had your halibut steak and the dishes are done and the sink has been brillo'd and the pans have been S.O.S.'d and the leftovers have been Saran-Wrapped—what do we do?

FELIX (*finishes clearing the table and puts everything on top of the bookcase*): Well, we read, we talk . . .

OSCAR (*takes off his pants and throws them on the floor*): No, no. *I* read and *you* talk! I try to work and you talk. I take a bath and you talk. I go to sleep and you talk. We've got your life arranged pretty good but I'm still looking for a little entertainment.

FELIX (*pulling the kitchen chairs away from the table*): What are you saying? That I talk too much?

OSCAR (*sits on the couch*): No, no. I'm not complaining. You have a lot to say. What's worrying me is that I'm beginning to listen.

FELIX (*pulls the table into the alcove*): Oscar, I told you a hundred times, just tell me to shut up. I'm not sensitive.

(*He pulls the love seat down into the room, and centers the table between the windows in the alcove.*)

OSCAR: I don't think you're getting my point. For a husky man, I think I've spent enough evenings discussing tomorrow's menu. The night was made for other things.

FELIX: Like what?

(*He puts two dining chairs neatly on one side of the table.*)

OSCAR: Like unless I get to touch something soft in the next two weeks, I'm in big trouble.

FELIX: You mean women?

(*He puts the two other dining chairs neatly on the other side of the table.*)

OSCAR: If you want to give it a name, all right, women!

FELIX (*picks up the two kitchen chairs and starts toward the landing*): That's funny. I know I haven't even *thought* about women in weeks.

OSCAR: I fail to see the humor.

FELIX (*stops*): No, that's really strange. I mean when Frances and I were happy, I don't think there was a girl on the street I didn't stare at for ten minutes. (*He crosses to the kitchen door and pushes it open with his back.*) I used to take the wrong subway home just following a pair of legs. But since we broke up, I don't even know what a woman looks like.

(*He takes the chairs into the kitchen.*)

OSCAR: Well, either I could go downstairs and buy a couple of magazines—or I could make a phone call.

FELIX (*from the kitchen, as he washes the dishes*): What are you saying?

OSCAR (*crosses to a humidor on a small table and takes out a cigar*): I'm saying let's spend one night talking to someone with higher voices than us.

FELIX: You mean go out on a date?

OSCAR: Yah . . .

FELIX: Oh, well, I—I can't.

OSCAR: Why not?

FELIX: Well, it's all right for you. But I'm still married.

OSCAR (*paces toward the kitchen door*): You can *cheat* until the divorce comes through!

FELIX: It's not that. It's just that I have no—no *feeling* for it. I can't explain it.

OSCAR: Try!

FELIX (*comes to the doorway with a brush and dish in his hand*): Listen, I intend to go out. I get lonely too. But I'm just separated a few weeks. Give me a little time.

(*He goes back to the sink.*)

OSCAR: There isn't any time left. I saw *TV Guide* and there's nothing on this week! (*He paces into and through the kitchen and out the kitchen door onto the landing.*) What am I asking you? All I want to do is have dinner with a couple of girls. You just have to eat and talk. It's not hard. You've eaten and talked before.

FELIX: Why do you need me? Can't you go out yourself?

OSCAR: Because I may want to come back here. And if we walk in and find you washing the windows, it puts a damper on things.

(He sits down.)

FELIX *(pokes his head out of the kitchen)*: I'll take a pill and go to sleep.

(He goes back into the kitchen.)

OSCAR: Why take a pill when you can take a girl?

FELIX *(comes out with an aerosol bomb held high over his head and circles around the room, spraying it)*: Because I'd feel guilty, that's why. Maybe it doesn't make any sense to you, but that's the way I feel.

(He puts the bomb on the bar and takes the silent butler and rag into the kitchen. He places them on the sink and busily begins to wipe the refrigerator.)

OSCAR: Look, for all I care you can take her in the kitchen and make a blueberry pie. But I think it's a lot healthier than sitting up in your bed every night writing Frances' name all through the crossward puzzles. Just for one night, talk to another girl.

FELIX *(pushes the love seat carefully into position and sits, weakening)*: But who would I call? The only single girl I know is my secretary and I don't think she likes me.

OSCAR *(jumps up and crouches next to FELIX)*: Leave that to me. There's two sisters who live in this building. English girls. One's a widow; the other's a divorcée. They're a barrel of laughs.

FELIX: How do you know?

OSCAR: I was trapped in the elevator with them last week. *(Runs to the telephone table, puts the directory on the floor, and gets down on his knees to look for the number.)* I've been meaning to call them but I didn't know which one to take out. This'll be perfect.

FELIX: What do they look like?

OSCAR: Don't worry. Yours is very pretty.

FELIX: I'm not worried. Which one is mine?

OSCAR *(looking in the book)*: The divorcée.

FELIX *(goes to OSCAR)*: Why do I get the divorcée?

OSCAR: I don't care. You want the widow?

(He circles a number on the page with a crayon.)

FELIX *(sitting on the couch)*: No, I don't want the widow. I don't even want the divorcée. I'm just doing this for you.

OSCAR: Look, take whoever you want. When they come in the door, point to the sister of your choice. *(Tears the page out of the book, runs to the bookcase and hangs it up.)* I don't care. I just want to have some laughs.

FELIX: All right. All right.

OSCAR *(crosses to the couch and sits next to FELIX)*: Don't say all right. I want you to promise me you're going to try to have a good time. Please, Felix. It's important. Say, "I promise."

FELIX *(nods)*: I promise.

OSCAR: Again!

FELIX: I promise!

OSCAR: And no writing in the book, a dollar thirty for the cab.

FELIX: No writing in the book.

OSCAR: No one is to be called Frances. It's Gwendolyn and Cecily.

FELIX: No Frances.

OSCAR: No crying, sighing, moaning or groaning.

FELIX: I'll smile from seven to twelve.

OSCAR: And this above all, no talk of the past. Only the present.

FELIX: And the future.

OSCAR: That's the new Felix I've been waiting for. *(Leaps up and prances around.)* Oh, is this going to be a night. Hey, where do you want to go?

FELIX: For what?

OSCAR: For dinner. Where'll we eat?

FELIX: You mean a restaurant? For the four of us? It'll cost a fortune.

OSCAR: We'll cut down on laundry. We won't wear socks on Thursdays.

FELIX: But that's throwing away money. We can't afford it, Oscar.

OSCAR: We have to eat.

FELIX *(moves to OSCAR)*: We'll have dinner here.

OSCAR: *Here?*

FELIX: I'll cook. We'll save thirty, forty dollars.

(He goes to the couch, sits and picks up the phone.)

OSCAR: What kind of a double date is that? You'll be in the kitchen all night.

FELIX: No, I won't. I'll put it up in the afternoon. Once I get my potatoes in, I'll have all the time in the world.

(He starts to dial.)

OSCAR *(pacing back and forth)*: What happened to the new Felix? Who are you calling?

FELIX: Frances. I want to get her recipe for London broil. The girls'll be crazy about it.

(He dials as OSCAR storms off toward his bedroom.)

ACT 2 / SCENE 2

(It is a few days later, about eight o'clock.

No one is on stage. The dining table looks like a page out of House and Garden. *It is set for dinner for four, complete with linen tablecloth, candles and wine glasses. There is a floral centerpiece and flowers about the room, and crackers and dip on the coffee table. There are sounds of activity in the kitchen.*

The front door opens and OSCAR *enters with a bottle of wine in a brown paper bag, his jacket over his arm. He looks about gleefully as he listens to the sounds from the kitchen. He puts the bag on the table and his jacket over a chair.)*

OSCAR *(calls out in a playful mood)*: I'm home, dear! *(He goes into his bedroom, taking off his shirt, and comes skipping out shaving with a cordless razor, with a clean shirt and a tie over his arm. He is joyfully singing as he admires the table.)* Beautiful! Just beautiful! *(He sniffs, obviously catching the aroma from the kitchen.)* Oh, yeah. Something wonderful is going on in that kitchen. *(He rubs his hands gleefully.)* No, sir. There's no doubt about it. I'm the luckiest man on earth. *(He puts the razor into his pocket and begins to put on the shirt.* FELIX *enters slowly from the kitchen. He's wearing a small dish towel as an apron. He has a ladle in one hand. He looks silently and glumly at* OSCAR, *crosses to the armchair and sits.)* I got the wine. *(He takes the bottle out of the bag and puts it on the table.)* Batard Montrachet. Six and a quarter. You don't mind, do you, pussycat? We'll walk to work this week. *(*FELIX *sits glumly and silently.)* Hey, no kidding, Felix, you did a great job. One little suggestion? Let's come down a little with the lights *(He switches off the wall brackets.)*—and up very softly with the music. *(He crosses to the stereo set in the bookcase and picks up some record albums.)* What do you think goes better with London broil, Mancini or Sinatra? *(*FELIX *just stares ahead.)* Felix? What's the matter? *(He puts the albums down.)* Something's wrong. I can tell by your conversation. *(He goes into the bathroom, gets a bottle of after-shave lotion and comes out putting it on.)* All right, Felix, what is it?

FELIX *(without looking at him)*: What is it? Let's start with what time do you think it is?

OSCAR: What time? I don't know. Seven thirty?

FELIX: Seven thirty? Try eight o'clock.

OSCAR *(puts the lotion down on the small table)*: All right, so it's eight o'clock. So?

(He begins to fix his tie.)

FELIX: So? You said you'd be home at seven.

OSCAR: Is that what I said?

FELIX *(nods)*: That's what you said. "I will be home at seven" is what you said.

OSCAR: Okay, I said I'd be home at seven. And it's eight. So what's the problem?

FELIX: If you knew you were going to be late, why didn't you call me?

OSCAR *(pauses while making the knot in his tie)*: I couldn't call you. I was busy.

FELIX: Too busy to pick up a phone? Where were you?

OSCAR: I was in the office, working.

FELIX: Working? Ha!

OSCAR: Yes. Working!

FELIX: I called your office at seven o'clock. You were gone.

OSCAR *(tucking in his shirt.)*: It took me an hour to get home. I couldn't get a cab.

FELIX: Since when do they have cabs in Hannigan's Bar?

OSCAR: Wait a minute. I want to get this down on a tape recorder, because no one'll believe me. You mean now I have to call you if I'm coming home later for dinner?

FELIX *(crosses to* OSCAR*)*: Not *any* dinner. Just the ones I've been slaving over since two o'clock this afternoon—to help save *you* money to pay your wife's alimony.

OSCAR *(controlling himself)*: Felix, this is no time to have a domestic quarrel. We have two girls coming down any minute.

FELIX: You mean you told them to be here at eight o'clock?

OSCAR *(takes his jacket and crosses to the couch, then sits and takes some dip from the coffee table)*: I don't remember what I said. Seven thirty, eight o'clock. What difference does it make?

FELIX *(follows* OSCAR*)*: I'll tell you what difference. You told me they were coming at seven thirty. You were going to be here at seven to help me with the hors d'oeuvres. At seven thirty they arrive and we have cocktails. At eight o'clock we have dinner. It is now eight o'clock. *My London broil is finished!* If we don't eat now the whole damned thing'll be *dried out!*

OSCAR: Oh, God, help me.

FELIX: Never mind helping *you.* Tell Him to save the meat. Because we got nine dollars and thirty-four cents worth drying up in there right now.

OSCAR: Can't you keep it warm?

FELIX *(pacing)*: What do you think I am, the Magic Chef? I'm lucky I got it to come out at eight o'clock. What am I going to do?

OSCAR: I don't know. Keep pouring gravy on it.

FELIX: What gravy?

OSCAR: Don't you have any gravy?

FELIX *(storms over to* OSCAR*)*: Where the hell am I going to get gravy at eight o'clock?

OSCAR *(getting up)*: I thought it comes when you cook the meat.

FELIX *(follows him)*: When you *cook the meat?* You don't know the first thing you're talking about. You have to make gravy. It doesn't come!

OSCAR: You asked my advice, I'm giving it to you.

(He puts on his jacket.)

FELIX: Advice? (*He waves the ladle in his face.*) You didn't know where the kitchen was till I came here and showed you.

OSCAR: You wanna talk to me, put down the spoon.

FELIX (*exploding in rage, again waving the ladle in his face*): Spoon? You dumb ignoramus. It's a ladle. You don't even know it's a ladle.

OSCAR: All right, Felix, get a hold of yourself.

FELIX (*pulls himself together and sits on the love seat*): You think it's so easy? Go on. The kitchen's all yours. Go make a London broil for four people who come a half hour late.

OSCAR (*to no one in particular*): Listen to me. I'm arguing with him over gravy.

(*The bell rings.*)

FELIX (*jumps up*): Well, they're here. Our dinner guests. I'll get a saw and cut the meat.

(*He starts for the kitchen.*)

OSCAR (*stopping him*): Stay where you are!

FELIX: I'm not taking the blame for this dinner.

OSCAR: Who's blaming you? Who even *cares* about the dinner?

FELIX (*moves to* OSCAR): *I* care. I take *pride* in what I do. And you're going to explain to them exactly what happened.

OSCAR: All right, you can take a Polaroid picture of me coming in at eight o'clock! Now take off that stupid apron because I'm opening the door.

(*He rips the towel off* FELIX *and goes to the door.*)

FELIX (*takes his jacket from a dining chair and puts it on*): I just want to get one thing clear. This is the last time I ever cook for you. Because people like you don't even appreciate a decent meal. That's why they have TV dinners.

OSCAR: You through?

FELIX: I'm through!

OSCAR: Then smile. (OSCAR *smiles and opens the door. The girls poke their heads through the door. They are in their young thirties and somewhat attractive. They are undoubtedly British.*) Well, hello.

GWENDOLYN (*to* OSCAR): Hallo!

CECILY (*to* OSCAR): Hallo.

GWENDOLYN: I do hope we're not late.

OSCAR: No, no. You timed it perfectly. Come on in. (*He points to them as they enter.*) Er, Felix, I'd like you to meet two very good friends of mine, Gwendolyn and Cecily . . .

CECILY (*pointing out his mistake*): Cecily and Gwendolyn.

OSCAR: Oh, yes, Cecily and Gwendolyn . . . er (*Trying to remember their last name.*) Er . . . Don't tell me. Robin? No, no. Cardinal?

GWENDOLYN: Wrong both times. It's Pigeon!

OSCAR: Pigeon. Right. Cecily and Gwendolyn Pigeon.

GWENDOLYN (*to* FELIX): You don't spell it like Walter Pidgeon. You spell it like "Coo-Coo" Pigeon.

OSCAR: We'll remember that if it comes up. Cecily and Gwendolyn, I'd like you to meet my roommate, and our chef for the evening, Felix Ungar.

CECILY (*holding her hand out*): Heh d'yew dew?

FELIX (*moving to her and shaking her hand*): How do you do?

GWENDOLYN (*holding her hand out*): Heh d'yew dew?

FELIX (*stepping up on the landing and shaking her hand*): How do you do?

(*This puts him nose to nose with* OSCAR, *and there is an awkward pause as they look at each other.*)

OSCAR: Well, we did that beautifully. Why don't we sit down and make ourselves comfortable?

(FELIX *steps aside and ushers the girls down into the room. There is ad libbing and a bit of confusion and milling about as they all squeeze between the armchair and the couch, and the* PIGEONS *finally seat themselves on the couch.* OSCAR *sits in the armchair, and* FELIX *sneaks past him to the love seat. Finally all have settled down.*)

CECILY: This is ever so nice, isn't it, Gwen?

GWENDOLYN (*looking around*): Lovely. And much nicer than our flat. Do you have help?

OSCAR: Er, yes. I have a man who comes in every night.

CECILY: Aren't you the lucky one?

(CECILY, GWENDOLYN *and* OSCAR *all laugh at her joke.* OSCAR *looks over at* FELIX *but there is no response.*)

OSCAR (*rubs his hands together*): Well, isn't this nice? I was telling Felix yesterday about how we happened to meet.

GWENDOLYN: Oh? Who's Felix?

OSCAR (*a little embarrassed, he points to* FELIX): He is!

GWENDOLYN: Oh, yes, of course, I'm so sorry.

(FELIX *nods that it's all right.*)

CECILY: You know it happened to us again this morning.

OSCAR: What did?

GWENDOLYN: Stuck in the elevator again.

OSCAR: Really? Just the two of you?

CECILY: And poor old Mr. Kessler from the third floor. We were in there half an hour.

OSCAR: No kidding? What happened?

GWENDOLYN: Nothing much, I'm afraid.

(CECILY *and* GWENDOLYN *both laugh at her latest joke, joined by* OSCAR. *He once again looks over at* FELIX, *but there is no response.*)

OSCAR (*rubs his hands again*): Well, this really is nice.

CECILY: And ever so much cooler than our place.

GWENDOLYN: It's like equatorial Africa on our side of the building.

CECILY: Last night it was so bad Gwen and I sat there in nature's own cooling ourselves in front of the open fridge. Can you imagine such a thing?

OSCAR: Er, I'm working on it.

GWENDOLYN: Actually, it's impossible to get a night's sleep. Cec and I really don't know what to do.

OSCAR: Why don't you sleep with an air conditioner?

GWENDOLYN: We haven't got one.

OSCAR: I know. But we have.

GWENDOLYN: Oh, you! I told you about that one, didn't I, Cec?

FELIX: They say it may rain Friday.

(They all stare at FELIX.*)*

GWENDOLYN: Oh?

CECILY: That should cool things off a bit.

OSCAR: I wouldn't be surprised.

FELIX: Although sometimes it gets hotter after it rains.

GWENDOLYN: Yes, it does, doesn't it?

(They continue to stare at FELIX.*)*

FELIX *(jumps up and picking up the ladle, starts for the kitchen)*: Dinner is served!

OSCAR *(stopping him)*: No, it isn't!

FELIX: Yes, it is!

OSCAR: No, it isn't! I'm sure the girls would like a cocktail first. *(to the girls)* Wouldn't you, girls?

GWENDOLYN: Well, I wouldn't put up a struggle.

OSCAR: There you are. *(to* CECILY*)* What would you like?

CECILY: Oh, I really don't know. *(to* OSCAR*)* What have you got?

FELIX: London broil.

OSCAR *(to* FELIX*)*: She means a drink. *(to* CECILY*)* We have everything. And what we don't have, I mix in the medicine cabinet. What'll it be?

(He crouches next to her.)

CECILY: Oh, a double vodka.

GWENDOLYN: Cecily, not before dinner.

CECILY *(to the men)*: My sister. She watches over me like a mother hen. *(to* OSCAR*)* Make it a *small* double vodka.

OSCAR: A small double vodka! And for the beautiful mother hen?

GWENDOLYN: Oh, I'd like something cool. I think I would like to have a double Drambuie with some crushed ice, unless you don't have the crushed ice.

OSCAR: I was up all night with a sledge hammer. I shall return!

(He goes to the bar and gets bottles of vodka and Drambuie.)

FELIX *(going to him)*: Where are you going?

OSCAR: To get the refreshments.

FELIX *(starting to panic)*: Inside? What'll *I* do?

OSCAR: You can finish the weather report.

(He exits into the kitchen.)

FELIX *(calls after him)*: Don't forget to look at my meat! *(He turns and faces the girls. He crosses to a chair and sits. He crosses his legs nonchalantly. But he is ill at ease and he crosses them again. He is becoming aware of the silence and he can no longer get away with just smiling.)* Er, Oscar tells me you're sisters.

CECILY: Yes. That's right.

(She looks at GWENDOLYN.*)*

FELIX: From England.

GWENDOLYN: Yes. That's right.

(She looks at CECILY.*)*

FELIX: I see. *(Silence. Then, his little joke.)* We're not brothers.

CECILY: Yes. We know.

FELIX: Although I am a brother. I have a brother who's a doctor. He lives in Buffalo. That's upstate in New York.

GWENDOLYN *(taking a cigarette from her purse)*: Yes, we know.

FELIX: You know my brother?

GWENDOLYN: No. We know that Buffalo is upstate in New York.

FELIX: Oh!

(He gets up, takes a cigarette lighter from the side table and moves to light GWENDOLYN's *cigarette.)*

CECILY: We've been there! Have you?

FELIX: No! Is it nice?

CECILY: Lovely.

*(*FELIX *closes the lighter on* GWENDOLYN's *cigarette and turns to go back to his chair, taking the cigarette, now caught in the lighter, with him. He notices the cigarette and hastily gives it back to* GWENDOLYN, *stopping to light it once again. He puts the lighter back on the table and sits down nervously. There is a pause.)*

FELIX: Isn't that interesting? How long have you been in the United States of America?

CECILY: Almost four years now.

FELIX *(nods)*: Uh huh. Just visiting?

GWENDOLYN *(looks at* CECILY*)*: No! We live here.

FELIX: And you work here too, do you?

CECILY: Yes. We're secretaries for Slenderama.

GWENDOLYN: You know. The health club.

CECILY: People bring us their bodies and we do wonderful things with them.

GWENDOLYN: Actually, if you're interested, we can get you ten per cent off.

CECILY: Off the price, not off your body.

FELIX: Yes, I see. *(He laughs. They all laugh. Suddenly he shouts toward the kitchen.)* Oscar, where's the drinks?

OSCAR *(offstage)*: Coming! Coming!

CECILY: What field of endeavor are you engaged in?

FELIX: I write the news for CBS.

CECILY: Oh! Fascinating!

GWENDOLYN: Where do you get your ideas from?

FELIX *(he looks at her as though she's a Martian)*: From the news.

GWENDOLYN: Oh, yes, of course. Silly me . . .

CECILY: Maybe you can mention Gwen and I in one of your news reports.

FELIX: Well, if you do something spectacular, maybe I will.

CECILY: Oh, we've done spectacular things but I don't think we'd want it spread all over the telly, do you, Gwen?

(They both laugh.)

FELIX *(he laughs too, then cries out almost for help)*: Oscar!

OSCAR *(offstage)*: Yeah, yeah!

FELIX *(to the girls)*: It's such a large apartment, sometimes you have to shout.

GWENDOLYN: Just you two baches have here?

FELIX: Baches? Oh, bachelors! We're not bachelors. We're divorced. That is, Oscar's divorced. I'm *getting* divorced.

CECILY: Oh. Small world. We've cut the dinghy loose too, as they say.

GWENDOLYN: Well, you couldn't have a *better* matched foursome, could you?

FELIX *(smiles weakly)*: No, I suppose not.

GWENDOLYN: Although technically I'm a widow. I was divorcing my husband, but he died before the final papers came through.

FELIX: Oh, I'm awfully sorry. *(Sighs.)* It's a terrible thing, isn't it? Divorce.

GWENDOLYN: It can be—if you haven't got the right solicitor.

CECILY: That's true. Sometimes they can drag it out for months. I was lucky. Snip, cut and I was free.

FELIX: I mean it's terrible what it can do to people. After all, what is divorce? It's taking two happy people and tearing their lives completely apart. It's inhuman, don't you think so?

CECILY: Yes, it can be an awful bother.

GWENDOLYN: But of course, that's all water under the bridge now, eh? Er, I'm terribly sorry, but I think I've forgotten your name.

FELIX: Felix.

GWENDOLYN: Oh, yes. Felix.

CECILY: Like the cat.

(FELIX takes his wallet from his jacket pocket.)

GWENDOLYN: Well, the Pigeons will have to beware of the cat, won't they?

(She laughs.)

CECILY *(nibbles on a nut from the dish)*: Mmm, cashews. Lovely.

FELIX *(takes a snapshot out of his wallet)*: This is the worst part of breaking up.

(He hands the picture to CECILY.)

CECILY *(looks at it)*: Childhood sweethearts, were you?

FELIX: No, no. That's my little boy and girl. *(CECILY gives the picture to GWENDOLYN, takes a pair of glasses from her purse and puts them on.)* He's seven, she's five.

CECILY *(looks again)*: Oh! Sweet.

FELIX: They live with their mother.

GWENDOLYN: I imagine you must miss them terribly.

FELIX *(takes back the picture and looks at it longingly)*: I can't stand being away from them. *(Shrugs.)* But—that's what happens with divorce.

CECILY: When do you get to see them?

FELIX: Every night. I stop there on my way home! Then I take them on the weekends, and I get them on holidays and July and August.

CECILY: Oh! Well, when is it that you miss them?

FELIX: Whenever I'm not there. If they didn't have to go to school so early, I'd go over and make them breakfast. They love my French toast.

GWENDOLYN: You're certainly a devoted father.

FELIX: It's Frances who's the wonderful one.

CECILY: She's the little girl?

FELIX: No, She's the mother. My wife.

GWENDOLYN: The one you're divorcing?

FELIX *(nods)*: Mm! She's done a terrific job bringing them up. They always look so nice. They're so polite. Speak beautifully. Never, "Yeah." Always, "Yes." They're such good kids. And she did it all. She's the kind of woman who— Ah, what am I saying? You don't want to hear any of this.

(He puts the picture back in his wallet.)

CECILY: Nonsense. You have a right to be proud. You have two beautiful children and a wonderful ex-wife.

FELIX *(containing his emotions)*: I know. I know. *(He hands CECILY another snapshot.)* That's her, Frances.

GWENDOLYN *(looking at the picture)*: Oh, she's pretty. Isn't she pretty, Cecy?

CECILY: Oh, yes, Pretty. A pretty girl. Very pretty.

FELIX *(takes the picture back)*: Thank you. *(Shows them another snapshot)*: Isn't this nice?

GWENDOLYN *(looks)*: There's no one in the picture.

FELIX: I know. It's a picture of our living room. We had a beautiful apartment.

GWENDOLYN: Oh, yes. Pretty. Very pretty.

CECILY: Those are lovely lamps.

FELIX: Thank you! *(Takes the picture)* We bought them in Mexico on our honeymoon. *(He looks at the picture again.)* I used to love to come home at night. *(He's beginning to break.)* That was my whole life. My wife, my kids—and my apartment.

(He breaks down and sobs.)

CECILY: Does she have the lamp now too?

FELIX *(nods)*: I gave her everything. It'll never be like that again. Never! I—I— *(He turns his head away.)* I'm sorry. *(He takes out a handkerchief and dabs his eyes.* GWENDOLYN *and* CECILY *look at each other with compassion.)* Please forgive me. I didn't mean to get emotional. *(Trying to pull himself together, he picks up a bowl from the side table and offers it to the girls.)* Would you like some potato chips?

(CECILY takes the bowl.)

GWENDOLYN: You mustn't be ashamed. I think it's a rare quality in a man to be able to cry.

FELIX *(puts a hand over his eyes)*: Please. Let's not talk about it.

CECILY: I think it's sweet. Terribly, terribly sweet.

(She takes a potato chip.)

FELIX: You're just making it worse.

GWENDOLYN *(teary-eyed)*: It's so refreshing to hear a man speak so highly of the woman he's divorcing! Oh, dear. *(She takes out her handkerchief.)* Now you've got me thinking about poor Sydney.

CECILY: Oh, Gwen. Please don't.

(She puts the bowl down.)

GWENDOLYN: It was a good marriage at first. Everyone said so. Didn't they, Cecily? Not like you and George.

CECILY *(the past returns as she comforts* GWENDOLYN*)*: That's right. George and I were never happy. Not for one single, solitary day.

(She remembers her unhappiness, grabs her handkerchief and dabs her eyes. All three are now sitting with handkerchiefs at their eyes.)

FELIX: Isn't this ridiculous?

GWENDOLYN: I don't know what brought this on. I was feeling so good a few minutes ago.

CECILY: I haven't cried since I was fourteen.

FELIX: Just let it pour out. It'll make you feel much better. I always do.

GWENDOLYN: Oh, dear; oh, dear; oh, dear.

(All three sit sobbing into their handkercheifs. Suddenly OSCAR *bursts happily into the room with a tray full of drinks. He is all smiles.)*

OSCAR *(like a corny M.C.)*: Is ev-rybuddy happy? *(Then he sees the maudlin scene.* FELIX *and the girls quickly try to pull themselves together.)* What the hell happened?

FELIX: Nothing! Nothing!

(He quickly puts his handkerchief away.)

OSCAR: What do you mean, nothing? I'm gone three minutes and I walk into a funeral parlor. What did you say to them?

FELIX: I didn't say anything. Don't start in again, Oscar.

OSCAR: I can't leave you alone for five seconds. Well, if you really want to cry, go inside and look at your London broil.

FELIX *(he rushes madly into the kitchen)*: Oh, my gosh! Why didn't you call me? I told you to call me.

OSCAR *(giving a drink to* CECILY*)*: I'm sorry, girls. I forgot to warn you about Felix. He's a walking soap opera.

GWENDOLYN: I think he's the dearest thing I ever met.

CECILY *(taking the glass)*: He's so sensitive. So fragile. I just want to bundle him up in my arms and take care of him.

OSCAR *(holds out* GWENDOLYN'S *drink. At this, he puts it back down on the tray and takes a swallow from his own drink)*: Well, I think when he comes out of that kitchen you may have to.

(Sure enough, FELIX *comes out of the kitchen onto the landing looking like a wounded puppy. With a protective kitchen glove, he holds a pan with the exposed London broil. Black is the color of his true love.)*

FELIX *(very calmly)*: I'm going down to the delicatessen. I'll be right back.

OSCAR *(going to him)*: Wait a minute. Maybe it's not so bad. Let's see it.

FELIX *(shows him)*: Here! Look! Nine dollars and thirty-four cents worth of ashes! *(Pulls the pan away. To the girls)* I'll get some corned beef sandwiches.

OSCAR *(trying to get a look at it)*: Give it to me! Maybe we can save some of it.

FELIX *(holding it away from* OSCAR*)*: There's nothing to save. It's all black meat. Nobody likes black meat!

OSCAR: Can't I even look at it?

FELIX: No, you can't look at it!

OSCAR: Why can't I look at it?

FELIX: If you looked at your watch before, you wouldn't have to look at the black meat now! Leave it alone!

(He turns to go back into the kitchen.)

GWENDOLYN *(going to him)*: Felix! Can *we* look at it?

CECILY *(turning to him, kneeling on the couch)*: Please?

(FELIX *stops in the kitchen doorway. He hesitates for a moment. He likes them. Then he turns and wordlessly holds the pan out to them,* GWENDOLYN *and* CECILY *inspect it wordlessly, and then turn away sobbing quietly.* (To OSCAR) How about Chinese food?

OSCAR: A wonderful idea.

GWENDOLYN: I've got a better idea. Why don't we just make pot luck in the kitchen?

OSCAR: A *much* better idea.

FELIX: I used up all the pots!

(*He crosses to the love seat and sits, still holding the pan.*)

CECILY: Well, then we can eat up in *our* place. We have tons of Horn and Hardart's.

OSCAR (*gleefully*): That's the best idea I ever heard.

GWENDOLYN: Of course it's awfully hot up there. You'll have to take off your jackets.

OSCAR (*smiling*): We can always open up a refrigerator.

CECILY (*gets her purse from the couch*): Give us five minutes to get into our cooking things.

(GWENDOLYN *gets her purse from the couch.*)

OSCAR: Can't you make it four? I'm suddenly starving to death.

(*The girls are crossing to the door.*)

GWENDOLYN: Don't forget the wine.

OSCAR: How could I forget the wine?

CECILY: And a corkscrew.

OSCAR: *And* a corkscrew.

GWENDOLYN: And Felix.

OSCAR: No, I won't forget Felix.

CECILY: Ta, ta!

OSCAR: Ta, ta!

GWENDOLYN: Ta, ta!

(*The girls exit.*)

OSCAR (*throws a kiss at the closed door*): You bet your sweet little crumpets, "Ta, Ta!" (*He wheels around beaming and quickly gathers up the corkscrew from the bar, and picks up the wine and the records.*) Felix, I love you. You've just overcooked us into one hell of a night. Come on, get the ice bucket. Ready or not, here we come.

(*He runs to the door.*)

FELIX (*sitting motionless*): I'm not going!

OSCAR: What?

FELIX: I said I'm not going.

OSCAR (*crossing to* FELIX): Are you out of your mind? Do you know what's waiting for us up there? You've just been invited to spend the evening in a two-bedroom hothouse with the Coo-Coo Pigeon Sisters! What do you mean you're not going?

FELIX: I don't know how to talk to them. I don't know

what to say. I already told them about my brother in Buffalo. I've used up my conversation.

OSCAR: Felix, they're crazy about you. They told me! One of them wants to wrap you up and make a bundle out of you. You're doing better than I am! Get the ice bucket.

(*He starts for the door.*)

FELIX: Don't you understand? I cried! I cried in front of two women.

OSCAR (*stops*): And they *loved* it! I'm thinking of getting hysterical. (*Goes to the door.*) Will you get the ice bucket?

FELIX: But why did I cry? Because I felt guilty. Emotionally I'm still tied to Frances and the kids.

OSCAR: Well, untie the knot for tonight, will you!

FELIX: I don't want to discuss it any more. (*Starts for the kitchen.*) I'm going to scrub the pots and wash my hair.

(*He goes into the kitchen and puts the pan in the sink.*)

OSCAR (*yelling*): Your greasy pots and your greasy hair can wait. You're coming upstairs with me!

FELIX (*in the kitchen*): I'm not! *I'm not!*

OSCAR: What am I going to do with two girls? Felix, don't do this to me. I'll never forgive you!

FELIX: I'm not going!

OSCAR (*screams*): All right, damn you, I'll go without you! (*And he storms out the door and slams it. Then it opens and he comes in again.*) Are you coming?

FELIX (*comes out of the kitchen looking at a magazine*): No.

OSCAR: You mean you're not going to make any effort to change? This is the person you're going to be—until the day you die?

FELIX (*sitting on the couch*): We are what we are.

OSCAR (*nods, then crosses to a window, pulls back the drapes and opens the window wide. Then he starts back to the door*): It's twelve floors, not eleven.

(*He walks out as* FELIX *stares at the open windows.*)

ACT 3

(*The next evening about 7:30 P.M. The room is once again set up for the poker game, with the dining table pulled down, the chairs set about it, and the love seat moved back beneath the windows in the alcove.* FELIX *appears from the bedroom with a vacuum cleaner. He is doing a thorough job on the rug. As he vacuums around the table, the door opens and* OSCAR *comes in wearing a summer hat and carrying a newspaper. He glares at* FELIX, *who is still vacuuming, and shakes his head contemptuously. He crosses behind* FELIX, *leaving his hat on the side table next to the armchair, and goes into his bedroom.* FELIX *is not aware of his presence. Then suddenly the power stops on the vacuum, as* OSCAR *has obviously pulled the plug in the bedroom.* FELIX *tries switching the button on and off a few times, then turns to go back into the bedroom. He stops and realizes what's happened as* OSCAR *comes back into the room.* OSCAR *takes a cigar out of his pocket and as he crosses in front of* FELIX *to the couch, he unwraps it and drops the wrappings carelessly on the floor. He then steps up on the couch and walks back and forth mashing down the pillows. Stepping down, he plants one foot on the armchair and then sits on the couch, taking a wooden match from the coffee table and striking it on the table to light his cigar. He flips the used match onto the rug and settles back to read his newspaper.* FELIX *has watched this all in silence, and now carefully picks up the cigar wrappings and the match and drops them into* OSCAR's *hat. He then dusts his hands and takes the vacuum cleaner into the kitchen, pulling the cord in after him.* OSCAR *takes the wrappings from the hat and puts them in the butt-filled ashtray on the coffee table. Then he takes the ashtray and dumps it on the floor. As he once more settles down with his newspaper,* FELIX *comes out of the kitchen carrying a tray with a steaming dish of spaghetti. As he crosses behind* OSCAR *to the table, he indicates that it smells delicious and passes it close to* OSCAR *to make sure* OSCAR *smells the fantastic dish he's missing. As* FELIX *sits and begins to eat,* OSCAR *takes a can of aerosol spray from the bar, and circling the table, sprays all around* FELIX, *then puts the can down next to him and goes back to his newspaper.)*

FELIX *(pushing the spaghetti away)*: All right, how much longer is this gonna go on?

OSCAR *(reading his paper)*: Are you talking to me?

FELIX: That's right, I'm talking to you.

OSCAR: What do you want to know?

FELIX: I want to know if you're going to spend the rest of your life not talking to me. Because if you are, I'm going to buy a radio. *(No reply.)* Well? *(No reply.)* I see. You're not going to talk to me. *(No reply.)* All right. Two can play at this game. *(Pause)* If you're not going to talk to me, I'm not going to talk to you. *(No reply.)* I can act childish too, you know. *(No reply.)* I can go on without talking just as long as you can.

OSCAR: Then why the hell don't you shut up?

FELIX: Are you talking to me?

OSCAR: You had your chance to talk last night. I begged you to come upstairs with me. From now on I never want to hear a word from that shampooed head as long as you live. That's a warning, Felix.

FELIX *(stares at him)*: I stand warned. Over and out!

OSCAR *(gets up, takes a key out of his pocket and slams it on the table)*: There's a key to the back door. If you stick to the hallway and your room, you won't get hurt.

(He sits back down on the couch.)

FELIX: I don't think I gather the entire meaning of that remark.

OSCAR: Then I'll explain it to you. Stay out of my way.

FELIX *(picks up the key and moves to the couch)*: I think you're serious. I think you're really serious. Are you serious?

OSCAR: This is my apartment. Everything in my apartment is mine. The only thing here that's yours is you. Just stay in your room and speak softly.

FELIX: Yeah, you're serious. Well, let me remind you that I pay half the rent and I'll go into any room I want.

(He gets up angrily and starts toward the hallway.)

OSCAR: Where are you going?

FELIX: I'm going to walk around your bedroom.

OSCAR *(slams down his newspaper)*: You stay out of there.

FELIX *(steaming)*: Don't tell me where to go. I pay a hundred and twenty dollars a month.

OSCAR: That was off-season. Starting tomorrow the rates are twelve dollars a day.

FELIX: All right. *(He takes some bills out of his pocket and slams them down on the table.)* There you are. I'm paid up for today. Now I'm going to walk in your bedroom.

(He starts to storm off.)

OSCAR: Stay out of there! Stay out of my room!

(He chases after him, FELIX *dodges around the table as* OSCAR *blocks the hallway.)*

FELIX *(backing away, keeping the table between them)*: Watch yourself! Just watch yourself, Oscar!

OSCAR *(with a pointing finger)*: I'm warning you. You want to live here, I don't want to see you, I don't want to hear you and I don't want to smell your cooking. Now get this spaghetti off my poker table.

FELIX: Ha! Ha, ha!

OSCAR: What the hell's so funny?

FELIX: It's not spaghetti. It's linguini!

(OSCAR picks up the plate of linguini, crosses to the doorway and hurls it into the kitchen.)

OSCAR: Now it's garbage!

(He paces by the couch.)

FELIX *(looks at OSCAR unbelievingly: what an insane thing to do)*: You are crazy! I'm a neurotic nut but *you are crazy!*

OSCAR: *I'm* crazy, heh? That's really funny coming from a fruitcake like you.

FELIX *(goes to the kitchen door and looks in at the mess. Turns back to OSCAR)*: I'm not cleaning that up.

OSCAR: Is that a promise?

FELIX: Did you hear what I said? I'm not cleaning it up. It's your mess. (*Looking into the kitchen again.*) Look at it. Hanging all over the walls.

OSCAR (*crosses to the landing and looks in the kitchen door*): I like it.

(*He closes the door and paces around.*)

FELIX (*fumes*): You'd just let it lie there, wouldn't you? Until it turns hard and brown and . . . Yich, it's disgusting. I'm cleaning it up.

(*He goes into the kitchen. OSCAR chases after him. There is the sound of a struggle and falling pots.*)

OSCAR: *Leave it alone!* You touch one strand of that linguini—and I'm gonna punch you right in your sinuses.

FELIX (*dashes out of the kitchen with OSCAR in pursuit. He stops and tries to calm OSCAR down*): Oscar, I'd like you to take a couple of phenobarbital.

OSCAR (*points*): Go to your room! Did you hear what I said? *Go to your room!*

FELIX: All right, let's everybody just settle down, heh?

(*He puts his hand on OSCAR's shoulder to calm him but OSCAR pulls away violently from his touch.*)

OSCAR: If you want to live through this night, you'd better tie me up and lock your doors and windows.

FELIX (*sits at the table with a great pretense of calm*): All right, Oscar, I'd like to know what's happened.

OSCAR (*moves toward him*): What's *happened?*

FELIX (*hurriedly slides over to the next chair*): That's right, Something must have caused you to go off the deep end like this. What is it? Something I said? Something I did? Heh? What?

OSCAR (*pacing*): It's nothing you said. It's nothing you did. It's *you!*

FELIX: I see. Well, that's plain enough.

OSCAR: I could make it plainer but I don't want to hurt you.

FELIX: What is it, the cooking? The cleaning? The crying?

OSCAR (*moving toward him*): I'll tell you exactly what it is. It's the cooking, cleaning and crying. It's the talking in your sleep, it's the moose calls that open your ears at two o'clock in the morning. I can't take it any more, Felix. I'm crackin' up. Everything you do irritates me. And when you're not here, the things I know you're gonna do when you come in irritate me. You leave me little notes on my pillow. I told you a hundred times, I can't stand little notes on my pillow. "We're all out of Corn Flakes. F.U." It took me three hours to figure out that F.U. was Felix Ungar. It's not your fault, Felix. It's a rotten combination.

FELIX: I get the picture.

OSCAR: That's just the frame. The picture I haven't even painted yet. I got a typewritten list in my office of the "Ten Most Aggravating Things You Do That Drive Me Berserk." But last night was the topper. Oh, that was the topper. Oh, that was the ever-loving lulu of all times.

FELIX: What are you talking about, the London broil?

OSCAR: No, not the London broil. I'm talking about those two lamb chops. (*He points upstairs.*) I had it all set up with that English Betty Boop and her sister, and I wind up drinking tea all night and telling them *your* life story.

FELIX (*jumps up*): Oho! so *that's* what's bothering you. That I loused up your evening!

OSCAR: After the mood you put them in, I'm surprised they didn't go out to Rockaway and swim back to England.

FELIX: Don't blame me. I warned you not to make the date in the first place.

(*He makes his point by shaking his finger in OSCAR's face.*)

OSCAR: Don't point that finger at me unless you intend to use it!

FELIX (*moves in nose to nose with OSCAR*): All right, Oscar, get off my back. Get off! Off!

(*Startled by his own actions, FELIX jumps back from OSCAR, warily circles him, crosses to the couch and sits.*)

OSCAR: What's this? A display of temper? I haven't seen you really angry since the day I dropped my cigar in your pancake batter.

(*He starts toward the hallway.*)

FELIX (*threateningly*): Oscar, you're asking to hear something I don't want to say. But if I say it, I think you'd better hear it.

OSCAR (*comes back to the table, places both hands on it and leans toward FELIX*): If you've got anything on your chest besides your chin, you'd better get it off.

FELIX (*strides to the table, places both hands on it and leans toward OSCAR. They are nose to nose*): All right, I warned you. You're a wonderful guy, Oscar. You've done everything for me. If it weren't for you, I don't know what would have happened to me. You took me in here, gave me a place to live and something to live for. I'll never forget you for that. You're tops with me, Oscar.

OSCAR (*motionless*): If I've just been told off, I think I may have missed it.

FELIX: It's coming now! You're also one of the biggest slobs in the world.

OSCAR: I see.

FELIX: And completely unreliable.

OSCAR: Finished?

FELIX: Undependable.

OSCAR: Is that it?

FELIX: And irresponsible.

OSCAR: Keep going. I think you're hot.

FELIX: That's it. I'm finished. *Now* you've been told off. How do you like that?

(He crosses to the couch.)

OSCAR *(straightening up)*: Good. Because now I'm going to tell *you* off. For six months I lived alone in this apartment. All alone in eight rooms. I was dejected, despondent and disgusted. Then *you* moved in—my dearest and closest friend. And after three weeks of close, personal contact—I am about to have a nervous breakdown! Do me a favor. Move into the kitchen. Live with your pots, your pans, your ladle and your meat thermometer. When you want to come out, ring a bell and I'll run into the bedroom. *(Almost breaking down.)* I'm asking you nicely, Felix—as a friend. Stay out of my way!

(And he goes into the bedroom.)

FELIX *(is hurt by this, then remembers something. He calls after him)*: Walk on the paper, will you? The floors are wet. (OSCAR *comes out of the door. He is glaring maniacally, as he slowly strides back down the hallway.* FELIX *quickly puts the couch between him and* OSCAR.) Awright, keep away. Keep away from me.

OSCAR *(chasing him around the couch)*: Come on. Let me get in one shot. You pick it. Head, stomach or kidneys.

FELIX *(dodging about the room)*: You're gonna find yourself in one sweet law suit, Oscar.

OSCAR: It's no use running, Felix. There's only eight rooms and I know the short cuts.

(They are now poised at opposite ends of the couch. FELIX *picks up a lamp for protection.)*

FELIX: Is this how you settle your problems, Oscar? Like an animal?

OSCAR: All right. You wanna see how I settle my problems. I'll show you. *(Storms off into* FELIX's *bedroom. There is the sound of falling objects and he returns with a suitcase.)* I'll show you how I settle them. *(Throws the suitcase on the table.)* There! That's how I settle them!

FELIX *(bewildered, looks at the suitcase)*: Where are you going?

OSCAR *(exploding)*: Not me, you idiot! You. You're the one who's going. I want you out of here. Now! Tonight!

(He opens the suitcase.)

FELIX: What are you talking about?

OSCAR: It's all over, Felix. The whole marriage. We're getting an annulment! Don't you understand? I don't want to live with you any more. I want you to pack your things, tie it up with your Saran Wrap and get out of here.

FELIX: You mean actually move out?

OSCAR: Actually, physically and immediately. I don't care where you go. Move into the Museum of Natural History. *(Goes into the kitchen. There is the crash of falling pots and pans.)* I'm sure you'll be very comfortable there. You can dust around the Egyptian mummies to your heart's content. But I'm a human, living person. *(Comes out with a stack of cooking utensils which he throws into the open suitcase.)* All I want is my freedom. Is that too much to ask for? *(Closes it.)* There, you're all packed.

FELIX: You know, I've got a good mind to really leave.

OSCAR *(looking to the heavens)*: Why doesn't he ever listen to what I say? Why doesn't he hear me? I know I'm talking—I recognize my voice.

FELIX *(indignantly)*: Because if you really want me to go, I'll go.

OSCAR: Then go. I want you to go, so go. When are you going?

FELIX: When am I going, huh? Boy, you're in a bigger hurry than Frances was.

OSCAR: Take as much time as she gave you. I want you to follow your usual routine.

FELIX: In other words, you're throwing me out.

OSCAR: Not in other words. Those are the perfect ones. *(Picks up the suitcase and holds it out to* FELIX.) I am throwing you out.

FELIX: All right, I just wanted to get the record straight. Let it be on *your* conscience.

(He goes into his bedroom.)

OSCAR: What? What? *(Follows him to the bedroom doorway.)* Let what be on my conscience?

FELIX *(comes out putting on his jacket and passes by* OSCAR): That you're throwing me out. *(Stops and turns back to him.)* I'm perfectly willing to stay and clear the air of our differences. But you refuse, right?

OSCAR *(still holding the suitcase)*: Right! I'm sick and tired of you clearing the air. That's why I want you to leave!

FELIX: Okay, as long as I heard you say the words, "Get out of the house." Fine. But remember, what happens to me is your responsibility. Let it be on *your* head.

(He crosses to the door.)

OSCAR *(follows him to the door and screams)*: Wait a minute, damn it! Why can't you be thrown out like a decent human being? Why do you have to say things like, "Let it be on your head"? I don't want it on my head. I just want you out of the house.

FELIX: What's the matter, Oscar? Can't cope with a little guilt feelings?

OSCAR (*pounding the railing in frustration*): Damn you. I've been looking forward to throwing you out all day long, and now you even take the pleasure out of that.

FELIX: Forgive me for spoiling your fun. I'm leaving now—according to your wishes and desires.

(*He starts to open the door*)

OSCAR (*pushes by* FELIX *and slams the door shut. He stands between* FELIX *and the door*): You're not leaving here until you take it back.

FELIX: Take what back?

OSCAR: "Let it be on your head." What the hell is that, the Curse of the Cat People?

FELIX: Get out of my way, please.

OSCAR: Is this how you left that night with Frances? No wonder she wanted to have the room repainted right away. (*Points to* FELIX's *bedroom*) I'm gonna have yours dipped in bronze.

FELIX (*sits on the back of the couch with his back to* OSCAR): How can I leave if you're blocking the door?

OSCAR (*very calmly*): Felix, we've been friends a long time. For the sake of that friendship. please say, "Oscar, we can't stand each other; let's break up."

FELIX: I'll let you know what to do about my clothes. Either I'll call—or someone else will. (*Controlling great emotion.*) I'd like to leave now.

(OSCAR, *resigned, moves out of the way.* FELIX *opens the door.*)

OSCAR: Where will you go?

FELIX (*turns in the doorway and looks at him*): Where? (*He smiles.*) Oh, come on, Oscar. You're not really interested, are you?

(*He exits.* OSCAR *looks as though he's about to burst with frustration. He calls after* FELIX.)

OSCAR: All right, Felix, you win. (*Goes out into the hall.*) We'll try to iron it out. Anything you want. Come back, Felix, Felix? Felix? Don't leave me like this—you louse! (*But* FELIX *is gone.* OSCAR *comes back into the room closing the door. He is limp. He searches for something to ease his enormous frustration. He throws a pillow at the door, and then paces about like a caged lion.*) All right, Oscar, get a hold of yourself! He's gone! Keep saying that over and over. He's gone. He's really gone! (*He holds his head in pain.*) He did it. He put a curse on me. It's on my head. I don't know what it is, but something's on my head. (*The doorbell rings and he looks*

up *hopefully.*) Please let it be him. Let it be Felix. Please give me one more chance to kill him.

(*Putting the suitcase on the sofa, he rushes to the door and opens it.* MURRAY *comes in with* VINNIE.)

MURRAY (*putting his jacket on a chair at the table*): Hey, what's the matter with Felix? He walked right by me with that "human sacrifice" look on his face again.

(*He takes off his shoes.*)

VINNIE (*laying his jacket on the love seat*): What's with him? I asked him where he's going and he said, "Only Oscar knows. Only Oscar knows." Where's he going, Oscar?

OSCAR (*sitting at the table*): How the hell should I know? All right, let's get the game started, heh? Come on, get your chips.

MURRAY: I have to get something to eat. I'm starving. Mmm, I think I smell spaghetti.

(*He goes into the kitchen.*)

VINNIE: Isn't he playing tonight?

(*He takes two chairs from the dining alcove and puts them at the table.*)

OSCAR: I don't want to discuss it. I don't even want to hear his name.

VINNIE: Who? Felix?

OSCAR: I told you not to mention his name.

VINNIE: I didn't know what name you meant.

(*He clears the table and places what's left of* FELIX's *dinner on the bookcase.*)

MURRAY (*comes out of the kitchen*): Hey, did you know there's spaghetti all over the kitchen?

OSCAR: Yes, I know, and it's not spaghetti; it's linguini.

MURRAY: Oh, I thought it was spaghetti.

(*He goes back into the kitchen.*)

VINNIE (*taking the poker stuff from the bookcase and putting it on the table*): Why shouldn't I mention his name?

OSCAR: Who?

VINNIE: Felix. What's happened. Has something happened?

(SPEED *and* ROY *come in the open door.*)

SPEED: Yeah, what's the matter with Felix?

(SPEED *puts his jacket over a chair at the table.* ROY *sits in the armchair.* MURRAY *comes out of the kitchen with a six-pack of beer and bags of pretzels and chips. They all stare at* OSCAR *waiting for an answer. There is a long pause and then he stands up.*)

OSCAR: We broke up! I kicked him out. It was my decision. I threw him out of the house. All right? I admit it. Let it be on my head.

VINNIE: Let what be on your head?

OSCAR: How should I know? *Felix put it there!* Ask him!

(*He paces around to the right.*)

MURRAY: He'll go to pieces. I know Felix. He's gonna try something crazy.

OSCAR (*turns to the boys*): Why do you think I did it? (MURRAY *makes a gesture of disbelief and moves to the couch, putting down the beer and the bags.* OSCAR *moves to him.*) You think I'm just selfish? That I wanted to be cruel? I did it for you—I did it for all of us.

ROY: What are you talking about?

OSCAR (*crosses to* ROY): All right, we've all been through the napkins and the ashtrays, and the bacon, lettuce and tomato sandwiches. But that was just the beginning. Just the beginning. Do you know what he was planning for next Friday night's poker game? As a change of pace. Do you have any idea?

VINNIE: What?

OSCAR: A Luau! An Hawaiian Luau! Spareribs, roast pork and fried rice. They don't play poker like that in Honolulu.

MURRAY: One thing has nothing to do with the other. We all know he's impossible, but he's still our friend, and he's still out on the street, and I'm still worried about him.

OSCAR (*going to* MURRAY): And I'm not, heh? I'm not concerned? I'm not worried. Who do you think sent him out there in the first place?

MURRAY: Frances!

OSCAR: What?

MURRAY: Frances sent him out in the first place. *You* sent him out in the second place. And whoever he lives with next will send him out in the third place. Don't you understand? It's Felix. He does it to himself.

OSCAR: Why?

MURRAY: I don't know why. *He* doesn't know why. There are people like that. There's a whole tribe in Africa who hit themselves on the head all day long.

(*He sums it all up with an eloquent gesture of resignation.*)

OSCAR (*a slow realization of a whole new reason to be angry*): I'm not going to worry about him. Why should I? He's not worrying about me. He's somewhere out on the streets sulking and crying and having a wonderful time. If he had a spark of human decency he would leave us all alone and go back to Blanche.

(*He sits down at the table.*)

VINNIE: Why should he?

OSCAR (*picks up a deck of cards*): Because it's his wife.

VINNIE: No, Blanche is your wife. His wife is Frances.

OSCAR (*stares at him*): What are you, some kind of wise guy?

VINNIE: What did I say?

OSCAR (*throws the cards in the air*): All right, the poker game is over. I don't want to play any more.

(*He paces around on the right.*)

SPEED: Who's playing? We didn't even start.

OSCAR (*turns on him*): Is that all you can do is complain? Have you given one single thought to where Felix might be?

SPEED: I thought you said you're not worried about him.

OSCAR (*screams*): I'm not worried, damn it! I'm not worried. (*The doorbell rings. A gleeful look passes over* OSCAR's *face.*) It's him. I bet it's him! (*The boys start to go for the door,* OSCAR *stops them.*) Don't let him in; he's not welcome in this house.

MURRAY (*moves toward the door*): Oscar, don't be childish. We've got to let him in.

OSCAR (*stopping him and leading him to the table*): I won't give him the satisfaction of knowing we've been worrying about him. Sit down. Play cards. Like nothing happened.

MURRAY: But, Oscar . . .

OSCAR: Sit down. Everybody. Come on, sit down and play poker.

(*They sit and* SPEED *begins to deal out cards.*)

VINNIE (*crossing to the door*): Oscar . . .

OSCAR: All right, Vinnie, open the door.

(VINNIE *opens the door. It is* GWENDOLYN *standing there.*)

VINNIE (*surprised*): Oh, hello. (*to* OSCAR) It's not him, Oscar.

GWENDOLYN: How do you do.

(*She walks into the room.*)

OSCAR (*crosses to her*): Oh, hello, Cecily. Boys, I'd like you to meet Cecily Pigeon.

GWENDOLYN: Gwendolyn Pigeon. Please don't get up. (*to* OSCAR) May I see you for a moment, Mr. Madison?

OSCAR: Certainly, Gwen. What's the matter?

GWENDOLYN: I think you know. I've come for Felix's things.

(OSCAR *looks at her in shock and disbelief. He looks at the boys, then back at* GWENDOLYN.)

OSCAR: Felix? My Felix?

GWENDOLYN: Yes. Felix Ungar. That sweet, tortured man who's in my flat at this moment pouring his heart out to my sister.

OSCAR (turns to the boys): You hear? I'm worried to death and he's up there getting tea and sympathy.

(CECILY rushes in draggging a reluctant FELIX with her.)

CECILY: Gwen, Felix doesn't want to stay. Please tell him to stay.

FELIX: Really, girls, this is very embarrassing. I can go to a hotel. (to the boys) Hello, fellas.

GWENDOLYN (overriding his objections): Nonsense. I told you, we've plenty of room, and it's a very comfortable sofa. Isn't it, Cecy?

CECILY (joining in): Enormous. And we've rented an air conditioner.

GWENDOLYN: And we just don't like the idea of you wandering around the streets looking for a place to live.

FELIX: But I'd be in the way. Wouldn't I be in the way?

GWENDOLYN: How could you possibly be in anyone's way?

OSCAR: You want to see a typewritten list?

GWENDOLYN (turning on him): Haven't you said enough already, Mr. Madison? (to FELIX) I won't take no for an answer. Just for a few days, Felix.

CECILY: Until you get settled.

GWENDOLYN: Please. Please say, "Yes," Felix.

CECILY: Oh, please—we'd be so happy.

FELIX (considers): Well, maybe just for a few days.

GWENDOLYN (jumping with joy): Oh, wonderful.

CECILY (ecstatic): Marvelous!

GWENDOLYN (crosses to the door): You get your things and come right up.

CECILY: And come hungry. We're making dinner.

GWENDOLYN (to the boys): Good night, gentlemen; sorry to interrupt your bridge game.

CECILY (to FELIX): If you'd like you can invite your friends to play in our flat.

GWENDOLYN (to FELIX): Don't be late. Cocktails in fifteen minutes.

FELIX: I won't.

GWENDOLYN: Ta, ta.

CECILY: Ta, ta.

FELIX: Ta, ta.

(The girls leave. FELIX turns and looks at the fellows and smiles as he crosses the room into the bedroom. The five men stare dumbfounded at the door without moving. Finally MURRAY crosses to the door.)

SPEED (to the others): I told you. It's always the quiet guys.

MURRAY: Gee, what nice girls.

(He closes the door. FELIX comes out of the bedroom carrying two suits in a plastic cleaner's bag.)

ROY: Hey, Felix, are you really gonna move in with them?

FELIX (turns back to them): Just for a few days. Until I find my own place. Well, so long, fellows. You can drop your crumbs on the rug again.

(He starts toward the door.)

OSCAR: Hey, Felix. Aren't you going to thank me?

FELIX (stopping on the landing): For what?

OSCAR: For the two greatest things I ever did for you. Taking you in and throwing you out.

FELIX (lays his suits over the railing and goes to OSCAR): You're right, Oscar. Thanks a lot. Getting kicked out twice is enough for any man. In gratitude, I remove the curse.

OSCAR (smiles): Oh, bless you and thank you, Wicked Witch of the North.

(They shake hands. The phone rings.)

FELIX: Ah, that must be the girls.

MURRAY (picking up the phone): Hello?

FELIX: They hate it so when I'm late for cocktails. (Turning to the boys.) Well, so long.

MURRAY: It's your wife.

FELIX (turning to MURRAY): Oh? Well, do me a favor, Murray. Tell her I can't speak to her now. But tell her I'll be calling her in a few days, because she and I have a lot to talk about. And tell her if I sound different to her, it's because I'm not the same man she kicked out three weeks ago. Tell her, Murray; tell her.

MURRAY: I will when I see her. This is Oscar's wife.

FELIX: Oh!

MURRAY (into the phone): Just a minute, Blanche.

(OSCAR crosses to the phone and sits on the arm of the couch.)

FELIX: Well, so long, fellows.

(He shakes hands with the boys, takes his suits and moves to the door.)

OSCAR (into the phone): Hello? Yeah, Blanche. I got a pretty good idea why you're calling. You got my checks, right? Good. (FELIX stops at the door, caught by OSCAR's conversation. He slowly comes back into the room to listen, putting his suits on the railing and sitting down on the arm of the armchair.) So now I'm all paid up. No, no, I didn't win at the track. I've just been able to save a little money. I've been eating home a lot. (Takes a pillow from the couch and throws it at FELIX.) Listen, Blanche, you don't have to thank me. I'm just doing what's right. Well, that's nice of you too. The apartment? No, I think you'd be shocked. It's in surprisingly good shape. *(FELIX throws the pillow back at OSCAR.)* Say, Blanche, did Brucey get the goldfish I sent him? Yeah, well, I'll speak to you again soon, huh? Whenever you want. I don't go out much any more.

FELIX *(gets up, takes his suits from the railing and goes to the door)*: Well, good night, Mr. Madison. If you need me again, I get a dollar-fifty an hour.

OSCAR *(makes a gesture to stop FELIX as he talks on the phone)*: Well, kiss the kids for me. Good night, Blanche. *(Hangs up and turns to FELIX.)* Felix?

FELIX *(at the opened door)*: Yeah?

OSCAR: How about next Friday night? You're not going to break up the game, are you?

FELIX: Me? Never! Marriages may come and go, but the game must go on. So long, Frances.

(He exits, closing the door.)

OSCAR *(yelling after him)*: So long, Blanche. *(The boys all look at OSCAR a moment.)* All right, are we just gonna sit around or are we gonna play poker?

ROY: We're gonna play poker.

(There is a general hubbub as they pass out the beer, deal the cards and settle around the table.)

OSCAR *(standing up)*: Then let's play poker. *(Sharply, to the boys.)* And watch your cigarettes, will you? This is my house, not a pig sty.

(He takes the ashtray from the side table next to the armchair, bends down and begins to pick up the butts. The boys settle down to play poker)

CURTAIN

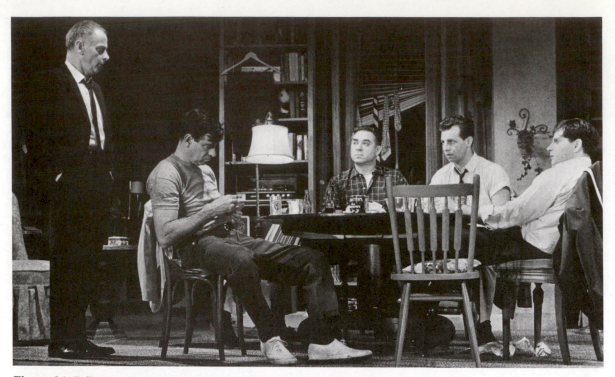

Figure 94. Felix (Art Carney, *standing*) peers at the hand being played by Oscar (Walter Matthau, *seated left*) in the poker game during the first act of the Plymouth Theater production of *The Odd Couple,* directed by Mike Nichols, New York, 1965. (Photograph: Henry Grossman.)

Figure 95. Felix (Art Carney, *standing*) pours a glass of beer, while Oscar (Walter Matthau, *seated right*) looks away in disgust during the poker game in the second act of the Plymouth Theater production of *The Odd Couple,* directed by Mike Nichols, New York, 1965. The spotlessness of the room in this figure should be compared with the messiness of the room in the preceding figure. (Photograph: Henry Grossman.)

Figure 96. Felix (Art Carney, *left*), concealing a ladle in his left hand, and Oscar (Walter Matthau, *right*), concealing Felix's towel behind his back, welcome the Pigeon sisters to dinner in the Plymouth Theater production of *The Odd Couple*, directed by Mike Nichols, New York, 1965. (Photograph: Henry Grossman.)

Staging of *The Odd Couple*

**REVIEW OF THE PLYMOUTH THEATER
PRODUCTION, 1965, BY WALTER KERR**

I'm sorry the Moscow Art players have returned to Russia. I'd like them to have seen the first-act poker game in "The Odd Couple."

I don't necessarily say they'd have learned anything from it. I just feel pretty sure they'd have liked it. It has so much interior truth. Director Mike Nichols has staged an absolute summer festival of warm beer, sprayed toward the ceiling like those terraced fountains municipal designers are so fond of, and I suppose we can credit author Neil Simon with providing the sandwiches. The sandwiches have been made of whatever was left over in host Walter Matthau's long-defrosted refrigerator: ("it's either very new cheese or very old meat" Mr. Matthau volunteers as he offers his cronies a choice between brown sandwiches and green) and the members of the party are happy enough to munch them as they gripe, growl, snarl, and roar over their hands, their wives, their lives, and the high cost of living.

This is where the art comes in. Instead of isolating each one of Mr. Simon's dozens of laugh-lines and milking it for all it's worth, director Nichols flings all the gags into the pot together, letting them clink and spin like so many chips, until everything overlaps and you can't tell life from lunacy. Nat Frey shuffles the pack as though he were crushing glass in his strong bare hands. John Fielder sings his piping little song about having to leave by twelve until it takes on the piercing sound of counterpoint from another planet. Sidney Armus and Paul Dooley fling their arms up and their cards down like men freshly accused of treason, and Mr. Matthau grunts and bellows in his homespun way to put a moose-like bass under the whole hot summer-night orchestration. The interplay is true, blue, and beautiful.

After the poker game comes the play, which is jim-dandy, ginger-peachy, and good. Mr. Matthau is a divorced man, which is why he is able to have all his friends in on Friday nights and also why the eight-room apartment looks like one of those village bazaars at which underprivileged citizens can exchange their old refuse. (Oliver Smith has caught in his setting just the right muddy and mottled note for ramshackle bachelor quarters, with the trousers back from the cleaners hanging where they ought to be, from the bookshelves, and with a nice fat hole burned in what used to be the best lampshade.)

Into the dissolute comfort and the brawling bliss of Mr. Matthau's menage comes a thin note of warning.

One friend, who turns out shortly to be Art Carney, hasn't shown up. News is received that he, too, has left his wife. Furthermore, he is threatening suicide, sort of. Now it is time for Mike Nichols to set his mother-hen actors pacing, pacing, pacing the floor, as they brood and cluck and worry inordinately about their deeply disturbed buddy. When Mr. Carney does finally appear, the rush to save him from himself—all windows are locked tightly against jumping, and he is scarcely allowed to go to the bathroom alone—is sympathetic, solicitous, and rough as a maddened hockey game. We may not have had as funny a first act since "The Acharnians."

Naturally, Mr. Matthau and Mr. Carney now settle down as roommates, making as nice a couple as you'd care to meet if they could only get along. Mr. Carney is death on dust and a fast man with an Aerosol bomb (one reason his wife threw him out is that he always insisted on recooking the dinner) and he drives Mr. Matthau stark, staring mad. In short, both of them might just as well have wives, and that constitutes the meat, the moral, and the malicious merriment of this brief encounter.

The contest thins out a bit, I am honor bound to say, during the second act, while Mr. Carney worries desperately over his London broil and reduces a couple of visiting pigeons (they're girls, they're sisters, and their name is Pigeon) to tears. But the repeated joke is at least a good joke, the Pigeon sisters ultimately prove to be funny and useful, Mr. Simon's comic invention keeps re-igniting, and the poker players are coming back, so I wouldn't even notice if I were you.

Now a word about Mr. Matthau, and I do hope the Moscow Art is listening. Mr. Matthau could play all of the parts in "Dead Souls" with one hand tied to one foot and without changing makeup. He is a gamut-runner, from grim to game to simple hysteria, and when he finally does have his long overdue nervous-breakdown, with his voice sinking into his throat like the sun in the western sea, he is magnificent. Of course, he is good, too, impersonating an orang-utan as he leaps furniture in his wild desire to make certain alterations in Mr. Carney's throat, and again when he shows his old pal the door (only to be haunted by the memory of that despairing face and by a parting remark that he comes to think of as The Curse of the Cat People). But perhaps our man is best of all when he is merely imitating contempt in his sneering dark eyes, with a baseball cap peaked backwards on his untidy head and his face curled in scorn until it looks like the catcher's mitt.

We mustn't overlook Mr. Carney, who is immensely funny quivering his lip like an agitated duck, clearing his ears by emitting foghorn hoots, and clawing his hands through what is left of his hair to indicate pride, despair and all of the seven other deadly virtues. His problem is tension ("It's tension. I get it from tension. I must be tense," he says) and ours is to keep from laughing through the next good line.

It's a good problem to have, and I urge you to drop in on "The Odd Couple" any night at all. Fridays included.

HAROLD PINTER

1930 —

Pinter, whose drama has come to be internationally known by critics as the "comedy of menace," is the son of a Portuguese-Jewish tailor who emigrated to London by way of eastern Europe early in the twentieth century. Pinter was born and raised in London's East End, where he attended the local grammar school and during his teens began writing poems, short stories, and dialogues for little magazines, as well as taking part in school theatrical productions. During the late 1940s, he spent a couple of terms at the Royal Academy of Dramatic Art, but he was put off by the sophistication of his fellow students and thus withdrew to start a professional career in acting, first in radio work during 1950, then with a professional company touring Ireland during 1951 and 1952. On returning to England, he continued acting in London and the provinces, under the pseudonym of David Baron, until 1957, when he wrote his first play, *The Room,* a one-act piece he did at the suggestion of a friend who was then studying drama at Bristol University. This eerie little play, which depicts an old couple suddenly beset by menacing visits and messages, clearly anticipated the inexplicably threatening situations that Pinter has dramatized repeatedly in his subsequent plays. During 1957, Pinter also wrote his first full-length work for the stage, *The Birthday Party,* and this time the menacing situation took the form of humiliating physical and verbal games inflicted on a retired pianist by two sinister men who turn up at his room on the afternoon of his birthday, then subject him to their birthday party games that evening, and finally carry him off with them the next morning.

When *The Birthday Party* opened in London in 1958, most critics found it "opaque" and charged that the characters spoke "in non-sequiturs, half-gibberish, and lunatic ravings." Although it closed after one week, *The Birthday Party* was revived six years later by the Royal Shakespeare Company in a highly successful production directed by Pinter himself. By then, Pinter had already achieved his first popular success with *The Caretaker* (1960), which dramatizes the comic but convulsive quarrels and competition that develop in a run-down house among the owner, his brain-damaged brother, and a devious tramp whom the brother has befriended. Several of his shorter plays, including *The Room, The Dumb Waiter* (1957), and *A Slight Ache* (1961) had also been successfully staged, while others, such as *A Night Out* (1960), *Night School* (1960), *The Collection* (1961), and *The Lover* (1963) had been filmed for television. By the mid-1960s, Pinter's screenplays for *The Servant* (1962) and *The Pumpkin Eater* (1964) had received major awards, and in 1965, *The Homecoming* opened in London, again in a highly successful production by the Royal Shakespeare Company. Given these astonishing dramatic accomplishments, it is hardly surprising that in 1966, Pinter was awarded the C.B.E. (Commander of the Order of the British Empire) by the Queen. All of Pinter's major plays have now received major productions first in London, then in New York, and his work is now no longer regarded as being quite so baffling and frustrating as it seemed twenty years ago.

Twenty years of discerning criticism about other dramatists of the absurd, such as Beckett, Genet, and Ionesco, have helped readers and playgoers to recognize Pinter's work as part of a widespread movement in contemporary drama away from clearly motivated characters and plots, as well as from entirely logical dialogue and events, to a theater in which the actions and utterances of characters, however preposterous or alarming, are interesting, even fascinating, because they can and do take place on stage. Pinter himself has also talked openly and helpfully about this aspect of his plays. For the audiences who came to the Royal Court Theater in 1960 to see *The Room* and *The Dumb Waiter,* he offered this brief statement revealing his approach to characterization:

> A character on the stage who can present no convincing argument or information as to his past experience, his present behaviour or his aspirations, nor give a comprehensive analysis of his motives is as legitimate and as worthy of attention as one who, alarmingly, can do all these things.

Pinter's view of character and motive also accounts for his special view of dialogue, which he also announced in his program notes for the Royal Court Theater:

> The more acute the experience, the less articulate its expression.

Given this concept of inarticulateness in the theater, Pinter was naturally led to his famous statement about "the two silences," which he formulated in a speech to a student drama festival in Bristol, in 1962:

> There are two silences. One when no word is spoken. The other when perhaps a torrent of language is employed. This speech is speaking of a language locked beneath it. That is its continual reference. The speech we hear is an indication of that we don't hear. It is a necessary avoidance, a violent, shy, anguished, or mocking smoke-screen which keeps the other in its place. When true silence falls we are still left with echo but are nearer nakedness. One way of looking at speech is to say it is a constant stratagem to cover nakedness.

Both these kinds of silence are, of course, true to general human experience, as Chekhov had clearly recognized in the dialogue of his plays seventy years earlier, but only in drama of the absurd, particularly in the plays of Pinter, have they become a pervasive theatrical element.

Both these silences occur throughout *The Homecoming*, and thus a recognition of them will usually help to make sense of what is happening in the play and between the characters. For example, when Lenny tells Ruth, whom he has just met, about "a certain lady" and "a certain proposal," both of which he rejected, he is not only telling a long anecdote, but also letting her know of his involvement in the world of pimps and prostitutes, and thus of his capacity for violence. His "torrent of language" is not only a reference to something else about himself, but also a tacit assertion of his having recognized her own lascivious disposition, even before she has said or done anything to reveal it. And when Ruth responds by saying quietly, "Have a sip. Go on. Have a sip from my glass. Sit on my lap. Take a long cool sip. Put your head back and open your mouth," she is not really talking about a glass of water, but returning his implicit sexual proposal. The other kind of silence, "when no word is spoken," may be seen near the beginning of the play, when Teddy returns home after being away for six years and first encounters his younger brother Lenny:

TEDDY: Hullo, Lenny.
LENNY: Hullo, Teddy.
   (Pause.)

The brevity of their greeting followed by that pause, that silence, quickly reveals their indifference, even their hostility, to one another.

Pinter's plays are distinguished not only by his use of language and silence, but also by his fascination with the dramatic situation of "two people sitting in a room." His early works, particularly *The Room, The Birthday Party,* and *The Caretaker,* are all set in a single room and explore the tensions that explode in that closed place and the menace that can intrude without warning. In commenting on this basic situation, Pinter has clearly related its application to ordinary human experience:

> A door can open at any moment and someone will come in. We'd love to know who it is, we'd love to know exactly what he has on his mind and why he comes in, but how often do we know what someone has on his mind or who this somebody is, and what goes to make him and make him what he is, and what his relationship is to others?

And throughout *The Homecoming,* he dramatizes the unanswerability of such questions. Why, for example, do Teddy and his wife, Ruth, suddenly come home to his father's house? Why does his father, Max, not know about his marriage to Ruth, not to mention their children? How does Max really feel about the son he insults and then offers to "cuddle and kiss"? And how does he feel about Ruth whom he labels "a stinking pox-ridden slut" when he first meets her and later praises as a "charming woman," "an intelligent and sympathetic woman"? Why does Teddy stand by silently when his brother Joey proceeds to make love to Ruth on the couch? Indeed, as the play proceeds, the questions about motivation and human relationships become even more troublesome. Why, for example, does Ruth so calmly and in such a businesslike way proceed to negotiate for a position of being resident prostitute to her husband's family? Why does Teddy offer no resistance at all, no plea for her to change her mind? These questions, Pinter would say, cannot really be answered. What is important and dramatically unforgettable in *The Homecoming* is that the events, bizarre as they may seem, do happen. And, in happening, they reveal a disturbing aspect of human experience, or at least a disturbing possibility in human experience.

When *The Homecoming* opened in London and later in New York, critics and audiences alike struggled to find explanations for the behavior they witnessed. Reviews of the New York production, reprinted following the text, reflect two contrasting views of the play: one believes that Pinter is "simply cheating us," the other argues that if we are willing to follow Pinter's vision, "we will have overcome our deadly habit of wanting what we expect." Two of the play's unexpected situations are pictured in photographs of the New York production, one showing Ruth about to offer Lenny a sip of water (see Figure 97), the other of Max insulting Ruth during their first encounter (see Figure 98). Debate about these and the other unexpected situations in the play raged for several months after it came to New York, and the *New York Times* went so far as to print a symposium of opinions under the title "What does *The Homecoming* Mean?" (February 5, 1967). Pinter's reply to that question can be found, perhaps, in the words of Ruth, when she breaks into a pseudo-philosophical argument that Lenny and Teddy are having about a table: "My lips move. Why don't you restrict . . . your observations to that? Perhaps the fact that they move is more significant . . . than the words which come through them. You must bear that . . . possibility . . . in mind."

THE HOMECOMING

BY HAROLD PINTER

CHARACTERS

MAX, *a man of seventy*
LENNY, *a man in his early thirties*
SAM, *a man of sixty-three*
JOEY, *a man in his middle twenties*
TEDDY, *a man in his middle thirties*
RUTH, *a woman in her early thirties*

SCENE

Summer. An old house in North London.
A large room, extending the width of the stage.

The back wall, which contained the door, has been removed. A square arch shape remains. Beyond it, the hall. In the hall a staircase ascending upper left, well in view. The front door upper right. A coatstand, hooks, etc.

In the room, a window, right. Odd tables, chairs. Two large armchairs. A large sofa, left. Against right wall a large sideboard, the upper half of which contains a mirror. Upper left, a radiogram.

ACT 1

(Evening.

    LENNY *is sitting on the sofa with a newspaper, a pencil in his hand. He wears a dark suit. He makes occasional marks on the back page.*

    MAX *comes in, from the direction of the kitchen. He goes to side-board, opens top drawer, rummages in it, closes it.*

    He wears an old cardigan and a cap, and carries a stick.

    He walks downstage, stands, looks about the room.)

MAX: What have you done with the scissors?

(Pause.)

    I said I'm looking for the scissors. What have you done with them?

(Pause.)

    Did you hear me? I want to cut something out of the paper.
LENNY: I'm reading the paper.
MAX: Not that paper. I haven't read that paper. I'm talking about last Sunday's paper. I was just having a look at it in the kitchen.

(Pause.)

    Do you hear what I'm saying? I'm talking to you! Where's the scissors?
LENNY *(looking up, quietly.)*: Why don't you shut up, you daft prat?

(MAX lifts his stick and points it at him.)

MAX: Don't you talk to me like that. I'm warning you.

(He sits in large armchair.)

    There's an advertisement in the paper about flannel vests. Cut price. Navy surplus. I could do with a few of them.

(Pause.)

    I think I'll have a fag. Give me a fag.

(Pause.)

    I just asked you to give me a cigarette.

(Pause.)

    Look what I'm lumbered with.

(He takes a crumpled cigarette from his pocket.)

    I'm getting old, my word of honour.

(He lights it.)

    You think I wasn't a tearaway? I could have taken care of you, twice over. I'm still strong. You ask your Uncle Sam what I was. But at the same time I always had a kind heart. Always.

(Pause.)

    I used to knock about with a man called Mac-Gregor. I called him Mac. You remember Mac? Eh?

(Pause.)

    Huhh! We were two of the worst hated men in the West End of London. I tell you, I still got the scars. We'd walk into a place, the whole room'd stand up, they'd make way to let us pass. You never heard such silence. Mind you, he was a big man, he was over six foot tall. His family were all MacGregors, they came all the way from Aberdeen, but he was the only one they called Mac.

(Pause.)

He was very fond of your mother, Mac was. Very fond. He always had a good word for her.

(*Pause.*)

Mind you, she wasn't such a bad woman. Even though it made me sick just to look at her rotten stinking face, she wasn't such a bad bitch. I gave her the best bleeding years of my life, anyway.

LENNY: Plug it, will you, you stupid sod, I'm trying to read the paper.

MAX: Listen! I'll chop your spine off, you talk to me like that! You understand? Talking to your lousy filthy father like that!

LENNY: You know what, you're getting demented.

(*Pause.*)

What do you think of Second Wind for the three-thirty?

MAX: Where?

LENNY: Sandown Park.

MAX: Don't stand a chance.

LENNY: Sure he does.

MAX: Not a chance.

LENNY: He's the winner.

(LENNY *ticks the paper.*)

MAX: He talks to me about horses.

(*Pause.*)

I used to live on the course. One of the loves of my life. Epsom? I knew it like the back of my hand. I was one of the best-known faces down at the paddock. What a marvellous open-air life.

(*Pause.*)

He talks to me about horses. You only read their names in the papers. But I've stroked their manes, I've held them, I've calmed them down before a big race. I was the one they used to call for. Max, they'd say, there's a horse here, he's highly strung, you're the only man on the course who can calm him. It was true. I had a . . . I had an instinctive understanding of animals. I should have been a trainer. Many times I was offered the job—you know, a proper post, by the Duke of . . . I forget his name . . . one of the Dukes. But I had family obligations, my family needed me at home.

(*Pause.*)

The times I've watched those animals thundering past the post. What an experience. Mind you, I didn't lose, I made a few bob out of it, and you know why? Because I always had the smell of a good horse. I could smell him. And not only the colts but the fillies. Because the fillies are more

highly strung than the colts, they're more unreliable, did you know that? No, what do you know? Nothing. But I was always able to tell a good filly by one particular trick. I'd look her in the eye. You see? I'd stand in front of her and look her straight in the eye, it was a kind of hypnotism, and by the look deep down in her eye I could tell whether she was a stayer or not. It was a gift. I had a gift.

(*Pause.*)

And he talks to me about horses.

LENNY: Dad, do you mind if I change the subject?

(*Pause.*)

I want to ask you something. That dinner we had before, what was the name of it? What do you call it?

(*Pause.*)

Why don't you buy a dog? You're a dog cook. Honest. You think you're cooking for a lot of dogs.

MAX: If you don't like it get out.

LENNY: I am going out. I'm going out to buy myself a proper dinner.

MAX: Well, get out! What are you waiting for?

(LENNY *looks at him.*)

LENNY: What did you say?

MAX: I said shove off out of it, that's what I said.

LENNY: You'll go before me, Dad, if you talk to me in that tone of voice.

MAX: Will I, you bitch?

(MAX *grips his stick.*)

LENNY: Oh, Daddy, you're not going to use your stick on me, are you? Eh? Don't use your stick on me, Daddy. No, please. It wasn't my fault, it was one of the others. I haven't done anything wrong, Dad, honest. Don't clout me with that stick, Dad.

(*Silence.*
MAX *sits hunched.* LENNY *reads the paper.*
SAM *comes in the front door. He wears a chauffeur's uniform. He hangs his hat on a hook in the hall and comes into the room. He goes to a chair, sits in it and sighs.*)

Hullo, Uncle Sam.

SAM: Hullo.

LENNY: How are you, Uncle!

SAM: Not bad. A bit tired.

LENNY: Tired? I bet you're tired. Where you been?

SAM: I've been to London Airport.

LENNY: All the way up to London Airport? What, right up the M4?

SAM: Yes, all the way up there.

LENNY: Tch, tch, tch. Well, I think you're entitled to be tired, Uncle.

SAM: Well, it's the drivers.

LENNY: I know. That's what I'm talking about. I'm talking about the drivers.

SAM: Knocks you out.

(Pause.)

MAX: I'm here, too, you know.

(SAM looks at him.)

I said I'm here, too. I'm sitting here.

SAM: I know you're here.

(Pause.)

SAM: I took a Yankee out there today . . . to the Airport.

LENNY: Oh, a Yankee, was it?

SAM: Yes, I been with him all day. Picked him up at the Savoy at half past twelve, took him to the Caprice for his lunch. After lunch I picked him up again, took him down to a house in Eaton Square—he had to pay a visit to a friend there—and then round about tea-time I took him right the way out to the Airport.

LENNY: Had to catch a plane there, did he?

SAM: Yes. Look what he gave me. He gave me a box of cigars.

(SAM takes a box of cigars from his pocket.)

MAX: Come here. Let's have a look at them.

(SAM shows MAX the cigars. MAX takes one from the box, pinches it and sniffs it.)

It's a fair cigar.

SAM: Want to try one?

(MAX and SAM light cigars.)

You know what he said to me? He told me I was the best chauffeur he'd ever had. The best one.

MAX: From what point of view?

SAM: Eh?

MAX: From what point of view?

LENNY: From the point of view of his driving, Dad, and his general sense of courtesy, I should say.

MAX: Thought you were a good driver, did he, Sam? Well, he gave you a first-class cigar.

SAM: Yes, he thought I was the best he'd ever had. They all say that, you know. They won't have anyone else, they only ask for me. They say I'm the best chauffeur in the firm.

LENNY: I bet the other drivers tend to get jealous, don't they, Uncle?

SAM: They do get jealous. They get very jealous.

MAX: Why?

(Pause.)

SAM: I just told you.

MAX: No, I just can't get it clear, Sam. Why do the other drivers get jealous?

SAM: Because (a) I'm the best driver, and because . . . (b) I don't take liberties.

(Pause.)

I don't press myself on people, you see. These big businessmen, men of affairs, they don't want the driver jawing all the time, they like to sit in the back, have a bit of peace and quiet. After all, they're sitting in a Humber Super Snipe, they can afford to relax. At the same time, though, this is what really makes me special . . . I do know how to pass the time of day when required.

(Pause.)

For instance, I told this man today I was in the second world war. Not the first. I told him I was too young for the first. But I told him I fought in the second.

(Pause.)

So did he, it turned out.

(LENNY stands, goes to the mirror and straightens his tie.)

LENNY: He was probably a colonel or something in the American Air Force.

SAM: Yes.

LENNY: Probably a navigator, or something like that, in a Flying Fortress. Now he's most likely a high executive in a worldwide group of aeronautical engineers.

SAM: Yes.

LENNY: Yes, I know the kind of man you're talking about.

(LENNY goes out, turning to his right.)

SAM: After all, I'm experienced. I was driving a dust cart at the age of nineteen. Then I was in long-distance haulage. I had ten years as a taxi-driver and I've had five as a private chauffeur.

MAX: It's funny you never got married, isn't it? A man with all your gifts.

(Pause.)

Isn't it? A man like you?

SAM: There's still time.

MAX: Is there?

(Pause.)

SAM: You'd be surprised.

MAX: What you been doing, banging away at your lady customers, have you?

SAM: Not me.

MAX: In the back of the Snipe? Been having a few crafty reefs in a layby, have you?

SAM: Not me.

MAX: On the back seat? What about the armrest, was it up or down?

SAM: I've never done that kind of thing in my car.
MAX: Above all that kind of thing, are you, Sam?
SAM: Too true.
MAX: Above having a good bang on the back seat, are you?
SAM: Yes, I leave that to others.
MAX: You leave it to others? What others? You paralysed prat!
SAM: I don't mess up my car! Or my . . . my boss's car! Like other people.
MAX: Other people? What other people?

(*Pause.*)

What other people?

(*Pause.*)

SAM: Other people.

(*Pause.*)

MAX: When you find the right girl, Sam, let your family know, don't forget, we'll give you a number one send-off, I promise you. You can bring her to live here, she can keep us all happy. We'd take it in turns to give her a walk round the park.
SAM: I wouldn't bring her here.
MAX: Sam, it's your decision. You're welcome to bring your bride here, to the place where you live, or on the other hand you can take a suite at the Dorchester. It's entirely up to you.
SAM: I haven't got a bride.

(SAM *stands, goes to the sideboard, takes an apple from the bowl, bites into it.*)

Getting a bit peckish.

(*He looks out of the window.*)

Never get a bride like you had, anyway. Nothing like your bride . . . going about these days. Like Jessie.

(*Pause.*)

After all, I escorted her once or twice, didn't I? Drove her round once or twice in my cab. She was a charming woman.

(*Pause.*)

All the same, she was your wife. But still . . . they were some of the most delightful evenings I've ever had. Used to just drive her about. It was my pleasure.
MAX (*softly, closing his eyes*): Christ.
SAM: I used to pull up at a stall and buy her a cup of coffee. She was a very nice companion to be with.

(*Silence.*
JOEY *comes in the front door. He walks into the room,*

takes his jacket off, throws it on a chair and stands. Silence.*)

JOEY: Feel a bit hungry.
SAM: Me, too.
MAX: Who do you think I am, your mother? Eh? Honest. They walk in here every time of the day and night like bloody animals. Go and find yourself a mother.

(LENNY *walks into the room, stands.*)

JOEY: I've been training down at the gym.
SAM: Yes, the boy's been working all day and training all night.
MAX: What do you want, you bitch? You spend all the day sitting on your arse at London Airport, buy yourself a jamroll. You expect me to sit here waiting to rush into the kitchen the moment you step in the door? You've been living sixty-three years, why don't you learn to cook?
SAM: I can cook.
MAX: Well, go and cook!
LENNY: What the boys want, Dad, is your own special brand of cooking, Dad. That's what the boys look forward to. The special understanding of food, you know, that you've got.
MAX: Stop calling me Dad. Just stop all that calling me Dad, do you understand?
LENNY: But I'm your son. You used to tuck me up in bed every night. He tucked you up, too, didn't he, Joey?

(*Pause.*)

He used to like tucking up his sons.

(LENNY *turns and goes toward the front door.*)

MAX: Lenny.
LENNY (*turning*): What?
MAX: I'll give you a proper tuck up one of these nights, son. You mark my word.

(*They look at each other.*
LENNY *opens the front door and goes out.*
Silence.*)

JOEY: I've been training with Bobby Dodd.

(*Pause.*)

And I had a good go at the bag as well.

(*Pause.*)

I wasn't in bad trim.
MAX: Boxing's a gentleman's game.

(*Pause.*)

I'll tell you what you've got to do. What you've got to do is you've got to learn how to defend yourself, and you've got to learn how to attack.

That's your only trouble as a boxer. You don't know how to defend yourself, and you don't know how to attack.

(*Pause.*)

Once you've mastered those arts you can go straight to the top.

(*Pause.*)

JOEY: I've got a pretty good idea . . . of how to do that.

(JOEY *looks round for his jacket, picks it up, goes out of the room and up the stairs.*
Pause.)

MAX: Sam . . . why don't you go, too, eh? Why don't you just go upstairs? Leave me quiet. Leave me alone.

SAM: I want to make something clear about Jessie, Max. I want to. I do. When I took her out in the cab, round the town, I was taking care of her, for you. I was looking after her for you, when you were busy, wasn't I? I was showing her the West End.

(*Pause.*)

You wouldn't have trusted any of your other brothers. You wouldn't have trusted Mac, would you? But you trusted me. I want to remind you.

(*Pause.*)

Old Mac died a few years ago, didn't he? Isn't he dead?

(*Pause.*)

He was a lousy stinking rotten loudmouth. A bastard uncouth sodding runt. Mind you, he was a good friend of yours.

(*Pause.*)

MAX: Eh, Sam . . .
SAM: What?
MAX: Why do I keep you here? You're just an old grub.
SAM: Am I?
MAX: You're a maggot.
SAM: Oh yes?
MAX: As soon as you stop paying your way here, I mean when you're too old to pay your way, you know what I'm going to do? I'm going to give you the boot.
SAM: You are, eh?
MAX: Sure. I mean, bring in the money and I'll put up with you. But when the firm gets rid of you—you can flake off.
SAM: This is my house as well, you know. This was our mother's house.

MAX: One lot after the other. One mess after the other.
SAM: Our father's house.
MAX: Look what I'm lumbered with. One cast-iron bunch of crap after another. One flow of stinking pus after another.

(*Pause.*)

Our father? I remember him. Don't worry. You kid yourself. He used to come over to me and look down at me. My old man did. He'd bend right over me, then he'd pick me up. I was only that big. Then he'd dandle me. Give me the bottle. Wipe me clean. Give me a smile. Pat me on the bum. Pass me around, pass me from hand to hand. Toss me up in the air. Catch me coming down. I remember my father.

(BLACKOUT.
LIGHTS UP.
Night.)
(TEDDY *and* RUTH *stand at the threshold of the room. They are both well dressed in light summer suits and light raincoats. Two suitcases are by their side. They look at the room.* TEDDY *tosses the key in his hand, smiles.*)

TEDDY: Well, the key worked.

(*Pause.*)

They haven't changed the lock.

(*Pause.*)

RUTH: No one's here.
TEDDY (*looking up*): They're asleep.

(*Pause.*)

RUTH: Can I sit down?
TEDDY: Of course.
RUTH: I'm tired.

(*Pause.*)

TEDDY: Then sit down.

(*She does not move.*)

That's my father's chair.
RUTH: That one?
TEDDY (*smiling*): Yes, that's it. Shall I go up and see if my room's still there?
RUTH: It can't have moved.
TEDDY: No, I mean if my bed's still there.
RUTH: Someone might be in it.
TEDDY: No. They've got their own beds.

(*Pause.*)

RUTH: Shouldn't you wake someone up? Tell them you're here?
TEDDY: Not at this time of night. It's too late.

(Pause.)

Shall I go up?

(He goes into the hall, looks up the stairs, comes back.)

Why don't you sit down?

(Pause.)

I'll just go up . . . have a look.

(He goes up the stairs, stealthily.
RUTH *stands, then slowly walks across the room.*
TEDDY *returns.)*

It's still there. My room. Empty. The bed's there. What are you doing?

(She looks at him.)

Blankets, no sheets. I'll find some sheets. I could hear snores. Really. They're all still here, I think. They're all snoring up there. Are you cold?
RUTH: No.
TEDDY: I'll make something to drink, if you like. Something hot.
RUTH: No, I don't want anything.

*(*TEDDY *walks about.)*

TEDDY: What do you think of the room? Big, isn't it? It's a big house. I mean, it's a fine room, don't you think? Actually there was a wall, across there . . . with a door. We knocked it down . . . years ago . . . to make an open living area. The structure wasn't affected, you see. My mother was dead.

*(*RUTH *sits.)*

Tired?
RUTH: Just a little.
TEDDY: We can go to bed if you like. No point in waking anyone up now. Just go to bed. See them all in the morning . . . see my father in the morning. . . .

(Pause.)

RUTH: Do you want to stay?
TEDDY: Stay?

(Pause.)

We've come to stay. We're bound to stay . . . for a few days.
RUTH: I think . . . the children . . . might be missing us.
TEDDY: Don't be silly.
RUTH: They might.
TEDDY: Look, we'll be back in a few days, won't we?

(He walks about the room.)

Nothing's changed. Still the same.

(Pause.)

Still, he'll get a surprise in the morning, won't he? The old man. I think you'll like him, very much. Honestly. He's a . . . well, he's old, of course. Getting on.

(Pause.)

I was born here, do you realize that?
RUTH: I know.

(Pause.)

TEDDY: Why don't you go to bed? I'll find some sheets. I feel . . . wide awake, isn't it odd? I think I'll stay up for a bit. Are you tired?
RUTH: No.
TEDDY: Go to bed. I'll show you the room.
RUTH: No, I don't want to.
TEDDY: You'll be perfectly all right up there without me. Really you will. I mean, I won't be long. Look, it's just up there. It's the first door on the landing. The bathroom's right next door. You . . . need some rest, you know.

(Pause.)

I just want to walk about for a few minutes. Do you mind?
RUTH: Of course I don't.
TEDDY: Well . . . Shall I show you the room?
RUTH: No, I'm happy at the moment.
TEDDY: You don't have to go to bed. I'm not saying you have to. I mean, you can stay up with me. Perhaps I'll make a cup of tea or something. The only thing is we don't want to make too much noise, we don't want to wake anyone up.
RUTH: I'm not making any noise.
TEDDY: I know you're not.

(He goes to her.)

(Gently.) Look, it's all right, really. I'm here. I mean . . . I'm with you. There's no need to be nervous. Are you nervous?
RUTH: No.
TEDDY: There's no need to be.

(Pause.)

They're very warm people, really. Very warm. They're my family. They're not ogres.

(Pause.)

Well, perhaps we should go to bed. After all, we have to be up early, see Dad. Wouldn't be quite right if he found us in bed, I think. *(He chuckles.)* Have to be up before six, come down, say hullo.

(Pause.)

RUTH: I think I'll have a breath of air.

TEDDY: Air?

(*Pause.*)

What do you mean?

RUTH (*standing*): Just a stroll.

TEDDY: At this time of night? But we've . . . only just got here. We've got to go to bed.

RUTH: I just feel like some air.

TEDDY: But I'm going to bed.

RUTH: That's all right.

TEDDY: But what am I going to do?

(*Pause.*)

The last thing I want is a breath of air. Why do you want a breath of air?

RUTH: I just do.

TEDDY: But it's late.

RUTH: I won't go far. I'll come back.

(*Pause.*)

TEDDY: I'll wait up for you.

RUTH: Why?

TEDDY: I'm not going to bed without you.

RUTH: Can I have the key?

(*He gives it to her.*)

Why don't you go to bed?

(*He puts his arms on her shoulders and kisses her. They look at each other, briefly. She smiles.*)

I won't be long.

(*She goes out of the front door.*
TEDDY *goes to the window, peers out after her, half turns from the window, stands, suddenly chews his knuckles.*
LENNY *walks into the room from upper left. He stands. He wears pyjamas and dressing-gown. He watches* TEDDY.
TEDDY *turns and sees him.*
Silence.)

TEDDY: Hullo, Lenny.

LENNY: Hullo, Teddy.

(*Pause.*)

TEDDY: I didn't hear you come down the stairs.

LENNY: I didn't.

(*Pause.*)

I sleep down here now. Next door. I've got a kind of study, workroom cum bedroom next door now, you see.

TEDDY: Oh. Did I . . . wake you up?

LENNY: No. I just had an early night tonight. You know how it is. Can't sleep. Keep waking up.

(*Pause.*)

TEDDY: How are you?

LENNY: Well, just sleeping a bit restlessly, that's all. Tonight, anyway.

TEDDY: Bad dreams?

LENNY: No, I wouldn't say I was dreaming. It's not exactly a dream. It's just that something keeps waking me up. Some kind of tick.

TEDDY: A tick?

LENNY: Yes.

TEDDY: Well, what is it?

LENNY: I don't know.

(*Pause.*)

TEDDY: Have you got a clock in your room?

LENNY: Yes.

TEDDY: Well, maybe it's the clock.

LENNY: Yes, could be, I suppose.

(*Pause.*)

Well, if it's the clock I'd better do something about it. Stifle it in some way, or something.

(*Pause.*)

TEDDY: I've . . . just come back for a few days.

LENNY: Oh yes? Have you?

(*Pause.*)

TEDDY: How's the old man?

LENNY: He's in the pink.

(*Pause.*)

TEDDY: I've been keeping well.

LENNY: Oh, have you?

(*Pause.*)

Staying the night then, are you?

TEDDY: Yes.

LENNY: Well, you can sleep in your old room.

TEDDY: Yes, I've been up.

LENNY: Yes, you can sleep there.

(LENNY *yawns.*)

Oh well.

TEDDY: I'm going to bed.

LENNY: Are you?

TEDDY: Yes, I'll get some sleep.

LENNY: Yes, I'm going to bed, too.

(TEDDY *picks up the cases.*)

I'll give you a hand.

TEDDY: No, they're not heavy.

(TEDDY *goes into the hall with the cases.*
LENNY *turns out the light in the room.*
The light in the hall remains on.
LENNY *follows into the hall.*)

LENNY: Nothing you want?

TEDDY: Mmmm?

LENNY: Nothing you might want, for the night? Glass of water, anything like that?

TEDDY: Any sheets anywhere?

LENNY: In the sideboard in your room.

TEDDY: Oh, good.

LENNY: Friends of mine occasionally stay there, you know, in your room, when they're passing through this part of the world.

(LENNY *turns out the hall light and turns on the first landing light.*

TEDDY *begins to walk up the stairs.*)

TEDDY: Well, I'll see you at breakfast, then.

LENNY: Yes, that's it. Ta-ta.

(TEDDY *goes upstairs.*
LENNY *goes off left.*
Silence.
The landing light goes out.
Slight night light in the hall and room.
LENNY *comes back into the room, goes to the window and looks out.*
He leaves the window and turns on a lamp.
He is holding a small clock.
He sits, places the clock in front of him, lights a cigarette and sits.
RUTH *comes in the front door.*
She stands still. LENNY *turns his head, smiles. She walks slowly into the room.*)

LENNY: Good evening.

RUTH: Morning, I think.

LENNY: You're right there.

(*Pause.*)

My name's Lenny. What's yours?

RUTH: Ruth.

(*She sits, puts her coat collar around her.*)

LENNY: Cold?

RUTH: No.

LENNY: It's been a wonderful summer, hasn't it? Remarkable.

(*Pause.*)

Would you like something? Refreshment of some kind? An aperitif, anything like that?

RUTH: No, thanks.

LENNY: I'm glad you said that. We haven't got a drink in the house. Mind you, I'd soon get some in, if we had a party or something like that. Some kind of celebration . . . you know.

(*Pause.*)

You must be connected with my brother in some way. The one who's been abroad.

RUTH: I'm his wife.

LENNY: Eh listen, I wonder if you can advise me. I've been having a bit of a rough time with this clock. The tick's been keeping me up. The trouble is I'm not all that convinced it was the clock. I mean there are lots of things which tick in the night, don't you find that? All sorts of objects, which, in the day, you wouldn't call anything else but commonplace. They give you no trouble. But in the night any given one of a number of them is liable to start letting out a bit of a tick. Whereas you look at these objects in the day and they're just commonplace. They're as quiet as mice during the daytime. So . . . all things being equal . . . this question of me saying it was the clock that woke me up, well, that could very easily prove something of a false hypothesis.

(*He goes to the sideboard, pours from a jug into a glass, takes the glass to* RUTH.)

Here you are. I bet you could do with this.

RUTH: What is it?

LENNY: Water.

(*She takes it, sips, places the glass on a small table by her chair.*
LENNY *watches her.*)

Isn't it funny? I've got my pyjamas on and you're fully dressed?

(*He goes to the sideboard and pours another glass of water.*)

Mind if I have one? Yes, it's funny seeing my old brother again after all these years. It's just the sort of tonic my Dad needs, you know. He'll be chuffed to his bollocks in the morning, when he sees his eldest son. I was surprised myself when I saw Teddy, you know. Old Ted. I thought he was in America.

RUTH: We're on a visit to Europe.

LENNY: What, both of you?

RUTH: Yes.

LENNY: What, you sort of live with him over there, do you?

RUTH: We're married.

LENNY: On a visit to Europe, eh? Seen much of it?

RUTH: We've just come from Italy.

LENNY: Oh, you went to Italy first, did you? And then he brought you over here to meet the family, did he? Well, the old man'll be pleased to see you, I can tell you.

RUTH: Good.

LENNY: What did you say?

RUTH: Good.

(*Pause.*)

LENNY: Where'd you go to in Italy?

RUTH: Venice.

LENNY: Not dear old Venice? Eh? That's funny. You

know, I've always had a feeling that if I'd been a soldier in the last war—say in the Italian campaign—I'd probably have found myself in Venice. I've always had that feeling. The trouble was I was too young to serve, you see. I was only a child, I was too small, otherwise I've got a pretty shrewd idea I'd probably have gone through Venice. Yes, I'd almost certainly have gone through it with my battalion. Do you mind if I hold your hand?

RUTH: Why?

LENNY: Just a touch.

(He stands and goes to her.)

Just a tickle.

RUTH: Why?

(He looks down at her.)

LENNY: I'll tell you why.

(Slight pause.)

One night, not too long ago, one night down by the docks, I was standing alone under an arch, watching all the men jibbing the boom, out in the harbour, and playing about with the yardarm, when a certain lady came up to me and made me a certain proposal. This lady had been searching for me for days. She'd lost track of my whereabouts. However, the fact was she eventually caught up with me, and when she caught up with me she made me this certain proposal. Well, this proposal wasn't entirely out of order and normally I would have subscribed to it. I mean I would have subscribed to it in the normal course of events. The only trouble was she was falling apart with the pox. So I turned it down. Well, this lady was very insistent and started taking liberties with me down under this arch, liberties which by any criterion I couldn't be expected to tolerate, the facts being what they were, so I clumped her one. It was on my mind at the time to do away with her, you know, to kill her, and the fact is, that as killings go, it would have been a simple matter, nothing to it. Her chauffeur, who had located me for her, he'd popped round the corner to have a drink, which just left this lady and myself, you see, alone, standing underneath this arch, watching all the steamers steaming up, no one about, all quiet on the Western Front, and there she was up against this wall—well, just sliding down the wall, following the blow I'd given her. Well, to sum up, everything was in my favour, for a killing. Don't worry about the chauffeur. The chauffeur would never have spoken. He was an old friend of the family. But . . . in the end I thought . . . Aaah, why go to all the bother . . . you know, getting rid of the corpse and all that, getting yourself into a state of tension. So I just gave her another belt in the nose and a couple of turns of the boot and sort of left it at that.

RUTH: How did you know she was diseased?

LENNY: How did I know?

(Pause.)

I decided she was.

(Silence.)

You and my brother are newly-weds, are you?

RUTH: We've been married six years.

LENNY: He's always been my favourite brother, old Teddy. Do you know that? And my goodness we are proud of him here, I can tell you. Doctor of Philosophy and all that . . . leaves quite an impression. Of course, he's a very sensitive man, isn't he? Ted. Very. I've often wished I was as sensitive as he is.

RUTH: Have you?

LENNY: Oh yes. Oh yes, very much so. I mean, I'm not saying I'm not sensitive. I am. I could just be a bit more so, that's all.

RUTH: Could you?

LENNY: Yes, just a bit more so, that's all.

(Pause.)

I mean, I am very sensitive to atmosphere, but I tend to get desensitized, if you know what I mean, when people make unreasonable demands on me. For instance, last Christmas I decided to do a bit of snow-clearing for the Borough Council, because we had a heavy snow over here that year in Europe. I didn't have to do this snow-clearing—I mean I wasn't financially embarrassed in any way—it just appealed to me, it appealed to something inside me. What I anticipated with a good deal of pleasure was the brisk cold bite in the air in the early morning. And I was right. I had to get my snowboots on and I had to stand on a corner, at about five-thirty in the morning, to wait for the lorry to pick me up, to take me to the allotted area. Bloody freezing. Well, the lorry came, I jumped on the tailboard, headlights on, dipped, and off we went. Got there, shovels up, fags on, and off we went, deep into the December snow, hours before cockcrow. Well, that morning, while I was having my mid-morning cup of tea in a neighbouring cafe, the shovel standing by my chair, an old lady approached me and asked me if I would give her a hand with her iron mangle. Her brother-in-law, she said, had left it for her, but he'd left it in the wrong room, he'd left it in the front room. Well, naturally, she wanted it in the back room. It was a present he'd given her, you see, a mangle, to iron out the washing. But he'd left it in the wrong room, he'd left it in the front room, well that was a silly place to leave it, it couldn't stay there. So I took time off to give her a hand. She only lived up the road. Well, the only trouble was when I got there I couldn't move this mangle. It must have weighed about half a ton. How this brother-in-law got it up there in the first place I can't even begin to envisage. So there I was, doing a bit of shoulders on with the mangle, risking a rupture, and this old lady just standing there, waving me on, not even lifting a little finger to give me a helping hand. So after a few minutes I said to her, now look here, why don't you stuff this iron mangle up your arse? Anyway, I said, they're out of date, you want to get a spin drier. I had a good mind to give her a workover there and then, but as I was feeling jubilant with the snow-clearing I just gave her a short-arm jab to the belly and jumped on a bus outside. Excuse me, shall I take this ashtray out of your way?

RUTH: It's not in my way.

LENNY: It seems to be in the way of your glass. The glass was about to fall. Or the ashtray. I'm rather worried about the carpet. It's not me, it's my father. He's obsessed with order and clarity. He doesn't like a mess. So, as I don't believe you're smoking at the moment, I'm sure you won't object if I move the ashtray.

(He does so.)

And now perhaps I'll relieve you of your glass.

RUTH: I haven't quite finished.

LENNY: You've consumed quite enough, in my opinion.

RUTH: No, I haven't.

LENNY: Quite sufficient, in my opinion.

RUTH: Not in mine, Leonard.

(Pause.)

LENNY: Don't call me that, please.

RUTH: Why not?

LENNY: That's the name my mother gave me.

(Pause.)

Just give me the glass.

RUTH: No.

(Pause.)

LENNY: I'll take it, then.

RUTH: If you take the glass . . . I'll take you.

(Pause.)

LENNY: How about me taking the glass without you taking me?

RUTH: Why don't I just take you?

(Pause.)

LENNY: You're joking.

(Pause.)

You're in love, anyway, with another man. You've had a secret liaison with another man. His family didn't even know. Then you come here without a word of warning and start to make trouble.

(She picks up the glass and lifts it toward him.)

RUTH: Have a sip. Go on. Have a sip from my glass.

(He is still.)

Sit on my lap. Take a long cool sip.

(She pats her lap. Pause.
She stands, moves to him with the glass.)

Put your head back and open your mouth.

LENNY: Take that glass away from me.

RUTH: Lie on the floor. Go on. I'll pour it down your throat.

LENNY: What are you doing, making me some kind of proposal?

(She laughs shortly, drains the glass.)

RUTH: Oh, I was thirsty.

(She smiles at him, puts the glass down, goes into the hall and up the stairs.
He follows into the hall and shouts up the stairs.)

LENNY: What was that supposed to be? Some kind of proposal?

(Silence.
He comes back into the room, goes to his own glass, drains it.
A door slams upstairs.
The landing light goes on.
MAX comes down the stairs, in pyjamas and cap. He comes into the room.)

MAX: What's going on here? You drunk?

(He stares at LENNY.)

What are you shouting about? You gone mad?

(LENNY pours another glass of water.)

Prancing about in the middle of the night shouting your head off. What are you, a raving lunatic?

LENNY: I was thinking aloud.

MAX: Is Joey down here? You been shouting at Joey?

LENNY: Didn't you hear what I said, Dad? I said I was thinking aloud.

MAX: You were thinking so loud you got me out of bed.

LENNY: Look, why don't you just . . . pop off, eh?

MAX: Pop off? He wakes me up in the middle of the night, I think we got burglars here, I think he's got a knife stuck in him, I come down here, he tells me to pop off.

(LENNY *sits down.*)

He was talking to someone. Who could he have been talking to? They're all asleep. He was having a conversation with someone. He won't tell me who it was. He pretends he was thinking aloud. What are you doing, hiding someone here?

LENNY: I was sleepwalking. Get out of it, leave me alone, will you?

MAX: I want an explanation, you understand? I asked you who you got hiding here.

(*Pause.*)

LENNY: I'll tell you what, Dad, since you're in the mood for a bit of a . . . chat, I'll ask you a question. It's a question I've been meaning to ask you for some time. That night . . . you know . . . the night you got me . . . that night with Mum, what was it like? Eh? When I was just a glint in your eye. What was it like? What was the background to it? I mean, I want to know the real facts about my background, I mean, for instance, is it a fact that you had me in mind all the time, or is it a fact that I was the last thing you had in mind?

(*Pause.*)

I'm only asking this in a spirit of inquiry, you understand that, don't you? I'm curious. And there's lots of people of my age share that curiosity, you know that, Dad? They often ruminate, sometimes singly, sometimes in groups, about the true facts of that particular night—the night they were made in the image of those two people *at it*. It's a question long overdue, from my point of view, but as we happen to be passing the time of day here tonight I thought I'd pop it to you.

(*Pause.*)

MAX: You'll drown in your own blood.

LENNY: If you prefer to answer the question in writing I've got no objection.

(MAX *stands.*)

I should have asked my dear mother. Why didn't I ask my dear mother? Now it's too late. She's passed over to the other side.

(MAX *spits at him.*
LENNY *looks down at the carpet.*)

Now look what you've done. I'll have to Hoover that in the morning, you know.

(MAX *turns and walks up the stairs.*
LENNY *sits still.*
BLACKOUT.
LIGHTS UP.
Morning.
JOEY *in front of the mirror. He is doing some slow limbering-up exercises. He stops, combs his hair, carefully. He then shadowboxes, heavily, watching himself in the mirror.*
MAX *comes in from upper left.*
Both MAX *and* JOEY *are dressed.* MAX *watches* JOEY *in silence.* JOEY *stops shadowboxing, picks up a newspaper and sits.*
Silence.)

MAX: I hate this room.

(*Pause.*)

It's the kitchen I like. It's nice in there. It's cosy.

(*Pause.*)

But I can't stay in there. You know why? Because he's always washing up in there, scraping the plates, driving me out of the kitchen, that's why.

JOEY: Why don't you bring your tea in here?

MAX: I don't want to bring my tea in here. I hate it here. I want to drink my tea in there.

(*He goes into the hall and looks toward the kitchen.*)

What's he doing in there?

(*He returns.*)

What's the time?

JOEY: Half past six.

MAX: Half past six.

(*Pause.*)

I'm going to see a game of football this afternoon. You want to come?

(*Pause.*)

I'm talking to you.

JOEY: I'm training this afternoon. I'm doing six rounds with Blackie.

MAX: That's not till five o'clock. You've got time to see a game of football before five o'clock. It's the first game of the season.

JOEY: No, I'm not going.

MAX: Why not?

(*Pause.*
MAX *goes into the hall.*)

Sam! Come here!

(MAX *comes back into the room.*

SAM *enters with a cloth.*)

SAM: What?

MAX: What are you doing in there?

SAM: Washing up.

MAX: What else?

SAM: Getting rid of your leavings.

MAX: Putting them in the bin, eh?

SAM: Right in.

MAX: What point you trying to prove?

SAM: No point.

MAX: Oh yes, you are. You resent making my breakfast, that's what it is, isn't it? That's why you bang round the kitchen like that, scraping the frying-pan, scraping all the leavings into the bin, scraping all the plates, scraping all the tea out of the teapot . . . that's why you do that, every single stinking morning. I know. Listen, Sam. I want to say something to you. From my heart.

(He moves closer.)

I want you to get rid of these feelings of resentment you've got towards me. I wish I could understand them. Honestly, have I ever given you cause? Never. When Dad died he said to me, Max, look after your brothers. That's exactly what he said to me.

SAM: How could he say that when he was dead?

MAX: What?

SAM: How could he speak if he was dead?

(Pause.)

MAX: Before he died, Sam. Just before. They were his last words. His last sacred words, Sammy. A split second after he said those words . . . he was a dead man. You think I'm joking? You think when my father spoke—on his death-bed—I wouldn't obey his words to the last letter? You hear that, Joey? He'll stop at nothing. He's even prepared to spit on the memory of our Dad. What kind of son were you, you wet wick? You spent half your time doing crossword puzzles! We took you into the butcher's shop, you couldn't even sweep the dust off the floor. We took MacGregor into the shop, he could run the place by the end of a week. Well, I'll tell you one thing. I respected my father not only as a man but as a number one butcher! And to prove it I followed him into the shop. I learned to carve a carcass at his knee. I commemorated his name in blood. I gave birth to three grown men! All on my own bat. What have you done?

(Pause.)

What have you done? You tit!

SAM: Do you want to finish the washing up? Look, here's the cloth.

MAX: So try to get rid of these feelings of resentment, Sam. After all, we are brothers.

SAM: Do you want the cloth? Here you are. Take it.

*(*TEDDY *and* RUTH *come down the stairs. They walk across the hall and stop just inside the room.*
The others turn and look at them. JOEY *stands.*
TEDDY *and* RUTH *are wearing dressing-gowns.*
Silence.
TEDDY *smiles.)*

TEDDY: Hullo . . . Dad . . . We overslept.

(Pause.)

What's for breakfast?

(Silence.)
*(*TEDDY *chuckles.)*

Huh. We overslept.

*(*MAX *turns to* SAM.*)*

MAX: Did you know he was here?

SAM: No.

*(*MAX *turns to* JOEY.*)*

MAX: Did you know he was here?

(Pause.)

I asked you if you knew he was here.

JOEY: No.

MAX: Then who knew?

(Pause.)

Who knew?

(Pause.)

I didn't know.

TEDDY: I was going to come down, Dad, I was going to . . . be here, when you came down.

(Pause.)

How are you?

(Pause.)

Uh . . . look, I'd . . . like you to meet . . .

MAX: How long you been in this house?

TEDDY: All night.

MAX: All night? I'm a laughing-stock. How did you get in?

TEDDY: I had my key.

*(*MAX *whistles and laughs.)*

MAX: Who's this?

TEDDY: I was just going to introduce you.

MAX: Who asked you to bring tarts in here?

TEDDY: Tarts?

MAX: Who asked you to bring dirty tarts into this house?

TEDDY: Listen, don't be silly—

MAX: You been here all night?

TEDDY: Yes, we arrived from Venice—

MAX: We've had a smelly scrubber in my house all night. We've had a stinking pox-ridden slut in my house all night.

TEDDY: Stop it! What are you talking about?

MAX: I haven't seen the bitch for six years, he comes home without a word, he brings a filthy scrubber off the street, he shacks up in my house!

TEDDY: She's my wife! We're married!

(Pause.)

MAX: I've never had a whore under this roof before. Ever since your mother died. My word of honour. *(to JOEY)* Have you ever had a whore here? Has Lenny ever had a whore here. They come back from America, they bring the slopbucket with them. They bring the bedpan with them. *(to TEDDY)* Take that disease away from me. Get her away from me.

TEDDY: She's my wife.

MAX *(to JOEY)*: Chuck them out.

(Pause.)

A Doctor of Philosophy. Sam, you want to meet a Doctor of Philosophy? *(to JOEY)* I said chuck them out.

(Pause.)

What's the matter? You deaf?

JOEY: You're an old man. *(to TEDDY)* He's an old man.

(LENNY walks into the room, in a dressing-gown. He stops. They all look round. MAX turns back, hits JOEY in the stomach with all his might. JOEY contorts, staggers across the stage. MAX, with the exertion of the blow, begins to collapse. His knees buckle. He clutches his stick. SAM moves forward to help him. MAX hits him across the head with his stick. SAM sits, head in hands. JOEY, hands pressed to his stomach, sinks down at the feet of RUTH. She looks down at him. LENNY and TEDDY are still. JOEY slowly stands. He is close to RUTH. He turns from RUTH, looks round at MAX. SAM clutches his head. MAX breathes heavily, very slowly gets to his feet. JOEY moves to him. They look at each other. Silence. MAX moves past JOEY, walks toward RUTH. He gestures with his stick.)

MAX: Miss.

(RUTH walks toward him.)

RUTH: Yes?

(He looks at her.)

MAX: You a mother?

RUTH: Yes.

MAX: How many you got?

RUTH: Three.

(He turns to TEDDY.)

MAX: All yours, Ted?

(Pause.)

Teddy, why don't we have a nice cuddle and kiss, eh? Like the old days? What about a nice cuddle and kiss, eh?

TEDDY: Come on, then.

(Pause)

MAX: You want to kiss your old father? Want a cuddle with your old father?

TEDDY: Come on, then.

(TEDDY moves a step toward him.)

Come on.

(Pause.)

MAX: You still love your old Dad, eh?

(They face each other.)

TEDDY: Come on, Dad. I'm ready for the cuddle.

(MAX begins to chuckle, gurgling. He turns to the family and addresses them.)

MAX: He still loves his father!

ACT 2

(Afternoon. MAX, TEDDY, LENNY and SAM are about the stage, lighting cigars. JOEY comes in from upper left with a coffee tray, followed by RUTH. He puts the tray down. RUTH hands coffee to all the men. She sits with her cup. MAX smiles at her.)

RUTH: That was a very good lunch.

MAX: I'm glad you liked it. *(to the others)* Did you hear that? *(to RUTH)* Well, I put my heart and soul into it, I can tell you. *(He sips.)* And this is a lovely cup of coffee.

RUTH: I'm glad.

(Pause.)

MAX: I've got the feeling you're a first-rate cook.

RUTH: I'm not bad.

MAX: No, I've got the feeling you're a number one cook. Am I right, Teddy?

TEDDY: Yes, she's a very good cook.

(Pause.)

MAX: Well, it's a long time since the whole family was together, eh? If only your mother was alive. Eh, what do you say, Sam? What would Jessie say if she was alive? Sitting here with her three sons. Three fine grown-up lads. And a lovely daughter-in-law. The only shame is her grandchildren aren't here. She'd have petted them and cooed over them, wouldn't she, Sam? She'd have fussed over them and played with them, told them stories, tickled them—I tell you she'd have been hysterical. *(to RUTH)* Mind you, she taught those boys everything they know. She taught them all the morality they know. I'm telling you. Every single bit of the moral code they live by—was taught to them by their mother. And she had a heart to go with it. What a heart. Eh, Sam? Listen, what's the use of beating round the bush? That woman was the backbone to this family. I mean, I was busy working twenty-four hours a day in the shop. I was going all over the country to find meat, I was making my way in the world, but I left a woman at home with a will of iron, a heart of gold and a mind. Right, Sam?

(Pause.)

What a mind.

(Pause.)

Mind you, I was a generous man to her. I never left her short of a few bob. I remember one year I entered into negotiations with a top-class group of butchers with continental connections. I was going into association with them. I remember the night I came home, I kept quiet. First of all I gave Lenny a bath, then Teddy a bath, then Joey a bath. What fun we used to have in the bath, eh, boys? Then I came downstairs and I made Jessie put her feet up on a pouffe—what happened to that pouffe, I haven't seen it for years—she put her feet up on the pouffe and I said to her, Jessie, I think our ship is going to come home, I'm going to treat you to a couple of items, I'm going to buy you a dress in pale corded blue silk, heavily encrusted in pearls, and for casual wear, a pair of pantaloons in lilac flowered taffeta. Then I gave her a drop of cherry brandy. I remember the boys came down, in their pyjamas, all their hair shining, their faces pink, it was before they started shaving, and they knelt down at our feet, Jessie's and mine. I tell you, it was like Christmas.

(Pause.)

RUTH: What happened to the group of butchers?

MAX: The group? They turned out to be a bunch of criminals like everyone else.

(Pause.)

This is a lousy cigar.

*(He stubs it out.
He turns to SAM.)*

What time you going to work?

SAM: Soon.

MAX: You've got a job on this afternoon, haven't you?

SAM: Yes, I know.

MAX: What do you mean, you know? You'll be late. You'll lose your job? What are you trying to do, humiliate me?

SAM: Don't worry about me.

MAX: It makes the bile come up in my mouth. The bile—you understand? *(to RUTH)* I worked as a butcher all my life, using the chopper and the slab, the slab, you know what I mean, the chopper and the slab! To keep my family in luxury. Two families! My mother was bedridden, my brothers were all invalids. I had to earn the money for the leading psychiatrists. I had to read books! I had to study the disease, so that I could cope with an emergency at every stage. A crippled family, three bastard sons, a slutbitch of a wife—don't talk to me about the pain of childbirth—I suffered the pain, I've still got the pangs—when I give a little cough my back collapses—and here I've got a lazy idle bugger of a brother won't even get to work on time. The best chauffeur in the world. All his life he's sat in the front seat giving lovely hand signals. You call that work? This man doesn't know his gearbox from his arse!

SAM: You go and ask my customers! I'm the only one they ever ask for.

MAX: What do the other drivers do, sleep all day?

SAM: I can only drive one car. They can't all have me at the same time.

MAX: Anyone could have you at the same time. You'd bend over for half a dollar on Blackfriars Bridge.

SAM: Me!

MAX: For two bob and a toffee apple.

SAM: He's insulting me. He's insulting his brother. I'm driving a man to Hampton Court at four forty-five.

MAX: Do you want to know who could drive? MacGregor! MacGregor was a driver.

SAM: Don't you believe it.

(MAX points his stick at SAM.)

MAX: He didn't even fight in the war. This man didn't even fight in the bloody war!

SAM: I did!

MAX: Who did you kill?

(Silence.
SAM gets up, goes to RUTH, shakes her hand and goes out of the front door.
MAX turns to TEDDY.)

Well, how you been keeping, son?

TEDDY: I've been keeping very well, Dad.

MAX: It's nice to have you with us, son.

TEDDY: It's nice to be back, Dad.

(Pause.)

MAX: You should have told me you were married, Teddy. I'd have sent you a present. Where was the wedding, in America?

TEDDY: No. Here. The day before we left.

MAX: Did you have a big function?

TEDDY: No, there was no one there.

MAX: You're mad. I'd have given you a white wedding. We'd have had the cream of the cream here. I'd have been only too glad to bear the expense, my word of honour.

(Pause.)

TEDDY: You were busy at the time. I didn't want to bother you.

MAX: But you're my own flesh and blood. You're my first born. I'd have dropped everything. Sam would have driven you to the reception in the Snipe, Lenny would have been your best man, and then we'd have all seen you off on the boat. I mean, you don't think I disapprove of marriage, do you? Don't be daft. *(to RUTH)* I've been begging my two youngsters for years to find a nice feminine girl with proper credentials—it makes life worth living. *(to TEDDY)* Anyway, what's the difference, you did it, you made a wonderful choice, you've got a wonderful family, a marvellous career . . . so why don't we let bygones be bygones?

(Pause.)

You know what I'm saying? I want you both to know that you have my blessing.

TEDDY: Thank you.

MAX: Don't mention it. How many other houses in the district have got a Doctor of Philosophy sitting down drinking a cup of coffee?

(Pause.)

RUTH: I'm sure Teddy's very happy . . . to know that you're pleased with me.

(Pause.)

I think he wondered whether you would be pleased with me.

MAX: But you're a charming woman.

(Pause.)

RUTH: I was . . .

MAX: What?

(Pause.)

What she say?

(They all look at her.)

RUTH: I was . . . different . . . when I met Teddy . . . first.

TEDDY: No you weren't. You were the same.

RUTH: I wasn't.

MAX: Who cares? Listen, live in the present, what are you worrying about? I mean, don't forget the earth's about five thousand million years old, at least. Who can afford to live in the past?

(Pause.)

TEDDY: She's a great help to me over there. She's a wonderful wife and mother. She's a very popular woman. She's got lots of friends. It's a great life, at the University . . . you know . . . it's a very good life. We've got a lovely house . . . we've got all . . . we've got everything we want. It's a very stimulating environment.

(Pause.)

My department . . . is highly successful.

(Pause.)

We've got three boys, you know.

MAX: All boys? Isn't that funny, eh? You've got three, I've got three. You've got three nephews, Joey. Joey! You're an uncle, do you hear? You could teach them how to box.

(Pause.)

JOEY *(to RUTH)*: I'm a boxer. In the evenings, after work. I'm in demolition in the daytime.

RUTH: Oh?

JOEY: Yes. I hope to be full time, when I get more bouts.

MAX *(to LENNY)*: He speaks so easily to his sister-in-law, do you notice. That's because she's an intelligent and sympathetic woman.

(He leans to her.)

Eh, tell me, do you think the children are missing their mother?

(She looks at him.)

TEDDY: Of course they are. They love her. We'll be seeing them soon.

(Pause.)

LENNY (*to* TEDDY): Your cigar's gone out.
TEDDY: Oh, yes.
LENNY: Want a light?
TEDDY: No. No.

(*Pause.*)

So has yours.
LENNY: Oh, yes.

(*Pause.*)

Eh, Teddy, you haven't told us much about your Doctorship of Philosophy. What do you teach?
TEDDY: Philosophy.
LENNY: Well, I want to ask you something. Do you detect a certain logical incoherence in the central affirmations of Christian theism?
TEDDY: That question doesn't fall within my province.
LENNY: Well, look at it this way . . . you don't mind my asking you some questions, do you?
TEDDY: If they're within my province.
LENNY: Well, look at it this way. How can the unknown merit reverence? In other words, how can you revere that of which you're ignorant? At the same time, it would be ridiculous to propose that what we *know* merits reverence. What we know merits any one of a number of things, but it stands to reason reverence isn't one of them. In other words, apart from the known and the unknown, what else is there?

(*Pause.*)

TEDDY: I'm afraid I'm the wrong person to ask.
LENNY: But you're a philosopher. Come on, be frank. What do you make of all this business of being and not-being?
TEDDY: What do you make of it?
LENNY: Well, for instance, take a table. Philosophically speaking. What is it?
TEDDY: A table.
LENNY: Ah. You mean it's nothing else but a table. Well, some people would envy your certainty, wouldn't they, Joey? For instance, I've got a couple of friends of mine, we often sit round the Ritz Bar having a few liqueurs, and they're always saying things like that, you know, things like: Take a table, take it. All right, I say, *take* it, *take* a table, but once you've taken it, what are you going to do with it? Once you've got hold of it, where you going to take it?
MAX: You'd probably sell it.
LENNY: You wouldn't get much for it.
JOEY: Chop it up for firewood.

(LENNY *looks at him and laughs.*)

RUTH: Don't be too sure though. You've forgotten something. Look at me. I . . . move my leg.

That's all it is. But I wear . . . underwear . . . which moves with me . . . it . . . captures your attention. Perhaps you misinterpret. The action is simple. It's a leg . . . moving. My lips move. Why don't you restrict . . . your observations to that? Perhaps the fact that they move is more significant . . . than the words which come through them. You must bear that . . . possibility . . . in mind.

(*Silence.*
TEDDY *stands.*)

I was born quite near here.

(*Pause.*)

Then . . . six years ago, I went to America.

(*Pause.*)

It's all rock. And sand. It stretches . . . so far . . . everywhere you look. And there's lots of insects there.

(*Pause.*)

And there's lots of insects there.

(*Silence.*
She is still.
MAX *stands.*)

MAX: Well, it's time to go to the gym. Time for your workout, Joey.
LENNY (*standing.*): I'll come with you.

(JOEY *sits looking at* RUTH.)

MAX: Joe.

(JOEY *stands. The three go out.*
TEDDY *sits by* RUTH, *holds her hand.*
She smiles at him.
Pause.)

TEDDY: I think we'll go back. Mmnn?

(*Pause.*)

Shall we go home?
RUTH: Why?
TEDDY: Well, we were only here for a few days, weren't we? We might as well . . . cut it short, I think.
RUTH: Why? Don't you like it here?
TEDDY: Of course I do. But I'd like to go back and see the boys now.

(*Pause.*)

RUTH: Don't you like your family?
TEDDY: Which family?
RUTH: Your family here.
TEDDY: Of course I like them. What are you talking about?

(*Pause.*)

RUTH: You don't like them as much as you thought you did?

TEDDY: Of course I do. Of course I . . . like them. I don't know what you're talking about.

(Pause.)

Listen. You know what time of thé day it is there now, do you?

RUTH: What?

TEDDY: It's morning. It's about eleven o'clock.

RUTH: Is it?

TEDDY: Yes, they're about six hours behind us . . . I mean . . . behind the time here. The boys'll be at the pool . . . now . . . swimming. Think of it. Morning over there. Sun. We'll go anyway, mmnn? It's so clean there.

RUTH: Clean.

TEDDY: Yes.

RUTH: Is it dirty here?

TEDDY: No, of course not. But it's cleaner there.

(Pause.)

Look, I just brought you back to meet the family, didn't I? You've met them, we can go. The fall semester will be starting soon.

RUTH: You find it dirty here?

TEDDY: I didn't say I found it dirty here.

(Pause.)

I didn't say that.

(Pause.)

Look. I'll go and pack. You rest for a while. Will you? They won't be back for at least an hour. You can sleep. Rest. Please.

(She looks at him.)

You can help me with my lectures when we get back. I'd love that. I'd be so grateful for it, really. We can bathe till October. You know that. Here, there's nowhere to bathe, except the swimming bath down the road. You know what it's like? It's like a urinal. A filthy urinal!

(Pause.)

You liked Venice, didn't you? It was lovely, wasn't it? You had a good week. I mean . . . I took you there. I can speak Italian.

RUTH: But if I'd been a nurse in the Italian campaign I would have been there before.

(Pause.)

TEDDY: You just rest. I'll go and pack.

(TEDDY goes out and up the stairs.
(She closes her eyes.
LENNY appears from upper left.

*He walks into the room and sits near her.
She opens her eyes.
Silence.)*

LENNY: Well, the evenings are drawing in.

RUTH: Yes, it's getting dark.

(Pause.)

LENNY: Winter'll soon be upon us. Time to renew one's wardrobe.

(Pause.)

RUTH: That's a good thing to do.

LENNY: What?

(Pause.)

RUTH: I always . . .

(Pause.)

Do you like clothes?

LENNY: Oh, yes. Very fond of clothes.

(Pause.)

RUTH: I'm fond . . .

(Pause.)

What do you think of my shoes?

LENNY: They're very nice.

RUTH: No, I can't get the ones I want over there.

LENNY: Can't get them over there, eh?

RUTH: No . . . you don't get them there.

(Pause.)

I was a model before I went away.

LENNY: Hats?

(Pause.)

I bought a girl a hat once. We saw it in a glass case, in a shop. I tell you what it had. It had a bunch of daffodils on it, tied with a black satin bow, and then it was covered with a cloche of black veiling. A cloche. I'm telling you. She was made for it.

RUTH: No . . . I was a model for the body. A photographic model for the body.

LENNY: Indoor work?

RUTH: That was before I had . . . all my children.

(Pause.)

No, not always indoors.

(Pause.)

Once or twice we went to a place in the country, by train. Oh, six or seven times. We used to pass a . . . a large white water tower. This place . . . this house . . . was very big . . . the trees . . . there was a lake, you see . . . we used to change and

walk down towards the lake . . . we went down a
path . . . on stones . . . there were . . . on this
path. Oh, just . . . wait . . . yes . . . when we
changed in the house we had a drink. There was
a cold buffet.

(*Pause.*)

Sometimes we stayed in the house but . . . most
often . . . we walked down to the lake . . . and did
our modelling there.

(*Pause.*)

Just before we went to America I went down
there. I walked from the station to the gate and
then I walked up the drive. There were lights on
. . . I stood in the drive . . . the house was very
light.

(TEDDY *comes down the stairs with the cases. He puts
them down, looks at* LENNY.)

TEDDY: What have you been saying to her?

(*He goes to* RUTH.)

Here's your coat.

(LENNY *goes to the radiogram and puts on a record of
slow jazz.*)

Ruth. Come on. Put it on.

LENNY (*to* RUTH): What about one dance before you
    go?

TEDDY: We're going.

LENNY: Just one.

TEDDY: No. We're going.

LENNY: Just one dance, with her brother-in-law, be-
    fore she goes.

(LENNY *bends to her.*)

Madam?

(RUTH *stands. They dance, slowly.*
TEDDY *stands, with* RUTH'S *coat.*
MAX *and* JOEY *come in the front door and into the room.
They stand.*
LENNY *kisses* RUTH. *They stand, kissing.*)

JOEY: Christ, she's wide open. Dad, look at that.

(*Pause.*)

She's a tart.

(*Pause.*)

Old Lenny's got a tart in here.

(JOEY *goes to them. He takes* RUTH'S *arm. He smiles at*
LENNY. *He sits with* RUTH *on the sofa, embraces and
kisses her.*
He looks up at LENNY.)

Just up my street.

(*He leans her back until she lies beneath him. He kisses
her.*
He looks up at TEDDY *and* MAX.)

It's better than a rubdown, this.

(LENNY *sits on the arm of the sofa. He caresses* RUTH'S
hair as JOEY *embraces her.*
MAX *comes forward, looks at the cases.*)

MAX: You going, Teddy? Already?

(*Pause.*)

Well, when you coming over again, eh? Look,
next time you come over, don't forget to let us
know beforehand whether you're married or
not. I'll always be glad to meet the wife. Honest.
I'm telling you.

(JOEY *lies heavily on* RUTH.
They are almost still.
LENNY *caresses her hair.*)

Listen, you think I don't know why you didn't
tell me you were married? I know why. You were
ashamed. You thought I'd be annoyed because
you married a woman beneath you. You should
have known me better. I'm broadminded. I'm a
broadminded man.

(*He peers to see* RUTH'S *face under* JOEY, *turns back to*
TEDDY.)

Mind you, she's a lovely girl. A beautiful woman.
And a mother too. A mother of three. You've
made a happy woman out of her. It's something
to be proud of. I mean, we're talking about a
woman of quality. We're talking about a woman
of feeling.

(JOEY *and* RUTH *roll off the sofa on to the floor.*
JOEY *clasps her.* LENNY *moves to stand above them. He
looks down on them. He touches* RUTH *gently with his
foot.*
RUTH *suddenly pushes* JOEY *away.*
She stands up.
JOEY *gets to his feet, stares at her.*)

RUTH: I'd like something to eat. (*To* LENNY.) I'd like a
    drink. Did you get any drink?

LENNY: We've got drink.

RUTH: I'd like one, please.

LENNY: What drink?

RUTH: Whisky.

LENNY: I've got it.

(*Pause.*)

RUTH: Well, get it.

(LENNY *goes to the sideboard, takes out bottle and glasses.*
JOEY *moves toward her.*)

Put the record off.

(*He looks at her, turns, puts the record off.*)

I want something to eat.

(*Pause.*)

JOEY: I can't cook. (*Pointing to* MAX.) He's the cook.

(LENNY *brings her a glass of whisky.*)

LENNY: Soda on the side?

RUTH: What's this glass? I can't drink out of this. Haven't you got a tumbler?

LENNY: Yes.

RUTH: Well, put it in a tumbler.

(*He takes the glass back, pours whisky into a tumbler, brings it to her.*)

LENNY: On the rocks. Or as it comes?

RUTH: Rocks? What do you know about rocks?

LENNY: We've got rocks. But they're frozen stiff in the fridge.

(RUTH *drinks.*
LENNY *looks round at the others.*)

Drinks all round?

(*He goes to the sideboard and pours drinks.*
JOEY *moves closer to* RUTH.)

JOEY: What food do you want?

(RUTH *walks round the room.*)

RUTH (*to* TEDDY): Have your family read your critical works?

MAX: That's one thing I've never done. I've never read one of his critical works.

TEDDY: You wouldn't understand them.

(LENNY *hands drinks all round.*)

JOEY: What sort of food do you want? I'm not the cook, anyway.

LENNY: Soda, Ted? Or as it comes?

TEDDY: You wouldn't understand my works. You wouldn't have the faintest idea of what they were about. You wouldn't appreciate the points of reference. You're way behind. All of you. There's no point in my sending you my works. You'd be lost. It's nothing to do with the question of intelligence. It's a way of being able to look at the world. It's a question of how far you can operate on things and not in things. I mean it's a question of your capacity to ally the two, to relate the two, to balance the two. To see, to be able to *see*! I'm the one who can see. That's why I can write my critical works. Might do you good . . . have a look at them . . . see how certain people can view . . . things . . . how certain people can maintain . . . intellectual equilibrium. Intellec-

tual equilibrium. You're just objects. You just . . . move about. I can observe it. I can see what you do. It's the same as I do. But you're lost in it. You won't get me being . . . I won't be lost in it.

(BLACKOUT.
LIGHTS UP.
Evening.
TEDDY *sitting, in his coat, the cases by him.* SAM.
Pause.)

SAM: Do you remember MacGregor, Teddy?

TEDDY: Mac?

SAM: Yes.

TEDDY: Of course I do.

SAM: What did you think of him? Did you take to him?

TEDDY: Yes. I liked him. Why?

(*Pause.*)

SAM: You know, you were always my favourite, of the lads. Always.

(*Pause.*)

When you wrote to me from America I was very touched, you know. I mean you'd written to your father a few times but you'd never written to me. But then, when I got that letter from you . . . well, I was very touched. I never told him. I never told him I'd heard from you.

(*Pause.*)

(*Whispering.*) Teddy, shall I tell you something? You were always your mother's favourite. She told me. It's true. You were always the . . . you were always the main object of her love.

(*Pause.*)

Why don't you stay for a couple more weeks, eh? We could have a few laughs.

(LENNY *comes in the front door and into the room.*)

LENNY: Still here, Ted? You'll be late for your first seminar.

(*He goes to the sideboard, opens it, peers in it, to the right and the left, stands.*)

Where's my cheese-roll?

(*Pause.*)

Someone's taken my cheese-roll. I left it there. (*To* SAM.) You been thieving?

TEDDY: I took your cheese-roll, Lenny.

(*Silence.*
SAM *looks at them, picks up his hat and goes out of the front door.*
Silence.)

LENNY: You took my cheese-roll?

TEDDY: Yes.

LENNY: I made that roll myself. I cut it and put the butter on. I sliced a piece of cheese and put it in between. I put it on a plate and I put it in the sideboard. I did all that before I went out. Now I come back and you've eaten it.

TEDDY: Well, what are you going to do about it?

LENNY: I'm waiting for you to apologize.

TEDDY: But I took it deliberately, Lenny.

LENNY: You mean you didn't stumble on it by mistake?

TEDDY: No, I saw you put it there. I was hungry, so I ate it.

(Pause.)

LENNY: Barefaced audacity.

(Pause.)

What led you to be so . . . vindictive against your own brother? I'm bowled over.

(Pause.)

Well, Ted, I would say this is something approaching the naked truth, isn't it? It's a real cards on the table stunt. I mean, we're in the land of no holds barred now. Well, how else can you interpret it? To pinch your younger brother's specially made cheese-roll when he's out doing a spot of work, that's not equivocal, it's unequivocal.

(Pause.)

Mind you, I will say you do seem to have grown a bit sulky during the last six years. A bit sulky. A bit inner. A bit less forthcoming. It's funny, because I'd have thought that in the United States of America, I mean with the sun and all that, the open spaces, on the old campus, in your position, lecturing, in the centre of all the intellectual life out there, on the old campus, all the social whirl, all the stimulation of it all, all your kids and all that, to have fun with, down by the pool, the Greyhound buses and all that, tons of iced water, all the comfort of those Bermuda shorts and all that, on the old campus, no time of the day or night you can't get a cup of coffee or a Dutch gin, I'd have thought you'd have grown more forthcoming, not less. Because I want you to know that you set a standard for us, Teddy. Your family looks up to you, boy, and you know what it does? It does its best to follow the example you set. Because you're a great source of pride to us. That's why we were so glad to see you come back, to welcome you back to your birthplace. That's why.

(Pause.)

No, listen, Ted, there's no question that we live a less rich life here than you do over there. We live a closer life. We're busy, of course. Joey's busy with his boxing, I'm busy with my occupation, Dad still plays a good game of poker, and he does the cooking as well, well up to his old standard, and Uncle Sam's the best chauffeur in the firm. But nevertheless we do make up a unit, Teddy, and you're an integral part of it. When we all sit round the backyard having a quiet gander at the night sky, there's always an empty chair standing in the circle, which is in fact yours. And so when you at length return to us, we do expect a bit of grace, a bit of je ne sais quoi, a bit of generosity of mind, a bit of liberality of spirit, to reassure us. We do expect that. But do we get it? Have we got it? Is that what you've given us?

(Pause.)

TEDDY: Yes.

(JOEY comes down the stairs and into the room, with a newspaper.)

LENNY *(to JOEY)*: How'd you get on?

JOEY: Er . . . not bad.

LENNY: What do you mean?

(Pause.)

What do you mean?

JOEY: Not bad.

LENNY: I want to know what you *mean*—by not bad.

JOEY: What's it got to do with you?

LENNY: Joey, you tell your brother everything.

(Pause.)

JOEY: I didn't get all the way.

LENNY: You didn't get all the way?

(Pause.)

(With emphasis.) You didn't get all the way? But you've had her up there for two hours.

JOEY: Well?

LENNY: You didn't get all the way and you've had her up there for two hours!

JOEY: What about it?

(LENNY moves closer to him.)

LENNY: What are you telling me?

JOEY: What do you mean?

LENNY: Are you telling me she's a tease?

(Pause.)

She's a tease!

(Pause.)

What do you think of that, Ted? Your wife turns out to be a tease. He's had her up there for two hours and he didn't go the whole hog.

JOEY: I didn't say she was a tease.

LENNY: Are you joking? It sounds like a tease to me, don't it to you, Ted?

TEDDY: Perhaps he hasn't got the right touch.

LENNY: Joey? Not the right touch? Don't be ridiculous. He's had more dolly than you've had cream cakes. He's irresistible. He's one of the few and far between. Tell him about the last bird you had, Joey.

(Pause.)

JOEY: What bird?

LENNY: The last bird! When we stopped the car . . .

JOEY: Oh, that . . . yes . . . well, we were in Lenny's car one night last week . . .

LENNY: The Alfa.

JOEY: And er . . . bowling down the road . . .

LENNY: Up near the Scrubs.

JOEY: Yes, up over by the Scrubs . . .

LENNY: We were doing a little survey of North Paddington.

JOEY: And er . . . it was pretty late, wasn't it?

LENNY: Yes, it was late. Well?

(Pause.)

JOEY: And then we . . . well, by the kerb, we saw this parked car . . . with a couple of girls in it.

LENNY: And their escorts.

JOEY: Yes, there were two geezers in it. Anyway . . .

(Pause.)

What we do then?

LENNY: We stopped the car and got out!

JOEY: Yes . . . we got out . . . and we told the . . . two escorts . . . to go away . . . which they did . . . and then we . . . got the girls out of the car . . .

LENNY: We didn't take them over the Scrubs.

JOEY: Oh, no. Not over the Scrubs. Well, the police would have noticed us there . . . you see. We took them over a bombed site.

LENNY: Rubble. In the rubble.

JOEY: Yes, plenty of rubble.

(Pause.)

Well . . . you know . . . then we had them.

LENNY: You've missed out the best bit. He's missed out the best bit!

JOEY: What bit?

LENNY *(to TEDDY)*: His bird says to him, I don't mind, she says, but I've got to have some protection. I've got to have some contraceptive protection. I haven't got any contraceptive protection, old Joey says to her. In that case I won't do it, she says. Yes you will, says Joey, never mind about the contraceptive protection.

(LENNY laughs.)

Even my bird laughed when she heard that. Yes, even she gave out a bit of a laugh. So you can't say old Joey isn't a bit of a knockout when he gets going, can you? And here he is upstairs with your wife for two hours and he hasn't even been the whole hog. Well, your wife sounds like a bit of a tease to me, Ted. What do you make of it, Joey? You satisfied? Don't tell me you're satisfied without going the whole hog?

(Pause.)

JOEY: I've been the whole hog plenty of times. Sometimes . . . you can be happy . . . and not go the whole hog. Now and again . . . you can be happy . . . without going any hog.

(LENNY stares at him.
MAX and SAM come in the front door and into the room.)

MAX: Where's the whore? Still in bed? She'll make us all animals.

LENNY: The girl's a tease.

MAX: What?

LENNY: She's had Joey on a string.

MAX: What do you mean?

TEDDY: He had her up there for two hours and he didn't go the whole hog.

(Pause.)

MAX: My Joey? She did that to my boy?

(Pause.)

To my youngest son? Tch, tch, tch, tch. How you feeling, son? Are you all right?

JOEY: Sure I'm all right.

MAX *(to TEDDY)*: Does she do that to you, too?

TEDDY: No.

LENNY: He gets the gravy.

MAX: You think so?

JOEY: No he don't.

(Pause.)

SAM: He's her lawful husband. She's his lawful wife.

JOEY: No he don't! He don't get no gravy! I'm telling you. I'm telling all of you. I'll kill the next man who says he gets the gravy.

MAX: Joey . . . what are you getting so excited about? *(to LENNY)* It's because he's frustrated. You see what happens?

JOEY: Who is?

MAX: Joey. No one's saying you're wrong. In fact everyone's saying you're right.

(Pause.
MAX *turns to the others.)*

You know something? Perhaps it's not a bad idea to have a woman in the house. Perhaps it's a good thing. Who knows? Maybe we should keep her.

(Pause.)

Maybe we'll ask her if she wants to stay.

(Pause.)

TEDDY: I'm afraid not, Dad. She's not well, and we've got to get home to the children.
MAX: Not well? I told you, I'm used to looking after people who are not so well. Don't worry about that. Perhaps we'll keep her here.

(Pause.)

SAM: Don't be silly.
MAX: What's silly?
SAM: You're talking rubbish.
MAX: Me?
SAM: She's got three children.
MAX: She can have more! If she's so keen.
TEDDY: She doesn't want any more.
MAX: What do you know about what she wants, eh, Ted?
TEDDY *(smiling)*: The best thing for her is to come home with me, Dad. Really. We're married, you know.

*(*MAX *walks about the room, clicks his fingers.)*

MAX: We'd have to pay her, of course. You realize that? We can't leave her walking about without any pocket money. She'll have to have a little allowance.
JOEY: Of course we'll pay her. She's got to have some money in her pocket.
MAX: That's what I'm saying. You can't expect a woman to walk about without a few bob to spend on a pair of stockings.

(Pause.)

LENNY: Where's the money going to come from?
MAX: Well, how much is she worth? What we talking about three figures?
LENNY: I asked you where the money's going to come from. It'll be an extra mouth to feed. It'll be an extra body to clothe. You realize that?
JOEY: I'll buy her clothes.
LENNY: What with?
JOEY: I'll put in a certain amount out of my wages.
MAX: That's it. We'll pass the hat round. We'll make a donation. We're all grown-up people, we've got a sense of responsibility. We'll put a little in the hat. It's democratic.

LENNY: It'll come to a few quid, Dad.

(Pause.)

I mean, she's not a woman who likes walking around in second-hand goods. She's up to the latest fashion. You wouldn't want her walking about in clothes which don't show her off at her best, would you?
MAX: Lenny, do you mind if I make a little comment? It's not meant to be critical. But I think you're concentrating too much on the economic considerations. There are other considerations. There are the human considerations. You understand what I mean? There are the human considerations. Don't forget them.
LENNY: I won't.
MAX: Well don't.

(Pause.)

Listen, we're bound to treat her in something approximating, at least, to the manner in which she's accustomed. After all, she's not someone off the street, she's my daughter-in-law!
JOEY: That's right.
MAX: There you are, you see. Joey'll donate, Sam'll donate. . . .

*(*SAM *looks at him.)*

I'll put in a few bob out of my pension, Lenny'll cough up. We're laughing. What about you, Ted? How much you going to put in the kitty?
TEDDY: I'm not putting anything in the kitty.
MAX: What? You won't even help to support your own wife? I thought he was a son of mine. You lousy stinkpig. Your mother would drop dead if she heard you take that attitude.
LENNY: Eh, Dad.

*(*LENNY *walks forward.)*

I've got a better idea.
MAX: What?
LENNY: There's no need for us to go to all this expense. I know these women. Once they get started they ruin your budget. I've got a better idea. Why don't I take her up with me to Greek Street?

(Pause.)

MAX: You mean put her on the game?

(Pause.)

We'll put her on the game. That's a stroke of genius, that's a marvellous idea. You mean she can earn the money herself—on her back?
LENNY: Yes.
MAX: Wonderful. The only thing is, it'll have to be

short hours. We don't want her out of the house all night.

LENNY: I can limit the hours.

MAX: How many?

LENNY: Four hours a night.

MAX (*dubiously*): Is that enough?

LENNY: She'll bring in a good sum for four hours a night.

MAX: Well, you should know. After all, it's true, the last thing we want to do is wear the girl out. She's going to have her obligations this end as well. Where you going to put her in Greek Street?

LENNY: It doesn't have to be right in Greek Street, Dad. I've got a number of flats all around that area.

MAX: You have? Well, what about me? Why don't you give me one?

LENNY: You're sexless.

JOEY: Eh, wait a minute, what's all this?

MAX: I know what Lenny's saying. Lenny's saying she can pay her own way. What do you think, Teddy? That'll solve all our problems.

JOEY: Eh, wait a minute. I don't want to share her.

MAX: What did you say?

JOEY: I don't want to share her with a lot of yobs!

MAX: Yobs! You arrogant git! What arrogance. (*to* LENNY) Will you be supplying her with yobs?

LENNY: I've got a very distinguished clientèle, Joey. They're more distinguished than you'll ever be.

MAX: So you can count yourself lucky we're including you in.

JOEY: I didn't think I was going to have to share her!

MAX: Well, you *are* going to have to share her! Otherwise she goes straight back to America. You understand?

(*Pause.*)

It's tricky enough as it is, without you shoving your oar in. But there's something worrying me. Perhaps she's not so up to the mark. Eh? Teddy, you're the best judge. Do you think she'd be up to the mark?

(*Pause.*)

I mean what about all this teasing? Is she going to make a habit of it? That'll get us nowhere.

(*Pause.*)

TEDDY: It was just love play . . . I suppose . . . that's all I suppose it was.

MAX: Love play? Two bleeding hours? That's a bloody long time for love play!

LENNY: I don't think we've got anything to worry about on that score, Dad.

MAX: How do you know?

LENNY: I'm giving you a professional opinion.

(LENNY *goes to* TEDDY.)

LENNY: Listen, Teddy, you could help us, actually. If I were to send you some cards, over to America . . . you know, very nice ones, with a name on, and a telephone number, very discreet, well, you could distribute them . . . to various parties, who might be making a trip over here. Of course, you'd get a little percentage out of it.

MAX: I mean, you needn't tell them she's your wife.

LENNY: No, we'd call her something else. Dolores, or something.

MAX: Or Spanish Jacky.

LENNY: No, you've got to be reserved about it, Dad. We could call her something nice . . . like Cynthia . . . or Gillian.

(*Pause.*)

JOEY: Gillian.

(*Pause.*)

LENNY: No, what I mean, Teddy, you must know lots of professors, heads of departments, men like that. They pop over here for a week at the Savoy, they need somewhere they can go to have a nice quiet poke. And of course you'd be in a position to give them inside information.

MAX: Sure. You can give them proper data. You know, the kind of thing she's willing to do. How far she'd be prepared to go with their little whims and fancies. Eh, Lenny. To what extent she's various. I mean if you don't know, who does?

(*Pause.*)

I bet you before two months we'd have a waiting list.

LENNY: You could be our representative in the States.

MAX: Of course. We're talking in international terms! By the time we've finished Pan-American'll give us a discount.

(*Pause.*)

TEDDY: She'd get old . . . very quickly.

MAX: No . . . not in this day and age! With the health service? Old! How could she get old? She'll have the time of her life.

(RUTH *comes down the stairs, dressed.*
She comes into the room.
She smiles at the gathering, and sits.
Silence.)

TEDDY: Ruth . . . the family have invited you to stay, for a little while longer. As a . . . as a kind of guest. If you like the idea I don't mind. We can manage very easily at home . . . until you come back.

RUTH: How very nice of them.

(Pause.)

MAX: It's an offer from our heart.

RUTH: It's very sweet of you.

MAX: Listen . . . it would be our pleasure.

(Pause.)

RUTH: I think I'd be too much trouble.

MAX: Trouble? What are you talking about? What trouble? Listen, I'll tell you something. Since poor Jessie died, eh, Sam? we haven't had a woman in the house. Not one. Inside this house. And I'll tell you why. Because their mother's image was so dear any other woman would have . . . tarnished it. But you . . . Ruth . . . you're not only lovely and beautiful, but you're kin. You're kith. You belong here.

(Pause.)

RUTH: I'm very touched.

MAX: Of course you're touched. I'm touched.

(Pause.)

TEDDY: But Ruth, I should tell you . . . that you'll have to pull your weight a little, if you stay. Financially. My father isn't very well off.

RUTH *(to* MAX*)*: Oh, I'm sorry.

MAX: No, you'd just have to bring in a little, that's all. A few pennies. Nothing much. It's just that we're waiting for Joey to hit the top as a boxer. When Joey hits the top . . . well . . .

(Pause.)

TEDDY: Or you can come home with me.

LENNY: We'd get you a flat.

(Pause.)

RUTH: A flat?

LENNY: Yes.

RUTH: Where?

LENNY: In town.

(Pause.)

But you'd live here, with us.

MAX: Of course you would. This would be your home. In the bosom of the family.

LENNY: You'd just pop up to the flat a couple of hours a night, that's all.

MAX: Just a couple of hours, that's all. That's all.

LENNY: And you make enough money to keep you going here.

(Pause.)

RUTH: How many rooms would this flat have?

LENNY: Not many.

RUTH: I would want at least three rooms and a bathroom.

LENNY: You wouldn't need three rooms and a bathroom.

MAX: She'd need a bathroom.

LENNY: But not three rooms.

(Pause.)

RUTH: Oh, I would. Really.

LENNY: Two would do.

RUTH: No. Two wouldn't be enough.

(Pause.)

I'd want a dressing-room, a rest-room, and a bedroom.

(Pause.)

LENNY: All right, we'll get you a flat with three rooms and a bathroom.

RUTH: With what kind of conveniences?

LENNY: All conveniences.

RUTH: A personal maid?

LENNY: Of course.

(Pause.)

We'd finance you, to begin with, and then, when you were established, you could pay us back, in instalments.

RUTH: Oh, no, I wouldn't agree to that.

LENNY: Oh, why not?

RUTH: You would have to regard your original outlay simply as a capital investment.

(Pause.)

LENNY: I see. All right.

RUTH: You'd supply my wardrobe, of course?

LENNY: We'd supply everything. Everything you need.

RUTH: I'd need an awful lot. Otherwise I wouldn't be content.

LENNY: You'd have everything.

RUTH: I would naturally want to draw up an inventory of everything I would need, which would require your signatures in the presence of witnesses.

LENNY: Naturally.

RUTH: All aspects of the agreement and conditions of employment would have to be clarified to our mutual satisfaction before we finalized the contract.

LENNY: Of course.

(Pause.)

RUTH: Well, it might prove a workable arrangement.

LENNY: I think so.

MAX: And you'd have the whole of your daytime free, of course. You could do a bit of cooking here if you wanted to.

LENNY: Make the beds.

MAX: Scrub the place out a bit.

TEDDY: Keep everyone company.

(SAM *comes forward.*)

SAM (*in one breath*): MacGregor had Jessie in the back of my cab as I drove them along.

(*He croaks and collapses.*
He lies still.
They look at him.)

MAX: What's he done? Dropped dead?

LENNY: Yes.

MAX: A corpse? A corpse on my floor? Get him out of here! Clear him out of here!

(JOEY *bends over* SAM.)

JOEY: He's not dead.

LENNY: He probably was dead, for about thirty seconds.

MAX: He's not even dead!

(LENNY *looks down at* SAM.)

LENNY: Yes, there's still some breath there.

MAX (*pointing at* SAM): You know what that man had?

LENNY: Has.

MAX: Has! A diseased imagination.

(*Pause.*)

RUTH: Yes, it sounds a very attractive idea.

MAX: Do you want to shake on it now, or do you want to leave it till later?

RUTH: Oh, we'll leave it till later.

(TEDDY *stands.*
He looks down at SAM.)

TEDDY: I was going to ask him to drive me to London Airport.

(*He goes to the cases, picks one up.*)

Well, I'll leave your case, Ruth. I'll just go up the road to the Underground.

MAX: Listen if you go the other way, first left, first right, you remember, you might find a cab passing there.

TEDDY: Yes, I might do that.

MAX: Or you can take the tube to Piccadilly Circus, won't take you ten minutes, and pick up a cab from there out to the Airport.

TEDDY: Yes, I'll probably do that.

MAX: Mind you, they'll charge you double fare. They'll charge you for the return trip. It's over the six-mile limit.

TEDDY: Yes. Well, bye-bye, Dad. Look after yourself.

(*They shake hands.*)

MAX: Thanks, son. Listen. I want to tell you something. It's been wonderful to see you.

(*Pause.*)

TEDDY: It's been wonderful to see you.

MAX: Do your boys know about me? Would they like to see a photo, do you think, of their grandfather?

TEDDY: I know they would.

(MAX *brings out his wallet.*)

MAX: I've got one on me. I've got one here. Just a minute. Here you are. Will they like that one?

TEDDY (*taking it*): They'll be thrilled.

(*He turns to* LENNY.)

Good-bye, Lenny.

(*They shake hands.*)

LENNY: Ta-ta, Ted. Good to see you. Have a good trip.

TEDDY: Bye-bye, Joey.

(JOEY *does not move.*)

JOEY: Ta-ta.

(TEDDY *goes to the front door.*)

RUTH: Eddie.

(TEDDY *turns.*
Pause.)

Don't become a stranger.

(TEDDY *goes, shuts the front door.*
Silence.
The three men stand.
RUTH *sits relaxed in her chair.*
SAM *lies still.*
JOEY *walks slowly across the room.*
He kneels at her chair.
She touches his head, lightly.
He puts his head in her lap.
MAX *begins to move above them, backwards and forwards.*
LENNY *stands still.*
MAX *turns to* LENNY.)

MAX: I'm too old, I suppose. She thinks I'm an old man.

(*Pause.*)

I'm not such an old man.

(*Pause.*)

(*To* RUTH) You think I'm too old for you?

(Pause.)

Listen. You think you're just going to get that big slag all the time? You think you're just going to have him . . . you're going to just have him all the time? You're going to have to work! You'll have to take them on, you understand?

(Pause.)

Does she realize that?

(Pause.)

Lenny, do you think she understands . . .

(He begins to stammer.)

What . . . what . . . what . . . we're getting at? What . . . we've got in mind? Do you think she's got it clear?

(Pause.)

I don't think she's got it clear.

(Pause.)

You understand what I mean? Listen, I've got a funny idea she'll do the dirty on us, you want to bet? She'll use us, she'll make use of us, I can tell you that! I can smell it! You want to bet?

(Pause.)

She won't . . . be adaptable!

(He falls to his knees, whimpers, begins to moan and sob. He stops sobbing, crawls past SAM's *body round her chair, to the other side of her.)*

I'm not an old man.

(He looks up at her.)

Do you hear me?

(He raises his face to her.)

Kiss me.

(She continues to touch JOEY's *head, lightly.* LENNY *stands, watching.)*

CURTAIN

Figure 97. Lenny (Ian Holm) offers Ruth (Vivien Merchant) a glass of water in the Royal Shakespeare Company production of *The Homecoming,* directed by Peter Hall, New York, 1967. (Photograph: Friedman-Abeles.)

Figure 98. Max (Paul Rogers, *left*) insults Ruth (Vivien Merchant) while *(left to right)* Joey (Terence Rigby), Sam (John Normington), Teddy (Michael Craig), and Lenny (Ian Holm) listen in the Royal Shakespeare Company production of *The Homecoming,* directed by Peter Hall, New York, 1967. (Photograph: Friedman-Abeles.)

Staging of *The Homecoming*

**REVIEW OF THE ROYAL SHAKESPEARE
COMPANY PRODUCTION, 1967, BY WALTER
KERR**

Harold Pinter's "The Homecoming" consists of a single situation that the author refuses to dramatize until he has dragged us all, aching, through a half-drugged dream.

The situation, when it is arrived at, is interesting in the way that Pinter's numbed fantasies are almost always interesting. A Doctor of Philosophy who actually teaches philosophy returns with his wife to the family home in North London, a home that looks like an emptied-out wing of the British Museum gone thoroughly to seed. (The few pieces of furniture are lonely in this cavern. The molding along the walls breaks off and gives up before it can reach the doorways, the carpet could be made of cement.)

A father and two brothers take one look at the wife and mistake (or do not mistake) her for a whore. She is silent, poised, leggy, self-contained. In due time the family decides that they would rather like to have a whore around, whatever about her husband and about the three children she has left behind in America. She might very well be kept available in a room at the top of the steep, forbidding staircase, and she could always pay her own keep by renting herself out a few nights a week.

They put the proposition to her, matter-of-factly, after she has obliged them by moving into trance-like dance with one of the brothers, brushing unfinished kisses across his lips and then obligingly draping herself to another brother's needs across a cold and impersonal sofa.

It is at this point that Mr. Pinter's most curious and most characteristic abilities as a diviner of unspecified demons come effectively into play. We are in an unconventional situation, and of course we know that. But our habits of mind—our compulsive attempts to try to deal with the world by slide rule—still continue to function, stubbornly. We expect even so bizarre a crisis to provoke logical responses: the husband will be humiliated or outraged, the wife will prove herself either a genuine wife or a genuine whore, and so on. We have the probabilities all ready in our heads.

But Mr. Pinter is not interested in the rational probabilities of the moment. He is interested in what *might* happen if our controlling expectations were suddenly junked, if flesh and heart and moving bone were freed from preconditioning and allowed simply to behave, existentially. The world might go another way—a surprising and ultimately unexplained way—if it went its own way, indifferent to philosophers.

Just how the tangle at the Music Box rearranges itself I won't say, because saying nails down what is meant to continue as movement. It's enough to report that for approximately 20 minutes during the final third of "The Homecoming" the erratic energies onstage display their own naked authority by forcing us to accept the unpredictable as though it were the natural shape of things.

During this time Vivien Merchant, as the wife who is hard-headed as she is enigmatic, cooly and with great reserve points out that her legs move, her underwear moves with her, her lips move. ("Perhaps the fact that they move is more significant than the words that come through them.") Husband Michael Craig draws on his donnish pipe with opaque detachment ("I won't be lost in it"), father Paul Rogers leers through sucked-in teeth that seem to have been borrowed from Bert Lahr, and poltergeist Iam Holm grins maliciously at the thought of all the tables that can be turned. The performing is cagey, studied, bristling with overtones. (A good half of Mr. Pinter's suspense invariably comes from the question that sticks in our heads: "What are these people *not* mentioning?").

Until the final moments of the evening, however, the playwright is simply cheating us, draining away our interest with his deliberate delay. He has no more vital material to offer here than he had, say, in the very much shorter "A Slight Ache," to which "The Homecoming" bears a strong resemblance.

But he is determined that we shall have two hours worth of improvisational feinting, and it leads him into a good bit of coy teasing giggly echoes of Ionesco ("You liked Venice, didn't you? You had a good week. I mean, I took you there. I can speak Italian") and calculated incidental violence that is without cumulative effect (the father spits at one son, rams another in the gut, canes his own paraffin-coated dullard of a brother).

Because none of this is of any growing importance to the ultimate confrontation, *everything* must seem to have its own arbitrary and artificial importance: the clink of a sugar lump on a saucer, the stiff, ritual crossing of trousered legs, the huddled lighting of four cigars, the effortful pronunciation of so much as a single word.

Holding too much back for too long, the play comes to seem afflicted by an arthritic mind and tongue, and while Peter Hall has directed the visiting members of England's Royal Shakespeare Company to make sleep-walking and strangled speech constitute a theatrical effect in and for itself, we are not engrossed by the eternal hesitation waltz, but seriously put off by it. The play agonizes over finding its starting point, and we share the prolonged agony without being certain that the conundrum is approaching a real core.

Mr. Pinter is one of the most naturally gifted dramatists to have come out of England since the war. I think he is making the mistake, just now, of supposing that the elusive kernel of impulse that will do for a 40-minute play will serve just as handily and just as suspensefully for an all-day outing. "The Homecoming," to put the matter as simply as possible, needs a second situation: We could easily take an additional act if the author would only scrap the interminable first. The tide must come in at least twice if we are to be fascinated so long by the shoreline.

REVIEW OF THE ROYAL SHAKESPEARE COMPANY PRODUCTION, 1967, BY RICHARD GILMAN

In all his plays, from *The Room,* which was written in 1957 as a more or less naïve exercise in the kind of drama Beckett and Ionesco had already made known, to his latest work, *The Homecoming,* Harold Pinter has been engaged with the question of what drama really is. It might be thought that the playwright, of all people, would know; yet if twentieth-century aesthetic developments have taught us anything, it is that the artist, rather than the public—which knows what it knows—is in continuing doubt about the nature of art. And since the theatre is the most immovable of all the arts, the most resistant to change, it is the playwright who has had to struggle most strenuously for new forms, against the heavy, unyielding conviction of nearly everybody else that there is no mystery about what plays are.

Plays are sequences of imagined events, recognizable to one degree or another as analogous to the events of life, and these events are participated in by "characters," whose interest and credibility are also measured by their potential actuality, their being possible to imagine in one or another way as existing in the world outside the drama. Beyond that, plays must "develop," must move steadily along, generally to a "higher" or "deeper" level, and must not, on pain of murderous responses from the audience, stop at any point—to give opportunity for reflection to gather new kinds of momentum, to simply be still, circular, without linear progression. What plays must do (the last stronghold of realism) is to trace a parabola for which life is thought to have provided the model.

Such, tightly stated, are the sovereign notions that still rule audiences, reviewers and commonplace playwrights alike. They learn nothing from the fact that nearly all the interesting drama of any period has taken place outside the textbook definitions. The complaint is still made against a play like *The Homecoming* that it is slow, illogical, unlifelike, wasteful of its opportunities—which are to be fast, logical, lifelike—and that its characters are not the sort one would expect or want to meet on one's daily round. (Get me Ivan Karamazov: Ivan, baby, we're having a party and we'd love you to . . .)

In Pinter's growth as a dramatist, which in a central way means progress toward colonizing hitherto unconsidered territories of the dramatic, shaping a redefinition, *on the stage,* of character, plot, action, etc., he has come unevenly but significantly to redirect procedures and techniques that had early threatened to congeal into mere negatives. His capacity for extracting ranges of implication from the most conventional varieties of speech themselves—incantatory, often, dreamlike yet anchored in the sharpest accuracy about how people really talk—his use of the most commonplace objects to undermine our complacency about the material world: all this was for the most part unsupported by imposing intellectual structure, any more solid knowledge or intuition than that traditions of perception and experience were not to be relied on.

From his first impact here, by way of rumor and the published early plays and then through *The Caretaker* when it arrived, we spoke of Pinter as a new presence, the master of striking if not quite trustworthy, because seemingly autonomous, effects. The world, his plays announced, is arbitrary, everything menaces, nothing is what it seems; he had broken into a new universe of drama, one in which language seldom coheres with gesture, terror is the obverse of humor, and habits of action conceal other kinds of action we can sense but never know.

In this universe, he once wrote in a program note, "there are no hard distinctions between what is real and what is unreal, nor between what is true and what is false." It is precisely its tendency to assume at some point that it knows what is real and unreal (which means what has up to now been *considered* so) that compels every art including drama continually to remonstrate with its own past, to repudiate its own inertia. This is the least that so-called avant-garde art does—but it has to do more. The peculiar giddiness, the sensations of disequilibrium and disturbed orientation which Pinter induced through his dislocations of the familiar—these, while enormously valuable, were not fully satisfying. For what was being let in through the holes he had punched in conventional dramaturgy? Not what meaning but what new and substanceful drama of his own?

The Homecoming, though flawed and marked by aesthetic problems not yet overcome, is the impressive culmination of a subtle process of change that set in midway in Pinter's career. It was toward a seemingly greater realism, a filling in the vacancies, in which abstract menace and unspecific fear lurked, that had resulted from his abandonment of accepted thematic developments, of ordinary psychologies and sociologies and the sequential narratives in which the stage has traditionally encased them. But this realism had nothing to do with an imitation of life or the conventions of popular drama, except that, in the latter case, it made a canny and partly ironic use of them.

The shift can be studied through Pinter's changing *mises en scène*. Moving into domestic settings, usually middle- or upper-middle class, he largely withdrew from those alarming locales of his earlier plays—the basement room of *The Dumbwaiter*, the seedy rooming house of *The Birthday Party*, the dementedly cluttered room of *The Caretaker*.

These theatrical sites were objectively disturbing, menacing in their own right, physical metaphors of violence which meant that their atmospheres tended to carry a disproportionate share of the plays' effects, tended in fact to consolidate those effects as the very essence of the works.

The setting of *The Homecoming* still possesses disquieting features in its great gray sparsely furnished room. But something crucial has happened. This new Pinter room no longer largely dictates what is to happen to its inhabitants but only reflects what has happened and will happen to them; its walls and furnishings have soaked up their emanations, for the center of dramatic reality has passed to them.

Yet it doesn't lie in them now in any way which we can organically connect with what we think of as domestic drama. If you think during the opening moments that you are watching a familiar battle scene, on the order of *Virginia Woolf,* or *Cat on a Hot Tin Roof,* you will be unprepared for what is to come and you may grow disgruntled, having expected, in the second act, denouement, completion, some satisfying rich ripe finale. But the play moves to its own logic, and it is not a tale; its characters are only tactically engaged in representing potentially real people, their strategic task being to incarnate, along the lines of the "characters" in *The Brothers Karamazov,* certain human faculties, dividing among themselves fundamental possibilities of attitude and approach to existence. They are their figures in a drama of the mind, which is not to say an intellectual drama, but one which makes no pretense (or only a pretense) of being a replica of actuality.

The relationship of the four men who occupy the stage at first is savage, almost cannibalistic, at the same time that it is self-lacerating. "Mind you she wasn't such a bad woman," Max, the roaring foulmouthed old man, says of his dead wife, "even though it made me sick just to look at her rotten stinking face, she wasn't a bad bitch." And he berates his coldly ironic son Lenny, the master of a stable of prostitutes, for "talking to your lousy filthy father like that."

Yet however straightforward, if extreme, their dialogue seems at first, its purpose is not to frame character or psychology, not as an English critic has pointed out, to reveal "inner life or intentions." Pinter's marvelously funny, splendidly violent or consciously banal dialogue is a matter of *kinds* of speech and therefore archetypes of being, warring with one another—Max's scatology, Lenny's wit, Max's pallid brother Sam's pinched rhetoric—as the faculties incarnated by the personages of the play similarly war. And the dialogue is there to serve the play, to serve its mostly immobile, nonanecdotal, ritualistic vision, not its presumed thesis, its "story" or concatenation of events.

That there is to be no plausible story quickly becomes apparent with the entrance of Teddy, Max's oldest son; a philosophy professor at an American university, he is returning for the first time in six years, with his wife Ruth, whom the others do not know of. Cooly elegant, enigmatic, sensual, Ruth immediately shifts the play to a new dimension. In the most Pinteresque of scenes, where language, objects and gestures unite to reinforce one another's elliptical and mythic condition, Ruth and Lenny clash. "I'll take it [a glass of water he has given her]," Lenny says, unaccountably threatening, to which she replies with deadly calm, "If you take the glass . . . I'll take *you.*"

From then on the play is about who takes whom,

that is to say, whose presence triumphs or yields, who, in the game of existence—not in that of society—are winners or losers. What loses most decisively is onlooking spectatorship, the propriety of consciousness when pitted against the absolutism of the physical self. In a world beyond morality, what is being sought for is a condition of authenticity, an immersion in what is. And to accomplish this, the play now leaves irrevocably behind it (the point at which the public grumbling starts) all verisimilitude, all pretense of being about a family, a social situation, people like you and me. Pinter is at the heart of his vision here, and if we follow him into it—attending to these characters who can no longer be mistaken for types or personalities but only seen as incarnations of possibility, of desire and refusal—we will have overcome our deadly habit of wanting what we expect.

When Ruth engages Lenny, and afterwards Joey, the naïve strongboy younger brother, in a sexual embrace which Teddy, her husband, watches with pipe-smoking professorial detachment, and when later the family proposes that Ruth stay with them, working for her keep as a prostitute—a proposal which leaves Teddy as unruffled as before—we are not in the presence of social behavior but of a dance of death—and life. Ruth's acceptance of the proposal is a movement toward the greater authenticity of the family, their closer proximity to genuine being. For Teddy is an abstract man, a figure of pure consciousness, an observer, while she is almost pure instinct and physicality.

In the key monologue of the play, the central speech which, as in all Pinter's work, offers the one irradiation of intention to light the rest of the play, Teddy tells the others:

"You wouldn't understand my works . . . You wouldn't appreciate the points of reference. You're way behind . . . It's nothing to do with the question of intelligence. It's a way of being able to look at the world. It's a question of how far you can operate on things and not in things . . . To see, to be able to *see!* I'm the one who can see . . . [I have] intellectual equilibrium . . . You're just objects. You just . . . move about. I can observe it. I can see what you do. It's the same as I do. But you're lost in it. You won't get me being . . . I won't be lost in it."

It is a brilliant piece of writing, one almost no other English-speaking playwright would be capable of. Fusing the most exact and compressed meanings with the most intense feeling, colloquial at the same time that it stretches to a more inclusive and nonrealistic level of speech, it exemplifies what is never considered in our public chatter about the theatre: that language can itself be dramatic, can *be* the play, not merely the means of advancing an anecdote, a decoration, or the emblem of something thought to be realer than itself.

Teddy's speech is followed by a longer one of Lenny's, an equally masterly piece of writing, opposing another rhythm and another mode of language as action to its predecessor. In it Lenny, the wit, the implicated observer, moral consciousness corrupted but still alive, throws at Teddy an image of America which in the conditions of the play, entirely transcends social criticism to become the truest kind of poetic fact:

"I will say you do seem to have grown a bit sulky . . . I'd have thought that in the United States of America, I mean with the sun and all that, the open spaces, on the old campus, in your position, lecturing, in the center of all the intellectual life out there, on the old campus, all the social whirl, all the stimulation of it all, all your kids and all that, to have fun with, down by the pool, the Greyhound buses and all that, tons of iced water, all the comforts of those Bermuda shorts and all that, on the old campus . . . I'd have thought you'd have grown more forthcoming . . . Listen, Ted, there's no question we lead a less rich life here than you do over there . . . We lead a closer life."

In the final movement of the play, this closer life is revealed to be partly one of fantasy. There is something crowded, rushed into being, somewhat arbitrary about this last section. Ruth takes command, promising in the manner of a contemporary fairy godmother to be whatever the men want her to be: for Joey a madonna figure, for Lenny, a whore, for Max a young and rejuvenating wife. A whole allegorical structure now rises shadowily into view. But it is too late, it has not been fully prepared for and therefore comes as an afterthought. Yet the main action of the play has been completed with Ruth's move toward the family and Teddy's devastating acceptance of it; to wish to do more, to want his dense, specific, precisely nonallegorical vision to yield up such further tenuous meanings is evidence that Pinter has not yet solved his major problem. And that is how to fuse meaning so securely with language, gesture and setting that it cannot be extrapolated from them. The taints of the old worn-out dramatic procedures—characters who represent action that points to something else—are still discernible in his work.

Yet, they are taints, not major infections. A struggle for the new is always more interesting than a successful appropriation of the old. *The Homecoming* is such a struggle, and nothing on Broadway in recent years comes close to matching it for the kind of excitement that our debased ad-man's vocabulary of critical appreciation ("*The Odd Couple* is the funniest play ever!") has so thoroughly disillusioned us about. The play itself, Peter Hall's direction and the Royal Shakespeare Company's acting ensemble offer examples of work in a dimension beyond anything we have been accustomed to.

PETER SHAFFER

1926–

Shaffer was born in Liverpool, raised in London, spent the war years working as a coal miner, and then attended Cambridge University, where he completed his degree with honors. He then turned to writing and did several detective novels with his twin brother Anthony, the author of *Sleuth,* before emigrating to New York, where he spent a couple of years working first in a library and then for a music publisher. While in New York, he started writing plays for television, and the BBC's production of two of these scripts brought him back to England in the mid-1950s and to full-time playwriting. His first stage play, *Five Finger Exercise* (1958), immediately established his reputation as a serious dramatist; it also established his abiding concern with the struggle of human beings to find beliefs worthy of acceptance.

The title of that first play suggests the practice scales with which a pianist begins, and Shaffer began, as have so many playwrights, with a conventional set and clearly recognizable characters: a typical upper middle-class English family whose affluence makes it possible for them to afford a comfortably furnished country house in which the play takes place, as well as a young German tutor, named Walter, for their teen-age daughter. Although presented as a realistic drama, firmly rooted in details of everyday living—in the apparent banalities, for example, of breakfast table conversation—*Five Finger Exercise* is, in fact, a serious dramatic revelation of the struggles and the perils in Walter's desire to belong to a family, in his search for "somewhere . . . where now and then good spirits can sit on the roof." This search, which ultimately destroys him, is thus a spiritual quest.

That desire also pervades the play that Shaffer wrote next, *The Royal Hunt of the Sun,* which was not produced until 1964 because its enormous cast and difficult staging problems caused directors and producers to shy away from the work. In this play, Shaffer turned from a comfortable English house to a stage representing both Spain and Peru, from a handful of characters to hordes of Spaniards and Indians, from breakfast and tea to conquest and massacre, from the search for a loving family to the quest for immortality, embodied in Pizarro, the Spanish conquerer of the Incas, yearning for "the source of life." Pizarro yearns, in particular, to believe in Atahuallpa, who claims that he is the Sun and who promises, "I will swallow death and spit it out of me," but after a spectacular scene in which Atahuallpa is strangled and then mourned, the stage is emptied, except for the old figure of Pizarro, sitting by the body of the dead Inca, waiting for him to come back to life. A similarly arresting and symbolic image occurs at the end of *Equus,* when Dysart kneels by the unconscious body of Alan and realizes that he, like Pizarro, has destroyed Alan's passion, everything that made him capable of ecstasy. *The Royal Hunt of the Sun* clearly anticipates *Equus* not only in dramatizing the ritual sounds and movements of religious ecstasy, but also in exposing the irrepressible tendency of human beings to destroy the sources of their belief.

Between *The Royal Hunt of the Sun* and *Equus,* Shaffer wrote five more plays, three one-acts and two full-length plays, in which he continued to explore the religious and philosophical problems of belief, largely in the realistic terms of his first play. But the most important dramatic precedents for *Equus* are to be found in theatrical sources much earlier than Shaffer's own work. In writing a play with a chorus, with figures wearing large masks and elevated shoes, with a series of short scenes between two actors, framed by narrative comment, Shaffer has used some of the most important elements of Greek tragedy. And it is appropriate that he should do so, for *Equus,* no less than Greek tragedy, is concerned with the problematic influence of spiritual belief in the world of human experience. Alan's "god" is an obsessive concern for him and Dysart, much as the gods are a continual source of preoccupation for the characters in Greek tragedy. And just as the characters in Greek tragedy often defy the authority of their gods—a defiance that inevitably brings them to catastrophe—so Dysart finds himself compelled to destroy Alan's god, though he recognizes that his own "God of Health" is also "lethal."

Shaffer's use of Greek dramatic precedents may be seen even in the structure of *Equus,* which has a detective-story plot similar to that of *Oedipus.* Just as Oedipus seeks the identity of his father's murderer and so moves inexorably toward a discovery of his own identity, Dysart find himself compelled to drive Alan into a relentless search through his own past for the reasons that first led the boy to create his "god" and then to multilate it by blinding the six horses. That archetypal pattern of probing the past to liberate the present may also be seen in Shaffer's remarks about the original source of the play that came from an anecdote he heard from a friend:

> He had given me no name, no place, and no time. I don't think he knew them. All I possessed was his report of a dreadful event, and the feeling it engendered in me. I knew very strongly that I wanted to interpret it in some entirely personal way. I had to create a mental world in which the deed could be made comprehensible.

In creating that world, Shaffer has chosen a series of images that repeatedly comment on each other. Although the setting is nominally the consulting-room of a psychiatrist in a provincial hospital, Shaffer's notes on the set describe it as "a square of wood set on a circle of wood. The square resembles a railed boxing ring." Later in the description, Shaffer indicates that the seats forming a backdrop to this platform-ring resemble those in a "dissecting theater." Yet in contrast to these images of modern conflict and scientific dissection, Dysart continually evokes in his dialogue the world of ancient Greece—sometimes a very nightmarish world in which he dreams that he is a priest carving up children, sometimes the world of artistic treasures, and sometimes, the most moving times, the world of "a thousand local Gods. And not just the old dead ones with names like Zeus—no, but living Geniuses of Place and Person!"

Reviews of the first New York production of 1974, reprinted following the text, clearly reveal that in the theater *Equus* works powerfully as a drama both of ritual and of complex human relationships. The scenes in which Alan relives his memories of being with the horses, from his first ride by the seashore to the midnight rides that constitute his worship of Equus (see Figure 99) are intensely haunting, for they blend the stylized grace of the horses' masks, hooves, and bodily movements with the passionate gestures of Alan as he touches, brushes, and rides his horse. Framing and counterpointing the ritual of the scenes with the horses is the realistic figure of Dysart (see Figure 100), at first clinical and detached, gradually becoming more and more involved with the boy's pain and pleasure. And framing both Alan and Dysart is the detached woman magistrate. But when the play ends, it is Dysart who speaks the words that epitomize the experience of the play, the same words spoken by Equus in the midnight ritual: "There is now, in my mouth, this sharp pain. And it never comes out."

EQUUS

BY PETER SHAFFER

CHARACTERS

MARTIN DYSART, *a psychiatrist*

ALAN STRANG

FRANK STRANG, *his father*

DORA STRANG, *his mother*

HESTHER SALOMON, *a magistrate*

JILL MASON

HARRY DALTON, *a stable owner*

A YOUNG HORSEMAN

A NURSE

SIX ACTORS–*including the* YOUNG HORSEMAN, *who also plays* NUGGET—*appear as* HORSES.

SCENE

The main action of the play takes place in Rokeby Psychiatric Hospital in Southern England.

The time is the present.

The play is divided into numbered scenes, indicating a change of time or locale or mood. The action, however, is continuous.

A NOTE ON THE PLAY

One weekend over two years ago, I was driving with a friend through bleak countryside. We passed a stable. Suddenly he was reminded by it of an alarming crime which he had heard about recently at a dinner party in London. He knew only one horrible detail, and his complete mention of it could barely have lasted a minute–but it was enough to arouse in me an intense fascination.

The act had been committed several years before by a highly disturbed young man. It had deeply shocked a local bench of magistrates. It lacked, finally, any coherent explanation.

A few months later my friend died. I could not verify what he had said, or ask him to expand it. He had given me no name, no place, and no time. I don't think he knew them. All I possessed was his report of a dreadful event, and the feeling it engendered in me. I knew very strongly that I wanted to interpret it in some entirely personal way. I had to create a mental world in which the deed could be made comprehensible.

Every person and incident in Equus is of my own invention, save the crime itself: and even that I modified to accord with what I feel to be acceptable theatrical proportion. I am grateful now that I have never received confirmed details of the real story, since my concern has been more and more with a different kind of exploration.

I have been lucky, in doing final work on the play, to have enjoyed the advice and expert comment of a distinguished child psychiatrist. Through him I have tried to keep things real in a more naturalistic sense. I have also come to perceive that psychiatrists are an immensely varied breed, professing immensely varied methods and techniques. Martin Dysart is simply one doctor in one hospital. I must take responsibility for him, as I do for his patient.

THE SET

A square of wood set on a circle of wood.

The square resembles a railed boxing ring. The rail, also of wood, encloses three sides. It is perforated on each side by an opening. Under the rail are a few vertical slats, as if in a fence. On the downstage side there is no rail. The whole square is set on ball bearings, so that by slight pressure from actors standing round it on the circle, it can be made to turn round smoothly by hand.

On the square are set three little plain benches, also of wood. They are placed parallel with the rail, against the slats, but can be moved out by the actors to stand at right angles to them.

Set into the floor of the square, and flush with it, is a thin metal pole, about a yard high. This can be raised out of the floor, to stand upright. It acts as a support for the actor playing Nugget, when he is ridden.

In the area outside the circle stand benches. Two downstage left and right, are curved to accord with the circle. The left one is used by Dysart as a listening and observing post when he is out of the square, and also by Alan as his hospital bed. The right one is used by Alan's parents, who sit side by side on it. (Viewpoint is from the main body of the audience.)

Further benches stand upstage, and accommodate the other actors. All the cast of Equus sits on stage the entire evening. They get up to perform their scenes, and return when they are done to their places around the set. They are witnesses, assistants–and especially a Chorus.

Upstage, forming a backdrop to the whole, are tiers of seats in the fashion of a dissecting theatre, formed into two railed-off blocks, pierced by a central tunnel. In these blocks sit members of the audience. During the play, Dysart addresses them directly from time to time, as he addresses the main body of the theatre. No other actor ever refers to them.

To left and right, downstage, stand two ladders on which are suspended horse masks.

The colour of all benches is olive green.

Above the stage hangs a battery of lights, set in a huge metal ring. Light cues, in this version, will be only of the most general description.

THE CHORUS

References are made in the text to the Equus Noise. I have in mind a choric effect, made by all the actors sitting round upstage, and composed of humming, thumping, and stamping–though never of neighing or whinnying. This Noise heralds or illustrates the presence of Equus the God.

THE HORSES

The actors wear track-suits of chestnut velvet. On their feet are light strutted hooves, about four inches high, set on metal horse-shoes. On their hands are gloves of the same colour. On their heads are tough masks made of alternating bands of silver wire and leather; their eyes are outlined by leather blinkers. The actors' own heads are seen beneath them: no attempt should be made to conceal them.

Any literalism which could suggest the cosy familiarity of a domestic animal–or worse, a pantomime horse–should be avoided. The actors should never crouch on all fours, or even bend forward. They must always–except on the occasion where Nugget is ridden–stand upright, as if the body of the horse extended invisibly behind them. Animal effect must be created entirely mimetically, through the use of legs, knees, neck, face, and the turn of the head which can move the mask above it through all the gestures of equine wariness and pride. Great care must also be taken that the masks are put on before the audience with very precise timing–the actors watching each other, so that the masking has an exact and ceremonial effect.

ACT 1 / SCENE 1

(*Darkness.*
Silence.
Dim light up on the square. In a spotlight stands ALAN STRANG, *a lean boy of seventeen, in sweater and jeans. In front of him, the horse* NUGGET. ALAN's *pose represents a contour of great tenderness: his head is pressed against the shoulder of the horse, his hands stretching up to fondle its head. The horse in turn nuzzles his neck.*
The flame of a cigarette lighter jumps in the dark. Lights come up slowly on the circle. On the left bench, downstage, MARTIN DYSART, *smoking. A man in his mid-forties.*)

DYSART: With one particular horse, called Nugget, he embraces. The animal digs its sweaty brow into his cheek, and they stand in the dark for an hour–like a necking couple. And of all nonsensical things–I keep thinking about the *horse*! Not the boy: the horse, and what it may be trying to do. I keep seeing that huge head kissing him with its chained mouth. Nudging through the metal some desire absolutely irrelevant to filling its belly or propagating its own kind. What desire could that be? Not to stay a horse any longer? Not to remain reined up for ever in those particular genetic strings? Is it possible, at certain moments we cannot imagine, a horse can add its sufferings together–the non-stop jerks and jabs that are its daily life–and turn them into grief? What use is grief to a horse?

(ALLAN *leads* NUGGET *out of the square and they disappear together up the tunnel, the horse's hooves scraping delicately on the wood.*
DYSART *rises, and addresses both the large audience in the theatre and the smaller one on stage.*)

You see, I'm lost. What use, I should be asking, are questions like these to an overworked psychiatrist in a provincial hospital? They're worse than useless: they are, in fact, subversive.

(*He enters the square. The light grows brighter.*)

The thing is, I'm desperate. You see, I'm wearing that horse's head myself. That's the feeling. All reined up in old language and old assumptions, straining to jump clean-hoofed on to a whole new track of being I only suspect is there. I can't see it, because my educated, average head is being held at the wrong angle. I can't jump because the bit forbids it, and my own basic force–my horsepower, if you like–is too little. The only thing I know for sure is this: a horse's head is finally unknowable to me. Yet I handle children's heads–which I must presume to be more complicated, at least in the area of my chief concern. ,.. In a way, it has nothing to do with this boy. The doubts have been there for years, piling up steadily in this dreary place. It's only the extremity of this case that's made them active. I know that. The *extremity* is the point! All the same, whatever the reason, they are now, these doubts, not just vaguely worrying–but intolerable ... I'm sorry. I'm not making much sense. Let me start properly: in order. It began one Monday last month, with Hesther's visit.

ACT 1 / SCENE 2

(*The light gets warmer.*
He sits. NURSE *enters the square.*)

NURSE: Mrs. Salomon to see you, Doctor.
DYSART: Show her in, please.

(NURSE *leaves and crosses to where* HESTHER *sits.*)

Some days I blame Hesther. She brought him to see me. But of course that's nonsense. What is he but a last straw? a last symbol? If it hadn't been him, it would have been the next patient, or the next. At least, I suppose. so.

(HESTHER *enters the square: a woman in her mid-forties.*)

HESTHER: Hello, Martin.

(DYSART *rises and kisses her on the cheek.*)

DYSART: Madam Chairman! Welcome to the torture chamber!

HESTHER: It's good of you to see me right away.

DYSART: You're a welcome relief. Take a couch.

HESTHER: It's been a day?

DYSART: No—just a fifteen year old schizophrenic, and a girl of eight thrashed into catatonia by her father. Normal, really . . . You're in a state.

HESTHER: Martin, this is the most shocking case I ever tried.

DYSART: So you said on the phone.

HESTHER: I mean it. My bench wanted to send the boy to prison. For life, if they could manage it. It took me two hours solid arguing to get him sent to you instead.

DYSART: Me?

HESTHER: I mean, to hospital.

DYSART: Now look, Hesther. Before you say anything else, I can take no more patients at the moment. I can't even cope with the ones I have.

HESTHER: You must.

DYSART: Why?

HESTHER: Because most people are going to be disgusted by the whole thing. Including doctors.

DYSART: May I remind you I share this room with two highly competent psychiatrists?

HESTHER: Bennett and Thoroughgood. They'll be as shocked as the public.

DYSART: That's an absolutely unwarrantable statement.

HESTER: Oh, they'll be cool and exact. And underneath they'll be revolted, and immovably English. Just like my bench.

DYSART: Well, what am I? Polynesian?

HESTHER: You know exactly what I mean! . . . (Pause.) Please, Martin. It's vital. You're this boy's only chance.

DYSART: Why? What's he done? Dosed some little girl's Pepsi with Spanish Fly? What could possibly throw your bench into two-hour convulsions?

HESTHER: He blinded six horses with a metal spike.

(A long pause.)

DYSART: Blinded?

HESTHER: Yes.

DYSART: All at once, or over a period?

HESTHER: All on the same night.

DYSART: Where?

HESTHER: In a riding stable near Winchester. He worked there at weekends.

DYSART: How old?

HESTHER: Seventeen.

DYSART: What did he say in Court?

HESTHER: Nothing. He just sang.

DYSART: Sang?

HESTHER: Any time anyone asked him anything.

(Pause.)

Please take him, Martin. It's the last favour I'll ever ask you.

DYSART: No, it's not.

HESTHER: No, it's not—and he's probably abominable. All I know is, he needs you badly. Because there really is nobody within a hundred miles of your desk who can handle him. And perhaps understand what this is about. Also . . . .

DYSART: What?

HESTHER: There's something very special about him.

DYSART: In what way?

HESTHER: Vibrations.

DYSART: You and your vibrations.

HESTHER: They're quite startling. You'll see.

DYSART: When does he get here?

HESTHER: Tomorrow morning. Luckily there was a bed in Neville Ward. I know this is an awful imposition, Martin. Frankly I didn't know what else to do.

(Pause.)

DYSART: Can you come in and see me on Friday?

HESTHER: Bless you!

DYSART: If you come after work I can give you a drink. Will 6.30 be all right?

HESTHER: You're a dear. You really are.

DYSART: Famous for it.

HESTHER: Goodbye.

DYSART: By the way, what's his name?

HESTHER: Alan Strang.

(She leaves and returns to her seat.)

DYSART (to audience): What did I expect of him? Very little, I promise you. One more dented little face. One more adolescent freak. The usual unusual. One great thing about being in the adjustment business: you're never short of customers.

(NURSE comes down the tunnel, followed by ALAN. She enters the square.)

NURSE: Alan Strang, Doctor.

(The boy comes in.)

DYSART: Hallo. My name's Martin Dysart. I'm pleased to meet you.

(He puts out his hand. ALAN does not respond in any way.)

That'll be all, Nurse, thank you.

ACT 1 / SCENE 3

(NURSE goes out and back to her place.
DYSART sits, opening a file.)

So: did you have a good journey? I hope they

gave you lunch at least. Not that there's much to choose between a British Rail meal and one here.

(ALAN *stands staring at him.*)

DYSART: Won't you sit down?

(*Pause. He does not.* DYSART *consults his file.*)

Is this your full name? Alan Strang?

(*Silence.*)

And you're seventeen. Is that right? Seventeen? . . . Well?

ALAN (*singing low*): Double your pleasure,
Double your fun
With Doublemint, Doublemint
Doublemint gum.

DYSART (*unperturbed*): Now, let's see. You work in an electrical shop during the week. You live with your parents, and your father's a printer. What sort of things does he print?

ALAN (*singing louder*): Double your pleasure
Double your fun
With Doublemint, Doublemint
Doublemint gum.

DYSART: I mean does he do leaflets and calendars? Things like that?

(*The boy approaches him, hostile.*)

ALAN (*singing*): Try the taste of Martini
The most beautiful drink in the world.
It's the right one—
The bright one—
That's Martini!

DYSART: I wish you'd sit down, if you're going to sing. Don't you think you'd be more comfortable?

(*Pause.*)

ALAN (*singing*): There's only one T in Typhoo!
In packets and teabags too.
Any way you make it, you'll find it's true:
There's only one T in Typhoo!

DYSART (*appreciatively*): Now that's a good song. I like it better than the other two. Can I hear that one again?

(ALAN *starts away from him, and sits on the upstage bench.*)

ALAN (*singing*): Double your pleasure
Double your fun
With Doublemint, Doublemint
Doublemint gum.

DYSART (*smiling*): You know I was wrong. I really do think that one's better. It's got such a catchy tune. Please do that one again.

(*Silence. The boy glares at him.*)

I'm going to put you in a private bedroom for a little while. There are one or two available, and they're rather more pleasant than being in a ward. Will you please come and see me tomorrow? . . . (*He rises.*) By the way, which parent is it who won't allow you to watch television? Mother or father? Or is it both? (*Calling out of the door.*) Nurse!

(ALAN *stares at him.* NURSE *comes in.*)

NURSE: Yes, Doctor?
DYSART: Take Strang here to Number Three, will you? He's moving in there for a while.
NURSE: Very good, Doctor.
DYSART (*to Alan*): You'll like that room. It's nice.

(*The boy sits staring at* DYSART. DYSART *returns the stare.*)

NURSE: Come along, young man. This way. . . . I said this way, please.

(*Reluctantly* ALAN *rises and goes to* NURSE, *passing dangerously close to* DYSART, *and out through the left door.* DYSART *looks after him, fascinated.*)

ACT 1 / SCENE 4

(NURSE *and patient move on to the circle, and walk downstage to the bench where the doctor first sat, which is to serve also as* ALAN's *bed.*)

NURSE: Well now: isn't this nice? You're lucky to be in here, you know, rather than the ward. That ward's a noisy old place.
ALAN (*singing*): Let's go where you wanna go— Texaco!
NURSE (*contemplating him*): I hope you're not going to make a nuisance of yourself. You'll have a much better time of it here, you know, if you behave yourself.
ALAN: Fuck off.
NURSE (*tight*): That's the bell there. The lav's down the corridor.

(*She leaves him, and goes back to her place.* ALAN *lies down.*)

ACT 1 / SCENE 5

(DYSART *stands in the middle of the square and addresses the audience. He is agitated.*)

DYSART: That night, I had this very explicit dream. In it I'm a chief priest in Homeric Greece. I'm wearing a wide gold mask, all noble and bearded, like the so-called Mask of Agamemnon found at Mycenae. I'm standing by a thick round stone and holding a sharp knife. In fact, I'm officiating at some immensely important ritual sacrifice, on which depends the fate of the crops or of a military expedition. The sacrifice is a herd of children: about five hundred boys and girls. I can see them stretching away in a long queue, right across the plain of Argos. I know it's Argos because of the red soil. On either side of me stand two assistant priests, wearing masks as well: lumpy, pop-eyed masks, such as also were found at Mycenae. They are enormously strong, these other priests, and absolutely tireless. As each child steps forward, they grab it from behind and throw it over the stone. Then, with a surgical skill which amazes even me, I fit in the knife and slice elegantly down to the navel, just like a seamstress following a pattern. I part the flaps, sever the inner tubes, yank them out and throw them hot and steaming on to the floor. The other two then study the pattern they make, as if they were reading hieroglyphics. It's obvious to me that I'm tops as chief priest. It's this unique talent for carving that has got me where I am. The only thing is, unknown to them, I've started to feel distinctly nauseous. And with each victim, it's getting worse. My face is going green behind the mask. Of course, I redouble my efforts to look professional—cutting and snipping for all I'm worth: mainly because I know that if ever those two assistants so much as glimpse my distress—and the implied doubt that this repetitive and smelly work is doing any social good at all—I will be the next across the stone. And then, of course—the damn mask begins to slip. The priests both turn and look at it—it slips some more—they see the green sweat running down my face—their gold pop-eyes suddenly fill up with blood—they tear the knife out of my hand . . . and I wake up.

ACT 1 / SCENE 6

(HESTHER *enters the square. Light grows warmer.*)

HESTHER: That's the most indulgent thing I ever heard.
DYSART: You think?
HESTHER: Please don't be ridiculous. You've done the most superb work with children. You must know that.
DYSART: Yes, but do the children?
HESTHER: Really!
DYSART: I'm sorry.
HESTHER: So you should be.
DYSART: I don't know why you listen. It's just professional menopause. Everyone gets it sooner or later. Except you.
HESTHER: Oh, of course. I feel totally fit to be a magistrate all the time.
DYSART: No, you don't—but then that's you feeling unworthy to fill a job. I feel the job is unworthy to fill me.

HESTHER: Do you seriously?
DYSART: More and more. I'd like to spend the next ten years wandering very slowly around the *real* Greece . . . Anyway, all this dream nonsense is your fault.
HESTHER: Mine?
DYSART: It's that lad of yours who started it off. Do you know it's his face I saw on every victim across the stone?
HESTHER: Strang?
DYSART: He has the strangest stare I ever met.
HESTHER: Yes.
DYSART: It's exactly like being accused. Violently accused. But what of? . . . Treating him is going to be unsettling. Especially in my present state. His singing was direct enough. His speech is more so.
HESTHER (*surprised*): He's talking to you, then?
DYSART: Oh yes. It took him two more days of commercials, and then he snapped. Just like that—I suspect it had something to do with his nightmares.

(NURSE *walks briskly round the circle, a blanket over her arm, a clipboard of notes in her hand.*)

HESTHER: He has nightmares?
DYSART: Bad ones.
NURSE: We had to give him a sedative or two, Doctor. Last night it was exactly the same.
DYSART (*to* NURSE): What does he do? Call out?
NURSE (*to desk*): A lot of screaming, Doctor.
DYSART (*to* NURSE): Screaming?
NURSE: One word in particular.
DYSART (*to* NURSE): You mean a special word?
NURSE: Over and over again. (*Consulting clipboard.*) It sounds like 'Ek'.
HESTHER: Ek?
NURSE: Yes, Doctor. Ek. . . . 'Ek!' he goes, 'Ek!'
HESTHER: How weird.
NURSE: When I woke him up he clung to me like he was going to break my arm.

(*She stops at* ALAN's *bed. He is sitting up. She puts the blanket over him, and returns to her place.*)

DYSART: And then he burst in—just like that—without knocking or anything. Fortunately, I didn't have a patient with me.
ALAN (*Jumping up*): *Dad!*
HESTHER: What?
DYSART: The answer to a question I'd asked him two days before. Spat out with the same anger as he sang the commercials.
HESTHER: Dad what?
ALAN: Who hates telly.

(*He lies downstage on the circle, as if watching television.*)

HESTHER: You mean his dad forbids him to watch?

DYSART: Yes.

ALAN: It's a dangerous drug.

HESTER: Oh, really!

(FRANK *stands up and enters the scene downstage on the circle. A man in his fifties.*)

FRANK (*to* ALAN): It may not look like that, but that's what it is. Absolutely fatal mentally, if you receive my meaning.

(DORA *follows him on. She is also middle-aged.*)

DORA: That's a little extreme, dear, isn't it?

FRANK: You sit in front of that thing long enough, you'll become stupid for life—like most of the population. (*to* ALAN) The thing is, it's a *swiz*. It seems to be offering you something, but actually it's taking something away. Your intelligence and your concentration, every minute you watch it. That's a true swiz, do you see?

(*Seated on the floor,* ALAN *shrugs.*)

I don't want to sound like a spoilsport, old chum—but there really is no substitute for reading. What's the matter: don't you like it?

ALAN: It's all right.

FRANK: I know you think it's none of my beeswax, but it really is you know . . . Actually, it's a disgrace when you come to think of it. You the son of a printer, and never opening a book! If all the world was like you, I'd be out of a job, if you receive my meaning!

DORA: All the same, times change, Frank.

FRANK (*reasonably*): They change if you let them change, Dora. Please return that set in the morning.

ALAN (*crying out*): No!

DORA: Frank! No!

FRANK: I'm sorry, Dora, but I'm not having that thing in the house a moment longer. I told you I didn't want it to begin with.

DORA: But dear, everyone watches television these days!

FRANK: Yes, and what do they watch? Mindless violence! Mindless jokes! Every five minutes some laughing idiot selling you something you don't want, just to bolster up the economic system. (*to* ALAN) I'm sorry, old chum.

(*He leaves the scene and sits again in his place.*)

HESTHER: He's a Communist, then?

DYSART: Old-type Socialist, I'd say. Relentlessly self-improving.

HESTHER: They're *both* older than you'd expect.

DYSART: So I gather.

DORA (*looking after* FRANK): Really, dear, you are very extreme!

(*She leaves the scene too, and again sits beside her husband.*)

HESTHER: She's an ex-school teacher, isn't she?

DYSART: Yes. The boy's proud of that. We got on to it this afternoon.

ALAN (*belligerently, standing up*): She knows more than you.

(HESTHER *crosses and sits by* DYSART. *During the following, the boy walks round the circle, speaking to* DYSART *but not looking at him.* DYSART *replies in the same manner.*)

DYSART (*to* ALAN): Does she?

ALAN: I bet I do too. I bet I know more history than you.

DYSART (*to* ALAN): Well, I bet you don't.

ALAN: All right, who was the Hammer of the Scots?

DYSART (*to* ALAN): I don't know: who?

ALAN: King Edward the First. Who never smiled again?

DYSART (*to* ALAN): I don't know: who?

ALAN: You don't know anything, do you? It was Henry the First. I know all the Kings.

DYSART (*to* ALAN): And who's your favourite?

ALAN: John.

DYSART (*to* ALAN): Why?

ALAN: Because he put out the eyes of that smarty little—

(*Pause.*)

(*sensing he has said something wrong.*) Well, he didn't really. He was prevented, because the gaoler was merciful!

HESTHER: Oh dear.

ALAN: *He was prevented!*

DYSART: Something odder was to follow.

ALAN: Who said 'Religion is the opium of the people'?

HESTHER: Good Lord!

(ALAN *giggles.*)

DYSART: The odd thing was, he said it with a sort of guilty snigger. The sentence is obviously associated with some kind of tension.

HESTHER: What did you say?

DYSART: I gave him the right answer. (*to* ALAN) Karl Marx.

ALAN: No.

DYSART (*to* ALAN): Then who?

ALAN: Mind your own beeswax.

DYSART: It's probably his dad. He may say it to provoke his wife.

HESTHER: And you mean she's religious?

DYSART: She could be. I tried to discover—none too successfully.

ALAN: Mind your own beeswax!

(ALAN *goes back to bed and lies down in the dark.*)

DYSART: However, I shall find out on Sunday.

HESTHER: What do you mean?

DYSART (*getting up*): I want to have a look at his home, so I invited myself over.

HESTHER: Did you?

DYSART: If there's any tension over religion, it should be evident on a Sabbath evening! I'll let you know.

(*He kisses her cheek and they part, both leaving the square.* HESTHER *sits in her place again;* DYSART *walks round the circle, and greets* DORA *who stands waiting for him downstage.*)

ACT 1 / SCENE 7

DYSART (*shaking hands*): Mrs. Strang.

DORA: Mr. Strang's still at the Press, I'm afraid. He should be home in a minute.

DYSART: He works Sundays as well?

DORA: Oh, yes. He doesn't set much store by Sundays.

DYSART: Perhaps you and I could have a little talk before he comes in.

DORA: Certainly. Won't you come into the living room?

(*She leads the way into the square. She is very nervous.*)

Please. . . .

(*She motions him to sit, then holds her hands tightly together.*)

DYSART: Mrs. Strang, have you any idea how this thing could have occurred?

DORA: I can't imagine, Doctor. It's all so unbelievable! . . . Alan's always been such a gentle boy. He loves animals! Especially horses.

DYSART: Especially?

DORA: Yes. He even has a photograph of one up in his bedroom. A beautiful white one, looking over a gate. His father gave it to him a few years ago, off a calendar he'd printed—and he's never taken it down . . . And when he was seven or eight, I used to have to read him the same book over and over, all *about* a horse.

DYSART: Really?

DORA: Yes, it was called Prince, and no one could ride him.

(ALAN *calls from his bed, not looking at his mother.*)

ALAN (*excited, younger voice*): Why not? . . . Why not? . . . Say it! In his voice!

DORA: He loved the idea of animals talking.

DYSART: Did he?

ALAN: *Say it! Say it! . . . Use his voice!*

DORA ('*proud*' voice): 'Because I am faithful!'

(ALAN *giggles.*)

'My name is Prince, and I'm a Prince among horses! Only my young Master can ride me! Anyone else—I'll *throw off*!'

(ALAN *giggles louder.*)

And then I remember I used to tell him a funny thing about falling off horses. Did you know that when Christian cavalry first appeared in the New World, the pagans thought horse and rider was one person?

DYSART: Really?

ALAN (*sitting up, amazed*): One person?

DORA: Actually they thought it must be a god.

ALAN: *A god!*

DORA: It was only when one rider fell off, they realized the truth.

DYSART: That's fascinating. I never heard that before. . . . Can you remember anything else like that you may have told him about horses?

DORA: Well, not really. They're in the Bible, of course. 'He saith among the trumpets, Ha, ha.'

DYSART: Ha, ha?

DORA: The Book of Job. Such a noble passage. *You* know—(*quoting*) 'Hast thou given the horse strength?'

ALAN (*responding*): 'Hast thou clothed his neck with thunder?'

DORA (*to* ALAN): 'The glory of his nostrils is terrible!'

ALAN: 'He swallows the ground with fierceness and rage!'

DORA: 'He saith among the trumpets—'

ALAN (*trumpeting*): 'Ha! Ha!'

DORA (*to* DYSART): Isn't that splendid?

DYSART: It certainly is.

ALAN (*trumpeting*): Ha! Ha!

DORA: And then, of course, we saw an awful lot of Westerns on the television. He couldn't have enough of those.

DYSART: But surely you don't have a set, do you? I understand Mr. Strang doesn't approve.

DORA (*conspiratorially*): He doesn't . . . I used to let him slip off in the afternoons to a friend next door.

DYSART (*smiling*): You mean without his father's knowledge?

DORA: What the eye does not see, the heart does not grieve over, does it? Anyway, Westerns are harmless enough, surely?

(FRANK *stands up and enters the square.* ALAN *lies back under the blanket.*)

(*to* FRANK) Oh, hallo dear. This is Dr. Dysart.

FRANK (*shaking hands*): How d'you do?

DYSART: How d'you do?

DORA: I was just telling the Doctor, Alan's always adored horses.

FRANK (*tight*): We assumed he did.

DORA: You know he did, dear. Look how he liked that photograph you gave him.

FRANK (*startled*): What about it?

DORA: Nothing dear. Just that he pestered you to have it as soon as he saw it. Do you remember? (*to* DYSART) We've always been a horsey family. At least my side of it has. My grandfather used to ride every morning on the downs behind Brighton, all dressed up in bowler hat and jodhpurs! He used to look splendid. Indulging in equitation, he called it.

(FRANK *moves away from them and sits wearily.*)

ALAN (*trying the word*): Equitation. . . .

DORA: I remember I told him how that came from *equus*, the Latin word for horse. Alan was fascinated by that word, I know. I suppose because he'd never come across one with two U's together before.

ALAN (*savouring it*): *Equus!*

DORA: I always wanted the boy to ride himself. He'd have so enjoyed it.

DYSART: But surely he did?

DORA: No.

DYSART: Never?

DORA: He didn't care for it. He was most definite about not wanting to.

DYSART: But he must have had to at the stables? I mean, it would be part of the job.

DORA: You'd have thought so, but no. He absolutely wouldn't, would he, dear?

FRANK (*dryly*): It seems he was perfectly happy raking out manure.

DYSART: Did he ever give a reason for this?

DORA: No. I must say we both thought it most peculiar, but he wouldn't discuss it. I mean, you'd have thought he'd be longing to get out in the air after being cooped up all week in that dreadful shop. Electrical and kitchenware! Isn't *that* an environment for a sensitive boy, Doctor? . . .

FRANK: Dear, have you offered the doctor a cup of tea?

DORA: Oh dear, no, I haven't! . . . And you must be dying for one.

DYSART: That would be nice.

DORA: Of course it would . . . Excuse me . . .

(*She goes out—but lingers on the circle, eavesdropping near the right door.* ALAN *stretches out under his blanket and sleeps.* FRANK *gets up.*)

FRANK: My wife has romantic ideas, if you receive my meaning.

DYSART: About her family?

FRANK: She thinks she married beneath her. I daresay she did. I don't understand these things myself.

DYSART: Mr. Strang, I'm fascinated by the fact that Alan wouldn't ride.

FRANK: Yes, well that's him. He's always been a weird lad, I have to be honest. Can you imagine spending your weekends like that—just cleaning out stalls—with all the things that he could have been doing in the way of Further Education?

DYSART: Except he's hardly a scholar.

FRANK: How do we know? He's never really tried. His mother indulged him. She doesn't care if he can hardly write his own name, and she a school teacher that was. Just as long as he's happy, she says . . .

(DORA *wrings her hands in anguish.* FRANK *sits again.*)

DYSART: Would you say she was closer to him than you are?

FRANK: They've always been thick as thieves. I can't say I entirely approve—especially I hear her whispering that Bible to him hour after hour, up there in his room.

DYSART: Your wife is religious?

FRANK: Some might say excessively so. Mind you that's her business. But when it comes to dosing it down the boy's throat—well, frankly, he's my son as well as hers. She doesn't see that. Of course, that's the funny thing about religious people. They always think their susceptibilities are more important than non-religious.

DYSART: And you're non-religious, I take it?

FRANK: I'm an atheist, and I don't mind admitting it. If you want my opinion, it's the Bible that's responsible for all this.

DYSART: Why?

FRANK: Well, look at it yourself. A boy spends night after night having this stuff read into him: an innocent man tortured to death—thorns driven into his head—nails into his hands—a spear jammed through his ribs. It can mark anyone for life, that kind of thing. I'm not joking. The boy was absolutely fascinated by all that. He was always mooning over religious pictures. I mean really kinky ones, if you receive my meaning. I had to put a stop to it once or twice! . . . (*Pause.*) Bloody religion—it's our only real problem in this house, but it's insuperable: I don't mind admitting it.

(*Unable to stand any more,* DORA *comes in again.*)

DORA (*pleasantly*): You must excuse my husband, Doctor. This one subject is something of an obsession with him, isn't it, dear? You must admit.

FRANK: Call it what you like. All that stuff to me is just bad sex.

DORA: And what has that got to do with Alan?

FRANK: Everything! . . . (*Seriously.*) Everything, Dora!

DORA: I don't understand. What are you saying?

(He turns away from her.)

DYSART *(calmingly)*: Mr. Strang, exactly how informed do you judge your son to *be* about sex?

FRANK *(tight)*: I don't know.

DYSART: You didn't actually instruct him yourself?

FRANK: Not in so many words, no.

DYSART: Did *you*, Mrs. Strang?

DORA: Well, I spoke a little, yes. I had to. I've been a teacher, Doctor, and I know what happens if you don't. They find out through magazines and dirty books.

DYSART: What sort of thing did you tell him? I'm sorry if this is embarrassing.

DORA: I told him the biological facts. But I also told him what I believed. That sex is not *just* a biological matter, but spiritual as well. That if God willed, he would fall in love one day. That his task was to prepare himself for the most important happening of his life. And after that, if he was lucky, he might come to know a higher love still . . . I simply . . . don't understand. . . . Alan! . . .

(She breaks down in sobs. Her husband gets up and goes to her.)

FRANK *(embarrassed)*: There now. There now, Dora. Come on!

DORA *(with sudden desperation)*: All right—laugh! Laugh, as usual!

FRANK *(kindly)*: No one's laughing, Dora.

(She glares at him. He puts his arms round her shoulders.)

No one's laughing, are they, Doctor?

(Tenderly, he leads his wife out of the square, and they resume their places on the bench. Lights grow much dimmer.)

ACT 1 / SCENE 8

(A strange noise begins. ALAN begins to murmur from his bed. He is having a bad nightmare, moving his hands and body as if frantically straining to tug something back. DYSART leaves the square as the boy's cries increase.)

ALAN: Ek! . . . Ek! . . . Ek! . . .

(Cries of Ek! on tape fill the theatre, from all around. DYSART reaches the foot of ALAN's bed as the boy gives a terrible cry—)

EK!

(—and wakes up. The sounds snap off. ALAN and the DOCTOR stare at each other. Then abruptly DYSART leaves the area and re-enters the square.)

ACT 1 / SCENE 9

*(Lights grow brighter.
DYSART sits on his bench, left, and opens his file. ALAN gets out of bed, leaves his blanket, and comes in. He looks truculent.)*

DYSART: Hallo. How are you this morning?

(ALAN stares at him.)

Come on: sit down.

(ALAN crosses the stage and sits on the bench, opposite.)

Sorry if I gave you a start last night. I was collecting some papers from my office, and I thought I'd look in on you. Do you dream often?

ALAN: Do *you?*

DYSART: It's my job to ask the questions. Yours to answer them.

ALAN: Says who?

DYSART: Says me. Do you dream often?

ALAN: Do you?

DYSART: Look—Alan.

ALAN: I'll answer if you answer. In turns.

(Pause.)

DYSART: Very well. Only we have to speak the truth.

ALAN *(mocking)*: Very well.

DYSART: So. So you dream often?

ALAN: Yes. Do you?

DYSART: Yes. Do you have a special dream?

ALAN: No. Do you?

DYSART: Yes. What was your dream about last night?

ALAN: Can't remember. What's yours about?

DYSART: I said the truth.

ALAN: That is the truth. What's yours about? The special one.

DYSART: Carving up children.

(ALAN smiles.)

My turn!

ALAN: What?

DYSART: What is your first memory of a horse?

ALAN: What d'you mean?

DYSART: The first time one entered your life, in any way.

ALAN: Can't remember.

DYSART: Are you sure?

ALAN: Yes.

DYSART: You have no recollection of the first time you noticed a horse?

ALAN: I told you. Now it's my turn. Are you married?

DYSART *(controlling himself)*: I am.

ALAN: Is she a doctor too?

DYSART: It's my turn.

ALAN: Yes, well what?

DYSART: What is Ek?

(Pause.)

You shouted it out last night in your sleep. I thought you might like to talk about it.

ALAN *(singing)*: Double your pleasure,

Double your fun!

DYSART: Come on, now. You can do better than that.

ALAN (*singing louder*): With Doublemint, Doublemint Doublemint gum!

DYSART: All right. Good morning.

ALAN: What d'you mean?

DYSART: We're finished for today.

ALAN: But I've only had ten minutes.

DYSART: Too bad.

(*He picks up a file and studies it.* ALAN *lingers.*)

Didn't you hear me? I said, Good morning.

ALAN: That's not fair!

DYSART: No?

ALAN (*savagely*): The Government pays you twenty quid an hour to see me. I know. I heard downstairs.

DYSART: Well, go back there and hear some more.

ALAN: *That's not fair!*

(*He springs up, clenching his fists in a sudden violent rage.*)

You're a—you're a—You're a swiz! . . . Bloody swiz! . . . Fucking swiz!

DYSART: Do I have to call Nurse?

ALAN: She puts a finger on me, I'll bash her!

DYSART: She'll bash you much harder, I can assure you. Now go away.

(*He reads his file.* ALAN *stays where he is, emptily clenching his hands. He turns away.*
A pause.
A faint hum starts from the CHORUS.)

ALAN (*sullenly*): On a beach. . . .

ACT 1 / SCENE 10

(*He steps out of the square, upstage, and begins to walk round the circle. Warm light glows on it.*)

DYSART: What?

ALAN: Where I saw a horse. Swizzy.

(*Lazily he kicks at the sand, and throws stones at the sea.*)

DYSART: How old were you?

ALAN: How should I know? . . . Six.

DYSART: Well, go on. What were you doing there?

ALAN: Digging.

(*He throws himself on the ground, downstage center of the circle, and starts scuffing with his hands.*)

DYSART: A sandcastle?

ALAN: Well, what else?

DYSART (*warningly*): And?

ALAN: Suddenly I heard this noise. Coming up behind me.

(*A young* HORSEMAN *issues in* slow motion *out of the tunnel. He carries a riding crop with which he is urging*

on his invisible horse, down the right side of the circle. The hum increases.)

DYSART: What noise?

ALAN: Hooves. Splashing.

DYSART: Splashing?

ALAN: The tide was out and he was galloping.

DYSART: Who was?

ALAN: This fellow. Like a college chap. He was on a big horse—urging him on. I thought he hadn't seen me. I called out: Hey!

(*The* HORSEMAN *goes into* natural time, *charging fast round the downstage corner of the square straight at* ALAN.)

and they just swerved in time!

HORSEMAN (*reining back*): Whoa! . . . Whoa there! *Whoa!* . . . Sorry! I didn't see you! . . . Did I scare you?

ALAN: No!

HORSEMAN (*looking down on him*): That's a terrific castle!

ALAN: What's his name?

HORSEMAN: Trojan. You can stroke him, if you like. He won't mind.

(*Shyly* ALAN *stretches up on tip-toe, and pats an invisible shoulder.*)

(*Amused.*) You can hardly reach down there. Would you like to come up?

(ALAN *nods, eyes wide.*)

All right, Come round this side. You always mount a horse from the left. I'll give you a lift. O.K.?

(ALAN *goes round on the other side.*)

Here we go, now. Just do nothing. Upsadaisy!

(ALAN *sets his foot on the* HORSEMAN's *thigh, and is lifted by him up on to his shoulders.*)

(*The hum from the* CHORUS *becomes exultant. Then stops.*)

All right?

(ALAN *nods.*)

Good. Now all you do is hold onto his mane.

(*He holds up the crop, and* ALAN *grips on to it.*)

Tight now. And grip with your knees. All right? All set? . . . Come on, then, Trojan. Let's go!

(*The* HORSEMAN *walks slowly upstage round the circle, with* ALAN's *legs tight round his neck.*)

DYSART: How was it? Was it wonderful?

(ALAN *rides in silence.*)

Can't you remember?

HORSEMAN: Do you want to go faster?

ALAN: Yes!

HORSEMAN: O.K. All you have to do is say 'Come on, Trojan—bear me away!' . . . Say it, then!

ALAN: Bear me away!

(*The* HORSEMAN *starts to run with* ALAN *round the circle.*)

DYSART: You went fast?

ALAN: Yes!

DYSART: Weren't you frightened?

ALAN: No!

HORSEMAN: Come on now. Trojan! Bear us away! Hold on! Come on now! . . .

(*He runs faster.* ALAN *begins to laugh. Then suddenly, as they reach again the right downstage corner,* FRANK *and* DORA *stand up in alarm.*)

DORA: Alan!

FRANK: Alan!

DORA: Alan, stop!

(FRANK *runs round after them.* DORA *follows behind.*)

FRANK: Hey, you! *You!* . . .

HORSEMAN: Whoa, boy! . . . Whoa! . . .

(*He reins the horse round, and wheels to face the parents. This all goes fast.*)

FRANK: What do you imagine you are doing?

HORSEMAN (*ironic*): 'Imagine'?

FRANK: What is my son doing up there?

HORSEMAN: Water-skiing!

(DORA *joints them, breathless.*)

DORA: Is he all right, Frank? . . . He's not hurt?

FRANK: Don't you think you should ask permission before doing a stupid thing like that?

HORSEMAN: What's stupid?

ALAN: It's lovely, dad!

DORA: Alan, come down here!

HORSEMAN: The boy's perfectly safe. Please don't be hysterical.

FRANK: Don't you be la-di-da with me, young man! Come down here. Alan. You heard what your mother said.

ALAN: No.

FRANK: Come down at once. Right this moment.

ALAN: No . . . NO!

FRANK (*in a fury*): I said—this moment!

(*He pulls* ALAN *from the* HORSEMAN'S *shoulders. The boy shrieks, and falls to the ground.*)

HORSEMAN: Watch it!

DORA: Frank!

(*She runs to her son, and kneels. The* HORSEMAN *skitters.*)

HORSEMAN: Are you mad? D'you want to terrify the horse?

DORA: He's grazed his knee. Frank—the boy's hurt!

ALAN: I'm not! I'm *not!*

FRANK: What's your name?

HORSEMAN: Jesse James.

DORA: Frank, he's bleeding!

FRANK: I intend to report you to the police for endangering the lives of children.

HORSEMAN: Go right ahead!

DORA: Can you stand, dear?

ALAN: Oh, *stop* it! . . .

FRANK: You're a public menace, d'you know that? How dare you pick up children and put them on dangerous animals.

HORSEMAN: Dangerous?

FRANK: Of course dangerous. Look at his eyes. They're rolling.

HORSEMAN: So are yours!

FRANK: In my opinion that is a dangerous animal. In my considered opinion you are both dangers to the safety of this beach.

HORSEMAN: And in my opinion, you're a stupid fart!

DORA: Frank, leave it!

FRANK: What did you say?

DORA: It's not important, Frank—really!

FRANK: *What did you say?*

HORSEMAN: Oh bugger off! Sorry, chum! Come on, Trojan!

(*He urges his horse straight at them, then wheels it and gallops off round the right side of the circle and away up the tunnel, out of sight. The parents cry out, as they are covered with sand and water.* FRANK *runs after him, and round the left side of the circle, with his wife following after.*)

ALAN: Splash, splash, splash! All three of us got covered with water! Dad got absolutely soaked!

FRANK (*shouting after the* HORSEMAN): Hooligan! Filthy hooligan!

ALAN: I wanted to laugh!

FRANK: Upper class riff-raff! That's all they are, people who go riding! That's what they *want*—trample on ordinary people!

DORA: Don't be absurd, Frank.

FRANK: It's why they do it. It's why they bloody do it!

DORA (*amused*): Look at you. You're covered!

FRANK: Not as much as you. There's sand all over your hair!

(*She starts to laugh.*)

(*Shouting.*) Hooligan! Bloody hooligan!

(*She starts to laugh more. He tries to brush the sand out of her hair.*)

What are you laughing at? It's not funny. It's not funny at all, Dora!

(She goes off, right, still laughing. ALAN *edges into the square, still on the ground.)*

It's just not funny! . . .

*(*FRANK *returns to his place on the beach, sulky. Abrupt silence.)*

ALAN: And that's all I remember.

DYSART: And a lot too. Thank you . . . You know, I've never been on a horse in my life.

ALAN *(not looking at him)*: Nor me.

DYSART: You mean, after that?

ALAN: Yes.

DYSART: But you must have done at the stables?

ALAN: No.

DYSART: Never?

ALAN: No.

DYSART: How come?

ALAN: I didn't care to.

DYSART: Did it have anything to do with falling off like that, all those years ago?

ALAN *(tight)*: I just didn't care to, that's all.

DYSART: Do you think of that scene often?

ALAN: I suppose.

DYSART: Why, do you think?

ALAN: 'Cos it's funny.

DYSART: Is that all?

ALAN: What else? My turn. . . . I told you a secret: now you tell me one.

DYSART: All right. I have patients who've got things to tell me, only they're ashamed to say them to my face. What do you think I do about that?

ALAN: What?

DYSART: I give them this little tape recorder.

(He takes a small tape recorder and microphone from his pocket.)

They go off to another room, and send me the tape through Nurse. They don't have to listen to it with me.

ALAN: That's stupid.

DYSART: All you do is press this button, and speak into this. It's very simple. Anyway, your time's up for today. I'll see you tomorrow.

ALAN *(getting up)*: Maybe.

DYSART: Maybe?

ALAN: If I feel like it.

(He is about to go out. Then suddenly he returns to DYSART *and takes the machine from him.)*

It's stupid.

(He leaves the square and goes back to his bed.)

ACT 1 / SCENE 11

DORA *(calling out)*: Doctor!

*(*DORA *re-enters and comes straight on to the square from*

the right. She wears an overcoat, and is nervously carrying a shopping bag.)*

DYSART: That same evening, his mother appeared.

DORA: Hallo, Doctor.

DYSART: Mrs. Strang!

DORA: I've been shopping in the neighbourhood. I thought I might just look in.

DYSART: Did you want to see Alan?

DORA *(uncomfortably)*: No, no . . . Not just at the moment. Actually, it's more you I wanted to see.

DYSART: Yes?

DORA: You see, there's something Mr. Strang and I thought you ought to know. We discussed it, and it might just be important.

DYSART: Well, come and sit down.

DORA: I can't stay more than a moment. I'm late as it is. Mr. Strang will be wanting his dinner.

DYSART: Ah. *(Encouragingly.)* So, what was it you wanted to tell me?

(She sits on the upstage bench.)

DORA: Well, do you remember that photograph I mentioned to you. The one Mr. Strang gave Alan to decorate his bedroom a few years ago?

DYSART: Yes. A horse looking over a gate, wasn't it?

DORA: That's right. Well, actually, it took the place of another kind of picture altogether.

DYSART: What kind?

DORA: It was a reproduction of Our Lord on his way to Cavalry. Alan found it in Reeds Art Shop, and fell absolutely in love with it. He insisted on buying it with his pocket money, and hanging it at the foot of his bed where he could see it last thing at night. My husband was very displeased.

DYSART: Because it was religious?

DORA: In all fairness I must admit it was a little extreme. The Christ was loaded down with chains, and the centurions were really laying on the stripes. It certainly would not have been my choice, but I don't believe in interfering too much with children, so I said nothing.

DYSART: But Mr. Strang did?

DORA: He stood it for a while, but one day we had one of our tiffs about religion, and he went straight upstairs, tore it off the boy's wall and threw it in the dustbin. Alan went quite hysterical. He cried for days without stopping—and he was not a crier, you know.

DYSART: But he recovered when he was given the photograph of the horse in its place?

DORA: He certainly seemed to. At least, he hung it in exactly the same position, and we had no more of that awful weeping.

DYSART: Thank you, Mrs. Strang. That *is* interesting . . . Exactly how long ago was that? Can you remember?

DORA: It must be five years ago, Doctor. Alan would have been about twelve. How is he, by the way?

DYSART: Bearing up.

(She rises.)

DORA: Please give him my love.

DYSART: You can see him any time you want, you know.

DORA: Perhaps if I could come one afternoon without Mr. Strang. He and Alan don't exactly get on at the moment, as you can imagine.

DYSART: Whatever you decide, Mrs. Strang . . . Oh, one thing.

DORA: Yes?

DYSART: Could you describe that photograph of the horse in a little more detail for me? I presume it's still in his bedroom?

DORA: Oh, yes. It's a most remarkable picture, really. You very rarely see a horse taken from that angle—absolutely head on. That's what makes it so interesting.

DYSART: Why? What does it look like?

DORA: Well, it's most extraordinary. It comes out all eyes.

DYSART: Staring straight at you?

DORA: Yes, that's right . . .

(An uncomfortable pause.)

I'll come and see him one day very soon, Doctor. Good-bye.

(She leaves, and resumes her place by her husband.)

DYSART *(to audience)*: It was then—that moment—I felt real alarm. What was it? The shadow of a giant head across my desk? . . . At any rate, the feeling got worse with the stable-owner's visit.

ACT 1 / SCENE 12

(DALTON comes in to the square: heavy-set: mid-fifties.)

DALTON: Dr. Dysart?

DYSART: Mr. Dalton. It's very good of you to come.

DALTON: It is, actually. In my opinion the boy should be in prison. Not in a hospital at the tax-payers' expense.

DYSART: Please sit down.

(DALTON sits.)

This must have been a terrible experience for you.

DALTON: Terrible? I don't think I'll ever get over it. Jill's had a nervous breakdown.

DYSART: Jill?

DALTON: The girl who worked for me. Of course, she feels responsible in a way. Being the one who introduced him in the first place.

DYSART: He was introduced to the stable by a girl?

DALTON: Jill Mason. He met her somewhere, and

asked for a job. She told him to come and see me. I wish to Christ she never had.

DYSART: But when he first appeared he didn't seem in any way peculiar?

DALTON: No, he was bloody good. He'd spend hours with the horses cleaning and grooming them, way over the call of duty. I thought he was a real find.

DYSART: Apparently, during the whole time he worked for you, he never actually rode.

DALTON: That's true.

DYSART: Wasn't that peculiar?

DALTON: Very . . . *If* he didn't.

DYSART: What do you mean?

(DALTON rises.)

DALTON: Because on and off, that whole year, I had the feeling the horses were being taken out at night.

DYSART: At night?

DALTON: There were just odd things I noticed. I mean too often one or other of them would be sweaty first thing in the morning, when it wasn't sick. Very sweaty, too. And its stall wouldn't be near as mucky as it should be if it had been in all night. I never paid it much mind at the time. It was only when I realised I'd been hiring a loony, I came to wonder if he hadn't been riding all the time, behind our backs.

DYSART: But wouldn't you have noticed if things had been disturbed?

DALTON: Nothing ever was. Still, he's a neat worker. That wouldn't prove anything.

DYSART: Aren't the stables locked at night?

DALTON: Yes.

DYSART: And someone sleeps on the premises?

DALTON: Me and my son.

DYSART: Two people?

DALTON: I'm sorry, Doctor. It's obviously just my fancy. I tell you, this thing has shaken me so bad, I'm liable to believe anything. If there's nothing else, I'll be going.

DYSART: Look: even if you were right, why should anyone do that? Why would any boy prefer to ride by himself at night, when he could go off with others during the day.

DALTON: Are you asking me? He's a loony, isn't he?

(DALTON leaves the square and sits again in his place. DYSART watches him go.)

ALAN: It was *sexy*.

DYSART: His tape arrived that evening.

ACT 1 / SCENE 13

(ALAN is sitting on his bed holding the tape-recorder. NURSE approaches briskly, takes the machine from him— gives it to DYSART in the square—and leaves again,

resuming her seat. DYSART *switches on the tape.*)

ALAN: That's what you want to know, isn't it? All right: it was. I'm talking about the beach. That time when I was a kid. What I told you about. . . .

(*Pause. He is in great emotional difficulty.*
DYSART *sits on the left bench listening, file in hand.* ALAN *rises and stands directly behind him, but on the circle, as if recording the ensuing speech. He never, of course, looks directly at the Doctor.*)

I was pushed forward on the horse. There was sweat on my legs from his neck. The fellow held me tight, and let me turn the horse which way I wanted. All that power going any way you wanted . . . His sides were all warm, and the smell . . . Then suddenly I was on the ground, where Dad pulled me. I could have bashed him . . .

(*Pause.*)

Something else. When the horse first appeared, I looked up into his mouth. It was huge. There was this chain in it. The fellow pulled it, and cream dripped out. I said 'Does it hurt?' And he said—the horse said—said—

(*He stops, in anguish.* DYSART *makes a note in his file.*)

(*desperately*) It was always the same, after that. Every time I heard one clop by, I had to run and see. Up a country lane or anywhere. They sort of pulled me. I couldn't take my eyes off them. Just to watch their skins. The way their necks twist, and sweat shines in the folds . . . (*Pause.*) I can't remember when it started. Mum reading to me about Prince who no one could ride, except one boy. Or the white horse in Revelations. 'He that sat upon him was called Faithful and True. His eyes were as flames of fire, and he had a name written that no man knew but himself' . . . Words like reins. Stirrup. Flanks . . . 'Dashing his spurs against his charger's flanks!' . . . Even the words made me feel— . . . Years, I never told anyone. Mum wouldn't understand. She likes Equita- tion'. Bowler hats and jodhpurs! 'My grand- father dressed for the horse,' she says. What does that mean? The horse isn't dressed. It's the most naked thing you ever saw. More than a dog or a cat or anything. Even the most broken down old nag has got its *life!* To put a bowler on it is *filthy!* . . . Putting them through their paces! Bloody gymkhanas! . . . No one understands! . . . Except cowboys. They do. I wish I was a cowboy. They're free. They just swing up and then it's miles of grass . . . I bet all cowboys are *orphans!* . . . I bet they are!

NURSE: Mr. Strang to see you, Doctor.

DYSART (*in surprise*): Mr. Strang? Show him up, please.

ALAN: No one ever says to cowboys 'Receive my meaning'! They wouldn't dare. Or 'God' all the time. (*Mimicking his mother.*) 'God sees you, Alan. God's got eyes everywhere—'

(*He stops abruptly.*)

I'm not doing any more! . . . I hate this! . . . You can whistle for anymore. I've had it!

(*He returns angrily to his bed, throwing the blanket over him.*
DYSART *switches off the tape.*)

ACT 1 / SCENE 14

(FRANK STRANG *comes into the square, his hat in his hand. He is nervous and embarrassed.*)

DYSART (*welcoming*): Hallo, Mr. Strang.
FRANK: I was just passing. I hope it's not too late.
DYSART: Of course not. I'm delighted to see you.
FRANK: My wife doesn't know I'm here. I'd be grate- ful to you if you didn't enlighten her, if you receive my meaning.
DYSART: Everything that happens in this room is confidential, Mr. Strang.
FRANK: I hope so . . . I hope so . . .
DYSART (*gently*): Do you have something to tell me?
FRANK: As a matter of fact I have. Yes.
DYSART: Your wife told me about the photograph.
FRANK: I know, it's not that! It's *about* that, but it's—worse. . . . I wanted to tell you the other night, but I couldn't in front of Dora. Maybe I should have. It might show her where all that stuff leads to, she drills into the boy behind my back.
DYSART: What kind of thing is it?
FRANK: Something I witnessed.
DYSART: Where?
FRANK: At home. About eighteen months ago.
DYSART: Go on.
FRANK: It was late. I'd gone upstairs to fetch some- thing. The boy had been in bed hours, or so I thought.
DYSART: Go on.
FRANK: As I came along the passage I saw the door of his bedroom was ajar. I'm sure he didn't know it was. From inside I heard the sound of this chanting.
DYSART: Chanting?
FRANK: Like the Bible. One of those lists his mother's always reading to him.
DYSART: What kind of list?
FRANK: Those Begats. So-and-so begat, you know. Genealogy.
DYSART: Can you remember what Alan's list sounded like?

FRANK: Well, the *sort* of thing. I stood there absolutely astonished. The first word I heard was . . .

ALAN (*rising and chanting*): *Prince!*

DYSART: Prince?

FRANK: Prince begat Prance. That sort of nonsense.

(ALAN *moves slowly to the center of the circle, downstage.*)

ALAN: And Prance begat Prankus! And Prankus begat Flankus!

FRANK: I looked through the door, and he was standing in the moonlight in his pyjamas, right in front of that big photograph.

DYSART: The horse with the huge eyes?

FRANK: Right.

ALAN: Flankus begat Spankus. And Spankus begat Spunkus the Great, who lived three score years!

FRANK: It was all like that. I can't remember the exact names, of course. Then suddenly he knelt down.

DYSART: In front of the photograph?

FRANK: Yes. Right there at the foot of his bed.

ALAN (*kneeling*): And Legwus begat Neckwus. And Neckwus begat Fleckwus, the King of Spit. And Fleckwus spoke out of his chinkle-chankle!

(*He bows himself to the ground.*)

DYSART: What?

FRANK: I'm sure that was the word. I've never forgotten it. Chinkle-chankle.

(ALAN *raises his head and extends his hands up in glory.*)

ALAN: And he said 'Behold—I give you Equus, my only begotten son!'

DYSART: Equus?

FRANK: Yes. No doubt of that. He repeated that word several times. 'Equus my only begotten son."

ALAN (*reverently*): Ek . . . wus!

DYSART (*suddenly understanding: almost 'aside'*): Ek. . . . Ek. . . .

FRANK (*embarrassed*): And then . . .

DYSART: Yes: what?

FRANK: He took a piece of string out of his pocket. Made up into a noose. And put it in his mouth.

(ALAN *bridles himself with invisible string, and pulls it back.*)

And then with his other hand he picked up a coat hanger. A wooden coat hanger, and—and—

DYSART: Began to beat himself?

(ALAN, *in mime, begins to thrash himself, increasing the strokes in speed and viciousness. Pause.*)

FRANK: You see why I couldn't tell his mother. . . . Religion. Religion's at the bottom of all this!

DYSART: What did you do?

FRANK: Nothing. I coughed—and went back downstairs.

(*The boy starts guiltily—tears the string from his mouth—and scrambles back to bed.*)

DYSART: Did you ever speak to him about it later? Even obliquely?

FRANK (*unhappily*): I can't speak of things like that, Doctor. It's not in my nature.

DYSART (*kindly*): No. I see that.

FRANK: But I thought you ought to know. So I came.

DYSART (*warmly*): Yes. I'm very grateful to you. Thank you.

(*Pause.*)

FRANK: Well, that's it . . .

DYSART: Is there anything else?

FRANK (*even more embarrassed*): There is actually. One thing.

DYSART: What's that?

FRANK: On the night that he did it—that awful thing in the stable—

DYSART: Yes?

FRANK: That very night, he was out with a girl.

DYSART: How d'you know that?

FRANK: I just know.

DYSART (*puzzled*): Did he tell you?

FRANK: I can't say any more.

DYSART: I don't quite understand.

FRANK: Everything said in here is confidential, you said.

DYSART: Absolutely.

FRANK: Then ask him. Ask him about taking a girl out, the very night he did it. . . . (*Abruptly.*) Goodbye, Doctor.

(*He goes.* DYSART *looks after him.* FRANK *resumes his seat.*)

ACT 1 / SCENE 15

(ALAN *gets up and enters the square.*)

DYSART: Alan! Come in. Sit down. (*Pleasantly.*) What did you do last night?

ALAN: Watched telly.

DYSART: Any good?

ALAN: All right.

DYSART: Thanks for the tape. It was excellent.

ALAN: I'm not making any more.

DYSART: One thing I didn't quite understand. You began to say something about the horse on the beach talking to you.

ALAN: That's stupid. Horses don't talk.

DYSART: So I believe.

ALAN: I don't know what you mean.

DYSART: Never mind. Tell me something else. Who introduced you to the stable to begin with?

(*Pause.*)

ALAN: Someone I met.

DYSART: Where?

ALAN: Bryson's.

DYSART: The shop where you worked?

ALAN: Yes.

DYSART: That's a funny place for you to be. Whose idea was that?

ALAN: Dad.

DYSART: I'd have thought he'd have wanted you to work with him.

ALAN: I haven't the aptitude. And printing's a failing trade. If you receive my meaning.

DYSART (amused): I see ... What did your mother think?

ALAN: Shops are common.

DYSART: And you?

ALAN: I loved it.

DYSART: Really?

ALAN (sarcastic): Why not? You get to spend every minute with electrical things. It's fun.

(NURSE, DALTON and the actors playing horses call out to him as CUSTOMERS, seated where they are. Their voices are aggressive and demanding. There is a constant background mumbling, made up of trade names, out of which can clearly be distinguished the italicized words, which are shouted out.)

CUSTOMER: *Philco!*

ALAN (to DYSART): Of course it might just drive you off your chump.

CUSTOMER: I want to buy a hot-plate. I'm told the *Philco* is a good make!

ALAN: I think it is, madam.

CUSTOMER: *Remington* ladies' shavers?

ALAN: I'm not sure, madam.

CUSTOMER: *Robex* tableware?

CUSTOMER: *Croydex?*

CUSTOMER: *Volex?*

CUSTOMER: *Pifco* automatic toothbrushes?

ALAN: I'll find out, sir.

CUSTOMER: Beautiflor!

CUSTOMER: Windowlene!

CUSTOMER: I want a *Philco* transistor radio!

CUSTOMER: This isn't a *Remington!* I wanted a *Remington!*

ALAN: Sorry.

CUSTOMER: Are you a dealer for *Hoover?*

ALAN: Sorry.

CUSTOMER: I wanted the heat retaining *Pifco!*

ALAN: *Sorry!*

(JILL comes into the square; a girl in her early twenties, pretty and middle class. She wears a sweater and jeans. The mumbling stops.)

JILL: Hallo.

ALAN: Hallo.

JILL: Have you any blades for a clipping machine?

JILL: Clipping?

JILL: To clip horses.

(Pause. He stares at her, open-mouthed.)

What's the matter?

ALAN: You work at Dalton's stables. I've seen you.

(During the following, he mimes putting away a pile of boxes on a shelf in the shop.)

JILL: I've seen you too, haven't I? You're the boy who's always staring into the yard around lunch-time.

ALAN: Me?

JILL: You're there most days.

ALAN: Not me.

JILL (amused): Of course it's you. Mr. Dalton was only saying the other day: 'Who's that boy keeps staring in at the door?' Are you looking for a job or something?

ALAN (eagerly): Is there one?

JILL: I don't know.

ALAN: I can only do weekends.

JILL: That's when most people ride. We can always use extra hands. It'd mainly be mucking out.

ALAN: I don't mind.

JILL: Can you ride?

ALAN: No ... No ... I don't want to.

(She looks at him curiously.)

Please.

JILL: Come up on Saturday. I'll introduce you to Mr. Dalton.

(She leaves the square.)

DYSART: When was this? About a year ago?

ALAN: I suppose.

DYSART: And she did?

ALAN: Yes.

(Briskly he moves the three benches to form three stalls in the stable.)

ACT 1 / SCENE 16

(Rich light falls on the square.
An exultant humming from the CHORUS.
Tramping is heard. Three actors playing horses rise from their places. Together they unhook three horse masks from the ladders to left and right, put them on with rigid timing, and walk with swaying horse-motion into the square. Their metal hooves stamp on the wood. Their masks turn and toss high above their heads–as they will do sporadically throughout all horse scenes—making the steel gleam in the light.
For a moment they seem to converge on the boy as he stands in the middle of the stable, but then they swiftly turn and take up positions as if tethered by the head, with their invisible rumps towards him, one by each bench. ALAN is sunk in this glowing world of horses. Lost in wonder, he starts almost involuntarily to kneel on the floor in

reverence—but is sharply interrupted by the cheery voice of DALTON, *coming into the stable, followed by* JILL. *The boy straightens up guiltily.*)

DALTON: First thing to learn is drill. Learn it and keep to it. I want this place neat, dry and clean at all times. After you've mucked out, Jill will show you some grooming. What we call strapping a horse.

JILL: I think Trooper's got a stone.

DALTON: Yes? Let's see.

(*He crosses to the horse by the left bench, who is balancing one hoof on its tip. He picks up the hoof.*)

You're right. (*to* ALAN) See this? This V here. It's what called a frog. Sort of shock-absorber. Once you pierce that, it takes ages to heal—so you want to watch for it. You clean it out with this. What we call a hoof-pick.

(*He takes from his pocket an invisible pick.*)

Mind how you go with it. It's very sharp. Use it like this.

(*He quickly takes the stone out.*)

See?

(ALAN *nods, fascinated.*)

You'll soon get the hang of it. Jill will look after you. What she doesn't know about stables, isn't worth knowing.

JILL (*pleased*): Oh yes, I'm sure!

DALTON (*handing* ALAN *the pick*): Careful how you go with that. The main rule is: anything you don't know—ask. Never pretend you know something when you don't. (*Smiling.*) Actually, the main rule is: enjoy yourself. All right?

ALAN: Yes, sir.

DALTON: Good lad. See you later.

(*He nods to them cheerfully, and leaves the square.* ALAN *clearly puts the invisible hoof-pick on the rail, downstage left.*)

JILL: All right, let's start on some grooming. Why don't we begin with him? He looks as if he needs it.

(*They approach* NUGGET, *who is standing to the right. She pats him.* ALAN *sits and watches her.*)

This is Nugget. He's my favorite. He's as gentle as a baby, aren't you? But terribly fast if you want him to be.

(*During the following, she mimes both the actions and the objects, which she picks up from the right bench.*)

Now this is the dandy, and we start with that. Then you move on to the body brush. This is the most important, and you use it with this curry-comb. Now you always groom the same way: from the ears downward. Don't be afraid to do it hard. The harder you do it, the more the horse loves it. Push it right through the coat: like this.

(*The boy watches in fascination as she brushes the invisible body of* NUGGET, *scraping the dirt and hair off on to the invisible curry-comb. Now and then the horse mask moves very slightly in pleasure.*)

Down towards the tail and right through the coat. See how he loves it? I'm giving you a lovely massage, boy, aren't I? . . . You try.

(*She hands him the brush. Gingerly he rises and approaches* NUGGET. *Embarrassed and excited, he copies her movements, inexpertly.*)

Keep it nice and easy. Never rush. Down towards the tail and right through the coat. That's it. Again. Down towards the tail and right through the coat. . . . Very good. Now you keep that up for fifteen minutes and then do old Trooper. Will you?

(ALAN *nods.*)

You've got a feel for it. I can tell. It's going to be nice teaching you. See you later.

(*She leaves the square and resumes her place.*
ALAN *is left alone with the horses.*
They all stamp. He approaches NUGGET *again, and touches the horse's shoulder. The mask turns sharply in his direction. The boy pauses, then moves his hand gently over the outline of the neck and back. The mask is re-assured. It stares ahead unmoving. Then* ALAN *lifts his palm to his face and smells it deeply, closing his eyes.*
DYSART *rises from his bench, and begins to walk slowly upstage round the circle.*)

DYSART: Was that good? Touching them.

(ALAN *gives a faint groan.*)

ALAN: Mmm.

DYSART: It must have been marvelous, being near them at last . . . Stroking them . . . Making them fresh and glossy'. . . Tell me . . .

(*Silence.* ALAN *begins to brush* NUGGET.)

How about the girl? Did you like her?

ALAN (*tight*): All right.

DYSART: Just all right?

(ALAN *changes his position, moving round* NUGGET's *rump so that his back is to the audience. He brushes harder.* DYSART *comes downstage around the circle, and finally back to his bench.*)

Was she friendly?

ALAN: Yes.

DYSART: Or stand-offish?
ALAN: Yes.
DYSART: Well which?
ALAN: What?
DYSART: Which was she?

(ALAN *brushes harder.*)

Did you take her out? Come on now: tell me. Did you have a date with her?
ALAN: What?
DYSART *(sitting)*: Tell me if you did.

(*The boy suddenly explodes in one of his rages.*)

ALAN *(yelling)*: TELL ME!

(*All the masks toss at the noise.*)

DYSART: What?
ALAN: *Tell me, tell me, tell me, tell me!*

(ALAN *storms out out of the square, and downstage to where* DYSART *sits. He is raging. During the ensuing, the horses leave by all three openings.*)

On and on, sitting there! Nosey Parker! That's all you are! Bloody Nosey Parker! Just like Dad. On and on and bloody on! Tell me, tell me, tell me! . . . Answer this. Answer that. Never stop!—

(*He marches round the circle and back into the square.* DYSART *rises and enters it from the other side.*)

ACT 1 / SCENE 17

(*Lights brighten.*)

DYSART: I'm sorry.

(ALAN *slams about what is now the office again, replacing the benches to their usual position.*)

ALAN: All right, it's my turn now. You tell me! Answer me!
DYSART: We're not playing that game now.
ALAN: We're playing what I say.
DYSART: All right. What do you want to know?

(*He sits.*)

ALAN: Do *you* have dates?
DYSART: I told you. I'm married.

(*Alan approaches him, very hostile.*)

ALAN: I know. Her name's Margaret. She's a dentist! You see, I found out! What made you go with her? Did you use to bite her hands when she did you in the chair?

(*The boy sits next to him, close.*)

DYSART: That's not very funny.
ALAN: Do you have girls behind her back?
DYSART: No.

ALAN: Then what? Do you fuck her?
DYSART: That's enough now.

(*He rises and moves away.*)

ALAN: Come on, tell me! Tell me, tell me!
DYSART: I said that's enough now.

(ALAN *rises too and walks around him.*)

I bet you don't. I bet you never touch her. Come on, tell me. You've got no kids, have you? Is that because you don't fuck?
DYSART *(sharp)*: Go to your room. Go on: quick march.

(*Pause.* ALAN *moves away from him, insolently takes up a packet of* DYSART's *cigarettes from the bench, and extracts one.*)

Give me those cigarettes.

(*The boy puts one in his mouth.*)

(*Exploding.*) Alan, *give them to me!*

(*Reluctantly* ALAN *shoves the cigarette back in the packet, turns and hands it to him.*)

Now go!

(ALAN *bolts out of the square, and back to his bed.* DYSART, *unnerved, addresses the audience.*)

Brilliant! Absolutely brilliant! The boy's on the run, so he gets defensive. What am *I*, then? . . . Wicked little bastard—he knew exactly what questions to try. He'd actually marched himself round the hospital, making enquiries about my wife. Wicked and—of course, perceptive. Ever since I made that crack about carving up children, he's been aware of me in an absolutely specific way. Of course, there's nothing novel in that. Advanced neurotics can be dazzling at that game. They aim unswervingly at your area of maximum vulnerability . . . Which I suppose is as good a way as any of describing Margaret.

(*He sits.* HESTHER *enters the square.*
Light grows warmer.)

ACT 1 / SCENE 18

HESTHER: Now stop it.
DYSART: Do I embarrass you?
HESTHER: I suspect you're about to.

(*Pause.*)

DYSART: My wife doesn't understand me, Your Honour.
HESTHER: Do you understand her?
DYSART: No. Obviously I never did.
HESTHER: I'm sorry. I've never liked to ask but I've always imagined you weren't exactly compatible.

(She moves to sit opposite.)

DYSART: We were. It actually worked for a bit. I mean for both of us. We worked for each other. She actually for me through a kind of briskness. A clear, red-headed, inaccessible briskness which kept me keyed up for months. Mind you, if you're kinky for Northern Hygenic, as I am, you can't find anything much more compelling than a Scottish Lady Dentist.

HESTHER: It's *you* who are wicked, you know!

DYSART: Not at all: She got exactly the same from me. Antiseptic proficiency. I was like that in those days. We suited each other admirably. I see us in our wedding photo: Doctor and Doctor Mac Brisk. We were brisk in our wooing, brisk in our wedding, brisk in our disappointment. We turned from each other briskly into our separate surgeries: and now there's damn all.

HESTHER: You have no children, have you?

DYSART: No, we didn't go in for them. Instead, she sits beside our salmon-pink, glazed brick fireplace, and knits things for orphans in a home she helps with. And I sit opposite, turning the pages of art books on Ancient Greece. Occasionally, I still trail a faint scent of my enthusiasm across her path. I pass her a picture of the sacred acrobats of Crete leaping through the horns of running bulls—and she'll say: 'Och, Martin, what an *absurred* thing to be doing! The Highland Games, now there's *norrmal sport!*' Or she'll observe, just after I've told her a story from the Iliad: 'You know, when you come to think of it, Agamemnon and that lot were nothing but a bunch of ruffians from the Gorbals, only with fancy names!' *(He rises.)* You get the picture. She's turned into a Shrink. The familiar domestic monster. Margaret Dysart: the Shrink's Shrink.

HESTHER: That's cruel, Martin.

DYSART: Yes. Do you know what it's like for two people to live in the same house as if they were in different parts of the world? Mentally, she's always in some drizzly kirk of her own inheriting: and I'm in some Doric temple—clouds tearing through pillars—eagles bearing prophecies out of the sky. She finds all that repulsive. All my wife has ever taken from the Mediterranean—from that whole vast intuitive culture—are four bottles of Chianti to make into lamps, and two china condiment donkeys labelled Sally and Peppy.

(Pause.)

(More intimately.) I wish there was one person in my life I could show. One instinctive, absolutely unbrisk person I could take to Greece, and stand in front of certain shrines and sacred streams and say 'Look! Life is only comprehensible through a thousand local Gods. and not just the old dead ones with names like Zeus—no, but living Geniuses of Place and Person! And not just Greece but modern England! Spirits of certain trees, certain curves of brick wall, certain chip shops, if you like, and slate roofs—just as of certain frowns in people and slouches . . . I'd say to them—'Worship as many as you can see—and more will appear!' . . . If I had a son, I bet you he'd come out exactly like his mother. Utterly worshipless. Would you like a drink?

HESTHER: No, thanks. Actually, I've got to be going. As usual . . .

DYSART: Really?

HESTHER: Really. I've got an Everest of papers to get through before bed.

DYSART: You never stop, do you?

HESTHER: Do you?

DYSART: This boy, with his stare. He's trying to save himself through me.

HESTHER: I'd say so.

DYSART: What am I trying to do to him?

HESTHER: Restore him, surely?

DYSART: To what?

HESTHER: A normal life.

DYSART: Normal?

HESTHER: It still means something.

DYSART: Does it?

HESTHER: Of course.

DYSART: You mean a normal boy has one head: a normal head has two ears?

HESTHER: You know I don't.

DYSART: Then what else?

HESTHER *(lightly)*: Oh, stop it.

DYSART: No, what? You tell me.

HESTHER *(rising: smiling)*: I won't be put on the stand like this, Martin. You're really disgraceful! . . . *(Pause.)* You know what I mean by a normal smile in a child's eyes, and one that isn't—even if I can't exactly define it. Don't you?

DYSART: Yes.

HESTHER: Then we have a duty to that, surely? Both of us.

DYSART: Touché. . . . I'll talk to you.

HESTHER: Dismissed?

DYSART: You said you had to go.

HESTHER: I do . . . *(She kisses his cheek.)* Thank you for what you're doing. . . . You're going through a rotten patch at the moment. I'm sorry . . . I suppose one of the few things one can do is simply hold on to priorities.

DYSART: Like what?

HESTHER: Oh—children before grown-ups. Things like that.

(He contemplates her.)

DYSART: You're really quite splendid.

HESTHER: Famous for it. Goodnight.

(She leaves him.)

DYSART *(to himself—or to the audience)*: Normal! . . . Normal!

ACT 1 / SCENE 19

(ALAN rises and enters the square. He is subdued.)

DYSART: Good afternoon.

ALAN: Afternoon.

DYSART: I'm sorry about our row yesterday.

ALAN: It was stupid.

DYSART: It was.

ALAN: What I said, I mean.

DYSART: How are you sleeping?

(ALAN shrugs.)

You're not feeling well, are you?

ALAN: All right.

DYSART: Would you like to play a game? It could make you feel better.

ALAN: What kind?

DYSART: It's called *Blink*. You have to fix your eyes on something: say, that little stain over there on the wall—and I tap this pen on the desk. The first time I tap it, you close your eyes. The next time you open them. And so on. Close, open, close, open, till I say Stop.

ALAN: How can that make you feel better?

DYSART: It relaxes you. You'll feel as though you're talking to me in your sleep.

ALAN: It's stupid.

DYSART: You don't have to do it, if you don't want to.

ALAN: I didn't say I didn't want to.

DYSART: Well?

ALAN: I don't mind.

DYSART: Good. Sit down and start watching that stain. Put your hands by your sides, and open the fingers wide.

(He opens the left bench and ALAN sits on the end of it.)

The thing is to feel comfortable, and relax absolutely . . . Are you looking at the stain?

ALAN: Yes.

DYSART: Right. Now try and keep your mind as blank as possible.

ALAN: That's not difficult.

DYSART: Ssh. Stop talking . . . On the first tap, close. On the second, open. Are you ready?

(ALAN nods. DYSART taps his pen on the wooden rail. ALAN shuts his eyes. DYSART taps again. ALAN opens them. The taps are evenly spaced. After four of them the sound cuts out, and is replaced by a louder, metallic sound, on tape. DYSART talks through this, to the audience—the light changes to cold—while the boy sits in front of him, staring at the wall, opening and shutting his eyes.)

The Normal is the good smile in a child's eyes—all right. It is also the dead stare in a million adults. It both sustains and kills—like a God. It is the Ordinary made beautiful: it is also the Average made lethal. The Normal is the indispensable, murderous God of Health, and I am his Priest. My tools are very delicate. My compassion is honest. I have honestly assisted children in this room. I have talked away terrors and relieved many agonies. But also—beyond question—I have cut from them parts of individuality repugnant to this God, in both his aspects. Parts sacred to rarer and more wonderful Gods. And at what length . . . Sacrifices to Zeus took at the most surely, sixty seconds each. Sacrifices to the Normal can take as long as sixty months.

(The natural sound of the pencil resumes. Light changes back.)

(to ALAN*)* Now your eyes are feeling heavy. You want to sleep, don't you? You want a long, deep sleep. Have it. Your head is heavy. Very heavy. Your shoulders are heavy. Sleep.

(The pencil stops. ALAN's eyes remain shut and his head has sunk on his chest.)

Can you hear me?

ALAN: Mmmm.

DYSART: You can speak normally. Say Yes, if you can.

ALAN: Yes.

DYSART: Good boy. Now raise your head, and open your eyes.

(He does so.)

Now, Alan, you're going to answer questions I'm going to ask you. Do you understand?

ALAN: Yes.

DYSART: And when you wake up, you are going to remember everything you tell me. All right?

ALAN: Yes.

DYSART: Good. Now I want you to think back in time. You are on that beach you told me about. The tide has gone out, and you're making sandcastles. Above you, staring down at you, is that great horse's head, and the cream dropping from it. Can you see that?

ALAN: Yes.

DYSART: You ask him a question. 'Does the chin hurt?'

ALAN: Yes.

DYSART: Do you ask him aloud?

ALAN: No.

DYSART: And what does the horse say back?

ALAN: 'Yes.'

DYSART: Then what do you say?

ALAN: 'I'll take it out for you.'

DYSART: And he says?

ALAN: 'It never comes out. They have me in chains.'

DYSART: Like Jesus?

ALAN: Yes!

DYSART: Only his name isn't Jesus, is it?

ALAN: No.

DYSART: What is it?

ALAN: No one knows but him and me.

DYSART: You can tell me, Alan. Name him.

ALAN: Equus.

DYSART: Thank you. Does he live in all horses or just some?

ALAN: All.

DYSART: Good boy. Now: you leave the beach. You're in your bedroom at home. You're twelve years old. You're in front of the picture. You're looking at Equus from the foot of your bed. Would you like to kneel down?

ALAN: Yes.

DYSART (*encouragingly*): Go on, then.

(ALAN *kneels.*)

Now tell me. Why is Equus in chains?

ALAN: For the sins of the world.

DYSART: What does he say to you?

ALAN: 'I see you.' 'I will save you.'

DYSART: How?

ALAN: 'Bear you away. Two shall be one.'

DYSART: Horse and rider shall be one beast?

ALAN: One person!

DYSART: Go on.

ALAN: 'And my chinkle-chankle shall be in thy hand.'

DYSART: Chinkle-chankle? That's his mouth chain?

ALAN: Yes.

DYSART: Good. You can get up . . . Come on.

(ALAN *rises.*)

Now: think of the stable. What is the stable? His temple? His Holy of Holies?

ALAN: Yes.

DYSART: Where you wash him? Where you tend him, and brush him with many brushes?

ALAN: Yes.

DYSART: And there he spoke to you, didn't he? He looked at you with his gentle eyes, and spake unto you?

ALAN: Yes.

DYSART: What did he say? 'Ride me? Mount me, and ride me forth at night?'

ALAN: Yes.

DYSART: And you obeyed?

ALAN: Yes.

DYSART: How did you learn? By watching others?

ALAN: Yes.

DYSART: It must have been difficult. You bounced about?

ALAN: Yes.

DYSART: But he showed you, didn't he? Equus showed you the way.

ALAN: No!

DYSART: He didn't?

ALAN: He showed me nothing! He's a mean bugger! Ride—or fall! That's Straw Law.

DYSART: Straw Law?

ALAN: He was born in the straw, and that is his law.

DYSART: But you managed? You mastered him?

ALAN: Had to!

DYSART: And then you rode in secret?

ALAN: Yes.

DYSART: How often?

ALAN: Every three weeks. More, people would notice.

DYSART: On a particular horse?

ALAN: No.

DYSART: How did you get into the stable?

ALAN: Stole a key. Had it copied at Bryson's.

DYSART: Clever boy.

(ALAN *smiles.*)

Then you'd slip out of the house?

ALAN: Midnight! On the stroke!

DYSART: How far's the stable?

ALAN: Two miles.

(*Pause:*)

DYSART: Let's do it! Let's go riding! . . . Now!

(*He stands up, and pushes in his bench.*)

You are there now, in front of the stable door.

(ALAN *turns upstage.*)

That key's in your hand. Go and open it.

ACT 1 / SCENE 20

(ALAN *moves upstage, and mimes opening the door.*
Soft light on the circle.
Humming from the CHORUS: *the Equus noise.*
The horse actors enter, raise high their masks, and put them on all together. They stand around the circle— NUGGET *in the mouth of the tunnel.*)

DYSART: Quietly as possible. Dalton may still be awake. Ssh . . . Quietly . . . Good. Now go in.

(ALAN *steps secretly out of the square through the central opening on to the circle, now glowing with a warm light. He looks about him. The horses stamp uneasily: their masks turn towards him.*)

You are on the inside now. All the horses are staring at you. Can you see them?

ALAN (*excited*): Yes!

DYSART: Which one are you going to take?

ALAN: Nugget.

(ALAN *reaches up and mimes leading* NUGGET *carefully round the circle downstage with a rope, past all the horses on the right.*)

DYSART: What colour is Nugget?

ALAN: Chestnut.

(*The horse picks his way with care.* ALAN *halts him at the corner of the square.*)

DYSART: What do you do, first thing?

ALAN: Put on his sandals.

DYSART: Sandals?

(*He kneels, downstage center.*)

ALAN: Sandals of majesty! . . . Made of sack.

(*He picks up the invisible sandals, and kisses them devoutly.*)

Tie them round his hooves.

(*He taps* NUGGET'*s right leg: the horse raises it and the boy mimes tying the sack around it.*)

DYSART: All four hooves?

ALAN: Yes.

DYSART: Then?

ALAN: Chinkle-chankle.

(*He mimes picking up the bridle and bit.*)

He doesn't like it so late, but he takes it for my sake. He bends for me. He stretches forth his neck to it.

(NUGGET *bends his head down.* ALAN *first ritually puts the bit into his own mouth, then crosses, and transfers it into* NUGGET'*s. He reaches up and buckles on the bridle. Then he leads him by the invisible reins, across the front of the stage and up round the left side of the circle.* NUGGET *follows obediently.*)

ALAN: Buckle and lead out.

DYSART: No saddle?

ALAN: Never.

DYSART: Go on.

ALAN: Walk down the path behind. He's quiet. Always is this bit. Meek and mild legs. At least till the field. Then there's trouble.

(*The horse jerks back. The mask tosses.*)

DYSART: What kind?

ALAN: Won't go in.

DYSART: Why not?

ALAN: It's his place of Ha Ha.

DYSART: What?

ALAN: Ha. Ha.

DYSART: Make him go into it.

ALAN (*whispering fiercely*): Come on! . . . Come on! . . .

(*He drags the horse into the square as* DYSART *steps out of it.*)

ACT 1 / SCENE 21

(NUGGET *comes to a halt staring diagonally down what is now the field. The Equus noise dies away. The boy looks about him.*)

DYSART (*from the circle*): Is it a big field?

ALAN: Huge!

DYSART: What's it like?

ALAN: Full of mist. Nettles on your feet.

(*He mimes taking off his shoes—and the string.*)

Ah!

DYSART (*going back to his bench*): You take your shoes off?

ALAN: Everything.

DYSART: All your clothes?

ALAN: Yes.

(*He mimes undressing completely in front of the horse. When he is finished, and obviously quite naked, he throws out his arms and shows himself fully to his God, bowing his head before* NUGGET.)

DYSART: Where do you leave them?

ALAN: Tree hole near the gate. No one could find them.

(*He walks upstage and crouches by the bench, stuffing the invisible clothes beneath it.* DYSART *sits again on the left bench, downstage beyond the circle.*)

DYSART: How does it feel now?

ALAN (*holds himself*): Burns.

DYSART: Burns?

ALAN: The mist!

DYSART: Go on. Now what?

ALAN: The Manbit.

(*He reaches again under the bench and draws out an invisible stick.*)

DYSART: Manbit?

ALAN: The stick for my mouth.

DYSART: Your mouth?

ALAN: To bite on.

DYSART: Why? What for?

ALAN: So's it won't happen too quick.

DYSART: Is it always the same stick?

ALAN: Course. Sacred stick. Keep it in the hole. The Ark of the Manbit.

DYSART: And now what? . . . What do you do now?

(*Pause. He rises and approaches* NUGGET.)

ALAN: Touch him!

DYSART: Where?

ALAN (*in wonder*): All over. Everywhere. Belly. Ribs. His ribs are of ivory. Of great value! . . . His flank is cool. His nostrils open for me. His eyes shine. They can see in the dark . . . *Eyes!*—

(*Suddenly he dashes in distress to the farthest corner of the square.*)

DYSART: *Go on!* . . . Then?

(*Pause.*)

ALAN: Give sugar.
DYSART: A lump of sugar?

(ALAN *returns to* NUGGET.)

ALAN: His Last Supper.
DYSART: Last before what?
ALAN: Ha Ha.

(*He kneels before the horse, palms upward and joined together.*)

DYSART: Do you say anything when you give it to him?
ALAN (*offering it*): Take my sins. Eat them for my sake . . . He always does.

(NUGGET *bows the mask into* ALAN's *palm, then takes a step back to eat.*)

And then he's ready.
DYSART: You can get up on him now?
ALAN: Yes!
DYSART: Do it, then. Mount him.

(ALAN, *lying before* NUGGET, *stretches out on the square. He grasps the top of the thin metal pole embedded in the wood. He whispers his god's name ceremoniallly.*)

ALAN: Equus! . . . Equus! . . . Equus!

(*He pulls the pole upright. The actor playing* NUGGET *leans forward and grabs it. At the same instant all the other horses lean forward around the circle, each placing a gloved hand on the rail.* ALAN *rises and walks right back to the upstage corner, left.*)

Take me!

(*He runs and jumps high on to* NUGGET's *back.*)

(*Crying out.*) Ah!
DYSART: What is it?
ALAN: Hurts!
DYSART: Hurts?
ALAN: Knives in his skin! Little knives—all inside my legs.

(NUGGET *mimes restiveness.*)

ALAN: Stay, Equus. No one said Go! . . . That's it. He's good. Equus the Godslave, Faithful and True. Into my hands he commends himself—naked in his chinkle-chankle. (*He punches.*) Stop it! . . . He wants to go so badly.
DYSART: Go, then. Leave me behind. Ride away now,

Alan. Now! . . . Now you are alone with Equus.

(ALAN *stiffens his body.*)

ALAN (*ritually*): Equus—son of Fleckwus—son of Neckwus—*Walk.*

(*A hum from the* CHROUS. *Very slowly the horses standing on the circle begin to turn the square by gently pushing the wooden rail.* ALAN *and his mount start to revolve. The effect, immediately, is of a statue being slowly turned round on a plinth. During the ride however the speed increases, and the light decreases until it is only a fierce spotlight on horse and rider, with the overspill glinting on the other masks leaning in towards them.*)

Here we go. The King rides out on Equus, mightiest of horses. Only I can ride him. He lets me turn him this way and that. His neck comes out of my body. It lifts in the dark. Equus, my Godslave! . . . Now the King commands you. Tonight, we ride against them all.
DYSART: Who's all?
ALAN: My foes and His.
DYSART: Who are your foes?
ALAN: The Hosts of Hoover. The Hosts of Philco. The Hosts of Pifco. The House of Remington and all its tribe!
DYSART: Who are His foes?
ALAN: The Hosts of Jodhpur. The Hosts of Bowler and Gymkhana. All those who show him off for their vanity. Tie rosettes on his head for their vanity! Come on, Equus. Let's get them! . . . *Trot!*

(*The speed of the turning square increases.*)

Stead-y! Stead-y! Stead-y! Stead-y! Cowboys are watching! Take off their stetsons. They know who we are. They're admiring us! Bowing low unto us! Come on now—show them! *Canter!* . . . CANTER!

(*He whips* NUGGET.)

And Equus the Mighty rose against All!
His enemies scatter, his enemies fall!
TURN!
Trample them, trample them,
Trample them, trample them,
TURN!
TURN!!
TURN!!!

(*The Equus noise increases in volume.*)

(*Shouting.*) WEE! . . . WAA! . . . WONDERFUL! . . .
I'm stiff! Stiff in the wind!
My mane, stiff in the wind!
My flanks! *My* hooves!
Mane on my legs, on my flanks, like whips!

Raw!
Raw!
I'm raw! Raw!
Feel me on you! *On* you! *On* you! *On* you!
I want to be *in* you!
I want to BE you forever and ever!—
Equus, I love you!
Now!—
Bear me away!
Make us One Person!

(He rides Equus frantically.)

   One Person! One Person! One Person! One Person!

(He rises up on the horse's neck, and calls like a trumpet.)

   Ha-HA! . . . Ha-HA! . . . Ha HA!

(The trumpet turns to great cries.)

   HA-HA! HA-HA! HA-HA! HA-HA! HA! . . .
HA! . . . HAAAAA!

(He twists like a flame.
Silence.
The turning square comes to a stop in the same position it
occupied at the opening of the Act.
Slowly the boy drops off the horse's back on the ground.
He lowers his head and kisses NUGGET's *hoof.*
Finally he flings back his head and cries up to him:)

   AMEN!

(NUGGET *snorts, once.)*

BLACKOUT

ACT 2 / **SCENE 22**

(Darkness.
Lights come slowly up on ALAN *kneeling in the night at*
the hooves of NUGGET. *Slowly he gets up, climbing lov-*
ingly up the body of the horse until he can stand and kiss
it. DYSART *sits on the downstage bench where he began*
Act 1.)

DYSART: With one particular horse, called Nugget, he
   embraces. He showed me how he stands with it
   afterwards in the night, one hand on its chest,
   one on its neck, like a frozen tango dancer, inhal-
   ing its cold sweet breath. 'Have you noticed,' he
   said, 'about horses: how they'll stand one hoof on
   its end, like those girls in the ballet?'

(ALAN *leads* NUGGET *out of the square.* DYSART *rises.*
The horse walks away up the tunnel and disappears. The
boy comes downstage and sits on the bench DYSART *has*
vacated. DYSART *crosses downstage and moves slowly up*
round the circle, until he reaches the central entrance to
the square.)

   Now he's gone off to rest, leaving me alone with

Equus. I can hear the creature's voice. It's calling
me out of the black cave of the Psyche. I shove in
my dim little torch, and there he stands—waiting
for me. He raises his matted head. He opens his
great square teeth, and says—*(mocking)* 'Why? . . .
Why Me? . . . Why—ultimately—Me? . . . do you
really imagine you can account for Me? Totally,
infallibly, inevitably account for Me? . . . Poor
Doctor Dysart!'

(He enters the square.)

   Of course I've stared at such images before. Or
been stared at by them, whichever way you look
at it. And weirdly often now with me the feeling
is that *they* are staring at *us*—that in some quite
palpable way they precede us. Meaningless, but
unsettling . . . In either case, this one is the most
alarming yet. It asks questions I've avoided all
my professional life. *(Pause.)* A child is born into
a world of phenomena all equal in their power to
enslave. It sniffs—it sucks—it strokes its eyes
over the whole uncomfortable range. Suddenly
one strikes. Why? Moments snap together like
magnets, forging a chain of shackles. Why? I can
trace them. I can even, with time, pull them
apart again. But why at the start they were ever
magnetized at all—just those particular moments
of experience and no others—I don't know. *And*
nor does anyone else. Yet *if* I don't know—if I can
never know that—then what am I doing here? I
don't mean clinically doing or socially doing—I
mean *fundamentally!* These questions, these
Whys, are fundamental—yet they have no place
in a consulting room. So then, do I? . . . This is
the feeling more and more with me—No Place.
Displacement. . . . 'Account for me,' says staring
Equus. 'First account for Me! . . .' I fancy this is
more than menopause.

(NURSE *rushes in.)*

NURSE: Doctor! . . . Doctor! There's a terrible scene
   with the Strang boy. His mother came to visit
   him, and I gave her the tray to take in. He threw
   it at her. She's saying the most dreadful things.

(ALAN *springs up, down left.* DORA *springs up, down*
right. They face each other across the bottom end of the
stage. It is observable that at the start of this Act FRANK *is*
not sitting beside his wife on their bench. It is hopefully not
observable that he is placed among the audience upstage,
in the gloom, by the central tunnel.)

DORA: Don't you dare! *Don't* you dare!
DYSART: Is she still there?
NURSE: Yes!

(He quickly leaves the square, followed by the NURSE.
DORA *moves towards her son.)*

DORA: Don't you look at me like that! I'm not a doctor, you know, who'll take anything. Don't you dare give me that stare, young man!

(She slaps his face. DYSART *joins them.)*

DYSART: Mrs. Strang!

DORA: I know your stares. They don't work on me!

DYSART *(to her)*: Leave this room.

DORA: What did you say?

DYSART: I tell you to leave here at once.

*(*DORA *hesitates. Then:)*

DORA: Goodbye, Alan.

(She walks past her son, and round into the square. DYSART *follows her. Both are very upset.* ALAN *returns to his bench and* NURSE *to her place.)*

ACT 2 / SCENE 23

(Lights up on the square.)

DYSART: I must ask you never to come here again.

DORA: Do you think I want to? Do you think I want to?

DYSART: Mrs. Strang, what on earth has got into you? Can't you see the boy is highly distressed?

DORA *(ironic)*: Really?

DYSART: Of course! He's at a most delicate stage of treatment. He's totally exposed. Ashamed. Everything you can imagine!

DORA *(exploding)*: *And me? What about me? . . . What do you think I am?* . . . I'm a parent, of course—so it doesn't count. That's a dirty word in here, isn't it, 'parent'?

DYSART: You know that's not true.

DORA: Oh, I know. I know, all right! I've heard it all my life. It's *our* fault. Whatever happens, *we* did it. Alan's just a little victim. He's really done nothing at all! *(Savagely.)* What do you have to do in this world to get any sympathy—blind animals?

DYSART: Sit down, Mrs. Strang.

DORA *(ignoring him: more and more urgently)*: Look, Doctor: you don't have to live with this. Alan is one patient to you: one out of many. He's my son. I lie awake every night thinking about it. Frank lies there beside me. I can hear him. Neither of us sleeps all night. You come to us and say Who forbids television? who does what behind whose back?—as if we're criminals. Let me tell you something. We're not criminals. We've done nothing wrong. We loved Alan. We gave him the best love we could. All right, we quarrel sometimes—all parents quarrel—we always make it up. My husband is a good man. He's an upright man, religion or no religion. He cares for his home, for the world, and for his boy. Alan had love and care and treats, and as much fun as any boy in the world. I know about loveless homes: I was a teacher. Our home wasn't loveless. I know about privacy too—not invading a child's privacy. All right, Frank may be at fault there—he digs into him too much—but nothing in excess. He's not a bully . . . *(Gravely.)* No, doctor. Whatever's happened has happened *because of Alan.* Alan is himself. Every soul is itself. If you added up everything we ever did to him, from his first day on earth to this, you wouldn't find why he did this terrible thing—because that's *him*: not just all of our things added up. Do you understand what I'm saying? I want you to understand, because I lie awake and awake thinking it out, and I want you to know that I deny it absolutely what he's doing now, staring at me, attacking me for what *he's* done, for what *he* is! *(Pause: calmer.)* You've got your words, and I've got mine. You call it a complex, I suppose. But if you knew God, Doctor, you would know about the Devil. You'd know the Devil isn't made by what mummy says and daddy says. The Devil's *there.* It's an old-fashioned word, but a true thing . . . I'll go. What I did in there was inexcusable. I only know he was my little Alan, and then the Devil came.

(She leaves the square, and resumes her place. DYSART *watches her go, then leaves himself by the opposite entrance, and approaches* ALAN.*)*

ACT 2 / SCENE 24

(Seated on his bench, the boy glares at him.)

DYSART: I thought you liked your mother.

(Silence.)

She doesn't know anything, you know. I haven't told her what you told me. You do know that, don't you?

ALAN: It was lies anyway.

DYSART: What?

ALAN: You and your pencil. Just a con trick, that's all.

DYSART: What do you mean?

ALAN: Made me say a lot of lies.

DYSART: Did it? . . . Like what?

ALAN: All of it. Everything I said. Lot of lies.

(Pause.)

DYSART: I see.

ALAN: You ought to be locked up. Your bloody tricks.

DYSART: I thought you liked tricks.

ALAN: It'll be the drug next. I know.

*(*DYSART *turns, sharply.)*

DYSART: What drug?

ALAN: I've heard. I'm not ignorant. I know what you get up to in here. Shove needles in people, pump them full of truth drug, so they can't help saying things. That's next, isn't it?

(Pause.)

DYSART: Alan, do you know why you're here?
ALAN: So you can give me truth drugs.

(He glares at him.
DYSART leaves abruptly, and returns to the square.)

ACT 2 / SCENE 25

(HESTHER comes in simultaneously from the other side.)

DYSART (agitated): He actually thinks they exist! And of course he wants one.
HESTHER: It doesn't sound like that to me.
DYSART: Of course he does. Why mention them otherwise? He wants a way to speak. To finally tell me what happened in that stable. Tape's too isolated, and hypnosis is a trick. At least that's the pretence.
HESTHER: Does he still say that today?
DYSART: I haven't seen him. I cancelled his appointment this morning, and let him stew in his own anxiety. Now I am almost tempted to play a real trick on him.
HESTHER (sitting): Like what?
DYSART: The old placebo.
HESTHER: You mean a harmless pill?
DYSART: Full of alleged Truth Drug. Probably an aspirin.
HESTHER: But he'd deny it afterwards. Same thing all over.
DYSART: No. Because he's ready to abreact.
HESTHER: Abreact?
DYSART: Live it all again. He won't be able to deny it after that, because he'll have shown me. Not just told me—but acted it out in front of me.
HESTHER: Can you get him to do that?
DYSART: I think so. He's nearly done it already. Under all that glowering, he trusts me. Do you realise that?
HESTHER (warmly): I'm sure he does.
DYSART: Poor bloody fool.
HESTHER: Don't start that again.

(Pause.)

DYSART (quietly): Can you think of anything worse one can do to anybody than take away their worship?
HESTHER: Worship?
DYSART: Yes, that word again!
HESTHER: Aren't you being a little extreme?
DYSART: Extremity's the point.
HESTHER: Worship isn't destructive, Martin. I know that.

DYSART: I don't. I only know it's the core of his life. What else has he got? Think about him. He can hardly read. He knows no physics or engineering to make the world real for him. No paintings to show him how others have enjoyed it. No music except television jingles. No history except tales from a desperate mother. No friends. Not one kid to give him a joke, or make him know himself more moderately. He's a modern citizen for whom society doesn't exist. He lives one hour every three weeks—howling in a mist. And after the service kneels to a slave who stands over him obviously and unthrowably his master. With my body I thee worship! . . . Many men have less vital with their wives.

(Pause.)

HESTHER: All the same, they don't usually blind their wives, do they?
DYSART: Oh, come on!
HESTHER: Well, do they?
DYSART (sarcastically): You mean he's dangerous? A violent, dangerous madman who's going to run round the country doing it again and again?
HESTHER: I mean he's in pain, Martin. He's been in pain for most of his life. That much, at least, you know.
DYSART: Possibly.
HESTHER: Possibly?! . . . That cut-off little figure you just described must have been in pain for years.
DYSART (doggedly): Possibly.
HESTHER: And you can take it away.
DYSART: Still—possibly.
HESTHER: Then that's enough. That simply has to be enough for you, surely?
DYSART: No!
HESTHER: Why not?
DYSART: Because it's his.
HESTHER: I don't understand.
DYSART: His pain. His own. He made it.

(Pause.)

(Earnestly.) Look . . . to go through life and call it yours—your life—you first have to get your own pain. Pain that's unique to you. You can't just dip into the common bin and say 'That's enough!' . . . He's done that. All right, he's sick. He's full of misery and fear. He was dangerous, and could be again, though I doubt it. But that boy has known a passion more ferocious than I have felt in any second of my life. And let me tell you something: I envy it.
HESTHER: You can't.
DYSART (vehemently): Don't you see? That's the Accusation! That's what his stare has been saying to me all the time. 'At least I galloped! When did you?'

. . . *(Simply.)* I'm jealous, Hesther. Jealous of Alan Strang.

HESTHER: That's absurd.

DYSART: Is it? . . . I go on about my wife. That smug woman by the fire. Have you thought of the fellow on the other side of it? The finicky, critical husband looking through his art books on mythical Greece. What worship has *he* ever known? Real worship! Without worship you shrink, it's as brutal as that . . . I shrank my *own* life. No one can do it for you. I settled for being pallid and provincial, out of my own eternal timidity. The old story of bluster, and do bugger-all . . . I imply that we can't have children: but actually, it's only me. I had myself tested behind her back. The lowest sperm count you could find. And I never told her. That's all I need—her sympathy with resentment . . . I tell everyone Margaret's the puritan, I'm the pagan. Some pagan! Such wild returns I make to the womb of civilization. Three weeks a year in the Peleponnese, every bed booked in advance, every meal paid for by vouchers, cautious jaunts in hired Fiats, suitcase crammed with Kao-Pectate! Such a fantastic surrender to the primitive. And I use that word endlessly: 'primitive.' 'Oh, the primitive world,' I say. 'What instinctual truths were lost with it!' And while I sit there, baiting a poor unimaginative woman with the word, that freaky boy tries to conjure the reality! I sit looking at pages of centaurs trampling the soil of Argos—and outside my window he is trying to *become* one, in a Hampshire field! . . . I watch that woman knitting, night after night—a woman I haven't *kissed* in six years—and he stands in the dark for an hour, sucking the sweat off his God's hairy cheek! *(Pause.)* Then in the morning, I put away my books on the cultural shelf, close up the kodachrome snaps of Mount Olympus, touch my reproduction statue of Dionysus for luck—and go off to hospital to treat him for insanity. Do you see?

HESTHER: The boy's in pain, Martin. That's all I see. In the end . . . I'm sorry.

(He looks at her. ALAN gets up from his bench and stealthily places an envelope in the left-hand entrance of the square, then goes back and sits with his back to the audience, as if watching television.
HESTHER rises.)

HESTHER: That stare of his. Have you thought it might not be accusing you at all?

DYSART: What then?

HESTHER: Claiming you.

DYSART: For what?

HESTHER *(mischievously)*: A new God.

(Pause.)

DYSART: Too conventional, for him. Finding a religion in Psychiatry is really for very ordinary patients.

(She laughs.)

HESTHER: Maybe he just wants a new Dad. Or is that too conventional too? . . . Since you're questioning your profession anyway, perhaps you ought to try it and see.

DYSART *(amused)*: I'll talk to you.

HESTHER: Goodbye.

(She smiles, and leaves him.)

ACT 2 / SCENE 26

(DYSART becomes aware of the letter lying on the floor. He picks it up, opens and reads it.)

ALAN *(speaking stiffly, as DYSART reads)*: 'It is all true, what I said after you tapped the pencil. I'm sorry if I said different. Post Scriptum: I know why I'm in here.'

(Pause.)

DYSART *(calling, joyfully)*: Nurse!

(NURSE comes in.)

NURSE: Yes, Doctor?

DYSART *(trying to conceal his pleasure)*: Good evening!

NURSE: You're in late tonight.

DYSART: Yes! . . . Tell me, is the Strang boy in bed yet?

NURSE: Oh, no, Doctor. He's bound to be upstairs looking at television. He always watches to the last possible moment. He doesn't like going to his room at all.

DYSART: You mean he's still having nightmares?

NURSE: He had a bad one last night.

DYSART: Would you ask him to come down here, please?

NURSE *(faint surprise)*: Now?

DYSART: I'd like a word with him.

NURSE *(puzzled)*: Very good, Doctor.

DYSART: If he's not back in his room by lights out, tell Night Nurse not to worry. I'll see he gets back to bed all right. And would you phone my home and tell my wife I may be in late?

NURSE: Yes, Doctor.

DYSART: Ask him to come straight away, please.

(NURSE goes to the bench, taps ALAN on the shoulder, whispers her message in his ear, and returns to her place. ALAN stands up and pauses for a second—then steps into the square.)

ACT 2 / SCENE 27

(He stands in the doorway, depressed.)

DYSART: Hallo.

ALAN: Hallo.

DYSART: I got your letter. Thank you. *(Pause.)* Also the Post Scriptum.

ALAN *(defensively)*: That's the right word. My mum told me. It's Latin for 'After-writing'.

DYSART: How are you feeling?

ALAN: All right.

DYSART: I'm sorry I didn't see you today.

ALAN: You were fed up with me.

DYSART: Yes. *(Pause.)* Can I make it up to you now?

ALAN: What'd you mean?

DYSART: I thought we'd have a session.

ALAN *(startled)*: Now?

DYSART: Yes! At dead of night! . . . Better than going to sleep, isn't it?

(The boy flinches.)

Alan—look. Everything I say has a trick or a catch. Everything I do is a trick or a catch. That's all I know to do. But they work—and you know that. Trust me.

(Pause.)

ALAN: You got another trick, then?

DYSART: Yes.

ALAN: A truth drug?

DYSART: If you like.

ALAN: What's it do?

DYSART: Make it easier for you to talk.

ALAN: Like you can't help yourself?

DYSART: That's right. Like you have to speak the truth at all costs. And all of it.

(Pause.)

ALAN *(slyly)*: Comes in a needle, doesn't it?

DYSART: No.

ALAN: Where is it?

DYSART *(indicating his pocket)*: In here.

ALAN: Let's see.

(DYSART solemnly takes a bottle of pills out of his pocket.)

DYSART: There.

ALAN *(suspicious)*: That really it?

DYSART: It is . . . Do you want to try it?

ALAN: No.

DYSART: I think you do.

ALAN: I don't. Not at all.

DYSART: Afterwards you'd sleep. You'd have no bad dreams all night. Probably many nights, from then on . . .

(Pause.)

ALAN: How long's it take to work?

DYSART: It's instant. Like coffee.

ALAN *(half believing)*: It isn't!

DYSART: I promise you . . . Well?

ALAN: Can I have a fag?

DYSART: Pill first. Do you want some water?

ALAN: No.

(DYSART takes one out on to his palm. ALAN hesitates for a second—then takes it and swallows it.)

DYSART: Then you can chase it down with this. Sit down.

(He offers him a cigarette, and lights it for him.)

ALAN *(nervous)*: What happens now?

DYSART: We wait for it to work.

ALAN: What'll I feel first?

DYSART: Nothing much. After a minute, about a hundred green snakes should come out of that cupboard singing the Hallelujah Chorus.

ALAN *(annoyed)*: *I'm serious!*

DYSART *(earnestly)*: You'll feel nothing. Nothing's going to happen now but what you want to happen. You're not going to say anything to me but what you want to say. Just relax. Lie back and finish your fag.

(ALAN stares at him. Then accepts the situation, and lies back.)

DYSART: Good boy.

ALAN: I bet this room's heard some funny things.

DYSART: It certainly has.

ALAN: I like it.

DYSART: This room?

ALAN: Don't you?

DYSART: Well, there's not much to like, is there?

ALAN: How long am I going to be in here?

DYSART: It's hard to say. I quite see you want to leave.

ALAN: No.

DYSART: You don't?

ALAN: Where would I go?

DYSART: Home. . . .

(The boy looks at him. DYSART crosses and sits on the rail upstage, his feet on the bench. A pause.)

Actually, I'd like to leave this room and never see it again in my life.

ALAN *(surprise)*: Why?

DYSART: I've been in it too long.

ALAN: Where would you go?

DYSART: Somewhere.

ALAN: Secret?

DYSART: Yes. There's a sea—a great sea—I love . . . It's where the Gods used to go to bathe.

ALAN: What Gods?

DYSART: The old ones. Before they died.

ALAN: Gods don't die.

DYSART: Yes, they do.

(Pause.)

There's a village I spent one night in, where I'd like to live. it's all white.

ALAN: How would you Nosey Parker, though? You wouldn't have a room for it any more.

DYSART: I wouldn't mind. I don't actually enjoy being a Nosey Parker, you know.

ALAN: Then why do it?

DYSART: Because you're unhappy.

ALAN: So are you.

(DYSART *looks at him sharply.* ALAN *sits up in alarm.*)

Oooh, I didn't mean that!

DYSART: Didn't you?

ALAN: Here—is that how it works? Things just slip out, not feeling anything?

DYSART: That's right.

ALAN: But it's so quick!

DYSART: I told you: it's instant.

ALAN (*delighted*): It's wicked, isn't it? I mean, you can say anything under it.

DYSART: Yes.

ALAN: Ask me a question.

DYSART: Tell me about Jill.

(*Pause. The boy turns away.*)

ALAN: There's nothing to tell.

DYSART: Nothing?

ALAN: No.

DYSART: Well, for example—is she pretty? You've never described her.

ALAN: She's all right.

DYSART: What colour hair?

ALAN: Dunno.

DYSART: Is it long or short?

ALAN: Dunno.

DYSART (*lightly*): You must know that.

ALAN: I don't remember. *I don't!*

(DYSART *rises and comes down to him. He takes the cigarette out of his hand.*)

DYSART (*firmly*): Lie back . . . Now listen. You have to do this. And now. You are going to tell me everything that happened with this girl. And not just *tell* me—*show* me. Act it out, if you like—even more than you did when I tapped the pencil. I want you to feel free to do absolutely anything in this room. The pill will help you. I will help you . . . Now, where does she live?

(*A long pause.*)

ALAN (*tight*): Near the stables. About a mile.

(DYSART *steps down out of the square as* JILL *enters it. He sits again on the downstage bench.*)

ACT 2 / SCENE 28

(*The light grows warmer.*)

JILL: It's called The China Pantry.

(*She comes down and sits casually on the rail. Her man-*

ner is open and lightly provocative. During these scenes ALAN *acts directly with her, and never looks over at* DYSART *when he replies to him.*)

When Daddy disappeared, she was left without a bean. She had to earn her own living. I must say she did jolly well, considering she was never trained in business.

DYSART: What do you mean, 'disappeared'?

ALAN (*to* DYSART): He ran off. No one ever saw him again.

JILL: Just left a note on her dressing table saying 'Sorry. I've had it.' Just like that. She never got over it. It turned her right off men. All my dates have to be sort of secret. I mean, she knows about them, but I can't ever bring anyone back home. She's so rude to them.

ALAN (*to* DYSART): She was always looking.

DYSART: At you?

ALAN (*to* DYSART): Saying stupid things.

(*She jumps off the bench.*)

JILL: You've got super eyes.

ALAN (*to* DYSART): Anyway, *she* was the one who had them.

(*She sits next to him. Embarrassed, the boy tries to move away as far as he can.*)

JILL: There was an article in the paper last week saying what points about boys fascinate girls. They said Number One is bottoms. I think it's eyes every time . . . They fascinate you too, don't they?

ALAN: Me?

JILL (*sly*): Or is it only horses' eyes?

ALAN (*startled*): What'd you mean?

JILL: I saw you staring into Nugget's eyes yesterday for ages. I spied on you through the door!

ALAN (*hotly*): There must have been something in it!

JILL: You're a real Man of Mystery, aren't you?

ALAN (*to* DYSART): Sometimes, it was like she knew.

DYSART: Did you ever hint?

ALAN (*to* DYSART): Course not!

JILL: I love horses' eyes. The way you can see yourself in them. D'you find them sexy?

ALAN (*outraged*): What? !

JILL: Horses.

ALAN: Don't be daft!

(*He springs up, and away from her.*)

JILL: Girls do. I mean, they go through a period when they pat them and kiss them a lot. I know *I* did. I suppose it's just a substitute, really.

ALAN (*to* DYSART): That kind of thing, all the time. Until one night . . .

DYSART: Yes? What?

ALAN (*to* DYSART: *defensively*): She did it! Not me. It

was her idea, the whole thing! . . . She got me into it!

DYSART: What are you saying? 'One night': go on from there.

(*A pause.*)

ALAN (*to* DYSART): Saturday night. We were just closing up.

JILL: How would you like to take me out?

ALAN: What?

JILL (*coolly*): How would you like to take me out to-night?

ALAN: I've got to go home.

JILL: What for?

(*He tries to escape upstage.*)

ALAN: They expect me.

JILL: Ring up and say you're going out.

ALAN: I can't.

JILL: Why?

ALAN: They expect me.

JILL: Look. Either we go out together and have some fun, or you go back to your boring home, *as usual,* and I go back to mine. That's the situation, isn't it?

ALAN: Well . . . where would we go?

JILL: The pictures! There's a skinflick over in Winchester! I've never seen one, have you?

ALAN: No.

JILL: Wouldn't you like to? *I* would. All those heavy Swedes, panting at each other! . . . What d' you say?

ALAN (*grinning*): Yeh! . . .

JILL: Good! . . .

(*He turns away.*)

DYSART: Go on, please.

(*He steps off the square.*)

ALAN (*to* DYSART): I'm tired now!

DYSART: Come on now. You can't stop there.

(*He storms round the circle to* DYSART, *and faces him directly.*)

ALAN: I'm *tired!* I want to go to bed!

DYSART (*sharply*): Well, you can't. I want to hear about the film.

ALAN (*hostile*): Hear what? . . . *What?* . . . It was bloody awful!

(*The actors playing horses come swiftly on to the square, dressed in sports coats or raincoats. They move the benches to be parallel with the audience, and sit on them—staring out front.*)

DYSART: Why?

ALAN: Nosey Parker!

DYSART: Why?

ALAN: *Because!* . . . Well—we went into the Cinema!

ACT 2 / SCENE 29

(*A burst of Rock music, instantly fading down. Lights darken.*
ALAN *re-enters the square.* JILL *rises and together they grope their way to the downstage bench, as if in a dark auditorium.*)

ALAN (*to* DYSART): The whole place was full of men. Jill was the only girl.

(*They push by a patron seated at the end, and sit side by side staring up at the invisible screen, located above the heads of the main audience. A spotlight hits the boy's face.*)

We sat down and the film came on. It was daft. Nothing happened for ages. There was this girl Brita, who was sixteen. She went to stay in this house, where there was an older boy. He kept giving her looks, but she ignored him completely. In the end she took a shower. She went into the bathroom and took off all her clothes. The lot. Very slowly. . . . What she didn't know was the boy was looking through the door all the time. . . . (*He starts to become excited.*) It was fantastic! The water fell on her breasts, bouncing down her. . . .

(FRANK *steps into the square furtively from the back, hat in hand, and stands looking about for a place.*)

DYSART: Was that the first time you'd seen a girl naked?

ALAN (*to* DYSART): Yes! You couldn't see everything, though. . . . (*Looking about him.*) All round me they were all looking. All the men—staring up like they were in church. Like they were a sort of congregation. And then—(*He sees his father.*) Ah!

(*At the same instant* FRANK *sees him.*)

FRANK: Alan!

ALAN: God!

JILL: What is it?

ALAN: *Dad!*

JILL: *Where?*

ALAN: At the back! *He saw me!*

JILL: You sure?

ALAN: Yes!

FRANK (*calling*): Alan!

ALAN: Oh God!

(*He tries to hide his face in the girl's shoulder. His father comes down the aisle toward him.*)

FRANK: Alan! You can hear me! Don't pretend!

PATRONS: Ssssh!

FRANK (*approaching the row of seats*): Do I have to come and fetch you out? . . . Do I? . . .

(Cries of 'Sssh!' and 'Shut up!')

Do I, Alan?

ALAN *(through gritted teeth)*: Oh fuck!

(He gets up as the noise increases. JILL *gets up too and follows him.)*

DYSART: You went?

ALAN *(to* DYSART*)*: What else could I do? He kept shouting. Everyone was saying Shut up!

(They go out, right, through the group of PATRONS—*who rise protesting as they pass, quickly replace the benches and leave the square.*
DYSART *enters it.)*

ACT 2 / SCENE 30

(Light brightens from the cinema, but remains cold: streets at night.
The three walk round the circle downstage in a line:
FRANK *leading, wearing his hat. He halts in the middle of the left rail, and stands staring straight ahead of him, rigid with embarrassment.*
ALAN *is very agitated.)*

ALAN *(to* DYSART*)*: We went into the street, all three of us. It was weird. We just stood there by the bus stop—like we were three people in a queue, and we didn't know each other. Dad was all white and sweaty. He didn't look at us at all. It must have gone on for about five minutes. I tried to speak. I said—*(to his father)* I—I—I've never been there before. Honest . . . Never . . . *(to* DYSART*)* He didn't seem to hear. Jill tried.

JILL: It's true, Mr. Strang. It wasn't Alan's idea to go there. It was mine.

ALAN *(to* DYSART*)*: He just went on staring, straight ahead. It was awful.

JILL: I'm not shocked by films like that. I think they're just silly.

ALAN *(to* DYSART*)*: The bus wouldn't come. We just stood and stood. . . . Then suddenly he spoke.

*(*FRANK *takes off his hat.)*

FRANK *(stiffly)*: I'd like you to know something. Both of you. I came here tonight to see the Manager. He asked me to call on him for business purposes. I happen to be a printer, Miss. A picture house needs posters. That's entirely why I'm here. To discuss posters. While I was waiting I happened to glance in, that's all. I can only say I'm going to complain to the council. I had no idea they showed films like that. I'm certainly going to refuse my services.

JILL *(kindly)*: Yes, of course.

FRANK: So long as that's understood.

ALAN *(to* DYSART*)*: Then the bus came along.

FRANK: Come along now, Alan.

(He moves away downstage.)

ALAN: No.

FRANK *(turning)*: No fuss, please. Say Goodnight to the young lady.

ALAN *(timid but firm)*: No. I'm stopping here . . . I've got to see her home . . . It's proper.

(Pause.)

FRANK *(as dignified as possible)*: Very well. I'll see you when you choose to return. Very well then . . . Yes . . .

(He walks back to his original seat, next to his wife. He stares across the square at his son—who stares back at him. Then, slowly, he sits.)

ALAN *(to* DYSART*)*: And he got in, and we didn't. He sat down and looked at me through the glass. And I saw . . .

DYSART *(soft)*: What?

ALAN *(to* DYSART*)*: His face. It was scared.

DYSART: Of you?

ALAN *(to* DYSART*)*: It was terrible. We had to walk home. Four miles. I got the shakes.

DYSART: You were scared too?

ALAN *(to* DYSART*)*: It was like a hole had been drilled in my tummy. A hole—right here. And the air was getting in!

(He starts to walk upstage, round the circle.)

ACT 2 / SCENE 31

(The girl stays still.)

JILL *(aware of other people looking)*: Alan . . .

ALAN *(to* DYSART*)*: People kept turning round in the street to look.

JILL: Alan!

ALAN *(to* DYSART*)*: I kept seeing him, just as he drove off. Scared of me. . . . And me scared of *him*. . . . I kept thinking—all those airs he put on! . . . 'Receive my meaning. Improve your mind!' . . . All those nights he said he'd be in late. 'Keep my supper hot, Dora!' 'Your poor father: he works so hard!' . . . Bugger! Old bugger! . . . Filthy old bugger!

(He stops, clenching his fists.)

JILL: Hey! Wait for me!

(She runs after him. He waits.)

What are you thinking about?

ALAN: Nothing.

JILL: Mind my own beeswax?

(She laughs.)

ALAN *(to* DYSART*)*: And suddenly she began to laugh.

JILL: I'm sorry. But it's pretty funny, when you think of it.

ALAN (*bewildered*): What?

JILL: Catching him like that! I mean, it's terrible—but it's very funny.

ALAN: Yeh!

(*He turns from her.*)

JILL: No, wait! . . . I'm sorry. I know you're upset. But it's not the end of world, is it? I mean, what was he doing? Only what we were. Watching a silly film. It's a case of like father like son, I'd say! . . . I mean, when that girl was taking a shower, you were pretty interested, weren't you?

(*He turns round and looks at her.*)

We keep saying old people are square. Then when they suddenly aren't—we don't like it!

DYSART: What did you think about that?

ALAN (*to* DYSART): I don't know. I kept looking at all the people in the street. They were mostly men coming out of pubs. I suddenly thought—*they all do it! All of them!* . . . They're not just Dads—they're people with pricks! . . . And Dad—he's just not Dad either. He's a man with a prick too. You know, I'd never thought about it.

(*Pause.*)

We went into the country.

(*He walks again.* JILL *follows. They turn the corner and come downstage, right.*)

We kept walking. I just thought about Dad, and how he was nothing special—just a poor old sod on his own.

(*He stops.*)

(*to* JILL: *realizing it*) Poor old sod!

JILL: That's right!

ALAN (*grappling with it*): I mean, what else has he got? . . . He's got mum, of course, but well—she—she—she—

JILL: She doesn't give him anything?

ALAN: That's right. I bet you . . . She doesn't give him anything. That's right . . . That's really right! . . . She likes Ladies and Gentlemen. Do you understand what I mean?

JILL (*mischievously*): Ladies and gentlemen aren't naked?

ALAN: That's right! Never! . . . *Never!* That would be disgusting! She'd have to put bowler hats on them! . . . Jodhpurs!

(JILL *laughs.*)

DYSART: Was that the first time you ever thought anything like that about your mother? . . . I mean, that she was unfair to your dad?

ALAN (*to* DYSART): Absolutely!

DYSART: How did you feel?

ALAN (*to* DYSART): Sorry. I mean for him. Poor old sod, that's what I felt—he's just like me! He hates ladies and gents just like me! Posh things—and la-di-da. He goes off by himself at night, and does his own secret thing which no one'll know about, just like me! There's no difference—he's just the same as me—just the same!—

(*He stops in distress, then bolts back a little upstage.*)

Christ!

DYSART (*sternly*): Go on.

ALAN (*to* DYSART): I can't.

DYSART: Of course you can. You're doing wonderfully.

ALAN (*to* DYSART): No, please. *Don't make me!*

DYSART (*firm*): Don't think: just answer. You were happy at that second, weren't you? When you realised about your dad. How lots of people have secrets, not just you?

ALAN (*to* DYSART): Yes.

DYSART: You felt sort of free, didn't you? I mean, free to do anything?

ALAN (*to* DYSART, *looking at* JILL): Yes!

DYSART: What was she doing?

ALAN (*to* DYSART): Holding my hand.

DYSART: And that was good?

ALAN (*to* DYSART): Oh, yes!

DYSART: Remember what you thought. *As if it's happening to you now. This very moment* . . . What's in your head?

ALAN (*to* DYSART): Her eyes. *She's* the one with eyes! . . . I keep looking at them, because I really want—

DYSART: To look at her breasts?

ALAN (*to* DYSART): Yes.

DYSART: Like in the film.

ALAN (*to* DYSART): Yes . . . Then she starts to scratch my hand.

JILL: You're really very nice, you know that?

ALAN (*to* DYSART): Moving her nails on the back. Her face so warm. Her eyes.

DYSART: You want her very much?

ALAN (*to* DYSART): Yes . . .

JILL: I love your eyes.

(*She kisses him.*)

(*Whispering.*) Let's go!

ALAN: Where?

JILL: I know a place. It's right near here.

ALAN: Where?

JILL: Surprise! . . . come on!

(*She darts away round the circle, across the stage and up the left side.*)

Come *on!*

ALAN (*to* DYSART): She runs ahead. I follow. And then— and then—!

(*He halts.*)

DYSART: What?

ALAN (*to* DYSART): I see what she means.

DYSART: What? . . . Where are you? . . . Where has she taken you?

ALAN (*to* JILL): *The Stables?*

JILL: Of course!

ACT 2 / SCENE 32

(*Chorus makes a warning hum.*
The horses actors enter, and ceremonially put on their masks—first raising them high above their heads.
NUGGET *stands in the central tunnel.*)

ALAN (*recoiling*): No!

JILL: Where else? They're perfect!

ALAN: No!

(*He turns his head from her.*)

JILL: Or do you want to go home now and face your dad?

ALAN: No!

JILL: Then come on!

(*He edges nervously past the horse standing at the left, which turns his neck and even moves a challenging step after him.*)

ALAN: Why not your place?

JILL: I can't. Mother doesn't like me bringing back boys. I told you. . . . Anyway, the Barn's better.

ALAN: No!

JILL: All that straw. It's cosy.

ALAN: No.

JILL: *Why not?*

ALAN: Them!

JILL: Dalton will be in bed . . . What's the matter? . . . Don't you want to?

ALAN (*aching to*): Yes!

JILL: So?

ALAN (*desperate*): Them! . . . Them! . . .

JILL: *Who?*

ALAN (*low*): Horses.

JILL: *Horses?* . . . You're really dotty, aren't you . . . What do you mean?

(*He starts shaking.*)

Oh, you're freezing . . . Let's get under the straw. You'll be warm there.

ALAN (*pulling away*): No!

JILL: What on earth's the matter with you? . . .

(*Silence. He won't look at her.*)

Look, if the sight of horses offends you, my lord,

we can just shut the door. You won't have to see them. All right?

DYSART: What door is that? In the barn?

ALAN (*to* DYSART): Yes.

DYSART: So what do you do? You go in?

ALAN (*to* DYSART): Yes.

ACT 2 / SCENE 33

(*A rich light falls.*
Furtively ALAN *enters the square from the top end, and* JILL *follows. The horses on the circle retire out of sight on either side.* NUGGET *retreats up the tunnel and stands where he can just be glimpsed in the dimness.*)

DYSART: Into the Temple? The Holy of Holies?

ALAN (*to* DYSART: *desperate*): What else can I do? . . . I can't say! I can't tell her . . .(*to* JILL) Shut it tight.

JILL: All right . . . You're crazy!

ALAN: Lock it.

JILL: Lock?

ALAN: Yes.

JILL: It's just an old door. What's the matter with you? They're in their boxes. They can't get out . . . Are you all right?

ALAN: Why?

JILL: You look weird.

ALAN: *Lock it!*

JILL: Sssh! D'you want to wake up Dalton? . . . Stay there, idiot.

(*She mimes locking a heavy door, upstage.*)

DYSART: Describe the barn, please.

ALAN (*walking round it: to* DYSART): Large room. Straw everywhere. Some tools . . . (*as if picking it up off the rail where he left it in Act 1.*) A hoof pick! . . .

(*He 'drops' it hastily, and dashes away from the spot.*)

DYSART: *Go on.*

ALAN (*to* DYSART): At the end this big door. Behind it—

DYSART: Horses.

ALAN (*to* DYSART): Yes.

DYSART: How many?

ALAN (*to* DYSART): Six.

DYSART: Jill closes the door so you can't see them?

ALAN (*to* DYSART): Yes.

DYSART: And then? . . . What happens now? . . . Come on, Alan. Show me.

JILL: See, it's all shut. There's just us . . . Let's sit down. Come on.

(*They sit together on the same bench, left.*)

Hallo.

ALAN (*quickly*): Hallo.

(*She kisses him lightly. He responds. Suddenly a faint trampling of hooves, off-stage, makes him jump up.*)

JILL: What is it?

(*He turns his head upstage, listening.*)

Relax. There's no one there. Come here.

(*She touches his hand. He turns to her again.*)

You're very gentle. I love that . . .

ALAN: So are you . . . I mean . . .

(*He kisses her spontaneously. The hooves trample again, harder. He breaks away from her abruptly toward the upstage corner.*)

JILL (*rising*): What is it?

ALAN: Nothing!

(*She moves toward him. He turns and moves past her. He is clearly distressed. She contemplates him for a moment.*)

JILL (*gently*): Take your sweater off.

ALAN: What?

JILL: I will, if you will.

(*He stares at her. A pause.*
She lifts her sweater over head: he watches—then unzips his. They each remove their shoes, their socks, and their jeans. Then they look at each other diagonally across the square, in which the light is gently increasing.)

ALAN: You're . . . You're very . . .

JILL: So are you. . . . (*pause*) Come here.

(*He goes to her. She comes to him. They meet in the middle, and hold each other, and embrace.*)

ALAN (*to* DYSART): She put her mouth in mine. It was lovely! *Oh, it was lovely!*

(*They burst into giggles. He lays her gently on the floor in the center of the square, and bends over her eagerly. Suddenly the noise of Equus fills the place. Hooves smash on wood.* ALAN *straightens up, rigid. He stares straight ahead of him over the prone body of the girl.*)

DYSART: Yes, what happened then, Alan?

ALAN (*to* DYSART: *brutally*): I put it in her!

DYSART: Yes?

ALAN (*to* DYSART): I put it in her.

DYSART: You did?

ALAN (*to* DYSART): Yes!

DYSART: Was it easy?

ALAN (*to* DYSART): Yes.

DYSART: Describe it.

ALAN (*to* DYSART): I told you.

DYSART: More exactly.

ALAN (*to* DYSART): I put it in her!

DYSART: Did you?

ALAN (*to* DYSART): All the way!

DYSART: Did you, Alan?

ALAN (*to* DYSART): All the way. I shoved it. I put it in her all the way.

DYSART: Did you?

ALAN (*to* DYSART): Yes!

DYSART: Did you?

ALAN (*to* DYSART): Yes! . . . Yes!

DYSART: Give me the TRUTH! . . . Did you? . . . *Honestly?*

ALAN (*to* DYSART): Fuck off!

(*He collapses, lying upstage on his face.* JILL *lies on her back motionless, her head downstage, her arms extended behind her. A pause.*)

DYSART (*gently*): What was it? You couldn't? Though you wanted to very much?

ALAN (*to* DYSART): I couldn't . . . see her.

DYSART: What do you mean?

ALAN (*to* DYSART): Only Him. Every time I kissed her—*He* was in the way.

DYSART: Who?

(ALAN *turns on his back.*)

ALAN (*to* DYSART): You *know* who! . . . When I touched her, I felt *Him*. Under me . . . His side, waiting for my hand . . . His flanks . . . I refused him. I looked. I looked right at her . . . and I couldn't do it. When I shut my eyes, I saw him at once. The streaks on his belly . . . (*With more desperation.*) I couldn't feel *her* flesh at all! I wanted the foam off his neck. His sweaty hide. Not flesh. *Hide! Horse-hide!* . . . Then I couldn't even kiss her.

(JILL *sits up.*)

JILL: What is it?

ALAN (*dodging her hand*): No!

(*He scrambles up and crouches in the corner against the rails, like a little beast in a cage.*)

JILL: Alan!

ALAN: Stop it!

(JILL *gets up.*)

JILL: It's all right . . . It's all right . . . Don't worry about it. It often happens—honest. . . . There's nothing wrong. I don't mind, you know . . . I don't at all.

(*He dashes past her downstage.*)

Alan, look at me . . . Alan? . . . Alan!

(*He collapses again by the rail.*)

ALAN: Get out! . . .

JILL: What?

ALAN (*soft*): Out!

JILL: There's nothing wrong: believe me! It's very common.

ALAN: *Get out!*

(*He snatches up the invisible pick.*)

GET OUT!

JILL: Put that down!

ALAN: Leave me alone!

JILL: Put that down, Alan. It's very dangerous. Go on, please—drop it.

(*He 'drops' it, and turns from her.*)

ALAN: You ever tell anyone. Just you tell . . .

JILL: Who do you think I am? . . . I'm your friend— Alan . . .

(*She goes toward him.*)

Listen: you don't have to do anything. Try to realize that. Nothing at all. Why don't we just lie together in the straw. And talk.

ALAN (*low*): Please . . .

JILL: Just talk.

ALAN: *Please!*

JILL: All right, I'm going . . . Let me put my clothes on first.

(*She dresses, hastily.*)

ALAN: You tell anyone! . . . Just tell and see . . .

JILL: *Oh, stop it!* . . . I wish you could believe me. It's not in the least important.

(*Pause.*)

Anyway, I won't say anything. You know that. You know I won't. . . .

(*Pause. He stands with his back to her.*)

Goodnight, then, Alan. . . . I wish—I really wish—

(*He turns on her, hissing. His face is distorted—possessed. In horrified alarm she turns—fumbles the door open— leaves the barn—shuts the door hard behind her, and dashes up the tunnel out of sight, past the barely visible figure of NUGGET.*)

ACT 2 / SCENE 34

(*ALAN stands alone, and naked.*
A faint humming and drumming. The boy looks about him in growing terror.)

DYSART: What?

ALAN (*to DYSART*): He was there. Through the door. The door was shut, but he was there! . . . He'd seen everything. I could hear him. He was laughing.

DYSART: Laughing?

ALAN (*to DYSART*): Mocking! . . . *Mocking* . . .

(*Standing downstage he stares up toward the tunnel. A great silence weighs on the square.*)

(*to the silence: terrified*) Friend . . . Equus the Kind . . . The Merciful! . . . *Forgive me!* . . .

(*Silence.*)

It wasn't me. Not really me. Me! . . . Forgive me! . . . Take me back again! Please! . . . PLEASE!

(*He kneels on the downstage lip of the square, still facing the door, huddling in fear.*)

I'll never do it again. I swear . . . I swear! . . .

(*Silence.*)

(*In a moan.*) Please!!! . . .

DYSART: And He? What does He say?

ALAN (*to DYSART: whispering*): 'Mine! . . . You're mine! . . . I am yours and you are mine!' . . . Then I see his eyes. They are rolling!

(*NUGGET begins to advance slowly, with relentless hooves, down the central tunnel.*)

'I see you. I see you. Always! Everywhere! Forever!'

DYSART: Kiss anyone and I will see?

ALAN (*to DYSART*): Yes!

DYSART: Lie with anyone and I will see?

ALAN (*to DYSART*): Yes!

DYSART: And you will fail! Forever and ever you will *fail!* You will see ME—and you will FAIL!

(*The boy turns round, hugging himself in pain. From the sides two more horses converge with NUGGET on the rails. Their hooves stamp angrily. The Equus noise is heard more terribly.*)

The Lord thy God is a Jealous God. He sees you. He sees you forever and ever, Alan. He sees you! . . . *He sees you!*

ALAN (*in terror*): Eyes! . . . White eyes—never closed! Eyes like flames—coming—coming! . . . God seest! God seest! . . . NO! . . .

(*Pause. He steadies himself. The stages begins to blacken.*)

(*Quieter.*) No more. No more, Equus.

(*He gets up. He goes to the bench. He takes up the invisible pick. He moves slowly upstage toward NUGGET, concealing the weapon behind his naked back, in the growing darkness. He stretches out his hand and fondles NUGGET's mask.*)

(*gently*) Equus . . . Noble Equus . . . Faithful and True . . . Godslave . . . Thou—God—Seest— NOTHING!

(*He stabs out NUGGET's eyes. The horse stamps in agony. A great screaming begins to fill the theatre, growing ever louder. ALAN dashes at the other two horses and blinds them too, stabbing over the rails. Their metal hooves join in the stamping.*
Relentlessly, as this happens, three more horses appear in cones of light: not naturalistic animals like the first three, but dreadful creatures out of nightmare. Their eyes

flare—their nostrils flare—their mouths flare. They are archetypal images—judging, punishing, pitiless. They do not halt at the rail, but invade the square. As they trample at him, the boy leaps desperately at them, jumping high and naked in the dark, slashing at their heads with arms upraised. The screams increase. The other horses follow into the square. The whole place is filled with cannoning, blinded horses—and the boy dodging among them, avoiding their slashing hooves as best he can. Finally they plunge off into darkness and away out of sight. The noise dies abruptly, and all we hear is ALAN yelling in hysteria as he collapses on the ground—stabbing at his own eyes with the invisible pick.

ALAN: Find me! . . . Find me! . . . Find me! . . . KILL ME! . . . KILL ME! . . .

ACT 2 / SCENE 35

(The light changes quickly to brightness.
DYSART enters swiftly, hurls a blanket on the left bench, and rushes over to ALAN. The boy is having convulsions on the floor. DYSART grabs his hands, forces them from his eyes, scoops him up in his arms and carries him over to the bench. ALAN hurls his arms round DYSART and clings to him, gasping and kicking his legs in dreadful frenzy. DYSART lays him down and presses his head back on the bench. He keeps talking—urgently talking—soothing the agony as he can.)

DYSART: Here . . . Here . . . Ssssh . . . Ssssh . . . Calm now . . . Lie back. *Just lie back!* Now breathe in deep. Very deep. In . . . Out . . . In . . . Out . . . That's it. . . . In. *Out . . . In . . . Out . . .*

(The boy's breath is drawn into his body with a harsh rasping sound, which slowly grows less. DYSART puts the blanket over him.)

Keep it going . . . That's a good boy . . . Very good boy . . . It's all over now, Alan. It's all over. He'll go away now. You'll never see him again, I promise. You'll have no more bad dreams. No more awful nights. Think of that! . . . You are going to be well. I'm going to make you well, I promise you. . . . You'll be here for a while, but I'll be here too, so it won't be so bad. Just trust me . . .

(He stands upright. The boy lies still.)

Sleep now. Have a good long sleep. You've earned it . . . Sleep. Just sleep. . . . I'm going to make you well.

(He steps backwards into the centre of the square. The light brightens some more.
A pause.)

DYSART: I'm lying to you, Alan. He won't really go that easily. Just clop away from you like a nice old nag. Oh, no! When Equus leaves—if he leaves at all—it will be with your intestines in his teeth. And I don't stock replacements . . . If you knew anything, you'd get up this minute and run from me fast as you could.

(HESTHER speaks from her place.)

HESTHER: The boy's in pain, Martin.
DYSART: Yes.
HESTHER: And you can take it away.
DYSART: Yes.
HESTHER: Then that has to be enough for you, surely? . . . In the end!
DYSART *(crying out)*: All right! I'll take it away! He'll be delivered from madness. *What then?* He'll feel himself acceptable! *What then?* Do you think feelings like his can be simply re-attached, like plasters? Stuck on to other objects we select? *Look at him!* . . . My desire might be to make this boy an ardent husband—a caring citizen—a worshipper of abstract and unifying God. My achievement, however, is more likely to make a ghost! . . . Let me tell you exactly what I'm going to do to him!

(He steps out of the square and walks round the upstage end of it, storming at the audience.)

I'll heal the rash on his body. I'll erase the welts cut into his mind by flying manes. When that's done, I'll set him on a nice mini-scooter and send him puttering off into the Normal world where animals are treated *properly*: made extinct, or put into servitude, or tethered all their lives in dim light, just to feed it! I'll give him the good Normal world where we're tethered beside them—blinking our nights away in a nonstop drench of cathode-ray over our shrivelling heads! I'll take away his Field of Ha Ha, and give him Normal places for his ecstasy—multi-lane highways driven through the guts of cities, extinguishing Place altogether, *even the idea of Place!* He'll trot on his metal pony tamely through the concrete evening—and one thing I promise you: he will never touch hide again! With any luck his private parts will come to feel as plastic to him as the products of the factory to which he will almost certainly be sent. Who knows? He may even come to find sex funny. Smirky funny. Bit of grunt funny. Trampled and furtive and entirely in control. Hopefully, he'll feel nothing at his fork but Approved Flesh. *I doubt, however, with much passion!* . . . Passion, you see, can be destroyed by a doctor. It cannot be created.

(He addresses ALAN directly, in farewell.)

You won't gallop any more, Alan. Horses will be quite safe. You'll save your pennies every week, till you can change that scooter in for a car, and put the odd fifty P on the gee-gees, quite forgetting that they were ever anything more to you than bearers of little profits and little losses. You will, however, be without pain. More or less completely without pain.

(*Pause.*
He speaks directly to the theatre, standing by the motionless body of ALAN STRANG, *under the blanket.*)

And now for me it never stops: that voice of Equus out of the cave—'Why me? . . . Why Me? . . . Account for Me!' . . . All right—I surrender! I say it . . . In an ultimate sense I cannot know what I do in this place—yet I do ultimate things. Essentially I cannot know what I do—yet I do essential things. Irreversible, terminal things. I stand in the dark with a pick in my hand, striking at heads!

(*He moves away from* ALAN, *back to the downstage bench, and finally sits.*)

I need—more desperately than my children need me—a way of seeing in the dark. What way is this? . . . *What dark is this?* . . . I cannot call it ordained of God: I can't get that far. I will however pay it so much homage. There is now, in my mouth, this sharp chain. And it never comes out.

(*A long pause.*
DYSART *sits staring.*)

BLACKOUT

Figure 99. Alan (Peter Firth) rides the Horse (David Combs) in the National Theatre Company production of *Equus,* directed by John Dexter and designed by John Napier, New York, 1974. (Photograph: Van Williams.)

Figure 100. Dysart (Anthony Hopkins), Alan (Peter Firth), and the Horse (David Combs) in the National Theatre Company production of *Equus,* directed by John Dexter and designed by John Napier, New York, 1974. (Photograph: Van Williams.)

Staging of *Equus*

REVIEW OF THE NATIONAL THEATER COMPANY
PRODUCTION, 1974, BY JOHN BEAUFORT

"Equus," the powerfully moving new British drama at the Plymouth Theater, brilliantly employs the elements of a clinical case history to probe a deep personal tragedy. At the same time that Dr. Martin Dysart (Anthony Hopkins) is untangling the mental disturbance that lies behind the commission of a horrible crime by teenage Alan Strang (Peter Firth), the doctor comes face to face with his own demons of frustration and despair.

Such is Peter Shaffer's skill as dramatist and humane observer that he is able to convey Alan's capacity for an ecstacy beyond anything of which Dysart is capable. In restoring Alan to mental health, the psychiatrist realizes he must exorcise the ecstacy along with the dark drives which led to Alan's vicious act of blinding six horses. As 'Equus" unfolds, Mr. Shaffer explores a variety of motives: Alan's freakish religious and sexual complexes; the domestic conflicts between a sensitive, conventionally respectable mother and an authoritarian, atheist father. How damagingly the discords of seeming family tranquility can aggravate the sensibilities of an impressionable child is one of the themes of this precisely designed and structured play.

In a program note, Mr. Shaffer comments as follows on "the dreadful event" which promoted its writing: "I knew very strongly that I wanted to interpret it in some entirely personal way. I had to create a mental world in which the deed could be made comprehensible." Even the crime itself the author "modified to accord with what I feel to be acceptable theatrical proportion."

"Equus" consistently respects this "theatrical proportion." In its most extravagant theatrical reach—the mimed movements of the horses and the simulated reenactment of Alan's secret nocturnal rides—the production does not exceed the artistic grasp of Mr. Shaffer and director John Dexter. Even the play's nude scene seems intended for more than merely sensational purposes.

In tracing the case history of Alan Strang, Mr. Shaffer illuminates the more complex ordeal of Martin Dysart. "Equus" (the word means "horse" in latin) might be called a psychological mystery play, since its technical process consists of exploring the genesis of a crime. The artistic achievement lies not merely in what the conflict unfolds but in what it suggests about the human mystery itself.

As a stunning piece of inventive play-making, "Equus" calls on all the resources of imagery, symbolism, and allusions that range from TV commercial jingles to mythical centaurs. Although the work is multilayered, the expression is a model of clarity. John Napier's visual design is spare and clinically functional: a central square platform in what is apparently a teaching-hospital lecture room, with tiers of spectators upstage. By slight rearrangement of leather benches, and with the aid of Andy Phillips's ingenious lighting, the scene becomes a room in the Strang's house, or the stable in which the crime occurs. Essential to the mounting tension and mythic atmosphere are the noble steeds, portrayed by human actors wearing wire-sculptured hooves and heads.

As the central figures, doctor and patient are admirably served by Mr. Hopkins and young Mr. Firth (the original Alan of the Old Vic production). The initial stand-off, the growing confidence, the turning of tables when Alan becomes interrogator—all the minutiae of an unfolding relationship are meticulously and expressively portrayed as the troubled man concentrates his professional skills on solving the plight of the troubled boy. An actor of tremendous inner resource, Mr. Hopkins reveals the torment of a frustrated professional with an unhappy marriage who has assuaged his frustrations in a love affair with ancient Greece. For his part, Mr. Firth displays the concealment, naivete, cunning, vivid perceptions, and dangerous neuroticism of the young patient.

"Equus" is brought arrestingly to stage life by a cast whose principals include Marian Seldes as an enlightened magistrate, Frances Sternhagen and Michael Higgins as Alan's perplexed parents, Roberta Maxwell as the boy's would-be girl friend, and Everett McGill doubling as rider and steed. "Equus" is a remarkable play stirringly acted.

A bare stage, a few actors, a standing ovation, and quite clearly Broadway had gotten a new popular success in Peter Shaffer's play "Equus," and a new star in the shock-headed, 21-year-old Peter Firth. Both play and star emerged last night at the Plymouth Theater.

Mr. Shaffer's play does an unusual thing. It asks why? Most plays tell us how. "Equus" is a psychological inquiry into a crime, a journey into someone's mind. It is a kind of highbrow suspense story, a psychic and mythic thriller, but also an essay in character and motive. It is the documentation of a crime.

One night in England—and the story has been based by Mr. Shaffer on a flimsily documented but apparently true incident—a young stable hand attacked six horses in their stable. He systematically put their eyes out. It seems motiveless. He loved horses. He almost worshipped them—yet one night, one by one, in a disgusting, purposeless scene of violence he blinded them. Why? The boy was sick. Of course, he was sick, but why?

The disturbed boy is placed in an institution under the care of a psychiatrist. The boy has perpetrated a crime that is not only senseless but also bizarre. The pattern of the crime runs not just contrary to nature but contain elements of grotesque fantasy. Why blind horses? A madman might kill them, wound them in some crazed passion, but to carefully if frenziedly blind six horses suggests a certain method in the madness.

The young criminal is obviously alienated. When he first meets the psychiatrist he refuses to answer any questions—his only response is to gabble-sing advertising jingles with a mocking despair. His mind is closed up by the secret of his tragedy. The psychiatrist decides to unclam it—to exorcise the ghost.

This is the story of the play. The psychiatrist painfully has to unravel the boy's background. He not only has to win his confidence, he also has to sustain his interest. First what was his family like? What were the events leading up to this obscene violence. Slowly the doctor investigates the facts and the circumstances, and pieces together the anatomy of an outrage. He does not have to judge. He is merely seeking the truth in the hope of freeing the boy from a demon.

The play Mr. Shaffer has created from all this is richly rewarding on a number of levels. It is by no means a clinical documentary, though it does have elements of this about it. Yet its nub is to be found in the doctor's relationship with the boy, and his growing realization that the boy has a fantasy love for horses. For it is a love, he actually finds in horses the spirit that Mr. Shaffer calls Equus, a deification of the horse as a life force, and the boy has entered realms of passion and, in a sense, reality, that his own humdrum existence has never known. He has an unkissed wife, an antiquarian interest in Greek relics and a whole tally of little, medium boredoms. He lives, as he recognizes, to a small if safe scale.

He comes to realize the uniqueness of the boy. "That boy," he says, "has known a passion more intense than any I felt all my life." He does not excuse, of course, the horrific results of that passion, but he is sheerly impressed by the Dionysiac strength of its existence. He can patch up the boy's tortured mind and psyche, and send it out on the street. But what will be lost in spiritual energy? "Passion can be destroyed by a doctor, it cannot be created."

The play is quite different from anything Mr. Shaffer has written before, and has, to my mind, a quite new sense of seriousness ot it. It has all of Mr. Shaffer's masterly command of the theater.

He has his theater set up here as a kind of bullring with a section of the audience actually sitting on stage, like confident graduate students watching a class. And most adroitly, he runs through many of the patterns of clinical psychiatry, from elementary hypnotism to the abreaction, whereby the patient reenacts circumstances of his trauma.

Mr. Shaffer was always a great juggler of the theater, whether it was in making his well-made play, such as "Five Finger Exercises" or Verdi spectacular in "The Royal Hunt of the Sun." But in "Equus" he has found a different métier. It is still a popularly intended play—it is essentially a Broadway vehicle for star actors—but it has a most refreshing and mind-opening intellectualism. It has the power of thought to it. Take one: "A child is born into a world of phenomena, all equal in their power to enslave." This, just as sample, has a quality of thoughtfulenss to it that is rare in the contemporary popular theater.

John Dexter has directed it beautifully. The staging catches just the right element of court drama, mystery thriller and philosophical exposition. The direction holds all the elements of the play together with consummate skill, and I was also impressed by the mimetic conception of the horses devised by Claude Chagrin. It is not easy to present men playing horses on stage without provoking giggles—here the horses live up to their reputed godhead.

The performances blaze with theatrical life. Oddly—and perhaps intentionally—Mr. Firth's performance as the victim-assailant is set apart from the rest, keyed into a kind of naturalism the others do not attempt.

It is a marvelous performance by a young man who has the makings of a great actor.

The rest are the background, yes, even the psychiatrist who by any count has the most important role, if only because it represents the playwright himself coming to terms with alientation. Anthony Hopkins, articulate and troubled is superb in opposition to the unyielding suspicion and wary tenseness of Mr. Firth.

It is a virtuoso performance gauged to a fraction.

The casting was exemplary, with Michael Higgins and Frances Sternhagen as the worried, guilty but uncomprehending parents, Roberta Maxwell as the young girl who involuntarily triggers the tragedy, and Marian Seldes as an admonishing psychiatrist.

This is a very fine and enthralling play. It holds you by the root of drama, and it adds immeasurably to the fresh hopes we have for Broadway's future.

CREDITS

Howard Taubman. Reviews of *Dutchman* and *The Cherry Orchard.* Copyright © 1980 by The New York Times Company. Reprinted by permission.

The Second Shepherds' Play, modernized version by Anthony Caputi. First published in *Masterworks of Drama*, Vol. II, D.C. Heath, 1968. Reprinted by permission of Anthony Caputi.

The Times Drama Critic. Reviews of *Othello* and *Miss Julie.* Reproduced from *The Times* by permission of The Times Newspapers Limited.

Irving Wardle. Review of *The Man of Mode.* Reprinted from *The Times* by permission of The Times Newspapers Limited.

Robert Waterhouse. Interview of the Director and Designer of *The Man of Mode.* Reprinted from *Plays and Players* by permission of Robert Waterhouse.

John Webster. *The Duchess of Malfi,* edited by J. Dennis Huston and Alvin B. Kernan. From *Classics of the Renaissance Theatre: Seven English Plays* by J. Dennis Huston and Alvin B. Kernan, copyright © 1969 by Harcourt Brace Jovanovich, Inc. Reprinted by permission of the publisher.

Tennessee Williams. *Cat on a Hot Tin Roof.* Copyright 1954, 1955, © 1971, 1975 by Tennessee Williams. All rights reserved. Reprinted by permission of New Directions. CAUTION: Professionals and amateurs are hereby warned that *Cat on a Hot Tin Roof,* being fully protected under the copyright laws of the United States of America, the British Empire including the Dominion of Canada, and all other countries of the Copyright Union, is subject to royalty. All rights, including professional, amateur, motion picture, recitation, lecturing, public reading, radio-broadcasting, and the rights of translation into foreign languages, are strictly reserved. Particular emphasis is laid on the question of readings, permission for which must be secured from the author's agent in writing. All inquiries should be addressed to the author's agent, Audrey Wood, c/o Ashley Famous Agency, 1303 Avenue of the Americas, New York, N.Y. 10019.

Thomas Willis. Review of *Volpone.* Copyrighted © by *Chicago Tribune.* Reprinted by permission of the publisher.